Fodor's 99

Europe

The complete guide, thoroughly up-to-date

Packed with details that will make your trip

What to see, what to skip

City strolls, countryside adventures

Smart lodging and dining options

Transportation tips, distances and directions

Key contacts, savvy travel tips

When to go, what to pack

Clear, accurate, easy-to-use maps

Fodor's Travel Publications, Inc.
New York • Toronto • London • Sydney • Auckland
www.fodors.com

Fodor's Europe

EDITOR: Nancy van Itallie

Editorial Contributors: Robert Andrews, Barbara Walsh Angelillo, Richard Berry, Tim Bird, Barbara Blechman, Toula Bogdanos, Bill Booth, David Brown, Jacqueline Brown, Jules Brown, Eleanore Boyse, Christine Cipriani, Peter Collis, Nancy Coons, Kathleen Cox, Fionn Davenport, Martha de la Cal, Bonnie Dodson, Chris Drake, Debbie Ebanks, Jon Eldan, Nigel Fisher, Robert Fisher, Judith Glynn, Brent Gregston, Kay Hammond, Nancy Hart, Simon Hewitt, Alannah Hopkin, Beth Ingpen, Gareth Jenkins, Nicola Keegan, Suzanne Rowan Kelleher, Laura Kidder, Michael Kissane, Ky Krauthamer, Martha Lagace, Jonathan Leff, Natasha Lesser, Mark Little, Alexander Lobrano, Andrew May, Dan Navid, Jennifer Paull, Ian Phillips, Ian Plenderleith, Karina Porcelli, Tatiana Repkova, Robert Rigney, Kristin Rimington, Caragh Rockwood, Rich Rubin, Patricia Rucidlo, Jurgen Scheunemann, Helayne Schiff, Marshall Schwartzmann (Gold Guide editor), Kate Sekules, George Semler, Katherine Semler, Eric Sjogren, Allison Stern, Gilbert Summers, Robert Tilley, Julie Tomasz, Goril Trondsen, Susan Tuttle-Laube, Annie Ward, Stephen Wolf

Editorial Production: Linda K. Schmidt

Maps: David Lindroth, *cartographer*; Steven Amsterdam, *map editor*

Design: Fabrizio La Rocca, *creative director*; Guido Caroti, *associate art director*; Jolie Novak, *photo editor*

Production/Manufacturing: Robert B. Shields

Cover Photograph: BKA Network/Aspen

Copyright

ISBN 0-679-00135-2

Special Sales

Fodor's Travel Publications are available at special discounts for bulk purchases for sales promotions or premiums. Special editions, including personalized covers, excerpts of existing guides, and corporate imprints, can be created in large quantities for special needs. For more information, contact your local bookseller or write to Special Markets, Fodor's Travel Publications, 201 East 50th Street, New York, NY 10022. Inquiries from Canada should be directed to your local Canadian bookseller or sent to Random House of Canada, Ltd., Marketing Department, 2775 Matheson Boulevard East, Mississauga, Ontario L4W 4P7. Inquiries from the United Kingdom should be sent to Fodor's Travel Publications, 20 Vauxhall Bridge Road, London SW1V 2SA, England.

PRINTED IN THE UNITED STATES OF AMERICA

10 9 8 7 6 5 4 3 2 1

CONTENTS

Italic entries are maps.

ON THE ROAD WITH FODOR'S

WHEN I PLAN A VACATION, the first thing I do is cast around among my friends and colleagues to find someone who's just been where I'm going. That's because there's no substitute for a recommendation from a good friend who knows your tastes, your budget, and your circumstances, someone who's just been there. Unfortunately, such friends are few and far between. So it's nice to know that there's *Fodor's Europe*.

In the first place, this book won't stay home when you hit the road. It will accompany you every step of the way, steering you away from wrong turns and wrong choices and never expecting a thing in return. It includes a wonderful, full-color map from Rand McNally, the world's largest commercial mapmaker. Most important of all, it's written and assiduously updated by the kind of people you *would* hit up for travel tips if you knew them. They're as choosy as your pickiest friend, except they've probably seen a lot more of Europe. In these pages, they don't send you chasing down every town and sight in Europe but have instead selected the best ones, the ones that are worthy of your time and money. Just tear out the map at the perforation, and join us on the road in Europe. Will this be the vacation of your dreams? We hope so.

Connections

We're pleased that the American Society of Travel Agents continues to endorse Fodor's as its guidebook of choice. ASTA is the world's largest and most influential travel trade association, operating in more than 170 countries, with 27,000 members pledged to adhere to a strict code of ethics reflecting the Society's motto, "Integrity in Travel." ASTA shares Fodor's devotion to providing smart, honest travel information and advice to travelers, and we've long recommended that our readers—even those who have guidebooks and traveling friends—consult ASTA member agents for the experience and professionalism they bring to your vacation planning.

On Fodor's Web site (www.fodors.com), check out the new Resource Center, an online companion to Chapter 1 of this book, complete with useful hot links to related sites. In our forums, you can also get lively advice from other travelers and more great tips from Fodor's experts worldwide.

How to Use This Book

Organization

The section following this one, **New and Noteworthy,** cues you in on trends and happenings. Following that is Chapter 1, the **Gold Guide,** Smart Travel Tips arranged alphabetically by topic. Under each listing you'll find tips and information that will help you accomplish what you need to in Europe. You'll also find addresses and telephone numbers of organizations and companies that offer destination-related services and detailed information and publications.

Chapters in *Europe 99* are in alphabetical order by country. Each covers the country's essential information A to Z, exploring, dining lodging, nightlife and the arts, shopping, and side trips in cities and regions. Sites in major cities accompanied by maps are arranged alphabetically, but they are numbered on the maps according to the suggested sequence of a walk or tour. Within regional sections, all restaurants and lodgings are grouped with the town. The A to Z list that ends all city or regional sections covers getting there and getting around. It also provides helpful contacts and resources.

Icons and Symbols

★ Our special recommendations
✕ Restaurant
🏨 Lodging establishment
✕🏨 Lodging establishment whose restaurant warrants a special trip
🦆 Good for kids (rubber duck)
☞ Sends you to another section of the guide for more information
✉ Address

☎ Telephone number
⏲ Opening and closing times
🎫 Admission prices for attractions that charge more than $10 or the equivalent (those we give apply to adults; substantially reduced fees are almost always available for children, students, and senior citizens); we indicate if the attraction does not charge admission.

Numbers in black circles ❸ that appear on the maps and in the margins correspond to one another.

Dining and Lodging

The restaurants and lodgings we list are the cream of the crop in each price range. Price charts appear in the country A to Z section following the introduction of each chapter.

Hotel Facilities

We always list the facilities that are available—but we don't specify whether you'll be charged extra to use them: When pricing accommodations, always ask what's included. In addition, assume that all rooms have private baths unless noted otherwise. In addition, when you book a room, be sure to mention if you have a disability or are traveling with children, if you prefer a private bath or a certain type of bed, or if you have specific dietary needs or other concerns. In addition, assume that all rooms have private baths unless otherwise noted.

Restaurant Reservations and Dress Codes

Reservations are always a good idea; we mention them only when they're essential or are not accepted. Book as far ahead as you can, and reconfirm as soon as you arrive. Unless otherwise noted, the restaurants listed are open daily for lunch and dinner. We mention dress only when men are required to wear a jacket or a jacket and tie. Look for an overview of local dining-out habits in the Dining section of the country A to Z list that follows the introduction of each chapter.

Credit Cards

The following abbreviations are used: **AE,** American Express; **DC,** Diners Club; **MC,** MasterCard; and **V,** Visa.

Don't Forget to Write

You can use this book in the confidence that all prices and opening times are based on information supplied to us at press time; Fodor's cannot accept responsibility for any errors. Time inevitably brings changes, so always confirm information when it matters—especially if you're making a detour to visit a specific place.

Were the restaurants we recommended as described? Did our hotel picks exceed your expectations? Did you find a museum we recommended a waste of time? Keeping a travel guide fresh and up-to-date is a big job, and we welcome your feedback, positive *and* negative. If you have complaints, we'll look into them and revise our entries when the facts warrant it. If you've discovered a special place that we haven't included, we'll pass the information along to our correspondents and have them check it out. So send us your thoughts via e-mail at editors@fodors.com (specifying the name of the book on the subject line) or on paper in care of the Europe editor at Fodor's, 201 East 50th Street, New York, New York 10022. In the meantime, have a wonderful trip!

Karen Cure

Karen Cure
Editorial Director

NEW AND NOTEWORTHY

A **NEW MONETARY CURRENCY** will make its debut on January 1, 1999, when the conversion to the **euro** begins for all members of the European Union. Some payment systems (mainly in trade) will begin using the euro immediately. The rates of conversion between the euro and local currencies will be irrevocably fixed, which should eliminate commission charges when exchanging currency. Consumers will continue to use chiefly their own national currency because euro banknotes and coins will not yet be available, but the gradual introduction of dual pricing of goods and services will enable people to slowly get used to the new money. Eventually, the euro will become a currency in its own right and participating national currencies will no longer be listed on foreign exchange markets. By January 1, 2002, at the latest, new euro banknotes and coins will be put into circulation and the old national currencies will be withdrawn. In Austria this will be done over a period of three months, after which euro banknotes and coins alone will have legal tender status.

Andorra

A new **gondola ski lift** has been installed in Ordino; a new golf course has opened up in Aravell (which is actually not in Andorra but just across the western border near La Seu d'Urgell); and the **summer music festival** has been upgraded and is becoming one of Europe's best.

Austria

The main musical event of 1999 is the 100th anniversary of the death of the king of the waltz, **Johann Strauss the Younger,** and the 150th anniversary of the death of his father. Austria is marking the year with a celebration of Strauss operettas and waltzes, and both the Vienna State Opera and the Volksoper will host performances of several of both composers' works. The highlight of the festival on the lake at Mörbisch in Burgenland will be a Strauss operetta. Getting tickets to the glamorous **Opernball** in Vienna depends on luck and speed. Earmark February 2, 1999, to take part in this quintessentially Viennese event.

New in the **Vienna art world** is the transformation of the rambling Messepalast building, near the Kunsthistorisches Museum, into a museum for post-1918 art, with works by Egon Schiele forming the nucleus of the collection.

Near the United Nations center in Vienna a massive new complex called **Donau City,** or Danube City, is under construction. It will house restaurants, shops, and movie theaters. The new four-star Forum Hotel, part of the Inter-Continental Hotel Group, is scheduled to open here in late 1998.

A new addition to Vienna's Stephansplatz is the **Jewish Welcome Center,** at Number 10. The Welcome Center provides information on where to visit important Jewish landmarks and former Jewish neighborhoods in the city.

Once every six years—and 1999 is a play year—just about the entire village of Thiersee in Tirol participates in its traditional **passion play,** May to October.

Baltic States

Although prices in Estonia, Latvia and Lithuania are rising, the Baltics are still some of the most cost-effective vacation spots for Europeans. The states are spending more and more on infrastructure improvements and Old Town maintenance. Estonia plows steadily forward in European Union talks—the only Baltic state chosen to begin negotiations—and Tallinn still has the best tourist infrastructure in the region. Riga, although struggling with its sometimes politically unpleasant neighbor Russia, is the most cosmopolitan of the three siblings, with new Greek and Indian restaurants opening as the National Opera mounts a revival. In 1998 Vilnius spruced up its historic district, one of the largest in Europe.

Belgium

In Brussels, the permanent **Magritte Museum** opens at 138 Esseghemstraat in the borough of Jette. This is the house where the artist lived until 1954, with the studio and living room restored and an exhibition of his paintings on the upper two floors. In Antwerp, the focus is on **Sir Anthony Van Dyck.** The largest collection of his works ever assembled is on show at the Royal Museum of Fine Arts from May 15 to August 15, 1999. Engravings and sketches are being exhibited at other venues in Antwerp, and a Van Dyck Walk has been laid out to show the way to other sites of special importance for an understanding of the background of the 17th-century master. A new **Booking Office** (☎ 0800/ 21 22 1) has opened in Brussels covering events all over the country. There is no charge for its services, and callers can enquire about what's on and prices before deciding to book. Payment is by direct debit or (for visitors) by major credit cards.

Bulgaria

The democratic Bulgarian goverment has finally succeeded in **stabilizing the lev,** pegged to the German mark, at around 1,700 leva to the dollar. The economy is improving, and new businesses, restaurants, hotels, and shops are opening up. The new Sofia **metro** runs from the city center straight out to a distant apartment-block neighborhood; new inner-city stops are slated for completion by the end of 1999.

Sofia's splendid Ottoman bath house, which had fallen into ruin and become a dangerous, dilapidated eye-sore, is being restored. The outside has been painted and restored and the towers are once again gilded. The inside is scheduled for completion in 1999.

The northeastern village of **Russe,** with Victorian buildings, fresh, colorful coats of paint, and numerous clean gardens and parks, has received an award as the loveliest Bulgarian city. Residents of the rival city of **Plovdiv,** known as the country's most historic intellectual center, are busy painting and landscaping as well.

The European Union is in the beginning stages of constructing two new **border crossing points** between Bulgaria and Greece, as well as **super-highways** linking the new border points with major towns by late 1999.

Cyprus

The difficult task of trying to **reunite** the north and south of the island continues, but remains so far without success. The Cyprus Tourism Organzation is currently recommending to the government programs for expansions to both Larnaca and Paphos airports, developing pedestrian areas in the main cities, and upgrading the standards for restaurants and hotel accommodations. Two important **highways** are due for **reconstruction**: One will extend the present route from Nicosia to Limassol all the way to Paphos; the second will link Ayia Napa and Paralimni to the present Nicosia–Larnaca highway.

Czech Republic

The Czech Republic, pursuing economic and cultural revitalization, aims for eventual membership in the EU and in NATO. Prague's Ruzyně airport has a spacious and spiffy **new terminal.** The arrival of visitors and long-term residents from all over the world has brought forth **new restaurants** offering Cajun, Indian, vegetarian, and other exotic fare alongside the traditional ones serving pork and dumplings.

Prague is a dream for classical-music lovers and opera fans. The annual mid-May–early June **Prague Spring Music Festival,** which even before the collapse of the Communist government was one of the great events on the European calendar, is attracting record numbers of music lovers. The less-hyped **Prague Autumn festival** has begun to bring in equally strong performers and orchestras, and the State Opera's annual **Verdi Festival** in August is gaining popularity.

Denmark

Both rail and auto routes of the **Great Belt** were well up and running by mid-1998. Still under construction, however, is the link across the Øresund between Denmark and Sweden. Completion is expected sometime in late-2000 to mid-2001.

Finland

In 1999 Finland takes over the **EU presidency,** bringing the country closer psychologically to the rest of Europe. **Price levels** have fallen, making this a more accessible and attractive option for visitors.

Vital to Helsinki's rising international profile has been the expansion and modernization of its **airport,** some 20 km (12 mi) north of town, which has emerged as a key transit point in traffic between the ex-Soviet bloc countries and East Asia, the United States, and western Europe. The futuristic Sanoma newspaper group building due to open in 1999 is an example of Helsinki's striking **architectural development** in the 1990s. Meanwhile, pride in older resources emerges in the renovation and reopening in 1999 of the 19th-century downtown **Kämp Hotel,** aiming to reclaim its status as one of the finest hotels in Scandinavia.

France

Not content with being the world's largest museum, the **Louvre** continues to expand: 11 new rooms of Persian and Arab antiquities opened in October 1997, followed in December by an extra-large exhibit space devoted to Greek, Roman, Egyptian, Etruscan, and Coptic art. The **Centre Pompidou** closed in October 1997 for a $120-million renovation program and will not reopen till the last day of the century—December 31, 1999. In the meantime, you can visit the **Atelier Brancusi** in front of the center—the reconstituted studios of avant-garde sculptor Constantin Brancusi. The **Bibliothèque Nationale François-Mitterrand,** the new national library building in Paris (which replaced the old national library, the Bibliothèque Nationale Richelieu, on rue Richelieu), has proved a popular addition to the southeast section of the city. The Tolbiac district around the new library was due to be united to central Paris by the express **Météor** métro line by late 1998.

Paris is gearing up for **L'An 2000** (The Year 2000) with a host of special events planned to celebrate the millennium. A digital clock on the Eiffel Tower is counting down the days to the end of the century and, more frenetically, the Genitron on place de la Bastille is ticking down the seconds.

In **Versailles,** the Musée des Carrosses, with its parade of historic royal carriages, is now open weekends in the Grandes Écuries. Out in the park, an ambitious tree-replacement scheme was launched in early 1998 to recapture Le Nôtre's original perspectives (the trees had grown too big and old).

After nearly a decade, the reopening of Bayonne's **Musée Basque,** which is dedicated to exhibits on Basque ethnography, is a big event. The exact date of reopening (the end of 1998 or 1999) is as yet undetermined; in the meantime, exhibits are being held at the Château Neuf.

France's **highways** continue to expand: the A26 from Paris, ultimately destined to reach the Channel, is in operation as far as Abbeville; the new A14 tollway opened between La Défense and Orgeval, easing traffic to the west of Paris; and a stretch of the E50 expressway between Angers and Saumur was completed, and is soon to be extended as far as Tours.

On the political front, France continues to prepare for the **euro,** the single European currency. Although notes and coins are not expected to be introduced until 2001, many banks and shops are already posting prices in euros as well as francs.

Germany

Tremendous changes are upon Germany as it faces repercussions from the September 1998 elections. Some political commentators believe these elections to be the most critical since the questionable 1933 vote that confirmed Adolf Hitler as chancellor. Pollsters in spring 1998 predicted that the Social Democrats under leader Gerhard Schröder would emerge strongest, to topple Chancellor Helmut Kohl. At press time (summer 1998), one thing seemed sure: With nearly 5 million Germans unemployed nationally, and reports of violence common in the industrial areas of eastern Germany, a major shift is indicated.

Great Britain

London's renaissance continues at full blast, with Tony Blair, the dynamic, young(ish) Labour Prime Minister and the National Lottery—which funds exciting projects—leading the way. London's art, style, dining, and fashion scenes are sizzling. England is in the grip of Millennium fever, which will only intensify as the numbers creep toward the big 2000. Among the several buildings due to open on or around the big day is the **Millennium Dome,** at Greenwich. This multimillion-pound multi-football-field-size structure designed by architect-provocateur Richard Rogers is to house a cornucopia of architectural installations.

The new **BBC Experience** is a guided tour of the Broadcasting House of the British Broadcasting Corporation, including the Marconi Collection of early audiovisual equipment and interactive bits where you can play at directing *EastEnders,* the popular Cockney TV soap, or cast yourself in a role on *Desert Island Discs*. Islington's first major museum, the new **Estorick Collection of Italian Art,** displays those naughty Futurists in a renovated Georgian building on Cannonbury Square. The new **British Library** won't be completely operational until mid-1999, but some services were available in 1998.

The performing arts Muses seem to be, for all intents and purposes, practically homeless in London these days. The world-renowned **Royal Opera House** is still shuttered, owing to an ongoing renovation. Its resident troupes are taking up temporary shelter, gypsylike, at other theaters in the interim. The English National Opera (**ENO**) has abandoned the Coliseum, its home since 1968. Possible sites for a new house, funded by the Lottery, include several places along the South Bank, King's Cross, or the sadly disused yet magisterial Battersea Power Station. In addition, the **Royal Shakespeare Theatre** will no longer offer a summer season, and the Old Vic theater may close, with the resultant eviction of some of London's livelier theater troupes.

In nearby Windsor, **renovations to Windsor Castle,** in the wake of the catastrophic fire of November 1992, have been completed. In Liverpool, the august National Trust has recently opened **a new Beatles landmark**—the childhood Merseyside home of Paul McCartney, located on Forthlin Road, in the Allerton section. Also in the city by the Mersey, the dockside **Tate Gallery** has re-opened after its long refit looking a lot better than before. In Bradford, Yorkshire, the **National Museum of Photography, Film, and Television** has been revitalized, bringing together its high-tech collection and associated Pictureville movie house under one roof.

A restyled **Manchester city center** is slowly emerging from the debris of the IRA bombing of 1996. Most major renovation projects should be completed during 1999 and the year 2000, and massive new retail outlets—Marks & Spencer certainly, possibly Harvey Nichols, plus a host of other new names—are beginning to put down roots. Over in Wales, work is proceeding with the construction of **Cardiff's new National Stadium,** with completion expected in time for the 1999 Rugby World Cup, which is the city is hosting.

Scotland's **Glasgow,** the **U.K. City of Architecture and Design for 1999,** showcases exhibitions from product and graphic design to architecture and interiors. Venues include Glasgow's galleries and museums, a new center for architecture and design called The Lighthouse (occupying a Charles Rennie Mackintosh–designed building) and other cutting-edge exhibition spaces city-wide.

Greece

Athens is urgently preparing for the **2004 Olympic Games.** Gaping construction sites line the extension of the **subway,** to be completed in 2000, and the new **airport** at Sparta will open in 2001, ready to handle 16 million passengers a year.

Throughout the city, squares, boulevards, and neoclassical mansions are being **renovated.** Cars have been banned from several streets in the historic center, as well as from several zones downtown. **Natural gas buses,** free to passengers, and **electric cars,** some equipped for individuals with special needs, now circulate in the historic center. The city is setting up **information booths** detailing local bus lines, **taxi** drivers are posting mandatory **fare scales** in three languages with suggested prices to landmarks, new signs at Piraeus harbor will indicate ferries' locations and sailing times, and **more tourist police** are being hired. The long-term plan is to link all major ancient sites, such as the Acropolis, the Temple of Olympian Zeus, and the ancient cemetery of Kerameikos by pedestrian networks to create a vast **archaeological park,** which should be more than half finished by 2004.

Making good use of grants available under the EU's Delors II structural aid package, many **hotel chains upgraded or expanded** in 1998, and there are plans for seven new hotels in Athens and the Attica plain alone, as well as more resorts like a 1,000-bed hotel, conference center and theme park in Loutra Killinis in the Peloponnese.

In the next two years Greece will spend more than 22 billion drachmas **upgrading museums and restoring archaeological sites.** By the end of the century, the Greek government and the EU will carry out restoration work on most of the monasteries of Mount Athos, including Xenofon Monastery, which celebrates its millennium in 1999. The aim is to ensure that Mount Athos, so long a pristine refuge for monks and increasingly a tourist destination, will not become a paradise lost.

At the prehistoric settlement of **Akrotiri on Santorini,** for decades covered by an eyesore of a protective shelter, a revolutionary new **shelter** has been designed that allows for natural light and ventilation. The design provides for visitor stations and exhibits tracing the ancients' daily lives.

The reopening of Athens's **Benaki Museum** and its tremendous collection is now scheduled for the summer of 1999. In northern Greece, **Kavala's archaeological museum** will take on greater significance when it completes its new wing at the end of 1999. It will be used to exhibit prehistoric and classical finds uncovered during the last 50 years in Macedonia and Thrace. **Archaeologists** have recently discovered a wealth of **finds in northern Greece,** including a brothel and bath house in Thessaloniki's ancient agora and a laurel-wreathed head from a statue of Emperor Trajan near the ancient city of Dion at the foothills of Mount Olympus.

The EU rewarded Greek **beaches** more **Blue Flags for cleanliness** than any other member country in 1998. On the other hand, the EU declared that freshwater quality in Greece's lakes and rivers had deteriorated.

Hungary

With NATO membership imminent and an invitation into the European Union on the more distant, but likely, horizon, Hungary stands at the center of Europe more and more prominently. Nineteen ninety-nine sees the country on the cusp of the **Magyar Millennium,** the 1,000th anniversary of Hungary's founding as a state. Improvements and restoration work on important sites throughout the country will come to full fruition for the celebration in the year 2000. Highlights include the construction of a new National Theater in Budapest, as well as the inauguration of several other cultural institutions honoring Hungary's artistic wealth and history, including a high-tech multimedia center and a Hungarian literature institute.

Grand old Budapest is seeing more and more improvements and development, from private restoration of crumbling, once-elegant buildings to city-funded infrastructure projects, such as the construction of a fourth metro line through southern Buda, begun in late 1998. More pedestrian-only zones are appearing, and new restaurants and shops are sprouting around the city.

Slowly but surely, Hungary continues to **improve its infrastructure.** Over the next several years, major highways will be upgraded and extended, the airport in Budapest will undergo a major expansion, and the antiquated telephone system will be overhauled. Travelers may witness these changes taking place but should not expect to reap their full benefits for some time to come.

At press time, Hungary's annual inflation rate had decreased from more than 25% to 16%, and with continued significant devaluation of the forint, exchange rates keep improving for visitors. Yet, while Hungary remains a bargain compared to Western Europe, strictly rock-bottom prices are a thing of the past as restaurant and hotel rates creep upward to compensate for the nation's shrinking currency.

Iceland

Work fast if you plan to welcome the year 2000 under Iceland's northern lights and man-made fireworks, because few rooms remain unclaimed in Reykjavík for **New Year's Eve 1999.** The capital is one of a select handful of **European Cultural Cities for the Year 2000.** The **3rd International Viking Festival** takes place in Hafnarfjörður, just south of Reykjavík, in 1999.

Tourism is now the second-largest foreign-currency earner for Iceland after fishing, leading to diversification and improved regulations within the tourism industry, with accompanying benefits for travelers. The Edda summer hotels are moving toward year-round operation, and independent hotels have formed several chains to better compete and cater to thrifty visitors all year round. Restaurateurs are also fine-tuning their menus to include more sophisticated dishes at modest prices.

Funding has been allotted to speed **pavement completion of the Ring Road** and reduce the number of single-lane bridges on it. Also, in 1998 a tunnel opened bypassing the large fjord, Hvalfjörður, north of Reykjavík. Icelanders are still studying the balance between public access to attractions and natural preservation, doing their best to give places like the fragile, wild highlands the benefit of the doubt.

Ireland

The roar of the Celtic Tiger—Ireland's booming economy—is as loud as ever, and the expansion of Dublin continues without any sign of abating. Amid all the new cafés, restaurants, and hotels in Ireland's capital, the most important cultural attraction is the new **Collins Barracks,** which now houses the decorative arts exhibits of the National Museum, part of an ongoing expansion project. For 1999, the city has unveiled the **Arthouse,** one of the world's first multimedia centers for the arts and home to a comprehensive database of many of Ireland's up-and-coming artists. Dublin's newest swanky hotel, the Merrion, is just one of many new hostelries meeting the tourist boom. Throughout the Republic, **new hotels** are opening in and near major hubs, including Cork City and Galway City. The **Adare Manor Golf Course** is one of several new courses opened recently.

By the end of 1999 a major **upgrading Ireland's national Routes** will be complete, with a significant portion of the work being done on the infrastructure in the Cork area. By 1999 a cross-river tunnel under the River Lee will funnel through traffic heading south away from the city center. Already innovations on the Dublin-Cork highway, including the by-passing of Newbridge, Portlaoise, Cahir, and Glanmire has reduced the Dublin–Cork road journey time by a third.

Limerick has been quietly transforming its inner city by opening stretches of its hitherto hidden river frontage on the mighty Shannon. One beneficiary of this new policy is the **Hunt Museum,** whose collection of artifacts from all major European civilizations has been relocated to the Old Custom House, a splendid 18th-century riverside building. The Shannon Bridge area has been revitalized with a series of bold, new, modern developments, including Steam Boat Quay, built to resemble a berthed ocean liner, which now houses a lively collection of restaurants and shops. The final touch to **Limerick's rejuvenation** will be the opening of the South Relief Road (scheduled for mid-1999), which will allow travelers from east to west and vice versa to avoid the center of the city entirely.

In **Northern Ireland,** the IRA cease-fire has been reestablished. On Good Friday 1998 all the major parties North and South signed a **historic agreement** proposing devolved government in the form of an Assembly for Northern Ireland, an end to the South's constitutional claim to the North, a North–South Council to oversee cooperation on matters of mutual interest, and adherence to the principle that Northern Ireland would not leave the U.K. without the consent of the people of the province. The U.K. and U.S. governments subsequently promised $600 million investment to the North, and in May 1998, 71% of the electorate backed the agreement in a referendum, thus paving the way for a life out of the shadow of a gun for the first time in three decades.

Italy

During 1999 in Rome the rush to finish public works and infrastructure planned for the **Jubilee Year of 2000** is evident in road works in progress and in the number of public buildings still covered with shrouds of restoration scaffolding. Among the Vatican facilities being constructed to handle the millions of pilgrims is an entirely new entrance to the Musei Vaticani, which will be near the former one on Viale Vaticano.

Rome loses one obelisk and gains another: The **Obelisk of Axum,** a victory trophy brought from Ethiopia by Mussolini and placed near the Circo Massimo, has been returned to its own country as a gesture of reconciliation. U.S. architect Richard Meier is putting up a new obelisk as part of his refurbishing of **Piazza dell'Augusteo** and the building containing the **Ara Pacis.**

You now have to pay a small entrance fee to visit 13 of **Venice**'s most interesting churches. The long-term restoration project for **Pompeii,** Italy's most-visited site, should be underway in 1999. The lack of maintenance and information at Pompeii has long been lamented.

The **telephone dialing system** in Italy has changed. You now must dial regional area codes even for local calls. For museumgoers, the happiest news has been the **extension of opening hours** of a number of major museums throughout Italy, now open roughly from 9 AM to 10 PM on weekdays and Saturday and from 9 to 8 or so on Sunday.

Thanks to the new ***Sicilia Jet*** passenger and car ferry, run by SNAV, you can now get from Naples to Palermo in only four hours.

Luxembourg

In Luxembourg City, a new, 4-km (2½ mi) **Vauban Walk** has been laid out for military history buffs. Like the Wenzel Walk, which explores the city's ancient fortifications, it starts from the Bock. Thence it leads through the Pfaffenthal to the 18th-century Austrian fortifications known as Les Trois Glands (The Three Acorns), which the towers indeed resemble. Right behind them, construction is in progress on the **Musée Grand Duc Jean,** dedicated to contemporary art and I.M. Pei–designed, scheduled to open in 2000.

Malta

Building is going on apace on Malta's quieter sister island, **Gozo,** making it more visitor-friendly than ever.

Netherlands

The Netherlands continues to be one of the most economically and socially stable countries in Europe. Though struggling with environmental issues, **Schiphol Airport** is set to expand. The addition of a 5th runway is part of a massive plan to create a whole new hub for road, rail, and air transport, right in the middle of the Randstad. There will also be ecologically friendly **country parks,** creating a green bridge between the coastal dunes and the country's Green Heart for indigenous wildlife and migratory birds. The **docklands** in both Amsterdam and Rotterdam are undergoing extensive **redevelopment** for both industrial and residential use.

Amsterdam's central **Museumplein,** once a major artery for traffic, is being transformed into a landscaped recreation area with stunning modernistic waterscapes as a backdrop for the extensions to both the Van Gogh Museum and the Stedelijk Museum of Modern Art that are currently being built. The **Rembrandt's House** museum has also just been given a new wing, providing display space for more of the old master's works, as well as for multimedia presentations. **Exhibitions** to watch for in 1999 include 17th- and 18th-century still lifes from June to September at the Rijksmuseum in Amsterdam.

Among the year's other important cultural events are the annual, multi-disciplinary **Holland Festival** throughout June, the world-famous **Holland Festival of Early Music** in Utrecht during the last week of August, and the three-day **North Sea Jazz Festival** in The Hague on the second weekend in July.

Norway

The 1997 Norwegian **elections** brought a surprise coalition of three centrist parties to power (Christian Democrat, Center, and Liberal) after a 10-year rule by the Labor Party, which still has 65 seats in Parliament compared to the 42 held by the Centrist coalition. The government is now headed by prime minister Kjell Magne Bondevik from the Christian Democrats. Norway's **economy** is doing very well, with the lowest unemployment figures in 10 years.

Oslo's **new international airport** at Gardermoen is scheduled to open on October 8, 1998, coinciding with the closing of Fornebu. A **new high-speed airport express train** carries passengers to and from Oslo Central Station at a speed of 210 km (130 mi) per hour.

The coastal town of Elesund celebrates its 150th anniversary with the opening of the **Atlantic Park,** a new indoor-outdoor aquarium with undersea life from the region, including sharks and seals. Another new attraction is the **Museum of Reconstruction** in Hammerfest, scheduled to open in July 1998 with exhibits on the forced evacuation, the devastation, and reconstruction of northern Norway during and after the Second World War. The **Norwegian Olympic Museum** is now open in Lillehammer with exhibits on the history of the Olympics.

Poland

More new hotels are opening and older ones are being refurbished. Prices, however, are rising quickly, particularly for visitor facilities at the upper end of the market. New Western-style restaurants, stores, and cafés have made traveling in Poland much easier and pleasanter, but key highway upgrades have progressed slowly. Poland's next major international goal is membership in the EU.

Portugal

Portugal's program to digitalize its **phone network** continues, with only about 2% of the country's phone numbers still to be changed. Not all recordings stating the new number are in English, so you may need the assistance of an international operator.

Although many new downtown stations of Lisbon's expanded **metro** (subway) system are open, additional stations will continue to open through the year 2000. The opening of a second bridge, the **Ponte Vasco de Gama,** has eased traffic congestion in and around the capital.

Development in Lisbon's **Chiado shopping district** continues, as the historic facades—destroyed in the 1988 fire—are slowly restored. At **Expo Urbe,** the capital's riverfront development site, Vasco da Gama Shopping, a huge shopping center with a multiscreen cinema, is due to open in April 1999. In addition, the Feri Internactional de Lisboa (FIL), or trade fair offices, move from Alcantara to Expo Urbe in 1999. **New hotels** are springing up throughout Lisbon. In addition to the Asia and the Oriente at Expo Urbe, and the new hotels in the Chiado, the Dom Pedro Lisboa, near Amoreiras, is also set for completion by 2000. In the Parque Eduardo VII, a **public swimming pool** is planned for alongside the new tennis courts.

Out along the **Estoril coast,** renovations and landscaping to the seawall and promenade should come to fruition during 1999. In a joint program with the EU, the **Algarve** region is currently replacing its many (and often confusing) road signs with clear, color-coded, easy-to-read signposts.

Romania

Following the election of Romania's first democratic government in November 1996, the country has slowly begun to move away from the era of the Ceauşescu dictatorship. The strict guidelines for its coveted admission to NATO and the EU have helped Romania to look realistically at what is necessary to rebuild the nation. The number of private establishments is increasing steadily. The government has agreed to discourage the country's long-standing policy of charging foreigners higher rates than Romanians. An increase in competition among travel agencies has helped to strengthen efforts to attract visitors.

Slovakia

A fast privatization process has been followed by numerous renovations of buildings of any historical value throughout the country. Since its 1993 separation from the Czechs, Slovakia has seen an increasing number of small, private pensions, restaurants, shops, and other facilities spring up not only in Bratislava and the High Tatras but also close to the country's numerous rivers, lakes, caves, spas, castles, and other scenic treasures, as unbound market forces awaken its citizens to seek self-determination.

Spain

The gleaming **Guggenheim Museum Bilbao,** designed by American architect Frank Gehry, has transformed Bilbao, capital of the Basque country, from an industrial blot to a Place to Be. This titanium landmark of modern art houses cubist, expressionist, surrealist, and geometrical and abstract expressionist works. In Catalonia the Spanish Ministry of Tourism is now operating a **Dali triangle,** which includes not only the Museu Dalí, in Figueres, but the artist's fishing shack in Port Lligat, near Cadaqués, and his castle in Pubol. Starting from Barcelona, the triangular tour of Dali's personal world covers roughly 140 miles and crosses some of the most beautiful countryside in Catalonia.

A timeless Madrid landmark has been revived after nearly a decade of disuse. Closed intermittently for almost 70 years due to successive disasters, such as fire and faulty engineering, the capital's **Teatro Real** underwent a massive refurbishment to open grandly in October 1997. Now replete with golden balconies, plush seats, and state-of-the-art stage equipment for operas and ballets, the theater is a modern concert hall with its vintage appeal intact.

Thanks to the **new network of four-lane highways** connecting the provincial capitals of Andalusia, driving **in southern Spain** is faster and safer. The new **AVE trains** speed from Madrid to Seville in 2½ hours and to Málaga in less than 4.

Sweden

The new **airport high-speed express train** starts operation between Stockholm and Arlanda Airport in 1999 at speeds of 160–200 km/h (100–125 mph), making the trip in only 20 minutes. It is scheduled to run 5 to 6 times per hour. Beginning in 1998, authorized guides will be available for English-language tours of the **Stockholm archipelago** through the Stockholm Information Service. In **Karlskrona,** a new **marine museum** opened in 1997.

Switzerland

Despite the departure of Fredy Girardet from the pantheon of European chefs, the Lac Léman (Lake Geneva) region has retained its status as the country's gastronomic center. **Philippe Rochat,** Girardet's protegé, and Gérard Rabaey lead the pack, with Bernard Ravet in Vufflens-le-Château close on their heels. Horst Petermann in Zürich, Roland Pierroz in Verbier, Roland Jöhri in Saint-Moritz and Georges Wenger in Le Noirmont still vie for the top of the national heap. One of the best chefs of recent years, however, is sadly gone; Basel-based Hans Stucki died in the winter of 1998.

One of the heights of the Swiss traditional festival calendar is the **Fête des Vignerons** (Winegrowers' Festival), from late July through early August of 1999. Based in Vevey, in the Vaud canton, the festival is held roughly every 25 years. Pageants and parades engulf the town—and on opening day there's a coronation for prize-winning wine growers followed by a tremendous banquet.

The **Vereina Tunnel,** stretching from Klosters to Susch/Lavin, is slated for completion in late fall 1999, smoothing the way for skiers headed for such Graubünden resorts as Saint-Moritz and Klosters. The railway will load cars and whisk away twice an hour from each terminal—an especially big blessing when the Flüela Pass is closed by snow.

Partly as a result of an intimidatingly strong **Swiss franc,** tourism hit a near-record low in 1997, with hotel and restaurant occupation diving to 1960s levels. Sadly, this resulted in more charming, little family-owned hotels knuckling under, unable to compete with international chains. However, in 1998 a dip in the Swiss franc's clout eased the pain for American visitors and tourism began to pick up again.

Turkey

Turkey's age-old search for identity took a new twist in early 1998 when the **pro-Islamic Welfare Party,** the largest party in parliament, was banned by the Turkish courts under pressure from the country's pro-Western establisment. The party had enjoyed considerable support among Turkey's poor. At press time the long-term impact of the banning of the party was still unclear.

The long-running struggle between Islamists and secularists for the soul of Turkey has left little time to tackle the country's **chronic inflation.** By early 1998 annual inflation in Turkey stood at over 100%, but in dollar terms it nevertheless remained one of the least expensive countries in Europe.

Turkey's increasing popularity as a tourist attraction has imposed a severe strain on its infrastructure, but many **new airports** are in the works. In early 1998, construction began on an additional terminal at Istanbul's Atatürk Airport and the foundations were laid for the city's second airport at Kürtköy on the Asian side of the city. In the Mediterranean resort of Antalya, a new international terminal with an annual capacity of 5 million tourists was expected to open in mid-1998. In late 1998 or early 1999 new airports were due to be completed in Cappadocia and the Black Sea town of Ordu.

As the millennium approaches, the Turkish Tourism Ministry has launched a major campaign for **"faith tourism,"** promoting visits to ancient Christian sites in Anatolia.

Europe

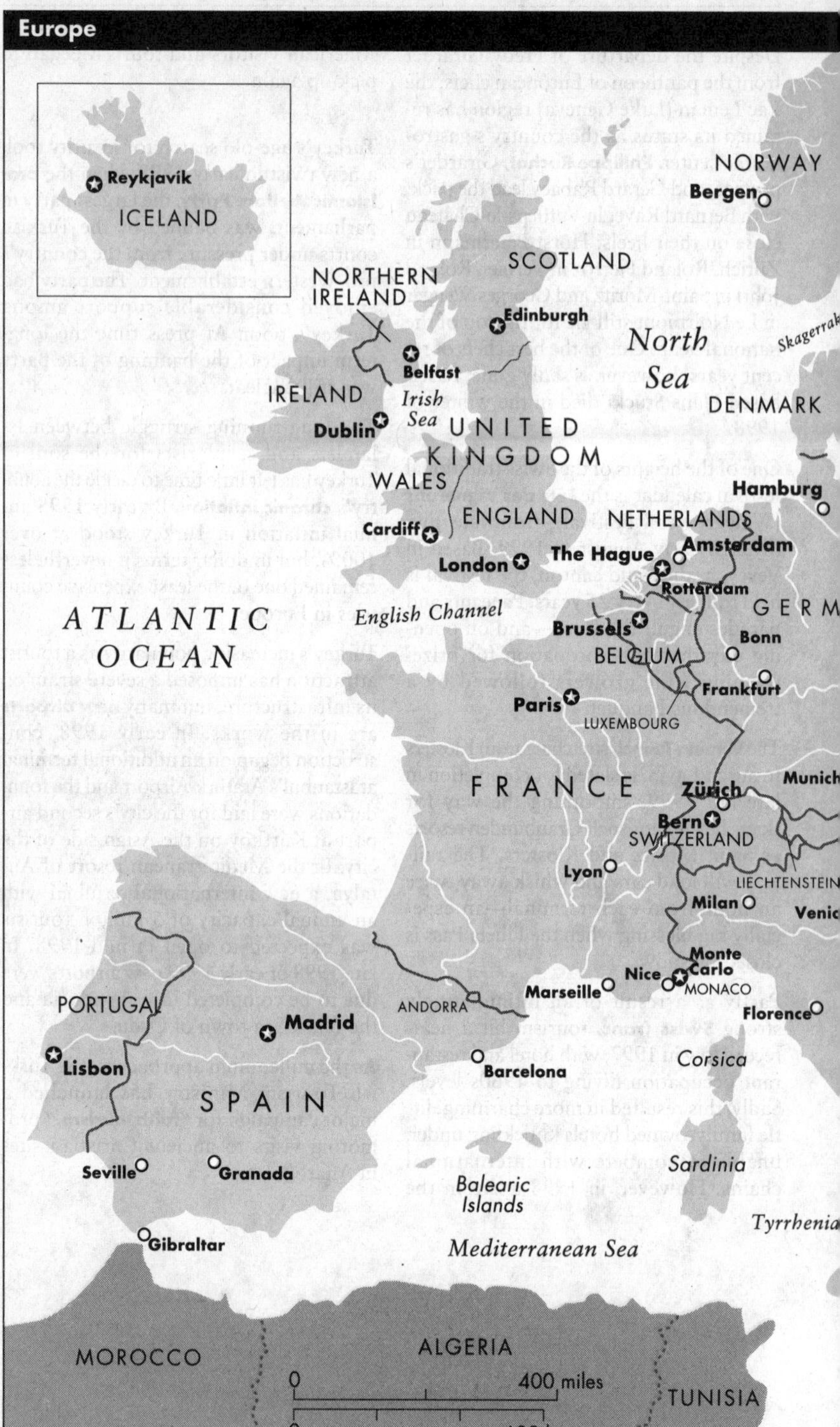
Reykjavík
ICELAND
NORWAY
Bergen
SCOTLAND
NORTHERN IRELAND
Edinburgh
North Sea
Skagerrak
Belfast
IRELAND
Irish Sea
DENMARK
Dublin
UNITED KINGDOM
WALES
Hamburg
ENGLAND
NETHERLANDS
Cardiff
Amsterdam
The Hague
London
Rotterdam
ATLANTIC OCEAN
English Channel
GERM
Brussels
Bonn
BELGIUM
Frankfurt
Paris
LUXEMBOURG
FRANCE
Zürich
Munich
Bern
SWITZERLAND
Lyon
LIECHTENSTEIN
Milan
Venic
Monte Carlo
Nice
MONACO
Marseille
ANDORRA
Florence
PORTUGAL
Madrid
Lisbon
Barcelona
Corsica
SPAIN
Sardinia
Seville
Granada
Balearic Islands
Tyrrhenia
Gibraltar
Mediterranean Sea
MOROCCO
ALGERIA
0
400 miles
TUNISIA
0
600 km

FINLAND
Gulf of Bothnia
Oslo
SWEDEN
Helsinki
Gulf of Finland
St. Petersburg
Tallinn
Stockholm
ESTONIA
Göteborg
Kattegat
Riga
LATVIA
Moscow
Copenhagen
LITHUANIA
Kaunas
Baltic Sea
RUSSIA
Vilnius
RUSSIA
Kaliningrad
Minsk
Berlin
POLAND
BELARUS
Warsaw
Kraków
Kiev
Prague
CZECH REPUBLIC
UKRAINE
SLOVAKIA
Vienna
Bratislava
Salzburg
MOLDOVA
Budapest
AUSTRIA
Chişinău
HUNGARY
SLOVENIA
Ljubljana
Zagreb
ROMANIA
CROATIA
Novi Sad
Bucharest
BOSNIA AND HERZEGOVINA
Belgrade
SERBIA
Black Sea
Adriatic Sea
Sarajevo
YUGOSLAVIA
KOSOVO
BULGARIA
MONTENEGRO
Rome
Priština
Sofia
Podgorica
Skopje
Istanbul
ITALY
MACEDONIA
Tiranë
Ankara
Naples
ALBANIA
TURKEY
GREECE
Aegean Sea
Ionian Sea
Athens
Sicily
CYPRUS
MALTA
Crete
Mediterranean Sea

World Time Zones

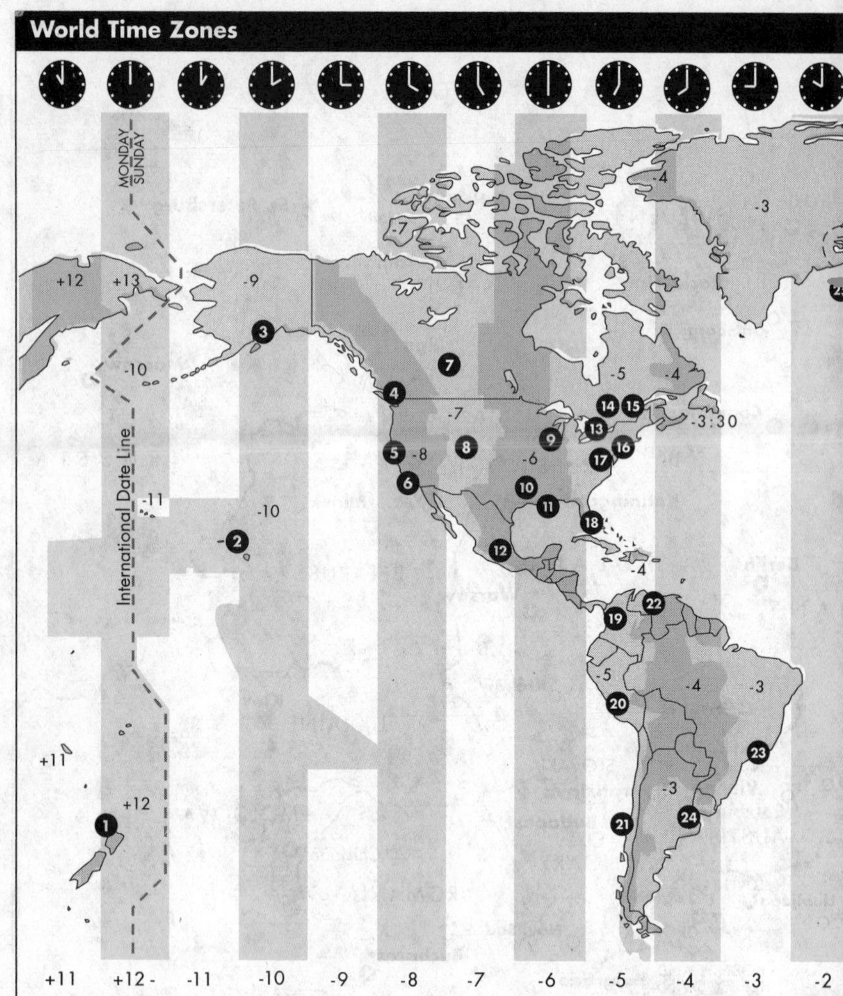

Numbers below vertical bands relate each zone to Greenwich Mean Time (0 hrs.). Local times frequently differ from these general indications, as indicated by light-face numbers on map.

Algiers, **29**
Anchorage, **3**
Athens, **41**
Auckland, **1**
Baghdad, **46**
Bangkok, **50**
Beijing, **54**
Berlin, **34**
Bogotá, **19**
Budapest, **37**
Buenos Aires, **24**
Caracas, **22**
Chicago, **9**
Copenhagen, **33**
Dallas, **10**
Delhi, **48**
Denver, **8**
Djakarta, **53**
Dublin, **26**
Edmonton, **7**
Hong Kong, **56**
Honolulu, **2**
Istanbul, **40**
Jerusalem, **42**
Johannesburg, **44**
Lima, **20**
Lisbon, **28**
London (Greenwich), **27**
Los Angeles, **6**
Madrid, **38**
Manila, **57**

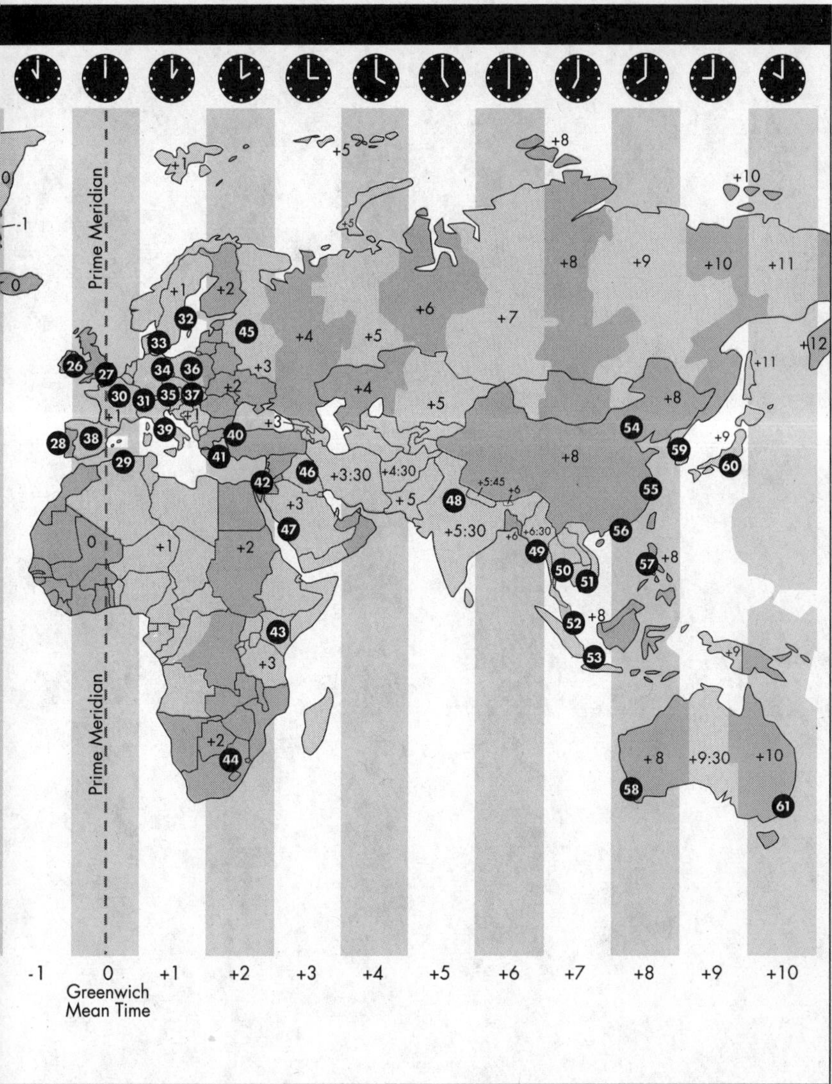

Mecca, **47**
Mexico City, **12**
Miami, **18**
Montréal, **15**
Moscow, **45**
Nairobi, **43**
New Orleans, **11**
New York City, **16**
Ottawa, **14**
Paris, **30**
Perth, **58**
Reykjavík, **25**
Rio de Janeiro, **23**
Rome, **39**
Saigon (Ho Chi Minh City), **51**
San Francisco, **5**
Santiago, **21**
Seoul, **59**
Shanghai, **55**
Singapore, **52**
Stockholm, **32**
Sydney, **61**
Tokyo, **60**
Toronto, **13**
Vancouver, **4**
Vienna, **35**
Warsaw, **36**
Washington, D.C., **17**
Yangon, **49**
Zürich, **31**

1 The Gold Guide

SMART TRAVEL TIPS A TO Z

Basic Information on Traveling in Europe, Savvy Tips to Make Your Trip a Breeze, and Companies and Organizations to Contact

AIR TRAVEL

BOOKING YOUR FLIGHT

Price is just one factor to consider when booking a flight: frequency of service and even a carrier's safety record are often just as important. Major airlines offer the greatest number of departures. Smaller airlines—including regional and no-frills airlines—usually have a limited number of flights daily. On the other hand, so-called low-cost airlines usually are cheaper, and their fares impose fewer restrictions, such as advance-purchase requirements. Safety-wise, low-cost carriers as a group have a good history—about equal to that of major carriers.

When you book, **look for nonstop flights** and **remember that "direct" flights stop at least once.** Try to **avoid connecting flights,** which require a change of plane. Two airlines may jointly operate a connecting flight, so ask if your airline operates every segment—you may find that your preferred carrier flies you only part of the way. International flights on a country's flag carrier are usually nonstop; U.S. airlines often fly direct.

Ask your airline if it offers electronic ticketing, which eliminates all paperwork. There's no ticket to pick up or misplace. You go directly to the gate and give the agent your confirmation number.

CARRIERS

When flying internationally, you must usually choose between a domestic carrier, the national flag carrier of the country you are visiting, and a foreign carrier from a third country. National flag carriers have the greatest number of nonstops. Domestic carriers may have better connections to your home town and serve a greater number of gateway cities. Third-party carriers may have a price advantage.

➤ U.S. AIRLINES: **American** (☎ 800/433–7300). **Continental** (☎ 800/525–0280). **Delta** (☎ 800/221–1212). **Northwest** (☎ 800/225–2525). **TWA** (☎ 800/221–2000). **United** (☎ 800/241–6522). **US Airways** (☎ 800/428–4322).

➤ EUROPEAN AIRLINES: Austria: **Austrian Airlines** (☎ 800/843–0002). Belgium: **Sabena Belgian World Airlines** (☎ 800/955–2000). The Czech Republic and Slovakia: **Czech Airlines** (CSA, ☎ 212/765–6022 or 800/223–2365). Denmark: **Scandinavian Airlines** (SAS, ☎ 800/221–2350). Finland: **Finnair** (☎ 800/950–5000). France: **Air France** (☎ 800/237–2747). Germany: **Lufthansa** (☎ 800/645–3880). Great Britain: **British Airways** (☎ 800/247–9297). **Virgin Atlantic** (☎ 800/862–8621). Greece: **Olympic Airways** (☎ 212/838–3600 or 800/223–1226). Hungary: **Malév Hungarian Airlines** (☎ 212/757–6446). Iceland: **Icelandair** (☎ 800/223–5500). Ireland: **Aer Lingus** (☎ 888/474–7424 or 800/223–6537). Italy: **Alitalia** (☎ 800/223–5730). Netherlands: **KLM Royal Dutch Airlines** (☎ 800/374–7747). Norway: **SAS** (☎ 800/221–2350). Poland: **LOT Polish Airlines** (☎ 212/869–1074). Portugal: **TAP Air Portugal** (☎ 800/221–7370). Romania: **Tarom Romanian Air Transport** (☎ 212/687–6013). Spain: **Iberia Airlines** (☎ 800/772–4642). Sweden: **SAS** (☎ 800/221–2350). Switzerland: **Swissair** (☎ 800/221–4750). Turkey: **THY Turkish Airlines** (☎ 212/339–9650).

➤ FROM CANADA: **Air Canada** (☎ 800/776–3000). **Air Transat** (☎ 905/678–1011).

➤ FROM THE U.K.: **British Airways** (✉ 156 Regent St., London W1R 5TA, ☎ 0345/222–111). **British Midland** (☎ 0181/745–7321 or 0345/554–554). **Air UK** (☎ 0345/666–777). **Debonair** (☎ 0541/500–

300. **Ryanair** (☎ 0541/569–569). **EasyJet** (☎ 0990/29–29–29 or 01582/44–55–55). **Virgin Express** (☎ 0800/89–11–99).

➤ FROM AUSTRALIA: **Qantas Airways** (☎ 13–12–11).

➤ FROM IRELAND: **Aer Lingus** (☎ 01/705–3333).

➤ FROM NEW ZEALAND: **Air New Zealand** (☎ 0800–737–000).

CHARTERS

Charters usually have the lowest fares but are the least dependable. Departures are infrequent and seldom on time, flights can be delayed for up to 48 hours or can be canceled for any reason up to 10 days before you're scheduled to leave. Itineraries and prices can change after you've booked.

In the U.S., the Department of Transportation's Aviation Consumer Protection Division has jurisdiction over charters and provides a certain degree of protection. The DOT requires that money paid to charter operators be held in escrow, so if you can't pay with a credit card, **always make your check payable to a charter carrier's escrow account.** The name of the bank should be in the charter contract. If you have any problems with a charter operator, contact the DOT (☞ Airline Complaints, *below*). If you buy a charter package that includes both air and land arrangements, remember that the escrow requirement applies only to the air component.

➤ CHARTER CARRIERS: **Tower Air** (☎ 800/34 TOWER).

CONSOLIDATORS

Consolidators buy tickets for scheduled international flights at reduced rates from the airlines, then sell them at prices that beat the best fare available directly from the airlines, usually without restrictions. Sometimes you can even get your money back if you need to return the ticket. Carefully read the fine print detailing penalties for changes and cancellations, and **confirm your consolidator reservation with the airline.**

➤ CONSOLIDATORS: **Cheap Tickets** (☎ 800/377–1000). **Up & Away Travel** (☎ 212/889–2345). **Discount Travel Network** (☎ 800/576–1600). **Unitravel** (☎ 800/325–2222). **World Travel Network** (☎ 800/409–6753).

COURIERS

When you fly as a courier, you trade your checked-luggage space for a ticket deeply subsidized by a courier service. It's all perfectly legitimate, but there are restrictions: You can usually book your flight only a week or two in advance, your length of stay may be set for a certain number of days, and you probably won't be able to book a companion on the same flight. Many courier associations also require a small membership fee.

Air Courier Association (✉ 15000 W. 6th Ave., Suite 203, Golden, CO 80401, ☎ 800/282–1202, www.aircourier.org).

International Association of Air Travel Couriers (✉ 220 South Dixie Highway #3, P.O. Box 1349, Lake Worth, FL, 33460, ☎ 561/582–8320, FAX 561/582–1581, www.courier.org).

Now Voyager Travel (✉ 74 Varick St., Suite 307, New York, NY 10013, ☎ 212/431–1616, FAX 212/219–1753 or 212/334–5243, www.nowvoyagertravel.com).

CUTTING COSTS

The least-expensive airfares to Europe are priced for round-trip travel and usually must be purchased in advance. It's smart to **call a number of airlines, and when you are quoted a good price, book it on the spot**—the same fare may not be available the next day. Airlines generally allow you to change your return date for a fee. If you don't use your ticket, you can apply the cost toward the purchase of a new ticket, again for a small charge. However, most low-fare tickets are nonrefundable. To get the lowest airfare, **check different routings.** Compare prices of flights to and from different airports if your destination or home city has more than one gateway. Also price off-peak flights, which may be significantly less expensive.

Travel agents, especially those who specialize in finding the lowest fares (☞ Discounts & Deals, *below*), can be especially helpful for booking a plane ticket. When you're quoted a price, **ask your agent if the price is likely to get any lower.** A wait-and-see strategy works best if your plans are flexible. If you must arrive and depart on certain dates, don't delay.

CHECK IN & BOARDING

Airlines routinely overbook planes, assuming that not everyone with a ticket will show up, but sometimes everyone does. When that happens, airlines ask for volunteers to give up their seats. In return these volunteers usually get a certificate for a free flight and are rebooked on the next flight out. If there are not enough volunteers, the airline must choose who will be denied boarding. The first to get bumped are passengers who checked in late and those flying on discounted tickets, so **get to the gate and check in as early as possible,** especially during peak periods.

Although the trend on international flights is to drop reconfirmation requirements, many airlines still ask you to reconfirm each leg of your international itinerary. Failure to do so may result in your reservation being canceled.

Always **bring a government-issued photo ID to the airport.** You may be asked to show it before you are allowed to check in.

For scheduled international flights, **arrive in time to check in one hour before departure**; for charter flights, allow two hours. If you just have hand luggage, you may be able to check in as late as 30 minutes before takeoff. If you're traveling Business Class, **ask about special deals,** such as check-in at designated hotels, or telephone check-in.

ENJOYING THE FLIGHT

For better service, **fly smaller or regional carriers,** which often have higher passenger-satisfaction ratings. Sometimes you'll find leather seats, more legroom, and better food.

For more legroom, **request an emergency-aisle seat.** Don't sit in the row in front of the emergency aisle or in front of a bulkhead, where seats may not recline.

If you don't like airline food, **ask for special meals when booking.** These can be vegetarian, low-cholesterol, or kosher, for example.

When flying internationally, try to maintain a normal routine, to help fight jet-lag. At night, **get some sleep.** By day, **eat light meals, drink water (not alcohol), and move around the cabin** to stretch your legs.

Many carriers have prohibited smoking on all of their international flights; others allow smoking only on certain routes or certain departures, so **contact your carrier regarding its smoking policy.**

HOW TO COMPLAIN

If your baggage goes astray or your flight goes awry, complain right away. Most carriers require that you **file a claim immediately.**

➤ AIRLINE COMPLAINTS: U.S. Department of Transportation **Aviation Consumer Protection Division** (✉ C-75, Room 4107, Washington, DC 20590, ☎ 202/366–2220). **Federal Aviation Administration Consumer Hotline** (☎ 800/322–7873).

AROUND EUROPE

Before booking, **compare different modes of transportation.** Many city pairs are so close together that flying hardly makes sense. For instance, it may take just half an hour to fly between London and Paris, but you must factor in time spent getting to and from the airports, plus check-in time. A 3-hour train ride from city center to city center seems a better alternative. It makes sense to **save air travel for longer distances**—say, between London and Rome, Paris and Vienna, Brussels and Stockholm—and do your local traveling from these hubs.

If you're flying so-called **national carriers,** full-fare tickets often remain the only kind available for one-way trips and restriction-free round-trips, and they are prohibitively expensive for most leisure travelers. On most European flights, your choice is between Business Class (which is what you get when paying full fare) and Economy (coach). Some flights are all Economy. First Class has ceased to exist in Europe. The most reasonable fares have long been non-refundable and non-transferable round trips (APEX fares), which require a Saturday night at the destination. But the near-monopoly that used to be enjoyed by these airlines is crumbling, and they have had to start offering less restrictive fares. Check before you fly.

Some national carriers reward transatlantic passengers with fixed-price flight coupons (priced at $100–$120) to destinations from their respective hubs and/or domestic or area air passes. These must be bought before leaving home. If you're young, **ask about youth stand-by fares,** which are available on a number of domestic and some international services.

Over the last few years, a substantial number of local airlines have been created to provide feeder services to major hubs and services between secondary city pairs. Do not, however, expect rock–bottom prices. **Seek advice from local branches of international travel agencies** like American Express or Carlson/Wagonlit.

Low-cost no-frills airlines base their fares on one-way travel, and a return ticket is simply twice the price. Advertised fares are always preceded by the word "from." To get the lowest fare, book two weeks ahead of time; it also helps to be flexible about your date of travel. In general, you have to book directly by calling the airline, credit card in hand. Some also accept reservations by fax. Reservation via Internet was not available at press time (spring 1998) but may well be possible within a year. You get a reservation number and pick up your boarding pass at the airport. Note that some flights use relatively distant secondary airports.

➤ NO-FRILLS CARRIER RESERVATIONS WITHIN EUROPE: Belgium: **Virgin Express** (☎ 32/2/752–0505) from Brussels to Milan, Rome, Nice, Madrid, Barcelona, Copenhagen, and London; from Rome to Barcelona and Madrid; and all Sabena flights to London, Barcelona and Rome. Ireland: **Ryanair** (☎ 01/844–4400 in Ireland; ☎ 0541/569–569, FAX 0541/580–588 in the U.K.) from Dublin to 12 U.K. destinations, to Paris (Beauvais) and Brussels (Charleroi); from London (Stansted, Luton, and Gatwick) to Dublin; from London (Stansted) to Stockholm (Skavsta) and Oslo (Torp). United Kingdm: **Debonair** (☎ 0541/500–300) from London (Luton) to Düsseldorf (Mönchengladbach), Barcelona, Copenhagen, Madrid, Munich, Nice, Milan (Bergamo), and Rome (Ciampino); from Munich to Copenhagen, Düsseldorf, Nice, Madrid, and Rome; from Barcelona to Madrid and Rome; and from northern Italian cities to Calabria. **EasyJet** (☎ 01582/700–059) from London (Luton) to Amsterdam, Barcelona, Nice, Palma de Mallorca and four Scottish destinations; from Liverpool to Amsterdam and Nice. **Go** (☎ 08456/054–321) from London (Stansted) to Rome, Milan, and Copenhagen.

AIRPORTS

ARRIVALS

Passport control has become a perfunctory affair within most of the European Union (EU). The nine signatories to the Schengen Agreement (Austria, Belgium, France, Germany, Italy, Luxembourg, The Netherlands, Portugal and Spain) have abolished passport controls for travelers within that area, but individual countries can temporarily suspend it.

The most notable exception is Great Britain, which has no intention of waiving its border controls. When a number of flights from the U.S. arrive at Heathrow or Gatwick close together in the morning, **be prepared for a longish wait** (though rarely as long as Europeans have to wait at JFK in New York).

The Green Channel/Red Channel customs system in operation at most Western European airports and other borders is basically an honor system. If you have nothing to declare, walk through the Green Channel, where there are only spot luggage checks; if in doubt, go through the Red Channel. If you fly between two EU-member countries, go through the new **Blue Channel,** where there are no customs officers except the one who glances at baggage labels to make sure only people off EU flights get through. On average, you need to **count on at least half an hour from deplaning to getting out of the airport.**

DUTY-FREE SHOPPING

If you're looking for good deals associated with duty-free airport shopping, **check out liquor and beauty products,** although prices vary considerably. The amount of liquor you may buy is restricted, generally to two bottles. Duty-free sales will cease within the EU on June 30, 1999, but will continue to be allowed for non-EU destinations.

Some airport concourses, notably in Amsterdam, Copenhagen, and Shannon, have practically been transformed into shopping malls, selling everything from electronics and chocolates to fashion and furs. These are tax-free rather than duty-free shops; if this is your last stop before leaving the EU there's no VAT and you can **avoid the tax-refund rigamarole.**

TRANSFERS

Some European airports (such as Paris Charles de Gaulle, Frankfurt, Amsterdam, Brussels, Geneva, and Zurich) have long been served by fast trains to the city center. The good news is that similar rapid transit systems are being completed at Copenhagen, Milan Malpensa, London Heathrow, Oslo Gardemoen, and Stockholm Arlanda, saving both time and money.

In a number of airports, unlicensed "taxi drivers" may accost you in the arrival hall; avoid them like the plague and make sure you **only get into taxicabs clearly designated as such.** Airports (like train and subway stations) are happy hunting grounds for pickpockets. Do not leave your baggage unguarded, hold your pocket book securely, and **do not let strangers distract you** so that another gang member can do the work; this is a favorite ploy.

➤ AIRPORT GUIDE: **Salk's Airport Transit Guide** (Magellan's, ☎ 800/962–4943) gives money-saving tips on transit links at 421 airports.

BIKE TRAVEL

Some ferry lines transport bicycles free, but others charge a nominal fee, so **shop around.** You can also transport your bicycle by air as checked baggage (☞ Bikes in Flight, *below*). Most European rail lines will transport bicycles free of charge or for a nominal fee, but **book ahead** with the main booking office.

Local and regional tourist information offices will have information about renting bicycles, camping sites, cycling tracks, and local bike tours. (For bike tours of Europe, ☞ Tour Operators, *below*).

BIKES IN FLIGHT

Most airlines will accommodate bikes as luggage, provided they are dismantled and put into a box. Call to see if your airline sells bike boxes (about $5; bike bags are at least $100) although you can often pick them up free at bike shops. International travelers can sometimes substitute a bike for a piece of checked luggage for free; otherwise, it will cost about $100. Domestic and Canadian airlines charge a $25–$50 fee.

BOAT & FERRY TRAVEL

Ferry routes for passengers and vehicles link the countries surrounding the North Sea, the Irish Sea, and the Baltic; Italy with Greece; and Spain, France, Italy, and Greece with their respective islands in the Mediterranean. Longer ferry routes—between, for instance, Britain and Spain or Scandinavia—can help you **reduce the amount of driving and often save time.** A number of modern ships offer improved comfort and entertainment ranging from one-armed bandits to gourmet dining and from swimming pools to magicians to keep the kids happy.

Ferry companies have responded differently to the challenge of the Channel Tunnel, which now has the largest market share. Hoverspeed, for instance, has taken over the Catamaran service run by Holyman Sally and invested in faster vessels. Stena Line and P&O have at long last received permission to merge their "short–sea" ferry operations (Dover–Calais and Newhaven–Dieppe) into a joint venture called P&O Stena Line. They will also reduce capacity, so the days of great bargains may come to an end.

➤ FERRY LINES: Ferry operators between the British Isles and the Continent include: **Brittany Ferries** (✉ Millbay Docks, Plymouth PL1 3EW, ☎ 0990/360–360) from Plymouth to Roscoff (Brittany) and Santander (Spain), from Poole to Cherbourg, and from Portsmouth to Caen and St. Malo; **Colour Line** (✉ International Ferry Terminal, Royal Quays, North Shields NE29 6EE, ☎ 01912/961313), from Newcastle to Bergen/Stavanger/Haugesund (Norway); **Hoverspeed Holyman** (✉ International Hoverport, Marine Parade, Dover, Kent CT17 9TG, ☎ 01304/240241), Dover–Calais, Dover–Oostend, Folkestone–Boulogne, and Liverpool–Dublin; **Irish Ferries** (✉ Reliance House, Water St., Liverpool L2 8TP, ☎ 0990/171–717), Holyhead–Dublin and Pembroke–Rosslare; also Rosslare (Ireland; reservations ☎ 01/661–0511) to Cherbourg, and Roscoff; **P&O European Ferries** (✉ Channel House, Channel View Rd., Dover, Kent CT17 9TJ, ☎ 0990/980–980), Portsmouth to Le Havre and Bilbao (Spain), and Cairnyarn (Scotland)–Larne (Belfast); **P&O North Sea Ferries** (✉ King George Dock, Hedon Rd., Hull HU9 5QA, ☎ 01482/377–177), from Hull to Zeebrugge (Belgium) and Rotterdam; P&O Stena Line (same address as P&O European Ferries), Dover–Calais, Newhaven–Dieppe and (trucks only) Dover–Zeebrugge (Belgium); **Scandinavian Seaways** (✉ Scandinavia House, Parkeston Quay, Harwich, Essex CO12 4QG, ☎ 01255/240240), from Harwich to Esbjerg (Denmark), Hamburg, and Gothenburg and from Newcastle to Amsterdam and (summer season) Gothenburg and Hamburg; **SeaFrance** (✉ Eastern Docks, Dover, Kent CT16 1JA, ☎ 01304/212–696), Dover–Calais; **Stena Line** (✉ Charter House, Park St., Ashford, Kent TN24 8EX, ☎ 0990/707–070), Harwich–Hoek of Holland, Holyhead–Dun Laoghaire (Dublin), Fishguard–Rosslare, and Stranraer (Scotland)–Belfast; and **Swansea Cork Ferries** (✉ Kings Dock, Swansea SA1 8RU, ☎ 01792/456116), Swansea–Cork (March–Jan.).

BUS TRAVEL

International bus travel is rapidly expanding in Europe, thanks to changing EU rules and the Channel Tunnel, but it still has some way to go before it achieves the status of a natural choice, except in Britain and Sweden. In other northern European countries, bus services exist mostly to supplement railroads. Some bus routes between northern Europe and the Mediterranean area cater mostly to low-income immigrants visiting their home countries.

Within several southern European countries—including Portugal, Greece, parts of Spain, and Turkey—the bus has supplanted the train as the main means of public transportation, and is often quicker and more comfortable, with more frequent service, than the antiquated national rolling stock. Be prepared to discover that the bus is more expensive. Competition among lines is keen, so **ask about air-conditioning and reclining seats before you book.**

National or regional tourist offices have information about bus services. For reservations on major lines before you go, **contact your travel agent at home.**

BUS LINES

Eurolines comprises 30 motor-coach operators of international scheduled services. They also transport passengers within each country. The 30-nation network serves 1500 cities with services ranging from twice-weekly to five times daily. Eurolines has its own coach stations in Paris (✉ 28 av. du Général de Gaulle at Bagnelot; Métro: Gallieni), Brussels (✉ 80 rue du Progrès, next to the Gare du Nord), and Amsterdam (✉ adjacent to the Amstel Railway Station). In other cities, coaches depart from railway stations or municipal bus terminals.

From the U.K., Eurolines links London with 400 destinations on the European Continent and Ireland, from Stockholm to Rome, from Dublin to Bucharest. All are via Calais, using either ferry services or Le Shuttle under the English Channel. Buses leave from Victoria Coach Station (adjoining the railway station). Services link up with the National Express network covering the U.K.

Eurobus operates "hop-on, hop-off" service on three different but interlinking one-way circuits in northern, central and southern Europe. Passes are valid for one to" four months from the first day of travel. Eurobus caters to a young market segment, but passengers older than 38 are accepted if they sign a waiver application stating that they know what they're in for. Pick-up points tend to be hostels on the outskirts of cities. Accommodations are not included, but on-board guides will help passengers with reservations if needed. There's a separately priced London/Paris link. Messages can be left with the reservations center and delivered next time the traveler hops on a bus.

Busabout is a new service that operates along similar principles, with a few wrinkles. Passes are not time limited and can be used throughout the April to October season. Starting from Paris, Zone 1 takes in Copenhagen and central Europe, Zone 2 extends south to Italy and Zone 3 to Spain. There are also links to London and Athens.

The same company offers **Bedabout**, providing accommodation in tent cities in 10 key locations at peak season when other low-budget accommodations tend to be fully booked; 10 nights cost $125.

➤ BUSABOUT: **Busabout (UK) Ltd.** (✉ 26/28 Paradise Road, Richmond, Surrey TW9 1SE, ☎ 0181/332–2900, FAX 0181/784–2824). Passes can be purchased at **Council Travel** (☞ *under* Students, *below*) and **STA Travel** (☞ *under* Students, *below*) offices in the U.S.

➤ EUROBUS: **Reservations center** (✉ Box 3026, Wokingham, Berkshire RG40 2YP, ☎ 800/387–6287 in the U.S., 0118/936–2320 in the U.K., FAX 0118/936–2322). Eurobus Passes can be obtained from **Council Travel** (☞ Students, *below*) and from **STA Travel** (☞ Students, *below*). In the U.K., they're available from any STA or campus travel agency.

➤ EUROLINES: **Eurolines** (✉ 52 Grosvenor Gardens, London SW1 OAU, ☎ 0990/143–219 or 0171/730–8235. Eurolines (UK) (✉ 4 Cardiff Rd., Luton LU1 1HX, ☎ 01582/404–511, FAX 01582/400–694). For **brochures and timetables,** contact the **Eurolines Pass Organization** (✉ Keizersgracht 317, 1016 EE Amsterdam, Netherlands, ☎ 020/625–3010, FAX 020/420–6904).

DISCOUNT PASSES

The **Eurolines Pass** allows unlimited travel between 40 European cities on scheduled bus services. A 30-day pass costs $339 ($299 for those under 26 or over 60); a 60-day pass costs $409 ($369). Passes can be bought from Eurolines offices and travel agents in Europe and from the companies listed below.

➤ AGENCIES: In the U.S.: **Eurolines Passes** can be purchased from **Rebel Tours** (✉ 2405 Kearney Ave., Valencia, CA 91355, ☎ 805/294–0944, FAX 805/294–0981), **DER Travel Services** (✉ 9501 W. Devon Ave., Rosemont, IL 60018, ☎ 800/782–2424 for reservations, 847/692–4141, FAX 888/712–5727), and from most Hosteling International and all STA offices (☞ Students, *below*).

CAMERAS & COMPUTERS

EQUIPMENT PRECAUTIONS

Always **keep your film, tape, or computer disks out of the sun.** Carry an extra supply of batteries, and **be prepared to turn on your camera, camcorder, or laptop** to prove to security personnel that the device is real. Always **ask for hand inspection of film,** which becomes clouded after successive exposure to airport X-ray machines, and **keep videotapes and computer disks away from metal detectors.**

TRAVEL PHOTOGRAPHY

➤ PHOTO HELP: **Kodak Information Center** (☎ 800/242–2424). ***Kodak Guide to Shooting Great Travel Pictures,*** available in bookstores or from Fodor's Travel Publications (☎ 800/533–6478; $16.50 plus $4 shipping).

CAR RENTAL

The great attraction of renting is obviously that you become independent of public transport. Cost-wise, you should **consider renting a car only if you are with at least one other person;** single travelers pay a tremendous premium. Car rental costs vary from country to country; rates in Scandinavia and Eastern Europe are particularly high. If you're visiting a number of countries with varying rates, it makes sense to **rent a vehicle in the cheapest country.** For instance, if you plan to visit Normandy, the same company that rents you a car for a weekly rate of $246 in Paris will rent you one for $159 in Brussels, adding a few hours to your trip but at a 35% savings.

Picking up a car at an airport is convenient but often costs extra (up to 10%) as rental companies pass along the fees charged to them by airports.

Rates in London begin at $39 a day and $136 a week for an economy car with air conditioning, a manual transmission, and unlimited mileage. Rates in Paris begin at $60 a day and $196 a week. Rates in Madrid begin at $37 a day and $132 a week. Rates in Rome begin at $49 a day and $167 a week. Rates in Frankfurt begin at $18 a day and $91 a week. These figures do not include tax on car rentals, which ranges from 15% to 21%.

➤ MAJOR AGENCIES: **Alamo** (☎ 800/522–9696 in the U.S. and Canada, 954/522–0000 in the U.K. and Ireland). **Avis** (☎ 800/331–1084 in U.S., 800/879–2847 in Canada, 0990/900500 in U.K., 02/9353–9000 in Australia, 649/525–1982 or 09/525–1982 in New Zealand). **Budget** (☎ 800/472–3325 in U.S., 800/268–8900 in Canada, 1442/276000 in the U.K., 39206/3666 in Australia, 09/375–2222 in New Zealand, 90/324668 in Ireland). **Dollar** (☎ 800/800–6000 in the U.S. and Canada; 113/242–2233 in the U.K., where it is known as Europcar; 1/668–1777 in Ireland, where it is known as Europcar; 292/231444 in Australia). **Hertz** (☎ 800/654–3001 in the U.S., 800/263–0600 in Canada, 0990/996699 in the U.K., 01/813–3550 in Ireland, 03/9222–2523 in Australia, 03/358–6777 in New Zealand). **National Car Rental** (☎ 800/227–3876; 01162/565656 in the U.K., 21/320755 in Ireland, 9/329–5000 in Australia).

CUTTING COSTS

To get the best deal, **book through a travel agent who is willing to shop around.**

Also **ask your travel agent about a company's customer-service record.** How has the company responded to late plane arrivals and vehicle mishaps? Are there often lines at the rental counter? During a holiday period, does a confirmed reservation guarantee you a car?

Be sure to **look into wholesalers,** companies that do not own fleets but rent in bulk from those that do and often offer better rates than traditional car-rental operations. Prices are best during off-peak periods. Rentals through wholesalers must be paid for before you leave the United States.

Short-term leasing can save you money if you need a rental for more than 17 days. Kemwel and Europe by Car are among the wholesalers offering such deals.

If you think you'll need a car in Europe but are unsure about when or where, ask your travel agent to check out Kemwel's CarPass. This gives the benefit of pre-paid vouchers with the flexibility of last-minute bookings in Europe. Unused vouchers are refunded.

➤ RENTAL WHOLESALERS: **Auto Europe** (☎ 207/842–2000 or 800/223–5555, FAX 800/235–6321). **Europe by Car** (☎ 212/581–3040 or 800/223–1516, FAX 212/246–1458). **DER Travel Services** (✉ 9501 W. Devon Ave., Rosemont, IL 60018, ☎ 800/782–2424, FAX 800/282–7474 for information or 800/860–9944 for brochures). **Kemwel Holiday Autos** (☎ 914/835–5555 or 800/678–0678, FAX 914/835–5126).

INSURANCE

When driving a rented car you are generally responsible for any damage to or loss of the vehicle. Before you rent, **see what coverage you already have** under the terms of your personal auto-insurance policy and credit cards.

Collision policies that car-rental companies sell for European rentals typically do not cover stolen vehicles. Before you buy additional coverage for theft, check with your credit-card company and personal auto insurance—you may already be covered. All car-rental companies operating in Italy require that you buy theft-protection policies.

REQUIREMENTS

Your own driver's license is acceptable virtually everywhere. An International Driver's Permit is a good idea, especially if your travel is likely to include Eastern Europe; it's available from the American or Canadian automobile association, and, in the United Kingdom, from the Automobile Association or Royal Automobile Club. These international permits are universally recognized, and having one in your wallet may save you a problem with the local authorities.

SURCHARGES

Before you pick up a car in one city and leave it in another, **ask about drop-off charges or one-way service fees,** which can be substantial. Note, too, that some rental agencies charge extra if you return the car before the time specified in your contract. To avoid a hefty refueling fee, **fill the tank just before you turn in the car,** but be aware that gas stations near the rental outlet may overcharge.

CAR TRAVEL

Unless you're in a rush to get from A to B, you will find it rewarding to **avoid the freeways and use the alternative and toll-free main routes.** Wherever you're driving, **be sure to carry a good road map.** You can purchase maps in bookshops and many newsstands at home and throughout Europe. City maps of major cities are generally available at service stations close to the destination.

➤ PUBLICATIONS: **Moto Europa** ($15.95 from Independent Publishers Group, ☎ 800/888–4741, FAX 312/337–5985), by Eric Bredesen, is a 320-page guide to motoring in Europe including illustrations of road signs, tables, and maps of ferry routes.

AUTO CLUBS

➤ IN AUSTRALIA: **Australian Automobile Association** (☎ 06/247–7311).

➤ IN CANADA: **Canadian Automobile Association** (CAA, ☎ 613/247–0117).

➤ IN NEW ZEALAND: **New Zealand Automobile Association** (☎ 09/377–4660).

➤ IN THE U.K.: **Automobile Association** (AA, ☎ 0990/500–600), **Royal Automobile Club** (RAC, ☎ 0990/722–722 for membership,.0345/121–345 for insurance).

➤ IN THE U.S.: **American Automobile Association** (☎ 800/564–6222).

BETWEEN THE U.K. & THE CONTINENT

Drivers traveling between Great Britain and the Continent can now **consider using Le Shuttle.** This Anglo-French name has been chosen for the train carrying cars, buses, motorbikes and trucks, plus their passengers, through the Channel Tunnel between Folkestone and Calais in 35 minutes. The shuttle trains operate continuously—three to four trains per hour—and reservations are not needed, but tickets may be bought in advance from travel agents or by credit card from **Le Shuttle** (☎ 800/388–3876 in the U.S., 0990/353–535 in the U.K.). Note that you must make advance reservations to benefit from promotional fares and special offers. *See* The Channel Tunnel, *below,* and Ferries, *above.*

BORDERS

Border controls have been abolished within the EU (except in the U.K., Ireland, Scandinavia, and Greece). The border posts are still standing, but drivers whiz through them without slowing down. Truck traffic is generally routed to separate checkpoints.

COSTS

Be prepared: Gasoline costs three to four times more than in the United States, due to heavy taxes. The better fuel economy of European cars offsets the higher price to some extent.

Motorway tolls can easily add $25 a day to your costs in driving through

France, and there are toll roads throughout southern Europe, as well as charges for many tunnels. When crossing borders into Switzerland, you're charged 40 Swiss francs (about $30) for a *vignette* that entitles you to use Swiss freeways for a year. To get a handle on costs, **ask the national tourist office or car rental firm about tolls before you travel.**

DOCUMENTATION

If you are driving a rented car, **be sure to carry the necessary papers provided by the rental company.** For U.K. citizens, if the vehicle is your own, you will need proof of ownership, a certificate of roadworthiness (known as a Ministry of Transport, or MOT, road vehicle certificate), up-to-date vehicle registration or tax certificate, and a Green Card proof of insurance, available from your insurance company (fees vary depending on destination and length of stay).

RULES OF THE ROAD

➤ SPEED LIMITS: Establishing a speed limit for German motorways has proved a tougher nut than any successive government could crack. On the rest of the Continent, the limit is generally 130 kph (80 mph), but the cruising speed is mostly about 140 kph (about 87 mph). In the United Kingdom, the speed limit is 70 mph (112 kph), but there, too, passing at considerably higher speed is not uncommon. For safe driving, **stay in the slower lane unless you want to pass, and make way for faster cars wanting to pass you.** Much of the time traffic is heavier than is common on U.S. freeways outside major city rush hours.

➤ SAFETY EQUIPMENT: You must carry a reflecting red triangle (to be placed well behind your car in case of breakdown). A first-aid kit and fire extinguisher are strongly recommended.

➤ SWITCHING SIDES: In the United Kingdom, the Republic of Ireland, Malta, Cyprus, and Gibraltar, cars drive on the left. In other European countries, traffic is on the right. If you're coming off Le Shuttle or ferries from Britain or Ireland to the Continent (or vice versa), beware the transition. Green signs indicate access to freeways everywhere except in France, where they are blue.

TRAFFIC

During peak vacation periods, main routes can be jammed with holiday traffic. In the United Kingdom, **try to avoid driving during any of the long bank-holiday (public holiday) weekends,** when motorways are invariably clogged. The tunnels carrying traffic between Italy and the countries to the north are often overburdened with truck traffic; cross the Alps on a weekend, if you can. In France, Spain, and Italy, huge numbers of people still take a fixed one-month vacation in August, so **avoid driving during *le départ,*** the first weekend in August, when vast numbers of drivers head south; or *le retour,* when they head back.

THE CHANNEL TUNNEL

Short of flying, the "Chunnel" is the fastest way to cross the English Channel: 35 minutes from Folkestone to Calais, 60 minutes from motorway to motorway, or 3 hours from London's Waterloo Station to Paris's Gare du Nord.

➤ CAR TRANSPORT: Le Shuttle (☎ 0990/353535 in the U.K.).

➤ PASSENGER SERVICE: In the U.K., **Eurostar** (☎ 0345/881881), **InterCity Europe** (✉:Victoria Station, London, ☎ 0171/834–2345, 0171/828–0892 for credit-card bookings). In the U.S., **BritRail Travel** (☎ 800/677–8585), **Rail Europe** (☎ 800/942–4866).

CHILDREN & TRAVEL

CHILDREN IN EUROPE

Be sure to plan ahead and **involve your youngsters** as you outline your trip. When packing, include things to keep them busy en route. On sightseeing days try to schedule activities of special interest to your children. If you are renting a car don't forget to **arrange for a car seat** when you reserve.

FLYING

If your children are two or older, **ask about children's airfares.** As a general rule, infants under two not occupying a seat fly at greatly reduced fares or even for free.

In general the adult baggage allowance applies to children paying half or more of the adult fare. When booking, **ask about carry-on allowances for those traveling with infants.** In general, for babies charged 10% of the adult fare you are allowed one carry-on bag and a collapsible stroller, which may have to be checked; you may be limited to less if the flight is full.

Experts agree that it's a good idea to use safety seats aloft for children weighing less than 40 pounds. Airlines, however, can set their own policies: U.S. carriers allow FAA-approved models but usually require that you buy a ticket, even if your child would otherwise ride free, since the seats must be strapped into regular seats. Airline rules vary, so it's important to **check your airline's policy about using safety seats during takeoff and landing.** Safety seats cannot obstruct the movement of other passengers in the row, so get an appropriate seat assignment as early as possible.

When making your reservation, **request children's meals or a free-standing bassinet** if you need them; the latter are available only to those seated at the bulkhead, where there's enough legroom. Remember, however, that bulkhead seats may not have their own overhead bins, and there's no storage space in front of you—a major inconvenience.

GROUP TRAVEL

When planning to take your kids on a tour, look for companies that specialize in family travel.

➤ FAMILY-FRIENDLY TOUR OPERATORS: **Grandtravel** (✉ 6900 Wisconsin Ave., Suite 706, Chevy Chase, MD 20815, ☎ 301/986–0790 or 800/247–7651) for people traveling with grandchildren ages 7–17. **Families Welcome!** (✉ 92 N. Main St., Ashland, OR 97520, ☎ 541/482–6121 or 800/326–0724, FAX 541/482–0660). **Rascals in Paradise** (✉ 650 5th St., Suite 505, San Francisco, CA 94107, ☎ 415/978–9800 or 800/872–7225, FAX 415/442–0289).

HOTELS

Most hotels in Europe allow children under a certain age to stay in their parents' room at no extra charge, but others charge them as extra adults; be sure to **ask about the cutoff age for children's discounts.**

Club Med has "Baby Clubs" (from age four months), "Mini Clubs" (for ages four to six or eight, depending on the resort), and "Kids Clubs" (for ages eight and up during school holidays) at many of its resort villages in France, Italy, Switzerland, and Spain.

➤ BEST CHOICES: **Club Med** (✉ 40 W. 57th St., New York, NY 10019, ☎ 800/258–2633).

CONSUMER PROTECTION

Whenever possible, **pay with a major credit card** so you can cancel payment or get reimbursed if there's a problem, provided that you can supply documentation. This is the best way to pay, whether you're buying travel arrangements before your trip or shopping at your destination.

If you're buying a package or tour, always **consider travel insurance** that includes default coverage (☞ Insurance, *below*). It's also a good idea to check with your local Better Business Bureau or your state or local Consumer Protection Office to learn whether they have received complaints against your tour operator.

➤ LOCAL BBBS: **Council of Better Business Bureaus** (✉ 4200 Wilson Blvd., Suite 800, Arlington, VA 22203, ☎ 703/276–0100, FAX 703/525–8277).

CRUISE TRAVEL

Europe is a major cruise center, with six seas (Aegean, Baltic, Black, Mediterranean, North, and Tyrrhenean) and the Atlantic Ocean. From the majesty of Norway's fjords to the ruins of ancient Greece, the region has more than one could possibly hope to see on one cruise vacation. **Select your ship as carefully as you choose your itinerary.** Cruises sail in Europe from April to November.

➤ CRUISE LINES: **Abercrombie & Kent** (✉ 1520 Kensington Rd., Oak Brook, IL 60521, ☎ 708/954–2944 or 800/323–7308); **Celebrity Cruises** (✉ 5201 Blue Lagoon Dr., Miami, FL 33126, ☎ 800/437–3111); **Clipper Cruise Line** (✉ 7711 Bonhomme Ave.,

St. Louis, MO 63105, ☎ 800/325-0010); **Crystal Cruises** (✉ 2121 Ave. of the Stars, Los Angeles, CA 90067, ☎ 800/446-6620); **Holland America Line** (✉ 300 Elliott Ave. W, Seattle, WA 98119, ☎ 800/426-0327); **Orient Lines** (✉ 1510 S.E. 17th St., Suite 400, Fort Lauderdale, FL 33316, ☎ 954/527-6660 or 800/333-7300); **Princess Cruises** (✉ 10100 Santa Monica Blvd., Los Angeles, CA 90067, ☎ 310/553-1770 or 800/774-6237 for brochures); **Radisson Seven Seas Cruises** (✉ 600 Corporate Dr., Suite 410, Fort Lauderdale, FL 33334, ☎ 800/333-3333); **Royal Caribbean International** (✉ 1050 Caribbean Way, Miami, FL 33132, ☎ 305/539-6000 or 800/255-4373 for brochures); **Royal Olympic Cruises** (✉ 1 Rockefeller Plaza, Suite 325, New York, NY 10020, ☎ 212/397-6400 or 800/872-6400; 800/368-3888 in Canada); **Seabourn Cruise Line** (✉ 55 Francisco St., San Francisco, CA 94133, ☎ 415/391-7444 or 800/929-9595); **Silversea Cruises** (✉ 110 E. Broward Blvd., Fort Lauderdale, FL 33301, ☎ 954/522-4477 or 800/722-9955); **Special Expeditions** (✉ 720 5th Ave., New York, NY 10019, ☎ 212/265-7740 or 800/762-0003); **Windstar Cruises** (✉ 300 Elliott Ave. W, Seattle, WA 98119, ☎ 800/258-7245).

CUSTOMS & DUTIES

When shopping, **keep receipts** for all of your purchases. Upon reentering the country, **be ready to show customs officials what you've bought.** If you feel a duty is incorrect, appeal the assessment. If you object to the way your clearance was handled, get the inspector's badge number. In either case, first ask to see a supervisor, then write to the appropriate authorities, beginning with the port director at your point of entry.

IN EUROPE

Since the EU's 1992 agreement on a unified European market, the same customs regulations apply to all 15 member states (Austria, Belgium, Denmark, Finland, France, Germany, Great Britain, Greece, Ireland, Italy, Luxembourg, the Netherlands, Portugal, Spain, and Sweden). If you arrive from another EU country, you do not have to pass through customs.

Duty-free allowances for visitors from outside the EU are the same whatever your nationality (but you have to be over 17): 200 cigarettes or 50 cigars or 100 cigarillos or 250 grams of pipe tobacco; 1 liter of spirits or 2 liters of fortified or sparkling wine or liqueurs; 2 liters of still table wine; 60 milliliters of perfume; 250 milliliters of toilet water (note: 1 U.S. quart equals 0.946 liters); plus $200 worth of other goods, including gifts and souvenirs. Unless otherwise noted in individual country chapters, there are no restrictions on the import or export of currency. These limits will continue in force after June 30, 1999, when duty-free shopping for travel within the EU will be abolished.

Duty-free shopping for travel **within** the EU until June 30, 1999, has been considerably relaxed: 300 cigarettes, or 400 cigarillos, or 200 cigars, or 1 kg of pipe tobacco; 10 liters of spirits, or 90 liters of wine, or 110 liters of beer.

See individual country chapters on non-EU countries for information on their import limits.

IN AUSTRALIA

Australian residents who are 18 or older may bring back $A400 worth of souvenirs and gifts (including jewelry), 250 cigarettes or 250 grams of tobacco, and 1,125 ml of alcohol (including wine, beer, and spirits). Residents under 18 may bring back $A200 worth of goods.

➤ INFORMATION: **Australian Customs Service** (Regional Director, ✉ Box 8, Sydney, NSW 2001, ☎ 02/9213-2000, FAX 02/9213-4000).

IN CANADA

Canadian residents who have been out of Canada for at least 7 days may bring in C$500 worth of goods duty-free. If you've been away less than 7 days but more than 48 hours, the duty-free allowance drops to C$200; if your trip lasts 24–48 hours, the allowance is C$50. You may not pool allowances with family members. Goods claimed under the C$500 exemption may follow you by mail; those claimed under the lesser exemptions must accompany you. Alcohol and tobacco products may be included in the 7-day and 48-hour exemptions but not in the 24-hour exemption. If you meet the age requirements of the province or territory through which you reenter Canada, you may bring in, duty-free, 1.14 liters (40 imperial ounces) of wine or liquor *or* 24 12-ounce cans or bottles of beer or ale. If you are 16 or older you may bring in, duty-free, 200 cigarettes and 50 cigars.

You may send an unlimited number of gifts worth up to C$60 each duty-free to Canada. Label the package UNSOLICITED GIFT—VALUE UNDER $60. Alcohol and tobacco are excluded.

➤ INFORMATION: **Revenue Canada** (✉ 2265 St. Laurent Blvd. S, Ottawa, Ontario K1G 4K3, ☎ 613/993–0534, 800/461–9999 in Canada).

IN NEW ZEALAND

Although greeted with a "Haere Mai" ("Welcome to New Zealand"), homeward-bound residents with goods to declare must present themselves for inspection. If you're 17 or older, you may bring back $700 worth of souvenirs and gifts. Your duty-free allowance also includes 4.5 liters of wine or beer; one 1,125-ml bottle of spirits; and either 200 cigarettes, 250 grams of tobacco, 50 cigars, or a combo of all three up to 250 grams.

➤ INFORMATION: **New Zealand Customs** (✉ Custom House, 50 Anzac Ave., Box 29, Auckland, New Zealand, ☎ 09/359–6655, ☎ 09/309–2978).

IN THE U.K.

If you are a U.K. resident and your journey was wholly within the European Union (EU), you won't have to pass through customs when you return to the United Kingdom. If you plan to bring back large quantities of alcohol or tobacco, check EU limits beforehand. From countries outside the EU, you may import, duty-free, 200 cigarettes or 50 cigars; 1 liter of spirits or 2 liters of fortified or sparkling wine or liqueurs; 2 liters of still table wine; 60 milliliters of perfume; 250 milliliters of toilet water; plus £136 worth of other goods, including gifts and souvenirs.

➤ INFORMATION: **HM Customs and Excise** (✉ Dorset House, Stamford St., London SE1 9NG, ☎ 0171/202–4227).

IN THE U.S.

U.S. residents may bring home $400 worth of foreign goods duty-free if they've been out of the country for at least 48 hours (and if they haven't used the $400 allowance or any part of it in the past 30 days).

U.S. residents 21 and older may bring back 1 liter of alcohol duty-free. In addition, regardless of your age, you are allowed 200 cigarettes and 100 non-Cuban cigars. Antiques, which the U.S. Customs Service defines as objects more than 100 years old, enter duty-free, as do original works of art done entirely by hand, including paintings, drawings, and sculptures.

You may also send packages home duty-free: up to $200 worth of goods for personal use, with a limit of one parcel per addressee per day (and no alcohol or tobacco products or perfume worth more than $5); label the package PERSONAL USE, and attach a list of its contents and their retail value. Do not label the package UNSOLICITED GIFT, or your duty-free exemption will drop to $100. Mailed items do not affect your duty-free allowance on your return.

Note that some states, such as New York, charge duty over and above that charged by the federal government; if you have exceeded the duty-free limits and have to pay U.S. duty, ask at your airport of entry about possible state duties; otherwise you may end up paying not only the state duty but also a hefty late penalty.

➤ INFORMATION: **U.S. Customs Service** (Inquiries, ✉ Box 7407, Washington, DC 20044, ☎ 202/927–6724; complaints, Office of Regulations and Rulings, ✉ 1301 Constitution Ave. NW, Washington, DC 20229; registration of equipment, Resource Management, ✉ 1301 Constitution Ave. NW, Washington DC 20229, ☎ 202/927–0540).

DISABILITIES & ACCESSIBILITY

ACCESS IN EUROPE

Getting around in many European cities and towns can be difficult if you're using a wheelchair, as cobblestone-paved streets and sidewalks are common in older, historic districts. Some that have been renovated have a flagstone track along with the cobblestones. Generally, newer facilities (including museums, transportation, hotels) provide easier access for people with disabilities.

MAKING RESERVATIONS

When discussing accessibility with an operator or reservations agent, **ask hard questions.** Are there any stairs, inside *or* out? Are there grab bars next to the toilet *and* in the shower/tub? How wide is the doorway to the room? To the bathroom? For the most extensive facilities meeting the latest legal specifications, **opt for newer accommodations,** which are more likely to have been designed with access in mind. Older buildings or ships may have more limited facilities. Be sure to **discuss your needs before booking.**

TRANSPORTATION

➤ COMPLAINTS: **Aviation Consumer Protection Division** (☞ Air Travel, *above*) for airline-related problems.

TRAVEL AGENCIES & TOUR OPERATORS

As a whole, the travel industry has become more aware of the needs of travelers with disabilities. In the U.S., the Americans with Disabilities Act requires that travel firms serve the needs of all travelers. Note, though, that some agencies and operators specialize in making travel arrangements for individuals and groups with disabilities.

➤ TRAVELERS WITH MOBILITY PROBLEMS: **Access Adventures** (✉ 206 Chestnut Ridge Rd., Rochester, NY 14624, ☎ 716/889–9096), run by a former physical-rehabilitation counselor. **Accessible Journeys** (✉ 35 W. Sellers Ave., Ridley Park, PA 19078, ☎ 610/521–0339 or 800/846–4537, FAX 610/521–6959), for escorted tours exclusively for travelers with mobility impairments. **CareVacations** (✉ 5019 49th Ave., Suite 102, Leduc, Alberta T9E 6T5, ☎ 403/986–6404, 800/648–1116 in Canada) has group tours and is especially helpful with cruise vacations. **Flying Wheels Travel** (✉ 143 W. Bridge St., Box 382, Owatonna, MN 55060, ☎ 507/451–5005 or 800/535–6790, FAX 507/451–1685), a travel agency specializing in customized tours and itineraries worldwide. **Hinsdale Travel Service** (✉ 201 E. Ogden Ave., Suite 100, Hinsdale, IL 60521, ☎ 630/325–1335), a travel agency that benefits from the advice of wheelchair traveler Janice Perkins.

➤ TRAVELERS WITH DEVELOPMENTAL DISABILITIES: **Sprout** (✉ 893 Amsterdam Ave., New York, NY 10025, ☎ 212/222–9575 or 888/222–9575, FAX 212/222–9768).

DISCOUNTS & DEALS

Be a smart shopper and **compare all your options** before making any choice. A plane ticket bought with a promotional coupon may not be cheaper than the least expensive fare from a discount ticket agency. For high-price travel purchases, such as packages or tours, keep in mind that what you get is just as important as what you save.

CLUBS & COUPONS

Many companies sell discounts in the form of travel clubs and coupon books, but these cost money. You must use participating advertisers to get a deal, and only after you recoup the initial membership cost or book price do you begin to save. If you plan to use the club or coupons frequently, you may save considerably. Before signing up, find out what discounts you get for free.

➤ DISCOUNT CLUBS: **Entertainment Travel Editions** (✉ 2125 Butterfield Rd., Troy, MI 48084, ☎ 800/445–4137; $20–$51, depending on destination). **Great American Traveler** (✉ Box 27965, Salt Lake City, UT 84127, ☎ 801/974–3033 or 800/548–2812; $49.95 per year). **Moment's Notice Discount Travel Club** (✉ 7301 New Utrecht Ave., Brooklyn, NY 11204, ☎ 718/234–6295; $25 per year, single or family). **Privilege Card International** (✉ 237 E. Front St., Youngstown, OH 44503,

☎ 330/746–5211 or 800/236–9732; $74.95 per year). **Sears's Mature Outlook** (✉ Box 9390, Des Moines, IA 50306, ☎ 800/336–6330; $19.95 per year). **Travelers Advantage** (✉ CUC Travel Service, 3033 S. Parker Rd., Suite 1000, Aurora, CO 80014, ☎ 800/548–1116 or 800/648–4037; $59.95 per year, single or family). **Worldwide Discount Travel Club** (✉ 1674 Meridian Ave., Miami Beach, FL 33139, ☎ 305/534–2082; $50 per year family, $40 single).

CREDIT-CARD BENEFITS

When you use your credit card to make travel purchases you may get free travel-accident insurance, collision-damage insurance, and medical or legal assistance, depending on the card and the bank that issued it. American Express, MasterCard, and Visa provide one or more of these services, so **get a copy of your credit card's travel-benefits policy.** If you are a member of an auto club, always **ask hotel and car-rental reservations agents about auto-club discounts.** Some clubs offer additional discounts on tours, cruises, and admission to attractions.

DISCOUNT RESERVATIONS

To save money, **look into discount-reservations services** with toll-free numbers, which use their buying power to get a better price on hotels, airline tickets, even car rentals. When booking a room, always **call the hotel's local toll-free number** (if one is available) rather than the central reservations number—you'll often get a better price. Always ask about special packages or corporate rates.

When shopping for the best deal on hotels and car rentals, **look for guaranteed exchange rates,** which protect you against a falling dollar.

➤ AIRLINE TICKETS: ☎ 800/359–4537 (800/FLY–4–LESS).

➤ HOTEL ROOMS: **Hotels Plus** (☎ 800/235–0909). **Hotel Reservations Network** (☎ 800/964–6835). **International Marketing & Travel Concepts** (☎ 800/790–4682). **Steigenberger Reservation Service** (☎ 800/223–5652). **Travel Interlink** (☎ 800/888–5898).

PACKAGE DEALS

Packages and guided tours can save you money, but don't confuse the two. When you buy a package, your travel remains independent, just as though you had planned and booked the trip yourself. Fly/drive packages, which combine airfare and car rental, are often a good deal. If you **buy a rail/drive pass,** you'll save on train tickets and car rentals. All Eurail- and Europass holders get a discount on Eurostar fares through the Channel Tunnel. A German Rail Pass is also good for travel aboard KD River Steamers on selected routes and on certain bus routes operated by Deutsche Touring/Europabus. Greek Flexipass options may include sightseeing, hotels, and plane tickets.

ELECTRICITY

To use your U.S.-purchased electric-powered equipment, **bring a converter and adapter.** The electrical current in Europe is 220 volts, 50 cycles alternating current (AC); wall outlets in most of Europe take plugs with two round prongs; Great Britain (and also Malta) uses plugs with three oblong prongs.

If your appliances are dual-voltage, you'll need only an adapter. Don't use 110-volt outlets, marked FOR SHAVERS ONLY, for high-wattage appliances such as blow-dryers. Most laptops operate equally well on 110 and 220 volts and so require only an adapter.

GAY & LESBIAN TRAVEL

Although big cities like Amsterdam and Paris have a visible and happening gay scene, most of Europe has a view of homosexuality similar to that found away from big cities in the U.S.

➤ INFORMATION SERVICES: **International Gay and Lesbian Travel Associations** (IGLTA; ✉ Box 4974, Key West, FL 33041, ☎ 800/448–8550). **International Lesbian and Gay Association** (IGLA; 81 rue Marché au Charbon, 1000 Brussels 1, Belgium, ☎ 02/502–2471).

➤ GAY- AND LESBIAN-FRIENDLY TOUR OPERATORS: **Hanns Ebensten Travel** (✉ 513 Fleming St., Key West, FL 33040, ☎ 305/294–8174, FAX 305/292–9665), one of the oldest operators in the gay market. **Toto Tours** (✉ 1326 W. Albion Ave., Suite 3W, Chicago, IL 60626, ☎ 773/274–8686 or 800/565–1241, FAX 773/274–8695), for groups.

➤ GAY- AND LESBIAN-FRIENDLY TRAVEL AGENCIES: **Corniche Travel** (✉ 8721 Sunset Blvd., Suite 200, West Hollywood, CA 90069, ☎ 310/854–6000 or 800/429–8747, FAX 310/659–7441). **Islanders Kennedy Travel** (✉ 183 W. 10th St., New York, NY 10014, ☎ 212/242–3222 or 800/988–1181, FAX 212/929–8530). **Now Voyager** (✉ 4406 18th St., San Francisco, CA 94114, ☎ 415/626–1169 or 800/255–6951, FAX 415/626–8626). **Yellowbrick Road** (✉ 1500 W. Balmoral Ave., Chicago, IL 60640, ☎ 773/561–1800 or 800/642–2488, FAX 773/561–4497). **Skylink Travel and Tour** (✉ 3577 Moorland Ave., Santa Rosa, CA 95407, ☎ 707/585–8355 or 800/225–5759, FAX 707/584–5637), serving lesbian travelers.

HEALTH

MEDICAL PLANS

No one plans to get sick while traveling, but it happens, so **consider signing up with a medical-assistance company.** Members get doctor referrals, emergency evacuation or repatriation, 24-hour telephone hot lines for medical consultation, cash for emergencies, and other personal and legal assistance. Coverage varies by plan, so **review the benefits of each carefully.**

➤ MEDICAL-ASSISTANCE COMPANIES: **International SOS Assistance** (✉ 8 Neshaminy Interplex, Suite 207, Trevose, PA 19053, ☎ 215/245–4707 or 800/523–6586, FAX 215/244–9617; ✉ 12 Chemin Riantbosson, 1217 Meyrin 1, Geneva, Switzerland, ☎ 4122/785–6464, FAX 4122/785–6424; ✉ 10 Anson Rd., 14-07/08 International Plaza, Singapore, 079903, ☎ 65/226–3936, FAX 65/226–3937).

INSURANCE

Travel insurance is the best way to **protect yourself against financial loss.** The most useful plan is a comprehensive policy that includes coverage for trip cancellation and interruption, default, trip delay, and medical expenses (with a waiver for preexisting conditions).

Without insurance, you will lose all or most of your money if you cancel your trip, regardless of the reason. Default insurance covers you if your tour operator, airline, or cruise line goes out of business. Trip-delay covers unforeseen expenses that you may incur due to bad weather or mechanical delays. Be sure to **compare the fine print** on trip-delay coverage when comparing policies.

For overseas travel, one of the most important components of travel insurance is its medical coverage. Supplemental health insurance will pick up the cost of your medical bills should you get sick or injured while traveling. U.S. residents should note that Medicare generally does not cover health-care costs outside the United States, nor do many privately issued policies. Residents of the United Kingdom can buy an annual travel-insurance policy valid for most vacations taken during the year in which the coverage is purchased. If you are pregnant or have a preexisting condition, make sure you're covered. British citizens should buy extra medical coverage when traveling overseas, according to the Association of British Insurers. Australian travelers should buy travel insurance, including extra medical coverage, whenever they go abroad, according to the Insurance Council of Australia.

Always **buy travel insurance directly from the insurance company**; if you buy it from a cruise line, airline, or tour operator that goes out of business you probably will not be covered for the agency or operator's default, a major risk. Before you make any purchase, **review your existing health and home-owner's policies** to find out whether they cover expenses incurred while traveling.

➤ TRAVEL INSURERS: In the U.S., **Access America** (✉ 6600 W. Broad St., Richmond, VA 23230, ☎ 804/285–3300 or 800/284–8300). **Travel Guard International** (✉ 1145 Clark St., Stevens Point, WI 54481, ☎ 715/

345–0505 or 800/826–1300). In Canada, **Mutual of Omaha** (✉ Travel Division, 500 University Ave., Toronto, Ontario M5G 1V8, ☎ 416/598–4083, 800/268–8825 in Canada).

➤ INSURANCE INFORMATION: In the U.K., **Association of British Insurers** (✉ 51 Gresham St., London EC2V 7HQ, ☎ 0171/600–3333). In Australia, the **Insurance Council of Australia** (☎ 613/9614–1077, FAX 613/9614–7924).

LODGING

APARTMENT & VILLA RENTALS

If you want a home base that's roomy enough for a family and comes with cooking facilities, **consider a furnished rental.** These can save you money, especially if you're traveling with a large group of people. Home-exchange directories list rentals (often second homes owned by prospective house swappers), and some services search for a house or apartment for you (even a castle if that's your fancy) and handle the paperwork. Some send an illustrated catalog; others send photographs only of specific properties, sometimes at a charge. Up-front registration fees may apply.

➤ RENTAL AGENTS: **At Home Abroad** (✉ 405 E. 56th St., Suite 6H, New York, NY 10022, ☎ 212/421–9165, FAX 212/752–1591). **Drawbridge to Europe** (✉ 5456 Adams Rd., Talent, OR 97540, ☎ 541/512–8927 or 888/268–1148, FAX 541/512–0978). **Europa-Let/Tropical Inn-Let** (✉ 92 N. Main St., Ashland, OR 97520, ☎ 541/482–5806 or 800/462–4486, FAX 541/482–0660). **Hideaways International** (✉ 767 Islington St., Portsmouth, NH 03801, ☎ 603/430–4433 or 800/843–4433, FAX 603/430–4444; membership $99). **Hometours International** (✉ Box 11503, Knoxville, TN 37939, ☎ 423/690–8484 or 800/367–4668). **Interhome** (✉ 124 Little Falls Rd., Fairfield, NJ 07004, ☎ 973/882–6864 or 800/882–6864, FAX 973/808–1742). **Property Rentals International** (✉ 1008 Mansfield Crossing Rd., Richmond, VA 23236, ☎ 804/378–6054 or 800/220–3332, FAX 804/379–2073). **Rental Directories International** (✉ 2044 Rittenhouse Sq., Philadelphia, PA 19103, ☎ 215/985–4001, FAX 215/985–0323). **Rent-a-Home International** (✉ 7200 34th Ave. NW, Seattle, WA 98117, ☎ 206/789–9377 or 800/488–7368, FAX 206/789–9379). **Vacation Home Rentals Worldwide** (✉ 235 Kensington Ave., Norwood, NJ 07648, ☎ 201/767–9393 or 800/633–3284, FAX 201/767–5510). **Villas and Apartments Abroad** (✉ 420 Madison Ave., Suite 1003, New York, NY 10017, ☎ 212/759–1025 or 800/433–3020, FAX 212/755–8316). **Villas International** (✉ 950 Northgate Dr., Suite 206, San Rafael, CA 94903, ☎ 415/499–9490 or 800/221–2260, FAX 415/499–9491).

HOME EXCHANGES

If you would like to exchange your home for someone else's, **join a home-exchange organization,** which will send you its updated listings of available exchanges for a year and will include your own listing in at least one of them. It's up to you to make specific arrangements.

➤ EXCHANGE CLUB: **HomeLink International** (✉ Box 650, Key West, FL 33041, ☎ 305/294–7766 or 800/638–3841, FAX 305/294–1148; $83 per year).

HOSTELS

No matter what your age, you can **save on lodging costs by staying at hostels.** In some 5,000 locations in more than 70 countries around the world, Hostelling International (HI), the umbrella group for a number of national youth hostel associations, offers single-sex, dorm-style beds and, at many hostels, "couples" rooms and family accommodations. Membership in any HI national hostel association, open to travelers of all ages, allows you to stay in HI-affiliated hostels at member rates (one-year membership is about $25 for adults; hostels run about $10–$25 per night). Members also have priority if the hostel is full; they're eligible for discounts around the world, even on rail and bus travel in some countries.

➤ HOSTEL ORGANIZATIONS: **Hostelling International—American Youth Hostels** (✉ 733 15th St. NW, Suite

840, Washington, DC 20005, ☎ 202/783-6161, FAX 202/783-6171). **Hostelling International—Canada** (✉ 400-205 Catherine St., Ottawa, Ontario K2P 1C3, ☎ 613/237-7884, FAX 613/237-7868). **Youth Hostel Association of England and Wales** (✉ Trevelyan House, 8 St. Stephen's Hill, St. Albans, Hertfordshire AL1 2DY, ☎ 01727/855215 or 01727/845047, FAX 01727/844126); membership in the U.S. $25, in Canada C$26.75, in the U.K. £9.30.

MONEY

CREDIT & DEBIT CARDS

Should you use a credit card or a debit card when traveling? Both have benefits. A credit card allows you to delay payment and gives you certain rights as a consumer (☞ Consumer Protection, *above*). A debit card, also known as a check card, deducts funds directly from your checking account and helps you stay within your budget. When you want to rent a car, you may still need an old-fashioned credit card. You can always *pay* for your car with a debit card, but some agencies will not allow you to *reserve* a car with a debit card.

Otherwise, the two types of plastic are virtually the same. Both will get you cash advances at ATMs worldwide if your card is properly programmed with your personal identification number (PIN). Both offer excellent, wholesale exchange rates. And both protect you against unauthorized use if the card is lost or stolen. Your liability is limited to $50, as long as you report the card missing.

➤ ATM LOCATIONS: **Cirrus** (☎ 800/424-7787). **Plus** (☎ 800/843-7587) for locations in the U.S. and Canada, or visit your local bank.

CURRENCY

The Euro, or single European currency, is being launched on January 1, 1999. In the beginning, it will function as a sort of alternative currency, and national bank notes and coins won't disappear for another three years. A great deal of belt-tightening has been going on in EU countries to meet the convergence criteria, notably through reducing budget deficits to less than 3%. Eleven EU nations are joining the system in the first wave—all but the U.K., Sweden, Denmark, and Greece.

EXCHANGING MONEY

For the most favorable rates, **change money through banks.** Although fees charged for ATM transactions may be higher abroad than at home, Cirrus and Plus exchange rates are excellent, because they are based on wholesale rates offered only by major banks. You won't do as well at exchange booths in airports or rail and bus stations, in hotels, in restaurants, or in stores, although you may find their hours more convenient. To avoid lines at airport exchange booths, **get a bit of local currency before you leave home.**

➤ EXCHANGE SERVICES: **Chase *Currency To Go*** (☎ 800/935-9935; 935-9935 in NY, NJ, and CT). **International Currency Express** (☎ 888/842-0880 on the East Coast, 888/278-6628 on the West Coast). **Thomas Cook Currency Services** (☎ 800/287-7362 for telephone orders and retail locations).

TRAVELER'S CHECKS

Do you need traveler's checks? It depends on where you're headed. If you're going to rural areas and small towns, go with cash; traveler's checks are best used in cities. Lost or stolen checks can usually be replaced within 24 hours. To ensure a speedy refund, buy your own traveler's checks—don't let someone else pay for them: irregularities like this can cause delays. The person who bought the checks should make the call to request a refund.

PACKING

LUGGAGE

How many carry-on bags you can bring with you is up to the airline. Most allow two, but the limit is often reduced to one on certain flights. Gate agents will take excess baggage—including bags they deem oversize—from you as you board and add it to checked luggage. To avoid this situation, make sure that everything you carry aboard will fit under your seat. Also, get to the gate early, and request a seat at the back of the plane; you'll probably board first, while the overhead bins are still empty. Since big, bulky baggage attracts the attention of gate agents and flight attendants on a busy flight, make sure your carry-on is really a carry-on. Finally, a carry-on that's long and narrow is more likely to remain unnoticed than one that's wide and squarish.

For international flights, note that baggage allowances may be determined not by piece but by weight—generally 88 pounds (40 kilograms) in first class, 66 pounds (30 kilograms) in business class, and 44 pounds (20 kilograms) in economy.

Airline liability for baggage is limited to $1,250 per person on flights within the United States. On international flights it amounts to $9.07 per pound or $20 per kilogram for checked baggage (roughly $640 per 70-pound bag) and $400 per passenger for unchecked baggage. You can buy additional coverage at check-in for about $10 per $1,000 of coverage, but it excludes a rather extensive list of items, shown on your airline ticket.

Before departure, **itemize your bags' contents** and their worth, and label the bags with your name, address, and phone number. (If you use your home address, cover it so that potential thieves can't see it readily.) Inside each bag, **pack a copy of your itinerary.** At check-in, **make sure that each bag is correctly tagged** with the destination airport's three-letter code. If your bags arrive damaged or fail to arrive at all, file a written report with the airline before leaving the airport.

PACKING LIST

You should **pack more for the season than for any particular dress code.** In general, northern and central Europe have cold, snowy winters, and the Mediterranean countries have mild winters, though parts of southern Europe can be bitterly cold, too. In the Mediterranean resorts **bring a warm jacket for mornings and evenings,** even in summer. The mountains usually are warm on summer days, but the weather is unpredictable, and the nights are generally cool.

For European cities, **pack as you would for an American city;** formal outfits for first-class restaurants and nightclubs, casual clothes elsewhere. Jeans are perfectly acceptable for sightseeing and informal dining. Sturdy walking shoes are appropriate for the cobblestone streets and gravel paths that fill many of the parks and surround some of the historic buildings. For visits to churches, cathedrals, and mosques, **avoid shorts and revealing outfits.** In Italy, women cover their shoulders and arms (a shawl will do). Women, however, no longer need to cover their heads in Roman Catholic churches. In Turkey, though, women must have a head covering; a long-sleeved shirt and a long skirt or slacks are required.

To discourage purse snatchers and pickpockets, **take a handbag with long straps** that you can sling across your body, bandolier-style, and with a zippered compartment for money.

If you stay in budget hotels, **take your own soap.**

In your carry-on luggage **bring an extra pair of eyeglasses or contact lenses** and **enough of any medication you take** to last the entire trip. You may also want your doctor to write a spare prescription using the drug's generic name, since brand names may vary from country to country. **Never put prescription drugs or valuables in luggage to be checked.** To avoid customs delays, carry medications in their original packaging. And don't forget to copy down and carry addresses of offices that handle refunds of lost traveler's checks.

PASSPORTS & VISAS

When traveling internationally, **carry a passport even if you don't need one** (it's always the best form of I.D.), and make **two photocopies of the data page** (one for someone at home and another for you, carried separately from your passport). If you lose your passport, call the nearest embassy or consulate and the local police.

ENTERING EUROPE

Citizens of the U.S., Canada, U.K., Ireland, Australia, and New Zealand need passports for travel in Europe.

Visas may also be required for visits to or through Turkey, Poland, Estonia, Latvia, Romania, Hungary, and the Czech and Slovak Republics even for short stays or train trips, and in some cases must be obtained before you'll be allowed to enter. Check with the nearest consulate of the country you'll be visiting for visa requirements. Austria and Italy require that you register with the local police shortly after arriving.

PASSPORT OFFICES

The best time to apply for a passport or to renew is during the fall and winter. Before any trip, be sure to check your passport's expiration date and, if necessary, renew it as soon as possible. (Some countries won't allow you to enter on a passport that's due to expire in six months or less.)

➤ AUSTRALIAN CITIZENS: **Australian Passport Office** (☎ 131–232).

➤ CANADIAN CITIZENS: **Passport Office** (☎ 819/994–3500 or 800/567–6868).

➤ NEW ZEALAND CITIZENS: **New Zealand Passport Office** (☎ 04/494–0700 for information on how to apply, 0800/727–776 for information on applications already submitted).

➤ U.K. CITIZENS: **London Passport Office** (☎ 0990/21010), for fees and documentation requirements and to request an emergency passport.

➤ U.S. CITIZENS: **National Passport Information Center** (☎ 900/225–5674; calls are charged at 35¢ per minute for automated service, $1.05 per minute for operator service).

SENIOR-CITIZEN TRAVEL

To qualify for age-related discounts, **mention your senior-citizen status up front** when booking hotel reservations (not when checking out) and before you're seated in restaurants (not when paying the bill). Note that discounts may be limited to certain menus, days, or hours. When renting a car, **ask about promotional car-rental discounts,** which can be cheaper than senior-citizen rates.

Radisson SAS Hotels in Europe offer discounts of 25% or more to senior citizens, subject to availability. You need a confirmed reservation.

➤ ADVENTURES: **Overseas Adventure Travel** (✉ Grand Circle Corporation, 625 Mt. Auburn St., Cambridge, MA 02138, ☎ 617/876–0533 or 800/221–0814, FAX 617/876–0455).

➤ EDUCATIONAL PROGRAMS: **Elderhostel** (✉ 75 Federal St., 3rd floor, Boston, MA 02110, ☎ 617/426–8056). **Folkways Institute** (✉ 14600 Southeast Aldridge Rd., Portland, OR 97236-6518, ☎ 503/658–6600 or 800/225–4666, FAX 503/658–8672). **Interhostel** (✉ University of New Hampshire, 6 Garrison Ave., Durham, NH 03824, ☎ 603/862–1147 or 800/733–9753, FAX 603/862–1113).

STUDENT TRAVEL

Students in Europe are entitled to a wide range of discounts on admission and transportation. An **International Student Identity Card** (☞ CIEE *in* Student I.D.s & Services, *below*) helps.

STUDYING ABROAD

Many U.S. colleges and universities have study-abroad programs or can link you up with one, and numerous institutions of higher learning in Europe accept foreign students for a semester or year's study. Check with your college administration or contact the CIEE (☞ Agencies, *below*) for contacts and brochures.

LODGING

If you're between 18 and 26, the Ibis hotel chain will let you have a room for $50 or less, provided you show up after 9 PM and they have a room free. You'll be asked for your student ID. Your chances are best on weekends. There are more than 400 Ibis hotels in Europe, most of them in France.

TRAVEL AGENCIES

➤ AGENCIES: **Council Travel** (✉ 205 E. 42nd St., New York, NY 10017, ☎ 212/822–2854). **STA Travel** (✉ U.S.: California (Berkeley, ☎ 510/642–3000); Illinois (Chicago, ☎ 312/786–9050); New York (Columbia University, ☎ 212/865–2700); Washington, D.C. (☎ 202/887–0912). Australia (Sydney, ☎ 29/368–1111 or

29/212–1255). Canada (Toronto, ☎ 416/977–5228; Vancouver, ☎ 604/681–9136).

➤ STUDENT I.D.S & SERVICES: **Council on International Educational Exchange** (✉ CIEE, 205 E. 42nd St., 14th floor, New York, NY 10017, ☎ 212/822–2600 or 888/268–6245, FAX 212/822–2699), for mail orders only, in the United States. **Travel Cuts** (✉ 187 College St., Toronto, Ontario M5T 1P7, ☎ 416/979–2406 or 800/667–2887) in Canada.

➤ STUDENT TOURS: **AESU Travel** (✉ 2 Hamill Rd., Suite 248, Baltimore, MD 21210, ☎ 410/323–4416 or 800/638–7640, FAX 410/323–4498). **Contiki Holidays** (✉ 300 Plaza Alicante, Suite 900, Garden Grove, CA 92840, ☎ 714/740–0808 or 800/266–8454, FAX 714/740–2034).

TAXES

VALUE-ADDED TAX (V.A.T.)

For information about value-added tax (VAT) refunds, *see* the individual country chapters. VAT varies from country to country; in some it's over 20%, so applying for a refund is always a worthwhile exercise. Shops displaying a tax-free shopping sign will explain what you need to do. For EU countries, have tax-refund forms from the store stamped at customs as you leave your final EU country; send the stamped form back to the stores, which will send you the refunds. You can also obtain a refund before leaving Europe if you've shopped at one of the 90,000 stores affiliated with the refund service **Europe Tax-free Shopping** (ETS; ✉ 233 S. Wacker Dr., Chicago, IL, ☎ 312/382–1101). You ask for a check at the store, have it validated at customs at the airport, and claim a cash refund (minus 20% handling) at an ETS booth.

TELEPHONES

Telephone systems in Europe are in flux; expect new area codes and extra digits in numbers. Country codes appear in the A to Z listing at the beginning of each country chapter.

COUNTRY CODES

When dialing a European number from abroad, drop the initial 0 from the local area code.

INTERNATIONAL CALLS

Consult individual country chapters for information on dialing international calls.

AT&T, MCI, and Sprint international access codes make calling the United States relatively convenient, but you may find the local access number blocked in many hotel rooms. First ask the hotel operator to connect you. If the hotel operator balks, ask for an international operator, or dial the international operator yourself. One way to improve your odds of being connected to your long-distance carrier is to travel with more than one company's calling card (a hotel may block Sprint, for example, but not MCI). If all else fails, call from a pay phone in the hotel lobby. Check individual country chapters for local access numbers or call your carrier for the number before you go.

➤ TO OBTAIN ACCESS CODES: **AT&T Direct** (☎ 800/435–0812). **MCI WorldPhone** (☎ 800/444–4141). **Sprint International Access** (☎ 913/624–5336).

TOUR OPERATORS

Buying a prepackaged tour or independent vacation can make your trip to Europe less expensive and more hassle-free. Because everything is prearranged, you'll spend less time planning.

Operators that handle several hundred thousand travelers per year can use their purchasing power to give you a good price. Their high volume may also indicate financial stability. But some small companies provide more personalized service; because they tend to specialize, they may also be more knowledgeable about a given area.

BOOKING WITH AN AGENT

Travel agents are excellent resources. In fact, large operators accept bookings made only through travel agents. It's a good idea to **collect brochures from several agencies,** because some agents' suggestions may be influenced by relationships with tour and package firms that reward them for volume sales. If you have a special interest, **find an agent with expertise in that area**; ASTA (☞ Travel Agencies, *below*) has a database of specialists worldwide.

Make sure your travel agent knows the accommodations and other services. Ask about the hotel's location, room size, beds, and whether it has a pool, room service, or programs for children, if you care about these. Has your agent been there in person or sent others you can contact?

Do some homework on your own, too: Local tourism boards can provide information about lesser-known and small-niche operators, some of which may sell only direct.

BUYER BEWARE

Each year consumers are stranded or lose their money when tour operators—even very large ones with excellent reputations—go out of business. So **check out the operator.** Find out how long the company has been in business, and ask several travel agents about its reputation. If the package or tour you are considering is priced lower than in your wildest dreams, **be skeptical.** Try to **book with a company that has a consumer-protection program.** If the operator has such a program, you'll find information about it in the company's brochure. If the operator you are considering does not offer some kind of consumer protection, then ask for references from satisfied customers.

In the U.S., members of the National Tour Association and United States Tour Operators Association are required to set aside funds to cover your payments and travel arrangements in case the company defaults. It's also a good idea to choose a company that participates in the American Society of Travel Agents' Tour Operator Program (TOP). This gives you a forum if there are any disputes between you and your tour operator; ASTA will act as mediator.

➤ TOUR-OPERATOR RECOMMENDATIONS: **American Society of Travel Agents** (☞ Travel Agencies, *below*). **National Tour Association** (✉ NTA, 546 E. Main St., Lexington, KY 40508, ☎ 606/226–4444 or 800/755–8687). **United States Tour Operators Association** (✉ USTOA, 342 Madison Ave., Suite 1522, New York, NY 10173, ☎ 212/599–6599 or 800/468–7862, FAX 212/599–6744).

COSTS

The more your package or tour includes, the better you can predict the ultimate cost of your vacation. Make sure you know exactly what is covered, and **beware of hidden costs.** Are taxes, tips, and service charges included? Transfers and baggage handling? Entertainment and excursions? These can add up.

Prices for packages and tours are usually quoted per person, based on two sharing a room. If traveling solo, you may be required to pay the full double-occupancy rate. Some operators eliminate this surcharge if you agree to be matched with a roommate of the same sex, even if one is not found by departure time.

GROUP TOURS

Among companies that sell tours to Europe, the following have a proven reputation and offer plenty of options. The classifications used below represent different price categories, and you'll probably encounter these terms when talking to a travel agent or tour operator. The key difference is usually in accommodations, which run from budget to better, and better-yet to best.

➤ SUPER-DELUXE: **Abercrombie & Kent** (✉ 1520 Kensington Rd., Oak Brook, IL 60521-2141, ☎ 630/954–2944 or 800/323–7308, FAX 630/954–3324). **Travcoa** (✉ Box 2630, 2350 S.E. Bristol St., Newport Beach, CA 92660, ☎ 714/476–2800 or 800/992–2003, FAX 714/476–2538).

➤ DELUXE: **Globus** (✉ 5301 S. Federal Circle, Littleton, CO 80123-2980, ☎ 303/797–2800 or 800/221–0090, FAX 303/347–2080). **Maupintour** (✉ 1515 St. Andrews Dr., Lawrence, KS 66047, ☎ 913/843–1211 or 800/255–4266, FAX 913/843–8351). **Tauck Tours** (✉ Box 5027, 276 Post Rd. W, Westport, CT 06881-5027, ☎ 203/226–6911 or 800/468–2825, FAX 203/221–6866).

➤ FIRST-CLASS: **Brendan Tours** (✉ 15137 Califa St., Van Nuys, CA

91411, ☎ 818/785–9696 or 800/421–8446, FAX 818/902–9876). **Caravan Tours** (✉ 401 N. Michigan Ave., Chicago, IL 60611, ☎ 312/321–9800 or 800/227–2826, FAX 312/321–9845). **CIE Tours** (✉ Box 501, 100 Hanover Ave., Cedar Knolls, NJ 07927-0501, ☎ 201/292–3899 or 800/243–8687). **Collette Tours** (✉ 162 Middle St., Pawtucket, RI 02860, ☎ 401/728–3805 or 800/340–5158, FAX 401/728–4745). **Delta Vacations** (☎ 800/872–7786). **DER Tours** (✉ 9501 W. Devon St., Rosemont, IL 60018, ☎ 800/937–1235, FAX 847/692–4141 or 800/282–7474, 800/860–9944 for brochures). **Gadabout Tours** (✉ 700 E. Tahquitz Canyon Way, Palm Springs, CA 92262–6767, ☎ 619/325–5556). **Insight International Tours** (✉ 745 Atlantic Ave., #720, Boston, MA 02111, ☎ 617/482–2000 or 800/582–8380, FAX 617/482–2884 or 800/622–5015). **Trafalgar Tours** (✉ 11 E. 26th St., New York, NY 10010, ☎ 212/689–8977 or 800/854–0103, FAX 800/457–6644). **TWA Getaway Vacations** (☎ 800/438–2929). **United Vacations** (☎ 800/328–6877).

➤ BUDGET: **Cosmos** (☞ Globus, *above*). **Trafalgar Tours** (☞ *above*).

PACKAGES

Like group tours, independent vacation packages are available from major tour operators and airlines. The companies listed below offer vacation packages in a broad price range.

➤ AIR/HOTEL: **American Airlines Vacations** (☎ 800/321–2121). **Celtic International Tours** (✉ 1860 Western Ave., Albany, NY 12203, ☎ 518/862–1810 or 800/833–4373). **Continental Vacations** (☎ 800/634–5555). **Delta Vacations** (☎ 800/872–7786). **DER Tours** (☞ Group Tours, *above*). **Five Star Touring** (✉ 60 E. 42nd St., #612, New York, NY 10165, ☎ 212/818–9140 or 800/792–7827, FAX 212/818–9142). **4th Dimension Tours** (✉ 7101 S.W. 99th Ave., #105, Miami, FL 33173, ☎ 305/279–0014 or 800/644–0438, FAX 305/273–9777). **TWA Getaway Vacations** (☎ 800/438–2929). **United Vacations** (☎ 800/328–6877). **US Airways Vacations** (☎ 800/455–0123).

➤ FLY/DRIVE: **American Airlines Vacations** (☎ 800/321–2121). **Delta Vacations** (☎ 800/872–7786). **United Vacations** (☎ 800/328–6877). Also contact **Budget World-Class Drive** (☎ 800/527–0700, 0800/181181 in the U.K.) for self-drive itineraries.

THEME TRIPS

Travel Contacts (✉ Box 173, Camberley, GU15 1YE, England, ☎ 01276/677–217, FAX 01276/63–477) presents over 150 tour operators in Europe.

➤ ADVENTURE: **Adventure Center** (✉ 1311 63rd St., #200, Emeryville, CA 94608, ☎ 510/654–1879 or 800/227–8747, FAX 510/654–4200). **Himalayan Travel** (✉ 110 Prospect St., Stamford, CT 06901, ☎ 203/359–3711 or 800/225–2380, FAX 203/359–3669). **Mountain Travel-Sobek** (✉ 6420 Fairmount Ave., El Cerrito, CA 94530, ☎ 510/527–8100 or 800/227–2384, FAX 510/525–7710). **Uniquely Europe** (1940 116th Ave. NE, Bellevue, WA 98004, ☎ 425/455–4445 or 800/927–3876, FAX 425/455–2111). **Wilderness Travel** (1102 Ninth St., Berkeley, CA 94710, ☎ 510/558–2488 or 800/368–2794).

➤ ART AND ARCHITECTURE: **Archeological Tours** (✉ 271 Madison Ave., Ste. 904, New York, NY 10016, ☎ 212/986–3054, FAX 212/370–1561). **Endless Beginnings Tours** (✉ 12650 Sabre Springs Pkwy., Ste. 207-105, San Diego, CA 92128, ☎ 619/679–5374 or 800/822–7855, FAX 619/679–5376). **Esplanade Tours** (✉ 581 Boylston St., Boston, MA 02116, ☎ 617/266–7465 or 800/426–5492, FAX 617/262–9829). **Five Star Touring** (☞ Packages, *above*). **Smithsonian Study Tours and Seminars** (✉ 1100 Jefferson Dr. SW, Room 3045, MRC 702, Washington, DC 20560, ☎ 202/357–4700, FAX 202/633–9250). In the United Kingdom, contact **Prospect Music & Art Tours Ltd.** (✉ 454–458 Chiswick High Rd., London W4 5TT, ☎ 0181/995–2151) and **Swan Hellenic** (✉ 77 New Oxford St., London WC1A 1PP, ☎ 0171/800–2200).

➤ BALLOONING: **Buddy Bombard European Balloon Adventures** (✉

333 Pershing Way, West Palm Beach, FL 33401, ☎ 561/837–6610 or 800/862–8537, FAX 561/837–6623). **Virgin Balloon Flights** (✉ 54 Linhope St., London NW1 6HL, ☎ 0171/706–1021).

➤ BARGE/RIVER CRUISES: **Abercrombie & Kent** (☞ Group Tours, *above*). **Alden Yacht Charters** (✉ 1909 Alden Landing, Portsmouth, RI 02871, ☎ 401/683–1782 or 800/662–2628, FAX 401/683–3668). **Etoile de Champagne** (88 Broad St., Boston, MA 02110, ☎ 800/280–1492, FAX 617/426–4689). **European Waterways** (✉ 140 E. 56th St., Ste. 4C, New York, NY 10022, ☎ 212/688–9489 or 800/217–4447, FAX 212/688–3778 or 800/296–4554). **Fenwick & Lang** (1940 116th Ave. NE, Bellevue, WA 98004, ☎ 425/455–4445 or 800/927–3876, FAX 425/455–2111). **KD River Cruises of Europe** (✉ 2500 Westchester Ave., Purchase, NY 10577, ☎ 914/696–3600 or 800/346–6525, FAX 914/696–0833). **Kemwel's Premier Selections** (✉ 106 Calvert St., Harrison, NY 10528, ☎ 914/835–5555 or 800/234–4000, FAX 914/835–5449). **Le Boat** (✉ 10 S. Franklin Turnpike, #204B, Ramsey, NJ 07446, ☎ 201/236–2333 or 800/922–0291). In the U.K.: **Top Deck Travel** (✉ 131–135 Earls Court Rd., London SW5 9RH, ☎ 0171/244–8641).

➤ BICYCLING: **Backroads** (✉ 801 Cedar St., Berkeley, CA 94710-1800, ☎ 510/527–1555 or 800/462–2848, FAX 510-527–1444). **Bike Riders** (✉ Box 254, Boston, MA 02113, ☎ 617/723–2354 or 800/473–7040, FAX 617/723–2355). **Butterfield & Robinson** (✉ 70 Bond St., Toronto, Ontario, Canada M5B 1X3, ☎ 416/864–1354 or 800/678–1147, FAX 416/864–0541). **Classic Adventures** (✉ Box 153, Hamlin, NY 14464-0153, ☎ 716/964–8488 or 800/777–8090, FAX 716/964-7297). **Easy Rider Tours** (✉ Box 228, Newburyport MA 01950, ☎ 978/463–6955 or 800/488–8332, FAX 978/463–6988). **Euro-Bike Tours** (✉ Box 990, De Kalb, IL 60115, ☎ 815/758–8851 or 800/321–6060). **Europeds** (✉ 761 Lighthouse Ave., Monterey, CA 93940, ☎ 800/321–9552, FAX 408/655–4501). **Himalayan Travel** (☞ Adventure, *above*). **Imagine Tours** (✉ Box 123, Davis, CA 95617, ☎ 530/758–8782 or 888/592–8687, FAX 530/758–8778). **Progressive Travels** (224 W. Galer Ave., Suite C, Seattle, WA 98119, ☎ 206/285–1987 or 800/245–2229, FAX 206/285–1988). **Rocky Mountain Worldwide Cycle Tours** (✉ 333 Baker St., Nelson, BC, Canada V1L 4H6, ☎ 250/354–1241 or 800/661–2453, FAX 250/354–2058). **Uniquely Europe** (☞ Adventure, *above*). **Vermont Bicycle Touring** (Box 711, Bristol, VT, 05443-0711, ☎ 800/245–3868 or 802/453–4811, FAX 802/453–4806).

➤ CRUISING: **EuroCruises** (✉ 303 W. 13th St., New York, NY 10014-1207, ☎ 800/688–3876, FAX 212/366–4747).

➤ FISHING: **Fishing International** (✉ Box 2132, Santa Rosa, CA 95405, ☎ 707/539–3366 or 800/950–4242, FAX 707/539–1320).

➤ FOOD AND WINE: **Annemarie Victory Organization** (✉ 136 E. 64th St., New York, NY 10021, ☎ 212/486–0353, FAX 212/751–3149). **Cuisine International** (✉ Box 25228, Dallas, TX 75225, ☎ 214/373–1161, FAX 214/373–1162). **Le Cordon Bleu** (✉ 404 Airport Executive Park, Nanuet, NY 10954, ☎ 914/426–7400 or 800/457–2433, FAX 914/426–0104). **Travel Concepts** (✉ 62 Commonwealth Ave., #3, Boston, MA 02116, ☎ 617/266–8450). **Winetrails** (✉ Greenways, Vann Lake, Ockley, Dorking RH5 5NT, ☎ 01306/712–111) has leisurely walks through the wine regions of Europe, with accommodations in family hotels, wine estates, and chateaux.

➤ GARDENS AND HOMES: **Coopersmith's England** (✉ Box 900, Inverness, CA 94937, ☎ 415/669–1914, FAX 415/669–1942). **Expo Garden Tours** (✉ 70 Great Oak, Redding, CT 06896, ☎ 203/938–0410 or 800/448–2685, FAX 203/938–0427).

➤ GOLF: **Francine Atkins Scotland Ireland** (✉ 2 Ross Court, Trophy Club, TX 76262, ☎ 817/491–1105 or 800/742–0355, FAX 817/491–2025). **Golf International** (✉ 275 Madison Ave., New York, NY 10016, ☎ 212/986–9176 or 800/833–1389,

FAX 212/986–3720). **ITC Golf Tours** (✉ 4134 Atlantic Ave., #205, Long Beach, CA 90807, ☎ 310/595–6905 or 800/257–4981). **Stine's Golftrips** (✉ 893 Towne Center Dr., Kissimmee, FL 34759, ☎ 407/933–0032 or 800/428–1940, FAX 407/933–8857). In the U.K.: **Green Card Golf Holidays** (✉ 11A Queensdale Rd., London W11 4QF, ☎ 0171/727–7287).

➤ HORSEBACK RIDING: **Cross Country International Equestrian Vacations** (✉ Box 1170, Millbrook, NY 12545, ☎ 800/828–8768, FAX 914/677–6077). **Equitour FITS Equestrian** (✉ Box 807, Dubois, WY 82513, ☎ 307/455–3363 or 800/545–0019, FAX 307/455–2354).

➤ LEARNING: **Fresh Pond Travel Vacations** (✉ 186 Alewife Brook Parkway, Cambridge, MA 02138, ☎ 617/661–9200 or 800/645–0001, FAX 617/661–3354). **IST Cultural Tours** (✉ 225 W. 34th St., New York, NY 10122-0913, ☎ 212/563–1202 or 800/833–2111, FAX 212/594–6953). **Smithsonian Study Tours and Seminars** (☞ Art and Architecture, *above*).

➤ MOTORCYCLE: **Beach's Motorcycle Adventures** (✉ 2763 W. River Pkwy., Grand Island, NY 14072-2053, ☎ 716/773–4960, FAX 716/773–5227). **Edelweiss Bike Travel** (Hartford Holidays Travel, 129 Hillside Ave., Williston Park, NY 11596, ☎ 516/746–6761 or 800/877–2784, FAX 516/746–6690).

➤ MUSIC: In the United Kingdom **Travel for the Arts** (✉ 117 Regent's Park Rd., London NW1 8UR, ☎ 0171/483–4466) arranges individual and group holidays to visit the musical highlights of regions throughout Europe. **Prospect Music & Art Tours Ltd.** (☞ Art and Architecture, *above*) has tours to many of the famous annual festivals—Verona, Savonlinna, Prague, Bregenz, and Munich among them.

➤ NATURAL HISTORY: **Earthwatch** (✉ Box 9104, 680 Mount Auburn St., Watertown, MA 02272, ☎ 617/926–8200 or 800/776–0188, FAX 617/926–8532) for research expeditions. **Naturequest** (934 Acapulco St., Laguna Beach, CA 92651, ☎ 714/499–9561 or 800/369–3033, FAX 714/499–0812). **Victor Emanuel Nature Tours** (✉ Box 33008, Austin, TX 78764, ☎ 512/328–5221 or 800/328–8368, FAX 512/328–2919).

➤ PERFORMING ARTS: **Dailey-Thorp Travel** (✉ 330 W. 58th St., #610, New York, NY 10019-1817, ☎ 212/307–1555 or 800/998–4677, FAX 212/974–1420). **Keith Prowse Tours** (✉ 234 W. 44th St., #1000, New York, NY 10036, ☎ 212/398–1430 or 800/669–7469, FAX 212/302–4251).

➤ SINGLES AND YOUNG ADULTS: **Club Europa** (✉ 802 W. Oregon St., Urbana, IL 61801, ☎ 217/344–5863 or 800/331–1882, FAX 217/344–4072). **Contiki Holidays** (✉ 300 Plaza Alicante, #900, Garden Grove, CA 92640, ☎ 714/740–0808 or 800/266–8454, FAX 714/740–0818). **Trafalgar Tours** (☞ Group Tours, *above*).

➤ SKIING: **Top Deck Travel** (☞ Barge/River Cruises, *above*). **Crystal Holidays** (✉ Crystal House, The Courtyard, Arlington Rd., Surbiton KT6 6BW, ☎ 0181/399–5144).

➤ SPAS: **Custom Spa Vacations** (✉ 1318 Beacon St., Brookline, MA 02146, ☎ 617/566–5144 or 800/443–7727, FAX 617/731–0599). **Great Spas of the World** (✉ 55 John St., New York, NY 10038, ☎ 212/267–5500 or 800/772–8463, FAX 212/571–0510). **Spa-Finders** (✉ 91 5th Ave., #301, New York, NY 10003-3039, ☎ 212/924–6800 or 800/255–7727). **Spa Trek Travel** (✉ 475 Park Ave. South, New York, NY 10016, ☎ 212/779–3480 or 800/272–3480, FAX 212/779–3471). In the U.K.: **Moswin Tours Ltd.** (✉ 21 Church St., Oadby, Leicester LE2 5DB, ☎ 0116/271–9922) counts spa resorts and city breaks among its programs.

➤ SPORTS: **Championship Tennis Tours** (✉ 8040 E. Morgan Trail #12, Scottsdale, AZ 85258, ☎ 602/443–9499 or 800/468–3664, FAX 602/443–8982). **Sportstours** (✉ Box 191072, Miami Beach, FL 33119, ☎ 800/879–8647, FAX 305/535–0008). **Steve Furgal's International Tennis Tours** (✉ 11828 Rancho

Bernardo Rd., #123-305, San Diego, CA 92128, ☎ 619/675–3555 or 800/258–3664). **Travel Concepts** (☞ Food and Wine, *above*).

➤ TRAIN TOURS: **Abercrombie & Kent** (☞ Group Tours, *above*). **Kemwel's Premier Selections** (☞ Barge/River Cruises, *above*).

➤ WALKING/HIKING: **Abercrombie & Kent** (☞ Group Tours, *above*). **Above the Clouds Trekking** (✉ Box 398, Worcester, MA 01602-0398, ☎ 508/799–4499 or 800/233–4499, FAX 508/797–4779). **Backroads** (☞ Bicycling, *above*). **Butterfield & Robinson** (☞ Bicycling, *above*). **Country Walkers** (✉ Box 180, Waterbury, VT 05676-0180, ☎ 802/244–1387 or 800/464–9255, FAX 802/244–5661). **Euro-Bike Tours** (☞ Bicycling, *above*). **Europeds** (☞ Bicycling, *above*). **Progressive Travels** (☞ Bicycling, *above*). **Ramblers Holidays Ltd.** (✉ Box 43, Welwyn Garden City, Hertfordshire AL8 6PQ, ☎ 01707/331–133). **Uniquely Europe** (☞ Adventure, *above*). **Walking the World** (✉ Box 1186, Fort Collins, CO 80522, ☎ 970/498–0500 or 800/340–9255, FAX 970/498–9100) specializes in tours for ages 50 and older.

➤ YACHT CHARTERS: **Huntley Yacht Vacations** (✉ 210 Preston Rd., Wernersville, PA 19565, ☎ 610/678–2628 or 800/322–9224, FAX 610/670–1767). **Lynn Jachney Charters** (✉ Box 302, Marblehead, MA 01945, ☎ 617/639–0787 or 800/223–2050, FAX 617/639–0216). **Ocean Voyages** (✉ 1709 Bridgeway, Sausalito, CA 94965, ☎ 415/332–4681 or 800/299–4444, FAX 415/332–7460). **Russell Yacht Charters** (✉ 404 Hulls Hwy., #175, Southport, CT 06490, ☎ 203/255–2783 or 800/635–8895). **SailAway Yacht Charters** (✉ 15605 S.W. 92nd Ave., Miami, FL 33157-1972, ☎ 305/253–7245 or 800/724–5292, FAX 305/251–4408).

TRAIN TRAVEL

Some national high-speed train systems have begun to link up to form the nucleus of a pan-European system. On a long journey, you still have to change trains a couple of times, for the national railways are jealously guarding their prerogatives. Deregulation, so far achieved only in Britain, is vigorously pushed by the European Commission. Even so, French TGV (Trains à Grande Vitesse), which serve most major cities in France, have been extended to Geneva, Lausanne, Bern, Zurich, Turin, and Milan. They link up with the latest generation of Italy's tilting Pendolino trains, also called Eurostar Italia. They extend beyond the country's borders with a service from Turin to Lyon and, in a joint venture with the Swiss Railways, from Milan to Geneva and Zurich. The TGV–like Thalys trains operate from Brussels to Paris on high-speed tracks and from Brussels to Amsterdam and Cologne on conventional track. Germany's equally fast ICE trains connect Hamburg and points in between with Basel, and Mannheim with Munich.

High-speed trains cover the distance from Paris to Marseille in just over 4 hours, Hamburg to Munich in less than 6, traveling at speeds of up to 190 mph on dedicated track and over 150 mph on old track. They have made both expensive sleeper compartments and budget *couchettes* (seats that convert into bunks) all but obsolete. Their other attraction is the comfort of a super-smooth ride. The flip side is the reservations requirement; rather than just hopping on the next train, you need to **reserve in advance or allow enough time to make a reservation at the station.**

Virtually all European systems, including the high-speed ones, operate a two-tier class system. First class costs substantially more and is usually a luxury rather than a necessity. Some of the poorer European countries retain a third class, but avoid it unless you're an adventure-minded budget traveler. For additional information on rail services and special fares, contact the national tourist office of the country (☞ Visitor Information, *below*).

DISCOUNT PASSES

Before you invest in a discount pass, ask for a comparison of the cost against the point-to-point fares on your actual itinerary. (Rates given in this section are for 1998, the latest available at press time.) EurailPasses provide unlimited first-class rail travel for the duration of the pass in 17 European countries: Austria, Belgium, Denmark, Finland, France, Germany, Greece, Hungary, the Irish Republic, Italy, Luxembourg, the Netherlands, Norway, Portugal, Spain, Sweden, and Switzerland (but not the United Kingdom). If you plan to rack up the miles, get a standard pass. These are available for 15 days ($538, £359), 21 days ($698, £468), one month ($864, £576), two months ($1,224, £816), and three months ($1,512, £1,008). Note that you will have to pay a supplement for certain high-speed trains—half the fare on Eurostar.

In addition to standard EurailPasses, check out special rail-pass plans. Among these are the Eurail Youthpass (in second class for those under-26, from $376/£251 to $1,059/£706), the Eurail Saverpass (which gives a discount for 2 or more people traveling together; a minimum of two persons Oct. through March, three April through Sept.; from $458/£305 to $1,286/£558 per person), and the Eurail Flexipass (which allows 10 or 15 travel days within a two-month period, $634/£423 and $836/£558 respectively).

If your plans call for only limited train travel, consider Europass, which costs less money than a EurailPass and is available in first class only for adults and second class only for travelers under 26. It has a number of conditions. It is valid only in France, Germany, Italy, Spain, and Switzerland, but "associated countries" can be added at an extra charge. These are Austria/Hungary, the Benelux area, Greece and Portugal. You also get a limited number of travel days, in a limited number of countries, during a specified time period. The other side of the coin is that a Europass costs a couple of hundred dollars less than the least expensive EurailPass. A Europass Adult ranges in price from $326 to $866 (£217 to £577), a Europass Youth from $216 to $599 (£144 to £399).

It used to be the rule that you had to **purchase your pass before you leave** for Europe. This remains the recommended option, but in case of need you can now buy a pass within six months of your arrival in Europe from Rail Europe in London (☎ 0990/300–003). Also remember that you need to **book seats ahead even if you are using a rail pass**; seat reservations are required on European high-speed trains, and are a good idea on other trains that may be crowded—particularly around Easter and at the beginning and end of European vacation periods. You will also need to purchase sleeper or couchette (sleeping berth) reservations separately.

European nationals and others who have resided in Europe for at least six months qualify for the **InterRail Pass.** It used to be exclusively for young people but can now also be purchased, at a premium, by older travelers. This entitles you to unlimited second-class travel within up to eight zones you have preselected. One zone for 22 days, for instance, costs UK£159 for -26's (£229 for 26+); all zones for one month, £259 (£349). InterRail Passes can be bought only in Europe at main railway stations.

➤ EURAIL & EURO PASSES: **CIT Tours Corp.** (✉ 15 West 44th St., 10th Floor, New York, NY 10036, ☎ 800/248–7245 for rail or 800/248–8687 for tours and hotels), **DER Travel Services** (☞ Discount Passes, Eurolines, *in* Bus Travel, *above*), **Rail Europe** (✉ 226–230 Westchester Ave., White Plains, NY 10604, ☎ 800/438–7245, FAX 800/432–1329; ✉ 2087 Dundas E., Suite 105, Mississauga, Ontario L4X 1M2, ☎ 905/602–4195), **Swissair's Swisspak** (☞ Tour Operators, Packages, *above*).

➤ PUBLICATION: **Guide to European Rail Passes** (Back Door, ✉ Box 2009, Edmonds, WA. 98020, ☎ 425/771–8304, FAX 425/771–0833; free), by Rick Steves, leads you through the maze of different passes. You can order passes from the same source.

INDIVIDUAL COUNTRY PASSES

Single-country passes are issued by most national railways, and the majority are sold by Rail Europe (☞ EurailPasses, *above*). ☞ *also* individual country chapters.

FROM THE U.K.

Sleek, high-speed Eurostar trains use the Channel Tunnel to link London (Waterloo) with Paris (Gare du Nord) in 3 hours and with Brussels (Gare du Midi) in 2 hours, 40 minutes. When the British build their high-speed rail link to London (St. Pancras), probably in 2003, another half-hour will be shaved off travel time. There are a minimum of 14 daily services to Paris and 10 to Brussels.

Many of the trains stop at Ashford (Kent), and all at the new Lille-Europe station in northern France, where you can change to French TGV trains to Brittany, southwest France, Lyon, the Alps, and the Riviera, eliminating the need to transit between stations in Paris.

Passengers headed for Germany and the Netherlands can buy through tickets via Brussels to Cologne (5½ hours) and Amsterdam (5 hours, 45 minutes). Eurostar does not accept EurailPasses but allows discounts of 40%–50% to passholders. Check for special prices and deals before you book. Or, if money is no object, you can choose the new Premium First Class (to Paris only), complete with limo delivery and pick-up at the stations, improved catering, and greater comfort.

Conventional boat trains from London are timed to dovetail with ferry departures at Channel ports. The ferries connect with onward trains at the main French, Belgian, Dutch and Irish ports. Be sure to ask when making your reservation which London railway station to use.

➤ EUROSTAR RESERVATIONS AND INFORMATION: Eurostar (☎ 800/942–4866 or 805/482–8210 in U.S.; ☎ 0345/303030 in the U.K.; ☎ 01233/617–575 from other countries). **Rail Europe** (179 Piccadilly and Victoria Station, London, reservations ☎ 0990/300–003).

SPECIAL TRAINS

The **Orient Express,** a glamorous recreation of a sumptuous past, takes two days to cover the distance from London to Venice, and if you want to know the price you can't afford it. The Swiss Railways operate special services that allow you to enjoy superb scenery and railway buffs to admire the equally superb railroad technology. The **Panoramic Express** takes 3 hours to travel from Montreux via Gstaad to Interlaken; the **Glacier Express** (7½ hours) runs from Zermatt to St. Moritz and also offers en-route gourmet dining as befits these famous resorts; and the **Bernina Express,** the most spectacular, runs from Chur over the 7,400-ft Bernina Pass (where you can turn around; each leg takes 2½ hours), or you can continue to Tirano in Italy (4 hours, with connections to Lugano and Milan). Holders of a Swisspass can travel on all three, but reservations are needed.

➤ THE ORIENT EXPRESS: Venice Simplon-Orient Express (✉ Sea Containers House, 20 Upper Ground, London SE1 9PF, ☎ 0171/805–5100, reservations, or ☎ 0870/607–6077, brochures; ☎ 800/524–2420, reservations in U.S.).

➤ SWISS SPECIALS: For information, contact the Swiss National Tourist Office (☞ Visitor Information, *below.*)

TIMETABLES

A good rail timetable is indispensable if you're doing extensive rail traveling. The Thomas Cook Timetables are updated monthly. There's also an annual summer edition (limited to Britain, France, and the Benelux).

➤ TO ORDER TIMETABLES: **Forsyth Travel Library** (☎ 800/367–7984, FAX 816/942–6969).

TRAVEL AGENCIES

A good travel agent puts your needs first. Look for an agency that has been in business at least five years, emphasizes customer service, and has someone on staff who specializes in your destination. In addition, **make sure the agency belongs to a professional trade organization,** such as ASTA in the United States. If your travel agency is also acting as your tour operator, *see* Buyer Beware in Tour Operators, *above.*

➤ LOCAL AGENT REFERRALS: **American Society of Travel Agents** (ASTA, ☎ 800/965–2782 24-hr hot line, FAX 703/684–8319). **Association of**

Canadian Travel Agents (✉ Suite 201, 1729 Bank St., Ottawa, Ontario K1V 7Z5, ☎ 613/521–0474, FAX 613/521–0805). **Association of British Travel Agents** (✉ 55–57 Newman St., London W1P 4AH, ☎ 0171/637–2444, FAX 0171/637–0713). **Australian Federation of Travel Agents** (☎ 02/9264–3299). **Travel Agents' Association of New Zealand** (☎ 04/499–0104).

TRAVEL GEAR

Travel catalogs specialize in useful items, such as compact alarm clocks and travel irons, that can **save space when packing.** They also offer dual-voltage appliances, currency converters, and foreign-language phrase books.

➤ CATALOGS: **Magellan's** (☎ 800/962–4943, FAX 805/568–5406). **Orvis Travel** (☎ 800/541–3541, FAX 540/343–7053). **TravelSmith** (☎ 800/950–1600, FAX 800/950–1656).

U.S. GOVERNMENT

Government agencies can be an excellent source of inexpensive travel information. When planning your trip, **find out what government materials are available.**

➤ ADVISORIES: **U.S. Department of State** (✉ Overseas Citizens Services Office, Room 4811 N.S., Washington, DC 20520; ☎ 202/647–5225 or FAX 202/647–3000 for interactive hot-line; ☎ 301/946–4400 for computer bulletin board); enclose a self-addressed, stamped, business-size envelope.

➤ PAMPHLETS: **Consumer Information Center** (✉ Consumer Information Catalogue, Pueblo, CO 81009, ☎ 719/948–3334 or 888/878–3256) for a free catalog with travel titles.

VISITOR INFORMATION

For general information before you go, contact the national tourism offices below.

➤ AUSTRIAN NATIONAL TOURIST OFFICE: **U.S.** (✉ Box 1142, Times Square Station, New York, NY 10108-1142, ☎ 212/944–6880, FAX 212/730–4568). **Canada** (✉ 2 Bloor St. E, Suite 3330, Toronto, Ontario M4W 1A8, ☎ 416/967–3381, FAX 416/967–4101; ✉ 1010 Ouest Rue, Sherbrooke, Ste. 1410, Montréal, Québec, H3A 2R7, ☎ 514/849–3709, FAX 514/849–9577; ✉ Granville Sq., 200 Granville St., Ste. 1380, Vancouver, British Columbia, V6C 1S4, ☎ 604/683–5808, FAX 604/662–8528). **U.K.** (14 Cork St., London, W1X 1PF, ☎ 0171/629–0461, FAX 0171/499–6038). **Australia and New Zealand** (✉ 36 Carrington St., 1st floor, Sydney, NSW 2000, ☎ 2/9299–3621, FAX 2/9299–3808). **Ireland** (✉ Merrion Hall, Strand Rd., Sandymount, P.O. Box 2506, Dublin, ☎ 283–0488, FAX 283–0531).

➤ BELGIAN NATIONAL TOURIST OFFICE: **U.S.** (✉ 780 3rd Ave., New York, NY 10017, ☎ 212/758–8130, FAX 212/355–7675). **Canada** (✉ Box 760 NDG, Montréal, Québec H4A 3S2, ☎ 514/484–3594, FAX 514/489–8965). **U.K.** (✉ 29 Prince St., London W1R 7RG, ☎ 0891/887–799, FAX 0171/629–0454). Calls cost 50p per minute peak rate or 45p per minute cheap rate.

➤ BRITISH TOURIST AUTHORITY: **U.S.:** Nationwide (✉ 551 5th Ave., Suite 701, New York, NY 10176, ☎ 212/986–2200 or 800/462–2748, FAX 212/986–1188); 24-hour fax information line (FAX 818/441–8265); Chicago (✉ 625 N. Michigan Ave., Suite 1510, 60611; walk-in service only). **Canada** (✉ 111 Avenue Rd., Suite 450, Toronto, Ontario M5R 3J8, ☎ 416/961–8124, FAX 416/961–2175). **U.K.** British Travel Centre (✉ 12 Regent St., London SW1Y 4PQ [no information by phone] or ✉ Thames Tower, Black's Rd., London W6 9EL, ☎ 0181/846–9000). **Australia** (✉ Level 16, Gateway, 1 Macquarie Place, Sydney, NSW 2000, ☎ 2/9377–4400, FAX 2/9377–4499). **New Zealand** (✉ Dilworth Bldg., Suite 305, 3rd floor, Corner of Queen & Customs Streets, Auckland 1, ☎ 9/303–1446, FAX 9/377–6965). **Ireland** (✉ 18-19 College Green, Dublin 2, ☎ 1670–8000, FAX 1670–8244).

➤ BULGARIAN NATIONAL TOURIST OFFICE: **U.S. and Canada** Balkan Tourist (authorized agent, ✉ 20 E. 46th St., Suite 1003, New York, NY 10017, ☎ 212/822–5900, FAX 212/822–5910). **U.K.** Balkan Holidays

(✉ 19 Conduit St., London W1R 9TD, ☎ 0171/491–4499).

➤ CYPRUS TOURIST OFFICE: **U.S. and Canada** (✉ 13 E. 40th St., New York, NY 10016, ☎ 212/683–5280, FAX 212/683–5282). **U.K.** (✉ 213 Regent St., London W1R 8DA, ☎ 0171/734–9822 or 0171/734–2593, FAX 0171/287-6534; North Cyprus Tourist Office, ✉ 28 Cockspur St., London SW1Y 5BN, ☎ 0171/930–5069).

➤ CZECH CENTER: **U.S. and Canada** (✉ 1109 Madison Ave., New York, NY 10028, ☎ 212/288–0830). **U.K.** (✉ 49 Southwark St., London SE1 1RU, ☎ 0171/378–6009, FAX 0171/403–2321; ✉ 30 Kensington Palace Gardens, London W8 4QY, ☎ 0171/243–7981, FAX 0171/727–9589).

➤ DANISH TOURIST BOARD: **U.S. and Canada** Scandinavia Tourism Inc. (✉ Box 4649 Grand Central Station, New York, NY 10163–4649, ☎ 212/949–2333, FAX 212/885–9710). **U.K.** (✉ 55 Sloane St., London SW1X 9SY, ☎ 0171/259–5959 or ☎ 0891/600–109 for 24-hour brochure line, FAX 0171/259–5955). Calls to the brochure line cost 50p per minute peak rate or 45p per minute cheap rate.

➤ ESTONIAN TOURIST OFFICE: **U.S.** Consulate (630 Fifth Ave., Suite 2415, New York, NY 10011, ☎ 212/247–7634, FAX 212/262–0893). **Canada** Consulate (958 Broadview Ave., Suite 202, Toronto, ON M4K 2R6, ☎ 416/461–0764,FAX 416/461–0448). **U.K.**. Embassy (16 Hyde Park Gate, London, SW7 5DG, ☎ 171/589–3428, FAX 171/589–3430).

➤ FINNISH TOURIST BOARD: **U.S. and Canada** Scandinavia Tourism Inc. (✉ Box 4649 Grand Central Station, New York, NY 10163-4649, ☎ 212/949–2333, FAX 212/885–9710). **U.K.** (✉ 30–35 Pall Mall, London SW1Y 5LP, ☎ 0171/839–4048, FAX 0171/321–0696).

➤ FRENCH GOVERNMENT TOURIST OFFICE: **U.S.** Nationwide (☎ 900/990–0040; costs 50¢ per minute); New York City (✉ 444 Madison Ave., 10022, ☎ 212/838–7800); Chicago (✉ 676 N. Michigan Ave., 60611, ☎ 312/751–7800); Beverly Hills (✉ 9454 Wilshire Blvd., 90212, ☎ 310/271–6665, FAX 310/276–2835). **Canada** (✉ 1981 Ave., McGill College, Suite 490, Montréal, Québec H3A 2W9, ☎ 514/288–4264, FAX 514/845–4868; ✉ 30 St. Patrick St., Suite 700, Toronto, Ontario M5T 3A3, ☎ 416/491–7622, FAX 416/979–7587). **U.K.** (✉ 178 Piccadilly, London W1V OAL, ☎ 0891/244–123, FAX 0171/493–6594). Calls cost 50p per minute peak rate or 45p per minute cheap rate.

➤ GERMAN NATIONAL TOURIST OFFICE: **U.S.** Nationwide (✉ 122 E. 42nd St., New York, NY 10168, ☎ 212/661–7200, FAX 212/661–7174). **Canada** (✉ 175 Bloor St. E, Suite 604, Toronto, Ontario M4W 3R8, ☎ 416/968–1570, FAX 416/968–1986). **U.K.** (✉ Nightingale House, 65 Curzon St., London W1Y 8NE, ☎ 0171/493–0081 or 0891/600–100 for brochures, FAX 0171/495–6129). **Australia** (✉ P.O. Box A980, Sydney, NSW 1235, ☎ 9267–8148, FAX 9267–9035). Calls to the brochure-line cost 50p per minute peak rate or 45p per minute cheap rate.

➤ GIBRALTAR INFORMATION BUREAU: **U.S. and Canada** (✉ 1156 15th St. NW, Suite 1100, Washington, DC 20005, ☎ 202/452–1108, FAX 202/872–8543). **U.K.** (✉ Arundel Great Court, 179 The Strand, London WC2R 1EH, ☎ 0171/836–0777, FAX 0170/240–6612).

➤ GREEK NATIONAL TOURIST ORGANIZATION: **U.S.:** Nationwide (✉ 645 5th Ave., New York, NY 10022, ☎ 212/421–5777, FAX 212/826–6940); Los Angeles (✉ 611 W. 6th St., Suite 2198, 90017, ☎ 213/626–6696, FAX 213/489–9744); Chicago (✉ 168 N. Michigan Ave., Suite 600, 60601, ☎ 312/782–1084, FAX 312/782–1091). **Canada** (✉ 1233 Rue de la Montagne, Suite 101, Montréal, Québec H3G 1Z2, ☎ 514/871–1535, FAX 514/871–1498; ✉ 1300 Bay St., Toronto, Ontario M5R 3K8, ☎ 416/968–2220, FAX 416/968–6533). **U.K.** (✉ 4 Conduit St., London W1R 0DJ, ☎ 0171/734–5997, FAX 0171/287–1369). **Australia** (✉ 51-57 Pitt St., Sydney, NSW 2000, ☎ 9241–1663, FAX 9235–2174.

➤ HUNGARIAN NATIONAL TOURIST OFFICE: **U.S. and Canada** (✉ 150 E. 58th St., New York, NY 10155, ☎

212/355–0240, FAX 212/207–4103). **U.K.** (✉ Embassy of the Republic of Hungary, Commercial Section, 46 Eaton Pl., London SW1X 8AL, ☎ 0171/823–1032 or 0171/823–1055, FAX 0171/823–1459).

➤ ICELAND TOURIST BOARD: **U.S. and Canada** Scandinavia Tourism Inc. (✉ Box 4649 Grand Central Station, New York, NY 10163–4649, ☎ 212/949–2333, FAX 212/885–9710). **U.K.** (✉ 172 Tottenham Court Rd., 3rd floor, London W1P 9LG, ☎ 0171/388–7550).

➤ IRISH TOURIST BOARD: **U.S.** (✉ 345 Park Ave., New York, NY 10154, ☎ 212/418–0800 or 800/223–6470, FAX 212/371–9052). **Canada** (✉ 160 Bloor St. E, Suite 1150, Toronto, Ontario M4W 1B9, ☎ 416/487–3335, FAX 416/929–6783). **U.K.** (✉ Ireland House, 150 New Bond St., London W1Y 0AQ, ☎ 0171/493–3201, FAX 0171/493–9065). **Australia** (✉ 5th floor, 36 Carrington St., Sydney, NSW 2000, ☎ 2929–9677, FAX 9299–6323). **Ireland** (✉ Baggot Street Bridge, Dublin 2,☎ 3531/605–7700, FAX 3531/605–7749).

➤ ITALIAN GOVERNMENT TOURIST BOARD (ENIT): **U.S.** Nationwide (✉ 630 5th Ave., New York, NY 10111, ☎ 212/245–4822, FAX 212/586–9249); Chicago (✉ 401 N. Michigan Ave., 60611, ☎ 312/644–0990, FAX 312/644–3019); Los Angeles (✉ 12400 Wilshire Blvd., Suite 550, 90025, ☎ 310/820–0098, FAX 310/820–6357). **Canada** (✉ 1 Pl. Ville Marie, Suite 1914, Montréal, Québec H3B 3M9, ☎ 514/866–7667, FAX 514/392–1429). **U.K.** (✉ 1 Princes St., London W1R 8AY, ☎ 0171/408–1254, FAX 0171/493–6695).

➤ LUXEMBOURG NATIONAL TOURIST OFFICE: **U.S. and Canada** (✉ 17 Beekman Pl., New York, NY 10022, ☎ 212/935–8888, FAX 212/935–5896). **U.K.** (✉ 122 Regent St., London W1R 5FE, ☎ 0171/434–2800, FAX 0171/734–1205).

➤ MALTA NATIONAL TOURIST OFFICE: **U.S. and Canada** (✉ 350 5th Ave., Suite 4412, New York, NY 10118, ☎ 212/695–9520, FAX 212/695–8229). **U.K.** (✉ 36–38 Piccadilly, London W1V 0PP, ☎ 0171/292–4900, FAX 0171/734–1880). **Ireland** (14 Leeson Park, Dublin 6, ☎ 0353/496–0244, FAX 0353/497–5183).

➤ MONACO GOVERNMENT TOURIST OFFICE AND CONVENTION BUREAU: **U.S. and Canada** (✉ 565 5th Ave., New York, NY 10017, ☎ 212/286–3330, FAX 212/286–9890). **U.K.** (✉ 3–18 Chelsea Garden Market, Chelsea Harbour, London SW10 0XF, ☎ 0171/352–9962, FAX 0171/352–2103).

➤ NETHERLANDS BOARD OF TOURISM: **U.S. and Canada** (✉ 225 N. Michigan Ave., Suite 1854, Chicago, IL 60601, ☎ 312/819–1500, FAX 312/819–1740; for brochures, ☎ 888/464–6552). **Canada** (✉ 25 Adelaide St. E, Suite 710, Toronto, Ontario M5C 1Y2; mailing address only). **U.K.** (✉ 25–28 Buckingham Gate, London SW1E 6LD, ☎ 0891/717–777, FAX 0171/828–7941). Calls cost 50p per minute peak rate or 45p per minute cheap rate.

➤ NORWEGIAN TOURIST BOARD: **U.S. and Canada** Scandinavia Tourism Inc. (✉ Box 4649 Grand Central Station, New York, NY 10163–4649, ☎ 212/949–2333, FAX 212/885–9710). **U.K.** (✉ Charles House, 5–11 Lower Regent St., London SW1Y 4LR, ☎ 0171/839–6255, FAX 0171/839–6041).

➤ POLISH NATIONAL TOURIST OFFICE: **U.S. and Canada** (✉ 275 Madison Ave., Suite 1711, New York, NY 10016, ☎ 212/338–9412, FAX 212/338–9283). **U.K.** (✉ 310–312 Regent St., Remo House, 1st floor, London W1R 5AJ, ☎ 0171/580–8811, FAX 0171/580–8866).

➤ PORTUGUESE NATIONAL TOURIST OFFICE: **U.S.** (✉ 590 5th Ave., 4th floor, New York, NY 10036, ☎ 212/354–4403, FAX 212/764–6137). **Canada** (✉ 60 Bloor St. W, Suite 1005, Toronto, Ontario M4W 3B4, ☎ 416/921–7376, FAX 416/921–1353). **U.K.** (✉ 2nd floor, 22–25A Sackville St., London W1X 2LY, ☎ 0171/494–1441 or 0891/600–370 [24-hour brochure line], FAX 0171/494–1868). Calls to the brochure line cost 50p per minute peak rate or 45p per minute cheap rate. **Ireland** (✉ 54 Dawson St., Dublin 2 ☎ 670–9133, FAX 670–9141).

➤ Romanian National Tourist Office: **U.S. and Canada** (✉ 342 Madison Ave., Suite 210, New York, NY 10173, ☎ 212/697–6971, FAX 212/697–6972). **U.K.** (✉ 83A Marylebone High St., London W1M 3DE, ☎ 0171/224–3692, FAX 0171/224–3692).

➤ Slovak Tourist Office: **U.S. and Canada:** Embassy of the Slovak Republic (✉ 2201 Wisconsin Ave., NW, Suite 250, Washington, DC 20007, ☎ 202/965–5160, FAX 202/965–5166); **U.K.:** Embassy of the Slovak Republic, Information Dept. (✉ 25 Kensington Palace Gardens, London W8 4QY, ☎ 0171/243–0830, FAX 0171/727–5821).

➤ Tourist Office of Spain: **U.S.:** Nationwide (✉ 666 5th Ave., 35th floor, New York, NY 10103, ☎ 212/265–8822, FAX 212/265–8864); Chicago (✉ 845 N. Michigan Ave., 60611, ☎ 312/642–1992, FAX 312/642–9817); Los Angeles (✉ 8383 Wilshire Blvd., Suite 960, 90211, ☎ 213/658–7188, FAX 213/658–1061); Miami (✉ 1221 Brickell Ave., Suite 1850, 33131, ☎ 305/358–1992, FAX 305/358–8223). **Canada** (✉ 2 Bloor St. W, 34th floor, Toronto, Ontario M4W 3E2, ☎ 416/961–3131, FAX 416/961–1992). **U.K.** (✉ 57–58 St. James's St., London SW1A 1LD, ☎ 0171/499–0901 or 0891/669–920 [24-hour brochure line], FAX 0171/629–4257); calls to the brochure line cost 50p per minute peak rate or 45p per minute cheap rate.

➤ Swedish Travel and Tourism Council: **U.S. and Canada:** Scandinavia Tourism Inc. (✉ Box 4649 Grand Central Station, New York, NY 10163–4649, ☎ 212/949–2333, FAX 212/885–9710). **U.K.** (✉ 73 Welbeck St., London W1M 8AN, ☎ 0171/935–9784, FAX 0171/935–5853).

➤ Swiss National Tourist Office: **U.S.:** New York (✉ 608 5th Ave., 10020, ☎ 212/757–5944, FAX 212/262–6116; El Segundo, CA (✉ 222 N. Sepulveda Blvd., Suite 1570, 90245, ☎ 310/335–5980, FAX 310/335–5982); Chicago (✉ 150 N. Michigan Ave., Suite 2930, 60601, ☎ 312/630–5840, FAX 312/630–5848). **Canada** (✉ 926 The East Mall, Etobicoke, Ontario M9B 6KI, ☎ 416/695–2090, FAX 416/695–2774). **U.K.** (✉ Swiss Centre, 1 New Coventry St., London W1V 8EE, ☎ 0171/734–1921, FAX 0171/437–4577).

➤ Turkish Tourist Office: **U.S.:** Nationwide (✉ 821 UN Plaza, New York, NY 10017, ☎ 212/687–2194, FAX 212/599–7568); Washington DC (✉ 1717 Massachusetts Ave. NW, Suite 306, 20036, ☎ 202/429–9844, FAX 202/429–5649). **Canada** (✉ 360 Albert St., Suite 801, Ottawa, Ontario K1R 7X7, ☎ 613/230–8654, FAX 613/230–3683). **U.K.** (✉ 1st floor, Egyptian House, 170–173 Piccadilly, London W1V 9DD, ☎ 0171/629–7771, FAX 0171/491–0773).

WHEN TO GO

For information about travel seasons and for the average daily maximum and minimum temperatures of the major European cities, *see* the A to Z section *in* each country chapter.

➤ Forecasts: **Weather Channel Connection** (☎ 900/932–8437), 95¢ per minute from a Touch-Tone phone.

2 Andorra

Andorra la Vella and Beyond

The coprincipality of Andorra has somehow carved itself a special niche in the world's imagination as a trout-fishing, through-the-looking-glass Pyrenean paradise. It may cause some disappointment when you find yourself in a 20-mile traffic jam of bargain hunters on the one road through the country.

The 191-square-mi tax haven, commercial oasis, and mountain hideaway drafted a constitution and held elections in 1993, converting one of Europe's last pockets of feudalism into a modern democratic state and member of the United Nations. The bishop of Urgell and the president of France assumed even more symbolic roles as the co-princes of this unique Pyrenean country. The area originally fell through the cracks between France and Spain when Charlemagne founded Andorra as an independent entity during his 8th-century battles with the Moors. In the 9th century, his heir, Charles the Bald, made the bishop of Urgell overlord of Andorra, a role contested by the French counts of Foix until a treaty providing for joint suzerainty was agreed upon in 1278. During the 16th century the French monarchy inherited these rights and eventually passed them on to the presidents of France.

This dual protection long allowed Andorra to thrive as a low-tax, duty-free haven. Europe's new semi-borderless unity, however, has changed this special status, and Andorra is now in the process of developing an improved tourist industry and a more conventional economy.

Winter sports, mountain climbing and hiking, and the architectural and cultural heritage represented by its many Romanesque chapels, bridges, and medieval farm and town houses are Andorra's once and future stock in trade, although numbered bank accounts will surely not be disappearing anytime soon.

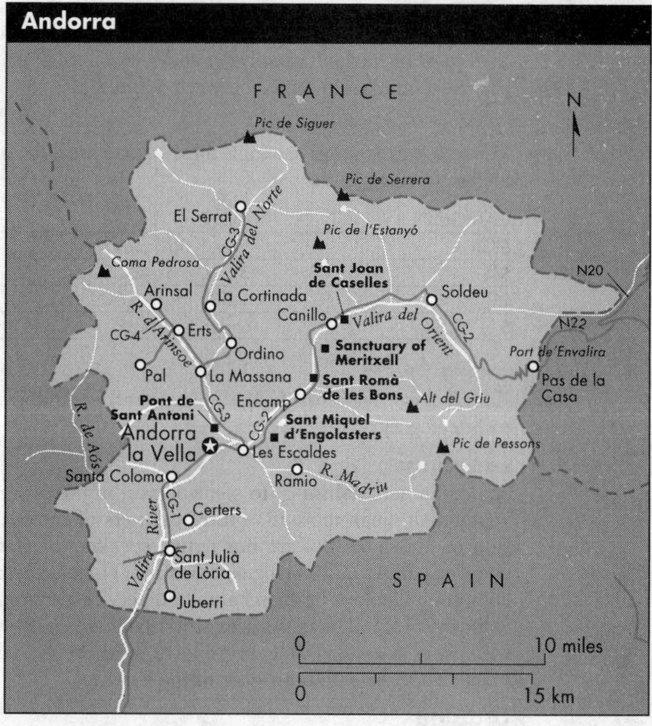

ANDORRA A TO Z

Customs

Andorra has traditionally been famous for its liberality regarding customs, duties, and visas. Non-Europeans need a passport to cross the border; Europeans enter with only an identity card. Now that the French–Spanish border is virtually a wave-by, Andorra's is less than a formality. Crossing out of Andorra, however, can be a problem. The French customs officers between Pas de la Casa and the Puymorens Tunnel sporadically stage mammoth roadblocks and may search anything. Spanish customs between Andorra la Vella and Seu d'Urgell can also be tricky. The established limits for all varieties of goods are specified in "Franquicias dels Viatgers," a leaflet in French, Catalan, and Spanish that is distributed by the Andorra National Tourist Office in Barcelona or Andorra la Vella (☞ Visitor Information, *in* Andorra Essentials, *below*). No one seems to mind how often you pass customs on a given day, however. So one way to score significant savings is to stay in a hotel on the Spanish side and make a half dozen trips through.

Dining

Andorra has never been a gastronomic paradise, but fine dining is on the rise. There are good restaurants serving French, Spanish, or Catalan cuisine and plenty of spots where you can eat hearty Pyrenean fare at no great cost. Local dishes worth trying include *trinchat,* a typical mountain specialty of potatoes and cabbage with bacon; *estofat d'isard* (stewed mountain goat); *truite de carreroles* (omelet with wild mushrooms); local cheeses, such as *formatge de tupí;* and *rostes amb mel* (ham baked with honey). Most restaurants offer prix-fixe menus, but some more expensive establishments are only à la carte.

MEALTIMES

True to the co-principality's predominantly Spanish culture, Andorrans eat late: Dinners don't usually get under way until 8:30 or 9, and lunch is a substantial meal served between 1 and 3:30.

RATINGS

The following ratings are for a three-course meal for one person, not including wine.

CATEGORY	COST
$$$$	over 5,000 ptas.
$$$	3,500 ptas.–5,000 ptas.
$$	1,500 ptas.–3,500 ptas.
$	under 1,500 ptas.

WHAT TO WEAR

Casual dress is acceptable in all restaurants in Andorra, regardless of price category.

Language

Andorran nationalism is, to some degree, in the process of being invented. Although more than three-quarters of the country's population of about 65,000 are not native speakers of Catalan, it is the co-principality's official language. Spanish, French, and English are also commonly spoken by merchants and service personnel. The establishment of Catalan as the area's first language has become a fact in the school system as well, as Andorra joins the more than 6 million Catalan-speakers on both sides of the Pyrenees.

Lodging

The number of Andorran hotels continues to increase, and standards are rising. The decor is usually functional, but service is friendly and the facilities are excellent.

Most hotels are open year-round. Reservations are necessary during July and August. Hotel rates often include at least two meals.

RATINGS

The following price ratings apply for two people in a double room.

CATEGORY	COST
$$$$	over 10,000 ptas.
$$$	7,500 ptas.–10,000 ptas.
$$	4,500 ptas.–7,500 ptas.
$	3,500 ptas.–4,500 ptas.

Mail

You can buy Andorran stamps with French francs or Spanish pesetas, though the postal service within the country is free. The Spanish post office in Andorra la Vella is at Carrer Joan Maragall 10; the French post office is at 1 rue Père d'Urg. There are no postal codes in Andorra, but be sure to write "Principat d'Andorra" to distinguish the country from the Spanish town of the same name. The abbreviation "s/n" in an address means that the building has no number.

Money Matters

CURRENCY

The Spanish peseta (pta.) is the major Andorran currency, but French francs are equally acceptable, and all prices are quoted in both currencies. For exchange rates and coinage information, ☞ *see* Currency *in* Chapters 11 *and* 28.

SAMPLE PRICES

Coca-Cola, 175 ptas.; cup of coffee, 125 ptas.; 1-mi taxi ride, 350 ptas.; ham sandwich, 500 ptas.

TIPPING

Restaurants and cafés almost always tack on a 10%–15% service charge; it's customary to leave a similar amount in addition to the charge, but this is optional.

WHAT IT WILL COST

Prices in Andorra are similar to those in neighboring France and Spain. The best bargains still available are products subject to state tax, such as tobacco, alcohol, perfume, and gasoline. Such staples as butter, cheese, and milk sold as surplus by member countries of the European Union (EU) are also cheaper in Andorra.

National Holidays

January 1; April 5 (Easter Monday); March 14 (Constitution Day); April 23 (St. George's Day); May 1 (Labor Day); May 19 (Pentecost Monday); June 23 (St. John); September 8 (La Verge de Meritxell); November 1 (All Saints' Day); Dec. 8 (Immaculate Conception); December 25; Dec. 26 (St. Stephen's Feast).

LOCAL HOLIDAYS

At Canillo, the third Saturday in July and the following Sunday and Monday; at Les Escaldes, July 25–27; at Sant Julià de Lòria, the last Sunday in July and the following Monday and Tuesday; at Andorra la Vella, the first Saturday, Sunday, and Monday in August; at Encamp and La Massana, August 15–17; at Ordino, September 16, 17.

Opening and Closing Times

Banks are open weekdays 9–1 and 3–5, and Saturday 9–noon. They are closed Sunday. Andorra is predominantly Catholic; most chapels and **churches** are kept locked around the clock, the key being left at the closest house. Check with the local tourist office. **Shops** are open daily 9–8, though many are closed between 1 and 4.

Telephoning

COUNTRY CODE

The country code for Andorra is 376.

INTERNATIONAL CALLS

For assistance, call the local operator at 111. To call Andorra from Spain, dial 07–376 and the six-digit local number; from France, dial 19–376.

LOCAL CALLS

For local directory assistance, dial 111. Andorra has no regional area codes. Most pay phones take phone cards issued by the telephone company, which may be purchased at *tabacs* (stores that sell tobacco and stamps).

Transportation

BY BUS

A bus service runs twice daily from Barcelona (✉ Ronda Universidad 4). In summer direct buses run from Perpignan and Toulouse to Andorra. The ride from Barcelona, Perpignan, or Toulouse to Andorra la Vella takes about three hours.

Minibuses connect the towns and villages, and fares are low; 150 ptas. will take you 5 km (3 mi). Details on fares and services are available at hotels and from tourist offices.

BY CAR

Road maintenance varies. The one main artery from France into Spain via Andorra la Vella is excellent and handles the heaviest traffic. Also superior is the spur north toward the ski resorts at La Massana and Ordino. Elsewhere, roads are narrow, winding, and best suited to four-wheel-drive vehicles or, higher up, mules. In winter, snow tires or chains are essential. Although the Puymorens Tunnel does not surface in Andorra, it does eliminate the switchbacks of the Puymorens mountain pass going through toward Spain from the northern entrance at L'Hospitalet, France. This pass is either dangerous or closed in bad weather and adds an extra 30 minutes to the Barcelona–Pas de la Casa trip. In good weather, though, don't miss this spectacularly scenic drive.

The fastest, most direct route from Barcelona to Andorra la Vella—with the fewest curves and the most tolls (about 4,500 ptas. in all)—runs through the Tunel del Cadí and the Cerdanya Valley via Bellver and La Seu d'Urgell. Slightly longer but cheaper, more beautiful, and often free of holdups is the western approach to La Seu d'Urgell via N-II to Igualada, then through Cervera, Pons, and Oliana on C-1311. The back way through Puigcerdà to Pas de la Casa is often a good way to avoid traffic. Andorra is 620 km (385 mi) from Madrid via Zaragoza, Lleida, and the C-1311, a six- to seven-hour drive.

BY PLANE

The nearest international airports are at Barcelona (200 km/125 mi) and, in France, at Perpignan (136 km/85 mi) and Toulouse-Blagnac (180 km/112 mi).

BY TRAIN

From Barcelona, take the train to Puigcerdà, then the bus to La Seu d'Urgell and Andorra la Vella; from Madrid, take the train to Lleida and then a bus to La Seu d'Urgell and Andorra la Vella. From Toulouse, take the train to Ax-les-Thermes and L'Hospitalet, where the bus to Pas de la Casa and Andorra la Vella meets the morning train. Alternatively, go on to Latour-de-Carol and take the bus from Puigcerdà to La Seu d'Urgell and Andorra la Vella.

ON FOOT

Mountainous Andorra is a playground for hikers and backpackers. The mountains are high and the terrain is wild, so a degree of care and experience is advisable. There are three long-distance trails: the GR7, which runs from the French border near Pas de la Casa to Les Escaldes on the road from Andorra la Vella to Spain; the GR11, also called the Ordino Route, a high-mountain trail that stretches across the central range; and the GR P1, a perimeter route running the crests around the Andorran border. There are 26 mountain refuges distributed throughout Andorra so you can plan day treks and travel light. Get details on treks and walks from tourist offices.

Weather

With a reliable snowfall from December to early April, Andorra has excellent ski resorts at Soldeu, Arinsal, Pal, Pas de la Casa–Grau Roig, and Ordino–Arcalis and a cross-country center at La Rabassa. Winter brings a huge influx of skiing buffs, but consumers are eager to take advantage of Andorra's tax- and duty-free shopping all year long. Holidays and weekends can make getting into, out of, or through Andorra a nightmare any time of year. In summer magnificent trails on the Grande Randonnée (GR) network and a score of shorter but still demanding routes draw hikers. In early April, the bird migrations from Africa begin, and the first flush of spring flowers livens the slopes and valleys. Be warned that even in summer the nighttime temperatures can drop to freezing.

CLIMATE

The following are the average daily maximum and minimum temperatures for Andorra.

Jan.	43F	6C	**May**	62F	17C	**Sept.**	71F	22C
	30	1		43	6		49	10
Feb.	45F	7C	**June**	73F	23C	**Oct.**	60F	16C
	30	1		39	4		42	6
Mar.	54F	12C	**July**	79F	26C	**Nov.**	51F	10C
	35	2		54	12		35	2
Apr.	58F	14C	**Aug.**	76F	24C	**Dec.**	42F	6C
	39	4		53	12		31	1

EXPLORING ANDORRA

Exploring Andorra takes time. The roads are narrow and steep, the views compel frequent stops, and every village is worth examining. If possible, do as much sight-seeing on foot as time permits.

Andorra la Vella

The capital's pivotal attraction, outside of its shops and restaurants, is the **Casa de la Vall** (House of the Valley) overlooking the town's main square. Constructed in 1580, this massive and medieval bulk of stone is the seat of the Andorran government. Charmingly rustic, the Casa de la Vall contains many notable religious frescoes, some of which were carefully moved here from village churches high in the Pyrenees. The kitchen is particularly interesting, with its splendid array of ancient copper pots and other culinary implements. ✉ *Carrer de la Vall s/n.* ⏲ *Tours weekdays 9–1 and 3–7; closed weekends.*

★ **Caldea** is an elaborate thermal spa complex barely 1 km (½ mi) from the center of Andorra la Vella, complete with steam rooms, Turkish baths, and snow patios. There are three restaurants, boutiques, an art gallery, and a cocktail bar open until 2 AM. Charges for the treatments vary; a five-day Andorra ski ticket will get you in for free. ✉ *Parc de la Mola 10, Les Escaldes,* ☎ *865777,* FAX *865656.*

$$$ ★ ✕ **Molí dels Fanals.** This quiet restaurant occupies an antique *borda* (a typical stone Andorran mountain refuge) with a fireplace and wooden paneling. The predominantly Catalan cuisine here uses consistently high-quality ingredients. Try the *magret de canard* (breast of duck) with grapes and port. ✉ *Carrer Dr. Vilanova 9 (Borda Casadet),* ☎ *821381. AE, DC, MC, V. Closed Mon. and last 2 wks in Aug. No dinner Sun.*

$$$ ★ ✕ **1900.** This small, beautifully decorated restaurant serves some of the best food in the co-principality, a blend of French, Spanish, and Andorran cuisines. It's fairly expensive for Andorra, but Chef Alain Despretz's inventive dishes are often worth it. ✉ *Plaça de la Unío 11,* ☎ *826716. AE, DC, MC, V. Closed Mon. and July.*

$$–$$$ ✕ **Borda Estevet.** A borda with a very Pyrenean feel, this simple spot offers a selection of Spanish and Andorran dishes, beef cooked and served *a la llosa* (on hot slabs of slate), and three private dining rooms in addition to the main dining room. ✉ *Ctra. Comella 2,* ☎ *864026. AE, DC, MC, V. Closed Sun. in Aug.*

$$–$$$ ★ ✕ **Versailles.** A tiny and authentic French bistro with only 10 tables, the Versailles is nearly always packed. The cuisine is primarily French with occasional Andorran specialties—such as *escudella barrejada,* a thick vegetable and meat soup, or *civet de jabali,* stewed wild boar. ✉ *Cap del Carrer 1,* ☎ *821331. AE, DC, MC, V.*

$$$$ ★ 🏨 **Andorra Palace.** The large, modern Palace is widely considered one of the capital's best hotels. The rooms are spacious and the furnish-

ings smartly contemporary. The outdoor terrace is a pleasant spot to relax and watch the bustle below. ✉ *Carrer de la Roda,* ☎ *821072,* FAX *828195. 140 rooms. Restaurant, pool. AE, DC, MC, V.*

$$$$ **Andorra Park.** The Park is a grand building away from the city's congestion of traffic and pedestrians. The American Bar is a popular watering hole for local society. There's a pretty garden, as well as a terrace, and the deluxe guest rooms have private balconies. ✉ *Carrer Les Canals 24,* ☎ *820979,* FAX *820983. 40 rooms. Restaurant, pool. AE, DC, MC, V.*

$$$$ **Hotel Eden Roc.** Besides having all the amenities of larger hotels, the smaller Eden Roc offers an exceptional dining room, a terrace, and attentive personal service. ✉ *Av. Dr. Mitjavila 1,* ☎ *821000,* FAX *860319. 56 rooms. Restaurant. AE, V.*

$$ **Florida.** For good value, try this cheerful hotel. There's no restaurant in-house, but several are nearby. ✉ *Carrer La Llacuna 15,* ☎ *820105,* FAX *861925. 52 rooms. AE, DC, MC, V.*

Les Escaldes

The spa town, now virtually one with Andorra la Vella, is a 15-minute ★ walk from the Casa de la Vall. The Romanesque church of **Sant Miquel d'Engolasters** stands on a ridge northeast of the capital and can be reached on foot—allow half a day for the round-trip—or by automobile up a mountain road. The views are well worth the climb.

$$$$ ★ ✕ **Roc Blanc.** Sleek, modern, and luxurious trappings—and a wealth of facilities to pamper the body, from mud baths to acupuncture—are what the Roc Blanc is all about. The rooms are large, there's a terrace, and the hotel's restaurants, Brasserie L'Entrecôte and El Pi, serve Andorran and international specialties. ✉ *Plaça Co-Princeps 5,* ☎ *821486,* FAX *860244. 250 rooms. Restaurant, 2 pools. AE, DC, MC, V.*

Encamp

Just beyond the town, which is 6 km (4 mi) northeast of Andorra la ★ Vella, is the 12th-century church of **Sant Romà de les Bons,** in a particularly picturesque setting combining medieval buildings and mountain scenery. ✉ *Old part of town.*

$$ **Hotel La Mola.** This friendly spot, midway between the ski slopes and the bright lights of Andorra la Vella, is a comfortable choice that has all the basic facilities at half the price of some of the better-known Andorran hotels. ✉ *Av. Co-Princep Episcopal 62,* ☎ *831181,* FAX *833046. 48 rooms. Restaurant, pool. AE, DC, MC, V.*

Canillo

The **Santuari de Meritxell** is the focal point of Andorran religious life. The Blessed Virgin of Meritxell is the principality's patron saint, yet, oddly enough for such a religious country, her patronage wasn't declared until the late 19th century. The original sanctuary was destroyed by fire in 1972; the new gray-stone building that replaced it looks remarkably like a factory, but the mountain setting is superb. ✉ *CG-2, between Encamp and Canillo.* *Free.* ⏲ *Wed.–Mon. 9–1 and 3–7.*

Just outside Canillo stands a **seven-armed Gothic cross** of stone (in fact, it has only six arms; one has been broken off).

The Romanesque church of **Sant Joan de Caselles,** 2 km (1½ mi) east of Canillo, is one of Andorra's treasures, with its ancient walls of stone that has turned a lovely dappled gingerbread color over the centuries. The bell tower is stunning: three stories of weathered stone punctuated by rows of round-arch windows. Inside the main building is a fine reredos (a wall or screen behind an altar) dating from 1525, that depicts the life of St. John the Evangelist.

La Massana

★ **Pont de Sant Antoni** (St. Anthony Bridge), a Romanesque stone bridge spanning a narrow river, is just 3 km (2 mi) north of Andorra la Vella on the CG-3 road toward La Massana. The rustic streets of the picturesque mountain town are good for strolling.

$$$$ ✕ **El Rusc.** A smallish flower-covered chalet 1 km (½ mi) from La Massana, El Rusc may be Andorra's top restaurant in both cost and quality. Chef Antoni Garrallá serves Basque cuisine and French and international specialties. Try the foie gras with onions or *besugo* (baked sea bream), a standard treat from the Basque country. ✉ *Ctra. d'Arinsal, La Massana,* ☎ *838200,* FAX *835180. Reservations essential. AE, DC, MC, V. Closed Mon. No dinner Sun.*

$$ ★ ✕ **La Borda de l'Avi.** This popular place specializes in lamb, goat, beef, quail, partridge, and trout cooked over coals. The three dining rooms can hold some 200 diners and, during the high season, often do. ✉ *La Massana,* ☎ *835154. AE, DC, MC, V.*

Ordino

The tiny village 5 km (3 mi) northeast of La Massana is known for its medieval church, **Sant Martíde la Cortinada.** Romanesque with Baroque altarpieces, the church also has 12th-century frescoes and unusual wooden furnishings. To see it properly, go at night between 7 and 8, when Mass is celebrated.

$$ 🏨 **Hotel Coma.** Surrounded by woods and meadows, this Swiss chalet–style hideaway just outside the village offers scenery, silence, and simple Andorran fare at affordable prices. ✉ *Ctra. General,* ☎ *835116,* FAX *837909. 48 rooms. Restaurant, pool. AE, DC, MC, V.*

La Cortinada

In this village is **Can Pal,** a fine example of medieval Andorran architecture. It is a privately owned manor house (strictly no admittance) with a dovecote attached. Note the turret perched high on the far side.

Santa Coloma

★ Santa Coloma's pre-Romanesque **Santa Coloma de les Bons** hermitage, the only Andorran church with a round tower, is the main attraction in this village 4 km (2½ mi) south of Andorra la Vella on CG-1. Parts of the church date from the 9th and 10th centuries. Twelfth-century Romanesque frescoes fill the interior walls, while an 18th-century Baroque altarpiece presides.

$$ ✕ **El Bon Racó.** Exactly what the name says it is—a good corner, nook, or retreat—it is a traditional borda in design. The place turns out fine local cuisine at encouraging prices. Try to arrive early; it fills quickly, especially on weekends. ✉ *Av. Salou 86,* ☎ *822085. AE, DC, MC, V.*

Pas de la Casa

This conglomeration of high-rises and supermarkets is a sort of Andorran Smuggler's Notch, traditionally a place for French and Spanish shoppers, merchants, and contrabandists to pull off a quick sting and then retreat back to their respective countries. Known to be colder and snowier than any other point around, Pas de la Casa is a favorite ski resort, especially for visitors from the Cerdanya valley in Spain.

$ ✕ **Le Grizzly.** This is a good French restaurant for lunch or dinner, especially during the ski season. The food, simple but well prepared, offers good value, with a choice of four prix-fixe menus from 1,000 ptas to 2,000 ptas. Try the *entrecôte* Roquefort (steak) and the thick Provençal soups. ✉ *Av. d'Encamp,* ☎ *855227. AE, DC, MC, V.*

Sant Julià de Lòria

Sant Julià de Lòria is the first parish you encounter coming into Andorra from Spain. It is the site of Andorra's only Nordic skiing facility. Around and above it are a number of unspoiled small villages.

$$$ ★ **Pol.** Gracefully modern surroundings and a friendly staff help make this hotel is popular. A garden and terrace are part of the Pol's appeal, and its dance club is a busy nightspot. ✉ *Av. Verge de Canólich 52,* ☎ *841122,* FAX *841852. 80 rooms. Restaurant. AE, MC, V.*

Shopping

Shopping has traditionally been one of Andorra's main attractions, but be careful: Not all the goods displayed are at bargain prices. The French and Spanish come to buy cigarettes, liquor, household items, and foodstuffs, but they often find electrical goods and cameras either flawed or lacking warranties and no cheaper than at home. Good buys are such consumables as gasoline, perfume, butter, cheese, cigarettes, wine, whiskey, and gin. For cameras, tape recorders, and other imported items, compare prices and models carefully. Ask for the *precio último* (final price) and insist politely on *el descuento,* the 10% discount to which you are entitled as a visitor to Andorra.

The main shopping area is **Andorra la Vella.** There are also stores in all the new developments and in the towns close to the frontiers, namely Pas de la Casa and Sant Julià de Lòria. The **Punt de Trobada** center (✉ Ctra. d'Espanya, ☎ 843433), 2 km (1¼ mi) from the Spanish border, is bright, modern, and immense. **La Casa del Formatge** in Les Escaldes (✉ Av. Carlemany s/n, ☎ 821689) has more than 500 different kinds of cheeses from all over the world.

Andorra Essentials

Consulates

U.S. (✉ Pg. Reina Elisenda 23, Barcelona, Spain, ☎ 93/2802227).**Canadian** (✉ Nuñez de Balboa 35, Madrid, Spain, ☎ 91/2259119). **U.K.** (✉ Apartado de Correos 12111, Barcelona, Spain, ☎ 93/3222151).

Emergencies

Police (☎ 110). **Ambulance**(☎ 118). **Doctor** (☎ 868000). Mountain rescue (112). **Dentist** (☎ 868000). **Pharmacy** (☎ 868000).

Guided Tours

Tours of Andorra la Vella and the surrounding countryside are offered by several firms; check with the tourist office for details or call **Excursion Nadal** (☎ 821138) or **Sol i Neu Excursion** (☎ 823653).

Travel Agency

Relax Travel Agency/American Express (✉ Mossen Tremosa 12, Andorra la Vella, ☎ 822044, FAX 827055).

Visitor Information

Andorra La Vella (Sindicat d'Iniciativa/National Tourist Office, ✉ Carrer Dr. Vilanova, ☎ 820214, FAX 825823; city tourist office, ✉ Plaça de la Rotonda, ☎ 827117). **Barcelona** (✉ Carrer Marià Cubí 15908021, ☎ 93/200–0655 or 93/200–0787). **Canillo** (Unió Pro-Turisme, ✉ Caseta Pro-Turisme, ☎ FAX 851002). **Encamp** (Unió Pro-Foment i Turisme, ✉ Plaça Consell General, ☎ 831405, FAX 831878). **Escaldes-Engordany** (Unió Pro-Turisme, ✉ Plaça dels Co-Prínceps, ☎ 820963). **La Massana** (Unió Pro-Turisme, ✉ Plaça del Quart, ☎ 835693). **Ordino** (Oficina de Turisme, ✉ Cruïlla d'Ordino, ☎ 836963). **Pas de la Casa** (Unió Pro-Turisme, ✉ C. Bernat III, ☎ 855292). **Sant Julià de Lòria** (Unió Pro-Turisme, ✉ Plaça de la Germandat, ☎ 841352).

3 Austria

Vienna, Danube Valley, Salzburg, Innsbruck

An oft-told story concerns an airline pilot whose prelanding announcement advised, "Ladies and gentlemen, we are on the final approach to Vienna Airport. Please make sure your seat belts are fastened, please refrain from smoking until you are inside the terminal, and please set your watches back 100 years."

Apocryphal or not, the pilot's observation suggests the allure of a country where tourists can sense something of what Europe was like before the pulse of the 20th century quickened to a beat that would have dizzied our great-grandparents. Today, the occasional bus driver still bows to you as if saluting a Hapsburg prince, and Lippizaner stallions still dance to Mozart minuets—in other words, Austria is a country that has not forgotten how to work, as well as waltz, in three-quarter time.

Look beyond the postcard clichés of dancing white horses, the zither strains, and the singing of the Vienna Boys Choir, however, and you'll find a conservative-mannered yet modern country, one of Europe's richest, in which the juxtaposition of old and new often creates excitement—even controversy. Vienna has its sumptuous palaces, but it is also home to an assemblage of U.N. organizations housed in a wholly modern complex. Tucked away between storybook villages are giant industrial plants, one of which turns out millions of compact discs for Sony. The world's largest penicillin producer is hidden away in a Tirolean valley. And those countless glittering crystal objects you see in jewelry and gift stores around the world originate in a small village outside of Innsbruck. By no means is the country frozen in a time warp: Rather, it is the contrast between the old and the new—experiencing an Andrew Lloyd Webber musical in the theater where Mozart's *Magic Flute* premiered—that makes Austria such a fascinating place to visit.

So, too, does the fact that, poised as it is between East and West, Austria shares a culture with Europe but has deep roots as well in the lands that lie beyond to the east. It was Metternich who declared that "Asia begins at the Landstrasse," referring to Vienna's crucial role as the meeting place of East and West for 2,000 years. Today, Vienna's spectacu-

Austria (Österreich)

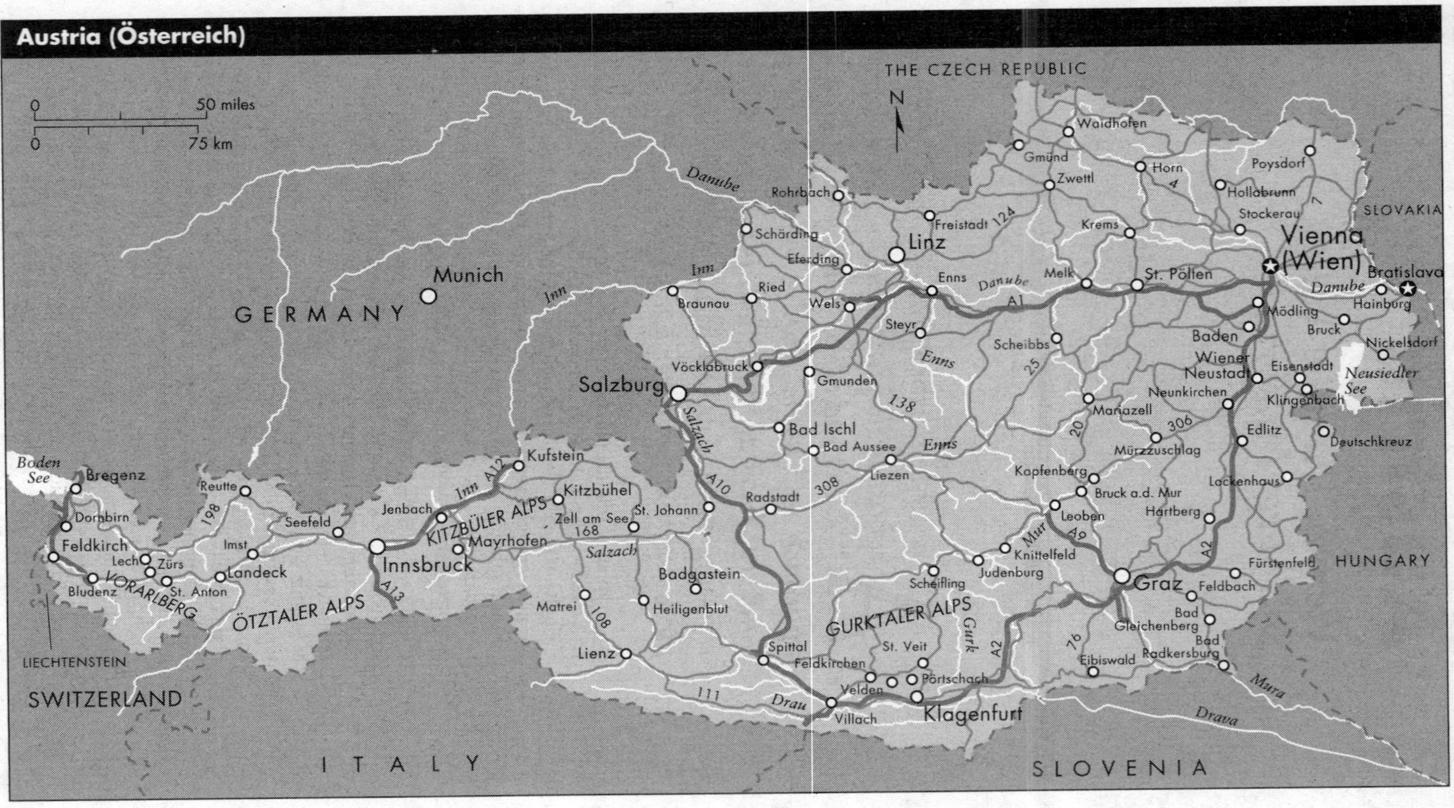

lar historical and artistic heritage—exemplified by the legacies of Beethoven, Freud, Klimt, and Mahler—lures travelers to this grande dame of a city. Between the Apfelstrudel and psychoanalysis, Schubert and sausages, lies a definite Old World charm that natives would be the last to underplay.

But as with most countries, the capital is only a small part of what Austria has to offer. A grand tour of the country reveals considerably more Austrias than the nine provinces would suggest: Salzburg—home every summer to one of the world's ritziest music festivals—is a departure point for the Salzkammergut lake country and the mountains of Land Salzburg; as the hub of the Alps, Innsbruck beckons skiers to explore the resorts of Lech, St. Anton, and Kitzbühel; finally, there's the Wachau, a stretch of the Danube Valley that easily rivals the scenery of the Rhine.

In the end, the way to get the most out of Austria is to come armed with a taste for history, an appreciation for the quirks in human nature, and a thirst for art and wonderful music. A taste for good wine comes in handy, too—as you'll discover when you're sitting in a wine garden in the heart of a lush vineyard, enjoying a mug of Grüner Veltliner to the gentle background music of a Schrammel quartet.

AUSTRIA A TO Z

Customs

Austria's duty-free allowances are as follows: 200 cigarettes or 50 cigars or 250 grams of tobacco; 2 liters of wine and 1 liter of spirits; 1 bottle of toilet water (about 250-milliliter size); and 50 milliliters of perfume for those ages 18 and over arriving from other European countries. Although Austria is a member of the European Union (EU), these limits may apply to EU citizens as well. Visitors arriving from the United States, Canada, or other non-European points may bring in twice the above amounts.

Dining

Take your choice among sidewalk *Wurstl* (frankfurter) stands, *Imbissstuben* (quick-lunch stops), cafés, *Heuriger* (wine taverns), self-service restaurants, modest *Gasthäuser* (neighborhood establishments featuring local specialties), and full-fledged restaurants in every price category. Most places post their menus outside. Shops (such as Eduscho) that sell coffee beans also offer coffee by the cup at prices considerably lower than those in cafés. Many Anker bakery shops also offer tasty *Schmankerl* (snacks) and coffee, and some offer a full breakfast. *Fleischer* or *Fleischhauer* (butchers) may also offer soup and a main course at noon. A growing number of shops and snack bars offer pizza by the slice. We recommend reservations for dinner.

MEALTIMES

A typical Austrian breakfast consists of rolls, cold cuts, cheese, and coffee. Unless dining out in the evening, lunch is usually the big meal of the day. *Jause* (coffee with cake) is taken in the late afternoon, and a light supper ends the day.

RATINGS

Prices are per person and include appetizer and a main course, usually with salad, and a small beer or glass of wine. Meals in the top price categories will include a dessert or cheese with coffee. Prices include taxes and service (but adding another 3%–5% to the bill as a tip is customary).

CATEGORY	MAJOR CITY	OTHER AREAS
$$$$	over AS800	over AS600
$$$	AS500–AS800	AS400–AS600
$$	AS200–AS500	AS170–AS400
$	under AS200	under AS170

WHAT TO WEAR

A jacket and tie are generally advised for restaurants in the top two price categories. Otherwise casual dress is acceptable. When in doubt, it's best to dress up.

Language

German is the official national language. In larger cities and most resort areas you will have no problem finding English speakers; hotel and restaurant employees, in particular, speak English reasonably well. Most younger Austrians speak at least passable English, and fluency is increasing.

Lodging

CAMPING

Most campsites are well equipped, with water and toilet facilities. Some have hookups for RVs. Few campsites are open year-round. Summer or winter, make reservations well in advance to be sure of a site. In addition to campsites, mountain cabins are available on an overnight basis to Alpine hikers. For information, contact **Österreichischer Alpenverein** (✉ Wilhelm-Greil-Str. 15, A-6020 Innsbruck, ☎ 0512/5954734, FAX 0512/575528). Information on camping is available from the National Tourist Office (☞ Visitor Information, *below*).

HOTELS

Austrian hotels and pensions are officially classified using from one to five stars. These grades broadly coincide with our own four-point rating system. No matter the category, standards for service and cleanliness are high. All hotels in the upper three categories have either a bath or shower in the room; even the most inexpensive accommodations provide hot and cold water. Accommodations include castles and palaces, conventional hotels, *Gasthöfe* (country inns), and the more modest pensions. In summer a reasonably priced option are the many student dormitories opened to guests of all ages.

RATINGS

All prices quoted here are for two people in a double room and include taxes. Although exact rates vary, a single room generally costs more than half the price of a comparable double. Breakfast at the roll-and-coffee level is often included in the room rate; full and sumptuous breakfast buffets, however, can be a supplementary charge. Keep in mind that hotels outside Vienna can offer comprehensive rates that include breakfast *and* dinner; these are often excellent deals, so inquire when booking.

CATEGORY	MAJOR CITY	OTHER AREAS
$$$$	over AS2,700	over AS1,800
$$$	AS1,200–AS2,700	AS1,000–AS1,800
$$	AS950–AS1,200	AS700–AS1,000
$	under AS950	under AS700

YOUTH HOSTELS

Hosteling is well developed, although most locations are outside city centers. For information, contact **Österreichischer Jugendherbergsverband** (Austrian Hostel Association; ✉ Schottenring 28, A-1010 Vienna, ☎ 01/533–5353, FAX 01/535–0861).

Mail

POSTAL RATES

Airmail letters and postcards to the United States and Canada cost AS13 minimum. Airmail letters and postcards to the United Kingdom cost AS7, and an aerogram costs AS13.

RECEIVING MAIL

American Express offices in Vienna, Linz, Salzburg, and Innsbruck will hold mail at no charge for those carrying an American Express credit card or American Express traveler's checks. The central American Express office in Vienna is ✉ Kärntner Strasse 21-23 , ☎ 01/515–40–0; in Linz, ✉ Bürgerstrasse 14, ☎ 0732/669013; in Salzburg, ✉ Mozartplatz 5-7, ☎ 0662/8080; in Innsbruck, ✉ Brixnerstrasse 3, ☎ 0512/582491.

Money Matters

COSTS

In recent years, Austria has become expensive, but since inflation is relatively low, at least prices remain fairly stable. Vienna and Salzburg are the most expensive cities, along with fashionable resorts at Kitzbühel, Seefeld, Badgastein, Velden, Zell am See, Pörtschach, St. Anton, Zürs, and Lech. Many smaller towns near these resorts offer virtually identical facilities at half the price. Drinks in bars and clubs cost considerably more than in cafés or restaurants. Austrian prices include service and tax.

CREDIT CARDS

Credit cards are not as widely used in Austria as they are in other European countries, and not all establishments that accept plastic take all cards. Some may require a minimum purchase if payment is to be made by card. Many restaurants take cash only. **American Express** has money machines in Vienna at its main office (✉ Kärntnerstr. 21–23) and at the airport. Many of the **Bankomat** money dispensers will also accept Visa cards if you have an encoded international PIN.

CURRENCY

The unit of currency is the Austrian schilling (AS), divided into 100 groschen. There are AS20, 50, 100, 500, 1,000, and 5,000 bills; AS1, 5, 10, and 20 coins; and 1-, 2-, 5-, 10-, and 50-groschen coins. The 1-, 2-, and 5-groschen coins are rare, and the AS20 coins are unpopular, though useful for some cigarette machines. The 500- and 100-schilling notes look similar; confusing the two can be an expensive mistake. At press time (spring 1998), the exchange rate was AS12.5 to the dollar, AS8.9 to the Canadian dollar, and AS21 to the pound sterling. You may bring in any amount of either foreign currency or schillings and take out any amount with you.

Exchange traveler's checks at a bank, a post office, or the American Express office to get the best rate. All charge a small commission; some smaller banks or "change" offices may give a poorer rate *and* charge a higher fee. All change offices at airports and at main train stations in major cities cash traveler's checks. In Vienna, bank-operated change offices with extended hours are found on Stephansplatz and at the main rail stations. The Bank Austria machines on Stephansplatz and at Kärntnerstrasse 51 (to the right of the Opera) and at the Raiffeisenbank on Kohlmarkt (at Michaelerplatz) change bills from other currencies into schillings, but rates are poor and a hefty commission is automatically deducted.

SAMPLE PRICES

Cup of coffee in a café or restaurant, AS35–AS45; ½ liter of draft beer, AS28–AS48; small glass of wine, AS35; Coca-Cola, AS28; open sandwich, AS25; theater ticket, AS200–AS300; concert ticket, AS250–AS500; opera ticket, AS600 and up; 1-mi taxi ride, AS35.

TIPPING

In restaurants, 10% service is included. Add anything from AS5 to AS50, depending on the restaurant and the size of the bill, or about 3–5%. Leave the actual tip by telling the waiter the total amount you wish to pay—that is, the bill plus the tip—then remit the tip with the payment to the waiter (do not leave it on the table). Railroad porters and hotel porters or bellhops get AS10 per bag. Doormen get AS20 for hailing a cab and assisting. Room service gets AS20 for snacks and AS20–AS40 for full meals; in more expensive establishments, expect to tip on the higher side. Maids get no tip unless you stay a week or more, or unless special service is rendered.

National Holidays

January 1; January 6 (Epiphany); Easter Monday; May 1 (May Day); Ascension; Pentecost; Corpus Christi; August 15 (Assumption); October 26 (National Day); November 1 (All Saints' Day); December 8 (Immaculate Conception); December 25–26. On the Dec. 8 holiday, banks and offices are closed but most shops are open.

Opening and Closing Times

Banks are open weekdays 8–noon or 12:30, and 1:30–3 or 4, closed Saturday. Hours vary from one city to another. Principal offices in cities stay open during lunch. **Museum** opening days and times vary considerably from one city to another and depend on the season, the museum's size, budgetary constraints, and assorted other factors. Monday is often a closing day. Your hotel or the local tourist office will have current details. **Shops** are open weekdays from 8 or 9 until 6, in shopping centers to 7:30, and Saturday until 5, although some may still close at noon or 1. Many smaller shops close for one or two hours at midday. Larger food markets are open weekdays from 7:30 to 7:30, Saturday to 5.

Shopping

SALES TAX REFUNDS

A value-added tax (VAT) of 20% is charged on all sales and is automatically included in prices. If you purchase goods worth AS1,000 or more and are not a citizen of an EU country, you can claim a refund of the tax either as you leave or after you've returned home. Ask the store clerk to fill out the necessary papers. Get them stamped at the airport or border crossing by customs officials (who may ask to see the goods). You can get an immediate refund of the VAT, less a service charge, at international airports or at main border crossings, or you can return the papers by mail to the shop(s). The VAT refund can be credited to your credit card account or remitted by check.

Telephoning

COUNTRY CODE

The country code for Austria is 43. When dialing an Austrian number from abroad, drop the initial 0 from the local area code.

INTERNATIONAL CALLS

It costs considerably more to telephone *from* Austria than it does *to* Austria. Calls from post offices are least expensive. To avoid hotel charges, call overseas and ask to be called back; use an international credit card, available from AT&T, Sprint, MCI, and others; or use access codes to reach operators for **AT&T** (☎ 022/903–011), **MCI** (☎ 022/903–012), **Sprint** (☎ 022/903–014), or **Canada Direct** (☎ 022/903–013). To make a collect call—you can't do this from pay phones—dial the operator and ask for an *R*-Gespräch (pronounced air-ga-*shprayk*).

For international information dial 1611 for European numbers or 1614 for overseas numbers. Most operators speak English; if yours doesn't, you'll be passed along to one who does.

LOCAL CALLS

Pay telephones take AS1, 5, 10, and 20 coins. The initial connection for a local call costs AS1; note that the initial call time is over *very* quickly, so have change handy. Emergency calls are free. Instructions are in English in most booths. Insert AS1 or more to continue the connection when you hear the tone warning that your time is up. If you will be making frequent phone calls, get a phone card at a post office. These work in all phones marked *Wertkartentelefon*. The cost of the call will be deducted from the card automatically. Cards cost AS190 for AS200 worth of calls, AS95 for AS100 worth, and AS48 for calls totaling AS50.

Phone numbers throughout Austria are currently being changed. A sharp tone indicates either no connection or that the number has been changed.

Visitor Information

Central Tourist Office (✉ Margaretenstr. 1, A-1040 Vienna, ☎ 01/211140, FAX 01/588–66–20) for phone inquiries and hotel assistance.

City Tourist Office (✉ Kärnterstr. 38, A-1010 Vienna) for walk-ins only.

Weather

Austria has two tourist seasons. The summer season technically starts around Easter, reaches its peak in July, and winds down in September. Aside from a few overly humid days when you may wish for wider use of air-conditioning, even Vienna is pleasant in summer, when the city literally moves outdoors. May, June, September, and October are the most temperate months, and the most affordable. The winter cultural season starts in October and runs into June; winter sports get under way in December and last until the end of April, although you can ski in certain areas well into June and on some of the highest glaciers year-round. Some events—the Salzburg Festival is a prime example—occasion a substantial increase in hotel and other prices.

CLIMATE

Summer can be warm; winter, bitterly cold. The southern region is usually several degrees warmer in summer, several degrees colder in winter. Winters north of the Alps can be overcast and dreary, whereas the south basks in winter sunshine. The following are the average daily maximum and minimum temperatures for Vienna.

Jan.	34F	1C	**May**	67F	19C	**Sept.**	68F	20C
	25	– 4		50	10		53	11
Feb.	38F	3C	**June**	73F	23C	**Oct.**	56F	14C
	28	– 3		56	14		44	7
Mar.	47F	8C	**July**	76F	25C	**Nov.**	45F	7C
	30	– 1		60	15		37	3
Apr.	58F	15C	**Aug.**	75F	24C	**Dec.**	37F	3C
	43	6		59	15		30	– 1

VIENNA

Vienna has been characterized as an "old dowager of a town"—an Austro-Hungarian empress, don't forget, widowed in 1918 by the Great War. It's not just the aristocratic and courtly atmosphere, with monumental doorways and facades of former palaces at every turn. Nor is it just that Vienna (Wien in German) has a higher proportion of middle-aged and older citizens than any other city in Europe, with a concomitant air of stability, quiet, and respectability. Rather, it's this factor—combined with a love of music; a discreet weakness for rich food (especially cakes); an adherence to old-fashioned and formal forms of address; a high, if unadventurous, regard for the arts; and a gentle mourning for lost glories—that preserves the stiff elegance of Old World dignity.

Exploring Vienna

Numbers in the margin correspond to points of interest on the Vienna map.

Most main sights are in the inner zone, the oldest part of the city, encircled by the Ring, once the course of the city walls and today a broad tree-lined boulevard. Carry a ready supply of AS10 coins; many places of interest have coin-operated tape-recording machines that provide English commentaries. As you wander around, train yourself to look upward; some of the most memorable architectural delights are found on upper stories and along roof lines. Note that addresses throughout the chapter ending with "-strasse" or "-gasse" (both meaning "street") are abbreviated "str." or "g." respectively (Augustinerstrasse will be "Augustinerstr."; Dorotheergasse will be "Dorotheerg.").

The Heart of Vienna

1 **Albertina.** Some of the greatest Old Master drawings—including Dürer's legendary *Praying Hands*—are housed in this unassuming building, home to the world's largest collection of drawings, sketches, engravings, and etchings. Dürer leads the list, but there are many other highlights, including works by Rembrandt, Michelangelo, and Correggio. The building is undergoing restoration and at press time (spring 1998) the collection is being housed in the Akademiehof, possibly for the next two years. The Akademiehof is across from the Secession (the building with the gold cabbage-shape ball on top). The closest U-bahn stop is Karlsplatz. Entrance to the collection is at Makartplatz 3. ✉ *Augustinerstr. 1,* ☎ *01/534–83–0.* ⏲ *Tues.–Fri. 10–6, weekends 10–4; may be closed in July and Aug.*

3 **Augustinerkirche** (St. Augustine's Church). The interior of this 14th-century church has undergone restoration; while much of the earlier Baroque ornamentation was removed in the 1780s, the gilt organ ornamentation and main altar remain as visual sensations. This was the court church; the Hapsburg rulers' hearts are preserved in a chamber here. The Augustinerkirche is a favorite on Sunday, when the 11 AM mass is sung in Latin. The church is on Josefsplatz, where much of Graham Greene's great spy story *The Third Man* was filmed (specifically in and around the **Palais Pallavicini** across the street). ✉ *Josefspl.*

18 **Donner Brunnen** (Donner Fountain). Marking the center of Neuer Markt square since 1739, this fountain is a Baroque showpiece, adorned with florid sculpted figures. The characters represent the main rivers that flow into the Danube. Empress Maria Theresa thought the figures were scandalously underclad and wanted them removed. ✉ *Neuer Markt.*

25 **Freud Museum.** The original famous couch is gone (there's a replica), but the apartment in which Sigmund Freud developed modern psychology and treated his first patients is otherwise generally intact. Other rooms include a reference library. ✉ *Bergg. 19,* ☎ *01/319–1596.* ⏲ *July–Sept., daily 9–6, Oct.–June, daily 9–4.*

★ 6 **Hofburg** (Imperial Palace). This centerpiece of Imperial Vienna is actually a vast complex comprising numerous buildings, courtyards, and must-sees. Start with the magnificent domed entry—**Michaelertor** (St. Michael's Gate), or the principal gateway to the Hofburg, named for the church diagonally opposite—and go through the courtyards to the vast grassy plaza, Heldenplatz (Hero's Square), on the front. The palace complex, with sections dating from the 13th through 18th centuries, includes the ☞ **Augustinerkirche**, the ☞ **Nationalbibliothek**—its central room is one of the most spectacular Baroque showpieces anywhere—and the ☞ **Hofburgkapelle**, home to the Vienna Boys Choir. Here, too, are the famous ☞ **Spanische Reitschule**—where the Lipizzaners go through their paces—and three fascinating museums: ☞ **Hofsilber-und Tafelkammer Museum**, the ☞ **Schauräume in der Hofburg**, and the ☞ **Schatzkammer**. The complex also houses the office of the federal presidency, a glittering chandelier-lit convention center, an elegant multipurpose hall (Redoutensaal), and private apartments as well as lesser government offices. The complex of the Hofburg is centered around the ☞ **Neue Berg** palace. ✉ *Hofburg; main streets circling the complex are the Opernring, Augustinerstr., Schauflerg., and Dr. Karl Renner-Ring Str.*

9 **Hofburgkapelle** (Court Chapel). Home to the renowned Vienna Boys Choir, this Gothic chapel dates to 1449. You'll need tickets to hear the angelic boys sing mass (alas, you can hear them but, due to the chapel layout, not see them) at 9:15 AM on Sunday mid-September through June; tickets are available from travel agencies at a substantial markup, at the chapel itself from 5 PM Friday (queue up by 4:30 and expect long lines), or by writing two months in advance to the Hofmusikkapelle, Hofburg, Schweizerhof, A-1010 Vienna. The City Tourist Office (☞ Visitor Information *in* Vienna Essentials, *below*) can sometimes help with ticket applications. Limited standing room is available for free; get to the chapel by at least 8:30 AM on Sunday for a shot at a spot. ✉ *Hofburg, Schweizer Hof,* ☎ *01/533–9927,* FAX *01/533–9927–75.*

★ 10 **Hofsilber-und Tafelkammer Museum** (Court Silver and Tableware Museum). See how royalty dined in this brilliant showcase of imperial table settings. Little wonder Marie Antoinette—who, as a child of Maria Theresa, grew up in Schloss Schönbrunn (☞ *below*)—got a taste for extreme luxury. You can get a combined ticket, which includes the imperial apartments around the corner. ✉ *Burghof inner court, Michaelertrakt,* ☎ *01/533–7570.* ⏲ *Daily 9–4:30.*

19 **Jüdisches Museum der Stadt Wien** (Jewish Museum). Housed in the former Eskeles town palace, the city's Jewish Museum offers permanent and changing exhibits that portray the richness of the Jewish culture and heritage that contributed so much to Vienna and Austria. Go to the top floor to view the staggering warehouse collection of Judaica. ✉ *Dorotheerg. 11,* ☎ *01/535–0431.* ⏲ *Sun.–Wed. and Fri. 10–6, Thurs. 10–9.*

17 **Kapuzinerkirche** (Capuchin Church). The ground-level church is nothing unusual, but the basement crypt holds the imperial vault known as the **Kaisergruft,** the final resting place of many sarcophagi of long-dead Hapsburgs. The oldest tomb is that of Ferdinand II; it dates from 1633. The most recent one is that of Empress Zita, widow of the last of the kaisers, who died in 1989. ✉ *Neuer Markt 1,* ☎ *01/512–6853–12.* ⏲ *Daily 9:30–4.*

★ 34 **Karlskirche** (St. Charles' Church). The classical Baroque facade and dome flanked by vast twin columns instantly identify the Karlskirche, one of the city's best-known landmarks. The church was built around 1715 by Fischer von Erlach. Its oval interior is surprisingly small, given the monumental exterior. The ceiling has airy frescoes, while the

Albertina, **1**
Am Hof, **26**
Augustinerkirche, **3**
Donner Brunnen, **18**
Freud Museum, **25**
Hofburg, **6**
Hofburgkapelle, **9**
Hofsilber-und Tafelkammer Museum, **10**
Hoher Markt, **29**
Hundertwasserhaus, **31**
Jüdisches Museum der Stadt Wien, **19**
Kapuzinerkirche, **17**
Karlskirche, **34**
Kunsthistorisches Museum, **13**
Looshaus, **14**
Maria am Gestade, **28**
Mozart Erinnerungsräume, **23**
Museum des 20 Jahrhunderts, **32**
Nationalbibliothek, **4**
Naturhistorisches Museum, **12**
Neue Burg, **11**
Pestsäule, **20**
Peterskirche, **21**
Ruprechtskirche, **30**
Sacher Hotel, **16**
Schatzkammer, **8**
Schauräume in der Hofburg, **7**
Schloss Belvedere, **33**
Schloss Schönbrunn, **35**
Schottenkirche, Museum im Schottenstift, **24**
Spanische Reitschule, **5**
Staatsoper, **15**
Stephansdom, **22**
Theater Museum, **2**
Uhrenmuseum, **27**

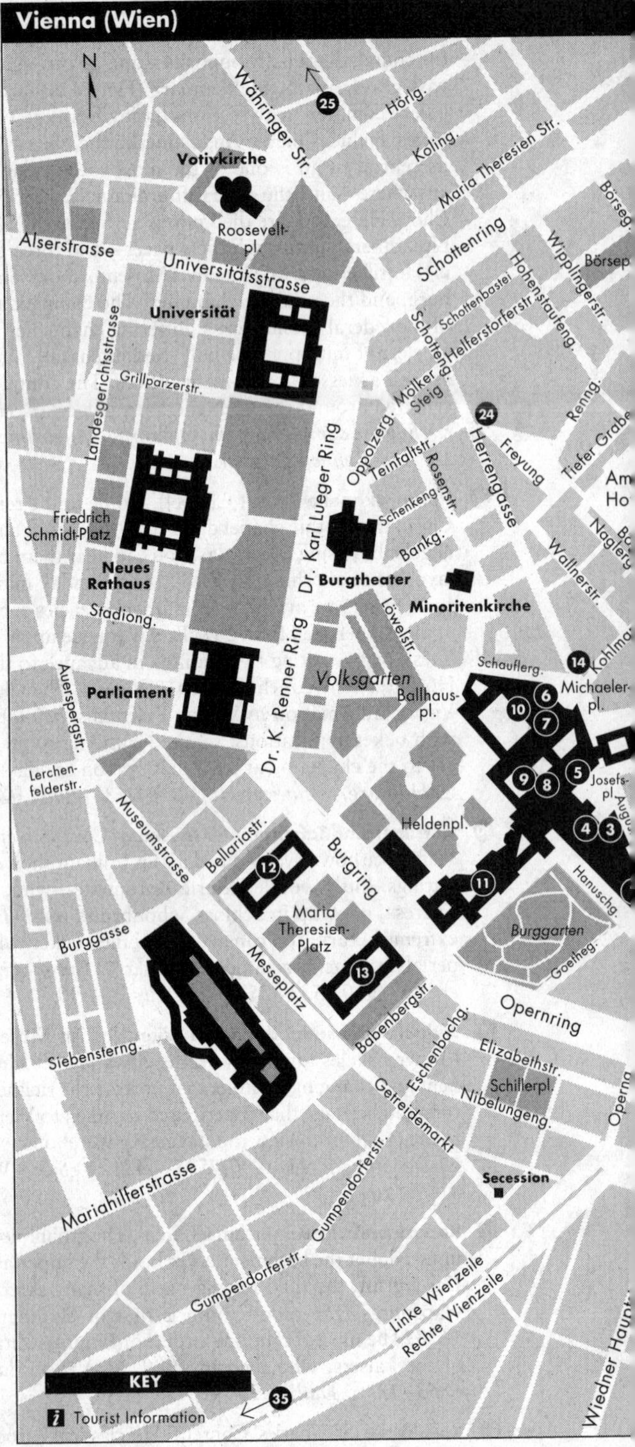

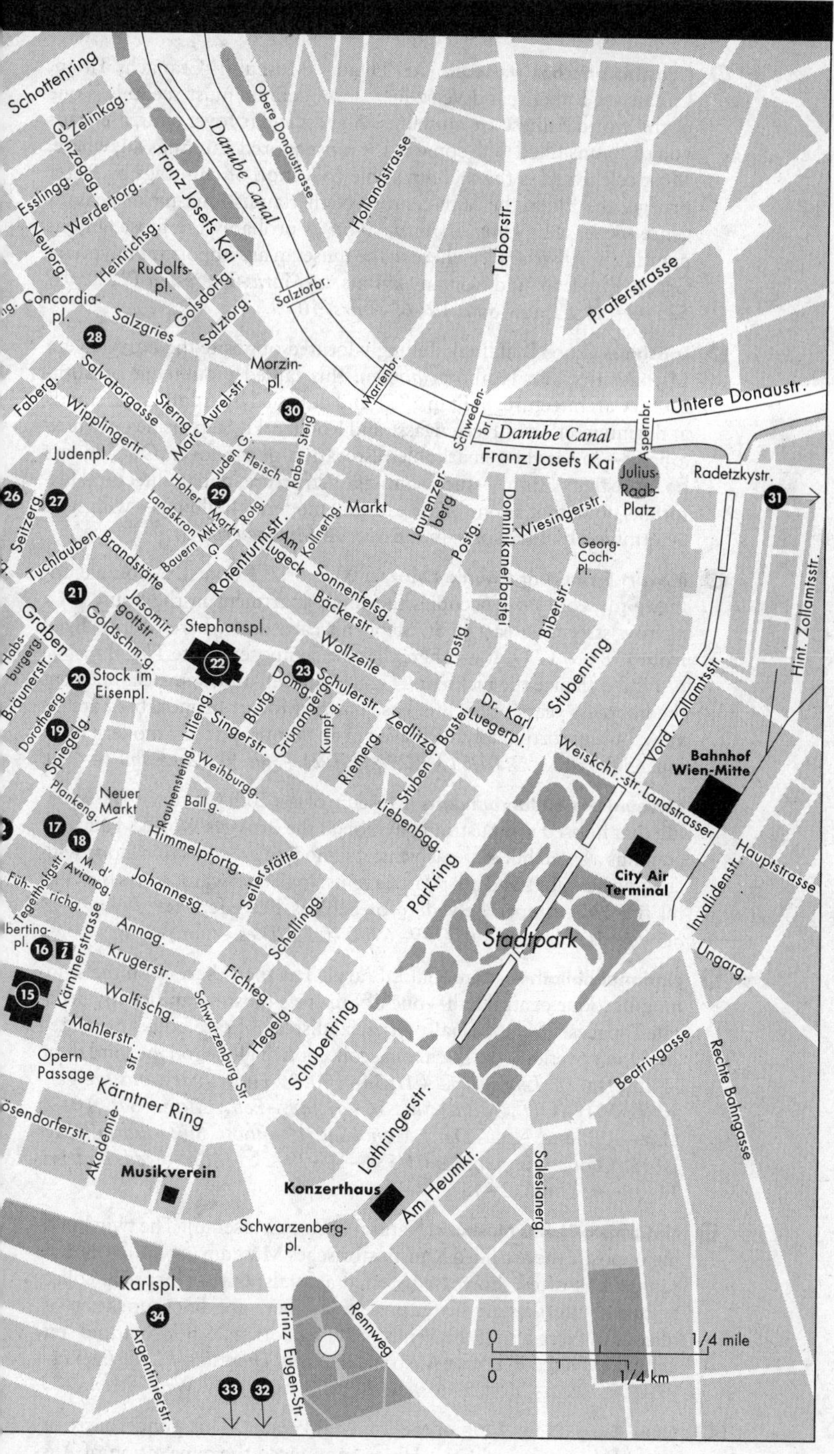
Schottenring
Zelinkag.
Gonzagag.
Esslingg.
Werdertorg.
Neutorg.
Heinrichsg.
Rudolfs-
pl.
Concordia-
pl.
Salzgries
Golsdorfg.
Salztorg.
Franz Josefs Kai
Danube Canal
Obere Donaustrasse
Salztorbr.
Hollandstrasse
Taborstr.
Praterstrasse
Marienbr.
Schweden-
br.
Danube Canal
Aspernbr.
Untere Donaustr.
Franz Josefs Kai
Julius-
Raab-
Platz
Radetzkystr.
Morzin-
pl.
Faberg.
Salvatorgasse
Wipplingerstr.
Sterng.
Marc Aurel-str.
Judenpl.
Juden G.
Fleisch
Raben Steig
Hoher
Markt
Landskron
Bauern Mkt.
Roig.
Markt
Laurenzer-
berg
Postg.
Dominikanerbastei
Wiesingerstr.
Georg-
Coch-
Pl.
Seitzerg.
Tuchlauben
Brandstätte
Rotenturmstr.
Am
Lugeck
Kollnerhg.
Sonnenfelsg.
Bäckerstr.
Postg.
Biberstr.
Hint. Zollamtsstr.
Graben
Jasomir-
gottstr.
Goldschm.g.
Stephanspl.
Wollzeile
Stubenring
Habs-
burgerg.
Bräunerstr.
Stock im
Eisenpl.
Dorotheerg.
Spiegelg.
Dom g.
Blutg.
Grünangerg.
Kumpf g.
Schulerstr.
Singerstr.
Liliengg.
Zedlitzg.
Stuben Bastei
Dr. Karl
Luegerpl.
Weiskchr.-str.
Vord. Zollamtsstr.
Bahnhof
Wien-Mitte
Landstrasser
Hauptstrasse
Plankeng.
Neuer
Markt
Rauhensteing.
Weihburgg.
Ballg.
Riemerg.
Liebenbgg.
Himmelpfortg.
M. d'
Avianog.
Tegetthoffstr.
Füh-
richg.
Johannesg.
Seilerstätte
Parkring
City Air
Terminal
Invalidenstr.
bertina-
pl.
Kärntnerstrasse
Annag.
Krugerstr.
Schellingg.
Stadtpark
Ungarg.
Walfischg.
Fichteg.
Schwarzenburg Str.
Hegelg.
Mahlerstr.
Schubertring
Opern
Passage
str.
Kärntner Ring
Beatrixgasse
Rechte Bahngasse
ösendorferstr.
Akademie-
Musikverein
Lothringerstr.
Konzerthaus
Am Heumkt.
Salesianerg.
Schwarzenberg-
pl.
Karlspl.
Argentinierstr.
Prinz Eugen-Str.
Rennweg
0
1/4 mile
0
1/4 km
15
16
17
18
19
20
21
22
23
26
27
28
29
30
31
32
33
34

Baroque altar is adorned with a magnificent sunburstlike array of gilded shafts. ✉ *Karlspl.*

★ ⓭ **Kunsthistorisches Museum** (Art History Museum). Cranach, Titian, Canaletto, Rubens, and Velázquez . . . A definite must-see, this is one of the world's finest art museums. A spectacular foyer staircase leads you to rooms filled with some of the most adored paintings anywhere. Most celebrated is the incomparable collection of paintings by Pieter Bruegel the Elder, the 16th-century Netherlandish master of peasant genre scenes. His *Hunters in the Snow* is probably the most famous painting in Austria. Elsewhere in the museum are important Egyptian, Greek, Etruscan, and Roman exhibits. ✉ *Maria-Theresien-Pl.,* ☎ *01/525–240.* ⏲ *Tues.–Sun. 10–6, Thurs. 10–9.*

⓮ **Looshaus** (Loos Building). Tellingly located opposite the Baroque-era Michaelertor (☞ Hofburg, *above*), this famed monument of 20th-century architecture, built in 1911 and designed by Adolf Loos, stands at the intersection of Herrengasse and Kohlmarkt. Step inside—it's now a bank—to see the remarkable restoration of the foyer. Outside, it's no more than a simple stucco-and-glass structure, but architectural historians point to it as one of the earliest "modern" buildings—with style determined by function—in Europe. ✉ *Michaelerpl. 3.*

㉓ **Mozart Errinerungsräume** (Mozart Memorial Rooms). A commemorative museum now occupies the small apartment in the house on a narrow street just east of St. Stephen's cathedral where Mozart lived from 1784 to 1787. It was here that the composer wrote *The Marriage of Figaro* (hence the nickname Figaro House), and, some claim, spent the happiest years of his life. Fascinating Mozart memorabilia are on view, but, unfortunately, displayed in an inappropriately modern fashion. ✉ *Domg. 5,* ☎ *01/513–6294.*⏲ *Tues.–Sun. 9–12:15 and 1–4:30.*

㉜ **Museum des 20 Jahrhunderts** (Museum of the 20th Century). The building that housed the Austrian pavilion at the Brussels World's Fair now contains a small but extremely tasteful modern art collection along with changing exhibits and art-related events. It is southward across the Gürtel from the Upper Belvedere of Schloss Belvedere (☞ *below*). ✉ *Schweizer Garten,* ☎ *01/799–6900–0.* ⏲ *Tues.–Sun. 10–6.*

★ ❹ **Nationalbibliothek** (National Library). The focus here is on the stunning Baroque central hall—one of Europe's most magnificently decorated spaces. There's usually a special display of rare books or related art. Don't overlook the fascinating collection of globes on the third floor. ✉ *Josefspl. 1. Library:* ☎ *01/534–100.* ⏲ *Hours vary, but are generally May–Oct., Mon.–Sat. 10–4; Jan.–Feb., Mon.–Sat. 10–2; Mar.–Apr. and Nov.–Dec., Mon.–Sat. 10–noon, Sun. and holidays 10–1. Globe museum:* ☎ *01/534–10–297.* ⏲ *Mon.–Wed. and Fri. 11–noon, Thurs. 2–3.*

⓬ **Naturhistorisches Museum** (Natural History Museum). The twin building opposite the art-filled Kunsthistorisches Museum (☞ *above*) houses ranks of assorted showcased stuffed animals, but such special collections as butterflies are better presented. There are dinosaur skeletons, of course. Here also is the Venus of Willendorf, a 25,000-year-old statuette discovered in Lower Austria. ✉ *Maria-Theresien-Pl.,* ☎ *01/521–77–0.* ⏲ *Wed.–Mon. 9–6; in winter, first floor only, Wed.–Mon. 9–3.*

⓫ **Neue Burg** (New Wing of the Imperial Palace). This ponderously ornate 19th-century edifice—Hitler announced the annexation of Austria from its balcony in 1938—now houses a series of museums, ranging from musical instruments (Beethoven's piano) to weapons (tons of armor) to the ethnological collections of the Museum für

Völkerkunde (Montezuma's headdress) and Ephesus (classical antiquity) museums. ✉ *Heldenpl. 1,* ☎ *01/521–77–0.* ⏲ *Wed.–Mon. 10–6. Ethnological Museum:* ⏲ *Wed.–Mon. 10–4.*

⑳ **Pestsäule** (Plague Column). Shooting up from the middle of the broad Graben Square like a geyser of whipped cream touched with gold, this heavily ornate Baroque-era column commemorates the Black Death of the plague epidemic of 1697. ✉ *Graben.*

㉑ **Peterskirche.** (St. Peter's Church). This Baroque jewel just off the Graben was erected by Johann Lukas von Hildebrandt in about 1730, and has what is probably the city's most theatrical interior. The pulpit is especially fine, with a highly ornate canopy, but florid and swirling decoration is everywhere. Many of the decorative elements are based on the tent form, a motif suggested by the encampment of Turkish forces beyond the city walls during the great siege of Vienna at the end of the 17th century. ✉ *Peterspl., just off the Graben.*

⑯ **Sacher Hotel.** Behind the Opera is Vienna's enduring plush red-and-gilt monument to the fin de siècle. Take a look into the grandly historic ground-floor complex—a veritable maze of gilded lobbies and bars. Who can pay a call and resist ordering up a slice of the original Sachertorte—the ultimate chocolate cake—in the hotel's noted café? ✉ *Philharmonikerstr. 4,* ☎ *01/514–56–0.*

★ ❽ **Schatzkammer** (Imperial Treasury). An almost overpowering display includes the magnificent crown jewels, the imperial crowns, the treasure of the Order of the Golden Fleece, regal robes, and other secular and ecclesiastical treasures. The imperial crown of the Holy Roman Empire is over 1,000 years old. This is one of the world's greatest collections of imperial regalia. ✉ *Hofburg, Schweizer Hof,* ☎ *01/533–7931.* ⏲ *Wed.–Mon. 10–6.*

❼ **Schauräume in der Hofburg** (Imperial Apartments). These rooms were the crystal-bedecked and tapestry-draped residence of Emperor Franz Josef and Empress Elisabeth. Among the exhibits is the exercise equipment used by the beautiful empress. Here, too, is the dress she was wearing when she was stabbed to death in 1898 by a demented Italian anarchist on the shore of Lake Geneva; the dagger marks are visible. State reception rooms are included in the tour. A combined admission with the Hofsilber-und Tafelkammer (Court Silver and Tableware Museum (☞ *above*) is available. ✉ *Michaelerpl. 1 entrance is under the Michaelertor dome (☞ above) from Michaelerpl.,* ☎ *01/533–7570.* ⏲ *Daily 9–4:30 (Thurs. until 9).*

★ ❺ **Spanische Reitschule** (Spanish Riding School). Probably the most famous interior in Vienna, the riding arena of the Spanish Riding School—wedding-cake white and crystal-chandeliered—is where the beloved white Lippizaner horses train and perform dressage when they are not stabled in stalls across the Reitschulgasse to the east side of the school. Due to renovations, the school entrance has been moved temporarily from Josefsplatz to the main courtyard next to the Swiss Gate, beyond the Michaelertor rotunda dome; when renovations are done, the main entrance will be moved back, so double-check. For performance schedules and tickets, write to the Spanische Reitschule (✉ Hofburg, A-1010,Vienna) *at least* three months in advance. There are generally full performances on Sunday at 10:45 AM from March through June, and from September into October. There are no performances in July and August. Evening performances are occasionally given on Wednesday at 7. The AmEx office sometimes has a few last-minute tickets, but expect a 22% service charge. Tickets for the few short training performances on Saturday morning at 10 are available only from ticket offices and travel agencies; a list of these agencies is available from the Austrian National Tourist Office. You can watch the 10 AM–noon training sessions Tuesday–Saturday during much of the performance season; tickets for these training sessions are available only at the door. ✉ *Michaelerpl. 1, Hofburg,* ☎ *01/533–9032,* FAX *01/535–0186.* *AS250–AS900, standing room AS200, Sat. morning training session with music AS250, other morning training sessions AS100.* ⏲ *Mar.–June and Sept.–mid-Dec; closed tour wks.*

15 **Staatsoper** (State Opera House). Considered one of the best opera houses in the world, the Staatsoper is a focus of Viennese social life as well. The house was almost totally destroyed in the last days of World War II (only the walls and front foyers were saved), but rebuilt in its present simpler elegance and reopened in 1955. Tickets for seats can be expensive and scarce, but one of the very best bargains in Vienna are the Staatsoper standing-room tickets, available for each performance at delightfully affordable prices—as low as AS50 ($4)! Backstage tours also are available: The tour schedule for the day is usually posted beside the door under the right front arcade, on the Kärntnerstrasse side (depending on the activities inside, there are usually tours at 2 and 3 PM). The repertory schedule here is one of the most ambitious in Europe; as many as four different operas are performed in a single week during the September–June season. ✉ *Opernring 2,* ☎ *01/514–4429–69.*

★ 22 **Stephansdom** (St. Stephen's Cathedral). The towering Gothic spires and gaudy 19th-century tile roof of the city's central landmark still dominate the skyline. The oldest parts of the structure are the 13th-century entrance, the soaring **Riesentor** (Great Entry), and the Heidentürme (Heathens' Towers). Inside, the church is mysteriously shadowy, filled with an array of monuments, tombs, sculptures, paintings, and pulpits. Despite extensive wartime damage—and numerous Baroque additions—the atmosphere seems authentically medieval. Climb the 343 steps of the south tower—Alte Steffl (Old Stephen) as the Viennese call it—for a stupendous view over the city. An elevator goes up the north tower to the Pummerin, a 22-ton bell cast in part from cannons captured from the Turks in 1683. If you take a 30-minute tour of the crypt, you can see the copper jars in which the entrails of the Hapsburgs are carefully preserved. ✉ *Stephanspl.,* ☎ *01/515–52–526.* ⏲ *Catacombs (guided tour only): Mon.–Sat. 10, 11, 11:30, 2, 2:30, 3:30, 4, 4:30; Sun. and holidays 2, 2:30, 3:30, 4, 4:30. North tower: Apr.–Sept., daily 9–6, Oct.–Mar., daily 8–5. South tower: daily 9–5:30.*

2 **Theater Museum.** Housed in the noted 18th-century Palais Lobkowitz—Beethoven was a regular visitor here—this museum covers the history of theater in Vienna and the rest of Austria. A children's museum in the basement—alas, open only by appointment—is reached by a slide! ✉ *Lobkowitzpl. 2,* ☎ *01/512–8800–0.* ⏲ *Tues.–Sun. 10–5.*

Other Corners of Vienna

26 **Am Hof.** The **Kirche am Hof** (Church of the Nine Choirs of Angels is its complete name, on the east side of Am Hof) is only one feature of this remarkable square, whose name simply translates as "at court." Most of the Baroque overlay both inside and out on the massive church dates from the 1600s. The somewhat dreary interior is curiously reminiscent of those of many Dutch churches. In the northeast corner of the square check out what is possibly the most ornate fire station in the world. You'll find an open-air antiques market in the square on Thursday and Friday in summer and frequent seasonal markets at other times. ✉ *Bounded by Tiefer Graben to the west, Nagelrg. to the south, and Seitzerg. to the west.*

29 **Hoher Markt.** This ancient cobblestone square with its imposing central monument celebrating the betrothal of Mary and Joseph sits atop **Roman ruins** (✉ Hoher Markt 3, ☎ 01/535–5606), remains of the 2nd-century Roman legion encampment. On the north side of Hoher Markt is the amusing **Anker-Uhr,** a clock that marks the hour with a parade of moving figures. The figures are identified on a plaque at the lower left of the clock; it's well worth passing by at noon to catch the show.

31 **Hundertwasserhaus** (Hundertwasser House). This famous structure is a masterpiece envisioned by artist Friedenreich Hundertwasser—an astonishing apartment complex marked by turrets, towers, unusual windows, and uneven floors. The nearby **KunstHaus Wien** (Vienna House of Art; ✉ KunstHaus Wien, Untere Weissgerberstr. 13, ☎ 01/712–0491) is an art museum designed by the artist; it offers a floor of Hundertwasser plus changing exhibits of other modern works. ✉ *Kegelg. and Köweng.* ⏲ *Daily 10–7.*

28 **Maria am Gestade** (St. Mary's on the Bank). When built around 1400, this was a church for fishermen from the nearby canal, hence the name. Note the arched stone doorway and the ornate carved stone latticework "folded hands" spire. ✉ *Salvatorg./Passauer Pl.*

30 **Ruprechtskirche** (St. Rupert's Church). Vienna's oldest church, dating from the 11th century, is small, damp, dark, and—unfortunately—usually closed. ✉ *Ruprechtspl.*

★ 33 **Schloss Belvedere** (Belvedere Palace). On a rise overlooking the city, this Baroque-era palace is one of the showpieces of Vienna. It was commissioned by Prince Eugene of Savoy and built by Johann Lukas von Hildebrandt in 1721–22. The palace consists of two separate buildings, one at the foot of the hill and the other at the top. The lavish gardens are among the finest showpieces of the Baroque style in landscaping found anywhere. The Upper Belvedere houses a gallery of 19th- and 20th-century Viennese art, featuring works by Klimt (including his world-famous painting *The Kiss*), Kokoschka, Schiele, Waldmüller, and Makart; the Lower Belvedere has a Baroque museum together with exhibits of Austrian art of the Middle Ages. Take Streetcar D toward the Südbahnhof to reach the Belvedere. ✉ *Prinz-Eugen-Str. 27,* ☎ *01/795–570.* ⏲ *Tues.–Sun. 10–5.*

★ 35 **Schloss Schönbrunn** (Schönbrunn Palace). The Versailles of Vienna, this magnificent Baroque residence has grandly formal gardens, and was built for the Hapsburgs between 1696 and 1713. The palace was originally conceived to top the hill behind the present palace, but the scheme was too costly and plans were changed, putting the palace on the lower ground and capping the hill with that touch of architectural genius, the Gloriette. The complex has been a summer residence for personages including Maria Theresa and Napoléon. Kaiser Franz Josef I was born and died here. His "office" (kept as he left it in 1916) is a touching reminder of his Spartan life. In contrast, other rooms are filled with truly spectacular imperial elegance. Six-year-old Mozart played here in the Hall of Mirrors for Maria Theresa and the court. The ornate reception areas are still used for state occasions. A guided tour leading through more than 40 of the palace's 1,441 rooms is the best way to see inside the palace (you can take a tour of just 20 rooms, but since the most dazzling salons start at No. 21, opt for the full tour). Other rooms are occasionally open independent of tours. Ask to see the **Berglzimmer,** ornately decorated ground-floor rooms generally not included in tours. To get to the palace, take the U4 subway line from the city center; it's an easy ride and just five stops from Karlsplatz. ✉ *Schönbrunner Schlosstr.,* ☎ *01/81113.* 🎫 *AS140 with guided tour;*

AS110 without tour (40 rooms). ⌚ *Nov.–Mar., daily 8:30–4:30; Apr.–Oct., daily 8:30–5.*

Once on the grounds of the Schönbrunn Palace, don't overlook the **Tiergarten** (zoo). It's Europe's oldest menagerie, established in 1752 to amuse and educate the court. It houses an extensive assortment of animals; the original Baroque enclosures now serve as viewing pavilions, with the animals housed in effective, modern settings. ☎ *01/877–9294.* ⌚ *Nov.–Jan., daily 9–4:30; Feb. and Oct., daily 9–5; Mar., daily 9–5:30; Apr., daily 9–6; May–Sept., daily 9–6:30.*

Pathways lead up through the formal gardens to the famous **Gloriette,** an 18th-century Baroque folly on the rise behind Schloss Schönbrunn built so that palace residents could enjoy superb views of the city. There's a café inside. ⌚ *Daily 9–5.*

The **Wagenburg** (Imperial Coach Collection), near the entrance to the palace grounds, displays splendid examples of bygone conveyances, from ornate children's sleighs to the grand carriages built to carry the coffins of deceased emperors in state funerals. ☎ *01/877–3244.* *AS30.* ⌚ *Apr.–Oct., daily 9–6; Nov.–Mar., Tues.–Sun. 10–4.*

If you have time, wander the grounds to discover the **Schöner Brunnen** (Beautiful Fountain) for which the Schönbrunn Palace is named; the re-created but convincing massive **Römische Ruinen** (Roman Ruins); the great glass **Palmenhaus** (Palmery), with its orchids and exotic plants; and the **Schmetterlinghaus** (Butterfly House), alive with unusual butterflies. *Palm House:* ✉ *Nearest entrance Hietzing,* ☎ *01/877–5087–406.* ⌚ *May–Sept., daily 9:30–5:30; Oct.–Apr., daily 9:30–4:30. Butterfly House:*☎ *01/877–5087–421.* ⌚ *May–Sept., daily 10–4:30; Oct.–Apr., daily 10–3.*

24 **Schottenkirche, Museum im Schottenstift** (Scottish Church and Museum). Despite its name, the monks who founded this church around 1177 were actually Irish, not Scots. The present imposing building dates from the mid-1600s. In contrast to the plain exterior, the interior bubbles with cherubs and angels. The Benedictines have set up a small but worthwhile museum of mainly religious art, including a late-Gothic winged altarpiece removed from the church when the interior was given a Baroque overlay. The museum entrance is in the courtyard. ✉ *Freyung 6,* ☎ *01/534–98–600.* ⌚ *Thurs.–Sat. 10–5, Sun. noon–5.*

27 **Uhrenmuseum** (Clock Museum). Tucked away on several floors of a lovely Renaissance structure is an amazing collection of clocks and watches. Try to be there when the hundreds of clocks strike the noon hour. ✉ *Schulhof 2,* ☎ *01/533–2265.* ⌚ *Tues.–Sun. 9–4:30.*

Vienna Environs

Wienerwald (Vienna Woods). You can reach a small corner of the legendary Vienna Woods by streetcar and bus: Take a streetcar or the U-2 subway line to Schottentor/University and, from there, Streetcar 38 (Grinzing) to the end of the line. To get into the woods, change in Grinzing to Bus 38A. This will take you to the Kahlenberg, which provides a superb view out over the Danube and the city. You can take the bus or hike to the Leopoldsberg, the promontory over the Danube from which Turkish invading forces were repulsed during the 16th and 17th centuries. Grinzing itself is a village out of a picture book. Unfortunately, much of the wine offered in its wine taverns, or Heuriger, is less than enchanting. For better wine and ambience, try the area around Pfarrplatz and Probusgasse in Hohe Warte—Streetcar 37, Bus 39A—or the suburb of Nussdorf—Streetcar D.)

Dining and Lodging

In recent years Vienna, once a culinary backwater, has produced a new generation of chefs willing to slaughter sacred cows and create a *Neue Küche,* a new Vienna cuisine. The movement is well past the "less is more" stage that nouvelle cuisine traditionally demands (and to which most Viennese vociferously objected), relying now on lighter versions of the old standbys and clever combinations of such traditional ingredients as liver pâtés and sour cream.

In a first-class restaurant you will pay as much as in most other Western European capitals. But you can still find good food at refreshingly low prices in the simpler restaurants, particularly at neighborhood *Gasthäuser* (rustic inns) in the suburbs. Remember if you eat your main meal at noon (as the Viennese do), you can take advantage of the luncheon specials available at most restaurants and in cafés. For details and price-category definitions, *see* Dining *in* Austria A to Z, *above*.

As for hotels, Vienna's first district (A-1010) is the best base for visitors because it's so close to most of the major sights, restaurants, and shops. This accessibility translates, of course, into higher prices. Try bargaining for discounts at the larger international chain hotels during the off-season. For details and price-category definitions, *see* Lodging *in* Austria A to Z, *above*.

$$$$ ★ ✕ **Korso.** A veritable gourmet temple, Korso has a sumptuous setting with elegant paneling and velvet and gold accents. For aficionados of the new Vienna cuisine, the decor is almost as delicious as the house specialties. Chef Reinhard Gerer produces exquisite variations on such Austrian standards as pork and beef by borrowing accents from Asian traditions. Sample the delicate Styrian lamb or fillet of venison. ✉ *Kärtner Ring 1,* ☎ *01/515–16–546. Reservations essential. Jacket and tie. AE, DC, MC, V. Closed 3 wks in Aug. No lunch Sat.*

$$$$ ★ ✕ **Le Siècle.** Most diners come for the pampered elegance and the variety of seafood, flown in fresh daily. Tempting items on the ever-changing menu might include marinated salmon with a dill mustard sauce to start, followed by a lightly fried turbot fillet with white asparagus and artichoke and truffle mousse. Desserts, such as the delicate citrus fruit terrine, are inspired and steer away from traditional heavy cakes and strudels. ✉ *Radisson/SAS Palais Hotel, Parkring 16,* ☎ *01/515–17–3440. Reservations essential. Jacket and tie. AE, DC, MC, V.*

$$$ ✕ **Do & Co.** The spectacular setting at the top of the modern Haas-Haus building smack in the middle of Stephansplatz would make this worthwhile for the view alone, but the food is also excellent and varied, with a nouvelle-Oriental slant featuring fragrant, tangy wok creations. For heartier appetites there are numerous meat choices, with the combination king crab and Uruguayan steak being most popular. There is also a fantastic, though pricey, sushi bar at lunchtime. In the evenings, book a table by the window so you can see the sunset over the spires of St. Stephen's, and in warm weather, ask for a table outside on the balcony. ✉ *In Haas-Haus, Stephanspl. 12,* ☎ *01/535–3969. Reservations essential. Jacket and tie. AE, DC, MC, V.*

$$$ ★ ✕ **Fadinger.** Near the *Börse* (the Vienna Stock Exchange), this unpretentious restaurant serves some of the best nouvelle Austrian cuisine in the city. The widely varied menu includes light-as-a-feather fish dishes, such as salmon in a crisp potato crust, as well as hearty, but never heavy, meat courses. The *Zwiebelrostbraten,* skirt steak topped with crisp fried onions, is outstanding. ✉ *Wipplingerstr. 29,* ☎ *01/533–4341. Reservations essential. No credit cards. Closed weekends.*

$$$ ✕ **Zu ebener Erde und erster Stock.** Ask for a table upstairs in this tiny, utterly charming original Biedermeier house, which serves excellent Austrian fare plus international specialties; the downstairs space is good for snacks. ✉ *Burgg. 13,* ☎ *01/523–6254. Reservations essential. Jacket and tie. AE, V. Closed Sun.–Mon. and late July–late Aug. No lunch Sat.*

$$ ✕ **Bei Max.** The decor is somewhat bland, but the tasty Carinthian specialties—*Käsnudeln* and *Fleischnudeln* (cheese and meat ravioli) in particular—keep this friendly restaurant packed. ✉ *Landhausg. 2 at Herreng.,* ☎ *01/533–7359. No credit cards. Closed weekends, last wk in July, first 3 wks in Aug.*

$$ ✕ **Figlmüller.** Known for its gargantuan schnitzel, which is so large it overflows the plate, Figlmüller is always packed with diners sharing benches and long tables. Food choices are limited and everything is à la carte. The small enclosed "greenhouse" in the passageway entry is more popular than the inside rooms. ✉ *Wollzeile 5 (passageway from Stephansdom),*☎ *01/512–6177. No credit cards. Closed Aug.*

$$ ★ ✕ **Lebenbauer.** This is Vienna's premier vegetarian restaurant and it even has a no-smoking room, rare in this part of Europe. Specialties include *Hirsegröstl* (millet hash with pumpkin seeds in an oyster mushroom sauce) and gluten-free pasta with smoked salmon and shrimp in a dill cream sauce. ✉ *Teinfaltstr. 3, near the Freyung,* ☎ *01/533–5556–0. AE, DC, MC, V.* ⏲ *Weekdays 11–3 and 5–10 , Sat. 11–2 . Closed Sat. evening, Sun., and first two weeks of Aug.*

$$ ★ ✕ **Livingstone.** If you're homesick for a hamburger and fries, this is the place to go. Buns are homemade and the Austrian beef is of the finest quality. But if the tropical-colonial setting straight out of a 1940s Bogart movie makes you want to try something more adventurous—such as pasta with smoked tofu, tiger shrimp, and squash, and green chili peppers in a garlic-ginger sesame oil sauce—you won't be disappointed. ✉ *Zelinkag. 4, near the Börse,* ☎ *01/533–3393. AE, DC, MC, V. No lunch.*

$$ ✕ **Melker Stiftskeller.** This is one of the city's half-dozen genuine *Weinkeller* (cellar wine taverns). The food selection is limited but good, featuring *Stelze* (crisp roasted pig's knuckle). ✉ *Schotteng. 3,* ☎ *01/533–5530. MC, V. Closed Sun. No lunch.*

$$ ✕ **Neu Wien.** As the name says, this is a taste of the new Vienna. The vaulted interior is enlivened by cheeky modern art. The eclectic menu changes frequently, but look for the herbed goat cheese salad with basil oil dressing, *Zanderfilet,* a crisp pike perch with a cream beet sauce, or veal with tagliatelle in a truffle sauce. ✉ *Bäckerstr. 5, near St. Stephen's,* ☎ *01/512–0999. Reservations essential. MC, V. Closed weekends in summer. No lunch.*

$ ★ ✕ **Gigerl.** It's hard to believe you're right in the middle of the city at this imaginative and charming wine restaurant that serves hot and cold buffets. The rooms are small and cozy but may get smoky and noisy when the place is full—which it usually is. The food is typical of wine gardens on the fringes of the city: roast meats, casserole dishes, cold cuts, salads. The wines are very good. The surrounding narrow alleys and ancient buildings add to the charm of the outdoor tables in summer. ✉ *Rauhensteing. 3,* ☎ *01/513–4431. AE, DC, MC, V. No lunch Sun.*

$ ★ ✕ **Königsbacher bei der Oper.** The space is intimate and tables are close, but portions are generous and the daily special (listed for the week) could be anything from roast pork to a ham-and-noodle casserole. Shaded outdoor tables are delightful in summer. ✉ *Walfischg. 5,* ☎ *01/513–1210. No credit cards. Closed Sun. No dinner Sat.*

$ ★ ✕ **Spatzennest.** This is simple, hearty Viennese cooking at its best, served on a quaint, cobblestone, pedestrian street in Old Vienna. Tasty dishes include schnitzel and roast chicken with spaetzle prepared with slivers of ham and melted cheese. It's especially delightful in summer, when tables are set outside. It can be smoky indoors. ✉ *Ulrichspl. 1, near the Volkstheater,* ☎ *01/520–1659. No credit cards. Closed Fri.–Sat.*

$$$$ ★ 🏨 **Bristol.** Opposite the Staatsoper (State Opera House), the Bristol is classic Viennese, preferred by many—particularly business travelers—for the service as well as the location. The bar is comfortable and the restaurants associated with the hotel are outstanding, especially Korso, which is one of the most beautiful dining salons to be found in Europe. Rooms are elegant and somewhat modern; rear and upper rooms are quieter. ✉ *Kärntner Ring 1, A-1010,* ☎ *01/515–16–0,* FAX *01/515–16–550. 142 rooms. 2 restaurants. AE, DC, MC, V.*

$$$$ ★ 🏨 **Das Triest.** This is a little off the beaten track, but still in easy walking distance to the city center. Redone by Sir Terence Conran, Das Triest is now Vienna's most chic hotel, giving guests the feeling that they are on board an ultra-sleek new ship, which is surprising, considering it was once a stable. ✉ *Wiedner Hauptstr. 12, A-1010,* ☎ *01/589–180,* FAX *01/589–1818. 73 rooms. Restaurant. AE, DC, MC, V.*

$$$$ ★ 🏨 **Imperial.** This former palace represents elegant old and new Vienna at its best—an appropriately luxurious setting for the crowned heads and off-duty celebrities that are frequent guests. The hotel's location on the Ring could hardly be better (noise is not a problem, thanks to double-paned windows) and the service throughout the hotel is superb. Be sure to visit the supremely intimate and sumptuously decorated bar that's hidden off the lobby as well as the peaceful and pretty Café Imperial (open for breakfast, lunch, and dinner). ✉ *Kärntner Ring 16, A-1010,* ☎ *01/501–10–0,* FAX *01/501–10–410. 128 rooms. Restaurant. AE, DC, MC, V.*

$$$$ 🏨 **Radisson/SAS Palais.** Two former fin de siècle palaces have come together to form this hotel that has a superb location on the Ring and Le Siècle (☞ Dining, *above*), arguably Vienna's best seafood restaurant. The staff is friendly and helpful. Ask for a room facing the Stadtpark. ✉ *Parkring 16, A-1010,* ☎ *01/515–170,* FAX *01/51–22–216. 246 rooms. 2 restaurants. AE, DC, MC, V.*

$$$$ ★ 🏨 **Sacher.** The Sacher is all about tradition and it remains one of the legendary addresses in Europe. Its opulent decor is highlighted by original oil paintings and other artwork. The Blue and Red bars are intimate and favored by guests and nonguests alike, as is the legendary café, home of the original Sacher torte. Guest rooms are spacious and elegantly appointed and the staff is particularly accommodating and soigné. ✉ *Philharmonikerstr. 4, A-1010,* ☎ *01/514–56–0,* FAX *01/514–57–810. 108 rooms. Restaurant. AE, DC, MC, V.*

$$$ 🏨 **Altstadt.** A real gem, this small hotel was once a patrician home. Rooms are large, with all the modern comforts, though they retain an antique feel. The English-style lounge has a fireplace and plump floral sofas. You're one streetcar stop or a pleasant walk from the main museums. ✉ *Kircheng. 41, A-1070,* ☎ *01/526–3399–0,* FAX *01/523–4901. 25 rooms with bath or shower. AE, DC, MC, V.*

$$$ 🏨 **Astoria.** Though the Astoria is one of Vienna's traditional old hotels, the rooms have been modernized considerably. The paneled lobby, however, has been preserved and retains an unmistakable Old World patina. The location is central, but because of the street musicians and late-night crowds in the pedestrian zone, rooms overlooking Kärntnerstrasse tend to be noisy in summer. ✉ *Fürichg. 1, A-1010,* ☎ *01/515–77–0,* FAX *01/515–7782. 108 rooms with bath or shower. Restaurant. AE, DC, MC, V.*

$$$ 🏨 **König von Ungarn.** This utterly charming centrally located hotel is tucked away in the shadow of the cathedral. Its historic facade belies the efficient modernity of the interior, from the atrium lobby to the guest rooms themselves. The bar is especially inviting, set in an enclosed courtyard. Insist on written confirmation of bookings. ✉ *Schulerstr. 10, A-*

1010, ☎ 01/515–84–0, FAX 01/515–84–8. 33 rooms with bath or shower. Restaurant. DC, MC, V.

$$$ **Mailberger Hof.** This is a favorite of opera stars, conductors, and others who want a central but quiet location. Some rooms have a kitchenette. The arcaded courtyard is appealingly relaxing. ✉ *Annag. 7, A-1010, ☎ 01/512–0641, FAX 01/512–0641–10. 40 rooms with bath or shower. Restaurant. AE, MC, V.*

$$$ **Opernring.** Spacious and homelike front rooms are less quiet but have great views across the Ring to the Staatsoper (State Opera House). Unusually personal attention and helpful management are added features in this Best Western affiliate. ✉ *Opernring 11, A-1010, ☎ 01/587–5518–0, FAX 01/587–5518–29. 35 rooms. AE, DC, MC, V.*

$$ ★ **Austria.** This older hotel is on a quiet side street in a historic area. ✉ *Wolfeng. 3/Fleischmarkt 20, A-1010, ☎ 01/515–23–0, FAX 01/515–23–506. 46 rooms, 42 with bath or shower. AE, DC, MC, V.*

$$ ★ **Pension Riedl.** On the upper floors of a lovely 19th-century building overlooking the Postsparkassenamt, is this Secession-style building designed by Otto Wagner. Rooms are nicely furnished and comfortable. Full breakfast is included. ✉ *Georg–Coch–Pl. 3/4/10 (near Julius–Raab Pl.), A-1010, ☎ 01/512–7919, FAX 01/512–79198. 8 rooms. Closed first 2 wks of Feb. DC, MC, V.*

$–$$ ★ **Kärntnerhof.** Though tucked away in a tiny, quiet side street, the Kärntnerhof is nevertheless centrally located. It's known for its particularly congenial staff. The rooms are functionally decorated but clean and serviceable. Rooms with shower only are in the $ category. ✉ *Grashofg. 4, A-1010, ☎ 01/512–1923–0, FAX 01/513–2228–33. 43 rooms, 41 with bath or shower. AE, DC, MC, V.*

$–$$ **Post.** Taking its name from the city's main post office, opposite, this is an older but updated hotel that offers a fine location, a friendly staff, and a good café. Rooms with shower only are serviceable and in the $ category. ✉ *Fleischmarkt 24, A-1010, ☎ 01/515–83–0, FAX 01/515–83–808. 107 rooms, 77 with bath or shower. AE, DC, MC, V.*

$ ★ **Kugel.** This older but freshly redecorated hotel is halfway between the Westbahnhof and the city center. Rooms are small but well furnished and the staff is helpful. ✉ *Siebensterng. 43, A-1070, ☎ 01/523–3355, FAX 01/523–1678. 38 rooms, 17 with bath or shower. Closed Jan.–early Feb. No credit cards.*

$ ★ **Reimer.** The Reimer is friendly and comfy and in a prime location just off the Mariahilferstrasse. Rooms have high ceilings and large windows. Breakfast is included. ✉ *Kircheng. 18, A-1070, ☎ 01/523–6162, FAX 01/524–3782. 14 rooms with bath or shower. MC, V.*

Nightlife and the Arts

The Arts

MUSIC

Most classical concerts are held in one of two places. The **Konzerthaus** (✉ Lothringerstr. 20, ☎ 01/712–4686, ticket window 01/712–1211, FAX 01/712–2872) is one. The **Musikverein** (✉ Dumbastr. 3, ☎ 01/505–86–8194, FAX 01/505–8681–94) is the other. Tickets can be bought at their box offices or ordered by phone (AE, DC, MC, V). Pop concerts are scheduled from time to time at the **Austria Center** (✉ Am Hubertusdamm 6, U-1 subway to Vienna International Center stop, ☎ 01/236–9150). Tickets to various musical events are sold through **Vienna Ticket Service** (☎ 01/588–85–0, FAX 01/588–3033) and the Salettl gazebo ticket office (☎ 01/588–85–81), which is open daily 10–7, on Kärntnerstrasse next to the Staatsoper (State Opera House). At the same office, same-day half-price tickets to many musical events—*but not the Staatsoper, Volksoper, or symphony concerts*—go on sale at 2 PM.

THEATER AND OPERA

Check the monthly program published by the city; posters also show opera and theater schedules. The **Staatsoper,** one of world's great opera houses, features major stars in its almost-nightly original-language performances. The **Volksoper** offers lighter operas, operettas, and musicals, all in German. Performances at the **Burgtheater** and **Akadamietheater** are also in German. Tickets for the Staatsoper, the Volksoper, and the Burg and Akademie theaters are available at the central ticket office to the left rear of the Staatsoper (Bundestheaterkassen, Hanuschg. 3, 01/514–44–2959, 01/514–44–2969; weekdays 8–6, weekends and holidays 9–noon). Tickets go on sale a month before performances. Unsold tickets can be obtained at the evening box office. Plan to be there at least one hour before the performance; students can buy remaining tickets at lower prices, so they are usually out in force. Tickets can be ordered three weeks or more in advance in writing (or by fax) or a month in advance from anywhere in the world by phone (01/513–1513). Standing room tickets for the Staatsoper are a great bargain.

Theater is offered in English at **Vienna's English Theater** (⊠ Josefsg. 12, ☎ 01/402–1260).The **International Theater** (⊠ Porzellang. 8, ☎ 01/319–6272) also has performances in English.

Nightlife

The central district for nightlife in Vienna is nicknamed the **Bermuda-Dreieck** (Bermuda Triangle). Centered around Judengasse/Seitenstettengasse, next to St. Ruprecht's, a small Romanesque church, the area is jammed with everything from good bistros to jazz clubs.

CABARETS

Most cabarets are expensive and unmemorable. One leading option is **Casanova** (⊠ Dorotheerg. 6, ☎ 01/512–9845), which emphasizes striptease. Another popular cabaret is **Moulin Rouge** (⊠ Walfischg. 11, ☎ 01/512–2130).

CAFÉS

A quintessential Viennese institution, the coffeehouse, or café, is club, pub, and bistro all rolled into one. To savor the atmosphere of the coffeehouses you must take your time: Set aside an afternoon, a morning, or at least a couple of hours, and settle down in one of your choice. There is no need to worry about overstaying your welcome, even over a single small cup of Mokka—although in some of the more opulent coffeehouses, this cup of coffee can cost as much as a meal.

Alte Backstube (⊠ Lange Gasse 34, ☎ 01/406–1101; AE, MC, V), in a gorgeous Baroque house—with a café in front and restaurant in back—was once a bakery and is now a museum as well. **Café Central** (⊠ Herreng. 14,☎ 01/535–4176–0) is where Stalin and Trotsky played chess; in the Palais Ferstel, it's one of Vienna's most beautiful cafés. **Cafe Landtmann** (⊠ Dr. Karl Leuger Str. 4, ☎ 01/532–0621), next to the dignified Burgtheater, with front-row views of the Ringstrasse, was reputedly Freud's favorite café. In May they offer a tempting selection of fresh strawberry tortes. A 200-year-old institution, **Demel** (⊠ Kohlmarkt 14, ☎ 01/535–1717–0) is the *grande dame* of Viennese cafés. Order a melange, brought with milk on the side in a dainty creamer, to go along with their Senegal torte, a scrumptious hazelnut cake. The elegant front rooms have more atmosphere than the airy modern atrium and are now reserved as no-smoking rooms. **Gerstner** (⊠ Kärtnerstr. 15, ☎ 01/496377) is in the heart of the bustling Kärntnerstrasse, and one of the more modern Viennese cafés. Popular here is the Bruegel torte, a marzipan pastry especially concocted for their branch in the Kunsthistorisches Museum. **Museum** (⊠ Friedrichstr. 6, ☎ 01/586–5202), with its original interior by the architect Adolf Loos, draws a mixed crowd and has lots of newspapers. **The Sacher** (✉ Philharmonikerstr. 4, ☎ 01/514–56–0) is hardly a typical Vienna café; more a shrine to plush gilt and marzipan, it's both a must-see and a must-eat. The world's ultimate chocolate cake is served here.

DISCOS

Atrium (✉ Schwarzenbergpl. 10, ☎ 01/505–3594) is open Thursday through Sunday and draws a lively young crowd. **Queen Anne** (✉ Johannesg. 12, ☎ 01/512–0203) is central, popular, and always packed. The **U-4** (✉ Schönbrunnerstr. 222, ☎ 01/815–8307) ranks high among the young set. **P 1** (✉ Rotg. 9, ☎ 01/535–9995) is another spot for the MTV crowd. Live bands, dancing, and snacks are offered at **Chattanooga** (✉ Graben 29A, ☎ 01/533–5000–0).

NIGHTCLUBS

A casual '50s atmosphere pervades the popular **Café Volksgarten** (✉ Burgring 1, ☎ 01/533–0518), in the city park of the same name; tables are set outdoors in summer. The more formal **Eden Bar** (✉ Lilieng. 2, ☎ 01/512–7450) is considered one of Vienna's classiest nightspots; don't expect to be let in unless you're dressed to kill.

WINE TAVERNS

For a traditional Viennese night out, head to one of the city's atmospheric *Heuriger,* or wine taverns, some of which date from as far back as the 12th century. You can often have full meals at these taverns, but the emphasis is mainly on drinking. The **Melker Stiftskeller** (☞ Dining, *above*) is one of the friendliest and most typical. Another wine-tavern option is the **Augustinerkeller** (✉ Augustinerstr. 1, ☎ 01/533–1026), open at lunchtime as well as evenings, in the same building as the Albertina collection. The **Esterházykeller** (✉ Haarhof 1, ☎ 01/533–3482), in a particularly mazelike network of rooms, has excellent wines. The **Zwölf Apostelkeller** (✉ Sonnenfelsg. 3, ☎ 01/512–6777), near St. Stephen's has rooms that are down, down, down underground.

Shopping

Boutiques

Famous name brands are found along the **Kohlmarkt** and **Graben** and their respective side streets, and the side streets off **Kärntnerstrasse.**

Folk Costumes

The main resource for exquisite Austrian *Trachten* (native dress) is **Loden-Plankl** (✉ Michaelerpl. 6, ☎ 01/533–8032).

Food and Flea Markets

The **Naschmarkt** (foodstuffs market; ✉ Between the Rechte and LinkeWienzeile; ⏲ weekdays 6 AM–mid-afternoon, Sat. 6–1) is a sensational open-air market offering specialties from around the world. The **Flohmarkt** (flea market) operates year-round beyond the Naschmarkt (subway U-4 to Kettenbrückeng.; Sat. 8–4) and is equally fascinating. An **Arts and Antiques Market** with better offerings operates on Saturday (2–6) and Sunday (10–6) alongside the Danube Canal near the Salztorbrücke. From late spring to early fall, check Am Hof square for antiques and collectibles on Thursday and Friday. Also look for the seasonal markets in Freyung Square opposite Palais Fersteal.

Shopping Districts

Many tourists first gravitate to **Kärntnerstrasse,** lined with luxury boutiques and large emporiums. Running neck and neck in popularity with the Kärntnerstrasse shopping avenue, however, is **Mariahilfer**

Strasse, where the Viennese do much of their in-town shopping in the many department and specialty stores.

Vienna Essentials

Arriving and Departing

BY CAR

Main access routes are the expressways to the west and south (Westautobahn A1, Südautobahn A2). Routes leading to the downtown area are marked ZENTRUM.

BY PLANE

All flights use Schwechat Airport (☎ 01/711–10–2231), about 16 km (10 mi) southwest of Vienna.

Between the Airport and Downtown. Buses leave the airport for the city air terminal, Wien-Mitte Landstrasse Hauptstrasse (✉ Am Stadtpark, ☎ 01/5800–33369), by the Hilton, on every half hour from 5 to 6:30 AM and every 20 minutes from 6:50 AM to 11:30 PM; after that, buses depart every hour until 5 AM. The S7 train (called the *Schnellbahn*) shuttles every half hour between the airport and the Landstrasse/Wien–Mitte (city center) and Wien–Nord (north Vienna) stations; the fare is AS34 and it takes about 35 minutes. Follow the picture signs of a train to the basement of the airport. Buses also run every hour (every half hour on weekends and holidays Apr.–Sept.) from the airport to the Westbahnhof (West Train Station) and the Südbahnhof (South Train Station). Be sure you get on the right bus! The one-way fare for all buses is AS70. A taxi from the airport to downtown Vienna costs about AS350–AS450; agree on a price in advance. Cabs (legally) do not meter this drive, as airport fares are more or less fixed (legally again) at about double the meter fare. The cheapest cab service is C+K Airport Service (☎ 01/1731, 01/689–6969), charging a set price of AS270. C+K will also meet your plane at no extra charge if you let them know in advance.

BY TRAIN

Vienna has four train stations. The principal station, the Westbahnhof, is for trains to and from Linz, Salzburg, and Innsbruck, and to and from Germany, France, and Switzerland. The Südbahnhof is for trains to and from Graz, Klagenfurt, Villach, and Italy. The Franz-Josefs-Bahnhof, or Nordbahnhof, is for trains to and from Prague, Berlin, and Warsaw. Go to the Wien–Mitte/Landstrasse Hauptstrasse station for local trains to and from the north of the city. Budapest trains use both the Westbahnhof and Südbahnhof, and Bratislava trains both Wien–Mitte and the Südbahnhof, so check.

Getting Around

Vienna is fairly easy to explore on foot; as a matter of fact, much of the heart of the city—the area within the Ring—is a pedestrian zone. Public transportation is comfortable, convenient, and frequent, though not cheap. **Tickets for buses, subways, and streetcars** are available in subway stations and from dispensers on buses and streetcars. Tickets in multiples of five are sold at cigarette shops—look for the sign TABAKTRAFIK—or at the window marked VORVERKAUF at such central stations as Karlsplatz or Stephansplatz. A block of five tickets costs AS85, a single ticket AS20. If you plan to use public transportation frequently, get a **24-hour ticket** (AS50), a **three-day tourist ticket** (AS130), or an **eight-day ticket** (AS265). Tariffs could be slightly higher in 1999. Maps and information in English are available at the Stephansplatz, Karlsplatz, and Praterstern U-bahn stations.

The Vienna Card, available for AS180 at tourist and transportation information offices and most hotels, will give you unlimited travel for 72 hours on city buses, streetcars, and the subway, reductions on selected museum entry fees, plus tips and discounts on various attractions and selected shopping throughout the city.

BY BICYCLE

Vienna has hundreds of kilometers of marked cycle routes, including reserved routes through the center of the city. Paved cycling routes parallel the Danube. For details, get the city brochure on cycling. Bicycles can be rented at a number of locations and can be taken on the Vienna subway (with the exception of the U-6 line) year-round all day Sunday and holidays, from 9 to 3, and after 6:30 on weekdays, and, from May through September, after 9 AM Saturday. You'll need a half-fare ticket for the bike (☞ By Subway, *below*).

BY BUS OR STREETCAR

Inner-city buses are numbered 1A through 3A and operate weekdays until about 7:40 PM, Saturday until 7 PM. Reduced fares are available for these routes (buy a **Kurzstreckenkarte;** it allows you four trips for AS34) as well as designated shorter stretches (roughly two to four stops) on all other bus and streetcar lines. Streetcars and buses are numbered or lettered according to route, and they run until about midnight. Night buses marked *N* follow 22 special routes every half hour between 12:30 AM and 4:30 AM. Get a route plan from any of the public transport or VORVERKAUF offices. The fare is AS25, payable on the bus unless you have a 24-hour, three-day, or eight-day ticket; then you need only pay an AS10 supplement. The central terminus is Schwedenplatz. Streetcars 1 and 2 run the circular route around the Ring, clockwise and counterclockwise, respectively.

BY CAR

Unless you know your way around the city, a car is more of a nuisance than a help. The center of the city is a pedestrian zone. Drive on the right. Seat belts are compulsory in front. Children under 12 must sit in the back, and smaller children must have a restraining seat. Speed limits are as posted; otherwise, 130 kph (80 mph) on expressways, 100 kph (62 mph) on other main roads, 50 kph (31 mph) in built-up areas. Some city areas have speed limits of 30 kph (19 mph). The right-of-way is for those coming from the right (especially in traffic circles) unless otherwise marked.

City on-street parking is a problem. Observe signs; tow-away is expensive. In winter, overnight parking is forbidden on city streets with streetcar lines. Overnight street parking in districts I, VI, VII, VIII, and IX is restricted to residents with stickers; check before you leave a car on the street, even for a brief period.

All vehicles using the autobahn (divided, mostly limited-access main highways, including the main highway from Vienna airport to the city) must display an autobahn-Vignette toll sticker on the inside of the windshield (to apply, contact the **ÖAMTC/Österreichischer Automobil-, Mororrad- und Touringclub,** ✉ Schubertring 3, A-1010, Vienna, ☏ 01/711997).

BY SUBWAY

Subway (U-bahn) lines—stations are marked with a huge blue U—are designated U-1, U-2, U-3, U-4, and U-6, and are clearly marked and color-coded. Trains run daily until about 12:30 AM. Additional services are provided by fast suburban trains, the S-bahn, indicated by a stylized blue *S* symbol. Both are tied into the general city fare system.

BY TAXI

Cabs can be flagged on the street if the FREI (free) sign is lit. You can also dial 60160, 31300, or 40100 to request one. All rides around town are metered. The initial fare is AS35, but expect to pay AS80–AS100 for an average city ride. There are additional charges for luggage, and a surcharge of AS16 is added at night, on Sunday, and for telephone orders. Tip the driver AS5–AS8 by rounding up the fare.

Contacts and Resources

EMBASSIES

U.S. embassy (✉ Boltzmanng. 16, ☎ 01/313–39); **consulate** (✉ Gartenbaupromenade, Parkring 12A, in the Marriott building, ☎ 01/313–39). **Canadian embassy** (✉ Laurenzerberg 2, on the 3rd floor of Hauptpost building complex, ☎ 01/531–38–01). **U.K. embassy and consulate** (✉ Jauresg. 10, near Schloss Belvedere, ☎ 01/71613–5151 for embassy and consulate).

EMERGENCIES

Police (☎ 133). **Ambulance** (☎ 144). **Doctor:** ask your hotel, or in an emergency, phone your embassy or consulate (☞ *above*). **Pharmacies:** in city center, open weekdays 8–6, Saturday 8–noon; in neighborhoods, weekdays 8–noon, 2–6. In each neighborhood, one pharmacy (Apotheke) in rotation is open all night and weekends; the address is posted on each area pharmacy.

ENGLISH-LANGUAGE BOOKSTORES

Big Ben Bookshop (✉ Serviteng. 4a, ☎ 01/319–6412). **British Bookshop** (✉ Weihburgg. 24–26, ☎ 01/512–1945–0). **Shakespeare & Co.** (✉ Sterng. 2, ☎ 01/535–5053).

GUIDED TOURS

Guided walking tours in English are available almost daily and include such topics as "Jewish Vienna." There are also tours that will take you to cultural events and nightclubs, and there are daytime bus trips to the Danube Valley, Salzburg, and Budapest, among other spots. Check with the City Tourist Office (☞ Visitor Information, *below*) or your hotel for details.

The following are city orientation tours. **Vienna Sightseeing Tours** (☎ 01/712–4683–0) offers a short highlights tour or a lengthier one to the Vienna Woods, Mayerling, and other sights near Vienna. Tours start in front of or beside the Staatsoper (State Opera House) on the Operngasse. **Cityrama** (☎ 01/533–4373) provides city tours with hotel pickup; tours assemble opposite the Inter-Continental Hotel (✉ Johannesg. 28). **CityTouring Vienna** (☎ 01/894–1417–0), with hotel pickup, starts from the city air terminal behind the Hilton Hotel (✉ Am Stadtpark). Prices are similar, but find out whether you will visit or just drive past Schönbrunn and Belvedere palaces and whether admission fees are included.

TRAVEL AGENCIES

American Express (✉ Kärntnerstr. 21–23, ☎ 01/515–40–0). **Österreichisches Verkehrsbüro** (Austrian Travel Agency; ✉ Opernring 3–5, ☎ 01/588–00–0). **Ökista** (✉ Reichstratstr. 13, next to the Rathaus, ☎ 01/402–1561).

VISITOR INFORMATION

City Tourist Office (✉ Kärntnerstr. 38, behind the Staatsoper ; ⏲ Daily 9–7).

THE DANUBE VALLEY

Austria contains some of the most beautiful stretches of the Danube (Donau), extending about 88 km (55 mi) west of Vienna. The river rolls through the celebrated Wachau—a gloriously scenic valley easily reached as part of an excursion from the country's capital. What the Wachau region offers is magnificent countryside, some of Austria's best food and wine, and comfortable—in some cases elegant—accommodations. Above the river are the ruins of ancient castles. The abbeys at Melk and Göttweig, with their magnificent libraries, dominate their settings. Vineyards sweep down to the river, which is lined with fruit trees that burst into blossom every spring. People here live close to the land, and at certain times of year vintners open their homes to sell their own wines and produce. Roadside stands offer flowers, fruits, vegetables, and wines. And this is an area of legend: The Danube shares with the Rhine the story of the mythical Nibelungen, defenders of Siegfried, hero of German myth.

The most delightful way to approach the Wachau is by boat, but car and train routes are also scenically splendid (☞ Getting Around *in* The Danube Valley Essentials, *below*). Our route out of Vienna follows the southern Danube bank, crossing at Melk and returning along the north bank. Vienna to Melk is about 112 km (70 mi), the return along the north bank about 109 km (68 mi).

Klosterneuburg

The massive **Stift Klosterneuburg** (abbey) dominating this market town was established in 1114; treasures in its museum include an enameled altar dating to 1181. The abbey is a major agricultural landowner in the region, and its extensive vineyards produce excellent wines. ✉ *Stiftspl. 1,* ☎ *02243/411–0, 02243/411–548 for Vinothek.* ⏲ *Guided tours every hr (winter schedule may vary) Mon.–Sat. 9–11 and 1:30–4:30, Sun. and holidays 11 and hourly 1:30–4:30.*

Göttweig

You will see **Stift Göttweig** high above the Danube Valley opposite Krems long before you reach it. This impressive 11th-century Benedictine abbey affords sensational panoramas of the Danube Valley; walk around the grounds and view the impressive chapel. ✉ *Rte. 303, on south bank of Danube, opposite Krems, Furth bei Göttweig,* ☎ *02732/85581–0.*

$$$$ ★ ✕ **Landhaus Bacher.** This is one of Austria's best restaurants, elegant but entirely lacking in pretension. Dining in the garden during summer adds to the experience. It's in Mautern, on the river bank opposite Krems. ✉ *Südtirolerpl. 208, Mautern,* ☎ *02732/82937–0,* FAX *02732/74337. Reservations essential. DC, V. Closed Mon. and Tues. Nov.–Apr., and mid-Jan.–mid-Feb. No lunch Mon. and Tues.*

$–$$ ✕ **Stiftskeller.** Have lunch at the abbey's restaurant. If the weather is clear, sit on the open terrace and enjoy magnificent views of the Danube in the distance. The local wines are excellent. ☎ *02732/84663. AE, DC, MC, V. Closed Nov.–Mar.*

Melk

The **Benediktinerstift Melk** (abbey) is one of the most impressive in Europe, commandingly situated above the Danube. This is one of Austria's monumental "not-to-be-missed" sights, with its library rich in art as well as books; the ceiling frescoes are particularly memorable. ✉ *Abt Berthold Dietmayr-Str. 1,* ☎ *02752/2307–32–0, or 12–232 for the Tourist Office.* ⏲ *May–Sept., daily 9–5; Apr. and Oct., daily 9–4; Nov.–Mar., daily tours at 11 and 2.*

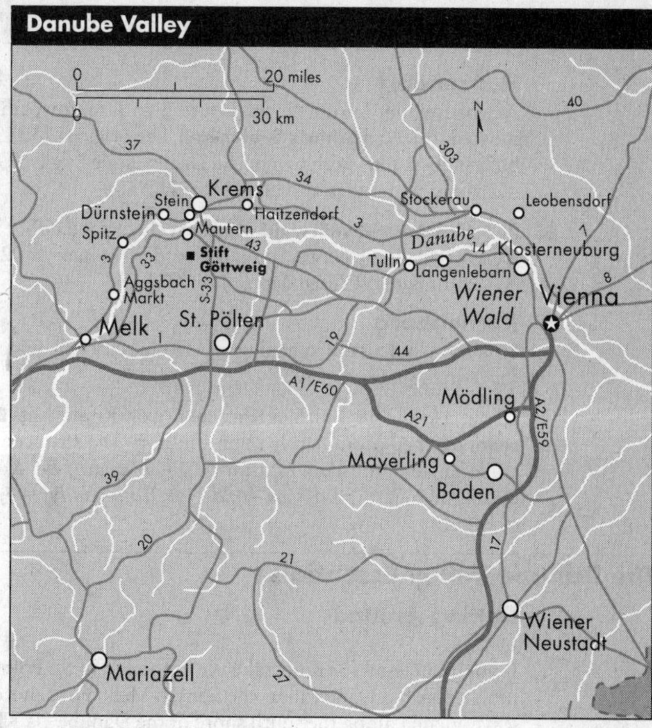

Dürnstein

Across the river from Melk, the romantic road hugs the Danube, heading north toward Dürnstein and Krems. The beautiful medieval town of Dürnstein is associated with Richard the Lionhearted, who was imprisoned in its now-ruined castle for 13 months. The town is also known for its fine hotels, restaurants, and wines, and its gloriously baroque Stiftskirche church.

$$$$ ★ **Richard Löwenherz.** This former cloister, justifiably a Romantik hotel member, sits above the Danube. Room furnishings include antiques and every comfort. The restaurant is excellent, as are the house wines. ✉ *Dürnstein 8, A–3061,* ☎ *02711/222,* FAX *02711/222–18. 40 rooms with bath or shower. Restaurant, bar, pool. AE, DC, MC, V. Closed Nov.–mid-Mar.*

Krems/Stein an der Donau

Remnants of the ancient city wall are prominent in this town over 1,000 years old, with its Renaissance, Gothic, and Baroque features. Krems and Stein sit at the center of Austria's foremost wine-growing region. Explore the town center, the churches, and the **Weinkolleg Kloster Und,** a wine museum in a beautifully restored cloister in Und, tucked between Krems and next-door Stein. ✉ *Undstr. 6,* ☎ *02732/73073–0,* FAX *02732/73074–85.* *AS130, including tasting.* *Mid-Jan.–Dec. 24, daily 11–7.*

Stein, with its 16th-century houses, is virtually part of adjacent Krems. Look for the former **Imperial Toll House** and 14th-century **Minoritenkirche,** a church that now serves as an exhibition showcase, just off the main street.

$$ **Alte Post.** A 16th-century house with an arcade courtyard, the Alte Post is conveniently positioned right in the center of Krems. In good weather the courtyard is used for dining. ✉ *Obere Landstr. 32, A–3500,*

Krems, ☏ 02732/82276–0, FAX 02732/84396. 26 rooms, most with bath. Restaurant (closed Wed.). No credit cards. Closed Jan.–mid-Mar.

Haitzendorf

A worthwhile detour off of Route 3 at Grafenwörth leads to the moated, turreted **Schloss Grafenegg.** The original 1533 castle was rebuilt in the 1800s with wonderful Disneyesque English Gothic Revival overtones, gargoyles and all. ☏ *02735/5500.*

$$ ✕ **Schlosstaverne Mörwald** offers excellent food either in the Biedermeier-style dining rooms or on the garden terrace. ☏ *02735/2616–0. No credit cards. Closed Mon., Jan.–Feb.*

Korneuburg

Stop for a look at the imposing neo-Gothic city hall, which towers over the town square.

About 3 km (2 mi) north of Korneuburg off Route 3 sits **Burg Kreuzenstein,** perched prominently upon a hilltop. The 19th-century castle includes a small museum of armor. ✉ *Leobendorf bei Korneuburg,* ☏ *02262/66102.* ⏲ *Mid-Mar.–mid-Nov. Tours daily 9–4, according to demand.*

The Danube Valley Essentials

Getting Around

BY CAR

If you're pressed for time, take the autobahn to St. Pölten, turn north onto Route S-33, and follow the signs to Melk. For a more scenic route, leave Vienna along the south shore of the Danube via Klosterneuburg and Greifenstein, taking Routes 14, 19, 43, and 33. Cross the Danube at Melk, then return to Vienna along the north bank of the river (Route 3).

BY TRAIN

Depart from the Westbahnhof for Melk, then take the bus along the north bank of the Danube to Dürnstein and Krems. Side bus trips can be made from Krems to Göttweig.

BY BOAT

Travel upstream, with stops at Krems, Dürnstein, Melk, and points between. Return to Vienna by boat or by train from Melk (combination tickets available). Check in Vienna with DDSG Blue Danube Schiffahrt (Handelskai 265, tel. 01/72750–222) for information about ferry schedules.

Contacts and Resources

GUIDED TOURS

Vienna travel agencies (☞ Vienna Essentials, *above*) offer tours of the Wachau ranging from one-day outings to longer excursions.

VISITOR INFORMATION

Lower Austria Tourist Office (✉ Heidenschuss 2, Vienna, ☏ 01/533–3114–0, FAX 01/535–0319). **Dürnstein** (✉ Parkpl. Ost, ☏ 02711/219, FAX 02711/442). **Klosterneuburg** (✉ Niedermarkt 4, Postfach 6, ☏ 02243/4440, FAX 02243/86773). **Krems/Stein an der Donau** (✉ Undstr. 6, ☏ 02732/801, FAX 02732/77650). **Melk**(✉ Babenbergerstr. 1, ☏ 02752/2307–32–0 or 02752/2312–232, FAX 02752/2307–37).

SALZBURG

Salzburg is best known as the birthplace of Wolfgang Amadeus Mozart, and receives its greatest number of visitors every summer during the annual music festival, the world-famous Salzburger Festspiele. Dominated by a fortress on one side and the Kapuzinerberg, a small mountain, on the other, this Baroque city is best explored on foot, for many of its most interesting areas are pedestrian precincts. Whereas Mozart rules over the festival months of July and August, visitors have long known that the city has innumerable other attractions as well. Art lovers call Salzburg the Golden City of the High Baroque; thanks to the powerful prince-archbishops of the Hapsburg era, few other places offer an equivalent abundance of Baroque splendor. American visitors also tour the city to the strains of music from the film that made Salzburg a household name in the United States, seeking out the many sites identifiable from the *Sound of Music* film. No matter what season you visit, be sure to bring an umbrella: Salzburg is noted for sudden, brief downpours.

Exploring Salzburg

Numbers in the margin correspond to points of interest on the Salzburg map.

The Salzach River separates Salzburg's old and "new" towns; for the best perspective on the old, climb the Kapuzinerberg (follow pathways from Linzergasse or Steingasse). For another postcard view, look toward the fortress through the Mirabell gardens, behind Mirabell palace. The sweeping panorama from the fortress itself offers the reverse of both perspectives. Wander along Getreidegasse, with its ornate wrought-iron shop signs and the Mönchsberg standing sentinel at the far end. Don't neglect the warren of interconnecting side alleys: These shelter a number of fine shops and often open onto impressive inner courtyards that are guaranteed to be overflowing with flowers in summer.

Don't forget to consider purchasing the Salzburg Card. **SalzburgKarten** are good for 24, 48, or 72 hours at AS190, AS270, and AS360, respectively, and allow no-charge entry to most museums and sights, use of public transport, and special discount offers.

14 **Alter Markt** (Old Market Square). Right in the heart of the Altstadt (Old City) is the Alter Markt, the old marketplace and center of secular life in past centuries. Salzburg's narrowest house is squeezed into the north side of the picturesque 17th-century square, filled in summer with flower stalls. Look into the former court pharmacy (Hofapotheke) for a touch of centuries past.

2 **Baroque Museum.** A focal point of the celebrated Mirabell Gardens is this museum, between Mirabellplatz and the Orangerie. Wander through the Baroque gardens behind the city's main theater complex, and enjoy a dramatic view of the Old City with the fortress in the background. ✉ *Orangeriegarten,* ☏ *0662/877432.* ⏲ *Tues.–Sat. 9–noon and 2–5, Sun. and holidays 9–noon.*

5 **Carolino Augusteum Museum** (Historical Museum). The worthwhile city museum is devoted to art, archaeology, and fascinating musical instruments. ✉ *Museumspl. 1,* ☏ *0662/843145.* ⏲ *Tues. 9–8, Wed.–Sun. 9–5.*

★ 10 **Dom** (Cathedral). The cathedral square setting is close to perfection, while the sheer mass of the cathedral itself gives a suggestion of the one-time power of the prince-archbishops who ruled the region. Don't overlook the great bronze doors as you enter. A small museum shows off centuries of church treasures. ✉ *Dompl. 1,* ☏ *0662/841162.* ⏲ *Mid-May–mid-Oct., Mon.–Sat. 10–5, Sun. and holidays 11–5.*

Alter Markt, **14**
Baroque Museum, **2**
Carolino Augusteum Museum, **5**
Dom, **10**
Festspielhaus, **7**
Festung Hohensalzburg, **11**
Franziskanerkloster, **9**
Kollegienkirche, **8**
Mozart-Wohnhaus, **1**
Mozarteum und Marionettentheater, **4**
Mozarts Geburtshaus, **15**
Residenz, **13**
Schloss Hellbrunn, **16**
Schloss Mirabell, **3**
Spielzeugmuseum, **6**
Stift St. Peter, **12**

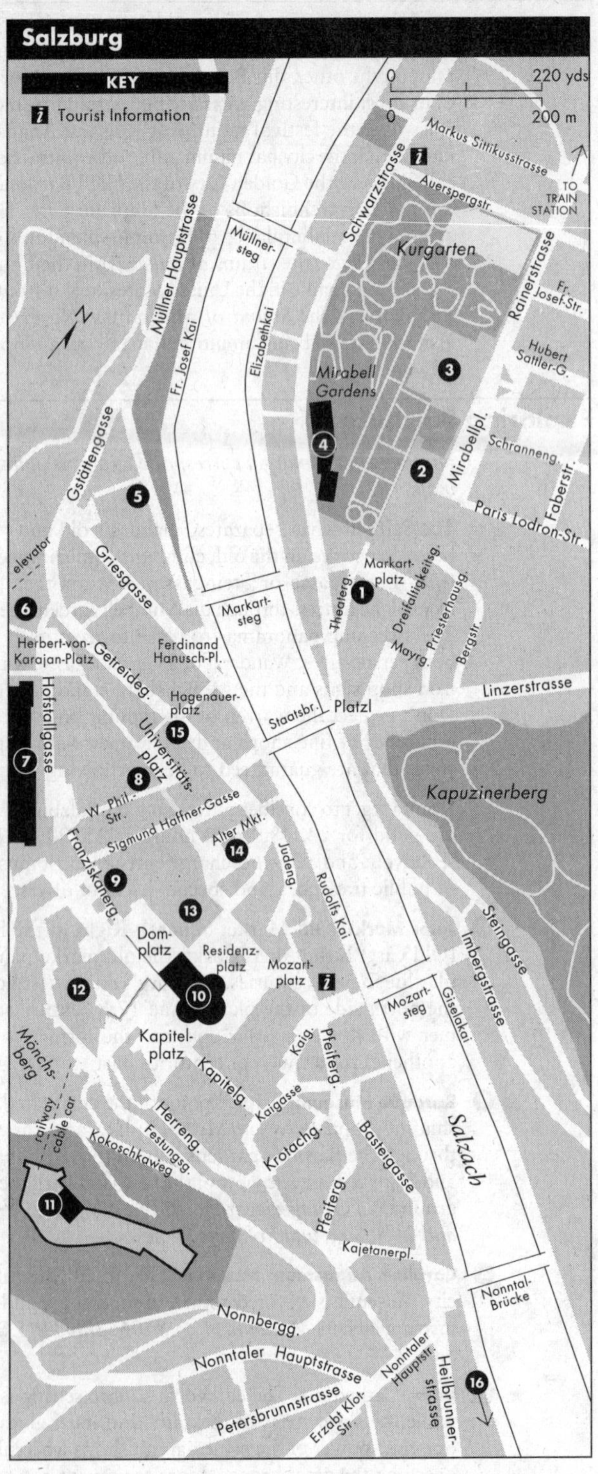

7 **Festspielhaus** (Festival Hall Complex). The three vast theaters and concert halls are cut into the mountain itself. This is the site of the celebrated Salzburg Music Festival and other musical special events. Occasional guided tours are given. ✉ *Hofstallg. 1,* ☎ *0662/80450, 0662/844501 for ticket office,* FAX *0662/848424.*

★ **11** **Festung Hohensalzburg** (Fortress Salzburg). To reach the 12th-century fortress that dominates the city, walk up the narrow Festungsgasse at the back end of Kapitalplatz. From here, you can either follow the footpath up the hill or take a five-minute ride on the funicular, or Festungsbahn. On a sunny day, a far more pleasurable—and strenuous!—route is to hike up Festungsgasse, turning frequently to enjoy the changing panorama of the city below. If it's a nice day, try to have a beer and snack at the terrace restaurant, which overlooks a *stunning* panorama.

Once at the fortress, you can wander around on your own or take a tour. The views are magnificent in all directions. A main attraction is **St. George's Chapel,** built in 1501. A year later, in 1502, the chapel acquired the 200-pipe barrel organ, which is played daily in summer at 7 AM, 11 AM, and 6 PM. ✉ *Mönchsberg 34,* ☎ *0662/842430.* 🎫 *Fortress AS35, fortress and tour AS65.* 🕓 *Nov.–Mar., daily 9–5; Apr.–June and Oct., daily 9–6; July–Sept., daily 8–7.*

9 **Franziskanerkloster** (St. Francis Monastery). An unusually graceful tall spire marks this 13th-century church, an eclectic mix of architectural styles with Romanesque and Gothic accents. The Baroque altar is by Fisher von Erlach. Check for mass—frequently one of Mozart's—on Sunday at 9. ✉ *Franziskanerg. 5,* ☎ *0662/843629–0.* 🕓 *Winter, daily 6:30–6; summer, daily 6:30 AM–8 PM.*

8 **Kollegienkirche** or Universitätskirche (Collegiate/University Church). Dating from 1707 and the work of Fischer von Erlach, this is one of the best examples of Baroque architecture anywhere. ✉ *Universitätspl.,* ☎ *0662/841–327–72.* 🕓 *Daily 9–6.*

1 **Mozart-Wohnhaus** (Mozart Residence). The house where the Mozart family lived for some years includes a small recital hall and the Mozart Audio and Film Museum. Combination tickets with Mozarts Geburtshaus (☞ *below*) are cheaper. ✉ *Makartpl. 8,* ☎ *0662/88940–0.* 🕓 *Daily 10–6; during summer festival (late July–Aug.), 9–6.*

4 **Mozarteum und Marionettentheater** (Mozart Center and Marionette Theater). This is the main research facility devoted to the work of Salzburg's most famous native son, Wolfgang Amadeus Mozart. Inside the complex are the Music Academy (☎ 0662/88908), the International Mozarteum Foundation (✉ Schwarzstr. 26, ☎ 0662/88940), whose courtyard contains the summerhouse (accessible only by special appointment) in which Mozart wrote *The Magic Flute,* and the **Marionettentheater,** home to the famed Salzburg Marionette Theater. The south end of the Mozarteum complex on Makartplatz includes the **Landestheater** (Provincal Theater; ☞ Opera, Music, and Art *in* The Arts, *below*) where operas, operetta, ballet, and dramas are staged during winter months when the larger festival buildings are closed. ✉ *Marionettentheater, Schwarzstr. 24,* ☎ *0662/872406–0,* FAX *0662/882141.* 🎫 *AS250–400.* 🕓 *Box office Mon.–Sat. 9–1 and 2 hrs before marionette performance; Salzburg season May–Sept., Dec. 25, Mozart Week (Jan.), Easter.*

★ **15** **Mozarts Geburtshaus** (Mozart's Birthplace). The house at the head of the tiny Hagenauerplatz in which the famed composer was born is now a museum, packed with Mozart memorabilia. Combination tickets with the Mozart-Wohnhaus (☞ *above*) are cheaper. ✉ *Getreideg. 9,*

☎ 0662/844313. ⏲ Daily 9–6; during summer festival (late July–Aug.), daily 9–7.

13 **Residenz** (Residence). The palatial complex gracing Residenzplatz includes the prince-archbishops' historic and sumptuous living quarters and ceremonial reception rooms. The **Residenzgalerie,** in the same building complex, has an outstanding collection of 16th- through 19th-century European art. Combination tickets can provide entry to both attractions. ✉ *Residenzpl. 1,* ☎ *0662/8042–2690; art collection,* ☎ *0662/840451. Residence:* ⏲ *Tours Sept.–June, daily at 10, 11, noon, 2, and 3; July–Aug., daily every 30 mins 10–4:30. Art Collection:* ⏲ *Apr.–Sept., daily 10–5; Oct.–Mar., Thurs.–Tues. 10–5.*

16 **Schloss Hellbrunn** (Hellbrunn Castle). Take Bus 55 from the city center about 5 km (3 mi) to Hellbrun, 6 km (4 mi) south of Salzburg, to reach this popular attraction. The castle was built during the 17th century, and its rooms have some fine trompe l'oeil decorations. To entertain Salzburg's great prince-archbishops, its gardens feature an ingenious system of **Wasserspiele**—hidden jets of water conceived by someone with an impish sense of humor: expect to get sprinkled by surprise. Admission only with a conducted tour. ✉ *Fürstenweg, 37, Hellweg,* ☎ *0662/820372.* ⏲ *Tours Apr. –Oct., daily 9–4:30; May–Sept., daily 9–5. Evening tours July–Aug., on the hr 6–10.*

The Hellbrunn park complex also includes the **Tiergarten** (zoo), outstanding for the way in which the animals have been housed in natural surroundings. You can also visit the small folklore museum in the **Monatsschlössl,** the historic hunting lodge. *Zoo:* ☎ *0662/820176.* ⏲ *Oct.–Mar., daily 8:30–4; Apr. and Sept., daily 8:30–5:30; May–Aug., daily 8:30–6. Folklore museum:* ⏲ *Apr.–Oct., daily 9–5.*

3 **Schloss Mirabell** (Mirabell Palace and Gardens). Built by Prince-Archbishop Wolf Dietrich for his mistress, the elegant complex now houses public offices, including that of the city's registrar; many couples come here to be married in the sumptuous setting. The foyer and staircase, decorated with cherubs, are splendid examples of Baroque excess. The gardens are world famous as the locale where the von Trapp children "Do-re-mi-ed" in *The Sound of Music.* ✉ *Mirabellpl., off Makartpl.,* ☎ *no phone.* ⏲ *Mon.–Thurs. 8–4, Fri. 8–1.*

6 **Spielzeugmuseum** (Toy Museum). Once a hospital, the Bürgerspital now houses a toy and musical instruments museum within its Renaissance arcades. There's a combined ticket with the Carolino Augusteum Museum (☞ *above*), cathedral excavations, and the Folklore Museum at Schloss Hellbrunn (☞ *above*). Nearby on Herbert-von-Karajan-Platz is the 15th-century royal **Pferdeschwemme** (Horse Drinking Trough). ✉ *Bürgerspitalg. 2,* ☎ *0662/847560.* ⏲ *Tues.–Sun. 9–5.*

12 **Stift St. Peter** (St. Peter's Abbey). Late-Baroque style marks this sumptuous edifice tucked beneath the mountain. The cemetery lends an added air of mystery to the monks' caves cut into the cliff. The catacombs attached to the church can be visited by guided tour. ✉ *St. Peter Bezirk, just off Kapitalpl.,* ☎ *0662/844576–0.* ⏲ *Tours daily at 10:30, 11:30, 1:30, 2:30, and 3:30.*

The Arts

Festivals

Information and tickets for the main **Salzburger Festspiele** (Salzburg Festival), held in late July–August, along with the performances of the Easter Festival (early April) and the Pentecost Concerts (late May), can be obtained from Salzburger Festspiele (✉ Postfach 140, A-5010

Salzburg, FAX 0662/846682). It's best to write or fax ahead, as it is difficult (but not impossible) to obtain tickets for festival performances once you are in Salzburg.

Opera, Music, and Art

Theater and opera are presented in the three auditoriums of the **Festspielhaus** (✉ Hofstallg. 1, ☎ 0662/844501–0 for ticket office, FAX 0662/848424). Opera, operettas, ballet, and drama are offered at the **Landestheater** ✉ Schwarzstr. 22, ☎ 0662/871–5120). Concerts are the specialty at the **Mozarteum** (✉ Schwarzstr. 26, ☎ 0662/873154). Chamber music has a grand venue at the **Schloss Mirabell** ✉ Mirabellpl., off Makartpl., ☎ 0662/848586 for tickets). Special art exhibitions are often held in the **Rupertinum** (✉ Wiener-Philharmoniker-Gasse 9). Another outstanding venue is the **Galerie Welz** (✉ Sigmund-Haffner-G. 16).

Dining and Lodging

Some of the city's best restaurants are in the leading hotels. This is a tourist town, and popular restaurants are always crowded, so make reservations well ahead, particularly during festival times. For details and price-category definitions, *see* Dining *in* Austria A to Z, *above.*

As for hotels, reservations are always advisable and are imperative at festival times (both Easter and summer). For details and price-category definitions, *see* Lodging *in* Austria A to Z, *above.*

$$$ ✕ **Bei Bruno.** A short walk from Schloss Mirabell, this intimate restaurant in the Bristol Hotel is a perfect choice for after-concert dining. The food is nouvelle Austrian, specializing in fresh fish, lightly prepared. ✉ *Makartpl. 4,* ☎ *0662/873557. AE, DC, MC, V.*

$$$ ✕ **Goldener Hirsch.** The traditional Austrian and international cuisine suit the preferences of the music and theater celebrities who regularly dine in these rustic rooms during festival months. Try the poached salmon on spinach mousse or game in season. The same kitchen serves the cheaper s'Herzl next door. ✉ *Getreideg. 37,* ☎ *0662/8485–11–861. Reservations essential. Jacket and tie. AE, DC, MC, V.*

$$$ ★ ✕ **Zum Eulenspiegel.** Delicious food matches the unique setting in this house, which is hundreds of years old. Tables are set with white linen in wonderful nooks and crannies reached by odd staircases. Try the potato goulash with chunks of sausage and beef in a creamy paprika sauce, or the house specialty, fish stew Provençale. These are served at lunch, or all day in the bar downstairs. ✉ *Hagenauerpl. 2,* ☎ *0662/843180. Reservations essential in the evening. MC, V. Closed Sun. late Mar.–Dec.*

$$ ✕ **St. Peter Stiftskeller.** People don't come here for the food, which is just so-so, but you can't beat the atmosphere, especially if you're lucky enough to get a table in the courtyard with its dramatic gray stone archways and vine-trellised walls. This is reportedly the oldest restaurant in Europe. ✉ *St. Peter District I/4,* ☎ *0662/841268. Reservations essential. AE, DC, MC, V.*

$$ ★ ✕ **Zum Fidelen Affen** (At the Faithful Ape). Across the river from the Altstadt, this small brew pub offers tasty Austrian dishes to go along with its own house beer. ✉ *Priesterhausg. 8,* ☎ *0662/877361. No credit cards.* ⏲ *Daily 5–11.*

$$ ✕ **Zum Mohren.** Arched ceilings in the lower rooms add atmosphere to this historic house. Duck and venison are specialties, in addition to such standards as Schnitzel, but you might find wild boar in season. ✉ *Judeng. 9,* ☎ *0662/842387. Jacket and tie. AE, MC, V. Closed Sun., holidays, and mid-June–mid-July.*

$ ✕ **Wilder Mann.** The atmosphere may be too smoky for some (choose the outside courtyard in summer), but the beamed ceiling and antlers are genuine, as are the food and value. Try the *Tellerfleisch* (boiled beef) or game in season. ✉ *Getreideg. 20/Griesg. 17 (passageway), ☎ 0662/841787. No credit cards. Closed Sun.*

$$$$ ★ **Goldener Hirsch.** This old-timer—800 years old and an inn since 1564—is conveniently set right in the heart of the Old City. Arched corridors, vaulted stairs, rustic furniture, and antiques provide a medieval atmosphere; the essential modern appliances stay ingeniously hidden. The restaurant (☞ Dining, *above*) is excellent. ✉ *Getreideg. 35–37, A-5020, ☎ 0662/8084, FAX 0662/843349. 71 rooms. Restaurant. AE, DC, MC, V.*

$$$$ **Hotel Bristol.** This is where Elizabeth Taylor and Richard Burton holed up in the '60s during the filming of *Where Eagles Dare*, and you can see why: Each room is decorated in a different sumptuous style. The staff is friendly and helpful. ✉ *Makartpl. 4, A-5020, ☎ 0662/873557, FAX 0662/873–5576. 60 rooms. Restaurant. AE, DC, MC, V.*

$$$$ **Österreichischer Hof.** The grande dame of Salzburg's hotels occupies a lovely riverside location, and the favored rooms give views of the fortress and the Old City. The house restaurants are good. ✉ *Schwarzstr. 5–7, A-5020, ☎ 0662/88977–0, FAX 0662/88977–551. 120 rooms, 118 with bath or shower. 4 restaurants. AE, DC, MC, V.*

$$$$ **Schloss Mönchstein.** This palatial mountain retreat is in its own magical world with gardens and hiking trails, yet just minutes from the city center. ✉ *Mönchsberg 26, A-5020, ☎ 0662/848559, FAX 0662/. 17 rooms. Restaurant. AE, DC, MC.*

$$$–$$$$ **Sheraton.** Favored rooms at the back overlook the Mirabell Gardens. ✉ *Auerspergstr. 4, A-5020, ☎ 0662/88999–0, FAX 0662/881776. 163 rooms. Restaurant, 2 indoor pools. AE, DC, MC, V.*

$$$ **Elefant.** This 12th-century structure in the middle of the Old City has been a hotel for 400 years and has an atmosphere of traditional comfort. The public rooms are tastefully decorated with Oriental carpets and Biedermeier furniture, but bedrooms are small and plain. ✉ *Sigmund-Haffner-Gasse 4, A-5020, ☎ 0662/843397, FAX 0662/840109–28. 36 rooms with bath or shower. Restaurant. AE, DC, MC, V.*

$$ ★ **Wolf.** The family touch reigns in this intimate, well-situated hotel. Spotless rooms have country decor. Book well ahead. ✉ *Kaig. 7, A-5020, ☎ 0662/843453–0, FAX 0662/842423–4. 15 rooms. AE.*

Shopping

Shopping centers around Griesgasse, Getreidegasse, and Alter Markt in the Old City, and Platzl and Linzer Strasse on the other side of the river. Look for quality handicrafts at **Salzburger Heimatwerk** (✉ Residenzpl. 9, ☎ 0662/844119).

Salzburg Essentials

Arriving and Departing

BY BUS

The central bus terminal (☎ 0662/167 for postal bus information; 0662/872150 for railway bus information) is in front of the train station, the Salzburg Hauptbahnhof, on the Südtirolerplatz.

BY CAR

Salzburg has several autobahn exits; study the map and decide which one is best for you. Parking is available in the cavernous garages under the Mönchsberg, near the city center, and in other garages around the city; look for the large blue P signs.

BY PLANE

All flights go via Salzburg Airport, 4 km (2 ½ mi) west of the city. For information, call the airport at 0662/8580. For passenger service and information about arrivals and departures, call 0662/851211.

Between the Airport and Downtown. Buses leave for the Salzburg train station at Südtirolerplatz every 15 minutes during the day, every half hour at night to 10 PM. Journey time is 18 minutes. Taxi fare runs about AS150–AS170.

BY TRAIN

Salzburg's main train station is at Südtirolerplatz. For train information, call ☎ 0662/1717; for telephone ticket orders and seat reservations, call 0662/1700.

Getting Around

Salzburg is compact and most distances are short. This is a city to explore on foot, but take an umbrella, as surprise showers are legendary.

BY BICYCLE

The city is compact, so a bicycle is useful only if you want to tackle some of the outlying areas. Marked bicycle paths will show the way.

BY BUS AND TROLLEYBUS

Service is frequent and reliable; route maps are available from the tourist office or your hotel. Save money by buying an **Umweltkarte** (available only in blocks of five), a 24-hour ticket that is good on all trolley and bus lines. For local transportation information, call ☎ 0662/620551–31.

BY CAR

Don't even think of it! The old part of the city is a pedestrian zone. Many other parts of the city have restricted parking (indicated by a blue pavement stripe), either reserved for residents with permits, or for a restricted period. Get parking tickets from coin-operated dispensers on street corners; instructions are also in English.

BY FIAKER

Fiakers, or horse-drawn cabs, are available on the Residenzplatz (☎ 0662/844772).

BY TAXI

At festival time, taxis are too scarce to hail on the street, so order through your hotel porter or phone 0662/8111 or 0662/1716.

Contacts and Resources

CONSULATES

U.S. (✉ Alter Markt 1/2/2, ☎ 0662/848776, FAX 0662/849777; ⏲ Mon., Wed., Fri. 9–noon). **U.K.** (✉ Joseph-Messner-Str. 24/20, ☎ 0662/648528; ⏲ Weekdays 9–noon).

EMERGENCIES

Police (☎ 133). **Ambulance** (☎ 144). **Pharmacies** (Apotheken) stay open nights and weekends on rotation; a sign is posted outside each pharmacy listing which are open.

ENGLISH-LANGUAGE BOOKSTORES

American Discount (✉ Alter Markt 1, ☎ 0662/845640) concentrates on popular paperbacks and magazines. Most good bookstores have some books in English.

GUIDED TOURS

Orientation. Guided bus tours of the city and its environs are given by: **Salzburg Sightseeing Tours** (✉ Mirabellpl. 2, ☎ 0662/881616); **Salzburg Panorama Tours** (✉ Schranneng. 2/2, ☎ 0662/883211–0); and **Bob's**

Special Tours (✉ Dreifaltigkeitsg. 3, ☎ 0662/872484, FAX 0662/8724844). Note that buses cannot enter much of the Altstadt (Old City).

Special-Interest. Many tour operators offer *Sound of Music* excursions through the city; those given by Bob's Special Tours (☞ *above*) are among the friendliest. All tour operators can organize chauffeur-driven tours for up to eight people. Your hotel will have details.

Walking. The city tourist office's folder "Salzburg—The Art of Taking it All In at a Glance" describes a one-day self-guided walking tour.

TRAVEL AGENCIES

American Express (✉ Mozartpl. 5–7, ☎ 0662/8080, FAX 0662/8080–9). **Thomas Cook/Wagon-Lits Travel** (✉ Münzg. 1, ☎ 0662/8422755–0, FAX 0662/8422755–5).

VISITOR INFORMATION

City Tourist Offices (Stadtverkehrsbüro) are in various areas of Salzburg. ✉ The one at Mozartpl. 5 is for walk-ins only. **Hauptbahnhof** (main train station) is at ✉ Bahnsteig 2A inside the station, ☎ 0662/88987. **Central Office** (☎ 0662/88987–0, FAX 0662/88987–32) is open for phone inquiries only. ⏲ Call Mon.–Thurs. 8–4, Fri. 8–2).

INNSBRUCK

Squeezed by mountains and sharing the valley with the Inn River, Innsbruck is compact and very easy to explore on foot. The medieval city—it received its municipal charter in 1239—owes much of its fame and charm to its unique location. To the north, the steep, sheer sides of the Alps rise like a shimmering blue-and-white wall from the edge of the city, an awe-inspiring backdrop for the mellow green domes and red roofs of the picturesque Baroque town.

Exploring Innsbruck

Numbers in the margin correspond to points of interest on the Innsbruck map.

Modern-day Innsbruck retains close associations with three historical figures: Emperor Maximilian I and Empress Maria Theresa (both responsible for much of the city's architecture), and Andreas Hofer, a Tyrolean patriot. You will find repeated references to these names as you tour the city and its historic core—the Altstadt.

OFF THE BEATEN PATH

Alpenzoo. This is a unique opportunity to see 150 species of Alpine animals in their natural habitat, some of which are extinct in the wild. To get there without a car, take Tram 1, Hungerburgbahn or Bus 0, N, D, or E, or the shuttle from Maria-Therisien Strasse in front of the Alter Landhaus and Hofburg. ✉ *Weiherburgg. 37,* ☎ *0512/292323.* 🎫 *AS70.* ⏲ *Daily 9–6, in winter 9–5.*

8 **Annasäule** (St. Anna's Column). This memorial commemorates the withdrawal of Bavarian forces in the war of the Spanish Sucsession in 1703 on St. Anna's Day. From here you'll have a classic view of Innsbruck, with the glorious mountains in the background. ✉ *Maria Theresien-Str.*

3 **Domkirche** (Cathedral). Built in 1722 and dedicated to St. James, the main attraction, aside from the interior with its dramatic painted ceilings, is the high-altar painting of the Madonna by Lucas Cranach the Elder, dating from about 1520. ✉ *Dompl. 6.* ⏲ *Sat.–Thurs. 6–noon, Fri. 2–5.*

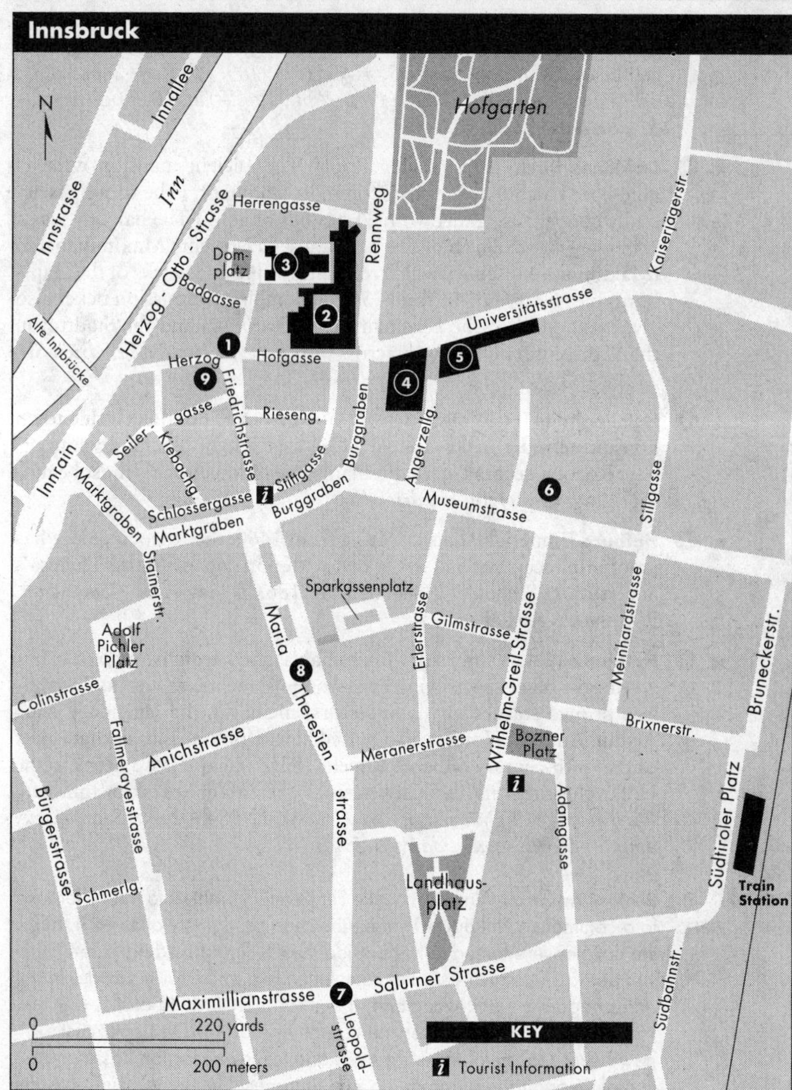

Annasäule, **8**
Domkirche, **3**
Ferdinandeum, **6**
Goldenes Dachl, **1**
Helblinghaus, **9**
Hofburg, **2**
Hofkirche, **4**
Tiroler Volkskunst-museum, **5**
Triumphpforte, **7**

6 **Ferdinandeum** (Tyrolean Provincal Museum). Austria's largest collection of Gothic art is here as well as paintings from the 19th and 20th centuries. ✉ *Museumstr. 15,* ☎ *0512/59489.* ⏲ *May–Sept., daily 10–5 and Thurs. 7 PM–9 PM; Oct.–Apr., Tues.–Sat. 10–noon and 2–5, Sun. and holidays 10–1.*

★ 1 **Goldenes Dachl** (The Golden Roof). The ancient mansion with its gold-roof balcony is the city's foremost landmark. (The roofing is actually copper tiles gilded with 31 pounds of gold.) The balcony was a reviewing stand. The building now houses a **Museum Maximilianeum** (Maximilian Museum), which recounts the life and works of the Hapsburg ruler between 1490 and 1519. A combined admission ticket also gives you entry to the Ferdinandeum (☞ *above*) and the Stadtturm, the 15th-century city tower, across the street. ✉ *Herzog Friedrich-Str. 21,* ☎ *0512/575962.* ⏲ *Daily 10–6.*

9 **Helblinghaus** (Helbling House). Dating from 1560, this Gothic town house received a make-over in 1730: a facade of blue-and-white ornate Rococo decoration that remains one of Innsbruck's most beautiful sights. ✉ *Herzog Friedrich-Str.*

★ 2 **Hofburg** (Imperial Palace). Dating from 1460, the Rococo palace has an ornate reception hall decorated with portraits of Maria Theresa's ancestors. ✉ *Rennweg 1,* ☎ *0512/587186.* ⏲ *May–Oct., Tues.–Sun. 9–5; Nov.–Apr., Tues.–Sat. 9–5.*

★ 4 **Hofkirche** (Court Church). Maximilian's mausoleum is surrounded by 24 marble reliefs portraying his accomplishments, as well as 28 oversize bronze statues of his ancestors, including the legendary King Arthur. Andreas Hofer is also buried here. Don't miss the ornate altar of the 16th-century **Silberne Kapelle** (Silver Chapel). Adjacent to the Hofkirche is the city's folk art museum, the Tiroler Volkskunstmuseum (☞ *below*). ✉ *Universitätsstr. 2,* ☎ *0512/584302.* ⏲ *Sept.–June, daily 9–5; July–Aug., daily 9–5:30.*

OFF THE BEATEN PATH

Schloss Ambras. When Archduke Ferdinand II wanted to marry for love to a commoner, Philippine Welser, the court grudgingly allowed it, but the couple were forced to live outside the city limits. Ferdinand revamped a 10th-century castle, completing it in 1556 for his bride. In acres of gardens and woodland, it is a curiously inviting castle, with cheery red and white shutters on its many windows. The upper castle now houses rooms of noble portraits and the lower section has a collection of weaponry and armor. Be sure to inspect Philippine's sunken bath, a luxury for its time. The Schloss is 2 mi southeast of the city. To reach it without a car, take Tram 3 to Ambras, or the shuttle (AS30 round-trip, leaves on the hour) from Maria-Therisien Str. 45. ✉ *Schloßstr. 20,* ☎ *0512/348446.* ⏲ *Apr.–Oct., Wed.–Mon. 10–5. Check with the tourist office for winter hours.* 🎟 *AS60.*

5 **Tiroler Volkskunstmuseum** (Tyrolean Folk Art Museum). In the Hofkirche complex (☞ *above*), this fascinating museum exhibits costumes and farmhouse rooms decorated in styles ranging from Gothic to Rococo. There's a combined ticket with the Hofburg. ✉ *Universitätsstr. 2,* ☎ *0512/584302.* ⏲ *Sept.–June, Mon.–Sat. 9–5, Sun. and holidays 9–noon; July–Aug., Mon.–Sat. 9–5:30, Sun. and holidays 9–noon.*

7 **Triumphpforte** (Triumphal Arch). Built in 1765, the arch celebrates the marriage of the later Kaiser Leopold II. ✉ *Maria-Theresien-Str.*

The Arts

Most hotels have a monthly calendar of events (in English). Tickets to most events are available at the City Tourist Office (☞ Innsbruck Essentials *in* Visitor Information, *below*). The leading venue for operas, musicals, and concerts is the **Tiroler Landestheater** (✉ Rennweg 2, ☎ 0512/520744). Other major performances are held at the **Kongresshaus** (✉ Rennweg 3, ☎ 0512/5936–0).

Dining and Lodging

Innsbruck gives you a chance to sample hearty Tyrolean cooking, such as *Tyroler G'röstl,* a tasty potato hash with onion and bacon, and *Schlutzkrapferln,* a local version of ravioli. Don't forget to check out some of the city's delightful coffeehouses. For details and price-category definitions, *see* Dining *in* Austria A to Z, *above.*

Many travelers use Innsbruck hotels as home bases for excursions into the surrounding countryside—just another reason why it's important to book far in advance for accommodations in this city. Most hotels offer or can arrange transport to ski areas. For details and price-category definitions, *see* Lodging *in* Austria A to Z, *above.*

$$$ ★ ✕ **Schwarzer Adler.** This cozy, romantic setting with rustic Tyrolean decor is a bit off the beaten track and expensive but worth it. Specialties include lobster ragout with tagliatelle in a red wine sauce and grilled fresh-water trout. ✉ *Kaiserjägerstr. 2,* ☎ *0512/587109. Reservations essential. Jacket and tie. AE, DC, MC, V. Closed Sun. and mid-Jan.*

$$ ✕ **Goethe-Stube.** The wine tavern of the city's oldest inn, the Goldener Adler (☞ *below*), is one of Innsbruck's best. It was here that Goethe (who lent his name to the tavern) sipped quantities of red South Tyrolean wine during his stays in 1786 and 1790. ✉ *Herzog Friedrich-Str. 6,* ☎ *0512/586334. Reservations essential. Jacket and tie. AE, DC, MC, V. No lunch.*

$$ ✕ **Hirschenstuben.** Old-fashioned hospitality and dark-wood trim are found in force at this charming local favorite. Game is particularly good here. ✉ *Kiesbachg. 5,* ☎ *0512/582979. Reservations essential. AE, DC, MC, V. Closed Sun.*

$$ ★ ✕ **Ottoburg.** You can sit in a bay window in one of the upstairs rooms overlooking the Altstadt at Ottoburg, which is in a medieval gray stone town house with charming red and white shutters, just down the street from the Goldenes Dachl. The lunch menu changes daily, but look for *Tyroler G'röstl,* potato hash with chunks of pork and slivered onion, including a side order of bacon-studded sauerkraut. ✉ *Herzog Friedrich-Str. 1A,* ☎ *0512/574652. Reservations essential. AE, DC, MC, V.*

$$ ★ ✕ **Tiroler Stuben.** This restaurant with a broad seasonal menu, including lots of vegetarian choices, is highly regarded by locals. Try the *Schlutzkrapferln,* Tyrolean ravioli stuffed with cheese, potatoes, and spinach, topped with melted butter and parmesan, or a simple, succulent roast chicken with potato salad. ✉ *Innrain 13 (Ursulinenhof), in Alpotel Tirol,* ☎ *0512/577931. AE, MC, V.*

$ ✕ **Gasthof Sailer.** A block from the train station, this quaint restaurant was assembled from the rooms of 17th-century Tyrolean farmhouses. Try the savory *Tyroler G'röstl* or the pillowy spinach spaetzle with ham and melted cheese. ✉ *Hotel SailerAdamg. 6–10,* ☎ *0512/5363. AE, MC, V.*

$$$$ ★ 🏨 **Goldener Adler.** An inn since 1390, it has a facade that looks medieval, and inside, passages and stairs twist. Readers have complained about closetlike rooms on upper floors, but it's ideally located in the heart of the Altstadt. The famous Goethe-Stube restaurant (☞ *above*) is on the premises. ✉ *Herzog Friedrich-Str. 6, A-6020,* ☎ *0512/*

586334, FAX *0512/584409. 40 rooms with bath or shower. 2 restaurants. AE, DC, MC, V.*

$$$ **Alpotel Tirol.** Abundant space, comfort, and modern style are the keys in this hotel on the edge of the Altstadt. The staff is particularly helpful. Many rooms have balconies overlooking the quiet garden and mountains. The Tiroler Stuben restaurant is unusually good (☞ *above*). ✉ *Innrain 13 (Ursulinenpassage), A-6020,* ☎ *0512/577931,* FAX *0512/577931–15. 75 rooms. Restaurant. AE, DC, MC, V.*

$$$ **Hotel Central.** Located halfway between the train station and the Altstadt (about a 10-minute walk from each), rooms are modern and spare, though spacious. The café (☞ *above*) is elegant and offers a tempting selection of pastries. ✉ *Gilmstr. 5, A-6020,* ☎ *0512/5920,* FAX *0512/580310. 87 rooms. Restaurant. AE, DC, MC, V.*

$$$ **Hotel Maria Theresia.** Ideally situated in the center of the shopping district, this hotel, part of the Best Western chain, is yet just a five-minute walk to the Altstadt. Rooms are comfortable and spacious. ✉ *Maria-Theresien-Str. 31, A-6020,* ☎ *0512/5933,* FAX *0512/575619. 105 rooms. Restaurant, bar. AE, DC, MC, V.*

$$ ★ **Weisses Kreuz.** Occupying an honored position just steps away from the famous Goldenes Dachl (☞ Exploring, *above*), the White Cross is a lovely inn that dates from 1465. Mozart stayed here in 1769. ✉ *Herzog Friedrich-Str. 31, A-6020,* ☎ *0512/59479,* FAX *0512/59479–90. 39 rooms, 28 with bath or shower. Restaurant. AE, V.*

$ **Binder.** A short streetcar trip (Line 3) from the center of town shouldn't be too high a price to pay for less-costly comfort at this small, friendly, family-run hotel. ✉ *Dr.-Glatz-Str. 20, A-6020,* ☎ *0512/33436–0,* FAX *0512/33436–99. 32 rooms, most with bath or shower. Café-bar. AE, DC, MC, V.*

$ **Tautermann.** You're within walking distance of the center in this spacious house sited above the city (take Bus A from the main station to Höttinger Kirchenplatz). The rooms are in natural woods and white, and service is friendly. ✉ *Stamser Feld/Höttingerg., A-6020,* ☎ *0512/281572,* FAX *0512/281572–10. 28 rooms. AE, DC, MC, V.*

Shopping

The main central shopping is concentrated around the Old City, along Maria-Theresien-Strasse, Maximilianstrasse, Anichstrasse, Burggraben, Museumstrasse, and Wilhelm-Greil-Strasse and their side streets. For local handicrafts, try **Tiroler Heimatwerk** (✉ Meraner Str. 2–4, ☎ 0512/582320).

Innsbruck Essentials

Arriving and Departing

BY BUS

The terminal (✉ Südtiroler-Pl., ☎ 0512/1717) is to the right of the main train station. Routes extend from here throughout the Tirol.

BY CAR

Exit from the east–west autobahn or from the Brenner autobahn running south to Italy.

BY PLANE

The airport is 4 km (2 mi) to the west of the city. For flight information, phone 0512/22525–304.

Between the Airport and Downtown. Buses (Line F) to the city center (✉ Maria-Theresien-Str.) run every 20 minutes and take about 20 minutes. Get your ticket from the bus driver; it costs AS20. Taxis should take no more than 10–15 minutes into town, and the fare is about AS120–AS150.

BY TRAIN

All trains stop at the city's main station at Südtiroler-Platz. For train information, call ☎ 0512/1717. For ticket reservations, call ☎ 0512/1700.

Getting Around

BY BUS AND STREETCAR

Service is frequent and efficient. Most bus and streetcar routes begin or end at Südtiroler-Platz, in front of the main train station. Bus is the most convenient way to reach the six major ski areas outside the city. Many hotels offer free transportation with direct hotel pickup; for those staying in the Old City, the buses leave from in front of the Tiroler Landestheater (☞ The Arts, *above*).

BY CAR

A car is a burden except for getting out of town. Much of the downtown area is a pedestrian zone or paid-parking only; get parking vouchers at tobacco shops, coin-operated dispensers, or the City Tourist Office (☞ Visitor Information, *below*).

BY TAXI

Taxis are not much faster than walking, particularly along the one-way streets and in the Altstadt. To order a radio cab, phone ☎ 0512/1718, 0512/5311, or 0512/45500.

Contacts and Resources

EMERGENCIES

Police (☎ 133). **Ambulance** (☎ 144). **Pharmacies** (Apotheken) stay open nights and weekends on a rotation system. Signs outside each pharmacy list which ones will be open.

GUIDED TOURS

Orientation. Bus tours lasting two hours cover the city's highlights and leave from the hotel information office at the railroad station (✉ Südtiroler-Pl.) daily at noon. In summer, additional buses are scheduled at 10 and 2, and there are shorter tours Monday through Saturday at 10:15, noon, 2, and 3:15. Your hotel or tourist office will have tickets and details.

TRAVEL AGENCIES

American Express (✉ Brixnerstr. 3, ☎ 0512/582491, FAX 0512/573385). **Wagons-Lits Travel** (✉ Brixnerstr. 2, ☎ 0512/520790, FAX 0512/520–7985).

Visitor Information

City Tourist Office (✉ Burggraben 3, ☎ 0512/5356, FAX 0512/535643; ⏲ Daily 8–7).

Österreichischer Alpenverein (✉ Wilhelm-Greil-Str. 15, ☎ 0512/59547–34, FAX 0512/575528; ⏲ Weekdays 8:30–6, Sat. 9–noon) is the place to go for information on Alpine huts and mountaineering. Pick up a free *Club Innsbruck* card at your hotel for no-charge use of ski buses and reduced-charge ski-lift passes. For big savings, buy the *Innsbruck Card,* which gives you free admission to all the museums, mountain cable cars, the Alpenzoo and Schloss Ambras, plus free bus and tram transportation. Cards are good for 24, 48, and 72 hours at AS200, AS280, and AS350, respectively.

4 Baltic States

Estonia, Latvia, Lithuania

Estonia, Latvia, Lithuania: These three small countries in northeastern Europe have weathered centuries of domination by Germans, Swedes, Russians, and Poles; fought countless battles to preserve, if nothing else, their dignity; and won their independence twice in this century alone. The three countries share a common terrain, history, and visa zone. Nevertheless, since breaking free of the Soviet Union in 1990 and 1991, the Baltics have been quietly reconstructing their individual national identities, societies, and economies, and each is quite resolute about its distinctness from the others.

While building sustainable democracies out of the rubble of post-Soviet republics, Estonia, Latvia, and Lithuania have pursued very different alliances. Estonia, with linguistic and geographic affinities to Helsinki, looks every bit as Scandinavian and Western as its neighbor across the Gulf of Finland. Latvia, with a huge Russian population, still retains some of the chaos of its eastern former nemesis but has emerged as the most cosmopolitan country of the three. Lithuania was slower in embracing the West but since 1996 has made great strides, renewing contacts and relations with Poland in an effort to hitch itself to the EU and NATO's rising star.

Although there aren't many world-famous attractions in the Baltics, the region's obscurity and remoteness may actually be the best thing about it. Another plus for the English-speaker is that it is becoming increasingly easy to roam the three Baltic capitals of Tallinn, Rīga, and Vilnius without encountering language barriers. The landscape itself is also free of barriers; everywhere in the Baltics you'll find unspoiled forests and beaches, as well as people whose initial aloofness toward strangers often gives way to genuine friendliness.

Baltic States
FINLAND
Helsinki
Gulf of Finland
Tallinn
Kohtla-Järve
Narva
Ivangorod
Rakvere
Narva
Narvskoe Vdchr.
ESTONIA
TO STOCKHOLM
Kärdla
Haapsalu
Hiiumaa
Käina
Rohukula
Heltermaa
Orjaku
Lihula
Baltic Sea
Trigi
Virtsu
Saaremaa
Orissaare
Paide
Jõgeva
RUSSIA
Põltsamaa
Peipsi järv
Vändra
Sauga
Sindi
Pärnu
Viljandi
Võrtsjärv
Tartu
Kihelkonna
Kuressaare
Pskovskoe ozero
Pskov
Võru
Valga
Sääre
TO STOCKHOLM
TO TRAVEMÜNDE
Gulf of Riga
Valmiera
Ostrov
Gauja National Park
Cēsis
Gulbene
Ventspils
Balvi
Līgatne
Talsi
Sigulda
Kuldīga
Jūrmala
Rīga
LATVIA
Madona
Kārsava
Tukums
Jelgava
Lielupe
Jēkabpils
Rēzekne
Liepāja
Venta
Bauska
Daugava
TO STOCKHOLM
Varduva
Subate
Krāslava
Palanga
Šiauliai
Daugavpils
Telšiai
TO KIEL
Panevėžys
Smyltinė
Klaipėda
Aukštaitija National Park
LITHUANIA
Juodkrante
Courland (Neringa) Spit
Nida
Ukmergė
Kaunas
Neris
Nemunas
N
Sovetsk
Rumšiškės
Kaliningrad
Trakai
Vilnius
RUSSIA
Marijampolė
BELARUS
Šeštokai
KEY
Rail Lines
Ferry Lines
Suwałki
Minsk
0
100 miles
0
150 km
POLAND

Baltic States A to Z

For country-specific details (money, phones, and so on), *see* the appropriate sections *below*; the following is general information on all three Baltic states.

Customs

Duty-free allowances are: 250 grams of tobacco, 1 liter of spirits, 1 liter of wine, and 10 liters of beer (3 liters of wine and 5 liters of beer in Lithuania).

The export of antiques and historic artifacts is strictly controlled. Contact the **Division of Export of Culture Objects** (☎ 2/448–501 or 2/446–578) in Estonia, the **Ministry of Culture** (☎ 721–4100) in Latvia, or the **Committee of Cultural Heritage** (☎ 2/724–005) in Lithuania. Generally a 10%–20% duty is charged on goods more than 50 years old and native to the country; up to 100% duty is charged on goods more than 100 years old made in a foreign country but bought in the Baltics.

Dining

Native dishes predominate: usually meat, potatoes, and root-vegetable salad. Nevertheless, the dining scene in the capitals has much improved in recent years and authentic Italian, Chinese, and, yes, even Indian food is available. Riga has the best international cuisine at the highest prices, with Tallinn a close second. The Vilnius dining scene offers more mid-range prices, though less variety.

RATINGS

Prices are for a three-course meal for one person, not including drinks or tip.

CATEGORY	COST
$$$	over $20
$$	$10–$20
$	under $10

WHAT TO WEAR

Casual dress is acceptable in all restaurants in the Baltics. However, jeans, sweat suits, and tennis shoes are generally not appropriate for high-priced establishments.

Embassies

ESTONIA

U.S. Embassy (✉ Kentmanni 20, Tallinn, ☎ 631–2021, FAX 631–2025). **Canadian Embassy** (✉ Toomkooli 13, Tallinn, ☎ 631–7978, FAX 631–3573). **British Embassy** (✉ Kentmanni 20, Tallinn, ☎ 631–3461, FAX 631–3354).

LATVIA

U.S. Embassy (✉ Raiņa 7, Riga, ☎ 722–0005, FAX 722–6530). **Canadian Embassy** (✉ Doma laukums 4, Riga, ☎ 783–0141 or 722–6315, FAX 783–0140). **British Embassy** (✉ Alunaña 5, Riga, ☎ 733–8126, FAX 733–8132).

LITHUANIA

U.S. Embassy (✉ Akmenų 6, Vilnius, ☎ 2/223–031, FAX 8/267–06084). **Canadian Embassy** (✉ Gedimino 64, Vilnius, ☎ 2/220–898, FAX 2/220–884). **British Embassy** (✉ Antakalnio 2, Vilnius, ☎ 2/222–070, FAX 2/727–579).

Lodging

All hotels listed have private bath or shower. Most have air-conditioning, but it's worth verifying for summertime reservations.

RATINGS

Prices are for two people sharing a double room and include breakfast.

CATEGORY	COST
$$$$	over $120
$$$	$80–$120
$$	$40–$80
$	under $40

Opening and Closing Times

Banks are open weekdays 9–4, but some open as early as 8 and close as late as 7. Most are closed on Saturday, but some stay open 9–3. **Museums** are generally open 11–5 and are closed on Monday and Tuesday. Some stay open until 6. **Shops** open between 10 and 11 and close between 5 and 7, with shorter hours on Saturday. Most shops are closed on Sunday.

Visas

American, Australian, British, Canadian, Irish, and New Zealand citizens can stay in Estonia visa-free for up to 90 days. Citizens of New Zealand and Ireland need visas to enter Lithuania. A 10-day visa can be issued at the airport for 80LTL if your country of citizenship does not have a Lithuanian embassy or consulate or you are a citizen of an EU country. Australians, Canadians, and New Zealanders need visas for Latvia; a 90-day visa can be purchased from consulates outside Latvia, and 10-day visas can be purchased for 12Ls upon arrival.

Visitor Information

Tallinn (✉ Raekoja plats 10, ☎ 631–3940, FAX 631–3941). **Riga** (✉ Skārņu 22, ☎ 722–1731 or 722–3113, FAX 722–7680). **Vilnius** (✉ Pilies 42, ☎ FAX 2/620–762).

Weather

Mid-summer in the capital cities sees an influx of tourists and an exodus by locals. For local color and temperate weather, visit in late spring or early autumn. Always be prepared for cold weather and rain.

CLIMATE

The Baltic states' climate is temperate, but tends to be cool and damp. Coastal regions tend to be colder by a few degrees in winter and warmer by a few in summer. The rainy season is in early summer. The snowy, cold winter season lasts from November through March. December, January, and February are the coldest months, with temperatures dipping below zero Celsius. The summer months, though warm, are generally wet, creating high humidity. August tends to see the smallest amount of rain in all three Baltic States. The following are the average daily temperatures for Estonia, Latvia, and Lithuania in that order.

Jan.	21F	–6.1C	**May**	17F	8.2C	**Sept.**	49F	9.4C
	27F	–3.0C		48F	9.0C		52F	11.2C
	22F	–5.4C		53F	11.5C		53F	11.4C
Feb.	15F	–9.4C	**June**	55F	12.9C	**Oct.**	64F	17.8C
	31F	–0.6C		60F	15.5C		46F	7.5C
	30F	–0.9C		61F	15.9C		46F	7.9C
Mar.	27F	–2.8C	**July**	59F	14.7C	**Nov.**	39F	4.0C
	31F	–0.4C		65F	18.1C		32F	–0.2C
	33F	0.4C		64F	18.0C		40F	4.5C
Apr.	9F	3.9C	**Aug.**	64F	17.8C	**Dec.**	27F	–3.0C
	37F	2.7C		65F	18.2C		10F	–12.1C
	39F	3.7C		66F	18.8C		19F	–7.4C

ESTONIA

The country's history is sprinkled liberally with long stretches of foreign domination, begun in 1219 with the Danes, followed without interruption by the Germans, Swedes, and Russians. Only after World War I, with Russia in revolutionary wreckage, was Estonia able to declare its independence. But shortly before the second world war, in 1940, that independence was usurped by the Soviets, who—save for a brief three-year occupation by Hitler's Nazis—proceeded to suppress all forms of national Estonian pride for the next 50 years. When Estonia finally regained independence in 1991, it was determined to put the stultifying occupations behind it.

In the early 1990s Estonia's own Riigikogu (Parliament), not some other nation's puppet ruler, handed down from the Upper City reforms that—though occasionally unpleasant—forced Estonia to blaze its post-Soviet trail to the European Union. In 1997 the country got the nod from Brussels to join the EU, an endorsement of Estonia's progress toward a sustainable market economy. Estonia's challenge in the next millennium is to strike a balance between its stunning but painful past and its promising but sometimes overwhelming future.

Estonia A to Z

Emergencies

Police (☎ 002). **Ambulance** (☎ 003). **Doctor: Tallinn Central Hospital** (☎ 620–7010); ESMED Medical Center (☎ 657–9118); Medica Arstikeskus (☎ 26/444–4231). **Dentist: Baltic Medical Partners** (☎ 631–1222); Kentmanni hambaravi (☎ 2/455–785). **Pharmacy: Koduapteek** (☎ 26/430–220); **Suur-Pärnu Apteek** (☎ 681–061).

Guided Tours

CDS Tours (✉ Raekoja plats 17, ☎ 627–6797, FAX 631–3666). **Estonian Holidays** (✉ Pärnu maantee 12, ☎ 631–4106, FAX 631–4109). **Baltic Tours** (✉ Aia 18, ☎ 630–0400, FAX 630–0411).

Language

Estonian, which belongs to the Finno-Ugric family, is the official language. However, many people in cities speak English perfectly. Most Estonians will ignore attempts to communicate in Russian, though the 30% of the population that is ethnically Russian is happy to speak it. Outside the city, sign language will have to do.

Mail

A 20-gram letter to the United States costs 7EEK, a postcard 6.70EEK. To Europe a 20-gram letter costs 5.50EEK, a postcard 5.20EEK. The **main post office** (✉ Narva 1, Tallin, ☎ 625–7300) is open weekdays 8–7, Saturday 9–5. Stamps are sold at post offices only.

Money Matters

COSTS

A cup of coffee or tea costs 10EEK; a glass of beer 20EEK–25EEK; a main dish at a local, medium-priced restaurant 50EEK to 60EEK. Admission to museums and galleries costs 10EEK or 20EEK.

CURRENCY

The monetary unit in Estonia is the kroon, which is divided into 100 senti. There are notes of 1, 2, 5, 10, 25, 50, 100, and 500EEK and coins of 5, 10, 20, and 50 senti and 1EEK. At press time (spring 1998) the rate of exchange was 14EEK to the U.S. dollar, 10EEK to the Canadian dollar, 24EEK to the pound sterling, 9EEK to the Australian dollar, and 8EEK to the New Zealand dollar. The Estonian kroon is pegged 8EEK to the German mark. National banks, with branches in all major and most minor cities, change cash and traveler's checks at fair commissions; most also give advances on a Visa or MasterCard. Credit cards are widely accepted in Estonia.

TIPPING

A 10% service charge is sometimes added and an 18% VAT is included in the price of dishes on the menu but may be listed separately on your bill. Tipping is not obligatory; for excellent service, add 5%.

National Holidays

January 1; February 24 (Independence Day); April 2 (Good Friday); April 4 (Easter); May 1 (May Day); May 31 (Whitsuntide); June 23 (Victory Day); June 24 (St. John's Day/Midsummer); December 25, 26.

Telephoning

COUNTRY CODE

The country code for Estonia is ☏ 372. For seven-digit phone numbers in Tallinn, there is no city code. For six-digit numbers dialed from abroad or outside the city, you must add an additional "2" for Tallinn.

INTERNATIONAL CALLS

To reach an **AT&T** long-distance operator, dial 8-008001001.

LOCAL CALLS

Pay phones take phone cards worth 30, 50, or 100 EEK. Buy cards at any kiosk. **Telephone information** (☏ 626–1111 or ☏ 631–3222).

Transportation

BY BOAT

Passenger ships—including frequent ferries and hydrofoils to nearby Helsinki—connect Tallinn with various Scandinavian cities.

BY BUS

Public transport costs 4EEK. Buy tickets from nearly any kiosk or from the driver. A single type of ticket is valid on buses, trolleys, and streetcars. Punch your ticket upon boarding or be fined 280EEK. Public transport operates 6 AM to midnight.

Domestic bus trips cost 40EEK–90EEK. For bus schedules call **Express Hotline**(☏ 631–3222).

BY CAR

An international or national driver's license bearing a photo is acceptable in Estonia. Drive on the right. Most roads are not up to Western standards, but major thoroughfares tend to be in better condition than secondary roads, where potholes and unpaved ways are common. Gas costs 7EEK per liter. Cars may be rented from 700EEK a day.

BY PLANE

There are no direct flights between Estonia and the United States. Estonian Air operates from Amsterdam, Copenhagen, Hamburg, Helsinki, London, Stockholm, and Vilnius. American carriers partnered with Finnair, Lufthansa, SAS, and Lot have good connections.

BY PRIVATE TAXI

Taxis operate 24 hours throughout the city. Taxis are expensive around hotels and ferry, bus, and train stations, cheaper within the city center; it's best to telephone for one. Taxi fares generally start at 6EEK or 8EEK and increase by 4EEK or 6EEK per km (½ mi) in the daytime, more at night or in bad weather. Drivers are bound by law to display an operating license and a meter. In-town journeys cost up to 50EEK. **Esra** (☏ 642–5425) and **Tulika** (☏ 655–2552 or 612–0000) are by and large trustworthy taxi companies.

Exploring Estonia

Tallinn

Tallinn's tiny Old Town, easily the most stunning and impressive in the region, if not Central Europe, has romantic towers, ankle-wrenching cobblestone streets, cozy nooks, city-wall cafés, and a dozen other attractions—all within one square kilometer. In the 1990s, Vanalinn (the lower Old Town)—historically the domain of traders, artisans, and ordinary citizens—has unfortunately sprouted glitzy neon signs and a profusion of pornography in otherwise charming alleys and sights.

The stately, sedate **Toompea** (Upper Town), a hillock that was the site of the original Estonian settlement, is on the burial mound of Kalev, the epic hero of Estonia. Toompea Castle, crowning the hill, is now the seat of the country's parliament and is not open to visitors.

The 19th-century Russian Orthodox **Aleksandr Nevski Khram** (Alexander Nevsky Cathedral), which houses the country's biggest bell, is symbol of the centuries of Russification this country has endured. ✉ *Lossi pl. 10, Toompea,* ☎ *2/443–484.* ⏲ *Daily 8–7:30.*

Housed in an 18th-century noble's house, the **Eesti Kunstimuuseum** (Estonian National Art Museum) contains an impressive array of Estonian art from the last 200 years. ✉ *Kiriku pl. 1, Toompea,* ☎ *2/449–340.* ⏲ *Wed.–Sun. 11–6.*

The Lutheran **Toomkirik,** the oldest church in the country, was founded by the occupying Danes in the 13th century. Leveled by a 1684 fire, it was rebuilt two years later. ✉ *Toom-Kooli 6, Toompea,* ☎ *2/444–140.* ⏲ *Daily 9:30–4:30.*

★ At the southern end of the Old Town looms the magnificent, six-story tower **Kiek-in-de-Kök** (Low German for "peep in the kitchen"), so called because during the 15th century one could peer into the kitchens of lower-town houses from here. The tower houses a museum of contemporary art and ancient maps and weapons. ✉ *Komandandi 1, Vanalinn,* ☎ *2/446–686.* ⏲ *Tues., Wed., Fri. 10:30–5:30, weekends 11–4.*

The 15th-century **Niguliste** (Church of St. Nicholas) is famed for its treasured frieze, Bernt Notke's (1440–1509) *Danse Macabre,* a 9-yard-long depiction of death. ✉ *Niguliste 13, Vanalinn,* ☎ *2/449903.* ⏲ *Thurs.–Sun. 11–6, Wed. 2–9.*

The stocky guardian of the northernmost point of the Old City, **Paks Margareeta** (Fat Margaret) is a 16th-century fortification named for a particularly hefty cannon it housed. Now it contains a **Maritime Museum,** with several exhibits detailing the tragic sinking of the MS *Estonia* ferry in 1994, which took with it 852 of the 989 people aboard. ✉ *Pikk 70, Vanalinn,* ☎ *641–1413.* ⏲ *Wed.–Sun. 10–6.*

★ For a completely raw and untranslated look at the country's musical past, peek into the **Teatri ja Muusikamuuseum** (Theater and Music Museum), where displays span the folksy and the freaky. ✉ *Müürivahe 12,* ☎ *2/442–132.* ⏲ *Wed.–Sun. 10–6.*

★ **Raekoja plats** (Town Hall Square) has a long, illustrious history of intrigue, executions, and salt (Tallinn's main export in the Middle Ages). Take a guided tour of the only surviving original Gothic **town hall** in Northern Europe. Old Thomas, its weather vane, has been atop the town hall since 1530. Across the square find the town **apothecary** (Raekoja plats 11). It dates from 1422. An L-shape stone marks the site of a 17th-century execution, where a priest was beheaded for killing a waitress who had offered him a rock-hard omelet. *Vanalinn,* ☎ *2/440–819.* ⏲ *Weekdays 10–4.*

DINING AND LODGING

$$$ ✕ **Tanduur.** One of the fanciest restaurants in the capital serves astoundingly good Indian food. The decor is quiet but authentic, the service excellent and unobtrusive. ✉ *Vene 7,* ☎ *631–3084. MC, V.*

$$ ✕ **Möökkala.** A superior seafood restaurant tucked away in an Old Town cellar, it has everything from crab salad to caviar to perch. The decor is an odd mix of ancient stone walls and passé pastel furnishings. ✉ *Rüütli 16/18,* ☎ *631–3583. MC, V.*

$$ ✕ **Toomkooli.** Enjoy such local dishes as reindeer with apple-cranberry jam in this snug hilltop dining room on Toompea. ✉ *Toom-Kooli 13,* ☎ *26/446613. AE, MC, V.*

$ ✕ **Creperie Chez Grigou.** Diminutive crepes with such fillings as ham, cheese, mushrooms, and zucchini or even banana are the focus here. Candlelight and soft jazz music greet a hip, laid-back clientele. ✉ *Müürivahe 23,* ☎ *631–4337. No credit cards.*

$ ✕ **Vanaema Juures.** Grandma's Place is a wonderful introduction to traditional Estonian cuisine amid independence-era furniture and 1920s music. It's good for a comfortable, cozy evening of potato pancakes or delightful meat dishes with potatoes. ✉ *Rataskaevu 10/12,* ☎ *631–3929 or 631–3928. Reservations essential. DC, MC, V.*

$$$$ 🏨 **Olümpia.** This high-rise offers a variety of rooms. Amenities include a conference hall, a top-floor sauna overlooking the city, and a splendid breakfast buffet. Request a room with a view of the Old Town. ✉ *Liivalaia 33, EE0001,* ☎ *631–5315,* FAX *631–5675. 405 rooms. 2 restaurants, pool. AE, DC, MC, V.*

$$$ 🏨 **Viru.** Formerly an Intourist hotel, this gray monolith on the edge of Old Town became Finnish in 1994. Besides offering rooms from standard to business class, the hotel has a sauna, a shopping center, a nightclub, and three bars. ✉ *Viru väljak 4, EE0001,* ☎ *630–1390,* FAX *630–1303. 434 rooms. 2 restaurants, pool. AE, DC, MC, V.*

$$ 🏨 **Hotel Central.** Winning service, a breakfast buffet, and a choice of special rooms for allergy sufferers are attractions here. It has Scandinavian-style decor. ✉ *Narva 7c, EE0001,* ☎ *633–9800,* FAX *633–9900. 124 rooms. Restaurant. AE, DC, MC, V.*

$$ 🏨 **Rataskaevu.** With homey independence-era furnishings, it has a radiating warmth missing from many hotels around town. You'll find plenty of living space and a central location. ✉ *Rataskaevu 7, EE0001,* ☎ *2/441–939,* FAX *2/443–688. Restaurant. MC, V.*

$ 🏨 **Eeslitall.** Right in the middle of Old Town, this budget hotel has sparely furnished rooms with common showers. Double rooms have a choice of one double bed or two singles. ✉ *Dunkri 4/6, EE0001,* ☎ *631–3755,* FAX *631–3210. 9 rooms. Restaurant. DC, MC, V.*

The Islands

Some 1,500 time machines float off the western coast of Estonia, embodying what the country was all about before World War II. Because the Soviets feared a mass exodus to the West, these islands have largely been off-limits for the past 50 years. They remain unspoiled today, practically frozen in a time long past. Only two islands, Saaremaa and Hiiumaa, are easily accessible, through port towns about 100 km (62 mi) south of Tallinn. **Kruessaare,** the capital of **Saaremaa,** is a town of only 16,000, but proudly lays claim to a fascinating and almost wholly intact **Gothic castle,** complete with turrets and moat. Some modest cliffs and fun-in-the-summer beaches round out a trip to the island. **Hiiumaa,** and its center of **Kärdla,** is quieter still, with nothing more audacious than some windmills and a few birds to disturb this perfect retreat from urban life.

LATVIA

Latvia, and particularly Riga, is fiercely distinct from the other two Baltic states in a number of ways. Although similar occupations plagued this country through the years, German influence was stronger here than elsewhere, as the 14th-century Knights of the Sword used this as their base of operations. And when the Soviets forcibly incorporated Latvia into the Soviet Union, in 1944, the effects of Russification—coupled with the White Russians who had been coming since 1710, when Russia first invaded Latvia—were more devastating here.

Today 45% of Latvia is Russian-speaking; in Riga, Russians, Ukrainians, and Belorussians are the majority. This has created a palpable tension: Latvians are angered because their culture has been suppressed for 50 years and because Russian continues to be used on the street; Russians are peeved that most of them have yet to be given citizenship in the country.

Latvia A to Z

Emergencies

Police (☎ 02). **Ambulance** (☎ 03). **Doctor:** Ars (☎ 720–1001 or 720–1007). **Dentist:** A+S Health Center (☎ 728–9516). **Pharmacy:** Kamēlijas aptieka (☎ 2/293–514).

Guided Tours

Latvia Tours (☎ 721–3652 or 722–3391).

Language

Latvian belongs to the Indo-European family of languages. The official language is Latvian. The unofficial language is Russian. Most Latvians will answer you if addressed in Russian.

Mail

A 20-gram letter to the United States costs 30s, a postcard 25s. To Europe a 20-gram letter costs 20s, a postcard 16s. The **main post office** (✉ Brīvības 19, Riga, ☎ 701–8738) is open 24 hours.

Money Matters

COSTS

A cup of coffee or tea costs 40s; a glass of local beer 1Ls; a medium-priced local dish will cost 1.50Ls to 2Ls. Admission to museums and galleries costs around 50s.

CURRENCY

The monetary unit in Latvia is the lat (Ls), which is divided into 100 santīmi(s). There are notes of 5, 10, 20, 50, 100, and 500 lat, coins of 1 and 2 lat and 1, 2, 5, 10, 20, and 50 santīmi. At press time (spring 1998) the rate of exchange was 60s to the U.S. dollar, 40s to the Canadian dollar, 1Ls to the pound sterling, 37s to the Australian dollar, and 32s to the New Zealand dollar. Banks, with branches in all major and most minor cities, change cash and traveler's checks at fair commissions; most also give advances on a Visa or MasterCard. Credit cards are widely accepted.

TIPPING

A service charge of 10% is sometimes added and an 18% VAT is automatically included. Tipping is not obligatory, but for excellent service, add 5%.

National Holidays

January 1; April 2 (Good Friday); April 4 (Easter); May 1 (Labor Day); June 23, 24 (St. John's Day/Midsummer); November 11 (Veteran's Day); November 18 (Independence Day - 1918); December 25, 26; December 31.

Telephoning

COUNTRY CODE

The country code for Latvia is 371.

INTERNATIONAL CALLS

To reach an **AT&T** long-distance operator, dial 700–7007.

LOCAL CALLS

Pay phones take phone cards worth 2, 5, or 10 Ls. Buy cards at any kiosk. For **telephone information** dial 707–7077 or 777–0777.

Transportation

BY BOAT

Passenger ships connect Riga with various Scandinavian ports.

BY BUS

Public transport costs 14s. Buy bus tickets from the conductor on the bus. Tram and trolleybus tickets can be purchased at kiosks. Public transport runs from 5:30 AM to 12:30 AM. Some routes have 24-hour service.

Domestic bus trips cost less than 5Ls. For bus schedules call 24-hour **Ekspress Hotline** (☏ 777–0777).

BY CAR

An international or national driver's license bearing a photo is acceptable in Latvia. Drive on the right. Roads are not up to Western standards. Gas costs 30s per liter. Cars may be rented from 40Ls a day; lower rates are available for longer rental terms.

BY PLANE

Air Baltic operates from Copenhagen, Frankfurt, Geneva, Helsinki, London, Stockholm, Tallinn, and Vilnius. Finnair and British Airways have good connections from the United States.

BY PRIVATE TAXI

Taxis operate 24 hours throughout Riga. They are expensive around hotels and ferry, bus, and train stations, cheaper within the city center; for best results, telephone for one. The official rate is 25s per km in the daytime and 35s at night or in bad weather. Drivers are bound by law to display an operating license and a meter. Stick to the state cabs with orange and black markings. Insist that the meter be turned on; if there is no meter, choose another taxi or decide on a price beforehand.

BY SERVICE TAXI

Shared taxis accommodate up to 10 people and are cheap and comfortable. They operate on virtually every bus and trolleybus line. Tariffs are 15s and 25s. Passengers may embark at any regular bus stop and disembark anywhere along the route.

BY TRAIN

Electric trains are by far the preferable mode of transport for getting around Latvia. Tickets cost less than 5Ls. For train schedule information call the 24-hour **Ekspress Hotline** (☏ 777–0777).

Exploring Latvia

Riga

Riga has an upscale, big-city feel unmatched in the region. The capital is almost as large as Tallinn and Vilnius combined and is the business center of the area. With a captive audience of high-rolling investors and Western businesspeople, original, high-quality restaurants and hotels have given Riga something to brag about.

Although Riga's Old Town is its calling card, it is also the city of Art Nouveau. Long avenues of complex and sometimes whimsical interwar Jugendstil facades hint at Riga's grand past. Many were designed by Mikhail Eisenstein, the father of Soviet director Sergei. This style dominates the city center; you can see the finest examples at Alberta 2, 2a, 4, 8, and 13.

Currently ensconced in scaffolding, the fiercely Gothic **Melngavlvju Nams** (Blackheads House) was built in 1344 as a hotel for wayfaring merchants (who wore black hats). Partially destroyed during World War II and leveled by the Soviets in 1948, it is being reconstructed for Riga's 800th anniversary in 2001. ✉ *Strēlnieku laukums.*

The **Brīvdabas muzejs** (Open-air Ethnographic Museum) is well worth the 9-km (5-mi) trek from downtown. At this 100-hectare living museum farmsteads and villages have been crafted to look like those in 18th- and 19th-century Latvia; folk-costumed workers engage in traditional activities (beekeeping, smithery, and so on). In early June the museum hosts a great crafts fair. ✉ *Brīvības 440,* ☎ *799–4510.* ⏲ *Daily 11–5.*

★ The central **Brīvības piemineklis** (Freedom Monument), a 1935 statue whose upheld stars represent Latvia's united peoples (the Kurzeme, Vidzeme, and Latgale), was the rallying point for many nationalist protests during the late 1980s and early 1990s. The monument, commemorating Latvia's interwar and contemporary independence, has an honor guard during the day. The woman on top is known as Milda. ✉ *Brīvības and Raiņa.*

In Doma laukums (Dom Square), the nerve center of the Old Town, though the Riga Stock Exchange and a number of outdoor cafés make the square important, it's the stately 1210 **Rīgas doms** (Rīga Cathedral) that dominates. Reconstructed over the years with bits of Romanesque, Gothic, and Baroque, this place of worship is astounding for its architecture as much as for its size. The massive 6,768-pipe organ is among the largest in Europe. Concert schedules are posted outside. ✉ *Doma laukums,* ☎ *721–3213.* ⏲ *Tues.–Fri. 1–5, Sat. 10–2.*

★ The **Okupācijas Muzejs** (Latvian Occupation Museum) details the devastation of Latvia at the hands of the Nazis and Soviets during World War II. It is one of the best museums in the Baltics, with no-punches-pulled exhibits. Ironically, in front of the museum is a monument dedicated to the Latvian sharpshooters who protected Lenin during the 1917 revolution. ✉ *Strēlnieku laukums 1,* ☎ *721–2715.* 🎫 *Free.* ⏲ *Tues.–Sun. 11–5.*

★ At **Rīgas Motormuzejs** (Motor Museum) the Western cars on display can impress, but the Soviet models—including Stalin's iron-plated limo and a Rolls Royce totalled by Brezhnev himself—are the most fun. ✉ *Eizenšteina 6,* ☎ *2/537–730.* ⏲ *Tues.–Sun. 10–6.*

Latvia's newly restored 18th-century **Nacionālā Opera Doms** (Opera House), where Richard Wagner once conducted is an imposing sight just off Freedom Square. ✉ *Box office, Teatra 10/12,* ☎ *722–5747.*

Towering **Pētera baznīca** (St. Peter's Church), originally built in 1209, had a long history of annihilation and conflagration before being destroyed most recently in 1941. Rebuilt by the Soviets, it lacks authenticity but has a good observation deck on the 200-ft spire. ✉ *Skārņu 19.* ⏲ *Tues.–Sun. 10–7.*

The **Trīs Brāļi** (Three Brothers)—a trio of houses on Mazä Pils—show what the city looked like before the 20th century. The three oldest houses in the capital (No. 17 is the oldest, dating from the 15th century) span several styles, from the medieval to the baroque. The middle house is the city's **architecture museum.** ✉ *Mazä Pils 17, 19, 21.*

The **Valsts mākslas muzejs** (National Art Museum) has several large halls of 19th- and 20th-century Latvian art. ✉ *Kr. Valdemara and Elizabetes,* ☎ *732–5021.* ⏲ *Wed.–Mon. 11–5.*

DINING AND LODGING

$$$ ✕ **Reformātu Klubs.** The international menu is tasty, but it's the nightly live jazz music that draws ex-pats. Candlelight glows in the sepia-tone dining room—the converted basement of a church hall. ✉ *Mārstaļu 10,* ☎ *721–0027. AE, DC, MC, V.*

$$$ ✕ **Vincents.** Named for the painter, this restaurant has fed the likes of Pierre Cardin, B. B. King, and Mstislav Rostropovitch. The menu is international, but always with a French flair. Try the mushroom gratin or the grilled goat cheese. ✉ *Elizabetes 19,* ☎ *733–2634. MC, V.*

$$ ✕ **Osiris.** A small restaurant next door to the Aperto Libro English-language bookstore, this is a favorite meeting spot of diplomats and ex-pats. It's famed for its weekend brunches; however, any meal is super here, from crepes to cutlets. ✉ *Kr. Barona 31,* ☎ *724–3002. MC, V.*

$$ ✕ **Pulkvedim Neviens Neraksta.** Named for the Gabriel Garcia Marquez novel *Nobody Writes to the Colonel,* this industrial-style bar/restaurant serves such imaginative dishes as garlic cream soup and flounder in guacamole sauce. Beware that at night the sedate atmosphere is traded for a more raucous one. ✉ *Peldu 26/28,* ☎ *721–3886.*

$$ ✕ **Rozamunde.** This restaurant captures pre-war Riga style with finesse. Enjoy live 1920s and 1930s music downstairs or live harp music upstairs. In either place the menu is a delicious assortment of Latvian dishes, with emphasis on meat with fruit sauces and Baltic herring. ✉ *Mazā Smilšu 8,* ☎ *722–7798. MC, V.*

$ ✕ **Räma.** The resident Hare Krishna community offers out-of-this-world vegetarian Indian fare in a preach-free environment. ✉ *Kr. Barona 56,* ☎ *2/274–134.*

$$$$ 🏨 **Hotel De Rome.** With warm and classy service, it is elegant and worth the cost. Rooms have a turn-of-the-century flavor. Amenities include conference facilities, business and travel service, an outstanding breakfast, and a roomy sauna. ✉ *Kaļķu 28, LV1050,* ☎ *708–7600,* FAX *708–7606. 90 rooms. 2 restaurants. AE, DC, MC, V.*

$$$$ 🏨 **Radisson SAS Daugava.** In this hotel across the river from Old Town, the simple, modern rooms have spectacular views. The staff is probably the most gracious in town. ✉ *Kugu 24, LV1050,* ☎ *706–1111,* FAX *706–1100. 361 rooms. Restaurant, pool. AE, DC, MC, V.*

$$$ 🏨 **Konventa Sēta.** In a charming complex of buildings dating from the Middle Ages, this hotel has rooms with a clean, white, Scandinavian aesthetic and medieval details. Ask for one with a view of the red roofs of Old Town. ✉ *Kalēju 9/11, LV1050,* ☎ *708–7501,* FAX *708–7506. 140 rooms. Restaurant. AE, DC, MC, V.*

$$$ 🏨 **Latvija.** An efficient and sleek modern hotel has evolved from what was once an Intourist hellhole. The VIP floors offer not only spectacular views but luxurious rooms. Standard rooms are well appointed. Amenities include guarded parking, a conference hall, a business center, and a Turkish sauna. ✉ *Elizabetes 55, LV1050,* ☎ *722–9020,* FAX *782–0240. 354 rooms. 3 restaurants. AE, DC, MC, V.*

$$ 🏨 **Raudi un Draugi.** Run by British-Latvians, this small hotel affords a great location for a low price; it's clean, efficiently run, and simple. Large rooms for families are available. ✉ *Mārstaļu 1/3, LV1050,* ☎ *722–0372,* FAX *724–2239. 47 rooms. MC, V.*

$ 🏨 **Saulīte.** Don't expect much, but the location (between the train station and Old Town) and cost make it an option. Renovated rooms are a tad overpriced but more comfortable. ✉ *Merķeļa 12, LV1050,* ☎ *722–4546. 33 rooms.*

Jūrmala

The Latvian name of this string of four small towns means "seaside" in English, and for a 20-km (12-mi) stretch that is exactly what you get. It was once a popular vacation spot for Communists, but mostly Latvians and local Russians enjoy the chilly Baltic sea here now. Recent efforts by the Swedes helped clean up the beaches. Frequent electric trains (crowded in summer) make the 40-minute trip out here.

Gauja National Park

Only about one hour east of the capital, it feels light-years away, populated by friendly people and a helpful forestry staff. Latvia's deepest river valley, at 280 ft, is little more than a dip, but the gently flowing Gauja and the 13th-century ruins of **Turaidas Castle** (built by the Knights of the Sword) near Sigulda provide plenty of amusement as well as a few local legends, ancient graffiti, a bobsled track, and bungie-jumping tourists. ✉ *53 km (33 mi) east of Riga, visitor center (in Sigulda): Raiņa,* ☎ *2/971–345.*

LITHUANIA

Lithuania was historically the invader, not the invaded. In 1386, the country formed a union with Poland, and over the following 400 years their kingdom stretched from the Baltic to the Black Sea. Though Poland took the leading role until the late 18th century, Lithuanians still remember their time as a European superpower. Russification ensued, followed by a short period of independence (during which Kaunas was the capital, as Vilnius was occupied by Poland). Although hundreds of thousands of Lithuanians were deported by the Soviets in the 1940s and 1950s, the result was not as devastating as in Latvia or Estonia—today 80% of the population is Lithuanian, with only 10% Russian-speaking. However, the Jewish population—which had thrived here since the 1400s—was almost entirely decimated during the Nazi occupation of World War II.

Lithuania A to Z

Emergencies

Police (☎ 02). **Ambulance** (☎ 03). **Doctor**: Baltic-American Clinic (☎ 2/742–020). **Dentist**: Dentalis (☎ 2/651–232). **Pharmacy**: Gedimino Vaistinė (☎ 2/610–135).

Guided Tours

Astrida (☎ 2/614–459) and **Piligrimas ir Kompanija** (☎ 8/299–54064) run two-hour walking tours in Riga.

Language

Lithuanian is the official language; however, English, Russian, and to a certain degree Polish are spoken in Riga. In provincial areas sign language will have to do.

Mail

A 20-gram letter to the United States costs 1.20Lt, a postcard 90c. To Europe a 20-gram letter costs 1Lt, a postcard 80c. The **main post office** (✉ Gedimino 7, ☎ 2/616–759) is open weekdays 8–8, Saturday 10–5.

Money Matters

COSTS

A cup of coffee or tea costs 3Lt; a glass of local beer 8Lt; a medium-priced dish at a local restaurant 12Lt to 15Lt. Admission to museums and galleries costs about 4Lt.

CURRENCY

The monetary unit in Lithuania is the litas, which is divided into 100 centas. There are notes of 1, 2, 5, 10, 20, 50, 100, and 200 litas and coins of 1, 2, 5, 10, 20, and 50 centas. At press time (spring 1998) the rate of exchange was 4Lt to the U.S. dollar, 2.78Lt to the Canadian dollar, 6.64Lt to the pound sterling, 2.56Lt to the Australian dollar, and 2.18Lt to the New Zealand dollar. National banks, with branches in all major and most minor cities, change cash and traveler's checks at fair commissions; most also give advances on a Visa card. Credit cards are accepted at better hotels and restaurants and Western-style grocery stores.

TIPPING

A service of charge of 7% is sometimes added and an 18% VAT is included in the price of dishes on the menu but may be listed separately on your bill. Tipping is not obligatory; if you've received excellent service, round up or add 5%.

National Holidays

January 1; January 13 (Defenders of Freedom Day); February 16 (Independence Day); March 11 (Restoration of Lithuania's Independence); April 4 (Easter); May 1 (Labor Day); June 14 (Day of Mourning and Hope); July 6 (Day of Statehood); August 23 (Black Ribbon Day); September 8 (Crowning of Vytautas the Great); October 25 (Constitution Day); November 1 (All Saints' Day); December 25, 26.

Telephoning

COUNTRY CODE

The country code for Lithuania is 370.

INTERNATIONAL CALLS

To reach an **AT&T** long-distance operator dial 8–196.

LOCAL CALLS

Rectangular pay phones accept magnetic strip cards worth 3.54 Lt, 7.08 Lt, 14.16 Lt, or 28.32 Lt. Square pay phones accept chip cards worth 7.08 L. Plans to make the magnetic strip phones compatible with chip phone cards are underway. Buy either kind of phone card from any post office or Lietuvos Spauda kiosk. For **telephone information** dial 2/704–000 or 2/757–009.

Transportation

BY BUS

Public transport costs 60c at kiosks and 75c from the driver. Buy tickets separately for buses and trolleybuses. Punch your ticket upon boarding or be fined 20Lt. Most public transport operates 5:30 AM to midnight.

Domestic bus trips cost between 8Lt and 40Lt. For bus schedules try **Infolinija** (☎ 2/704–000) or the bus station (☎ 2/262–482).

BY CAR

An international or national driver's license bearing a photo is acceptable in Lithuania. Drive on the right. Main roads tend to be in good condition, better than those in Latvia or Estonia; however, secondary roads are commonly unpaved and have potholes. Gas costs 2Lt per liter. Cars may be rented from 250Lt a day; lower rates are available for longer rental terms.

BY PLANE

There are no direct flights between Lithuania and the United States. Lithuanian Airlines operates from Amsterdam, Berlin, Copenhagen, Frankfurt, Helsinki, London, Paris, Stockholm, and Warsaw. American carriers partnered with Lufthansa or SAS have good connections from the United States to Lithuania.

BY PRIVATE TAXI

Taxis operate 24 hours throughout the city. Taxis are, by and large, fair, but can be expensive around hotels and the bus and train station. It's best to telephone for one. Taxi fares generally start at 1.30Lt and increase by 1Lt to 1.30Lt per km in the daytime, more at night or in bad weather. Drivers are bound by law to display an operating license and a meter. In-town journeys cost up to 10Lt. **Express Taxi** (☎ 2/631–111 or 2/250–000) is the most trustworthy taxi company in town.

BY TRAIN

Domestic train trips cost between 8Lt and 40Lt. For schedules call the **train station** (☎ 2/630–086). Beware that certain trains running from Vilnius to Poland cross Belarus. Avoid these trains, as you need a Belarusian transit visa to cross a mere 48 km (30 mi) of Belarus along the way. Due to their slowness and lack of comfort, trains tend to be less popular than buses.

Exploring Lithuania

Vilnius

What Vilnius has is *soul.* Good jazz is a way of life here. Missing the fine dining of Riga, it compensates with a few relaxed eateries that make their customers regulars. Though the Old Town is somewhat shabby around the edges—it is, after all, the biggest in Central and Eastern Europe—those structures that have been renovated shine, and some that haven't been renovated possess a living pulse as homes for the city's artsy squatters.

Founded by Lithuanian Grand Duke Gediminas in the 14th century, Vilnius was an important center of Lithuanian, Polish, and Jewish culture until World War II. Now this former "Jerusalem of the East" is Lithuania's bustling capital—a national symbol to extradited Poles, a ghost town to the 150,000 Jews who once lived here, and home to 100,000 displaced Russians. It has museums, lush parks, a wealth of baroque churches, and myriad courtyards, many of which have been converted into cafés and jazz clubs.

★ Vilnius's main cathedral, **Arkikatedra Bazilika,** has been a major national symbol for centuries; inside is the dazzling 17th-century Chapel of St. Kazimieras. Originally a temple to Perkūnas, one of Lithuania's many pagan gods, the building became a church during the 13th century, when Lithuania converted from Paganism to Christianity; it was the last European country to do so. The cathedral was used for other purposes under communism and althoughthe church reclaimed the cathedral in the 1980s, it wasn't until 1996 that the statues atop the portal were replaced. ✉ *Katedros 1,* ☎ *2/611–127.*

★ The **Aušros Vartai** (Gates of Dawn), the main entrance to the Old Town, is the only one remaining of Vilnius's nine 16th-century gates. Beyond it to the right, a door leads to the **Chapel of Our Lady of Vilnius,** a room whose walls are covered with small metal and silver hearts and which contains an icon of the Virgin Mary renowned for its healing powers. Many of the devout climb on their knees up the steps to this holy place, converted into a chapel in 1671 and remade in neoclassical style in 1829. ✉ *Aušros Vartų.*

Wind past the good-natured, beer-drinking youth of Kalnų Parkas and mount Castle Hill, topped by the 13th-century **Gedimino bokštas** (Gedimino Tower), once part of the city's fortifications. Inside the tower is the **Vilniaus pilies muziejus** (Vilnius Castle Museum), which has outstanding city views. To the east you can see the **Trijų Kryžių Kalnas** (Hill of Three Crosses), which are said to commemorate seven Franciscan monks killed on the hill by pagans; four of them were thrown into the river below (hence only three crosses). ✉ *Arsenalo 5,* ☎ *2/617–453.* ⏲ *Wed.–Sun. 11–6.*

During the early 1900s Vilnius was Europe's major center of Yiddish education and literature. By the end of World War II, all but 600 of Vilnius's 100,000 Jews had been killed, most of them at the nearby Paneriai death camp. Today the **Jewish quarter** contains almost no trace of the once-thriving culture. The single remaining **synagogue** (Pylimo 39) survived only because the Nazis used it as a medical-supply warehouse. The best way to learn about Vilnius's Jewish heritage is to visit the **Valstybinis žydų muziejus** (State Jewish Museum). ✉ *Pylimo 4,* ☎ *2/617–917.* ⏲ *Weekdays 11–5.*

★ The most fascinating and disturbing sight in the New Town is the **Genocido Aukų Muziejus** (KGB Museum), where plaques take you through a litany of horrors in the basement of the former KGB prison. Hundreds of Lithuanians were killed here, with hundreds of thousands deported to Siberia by the Soviet regime during the 1940s and '50s. ✉ *Aukų 4,* ☎ *2/622–449.* ⏲ *Daily 10–5.*

Don't miss the amazing Gothic facade of the 16th-century **Šv Onos Bažnyčia** (St. Anne's Church), created using 33 different types of brick. It's said that when Napoléon passed through town, he wanted to take the church back to Paris "in the palm of his hand." ✉ *Maironio 8,* ☎ *2/611–236.*

The baroque 17th-century **Šv Kazimiero bažnyčia** (St. Casimir's Church) is named for the city's patron saint, Prince Casimir Jagiellon. During Russia's reign a cupola replaced the familiar crown; under the Soviets this church was converted into a museum of atheism. ✉ *Didžioji 34,* ☎ *2/221–715.*

Šv Petro ir Povilo (Church of Saints Peter and Paul) has an astounding baroque interior, with nearly 2,000 ornate, white-stucco figures and an extraordinary boat-shape chandelier. ✉ *Antakalnio 1,* ☎ *2/740–229.*

The best collection of Lithuanian fine art is at the **Vilniaus Paveikslų Galerija** (Vilnius Picture Gallery), which displays 16th- to 19th-century paintings, as well as a number of sculptures and some early pottery and folk art. The interior, which was a palace from the 17th through the 19th centuries, has been handsomely restored. ✉ *Didžioji 4,* ☎ *2/220–841.* ⏲ *Tues.–Sun. noon–6.*

Vilniaus Universiteto (Vilnius University), founded by the Jesuits in 1579, is a fascinating complex of tunnels and some 13 courtyards. Highlights include the **observatory,** with its 18th-century zodiac engravings, and **St. John's Church** (☎ 2/611–795; ⏲ Wed.–Sun. 10–6), a Gothic structure begun in 1387. ✉ *Šv Jono 12.*

DINING AND LODGING

$$$ ✕ **Freskos.** The pleasant dining room is filled with antiques and props from the opera and theater. Mellow music and soft lighting accompany such delights as pepper steak or grilled chicken breast salad. There's also a salad bar and local beer. ✉ *Didžioji 31,* ☎ *2/618–133. MC, V.*

$$ ✕ **Aludė Stikliai Taverna.** The collection of dining rooms is reminiscent of a Bavarian beer hall, but the food here is Eastern European, from *cepeliniai* (potatoes stuffed with meat) to goulash. A live folk band plays on weekends. ✉ *Gaono 7,* ☎ *2/627–971. AE, MC, V.*

$$ ✕ **Da Antonio.** A welcome addition to the ailing fine-dining scene in Vilnius, this restaurant is upscale but relaxed. The fare is Italian: great pies, pastas, and meat dishes, and the city's top cup of cappuccino. ✉ *Vilniaus 23,* ☎ *2/620–109. MC, V.*

$$ ✕ **Ritos Sleptuve.** Lithuanian-American Rita Dapkus, who gave up political life to start cooking, serves authentic Chicago-style pizza, great steaks, or Vilnius's best burger. ✉ *Goštauto 8,* ☎ *2/626–117. AE, MC, V.*

$ ✕ **Amatininkų Užeiga.** Though this cozy restaurant is open until 5 AM, its real forte is authentic and original Lithuanian food. Choose from a variety of dishes from stews to roasted meats not found on most Vilnius menus. The decor oozes fin-de-siecle charm, with wicker baskets, wooden furniture, and wrought-iron everything. ✉ *Didžioji 19/2,* ☎ *2/617–968. MC, V.*

$$$$ 🏨 **Raddisson SAS Astorija Hotel Vilnius.** Radisson-quality rooms have a touch of the antique thrown in. This hotel sets the standard for service in Vilnius. The building is turn of the century, with an unbeatable location. ✉ *Didžioji 35/2,* ☎ *2/220–110,* FAX *2/221–762. 61 rooms. Restaurant. AE, DC, MC, V.*

$$$$ 🏨 **Stikliai.** Rooms here are lavish and elegant, with a hint of British colonial meets Martha Stewart: comfortable, with lots of flower prints, antique baskets and knickknacks. Service is impeccable and amenities include sauna and guarded parking. ✉ *Gaono 7, 2001,* ☎ *2/627–971,* FAX *2/223–870. 29 rooms. 2 restaurants. AE, MC, V.*

$$$ 🏨 **Narutis.** On the only pedestrian street in Vilnius, this Old Town hotel has spacious, well-appointed rooms. Though the building dates from the 16th century, it has been thoroughly restored. Amenities include a sauna and workout facilities. ✉ *Pilies 24, 2001,* ☎ *2/222-894,* FAX *2/622–882. 30 rooms. 2 restaurants. AE, MC, V.*

$$$ 🏨 **Villon.** Although 20 minutes from town, this deluxe hotel/spa offers a free shuttle. Amenities include a satisfying breakfast buffet, a conference hall, a full-service spa, and a fitness center with Turkish and Finnish saunas. ✉ *P.O. Box 2590, 2015. 19 km (12 mi) north of Vilnius on Riga-Vilnius hwy,* ☎ *2/505–200,* FAX *2/651–385. 65 rooms. 2 restaurants, pool. AE, DC, MC, V.*

$$ 🏨 **Šauni Vietelė.** This tiny hotel has rooms whose furnishings date back to the late, and very Soviet, 1980s, but it's smack in the center of the Old Town. ✉ *Panciškonų 3/6, 2001,* ☎ *2/623–191,* FAX *2/224–110. 4 rooms. Restaurant. MC, V.*

$ 🏨 **Filaretai.** The local IYH hostel has a little too much residual Communist left over. The ambience is always youthful and friendly, but the facilities and location could be better. ✉ *Filaretų 17,* ☎ *2/696–627,* FAX *2/220–149. 40 spaces.*

Neringa

Also known as the Courland Spit, this tiny 100-km- (60-mi-) long fingernail of land ranks among Europe's most fascinating natural features. Although only half of the spit is Lithuanian—the other half belongs to the Russian exclave of Kaliningrad—there's plenty of space for playing on the beach, rolling down the Sahara-like sand dunes, or relaxing in one of the vacation houses. Thomas Mann used to summer here. Of the two tiny villages on the spit, **Nida,** about 50 km (31 mi) down the two-lane road, is the more developed, with the biggest dunes and the most popular beach. The sleepy town of **Juodkrante,** 25 km (15 mi) out on the spit, feels less like a resort. To reach the spit, drive 312 km (193 mi) west from Vilnius to Klaipeda, then take a ferry across.

5 Belgium

Brussels, Antwerp, Ghent, Brugge

Belgium is a connoisseur's delight. The land of Bruegel and Van Eyck, Rubens and Van Dyck, and Ensor and Magritte is where their best work can still be seen. Belgian culture was and remains that of a bourgeois, mercantile society. Feudal lords may have built Belgium's many castles, and prelates its splendid churches, but merchants and craftsmen are responsible for the guild houses and sculpture-adorned town halls of Brussels, Antwerp, Ghent, and Brugge.

This small country offers surprising variety, from the beaches and dunes of the North Sea coast and the tree-lined canals and big sky of the "platte (flat) land" to the rolling Bruegel country around Brussels and the sheer cliffs and dense woods of the Ardennes. It has been fought over for centuries by invaders from all points of the compass. Julius Caesar called the Belgians the bravest of the tribes that defied the Roman legions. His conquerors were followed by Huns and Vikings, the Spanish, and the French. The Battle of the Golden Spurs, in 1302, when mounted French knights were defeated by Flemish foot soldiers, is still commemorated in Flanders as the date when the Flemish identity came into its own. The greatest battleground, though, was Waterloo, just south of Brussels, where Napoléon was defeated in 1815.

Independence came in 1830, and Belgium was able to start forging a national identity. The Belgians are inveterate individualists—witness the endless variations of Art Nouveau in the town houses of the Belle Epoque that line many a prosperous street. The art of living well has been cultivated in Belgium since the days of its great Burgundian wedding feasts, when members of the ruling dynasty of Burgundy were joined in wedlock with other Royal houses. The country continues to claim an amazing number of gourmet restaurants. Whole families can often be seen celebrating a first communion, an engagement, or a birthday in an expensive restaurant. That generosity of spirit is also manifested

Belgium (Belgique, Belgien)

in the comfortable proportions of private homes and the spaciousness of public squares and avenues.

Belgium packs just over 5 million Dutch-speaking Flemings and almost as many French-speaking Walloons into a country the size of Vermont. The presence of two language cultures enriches its intellectual life but also creates constant political tension, even though in the 1990s the country became a federation of three largely self-governing regions—Flanders, Wallonia, and the City of Brussels, which is bilingual and multicultural.

Belgium's neutrality was violated during both world wars, when much of its architectural heritage was destroyed and great suffering was inflicted by the occupying forces. This may be why Belgium staunchly supports the European Union (EU), which, if it has done nothing else, has guaranteed peace in Western Europe for the past 50 years. As the home of most EU institutions, Brussels has to some become a synonym for a faceless bureaucracy, but this is unfair to both the city and the so-called Eurocrats. A rigid austerity program has enabled Belgium to reduce its national debt sufficiently to qualify for the European Common Currency, whose gradual introduction will begin in 1999. In other respects, Belgium has long been known for its laissez-faire attitudes. However, deficiencies in the judiciary and the police have recently come to light, and there is now strong support for reforms that are slowly—too slowly for many—being introduced. A change in attitudes to civic responsibility and a commitment to fashioning unity out of diversity are the major challenges facing Belgium today.

BELGIUM A TO Z

Customs

Since the EU's 1992 agreement on a unified European market, the limits to what visitors from EU countries may bring in have become generous to the point of being meaningless. For details on imports and duty-free limits, *see* Customs & Duties *in* Chapter 1.

Dining

Nearly all Belgians take eating seriously and are discerning about fresh produce and innovative recipes. At the top end of the scale, the *menus de dégustation* (tasting menus) offer a chance to sample a large selection of the chef's finest dishes. A number of brasseries and neighborhood restaurants have risen to the challenge of making going out affordable, and an animated ambience more than makes up for a more limited choice of dishes.

Belgian specialties include *lapin à la bière* (rabbit in beer), *faisan à la brabançonne* (pheasant with braised endives), *waterzooi* (a rich chicken or fish hot pot), and *moules marinières* with *frites* (marinated mussels, served with french fries). Belgians love their frites so much that they think they invented them. Other local specialties are the marvelous asparagus from Mechelen, at its best in May; and tiny, sweet shrimps (Flanders). For lunch, cold cuts, *croque-monsieur* (toasted ham-and-cheese sandwich), and *jambon d'Ardennes* (Ardennes ham) are popular, as is creamy *fromage blanc* (similar to cottage cheese) with radishes and spring onions on rye.

Prix-fixe menus are widely available and often represent considerable savings. Menus and prices are always posted outside.

MEALTIMES

Most hotels serve breakfast until 10. Belgians usually eat lunch between 1 and 3, some making it quite a long, lavish meal. However, the main meal of the day is dinner, which most Belgians eat between 7 and 10; peak dining time used to be about 8 but is now creeping closer to 9:30.

RATINGS

Prices are per person, à la carte, and include a first course, main course, dessert, 16% service, and a whopping 21% value added tax, but no wine. Look for fixed-price menus; if you sacrifice choice, you can eat for less than BF500 in many good restaurants. Restaurant prices are roughly the same in Brussels and other cities.

CATEGORY	COST
$$$$	over BF3,500
$$$	BF2,500–BF3,500
$$	BF1,500–BF2,500
$	under BF1,500

WHAT TO WEAR

Jacket and tie are required only in the most expensive establishments. Younger Belgians favor stylish, casual dress in most restaurants.

Language

Language is a sensitive subject that leads to frequent political crises. There are three national languages in Belgium: French, spoken primarily in the south of the country (Wallonia); Flemish, spoken in the north; and German, spoken in a small area in the east. Brussels is bilingual, with both French and Flemish officially recognized, though French predominates. Many people speak English in Brussels and in the north (Flanders); in Wallonia, English speakers tend to be thin on the ground.

Lodging

As the capital of Europe, Brussels attracts high-powered visitors, and many luxury hotels have been built to accommodate them. Over weekends and during July and August, business travelers are few and far between, so prices come down to BF5,000 or less. New hotels catering to cost-conscious travelers have also been built, where doubles cost less than BF3,000.

BED-AND-BREAKFAST

This has recently become a much more attractive option, thanks to self-regulation and higher standards. Local tourist offices (☞ Visitor Information *in* Contacts and Resources in each region, *below*) have the details.

CAMPING

Belgium is well supplied with camping and caravan (trailer) sites. For details contact the **Royal Camping and Caravaning Club of Belgium** (✉ Av. Villa 5, 1060 Brussels, ☎ 02/537–3681).

HOTELS

You can trust Belgian hotels, almost without exception, to be clean and of a high standard. The more ritzy hotels in city centers tend to be like luxury hotels around the globe. Smaller, family-owned hotels are much more personal, with Brugge being especially well endowed with romantic hideaways. **BTR** (Belgian Tourist Reservations; ✉ Bd. Anspach 53, 1000 Brussels, ☎ 02/513–7484, FAX 02/513–9277) handles reservations free of charge.

RATINGS

Hotel prices, including a 16% service charge and 6% sales tax, are usually posted in each room. All prices are for two people in a double room.

CATEGORY	BRUSSELS	OTHER CITIES
$$$$	BF9,000–BF12,500	BF7,500–BF10,000
$$$	BF6,500–BF9,000	BF5,500–BF7,500
$$	BF3,500–BF6,500	BF2,500–BF5,500
$	under BF3,500	under BF2,500

YOUTH HOSTELS

For information about youth hostels in Brussels and Wallonia, contact **Les Auberges de Jeunesse** (✉ Rue Van Oost 52, 1030 Brussels, ☎ 02/215–3100). For Flanders, contact **Vlaamse Jeugdherbergcentrale** (✉ Van Stralenstraat 40, 2060 Antwerp, ☎ 03/232–7218). The youth organization **Acotra World** (✉ Rue du Marché-aux-Herbes 110, ☎ 02/512–8607) specializes in travel arrangements for young people.

Mail

POSTAL RATES

First-class (airmail) letters and postcards to the United States cost BF34, second-class (surface) BF20. Airmail letters and postcards to the United Kingdom cost BF17. All international first-class mail must be marked with a blue A-PRIOR sticker (available in post offices).

Money Matters

COSTS

Costs in Brussels are on a par with those in London and New York. All taxes and service charges are included in hotel and restaurant bills. Restaurant prices are inflated by value-added tax. Gasoline prices are high, but the highways are toll-free.

CURRENCY

The unit of currency in Belgium is the franc (BF). There are bills of 100, 200, 500, 1,000, 2,000, and 10,000 francs, and coins of 1, 5, 20, and 50 francs. At press time (spring 1998), the exchange rate was BF37 to the U.S. dollar, BF25 to the Canadian dollar, BF60 to the pound sterling, BF23 to the Australian dollar, and BF20 to the New Zealand dollar.

SAMPLE PRICES

A cup of coffee in a café will cost BF45–BF60; a glass of beer, BF50–BF85; and a glass of wine, about BF100. The average bus/metro/tram ride costs BF50, theater tickets cost about BF500, and movie tickets about BF250.

National Holidays

January 1; April 5 (Easter Monday); May 1 (May Day); May 13 (Ascension); May 24 (Pentecost Monday); July 21 (National Day); August 15 (Assumption); November 1 (All Saints' Day); November 11 (Armistice Day); December 25.

Opening and Closing Times

Banks are open weekdays 9–4; some close for an hour at lunch. Exchange facilities (Bureaux de Change) are usually open on weekends, but you'll get a better rate in banks during the week. **Museums** are generally open 10–5 six days a week. Many are closed on Monday. **Shops** are open weekdays and Saturday 10–6 and generally stay open later on Friday. Bakeries are open Sunday and closed Monday.

Shopping

VALUE-ADDED TAX REFUNDS

☞ Taxes *in* Smart Travel Tips A to Z, *above*. There are simpler variations, but they require trust. One often suggested by diamond jewelers in Antwerp is that you pay the full amount by credit card. After you have had the invoice stamped by customs at your last port of call in the EU, you mail it back to the store before boarding your plane, and the VAT amount will immediately be credited to your card account.

Telephoning

COUNTRY CODE

The country code for Belgium is 32. When dialing Belgium from outside the country, drop the first zero in the regional telephone code.

INTERNATIONAL CALLS

Buy a high-denomination telecard and make a direct call from a phone booth. For credit card and collect calls, dial **AT&T** (☏ 0800–10010), **MCI** (☏ 0800–10012), or **Sprint** (☏ 0800–10014).

LOCAL CALLS

Pay phones work mostly with telecards, available at post offices and at many newsstands. An average local call costs BF20. Some phones are coin-operated and take 5- and 20-franc coins.

Tipping

A service charge is always included in restaurant and hotel bills. The tip is also included in taxi fares. Railway porters expect a minimum of BF60 per suitcase. For bellhops and doormen, BF100 is adequate. Give movie ushers BF20, whether or not they show you to your seat. Tip washroom attendants in public places BF10.

Transportation

BY BICYCLE

You can rent a bicycle from Belgian Railways at 48 stations throughout the country; train travelers get reduced rates. These bikes are serviceable, but not the state-of-the-art mountain bikes you can rent in specialized outlets. Bicycling is especially easy in the flat northern and coastal areas ; in the hilly south and east it becomes a much more muscular activity. There are bicycle lanes in many Flemish cities, but bicycling in Brussels takes a lot of guts.

BY BUS

Intercity bus service is not well developed, with bus routes often operated as an adjunct to the train. For details check your local tourist office or train station.

BY CAR

Parking. On-street parking often requires you to display a ticket dispensed from machines generally located in the middle of the block. These are not always readily seen, so take care. Old-fashioned meters taking 5- or 20-franc coins still line some streets. Parking garages provide an expensive option.

Road Conditions. Belgium has an excellent system of toll-free expressways, most of them illuminated at night, and the main roads are generally very good. Road numbers for main roads have the prefix *N*; expressways, the prefix *A* or *E*. Watch out for potholes in some city streets.

Road Signs. Road signs are written in the language of the region, so you need to know that Antwerp is Antwerpen in Flemish and Anvers in French; likewise, Brugge is Bruges in French and Brussels is Bruxelles in French and Brussel in Flemish; Ghent is Gent (Flemish) and Gand (French). Even more confusing, Liège and Luik are the same place, as are Louvain and Leuven, and Namur and Namen. Yet more difficult is Mons (French) and its Flemish equivalent, Bergen, or Tournai (French), which becomes Doornik in Flemish.

Rules of the Road. Drive on the right and pass on the left; passing on the right is forbidden, although the occasional impatient driver may do it. Seat belts are compulsory in both front and rear seats. Every car must have a warning triangle to be used in the event of a breakdown or accident. At intersections, traffic on the right has right-of-way. Adhere strictly to this rule, as there are few stop or yield signs. Two new rules have been introduced (although some drivers don't seem to have heard of them): pedestrians have priority on marked crossings, and vehicles in traffic circles have priority over those entering them. Buses and streetcars have priority over cars. Maximum speed limits are 130 kph (80 mph) on highways, 90 kph (55 mph) on major roads, and 50 kph (30 mph) in cities.

BY PLANE

There are no domestic air services.

BY TRAIN

Fast and frequent trains connect all main towns and cities. If you intend to travel often, buy a **Benelux Tourrail Ticket,** which allows unlimited travel throughout Belgium, Luxembourg, and the Netherlands for any five days during a one-month period. The **Belgian Tourrail Ticket** allows unlimited travel for five days in a one-month period. Young people from 12 to 26 can purchase a **Go Pass** valid for 10 one-way trips in a six-month period on the Belgian rail network.

Special weekend round-trip tickets are valid from Friday morning to Monday night: A 40% reduction is available on the first traveler's ticket and a 60% reduction on companions' tickets. Sample full-price round-trip fares (second class) from Brussels are: to Antwerp, BF380; to Brugge, BF740; and to Ghent, BF470.

Visitor Information

Each region has its own tourist office. The **national Flemish office** (☎ 02/504–0355) and the **national French-speaking office** (☎ 02/504–0205) are at the same address in Brussels and share a ground-floor **Tourist Information Office** (✉ Rue Marché-aux-Herbes 63, ☎ 02/504–0390).

Weather

The tourist season runs from early May to late September and peaks in July and August, when the weather is warmest. May and September offer the advantage of generally clear skies and smaller crowds.

CLIMATE

Temperatures range from around 65°F in May to an average of 73°F in July and August. In winter they drop to an average of about 40°F to 45°F. Snow is unusual except in the mountains of the Ardennes, where cross-country and alpine skiing are popular.

The following are the average daily maximum and minimum temperatures for Brussels.

Jan.	40F	4C	**May**	65F	18C	**Sept.**	69F	21C
	30	– 1		46	8		51	11
Feb.	44F	7C	**June**	72F	22C	**Oct.**	60F	15C
	32	0		52	11		45	7
Mar.	51F	11C	**July**	73F	23C	**Nov.**	48F	9C
	36	25		4	12		38	3
Apr.	58F	14C	**Aug.**	72F	22C	**Dec.**	42F	6C
	41	5		54	12		32	0

BRUSSELS

Brussels remains at heart a comfortable provincial city. It is remarkably unaffected by its status as "the capital of Europe" and by the influx of international experts who staff the institutions of the European

Union and NATO. A stone's throw away from steel and glass towers are cobbled streets, where the demands of modern life have had little impact. Away from the winding alleys of the city center, parks and squares are plentiful, and the park of the Bois de la Cambre at the end of fashionable Avenue Louise leads straight into a forest as large as the city itself. In Brussels, Art Nouveau flourished as nowhere else, and its spirit lives on. Town houses are gloriously different from one another, which makes walking down most any residential street a joyous adventure.

Exploring Brussels

You need to give yourself at least two days to explore the many riches of Brussels, devoting one day to the Old Town (whose cobblestones call for comfortable walking shoes), and the other to the great museums and uptown shopping streets.

Around the Grand'Place

Numbers in the margin correspond to points of interest on the Brussels map.

9 **Cathédrale St-Michel et Ste-Gudule.** The names of the archangel and an obscure 7th-century local saint have been joined together for the cathedral of Brussels. Begun in 1226, it combines architectural styles from the Romanesque to full-blown Gothic. The chief treasures are the stained-glass windows designed by Bernard van Orley, an early 16th-century court painter. In summer the great west window is floodlighted from within to reveal its glories. The ornately carved pulpit (1699) depicts Adam and Eve being expelled from the Garden of Eden. In the crypt are remnants of the original church. The huge construction is again gleaming white after the removal of centuries of grime. The interior restoration of the nave is complete, but the choir is not yet accessible. ✉ *Parvis Ste-Gudule,* ☎ *02/217–8345.* ⏲ *Nov.–Mar., Mon.–Sat. 7–7, Sun. 8–6; Apr.–Oct., Mon.–Sat. 7–7, Sun. 8–7.*

★ 7 **Centre Belge de la Bande Dessinée** (Belgian Comic-Strip Center). This unique museum celebrates the comic strip, focusing on such famous Belgian graphic artists as Hergé, Tintin's creator; Morris, the progenitor of Lucky Luke; and many others. Temporary exhibitions feature other practitioners of the "seventh art." There's also a lending library and bookshop. The display is housed in a splendid Art Nouveau building from 1903, designed down to the smallest detail by that movement's leading figure, Victor Horta (1861–1947). ✉ *Rue des Sables 20,* ☎ *02/219–1980.* ⏲ *Tues.–Sun. 10–6.*

5 **Galeries St-Hubert.** This oldest and most elegant of covered shopping arcades was constructed in 1847 and is filled with upscale shops, restaurants, and theaters. Recently spruced up and renovated, it is now particularly attractive. Diffused daylight penetrates the gallery from the glassed arches high above, flags of many nations billow ever so slightly, and neoclassical gods and heroes in their sculpted niches look down on the crowded shopping scene below. Midway through the gallery, it is traversed by the **Rue des Bouchers,** which, with its side streets, forms the main restaurant area in the heart of the tourist maelstrom. Caveat: The more lavish the display of food outside, the poorer the cuisine inside. ✉ *Between Rue du Marché-aux-Herbes and Rue d'Arenberg.*

★ 1 **Grand'Place.** In one of his more pointless military exercises, France's "Sun King," Louis XIV, had the Grand'Place bombarded with red-hot cannon balls in 1695. The resulting fires destroyed all but the Town Hall. The ornate Baroque guild houses of the Grand'Place, with their burnished facades, were built shortly after the French bombardment. They are topped by gilded statues of saints and heroes so vividly rendered that they seem to call out to each other. Thus the end result of Louis XIV's folly is Europe's most sumptuous market square, the jewel of Brussels. There is a daily flower market from spring to fall and a Sunday-morning bird market. On summer nights, music and colored light flood the entire square. Shops and taverns occupy most ground floors, but one serves its original purpose. This is the Maison des Brasseurs, which houses the **Brewery Museum** (⊠ Grand'Place 10, ☎ 02/511–4987). The Grand'Place comes enchantingly alive during local festivals, such as the *Ommegang*, a magnificent historical pageant re-creating Emperor Charles V's reception in the city (first Tuesday and Thursday in July) and the European Christmas Market, with stalls representing many different nations and a life-size crèche with real animals.

2 **Hôtel de Ville** (Town Hall). Dominating the Grand'Place, the Town Hall is 500 years older than the guild houses that line the square. Over the gateway are statues of the prophets and effigies of long-gone dukes and duchesses. The slender central tower, combining boldness and light, is topped by a statue of St. Michael crushing a figure of the devil under his feet. During the current restoration, the weather-worn St. Michael was airlifted off the top of the tower and another archangel flown in to replace him. The halls are embellished with some of the finest examples of Brussels and Mechelen tapestries. ⊠ *Grand'Place,* ☎ *02/279–4365.* ⊙ *English-speaking tours Tues. 11:30 and 3:15, Wed. 3:15, Sun. 12:15. No individual visits.*

3 **Maison du Roi** (King's House). Despite the name, no king ever lived in the 16th-century palace facing the Town Hall on the Grand'Place. It contains the **Musée de la Ville de Bruxelles** (City Museum), whose collections include Gothic sculptures, porcelain, and silverware, as well as a number of paintings, such as Bruegel's *Marriage Procession.* On the top floor is an extravagant wardrobe of more than 600 costumes for Manneken Pis, Brussels's naughty trademark, starting with one donated by the self-same Louis XIV who destroyed the original Grand'-Place. ⊠ *Grand'Place,* ☎ *02/279–4355.* ⊙ *Mon.–Thurs. 10–12:30 and 1:30–5 (Oct.–Mar. until 4), weekends 10–1.*

4 **Manneken Pis.** Originally this was one of many public fountains. The first mention of him dates from 1377, but the present version, a small bronze statue of a chubby little boy peeing, was made by Jerome Duquesnoy in 1619. The statue of "Brussels's Oldest Citizen" is in fact a copy; the original was kidnapped by 18th-century French soldiers. ⊠ *3 blocks southwest of Grand'Place, corner of Rue de l'Etuve and Rue du Chêne.*

6 **Théâtre de Marionettes Toone** (Toone Marionette Theater). Brussels folklore lives in this tiny puppet theater, with an adjoining pub and a small museum. The puppeteers irreverently tackle anything from *Hamlet* to the *Three Musketeers* in the broadest of Brussels dialect. For the benefit of visitors, there are occasional performances in more widely understood languages, such as French, Dutch, and even English. ⊠ *L'Impasse Schuddeveld off Petite Rue des Bouchers,* ☎ *02/511–7137.* 🎫 *BF400.* ⊙ *Daily; performances Fri. and Sat. 8:30 PM.*

8 **Vismet** (Fish Market). The river has been channeled underground, but the many seafood restaurants remain, making this a pleasantly animated area, highly popular with the *Bruxellois* (residents of Brussels). There's one seafood restaurant after the other on both of the former wharves, and when the weather is good they all set up tables and chairs on the wide promenade that separates them. ⊠ *Quai au Bois-à-Brûler and Quai aux Briques.*

Autoworld, **18**
Cathédrale St-Michel et Ste-Gudule, **9**
Centre Belge de la Bande Dessinée, **7**
European Union Institutions, **19**
Galeries St-Hubert, **5**
Grand'Place, **1**
Grand Sablon, **17**
Hôtel de Ville, **2**
Hôtel Hannon, **21**
Maison d'Erasme, **23**
Maison du Roi, **3**
Manneken Pis, **4**
Mini-Europe, **24**
Musée d'Art Ancien, **13**
Musée d'Art Moderne, **11**
Musée Horta, **22**
Musée Instrumental, **16**
Musée Royal de l'Afrique Centrale, **20**
Old England, **10**
Palais Royal, **14**
Petit Sablon, **15**
Place Royale, **12**
Théâtre de Marionettes Toone, **6**
Vismet, **8**

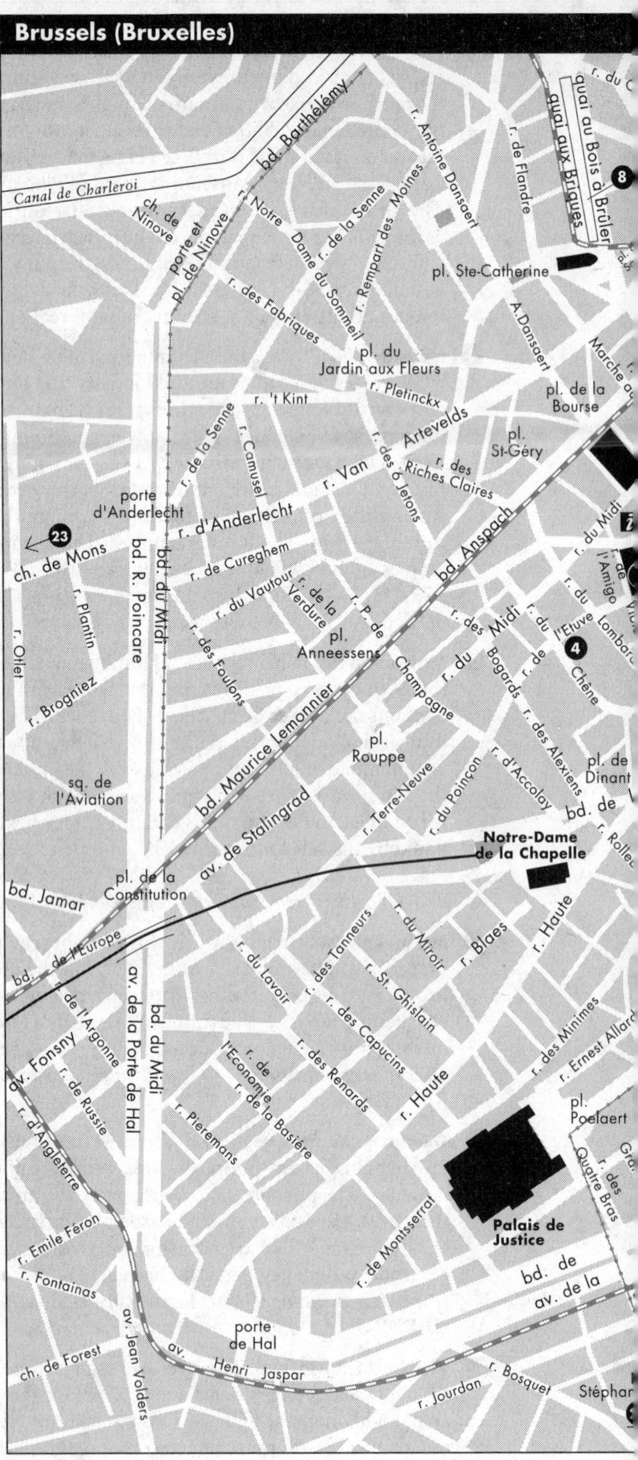

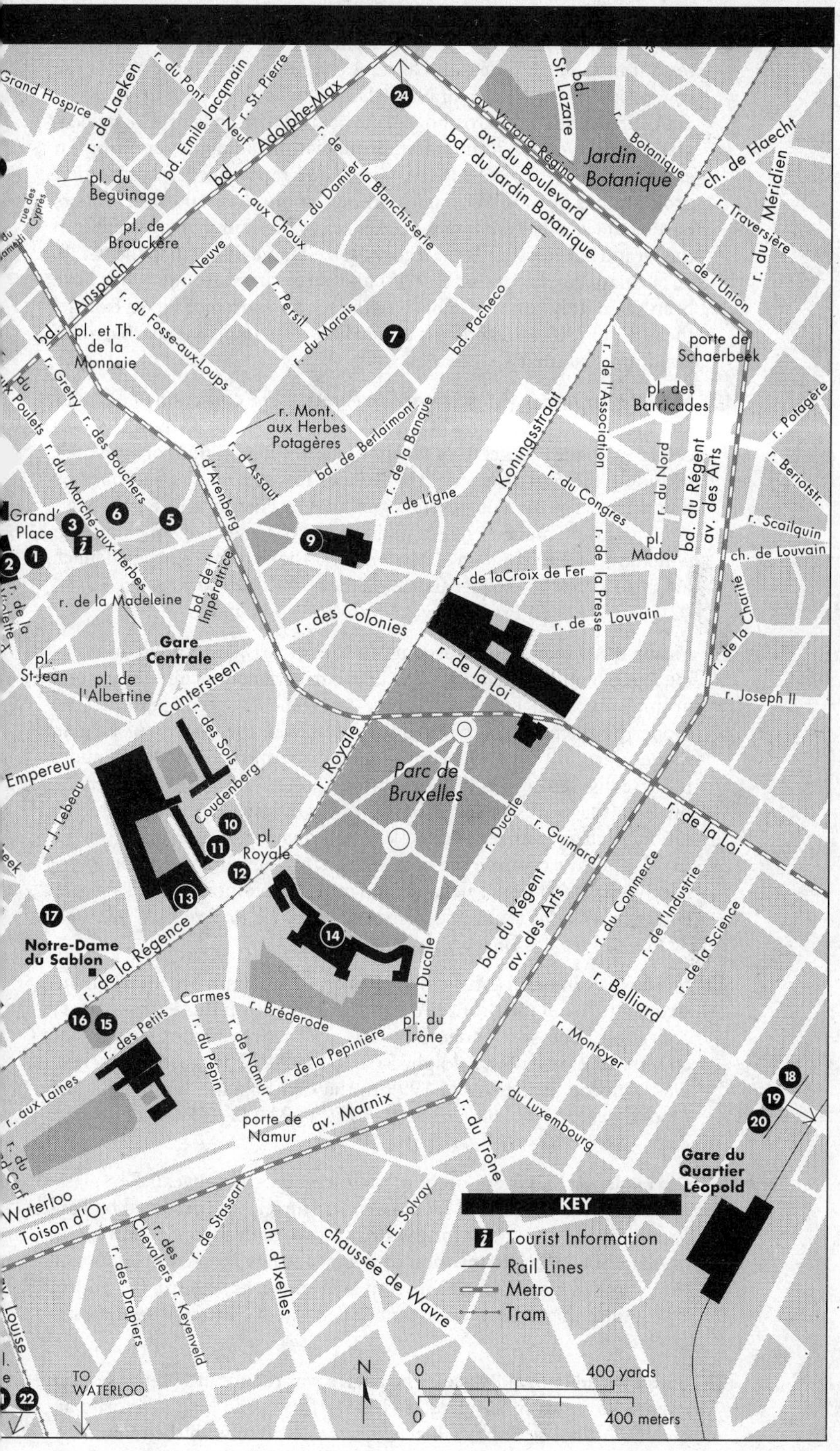
Grand Hospice
r. de Laeken
r. du Pont Neuf
bd. Emile Jacqmain
r. St. Pierre
bd. Adolphe-Max
pl. du Beguinage
pl. de Brouckère
bd. Anspach
pl. et Th. de la Monnaie
r. Neuve
r. aux Choux
r. du Damier
r. de la Blanchisserie
r. du Fosse-aux-Loups
r. Persil
r. du Marais
bd. Pacheco
r. Mont. aux Herbes Potagères
r. d'Assaut
bd. de Berlaimont
r. de la Banque
r. de Ligne
r. d'Arenberg
r. des Bouchers
r. du Marché-aux-Herbes
r. Gretry
Grand' Place
r. de la Madeleine
bd. de l'Impératrice
Gare Centrale
pl. St-Jean
pl. de l'Albertine
Cantersteen
Empereur
r. des Sols
Coudenberg
pl. Royale
r. Royale
r. des Colonies
r. de la Loi
r. de laCroix de Fer
r. de Louvain
Parc de Bruxelles
r. Ducale
r. Guimard
Koningsstraat
r. de l'Association
r. du Congres
r. de la Presse
r. du Nord
pl. Madou
bd. du Régent
av. des Arts
pl. des Barricades
porte de Schaerbeek
St. Lazare
bd.
Jardin Botanique
r. Botanique
av. Victoria Régina
av. du Boulevard
bd. du Jardin Botanique
ch. de Haecht
r. du Méridien
r. Traversière
r. de l'Union
r. Potagère
r. Beriotstr.
r. Scailquin
ch. de Louvain
r. de la Charité
r. Joseph II
r. du Commerce
r. de l'Industrie
r. de la Science
r. Belliard
r. Montoyer
r. du Luxembourg
r. J. Lebeau
Notre-Dame du Sablon
r. de la Régence
Carmes
r. Bréderode
r. des Petits
r. du Pépin
r. de Namur
r. de la Pepiniere
pl. du Trône
r. aux Laines
porte de Namur
av. Marnix
r. du Trône
Waterloo
Toison d'Or
r. des Chevaliers
r. de Stassart
ch. d'Ixelles
r. E. Solvay
chaussée de Wavre
r. des Drapiers
r. Keyenveld
Louise
TO WATERLOO
Gare du Quartier Léopold
KEY
Tourist Information
Rail Lines
Metro
Tram
N
0
400 yards
0
400 meters

Around the Place Royale

★ 17 **Grand Sablon.** The city's most sophisticated square is alive with cafés, restaurants, art galleries, and antiques shops. At the upper end of the square stands the church of **Notre Dame du Sablon,** built in flamboyant Gothic style by the crossbowmen who used to train here. The stained-glass windows are illuminated from within at night, creating an extraordinary effect of kindly warmth. A much-needed restoration program has begun. Weekend mornings, more than 100 stall holders participate in a lively antiques market below the church. Downhill from the Grand Sablon stands the **Eglise Notre-Dame de la Chapelle** (✉ Pl. de la Chapelle). Its Gothic exterior and surprising Baroque belfry have been splendidly restored. This was the parish church of Pieter Bruegel the Elder (1520–69), and he is buried here in an imposing marble tomb amid much statuary.

13 **Musée d'Art Ancien** (Museum of Ancient Art). The collection of old masters focuses on Flemish and Dutch paintings from the 15th to the 19th centuries. In the Bruegel Room is one of the finest collections of his works, including the *Fall of Icarus;* The Rubens Room contains paintings by that master. The museum displays paintings by Hieronymus Bosch, Matsys, Van Dyck, and others. An underground passage links the museum with the adjacent Museum of Modern Art. The two have staggered lunch hours so as not to inconvenience visitors. ✉ *Rue de la Régence 10,* ☎ *02/508–3211.* 🎫 *Free.* ⏲ *Tues.–Sun. 10–noon and 1–5.*

★ 11 **Musée d'Art Moderne** (Museum of Modern Art). Housed in an exciting feat of modern architecture, it descends seven floors into the ground around a central light well. There are some excellent paintings by modern French artists, but the surprise lies in the quality of Belgian modern art: not only Magritte's luminous fantasies, Delvaux's nudes in surrealist settings, and James Ensor's hallucinatory carnival scenes, but also the works of several artists who deserve much wider recognition, such as Spilliaert, Permeke, Brusselmans, and Wouters from the first half of the century; the post-war COBRA group, including Pierre Alechinsky and Henri Michaux; and on to contemporary works. Note: entrance is via the ☞ **Musée d'Art Ancien.** ✉ *Pl. Royale 1,* ☎ *02/508–3211.* 🎫 *Free.* ⏲ *Tues.–Sun. 10–1 and 2–5.*

16 **Musée Instrumental** (Musical Instruments Museum). Six thousand instruments, from the Bronze Age to today, make up this extraordinary collection. The saxophone family is well represented, as befits the country of its inventor, Adolphe Sax (1814–94). The museum is scheduled to move at the end of 1999 to the Old England building, a few blocks away. ✉ *Pl. du Petit Sablon 17,* ☎ *02/511–3595.* 🎫 *Free.* ⏲ *Tues.–Sat. 9:30–4:45 (Sat. from 10* AM*).*

★ 10 **Old England.** This is one of the masterpieces of Art Nouveau. The glass-and-steel building, with a fanciful corner turret, was designed by Paul Saintenoy (1862–1952) for the British-owned department store, Old England, in 1899. Renovation of the facade has been completed, and the Musical Instruments Museum will move in toward the end of 1999; until then, the interior cannot be visited. ✉ *Rue Montagne-de-la-Cour 94.*

14 **Palais Royal** (Royal Palace). The palace was rebuilt in 1904 to suit the expansive tastes of Leopold II (1835–1909). The king's favorite architect, Alphonse Balat, achieved his masterpiece with the monumental stairway and the Throne Hall. ✉ *Pl. des Palais,* ☎ *02/551–2020.* 🎫 *Free.* ⏲ *July 22–mid-Sept., Tues.–Sun. 9:30–3:30.*

15 **Petit Sablon.** The benches in this peaceful garden square offer welcome respite after the busy Grand Sablon. Statues of the counts Egmont and

Hoorn, who were executed by the Spanish in 1568, hold pride of place. The square is surrounded by a magnificent wrought-iron fence, topped by 48 small statues representing Brussels's medieval guilds. Each craftsman carries an object that reveals his trade: The furniture maker holds a chair; the wine merchant, a goblet. ✉ *Rue de la Régence.*

⓬ **Place Royale.** This white, symmetrical square is neoclassical Vienna transposed to Brussels during the Austrian reign in the late 18th century. From here you have a superb view over the lower town. The Coudenberg Palace once stood here. Underneath the square, excavations have revealed the "Aula Magna" (soon to become accessible to the public), where the Flanders-born King of Spain and Holy Roman Emperor Charles V (1500–58) was crowned and where he also announced his abdication two years before his death. The name of the palace lives on in the 18th-century church, St-Jacques-sur-Coudenberg. In the center of the square stands the equestrian statue of Godefroy de Bouillon (1060–1100), leader of the First Crusade and ruler of Jerusalem.

Elsewhere in Brussels

⓲ **Autoworld.** This mecca for vintage car aficionados comprises a collection of 450 vehicles. The surprise star of the show is the Belgian-made Minerva, a luxury car from the early '30s. ✉ *Parc du Cinquantenaire 11,* ☎ *02/736–4165.* ⏲ *Daily 10–6 (Nov.–Mar. until 5).*

⓳ **European Union Institutions.** The various offices of the European Commission are centered on Rond Point Schuman (Metro: Schuman.) The rounded glass summit of the new **European Parliament** building (✉ Rue Wiertz 43) looms behind the Gare de Luxembourg.

㉑ **Hôtel Hannon** (Hannon Mansion). The flowering of Art Nouveau produced this handsome and original town house by Jules Brunfaut (1903). In the interior note the staircase with its romantic fresco, and the stained glass. ✉ *Av. de la Jonction 1,* ☎ *02/538–4220.* ⏲ *Tues.–Sun. 1–6; closed July 15–Aug. 15. Near Musée Horta; trams 91 and 92 from Place Louise.*

★ ㉓ **Maison d'Erasme** (The Erasmus House). The remarkable redbrick 15th-century house where Erasmus (1466–1536), the great humanist, lived in 1521 stands in the middle of a nondescript neighborhood. Every detail is authentic, with period furniture, paintings by Holbein and Hieronymus Bosch, prints by Albrecht Dürer, and early editions of Erasmus's works, including *In Praise of Folly.* ✉ *Rue du Chapitre 31,* ☎ *02/521–1383.* ⏲ *Wed.–Thurs. and Sat.–Mon., 10–noon and 2–5. Metro: St-Guidon.*

㉔ **Mini-Europe.** This highly popular family attraction comprises 300 models (on a 1:25 scale) of famous European buildings, monuments, and technical achievements. ✉ *Bd. du Centenaire 20,* ☎ *02/478–0550.* 🎟 *BF390.* ⏲ *Apr.–Dec., daily 10–6 (July–Aug. until 8). Metro: Heysel.*

★ ㉒ **Musée Horta** (Horta Museum). Victor Horta (1861–1947), the Belgian master of Art Nouveau, designed this building for himself and lived and worked here until 1919. From cellar to attic—the staircase is a great work of art—every detail of the house displays the exuberant curves of the Art Nouveau style. It was Horta's aim to put nature and light back into daily life, and here his floral motifs give a sense of opulence and spaciousness where in fact space is very limited. ✉ *Rue Américain 25,* ☎ *02/537–1692.* ⏲ *Tues.–Sat. 2–5:30. Bus 91 or 92 from Place Louise.*

⓴ **Musée Royal de l'Afrique Centrale** (Royal Museum of Central Africa). King Leopold II (1835–1909) didn't do things by halves. He was sole owner of the Congo, later Zaire, and now the Republic of Congo—in hindsight an unfortunate colonial adventure, which brought great wealth to the exploiters and untold misery to the exploited. He built a museum outside Brussels to house some 250,000 objects emanating from his domain, as well as an avenue leading to the attractive site. The museum has since become a leading research center for African studies, with 13 specialized libraries. ✉ *Leuvensesteenweg 13, Tervuren,* ☎ *02/769–5211.* ⏲ *Tues.–Sun. 10–5. Tram 44 from Square Montgomery.*

Dining and Lodging

You cân eat as well in Brussels as anywhere else in the world, but one restaurant meal a day is as much as most can manage. Brussels's 3,000-odd restaurants are supplemented by a multitude of fast-food establishments and snack bars, and most cafés also offer *petite restauration* (light meals)—omelets, pastas, and the like. It is *always* advisable to check out prix-fixe menus, especially in top-dollar restaurants. They sometimes cost only half of what you would pay dining à la carte. There's much less smoking than in the past, but dedicated no-smoking areas are rare.

The main hotel districts are in the Grand'Place area and in the Avenue Louise shopping area. Finding accommodations is not difficult, but if you have a problem, go to the T.I.B. tourist office in the Hôtel de Ville at the Grand'Place. A deposit is required (deductible from the final hotel bill). Weekend and summer rebates are available in almost all hotels; be sure to check when you book. New hotels have set aside rooms or floors for nonsmokers and offer a limited number of rooms equipped for the needs of people with disabilities.

$$$$ ★ ✕ **Comme Chez Soi.** Pierre Wynants, with his second-in-command, Lionel Rigolet, runs a restaurant where the kitchen is larger than the Art Nouveau dining room. One all-time favorite, fillet of sole with a white wine mousseline and shrimp, is always on the menu. A new creation is warm oysters with Belgian endives and bacon. Many dishes are served for a minimum of two persons. You'll be happier here if you can go as a party of four; tables for two are too close for comfort. Be sure to reserve well ahead of time. ✉ *Pl. Rouppe 23,* ☎ *02/512–2921. Reservations essential. Jacket and tie. AE, DC, MC, V. Closed Sun., Mon., July.*

$$$$ ✕ **Maison du Cygne.** With decor to match its classical cuisine, this restaurant is set in a 17th-century guildhall on the Grand'Place. The formal dining room upstairs has paneled walls hung with old masters, and a small room on the mezzanine floor contains two priceless Bruegels. Service is flawless in the grand old manner. The food is dependable but not the main attraction; rack of lamb and braised turbot are specialties. ✉ *Rue Charles Buyls 2,* ☎ *02/511–8244. Reservations essential. Jacket and tie. AE, DC, MC, V. Closed Sun. and 3 wks in Aug. No lunch Sat.*

$$$$ ★ ✕ **Sea Grill.** Gigantic etched-glass murals convey the cool of the Arctic fjords that provide many of the ingredients for this seafood restaurant, one of Belgium's best. The young chef, Yves Mattagne, has gone from strength to strength with such dishes as ravioli stuffed with smoked langoustines and served with sun-dried tomato butter. Classics include whole sea bass baked in salt and Brittany lobster pressed at your table. ✉ *Radisson SAS Hotel, Rue du Fossé-aux-Loups 47,* ☎ *02/227–3120. Jacket and tie. AE, DC, MC, V. Closed Sun., Easter wk, and 4 wks in July/Aug. No lunch Sat.*

$$$ ★ ✕ **Ogenblik.** With green-shade lamps over marble-top tables, sawdust on the floor, ample servings, and a great ambience, Ogenblik is a

true (but expensive) bistro. The long and imaginative menu changes frequently but generally includes such specialties as mille-feuille with lobster and salmon, and saddle or leg of lamb with fresh, young vegetables. ✉ *Galerie des Princes 1,* ☎ *02/511–6151. Reservations not accepted after 8* PM. *AE, DC, MC, V. Closed Sun.*

$$ ✕ **Aux Armes de Bruxelles.** This restaurant is one of the few to escape the "tourist trap" label in this hectic little street. The three rooms have a lively atmosphere: The most popular section overlooks the street theater outside, but locals prefer the cozy rotunda. Among the specialties are tomatoes stuffed with freshly peeled shrimps, waterzooi, and mussels in white wine. ✉ *Rue des Bouchers 13,* ☎ *02/511–2118. AE, DC, MC, V. Closed Mon. and June.*

$$ ✕ **L'Idiot du Village.** Walls and ceiling in the front room are cornflower blue and in the back room oxblood red; the paintings are surrealist and the chandelier multicolored in this old-town eatery, vastly popular with a young clientele. Goose liver marbled with prunes, salmon-stuffed cannelloni, and roast suckling pig are popular items on the menu. ✉ *Rue Notre-Seigneur 19,* ☎ *02/502–5582. Reservations essential. AE, MC, V. Closed weekends and mid-July–mid-Aug.*

$ ✕ **Au Vieux St-Martin.** When neighboring eateries on Grand Sablon are empty, this one remains busy, and you're equally welcome whether you order a full meal or a cup of coffee. Belgian specialties dominate the menu, and portions are generous. The restaurant claims to have invented the now ubiquitous *filet américain,* the well-seasoned Belgian version of steak tartare. The walls are hung with bright contemporary paintings, and picture windows face the pleasant square. ✉ *Pl. du Grand Sablon 38,* ☎ *02/512–6476. Reservations not accepted. No credit cards.*

$ ✕ **Chez Jean.** This old-timer next to the Grand'Place is celebrating 65 years of serving good, honest Belgian food: shrimp croquettes, waterzooi, salmon-and-endives cooked with a dash of beer. Waitresses in black and white provide friendly service. ✉ *Rue des Chapeliers 6,* ☎ *02/511–9815. AE, DC, MC, V.*

$ ★ ✕ **Falstaff.** Some things never change, and Falstaff used to be one of them. There is now an up-market Falstaff Gourmand (Rue des Pierre 38) where the food is fancier and prices higher. But old-timers stick with the original, a huge tavern, with an Art Nouveau interior, that fills up for lunch and keeps going until 5 AM, with an ever-changing crowd, from students to pensioners. Cheerful waitresses take your orders for onion soup, filet mignon, salads, and other straightforward dishes. ✉ *Rue Henri Maus 19,* ☎ *02/511–8789. AE, DC, MC, V.*

$ ✕ **Léon de Bruxelles.** Even though prices have been edging upward lately, Léon continues to do a land-office business and has over the years expanded into a row of eight old houses. Heaping plates of mussels and other Belgian specialties, such as eels in a green sauce, are served nonstop from noon to midnight, accompanied by what may be the best french fries in town. ✉ *Rue des Bouchers 18,* ☎ *02/511–1415. Reservations not accepted. AE, DC, MC, V.*

$ ✕ **Le Pain Quotidien.** These bakeries-cum-snack bars have spread like wildfire all over Brussels (and even to New York and Boston in the U.S.) with the same formula: copious salads and delicious open sandwiches on farm-style bread, served at a communal table from 7 AM to 7 PM. Service at peak hours tends to be slow. ✉ *Rue des Sablons 11,* ☎ *02/513–5154;* ✉ *Rue Antoine Dansaert 16,* ☎ *02/502–2361; and other locations. Reservations not accepted. No credit cards.*

$ ★ ✕ **Les Salons de Wittamer.** The elegant upstairs rooms at Brussels's best-known patisserie have been converted into a stylish breakfast and lunch restaurant, topped off with the establishment's celebrated pastry or ice-cream concoctions. ✉ *Pl. du Grand Sablon 12,* ☎ *02/511–9339. AE, DC, MC, V. Closed Mon.*

$$$$ **Brussels Hilton.** The 27-story Hilton was one of the first high-rises in Brussels back in the '60s and remains a distinctive landmark. Corner rooms are the most desirable. The second-floor Maison du Boeuf restaurant is much appreciated by Brussels gourmets, and the Café d'Egmont (open around the clock) is also highly popular. Centrally located, the hotel is next to the main luxury shopping area and overlooks the Parc d'Egmont. ✉ *Bd. de Waterloo 38, 1000,* ☎ *02/504–1111,* FAX *02/504–2111. 389 rooms, 39 suites. 2 restaurants. AE, DC, MC, V.*

$$$$ **Conrad.** Opened in 1993, the Conrad, seeking to combine the European grand hotel tradition with American tastes and amenities, has quickly become *the* place to stay for visiting dignitaries. Rooms come in many different shapes but are uniformly spacious, with three telephones, bathrobes, and in-room checkout. The Maison de Maître restaurant maintains the same high standard, and the large bar is pleasantly clublike. ✉ *Av. Louise 71, 1050,* ☎ *02/542–4242,* FAX *02/542–4342. 244 rooms, 25 suites. 2 restaurants. AE, DC, MC, V.*

$$$$ ★ **Le Méridien.** Opened in 1995, Le Méridien is Brussels's newest luxury hotel. The marble and gilt-edged lobby recalls Parisian hotel palaces, and the restaurant sets out brightly colored Limoges china. Rooms, in dark blue or green, come with three telephones, large desks, and modem jacks. Doors don't slam behind you if you step into the corridor, a technological achievement of sorts. ✉ *Carrefour de l'Europe 3, 1000,* ☎ *02/548–4211,* FAX *02/548–4080. 212 rooms, 12 suites. Restaurant. AE, DC, MC, V.*

$$$$ **Radisson SAS.** This 1990 hotel has guest rooms decorated with great panache in four different styles: Scandinavian, Asian, Italian, and Art Deco. A portion of the city wall from 1134 forms part of the atrium. ✉ *Rue du Fossé-aux-Loups 47, 1000,* ☎ *02/219–2828,* FAX *02/219–6262. 258 rooms, 23 suites. 2 restaurants. AE, DC, MC, V.*

$$$ ★ **Amigo.** Although it was built in the 1950s, this family-owned hotel off the Grand'Place has the charm of an older age. It's a favorite among the titled and famed who relish privacy. Each room is individually decorated, often in silk, velvet, and brocades. The good news is that most of the rooms have been refurbished, with new marble bathrooms. The bar is very pleasant, and a new chef has been hired for the renovated dining room. The 60-odd rooms that have not been refurbished are the least expensive. ✉ *Rue d'Amigo 1, 1000,* ☎ *02/547–4747,* FAX *02/513–5277. 156 rooms, 27 suites. Restaurant. AE, DC, MC, V.*

$$$ **Metropole.** A major restoration has returned the Metropole to the palace it was during the Belle Epoque. The lobby sets the tone, with its high coffered ceiling, chandeliers, and Oriental rugs. The theme extends seamlessly to the bar with its deep leather sofas, to the gourmet restaurant, and to the café, which opens onto a heated terrace on the busy Place Brouckère. Most guest rooms have been discreetly done over in pastel shades and art deco style, but the very high ceilings take getting used to. ✉ *Pl. de Brouckère 31, 1000,* ☎ *02/217–2300,* FAX *02/218–0220. 404 rooms, 6 suites. 2 restaurants. AE, DC, MC, V.*

$$ **Le Dixseptième.** This stylish 18th-century hotel was originally the residence of the Spanish ambassador. Suites are up a splendid Louis XV staircase, and the standard rooms surround an interior courtyard. Whitewashed walls, bare floors, exposed beams, and colorful textiles are the style here. Some rooms have kitchenettes; suites have working fireplaces and fax machines, and there's one with a separate office. ✉ *Rue de la Madeleine 25, 1000,* ☎ *02/502–5744,* FAX *02/502–6424. 12 rooms, 13 suites. AE, DC, MC, V.*

$$ **Forum.** Decorated from top to bottom in postmodern art deco, the Forum stands on a pleasantly green residential street, near the Horta Museum and other Art Nouveau buildings. Rooms in the back face a leafy garden. The Italian restaurant spills out over the sidewalk. ✉ *Av.*

du Haut-Pont 2, 1060, ☎ *02/340–3400,* FAX *02/347–0054. 78 rooms. Restaurant. AE, DC, MC, V.*

$ **Bed & Brussels.** This upscale B&B accommodations service arranges stays with 100 host families, most of them with room to spare after children have flown the coop. Many rooms come with private bath, and breakfast with the hosts is included. ✉ *Rue Gustave Biot 2, 1050,* ☎ *02/646–0737,* FAX *02/644–0114. No credit cards.*

$ **Matignon.** Only the Belle Epoque facade of this family-owned-and-operated hotel opposite the Bourse was preserved when it was converted into a hotel in 1993. The lobby is tiny to make room for the large café-brasserie. Business has been good enough for the proprietors to buy and refurbish the building next door. Rooms are small but have large beds. The eight duplex suites are good value for families. ✉ *Rue de la Bourse 10, 1000,* ☎ *02/511–0888,* FAX *02/513–6927. 37 rooms, 8 suites. Restaurant. AE, DC, MC, V.*

$ **Mozart.** The entrance to the Mozart, which opened in 1993, is between two Greek pita joints; the reception is up a flight of stairs. The lack of an elevator is a drawback, but the spacious, oak-beamed rooms, in shades of salmon, are attractive; each has a refrigerator and a shower. Complimentary breakfast is served in a cozy nook. The owners also run the inexpensive restaurant, Boccaccio, across the street. ✉ *Rue Marché aux Fromages 15a, 1000,* ☎ *02/502–6661,* FAX *02/502–7758. 23 rooms with shower. AE, DC, MC, V.*

$ ★ **Welcome Hotel/Truite d'Argent.** Among the charms of the smallest hotel in Brussels are the young owners, Michel and Sophie Smeesters. The six rooms, with king- or queen-size beds, are as comfortable as those in far more expensive establishments. This hotel is much in demand, so book early. There's a charming breakfast room, and around the corner on the fish market Michel doubles as chef of the excellent seafood restaurant La Truite d'Argent, where hotel guests get a discount. ✉ *Rue du Peuplier 5, 1000,* ☎ *02/219–9546,* FAX *02/217–1887. 6 rooms. Restaurant. AE, DC, MC, V.*

Nightlife and the Arts

The Arts

The best way to find out what's going on is to buy a copy of the English-language weekly magazine, the *Bulletin.* It's published every Thursday and sold at newsstands for BF85.

FILM

Movies are mainly shown in their original language. Complete listings appear in the *Bulletin.* The Acropole (✉ Galeries de la Toison d'Or), the new UCG complex (✉ Pl. de Brouckère), and the multiscreen Kinepolis (✉ Av. du Centenaire 1) have comfortable armchairs and **first-run movies.** For unusual movies or screen classics, visit the **Musée du Cinéma** (Cinema Museum), where three movies with sound and two silents are shown daily. ✉ *Rue Baron Horta 9,* ☎ *02/507–8370.* 🎫 *BF90 (BF60 if bought 24 hrs in advance).*

MUSIC

Major symphony concerts and recitals are held at the **Palais des Beaux-Arts** (✉ Rue Ravenstein 23, ☎ 02/507–8200). Chamber music is best enjoyed at the intimate **Conservatoire Royal de Musique** (✉ Rue de la Régence 30, ☎ 02/507–8200). Free Sunday morning and lunchtime concerts take place at various churches, including the Cathédrale St-Michel et Ste-Gudule (☞ Exploring Brussels, *above*) and the Petite Eglise des Minimes (✉ Rue des Minimes 62). **Forest National** (✉ Av. du Globe 36, ☎ 02/347–0355) hosts rock and pop concerts.

OPERA AND DANCE

The national opera company, based at the handsome **Théâtre Royal de la Monnaie** (✉ Pl. de la Monnaie, ☎ 02/218–1202), stages productions of international quality under up-and-coming music director Antonio Pappano. Tickets cost BF300–BF3,100. Touring dance and opera companies often perform at the **Cirque Royal** (✉ Rue de l'Enseignement 81, ☎ 02/218–2015).

THEATER

The most attractive theater in town is the **Théâtre Royal du Parc** (✉ Rue de la Loi 3, ☎ 02/512–2339), which stages productions of Molière and other French classics. Avant-garde theater is performed at: **Théâtre Varia** (✉ Rue du Sceptre 78, ☎ 02/640–8258) and at the recently refurbished **Théâtre de Poche** (✉ Chemin du Gymnase, in Bois de la Cambre, ☎ 02/649–1727).

Nightlife

BARS

There's a café on virtually every corner in Brussels, and all of them serve beer from morning to late at night. Some of the most authentic, with old-style Flemish wooden furniture and fittings, are around the Grand'-Place. **Le Cerf** (✉ Grand'Place 20, ☎ 02/511–4791), is particularly pleasant. An appealing uptown outpost is **Nemrod** (✉ Bd. de Waterloo 61, ☎ 02/511–1127). **La Fleur en Papier Doré** (✉ Rue des Aléxiens 53, ☎ 02/511–1659) is a quiet bar with surrealist decor that attracts an artsy crowd. **Cirio** (✉ Rue de la Bourse 18, ☎ 02/512–1395) is a pleasant old Art Nouveau bar. **Rick's Café Américain** (✉ Av. Louise 344, ☎ 02/647–7530), a favorite with the American and British expat community, packs them in three deep at the bar at lunch. It serves great burgers and Tex-Mex fare. **Henry J. Bean's** (✉ Rue du Montagne-aux-Herbes-Potagères 40, ☎ 02/219–2828), a 1950s-style bar and grill, attracts mostly the young.

DANCE CLUBS

In all the clubs the action starts after midnight. **Griffin's** (✉ Rue Duquesnoy 5, ☎ 02/505–5555), at the Royal Windsor Hotel, appeals to young adults and business travelers. The trendy favor **Jeux d'Hiver** (✉ Chemin du Croquet 1A, ☎ 02/649–0864), a members-only club in the Bois de la Cambre; you'll be admitted if you look the part. **Le Garage** (✉ Rue Duquesnoy 16, ☎ 02/512–6622) draws a young crowd (Sun. gays only). **Le Mirano Continental** (✉ Chaussée de Louvain 38, ☎ 02/218–5772) attracts a self-styled jet set.

JAZZ

Most of Brussels's dozen or so jazz haunts lead a double life and feature live music only on certain nights; check before you go. **New York Café Jazz Club** (✉ Chaussée de Charleroi 5, ☎ 02/534–8509) is an American restaurant by day and a modern jazz hangout by night. **Sounds** (✉ Rue de la Tulipe 28, ☎ 02/512–9250), a big café, emphasizes jazz rock and other modern trends. **Travers** (✉ Rue Traversière 11, ☎ 02/218–4086), a café-cum-jazz club, has sounds from swing to modern jazz.

Shopping

Gift Ideas

Belgium is where the *praline*—rich chocolate filled with flavored creams, liqueur, or nuts—was invented. Try Godiva, Neuhaus, or the lower-priced Leonidas, available at shops throughout the city. Exclusive handmade pralines can be bought at **Wittamer** (✉ Pl. du Grand Sablon 16, ☎ 02/512–3742). **Le St. Aulaye** (Rue Jean Chapelie 4, ☎ 02/345–7785) is an excellent pâtisserie with a sideline in superb chocolates. **Mary** (Rue Royal 73, ☎ 02/217–4500) is devoted exclusively to the art of the chocolatier.

Only the Val-St-Lambert mark guarantees handblown, hand-carved **crystal** tableware. Many stores sell crystal, including **Art and Selection** (✉ Rue Marché-aux-Herbes 83, ☎ 02/511–8448) near the Grand'Place.

In shopping for **lace,** be sure to ask the store assistant outright whether it is handmade Belgian or made in East Asia. **Maison F. Rubbrecht** (✉ Grand'Place, ☎ 02/512–0218) sells authentic Belgian lace. For a large choice of old and modern lace, try **Manufacture Belge de Dentelles** (✉ Galerie de la Reine 6–8, ☎ 02/511–4477).

Markets

On Saturday (9–5) and Sunday (9–1), the upper end of the Grand Sablon square becomes an **antiques market** with well over 100 stalls. The **Vieux Marché** (Old Market; ✉ Place du Jeu de Balle) is a flea market worth visiting for the authentic atmosphere of the working-class Marolles district. The market is open daily 7–2. If you hope to make real finds, get there early in the morning.

Shopping Districts

The shops in the **Galeries St-Hubert** sell mostly luxury goods or gift items. **Rue Neuve** and the **City 2** mall are good for less expensive boutiques and department stores. Avant-garde clothes by the recently famous Antwerp Six and their followers are sold in boutiques in the **Rue Antoine Dansaert.**

Uptown, **Avenue Louise,** with the arcades Galerie Louise and Espace Louise, counts a large number of boutiques selling expensive men's and women's wear, accessories, leather goods, and jewelry. The **Boulevard de Waterloo** is home to the same fashion names as Bond Street and Rodeo Drive. The **Grand Sablon** has more charm; this is the center for antiques and oriental carpets and for art galleries.

Side Trip

Waterloo, where Napoléon was finally defeated by the British and German armies on June 18, 1815, lies 19 km (12 mi) to the south of the city; take a bus from Place Rouppe or a train from Gare Centrale to Waterloo station. The Waterloo Tourist Office (✉ Chaussée de Bruxelles 149, ☎ 02/354–9910) is in the center of town.

The **Wellington Museum,** in the building where the general established his headquarters, displays maps and models of the battle and military memorabilia. ✉ *Ch. de Bruxelles 147,* ☎ *02/354–7806.* ⏲ *Apr.–Sept., daily 9:30–6:30; Oct.–Mar., daily 10:30–5.*

Just south of town is the actual battlefield. Start at the **Visitors' Center,** which has an audiovisual presentation that shows scenes of the battle. You can also book guides to take you around the battlefield. ✉ *Rte. du Lion 252–254, Braine–l'Alleud,* ☎ *02/385–1912.* 🎟 *BF300.* ⏲ *Apr.–Oct., daily 9:30–6:30; Nov.–Mar., daily 10:30–4. Guides 1815:* ✉ *Rte. du Lion 250,* ☎ *02/385–0625.* 🎟 *BF1,400, 1 hr; BF2,200, 3 hrs.*

Overlooking the battlefield is the **Butte de Lion,** a pyramid-shape monument erected by the Dutch. After climbing 226 steps, you will be rewarded with a great view of the site, especially the quadrangular fortified farms where British troops broke the French assault.

Brussels Essentials

Arriving and Departing

BY BUS

Eurolines (✉ Place de Brouckère 50, ☎ 02/217–0025) operates up to three daily express services from and to Amsterdam, Berlin, Frankfurt, Paris, and London. The Eurolines Coach Station (✉ Rue du Progrès 80, ☎ 02/203–0707) in Brussels adjoins the Gare du Nord.

BY CAR

If you use Le Shuttle under the English Channel or a ferry arriving in Calais, note that the E40 (via Oostende and Brugge) now connects with the French expressway, cutting driving time from Calais to Brussels to under two hours.

BY FERRY

Holyman Hoverspeed (☎ 01304/240241 in the U.K.; ☎ 059/559955 in Belgium) operates catamaran and ferry services between Dover and Oostende, carrying cars and foot passengers. Travel time by catamaran is less than two hours, by ferry about four hours. Trains at either end connect with London and Brussels.

P&O North Sea Ferries (☎ 01482/377177 in the U.K.; ☎ 050/543430 in Europe) operates an overnight conventional ferry service between Hull and Zeebrugge.

BY PLANE

All international flights arrive at Brussels National Airport at Zaventem (sometimes called simply Zaventem), about a 30-minute drive or a 16-minute train trip from the city center. For flight information, call 0900–00747.

Between the Airport and Downtown. Trains depart from the airport for the Gare du Nord (North Station) and the Gare Centrale (Central Station) every 20 minutes. The trip takes 16 minutes and costs BF110 (first class) and BF85 (second class). A taxi to the city center takes about a half hour and costs about BF1,000.

BY TRAIN

Ten **Eurostar** (☎ 02/555–2525 for information; ☎ 0900/10–177 for telephone sales, MC and V only) passenger trains a day link Brussels's Gare du Midi with London's Waterloo station via the Channel Tunnel in two hours, 40 minutes. A one-way trip costs BF6,700 in business class, BF4,200 in economy; rail pass holders qualify for 50% discounts.

All rail services between Brussels and Paris are now operated with new **Thalys** high-speed trains, which have slashed travel time between the two cities to one hour, 25 minutes. A one-way trip costs BF2,990 in "Confort 1", BF1,900 in "Confort 2." Reservations are required (☎ 0800/95–777 for information, ☎ 0900/10–177 for reservations). Thalys trains, traveling at lower speeds on conventional tracks, also link Brussels with Amsterdam and Cologne.

Getting Around

BY METRO, TRAM, AND BUS

The metro (subway), trams (streetcars), and buses run as parts of the same system. All are clean and efficient, and a single ticket costs BF50. The best buy is a 10-trip ticket for BF330 or a one-day card costing BF130. Tickets are sold in any metro station or at newsstands. Single tickets can be purchased on the bus.

BY TAXI

To call a cab, phone **Taxis Verts** (☎ 02/349–4949) or catch one at a cab stand. It's not possible to hail cruising taxis. Typical downtown rides cost BF250–BF500. Tips are included in the fare.

Contacts and Resources

EMBASSIES

U.S. (✉ Bd. du Régent 27, 1000 Brussels, ☎ 02/513–3830). **Canadian** (✉ Av. de Tervuren 2, 1040 Brussels, ☎ 02/741–0611). **U.K.** (✉ Rue d'Arlon 85, 1040 Brussels, ☎ 02/287–6211). **Australian** (Rue Guimard 6–8, 1040 Brussels, ☎ 02/286–0500). **New Zealand** (Bd. du Régent 47, 1000 Brussels, ☎ 02/512–1040).

EMERGENCIES

Police (☎ 101). **Ambulance and Fire Brigade** (☎ 100). **Doctor** (☎ 02/479–1818). **Dentist** (☎ 02/426–1026). **Pharmacy:** For information about all-night and weekend services, call ☎ 02/479–1818.

ENGLISH-LANGUAGE BOOKSTORES

Librairie de Rome (✉ Av. Louise 50b, ☎ 02/511–7937. **Sterling Books** (✉ Rue du Fossé-aux-Loups 38, ☎ 02/223–6223). **W. H. Smith** (✉ Bd. Adolphe Max 71–75, ☎ 02/219–2708).

GUIDED TOURS

Orientation. De Boeck Sightseeing (✉ Rue de la Colline 8, Grand'Place, ☎ 02/513–7744) operates city tours (BF750) with multilingual cassette commentary. Passengers are picked up at major hotels and at the tourist office in the Grand'Place. More original tours are run by **Chatterbus** (✉ Rue des Thuyas 12, ☎ 02/513–8940 for reservations). Tours include visits on foot or by minibus to the main sights (BF600) and a walking tour with a visit to a bistro (BF250). Tours are operated early June–September. **Walking Tours** organized by the tourist office (BF350) depart from the T.I.B. in the Town Hall (May–Sept., Mon.–Sat. at 10).

Side Trips. De Boeck Sightseeing Tours (☞ *above*) visits Antwerp, the Ardennes, Brugge, Ghent, Ieper, and Waterloo.

Special-Interest Bus Tours. Expertly guided half-day English-language coach tours are organized by **ARAU** (✉ Bd. Adolphe Max 55, ☎ 02/219–3345, information and reservations; 🎫 BF600) from March through November, including "Brussels 1900: Art Nouveau" (every Sat. AM) and "Brussels 1930: Art Deco" (every 3rd Sat.). Tours begin in front of Hotel Métropole on Place Brouckère.

TRAVEL AGENCIES

American Express (✉ Bd. du Souverain 100, 1170 Brussels, ☎ 02/676–2727). **Carlson Wagonlit Travel**(✉ Bd. Clovis 53, 1040 Brussels, ☎ 287–8110).

VISITOR INFORMATION

Tourist Information Brussels (T.I.B.; ✉ Hôtel de Ville, Grand'Place, ☎ 02/513–8940); here you can buy a **Tourist Passport** (BF300)—a one-day transport card and BF1,000 worth of museum admissions.

ANTWERP

Antwerp's real, Flemish name is Antwerpen, close enough to be confused with *handwerpen,* and thereby hangs a tale. The Roman soldier Silvius Brabo is said to have cut off and flung into the water the hand of the giant who exacted a toll from boatmen on the river. *Hand* is hand, and *werpen* means throwing. True or not, the tale explains the presence of severed hands on Antwerp's coat of arms.

Great prosperity came to Antwerp in the 16th century, during the reign of Charles V, Holy Roman Emperor and King of Spain (1500–58). A hundred years later Rubens and his contemporaries made their city an equally important center of the arts. Craftsmen began practicing diamond cutting at about this time, and the city is still the world leader in the diamond trade, with an annual turnover of more than $20 billion. In spite of being 88 km (55 mi) up the River Scheldt, it has also become Europe's second-largest port and number three in the world. Antwerp is the principal city of Flanders, and the Antwerpers, convinced they are a cut above most others, don't mind at all their Spanish-derived nickname: They are known as the *Sinjoren* (señores).

Exploring Antwerp

Numbers in the margin correspond to points of interest on the Antwerp map.

The Old City—a short subway ride from the Central Station—is the heart of Antwerp and best explored on foot. Rubens and his contemporaries and friends seem to be everywhere, in churches, art museums, and splendid Renaissance mansions. But Antwerp is also known as the City of Madonnas. Lift your eyes, and on many a street corner you'll see a statuette of Our Lady.

8 **Bourlaschouwburg** (Bourla Theater). Dating from the 1830s, this handsome neoclassic theater was allowed to fall into neglect before being restored to gold-and-velvet glory in 1995. ✉ *Komedieplaats 18,* ☎ *03/231–0750.*

12 **Centraal Station** (Central Station). A railway station may not be on everybody's must-see list, but this one is special. Leopold II (1835–1909), a monarch not given to understatement, had it built as a neo-Baroque cathedral to the railway age, with splendid staircases and a magnificently vaulted ticket-office hall. ✉ *Koningin Astridplein,* ☎ *03/233–3915.*

11 **Dierentuin** (Antwerp Zoo). The residents are housed in style in this huge, well-designed complex: giraffes and oryxes in an Egyptian temple, rhinoceroses in a Moorish villa, okapis around an Indian temple. There's also a winter garden, a planetarium, an aquarium, a dolphin pool, and a good restaurant. ✉ *Koningin Astridplein 26,* ☎ *03/231–1640.* *BF450.* ⏲ *July–Aug., daily 8:30–6:30; Sept.–Feb., daily 9–5; Mar.–June, daily 8:30–6.*

1 **Grote Markt.** The heart of the Old City, a three-sided square, is dominated by a huge fountain that splashes water over much of it. The fountain is topped by a statue of Silvius Brabo, the giant-killer. The Renaissance **Stadhuis** (City Hall), built when only Antwerp and Paris had more than 100,000 inhabitants, flanks one side of the square, and guild houses the other two.

6 **Koninklijk Museum voor Schone Kunsten** (Royal Museum of Fine Arts). This huge museum contains more than 1,500 paintings by old masters, including magnificent works by Rubens, Van Dyck, Jordaens, Hals, and Bruegel. The largest-ever exhibition of paintings by native son Sir Anthony Van Dyck (1599–1641) is being staged here May 15 to August 15, 1999. The second floor houses an outstanding collection of Flemish paintings from the 15th and 16th centuries; the first floor has more modern paintings. The museum is a short tram ride south of the Old City. ✉ *Leopold de Waelplaats 1–9,* ☎ *03/238–7809.* ⏲ *Tues.–Sun. 10–4:45.*

★ 7 **Museum Mayer van den Bergh.** A passionate collector, Mayer van den Bergh amassed almost 4,000 works of art, and the best of them are

Antwerp (Antwerpen)

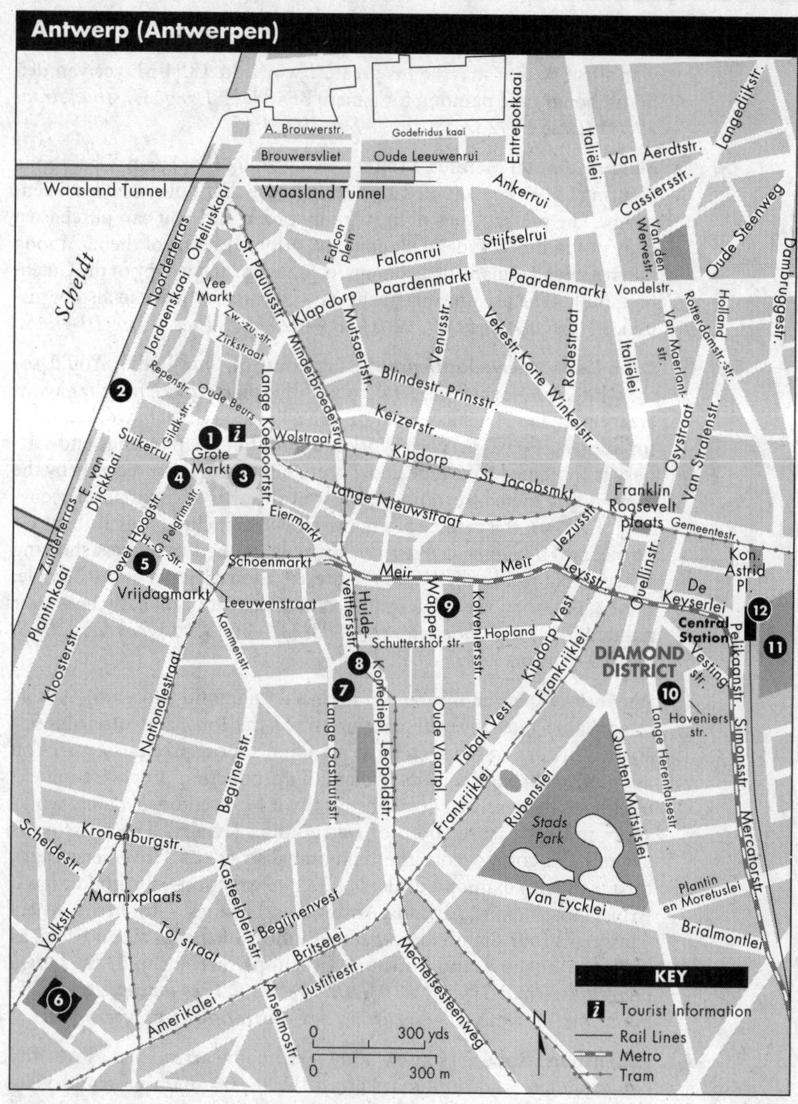

Bourlaschouwburg, **8**
Centraal Station, **12**
Dierentuin, **11**
Grote Market, **1**
Koninklijk Museum voor Schone Kunsten, **6**
Museum Mayer van den Bergh, **7**
Museum Plantin-Moretus, **5**
Onze-Lieve-Vrouwekathedraal, **3**
Provinciaal Diamantmuseum, **10**
Rubenshuis, **9**
Steen, **2**
Vlaeykensgang, **4**

displayed in the small museum that bears his name. The masterpiece is Bruegel's *Dulle Griet* (referred to in English as *Mad Meg*), an antiwar allegory that may be his greatest work. In 1894 Mayer van den Bergh bought the painting for a mere BF488. ✉ *Lange Gasthuisstraat 19,* ☎ *03/232–4237.* ⏲ *Tues.–Sun. 10–4:45.*

★ ❺ **Museum Plantin-Moretus.** Printer to King Philip II of Spain, Christophe Plantin (1514–89) founded a printing house that flourished for 3 centuries. The presses are still in working order, and you can purchase a copy of Plantin's "Ode to Happiness" printed on one of them. Among the treasures are many first editions, engravings, and a copy of the Gutenberg Bible. The private apartments and editorial offices can also be visited. ✉ *Vrijdagmarkt 22,* ☎ *03/233–0294.* ⏲ *Tues.–Sun. 10–4:45.*

★ ❸ **Onze-Lieve-Vrouwekathedraal** (Cathedral of Our Lady). You'll see the white, 400-ft spire of Antwerp's Gothic masterpiece from far away. Starting in 1352, a succession of remarkable architects worked on it for almost 200 years. Their work remains, but the paintings and statuary it contained have repeatedly been plundered, most recently by the army of the French revolution. Most of the artwork was never recovered. Even so, the cathedral's many treasures include four Rubens altarpieces. His *Descent from the Cross* is flanked by panels showing Mary's visit to Elizabeth and the presentation of Jesus in the Temple; these are among the tenderest and most delicate Biblical scenes ever painted. ✉ *Handschoenmarkt,* ☎ *03/231–3033.* ⏲ *Weekdays 10–5, Sat. 10–3, Sun. 1–4.*

❿ **Provinciaal Diamantmuseum** (Provincial Diamond Museum). At this remarkable museum, the exhibits trace the long and often bloodstained history of the search for mankind's most precious gems. You are guided through the entire diamond production process, from extraction to the sparkling gem. There's also a 19th-century diamond workshop and a treasure room of outstanding jewelry. The museum is around the corner from the **diamond district** (✉ Hoveniersstraat), thronged with diamond dealers of every extraction—Orthodox Jews, Armenians, Indians, Africans, Australians, Lebanese—for here is where Antwerp's four diamond *bourses* and most of the diamond firms, as well as polishing and cutting workshops, are located. ✉ *Lange Herentalsestraat 31–33,* ☎ *03/202–4890.* *Free (except special exhibitions).* ⏲ *Daily 10–5; cutting demonstrations Sat. afternoon.*

❾ **Rubenshuis** (Rubens House). In this setting the artist lived as wealthy court painter and diplomat. From the mezzanine one could view Rubens and his pupils at work. He lived on this site from 1610 until his death in 1640. The patrician mansion is a reconstruction, but it does give a vivid impression of his life and times. There are a few Rubens originals in the house, but nothing like the 300 paintings that his widow promptly disposed of when he died. ✉ *Wapper 9,* ☎ *03/232–4751.* ⏲ *Tues.–Sun. 10–4:45.*

❷ **Steen.** This 9th-century fortress is the oldest building in Antwerp. It was used as a prison for centuries, and the crucifix where condemned men said their final prayers is still in place. The Steen now houses the **National Maritime Museum.** ✉ *Steenplein,* ☎ *03/232–0850.* ⏲ *Tues.–Sun. 10–5.*

❹ **Vlaeykensgang.** Time has stood still in this cobblestone alley in the center of town, which captures the mood and style of the 16th century. There's no better place to linger on a Monday night, when the carillon concert rings out from the Cathedral.

Dining and Lodging

The Flemish and the Dutch may share the same language, but when it comes to cuisine, they are poles apart. Dining in Antwerp's many fine restaurants has a distinctly French flavor, making full use of the excellent ingredients from the surrounding sea and farmland. Naturally, seafood has pride of place on the dinner tables of this port city. For price-category definitions, ☞ Dining *in* Belgium A to Z, *above.*

The Antwerp City Tourist Office (☞ Antwerp Essentials, *below*) keeps track of the best hotel prices and can make reservations for you up to a week in advance. Write or fax for a reservation form. It also maintains a list of some 25 recommended bed-and-breakfast accommodations from BF1,200 to BF2,000. For details and price-category definitions, *see* Lodging *in* Belgium A to Z, *above.*

$$$$ ✕ **'t Fornuis.** In the heart of Old Antwerp, this old and cozy restaurant, decorated in traditional Flemish style, serves arguably the best food in the city at the steepest prices. Suckling lamb is one specialty, truffled sweetbreads with green cabbage another. ✉ *Reyndersstraat 24,* ☎ *03/233–9903. Reservations essential. Jacket and tie. AE, DC, MC, V. Closed weekends and 3 wks in Aug.*

$$$ ★ ✕ **De Matelote.** The gifted chef at this tiny restaurant in a narrow, Old City street concocts such inventive dishes as grilled asparagus with fresh morels and a poached egg, or langoustines in a light curry sauce. The chef knows how to ennoble fish like brill or skate, and local gourmets consider this the best fish restaurant in town. For dessert, try the outstanding crème brûlée. ✉ *Haarstraat 9,* ☎ *03/231–3207. Reservations essential. Jacket and tie. AE, DC, MC, V. Closed Sun., 2 wks in Jan. and July.*

$$$ ★ ✕ **Neuze Neuze.** Five tiny houses have been cobbled together to create a handsome, split-level restaurant with whitewashed walls, dark-brown beams, and a blazing fireplace. The chef produces such inventive and contemporary dishes as sautéed goose liver with caramelized pineapple, or sea scallops with endives in a white beer sauce. ✉ *Wijngaardstraat 19,* ☎ *03/232–5783. AE, DC, MC, V. Closed Sun. and 2 wks in summer. No lunch Sat.*

$$ ✕ **Hungry Henrietta.** Father and son run this Antwerp institution, next to the church where Rubens is buried. It's a stylish place, and in good weather you can dine in the garden. Fillet of salmon with endives, quail salad, and leg of lamb are on the menu. ✉ *Sint-Jacobsstraat 17,* ☎ *03/232–2928. AE, DC, MC, V. Closed weekends, 2 wks at Easter, Aug.*

$$ ★ ✕ **Sir Anthony Van Dijk.** On Antwerp's most famous and romantic alley, the stylish brasserie has tables grouped around stone pillars under high, massive beams. The fare includes such items as salad liègeoise with smoked salmon and caramelized onions, duck à l'orange, and tuna steak. There are two seatings a night. ✉ *Vlaeykensgang, Oude Koornmarkt 16,* ☎ *03/231–6170. Reservations essential. AE, DC, MC, V. Closed Sun., 3 wks in Aug.*

$ ✕ **Foyer.** If you don't get the chance to witness a performance at the Bourla Theater, you owe it to yourself to take in its Foyer. This very handsome café-restaurant serves a buffet lunch and snacks from noon to midnight. ✉ *Komedieplaats 18,* ☎ *03/253–5517. Reservations not accepted. No credit cards.*

$ ✕ **Kiekekot.** Antwerp students satisfy their craving for spit-roasted chicken and french fries at this no-frills "chicken coop," which offers a juicy half chicken for about $7, little more than its retail price, from 6 PM to 4 AM (Fri. and Sat. until 6 AM). ✉ *Grote Markt 35,* ☎ *03/232–1502. No credit cards. Closed Tues.*

$ ✕ **Ulcke van Zurich.** Much favored by the young-at-heart, this trendy dinner spot in the Old Town serves chicken salad, spareribs, or chicken-liver mousse with port every night from 6 PM until late. ✉ *Oude Beurs 50,* ☎ *03/234-0494. Reservations essential. No credit cards.*

$ ✕ **Zuiderterras.** A stark glass-and-black-metal construction, this riverside café and restaurant was designed by avant-garde architect bOb (his spelling) Van Reeth. Here you can have a light meal for about $15 and enjoy seeing the river traffic on one side and, on the other, a view of the cathedral and the Old Town. ✉ *Ernest Van Dijckkaai 37,* ☎ *03/234–1275. Reservations not accepted. AE, DC, MC, V.*

$$$$ **Antwerp Hilton.** The five stories of the Hilton (from 1993) are architecturally compatible with the much older buildings on Groenplaats, to the extent that you almost don't see the hotel. Rooms are equipped with three telephones, safes, and desks. Afternoon tea is served in the marble-floor lobby, and if you want to throw a party, there's a ballroom for 1,000 guests. The restaurant, Het Vyfde Seizoen, will satisfy gourmets. ✉ *Groenplaats, 2000,* ☎ *03/204–1212,* FAX *03/204–1213. 199 rooms, 12 suites. 2 restaurants. AE, DC, MC, V.*

$$$$ ★ **De Witte Lelie.** Three step-gabled 17th-century houses have been combined to make the White Lily Antwerp's most exclusive hotel (opened in 1993). Personal service is the watchword in the 10-room hotel, decorated mostly in white, with colorful carpets and modern art on the walls. Decanters of sherry and port await guests in all rooms, and sumptuous breakfasts are served on a loggia opening up on the inner courtyard. ✉ *Keizerstraat 16-18, 2000,* ☎ *03/226–1966,* FAX *03/234–0019. 7 rooms, 3 suites. Breakfast room. AE, DC, MC, V.*

$$$ **Classic Hotel Villa Mozart.** This small, modern hotel in an old building in a pedestrian area could not be more central: next door to the cathedral. The rooms, equipped with business-class features, air-conditioning, and electronic safes, are slightly cramped, but many overlook the cathedral. ✉ *Handschoenmarkt 3, 2000,* ☎ *03/231–3031,* FAX *03/231–5685. 25 rooms. Restaurant. AE, DC, MC, V.*

$$ ★ **Firean.** An Art Deco gem built in 1929, Firean offers the personal service of a family-operated hotel. Rooms are decorated in pastels, offset by rich fabrics. There's a tiny bar-cum–breakfast room, where eggs are served in floral-print cozies. The location is not central, but a tram to the Old Town runs outside the door. ✉ *Karel Oomsstraat 6, 2018,* ☎ *03/237–0260,* FAX *03/238–1168. 11 rooms, 6 in annex next door. AE, DC, MC, V.*

$$ **Hyllit.** The Hyllit (1995) stands on the corner of De Keyserlaan, Antwerp's prestige shopping street, with its entrance on Appelmansstraat, the gateway to the diamond district (reception on second floor). Rooms are decorated in muted colors and equipped with office-type desks; suites have a fax as well. There's a roof-top buffet breakfast room and full room service. ✉ *De Keyserlei 28–30, 2018,* ☎ *03/202–6800,* FAX *03/202–6890. 24 rooms, 56 suites. Breakfast room. AE, DC, MC, V.*

$ **Pension Cammerpoorte.** In this simple but pleasant hotel, the rooms (some with a view of the cathedral) are decorated in bright pastels and sad-clown art. A buffet breakfast, included in the price, is served in the tidy brick-and-lace café downstairs. There's no elevator. ✉ *Steenhouwersvest 55, 2000,* ☎ *03/231–2836,* FAX *03/226–2968. 9 rooms with shower. AE, DC, MC, V.*

Shopping

To the fashion-conscious, Antwerp has become a center second only to Milan, thanks to a group of designers who burst on the scene as the Antwerp Six. Inspired by their success, other young designers of fashion items have achieved prominence; check out the boutiques along

Huidewetterstraat and Schuttershofstraat. Ready-to-wear by Ann Demeulemeester and Dirk Bikkenbergs can be found at **Louis** (⊠ Lombardenstraat 2, ☎ 03/232–9872). **Dries Van Nooten** (⊠ Kammenstraat 18, ☎ 03/233–9437) has his own beautiful new boutique.

If you plan to invest in diamonds, it makes sense to do so in the world's leading diamond center. If you're not an expert, your best bet is **Diamondland** (⊠ Appelmansstraat 33a, ☎ 03/234–3612), in whose spectacular showrooms you can see both loose and mounted diamonds. Among the hundreds of diamond jewelers, three stand out: **Frohmann Fréres** (Pelikaanstraat 54, ☎ 03/231–1643); **J. Katz** (⊠ Appelmansstraat 19, ☎ 03/231–9780); and **Slaets** (⊠ De Keyserlei 46–48, ☎ 03/233–5373).

Antwerp Essentials

Arriving and Departing

BY CAR

Expressways from Amsterdam, Eindhoven, Aachen, Liège, Brussels, and Ghent converge on Antwerp's inner-city ring expressway. It's a 10-lane racetrack, so be sure you maneuver into the correct lane well before you exit.

BY PLANE

Antwerp International Airport (☎ 03/218–1211 for flight information) is 3 km (2 mi) southeast of the city. There are several flights a day to and from London City Airport. Most passengers arrive via Brussels National Airport (Zaventem), which is linked with Antwerp by hourly bus service (50 minutes one-way).

Between Antwerp Airport and Downtown. Buses to Antwerp's Centraal Station leave about every 20 minutes; travel time is about 15 minutes.

BY TRAIN

Frequent fast trains run between Antwerp (Centraal Station (☎ 03/233–3915) and Brussels; the trip takes 35 minutes.

Getting Around

In the downtown area, the tram is the most convenient means of transportation. Some lines have gone underground (look for signs marked M); the most useful line runs between Centraalstation (metro stop Diamant) and the Groenplaats (for the old city). A single ride costs BF40, a 10-ride ticket BF280, and a day pass BF110. For detailed transportation maps, stop at the tourist office.

Contacts and Resources

GUIDED TOURS

Orientation. Touristram (Groenplaats, ☎ 03/480–9388) operates 50-minute tram tours with cassette commentary in the Old City and old harbor area. Tickets (BF125) are sold on the tram. Qualified **personal guides** can be engaged through the City Tourist Office, which requires a couple of days' notice. The price for two hours is BF1,500.

Special Interest. Flandria (☎ 03/231–3100) operates 50-minute boat trips on the River Scheldt, departing from the Steenplein pontoon (next to the Steen) from Easter through September (BF250), as well as boat tours of the enormous port (2½ hours), which leave from Quay 13 near Londonstraat, May–August (BF400).

VISITOR INFORMATION

Toerisme Stad Antwerpen (Antwerp City Tourist Office; ⊠ Grote Markt 15, ☎ 03/232–0103, FAX 03/231–1937).

GHENT

Ghent—spelled Gent in Flemish and known to French speakers as Gand—is the home of one of the world's greatest works of art, Van Eyck's *Adoration of the Mystic Lamb.* This dynamic modern city has a center straight out of the Middle Ages. It was weavers from Ghent, joined by others from Brugge, who took up arms to defeat the French cavalry in 1302. Charles V (1500–58), destined to become Holy Roman Emperor and King of Spain, was born here, but that did not prevent an uprising against Spanish rule from being cruelly crushed. Centuries later, a weaver saved Ghent from decline by stealing a newfangled spinning mule from England and starting Ghent's industrial revolution. Later, socialists battled here for workers' rights, and Ghent became the site of Belgium's first Flemish-speaking university.

Exploring Ghent

The best spot to start a walk around the center is Sint-Michielsbrug (St. Michael's Bridge), with its view of Ghent's three glorious medieval steeples. The closest is the early Gothic Sint-Niklaaskerk (St. Nicholas's Church); behind it is the Belfort (Belfry) from 1314. In the background rises the honey-color tower of Sint-Baafskathedraal (St. Bavo's Cathedral) in Brabant Gothic. The classic walk around the Old City takes you up to the Castle of the Counts, and then, on the opposite shore of the River Leie, to the Town Hall and the Cathedral. Many historic buildings are lit up every night from May through October (and Friday and Saturday nights the rest of the year), making an evening walk a memorable experience.

Belfort (The Belfry). Three hundred feet high, it symbolizes the power of the guilds during the 14th century. The spire was added in 1913, based on the original plans. A 52-bell carillon hangs on the fifth floor. ✉ *Sint-Baafsplein,* ☎ *09/233–3954.* ⏲ *Mid-Apr.–mid-Nov., daily 10–12:30 and 2–5:30. Guided visits at 10 mins past the hr.*

★ **Graslei.** This pier along the Leie River, between St. Michael's Bridge and Gras Bridge, is best seen from the Korenlei across the river. Once the center of Ghent's trade, it is lined with a row of Baroque guild houses and other buildings, among them the 12th-century **Koornstapelhuis** (Granary), used for 600 years.

Gravensteen. The ancient Castle of the Counts of Flanders hulks up like an enormous battleship near the confluence of the Leie with the Lieve Canal, the 700-year-old waterway that links the city with Brugge. First erected in 1180, the castle has been rebuilt a number of times, most recently during the 19th century. Its display of torture instruments and its dungeon indicate how feudal justice was meted out. The spinning mules that made Ghent a textile center to rival Manchester were first installed here. ✉ *Sint-Veerleplein,* ☎ *09/225–9306.* ⏲ *Apr.–Sept., daily 9–6; Oct.–Mar., daily 9–5.*

★ **Sint-Baafskathedraal** (St. Bavo's Cathedral). In the De Villa Chapel is the stupendous 24-panel *Adoration of the Mystic Lamb,* completed on May 6, 1432, by Jan Van Eyck (1389–1441), who is said to have invented the technique of painting with oil. His brother Hubert worked on the painting for four years until his death in 1426, and Jan was brought from Brugge to finish it. Its central panel is based on Revelation 14:1: "And I looked, and, lo, a Lamb stood on Mt. Sion, and with him a hundred forty and four thousand." Van Eyck used a miniaturist technique to express the universal; realism, to portray spirituality. To the medieval viewer, the painting was a theological summation of all things revealed about the relationship between God and the world. Over the centuries, the painting has been stolen and recovered a number of times. The cathedral has several other treasures, notably a Rubens masterpiece, *The Vocation of St. Bavo,* in which the artist painted himself as a convert in a red cloak. ✉ *Sint-Baafsplein. Cathedral:* ⌚ *Daily 8:30–6. No visits during services.* ⌚ *Apr.–Oct., Mon.–Sat. 9:30–noon and 2–6, Sun. 1–6; Nov.–Mar., Mon.–Sat., 10:30–noon and 2:30–4, Sun. 2–5*

Stadhuis (Town Hall). You notice immediately that this building reflects two distinct architectural styles. The older Gothic section, with its lacelike tracery, was begun early in the 16th century. The structure was finished at the end of the same century in a more sober Renaissance style. ✉ *Botermarkt,* ☎ *09/266–5288.* ⌚ *Guided visits only, May–Oct., Mon.–Thurs. at 3.*

Dining and Lodging

Ghent's contribution to Belgian gastronomy is a creamy fish and vegetable stew called waterzooi, and it's on most menus. For price-category definitions, *see* Dining *in* Belgium A to Z, *above.*

A number of Ghent hotels catering to exhibition and trade fair visitors stand near the Expo Center. There are not so many in the Old Town, but they do include the oldest hotel in Europe. For price-category definitions, *see* Lodging *in* Belgium A to Z, *above.*

$$$ ★ ✕ **Waterzooi.** This tiny restaurant stands on a square distinguished by 16th- and 17th-century buildings. It serves such specialties as turbot with goose liver and asparagus, and lobster-filled ravioli with tarragon. ✉ *Sint-Veerleplein 2,* ☎ *09/225–0563. Reservations essential. Jacket and tie. AE, DC, MC, V. Closed Wed., Sun., and 3 wks in Aug.*

$$ ★ ✕ **'t Buikske Vol.** Patershol, formerly a district where textile workers lived, has become a charming residential area. Probably the best among nouveau-chic Patershol's trendy eateries, the Buikske Vol delights diners with such well-prepared dishes as grilled turbot and roast lobster. ✉ *Kraanlei 17,* ☎ *09/225–1880. Jacket and tie. AE, MC, V. Closed Sun., Wed., Easter wk, and 1st ½ Aug. No lunch Sat.*

$$ ★ ✕ **Het Cooremetershuis.** One flight up in an ancient guild house on the Graslei is this venturesome little restaurant. It's noted for such well-executed contemporary dishes as marinated salmon with soy shoots and fillet of lamb with oriental spices. ✉ *Graslei 12,* ☎ *09/223–4971. Reservations essential. Jacket and tie. AE, DC, MC, V. Closed Wed., Sun., and July 15–Aug. 15.*

$–$$ ✕ **Pakhuis.** An old warehouse has been skillfully converted into an enormously popular Parisian-style brasserie, with marble-top tables, parquet flooring, and a huge oak bar as the centerpiece. There's an oyster-and-shellfish bar to supplement such basic brasserie fare as knuckle of ham with mustard and steak tartare. ✉ *Schuurkenstraat 4,* ☎ *09/223–5555. AE, DC, MC, V. Closed Sun.*

$ ✕ **Taverne Keizershof.** Touristy taverns are much the same all over Belgium, but this one is popular with locals—always a good sign. The daily plates are large portions of good, solid foods, and all-day snacks include toasted sandwiches and spaghetti. ✉ *Vrijdagmarkt 47,* ☎ *09/223–4446. MC, V. Closed Sun.*

$$$ 🏨 **Sofitel.** The Ghent outpost of this comfortable, top-of-the-line French hotel chain, decorated in warm brown and beige, is excellently situated in the heart of the Old City. ✉ *Hoogpoort 63, 9000,* ☎ *09/233–3331,* FAX *09/233–1102. 126 rooms, 1 suite. Restaurant. AE, DC, MC, V.*

$$ **Gravensteen.** This handsome 19th-century mansion has been restored in Second Empire style. Rooms are freshly furbished, and 10 more luxurious rooms have been added (surcharge BF1,300). The canal-front location, close to the Castle of the Counts, is a great plus. ✉ *Jan Breydelstraat 35, 9000,* ☎ *09/225–1150,* FAX *09/225–1850. 27 rooms. AE, DC, MC, V.*

$$ **Sint-Jorishof.** Napoléon stayed here, and so, before him, did Mary of Burgundy and Emperor Charles V, for this is the oldest hotel in Europe. Much of its Gothic spirit has been preserved, especially in the reception area and the restaurant, which serves classic French fare. There are only four rooms in the main building. The rest are in an almost equally ancient annex across the street; seven, renovated, are higher priced. ✉ *Botermarkt 2, 9000,* ☎ *09/224–2424,* FAX *09/224–2640. 4 rooms in main building, 24 in annex. Restaurant. AE, DC, MC, V.*

$ ★ **Erasmus.** From the flagstone and wood-beam library-lounge to the stone mantels in the bedrooms, every inch of this noble 16th-century house has been scrubbed, polished, and bedecked with period ornaments. Even the tiny garden has been carefully manicured. ✉ *Poel 25, 9000,* ☎ *09/224–2195,* FAX *233–4241. 12 rooms. AE, DC, MC, V.*

Ghent Essentials

Arriving and Departing

BY CAR

Ghent is just off the six-lane E40 from Brussels, which continues to Brugge and the coast. Traffic can be bumper-to-bumper on summer weekends. It is generally lighter on the E17 from Antwerp, which continues to Lille and Paris.

BY TRAIN

Nonstop trains depart on the hour and 27 minutes past the hour from Gare du Midi in Brussels (☎ 02/203–3640 or 09/221–4444). Travel time to Ghent is 28 minutes.

Getting Around

Most of the sights are within a radius of ½ mi from the Town Hall, and by far the best way to see them is on foot. You can rent bikes at the train station, but car traffic is fairly heavy.

Contacts and Resources

GUIDED TOURS

Sightseeing boats (BF150, ⏲ Easter–Oct.) depart from landing stages at Graslei (☎ 09/282–9248) and Korenlei (☎ 09/223–8853) for 35-minute trips. Your Ghent experience can be much enhanced by a personal guide. Call **Gidsenbond van Gent** (Association of Ghent Guides; ☎ 09/233–0772, FAX 09/233–0865). The charge is BF1,500 for the first two hours; BF750 per additional hour.

VISITOR INFORMATION

Dienst voor Toerisme (Tourist Office; ✉ Belfort, Botermarkt 17a, ☎ 09/266–5232).

BRUGGE

Brugge (or Bruges, as it is known to French and most English speakers) represents the flowering of the Middle Ages. The city had the good fortune to be linked with the North Sea by a navigable waterway and became a leading member of the Hanseatic League during the 13th century. Splendid marriage feasts were celebrated here; that of Charles the Bold, Duke of Burgundy (1433–77), to Margaret of York in 1468 is commemorated in the annual Holy Blood Procession. Disaster struck when the link with the sea silted up during the 15th century, but this past misfortune is responsible for Brugge's present glory. Little has changed in this city of interlaced canals overhung with humpback bridges.

Exploring Brugge

Numbers in the margin correspond to points of interest on the Brugge (Bruges) map.

The center of Brugge is virtually reserved for pedestrians; you need to remember that cobbled streets call for good walking shoes. It's a fact that Brugge draws large numbers of visitors, but there's always a quiet corner away from the madding crowd. Try to do your exploring in the early evening when the trippers have left and Brugge is at its most magical.

★ 9 **Begijnhof** (Beguinage). The Begijnhof has been an oasis of peace for 750 years. The first Beguines were widows of fallen crusaders. They were not nuns but lived a devout life while serving the community. The close of small, whitewashed houses where they lived has retained its serenity. Although the last Beguines left in 1930, a Benedictine community has replaced them, and you may join them, discreetly, for vespers in their small church. ⊠ *Off Wijngaardstraat,* ☎ *050/330011.* ⊙ *Mar.–Nov., daily 10:30–noon and 1:45–5; Dec.–Feb., Wed.–Thurs. and weekends 2:45–4:45, Fri. 1:45–6.*

1 **Belfort** (The Belfry). There's a panoramic view of the town from the top of the 270-ft-high (366 steps!) Belfort, which dominates the Markt, the city's ancient market square. The Belfort has a carillon notable even in Belgium, where they are a matter of civic pride. On summer evenings, the Markt is brightly lighted. ⊠ *Markt 7.* ⊙ *Apr.–Sept., daily 9:30–5; Oct.–Mar., daily 9:30–12:30 and 1:30–5. Carillon concerts: Oct.–mid-June, Wed. and weekends 2:15–3; mid-June–Sept., Mon., Wed., and Sat. 9 PM–10 PM, Sun. 2:15–3.*

6 **Brangwyn Museum.** The institution is named for a Brugge-born English artist, Frank Brangwyn (1867–1956), many of whose paintings of Brugge are on view here. The ground floor is occupied by the **Kantmuseum** (Lace Museum), containing outstanding examples of a craft long and lovingly practiced in Brugge. ⊠ *Dijver 16,* ☎ *050/448711.* ⊙ *Apr.–Sept., daily 9:30–5; Oct.–Dec. and Feb.–Mar., Wed.–Mon. 9:30–12:30 and 2–5.*

★ 2 **Burg.** This magic, medieval square is the focal point of ancient Brugge. The **Stadhuis** (Town Hall), a jewel of Gothic architecture in white sandstone from the 14th century, has an ornate facade adorned with a multitude of statues. It is linked with the graceful, Renaissance **Oude Griffie** (Old Recorder's House) by a bridge arching over the narrow Blinde Ezelstraat, which leads down to the canal. ⊠ *Stadhuis: Burg 12.* ⊙ *Apr.–Sept., daily 9:30–5; Oct.–Mar., daily 9:30–12:30 and 2–5.*

★ 5 **Groeninge Museum.** Set back from the canal in a diminutive park, this small museum enjoys a worldwide reputation for its superb and wide-ranging collection of Flemish Primitives, including Van Eyck's *Virgin and Canon Van der Paele,* in which the prelate is so realistically rendered that physicians can diagnose the illness he suffered from; Memling's *Moreel Triptych,* arguably his most intensely spiritual work; Hieronymus Bosch's surrealistic *Last Judgment*; and Pieter Bruegel's *Preaching of John the Baptist.* ⊠ *Dijver 12,* ☎ *050/448711.* ⊙ *Apr.–Sept., daily 9:30–5; Oct.–Mar., Wed.–Mon. 9:30–12:30 and 2–5.*

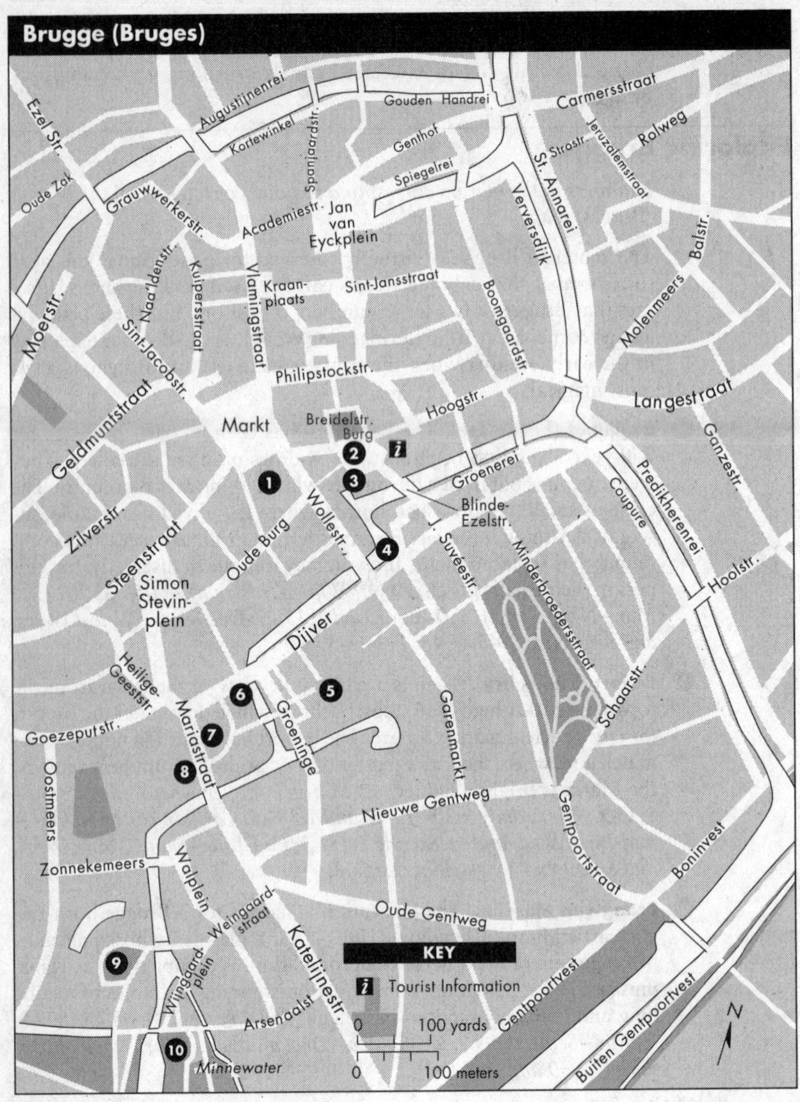

Begijnhof, **9**
Belfort, **1**
Brangwyn Museum, **6**
Burg, **2**
Groeninge Museum, **5**
Heilig-Bloed Basiliek, **3**
Memling Museum, **8**
Minnewater, **10**
Onze-Lieve Vrouwekerk, **7**
Reien, **4**

3 **Heilig-Bloed Basiliek** (Basilica of the Holy Blood). The Basilica stands on a corner of the Burg, next to the Town Hall. The Lower Chapel has kept its pure, austere 12th-century Romanesque character. The upper chapel, however, was rebuilt in Gothic style during the 15th century and was later decorated with 19th-century murals. The phial thought by some of the faithful to contain a few drops of the blood of Christ is exposed here every Friday. The **Heilig-Bloed Museum** (Museum of the Holy Blood) has a reliquary and exhibits of vestments and paintings. The **Procession of the Holy Blood** on Ascension Day (May 13 in 1999) combines religious and historical pageantry. ✉ *Burg. Museum* ⏲ *Apr.–Sept., daily 9:30–noon and 2–6; Oct.–Mar., daily 10–noon and 2–4. Closed Wed. afternoon.*

★ 8 **Memling Museum.** The museum is dedicated to the work of one of Brugge's most famous sons, the painter Hans Memling (?1440–94), perhaps the greatest and certainly the most spiritual of all early Flemish painters. The six masterpieces in the museum include the altarpiece *St. John the Baptist and St. John the Evangelist* and the fabulous miniatures adorning the St. Ursula shrine. The museum is housed in the former **Sint-Janshospitaal,** where the sick were nursed for 7 centuries. The 17th-century pharmacy can be visited. ✉ *Mariastraat 38,* ☎ *050/448711.* ⏲ *Apr.–Sept., daily 9:30–5; Oct.–Mar., Thurs.–Tues. 9:30–12:30 and 2–5.*

10 **Minnewater.** The enchanting body of water was once the city harbor and more recently has been known as the Lake of Love. The adjoining 16th-century lockkeeper's house is usually surrounded by white swans, the symbol of the city. ✉ *Off Wijngaardplein.*

7 **Onze-Lieve-Vrouwekerk** (Church of Our Lady). At 381 ft, the spire tower is Belgium's tallest. Inside, you'll find a notable collection of paintings and carvings—including Michelangelo's small *Madonna and Child*—and splendid tombs with the effigies of Duke Charles the Bold of Burgundy, who died on the battlefield in 1477 and his daughter, Mary, who married into the Hapsburg family and died in a riding accident at the age of 25. ✉ *Gruuthusestraat.* ⏲ *Mon.–Sat. 10–11:30 and 2:30–5 (until 4 on Sat.), Sun. 2:30–5 (Oct.–Mar. until 4:30).*

★ 4 **Reien** (Canals). The canals of Brugge with their old, arching stone bridges, to be explored both by boat and on foot along the quays, give the city its special character. From **Steenhouwersdijk** you see the brick rear gables, which are all that remains of the old county hall. Next to the little **Huidenvettersplein,** with its 17th-century guild houses, is **Rozenhoedkaai;** from here the view of the heart of Brugge includes the pinnacles of the Town Hall, the Basilica, and the Belfry.

Dining and Lodging

In some of Brugge's quiet streets stand restaurants that rank with Belgium's finest; the choice as well as the number of eating places is staggering. The Markt, however, is ringed with unremarkable restaurants catering to the tourist trade. For details and price-category definitions, ☞ Dining *in* Belgium A to Z, *above.*

In proportion to its size, Brugge has a large number of hotels, many of them romantic, canal-side residences, for this is a town where people like to come for a second honeymoon. Prices are relatively high, but so are the standards. Many hotels offer good value-for-money package deals. For details and price-category definitions, ☞ Lodging *in* Belgium A to Z, *above.*

$$$$ ★ ✕ **De Karmeliet.** Owner-chef Geert Van Hecke, one of Belgium's best, works in this lovely 18th-century house. His inventive, elaborate kitchen serves a festival of flavors: goose liver with truffled potatoes, roast langoustines with endives in an apple-and-curry juice, vanilla raviolis. ✉ *Langestraat 19, ☎ 050/338259. Reservations essential. Jacket and tie. AE, DC, MC, V. Closed Mon., 2 wks June–July and Jan. No dinner Sun.*

$ ✕ **Straffe Hendrik.** This daytime pub is attached to the brewery, dating from 1546, that produces the potent, crystal-clear, natural beer of the same name. It also serves quite acceptable pub grub, and you can tour the facilities. The square is among Brugge's most charming. ✉ *Walplein 26, ☎ 050/332697. No credit cards.*

$ ✕ **Taverne Oud Handbogenhof.** Here's an authentic Flemish inn, with a big courtyard shaded by linden trees. It's much favored by locals, always a good sign. Specialties are spareribs with garlic sauce and salmon with scallops and shrimps in white sauce. ✉ *Baliestraat 6, ☎ 050/331945. MC, V. Closed Mon., 1st wk July, Jan. No lunch Tues.*

$ ✕ **Tom Pouce.** This old tearoom has a superb location, right on the Burg. It serves lunch but is better known for warm apple strudel, airy waffles, and light, eggy pancakes. ✉ *Burg 17, ☎ 050/330336. Reservations not accepted. AE, DC, MC, V. Closed Mon.*

$$$ ✕🏨 **'t Bourgoensche Cruyce.** In a romantic canal-side setting, this restaurant has salmon-and-copper decor that is reflected in the water. The cuisine is equally romantic: panfried langoustines with wild mushrooms, tornedos of salmon with bacon, burbot medallions with coriander and caramelized leeks. Reservations and jacket and tie are essential; the restaurant is closed Tuesday and Wednesday and the first week in July. The establishment has eight cozy guest rooms furnished in traditional Flemish style; four face the canal. ✉ *Wollestraat 41, ☎ 050/337926, FAX 050/341968. 8 rooms. Restaurant. AE, DC, MC, V. Mid-Nov.–mid-Dec.*

$$$ ✕🏨 **Die Swaene.** This hotel has "romantic" written all over it: canal-side location, oxblood wallpaper, four-poster beds, candles, and marble nymphs in every nook and cranny.The restaurant ($$$$) is a serious contender as one of the best in this gourmet city: goose liver, sweetbreads, and grilled turbot are among its treats. It is closed Wednesday, three weeks in July, and three weeks in January and does not serve lunch on Thursday. ✉ *Steenhouwersdijk 1, 8000, ☎ 050/342798, FAX 050/3336674.19 rooms, 2 suites. Restaurant, pool. AE, DC, MC, V.*

$$ ✕🏨 **De Castillion.** This restaurant and hotel was the residence of 18th-century bishop Jean-Baptiste de Castillion. Predinner drinks and postprandial coffee are served in a handsome Art Deco salon. Fillet of venison in a Pomerol stock and a combination of burbot and scampi on a bed of tagliatelle with a curry sauce are among the offerings. Reservations and jacket and tie are required in the restaurant; there's no dinner on Sunday and no lunch Monday and Tuesday. The rooms in the hotel side vary considerably in size and price. Their decor ranges from rustic to modern. ✉ *Heilige Geeststraat 1, ☎ 050/343001, FAX 050/339475. 18 rooms, 2 suites. Restaurant. AE, DC, MC, V.*

$$$ ★ 🏨 **De Tuileriëen.** A mansion with Venetian glass windows was converted into this patrician hotel and decorated with discreet antique reproductions. The breakfast room has a coffered ceiling. Canal-side rooms have great views; courtyard rooms are quieter. ✉ *Dijver 7, 8000, ☎ 050/343691, FAX 050/340400. 24 rooms, 1 suite. Pool. AE, DC, MC, V.*

$$$ 🏨 **Walburg.** One of Brugge's grandest 19th-century town houses, a few blocks from the Burg, was converted into a hotel in 1996. The rooms, decorated in different color schemes, with period Marie Antoinette furniture and marble bathrooms, are a generous 750 square ft—and the suite twice as large. ✉ *Boomgaardstraat 13, 8000, ☎ 050/349414, FAX 050/336884. 12 rooms, 1 suite. Restaurant, bar. AE, DC, MC, V.*

$$ ★ **Egmond.** Every room in this manorlike inn on Minnewater has garden views, as well as parquet floors and the odd fireplace or dormer ceiling. The hotel is a pleasant retreat from the bustle of the center, 10 minutes away. The bathrooms, an afterthought, are tiny. ✉ *Minnewater 15, 8000,* ☎ *050/341445,* FAX *050/342940. 8 rooms. No credit cards.*

$ ★ **De Pauw.** At this spotless, family-run hotel, the warmly furnished rooms have names rather than numbers, and breakfast comes with six different kinds of bread, cold cuts, and cheese. The two rooms that share a shower down the hall are a super value. ✉ *Sint-Gilliskerkhof 8, 8000,* ☎ *050/337118,* FAX *050/345140. 8 rooms (6 with bath). AE, DC, MC, V.*

Brugge Essentials

Arriving and Departing

BY CAR

Brugge is about an hour's drive from Brussels on the E40 motorway to the coast. Holiday weekend traffic is often heavy. Unless you are driving to a hotel, leave your car at one of the parking lots or garages at the entrance to the Old City.

BY TRAIN

Trains run hourly at 28 and 59 minutes past the hour from Brussels (Gare du Midi) to Brugge. The station is south of the canal that circles the downtown area; for train information, call 050/382382. Travel time from Brussels is 53 minutes.

Getting Around

The center of Brugge is best explored on foot, as car and bus access is severely restricted. This makes for bicycle heaven; ask the tourist office (☞ *below*) for information on where to rent one.

Contacts and Resources

GUIDED TOURS

Boat trips along the city canals are run by several companies and depart from five separate landings. Boats ply the waters March–November, daily 10–6. They leave every 10–15 minutes, and a 30-minute trip costs BF170. The **horse-drawn carriages** that congregate in the Markt are an expensive way of seeing the sights. They are available March–November, daily 10–6; a 35-minute trip will cost BF900. The carriages take up to five people. Fifty-minute **minibus tours** of the city center leave every hour on the hour from the Markt in front of the post office. Commentaries are given in seven languages (individual headphones) and cost BF380.

VISITOR INFORMATION

Toerism Brugge (Brugge Tourist Office; ✉ Burg 11, ☎ 050/448686, FAX 050/448600). Contact them well in advance for tickets to the Holy Blood Procession (Heilig-Bloed Basiliek, *above*).

6 Bulgaria

Sofia, the Black Sea Coast, Inland Bulgaria

Bulgaria, with mountains and seasides, modern cities and medieval villages, is an enigmatic land where rustic beauty exists alongside decaying remnants of a communist past. Lying in the eastern half of the Balkan Peninsula, Bulgaria was the closest ally of the former Soviet Union and has always presented a mysterious image to the West. Their alliance ended in 1989 with the overthrow of Communist party head Todor Zhivkov. Since then, Bulgaria, which is striving to become a member of the European Union, has struggled toward democracy and a free-market economy.

Except for a brief reign by the opposition party in 1992, the Socialist party (containing many members from the former Communist party) has held power since 1989. However, corruption, massive unemployment, and skyrocketing inflation resulting in a decreasing standard of living have severely tested the patience of Bulgarians for years. The national desire for change was reflected in the victory of opposition candidate Peter Stoyanov in the presidential elections of late 1996. In January of 1997, as the lev plunged, the people of Bulgaria took to the streets. Month-long protests and strikes immobilized the country and forced the government to hold early elections (the ruling Socialist party still officially had two years to go in power). April 1997 elections gave the opposition coalition (UDF; Union of Democratic Forces) a plurality. Though the lev has stabilized, it is still doubtful that the fledgling government will pull Bulgaria out of the economic crisis that's made it one of the poorest countries in Europe. Visitors, however, are not likely to be affected by the plight of the economy. Foods and goods are plentiful and, for those living on a Western salary, very inexpensive.

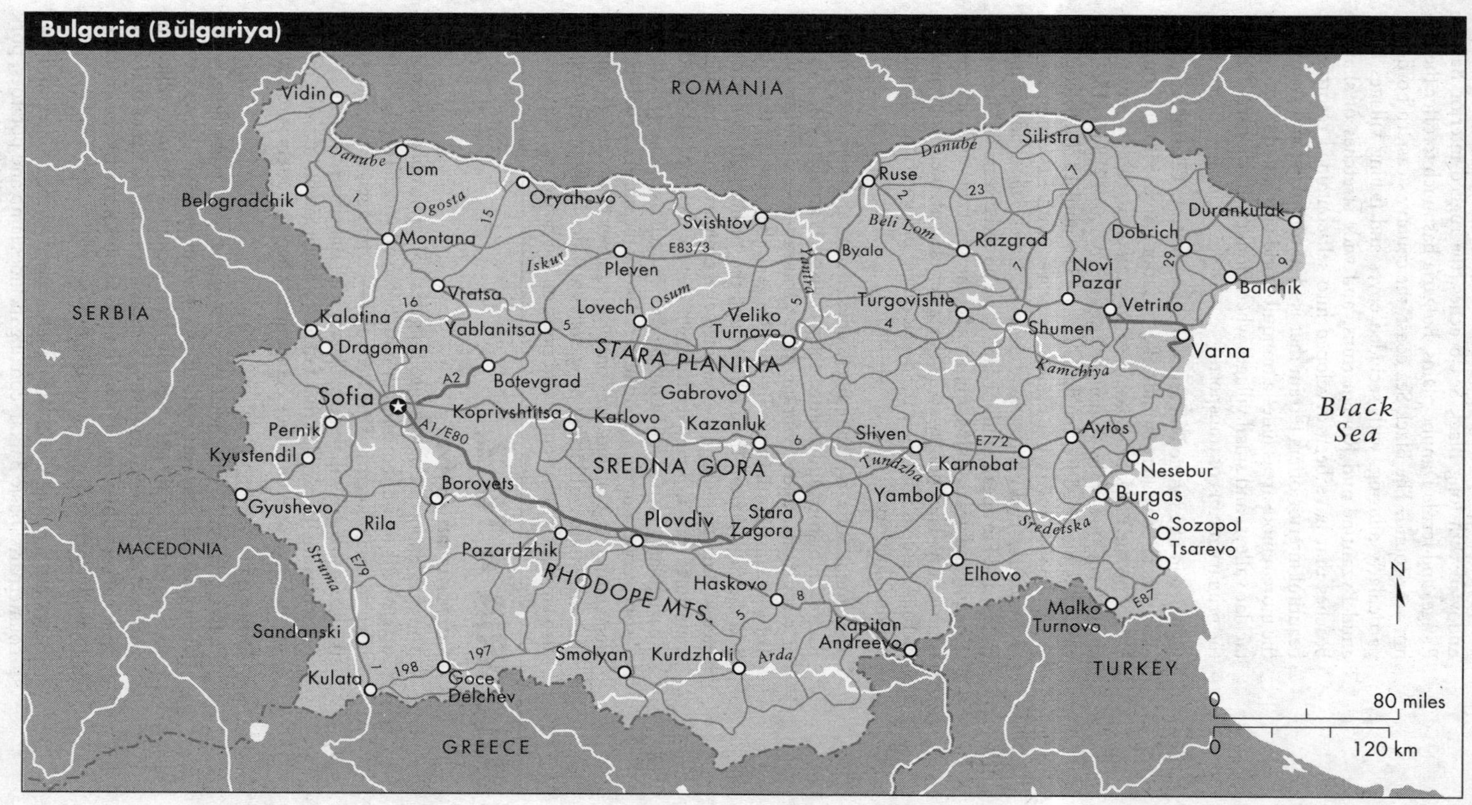
Bulgaria (Bŭlgariya)
ROMANIA
SERBIA
MACEDONIA
GREECE
TURKEY
Black Sea
Vidin
Lom
Belogradchik
Oryahovo
Montana
Svishtov
Pleven
E83/3
Byala
Ruse
Silistra
Razgrad
Dobrich
Durankulak
Balchik
Novi Pazar
Vetrino
Varna
Shumen
Turgovishte
Veliko Turnovo
Lovech
Yablanitsa
Vratsa
Kalotina
Dragoman
Botevgrad
Sofia
Pernik
Kyustendil
Gyushevo
Rila
Koprivshtitsa
Karlovo
Kazanluk
Gabrovo
STARA PLANINA
SREDNA GORA
Sliven
Karnobat
Aytos
Nesebur
Burgas
Sozopol
Tsarevo
Yambol
Stara Zagora
Plovdiv
Borovets
Pazardzhik
RHODOPE MTS.
Haskovo
Elhovo
Malko Turnovo
Kapitan Andreevo
Kurdzhali
Smolyan
Goce Delchev
Sandanski
Kulata
Danube
Ogosta
Iskur
Osum
Yantra
Beli Lom
Kamchiya
Tundzha
Sredetska
Arda
Struma
A1/E80
A2
E772
E87
E79
1
2
4
5
6
7
8
9
15
16
23
29
197
198
N
0
80 miles
0
120 km

Endowed with long Black Sea beaches, the rugged interior Balkan Range, and fertile Danube plains, Bulgaria has much to offer the visitor year-round. The Black Sea coast, the country's eastern border, is particularly alluring, with secluded coves and fishing villages built amid Byzantine and Roman ruins, and wide stretches of shallow beaches that have been developed into self-contained resorts. The beautiful interior offers terrain that is ideal for hiking and skiing. In the more remote areas hides a tranquil world of forested ridges, spectacular valleys, and small villages where donkey-drawn carts are still the primary means of transport.

Founded in 681 by the Bulgars, a Turkic tribe from Central Asia, Bulgaria was already a crossroads of civilization. Archaeological finds in Varna, on the Black Sea coast, give proof of civilization from as early as 4600 BC. Part of the Byzantine Empire from AD 1018 to 1185, Bulgaria was occupied by the Turks from 1396 until 1878. Today, Bulgaria remains a dizzying blend of cultures, with Eastern-influenced architecture, Turkish fast-food aromas, Greek ruins, Soviet monuments, and European outdoor cafés. Five hundred years of Muslim occupation and nearly half a century of communist rule did not wipe out Christianity. The country's 120 monasteries, with their icons and numerous frescoes, chronicle the development of Bulgarian cultural and national identity.

The capital, Sofia, is picturesquely situated in a valley near Mt. Vitosha. Rich with history and culture, the city also has good hotels, a variety of restaurants, and a vibrant Mediterranean-style nightlife. Veliko Turnovo, just north of the Balkan Range in the center of the country and the capital from the 12th through the 14th centuries during the Second Bulgarian Empir still has medieval ramparts and vernacular architecture. Plovdiv, a university town, lies southeast of Sofia and has a particularly picturesque Old Quarter as well as one of the world's best-preserved Roman amphitheaters. Varna, the site of one of Europe's first cultural settlements, was once the summer beach playground for the entire Eastern Bloc but now draws a wider array of visitors. It is also among the most important ports on the Black Sea.

BULGARIA A TO Z

Customs on Arrival

You may import duty-free into Bulgaria 250 grams of tobacco products, plus 1 liter of hard liquor and 2 liters of wine. Travelers are advised to declare items of greater value—computers, camcorders, and the like—so there will be no problems with Bulgarian customs officials on departure. Be advised that failure to declare items of value can result in a fine or even police detainment when you attempt to leave.

Dining

In Bulgaria you have a choice between predictable hotel dining, which often includes international cuisines, and more adventurous outings to private restaurants or cafés where the menu may be in Cyrillic. The best bets are the small folk-style restaurants called mehanas that serve regional specialties. In a crowded mehana, it is perfectly acceptable to sit with others if there are no free tables.

Bulgarian national dishes are closely related to their Greek and Slav counterparts: basic Balkan cooking includes lamb and potatoes, pork sausages called *kebapche,* and a popular salad called *shopska salata* made with feta-style sheep cheese, tomatoes, cucumbers, peppers, and onions. Bulgaria produces sumptuous fruits and vegetables. Try the rich, amber-color *bolgar* grapes and orange-red apricots. Bulgaria invented *kiselo mlyako* (yogurt), and there is excellent *tarator* (cold yogurt soup with sliced cucumber and garlic) in summer. *Banitsa* (butter, cheese, and phyllo dough pastry) is often eaten for breakfast. Syrupy baklava and chocolate or *palachinki* (nut- and honey-stuffed crepes) are favorite desserts.

Bulgarian wines are good, usually full-bodied, dry, and inexpensive. The national drink is *rakia*—either *slivova* (plum) or *grozdova* (grape) brandy—but other hard alcohol and beer are popular, too. Coffee is strong and is often drunk along with a cold beverage, such as cola or a lemon drink. Tea is taken with lemon rather than milk.

RATINGS

Prices are per person and include a first course, main course, dessert, and tip, but no alcohol.

CATEGORY	COST
$$$$	over 20,000 leva
$$$	12,000 leva–20,000 leva
$$	7,000 leva–12,000 leva
$	under 7,000 leva

WHAT TO WEAR

In Sofia, formal dress (jacket and tie) is customary at $$$$ restaurants. Casual dress is appropriate elsewhere.

Language

The official language, Bulgarian, is written in Cyrillic and is close to Old Church Slavonic, the root of all Slavic languages. English, though becoming popular with the young, is rarely understood outside major hotels and restaurants. It is essential to remember that in Bulgaria a nod of the head means "no" and a shake of the head means "yes."

Lodging

There is a wide choice of accommodations, ranging from the old, state-run hotels—most of them dating from the '60s and '70s—to new, private hotels, apartment rentals, rooms in private homes, and campsites. Although hotels are improving, the older ones still tend to suffer from temperamental wiring and erratic plumbing; pack a universal drain plug, as plugs are often missing in bathrooms.

HOTELS

Until recently most hotels used by Western visitors were owned by Balkantourist and Interhotels. At press time many of the government-owned or -operated hotels were on the verge of privatization. During the conversion hotels may be closed for renovation. Private hotels are opening as well. Outside Sofia call ahead to hotels to get the latest information. Most hotels have restaurants and bars; the large, modern ones have swimming pools, shops, and other facilities.

PRIVATE ACCOMMODATIONS

Staying in private homes, with arrangements made by private-room agencies, is becoming a popular alternative to hotels; it not only cuts costs but also means increased contact with Bulgarians. Booking offices are located in most main tourist areas. In Sofia contact **Balkantour Ltd.** (✉ 27 bul. Stamboliiski, ☎ 02/988–55–43). **Balkan Tourist** (✉ 1 bul. Vitosha, ☎ 02/87–51–92) can help with Sofia lodgings. Bring your own towels, soap, and other necessities.

RENTED ACCOMMODATIONS

Rented accommodations are a growth industry, with planned modern complexes as well as picturesque cottages. Cooking facilities tend to be meager, and meal vouchers are included in the deal. An English-speaking manager is generally on hand. Such accommodations usually aren't offered in Sofia but can often be found on the Black Sea coast and in Plovdiv and Veliko Turnovo. Check with the agencies listed under Visitor Information (☞ *below*).

RATINGS

Prices are for two people in a double room with half board (breakfast and a main meal). At the leading hotels you can pay in either U.S. dollars or leva; the less expensive hotels accept only leva. Foreign currency can be exchanged for leva at the reception desk in most hotels. The price categories below are listed in U.S. dollars, as that is how hotel prices are usually quoted.

CATEGORY	SOFIA	OTHER AREAS
$$$$	over $200	over $100
$$$	$130–$200	$70–$100
$$	$70–$130	$40–$70
$	under $70	under $40

Mail

Letters up to 10 grams to North America cost 860 leva; to the United Kingdom, 700 leva. Rates change constantly with inflation, so ask for the current price at the post office.

Money Matters

COSTS

Bulgarians are facing increasing economic hardship due to rising prices and the devaluation of the lev; the favorable exchange rate makes prices seem extremely low by international standards. The greatest expense is lodging, but if you choose the more moderate hotels, accommodations won't be very expensive. It is possible to cut costs even more by staying in a private room in a Bulgarian house or apartment. Such expenses as taxi and public transport fares, museum and theater admissions, and meals in most restaurants are quite low.

CREDIT CARDS

The major international credit cards are accepted in a few larger stores and in the most expensive hotels and restaurants, but the list of accepted cards may not be correctly posted. Before you place an order, check to see whether or not you can use your card.

CURRENCY

The unit of currency in Bulgaria is the lev (plural leva). There are bills of 100, 200, 500, 1,000, 2,000, 5,000, 10,000, 20,000, and 50,000 leva. Bills smaller than 100 still exist, but their use is illegal as of 1998, so don't accept change in 20 or 50 leva bills. Ask for coins. Although prices are sometimes quoted in dollars, all goods and services (except the most expensive hotels and international airline tickets) must be paid for in leva. It is illegal to import or export large amounts of Bulgarian currency. You may import any amount of foreign currency, including traveler's checks, and exchange foreign currency at banks, hotels, airports, border posts, and the plentiful private exchange offices (which offer the best rates and take no commission), all of which quote their daily selling and buying rates. Bring new, clean U.S. bills, as counterfeiting is a recent phenomenon, and torn or marked currency will be turned away. Though it is possible to change traveler's checks at a few select locations, such as the airport and some major hotels, commissions are exorbitant. In small towns traveler's checks are worthless. ATMs exist but rarely work. The value of the lev continues to fluctuate, and the exchange rate and price information quoted here may be outdated very quickly. At press time the rate quoted by the Bulgarian State Bank is 1,770 leva to the U.S. dollar, 1,240 leva to the Canadian dollar, 2,960 leva to the pound sterling, 1,130 leva to the Australian dollar, and 974.6 leva to the New Zealand dollar.

SAMPLE PRICES

Because of fluctuating exchange rates, the following price list can be used only as a rough guide. A trip on a tram, trolley, or bus, 200 leva; theater ticket, 2,000–7,500 leva; coffee in a moderate restaurant, 300 leva; bottle of wine in a moderate restaurant, 4,000–9,000 leva; museum admission, 500–2,000 leva.

TIPPING

Tips of 10% of the bill are appropriate for waiters and taxi drivers; hotel employees also receive tips.

National Holidays

January 1; March 3 (Liberation Day); April 22, 23 (Orthodox Easter); May 1 (Labor Day); May 24 (Saints Cyril and Methodius—creators of the Cyrillic alphabet—Commemoration Day); December 24–26.

Opening and Closing Times

Banks are open weekdays 9–3. **Museums** are usually open 9–5 but are often closed on Monday or Tuesday. **Shops** are open Monday through Saturday 9–7. Some shops are open on Sunday. A few *denonoshni magazini* (day and night minimarkets) in the city center are open around the clock.

Passports and Visas

All visitors need a valid passport. Americans do not need visas when traveling as tourists for 30 days or less but are required to pay a $23 border tax upon entering the country. Other tourists, traveling independently, should inquire about visa requirements at a Bulgarian embassy or consulate before entering the country. Many package tours are exempt from the visa requirement. All tourists are given a "statistical card." This must be stamped everywhere you spend the night and is collected at the border as you leave the country. If you plan on staying in private homes rather than in hotels, you are required by law to register at the local police station within 48 hours of entering the county, or you risk a $100 fine at departure.

Telephoning

Local calls cost 2 leva and can be made from your hotel, from pay phones, or from the two types of card phones, *Betkom* and *Bulfon,* both of which can also be used for long-distance calls throughout Bulgaria and Europe. Phone cards can be purchased at post offices, hotels, and numerous street kiosks. Calls to the United States can be made from Bulfon or Betkom phones by using a local calling card to reach the international operator and then a long-distance calling card to reach the States. They can also be made from your hotel, for a surcharge, or placed from a post office. In Sofia direct-dial calls to the United States can also be made from the international phone office (½ block west of the main post office). To place a call using an **AT&T USA Direct** international operator, dial 00–800–0010.

COUNTRY CODE

For international calls to Bulgaria, the country code is 359. The access code for Sofia is 2 from outside Bulgaria and 02 from within the country.

Transportation

Bulgaria uses the following abbreviations in addresses: *ul.* (*ulitsa*) is street; *bul.* (*bulevard*) is boulevard; *pl.* (*ploshtad*) is square.

BY BOAT

Modern luxury vessels cruise the Danube from Passau in Austria to Ruse. Hydrofoils link main communities along the Bulgarian stretches of the Danube and the Black Sea, and there are coastal excursions from some Black Sea resorts. A ferry from Vidin to Calafat links Bulgaria with Romania. Contact a travel agent for reservations.

BY BUS

An increasing number of private bus firms link all the major towns. Buses tend to be luxurious, air-conditioned, and faster than trains. Bus stations are generally close to the train station. Buy tickets a day or two in advance. Within the cities a regular system of trams and trolley buses operates for a single fare of 200 leva. In Sofia booths at bus stops sell tickets; outside the city you can pay the driver. **Group Travel** (✉ Novotel Europa Sofia, 131 bul. Maria Luisa, 11202 Sofia) is the chief bus service in the country.

BY CAR

For motorist information contact the main office of the **Bulgarian Automobile Touring Association** (SBA; ✉ 3 ul. Pozitano Sofia, ☎ 02/980–33–08).

Breakdowns. In case of breakdown call 146. The **SBA** trucks carry essential spares. Fiat, Ford, Volkswagen, Peugeot, and Mercedes-Benz all have car-service operations in Bulgaria.

Car Rental. Three international car-rental firms have offices in Sofia and other major towns: **Eurodollar** (Hotel Kempinski Zografski, ✉ 100 bul. James Bourchier, ☎ 02/68–32–51). **Avis** (Sheraton Sofia Hotel, ✉ 5 pl. St. Nedelya, ☎ 02/988–81–67; Sofia airport, ☎ 02/73–80–23). **Hertz** (☎ 02/980–04–61 reservations, ☎ 02/79–14–77 airport). Two agencies rent cars with drivers: **Balkantour** (✉ 27 bul. Stamboliiski, ☎ 02/988–55–43). **Balkantourist** (✉ 1 bul. Vitosha, ☎ 02/87–51–92).

Gasoline. Stations are regularly spaced on main roads but may be few and far between. All are marked on Balkantourist's motoring map and sell unlimited quantities of fuel.

Parking. Bulgaria's parking laws are liberal, and if there's not a place on the street, you can often park on the sidewalk. Just be sure you're not blocking a driveway or another car, and never park where there's a NO PARKING sign (a red circle with a line through it). If you are in doubt, check with the hotel, restaurant, or sight you are visiting.

Road Conditions. Main roads are generally well engineered, although some routes are poor and narrow for the volume of traffic they have to carry. A large-scale expressway construction program has begun to link the main towns. Completed stretches run from Kalotina—on the Serbian border—to Sofia, and from Sofia to Plovdiv.

Rules of the Road. Drive on the right, as in the United States. The speed limit is 50 or 60 kph (31 or 36 mph) in built-up areas, and 80 kph (50 mph) elsewhere, except on highways, where it is 120 kph (70 mph). The limits for a car towing a trailer are 50 kph (31 mph), 70 kph (44 mph), and 100 kph (62 mph), respectively. Balkantourist recommends that you take out collision, or Casco, insurance. You are required to carry a first-aid kit, fire extinguisher, and breakdown triangle in the vehicle. Front seat belts must be worn. The drunk-driving laws are strict—you are expected not to drive after you have had more than one drink. If you're pulled over, be prepared to pay on the spot a fine determined by the officer.

BY PLANE

Balkan Airlines (✉ 12 pl. Narodno Subranie Sofia, ☎ 02/68–41–48) has regular services to Varna and Burgas, the biggest ports on the Black Sea. Group-travel and air-taxi services are available through privately run **Hemus Air** (✉ Sofia International Airport, ☎ 02/65–85–77). Business flights to other destinations in the country are also arranged by Hemus Air.

BY TRAIN

Buy tickets in advance at the ticket office in Sofia (in the underpass below the National Palace of Culture) if you want to avoid long lines at the station. In other cities get your tickets at the station. It's best to take an *ekspresni* (express) or *burzi* (fast) train, as they are the fastest and most comfortable. *Putnicheski* (slow) trains are very old and painfully slow. Trains tend to be crowded; seat reservations are obligatory on expresses. *Purva clasa* (first class) is not much more expensive than second class and is worth it. From Sofia there are six main routes—to Varna or Burgas on the Black Sea coast, to Plovdiv and beyond to the Turkish border, to Dragoman and the Serbian border, to Kulata and the Greek border, and to Ruse on the Romanian border. The main lines are powered by electricity.

Visitor Information

Balkan Tour Sofia (✉ 27 bul. Stamboliiski, ☎ 02/988–55–43. **Balkan Tourist** (✉ 1 bul. Vitosha, ☎ 02/87–51–92.

Weather

The ski season lasts from mid-December through March; the Black Sea coast season runs from May through October, reaching its crowded peak in July and August. Fruit trees blossom in April and May; in May and early June the blossoms are gathered in the Valley of Roses (you have to be up early to watch the harvest); in October the fall colors are at their best.

CLIMATE

Summers are warm; winters are crisp and cold. The coastal areas enjoy considerable sunshine. March and April are the wettest months inland. Even when the temperature climbs, the Black Sea breezes and the cooler mountain air prevent the heat from being overwhelming.

The following are the average daily maximum and minimum temperatures for Sofia.

<table>
<tr><td>Jan.</td><td>35F</td><td>2C</td><td>May</td><td>69F</td><td>21C</td><td>Sept.</td><td>70F</td><td>22C</td></tr>
<tr><td></td><td>25</td><td>– 4</td><td></td><td>50</td><td>10</td><td></td><td>52</td><td>11</td></tr>
<tr><td>Feb.</td><td>39F</td><td>4C</td><td>June</td><td>76F</td><td>24C</td><td>Oct.</td><td>63F</td><td>17C</td></tr>
<tr><td></td><td>27</td><td>– 3</td><td></td><td>56</td><td>14</td><td></td><td>46</td><td>8</td></tr>
<tr><td>Mar.</td><td>50F</td><td>10C</td><td>July</td><td>81F</td><td>27C</td><td>Nov.</td><td>48F</td><td>9C</td></tr>
<tr><td></td><td>33</td><td>1</td><td></td><td>60</td><td>16</td><td></td><td>37</td><td>3</td></tr>
<tr><td>Apr.</td><td>60F</td><td>16C</td><td>Aug.</td><td>79F</td><td>26C</td><td>Dec.</td><td>38F</td><td>4C</td></tr>
<tr><td></td><td>42</td><td>5</td><td></td><td>59</td><td>15</td><td></td><td>28</td><td>– 2</td></tr>
</table>

SOFIA

Bulgaria's bustling capital is set on the high Sofia Plain, ringed by mountain ranges: the Balkan Range to the north; the Lyulin Mountains to the west; part of the Sredna Gora Mountains to the southeast; and, to the southwest, Mt. Vitosha—the city's playground—which rises to more than 7,600 ft. The area has been inhabited for about 7,000 years, but your first impression may be of a city besieged by urban development dominated by an expanse of nightmarish Socialist-era block housing.

This soon gives way to spacious parks, open-air cafés, and broad streets filled with an incongruous mix of Western sports cars and old-fashioned farmer's wagons laden with firewood. As recently as the 1870s Sofia was part of the Ottoman Empire, and one mosque still remains. Most of the city, however, was planned after 1880, and following the destruction of World War II, many of the main buildings were rebuilt in the Socialist style.

Exploring Sofia

Numbers in the margin correspond to points of interest on the Sofia map.

There are enough intriguing museums and high-quality musical performances to merit a lengthy stay, but if time is short, you need only two days to see the main city sights and another day to enjoy the serenity of Mt. Vitosha.

6 **Banya Bashi Dzhamiya** (Banya Bashi Mosque). This distinctive building, consisting of a large dome and a lone minaret, a legacy from the centuries of Turkish rule, was built during the 16th century and closed between the mid-1980s and 1993. Now that it is open for worship, loudspeakers on the minaret call the city's Muslim minority to prayer. ✉ *Bul. Maria Luiza at ul. Triyaditsa.*

17 **Borisova Gradina** (Boris's Garden). Dilapidated benches, stray dogs, overflowing garbage dumpsters, an empty lake, a dry fountain, and neglected statues of communist leaders mar this former haven. Nevertheless, it is huge, central, and important to the city's inhabitants. The wild woods surrounding it are a good place for a stroll. In summer, ice-cream vendors, children riding around in rented battery-operated minicars, a first-class outdoor disco, and a surprisingly pristine public pool with water slides for children, bring life to the deteriorated park. ✉ *Bul. Bulgaria between bul. Tsar Osvoboditel and bul. Dragan Tsankov.*

★ 15 **Hram-pametnik Alexander Nevski** (Alexander Nevski Memorial Church). The neo-Byzantine structure with glittering onion domes, whose image you may recognize from almost every piece of tourist literature, really does dominate the city. It was built by the Bulgarian people at the beginning of the 20th century as a mark of gratitude to their Russian liberators. Inside are decorations in alabaster, onyx, and Italian marble; Venetian mosaics; magnificent frescoes; and space for a congregation of 5,000. Attend a service to hear the superb choir, and, above all, don't miss the fine collection of icons in the **Crypt Museum.** ✉ *Pl. Alexander Nevski,* ☎ *02/981–57–75.* ⏲ *Wed.–Mon. 10–5.*

10 **Mavsolei Georgi Dimitrov** (Georgi Dimitrov Mausoleum). Until 1990 this building contained the embalmed body of the first general secretary of the Bulgarian Communist party, who died in Moscow in 1949. His remains have been moved to the Central Cemetery, and there is talk of either converting the mausoleum into a museum or tearing it down. ✉ *South side of pl. Alexander Batenberg.*

16 **Narodno Subranie** (National Assembly). During the January 1997 uprising, CNN immortalized this building by repeatedly broadcasting clips of Bulgarian protesters smashing the windows and attempting to drag barricaded members of the Socialist parliament onto the plaza. Topped by the Bulgarian national flag, this squat building is adorned with an inscription reading "Unity makes strength," referring to the unification of the country in 1885, a few years after the defeat of the Turks. In front of the building is a monument to the Russians, who helped in the bat-

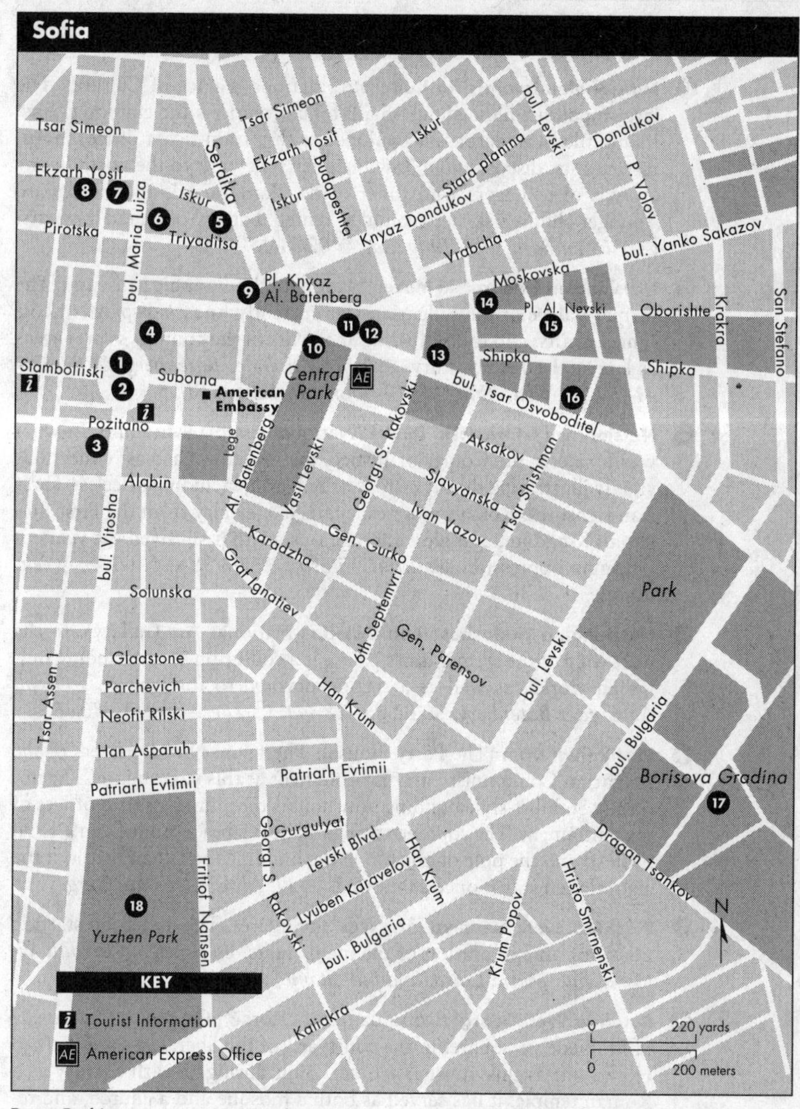

Banya Bashi Dzhamiya, **6**
Borisova Gradina, **17**
Hram-pametnik Alexander Nevski, **15**
Mavsolei Georgi Dimitrov, **10**
Narodno Subranie, **16**
Natsionalen Dvorets na Kulturata, **18**
Natsionalen Etnografski Muzei, **12**
Natsionalen Istoricheski Muzei, **3**
Natsionalna Hudozhestvena Galeria, **11**
Partiyniyat Dom, **9**
Ploshtad Sveta Nedelya, **1**
Rotonda Sveti Georgi, **4**
Tsentralna Sinagoga, **8**
Tsentralnata Banya, **5**
Tsentralni Hali, **7**
Tsurkva Sveta Nedelya, **2**
Tsurkva Sveta Sofia, **14**
Tsurkva Sveti Nikolai, **13**

tle against the Turks, surmounted by an equestrian statue of Russian Tsar Alexander II. ✉ *bul. Tsar Osvoboditel at pl. Narodno Subranie.*

⓲ **Natsionalen Dvorets na Kulturata** (National Palace of Culture). The large modern building houses halls for conventions and cultural events. Its multilevel underpass is equipped with a train-ticket office, shops, restaurants, discos, and a bowling alley. The park to the north draws crowds of teenagers who roller blade, skate board, and ride bikes. Younger children skitter around in rented, battery-operated minicars. ✉ *Yuzhen Park, 1 pl. Bulgaria,* ☎ *02/5–15–01.*

⓬ **Natsionalen Etnografski Muzei** (National Ethnographic Museum). The former palace of the Bulgarian tsar currently houses displays of costumes, crafts, and tools illustrating the life of the country's rural areas as late as the 19th century. ✉ *1 pl. Alexander Batenberg,* ☎ *02/87–41–91.* ⊙ *Wed.–Sun. 10:30–noon and 1:30–5:30.*

★ ❸ **Natsionalen Istoricheski Muzei** (National History Museum). In what was formerly the Courts of Justice, the museum has vast collections vividly illustrating the art history of Bulgaria, including priceless Thracian treasures, Roman mosaics, enameled jewelry from the First Bulgarian Kingdom, and glowing religious art that survived the years of Ottoman oppression. ✉ *2 bul. Vitosha,* ☎ *02/88–41–60.* ⊙ *Weekdays 9:30–4:30.*

⓫ **Natsionalna Hudozhestvena Galeria** (National Art Gallery). In the west wing of the former tsar's palace is a collection of outstanding Bulgarian works, as well as a section devoted to foreign art. ✉ *1 pl. Alexander Batenberg,* ☎ *02/89–28–41.* ⊙ *Tues.–Sun. 10:30–6.*

❾ **Partiyniyat Dom** (The Party House). The former headquarters of the Bulgarian Communist party is prominent at this vast square. The imposing Stalinist-style building now houses the administrative offices of the parliament. The southern walls still bear smoke stains from a 1990 protest, and the pole on the top of the building looks bare without the gigantic red star it once supported. ✉ *Pl. Alexander Batenberg.*

❶ **Ploshtad Sveta Nedelya** (St. Nedelya Square). This is a good starting point for an exploration of the main sights. ✉ *Bordered by bul. Vitosha, bul. Maria Luiza, and bul. Stamboliiski.*

❹ **Rotonda Sveti Georgi** (Rotunda of St. George). On the northeast side of St. Nedelya Square, in the courtyard of the Sheraton Sofia Balkan Hotel, stands this unusual artifact. Built during the 4th century as a Roman temple, it has served as both a mosque and a church, and recent restoration has revealed medieval frescoes. It is not open to the public. ✉ *2 pl. St. Nedelya.*

❽ **Tsentralna Sinagoga** (Central Synagogue). This spectacular structure is topped with an enormous dome and is surrounded by five smaller domes and six towers. Constructed in a Moorish style in 1909, it has recently been renovated after decades of disuse. ✉ *Ul. Ekzarh Yosif.* ⊙ *Daily 11–2, 4–6.*

❺ **Tsentralnata Banya** (The Central Baths). For years this former Ottoman mineral bathhouse was in ruins, occupied by vagrants. Renovations, begun in 1997, have restored the splendid building, and the domes gleam once again. It is still closed to the public, but hot mineral water flows at the spring in the adjacent park where Sofians line up to fill plastic bottles with the water, which supposedly cures respiratory diseases and ensures longevity. ✉ *Bul. Maria Luiza at ul. Triyaditsa.*

❼ **Tsentralni Hali** (Central Market Hall). Once one of the most beautiful buildings in Sofia, the hall served as the central market during communist times. After falling into ruin, it is now a shell of its former self and is currently closed for renovations. ✉ *Bul. Maria Luiza at ul. Ekzarh Yosif.*

❷ **Tsurkva Sveta Nedelya** (St. Nedelya Church). This 19th-century church, with its huge dome ringed by little windows, dominates the south side of St. Nedelya Square. It is the latest in a series of churches that have occupied the site since the Middle Ages. Behind it is bulevard Vitosha, a lively pedestrian street with plenty of stores, cafés, and restaurants. ✉ *Pl. St. Nedelya.*

⓮ **Tsurkva Sveta Sofia** (Church of St. Sofia). This simple brick edifice dates from the 6th century and in the mid-14th century became the namesake for the city of Sofia. ✉ *North side of pl. Alexander Nevski.*

⓭ **Tsurkva Sveti Nikolai** (Church of St. Nicholas). This ornate Russian structure was erected between 1912 and 1914. ✉ *Bul. Tsar Osvoboditel at ul. Rakovski.*

Dining and Lodging

Suddenly Sofia is teeming with new restaurants and cafés, offering high-quality but inexpensive international cuisines. Still, if you can tolerate cigarette smoke and crowded seating, the most authentic eating experience is in a mehana, or tavern, where the music is loud, and diners relax for hours over rakia and salads. For details and price-category definitions, *see* Dining *in* Bulgaria A to Z, *above.*

The hotels below are comfortable, with a high standard of cleanliness, and are open year-round. You shouldn't have trouble finding a room, even if you arrive in town without a reservation. If you want help finding a room, **Balkantourist** (✉ 1 bul. Vitosha, ☎ 02/87–51–92) will book you in a state-owned hotel. For details and price-category definitions, *see* Lodging *in* Bulgaria A to Z, *above.*

$$$$ ✕ **Krim.** This Russian restaurant serves the best beef Stroganoff in town. It also has a delectable caviar and lox platter that goes well with a superb selection of chilled vodkas. Expect to pay western prices for the lox and caviar spread. ✉ *17 ul. Slavyanska,* ☎ *02/87–01–31. No credit cards.*

$$$$ ✕ **Nad Aleyata, Zad Shkafut** (Beyond the Alley, Behind the Cupboard). In a beautiful old house this small, casually elegant restaurant serves such delicious and innovative Bulgarian and European dishes as Chicken Kiev, Russian salad, veal medallions, beef with béchamel sauce, and grilled pork stuffed with mushrooms and cheese. Popular with local diplomats, it offers a large selection of salads and an excellent wine list. The staff speaks English, there are menus in English, and it is one of the few places that provide the kind of western service that foreigners tend to expect—such as taking back a cold or under-cooked dish. ✉ *31 ul. Budapeshta,* ☎ *02/83–55–81. Reservations essential. No credit cards.*

$$$$ ✕ **33 Stoli** (33 Chairs). Classy and intimate, this candle-lit cellar has a changing menu specializing in such fine European cuisine as frogs' legs and Swiss fondue, as well as a wide range of appetizers and salads. The wine list is comprehensive, and the desserts are irresistible. Try *shokolade palachinka sus presni plodove* (chocolate crepe with fresh fruit). And, yes, there really are only 33 chairs. ✉ *14 ul. Assen Zlatarov,* ☎ *02/44–29–81. Reservations essential. No credit cards.*

$$$ ✕ **Bai Gencho.** A favorite with Sofians, this traditional Bulgarian mehana provides the classic tavern experience with the added elegance of candles, fresh flowers on each table, and a warm basement fireplace. The *etspetsialitet na gotvachka za dvama* (mixed grill of sausages, steaks, and shish kebabs), the chef's specialty for two people, is a carnivore's dream. ✉ *ul. Kniaz Alexander Dondukov 15,* ☎ *02/81–74–54. Reservations essential. No credit cards.*

$$$ ✕ **The Golden Dragon.** Near the opera house this small Shanghai restaurant has drawn faithful regulars who come for the spicy dumplings and informal friendly atmosphere. Don't expect a "NO MSG" promise on the menu, but do expect tasty food and fast service. ✉ *166A ul. Rakovski,* ☎ *02/88–80–30. No credit cards.*

$$$ ✕ **Mexicano (Casa del Arquitecto).** Pseudo-Mexican food and Cuban strolling musicians make this quirky place popular. It also serves traditional Bulgarian dishes, including a spicy moussaka. In summer the outdoor candle-lit patio, with its canopy of leafy trees, draws crowds who put up with the inflated prices and snobby service. ✉ *11 ul. Krakra,* ☎ *02/44–65–98 or 02/44–17–24. No credit cards.*

$$ ✕ **Art Club Lucky.** A trendy café and renowned Mafia hangout, Art Club Lucky serves excellent pizzas, quiches, salads, and sandwiches. Bright windows facing lively ulitsa Tsar Shishman make it an ideal spot for a daytime cappuccino and delicious dessert while you people-watch. ✉ *38 ul. Gurko,* ☎ *02/980–77–12. No credit cards.*

$$ ✕ **Baalbeck.** Local businesspeople like this Middle Eastern restaurant just off central Slaveikov Square. Though it's seedy in appearance, it prepares fast lunches of delicious falafel, hummus, and tabouli. Sit downstairs for a quick bite wrapped in pita bread to go, or dine upstairs if you want your *doner kebap* (a lamb, beef, or chicken skewer) on a plate, accompanied by a fork and knife, with the pita bread on the side. ✉ *6 Vasil Levski. No credit cards.*

$$$$ 🏨 **Castle Hotel Hrankov.** Escape the city to this new hotel at the foot of Mt. Vitosha. Something of a cross between a beige-and-white mountain chalet and a castle (with such architectural elements as turrets and oversize doorways), the Hrankov has picture windows facing the mountain, and plush carpets, chandeliers, and a clean bright ambience. The most attractive hotel in Sofia, it can also claim the best fitness center in the city, complete with squash courts, an Olympic-size swimming pool, tennis courts, and ski facilities. ✉ *53 Krusheva Gradina, Dragalevtsi 1415,* ☎ *02/91–909,* FAX *02/67–29–85. 360 rooms. 4 restaurants, pool, nightclub, casino. AE, DC, MC, V.*

$$$$ ★ 🏨 **Hotel Kempinski Zografski–Sofia.** Acquired in 1997 by the classy Kempinksi hotel chain, the former Intercontinental is a towering, luxurious hotel designed in Japanese minimalist style. Guest rooms are rather basic for a luxury listing; big beds, televisions, large bathrooms with bathtubs, mini-refrigerators and desks. With audiovisual and simultaneous translation facilities available, it is a good choice for business conferences. The hotel also has a shopping arcade and the most expensive restaurant in the entire country, Sakura, Bulgaria's one and only spot for sushi. ✉ *100 bul. James Bourchier, 1407,* ☎ *02/68–32–51,* FAX *02/68–12–25. 454 rooms. 5 restaurants, pool. AE, DC, MC, V.*

$$$$ 🏨 **Hotel Maria Luiza.** The closest thing Sofia has to a modern yet cozy bed and breakfast, this upscale private hotel has comfortable, cheery rooms, business facilities, an excellent location, and a friendly staff. On busy Maria Luiza Bulevard, the hotel is a narrow six stories, wedged between cafés, shops, and apartments—all of which are part of a renovated stretch of turn-of-the-century buildings. It is painted in bright blues and purples, and rooms are modern and airy. Fruit baskets and chocolates greet guests in the rooms, windows face out toward the Banya Bashi Mosque, and the bathrooms have big, glass western-style showers. ✉ *29 bul. Maria Luiza, 1000,* ☎ *02/9–10–44,* FAX *02/980–33–55. 21 rooms with bath or shower. Restaurant. AE, DC, MC, V.*

$$$$ ★ **Sheraton Sofia Hotel Balkan.** The former Grand Hotel Balkan, converted to Sheraton standards, is a first-class hotel with a central location that is hard to match. Rooms are basic and businesslike with dark decor. Suites are much more lavish, with brighter decor, bigger bathtubs, and views of the Plaza Sveta Nedelya. It also has excellent restaurants and other facilities. ✉ *5 pl. St. Nedelya, 1000,* ☎ *02/981–65–41,* FAX *02/980–64–64. 187 rooms. 3 restaurants. AE, DC, MC, V.*

$$$ **Bulgaria.** Despite its central location, this small hotel is quiet and old-fashioned. Dark and decorated with antiques, it is private, somber, and serious. Guests are more likely to be Eastern European business travelers than westerners or tourists on holiday. ✉ *4 bul. Tsar Osvoboditel, 1000,* ☎ *02/87–19–77 or 02/87–01–91,* FAX *02/88–41–77. 85 rooms with bath or shower. Restaurant. No credit cards.*

$$$ **Novotel Europa.** This member of the prestigious French Novotel chain is on one of Sofia's main boulevards, near the train station, and not far from the center of the city. The shiny white high-rise is ultramodern for Sofia; it has neon lights and gambling in the lobby. Card keys open doors to slick, cookie-cutter rooms, which include minibars, televisions, and small clean bathrooms. Among its many facilities are a conference center and a casino. ✉ *131 bul. Maria Luiza, 1202,* ☎ *02/3–12–61,* FAX *02/32–00–11. 600 rooms. 2 restaurants. AE, DC, MC, V.*

$$ **Grand Hotel Sofia.** Just south of the Russian Liberation monument, this central, five-story Interhotel is comfortable, pleasant, and intimate. Guest rooms are reminiscent of past decades in the Eastern Block. The decor is austere, and the amenities are basic—TV, phone, bath, and shower. Suites, however, are far better; some include office and kitchen areas. The Panorama Restaurant affords a fine view of Sofia but provides mechanical, unfriendly service. Its retro '70s nightclub hosts amateur beauty contests that are titled "Beauties of Bulgaria" and "Miss Striptease." Still popular with former Communist leaders, the stately hotel transports you back to Bulgaria before MTV. ✉ *4 pl. Narodno Subranie, 1000,* ☎ *02/87–88–21,* FAX *02/88–13–08. 106 rooms. 2 restaurants. AE, DC, MC, V.*

$$ **Rila.** A rather unattractive, squat structure in the center of the city, the Rila has basic rooms (bed, bath, TV, phone, desk, and shower) decorated in drab brown and orange. It has a Bulgarian tavern, a bingo parlor, and a cafeteria. It is frequented mostly by other Eastern Europeans. ✉ *6 ul. Kaloyan, 1000,* ☎ *02/980–88–65,* FAX *02/981–33–86. 138 rooms with bath or shower. Restaurant. AE, DC, MC, V.*

$$ **Sun Hotel.** Cozy and comparatively inexpensive, this private hotel offers small but comfortable rooms and a business center in a beautiful old building with lots of character. Beware of the location. It is directly across from the Lion's Bridge, Sofia's most notorious red-light district and hunting ground for pickpockets. ✉ *89 bul. Maria Luiza, 1000,* ☎ *02/83–36–70,* FAX *02/83–53–89. 16 rooms with bath or shower. No credit cards.*

Nightlife and the Arts

The Arts

The standard of music in Bulgaria is high, whether it's performed in opera houses, symphony halls, or at concerts of folk music with its close harmonies and colorful stage displays. For a list of cultural events in Sofia, pick up a copy of *Sofia City Info Guide* at the American Express office (☞ Sofia Essentials, Contacts and Resources, *below*), or look for at hotels. Newsstands in Sofia now carry two helpful English-language newspapers: the *Sofia Independent* and the *Sofia Echo,* which publish current news and entertainment listings. For ballet and opera tickets, go to the **National Opera House** (✉ 1 ul. Vrabcha). Buy concert and symphony tickets at the **Bulgarian Concert Hall** (✉ 1 ul. Benkovski).

There are a number of good art galleries: The **City Art Gallery** (✉ 1 ul. Gen. Gurko, ☎ 02/87–21–81) has permanent exhibits of both 19th-century and modern Bulgarian paintings as well as changing exhibits showcasing contemporary artists. The art gallery of the **Sts. Cyril and Methodius International Foundation** (✉ pl. Alexander Nevski, ☎ 02/80–44–37; ⏲ Wed.–Mon. 10:30–6) has a collection of Indian, African, Japanese, and Western European paintings and sculptures. The art gallery of the **Union of Bulgarian Artists** (✉ 6 ul. Shipka, ☎ 02/44–61–15; ⏲ daily 10:30–6) has exhibitions of contemporary Bulgarian art.

Most movie theaters show recent foreign films in their original languages with Bulgarian subtitles: **Dom na Kinoto** (House of Cinema; ✉ 37 ul. Ekzarh Yosif, ☎ 02/88–06–76). **Serdika** (✉ pl. Pametnik V. Levski, ☎ 02/43–17–97). **Vitosha** (✉ 62 bul. Vitosha, ☎ 02/988–58–78).

Nightlife

BARS AND NIGHTCLUBS

La Strada Jazz Club (✉ 4 ul. 6 Septemvri, ☎ no phone) draws a more sophisticated, international crowd. The **703 Club** (✉ 38B ul. Gurko, at ul. Tsar Shishman, ☎ 02/981–97–75) is a contemporary bar for the trendy twentysomething crowd. For live music, check out the lineup at **Swingin' Hall** (✉ 8 bul. Dragan Tsankov, ☎ 02/66–63–23).

CASINOS

You can try your luck at the **International Casino Club Sheraton** (✉ 5 pl. St. Nedelya, ☎ 02/80–60–30). **Las Vegas** (Novotel Europa, ✉ 131 bul. Maria Luiza, ☎ 02/931–00–72) also offers gambling.

DISCOS

Aliby 1 (✉ Borisova Gradina, ☎ no phone) is Sofia's hippest summertime club, where a college crowd gathers under an enormous tent to dance to electronic music in a carnival atmosphere. **Aliby 2** (✉ Yuzhen Park, ☎ no phone) is the winter-time sister disco to the favorite summer outdoor nightspot. **Neron** (✉ 1 pl. Bulgaria, ☎ 02/80–34–38), in the National Palace of Culture, is a huge, flashy underground disco popular with the local Mafia. Metal detectors screen for guns as you enter, and you must check your mobile phone with your coat. **Spartacus** (in the underpass in front of Sofia University) is Sofia's first gay club, attracting the city's avant garde, both gay and straight.

Shopping

Department Stores

The drab yet well-stocked Tsentralen Universalen Magazin—**TSUM** (Central Department Store, ✉ 2 bul. Maria Luiza) is Sofia's biggest department store.

Gifts and Souvenirs

The **Bulgarian Folk Art Shop** (✉ 14 bul. Vitosha) carries an excellent assortment of national arts. **Prizma Store** (✉ 1 ul. Vasil Levski) offers many souvenirs. There is a good selection of arts and crafts at the shop of the **Union of Bulgarian Artists** (✉ 6 ul. Shipka). If you are interested in furs or leather, try the shops along bulevard Vitosha, bulevard Levski, and bulevard Tsar Osvoboditel. For recordings of Bulgarian music, go to the underpass below the National Palace of Culture (☞ Exploring

Sofia, *above*), where there are stalls selling music, as well as the **Balkanton** music store. The outdoor **arts and crafts market** around Alexander Nevsky Cathedral specializes in lace and linen at reasonable prices. For a large variety of **crafts and souvenirs,** visit the underpass between St. Nedelya Church and the Central Department Store.

Shopping Districts

Bulevard Vitosha is a lively street with many upscale shops. Moderately priced and stylish boutiques are on **ulitsa Graf Ignatiev.** The quintessential shopping excursion in Sofia is to the outdoor **Zhenski Pazaar** (✉ ul. Stefan Stambolov, between ul. Tsar Simeon and bul. Slivnitsa), the women's market, so-called for the endless stalls worked by women from neighboring villages who commute in daily to hawk everything from homemade brooms and lace to produce and used electronic equipment.

Side Trips

Both Boyana (8 km/5 mi southwest of Sofia) and Dragalevtsi (9 km/5½ mi south of Sofia) are pleasant day trips to the Mt. Vitosha vicinity and can be reached by Bus 64 from Sofia.

Boyana

The little medieval **Boyana Church** is well worth a visit, as is the small, elegant restaurant of the same name, next door. The church is closed for restoration, but a replica, complete with copies of the exquisite 13th-century frescoes, is open to visitors. ✉ *ul. Belite Brezi.* ⏲ *Daily, approx. noon–4.*

$ ✕ **Chepishev.** At the foot of Mt. Vitosha this eatery offers Bulgarian specialties and live folk music in the evenings. ✉ *Boyana district, 25 ul. Kumata,* ☎ *02/56–50–35. No credit cards.*

Dragalevtsi

The **Dragalevtsi Monastery** stands in beech woods above the village. The complex is still used as a convent, but you can visit the 14th-century church with its outdoor frescoes. ✉ *3 km (2 mi) past Vodenicharski Mehani Restaurant, Dragalevtsi.*

You can take chairlifts (✉ beside Vodenicharski Mehani Restaurant) from Dragalevtsi to the delightful resort complex of **Aleko.** From Aleko you can continue on foot for about an hour to the top of **Rezen Maluk,** the nearest peak. There are well-marked walking and ski trails in the area.

$$ ✕ **Vodenicharski Mehani.** The English translation is "Miller's Tavern," which is appropriate, as it's made up of three old mills linked together. It stands at the foot of Mt. Vitosha. A folklore show and a menu of Bulgarian specialties provide a tourist-friendly but authentic atmosphere. Try the *gyuvech* (potatoes, tomatoes, peas, and onions baked in an earthenware pan). ✉ *Dragalevtsi district (Bus 64), at southern end of town next to chairlift,* ☎ *02/67–10–21 or 02/67–10–01. No credit cards.*

Sofia Essentials

Arriving and Departing

BY CAR

From Serbia, the main routes are E-80, going through the border checkpoint at Kalotina on the Niš-Sofia road, or E-871, going through the checkpoint at Gyueshevo. From Greece, take E-79, passing through the checkpoint at Kulata; from Turkey, take E-80, passing through checkpoint Kapitan-Andreevo. Border crossings to Romania are at Vidin on E-79 and at Ruse on E-97 and E-85.

BY PLANE

All international flights arrive at Sofia airport. For information on international flights, call 02/79–80–35 or 02/72–06–72; for domestic flights, 02/72–24–14.

Between the Airport and Downtown. Bus 84 from Sofia University serves the airport. At the airport taxi stand fares to the center are fixed at $20. If you speak some Bulgarian and know where you're going, private taxis outside the terminal will get you there for less than half the official price. Agree on the fare before starting.

BY TRAIN

Tsentralna Gara (Central Station; northern edge of city, ☎ 02/3–11–11 or 02/843–33–33). Ticket offices (in underpass below National Palace of Culture, ✉ 1 pl. Bulgaria, ☎ 02/59–01–36; Rila International Travel Agency, ✉ 5 ul. Gurko, ☎ 02/87–07–77). There is a taxi stand at the station.

Getting Around

The main sights are centrally located, so the best way to see the city is on foot.

BY BUS

Buses, trolleys, and trams run fairly often. Buy a ticket from the ticket stand near the streetcar stop and punch it into the machine on board. (Watch how other people do it.) For information (in Bulgarian), call 02/312–42–63 or 02/88–13–53.

BY RENTAL CAR

You can hire a car with a driver through Balkantourist, Balkantour Ltd., or your hotel (☞ Car Rental *in* Bulgaria A to Z, *above*); you can also rent a car at the airport.

BY TAXI

It is easy to find cabs in Sofia. Hail them in the street or at a stand—or ask the hotel to call one. Always take a taxi with a phone number written on the side. The rate should be 300 leva–400 leva per kilometer. There is a 10-leva surcharge for taxis ordered by phone in Sofia (☎ 2121, 1280, or 1282). To tip, round out the fare by 5%–10%.

Contacts and Resources

EMBASSIES

United States (✉ 1 ul. Suborna, ☎ 02/980–52–41). **United Kingdom** (✉ 38 bul. Levski, ☎ 02/980–1220).

EMERGENCIES

Police: ☎ 166. **Fire:** ☎ 160. **Ambulance:** ☎ 150. **Doctor:** Pirogov Emergency Hospital (☎ 02/5–15–31). **Pharmacy:** Apteka (✉ 5 pl. St. Nedelya, ☎ 02/87–59–89) is open daily 24 hours.

GUIDED TOURS

Orientation. Guided tours of Sofia and environs are arranged by Balkantourist or Balkantour Ltd. (☞ Visitor Information, *below*) or by many of the major hotels. Among the possibilities are three- to four-hour tours of the principal city sights by car or minibus or a longer four- to five-hour tour that goes as far as Mt. Vitosha.

Excursions. Balkantourist and Balkantour Ltd. (☞ Visitor Information, *below*) offer special-interest tours of various lengths, using Sofia as the point of departure. There are trips to the most beautiful monasteries, to museum towns, to sports areas and spas, and to other places of exceptional scenic or cultural interest.

TRAVEL AGENCIES

American Express (✉ 1 ul. Vasil Levski, ☎ 02/981–42–01). **Carlson Wagonlit Travel** (✉ 10 ul. Lege, ☎ 02/980–81–26).

VISITOR INFORMATION

Balkantourist (✉ 1 bul. Vitosha, ☎ 02/87–51–92). **Balkantour Ltd.** (✉ 27 bul. Stamboliiski, ☎ 02/988–55–43).

THE BLACK SEA COAST

Bulgaria's most popular resort area attracts visitors from all over Europe. Its sunny, sandy beaches are backed by the easternmost slopes of the Balkan Range and, to the south, by the Strandzha Mountains. Although the tourist centers tend to be huge, state-built complexes with a somewhat lean feel, they have modern amenities. Slânčer Brjag (Sunny Beach), the largest of the resorts, with more than 100 hotels, has plenty of children's amusements and play areas.

The historic port of Varna is a good center for exploration. It is a focal point of land and sea transportation for the region and has museums, a variety of restaurants, and a lively nightlife in summer. The nearby fishing villages of Nesebâr and Sozopol to the south are more attractive and tranquil. Hotels tend to be scarce in these villages, but private lodgings are easily arranged through local accommodation agencies. All resorts offer facilities for water sports. Tennis and horseback riding are also available. The Black Sea resorts (Albena, Dyuni, Slânčer Brjag) are closed from November through April.

Varna

Bulgaria's third-largest city is easily reached by rail (about 7½ hours by express) or road from Sofia. If you plan to drive, allow time to see the **Pobiti Kamuni** (Stone Forest), just off the Sofia–Varna road between Devnya and Varna. The unexpected groups of monumental petrified tree trunks are thought to have been formed when the area was inundated by the Lutsian Sea. The ancient city of Varna, named Odyssos by the Greeks, became a major Roman trading center and is now an important shipbuilding and industrial city. With its beaches and tourism, Varna has become cosmopolitan and already holds an international Film Festival each August.

The **Archeologicheski Muzei** (Archaeological Museum) is one of the great—if lesser known—museums of Europe. The splendid collection includes the world's oldest gold treasures from the Varna necropolis of the 4th millennium BC, as well as Thracian, Greek, and Roman artifacts and richly painted icons. ✉ *41 bul. Maria Luiza, located in the park,* ☎ *052/23–70–57 or 052/212–41.* ⏲ *Tues.–Sat. 10–5.*

The pedestrian-only **ploshtad Nezavisimost** marks the center of town. To the east, **ulitsa Knyaz Boris I** is lined with shops, cafés, and restaurants.Take a look at the lavish murals in the monumental **Tsurkva Yspenie Bogorodichno** (Cathedral of the Assumption), built between 1880 and 1886. ✉ *Pl. Mitropolit Simeon.*

Running north from the cathedral is **ulitsa Vladislav Varnenchik,** with shops, movie theaters, and eateries. In the city gardens stands the **starata chasovnikuh kula** (Old Clock Tower; ✉ pl. Nezavisimost), built in 1880 by the Varna Guild Association. The magnificent Baroque **Stoyan Buchvarov Dramatichen Teatur** (Stoyan Bucharov Drama Theater; ✉ pl. Nezavisimost) presents local and national theater productions, as well as opera and symphonic concerts.

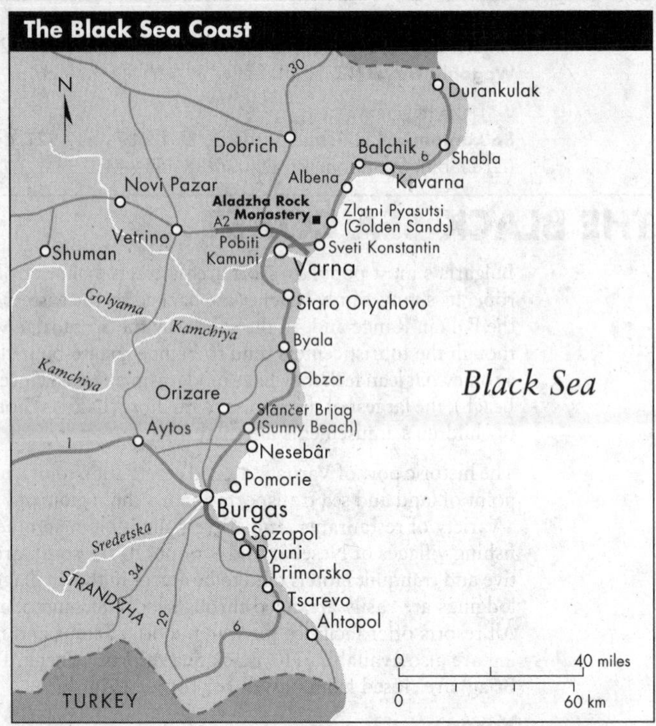

The 1602 **Tsurkva Sveta Bogoroditsa** (Church of the Holy Virgin) is worth a look for its beautifully carved iconostasis. ✉ *Ul. Han Krum at ul. Knyaz Alexander Batenberg.*

Wander through the remains of the **Rimski Termi** (Roman Baths), dating from the 2nd through the 3rd centuries. Signs in English detail the various steps of the bath ritual. ✉ *ul. Han Krum just south of Tsurkva Sveta Bogoroditsa.*

The restored **ulitsa Stari Druzhi** is comfortingly lined with restaurants, taverns, and coffeehouses. The **Morski Muzei** (Marine Museum) has displays of the early days of navigation on the Black Sea and the Danube. ✉ *2 bul. Primorski,* ☎ *052/22–26–55.* ⏲ *Weekdays 8–4.*

In the extensive and luxuriant **Primorski Park** (Seaside Park) are restaurants, an open-air theater, and the fascinating **Copernicus Astronomy Complex** (☎ 052/22–28–90; ⏲ weekdays 8–noon and 2–5) near the main entrance. ✉ *Southern end of bul. Primorski.*

$$ ✕ **Horizont.** This restaurant in the north end of Primorski Park has a wide selection of seafood as well as a view of the Black Sea from its outside tables. It's not too busy during the day, but at night the live Greek music draws a crowd. ✉ *Ul. Morska Gradina, just inside the front entrance to the park,* ☎ *052/88–45–30. No credit cards.*

$$ ✕ **Orbita.** This cheap hole-in-the-wall is extremely popular with the locals, who come here for the lentil soup, grilled kebabs with potatoes, or stewed Bulgarian sausage in a crock pot. ✉ *25 bul. Tsar Osvoboditel, in Hotel Orbita, off bul. Knyaz Boris I,* ☎ *052/22–52–75. No credit cards.*

$$ ★ 🏨 **Cherno More.** A dark four-story structure, it stands on a bright, tree-lined street packed with cafés, bars, and shops. Although its decor is a bit dated, this is still one of the more modern hotels in Varna. Rooms are spartan: low beds, fading carpet, inexpensive wooden furniture, and small bathrooms. You can expect panoramic vistas from the top floors of the 22-story tower. ✉ *33 bul. Slivnitsa, 9000,* ☎ *052/23–21–15. 230 rooms with bath or shower. 3 restaurants. AE, DC, MC, V.*

Albena

The newest and most modern Black Sea resort has a long, wide beach and clean sea. Some of its 35 hotels have extensive hydrotherapy facilities. The contemporary conveniences of this present-day tourist village come with a smaller dose of local charm, inflated prices, and menus and street signs in German and Russian. This is a resort for people seeking amenities but not necessarily the true Bulgaria.

$$ ✕ **Bambuka** (Bamboo). This open-air restaurant serves international and Bulgarian cuisines and seafood. ✉ *Albena,* ☎ *05722/24–04. No credit cards.*

$$$ **Dobrudzha Hotel.** The mineral-water health spa is the main attraction at this big, comfortable hotel. ✉ *Albena 9620,* ☎ *05722/20–20,* FAX *05722/22–16. 275 rooms. 3 restaurants, 2 pools. AE, DC, MC, V.*

Slânčer Brjag

This popular resort, known as **Sunny Beach** in English, is enormous and offers safe beaches, gentle tides, and facilities for children. It has a variety of beachside restaurants, kiosks, and playgrounds. Rapid socialist construction left behind enormous and ugly hotels that line a gorgeous crescent-shape beach.

$$ ✕ **Hanska Shatra** (Tent Inn). In the coastal hills above the sea, this combination restaurant and nightclub has been built to resemble the tents of the *Hans* (Bulgarian rulers) of old. It has entertainment well into the night. ✉ *4¾ km (3 mi) west of Slunchev Bryag,* ☎ *0554/28–11. No credit cards.*

$$ ✕ **Ribarska Hizha** (Fisherman's Hut). The lively beachside restaurant specializes in fried fish and has music until 1 AM. ✉ *Northern end of Slunchev Bryag,* ☎ *0554/21–86. No credit cards.*

$$ **Chaika.** Among the bargain hotels, the Chaika offers the best location, just off the cleanest and prettiest stretch of beach and close to the best restaurants and cafés. ✉ *Slunchev Bryag 8240,* ☎ *0554/23–08. 36 rooms with bath or shower. No credit cards.*

$$ ★ **Globus.** Popular with tour groups and usually full, with a lively, holiday atmosphere, the Globus is considered by many to be the best in the resort. The rooms are brighter, cleaner, and more modern (with bigger, better-equipped bathroom facilities, such as enclosed showers) than those in many other hotels. ✉ *Slunchev Bryag 8240,* ☎ *0554/22–45. 100 rooms with bath or shower. Restaurant, pool. AE, DC, MC, V.*

Nesebâr

★ Just 10 minutes by bus or car south of Sunny Beach is a painter's and poet's retreat. It would be hard to find a town that exudes a greater sense of age than this ancient settlement, founded by the Greeks 25 centuries ago on a rocky peninsula reached by a narrow causeway. Among its vine-covered houses are richly decorated medieval churches. Don't miss the frescoes and the dozens of small, private, cozy pubs.

Burgas

Bulgaria's second main port on the Black Sea, Burgas is industrial, chaotic, and polluted, with heavy traffic, several oil refineries, and huge ships anchored off its coast. There is one place that does offer a reasonable night's stay: **Primorska Gradina** (Seaside Park), with its expansive beach and pedestrian alleyways winding through the adjacent gardens.

$$ ✕ **Cheren Peter.** This elegant and inexpensive hideaway is intimate, sparkling clean, and popular. The cuisine is Bulgarian—everything from a big *ovcharska salata* (shepherd salad: tomatoes, cucumbers, mushrooms, peppers, feta cheese, and boiled eggs) to moussaka, grilled meats, and dessert crepes. You can relax here over an excellent bottle of the local Burgas Cabernet. ✉ *26 ul. Gurko,* ☎ *no phone. No credit cards.*

$$ 🏨 **Bulgaria.** The Bulgaria is a high-rise Interhotel in the center of town. Rooms are modern but basic, with televisions, showers, and desks. Popular with tour groups and business travelers, it has its own nightclub with floor show and a restaurant set in a mock winter garden. ✉ *21 ul. Aleksandrovska, 8000,* ☎ *056/4–28–20,* FAX *056/4–72–91. 200 rooms with bath or shower. Restaurant. DC, MC, V.*

Sozopol

★ Nestled in Byzantine ruins, the fishing port of Sozopol, with narrow, cobbled streets leading down to the harbor, was Apollonia, the oldest of the Greek colonies in Bulgaria. It is now a popular haunt for Bulgarian and, increasingly, foreign writers and artists, who find private accommodations (through Lotos, ✉ ul. Ropotamo, ☎ 05514/429) in the rustic Black Sea–style houses, so picturesque with their rough stone foundations and unpainted wood slats on the upper stories. It also hosts the **Apollonia Arts Festival** each September, which draws musicians, playwrights, painters, dancers, and actors from all of Europe.

Black Sea Coast Essentials

Getting Around

Buses make frequent runs up and down the coast. **Cars** and **bicycles** can be rented. A **hydrofoil** service links Varna, Nesebur, Burgas, and Sozopol. A regular **boat** service travels the Varna–Sveti Konstantin (St. Konstantin)–Zlatni Pyasutsi (Golden Sands)–Albena–Balchik route.

Guided Tours

A wide range of excursions can be arranged from all resorts. There are bus excursions to Sofia from Albena, and Slunchev Bryag; a one-day bus and boat trip along the Danube from neighboring resorts Zlatni Pyasutsi and Sveti Konstantin, as well as Albena; and a multiday bus tour of Bulgaria, including the Valley of Roses, departing from Zlatni Pyasutsi, Sveti Konstantin, and Albena. All tours are run by local tourist agencies (☞ Visitor Information, *below,* or check with your hotel information desk).

Visitor Information

Albena (☎ 05722/27–21). **Burgas** (Hotel Primorets, ✉ 1 ul. Knyaz Batenberg, ☎ 056/4–54–96). **Nesebâr** (☎ 0554/58–30). **Slânčer Brjag** (☎ 0554/23–25). **Varna** (Varnenski Bryag, ✉ 3 ul. Moussala, ☎ 052/22–55–24 or 052/22–22–72).

INLAND BULGARIA

Inland Bulgaria is less well known to outsiders than the capital and the coast, but if you're willing to put up with limited hotel facilities and the sometimes complicated public transportation, you'll find plenty to photograph or simply savor. Wooded and mountainous, the interior is dotted with attractive museum villages (entire settlements listed for preservation because of their historic cultural value) and ancient towns. The foothills of the Balkan Range, marked Stara Planina (old mountains) on most maps, lie parallel to the lower Sredna Gora Mountains, with the verdant Rozova Dolina (Valley of Roses) between them. In the Balkan range is the ancient capital of Veliko Turnovo; south of the Sredna Gora stretches the fertile Thracian plain, home to Bulgaria's second-largest city, Plovdiv. Between Sofia and Plovdiv is the enchanting old town of Koprivshtitsa. To the south, in the Rila Mountains, is Borovets, the first of the mountain resorts. A round-trip covering all these towns, with a side excursion to Rila Monastery, can be made in four or five days.

Koprivshtitsa

★ One of Bulgaria's showpiece villages, Koprivshtitsa is set in mountain pastures and pine forests, about 3,050 ft up in the Sredna Gora range. It is 105 km (65 mi) from Sofia, reached by a minor road south from the Sofia–Kazanluk expressway. Koprivshtitsa became a prosperous trading center with close ties to Istanbul during the 19th century. The architecture of this period, called the National Revival or Bulgarian Renaissance style, is marked by carved woodwork on broad verandas and overhanging eaves, brilliant colors, and courtyards with studded wooden gates. For centuries artists, poets, and wealthy merchants have made their homes here, and many of the historic houses are now open as museums. The town has been well preserved and revered by the Bulgarians as a symbol of freedom since April 1876, when the people of Koprivshtitsa sparked the rebellion that led to the end of Turkish occupation.

$ ✕ **Byaloto Kouche** (The White Dog). Uphill from the town square, this intimate, family-owned restaurant is decorated in the National Revival style and offers traditional Bulgarian dishes. ✉ *Ul. Generilo 2,* ☎ *07184/22–50. No credit cards.*

$ 🏨 **Hotel Byaloto Kouche.** This charming inn offers rustic rooms furnished in the traditional National Revival style, with woven rugs and low beds. One room has a fireplace, but none have adjoining baths. ✉ *Ul. Generilo 2, 2090,* ☎ *07184/22–50. 6 rooms without bath. Restaurant. No credit cards.*

$ 🏨 **Koprivshtitsa.** This good-value hotel, popular with vacationing Bulgarians, is just across the river from the center of town. ✉ *12 ul. G. Benkovski, 2090,* ☎ *07184/21–82. 30 rooms with bath or shower. No credit cards.*

Klisura

The town lies at the beginning of the Valley of Roses. Here the famous Bulgarian rose water and attar, or essence, are produced. Each May and June, the whole valley is awash in fragrance and color.

Troyan

A few miles from town stands the **Troyanski Monastir** (Troyan Monastery), built during the 1600s in the heart of the mountains. Its church was painstakingly remodeled during the 19th century, and its icons, wood carvings, and frescoes are classic examples of National Revival art. ✉ *5 km (3 mi) east of Troyan.* ⏲ *Daily 8–6.*

Veliko Târnovo

This town of panoramic vistas, about 200 km (124 mi) northeast of Sofia, rises up against steep mountain slopes through which the Yantra River runs its jagged course. From the 12th through the 14th centuries, Veliko Târnovo was the capital of the Second Bulgarian Kingdom. Damaged by repeated Ottoman attacks, and again by an earthquake in 1913, it has been reconstructed and is now a museum city of marvelous relics. Ideally, you should begin at a vantage point above the town in order to get an overview of its design and character.

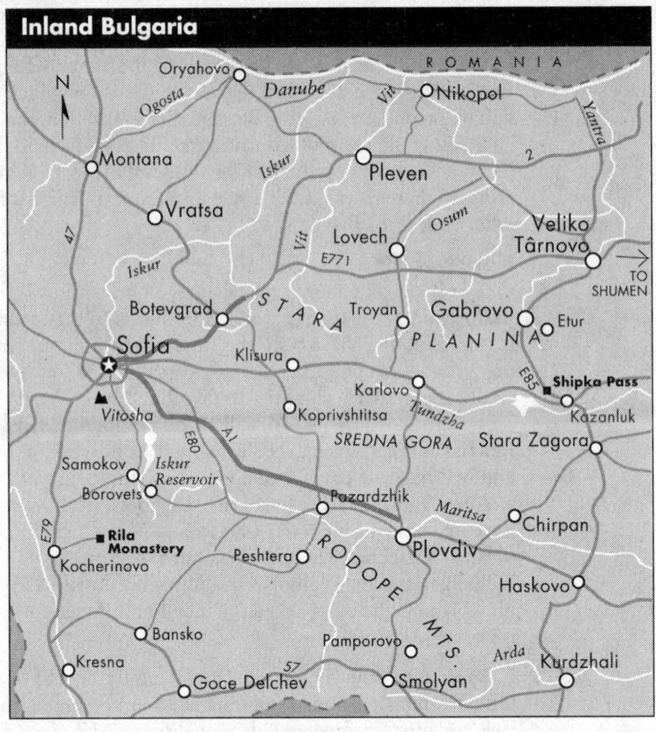

Tsarevets, a hill on the east end of town, almost encircled by the Yantra River, is where the palace and patriarchate of the Second Bulgarian Kingdom stood. The area is under restoration, and steep paths and stairways provide opportunities to view the extensive ruins of the royal palace. Thursday through Saturday in the summer, the hill is illuminated at 10 PM with a spectacular laser light show. The prominent feature on the south side of Tsarevets is **Balduinova Kula** (Baldwin's Tower), the 13th-century prison of Baldwin of Flanders, onetime Latin emperor of Constantinople. On the west side of the hill stands the 13th-century **Tsurkva na Chetirideset Muchenitsi** (Church of the Forty Martyrs), with its Turnovo-school frescoes and two inscribed columns, one dating from the 9th century. On the north side of Tsarevets, the **Tsurkva na Sveti Petur i Pavel** (Church of Sts. Peter and Paul) has vigorous murals both inside and out. Across the river to the west, reached by a bridge near the Forty Martyrs, the restored **Tsurkva na Sveti Dimitur** (Church of St. Dimitrius) was built on the spot where the Second Bulgarian Kingdom was proclaimed in 1185.

Near the center of town is **ulitsa Samovodene,** lined with restored crafts workshops—a fascinating place to linger and a good place to find souvenirs, Turkish candy, or a charming café.

In a large, National Revival–style house, the **Muzei Vuzrazhdanei Uchereditelno Subranie** (Museum of the National Revival and Constitutional Assembly) has three floors of exhibits. The first floor holds a collection of medieval icons and local craftwork; the second has photos and documents detailing the national liberation movement; the third houses the hall where the first Bulgarian parliament drafted the country's first constitution. ✉ *2 ul. Nicola Picolo,* ☎ *062/2-98-21.* ⏲ *Wed.–Sun. 8–noon and 1–5.*

$ ✕ **Bolyarska Izba** (Bolyar's Hut). In the center of the busy district just north of the river, this unpretentious eatery is a favorite with locals, many of whom order the house *sarmi* (vine leaves stuffed with pork). ✉ *ul. St. Stambolov,* ☏ *no phone. No credit cards.*

$$$$ 🏨 **Veliko Târnovo.** Right in the middle of the most historic part of the town, this modern Interhotel offers some of the best facilities in its class. Rooms, though not bright, are big and airy with all the amenities, such as televisions, phones, desks, modern bathrooms. Compared with other hotels in the town, it is the cleanest and most comfortable. ✉ *2 ul. Al. Penchev, 5000,* ☏ *062/3–05–71. 195 rooms with bath or shower. 2 restaurants, pool. AE, DC, MC, V.*

$$ 🏨 **Etur.** Despite its dark and state-owned atmosphere, this moderate-size hotel is still good value and the best base for sightseeing within the city. ✉ *1 ul. Ivailo, 5000,* ☏ *062/2–18–38. 80 rooms with shower. Restaurant. AE, DC, MC, V.*

$$ 🏨 **Yantra.** The Yantra has some of the best views in town, looking across the river to Tsarevets. It also has a decent restaurant with a balcony that provides the best vantage point on the great vista. ✉ *1 pl. Velchova Zavera, 5000,* ☏ *062/2–03–91. 60 rooms, most with shower. Restaurant. AE, DC, MC, V.*

Shumen

You can go far back in time by visiting the ruins of the two capitals of the First Bulgarian Kingdom near here. The fortifications at **Pliska,** 23 km (14 mi) northeast of Shumen, date from AD 681. At **Veliki Preslav,** 21 km (13 mi) southwest of Shumen, ruins from the second capital date from 893 to 927. The 8th- to 9th-century **Madara Horseman,** a rather eroded bas-relief of a rider slaying a lion, appears 18 km (11 mi) east of Shumen on a sheer cliff face.

Etur

The mill in this museum village is still powered by a stream, and local craftspeople continue to be trained in traditional skills.

Shipka Pass

A mighty monument on the peak honors the thousands of Russian soldiers and Bulgarian volunteers who died here in 1877, during the Russian-Turkish Wars.

Kazanluk

In this town at the eastern end of the Valley of Roses, you can trace the history of rose cultivation, Bulgaria's oldest industry. Each June the town hosts the Festival of Roses, which features folk dancing, art exhibits, and rose-picking demonstrations. There is also a highly decorated replica of a Thracian tomb of the 3rd or 4th century BC, set near the original, which remains closed for its preservation.

Plovdiv

★ Bustling with college students and new businesses, Bulgaria's second-largest city, Plovdiv, is one of the oldest settlements in Europe and now a major industrial, cultural, and intellectual center. Closed to cars to preserve the original cobble work, the breathtaking, lantern-lit **starata grad** (old town), lies on the hillier southern side of the Maritsa River.

Each year the new section of the city hosts the Annual Trade Fair at the Plovdiv Fairgrounds.The **Natsionalen Etnografski Muzei** (National Ethnographic Museum) is in the much-photographed former home of a Greek merchant, Arghir Kuyumdzhioglu. It is an elegant example of the National Revival style, which made its first impact in Plovdiv. The museum is filled with artifacts from that fertile period. ✉ *2 ul. Chomakov,* ☏ *032/22–56–56.* ⏲ *Tues.–Sun. 9–noon and 2–5.*

Below the medieval gateway of Hisar Kapiya, the **Georgiadieva Kushta** (Georgiadi House) is a grandiose example of National Revival–style architecture; it also contains a small museum dedicated to the April 1876 uprising against the Turks. ✉ *1 ul. Starinna.* ⏲ *Wed.–Sun. 9:30–12:30 and 2–5.*

The steep, narrow **ulitsa Strumna** is lined with workshops and boutiques, some reached through little courtyards. Beyond the railings and past the jewelry and leather vendors in the center of Stamboliiski Square stand the remains of a 2nd-century **Rimski stadion** (Roman stadium). ✉ *Ul. Saborna and ul. Knyaz Alexander I.*

The old **Kapana District** (✉ northwest of pl. Stamboliiski) has narrow, winding streets and restored shops and cafés. The exquisite hilltop **Rimski amfiteatur** (Roman amphitheater), only discovered and excavated in 1981, has been sensitively renovated. In summer the majestic and timeless theater is frequently used for dramatic and musical performances. ✉ *Ul. Tsar Ivailo.*

The **Natsionalen Archeologicheski Muzei** (National Archaeological Museum) holds a replica of the 4th-century BC Panagjuriste Gold Treasure and a wealth of ancient Thracian artifacts from Plovdiv and the surrounding region. ✉ *1 pl. Suedinenie.* ⏲ *Tues.–Sun. 9–12:30 and 2–5:30.*

$$$ ✕ **Puldin.** On a hill in the center of old town, this folk restaurant has a romantic subterranean dining room complete with a waterfall and live piano music. Order the excellent *pulneni chushki* (peppers stuffed with meat, spices, and rice) served with yogurt for a taste of Bulgarian home cooking. ✉ *3 ul. Knyaz Tseretelev,* ☎ *032/23–17–20. AE, DC, MC, V.*

$$ ✕ **Alafrangite.** This charming mehana is in a restored 19th-century house with carved wood ceilings and a vine-covered courtyard in the old part of town. One of the specialities is *kuopoolu* (vegetable pureé of baked eggplant, peppers, and tomatoes). ✉ *17 ul. Nektariev,* ☎ *032/22–98–09 or 032/26–95–95. No credit cards.*

$$ ✕ **Restaurant Starata Kushta.** In a renovated Renaissance house in the old quarter, this restaurant presents such traditional fare as *cirene po shopski* (hot feta cheese with herbs, tomatoes, and peppers in a crock pot). ✉ *19 ul. Nektariev,* ☎ *032/26–68–42. No credit cards.*

$$$ 🏨 **Trimontsium.** This central Interhotel built during the 1950s is comfortable and ideal for exploring the old town. ✉ *2 ul. Kapitan Raicho, 4000,* ☎ *032/2–34–91. 163 rooms with bath or shower. Restaurant. AE, DC, MC, V.*

$$ 🏨 **Hotel S and M** This brand-new family-run bed and breakfast (opened in 1997) just outside the old town has bright, airy rooms with bay windows and private baths.✉ *28, Hristo Duckmedjiev, 4000,* ☎ *032/26–01–35. 4 rooms. Café. AE, MC, V.*

$$ 🏨 **Novotel Plovdiv.** The large, modern, and well-equipped Novotel lies across the river from the main town, near the fairgrounds. ✉ *2 ul. Zlatyu Boyadzhiev, 4000,* ☎ *032/65–25–05 or 032/55–19–79. 322 rooms. Restaurant, pool. AE, DC, MC, V.*

Borovets

Slightly more than 4,300 ft up the northern slopes of the Rila Mountains, this is an excellent walking center and winter sports resort. It is well equipped with hotels, folk-style taverns, and ski schools. The winding mountain road leads back to Sofia, 70 km (43 mi) from here, past Iskur Reservoir, the largest lake in the country.

Rila

★ **Rila Monastery,** founded by Ivan of Rila during the 10th century, lies in a steep, forested valley past the village of Rila. The monastery has suffered so frequently from fire that most of it is now a grand National Revival reconstruction, although a rugged 14th-century tower has survived. The atmosphere in this striking mountain retreat, populated by many storks, is still heavy with a sense of the past—although part of the complex has been turned into a museum and some of the monks' cells are now guest rooms. You can see 14 small chapels with frescoes from the 15th and 17th centuries, a lavishly carved altarpiece in the new Church of the Assumption, the sarcophagus of Ivan of Rila, icons, and ancient manuscripts—a reminder that this was a stronghold of Christian art and learning during the centuries of Ottoman rule.

Inland Bulgaria Essentials

Getting Around

Rail and bus services cover all parts of inland Bulgaria, but the best bet is to rent a car. To hire a driver check with Balkantourist or Balkantour Ltd. in Sofia (☞ Visitor Information *in* Sofia Essentials, *above*).

Guided Tours

Organized tours set out from Sofia, each covering different points of interest. Check with your Sofia hotel information desk or with Balkantourist or Balkantour Ltd. for specific information (☞ Visitor Information *in* Sofia Essentials, *above*).

Visitor Information

Plovdiv (Puldin Tours, ✉ 106 bul. Bulgaria, ☎ 032/55–38–48). **Veliko Târnovo** (E.A.D. Yantra, ✉ 2 ul. Al. Penchev, ☎ 062/3–05–71).

7 Cyprus

The Republic of Cyprus, Northern Cyprus

The Mediterranean island of Cyprus was once a center for the cult of the Greek goddess Aphrodite. Wooded and mountainous, with a 751-km-long (466-mi-long) coastline, Cyprus lies just off the southern coast of Turkey. Fruits grow here in abundance, and fish are plentiful. The summers are hot and dry, the springs gentle. Winter snow in the Troodos Mountains permits skiing in the morning and sunbathing on a beach in the afternoon.

Cyprus's strategic position in the eastern Mediterranean has made it subject to regular invasions by powerful empires. Greeks, Phoenicians, Assyrians, Egyptians, Persians, Romans, and Byzantines—all have ruled here. In the Middle Ages King Richard I of England took Cyprus from the Byzantine Empire by force and gave it to Guy of Lusignan. Guy's descendants ruled the island until the late 15th century, when it was annexed by the Venetians. From the 16th century through the 19th century it was ruled by the Turks. It became a British colony in 1914.

Vestiges of the diverse cultures that have ruled here dot the island. Many fortifications built by the Crusaders and the Venetians still stand. The tomb of the prophet Muhammad's aunt (Hala Sultan Tekke), on the shore of the great salt lake near Larnaca Airport, is one of Islam's most important shrines. A piece of the true cross is said to be kept in the monastery of Stavrovouni, and Paphos has the remains of a pillar to which St. Paul was allegedly tied when he was beaten for preaching Christianity.

The upheavals are not over. Following independence in 1960, the island became the focus of contention between Greeks and Turks. Currently nearly 80% of the population is Greek and 18% Turkish. Since 1974 Cyprus has been divided by a thin buffer zone—occupied by United Nations (UN) forces—between the Turkish Cypriot north and the Greek Cypriot south. The zone cuts right through the capital city of Nicosia. Talks aimed at uniting the communities into one bizonal federal state have been going on for years. The U.S. government is now involved in trying to resolve the dispute, and with the Republic of Cyprus anxious to join the European Union, governments from that organization's member countries are taking a greater interest, too. Both communities have comfortable tourist facilities, but entry through the northern part, which is recognized only by Turkey, makes access to the south impossible.

THE REPUBLIC OF CYPRUS

Republic of Cyprus A to Z

Customs

Duty-free allowances are: 250 grams of tobacco, 1 liter of spirits, 750 milliliters of wine, 300 milliliters of perfume, and up to C£50 in other goods.

The export of antiques and historic artifacts is strictly forbidden unless a license is obtained from the Department of Antiquities in Nicosia.

Dining

The top hotels offer a good variety of both local and international food at competitive prices; large buffets are especially popular. Meals in local restaurants or tavernas usually start with a variety of *mezes* (appetizers), followed by kebabs, dolmas, stews, fresh fish, and various lamb dishes. Meals end with fruit or honey pastries and Greek coffee. By law, all establishments must display a menu with government-approved prices, which include the 10% service charge and 8% value added tax. Food is relatively cheap and the quality is good.

RATINGS

Prices are for a three-course meal for one person, not including drinks or tip.

CATEGORY	COST
$$$	OVER C£12
$$	C£6–C£12
$	UNDER C£6

WHAT TO WEAR

Casual dress is acceptable in most restaurants in Cyprus, regardless of price category, although those in major hotels may require more formal clothing.

Embassies or High Commissions

U.S. Embassy (✉ Metochiou Ploutarchou, Box 4536, Engomi, Nicosia, ☎ 02/476100, FAX 02/465944). **Consulate of Canada** (✉ 15 Them Dervis St., Box 2125, Nicosia, ☎ 02/451630, FAX 02/459096). **British High Commission** (✉ Alexander Pallis St., Nicosia, ☎ 02/473131–7, FAX 02/367198).

Emergencies

Ambulance, Fire Brigade, and **Police** (☎ 199). **Doctor:** Nicosia General Hospital (☎ 02/451111); Limassol Hospital (☎ 05/330333); Paphos Hospital (☎ 06/240111). **Pharmacies** (open during normal shopping hours; for information in English about those open until late at night and during holidays, ☎ 1412 in Nicosia, 1415 in Limassol, 1414 in Larnaca, or 1416 in Paphos).

Guided Tours

Guided tours are often the best way to see Cyprus and learn about its rich history. Try **National Sightseeing Tours** (✉ c/o Louis Tourist Agency, 54–58 Evagoras Ave., Nicosia, ☎ 02/442114) for half-day and full-day trips—expect to pay C£7–C£19. Night tours typically include dinner at a local taverna, folk dancing, and bouzouki music. In

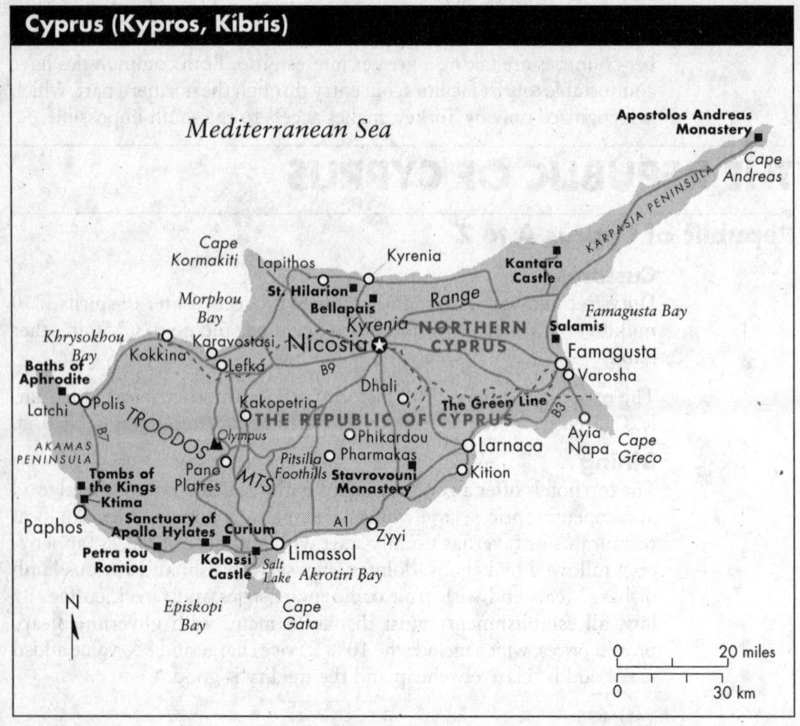

seaside resorts almost any hotel or travel agency will arrange coastal cruises with varying destinations and durations, some serving meals on board.

Language

Greek is the main language, but English is widely spoken in hotels, tavernas, and other tourist haunts. Off the beaten path, sign language may have to do.

SPELLING

The Republic of Cyprus government has carried out a controversial exercise to spell all place names as they are pronounced in Greek. Hence Nicosia becomes Lefkosia, Larnaca is Larnaka, Limassol is Lemesos, and Paphos is Pafos. Internationally, the original names remain, and in Cyprus both spellings are currently in use. To avoid confusion we have retained the original spellings.

Lodging

All hotels listed have private bath or shower, but check when making reservations. Most have at least partial air-conditioning. In resort areas hotel/apartments are a convenient choice for groups or families—many have kitchens.

RATINGS

Prices are for two people sharing a double room and include breakfast.

CATEGORY	COST
$$$$	OVER C£80
$$$	C£60–C£80
$$	C£40–C£60
$	UNDER C£40

Mail

A 20-gram letter to the United States costs 36¢, a postcard, 31¢. To Europe a 20-gram letter costs 31¢, and a postcard 26¢. Post offices are open weekdays 7:30–2:30. Stamps are also sold at hotels, newsstands, and kiosks. Every item of mail must carry a separate 1¢ refugee stamp, which is included in the above costs.

Money Matters

COSTS

A cup of coffee or tea costs Cyprus 60¢–C£1; a glass of beer 75¢–C£1; a kebab around C£1.25–C£1.75; a bottle of local wine C£1.75–C£4.50. Admission to museums and galleries costs 50¢–C£1.

CURRENCY

The monetary unit in the Republic of Cyprus is the Cyprus pound (C£), which is divided into 100 cents. There are notes of C£20, C£10, C£5, and C£1 and coins of 50, 20, 10, 5, 2, and 1 Cyprus cents. At press time (spring 1998) the rate of exchange was C£0.52 to the U.S. dollar, C£0.36 to the Canadian dollar, and C£0.87 to the pound sterling, C£0.34 to the Australian dollar, and C£0.29 to the New Zealand dollar.

TIPPING

A service charge of 10% and an 8% VAT are automatically included in all bills. If service has been especially good, add 5%.

National Holidays

January 1; January 6 (Epiphany); February 22 (Green Monday); April 1 (National Day); April 9–13 (Greek Orthodox Easter); May 1 (May Day); May 31 (Pentecost Monday); August 15 (Assumption); October 1 (Cyprus Independence Day); October 28 (Greek National Day); December 25, 26.

Opening and Closing Times

Banks are open September–June, weekdays 8:30–12:30 and Monday afternoons 3:15–4:45; July and August, weekdays 8:15–12:30. Some have special afternoon tourist services and will cash traveler's checks weekdays 3–6 in winter, 4–7 in summer, and Saturday 8:30–noon year-round. **Museum** hours vary greatly. It pays to check ahead. Generally, museums are closed for lunch and on Sunday. Most ancient monuments are open from dawn to dusk. **Shops** open between 8 and 9 and close at 6 PM November–March, 7 PM April–May and mid-September–October, 7:30 PM June–mid-September. Between June and mid-September, they close for the afternoon summer break 1–4, and throughout the year at 2 on Wednesday and Saturday, and all day Sunday. However, in tourist areas many shops open until late at night and on Sunday during the summer.

Telephoning

COUNTRY CODE

The country code for Cyprus is 357.

INTERNATIONAL CALLS

To reach an AT&T long-distance operator, dial 080–90010; for MCI, 080–90000; for Sprint, 080–90001. Public phones may require the deposit of a coin or use of a phone card when you call these services.

LOCAL CALLS

Pay phones take 2¢, 5¢, 10¢, and 20¢ coins, but most popular these days are those taking Telecards. These have values of C£3, C£5, or C£10 and can be purchased at post offices, banks, souvenir shops, and kiosks. Cheaper rates apply from 10 PM to 8 AM and all day Sunday. For telephone information dial 192 in all towns.

Transportation

BY BOAT

Passenger ships connect Cyprus (Limassol and Larnaca) with various Greek, Italian, Egyptian, and Middle Eastern ports.

BY BUS

This is the cheapest form of transportation in urban areas; the fare is 40¢. Buses operate every half hour and cover an extensive network. In Nicosia, buses run until 7:30 PM (6:30 PM in winter). In tourist areas during the summer services are extended until midnight.

Intercity bus fares range between C£2 and C£3. For information on the Nicosia–Limassol–Paphos route, call 02/463989; for the Limassol–Larnaca–Ayia Napa route, dial 04/654890.

BY CAR

An international or national license is acceptable in Cyprus. Drive on the left. Main roads between large towns are good. Minor roads can be unsurfaced, narrow, and winding. Gas costs about 37¢ per liter. Cars may be rented from C£20 per day; lower rates are available off season.

BY PLANE

There are no direct flights between Cyprus and the United States. Cyprus Airways and British Airways fly direct from London, Birmingham, and Manchester to Larnaca and Paphos. Cyprus Airways also operates from Amsterdam, Athens, Frankfurt, Milan, Munich, Paris, Vienna, and Zurich. Alitalia flies from Rome. United Airlines and Swissair have good connections.

BY PRIVATE TAXI

Private taxis operate 24 hours throughout the island. They are generally very cheap within towns but far more expensive than service taxis between towns. Telephone from your hotel or hail one in the street. Urban taxis have an initial charge of 65¢ and charge 22¢ per km (½ mi) in the daytime, more at night. Drivers are bound by law to display and run a meter. In-town journeys range from C£1.50 to about C£3.

BY SERVICE TAXI

Shared taxis accommodate four–seven passengers and are a cheap, fast, and comfortable way of traveling between towns. Taxis operate between the main towns: Nicosia, Limassol, Larnaca, and Paphos. Tariffs are from C£1.65 to C£4.25. Seats must be booked by phone, and passengers may embark/disembark anywhere within the town boundaries. The taxis run every half hour (Mon.–Sat. 5:45 AM–6:30 PM). Sunday service is less frequent and rides must be booked one day ahead. Contact the Kypros Taxi Office (☎ 02/464811), Karydas (☎ 02/463126), or Kyriakos (☎ 02/444141).

Visas

No visas are necessary for holders of valid passports from the United States, Canada, the United Kingdom, or mainland European countries.

VISITOR INFORMATION

Nicosia (national office, ✉ 19 Limassol Ave., ☎ 02/337715, FAX 02/331644; local, ✉ Laiki Yitonia, ☎ 02/444264). **Larnaka** (✉ Democratias Sq., ☎ 04/654322). **Limassol** (✉ Spyros Araouzos St., ☎ 05/362756). **Paphos** (✉ Gladstone St., ☎ 06/232841).

Weather

The tourist season runs throughout the year, though prices tend to be lower from November through March. Spring and fall are best, usually warm enough for swimming but not uncomfortably hot.

CLIMATE

The rainy season is in January and February, and it often snows in the highest parts of the Troodos Mountains from January through March. January and February can be cold and wet; July and August are always very hot and dry. The following are the average daily maximum and minimum temperatures for Nicosia.

Jan.	59F	15C	**May**	85F	29C	**Sept.**	92F	33C
	42	5		58	14		65	18
Feb.	61F	16C	**June**	92F	33C	**Oct.**	83F	28C
	42	5		65	18		58	14
Mar.	66F	19C	**July**	98F	37C	**Nov.**	72F	22C
	44	7		70	21		51	10
Apr.	75F	24C	**Aug.**	98F	37C	**Dec.**	63F	17C
	50	10		69	21		45	7

Exploring the Republic of Cyprus

Nicosia

The capital is twice divided. Its picturesque Old City is contained within 16th-century Venetian fortifications that separate it from the wide, tree-lined streets, large hotels, and high-rises of the modern section. The second division is political and more noticeable. The so-called Green Line (set up by the United Nations) divides the island between the Republic of Cyprus and Turkish-occupied Northern Cyprus. It is possible, at press time (spring 1998), to arrange a day trip from the Greek to the Turkish sector through the official checkpoint in Nicosia (Ledra Palace), though it is essential to return by 5 PM. Visits in the other direction are not permitted.

★ In the Greek sector **Laiki Yitonia,** at the southern edge of the Old City, is an area of winding alleys and traditional architecture that is being completely renovated. Among its important sites is the **Archbishopric,** which houses several museums. Tavernas, cafés, and crafts workshops line the shaded, cobbled streets. Just to the west lies Ledra Street, where modern shops alternate with yet more crafts shops. Head north to visit the tiny Greek Orthodox **Tripiotis** church (Solonos 47–49), with its ornately carved golden iconostasis and silver-covered icons, which dates from 1690.

The **Leventis Museum** in Laiki Yitonia traces the city's history from 3000 BC to the present, with exhibits on crafts and daily life. ✉ *17 Ippocratous St.,* ☏ *02/451475.* *Free.* ⏲ *Tues.–Sun. 10–4:30.*

Housed in a wing of the archiepiscopal palace built in 1960 in neo-Byzantine style, the **Archbishop Makarios III Cultural Foundation** consists of the **Byzantine Art Museum,** with fine displays of icons spanning 1,000 years, and the **Greek War of Independence Gallery,** with a collection of maps, paintings, and mementos of 1821. ✉ *Archbishop Kyprianou Sq.,* ☏ *02/430008.* ⏲ *Weekdays 9–4:30, Sat. 8–noon.*

The **Museum of the National Struggle** has dramatic displays of the Cypriot campaigns against the British during the pre-independence years 1955–59. ✉ *Archbishop Kyprianou Sq.,* ☏ *02/304550.* ⏲ *Weekdays 8–6.*

★ The **Cyprus Folk Art Museum,** housed in the 14th-century part of the archiepiscopal palace, has demonstrations of ancient weaving techniques and displays of ceramics and olive and wine presses. ✉ *Archbishop Kyprianou Sq.,* ☏ *02/432578.* ⏲ *Weekdays 8:30–4, Sat. 8:30–1.*

Don't miss **Ayios Ioannis** (St. John's) Cathedral, built in 1662 within the courtyard of the archiepiscopal palace. Look for the 18th-century wall paintings illustrating important moments in Cypriot religious history and including a depiction of the tomb of St. Barnabas. ✉ *Archbishop Kyprianou Sq.*

The **Famagusta Gate,** now a cultural center, houses exhibitions, a lecture hall, and a theater. ✉ *Athina St.,* ☎ *02/430877.* ⏲ *Weekdays 8–1 and 4–7.*

★ Outside the city walls near the western Paphos Gate stands the **Cyprus Museum.** It has extensive archaeological displays ranging from Neolithic to Roman times. This stop is essential to an understanding of the island's ancient sites. ✉ *Museum St.,* ☎ *02/305320.* ⏲ *Mon.–Sat. 9–5, Sun. 10–1.*

The neoclassical **Municipal Theater** (✉ Museum St.) seats 1,200 people and stages events throughout the year, including Greek-language dramas and concerts. The lush **Municipal Gardens** (✉ opposite Cyprus Museum) are a well-maintained oasis of greenery in the city.

$$$ ✕ **Plaka Tavern.** One of the oldest eating establishments in the city, in the heart of Engomi, offers up to 30 different meze dishes, including some unusual items, such as snails and okra with tomatoes. Although it's mezes only, there's enough variety to satisfy every palate and size of appetite. ✉ *8 Stylianou Lena,* ☎ *02/446498. AE, DC, MC, V.*

$$$ ✕ **Trattoria Romantica.** The fare, like the owner, is Italian, and the atmosphere is distinctly friendly, with no shortage of advice available on any topic relating to Cyprus. There's a roaring fire in winter and service in the courtyard outside during the summer. ✉ *13 Evagora Pallikaridi,* ☎ *02/376161. AE, DC, MC, V. Closed Sun.*

$$ ✕ **Cellari.** This romantic, candlelit inn is lent a festive touch by a pair of guitarists strumming mellow Greek and Cypriot favorites. The excellent traditional local cooking produces such dishes as *souvla* (marinated lamb chunks cooked over charcoal). ✉ *22 Korai St.,* ☎ *02/448338. No credit cards.*

$$$$ 🏨 **Cyprus Hilton.** The Hilton is among the island's best hotels, with extensive sports facilities, a skylit indoor pool, dancing, and more. An executive wing with 84 rooms offers separate check-in, a business center, a club room, and exercise rooms. ✉ *Archbishop Makarios Ave., Box 2023,* ☎ *02/377777,* FAX *02/377788. 314 rooms. 2 restaurants, 2 pools. AE, DC, MC, V.*

$$$ 🏨 **Holiday Inn.** In the Old City, near commercial and historic districts, this member of the chain opened in 1995. Its amenities include Japanese, international, and health-food restaurants and a rooftop pool with a garden. ✉ *70 Regina St., Box 1212,* ☎ *02/475131,* FAX *02/473337. 140 rooms. 4 restaurants, 2 pools. AE, DC, MC, V.*

$$ 🏨 **Cleopatra Hotel.** This hostelry offers a convenient location, cordial service, and well-prepared food served poolside. ✉ *8 Florina St., Box 1397,* ☎ *02/445254,* FAX *02/452618. 90 rooms. Restaurant, pool. AE, DC, MC, V.*

Ayia Napa

Once a small fishing village, 30 km (19 mi) east of Larnaca, it is anchored by a 16th-century monastery and renowned for its white, sandy beaches and views of the brilliant sea. Today its many restaurants and hotels reflect the town's transformation into Cyprus's premier vacationland. Ayia Napa maintains the flavor of its historic past, however, and beneath the monastery's 14th-century sycamore tree, you can still enjoy the panoramic view of the Mediterranean.

$$$ **Nissi Beach.** This modern, fully air-conditioned, family-style hotel is set in magnificent gardens overlooking a sandy beach 3 km (2 mi) outside town. Some accommodations are in bungalows, which do not have kitchens. ✉ *Nissi Ave., Box 10,* ☎ *03/721021,* FAX *03/721623. 270 rooms, 166 bungalows. Restaurant, pool. AE, DC, MC, V.*

$$ **Pernera Beach Sun Hotel.** This budget hotel has a view of the beach. All rooms are air-conditioned. ✉ *Pernera Beach, Box 38,* ☎ *03/831011,* FAX *03/831020. 156 rooms. AE, DC, MC, V.*

Larnaca

The seaside resort with its own airport, 51 km (32 mi) southeast of Nicosia, is famous as the burial place of Lazarus and for its flamboyant Whitsuntide celebration, Cataklysmos. It has fine beaches, palm trees, and a modern harbor and marina, the starting point for boat trips. In the marina district the **Larnaca Museum** displays treasures, including outstanding sculptures and Bronze Age seals. ✉ *Kimon and Kilkis Sts.,* ☎ *04/630169.* ⏲ *Weekdays 7:30–2:30.*

Kition, the old Larnaca of biblical times, was one of the most important ancient city-kingdoms. Architectural remains of temples date from the 13th century BC. ✉ *Kyman St., north of Larnaca Museum.* ⏲ *Weekdays 7:30–2:30 and 3–5.*

The **Pierides Collection** is a private assemblage of more than 3,000 pieces distinguished by its Bronze Age terra-cotta figures. ✉ *Paul Zenon Kitieos St. 4, near Lord Byron St.,* ☎ *04/651345.* ⏲ *Mon.–Sat. 9–1, Sun. 10–1 and 3–6.*

The 17th-century **Turkish fort** contains finds from Hala Sultan Tekke (☞ *below*) and Kition (☞ *above*). ✉ *Within sight of marina on seafront.* ⏲ *May–Sept., Mon.–Wed. and Fri. 7:30–2:30, Thurs. 7:30–2:30 and 4–7; Nov.–Feb., Mon.–Wed. and Fri. 7:30–2:30, Thurs. 7:30–2:30 and 3–6.*

In the town center stands one of the island's more important churches, **Ayios Lazarus,** resplendent with icons. It has a fascinating crypt containing Lazarus's sarcophagus. ✉ *Plateia Agiou Lazarou.*

South of Larnaca on the airport road is the 2½-sq-mi **Salt Lake.** In winter it's a refuge for migrating birds. On the lake's edge a mosque stands ★ in an oasis of palm trees guarding the **Hala Sultan Tekke**—burial place of the prophet Muhammad's aunt, Umm Haram, and an important Muslim shrine. ✉ *Salt Lake.* 🎟 *Free.* ⏲ *June–Sept., daily 7:30–7:30; Oct.–May, daily 7:30–5.*

The 11th-century **Panayia Angeloktistos** church, 11 km (7 mi) south of Larnaca, has extraordinary Byzantine wall mosaics that date from the 6th and 7th centuries. ✉ *Rte. B4, Kiti.* ⏲ *Daily 9–5.*

On a mountain 40 km (25 mi) west of Larnaca stands the **Stavrovouni** (Mountain of the Cross) monastery. It was founded by St. Helena (mother of Emperor Constantine) in AD 326, though the present buildings date from the 19th century. The views of the island from here are splendid. Ideally, the monastery should be visited in a spirit of pilgrimage rather than sightseeing, out of respect for the monks. Male visitors are allowed inside the monastery daily from sunrise to sunset, except between noon and 3 (noon and 1 in winter). The monks have decreed that female visitors may be admitted only on Sunday morning.

$$$ ✕ **The Kampanario.** This renovated old house with its cheery atmosphere specializes in good steaks and fresh fish, especially trout. Its bar provides a popular meeting point, and the spacious garden is especially attractive in summer. ✉ *10 Nic. Mylonas St.,* ☎ *04/626110. AE, DC, MC, V.*

$$ ✕ **Monte Carlo.** The outdoor seating at this spot on the road to the airport is on a balcony extending over the sea. Service is efficient, and the dining area is clean. Particularly worthy Cypriot dishes are the fish and meat mezes and casseroles. ✉ *28 Piale Pashia,* ☎ *04/653815. AE, DC, MC, V.*

$$$$ **Golden Bay.** Comfort is paramount at this beach hotel east of the town center. All rooms have balconies and views of the sea. The extensive sports facilities make it an ideal spot for summer or winter vacations. ✉ *Larnaca-Dhekelia Rd., Box 741,* ☎ *04/645444,* FAX *04/645451. 194 rooms. 2 restaurants, 2 pools. AE, DC, MC, V.*

$$ **Pasithea.** This apartment/hotel near Salt Lake is a short stroll from the sandy beach. The management is friendly, and the one-bedroom apartments are spacious. ✉ *4 Michael Angelou, Box 309,* ☎ *04/658264,* FAX *04/625848. 14 apartments. AE, DC, MC, V.*

$ **Cactus Hotel.** The Cactus, near the airport, has a restaurant and bar. It's 20 minutes from the seafront and Larnaca's tavernas. ✉ *6–8 Shakespeare St., Box 188,* ☎ *046/27400,* FAX *046/26966. 58 rooms. Restaurant, pool. AE, MC, V.*

Phikardou

The museum village, a half-hour drive south of Nicosia off the road to Pharmakas, is being restored to its appearance at the beginning of the 20th century. Many of these rural houses, outstanding examples of folk architecture, have remarkable woodwork; they also contain the household furnishings used a century ago. Official tour guides are available in the village. ✉ *1½ km (1 mi) east of Gourri (Machairas Alicosia Rd. via Klirou),* ☎ *02/337715 in Nicosia for information.* ⏲ *Year-round; hrs vary.*

Limassol

A commercial port and wine-making center on the south coast, Limassol, 75 km (47 mi) from Nicosia, is a bustling, cosmopolitan town. Luxury hotels, apartments, and guest houses stretch along 12 km (7 mi) of seafront. The town's nightlife is the liveliest on the island. In central Limassol the elegant, modern shops of Makarios Avenue contrast with those of the old part of town, where you'll discover local handicrafts.

Limassol Fort, a 14th-century castle, was built on the site of an earlier Byzantine fortification. According to tradition, Richard the Lion-Hearted was married here in 1191. The **Cyprus Medieval Museum** is housed in the castle and displays a variety of medieval armor and relics. ✉ *Near old port,* ☎ *05/330132.* ⏲ *Weekdays 7:30–5, Sat. 9–5, Sun. 10–1.*

For a glimpse of Cypriot folklore, visit the **Folk Art Museum.** The collection includes national costumes and fine examples of weaving and other crafts. ✉ *Agiou Andreou 253,* ☎ *05/362303.* ⏲ *Mon. and Wed.–Fri. 8:30–1:30 and 4–7 (winter 3–5:30); Tues. 8:30–1:30.*

At the annual **Limassol Wine Festival** in September, local wineries offer free samples and demonstrate traditional grape-pressing methods. There are open-air music and dance performances. You can take a side trip to the **KEO Winery,** just west of the town, which welcomes visitors daily. ✉ *Roosevelt Ave., toward the new port,* ☎ *05/362053.* 🎫 *Free.* ⏲ *Tours weekdays, 10.*

★ **Kolossi Castle,** a Crusader fortress of the Knights of St. John, is 15 minutes by car west of Limassol. This notable piece of military architecture was constructed during the 13th century and rebuilt during the 15th. ✉ *Road to Paphos.* ⏲ *June–Sept., daily 7:30–7:30; Oct.–May, daily 7:30–5.*

Kourion (Curium), west of Limassol, has numerous Greek and Roman ruins. There is an **amphitheater,** where classical and Shakespearean plays are sometimes staged. Next to the theater is the **Villa of Eustolios,** a summerhouse built by a wealthy Christian. A nearby **Roman stadium** has been partially rebuilt. Three kilometers (2 mi) farther is the **Apollo Hylates** (Sanctuary of Apollo of the Woodlands), an impressive archaeological site. ✉ *Main Paphos Rd.* ⏲ *Daily 7:30–sunset (winter 7:30–5:30).*

$$$ ✕ **Scottis Steak House.** Just off the city's main thoroughfare, Makarios Avenue, this restaurant's plain-looking exterior hides some of the best steaks available in Cyprus, all served with tasty fresh vegetables. ✉ *38 Souli St.,* ☎ *05/335173. AE, DC, MC, V.*

$$ ✕ **Porta.** A varied menu of international and Cypriot dishes, such as foukoudha barbecue (grilled strips of steak) and trout baked in prawn and mushroom sauce, is served in this restored warehouse. On many nights you'll be entertained by soft, live music. ✉ *17 Yenethliou Mitella, Old Castle,* ☎ *05/360339. MC, V.*

$$$$ **Le Meridien.** The striking lobby of this spacious, luxurious hotel is pink marble and glass. You'll find all the amenities expected in a first-class hotel, as well as the island's largest swimming pool. The water-sport options include scuba diving. ✉ *Old Limassol–Nicosia Rd., Box 6560,* ☎ *05/634000,* FAX *05/634222. 191 rooms, 60 villas. 3 restaurants, pool. AE, DC, MC, V.*

$$ **Azur Beach.** This fine apartment/hotel has a good sandy beach and helpful management. ✉ *Potamios Yermasoyias, Box 1318,* ☎ *05/322667,* FAX *05/321897. 24 1-bedroom apartments, 12 studios, 60 rooms. 2 restaurants. DC, MC, V.*

$ **Continental.** A great sea view adds to the appeal of this family hotel close to the castle. ✉ *137 Spyros Araouzos Ave., Box 398,* ☎ *05/362530,* FAX *05/373030. 30 rooms. AE, V.*

Troodos Mountains

North of Limassol, the Troodos Mountains, which rise to 1,950 m (6,500 ft), are popular in summer for their shady cedar and pine forests and their cool springs. Small, painted churches in the Troodos and Pitsilia Foothills are rich examples of a rare indigenous art form. **Asinou Church,** near the village of Nikitari, and **Agios Nikolaos tis Stegis** (St. Nicholas of the Roof), south of Kakopetria, are especially noteworthy. Nearby is the **Tall Trees Trout Farm,** an oasis serving delicious meals of fresh fish. In winter, skiers take over. **Platres,** in the foothills of Mt. Olympus, is the principal resort. Be sure to visit the **Kykkos** monastery, founded in 1100, whose prized icon of the Virgin is reputed to have been painted by St. Luke.

Petra tou Romiou

The legendary **birthplace of Aphrodite** is just off the main road between Limassol and Petra. Signs in Greek point to the spot.

Paphos

In the west of the island 142 km (88 mi) southwest of Nicosia, the town combines superb sea swimming with archaeological sites and a rich history. Near the birthplace of Aphrodite (☞ *above*)—Greek goddess of love and beauty—it has a modern center with numerous ancient sights.

The **Paphos District Museum** is famous for its pottery, jewelry, and statuettes from Cyprus's Roman villas. ✉ *43 Grivas Dighenis Ave., Ktima,* ☎ *06/240215.* ⏲ *Weekdays 7:30–2:30 and 4–6 (winter 7:30–2 and 3–5), weekends 10–1.*

★ There are notable icons in the **Byzantine Museum** in the archiepiscopal palace. ✉ *7 Andreas Ioannou St.,* ☎ *06/232092.*

The charming **Ethnographical Museum** provides a fascinating review of historical times with various rooms of typical old homes carefully re-created in their original state, including furnishings, fabrics, and kitchen and agricultural utensils. ✉ *1 Exo Vrysi,* ☎ *06/232010.* ⏲ *Daily 9–1 and 3–7 (winter 9–1 and 2–5).*

Don't miss the elaborate **Roman mosaics** in the **Roman Villa of Theseus**, the **House of Dionysos**, and the **House of Aion.** The mosaics are among the finest in the eastern Mediterranean. The town bus stops nearby. ✉ *Kato Paphos (New Paphos), near the harbor.* ⏲ *Daily 7:30–sunset (winter 7:30–5:30).*

★ The **Tombs of the Kings,** an early necropolis, date from 300 BC. Though the coffin niches are empty, a powerful sense of mystery remains. ✉ *Kato Paphos (New Paphos).* ⏲ *Summer, daily 7:30–sunset; winter, daily 7:30–5:30.*

$$ ✕ **Chez Alex.** A well-established tavern, it serves only fresh fish (which varies according to the catch of the day) and fish mezes. ✉ *7 Constantia St., Kato Paphos,* ☎ *06/234767. AE, DC, MC, V.*

$$ ✕ **Corallo Restaurant.** Sheltered from the main road by grapevines, this traditional, family-run restaurant is just outside Paphos on the northern coastal road toward Coral Bay. The veal is recommended, as is the swordfish, a house specialty. Meals are served with homegrown vegetables. ✉ *Peyia,* ☎ *06/621052. DC, MC, V.*

$$$ 🏨 **Paphos Beach.** Surrounded by attractive gardens, this hotel has many facilities. Water sports are important as well. Accommodations are either in the main hotel or in spacious bungalows on the grounds. ✉ *Posidonos St., Box 136,* ☎ *06/233091,* FAX *06/242818. 224 rooms, 20 bungalows. 3 restaurants, pool. AE, DC, MC, V.*

$$ 🏨 **Amalthea Hotel.** This hotel on the beach amid banana groves has a friendly, personal atmosphere fostered by the resident owner-managers. The impressive, open lobby, furnished with gray leather couches and large plants, overlooks the water, and the rooms have balconies with sea views. ✉ *Kissonerga Rd., Box 323,* ☎ *06/247777,* FAX *06/245963. 168 rooms. Restaurant, 2 pools. AE, DC, MC, V.*

$$ 🏨 **Hilltop Gardens Hotel Apartments.** All apartments have a view of the sea, just 500 yards away. The decor is a pleasant mixture of traditional Cypriot village style, including wooden furniture, and modern touches. ✉ *Off Tombs of the Kings Rd., Box 185,* ☎ *06/243111,* FAX *06/248229. 48 apartments. Pool. AE, DC, MC, V.*

Polis

Just past the town's fishing harbor of Latchi and 48 km (30 mi) north of Paphos, are the **Baths of Aphrodite,** where the goddess is said to have seduced her swains. The wild, undeveloped Akamas Peninsula is perfect for a hike.

NORTHERN CYPRUS

There are two important things to bear in mind in Northern Cyprus. One is to obey the "no photographs" signs wherever they appear. The other is to note that as Turkish is the language used here, Turkish names designate the cities and towns: Nicosia is known as Lefkoşa, Kyrenia as Girne, and Famagusta as Gazimagusa. A useful map showing these and other Turkish names is available free from tourist offices.

Northern Cyprus A to Z

Money Matters

COSTS

Prices for food and accommodations tend to be lower than those in the Republic of Cyprus. Wine and spirits, on the other hand, are imported from Turkey, and drinks will be slightly more expensive.

CURRENCY

The monetary unit in Northern Cyprus is the Turkish lira (TL). There are bills for 5,000,000; 1,000,000; 500,000; 250,000; 100,000; 50,000; and 20,000 TL and coins for 10,000; 5,000; 2,500; and 1,000 TL. The Turkish lira is subject to considerable inflation, so most of the prices in this section are quoted in U.S. dollars.

SAMPLE PRICES

A cup of coffee costs around $1, a glass of beer about $1.50. Wine is around $3 per glass. An 80-km (50-mi) taxi ride costs about $30. Admission to museums costs about $1.

Opening and Closing Times

In the hot summer months (May–September), weekday museum hours are usually 8–1:30 and 4–6, but check before you visit.

Transportation

BY BUS AND DOLMUŞ

Buses and the shared dolmuş (taxis) are the cheapest forms of transportation. Service is frequent on main routes. A bus from Nicosia to Kyrenia costs about 90¢, and to Famagusta about $1.50. A seat in a dolmuş for the same trips would cost about $1.50 and $3, respectively.

BY CAR

☞ By Car *in* Republic of Cyprus, *above*.

BY PLANE

Cyprus Turkish Airlines, Istanbul Airlines, and Turkish Airlines run all flights via mainland Turkey, usually with a change of plane at Istanbul. There are also direct flights from Adana, Ankara, Antalya, and İzmir to Ercan Airport near Nicosia. Ferries run from Mersin and Tasucu in Turkey to Famagusta and Kyrenia, respectively. It is not possible to enter Northern Cyprus from the Republic except for a day trip from Nicosia, and it is not possible to enter Cyprus from Northern Cyprus.

Visitor Information

Department of Tourism Marketing (Selçuklu Caddesi, Lefkoşa/Nicosia, ☎ 90/392/228–3666, FAX 90/392/228–5625; postal address, Selçuklu Cad., Lefkoşa-KKTC, Mersin–10, Turkey). Regional tourism offices: Gazimagusa, Girne, and Lefkoşa.

Weather

☞ Weather *in* Republic of Cyprus A to Z, *above*.

Exploring Northern Cyprus

Lefkoşa (Nicosia)

The Turkish half of the city is the capital of Northern Cyprus. In addition to Venetian fortifications (☞ Exploring the Republic of Cyprus, *above*), it contains the **Selimiye Mosque** (✉ Selimiye St.), originally the 13th-century Cathedral of St. Sophia and a fine example of Gothic architecture to which a pair of minarets has been added. Near the Girne Gate is the **Mevlevi Tekke ve Etnografy Müzesi** (Mevlevi Shrine and Ethnographic Museum), the former home of the Mevlevi Dervishes, a Sufi order popularly known as Whirling Dervishes. The building now houses a museum of Turkish history and culture. ✉ *Girne St.* ⏲ *Weekdays 8–1 and 2–5, Sat. 8–1, Sun. 10–1.*

A walk around the Old City, within the encircling walls, is rich with glimpses from the Byzantine, Lusignan, and Venetian past. A great deal of restoration and reconstruction work is being undertaken, especially in the parts of the city beyond the walls.

Girne (Kyrenia)

Of the coastal resorts, Girne, with its yacht-filled harbor, is the most appealing. There are excellent beaches to the east and west of the town. **Girne Castle,** overlooking the harbor, is Venetian. It now houses the Batık Gemi Müzesi (Shipwreck Museum), whose prize possession is the remains of a ship that sank around 300 BC. ⏲ *Weekdays 8–1 and 2–5, Sat. 8–1, Sun. 10–1.*

It is well worth making two short excursions from Girne. The fantastic ruins of the **Castle of St. Hilarion** stand on a hilltop 11 km (7 mi) to the southwest. It's a strenuous walk, so take a taxi; the views are breathtaking. The ruins of the former **Abbey of Bellapais,** built during the 12th century by the Lusignans, are just as impressive. They lie on a mountainside 6 km (4 mi) to the southeast.

Gazimagusa (Famagusta)

The chief port of Northern Cyprus, Gazimagusa, has massive and well-preserved Venetian walls and the late-13th-century Gothic Cathedral of St. Nicholas, now Lala Mustafa Pasha Mosque. The Old Town, within the walls, is the most intriguing part to explore.

Salamis, north of Gazimagusa, is an ancient ruined city and perhaps the most dramatic archaeological site on the island. St. Barnabas and St. Paul arrived in Salamis and established a church near here. The present ruins date largely from the 12th-century Lusignan rulers of Cyprus, who came from France, but Salamis does contain relics of earlier civilizations, including Greek and Roman settlements. The setting is beautiful, and some of the ruins are overgrown, filling the place with a sense of mystery.

8 Czech Republic

Prague, Side Trips: Bohemia and Moravia

For all its history, the Czech Republic is a very young nation. After a dramatic but peaceful revolution overthrew a Communist regime that had been in power for 40 years, Czechoslovakia split in 1993 as its two constituent republics, Czech and Slovak, parted ways to form independent countries.

To international observers, the rush to split the republics came as a surprise. Formed from the ruins of the Austro-Hungarian empire at the end of World War I, Czechoslovakia appeared to withstand the threat of divisive nationalism and brought stability to the potentially volatile region. During the difficult 1930s, the Czechoslovak republic stood as the model democracy in central Europe. In the 1960s a courageous Slovak, Alexander Dubček, led the 1968 Prague Spring, an intense period of national renewal. Students and opponents of the Communist regime in both Prague and Bratislava toppled the ruling party in 1989.

In time, however, the separatist forces triumphed. Czechoslovakia proved to be an artificial creation that masked important and long-standing cultural differences between two outwardly similar peoples. The old Czech Lands of Bohemia and Moravia, whose territory makes up most of the Czech Republic, can look to a rich cultural history that goes back a millennium, and they played pivotal roles in the great religious and social conflicts of European history. Slovakia, by contrast, languished for centuries as an agrarian outpost of the Hungarian empire. Given the state of the Slovaks' national ego, independence was probably inevitable.

Today, travelers have rediscovered Prague, while Prague is rediscovering the world. Since the 1989 revolution, the Czech capital has become one of Europe's top destinations. Forget old impressions of neglect and melancholy; Prague exudes an atmosphere of enthusiasm and provides such conveniences as English-language newspapers, attentive service, and restaurateurs who will try to find you a seat even if you don't have a reservation. Musicians and writers find new inspiration in the city that once harbored Mozart and Kafka. Spectacu-

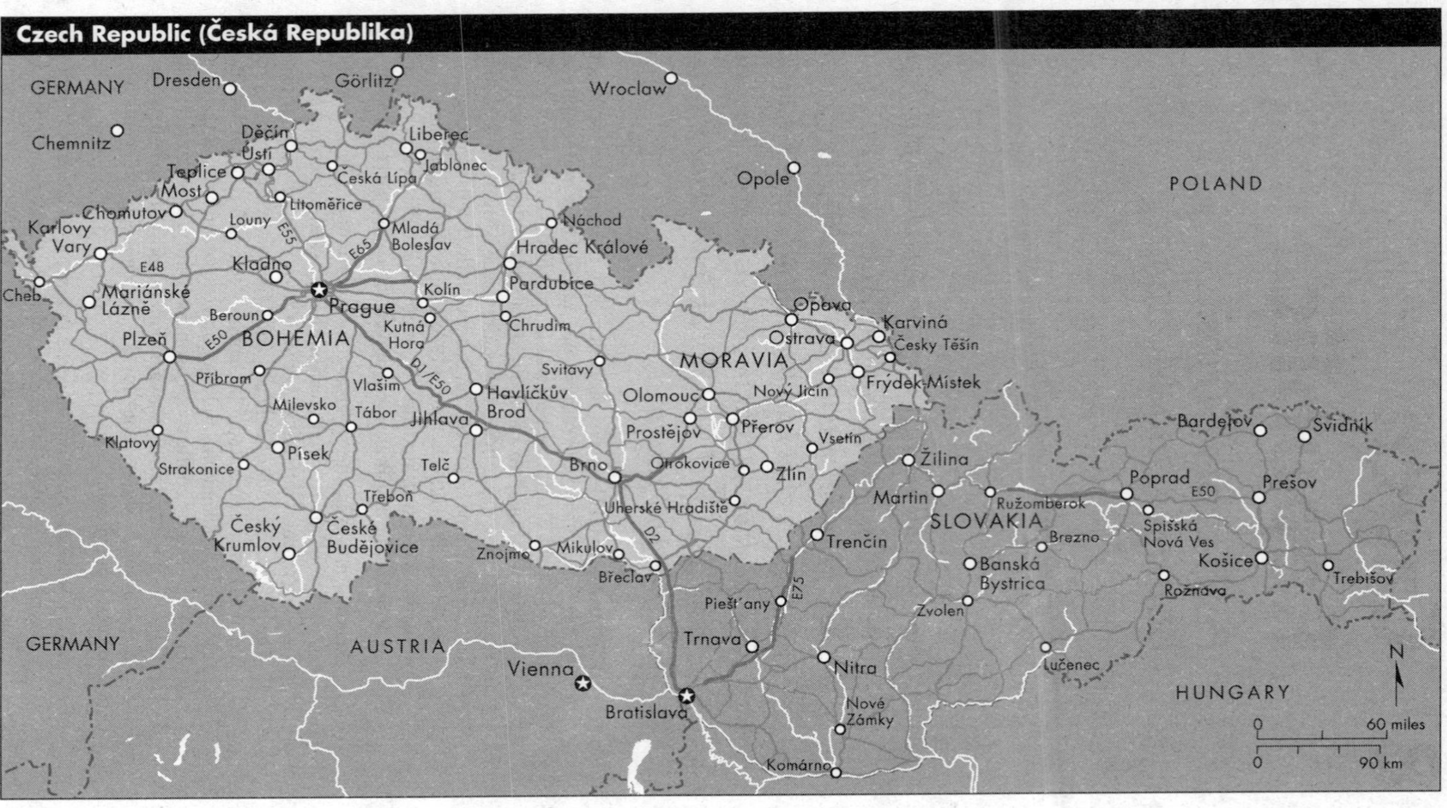

Czech Republic (Česká Republika)
GERMANY
POLAND
AUSTRIA
HUNGARY
SLOVAKIA
BOHEMIA
MORAVIA
Prague
Bratislava
Vienna
Chemnitz
Dresden
Görlitz
Wroclaw
Opole
Cheb
Karlovy Vary
Mariánské Lázně
Chomutov
Most
Teplice
Ústí
Děčín
Louny
Litoměřice
Česká Lípa
Liberec
Jablonec
Mladá Boleslav
Kladno
Beroun
Plzeň
Příbram
Klatovy
Strakonice
Písek
Milevsko
Tábor
Vlašim
Český Krumlov
České Budějovice
Třeboň
Kolín
Kutná Hora
Náchod
Hradec Králové
Pardubice
Chrudim
Svitavy
Havlíčkův Brod
Jihlava
Telč
Znojmo
Mikulov
Břeclav
Brno
Uherské Hradiště
Otrokovice
Prostějov
Olomouc
Přerov
Zlín
Vsetín
Nový Jičín
Opava
Ostrava
Karviná
Česky Těšín
Frýdek-Místek
Žilina
Martin
Trenčín
Piešťany
Trnava
Nitra
Nové Zámky
Komárno
Zvolen
Banská Bystrica
Ružomberok
Brezno
Lučenec
Poprad
Spišská Nová Ves
Rožňava
Košice
Prešov
Bardejov
Svidník
Trebišov
E48
E50
E55
E65
D1/E50
D2
E75
N
0
60 miles
0
90 km

lar Gothic, Baroque, and Art Nouveau treasures stand in glorious counterpoint to the drab remnants of socialist architecture that exist in the city.

Outside the capital you can discover everything from imperial spas to modern industrial cities. Don't pass up the lovely towns and castles of southern Bohemia: the Renaissance river town of Český Krumlov ranks among Central Europe's grandest sights. Expect improved services as compared with only a couple of years ago, although prices are rising along with standards.

CZECH REPUBLIC A TO Z

Customs

You may import duty free 200 cigarettes, 50 cigars, 1 liter of spirits, 2 liters of wine, and gifts with a total value of 1,000 Kč. Goods worth up to 3,000 Kč (aprox. 90 USD) are not liable to duty upon arrival. Items of greater value (jewelry, computers, and so on) should be declared on arrival so that there will be no problems with customs officials on departure.

You may only export antiques that are certified as not of historical value. Reputable dealers will advise. Play safe, and also save your receipts.

Dining

Dining options include restaurants; the *vinárna* (wine cellar), which covers anything from inexpensive wine bars to swank restaurants; the more down-to-earth *pivnice* or *hospody* (beer taverns); cafeterias; and a growing number of coffee shops and snack bars. Eating out is popular. Make reservations at all but the humblest places during high season. Privatization has brought more culinary variety, especially in Prague. Be wary of food bought from street vendors, as cases of salmonella are on the rise.

Prague ham makes a favorite first course. The most typical main dish is roast pork (or duck or goose) with sauerkraut. Also try the outstanding trout, carp, and other freshwater fish. Crepes, here called *palačinky*, are ubiquitous and may come with savory or sweet fillings. Dumplings in various forms, generally with a rich gravy, accompany many dishes. A typical Czech breakfast is cold cuts and spreadable cheese or jam with rolls, washed down with coffee.

MEALTIMES

Lunch is usually from 11:30 to 2 or 3; dinner from 6 to 9:30 or 10. Some places are open all day, and you'll find it easier to get a table during off-hours.

RATINGS

Prices are reasonable by American standards, even in some of the more expensive restaurants. Czechs don't normally go for three-course meals, and the following prices apply only if you're having a first course, main course, and dessert (prices are per person, excluding wine and tip).

CATEGORY	PRAGUE	OTHER AREAS
$$$$	over 1,440 Kč	over 1,260 Kč
$$$	900 Kč–1,440 Kč	720 Kč–1,260 Kč
$$	540 Kč–900 Kč	360 Kč–720 Kč
$	under 540 Kč	under 360 Kč

WHAT TO WEAR

A jacket and tie are recommended for $$$$ and $$$ restaurants. Informal dress is appropriate elsewhere.

Language

You'll find a growing number of English speakers, especially among young people and those associated with the tourist industry. German is generally understood throughout the country.

Lodging

Accommodations in the Czech Republic range from hotels, motels, private lodgings, and hostels to campsites. Renovated older properties have great character and style. There is still a shortage of hotel rooms during the peak season, so make reservations well in advance. Many private room agencies offer a variety of lodgings. The standards of facilities and services in the less expensive categories hardly match those in the West, so don't be surprised by faulty plumbing or indifferent reception clerks. Unless otherwise noted, rooms include bath.

CAMPING

Maps showing the locations of the many campgrounds around the country are available at bookstores and tourist offices. Several campgrounds in Prague operate year-round; a list is available from the Prague Information Service (PIS) (☞ Visitor Information *in* Prague Essentials, *below*).

HOTELS

These are officially graded with from one to five stars, using the international classification system. Outside Prague and the spa resorts, few hotels carry more than three stars.

Bills can be paid in koruny (check to see if your hotel insists on hard currency; some hotels refuse to accept credit cards). Breakfast is often included in the room price.

PRIVATE LODGINGS

Many travel agencies in Prague offer accommodation in private homes. Such rooms are invariably cheaper and often more comfortable than hotel rooms, though you may have to sacrifice some privacy. The largest room-finding service is probably **AVE** (☎ 02/2422–3226) in the main and Holešovice train stations and at the airport (all branches are open daily). Insist on a room in the city center, however, or you may find yourself in a dreary, far-off suburb. Another helpful agency is **City of Prague Accommodation Service** (✉ Haštalská 7, ☎ 02/231–6663). Elsewhere, look along main roads for signs that read ROOM FREE, or in German, ZIMMER FREI or PRIVATZIMMER. Offices of the travel bureau Čedok and the Prague Information Service (PIS) (☞ Visitor Information *in* Prague Essentials, *below*) can also help you find private accommodations.

RATINGS

Prices are for double rooms, generally including breakfast. Prices at the lower end of the scale apply to low season. Expect a 15%–25% rate increase at certain periods, such as Christmas, New Year's, Easter, or during festivals.

CATEGORY	PRAGUE	OTHER AREAS
$$$$	over 5,200 Kč	over 2,600 Kč
$$$	2,600 Kč–5,200 Kč	1,300 Kč–2,600 Kč
$$	1,300 Kč–2,600 Kč	650 Kč–1,300 Kč
$	under 1,300 Kč	under 650 Kč

YOUTH HOSTELS

IYH members can book reservations at any of 25-odd hostels across the country, including three in Prague (350 Kč and up, including breakfast), at **KMC** (✉ Karoliny Světlé 30, 160 00 Prague 6, ☎ 02/9000–1458). IYH cards are also sold here (200 Kč) and at **CKM Youth Travel Service** (✉ Žitná 12, Prague, ☎ 02/2491–5767).

In Prague most hostels are open to anyone, and generally operate year-round. One of these is **Hostel Estec** (✉ Vaníčkova 5, 160 00 Prague 6, ☎ 02/5721–5263, FAX 02/527343). Ask at accommodation agencies about hostels outside Prague. Rates start at 300 Kč per person at hostels not affiliated with IYH.

Mail

POSTAL RATES

First-class (airmail) letters to the United States and Canada cost 11 Kč up to 20 grams, postcards 7 Kč. First-class (airmail) letters to the United Kingdom cost 8 Kč up to 20 grams, postcards 5 Kč.

RECEIVING MAIL

Mail can be labeled "poste restante" and sent to the main post office in Prague (✉ Jindřišská 14, Prague) or to any other main post office. There's no charge. The American Express office (✉ Václavské náme 56/Wenceslas Sq. 56, Prague) will hold letters to cardholders or holders of American Express traveler's checks for up to a month free of charge.

Money Matters

COSTS

Costs are highest in Prague and only slightly lower in the main Bohemian resorts and spas, though even in these places you can now find inexpensive accommodations in private homes. The least expensive area is southern Moravia.

CURRENCY

The unit of currency in the Czech Republic is the crown, or *koruna* (plural *koruny*), written as Kč, and divided into 100 *haléřů* (hellers). There are bills of 20, 50, 100, 200, 500, 1,000, and 5,000 koruny and coins of 10, 20, and 50 hellers and 1, 2, 5, 10, 20, and 50 koruny. At press time (spring 1998), the rate of exchange was 32 Kč to the U.S. dollar, 23 Kč to the Canadian dollar, 54 Kč to the pound sterling, 21 Kč to the Australian dollar, and 18 Kč to the New Zealand dollar. Banks and ATMs give the best rates. Banks and private exchange outlets, which litter Prague's tourist routes, charge either a set fee or a percentage of the transaction or both, and for small transactions (US$100 or less) the charge at a bank may be more than you would pay for the same transaction at a private exchange outlet. It's wise to compare. The koruna is fully convertible and can be purchased outside the country and changed into other currencies, but you should keep your receipts and convert your koruny before you leave the country just to be sure.

SAMPLE PRICES

Cup of coffee, 30 Kč; beer (½ liter), 10 Kč–25 Kč; Coca-Cola, 20 Kč; ham sandwich, 30 Kč; 1-mi taxi ride, 50 Kč–100 Kč. Museums and castles admission 20 Kč–300 Kč.

TIPPING

A service charge is rarely added to restaurant bills. Give a tip for good service directly to the waiter when you pay your bill. As a rule of thumb, round up to the nearest multiple of 10 (i.e., if the bill comes to 83 Kč, give the waiter 90 Kč). Give 10% on big or group tabs. For taxis, consider 10% a reasonable tip. In the better hotels doormen should get 20 Kč for each bag they carry to the check-in desk; bellhops get up to 40 Kč each for taking them up to your rooms. In $$ or $ hotels plan to lug your own baggage.

National Holidays

January 1; April 4 and 5 (Easter Sunday and Monday); May 1 (Labor Day); May 8 (Liberation Day); July 5 (Sts. Cyril and Methodius); July 6 (Jan Hus); October 28 (Czech National Day); December 24–26.

Opening and Closing Times

Banks are open weekdays 8–5. **Museums** are usually open Tuesday–Sunday 10–5. **Shops** are generally open weekdays 9–6; some close for lunch between noon and 2. Many are also open till noon or later on Saturday.

Passports and Visas

Americans, Canadians, British citizens, and Australians are required to have a valid passport for stays of up to 30 days in the Czech Republic. Australians also need tourist visas to enter the Czech Republic; the visa is free if obtained at a Czech embassy or consulate outside the Czech Republic; at the Czech Republic border, it costs 1,600 Kc.

Telephoning

To use a public phone buy a phone card at a newsstand or tobacconist. Cards cost 100 Kč for 50 units or 190 Kč for 100 units. To place a call lift the receiver, insert the card, and dial.

COUNTRY CODE

A new country code—420, replacing the old code, 42—went into service in 1997.

INTERNATIONAL CALLS

Some special international pay phone booths in central Prague will take 5 Kč coins or accept phone cards that allow automatic dialing. You will also find coin and card booths at the main post office (⊠ Jindřišská 14), near Václavské náměstí (Wenceslas Square). The international dialing code is 00. Dial 0132 for international inquiries to the United States, Canada, or the United Kingdom. To place a call via an **AT&T USA Direct** international operator, dial 0042–000101; for **MCI,** dial 0042–000112; for **Sprint,** dial 0042–087187. International rates vary according to destination.

LOCAL CALLS

Local calls cost one unit.

Transportation

Traveling in the Czech Republic is relatively simple once you know the basic street sign words: *ulice* (street), abbreviated to *ul.* (note that common usage often drops ulice in a printed address), *náměstí* (square), abbreviated to *nám.*, and *třída* (avenue). In most cases blue signs on buildings mark the street address.

BY BUS

An excellent bus network provides quicker service than trains at somewhat higher prices (though they are still low by western standards). Buses are always full. Reserve your seat in advance, especially on long-distance routes. Seat reservations are called *Místenka.*

BY CAR

Breakdowns. The Yellow Angels (☎ 123 or 124) operate a patrol service on main highways. The emergency number for motorists is ☎ 154.

Gasoline. At about 93 Kč ($2.60) a gallon, gasoline is expensive. Look for service stations along main roads on the outskirts of towns and cities. Lead-free gasoline, known as "natural," is sold at all stations.

Road Conditions. Main roads are usually good, if sometimes narrow. An expressway links Plzeň, Prague, Brno, and Bratislava. If you plan to do much exploring, pick up an *Auto Atlas,* available in most bookstores and souvenir shops.

Rules of the Road. Drive on the right. Speed limits are 60 kph (37 mph) in urban areas, 90 kph (55 mph) on open roads, and 110 kph (68 mph) on expressways. Seat belts are compulsory outside urban areas; drinking and driving is strictly prohibited. A permit is required to drive on expressways and other four-lane highways. It costs 800 Kč and is sold at border crossings and some service stations.

BY PLANE

Good air service links Prague with several other towns, including Ostrava in Moravia and Bratislava and Poprad (for the High Tatras) in Slovakia. Prices are reasonable. Make reservations at Čedok offices or directly at **ČSA,** Czech Airlines (☎ 02/2010–4310).

BY TRAIN

The country has an extensive rail network. As elsewhere in Eastern Europe, expect relatively low fares and crowded trains. You have to pay a small supplement on EuroCity (EC) and InterCity (IC) trains. Most long-distance trains have dining cars; overnight trains between main centers have sleeping cars.

Visitor Information

Many towns have an information office ("Infocentrum") or private tourist bureau, often in the main square. The ubiquitous Čedok (main office in Prague, ✉ Na Příkopě 18, 111 35 Prague 1, ☎ 02/2419–7111), now a private travel agency, has offices in all larger towns.

Weather

Organized sightseeing tours run from April or May through October (year-round in Prague). Some monuments, especially castles, either close entirely or open for shorter hours in winter. Hotel rates may drop during the off-season except during festivals. May, the month of fruit blossoms, is the time of the Prague Spring International Music Festival. Be prepared for huge crowds at Prague sites in the summer.

CLIMATE

The following are the average daily maximum and minimum temperatures for Prague.

Jan.	36F	2C	**May**	66F	19C	**Sept.**	68F	20C
	25	– 4		46	8		50	10
Feb.	37F	3C	**June**	72F	22C	**Oct.**	55F	13C
	27	– 3		52	11		41	5
Mar.	46F	8C	**July**	75F	24C	**Nov.**	46F	8C
	32	0		55	13		36	2
Apr.	58F	14C	**Aug.**	73F	23C	**Dec.**	37F	3C
	39	4		55	13		28	– 2

PRAGUE

Poets, philosophers, and the Czech-in-the-street have long sung the praises of Praha (Prague), also referred to as the "Golden City of a Hundred Spires." Like Rome, Prague is built on seven hills, which slope gently or tilt precipitously down to the Vltava (Moldau) River. The riverside location, enhanced by a series of graceful bridges, makes a great setting for two of the city's most notable features: its extravagant, fairytale architecture and its memorable music. Mozart claimed that no one understood him better than the citizens of Prague, and he was only one of several great masters who lived or lingered here.

It was under Karel IV (Charles IV), during the 14th century, that Prague first became the seat of the Holy Roman Empire—virtually the capital of Western Europe—and acquired its distinctive Gothic imprint. At times you'll need to look quite hard for this medieval inheritance;

it's still here, though, under the overlays of graceful Renaissance and exuberant Baroque.

Prague escaped serious wartime damage, but it didn't escape neglect. During the last decade, however, artisans and their workers have restored dozens of the city's historic buildings with care and sensitivity.

Exploring Prague

Shades of the five medieval towns that combined to form Prague linger in the divisions of its historic districts. On the flat eastern shore of the Vltava River are three areas arranged like nesting boxes: **Josefov** (the old Jewish Quarter) within **Staré Město** (Old Town) within **Nové Město** (New Town). **Malá Strana** (the Lesser Quarter) and **Hradčany** (Castle District) perch along the river's hillier west bank. Spanning the Vltava is **Karlův most** (the Charles Bridge), which links the Old Town to the Lesser Quarter; everything within the historic center can be reached on foot in a half hour or less from here.

Nové Město and Staré Město (New Town and Old Town)

Numbers in the margin correspond to points of interest on the Prague map.

11 **Betlémská kaple** (Bethlehem Chapel). The martyr and national hero Jan Hus thundered his humanitarian teachings from the chapel pulpit during the early 15th century. The structure was reconstructed in the 1950s, but the little door through which Hus came to the pulpit is original, as are some of the inscriptions on the wall. ✉ *Betlémské nám.* ⏲ *Apr.–Sept. daily 9–6; Oct.–Mar. daily 9–5.*

3 **Celetná ulice.** Medieval kings set off along this street on their way to their coronation at Prague Castle. The **Royal Route** includes this street, passing the Gothic spires of the Týn Church in Old Town Square; it then crosses Charles Bridge and goes up to the castle. As you explore the route, you can study every variety of Romanesque, Gothic, Renaissance, and Baroque architecture.

10 **Clam-Gallas palác** (Clam-Gallas Palace). Squatting on a constricted site in the heart of the Old Town is this pompous Baroque palace, designed by the great Viennese architect J. B. Fischer von Erlach. All the sculptures, including the Titans that struggle to support the two doorways, are the work of one of the great Bohemian Baroque artists, Matthias Braun. Take a peek inside at the superb staircase. ✉ *Husova 20.*

4 **Dům U černé Matky Boží** (House of the Black Madonna). This Cubist building adds a decided jolt to the architectural styles along Celetná ulice. In the second decade of this century, several leading Czech architects boldly applied Cubism's radical reworking of visual space to structures. The Black Madonna, designed by Josef Gočár, is unflinchingly modern yet topped with an almost Baroque tile roof. ✉ *Celetná ul. (at Ovocný trh).* ⏲ *Tues.–Sun. 10–6.*

2 **Na Příkopě.** Once part of the moat surrounding the Old Town, this street is now an elegant (in places) pedestrian mall. It leads from the bottom of Wenceslas Square to the **Obecní dům** (Municipal House), Prague's most lavish Art Nouveau building, which reopened in 1997 after a controversial, two-year refurbishment. A bridge links it to the Prašná brána (Powder Tower), a 19th-century neo-Gothic restoration of the medieval original. ✉ *Nám. Republiky.*

★ 5 **Staroměstské náměstí** (Old Town Square). The old commercial center of the Old Town is now a remarkably harmonious hub—architecturally beautiful and relatively car-free and quiet. Looming over the center, the twin towers of **Kostel Panny Marie před Týnem** (the Church of the Virgin Mary before Týn) still look forbidding even though their grimy stones have been cleaned and Disneyesque lighting has been installed in the spires. The large Secession-style **sculptural group** in the square's center commemorates the martyr Jan Hus, whose followers completed the Týn Church during the 15th century. The white Baroque **Kostel svatého Mikuláše** (Church of St. Nicholas) is tucked into the square's northwest angle. It was built by Kilian Ignatz Dientzenhofer, co-architect also of the Lesser Quarter's church of the same name. Every hour, mobs converge on the famous Clock Tower of the **Staroměstská radnice** (Old Town Hall) as the clock's 15th-century mechanism activates a procession that includes the 12 Apostles. Note the skeleton figure of Death that tolls the bell.

❽ **Staronová synagóga** (Old-New Synagogue). A small congregation still attends the little Gothic Old-New Synagogue, one of Europe's oldest surviving houses of Jewish prayer. Men are required to cover their heads upon entering; skull caps can be bought for a small fee at the door. ⊠ *Červená at Pařížská.* ⊙ *Sun.–Thurs. 9–5, Fri. 9–2.*

★ ❾ **Starý židovský hřbitov** (Old Jewish Cemetery). The crowded cemetery is part of **Josefov,** the former Jewish quarter. Here, ancient tombstones lean into one another; below them, piled layer upon layer, are thousands of graves. Many gravestones—they date from the mid-14th to the late 17th centuries—are carved with symbols indicating the name, profession, and attributes of the deceased. If you visit the tomb of the 16th-century scholar Rabbi Löw, you may see scraps of paper covered with prayers or requests stuffed into the cracks. In legend the rabbi protected Prague's Jews with the help of a *golem,* or artificial man; today he still receives appeals for assistance. ⊠ *Entrance at Pinkas Synagogue, Široká 3.*

❶ **Václavské náměstí** (Wenceslas Square). In the Times Square of Prague hundreds of thousands voiced their disgust for the Communist regime in November 1989 at the outset of the "Velvet Revolution." The "square" is actually a broad boulevard that slopes down from the **Národní muzeum** (National Museum) and the equestrian **statue of St. Václav** (Wenceslas).

❻ **Výstara Franze Kafky** (Franz Kafka's birthplace). Since the 1989 revolution, Kafka's popularity has soared, and the works of this German Jewish writer are now widely available in Czech. A small museum in the house displays photos, editions of Kafta's books, and other memorabilia. (Kafka's grave lies in the overgrown New Jewish Cemetery at the Želivského Metro stop.) ⊠ *U radnice 5.* ⊙ *Tues.–Fri. 10–6, Sat. 10–5.*

❼ **Židovské muzeum (Jewish Museum).** The rich exhibits in the Josefov's Pinkas Synagogue, Maisel Synagogue, Klaus Synagogue, and Ceremonial Hall, along with the Old Jewish Cemetery, make up the museum. Jews, forced to fulfill Adolf Hitler's plan to document the lives of the people he was trying to exterminate, gathered the collections. They include ceremonial objects, textiles, and displays covering the history of Bohemia's and Moravia's Jews. The interior of the Pinkas Synagogue is especially poignant, as it is painted with the names of 77,297 Jewish Czechs killed during World War II. Communists closed the building and allowed it to decay; now, however, the lists have been restored. *Museum ticket offices:* ⊠ *U starého hřbitova 3a and Široká 3.* ⊙ *Sun.–Fri. 9–6 (9–4 in winter; last tour of cemetery at 3 in winter). Closed Sat. and religious holidays.*

Prague (Praha)

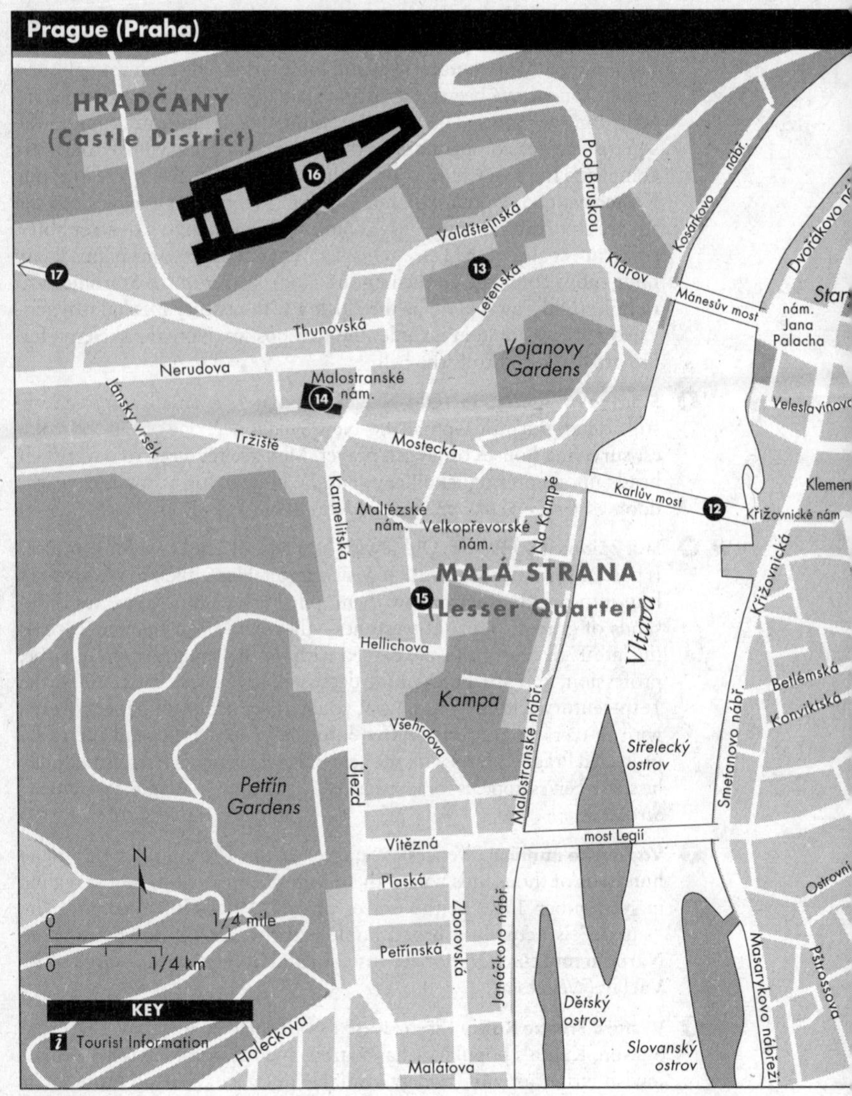

Betlémská kaple, **11**
Celetná ulice, **3**
Chrám svatého Mikuláše, **14**
Clam-Gallas palác, **10**
Dům U černé Matky Boží, **4**
Karlův most, **12**
Loreta, **17**
Malá Strana, **15**
Na Příkopě, **2**
Pražský hrad, **16**
Staroměstské náměstí, **5**
Staronová synagóga, **8**
Starý židovský hřbitov, **9**
Václavské náměstí, **1**
Valdštejnská zahrada, **13**
Výstara Franze Kafky, **6**
Židovské Muzeum, **7**

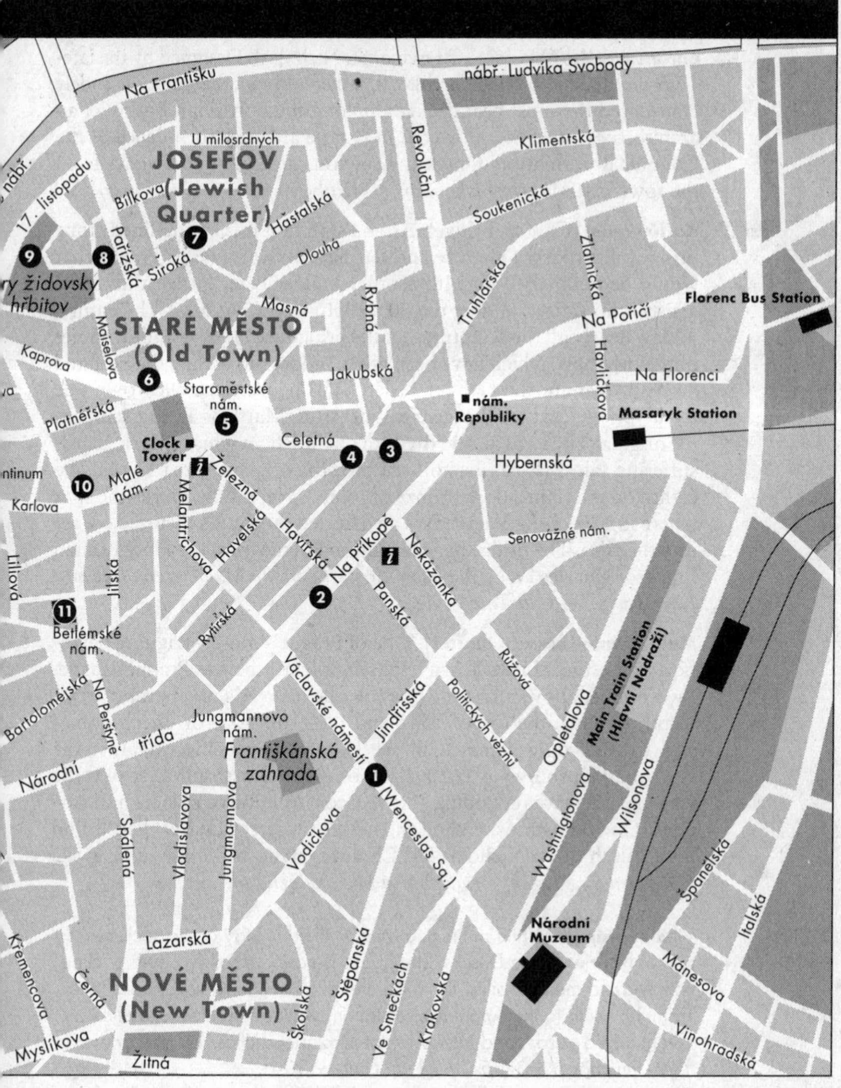

nábř. Ludvíka Svobody
Na Františku
U milosrdných
JOSEFOV (Jewish Quarter)
17. listopadu
Bílkova
Pařížská
Široká
Haštalská
Dlouhá
Revoluční
Klimentská
Soukenická
Zlatnická
Truhlářská
Rybná
Masná
ry židovsky hřbitov
Maiselova
STARÉ MĚSTO (Old Town)
Kaprova
Jakubská
Na Poříčí
Havlíčkova
Florenc Bus Station
Na Florenci
Masaryk Station
Staroměstské nám.
nám. Republiky
Platnéřská
Clock Tower
Celetná
Hybernská
Malé nám.
Karlova
Železná
Melantrichova
Havelská
Havířská
Na Příkopě
Nekázanka
Senovážné nám.
Liliová
Jilská
Panská
Betlémské nám.
Rytířská
Růžová
Main Train Station (Hlavní Nádraží)
Bartolomějská
Na Perštýně
Václavské náměstí
Jindřišská
Politických vězňů
Opletalova
Jungmannovo nám.
Národní
třída
Františkánská zahrada
(Wenceslas Sq.)
Vodičkova
Washingtonova
Wilsonova
Spálená
Vladislavova
Jungmannova
Španělská
Italská
Lazarská
Národní Muzeum
Křemencova
Černá
NOVÉ MĚSTO (New Town)
Školská
Štěpánská
Ve Smečkách
Krakovská
Mánesova
Vinohradská
Myslíkova
Žitná

Karlův most and Malá Strana (Charles Bridge and the Lesser Quarter)

⓮ **Chrám svatého Mikuláše** (Church of St. Nicholas). Designed by the late-17th-century Dietzenhofer architects, father and son, this edifice is widely considered the most beautiful example of the Bohemian Baroque, an architectural style that flowered in Prague after the turbulence of the Counter-Reformation. On clear days you can enjoy great views from the tower. ✉ *Malostranské nám.* ⏲ *Daily 9–4 (9–6 in summer).*

★ ⓬ **Karlův most** (Charles Bridge). As you stand on this statue-lined stone bridge, unsurpassed in grace and setting, you see views of Prague that would be familiar to its 14th-century builder Peter Parler and to the artists who started adding the 30 sculptures during the 17th century. Today, nearly all the sculptures on the bridge are fakes—skillful copies of the originals, which have been taken indoors to escape the polluted air. Still, examine the 12th on the left (starting from the Old Town side of the bridge), which depicts St. Luitgarde (Matthias Braun sculpted the original, circa 1710), and the 14th on the left, in which a Turk guards suffering saints (F. M. Brokoff sculpted the original, circa 1714). The eighth on the right side, a bronze of John of Nepomuk, marks the spot where in 1393 King Václav IV's men hurled the saint's tortured corpse into the river. The bridge itself is a gift to Prague from the Holy Roman Emperor Charles IV. ✉ *Between Mostecká ul. on Mala Strana side and Karlova ul. on Old Town side.*

⓯ **Malá Strana** (Lesser Quarter). One of Prague's most intriguing neighborhoods, the "Little Town" lolls indolently below Prague Castle. Two events, above all, made possible the quarter's aristocratic architectural visage: the fire of 1541 and the expulsions of Czech nobles and townspeople defeated in the Protestant rebellion against the Catholic Hapsburgs in 1620. Each of these catastrophes cleared the way for extensive rebuilding and new construction of palaces and gardens. On Malostranské náměstí (Lesser Quarter Square), you'll find the **Church of St. Nicholas** (☞ Chrám svatého Mikuláše, *above*). ✉ *Bordered by Pražský hrad, Petřín Hill, Vítězná ul.*

OFF THE BEATEN PATH — **Villa Bertramka** While in Prague Mozart liked to stay at the secluded estate of his friends the Dušeks. The house is now a small museum packed with Mozart memorabilia. From Karmelitská ulice in Malá Strana, take Tram 12 south to the Anděl Metro station; walk down Plzeňská ulice a few hundred yards, and take a left at Mozartova ulice. ✉ *Mozartova ul. 169, Smíchov,* ☎ *02/543893.* ⏲ *Daily 9:30–6.*

⓭ **Valdštejnská zahrada** (Wallenstein Gardens). This is one of the most elegant of the many sumptuous Lesser Quarter gardens. During the 1620s the Hapsburgs' victorious commander, Czech nobleman Albrecht of Wallenstein, demolished a wide swath of existing structures in order to build his oversize palace with its charming walled garden. A covered outdoor stage of late-Renaissance style dominates the western end. ✉ *Entrance at Letenská 10.* 🎫 *Free.* ⏲ *May–Sept., daily 9–7.*

Pražský hrad and Hradčany (Prague Castle and the Castle District)

⓱ **Loreta.** This Baroque church and shrine are named for the Italian town to which angels supposedly transported the Virgin Mary's house from Nazareth to save it from the infidel. The glory of its fabulous treasury is the monstrance, the *Sun of Prague,* with its 6,222 diamonds. Arrive on the hour to hear the 27-bell carillon. ✉ *Loretánské nám. 7.* ⏲ *Tues.–Sun. 9–noon and 1–4:30.*

★ 16 **Pražský hrad** (Prague Castle). From its narrow hilltop, the monumental castle complex has witnessed the changing fortunes of the city for more than 1,000 years. The castle's physical and spiritual core, **Chrám svatého Víta** (St. Vitus Cathedral), took from 1344 to 1929 to build, so you can trace in its lines architectural styles from high Gothic to Art Nouveau. The eastern end, mostly the work of Peter Parler, builder of the Charles Bridge, is a triumph of Bohemian Gothic. "Good King" Wenceslas (in reality a mere prince, later canonized) has his own chapel in the south transept, dimly lit and decorated with fine medieval wall paintings. Four silver angels hover over the tomb of St. John of Nepomuk, whose statue adorns many a Central European bridge, including the Charles Bridge. Note the fine 17th-century carved wooden panels on either side of the chancel. The left-hand panel shows a view of the castle and town in November 1620 as the defeated Czech Protestants flee into exile. The three easternmost chapels house tombs of Czech princes and kings of the 11th to the 13th centuries, while Charles IV and Rudolf II lie in the crypt, the former in a bizarre modern sarcophagus.

Behind St. Vitus's, don't miss the miniature houses of **Zlatá ulička** (Golden Lane). Its name, and the apocryphal tale of how Holy Roman Emperor Rudolf II used to lock up alchemists here until they transmuted lead into gold, may come from the gold-beaters who once lived here. Knightly tournaments often accompanied coronation ceremonies in the **Královský palác** (Royal Palace), next to the cathedral, hence the broad Riders' Staircase leading up to the grandiose **Vladislavský sál** (Vladislav Hall), with its splendid late-Gothic vaulting and Renaissance windows. Oldest of all the castle's buildings, though much restored, is the complex of **Bazilika svatého Jiří** (St. George's Basilica and Convent). The basilica's cool Romanesque lines hide behind a glowing salmon-color Baroque facade. The ex-convent houses a superb collection of Bohemian art from medieval religious sculptures to Baroque paintings. The castle **ramparts** afford glorious vistas of Prague's fabled hundred spires rising above the rooftops. ✉ *Main castle ticket office in Second Courtyard.* 🎫 *Tickets valid 3 days; admits visitors to cathedral, Royal Palace, and St. George's Basilica (but not convent gallery) and Powder Tower:* ☞ *Nové Město and Staré Město (New Town and Old Town), above.* ⏲ *Daily 9–5 (9–4 in winter); castle gardens, Apr.–Oct.*

Dining and Lodging

Eating out is important to Prague residents, so restaurants are well attended. Make reservations whenever possible. For details and price-category definitions, *see* Dining, *in* The Czech Republic A to Z, *above*.

Many of Prague's older hotels have been renovated, and new establishments in old buildings ornament the Old Town and Lesser Quarter. Very few hotel rooms in the more desirable districts go for less than $100 per double room in high season; most less-expensive hotels are far from the center of Prague. Private rooms and pensions remain the best budget deal. For details and price-category definitions, *see* Lodging *in* The Czech Republic A to Z, *above*.

$$$$ ✕ **Jewel of India.** Although generally Asian cooking is not Prague's forte, here is a spot worth seeking out for Northern Indian tandooris and other moderately spiced specialties, including some vegetarian dishes. The decor is luxurious without being stuffy, with rich colors and thick carpeting. ✉ *Pařížská 20, Staré Město,* ☎ *02/2481–1010. Reservations essential. AE, MC, V.*

$$$$ ★ ✕ **La Perle de Prague.** This French restaurant, which opened in 1996, continues to be one of Prague's most glamorous spots. The location doesn't hurt: atop the love-it-or-hate-it "Fred and Ginger" building, co-designed by Frank Gehry, whose two contrasting wings swoop and sway toward one another like a dancing couple. The nouvelle cuisine Parisian dishes are excellent: superb soups, young rabbit in mustard sauce, sea bream à la Badiane, and tournedos de boeuf with Bearnaise sauce. For dessert, there is a chocolate plate to die for (an assortment of tiny treats—tartelettes, ice cream, and so on—served in a fanciful style). ✉ *Raší Building, Rašínovo nábřeží 80 (at Resslova),* ☎ *02/2198–4160. Reservations essential. AE, DC, MC, V.*

$$$$ ★ ✕ **Opera Grill.** Though called a grill, this is a stylish little restaurant, complete with antique Meissen candelabra and such Czech specialties as *svíčková* (beef in a delectable cream sauce with a hint of lemon) and roast duck with dumplings. ✉ *K. Světlé 35, Staré Město,* ☎ *02/265508. Reservations essential. AE, MC, V. Dinner only.*

$$$$ ✕ **U Zlaté Hrušky.** Careful restoration has returned this restaurant to its original 18th-century style. It specializes in Moravian wines, which are well matched with fillet steaks and goose liver. ✉ *Nový Svět 3, Hradčany,* ☎ *02/2051–5356. Reservations essential. AE, V.*

$$$ ✕ **U Mecenáše.** This wine restaurant manages to be both medieval and elegant despite the presence of an ancient gallows. Try to get a table in the back room. The chef specializes in thick, juicy steaks, served with a variety of sauces. ✉ *Malostranské nám. 10, Malá Strana,* ☎ *02/533881. Reservations essential. AE, MC, V. Dinner only.*

$$$ ★ ✕ **U Modré Kachničky.** The exuberant, eclectic decor is as attractive as the Czech and international dishes served, which include steaks, duck, and game in the autumn, and Bohemian trout and carp specialties. ✉ *Nebovidská 6, Malá Strana,* ☎ *02/5732–0308. Dinner reservations essential. AE, V.*

$$ ✕ **La colline oubliée.** In "The Forgotten Hill," savor authentic *brik* (spicy ratatouille or ground meat in pastry) and *amekful* (flavorful vegetables and steamed grain), as well as all-you-can eat couscous served by charming waiters from North Africa. You may even be whisked into the kitchen for a sample of the offerings. The decor in this intimate restaurant is bright and cheerful, as is the music; the Old Town location is ideal, just off Pařížská street. ✉ *Elišky Krásnohorské 11, Staré Město,* ☎ *02/2329522. AE, V.*

$$ ✕ **Oscar's.** You can enjoy juicy barbecued ribs in Prague at this spacious and informal basement restaurant tucked inside the elegant Tynsky Court (just off Old Town Square). Huge portions of burgers, nachos, salads, hearty sandwiches, and potato skins help distract diners from the restaurant's cute but kitschy theme, which highlights Academy Award–winning movies in everything from decor to names of sandwiches. ✉ *Týnský dvur, Týn 1, Staré Město,* ☎ *02/2489–5404. AE, MC, V.*

$$ ★ ✕ **Palffy palác.** The faded charm of an old-world palace makes this a lovely, romantic spot for a meal. Very good continental cuisine is served with elegance that befits the surroundings. Try the potatoes au gratin or chicken stuffed with goat cheese. Surprisingly, brunches here are not worth the price. Dining is also possible on the terrace in summer. ✉ *Valdštejnská 14, Malá Strana,* ☎ *02/5731–2243. AE, MC, V.*

$$ ✕ **Pezinok.** You'll get good, filling Slovak fare at this relaxed, no-frills restaurant behind Národní třída in the New Town. The homemade sausage, accompanied by hearty wine, is excellent. ✉ *Purkyňova 4, Nové Město,* ☎ *02/291996. AE, MC, V.*

$$ ✕ **U Lorety.** You can hear the carillon from neighboring Loreta church in this otherwise quiet spot. The service here is discreet but attentive, the tables are private, and the food is consistently good. Venison and steak are specialties. ✉ *Loretánské nám. 8, Hradčany,* ☎ *02/5732–0073. No credit cards.*

$–$$ ✕ **Novoměstský pivovar.** Always packed with out-of-towners and locals alike, this microbrewery-restaurant is a maze of rooms, some painted in mock-medieval style, others decorated with murals of Prague street scenes. Pork knuckle *(vepřové koleno)* is a favorite dish. The beer is the cloudy, fruity, fermented style exclusive to this venue. ✉ *Vodičkova 20, Prague 1,* ☎ *02/2423–3533. AE, MC, V.*

$ ✕ **Bohemia Bagel.** Okay, it's not New York, but the American-owned and child-friendly Bohemia Bagel still serves a good assortment of fresh bagels from raisin-walnut to "supreme" with all kinds of spreads and toppings. The thick soups are among the best in Prague for the price, and the bottomless cups of coffee (from gourmet blends) are a further draw. The casual setting makes it a popular choice for weekend brunches, too. ✉ *Újezd 16, Malá Strána,* ☎ *02/531002. No credit cards.*

$ ✕ **Česká hospoda v Krakovské.** Right off Wenceslas Square, this clean pub noted for its excellent traditional fare is the place to try Bohemian duck: It's cooked just right and offered at an excellent price. Pair it with cold Krušovice beer. ✉ *Krakovská 20, Nové Město,* ☎ *02/2221–0204. No credit cards.*

$ ★ ✕ **Slávia kavárna.** This legendary hangout for the best and brightest of the Czech arts world—from composer Bedřich Smetana and poet Jaroslav Seifert to then-dissident Václav Havel—is back in business after real-estate wrangles held it hostage for most of the '90s. Its Art Deco decor is a perfect backdrop for people-watching, and the vistas (the river and Prague Castle on one side, the National Theater on the other) are a compelling reason to linger over an espresso. Although the Slávia is principally a café, you can also order a light meal here. ✉ *Smetanovo nábřeží 1012/2, Nové Městođ,* ☎ *02/2422–0957. No credit cards.*

$ ✕ **U Zlatého Tygra.** This crowded hangout is the last of a breed of authentic Czech pivnice. The smoke and stares preclude a long stay, but it's still worth a visit for such pub staples as ham and cheese plates or roast pork. The service is surly, but the beer is good. ✉ *Husova 17, Staré Město,* ☎ *02/2422–9020. Reservations not accepted. No credit cards.*

$ ✕ **Vltava.** In this riverside retreat you'll find classic Bohemian fish dishes, served in big portions. Try the simple preparations—like carp or trout sautéed in butter with slivered almonds. ✉ *On quay below Rašínovo nábřeží, near Palackého Bridge,* ☎ *02/294964. No credit cards.*

$$$$ 🏨 **Diplomat.** Completed in 1990 as part of a joint venture with an Austrian company, the Diplomat fuses style with Western efficiency. A 10-minute taxi or subway ride from the Old Town, it's close to the airport. The hotel is modern and tasteful, with a huge, sunny lobby and comfortable rooms. ✉ *Evropská 15, 160 00 Prague 6,* ☎ *02/2439–4111,* FAX *02/2439–4215. 387 rooms. 2 restaurants. AE, DC, MC, V.*

$$$$ ★ 🏨 **Dům U Červeného Lva.** On Mala Strana's main, historic thoroughfare, a five-minute walk from Prague Castle's front gates, the Baroque House at the Red Lion is an intimate, immaculately kept hotel. The spare but comfortable guest rooms have parquet floors, 17th-century painted-beam ceilings, superb antiques, and all-white bathrooms with brass fixtures. The two top-floor rooms can double as a suite. Note: There is no elevator, and stairs are steep. ✉ *Nerudova 41, 118 00 Prague 1,* ☎ *02/537–239 or 02/538–192,* FAX *02/538–193. 11 rooms. 2 restaurants. AE, MC, V.*

$$$$ ★ 🏨 **Hoffmeister.** On a picturesque (if a bit busy) corner near the Malostranská Metro station, this is one of the most stylish small hotels in the city. Rooms, done in a soothing palette of blues, grays, and purples, have finely crafted wood built-ins and luxuriously appointed bathrooms. Museum-quality prints by the proprietor's father hang throughout the hotel. ✉ *Pod Bruskou 9, 118 00 Prague 1,* ☎ *02/538380,* FAX *02/530959. 42 rooms. Restaurant. AE, DC, MC, V.*

$$$$ ★ **Palace Praha.** The Art Nouveau–style Palace is Prague's most elegant and luxurious hotel, though it now faces tougher competition from other equally luxurious hotels. Rooms have high ceilings, marble baths with phones, and minibars with complimentary snacks and beverages. Its central location just off Wenceslas Square offers more convenience than local character. ✉ *Panská 12, 110 00 Prague 1,* ☎ *02/2409–3111,* FAX *02/2422–1240. 125 rooms. Restaurant. AE, DC, MC, V.*

$$$ **Hotel Ibis Praha Karlín.** Renovated by its new owner, the Ibis chain, in spring 1998, the hotel has rooms decorated in standard Ibis style: blue floral curtains and bedspreads, dark carpeting, white modern functional furniture, and white walls. In a rather run-down residential neighborhood, it is near two tram lines and a Metro station (Křižíkova), which provide quick transport to the center and the Florenc bus terminal. ✉ *Šaldova 54, 186 00 Prague 8,* ☎ *02/2481–1718,* FAX *02/2481–2681. 210 rooms. Restaurant. AE, MC, V.*

$$$ **Kampa.** An early Baroque armory-turned-hotel, the Kampa is tucked away in a residential corner of the Lesser Quarter. The rooms are clean, if spare, but the bucolic setting one block from the river as well as a lovely park compensate for its relative remoteness from commercial districts. ✉ *Všehrdova 16, 118 00 Prague 1,* ☎ *02/5732–0508, 5732–0404,* FAX *02/5732–0262. 85 rooms. Restaurant. AE, DC, MC, V.*

$$$ **Opera.** Once the lodging of choice for divas performing at the nearby State Theater, the Opera greatly declined under the Communists. The mid-'90s saw the grand fin de siècle facade rejuvenated with a perky pink-and-white paint job and the installation of bathrooms and TVs in all rooms. Comfy wing chairs add to the rooms, which are decorated in tan and white. ✉ *Těšnov 13, 110 00 Prague 1,* ☎ *02/231–5609,* FAX *02/231–1477. 66 rooms with bath. Restaurant, bar. AE, DC, MC, V.*

$$ **Central.** Quite conveniently, this hotel lives up to its name, with a site near Celetná ulice and Náměstí Republiky. Rooms are sparely furnished, but all have baths. The Baroque glories of the Old Town are steps away. ✉ *Rybná 8, 110 00 Prague 1,* ☎ *02/2481–2041,* FAX *02/232–8404. 62 rooms. Restaurant . MC, V.*

$ **Balkan.** The hotel is a spiffy yellow building on an otherwise drab street not far from the Lesser Quarter. Rooms are small, simple, clean: white speads and walls, tan paneling, lacy curtains. Request a room at the back, as the hotel is on a major street. The lobby is small and basic, nothing to linger in. However, the Balkan remains absurdly affordable for a Prague hotel and is one block from the tram stop (direct trams to Wenceslas Square). ✉ *Svornosti 28, 150 00 Prague 5,* ☎ FAX *02/540777. 24 rooms. Breakfast not included. Restaurant. AE.*

$ **Pension Unitas.** Operated by the Christian charity Unitas in an Old Town convent, the sparely furnished rooms at this well-run establishment used to serve as interrogation cells for the Communist secret police. (Václav Havel was once a "guest.") Conditions, though more comfortable, are far from luxurious. Note that an adjacent 3-star hotel, Cloister Inn, uses the same address and phone number. ✉ *Bartolomějská 9, 110 00 Prague 1,* ☎ *02/2327700,* FAX *02/2327709. 40 rooms without bath. Reserve well in advance, even for off-season. Restaurant. AE, MC, V.*

$ **Penzion Sprint.** Basic, clean, no-frills rooms, most of which have their own bathrooms (however tiny), make the Sprint a fine budget choice. The rustic-looking pension is on a quiet residential street in the outskirts of Prague about 20 minutes from the airport; tram 18, however, rumbles directly to Old Town. ✉ *Cukrovárnická 62, 160 00 Prague 6,* ☎ *02/312–3338,* FAX *02/312–1797. 12 rooms, most with bath. AE, MC, V.*

Nightlife and the Arts

The Arts

Prague's cultural life is one of its top attractions—and its citizens like to dress up for it and participate; performances can be booked far ahead. You can get a monthly program of events from the PIS (☞ Visitor Information, *below*), Čedok (☞ Visitor Information, *below*), or hotels. The English-language newspaper *The Prague Post* carries detailed entertainment listings. The main ticket agencies are **Bohemia Ticket International** (✉ Salvátorská 6, ☎ 02/2422–7832) and **Ticketpro** (☎ 02/2481–4020, credit card orders accepted). For major concerts, opera, and theater, it's much cheaper to buy tickets at the box office.

CONCERTS

Performances are held in many palaces and churches. Too often, programs lack originality (how many different ensembles can play the *Four Seasons* at once?), but the settings are lovely and the acoustics can be superb. Concerts at the **churches of St. Nicholas** in both the Old Town Square and the Lesser Quarter are especially enjoyable. At **St. James's Church** on Malá Stupartská (Old Town) cantatas are performed amid a flourish of Baroque statuary. At the Prague Castle's **Garden on the Ramparts,** music in summer comes with a view.

The excellent Czech Philharmonic plays in the intimate, lavish Dvořák Hall in the **Rudolfinum** (✉ Nám. Jana Palacha, ☎ 02/2489–3111). The lush home of the Prague Symphony, **Smetana Hall,** reopened in 1997 along with the rest of the Obecní dům building (✉ Nám. Republiky 5, ☎ 02/2200–2336).

OPERA AND BALLET

Opera is of an especially high standard in the Czech Republic. One of the main venues in the grand style of the 19th century is the beautifully restored **National Theater** (✉ Národní třída 2, ☎ 02/2421–5001). The **State Opera of Prague** (✉ Wilsonova 4, ☎ 02/265353; formerly the Smetana Theater) is another historic site for opera lovers. The **Theater of the Estates** (✉ Ovocný trh 1, ☎ 02/2421–5001) hosts opera, ballet, and theater performances. Mozart conducted the premiere of *Don Giovanni* here.

PUPPET SHOWS

This traditional form of Czech entertainment, generally adaptations of operas performed to recorded music, has been given new life thanks to productions at the **National Marionette Theater** (✉ Žatecká 1, ☎ 02/2324565).

THEATER

Theater thrives in the Czech Republic. A dozen or so professional companies play in Prague to packed houses. Nonverbal theater abounds as well, notably "black theater," a melding of live acting, mime, video, and stage trickery that, despite signs of fatigue, continues to draw crowds. The popular **Archa Theater** (✉ Na Poříčí 26, ☎ 02/232–8800) offers avant-garde and experimental theater, music, and dance and hosts world-class visiting ensembles, including the Royal Shakespeare Company. **Laterna Magika** (Magic Lantern; ✉ Národní třída 4, ☎ 02/2491–4129) is one of the more established producers of black theater extravaganzas.

Nightlife

DISCOS AND CABARET

Discos catering to a young crowd blast sound onto lower Wenceslas Square. Corona Club and Latin Café (✉ Novotného lávká, ☎ 02/2108–2357) has Latin, Gypsy, and other dance-friendly music. A classier act, where the newest dance music plays, is the ever-popular **Radost FX** (✉ Bělehradská 120, Prague 2, ☎ 02/251210).

JAZZ AND ROCK CLUBS

Jazz clubs are a Prague institution, although foreign customers keep them in business. Excellent Czech groups play the tiny **AghaRTA** (✉ Krakovská 5, ☎ 02/2221–1275); arrive well before the 9 PM show time to get a seat with a sight line. **Malostranská Beseda** (✉ Malostranské nám. 21, ☎ 02/539024) is a funky hall for rock, jazz, and folk. **Reduta** (✉ Národní třída 20, ☎ 02/2491–2246), the city's best-known jazz club for three decades, features mostly local talent. Hip locals congregate at **Roxy** (✉ Dlouhá 33, ☎ 02/2481–0951) for everything from punk to funk to New Age tunes.

Shopping

Many of the main shops are in and around Old Town Square and Na Příkopě, as well as along Celetná ulice and Pařížská. On the Lesser Quarter side, Nerudova has the densest concentration of shops.

Department Stores

The biggest department store is **Kotva** (✉ Nám. Republiky 8), which grows flashier and more expensive every year. **Bílá Labuť** (✉ Na poříčí 23) and **Tesco** (✉ Národní třída 26) are good-value options.

Specialty Shops

Dila addresses include: Shops specializing in Bohemian crystal, porcelain, ceramics, and antiques abound in Old Town and Malá Strana, and on Golden Lane at Prague Castle. (Every other shop sells these items in the main tourist areas.) Look for the name **Dílo** (✉ Melantrichova 17, Old Town; Mostecká 17, Malá Strana) for glass and ceramic sculptures, prints, and paintings by local artists. **Lidová Řemesla** (✉ Jilská 22, Old Town; Nerudova 23, Malá Strana) (folk art) shops in the Old Town stock wooden toys, elegant blue-and-white textiles, and gingerbread Christmas ornaments. **Moser** (✉ Na Příkopě 12) is the source for glass and porcelain.

Side Trips

The castle and spa region of Bohemia or the history-drenched villages of Moravia make excellent (and convenient) excursions from Prague. Buses or trains link the capital with every corner of the Bohemian region; transportation to towns in Moravia takes longer (three hours or more from the capital) but is also dependable.

Bohemia's Spas and Castles

The Bohemian countryside is a restful world of gentle hills and thick woods. It is especially beautiful during fall foliage season or in May, when the fruit trees that line the roads are in blossom. Two of the most famous of the Czech Republic's scores of spas lie in such settings: Karlovy Vary (Karlsbad) and Mariánské Lázně (Marienbad). During the 19th and early 20th centuries, European royalty and aristocrats came to ease their overindulged bodies (or indulge them even more!) at these spas.

South Bohemia, a country of lonely castles, green hills, and quiet fish ponds, is peppered with exquisite medieval towns, many of which are undergoing much-needed rehabilitation. In such towns as Tábor, the Hussite reformist movement was born during the early 15th century, sparking a series of religious conflicts that engulfed all of Europe. Countering the Hussites from Český Krumlov was the powerful Rožmberk family, who scattered castles over the countryside and cre-

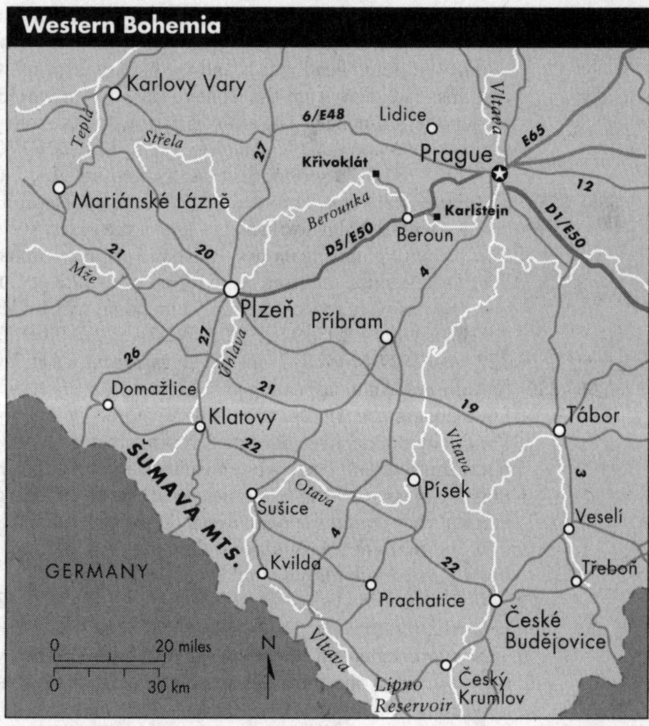

ated lake-size "ponds" in which to breed highly prized carp, still the focus of a Czech Christmas dinner.

Praguers love to spend weekends in the **Berounka Valley.** Two magnificent castles, Karlštejn and Křivoklát, rise up over the river.

Karlštejn, less than an hour from Prague off Route E50 (direction Beroun), is an admirable restoration of the 14th-century castle built by Charles IV. It protects the crown jewels of the Holy Roman Empire, housed in the castle's stunning **Kaple svatého kříže** (Chapel of the Holy Rood). The chapel is filled with 128 Gothic paintings and 2,000 dazzling gems. ✉ *Karlštejn,* ☎ *0311/684617.* ⏲ *Nov.–Mar., Tues.–Sun. 9–noon and 1–4 (Apr. and Oct. 1–5; May, June, and Sept. 1–6; July and Aug. 1–7).*

The main attractions of **Křivoklát** are its glorious woodlands, a favorite royal hunting ground in times past. The castle is about an hour from Prague. ✉ *Křivoklát.* ⏲ *Apr.–May and Sept.–Dec., Tues.–Sun. 9–4; June–Aug., Tues.–Sun. 9–6.*

★ **Karlovy Vary,** or Karlsbad, was named for the Holy Roman Emperor Charles IV. While he was in pursuit of a deer during a hunt, the animal supposedly led him to the main spring of Vřídlo. Over the years the spa attracted not only many of the crowned heads and much of the blue blood of Europe, but also leading musicians and writers. Confident bourgeois architecture in a deep, forested valley makes it an indisputably picturesque town. The waters from the spa's 12 springs are uniformly foul-tasting: Sip them while nibbling rich Karlovy Vary *oplatky* (wafers), then resort to the "13th spring," Karlovy Vary's tangy herbal liqueur known as Becherovka. Karlovy Vary is about two hours from Prague by car on route E48.

$$$$ 🏨 **Dvořák.** Opened in 1991, this Austrian-built hotel in the center of town offers imaginative decor, with whimsical white furniture (as if from a stage set: fluted headboards and the like), pale peach walls, and lacy curtains. The view from the front rooms, over a whole stretch of the colonnade, is amazing. The lobby is bright, and the staff is cheerful and utterly professional. ✉ *Nova louka 11, 360 21,* ☎ *017/322–4145,* FAX *017/322–2814. 76 rooms, 3 suites. Restaurant. AE, DC, MC, V.*

$$$–$$$$ ★ 🏨 **Grandhotel Pupp.** Founded in 1701, the Pupp still has a fine 18th-century hall, the Slavností sál. It's one of the oldest surviving hotels in Europe, with glittering names—past and present—in its guest register. For more elegance, request a room furnished in 19th-century period style: other rooms were redecorated in a functional way under communism. ✉ *Mírové nám. 2, 360 91,* ☎ *017/310–9111,* FAX *017/310–9620 or 322–4032. 214 rooms, 10 suites. 2 restaurants. AE, DC, MC, V.*

$$–$$$ 🏨 **Thermal.** An unappealing gray high-rise on first view, the Thermal, built during the 1970s, is solidly anchored at one end of Karlovy Vary's colonnade. Even though its rooms are not special—narrow, simply furnished with basic white furniture and lots of mirrors to add an illusion of space—the balconies of all front-facing rooms afford a magical view over the entire colonnade and the rolling hills of the town. The Thermal's heated outdoor swimming pool, built into a hillside and open year round, allows similar gorgeous vistas. ✉ *I. P. Pavlova 11, 360 00 Karlovy Vary,* ☎ *017/321–1111,* FAX *017/322–6992. 145 rooms. 2 restaurants, pool. AE, DC, MC, V.*

The sanatoriums and colonnades of **Mariánské Lázně** (Marienbad) are impressively arrayed around an oblong park; it's not hard to conjure up visions of Chopin or Goethe retreating here from the comparatively noisy Karlovy Vary. Nowadays, the town has one of the Czech Republic's best golf courses and hosts a PGA European Tour event. Mariánské Lázně is about three hours from Prague, on Route 21 off Route E50.

$$$–$$$$ 🏨 **Palace.** Built during the spa's heyday in 1875, this elegant five-story building is just within the resort center. Turrets sprout at the top of the bright white and canary yellow hotel, and the myriad balconies have swirling metal railings. Chandeliers and gold-color plating glisten in the public rooms. The comfortable guest rooms are less ostentatious, decorated in peach tones, with simple light fixtures and fluted white furniture. No-smoking rooms are available. ✉ *Hlavní třída 67, 353 01 ,* ☎ *0165/622222,* FAX *0165/624262. 49 rooms, 11 suites. 2 restaurants. AE, DC, MC, V.*

$$$ 🏨 **Bohemia.** At this renovated spa resort beautiful crystal chandeliers in the main hall set the stage for a comfortable and elegant stay. The rooms are well appointed and completely equipped, though you may want to be really decadent and request one of the enormous suites overlooking the park. The helpful staff can arrange spa treatments and horseback riding. ✉ *Hlavní třída 100, 353 01 Mariánské Lázně,* ☎ *0165/623251,* FAX *0165/622943. 73 rooms, 4 suites. 2 restaurants. AE, DC, MC, V.*

★ Once the main seat of the Rožmberks, Bohemia's noblest family, **Český Krumlov,** about four hours from Prague on Route 159 from Route E55, is an enchanting town with its imposing Renaissance castle (✉ Hrad, ☎ 0337/711465; ⏲ Apr., Oct. 9–4; May–Aug. 8–5; Sept. 9–5) complete with romantic elevated walkways, a round, pastel-hued tower, and an 18th-century theater that still hosts performances. The Vltava River snakes through the town, which has steeply stacked steps on either bank linking various levels and twisting narrow lanes that converge on **Náměstí Svornosti**, the Old Town's main square. A number of notable Renaissance houses add an air of formality to the overall effect of this exquisite place. The **Egon Schiele Center (Mezinárodní kul-**

turní centrum Egona Schieleho) exhibits the work of the painter Schiele, a frequent visitor to the town, and other 20th-century artists. ✉ *Široká 70–72,* ☎ *0337/61349, 61352.* ⏲ *Daily 10–6 (11–5 in low season).*

$$$ ★ ✕🏨 **Na louži.** Homey wooden shutters on street level set the old-but-cared-for atmosphere of this friendly pub-restaurant and the five small rooms upstairs, which are furnished with cozy country-style beds and wardrobes, and are immaculate. ✉ *Kájovská 66, 381 01,* ☎ FAX *0337/711280. 5 rooms. Restaurant. No credit cards.*

$$$ 🏨 **Růže.** The heavy stone exterior clearly shows its Renaissance monastery past, but the lobby is modern. Most of the (smallish) rooms were modernized in the '70s with violet as the color of choice; they have charmingly tiny gothic windows. Some face the Old Town and castle or the river. ✉ *Horní ul. 153, 381 01,* ☎ *0337/711141,* FAX *0337/711128. 50 rooms, 38 with bath. Restaurant. AE, DC, MC, V.*

After Jan Hus's death at the stake in 1415, his proto-Protestant followers established an egalitarian commune on a fortified bluff above the Lužnice river. Jan Žižka, a one-eyed general, led the zealots of **Tábor,** (1½ hr from Prague on Route E55) and shaped them into Europe's most feared army. The town itself became a weapon of defense: Its twisting streets were designed to confuse the enemy. A labyrinth of tunnels and cellars below the town served both as living quarters and as a link with the outer defenses. The story is told in the **Husitské muzeum** (Hussite Museum) just off Žižkovo náměstí. ✉ *Křivkova 31.* ⏲ *Apr.–Nov. 8:30–4 (in winter on request).*

Moravian Towns

Moravia, with its peaceful villages and small towns, is the easternmost of the historic Czech Lands, sharing a lightly populated border with Bohemia. About three hours southeast of Prague on Route 406 (from E50 and 19) is the tiny village of Telč, one of the most beautiful towns in an area with stiff competition. Farther southeast, limestone crags tower over the sleepy town of Mikulov.

A former center of Jewish life and learning in the Hapsburg empire, **Mikulov** (about 4 hr southeast of Prague on Route 620 off E55) now bears few traces of its scholarly past. Today, the town is known for its wine making. If your visit coincides with the grape harvest in October, head for the hills surrounding the town—tradition dictates that a knock on the door of a private *sklípek* (wine cellar) will lead to a tasting session. The town's Baroque-and-Gothic **Zámek Mikulov** (château) contains a wine-making museum where you can see a 22,000-gallon wine cask from 1643. ☎ *0625/2255.* ⏲ *Apr.–Oct., Tues.–Sun. 9–4.*

$–$$$ 🏨 **Rohatý Krokodýl.** This classic hotel is perfectly in keeping with the town's look in that it is a long, low white building on a street that dates back to the Renaissance. The furnishings are simple, modern, and very clean. There's a room to fit every budget. ✉ *Husova 8, 692 01,* ☎ *0625/2692, 3695. 10 rooms, 3 suites. Restaurant. AE, MC, V.*

Amid the farmlands and industrial centers of middle Moravia, **Olomouc,** three hours from Prague on Route 462 off E50, comes as an unexpected joy. The city retains its rambling Old Town, partially circled by high brick fortifications. The Renaissance town hall and the tall, impossibly ornate Trinity column compete for attention on **Horní náměstí,** the main square. At the eastern end of the Old Town are the neo-Gothic **Dóm svatého Václava** (Cathedral of St. Wenceslas, ✉ Václavské nám.) and a ruined 12th-century **palace** (✉ Dómská ul.) with an exquisite row of Romanesque stone windows.

$$$ 🏨 **Národní Dům.** This architecturally lavish turn-of-the-century hotel is a good, centrally located choice, though it could use some refurbishing. The room furnishings are also lavish, perhaps too much so: white faux Louis XVI style with gold-color leaf trim everywhere. The large café serves that Czech rarity: a filling breakfast. ✉ *Třída 8 května 21, 772 00,* ☎ *068/522–4806,* FAX *068/522–4808. 55 rooms, 45 with bath or shower. Restaurant. AE, DC, MC, V.*

It is a surprise to come upon trim little **Telč,** with its neat, formal architecture, nestled in such bucolic countryside. Only the Renaissance facades, each fronted by arcades and topped with rich gables, are visible, and although they are colorful, cute, and well maintained, often the buildings behind them are falling apart. The Renaissance theme carries over to the **Zámek Telč** (château), whose architecture and decoration form a rare pre-Baroque example of stylistic unity. ☎ *066/962943.* ⏲ *Apr.–Oct., Tues.–Sun. 9–4.*

Prague Essentials

Arriving and Departing

BY BUS

The Czech bus network **(CHAD)** operates from a station (✉ Křižíkova 4, ☎ 02/1034) near the main train station. Take Metro B or C to Florenc.

BY PLANE

All international flights arrive at Prague's Ruzyně Airport, about 20 km (12 mi) from downtown. For arrival and departure times, call 02/367814.

Between the Airport and Downtown. The private Cedaz minibus shuttle links the airport and Náměstí Republiky, a downtown square near the Old Town. Shuttles run every 30–60 minutes between 5:30 AM and 9 PM daily. The trip costs 90 Kč one-way and takes about 30 minutes. The cheapest way to get into Prague is by regular Bus 119; the cost is 12 Kč, but you'll need to change to the subway at the Dejvická station to reach the center. By taxi, expect to pay 500 Kč.

BY TRAIN

The main station for international and domestic routes is Hlavní Nádraží (✉ Wilsonova ul.), not far from Wenceslas Square. Some international trains arrive at and depart from Nádraží Holešovice (✉ Vrbenského ul.), on the same Metro line (C) as the main station. Call 02/2422–4200, 02/2461–4030, or 2461–4031 for domestic and international schedules for both stations.

Getting Around

BY CAR

In the center of the city parking meters with green stripes let you park up to six hours; an orange stripe indicates a two-hour parking limit. Avoid the blue-marked spaces, which are reserved for local residents. (Parking boots may be attached to offending vehicles.) There is an underground lot on Alšovo nábřeží, near Old Town Square.

BY PUBLIC TRANSPORT

Public transportation is a bargain. *Jízdenky* (tickets) can be bought at hotels, newsstands, and from dispensing machines in Metro stations. Transport passes for unlimited use of the system for one day (70 Kč) up to 15 days (280 Kč) are sold at some newsstands and at the windows marked DP or *Jízdenky* in the main Metro stations. Be sure to validate your pass by signing it where indicated. A basic 12-Kč ticket allows one hour's travel, with unlimited transfers (90 minutes on weekends and between 8 PM and 5 AM weekdays) on the Metro, tram, and bus network within the city limits. Cheaper 8-Kč tickets are good for a tram or bus ride up to 15 minutes without transferring, or 30 minutes on the Metro including transfers between lines; on the Metro, though, you cannot travel more than four stops from your starting point. For the Metro punch the ticket in the station before getting onto the escalators; for buses and trams punch the ticket inside the vehicle.

Subway. Prague's three modern Metro lines are easy to use and relatively safe. They provide the simplest and fastest means of transportation, and most new maps of Prague mark the routes. The Metro runs from 5 AM to midnight, seven days a week.

Tram and Bus. Trams are often more convenient than the Metro for short hops. Most bus lines connect outlying suburbs with the nearest Metro station. Trams 50–59 and buses numbered 500 and above run all night after the Metro shuts down.

BY TAXI

Each of Prague's countless taxi operators is allowed to set its own fares; the rates should be posted on the cab doors. The average basic charge is 20–30 Kč and per-kilometer rates range from 15 Kč to 30 Kč. Taxi scams are common. Avoid taxi stands in heavily touristed areas. Instead, hail cabs from the street or order them in advance by telephone. Two established firms with telephone dispatchers are **AAA** (☎ 02/1080) and **Profitaxi** (☎ 02/1035). Some larger hotels have their own fleets, which are a little more expensive.

Contacts and Resources

EMBASSIES AND CONSULATE

United States (✉ Tržiště 15, Malá Strana, ☎ 02/5732–0663). **Canadian** (✉ Mickiewiczova 6, Hradčany, ☎ 02/2431–1108). **United Kingdom** (✉ Thunovská 14, Malá Strana, ☎ 02/5732–0355). **Australian Consulate** (The Honorary Consulate and Trade Commission of Australia, ✉ Na Ořechovce 38,☎ 02/2431–0071, 02/2431–0743).

EMERGENCIES

Police (☎ 158). **Ambulance** (☎ 155). **Foreigners' Department of Na Homolce Hospital** (weekdays ☎ 02/5292–2146, evenings and weekends ☎ 02/5292–2191 or 5721–1111). **First Medical Clinic of Prague** (☎ 02/292286, 2421–6200; 24-hr emergency ☎ 02/0601–225050, mobile phone). **American Medical Center** (☎ 02/807756, weekdays). Be prepared to pay in cash for medical treatment, whether you are insured or not. **24-Hour Pharmacies** (✉ Lékárna U Anděla, ☎ 02/537039; ✉ Lékárna U svaté Ludmily, ☎ 02/2423–7207).

ENGLISH-LANGUAGE BOOKSTORES

Globe Bookstore and Coffeehouse (✉ Janovského 14, Prague 7). **U Knihomola** (✉ Mánesova 79, Prague 2). **Knihkupectví U černé Matky Boží** (✉ Celetná ul. at Ovocný trh; good for hiking maps and atlases; go downstairs). **Big Ben Bookshop** (✉ Malá Štupartská 5, Prague 1).

GUIDED TOURS

Excursions. Čedok's (☞ Visitor Information, *below*) one-day tours out of Prague include excursions to the lovely medieval town of Kutná Hora, the unusual sandstone formations of the "Bohemian Paradise" region, famous spa towns and castles, wineries, and the Terezín ghetto.

Orientation. Čedok offers a daily three-hour tour of the city, starting at 10 AM from the Čedok (☎ 02/231–8255) offices at Na Příkopě 18 and Pařížská 6. From April through October, the organization also operates an afternoon tour, starting at 2. Both tours cost about 500 Kč. **Martin-Tour** (☎ 02/2421–2473) offers a similar tour departing from Náměstí Republiky and three other Old Town points four times daily.

PIS (☏ 02/2448–2018, 264020) arranges guided tours at its Na Příkopě and Old Town Square locations.

Personal Guides. Contact Čedok (☞ Visitor Information, *below*) or PIS(☞ Visitor Information, *below*) to arrange a personal walking tour of the city. Prices start at around 400 Kč per hour.

Special-Interest. For cultural tours call Čedok (☞ Visitor Information, *below*). These include visits to the Jewish quarter, performances of folk troupes, Laterna Magika (☞ Nightlife and the Arts, *above*), opera, and concerts. Shalom (☏ 02/2481–2325) specializes in tours of the Jewish quarter.

TRAVEL AGENCIES

American Express (✉ Václavské nám. 56, ☏ 02/2421–9992, FAX 02/2221–1131). **Thomas Cook** (✉ Národní třída 28, ☏ 02/2110–5276).

VISITOR INFORMATION

The main **Čedok** office (✉ Na Příkopě 18, near Wenceslas Sq., ☏ 02/2419–7111; other branches at Rytířská 16 and Pařížská 6). **Prague Information Service** (PIS; ✉ Na Příkopě 20 and Staroměstské náměstí [Old Town Square] 22, ☏ 02/2448–2018, 02/264020).

The English-language weekly, *The Prague Post,* lists current events and entertainment programs.

The **Czech Tourist Authority** (✉ Národní třída 37, ☏ FAX 02/2421–1458) provides information on tourism outside Prague. Tourist bureaus are also found in: **Český Krumlov** (✉ Čedok, Latrán 79, ☏ 0337/711406, 711607; ✉ Infocentrum, Nám. Svornosti 1, ☏ 0337/711183). **Karlovy Vary** (✉ Ul. Dr. Bechera 21–23, ☏ 017/22281). **Mariánské Lázně** (✉ Infocentrum, Hlavní 47, ☏ 0165/5330, 5892, 3757). **Mikulov** (✉ Regional Tourist Center, Námtřıda 32, ☏ 0625/2855). **Olomouc** (✉ Horní nám, ☏ 068/551–3385). **Tábor** (✉ Žižkovo nám., ☏ 0361/252385). **Telč** (✉ Town hall, Nám. Zachariáše z Hradce 10, ☏ 066/962233).

9 Denmark

Copenhagen, Fyn and the Central Islands, Jylland and the Lakes

*Ebullience and a sense of humor have always been Danish trademarks. Though one might expect a country comprising more than 400 islands to develop an island mentality, the Danes are famous for their friendliness. They even have a word—*hyggelig*—for the feeling of well-being that comes from their own brand of cozy hospitality.*

The stereotype of melancholic Scandinavia simply doesn't hold here: neither in the café-studded streets of the larger cities, where musicians and fruit vendors hawk their wares to passersby, nor in the tiny coastal towns, where the fishing boats are as brightly painted as fire trucks. Even the country's indoor/outdoor museums, where history is brought to life in clusters of reconstructed structures out in the open, indicate that Danes don't choose to keep experience behind glass.

This is a land of well-groomed agriculture, where every available acre is planted in orchards or crops. Nowhere are you far from water as you drive on and off the ferries and bridges linking the three regions of Jylland (Jutland), Fyn (Funen), and Sjælland (Zealand).

The surrounding sea has shaped Denmark's history. The Vikings, unparalleled seafarers, had seen much of the world by the 8th century. Today the Danes remain expert navigators, using their 4,480 km (2,800 mi) of coastline both for sport—there are regattas around Sjælland and Fyn—and for fishing and trading. Copenhagen is also proving itself as one of the most popular cruise ports in northern Europe.

Long one of the world's most liberal countries, Denmark has a highly developed social welfare system. Hefty taxes are the subject of grumbling and jokes, but Danes remain proud of their state-funded medical and educational systems.

The country that gave the world Isak Dinesen, Hans Christian Andersen, and Søren Kierkegaard has a long-standing commitment to culture and the arts. In what other nation does the royal couple translate the writings of Simone de Beauvoir or the queen design costumes for the bal-

Denmark (Danmark)

let? The Royal Danish Ballet is world renowned, and even in the provinces there are numerous theater groups and opera houses.

Perhaps Denmark's greatest charm is its manageable size—about half that of Maine (53,485 sq km/33,215 sq mi). The combined ferry and train ride from Esbjerg, on the western coast of Jylland, to Copenhagen, on the eastern coast of Sjælland, takes just over three hours. From the capital you can make comfortable, unhurried expeditions by boat, car, bus, or train to explore one of the world's most civilized countries.

DENMARK A TO Z

Customs

For details on imports and duty-free limits, *see* Customs & Duties *in* Chapter 1.

Dining

Danes take their eating seriously, and Danish food, however simple, is excellent, with an emphasis on fresh ingredients, few spices, and careful presentation. Fish and meat are both of top quality in this fishing and farming country, and both are staple ingredients of the famous *smørrebrød* (open-faced sandwiches). Some smørrebrød are huge meals in themselves: Innocent snackers can find themselves faced with a dauntingly large (but nonetheless delicious) mound of fish or meat, slathered with condiments, all atop either *rugbrød* (rye bread) or *franskbrød* (French bread). Another specialty is *wienerbrød,* a confection far superior to anything billed as "Danish pastry" elsewhere.

All Scandinavian countries have versions of the cold table, but Danes claim that theirs, *det store kolde bord,* is the original and the best. It's a celebration meal; the setting of the long table is a work of art—often with lighted candles and silver platters—and the food itself is a minor miracle of design and decoration.

In hotels and restaurants the cold table is served at lunch only, though you will find a more limited version at hotel breakfasts—a good bet for budget travelers, since you can eat as much as you like.

Denmark boasts more than 50 varieties of beer, made by as many breweries; the best-known suds are Carlsberg and Tuborg, both made by the same company. If you like harder stuff, try *snaps,* the aquavit traditionally drunk with cold food, especially herring. A note about smoking: Danes, like many Europeans, regard smoking as an inalienable right. Militant insistence that they abstain will be regarded as either hysteria or comedy. A polite tone requesting they blow their smoke away from you may prove more effective.

MEALTIMES

The Danes start work early, which means they generally eat lunch at noon. Evening meals are also eaten early, so make sure you have dinner reservations for 9 at the latest. Bars and cafés stay open later, and most offer at least light fare.

RATINGS

Meal prices vary little between town and country. While approximate price ranges are given below, remember that careful ordering, especially when it comes to beer, wine, and liquor, can get you a moderate ($$) meal at a very expensive ($$$$) restaurant. Prices are per person and include a first course, main course, and dessert, plus taxes and tip, but not wine.

CATEGORY	COPENHAGEN	OTHER AREAS
$$$$	over DKr400	over DKr350
$$$	DKr200–DKr400	DKr 200–DKr350
$$	DKr120–DKr200	DKr100–DKr200
$	under DKr120	under DKr100

WHAT TO WEAR

The Danes are a fairly casual lot, and few restaurants require a jacket and tie. Even in the most chic establishments, the tone is elegantly casual.

Language

Danish is a difficult tongue for foreigners—except those from Norway and Sweden—to understand, let alone speak. Danes are good linguists, however, and almost everyone, except perhaps elderly people in rural areas, speaks English well in addition to a third language, usually French or German.

Lodging

Accommodations in Denmark range from the spare and comfortable to the resplendent. Even inexpensive hotels have invested in good materials and good, firm beds in simple designs. However, when you make reservations, pin down details so that you get what you want. Many hotels are in century-old buildings; room sizes, even in top hotels, can vary enormously; the smallest have sloping ceilings and cubby-hole size doubles. Also ask about noise caused by traffic or adjacent rooms. If you have preferences, ask for them specifically and get a confirmation in writing. The staff at the hotels will almost always try to accommodate you. Also, many Danes prefer a shower to a bath, so if you particularly want a tub, ask for it, but be prepared to pay more. Except in the case of rentals, breakfast and taxes are usually included in prices, though this seems to be changing. Check when making a reservation.

CAMPING

Denmark has more than 500 approved campsites, with a rating system of one, two, or three stars. To camp you need an International Camping Carnet or Danish Camping Pass (available at any campsite and valid for one year). For more details on camping and discounts for groups and families, contact **Campingrådet** (☏ Hesseløg. 16, DK 2100 Copenhagen Ø, ☏ 39/27–88–44).

FARM VACATIONS

This is perhaps the best way to see how the Danes live and work. You stay on a farm and share meals with the family; you can even get out and help with the chores. The minimum stay is three nights; bed and breakfast is about DKr150, and half board (an overnight with breakfast and one hot meal) runs DKr245. (Full board, an overnight with three meals, can be arranged.) There is a 50% discount for children under 11. Contact **Ferie på Landet** (Holiday in the Country; ✉ Ceresvej 2, DK 8410 Rønde, Jylland, ☏ 70/10–41–90, FAX 86/37–35–50) for details.

HOTELS

Luxury hotels in the city or countryside offer rooms of a high standard; in a manor-house hotel you may find yourself sleeping in a four-poster bed. Less expensive accommodations, however, are uniformly clean and comfortable.

INNS

A cheaper and charming alternative to hotels are the old stagecoach *kroer*—inns scattered throughout Denmark. You can save money by contacting **Kro Ferie** (Inn Holiday, ✉ Vejlevej 16, DK 8700 Horsens, Jylland, ☎ 75/64–87–00) to invest in a book of Inn Checks, valid at 84 inns. Each check costs about DKr600 per couple and includes one overnight stay in a double room, breakfast included. Family checks, for three (DKr675) and four (DKr755), are also available. Order a free catalogue from Kro Ferie and choose carefully; the organization includes some chain hotels bereft of even a smidgen of inn-related charm. Some establishments also tack a DKr125 surcharge on the price of a double.

RENTALS

Many Danes rent out their summer homes—an ideal option if you want to see the countryside in a more relaxed way. A simple house with room for four costs from DKr1,000 per week to twice that much during the summer high season. Contact the Danish Tourist Board (☞ Visitor Information, *below*) for details.

RATINGS

Prices are for two people in a double room and include service and taxes and usually breakfast.

CATEGORY	COPENHAGEN	OTHER AREAS
$$$$	over DKr1,100	over DKr850
$$$	DKr800–DKr1,100	DKr650–DKr850
$$	DKr670–DKr800	DKr450–DKr650
$	under DKr670	under DKr450

YOUTH HOSTELS

The 101 youth hostels in Denmark are open to everyone regardless of age. If you have an International Youth Hostels Association card (obtainable before you leave home), the rate is roughly DKr90 for a single bed; DKr150–DKr300 for a private double room. Without the card, there's a surcharge of DKr25 per person. For more information contact **Danhostel Danmarks Vandrehjem** (✉ Vesterbrog. 39, DK 1620 Copenhagen V, ☎ 31/31–36–12, FAX 31/31–36–26) or American Youth Hostels (☞ Students *in* Chapter 1).

Mail

POSTAL RATES

Surface and airmail letters, aerograms, and postcards to the United States and Canada cost DKr5.25 for 20 grams. Letters and postcards to the United Kingdom and other EU countries cost DKr4. Stamps are sold at post offices and some shops.

RECEIVING MAIL

If you do not know where you will be staying, your mail can be addressed to "poste restante" and sent to any post office. If no post office is specified, letters will be sent to the main post office in Copenhagen (✉ Tietgensg. 37, DK 1704). American Express holds mail free of charge for cardholders and those carrying its traveler's checks; others are charged a small fee.

Money Matters

COSTS

Denmark's economy is stable, and inflation remains reasonably low, without wild fluctuations in exchange rates. The standard and the cost of living is high, especially for such luxuries as hard alcohol and cigarettes. Prices are highest in Copenhagen; the least expensive areas are Fyn and Jylland.

CURRENCY

The monetary unit in Denmark is the krone (kr., DKr, or DKK), which is divided into 100 øre. At press time (spring 1998), the krone stood at DKr6.8 to the U.S. dollar, DKr4.7 to the Canadian dollar, DKr11.2 to the pound sterling, DKr4.3 to the Australian dollar, and DKr3.7 to the New Zealand dollar. Most well-known credit cards are accepted in Denmark, though the American Express card is accepted less frequently than others. Traveler's checks can be cashed in banks and in many hotels, restaurants, and shops.

SAMPLE PRICES

Cup of coffee, DKr14–DKr25; bottle of beer, DKr15–DKr30; soda, DKr10–DKr15; ham sandwich, DKr22–DKr40; 1-mi taxi ride, DKr30.

TIPPING

The egalitarian Danes do not expect to be tipped. The exceptions are hotel porters, who get around DKr5 per bag; you should also leave DKr1 or DKr2 for the use of a public toilet if there is an attendant.

National Holidays

January 1; April 4–5 (Easter); April 23–24 (Pentecost); April 30 (Common Prayer); May 13 (Ascension); June 5 (Constitution Day; shops close at noon); and December 24–26.

Opening and Closing Times

Banks in Copenhagen are open weekdays 9:30–4 and Thursday until 6. Several *bureaux de change,* including the ones at Copenhagen's central station and airport, stay open until 10 PM. Outside Copenhagen, banking hours vary. **Museums** are generally open 10–3 or 11–4 and closed Monday. In winter opening hours are shorter, and some museums close for the season. Check the local papers or ask at tourist offices. **Small shops** and boutiques are open weekdays 10–5:30; most stay open Thursday and Friday until 7 or 8 and close on Saturday at 1 or 2. On the first and last Saturday of every month, most shops stay open until 4 or 5. In response to increasingly liberal laws, shop hours keep changing. Some stores are even able to get around the rules and stay open Sunday. Call to double-check weekend opening hours for specific stores to avoid disappointment.

Shopping

SALES-TAX REFUNDS

Visitors from a non-EU country can save about 20% on purchases over DKr300 by obtaining a refund of the value-added tax (VAT) at the more than 1,500 shops displaying TAX FREE signs. If the shop sends your purchase directly to your home address, you pay only the sales price, exclusive of VAT. If you want to take the goods home yourself, pay the full price in the shop and get a VAT refund at the Danish duty-free shopping center at the Copenhagen airport. Get a copy of the *Tax-Free Shopping Guide* from the tourist office (☞ Visitor Information, *below*).

Telephoning

COUNTRY CODE

The country code for Denmark is 45.

INTERNATIONAL CALLS

Dial 00, then the country code, area code, and the desired number. To reach an **AT&T** long-distance operator, dial 800/10010; for **MCI,** dial 800/10022; and for **Sprint,** 800/10877.

LOCAL CALLS

Pay phones take 1-, 2-, 5-, and 10-DKr coins. You must use area codes even when dialing a local number. Calling cards, which are sold at Danish State Railways stations, post offices, and some kiosks, cost DKr25, DKr50, or DKr100, and may be used at certain phones.

OPERATORS AND INFORMATION

To ask an operator, most of whom speak English, for local assistance, dial 118; for an international operator, dial 113.

Transportation

BY BICYCLE

Some say the Danes have the greatest number of bikes per capita in the world. Indeed, with its flat landscape and uncrowded roads, Denmark is a cyclist's paradise. You can rent bikes at some train stations and many tourist offices, as well as from private firms. Contact the **Danish Cyclists' Association** (Dansk Cyklist Forbund, ✉ Rømersg. 7, DK 1362 Copenhagen, ☎ 33/32–31–21) for additional information. The Danish Tourist Board (☞ Visitor Information, *below*) publishes the pamphlet "Cycling Holiday in Denmark." You'll also see Bycykler (City Bikes) parked at special bike stands around town; the one at the top of Nyhavn usually has a couple available. Deposit DKr20 and pedal away. Though the bikes are often dented, they do function. You'll get your deposit back when you return the bike.

BY BOAT

There is frequent service to Germany, Poland, Sweden, Norway, and the Faroe Islands (in the Atlantic Ocean, north of Scotland), as well as to Britain. Domestic ferries provide service between Jylland, Fyn, and Sjælland and to the smaller islands, 100 of which are inhabited. Danish State Railways and several private shipping companies publish timetables in English; you should reserve on both domestic and overseas routes. Ask about off-season discounts.

BY CAR

Roads here are good and largely traffic-free (except around Copenhagen); you can reach many islands by toll-free bridges.

Breakdowns. Members of organizations affiliated with Alliance International de Tourisme (AIT), including American AAA and British AA, can get technical and legal assistance from the **Danish Motoring Organization** (FDM, ✉ Firskovvej 32, DK 2800 Lyngby, ☎ 45/27–07–07). All highways have emergency phones, and you can also phone your car-rental company for help. If you cannot drive your car to a garage for repairs, the rescue corps, **Falck** (☎ 44/92–22–22), can help anywhere, night or day.

Gasoline. Gas costs about DKr6 a liter.

Parking. In areas with signs reading PARKERING/STANDSNING FORBUDT (no parking and no stopping) you are allowed a three-minute grace period to load and unload. In towns automatic parking-permit machines are used. Drop in coins, push the silver button, and a ticket marked with the expiration time will drop down. Display the ticket clearly on the dashboard. Parking for an hour costs DKr6–Dkr15 in Copenhagen, DKr7 elsewhere. In some areas signs post parking regulations. All cars have a plastic dial on the inside of their windshields. Set the dial to the time you leave your car.

Rules of the Road. To drive you will need a valid license, and if you're using your own car it must have a certificate of registration and national plates. A triangular hazard-warning sign is compulsory in every car and is provided with rentals. The driver and all passengers must wear seat belts. Headlights must always be on—even in the daytime. Motorcyclists must always wear helmets and use headlights. All drivers must pay attention to cyclists, who use the outer right lane and have the right-of-way.

Drive on the right and give way to traffic from the left. A red-and-white triangular yield sign, or a line of white triangles across the road, means you must yield to traffic on the road you are entering. Do not turn right on a red light. Speed limits are 50 kph (30 mph) in built-up areas; 100

kph (60 mph) on highways; and 80 kph (50 mph) on other roads. If you are towing a trailer, you must not exceed 70 kph (40 mph). Speeding, and drinking and driving, especially, are punished severely.

BY TRAIN AND BUS

Traveling by train or bus is easy, as **Danish State Railways** (DSB, ☏ 70/13–14–15 for information) and a few private companies cover the country with a dense network of train services, supplemented in remote areas by buses. Hourly intercity trains connect the main towns in Jylland and Fyn with Copenhagen and Sjælland, using high-speed diesels, called IC-3s, on the most important stretches. All these trains make the seven-minute tunnel crossing of the Store Bælt (Great Belt), the waterway separating Fyn and Sjælland. Seat reservations on intercity trains and IC-3s are optional, but you must have a reservation if you plan to cross the Great Belt. Buy tickets at stations for trains, buses, and connecting ferry crossings (buses allow you to buy tickets on board). For most cross-country trips, children between 4 and 11 accompanied by an adult travel free, though they must have a seat reservation (DKr15). Ask about discounts for senior citizens and groups.

Fares. The **ScanRail** pass affords unlimited train travel throughout Denmark, Finland, Norway, and Sweden, as well as restricted ferry passage in and beyond Scandinavia. It is available for five days of travel within 15 days, 10 days within a month, or one month. In the United States call RailEurope (☏ 800/438–7245), or DER (☏ 800/782–2424), which also offers a 21-day pass. Buy your tickets in the United States: Though they are available in Denmark, they are more expensive. Various discounts are offered to holders of the pass by hotel chains and other organizations; ask DER, RailEurope, or your travel agent for details.

Visitor Information

The main tourist information office is the **Danish Tourist Board** (✉ Danmarks Turistråd, Bernstoffsg. 1, DK 1577 Copenhagen V, ☏ 33/11–13–25). On the Tivoli grounds, it is open May–mid-Sept., daily 9–9; mid-Sept.–Apr., weekdays 9–4:30, Sat. 9–2, closed Sun. There are additional offices in Helsingør, Hillerød, Køge, Roskilde, Gilleleje, Hundersted, and Tisvildeleje. Youth information is available in Copenhagen at **Huset** (✉ Rådhusstraede 13, ☏ 33/15–65–18).

Weather

Most travelers visit Denmark during the warmest months, July and August, but there are advantages to going in May, June, or September, when sights are less crowded and many establishments offer off-season discounts. However, few places in Denmark are ever unpleasantly crowded, and when the Danes make their annual exodus to the beaches, the cities have even more breathing space. In the winter months days are short and dark, and important attractions, including Copenhagen's Tivoli Gardens, are closed for most of the season. It's worth noting, however, that winter holidays are beautiful and especially cozy—even Tivoli reopens with its special Christmas market.

CLIMATE

The following are the average daily maximum and minimum temperatures for Copenhagen.

Jan.	36F	2C	**May**	61F	16C	**Sept.**	64F	18C
	28	– 2		46	8		51	11
Feb.	36F	2C	**June**	67F	19C	**Oct.**	54F	12C
	28	– 2		52	11		44	7
Mar.	41F	5C	**July**	71F	22C	**Nov.**	45F	7C
	31	– 1		57	14		38	3
Apr.	51F	11C	**Aug.**	70F	21C	**Dec.**	40F	4C
	38	3		56	14		34	1

COPENHAGEN

If you arrive in Copenhagen Airport on the isle of Amager, as you taxi into the city you are met with no startling skyline, no seething metropolis. Instead, elegant spires and cobbled streets characterize Scandinavia's most populous capital and one of its oldest towns. It is not divided like most other cities into single-purpose districts; instead it is a rich, multilayered capital where people work, play, shop, and live throughout its central core. Surrounded by water, be it sea or canal, and connected by bridges and drawbridges, it has a maritime atmosphere that is indelible.

Copenhagen

Numbers in the margin correspond to points of interest on the Copenhagen map.

When Denmark ruled Norway and Sweden during the 15th century, Copenhagen was the capital of all three countries. Today it is still a lively northern capital, with about 1 million inhabitants. It's a city meant for walking, the first in Europe to recognize the value of pedestrian streets in fostering community spirit. As you stroll through the cobbled streets and squares, you'll find that Copenhagen combines the excitement and variety of big-city life with a small-town atmosphere. If there's such a thing as a cozy metropolis, this is it.

In Copenhagen you're never far from water, whether sea or canal. The city itself is built upon two main islands, Slotsholmen and Christianshavn, connected by drawbridges. The ancient heart of the city is intersected by two heavily peopled walking streets—part of the five such streets known collectively as Strøget—and around them curls a maze of cobbled streets packed with tiny boutiques, cafés, and restaurants—all best explored on foot. In summer, when Copenhagen moves outside, the most engaging views of city life are from sidewalk cafés in the sunny squares. Walk down Nyhavn Canal, formerly haunted by a fairly salty crew of sailors, now gentrified and filled with chic restaurants.

16 **Amalienborg** (Amalia's Castle). During the fall and winter, when the royal family has returned to its principal residence since 1784, the Royal Guard and band march through the city at noon to change the palace guard. Amelienborg's other main attraction is the second division of the Royal Collection (the first is at Rosenborg), housed inside the **Amalienborg Museum.** Among the collection's offerings are the study of King Christian IX (1818–1906) and the drawing room of his wife, Queen Louise. Also included are a set of Rococo banquet silver, highlighted by a bombastic Viking ship centerpiece, and a small costume exhibit. Afterward, you can view visiting yachts along the castle's harbor, as well as the modern sculptures and manicured flower beds of **Amalienhaven** (Amalia's Gardens). ✉ *Amalienborg Pl.,* ☎ *33/12–21–86.* ⏲ *May–late Oct., daily 11–4; late Oct.–Apr., Tues.–Sun. 11–4.*

Amalienborg, **16**
Børsen, **10**
Botanisk Have, **25**
Carlsberg Bryggeri, **32**
Christiansborg Slot, **5**
Den Lille Havfrue, **20**
Frihedsmuseet, **18**
Helligånds Kirken, **31**
Hirschsprungske Samling, **27**
Kastellet, **19**
Københavns Synagoge, **22**
Kongelig Teater, **13**
Kongelige Bibliotek, **7**
Kunstindustrimuseet, **17**
Lurblæserne, **2**
Marmorkirken, **15**
Nationalmuseet, **4**
Nikolaj Kirken, **12**
Ny Carlsberg Glyptotek, **30**
Nyhavn, **14**
Rådhus Pladsen, **1**
Rosenborg Slot, **24**
Rundetårn, **23**
Statens Museum for Kunst, **26**
Strøget, **3**
Teatermuseum, **8**
Thorvaldsen Museum, **6**
Tivoli, **29**
Tøjhusmuseet, **9**
Tycho Brahe Planetarium, **28**
Vor Frelsers Kirken, **11**
Vor Frue Kirken, **21**

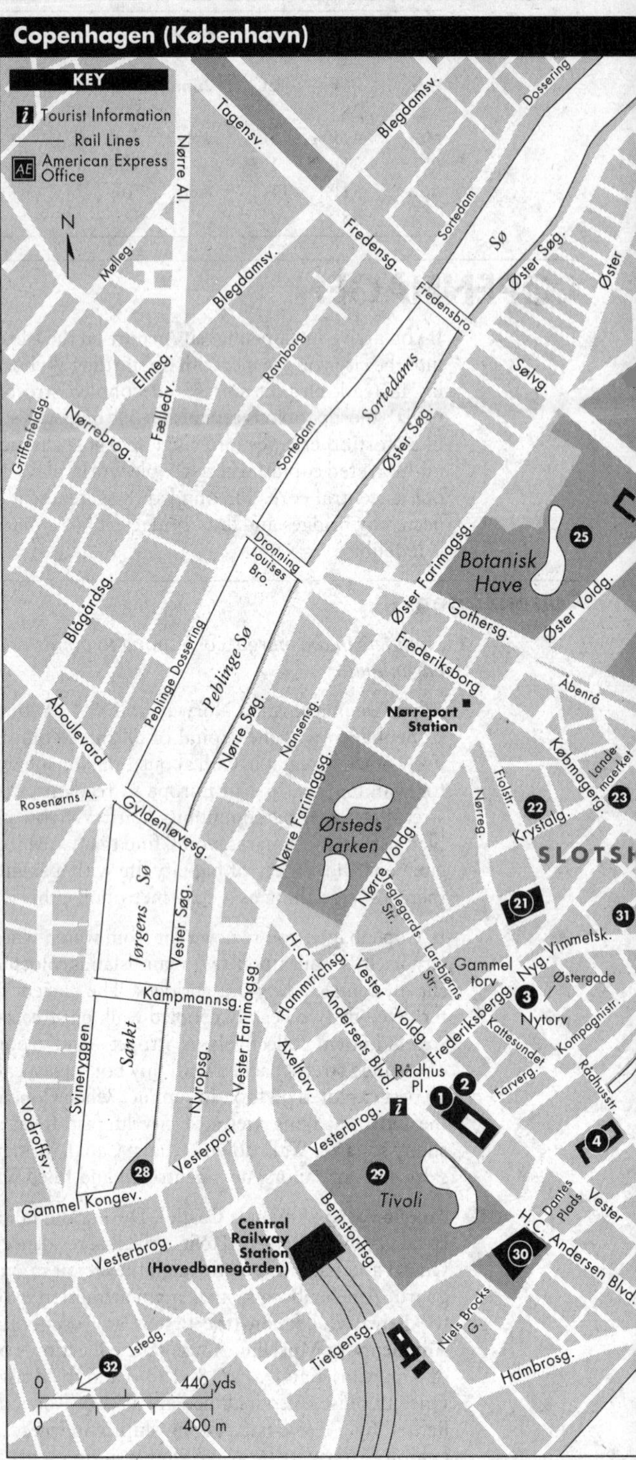

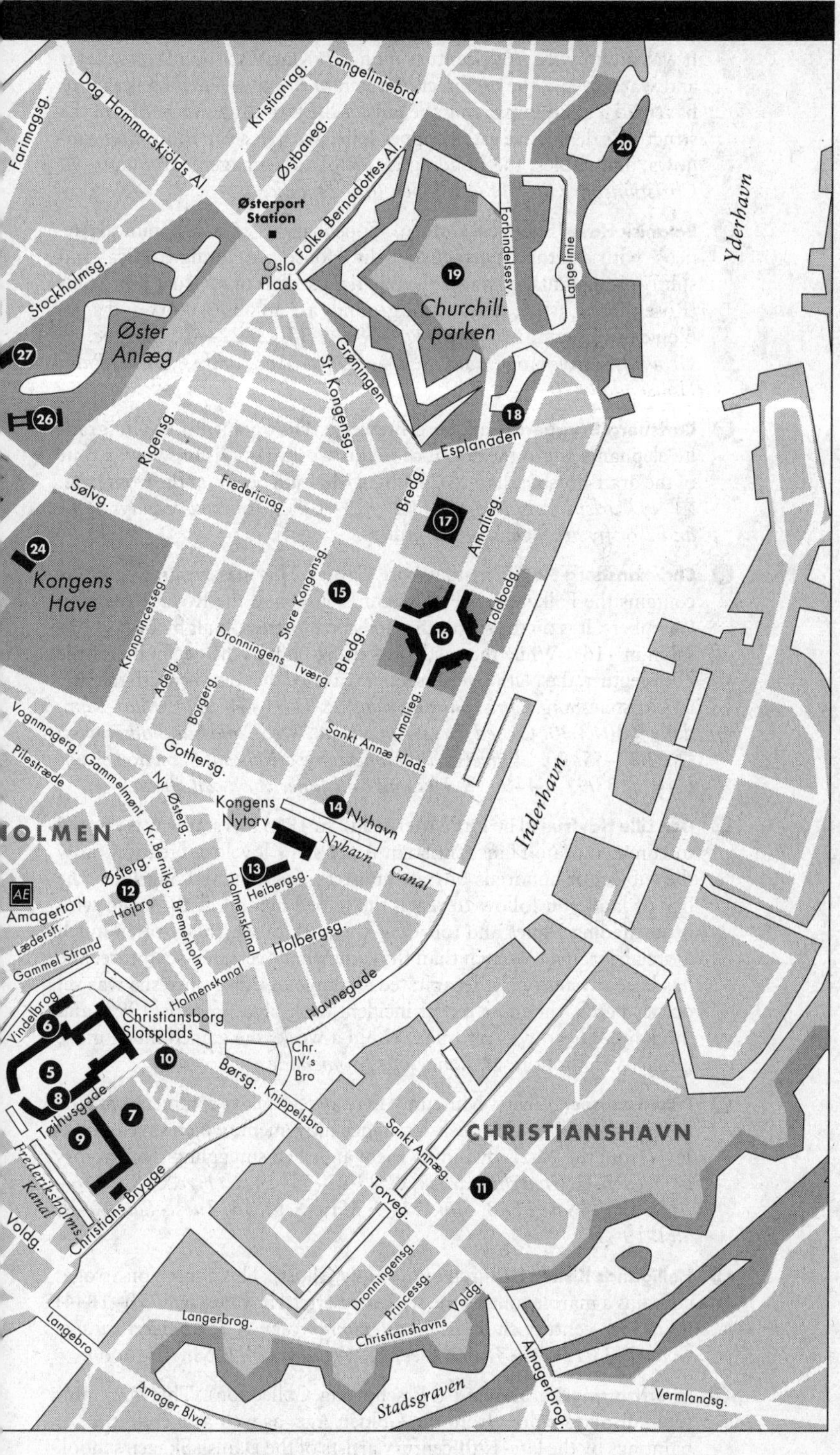

Langeliniebrd.
Kristianiag.
Dag Hammarskjölds Al.
Farimagsg.
Østbaneg.
Folke Bernadottes Al.
Østerport Station
Oslo Plads
Stockholmsg.
Øster Anlæg
Churchill-parken
Forbindelsesv.
Langelinie
Yderhavn
Grøningen
St. Kongensg.
Esplanaden
Rigensg.
Sølvg.
Fredericiag.
Bredg.
Amalieg.
Kongens Have
Kronprincesseg.
Store Kongensg.
Toldbodg.
Dronningens Tværg.
Adelg.
Borgerg.
Vognmagerg.
Gammelmønt
Pilestræde
Gothersg.
Sankt Annæ Plads
Ny Østerg.
Kongens Nytorv
Nyhavn
Nyhavn Canal
Inderhavn
OLMEN
Kr. Bernikg.
Østerg.
Amagertorv
Højbro
Bremerholm
Holmenskanal
Heibergsg.
Læderstr.
Gammel Strand
Holbergsg.
Havnegade
Vindelbrog
Christiansborg Slotsplads
Chr. IV's Bro
Børsg.
Knippelsbro
Tøjhusgade
Frederiksholms Kanal
Christians Brygge
Sankt Annæg.
CHRISTIANSHAVN
Torveg.
Voldg.
Dronningensg.
Princessg.
Christianshavns Voldg.
Langerbrog.
Langebro
Amager Blvd.
Stadsgraven
Amagerbrog.
Vermlandsg.

10 **Børsen** (the Stock Exchange). This edifice is believed to be the oldest such structure still in use, though it functions only on special occasions. It was built by the 16th-century monarch King Christian IV, a scholar and warrior, and the architect of much of the city. The king is said to have had a hand in twisting the tails of the four dragons that form the structure's distinctive green copper spire. With its steep roofs, tiny windows, and gables, the building is one of Copenhagen's treasures. ✉ *Christiansborg Slotspl. Not open to the public.*

25 **Botanisk Have** (Botanical Garden). Copenhagen's 25-acre botanical gardens, with a rather spectacular Palm House containing tropical and subtropical plants, upstages the palatial gardens of ☞ **Rosenborg Slot** (Rosenborg Castle). Also on the grounds are an observatory and a geological museum. ✉ *Gothersg. 128,* ☎ *33/32–22–40.* *Free.* ⏲ *Grounds: May–Aug., daily 8:30–6; Sept.–Apr., daily 8:30–4. Palm House: daily 10–3.*

32 **Carlsberg Bryggeri** (Carlsberg Brewery). Four giant Bornholm granite elephants guard the entrance to this world-famous brewery; a tour of the draft-horse stalls and **Carlsberg Museum** begins at the front gate. ✉ *Ny Carlsbergvej 140,* ☎ *33/27–13–14.* ⏲ *Tours: weekdays at 11 and 2 or by arrangement for groups.*

★ 5 **Christiansborg Slot** (Christiansborg Castle). This massive gray complex contains the Folketinget (Parliament House) and the Royal Reception Chambers. It is on the site of the city's first fortress, built by Bishop Absalon in 1167. While the castle was being built at the beginning of the 20th century, the National Museum excavated the ruins beneath the site. ✉ *Christiansborg. Christiansborg ruins:* ☎ *33/92–64–92;* ⏲ *May–Sept., daily 9:30–3:30. Closed Oct.–Apr., Mon., Wed., and Sat. Folketinget:* ☎ *33/37–55–00;* *Free;* ⏲ *Tour times vary; call ahead. Reception chambers:* ☎ *33/92–64–92.* ⏲ *Hrs and tour times vary; call ahead.*

20 **Den Lille Havfrue** (The Little Mermaid). In 1913 this statue was erected to commemorate Hans Christian Andersen's lovelorn creation, now the subject of hundreds of travel posters. On Sunday **Langelinie,** the lick of land you follow to reach the famed nymph, is thronged with promenading Danes and tourists—the pack of which are often much more absorbing to watch than the somewhat overrated sculpture. She has been mysteriously decapitated a couple of times since she was set on her perch; the most recent incident took place in early 1998, and though her head was returned within a week, she gained much more publicity without it. ✉ *Langelinie promenade.*

18 **Frihedsmuseet** (Liberty Museum). Evocative displays commemorate the heroic World War II Danish resistance movement, which saved 7,000 Jews from the Nazis by hiding them and then smuggling them across to Sweden. ✉ *Churchillparken,* ☎ *33/13–77–14.* *Free.* ⏲ *Sept. 16–Apr., Tues.–Sat. 11–3, Sun. 11–4; May–Sept. 15, Tues.–Sat. 10–4, Sun. 10–5.*

31 **Helligånds Kirken** (Church of the Holy Ghost). This church on Strøget contains a marble font by the sculptor Bertel Thovaldsen (1770–1844) in its 18th-century choir. ✉ *Niels Hemmingsensg. 5, Amagertorv section,* ☎ *33/12–95–55.* *Free.* ⏲ *Weekdays 9–1, Sat. 10–noon.*

27 **Hirschsprungske Samling** (Hirschprung Collection). This cozy museum displays works from the Golden Age, as well as a collection of paintings by the late-19th-century artists of the Danish Skagen school. It also contains interiors with furnishings from the artists' homes. ✉ *Stockholmsg. 20,* ☎ *31/42–03–36.* *Free.* ⏲ *Thurs.–Mon. 11–4, Wed. 11–9.*

19 **Kastellet** (The Citadel). Once surrounded by two rings of moats, this building was the city's main fortress during the 18th century, but, in a grim reversal during World War II, the Germans used it as their headquarters during their occupation of Denmark. The lovely green area around it, cut throughout with walking paths, is a favorite among the Danes, who flock here on weekends. If you have time, walk past the spired **St. Alban's,** an English church that stands at Churchillparken's entrance. ✉ *Churchillparken. Grounds:* ⏲ *Daily 6 AM–sunset.*

22 **Københavns Synagoge** (Copenhagen Synagogue). This synagogue was designed by the contemporary architect Gustav Friedrich Hetsch, who borrowed from the Doric and Egyptian styles in creating the arklike structure. ✉ *Krystalg. 12.* ⏲ *Daily services 4:15.*

13 **Kongelig Teater** (Royal Theater). The home of Danish opera and ballet as well as theater occupies the southeast side of Kongens Nytorv. The Danish Royal Ballet remains one of the world's great companies, with a repertory ranging from classical to modern. On the western side of the square you'll see the stately facade of the **D'Angleterre,** the grandest of Copenhagen's hotels. ✉ *Tordenskjoldsg. 3,* ☎ *33/69–69–69. Not open for tours.*

7 **Kongelige Bibliotek** (Royal Library). This library houses the country's largest collection of books, newspapers, and manuscripts. Look for early records of the Viking journeys to America and Greenland and the statue of the philosopher Søren Kierkegaard in the garden. A marble annex next door, which opens in the fall of 1999, has special reading rooms, a ground-floor performance space, and a bookstore. ✉ *Christians Brygge 8,* ☎ *33/47–47–47.* 🎫 *Free.* ⏲ *June–Aug., weekdays 9–7, Sat. 10–7; Sept.–May, Mon. 9–7, Tues.–Thurs. 9–9, Fri. 9–7, Sat. 10–7.*

17 **Kunstindustrimuseet** (Museum of Decorative Art). The highlights of this museum's collection are a large selection of European and Asian handicrafts, as well as ceramics, silver, and tapestries. The quiet library full of design tomes and magazines doubles as a primer for Danish functionalism with its Le Klint paper lamp shades and wooden desks. ✉ *Bredg. 68,* ☎ *33/14–94–52.* ⏲ *Permanent exhibition: Tues.–Sun. 1–4; special exhibitions: Tues.–Sat. 10–4, Sun. 1–4.*

2 **Lurblæserne** (Lur Blower Column). Topped by two Vikings blowing an ancient trumpet called a *lur,* this column displays a good deal of artistic license—the lur dates from the Bronze Age, 1500 BC, whereas the Vikings lived a mere 1,000 years ago. The monument is a starting point for sightseeing tours of the city. ✉ *East side of Rådhus Pl.*

15 **Marmorkirken** (The Marble Church). The ponderous Frederikskirke, commonly called the Marmorkirken, is a Baroque church begun in 1749 in high-priced Norwegian marble that lay unfinished (because of budget constraints) from 1770 to 1874. It was finally completed and consecrated in 1894. Perched around the exterior are 16 statues of various religious leaders from Moses to Luther, and below them stand sculptures of outstanding Danish ministers and bishops. ✉ *Frederiksgade 4,* ☎ *33/15–01–44.* 🎫 *Free.* ⏲ *Weekdays 11–2, Sat. 11–4, Sun. noon–4, with service at 10:30.*

4 **Nationalmuseet** (National Museum). On Ny Vestergade you'll find the entrance to this museum with extensive collections chronicling Danish cultural history to modern times and displays of Egyptian, Greek, and Roman antiquities. You can see Viking Runic stones in the Danish cultural history section. ✉ *Ny Vesterg. 10,* ☎ *33/13–44–11.* ⏲ *Tues.–Sun. 10–5.*

12 **Nikolaj Kirken** (St. Nicholas Church). In Østergade, the easternmost of the streets that make up Strøget, you cannot miss the green spire of St. Nicholas Church. The present structure was built in the 20th century; the previous one, dating from the 13th century, was destroyed by fire in 1728. Today the building is no longer a church but an art gallery and exhibition center. ✉ *Nikolaipl.,* ☎ *33/93–16–26.* 🎫 *Changing admission for special exhibitions.* ⏲ *Daily noon–5.*

★ 30 **Ny Carlsberg Glyptotek** (New Carlsberg Sculpture Museum). This elaborate neoclassical building houses an impressive collection of works by Gauguin, Degas, and other Impressionists. The French, Egyptian, Greek, and Roman sculpture is one of the most impressive collections of antiquities and sculpture in northern Europe. ✉ *Dantes Pl. 7,* ☎ *33/41–81–41.* 🎫 *Free Wed. and Sun.* ⏲ *Tues.–Sun. 10–4.*

★ 14 **Nyhavn** (New Harbor). After a long tour, relax with a beer in one of the most gentrified parts of the city, longtime haunt of sailors. Now restaurants and cafés outnumber tattoo shops. The name refers to both the street and the canal leading southeast out of Kongens Nytorv—but to Danes, it could as well mean the general feeling of tipsy euphoria that erupts here every warm, sunny day. Long into the hot summer nights, the area still gets rowdy, with Scandinavians reveling against the backdrop of a fleet of old-time sailing ships and well-preserved 18th-century buildings. Hans Christian Andersen lived at numbers 18 and 20. Nearer to the harbor are old shipping warehouses, including two—Nyhavn 71 and the Admiral—that have been converted into comfortable hotels. ✉ *East of Kongens Nytorv.*

★ 1 **Rådhus Pladsen** (City Hall Square). This hub of Copenhagen's commercial district is the best place to start a stroll. The Renaissance-style building dominating it is the **Rådhus** (City Hall), completed in 1905. A statue of Copenhagen's 12th-century founder, Bishop Absalon, sits atop the main entrance. Inside, you can see the first World Clock, an astrological timepiece invented and built by Jens Olsen and set in motion in 1955. If you're feeling energetic, take a guided tour partway up the 350-ft **tower** for a panoramic view. ✉ *Square in Strøget at eastern end of Vesterbrog, and western end of Frederiksbergg.,* ☎ *33/66–25–82.* ⏲ *Rådhus Pl.: Mon.–Wed., Fri. 9:30–3, Thurs. 9:30–4, Sat. 9:30–1. Tours in English, weekdays at 3, Sat. at 10. Tower tours: Mon.–Sat. at noon; additionally June–Sept. at 10 and 2. Call to confirm hrs.*

★ 24 **Rosenborg Slot** (Rosenborg Castle). This Renaissance palace—built by jack of all trades Christian IV—houses the Crown Jewels, as well as a collection of costumes and royal memorabilia. Don't miss Christian IV's pearl-studded saddle. ✉ *Øster Voldg. 4A,* ☎ *33/15–32–86.* ⏲ *Castle: late-Oct.–Apr., Tues., Fri., and Sun. 11–2; treasury: Tues.–Sun. 11–3; both: May, Sept.–late-Oct., daily 11–3; June–Aug., daily 10–4.*

23 **Rundetårn** (Round Tower). It is said that Peter the Great of Russia drove a horse and carriage up the 600 ft of the inner staircase of this round tower, built as an observatory in 1642 by Christian IV. It's a formidable walk, but the view is worth it. At the base of the tower is the university church, Trinitas; halfway up the tower you can take a break at the tower's art gallery. ✉ *Købmagerg. 52A,* ☎ *33/93–66–60.* ⏲ *Tower: Sept.–May, Mon.–Sat. 10–5, Sun. noon–4; June–Aug., Mon.–Sat. 10–8, Sun. noon–8. Observatory and telescope, with astronomer on hand to answer questions, mid-Oct.–mid-Mar., Tues.–Wed. 7 PM–10 PM.*

26 **Statens Museum for Kunst** (National Art Gallery). This museum reopens in the fall of 1999 with a complete refurbishment of the original 100-year-old building and a new, modern building that doubles the exhibition space. Though the collection remains the same—including works

of Danish art from the Golden Age (early 19th century) to the present, as well as paintings by Rubens, Dürer, the Impressionists, and other European masters—the space also includes a children's museum, an amphitheater, a documentation center and study room, a bookstore, and a restaurant. ✉ *Sølvg. 48–50,* ☎ *33/91–21–26.* ⊙ *Tues.–Sun. 10–4:30, Wed. until 9.*

3 **Strøget.** Frederiksberggade is the first of the five pedestrian streets that make up Strøget, Copenhagen's shopping district and promenade area. Walk past the cafés and trendy boutiques to the double square of **Gammeltorv** and **Nytorv,** where, farther along, the street is paved with mosaic tiles. Outside the posh displays of the fur and porcelain shops the sidewalks have the festive aura of a street fair. **Kongens Nytorv** (King's New Market) is the square marking the end of Strøget.

8 **Teatermuseum** (Theater Museum). Built in 1767 in the Royal Court, this museum is devoted to exhibits on theater and ballet history. You can wander around the boxes, stage, and dressing rooms to see where it all happened. ✉ *Christiansborg Ridebane 18,* ☎ *33/11–51–76.* ⊙ *Wed. 2–4, weekends noon–4.*

★ 6 **Thorvaldsen Museum.** The 19th-century Danish sculptor Bertel Thorvaldsen, whose tomb stands in the center of the museum, was greatly influenced by the statues and reliefs of classical antiquity. In addition to his own works, the collection includes paintings and drawings by other artists illustrating the influence of Italy on the artists of Denmark's Golden Age. ✉ *Porthusg. 2,* ☎ *33/32–15–32.* 🎫 *Free.* ⊙ *Tues.–Sun. 10–5.*

★ 29 **Tivoli.** In the 1840s the Danish architect Georg Carstensen persuaded King Christian VIII that an amusement park would be the perfect opiate for the masses, arguing that "when people amuse themselves, they forget politics." In the season from May through September, about 4 million people come through the gates. Tivoli is more sophisticated than a mere funfair: It offers a pantomime theater and an open-air stage, elegant restaurants, and frequent classical, jazz, and rock concerts in addition to a museum chronicling its own history. On weekends there are elaborate fireworks displays. Try to see Tivoli at least once by night, when the trees are illuminated along with the Chinese Pagoda and the main fountain. In recent years Tivoli has also been opened a month before Christmas with a gift and decorations market and a children's theater, albeit in Danish. Most of the restaurants are also open. ✉ *Vesterbrog. 3,* ☎ *33/15–10–01.* ⊙ *May–mid-Sept., daily 11 AM–midnight.*

9 **Tøjhusmuseet** (Royal Armory). The Renaissance structure was built by King Christian IV, a scholar and a warrior as well as the architect of much of the city. It houses impressive displays of uniforms, weapons, and armor in an arched hall 200 yards long. ✉ *Tøjhusg. 3,* ☎ *33/11–60–37.* ⊙ *Tues.–Sun. 10–4.*

28 **Tycho Brahe Planetarium.** This modern cylindrical building is filled with astronomy exhibits and an Omnimax theater that takes visitors on a simulated journey up into space and down into the depths of the seas. Because these films can be disorienting, planetarium officials do not recommend them for children under 7. ✉ *Gammel Kongevej 10,* ☎ *33/12–12–24.* 🎫 *Exhibition and theater Dkr65. Reservations advised for theater.* ⊙ *Daily 10:30–9.*

11 **Vor Frelsers Kirken** (Our Savior's Church). Local legend has it the staircase encircling the fantastic green-and-gold spire of this 1696 Gothic structure was built curling the wrong way around and that when its architect reached the top and saw what he had done, he jumped. ✉

Skt. Annæg. 9, ☎ 31/57–63–25. Free. ⏲ Weekdays 9–1. Closed during services and special functions; call ahead.

21 **Vor Frue Kirken** (Church of Our Lady). Though this has been Copenhagen's cathedral since 1924, the site itself has been a place of worship since the 13th century, when Bishop Absalon built a chapel here. The spare, neoclassical facade is a 19th-century innovation repairing damage suffered during Nelson's bombing of the city in 1801. If the church is open, you can see Thorvaldsen's marble sculptures of Christ and the Apostles. Afterwards, if you're on your way to the Nørreport train station, you'll pass the stoic, columned **Copenhagen University.** It was built during the 19th century on the site of the medieval bishops' palace. ✉ *Pilestræde 67, ☎ 33/14–41–28. ⏲ Irregular hrs; call ahead.*

Dining and Lodging

Food remains one of the great pleasures in Copenhagen, a city with more than 2,000 restaurants. Traditional Danish fare spans all the price categories: You can order a light lunch of smørrebrød, snack from a store kolde bord, or dine out on lobster and Limfjord oysters. If you are strapped for cash, you can enjoy fast food Danish style, in the form of *pølser* (hot dogs) sold from trailers on the street. Team any of this with some pastry from a bakery (the shops displaying an upside-down gold pretzel), and you've got yourself a meal on the go. Many restaurants close for Christmas, roughly from December 24 through December 31. For details and price-category information, *see* Dining *in* Denmark A to Z, *above*.

Copenhagen is well served by a wide range of hotels, which are almost always clean, comfortable, and well run. Most Danish hotels include a substantial breakfast in the room rate, but this isn't always the case. Summertime reservations are a good idea, but if you should arrive without one, try the hotel booking service at the Danish Tourist Board (☞ Visitor Information *in* Copenhagen Essentials, *below*). They can also give you a "same-day, last-minute price," which is about DKr320 to DKr400 for a double hotel room. This service will also locate rooms in private homes, with rates starting at about DKr260 for a double. Try the **Huset** (Use It) lodging service (✉ Rådhusstr. 13, ☎ 33/15–65–18) for budget accommodations. For details and price-category definitions, *see* Lodging *in* Denmark A to Z, *above*.

$$$$ ★ ✕ **Kong Hans Kaelder.** Five centuries ago this was a Nordic vineyard, but now it's one of Scandinavia's finest restaurants—though change is afoot. After 17 years as the restaurant's head chef, Daniel Letz is passing the torch to Thomas Rode Andersen. No major restructuring is planned; rather the staff promises to continue serving superb, French-inspired dishes. The setting is subterranean and mysterious, with white-washed, arching ceilings, candles, and wood carvings. ✉ *Vingårdstr. 6, ☎ 33/11–68–68. AE, DC, MC, V. Closed Sun. last 2 wks in July, and Easter week. No lunch.*

$$$$ ✕ **Krogs.** This elegant canal-front restaurant commands a loyal clientele, both foreign and local. It's decorated with pale green walls and paintings of old Copenhagen. The menu (printed in five languages) lists such specialties as a rich, dark bouillabaisse and a generous cold platter heaped with sea scallops, lobster, and local fish. ✉ *Gammel Strand 38, ☎ 33/15–89–15. Reservations essential. AE, DC, MC, V.*

$$$$ ★ ✕ **Sct. Gertruds Kloster.** The history of this monastery goes back 700 years. The dining room, bedecked with hundreds of icons, is illuminated by 2,000 candles. The extensive French menu lists such specials as fillet of halibut with lobster glacé and duck breast in tarragon sauce.

✉ *Hauser Pl. 32,* ☎ *33/14–66–30. Reservations essential. AE, DC, MC, V. No lunch.*

$$$ ★ ✕ **Els.** When it opened in 1853, the intimate Els was the place to be seen before the theater, and the painted Muses on the walls still watch diners rush to make an 8 o'clock curtain. Antique wooden columns and Royal Copenhagen tile tables complement a nouvelle Danish and French menu that changes daily, offering game, fish, and market-fresh produce. ✉ *Store Strandstr. 3,* ☎ *33/14–13–41. Reservations essential. AE, DC, MC, V.*

$$$ ✕ **L'Alsace.** In the cobbled courtyard of Pistolstraede and hung with paintings by Danish surrealist Wilhelm Freddie, this restaurant is peaceful and quiet, attracting such diverse diners as Queen Margrethe and Pope Paul II. The hand-drawn menu includes a hearty *choucroute* (sauerkraut) with sausage and pork, plus superb fruit tarts and cakes for dessert. ✉ *Ny Østerg. 9,* ☎ *33/14–57–43. AE, DC, MC, V. Closed Sun.*

$$$ ✕ **Pakhuskælderen.** Surrounded by thick white walls and raw timbers, the Nyhavn 71 hotel's (☞ Lodging, *below*) intimate restaurant attracts a mix of business and holiday guests. In recent years it has moved away from being exclusively of the seafood school and now is known for its fresh, classically prepared range of Danish-French specialties. ✉ *Nyhavn 71,* ☎ *33/11–85–85. Reservations essential. AE, DC, MC, V. Closed Sun. No lunch.*

$$ ✕ **Copenhagen Corner.** Diners here are treated to a superb view of the Rådhus Pladsen, as well as to a terrific store kolde bord, both of which compensate for the often harried staff. Specialties include fried veal with bouillon gravy and fried potatoes; entrecôte in garlic and bordelaise sauce, served with creamed potatoes; and a herring plate with three types of spiced and marinated herring and boiled potatoes. ✉ *Rådhus Pl.,* ☎ *33/91–45–45. AE, DC, MC, V.*

$$ ✕ **El Meson.** Ceiling-hung pottery, knowledgeable waiters, and a top-notch menu make this Copenhagen's best Spanish restaurant. Choose carefully for a moderately priced meal, which might include beef spiced with spearmint, lamb with honey sauce, or paella for two. ✉ *Hauser Pl. 12,* ☎ *33/11–91–31. AE, DC, MC, V. Closed Sun. No lunch.*

$$ ✕ **Havfruen.** A life-size wooden mermaid swings decorously from the ceiling in this small, rustic fish restaurant in Nyhavn. Natives love the maritime-bistro ambience and the daily evolving French and Danish menu. ✉ *Nyhavn 39,* ☎ *33/11–11–38. DC, MC, V. Closed Sun.*

$$ ★ ✕ **Ida Davidsen.** Five generations old (counting Ida's children Oscar and Ida Maria), this world-renowned lunch spot has become synonymous with smørrebrød. Choose from these creative open-face sandwiches, piled high with such ingredients as pâté, bacon, and steak tartare, or even kangaroo, or opt for smoked duck served with a beet salad and potatoes. ✉ *St. Kongensg. 70,* ☎ *33/91–36–55. Reservations essential. AE, DC, MC, V. Closed weekends and July. No dinner.*

$$ ✕ **Peder Oxe.** This countrified, lively bistro welcomes you with rustic antiques, 15th-century Portuguese tiles, and damask-covered tables set with heavy cutlery. Grilled steaks and fish—and some of the best burgers in town—come with an excellent salad bar. ✉ *Gråbrødretorv 11,* ☎ *33/11–00–77. DC, MC, V.*

$$ ✕ **Victor.** This French-style corner café has great people-watching and bistro fare. It's best during weekend lunches, when Danes gather for such specialties as rib roast, homemade pâté, smoked salmon, and cheese platters. Careful ordering here can get you an inexpensive meal. Unfortunately, the waiters can be obnoxious. ✉ *Ny Østerg. 8,* ☎ *33/13–36–13. AE, DC, MC, V.*

$ ✕ **Flyvefisken.** Silvery stenciled fish swim along blue-and-yellow stenciled walls in this funky Thai eatery. Among the city's more experimental (and spicy) restaurants, it offers chicken with cashews, spicy shrimp soup with lemongrass, and herring shark in basil sauce. A less-expensive health-food café is in the basement. ✉ *Larsbjørnsstr. 18,* ☎ *33/14–95–15. AE, DC, MC, V. Closed Sun.*

$ ✕ **Quattro Fontane.** On a corner west of the lakes, one of Copenhagen's busiest Italian restaurants is a noisy, two-story affair, packed tight with marble-top tables and a steady flow of young Danes. Chatty Italian waiters serve cheese or beef ravioli, cannelloni, linguine with clam sauce, and thick pizzas. ✉ *Guldbersg. 3,* ☎ *31/39–39–31. Reservations essential weekends. No credit cards.*

$ ★ ✕ **Riz Raz.** On a corner off Strøget, this Middle Eastern restaurant packs in young and old, families, and singles every night and on weekends. The very inexpensive all-you-can-eat buffet is heaped with healthy dishes, including lentils, falafel, bean salads, and occasionally pizza. ✉ *Kompagnistr. 20,* ☎ *33/15–05–75. Reservations essential weekends. DC, MC, V.*

$$$$ ★ **D'Angleterre.** The grande dame of Copenhagen hotels has undergone major changes this century, but the hotel still retains its Old World, old-money aura. The rooms are done in pinks and blues, with overstuffed chairs and antique escritoires and armoires. Bathrooms sparkle with brass, mahogany, and marble. If you are a light sleeper, choose your room carefully; some guests complain of noise from the nearby bars, as well as early-morning deliveries. ✉ *Kongens Nytorv 34, DK 1051 KBH K,* ☎ *33/12–00–95,* FAX *33/12–11–18. 110 rooms, 20 suites. 2 restaurants, pool. AE, DC, MC, V.*

$$$$ **Nyhavn 71.** In a 200-year-old warehouse, this quiet hotel is a good choice for privacy seekers. It overlooks the old ships of Nyhavn, and the maritime interiors have been preserved with their original plaster walls and exposed brick. Rooms are tiny but cozy, with warm woolen spreads, dark woods, soft leather furniture, and crisscrossing timbers—though this may all be changing soon. At press time (spring 1998), the hotel was beginning room renovations, but promising there would be no major changes in the atmosphere. ✉ *Nyhavn 71, DK 1051 KBH K,* ☎ *33/11–85–85,* FAX *33/93–15–85. 82 rooms. Restaurant. AE, DC, MC, V.*

$$$$ **SAS Scandinavia.** Near the airport, this is one of northern Europe's largest hotels and Copenhagen's token skyscraper. An immense lobby, with cool, recessed lighting and streamlined furniture, gives access to the city's first (and only) casino. Guest rooms are large and somewhat institutional but offer every modern convenience. Breakfast is not included in the rates. ✉ *Amager Blvd. 70, DK 2300 KBH S,* ☎ *33/11–24–23,* FAX *31/57–01–93. 542 rooms, 52 suites. 4 restaurants, pool. AE, DC, MC, V.*

$$$ **Kong Frederik.** West of Rådhus Pladsen, near Strøget, this intimate hotel is a cozy version of its big sister, D'Angleterre (☞ *above*). The sunny Queen's Garden restaurant serves a breakfast buffet (not included in the rate); rooms are elegant with Oriental vases, mauve carpets, and plain blue spreads. ✉ *Vester Voldg. 25, DK 1552 KBH K,* ☎ *33/12–59–02,* FAX *33/93–59–01. 110 rooms, 17 suites. Restaurant. AE, DC, MC, V.*

$$$ **Neptun.** The centrally situated Neptun has been in business for nearly 150 years and shows no signs of flagging. Guest rooms decorated with blond wood are favored by Americans. Though charming, this Best Western Hotel can become very busy with tour groups. Moreover, because it is housed in a old building, room sizes vary greatly, and so does the noise from the street. Ask for details when booking a room. ✉ *Skt. Annæ Pl. 18, DK 1250 KBH K,* ☎ *33/13–89–00,* FAX *33/14–12–50. 123 rooms, 14 suites. Restaurant. AE, DC, MC, V.*

$$$ **The Phoenix.** This luxury hotel welcomes guests with automatic glass doors, crystal chandeliers, and gilt touches everywhere. The staff

switches languages as they register business and cruise guests. Suites and executive-class rooms have Biedermeier-style furniture and 18-karat-gold bathroom fixtures, but the standard rooms are very small, at barely 9′ by 15′. If you're a light sleeper, ask for a room above the second floor to avoid street noise. ✉ *Bredg. 37, DK 1260 KBH K,* ☎ *33/95–95–00,* FAX *33/33–98–33. 208 rooms, 7 suites. Restaurant. AE, DC, MC, V.*

$$ **Ascot.** A charming old building downtown, this family-owned hotel has a classically columned entrance and an excellent breakfast buffet. Rooms have colorful geometric-pattern bedspreads and cozy bathrooms. A few have kitchenettes. Repeat guests often ask for their regular rooms. ✉ *Studiestr. 61, DK 1554 KBH K,* ☎ *33/12–60–00,* FAX *33/14–60–40. 113 rooms, 30 apartments. Restaurant (breakfast only). AE, DC, MC, V.*

$$ **Copenhagen Admiral.** Overlooking old Copenhagen and Amalienborg, the monolithic Admiral, once a grain warehouse, now affords historic but airy accommodations. With massive stone walls broken by rows of tiny windows, it's one of the less expensive top hotels, though in recent years it's been upping both frills and prices. Guest rooms are spare, with jutting beams and modern prints. ✉ *Toldbodg. 24–28, DK 1253 KBH K,* ☎ *33/11–82–82,* FAX *33/32–55–42. 365 rooms. Restaurant, bar, sauna, nightclub, shop, meeting rooms. AE, DC, MC, V.*

$$ **Triton.** Despite seedy surroundings, this streamlined hotel attracts a cosmopolitan clientele thanks to a central location in Vesterbro. The large rooms, in blond wood and warm tones, have new bathrooms and state-of-the-art fixtures. The buffet breakfast included in the price is exceptionally generous, the staff friendly. There are also family rooms, each with a separate bedroom and foldout couch. ✉ *Helgolandsg. 7–11, DK 1653 KBH K,* ☎ *31/31–32–66,* FAX *31/31–69–70. 123 rooms. Restaurant (breakfast only). AE, DC, MC, V.*

$ **Cab-Inn Scandinavia.** Winter business travelers and kroner-pinching summer backpackers and families alike flock to Copenhagen's answer to Japanese-style hotel minirooms. More cozy than futuristic, shiplike "berths" are brightly decorated, all with standard furnishings, including a small wall-hung desk with chair. Around the corner, at Danasvej 32, is a sister hotel, the Cab-Inn Copenhagen, with 86 rooms. ✉ *Vodroffsvej 55, DK 1900 FR C,* ☎ *35/36–11–11,* FAX *35/36–11–14. 201 rooms with shower. AE, DC, MC, V.*

$ **Missionhotellet Nebo.** This budget hotel is between the main train station and Istedgade's seediest porn shops. Nonetheless, it's a prim hotel, comfortable and well maintained by a friendly staff. The dormlike guest rooms are furnished with industrial carpeting, polished pine furniture, and soft duvet covers. Baths, showers, and toilets are clustered at the center of each hallway, and the breakfast restaurant downstairs has a tiny courtyard. ✉ *Istedg. 6, DK 1650 KBH V,* ☎ *31/21–12–17,* FAX *31/23–47–74. 96 rooms, 40 with bath. AE, DC, MC, V.*

Nightlife and the Arts

Copenhagen This Week has good information on musical and theatrical happenings, as well as on special events and exhibitions. Concert and festival information is available from the **Dansk Musik Information Center** (DMIC; ✉ Gråbrødretorv 16, ☎ 33/11–20–66). Copenhagen's main theater and concert season runs from September through May, and tickets can be obtained either directly from theaters and concert halls or from ticket agencies; ask your hotel concierge for advice. **Billetnet** (✉ Main post office: Tietgensg. 37, ☎ 38/88–70–22), a box-office service available at all large post offices, has tickets for most major events. Keep in mind that same-day purchases at the box office **ARTE**

(☒ near Nørreport station) are half price. There is no phone number, so you must show up in person.

The Arts

FILM AND TELEVISION

Copenhagen natives are avid **movie** buffs, and as the Danes rarely dub films or television imports, you can often see original American and British movies and TV shows with Danish subtitles.

MUSIC

Tivoli Concert Hall (☒ Vesterbrog. 3, ☎ 33/15–10–12) offers more than 150 concerts each summer, presenting a host of Danish and foreign soloists, conductors, and orchestras.

THEATER

The **Royal Theater** (☒ Kongens Nytorv, ☎ 33/14–10–02) regularly holds theater, ballet, and opera performances. For English-language theater, try to catch a performance of the professional **London Toast Theatre** (☎ 31/22–86–86).

Nightlife

Many of the city's restaurants, cafés, bars, and clubs stay open after midnight, some as late as 5 AM. Copenhagen is famous for jazz, but you'll find nightspots catering to musical tastes ranging from bop to ballroom music. In the inner city most discos open at 11 PM, have a cover charge (about DKr40), and pile on steep drink prices. A few streets behind the railway station is Copenhagen's red-light district, where sex shops share space with grocers. Although the area is fairly well lighted and lively, women may feel uncomfortable here alone at night.

JAZZ

Many of Copenhagen's sophisticated jazz clubs have closed in the past couple of years. **La Fontaine** (☒ Kompagnistr. 11, ☎ 33/11–60–98) is Copenhagen's quintessential jazz dive, with sagging curtains, impenetrable smoke, crusty lounge lizards, and the random barmaid nymph; for jazz lovers the bordello mood and Scandinavian jazz talent make this a must. **Copenhagen Jazz House** (☒ Niels Hemmingsensg. 10, ☎ 33/15–26–00) is infinitely more upscale than La Fontaine, attracting European and some international talent to its chic, modern barlike ambience. **Tivoli Jazzhouse Mantra** (☒ Vesterbrog. 3, ☎ 33/11–11–13), Tivoli's jazz club, lures some of the biggest names in the world.

NIGHTCLUBS AND DANCING

The young set gets down on the disco floor in the fashionable **Park Café** (☒ Østerbrog. 79, ☎ 35/26–63–42). The mellower folks come for brunch when the place transforms back to its Old World roots, or to check out the movie theater next door. **Rosie McGees** (☒ Vesterbrog. 2A, ☎ 33/32–19–23) is a very popular English-style pub with Mexican food and dancing. **Sabor Latino** (☒ Vester Voldg. 85, ☎ 33/11–97–66) is the UN of discos, with an international crowd dancing to salsa and other Latin beats. Among the most enduring clubs is **Woodstock** (☒ Vesterg. 12, ☎ 33/11–20–71), where a mixed audience grooves to '60s classics.

Shopping

Strøget's pedestrian streets are synonymous with shopping.

Specialty Shops

Just off Østergade street is **Pistolstræde,** a typical old courtyard filled with intriguing boutiques. Farther down the street toward the town hall square is a compound that includes several important stores: **Georg Jensen** (☒ Amagertorv 4 and Østerg. 40, ☎ 33/11–40–80), one of the world's finest silversmiths, gleams with a wide array of silver patterns and jewelry. Don't miss the **Georg Jensen Museum** (✉ Amagertorv 6, ☎ 33/14–02–29), which showcases glass and silver creations ranging from tiny, twisted-glass shot glasses to an $85,000 silver fish dish. **Royal Copenhagen Porcelain** (✉ Amagertorv 6, ☎ 33/13–71–81) carries both old and new china, plus porcelain patterns and figurines.

A. C. Bang (✉ Østerg. 27, ☎ 33/15–17–26) upholds its Old World, old-money aura with impeccable quality; midsummer and after-Christmas fur sales offer real savings. **Bang & Olufsen** (✉ Østerg. 3–5, ☎ 33/15–04–22) offers reasonable prices in its own upscale shop. Along Strøget, at furrier **Birger Christensen** (✉ Østerg. 38, ☎ 33/11–55–55), you can peruse designer clothes and chic furs. **FONA** (✉ Østerg. 47, ☎ 33/15–90–55) carries stereo equipment, including the superior design and sound of Bang & Olufsen. **Illum** (✉ Østerg. 52, ☎ 33/14–40–02) is a department store that has a fine basement grocery store and eating arcade. Don't confuse Illum with **Illums Bolighus** (✉ Amagertorv 10, ☎ 33/14–19–41), where designer furnishings, porcelain, quality clothing, and gifts are displayed in near-gallery surroundings. **Magasin** (✉ Kongens Nytorv 13, ☎ 33/11–44–33), one of the largest department stores in Scandinavia, offers all kinds of clothing and gifts, as well as an excellent grocery department.

Side Trips

Heslingør

Shakespeare immortalized both the town and the castle when he chose Helsingør's **Kronborg Slot** (Kronborg Castle) as the setting for *Hamlet.* Completed in 1585, the present gabled and turreted structure is about 600 years younger than the fortress we imagine as the setting of Shakespeare's tragedy. Inside are a 200-ft-long dining hall, the luxurious chapel, and the royal chambers. The ramparts and 12-ft-thick walls are a reminder of the castle's role as a coastal bulwark—Sweden is only a few kilometers away. Helsingør town—about 47 km (29 mi) north of Copenhagen—possesses a number of picturesque streets with 16th-century houses. Frequent trains stop at Helsingør station, and then it's a 20-minute walk around the harbor to the castle. ✉ *Kronborg Slot,* ☎ *49/21–30–78.* ⏲ *Easter and May–Sept., daily 10:30–5; Oct. and Apr., Tues.–Sun. 11–4; Nov.–Mar., Tues.–Sun. 11–3.*

Humlebæk

★ **Louisiana** is a world-class modern art collection housed in a spectacular building in Humlebæk—part of the "Danish Riviera" on the North Sjælland coast. Even if you can't tell a Rauschenberg from a Rembrandt, you should make the 35-km (22-mi) trip to see the setting: It's an elegant, rambling structure set in a large park with views of the sound, and, on a clear day, Sweden. The children's wing houses pyramid-shape chalkboards, kid-proof computers, and weekend activities under the guidance of an artist or museum coordinator. It's a half-hour train ride from Copenhagen to Humlebæk. A 10-minute walk from the station, the museum is also accessible by the E4 highway and the more scenic Strandvejen, or coastal road. ✉ *Gammel Strandvej 13,* ☎ *49/19–07–19.* *Combined train fare (from Copenhagen) and admission DKr94 available from DSB (☞ Arriving and Departing by Train* in *Copenhagen Essentials,* below*); prices higher for special exhibitions.* ⏲ *Daily 10–5, Wed. 10–10.*

Roskilde

For a look into the past, head 30 km (19 mi) west of Copenhagen to the bustling market town of Roskilde. A key administrative center during Viking times, it remained one of the largest towns in northern Europe through the Middle Ages. Today the legacy of its 1,000-year history lives on in its spectacular cathedral. Built on the site of one of Denmark's first churches, the **Domkirke** (cathedral) has been the burial place of Danish royalty since the 15th century. The combined effect of their tombs is striking—from the magnificent shrine of Christian IV to the simple brick chapel of Frederik IX. ✉ *Domkirkepl.,* ☎ *46/35–27–00.* ⏲ *Subject to change; call ahead.*

A 10-minute walk south and through the park takes you to the water ★ and to the **Vikingeskibshallen** (Viking Ship Museum). Inside are five exquisitely reconstructed Viking ships, discovered at the bottom of Roskilde Fjord in 1962. Detailed placards in English chronicle Viking history. There are also English-language films on the excavation and reconstruction. ✉ *Strandengen,* ☎ *46/35–65–55.* ⏲ *Apr.–Oct., daily 9–5; Nov.–Mar., daily 10–4.*

Copenhagen Essentials

Arriving and Departing

BY PLANE

The main airport for both international and domestic flights is Copenhagen Airport, 10 km (6 mi) southeast of town.

Between the Airport and Downtown. Bus service to the city is frequent. The airport bus to the central station leaves every 15 minutes: The trip takes about 25 minutes; the fare is about DKr39 (pay on the bus). Public buses cost about DKr16 and run as often but take longer. Bus 250S takes you to Rådhus Pladsen, the city hall square. A taxi ride takes 15 minutes and costs about DKr120.

BY TRAIN

Copenhagen's clean and convenient central station, **Hovedbanegården** (✉ Just south of Vesterbrog., ☎ 33/14–88–00), is the hub of the country's train network. Intercity express trains leave hourly, on the hour, from 6 AM to 10 PM for principal towns in Fyn and Jylland. Find out more from DSB Information (☎ 70/13–14–15) at the central station. You can make reservations at the central station as well as most other stations, and through travel agents. Public shower facilities at the central station are open 4:30 AM–2 AM and cost DKr15.

Getting Around

BY BICYCLE

More than half the 5 million Danes are said to ride bikes, which visitors use as well. Bike rental costs DKr25 to DKr60 a day, with a deposit of DKr100 to DKr200. Contact **Københavns Cykler** (✉ Central Station, ☎ 33/33–86–13) or **Østerport Cykler** (✉ Oslo Plads, ☎ 33/33–85–13).

BY BUS AND SUBURBAN TRAIN

The best bet for visitors is the **Copenhagen Card,** affording unlimited travel on buses and suburban trains (S-trains), admission to some 60 museums and sights around metropolitan Copenhagen, and a reduction on the ferry crossing to Sweden. Buy the card, which costs about DKr140 (24 hours), Dkr255 (48 hours), or DKr320 (72 hours)—half price for children ages 5 to 11—at tourist offices or hotels or from travel agents.

Buses and suburban trains operate on the same ticket system and divide Copenhagen and environs into three zones. Tickets are validated on the time system: On the basic ticket, which costs DKr10 for an hour, you can travel anywhere in the zone in which you started. You can buy a discount *klip cort* (clip card), equivalent to 10 basic tickets, for DKr70. Call the 24-hour information service for zone information: ☎ 36/45–45–45 for buses, ☎ 70/13–14–15 for S-trains (wait for the Danish message to end and a live operator will answer). Buses and S-trains run from 5 AM (6 AM on Sunday) to 12:30 AM. A reduced network of buses drives through the night.

BY CAR

Copenhagen is a city for walkers, not drivers. The charm of its pedestrian streets is paid for by a complicated one-way road system and difficult parking. Leave your car in the garage: Attractions are relatively close together, and public transportation is excellent.

BY TAXI

The computer-metered Mercedes and Volvos are not cheap. The base charge is DKr15, plus DKr8–DKr10 (DKr 11 at night) per km (½ mi). A cab is available when it displays the sign FRI (free); you can either hail a cab (though this can be difficult outside the center), pick one up at a taxi stand, or call ☎ 31/35–35–35 (surcharge of DKr20).

Contacts and Resources

EMBASSIES

United States (✉ Dag Hammarskjöldsallé 24, ☎ 35/55–31–44). **Canadian** (✉ Kristen Benikowsg. 1, ☎ 33/44–52–00). **United Kingdom** (✉ Kastelsvej 40, ☎ 35/26–46–00).

EMERGENCIES

Police, fire, ambulance (☎ 112). **Auto Rescue/Falck** (☎ 31/14–22–22). **Doctor** (Weekdays 8–4, ☎ 33/936300; daily after 4 PM, ☎ 38/84–00–41; fees payable in cash only; night fees around DKr120–DKr350). **Dentist:** Dental Emergency Service (✉ Tandlægevagten 14, Oslo Pl., near Østerport station, ☎ no phone; emergencies only; cash only). **Pharmacies** open 24 hours: **Steno Apotek** (✉ Vesterbrog. 6C, ☎ 33/14–82–66); **Sønderbro Apotek** (✉ Amagerbrog. 158, Amager area, ☎ 32/58–01–40).

ENGLISH-LANGUAGE BOOKSTORES

Boghallen (✉ Rådhus Pl. 37, ☎ 33/11–85–11, ext. 309). **Arnold Busck** (✉ Købmagerg. 49, ☎ 33/12–24–53).

GUIDED TOURS

Orientation. The boat "Harbor and Canal Tour" leaves from Gammel Strand and the east side of Kongens Nytorv; it runs from May through mid-September, daily every half hour from 10 to 5. The following bus tours, conducted by **Copenhagen Excursions** (☎ 31/54–06–06), leave from the Lur Blowers' Column in Rådhus Pladsen: "City Tour" (mid-June–mid-Sept., daily at 9:30, 1, and 3); "Grand Tour of Copenhagen" (daily at 11; Apr.–Sept., additional tour daily at 1:30; Oct.–Mar., Sat. at 1:30); "Royal Tour of Copenhagen" (June–mid-Sept., Tues. and Sat. at 10); "City and Harbor Tour" (combined bus and boat; mid-May–mid-Sept., daily at 9:30; mid-June–mid-Sept., additional tour daily at 3). Tickets are available aboard the bus and boat or from travel agencies.

Personal Guides. The Danish Tourist Board (☞ Visitor Information, *below*) can recommend multilingual guides for individual needs; travel agents have details on hiring a limousine and guide.

Regional. The Danish Tourist Board (☞ Visitor Information, *below*) has full details relating to excursions outside the city, including visits to castles (such as Hamlet's castle), the Viking Ship Museum, and Sweden.

Special-Interest. The "Royal Copenhagen Porcelain" tour (✉ Smalleg. 45, ☎ 31/86–48–59) is given on weekdays at 9, 10, and 11. If you're a beer aficionado, try the "Carlsberg Brewery Tour" (☞ Exploring Copenhagen, *above*).

Walking. The Danish Tourist Board (☞ Visitor Information, *below*) supplies maps and brochures and can recommend a walking tour.

TRAVEL AGENCIES

American Express (✉ Amagertorv 18, ☎ 33/12–23–01). **Spies** (✉ Nyropsg. 41, ☎ 33/32–15–00) arranges charter flights and accommodations all over Europe.

VISITOR INFORMATION

Danish Tourist Board (✉ Danmarks Turistråd, Bernstoffsg. 1, Tivoli Grounds, DK 1577 KBH V, ☎ 33/11–13–25).

FYN AND THE CENTRAL ISLANDS

It was Hans Christian Andersen, the region's most famous native, who dubbed Fyn (Funen) the "Garden of Denmark." Part orchard, part farmland, Fyn is sandwiched between Sjælland and Jylland, and with its tidy, rolling landscape, seaside towns, manor houses, and castles, it is one of Denmark's loveliest islands. Its capital—1,000-year-old Odense, in the north—is the birthplace of Hans Christian Andersen; his life and works are immortalized here in two museums. Fyn is also the site of two of Denmark's best-preserved castles: 12th-century Nyborg Slot, in the east, and 16th-century Egeskov Slot, near Svendborg, in the south. From Svendborg it's easy to hop on a ferry and visit some of the smaller islands, such as Tåsinge, Langeland, and Ærø, whose main town, Ærøskøbing, with its twisting streets and half-timber houses, seems caught in a time warp.

Fyn has a wide range of hotels and inns, many of which offer off-season (October through May) rates, as well as special weekend deals. The islands are also furnished with numerous campsites and youth hostels, all clean and attractively located. Some, like Odense's youth hostel, are set in old manor houses. Contact local tourist offices for information (☞ Visitor Information *in* Fyn and the Central Islands, *below*).

Nyborg

This 13th-century town was Denmark's capital during the Middle Ages, as well as an important stop on a major trading route between Sjælland and Jylland. From 1200 to 1413, Nyborg housed the Danehof, the early Danish parliament. Nyborg's major landmark is its 12th-century **Nyborg Slot** (Nyborg Castle). It was here that Erik Glipping granted the first Danish constitution, the Great Charter, in 1282. ✉ *Slotspl.,* ☎ *65/31–02–07.* ⏲ *Mar.–May, Tues.–Sun. 10–3; June–Aug., daily 10–5; Sept.–Oct., Tues.–Sun. 10–3.*

$$$ 🏨 **Hesselet.** This modern hotel looks like a brick slab outside, but inside it's a refined English-cum-Asian sanctuary. The guest rooms are furnished with cushy, modern furniture, and most have splendid views. ✉ *Christianslundsvej 119, DK 5800,* ☎ *65/31–30–29,* FAX *65/31–29–58. 43 rooms, 3 suites. Restaurant, indoor pool. AE, DC, MC, V.*

Kerteminde

Coastal Kerteminde is Fyn's most important fishing village and a picturesque summer resort. Stroll down Langegade to see its half-timber houses.

$$$ ✕ **Rudolf Mathis.** You can enjoy delectable fish and seafood specialties and a splendid view of Kerteminde Harbor at this traditional Dan-

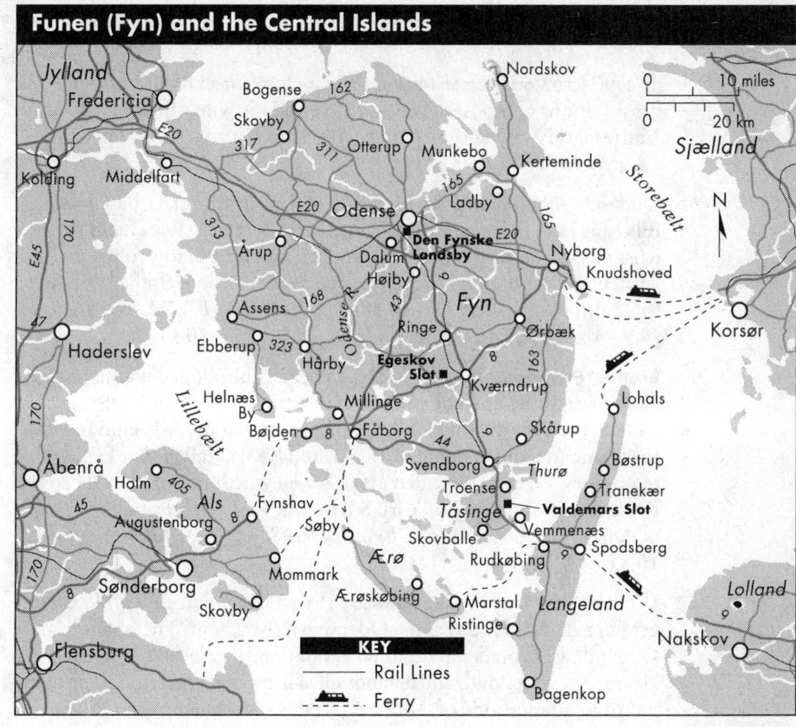

ish restaurant. ✉ *Dosseringen 13, 13 km (8 mi) northeast of Odense on Rte. 165,* ☎ *65/32–32–33. AE, DC, MC, V. Closed Mon. Jan.–Mar., and Sun. Oct. and Dec.*

Ladby

If you're a Viking enthusiast, stop in the village of Ladby to see the **Ladbyskibet** (Ladby ship), the 1,100-year-old underground remains of a Viking chieftain's burial, complete with his 72-ft-long ship. The warrior was equipped for his trip to Valhalla (the afterlife) with his weapons, 4 hunting dogs, and 11 horses. ✉ *Vikingevej 123,* ☎ *65/32–16–67.* ⏲ *Mar.–mid-May, daily 10–4; mid-May–mid-Sept., daily 10–6; mid-May–Oct., daily 10–4; Nov.–Feb., weekends 11–3.*

Odense

Plan on spending at least one night in Denmark's third-largest city. In addition to its museums and pleasant pedestrian streets, Odense is an especially charming provincial capital. If you can't take quaintness, don't go to the **H. C. Andersens Hus** (Hans Christian Andersen Museum). The surrounding area has been carefully preserved, with cobbled pedestrian streets and low houses with lace curtains. Inside, exhibits use photos, diaries, drawings, and letters to convey a sense of the man and the time in which he lived. Attached to the museum is an extensive library with Andersen's works in more than 127 languages (he was in fact one of the most widely published authors in the history of literature), where you can listen to fairy tales on tape. The museum includes child-friendly exhibits. ✉ *Hans Jensenstr. 37–45,* ☎ *66/13–13–72, ext. 4611.* ⏲ *Sept.–May, Tues.–Sun. 10–4; June–Aug., daily 9–6.*

Families with little ones and fantasy-minded bigger ones should head to **Børnekulturehuset Fyretøjet** (Children's Culture House, The Tinderbox). This new museum includes walk-through fairy-tale exhibits, as well as studios where children can draw and write their own tales and plays and then dress up and perform them. ✉ *Hans Jensenstr. 21,* ☎ *66/14–44–11.* ⏲ *Sept.–June, Tues.–Sun. 10–4; July–Aug., daily 10–5.*

The modern **Carl Nielsen Museum** has multimedia exhibits of Denmark's most famous composer (1865–1931) and his wife, the sculptor Anne Marie Carl Nielsen (1863–1945). ✉ *Claus Bergsg. 11,* ☎ *66/13–13–72, ext. 4671.* ⏲ *Tues.–Sun. 10–4.*

Odense's **Møntergården** (Museum of Cultural and Urban History) fills four houses representing Danish architectural styles from the Renaissance to the 18th century, all grouped around a shady, cobbled courtyard. Inside are dioramas, an extensive coin collection, clothed dummies, toys, and tableaus. ✉ *Overg. 48–50,* ☎ *66/13–13–72, ext. 4611.* ⏲ *July–Aug., daily 10–5; Sept.–June, Tues.–Sun. 10–5.*

Brandts Passage, off Vestergade, is a heavily boutiqued walking street. At the end of it, in what was once a textile factory, is a four-story art ★ gallery, the **Brandts Klædefabrik,** incorporating the **Museum for Photographic Art,** the **Graphic Museum,** and **Kunst Hallen** (Art Hall), with temporary exhibits for video art. It's well worth the short walk to see Fyn's rendition of a New York SoHo loft. ✉ *37–43 Brandts Passage,* ☎ *66/13–78–97.* ⏲ *Sept.–June, Tues.–Sun. 10–5; July–Aug., daily 10–5.*

Don't neglect **Den Fynske Landsby** (Fyn Village); an enjoyable way to get here is to travel down the Odense River by boat. The open-air museum village is made up of 20 farm buildings, including workshops, a vicarage, a water mill, and a windmill. There's a theater, too, with summertime adaptations of Andersen's tales. ✉ *Sejerskovvej 20,* ☎ *66/13–13–72, ext. 4642.* ⏲ *Apr.–May and Sept.–Oct., daily 10–5; June–Aug. daily 10–7; Nov.–Mar., Sun. and holidays 10–4.*

$$ ✕ **Le Provence.** A few minutes from the pedestrian street, this restaurant, with its cozy orange-and-yellow–clad dining room, puts a Danish twist on Provençal cuisine, with such specialties as venison in blackberry sauce and duck breast cooked in sherry. ✉ *Pogstr. 31,* ☎ *66/12–12–96. DC, MC, V.*

$ ✕ **Målet.** A lively crowd calls this sports club its neighborhood bar. Next to steaming plates of schnitzel served in a dozen ways, soccer is the delight of the house. ✉ *Jernbaneg. 17,* ☎ *66/17–82–41. Reservations not accepted. No credit cards.*

$$$$ **Grand Hotel.** They don't make spacious, gracious places like this anymore. Dating from 1897, the Grand offers spruced-up fin de siècle elegance. The lobby decor is cool and green, with a sweeping staircase and a spectacular Pompeian-red dining room. Guest rooms are ample and comfortable. ✉ *Jernbaneg. 18, DK 5000,* ☎ *66/11–71–71,* FAX *66/14–11–71. 137 rooms. Restaurant. AE, DC, MC, V.*

$$ **Hotel Ansgar Slotsgaarden.** Though completely renovated in 1995, this hotel still maintains a cozy, modest, English-style ambience. The rooms—done in rather dark colors—have a mix of old and new furniture. ✉ *Østre Stationsvej 32, DK 5000,* ☎ *66/11–96–93,* FAX *66/11–96–75. 44 rooms. Restaurant. AE, MC, V.*

$ **Hotel Ydes.** If you're a student or budget-conscious and tired of barracks-type accommodations, this bright, colorful hotel is a good bet. The plain, white, hospital-style rooms are clean and comfortable. ✉ *Hans Tausensg. 11, DK 5000,* ☎ *66/12–11–31. 30 rooms, 24 with shower. Restaurant. AE, DC, MC, V.*

Fåborg

Four times a day, the lovely little 12th-century town of Fåborg echoes with the dulcet chiming of the Klokketårnet (Bell Tower)'s carillon, the largest in Fyn. Dating from 1725 the **Gamla Gård** (Old Merchant's House) chronicles the cultural history of Fyn. ✉ *Holkeg. 1,* ☎ *62/61–33–38.* ⏲ *Mid-May–Sept., daily 10:30–4:30.*

The **Fåborg Museum for Fynsk Malerkunst** (Fyn Painting Museum) displays the compositions—dating mainly from 1880 to 1920—of Fyn painters, filled with the dusky light that so often illuminates Scandinavian painting. ✉ *Grønneg. 75,* ☎ *62/61–06–45.* ⏲ *Apr.–May and Sept.–Oct., daily 10–4; June–Aug., daily 10–5; Nov.–Mar., daily 11–3.*

$$$$ **Falsled Kro.** Once a smuggler's hideaway, this 500-year-old institution is one of Denmark's most elegant inns. A favorite among well-heeled Europeans, it has sumptuously appointed cottages with European antiques and stone fireplaces. The restaurant combines French and Danish cuisines, employing ingredients from its own garden and markets in faraway Lyon. ✉ *Assensvej 513, DK 5642 Millinge, 13 km (8 mi) northwest of Fåborg on the Millinge-Assens Hwy.,* ☎ *62/68–11–11,* FAX *62/68–11–62. 14 rooms, 3 apartments. Restaurant. AE, DC, MC. Closed Jan.–Feb.*

$$$ **Steensgård Herregårdspension.** A long avenue of beeches leads to this 700-year-old moated manor house 7 km (4½ mi) northwest of Fåborg. Rooms are elegant, with antiques, four-poster beds, and yards of silk damask. The fine restaurant serves wild game from the manor's own preserve. ✉ *Steensgård 4, DK 5642 Millinge,* ☎ *62/61–94–90,* FAX *62/61–78–61. 15 rooms, 13 with bath. Restaurant, tennis, horseback riding. AE, DC, MC, V. Closed Jan.*

Ærø

Take the car ferry to **Søby** at the northern tip of Ærø island, the "Jewel of the Archipelago," where roads wend through fertile fields and past thatched farmhouses. South from Søby is the charming town of **Ærøskøbing,** on the island's north coast. Once you've spent an hour walking through its cobbled 17th- and 18th-century streets, you'll understand its great appeal.

$$ **Ærøhus.** A half-timber building with a steep red roof, the Ærøhus looks like a rustic cottage on the outside and a great aunt's house on the inside. Hanging pots and slanted walls characterize the public areas; pine furniture and cheerful curtains and duvets keep the guest rooms simple and bright. In an annex are apartments, all with kitchenettes. The garden's eight cottages have small terraces. ✉ *Vesterg. 38, DK 5970 Ærøskøbing,* ☎ *62/52–10–03,* FAX *62/52–21–23. 30 rooms, 18 with bath; 8 cottages; 37 apartments. Restaurant. Closed Dec. 24 and Jan.*

Svendborg

The southernmost town in Fyn is the gateway to the country's southern islands. ★ Just north of Svendborg is **Egeskov Slot** (Egeskov Castle), one of the best-preserved island castles in Europe. Egeskov means "oak forest," and an entire one was felled around 1540 to form the piles on which the rose-stone structure was erected. The park contains noteworthy Renaissance, Baroque, English, and peasant gardens and an antique-car museum. Though this is still a private home, a few rooms, including the trophy-filled hunting room, are open to the public. ✉ *Egeskovg. 18, Kværndrup (15 km/9 mi north of Svendborg),* ☎ *62/27–10–16.* *Castle and museum, DKr100.* ⏲ *Castle: May–June, Aug.–Sept., daily 10–5; July, daily 10–7; museum: May and Sept., daily 10–5; June and Aug., daily 9–6; July, daily 9–8.*

$ ✕ **Ærø.** A dim hodgepodge of ship parts and maritime doodads, this harborside restaurant is peopled by brusque waitresses and serious local trenchermen. Though refurbished a couple of years back, it retains its maritime decor while the menu remains staunchly old-fashioned, focusing on *frikadeller* (fried meatballs), fried *rødspætte* (plaice) with hollandaise sauce, and dozens of smørrebrød options. ✉ *Brøg. 1 ved Ærøfærgen,* ☎ *62/21-07-60. DC, MC, V. Closed Sun.*

Troense

On the island of Tåsinge, pretty Troense is one of Denmark's best-preserved villages. Once the home port for countless sailing ships, both Viking and, later, commercial, today the harbor is stuffed with pleasure yachts. Dating from around 1640, **Valdemars Slot** (Valdemars Castle), now a sumptuously furnished home, is one of Denmark's oldest privately owned castles. Upstairs rooms are appointed to the smallest detail. Downstairs is the castle church, illuminated only by candlelight. There's a restaurant (☞ *below*) beneath the church. The sister café overlooks Lunkebugten, a bay with one of south Fyn's best stretches of beach. ✉ *Slotsalleen 100, Troense,* ☎ *62/22-61-06.* ⏲ *May and Sept.-Oct., daily 10-5; June-Aug. daily 10-6.*

$$$ ✕ **Restaurant Valdemars Slot.** Beneath the castle, this domed restaurant is all romance and prettiness, with pink carpet and candlelight. Fresh ingredients from France and Germany and wild game from the castle's preserve are the essentials for an ever-changing menu, which includes such specialties as wild venison with cream sauce and duck breast à l'orange. The less expensive café, Den Grå Dame, serves traditional Danish food. ✉ *Slotsalleen 100, Troense,* ☎ *62/22-59-00. AE, MC, V. Closed Nov.-Mar. except to groups of 4 or more with several days' notice.*

Langeland

Tåsinge is connected with the island of Langeland by a causeway bridge. The largest island in the southern archipelago, Langeland is rich in relics of the past, and the beaches are worth scouting out.

Fyn and the Central Islands Essentials

Getting Around

The best starting point is Nyborg, on Fyn's east coast, just across the Great Belt from Korsør, on Sjælland. "The other Chunnel"—this one connecting Sjælland to Fyn—opened for rail traffic in 1997 and for cars in 1998. From Nyborg the easiest way to travel is by car, though public transportation is good. Distances on Fyn and its islands are short, but there is much to see and you can easily spend two or three days here, circling the islands from Nyborg or using Odense or Svendborg as a base from which to make excursions.

Guided Tours

Odense has a two-hour tour that operates Monday through Saturday during July and August and focuses on native son Hans Christian Andersen; contact the Danish Tourist Board (☞ *below*) for details.

A day trip to Odense leaves from Copenhagen's city hall square at 9 AM every Sunday from mid-May to mid-September. Lasting about 11 hours, the trip includes stops at several picturesque villages and a lightning-speed visit to Egeskov Castle.

Visitor Information

Nyborg (✉ Torvet 9, ☎ 65/31-02-80). **Odense** (✉ Rådhuset, ☎ 66/12-75-20). **South Fyn Tourist Board** (✉ Centrumpl., Svendborg, ☎ 62/21-09-80).

JYLLAND AND THE LAKES

A region of carefully groomed pastures punctuated by stretches of rugged beauty, the peninsula of Jylland (Jutland) is the only part of Denmark that is attached to the mainland of Europe; its southern boundary forms the frontier with Germany. Moors and sand dunes cover a tenth of the peninsula—the windswept landscapes of Isak Dinesen's short stories can be seen in the northwest—and the remaining land is devoted to agriculture and forestry. On the east side of the peninsula, facing Fyn, well-wooded fjords run inland for miles. Beyond rustic towns and stark countryside, Jylland possesses gracious castles, parklands, and the famed Legoland. Ribe, Denmark's oldest town, lies to the south; to the east is Århus, Denmark's second-largest city, with superb museums and a new concert hall. If you are in this region directly after touring Fyn, head northwest from Odense through Middlefart and then on to Vejle. By train, either from Odense or Copenhagen, the starting point is Kolding, to the south of Vejle.

Kolding

Don't miss the well-preserved 13th-century **Koldinghus** castle, a royal residence during the Middle Ages. Rebuilt during the 15th century, it was destroyed by fire in the early 1800s. Modern restoration took nearly 20 years, ending in 1993. Perched at the edge of the Kolding Fjord is a massive redbrick quadrangle centered on a courtyard. The castle floors are made of raw oak, and its walls are alternately spare and white or lined with iron plates. The construction reveals how Danish design bridges the old and the new: The building was awarded the European Nostra Prize in 1993 for restoration. ✉ *Rådhusstr.,* ☎ *75/50–15–00.* ⏲ *Daily 10–5.*

The **Geografiske Have** (Geographical Garden) has a rose garden with more than 120 varieties, as well as some 2,000 other plants from all parts of the world, arranged geographically. ⏲ *June and Aug., daily 9–7; July, daily 9–8; Sept.–May, daily 10–6.*

Vejle

Beautifully positioned on the fjord amid forest-clad hills, Vejle looks toward the Kattegat, the strait that divides Jylland and Fyn. You can hear an old Dominican monastery clock chiming the hours; the clock survives, but the monastery itself was long ago torn down to make room for the town's imposing 19th-century city hall.

$$$$ 🏨 **Munkebjerg.** Seven kilometers (4½ mi) southeast of town, surrounded by a thick beech forest and majestic views of the Vejle Fjord, this elegant hotel attracts guests who prefer privacy. Rooms overlook the forest and are furnished in blond pine and soft green; the lobby is rustic. There are also two top-notch restaurants, one specializing in French cuisine, the other in very Danish fare. ✉ *Munkebjergvej 125, DK 7100,* ☎ *76/42–85–00,* FAX *75/72–08–86. 148 rooms. 2 restaurants, café, pool, sauna, golf course, tennis court, exercise room, horseback riding, jogging, biking, casino, heliport. AE, DC, MC, V.*

Jelling

Here lie two 10th-century burial mounds, all that remains from the court of King Gorm the Old and his wife, Thyra. Between the mounds are the Jelling **Runestener** (runic stones), one of which, "Denmark's Certificate of Baptism," is decorated with the oldest known figure of Christ in Scandinavia. The stone was erected by Gorm's son, King Harald Bluetooth, who brought Christianity to the Danes in AD 960.

Jutland (Jylland)

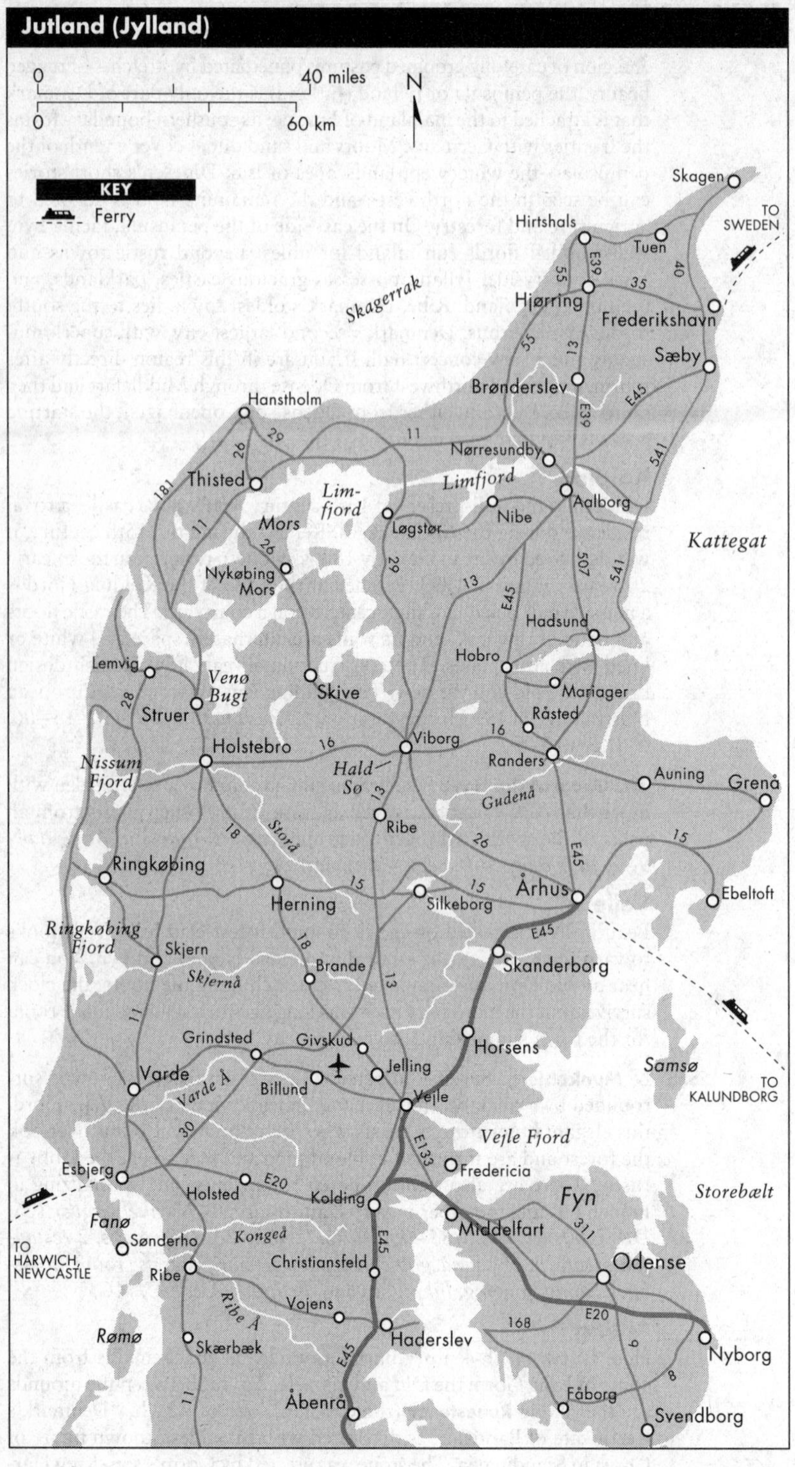

Silkeborg

An exploration of the region between Silkeborg, on the banks of the Gudenå in Jylland's lake district, and Skanderborg to the east will reveal some of Denmark's loveliest scenery. The best way to explore the area is by water; the Gudenå winds its way some 160 km (100 mi) through lakes and wooded hillsides down to the sea. You can take one of the excursion boats or, better still, a rare old coal-fired paddle steamer, the ***Hjejlen,*** which runs in summer and is based at Silkeborg. Ever since 1861 it has been paddling its way through narrow stretches of fjord where the treetops meet overhead to the foot of Denmark's highest hill, the Himmelbjerget, which rises all of 438 ft at Lake Julso. You can clamber up the narrow paths through the heather and trees to the top of the hill, where there is an 80-ft tower erected in 1875 in memory of King Frederik VII. ✉ *Havnen, Silkeborg,* ☎ *86/82–07–66 (reservations).* 🎫 *Round-trip tickets DKr39–DKr76.* ⏲ *Departs Silkeborg Harbor 10 and 1:45 Sun. in June, daily mid-June–July.*

One of Silkeborg's chief attractions can be seen in the **Kulturhistoriske Museum** (Museum of Cultural History)—the 2,200-year-old Tollund Man, whose corpse was preserved by the natural chemicals in a nearby bog. ✉ *Hovedgaardsvej 7,* ☎ *86/82–14–99.* ⏲ *Mid-Apr.–late Oct., daily 10–5; late Oct.–mid-Apr., Wed. and weekends noon–4.*

Århus

Denmark's second-largest city is at its liveliest during the 10-day **Århus Festival** in September, which brings together everything from classical concerts to jazz and folk music, clowning, theater, exhibitions, beer tents, and sports. The town's cathedral, the 15th-century **Domkirke,** is Denmark's longest church; it contains a beautifully executed three-panel altarpiece. Look up at the whimsical sketches on the ceiling. ✉ *Bispetorv,* ☎ *86/12–38–45.* ⏲ *Jan.–Apr., Mon.–Sat. 10–3; May–Sept., Mon.–Sat. 9:30–4, Oct.– Dec., Mon.–Sat. 10–3. Closed Sun. and holidays for services.*

Århus's 13th-century **Vor Frue Kirken** (Church of Our Lady), formerly attached to a Dominican abbey, has an eerie but interesting crypt church rediscovered in 1955 and dating from 1060, one of the oldest preserved stone churches in Scandinavia. The vaulted space contains a replica of an old Roman crucifix. ✉ *Frue Kirkepl.,* ☎ *86/12–12–43,* ⏲ *Sept.–Apr., weekdays 10–2, Sat. 10–noon; May–Aug., weekdays 10–4, Sat. 10–2. Closed Sun. and holidays for services.*

The town's open-air museum, the **Gamle By** (Old Town), is composed of 65 half-timber houses, a mill, and a millstream. The meticulously re-created period interiors range from the 15th to the early 20th centuries. ✉ *Viborgvej,* ☎ *86/12–31–88.* ⏲ *Jan.–Mar. and Nov., daily 11–3; Apr., Oct., and Dec., daily 10–4; May and Sept., daily 9–5; June–Aug., daily 9–6.*

★ In a 250-acre forest just south of Århus, the indoor-outdoor **Moesgård Forhistorisk Museum** (Prehistoric Museum) displays ethnography and archaeology, including the Grauballe Man, an eerie, well-preserved corpse from 2,000 years ago. Take the Prehistoric Trail through the forest, which leads past Stone and Bronze Age displays to some reconstructed houses from Viking times. ✉ *Ny Moesgård Allé 20, Højbjerg,* ☎ *89/42–11–00.* ⏲ *Oct.–Mar., Tues.–Sun., 10–4; Apr.–Sept., daily 10–5.*

$ ✕ **Rio Grande.** Full of the standard-issue blankets, straw hats, and bright colors ubiquitous in Mexican restaurants all over the world, Rio Grande is a favorite with youngsters, families, and even businesspeople. Heaping plates of tacos, enchiladas, and chili are a good value—and tasty, too. ✉ *Vesterg. 39,* ☎ *86/19–06–96. AE, MC, V.*

$$$$ 🏨 **Royal Hotel.** Open since 1838, Århus's grand hotel has hosted such greats as Arthur Rubinstein and Marian Andersen. Guests are welcomed into a stately lobby appointed with Chesterfield sofas, modern paintings, and a winding staircase leading to the accommodations above. The plush rooms vary in style and decor, but all have rich drapery, velour- and brocade-covered furniture, and marble bathrooms. ✉ *Store Torv 4, DK 8100,* ☎ *86/12–00–11,* FAX *86/76–04–04. 98 rooms, 7 suites. Restaurant. AE, DC, MC, V.*

$ 🏨 **Youth Hostel Pavilionen.** As in all Danish youth and family hostels, rooms here are clean, bright, and functional, and the secluded, wooded setting near the fjord is downright beautiful. Keep in mind that it does get noisy, with carousing business parties mixed in with budget-conscious backpackers. ✉ *Marienlundsvej 10, DK 8240,* ☎ *86/16–72–98,* FAX *86/10–55–60. 30 rooms, 11 with shower; 4 communal showers and toilets. Cafeteria (breakfast only), kitchen. AE, MC, V. Closed mid-Dec.–mid-Jan.*

Aalborg

This city guards the narrowest point of the Limfjord, the great waterway of northern Jylland and the gateway between north and south. Here you'll find charming combinations of new and old; twisting lanes filled with medieval houses and, nearby, broad modern boulevards. Jomfru Ane Gade, a tiny cobbled street in the center of Aalborg, is lined with restaurants, inns, and sidewalk cafés. The magnificent five-story **Jens Bangs Stenhus** (Jens Bang's Stone House; ✉ Østerågade 9, ☎ 98/12–50–56), dating from 1624, has an atmospheric restaurant and an excellent wine cellar. The Baroque cathedral, **Budolfi Kirken** (✉ Gammel Torv), is consecrated to the English St. Butolph. The 15th-century **Helligandsklosteret** (Monastery of the Holy Ghost; ✉ Gammel Torv, next to Budolfi Kirken), one of Denmark's best preserved, is now a home for the elderly.

$$ ★ ✕ **Duus Vinkælder.** This amazing cellar is part alchemist's dungeon, part neighborhood bar. Though most people come for a drink before or after dinner, you can also get a light bite. In summer the menu is chiefly smørrebrød, but during the winter you can order such grilled specialties as pølser, frikadeller, *biksemad* (cubed potato, meat, and onion hash) and the restaurant's specialty, pâté. ✉ *Østerå 9,* ☎ *98/12–50–56. Reservations essential. No credit cards. Closed Sun.*

$$ ✕ **Spisehuset Kniv og Gaffel.** In a 400-year-old building parallel to Jomfru Ane Gade, the busy Knife and Fork is crammed with oak tables balancing on crazy slanting floors and lit by candles. Its year-round courtyard is a veritable greenhouse. Young waitresses negotiate the mayhem to deliver inch-thick steaks, the house specialty. ✉ *Maren Turisg. 10,* ☎ *98/16–69–72. DC, MC, V. Closed Sun.*

$$$$ 🏨 **Helnan Phønix.** At a central location in a sumptuous old mansion, this hotel is popular with international and business guests. Rooms are luxuriously furnished with plump chairs and polished dark-wood furniture; in some the original raw beams are still intact. The Brigarden restaurant serves excellent Danish cuisine. ✉ *Vesterbro 77, DK 9000,* ☎ *98/12–00–11,* FAX *98/16–31–66. 208 rooms, 2 suites. Restaurant, bar, sauna. AE, DC, MC, V.*

Skagen

The picturesque streets and luminous light of the town have inspired both painters and writers. Here the Danish artist Holger Drachmann (1846–1908) and his friends founded what has become known as the Skagen school of painting; you can see their work in the **Skagens Mu-**

seum. ✉ *Brøndumsvej 4,* ☎ *98/44–64–44.* ⏲ *Apr. and Oct., Tues.–Sun. 11–4; May and Sept., daily 10–5; June–Aug., daily 10–6; Nov.–Mar., Wed.–Fri. 1–4, Sat. 11–4, Sun. 11–3.*

$$$ **Brøndums Hotel.** A few minutes from the beach, this 150-year-old gabled inn is furnished with antiques and Skagen-school paintings. The 21 guest rooms in the main building, without TVs or phones, are old-fashioned, with wicker chairs and Oriental rugs, and pine and four-poster beds. Some are beginning to show their age, but 25 annex rooms are more modern. The hotel has a fine Danish-French restaurant with a lavish cold table. ✉ *Anchersvej 3, DK 9990,* ☎ *98/44–15–55,* FAX *98/45–15–20. 46 rooms, 12 with bath. Restaurant. AE, DC, MC, V.*

Viborg

Dating from the 8th century, the town started out as a trading post and a place of pagan sacrifice. Later it became a center of Christianity, with monasteries and its own bishop. The 1,000-year-old **Haervejen,** the old military road that starts near here, was once Denmark's most important connection with the outside world. Legend has it that during the 11th century, King Canute set out from Viborg to conquer England, which he subsequently ruled from 1016 to 1035. Built in 1130, Viborg's **Domkirke** (cathedral; ✉ Mogensg., ☎ 86/62–10–60) was once the largest granite church in the world. The crypt, restored and reopened in 1876, is all that remains of the original building. Its 20th-century biblical frescoes were painted by Danish artist Joakim Skovgaard.

Hald Sø

There's terrific walking country beside Hald Sø (Hald Lake) and on the nearby heatherclad **Dollerup Bakker** (Dollerup Hills). At a small kiosk near the lake that sells snacks and sweets you can pick up a map.

Herning

In this old moorland town, you'll find a remarkable circular building with an exterior frieze by Carl-Henning Pedersen (born 1913); it houses the **Carl–Henning Pedersen and Else Afelt Museum.** Just next door is the **Herning Art Museum.** The concave outer wall of the collar-shape building, a shirt factory until 1977, is lined with another enormous frieze 722 ft long. The two museums are set within a sculpture park. ✉ *Uldjydevej 3,* ☎ *97/12–10–33.* ⏲ *May–Oct., Tues.–Fri. noon–5, weekends 10–5; Nov.–Apr., Tues.–Sun. noon–5.*

Ribe

The medieval center in Denmark's oldest town is preserved by the Danish National Trust. From May to mid-September, a night watchman walks around the town telling of its ancient history and singing traditional songs. Visitors can join him in the main square each night at 10.

$$$ **Hotel Dagmar.** In the middle of Ribe's quaint center, this cozy, half-timber hotel encapsulates the charm of the 16th century, with stained-glass windows, frescoes, sloping floors, and carved chairs. The lavish rooms are all appointed with antique canopy beds, fat armchairs, and chaise longues. The fine French restaurant serves such specialties as fillet of salmon in sorrel cream sauce and marinated *foie gras de canard* (duck liver). ✉ *Torvet 1, DK 6760,* ☎ *75/42–00–33,* FAX *75/42–36–52. 50 rooms. Restaurant. AE, DC, MC, V.*

Billund

★ **Legoland** is a park filled with scaled-down versions of cities, towns, and villages, working harbors and airports, a Statue of Liberty, a statue of Sitting Bull, a Mt. Rushmore, a safari park, even a Pirate Land—all constructed of millions of Lego bricks. There are also exhibits of toys from pre-Lego days, including Legoland's showpiece, Titania's Palace, a sumptuous dollhouse built in 1907 by Sir Neville Wilkinson for his daughter. Legoland bought it at an auction in 1978 for an undisclosed, but steep, price. The park also has a massive theme-building-ride-restaurant extravaganza that's much better experienced than described. It all takes place within the double-football-field-size Castleland, where guests arrive through a serpentine dragon ride. Naturally, everything is made of Lego bricks, from the castle itself to the wizards and warlocks, dragons and knights that inhabit it. That is until you get to the theme restaurant, The Knight's Barbeque, where waiters in Middle Ages garb hustle skewered haunches of beef, "loooong sausages," and typical fare of the period. ✉ *Legoland,* ☎ *75/33–13–33.* 🎫 *DKr110–DKr130.* ⏲ *Apr.–Sept., daily 10–8.*

Jylland and the Lakes Essentials

Getting Around

Although there is good train and bus service between all the main cities, this region is best visited by car. The delightful offshore islands are suitable only if you have ample time, as many involve an overnight stay.

Guided Tours

Guided tours are scarce in these parts; stop by any tourist office for maps and suggestions for a walking tour. Århus also offers a "Round and About the City" tour, which leaves from the tourist office (☞ Visitor Information, *below*) daily at 10 AM from mid-June to mid-August.

Visitor Information

Aalborg (✉ Østerå 8, ☎ 98/12–60–22). **Århus** (✉ Rådhuset, ☎ 86/12–16–00). **Billund** (✉ c/o Legoland A/S, ☎ 75/33–19–26). **Herning** (✉ Bredg. 2, ☎ 97/12–44–22). **Kolding** (✉ Axeltorv 8, ☎ 75/53–21–00). **Randers** (✉ Erhvervens Hus, Tørvebryggen 12, ☎ 86/42–44–77). **Ribe** (✉ Torvet 3–5, ☎ 75/42–15–00). **Silkeborg** (✉ Åhavevej Haven, Godthåbsvej 4, ☎ 86/82–19–11). **Vejle** (✉ Sønderg. 14, ☎ 75/82–19–55). **Viborg** (✉ Nytorv 9, ☎ 86/61–16–66).

10 Finland

Helsinki, The Lakelands, Finnish Lapland

If you like majestic open spaces, fine architecture, and civilized living, Finland is for you. It is a land of lakes—187,888 at the last count—and forests, where nature is so prized that even the designs of urban centers reflect the functional architecture of the countryside.

The music of Sibelius echoes the mood of this Nordic landscape. Both can swing from the somber nocturne of midwinter darkness to the tremolo of sunlight slanting through pine and bone-white birch, ending with the diminuendo of a sunset as it fades into the next day's dawn. Similarly, the Finnish people reflect the changing moods of their land and climate. Their affinity with nature has produced some of the world's greatest designers and architects. Many American cities have buildings designed by Alvar Aalto and the Saarinens, Eliel and his son Eero. Eliel and his family moved to the United States in 1923 and became American citizens—but it was to a lonely Finnish seashore that Saarinen had his ashes returned.

Until 1917 Finland (the Finns call it *Suomi*) was under the domination of Sweden and Russia. After more than 600 years under the Swedish crown and 100 under the tsars, the country bears marks of the two cultures, such as a small (6%) but influential Swedish-speaking minority and a scattering of onion-dome Russian Orthodox churches.

The Finns themselves, neither Scandinavian nor Slavic, are descendants of the wandering Finno-Ugric peoples, who settled on the swampy shores of the Gulf of Finland before the Christian era. Finnish is one of the Finno-Ugric languages; it is related to Estonian and, distantly, to Hungarian.

There is a tough, resilient quality to the Finns. No other people fought the Soviets to a standstill as the Finns did in the Winter War of 1939–40. This resilience, in part, stems from the turbulence of the country's past, but it also comes from the people's strength and determination to work the land and survive the long, dark winters. They are stubborn, self-sufficient, and patriotic, yet not aggressively nationalistic. They mainly take pride in finding ways to live independently and in peace. In 1995 Finland joined the European Union, aiming for greater economic and political security.

The atmosphere in the capital, Helsinki with its outdoor summer bars and cafés and multilingual population, is far more cosmopolitan than was the case a decade ago. A conspicuous influx of Russians and Estonians is also evidence of Finland's new, more open relationship with its eastern neighbors.

Efficiency and value for money of its extensive public transport system makes it easy and viable to cover its beautiful expanses of lakeland and forest. Mobile telephones here are a standard accessory, and Internet and e-mail connections are more numerous per head of population than anywhere else. Technologically and culturally, this is a sophisticated country. Just the same, Finland is home to only 5.1 million inhabitants, and they continue to treasure their vast silent spaces. They won't always appreciate back-slapping familiarity—least of all in the sauna, widely regarded in the land that gave the traditional bath its name as a spiritual, as well as a cleansing, experience. But Finnish friendship, once nurtured, has a sincere and durable quality.

FINLAND A TO Z

Customs

For details on imports and duty-free limits, *see* Customs & Duties *in* Chapter 1.

Dining

As in other parts of Scandinavia, the *seisovapöytä* (buffet table) is often a work of art as well as a feast. Some special Finnish dishes are *poronkäristys* (reindeer casserole); salmon, herring, and various freshwater fish; and *lihapullat* (meatballs with a tasty sauce). Crayfish parties are popular between the end of July and early September. For a delicious dessert, try *lakka* (cloudberries), which grow in the midnight sun above the Arctic Circle and are frequently used in sauces for ice cream. Most restaurants close for major holidays.

MEALTIMES

The Finns eat early; lunch runs from 11 or noon to 1 or 2, dinner from 4 to 7 (a bit later in Helsinki).

RATINGS

Prices are per person and include first course, main course, dessert, and *palvelupalkkio* (service charge), which is included on the check. If you want to leave an additional tip—though it really isn't necessary—round the figure off to the nearest FIM 5 or FIM 10.

If you select the prix-fixe menu, which usually covers two courses and coffee and is served at certain hours in many establishments, the cost of the meal can be as little as half the prices shown below.

CATEGORY	HELSINKI	OTHER AREAS
$$$$	over FIM 200	over FIM 170
$$$	FIM 150–FIM 200	FIM 140–FIM 170
$$	FIM 80–FIM 150	FIM 80–FIM 140
$	under FIM 80	under FIM 80

WHAT TO WEAR

Except for the most elegant establishments, where a jacket and tie are preferred, casual attire is acceptable for restaurants in all price categories; jeans are not allowed in some more expensive dining rooms.

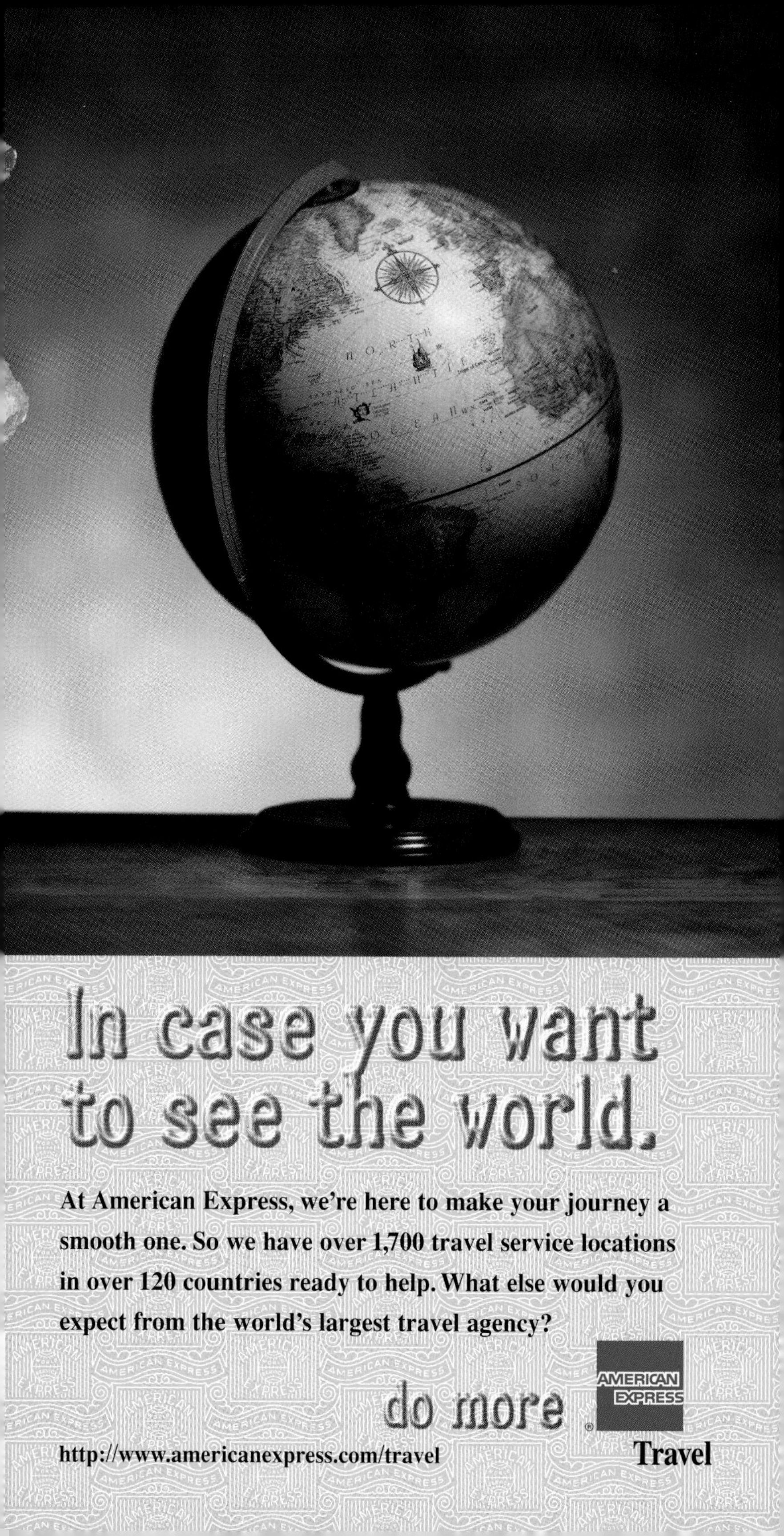

In case you want to see the world.
At American Express, we're here to make your journey a smooth one. So we have over 1,700 travel service locations in over 120 countries ready to help. What else would you expect from the world's largest travel agency?
do more
AMERICAN EXPRESS
Travel
http://www.americanexpress.com/travel

Finland (Suomi)

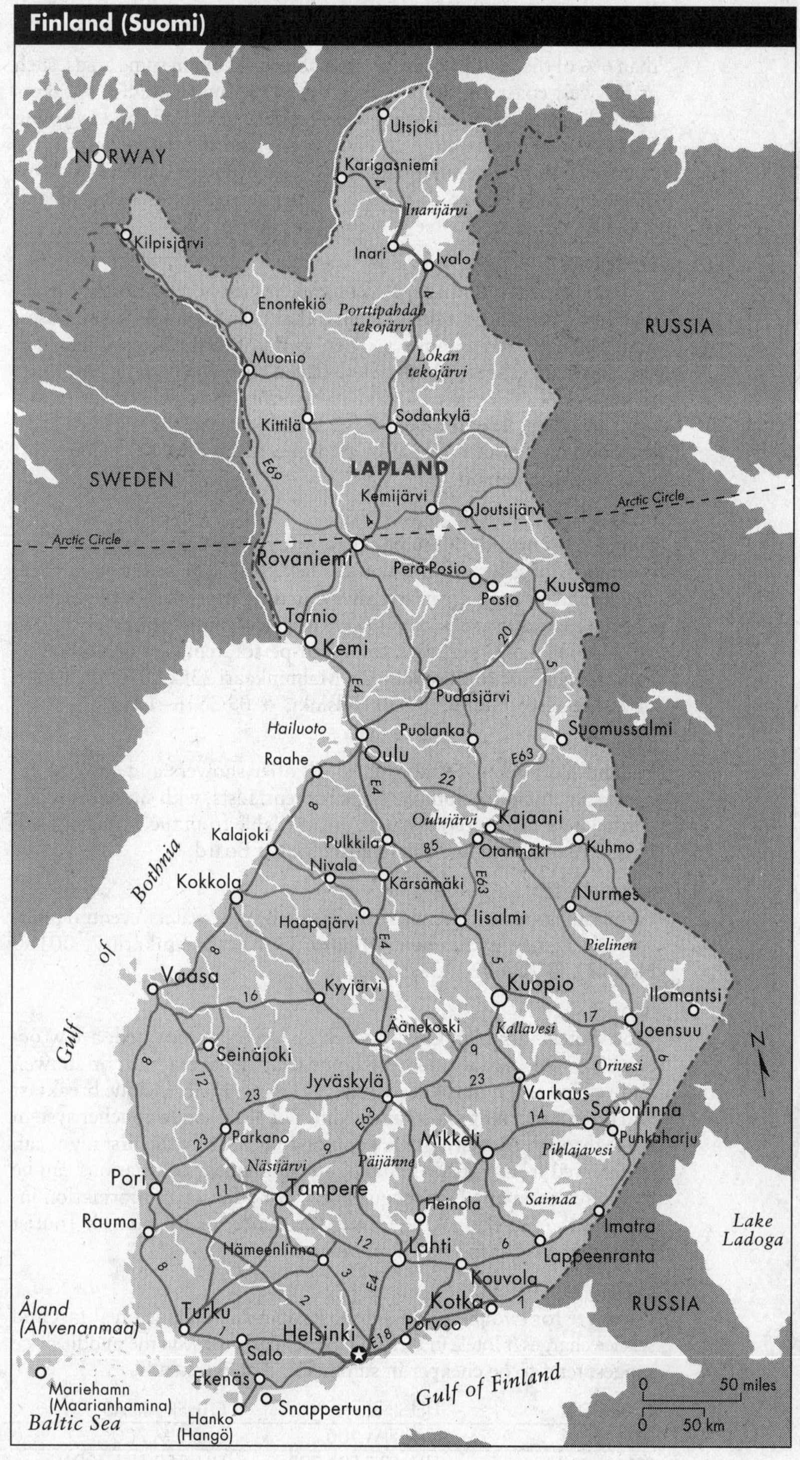
NORWAY
SWEDEN
RUSSIA
RUSSIA
Utsjoki
Karigasniemi
Inarijärvi
Inari
Ivalo
Kilpisjärvi
Enontekiö
Porttipahdan tekojärvi
Lokan tekojärvi
Muonio
Kittilä
Sodankylä
LAPLAND
E69
Kemijärvi
Joutsijärvi
Arctic Circle
Arctic Circle
Rovaniemi
Perä-Posio
Posio
Kuusamo
Tornio
Kemi
E4
Pudasjärvi
Hailuoto
Puolanka
Suomussalmi
Raahe
Oulu
E63
22
Oulujärvi
Kajaani
Kalajoki
Pulkkila
85
Otanmäki
Kuhmo
Gulf of Bothnia
Kokkola
Nivala
Kärsämäki
Nurmes
Haapajärvi
Iisalmi
Pielinen
Vaasa
Kyyjärvi
Kuopio
Ilomantsi
16
17
Joensuu
Äänekoski
Kallavesi
Seinäjoki
Orivesi
Jyväskylä
23
Varkaus
Savonlinna
Parkano
E63
14
Punkaharju
Mikkeli
Pihlajavesi
Näsijärvi
Päijänne
Pori
Tampere
Heinola
Saimaa
Rauma
Imatra
Lake Ladoga
Hämeenlinna
Lahti
Lappeenranta
Kouvola
Kotka
Åland (Ahvenanmaa)
Turku
Porvoo
Helsinki
E18
Salo
Ekenäs
Mariehamn (Maarianhamina)
Snappertuna
Gulf of Finland
Hanko (Hangö)
Baltic Sea
N
0 50 miles
0 50 km

Language

The official languages of Finland are Finnish and Swedish. A little more than 6% of the total population speak Swedish, but in some areas, such as the west coast and in pockets close to Helsinki, Swedish speakers form a local majority. English is widely spoken in Helsinki and by young Finns around the country. In Finnish Lapland the native Sami (pronounced Sah-me) population speaks three different dialects of a language distantly related to Finnish. Note that the Finnish letters ä and ö and the Swedish å come at the end of the alphabet.

Lodging

Finland offers a full range of accommodations: hotels, motels, boardinghouses, bed-and-breakfasts, rental chalets and cottages, farmhouses, youth hostels, and campsites. There is no official rating system, but standards are generally high. If you haven't reserved a room before arriving in Helsinki, you can make reservations through a travel agency or at the **Hotel Booking Center** (✉ Rautatieasema, ☎ 09/171–133); the booking service is free if by phone; a fee of FIM 12 is charged if you appear in person.

BOARDINGHOUSES AND RENTALS

Found only outside Helsinki, these provide the least expensive accommodations; local tourist offices have lists. The selection is huge; chalets and cottages are nearly always in delightful lakeside or seashore settings. Comfortable (not luxurious) accommodations cost FIM 1,000–FIM 3,500 per week for a four-person rental. A central reservations agency is **Lomarengas** (✉ Malminkaari 23C, 00700 Helsinki, or ✉ Eteläesplanadi 4, 00130 Helsinki, ☎ 09/3516–1321).

CAMPING

Finland has about 350 campsites. All offer showers and cooking facilities, and many include cottages for rent. Lists, with sites graded according to a three-grade system, are available from the Finnish Youth Hostel Association and the Finnish Tourist Board.

FARMHOUSES

Farmhouses are in attractive settings, usually near water. A central reservations agency is **Suomen 4H-liitto** (✉ Abrahaminkatu 7, 00180 Helsinki, ☎ 09/642–233).

HOTELS

Most hotels in Finland are modern or recently renovated; a few occupy fine old manor houses. Rooms usually have a bath or shower, and virtually all hotels have saunas. Prices generally include breakfast and often a morning sauna and swim. The **Finncheque** voucher system (June through August), offers good discounts. Only the first night can be reserved from outside Finland, but subsequent reservations can be made free from any Finncheque hotel. For additional information inquire at the Hotel Booking Center (☞ *above*) or the Finnish Tourist Board (☞ Visitor Information, *below*).

RATINGS

Prices are for two people in a double room and include breakfast and service charges. Hotels in Helsinki, particularly those in the middle price ranges, tend to be cheaper in summer and on weekends.

CATEGORY	HELSINKI	OTHER AREAS
$$$$	over FIM 900	over FIM 700
$$$	FIM 600–FIM 900	FIM 550–FIM 700
$$	FIM 400–FIM 600	FIM 400–FIM 550
$	under FIM 400	under FIM 400

SUMMER HOTELS

Some university student housing is turned into "summer hotels" from June through August; they offer modern facilities at slightly lower-than-average prices. The Finnish Youth Hostel Association publishes "Hostel-lit," which lists summer hotels as well as youth hostels. Free copies are available at the Finnish Tourist Board (☞ Visitor Information, *below*) and the Finnish Youth Hostel Association (☞ *below*).

YOUTH HOSTELS

Hostels range from empty schools to small manor houses. The Finnish Tourist Board (☞ Visitor Information, *below*) and the Finnish Youth Hostel Association (YHA; ✉ Yrjönkatu 38B, 00100 Helsinki, ☎ 09/694–0377) can provide a list of hostels. There are no age restrictions, and prices range from FIM 60 to FIM 180 per bed, with a discount of FIM 15 for YHA members.

Mail

POSTAL RATES

Airmail rates to North America are FIM 3.40 for postcards or letters weighing up to 20 grams. Letters to the United Kingdom and the rest of the European Union cost FIM 3.20.

RECEIVING MAIL

If you're uncertain about where you'll be staying, have mail sent to you marked "poste restante" and addressed to the post office in the appropriate town (Helsinki's main post office: ✉ Mannerheimintie 11, 00100). American Express offers free mail service to cardholders (Clients' Mail, American Express, Mikonkatu 2D, 00100 Helsinki).

Money Matters

COSTS

Prices are highest in Helsinki. Taxes are already included in hotel and restaurant charges. The prices of many goods include an 18% sales tax; the tax on food is less (☞ Shopping, *below*).

CURRENCY

The unit of currency in Finland is the Finnish mark, divided into 100 penniä. There are bills of FIM 20, 50, 100, 500, and 1,000. Coins are 10 and 50 penniä, and FIM 1, FIM 5, and FIM 10. At press time (spring 1998), the exchange rate was about FIM 5.4 to the U.S. dollar, FIM 3.8 to the Canadian dollar, FIM 9 to the pound sterling, FIM 3.4 to the Australian dollar, and FIM 2.9 to the New Zealand dollar. Finland is prepared to be one of the "first wave" countries in the European Monetary Union project. Credit cards are widely accepted, even in many taxicabs. Traveler's checks can be cashed only in banks.

Finland is making advances in the use of a "smart" prepaid electronic cash card, called the Avant card, that processes even the smallest of anonymous cash transactions; at press time such transactions could be made at designated public pay phones, vending machines, and McDonald's, of all places. Disposable prepaid cards can be purchased at kiosks. Reloadable purse cards, available to customers of major Finnish banks in 1998, will eventually be integrated with existing ATM and debit cards.

SAMPLE PRICES

Cup of coffee, FIM 8; glass of beer, FIM 15–FIM 25; soft drink, FIM 10; ham sandwich, FIM 15–FIM 20; 1-mi taxi ride, FIM 30.

TIPPING

You can give taxi drivers small coins. Train and airport porters have a fixed charge. It's not necessary to tip hotel doormen for carrying bags to the check-in counter, but give bellhops FIM 5–FIM 10 for carrying bags to your room. The coat-check room fee of FIM 5 is usually clearly posted; if not, give FIM 10, depending on the number in your party. FIM 5 is a standard tip for minor services.

National Holidays

January 1; January 6 (Epiphany); April 2–5 (Good Friday, Easter, and Easter Monday); May 1 (May Day); May 13 (Ascension); May 31 (Pentecost/Whit Sunday); June 26–27 (Midsummer's Eve and Day); October 31–November 1 (All Saints' Day); December 6 (Independence Day); December 25–26.

Opening and Closing Times

Banks are open weekdays 9:15–4:15. Opening hours for **museums** vary considerably, so check individual listings. Many museums in the countryside are open only in summer. **Shops** are generally open weekdays 9–6, Saturday 9–2. Department stores and supermarkets stay open until 8 on weekdays. Shops may also open on Sunday during June, July, and August and on four other Sundays in the year—usually in December for Christmas shopping. Shops in the tunnel complex beneath the main railway station are open daily, including holidays, until 10 PM.

Shopping

Non-EU residents who purchase goods worth more than FIM 100 in any shop marked "tax free for tourists" can get a 12%–16% refund. Show your passport and the store will give you a check for the appropriate amount, which you can cash at your final point of departure from the EU.

Telephoning

COUNTRY CODE

The country code for Finland is 358.

INTERNATIONAL CALLS

You can dial Britain and North America directly from anywhere in Finland. Calls to other countries can be made from a telegraph office; these, marked TELE or LENNÄTIN, are usually next to the post office. An operator will assign you a private booth and collect payment at the end of the call. To dial numbers from outside Finland, omit the "0" at the beginning of the city code. To make a direct international phone call from Finland, dial 00, or 999, or 990, then the appropriate country code and phone number. To reach an **AT&T** long-distance operator, dial 9800–10010; for **MCI,** dial 9800–10280; for **Sprint,** dial 9800–10284. For **directory assistance** abroad, dial 020–208.

LOCAL CALLS

To avoid exorbitant hotel surcharges on calls, use public pay phones, and have some FIM 1 and FIM 5 coins ready. Some pay phones only accept a phone card, the *Tele Kortti* or *HPY Kortti,* available at post offices, R-kiosks, and some grocery stores. They come in increments of FIM 30, FIM 50, FIM 100, and FIM 150. For information about telephone service, call HPY/HTF at 6061 or Tele at 02–0401. For directory assistance dial 118 or 10013.

Transportation

BY BICYCLE

Well-marked cycle paths run into the heart of Helsinki and other towns and cities, making cycling safe and fast. Bikes can be rented at some youth hostels. The **Finnish Youth Hostel Association** (✉ Yrjönkatu 38B, 00100 Helsinki, ☎ 09/694–0377) offers accommodation packages to tie in with visitors' cycling tours for FIM 1,250 (7 days) or FIM 2,200 (14 days).

BY BOAT

Helsinki and Turku have regular sea links with the Finnish Åland Islands in the Baltic Sea. From mid-June to mid-August you can cruise the lakes of the Finnish interior. Complete timetables are available from the Finnish Tourist Board (☞ Visitor Information, *below*).

BY BUS

Finland's bus system can take you virtually anywhere. A Coach Holiday Ticket, available from bus stations and travel agencies, entitles you to 1,000 km (625 mi) of bus travel within two weeks for FIM 350.

BY CAR

Breakdowns and Accidents. The Automobile and Touring Club of Finland (Autoliitto; ✉ Hämeentie 105 A, 00550 Helsinki, ☎ 09/774–761) operates a 24-hour information service (☎ 09/7747–6400; 9700–8080 on weekends) for club members and members of foreign auto clubs. If an accident requires an ambulance or fire squad, call the national emergency number, ☎ 112. Report accidents without delay to the Finnish Motor Insurers' Center (Liikennevakuutuskeskus; ✉ Bulevardi 28, 00120 Helsinki, ☎ 09/680–401) as well as to the police (☎ 10022).

Gasoline. Gasoline costs about FM 5.54 per liter.

Parking. Finding parking is difficult only in some city centers. Major cities offer multistory garages; most towns have on-street meters. In Helsinki there is no free on-street parking. In areas with no meters drivers must display a *pysäköintilippu* (parking voucher), for sale at R-kiosks and gas stations, on their dashboard. Illegally parked cars may be towed.

Road Conditions. Finland has an expanding network of efficient major roads, some of which are multilane. In the north, you can expect long stretches of dirt road, which become difficult to negotiate during the spring thaw. Away from the larger towns, traffic is light, but take elk and reindeer warning signs seriously.

Rules of the Road. Drive on the right. At intersections cars coming from the right have the right-of-way. Speed limits (usually marked) are 50 kph (30 mph) in built-up areas and 80–100 kph (50–62 mph) in the country and on main roads, 120 kph (74 mph) in summer on some highways. Low-beam headlights must be used at all times outside city areas, seat belts are compulsory (for all seats), and you must carry a warning triangle in case of a breakdown.

BY PLANE

Finnair (☎ 09/818–800) operates an elaborate network of flights linking 25 towns in Finland. Finnair grants visitors under age 25 a 50-percent Youth Discount on flights booked ahead. These tickets are available in most countries and in Finland at major travel agencies.

BY TRAIN

Finland's comfortable and clean rail system extends to all main centers of the country. A special **Finnrail Pass** entitles you to unlimited travel for 3, 5, or 10 days within a four-week period. In Finland the Finnrail Pass is available from VR Finnish Railways (☎ 09/707–3700). In the United States and Canada it can be purchased from Rail Europe (☎ 800/438–7245), and in the United Kingdom, from Norvista (☎ 0171/409–7334). The **ScanRail** pass allows unlimited train travel throughout Denmark, Finland, Norway, and Sweden, as well as restricted ferry passage in and beyond Scandinavia. Certain hotel chains and organizations offer discounts to passholders. The pass is available for 5 days of travel within 15 days, 10 days within a month, or one month. In the United States call Rail Europe (☞ *above*), or DER (☎ 800/782–2424), which also offers a 21-day pass.

Visitor Information

Finnish Tourist Board **Tourist Information Office** (✉ Eteläesplanadi 4, 00100 Helsinki, ☎ 09/417–6911).

Weather

The summer season from mid-June to mid-August is marked by long hours of sunlight and cool nights. Though many establishments and sights close or drastically reduce hours off-season, the advantages to off-season travel are many: avoiding the mosquitoes, especially fearsome in the north; spectacular fall foliage; and cross-country skiing.

CLIMATE

You can expect warm days in Helsinki from mid-May, and in Lapland from mid-June. Hot weather, with temperatures well into the 80s, is not uncommon in July and August. The midnight sun can be seen from May through July, depending on the region. For a period in midwinter, the northern lights in Lapland almost make up for the fact that the sun does not rise at all. Even in Helsinki, summer nights are brief and never really dark; in midwinter daylight lasts only a few hours.

The following are average daily maximum and minimum temperatures for Helsinki.

Jan.	30F	– 1C	**May**	64F	18C	**Sept.**	53F	11C
	26	– 3		48	9		39	4
Feb.	34F	1C	**June**	60F	16C	**Oct.**	46F	8C
	24	– 4		48	9		36	2
Mar.	36F	2C	**July**	68F	20C	**Nov.**	32F	0C
	26	– 3		55	13		26	– 3
Apr.	46F	8C	**Aug.**	64F	18C	**Dec.**	32F	0C
	32	0		53	12		24	– 4

HELSINKI

Built on the peninsulas and islands of the Baltic shoreline, Helsinki is a city of the sea. Streets curve around bays, bridges arch between islands, and ferries carry traffic to islands farther offshore. The smell of the sea hovers over the city, and there is a constant bustle in the city's harbors as the huge ships that ply the Baltic drop and lift anchor.

Helsinki has grown dramatically since World War II; it now accounts for about one-sixth of Finland's population. The city covers a total of 1,140 square km (433 square mi), including some 315 islands. Most of Helsinki's sights, hotels, and restaurants, however, are crowded onto a single peninsula.

During the 16th century the Swedish king Gustav Vasa, at that time ruler of Finland as well, was determined to woo trade away from the Estonian city of Tallinn and the Hanseatic League. Helsinki was founded next to the rapids of the Vantaa River on June 12, 1550, by a group of Finns who had settled here upon the king's orders.

Over the next three centuries, Turku, on Finland's west coast, was the country's capital and intellectual center. Helsinki took center stage only when Sweden ceded Finland to Russia in 1809. Tsar Alexander I turned Finland into an autonomous grand duchy, proclaiming Helsinki its capital in 1812. About the same time, much of Turku burned to the ground, and the university was forced to move to Helsinki. From then on Helsinki's position as Finland's first city was assured.

Just before the tsar's proclamation, a fire destroyed many of Helsinki's traditional wooden buildings, making it necessary to build a new city center. The German-born architect Carl Ludvig Engel was entrusted with the project, and thanks to him Helsinki has some of the purest neoclassical architecture in the world. Add to this foundation the stunning outlines of the Jugendstil (Art Nouveau) period of the early 20th century and more modern buildings designed by native Finnish architects, and you have a capital city as architecturally eye-catching as it is unlike those of the rest of Europe.

Exploring Helsinki

Numbers in the margin correspond to points of interest on the Helsinki map.

16 **Eduskuntatalo** (Parliament House). The imposing, colonnaded, red-granite structure was built between 1927 and 1931. The legislature has one of the highest proportions of women in the world. ✉ *Mannerheimintie 30,* ☎ *09/4321.*

18 **Finlandiatalo** (Finlandia Hall). The inland lake Töölönlahti forms the backdrop for one of Helsinki's major cultural sites, architect Alvar Aalto's Finlandiatalo completed in 1971. ✉ *Karamzininkatu 4,* ☎ *09/40241.* ⏲ *Concerts are usually held Wed. and Thurs. nights.*

Kaivopuisto (Well Park). This elegant district was favored by Russian high society during the 19th century. Now it is a residential area for diplomats and a popular strolling ground. ✉ *Close to ferry terminals.*

Katajanokka. Here 19th-century brick warehouses have been converted into boutiques, galleries, crafts studios, and restaurants. ✉ *Harbor district east of Kanavaranta and the Greek Orthodox cathedral.*

★ 1 **Kauppatori** (Market Square). The colorful, bustling market beside the South Harbor attracts customers for freshly cut flowers, fruit, and vegetables trucked in from the hinterland, as well as handicrafts from small country villages—all sold by vendors in bright orange tents. Closer to the dock are fresh fish from the waters of the Baltic. You can't miss the curvaceous ***Havis Amanda*** statue watching over the busy square. ✉ *Eteläranta and Pohjoisesplanadi.* ⏲ *Market: Mon.–Sat. 7–2 year-round; June–Aug. arts and crafts, 3:30–8.*

2 **Kaupungintalo** (City Hall). The light blue building on Pohjoisesplanadi (North Esplanade), the political center of Finland, is the home of city government offices. ✉ *Pohjoisesplanadi 1,* ☎ *09/1691.*

23 **Korkeasaari Eläintarha** (Helsinki Zoo). Here snow leopards and reindeer enjoy the cold Finnish climate. The zoo is entirely within the limits of the small Korkeasaari Island, but the winding paths make the zoo seem much larger than it actually is. Outdoor play equipment is an added attraction for children. The ferry departs approximately every 30 minutes from the South Harbor. Alternatively, you can take the metro to the Kulosaari stop, cross under the tracks, and then follow the signs 20 minutes to the zoo. ✉ *Korkeasaari Island,* ☎ *09/19981.* *FIM 20.* ⏲ *Jan.–Feb., daily 10–4; Mar.–Apr., daily 10–6; May–Sept., daily 10–8; Oct.–Dec., daily 10–4.*

14 **Mannerheimin patsas** (statue of Marshal Mannerheim). In front of the main post office, the equestrian gazes down Mannerheimintie, named in his honor. No man in Finnish history is so revered as Baron Carl Gustaf Mannerheim, the military and political leader who guided Finland through the first half of the 20th century. ✉ *Mannerheimintie.*

15 **Nykytaiteenmuseo** (Museum of Contemporary Art). This striking new building, designed by American architect Steven Holl, opened in spring 1998 to a mixed reaction. Some praised the boldness of its curved steel

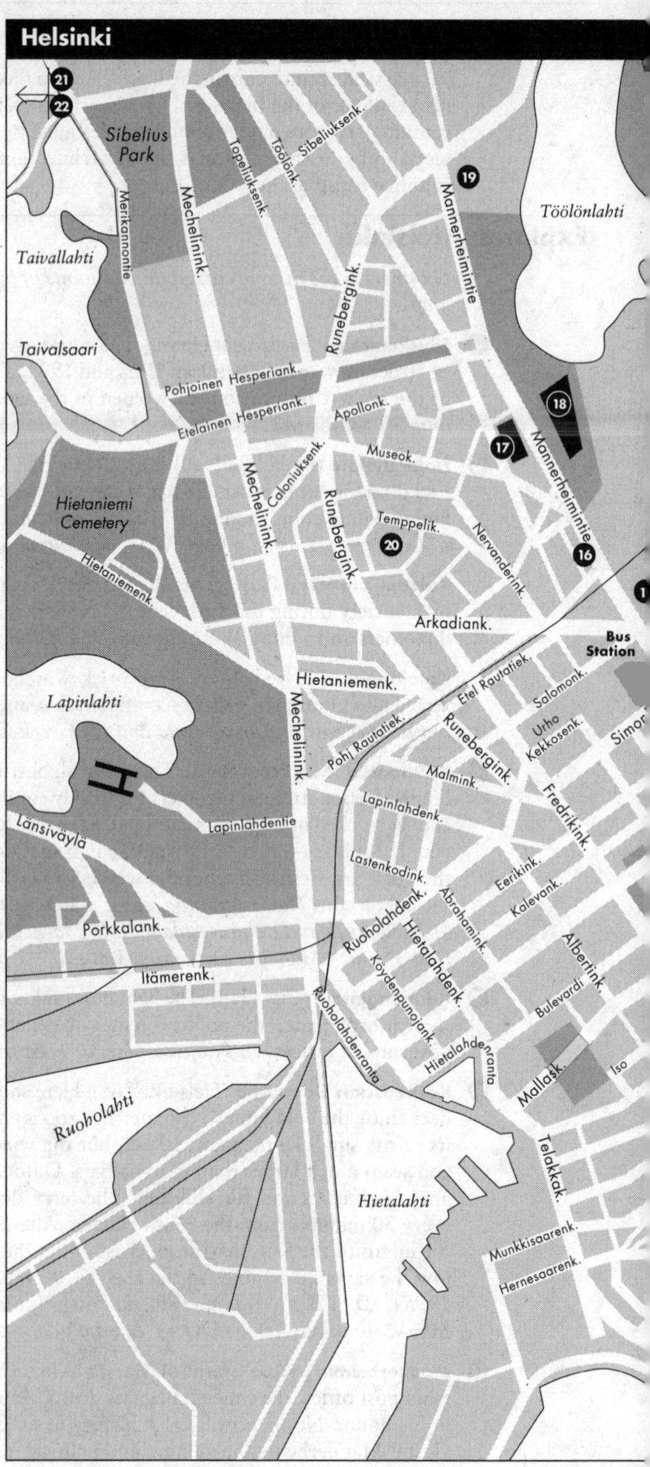
Helsinki
Sibelius Park
Taivallahti
Taivalsaari
Töölönlahti
Hietaniemi Cemetery
Lapinlahti
Ruoholahti
Hietalahti
Bus Station
Sibeliuksenk.
Topeliuksenk.
Töölönk.
Merikannontie
Mechelinink.
Mannerheimintie
Runeberginк.
Pohjoinen Hesperiank.
Etelainen Hesperiank.
Apollonk.
Museok.
Caloniuksenk.
Temppelik.
Nervanderink.
Hietaniemenk.
Arkadiank.
Etel Rautatiek.
Pohj Rautatiek.
Salomonk.
Urho Kekkosenk.
Simon
Malmink.
Fredrikink.
Lapinlahdenk.
Lapinlahdentie
Länsiväylä
Lastenkodink.
Eerikink.
Abrahamink.
Kalevank.
Ruoholahdenk.
Hietalahdenk.
Albertink.
Porkkalank.
Itämerenk.
Köydenpunojank.
Ruoholahdenranta
Hietalahdenranta
Bulevardi
Mallask.
Iso
Telakkak.
Munkkisaarenk.
Hernesaarenk.

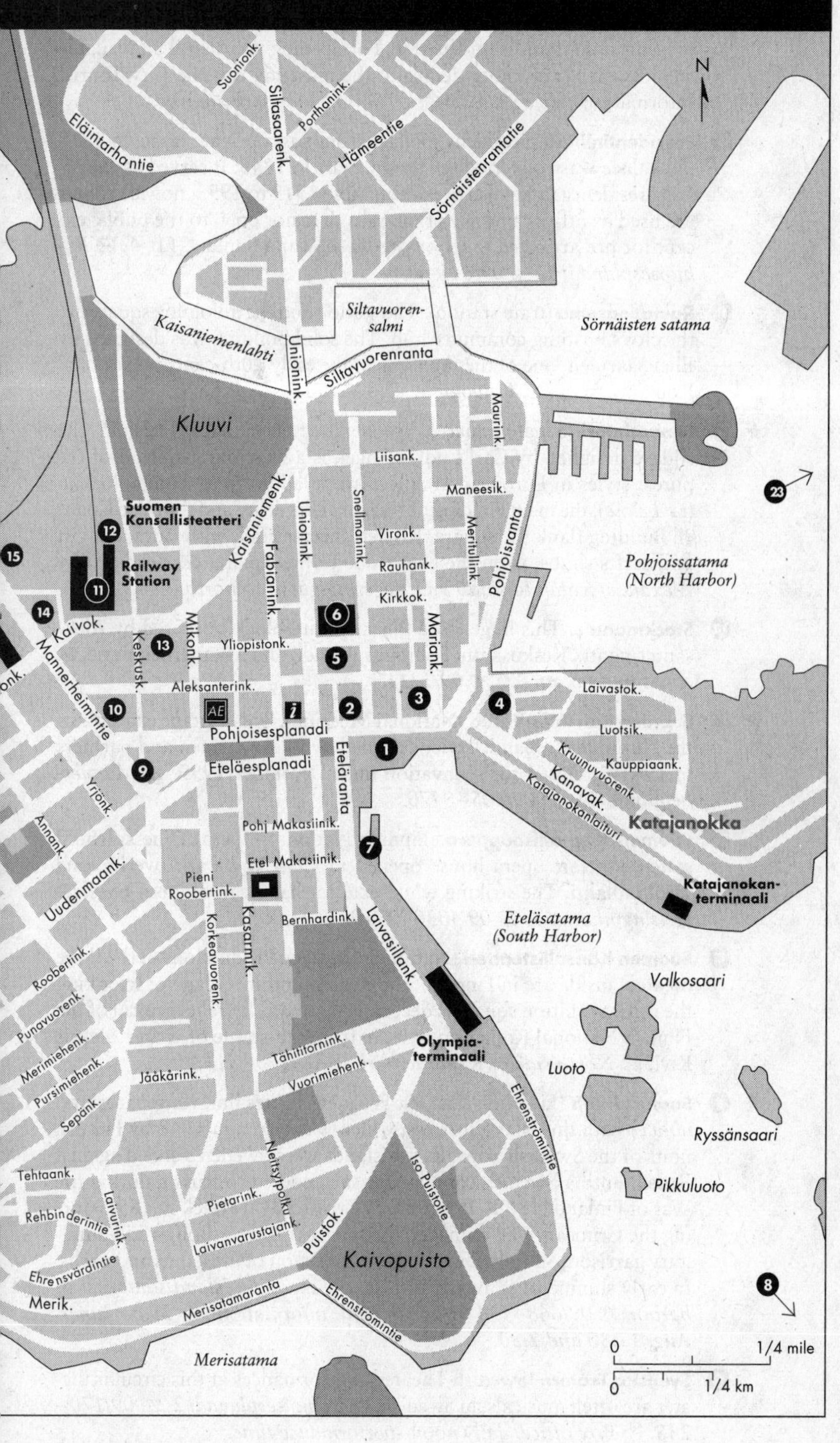

Suonionk.
Siltasaarenk.
Porthanink.
Eläintarhantie
Hämeentie
Sörnäistenrantatie
Siltavuorensalmi
Sörnäisten satama
Kaisaniemenlahti
Unionink.
Siltavuorenranta
Kluuvi
Maurink.
Liisank.
Maneesik.
Snellmanink.
Meritullink.
Pohjoisranta
Suomen Kansallisteatteri
Kaisaniemenk.
Vironk.
Rauhank.
Kirkkok.
Fabianink.
Railway Station
Pohjoissatama (North Harbor)
Kaivok.
Mannerheimintie
Keskusk.
Mikonk.
Yliopistonk.
Mariank.
Aleksanterink.
AE
Pohjoisesplanadi
Eteläesplanadi
Eteläranta
Laivastok.
Luotsik.
Kruunuvuorenk.
Kauppiaank.
Kanavak.
Katajanokanlaituri
Katajanokka
Yrjönk.
Annank.
Pohj Makasiinik.
Etel Makasiinik.
Uudenmaank.
Pieni Roobertink.
Korkeavuorenk.
Kasarmik.
Bernhardink.
Laivasillank.
Katajanokanterminaali
Eteläsatama (South Harbor)
Roobertink.
Valkosaari
Punavuorenk.
Merimiehenk.
Pursimiehenk.
Jääkärink.
Tähtitornink.
Vuorimiehenk.
Olympiaterminaali
Luoto
Ehrenströmintie
Sepänk.
Ryssänsaari
Neitsytpolku
Iso Puistotie
Tehtaank.
Pikkuluoto
Laivurink.
Pietarink.
Rehbinderintie
Laivanvarustajank.
Puistok.
Kaivopuisto
Ehrensvärdintie
Merik.
Merisatamaranta
Ehrenströmintie
Merisatama
0
1/4 mile
0
1/4 km
N

shell, others condemned it for its encroachment on the territory of the Mannerheim statue. The wealth of Finnish art (from the 1960s to the present) it contains is undeniable. For opening times (still unavailable at press time) and other details of the museum, call the City Tourist Information office (☎ 09/169-3757). ✉ *Mannerheimintie.*

3 **Presidentinlinna** (President's Palace). Built as a private home in 1818 the palace was converted for use by czars in 1843. It served as the official residence of Finnish presidents from 1919 to 1993; now its rooms are used as offices and reception halls. It is not open to the public except for pre-arranged tours on Wednesday and Sunday, 11–4. ✉ *Pohjoisesplanadi 1,* ☎ *09/641–200.*

11 **Rautatieasema** (train station). The station and the adjoining square are the city's bustling commuter hub. The solid building was designed by Eliel Saarinen, one of the founders of the early 20th-century National Romantic style. ✉ *Kaivokatu,* ☎ *09/7071.*

★ 5 **Senaatintori** (Senate Square). The heart of neoclassical Helsinki, the square designed by Carl Ludvig Engel, is a harmonious blend of the purest styles in European architecture. In addition to **Tuomiokirkko** (☞ *below*), the main building of Helsinki University and the State Council Building flank the square. **Kiseleff Bazaar Hall,** with cafés and gift and crafts shops, is on the south side of the square. ✉ *Bordered by Alexandersgatan to south and Regeringsgatan to north.*

10 **Stockmann's.** This huge store fills an entire block bordered by Aleksanterinkatu, Keskuskatu, Pohjoisesplanadi, and Mannerheimintie. ✉ *Aleksanterinkatu 32,* ☎ *09/1211.*

★ 17 **Suomen Kansallismuseo** (National Museum). This vintage example of the National Romantic style, designed by Eliel Saarinen and partners in 1901, is closed for renovation until December 1999. ✉ *Mannerheimintie 34,* ☎ *09/405–0470.*

19 **Suomen Kansallisooppera** (Finnish National Opera). The splendid state-of-the-art opera house opened in 1993 in a park overlooking Töölöndlahti. The striking white exterior has clean modern lines. ✉ *Helsinginkatu 58,* ☎ *09/4030–2350.*

12 **Suomen Kansallisteatteri** (National Theater). Productions in the three theaters inside are in Finnish. The elegant granite facade overlooking the railway station square is decorated with quirky relief typical of the Finnish National Romantic style. In front is a statue of writer Aleksis Kivi. ✉ *North side of Rautatientori,* ☎ *09/173–311.*

★ 8 **Suomenlinna** (Finland's Castle). Frequent ferries link Kauppatori (☞ *above*) with this island fortress, which was begun in 1748 by Finnish units of the Swedish army. Its six islands were Sweden's shield against Russia until a Swedish commander surrendered to Russia during the War of Finland (1808–19). A heavy British naval attack in 1855, during the Crimean War, damaged the fortress. Today, though still a military garrison, Suomenlinna is also a collection of museums and parks. In early summer it is awash with purple lilacs. ✉ *Island southeast of harbor,* ☎ *09/668–154 (castle and tour information).* ⏲ *Tours: June–Aug. 12:30 and 2:30.*

9 **Svenska Teatern** (Swedish Theater). Performances at this circular theater are often musicals, in Swedish. ✉ *Pohjoisesplanadi 2,* ☎ *09/170–238.* ⏲ *Box office: daily noon–performance time.*

★ 20 **Temppeliaukion Kirkko** (Temple Square Church). In a labyrinth of streets west of the Opera, the strikingly modern church is carved out of rock and topped with a copper dome. ✉ *Lutherininkatu 3,* ☎ *09/494–698,*

⏲ *Weekdays 10–8, Sat. 10–6, Sun. 11:30–1:45 and 3:20–5:30. Closed Tues. 12:45–2 and during weddings, concerts, and services.*

❻ **Tuomiokirkko** (Lutheran Cathedral). The domed cathedral built in 1852 and now a symbol of Helsinki dominates the Senaatintori. ✉ *Yliopistonkatu 7.* ⏲ *June–Aug., weekdays 9–5, Sat. 9–7, Sun. 9–8; Sept.–May, weekdays 10–4, Sat. 10–7, Sun. 10–4.*

★ ❹ **Uspenskin Katedraali** (Uspenski Cathedral). The redbrick Orthodox cathedral looms over the east side of Kauppatori. ✉ *Kanavakatu 1,* ☎ *09/634–267.* ⏲ *May–Sept., Mon. and Wed.–Fri. 9:30–4, Tues. 9:30–6, Sat. 10–4, Sun. noon–3; Oct.–Apr., Tues. and Thurs. 9–2, Wed. noon–6, Fri. noon–4, Sun. noon–3.*

⓭ **Valtion Taidemuseo** (Finnish National Gallery). The best traditional Finnish art is housed in this complex, which includes the **Ateneum,** with Finnish art from the 18th century to the 1960s, as well as changing shows, an excellent bookshop, and a café. ✉ *Kaivokatu 2–4,* ☎ *09/173–361.* ⏲ *Tues. and Fri. 9–6, Wed. and Thurs. 9–9, weekends 11–5.*

❼ **Vanha Kauppahalli** (Old Market Hall). On the western shore of the South Harbor, near the huge ferry dock for boats from Sweden, Poland, and Estonia, the brick market hall is worth a visit for its amazing spreads of meat, fish, and other delights. ✉ *Eteläranta, along the South Harbor.* ⏲ *Weekdays 8–5, Sat. 8–2.*

Elsewhere in Helsinki

㉑ **Seurasaaren Ulkomuseo** (Seurasaari Outdoor Museum). For a taste of the Finnish countryside within the city, this museum showcases traditional rural architecture and lifestyles on a wooded island. A highlight is the ornate **Karunan kirkko** (Karuna Church) from 1686. Seurasaari also has a restaurant and several beaches, including a secluded clothing-optional strand. A long, picturesque bridge connects the island to the city mainland. ✉ *Seurasaari, island 3 km/2 mi west of city center; Bus 24 from Swedish Theater,* ☎ *09/484–712.* ⏲ *Island: accessible anytime. Museum:* ⏲ *June–Aug. Thurs.–Tues. 11–5, Wed. 11–7; Sept.–May, daily 11–5.*

㉒ **Gallen-Kallela Museum.** Akseli Gallen-Kallela (1865–1931), one of Finland's greatest artists, lived in this studio-home. To get to the estate, take Tram 4 from in front of the City Sokos department store on Mannerheimintie. From the Munkkiniemi stop transfer to Bus 33, or walk the 2 km (1¼ mi) through the woods. ✉ *Gallen-Kallelantie 27, Tarvaspää Espoo,* ☎ *09/513–388.* ⏲ *Mid-May–Aug., Mon.–Thurs. 10–8, Fri.–Sun. 10–5; Sept.–mid-May, Tues.–Sat. 10–4, Sun. 10–5.*

Dining and Lodging

Although Russian restaurants are among the star attractions here, seek out Finnish specialties—pheasant, reindeer, hare, and grouse—accompanied by wildberries and exotic mushrooms. Many expensive establishments close on weekends. For details and price-category information, *see* Dining *in* Finland A to Z, *above.*

Helsinki's hotels have a reputation for being extremely expensive, but this is true only of the very top stratum. Special summer and weekend offers are common. Generous breakfast buffets are nearly always included in the room price. The standards of cleanliness are high, and the level of service usually corresponds to the price. Most hotels cater to business travelers, but standard rooms tend to be small, even at more expensive hotels. For details and price-category information, *see* Lodging *in* Finland A to Z, *above.*

$$$$ ★ ✕ **Alexander Nevski.** In a city famed for fine Russian cuisine, Alexander Nevski has the best. Echoing the Russian-French style of 19th-century St. Petersburg, the decor is dominated by palm trees and shades of green. Sample the game specialties—often baked in clay pots—and blinis. ✉ *Pohjoisesplanadi 17,* ☎ *09/639–610. AE, DC, MC, V.*

$$$$ ✕ **Amadeus.** In an old town house with an old-fashioned, intimate, 19th-century interior near the South Harbor, Amadeus specializes in such game dishes as snow grouse, wild duck, and reindeer fillets. ✉ *Sofiankatu 4,* ☎ *09/626–676. AE, DC, MC, V. Closed Sun.*

$$$$ ✕ **Havis Amanda.** Across the street from the *Havis Amanda* statue, this neat and gracious restaurant, with its sophisticated turn-of-the-century interior, is a seafood institution. Don't pass up the flamed cloudberry crepes served with ice cream for dessert. ✉ *Unioninkatu 23,* ☎ *09/666–882. AE, DC, MC, V. Closed Sun.*

$$$$ ✕ **Töölönranta.** Right behind the National Opera House, the new upmarket Töölönranta gathers in plenty of opera goers. The innovative water-cooled wok is the source of stir-fried specials and, like the rest of the kitchen area, is open to view from the restaurant. The patio catches the evening sun. ✉ *Töölönlahdenranta,* ☎ *09/499–571.*

$$$ ★ ✕ **Bellevue.** Established in 1917, it is one of Helsinki's oldest Russian restaurants, in both decor and cuisine. The fillet à la Novgorod (a traditional ox fillet prepared with carrots, barley, and sauerkraut) and chicken Kiev are the authentic articles here. ✉ *Rahapajankatu 3,* ☎ *09/179–560. AE, DC, MC, V. No lunch weekends.*

$$$ ✕ **Sipuli.** In a brick warehouse dating from the late 19th century, Sipuli takes its name from the golden onion-shape cupolas that adorn the Russian Orthodox Uspenski Cathedral nearby. The food is French in style with a Finnish flair. ✉ *Kanavaranta 3,* ☎ *09/179–900. AE, DC, MC, V. Closed weekends. No lunch.*

$$$ ✕ **Troikka.** The Troikka takes you back to tsarist times in decor, paintings, and music. Try the *pelmeny* (small meat pastries). ✉ *Caloniuksenkatu 3,* ☎ *09/445–229. AE, DC, MC, V. Closed Sun., weekends in July.*

$$$ ✕ **Villa Thai.** Patrons have a choice between western and Thai-style seating for authentic Thai food in elegant and comfortable surroundings. ✉ *Bulevardi 28,* ☎ *09/680–2778. AE, DC, MC, V.*

$$ ✕ **Kuu.** For the true character of Helsinki, try simple, friendly, and atmospheric restaurants as Kuu (moon). It has retained its local character and clientele. The menu combines Finnish specialties with creative international fare. ✉ *Töölönkatu 27,* ☎ *09/2709–0973. AE, DC, MC, V.*

$$ ★ ✕ **Kynsilaukka.** Most imaginative and dominated by garlic—there's even garlic beer—this restaurant appeals to the senses with fresh, beautifully prepared food. Stellar dishes might be cold marinated reindeer or pancakes with cloudberry sauce and ice cream. ✉ *Fredrikinkatu 22,* ☎ *09/651–939. AE, DC, MC, V.*

$$ ✕ **Maxill.** This café-bar hybrid earned its reputation by serving absolutely the best omelets in town. The atmosphere is young and trendy, in keeping with the other shops and restaurants in this colorful, lively street. ✉ *Korkeavuorenkatu 4,* ☎ *09/638–873. AE, DC, MC, V.*

$$ ✕ **Wellamo.** Unbeatable for cheerful intimacy and local character, this restaurant is tucked away on the Katajanokka promontory, not far from the icebreaker quay. Be sure to book in advance: it can fill up quickly. Spontaneous piano recitals are possible, and there is usually a small art show decorating the walls. The simple but hearty menu includes fried Baltic herrings, as well as fried camembert among the quirky desserts. ✉ *Vyökatu 9,* ☎ *09/663–139. AE, DC, MC, V. Closed Mon.*

$ ✕ **Ravintola Mechelin.** This is the restaurant associated with Helsinki's catering school. The emphasis is on Finnish food, with myriad salmon options. ✉ *Perhonkatu 11,* ☎ *09/4056–2118. AE, DC, MC, V.*

$ ✕ **Zucchini.** For a vegetarian lunch or just coffee and dessert, Zucchini is a cozy hideaway with quiet music, magazines, and a few sidewalk tables. Pizzas, soups, and salads are all tasty here. ✉ *Fabianinkatu 4,* ☎ *09/622–2907. DC, MC, V. No dinner.*

$$$$ **Arctia Hotel Marski.** Thoroughly renovated and reopened in spring 1997, the Marski is opposite the Stockmann department store. The suites are the last word in modern luxury, and all rooms are soundproof, shutting out traffic noise. ✉ *Mannerheimintie 10, 00100,* ☎ *09/68061. 236 rooms, 6 suites. Restaurant. AE, DC, MC, V.*

$$$$ ★ **Inter-Continental Helsinki.** Modern and centrally located, it's close to Finlandia Hall and the Finnish National Opera. ✉ *Mannerheimintie 46, 00260,* ☎ *09/40551,* FAX *09/405–5255. 552 rooms. 2 restaurants, pool. AE, DC, MC, V.*

$$$$ **Kalastajatorppa.** In the posh western Munkkiniemi neighborhood, this hotel catered to U.S. presidents Ronald Reagan in 1988 and George Bush in 1990 and 1992. The best rooms are in the seaside annex, and all are large and airy. Rooms in the main building may be equipped with bath and terrace or with showers only; prices vary accordingly. ✉ *Kalastajatorpantie 1, 00330,* ☎ *09/458–152 or 09/45811,* FAX *09/458–1683. 235 rooms, 8 suites. 2 restaurants, 2 indoor pools. AE, DC, MC, V. Closed Dec.*

$$$$ **Radisson SAS Hotel Hesperia.** Having undergone extensive renovation and a change of ownership, the Hesperia, built in 1972, remains Finnish with a modern flair. It's just a short stroll from the center of the city. ✉ *Mannerheimintie 50, 00260,* ☎ *09/43101,* FAX *09/431–0995. 383 rooms. Restaurant, pool. AE, DC, MC, V.*

$$$$ ★ **Strand Inter-Continental.** On the waterfront, the hotel has granite and marble in the lobby and designer-modern bedrooms. There is a choice of cuisines—Pamir's elegant gourmet offerings of seafood, steak, and game, or the Atrium Plaza's buffet for light meals. ✉ *John Stenbergin ranta 4, 00530,* ☎ *09/39351,* FAX *09/393–5255. 200 rooms. 2 restaurants, pool. AE, DC, MC, V.*

$$$ **Cumulus Airport Hotel Rantasipi.** Proximity to the airport and a shuttle for the 3¼ km (2 mi) to town are the keys to this hotel. Rooms are rather small. ✉ *Robert Huberintie 4, 01510 Vantaa,* ☎ *09/4157–7100,* FAX *09/822–846. 300 rooms. Restaurant, pool. AE, DC, MC, V.*

$$$ ★ **Cumulus Seurahuone.** This traditional hotel was built in 1914 and renovated in 1992. Rooms range from sleek modern to formal classic with crystal chandeliers and brass bedsteads. The street-side rooms are not always quiet. ✉ *Kaivokatu 12, 00100,* ☎ *09/69141,* FAX *09/691–4010. 118 rooms. Restaurant. AE, DC, MC, V.*

$$$ **Grand Marina.** This renovated early 19th-century customs warehouse sits in the posh Katajanokka Island neighborhood. Friendly service and ample modern facilities have made the hotel a success. ✉ *Katajanokanlaituri 7, 00160,* ☎ *09/16661,* FAX *09/664–764. 462 rooms. 5 restaurants. AE, DC, MC, V.*

$$$ **Rivoli Jardin.** The small but richly designed rooms in this central town house overlook a quiet courtyard. Breakfast is served each morning in the winter garden. ✉ *Kasarmikatu 40, 00130,* ☎ *09/177–880,* FAX *09/656–988. 53 rooms. AE, DC, MC, V.*

$$$ **Torni.** The original part of this hotel, built in 1903, has striking views of Helsinki from the higher floors; the Atelier Bar has some of the best available views of the city. Old-section rooms on the courtyard have extra charm: some have high ceilings with original carved-wood details and wooden writing desks. ✉ *Yrjönkatu 26, 00100,* ☎ *09/131–131,* FAX *09/131–1361. 154 rooms with bath or shower, 9 suites. 2 restaurants. AE, DC, MC, V. Closed Dec. 25.*

$$ **Arthur.** A property of the Helsinki YMCA, on a quiet, central street, it is unpretentious and comfortable. ✉ *Vuorikatu 19, 00100,*

☎ *09/173–441,* FAX *09/626–880. 143 rooms. Restaurant. AE, DC, MC, V.*

$$ **Aurora.** About 1½ km (1 mi) from the city center, just opposite the Linnanmäki amusement park, it has reasonable prices, cozy rooms, and good facilities. ✉ *Helsinginkatu 50, 00530,* ☎ *09/770–100,* FAX *09/7701–0200. 70 rooms. Restaurant. AE, DC, MC, V.*

$$ **Cumulus Merihotelli.** Standing right on the seafront, the Merihotelli is a 10-minute walk from the center of town. Rooms are somewhat small and modern; those with a sea view get some traffic noise. ✉ *John Stenbergin ranta 6, 00530,* ☎ *09/69121,* FAX *09/691–2214. 87 rooms. 2 restaurants. AE, DC, MC, V.*

$$ **Marttahotelli.** Run by a country women's association, the hotel has small but pleasantly decorated rooms. It is only a 10-minute walk from the railway station. ✉ *Uudenmaankatu 24, 00120,* ☎ *09/646–211,* FAX *09/680–1266. 45 rooms. AE, DC, MC, V.*

$ **Academica.** This summer hotel is a standard student dormitory during the school year. Its simple rooms and the impressive array of exercise facilities make this an excellent value. ✉ *Hietaniemenkatu 14, 00100,* ☎ *09/402–0206,* FAX *09/441–201. 115 rooms. Pool. AE, DC, MC, V. Closed Sept.–May 2.*

Nightlife and the Arts

The Arts

For a list of events pick up *Helsinki This Week*, available in hotels and tourist offices. In summer the guide lists a telephone number for recorded program information in English. Published every two months, *Helsinki Happens* also lists events and provides more detailed cultural background. Tickets are available from **Lippupalvelu** (✉ Mannerheimintie 5, ☎ 9600–4600 for cultural events, ☎ 9700–4700 for sports, ☎ 09/6138–6232 from abroad). Call **Tiketti** (✉ Yrjönkatu 29C, ☎ 9700–4202) for small concerts at clubs and restaurants.

CONCERTS

Finlandiatalo (Finlandia Hall; ✉ Karamzininkatu 4, ☎ 09/40241) is the home of the Helsinki Philharmonic. **Savoy Theater** (✉ Kasarminkatu 46–48, ☎ 09/169–3703) presents ballet and world music. The **Sibelius Academy** (✉ Pohjois Rautatiekatu 9, ☎ 09/405–441) hosts frequent performances, usually by students. **Temppeliaukio Kirkko** (Temppeliaukion Church; ✉ Lutherinkatu 3, ☎ 09/494–698) is a favorite venue for choral and chamber music.

FESTIVALS

Many festivals are scheduled throughout the country, especially in summer. For information contact Finland Festivals (✉ Uudenmaankatu 36D, 00120 Helsinki, ☎ 09/621–4224, FAX 09/612–1007). The **Helsinki Festival** (✉ Rauhankatu 7E, 00170 Helsinki; ☎ 09/135–4522, FAX 09/278–1578) is among the largest in the Nordic area. Over two weeks in August and September, scores of music, dance, and poetry performances and art exhibits take place.

THEATER

Summertime productions (in Finnish or Swedish) in such bucolic settings as Suomenlinna Island, Keskuspuisto Park, Mustikkamaa Island, and the Rowing Stadium (operettas) make enjoyable entertainment. Check *Helsinki This Week* for listings. Also try the splendid **Suomen Kansallisooppera** (Finnish National Opera; ✉ Helsinginkatu 58, ☎ 09/4030–2211; ☞ Exploring Helsinki, *above*).

Nightlife

BARS AND LOUNGES

Helsinki This Week (☞ The Arts, *above*) lists all the pubs and clubs. **Cantina West** (✉ Kasarmikatu 23, ☎ 09/622–1500) is a Tex-Mex bar and restaurant with live music nightly. One of Helsinki's most popular nightspots is **Happy Days** (✉ Pohjoisesplanadi 2, ☎ 09/657–700), known for its burgers and outdoor summer terrace. Founded in 1867, **Kappeli** (✉ Eteläesplanadi 1, ☎ 09/179–242) brews its own beer. **Kaarle XII** (✉ Kasarmikatu 40, ☎ 09/171–312) is in one of Helsinki's striking Jugendstil buildings: the young and beautiful are drawn here for crowded socializing and frantic dancing on weekends. At **Storyville** (✉ Museokatu 8, ☎ 09/408–007), Finnish and foreign jazz musicians complement New Orleans–style cuisine.

The Irish bar craze has caught on in a big way in Helsinki. The choice includes **Molly Malone's** (Kaisaniemenkatu 1C, 09/171-272), **Mulligan's** (Mannerheimintie 10, 09/680–6296), **O'Malley's** (Yrjökatu 28, 09/131–131), and **Richard O'Donoghue's** (Rikhardinkatu 4, 09/622–5992). For beer, head for the two **William K** bars (✉ Annankatu 3, ☎ 09/680–2562 and ✉ Mannerheimintie 72, ☎ 09/409–484) for excellent selections of ales, bottled and on tap, from all over the world.

NIGHTCLUBS

Fennia (✉ Mikonkatu 17, ☎ 09/666–355) has dancing and live music on weekends. Helsinki's largest and most famous club is the **Hesperia Nightclub** (Radisson SAS Hotel Hesperia, ✉ Kivelänkatu 2, ☎ 09/43101). **Kaivohuone** (✉ Kaivopuisto/Well Park, ☎ 09/177–881) is a summertime favorite in an attractive park setting. The line outside the street level entrance to **Tenth Floor** (✉ Asema-aukio, ☎ 09/1311–8232) testifies to its popularity with the trendy dance-and-party crowd.

Shopping

Department Stores

Stockmann's (☞ Exploring Helsinki, *above*).

Markets

In good weather you'll find a variety of goods at the **Hietalahti Flea Market** (✉ on Hietalahti at west end of Bulevardi). **Kauppatori** (Market Square; ☞ Exploring Helsinki, *above*) next to the South Harbor is an absolute must year-round.

Shopping Districts

Helsinki's prime shopping districts run along **Pohjoisesplanadi** (North Esplanade) and **Aleksanterinkatu** in the city center. Along **Pohjoisesplanadi** and **Eteläesplanadi** (✉ Bordering the gardens), you'll find Finland's design houses. You can find a number of antiques shops in the neighborhood called **Kruununhaka** (✉ behind Senate Square).

Specialty Shops

Forum (✉ Mannerheimintie 20, ☎ 09/694–1498) is a modern, multistory shopping mall carrying clothing, gifts, books, and toys. The **Kiseleff Bazaar Hall** (✉ Aleksanterinkatu 22–28) has shops specializing in handicrafts, toys, knitwear, and children's items. You can shop until 10 PM in stores along the **Tunneli** (✉ underneath the train station).

Aarikka (✉ Pohjoisesplanadi 27, ☎ 09/652–277; ✉ Eteläesplanadi 8, ☎ 175–462) offers wooden jewelry, toys, and gifts. **Artek** (✉ Eteläesplanadi 18, ☎ 09/613–250) is known for its Alvar Aalto–designed furniture and ceramics. **Hackman Shop Arabia** (✉ Pohjoisesplanadi 25, ☎ 0204/393–501) sells Finland's Arabia china and Iittala glass. **Kalevala Koru** (✉ Unioninkatu 25, ☎ 09/171–520) specializes in jewelry based on ancient Finnish designs. **Marimekko** (✉ Pohjoisesplanadi 31, ☎ 09/177–944; ✉ Eteläesplanadi 14, ☎ 170–704) sells women's clothing, household items, and gifts made from its textiles. **Pentik** (✉ Pohjoisesplanadi 27, ☎ 09/625–558) has artful leather goods.

Side Trip from Helsinki

Hvitträsk, a dramatic and romantic villa designed by Eliel Saarinen and his partners Herman Gesellius and Armas Lindgren, was their shared home and studio from the turn of the century and is now a museum. This forested estate 30 km (19 mi) west of Helsinki has exhibits, a restaurant, a café, a shop, and a lakeside sauna with swimming. Bus 166 will take you from Helsinki's main bus station, or take the train to Luoma and follow the signs, about 2 km (1 mi), or to Masala and take a taxi. *✉ Luoma, Kirkkonummi, ☎ 09/221–9230. ⏲ June–Aug., weekdays 10–7; Sept.–May weekdays 11–5; closed Mon. Nov.–Apr.*

Helsinki Essentials

Arriving and Departing

BY BOAT

The **Finnjet-Silja and Viking Line** (✉ Mannerheimintie 12, ☎ 09/123–577) terminal for ships arriving from Travemünde, Germany, and Stockholm is at Katajanokanlaituri (✉ east side of South Harbor). **Silja Line** (✉ Mannerheimintie 2, ☎ 09/18–041) ships from Stockholm, Sweden, arrive at Olympialaituri (✉ west side of South Harbor).

BY BUS

The main long-distance bus station is **Linja-autoasema** (✉ off Mannerheimintie, between Salomonkatu and Simonkatu). Many local buses arrive and depart from **Rautatientori** (Railway Station Square). For information on long-distance transport, call ☎ 9600–4000.

BY PLANE

All international flights arrive at **Helsinki–Vantaa Airport** (✉ 20 km/12 mi north of Helsinki, ☎ 9600–8100, information).

Between the Airport and Downtown. Finnair buses make the trip between Helsinki–Vantaa Airport and the city center two–three times an hour, stopping behind the Inter-Continental Helsinki and at the Finnair Terminal next to the train station. The ride takes about 35 minutes and costs FIM 24. A local bus service (Bus 615) will also take you to the train station and costs FIM 15 for the 40-minute ride. Expect to pay between FIM 100 and FIM 140 for a taxi into the city center. If you are driving, follow the well-placed signs to Highway 137 (Tuusulantie) and KESKUSTA (downtown Helsinki).

BY TRAIN

Helsinki's main rail gateway is the **Rautatieasema** (train station; ✉ City center, off Kaivokatu, ☎ 09/707–5700, information).

Getting Around

The center of Helsinki is compact and best explored on foot. If you want to use public transportation, your best buy is the **Helsinki Kortti** (Helsinki Card), which offers unlimited travel on city public transportation, free entry to many museums, a free sightseeing tour, and a variety of other discounts. It's available for one, two, or three days. You can buy it at some hotels and travel agencies, Stockmann's department store, and the Helsinki City Tourist Office. The **Helsinki City Transport tourist ticket** entitles you to unlimited travel on all buses, trams, subways, and local trains in Helsinki. It is valid for one, three, or five days and costs FIM 25, FIM 50, or FIM 75. For timetable and ticket information related to Helsinki's comprehensive, punctual, and generally efficient public transport system, call the 24-hour line (in Finland), ☎ 0100–111.

BY BOAT

In summer regular boat service links the South Harbor Kauppatori (Market Square) with the Suomenlinna and Korkeasaari, site of Helsinki Zoo. Schedules and prices are listed on signboards at the harbor.

BY BUS, STREETCAR, LOCAL TRAIN, OR SUBWAY

Tickets may be purchased at subway stations, R-kiosks, and shops displaying the Helsinki city transport logo (two curving black arrows on a yellow background). Standard single tickets valid on all transport, and permitting transfers within the whole network for within an hour of the time stamped on the ticket, cost FIM 10, and can be bought on trams and buses. Single tickets bought beforehand, at the City Transport office in the railway station tunnel or at one of the many R-kiosk shops, for example, cost FIM 8. A 10-trip ticket sold at R-kiosks costs FIM 75. Most of Helsinki's major points of interest, from Kauppatori to the Opera House, are along the 3T tram line; the Helsinki City Tourist Office (☞ Visitor Information, *below*) distributes a free pamphlet called "Helsinki Sightseeing: 3T."

Helsinki's subway (Metro) line runs from Ruoholahti, just west of the city center, to Mellunmäki, in the eastern suburbs. It operates Monday through Saturday from 5:25 AM, and Sunday from 6:30 AM to 11:20 PM.

BY TAXI

Taxis are all marked TAKSI. Meters start at FIM 30, the fare rising on a kilometer basis. A listing of all taxi companies appears in the white pages; they charge from the point of dispatch. The main phone number for taxi service is ☎ 700–700. Be sure to request a cab that accepts credit cards when ordering a taxi by phone. Car services have a minimum charge and should be ordered well in advance.

Contacts and Resources

EMBASSIES

United States (✉ Itäinen Puistotie 14, ☎ 09/171–931). **Canadian** (✉ Pohjoisesplanadi 25B, ☎ 09/171–141). **United Kingdom** (✉ Itäinen Puistotie 17, ☎ 09/228–65100).

EMERGENCIES

Ambulance (☎ 112). **Doctor** (☎ 10023). **Dentist** (☎ 09/736–166). **General** (☎ 112). **Police** (☎ 112 or 10022). **Twenty-four-hour Pharmacy** Yliopiston Apteekki (✉ Mannerheimintie 96, ☎ 02/032–0200).

ENGLISH-LANGUAGE BOOKSTORES

Akateeminen Kirjakauppa (Academic Bookstore; ✉ Pohjoisesplanadi 39, ☎ 09/12141). **Suomalainen Kirjakauppa** (Finnish Bookstore; ✉ Aleksanterinkatu 23, ☎ 09/651–855).

GUIDED TOURS

Boat. J. L. Runeberg (✉ Departs from Kauppatori, ☎ 019/524–3331) has all-day boat tours to the charming old wooden town of Porvoo, with departures at 10 AM six days a week May 31–September 13.

Orientation. Suomen Turistiauto (✉ Kaupintie 8, ☎ 09/588–5116; ✉ Silja Line, South Harbor). **Ageba Travel Agency** (✉ Pohjoisranta 4, 00170 Helsinki, ☎ 09/615–0155).

TRAVEL AGENCIES

American Express (✉ Area Travel Agency, Mikonkatu 2D, 00100 Helsinki, ☎ 09/628–788). **Finland Travel Bureau** (Suomen Matkatoimisto; ✉ Kaivokatu 10A, PL 319, 00100 Helsinki, ☎ 09/18261);

Finnway Inc. (✉ 228 E. 45th St., 14th fl., New York, NY 10017, ☎ 212/818–1198); **Norvista** (✉ 227 Regent St., London W1R 8PD, ☎ 0171/409–7334).

VISITOR INFORMATION

Helsinki City Tourist Office (✉ Pohjoisesplanadi 19, ☎ 09/169–3757). The Finnish Tourist Board **Tourist Information Office** (✉ Eteläesplanadi 4, ☎ 09/417–6911).

SOUTH COAST

A magical world of 30,000 islands stretches along Finland's coastline, forming a magnificent archipelago in the Gulf of Finland and the Baltic. On the coast, Turku, the former Finnish capital, was the main gateway through which cultural influences reached Finland over the centuries. Westward from Turku lies the rugged and fascinating Åland Islands group, an autonomous province of its own. Many of Finland's oldest towns, chartered by Swedish kings, lie in the southwest—hence the predominance of the Swedish language here. It is a region of flat, often mist-soaked rural farmlands where the larger villages are highly picturesque, with their traditional wooden houses.

Snappertuna

Snappertuna, 70 km (43 mi) west of Helsinki, is a farming town with a proud hilltop church, a charming homestead museum, and a castle set in a small dale. The handsome, restored ruin of **Raaseporin Linna** (Raseborg Castle) is believed to date from the 12th century. In summer concerts, dramas, and old-time market fairs are staged here. Guided tours are arranged by the local tourist office (☎ 019/278–6540) ✉ *Keskuskatu 90,* ☎ *019/234–015.* *FM 5.* *May–Aug., daily 10–8* .

Tammisaari

Tammisaari (Ekenäs in Swedish) has a colorful Old Quarter, 18th- and 19th-century buildings, and a lively marina. In summer the sun glints off the water and marine traffic is at its peak. The **Tammisaaren Museo** (Tammisaari Museum) is the provincial museum of western Uusimaa and provides a taste of the region's culture and history. ✉ *Kustaa Vaasan katu 13,* ☎ *019/263–3161.* *May 20–July, Tues.–Sun. 11–4; Aug.–May 19, Tues.–Thurs. 6 PM–8 PM.*

$$$ **Ekenäs Stadshotell and Restaurant.** This modern, airy hotel is set amid fine lawns and gardens right in the heart of Tammisaari. The rooms, each with its own balcony, have wide picture windows and comfortable modern furnishings, all in pale and neutral colors. The restaurant offers Continental food and Swedish-Finnish seafood specialties prepared by a veteran chef. ✉ *Pohjoinen Rantakatu 1, 10600 Tammisaari,* ☎ *019/241–3131, 019/246–1550,* FAX *019/246–1550. 6 rooms, 2 suites. Restaurant, indoor pool. AE, DC, MC, V.*

Hanko

In the coastal town of Hanko (Hangö), you'll find long stretches of beach—about 30 km (19 mi) in total—and some of the most fanciful private homes in Finland, their porches edged with gingerbread iron- and woodwork, and crazy towers sprouting from their roofs. Hanko is also a popular sailing center, with Finland's largest guest harbor.

Fortified in the 18th century, Hanko lost its defenses to the Russians in 1854, during the Crimean War. Later Hanko became a popular spa town for Russians, then the port from which more than 300,000 Finns emigrated to North America between 1880 and 1930.

Turku

Founded at the beginning of the 13th century, Turku is the nation's oldest city and was the original capital of Finland. The city has a long history as a commercial and intellectual center; the site of the first Finnish university, it now has two major universities, the Finnish University of Turku and the Swedish-speaking Åo Akademi. With a population of more than 160,000, Turku is the fifth-largest city in Finland and has commercial significance in its year-round harbor, from which ferries depart daily to Stockholm and the beautiful Åland archipelago.

The 700-year-old **Turun Tuomiokirkko** (Turku Cathedral) remains the seat of the archbishop of Finland. Although it was partially gutted by fire in 1827, the cathedral has been completely restored. The cathedral museum includes a collection of medieval church vestments, silver chalices, and wooden sculptures. ✉ *Turun Tuomiokirkko,* ☎ *02/251–0651.* 🎫 *Free.* ⏲ *Mid-Apr.–mid-Sept., daily 9–8; mid-Sept.–mid-Apr., daily 9–7.*

Where the Aura flows into the sea stands **Turun Linna** (Turku Castle), one of the city's most important historical monuments. The oldest part of the fortress was built at the end of the 13th century, and the newer part dates from the 16th century. The castle was damaged by bombing in 1941; restoration was completed in 1961. The vaulted chambers themselves give you a sense of the domestic lives of the Swedish royals. A good gift shop and a pleasant café are on the castle grounds. ✉ *Linnankatu 80,* ☎ *02/262–0300.* 🎫 *FIM 20.* ⏲ *Mid-Apr.–mid-Sept., daily 10–6; mid-Sept.–mid-Apr., Mon. 2–7, Tues.–Sun. 10–3.*

The **Luostarinmäki Handicrafts Museum** is an authentic collection of wooden houses and buildings containing shops and workshops where traditional crafts are demonstrated and sold. ✉ *Vartiovuorenkatu 4,* ☎ *02/262–0350.* 🎫 *FM 20.* ⏲ *Mid-Apr.–mid-Sept., daily 10–6; mid-Sept.–mid-Apr., daily 10–3. Closed Mon.*

The **Aboa Vetus/Ars Nova Museum** is a unique combination of history and art. The concept for the museum, begun as a straightforward extension of the then Villa von Rettig art museum, changed when workers excavated medieval archaeological remains. Modern art in the old Villa includes paintings by Auguste Herbin (1882–1960) and Max Ernst and the *Swordsman* by Picasso. The preserved excavations in the Aboa Vetus section date from as early as the 15th century. ✉ *Itäinen Rantakatu 4-6,* ☎ *02/250–0552.* 🎫 *FIM 50, combined ticket for both museums; FIM 35 for separate museums.* ⏲ *May–Sept., daily 11–7; rest of yr, closed Mon.*

The **Turun Taidemuseo** (Turku Art Museum) holds some of Finland's most famous paintings, including works by Akseli Gallen-Kallela, and a broad selection of turn-of-the-century Finnish art and modern multimedia works. ✉ *Aurakatu 26, Puolanpuisto,* ☎ *02/233–0954.* 🎫 *About FM 30 (varies according to current exhibit).* ⏲ *Apr.–Sept., Tues., Fri., Sat. 10–4, Wed., Thurs. 10–7, Sun. 11–6; Oct.–Mar., Tues.–Sat. 10–4, Sun. 11–6.*

$$$ ✕ **Calamare.** At this hotel restaurant, try the Delicacy Plate, with Baltic herring, roe in mustard sauce, shrimp, fillet of beef, egg, and marinated mushrooms. Calamare has impressive views of the Auajoki River and a Mediterranean atmosphere with Roman-style statues and palm trees. ✉ *Linnankatu 32,* ☎ *02/336–2126. AE, DC, MC, V.*

$$$ ✕ **Julia.** French country fare is the specialty in this informal and cozy restaurant where you can enjoy a tasty meal by the warmth of a fireplace. ✉ *Eerikinkatu 4,* ☎ *02/336–3251. AE, DC, MC, V. Closed Sun.*

$$ ✕ **Suomalainen Pohja.** Next to the Turku Art Museum this restaurant has a splendid view of an adjacent park. Seafood, poultry, and game dishes are good here; try the fillet of reindeer with sautéed potatoes or the cold smoked rainbow trout with asparagus. ✉ *Aurakatu 24,* ☎ *02/251–2000. AE, DC, MC, V. Closed weekends.*

$$ **Park Hotel.** The castlelike Park Hotel in the heart of Turku is one of Finland's most unusual lodgings. Its high-ceiling rooms have antique furniture. ✉ *Rauhankatu 1, 20100 Turku,* ☎ *02/251–9666 or 02/251–9696. 21 rooms. Restaurant. AE, DC, MC, V.*

South Coast Essentials

Getting Around

Turku offers a special 24-hour Tourist Ticket (FIM 20) for unlimited public transport access; it's available from the city tourist information office: ☞ Visitor Information, *below*.

BY BUS

Regular daily bus services operate between Helsinki and Turku. The trip takes about 2½ hours.

BY CAR

The main route between Helsinki and Turku is fast and normally traffic-free. A parallel, more picturesque route to the south takes you at a leisurely pace through the smaller towns closer to the coast itself.

BY PLANE

Turku Airport is about 7 km (4 mi) from the city center. Finnair domestic flights run to Helsinki, Mariehamn, and Stockholm.

BY BOAT

Passenger/car ferries depart daily from Turku's harbor for Stockholm and Åland: call **Silja Line** (☎ 09/18–041) or **Viking Line** (☎ 09/12351) for details and timetables.

BY TRAIN

Turku is served by fast train services to Helsinki and Tampere several times a day. The Pendolino high-speed train also operates between Helsinki and Turku, cutting travel time to under two hours.

Guided Tours

South West Finland Tours (✉ Läntinen Rantakatu 13, 20100 Turku, ☎ 02/251–7333, FAX 02/251–7328). **Finland Travel Bureau** (☞ Travel Agencies *in* Contacts and Resources *in* Helsinki Essentials, *above*).

Visitor Information

Turku (✉ City Tourist Information Office, Aurakatu 4, 20100 Turku, ☎ 0600/9–5515 from Finland, 358/2/233–6366 from abroad).

THE LAKELANDS

In southeastern and central Finland, the light has a softness that seems to brush the forests, lakes, and islands, changing the landscape throughout the day. For centuries this beautiful region was a much-contested buffer between the warring empires of Sweden and Russia. The Finns of the Lakelands prevailed by sheer *sisu* (guts), and now their descendants thrive amid the rough beauty of the terrain.

Savonlinna

The center of Savonlinna is a series of islands linked by bridges. An open-air market flourishes alongside the main passenger quay. Savonlinna was once the hub of the passenger fleet serving Saimaa, the largest lake system in Europe. Now cruise boats dominate lake traffic.

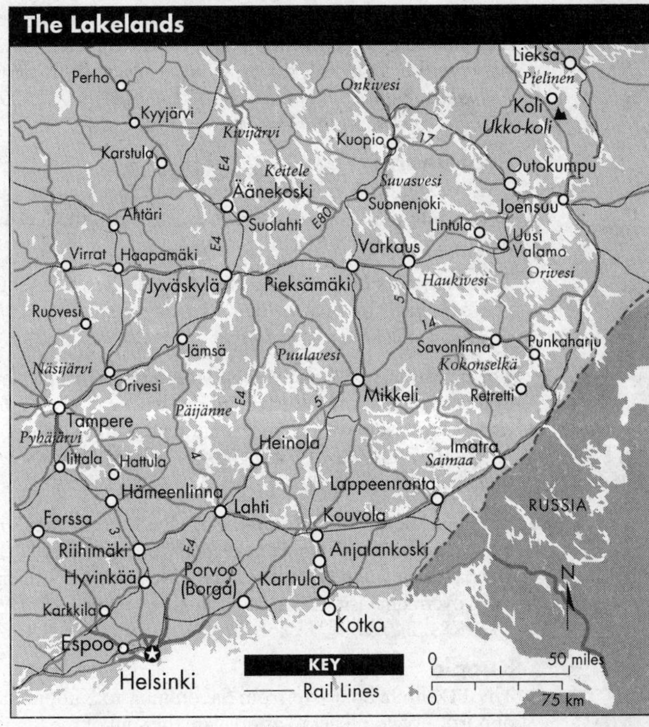

★ First built in 1475 to protect Finland's eastern border, the castle **Olavinlinna** rises majestically out of the lake retaining its medieval character. It is one of Scandinavia's best-preserved historic monuments. The **Savonlinna Opera Festival** is held in the courtyard each July. Make reservations well in advance for both the opera and hotel rooms; contact the Savonlinna Tourist Service (☎ 015/273–492, FAX 015/514–449). ✉ *10-minute walk southeast from quay,* ☎ *015/531–164.* 🎫 *Castle admission includes guided tours in English on the hr.* ⏲ *June–Aug., daily 10–5; Sept.–May, daily 10–3.*

Near Olavinlinna is the **Savonlinnan maakunta museo** (Savonlinna Provincial Museum), to which belong the 19th century steam schooners, the SS *Salama,* the SS *Mikko,* and the SS *Savonlinna.* ✉ *Near Olavinlinna.* ⏲ *Aug.–June, Tues.–Sun. 11–5; July, Tues.–Sun. 10–8.*

$$$ ✕ **Rauhalinna.** This romantic turn-of-the-century timber villa was built by a general in the Imperial Russian Army. From town it's 16 km (10 mi) by road, 40 minutes by boat. Both food and atmosphere are Old Russian, touched by Finnish accents. ✉ *Lehtiniemi,* ☎ *015/523–119. Reservations essential. AE, DC, MC, V. Closed Aug. 7–July 3.*

$$ ✕ **Majakka.** Centrally located, Majakka goes in for home cooking and a family atmosphere. ✉ *Satamakatu 11,* ☎ *015/531–456. Festival-season reservations essential. AE, DC, MC, V.*

$ ✕ **Paviljonki.** An affiliate of the Savonlinna restaurant school, this convenient spot just 1 km (½ mi) west of the city serves classic Finnish dishes. ✉ *Rajalahdenkatu 4,* ☎ *015/574–9303. DC, MC, V.*

$$$–$$$$ 🏨 **Seurahuone.** In this hotel near the market and passenger harbor, rooms are small but modern. The open-air summer restaurant has views of the harbor and the market. ✉ *Kauppatori 4–6, 57130,* ☎ *015/5731,* FAX *015/273–918. 84 rooms. 6 restaurants. AE, DC, MC, V.*

$$$ **Casino Spa.** The Casino Spa has a bucolic lakeside setting on an island linked by a pedestrian bridge to the center of town. Rooms are basic with brown cork floors, white walls, and simple furnishings. ✉ *Kylpylaitoksentie, Kasinosaari, 57130,* ☎ *015/57500,* FAX *015/73-950. 80 rooms. Restaurant, pool. AE, DC, MC, V.*

Punkaharju

This breathtaking ridge of pine-covered rocks, rising out of the water to separate the lakes on either side, predates the Ice Age. At times it narrows to only 25 ft.

Take an excursion to **Taidekeskus Retretti** (Retretti Art Center), which you can reach by boat or bus. ✉ *Just south of Punkaharju,* ☎ *015/644-253.* *FIM 65.* *June 4-Aug. 20, daily 10-6.*

The nearby **Lusto Finnish Forest Museum** has displays on every aspect of forestry, from the industrial to the artistic, and all sides of Finland's close relationship with its most abundant natural resource. ✉ *Lustontie 1, 58450, Punkaharju,* ☎ *015/345-100.* *May-Sept., daily 10-6; Oct.-Apr., Tues.-Sun. 10-5.*

$$$ **Punkaharju National Hotel.** Near the Retretti Art Center, the building was constructed as a gamekeeper's lodge for Tsar Nicholas I in 1845 but has been enlarged and restored. Now it's a restful spot for a meal or an overnight visit. ✉ *Punkaharju 2, 58450,* ☎ *015/739-611,* FAX *015/441-784. 24 rooms, 15 cottages. Restaurant. AE, DC, MC, V.*

Kuopio

The 11½-hour boat trip from Savonlinna to Kuopio may be the best opportunity you'll get to appreciate the soul of the Finnish Lakelands. Meals are available on board. The boat arrives at Kuopio's passenger harbor, where you'll find a small evening market daily from 3 to 10.

★ Kuopio's tourist office is close to the **Tori** (marketplace) one of the most colorful outdoor markets in Finland. ✉ *City center.* *Apr.-Sept., weekdays 7-5, Sat. 7-2; Oct.-Mar., weekdays 7-2.*

The **Ortodoksinen Kirkkomuseo** (Orthodox Church Museum) has an unusual collection of religious art from the monasteries of Karelia (the formereastern province of Finland). ✉ *Karjalankatu 1,* ☎ *017/287-2244.* *May-Aug., Tues.-Sun. 10-4; Sept.-Apr., weekdays noon-3, weekends noon-5.*

Valamon Luostari (Valamo Monastery) is a center for Russian Orthodox religious and cultural life in Finland. Precious 18th-century icons and other sacred objects are housed in the main church and in the icon conservation center. On the grounds are a café-restaurant, hotel and hostel accommodations. ✉ *Uusi Valamo,* ☎ *017/570-111.* *Free.* *Oct.-Feb., daily 8 AM-9 PM; Mar.-Sept., daily 7 AM-9 PM.*

Puijo Näkötorni (Puijo Tower) is best visited at sunset, when the lakes shimmer with reflected light. It has two observation decks and a revolving restaurant on top from which you can enjoy the marvelous views. ✉ *3 km/2 mi northwest of Kuopio,* ☎ *017/209-103.* *Free Sept.-Apr.* *May-Aug., daily 11-11; Sept.-Apr., daily 11-9.*

$$$ ✕ **Musta Lammas.** The attractive restaurant in what was once a beer cellar, serves Finnish dishes. The specialty is the smoked *muikku*—a kind of whitefish—with sour cream and mashed potatoes. ✉ *Satamakatu 4,* ☎ *017/262-3494. AE, DC, MC, V. Closed Sun.*

$$ ✕ **Sampo.** The specialty here is whitefish. The atmosphere is unpretentious and lively, and the location in the town center is convenient. ✉ *Kauppakatu 13,* ☎ *017/261-4677. AE, DC, MC, V.*

$$$ **Arctia Hotel Kuopio.** The best equipped of local hotels, the Arctia has all the advantages of a lakefront location while being close to the center of town. Rooms are spacious by European standards, with large beds and generous towels. ✉ *Satamakatu 1, 70100,* ☎ *017/195–111,* FAX *017/195–170. 134 rooms. Pool. AE, DC, MC, V.*

$$ **Hotel-Spa Rauhalahti.** Sports-oriented travelers and families flock to this high-energy setting. Close to the lakeshore and 4¾ km (3 mi) from the town center, Rauhalahti offers lively activities and conveniences for all ages and interests . ✉ *Katiskaniementie 8, 70700,* ☎ *017/473–111,* FAX *017/473–470. 106 rooms, 20 apartments, 26 hostel rooms. 3 restaurants. AE, DC, MC, V.*

Tampere

The city is a traditional center of industry—notably cotton and textile manufacture. But Tampere has its own special character, combining the cultural sophistication worthy of a city with twice its 200,000 population with an endearing intimacy.

From about the year 1000, this part of Finland was a base from which traders and hunters set out on their expeditions to the north. It was not until 1779 that a Swedish king, Gustav III, founded Tampere. A Scotsman by the name of James Finlayson came to the city in 1882 and established a factory for spinning cotton. The firm of Finlayson is still one of the country's large industrial enterprises.

An isthmus, little more than 1 km (½ mi) wide at its narrowest point, separates the lakes Näsijärvi and Pyhäjärvi, and at one spot the waters of one rush through to the other down the Tammerkoski Rapids. Their natural beauty has been preserved despite the factories on either bank, and the distinctive public buildings of the city grouped around them add to the overall effect.

The **Amurin Työläismuseokortteli** (Amuri Museum of Workers' Housing) consists of more than 30 wooden houses, plus a sauna, a bakery, a haberdashery, and more from the 1880s to the 1970s. ✉ *Makasiininkatu 12,* ☎ *03/214–1633.* ⏲ *Mid-May–mid-Sept., Tues.–Sat. 9–5, Sun. 11–5.*

The **Lenin Museo** (Lenin Museum) commemorates the first meeting of Lenin and Stalin in Tampere with photos and memorabilia. ✉ *Hämeenpuisto 28, 3rd fl.,* ☎ *03/276–8100.* ⏲ *Weekdays 9–6, weekends 11–4.*

On the east side of town the modern **Kalevan Kirkko** (Kaleva Church) is a soaring monument to light and space designed by Reima Pietilä. ✉ *Lissanpuisto 1.* ⏲ *May–Aug., daily 10–5; Sept.–Apr., daily 11–3.*

Among Reima Pietilä's many unusual structures in Tampere is the **Tampere pääkirjasto** (Tampere Central Library), which houses an exhibit celebrating the Moomintroll books of Finnish author Tove Jansson. ✉ *Hämeenpuisto 20,* ☎ *03/219–6578.* ⏲ *Tues.–Fri. 9–5, weekends 10–6.*

The **Tuomiokirkko** (cathedral), built in 1907, displays some of the best-known masterpieces of Finnish mural art. ✉ *Tuomiokirkonkatu.* ⏲ *May–Aug., daily 10–6; Sept.–Apr., daily 11–3.*

The **Särkänniemi peninsula** holds many attractions. **Särkänniemen Huvikeskus** (Särkäniemi Amusement Center) is a major recreation complex made up of an amusement park, a children's zoo, a planetarium, and a well-planned aquarium with a separate "dolphinarium." Within Särkäniemi, the **Sara Hildénin Taidemuseo** (Sara Hildén Art Museum) is a striking example of Finnish architecture, displaying works by such modern artists as Chagall, Klee, Miró, and Picasso. ✉ *Särkänniemi. Hildén Museum:* ☎ *03/214–3134;* ☎ *03/248–8111 (main complex information).* *Joint admission: FIM 130.* ⏲ *Daily 11–6.*

Särkänniemi claims Finland's tallest structure, the 550-ft **Näsinneula Observation Tower,** which dominates the Tampere skyline. At the top are an observatory and a revolving restaurant. The contrast between the industrial maze of Tampere at your feet and the serenity of the lakes stretching out to meet the horizon is unforgettable. ✉ *Särkänniemi.* ☎ *03/248–8111 (main complex information).* ⏲ *Observation tower: June–Aug., daily 10–10; Sept.–May, daily 10–4.*

On the **"Poet's Way"** boat tour along Lake Näsijärvi, the boat passes through the agricultural parish of Ruovesi, where J. L. Runeberg, Finland's national poet, once lived. Many artists and writers spend their summers by the straits of Visuvesi. ✉ *Finnish Silverline and "Poet's Way," Verkatehtaankatu 2,* ☎ *03/212–4804.* *Round-trip fare: FIM 310.*

$$$ ✕ **Tiiliholvi.** Fish, meat, and game dishes are the specialties of this romantic converted cellar. ✉ *Kauppakatu 10,* ☎ *031/212–1220. AE, DC, MC, V. Closed Sun.*

$$ ✕ **Astor.** Dark wood and red tones create a pleasant ambience in which to try the kitchen's renowned reindeer and snow grouse dishes. In the evening, candlelight and live piano music add still more charm. ✉ *Aleksis Kivenkatu 26,* ☎ *03/213–3522. AE, DC, MC, V.*

$$ ★ ✕ **Silakka.** In a casual atmosphere, Silakka (which means Baltic herring) serves excellent Finnish fish specialties. ✉ *Koskikeskus, Hatanpään valtatie 1,* ☎ *03/214–9740. DC, MC, V.*

$$$$ **Sokos Hotel Ilves.** Soaring above newly gentrified old warehouses near the city center, the hotel has rooms above the sixth floor with spectacular views of the city and Pyhäjärvi and Näsijärvi lakes. ✉ *Hatanpään valtatie 1, 33100,* ☎ *03/262–6262,* FAX *03/262–6264. 336 rooms. 4 restaurants, pool. AE, DC, MC, V.*

$$$ **Cumulus Koskikatu.** Overlooking the tame rapids of Tammerkoski, Cumulus Koskikatu is central and modern. The Finnair terminal is in the same building. ✉ *Koskikatu 5, 33100,* ☎ *03/242–4111,* FAX *03/242–4399. 227 rooms. Restaurant, pool. AE, DC, MC, V.*

$ **Domus Summer Hotel.** About 1½ km (1 mi) from the center of town this hotel is a good value. ✉ *Pellervonkatu 9, 33540,* ☎ *03/255–0000,* FAX *03/317–1200. 127 rooms. Pool. MC, V. Closed Sept.–May.*

Iittala

The **Iittala Lasikeskus** (Iittala Glass Center) offers museum tours and has a shop. The magnificent glass is produced by top designers, and the seconds are bargains you won't find elsewhere. ✉ *14500 Iittala,* ☎ *03/535–6230.* ⏲ *Museum: May–Aug., daily 10–6; Sept.–Apr., daily 10–6. Shop: May–Aug., daily 10–8; Sept.–Apr., daily 10–6.*

Hämeenlinna

Hämeenlinna's secondary school has educated many famous Finns, among them composer Jean Sibelius (1865–1957). The only surviving timber house in the town center is **Sibeliuksen syntymäkoti** (Sibelius's birthplace), a modest dwelling built in 1834. One of the rooms houses the harmonium Sibelius played as a child. ✉ *Hallituskatu 11,* ☎ *03/621–2755.* ⏲ *May–Aug., daily 10–4; Sept.–Apr., daily noon–4.*

Hämeen Linna (Häme Castle) is Finland's oldest castle: Swedish crusaders began building it during the 13th century. In modern times the castle has served in turn as a granary and as a prison. It is now restored and open to the public for tours and exhibitions. The castle sits on the lakeshore 1 km (½ mi) north of Hämeenlinna's town center. ✉ *Kus-*

taa II:n katu 6, ☎ 03/675–6820. ⏲ May–Aug. 14, daily 10–6; Aug. 15–Apr., daily 10–4. Closed some holidays.

Hattula

The interior of medieval **Hattulan Kirkko** (Hattula Church), 6 km (4 mi) north of Hämeenlinna in Hattula has frescoes of biblical scenes in which the vicious little devils and soulful saints are still as vivid as when they were first painted around 1510. ✉ *Hattula,* ☎ *03/672–3383 during opening hrs; 03/637–2477 at other times.* ⏲ *May 14–Aug. 14, daily 11–5; other times by appointment.*

Riihimäki

The **Suomen Lasimuseo** (Finnish Glass Museum) in Riihimäki, 35 km (22 mi) south of Hämeenlinna, has an outstanding display of the history of glass from early Egyptian times to the present, artfully arranged in an old glass factory. ✉ *Tehtaankatu 23, Riihimäki,* ☎ *019/741–494.* ⏲ *May–Aug., daily 10–6; Sept.–Apr., Tues.–Sun. 10–6.*

$$ ✕ **Bistro Park.** In a renovated old timber building, Bistro Park offers Finnish and international fare. ✉ *Kirkkorinne 2,* ☎ *03/612–1606. DC, MC, V.*

$$$ ★ **Rantasipi Aulanko.** One of Finland's top hotels sits on the lakeshore in a beautifully landscaped park 6½ km (4 mi) from town. All rooms have wall-to-wall carpeting and overlook the golf course, the park, or the lake.✉ *Aulanko Puisto (Aulanko Park), 13210,* ☎ *03/658–801,* FAX *03/682–1922. 245 rooms. Pool. AE, DC, MC, V.*

The Lakelands Essentials

Getting Around

In Tampere you can buy a 24-hour **Tourist Ticket** from the city tourist office (☞ Visitor Information, *below*) that allows unlimited travel on city transportation.

BY BUS

Buses are the best form of public transport into the region, with frequent connections to lake destinations from most major towns. It is a six-hour ride from Helsinki to Savonlinna.

BY CAR

The region is vast, so the route you choose will depend on your destination. Consult the Finnish Automobile Association or tourist boards for route advice.

BY PLANE

Airports in the Lakelands are at Tampere, Mikkeli, Jyväskylä, Varkaus, Lappeenranta, Savonlinna, Kuopio, and Joensuu.

BY TRAIN

Trains run from Helsinki to Lahti, Mikkeli, Imatra, Lappeenranta, Joensuu, and Jyväskylä.

Guided Tours

Friendly Finland Tours (Finland Travel Bureau, ☞ Travel Agencies *in* Contacts and Resources *in* Helsinki Essentials, *above*).

Visitor Information

Hämeenlinna (✉ Sibeliuksenkatu 5A, 13100, ☎ 03/621–2388). **Kuopio** (✉ Haapaniemenkatu 17, 70110, ☎ 017/182–584). **Savonlinna** (✉ Puistokatu 1, 57100, ☎ 015/273–492). **Tampere** (✉ Verkatehtaankatu 2, 33211, ☎ 03/212–6652).

FINNISH LAPLAND

Lapland is a region of great silences with endless forests and fells. Settlers in Finnish Lapland have walked gently and left the landscape almost unspoiled. The oldest traces of human habitation in Finland have been found in Lapland, where hoards of Danish, English, and even Arabian coins indicate active trading many centuries ago. Until the 1930s, Lapland was still largely unexploited, and any trip to the region was an expedition. Its isolation ended when the Arctic Highway was completed, connecting Rovaniemi with the Arctic Sea.

Only about 4,500 native Sami still live in Lapland; the remainder of the province's population of 220,000 is Finnish. Recent grass-roots efforts to preserve Sami language and traditions have been largely successful. Sami craftspeople create beautiful objects and clothing out of the materials readily at hand: wood, bone, and reindeer pelts.

Winter in Lapland is full of fascinating experiences, from the northern lights to reindeer roundups. Summer has the blessing of daylight for up to 24 hours, and beautiful weather typically accompanies the nightless days. In early fall the colors are spectacular.

Exploring Lapland

Rovaniemi

Rovaniemi is the Lapland administrative and communications hub. Nearly razed by the retreating German army in 1944, Rovaniemi is today a modern university town and business center strongly influenced by Alvar Aalto's architecture. In the process of rebuilding, the city grew from a population of 8,000 to around 34,000. One notable structure is the **Lappia-Talo** (Lappia House; ✉ Hallituskatu 11, ☎ 016/322–2944), an Aalto-designed concert and congress center with the world's northernmost professional theater.

★ You can get a good instant introduction to the region and its natural history at the **Arktikum** (Arctic Research Center), 1 km (½ mi) north of Lappia-Talo. The Arktikum houses the Museum of the Province of Lapland, with exhibits on Sami culture. ✉ *Pohjoisranta 4,* ☎ *016/317–840.* ⏲ *May–Aug., daily 10–6; Sept.–Apr., Tues.–Sun. 10–6.*

$$ ✕ **Fransmanni.** In the Vaakuna Hotel in downtown Rovaniemi, the restaurant specializes in international, Finnish, and Sami dishes. ✉ *Koskikatu 4,* ☎ *016/332–211. AE, DC, MC, V.*

$$ ✕ **Ounasvaaran Pirtit.** This town favorite, a small restaurant decorated in traditional Lapp wooden style and focused on a welcoming open fireplace, serves traditional Finnish and Sami fare. ✉ *Antinmukka 4,* ☎ *016/369–056. Reservations essential. MC, V.*

$$$ ★ 🏨 **Sky Hotel Ounasvaara.** The views of the town and the surrounding area are fantastic from this tranquil, full-service hotel perched on a hilltop 3 km (2 mi) from town. ✉ *96400,* ☎ *016/335–3311,* FAX *016/318–789. 69 rooms, 47 with sauna. Restaurant. AE, DC, MC, V.*

$$$ 🏨 **Sokos Hotel Vaakuna.** Opened in 1992, the Vaakuna has small rooms painted in pastel shades. The club here is a center of Rovaniemi nightlife. ✉ *Koskikatu 4, 96200,* ☎ *016/332–211,* FAX *016/332–2199. 157 rooms, 2 suites. 3 restaurants. AE, DC, MC, V.*

$$ 🏨 **Pohjanhovi.** With its pleasant location overlooking the Kemi River, this hotel is an old favorite with travelers to the north. It has been expanded and modernized over the years. ✉ *Pohjanpuistikko 2, 96200,* ☎ *016/33711,* FAX *016/313–997. 216 rooms. Pool. AE, DC, MC, V.*

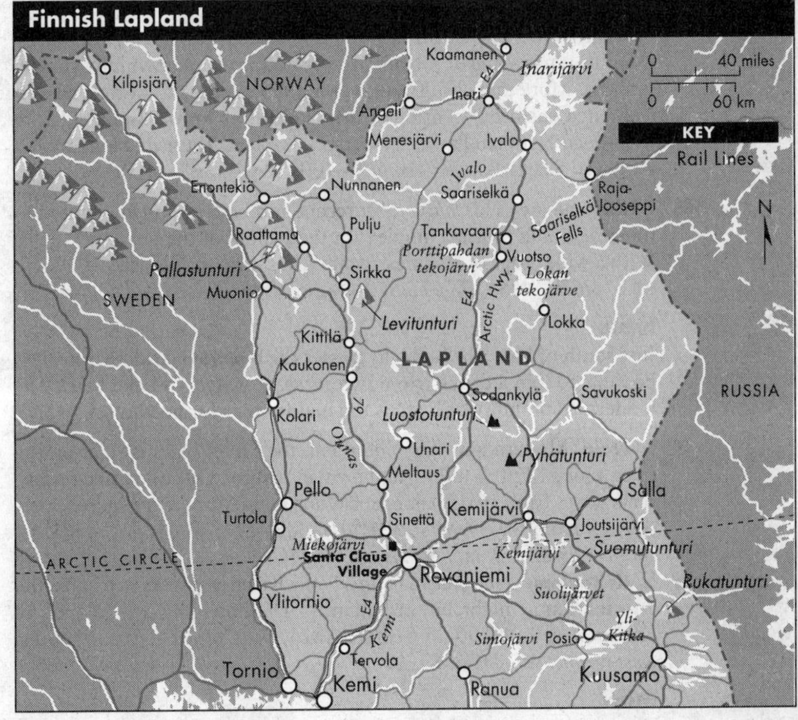

$$ 🏨 **Rudolf.** Renovated since 1995, the former Gasthof is still a comfortable small hotel with a traditional restaurant. ✉ *Koskikatu 41, 96100,* ☎ *016/302–3222,* FAX *016/342–3226. 41 rooms. Restaurant, pool. AE, DC, MC, V.*

$ 🏨 **Oppipoika.** As a branch of the Hotel School of Rovaniemi, this place focuses on service. Rooms are spacious and comfortable, but the real reason to come here is the food, featuring a variety of Lapland specialties. ✉ *Korkalonkatu 33, 96200,* ☎ *016/338–8111,* FAX *016/346–969. 40 rooms. Restaurant, bar, pool. AE, DC, MC, V.*

Arctic Circle

★ Right where the Arctic Circle intersects with the Arctic Highway is **Santa Claus Village,** where you can shop for gifts at any time of year and have your purchases and postcards shipped and marked with a special Santa Claus Land stamp. ✉ *Arctic Hwy. at Arctic Circle, 96930,* ☎ *016/356–2157,* FAX *016/348–1418.* 🎫 *Free.* ⏲ *June–Aug., daily 8–8; Sept.–May, daily 10–5.*

Tankavaara

Tankavaara is the most accessible and best developed of several gold-panning areas. The **Kultamuseo** (Gold Museum) tells the centuries-old story of Lapland's hardy fortune seekers. In the summer months authentic prospectors will show you how to wash gold dust and tiny nuggets from the dirt of an ice-cold stream. ✉ *Arctic Hwy. 4, Kultakylä,* ☎ *016/626–158.* ⏲ *June–Aug. 15, daily 9–6; Aug. 16–Sept., daily 9–5; Oct.–May, daily 10–4.*

$$ ✕ **Wanha Waskoolimies.** Sami specialties predominate at this attractive café/restaurant at the Gold Museum; try the gold prospector's reindeer beefsteak. ✉ *Tankavaaran kultakylä,* ☎ *016/626–158. DC, V.*

Saariselkä

From here you can set off into the true wilderness; during the snowy months, it has some of the finest cross-country and downhill skiing in Finland. More than 2,500 square km (965 square mi) of this magnificent area has been set aside as **Urho Kekkosen kansallispuisto** (Urho Kekkonen National Park; ✉ Northern Lapland Tourism, Honkapolku 3, 99830 Saariselkä, ☎ 016/668–400, FAX 016/668–405).

$$$ **Riekonlinna.** This is the most recent and best-equipped addition to the developing tourist complex on the fringes of the wilderness fells. With a wide range of facilities, it caters to sports enthusiasts. ✉ *99830,* ☎ *016/679–4455,* FAX *016/679–4456. 124 rooms. AE, DC, MC, V.*

Ivalo

Just south of here, the highway passes the **Ivalojoki** (Ivalo River). It is possible to join a canoe trip down its swift waters to Lake Inari. The modern community of Ivalo is the main center for northern Lapland.

$$ **Ivalo.** Modern and fully equipped, the Hotel Ivalo is right on the river about 1 km (½ mi) from the village center. One of its two restaurants serves Lapland specialties, including *poronkäristys,* a reindeer casserole. ✉ *Ivalontie 34, 99800,* ☎ *016/688–111,* FAX *016/661–905. 94 rooms. 2 restaurants, pool. AE, DC, MC, V.*

$ **Kultahippu.** Here, next to the Ivalo River, you can patronize the "northernmost nightclub in Finland." The hotel has cozy rooms. ✉ *Petsamontie 1, 99800,* ☎ *016/661–825,* FAX *016/662–510. 30 rooms. Restaurant. AE, DC, MC, V.*

Inari

The huge island-studded expanses of Inarijärvi (Lake Inari), north of Ivalo, offer endless possibilities for wilderness exploration. Lakeside Inari, home of the Sami Parliament, is a good base for summer boat excursions. Information and permits for camping, fishing, and other activities can be obtained from the **Visitor Centre** (✉ Box 75, 99871 Inari, ☎ 016/665–212).The **Saamelaismuseo** (Sami Museum), on the village outskirts, covers all aspects of Sami culture—traditional and contemporary—and the natural phenomena of the region. ✉ *Inari,* ☎ *016/671–014.* ⏲ *June–Aug. 10, daily 8 AM–10 PM; Aug. 11–31, daily 8–8; Sept. 1–20, daily 9–3:30.*

$$ **Inarin Kultahovi.** This renovated old inn stands on the wooded bank of a swiftly flowing river. ✉ *99870,* ☎ *016/671–221,* FAX *016/671–250. 29 rooms. Restaurant. DC, MC, V.*

Lapland Essentials

Getting Around

All but the most remote towns are accessible by bus, train, or plane.

BY BUS

Buses leave five times daily from Rovaniemi to Inari (five hours) and Ivalo (four hours). Taxi stands are at most bus stations.

BY CAR

The Arctic Highway will take you north from Rovaniemi at the Arctic Circle to Inari, just below the 69th parallel.

BY PLANE

Finnair domestic flights link Oulu and Rovaniemi with Ivalo, Enontekiö, Kemi, and Sodankylä. **Finnair** also has daily flights directly from Helsinki to Kuusamo. The SAS-owned **Air Botnia** (☎ 09/870–2530) also serves Lapland's airports.

Guided Tours

Friendly Finland Tours (Finland Travel Bureau, ☞ Travel Agencies *in* Contacts and Resources *in* Helsinki Essentials, *above*).

Visitor Information

Inari (✉ Honkapolku 3, 99830, ☎ 016/668–400). **Rovaniemi** (✉ Koskikatu 1, 96200, ☎ 016/346–270). **Saariselkä** (✉ Saariselkätie, PL 22, 99831, ☎ 016/668–122). **Sodankylä** (✉ Jäämerentie 9, 99600, ☎ 016/613–474).

11 France

Paris, the Ile-de-France, the Loire Valley, Normandy, Burgundy and Lyon, Provence, the Riviera

Like the new 190-mph TGV speeding toward the Channel Tunnel, France is on the move. This is particularly evident in Paris: In the last two decades no other European capital has seen as much pharaonic building. I. M. Pei's glass pyramid at the Louvre and the postmodern Grande Arche de la Défense are just two examples of the architecturally dramatic monuments that have shocked purists and set the city abuzz.

But traditionalists need not worry: France's attachment to its heritage persists, as major restorations of the Champs-Elysées and the Tuileries Gardens in Paris prove. The world's most magnificent châteaux—Versailles and Fontainebleau in the Ile-de-France, Cheverny and Chambord in the Loire Valley—remain testaments to France's illustrious nobility. The spires of Chartres and Claude Monet's gardens in Giverny still demonstrate France's glorious artistic and architectural legacy.

It's easy to see this grand France of dreams: The Loire Valley and the Ile-de-France are easily accessible from Paris. To really experience France, however, you must travel even farther afield. Go west to Normandy, home of Camembert, Calvados (apple brandy), the D-day landings, and dramatic Mont-St-Michel on its peak overlooking the English Channel (*La Manche* to the French). Head southeast to Burgundy, famed for its wine, and explore the towering Rhône Valley and the hills of Beaujolais, en route to Lyon, a city that competes with Paris—and Dijon—for the title of France's gastronomic capital. Then wend your way south to Provence, to find warm colors and the sweet smell of lavender; and to the Riviera, for the stars, the sun, and the beaches along the bright blue waters of the Mediterranean.

Although life in France is changing—as witnessed by an expanding view toward the global marketplace, an increase in the number of chain stores, and the influx of immigrants transforming the face of the country—the French still maintain, and sometimes furiously defend, the importance of *joie de vivre*. People continue to spend hours in their favorite café, buy baguettes from their local *boulangerie* (bakery), and enjoy long meals over fine wine and conversation.

The best way to get by in France is to try out a little French—a simple *"bonjour"* (good day) or a *"Parlez-vous anglais?"* (Do you speak English?) will carry you a long away. Do as the French do. You'll be surprised, for instance, at how quickly a surly waiter will melt if you fight a smirk with a smirk. Take time out from your busy sightseeing schedule to match that French passion for the daily rituals. Linger over a coffee in the afternoon or a bottle of wine at dinner and your own experience will be all the more authentic and satisfying.

FRANCE A TO Z

Customs on Arrival

For details on imports and duty-free limits, *see* Customs & Duties *in* Chapter 1.

Dining

Eating in France is serious business, at least for two of the three meals each day. For a light meal try an informal brasserie (steak and french fries remain the classic), a picnic (a baguette with ham, cheese, or pâté is a perfect combination), or one of the fast-food outlets that have sprung up in urban areas during recent years. Reservations are advised at most restaurants, particularly in summer.

French breakfasts are relatively modest—strong coffee, fruit juice if you insist, and croissants. International chain hotels are likely to offer American or English breakfasts, but in cafés you will probably be out of luck if this is what you want.

MEALTIMES

Dinner is the main meal and usually begins at 8. Lunch begins at noon in the countryside, and 12:30 or 1 (seldom later) in towns.

PRECAUTIONS

Tap water is perfectly safe, though not always very palatable (least of all in Paris). Mineral water is a good alternative; there is a vast choice of *eaux plates* (plain) as well as *eaux gazeuses* (fizzy).

RATINGS

Prices are per person and include a first course, main course, and dessert plus tax (20.6%) and service (which are always included in displayed prices), but not wine.

CATEGORY	MAJOR CITY	OTHER AREAS
$$$$	over 600 frs	over 500 frs
$$$	300 frs–600 frs	250 frs–500 frs
$$	175 frs–300 frs	125 frs–250 frs
$	under 175 frs	under 125 frs

WHAT TO WEAR

Jacket and tie are recommended for $$$$ and $$$ restaurants, and at some of the more stylish $$ restaurants as well. When in doubt, it's best to dress up. Otherwise casual dress is appropriate.

Language

The French study English for a minimum of four years at school and, although few are fluent, their English is probably better than the French of most Americans. English is widely understood in major tourist areas, and in most hotels there is likely to be at least one person who can converse with you. Even if your own French is rusty, try

France

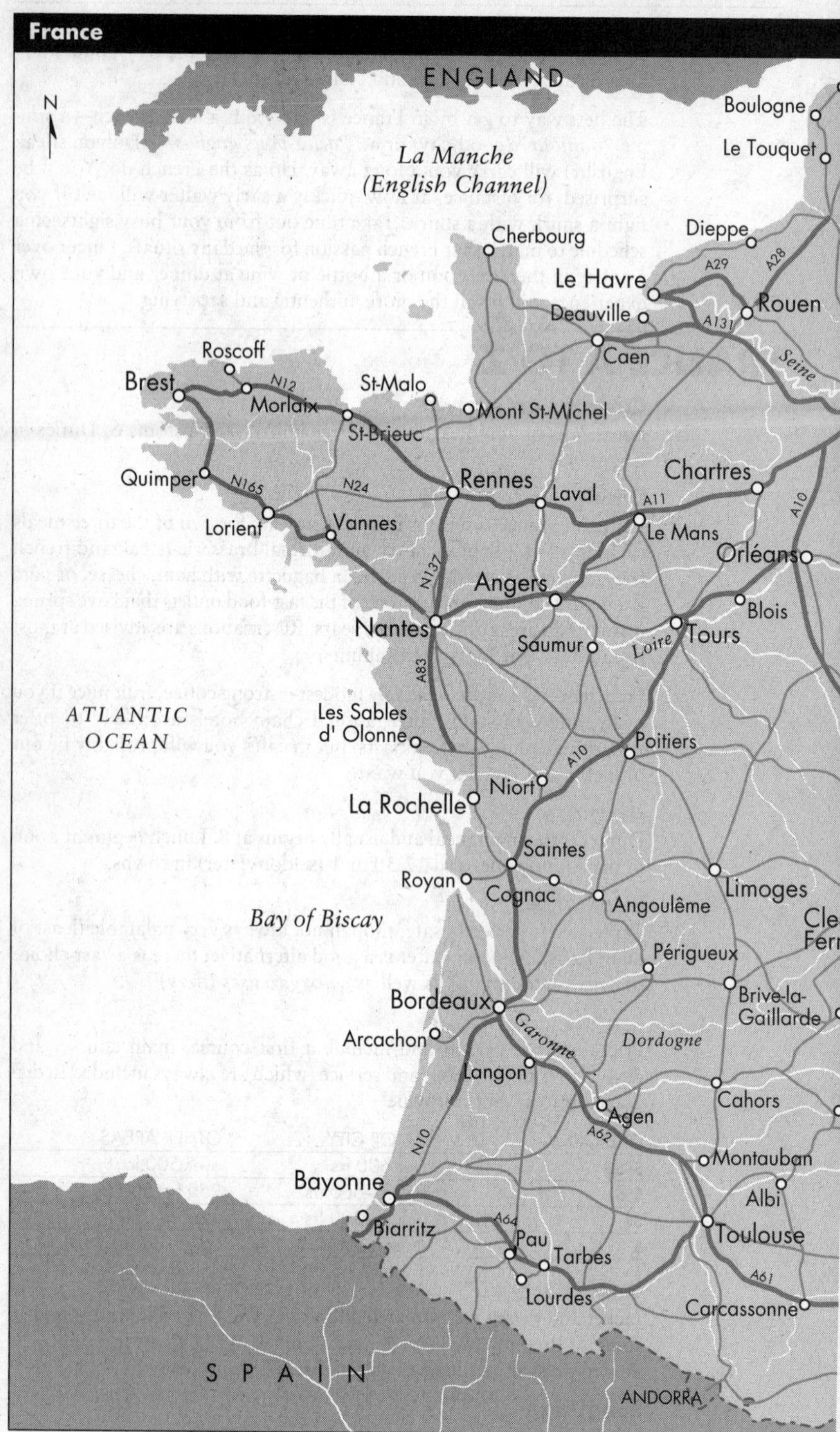
ENGLAND
N
La Manche
(English Channel)
Boulogne
Le Touquet
Dieppe
Cherbourg
Le Havre
A29
A28
Rouen
Deauville
A131
Caen
Seine
Roscoff
Brest
N12
Morlaix
St-Malo
Mont St-Michel
St-Brieuc
Quimper
N165
N24
Rennes
Laval
Chartres
A11
A10
Lorient
Vannes
Le Mans
Orléans
N137
Angers
Blois
Nantes
Saumur
Loire
Tours
A83
ATLANTIC
OCEAN
Les Sables
d' Olonne
Poitiers
A10
Niort
La Rochelle
Saintes
Royan
Cognac
Angoulême
Limoges
Bay of Biscay
Périgueux
Brive-la-
Gaillarde
Bordeaux
Garonne
Arcachon
Dordogne
Langon
Cahors
Agen
A62
N10
Montauban
Bayonne
Albi
Biarritz
A64
Toulouse
Pau
Tarbes
A61
Lourdes
Carcassonne
SPAIN
ANDORRA

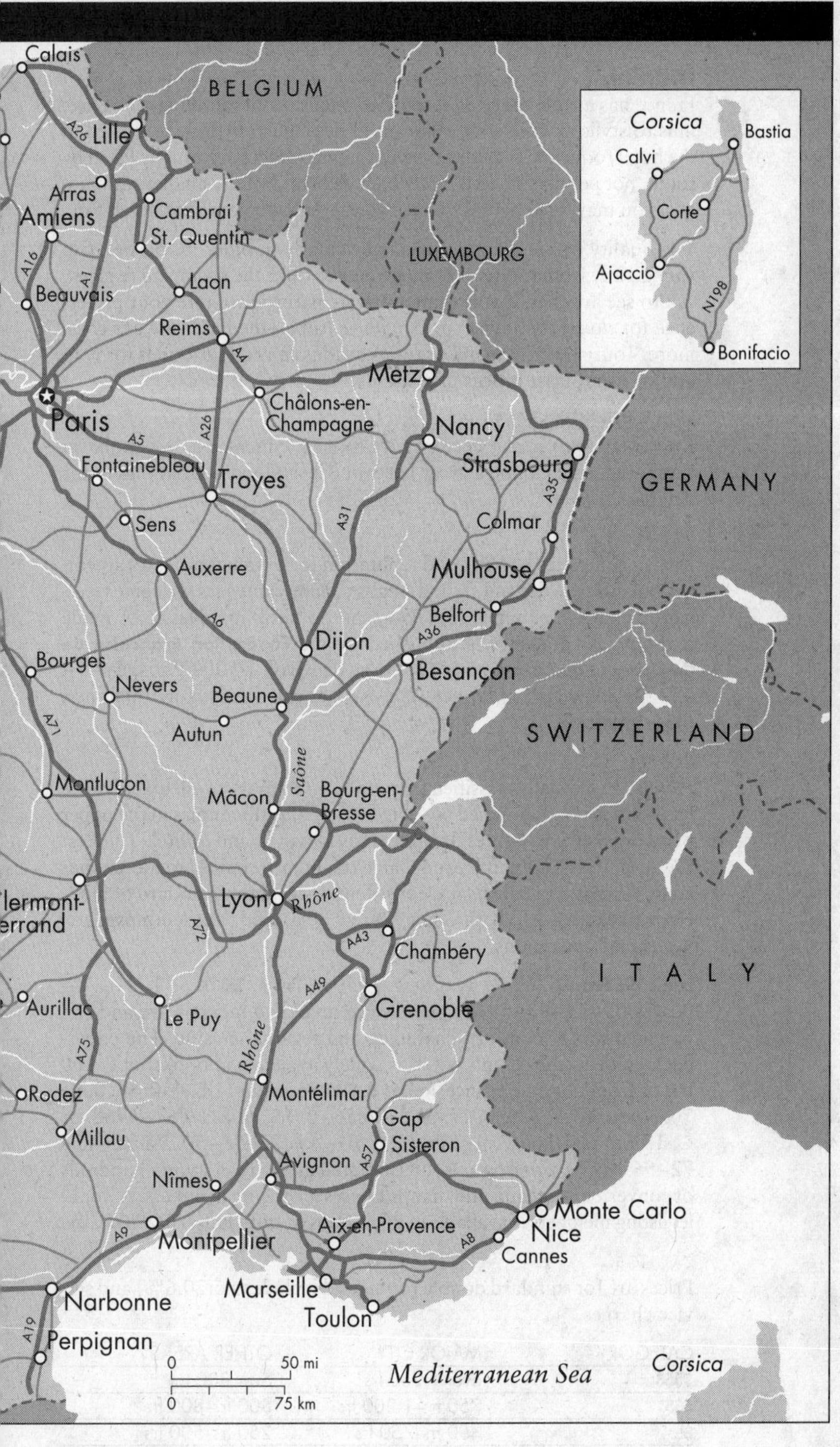

Calais
BELGIUM
Lille
A26
Arras
Amiens
Cambrai
St. Quentin
A16
A1
Beauvais
Laon
Reims
A4
LUXEMBOURG
Metz
Paris
Châlons-en-Champagne
A5
A26
Nancy
Strasbourg
Fontainebleau
Troyes
GERMANY
A35
A31
Sens
Colmar
Auxerre
Mulhouse
Belfort
A6
A36
Dijon
Besançon
Bourges
Nevers
Beaune
Autun
SWITZERLAND
A71
Saône
Montluçon
Mâcon
Bourg-en-Bresse
lermont-errand
Lyon
Rhône
A72
A43
Chambéry
ITALY
A49
Aurillac
Le Puy
Grenoble
A75
Rhône
Rodez
Montélimar
Gap
Millau
Sisteron
A57
Avignon
Nîmes
Monte Carlo
Nice
Cannes
A9
Montpellier
Aix-en-Provence
A8
Marseille
Narbonne
Toulon
A19
Perpignan
0
50 mi
0
75 km
Mediterranean Sea
Corsica
Corsica
Bastia
Calvi
Corte
Ajaccio
N198
Bonifacio

to master a few words: People will greatly appreciate that you are at least making an effort to speak their beloved language.

Lodging

France has a wide range of accommodations, from rambling old village inns to stylishly converted châteaux. Prices must, by law, be posted in the hotel room and include taxes and service. Prices are usually listed by room, not per person, and rarely include breakfast. In smaller rural hotels, you may be expected to have your evening meal at the hotel, too.

The quality of accommodations, particularly in older properties, can vary greatly from room to room; if you don't like the room you're given, ask to see another. If you want a private bathroom, state your preference for *douche* (shower) or *baignoire* (tub)—the latter always costs more. Tourist offices in major train stations can reserve hotels for you, and so can tourist offices in most towns.

BED-AND-BREAKFASTS

Known as *chambres d'hôte* or *gîtes,* these are increasingly popular in rural areas and can be a great bargain. Check local tourist offices for details.

CAMPING

French campsites have a good reputation for organization and amenities but are crowded in July and August. Many campsites welcome reservations, and in summer, it makes sense to book in advance. A guide to France's campsites is published by the **Fédération Française de Camping et de Caravaning** (✉ 78 rue de Rivoli, 75004 Paris, ☎ 01–42–72–84–08). You can get a copy sent to you directly for 100 francs, plus shipping.

HOTELS

Hotels are officially classified from one-star to four-star-deluxe. France has—but is not dominated by—big hotel chains: Examples in the upper price bracket are Frantel, Holiday Inn, Novotel, and Sofitel. The Best Western, Ibis, Campanile, and Climat de France chains are more moderate. Chains typically have a consistently acceptable standard of modern features (modern bathrooms, TV, etc.), but tend to lack atmosphere, with some exceptions.

Logis de France (✉ 83 av. d'Italie, 75013 Paris, ☎ 01–45–84–70–00, FAX 01–45–83–59–66) hotels are small and inexpensive and can be relied on for comfort, character, and regional cuisine. The paperback guide to the chain's hotels is widely available in bookshops (100 frs) or from Logis de France. **Relais & Châteaux** (✉ 11 E. 44th St., Suite 707, New York, NY10017, ☎ 212/856–0115, FAX 212/867–4968, or ✉ 15 rue Galvani, 75017 Paris, ☎ 01–45–72–96–50, FAX 01–45–72–96–69) is a prestigious international group that counts hundreds of converted châteaux and manor houses among its members. A booklet listing members is available in bookshops or from Relais & Châteaux.

RATINGS

Prices are for standard double rooms and include tax (20.6%) and service charges.

CATEGORY	MAJOR CITY	OTHER AREAS
$$$$	over 1,200 frs	over 800 frs
$$$	750 frs–1,200 frs	500 frs–800 frs
$$	450 frs–750 frs	250 frs–500 frs
$	under 450 frs	under 250 frs

RENTALS

Renting a gîtes ruraux—a furnished cottage, chalet, or apartment—for a week or month can save families and small groups money. There are also more luxurious properties for rent, economical only when your party is large, as well as apartments. The **French Government Tourist Offices** in New York or London (☞ Visitor Information, *below*) are good sources for information about gîte and villa rentals. The **Fédération Nationale des Gîtes de France** (✉ 59 rue St-Lazare, 75009 Paris, ☎ 01–49–70–75–75, FAX 01–42–81–28–53) has a list of gîtes for rent: indicate the region that interests you or order the annual nationwide guide (115 francs).

Interhome (✉ 124 Little Falls Rd., Fairfield, NJ 07004, ☎ 201/882–6864, FAX 201/808–1742) lists houses and apartments for rent. Apartment and villa listings are also available through **Villas and Apartments Abroad** (✉ 420 Madison Ave., Suite 1003, New York, NY 10017, ☎ 212/759–1025 or 800/433–3020, FAX 212/755–8316).

YOUTH HOSTELS

Since it is possible to find simple, clean, comfortable accommodations for under 350 francs, you may think twice before staying in a youth hostel, though some of the ones in France are quite nice and even have double rooms. Age restrictions may apply, however. Contact **Fédération Unie des Auberges de Jeunesse** (✉ 27 rue Pajol, 75018 Paris, ☎ 01–44–89–87–27, FAX 01–44–89–87–10).

Mail

POSTAL RATES

Letters and postcards to the United States and Canada cost 4.40 francs for 20 grams. Letters to the United Kingdom cost 3 francs for up to 20 grams, as do letters within France. Postcards cost 2.70 francs within France and to EU countries. Stamps can be bought in post offices (La Poste) and cafés sporting a red TABAC sign outside.

RECEIVING MAIL

If you're uncertain where you'll be staying, have mail sent to American Express (if you're a card member) or Thomas Cook; mail labeled "poste restante" is also accepted at most French post offices.

Money Matters

COSTS

France can be expensive, but many travel basics—hotels, restaurants, plane and train tickets—are affordable if you plan ahead, take advantage of prix-fixe menus, and stay in smaller, family-run places. Prices are highest in Paris and on the Riviera. But even in these areas, you can find pleasant accommodations and excellent food for surprisingly reasonable prices.

All taxes must be included in posted prices in France. The initials TTC (*toutes taxes comprises,* which means taxes included) are sometimes included on price lists, but they are superfluous. Restaurant and hotel prices must *by law* include taxes and service charges: If they are tacked onto your bill as additional items, you should complain.

CURRENCY

The unit of French currency is the franc, subdivided into 100 centimes. Bills are issued in denominations of 50, 100, 200, and 500 francs (frs); coins are 5, 10, 20, and 50 centimes and 1, 2, 5, 10, and 20 francs. The small, copper-color 5-, 10-, and 20-centime coins have considerable nuisance value, but they can be used for tips in bars and cafés. International credit cards and traveler's checks are widely accepted throughout France, except in rural areas. At press time (spring 1998), the U.S. dollar bought 6 francs, the Canadian dollar 4.13 francs, the pound sterling 9.7 francs, the Australian dollar 3.8 francs, and the New Zealand dollar 3.2 francs.

SAMPLE PRICES

Prices vary greatly depending on the region, proximity to tourist sights, and—believe it or not—whether you're sitting down or standing up in a café! Here are a few samples: cup of coffee, 5–12 francs; glass of beer, 10–20 francs; soft drink, 10–20 francs; ham sandwich, 15–25 francs; 1½-km (1-mi) taxi ride, 35 francs.

TIPPING

The bill in a bar or restaurant will include service, but it is customary to leave some small change unless you're dissatisfied. The amount varies, from 30 centimes for a beer to 10 francs after a meal. Tip taxi drivers and hairdressers about 10%. Give ushers in theaters 1–2 francs. Cloakroom attendants will expect nothing if there is a sign saying POURBOIRE INTERDIT (tipping forbidden); otherwise give them 5 francs. Washroom attendants usually get 2 francs—a sum that is often posted. Bellhops should get 10 francs per item.

If you stay in a moderately priced hotel for more than two or three days, it is customary to leave something for the chambermaid—perhaps 10 francs per day. Expect to tip 10 francs for room service—but nothing is expected if breakfast is routinely served in your room.

Service station attendants get nothing for giving you gas or oil, and 5 or 10 francs for checking tires. Train and airport porters get a fixed sum (6–10 frs) per bag. Museum guides should get 5–10 francs after a guided tour. Tip tour guides (and bus drivers) 10 francs or more after an excursion.

National Holidays

January 1; April 15 (Easter Monday); May 1 (Labor Day); May 8 (VE Day); May 13 (Ascension); May 24 (Pentecost Monday); July 14 (Bastille Day); August 15 (Assumption); November 1 (All Saints' Day); November 11 (Armistice); December 25.

Opening and Closing Times

Banks are open weekdays 9:30–4:30, with variations. Most close for at least an hour at lunch. **Museums** are closed one day a week (often Monday or Tuesday) and on national holidays. Usual hours are from 9:30 to 5 or 6. Many museums close for lunch (noon–2); on Sunday many are open afternoons only. **Shops** in big towns are open from 9 or 9:30 to 7 or 8 without a lunch break; though still rare, an increasing number are now open on Sunday. Smaller shops often open earlier and close later, but take a lengthy lunch break (1–4). This siesta-type schedule is more typical in the south of France. Corner grocery stores frequently stay open until around 10 PM.

Precautions

Beware of thieves and pickpockets! Though no one likes to talk about it, burglaries, once confined to major cities, have spread into the countryside.

Shopping

BARGAINING

People don't usually bargain in shops where prices are clearly marked, but they do at outdoor markets and flea markets.

SALES-TAX REFUNDS

A value-added tax of 20.6%, known in France as the TVA, is imposed on most consumer goods. Non-European Union residents, aged 15 and over, can reclaim part of this tax. To qualify, your purchases in a single shop must total at least 2,000 francs. The amount of the refund varies from shop to shop, but usually hovers between 13% and 16%. The major department stores have simplified the refund process with special desks where the *bordereaux* (export sales invoices) are prepared.

Telephoning

French phone numbers have ten digits. All phone numbers have a two-digit prefix determined by zone: Paris and the Ile de France, 01; the northwest, 02; the northeast, 03; the southeast, 04; and the southwest, 05.

COUNTRY CODE

The country code for France is 33 and for Monaco 337. To call France from the United States, dial 011 (for all international calls), then dial 33 (the country code), and the number in France, minus any initial 0. To dial France from the United Kingdom, dial 00–33, then dial the number in France, minus any initial 0.

INTERNATIONAL CALLS

To call a foreign country from France, dial 00 and wait for the tone, then dial the country code, area code, and number. You can also contact your long distance carrier directly and charge your call to your calling card or make a collect call. **AT&T**: 08–00–99–00–11. **MCI**: 08–00–99–00–19. **Sprint**: 08–00–99–00–87.

LOCAL AND REGIONAL CALLS

To make calls within a region or to another region in France, simply dial the full, 10-digit number. A local call in France costs 74 centimes per three minutes; half-price rates apply between 9:30 PM and 8 AM and between 1:30 PM Saturday and 8 AM Monday. Dial 12 for local operators.

Telephone booths can almost always be found at post offices, cafés, and métro stations. Some French pay phones take 1-, 2-, and 5-franc coins (1-fr minimum), but most phones are now operated by *télécartes* (phone cards), sold in post offices, métro stations, and cafés with red TABAC signs by unit (cost: 48 francs for 50 units; 96 francs for 120 units).

Transportation

BY BOAT

Canal and river vacations are popular: You can either take an organized cruise or rent a boat and plan you own leisurely route. Contact a travel agent for details or ask for a "Tourisme Fluvial" brochure in any French tourist office.

BY BUS

Because of the excellent train service, long-distance buses are rare; they're found mainly where train service is scarce. Bus tours are organized by **SNCF** (☞ By Train, *below*). Long-distance routes to many European cities are covered by **Eurolines** (✉ 28 av. Général-de-Gaulle, 93170 Bagnolet, ☎ 01–49–72–51–51, métro: Galliéni).

BY CAR

Breakdowns. If your car breaks down on a highway, go to a roadside emergency telephone and call the breakdown service. If you have a breakdown anywhere else, find the nearest garage or contact the police (dial 17).

Gasoline. Gas is expensive, especially on expressways and in rural areas. Don't let your tank get too low—you can go for many miles in the country without passing a gas station—and keep an eye on pump prices as you go. These vary enormously; from 6.10 to 7 francs per liter. The cheapest gas can be found at *hypermarchés* (super stores).

Parking. Parking is a nightmare in Paris and often difficult in other large towns. Meters and ticket machines (pay and display) are common: Make sure you have a supply of 1-, 2-, 5-, and 10-franc coins. Parking is free during August in most of Paris, but be sure to check the signs. In smaller towns parking may be permitted on one side of the street only—alternating every two weeks—so pay attention to signs.

Road Conditions. France's roads are classified into five types, numbered and prefixed *A, N, D, C,* or *V.* Roads marked *A* (Autoroutes) are expressways. There are excellent links between Paris and most French cities, but poor ones between the provinces (the principal exceptions being A26 from Calais to Reims, A62 between Bordeaux and Toulouse, and A9/A8 the length of the Mediterranean coast). It is often difficult to avoid Paris when crossing France—just try to steer clear of the rush hours (7–9:30 AM and 4:30–7:30 PM). A *péage* (toll) must be paid on most expressways: The rate varies but can be steep. The *N* (Route Nationale) roads—which are sometimes divided highways—and *D* (Route Départementale) roads are usually wide and fast, and driving along them can be a real pleasure. Don't be daunted by smaller (*C* and *V*) roads, either. The yellow regional Michelin maps—on sale throughout France—are invaluable.

Rules of the Road. You may use your own driver's license in France, but you must be able to prove you have third-party insurance. Drive on the right and yield to drivers coming from the right if there is no solid white line. Seat belts are obligatory for all passengers, and children under 12 may not travel in the front seat. Speed limits are 130 kph (80 mph) on expressways, 110 kph (70 mph) on divided highways, 90 kph (55 mph) on other roads, 50 kph (30 mph) in towns. French drivers break these limits and police dish out hefty on-the-spot fines with equal abandon.

BY PLANE

The major gateways to France are **Orly** (☎ 01–49–75–15–15) and **Charles de Gaulle** (☎ 01–48–62–22–80), also known as Roissy, airports in Paris. Flying time is 7½ hours from New York, 9 hours from Chicago, and 11 hours from Los Angeles. Many major airlines also have (less frequent) flights to Lyon, Nice, Marseille, Bordeaux, and Toulouse.

Domestic air travel in France is less expensive than it used to be, and there are more airline companies flying all over the country. Train service, however, may be faster when you consider time spent getting to and from the airport. Most domestic flights from Paris leave from Orly on **Air Inter-Europe** (☎ 800/237–2747 in the U.S., 01–45–46–90–00 in France), a subsidiary of Air France; it flies all over the country. **Air Liberté** (☎ 08–03–80–58–05) flies from Paris to the Riviera and the southwest region of France.

BY TRAIN

SNCF (✉ 88 rue St-Lazare, 75009 Paris, ☎ 08–36–35–35–35), the French national railroad, is fast, punctual, comfortable, and comprehensive. The fast TGV (*Trains à Grande Vitesse*), with a top speed of 304 kph (190 mph), are the best domestic trains, heading southeast from Paris to Lyon, the Riviera, and Switzerland; west to Nantes; southwest to Bordeaux; and north to Lille and Brussels. TGVs require a seat reservation, and prices vary considerably depending on the time of travel. For instance, the cost of a second-class ticket for the Paris-Lyon route—to which double-decker trains were introduced in 1997—ranges from 259 francs around lunchtime up to 384 francs during the morning and evening rush hours. You must always make a seat reservation for the TGV—easily obtained at the ticket window or from an automatic machine. Seat reservations are reassuring but seldom necessary on other French trains, except at holiday times.

You must punch your train ticket in one of the orange machines you'll encounter alongside platforms. Slide your ticket in face up and wait for a "clink" sound. (The small yellow tickets and automatic ticket barriers used for most suburban Paris trains are similar to those in the métro/RER.) The ticket collectors will present you with an on-the-spot fine of 100 francs if your ticket hasn't been validated before boarding.

On overnight trains you choose between wagons-lits (private sleeping cars), which are expensive, and *couchettes* (bunks), which sleep six to a compartment in second class and four to a compartment in first class (sheet and pillow provided) and are cheaper (90 frs). Ordinary compartment seats do not pull together to enable you to lie down. In summer special night trains from Paris to Spain and the Riviera are geared for a younger market, with discos and bars.

Fares. If France is your only destination in Europe, consider purchasing a **France Rail Pass,** which allows three days of unlimited train travel in a one-month period. Prices range from $120 to $198 for one or two adults in first or second class. Additional days may be added for $30 a day in either class. Other options include the France Rail 'n Drive Pass (combining rail and rental car), France Rail 'n Fly Pass (rail travel and one air journey within France), and the France Fly Rail 'n Drive Pass (a rail, air, and rental-car program all in one).

France is one of 17 countries in which you can use **Eurailpasses,** which provide unlimited first-class rail travel, in all of the participating countries, for the duration of the pass. If your plans call for only limited train travel, look into a **Europass,** which costs less money than a Eurailpass.

Various reduced-fare passes are available from major train stations in France and from SNCF travel agents. If you are planning to do a lot of traveling by train in France, consider buying a special **France Vacances** card (1,018 frs for four days, 1,622 frs for nine days). When traveling together, two people (who don't have to be a couple) can save money with the **Prix Découverte à Deux.** Just say you're traveling together when you make a reservation or buy the tickets, and you will get a 25% discount during "périodes bleus" (blue periods; weekdays and not on or near any holidays). Senior citizens (over 60) qualify for the **Carte Vermeil** (279 frs for four trips), and young people (under 26) qualify for the **Carte 12/25 ans** (270 frs). You can get 50% discounts in blue periods (most of the time) and 20% most of the rest of the time (white periods: noon Friday to noon Saturday; 3 PM Sunday to noon Monday). Calendars are available at stations. The **Carte Kiwi 4 x 4** (291 frs) enables children and up to four accompanying adults to make four trips at half price. Other discounts are available if you book 30 or 8 days before traveling (**J30** or **J8**). If you don't benefit from any of these reductions and plan on traveling at least 1,000 km (620 mi) round-trip (including several stops), look into purchasing a **Billet Séjour.** This ticket gives you a 25% reduction if you stay over a Sunday and travel only during blue periods.

BY BICYCLE

The French are great bicycling enthusiasts—witness the Tour de France—and there are many good bicycling routes in France. For 44 francs a day (55 francs for a 10-gear touring bike) you can rent a bike from one of 30 train stations; you need to show your passport and leave a deposit of 1,000 francs or a Visa or MasterCard. Bikes may be taken as accompanied luggage from any station in France; some trains in rural areas don't even charge for this. Tourist offices supply details on the more than 200 local shops that rent bikes, as well as mountain bikes (known as VTT or *Vélo Touts Terrains*), or you can get the SNCF brochure "Guide du Train et du Vélo" from any station.

Visas

Citizens of the United States, Canada, and Britain do not need a visa for visits to France of less than three months. A valid passport is required.

Visitor Information

The French Government Tourist Office has a number of branches in the United States, Canada, and the United Kingdom. **France On-Call** (☎ 202/659–7779, ⏲ weekdays 9–9). **New York City** (✉ 444 Madison Ave., New York, NY 10022, ☎ 212/838–7800). **Chicago** (✉ 676 N. Michigan Ave., Chicago, IL60611, ☎ 312/751–7800). **Beverly Hills** (✉ 9454 Wilshire Blvd., Beverly Hills, CA 90212, ☎ 310/271–6665, FAX 310/276–2835). **Canada** (✉ 1981 Ave. McGill College, Suite 490, Montréal, Québec H3A 2W9, ☎ 514/288–4264, FAX 514/845–4868. **United Kingdom** ✉ 178 Piccadilly, LondonW1V 0AL, ☎ 0171/629–2869, FAX 0171/493–6594; calls cost 50p per minute peak rate or 45p per minute cheap rate).

Weather

June and September, free of the midsummer crowds, are the best months to be in France. June has the advantage of long daylight hours, and slightly cheaper prices and many warm days (often lasting well into October) make September attractive. The second half of July and all of August are spoiled by inflated prices and huge crowds on the beaches, and the heat can be stifling in southern France. Paris, though pleasantly deserted, can be stuffy and polluted in August, too. Anytime between March and November offers a good chance to soak up the sun on the Riviera. The weather in Paris and the Loire is unappealing before Easter (lots of rain and chilly temperatures). If you're dreaming of Paris in the springtime, May (not April) is your best bet.

CLIMATE

North of the Loire (including Paris), France has a northern European climate—cold winters, pleasant if unpredictable summers, and frequent rain. Southern France has a Mediterranean climate: mild winters, long, hot summers, and sunshine throughout the year. The more Continental climate of eastern and central France is a mixture of these two extremes: Winters can be very cold and summers very hot. France's Atlantic coast has a temperate climate even south of the Loire, with the exception of the much warmer Biarritz.

The following are the average daily maximum and minimum temperatures for Paris and Marseille.

PARIS

Jan.	43F	6C	**May**	68F	20C	**Sept.**	70F	21C
	34	1		49	10		53	12
Feb.	45F	7C	**June**	73F	23C	**Oct.**	60F	16C
	34	1		55	13		46	8
Mar.	54F	12C	**July**	76F	25C	**Nov.**	50F	10C
	39	4		58	15		40	5
Apr.	60F	16C	**Aug.**	75F	24C	**Dec.**	44F	7C
	43	6		58	15		36	2

MARSEILLE

Jan.	50F	10C	**May**	71F	22C	**Sept.**	77F	25C
	35	2		52	11		58	15
Feb.	53F	12C	**June**	79F	26C	**Oct.**	68F	20C
	36	2		58	14		51	10
Mar.	59F	15C	**July**	84F	29C	**Nov.**	58F	14C
	41	5		63	17		41	5
Apr.	64F	18C	**Aug.**	83F	28C	**Dec.**	52F	11C
	46	8		63	17		37	3

PARIS

If there's a problem with a trip to Paris, it is the embarrassment of riches that faces you. A city of vast, noble perspectives and winding, hidden streets, Paris remains a combination of the pompous and the intimate. Whether you've come looking for sheer physical beauty, cultural and artistic diversions, world-famous dining and shopping, history, or simply local color, you will find it here in abundance.

Exploring Paris

Numbers in the margin correspond to points of interest on the Paris map.

Paris is a compact city. With the exceptions of the Bois de Boulogne and Montmartre, you can easily walk from one sight to the next. The city is divided in two by the River Seine, with two islands (Ile de la Cité and Ile St-Louis) in the middle. The south—or Left—Bank has a more intimate, bohemian flavor than the haughtier Right Bank. The east–west axis from Châtelet to the Arc de Triomphe, via the rue de Rivoli and the Champs-Elysées, is the principal thoroughfare for sightseeing and shopping on the Right Bank.

A special **Carte Musées et Monuments** pass, allowing access to most Paris museums and monuments, can be obtained from museums or major métro stations (one-day pass, 70 frs; three days, 140 frs; five days, 200 frs). Note, however, that this pass may only be useful to you if you plan to see a lot of museums in the allotted days.

If time is a problem, try to get in several "musts": Explore Notre-Dame and the Latin Quarter; head to place de la Concorde and enjoy the vista from the Champs-Elysées to the Louvre; then take a boat along the Seine for a waterside rendezvous with the Eiffel Tower. You could finish off with dinner in Montmartre and consider it a day well spent.

From the Arc de Triomphe to the Louvre

1 **Arc de Triomphe** (Triumphal Arch). This 164-ft arch was planned by Napoléon to celebrate his military successes. Yet when Empress Marie-Louise entered Paris in 1810, it was barely off the ground. Napoléon had been dead for 15 years when the Arc de Triomphe was finished in 1836. The arch looms over place Charles-de-Gaulle, referred to by Parisians as **L'Étoile** (The Star), one of Europe's most chaotic traffic circles. Short of a death-defying dash, your only way to get over to the Arc de Triomphe is to take the pedestrian underpass. France's Unknown Soldier is buried beneath the archway; the flame is rekindled every evening at 6:30. Halfway up the arch is a small museum devoted to its history. ✉ *Pl. Charles-de-Gaulle,* ☎ *01–43–80–31–31.* ⏲ *Daily 10–5:30; Oct.–Easter, daily 10–5. Closed public holidays. Métro, RER: Charles-de-Gaulle–Étoile.*

4 **Champs-Elysées.** The cosmopolitan pulse of Paris beats strongest along this gracefully sloping, 2-km (1¼-mi) avenue, originally laid out in the 1660s by André Le Nôtre as a garden sweeping away from the Tuileries. There isn't much sign of that pastoral past these days, as you stroll by the cafés, restaurants, airline offices, car showrooms, movie theaters, and chic arcades that occupy its upper half. *Métro: George-V, Franklin-D.-Roosevelt, Champs-Elysées–Clemenceau.*

5 **Grand Palais** (Grand Palace). This so-called palace was built for the World Exhibition of 1900 and now houses temporary exhibitions. Unfortunately the main hall, with its Art Nouveau iron banisters and striking glass roof, is closed for renovation until the end of the century; but you can still visit the **Palais de la Découverte** (Palace of Discovery), with scientific and mechanical exhibits and a **planetarium.** ⊠ *Av. Winston-Churchill,* ☎ *01–44–13–17–17.* ⏲ *Palais de la Découverte: Tues.–Sat. 9:30–6, Sun. 10–7. Métro: Franklin-D.-Roosevelt.*

17 **Jardin des Tuileries** (Tuileries Garden). This enormous formal garden is lined with trees, ponds, and statues. Standing guard on either side as you arrive from place de la Concorde are two museums, the **Musée Jeu de Paume** and the **Musée de l'Orangerie,** identical buildings erected during the mid-19th century (☞ *below*). At the far end of the Tuileries, leading toward the Louvre, is the **Arc du Carrousel,** a dainty triumphal arch erected more quickly (1806–08) than its big brother at the far end of the Champs-Elysées. *Métro: Concorde.*

★ 18 **Louvre.** Once a royal palace, now the world's largest and most famous museum, the Louvre has been given fresh purpose by a decade of expansion, renovation, and reorganization, symbolized by I. M. Pei's daring glass pyramid that now serves as the entrance to both the museum and an underground shopping arcade, the **Carrousel du Louvre.**

The Louvre was begun as a fortress around 1200, but the earliest parts still in use date from the 1540s. Building was a regular process until the reign of Napoléon III in the 1860s. Then, the Louvre was even larger; a wing facing the Tuileries Gardens was razed by rampaging revolutionaries during the bloody Paris Commune of 1871.

Pei's new Louvre has emerged less cramped and more rationally organized. Yet its sheer variety can intimidate. The main tourist attraction is Leonardo da Vinci's *Mona Lisa* (known in French as *La Joconde*), painted in 1503. It's smaller than you might have imagined, kept behind glass, and invariably encircled by a mob of tourists. Turn your attention instead to some less-crowded rooms and galleries nearby, where Leonardo's fellow Italians are strongly represented: Fra Angelico, Giotto, Mantegna, Raphael, Titian, and Veronese. El Greco, Murillo, and Velázquez lead the Spanish; Van Eyck, Rembrandt, Frans Hals, Bruegel, Holbein, and Rubens underline the achievements of northern European art. English paintings are highlighted by works of Lawrence, Reynolds, Gainsborough, and Turner. Highlights of French painting include works by Poussin, Fragonard, Chardin, Boucher, and Watteau—together with David's *Coronation of Napoléon,* Géricault's *Raft of the Medusa,* and Delacroix's *Liberty Guiding the People.*

Famous statues include the soaring *Victory of Samothrace,* the celebrated *Venus de Milo,* and the realistic Egyptian *Seated Scribe.* New rooms for ancient Persian, Arab, and Greek art were opened in 1997. Also be sure to inspect the Gobelin tapestries, the Crown Jewels (including the 186-carat Regent diamond), and the 9th-century bronze statuette of Emperor Charlemagne. ⊠ *Palais du Louvre,* ☎ *01–40–20–53–17 for information.* ⏲ *Mon. and Wed. 9 AM–9:45 PM, Thurs.–Sun. 9–6. Métro: Palais Royal.*

9 **Musée du Jeu de Paume.** Home to the Impressionists before their move to the Musée d'Orsay across the Seine, the Jue de Paume (literally, palm game—a forerunner of tennis) Museum is now an airy, austere, white-walled center for contemporary art. ⊠ *Pl. de la Concorde,* ☎ *01–42–60–69–69.* ⊙ *Tues. noon–9:30, Wed.–Fri. noon–7, weekends 10–7. Métro: Concorde.*

8 **Musée de l'Orangerie** (Orangery Museum). This museum bordering the Jardins des Tuileries contains fine early 20th-century French works by Monet (including some of his *Water Lilies*), Renoir, Marie Laurencin, and others. ⊠ *Pl. de la Concorde,* ☎ *01–42–97–48–16.* ⊙ *Wed.–Mon. 9:45–5:15.*

6 **Petit Palais** (Little Palace). Directly opposite the main entrance to the Grand Palais, and built at the same time (1900), this building is now home to an attractively presented collection of French paintings and furniture from the 18th and 19th centuries. ⊙ *Tues.–Sun. 10–5:40,* ☎ *01–42–65–12–73. Métro: Champs-Elysées–Clemenceau.*

7 **Place de la Concorde.** Flanked by elegant neoclassical buildings, this huge square is often choked with traffic and perhaps at its most scenic come nightfall. Over 1,000 people, including Louis XVI and Marie-Antoinette, were guillotined here in the early 1790s. The obelisk, a gift from the viceroy of Egypt, originally stood at Luxor and was erected here in 1833. *Métro: Concorde.*

From the Eiffel Tower to Pont de l'Alma

47 **Hôtel des Invalides.** The Invalides, soaring above expansive if hardly manicured lawns, was founded by Louis XIV in 1674 to house wounded (or "invalid") war veterans. Although only a few old soldiers live here today, the military link remains in the form of the **Musée de l'Armée**—a vast, though musty military museum with a collection of arms, armor, and uniforms. The **Musée des Plans-Reliefs** contains a fascinating collection of scale models of French towns, dating from the days of military architect Vauban in the 17th century. The Invalides, itself, is an outstanding Baroque ensemble, designed by Bruand and Hardouin-Mansart. Its church, the **Église du Dôme,** possesses the city's most elegant dome as well as the tomb of Napoléon. ⊠ *Esplanade des Invalides,* ☎ *01–44–42–37–67.* ⊙ *Daily 10–6 (Oct.–Mar. 10–5). Métro: Latour-Maubourg.*

50 **Musée d'Art Moderne de la Ville de Paris** (City of Paris Museum of Modern Art). Both temporary exhibits and a permanent collection of top-quality 20th-century art can be found at this modern art museum. It takes over, chronologically speaking, where the Musée d'Orsay leaves off. ⊠ *11 av. du Président-Wilson,* ☎ *01–53–67–40–00.* 🎫 *27 frs.* ⊙ *Tues.–Sun. 10–5:30, Wed. 10–8:30. Métro: Iéna.*

49 **Palais de Chaillot** (Chaillot Palace). This honey-color, Art Deco culture center facing the Seine, perched atop tumbling gardens with sculpture and fountains, was built in the 1930s. It houses three museums: the **Musée des Monuments Français** (French Monuments Museum), whose painstaking replicas of statues and archways form an excellent introduction to French medieval architecture; the **Musée de la Marine** (Maritime Museum), with a salty collection of seafaring paraphernalia; and the **Musée de l'Homme** (Museum of Mankind), an anthropology museum with an array of prehistoric artifacts. ⊠ *Pl. du Trocadéro.* ⊙ *Daily 10–5. Métro: Trocadéro.*

48 **Tour Eiffel** (Eiffel Tower). What is now the worldwide symbol of Paris nearly became 7,000 tons of scrap-iron when its concession expired in 1909. Only its potential use as a radio antenna saved the day. Architect

Paris

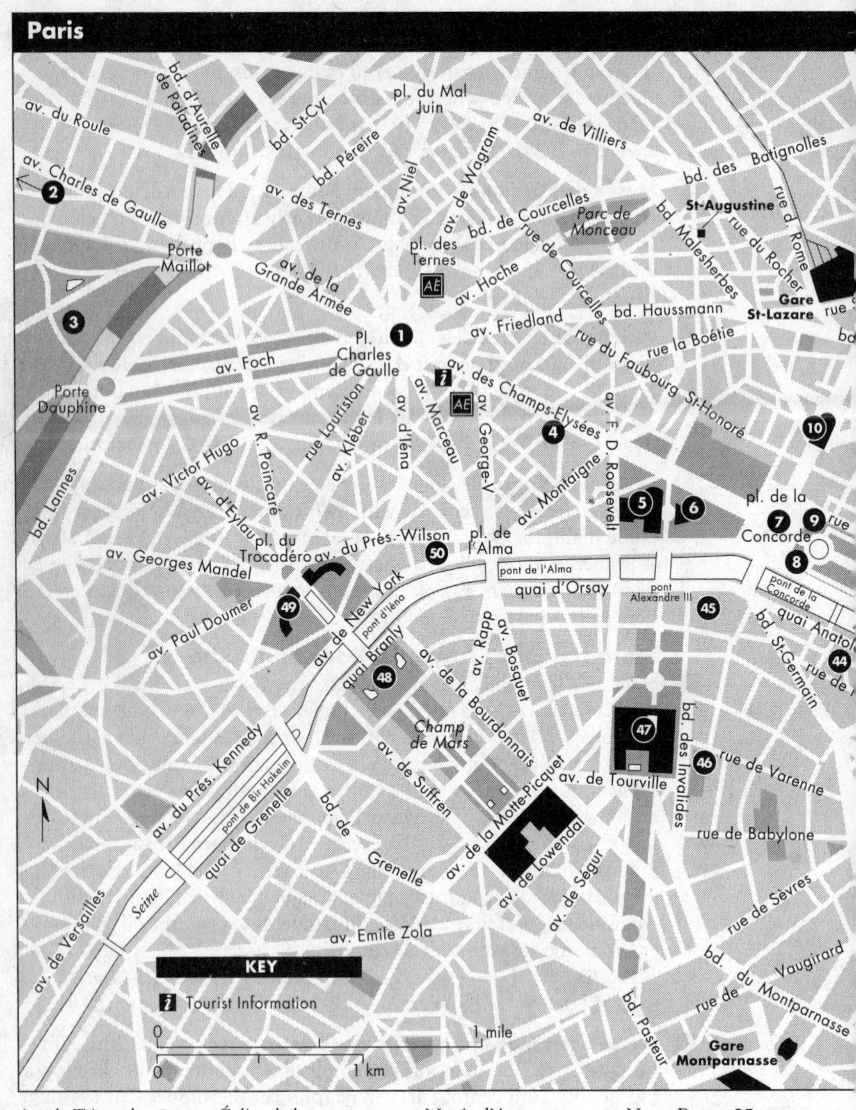

Arc de Triomphe, **1**
Arènes de Lutèce, **31**
Bercy, **27**
Bibliothèque François-Mitterrand, **29**
Bois de Boulogne, **3**
Bois de Vincennes, **28**
Centre Pompidou, **22**
Champs-Elysées, **4**
Cimetière du Père-Lachaise, **26**
La Conciergerie, **36**
La Défense, **2**
Église de la Madeleine, **10**
Grand Palais, **5**
Grands Magasins, **12**
Les Halles, **21**
Hôtel des Invalides, **47**
Hôtel de Ville, **34**
Ile St-Louis, **32**
Jardin du Luxembourg, **41**
Jardin des Plantes, **30**
Jardin des Tuileries, **17**
Louvre, **18**
Musée d'Art Moderne de la Ville de Paris, **50**
Musée du Jeu de Paume, **9**
Musée National du Moyen-Age, **37**
Musée de l'Orangerie, **8**
Musée d'Orsay, **44**
Musée Picasso, **23**
Musée Rodin, **46**
Notre-Dame, **35**
Opéra Garnier, **11**
Palais Bourbon, **45**
Palais de Chaillot, **49**
Palais-Royal, **19**
Panthéon, **39**
Parc de la Villette, **15**
Petit Palais, **6**
Place de la Bastille, **25**
Place de la Concorde, **7**
Place du Tertre, **13**
Place Vendôme, **16**

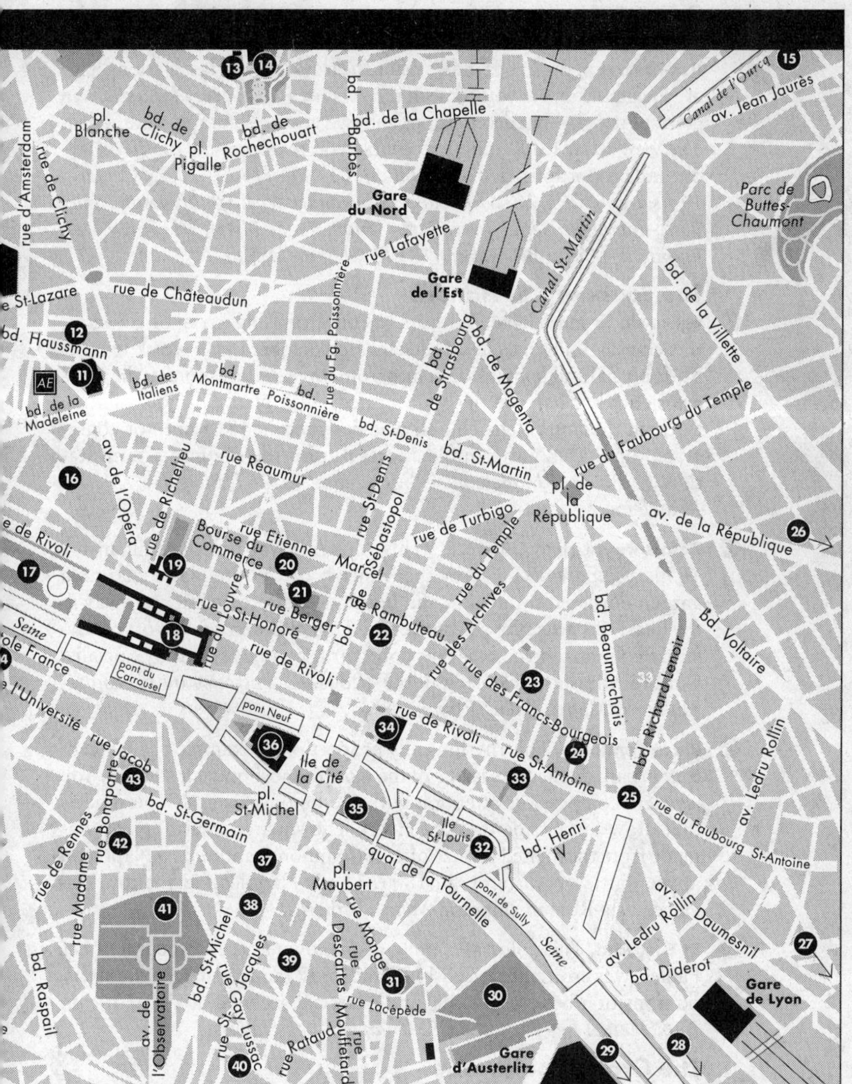

Place des Vosges, **24**
Sacré-Coeur, **14**
St-Eustache, **20**
St-Germain-des-Prés, **43**
Saint-Paul–Saint-Louis, **33**
St-Sulpice, **42**
La Sorbonne, **38**
Tour Eiffel (Eiffel Tower), **48**
Val de Grâce, **40**

Gustave Eiffel, whose skill as an engineer earned him renown as a builder of iron bridges, created his Tower for the World Exhibition of 1889. Restoration in the 1980s didn't make the elevators any faster—long lines are inevitable unless you come in the evening (when every girder is lit in glorious detail)—but decent shops and two good restaurants were added. The view from 1,000 ft up will enable you to appreciate the city's layout and proportions. ⊠ *quai Branly,* ☎ *01–44–11–23–23.* 🎫 *On foot, 14 frs; by elevator, 20–57 frs, depending on the level.* ⏲ *July–Aug., daily 9 AM–midnight; Sept.–June, Sun.–Thurs. 9 AM–11 PM, Fri., Sat. 9 AM–midnight. Métro: Bir-Hakeim, RER: Champ-de-Mars.*

The Faubourg St-Honoré

10 **Église de la Madeleine.** With its uncompromising array of columns, this church, known as La Madeleine, looks more like a Greek temple. The only natural light inside comes from three shallow domes; the walls are richly but harmoniously decorated, with plenty of gold glinting through the murk. The church was designed in 1814 but not consecrated until 1842, after futile efforts to turn the site into a train station. ⊠ *Pl. de la Madeleine.* ⏲ *Mon.–Sat. 7:30–7, Sun. 8–7. Métro: Madeleine.*

19 **Palais-Royal** (Royal-Palace). This former royal palace, built in the 1630s and now occupied by the Ministry of Culture, has a charming garden bordered by arcades and boutiques, discreetly tucked away in the heart of Paris. Not so discreet are Daniel Buren's sawn-off candy-stripe columns in the adjacent courtyard, commissioned by Socialist Culture Minister Jack Lang in the 1980s. ⊠ *Entrance on pl. André-Malraux. Métro: Palais-Royal.*

16 **Place Vendôme.** This rhythmically proportioned example of 17th-century urban architecture is one of the world's most opulent squares. Top jewelers compete for attention with the limousines and supermodels that draw up outside the Ritz Hotel. The square's central pillar was made from the melted bronze of 1,200 cannons captured by Napoléon at the Battle of Austerlitz in 1805. That's Napoléon at the top, disguised as a Roman emperor. *Métro: Tuileries.*

20 **St-Eustache.** This colossal church, also known as the Cathedral of Les Halles, was erected between 1532 and 1637, and testifies to the stylistic transition between Gothic and Classical architecture. ⊠ *2 rue du Jour. Métro: Les Halles, RER: Châtelet–Les Halles.*

The Grand Boulevards

12 **Grands Magasins** (Department Stores). Paris's most venerable department stores can be found behind the Opéra: **Galeries Lafayette** has an elegant turn-of-the-century glass dome; **Au Printemps** has an excellent view from its rooftop cafeteria. ⊠ *Bd. Haussmann. Métro: Havre-Caumartin.*

21 **Les Halles.** Since the city's much-lamented central glass-and-iron market halls were torn down during the late '60s, the area has been transformed into a trendy—albeit slightly seedy—shopping complex, Le Forum des Halles, with an extensive topiary garden basking in the shadow of the nearby **Bourse du Commerce** (Commercial Exchange) and bulky church of **St-Eustache** (☞ Faubourg St-Honoré, *above*). *Métro/RER: Les Halles.*

11 **Opéra Garnier.** The original Paris opera house was the flagship building of the Second Empire (1851–70), and its design mirrors the period's flaunt-it philosophy. Architect Charles Garnier fused elements of neoclassical architecture—bas-reliefs on facades and columns—in an exaggerated combination imbued with as much subtlety as a Wag-

nerian cymbal crash. You can visit the lavishly upholstered auditorium, with its delightful ceiling painted by Marc Chagall in 1964. The stage is the largest in the world, accommodating up to 450 players. ✉ *Pl. de l'Opéra,* ☎ *01–47–42–07–02.* ⏲ *Daily 10–5. Métro: Opéra.*

The Marais and the Bastille

27 **Bercy.** This colorful district, tucked away on the Right Bank of the Seine, south of the Gare de Lyon in the 12e arrondissement and opposite the new national library, was for centuries filled with warehouses storing wine from the provinces. The old warehouses have been replaced by the **Parc de Bercy,** a witty, state-of-the art garden. The mighty glass wall of the new **Ministère des Finances** (Finance Ministry) looms up at one end, beyond the sloping, grass-walled **Palais Omnisports** indoor stadium. Nearby, Frank Gehry's quirky, cubistic former **American Center** sounds a mournful note; it closed in 1996 for lack of funds. ✉ *rue de Bercy. Métro: Bercy.*

22 **Centre Pompidou** (Pompidou Center). The futuristic, funnel-top Pompidou Center—known to Parisians as Beaubourg, after the surrounding district—was built in the mid-1970s and named in honor of former French president Georges Pompidou (1911–74). The Center was soon attracting over 8 million visitors a year—five times more than intended. Hardly surprising, then, that it was soon showing signs of fatigue. In 1996 the government stepped in and took drastic action: shutting the Center until December 1999 and embarking on top-to-bottom renovation. A canvas teepee has been erected on the sloping esplanade in front of the Center, with a battery of computer screens to outline its future plans. Alongside you can visit the **Atelier Brancusi** (Brancusi's Studio), four reconstituted glass-fronted rooms of Romanian-born sculptor Constantin Brancusi, crammed with smooth, stylized works from throughout his career. ✉ *Pl. Georges-Pompidou,* ☎ *01–44–78–12–33.* ⏲ *Atelier Brancusi: Wed.–Mon. noon–10. Métro: Rambuteau.*

26 **Cimetière du Père-Lachaise** (Father Lachaise Cemetery). Cemeteries may not be your idea of the ultimate attraction, but this one is the largest and most interesting in Paris. It forms a veritable necropolis with cobbled avenues and tombs competing in pomposity and originality. Leading incumbents include Frédéric Chopin, Marcel Proust, Jim Morrison, Edith Piaf, and Gertrude Stein. Get a map at the entrance and track them down. ✉ *Entrances on rue des Rondeaux, bd. de Ménilmontant, and rue de la Réunion.* ⏲ *Apr.–Sept., daily 8–6; Oct.–Mar., daily 8–5. Métro: Père-Lachaise, Gambetta, Philippe-Auguste.*

34 **Hôtel de Ville** (City Hall). Overlooking the Seine, the City Hall has only been the office of the mayor since 1977—when the seat was first created in Paris. The square in front of the Hôtel de Ville was once the site of public executions. During the Commune of 1871, the Hôtel de Ville was burned to the ground. Today's exuberant building, based closely on the 16th-century Renaissance original, went up between 1874 and 1884. ✉ *Pl. de l'Hôtel-de-Ville.* ⏲ *For special exhibitions. Métro: Hôtel-de-Ville.*

★ 23 **Musée Picasso** (Picasso Museum). The Hôtel Salé, an elegant mansion in the heart of the Marais, was comprehensively restored by the French government in the 1980s to receive an extensive collection of little-known paintings, drawings, and engravings donated to the state by Picasso's heirs in lieu of death duties. ✉ *5 rue Thorigny,* ☎ *01–42–71–25–21.* ⏲ *Wed.–Mon. 9:30–6. Métro: Chemin-Vert.*

25 **Place de la Bastille.** Nothing remains of the fortress stormed at the outbreak of the French Revolution, but just to mislead you, there's a soaring gilt-edge column, topped by the figure of Liberty, commemo-

rating Parisians killed . . . in the long-forgotten uprising of 1830. Also on the square is the modern, glass-fronted **Opéra de la Bastille** (Bastille Opera) opened in 1989 in commemoration of the Revolution's bicentennial. Rather more appealing is the **Viaduc des Arts** (Arts Viaduct) that leads off down avenue Daumesnil: a disused railway viaduct converted into boutiques below and a walkway on top. *Métro: Bastille.*

★ 24 **Place des Vosges.** Built in 1605, this is the oldest square in Paris. Its harmonious proportions, soft pink brick, and cloisterlike arcades give it an aura of calm. In the far corner is the **Maison de Victor Hugo** (Victor Hugo House), containing souvenirs of the great poet's life and many of his surprisingly able paintings and ink drawings. ✉ *Maison de Victor Hugo: 6 pl. des Vosges.* ⏲ *Tues.–Sun. 10–5:45. Métro: St-Paul.*

33 **St-Paul–St-Louis.** This stately Baroque church in the Marais (1627–41) has one of the city's earliest domes, and a compelling, if melodramatic, vision of *Christ on the Mount of Olives* (1826) high up in the north transept, by a youthful Delacroix. ✉ *Rue St-Antoine. Métro: St-Paul.*

The Islands and the Latin Quarter

31 **Arènes de Lutèce** (Lutèce Arena). This Gallo-Roman arena was rediscovered only in 1869; it has since been landscaped and excavated to reveal parts of the original amphitheater, but remains one of the lesser-known points of interest in Paris. ⏲ *During daylight hrs. Métro: Monge.*

29 **Bibliothèque François-Mitterrand** (François Mitterrand Library). The last of late president Mitterrand's grand building projects opened in early 1997. Architect Dominique Perault's controversial design features four soaring 24-story L-shape towers (meant to resemble open books) around a stunning interior courtyard—sunk beneath ground level. ✉ *11 quai François-Mauriac,* ☎ *01–53–79–53–79.* ⏲ *Tues.–Sat. 10–7, Sun. noon–6. Métro: Quai de la Gare.*

36 **La Conciergerie.** This former prison has a superb vaulted 14th-century hall, the **Salles des Gens d'Armes** (Hall of the Men-at-Arms), that often hosts temporary exhibitions. The **Tour de l'Horloge** (Clock Tower) near the entrance on the quai de l'Horloge has a clock that has been ticking off time since 1370. ✉ *Entrance on quai de l'Horloge.* ⏲ *Daily 9:30–6:30 (Oct.–Mar. 10–5). Métro: Cité.*

32 **Ile St-Louis** (St-Louis Island). The city's second and smaller island, barely 650 yards long, was developed as an upscale property venture during the 17th century, and remains largely residential. From its eastern tip you can admire the curving glass facade of Jean Nouvel's Institut du Monde Arabe (Insitute of the Arab World) on the Left Bank. *Métro: Pont-Marie.*

30 **Jardin des Plantes** (Botanical Garden). Established here since the 17th century, Paris's Botanical Garden has a zoo, an aquarium, a maze, an alpine garden, hothouses, and several natural history museums: the **Musée Entomologique** (insects); the **Musée Paléontologique** (fossils and prehistoric animals); and the **Musée Minéralogique** (minerals). Don't miss the **Grande Galerie de l'Évolution** (Great Hall of Evolution) for its mind-blowing collection of stuffed and mounted animals (some now extinct). ✉ *36 rue Geoffroy-St-Hilaire.* ⏲ *Museums: Wed.–Mon. 9–11:45 and 1–4:45. Grande Galerie de l'Évolution: Wed.–Mon. 10–5, Thurs. 10–10. Métro: Monge.*

37 **Musée National du Moyen-Age** (National Museum of the Middle Ages). This museum, housed in the Hôtel de Cluny, is devoted to the late Middle Ages and Renaissance. Look for the *Lady with the Uni-*

corn tapestries and the beautifully displayed medieval statues. The gardens contain remnants of Roman baths. ⊠ *6 pl. Paul-Painlevé,* ☎ *01–53–73–78–00.* ⏲ *Wed.–Mon. 9:30–5:45. Métro: Cluny–La Sorbonne.*

35 **Notre-Dame.** Notre-Dame Cathedral, Paris's historic and geographic heart, has been a place of worship for more than 2,000 years; the present building is the fourth on this site. It was begun in 1163, making it one of the earliest Gothic cathedrals, but wasn't finished until 1345. The facade seems perfectly proportioned until you notice that the north (left) tower is wider than the south. The interior is at its lightest and least cluttered in the early morning. Bay-by-bay cleaning is gradually revealing the original honey color of the stone. Window space is limited and filled with shimmering stained glass; the circular rose windows in the transept are particularly delicate. The 387-step climb up the towers is worth the effort for a perfect view of the famous gargoyles and the heart of Paris. ⊠ *Pl. du Parvis.* ⏲ *Cathedral: daily 10–5. Treasury (religious and vestmental relics): Mon.–Sat. 10–6, Sun. 2–6. Métro: Cité.*

39 **Panthéon.** This Temple to the Famous started life as a church; its huge dome recalls that of St-Paul's in London, but dates from nearly a century later (1758–89). Since the Revolution, the crypt has contained the remains of such national heroes as Voltaire, Rousseau, and Zola. The austere interior is ringed with Puvis de Chavannes's late-19th-century frescoes, relating the life of Geneviève, patron saint of Paris. ⊠ *Pl. du Panthéon,* ☎ *01–43–54–34–51.* ⏲ *Daily 10–5:30. Métro: Cardinal-Lemoine.*

38 **La Sorbonne.** Students at Paris's ancient university—one of the oldest in Europe—used to listen to lectures in Latin, which explains why the surrounding area is known as the Quartier Latin (Latin Quarter). You can visit the main courtyard and peek into the lecture halls if they're not in use. The Baroque chapel is only open during exhibitions. ⊠ *Rue de la Sorbonne. Métro: Cluny–La Sorbonne.*

Ste-Chapelle (Holy Chapel). This chapel was built by St-Louis (Louis IX) in the 1240s to house the Crown of Thorns he had just bought from Emperor Baldwin of Constantinople. The building's lead-covered wood spire, rebuilt in 1854, rises 246 ft. The somewhat garish lower chapel is less impressive than the upper one, whose walls consist of little else but dazzling 13th-century stained glass. ⊠ *In the Palais de Justice.* ⏲ *Daily 9:30–6:30 (Oct.–Mar. 10–5). Métro: Cité.*

40 **Val de Grâce.** This domed church was designed by François Mansart and Jacques Lemercier, and erected in 1645–67 (after the Sorbonne church but before the Invalides). Its two-tier facade, with capitals and triangular pedestals, was inspired by the Counter-Reformation Jesuit architectural style, found more often in Rome than in Paris. ⊠ *1 pl. Alphonse-Laveran. RER: Port-Royal.*

From Orsay to St-Germain

41 **Jardin du Luxembourg** (Luxembourg Garden). Paris's most famous Left Bank park has tennis courts, colorful flower beds, tree-lined alleys, and a large pond (with toy boats for hire alongside). The **Palais du Luxembourg** (Luxembourg Palace), built by Queen Maria de' Medici at the beginning of the 17th century in answer to Florence's Pitti Palace, houses the French Senate and is not open to the public. *Métro: Odéon; RER: Luxembourg.*

★ 44 **Musée d'Orsay** (Orsay Museum). This museum is one of Paris's star attractions, thanks to its imaginatively housed collections of the arts (mainly French) spanning the period 1848–1914. Exhibits take up three floors, but your immediate impression may be of one single, vast hall.

This is not surprising: The museum was originally built in 1900 as a train station. The chief artistic attraction is its Impressionist collection. Other highlights include Art Nouveau furniture, a faithfully restored Belle Epoque restaurant, and a model of the Opéra quarter beneath a glass floor. ✉ *1 rue Bellechasse,* ☎ *01–40–49–48–14.* ⏲ *Tues., Wed., Fri., Sat. 10–5:30; Thurs. 10–9:30; Sun. 9–5:30. Métro: Solférino; RER: Musée d'Orsay.*

46 **Musée Rodin** (Rodin Museum). The splendid, 18th-century Hôtel Biron makes a gracious setting for the sculpture of Auguste Rodin (1840–1917). There's also a pretty garden filled with Rodin sculptures and hundreds of rosebushes. ✉ *77 rue de Varenne,* ☎ *01–47–05–01–34.* ⏲ *Tues.–Sun. 10–5. Métro: Varenne.*

45 **Palais Bourbon.** The 18th-century home of the **Assemblée Nationale** (French National Legislature) is only open during temporary exhibitions, but its colonnaded facade, commissioned by Napoléon, is a handsome sight across the Seine from place de la Concorde. ✉ *Pl. du Palais-Bourbon. Métro: Assemblée Nationale.*

43 **St-Germain-des-Prés.** The oldest church in Paris was first built to shelter a relic of the true cross, brought back from Spain in AD 542. The chancel was enlarged and the church consecrated by Pope Alexander III in 1163 (the church tower dates from this period). ✉ *Pl. St-Germain-des-Prés.* ⏲ *Weekdays 8–7:30, weekends 8 AM–9 PM. Métro: St-Germain-des-Prés.*

42 **St-Sulpice.** Stand back and admire the impressive 18th-century facade of this enormous 17th-century church, known as the Cathedral of the Left Bank. The unequal, unfinished towers strike a quirky, fallible note at odds with the chillingly impersonal interior, embellished only by the masterly wall paintings by Delacroix—notably *Jacob and the Angel*—in the first chapel on the right. ✉ *Pl. St-Sulpice. Métro: St-Sulpice.*

Montmartre

13 **Place du Tertre.** This folksy, tumbling square is the hub of Montmartre, humming most of the time with tourists and would-be painters. Its old-time charm is best appreciated over breakfast, before they all arrive. The understated facade of **St-Pierre de Montmartre** emerges sleepily around one corner of the square, as the bombastic bell-tower of the Sacré-Coeur belts out a morning call behind. *Métro: Anvers.*

14 **Sacré-Coeur.** If you start at the Anvers métro station and head up rue de Steinkerque (full of budget clothing shops), you will be greeted by the most familiar and spectacular view of the Sacré-Coeur, perched proudly atop the Butte Montmartre. The basilica was built in a bizarre, mock-Byzantine style between 1876 and 1910; although no favorite with aesthetes, it has become a major Paris landmark. It was constructed as an act of national penitence after the disastrous Franco-Prussian War of 1870—a Catholic show of strength at a time of bitter church-state conflict. ✉ *Pl. du Parvis-du-Sacré-Coeur. Métro: Anvers.*

On the Fringe

3 **Bois de Boulogne.** Class and style have been associated with "Le Bois" (The Wood) ever since it was landscaped into an upper-class playground by Haussmann in the 1850s. The attractions of this sprawling 2,200-acre wood include cafés, restaurants, racetracks, gardens, waterfalls, and two lakes. An inexpensive ferry crosses frequently to the idyllic island in the larger of the lakes, the **Lac Inférieur,** and rowboats can be rented nearby. Fairground stalls, a folly, a small zoo, and a miniature railway await youngsters at the **Jardin d'Acclimatation** (Zoo/Amuse-

ment Park). ⊠ *Jardin d'Acclimatation: bd. des Sablons,* ☎ *01–40–67–90–82.* ⏲ *Daily 10–6. Métro: Les Sablons, Porte-Maillot.*

28 **Bois de Vincennes.** This less touristy east Paris counterweight to the Bois de Boulogne has a zoo, a racetrack, and an extensive flower garden, the **Parc Floral.** You can also rent rowboats here and take them out to the two islands in **Lac Daumesnil** or to the three in **Lac des Minimes.** In addition, you can visit the **Château de Vincennes,** an imposing, high-walled castle surrounded by a dry moat and dominated by a 170-ft keep. It contains a replica of the Ste-Chapelle on Ile de la Cité. ⊠ *Château de Vincennes: av. de Paris; Parc Floral: rte. de la Pyramide.* ⏲ *Château daily 10–5; park daily 9:30–5. Métro: Château de Vincennes.*

2 **La Défense.** If you're interested in modern architecture, you'll be stimulated by the variety of skyscrapers clustered around the sculpture-littered plaza in this contemporary suburb, just west of Paris. The most famous building is the **Grande Arche,** a huge hollow cube crowning the famous vista that extends from the Louvre via the Arc de Triomphe. Tubular glass elevators whisk you to the top. ⏲ *Grande Arche: daily 10–5. Métro: Grande Arche de La Défense.*

15 **Parc de la Villette** (La Villette Park). This 130-acre site in northeast Paris has been imaginatively landscaped, with sweeping lawns, playground, moats, canopied walkways, and brightly painted pavilions. Chief attractions are the spherical **Géode** cinema; the iron and glass **Grande Halle** (Big Hall) arts center; the **Cité de la Musique** (Music Center), with its outstanding collection of musical instruments; and the **Cité des Sciences et de l'Industrie** (Industry and Science Museum), which tries to do for science and industry what the Pompidou Center does for modern art. ⊠ *221 av. Jean-Jaures, 30 av. Corentin-Cariou. Museums closed Mon. Métro: Porte de Pantin, Porte de la Villette.*

Dining

Left Bank

$$$ ★ ✕ **Le Violon d'Ingres.** Christian Constant, former head chef of the Hôtel Crillon, has created a hit with his own well-heeled bistro. The regularly revised menu may include such dishes as cream of pumpkin soup with sheep's cheese, and guinea hen on a bed of diced turnips. ⊠ *135 rue St-Dominique,* ☎ *01–45–44–15–05. Reservations essential. AE, DC, MC, V. Closed weekends. Métro: École-Militaire.*

$$ ✕ **Campagne et Provence.** On the quai across from Notre-Dame, this pleasant little restaurant serves Provençal cuisine including grilled John Dory with preserved fennel, and peppers stuffed with cod and eggplant. ⊠ *25 quai de la Tournelle, 5e,* ☎ *01–43–54–05–17. MC, V. Closed Sun. No lunch Sat., Mon. Métro: Maubert-Mutualité.*

$$ ★ ✕ **Philippe Detourbe.** Sample Detourbe's spectacular food at remarkably good prices amid black lacquer, mirrors, and Burgundy velvet upholstery. The menu of contemporary French cooking changes with every meal. ⊠ *8 rue Nicolas Charlet, 15e,* ☎ *01–42–19–08–59. Reservations essential. MC, V. Closed Sun. No lunch Sat. Métro: Pasteur.*

$–$$ ✕ **Au Bon Accueil.** Book a table at this popular bistro as soon as you get to town. The excellent *cuisine du marché* (menu based on what's in the markets that day) has made it a hit, as have the delicious, homemade desserts. ⊠ *14 rue de Montessuy, 7e,* ☎ *01–47–05–46–11. Reservations essential. MC, V. Closed Sun. Métro, RER: Pont l'Alma.*

$ ✕ **Le Bouillon Racine.** Originally a *bouillon,* a Parisian soup restaurant popular at the turn of the century, this two-story place is now a delightfully renovated Belle Epoque oasis with a good Franco-Belgian menu. ⊠ *3 rue Racine, 6e,* ☎ *01–44–32–15–60. Reservations essential. AE, MC, V. Closed Sun. Métro: Odéon.*

$ ✕ **Chantairelle.** Not only is delicious south-central Auvergne cuisine served at this restaurant, but the owners also offer a full regional experience. Hence the decor: recycled barn timbers and essential oils diffusing local scents. The food is hearty and the portions copious. ✉ *17 rue Laplace, 5e, ☎ 01–46–33–18–59. MC, V. Closed Sun. No lunch Sat. Métro: Maubert-Mutualité.*

$ ✕ **Le Terroir.** A jolly crowd of regulars makes this little bistro festive. The solidly classical menu includes an assortment of salads, and calves' liver, or monkfish with saffron. ✉ *11 bd. Arago, 13e, ☎ 01–47–07–36–99. AE, MC, V. Closed Sun. No lunch Sat. Métro: Les Gobelins.*

Right Bank

$$$$ ★ ✕ **Pierre Gagnaire.** Legendary chef Pierre Gagnaire's cooking is at once intellectual and poetic—unexpected tastes and textures are brought together in a sensational experience. The only drawback is the amateurish service and the puzzlingly brief wine list. ✉ *6 rue de Balzac, 8e, ☎ 01–44–35–18–25. Reservations essential. AE, DC, MC, V. Closed Sun. Métro: Charles-de-Gaulle–Etoile.*

$$$$ ✕ **Le Grand Véfour.** Luminaries from Napoléon to Colette to Jean Cocteau frequented this intimate and sumptuous address under the arcades of the Palais-Royal. Chef Guy Martin impresses with his unique blend of such sophisticated yet rustic dishes as roast lamb in a juice of herbs. ✉ *17 rue Beaujolais, 1er, ☎ 01–42–96–56–27. Reservations essential 1 wk in advance. Jacket and tie. AE, DC, MC, V. Closed weekends and Aug. Métro: Palais-Royal.*

$$$$ ★ ✕ **Guy Savoy.** Top chef Guy Savoy's other five bistros have not distracted him too much from his handsome luxury restaurant near the Arc de Triomphe. The oysters in aspic, and grilled pigeon reveal the magnitude of his talent. ✉ *18 rue Troyon, 17e, ☎ 01–43–80–40–61. AE, MC, V. Closed Sun. No lunch Sat. Métro: Charles de Gaulle–Étoile.*

$$$ ✕ **Le Cercle Ledoyen.** For about 250 francs a dinner—wine included—you can sample renowned chef Ghislaine Arabian's northern French cuisine at this luxury brasserie. The handsome, curved dining room with a view of the surrounding park is a pleasure year-round, and the terrace is a special treat in warm weather. ✉ *1 av. Dutuit, 8e, ☎ 01–47–42–23–23. AE, DC, MC, V. Closed Sun. Métro: Champs-Elysées–Clemenceau.*

$$ ✕ **Chardenoux.** A bit off the beaten path but well worth the effort, this cozy neighborhood bistro with etched-glass windows, dark bentwood furniture, and a long zinc bar attracts a cross-section of savvy Parisians. The traditional cooking is first-rate, from the delicious foie gras salad to the veal chop with morels. ✉ *1 rue Jules-Valles, 11e, ☎ 01–43–71–49–52. AE, V. Closed weekends, Aug. Métro: Charonne.*

$$ ✕ **Chez Georges.** The traditional bistro cooking is good—herring, sole, kidneys, steak, and *frites* (fries)—but the atmosphere is better. A wood-paneled entry leads you to an elegant and unpretentious dining room where one long, white-clothed stretch of table lines the mirrored walls. ✉ *1 rue du Mail, 2e, ☎ 01–42–60–07–11. AE, DC, MC, V. Closed Sun. and Aug. Métro: Sentier.*

$$ ★ ✕ **Le Repaire de Cartouche.** Near the Cirque d'Hiver in the Bastille, this split-level, '50s-style bistro with dark-wood decor is the latest good-value sensation in Paris. Young chef Rodolphe Paquin is a creative and impeccably trained cook who does a stylish take on earthy French regional dishes. ✉ *99 rue Amelot, 11e, ☎ 01–47–00–25–86. AE, MC, V. Reservations essential. Closed Sun., dinner Mon. Métro: Filles du Calvaire.*

$–$$ ✕ **Chez Michel.** If you're willing to go out of your way for excellent food at fair prices, even if the decor and the neighborhood are drab, then this place is for you. Chef Thierry Breton pulls a stylish crowd with his wonderful cuisine du marché and dishes from his native Brittany, including lasagna stuffed with chèvre cheese. ✉ *10 rue Belzunce, 10e, ☎ 01-44-53-06-20. Reservations essential. MC, V. Closed Sun., Mon. No lunch Sat. Métro: Gare du Nord.*

$ ✕ **Le Moi.** At this superb Vietnamese restaurant near the Opéra, sample *nems* (deep-fried mini spring rolls); steamed dumplings; and chicken, beef, and seafood salads enlivened with lemongrass and lemon basil. Service is prompt and friendly. ✉ *5 rue Danou, 1er, ☎ 01-47-03-92-05. MC, V. Closed Sun. No lunch Sat. Métro: Opéra.*

Lodging

Left Bank

$$$$ **Montalembert.** Whether appointed with traditional or contemporary furnishings, rooms at the Montalembert are all about simple lines and chic luxury. Ask about special packages if you're staying for more than three nights. ✉ *3 rue de Montalembert, 75007, ☎ 01-45-49-68-68, 800/628-8929 in the U.S., FAX 01-45-49-69-49. 50 rooms and 6 suites. Restaurant, bar, air-conditioning, in-room modem lines, in-room safes, room service, in-room VCRs, baby-sitting, meeting rooms. AE, DC, MC, V. Métro: Rue du Bac.*

$$$$ ★ **Relais St-Germain.** The interior-designer owners of this hotel have exquisite taste and a superb respect for tradition and detail. Moreover, the rooms are at least twice the size of those at other area hotels. Much of the furniture was selected with a knowledgeable eye from the city's *brocantes* (second-hand dealers). Breakfast is included. ✉ *9 carrefour de l'Odéon, 75006, ☎ 01-43-29-12-05, FAX 01-46-33-45-30. 21 rooms, 1 suite. AE, DC, MC, V. Métro: Odéon.*

$$$ **Jardin du Luxembourg.** Blessed with a charming staff and a stylish look, this hotel is one of the most sought-after in the Latin Quarter. Rooms are a bit small (common for this neighborhood) but intelligently furnished to save space, and warmly decorated *à la provençale.* Ask for one with a balcony overlooking the street; the best, No. 25, has a peekaboo view of the Eiffel Tower. ✉ *5 impasse Royer-Collard, 75005, ☎ 01-40-46-08-88, FAX 01-40-46-02-28. 27 rooms. Air-conditioning, no-smoking rooms, in-room safes, sauna. AE, DC, MC, V. Métro: Luxembourg.*

$$–$$$ ★ **Le Tourville.** Here is a rare find: an intimate, upscale hotel at affordable prices. Each room has crisp, virgin-white damask upholstery set against pastel or ocher walls, a smattering of antiques, original artwork, and fabulous old mirrors. ✉ *16 av. de Tourville, 75007, ☎ 01-47-05-62-62, 800/528-3549 in the U.S., FAX 01-47-05-43-90. 27 rooms and 3 junior suites. Bar, air-conditioning, no-smoking rooms, laundry service. AE, DC, MC, V. Métro: École Militaire.*

$$ **Atelier Montparnasse.** This Art Deco–inspired gem was designed with style and comfort in mind. Rooms are tastefully decorated and spacious; one sleeps three; bathrooms feature mosaic reproductions of famous French paintings. The hotel is within walking distance of the Luxembourg Gardens and St-Germain-des-Prés. ✉ *49 rue Vavin, 75006, ☎ 01-46-33-60-00, FAX 01-40-51-04-21. 17 rooms. AE, DC, MC, V. Métro: Vavin.*

$$ **Latour Maubourg.** In the bourgeois heart of the smart seventh arrondissement, a stone's throw from Invalides, this friendly hotel has been inked into many a traveler's journal. Decor is homey and unpretentious, and with just 10 rooms, the accent is on intimacy and personalized service. ✉ *150 rue de Grenelle, 75007, ☎ 01-47-05-16-16, FAX 01-47-05-16-14. 9 rooms and 1 suite. In-room safes. MC, V. Métro: Latour Maubourg.*

$ ★ **Familia.** The hospitable Gaucheron family bend over backwards for you. About half the rooms feature romantic sepia frescoes of celebrated Paris scenes; others are appointed with exquisite Louis XV–style furnishings, or nice mahogany pieces. Book a month ahead for one with a walk-out balcony on the second or fifth floor. ✉ *11 rue des Écoles, 75005,* ☎ *01–43–54–55–27,* FAX *01–43–29–61–77. 30 rooms, 16 with shower. AE, MC, V. Métro: Cardinal Lemoine.*

Right Bank

$$$$ **Costes.** Jean-Louis and Gilbert Costes's sumptuous hotel is the darling of the fashion and media set. Conjuring up the palaces of Napoléon III, rooms are swathed in rich garnet and bronze tones and contain a luxurious mélange of patterned fabrics, heavy swags, and enough brocade and fringe to blanket the Champs-Elysées. ✉ *239 rue St-Honoré, 75001,* ☎ *01–42–44–50–50,* FAX *01–42–44–50–01. 85 rooms. Restaurant, bar, air-conditioning, in-room modem lines, in-room safes, no-smoking rooms, room service, indoor pool, sauna, exercise room, laundry service. AE, DC, MC, V. Métro: Tuileries.*

$$$$ ★ **Lancaster.** The Lancaster—one of Paris's most venerable institutions—has been meticulously transformed into one of the city's most modish luxury hotels, and is now part of the Savoy group. A seamless blend of the traditional and the contemporary, the overall feel is one of timeless elegance. ✉ *7 rue de Berri, 75008,* ☎ *01–40–76–40–76, 800/63-SAVOY in the U.S.,* FAX *01–40–76–40–00. 60 rooms and 10 suites. Restaurant, bar, air-conditioning, in-room modem lines, in-room safes, room service, in-room VCRs, sauna, exercise room, baby-sitting, laundry service, meeting rooms. AE, DC, MC, V. Métro: George-V.*

$$$$ **Pavillon de la Reine.** This magnificent mansion, reconstructed from original plans, is on the place des Vosges. It's filled with Louis XIII–style fireplaces and antiques. Ask for a duplex with French windows overlooking the first of two flower-filled courtyards behind the historic Queen's Pavilion. ✉ *28 pl. des Vosges, 75003,* ☎ *01–40–29–19–19, 800/447–7462 in the U.S.,* FAX *01–40–29–19–20. 30 rooms and 25 suites. Bar, breakfast room, air-conditioning, room service, laundry service, free parking. AE, DC, MC, V. Métro: Bastille, St-Paul.*

$–$$$ **Louvre Forum.** This friendly hotel is a find: Smack in the center of town, it has clean, comfortable, well-equipped rooms (with satellite TV) at extremely reasonable prices. ✉ *25 rue du Bouloi, 75001,* ☎ *01–42–36–54–19,* FAX *01–42–33–66–31. 27 rooms, 16 with shower. AE, DC, MC, V. Métro: Louvre.*

$$ **Bretonnerie.** This small hotel is in a 17th-century *hôtel particulier* (town house) on a tiny street in the Marais. Rooms are decorated in Louis XIII style, complete with upholstered walls, but vary considerably in size from spacious to cramped. ✉ *22 rue Ste-Croix-de-la-Bretonnerie, 75004,* ☎ *01–48–87–77–63,* FAX *01–42–77–26–78. 27 rooms and 3 suites. In-room safes. MC, V. Métro: Hôtel de Ville.*

$$ ★ **Caron de Beaumarchais.** The theme of this intimate jewel is the work of Caron de Beaumarchais, who wrote the *Marriage of Figaro* in 1778. Rooms are faithfully decorated to reflect the taste of 18th-century French nobility. The second- and fifth-floor rooms with balconies are the largest; those on the sixth floor have beguiling views across Right Bank rooftops. ✉ *12 rue Vieille-du-Temple, 75004,* ☎ *01–42–72–34–12,* FAX *01–42–72–34–63. 19 rooms, 2 with shower. AE, DC, MC, V. Métro: Hôtel de Ville.*

$ **Castex.** In a Revolution-era building in the Marais, this hotel is a bargain hunter's dream. Rooms are low on frills but squeaky clean, the owners are extremely friendly, and the prices are rock-bottom, which ensures that the hotel is often booked months ahead by a largely young, American clientele. There's no elevator, and the only TV is on the ground floor. ✉ *5 rue Castex, 75004,* ☎ *01–42–72–31–52,* FAX *01–42–72–57–91. 27 rooms, 23 with shower. MC, V. Métro: Bastille.*

Nightlife and the Arts

Look for the weekly magazines *Pariscope, L'Officiel des Spectacles,* and *Figaroscope,* which contain detailed entertainment listings. The Paris Tourist Office has a **24-hour English-language hot line** (☎ 01–49–52–53–56) with information about weekly events. Buy tickets at the place of performance; otherwise, try hotels or such travel agencies as **Paris-Vision** (✉ 1 rue Auber, 9e, ☎ 01–40–06–01–00, métro Opéra). Tickets for most concerts can be bought at **FNAC** (✉ 1–5 rue Pierre Lescot, Forum des Halles, 1e, ☎ 01–40–41–40–00, métro Châtelet–Les Halles). Half-price tickets for many same-day theater performances are available at the **Kiosques Théâtre** (✉ across from 15 pl. de la Madeleine, métro Madeleine, and in front of the Gare Montparnasse at ✉ pl. Raoul Dautry, 14e, métro Montparnasse-Bienvenue). It's open Tuesday–Sunday 12:30–7:30; expect a line.

The Arts

Getting a ticket for an opera or ballet performance is not always easy and may require luck, preplanning, or a well-connected hotel receptionist. Beware of scalpers: Counterfeit tickets have been known to be sold. Inexpensive organ or chamber music concerts proliferate in churches throughout the city.

CLASSICAL MUSIC AND OPERA

Following are other venues for fine orchestral concerts and recitals: **Cité de la Musique** (✉ parc de la Villette, 221 av. Jean-Jaurès, 19e, ☎ 01–44–84–44–84, métro Porte de Pantin); **Salle Pleyel** (✉ 252 rue du Faubourg-St-Honoré, 8e, ☎ 01–45–61–53–00, métro Ternes); and the **Théâtre des Champs-Elysées** (✉ 15 av. Montaigne, 8e, ☎ 01–49–52–50–50, métro Alma-Marceau). The **Opéra de la Bastille** (✉ pl. de la Bastille, 12e, ☎ 08–36–69–78–68, métro Bastille) has replaced the 19th-century Opéra Garnier as the main Paris operatic venue since opening in 1989.

DANCE

Opéra Garnier (✉ pl. de l'Opéra, 9e, ☎ 08–36–69–78–68, métro Opéra), the "old Opéra," now concentrates on dance: In addition to being the home of the well-reputed Paris Ballet, it also bills a number of major foreign troupes. The **Théâtre de la Ville** (✉ 2 pl. du Châtelet, 4e, métro Châtelet and 31 rue des Abbesses, 18e, métro Abbesses, ☎ 01–42–74–22–77 for both) is the place for contemporary dance.

FILM

There are hundreds of movie theaters in Paris, and some of them, especially in such principal tourist areas as the Champs-Elysées, Les Halles, Odéon and the boulevard des Italiens near the Opéra, run English films marked *"version originale"* (v.o., i.e., not dubbed). Admission is around 40–50 francs, with reduced rates on Monday. Classics and independent films often play in Latin Quarter theaters. Movie fanatics should check out the **Cinémathèque Française** (✉ 42 bd. de Bonne-Nouvelle, 10e, ☎ 01–47–04–24–24, métro Bonne-Nouvelle), where classic French and international films are shown Wednesday–Sunday.

THEATER

There is no Parisian equivalent to Broadway or the West End, although a number of theaters line the grand boulevards between the Opéra and République. Shows are mostly in French. The **Comédie Française** (✉ pl. André-Malraux, 1er, ☎ 01–44–58–15–15, métro Palais-Royal) performs distinguished classical drama by Racine, Molière, and

Corneille. The **Théâtre de la Huchette** (✉ 23 rue de la Huchette, 5e, ☎ 01–43–26–38–99, métro St-Michel) is a tiny venue where Ionesco's short plays make a deliberately ridiculous mess of the French language. The **Théâtre de l'Odéon** (✉ pl. de l'Odéon, 6e, ☎ 01–44–41–36–36, métro Odéon) has made pan-European theater its primary focus.

Nightlife

BARS AND CLUBS

The hottest area at the moment is around Ménilmontant. Nightlife is still hopping in and around the Bastille, and the Left Bank has a bit of everything. The Champs-Elysées is making a comeback, though the clientele remains predominantly foreign. Gay and lesbian bars and clubs are mostly concentrated in the Marais (especially around rue Ste-Croix-de-la-Bretonnerie) and include some of the most happening addresses in the city.

If you want to dance the night away, the best addresses are the trendy **Les Bains** (✉ 7 rue du Bourg-l'Abbé, 3e, ☎ 01–48–87–01–80, métro Etienne-Marcel); super chic **Le Cabaret** (✉ 68 rue Pierre-Charron, 8e, ☎ 01–42–89–44–14, métro Franklin-D.-Roosevelt); and the predominantly gay **Queen** (✉ 102 av. des Champs-Elysées, 8e, ☎ 01–53–89–08–90, métro George V).

Barfly (✉ 49–51 av. George V, 8e, ☎ 01–53–67–84–60, métro George V) has its followers among the business and fashion crowd who come to this place to see and be seen. **Buddha Bar** (✉ 8 rue Boissy d'Anglas, 8e, ☎ 01–53–05–90–00, métro Concorde) has a spacious mezzanine bar that overlooks the dining room where cuisines, east and west, meet somewhere in California. **Café Charbon** (✉ 109 rue Oberkampf, 11e, ☎ 01–43–57–55–13, métro St-Maur/Parmentier) is a beautifully restored 19th-century café, whose trend-setting clientele chats to jazz in the background.

La Champmeslé (✉ 4 rue Chabanais, 2e, ☎ 01–42–96–85–20, métro Bourse) is the hub of lesbian nightlife with a dusky back room reserved exclusively for women. **China Club** (✉ 50 rue de Charenton, 12e, ☎ 01–43–43–82–02, métro Ledru-Rollin) has three floors of bars and a restaurant with lacquered furnishings and a colonial Orient theme. **Le Moloko** (✉ 26 rue Fontaine, 9e, ☎ 01–48–74–50–26, métro Blanche) is a popular, smoky, late-night bar with several rooms, a mezzanine, and a small dance floor.

CABARET

Paris's cabarets are household names, shunned by Parisians and beloved of foreign tourists, who flock to the shows. You can dine at many of them; prices range from 200 francs (simple admission plus one drink) to more than 800 francs (dinner plus show). **Crazy Horse** (✉ 12 av. George V, 8e, ☎ 01–47–23–32–32, métro Alma-Marceau) is one of the best-known clubs for pretty dancers and raunchy routines. **Lido** (✉ 116 bis av. des Champs-Elysées, 8e, ☎ 01–40–76–56–10, métro George-V) stars the famous Bluebell Girls; the owners claim that no show in Las Vegas rivals it for special effects. **Moulin Rouge** (✉ pl. Blanche, 18e, ☎ 01–46–06–00–19, métro Blanche), the old favorite at the foot of Montmartre, mingles the Doriss Girls, a horse, and the cancan in an extravagant spectacle.

JAZZ CLUBS

The French take jazz seriously, and Paris is one of the great jazz cities of the world. For nightly schedules consult the specialty magazines *Jazz Hot* or *Jazz Magazine*. Nothing gets going till 10 or 11 PM, and entry prices vary widely from about 40 francs to over 100 francs.

The **New Morning** (✉ 7 rue des Petites-Ecuries, 10e, ☎ 01–45–23–51–41, métro Château-d'Eau) is a premier spot for serious fans of avant-garde jazz, folk, and world music; decor is spartan, the mood reverential. The greatest names in French and international jazz have been playing at **Le Petit Journal** (✉ 71 bd. St-Michel, 5e, ☎ 01–43–26–28–59, RER Luxembourg) for decades. Sundays are devoted to the blues. **Le Petit Opportun** (✉ 15 rue des Lavandières-Ste-Opportune, 1er, ☎ 01–42–36–01–36, métro Châtelet), in a converted bistro, sometimes features top-flight American soloists with French backup.

ROCK CLUBS

Lists of upcoming concerts are posted on boards in the FNAC stores. Following are the best places to catch big French and international stars: **Palais Omnisports de Paris-Bercy** (✉ rue de Bercy, 12e, ☎ 01–44–68–44–68, métro Bercy); and **Zenith** (✉ Parc de la Villette, 19e, ☎ 01–42–08–60–00, métro Porte-de-Pantin). For emerging talent and lesser known groups, try : **Bataclan** (✉ 50 bd. Voltaire, 11e, ☎ 01–47–00–30–12, métro Oberkampf); or **Elysée Montmartre** (✉ 72 bd. Rochechouart, 18e, ☎ 01–44–92–45–45, métro Anvers).

Shopping

Antiques

Antiques dealers proliferate in the **Carré Rive Gauche** (✉ between St-Germain-des-Prés and the Musée d'Orsay). There are also several antiques dealers around the **Drouot** auction house (✉ corner of rue Rossini and rue Drouot, 9e, métro Richelieu-Drouot) near the Opéra . The **Louvre des Antiquaires** (✉ pl. du Palais-Royal, 1er, métro Palais-Royal) is a stylish shopping mall devoted primarily to antiques. At the **Village Suisse** (✉ 78 av. de Suffren, 15e, métro La Motte–Picquet-Grenelle), near the Champ de Mars, over 100 dealers are grouped together.

Boutiques

Only Milan can compete with Paris for the title of Capital of European Chic. The top designer shops are found on **avenue Montaigne, rue du Faubourg-St-Honoré,** and **place des Victoires.** The areas surrounding **St-Germain-des-Prés** on the Left Bank is a mecca for small specialty shops and boutiques, and has recently seen an influx of the elite names in haute couture. Scores of trendy boutiques can be found in the **Bastille** and **Les Halles.** Between the pre-Revolution mansions and tiny kosher food stores that characterize the **Marais** are numerous gift shops and clothing stores. The streets to the north of the Marais, close to the Arts-et-Métiers métro stop, are historically linked to the cloth trade, and some shops sell garments at wholesale prices. Also search for bargains along the streets around the foot of Montmartre, or in the designer discount shops (Cacharel, Rykiel, Dorotennis) along **rue d'Alésia** in Montparnasse.

Department Stores

Au Bon Marché (✉ 22 rue de Sèvres, 7e, métro Sèvres-Babylone) is the leading department store on the Left Bank. **Au Printemps** (✉ 64 bd. Haussmann, 9e, métro Havre-Caumartin) is perhaps the most famous Paris department store; its distinctive narrow domes add an Art Nouveau touch to boulevard Haussmann. **Galeries Lafayette** (✉ 40 bd. Haussmann, 9e, métro Chaussée-d'Antin) has a comprehensive array of fashionable goods beneath its shimmering turn-of-the-century glass cupola. **La Samaritaine** (✉ 19 rue de la Monnaie, 1er, métro Pont-Neuf) occupies several buildings near the Louvre; building No. 2 is an airy Art Nouveau emporium overlooking the Seine.

Food and Flea Markets

Every *quartier* (neighborhood) has at least one open-air food market. Sunday morning till 1 PM is usually a good time to go; they are likely to be closed Monday. The **Marché aux Puces de St-Ouen** (métro Porte de Clignancourt), just north of Paris, is one of Europe's largest flea markets; it's open Saturday–Monday. Best bargains are to be had early in the morning. There are also smaller flea markets at the **Porte de Vanves** and **Porte de Montreuil** (weekends only).

Gift Ideas

Old prints are sold by ***bouquinistes*** (secondhand booksellers) in stalls along the banks of the Seine. **Guerlain** (✉ 47 rue Bonaparte, 6e, métro Mabillon) sells legendary French perfumes. The **Musée des Arts Décoratifs** (✉ 107 rue de Rivoli, 1er, métro Palais-Royal) has state-of-the-art home decorations. **Le Cave Augé** (✉ 116 bd. Haussmann, 8e, métro St-Augustin) is one of the best wine shops in Paris. **Fauchon** (✉ 30 pl. de la Madeleine, 8e, métro Madeleine) is an upscale grocery with regional specialty foods, herbs, and pâtés. **Hédiard** (✉ 21 pl. de la Madeleine, 8e, métro Madeleine) is a super-deluxe delicatessen with a wide choice of French specialties.

Paris Essentials

Arriving and Departing

BY BUS

Long-distance bus journeys within France are uncommon, which may be why Paris has no central bus depot. But if you do need to take a bus in France, contact **Eurolines** (✉ 28 av. du Général-de-Gaulle, Bagnolet, ☎ 01–49–72–51–51).

BY CAR

In a country as highly centralized as France, it is no surprise that expressways converge on the capital from every direction: A1 from the north (225 km/140 mi to Lille); A13 from Normandy (225 km/140 mi to Caen); A4 from the east (499 km/310 mi to Strasbourg); A10 from the southwest (579 km/360 mi to Bordeaux); and A7 from the Alps and Riviera (466 km/290 mi to Lyon). Each connects with the *périphérique*, the beltway. Exits are named by "porte" (gateway) and are not numbered. The "Périphe" can be fast—but gets very busy; try to avoid it between 7:30 and 10 AM and between 4:30 and 7:30 PM.

BY PLANE

International flights arrive at either **Charles de Gaulle Airport** (also called Roissy), 24 km (15 mi) northeast of Paris, or at **Orly Airport,** 16 km (10 mi) south of the city. Both airports have two terminals.

Between the Airport and Downtown. Both airports have their own train stations from which you can take the **RER** to Paris. The advantages of this are speed, price (47 frs to Paris from Roissy, 57 frs from Orly on the shuttle-train Orlyval), and the RER's direct link with the métro system. The disadvantage is having to lug your bags around. **Taxi** fares from both airports to Paris range from 150 to 250 francs, with a 6-franc surcharge per bag. The **Paris Airports Service** takes you by eight-passenger van to your destination in Paris from de Gaulle: 140 francs (one person) or 170 francs (two); Orly: 110 francs (one), 130 francs (two), less for groups. You need to book at least two days in advance (there are English-speaking clerks); call ☎ 33–1/49–62–78–78 or fax FAX 33–1/49–62–78–79.

From Roissy **Air France Buses** (open to all) leave every 15 minutes from 5:40 AM to 11 PM. The fare is 55 francs and the trip takes from 40 minutes to 1½ hours during rush hour. You arrive at the Arc de Triomphe or Porte Maillot, on the Right Bank by the Hôtel Concorde-Lafayette. From Orly, buses operated by Air France leave every 12 minutes from 6 AM to 11 PM and arrive at the Air France terminal near Les Invalides on the Left Bank. The fare is 40 francs, and the trip takes between 30 and 60 minutes, depending on traffic. Alternatively, the **Roissybus,** operated by Paris Transport Authority (RATP), runs directly to and from rue Scribe, by the Opéra, every 15 minutes and costs 45 francs. RATP also runs the **Orlybus** to and from Denfert-Rochereau and Orly every 15 minutes for 30 francs; the trip takes around 35 minutes.

BY TRAIN

Paris has five international stations: **Gare du Nord** (for northern France, northern Europe, and England via Calais or the Channel Tunnel); **Gare de l'Est** (for Strasbourg, Luxembourg, Basel, and central Europe); **Gare de Lyon** (for Lyon, Marseille, the Riviera, Geneva, and Italy); **Gare d'Austerlitz** (for the Loire Valley, southwest France, and Spain); and Gare St-Lazare (for Normandy and England via Dieppe). The **Gare Montparnasse** serves western France (mainly Nantes and Brittany) and is the terminal for the TGV Atlantic service from Paris to Bordeaux. For train information call ☏ 08–36–35–35–35 . You can reserve tickets at any Paris station regardless of the destination. Go to the Grandes Lignes counter for travel within France or to the Billets Internationaux desk if you're heading out of France.

Getting Around

Paris is relatively small as capital cities go, and most of its prize monuments and museums are within walking distance of one another. A river cruise is a pleasant way to get an overview. The most convenient form of public transportation is the métro; buses are a slower alternative, though they do allow you to see more of the city. Taxis are not very expensive, but are not always so easy to find. Car travel within Paris is best avoided because finding parking is difficult and there is often a lot of traffic.

BY BUS

Most buses run from around 6 AM to 8:30 PM; some continue until midnight. Noctambus (night buses) operate from 1 AM to 6 AM between Châtelet and nearby suburbs. They can be stopped by hailing them at any point on their route. You can use your métro tickets on the buses, or you can buy a one-ride ticket on board. You need to show weekly/monthly/special tickets to the driver; if you have individual tickets, state your destination and be prepared to punch one or more tickets in the red and gray machines on board the bus.

BY MÉTRO

There are 13 métro lines crisscrossing Paris and the nearby suburbs, and you are seldom more than a five-minute walk from the nearest station. It is essential to know the name of the last station on the line you take, since this name appears on all signs within the system. A connection (you can make as many as you please on one ticket) is called a *correspondance.* At junction stations illuminated orange signs bearing the names of each line terminus appear over the corridors that lead to the various correspondances.

The métro runs from 5:30 AM to 1:15 AM. Some lines and stations in the seedier parts of Paris are a bit risky at night—in particular, Line 2 (Porte-Dauphine–Nation) and the northern section of Line 13 from St-Lazare to St-Denis/Asnières. The long, bleak corridors at Jaurès and Stalingrad are a haven for pickpockets and purse snatchers. But the Paris métro is relatively safe, as long as you don't walk around with your wallet in your back pocket or travel alone (especially women) late at night.

Paris Métro

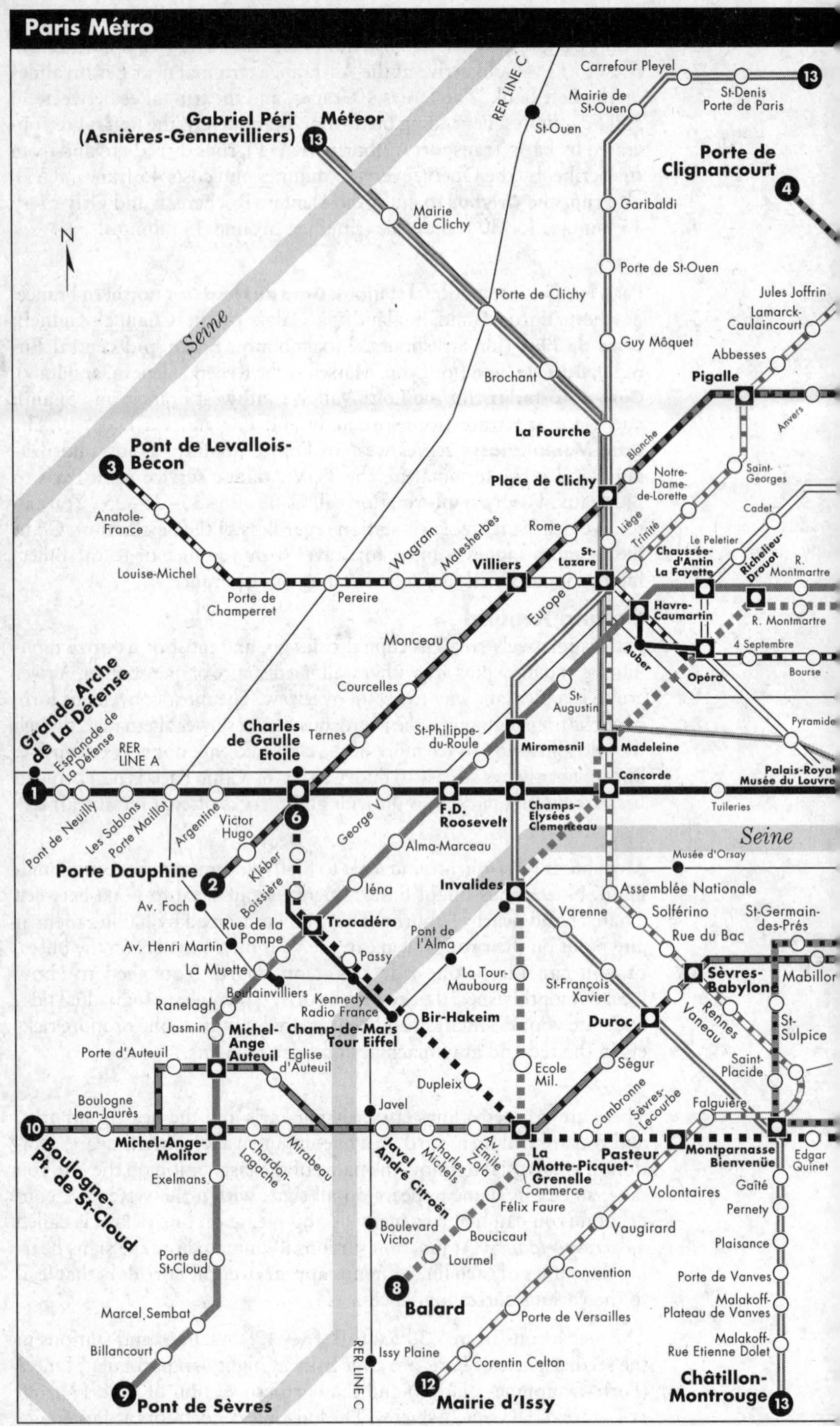
Gabriel Péri
(Asnières-Gennevilliers)
Méteor
RER LINE C
St-Ouen
Carrefour Pleyel
Mairie de
St-Ouen
St-Denis
Porte de Paris
Porte de
Clignancourt
Mairie
de Clichy
Garibaldi
Porte de St-Ouen
Porte de Clichy
Jules Joffrin
Lamarck-
Caulaincourt
Seine
Guy Môquet
Brochant
Abbesses
Pigalle
Anvers
La Fourche
Blanche
Pont de Levallois-
Bécon
Saint-
Georges
Notre-
Dame-
de-Lorette
Place de Clichy
Cadet
Anatole-
France
Rome
Liège
Trinité
Le Peletier
Chaussée-
d'Antin
La Fayette
Richelieu-
Drouot
R.
Montmartre
Wagram
Malesherbes
St-
Lazare
Louise-Michel
Villiers
Porte de
Champerret
Pereire
Europe
Havre-
Caumartin
R. Montmartre
Monceau
Auber
4 Septembre
Opéra
Bourse
Courcelles
St-
Augustin
Grande Arche
de La Défense
Esplanade de
La Défense
RER
LINE A
Charles
de Gaulle
Etoile
Ternes
St-Philippe-
du-Roule
Miromesnil
Madeleine
Pyramides
Palais-Royal
Musée du Louvre
Concorde
Pont de Neuilly
Les Sablons
Porte Maillot
Argentine
Victor
Hugo
George V
F.D.
Roosevelt
Champs-
Elysées
Clemenceau
Tuileries
Seine
Porte Dauphine
Kléber
Alma-Marceau
Musée d'Orsay
Boissière
Iéna
Invalides
Assemblée Nationale
Av. Foch
Rue de la
Pompe
Trocadéro
Pont de
l'Alma
Varenne
Solférino
St-Germain-
des-Prés
Av. Henri Martin
Passy
Rue du Bac
La Muette
La Tour-
Maubourg
St-François
Xavier
Sèvres-
Babylone
Mabillon
Boulainvilliers
Kennedy
Radio France
Bir-Hakeim
Ranelagh
Champ-de-Mars
Tour Eiffel
Duroc
Rennes
Vaneau
St-
Sulpice
Jasmin
Michel-
Ange
Auteuil
Eglise
d'Auteuil
Porte d'Auteuil
Ecole
Mil.
Ségur
Saint-
Placide
Dupleix
Boulogne
Jean-Jaurès
Javel
Cambronne
Sèvres-
Lecourbe
Falguière
Michel-Ange-
Molitor
Chardon-
Lagache
Mirabeau
Javel
André Citroën
Charles
Michels
Av.
Emile
Zola
La
Motte-Picquet-
Grenelle
Pasteur
Montparnasse
Bienvenüe
Edgar
Quinet
Boulogne-
Pt. de St-Cloud
Exelmans
Commerce
Volontaires
Gaîté
Félix Faure
Pernety
Boulevard
Victor
Boucicaut
Vaugirard
Plaisance
Porte de
St-Cloud
Lourmel
Convention
Porte de Vanves
Balard
Malakoff-
Plateau de Vanves
Marcel Sembat
Porte de Versailles
Malakoff-
Rue Etienne Dolet
Billancourt
Issy Plaine
Corentin Celton
RER LINE C
Châtillon-
Montrouge
Pont de Sèvres
Mairie d'Issy

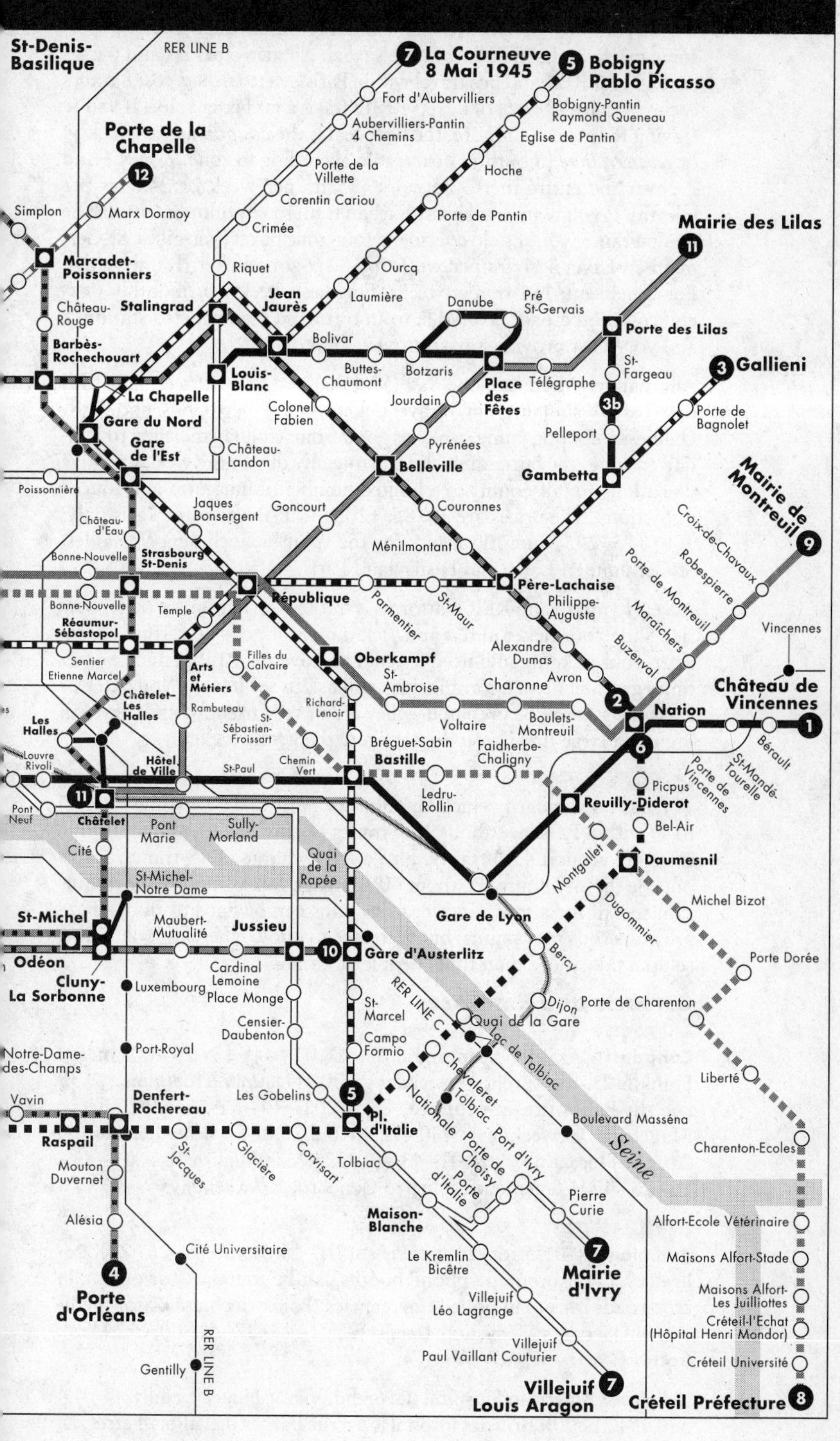
St-Denis-Basilique
RER LINE B
7 La Courneuve 8 Mai 1945
5 Bobigny Pablo Picasso
Fort d'Aubervilliers
Bobigny-Pantin Raymond Queneau
Aubervilliers-Pantin 4 Chemins
Eglise de Pantin
Porte de la Chapelle
12
Porte de la Villette
Hoche
Corentin Cariou
Simplon
Marx Dormoy
Crimée
Porte de Pantin
Mairie des Lilas
11
Marcadet-Poissonniers
Riquet
Ourcq
Château-Rouge
Stalingrad
Jean Jaurès
Laumière
Danube
Pré St-Gervais
Porte des Lilas
Barbès-Rochechouart
Bolivar
Louis-Blanc
Buttes-Chaumont
Botzaris
Place des Fêtes
Télégraphe
St-Fargeau
3 Gallieni
La Chapelle
Colonel Fabien
Jourdain
3b
Porte de Bagnolet
Gare du Nord
Gare de l'Est
Château-Landon
Pyrénées
Pelleport
Belleville
Gambetta
Poissonnière
Mairie de Montreuil
Jaques Bonsergent
Goncourt
Couronnes
Château-d'Eau
Croix-de-Chavaux
Ménilmontant
9
Bonne-Nouvelle
Strasbourg St-Denis
Robespierre
Porte de Montreuil
République
Père-Lachaise
Bonne-Nouvelle
Temple
Parmentier
St-Maur
Philippe-Auguste
Maraîchers
Vincennes
Réaumur-Sébastopol
Sentier
Arts et Métiers
Filles du Calvaire
Oberkampf
Alexandre Dumas
Buzenval
Etienne Marcel
St-Ambroise
Avron
Château de Vincennes
Châtelet-Les Halles
Charonne
Les Halles
Rambuteau
Richard-Lenoir
Voltaire
Boulets-Montreuil
2
Nation
1
St-Sébastien-Froissart
Bréguet-Sabin
Faidherbe-Chaligny
Bérault
Louvre Rivoli
Hôtel de Ville
Chemin Vert
Bastille
6
St-Mandé-Tourelle
St-Paul
Picpus
Porte de Vincennes
11
Ledru-Rollin
Reuilly-Diderot
Pont Neuf
Châtelet
Pont Marie
Sully-Morland
Bel-Air
Cité
Quai de la Rapée
Montgallet
Daumesnil
St-Michel-Notre Dame
Michel Bizot
St-Michel
Dugommier
Maubert-Mutualité
Jussieu
Gare de Lyon
Odéon
10
Gare d'Austerlitz
Bercy
Porte Dorée
Cluny-La Sorbonne
Cardinal Lemoine
Luxembourg
Place Monge
RER LINE C
Dijon
Porte de Charenton
St-Marcel
Quai de la Gare
Censier-Daubenton
Campo Formio
Lac de Tolbiac
Notre-Dame-des-Champs
Port-Royal
Chevaleret
Liberté
Vavin
Denfert-Rochereau
Les Gobelins
5
Nationale
Tolbiac
Port d'Ivry
Boulevard Masséna
Pl. d'Italie
Raspail
St-Jacques
Glacière
Corvisart
Porte de Choisy
Seine
Charenton-Ecoles
Mouton Duvernet
Tolbiac
Porte d'Italie
Pierre Curie
Alésia
Maison-Blanche
Alfort-Ecole Vétérinaire
Cité Universitaire
7
Maisons Alfort-Stade
4
Porte d'Orléans
Le Kremlin Bicêtre
Mairie d'Ivry
Villejuif Léo Lagrange
Maisons Alfort-Les Juilliottes
Créteil-l'Echat (Hôpital Henri Mondor)
RER LINE B
Villejuif Paul Vaillant Couturier
Gentilly
Créteil Université
Villejuif Louis Aragon
7
Créteil Préfecture
8

The métro connects at several points in Paris with RER trains that race across Paris from suburb to suburb: RER trains are a sort of supersonic métro and can be great time-savers. All métro tickets and passes are valid for RER and bus travel within Paris. Métro tickets cost 8 francs each, though a *carnet* (10 tickets for 48 frs) is a far better value. If you're staying for a week or more, the best deal is the *coupon jaune* (weekly) or *carte orange* (monthly) ticket, sold according to zone. Zones 1 and 2 cover the entire métro network (75 frs per week or 243 frs per month). If you plan to take a suburban train to visit monuments in the Ile-de-France, you should consider a four-zone ticket (Versailles, St-Germain-en-Laye; 131 frs per week) or a six-zone ticket (Rambouillet, Fontainebleau; 181 frs per week). For these weekly or monthly tickets, you need a pass (available from train and major métro stations), and you must provide a passport-size photograph.

Alternatively there are one-day (Mobilis) and two-, three-, and five-day (Paris Visite) unlimited travel tickets for the métro, bus, and RER. Unlike the coupon jaune, which is good from Monday morning to Sunday evening, the latter are valid starting any day of the week and give you admission discounts to a limited number of museums and tourist attractions. The prices are 30, 85, 120, and 170 francs for Paris only; 100, 175, 245, and 300 francs for the suburbs, including Versailles, St-Germain-en-Laye, and Disneyland Paris.

Access to métro and RER platforms is through an automatic ticket barrier. Slide your ticket in flat and pick it up as it pops up farther along. Keep your ticket; you'll need it again to leave the RER system. Sometimes green-clad métro authorities will ask to see it when you enter or leave the station: Be prepared—they aren't very friendly, and they will impose a large fine if you do not show them your ticket.

BY TAXI

There is no standard vehicle or color for Paris taxis. Daytime rates (7 to 7) within Paris are about 2.80 francs per km (½ mi), and nighttime rates are around 4.50 francs, plus a basic charge of 13 francs. Rates outside the city limits are about 40% higher. Ask your hotel or restaurant to call for a taxi, since cruising cabs can be hard to find. There are numerous taxi stands, but you have to know where to look. Taxis seldom take more than three people at a time.

Contacts and Resources

EMBASSIES

Canada (✉ 35 av. Montaigne, 8e, ☎ 01–44–43–29–00, métro Franklin-D.-Roosevelt, ⏲ weekdays 8:30–11). **United Kingdom** (✉ 35 rue du Faubourg-St-Honoré, 8e, ☎ 01–44–51–31–00, métro Madeleine, ⏲ weekdays 9:30–12:30 and 2:30–5). **United States** (✉ 2 rue St-Florentin, 1er, ☎ 01–43–12–22–22 in English or ☎ 01–43–12–23–47 in emergencies, métro Concorde, ⏲ weekdays 9–3).

EMERGENCIES

Ambulance (☎ 15 for emergencies or 01–15 or 43–78–26–26). **Police** (☎ 17). Automatic phone booths can be found at various main crossroads for use in police emergencies (Police-Secours) or for medical help (Services Médicaux). **Dentist** (☎ 01–43–37–51–00, ⏲ 24 hrs). **Doctor** (☎ 01–47–07–77–77).

Hospitals: American Hospital (✉ 63 bd. Victor-Hugo, Neuilly, ☎ 01–47–45–71–00); British Hospital (✉ 3 rue Barbès, Levallois-Perret, ☎ 01–47–58–13–12).

Pharmacies: Dhéry (✉ Galerie des Champs, 84 av. des Champs-Elysées, ☎ 01–45–62–02–41; ⏲ 24 hrs); **Pharmacie des Arts** (✉ 106 bd. Montparnasse, 6e, ☎ 01–43–35–44–88; ⏲ until midnight).

ENGLISH-LANGUAGE BOOKSTORES

Most newsstands in central Paris sell *Time, Newsweek,* and the *International Herald Tribune,* as well as the English dailies. Some English-language bookstores include: **W. H. Smith** (✉ 248 rue de Rivoli); **Brentano's** (✉ 37 av. de l'Opéra); and **Shakespeare & Co.** (✉ rue de la Bûcherie).

GUIDED TOURS

Bicyling Tours: Paris à Vélo (✉ 37 bd Bourdon, 4e, ☎ 01–48–87–60–01) organizes three-hour cycling tours around Paris and rents bikes for 80 francs a day.

Boat Tours: Boat rides along the Seine are a must if it's your first time in Paris. The price for a 60-minute trip is usually around 40 francs. Boats depart in season every half hour from 10:30 to 5 (less frequently in winter). The **Bateaux Mouches** leave from the Pont de l'Alma, at the bottom of avenue George-V. The **Vedettes du Pont-Neuf** set off from the square du Vert-Galant on the western edge of the Ile de la Cité.

Bus Tours: Bus tours of Paris provide a good introduction to the city. Tours usually start from the tour company's office and are generally given in double-decker buses with either a live guide or tape-recorded commentary. They last two to three hours and cost about 150 francs. Tour operators also have a variety of theme tours (historic Paris, modern Paris, Paris by night) that last from 2½ hours to all day and cost up to 390 francs. **Cityrama** (✉ 147 rue St-Honoré, 1er, ☎ 01–44–55–61–00) is one of the largest bus operators in Paris. For an intimate tour of the city, Cityrama also runs minibus excursions that pick you up and drop you off at your hotel. **Paris Vision** (✉ 214 rue de Rivoli, 1er, ☎ 01–42–60–31–25) is another large bus tour operator.

Excursions: Cityrama and **Paris Vision** (☞ Bus Tours, *above*) organize half- and full-day trips to Chartres, Versailles, Fontainebleau, the Loire Valley, and Mont-St-Michel at a cost of between 195 and 950 francs.

Personal Guides: Tours of Paris or the surrounding areas by limousine or minibus for up to seven passengers for a minimum of three hours can be organized. The cost starts at about 250 francs per hour. Contact **International Limousines** (✉ 182 bd. Pereire, 17e, ☎ 01–53–81–14–14) or **Paris Bus** (✉ 22 rue de la Prévoyance, Vincennes, ☎ 01–43–65–55–55).

Walking Tours: Numerous special-interest tours concentrate on historical or architectural topics. Most are in French and cost between 40 and 60 francs. Details are published in the weekly magazines *Pariscope* and *L'Officiel des Spectacles* under the heading "Conférences."

TRAVEL AGENCIES

American Express (✉ 11 rue Scribe, 75009 Paris, ☎ 01–47–77–77–07). **Wagons-Lits** (✉ 32 rue du Quatre-Septembre, 75002 Paris, ☎ 01–44–94–20–67).

VISITOR INFORMATION

The **Paris Tourist Office** (✉ 127 av. des Champs-Elysées, ☎ 01–49–52–53–54; 01–49–52–53–56 for recorded information in English) is open daily 9–8. It has branches at all mainline train stations except Gare St-Lazare.

ILE-DE-FRANCE

The region surrounding Paris is called Ile-de-France, although it isn't actually an *île* (island). But the area is figuratively isolated from the rest of France by three rivers—the Seine, the Oise, and the Marne—that weave meandering circles around its periphery. If you are visiting Paris—and France—for the first time, this is an excellent place to get a taste of French provincial life, with its palpably slower pace.

Parts of the area are fighting a losing battle against the encroaching capital, but you can still see the countryside that was the inspiration for the Impressionists and other 19th-century painters, as well as the wealth of architecture dating from the Middle Ages and Renaissance. The most famous sights are Chartres—one of the most beautiful French cathedrals—and Versailles, the monumental château of Louis XIV, the Sun King. Before the completion of Versailles, king and court resided in the delightful château of St-Germain-en-Laye, west of Paris—an easy day trip from the capital, as are the châteaux of Vaux-le-Vicomte, Rambouillet, and Fontainebleau, and Disneyland Paris.

The region can be covered in a series of loops: Travel west from Paris to see Versailles, Rambouillet, and Chartres; east to Disneyland; and southeast to Fontainebleau, Barbizon, and Vaux-le-Vicomte. Most of these sights are under 80 km (50 mi) away from Paris, including Disneyland, which is just 32 km (20 mi) east of the city via A4 (or take the RER-A train, stopping at Marne-la-Vallée-Chessy). Chartres and Giverny are a little farther away, but they're still easily manageable—and particularly enjoyable—side trips from the capital.

Versailles

Versailles is the location of one of the world's grandest palaces—and in fact, a grand town, since the château's opulence had to have a setting to match. Wide, tree-lined avenues, broader than the Champs-Elysées and bordered by massive 17th-century mansions, lead directly to the palace. From the imposing place d'Armes, you enter the Cour d'Honneur, a sprawling cobbled forecourt. Right in the middle, the statue of Louis XIV, the Sun King, stands triumphant, surveying the town built to house those of the 20,000 noblemen, servants, and hangers-on who weren't quick enough to grab one of the 3,000 beds in the château.

★ The **Château de Versailles** took 50 years to complete. Hills were flattened, marshes drained, forests transplanted, and water from the Seine river was channeled from several miles away to supply the magnificent fountains. Visit the **Grands Appartements** (Grand Suites), rooms that made up the royal living quarters, and the famous **Galerie des Glaces** (Hall of Mirrors), where the controversial Treaty of Versailles, asserting Germany's responsibility for World War I, was signed in 1919. Both can be visited without a guide, but you can get an audio tour in English. There are also guided tours of the **Petits Appartements** (Small Suites), where the royal family and friends lived in relative intimacy, and the magnificent opera house—one of the first oval rooms in France, built on the *aile nord* (north wing) for Louis XV in 1770.

The château's vast **park** is a masterpiece of formal landscaping. At one end of the Petit Canal, which crosses the Grand Canal at right angles, is the **Grand Trianon,** a scaled-down pleasure palace built in the 1680s. The **Petit Trianon,** nearby, is a sumptuously furnished 18th-century mansion, commissioned by Louis XV; Marie-Antoinette would flee here to avoid the stuffy atmosphere of the court. Nearby, she built a model village, complete with dairy and mill, where she and her companions led a make-believe bucolic life. ☎ *01–30–84–74–00.* ⏲ *Château: Apr.–*

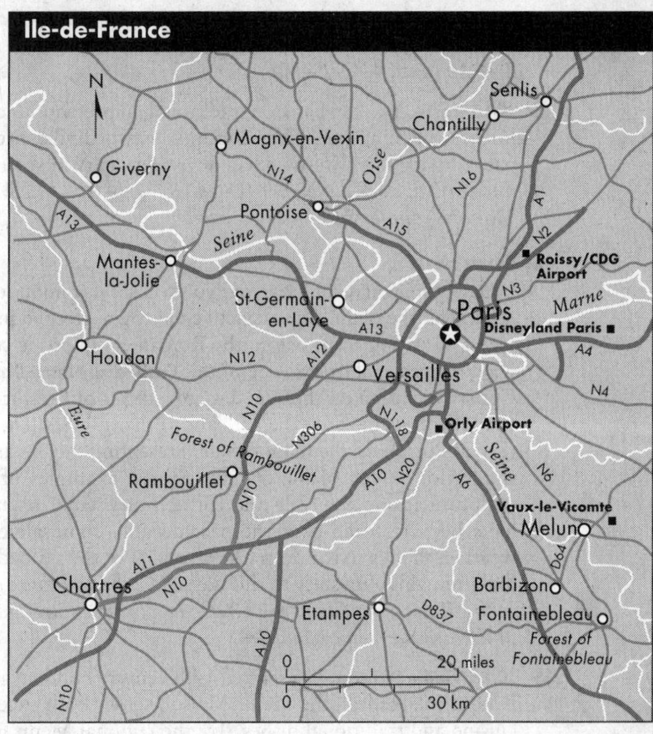

Sept., Tues.–Sun. 9–6:30, Oct.–Mar., Tues.–Sun. 9–5:30. Galerie des Glaces: ⏲ *9:45–5. Opéra:* ⏲ *9:45–3:30. Tours of Petits Appartements and opera house every 15 mins. Park:* ⏲ *7–dusk. Grand Trianon and Petit Trianon:* ⏲ *Tues.–Fri. 10–12:30 and 2–5:30, weekends 10–5:30.*

$$$$ ✕ **Trois Marches.** Don't miss Gerard Vié's nouvelle cuisine at one of the best restaurants in town. The view of the château park and the setting—in the sumptuous Trianon Palace Hotel—add to the experience. ✉ *1 bd. de la Reine,* ☎ *01–39–50–13–21. Reservations essential. Jacket and tie. AE, DC, MC, V. Closed Sun., Mon., and Aug.*

$$ ✕ **Quai No. 1.** Barometers, sails, and model boats fill this small, charming seafood restaurant. In summer you can enjoy your meal on the terrace. Home-smoked salmon and sauerkraut with fish are specialties; any dish on the two prix-fixe menus is a good value. ✉ *1 av. de St-Cloud,* ☎ *01–39–50–42–26. MC, V. Closed Mon. No dinner Sun.*

Rambouillet

The small town of Rambouillet is home to a château, a park, and 34,000 acres of forest. Since 1897 the **Château de Rambouillet** has been a summer residence of the French president; today it is also used as a site for international summits. You can't visit the château if the president is in residence—fortunately, that's not often. French kings have lived in the château since it was built in 1375. Highlights include the wood-paneled apartments, especially the **Boudoir de la Comtesse** (Countess's Dressing Room); the marble-walled **Salle de Marbre** (Marble Room), dating from the Renaissance; and the **Salle de Bains de Napoléon** (Napoléon's Bathroom), adorned with Pompeii-style frescoes. The **park** stretches way behind the château, and includes the Jardin d'Eau (Water Garden), an English-style garden, and the **Laiterie de la Reine** (Queen's Dairy), belonging to Marie-Antoinette. This was another of her attempts to "get back to nature." ☎ *01–34–94–28–00.* ⏲ *Daily 10–11:30 and 2–5:30; park: sunrise–sunset; laiterie: Wed.–Mon. 10–11:30 and 2–4:30 (until 4, Oct.–Mar.).*

$ ✕ **La Poste.** You can bank on traditional, unpretentious cooking at this former coaching inn. The restaurant's two dining rooms are often packed with a lively crowd. Game is a specialty in season. ✉ *101 rue du Général-de-Gaulle,* ☎ *01–34–83–03–01. AE, MC, V. Closed Mon. No dinner Sun.*

Chartres

Long before you reach Chartres, you will see its famous cathedral towering over the plain. The attractive old town, steeped in religious history and dating from before the Roman conquest, is still laced with ★ winding medieval streets. The Gothic **Cathédral Notre-Dame** is the sixth Christian church on the site; despite a series of fires, it has remained virtually the same since the 12th and 13th centuries. The **Portail Royal** (Royal Portal) on the main facade, presenting the life and triumph of the Savior, is one of the country's finest examples of Romanesque sculpture. Inside, the 12th- and 13th-century windows, many of which have been restored over the past decade, come alive even in dull weather, thanks to the deep Chartres blue of the stained glass: Its formula remains a mystery to this day. ⏲ *Cathedral tours available. Ask at the Maison des Clercs (✉ 18 rue du Cloître-Notre-Dame).* ⏲ *Tours in English daily noon and 2:45.*

$$$ ✕ **La Vieille Maison.** In a refitted 14th-century building a stone's throw from the cathedral, the Vieille Maison serves both excellent nouvelle cuisine and traditional dishes. Try the regional Menu Beauceron, for the homemade foie gras and duck dishes. ✉ *5 rue au Lait,* ☎ *02–37–34–10–67. AE, MC, V. Closed Mon. No dinner Sun.*

$$ ✕ **Buisson Ardent.** This attractive restaurant, in an old, oak-beamed building opposite the Vieille Maison, serves such dishes as chicken ravioli with leeks or rolled beef with spinach. ✉ *10 rue au Lait,* ☎ *02–37–34–04–66. AE, DC, MC, V. No dinner Sun.*

$$$ 🏨 **Grand Monarque.** The most popular rooms in this 18th-century coaching inn are in a separate turn-of-the-century building overlooking a garden. The hotel also has an excellent restaurant with a good choice of prix-fixe menus for 152, 210, and 275 francs. ✉ *22 pl. des Épars, 28000,* ☎ *02–37–21–00–72,* FAX *02–37–36–34–18. 54 rooms. Restaurant. AE, DC, MC, V.*

Giverny

This small village is a place of pilgrimage for art lovers enticed by the ★ **Maison et Jardin de Claude Monet** (Claude Monet House and Garden). The house where Monet worked and lived for over 40 years has been faithfully restored; the kitchen with its cool blue tiles and the buttercup-yellow dining room are particularly striking. However, the real pull is the colorful **garden** and especially the famous lily pond with its Japanese bridge, which was one of Monet's favorite subjects. ✉ *84 rue Claude-Monet,* ☎ *02–32–51–94–65.* ⏲ *Apr.–Oct., Tues.–Sun. 10–noon and 2–6.*

Fontainebleau

During the early 16th century the flamboyant François I transformed the medieval hunting lodge of Fontainebleau into a magnificent Re- ★ naissance palace, the **Château de Fontainebleau.** His successor, Henry II, covered the palace with his initials, woven into the *D* for his mistress, Diane de Poitiers. When he died, his queen, Catherine de' Medici, carried out further alterations, later continued under Louis XIV. However, it was Napoléon who made a Versailles, as it were, out of the château by spending lavishly to restore the neglected property to its former glory. Before he was exiled to Elba, he bade farewell to his Old Guard in the courtyard now known as the **Cour des Adieux** (Court of Farewell), with its elegant horseshoe staircase. Ask the curator to let you see the **Cour Ovale** (Oval Court), the oldest and perhaps most interesting courtyard. It stands on the site of the original 12th-century fortified building, of which only the keep remains.

The **Grands Appartements** (Royal Suites, or State Rooms) are the main attractions of any visit to the château; these include the **Galerie de François I** (Gallery François I) and a covered bridge (built 1528–30) looking out over the Cour de la Fontaine. The magnificent **Salle de Bal** (Ballroom) is nearly 100 ft long, with wood paneling, 16th-century frescoes and gilding, and, reputedly, the first coffered ceiling in France, its intricate pattern echoed by the splendid 19th-century parquet floor. If you're here on a weekday, you may also be able to join a guided tour (in French) of the **Petits Appartements** (Small, or Private Suites), used by Napoléon and Joséphine, and the **Musée Napoléon** (Napoléon Museum), which has some mementos, including the leader's imperial uniform. ✉ *Pl. du Général-de-Gaulle,* ☎ *01–60–71–50–70.* ⏲ *Wed.–Mon. 9:30–5. Call ahead for tour schedule.*

$$$$ ★ ✕🏨 **Aigle-Noir.** This may be Fontainebleau's costliest hotel, but you can't go wrong if you request one of the rooms overlooking either the garden or the château. Late 18th- or early 19th-century reproduction furniture evokes a Napoleonic mood. The restaurant, Le Beauharnais, serves subtle, imaginative cuisine; reservations are essential and jacket and tie are required. ✉ *27 pl. Napoléon-Bonaparte, 77300,* ☎ *01–64–22–32–65,* FAX *01–64–22–17–33. 56 rooms. Restaurant, pool. AE, DC, MC, V.*

$$ 🏨 **Londres.** The balconies of this tranquil hotel look out over the palace and the Cour des Adieux; the 1830 facade is preserved by government order. Inside, the decor is dominated by Louis XV furniture. ✉ *1 pl. du Général-de-Gaulle, 77300,* ☎ *01–64–22–20–21,* FAX *01–60–72–39–16. 22 rooms. Restaurant. AE, DC, MC, V. Closed mid-Dec.–early Jan.*

Barbizon

This delightful village is scarcely more than a main street lined with restaurants and boutiques, but a group of landscape painters, including Camille Corot, Jean-François Millet, and Théodore Rousseau, put it on the map in the mid-19th century. Two artists' studios are open to the public—the **Atelier Millet** (✉ 27 Grand-Rue) and the **Atelier Rousseau** (✉ 55 Grand-Rue).

Corot and company would often repair to the Auberge du Père Ganne after painting; the inn still stands, and is now the **Musée de l'École de Barbizon** (Barbizon School Museum). The museum contains documents of the village as it was during the 19th century as well as a few original works by the landscapists—including some paintings done on the inn's walls and furniture. ✉ *92 Grande-Rue,* ☎ *01–60–66–22–27.* ⏲ *Wed.–Mon. 10–12:30 and 2–5.*

$–$$ ✕ **Le Relais.** Enjoy the large portions of delicious specialties—particularly the beef and the game (in season). In summer you can eat in the shade of lime and chestnut trees on the large terrace. ✉ *2 av. du Général-de-Gaulle,* ☎ *01–60–66–40–28. Weekend reservations essential. MC, V. Closed Wed. No dinner Tues.*

$$ ★ 🏨 **Auberge des Alouettes.** Two acres of grounds stretch around this delightful 19th-century inn. The interior has been decorated in '30s style, but many rooms still have their original oak beams. The restaurant, on a large open terrace, features nouvelle cuisine in sizable portions. Weekend dinner reservations are essential. ✉ *4 rue Antoine-Barye, 77630,* ☎ *01–60–66–41–98,* FAX *01–60–66–20–69. 22 rooms. Restaurant. AE, DC, MC, V.*

Vaux-le-Vicomte

★ The **Château de Vaux-le-Vicomte** is one of the greatest monuments of 17th-century France. Too grand for some: When owner Nicolas Fouquet, the royal finance minister, threw a housewarming party in 1661, Sun King Louis XIV threw a fit of jealousy, hurled Fouquet in the slammer on trumped-up fraud charges, and promptly began building Versailles to prove just who was boss—after signing up Fouquet's architectural supergroup (Louis Le Vau for design, André Le Nôtre in the gardens, and Charles Le Brun on all lead murals). From your point of view, though, Fouquet's *folie de grandeur* will probably be a treat. ☎ *01–64–14–41–90.* 🎫 *Château: 56 frs; Candlelight visits: 75 frs.* ⏲ *Apr.–Oct., daily 10–6; Mar. and early–mid-Nov., daily 11–1 and 2–5. Candlelight visits May–Oct., Sat. 8:30 PM–11 PM.*

Disneyland Paris

Get a dose of American pop culture in between visits to the Louvre and the Left Bank. Disneyland Paris is east of the capital, in Marne-la-Vallée, and easily accessible by RER from the city.

The theme park, less than 1½ km (½ mi) across, is ringed by a railroad with whistling steam engines. In the middle of the park is the soaring Sleeping Beauty Castle, surrounded by a plaza from which you can enter each of the "lands": **Frontierland, Adventureland, Fantasyland,** and **Discoveryland.** In addition **Main Street U.S.A.** connects the castle to the entrance. Also included in the complex is **Disney Village,** an entertainment center with restaurants, a theater, dance clubs, shops, a post office, and a tourist office. ☎ *01–60–30–60–30.* 🎫 *Apr.–Sept. and Christmas period: 200 frs (380 frs for 2-day Passport, 515 frs for 3-day Passport); Oct.–Mar., except Christmas period: 160 frs (305 frs for 2-day Passport, 415 frs for 3-day Passport); includes admission to all individual attractions within the park but not meals. AE, DC, MC, V.* ⏲ *Mid-June–mid-Sept., daily 9 AM–10 PM; mid-Sept.–mid-June, daily 10–6; Dec. and spring school holidays, daily 9–8.*

$–$$ ✕ **Disneyland Restaurants.** The park is peppered with places to eat, ranging from snack bars and fast-food joints to full-service restaurants—all with a distinguishing theme. Eateries serve nonstop as long as the park is open. ☎ *01–60–45–65–40. Sit-down restaurants: AE, DC, MC, V; counter-service restaurants: no credit cards.*

$$–$$$$ 🏨 **Disneyland Hotels.** The resort has 5,000 rooms in six hotels, all a short distance from the park, ranging from the luxurious Disneyland Hotel to the not-so-rustic Camp Davy Crockett. Free transportation to the park is available at every hotel. To book a room contact the Central Reservations Office. ✉ *Central Reservations Office, Box 100, 77777 Marne-la-Vallée cedex 4,* ☎ *01–60–30–60–30, 407/934–7639 in the U.S.,* FAX *01–49–30–71–00 All hotels have at least 1 restaurant and indoor swimming pool. AE, DC, MC, V.*

Ile-de-France Essentials

Getting Around

The region is reached easily from Paris by car and by regular suburban train services. But you might find it convenient to group some sights together: Versailles, Rambouillet, and Chartres are all on the Paris–Chartres train line; Fontainebleau, Barbizon, and Vaux-le-Vicomte are all within a few miles of each other.

BY CAR

Expressway A13, from the Porte d'Auteuil, links Paris to Versailles. You can get to Chartres on A10 from Porte d'Orléans. For Fontainebleau take A6 from Porte d'Orléans or, for a more attractive route through the Forest of Sénart and the northern part of the Forest of Fontainebleau, take N6 from Porte de Charenton via Melun. Vaux-le-Vicomte is 6 km (4 mi) northeast of Melun via N36 and D215. The 32-km (20-mi) drive along the A4 expressway from Paris to Disneyland Paris takes about 30 minutes, longer in heavy traffic. Disneyland is 4 km (2½ mi) off the A4; follow the signs for the park.

BY TRAIN

Three lines connect Paris with Versailles; on each the trip takes about 30 minutes. The best is RER-C5 to Versailles Rive Gauche station. Trains from Gare St-Lazare go to Versailles Rive Droite. Trains from Gare Montparnasse go to Versailles Chantiers and then on to Rambouillet and Chartres. Fontainebleau is served by 20 trains a day from Gare de Lyon; buses for Barbizon leave from the main post office in Fontainebleau. The RER-A4 line goes to Disneyland Paris. Vaux-le-Vicomte is a 7-km (4-mi) taxi ride from the nearest station at Melun, served by regular trains from Paris and Fontainebleau. The taxi ride costs about 80–100 francs.

Guided Tours

Following are two private companies that organize regular half-day and full-day tours from Paris to Chartres, Fontainebleau, Barbizon, and Versailles with English-speaking guides. Tours are subject to cancellation, and reservations are suggested. **Cityrama** (✉ 147 rue St-Honorê, Paris, 1er, ☎ 01–44–55–61–00). **Paris Vision** (✉ 214 rue de Rivoli, Paris, 1er, ☎ 01–42–60–31–25).

Visitor Information

Barbizon (✉ 55 Grande Rue, ☎ 01–60–66–41–87). **Chartres** (✉ pl. de la Cathédrale, ☎ 02–37–21–50–00). **Disneyland Paris** (✉ B.P. 100, 77777 Marne-la-Vallée cedex , ☎ 01–60–30–60–30). **Fontainebleau** (✉ 4 rue Royale , ☎ 01–60–74–99–99). **Rambouillet** (✉ 8 pl. de la Libération, ☎ 01–34–83–21–21). **Versailles** (✉ 7 rue des Réservoirs, ☎ 01–39–50–36–22).

THE LOIRE VALLEY

The Loire is the longest river in France, rising near Le Puy in the east of the Massif Central and pursuing a broad northwest curve on its 1,000-km (620-mi) course to the Atlantic near Nantes. The meandering Loire has two distinct faces: fast-flowing and spectacular in spring, sluggish and sandy in summer. Château country encompasses the 225-km (140-mi) stretch between Orléans, 113 km (70 mi) south of Paris, and Angers, 96 km (60 mi) from the Atlantic coast. Thanks to its mild climate and lush meadowland, this area is known as the Garden of France.

To the north lies the vast grain plain of the Beauce; to the southeast the marshy, forest-covered Sologne, renowned for mushrooms, asparagus, and game. The star attractions along the rocky banks of the Loire and its tributaries—the Rivers Cher, Indre, Vienne, and Loir (with no *e*)—are the famous châteaux: stately houses, castles, and fairy-tale palaces, where Renaissance elegance is often combined with fortresslike medieval mass. The Loire Valley was fought over by France and England during the Middle Ages until, inspired by Joan of Arc, the "Maid of Orléans" (scene of her most rousing military successes), France finally managed to expel the English.

The Loire Valley (Val de Loire)

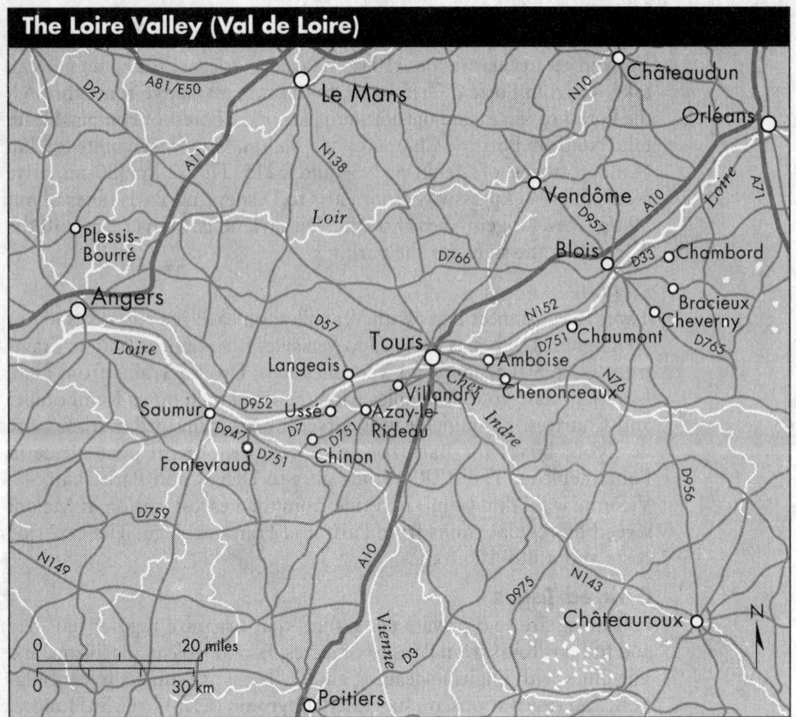

The Loire Valley's golden age came under François I (1515–47), France's flamboyant contemporary of England's Henry VIII. He hired Renaissance craftsmen from Italy and hobnobbed with the aging Leonardo da Vinci, his guest at Amboise. You can see his salamander emblem in many châteaux.

Most of the sights covered here are close to the Loire River along the 170-km (105-mi) stretch between Blois and Angers. If you're coming from Paris, Châteaudun and Vendôme make good stops en route to Blois. Tours, 58 km (36 mi) west of Blois, is the region's major city. Saumur, Chinon, and Amboise are the other main historic towns.

Châteaudun

The **Château de Châteaudun** is a colossal castle, resplendent and impregnable on a steep promontory 200 ft above the Loir. The round, 12th-century Grosse Tour (Big Tower) is one of France's beefiest keeps, with walls over 12 ft thick. In the chapel alongside are 15 lifelike statues, mainly of saints, sculpted locally during the late 15th century. ☎ *02–37–94–02–90.* ⏲ *Mid-Mar.–Sept., daily 9–12:30 and 2–6; Oct.–mid-Mar., daily 10–12:30 and 2–5.*

Vendôme

At Vendôme the Loir River (not to be confused with the larger and more famous Loire to the south) splits into many arms, giving the town a canal-like charm that harmonizes with its old streets and bridges. The large but little-known main church, the **Église de la Trinité,** is an encyclopedia of different styles, with brilliantly carved choir stalls and an exuberant west front. It is the work of Jean de Beauce, best known for his spire at Chartres Cathedral. Vendôme also has a ruined castle with ramparts and pleasant, uncrowded gardens, open from 9 to dusk.

Blois

With its forest of towers and tumbling alleyways, Blois is the most attractive of the major Loire towns. It is best known for its massive **Château de Blois,** a mixture of four different styles: Feudal (13th century), Gothic-Renaissance Transition (circa 1500), Renaissance (circa 1520), and Classical (circa 1635). ☎ *02–54–74–16–06.* ⏲ *Apr.–Aug., daily 9–6; Sept.–Mar., daily 9–12:30 and 2–5:30.*

$$ ✕ **Rendez-vous des Pêcheurs.** On the right bank of the Loire below the castle, this extremely modest restaurant is an excellent value. Chef Eric Reithler creates inventive fish-based specialties. ✉ *27 rue de Foix,* ☎ *02–54–74–67–48. MC, V. Closed Sun. No dinner Mon.*

$$ ✕🏨 **Médicis.** Your best bet in Blois, this smart, friendly hotel, 1,000 yards from the château, has comfortable, soundproof, air-conditioned rooms. Each is furnished differently, but all share the same joyous color scheme. Chef-owner Christian Garanger's cooking is innovative classical—*coquilles St-Jacques* (scallops) with a pear fondue, for instance. ✉ *2 allée François-I, 41000,* ☎ *02–54–43–94–04,* FAX *02–54–42–04–05. 12 rooms, 1 suite. Restaurant. AE, DC, MC, V. Closed Jan.*

Chambord

★ The largest of the Loire châteaux, the palatial **Château de Chambord** (begun in 1519) is in the heart of a vast forest packed with game. There's another forest on the roof: 365 chimneys and turrets, representing architectural self-indulgence at its least squeamish. Grandeur or a mere 440-room folly? Judge for yourself, and don't miss the superb spiral staircase or the chance to saunter over the rooftop terrace. ☎ *02–54–50–40–28.* ⏲ *Apr.–Aug., daily 9:30–6:30; Sept.–Mar., daily 9:30–5:15.*

$$ 🏨 **Grand St-Michel.** Considering its location across from the château, the St-Michel is reasonably priced, especially if you obtain a room with one of the splendid views of the château and the forest backdrop. ✉ *103 pl. St-Michel, 41250,* ☎ *02–54–20–31–31,* FAX *02–54–20–36–40. 39 rooms, 31 with bath or shower. Restaurant. MC, V. Closed mid-Nov.–late Dec.*

Chaumont-sur-Loire

Chaumont is best known for its sturdy castle with famous stables and magnificent panorama of the Loire.The sturdy riverside **Château de Chaumont** was built between 1465 and 1510—well before Benjamin Franklin became a regular visitor. The stables—where purebreds dined like royalty—show the importance attached to fine horses, for hunting or just prestige. ☎ *02–54–51–26–26.* ⏲ *Apr.–Sept., daily 9:30–6:30; Oct.–Mar., daily 10–5.*

Amboise

This bustling town has two star attractions. The **Château d'Amboise,** dating from 1500, has splendid grounds, a rich interior, and fine views of the river from the battlements. But it wasn't always so peaceful: In 1560, more than 1,000 Protestant "conspirators" were hanged from these battlements during the Wars of Religion. ☎ *02–47–57–00–98.* ⏲ *July–Aug., daily 9–6:30; Sept.–June, daily 9–noon and 2–5.*

The **Clos-Lucé,** a 15th-century brick manor house, was the last home of Leonardo da Vinci. Invited to stay here by François I, Leonardo died here in 1519. His engineering genius is illustrated by models based on his plans and sketches. ✉ *2 rue du Clos-Lucé,* ☎ *02–47–57–62–88.* ⏲ *Apr.–Oct., daily 9–6; Nov.–Mar., daily 10–5.*

$–$$ ✕🏨 **Le Blason.** This delightful, small hotel is behind the château. Ask for Room 109 or 229. The pretty little restaurant has a seasonal menu that begins at 95 francs and might include roast lamb with garlic or medallions of pork. ✉ *11 pl. Richelieu, 37400,* ☎ *02-47-23-22-41,* FAX *02-47-57-56-18. 29 rooms. Restaurant. AE, DC, MC, V.*

Chenonceaux

The small village of Chenonceaux, on the River Cher, is best known as the site of the "most romantic" of all the Loire châteaux. The early 16th-century **Château de Chenonceau** (without the *x*) straddles the tranquil River Cher like a bridge. It is surrounded by elegant gardens and plane trees. Inside, note the fine paintings, colossal fireplaces, and richly worked ceilings. A museum with wax figures depicting scenes from the château's history is in an outbuilding. ☎ *02-47-23-90-07.* ⏲ *Mid-Mar.–mid-Sept., daily 9–7; mid-Sept.–mid-Mar., daily 9–5.*

$$ ★ **Bon Laboureur.** Since 1882, through four generations of the Jeudi family, this inn has become an elegant hotel. Rooms in the old house are comfortably traditional; those in the former stables are larger and more modern; the biggest are in the converted manor house across the street. Dine on excellent turbot with hollandaise or the *poêlée de St-Jacques* (sautéed scallops) with fresh wild mushrooms. ✉ *6 rue du Dr-Bretonneau, 37150,* ☎ *02-47-23-90-02,* FAX *02-47-23-82-01. 36 rooms. Restaurant, pool. AE, DC, MC, V. Closed mid-Nov.–mid-Dec.*

Tours

The largest city along the Loire, with 250,000 inhabitants, Tours was extensively damaged in World War II. But the timber-framed houses in the medieval center of Tours, the attractive old quarter around place Plumereau, were tastefully restored.

★ The **Cathédrale St-Gatien** (1239–1484) numbers among France's most impressive churches. The influence of local Renaissance sculptors and craftsmen is evident on the ornate facade. The stained glass in the choir is particularly delicate; some of it dates from 1320. ✉ *rue Lavoisier.*

$$$ ★ **Domaine de la Tortinière.** This turreted mid-19th century mansion stands proudly on a hill amid vast fields and woodland, 12 km (7 mi) south of Tours on N10 near Montbazon. Rooms vary in styles, ranging from conventionally old-fashioned to brashly modern. The spacious restaurant looks out over the gardens. Salmon, pigeon, and rabbit with truffles are menu highlights. ✉ *10 rte. de Ballan, 37250 Veigné,* ☎ *02-47-34-35-00,* FAX *02-47-65-25-70. 14 rooms. Restaurant. AE, MC, V. Closed mid-Dec.–Feb.*

$$$ **Univers.** Rooms in this old hotel are all slightly different and all cleverly designed; most look onto the garden. Wood paneling and soft colors give them warmth. The lobby has murals depicting some famous guests, among them Winston Churchill and Maurice Chevalier. ✉ *5 bd. Heurteloup, 37000,* ☎ *02-47-05-37-12,* FAX *02-47-61-51-80. 80 rooms, 8 suites. Restaurant. AE, DC, MC, V.*

Villandry

The **Château de Villandry,** near the River Cher, is known for its pains-★ takingly relaid 16th-century **gardens,** with long avenues of 1,500 manicured lime trees. The château interior was restored in the mid-19th century. Note the painted and gilded ceiling from Toledo and the collection of Spanish pictures. ☎ *02-47-50-02-09.* ⏲ *June–Sept., château daily 9–6, gardens daily 9–8; Oct.–May, château daily 9:30–12:30 and 2–5:30, gardens daily 9–dusk.*

Langeais

Across the Loire from Villandry is the small, old village of Langeais, which seems to be crushed underfoot by its massive castle. The **Château de Langeais,** built during the 1460s and never altered, is one of the Loire's most uncompromising castles. Its apartments contain a superb collection of tapestries, chests, and beds. ☎ *02-47-96-72-60.* ⏲ *Easter-Oct., daily 9-6:30; Nov.-Easter, Tues.-Sun. 9-noon and 2-5.*

Azay-le-Rideau

One of the region's prettiest châteaux is the early 16th century **Château d'Azay-le-Rideau.** Its high roof and cheerful corner turrets are reflected in the River Indre, which surrounds the château like a lake. This graceful ensemble compensates for the château's spartan interior, as does the charm of the surrounding village. ☎ *02-47-45-42-04.* ⏲ *Apr.-Sept., daily 9:30-6; Oct.-Mar., daily 9:30-noon and 2-5.*

Ussé

The **Château d'Ussé**—actually in the village of Rigny-Ussé—claims to be the setting of the French fairy-tale *Sleeping Beauty.* Its bristling turrets, terraces, and forest backcloth are undeniably romantic. Be sure to also visit the dainty Renaissance chapel in the park. ☎ *02-47-95-54-05.* ⏲ *Mid-Feb.-mid-Nov., daily 9-noon and 2-6.*

Chinon

Chinon is an ancient town nestled by the River Vienne, with a rock-of-ages castle patrolling the horizon. The 12th-century **Château de Chinon,** with walls 400 yards long, is mainly in ruins, though there's a small museum in the **Logis Royal** (Royal Chambers). The **Tour de l'Horloge** (Clock Tower), whose bell has sounded the hours since 1399, contains the **Musée Jeanne d'Arc** (Joan of Arc Museum). There are panoramic views of the Vienne river valley from the ramparts. ☎ *02-47-93-13-45.* ⏲ *Nov.-mid-Mar., daily 9-noon and 2-5; mid-Mar.-June and Sept., daily 9-6; July-Aug., daily 9-7; Oct., daily 9-5.*

$$$ ✕▦ **Château de Marçay.** In this 15th-century château, 6 km (4 mi) south of Chinon via D49 and D116, Pascal Bodin prepares excellent cuisine—carpaccio of duck, and tournedos of salmon in a Chinon wine sauce. Rooms are furnished with antiques; beams and gables add warmth. Those on the ground floor in the west wing have private patios; the ones in the pavilion near the château, though pleasantly furnished, have less charm. ✉ *37500 Marçay,* ☎ *02-47-93-03-47,* FAX *02-47-93-45-33. 35 rooms (27 in château). Restaurant, pool. AE, DC, MC, V. Closed Feb.-mid-Mar.*

Fontevraud

This quiet village is dominated by its medieval **Abbaye,** where English kings Henry II and Richard the Lionhearted are buried. The church, cloisters, Renaissance chapter house, long-vaulted refectory, and octagonal kitchen are still standing. Guided tours are in French, but you can get a brochure in English. ☎ *02-41-51-71-41.* ⏲ *May-mid-Sept., daily 9-noon and 2-6:30; mid-Sept.-Apr., daily 9:30-noon and 2-5.*

Saumur

The prosperous town of Saumur is famous for its riding school, wines, and castle. The **Château de Saumur**—a white 14th-century castle—towers above the river. It is home to two outstanding museums: the **Musée des Arts Décoratifs** (Decorative Arts Museum), featuring porcelain and enamels; and the **Musée du Cheval** (Horse Museum), with saddles, stirrups, skeletons, and Stubbs engravings. ☎ *02-41-40-24-40.* ⏲ *July-Sept., daily 9-6:30; Oct. and Apr.-June, daily 9-11:30 and 2-6; Nov.-Mar., Wed.-Mon. 9:30-noon and 2-5:30.*

$$ ✕▦ **Anne d'Anjou.** Close to the center of town, this hotel facing the river has a view of the château (floodlit at night) perched above. Inside the 18th-century building, the simple rooms are filled with both old furniture and contemporary decor; Room 102 has wood-panel paintings and Empire furnishings. The restaurant, Les Ménestrels, serves traditional cuisine. ✉ *32 quai Mayaud, 49400,* ☎ *02–41–67–30–30,* FAX *02–41–67–51–00. 50 rooms. Restaurant. AE, DC, MC, V.*

Angers

This historic city on the River Maine, just north of the Loire, is dominated by its castle. The feudal **Château d'Angers,** built by St-Louis (1228–38), has a dry moat, drawbridge, and 17 round towers along its 1-km-long (½-mi-long) walls. A gallery houses an exquisite tapestry ★ collection, notable for the blockbuster **Apocalypse Tapestry,** gorily evoking scenes from the Book of Revelation. It was woven in Paris around 1380 and restored to almost pristine glory in 1996. ☎ *02–41–87–43–47.* ⏲ *July–Aug., daily 10–7; Sept.–June, daily 10–5.*

$ ✕ **La Treille.** For traditional, simple fare, try this small, two-story mom-and-pop restaurant just off the place Ste-Croix (next to the cathedral). The prix-fixe menu may start with a *salade au chèvre chaud* (warm goat cheese salad), followed by confit of duck, and an apple tart. The upstairs dining room has a party atmosphere; downstairs is better for quiet conversation. ✉ *12 rue Montault,* ☎ *02–41–88–45–51. MC, V. Closed Sun.*

$$$ ✕🏨 **Pavillon Le Quéré.** Paul Le Quéré's luxurious hotel complements his fine restaurant in a mansion off the main avenue. Rooms were decorated by his wife, Martine, in classic modern style. The chef happily juggles tradition and modern innovations. ✉ *3 bd. du Maréchal-Foch, 49100,* ☎ *02–41–20–00–20,* FAX *02–41–20–06–20. 6 rooms, 4 suites. Restaurant. AE, DC, MC, V.*

The Loire Valley Essentials

Getting Around

The easiest way to visit the Loire châteaux is by car; N152 hugs the riverbank and offers excellent sightseeing possibilities. Trains run along the Loire Valley every two hours, supplemented by local bus services. A peaceful way to explore the region is to rent a bicycle at one of the SNCF train stations.

Guided Tours

Bus tours of the main châteaux leave daily in summer from Tours, Blois, Angers, Orléans, and Saumur: Ask at the relevant tourist office for latest times and prices. Most châteaux insist that you follow one of their tours; try to get a booklet in English before joining the tour, as most are in French.

Visitor Information

Angers (✉ pl. du Président-Kennedy, ☎ 02–41–23–51–11). **Blois** (✉ 3 av. du Dr-Jean-Laigret, ☎ 02–54–74–06–49). **Orléans** (✉ pl. Albert-1er, ☎ 02–38–24–05–05). **Tours** (✉ 78 rue Bernard-Palissy, ☎ 02–47–70–37–37).

NORMANDY

Jutting out into the Channel, Normandy has had more connections with the English-speaking world than any other part of France, from William the Conqueror to D Day. Visitors flock here not only to see historic monuments but to relax in the rich countryside amid apple orchards, lush meadows, and sandy beaches.

The historic cities of Rouen and Caen, capitals of Upper and Lower Normandy, respectively, are full of churches, well-preserved buildings, and museums. The Seine Valley is lined with abbeys and castles from all periods; along the coast are remnants of the D-Day landings. Normandy also has one of France's most enduring tourist attractions:

Mont-St-Michel, a remarkable Gothic abbey perched on a rocky mount off the Cotentin peninsula.

Étretat and Fécamp on the Alabaster Coast and Deauville, Trouville, and Honfleur on the Côte Fleurie (Flower Coast) are among Normandy's many seaside resorts. Normandy is also recognized as one of France's finest gastronomic regions for its excellent cheeses, cider, Calvados, and wide range of seafood dishes.

A13 and N13, linking Rouen to Caen, Bayeux, and Cherbourg, are the backbones of Normandy. The expressway goes as far as Caen; it is fast highway thereafter.

Les Andelys

In one of the most picturesque loops of the Seine, the small town of Les Andelys is set against magnificent chalky cliffs. Dominating the town are the imposing ruins of the **Château Gaillard,** a castle built in 1196 by Richard the Lionhearted, king of England and duke of Normandy. It overlooks Les Andelys from the top of the river's chalky cliffs, with spectacular views in both directions. ✉ *Rue Richard-Coeur-de-Lion,* ☎ *02–32–54–41–93.* ⏲ *Mid-Mar.–mid-Nov., Thurs.–Mon. 10–12:30 and 2–5, Wed. 2–5.*.

Rouen

Numbers in the margin correspond to points of interest on the Rouen map.

Although blitzed during World War II, Rouen retains much medieval charm. The square where Joan of Arc was burned at the stake in 1431 has been transformed beyond recognition, but the adjacent rue du Gros-Horloge, with its giant Renaissance clock built in 1527, will fire your imagination.

1 You may be familiar with the facade of Rouen's **Cathédrale Notre-Dame** from Claude Monet's famous series of paintings. The facade has suffered badly from war since Monet's days, but the two towers, the older, 12th-century Tour St-Romain and the more intricate Tour de Beurre, retain lofty appeal. The huge metal spire over the crossing is a 19th-century appendage of dubious distinction. Inside, note the 160-ft tower above the crossing on its four massive pillars, and the richly carved staircase in the north transept. ✉ *Pl. de la Cathédrale.* ⏲ *Mon.–Sat. 8–7, Sun. 8–6.*

2 The modern, fish-shape **Église de Jeanne d'Arc** (Church of Joan of Arc), built in the old market square on the site of Joan of Arc's execution, showcases some pleasantly incongruous 16th-century stained glass, rescued from a church bombed in 1944. ✉ *Pl. du Vieux-Marché.* ⏲ *Daily 10–12:15 and 2–6, except Fri. and Sun. mornings.*

3 The Renaissance **Palais de Justice** (Law Courts), the most impressive civic building in Rouen, date from the early 16th century. The facade bristles with a forest of turrets, pinnacles, gables, and buttresses. ✉ *34–36 rue des Juifs,* ☎ *02–35–52–88–70.*

4 The Flamboyant Gothic church of **St-Maclou** has an unusual five-gable facade, riotous stonework, and intricately carved bronze and wood Renaissance doors. ✉ *Pl. St-Maclou.* ⏲ *Mon.–Sat. 10–noon and 2:30–6; Sun. 3–5:30.*

5 **Abbaye St-Ouen,** an airy, beautifully proportioned 14th-century abbey-church, has splendid medieval stained glass and one of France's most sonorous 19th-century organs. ✉ *Pl. du Général-de-Gaulle.* ⏲ *Mid-Mar.–Oct., Wed.–Mon. 8–noon and 2–6; Nov.–mid-Dec. and mid-Jan.–mid-Mar., Wed., Sat., and Sun. 10–12:30 and 2–6.*

Normandy (Normandie)

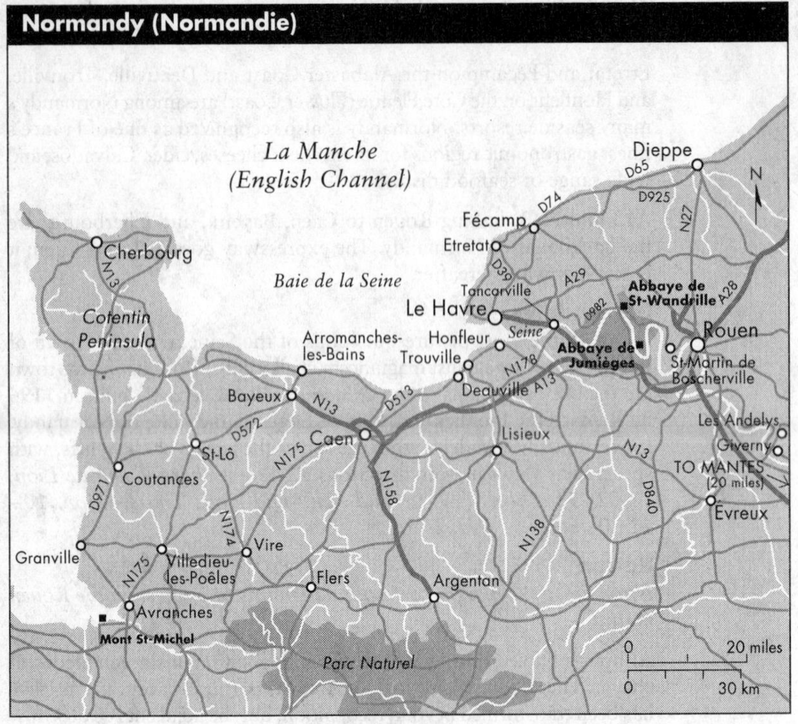

6 The church of **St-Godard.** A painted wooden ceiling and fine medieval stained glass, especially the *Tree of Jesse* dating from 1506, distinguish this church. ✉ *Pl. St-Godard,* ☎ *02–35–71–47–12.*

7 The **Musée des Beaux-Arts** (Fine Arts Museum) specializes in 17th- and 19th-century French painting, with an emphasis on works by local artists and a collection of macabre paintings by Rouen-born painter Théodore Géricault. ✉ *26 bis rue Jean-Lecanuet,* ☎ *02–35–71–28–40.* ⏲ *Wed.–Mon. 10–6.*

8 The curious **Musée Le Secq des Tournelles** (Wrought Ironwork Museum), housed in the disused church of St-Laurent, claims to have the world's finest collection of wrought iron. ✉ *rue Jacques-Villon,* ☎ *02–35–07–31–74.* ⏲ *Wed.–Mon. 10–1 and 2–6.*

9 At the **Musée de la Céramique** (Ceramics Museum), you can see examples of local earthenware; Rouen used to be a renowned faience-making center, reaching its heyday in the early 18th century. ✉ *rue Faucon,* ☎ *02–35–07–31–74.* ⏲ *Wed.–Mon. 10–1 and 2–6.*

10 The name of the pedestrian rue du Gros-Horloge, Rouen's most popular street, comes from the **Gros-Horloge** itself, a giant Renaissance clock; in 1527 the Rouennais had a splendid arch built especially for it. A 15th-century belfry offers the chance to study the iron mechanism. ✉ *rue du Gros-Horloge.* ⏲ *Wed.–Mon. 10–1 and 2–6.*

$$$ ✕ **La Couronne.** Built in 1345, La Couronne is supposedly the oldest inn in France. Amid the oak beams, leather upholstery, and woodwork, there's a sculpture collection. The traditional cuisine features homemade foie gras and turbot in flaky pastry. Keep to the "menu Normand" or expect a hefty bill. ✉ *31 pl. du Vieux-Marché,* ☎ *02–35–71–66–66. Reservations essential. AE, DC, MC, V.*

Abbaye St-Ouen, **5**
Cathédrale Notre-Dame, **1**
Église de Jeanne d'Arc, **2**
Gros-Horloge, **10**
Musée de la Céramique, **9**
Musée des Beaux Arts, **7**
Musée Le Secq des Tournelles, **8**
Palais de Justice, **3**
St-Godard, **6**
St-Maclou, **4**

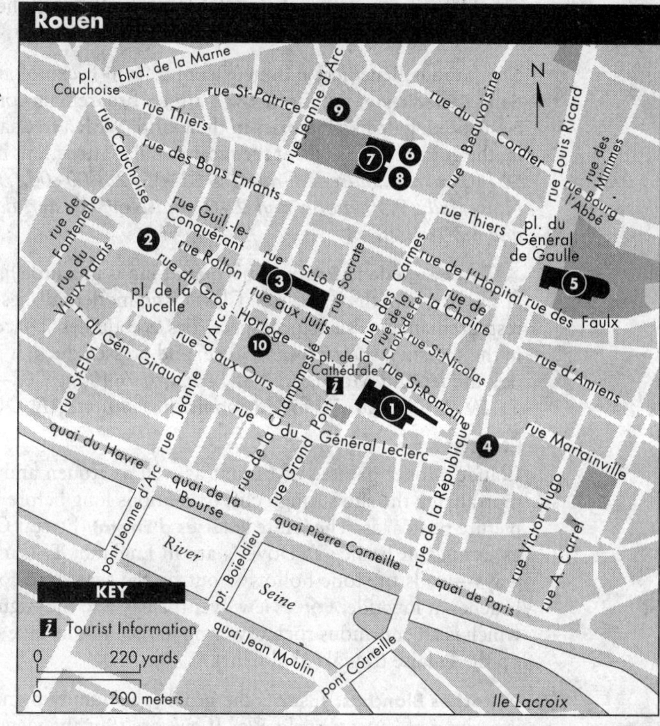

$$–$$$ **Mercure Rouen-Centre.** In the jumble of narrow streets near the cathedral (a challenge if you arrive by car), this modern hotel has small, comfortable rooms that are breezily furnished in pastels. It's not particularly charming, but it's central and there's a bar for an evening aperitif. ✉ *7 rue de la Croix-de-Fer, 76000,* ☎ *02–35–52–69–52,* FAX *02–35–89–41–46. 125 rooms. AE, DC, MC, V.*

$–$$ **Hôtel de la Cathédrale.** This appealing hotel is in a medieval building on a narrow pedestrian street behind the cathedral (you can sleep soundly: The cathedral bells don't boom out the hour at night). Rooms are petite, but neat and comfortable. ✉ *12 rue St-Romain, 76000,* ☎ *02–35–71–57–95,* FAX *02–35–70–15–54. 25 rooms. MC, V.*

Abbaye de Jumièges

The **Abbaye de Jumièges,** once a powerful Benedictine center, was founded in the 7th century but dismantled during the Revolution. The ruins are substantial and spectacular, and you can also visit the remains of the chapter house and several chapels. ✉ *24 rue Guillaume-le-Conquérant,* ☎ *02–35–37–24–02.* ⌚ *Apr.–Sept., daily 9–7; Oct.–Mar., daily 9:30–12:30 and 2–5:30.*

Abbaye de St-Wandrille

The **Abbaye de St-Wandrille** was founded in 649, and still has a Benedictine community. Arrive early in the morning to hear the Gregorian chants at Mass. ☎ *02–35–96–23–11.* ⌚ *Guided tour at 3 and 4 weekdays, 11:30 Sun.*

Fécamp

Fécamp, at the foot of the highest cliffs in Normandy, was the region's first place of pilgrimage. Legend has it that in the first century, an abandoned boat washed ashore here with a bottle containing Christ's blood.

The 11th-century **Église de la Trinité** was built for all the pilgrims. ✉ *Rue Leroux.* ⏲ *Guided tours May–Oct., Sun. at 11, 3, and 5.*

The famous Bénédictine liqueur comes from Fécamp, and the **Palais de la Bénédictine,** rebuilt in 1892 after a fire, remains one of the fanciest-looking drinks factories in the world. With a free sample thrown in, the guided tour is one of the most popular attractions in Normandy. ✉ *110 rue Alexandre-le-Grand,* ☎ *02–35–28–00–06.* ⏲ *Easter–mid-Nov., daily 9:30–noon and 2–6; mid-Nov.–Easter, daily 10–1:30 and 3:30–4:30.*

$$ ✕ **Auberge de la Rouge.** This quaint inn is in a little hamlet 1 ½ km (1 mi) or so south of Fécamp. Classic and modern dishes served at the restaurant include such local specialties as coquilles St-Jacques (scallops in the shell in a sherry cream sauce) and pressed duck; it is closed Sunday dinner and Monday. ✉ *St-Léonard, 76400,* ☎ *02–35–28–07–59,* FAX *02–35–28–70–55. 8 rooms. Restaurant. AE, DC, MC, V.*

Étretat

Claude Monet painted at Étretat as well as Rouen and Giverny, immortalizing the site's rough cliff formations long before the advent of picture postcards. The white **Falaises d'Étretat** (Étretat Cliffs) are just as famous in France as Dover's are in England. Two immense archways—walls of stone hollowed out by the sea—lead to neighboring beaches at low tide. For a view over the bay and the **Aiguille** (Needle), which is an enormous rock towering in the middle, take the little path up the **Falaise d'Aval** (Aval Cliff).

$$ ✕ **Roches Blanches.** Just off the beach, this family-owned restaurant is a concrete, post–World War II eyesore. But the views and the superbly fresh seafood are another story. Be sure to try the veal escalope flambéed in Calvados, and the mussels. ✉ *rue Abbé-Cochet,* ☎ *02–35–27–07–34. Reservations essential. MC, V. Closed Wed. in summer, Tues.–Thurs. Oct.–Mar.*

$$ **Donjon.** This charming little château, in a park overlooking the town, has a lovely view of the bay. Rooms are individually furnished, spacious, comfortable, and quiet. Reliable French cuisine is served with flair in the cozy, romantic restaurant. ✉ *chemin de St-Clair, 76790,* ☎ *02–35–27–08–23,* FAX *02–35–29–92–24. 10 rooms, 7 with bath. Restaurant, pool. AE, DC, MC, V.*

Honfleur

Toward the end of the last century, pretty Honfleur, once an important port for maritime expeditions, became a favorite spot for vacationers and painters, including the Impressionists. In summer or on weekends, be prepared for lines at restaurants and cafés. Its lively cobbled streets, harbors full of colorful yachts, and the **Église Ste-Catherine**—a 15th-century wooden church—make it the most picturesque town on the Normandy coast.

$$$ ✕ **Absinthe.** A magnificent 17th-century dining room is the setting for nouvelle and traditional cuisine, with an accent on seafood. In warm weather dine on the quayside terrace. There's also a pub, the Ivanhoe. ✉ *10 quai de la Quarantaine,* ☎ *02–31–89–39–00. AE, DC, MC, V. Closed 2nd ½ Nov.*

$$–$$$ ✕ **Assiette Gourmande.** When Chef Gérard Bonnefoy comes into the dining room at Honfleur's unsung top restaurant, he decides what you would enjoy after a few minutes of conversation. Hopefully you will be lucky to have the superb coquilles St-Jacques grilled with sautéed asparagus in a raspberry vinaigrette and orange sauce. ✉ *2 quai des Passagers,* ☎ *02–31–89–24–88. AE, DC, MC, V. Closed Tues. No dinner Mon. off-season.*

$$ ★ **Cheval Blanc.** Owners Alain Petit and his wife run this friendly inn in a renovated 15th-century building on the harbor front. Rooms offer fine views of the port; No. 34 (slightly more expensive than the others) has gabled ceilings, a small sitting area, and a whirlpool bath. ✉ *2 quai des Passagers, 14600,* ☎ *02–31–81–65–00,* FAX *02–31–89–52–80. 33 rooms, 14 with bath. MC, V. Closed Jan.*

Trouville–Deauville

Although separated only by the little River Touques, the popular resorts of Trouville and Deauville are vastly different in mood. Deauville is the fancier of the two, with its palaces, casino, horse racing, and film festival. Some would say all the style is artificial: The town was built from scratch in the 1860s, and is invaded each weekend by wealthy Parisians. Neighboring Trouville retains an active fishing fleet and working population, and is less damaging to the wallet. Its beach is arguably larger and more scenic, tucked in beneath a corniche.

$$$$ ✕ **Normandy.** The fashionable and monied from Paris have been attracted to this hotel, with its traditional Norman facade and underground passage to the casino, since it opened in 1912. Request a room with a sea view. The gourmet restaurant, La Potinière, and the large dining room both serve mouthwatering variations of Norman cuisine. *38 rue Jean-Mermoz, 14800 Deauville,* ☎ *02–31–98–66–22, 800/223–5652 for U.S. reservations,* FAX *02–31–98–66–23. 271 rooms. 2 restaurants, indoor pool, sauna. AE, DC, MC, V.*

$–$$ **Carmen.** This straightforward, unpretentious little hotel is around the corner from the casino and a block from the sea. Rooms range from plain and inexpensive to comfortable and moderate. The owners, the Bude family, are on hand to give advice. *24 rue Carnot, 14360 Trouville,* ☎ *02–31–88–35–43,* FAX *02–31–88–08–03. 18 rooms. Restaurant. AE, DC, MC, V. Closed Jan.–mid-Feb., and 10 days in Oct.*

Caen

Caen, a few miles inland, is the capital of Lower Normandy and one of the region's few cities. It was badly bombed in 1944 but has been rebuilt with care.

William the Conqueror was responsible for Caen's large **Château,** an impregnable-looking fortress glowering down from a hill above the city center. Its ramparts now encircle a public garden containing two museums, the **Musée de Normandie** (a museum of regional history) and the **Musée des Beaux-Arts** (Fine Arts Museum with a choice collection of old masters). William and his queen, Mathilda, also built Caen's "his ★ and hers" **abbeys:** the **Abbaye aux Dames** (Women's Abbey), now a hospital (only the church is open to visitors); and the **Abbaye aux Hommes** (Men's Abbey), with a cathedral-size church. Guided tours are given hourly.

A good introduction to the Normandy landings of June 1944 is available at the **Mémorial,** a museum on the north side of the city. ✉ *Esplanade Dwight-D.-Eisenhower,* ☎ *02–31–06–06–44.* *65 frs.* ⏲ *Jan.–June and Sept.–Dec., daily 9–7; July–Aug., daily 9–9.*

$$$ ✕ **Bourride.** Michel Bruneau, owner and chef of this famous restaurant on one of the town's oldest streets, bases his inventive recipes almost exclusively on local and regional produce. Specialties include skate caramelized in honey and cider, and meat pastry cooked in cider vinegar. ✉ *15 rue du Vaugueux,* ☎ *02–31–93–50–76. AE, DC, MC, V. Closed Sun., Mon., most of Jan., and Aug. 15–31.*

$$ ✕ **Dauphin.** Rooms in this old priory are small but clean; many overlook a quiet courtyard. The restaurant serves excellent Norman dishes, emphasizing seafood with unusually light sauces. ✉ *29 rue Gémare,*

14000, ☎ 02–31–86–22–26, FAX 02–31–86–35–14. 21 rooms. Restaurant. AE, DC, MC, V.

Bayeux

Bayeux, a few miles inland from the D-Day beaches, was the first French town freed by the Allies in June 1944. It's known primarily as the home ★ of **La Tapisserie de la Reine Mathilde** (Queen Mathilde's Tapestry, more commonly known as The Bayeux Tapestry), which tells the epic story of William's conquest of England in 1066. You can rent headphones in English (5 frs) to have the tapestry commented to you scene by scene. ✉ *13 bis rue de Nesmond,* ☎ *02–31–51–25–50.* ⏲ *May–mid-Sept., daily 9–6:30; mid-Sept.–Apr., daily 9:30–12:30 and 2–6.*

The **Musée Baron Gérard** (Baron Gerard Museum) has a fine collection of Bayeux porcelain and lace, ceramics from Rouen, a marvelous array of apothecary jars from the 17th and 18th centuries, and furniture and paintings from the 16th to 19th centuries. ✉ *1 rue de la Chaine,* ☎ *02–31–92–14–21.* ⏲ *June–mid-Sept., daily 9–7; mid-Sept.–May, daily 10–12:30 and 2–6. Last admission 30 mins before closing. Closed 2 wks in Jan.*

Dominating the heart of Bayeux is the **Cathédrale Notre-Dame,** a harmonious mixture of Norman (Romanesque) and Gothic architecture. Note the portal on the south side of the transept, which depicts the assassination of English Archbishop Thomas à Becket in Canterbury Cathedral in 1170. ✉ *Rue de Bienvenu.*

The **Musée de la Bataille de Normandie** (Battle of Normandy Museum), overlooking the British Military Cemetery, traces the Allied advance against the Nazis in 1944. ✉ *Bd. Général-Fabian-Ware,* ☎ *02–31–92–93–41.* ⏲ *May–mid-Sept., daily 9–6:30; mid-Sept.–Apr., daily 10–noon and 2–6.*

$$ ✕ **Les Quatres Saisons.** This restaurant, in the Grand Hotel du Luxembourg, is the best in town. Chef Daniel Rivièνe's classical repertoire from Normandy includes chicken roasted with cider, and veal in a sauce strongly scented with Calvados. ✉ *25 rue des Bouchers,* ☎ *02–31–92–00–04. AE, DC, MC, V.*

$ ✕ **L'Amaryllis.** This small, simply decorated restaurant with fewer than 15 tables serves good, reasonably priced Norman fare. For 105 francs you can get a three-course dinner that might include a half dozen oysters, sole with a cider-based sauce, and dessert. ✉ *32 rue St-Patrice,* ☎ *02–31–22–47–94. AE, DC, MC, V. Closed Mon. and mid-Dec.–mid-Jan.*

$$$ ✕🏨 **La Chenevière.** In a late-19th-century grand manor in parkland between Bayeux and the coast, this elegant hotel has rooms with modern furnishings, floor-to-ceiling windows, and flowered bedspreads that add a splash of color. Chef Claude Espraben's Norman dishes are worth the detour. ✉ *Les Escures, 14520 Commes (9 km/5½ mi north of Bayeux via D6),* ☎ *02–31–51–25–25,* FAX *02–31–51–25–20. 19 rooms. Restaurant. AE, MC, V.*

$$ 🏨 **Churchill.** This friendly, family-run inn in an old town house is within walking distance of Bayeux's major attractions. Rooms vary in shape and size. Furnishings are modest and functional. ✉ *14 rue St-Jean, 14400,* ☎ *02–31–21–31–80,* FAX *02–31–21–41–66. 31 rooms. AE, DC, MC, V. Closed mid-Nov.–mid-Mar.*

Arromanches-les-Bains

Not much remains to mark the furious fighting waged hereabouts. In the bay off Arromanches, however, some elements of the floating harbor are still visible. A few hundred yards out to sea you can see the concrete vestiges of **Mulberry B,** an artificial port built for the landings. (American troops landed farther up the coast on Omaha Beach at Mulberry A, which was destroyed by a storm a few months later.)

The **Musée du Débarquement** (Normandy Landings Museum) on the seafront shows the D-Day landing plan and a film (in English) about the operation. ✉ *Pl. du 6-Juin,* ☎ *02–31–22–34–31.* ⏲ *May–Sept., daily 9–7; Oct.–Apr., daily 9:30–4:30.*

★ Mont-St-Michel

The fabled Mont-St-Michel, an offshore rock crowned by the spire of a medieval abbey, is perhaps the most spectacular site in France—and certainly the most visited outside Paris. The best views can be had on the road from Avranches, to the east. The mount's fame comes not just from its location—until the causeway was built, it was cut off from the mainland at high tide—but also from the dramatic nature of its construction during the 8th century, when tons of granite were brought from the nearby Chausey Islands and hauled up the 265-ft peak. It has been a pilgrimage center ever since.

For most of the year Mont-St-Michel—officially a small village with a permanent population of less than 100—is surrounded by sandy beach. The best time to see it is during the high tides of spring and fall, when the sea comes pounding in—dangerously fast—and encircles the mount. **La Merveille** (The Wonder) is the name given to the collection of Gothic buildings on top. What looks like a fortress is in fact a series of architectural layers that trace the evolution of French architecture from Romanesque to late Gothic. You can join a guided tour (in English). ☎ *02–33–60–14–14.* ⏲ *May–Sept., daily 9:30–11:30 and 1:30–6; Oct.–Apr., Wed.–Mon. 9:30–4:30.*

$$$ ✕🏨 **Terrasses Poulard.** In this slightly overpriced collection of town houses, each room is named after a famous Norman personality and decorated accordingly. Several have breathtaking views of the bay; others look out onto a little garden. The restaurant, crowded with American, British, and Canadian tourists, has its best views upstairs. ✉ *Grande Rue, 50116,* ☎ *02–33–60–14–09,* FAX *02–33–60–37–31. 29 rooms. Restaurant. AE, DC, MC, V.*

$$ 🏨 **Le Manoir de la Roche Turin.** Only 9 km (6 mi) east of Mont-St-Michel, this small ivy-clad manor house is an appealing alternative to high-priced hotels. Rooms are pleasantly old-fashioned; bathrooms are modern. ✉ *34 route de la Roche-Turin, 50220 Courtils,* ☎ *02–33–70–96–55,* FAX *02–33–48–35–20. 11 rooms with bath, 1 suite. Restaurant. MC, V. Closed mid-Nov.–mid-Mar.*

Normandy Essentials

Getting Around

Normandy is best visited by car. Though trains leave regularly from Paris to Rouen, Caen, and Bayeux, limited train connections make cross-country traveling difficult. And visiting many of the historic monuments and towns—such as Honfleur, which has no train station—means using buses, which don't always run so frequently.

Guided Tours

One-day excursions (990 frs) to Mont-St-Michel from Paris are organized by the following: **Cityrama** (✉ 147 rue St-Honoré, 75001 Paris, ☎ 01–44–55–61–00) and **Paris Vision** (✉ 214 rue de Rivoli, 75001 Paris, ☎ 01–42–60–31–25).

Visitor Information

Les Andelys (✉ rue Philippe Auguste, ☎ 02–32–54–41–93). **Bayeux** (✉ 3 rue St-Jean, ☎ 02–31–51–28–28). **Caen** (✉ 12 pl. St-Pierre,

☎ 02–31–27–14–14). **Deauville** (✉ rue Victor-Hugo, ☎ 02–31–14–40–00). **Étretat** (✉ pl. Maurice-Guillard, ☎ 02–35–27–05–21). **Fécamp** (✉ 113 rue Alexandre-le-Grand, ☎ 02–35–28–51–01). **Honfleur** (✉ 9 rue de la Ville, ☎ 02–31–89–23–30). **Mont-St-Michel** (✉ Corps de Garde des Bourgeois, ☎ 02–33–60–14–30). **Rouen** (✉ 25 pl. de la Cathédrale, ☎ 02–32–08–32–40).

BURGUNDY AND LYON

For a region whose powerful medieval dukes held sway over large tracts of Western Europe and whose current image is closely allied to its expensive wine, Burgundy is a place of surprisingly rustic, quiet charm. Its leading religious monument is the Romanesque basilica at Vézelay, once an important pilgrimage center, and today a tiny village hidden in rolling hills.

The heart of Burgundy is the dark, brooding Morvan Forest. Dijon, the region's only city, retains something of its medieval opulence, but its present reputation is essentially gastronomic. Top restaurants abound, and local industries produce mustard, cassis, snails, and—of course—wine. The vineyards leading down toward Beaune are among the world's most distinguished and picturesque. The vines continue to flourish as you head south along the Saône Valley, through the Mâconnais and Beaujolais, toward Lyon, one of France's most appealing cities.

Burgundy is best visited by car. Its meandering country roads invite leisurely exploration. There are few big towns, and traveling around by train is unrewarding, especially as the infrequent cross-country trains steam along at the speed of a legendary Burgundy snail. However, the TGV (high speed trains) zip out of Paris to Dijon (75 minutes), Mâcon (100 minutes), and Lyon (2 hours).

It makes sense for Sens to be your first stop on the way down to Burgundy, as it is just 120 km (75 mi) southeast of Paris on N6—a fast, pretty road that hugs the Yonne Valley south of Fontainebleau. Take the autouroute, A6, if you are in a hurry. Zigzag across N6 and A6, taking the smaller roads that lead off them. A6, which turns into A7, is the highway to the Mediterranean and will take you close to Auxerre, Dijon, Beaune, Mâcon, and Lyon, then down the Rhone valley to Provence.

Sens

Sens is home to France's senior archbishop and is dominated by the 12th-century **Cathédrale St-Étienne.** This is one of the oldest cathedrals in France and has a foursquare facade topped by towers and an incongruous little Renaissance campanile. The vast, harmonious interior contains outstanding stained glass of various periods.

The 13th-century **Palais Synodal** (Synodal Palace), alongside the Cathédrale St-Étienne, with six grand windows and a vaulted hall, provides a first encounter with Burgundy's multicolor tile roofs; from its courtyard there is a fine view of the cathedral's south transept, constructed in the fluid Flamboyant Gothic style of the 16th century. It's now a museum with an emphasis on archaeological finds from the Gallo-Roman period as well as statues, mosaics, and tapestries. ✉ *Rue des Déportés de la Résistance.* ⏲ *June–Sept., daily 10–noon and 2–6; Oct.–May, Wed. and weekends 10–noon and 2–6, Mon., Thurs., and Fri. 2–6.*

$$ ★ ✕🏨 **Paris et Poste.** This hotel, a former staging post, is a pleasant stop on the way from Paris to Burgundy. Rooms are comfortably large; the quietest are on the inner courtyard. The helpful staff and big breakfasts (rare in France) create a sense of well-being, confirmed by the robust

Burgundy (Bourgogne)

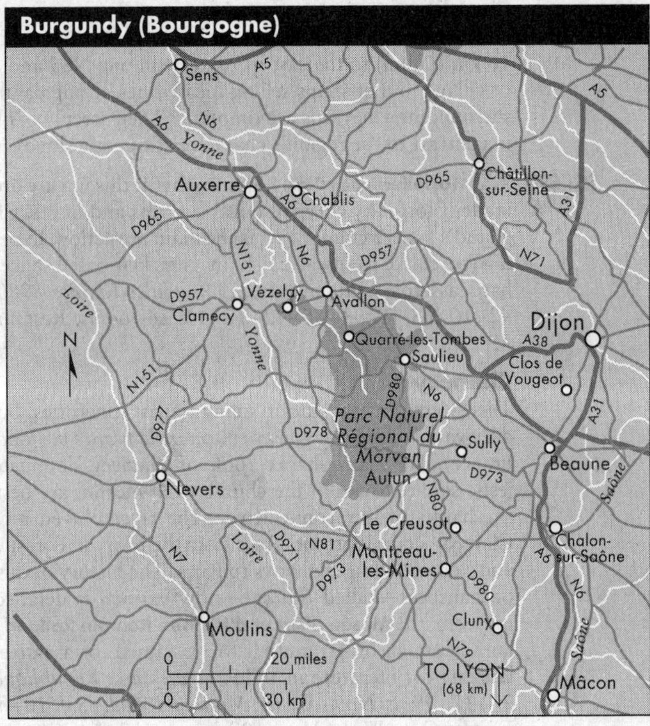

dinner. ✉ *97 rue de la République, 89100,* ☎ *03–86–65–17–43,* FAX *03–86–64–48–45. 25 rooms. Restaurant, bar. AE, DC, MC, V.*

Auxerre

Auxerre is a small, peaceful town perched on a steep hill overlooking the River Yonne. Its main feature is the muscular **Cathédrale St-Étienne** rising majestically from the squat houses around it. It was built between the 13th and 16th centuries and has a powerful north tower similar to that at Clamecy. ✉ *Pl. St-Étienne,* ☎ *03–86–52–31–68.* ⏲ *Easter–Nov., Mon.–Sat. 9–noon and 2–6, Sun. 2–6. A 75-minute son et lumière focusing on Roman Gaul is presented every evening June–Sept.*

The town's most interesting church is the former **Abbaye de St-Germain,** which contains a crypt dating from the 9th century. ✉ *Pl. St-Germain,* ☎ *03–86–51–09–74.* ⏲ *Guided crypt tours Wed.–Mon. 9–11:30 and 2–5:30.*

$$ ✕ **Jardin Gourmand.** As its name implies, the Jardin Gourmand has a pretty garden where you can eat *en terrasse* in warm weather. The interior, accented by light-color oak, is equally congenial. The cuisine is innovative—try the duck with black currants. ✉ *56 bd. Vauban,* ☎ *03–86–51–53–52. MC, V. Closed Mon. No lunch Tues.*

$$$ ★ **La Borde.** On rich Burgundy farmlands a couple miles out of the tiny village of Leugny (20 km/12 mi southwest of Auxerre), the Duclos offer four delightful, large rooms with exposed beams in a former granary of a manorial estate. Table d'hôte meals with free-flowing local Burgundy wine are served across the courtyard at the main house. ✉ *89130 Leugny (20 km/12 mi southwest of Auxerre on D50 east of Toucy),* ☎ *03–86–47–64–28,* FAX *03–86–47–60–28. 4 rooms. No credit cards.*

Chablis

Famous for its dry white wine, Chablis makes an attractive excursion 16 km (10 mi) to the east of Auxerre, along N65 and D965. Beware of village tourist shops selling local wines at unpalatable prices. The surrounding vineyards are dramatic: Their steeply banked hills stand in contrast to the region's characteristic gentle slopes.

$$–$$$ ★ ✕🏨 **Hostellerie des Clos.** Guest rooms at this inn are ordinary, but are made colorful by cheerful floral curtains and quilts. Chef Michel Vignaud's superb culinary art is the main attraction. Experience his *sandre* (perchlike freshwater fish) in a chicken-based sauce, or the robust hare casserole (autumn only). ✉ *Rue Jules-Rathier, 89800,* ☎ *03–86–42–10–63,* FAX *03–86–42–17–11. 26 rooms. Restaurant. AE, DC, MC, V.*

Clamecy

This sleepy town is not on many tourist itineraries, but its tumbling alleyways and ancient houses epitomize *la France profonde* (classic rural France). The many-shaped roofs of Clamecy, dominated by the majestic square tower of the church of **St-Martin,** are best viewed from the banks of the Yonne River. The river played a crucial role in Clamecy's development: Trees from the Morvan Forest were cut down and floated in huge convoys to Paris. The history of this curious form of transport—called *flottage*—now extinct, is detailed in the town museum, the **Musée d'Art et d'Histoire Romain Rolland** (Romain Rolland Museum of Art and History), named for a native son, a Nobel laureate for literature in 1915. ✉ *av. de la République,* ☎ *03–86–27–17–99.* ⏲ *Nov.–Easter, Mon. and Wed.–Sat. 10–noon and 3–6; Easter–Oct., Wed.–Mon. 10–noon and 2–6.*

Vézelay

Burgundy's leading religious monument is the Romanesque basilica in Vézelay, once an important pilgrimage center, and today a tiny village hidden in rolling hills. The **Basilique Ste-Madeleine** is perched on a rocky crag, with commanding views of the surrounding countryside. It rose to fame during the 11th century as the resting place of the relics of St. Mary Magdalene and became a departure point for the great pilgrimages to Santiago de Compostela in northwest Spain. The church was rescued from decay by the 19th-century Gothic Revival architect Eugène Emmanuel Viollet-le-Duc and counts as one of the foremost Romanesque buildings in existence. ✉ *Pl. de la Basilique,* ☎ *03–86–33–27–73.* ⏲ *8–8, except Mon.–Sat. 12:15–1:15 and 5:15–7:15, and Sun. 10:30–12:30.*

$$$$ ✕🏨 **L'Espérance.** In St-Père-sous-Vézelay, a neighboring village, enjoy chef Marc Meneau's subtle and original cuisine at one of France's premier restaurants (closed Tues., Wed. lunch, and Feb.; reservations and jacket and tie are required). A second restaurant, Le Pré des Marguerites, serves simpler, more traditional, less expensive fare. Rooms in the main house are pretty, but rather small; the others, in nearby buildings, are slightly larger. ✉ *St-Père-sous-Vézelay, 89450,* ☎ *03–86–33–20–45,* FAX *03–86–33–26–15. 40 rooms. 2 restaurants.*

Avallon

Avallon's location, on a promontory, is spectacular, and the old streets and ramparts are great places to stroll. At the venerable church of **St-Lazarus,** you can see how the imagination of medieval stone carvers ran riot with the portals.

$$ ✕🏨 **Moulin des Ruats.** In an old flour mill just southwest of Avallon on D427 is this popular hotel with rustic rooms. Most have a balcony and look out onto the Cousin River. Ask for one of the most recently

renovated ones. Traditional Bourgogne dishes with a strong Provençal accent are served. Most popular is the 230-franc menu; go for simple rather than complex dishes. ✉ *Vallée du Cousin, 89200,* ☎ *03–86–34–07–14,* FAX *03–86–31–65–47. 27 rooms, some with bath or shower. Restaurant. AE, DC, MC, V. Closed Nov.–Feb.*

Parc Naturel Régional du Morvan

If you're in no rush to get to Dijon, take time to explore the northern part of the huge Morvan Regional Park; roads and trails in the park twist and turn past lovely lakes, hills, and forests. This is where Parisians come to hike the well-marked trails and spend nights in small gîtes (rustic bed-and-breakfasts or refuges). Horseback riding is also popular, and some gîtes having stabling facilities. One of the small towns just inside the park (from Avallon, on N6, take D944, then turn left on D10) is **Quarré-les-Tombes**—so called because of the empty prehistoric stone tombs discovered locally and eerily arrayed around the church. The **Rocher de la Pérouse,** 8 km (5 mi) from Quarré-les-Tombes, is an outcrop worth climbing for the view of the Cousin Valley. To leave the park continue to Saulieu via N6, D264, and D977.

Saulieu

Saulieu's reputation belies its size (just 3,000 inhabitants). It is renowned for good food (Rabelais, that 16th-century authority, extolled its hospitality) and Christmas trees (a million are harvested each year). The abbey church of **St-Andoche** is almost as old as Vézelay's, though less imposing and more restored. Next to the church is the town museum, the **Musée François Pompon,** which contains a room devoted to Pompon, the sculptor of Art Deco animals; another dedicated to local gastronomic lore (historic menus and preparation techniques); and a collection of Gallo-Roman funeral stones and sacred art. ✉ *Rue Sallier,* ☎ *03–80–64–19–51.* ⏲ *Apr.–Sept., Wed.–Mon. 10–12:30 and 2–6 (until 5:30 Oct.–Mar.).*

Dijon

Dijon is both the capital of Burgundy and of gastronomy. Testimony
★ to Dijon's bygone splendor is the **Palais des Ducs** (Ducal Palace), now one of France's leading art museums. The tombs of Philip the Bold and John the Fearless head a rich collection of medieval objects and Renaissance furniture. ✉ *Pl. de la Ste-Chapelle,* ☎ *03–80–74–52–70.* ⏲ *Wed.–Mon. 10–6.*

With its 13th-century stained glass, elegant towers, and delicate nave stonework, **Notre-Dame** (✉ rue de la Préfecture) church is one of the city's highlights. Among the city's oldest churches is the **Cathédral St-Bénigne,** (✉ pl. St-Bénigne), with its uncommonly austere interior. The relatively new church of **St-Michel** (✉ pl. St-Michel) is notable for its chunky Renaissance facade. Don't miss the exuberant 15th-century gateway at the **Chartreuse de Champmol** (✉ just off avenue Albert I beyond the train station)—all that remains of a former charterhouse. Next to the Chartreuse de Champmol is the **Puits de Moïse,** the so-called Well of Moses, with six large, realistic medieval statues.

A leisurely trip south of Dijon in the direction of Beaune takes you through some of the world's most famous **vineyards.** Route D122 wends its way past such properties as Gevrey-Chambertin and Chambolle-Musigny, then joins N74 at Chambolle-Musigny.

$ ✕ **Bistrot des Halles.** Of the many restaurants in this area, this one is the best value. Well-prepared dishes range from escargots to sautéed fresh fish in a beurre blanc. Dine at the sidewalk tables or inside, where traditional decor of mirrors and polished wood dominates. ✉ *10 rue Bannelier,* ☎ *03–80–49–94–15. MC, V. Closed Sun. dinner.*

$$–$$$ ✕🏨 **Chapeau Rouge.** If you want a quiet, tasteful room close to the cathedral, this is a good choice. Snails, pigeon, and veal in mustard top the list of regional specialties at the restaurant; reservations are essential. ✉ *5 rue Michelet, 21000,* ☎ *03–80–30–28–10,* FAX *03–80–30–33–89. 29 rooms. Restaurant. AE, DC, MC, V.*

$ ✕🏨 **Hostellerie du Sauvage.** In a courtyard off a busy street in Dijon's old quarter is this small, charming hotel. Rooms are old-fashioned and far from stylish, but they offer a quiet night's sleep. The restaurant, which has sunken beams and open fireplaces, attracts both guests and locals. ✉ *64 rue Mange, 21000,* ☎ *03–80–41–31–21,* FAX *03–80–42–06–07. 23 rooms. Restaurant. MC, V.*

Clos du Vougeot

Come to Vougeot to see its castle. Constructed by Cistercian monks during the 12th century and completed during the Renaissance, the **Château du Clos de Vougeot** is famous as the seat of Burgundy's elite company of wine lovers, the Confrérie des Chevaliers du Tastevin, who gather here in November at the start of an annual three-day festival, Les Trois Glorieuses. ✉ *Château du Clos de Vougeot,* ☎ *03–80–62–86–09.* ⏲ *Apr.–Sept., weekdays and Sun. 9–7, Sat. 9–6:30; Oct.–Mar., weekdays and Sun. 9–11:30 and 2–5:30, Sat. 9–5.*

Beaune

Despite the hordes of tourists, Beaune remains one of the most attractive ★ French provincial towns. The **Hospices de Beaune** (or Hôtel Dieu), founded in 1443 as a hospital, owns some of the region's finest vineyards. Its history is retraced in a museum that also has Rogier van der Weyden's medieval Flemish masterpiece *The Last Judgment* and tapestries. ✉ *Hospices de Beaune,* ☎ *03–80–24–45–00.* ⏲ *Apr.–mid-Nov., daily 9–6:30; mid-Nov.–Mar., daily 9–11:30 and 2–5:30.*

Tapestries, relating the life of the Virgin, hang in Beaune's main church, the **Collégiale Notre-Dame,** dating from 1120. ✉ *Just off av. de la République.*

There are few more delightful experiences than a visit to the candlelit cellars of the **Marché aux Vins** (Wine Market). Here—for the price of admission—you can taste as many of the regional wines as you wish. ✉ *7 rue Nicolas Rolin,* ☎ *03–80–22–27–69 or 03–80–22–25–68.* 🎫 *Entry and tasting: 50 frs.* ⏲ *Easter–3rd weekend in Nov., daily 9:30–noon and 2:30–6:30; late-Nov.–Easter, daily 9:30–noon and 2:30–6.*

$$ ✕ **L'Écusson.** Despite its unimpressive exterior, this is a friendly, comfortable, thick-carpeted restaurant with four prix-fixe menus of outstanding value. For around 200 francs you can have rabbit terrine followed by leg of duck in oxtail sauce, cheese, and dessert. ✉ *2 rue du Lieutenant-Dupuis,* ☎ *03–80–24–03–82. AE, DC, MC, V. Closed Sun., mid-Feb.–mid-Mar.*

$$ ★ ✕ **La Grilladine.** Chef Pierre Lenko's fare at this small, warm restaurant is not elaborate, but it is good, hearty Burgundy cooking. ✉ *17 rue Maufoux,* ☎ *03–80–22–22–36. MC, V. Closed Mon., and 2 wks in the winter (usually end of Nov.–mid-Dec.).*

$$$ ★ 🏨 **Le Cep.** This top hotel in two old town houses (the oldest is circa 1547) is only five minutes from the main square. The spacious rooms have antiques; those facing the courtyard are quieter. Service can become a little harried when tour groups, albeit of fairly small size, check in and out. ✉ *27 rue Maufoux, 21200,* ☎ *03–80–22–35–48,* FAX *03–80–22–76–80. 53 rooms. Restaurant. AE, DC, MC, V.*

$$ 🏨 **Hôtel de la Cloche.** In the heart of town, this welcoming hotel in a 15th-century residence has neat rooms decorated with care. The best have full baths; the smaller, delightful attic rooms have shower only.

✉ *40–42 rue du Faubourg-Madeleine, 21200,* ☎ *03–80–24–66–33,* FAX *03–80–24–04–24. 22 rooms. Restaurant. MC, V.*

Sully

The turreted Renaissance **Château de Sully** stands in a stately park, surrounded by a moat. A monumental staircase leads to the north front and a broad terrace. Marshal MacMahon, president of France from 1873 to 1879, was born here in 1808. ☎ *03–85–82–10–27.* ⏲ *Château: 45-min guided tours June–Sept. (call for times). Grounds: daily 10–noon and 2–6.* 🎫 *Guided tours: 35 frs. Grounds: 15 frs.*

Autun

Autun has been an important town since Roman times, as you can detect from the well-preserved archways Porte St-André and Porte d'Arroux, and the Théâtre Romain, once the largest arena in Gaul.

★ Autun's principal monument is the **Cathédrale St-Lazarus,** a curious Gothic cathedral redone in the Classical style by 18th-century clerics trying to follow fashion. Note the majestic picture by Ingres, the *Martyrdom of St-Symphorien,* in one of the side chapels. ✉ *Pl. St-Louis.*

The **Musée Rolin,** across from the cathedral, contains several fine paintings from the Middle Ages. ✉ *Pl. St-Louis,* ☎ *03–85–52–09–76.* ⏲ *Nov.–Mar., Mon. and Wed.–Sat. 10–noon and 2–6, Sun. 10–noon and 2–5; Apr.–Sept., Wed.–Mon. 9:30–noon and 1:30–6; Oct., Mon. and Wed.–Sat. 10–noon and 2–5, Sun. 10–noon and 2:30–5.*

$$ ✕🏨 **St-Louis.** This comfortable hotel on a quiet street dates from the 17th century, but the well-designed wrought-iron furnishings are imported from Mexico and the manager hails from North America. The pleasant patio-garden is a delight and La Rotonde is one of Autun's top restaurants. ✉ *6 rue de l'Arbalète, 71400,* ☎ *03–85–52–01–01,* FAX *03–85–86–32–54. 52 rooms. Restaurant. AE, DC, MC, V.*

Cluny

The village of Cluny is famous for its medieval abbey, which was once the center of a vast Christian empire and is now a tourist mecca. Founded in the 10th century, the **Ancienne Abbaye** was the biggest church in Europe until the 16th century, when St. Peter's was built in Rome. The ruins give an idea of its original grandeur. Note the **Clocher de l'Eau-Bénite,** a majestic bell tower, and the 13th-century **farinier** (flour mill) with its fine chestnut roof and collection of statues. A small **museum** displays religious paintings, sculptures, and the remains of the *bibliothèque des moines* (monks' library). ☎ *03–85–59–12–79.* ⏲ *Abbey and museum: Nov.–Mar., daily 10:30–11:30 and 2–4; Apr.–June, daily 9:30–noon and 2–6; July–Sept., daily 9–7; Oct., daily 10–noon and 2–5. Museum closed Tues.*

$$$ ✕🏨 **Bourgogne.** Get into the medieval mood of Cluny at this old-fashioned hotel, right next door to the abbey. There is a small garden and an atmospheric restaurant (closed lunch Wednesday) with sober pink decor and refined cuisine: foie gras, snails, and fish with ginger. ✉ *Pl. de l'Abbaye, 71250,* ☎ *03–85–59–00–58,* FAX *03–85–59–03–73. 14 rooms. Restaurant. AE, DC, MC, V. Closed Mon. and mid-Nov.–mid-Feb.*

$ ✕🏨 **Hôtel de l'Abbaye.** This modest hotel is just five minutes from Cluny center. Request one of the three rooms to the right of the dining room. The restaurant serves reasonably priced local cuisine. ✉ *Av. Charles-de-Gaulle, 71250,* ☎ *03–85–59–11–14,* FAX *03–85–59–09–76. 14 rooms, 9 with bath. Restaurant. MC, V. Closed mid-Jan.–mid-Feb.*

Lyon

Lyon, one of France's "second" cities, is easily accessible by car or train. Much of the city has an enchanting air of untroubled prosperity, and the dining choices are plentiful. It's easy to walk its pedestrian streets and explore its sights. If you have a few days, you can visit Vieux Lyon (Old Lyon) on the western bank of the Saône River, the old Roman district of Fourvière above it, and La Presqu'île (Almost Island) between the Saône and the Rhone, which is the main downtown area for shopping, restaurants, bars, and theaters. For 90 francs buy the three-day "Clés de Lyon" museum pass.

It's easy to get around the city on the subway. A single ticket costs 8 francs, a 10-ticket book 68 francs. A day pass for bus and métro is 24 francs (available from bus drivers and machines in the métro).

The cliff-top silhouette of the **Basilique de Notre-Dame-de-Fourvière** is the city's most striking symbol: The 19th-century basilica is an exotic mishmash of styles with an interior that's pure overkill. Climb the observatory heights for the view, instead, and then go to the nearby Roman remains. ✉ *Pl. de Fourvière.* ⏲ *Basilica: daily 8–noon and 2–6. Observatory: Easter–Oct., daily 10–noon and 2–6; Nov.–Easter, weekends 10–noon and 2–5.*

Two ruined, semicircular **Théâtres Romains** (Roman Theaters) are tucked into the hillside, just down from the summit of Fourvière. The **Grand Théâtre,** the oldest Roman theater in France, was built in 15 BC. The smaller **Odéon** was designed for music and poetry performances. ✉ *Colline Fourfière.* ⏲ *Daily 9–dusk.*

The best Lyon museum is the **Musée des Beaux-Arts** (Fine Arts Museum). It houses sculpture, classical relics, and an extensive collection of old masters and Impressionists. ✉ *20 pl. des Terreaux,* ☎ *04–72–10–17–40.* ⏲ *Wed.–Sun. 10:30–6.*

$$ ★ ✕ **Les Muses.** High up under the glass vault of the Opéra de Lyon is this small restaurant run by Philippe Chavent. The nouvelle cuisine makes it hard to choose, but don't pass up the salmon in butter sauce with watercress mousse. The best value at dinner is the 159-franc menu. ✉ *Opéra de Lyon,* ☎ *04–72–00–45–58. Reservations essential. AE, V.*

$ ✕ **Brunet.** Tables are crammed together in this tiny bouchon where the decor is limited to past menus inscribed on mirrors and a few photographs. The food is good, traditional Lyonnais fare; besides the mandatory andouillette sausage and tripe, there is usually excellent roast pork on the 98-franc menu. ✉ *23 rue Claudia,* ☎ *04–78–37–44–31. MC, V. Closed July–Aug., Sun. in June, Sun. and Mon. Sept.–May.*

$$$$ 🏨 **La Cour des Loges.** Four Renaissance mansions have been transformed into this stylish hotel. The immense courtyard, spiral stone staircases, and exposed roof beams lend a courtly ambience. Rooms, varying in size and price, have contemporary or classic decor (No. 62 is particularly attractive). ✉ *6 rue du Boeuf, 69005,* ☎ *04–78–42–75–75,* FAX *04–72–40–93–61. 63 rooms. Pool. AE, DC, MC, V.*

$$–$$$ 🏨 **Grand Hotel des Beaux-Arts.** Half the rooms at this hotel are "inspired worlds" where a particular artist has developed a theme through his paintings. This is a brave concept, but should you want a more standard sleeping environment, other rooms are more traditionally furnished. ✉ *73 rue du Président Édouard-Herriot, pl. des Jacobins, 69002,* ☎ *78–38–09–50,* FAX *78–42–19–19. 80 rooms. AE, DC, MC, V.*

Burgundy and Lyon Essentials

Getting Around

Larger towns can be reached by train, but to get to smaller towns you need a car. A6 speeds south from Paris to Lyon (463 km/287 mi) away. Regional roads are fast and well maintained. The TGV to Lyon leaves from Paris (Gare de Lyon) hourly and arrives in just two hours. There are also six TGVs daily between Charles de Gaulle airport and Lyon. From Lyon there is frequent train service to other points. In addition buses leave Lyon for smaller towns in the region. The international airport for the region is in **Satolas** (☏ 04–72–22–72–21 for flight information), 26 km (16 mi) east of Lyon. Air Inter and other major airlines have connecting services from Paris.

Guided Tours

Write to the **Comité Régional de Tourisme** (✉ B.P. 1602, 21035 Dijon) for information on regional tours using Dijon as a base, including wine tastings and visits to the famous religious centers.

Visitor Information

Auxerre (✉ 1 quai de la République, ☏ 03–86–52–06–19). **Beaune** (✉ rue de l'Hôtel-Dieu, ☏ 03–80–26–31–30). **Dijon** (✉ 29 pl. Darcy, ☏ 03–80–30–35–39). **Lyon** (✉ pl. Bellecour, ☏ 04–78–42–25–75). **Sens** (✉ pl. Jean-Jaurès, ☏ 03–86–65–19–49).

PROVENCE

As you approach Provence there is a magical moment when the north is finally left behind: Cypresses and red-tile roofs appear; you hear the screech of cicadas and catch the scent of wild thyme and lavender—and all of this is against a backdrop of harsh, brightly lit landscapes that inspired the paintings of Paul Cézanne and Vincent van Gogh. Roman remains litter the ground in well-preserved profusion. The theater and triumphal arch at Orange, the amphitheaters at Nîmes and Arles (both are still used for spectacles that include bullfighting), the aqueduct at Pont du Gard, and the mausoleum at St-Rémy-de-Provence are considered the best of their kind in existence.

A number of towns have grown up along the Rhône Valley owing to its historical importance as a communications artery. The biggest is bustling Marseille; Orange, Avignon, Tarascon, and Arles have more picturesque charm. The Camargue, on the other hand, is the marshy realm of birds and beasts, though its coast attracts flocks of vacationers. North of Marseille lies Aix-en-Provence, with an old-time elegance that reflects its former role as regional capital. Extending the traditional boundaries of Provence westward, historic Nîmes has been included. The Riviera is also part of this region but has an identity of its own (☞ The Riviera, *below*).

Orange

Orange is a small, pleasant town that sinks into total siesta somnolence during hot afternoons, but at other times buzzes with visitors keen ★ on admiring its Roman remains. The magnificent, semicircular **Théâtre Antique** (Ancient Theater), in the center of town, is the best-preserved remains of a theater from the ancient world. It was built just before the birth of Jesus and still accommodates 7,000 spectators for open-air concerts and operatic performances. The **Parc de la Colline St-Eutrope,** the banked garden behind the theater, yields a fine view of the theater and the 6,000-ft Mont Ventoux to the east. Orange also has the third-highest Roman arch still standing. The 70-ft **Arc de Triomphe** (Triumphal Arch) was probably built around AD 25 in honor of the Gallic Wars. ✉ *Pl. des Frères-Mounet,* ☏ *04–90–34–70–88.* ⏲ *Apr.–Oct., daily 9–6:30; Nov.–Mar., daily 9–noon and 1:30–5.*

$$–$$$ ★ ✕ **Le Pigraillet.** One of Orange's best lunch spots is Le Pigraillet, at the far end of the gardens behind the theater. You can eat outside or find shelter from the mistral in the glassed-in terrace. The modern cuisine includes crab ravioli, and foie gras in port. ✉ *Chemin de la Colline St-Eutrope,* ☏ *04–90–34–44–25. MC, V. Closed Jan.–Feb. and Mon.*

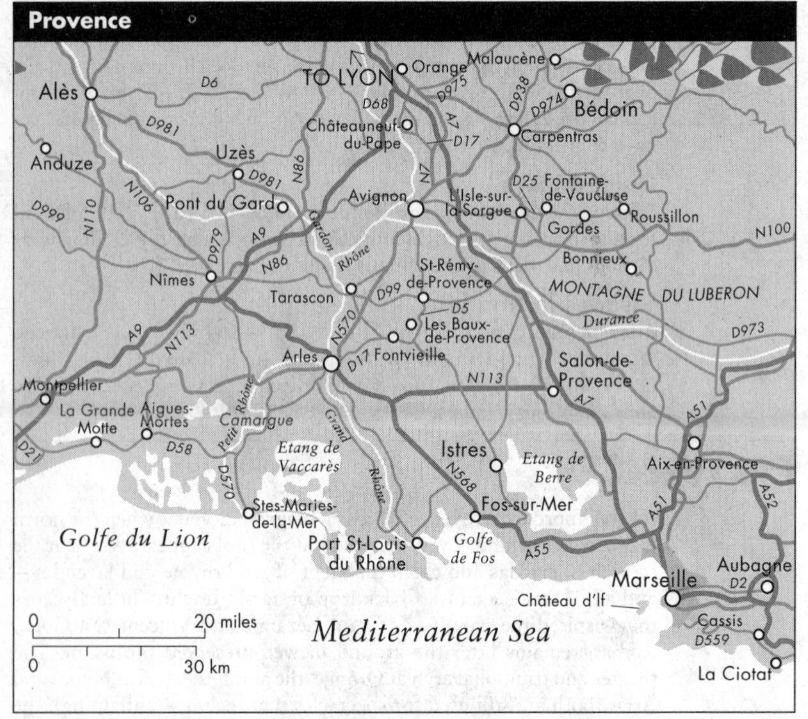

$$ 🏨 **Arène.** This stylish old hotel, on a venerable, shady square lined with plane trees, prides itself on providing a warm welcome, attentive service, and large, air-conditioned rooms. ✉ *Pl. de Langes, 84100,* ☎ *04–90–34–10–95,* FAX *04–90–34–91–62. 30 rooms. Air-conditioning. AE, DC, MC, V. Closed Nov.–mid-Dec.*

Avignon

A warren of medieval alleys nestling behind a protective ring of stocky towers, Avignon is where seven exiled popes camped between 1309 and 1377 after fleeing from the corruption of Rome. The most dominant building within the town walls is the colossal **Palais des Papes** (Papal Palace). It's really two buildings: the severe **Palais Vieux** (Old Palace), built between 1334 and 1342 by Pope Benedict XII, a member of the Cistercian order, which frowned on frivolity, and the more decorative **Palais Nouveau** (New Palace), built in the following decade by the arty, lavish Pope Clement VI. The Great Court, where you enter, links the two. ✉ *Pl. du Palais-des-Papes,* ☎ *04–90–27–50–73.* ⏲ *Mar.–Oct., daily 9–7; Nov.–Mar., daily 9–12:45 and 2–6.*

The 12th-century **Cathédral** near the Palais des Papes contains the Gothic tomb of Pope John XII. Beyond the cathedral is the **Rocher des Doms** (Bluff of the Doms), a large garden where there are fine views of Avignon and the Rhône.

The medieval **Petit Palais** (Small Palace) was once home to cardinals and archbishops. Nowadays it contains an outstanding collection of Old Masters. ✉ *21 pl. du Palais,* ☎ *04–90–86–44–58.* ⏲ *Wed.–Mon. 9:30–noon and 2–6.*

The 12th-century **Pont St-Bénezet** (St-Bénezet Bridge) of "Sur la Pont d'Avignon" fame, is an easy walk from the Petit Palais if you want a demi-inspection of the bridge—only half of it now remains. ☎ *04–*

90–85–60–16. ⏲ Apr.–Sept., daily 9–6:30; Oct.–Mar., Tues.–Sun. 9–1 and 2–5.

In the shop-lined streets of old Avignon is the **Musée Lapidaire,** with a variety of archaeological finds. ✉ *27 rue de la République,* ☎ *04–90–85–75–38.* ⏲ *Wed.–Mon. 10–noon and 2–6.*

The **Musée Calvet,** an 18th-century town house, contains an extensive collection of mainly French paintings from the 16th century on. Greek, Roman, and Etruscan statuettes are also displayed. ✉ *65 rue Joseph-Vernet,* ☎ *04–90–86–33–84.* ⏲ *Wed.–Mon. 10–noon and 2–6.*

$$$ ★ ✕ **Hiély-Lucullus.** This restaurant is among the top 50 in France. The dining room, run with aplomb by Mme. Hiély, is charmingly quiet and dignified. Traditional delicacies include crayfish tails in scrambled eggs inside a puff-pastry case. ✉ *5 rue de la République,* ☎ *04–90–86–17–07. Reservations essential. AE, V. Closed most of Jan., last 2 wks in June, and Mon. No lunch Tues.*

$ ✕ **NaniType.** By 12:30 all the tables are occupied at this centrally located spot off rue de la République. The reasons are good: The price is right—about 55 francs for one large course and 30 francs for a carafe of wine; and the food is wholesome, from seafood salad to andouillette with french fries. ✉ *29 rue Théodore Aubanel,* ☎ *04–90–82–60–90. No credit cards. Closed dinner Sun.–Wed., Nov.–May.*

$$$ ✕🏨 **Europe.** This noble 16th-century town house became a hotel in Napoleonic times. The spacious guest rooms are filled with period furniture. The restaurant, La Vieille Fontaine (closed Sat. lunch and Sun.), serves respectable regional cuisine, which you can eat outside in the stone courtyard. ✉ *12 pl. Crillon, 84000,* ☎ *04–90–82–66–92,* FAX *04–90–85–43–66. 47 rooms. Restaurant. AE, DC, MC, V.*

$ 🏨 **Hôtel Colbert.** This very reasonably priced hotel is 50 yards from the tourist office. Rooms are small but air-conditioned. ✉ *7 rue Agricol Perdiquier, 84000,* ☎ *04–90–86–20–20. 15 rooms, most with shower. Air-conditioning. No credit cards.*

Pont du Gard

West of Avignon is the well-preserved Pont du Gard, a huge, three-tier aqueduct, erected 2,000 years ago as part of a 48-km (30-mi) canal supplying water to Roman Nîmes. Its setting, spanning a rocky gorge 150 ft above the River Gardon, is nothing less than spectacular.

Nîmes

Few towns have preserved such visible links with their Roman past as Nîmes, which is 20 km (12½ mi) southwest of the Pont du Gard (via N86). A three-day, 60-franc "passport," available from the tourist office, admits you to the town's museums and monuments.

★ Start at the **Arènes** (Arena), with a seating capacity of 21,000. An inflatable roof covers it in winter, when various exhibits and shows occupy the space; bullfights and tennis tournaments are held in summer. ✉ *Bd. Victor-Hugo,* ☎ *04–66–67–29–11.* ⏲ *May–Mar., daily 9–noon and 2–6. Apr. guided visits only.*

Take rue de la Cité-Foulc, behind the Arènes, to the **Musée des Beaux-Arts** (Fine Arts Museum), where you can admire a vast Roman mosaic, as well as works by Poussin, Bruegel, Rubens, and Rodin. ✉ *Rue de la Cité-Foulc,* ☎ *04–66–67–38–21.* ⏲ *Tues.–Sat. 11–6.*

The **Musée Archéologique et d'Histoire Naturelle** (Museum of Archaeology and Natural History) is rich in local archaeological finds. ✉ *Bd. de l'Amiral-Courbet,* ☎ *04–66–67–25–57.* ⏲ *Tues.–Sun. 11–6.*

The **Cathédral Notre-Dame et St-Castor** (✉ pl. Aux Herbes), an uninspired 19th-century reconstruction, is of less interest than either of the surrounding pedestrian streets.

The **Musée du Vieux Nîmes** (Museum of Old Nîmes), in a 17th-century bishop's palace, has a vibrant display of embroidered garments and woolen shawls. ✉ *Pl. aux Herbes,* ☎ *04–66–36–00–64.* ⌚ *Tues.–Sun. 11–6.*

North of the cathedral is the **Maison Carrée** (Square House). This former Roman temple, dating from the 1st century AD, is now a gallery for exhibitions. So classically delightful are the lines of this temple that Thomas Jefferson had it copied for Virginia's state capitol. ✉ *Bd. Victor-Hugo.* ⌚ *May–Oct., daily 9–7; Nov.–Apr., daily 9–6.*

The formal **Jardin de la Fontaine** (Fountain Garden) contains the shattered remnant of a Roman ruin, known as the **Temple de Diane.** At the far end of the garden is the **Tour Magne**—a stumpy tower that provides fine views of Nîmes. ✉ *Quai de la Fontaine,* ☎ *04–66–67–29–11.* ⌚ *May–Oct., daily 9–7; Nov.–Apr., daily 9–12:30 and 1:30–6.*

$ ★ ✕ **Nicolas.** Locals have long known about this homey place, which is always packed. A friendly, frazzled staff serves up delicious bourride and other local specialties—all at unbelievably low prices. ✉ *1 rue Poise,* ☎ *04–66–67–50–47. AE, MC, V. Closed Mon., 1st 2 wks in July, and mid-Dec.–1st wk in Jan.*

$$–$$$ ✕🏨 **Impérator.** This little palace-hotel, just a few minutes' walk from the Jardin de la Fontaine, is Nîmes's best. Though it's totally modernized, most rooms retain a quaint Provençal feel. The fine restaurant, L'Enclos de la Fontaine (closed Sat. lunch), is Nîmes's most fashionable eating place. The prix-fixe menus are bargains. ✉ *15 rue Gaston-Boissier, 30900,* ☎ *04–66–21–90–30,* FAX *04–66–67–70–25. 62 rooms. Restaurant. AE, DC, MC, V.*

The Camargue

The Camargue is a haunting, desolate marshy wilderness of endless horizons, vast pools, low flat plains, and innumerable species of migrating birds overhead. Spend an hour at **Stes-Maries-de-la-Mer,** the Camargue's main town and now a resort with good sandy beaches. The town is home to a tiny, dark fortress-church that guards caskets containing relics of the "Holy Maries" for whom the town was named.

Arles

On the northern border of the Camargue is Roman Arles. For 55 francs you can purchase a joint ticket to all the monuments and museums. Its most notable sight is the 26,000-capacity **Arènes** (Arena), built in the 1st century AD for circuses and gladiator combats. ✉ *Rond-Point des Arènes,* ☎ *04–90–96–03–70.* ⌚ *June–Sept., daily 8:30–7; Nov.–Mar., daily 9–noon and 2–4:30; Apr.–May and Oct., daily 9–12:30 and 2–6:30.*

Close by are the scanty remains of Arles's **Théâtre Antique** (Roman Theater); the bits of marble column scattered around the grassy enclosure hint poignantly at the theater's onetime grandeur. ✉ *Rue du Cloître,* ☎ *04–90–96–93–30 for ticket information.* ⌚ *June–Sept., daily 8:30–7; Nov.–Mar., daily 9–noon and 2–4:30; Apr.–May and Oct., daily 9–12:30 and 2–6:30.*

Across from the Espace Van Gogh, where the artist was once hospitalized, is the **Cryptoporticus.** A double horseshoe-shape cavern beneath the former Roman forum built during the 1st century, it's surprisingly vast: 295 ft long and 197 ft wide, with galleries on three sides of the rectangle. Aside from stabilizing the forum and giving its grand monuments support, the gallery was probably used as a granary. ✉ *Rue Balze.* ⏲ *June–Sept., daily 8:30–7; Nov.–Mar., daily 9–noon and 2–4:30; Apr.–May and Oct., daily 9–12:30 and 2–6:30.*

The **Muséon Arlaten** is housed in a 16th-century mansion. Displays include costumes and headdresses, puppets, and waxworks, lovingly assembled by the great 19th-century Provençal poet, Frédéric Mistral. ✉ *29 rue de la République,* ☎ *04–90–96–08–23.* ⏲ *June–Sept., daily 8:30–7; Nov.–Mar., Tues.–Sun. 9–noon and 2–4:30; Apr.–May and Oct., Tues.–Sun. 9–12:30 and 2–6:30.*

The fountains of the **Jardin d'Hiver** (Winter Garden) figure in several of van Gogh's paintings. Firebrand Dutchman Vincent van Gogh produced much of his best work—and chopped off his ear—in Arles during a frenzied 15-month spell (1888–90) just before his suicide at 37. ✉ *East end of the bd. des Luces.*

At the **Alyscamps** empty Roman tombs and sarcophagi line the allée des Sarcophages. ☎ *04–90–49–36–87.* ⏲ *Daily 9–5.*

Alongside the Rhône and a little to the west of downtown is the new **Musée de l'Arles Antique** (Museum of Arles Antiquities). Presented here are historical artifacts excavated in the region of Arles. Most of the 1,300 objects displayed are of Roman origin. ✉ *Presque'île du Cirque Romain, south side of town (across highway N113), by the Rhône,* ☎ *04–90–19–88–89.* ⏲ *Apr.–Sept., daily 9–7; Oct.–Mar., Wed.–Mon. 10–6.*

$$ ✕ **Le Vaccarès.** In this elegant restaurant overlooking place du Forum, Bernard Dumas serves Provençal classics with an inventive touch. His seafood creations are particularly good: Try the mussels dressed in herbs and garlic. ✉ *11 rue Favorin,* ☎ *04–90–96–06–17. MC, V. Closed mid-Jan.–mid-Feb. and Mon. No dinner Sun.*

$$$ ★ 🏨 **Arlatan.** Follow the signposts from place du Forum to the picturesque street where this 15th-century house is built on the site of a 4th-century basilica. Antiques, pretty fabrics, sumptuous tapestries, and elegant furniture lend it a gracious atmosphere. ✉ *26 rue du Sauvage, 13200,* ☎ *04–90–93–56–66,* FAX *04–90–49–68–45. 51 rooms. AE, DC, MC, V.*

$ 🏨 **Hôtel Gauguin.** The rooms, painted in fresh yellows and blues, are small, but so is the price. Those with full bathrooms cost a little more. Ask for a room in front, looking onto the square. The welcoming owner, Mme. Dugand, is happy to try her English. ✉ *5 pl. Voltaire, 13200,* ☎ *04–90–96–14–35,* FAX *04–90–18–98–87. 18 rooms, 7 with shared baths, 11 with shower. MC, V.*

Tarascon

The mythical Tarasque, a monster that would emerge from the Rhône to gobble up children and cattle, came from Tarascon, north of Arles. Supposedly it has been killed, but drive carefully. The town's formidable 12th-century **Château** has massive stone walls that tower 150 ft above the Rhône, among the most daunting in France. ☎ *04–90–91–01–93.* 🎫 *28 frs.* ⏲ *July and Aug., daily 9–7; Sept.–June, daily 9–noon and 2–6 (Oct.–Mar. until 5).*

$$ 🏨 **Hôtel de Provence.** Rooms vary at this pleasant, traditional hotel with enthusiastic owners. Especially pleasant are those on the large balcony, where breakfast is served. The ones on the other side of the building only have views of other houses. ✉ *7 bd. Victor Hugo, 13150,* ☎ *04–90–91–06–43,* FAX *04–90–43–58–13. 11 rooms. MC, V.*

St-Rémy-de-Provence

Founded during the 6th century BC, St-Rémy de Provence was known as Glanum to the Romans. Its Roman **Mausolée** (Mausoleum) was erected around AD 100 to the memory of Caius and Lucius Caesar, grandsons of the emperor Augustus. The nearby **Arc Municipal** (Municipal Arch) is a few decades older and has suffered heavily; the upper half has crumbled away, although you can still make out some of the stone carvings.

Excavations of **Glanum** began in 1921, and a tenth of the original Roman town has now been unearthed. The remains are less spectacular than the arch and mausoleum but are still fascinating. ☎ *04–90–92–23–79.* ⏲ *Apr.–Sept., daily 9–noon and 2–6; Oct.–Mar., daily 9:30–noon and 2–5.*

You can examine many of the finds from Glanum—statues, pottery, and jewelry—at the **Musée Archéologique** (Archaeology Museum) in the center of St-Rémy. ✉ *Hôtel de Sade, rue Parage,* ☎ *04–90–92–64–04.* ⏲ *June–Sept., daily 9–noon and 2–6; Apr.–May and Oct., weekends 10–noon, weekdays 3–6; closed Nov.–Mar.*

$$$–$$$$ ✕🏨 **Domaine de Valmouraine.** Hospitable owner Judith McHugo, who speaks excellent English and French, has turned this Provençale manor into a home-away-from-home. The young chef expresses his creativity in the restaurant with recipes using fresh hare and seafood from the Mediterranean. ✉ *Petite route des Baux (D27), 13210,* ☎ *04–90–92–44–62,* FAX *04–90–92–37–32. 14 rooms. Restaurant, pool, 2 tennis courts. AE, DC. MC, V.*

Les Baux-de-Provence

Hilly D5 heads south from St-Rémy-de-Provence to the striking medieval village of Les Baux-de-Provence, perched high above the surrounding countryside of vines, olive trees, and bauxite quarries. Half of Les Baux is composed of tiny climbing streets and ancient stone houses inhabited, for the most part, by local craftsmen. The other half, the Ville Morte (Dead Town), is a mass of medieval ruins.

The Luberon

The Luberon Mountains have enchanting weathered hills with cozy gorges and small, charming villages. The north face of this mountain range is forested and rugged; the south face is more cultivated and peaceful. At **L'Isle-sur-la-Sorgue,** the River Sorgue once turned the waterwheels of the town's silk factories. Some of the waterwheels are still in place. Tiny D25 leads east from L'Isle-sur-la-Sorgue to **Fontaine-de-Vaucluse,** where the Sorgue emerges from underground imprisonment: Water shoots up from a cavern as the emerald-green river sprays and cascades at the foot of steep cliffs. Through a gorge and up the Col de Murs lies **Gordes,** a golden-stone village perched dramatically on its own hill. The picturesque hilltop village of **Roussillon,** whose houses are built with a distinctive orange- and pink-color stone, makes a great photograph from the valley below. **Bonnieux** is one of several wondrous hillside villages in the Vaucluse. From the terrace of the old church there is a sweeping view that takes in Gordes, Roussillon, and the ruined château of Lacoste, once home to the notorious marquis de Sade.

$$$ ✕ **Comptoir du Victuailler.** There are only 10 tables at this tiny restaurant in the center of Gordes. Elegantly simple meals contain only the freshest local capon, guinea fowl, asparagus, and truffles. ✉ *Pl. du Château,* ☎ *04–90–72–01–31. Reservations essential. MC, V. Closed mid-Nov.–mid-Dec., mid-Jan.–mid-Mar., and Wed. Sept.–May. No dinner Tues.*

$$–$$$ 🏨 **Les Romarins.** While you breakfast on a sheltered terrace in the morning sun, you can gaze across the valley at Gordes. The small inn has clean, well-lighted rooms and a spacious feel—ask for No. 1 in the main building, from whose white-curtain windows you can see forever, or the room with a terrace in the atelier. ✉ *Rte. de Sénanque, 84220 Gordes,* ☎ *04-90-72-12-13,* FAX *04-90-72-13-13. 10 rooms. Pool. AE, MC, V.*

$$ **Hostellerie du Prieuré.** In a former 17th-century priory, this hotel retains its architectural authenticity and is filled with a mix of antiques and collectibles. A few rooms, such as No. 9, have a private balcony; others have a view of the garden. It's efficiently and enthusiastically run by Mme. Caroline Coutaz. ✉ *84480 Bonnieux,* ☎ *04-90-75-80-78,* FAX *04-90-75-96-00. 10 rooms. Restaurant. MC, V.*

Aix-en-Provence

★ Few towns are as well preserved as the traditional capital of Provence: elegant Aix-en-Provence, birthplace of the Impressionist Paul Cézanne (1839–1906) and the novelist Émile Zola (1840–1902). The celebrated, graceful, lively avenue **cours Mirabeau** is the town's nerve center. It divides Old Aix in half, with narrow medieval streets to the north and 18th-century mansions to the south (particularly along rue Espariat). The sumptuous Hôtel Boyer d'Eguilles, erected in 1675, is worth a visit for its fine woodwork and murals, but is best known as the **Muséum d'Histoire Naturelle** (Natural History Museum). The highlight is the rare collection of dinosaur eggs, accompanied by life-size models of the dinosaurs that roamed locally 65 million years ago. ✉ *6 rue Espariat,* ☎ *04-42-26-23-67.* ⏲ *Mon.–Sat. 10–noon and 2–6, Sun. 2–6.*

The sculpted facade of the **Hôtel d'Albertas** (✉ 10 rue Espariat), built in 1707, is worth a look. Rue Aude is also lined with ancient town houses. Notice the **Hôtel de Ville** and the 16th-century **Tour de l'Horloge** (former town belfry) next to it. Toward the far end of rue Aude (now known as rue Gaston-de-Saporta) is the **Cathédrale St-Sauveur,** with a remarkable 15th-century triptych by Nicolas Froment, the *Tryptique du Buisson Ardent* (Burning Bush). The Archbishop's Palace is next to the cathedral and now houses the **Musée des Tapisseries** (Tapestry Museum). Its highlight is a magnificent suite of 17 tapestries made in Beauvais that date, like the palace itself, from the 17th and 18th centuries. Nine woven panels illustrate the adventures of Don Quixote. ✉ *28 pl. des Martyrs de la Résistance,* ☎ *04-42-23-09-91.* ⏲ *Wed.–Mon. 10–noon and 2–5:45.*

Drop into the **Musée-Atelier de Paul Cézanne** (Cézanne's Studio). No major pictures are on display here, but his studio remains as he left it at the time of his death in 1906. ✉ *9 av. Paul-Cézanne,* ☎ *04-42-21-06-53.* ⏲ *Wed.–Mon. 10–noon and 2–5.*

Several of Cézanne's oils and watercolors can be found at the **Musée Granet.** ✉ *13 rue Cardinale, pl. St-Jean de Malte,* ☎ *04-42-38-14-70.* ⏲ *Wed.–Mon. 10–noon and 2–6.*

$$$ ★ ✕ **Le Clos de la Violette.** Aix's best restaurant is in a residential district north of the old town. Chef Jean-Marc Banzo uses only fresh, local ingredients in his nouvelle and traditional recipes. Try the *saumon vapeur* (aromatic steamed salmon). The weekday lunch menu is moderately priced. ✉ *10 av. de la Violette,* ☎ *04-42-23-30-71. Jacket required. AE, MC, V. Closed Sun., early Nov., and most of Mar. No lunch Mon.*

$$–$$$ **Nègre-Coste.** This elegant 18th-century town house has been modernized but still has luxurious Old World decor. Rooms in front are noisiest, but they are also sunnier, larger, and better furnished and have a view. ✉ *33 cours Mirabeau, 13100,* ☎ *04-42-27-74-22,* FAX *04-42-26-80-93. 37 rooms. AE, DC, MC, V.*

Marseille

Marseille, the Mediterranean's largest port, is not crowded with tourist goodies, nor is its reputation as a big dirty city entirely unjustified. But it still has more going for it than many realize: a craggy mountain hinterland that provides a spectacular backdrop, superb coastal views of nearby islands, and the sights and smells of a Mediterranean melting pot. The picturesque **Vieux Port** (Old Harbor) is the heart of Marseille; avenue Canebière leads to the water's edge. A short way down the quay on the right (as you look out to sea) is the elegant 17th-century **Hôtel de Ville** (Town Hall). Just behind the Town Hall is the Maison Diamantée, a 16th-century mansion housing the **Musée du Vieux Marseille** (Old Marseille Museum), displaying costumes, pictures, and figurines. ✉ *2 rue de la Prison,* ☎ *04–91–55–10–19.* ⏲ *Apr.–Sept., Tues.–Sun. 11–6; Oct.–Mar. 10–5.*

The various domes of Marseille's pompous, striped neo-Byzantine **Cathédral de la Major** look utterly incongruous against the backdrop of industrial docks. ✉ *Esplanade de la Tourette.*

The grid of narrow, tumbledown streets leading off rue du Panier is called simply *Le Panier* (The Basket). Apart from the colorful, sleazy ambience, Le Panier is worth visiting for the elegantly restored 17th-century hospice now known as the **Musée de la Vieille-Charité** (Museum of the Ancient Hospice). Excellent art exhibitions are held here. ✉ *2 rue de la Charité,* ☎ *04–91–14–58–80.* ⏲ *Tues.–Sun. 11–6 in summer, 10–5 in winter.*

Make the climb up to the church of **Notre-Dame de la Garde** with its great gilded statue of the Virgin standing sentinel over the old port, 500 ft below. The church's interior is generously endowed with bombastic murals, mosaics, and marble. ✉ *Pl. du Colonel-Edon,* ☎ *04–91–13–40–80.* ⏲ *Daily 7–7 in winter; 7–8 in summer.*

Take time to drive the scenic 5-km (3-mi) coast road (corniche du Président-J.-F.-Kennedy) linking the Vieux Port to the **Plages Prado** (Prado Beaches) in the swanky part of southern Marseille. From the corniche du Président-J.-F.-Kennedy there are breathtaking views across the sea toward the rocky **Îles de Frioul,** which can be visited by ferries that leave from Vieux Port frequently throughout the day. On one of these is the **Château d'If,** to which Alexandre Dumas condemned his fictional hero, the count of Monte Cristo.

$$ ★ ✕ **Chez Madie.** Every morning Madie Minassian, the colorful *patronne,* scours the fish market for the freshest specimens. They end up in her bouillabaisse, fish soup, *favouilles* sauce (made with tiny crabs), and other savory dishes. ✉ *138 quai du Port,* ☎ *04–91–90–40–87. AE, DC, MC, V. Closed Mon. and most of Aug. No dinner Sun.*

$$$ 🏨 **Mercure Vieux Port.** Right on the Vieux Port, a few steps from the end of La Canebière, is this 200-year-old former coaching inn. The feel is of charming Old World opulence. The best rooms look out onto the harbor. ✉ *4 rue Beauvau, 13001,* ☎ *04–91–54–91–00, 800/223–9868 for U.S. reservations, 0171/621–1962 in the U.K.,* FAX *04–91–54–15–76. 71 rooms. AE, DC, MC, V.*

Provence Essentials

Getting Around

Provence's key attractions are not far apart. Traveling by car is the most rewarding way to get around, especially if you want to go to the smaller villages and explore the landscape. Speedy highways descend from Lyon and split at Orange to go to Nîmes and Montpellier or Aix-en-Provence and Marseille en route to the Riviera. If you're limited to public transportation, Avignon makes the best base for both train and bus connections. Avignon is where the TGV from Paris and Lyon splits for either the run down to Marseille or Montpellier. From Marseille trains run along the coast to Nice and Monaco.

Guided Tours

The regional tourist offices' "52 Week" program pools 52 tours offered by various agencies throughout the year, touching on wine tasting, sailing, hang gliding, golfing, gastronomy, and cultural exploration. Contact **Loisirs-Acceuil** (✉ Domaine de Vergon, 13370, Mallemort, ☎ 01–90–59–18–05) for details.

Visitor Information

Aix-en-Provence (✉ 2 pl. du Général-de-Gaulle, ☎ 04–42–16–11–61). **Arles** (✉ esplanade Charles-de-Gaulle, ☎ 04–90–18–41–21). **Avignon** (✉ 41 cours Jean-Jaurès, ☎ 04–90–82–65–11). **Marseille** (✉ 4 La Canebière , ☎ 04–91–13–89–00). **Montpellier** (✉ pl. René-Devic, ☎ 04–67–58–67–58). **Nîmes** (✉ 6 rue Auguste, ☎ 04–66–67–29–11).

THE RIVIERA

Few places in the world have the same pull on the imagination as France's fabled Riviera, the Mediterranean coastline stretching from St-Tropez in the west to Menton on the Italian border. Cooled by the Mediterranean in the summer and warmed by it in winter, the climate is almost always pleasant. Avoid the area in July and August, however, unless you love crowds.

The Riviera's coastal resorts may live exclusively for the tourist trade and have often been ruined by high-rises, but the hinterlands remain relatively untarnished. The little villages perched high on the hills behind medieval ramparts seem to belong to another century. One of them, St-Paul-de-Vence, is the home of the Maeght Foundation, one of the world's leading museums of modern art. Artists have played a considerable role in popular conceptions of the Riviera, and their presence is reflected in the number of art museums: the Musée Picasso in Antibes, the Musée Renoir and the Musée d'Art Moderne Méditerranée in Cagnes-sur-Mer, and the Musée Jean Cocteau in Menton. Wining and dining are special treats on the Riviera; bouillabaisse, a spicy fish stew, is the most popular regional specialty.

Although the tiny principality of Monaco, which lies between Nice and Menton, is a sovereign state, with its own army and police force, its language, food, and way of life are French.

The distance between St-Tropez and the border with Italy is only 120 km (75 mi), so most places are, in fact, within a day's journey. For the drama of mountains and sea, take one of the famous Corniche roads, which traverse the coastline at various heights over the Mediterranean and are especially spectacular from Nice to the Italian frontier (☞ Getting Around, *below*).

St-Tropez

St-Tropez was just another pretty fishing village until it was "discovered" in the 1950s by the "beautiful people," a fast set of film stars, starlets, and others who scorned bourgeois values while enjoying bourgeois bank balances. Today, its summer population swells from 6,000 to 60,000, and the top hotels and nightclubs are jammed. In winter it's hard to find a restaurant open. The best times to visit, therefore, are early summer or fall. May and June are perhaps the best months, when the town lets its hair down during two local festivals.

The **Vieux Port** (Old Harbor) is the liveliest part of town. It's easy to kill time here on a café terrace, watching the rich and famous on their gleaming yachts. Between the old and new harbors, in a cleverly converted chapel, is the **Musée de l'Annonciade,** housing paintings by artists drawn to St-Tropez between 1890 and 1940, including Signac, Ma-

The Riviera (Côte d'Azur)

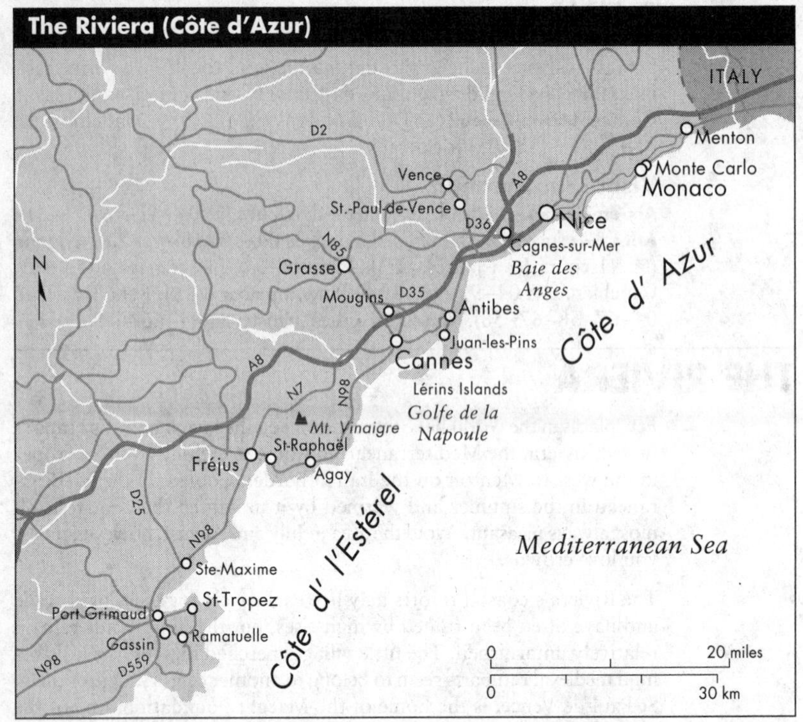

tisse, Derain, and Van Dongen. ✉ *Quai de l'Épi,* ☎ *04–94–97–04–01.* ⏲ *June–Sept., Wed.–Mon. 10–noon and 3–7; Oct.–May, Wed.–Mon. 10–noon and 2–6.*

Across the place de l'Hôtel de Ville lies the **Vieille Ville** (Old Town), where twisting streets, designed to break the impact of the terrible mistral (the cold, dry, northerly wind common to this region), open onto ★ tiny squares and fountains. The long climb up to the **Citadelle** rewards you with a splendid view across the gulf to Ste-Maxime, a quieter if heavily built-up and less posh family resort with a decent beach and reasonably priced hotels.

St-Tropez is also a good base for visiting **Port Grimaud,** a pastiche of an Italian fishing village (take D558). Easily visited from St-Tropez is the old Provençal town of **Ramatuelle** on a rocky spur 440 ft above the sea. Six kilometers (4 mi) north of Ramatuelle is the hilltop village of **Gassin,** a charming place to escape the heat of the shoreline.

$$$$ ✕🏨 **Byblos.** At this unique hotel, the luxury rooms and suites are built, like a miniature Provençal village, around tile courtyards, fragrant with magnolia and orange trees. Each one is differently decorated with amusing touches and subtle lighting. Les Caves du Roy, one of two nightclubs, and Les Arcades, the restaurant run by Philippe Audibert, are among the best in town. ✉ *Av. Paul Signac, 83990,* ☎ *04–94–56–68–00,* FAX *04–94–56–68–01. 47 rooms, 55 suites. Restaurant, pool. AE, DC, MC, V. Closed mid-Oct.–mid-Mar.*

Fréjus

Fréjus was founded by Julius Caesar as Forum Julii in 49 BC. The Roman remains are modest but impressive, and consist of part of the theater, an arena, a long series of chunks of aqueduct, and city walls. In the ★ heart of the atmospheric hilltop old town is the **Cathédrale.** Though it dates from the 10th century, its richly worked choir stalls belong to the 15th century. ✉ *Pl. Formigé.* ⏲ *Oct.–Mar., Tues.–Sun. 9–noon and 2–5; Apr.–Sept., daily 9–noon and 2–5.*

Cannes

In 1834 a chance event was to change the town of Cannes forever. Lord Brougham, Britain's lord chancellor, was en route to Nice when an outbreak of cholera forced the authorities to freeze all travel. Trapped in Cannes, he fell in love with the place and built himself a house to use as an annual refuge from the British winter. The English aristocracy, czars, kings, and princes soon caught on, and Cannes became a community for the international elite. Grand palace hotels were built to cater to them, and Cannes came to symbolize dignified luxury. Today, Cannes is also synonymous with the International Film Festival.

Stroll along the seafront on **La Croisette,** and elegant promenade with splendid views of the Napoule Bay. All along the promenade are cafés, boutiques, and luxury hotels. Speedboats and waterskiers glide by; little waves lick the beach, lined with prostrate bodies. Almost all beaches are private, but that doesn't mean you can't use them, only that you must pay for the privilege. Behind the promenade lies the town, and beyond, the hills with the villas of the very rich. Only a few steps in-
★ land is the Old Town, known as **Le Suquet,** with its steep, cobbled streets and its 12th-century watchtower.

$$ ✕ **Chez Astoux.** For seafood, this stands out among the other restaurants on the block. The ambience is simple but elegant, both on the terrace and inside. Locals go to the seafood stall and restaurant next door, Astoux & Brun, to save money and bring home fish. ✉ *43 rue Félix-Faure,* ☎ *04–93–39–06–22. AE, DC, MC, V.*

$ ✕ **Bouchon d'Objectif.** Popular and unpretentious, this tiny bistro
★ serves inexpensive Provençal fare prepared with a sophisticated twist. Watch for terrine of hare with sultanas and Armagnac, or a trio of fresh fish with aioli. An ever-changing display of photography adds a hip touch to the simple ocher-and-aqua setting. ✉ *6 rue Maréchal Joffre,* ☎ *04–93–39–98–38. AE, MC, V. Closed Mon.*

$ ✕ **Montagard.** This extraordinary newcomer serves elegant, imagina-
★ tive vegetarian cuisine—nearly nonexistent in France—in a chic, low-key setting, and at startlingly low prices (the copious three-course quick-lunch menu is only 95 francs). ✉ *6 rue Maréchal Joffre,* ☎ *04–93–39–98–38. MC, V. Closed Sun., and lunch Mon.*

$$$ 🏨 **Majestic.** Unlike most luxury hotels lining La Croisette, this one has a less blatantly luxurious charm (though prices are mega-deluxe). Rooms are spacious and traditional, but refreshingly decorated in pastels. ✉ *14 La Croisette, 06400,* ☎ *04–92–98–77–00,* FAX *04–93–38–97–90. 264 rooms. Restaurant, air-conditioning, pool. AE, DC, MC, V. Closed mid-Nov.–Dec.*

$$ 🏨 **Molière.** Plush, intimate and low-keyed, this low-priced hotel has
★ small rooms in cool shades of peach and indigo. Nearly all overlook a vast enclosed front garden, with mature palms and cypress shading terrace tables. ✉ *5 rue Molière, 06400,* ☎ *04–93–68–16–16,* FAX *04–93–68–29–57. AE, MC, V. Closed mid-Nov.–late Dec.*

$ 🏨 **Albert Ier.** In a quiet residential area above the Forville market, this neo-Art Deco mansion offers pretty pastels, tidy tile baths, and an enclosed garden setting. You can have breakfast on the flowered, shady terrace or in the family-style salon. It's a 10-minute walk downhill to La Croisette and the beach. ✉ *68, av. de Grasse, 06400,* ☎ *04–93–39–24–04,* FAX *04–93–38–83–75. 11 rooms. MC, V.*

Grasse

Grasse is perched in the hills behind Cannes. Take N85 or just follow your nose to the town that claims to be the perfume capital of the world. A good portion of its 40,000 inhabitants work at distilling and extracting scent from the tons of roses, lavender, and jasmine produced here every year. The various perfumers are only too happy to guide you around their fragrant establishments. **Fragonard** (✉ 20 bd. Fragonard, ☎ 04–93–36–44–65) is the best known. The old town is attractive, with its narrow alleys and massive, somber **Cathédrale.** Three of the paintings inside the cathedral are by Rubens and one is by Fragonard, who lived here for many years.

Mougins

From quaint, fortified, hilltop Mougins, with its cluster of ancient houses dating from the 15th century, you can see Cannes and the Golfe de Napoule. Unfortunately, Mougin's popularity means that you have to park at the bottom of the hill and hike into the old village, which is a little hard to find behind the new houses and shopping centers that form Cannes's suburban sprawl. Don't be misled by signs for Mougins-le-Haut, a huge real-estate development that has become a village in its own right. Be sure to stop in at the **Notre-Dame-de-Vie** hermitage, one of the village's most interesting sights. Also look out for the **Chapelle St-Barthelmy** with its 17th-century bell tower roofed in colored tiles.

$$$$ ✕ **Le Moulin de Mougins.** Roger Vergé's fine restaurant (reservations essential; closed Thurs. lunch and Mon.) is in a converted mill a short distance west of Mougins on D3. The cuisine, now created in partnership with chef Serge Chollet, ranges from seemingly simple salads to rich sauces for lobster, salmon, or turbot. The atmosphere is surprisingly informal. There are five elegantly rustic guest rooms as well. ✉ *Quartier Notre-Dame-de-Vie, 424 chemin du Moulin, 06250,* ☎ *04–93–75–78–24,* FAX *04–93–90–18–55. 3 rooms, 2 apartments. Restaurant. AE, DC, MC, V. Closed Feb.–Mar.*

Antibes

On the east side of Cannes and Napoule Bay are Antibes and Juan-les-Pins, two villages that flow into one another with no perceptible boundary on either side of the peninsula, the Cap d'Antibes. Antibes, an older village, dates from the 4th century BC, when it was a Greek trading port. Until recently, the town was renowned throughout Europe for its commercial flower and plant production, today somewhat diminished. Every morning except Monday, the market on the Cours Masséna comes alive with the colors of roses, carnations, anemones, and tulips.

The Grimaldis, the family that rules Monaco, built the **Château Grimaldi** during the 12th century on the remains of a Roman camp. Today, the château's main attraction is the **Musée Picasso** (Picasso Museum), a bounty of paintings, ceramics, and lithographs inspired by the sea and Greek mythology. ✉ *Pl. du Château,* ☎ *04–93–90–54–20.* ⏲ *June–Sept., Wed.–Mon. 10–6; Oct.–May, Wed.–Mon. 10–noon and 2–6.*

$$ ★ ✕ **Le Brûlot.** One street back from the thriving market, this bistro is one of the busiest in Antibes. Burly Chef Christian Blancheri horses anything from suckling pigs to apple pies in and out of his roaring wood oven, and it's all delicious. ✉ *3 rue Frédéric Isnard,* ☎ *04–93–34–17–76. MC, V. Closed Sun., Mon. lunch, last 2 wks of Aug., last wk of Dec.–1st wk Jan.*

$$$$ ✕🏨 **Juana.** At this luxuriously renovated '30s hotel run by the second generation of the Barrache family, service is extremely attentive and thoughtful. Rooms are large and individually decorated. Chef Christian Morisset wins praise for his fine seafood and lamb at La Terrasse, one of the best restaurants on the Côte d'Azur. ✉ *av. Georges-Gallice, 06160 Juan-les-Pins,* ☏ *04-93-61-08-70,* FAX *04-93-61-76-60. 45 rooms. Restaurant, pool. AE, MC, V. Closed late-Oct.-mid-Apr.*

$$ ★ ✕🏨 **Auberge Provençale.** Rooms in this onetime abbey, complete with beams and canopied beds, have just had a face-lift, which only enhanced their charm. The dining room (closed Mon., no lunch Tues.) and the covered garden are decorated with the same impeccable taste. Cuisine includes fine bouillabaisse, fresh seafood, and grilled lamb and duck. ✉ *61 pl. Nationale, 06600,* ☏ *04-93-34-13-24,* FAX *04-93-34-89-88. 6 rooms. Restaurant. AE, DC, MC, V.*

Nice

Numbers in the margin correspond to points of interest on the Nice map.

With a population of 350,000, its own university, a new congress hall, and a nearby science park, Nice is the undisputed capital of the Riviera. Founded by the Greeks as Nikaia, it has lived through several civilizations and was attached to France only in 1860. It consequently has a profusion of Greek, Italian, British, and French styles. Tourism may not be the main business of Nice, but it is a deservedly popular center. There is an eclectic mixture of old and new architecture, an opera house, museums, flourishing markets, and regular concerts and festivals, including the Mardi Gras festival and the Battle of Flowers.

1 The **place Masséna** is a fine square built in 1815 to celebrate a local
hero: one of Napoléon's most successful generals. Just west of place
2 Masséna are the fountains and gardens of the **Jardin Albert I.** A short
3 stroll from the garden takes you to the **Promenade des Anglais** (English Promenade), built by the English community here in 1824. The promenade is very busy, but it's a pleasant strand between town and sea with fine views of the Baie des Anges (Bay of Angels).

4 The **Palais Masséna** (Masséna Palace) is a museum with exhibits concerned with the Napoleonic era. ✉ *65 rue de France,* ☏ *04-93-88-11-34.* 🎫 *25 frs.* ⏲ *Tues.-Sun. 10-noon and 2-6.*

West of the Palais Masséna, along rue de France, and right, up avenue
5 des Baumettes, is the **Musée des Beaux-Arts Jules-Chéret** (Jules Chéret Fine Arts Museum), built in 1878 as a palatial mansion for a Russian princess. The rich collection has works by Renoir, Degas, Monet; sculptures by Rodin; and ceramics by Picasso. ✉ *33 av. des Baumettes,* ☏ *04-93-44-50-72.* ⏲ *May-Sept., Tues.-Sun. 10-noon and 2-6; Oct.-Apr., Tues.-Sun. 10-noon and 2-5.*

The Cours Saleya flower market and the narrow streets in Vieux Nice (Old Nice) are the prettiest parts of Nice: While you're market-brows-
★ 6 ing, stop in to see the 18th-century **Chapelle de la Miséricorde,** renowned for its ornate Baroque interior and sculpted decoration. At the north-
7 ern extremity of the old town is the vast **place Garibaldi**—all yellow-ocher buildings and formal fountains. Along the boulevard Jean-Jaurès,
8 the **Musée d'Art Modern** (Modern Art Museum) has an outstanding collection of French and international abstract and figurative art from the late 1950s onward. ✉ *Promenade des Arts,* ☏ *04-93-62-61-62.* ⏲ *Wed.-Mon. 11-6, Fri. 11-10.*

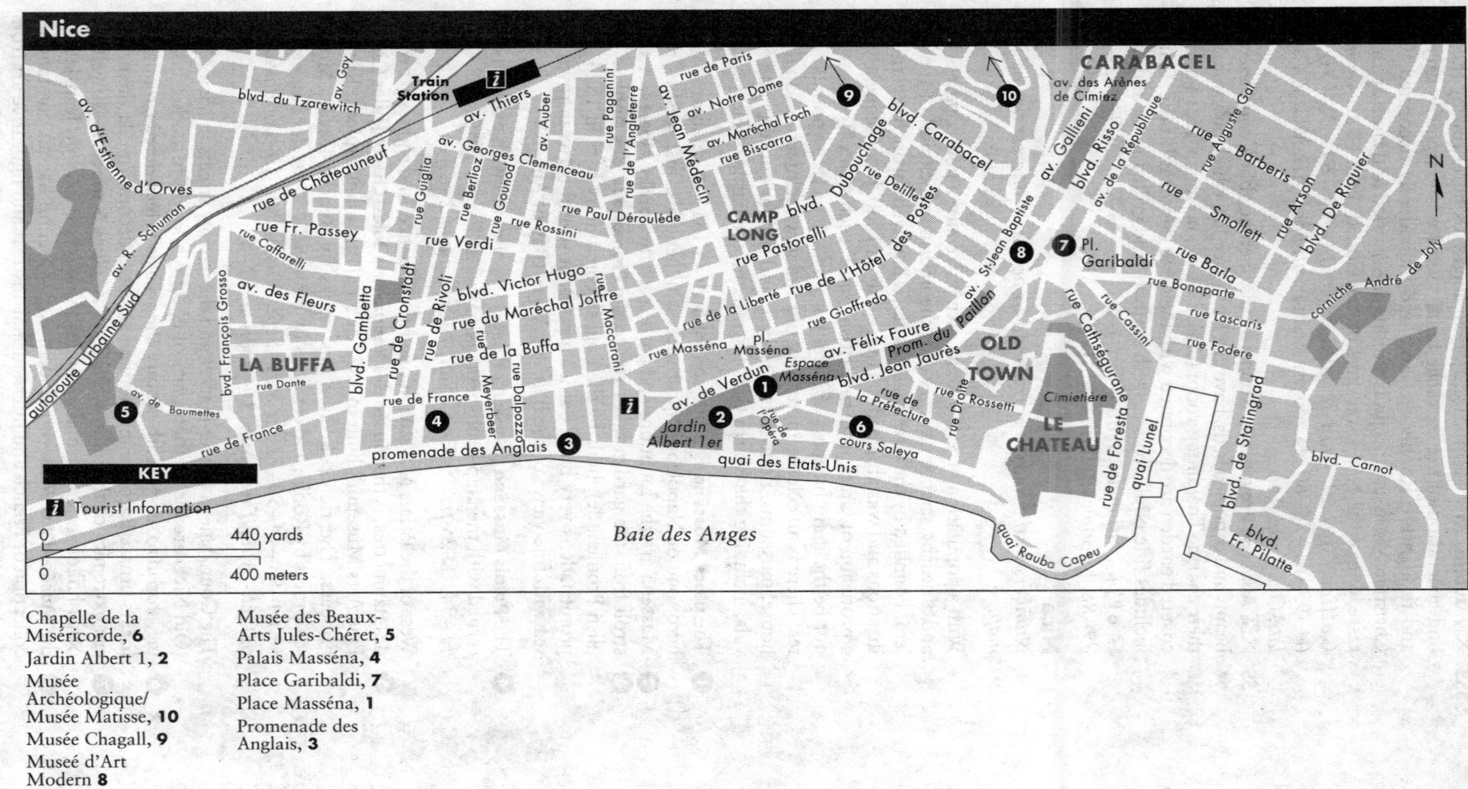

Chapelle de la Miséricorde, **6**
Jardin Albert 1, **2**
Musée Archéologique/ Musée Matisse, **10**
Musée Chagall, **9**
Museé d'Art Modern **8**
Musée des Beaux-Arts Jules-Chéret, **5**
Palais Masséna, **4**
Place Garibaldi, **7**
Place Masséna, **1**
Promenade des Anglais, **3**

9 The **Musée Chagall** (Chagall Museum) is off the boulevard de Cimiez, near the Roman ruins. Housed here is the Chagall collection, including the 17 huge canvases of *The Message of the Bible,* which took 13 years to complete. ✉ *Av. du Dr-Ménard,* ☎ *04–93–53–87–20.* ⌚ *July–Sept., Wed.–Mon. 10–6; Oct.–June, Wed.–Mon. 10–5.*

A 17th-century Italian villa amid Roman remains contains two muse-
10 ums. The **Musée Archéologique** (Archaeology Museum), with a plethora of ancient objects, and the **Musée Matisse** (Matisse Museum) with paintings and bronzes by Henri Matisse (1869–1954). ✉ *164 av. des Arènes-de-Cimiez. Musée Matisse:* ☎ *04–93–81–08–08.* ⌚ *Apr.–Oct., Wed.–Mon. 10–6; Nov.–Mar. 10–5. Musée Archéologique:* ☎ *04–93–81–59–57.* ⌚ *Apr.–Sept., Tues.–Sun. 10–noon and 2–6; Oct.–Mar., 10–1 and 2–5.*

$$$ ✕ **Ane-Rouge.** Popular with locals, this tiny, family-run restaurant has been *the* place for Nice's best fish and seafood for generations. ✉ 7 *quai des Deux-Emmanuel,* ☎ *04–93–89–49–63. AE, DC, MC, V. Closed Wed. in winter.*

$$ ★ ✕ **La Mérenda.** The back-to-bistro boom climaxed here when Dominique Le Stanc retired his crown at the Negresco to take over this tiny, unpretentious landmark of Provençal cuisine. Now he and his wife work in the miniature open kitchen creating the ultimate versions of stuffed sardines, pistou, and quintessential stockfish (the local lutefisk). Stop by in person to reserve entry to the inner sanctum. ✉ *4 rue de la Terrasse,* ☎ *No phone. No credit cards. Closed weekends.*

$–$$ ✕ **La Cambuse.** This little bistro on the cours Saleya next to the lovely Chapelle de la Miséricorde is a winner. Aptly named for a ship's storeroom, this sunny place serves fresh seafood and wonderful steamed vegetable dishes on elevated platters. ✉ *5 cours Saleya,* ☎ *04–93–80–12–31. MC, V. Closed Sun.*

$$$$ ★ ✕🏨 **Château des Ollières.** The genteel owner of this fantastical neo-Moroccan palace, once the dream-house of Prince Lobnov-Rostowsky, has financed its meticulous restoration by conceding to modern commerce. Its eight rooms are furnished with period details—herringbone parquet, crown moldings, and chandeliers. Deluxe rooms have vast marble baths and fine old furniture; standard rooms are filled with toile de Jouy . The candlelit restaurant functions as a table d'hôte—one prix-fixe menu each day. ✉ *39 av. des Baumettes, 06000,* ☎ *04–92–15–77–99,* FAX *04–93–88–35–68. 8 rooms. Restaurant. AE, MC, V.*

$ ★ 🏨 **Hôtel Félix.** In the heart of the city and a block from the beach, this tiny hotel is owned by a hard-working couple (both fluent in English) who go out of their way to make you feel welcome. Rooms are compact, but neat and bright so they don't feel so small. Some have tiny balconies. ✉ *41 rue Masséna, 06000,* ☎ *04–93–88–67–73,* FAX *04–93–16–15–78. 14 rooms. AE, DC, MC, V.*

Monaco

Numbers in the margin correspond to points of interest on the Monaco map.

Sixteen kilometers (10 mi) along the coast east of Nice is Monaco. Though there is no frontier, it is a different country; when dialing numbers from outside Monaco, including France, you must prefix the call with "377." For more than a century Monaco's livelihood was cen-
★ 1 tered beneath the copper roof of its splendid **Casino.** The oldest section dates from 1878 and was conceived by Charles Garnier, architect of the Paris opera house. It's as elaborately ornate as anyone could wish. ✉ *Pl. du Casino,* ☎ *92–16–21–21. Persons under 21 not admitted.* 🎫 *European rooms, 50 frs; English Club and Monte-Carlo Sporting*

Club rooms, 100 frs.; American room, free. ⏲ *Daily noon–4* AM. *Closed May 1.*

❷ The **Musée National des Automates et Poupées d' Autrefois** (Antique Dolls and Automatons Museum, sometimes simply called the Musée National) has 18th- and 19th-century dolls and mechanical figures, the latter shamelessly showing off their complex inner workings. It's magically set in a 19th-century seaside villa (designed by Garnier). ⊠ *17 av. Princesse-Grace,* ☎ *93–30–91–26.* ⏲ *Daily except holidays: Easter–Aug., 10–6:30; Sept.–Easter, 10–12:15 and 2:30–6:30.*

Monaco Town, the principality's old quarter, has many vaulted passageways and exudes an almost tangible medieval feel. The magnifi-
❸ cent **Palais du Prince** (Prince's Palace), a grandiose Italianate structure with a Moorish tower, was largely rebuilt in the last century. Here, since 1297, the Grimaldi dynasty has lived and ruled. The spectacle of the **Changing of the Guard** occurs each morning at 11:55; inside, guided tours take you through the state apartments and a wing containing the **Palace Archives** and **Musée Napoléon** (Napoleonic Museum), which remains open throughout the year. ⊠ *Pl. du Palais,* ☎ *93–25–18–31.* ⏲ *June–Oct., daily 9:30–6:30; Musée Napoléon and Palace Archives: Tues.–Sun. 9:30–6:30.*

❹ Monaco's **cathedral,** is a late-19th-century neo-Romanesque confection in which Philadelphia-born Princess Grace lies entombed in splendor along with past members of the Grimaldi dynasty. ⊠ *4 rue Colonel Bellando de Castro.*

Next to the St-Martin Garden, which contains an evocative bronze monument in memory of Prince Albert I (Prince Rainier's great-grandfather, the one in the sou'wester and flying oilskins, benignly guiding a ship's
❺ wheel), is the **Musée Océanographique** (Oceanography Museum and Aquarium). The museum is also an internationally renowned research institute founded by Prince Albert; the well-known underwater explorer Jacques Cousteau (1910–97) was the director. The aquarium is the undisputed highlight. ⊠ *Av. St-Martin,* ☎ *93–15–36–00.* 🎫 *60 frs.* ⏲ *July–Aug., daily 9–8; Sept.–June, daily 9:30–7 (6 in winter).*

Before heading back inland, take a stroll to the eastern tip of the rock,
❻ to the **Fort Antoine Theater** (⊠ Av. de la Quarantaine, ☎ 93–30–19–21), a converted 18th-century fortress that is covered in ivy and flowering myrtle and thyme. In summer this open-air theater seats 350.

❼ The Moneghetti area is the setting for the **Jardin Exotique** (Exotic Plants Garden), where 600 varieties of cacti and succulents cling to the rock face. Your ticket to the Jardin Exotique also allows you to explore the
❽ caves next door, and to visit the adjacent **Musée d'Anthropologie Préhistorique** (Museum of Prehistoric Anthropology). ⊠ *Bd. du Jardin Exotique,* ☎ *93–15–80–06.* ⏲ *Mid-May–mid-Sept., daily 9–7; mid-Sept.–mid-May, daily 9–6. Closed Nov. 19 and Dec. 25.*

$$$$ ★ ✕ **Louis XV.** At this strong contender for the best-in-Monaco award (some say the best in Europe), the opulent decor and chef Alain Ducasse's beautifully conceived "country cooking," such as ravioli with foie gras and truffles, contribute to the formal atmosphere. ⊠ *Hôtel de Paris, pl. du Casino,* ☎ *92–16–30–01. Reservations essential. AE, DC, MC, V. Closed Tues. and Wed. (except dinner July–Aug.), mid-Feb.–early Mar., and late-Nov.–late-Dec.*

$$–$$$ ✕ **Port.** Harbor views from the terrace and top-notch Italian food make Port a good choice. A large, varied menu includes homemade pasta, seafood, and fish risotto. ⊠ *Quai Albert I,* ☎ *93–50–77–21. AE, DC, MC, V. Closed Mon. and Nov.*

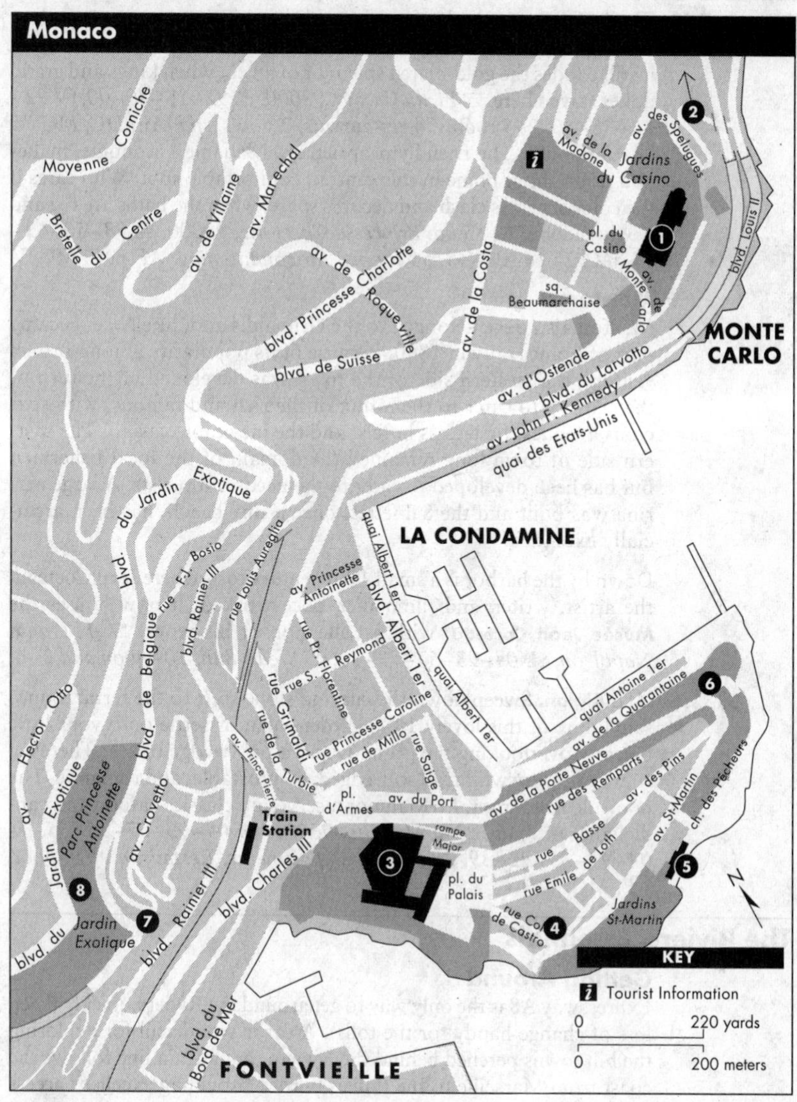

Casino, **1**
Cathedral, **4**
Fort Antoine Theater, **6**
Jardin Exotique, **7**
Musée d'Anthropologie Préhistorique, **8**
Musée National des Automates et Poupées d'Autrefois, **2**
Musée Océanographique, **5**
Palais du Prince, **3**

$$$$ ★ 🏨 **Hôtel de Paris.** At this famed establishment, elegance, expense, luxury, dignity, and Old World charm are the watchwords. Built in 1864, it still exudes the gold-plated splendor of an era when kings and grand dukes stayed here. ✉ *Pl. du Casino, 98000,* ☎ *92–16–30–00,* FAX *92–16–38–50. 245 rooms. 4 restaurants, 2 pools, spa. AE, DC, MC, V.*

$$ 🏨 **Alexandra.** The friendly proprietress, Madame Larouquie, makes you feel right at home in this central, comfortable spot. Who cares if the color schemes clash and decor is spare, when the baths are big and newly redone? ✉ *35 bd. Princesse-Charlotte, 98000,* ☎ *93–50–63–13,* FAX *92–16–06–48. 55 rooms. Air-conditioning. AE, DC, MC, V.*

Menton

Menton also once belonged to the Grimaldis and, like Nice, became part of France only in 1860. Because of its popularity among British visitors, the western side of the town was developed at the turn of the century to cater to the influx of the rich and famous, with spacious avenues, first-class hotels, and the inevitable casino. The eastern side of town long remained the domain of the local fishermen but has been developed to cater to the needs of tourists. A large marina was built and the **Sablettes,** once a tiny beach, has been artificially extended.

Down by the harbor is a small 17th-century fort, where Jean Cocteau, the artist, writer, and filmmaker, once worked. It now houses the **Musée Jean Cocteau,** with a collection of his work. ✉ *111 quai Napoléon,* ☎ *04–93–57–72–30.* ⏲ *Wed.–Sun. 10–noon and 2–6.*

$$–$$$ ★ ✕🏨 **Aiglon.** Sweep down the curving stone stair to the terrazzo mosaic lobby of this lovely 1880 garden-villa; or settle onto your little balcony overlooking the grounds and a tiny wedge of sea. There's a room for every whim, all soft-edged, comfortable, and romantic. The poolside restaurant, Le Riaumont, serves up classic seafood and candlelight. ✉ *7, av. de la Madone, 06502,* ☎ *04–93–57–55–55,* FAX *04–93–35–92–39. 28 rooms, 2 apartments. Restaurant, bar, pool. AE, MC, V.*

The Riviera Essentials

Getting Around

Expressway A8 is the only way to get around the Riviera quickly (keep lots of change handy for the tolls). A car is wonderful for exploring the hill towns perched behind the Riviera, but a train line follows the coast from Marseille to the Italian border, providing excellent access to the seaside resorts. Local buses (marked GARE ROUTIÈRE) or guided tours (☞ *below*) are needed to visit Grasse, Vence, and other inland areas if you're traveling by public transportation.

Guided Tours

SNCF runs many organized tours (contact the Nice Tourist Office) to areas otherwise hard to reach: St-Paul-de-Vence, Upper Provence, and the Verdon Gorges. Boats operate from Nice to Marseille; from St-Tropez to the charming Hyères Islands; and from Antibes, Cannes, and Juan-les-Pins to the Lérins Islands.

Visitor Information

Antibes (✉ 11 pl. Général-de-Gaulle, ☎ 04–92–90–53–00). **Cagnes-sur-Mer** (✉ 6 bd. du Mal-Juin , ☎ 04–93–20–61–64). **Cannes** (✉ Palais des Festivals La Croisette, ☎ 04–93–39–01–01). **Fréjus** (✉ 325 rue Jean-Jaurès, ☎ 04–93–39–24–53). **Grasse** (✉ 22 cours Honoré-Cresp, ☎ 04–93–36–03–56). **Juan-les-Pins** (✉ 51 bd. Charles-Guillaumont, ☎ 04–92–90–53–05). **Menton** (✉ Palais de l'Europe, av. Boyer, ☎ 04–93–57–57–00). **Monaco** (✉ 2a bd. des Moulins, ☎ 92–16–61–16). **Nice** (✉ av. Thiers, ☎ 04–93–87–07–07; ✉ 5 av. Gustave-V, ☎ 04–93–87–60–60). **St-Paul-de-Vence** (✉ Maison Tour, rue Grande, ☎ 04–93–32–86–95). **St-Tropez** (✉ quai Jean-Jaurès, ☎ 04–94–97–45–21). **Vence** (✉ pl. du Grand-Jardin, ☎ 04–93–58–06–38).

12 Germany

Munich, Frankfurt, the Black Forest, the Rhine, Hamburg, Berlin, Saxony and Thuringia

Today one country exists where there used to be two, and although the 40-year division was an artificial one, the differences that developed will take many years to even out. Technically, Germany is already one country: the same language, the same currency, the same federal political structure. But some of the differences can be quirky.

The bid to quickly rejuvenate former East Germany and provide its 17 million inhabitants with better standards of living has so far proved difficult, while costing western German taxpayers billions of Deutschmarks. By the end of 1992, the effects of reunification had virtually stopped the great German economic locomotive, resulting in higher prices and the threat of higher taxes—and causing much grumbling in western Germany. Inflation had been cut to less than 2% by 1997, and stayed that low in 1998, but at the expense of many jobs. More than 4.5 million Germans—roughly 12% of the adult population—were out of work at the beginning of the critical 1998 election year, with no relief in sight.

In the eastern part of the country, most Germans still earn less than their fellow citizens to the west. But many basic living costs are lower. Overall, eastern German shops are less numerous and elegant, but they are filled with the sort of material goods that were unobtainable under the Communist regime.

Eastern Germany's emergence from communism has not so much inspired a new sense of nationhood as it has revived regional traditions and identities. The villages south of Leipzig and Dresden have more in common with their neighbors in northern Bavaria, from whom they were cut off for four decades, than with Berlin bureaucrats.

Germans tend to rise very early; they may be found hammering away at a building site by 7 AM or seated at an office desk by 8 AM, but they take their leisure time just as seriously. Annual vacations of up to six weeks are the norm, and secular and religious festivals occupy at least another 12 days. Every town and village, and many a city neighborhood, manages at least one "Fest" a year, when the beer barrels are rolled out and sausages are thrown on the grill. The seasons have their own festivities: Fasching (carnival) heralds the end of winter, countless beer gardens open up with the first warm rays of sunshine; fall is celebrated with the Munich Oktoberfest; and Advent brings Christkindlmärkte, colorful pre-Christmas markets held in town and city squares.

The great outdoors has always been an important escape for Germans. A Bavarian mountain inn, the glow of its lights reflected on the blanket of snow outside, may be only a short drive from Munich. The busy industrial city of Stuttgart lies at the gateway to the Schwarzwald (Black Forest), the popular region of spas, hiking trails, and tempting cake. Berlin is surrounded by its own lakes and green parklands. The transportation system that links these various regions is a godsend to the visitor, as German trains are fast, clean, and punctual. However, a drive on a speed limit–free autobahn will give you an idea of just how fast all those BMW and Mercedes sports cars are meant to go.

GERMANY A TO Z

Customs

For details on imports and duty-free limits, *see* Customs & Duties *in* Chapter 1.

Dining

In fact, the range of dining experiences in Germany is vast: everything from high priced nouvelle cuisine to plenty of sausages. Seek out local restaurants if atmosphere and regional specialties are your priority. Beer restaurants in Bavaria, *Apfelwein* (alcoholic apple cider) taverns in Frankfurt, and *Kneipen*—the pubs-cum-local-cafés on the corner—in Berlin nearly always offer the best value and atmosphere. But throughout the country you'll find *Gaststätten, Gasthäuser,* and/or *Gasthöfe*—local inns—where atmosphere and regional specialties are always available. Likewise, just about every town will have a *Ratskeller,* a cellar restaurant in the town hall, where exposed beams, huge fireplaces, sturdy tables, and immense portions are the rule.

The natural accompaniment to German food is either beer or wine. Munich is the beer capital of Germany, though there's no part of the country where you won't find the amber nectar. Say *"Helles"* or *"Export"* if you want light beer; *"Dunkles"* if you want dark beer. In Bavaria try the sour but refreshing beer brewed from wheat, called *Weissbier.*

Germany is also a major producer of wine, and much of it is of superlative quality. Try the house wine in most restaurants or an earthenware pitcher of cold Mosel wine. If you want something more expensive, remember that all wines are graded in one of three basic categories: *Tafelwein* (table wine); *Qualitätswein* (fine wine); and *Qualitätswein mit Prädikat* (top-quality wine).

MEALTIMES

Breakfast, served from 6:30 to 10 (in some cafés and Kneipen, until as late as 2 or 4 PM), is often a substantial meal, with cold meats, cheeses, rolls, and fruit. Many city hotels offer Sunday brunch, and the custom is rapidly catching on. Lunch is served from around 11:30 (especially in rural areas) to around 2; dinner is generally from 6 until 9:30, or earlier in some quiet country areas. Big-city hotels and popular restaurants serve later. Lunch tends to be the main meal, a fact reflected in the almost universal appearance of a lunchtime *Tageskarte,* or suggested menu; try it if you want maximum nourishment for minimum outlay.

Germany (Deutschland)
0
100 miles
0
150 km
North Sea
Baltic Sea
DENMARK
POLAND
HOLLAND
N
Rügen
Fehmarn
Elbe
Oder
Neisse
Ems
FORMER BORDER BETWEEN EAST AND WEST GERMANY
Flensburg
Husum
Kiel
Neustadt
Rostock
Barth
Stralsund
Greifswald
Anklam
Wismar
Lübeck
Güstrow
Teterow
Schwerin
Neubrandenburg
Waren
Neustadt-Glewe
Neustrelitz
Ludwigslust
Pritzwalk
Perleberg
Wittenberge
Neuruppin
Salzwedel
Oranienburg
Stendal
Berlin
Potsdam
Brandenburg
Frankfurt
Cuxhaven
Caroliensiel
Norden
Wilhelmshaven
Bremerhaven
Emden
Hamburg
Oldenburg
Bremen
Meppen
Hannover
Wolfsburg
Osnabrück
Rheine
Braunschweig
Minden
Magdeburg
Bielefeld
Hildesheim
Lübben
Halberstadt
Münster
Bernburg
Dessau
Wittenberg
Cottbus
Bitterfeld
Essen
Göttingen
Nordhausen
Duisberg
Dortmund
Halle
Leipzig
Hagen
Düsseldorf
Kassel
Mühlhausen
Meissen
Görlitz

Köln
Aachen
Bonn
Siegen
Marburg
Alsfeld
Bad
Fulda
Giessen
BELGIUM
Rhine
Koblenz
Wiesbaden
Mainz
Frankfurt-am-Main
Mosel
Bingen
Bad Kreuznach
LUX.
Trier
Darmstadt
Main
Mannheim
Ludwigshafen
Heidelberg
Saarbrücken
Speyer
Karlsruhe
Heilbronn
Stuttgart
Baden-Baden
Tübingen
Offenburg
Rhein
FRANCE
Freiburg
Tuttlingen
Rheinfelden
Konstanz
Bodensee
Friedrichshafen
Wangen
Ravensburg
Biberach
Memmingen
Ulm
Neu-Ulm
Danube
Augsburg
Munich
Isar
Inn
Garmisch-Partenkirchen
Bad Reichenhall
Berchtesgaden
SWITZERLAND
AUSTRIA
Eisenach
Erfurt
Weimar
Gera
Dresden
Görlitz
Chemnitz
Zwickau
Saalfeld
Suhl
Meiningen
Plauen
Hof
Coburg
Münchberg
Bamberg
Bayreuth
THE CZECH REPUBLIC
Würzburg
Rothenburg-o-d-Tauber
Fürth
Nürnberg
Regensburg
Straubing
Deggendorf
Passau
Danube

RATINGS

The following chart gives price ranges for restaurants in the western part of Germany. Food prices in the former East Germany are still somewhat unstable, although in the bigger cities many of the better-quality restaurants already mimic rates in western Germany. Generally speaking, the prevailing price structure in the eastern part of the country, except for restaurants in the priciest hotels, falls into the $ to $$$ categories listed below. Bills in simple restaurants in country areas of the eastern region will, however, still come well below DM 35. Prices are per person and include a first course, main course, dessert, and tip and 10% tax.

CATEGORY	MAJOR CITIES AND RESORTS	OTHER AREAS
$$$$	over DM 100	over DM 90
$$$	DM 75–DM 100	DM 55–DM 90
$$	DM 50–DM 75	DM 35–DM 55
$	under DM 50	under DM 35

WHAT TO WEAR

Jacket and tie are advised for restaurants in the $$$ and $$$$ categories. Casual dress is appropriate elsewhere.

Language

English has long been taught in high schools in the western part of Germany. Consequently, many people under age 40 speak some English. Older people in rural areas are less familiar with English, although some may remember the language from contacts with American and British forces who occupied portions of the country after World War II.

Among Germany's many dialects, probably the most difficult to comprehend is Bavaria's, which is like another language. Nonetheless, except for older people in remote, rural districts, virtually everyone can also speak *Hochdeutsch*, the German equivalent of Oxford English. Hochdeutsch is always used on TV and radio.

Lodging

The standard of **German hotels,** from top-notch luxury spots (of which the country has more than its fair share) to the humblest pension, is excellent. You can expect courteous service; clean and comfortable rooms; and, in rural areas especially, considerable old-German atmosphere.

In addition to hotels proper the country has numerous *Gasthöfe* or *Gasthäuser* (country inns); pensions or *Fremdenheime* (guest houses); and, at the lowest end of the scale, *Zimmer,* meaning rooms, normally in private houses. Look for the sign ZIMMER FREI (rooms free) or ZU VERMIETEN (for rent). A red sign reading BESETZT means there are no vacancies.

Lists of hotels are available from the **German National Tourist Office** (✉ Beethovenstr. 69, D-60325 Frankfurt/Main 1, ☎ 069/974640), and from all regional and local tourist offices. Tourist offices will also make reservations for you—they usually charge a nominal fee—but may have difficulty doing so after 4 PM in peak season and on weekends. There is also an excellent, nationwide reservations service, **Turistische Informations-und Buchungssystem** (TIBS, ✉ Freiburg im Briesgau, ☎ 0761/885810, FAX 0761/8858129), which is open weekdays 9–6 and Saturday 9–1.

Most hotels have restaurants, but those describing themselves as *Garni* will provide breakfast only. Many larger hotels offer no-smoking rooms, and some even offer no-smoking floors, so ask. One other point to note is that in Germany the distinction is made between standard rooms, suites, and apartments. We classify an apartment as having two separate rooms and cooking facilities; otherwise a larger-than-standard unit with a sitting room is considered a suite.

Tourist accommodations in eastern Germany are blossoming under private enterprise. The formerly state-owned Interhotel chain (34 hotels with several thousand rooms) has been dismantled, its components sold individually. The addition of new properties is also moderating the high room rates, which have been the rule in the east. Accommodations remain fairly scarce at the top- and middle-quality levels. If you want to stay in good hotels in eastern Germany, book well in advance (Berlin is the notable exception). Hotel rooms in the cities are in demand year-round because of the high rate of business travel. Traditional inn accommodations have become run down during the past 40 years—still, you may well come across the odd gem.

CAMPING

There are 2,600 campsites in Germany, about 1,600 of which are listed by the **German Camping Club** (DCC, ✉ Mandlstr. 28, D-80802 Munich, ☎ 089/380–1420). The German National Tourist Office also publishes a listing of sites. Most are open from May through October, with about 400 staying open year-round. They tend to become crowded during the summer, so it's always worthwhile to make reservations a day or two ahead. Prices range from DM 15 to DM 20 per night for two adults, a car, and a trailer (less for tents).

CASTLE HOTELS

Germany's Schloss, or castle, hotels are privately owned and run, and prices are mostly moderate; some of the simpler establishments, however, may lack a little in the way of comfort, and furnishings can be basic. On the whole they're delightful, with antiques, imposing interiors, and out-of-the-way locations. For a brochure listing castle hotels in Germany, contact **European Castle Hotels** (✉ Postfach 1111, D-67142 Deidesheim an der Weinstrasse, ☎ 06326/7000, FAX 06326/700022).

FARM VACATIONS

Taking an *Urlaub auf dem Bauernhof* (farm vacation) has increased dramatically in popularity over the past four or five years. Almost every regional tourist office has listings of farms, by area, offering bed and breakfast, apartments, or whole farmhouses to rent. The **German Agricultural Association** (DLG; ✉ Eschborner Landstr. 122, D-60489 Frankfurt/Main, ☎ 069/247–880) produces an annual listing of more than 1,500 farms, all of them inspected and graded, that offer accommodations. The brochure costs DM 15.50.

RATINGS

Breakfast is usually, but not always, included in room rate, so check before you book. Major hotels in cities often have lower rates on weekends or in other periods when business is quiet. If you're lucky, you can find reductions of up to 60%. Likewise, rooms reserved after 10 PM will often carry a discount.

The following chart is for hotels throughout Germany. In Berlin hotel price categories are about DM 50 higher than those for major cities, indicated below. Prices are for standard double rooms and include tax.

CATEGORY	MAJOR CITIES AND RESORTS	OTHER AREAS
$$$$	over DM 300	over DM 200
$$$	DM 200–DM 300	DM 160–DM 200
$$	DM 140–DM 200	DM 100–DM 160
$	under DM 140	under DM 100

RENTALS

Apartments and hotel homes, most accommodating from two to eight guests, can be rented throughout Germany. Rates are reasonable, with reductions for longer stays. Rates for short- or medium-term stays usually include charges for gas and electricity. Local and regional tourist offices have lists of apartments in their areas; otherwise contact the German National Tourist Office (☞ *above*).

RINGHOTELS

Ringhotels (✉ Belfortstr. 6–8, D-81667 Munich, ☎ 089/458–7030) groups 130 individually owned and managed hotels in the medium price range. Many are in the countryside or in pretty villages. Package deals of two–three days are available.

ROMANTIK HOTELS

Among the most delightful places to stay and eat in Germany are the aptly named Romantik Hotels and Restaurants. All are in historic buildings—this is a precondition of membership—and are personally run by the owners. The emphasis generally is on solid comfort, good food, and style. A listing of Romantik Hotels is available in the United States from the German National Tourist Office (✉ Visitor Information *in* Chapter 1).

YOUTH HOSTELS

Germany's 500 *Jugendherberge* (youth hostels) are among the most efficient and up-to-date in Europe. Many are in castles. There's an age limit of 27 in Bavaria; elsewhere, there are no restrictions, though those under 20 take preference if space is limited. It's advisable to be a member of a national hosteling association or Hostelling International (HI), although nonmembers are admitted on payment of a nightly premium of DM 6–DM 7 over the normal rate for the first six nights, after which visitors pay the normal rate (DM 15–DM 38). The **Deutsches Jugendherbergswerk Hauptverband** (✉ Postfach 1455, D-32704 Detmold, ☎ 05231/74010 or 05231/993655) provides a complete list of German hostels for DM 14.80 and has information on regional offices around the country. Hostels must be reserved well in advance for midsummer, especially in eastern Germany. Bookings for hostels can be made only by calling hostels directly.

Mail

POSTAL RATES

Airmail letters to the United States and Canada cost DM 3; postcards cost DM 2. Airmail letters to the United Kingdom cost DM 1.10; postcards cost DM 1.

RECEIVING MAIL

You can arrange to have mail sent to you in care of any German post office; have the envelope marked "Postlagernd." This service is free. Alternatively, if you have an American Express card or have booked a vacation with American Express you can have mail sent to any American Express office in Germany; there's no charge.

Money Matters

COSTS

Inflation has crept up in the 1990s (although at press time—spring 1998—the annual rate of inflation was being held below 2%). The most expensive areas to visit are the major cities, notably Berlin, Frankfurt, Hamburg, and Munich. The cost of living is still somewhat lower in eastern Germany, and some of these lower costs benefit tourists. But a growing number of places in eastern Germany that cater specifically to visitors are now charging western Germany rates.

CURRENCY

Although the new European monetary unit, the Euro, officially makes its appearance in 1999, it won't replace the Deutschmark as a currency until the year 2002. In 1999 Deutschmark banknotes and coins will still be the means of exchange. The Deutschmark, written DM and generally referred to as the mark, is divided into 100 pfennige. There are bills of 5 (rare), 10, 20, 50, 100, 200, 500, and 1,000 marks and coins of 1, 2, 5, 10, and 50 pfennige and 1, 2, and 5 marks. At press time (spring 1998), the mark stood at DM 1.80 to the U.S. dollar, DM 1.26 to the Canadian dollar, and DM 2.98 to the pound sterling.

SAMPLE PRICES

Cup of coffee in a café, DM 3.50, in a stand-up snack bar DM 1.80; mug of beer in a beer hall, DM 4.50, bottle of beer from a supermarket, DM 1.50; soft drink, DM 2; ham sandwich, DM 4; 3-km (2-mi) taxi ride, DM 13.

TIPPING

Overtipping is as frowned upon as not tipping at all. In restaurants service is included (under the heading *Bedienung*, at the bottom of the check), and it is customary to round out the check to the next mark or two, a practice also commonplace in cafés, beer halls, and bars. For taxi drivers, also round out to the next mark or two: for DM 11.20, make it DM 12; for DM 11.80, make it DM 13. Railway and airport porters (if you can find any) have their own scale of charges, but round out the requested amount to the next mark. Hotel porters get DM 1 per bag. Doormen are tipped the same amount for small services, such as calling a cab. Room service should be rewarded with at least DM 2 every time you use it. Maids should get about DM 1 per day. Double all these figures at luxury hotels. Service-station attendants get 50 pf or DM 1 for checking oil and tires or cleaning windshields.

National Holidays

January 1; January 6 (Epiphany—Bavaria, Baden-Württemberg, and Sachsen-Anhalt only); April 2 (Good Friday); April 5 (Easter Monday); May 1 (Worker's Day); May 13 (Ascension); May 24 (Pentecost Monday); June 3 (Corpus Christi—south Germany only); August 15 (Assumption Day—Bavaria and Saarland only); October 3 (German Unity Day); November 1 (All Saints' Day); December 24–26.

Opening and Closing Times

Banks. Times vary from state to state and city to city, but banks are usually open weekdays from 8:30 or 9 to 2 or 3 (5 or 6 on Thursday). Some banks close from 12:30 to 1:30. Branches at airports and main train stations open as early as 6:30 AM and close as late as 10:30 PM. **Museums** are generally open from Tuesday through Sunday 9–5. Some close for an hour or more at lunch, and some are open on Monday. Many stay open until 8 or 9 on Wednesday and/or Thursday. Larger **shops** and department stores open weekdays 9:30–8, and Saturday 9:30–4, owing to legislation passed in 1996. Many smaller shops, however, cling to the previous hours, closing around 6 PM.

Shopping

SALES TAX

German goods carry a 17% value-added tax (VAT). You can claim the tax back either as you leave the country or once you've returned home. When you make a purchase, ask the shopkeeper for a form known as an *Ausfuhr-Abnehmerbescheinigung*; he or she will help you fill it out. As you leave the country present the form, plus the goods and receipts, to German customs, which will give you an official export certificate or stamp and point you in the direction of a refund point where you can recover the tax in cash. Alternatively, send the form back to the shop, and it will send the refund.

Telephoning

COUNTRY CODE

Germany's country code is 49. When dialing a number in Germany from outside the country, drop the initial 0 in the regional code.

INTERNATIONAL CALLS

These can be made from public phones bearing the sign INLANDS UND AUSLANDSGESPRÄCHE. Using DM 5 coins is best for long-distance dialing; a four-minute call to the United States costs DM 15. To avoid weighing yourself down with coins, use a phone card or make international calls from post offices; even those in small country towns will have a special booth for international calls. You pay the clerk at the end of your call, adding a DM 2 service fee. To reach an **AT&T** long-distance operator, dial 0130–0010; for **MCI,** dial 0130–0012; for **Sprint,** 0130–0013. Dial 0010 for a local operator who handles international calls.

LOCAL CALLS

Since reunification, all phones in the east and west use the same coins: 10 pf, DM 1, and DM 5 for long-distance calls. A local call from a call-box costs 30 pf and lasts six minutes. Card phones are rapidly replacing coin-operated phones: Cards cost DM 12 or DM 50 (the latter good for DM 60 worth of calls) and can be purchased at all post offices and many exchange places. If you need an operator, dial 010.

Transportation

BY BICYCLE

Bicycles can be rented at more than 130 train stations throughout Germany from April through October. The cost is DM 11 or DM 13 (with gears) per day, DM 7 or DM 9 if you have a valid rail ticket. You can pick up a bike at one station and return it to another, provided both stations rent bikes. Mountain bikes can be rented for DM 20 a day at the Garmisch-Partenkirchen station and three other Alpine stations (Immenstadt, Oberstdorf, and Sonthoten). You will need to buy a *Fahrradkarte,* or bicycle ticket (DM 5.60 for journeys up to 100 km; DM 9.40 for longer trips), to take your bike on the train; InterCity Express trains do not carry bikes. Most cities also have companies that rent bikes for about DM 15 per day or DM 80–DM 90 a week.

BY BOAT

You can cruise rivers and lakes throughout Germany. The biggest fleet belongs to the Köln-based **Köln-Düsseldorfer** (KD) line. **KD River Cruises of Europe** (Rhine Cruise Agency, ✉ 2500 Westchester Ave., Purchase, NY 10577, ☏ 914/696–3600) and **KD German Rhine Line** (✉ Frankenwerft 15, D-50667 Köln, ☏ 0221/208–8288) operate on the Rhine, Mosel, Saar, Neckar, Danube, Elbe, and Main rivers.

Services on the 160-km (100-mi) stretch of the Danube (Donau) between the spectacular Kelheim Gorge and Passau on the Austrian border are operated by **Donauschiffahrt Wurm & Köck** (✉ Höllg. 26, D-94032 Passau, ☏ 0851/929–292). The Bodensee (Lake Constance), the largest lake in Germany, has up to 40 ships crisscrossing it in summer. **Deutsche Bahn** (✉ Bodensee-Schiffsbetriebe, Hafenstr. 6, D-78462 Konstanz) also has information on cruises. For details on regular summer cruises on Bavaria's five largest lakes—Ammersee, Chiemsee, Königsee, Tegernsee, and Starnbergersee—contact local tourist offices.

BY BUS

Long-distance bus services in Germany are part of the Europe-wide Europabus network. Services are neither as frequent nor as comprehensive as those on the rail system, so make reservations. All Europabus services have a bilingual attendant and offer small luxuries that you won't find on the more basic, though still comfortable, regular services. For details and reservations contact DTG (☞ By Train, *below*). Travel agents and Deutsche Touring offices in Köln, Hannover, Hamburg, Munich, Nürnberg, and Wuppertal can also take reservations. Rural bus services are operated by local municipalities and some private firms, as well as by Deutsche Bahn and the post office.

BY CAR

Breakdowns. The **ADAC** (✉ Am Westpark 8, D-81373 Munich, ☎ 089/76760), the major German automobile organization, gives free help and advice to tourists, though you have to pay for any spare parts you need, plus labor and mileage if a tow truck has to be called. All autobahns have regularly spaced telephones at which you can call for help.

Gasoline. Leaded and unleaded gas and diesel are generally available all over Germany, although leaded fuel is gradually being phased out and is unobtainable at many gas stations. The price of a liter of gas may range from DM 1.20 to DM 1.70, depending on the grade.

Parking. Daytime parking in cities is very difficult. If you can find a parking lot, use it or you'll risk having your car towed. Parking restrictions are not always clearly marked and can be hard to understand when they are. At night parking-meter spaces are free.

Road Conditions. The autobahn system in Germany is of the highest standard. These roads are marked either A (on blue signs), meaning inter-German highways, or E (on green signs), meaning they form part of the Europe-wide *Europastrasse* network. All autobahns are toll-free. Local roads are called *Bundesstrassen* and are marked by their number on a yellow sign. All local roads are single lane and slower than autobahns.

Rules of the Road. Officially, there's no speed limit on autobahns, although you'll find signs recommending that motorists stay below 130 kph (80 mph). You'll also find blue signs on autobahns stating the recommended minimum speed on that stretch. Germans are fast drivers, and autobahn speeds of more than 160 kph (100 mph) are common. Unless you're driving at that speed, stay in the right-hand lane on autobahns, using the faster-paced left-hand lanes only for passing. There are speed limits on other roads—100 kph (60 mph) on Bundesstrassen, 80 kph (50 mph) on country roads, between 30 kph (18 mph) and 60 kph (36 mph) in built-up urban areas. Fines for exceeding the speed limit can be heavy. Penalties for driving under the influence of alcohol are even more severe, so make sure to keep within the legal limit—equivalent to the consumption of two small beers or a glass of wine.

BY PLANE

Germany's national airline, **Lufthansa** (☎ 800/645–3880 in the U.S., ☎ 0171/495–2044 in Great Britain, ☎ 0180/380–3803 in Germany), serves all major cities. **LTU International Airways** (☎ 800/546–7334 in the U.S., ☎ 0211/941–8888 in Germany) has connections between Düsseldorf and Munich and between Frankfurt and Munich. Regular fares are high, but you can save up to 40% with *Flieg und Spar* (fly-and-save) specials; several restrictions apply, such as a DM 100 penalty for changing flights. A British Airways subsidiary, **Deutsche BA** (based at Munich's Franz Josef Strauss Airport, ☎ 089/9759–1500), competes with Lufthansa on many domestic routes, including those between Berlin and Munich, Munich and Hamburg, and Köln/Bonn and Düsseldorf. Deutsche BA fares are often substantially lower than Lufthansa's.

BY TRAIN

The German railway system is being privatized, so routes and timetables may change in some areas. The two separate rail networks of the former East and West Germany merged in 1994 into one entity known as **Deutsche Bahn** (DB), or German Rail, bringing Berlin and the cities of the old DDR much closer to the main railheads of the west.

Train journeys between the centers of many cities—Munich–Frankfurt, for example—can be completed faster by rail than by plane. All overnight InterCity services and the slower D-class trains have sleepers, with a first-class service that includes breakfast in bed. All InterCity trains have restaurant cars, and InterCity and EuroCity trains have either restaurant cars or trolley service. Seat reservations (highly advisable on InterCity, EuroCity, and InterCity Express trains) cost DM 3. Bikes cannot be transported on InterCity Express services, but InterCity, EuroCity, and most D-class trains have onboard storage, and InterRegio trains even have compartments where cyclists can travel next to their bikes.

Fares. The **German Rail Pass,** not available to Germans, allows travel over the entire German rail network for 5, 10, or 15 days within a single month. It can be purchased for first- or second-class travel. A **Twin Pass** discounts these rates for two people traveling together. A **Youth Pass,** sold to those age 12–25, is for second-class travel. These passes are also valid on all buses operated by the Deutsche Bahn, as well as on tour routes along the Romantic and Castle roads served by **Deutsche Touring Gesellschaft** (DTG, ✉ Am Römerhof 17, D-60486 Frankfurt/Main, ☎ 069/79030) and Rhine, Main, and Mosel river cruises operated by the **Köln-Düsseldorfer (KD) German Rhine Line** (☞ By Boat, *above*). Passes are sold by travel agents and **DER Tours** (✉ Box 1606, Des Plaines, IL 60017, ☎ 800/782–2424) in the United States and by Deutsche Bahn in Germany.

The popular **Inter Rail** ticket can be complicated, but there are big savings for young travelers (26 years old or younger) touring just one area of Europe. Young travelers intending to tour only Germany can get an even better deal with a **Euro Domino** ticket, but you must purchase the ticket outside Germany. No age limit is linked to other special deals, such as the Sparpreis and ICE-Super Sparpreis, which offer big savings on return journeys made on off-peak days.

If you intend to stay in one region of Germany, you can save on fares by buying a *FerienTicket* (Holiday Ticket), valid for unlimited train travel in any one region for one, two, or three weeks. The ticket costs DM 40 for one week, DM 60 for two weeks, and DM 80 for three weeks.

Weather

The main tourist season in Germany runs from May to late October, when the weather is best. Hundreds of folk festivals take place during this period. Winter-sports season in the Bavarian Alps runs from Christmas to mid-March. Prices are generally higher in summer. Most resorts have *Zwischensaison* (between season) and *Nebensaison* (edge-of-season) rates, and tourist offices can provide lists of hotels offering *Pauschalangebote* (special low-price inclusive weekly packages). Similarly, many winter resorts lower their rates for the periods immediately before and after the Christmas and New Year's high season (*weisse Wochen,* or "white weeks"). In the colder months, weather can be gloomy, and, except at ski resorts and in the larger cities, many attractions are closed.

CLIMATE

Germany's climate is generally temperate. Winters vary from mild and damp to very cold and bright. Summers are usually sunny and warm, though you should be prepared for a few cloudy and wet days. In Alpine regions spring often comes late, with snow flurries well into April. Fall is sometimes spectacular in the south: warm and soothing. Only in southern Bavaria (Bayern) will you find strikingly variable weather, which is caused by the *Föhn,* a warm Alpine wind that brings sudden barometric changes and gives rise to clear but oppressive conditions in summer and causes snow to disappear overnight in winter.

The following are the average daily maximum and minimum temperatures for Munich.

Jan.	35F	1C	**May**	64F	18C	**Sept.**	67F	20C
	23	– 5		45	7		48	9
Feb.	38F	3C	**June**	70F	21C	**Oct.**	56F	13C
	23	– 5		51	11		40	4
Mar.	48F	9C	**July**	74F	23C	**Nov.**	44F	7C
	30	– 1		55	13		33	0
Apr.	56F	14C	**Aug.**	73F	23C	**Dec.**	36F	2C
	38	3		54	12		26	– 3

MUNICH

People who live in other parts of Germany sometimes refer to Munich (München in German) as the nation's "secret capital." Flamboyant, easygoing Munich, city of beer and Baroque, is starkly different from the sometimes stiffly Prussian-influenced Berlin; the gritty and industrial Hamburg; or the hard-headed, commercially driven Frankfurt. This is a city to visit for its good-natured and relaxed charm—Gemütlichkeit, they call it here. Munich is a crazy mix of high culture (witness its world-class opera house and art galleries) and wild abandon (witness the vulgar frivolity of the Oktoberfest). Its citizenry seems determined to perpetuate the lifestyle of the 19th-century king Ludwig I, the Bavarian ruler who brought so much international prestige to his home city after declaring: "I want to make out of Munich a town that does such credit to Germany that nobody knows Germany unless he has seen Munich." He kept his promise with an architectural and artistic renaissance—before abdicating in the wake of a wild romance with an Irish-born dancing girl, Lola Montez.

Exploring Munich

Numbers in the margin correspond to points of interest on the Munich map.

Munich is unique among German cities because it has no identifiable, homogeneous Old Town center. The historic heart of the city is a quiet courtyard unknown to most tourists, while clusters of centuries-old buildings that belong to Munich's origins are often separated by postwar developments of sometimes singular ugliness.

★ 19 **Alte Pinakothek** (Old Picture Gallery). This major art gallery contains some of the world's most celebrated old master paintings, including works by Dürer, Rembrandt, Rubens, and Murillo. Built by Leo von Klenze at the beginning of the 19th century to house Ludwig I's collections, the towering brick edifice is also an architectural treasure in its own right. After extensive renovations, the museum reopened in late 1997 and now displays its treasures in the high style they deserve. ✉

Barestr. 27, ☎ 089/238–05215. ⏲ Wed., Fri., and weekends 9–5; Tues. and Thurs. 9–8.

❽ **Altes Rathaus** (Old Town Hall). The 1474 medieval building has a fine assembly room used for official functions. Its tower provides a satisfyingly atmospheric setting for a little toy museum. ✉ *Marienpl.,* ☎ *089/233–22347.* ⏲ *Daily 10–5:30.*

★ ❾ **Asamkirche** (Asam Church). Some consider the Asamkirche a preposterously overdecorated jewel box; others find it one of Europe's finest late-Baroque churches. It was built around 1730 by the Asam brothers—Cosmas Damian and Egid Quirin—next door to their home, the Asamhaus. They dedicated it to St. John Nepomuk, a 14th-century monk. Inside, there is a riot of decoration: frescoes, statuary, rich rosy marble, billowing stucco clouds, and gilding everywhere. ✉ *Sendlingerstr.* ⏲ *Daily 9–5:30.*

❸ **Bürgersaal.** Behind the modest facade of this unassuming building is an unusual split-level interior. The main Oberkirche (upper level) consists of a richly decorated Baroque oratory. The Unterkirche (lower level) is a cryptlike chapel containing the tomb of the courageous Jesuit priest Rupert Mayer, an outspoken opponent of the Nazis. ✉ *Neuhauserstr. 14,* ☎ *089/223–884.* ⏲ *Oberkirche: Mon.–Sat. 11–1, Sun. 9–12:30; Unterkirche: Mon.–Sat. 6:30 AM–7 PM, Sun. 7–7.*

⓱ **Englischer Garten** (English Garden). Count Rumford, a refugee from the American War of Independence, designed this seemingly endless park (5 km/3 mi long and more than ½ km/¼ mi wide). He was born in England, but it wasn't his English ancestry that determined the park's name as much as its open, informal nature, a style favored by 18th-century English aristocrats. Here you can rent boats, relax in beer gardens (the most famous is at the foot of a Chinese Pagoda), ride your bike (or ski in winter), or simply stroll. Ludwig II loved to wander incognito along the English Garden's serpentine paths. A large section of the park right behind the **Haus der Kunst**(☞ *below*) has been designated a nudist area. ✉ *Bordering the eastern side of Schwabing.*

⓯ **Feldherrnhalle** (Hall of Generals). This local open-air hall of fame was modeled on the 14th-century Loggia dei Lanzi in Florence. During the '30s and '40s it was a key Nazi shrine, marking the site of Hitler's abortive rising, or putsch, which took place in 1923. All who passed it had to give the Nazi salute. ✉ *South end of Odeonspl.*

★ ❺ **Frauenkirche** (Church of Our Lady). This soaring Gothic redbrick masterpiece has two incongruous towers topped by onion-shape domes, symbols of the city (perhaps because they resemble brimming beer mugs, cynics claim). The church was built between 1474 and 1494, and the towers were added in 1524–21. The cathedral's interior is stark. The crypt houses the tombs of numerous Wittelsbachs, the family that ruled Bavaria for 7 centuries until forced to abdicate in 1918. ✉ *Frauenpl.,* ☎ *089/290–0820.*

❶ **Hauptbahnhof** (Main Train Station). It contains the city tourist office, with maps and helpful information on events around town. ✉ *Bayerstr.,* ☎ *089/239–1256.*

⓲ **Haus der Kunst** (House of Art). Munich's leading modern art gallery is housed in one of the city's few remaining Nazi-era monuments, opened officially in 1938 by Hitler himself. The gallery contains some outstanding 20th-century art, including works by Kandinsky and Klee. ✉ *Prinzregentenstr. 1,* ☎ *089/2112–7137.* ⏲ *Tues., Wed., Fri., and weekends 10–5, Thurs. 10–8.*

⓭ **Hofgarten** (Royal Garden). Two sides of the pretty, formal garden that was once part of the royal palace grounds are bordered by arcades designed in the 19th century by the royal architect Leo von Klenze. ⊠ *Hofgartenstr., north of the Residenz.*

❷ **Karlsplatz** (Charles Square). Known locally as Stachus, this busy intersection has one of Munich's most popular fountains, a circle of water jets that cool city shoppers and office workers on hot summer days. The semicircle of yellow-front buildings that backs the fountain, with their high windows and delicate cast-iron balconies, gives the area a southern, almost Mediterranean, air. ⊠ *At the meeting point of Sonnenstr., Bayerstr., Schützenstr., Luisenstr., Prielmayerstr., and Neuhauserstr.*

★ ❻ **Marienplatz** (Square of Our Lady). Surrounded by shops, restaurants, and cafés, this square is named after the 1638 gilt statue of the Virgin Mary that has been watching over it for nearly 4 centuries. ⊠ *Bordered by Kaufingerstr., Rosenstr., Weinstr., and Dienerstr.*

❹ **Michaelskirche** (St. Michael's Church). One of the most magnificent Renaissance churches in Germany, this spacious and handsome structure is decorated throughout in plain white stucco. It was built during the late 16th century for the Jesuits and was closely modeled on Il Gesù, the Jesuit church in Rome. ⊠ *Neuhauserstr. 6,* ☎ *089/551–99257.* ⏲ *Mon.–Wed., Fri., Sat. 8:30–7, Thurs. 8:30–9, Sun. 6 AM–10 PM. Guided tours Wed. at 2.*

⓬ **Nationaltheater** (National Theater). Constructed at the beginning of the 19th century and twice destroyed, this neo-Classical opera house with state-of-the-art facilities is the home of the world-famous Bavarian State Opera and Ballet companies. ⊠ *Maximilianstr. 1,* ☎ *089/218–51920.*

⓴ **Neue Pinakothek** (New Picture Gallery). The original art gallery that King Ludwig I built to house his "modern" collections (meaning, of course, 19th-century works) was destroyed during World War II and replaced by a new exhibition hall in 1981. The low, brick structure—some have compared it to a Florentine palazzo—is a superb, skylit setting for one of the finest collections of European 19th-century paintings and sculpture in the world. ⊠ *Barerstr. 29, near Königspl.,* ☎ *089/238–05195.* ⏲ *Wed., Fri., and weekends 10–5; Tues., Thurs. 10–8.*

❼ **Neues Rathaus** (New City Hall). Munich's present city hall was built between 1867 and 1908 in the fussy, turreted, neo-Gothic style so beloved by King Ludwig II. At 9 AM and 11 AM daily (also May–Oct. at 5 PM and 9 PM), the Glockenspiel, or chiming clock, in the central tower swings into action with two tiers of dancing and jousting figures. An elevator whisks visitors to an observation point near the top of one of the towers. ⊠ *Marienpl.,* ☎ *089/2331.* ⏲ *Tower Apr.–Oct., Mon.–Thurs. 9–4, Fri. 9–1.*

⓫ **Residenz** (Royal Palace). This mighty yet somber palace dating from the 14th century was the home of the Wittelsbach dukes for more than 3 centuries. Its main attractions are the glittering Schatzkammer, or treasury, and glorious Rococo theater. ⊠ *Max-Joseph-Pl. 3,* ☎ *089/290–671.* ⏲ *Treasury: Tues.–Sun. 10–4:30. Cuvilliés Theater: Mon.–Sat. 2–5, Sun. 10–5.*

⓰ **Siegestor** (Victory Arch). The monument has Italian origins—it was modeled on the Arch of Constantine in Rome—and was built to honor the achievements of the Bavarian army during the Wars of Liberation (1813–15). ⊠ *At start of Leopoldstr.*

⓮ **Theatinerkirche** (Theatine Church). This handsome, yellow-stucco church was built for the Theatine monks in the mid-17th century,

Alte Pinakothek, **19**
Altes Rathaus, **8**
Asamkirche, **9**
Bürgersaal, **3**
Englischer Garten, **17**
Feldherrnhalle, **15**
Frauenkirche, **5**
Hauptbahnhof, **1**
Haus der Kunst, **18**
Hofgarten, **13**
Karlsplatz, **2**
Marienplatz, **6**
Michaelskirche, **4**
Nationaltheater, **12**
Neue Pinakothek, **20**
Neues Rathaus, **7**
Residenz, **11**
Siegestor, **16**
Theatinerkirche, **14**
Viktualienmarkt, **10**

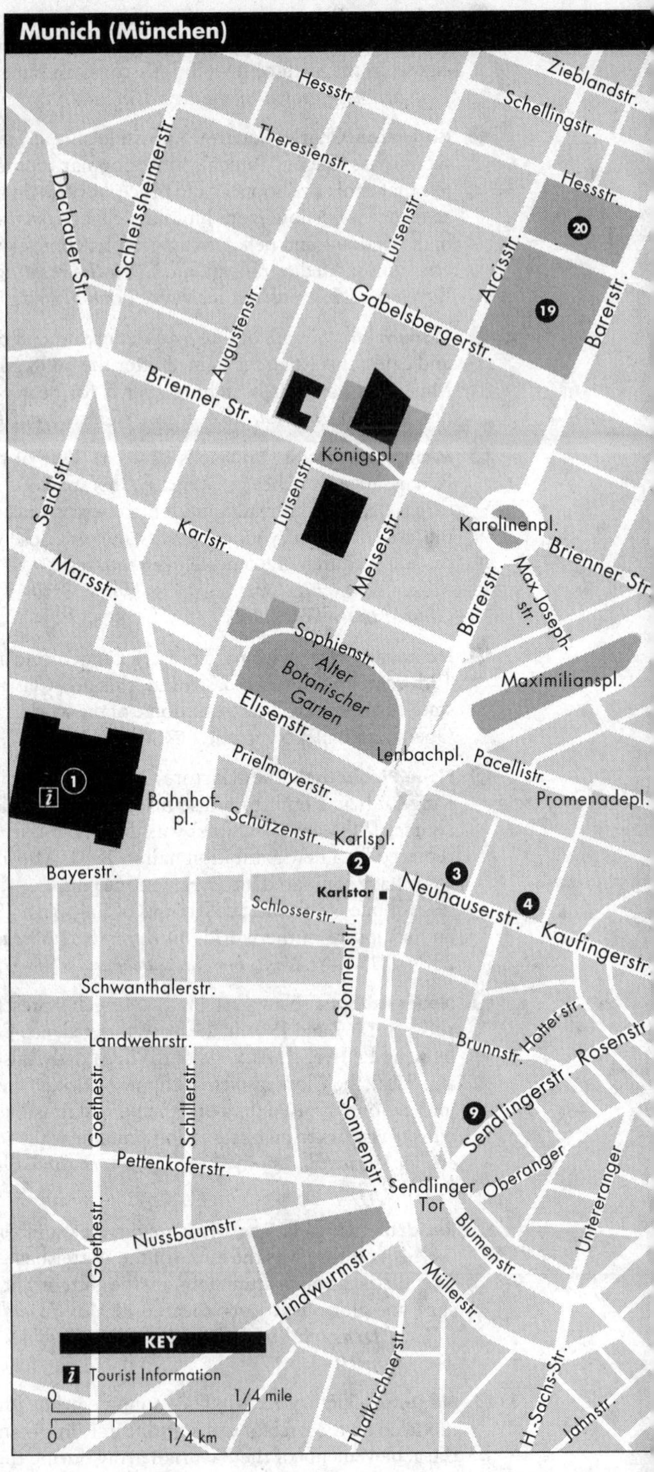

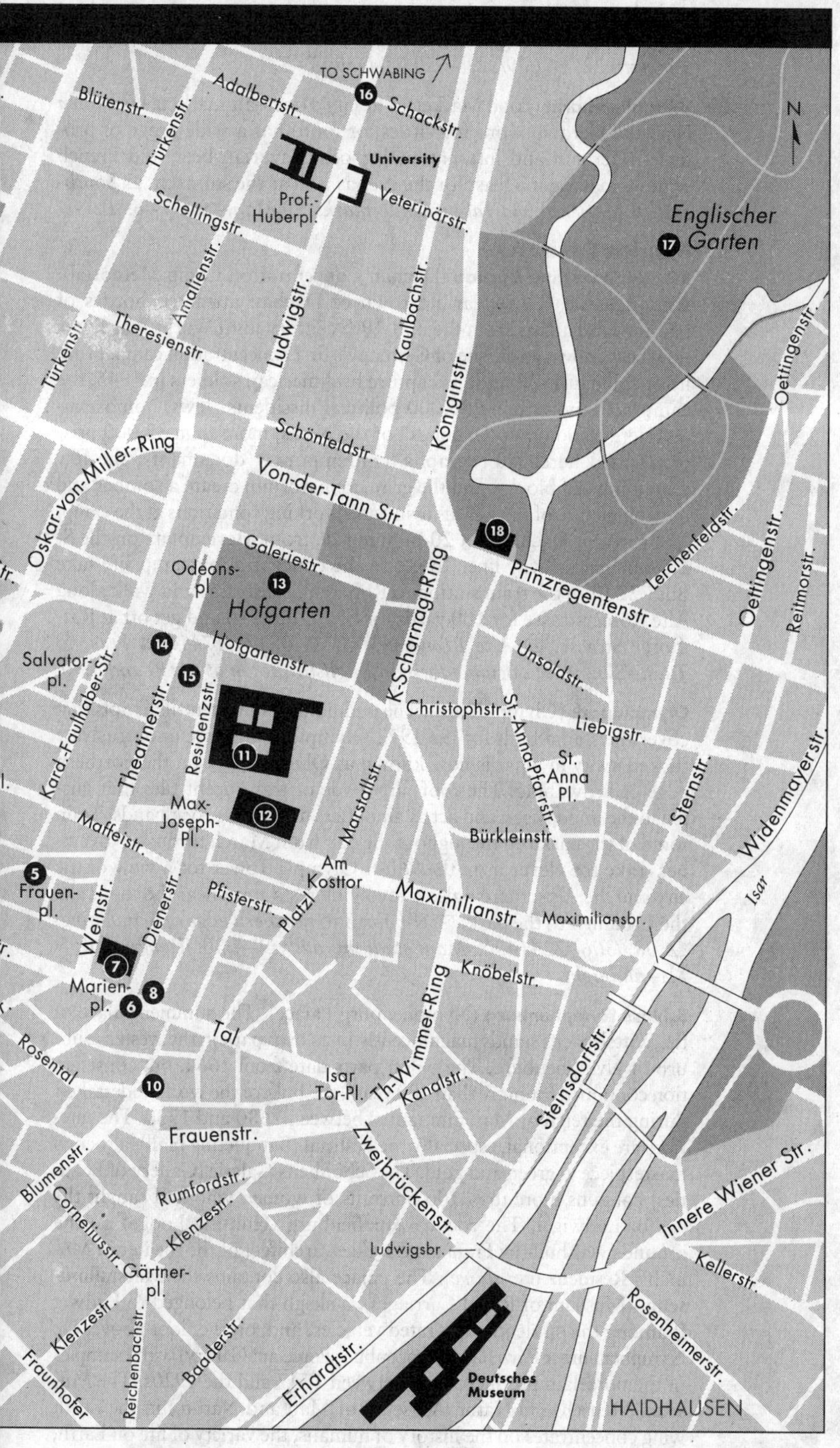
TO SCHWABING
Blütenstr.
Adalbertstr.
Schackstr.
Türkenstr.
University
Veterinärstr.
Prof.-
Huberpl.
Schellingstr.
Englischer
Garten
Amalienstr.
Ludwigstr.
Kaulbachstr.
Theresienstr.
Türkenstr.
Königinstr.
Oettingenstr.
Schönfeldstr.
Oskar-von-Miller-Ring
Von-der-Tann Str.
Galeriestr.
Odeons-
pl.
Hofgarten
K.-Scharnagl-Ring
Prinzregentenstr.
Lerchenfeldstr.
Oettingenstr.
Reitmorstr.
Salvator-
pl.
Hofgartenstr.
Unsoldstr.
Kard.-Faulhaber-Str.
Theatinerstr.
Residenzstr.
Christophstr.
St.-Anna-pfarrstr.
Liebigstr.
St.
Anna
Pl.
Sternstr.
Widenmayerstr.
Max-
Joseph-
Pl.
Marstallstr.
Maffeistr.
Bürkleinstr.
Frauen-
pl.
Am
Kosttor
Maximilianstr.
Isar
Pfisterstr.
Platzl
Maximiliansbr.
Weinstr.
Dienerstr.
Knöbelstr.
Marien-
pl.
Th.-Wimmer-Ring
Tal
Rosental
Isar
Tor-Pl.
Kanalstr.
Steinsdorfstr.
Frauenstr.
Zweibrückenstr.
Blumenstr.
Rumfordstr.
Corneliusstr.
Klenzestr.
Innere Wiener Str.
Ludwigsbr.
Kellerstr.
Gärtner-
pl.
Rosenheimerstr.
Klenzestr.
Reichenbachstr.
Baaderstr.
Erhardtstr.
Deutsches
Museum
Fraunhofer
HAIDHAUSEN

though its striking facade, with twin eye-catching domes, was added only in the following century. The interior is austerely white. ✉ *Theatinerstr. 22,* ☎ *089/221–650.* ⏲ *Daily 7–7.*

★ ⑩ **Viktualienmarkt** (Food Market). The city's open-air market (*Viktualien* is an old German word for vittles, or food) has a wide range of produce—German and international goods, Bavarian beer, and French wines—making it a feast for the eyes as well as the stomach. ✉ *Southeast of Marienpl. via Tal or Rindermarkt.* ⏲ *Mon.–Sat. 7–6:30.*

Munich Environs

KZ-Gedenkstätte Dachau (Dachau Concentration Camp Memorial). Although the 1,200-year-old town of Dachau attracted hordes of painters and artists from the mid-19th century until World War I, it is now best known as the site of Germany's first concentration camp. From its opening in 1933 until its capture by American soldiers in 1945, the camp held more than 206,000 political dissidents, Jews, homosexuals, clergy, and other "enemies" of the Nazis; more than 32,000 prisoners died here. Photographs, contemporary documents, the few remaining cell blocks, and the grim crematorium create a somber and moving picture of the vicious living and working conditions at the camp. The town of Dachau is a 20-minute ride from Marienplatz on the S-2 suburban railway line. To get to the concentration camp site take Bus 722 from the train station to Robert-Boschstrasse and walk along Alte Römerstrasse for 100 yards, or board Bus 720 and get off at Ratiborer Strasse. ✉ *Alte Römerstr. 75,* ☎ *08121/1741.* 🎫 *Free.* ⏲ *Tues.–Sun. 9–5; documentary (in English) shown at 11:30 and 3:30.*

Olympiapark (Olympic Park). The undulating circus-tent-like roofs that cover the stadia built for the 1972 Olympic Games are unobtrusively tucked away in what is now known as Olympiapark on the northern edge of Schwabing. The roofs are made of translucent tiles that glisten in the midday sun and act as amplifiers for visiting rock bands. Train tours of the park run throughout the day from March through November. Take the elevator up the 960-ft Olympia Tower for a view of the city and the Alps; there's also a revolving restaurant near the top. Take the U-bahn 3 to the park. ✉ *U-bahn 3 to northern edge of Schwabing,* ☎ *089/306–72414.* ⏲ *Main stadium: daily 9–4:30. Tower: daily 9 AM–midnight.*

Schloss Nymphenburg (Nymphenburg Palace). The summer palace of the Wittelsbachs stands magnificently in its own park in the western suburb of Nymphenburg. The oldest parts date from 1664, but construction continued for more than 100 years, the bulk of the work undertaken during the reign of Max Emmanuel between 1680 and 1730. The interiors are exceptional, especially the **Festsaal** (Banqueting Hall), a rococo masterpiece in green and gold. The **Schönheits Galerie** (Gallery of Beauties) contains more than 100 portraits of women who had caught the eye of Ludwig I. The rococo **Amalienburg** (Hunting Lodge) on the grounds was built by François Cuvilliés, architect of the theater in Munich's **Residenz** (☞ *above*). The palace also contains the **Marstallmuseum** (Museum of Royal Carriages), a sleigh that belonged to Ludwig II among the opulently decorated vehicles, and, on the floor above, the **Nymphenburger Porzellan** (Nympenburg Porcelain Gallery) with examples of the porcelain produced here between 1747 and the 1920s. The **Museum Mensch und Natur** (Museum of Man and Nature) in the north wing concentrates on the history of humans, the variety of life on Earth, and our place in the environment. ✉ *U-bahn 1 from Hauptbahnhof to Rotkreuzpl., then pick up Tram 12, heading for Amalienburg,* ☎ *089/179–080.* ⏲ *Apr.–Sept., Tues.–Sun. 9–12:30 and 1:30–5; Oct.–Mar., Tues.–Sun. 10–12:30 and 1:30–4; gardens daily year-round.*

Dining and Lodging

Munich claims some of Europe's best chefs, purveyors of French nouvelle cuisine in some of the most noted—and pricey—restaurants in Germany. For local cuisine, Munich's wood-paneled, flagstone beer restaurants and halls serve food as sturdy as the large measure of beer that comes to your table almost automatically. Münchners love to eat just as much as they love to drink their beer, and the range of food is as varied and rich as the local breweries' output. For details and price-category definitions, *see* Dining *in* Germany A to Z, *above*.

Though Munich has a vast number of hotels in all price ranges, many are full year-round. If you plan to visit during the "fashion weeks" (Mode Wochen) in March and September or during the Oktoberfest at the end of September, make reservations at least several months in advance. Munich's tourist offices will handle only written or personal requests for reservations assistance. Write or fax the Fremdenverkehrsamt (✉ Sendlingerstr. 1, D-80313 Munich, FAX 089/239–1313). Your best bet for finding a room if you haven't reserved one is the tourist office at the Hauptbahnhof, by the Bayerstrasse entrance. There is a small fee.

Consider staying in a suburban hotel—where rates are often, but not always, lower—and taking the 15-minute U-bahn or S-bahn ride into town. The city tourist office's "Key to Munich" packages include reduced-rate hotel reservations, sightseeing tours, theater admissions, and low-cost travel on the U- and S-bahn. For details and price-category definitions, *see* Lodging *in* Germany A to Z, *above*.

$$$$ ★ ✕ **Königshof.** On the second floor of the postwar Königshof Hotel and overlooking the Karlstor at the northern entrance to the pedestrian-only center, the Königshof is without doubt Munich's most opulent restaurant. The neo-Baroque style includes ceiling frescoes, subdued chandelier lighting, and heavy drapery. Nouvelle cuisine is served—breast of goose with truffles, for example, or veal in basil cream and mushroom sauce. ✉ *Karlspl. 25,* ☎ *089/551–36142. AE, DC, MC, V.*

$$$ ✕ **Lenbach.** Michael Käfer's latest spectacular addition to the restaurant scene is not for the shy: Guests enter the vast dining area along a floor-lit catwalk. Britain's number-one restaurant designer, Sir Terence Conran, was given a 100-year-old city palace to work on and clearly had a ball. The high, vaulted ceilings, marble pillars, art nouveau wrought-iron and rich stucco were blended with Conran's typical minimalist decoration, all under the general theme of the "Seven Deadly Sins." The seafood is outstanding and is a feature of a daily buffet in the chandelier-hung main lobby. The bar, by the way, is Munich's longest. ✉ *Ottostr. 6,* ☎ *089/549–1300. Jacket and tie. AE, MC, V.*

$$$ ★ ✕ **Preysing Keller.** The food here is light and sophisticated but with recognizably Teutonic touches. The over-restored restaurant is in a 16th-century cellar. It's the food, the extensive wine list, and the perfect service that make this place special. ✉ *Innere-Wiener-Str. 6,* ☎ *089/458–45260. Reservations essential. No credit cards. Closed Sun.*

$$–$$$ ✕ **Dukatz.** Join the Munich literati and glitterati in the severely intellectual surroundings of the *Literaturhaus* (House of Literature). The restaurant hums with talk of publishing contracts and literary gossip. Its excellent cuisine combines traditional German with a light Gallic touch: lamb's tripe melting in a rich champagne sauce, for instance, or stuffed pig's trotters with truffles. The light and airy café-bar has a pile of American and British daily papers. ✉ *Salvatorpl. 1,* ☎ *089/291–9600. Reservations essential. No credit cards. Closed Sun. dinner.*

$$ ✕ **Augustiner Keller.** This 19th-century establishment is the flagship beer restaurant of one of Munich's oldest breweries, Augustiner. The decor of the two baronial hall-like rooms emphasizes wood—from the

refurbished parquet floors to the wooden barrels from which the beer is drawn. Bavarian specialties such as *Tellerfleisch*—cold roast beef with lashings of horseradish, served on a big wooden board—fill the daily menu. ✉ *Arnulfstr. 52,* ☎ *089/594–393. AE, DC, MC, V.*

$$ ✕ **Bamberger Haus.** This historic villa on the edge of Schwabing's Luitpold Park has a rambling, vaulted beer-cellar and a slightly faded upstairs dining room. You dine beneath crystal chandeliers and under the gaze of Baroque statuary. Some of the vegetarian dishes on the imaginative menu, such as finely prepared vegetables au gratin, are incredibly cheap and filling. ✉ *Brunnerstr. 2,* ☎ *089/308–8966. AE, MC, V.*

$$ ✕ **Dürnbräu.** A fountain plays outside this picturesque old Bavarian inn. Inside, it's crowded and noisy. Expect to share a table; your fellow diners will range from business sorts to students. The food is resolutely traditional. Try the cream of spinach soup and the boiled beef. ✉ *Dürnbräug. 2,* ☎ *089/222–195. AE, DC, MC, V.*

$$ ✕ **Grüne Gans.** This small, chummy restaurant near the Viktualienmarkt is popular with local entertainers, whose photographs clutter the walls. International fare with regional German influences dominates the menu. Try the chervil cream soup, followed by calves' kidneys in tarragon sauce. ✉ *Am Einlass 5,* ☎ *089/266–228. Reservations essential. No credit cards. Closed lunch and Sun.*

$$ ✕ **Weinhaus Neuner.** Originally a seminary, this early 18th-century building houses Munich's oldest surviving wine hostelry, in the Neuner family since 1852. The high-ceiling dining rooms are lined with dark oak paneling. Look for the herb-filled pork fillets with noodles, and veal with Morchela mushroom sauce. ✉ *Herzogspitalstr. 8,* ☎ *089/260–3954. Reservations essential. AE, DC, MC. Closed Sun. and holidays.*

$ ★ ✕ **Altes Hackerhaus.** This upscale beer restaurant on one of Munich's ritziest shopping streets is full of bric-a-brac and mementos that hark back to its origins as a medieval brewery. Since 1570, beer has been brewed or served here at the birthplace of one of the city's largest breweries—Hacker-Pschorr. Duck into one of the cozy little rooms and choose from the selection of hearty soups, then try a plate of *Käsespätzle* (egg noodles with melted cheese). ✉ *Sendlingerstr. 14,* ☎ *089/260–5026. AE, DC, MC, V.*

$ ✕ **Brauhaus zur Brez'n.** This hostelry bedecked in the blue and white of the Bavarian flag spreads over three floors. Everyone from local business lunchers to hungry night owls chooses from a big all-day menu of traditional roasts, to be washed down with a choice of three draft beers. ✉ *Leopoldstr. 72,* ☎ *089/390–092. No credit cards.*

$ ✕ **Franziskaner.** Vaulted archways, cavernous rooms interspersed with intimate dining areas, bold blue frescoes on the walls, and long wooden tables create a spic-and-span medieval atmosphere. Besides the late-morning *Weisswurst* (a delicate white sausage), look for *Ochsenfleisch* (boiled ox meat) and dumplings. ✉ *Perusastr. 5,* ☎ *089/231–8120. Reservations not accepted. AE, DC, MC, V.*

$ ✕ **Hofbräuhaus.** The cavernous, smoky, stone vaults of the Hofbräuhaus contain crowds of singing, shouting, swaying beer drinkers. If you're not here solely to drink, try the Bavarian food in the more subdued upstairs restaurant, where the service is not so brusque. It's between Marienpl. and Maximilianstrasse. ✉ *Platzl 9,* ☎ *089/221–676. Reservations not accepted. MC, V.*

$ ✕ **Hundskugel.** History practically oozes from the crooked walls at this tavern, Munich's oldest, which dates from 1440. Order *Spanferkel*—roast suckling pig—if it's on the menu; this is simple Bavarian fare at its best. ✉ *Hotterstr. 18,* ☎ *089/264–272. No credit cards. Closed Sun.*

$ ★ ✕ **Pfälzer Weinprobierstube.** A warren of stone-vault rooms of various sizes, wooden tables, glittering candles, dirndl-clad waitresses, and a vast range of wines provide a backdrop for food that's reliable rather than spectacular. Local specialties predominate. ✉ *Residenzstr. 1,* ☎ *089/225–628. Reservations not accepted. No credit cards.*

$$$$ 🏨 **Bayerischer Hof.** This is one of Munich's most traditional luxury hotels. Public rooms are decorated with antiques, fine paintings, marble, and painted wood. Old-fashioned comfort and class abound in the older rooms; some of the newer rooms are less ornate but functional. ✉ *Promenadepl. 2–6, D-80333,* ☎ *089/21200,* FAX *089/212–0906. 383 rooms, 45 apartments. 3 restaurants, pool. AE, DC, MC, V.*

$$$$ ★ 🏨 **Kempinski Hotel Vier Jahreszeiten.** Close to the heart of the city, the Vier Jahreszeiten—Four Seasons—has been playing host to the world's wealthy and titled for more than a century. Elegance and luxury set the tone; many rooms have handsome antique pieces. ✉ *Maximilianstr. 17, D-80539,* ☎ *089/21250, 516/794–2670 reservations in the U.S.,* FAX *089/2125–2000. 268 rooms, 30 suites, 1 presidential suite, 17 apartments. 2 restaurants, pool. AE, DC, MC, V.*

$$$$ ★ 🏨 **Rafael.** A character-laden lodging in the heart of the Old Town (close to the Hofbräuhaus), the Rafael, which opened in 1989, retains many of the architectural features of its building's late-19th-century origins, including a sweeping staircase and stucco ceilings. In 1995, Britain's Prince Charles stayed here. Rooms are individually furnished and extravagantly decorated. The hotel restaurant, Mark's, has made a name for itself with its new German cuisine. ✉ *Neuturmstr. 1, D-80331,* ☎ *089/290–980,* FAX *089/222–539. 54 rooms, 19 suites. Restaurant, pool. AE, DC, MC, V.*

$$$–$$$$ 🏨 **Eden Hotel Wolff.** Chandeliers and dark-wood paneling in the public rooms underline the old-fashioned elegance of this downtown favorite. Across from the train station and the airport bus terminal. The rooms are comfortable, and most are spacious. Dine on excellent Bavarian specialties in the intimate Zirbelstube restaurant. ✉ *Arnulfstr. 4, D-80335,* ☎ *089/551–150,* FAX *089/5511–5555. 209 rooms, 2 suites. Restaurant. AE, DC, MC, V.*

$$$–$$$$ 🏨 **Torbräu.** In the shadow of one of Munich's ancient city gates, this snug hotel offers comfortable rooms decorated in plush and ornate Italian style. There's an Italian restaurant and a coffee shop that bakes its own cakes. ✉ *Tal 41, D-80331,* ☎ *089/225–016,* FAX *089/225–019. 83 rooms, 3 suites. Restaurant. AE, MC, V.*

$$$ 🏨 **Adria.** This modern, comfortable hotel is in the middle of Munich's museum quarter. Rooms are large and tastefully decorated, with old prints on the pale pink walls, Oriental rugs on the floors, and flowers beside the large double beds. A spectacular breakfast buffet (including a glass of sparking wine) is included in the room rate. ✉ *Liebigstr. 8a, D-80538,* ☎ *089/293–081,* FAX *089/227–015. 46 rooms. AE, MC, V.*

$$$ ★ 🏨 **Pannonia Hotel Königin Elisabeth.** Northwest of the city center, in a 19th-century neoclassical building, the Elisabeth was completely restored and opened for the first time as a hotel in 1989. It is modern and bright, with an emphasis on the color pink. The restaurant offers Hungarian specialties. ✉ *Leonrodstr. 79, D-80636,* ☎ *089/126–860,* FAX *089/1268–6459. 79 rooms. Restaurant. AE, DC, MC, V.*

$$ 🏨 **Hotel Europa.** Fodor's readers get a special deal at this large but friendly hotel near the main railroad station. The hotel is on a busy shopping street so try for a room overlooking the small back garden and terrace, where you can also take breakfast in fine weather. All rooms are furnished in modern, brightly colored fabrics and light woods and veneers. ✉ *Dachauerstr. 115, D–80335,* ☎ *089/542–420,* FAX *089/542–42500. 180 rooms. Restaurant. AE, MC, V.*

$ 🏨 **Hotel-Pension am Siegestor.** An ancient, wood-paneled elevator conveys you in style to the fourth-floor reception area of this charming little hotel between Schwabing's main boulevard and the university quarter. Rooms on the fifth floor, tucked up under the eaves, are particularly cozy. None has private bath, but each floor has its own bathroom. ✉ *Akademiestr. 5, D–80799,* ☎ *089/399–550 or 089/399–551,* FAX *089/343–050. 20 rooms with shared bath. No credit cards.*

$ **Hotel-Pension Beck.** American and British guests receive a particularly warm welcome from the Anglophile owner of the rambling, friendly Beck. Rooms are furnished in pinewood. The pension is near museums and the Englischer Garten. ✉ *Thierschstr. 36, D-80538,* ☎ *089/220–708 or 089/225–768,* FAX *089/220–925. 44 rooms, 5 with shower. No credit cards.*

Nightlife and the Arts

The Arts

Details of concerts and theater performances are available from the "Vorschau" or "Monatsprogramm" booklets obtainable at most hotel reception desks. Some hotels will make ticket reservations; otherwise book tickets at the two kiosks on the concourse below Marienplatz, or use one of the ticket agencies in the city center: **Max Hieber Konzertkasse** (✉ Liebfrauenstr. 1, ☎ 089/290–08014) or the **Residenz Bücherstube** (✉ Residenzstr. 1, ☎ 089/220–868 concert tickets only).

CONCERTS

Munich's Philharmonic Orchestra performs in Germany's biggest concert hall, the **Gasteig Cultural Center** (✉ Rosenheimerstr. 5, ☎ 089/5481–8181). Tickets can be purchased at the box office. The Bavarian Radio Orchestra also performs Sunday concerts here. In summer, concerts are held at Schloss Nymphenburg and in the open-air interior courtyard of the Residenz (☞ Exploring Munich, *above*).

DANCE

The ballet company of the Bavarian State Opera performs at the **Nationaltheater** (✉ Maximilianstr. 11, ☎ 089/2185–1920). Ballet productions are also staged at the attractive late-19th-century **Staatstheater am Gärtnerplatz** (✉ Gärtnerpl. 3, ☎ 089/201–6767).

OPERA

Munich's Bavarian State Opera company is world famous, and tickets for major productions in its permanent home, the **Nationaltheater** (✉ Maximilianstr. 11, ☎ 089/2185–1920), are difficult to obtain; the box office takes reservations one week in advance only. Book far in advance through the tourist office (☞ Visitor Information, *below*) for the annual opera festival held in July and August.

THEATER

The Bavarian state-supported Residenz Theater (Royal Theater), concentrates on the classics. The Kammerspiele is financed mostly by the city government. More than 20 other theater companies (some of them performing in basements) are to be found throughout the city. Regular English-language productions, featuring the American Drama Group Europe, are staged at the **Theater an der Leopoldstrasse** (✉ Leopoldstr. 17, ☎ 089/380–14032) or in the auditorium of **America House** (Amerikahaus; ✉ Karolinenpl. 3, ☎ 089/552–5370). The English-language productions are also staged from time to time at the **Theater im Karlshof** (✉ Karlstr. 43, ☎ 089/596–611).

Nightlife

BARS, CABARET, NIGHTCLUBS

Schumann's (✉ Maximilianstr. 36, ☎ 089/229–268) has a shabby New York bar look, but the clientele is Munich chic. **Käfers am Odeonsplatz** (✉ Odeonspl. 3, ☎ 089/290–7530) attracts a similarly smart and contact-happy crowd. Munich's media types have turned the **Alter Simpl** (✉ Turkenstr. 57, ☎ 089/272–3083) into an unofficial press club.

O'Reilly's Irish Cellar Pub (✉ Maximilianstr. 29, ☎ 089/292–311) serves genuine Irish Guinness. Great Caribbean cocktails and a powerful Irish-German Black and Tan (Guinness and strong German beer) are served at the English nautical-style **Pusser's** bar (✉ Falkenturmstr. 9, ☎ 089/220–500). The **Havana** (✉ Herrnstr. 3, ☎ 089/291–884) does its best to look like a run-down Cuban dive, drawing a chic clientele. At the **Wunderbar** (✉ Hochbrückenstr. 3, ☎ 089/295–118) on Tuesday nights telephones are installed on the tables and at the bar, and the place hums like a stygian switchboard.

DISCOS

Munich has a spectacular new disco center: the **Kunstpark Ost** (✉ Grafingerstr. 6, ☎ 089/490–72113), a former pasta factory with 13 "entertainment areas," including several discos and music bars. Discos abound in the side streets off **Freilitzschstrasse,** surrounding Münchener Freiheit in Schwabing. Tops of the lot (quite literally) is the **Skyline** (✉ Münchner Freiheit, ☎ 089/333–131), at the top of the Hertie department store building Münchner Freiheit. The **Nachtcafe** (✉ Maximilianspl. 5, ☎ 089/595–900), is open all night on weekends. At **Maximilian's** (✉ Maximilianspl. 16, ☎ 089/223–252), the chic crowd packs a throbbing cellar into the early hours. **P1** (✉ Haus der Kunst, Prinzregentenstr. 1, ☎ 089/294–252) is the queen of them all, a place to see and be seen, with a series of tiny dance floors and a great sound system.

JAZZ CLUBS

The **Unterfahrt** (✉ Kirchenstr. 96, ☎ 089/448–279), in Munich's latest "quartier Latin," Haidhausen, has traditional and mainstream jazz. Munich's longest-established jazz haunt, the **Podium** (✉ Wagnerstr. 1, ☎ 089/399–482), has taken to offering rock music as well as traditional jazz; it's packed nightly.

Shopping

Antiques

Blumenstrasse, Ottostrasse, Türkenstrasse, and Westenriederstrasse all have antiques shops. The open-air **Auer Dult fairs** sell antiques; they're held on Mariahilfplatz at the end of April, July, and October (Streetcar 25).

Department Stores

Most of the city's major department stores are along Maffeistrasse, Kaufingerstrasse, and Neuhauserstrasse. **Hertie** (✉ Bahnhofpl. 7, ☎ 089/55120) is the largest and, some claim, the best department store in the city; it has a stylish delicatessen with champagne bar and bistro. **Kaufhof** has two central Munich stores (✉ Karlspl. 2, opposite Hertie, ☎ 089/51250; ✉ corner of Marienpl., ☎ 089/231–851); both offer a wide range of goods in the middle price range. **Karstadt** (✉ Neuhauserstr. 18, ☎ 089/290–230) is a high-class department store, with a very wide range of Bavarian arts and crafts.

Gift Ideas

Munich is a city of beer, and beer mugs and coasters make an obvious gift to take home. Many shops specialize in beer-related souvenirs, but **Ludwig Mory** (✉ Marienpl. 8, ☎ 089/224–542) is about the best. Munich is also the home of the famous **Porzellan Manufaktur Nymphenburg** (Nymphenburg Porcelain Factory; ✉ corner of Odeonspl. and Briennerstr., ☎ 089/282–428; ✉ Nördliche Schlossrondell 8, in front of Schloss Nymphenburg, ☎ 089/1791–9710).

Shopping Districts

Munich has an immense **central shopping area,** 2 km (1 mi) of pedestrian streets stretching from the train station to Marienplatz and north to Odeonsplatz. The two main streets here are Neuhauserstrasse and Kaufingerstrasse. For **upscale shopping** Maximilianstrasse, Residenzstrasse, and Theatinerstrasse are unbeatable and contain a fine array of classy and tempting stores. **Schwabing,** north of the university, has several of the city's most intriguing and offbeat shopping streets—Schellingstrasse and Hohenzollernstrasse are two to try.

Munich Essentials

Arriving and Departing

BY BUS

Munich has no central bus station. Long-distance buses arrive at and depart from the north side of the train station on Arnulfstrasse.

BY CAR

From the north (Nürnberg, Frankfurt), leave the autobahn at the Schwabing exit and follow the STADTMITTE signs. The autobahn from Stuttgart and the west ends at Obermenzing; again, follow the STADTMITTE signs. The autobahns from Salzburg and the east, from Garmisch and the south, and from Lindau and the southwest all join up with the city beltway, the Mittlerer Ring. The city center is well posted.

BY PLANE

Munich's **Franz Josef Strauss (FJS) Airport,** named for a former state premier, is 28 km (17 mi) northeast of the city center.

Between the Airport and Downtown. The S-8 and S-1 **S-bahn** (suburban train lines) link FJS Airport with the city's main train station (Hauptbahnhof). Trains depart in both directions every 10 minutes from 3:55 AM to 12:55 AM daily. Intermediate stops are made at the Ostbahnhof (good for hotels located east of the River Isar) and city-center stations such as Marienplatz. The 38-minute trip costs DM 10.80 if you purchase a multi-use strip ticket (☞ Getting Around, *below*) and use 8 strips; otherwise an ordinary one-way ticket is DM 12.80 per person. A tip for families: Up to five people (maximum of two adults) can travel to or from the airport for only DM 24 after 9 AM by buying a Tageskarte (☞ Getting Around, *below*).

Bus service is slower and more expensive (DM 15) than the S-bahn; only use it if you're carrying a great deal of luggage. A **taxi** will cost between DM 80 and DM 100. If you are **driving** from the airport into the city, follow the MÜNCHEN autobahn signs to A92 and A9. Once on the A92, watch carefully for the signs to Munich; a relatively high number of motorists miss the sign and end up headed toward Stuttgart.

BY TRAIN

All long-distance services arrive at and depart from the main train station, the Hauptbahnhof. Trains to and from destinations in the Bavarian Alps usually use the adjoining Starnbergerbahnhof. For information on train times call 089/19419. For tickets and information go to the station or to the ABR travel agency on Bahnhofplatz.

Getting Around

BY PUBLIC TRANSPORTATION

Downtown Munich is only about 1.6 km (1 mi) square, so it can easily be explored on foot. Other areas—Schwabing, Nymphenburg, the Olympiapark—are best reached on the efficient and comprehensive **public transportation network,** which incorporates buses, streetcars, U-bahn (subways), and S-bahn (suburban trains). Tickets are good for the entire network, and you can break your trip as many times as you like using just one ticket, provided you travel in one direction within a given period of time. If you plan to make only a few trips, buy *Streifenkarten* (strip tickets)—blue for adults, red for children. At press time (spring 1998), an 11-strip ticket cost DM 15. All tickets must be validated by time, punching them in the automatic machines at station entrances and on all buses and streetcars.

The best buy is the *Tageskarte* (all-day ticket): Up to two adults and three children can use this ticket for unlimited journeys between 9 AM and the end of the day's service (about 2 AM). It costs DM 12 for the inner zone, which covers central Munich. A Tageskarte for the entire system, extending to the Starnbergersee and Ammersee, costs DM 24. Holders of a Eurail Pass, a Youth Pass, an InterRail Card, or a DB Tourist Card travel free on all S-bahn trains.

BY TAXI

Munich's cream-color taxis are numerous. Hail them in the street or call 089/21610 or 089/19410. Rates start at DM 5 and rise by DM 2.20 per km (about DM 4 per mi). There are additional charges of DM 2 if a taxi is ordered by telephone and DM 1 per piece of luggage. Plan to pay about DM 13 for a short trip within the city.

Contacts and Resources

CONSULATES

United States (✉ Königinstr. 5, ☎ 089/28880). **Canadian** (✉ Tal 29, ☎ 089/290–650). **United Kingdom** (✉ Bürkleinstr. 10, ☎ 089/211–090).

EMERGENCIES

Police (☎ 110). **Fire Department and Paramedical Aid** (☎ 112). **Ambulance and emergency medical attention** (☎ 089/19222). **Dentist** (☎ 089/723–3093). **Pharmacies: Internationale Ludwigs-Apotheke** (✉ Neuhauserstr. 11, ☎ 089/260–3021); **Europa-Apotheke** (✉ Schützenstr. 12, near the Hauptbahnhof, ☎ 089/595–423).

ENGLISH-LANGUAGE BOOKSTORES

The **Anglia English Bookshop** (✉ Schellingstr. 3, ☎ 089/283–642). **Hugendubel** (✉ Marienpl. 22, ☎ 089/22890; ✉ Karlspl. 3, ☎ 089/552–2530).

GUIDED TOURS

Orientation. City bus tours are operated by **Panorama Tours** (✉ Arnulfstr. 8, ☎ 089/591–504). Tours run daily and take in the city center, the Olympiapark, and Schloss Nymphenburg. Departures are at 10 AM and 2:30 PM (and 11:30 AM in midsummer) from outside the Hertie department store across from the Hauptbahnhof, the main train station. The cost ranges from DM 15 to DM 27 per person.

Walking and Cycling. Münchner Stadtrundgänge has a Central Munich walking tour that starts daily at 9:30 at the Mariensäule column in the center of the Marienplatz; cost: DM 10. **Radius Touristik** (✉ Arnulfstr. 3, opposite platforms 30–36 in the Hauptbahnhof main concourse, ☎ 089/596–113) has bicycle tours from May through the beginning of October at 10:15 and 2; cost, including bike rental: DM 15. **City Hopper Touren** (☎ 089/272–1131) tours of the city, including bike rentals, cost DM 40 per person in a group of two to DM 20 for larger groups. **Mike's Bike Tours** (☎ 089/651–4275) organizes tours of the city by English-speaking guides daily March through November, starting from the Altes Rathaus at 11:30 and 4. The DM 28 cost includes bike rental and, in fine weather, a beer-garden stop.

Excursions. Panorama Tours (✉ Arnulfstr. 8, ☎ 089/591–504) organizes bus trips to most leading tourist attractions outside the city, including the "Royal Castles Tour" (Schlösserfahrt) of "Mad" King Ludwig's dream palaces; cost: DM 75.

TRAVEL AGENCIES

American Express (✉ Promenadepl. 6, ☎ 089/290–900). **ABR** (☎ 089/12040), the official Bavarian travel, has outlets all over Munich.

VISITOR INFORMATION

Rathaus (✉ City Hall on Marienpl., ☎ 089/233–30273). **Hauptbahnhof** (Main Train Station, ✉ Bahnhofpl. 2, next to ABR travel agency, ☎ 089/233–30256). **Franz Josef Strauss Airport** (☎ 089/9759–2815).

FRANKFURT

At first glance Frankfurt-am-Main doesn't seem to offer much to the tourist. Virtually flattened by bombs during the war, it now bristles with skyscrapers, the visible signs of the city's role as Germany's financial capital. Originally a Roman settlement, Frankfurt later served as one of Charlemagne's two capitals (the other being Aachen). Still later, the electors of the Holy Roman Empire met here to choose and crown the emperor. It was also the birthplace of the poet and dramatist Johann Wolfgang von Goethe (1749–1832).

Exploring Frankfurt

Numbers in the margin correspond to points of interest on the Frankfurt map.

The neighborhood around the Hauptbahnhof (main train station), site of many of the major hotels, is mostly devoted to business and banking. If you want a sense of the past, or to let the good times roll, head to the Old Town with its restored medieval quarter and to Sachsenhausen across the river, where the pubs and museums greatly outnumber the banks.

13 **Alte Oper** (Old Opera House). Built between 1873 and 1880 and destroyed during World War II, Frankfurt's Old Opera House has been beautifully reconstructed in the style of the original. Kaiser Wilhelm II traveled from Berlin for the gala opening in 1880. ✉ *Opernpl.,* ☎ *069/134–0405.*

14 **Börse** (Stock Exchange). The Börse was founded by Frankfurt merchants in 1558 to establish some order in their often chaotic dealings, but the present building dates from the 1870s. This center for Germany's stock and money market also has a visitors gallery. ✉ *Börsepl.,* ☎ *069/21010.* *Free.* *Weekdays 10:30–1:30.*

12 **Fressgasse** (Pig-Out Alley). The proper name of one of the city's liveliest thoroughfares is Grosse Bockenheimer Strasse, but Frankfurters have given it this sobriquet because of the amazing choice of delicatessens, wine merchants, cafés, and restaurants to be found here. ✉ *East of Opernpl.*

★ 11 **Goethehaus und Goethemuseum** (Goethe's House and Museum). The birthplace of Germany's most famous poet is furnished with many original pieces that belonged to his family. Although the original house was destroyed by Allied bombing, it has been carefully rebuilt and restored in every detail as the young Goethe would have known it. The adjoining museum contains works of art that inspired Goethe (he was an amateur painter) and works associated with his literary contemporaries. ✉ *Grosser Hirschgraben 23–25,* ☎ *069/138–800.* *DM 7.* *Apr.–Sept., Mon.–Sat. 9–5:30, Sun. 10–1; Oct.–Mar., Mon.–Sat. 9–4, Sun. 10–1.*

1 **Hauptwache.** This square serves as the hub of the city's transportation network. It is named Hauptwache (main guard), an attractive Baroque

building with a steeply sloping roof that was constructed on the square as a municipal guardhouse in 1729. Today it houses a café and a tourist information office. ⊠ *At junction of Zeil and Grosse Eschenheimer Str.*

19 **Jüdisches Museum** (Jewish Museum). Housed in the former Rothschild Palace, this museum tells the story of Frankfurt's Jewish quarter. Prior to the Holocaust it was the second largest Jewish neighborhood in Germany. ⊠ *Untermainkai 14–15,* ☎ *069/2123–5000.* ⊙ *Tues.–Sun. 10–5, Wed. 10–8.*

10 **Karmeliterkloster** (Carmelite Church and Monastery). Secularized in 1803, the church and buildings were renovated in the 1980s and now contain the **Museum für Vor- und Frügeschichte** (Museum of Prehistory and Early History). The main cloister has a **gallery** that houses rotating modern art exhibitions and the largest religious fresco north of the Alps, a 16th-century representation of Christ's birth and death. *Museum für Vor- und Frühgeschichte:* ⊠ *Karmeliterg. 1,* ☎ *069/2123–5896.* ⊙ *Tues. and Thurs.–Sun. 10–5, Wed. 10–8.* Gallery: ⊠ *Münzg. 9.* ⊙ *Tues.–Sun. 11–6.*

3 **Katharinenkirche** (St. Catherine's Church). Originally built between 1678 and 1681, it was the first independent Protestant church in the Gothic style. The first Protestant sermon in Frankfurt was given here. ⊠ *Corner of An der Hauptwache and Katherinenpfad.* ⊙ *Daily 10–5.*

16 **Kuhhirtenturm** (Shepherd's Tower). Built during the 15th century, this is the last of nine towers that formed part of the fortifications for **Sachsenhausen** (☞ *below*). The composer Paul Hindemith lived in the tower from 1923 to 1927 while working at the Frankfurt Opera. ⊠ *Grosse Ritter G. at Sachsenhaüser Ufer.*

9 **Leonhardskirche** (St. Leonard's Church). This beautifully preserved 13th-century building with five naves has some fine old stained glass. The hanging, ornately carved piece of the ceiling vault was already a major Frankfurt tourist attraction during the 17th century. ⊠ *Corner of Leonhardstr. and Untermainkai.* ⊙ *Wed., Fri., and Sat. 10–noon and 3–6; Tues. and Thurs. 10–noon and 3–6:30; Sun. 9–1 and 3–6.*

15 **Museum für Moderne Kunst** (Museum of Modern Art). In a distinctive triangular building designed by Austrian architect Hans Hollein, the collection has American Pop art and works by such German artists as Gerhard Richter and Joseph Beuys. ⊠ *Domstr. 10,* ☎ *069/2123–0447.* *DM 7.* ⊙ *Tues. and Thurs.–Sun. 10–5, Wed. 10–8.*

8 **Nikolaikirche** (St. Nicholas's Church). This small red sandstone church dates from the late 13th century. The wonderful chimes of the glockenspiel carillon ring out three times a day. ⊠ *South side of Römerberg.* ⊙ *Mon.–Sat. 10–5. Carillon chimes daily at 9, noon, and 5.*

4 **Paulskirche** (St. Paul's Church). The first all-German parliament meeting, in 1848, took place at this church. The parliament lasted a year, having done little more than offer the Prussian king the crown of Germany. Today the church is used mainly for formal ceremonial events. ⊠ *Paulspl.* ⊙ *Daily 11–3.*

6 **Römer** (City Hall). Its gabled Gothic facade with an ornate balcony is widely known as the city's official emblem. The mercantile-minded Frankfurt burghers used the complex of three patrician buildings not only for political and ceremonial purposes but also for trade fairs and other commercial ventures. Banquets to celebrate the coronations of the Holy Roman emperors were mounted starting in 1562 in the **Kaisersaal** (Imperial Hall). Impressive, full-length, 19th-century portraits of

Frankfurt

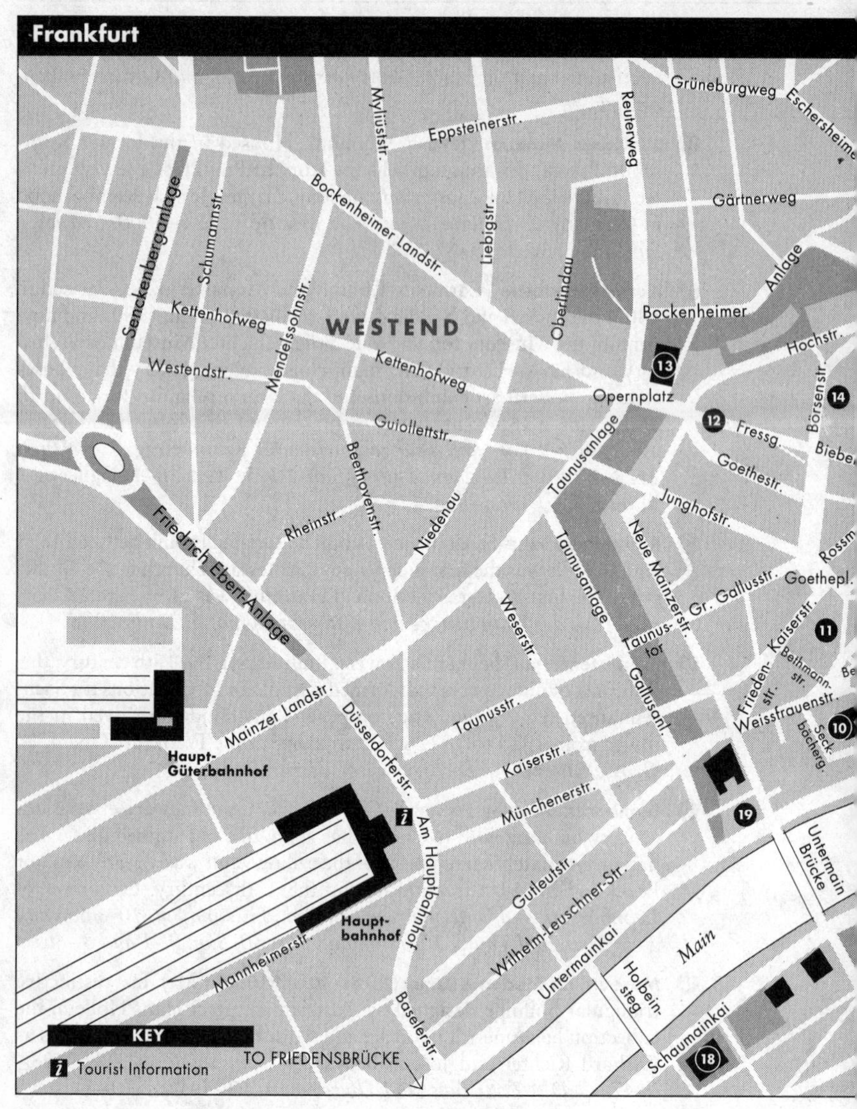

Alte Oper, **13**
Börse, **14**
Fressgasse, **12**
Goethehaus und Goethemuseum, **11**
Hauptwache, **1**
Jüdisches Museum, **19**
Karmeliterkloster, **10**
Katharinenkirche, **3**
Kuhhirtenturm, **16**
Leonhardskirche, **9**
Museum für Moderne Kunst, **15**
Nikolaikirche, **8**
Paulskirche, **4**
Römer, **6**
Römerberg Square, **5**
Sachsenhausen, **17**
St. Bartholomäus, **7**
Städelsches Kunstinstitut und Städtische Galerie, **18**
Zeil, **2**

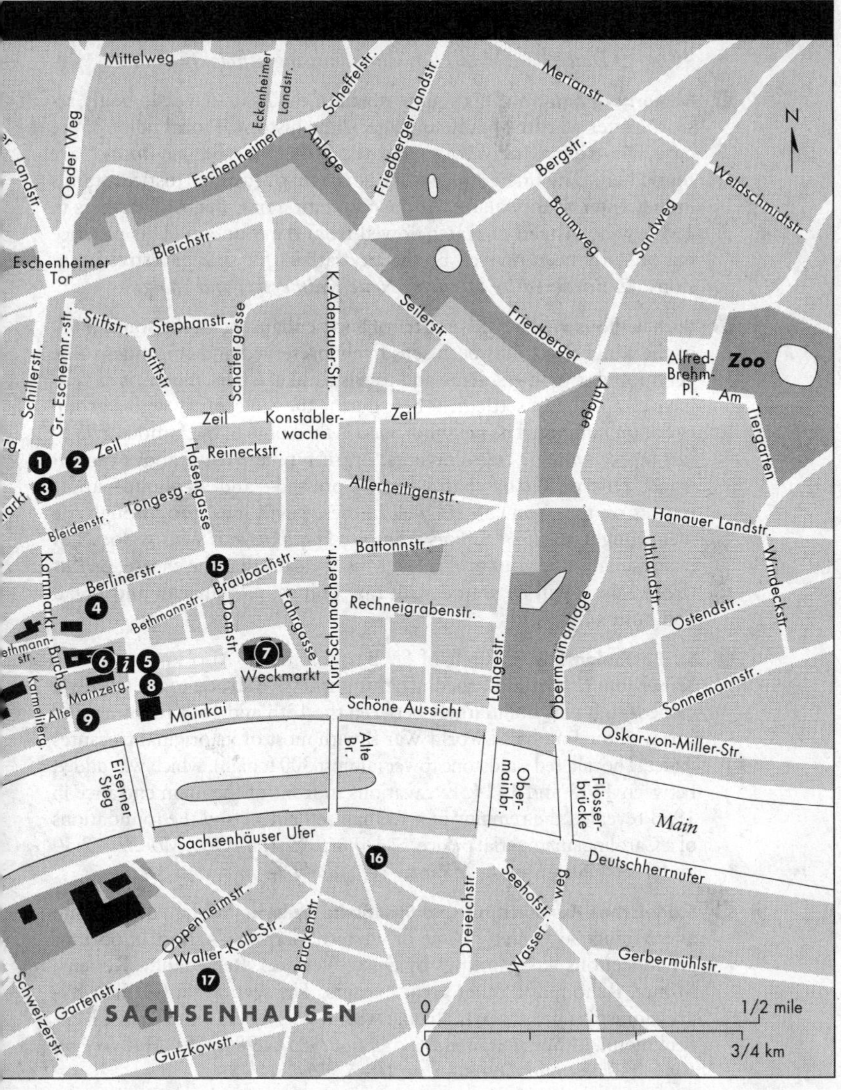
Mittelweg
Eckenheimer Landstr.
Scheffelstr.
Merianstr.
Oeder Weg
Eschenheimer Anlage
Friedberger Landstr.
Bergstr.
Weldschmidtstr.
Baumweg
Sandweg
Eschenheimer Tor
Bleichstr.
K.-Adenauer-Str.
Seilerstr.
Friedberger Anlage
Stiftstr.
Stephanstr.
Schäfergasse
Alfred-Brehm-Pl.
Zoo
Am Tiergarten
Schillerstr.
Gr. Eschenmr.-str.
Zeil
Konstablerwache
Reineckstr.
Allerheiligenstr.
Hanauer Landstr.
Töngesg.
Hasengasse
Bleidenstr.
Battonnstr.
Uhlandstr.
Windeckstr.
Kornmarkt
Berlinerstr.
Braubachstr.
Fahrgasse
Kurt-Schumacherstr.
Recheneigrabenstr.
Obermainanlage
Ostendstr.
Bethmannstr.
Domstr.
Langestr.
Weckmarkt
Buchg.
Mainzerg.
Karmeliterg.
Alte
Mainkai
Schöne Aussicht
Sonnemannstr.
Oskar-von-Miller-Str.
Eiserner Steg
Alte Br.
Obermainbr.
Flösserbrücke
Main
Sachsenhäuser Ufer
Deutschherrnufer
Oppenheimstr.
Walter-Kolb-Str.
Brückenstr.
Dreieichstr.
Seehofstr.
Wasserweg
Gerbermühlstr.
Gartenstr.
Schweizerstr.
SACHSENHAUSEN
Gutzkowstr.
0
1/2 mile
0
3/4 km
1
2
3
4
5
6
7
8
9
15
16
17

the 52 emperors of the Holy Roman Empire line the walls of the reconstructed banquet hall. ✉ *West side of Römerberg,* ☎ *069/2123–4814.* ⌚ *Daily 10–1 and 2–5. Closed during official functions.*

5 **Römerberg Square.** This square north of the Main River, lovingly restored after wartime bomb damage, is the historical focal point of the city. The **Römer** (☞ *above*) and the **Nikolaikirche** (☞ *above*) are found here. The fine 16th-century Fountain of Justitia (Justice) stands in the center of the square. At the coronation of Emperor Matthias in 1612, wine instead of water flowed from the fountain. This practice has recently been revived by the city fathers for special festive occasions. ✉ *Bordered by Domstr., Neue Krämerstr., and Saalg..*

★ 17 **Sachsenhausen.** The old quarter of Sachsenhausen, on the south bank of the Main River, has been sensitively preserved and continues to be very popular with residents and tourists alike. Charlemagne is said to have established a settlement here during the 8th century with a group of Saxon families. The neighborhood is the home of the famous *Ebbelwei* (apple wine or cider) taverns. A green pine wreath above the entrance tells passersby that a freshly pressed—and alcoholic—apple juice is on tap. You can eat well in these small inns, too, though the menu might seem odd. For example, *Handkas mit Musik* does not promise music at your table. The Musik means that the cheese, or *Kas* (from Käse), will be served with raw onions, oil, vinegar, and bread and butter.

7 **St. Bartholomäus** (Church of St. Bartholomew). Also known as the Kaiserdom (Imperial Cathedral), this impressive structure isn't really a cathedral. It was built largely between the 13th and 15th centuries and survived the bombs of World War II with most of its original treasures intact. The tall, red sandstone tower (almost 300 ft high), which was added between 1415 and 1514. Excavations in front of the main entrance in 1953 revealed the remains of a Roman settlement and the foundations of a Carolingian imperial palace. ✉ *Domstr.* ⌚ *Apr.–Oct., Mon. 9–12:30 and 3–6, Tues.–Sun. 8–6; Nov.–Feb., daily 9–noon and 3–5.*

★ 18 **Städelsches Kunstinstitut und Städtische Galerie** (Städel Art Institute and Municipal Gallery). One of western Germany's most important art collections has paintings by Dürer, Vermeer, Rembrandt, Rubens, Monet, Renoir, and other great masters. The section on German Expressionism is particularly strong, with works by Frankfurt artist Max Beckmann. ✉ *Schaumainkai 63,* ☎ *069/605–0980.* 🎫 *DM 8, free on Wed.* ⌚ *Tues. and Thurs.–Sun. 10–5, Wed. 10–8.*

2 **Zeil.** The heart of Frankfurt's shopping district is this ritzy pedestrian thoroughfare, which city officials claim is the country's busiest shopping street; it has an unrivaled annual turnover of more than a billion marks. ✉ *East of Hauptwache.*

Dining and Lodging

Several Frankfurt restaurants close for the school summer vacation break between mid-June and mid-September. Check to avoid disappointment. For details and price-category definitions, *see* Dining *in* Germany A to Z, *above.*

Businesspeople descend on Frankfurt year-round, so most hotels in the city are expensive (many offer significant reductions on weekends) and are frequently booked up well in advance. The majority of the larger hotels are around the main train station, a 15- to 20-minute walk from the Old Town. For details and price-category definitions, *see* Lodging *in* Germany A to Z, *above.*

$$$ ★ ✕ **Brückenkeller.** Magnificent German specialties are served in an antique arched cellar. The food is unmistakably Teutonic yet light and delicate, with such dishes as cream of cucumber soup, or veal in tomato vinaigrette. The caves hold around 85,000 bottles; don't be shy about asking to see them. ✉ *Schützenstr. 6,* ☎ *069/298–0070. Jacket and tie. AE, DC, MC, V. Closed Sun.*

$$$ ✕ **Erno's Bistro.** Small, chic, and popular with visiting power brokers, Erno's has become something of a Frankfurt institution. The menu has classy nouvelle specialties, with fish—flown in daily, often from France—predominating. The waiters speak English. ✉ *Liebigstr. 15,* ☎ *069/721–997. Reservations essential. AE, DC, MC, V. Closed weekends and July–early Aug.*

$$$ ★ ✕ **Humperdinck.** Alfred Friedrich, one of Frankfurt's leading chefs, launched his own business in an elegant, neo-Baroque setting. He regales the lucky diners at his 15 tables with some of the most creative cooking in Frankfurt; rabbit salad with marinated mushrooms, and sea bass with fennel are typical entrées, followed by wild strawberries in cream. ✉ *Grüneburgweg 95 at the corner of Liebigstr.,* ☎ *069/9720–3154. Jacket and tie. AE, MC, V.*

$$ ✕ **Altes Zollhaus.** In this beautiful, 200-year-old half-timber house, you can sample very good versions of traditional German specialties. Try a game dish. In summer you can eat in the beautiful garden. ✉ *Friedberger Landstr. 531,* ☎ *069/472–707. AE, DC, MC, V. Closed Mon. No lunch.*

$$ ✕ **Charlot.** The French cuisine of this very popular restaurant acquired an Italian touch with the arrival of chef Mario. The Alte Oper is just across the street, so after the curtain falls you'll be fighting with the music buffs for a place in the French bistro–style dining rooms, spread over two floors. ✉ *Opernpl. 10,* ☎ *069/287–007. AE, DC, MC, V. No lunch Sun.*

$$ ✕ **Jaspers.** This is technically a French restaurant, but the many Alsatian specialties give it a German flair. Some better dishes include fish soup with croutons, and snails in Calvados sauce over spinach. The high level of service and cooking puts many better known and more expensive restaurants to shame. ✉ *Schifferstr. 8 (just off Affentorpl.), Sachsenhausen,* ☎ *069/614–117. AE, DC, V. Closed Sun.*

$ ✕ **Café GegenwART.** "Gegenwart" means "the present," and the emphasis on ART means there are always works of local artists exhibited in this friendly, bustling café. The cuisine is also artfully presented. Try the freshly caught angler fish or the tomato fondue when available. ✉ *Bergerstr. 6,* ☎ *069/497–0544. No credit cards.*

$ ✕ **Germania.** This noisy, smoky, apple-cider tavern, one of Sachsenhausen's most authentic, is filled with long wooden tables at which locals rub—and bend—elbows. Good traditional grub and great cider, but absolutely no beer! ✉ *16 Textorstr., Sachsenhausen,* ☎ *069/613–336. No credit cards. Closed Mon.*

$ ✕ **Melange.** This festive, largely vegetarian restaurant is typically packed with students and professors from the nearby university. ✉ *Jordanstr. 19,* ☎ *069/701–287. No credit cards.*

$ ★ ✕ **Wagner.** The kitchen produces the same hearty German dishes as other apple-wine taverns only better. Try the *Tafelspitz mit Frankfurter Grüner Sosse* (stewed beef with a sauce of green herbs) or come on Friday for fresh fish. Beer and wine are served as well as cider. This Sachsenhausen classic succeeds in being trendy, touristy, and traditional all at once. ✉ *Schweizer Str. 71, Sachsenhausen,* ☎ *069/612–565. Reservations not accepted. No credit cards.*

$$$$ ★ 🏨 **Gravenbruch Kempinski.** The atmosphere of the 16th-century manor house that this elegant, sophisticated hotel was built around still remains at this parkland sight in leafy Neu Isenburg (a 15-minute drive

south of Frankfurt). Some of its luxuriously appointed rooms and suites are arranged as duplex penthouse apartments. Make sure you get a room overlooking the lake. ✉ *D-63243 Neu Isenburg,* ☎ *06102/5050,* FAX *06102/505–445. 287 rooms. 2 restaurants, indoor and outdoor pools. AE, DC, MC, V.*

$$$$ **Hessischer Hof.** This former palace is still owned by a prince of Hesse, and fine antiques are deftly positioned in many guest rooms. One of the two bars, Jimmy's, numbers among Frankfurt's best, and the hotel restaurant, Sevres, is prized for its haute cuisine and refined ambiance. ✉ *Friedrich-Ebert-Anlage 40, D-60235,* ☎ *069/7540–2924,* FAX *069/754–0924. 117 rooms. Restaurant. AE, DC, MC, V.*

$$$$ ★ **Steigenberger Hotel Frankfurter Hof.** The Victorian Frankfurter Hof is one of the city's oldest hotels. The atmosphere throughout is one of old-fashioned, formal elegance, with burnished woods, fresh flowers, and thick-carpeted hush. Kaiser Wilhelm once slept here. ✉ *Am Kaiserpl., D-60311,* ☎ *069/21502,* FAX *069/215–900. 347 rooms, 10 suites. 4 restaurants. AE, DC, MC, V.*

$$$ **Hotel Robert Mayer.** In a turn-of-the-century villa, each room has been decorated by a different Frankfurt artist, with furniture designs by the likes of Rietveld and Frank Lloyd Wright. The room designed by Therese Traube contrasts abstract newspaper collage with a replica Louis 14th armchair. Breakfast is included in the price of the room. ✉ *Robert-Mayer-Str. 44, D–60486,* ☎ *069/970910. 11 rooms, 1 suite. AE, DC, MC, V.*

$$ **Maingau.** You'll find this pleasant hotel-restaurant in the middle of the lively Sachsenhausen quarter and its cheery apple-wine taverns. Rooms are modest but spotless, comfortable, and equipped with TVs; the room rate includes a substantial breakfast buffet. Chef Stephan Döpfner has made the restaurant, Maingau-Stube, one of Frankfurt's best. ✉ *Schifferstr. 38–40, D-60594,* ☎ *069/617–001,* FAX *069/620–790. 100 rooms. Restaurant. AE, MC.*

$$ **Westend.** French antiques are at every turn in this small, elegant, family-run establishment. It's also very popular with media types. ✉ *Westendstr. 15, Frankfurt am Main, D–60325,* ☎ *069/ 746–702,* FAX *069/745–396. 15 rooms. AE, MC, V.*

$ **Hotel-Schiff *Peter Schlott*.** The hotel ship is moored on the Main River in the suburb of Höchst, a 15-minute train or tram ride from the city center. Guest cabins are on the small side, but the river views more than compensate. ✉ *Mainberg, D-65929,* ☎ *069/315–480,* FAX *069/307–671. 19 rooms, 10 with shower. Restaurant. AE, MC.*

$ **Waldhotel Hensels Felsenkeller.** Helmut Braun's hotel backs onto the woods that ring Frankfurt, and the city center is just a 15-minute train ride away (the nearest stop is a three-minute walk). Rooms are basic; the less expensive ones have shared showers. ✉ *Buchrainstr. 95, D–60599, Frankfurt am Main,* ☎ *069/652–086,* FAX *069/658–379. 15 rooms, 7 with bath. Restaurant. MC.*

Frankfurt Essentials

Arriving and Departing

BY BUS

Long-distance buses connect Frankfurt with more than 200 other European cities. Buses leave from the south side of the Hauptbahnhof. Tickets and information are available from **Deutsche Touring GmbH** (✉ Am Römerhof 17, ☎ 069/79030).

BY CAR

Frankfurt is the junction of many major **autobahns,** of which the most important are the A-3, running south from Köln and then on to

Würzburg, Nürnberg, and Munich; and the A-5, running south from Giessen and then on to Mannheim, Heidelberg, Karlsruhe, and the Swiss-German border at Basel. A complex series of beltways surrounds the city. If you're driving to Frankfurt on the A-5 from either north or south, exit at Nordwestkreuz and follow A-66 to the Nordend district, just north of downtown. Driving south on A-3, exit onto A-66 and follow the signs to Frankfurt-Höchst and then the Nordend district. Driving north on A-3, exit at Offenbach onto A-661 and follow the signs for FRANKFURT-STADTMITTE (City Center).

BY PLANE

Frankfurt Airport, the busiest and biggest airport in mainland Europe, is about 10 km (6 mi) southwest of the city.

Between the Airport and Downtown. Getting into Frankfurt from the airport is easy. The S-8 (S-bahn) runs from the airport to downtown, stopping at the Hauptbahnhof (main train station) and then at the centrally located Hauptwache square. Trains run every 15 minutes and the ride takes about as long; the one-way fare is DM 5.80. InterCity and InterCity Express (ICE) trains to and from most major western German cities also stop at the airport. Taxis from the airport downtown take about 20 minutes (double that in rush hour); the fare averages DM 40. If you're driving, take the B43 main road, following signs for STADTMITTE.

BY TRAIN

EuroCity and InterCity trains connect Frankfurt with all other German cities and many major European ones. The InterCity Express (ICE) line links Frankfurt with Hamburg, Munich, and several other major German cities. All long-distance trains arrive at and depart from the Hauptbahnhof. For information call **Deutsche Bahn** (German Railways; ☎ 069/19419) or ask at the information office in the station.

Getting Around

BY PUBLIC TRANSPORTATION

Frankfurt's efficient, well-integrated **public transportation system** consists of the U-bahn (subway), S-bahn (suburban railway), and Strassenbahn (streetcars). During rush hours the subway is sometimes the fastest way to get around. Fares for the entire system are uniform but based on a complicated zone system. A day ticket for unlimited travel in the inner zone costs DM 9. The Frankfurt tourist office sells a Frankfurt Card (DM 10 for one day, DM 15 for two days) entitling you to unlimited inner-zone travel and half-off admission to 15 museums. Tickets may be purchased from automatic vending machines accepting coins and notes at all stations and at most street newsstands; on buses and streetcars, they can also be purchased from the driver. For further information or assistance call 069/269–462.

BY TAXI

Cabs are not always easy to hail from the sidewalk; some stop, others will pick up only from the city's numerous taxi stands or outside hotels or the train station. Fares start at DM 3.50 and increase by DM 2.15–DM 2.55 per km (½ mi), depending on the time of day. You can call 069/250–001 or 069/230–033 for a taxi to come get you.

Contacts and Resources

CONSULATES

United States (✉ Siesmayerstr. 21, ☎ 069/75350). **Canadian** (✉ Friedrich-Wilhelm Str. 18, D-53113 Bonn, ☎ 0228/968–3903). **United Kingdom** (✉ Bockenheimer Landstr. 42, ☎ 069/170–0020).

EMERGENCIES

Police (☎ 110). **Fire** (☎ 112). **Medical Emergencies** (☎ 069/7950–2200 or 069/19292). **Pharmacies** (☎ 069/11500). **Dental Emergencies** (☎ 069/660–7271).

ENGLISH-LANGUAGE BOOKSTORES

The **British Bookshop** (✉ Börsenstr. 17, ☎ 069/280–492). The **American Book Center** (✉ Jahnstr. 36, ☎ 069/552–816).

GUIDED TOURS

Orientation. Two-and-a-half-hour **bus tours** that take in all the main sights with English-speaking guides, as well as special tours by prior arrangement, are offered throughout the year by the **main tourist office** (✉ Römerberg 27, ☎ 069/2123–8953). **Gray Line** (☎ 069/230–492) offers two-hour city tours; the price (💰 DM 50) includes a typical Frankfurt snack. The **city transit authority** (☎ 069/2132–2425) runs a brightly painted old-time streetcar—the *Ebbelwei Express* (Cider Express)—on weekend and holiday afternoons. Departures are from the Bornheim-Mitte U- and S-bahn station and the fare is DM 4.

Excursions. Deutsche Touring GmbH (✉ Am Römerhof 17, ☎ 069/790–3268) offers excursions outside Frankfurt. The **Deutsche Bahn,** German Railways, organizes a number of trips, described in a brochure, "Der Schöne Tag," available at the main train station and the DER tourist office (☞ Travel Agencies, *below*). Pleasure boats of the Primus Line cruise the Main and Rhine rivers from Frankfurt, sailing as far as the Lorelei and back in a day; for schedules and reservations contact **Frankfurter Personenschiffahrt** (✉ Mainkai 36, ☎ 069/281–884).

TRAVEL AGENCIES

American Express (✉ Kaiserstr. 8, ☎ 069/210–548).

VISITOR INFORMATION

Main tourist office (✉ Römerberg 27, ☎ 069/2123–8800; mailing address: ✉ Verkehrsamt Frankfurt/Main, Kaiserstr. 52, D-60329, ☎ 069/2123–8800). **Hauptbahnhof** (Main Train Station; ✉ Am Hauptbahnhof, opposite Track 23, ☎ 069/2123–8849). **Frankfurt Airport** (FAG Flughafen-Information, first floor of Arrivals Hall B; DER Deutsches Reisebüro, Arrivals Hall B-6).

THE BLACK FOREST

Only a century ago the Black Forest (Schwarzwald) was one of the wildest stretches of countryside in Europe. But then the deep hot springs first enjoyed by the Romans were rediscovered, and small forgotten villages became wealthy spas. Today, the region is friendly and hospitable, still extensively forested but with large, open valleys and stretches of verdant farmland. The Black Forest is the southernmost German wine region and the custodian of some of the country's best traditional foods. Black Forest smoked ham and Black Forest cake are world famous. The region retains its vibrant clock-making tradition, and local woodcarvers can still be found.

You can tour the region by all means of transportation, taking in parts of the Black Forest High Road, Low Road, Spa Road, Wine Road, and Clock Road. Crossing all the regions of the Black Forest, these roads start in the north in Pforzheim and go as far south as Staufen (approximately 200 km/125 mi) before descending into the Rhine Valley and returning north along the Rhine River to Baden-Baden (approximately 90 km/56 mi).

The Black Forest (Schwarzwald)

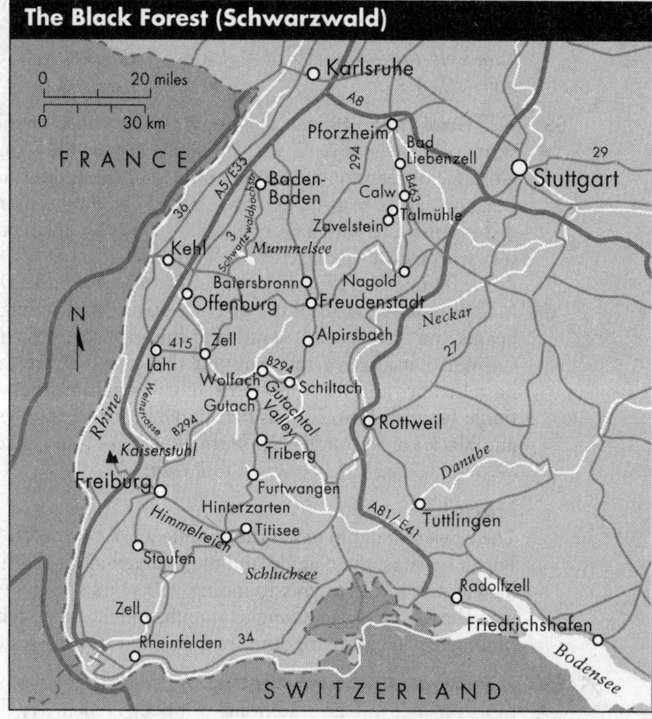

Pforzheim

The ancient Roman city, almost completely destroyed by wartime bombing, is an example of careful reconstruction. The **Schmuckmuseum** (Jewelry Museum) in the Reuchlinhaus is the world's finest museum collection of jewelry. ✉ *Jahnstr. 42,* ☎ *07231/392–126.* ⏲ *Tues.–Sun. 10–5.*

$$ ✕ **Silberburg.** This rustic restaurant offers classic and regional cooking. Ask to see the *Tagesempfehlungen*—the chef's daily recommendations. ✉ *Dietlingerstr. 27,* ☎ *07231/41159. Reservations essential. AE, DC, MC, V. Closed Mon. and 3 wks in Aug.*

Bad Liebenzell

The first stop on B463 is one of the Black Forest's oldest spas, with the remains of 15th-century installations. You can take the waters at the **Paracelsusbad lido complex** (Paracelsus Swimming Pool Center) on the Nagold riverbank. ☎ *07052/408–250.* 🎫 *DM 12 for 3 hrs.* ⏲ *Apr.–Oct., Tues., Wed., Fri.–Sun. 7:30 AM–9 PM, Mon., Thurs. 7:30–5; Nov.–Mar., Tues., Wed., Fri.–Sun. 8:30–8, Mon., Thurs. 8:30–5.*

$$$ ✕🏨 **Kronen Hotel.** A large modern wing updates this comfortable hotel. The kitchen, which provides the food for the hotel's three different restaurants, prides itself on serving healthful cuisine with lots of fresh vegetables and herbs, whole-grain products, and fruit. ✉ *Badweg 7, D-75378,* ☎ *07052/4090,* FAX *07052/409–420. 43 rooms. 3 restaurants. AE, DC, V.*

Calw

Lovely Calw (pronounced "calve") lies south of Bad Liebenzell. Its famous native son, the novelist and poet Hermann Hesse, called it the "most beautiful [town] of all I know."

The **Neubulach silver mine** was once the most productive in the Black Forest; it closed in 1924 and is now a museum open to visitors. ✉ *Talmühle turnoff south of Calw,* ☎ *07053/969510.* ⏲ *Apr.–Oct., daily 10–4:15.*

$$$ ★ ✕🏨 **Hotel Kloster Hirsau.** This country-house hotel on the wooded outskirts of Calw stands on the site of a 900-year-old monastery, whose Gothic cloisters are still largely intact. In the restaurant, owner-chef Joachim Ulrich's menu changes daily. The emphasis is on regional dishes enhanced with a French touch such as Swabian farmhouse noodles with truffle vinaigrette. ✉ *Wildbaderstr. 2, D-75365,* ☎ *07051/5621,* FAX *07051/51795. 43 rooms. Restaurant, pool. DC, MC, V.*

$$ ✕🏨 **Ratsstube.** Most of the original features, including 16th-century beams and brickwork, are intact at this historic house in the center of Calw. Rooms aren't spacious but they are brightly decorated with pastel colors and floral patterns. The restaurant offers sturdy, traditional German fare, such as marinated beef and noodles, thick soups, and Black Forest sausage. ✉ *Marktpl. 12, D-75365,* ☎ *07051/92050,* FAX *07051/70826. 13 rooms. Restaurant. AE, D, V.*

Nagold

The town of Nagold lies at the confluence of two gently flowing Black Forest streams, the Nagold and the Waldach. The elliptical street plan harks back to the town's founding 750 years ago; half-timber buildings, the Romanesque Remigius church, and the modest, hilltop remains of a medieval castle are other reminders of its long history.

$$–$$$ ★ ✕ **Romantik Restaurant Alte Post.** At this centuries-old inn, the menu ranges from Swabian traditional to pricey French. Try the local dishes such as veal in a rich mushroom sauce or, in season, venison in the Baden-Baden style. For snacks, enjoy the local beer and a plate of Black Forest smoked ham or a pot of strong coffee and a slice of delectable Black Forest cake. ✉ *Bahnhofstr. 2,* ☎ *07452/4048. Reservations essential. AE, DC, MC, V. Closed 2 wks in Jan. and 2 wks in July–Aug. No lunch Fri.*

$$–$$$ 🏨 **Hotel Post Gästehaus.** Run by the former proprietors of the adjacent Alte Post restaurant, this hotel is made up of an old coaching inn and modern additions. It offers a high degree of comfort—and homemade preserves for breakfast. ✉ *Bahnhofstr. 3, D-72202,* ☎ *07452/4048,* FAX *07452/4040. 24 rooms. AE, DC, MC, V.*

Freudenstadt

This small town lies south of Nagold in the middle of lush farmland. Flattened in the war, it was painstakingly restored. The main square, one of Germany's largest, is surrounded by arcaded houses. Don't miss the imposing **Protestant parish church.** Its L-shape ground plan was a daring innovation in the early 17th century, when it was built.

$$ ✕ **Ratskeller.** If it's cold outside, ask for a place near the Ratskeller's *Kachelofen,* a large, traditional, tile stove. Swabian dishes and venison are prominent on the menu, but if the homemade trout roulade with crab sauce is available, go for it. ✉ *Marktpl. 8,* ☎ *07441/2693. MC, V. Closed Mon.*

$$ ★ ✕ **Warteck.** Unless you arrive in the dead of winter, you'll find flowers everywhere here, even in the nooks and crannies between the leaded windows. Try the succulent lamb in meadow herbs, venison with Swabian noodles, or veal in mushroom sauce. In season the asparagus is dressed in an aromatic hazelnut vinaigrette. ✉ *Stuttgarter Str. 14, D-72250,* ☎ *07441/7418. DC, V. Closed Tues. and Nov.–3 wks after Easter.*

$$$ ★ ✕🏨 **Schwarzwaldhotel Birkenhof.** Old-fashioned comfort and a woodland setting complement a wide range of sports facilities at this superbly equipped hotel. The two restaurants offer a choice between classic French

cuisine and sturdy Black Forest fare. ✉ *Wildbaderstr. 95, D-72250,* ☎ *07441/8920,* FAX *07441/4763. 57 rooms. Restaurant, indoor pool. AE, DC, MC, V.*

$$–$$$ ✕🏨 **Bären.** Owned by the same family since 1878, the sturdy old Gasthof strives to maintain tradition and service with a personal touch. Rooms are modern but homey with farmhouse-style bedsteads and cupboards. The beam-ceiling restaurant is a favorite with the locals; its menu combines heavy German dishes (roasts and hearty sauces) and lighter international fare. ✉ *Langestr. 33, D-72250,* ☎ *07441/2779,* FAX *07441/2887. 33 rooms. Restaurant. No credit cards.*

Baiersbronn

This mountain resort (7 km/4 mi northwest of Freudenstadt), in the midst of the northern Black Forest, is blessed with two of Germany's leading hotel-restaurants—both for hospitality and cuisine. Skiing, golf, and horseback riding are among the area's activities.

$$$$ ★ ✕🏨 **Bareiss.** The luxury hotel has dark-wood furniture, and tapestry-papered walls are warmly lit by candles and traditional lamps. Restaurant Bareiss (closed Mon. and Tues.), serves light, classic cuisine and carefully selected wines (30 brands of champagne alone). The hotel is among the most luxurious and best-equipped in the Black Forest. Suites have their own sauna, solarium, and whirlpool baths. ✉ *Gärtenbühlweg 14, D-07442 Mitteltal/Baiersbronn,* ☎ *07442/470,* FAX *07442/47320. 51 rooms, 42 apartments, 7 suites. 2 restaurants, 3 pools. AE, DC, MC, V.*

$$$$ ★ ✕🏨 **Traube Tonbach.** The award-winning luxurious mountain hotel has three outstanding restaurants—Schwarzwaldstube (closed Mon. and Tues.), the Köhlerstube, and the Bauernstube. In the latter two you dine beneath beamed ceilings. The hotel is a harmonious blend of old and new, each room enjoying sweeping views of the Black Forest. Guests are nearly outnumbered by a small army of extremely helpful and friendly staff. ✉ *Tonbachstr. 237, D-72270,* ☎ *07442/4920,* FAX *07442/492-692. 134 rooms, 58 apartments, 8 suites. 3 restaurants, 3 pools. AE, DC, MC, V.*

$$ ✕🏨 **Hotel Lamm.** The half-timber exterior of this 200-year-old building presents a clear picture of the traditional Black Forest hotel within. Rooms are furnished with heavy oak fittings and some fine antiques. In its beamed restaurant you can order fish taken from the hotel's trout pools. ✉ *Ellbacherstr. 4, D-072270 Mitteltal/Baiersbronn,* ☎ *07442/4980,* FAX *07442/49878. 48 rooms. Restaurant, pool. AE, DC, MC, V.*

Wolfach

★ South of Freudenstadt on B294, Wolfach has a glass factory, the **Dorotheen-Glashütte,** that is one of the last of its kind—glass is blown by centuries-old techniques once common throughout the region. ✉ *Glashüttenweg 4,* ☎ *07834/751.* ⏲ *Weekdays 9–4:30, Sat. 9–2.*

Gutach

Gutach is best known for the **Vogtsbauernhof,** an outdoor museum consisting of old Black Forest buildings. The town lies in Gutachtal, south of Wolfach, a valley famous for its traditional costumes, and if you're here at the right time (holidays and some Sundays), you'll see the married women sporting black pom-poms on their hats to denote their matronly status (red pom-poms are for the unmarried).

$$–$$$ ★ ✕🏨 **Romantik Hotel Stollen.** The flower-bedecked balconies and low roofs of this hotel disguise a distinctive and luxurious interior, where understated comfort—some rooms have four-poster beds—is combined with attentive service. The restaurant, complete with a roaring log fire, serves regional food with nouvelle touches. ✉ *Elzacherstr. 2, D-79261*

Gutach im Elztal, 21 km (15 mi) northeast of Freiburg, ☎ *07685/207,* FAX *07685/1550. 11 rooms, 1 suite. Restaurant. AE, MC, V.*

Triberg

★ This town is the site of Germany's highest **waterfalls,** plunging nearly 509 ft. The area around the falls is also renowned for pom-pom hats, straw-covered farmhouses, cuckoo clocks, and mountain railways. The ride on **Schwarzwaldbahn** (Black Forest Railway) Offenburg-Villingen line, which passes through Triberg, is one of the most scenic in all of Europe.

The **Schwarzwaldmuseum** (Black Forest Museum) has exhibits related to Black Forest culture. The oldest clock dates from 1640; its simple wooden mechanism is said to have been carved with a bread knife. ✉ *Wallfahrtstr. 4,* ☎ *077722/4434.* ⊙ *May–Oct., daily 9–6; Nov. 1–15 and mid-Dec.–Apr., daily 10–5; mid-Nov.–mid-Dec., weekends 10–5.*

$$–$$$ ✕🏨 **Park Hotel Wehrle.** The Wehrle family has owned this enchanting building in the center of town since 1707; its vine-covered facade dominates the marketplace. The comfortable rooms are individually furnished, the service is impeccable and the restaurant is outstanding. ✉ *Am Marktpl. 1, D-78098,* ☎ *07722/86020,* FAX *07722/860–290. 67 rooms, 2 apartments, 2 suites. 2 indoor and outdoor pools. AE, DC, MC, V.*

Furtwangen

Clock enthusiasts come to Furtwangen to visit its **Uhren Museum** (Clock Museum), the largest of its kind in Germany, charting the development of Black Forest clocks, the cuckoo clock taking pride of place. Its collection includes an astronomical timepiece weighing more than a ton. ✉ *Gerwigstr. 11,* ☎ *07723/920–117.* ⊙ *Apr.–Oct., daily 9–5; Nov.–Mar., daily 10–5.*

Titisee

The 2½-km-long (1½-mi-long) lake, set in a mighty forest, is the star attraction of the Black Forest's lakeland region. It becomes invariably crowded in summer with boats and windsurfers. Boats and boards can be rented at several points along the shore.

$$ ✕🏨 **Romantik Hotel Adler Post.** In the Neustadt district of Titisee, about 5 km (3 mi) from the lake, the solid old building has been in the possession of the Ketterer family for more than 140 years. The guest rooms are comfortably and traditionally furnished. The hotel's restaurant is noted for its regional cuisine. ✉ *Hauptstr. 16, D-79822 Titisee–Neustadt,* ☎ *07651/5066,* FAX *07651/3729. 24 rooms, 4 apartments. Restaurant, pool. AE, DC, MC, V. Closed mid-Mar.–early Apr.*

Hinterzarten

This lovely 800-year-old town is the most important resort in the southern Black Forest. Some buildings date from the 12th century, among them **St. Oswald's church,** built in 1146. Hinterzarten's oldest inn, **Weisses Rossle,** has been in business since 1347.

$$$ ✕🏨 **Park Hotel Adler.** The hotel, established in 1446, has been managed by the same family for 14 generations. It stands on nearly 2 acres of grounds that are ringed by the Black Forest. Marie Antoinette once ate here, and the highest standards are maintained in the French restaurant and a paneled 17th-century dining room. All rooms are sumptuously appointed. ✉ *Adlerpl. 3, D-79856,* ☎ *07652/1270,* FAX *07652/127–717. 46 rooms, 32 suites. 2 restaurants, pool. AE, DC, MC, V.*

Schluchsee

The largest of the Black Forest lakes, mountain-enclosed Schluchsee is a diverse resort, where swimming, windsurfing, fishing, and, in winter, skiing are the preferred sports.

Freiburg

Perched on the western slopes of the Black Forest, this is now one of the region's largest and loveliest cities; it was founded as a free market town during the 12th century. Towering over Freiburg's rebuilt medieval streets is its most famous landmark, the **Münster** (Cathedral). ★ This church took 3 centuries to build and has one of the finest spires in the world. ✉ *Münsterpl.,* ☎ *0761/31099.* *Tours: DM 8.* *Münster tours: Mon. and Fri. 2:30, Wed., Thurs., and weekends 10:30.*

On weekdays **Münsterplatz** (Cathedral Square), the square in front of the cathedral, becomes a mass of color and movement; it's the town market, where you can buy everything from herbs to hot sausage. The Kaufhaus, a 16th-century market house, overlooks it.

$$–$$$ ✕ **Oberkirchs Weinstuben.** Right across from the Gothic cathedral and next to the Renaissance Kaufhaus, this wine cellar is a bastion of tradition and local Gemütlichkeit. Approximately 20 Baden wines are served by the glass, from white Gutedel to red Spätburgunder. The proprietor personally bags some of the game that ends up in the kitchen. Fresh trout is another specialty. ✉ *Münsterpl. 22,* ☎ *0761/31011. V. Closed Sun., public holidays, and Jan. 10–Feb. 2.*

$$ ✕ **Kleiner Meyerhof.** This has Weinstube atmosphere with more places to sit. It's a good spot to try regional specialties at comfortable prices. In fall and winter come for goose and wild game. ✉ *Rathausg. 27,* ☎ *0761/26941. MC. Closed Sun. June–Aug.*

$$ ✕ **Kühler Krug.** Venison dominates the proceedings at this restaurant, which has even given its name to a distinctive saddle-of-venison dish. There's also an imaginative range of freshwater fish available. ✉ *Torpl. 1,* ☎ *0761/29103. MC. Closed Mon. and 3 wks in June. No lunch Tues.*

$$ ✕ **Markgräfler Hof.** Even the French make the pilgrimage to dine in Hans Leo Kempchen's restaurant, in this traditional old hotel within Freiburg's quaint pedestrian zone. Kempchen rewards travelers with special gourmet menus and unbeatable two-day deals that include accommodations, a wine tasting, and a guided tour of the city. Call well in advance to reserve rooms. ✉ *Gerberau 22, D-79098,* ☎ *0761/32540,* FAX *0761/37947. 18 rooms. Restaurant. AE, DC, MC, V.*

$ ✕ **Freiburger Salatstuben.** Healthy vegetarian food is prepared in creative ways—try the homemade whole-wheat noodles with cauliflower in a pepper cream sauce—and served cafeteria style. It gets crowded at peak hours with students from the university up the street. ✉ *Am Martinstor-Löwenstr. 1,* ☎ *0761/35155. No credit cards. Closed Sat. dinner, Sun., public holidays.*

$$$–$$$$ ★ ✕ **Colombi.** Freiburg's most luxurious hotel also has the city's finest and most original restaurant (closed Sun.). In the rustic section you can order hearty local dishes, such as lentil soup and venison, while its more elegant section's menu combines traditional meat and fish dishes with innovative sauces. The two reconstructed 18th-century farmhouse guest cottages are stunningly furnished and decorated with antiques. ✉ *Am Colombi Park/Rotteckring 16, D-79098,* ☎ *0761/21060,* FAX *0761/31410. 80 rooms, 12 suites. Restaurant. AE, DC, MC, V.*

$$$ ★ ✕ **Zum Roten Bären.** Now a showpiece of the Ring group, this inn, which dates from 1311, has very comfortable lodging and excellent dining in a cozy warren of four restaurants and taverns. You can tour the two basement floors of cellars, dating from the original 12th-cen-

tury foundation of the town of Freiburg and now well stocked with fine wines. ✉ *Oberlinden 12, D-79098,* ☎ *0761/36913,* FAX *0761/36916. 19 rooms, 3 apartments. Restaurant. AE, DC, MC, V.*

$$ **Rappen Hotel.** The Rappen is in the center of the traffic-free Old Town overlooking the marketplace and the cathedral (and overhearing the bustle of the former and the bells of the latter). A farmhouse theme dominates here, with rustic furnishings in every room. The countrified but comfortable restaurant offers more than 200 regional wines. ✉ *Am Münsterpl. 13, D-79098,* ☎ *0761/31353,* FAX *0751/382–252. 25 rooms, 13 with bath. Restaurant. AE, DC, MC, V.*

Staufen

This small town, some 19 km (12 mi) south of Freiburg, claims the inquisitive Dr. Faustus as one of its early burghers. Faustus, who reputedly made a pact with the Devil, was the subject of Goethe's 1808 drama, *Faust.*

The Weinstrasse

From Staufen turn northward toward Baden-Baden along the Weinstrasse (Wine Road) skirting the French border to your left, through the southernmost vineyards of Germany. These produce the prized Baden wine. All the vineyards along the Wine Road offer tastings, so don't hesitate to drop in and try one or two.

The Schwarzwaldhochstrasse

Leave the Wine Road at the town of Lahr and head inland, on B415, through the narrow Schuttertal valley to Zell, and from there to the Schwarzwaldhochstrasse (Black Forest High Road). This is the land of fable and superstition, and if you're here during the misty days of autumn, stop off at the mystery-shrouded lake called the **Mummelsee.**

Baden-Baden

★ The fashionable Baden-Baden, idyllically set in a wooded valley of the northern Black Forest, sits atop the extensive underground hot springs that gave the city its name (*Bad* means baths). The Romans first exploited the springs, which were then rediscovered by wealthy travelers a couple of centuries ago. By the end of the 19th century, there was scarcely a crowned head of Europe who had not dipped into the healing waters of Baden-Baden.

One of the grand buildings of Baden-Baden's Belle Epoque is the pillared **Kurhaus** (Spa), home of Germany's first casino, which opened its doors in 1853. Visitors are required to sign a declaration that they enter with sufficient funds to settle subsequent debts! Passports are necessary as proof of identity. ✉ *Werderstr.,* ☎ *07221/21060.* 🎫 *DM 5.* ⏲ *Sun.–Fri. 2–2, Sat. 2 PM–3 AM.* ⏲ *Apr.–Sept., daily 9:30–noon; Oct.–Mar., 10–noon. Jacket and tie.*

At Baden-Baden's famous Roman baths, the **Friedrichsbad**, you take the waters just as the Romans did nearly 2,000 years ago—nude. The remains of the Roman baths that lie beneath the Friedrichsbad can be visited from April through October. ✉ *Römerpl. 1,* ☎ *07221/275–920.* 🎫 *DM 28 for 3 hrs (DM 48 with massage).* ⏲ *Mon.–Sat. 9 AM–10 PM, Sun. 2–10. Children under 18 not admitted.*

The **Caracalla-Therme** (Caracalla Baths) are a huge, modern complex with five indoor pools, two outdoor pools, numerous whirlpools, a solarium, and a "sauna landscape"—you look out through windows at the countryside while you bake. ✉ *Römerpl. 11,* ☎ *07221/275–940.* 🎫 *DM 18 for 2 hrs, DM 24 for 3 hrs.* ⏲ *Daily 8 AM–10 PM.*

$$$ ✕ **Stahlbad.** The Gallo-Germanic menu here is echoed by the restaurant's furnishings—19th-century French oils adorn the walls, and

French and German china are reflected in the mahogany gleam of antique tables and sideboards. An abundance of green velvet catches the tone of the parklike grounds of the stately house that accommodates this elegant restaurant. ✉ *Augustapl. 2,* ☎ *07221/24569. AE, DC, MC, V. Closed Mon.*

$$$ ★ ✕🏨 **Der Kleine Prinz.** Each room of this beautifully modernized 19th-century mansion is decorated in a different style, from romantic Art Nouveau to Manhattan modern. Chef Berthold Krieger combines nouvelle cuisine flair with unmistakable German thoroughness, elevating the restaurant (closed first two weeks of January) to a leading position in demanding Baden-Baden. ✉ *Lichtentalerstr. 36, D-76530,* ☎ *07221/3464,* FAX *07221/38264. 25 rooms, 14 suites. Restaurant. AE, DC, MC, V.*

$$ ✕🏨 **Gasthaus zur Traube.** Regional specialties, such as smoked bacon and homemade noodles, head the menu in this cozy inn, south of the city center in the Neuweier district. If you like the food, you can also spend the night in one of the neatly furnished and moderately priced rooms. The restaurant is closed Wednesday. ✉ *Mauerbergstr. 107, D-76534,* ☎ *07223/57216,* FAX *072336764. 18 rooms. Restaurant. MC, V.*

$$$$ 🏨 **Brenner's Park Hotel.** This exceptional, stately mansion is set in spacious, private grounds. All rooms are luxuriously furnished and appointed. ✉ *Schillerstr. 6, D-76530,* ☎ *07221/9000,* FAX *07221/38772. 68 rooms, 32 suites. 2 restaurants, pool. AE, DC, MC.*

$ 🏨 **Hotel am Markt.** The Bogner family has run the place for more than three decades—a relatively short amount of time for this 250-plus-year-old building. It's friendly, popular, and right in the center of town. ✉ *Marktpl. 17–18, D-76530,* ☎ *07221/22747,* FAX *07221/391–887. 28 rooms, 14 with bath. Restaurant. AE, DC, MC, V.*

The Black Forest Essentials

Getting Around

The **Rhine Valley autobahn,** the A5, runs the entire length of the Black Forest and connects at Karlsruhe with the rest of the German expressway network. Well-paved, single-lane highways traverse the region. A main **north–south train line** follows the Rhine Valley, carrying EuroCity and InterCity trains that call at hourly intervals at Freiburg and Baden-Baden, connecting them directly with Frankfurt and many other German cities. Local lines connect most Black Forest towns, and two local east–west services, the Black Forest Railway and the Höllental Railway, are spectacular scenic runs. The nearest **airports** are in Stuttgart; Strasbourg, in the neighboring French Alsace; and the Swiss border city of Basel, just 64 km (40 mi) from Freiburg.

Guided Tours

Guided **bus tours** of the Black Forest begin in Freiburg; contact the visitor information office (☞ *below*). A choice of 25 one-day tours includes the French Alsace region, the Swiss Alps, and various attractions in the Black Forest itself. Prices start at DM 32 and include English-speaking guides.

Visitor Information

The **Fremdenverkehrsverband** (regional tourist authority; ✉ Bertoldstr. 45, D-79098 Freiburg, ☎ 0761/31317) offers a series of scenic routes covering every important attraction.

Baden-Baden (✉ Augustapl. 8, D-76530, ☎ 07221/275–200). **Freiburg** (✉ Rotteckring 14, D-79098, ☎ 0761/368–9090). **Freudenstadt** (✉ Promenadenpl. 1, D-72250, ☎ 07741/8640). **Pforzheim** (✉ Marktpl. 1, D-75175, ☎ 07231/39900).

THE RHINE

For the Romans, who established forts and colonies along its western bank, the Rhine was the frontier between civilization and the barbaric German tribes. Roman artifacts can be seen in museums throughout the region. In the Middle Ages the river's importance as a trade artery made it the focus of conflict between princes, nobles, and archbishops. Many of the picturesque castles that crown its banks were the homes of robber barons who held up passing ships and exacted tolls to finance even grander fortifications.

For poets and composers the Rhine—or *Vater Rhein* (Father Rhine), as the Germans call it—has been an endless source of inspiration. As legend has it, the Lorelei, a treacherous, craggy rock, was home to a beautiful and bewitching maiden who lured sailors to a watery grave. The Rhine does not belong to Germany alone, but the German span of it has the most spectacular scenery—especially the 190-km (120-mi) stretch between Mainz and Köln (Cologne) known as the Middle Rhine. This is a land of steep and thickly wooded hills, vineyards, tiny villages hugging the banks, and a succession of brooding castles.

Köln

The largest German city on the Rhine is Köln (Cologne), first settled by the Romans in 38 BC. The Franks and Merovingians followed the Romans before Charlemagne restored the city's fortunes during the 9th century, appointing its first archbishop and ensuring its ecclesiastical prominence for centuries.

By the Middle Ages Köln was the largest city north of the Alps, and, as a member of the powerful Hanseatic League, it was more important commercially than either London or Paris. Ninety percent of the city was destroyed in World War II, and the rush to rebuild it after the war shows in some of the blocky, uninspired architecture. Still, attempts were made to restore many of its old buildings. Whatever the city's aesthetic drawbacks, the Altstadt (Old Town), within the line of the medieval city walls, has great charm, and at night it throbs with life.

★ Towering over the Old Town is the **Kölner Dom** (Cologne Cathedral), an extraordinary Gothic edifice, dedicated to St. Peter and the Virgin. At 515 ft high, the two western towers of the cathedral were by far the tallest structures in the world when they were finished. The length of the building is 469 ft; the width of the nave is 148 ft; and the highest part of the interior is 139 ft. The cathedral was built to house what were believed to be the relics of the Magi, the three kings or wise men who paid homage to the infant Jesus. Today the relics are kept just behind the altar, in the same enormous gold-and-silver **reliquary** in which they were originally displayed. The other great treasure of the cathedral is the **Gero Cross,** a monumental oak crucifix dating from 971. Impressive for its simple grace, it's in the last chapel on the left as you face the high altar. Still more treasures can be seen in the **Schatzkammer** (Cathedral Treasury), including the silver shrine of Archbishop Engelbert, who was stabbed to death in 1225. ⊠ *Dompl.,* ☎ *0221/135–130.* ⏲ *Mon.–Sat. 9–5, Sun. 1–5.*

★ If your priority is painting, visit the ultramodern **Wallraf-Richartz-Museum/Museum Ludwig** complex across the square from the Dom. Together, they form the largest art collection in the Rhineland. The Wallraf-Richartz-Museum's pictures span the years 1300–1900, with Dutch and Flemish schools particularly well represented (Rubens, who spent his youth in Köln, has a place of honor). The Museum Ludwig is devoted exclusively to 20th-century art. ⊠ *Bischofsgartenstr. 1,* ☎

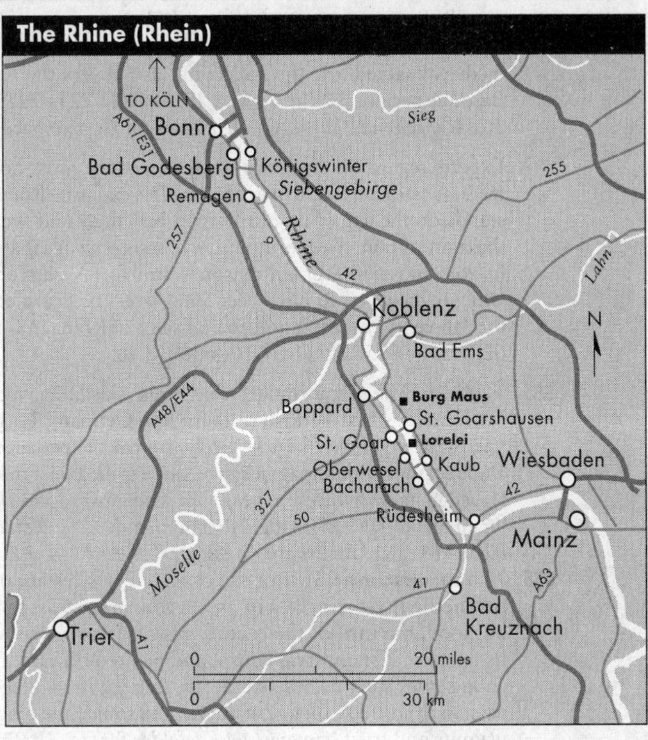

0221/221–2379. ✉ *Both museums: DM 10.* ⏲ *Tues.–Fri. 10–6, weekends 11–6.*

★ Opposite the Dom is the **Römisch-Germanisches Museum** (Roman-German Museum), built from 1970 to 1974 around the Dionysus mosaic that was uncovered at the site during the construction of an air-raid shelter in 1941. The huge mosaic, more than 300 ft square, once covered the dining-room floor of a wealthy Roman trader's villa. ✉ *Roncallipl. 4,* ☎ *0221/ 221–4438.* ⏲ *Tues.–Fri. 10–4, weekends 11–4.*

The **Altes Rathaus** (Old Town Hall), stands in the **Alter Markt** (Old Market Square) south of the Dom. This is the oldest town hall in Germany; there was a seat of local government here in Roman times, and directly below the current Rathaus are the remains of the Roman city governor's headquarters, the Praetorium. Go inside to see the 14th-century **Hansa Saal**, a meeting hall whose tall Gothic windows and barrel-vaulted wooden ceiling are potent expressions of medieval civic pride. The figures of the prophets, standing on pedestals at one end, are all from the early 15th century. ✉ *Alter Markt,* ☎ *0221/221–3345 for tour information.*

Gross St. Martin (Great St. Martin), the most outstanding of Köln's 12 Romanesque churches, has a massive 13th-century tower, distinctive turrets, and an imposing central spire. ✉ *Lintg.* ⏲ *Daily 9–5.*

Gross St. Martin is the parish church of Köln's colorful old section, the **Martinsviertel** (St. Martin's Quarter), an attractive combination of reconstructed, high-gabled medieval buildings, winding alleys, and tastefully designed modern apartments and business quarters. Head here at night—the place comes alive at sunset.

The 12th-century **Cäcilienkirche** (St. Cecilia Church) lies at the edge of the Martinsviertel. Its cool, well-lighted interior now houses one of the world's finest museums of medieval Christian art, the **Schnütgen Museum.** Although the main emphasis of the museum falls on early and medieval sacred art, the collection also covers the Renaissance and Baroque periods. ✉ *Cäcilienstr. 29,* ☎ *0221/221–2310.* ⏲ *Tues.–Fri. 10–4, weekends 11–4. Guided tours (in German) Sun. at 11.*

Experts regard **St. Gereon's** to be one of the most noteworthy early medieval structures still in existence. This exquisite Romanesque church stands on the site of an old Roman burial ground six blocks west of the train station. An enormous dome rests on walls that were once clad in gold mosaics. Roman masonry still forms part of the structure, which is believed to have been built over the grave of its namesake, the 4th-century martyr and patron saint of Köln. ✉ *Gereonshof 4,* ☎ *0221/579–0950.* ⏲ *Daily 10–noon, 3–6.*

$$$ ✕ **Bizim.** The extraordinary chef, Enis Akisik, has made his Bizim a candidate for best Turkish restaurant in Germany. Forget shish kebab and prepare yourself for a leisurely, gourmet experience that might include scampi with tarragon sauce, quail grilled on a rosemary spit and served in its own juices, or veal with wild mushrooms. The four-course lunch menu (DM 55) is highly recommended. ✉ *Weideng. 47–49,* ☎ *0221–131581. Reservations essential. Sat.–Mon. AE, D.*

$$$ ✕ **Le Moissonnier.** Part of the charm of this restaurant—among the best in the city—is its lack of pretension. In contrast to the gray neighborhood, the turn-of-the-century bistro decor radiates warmth from its mirrors, Tiffany-style lamps, and painted flowers. Chef Eric Menchon serves such dishes as crayfish sautéed in vanilla oil, a gourmet version of stuffed cabbage with veal and squid, and ginger parfait with walnuts and fried bananas. ✉ *Krefelder Str. 25,* ☎ *0221/729479,* FAX *0221/7325461. Reservations essential. No credit cards. Closed Sun.*

$$ ✕ **Früh am Dom.** For real down-home German food, few places compare with this former brewery. Bold frescoes on the vaulted ceilings establish the mood, and such dishes as *Hämmchen* (pork shank) provide an authentically Teutonic experience. ✉ *Am Hof 12–14,* ☎ *0221/258–0389. No credit cards.*

$$$$ ✕🏨 **Dom-Hotel.** The Dom is in a class of its own. Old-fashioned, formal, and gracious, with a stunning location right by the cathedral, it offers elegance and discreetly efficient service. The antiques-filled bedrooms, generally in Louis XV or Louis XVI style, are subdued in color, high-ceilinged, and spacious. Each room is individually furnished. In the glassed-in Atelier am Dom you can enjoy views of the cathedral while dining on anything from wild boar served with chanterelle ragout to tofu piccata with ratatouille and curried rice. ✉ *Domkloster 2A, D-50667,* ☎ *0221/20240,* FAX *0221/202–4444. 126 rooms. 2 restaurants. AE, DC, MC, V.*

$$$$ ★ ✕🏨 **Excelsior Hotel Ernst.** The Empire-style lobby in sumptuous royal blue, bright yellow, and gold is striking, and a similar, boldly conceived grandeur extends to all the public rooms in this 1863 hotel. Old master paintings (including a Van Dyck) are everywhere; you'll be served breakfast in a room hung with Gobelin tapestries. Guest rooms are intimate in scale, with spectacular marble bathrooms and ultramodern fixtures. The lacquered-wood-paneled restaurant serves classic French cuisine imaginatively prepared. ✉ *Trankg. 1–5, D-50667,* ☎ *0221/2701,* FAX *0221/135–150. 160 rooms. Restaurant. AE, DC, MC, V.*

$$$$ ★ 🏨 **Hotel im Wasserturm.** What used to be Europe's tallest water tower is now an 11-story luxury hotel-in-the-round, opened at the end of 1989. The neoclassic look of the brick exterior was retained by order of Cologne conservationists. The ultramodern interior was the work of the French designer Andrée Putman. The 11th-floor restaurant has a view of the city. ✉ *Kayg. 2, D–50676,* ☎ *0221/20080,* FAX *0221/200–8888. 48* *rooms, 40 suites and maisonettes. Restaurant, café, room service, sauna. AE, DC, MC, V.*

$$ 🏨 **Chelsea.** This hotel has a strong following among artists and art dealers, and decor that is a cross between Rietveld, Philippe Stark, and a half dozen others. The bathrooms and bathtubs are luxuriously roomy and there is no end of mirrors. Breakfast is served until noon. It's not right in the city center but is just 20 minutes away by foot, 10 by subway or tram. ✉ *Fischmarkt 1-3, D–50667,* ☎ *0221/257–7862,* FAX *0221/257–4232. 32 rooms. Restaurant. AE, DC, MC, V.*

$$ 🏨 **Stapelhäuschen.** One of the few houses along the riverbank to have survived World War II bombings, this is among the very oldest buildings in Köln. You can't beat the location, overlooking the river and right by Gross St. Martin; rooms make up in quaintness for what they lack in luxury. ✉ *Fischmarkt 1–3, D-50667,* ☎ *0221/257–7862,* FAX *0221/257–4232. 55 rooms. MC, V.*

Bonn

Not far south of Köln is the staid city of Bonn, the former capital of West Germany, now preparing to hand most of its legislative and administrative functions over to Berlin. The city has a vintage, late-Romanesque, 900-year-old **Münster** (Cathedral) with a massive octagonal main tower, a soaring spire, and an ornate rococo pulpit inside. ✉ *Münsterpl.,* ☎ *0228/633–344.* ⏱ *Daily 7–7.*

★ The **Beethovenhaus** (Beethoven Museum) displays scores, a grand piano, and ear trumpets in the house where the composer was born. ✉ *Bonng. 20,* ☎ *0228/635–188.* 🎫 *DM 8.* ⏱ *Apr.–Sept., Mon.–Sat. 10–5, Sun. 11–4; Oct.–Mar., Mon.–Sat. 10–4, Sun. 10–1.*

The **Kunst- und Austellungshalle der Bundesrepublik Deutschland** (Art and Exhibition Hall of the German Federal Republic) is a space for major traveling exhibitions. ✉ *Friedrich-Ebert-Allee 2,* ☎ *0228/9171200.* 🎫 *Free.* ⏱ *Tues.–Sun. 10–7.*

In the town of Königswinter (12 km/7 mi northeast of Bonn) is one of the most-visited castle sites on the Rhine, the **Drachenfels.** The ruins of the Drachenfels crown the highest hill in the Siebengebirge (Seven Hills), commanding a spectacular view of the river. The castle was built during the 12th century by the archbishop of Köln.

$$ ✕ **Gasthaus Sutorius.** Just across from the church of St. Margaretha in Königswinter, this wine tavern serves refined variations on traditional German dishes, along with an intelligent selection of local wines. In summer, food is served outdoors beneath the lime trees. ✉ *Oelinghovener Str. 7, Königswinter,* ☎ *02244/4749. AE, D. Closed Mon. No lunch Tues.–Sat.*

$$ ✕ **Haus Daufenbach.** Behind Bonn's stark white exterior of Daufenbach, the mood is rustic, with simple wooden furniture and antlers on the walls. Specialties include *Spanferkel* (suckling pig) and a range of imaginative salads. Wines come from the restaurant's own vineyards. ✉ *Brüderg. 6,* ☎ *0228/637–944. No credit cards. Closed Mon. No dinner Sun. in summer.*

$ ✕ **Em Höttche.** Travelers have been dining at this rustic tavern since the late 14th century; today it offers one of the best-value lunches in town. The food is hearty, and the portions are large. ✉ *Markt 4,* ☎ *0228/690–009. Reservations not accepted. No credit cards.*

$$$$ 🏨 **Domicil.** A group of buildings around a courtyard has been stylishly converted into a hotel of great charm and comfort. The rooms are decorated in styles from fin-de-siècle romantic to Italian modern. ✉ *Thomas-Mann-Str. 24–26, D-53115,* ☎ *0228/729–090,* FAX *0228/691–207. 42 rooms. Restaurant. AE, DC, MC, V. Closed Dec. 25–Jan. 1.*

$$ 🏨 **Rheinland.** This modest lodging has the advantage of being a short walk from the center of the Old Town. Rooms are comfortable, and a good buffet breakfast greets the day. ✉ *Berliner Freiheit 11, D-53111,* ☎ *0228/658–096,* FAX *0228/472–844. 31 rooms. AE, MC.*

$$ 🏨 **Sternhotel.** For good value, solid comfort, and a central location in the Old Town, the family-run "Star" is tops. Rooms can be small, but all are pleasantly furnished. Snacks are available at the bar. ✉ *Markt 8, D-53111,* ☎ *0228/72670,* FAX *0228/726–7125. 81 rooms. AE, DC, MC, V.*

Koblenz

This ancient city began as a Roman camp more than 2,000 years ago. The **Deutsches Eck,** or "Corner of Germany," is the tip of the sharp peninsula separating the two rivers. On summer evenings concerts are held in the nearby Blumenhof Garden. Most of the city's historic churches are also within walking distance of the Deutsches Eck. The **Liebfrauenkirche** (Church of Our Lady) completed in the 13th century but later much modified, incorporates Romanesque, late-Gothic, and Baroque elements. ✉ *An der Liebfrauenkirche.* ⏲ *Daily 7–6.*

The city's most important church, **St. Kastor Kirche** (St. Castor Church) combines Romanesque and Gothic elements and contains some unusual altar tombs and rare Gothic wall paintings. ✉ *Kastorhof.* ⏲ *Daily 7–6.*

St. Florin Kirche, a Romanesque church built around 1100, was remodeled in the Gothic style during the 14th century. Gothic windows and a vaulted ceiling were added during the 17th century. The vaults beneath St. Florin's contain an interesting assortment of Roman remains. ✉ *St. Florins Markt at Auf der Danne Str.*

Much of the **Altstadt** (Old Town) of Koblenz is now a pedestrian district, an attractive area for a leisurely stroll. Many of the ancient cellars beneath the houses have been rediscovered and now serve as wine bars and jazz clubs.

The **Museum Ludwig** presents rotating exhibitions of contemporary art, much of it from the enormous collection of Koblenz-born tycoon Peter Ludwig. ✉ *Danziger Freiheit 1,* ☎ *0261/304–040.* ⏲ *Tues., Wed., Fri., and Sat. 11–5; Thurs. 11–8; Sun. 11–6.*

The **Mittelrhein Museum** (Middle Rhine Museum) displays Rhenish art and artifacts from the Middle Ages to the present day. ✉ *15 Florinsmarkt,* ☎ *0261/129–2502.* ⏲ *Tues. and Thurs.–Sat. 11–5, Wed. 11–7, Sun. 11–6.*

Across the river from Koblenz, on the Rhine's east bank, towers the city's most spectacular castle, **Festung Ehrenbreitstein** (Ehrenbreitstein Fortress). The fortifications of this vast structure date from the 1100s, although the bulk of it was built much later, during the 16th and 17th centuries. To reach the fortress take the *Sesselbahn* (cable car) or, try walking up. ☎ *0261/97030.* 🎫 *Castle: Free.* ⏲ *Daily 9–12:30 and 1–5.* 🎫 *Cable car: DM 8.* ⏲ *June–Aug., daily 9–6; Sept., daily 10–6; Easter–May, daily 10–5.*

$$ ✕ **Wacht am Rhein.** The name of this attractive riverside restaurant, Watch on the Rhine, sums it up. In summer take a table on the terrace and watch the river traffic pass by; in winter choose a window table and dine with the Rhine outside and the atmospheric warmth of the fin de siècle fittings and furnishings inside. Fish is the basis of the extensive menu. ✉ *Adenauer-Ufer 6,* ☎ *0261/15313. AE.*

$$$ ★ ✕🏨 **Kurfürstliches Amtshaus.** The yellow walls of the former castle rise above the town of Daun in the picturesque Eifel, a region of volcanic

lakes just outside Koblenz. Inside are comforts both baronial and modern. Most bedrooms have views of the surrounding hills and woods. The heated swimming pool uses water from the local springs. The restaurant, "Graf Leopold," has a noted German chef who excels at both traditional and creative Asian-accented dishes. ✉ *Auf dem Burgberg D–54550,* ☎ *06592/3031,* FAX *06592/4942. 35 rooms, 1 suite. Restaurant, solarium, pool, sauna. AE, DC, V.*

$$–$$$ **Kleiner Reisen.** This is a well-run, straightforward hotel that gives value for the money. Another plus is the quiet riverside location that's still within walking distance of the train station and Old Town. ✉ *Kaiserin-Augusta-Anlagen 18, D-56068,* ☎ *0261/32077,* FAX *0261/160–725. 27 rooms. AE, DC, MC, V.*

Rhine Gorge

Between Koblenz and Mainz, the Rhine flows through the 64-km (40-mi) Rhine Gorge. It is here that the Rhine lives up to its legends and lore, and where in places the river narrows to a mere 200 yards. Vineyards occupy every inch of available soil on the steep, terraced slopes. High above, ancient castles crown the rocky shelves.

South of Koblenz, at a wide, western bend in the river, lies the quiet old town of **Boppard,** once a bustling city of the Holy Roman Empire. Now the remains of its Roman fort and castle are used to house a museum of Roman artifacts and geological specimens. There are also several notable churches, including the **Karmeliterkirche** (Carmelite Church), with its fine Baroque altar, and the Romanesque church of **St. Severus.** From Boppard there is a wonderful view across the Rhine to the ruined castles of **Liebenstein** and **Sterrenberg.**

★ **Marksburg** castle is on the opposite bank of the river, 500 ft above the town of Braubach. Built during the 12th century to protect silver and lead mines in the area, it is the only castle in the entire Middle Rhine Valley to have survived the centuries without ever being destroyed. Within its massive walls are a collection of weapons and manuscripts, a medieval botanical garden, and a restaurant. ☎ *02627/206.* *DM 7.* ⏲ *Easter–Oct., daily 10–5; Nov.–day before Easter, daily 11–4.*

$$$ **Bellevue Rheinhotel.** This is one of the Rhineland's most majestic hotels, an imposing turn-of-the-century building whose elegant white-and-yellow facade, under steep slate eaves, faces directly onto the river. ✉ *Rheinallee 41–42, D-56154,* ☎ *06742/1020,* FAX *06742/102–602. 94 rooms. Restaurant, pool. AE, DC, MC, V.*

St. Goar

South of Boppard, this little town is crowded against the steep gorge cliff and shadowed by the imposing ruin of **Burg Rheinfels** (Rhine Cliff Castle), built during the mid-13th century. The ruins are now being restored, and a luxury hotel has been built on the site. ☎ *06741/802–0.* *DM 5.* ⏲ *Apr.–Oct., daily 9–6; Nov.–Mar., daily 10–4.*

Just across from the town of St. Goar, on the east bank of the Rhine, lies its sister village, **St. Goarshausen** (an hourly ferry service links the city to St. Goar). **Burg Katz** (Cat Castle), a massive 13th-century fortress towers over St. Goarshausen. The top of the cliff offers a lovely view of the famous Lorelei rock.

Only a few kilometers from St. Goarshausen is the legendary **Lorelei rock.** To get to the Lorelei follow the road marked with LORELEI-FELSEN signs. Here the Rhine takes a sharp turn around a rocky, shrub-covered headland. This is the narrowest and shallowest part of the Middle Rhine, full of treacherous currents. According to legend the beautiful maiden, Lore, sat on the rock here, combing her golden hair and singing a song so irresistible that passing sailors forgot the navigational hazards and were swept to their deaths.

$$ ✕ **Roter Kopf.** This is a historic wine restaurant brimming with rustic Rhineland atmosphere. ✉ *Burgstr. 5, St. Goarshausen,* ☏ *06771/2698. No credit cards.*

$$$ ★ ✕🏨 **Auf Schönburg.** Above the Rhine and the town of Oberwesel, stands this ancient castle-turned-hotel. The modernized rooms are decorated with antiques. The wooden-beamed restaurant serves such satisfying dishes as lentil soup with mushroom ravioli or rack of lamb in an herb crust. ✉ *Burg Schönburg, D–55430,* ☏ *06744/93930,* FAX *06744/1613. 20 rooms. Restaurant. Closed Jan.–Mar. AE, DC, MC, V.*

$$$ ★ 🏨 **Schlosshotel-Burg Rheinfels.** High above St. Goar, on a hill commanding spectacular river views, the Schlosshotel-Burg Rheinfels rises from the ruins of the adjacent castle (☞ *above*). ✉ *Schlossberg 47, D-56329 St. Goar,* ☏ *06741/8020,* FAX *06741/802802. 58 rooms. Restaurant, pool. AE, DC, MC, V.*

$ 🏨 **Hermannsmühle.** This warm, rustic, chalet-style hotel just outside St. Goarshausen has heavy furniture decorated with painted floral patterns. ✉ *Forstbachstr. 46, D-56346 St. Goarshausen,* ☏ *06771/7317. 10 rooms. Restaurant. MC, V. Closed mid-Nov.–Feb.*

Kaub

This medieval village, south of the Lorelei on the east side of the river, is one of the most-photographed sites of the Middle Rhine region because of its unusual castles. Bristling with sharp-pointed towers, the **Pfalzgrafenstein** castle on a tiny island in the middle of the Rhine has the appearance of a small sailing ship. During the 14th century the resident Pfalzgraf, or Count Palatine, was said to have strung chains across the Rhine to stop riverboats and collect his tolls. A special boat takes visitors to the island. ⏲ *Ferry trips every ½-hr 9–1 and 2–5 (in season).*

On a hillside above Kaub perches a small castle, **Burg Gutenfels** (Good Cliff Castle). Built during the 13th century, Gutenfels was renovated completely at the end of the 18th century and is now a hotel (☞ *below*).

$$$ 🏨 **Burg Gutenfels.** The terrace of this luxurious castle hotel offers one of the finest views in the Rhine Valley. Wines come from the hotel's own vineyard. Be sure to reserve well in advance. ✉ *D-56349 Kaub am Rhein,* ☏ *06774/220,* FAX *06774/1760. 10 rooms. Restaurant. AE, DC, MC, V.*

Bacharach

This picturesque little village, encircled by 15th-century walls, is the best-preserved town of the Middle Rhine. Bacharach is an important trading center for the region's vintages.

$$ ✕🏨 **Altkölnischer Hof.** This small but cozy half-timber hotel was built at the turn of the century. Its rustic restaurant serves typical local dishes and some excellent wines. ✉ *Blücherstr. 2, D-55422,* ☏ *06743/1339,* FAX *06743/2793. 18 rooms. Restaurant. AE, V. Closed Nov.–Mar.*

Rüdesheim

At the center of the Rhine Gorge region, lies this famous wine town. According to legend, its first vines were planted by Charlemagne. More recent vintages can be enjoyed in the many taverns lining **Drosselgasse,** a narrow, colorful street in the heart of town. Rüdesheim is the most popular destination on the Rhine—be sure to reserve well in advance.

$$–$$$ ★ ✕ **Krone.** The restaurant of the 450-year-old Krone ranks among the most outstanding in the region. Chef Herbert Pucher's terrines and pâtés draw regular customers from as far away as Frankfurt. His fish dishes

are supreme, and the Rhine wines are the best. ✉ *Rheinuferstr. 10, Assmannshausen,* ☎ *06722/4030,* FAX *06722/3049. AE, DC, MC, V.*

$$$–$$$$ **Hotel Jagdschloss Niederwald.** This is not so much a place to overnight as it is a luxury resort hotel. It's in the hills 5 km (3 mi) outside Rüdesheim, with views over the Rhine and the Rhine Gorge. The former hunting lodge of the dukes of Hesse, it has a lavish, baronial atmosphere. ✉ *Auf dem Niederwald 1, D-65383,* ☎ *06722/1004,* FAX *06722/47970. 52 rooms. Restaurant, pool. AE, DC, MC, V. Closed Jan.–mid-Mar.*

$$ **Rüdesheimer Hof.** For a taste of Rhine Gorge hospitality, try this typical inn. There's a terrace for summer dining on excellent local specialties, which you can enjoy along with any of the many wines offered. ✉ *Geisenheimerstr. 1, D-65385,* ☎ *06722/2011,* FAX *06722/48194. 42 rooms. Restaurant. AE, DC, MC, V. Closed mid-Nov.–mid-Feb.*

Mainz

This bustling modern city of nearly 200,000 lies on the west bank of the Rhine, at the mouth of the Main River. Once the seat of powerful archbishops, the city still has as its focal point the **Dom** (Cathedral), one of the finest Romanesque churches in Germany, dating mostly from the late 11th century through the 13th century, with an imposing Baroque spire added in the 18th century. ✉ *Domstr. 3,* ☎ *06131/253–344.* *DM 8.* *Mon.–Wed. and Fri. 10–4, Thurs. 10–5, Sat. 10–2.*

★ The **Gutenberg Museum** honors the printing pioneer Johannes Gutenberg, who first experimented with moveable type around 1450 in Mainz. The museum houses his press and one of the Bibles he printed. ✉ *Liebfrauenpl. 5,* ☎ *06131/122–640.* *DM 5.* *Tues.–Sat. 10–6, Sun. and holidays 10–1. Closed Jan.*

The **Römisch-Germanisches Museum** (Roman-German Museum) in the Kurfürstliches Schloss (Elector's Palace), contains a notable collection of archaeological finds from a Roman settlement and two ancient Roman ships unearthed in 1981. ✉ *Rheinstr.,* ☎ *06131/232–231.* *Free.* *Tues.–Sun. 10–5.*

★ The **Mittelrheinische Landesmuseum** (Middle Rhine Provincial Museum) is just three blocks off the riverfront. The museum covers the culture of the Middle Rhine region from the Stone Age to the present. Its remarkable collection of Roman altars and tombstones includes the **Jupitersäle** (Jupiter's Pillar), a beautifully preserved column dedicated to the Roman god Jupiter. ✉ *Grosse Bleiche 49-51,* ☎ *06131/236298.* *DM 5.* *Tues. 10–8, Wed.–Sun. 10–5.*

The Gothic church of **St. Stephan** stands on a hilltop to the south; in its choir are six stained-glass windows by French artist Marc Chagall. ✉ *Kleine Weissg. 12,* ☎ *06131/231–640.* *Feb.–Nov., weekdays 10–noon and 2–5; Dec.–Jan., weekdays 10–noon and 2–4:30.*

$$ ✕ **Rats und Zunftstuben Heilig Geist.** Although the decor is predominantly modern, this popular restaurant also incorporates some Roman remains and offers a traditional atmosphere. The cuisine is hearty German fare. ✉ *Renteng. 2,* ☎ *06131/225–757. Reservations essential. AE, DC, MC, V. Closed Sun.*

$ ✕ **HDW.** You can sample 45 kinds of wine by the glass from 11 German wine regions at this "House of German Wine." The kitchen takes a modern approach to traditional food, including hearty local specialties. ✉ *Gutenbergpl. 3,* ☎ *06131/221–300. No credit cards.*

$$$ ★ ✕ **Hilton International.** A terrific location by the Rhine and high standards of service and comfort make the Hilton the top accommodation choice in Mainz, despite a distinct lack of old German atmosphere. The hotel has a casino. ✉ *Rheinstr. 68, D-55116,* ☎ *06131/2450,* FAX *06131/245–589. 433 rooms. 2 restaurants. AE, DC, MC, V.*

$ **Hotel Stadt Coblenz.** In the heart of the town this attractive hotel offers budget rooms (bath in the hall)—ask for a room facing the back. The rustic restaurant serves local and German specialties. ✉ *Rheinstr. 49, D-55116,* ☎ *0631/227–602. Restaurant. No credit cards.*

The Rhine Essentials

Getting Around

BY BICYCLE

Tourist offices in all the larger towns will provide information and route maps. **Deutsche Bahn** (☎ 069/19419) rents bikes at numerous stations. Ask for the "*Fahrrad am Bahnhof*" ("Bikes for Rent") brochure at any station.

BY BOAT

Köln-Düsseldorfer Rheinschiffahrt (✉ Frankenwerft 15, D-50667 Köln, ☎ 0221/208–8288) has daily cruises between Köln and Frankfurt from Easter to late October. **JFO CruiseService Corp.** (✉ 2500 Westchester Ave., Purchase, NY 10577, ☎ 914/696–3600 or 800/346–6525 in the U.S.) organizes Rhine cruises. **KD River Cruises of Europe** (✉ 323 Geary St., Suite 603, San Francisco, CA 94102, ☎ 415/392–8817 or 800/346–6525) offers daily cruises and trips up the Mosel as far as Trier. From March through November the **Hebel-Line** (☎ 06742/2420) in Boppard cruises the Lorelei Valley; night cruises have music and dancing. For information about Neckar River excursions contact **Neckar Personen Schiffahrt** (☎ 0711/541–073 or 0711/541–074).

BY CAR

For information about Rhineland's comprehensive highway network contact the **Automobilclub von Deutschland** (German Automobile Club, ✉ Lyonerstr. 16, D-60528 Frankfurt-am-Main, ☎ 069/66060).

BY TRAIN

One of the best ways to visit the Rhineland in very limited time is to take the scenic, two-hour train journey from Mainz north to Köln along the western bank of the river. Contact **Deutsche Bahn** (German Railways; ✉ Friedrich-Ebert-Anlage 43, Frankfurt, ☎ 069/19419), or get details at any central train station travel office.

Guided Tours

In addition to a number of special-interest cruises, **KD River Cruises of Europe** (☞ By Boat *in* Getting Around, *above*) operates a series of guided excursions covering the towns along its routes. The local shipping company, **Personenschiffahrt Merkelbach** (✉ Emserstr. 87, D-56076 Koblenz-Pfaffendorf, ☎ 0261/76810), has guided river tours. **Rhein und Moselschiffahrt Gerhard Colée-Hölzenbein** (✉ Rheinzollstr. 4, D-56068 Koblenz, ☎ 0261/37744) organizes guided tours of the Mosel and Rhine rivers. The **tourist offices** in Mainz, Köln, and Koblenz (☞ Visitor Information, *below*) offer English-language tours of their respective cities.

Visitor Information

For general information on the region contact the **Fremdenverkehrsverband Rheinland-Pfalz** (Rhineland Tourist Board, ✉ Löhrstr. 103, Postfach 1420, D-56014 Koblenz, ☎ 0261/915–200).

Bacharach (Fremdenverkehrsamt, ✉ Oberstr. 1, D-55422, ☎ 06743/2968). **Boppard** (Verkehrsamt, ✉ Karmeliterstr. 2, D-54154, ☎ 06742/10319). **Koblenz** (Fremdenverkehrsamt Pavillon am Hauptbahnhof, ✉ Postfach 2080, D-56020, ☎ 0261/31304). **Köln** (Verkehrsamt, ✉ Unter Fettenhennen 19, D-50667, ☎ 0221/221–3340). **Mainz** (✉ Tourist-Zentrale Mainz, Im Brückenturm amd Rathaus, D–55116, ☎ 06131/

286–210). **Rüdesheim** (Verkehrsamt, ✉ Rheinstr. 16, D-65385, ☎ 06722/2962). **St. Goarshausen** (Verkehrsamt, ✉ Bahnhofstr. 8, D-56346, ☎ 06771/9100).

HAMBURG

Hamburg is a city on water: the great River Elbe, which flows into the North Sea; the smaller River Alster, which has been dammed to form two lakes, the Binnenalster and Aussenalster; and many canals. Once a leading member of the Hanseatic League, which dominated trade on the North Sea and the Baltic during the Middle Ages, the city is a major port, with 33 individual docks and 500 berths for oceangoing vessels, and Germany's gateway to the world.

Exploring Hamburg

Numbers in the margin correspond to points of interest on the Hamburg map.

Within the remaining traces of its old city walls, downtown Hamburg combines the seamiest, steamiest streets of dockland Europe with sleek avenues. The city is easy to explore on foot.

★ ❷ **Alter Botanischer Garten** (Old Botanical Gardens). This green and open park in Wallringpark specializes in rare and exotic plants. Tropical and subtropical species are grown under glass in hothouses, with specialty gardens—including herbal and medicinal—clustered around an old moat. ✉ *Stephanspl.,* ☎ *040/232–327.* 🎟 *Free.* ⏲ *Daily 8–6.*

❾ **Bismarck-Denkmal** (Bismarck Memorial). The colossal 111-ft granite monument, erected between 1903 and 1906, is a mounted statue of Chancellor Bismarck, the Prussian "Iron Chancellor," who was the force behind the unification of Germany. ✉ *Helgoländer Allee.*

❽ **Blankenese.** This city suburb has the character of a quaint fishing village. Along the north bank of the Elbe is one of the finest walks Hamburg has to offer. The walk is a long one, about 13 km (8 mi) from the St. Pauli Landungsbrücken to the attractive waterside area of Blankenese. A ferry connects Blankenese with Hamburg's St. Pauli district, but there are S-bahn stations and bus stops along the way, to give you a speedy return to the downtown area.

★ ❼ **Erotic Art Museum.** Sexually provocative art from 1520 to the present, 500 original works in all, is showcased here. The collection is presented with great taste and decorum in an attractively renovated four-story building. Special exhibits of modern erotic photography or comic art are staged in a different building on Bernhard-Nocht-Strasse. ✉ *Nobistor 10a at Reeperbahn and Bernhard-Nocht-Str. 69,* ☎ *040/3174–757. Minimum age 18.* 🎟 *DM 15, combined ticket for both exhibitions DM 20.* ⏲ *Sun.–Thurs. 10 AM–midnight, Fri., Sat. 10AM–1AM. U-bahn: St. Pauli.*

★ ❺ **Fischmarkt** (Fish Market). Freshly caught fish are only part of a compendium of wares on sale at the popular Fischmarkt in Altona. In fact you can find almost anything—from live parrots and palm trees to armloads of flowers and bananas, valuable antiques to second-, third-, and fourth-hand junk. ✉ *Between Grosse Elbestr. and St. Pauli Landungsbrücken.* ⏲ *Apr.–Sept., Sun. 5 AM–10 AM; Oct.–Mar., Sun. 7 AM–10 AM.*

❶ **Hauptbahnhof** (Central Train Station). This train station's impressive architecture of steel and glass is a breathtaking example of imperial German pride. It was opened in 1906 and completely renovated in 1991. The enormous 394-ft-long cast-iron-and-glass building is accentuated

Hamburg

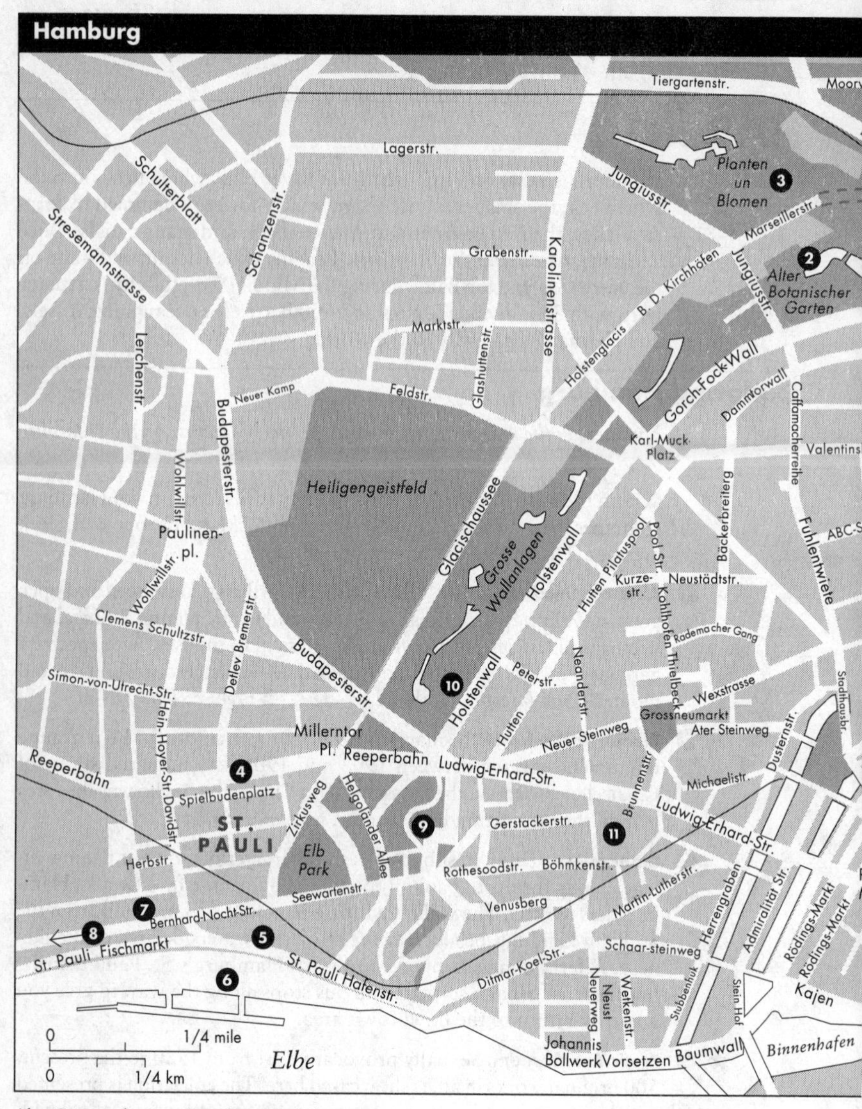

Alter Botanischer Garten, **2**
Bismarck-Denkmal, **9**
Blankenese, **8**
Erotic Art Museum, **7**
Fischmarkt, **5**
Hauptbahnhof, **1**
Jungfernstieg, **14**
Kunsthalle, **15**
Landungsbrücken, **6**
Museum für Hamburgische Geschichte, **10**
Planten un Blom, **3**
Rathaus, **13**
Rathausmarkt, **12**
Reeperbahn, **4**
St. Michaliskirche, **11**

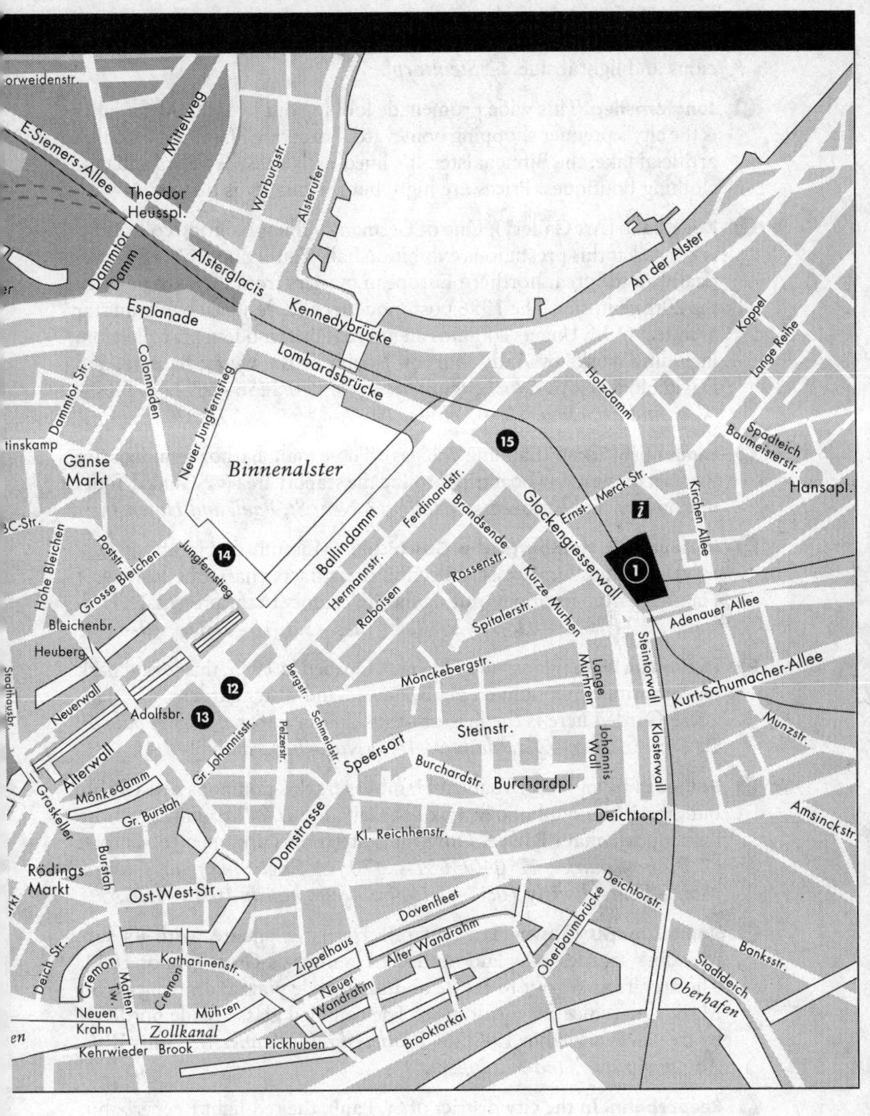

orweidenstr.
E-Siemers-Allee
Mittelweg
Theodor Heusspl.
Warburgstr.
Alsterufer
Dammtor Damm
Alsterglacis
An der Alster
Esplanade
Kennedybrücke
Koppel
Lombardsbrücke
Lange Reihe
Colonnaden
Dammtor Str.
Neuer Jungfernstieg
Holzdamm
Spadteich
Baumeisterstr.
tinskamp
Gänse Markt
Binnenalster
15
Ferdinandstr.
Brandsende
Glockengiesserwall
Ernst-Merck Str.
Kirchen Allee
Hansapl.
i
BC-Str.
Poststr.
Jungfernstieg
14
Ballindamm
Hermannstr.
Rossenstr.
Kurze Murhen
1
Hohe Bleichen
Grosse Bleichen
Raboisen
Spitalerstr.
Adenauer Allee
Bleichenbr.
Heuberg
Bergstr.
Mönckebergstr.
Lange Murhren
Steintorwall
Kurt-Schumacher-Allee
Stadthausbr.
Neuerwall
12
Adolfsbr.
13
Schmiedstr.
Steinstr.
Johannis Wall
Klosterwall
Munzstr.
Alterwall
Gr. Johannisstr.
Pelzerstr.
Speersort
Burchardstr.
Burchardpl.
Mönkedamm
Graskeller
Gr. Burstah
Domstrasse
Deichtorpl.
Amsinckstr.
Kl. Reichhenstr.
Rödings Markt
Burstah
Ost-West-Str.
Deichtorstr.
Dovenfleet
Oberbaumbrücke
Banksstr.
Deich Str.
Cremon
Katharinenstr.
Zippelhaus
Alter Wandrahm
Stadtdeich
Oberhafen
Matten Tw.
Cremon
Neuer Wandrahm
Neuen Krahn
Mühren
Zollkanal
Brooktorkai
Kehrwieder
Brook
Pickhuben

by a 460-ft-wide glazed roof that is supported only by pillars at each end. The largest structure of its kind in Europe, it is remarkably spacious and light inside. ✉ *Steintorpl.*

⓮ **Jungfernstieg.** This wide promenade looking out over the Alster lakes is the city's premier shopping boulevard, bordering Hamburg's smaller artificial lake, the Binnenalster. It's lined with classy jewelers and chic clothing boutiques. Prices are high, but the quality is first-rate.

★ ⓯ **Kunsthalle** (Art Gallery). One of Germany's finest painting collections is housed at this prestigious exhibition hall. You'll find works by practically all the great northern European masters from the 14th through the 20th centuries. The 1996 post-modern cube, designed by Berlin star architect O.M. Ungers contains an international modern art collection, including works by Andy Warhol, Joseph Beuys, Georg Baselitz, and David Hockney. ✉ *Glockengiesserwall,* ☎ *040/2486–2612.* ⏲ *Tues.–Wed. and Fri.–Sun. 10–6, Thurs. 10–9.*

❻ **Landungsbrücken** (Landing Bridges). These main harbor terminals are the start of the many boat trips around the seaport area (☞ Guided Tours *in* Contacts and Resources, *below*). ✉ *Near St. Pauli and Hafenstr.*

❿ **Museum für Hamburgische Geschichte** (Museum of Hamburg History). The museum's vast collection of artifacts charts the history of Hamburg from its origins during the 9th century to the present. ✉ *Holstenwall 24,* ☎ *040/3504–2360.* ⏲ *Tues.–Sat. 10–5, Sun. 10–6.*

❸ **Planten un Blom** (Plants and Flowers). Opened in 1935, this restful park has beautifully maintained plant, flower, and water gardens. The Japanese Garden here is the largest of its kind in Europe. ✉ *Stephanspl.* 🎫 *Free.* ⏲ *Mar.–Oct., daily 9–4:45; Nov.–Feb., daily 9–3:45.*

★ ⓭ **Rathaus** (Town Hall). To most Hamburgers this pompous neo-Gothic building is the symbolic heart of the city. It has 647 rooms, six more than Buckingham Palace. Only the state rooms are open to visitors. ✉ *Rathausmarkt,* ☎ *040/3681–2470.* ⏲ *English-language tours: Mon.–Thurs. hourly 10:15–3:15, Fri.–Sun. hourly 10:15–1:15.*

⓬ **Rathausmarkt** (Town Hall Square). The large square, with its surrounding arcades, was laid out after Hamburg's Great Fire of 1842. The architects set out to create an Italian-style piazza, drawing on St. Mark's in Venice for inspiration. The rounded glass arcade bordered by trees was added in 1982. ✉ *Bordered by Johannesstr., Alter Wall, Adolphsbrücke, and Adolphspl.*

❹ **Reeperbahn.** In the city district of St. Pauli, the red-light Reeperbahn, its major thoroughfare, offers a broad menu of entertainment in addition to the striptease and sex shows. Beyond this strip, St. Pauli is dominated by its waterfront at the river Elbe, giving this part of Hamburg a maritime, though run-down, appeal.

★ ⓫ **St. Michaliskirche** (St. Michael's Church). The finest Baroque church in northern Germany serves as Hamburg's principal Protestant house of worship. St. Michael's has a distinctive 433-ft brick-and-iron tower bearing the largest tower clock in Germany, 26 ft in diameter. Just above the clock is the viewing platform, which affords a magnificent panorama of the city, the Elbe River, and the Alster Lakes. ✉ *Krayenkamp 10,* ☎ *040/3767–8100.* ⏲ *Apr.–Sept., Mon.–Sat. 9–6, Sun. 11:30–5:30; Oct.–Mar., Mon.–Sat. 10–4:30, Sun. 11:30–4:30.*

Dining and Lodging

Hamburg restaurants range from simple harborside taverns to sophisticated upscale establishments, and many of them serve fresh seafood, cooked in the traditional northern German way. A flotilla of boats brings a wide variety of fish to Hamburg's harbor. One of the most celebrated of the robust local specialties is *Aalsuppe* (eel soup), a tangy concoction resembling bouillabaisse. *Räucheraal* (smoked eel) is also worth sampling. Another popular dish is the sailors' favorite *Labskaus,* a stew made from pickled meat, potatoes, and sometimes herring; it is usually garnished with a fried egg, sour pickles, and plenty of beets. For details and price-category definitions, *see* Dining *in* Germany A to Z, *above.*

The city has a full range of hotels, from luxury properties to simple pensions. The nearly year-round conference and convention business keeps most rooms booked, and rates are high, although special weekend reductions are common. The tourist office can help you with reservations; try the HAM-Hotline (☎ 040/3005–1300) to book a room. A fee of DM 5 is charged when you make your reservation; this is then deducted from your hotel bill. For details and price-category definitions, *see* Lodging *in* Germany A to Z, *above.*

$$$$ ✕ **Landhaus Dill.** A fine fin de siècle building with views of the Elbe houses this stylish restaurant, with crisp linen on the tables, glistening tile floors, and exquisite entrées. The lobster salad is prepared at your table, and the rack of lamb comes hot from the kitchen with an aromatic thyme sauce. ✉ *Elbchaussee 94,* ☎ *040/390–5077. Jacket and tie. AE, DC, MC, V. Closed Mon.*

$$$ ★ ✕ **Landhaus Scherrer.** A popular, country house–style restaurant in the city's Altona district, Scherrer fuses sophisticated nouvelle specialties with more down-to-earth local dishes. ✉ *Elbchaussee 130,* ☎ *040/880–1325. Jacket and tie. AE, DC, MC, V. Closed Sun. and holidays.*

$$$ ★ ✕ **Nil.** This is one of the new hip places where the media scene, the intellectual and cultural elite of Hamburg, gathers. Nestled in an old '50s-style shoe shop, it spans three floors. The kitchen turns out high-powered seafood and modern German fare such as *Rinderfilet mit Walnuß-Rosmarinkruste, Schwarzwurzeln und Madeirasauce* (filleted beef in a walnut-rosemary crust, with Madeira sauce) or *Zander in Nussbutter mit Weinkraut und glasierten Trauben* (zander in nut butter with wine cabbage and glacéed grapes). ✉ *Neuer Pferdemarkt 5,* ☎ *040/4397–823. Reservations essential for dinner. AE, DC, MC, V.*

$$$ ★ ✕ **Peter Lembcke.** There's no better place to eat eel soup or the traditional Hamburg *Labskaus*—a stew made from pickled meat, potatoes, and (sometimes) herring—than this small, traditional restaurant just north of the train station. ✉ *Holzdamm 49,* ☎ *040/243–290. AE, DC, MC, V. Closed Sun. and holidays. No lunch Sat.*

$$$ ★ ✕ **Rive.** Fresh seafood, including oysters and clams, are served right at the harbor, in a building representing a ship, where mostly media people hang out enjoying spectacular views. ✉ *Van der Smissen Str. 1, Kreuzfahrt-Center,* ☎ *040/3805–919. Reservations essential. AE.*

$$ ✕ **Ahrberg.** Next to the river in Blankenese, the Ahrberg has a pleasant terrace for summer dining and a cozy, wood-paneled dining room for colder days. The menu features a range of traditional German dishes and seafood specialties—often served together. Try the shrimp and potato soup and the fresh carp in season. ✉ *Strandweg 33, Blankenese,* ☎ *040/860–438. AE, MC. Closed Sun.*

$$ ★ ✕ **Eisenstein.** This place, housed in a 19th-century industrial complex with high ceilings and dark red brick walls, is very rustic. The crowd is joyful and mostly stylish. A sure bet are the daily Italian-Mediterranean dishes, including pasta and pizzas, but also duck, pheasant, and an amazing assortment of fine wines from around the world. ✉ *Friedensallee 9,* ☎ *040/3904–606. Reservations essential for dinner. No credit cards.*

$$ ✕ **Fischerhaus.** Hamburg's famous fish market is right outside the door of this traditional old restaurant, which accounts for the variety and quality of seafood dishes on its menu. Meat-eaters are also catered to, and the soups (especially fish soup) are legendary. It's always busy, so be sure to reserve a table and arrive on time. ✉ *St. Pauli Fischmarkt 14,* ☎ *040/314–053. AE, DC, MC, V.*

$$$$ ★ **Kempinski Hotel Atlantic Hamburg.** The sumptuous Atlantic has been a focal point of Hamburg's social scene since it opened in 1909. Rooms, whether traditionally furnished or more modern, exude an understated luxury, and suites are just short of palatial; the service is swift and hushed. ✉ *An der Alster 72-79, D-20099,* ☎ *040/28880,* FAX *040/24729. 254 rooms, 13 suites. 2 restaurants. AE, DC, MC, V.*

$$$$ ★ **Vier Jahreszeiten.** This handsome 19th-century town house hotel offers scenic views of the Binnenalster and is rated, with its old-style rooms, impeccable service, and excellent food, among the world's best. ✉ *Neuer Jungfernstieg 9–14, D-20354,* ☎ *040/34940,* FAX *040/349–4602. 158 rooms, 23 suites. 3 restaurants. AE, DC, MC, V.*

$$$ **Aussen Alster.** Crisp and contemporary in design, this boutique hotel gives personal attention to its guests. Rooms are compact; most have a full bathroom, and a few have a shower only. The cool, modern decor is warmed by a fireplace and a friendly bar. ✉ *Schmilinskystr. 11, D-20099,* ☎ *040/241–557,* FAX *040/280–3231. 27 rooms. Restaurant. AE, DC, MC, V.*

$$$ **Hotel Prem.** Most guests here are repeats who have their favorite rooms; no two rooms are the same. The Adenauer Suite (named for the former West Germany's then-chancellor, who stayed here), for example, is traditionally furnished, including an antique chaise longue and a period writing desk in a small alcove with a lake view. ✉ *An der Alster 9, D–20099,* ☎ *040/2417–2628,* FAX *040/2803–851. 44 rooms, 11 suites. Restaurant. AE, DC, MC, V.*

$$ **Kronprinz.** For its down-market location (on a busy street opposite the railway station) and its moderate price, the Kronprinz is a surprisingly attractive hotel. Rooms are individually styled, modern but homey; ask for Number 45, with its mahogany and red-plush decor. ✉ *Kirchenallee 46, D-20099,* ☎ *040/243–258,* FAX *040/280–1097. 69 rooms. Restaurant. AE, DC, MC, V.*

$$ ★ **Wedina.** Rooms at this small hotel are neat, compact, and completely renovated. When making a reservation, ask for a room in the stylish 100-year-old-plus "Yellow House," which is rustic Italian in style and has an elegant parquet floor. ✉ *Gurlittstr. 23, D-20099,* ☎ *040/243–011,* FAX *040/280–3894. 27 rooms. Pool. AE, DC, MC, V.*

Nightlife and the Arts

From about 10 PM on, the Reeperbahn really shakes into life, and *everything* is for sale. Among the Reeperbahn's even rougher side streets, the most notorious is the Grosse Freiheit, which means "Great Freedom." This area is not just a red-light district, however. Side streets are rapidly filling up with a mixture of yuppie bars, restaurants, and theaters that are somewhat more refined than the seamen's bars and sex shops. The Hans-Albers-Platz is a center of this revival. The bar **La Paloma** (✉ Gerhardstr. 2, ☎ 040/314–512) is stylish. The **Hans-Albers-Ecke** (✉ Hans-Albers-Pl., ☎ 040/317–5960) is an old sailors' hangout. The **Theater Schmidt** (✉ Spielbudenpl. 27–28, ☎ 040/3177–8899) presents variety shows most evenings to a packed house.

Hamburg Essentials

Arriving and Departing

BY BUS

Hamburg's bus station, the **Zentral-Omnibus-Bahnhof** (ZOB; ☎ 040/247–575), is right behind the Hauptbahnhof (☞ By Train, *below*). For more information contact the Deutsche Touring-Gesellschaft (✉ Am Römerhof 17, D-60486 Frankfurt/Main, ☎ 069/79030).

BY CAR

Hamburg is easier to handle by car than are many other German cities and is relatively uncongested with traffic. Incoming autobahns connect with Hamburg's three beltways, which then take you easily to the downtown area. Follow the signs for STADTZENTRUM (downtown).

BY PLANE

Fuhlsbüttel, Hamburg's international airport, is 11 km (7 mi) northwest of the city. Lufthansa connects Hamburg with all other major German cities and European capitals.

Between the Airport and Downtown. An Airport-City-Bus runs nonstop between the airport and Hamburg's Hauptbahnhof daily at 20-minute intervals. Buses run from 5:40 AM to 10:30 PM. Tickets are DM 8 per person. The Airport-Express (Bus 110) runs every 10 minutes between the airport and the Ohlsdorf U- and S-bahn stations, a 17-minute ride from the main train station. The fare is DM 10. If you're picking up a rental car at the airport, follow the signs to STADTZENTRUM (downtown).

BY TRAIN

Hamburg is a terminus for main-line service to northern Germany. There are two principal stations: the Hauptbahnhof (main train station; ✉ Adenauerallee 78, ☎ 040/19419), and Hamburg-Altona.

Getting Around

BY PUBLIC TRANSPORTATION

The comprehensive **city and suburban transportation system** includes the U-bahn (subway) network, which connects efficiently with the S-bahn (suburban train lines), and an exemplary bus service. Tickets cover travel by all three, as well as by harbor ferry. The one- and three-day Hamburg CARD allows free travel on all public transportation within the city, free admission to state museums, and discounts of approximately 30% on most bus, train, and boat tours. For information about this card inquire at tourist offices (☞ Visitor Information, *below*). Information on the public-transportation system can be obtained directly from the **Hamburg Passenger Transport Board** (HVV; ✉ Steinstr. 1, ☎ 040/322–911 or 040/19449).

BY TAXI

Taxi meters start at DM 3.60, and the fare is DM 2.20 per km (½ mi), plus 50 pfennigs for each piece of luggage. To order a taxi call 040/441–011, 040/686–868, or 040/611–061.

Contacts and Resources

CONSULATES

U.S. Consulate General (✉ Alsterufer 28, ☎ 040/411–710). **British Consulate General** (✉ Harvestehuder Weg 8a, ☎ 040/448–0320).

EMERGENCIES

Police (☎ 110). **Ambulance and Fire Department** (☎ 112). **Medical Emergencies** (☎ 040/228–022). **Dentist** (☎ 040/11500).

ENGLISH-LANGUAGE BOOKSTORE

Try **Frensche International** (✉ Spitalerstr. 26c, ☎ 040/327–585).

GUIDED TOURS

Orientation. Bus tours of the city, with an English-speaking guide, leave from Kirchenallee (in front of the Hauptbahnhof) at regular intervals. The 1¾-hour tour costs DM 26. For an additional DM 11, tours can be combined with a one-hour boat trip around Hamburg harbor. For more information contact a city tourist office (☞ Visitor Information, *below*).

Boat. Tours of the harbor leave every half hour in summer, less frequently during the winter, from Piers (Landungsbrücken) 1, 2, 3, and 7. The one-hour tour costs DM 15. A special harbor tour with an English-speaking guide leaves Pier 1 at 11:15 daily from March through November (same price). The Störtebeker line (☎ 040/2274–2375) has a special party boat on which you can wine, dine, and dance. For additional information on harbor tours call 040/311–7070, 040/313–130, 040/313–959, or 040/314–611. Fifty-minute cruises of the Binnenalster and Aussenalster leave from the Jungfernstieg.

TRAVEL AGENCIES

American Express (✉ Ballindamm 39, ☎ 040/309–080), and at the Airport Fuhlsbüttel (✉ terminal 4, level 2, ☎ 040/5005–980). **Hapag-Lloyd** (✉ Verkehrspavillon Jungfernstieg, ☎ 040/3258–5640).

VISITOR INFORMATION

Hauptbahnhof (Central Train Station, ✉ Steintorpl., ☎ 040/3005–1200). **St. Pauli Landungsbrücken** (✉ boat landings, between piers 4 and 5; ☎ 040/300–51200).

BERLIN

The year 1999 will establish Berlin's role as capital of Germany, as the Federal Parliament moves to the city. Due to burgeoning building development, the city is still the Continent's largest construction site. As ever, life here is literally on the razor's edge.

Exploring Berlin

Visiting Berlin is still a bittersweet experience, as so many of the triumphs and tragedies of the past are tied up with the bustling present. The result can be either dispiriting or exhilarating. By European standards, Berlin isn't too old. Although already a royal residence during the 15th century, Berlin really came into its own 3 centuries later, under the rule of King Friedrich II—Frederick the Great—whose liberal reforms and artistic patronage led the way as the city developed into a major cultural capital.

What Berlin was forced to endure during the 20th century would have crushed the spirit of most other cities. Hitler and his supporters destroyed the city's reputation for tolerance and plunged Berlin headlong into the war that led to the wholesale destruction of monuments and houses. And after World War II, Berlin was still to face the bitter division of the city and the construction of the infamous Wall in 1961.

Downtown Berlin

Numbers in the margin correspond to points of interest on the Downtown Berlin map.

★ 13 **Ägyptisches Museum** (Egyptian Museum). This small but outstanding museum is home to the beautiful portrait sculpture head of Nefertiti. The 3,300-year-old queen is the centerpiece of a fascinating collection of Egyptian antiquities that includes some of the finest preserved mummies outside Cairo. ✉ *Schloss-Str. 70,* ☎ *030/320–911.* ⏲ *Mon.–Thurs. 9–5, weekends 10–5.*

★ 9 **Berliner Mauer** (Berlin Wall). One of only four still-standing sections of the Berlin Wall has been left here, in the city's historic heart. ✉ *Along Niederkirchnerstr.*

★ 6 **Brandenburger Tor** (Brandenburg Gate). Berlin's premier historic landmark was built in 1788 to celebrate the triumphant Prussian armies. The monumental gate was cut off from West Berlin by the Wall, and it became a focal point of celebrations marking the reunification of Berlin and of all Germany. The square behind the gate, the **Pariser Platz**, has regained its pre-war design. Among the new buildings erected here between 1996 and 1998 is the American Embassy. You'll reach the gate by walking along Strasse des 17. Juni (June 17th Street). ✉ *Under den Linden at Pariser Pl.*

14 **Dahlemer Museen** (Dahlem Museums). This unique complex of six museums includes the **Museum fur Völkerkunde** (Ethnographic Museum), internationally famous for its arts and artifacts from Africa, Asia, the South Seas, and the Americas, and the **Skulpturensammlung** (Sculpture Collection), which houses Byzantine and European sculpture from the 3rd through the 18th centuries. *Please note:* Due to the reorganization of Berlin's major state museums, both the Museum für Völkerkunde and the Skulpturensammlung, as well as parts of the other four museums at the Dahlem location, will be closed in 1999. ✉ *Lansstr. 8 and Arnimalle 23–27, subway line U-2 to Dahlem-Dorf station,* ☎ *030/83011.* ⏲ *Tues.–Fri. 9–5, weekends 10–5.*

15 **Grunewald** (Green Forest). Together with its Wannsee lakes, this splendid forest is the most popular green retreat for Berliners, who come out in force, swimming, sailing their boats, tramping through the woods, and riding horseback. In winter a downhill ski run and even a ski jump operate on the modest slopes of Teufelsberg hill. Excursion steamers ply the water wonderland of the Wannsee, the Havel River, and the Müggelsee (☞ Guided Tours *in* Berlin Essentials, *below*). ✉ *Southwest of downtown western Berlin.*

★ 11 **Haus am Checkpoint Charlie** (House at Checkpoint Charlie–The Wall Museum). The history of the events leading up to the Wall's construction can be followed in the museum that arose at its most famous crossing point, at Friedrichstrasse, the second cross street heading east. Checkpoint Charlie, as it was known, disappeared along with the Wall. ✉ *Friedrichstr. 44,* ☎ *030/251–1031.* 🎫 *DM 7.50.* ⏲ *Daily 9 AM–10 PM.*

★ 2 **Kaiser-Wilhelm-Gedächtniskirche** (Kaiser Wilhelm Memorial Church). This landmark had come to symbolize West Berlin, and it still is a dramatic reminder of the futile destructiveness of war. The shell of the tower is all that remains of the church that was built at the end of the 19th century and dedicated to Kaiser Wilhelm I. Surrounding the tower are the new church and bell tower. ✉ *Breitscheidpl.,* ☎ *030/218–5023.* 🎫 *Free.* ⏲ *Old Tower, Mon.–Sat. 10–4; Memorial Church, daily 9–7. Closed holidays.*

★ 8 **Kulturforum** (Cultural Forum). With its unique ensemble of museums, galleries, and libraries, the complex is considered one of Germany's cultural jewels. It includes the **Philharmonie** (Philharmonic Hall), home of the Berlin Philharmonic orchestra. ✉ *Matthäikirchstr. 1,* ☎ *030/2548–8132.* ⏲ *Box office: weekdays 3:30–6, weekends 11–2.*

The **Kunstgewerbemuseum** (Museum of Decorative Arts) displays arts and crafts of Europe from the Middle Ages to the present. ✉ *Matthäikirchpl. 10,* ☎ *030/266–2911.* 🎫 *DM 8 (day card covers 1-day admission to all museums at Kulturforum and is available at all museums.* ⏲ *Tues.–Fri. 9–5, weekends 10–5.*

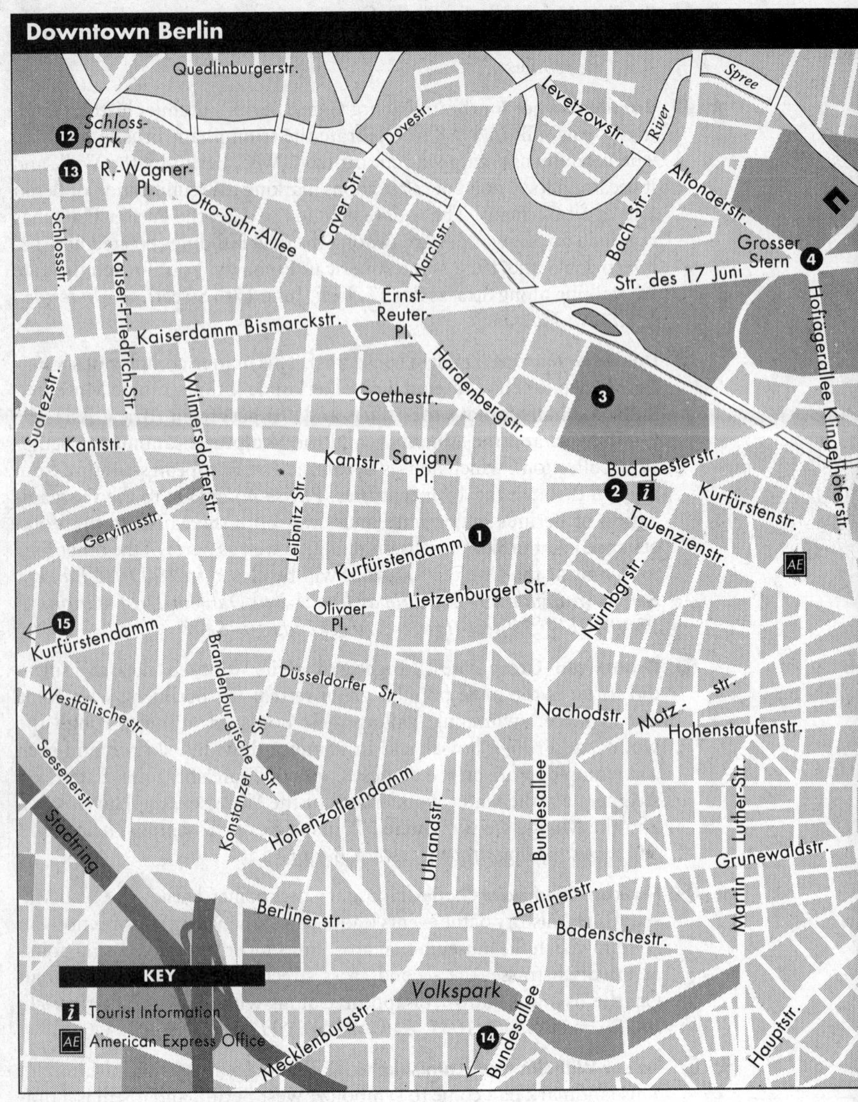

Ägyptisches Museum, **13**
Berliner Mauer, **9**
Brandenburger Tor, **6**
Dahlemer Museen, **14**
Grunewald, **15**
Haus am Checkpoint Charlie, **11**
Kaiser-Wilhelm-Gedächtniskirche, **2**
Kulturforum, **8**
Kurfürstendamm, **1**
Potsdamer Platz, **7**
Prinz-Albrecht-Gelände, **10**
Reichstag, **5**
Schloss Charlottenburg, **12**
Siegessäule, **4**
Zoologischer Garten, **3**

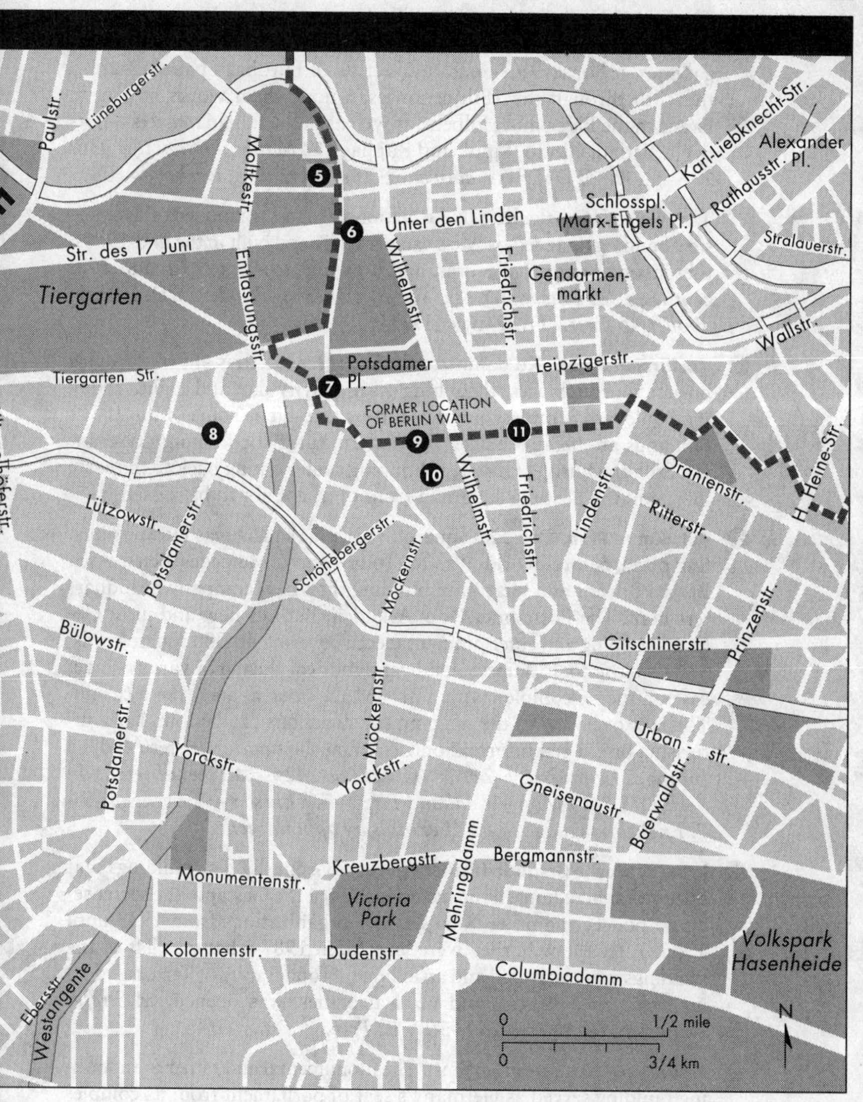

Paulstr.
Lüneburgerstr.
Moltkestr.
Entlastungsstr.
Str. des 17 Juni
Tiergarten
Tiergarten Str.
Unter den Linden
Wilhelmstr.
Friedrichstr.
Schlosspl.
(Marx-Engels Pl.)
Karl-Liebknecht-Str.
Alexander Pl.
Rathausstr.
Stralauerstr.
Gendarmenmarkt
Wallstr.
Potsdamer Pl.
Leipzigerstr.
FORMER LOCATION OF BERLIN WALL
Oranienstr.
Ritterstr.
Lindenstr.
H. Heine-Str.
Lützowstr.
Potsdamerstr.
Schönebergerstr.
Möckernstr.
Bülowstr.
Gitschinerstr.
Prinzenstr.
Urban str.
Yorckstr.
Gneisenaustr.
Baerwaldstr.
Bergmannstr.
Mehringdamm
Kreuzbergstr.
Monumentenstr.
Victoria Park
Kolonnenstr.
Dudenstr.
Columbiadamm
Volkspark Hasenheide
Eberstr.
Westangente
0
1/2 mile
0
3/4 km
N

The **Gemäldegalerie** (painting gallery) reunites formerly separated collections from eastern and western Berlin. One of Germany's finest art galleries, it houses an extensive selection of European paintings from the 13th through the 18th centuries, among them works by Dürer, Cranach the Elder, and Holbein, as well as of the Italian masters—Botticelli, Titian, Giotto, Lippi, and Raphael. ✉ *Matthäikirchpl.,* ☎ *030/266–2002.* *DM 8 (☞ above).* ⏲ *Tues.–Fri. 9–5, weekends 10–5.*

The **Neue Nationalgalerie** (New National Gallery), a modern glass-and-steel building designed by Mies van der Rohe and built in the mid-1960s, presents paintings, sculptures, and drawings from the 19th and 20th centuries. ✉ *Potsdamer Str. 50,* ☎ *030/266–2662.* *DM 8 (☞ above).* ⏲ *Tues.–Fri. 9–5, weekends 10–5.*

★ ❶ **Kurfürstendamm.** Ku'damm, as the Berliners call it, is one of Europe's busiest thoroughfares, throbbing with activity day and night. Today the boulevard is undergoing a vigorous face-lift as some of the 1950s buildings are being replaced by modern, futuristic-looking skyscrapers. Still, the **Europa Center,** a shopping center dating back to the early '60s, and the bustling square in front of it, are not to be missed.

★ ❼ **Potsdamer Platz** (Potsdam Square). This huge square was Europe's busiest plaza before World War II. Today Sony, Mercedes Benz, Asea Brown Boveri, and Hertie are building their new company headquarters here. The **Potsdamer Platz Arkaden,** Berlin's new and most elegant shopping and entertainment mecca covering 40,000 square yards, houses close to 150 upscale shops, a musical theater, a variety stage, cafés, a movie complex with a 3D-IMAX cinema, and even a casino. The best overview of the ongoing constructions can be found at a futuristic, bright-red **Information Center,** at the square's eastern end. ✉ *Infobox, Leipziger Pl. 21,* ☎ *030/2266–2424.* *Free, observation deck DM 2.* ⏲ *Mon.–Wed. and Fri. 9–7, Thurs. 9–9, weekends 9–7. English-language tours of exhibit by appointment.*

❿ **Prinz-Albrecht-Gelände** (Prince Albrecht Grounds). The buildings that once stood here housed the headquarters of the Gestapo, the secret security police, and other Nazi security organizations from 1933 until 1945. After the war, they were leveled; in 1987 what was left of the buildings was excavated and an exhibit, "Topography of Terrors," documenting their history and Nazi atrocities, was opened. ✉ *Stresemannstr. 110,* ☎ *030/254–509.* *Free.* ⏲ *Daily 10–6.*

❺ **Reichstag** (German Parliament). The monumental and rather grim-looking building served as Germany's seat of parliament from its completion in 1894 until 1933, when it was gutted by fire under suspicious circumstances. The Bundestag, the lower house of parliament, will again convene here. The building opens to the public in late 1998. ✉ *Pl. der Republik.*

★ ⓬ **Schloss Charlottenburg** (Charlottenburg Palace). Built at the end of the 17th century by King Frederick I for his wife, Queen Sophie Charlotte, this grand palace and its magnificent gardens were progressively enlarged for later royal residents and now include museums. ✉ *Luisenpl., U-7 subway line to Richard-Wagner-Pl. station. From the station walk east along Otto-Suhr-Allee,* ☎ *030/320–911.* ⏲ *Tues.–Fri. 9–5, weekends 10–5.*

❹ **Siegessäule** (Victory Column). The memorial erected in 1873 to commemorate four Prussian military campaigns, is at the center of the 630-acre **Tiergarten** (Animal Park), the former hunting grounds of the Great Elector. From its 285 steps to its 213-ft summit, you'll be rewarded with a fine view of Berlin. ✉ *Am Grossen Stern,* ☎ *030/391–2961.* ⏲ *Mon. 1–6, Tues.–Sun. and holidays 9–6.*

★ 3 **Zoologischer Garten** (Zoological Gardens). Berlin's zoo has the world's largest variety of individual types of fauna along with a fascinating aquarium. ✉ *Hardenbergpl. 8 and Budapester Str. 34,* ☎ *030/254–010.* 🎟 *Zoo DM 11, aquarium DM 11, combined ticket DM 18.* ⏲ *Zoo, daily 9–6:30 or until dusk in winter; aquarium, daily 9–6.*

Historic Berlin

Numbers in the margin correspond to points of interest on the Historic Berlin map.

22 **Berliner Dom** (Berlin Cathedral). The impressive 19th-century cathedral with its enormous green copper dome is one of the great ecclesiastical buildings in Germany. Its main nave was reopened in June 1993 after a 20-year renovation. More than 80 sarcophagi of Prussian royals are on display in the cathedral's catacombs. ✉ *Am Lustgarten,* ☎ *030/202–69136.* 🎟 *Balcony DM 5, museum free.* ⏲ *Church Mon.–Sat. 9–6:30, Sun. 11:30–6:30; balcony Mon.–Sat. 10–6, Sun. 11:30–6; museum Wed.–Sun. 10–6.*

25 **Berliner Rathaus** (Berlin City Hall). After the city's reunification this pompous symbol of Berlin's 19th-century urban pride again became the seat of the city government. ✉ *Jüdenstr. at Rathausstr.,* ☎ *030/24010.* 🎟 *Free.* ⏲ *Weekdays 9–6.*

20 **Deutsches Historisches Museum** (German Historical Museum). The one-time Prussian Zeughaus (arsenal), a magnificent Baroque building constructed in 1695–1730, houses Germany's National History Museum, a compendium of German history from the Middle Ages to the present. ✉ *Unter den Linden 2,* ☎ *030/215–020.* 🎟 *Free.* ⏲ *Thurs.–Tues. 10–6. Tours by appointment only. English-speaking guides available for DM 60.*

24 **Fernsehturm** (TV Tower). At 1,198 ft high, eastern Berlin's TV tower is 710 ft *taller* than western Berlin's. Its observation deck affords the best view of Berlin; the city's highest café, which revolves, is also up here. ✉ *Alexanderpl.,* ☎ *030/242–3333.* ⏲ *Daily 9 AM–midnight.*

★ 16 **Friedrichstrasse** (Frederick Street). For a sense of times past and new, head south on historic Friedrichstrasse, where you'll pass various new business and shopping buildings, including the **Friedrichstadtpassagen,** a gigantic shopping and business complex. At the corner of Französische Strasse is the French department store **Galeries Lafayette.** ✉ *Französische Str. 23,* ☎ *030/209–480.*

17 **Gendarmenmarkt** (Gendarme Market). With its beautifully reconstructed **Schauspielhaus** (Theatre)—built in 1818, and now one of the city's main concert halls—and twin **Deutscher** (German) and **Französischer** (French) cathedrals, this historic square is one of Europe's finest piazzas. The French cathedral houses a museum displaying the history of Huguenot immigrants in Berlin while the German cathedral showcases an official exhibit on German history. ✉ *Deutscher Dom, Gendarmenmarkt 1,* ☎ *030/2273–2141.* 🎟 *Free.* ⏲ *Tues.–Sun. 10–5.* ✉ *Französischer Dom, Gendarmenmarkt,* ☎ *030/229–1760.* ⏲ *Tues.–Sat. noon–5, Sun. 11–5.*

★ 28 **Hamburger Bahnhof** (Hamburg Train Station). Berlin's newest museum for contemporary art is housed in an early 19th-century structure, once a major train station. Remodeled and given a huge and spectacular new wing—a stunning interplay of glass, steel, color, and sunlight—it displays an outstanding private collection of works by German artists Joseph Beuys

Historic Berlin

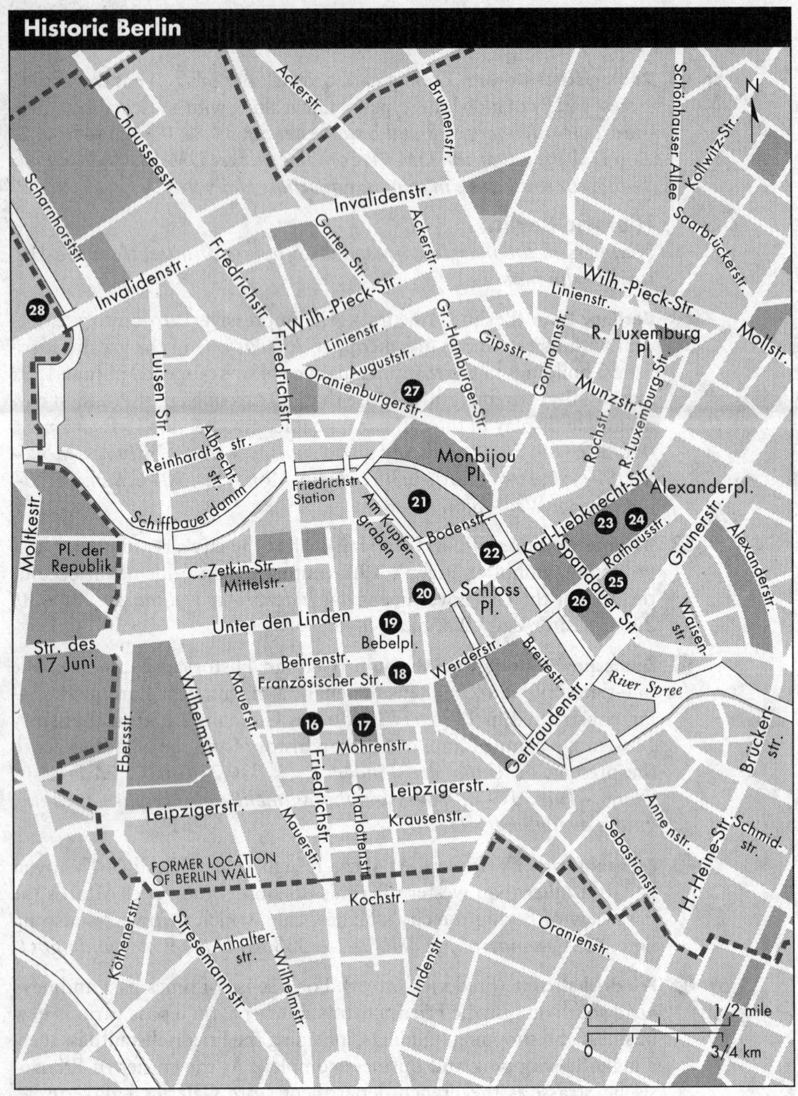

Berliner Dom, **22**
Berliner Rathaus, **25**
Deutsches Historisches Museum, **20**
Fernsehturm, **24**
Friedrichstrasse, **16**
Gendarmenmarkt, **17**
Hamburger Bahnhof, **28**
Museumsinsel, **21**
Neue Synagoge, **27**
Nikolaiviertel, **26**
St. Hedwigs-kathedrale, **18**
St. Marienkirche, **23**
Staatsoper Unter den Linden, **19**

and Anselm Kiefer as well as paintings by Andy Warhol, Cy Twombly, Robert Rauschenberg, and Robert Morris. ✉ *Invalidenstr. 50–51,* ☎ *030/3978–340.* 🎫 *DM 12.* 🕐 *Tues.–Fri. 10–6, weekends 11–6.*

★ 21 **Museumsinsel** (Museum Island). This unique complex contains four world-class museums. The **Altes Museum** (Old Museum; entrance on Lustgarten) is an austere neoclassical building, decorated with red marble. The collections here include postwar art from some of Germany's most prominent artists and numerous works by the old masters. The **Alte Nationalgalerie** (Old National Gallery; Bodestrasse), displays 19th- and 20th-century paintings and sculptures. The **Pergamonmuseum** (Am Kupfergraben), one of Europe's greatest museums, takes its name from its principal exhibit, the Pergamon Altar, a monumental Greek sculpture dating from 180 BC that occupies an entire city block. To the north is the **Bodemuseum** (Am Kupfergraben; entrance on Monbijoubrücke), with an outstanding collection of early Christian, Byzantine, and Egyptian art. *Please note:* Due to reconstruction and a major reorganization of the Museum Island's collections, the Bodemuseum and parts of the Alte Nationalgalerie are closed to the public through the year 2001. ✉ *Museumsinsel; right from Unter den Linden along Spree Canal via Am Zeughaus and Am Kupfergraben;* ☎ *030/209–050 for all museums.* 🎫 *DM 8, free 1st Sun. of month.* 🕐 *Tues.–Sun. 10–6.*

27 **Neue Synagoge** (New Synagogue). Completed in 1866, in Middle Eastern style, this was one of Germany's most beautiful synagogues until it was seriously damaged on *Kristallnacht,* November 9, 1938, when synagogues and Jewish stores across Germany were vandalized, looted, and burned. Today the outside is perfectly restored, and the interior is connected to the **Centrum Judaicum** (Jewish Center)—an institution of Jewish culture and learning that frequently stages exhibitions and other cultural events. ✉ *Oranienburger Str. 28/30,* ☎ *030/2840–1316.* 🕐 *Sun.–Thurs. 10–6, Fri. 10–2.*

26 **Nikolaiviertel** (Nikolai Quarter). Berlin's oldest historic quarter has been handsomely rebuilt and is now filled with delightful shops, cafés, and restaurants. On the quarter's Nikolaikirchplatz is Berlin's oldest building, the **Nikolaikirche** (St. Nicholas Church), dating from 1230. ✉ *Nikolaikirchpl.,* ☎ *030/2380–900.* 🎫 *DM 3.* 🕐 *Tues.–Sun. 10–6.*

18 **St. Hedwigskathedrale** (St. Hedwig's Cathedral). When Berlin's premier Catholic church was erected in 1747, it was the first to be built in resolutely Protestant Berlin since the Reformation of the 16th century. ✉ *Hinter der Katholischen Kirche 3,* ☎ *030/203–4810.* 🕐 *Weekdays 10–5, Sun. 1–5.*

23 **St. Marienkirche** (Church of St. Mary). This medieval church, one of the finest in Berlin, is worth a visit for its late-Gothic fresco *Der Totentanz* (*Dance of Death*). ✉ *Karl-Liebknecht-Str. 8,* ☎ *030/242–4467.* 🕐 *Mon.–Thurs. 10–noon and 1–5, Sat. noon–4:30, Sun. noon–5. Free tours Mon.–Thurs. at 1, Sun. at 11:45.*

19 **Staatsoper Unter den Linden** (German State Opera). This lavishly restored hall is Berlin's prime opera house. ✉ *Unter den Linden 7,* ☎ *030/2035–4555.* 🕐 *Box office: weekdays 10–6, weekends 2–6. Reservations by phone: weekdays 10–8, weekends 2–8.*

Dining and Lodging

Dining in Berlin can mean sophisticated nouvelle creations in upscale restaurants or hearty local specialties in atmospheric and inexpensive inns. Typical are *Eisbein mit Sauerkraut,* (knuckle of pork with sauerkraut), *Spanferkel* (suckling pig), *Berliner Schüsselsülze* (potted meat in aspic), *Schlachterplatte* (mixed grill), and *Currywurst* (chubby and very spicy frankfurters sold at wurst stands). For details and price-category definitions, *see* Dining *in* Germany A to Z, *above*.

Year-round business conventions and the influx of summer tourists mean you should make reservations for hotels well in advance. For lodging in Berlin add DM 50 to the price chart categories given in Lodging *in* Germany A to Z, *above*.

$$$$ ★ ✕ **Bamberger Reiter.** At one of the city's best restaurants, Tyrolean chef Franz Raneburger relies heavily on fresh market produce for his *Neue Deutsche Küche* (new German cuisine), so the menu changes from day to day. ✉ *Regensburger Str. 7,* ☎ *030/218–4282. Reservations essential. AE, DC, V. Closed Sun., Mon., Jan. 1–15.*

$$$ ★ ✕ **Borchardt.** At this fashionable meeting place, columns, red plush benches, and an Art Nouveau mosaic create the impression of a 1920s salon. Entrées are prepared with a French accent. ✉ *Französische Str. 47,* ☎ *030/203–971–17. Reservations essential. AE, V.*

$$$ ✕ **Paris Bar.** This trendy restaurant in Charlottenburg attracts a polyglot clientele of film stars, artists, entrepreneurs, and executives. The cuisine is high-powered, but medium-quality French. ✉ *Kantstr. 152,* ☎ *030/313–8052. AE.*

$$$ ★ ✕ **Rockendorf's.** The city's premier restaurant has only fixed-price menus, some with up to nine courses. Exquisitely presented, the mainly nouvelle specialties are sometimes fused with classic German cuisine. The wine list—with 800 choices—has the appropriate accompaniment to any menu. ✉ *Düsterhauptstr. 1,* ☎ *030/402–3099. Reservations essential. AE, DC, MC, V. Closed Sun., Mon., 3–4 wks in summer, and Dec. 25–Jan. 6.*

$$$ ★ ✕ **VAU.** Still a newcomer to Berlin's hip restaurant scene, the VAU serves excellent German fish and game dishes prepared by chef Kolja Kleeberg. Among his creations are combinations such as *Lammhaxe mit Schmorgemüse* (leg of lamb with braised vegetables) or *Steinbutt mit Kalbbries auf Rotweinschalotten* (turbot with veal sweetbread on shallots in red wine). The VAU's cool interior is all style and modern art. ✉ *Jägerstr. 54/55,* ☎ *030/2029–730. Reservations essential. AE, DC, MC, V. Closed Sun.*

$$ ★ ✕ **Reinhard's.** Berliners of all stripes meet here in the Nikolai Quarter to enjoy the carefully prepared entrées and to sample spirits from the amply stocked bar. *Adlon* (honey-glazed breast of duck) is one of the house specialties. Due to its success, Reinhard's has opened a second restaurant on the Ku'damm. It's much smaller but more elegant and one of the trendiest places in town. ✉ *Poststr. 28,* ☎ *030/242–5295;* ✉ *Kurfürstendamm 190,* ☎ *030/881–1621. Reservations essential on weekends. AE, DC, MC, V. Closed Dec. 24.*

$$ ✕ **Turmstuben.** Tucked away below the cupola of the French Cathedral on the north side of the beautiful Gendarmenmarkt, this restaurant is approached by a long, winding staircase. At the top of the stairs is one of Berlin's most original and attractive restaurants. The menu is short, but there's an impressive wine list. ✉ *Gendarmenmarkt 5,* ☎ *030/2044–888. Weekend reservations essential. AE, MC, V.*

$ ✕ **Alt-Cöllner Schankstuben.** A tiny restaurant and pub are contained within this charming, historic Berlin house. The menu is relatively limited, but the quality, like the service, is good. ✉ *Friedrichsgracht 50,* ☎ *030/2011–299. AE, DC, MC, V.*

$ ✕ **Blockhaus Nikolskoe.** Prussian King Frederick Wilhelm III built this Russian-style wooden lodge for his daughter Charlotte, wife of Russia's Tsar Nicholas I. It's on the eastern edge of Glienicke Park, with an open terrace (in summer) overlooking the Havel River. The Blockhaus features game dishes. ✉ *Nikolskoer Weg 15,* ☎ *030/805–2914. DC, MC, V. Closed Thurs.*

$ ★ ✕ **Café Oren.** This popular vegetarian eatery is next to the Neue Synagoge, not far from Friedrichstrasse. The restaurant buzzes with loud chatter all evening, and the atmosphere and service are welcoming and friendly. The extensive menu offers mostly Israeli and Middle Eastern fare—including delicious, filled "Moroccan Cigars." ✉ *Oranienburger Str. 28,* ☎ *030/282–8228. AE, MC, V.*

$ ✕ **Zur Letzten Instanz.** Established in 1621, Berlin's oldest restaurant combines the charming atmosphere of old-world Berlin with a limited (but tasty) choice of dishes. The emphasis here is on beer, both in the recipes and in the mug. Service can be erratic, though engagingly friendly. ✉ *Waisenstr. 14–16,* ☎ *030/242–5528. AE, DC, MC, V.*

$$$$ **Bristol Hotel Kempinski.** This grand hotel in the heart of the city has the best of Berlin's shopping on its doorstep. All the rooms and suites are luxuriously decorated and equipped, with marble bathrooms, air-conditioning, cable TV, and English-style furnishings. Children under 12 stay for free if they share their parents' room. ✉ *Kurfürstendamm 27, D-10719,* ☎ *030/884–340,* FAX *030/883–6075. 301 rooms, 52 suites. 2 restaurants, pool. AE, DC, MC, V.*

$$$$ ★ **Four Seasons Hotel Berlin.** This winner combines turn-of-the-century luxury with smooth and modern service. The facade may look rather modernistic, beside the surrounding sober Prussian architecture, but behind the walls of this first-class hotel, thick red carpets, heavy crystal chandeliers, and a romantic restaurant, including an open fireplace, make for a sophisticated and serene atmosphere. ✉ *Charlottenstr. 49, D-10117,* ☎ *030/20338,* FAX *030/2033–6166. 162 rooms, 42 suites. Restaurant. AE, DC, MC, V.*

$$$$ ★ **Grand Hotel Esplanade.** The Grand Hotel Esplanade exudes luxury. Uncompromisingly modern architecture, chic rooms, and works of art by some of Berlin's most acclaimed artists are some of its delights. ✉ *Lützowufer 15, D-10785,* ☎ *030/254–780,* FAX *030/265–1171. 369 rooms, 33 suites. 3 restaurants, pool. AE, DC, MC, V.*

$$$$ ★ **Hotel Adlon Berlin.** Berlin's first-class hotel has to live up to its almost mythical predecessor, the old Hotel Adlon, which, until its destruction during World War II, was considered to be Europe's premier resort. The new Adlon has impeccable service and an international guest list. Guest rooms are furnished in '20s style with dark-wood trimmings and bathrooms in black granite and bright marble. Some of the rooms overlook Unter den Linden and the Brandenburger Tor. ✉ *Unter den Linden 77, D–10117,* ☎ *030/22610,* FAX *030/2261–1116. 290 rooms, 47 suites. 2 restaurants, pool. AE, DC, MC, V.*

$$$$ **Inter-Continental Berlin.** Rooms and suites are all of the highest standard and their decor shows exquisite taste. The lobby is a quarter the size of a football field, opulently furnished, and just the place for afternoon tea and pastries. ✉ *Budapester Str. 2, D-10787,* ☎ *030/26020,* FAX *030/2602–80760. 511 rooms, 70 suites. 3 restaurants, pool. AE, DC, MC, V.*

$$$$ **Steigenberger Berlin.** The Steigenberger group's exemplary Berlin hotel is only a few steps from the Ku'damm but remarkably quiet. All rooms have elegant maple-wood furniture. Luxury rooms of the executive club provide late check-in, complimentary ironing and shoeshine service, a special lounge, and a small breakfast. ✉ *Los-Angeles-Pl. 1, D-10789,* ☎ *030/21270,* FAX *030/212–7799. 397 rooms, 11 suites. 2 restaurants, pool. AE, DC, MC, V.*

$$$$ **Westin Grand Hotel.** Since the takeover of former East Berlin's top hotel by the Westin Hotel Group in 1997, the Grand Hotel has undergone a major modernization. Its neoclassical pink-marble lobby, with a soaring six-story atrium, has polished brass accents, stucco work, and

rich wall coverings. Standard rooms are tastefully decorated in muted tones; bathrooms have large tubs. ✉ *Friedrichstr. 158–164, D–10117,* ☎ *030/20270,* FAX *030/2027–3362. 323 rooms, 35 suites. 6 restaurants, pool. AE, DC, MC, V.*

$$$ ★ **Estrel Residence Congress Hotel.** Europe's biggest hotel may seem huge and anonymous, but it's definitely the only way to get upscale rooms and service for less money. In the unappealing working-class district of Neukölln, it's some 20 minutes from downtown. The modern hotel does offer all amenities you can think of with quiet efficiency and comfort. Rooms are decorated with Russian art. The lobby hall is a breathtakingly bright atrium with a greenhouse atmosphere. ✉ *Sonnenallee 225, D–12057,* ☎ *030/68310,* FAX *030/6831–2345. 1,050 rooms, 75 suites. 9 restaurants, pool. AE, DC, MC, V.*

$$$ **Forum Hotel Berlin.** With its 40 stories, the Forum Hotel competes with the nearby TV tower for the title of premier downtown landmark. As one of the city's largest hotels, it is understandably somewhat impersonal. Most floors have undergone extensive renovation; when booking, ask for a newly decorated room. The high-level dining room, Panorama 37, has good food and stunning views. ✉ *Alexanderpl. 8, D-10178,* ☎ *030/23890,* FAX *030/2389–4305. 995 rooms, 12 suites. 2 restaurants. AE, DC, MC, V.*

$$ ★ **Riehmers Hofgarten.** Surrounded by the bars and restaurants of the colorful Kreuzberg district, this hotel has fast connections to the center of town. The 19th-century building's high-ceiling rooms are stylishly furnished. ✉ *Yorckstr. 83, D-10965,* ☎ *030/781–011,* FAX *030/786–6059. 21 rooms. Restaurant. AE, DC, MC, V.*

$ ★ **Gendarm Garni Hotel.** At this well-run hotel near the Gendarmenmarkt, the neat rooms are pleasantly furnished. The view and the large living room of the corner suite make it one of the better deals in town (DM 215). ✉ *Charlottenstr. 60, D-10117,* ☎ *030/200–4180,* FAX *030/208–2482. 25 rooms, 4 suites. AE, MC, V.*

Nightlife and the Arts

The Arts

The quality of opera and classical concerts in Berlin is high. Tickets are available at the theaters' own box offices, either in advance or an hour before the performance, at many hotels, and at numerous ticket agencies: **Showtime Konzert- und Theaterkassen** at the KaDeWe (✉ Tauentzienstr. 21, ☎ 030/217–7754); **Wertheim** (✉ Kurfürstendamm 181, ☎ 030/8822500); **Theaterkonzertkasse City Center** (✉ Kurfürstendamm 16, ☎ 030/882–6563); and **Hekticket office** at Alexanderplatz (✉ Rathausstr. 1 and Kurfürstendamm 14, ☎ 030/2431–2431). Detailed information about what's going on in Berlin can be found in *Berlin–the magazine,* an English-language monthly cultural magazine published by Berlin's Tourism Board; *Berlin Programm,* a monthly tourist guide to Berlin arts, museums, and theaters; and the magazines *prinz, tip,* and *zitty,* which appear every two weeks and provide full arts listings.

CONCERTS

The Berlin Philharmonic, one of the world's leading orchestras, performs in the **Philharmonie** (✉ Matthäikirchstr. 1, ☎ 030/254–880 or 030/2548–8132). A more historic venue is the **Konzerthaus Berlin** (✉ Gendarmenmarkt, ☎ 030/2030–92101).

MUSICALS

For musicals check out: **Estrel Festival Center** (✉ Sonnenallee 225/ Ziegrastr. 21–29, ☎ 030/6831–6831); **Theater des Westens** (✉ Kantstr. 12, ☎ 030/882–2888); **Metropol Theater** (✉ Friedrichstr. 101, ☎ 030/2024–6117); **Schiller-Theater** (✉ Bismarckstr. 110, ☎ 030/3111–

3111); and **Space Dream Musical Theater** (✉ Tempelhof Airport, Clumbiadamm 2–6, ☎ 030/6951–2802).

Please note: Berlin's largest musical theater is likely to open in 1999 at the Potsdamer Platz Arkaden. At press time, however, information was still unavailable. Contact Berlin tourist information office (☞ *below*) for more details.

OPERA AND BALLET

The **Deutsche Oper** (German Opera House; ✉ Bismarckstr. 35, ☎ 030/343–8401), by the U-bahn stop of the same name, is home to both opera and ballet. The grand **Staatsoper Unter den Linden** (German State Opera; ✉ Unter den Linden 7, ☎ 030/2035–4555) is Berlin's main opera venue. **Komische Oper** (Comic Opera House; ✉ Behrenstr. 55–57, ☎ 030/4702–1000) schedules opera performances regularly.

VARIETY SHOWS

During the past few years Berlin has become Germany's prime hot spot for variety shows. The world's largest circus is at the **Friedrichstadtpalast** (✉ Friedrichstr. 107, ☎ 030/2326–2474). Small but classy in style is the **Wintergarten** (✉ Potsdamer Str. 96, ☎ 030/2308–8230 or 030/2500–8863), a romantic homage to the '20s. Equally intimate and intellectually entertaining is the **Bar jeder Vernuft** (✉ Schaperstr. 24, ☎ 030/8831–582). More than hilarious and constantly sold out are the shows at the **Chamäleon Varieté** (✉ Rosenthaler Str. 40/41, ☎ 030/2827–118).

Nightlife

With more than 6,000 Kneipen (pubs), bars, and clubs, nightlife in Berlin is no halfhearted affair. It starts late (from 9 PM) and runs until breakfast. Almost 50 Kneipen have live music of one kind or another, and there are numerous small cabaret clubs and discos. The heart of this nocturnal scene used to be the Kurfürstendamm, but today most of the best bars and Kneipen can be found around Savignyplatz in Charlottenburg, Nollendorfplatz and its side streets in Schöneberg, and along Oranienstrasse and Wienerstrasse in Kreuzberg. In eastern Berlin nighthawks come together around Kollwitzplatz in the Prenzlauer Berg district, along Oranienburger Strasse, and around Rosenthaler Platz and Hackesche Höfe in Mitte.

Berlin is a major center for jazz in Europe. If you're visiting in the fall, call the tourist office (☞ *below*) for details on the annual international Jazz Fest. Throughout the year a variety of jazz groups appear at the **A-Trane** (✉ Pestalozzistr. 105, ☎ 030/3132–550), **Eierschale** (✉ Podbielskiallee 50, ☎ 030/832–7097), and **Quasimodo** (✉ Kantstr. 12a, ☎ 030/312–8086).

Shopping

Antiques

On weekends from 10 to 5, the colorful and lively antiques and handicrafts fair on **Strasse des 17. Juni** swings into action. Not far from **Wittenbergplatz,** several streets are strong on antiques, including Eisenacher Strasse, Fuggerstrasse, Keithstrasse, Kalckreuthstrasse, Motzstrasse, and Nollendorfstrasse.

Department Stores

One of Berlin's classiest department stores is the **Kaufhaus des Westens** (KaDeWe; ✉ Tauentzienstr. 21, ☎ 030/21210); be sure to check out the food department, which occupies the whole sixth floor. Downtown Berlin's **Wertheim** (✉ Kurfürstendamm 181, ☎ 030/8800–3206) is neither as big nor as attractive as KaDeWe, but it nonetheless has a large selection of fine wares. The popular **Galeries Lafayette** (✉ Französische Str. 23, ☎ 030/209–480) carries almost exclusively French products, including designer clothes, perfume, and French produce. The main department store in eastern Berlin is **Kaufhof** (✉ north end of Alexanderpl., ☎ 030/247–430).

Gift Ideas

Fine porcelain is still produced at the former Royal Prussian Porcelain Factory, now called **Staatliche Porzellan Manufaktur** (State Porcelain Factory) or KPM. This delicate, handmade, hand-painted china is sold at KPM's store (✉ Kurfürstendamm 26A, ☎ 030/8867–210), but it may be more fun to visit the factory salesroom (✉ Wegelystr. 1, ☎ 030/390–090), where seconds are sold at reduced prices. If you long to have the Egyptian queen Nefertiti on your mantelpiece at home, try the **Gipsformerei der Staatlichen Museen Preussicher Kulturbesitz** (Plaster Sculpture of the Prussian Cultural Foundation State Museums; ✉ Sophie-Charlotte-Str. 17, ☎ 030/321–7011), which sells plaster casts of this and other museum treasures.

Shopping Districts

The liveliest and most famous shopping area in west Berlin is the **Kurfürstendamm** and its side streets, especially between Breitscheidplatz and Olivaer Platz. The **Europa Center** at Breitscheidplatz encompasses more than 100 stores, cafés, and restaurants—but this is not a place to bargain hunt. Running east from Breitscheidplatz is **Tauentzienstrasse,** another shopping street. The **Potsdamer Platz Arkaden,** the city's newest shopping mall on Potsdamer Platz, is also its fanciest. **Eastern Berlin** has major shopping districts along Friedrichstrasse, Unter den Linden, and in the area around Alexanderplatz.

Berlin Essentials

Arriving and Departing

BY BUS

Long-distance bus services link Berlin with numerous other German and European cities. For travel details, if you're in Berlin, call the main bus station (✉ Messedamm, ☎ 030/301–8028); if you're in other parts of Germany, inquire at the local tourist office.

BY CAR

The eight roads linking the western part of Germany with Berlin have been incorporated into the country-wide autobahn network, but be prepared for large traffic jams, particularly on weekends.

BY PLANE

Tegel (☎ 030/41010) airport is only 7 km (4 mi) from downtown. Delta, United, Air France, British Airways, Deutsche BA, Lufthansa, and some charter specialists regularly fly to Tegel. Because of increased air traffic at Tegel following unification, the former military airfield at **Tempelhof** (☎ 030/691–510), even closer to downtown, is used for commuter plane traffic. **Schönefeld** (☎ 030/60910) airport is about 24 km (15 mi) outside the downtown area; it is used primarily for charter flights to Asia and southern and eastern Europe.

Between the Airports and Downtown. Buses 109 and X09 run every 10 minutes between **Tegel** airport and downtown. The journey takes 30 minutes; the fare is DM 3.90 and covers all public transportation throughout Berlin. A taxi costs about DM 25. If you're driving from the airport, follow signs for the STADTAUTOBAHN (City Freeway). **Tempelhof** is right on the U-6 subway line, in the center of the city. A shuttle bus leaves **Schönefeld** airport every 10–15 minutes for the nearby S-bahn station. S-bahn trains leave every 20 minutes for the Friedrichstrasse and Zoologischer Garten stations. The trip takes about 30 minutes, and you can get off at whatever stop is nearest your hotel; The fare is DM 3.60. Taxi fare to your hotel is about DM 40–DM 55, and the trip takes about 40 minutes. By car follow the signs for BERLIN-ZENTRUM (Downtown Berlin).

BY TRAIN

There are six major rail routes to Berlin from the western part of the country (from Hamburg, Hannover, Köln, Frankfurt, Munich, and Nürnberg), and the network has expanded considerably, making the rest of eastern Germany more accessible. For information call **Deutsche Bahn** (☎ 030/19419) or inquire at the local main train station.

Getting Around

BY PUBLIC TRANSPORTATION

The city has an excellent **public transportation system:** a combination of U-bahn and S-bahn lines, buses, and streetcars (in eastern Berlin only). For DM 3.60, you can buy a ticket that covers travel on the entire downtown system (fare zones A and B) for two hours. If you are just making a short trip, buy a **Kurzstreckentarif.** It allows you to ride six bus stops or three U-bahn or S-bahn stops for DM 2.50. The **Day Card,** for DM 7.50 (no children's discount), is valid until 3 AM of the day following validation. The **Group Day Card,** for DM 20, offers the same benefits for two adults and up to three children.

If you're staying for more than a few days, the **Tourist Pass,** valid for a week and costing DM 40, is the best bargain. The **BerlinWelcomeCard,** at DM 16 for a day (DM 29 for two days), entitles one adult and up to three children to unlimited travel as well as free or reduced sightseeing trips and admission to museums, theaters, and other events and attractions. If you're caught without a ticket, the fine is DM 60. Tickets are available from vending machines at U-bahn and S-bahn stations or from bus drivers. For information call the **Berliner Verkehrsbetriebe** (BVG; Berlin Public Transportation; ☎ 030/19449) or go to the information office on Hardenbergplatz, directly in front of the Bahnhof Zoo train station.

Please note: Subway fares quoted above were those available in spring 1998. Fares are likely to rise during the latter half of 1998, and ticket regulations will likely be different in 1999.

BY TAXI

The base rate is DM 4, after which prices vary according to a complex tariff system. If your ride will be short, ask in advance for the special Kurzstreckentarif, which is DM 5 for rides of less than 2 km (1 mi) or five minutes. Figure on paying around DM 15 for a ride the length of the Kurfurstendamm. Hail cabs in the street or at taxi stands, or order one by calling 030/9644, 030/210–202, 030/691–001, or 030/261–026. U-bahn employees will call a taxi for passengers after 8 PM.

A new service offered in the downtown areas is *Velotaxis*, a rickshaw service system operating along Kurfürstendamm and Unter den Linden. Just hail one of the orange- or red-color bicycle cabs on the street or look for the VELOTAXI STAND signs along the boulevards mentioned. The fare is DM 2 (for up to 1 km/½ mi), DM 5 for a tour between sightseeing landmarks (for example, Europa Center to the Brandenburger Tor), and DM 15 for 30 minutes of individual travel. Velotaxis operate from April through October, 1 PM–8 PM only. For more information call 030/4435–8990.

Contacts and Resources

CONSULATES

United States (✉ Neustädtische Kirchstr. 4–5, ☎ 030/2385–174). **Canadian** (✉ International Trade Center, Friedrichstr. 95, ☎ 030/261–1161). **United Kingdom** (✉ Unter den Linden 32–34, ☎ 030/201–840). **Ireland** (✉ Ernst-Reuter-Pl. 10, ☎ 030/3480–0822).

Please note: The embassies listed above are branch offices of the embassies' head offices in Bonn. By the year 2000, the United States, among other nations, will have moved their main offices to new facilities in Berlin. Phone numbers and addresses shown above are likely to change in 1999.

EMERGENCIES

Police (☎ 030/110). **Ambulance** (☎ 030/112). **Ambulance and emergency medical attention** (☎ 030/310–031). **Dentist and emergency pharmaceutical assistance** (☎ 030/01141).

ENGLISH-LANGUAGE BOOKSTORES

Hugendubel (✉ Tauentzienstr. 13, ☎ 030/214060), **Dussmann Kulturkaufhaus** (✉ Friedrichstr. 90, ☎ 030/20250), **Marga Schoeller** (✉ Knesebeckstr. 33, ☎ 030/881–1112), and **Buchhandlung Kiepert** (✉ Hardenbergstr. 4–5, ☎ 030/311–0090) sell English-language publications.

GUIDED TOURS

Orientation. Severin & Kühn (✉ Kurfürstendamm 216, ☎ 030/8804–190); **Berliner Bären Stadtrundfahrt** (BBS, ✉ Seeburgerstr. 19b, ☎ 030/3519–5270); **Berolina Stadtrundfahrten** (✉ Kurfürstendamm 22, corner Meinekestr., ☎ 030/8856–8030); and **Bus Verkehr Berlin (BVB,** ✉ Kurfürstendamm 225, ☎ 030/885–9880) offer more or less identical tours in English, covering all the major sights in Berlin, as well as day tours to Potsdam and Dresden. The Berlin tours cost DM 25–DM 45, those to Potsdam and Sanssouci Palace, the favorite residence of Frederick the Great, DM 54.

Boat. Berlin is a city of waterways, and boat trips can be made on the Spree River, on the canals that connect the city's network of big lakes, and on the lakes themselves. For details contact the main city tourist office (☞ Visitor Information, *below*).

TRAVEL AGENCIES

American Express Reisebüro (✉ at Wittenbergpl., Bayreuther Str. 37, ☎ 030/2149–8363; ✉ Uhlandstr. 173, ☎ 030/882–7575; ✉ Friedrichstr. 172, ☎ 030/238–4102). **American Lloyd** (✉ Kurfürstendamm 209, ☎ 030/20740).

VISITOR INFORMATION

The **Berlin Tourismus Marketing GmbH** (main tourist office; Europa Cente; Brandenburger Tor; Tegel Airport; by mail, Berlin Tourismus Marketing ✉ Am Karlsbad 11, D-10785 Berlin).

Berlin-Hotline (☎ 030/250–025, FAX 2500–2424).

SAXONY AND THURINGIA

Saxony and Thuringia—the names alone conjure up images of kingdoms and forest legends, of cultural riches and booming industrial enterprises. Since German reunification, Saxony has thrown open its doors to visitors to its capital, Dresden, and to sites such as the renowned porcelain factory in Meissen. Tourists are proudly conducted around the world-famous porcelain factory in Meissen. Leipzig's true fame lies in its music and literary tradition, proudly upheld by the Gewandhaus Orchestra and by its annual book fair.

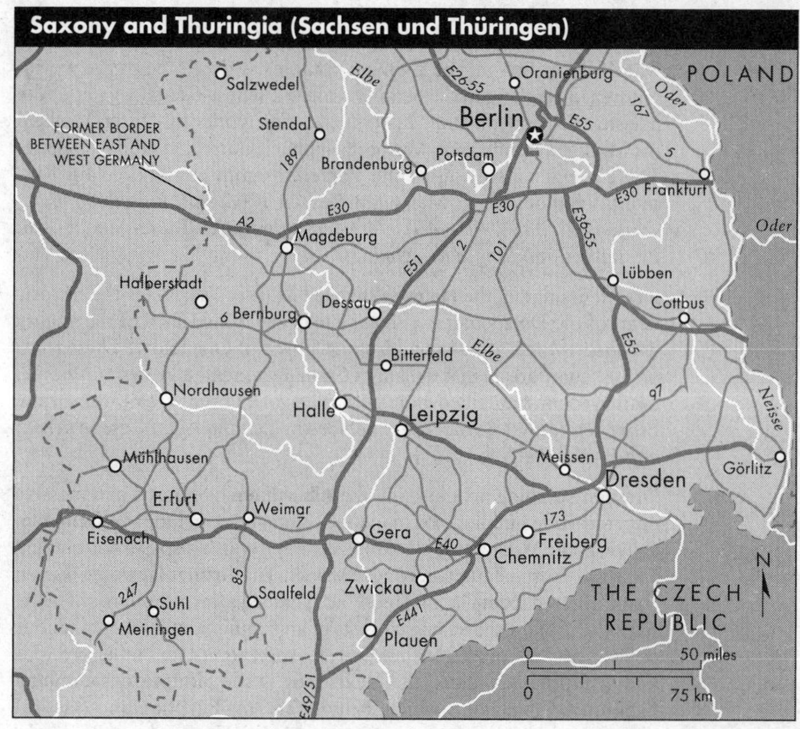

During the 14th century, Thuringia was known as the Rynestig or Rennsteig (literally, "fast trail"), when it attracted traders from the dark forested depths of the Thüringer Wald (forest) to the prospering towns of Erfurt (today the state capital), Eisenach, and Weimar, then already 600 years old. It was in Weimar in 1777 that the privy councillor and poet Johann Wolfgang von Goethe was inspired by the pristine beauties of the 168 km (104 mi) of the Rennsteig to write that "tranquillity crowns all its peaks."

Dresden

Saxony's capital city is superbly sited on the banks of the Elbe River. Although it suffered appalling damage during World War II, it has been lovingly rebuilt. Italianate influences abound, most pronounced in the glorious rococo and Baroque buildings in pastel shades of yellow and green.

The magnificent **Semperoper** (Semper Opera House) was built in 1838–41 by architect Gottfried Semper. The sumptuous interior is covered in marble, velvet, and brocade in shades of crimson, white, and gold. Wagner's *The Flying Dutchman* and *Tannhäuser* (conducted by the composer) and nine operas by Richard Strauss have all premiered here. Tickets to opera performances here are reasonably priced but hard to get; they're often included in package tours. Try booking through your travel agent before you go or ask at your hotel. As a last resort, line up at the evening box office, the Abendkasse, left of the main entrance, about ½ hour before the performance; there are usually a few dozen tickets available. Guided tours of the opera house (in German) start at the entrance facing the Elbe River. ✉ *Theaterpl.*, ☎ *0351/491–1496, 0351/49110, 0351/491–1716 (tickets).* 🎫 *Tours: DM 8.* ⏲ *Tours: daily 2–3.*

★ The largely 18th-century **Zwinger** palace complex is among the greatest examples of Baroque architecture in Europe. Completely enclosing a central courtyard of lawns and pools, six linked pavilions are decorated with a riot of garlands, nymphs, and other Baroque ornamentation and sculpture, created under the direction of Matthäus Daniel Pöppelmann.The Zwinger complex is the home of the world-renowned **Sempergalerie** (Semper Gallery), whose Gemäldegalerie Alte Meister (Gallery of Old Masters) contains works by Dürer, Holbein the Younger, Rembrandt, Vermeer, Raphael, Correggio, and Canaletto. The Zwinger also houses the Porzellansammlung (Porcelain Museum)—famous for its Meissen pieces. ✉ *Theaterpl., follow Sophienstrasse,* ☎ *0351/491–4619.* ⏲ *Sempergalerie: Tues.–Sun. 10–6. Porzellansammlung: Fri.–Wed. 10–6.*

Despite its name, the **Neumarkt** (New Market), serves as the historic heart of old Dresden; it is also the site of the ruined shell of the mighty baroque church, the **Frauenkirche** (Church of Our Lady). These ruins on the square are all that remain of Germany's greatest Protestant church, destroyed in the Allied bombing raids of February 1945 and now being rebuilt. ✉ *Bordered by Schlosstr., Landhausstr., Tzschirnerpl., and Brühlsche G.*

Dresden's leading art museum, the **Albertinum,** is housed in a massive imperial-style building. Permanent exhibits here include the **Gemäldegalerie Neue Meister** (New Masters Gallery), which displays outstanding 19th- and 20th-century European works. The **Grünes Gewölbe** (Green Vault; entered from Georg-Treu-Platz); named after a green room in the palace of August the Strong consists of an exquisite collection of unique objets d'art fashioned from gold, silver, ivory, amber, and other precious and semiprecious materials. Next door is the **Skulpturensammlung** (Sculpture Collection), which includes ancient Egyptian and classical objects and Italian Mannerist works. ✉ *Am Neumarkt at Brühlsche Terrasse,* ☎ *0351/4914–730.*⏲ *Mon.–Wed. and Fri.–Sun. 10–6.*

The 16th-century Johanneum, once the royal stables, now houses the **Verkehrsmuseum** (Transport Museum), a collection of historic vehicles, including vintage automobiles and engines. On the outside wall of the Johanneum is a prime example of Meissen porcelain art: a 335-ft-long mural of a royal procession. ✉ *Am Neumarkt,* ☎ *0351/86440.* ⏲ *Tues.–Sun. 10–5.*

The **Katholische Hofkirche** (Catholic Court Church), also known as the Cathedral of St. Trinitas, is Saxony's largest church, consecrated in 1754. In the crypt are the tombs of 49 Saxon rulers and a precious vessel containing the heart of August the Strong. ✉ *Schlosspl.,* ☎ *0351/495–1233.* 🎫 *Free.* ⏲ *Weekdays 9–5, Sat. 10–5, Sun. noon–5.*

Freital, 9 km (5.6 mi) southwest of Dresden, is where Dresden's renowned porcelain is made, at the **Sächsische Porzellanmanufaktur Dresden**. You can find exquisite examples of the porcelain in all Dresden department stores, and in Freital, you can visit a showroom and shop. ✉ *Bachstr. 16,* ☎ *0351/647–130.* ⏲ *Weekdays 9–6.*

$$ ✕ **Italienisches Dörfchen.** This Baroque structure on the Elbe was built to house Italian craftsmen working on the nearby Hofkirche. It has been cleverly and tastefully converted into a restaurant and café, with a shady beer garden and fine river views. The Italian influence is still in evidence—in the decor and on the menu, where pasta dishes are heavily favored. ✉ *Theaterpl. 3,* ☎ *0351/498160. AE, DC, MC, V.*

$–$$ ✕ **Haus Altmarkt.** The choice of cuisine in this busy corner of the colonnaded Altmarkt (Old Market Square) is enormous—the upscale Amadeus restaurant on the first floor, a jolly, bistrolike café, and, downstairs, a vaulted restaurant with a secluded bar. The Zum Humpen restaurant is the best value. ✉ *Wilfdrufferstr. 19–21,* ☎ *0351/495–1212. AE, MC, V.*

$$$$ **Hotel am Terrassenufer.** Canaletto painted the same vistas that latter-day guests can enjoy from within this sleek, 12-story hotel on the Elbe River terrace; all rooms have panoramic views of the river and the Old Town, and on clear days even to the hills of the Sächsische Schweiz, a mountain region south of Dresden. The rooms have bright cherry-wood veneer furniture and fresh pastel color schemes. ✉ *Am Terrassenufer 12, D-01067,* ☎ *0351/440–9500,* FAX *0351/440–9600. 190 rooms, 6 suites. Restaurant. AE, DC, MC, V.*

$$$$ ★ **Kempinski Hotel Taschenbergpalais Dresden.** Destroyed in wartime bombing but now rebuilt, the historic Taschenberg Palace—the work of architect Matthäus Daniel Pöppelmann—reopened a hotel in early 1995. It provides expensive pampering in the romantic heart of old Dresden. ✉ *Am Taschenberg 3, D-01067,* ☎ *0351/49120,* FAX *0351/491–2812. 188 rooms, 25 suites. 2 restaurants, pool. AE, DC, MC, V.*

$$$$ **Westin Bellevue Dresden.** Across the river from the Zwinger palace, the opera, and the main museums, this modern hotel cleverly incorporates an old restored mansion. The views of the historic center are terrific, the rooms are luxurious, and the service is good. ✉ *Grosse-Meissner-Str. 15, D-01097,* ☎ *0351/8050,* FAX *0351/8051–699. 323 rooms, 16 suites. 3 restaurants, pool. AE, DC, MC, V.*

$$$ ★ ✕ **artotel Dresden.** The artotel keeps the promise of its rather unusual name, with all modern art and designs by Italian interior architect Denis Santachiara. Inside are more than 600 works of art by Dresden-born painter and sculptor A.R. Penck. Apart from offering art, the hotel's heavily styled rooms and service have genuine first-class appeal at considerably lower prices. ✉ *Astra-Allee 33, D–01067,* ☎ *0351/49220,* FAX *0351/492–2777. 158 rooms, 16 suites. 3 restaurants, pool. AE, DC, MC, V.*

$$ ✕ **Hotelschiff Florentina.** From your cabin window in this cleverly converted "hotel ship" you have a better view of the Elbe and Dresden than from many of the luxury hotels along the banks. Accommodation is understandably a bit cramped, although all the cabins have satellite TV and bathrooms with showers. ✉ *Terrassenufer, D-01069,* ☎ *0351/459–0169,* FAX *0351/459–5036. 64 cabins. Restaurant. AE, DC, MC, V.*

Leipzig

With a population of about 560,000, Leipzig is the second-largest city (after Berlin) in eastern Germany. Since the Middle Ages, it has been an important market town and a center for printing, book publishing, and the fur business. Nowadays, its various industrial fairs held throughout the year maintain Leipzig's position as a commercial center. Yet it is music and literature that most people associate with Leipzig; Johann Sebastian Bach (1685–1750) was the organist and choir director at St. Thomas's church, and the composer Richard Wagner was born in Leipzig in 1813. One of the greatest battles of the Napoleonic Wars, and one that led to the ultimate defeat of the French general—the Battle of the Nations—was fought here in 1813.

Hauptbahnhof (Main Train Station) with its 26 platforms, majestic staircase, great arched ceiling, and more than 150 upscale shops, is Europe's largest and unique among German railway stations. ✉ *Willy-Brandt-Pl.,* ☎ *0341/19419.*

Leipzig's showpiece is its **Markt,** an old market square only slightly smaller than St. Mark's Square in Venice. Small streets leading off from the Markt on all sides attest to Leipzig's rich trading past. Tucked in among them are glass-roofed arcades of surprising beauty and elegance. One side of the Markt is occupied completely by the recently restored Renaissance **Altes Rathaus** (Old City Hall), which now houses the **Stadtgeschichtliches Museum** (City History Museum), where Leipzig's past is well documented. ✉ *Markt 1,* ☎ *0341/965–130.* ⏲ *Tues.–Fri. 10–6, weekends 10–4.*

Mädlerpassage (Mädler Mall) is Leipzig's finest shopping arcade, where the ghost of Goethe's Faust lurks in every marble corner. Here you'll find the famous Auerbachs Keller restaurant (☞ Dining and Lodging, *below*), where Goethe set a scene in *Faust.* ✉ *Grimmaischestr.*

★ At **Thomaskirche** (St. Thomas's Church), Johann Sebastian Bach worked for 27 years, composing most of his cantatas for the church's boys' choir. ✉ *Thomaskirchhof (just off Grimmaischestr.),* ☎ *0341/9602–855.* 🎫 *Free.* ⏲ *Apr.–Oct., daily 8–6; Nov.–Mar., daily 9–5.*

★ **Nikolaikirche** (St. Nicholas's Church) is more impressive inside than out; it has an ornate 16th-century pulpit and an unusual diamond-pattern ceiling supported by classical pillars crowned with palm-tree-like flourishes. The church also has played a central part in Leipzig's history—demonstrations here are credited with helping to bring down the Communist regime. ✉ *Nikolaikirchhof,* ☎ *0341/960–5270.* 🎫 *Free.* ⏲ *Daily 10–6.*

The **Grassimuseum,** a fine example of German Art Deco, was built between 1925 and 1929 to house three important museums: the newly renovated **Museum für Kunsthandwerk** (Museum of Arts and Crafts; ⏲ Tues.–Sun. 10–6, Wed. noon–8); the **Museum für Völkerkunde zu Leipzig** (Ethnological Museum; ⏲ Tues.–Fri. 10–5:30, weekends 10–4); and the **Musikinstrumenten-Museum** (Musical Instruments Museum; ✉ enter from Täubchenweg 2., ⏲ Tues.–Fri. 10–5, Sat. 10–5, Sun. 10–1). *Grassimuseum:* ✉ *Johannespl. 5–11,* ☎ *0341/21420.*

★ The city's most outstanding museum, the **Museum der Bildenden Künste** (Museum of Fine Arts), is an art gallery of international stature, especially strong in German and Dutch painting. ✉ *Grimmaische Str. 1–7,* ☎ *0341/216–9914.* ⏲ *Tues. and Thurs.–Sun. 10–6, Wed. 1–9:30.*

The modernistic **Opernhaus** (Opera House; ✉ Augustuspl. 12, ☎ 0341/126–1261), is a center of the city's music life. The **Neues Gewandhaus** (✉ Augustuspl. 8, ☎ 0341/127–0280) is home to a first-class orchestra.

$$ ★ ✕ **Auerbachs Keller.** Established in 1530, this restaurant was made famous by Goethe's *Faust* and became an indispensable part of Leipzig life. Regional dishes from Saxony, often with Faustian names, head the menu. ✉ *Mädlerpassage, Grimmaische Str. 2–4,* ☎ *0341/216–1040. Reservations essential. Jacket and tie. AE, MC, V.*

$$ ✕ **Deutscher Hof.** The beamed and paneled hotel restaurant is a fine example of Leipzig Jugendstil, with elegant woodwork and glass. The menu is heartily Saxon with an international touch. ✉ *Waldstr. 31–33,* ☎ *0341/71100. AE, DC, MC, V. Closed Sun.*

$$ ★ ✕ **Paulaner Restaurant.** Munich's Paulaner brewery has transformed a historic corner of Leipzig into a vast complex combining a restaurant, banquet hall, café, and beer garden. There's something for everybody here, from intimate dining to noisy Bavarian-style tavern-table jollity. ✉ *Klosterg. 3–5,* ☎ *0341/211–3115. AE, MC, V.*

$$ ✕ **Zill's Tunnel.** In the barrel-vaulted ground-floor restaurant, foaming glasses of excellent local beer are served by the friendly staff. The menu offers Old Saxon descriptions of traditional dishes. ✉ *Barfussgässchen 9,* ☎ *0341/960–2078. AE, MC, V.*

$$$$ ✕🏨 **Hotel Inter-Continental Leipzig.** The imposing high-rise "Interconti" is one of the city's luxury hotels. The service is outstanding, but the place lacks true atmosphere, despite a Japanese restaurant and garden. Rooms in this Japanese-built lodging offer every luxury, including bathrooms with marble floors and walls. ✉ *Gerberstr. 15, D-04105,*

☎ *0341/9880,* FAX *0341/988–1229. 447 rooms, 26 suites. 3 restaurants, pool. AE, DC, MC, V.*

$$$$ ★ ✕🏨 **Kempinski Hotel Fürstenhof Leipzig.** The city's newest and most luxurious hotel is located in the *Löhr-Haus,* one of Leipzig's most precious old mansions, which was restored by the Kempinski group. The 19th-century-style banquet section is stunning with red wallpaper and dark magagoni wood. The spacious rooms are decorated with modern designer furniture. The fitness and swimming pool sections are among the best in eastern Germany. ✉ *Tröndlinring 8, D–04105,* ☎ *0341/1400,* FAX *0341/1403–700. 84 rooms, 8 suites. Restaurant, pool. AE, DC, MC, V.*

$$$ ★ ✕🏨 **Renaissance Leipzig Hotel.** One of the largest hotels in this city of fairs, this one in the heart of old Leipzig is mostly chosen by business travelers for its quiet, yet not intimate, atmosphere, and its large, elegant rooms. If you reserve a room on the CLUB floor, for about DM 40 a day you get a free continental breakfast and access to the CLUB-Lounge. The hotel's restaurant, Four Seasons, offers light Asian cuisine. ✉ *Querstr. 12, D–04103,* ☎ *0341/12920,* FAX *0341/1292–800. 295 rooms, 61 suites. Restaurant, pool. AE, DC, MC, V.*

$$$ 🏨 **Holiday Inn Garden Court.** The former, and slightly seedy, Hotel Zum Löwen is now a smart and very comfortable hotel. Unchanged is the excellent location, across from Leipzig's main railway station. Rooms tend to be small but lack nothing in terms of comfort and facilities. ✉ *Rudolf-Breitscheid-Str. 3, D-04105,* ☎ *0341/125–100,* FAX *0341/125–1100. 121 rooms, 9 suites. Restaurant. AE, DC, MC, V.*

Weimar

Weimar sitting prettily on the Ilm River between the Ettersberg and Vogtland hills, has a place in German political and cultural history all out of proportion to its size (population 63,000). Goethe and the poet and dramatist Friedrich von Schiller were neighbors here, Carl Maria von Weber (1786–1826) wrote some of his best music here, and later it was here that Liszt presented the first performance of Wagner's *Lohengrin.* Walter Gropius founded his Bauhaus design school in Weimar in 1919, and it was here in 1919–20 that the German National Assembly drew up the constitution of the Weimar Republic.

Theaterplatz, in front of the National Theater, has a statue that shows Goethe placing a patronizing hand on the shoulder of the younger Schiller. ✉ *Bordered by Dingelstedstr., Gropiusstr., Heinrich-Heine-Str., Schillerstr., and Schützeng.*

★ The **Goethehaus** (Goethe House) was Goethe's home for 47 of his 57 years in Weimar. The museum it contains is testimony not only to the great man's literary might but also to his interest in the sciences, particularly medicine, and his administrative skills (and frustrations) as Weimar's exchequer. ✉ *Frauenplan 1, 2 blocks south of Theaterpl.,* ☎ *03643/545–320.* ⏲ *Mar.–Oct., Tues.–Sun. 9–6; Nov.–Feb., Tues.–Sun. 10–4.*

On a tree-shaded square around the corner from Goethe's house is the green-shutter **Schillerhaus** (Schiller House), in which Friedrich Schiller and his family spent an all-too-brief but happy three years (the poet died here in 1805). His study, dominated by the desk at which he probably completed *Wilhelm Tell,* is tucked up underneath the mansard roof. ✉ *Schillerstr. 17,* ☎ *03643/545–350.* ⏲ *Mar.–Oct., Mon. and Wed.–Sun. 9–6; Nov.–Feb., Mon. and Wed.–Sun. 9–4.*

Weimar's 16th-century castle, the **Stadtschloss** (City Palace), has a restored classical staircase, festival hall, and falcon gallery. The castle's impressive art collection includes paintings by Cranach the Elder and early 20th-century works by such artists as Böcklin, Liebermann, and Beckmann. ✉ *Burgpl. 4, around the corner from the* *market square,* ☎ *03643/5460.* ⏲ *Sept.–Mar., Tues. 10–4:30; Apr.–Aug., Tues.–Sun. 10–6.*

Goethe and Schiller are buried in the leafy **Historischer Friedhof** (Historic Cemetery), where virtually every gravestone commemorates a famous citizen. The writers' tombs are in the vault of the chapel. ✉ *A short walk south past Goethe Haus and Wieland Pl.* ⏲ *Mar.–Oct., Wed.–Mon. 9–1 and 2–5; Nov.–Feb., Wed.–Mon. 9–1.*

Goethe's beloved **Gartenhaus** (Garden House), a country cottage where he spent many happy hours and wrote much poetry and began his masterpiece, *Iphigenie,* is set amid parkland on the banks of the river Ilm. You can soak up the rural atmosphere on footpaths along the peaceful little river. ✉ *Goethepark,* ☎ *03642/545–375.* ⏲ *Mar.–Oct., Mon. and Wed.–Sun. 9–6; Nov.–Feb., Mon. and Wed.–Sun. 9–4.*

North of Weimar, in the Ettersberg Hills, is a blighted patch of land that contrasts cruelly with the verdant countryside that so inspired Goethe: ★ **Buchenwald,** where, between 1937 and 1945 some 65,000 men, women, and children from 35 countries met their deaths from disease, starvation, or gruesome medical experiments. ✉ *Buchenwald Str., take public bus No. 6 from Goethepl.,* ☎ *03643/4300.* *Free.* ⏲ *May–Sept., Tues.–Sun. 9:45–5:15; Oct.–Apr., Tues.–Sun. 8:45–4:15.*

$$ ✕ **Hotel Thüringen.** The plush elegance of the hotel's restaurant, complete with velvet drapes and chandeliers, makes it seem expensive, but the menu of international and regional dishes, such as Thüringer roast beef, is remarkably moderately priced. ✉ *Brennerstr. 42,* ☎ *03643/903–675. AE, DC, MC, V.*

$ ✕ **Scharfe Ecke.** Thuringia's traditional *Knödeln* (dumplings) are best here. But be patient; they are made to order and take at least 20 minutes to prepare. The Knödeln come with just about every dish, from roast pork to venison stew. And the ideal accompaniment to any of the choices here is the locally brewed beer. ✉ *Eisfeld 2,* ☎ *03643/202–430. No credit cards. Closed Mon.*

$$$$ 🏨 **Kempinski Hotel Elephant.** The historic Elephant, dating from 1696, is now a member of the Kempinski group, which has kept the original charm that made the hotel one of Germany's most famous, even in the communist years. Goethe, Schiller, and Liszt are some of the illustrious names in the hotel register. Book well in advance. ✉ *Markt 19, D-99423,* ☎ *03643/8020,* FAX *03643/802–610. 97 rooms, 5 suites. 2 restaurants. AE, DC, MC, V.*

$$$$ 🏨 **Weimar Hilton.** Weimar's most modern hotel combines luxury with sleek and smooth-running service. The riverside Belvedere Park that Goethe helped to plan is just across the road. Weimar's center is quite a hike in the other direction, but buses are frequent. ✉ *Belvederer Allee 25, D-99425,* ☎ *03643/7220,* FAX *03643/722–741. 294 rooms, 6 suites. 2 restaurants, pool. AE, DC, MC, V.*

$$ 🏨 **Amalienhof VCH Hotel.** Book far ahead to secure a room here. The officially protected building began life in 1826 as a church hostel, but subsequent remodeling turned it into a comfortable, cozy, and friendly little hotel, central to Weimar's chief attractions. Double rooms are furnished with high-class antique reproductions, while public rooms have the real thing. ✉ *Amalienstr. 2, D-99423,* ☎ *03643/5490,* FAX *03643/549–110. 22 rooms, 9 apartments. AE, MC, V.*

Saxony and Thuringia Essentials

Getting Around

BY BOAT

The **Weisse Flotte** (White Fleet) of inland boats, including paddle side-wheelers, ply the River Elbe, starting in Dresden or at the beautiful forested border town of Bad Schandau and proceeding on into the Czech Republic. For details contact the tour operator (✉ Sächsische Dampfschiffahrt, Hertha-Lindner-Str. 10, D-01067 Dresden, ☎ 0351/866–090). **KD River Cruises of Europe** (✉ 2500 Westchester Ave., Purchase, NY 10577, ☎ 914/696–3600; ✉ 323 Geary St., Suite 603, San Francisco, CA 94102, ☎ 415/392–8817) operates luxury cruises in both directions on the Elbe from May through October.

BY BUS AND STREETCAR

Within Saxony and Thuringia, most areas are accessible by bus, but service is infrequent and is chiefly to connect with rail lines. In Dresden, Leipzig, and Weimar, public buses and streetcars are cheap and efficient.

BY CAR

Some 1,600 km (1,000 mi) of autobahn and 11,300 km (7,000 mi) of secondary roads crisscross the five new federal states in the east. Resurfacing of some of the communist-built highways has now resulted in the lifting of the previous strictly enforced 100 kph (62 mph) speed limits on autobahns. Gas stations can be scarce on back roads.

BY TAXI

Taxis in Dresden are inexpensive. Leipzig has more cabs than any other eastern German city because of the number needed to cope with peak traffic at fair time. Weimar's chief attractions are within walking distance, but you may want to take a taxi from the main train station, which is somewhat removed from the city center.

BY TRAIN

InterCity, EuroCity, and InterCity Express **trains** connect Dresden and Leipzig with Berlin and other major German cities, with InterRegio services completing the express network; older and slower D- and E-class trains connect smaller towns.

Leipzig has an **S-bahn** system. Tickets must be obtained in advance, at various prices according to the number of rides in a block. Get S-bahn tickets at the main railway station.

Guided Tours

In **Dresden** every day there are 10 guided tours by bus, tram, or open carriage, at least two steamer trips on the Elbe, and four tours of the city on foot. Consult the tourist office (☞ *below*) before setting off. The tourist office also sells a one-day Dresden Card (DM 11, or DM 20 for 48 hours) covering various museum admissions and transportation.

The visitor information office in **Leipzig** (☞ *below*) leads regularly scheduled bus and tram tours of the city; reservations are advised (☎ 0341/79590). Walking tours start from the main tourist office (☞ Visitor Information, *below*) at 4 PM.

Walking tours of **Weimar** start from outside the main tourist office (☞ Visitor Information, *below*), daily at 11 and 4. The tourist office can also arrange individual tours.

Visitor Information

Dresden (✉ Tourist-Information, Prager Str. 10, D-01069, ☎ 0351/491–920). **Leipzig** (✉ Leipzig Tourist Service e.V., Sachsenpl. 1, D-06108, ☎ 0341/7401–260/265). **Weimar** (✉ Tourist-Information, Markt 10, D-99421, ☎ 03643/24000).

13 Great Britain

London, Windsor to Bath, Cambridge, York, the Lake District, Edinburgh

When you visit London, chances are you'll glimpse St. Paul's Cathedral riding high and white over the rooftops of the city skyline, just as it does in Canaletto's 18th-century views of the Thames. The great cathedral, cleaned, glows honey-gold, breathtakingly floodlit by night, making architect Christopher Wren's detail and proportion evident once again. Then, on second glance, you'll note that St. Paul's is being nudged by modern, glittering skyscrapers, with glass and steel tower blocks marching two abreast the length of London Wall. The juxtaposition should give you pause: Clearly, when you come to see the sights of Britain, you ought not to miss the greatest sight of all, which is the unconquered, nearly 2,000-year-long continuity of English society.

From Baroque-era cathedrals to the latest Postmodern structures, from prehistoric Stonehenge to Regency Bath, from one-pub Cotswold villages to London's Mod Brit restaurants, Great Britain is a spectacular tribute to the strength—and flexibility—of tradition. Here in this "green and pleasant land," you'll find soaring medieval cathedrals, evidence of the faith of the churchmen and masons who built them; grand country mansions of the aristocracy filled with treasures—paintings, furniture, tapestries—and set in elegantly landscaped grounds; and grim fortified castles, whose gray-stone walls held fast against all challengers. But there is more to Britain than a historical theme park aspect: many of the pleasures of exploration derive from the ever-changing variety of its countryside. A day's drive from York, for example, will take you through stretches of wild, heather-covered moorland, ablaze with color in the fall; or past the steep, sheep-dotted mountainsides of the Dales, in which isolated hamlets are scattered.

Wandering off the beaten track will also allow you to discover Britain's many distinctive rural towns and villages, which move at a notably slower pace than do the metropolitan centers. A medieval parish church, a high street of 18th-century buildings accented by occasional survivors from earlier centuries, and perhaps a grandiose Victorian town hall, all still in use today, help to convey a sense of a living past. This direct continuity of past into present can be generously experienced in such a celebrated place as Stratford-upon-Avon. It's even more evident in such communities as the little town of Chipping Campden, set in the rolling Cotswold Hills, or Bury St. Edmunds, in the gentle Suffolk countryside east of Cambridge. In such places the visitor's understanding is often aided by small museums devoted to local history, full of intriguing artifacts and information on trade, traditions, and social life. These towns are likely places to look for specialty goods, including knitwear, pottery, and glass, the result of a 1990s renaissance in craftsmanship.

In contrast is the dazzling—at times hectic—pace of life in London. Today, Britain's swinging-again capital is much in the news and the city's sizzling art, dining, style, and fashion scenes have done much to transform London's stodgy and traditional image. Thanks to such figures as artist Damien Hirst, designer-provocateur Alexander McQueen, and, of course, Tony Blair, the new young(ish) Prime Minister, the New London continues to make headlines around the world. Yet here, too, the links with the past are plain to see. For instance, despite all the rebuilding of the 1980s and 1990s, the basic street pattern of the City (the financial quarter between St. Paul's Cathedral and the Tower of London) remains the one that evolved in the Middle Ages. Still standing is much of the work of Christopher Wren, the master architect chiefly responsible for reconstruction after the disastrous Great Fire of 1666. Most notable of these works is St. Paul's itself. Here again, exploration off the beaten path will reward you with the discovery of a London relatively untouched by tourists.

Finally, it is important to remember that Great Britain consists of three nations—England, Scotland, and Wales—and that 648 km (400 mi) north of London lies the capital city of Edinburgh, whose streets and monuments bear witness to the often turbulent and momentous history of the Scottish people.

GREAT BRITAIN A TO Z

Customs

For details on imports and duty-free limits, *see* Customs & Duties *in* Chapter 1.

Dining

British food used to be put down for its lack of imagination and its mediocrity. Today, numerous chefs have taken such giant steps that London is now one of the world's greatest cities for dining out. Across Britain, the problem may be not so much bad food as expensive food—you might want to check prices on the menu, which, by law, must be displayed outside the restaurant, before stepping inside. The best of traditional British cooking, deeper into the country, uses top-quality, fresh, local ingredients: wild salmon; spring lamb; distinctive handmade cheeses; myriad, almost forgotten, fruit varieties; and countless types of seasonal vegetables. Nearly all restaurant menus include vegetarian dishes, and interesting ethnic cuisines, especially Asian, can be found in the main street of even the smaller towns and villages.

ORKNEY ISLANDS
Thurso
John O'Groats
Wick
A9
A897
OUTER HEBRIDES
Stornoway
Lewis
Ullapool
Dornoch
Moray Firth
Harris
North Uist
Banff
Peterhead
Portree
Inverness
South Uist
Kyle of Lochalsh
Loch Ness
Skye
Aviemore
Braemar
Aberdeen
Fort William
Montrose
Coll
INNER HEBRIDES
SCOTLAND
Dundee
Perth
Firth of Tay
Tiree
Mull
Oban
Callander
St. Andrew's
ATLANTIC OCEAN
Dunfermline
Firth of Forth
Stirling
Edinburgh
Islay
Jura
Greenock
M8
Glasgow
Lanark
Berwick-upon-Tweed
Arran
A68
Campbeltown
Ayr
Kilmarnock
A77
Dumfries
Londonderry
Newcastle-upon-Tyne
Stranraer
Carlisle
NORTHERN IRELAND
Kirkcudbright
Sunderland
Bangor
Durham
Middlesbrough
M1
Belfast
Portadown
Keswick
Whitby
Unst
Yell
SHETLAND ISLANDS
Mainland
Lerwick
Mainland
Kirkwall
ORKNEY ISLANDS
Hoy
North Sea
N

Armagh
Isle of Man
Kendal
M6
Scarborough
A1
Lancaster
York
Blackpool
Bradford
Leeds
Kingston-upon-Hull
Irish Sea
M62
Bolton
Manchester
Grimsby
Liverpool
Birkenhead
Doncaster
REPUBLIC OF IRELAND
Dublin
Holyhead
Sheffield
A16
Anglesey
Llandudno
Skegness
ENGLAND
Lincoln
Boston
The Wash
Cromer
Stoke-on-Trent
Nottingham
Derby
Norwich
Shrewsbury
Stamford
Great Yarmouth
Wolverhampton
Leicester
Peterborough
Aberystwyth
Birmingham
Lowestoft
Coventry
Cambridge
Bury St. Edmunds
WALES
Stratford
St. George's Channel
Northampton
Fishguard
Banbury
M40
M1
A1/M1
M11
Ipswich
Harwich
Gloucester
Colchester
Oxford
LONDON
Swansea
Newport
Swindon
Pembroke
Bristol
M4
Windsor
Cardiff
Reading
M3
M2
Canterbury
Bath
Bristol Channel
Maidstone
Dover
Winchester
Reigate
Tunbridge Wells
Folkestone
Barnstaple
Taunton
M5
Salisbury
Southampton
Strait of Dover
Brighton
0
50 miles
100 miles
Yeovil
Dorchester
Bude
0
50 km
100 km
150 km
Exeter
Bournemouth
Portsmouth
Isle of Wight
Bodmin
Torquay
Plymouth
English Channel
Penzance
Scilly Isles
Falmouth
Land's End
FRANCE

MEALTIMES

These vary somewhat, depending on the region of the country you are visiting. But in general breakfast is served between 7:30 and 9 and lunch between noon and 2 (in the North the latter meal is called dinner). Tea—a famous British tradition and often a meal in itself—is generally served between 4 and 5:30. Dinner or supper is served between 7:30 and 9:30, sometimes earlier, but rarely later outside the metropolitan areas. High tea, at about 6, replaces dinner in some areas—especially in Scotland—and in large cities, pre- and after-theater suppers are often available. Note that many upscale restaurants close for 10 days during Easter and/or Christmas and for several weeks in July, August, or September. Call ahead.

RATINGS

Prices quoted here are per person and include a first course, a main course, and dessert, but not wine or service.

CATEGORY	LONDON AND SOUTHERN ENGLAND	OTHER AREAS
$$$$	OVER £50	OVER £40
$$$	£35–£50	£25–£40
$$	£25–£35	£15–£25
$	UNDER £25	UNDER £15

WHAT TO WEAR

Jacket and tie are suggested for the more formal restaurants in the top price categories, but, in general, casual chic or informal dress is acceptable in most establishments.

Lodging

Britain offers a wide variety of accommodations, ranging from enormous, top-quality, top-price hotels to simple, intimate farmhouses and guest houses. Note that many smaller establishments close for 10 days during Christmas and sometimes for several weeks in July or August. Call ahead.

BED-AND-BREAKFASTS

In Britain these are small, simple establishments, not the upscale option Americans know by this name. They offer modest, inexpensive accommodations, usually in a family home. Few rooms have private bathrooms, and most B&Bs offer no meals other than breakfast. Guest houses are a slightly larger, somewhat more luxurious, version. Both provide the visitor with an excellent glimpse of everyday British life.

CAMPING

Britain offers an abundance of campsites. Some are large and well equipped; others are merely small farmers' fields, offering primitive facilities. For information contact the British Tourist Authority in the United States (☞ Visitor Information *in* Chapter 1) or the **Camping and Caravanning Club** (⊠ Greenfields House, Westwood Way, Coventry CV4 8JH, ☎ 01203/694995).

FARMHOUSES

Farmhouses rarely offer professional hotel standards, but they have a special appeal: the rustic, rural experience. Prices are generally very reasonable. A car is vital for a successful farmhouse stay. The **Farm Holiday Bureau** (⊠ National Agricultural Centre, Stoneleigh Park, Kenilworth, Warwickshire CV8 2LZ, ☎ 01203/696909), a network of farming and country people who offer B&B accommodation, is a good source for regional tourist board inspected and approved properties. These properties are listed in the "Stay on a Farm" guide, produced by the Bureau.

HISTORIC BUILDINGS

To spend your vacation in a Gothic temple, an old lighthouse on an isolated island, or maybe in an apartment at Hampton Court Palace, contact one of the half-dozen organizations in Great Britain that have specially adapted, modernized historic buildings to rent. A leading charity that rents such buildings is **The Landmark Trust** (✉ Shottesbrooke, Maidenhead, Berkshire SL6 3SW, ☎ 01628/825925); these properties do not have TVs. The **National Trust** (✉ Box 536, Melksham, Wiltshire SN12 8SX, ☎ 01225/705676) is another heritage charity that rents historic buildings. A noted source of such rentals is **Portmeirion Cottages** (✉ Hotel Portmeirion, Gwynedd, Wales LL48 6ET, ☎ 01766/770228). The rather upscale **Rural Retreats** (✉ Retreat House, Station Rd., Blockley, Moreton-in-Marsh, Gloucestershire GL56 9DZ, ☎ 01386/701177) has a number of these properties.

HOLIDAY COTTAGES

Furnished apartments, houses, cottages, and trailers are available for weekly rental in all areas of the country. These vary from quaint, cleverly converted farmhouses to brand-new buildings set in scenic surroundings. The British Tourist Authority booklet, "Self Catering Holiday Homes," is available from the BTA office in New York. Lists of rental properties are available free of charge from local Tourist Information Centres in Britain. Discounts of up to 50% apply during the off-season (October through March).

HOTELS

British hotels vary greatly, and there is no reliable official system of classification. Most have rooms with private bathrooms, although there are still many—usually older hotels—that offer some rooms with only washbasins; in this case, showers and bathtubs (and toilets) are usually just down the hall. Many also have "good" and "bad" wings. Be sure to check the room before you take it. Generally, British hotel prices include breakfast, but beware: Many offer only a Continental breakfast—often little more than tea and toast. A hotel that includes a traditional British breakfast in its rates is usually a good bet. Hotel prices in London can be significantly higher than in the rest of the country, and sometimes the quality does not reflect the extra cost. Tourist information centers all over the country will reserve rooms for you, usually for a small fee. A great many hotels offer special weekend and off-season bargain packages.

RATINGS

Prices are for two people in a double room and include all taxes.

CATEGORY	LONDON AND SOUTHERN ENGLAND	OTHER AREAS
$$$$	OVER £180	OVER £110
$$$	£120-£180	£60-£110
$$	£70-£120	£50-£60
$	UNDER £70	UNDER £50

UNIVERSITY HOUSING

In larger cities and in some towns, certain universities offer their residence halls to paying vacationers. The facilities available are usually compact sleeping units, and they can be rented on a nightly basis. For information contact the **British Universities Accommodation Consortium** (✉ Box 1450, University Park, Nottingham NG7 2RD, ☎ 01159/504571).

YOUTH HOSTELS

The more than 350 youth hostels throughout England, Wales, and Scotland range from very basic to very good. Many are in remote and beautiful areas; others are on the outskirts of large cities. Despite the name, there is no age restriction. The accommodations are inexpensive and generally reliable and usually include cooking facilities. For additional information contact the **YHA Headquarters** (✉ Trevelyan House, 8 St. Stephen's Hill, St. Albans, Hertfordshire AL1 2DY, ☎ 01727/855215).

Mail

POSTAL RATES

Airmail letters to the United States and Canada cost 43p for 10 grams; postcards, 37p; aerograms, 36p. Letters and postcards to Europe weighing up to 20 grams cost 31p (26p to EU-member countries). Letters within the United Kingdom: first-class, 26p; second-class and postcards, 20p. These rates are current at press time.

RECEIVING MAIL

If you're uncertain where you'll be staying, you can arrange to have your mail sent to American Express (✉ 6 Haymarket, London SW1Y 4BS). The service is free to cardholders and AmEx travelers' check holders; all others pay a small fee. You can also collect letters at London's Main Post Office. Ask to have them addressed as the recipient's name appears on their passport, to "Poste Restante" or "To Be Called For" and mailed to the Main Post Office, Trafalgar Square, 24-28 William IV Street, London WC2N 4DL. For collection, hours are Monday–Saturday 8:30 AM–9 PM. You'll need your passport or other official form of identification. This service can be arranged at post offices throughout Britain.

Money Matters

COSTS

In general, transportation in Britain is expensive in comparison with that in other countries. You would be well advised to take advantage of the many reductions and special fares available on trains, buses, and subways. Always ask about these when buying your ticket.

London now ranks with Tokyo as one of the world's most expensive hotel capitals. Finding budget accommodations—especially during July and August—can be difficult; you should try to book well ahead if you are visiting during these months. Many London hotels offer special off-season (October–March) rates, however. Dining out at top-of-the-line restaurants can be prohibitively expensive, but there are new chains of French-Italian style café-brasseries, along with a large number of pubs and ethnic restaurants that offer excellent food at reasonable prices. Fast-food facilities of every nationality are widespread.

Remember that the gulf between prices in the capital and outside is wide. Be prepared to pay a value-added tax (VAT) of 17½% on almost everything you buy; in nearly all cases it is included in the advertised price.

CURRENCY

The British unit of currency is the pound sterling, divided into 100 pence (p). Bills are issued in denominations of 5, 10, 20, and 50 pounds (£). Coins are £1, £2, 50p, 20p, 10p, 5p, 2p, and 1p; the 10p and 5p are the size of a quarter and a dime, respectively. Scottish banks issue Scottish currency, of which all coins and notes—with the exception of the £1 notes—are accepted in England. At press time the pound stood at approximately £.61 to the U.S dollar, £.42 to the Canadian dollar, £.39 to the Australian dollar, and £.33 to the New Zealand dollar.

Traveler's checks are widely accepted in Britain, and many banks, hotels, and shops offer currency-exchange facilities. You will have to pay a £2 commission fee wherever you change them; banks offer the best rates, yet even these fees vary. If you are changing currency, you will have to pay (on top of commission) based on the amount you are changing. In London and other big cities, *bureaux de change* abound, but it definitely pays to shop around: they charge a flat fee and it's often a great deal more than that at other establishments, such as banks. American Express foreign exchange desks do not charge a commission fee on AmEx traveler's checks. Credit cards are universally accepted, too. The most commonly used are MasterCard and Visa.

SAMPLE PRICES

For London: cup of coffee, £1–£2; pint of beer, £1.80–£2.20; glass of wine, £2–£4; soda, 80p–£1.50; 2-km (1-mi) taxi ride, £3; ham sandwich, £1.75–£3.50.

TIPPING

Some restaurants and most hotels add a service charge of 10%–15% to the bill. If this has been done, you're under no obligation to tip further. If no service charge is indicated, add 10%–15% to your total bill, unless you are totally unhappy with the service given. Taxi drivers should also get 10%–15%, although it's not obligatory. You are not expected to tip theater or cinema ushers, elevator operators, or bartenders in pubs. Hairdressers and barbers should receive 10%–15%.

National Holidays

Parliament isn't the only institution to decide which days are national holidays: Some holidays are actually subject to royal proclamation. England and Wales: January 1; April 2 (Good Friday); April 5 (Easter Monday); May 3 (Early May Bank Holiday); May 31 (Spring Bank Holiday); August 30 (Summer Bank Holiday); December 25–26, 28 (in lieu of December 26). Scotland: January 1–2; April 2; May 3; May 31; August 30 (Summer Bank Holiday); December 25–26, 28 (in lieu of December 26).

Opening and Closing Times

Banks. Most banks are open weekdays 9:30–4:30. Some have extended hours on Thursday evening, and a few are open on Saturday morning. **Museums.** Museum hours vary considerably from one part of the country to another. In large cities most are open Tuesday–Saturday 10–5; many are also open on Sunday afternoon. The majority close one day a week. Be sure to double-check the opening times of historic houses, especially if the visit involves a special trip; most stately houses in the countryside are closed November–March. **Shops.** Usual business hours are Monday–Saturday 9–5:30, but many shops are open Sunday. Outside the main centers most shops close at 1 PM once a week, often Wednesday or Thursday. In small villages many also close for lunch. In large cities—especially London—department stores stay open for late-night shopping (usually until 7:30 or 8) one day midweek.

Shopping

SALES-TAX REFUNDS

Foreign visitors from outside Europe can avoid Britain's 17½% value-added tax (VAT) by taking advantage of the following two schemes. By the Direct Export method, the shopkeeper arranges the export of the goods and does not charge VAT at the point of sale. This means that the purchases are sent on to your home separately. If you prefer to take your purchase with you, try the Retail Export scheme, run by most large stores: The special Form 407 (provided only by the retailer) is attached to your invoice. You must present the goods, form, and invoice to the customs officer at the last port of departure from the EU. Allow plenty of time to do this at the airport as there are often long lines. The form is then returned to the store and the refund forwarded to you, minus a small service charge. For inquiries call the local Customs & Excise office listed in the telephone directory.

Telephoning

COUNTRY CODE

When you're dialing overseas, the United Kingdom's country code is 44. When dialing a number in Britain from abroad, drop the initial 0 from the local area code.

INTERNATIONAL CALLS

The cheapest way to make an overseas call is to dial it yourself. But be sure to have plenty of coins or phone cards close at hand. After you have inserted the coins or card, dial 00 (the international code), then the country code—for the United States, it is 1—followed by the area code and local number. To reach an **AT&T** long-distance operator, dial 0500/890011; for **MCI,** dial 0800/890222, and for **Sprint,** dial 0800/890877 (from a British Telecom phone) or 0500/890877 (from a Mercury Communications phone). To make a collect or other operator-assisted call, dial 155.

LOCAL CALLS

Public telephones are plentiful in British cities, especially London. Other than on the street, the best place to find a bank of pay phones is in a hotel or large post office; pubs and stations usually have a pay phone, too. British Telecom is gradually replacing the distinctive red phone booths with generic glass and steel cubicles, but the traditional boxes still remain in the countryside where the modern versions do not suit the surroundings. The workings of coin-operated telephones vary, but there are usually instructions in each unit. Most take 10p, 20p, 50p, and £1 coins. A phone card is also available; it comes in denominations of 10, 20, 50, and 100 units and can be bought in a number of retail outlets. Card phones, which are clearly marked with a special green insignia, will not accept coins. You can often use your credit card, although this is a more expensive option.

A local call before 6 PM costs 15p for three minutes; this doubles to 30p for the same from a pay phone. A daytime call to the United States will cost 24p a minute on a regular phone (weekends are cheaper); 80p on a pay phone. Each large city or region in Britain has its own numerical prefix, which is used only when you are dialing from outside the city. In provincial areas the dialing codes for nearby towns are often posted in the booth.

OPERATORS AND INFORMATION

For information anywhere in Britain, dial 192. For the operator, dial 100. For assistance with international calls, dial 155.

Transportation

BY BICYCLE

Most towns—including London—offer bike-rental facilities. Any bike shop or tourist information center should be able to direct you to the nearest rental firm. Rental fees can be as little as £5 per day, plus a fairly large deposit, though this can often be put on your credit card. If you're planning a tour and would like information on rental shops and special holidays for cyclists, contact a British Tourist Authority office in the United States before you leave home. In Britain contact the **Cyclists' Touring Club** (✉ Cotterell House, 69 Meadrow, Godalming, Surrey GU7 3HS, ☎ 01483/417217).

BY BOAT

Britain offers more than 2,430 km (1,500 mi) of navigable inland waterways—rivers, lakes, canals, locks, and loughs—for leisure travel. Particular regions, such as the Norfolk Broads in East Anglia, the Severn Valley in the West Country, and the lochs and canals of Scotland are especially inviting. Although there are no regularly scheduled waterborne services, hundreds of yachts, canal boats, and motor cruises are available throughout the year. The **British Tourist Authority's** free booklet "Inland Waterway Holidays" is a good source of information (available only from offices outside the United Kingdom). The **Inland Waterways Association** (✉ 114 Regents Park Rd., London NW1 8UQ, ☎ 0171/586–2510) is a popular source for maps and guide books. **British Waterways** (✉ Willow Grange, Church Rd., Watford WD1 3QA, ☎ 01923/226422) can assist with information. For boat-rental operators along Britain's several hundred miles of historic canals and waterways, contact the **Association of Pleasure Craft Operators** (✉ 35A High St., Newport, Shropshire TF10 7AT, ☎ 01952/813572).

BY BUS

Buses provide the most economical form of public transportation in Britain. Prices are invariably half those of train tickets, and the network is just as extensive. In recent years both short- and long-distance buses have improved immeasurably in speed, comfort, and frequency. There is one important semantic difference to keep in mind when discussing bus travel in Britain. **Buses** (either double- or single-decker) are generally part of the local transportation system in towns and cities and make frequent stops. **Coaches,** on the other hand, are comparable to American Greyhound buses and are used only for long-distance travel.

National Express offers the largest number of routes of any coach operator in Britain. It also offers a variety of discount tickets, including the **Discount Coachcard** and the **Tourist Trail Pass** for overseas visitors. The Discount Coachcard (£8) provides a 30% reduction on journeys made within a year and is only available to students and those under 25 years or over 50. The Tourist Trail Pass offers discounted rates for several ranges of days' travel. Passes can be bought from travel agents in the United States through British Travel International (✉ Box 299, Elkton, Virginia 22827, ☎ 540/298–2332); in London, at the Victoria Coach Station (✉ Buckingham Palace Rd., SW1 9TP, ☎ 0171/730–3466) or at any of 2,000 National Express agents in the United Kingdom. Information about all services can be obtained from the National Express Information Office at Victoria Coach Station (☎ 0990/808080) or from **Scottish Citylink** (✉ St. Andrew Sq., ☎ 0990/505050) in Edinburgh.

BY CAR

Breakdowns. There is a 24-hour breakdown service (☎ 01800/887766) run by the Automobile Association (AA). Most motorways have emergency phones along the route that connect the caller to the nearest police station. If driving extensively through Britain, membership in the AA can be useful for many reasons; sign on through car-rental agents (or ☎ 0990/500600).

Gasoline. In Britain gas (called petrol) pumps now measure in liters. Petrol is rarely sold here in gallons; if you do come across gallons, remember that there are 5 American gallons to 4 British gallons—for that amount, you will get about 20 liters. At press time the price of gasoline was about £2.80 per U.S. gallon, and £2.50 for lead-free. The price generally rises in spring and autumn with government tax rises, and you'll find the cheapest prices at the supermarket pumps. Although you can still buy leaded gas at most stations, the trend is for greener, cleaner lead-free, which is slightly cheaper.

Parking. Parking in London and in other large cities can be a nightmare. On-street meters are hard to find and can be very expensive. Cheaper pay-and-display lots (the driver inserts money into a machine to receive a sticker for the car with the amount of time allowed for parking) are common in smaller towns and suburban areas. But wherever you are, in town or city, beware of yellow or red lines. A single yellow line denotes no parking during the daytime. Double yellow lines or red lines indicate a more extensive prohibition on stopping. The exact times can always be ascertained from nearby signs, usually attached to lampposts. Illegal parking can result in having your vehicle removed or its wheel clamped, which can lead to a great deal of inconvenience as well as a hefty fine. Be sure to check street signs carefully before parking. In central London, where there is a good bus and underground service and taxis are plentiful, the use of a car is not recommended. If you must drive, an indispensable insider's reference book is the *London Parking Guide* (£4.99, Two Heads Publishing), available at good bookstores.

Road Conditions. Britain has superhighways (called motorways) running almost the length of the country, with links connecting them in the South, West, Midlands, and North. Motorways, given the prefix *M* on maps and road signs and shown in blue, have two or three lanes in each direction and are designed for high-speed rather than scenic travel. The main north–south road between London and the north is the M1. Other principal routes are the M3, from southwest London to the south coast and channel port ferries; M4 covers the route from London to Wales via Bristol and is heavily congested by weekenders escaping from the city; M5, running from the Midlands to the deep southwest peninsula; M6, from the Midlands north to Scotland; M11 serves eastward to Cambridge; M20 for southeast to Folkestone ferries and the Eurotunnel; M40 for northwest to Oxford, Stratford, and the Midlands. Encircling London is the M25, which provides access to many of the aforementioned motorways and links into the capital and is, therefore, heavily traveled during work rush hours, with a lull during the day. Be ready for lengthy rush-hour jams and heavy traffic during holiday weekends.

The other primary roads are A roads. Shown on maps as red and green lines, they connect town to town. Some bypass town centers and have fast stretches of divided (2-lane dual carriageway) highway. These are shown as thicker, black-edged lines on maps. Most other routes, yellow B roads, are the early roads once designed for horses and carriages. Although they—and the even narrower, winding white unclassified village roads—will allow you to see much more of the real Britain, your journey could end up taking twice the time. In remote country areas, road travel can be slow, especially in an icy winter. Good planning maps are available from the **AA** (Automobile Association) and the **RAC** (Royal Automobile Club); for in-depth exploring try the Ordnance Survey 1:50,000-series maps. These show every road, track, and footpath in the country. You might also consult the very useful Ordnance Survey *Motoring Atlas,* available at many bookstores.

Rules of the Road. You can use either your driver's license or an International Driving Permit in Britain. Drive on the left-hand side of the road and pay close attention to the varying—and abruptly changing—speed limits. Seat belts are obligatory for front-seat passengers (and back-seat ones when the cars are fitted with them). In general, speed limits are 30 mph in the center of cities and built-up areas, 40 mph in suburban areas, 70 mph on motorways, divided highways, and dual carriageways, and 60 mph on all other roads.

BY PLANE

Britain offers an extensive network of internal air routes, run by about six different airlines. Hourly shuttle services operate every day between

London and Glasgow, Edinburgh, Belfast, and Manchester. Seats are available on a no-reservations basis, and you can generally check in about half an hour before flight departure time. Keep in mind, however, that with fast trains and relatively short distances, it is often much cheaper—and not much more time-consuming—to travel by train.

BY TRAIN

Britain's rail system is somewhat overpriced, but it is one of the fastest, safest, and most comfortable rail services in the world. The beloved—and loathed—**British Rail (BR)** has now been broken up into individual private operators. For better or worse, only time will tell. If you need answers on train travel questions before you arrive in Great Britain, the overseas numbers to dial are 0161/236–3522 or 0171/928–5151. Once in Great Britain, the main central information number is 345/484950.

The country's principal—and most efficient—service is National Railways (using the old BR InterCity network of tracks and rolling stock), linking London with every major city in the country. The most modern high-speed trains travel up to 140 mph and offer comfortable, fully air-conditioned cars, both first- and second-class, with restaurant or buffet facilities. Local train services are not quite as reliable, particularly around such congested city centers as London. In general, seat reservations are not necessary except during peak vacation periods and on popular medium- and long-distance routes. Charges for reserving a standard-class seat start from £1, although reservations may be free over some routes.

Fares. Rail fares are high when compared with those in other countries. However, the network does offer a wide, and often bewildering, range of ticket reductions, and these can make a tremendous difference. The information office in each station can help you make the right choice. Information and tickets can also be obtained from Rail Travel Centres within the larger train stations and from selected travel agents displaying the double-arrow British Rail logo.

One of the best bargains available to overseas visitors is the **BritRail Pass** or the **BritRail Flexi Pass,** the U.K. equivalent of the Eurail ticket. It provides unlimited standard and first-class travel over the entire rail network for periods of 8, 15, or 22 days, or for one month. These passes can be purchased only outside Britain, either in the United States, before you leave, or in one of 46 other countries. British Rail still has an information office in New York City (✉ BritRail Travel International, 1500 Broadway, New York, NY 10036, ☎ 212/575–2542).

If you are planning to travel only short distances, be sure to buy inexpensive **same-day return tickets** ("cheap day returns"). These cost only slightly more than ordinary one-way ("single"), standard-class tickets but can be used *only* after 9:30 AM and on weekends. Other special offers are regional **Rover** tickets, giving unlimited travel within local areas, and **Saver** returns, allowing greatly reduced round-trip travel during off-peak periods. Inquire at main rail stations for details about reduced-price tickets to specific destinations.

ON FOOT

Many organizations conduct group walking holidays during the summer months. These are especially popular in the Welsh mountains, the Lake District, Dartmoor, and Exmoor. Details are available from the British Tourist Authority (☞ Visitor Information *in* Chapter 1).

Visitor Information

For National Tourist Board addresses and phone numbers, *see* Visitor Information *in* Chapter 1. For regional and city tourist boards, *see* Visitor Information *in* the Essentials directory for the relevant geographic region, *below*.

Weather

The main tourist season runs from mid-April to mid-October. In recent years, however, parts of the winter—especially December—have been almost as busy. Winter is also the height of London's theater, ballet, and opera season. Springtime reveals the countryside at its most verdant and beautiful, while fall offers soft vistas of reds, browns, and golden color. May, September, and October are the months to visit the northern moorlands—when the ground is carpeted with the purple hues of heathers—and Scottish highlands, while June is best for Wales and the Lake District. Most British people take their vacations during July and August, when costs are high and accommodations are at a premium.

CLIMATE

On the whole, Britain's winters are rarely bitter, except in the north and Scotland. Recent summers have been scorchers all over the country. Wherever you are, and whatever the season, be prepared for sudden changes. What begins as a brilliant, sunny day often turns into a damp and dismal one by lunchtime. Take an umbrella and raincoat wherever you go, particularly in Scotland, where the temperatures can be somewhat cooler.

The following are the average daily maximum and minimum temperatures for London.

Jan.	43F	6C	**May**	62F	17C	**Sept.**	65F	19C
	36	2		47	8		52	11
Feb.	44F	7C	**June**	69F	20C	**Oct.**	58F	14C
	36	2		53	12		46	8
Mar.	50F	10C	**July**	71F	22C	**Nov.**	50F	10C
	38	3		56	13		42	6
Apr.	56F	13C	**Aug.**	71F	22C	**Dec.**	45F	7C
	42	6		56	13		38	3

LONDON

If London contained only its famous landmarks—Buckingham Palace, Big Ben, Parliament, the Tower of London—it would still rank as one of the world's great destinations. It is a vast city of living history, whose story is still emerging in big events, like the death of Princess Diana in 1997, and small, like the opening of what seems like the millionth new restaurant. A city that loves to be explored, London beckons with great museums, royal pageantry, and history-steeped houses. Marvel at the Duke of Wellington's house, track Jack the Ripper's shadow in Whitechapel, then get Beatle-ized at Abbey Road. East End, West End, you'll find London is a dickens of a place.

Exploring London

Traditionally London has been divided between the City, to the east, where its banking and commercial interests lie, and Westminster, to the west, the seat of the royal court and of government. It is in these two areas that you will find most of the grand buildings that have played a central role in British history: the Tower of London and St. Paul's Cathedral, Westminster Abbey and the Houses of Parliament, Buckingham Palace, and the older royal palace of St. James's.

Visitors who restrict their sightseeing to the well-known tourist areas miss much of the best the city has to offer. Within a few minutes' walk of Buckingham Palace, for instance, lie St. James's, and Mayfair, two neighboring quarters of elegant town houses built for the nobility during the 17th and early 18th centuries and now notable for the shopping opportunities they house. The same lesson applies to The City, where, tucked away in quiet corners, stand many of the churches Christopher Wren built to replace those destroyed during the Great Fire of 1666.

Other parts of London worth exploring include Covent Garden, a former fruit and flower market converted into a lively shopping and entertainment center where you can wander for hours enjoying the friendly bustle of the streets. Hyde Park and Kensington Gardens, by contrast, offer a great swath of green parkland across the city center, preserved by past kings and queens for their own hunting and relaxation. A walk across Hyde Park will bring you to the museum district of South Kensington, with three major national collections: the Natural History Museum, the Science Museum, and the Victoria & Albert Museum, which specializes in the fine and applied arts.

The south side of the River Thames has its treats as well. A short stroll across Waterloo Bridge brings you to the South Bank Arts Complex, which includes the National Theatre, the Royal Festival Hall, the Hayward Gallery (with changing exhibitions of international art), the National Film Theatre, and the Museum of the Moving Image (MOMI)—a must for movie buffs. Here also are the exciting reconstruction of Shakespeare's Globe theater and its sister museum; and the future home, at Bankside Power Station, of the Tate Gallery of Modern Art—due for completion for the millennium. The views from the South Bank are stunning—to the west are the Houses of Parliament and Big Ben; to the east the dome of St. Paul's is just visible on London's changing skyline. London, although not simple of layout, is a rewarding walking city, and this remains the best way to get to know its nooks and crannies. The infamous weather may not be on your side, but there's plenty of indoor entertainment to keep you amused if you forget the umbrella!

Westminster

Numbers in the margin correspond to points of interest on the London map.

Westminster is the royal backyard—the traditional center of the royal court and of government. Here, within 1 km (½ mi) or so of one another, are nearly all London's most celebrated buildings, and there is a strong feeling of history all around you. Generations of kings and queens have lived here since the end of the 11th century—including the current monarch. The Queen resides at Buckingham Palace through most of the year; during summer periods when she visits her country estates, the palace is partially open to visitors.

17 **Banqueting House.** On the right side of the grand processional avenue known as Whitehall—site of many important government offices—stands this famous monument of the English Renaissance period. Designed by Inigo Jones in 1625 for court entertainments, it is the only part of Whitehall Palace, the monarch's principal residence during the 16th and 17th centuries, that was not burned down in 1698. It has a magnificent ceiling by Rubens, and outside is an inscription that marks the window through which King Charles I stepped to his execution. ✉ *Whitehall,* ☎ *0171/930–4179.* 🎫 *£3.25.* ⏲ *Tues.–Sat. 10–5, Sun. 2–5.*

8 **Buckingham Palace.** Supreme among the symbols of London, indeed of Britain generally, and of the royal family, Buckingham Palace tops

London

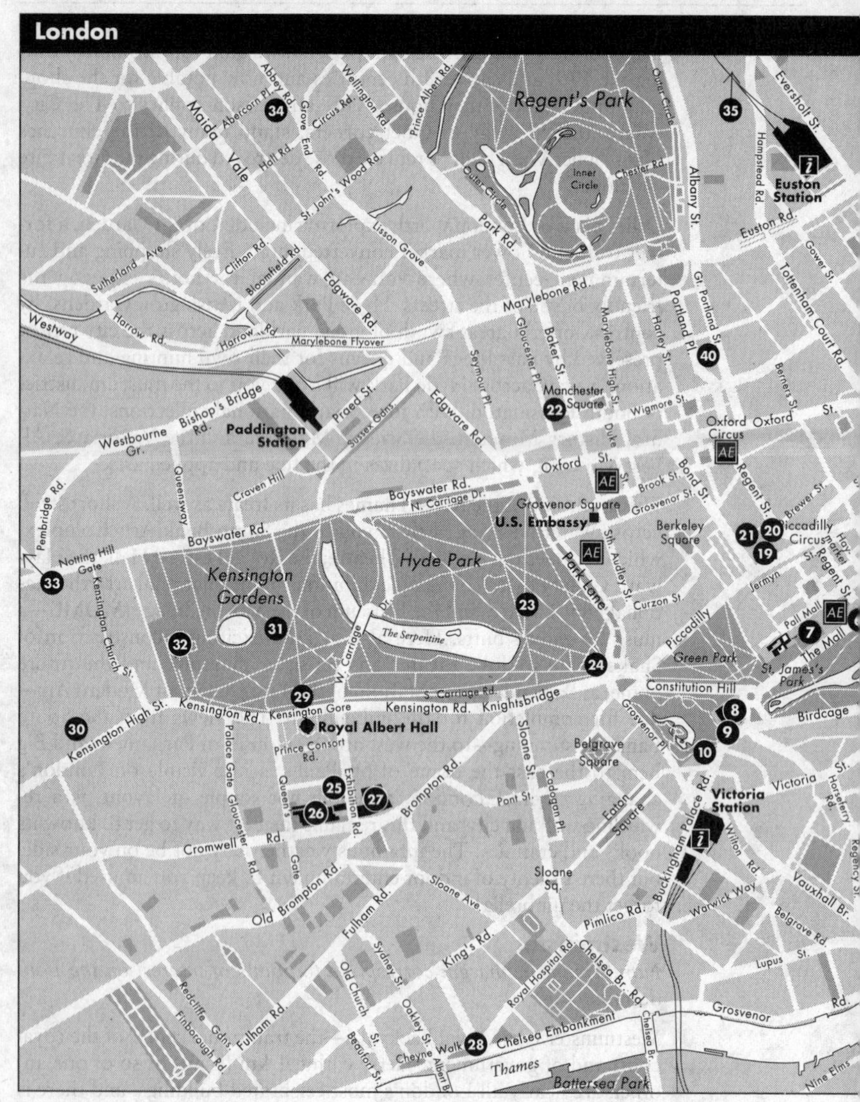

Regent's Park
Inner Circle
Outer Circle
Chester Rd.
Park Rd.
Albany St.
Hampstead Rd.
Eversholt St.
Euston Station
Euston Rd.
Gower St.
Tottenham Court Rd.
Maida Vale
Abercorn Pl.
Abbey Rd.
Grove End Rd.
Circus Rd.
Wellington Rd.
Prince Albert Rd.
Hall Rd.
St. John's Wood Rd.
Lisson Grove
Clifton Rd.
Bloomfield Rd.
Sutherland Ave.
Edgware Rd.
Harrow Rd.
Westway
Marylebone Flyover
Marylebone Rd.
Gloucester Pl.
Baker St.
Marylebone High St.
Harley St.
Portland Pl.
Gt. Portland St.
Berners St.
Seymour Pl.
Manchester Square
Wigmore St.
Oxford Circus
Oxford St.
Bishop's Bridge Rd.
Westbourne Gr.
Paddington Station
Praed St.
Sussex Gdns.
Queensway
Craven Hill
Pembridge Rd.
Bayswater Rd.
N. Carriage Dr.
Grosvenor Square
U.S. Embassy
Brook St.
Grosvenor St.
Bond St.
Regent St.
Brewer St.
Berkeley Square
Piccadilly Circus
Haymarket
Notting Hill Gate
Kensington Church St.
Kensington Gardens
Hyde Park
The Serpentine
W. Carriage Dr.
Park Lane
Sth. Audley St.
Curzon St.
Jermyn St.
Pall Mall
The Mall
Piccadilly
Green Park
St. James's Park
Constitution Hill
Birdcage
S. Carriage Rd.
Kensington High St.
Kensington Rd.
Kensington Gore
Knightsbridge
Royal Albert Hall
Prince Consort Rd.
Palace Gate
Gloucester Rd.
Queen's Gate
Exhibition Rd.
Brompton Rd.
Sloane St.
Cadogan Pl.
Pont St.
Grosvenor Pl.
Belgrave Square
Eaton Square
Victoria Station
Victoria St.
Horseferry Rd.
Buckingham Palace Rd.
Wilton Rd.
Regency St.
Cromwell Rd.
Old Brompton Rd.
Sloane Ave.
Sloane Sq.
Warwick Way
Vauxhall Br.
Belgrave Rd.
Pimlico Rd.
Lupus St.
Fulham Rd.
Sydney St.
Old Church St.
King's Rd.
Royal Hospital Rd.
Chelsea Br. Rd.
Grosvenor Rd.
Redcliffe Gdns.
Finborough Rd.
Oakley St.
Beaufort St.
Albert Br.
Cheyne Walk
Chelsea Embankment
Chelsea Br.
Thames
Battersea Park
Nine Elms
AE

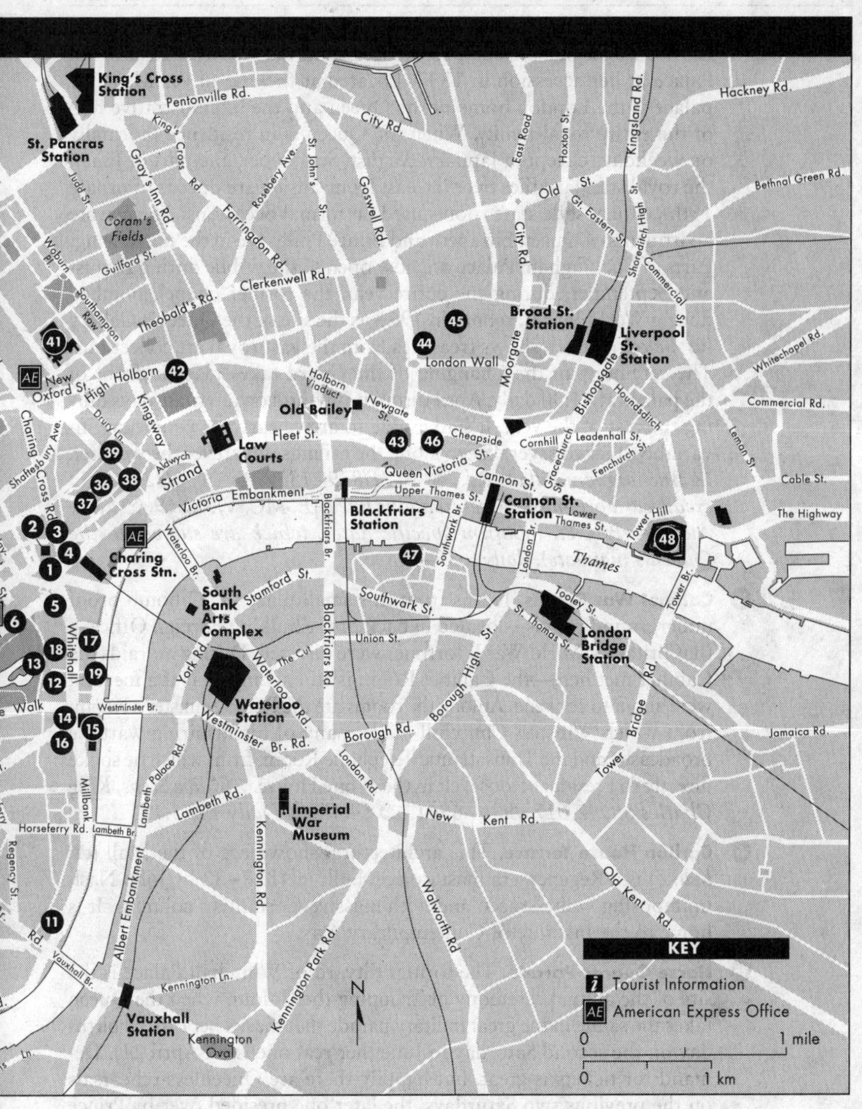

Royal Academy of Arts, **19**
Royal Mews, **10**
Royal Opera House, **39**
St. James's Palace, **7**
St. Martin-in-the-Fields, **4**
St. Mary-le-Bow, **46**
St. Paul's Cathedral, **43**
St. Paul's Church, **37**
Science Museum, **25**
Shakespeare's Globe, **47**
Sir John Soane's Museum, **42**
Tate Gallery, **11**
Ten Downing Street, **13**
Theatre Museum, **38**
Tower of London, **48**
Trafalgar Square, **1**
Victoria & Albert Museum, **27**
Wallace Collection, **22**
Westminster Abbey, **16**

many must-see lists—although the building itself is no masterpiece and has housed the monarch only since Victoria moved here from Kensington Palace at her accession in 1837. Located at the end of the Mall, the palace is the London home of the Queen and the administrative hub of the entire royal family. When the Queen is in residence (normally on weekdays except in January, August, September, and part of June), the royal standard flies over the east front. Inside are dozens of ornate 19th-century-style state rooms used on formal occasions. The private apartments of Queen Elizabeth and Prince Philip are in the north wing. Parts of Buckingham Palace are now open to the public during August and September; during the entire year, the former chapel, bombed during World War II, rebuilt in 1961, is the site of the **Queen's Gallery** (☞ *below*), which shows treasures from the vast royal art collections. The ceremony of the **Changing of the Guard** takes place in front of the palace at 11:30 daily, April through July, and on alternate days during the rest of the year. It's advisable to arrive early, as people are invariably stacked several deep along the railings, whatever the weather. ✉ *Buckingham Palace Rd.,* ☎ *0171/839–1377;* ☎ *0171/321–2233 credit-card pre-booking reservations line (AE, MC, V).* 💷 *£9.* ⏲ *Early Aug.–early Oct. (confirm specific dates, which are subject to the Queen's mandate), daily 9:30–4.*

12 **Cabinet War Rooms.** It was from this small maze of 17 bomb-proof underground rooms—located in back of the hulking Foreign Office—that Britain's World War II fortunes were directed. During air raids the Cabinet met here—the Cabinet Room is still arranged as if a meeting were about to convene. Among the rooms are the Prime Minister's Room, from which Winston Churchill made many of his inspiring wartime broadcasts, and the Transatlantic Telephone Room, from which he spoke directly to President Roosevelt in the White House. ✉ *Clive Steps, King Charles St.,* ☎ *0171/930–6961.* 💷 *£4.40.* ⏲ *Daily 10–5:15.*

6 **Carlton House Terrace.** This architectural showpiece of the Mall (☞ *below*) is a Regency-era masterpiece, built in 1827–32 by John Nash in imposing white-stucco and with massive Corinthian columns. It is home to the Institute of Contemporary Arts.

18 **Horse Guards Parade.** The former tiltyard of Whitehall Palace is the site of the annual ceremony of Trooping the Colour, when the Queen takes the salute in the great military parade that marks her official birthday on the second Saturday in June (her real one is on April 21). Demand for tickets is great, but happily there are Queenless rehearsals on the previous two Saturdays, the later one presided over by Prince Charles; for information, call 0171/414–2497. There is also a daily guard-changing ceremony outside the guard house, on Whitehall, at 11 AM (10 on Sunday)—one of London's best photo-ops. ✉ *Whitehall, opposite Downing St.*

15 **Houses of Parliament.** The Houses of Parliament are among the city's most famous and photogenic sights. The Clock Tower keeps watch on Parliament Square, in which stand statues of everyone from Richard the Lionhearted to Abraham Lincoln, and, across the way, Westminster Abbey. Also known as the **Palace of Westminster,** this was the site of the monarch's main residence from the 11th century until 1512; the court then moved to the newly built Whitehall Palace. The only parts of the original building to have survived are the Jewel Tower and **Westminster Hall,** which has a fine hammer-beam roof. The rest of the structure was destroyed in a disastrous fire in 1834 and was rebuilt in the newly popular mock-medieval Gothic style to the delight of millions. The architect, Augustus Pugin, designed the entire place, right down to the Gothic umbrella stands. This newer part of the palace contains the debating cham-

bers and committee rooms of the two Houses of Parliament—the Commons (whose members are elected) and the Lords (whose members are appointed or inherit their seats). There are no tours of the palace, but the public is admitted to the Public Gallery of each House; expect to wait in line for several hours (the line for the Lords is generally much shorter than that for the Commons). The most famous features of the palace are its towers. At the south end is the 336-ft **Victoria Tower.** At the other end is **St. Stephen's Tower,** or the Clock Tower, better known, but inaccurately so, as **Big Ben;** that name properly belongs to the 13-ton bell in the tower on which the hours are struck. Big Ben himself was probably Sir Benjamin Hall, commissioner of works when the bell was installed in the 1850s. A light shines from the top of the tower during a night sitting of Parliament. ✉ *St. Stephen's Entrance, St. Margaret St., SW1,* ☎ *0171/219–3000.* 🎫 *Free.* 🕓 *Commons: Mon.–Thurs. 2:30–10, Fri. 9:30–3; Lords: Mon.–Thurs. 2:30–10.*

❺ **The Mall.** The splendid and imperial **Admiralty Arch** guards the entrance to The Mall, the noted ceremonial way that leads alongside **St. James's Park** to Buckingham Palace. The Mall takes its name from a game called *palle maille,* a version of croquet that James I imported from France, and Charles II popularized during the late 1600s. The park was developed by successive monarchs, most recently by George IV in the 1820s, having originally been used for hunting by Henry VIII. Join office workers relaxing with a lunchtime sandwich, or stroll here on a summer's evening when the illuminated fountains play and Westminster Abbey and the Houses of Parliament are floodlit. Toward Buckingham Palace, along The Mall, you'll pass the foot of the imposing **Carlton House Terrace** (☞ *above*).

★ ❼ **National Gallery.** Generally ranked right after the Louvre, the National Gallery is one of the world's greatest museums. Occupying the long neoclassical building on the north side of Trafalgar Square (☞ *below*), it contains works by virtually every famous artist and school from the 14th to the 19th centuries. Its galleries overflow with masterpieces, including Jan van Eyck's *Arnolfini Marriage,* Leonardo da Vinci's *Burlington Virgin and Child,* Velásquez's *The Toilet of Venus* (known as "The Rokeby Venus"), and Constable's *Hay Wain.* The gallery is especially strong on Flemish and Dutch masters, Rubens and Rembrandt among them, and on Italian Renaissance works. The museum's Brasserie is an excellent spot for lunch. ✉ *Trafalgar Sq.,* ☎ *0171/839–3321; 0171/839–3526 (recorded general information).* 🎫 *Free; admission charge for special exhibitions.* 🕓 *Mon.–Sat. 10–6, Sun. 2–6; June–Aug., also Wed. until 8.*

❽ **National Portrait Gallery.** This fascinating collection contains portraits of well-known (and not so well-known) Britons, including monarchs, statesmen, and writers. ✉ *2 St. Martin's Pl., at foot of Charing Cross Rd.,* ☎ *0171/306–0055.* 🎫 *Free.* 🕓 *Weekdays 10–5, Sat. 10–6, Sun. 2–6.*

❾ **Queen's Gallery.** This is the former chapel at the south side of Buckingham Palace (☞ *above*). On display here are smaller shows drawn from the royal collections, such as Michelangelo drawings; call for information on current exhibits. ✉ *Buckingham Palace Rd.,* ☎ *0171/799–2331.* 🎫 *£3.50; combined ticket for Queen's Gallery and Royal Mews: £6.20.* 🕓 *Tues.–Sat. 10–5, Sun. 2–5.*

❿ **Royal Mews.** Unmissable children's entertainment, this museum is the home of Her Majesty's Coronation Coach. Here, some of the queen's horses are stabled and the elaborately gilded state coaches are on view. ✉ *Buckingham Palace Rd.,* ☎ *0171/799–2331.* 🎫 *£3.70; combined* *ticket with Queen's Gallery: £6.* ⏲ *Oct. 7–Dec. 23 and Jan. 6–Mar. 24, Wed. noon–4; Apr. 1–Sept. 30, Tues.–Thurs. noon–4.*

❹ **St. Martin-in-the-Fields.** Soaring above Trafalgar Square, this landmark church may seem familiar to many Americans because James Gibbs's classical-temple-with-spire design became a pattern for churches in early Colonial America. Built in about 1730, the distinctive neoclassical church is the site for regular lunchtime music recitals. ✉ *Trafalgar Sq.,* ☎ *0171/930–0089, 0171/839–8362 credit-card bookings for evening concerts.* ⏲ *Church daily 8–8; crypt Mon.–Sat. 10–8, Sun. noon–6.*

⓫ **Tate Gallery.** By the river to the north of Chelsea, on traffic-laden Millbank, the Tate Gallery of Modern British Art is the greatest museum devoted to British painting and sculpture. "Modern" is slightly misleading, as one of the three collections here consists of British art from 1545 to the present, including works by William Hogarth, Thomas Gainsborough, Sir Joshua Reynolds, and George Stubbs from the 18th century; and by John Constable, William Blake, and the Pre-Raphaelite painters from the 19th century (don't miss Sir John Everett Millais' unforgettable *Ophelia*). Also from the 19th century is the second of the Tate's collections, the incredible Turner Bequest, consisting of the personal collection of England's greatest romantic painter, J. M. W. Turner. About a 20-minute walk south of the Houses of Parliament, the Tate is also accessible if you tube it to the Pimlico stop, then take a five-minute walk through Chelsea to the museum. ✉ *Millbank, SW1,* ☎ *0171/821–1313 or 0171/821–7128.* 🎫 *Free; special exhibitions £3–£7.* ⏲ *Mon.–Sat. 10–5:50, Sun. 2–5:50. Tube: Pimlico.*

⓭ **Ten Downing Street.** As you walk along Whitehall, past government offices, you'll note, on the north side of the street, the entrance to Downing Street, a row of unassuming 18th-century houses. The prime minister's office is at No. 10 (with a private apartment on the top floor). The chancellor of the exchequer, the finance minister, occupies No. 11. The street is now gated off from the main thoroughfare. Not far away in the middle of Whitehall is the **Cenotaph,** a stone national memorial to the dead of both world wars. At 11 AM on the Sunday closest to the 11th day of the 11th month, the Queen and other dignitaries lay flowers in tribute here..

❶ **Trafalgar Square.** This is the center of London, by dint of a plaque on the corner of the Strand and Charing Cross Road from which distances on U.K. signposts are measured. It is the home of the **National Gallery** (☞ *above*) and of one of London's most distinctive landmarks, **Nelson's Column,** a tribute to one of England's favorite heroes, Admiral Lord Horatio Nelson, who routed the French at the Battle of Trafalgar in 1805. Permanently alive with Londoners and tourists alike, roaring traffic, and pigeons, it remains London's "living room"—great events, such as New Year's, royal weddings, elections, sporting triumphs—will always see the crowds gathering in the city's most famous square.

★ ⓰ **Westminster Abbey.** This is the most ancient of London's great churches and the most important, for it is here that Britain's monarchs are crowned. Most of the abbey dates largely from the 13th and 14th centuries. The main nave is packed with atmosphere and memories, as it has witnessed many splendid coronation ceremonies, royal weddings, and more recently, the funeral of Diana, Princess of Wales. It is also packed with crowds—so many, in fact, that the Abbey has now started to charge admission to the main nave (always free, of course, for participants in religious services). **Henry VII's Chapel,** an exquisite example of the heavily decorated late-Gothic style, was not built until the early 1600s, and the twin towers over the west entrance are an 18th-century addition. There is much to see inside, including the tomb of the Unknown Warrior, a nameless World War I soldier buried, in memory of the war's victims, in earth brought with his corpse from France; and the famous Poets' Corner, where England's great writers—Milton, Chaucer, Shakespeare, et al—are memorialized, and some are actually buried. Behind the high altar are the royal tombs, including those of Queen Elizabeth I; Mary, Queen of Scots; and Henry V. In the Chapel of Edward the Confessor stands the Coronation Chair. Among the royal weddings that have taken place here are those of the present queen and most recently, in 1986, the (ill-starred) duke and duchess of York.It is all too easy to forget, swamped by the crowds trying to see the abbey's sights, that this is a place of worship. Early morning is a good moment to catch something of the building's atmosphere. Better still, take time to attend a service. Note that photography is not permitted except Wednesday 6 PM–8 PM. ✉ *Broad Sanctuary,* ☎ *0171/222–5152.* 🎟 *£5.* 🕙 *Mon., Tues., Thurs., and Fri. 9–4; Wed. 9–7:45; Sat. 9–2 and 3:45–5; Sun. all day for services only. Undercroft, Pyx Chamber, Chapter House, and Treasury daily 10:30–4. Closed Sun. except for religious services; Henry VII Chapel closed Sun.*

St. James's and Mayfair

These are two of London's most exclusive neighborhoods, where the homes are fashionable and the shopping is world-class. You can start by walking west from Piccadilly Circus along Piccadilly, a busy street lined with some very English shops (including Hatchards, the booksellers; Swaine, Adeney Brigg, the equestrian outfitters; and Fortnum & Mason, the department store that supplies the Queen's groceries).

24 **Apsley House.** Once known, quite simply, as No. 1, London, this was long celebrated as the best address in town. Built by Robert Adam in the 1770s, this was where the Duke of Wellington lived from the 1820s until his death in 1852. It has been kept as the Iron Duke liked it, his uniforms and weapons, his porcelain and plate, and his extensive art collection, displayed heroically in opulent 19th-century rooms. Unmissable, in every sense, is the gigantic Canova statue of a nude (but fig-leafed) Napoléon Bonaparte, Wellington's archenemy. ✉ *149 Piccadilly,* ☎ *0171/499–5676.* 🎟 *£4.* 🕙 *Tues.–Sun. 11–5.*

40 **BBC Experience.** To celebrate its 75th anniversary, the BBC—the folks who brought you all those wonderful Masterpiece Theater TV shows—has just opened the doors of its own in-house museum. There's an audiovisual show, an interactive section—want to try making your own director's cut of a segment of *EastEnders*?—and, of course, a massive gift shop. This museum will probably be deluged by natives for the first few years—conveniently, admission is on a pre-booked and timed system. ✉ *Broadcasting House, Portland Pl., W1,* ☎ *0870/603–0304, 01222/55771 outside U.K.* 🎟 *Free.* 🕙 *Daily 9:30–5:30. Tube: Oxford Circus.*

Bond Street. Divided into two parts, Old and New (though both are some 300 years old), Bond is the classiest shopping street in London, the home of haute couture, with such famous names as Gucci, Hermès, and Chanel, and costly jewelry from such shops as Asprey, Tiffany, and Cartier.

20 **Burlington Arcade.** This perfectly picturesque covered walkway dates from 1819. Here, shops sell cashmere sweaters, silk scarves, handmade chocolates, and leather-bound books. If not the choice shopping spot it once was, it still makes a great photo-op, particularly if you can snap the uniformed beadle (he ensures that no one runs, whistles, or sings here) on duty. ✉ *Off Piccadilly.*

21 **Museum of Mankind.** Behind the Royal Academy, this magnificently florid Victorian edifice contains the British Museum's ethnographic collection (though this will soon be transferred to the British Museum when the British Library moves to its new premises in St. Pancras). There are displays on the South Seas, the Arctic, and other regions of the world. ✉ *6 Burlington Gardens,* ☎ *0171/323–8043.* 🎟 *Free.* 🕓 *Mon.–Sat. 10–5, Sun. 2:30–6.*

19 **Royal Academy of Arts.** On the north side of Piccadilly, the grand marble pile of **Burlington House** contains the offices of many learned societies and the headquarters of the Royal Academy. The RA, as it is generally known, stages major visiting art exhibitions. Once most famous for its Summer Exhibition (May–Aug.)—a chaotic hodgepodge of works by living and mostly conservative British artists—the RA has now adopted an impressive schedule of temporary art exhibitions that ranks among the most prestigious and cutting-edge in the country; inquire about current calendar of events. ✉ *Burlington House,* ☎ *0171/439–7438 or 0171/439–4996 (recorded information).* 🎟 *Admission varies according to exhibition.* 🕓 *Daily 10–6.*

7 **St. James's Palace.** This historic abode has for centuries been a useful royal address and, today, it still is, as it is the current residence of the future King Charles III (if the current Prince of Wales makes it to Westminster Abbey). Although the earliest parts of the lovely brick building date from the 1530s, it had a relatively short career as the center of royal affairs—from the destruction of Whitehall Palace in 1698 until 1837, when Victoria became queen and moved the royal household down the road to Buckingham Palace. Today, the Palace is closed to the public, but your viewfinder will love the picturesque exterior and regimental guard on duty. ✉ *Friary Court, Pall Mall.*

22 **Wallace Collection.** A palatial town house museum, the Wallace is important, exciting, under-visited—and free. As at the Frick Collection in New York, the setting here, Hertford House, is part of the show—built for the Duke of Manchester, and now stuffed with armor, exquisite furniture, and great paintings, including Bouchers, Watteaus, and Fragonard's *The Swing*. Don't forget to smile back at Frans Hals's *Laughing Cavalier* in the Big Gallery. ✉ *Hertford House, Manchester Sq.,* ☎ *0171/935–0687.* 🎟 *Free.* 🕓 *Mon.–Sat. 10–5, Sun. 2–5.*

Hyde Park, Kensington, and Beyond

When in need of elbow room, Londoners head for their green "lungs"—Hyde Park and Kensington Gardens. Viewed by natives as their own private backyards, they form an open swath across central London. In and around them are some of London's most noted museums and monuments.

29 **Albert Memorial.** This florid monument of the 19th century commemorates Queen Victoria's much-loved husband, Prince Albert, who died in 1861 at the age of 42. The monument, itself the epitome of high Victorian taste, commemorates the many socially uplifting projects of the prince, among them the Great Exhibition of 1851, whose catalog he is holding. The Memorial, which has been badly eroded by pollution, is currently being restored. It's directly opposite the Royal Albert Hall. ✉ *Kensington Gore.*

28 **Cheyne Walk.** The most beautiful spot in Chelsea—one of London's most arty (and expensive) residential districts—this Thamesside street is adorned with Queen Anne houses and legendary addresses. Author George Eliot died at No. 4 in 1880; Pre-Raphaelite artist Dante Gabriel Rossetti lived at No. 16. Two other resident artists were James McNeill Whistler and J.M.W. Turner.

23 **Hyde Park.** Along with the smaller St. James's and Green Parks to the east, Hyde Park started as Henry VIII's hunting grounds. Nowadays, it remains a tranquil oasis from urban London—-tranquil, that is, except for Sunday morning, when the soapbox orators take over **Speakers' Corner,** near the northeast corner of the park. Not far away, along the south side of the park, is **Rotten Row.** It was Henry VIII's royal path to the hunt—hence the name, a corruption of *route du roi.* It's still used by the Household Cavalry, the queen's guard. You can see them leave, in full regalia, plumed helmets and all, at around 10:30, or await the return of the exhausted ex-guard about noon. ✉ *Bounded by the Ring, Bayswater Rd., Park La., and Knightsbridge.*

31 **Kensington Gardens.** More formal than neighboring Hyde Park, Kensington Gardens was first laid out as palace grounds and adjoins Kensington Palace (☞ *below*). George Frampton's 1912 **Peter Pan,** a bronze of the boy who lived on an island in the Serpentine and never grew up, overlooks the Long Water. His creator, J. M. Barrie, lived at 100 Bayswater Road, not 500 yards from here. At the **Round Pond,** you can feed the swans. Nearby is boating and swimming in the **Serpentine,** an S-shape lake. Refreshments can be had at the lakeside tearooms. The **Serpentine Gallery** (☎ 0171/402–6075) holds noteworthy exhibitions of modern art. ✉ *Bounded by The Broad Walk, Bayswater Rd., the Ring, and Kensington Rd.*

32 **Kensington Palace.** This has been a royal home since the late 17th century. From the outside it looks less like a palace than a country house, which it was until William III bought it in 1689. Queen Victoria spent a less-than-happy childhood at Kensington Palace, Princess Diana a less-than-happy marriage. Called the "royal ghetto," the palace is home to many Windsors (they live in a distant section cordoned off to the public). Kensington Palace's state apartments have been restored to how they were in Princess Victoria's day. Drop in on the Orangery here for a very elegant cup of tea. ✉ *Kensington Gardens,* ☎ *0171/937–9561.* 🎫 *£5.50.* ⏲ *May–Dec., daily 10–3:30.*

30 **Linley Sambourne House.** Stuffed with Victorian and Edwardian antiques, fabrics, and paintings, this is one of the most charming 19th-century London houses extant—little wonder it was filmed for Merchant/Ivory's *A Room with A View.* During the 1870s this was home to the political cartoonist Edward Linley Sambourne. ✉ *18 Stafford Terr.,* ☎ *0181/994–1019.* 🎫 *£3.* ⏲ *Mar.–Oct., Wed. 10–4, Sun. 2–5.*

26 **Natural History Museum.** Housed in an ornate late-Victorian building with striking modern additions, this museum features displays on such topics as human biology and evolution, designed to challenge visitors to think for themselves. ✉ *Cromwell Rd.,* ☎ *0171/938–9123; 0142/692–7654 (recorded information).* 🎫 *£6; free weekdays 4:30–5:50 and weekends 5–5:50.* ⏲ *Mon.–Sat. 10–6, Sun. 2:30–6.*

33 **Portobello Road.** North of Kensington Gardens is the lively **Notting Hill** district, full of restaurants and cafés where some of London's most stylish, trendsetting people gather. The best-known attraction in this area is Portobello Road, where the lively antiques and bric-a-brac market is held each Saturday (arrive at 6 AM for the best finds); the southern end is focused on antiques, the northern end on food, flowers, and secondhand clothes. The street is also full of regular antiques shops that are open most weekdays. ✉ *Pembridge Rd., Notting Hill Gate.*⏲ *Antiques market Sat. 6–4.*

25 **Science Museum.** The leading national collection of science and technology, this museum has extensive hands-on exhibits on outer space,

astronomy, and hundreds of other subjects. ⊠ *Exhibition Rd.,* ☎ *0171/938–8000.* 🎫 *£5.95.* ⏲ *Mon.–Sat. 10–6, Sun. 11–6.*

★ 27 **Victoria & Albert Museum.** The V&A, as it is commonly known, originated during the 19th century as a museum of the decorative arts and has extensive collections of costumes, paintings, jewelry, and crafts from every part of the globe. Don't miss the sculpture court, the vintage couture collections, and the great Raphael Room. ⊠ *Cromwell Rd.,* ☎ *0171/938–8500.* 🎫 *£5; free after 4:30, except Wed.* ⏲ *Mon. noon–5:50, Tues.–Sun. 10–5:50; Wed. Late View 4:30–9:30.*

Covent Garden

The Covent Garden district—which lies just to the east of Soho—has gone from a down-at-heels area to one of the busiest, most raffishly enjoyable parts of the city. Continental-style open-air cafés create a very un-English atmosphere, with vintage fashion boutiques, art galleries, and street buskers attracting crowds.

36 **Covent Garden.** You could easily spend several hours exploring the block of streets north of the Strand known as Covent Garden. The heart of the area is a former wholesale fruit and vegetable market—made famous as one of Eliza Doolittle's haunts in *My Fair Lady*—established in 1656. **The Piazza,** the Victorian Market Building, is now a vibrant shopping center, with numerous boutiques, crafts shops, and cafés. On the south side of the market building is the **Jubilee market,** with crafts and clothing stalls. The section is anchored by **St. Paul's Church** (☞ *below*) and the **Royal Opera House** (now undergoing extensive renovations; ☞ *below*). For interesting specialty shops, head north of the Market Building. Shops on **Long Acre** sell maps, art books and materials, and clothing; shops on **Neal Street** sell clothes, pottery, jewelry, tea, housewares, and goods from East Asia. ⊠ *Bounded by the Strand, Charing Cross Rd., Long Acre, and Drury La.*

39 **Royal Opera House.** Until 2001, the home of the Royal Ballet and the Royal Opera Company will be closed for extensive renovations. These legendary resident troupes will be performing elsewhere (☞ The Arts, *below*). ⊠ *Bow St.*

37 **St. Paul's Church.** A landmark of the Covent Garden market area, this 1633 church, designed by Inigo Jones, is known as the Actors' Church. Inside are numerous memorials to theater people. Look for the open-air entertainers performing under the church's portico. ⊠ *Bedford St.*

38 **Theatre Museum.** A comprehensive collection of material on the history of the English theater, this museum traces the history not merely of the classic drama but also of opera, music hall, pantomime, and musical comedy. A highlight is the re-creation of a dressing room filled with memorabilia of former stars. ⊠ *Russell St.,* ☎ *0171/836–7891.* 🎫 *£3.50.* ⏲ *Tues.–Sun. 11–7.*

Bloomsbury

Bloomsbury is a semiresidential district to the north of Covent Garden that contains some spacious and elegant 17th- and 18th-century squares. It could be called the intellectual center of London, as both the British Museum and the University of London are here. The area also gave its name to the Bloomsbury Group, a clique of writers and painters who thrived here during the early 20th century.

★ 41 **British Museum.** Known as "Mankind's attic," this fabled museum houses a vast and priceless collection of treasures, including Egyptian, Greek, and Roman antiquities; Renaissance jewelry; pottery; coins; glass; and drawings from virtually every European school since the 15th century. It's best to pick out one section that particularly interests you—to try to see everything would be an overwhelming and exhausting task. Some of the highlights are the **Elgin Marbles,** sculptures that formerly decorated the Parthenon in Athens; the **Rosetta Stone,** which helped archaeologists to interpret Egyptian hieroglyphs; and a copy of the **Magna Carta,** the charter signed by King John in 1215 to which is ascribed the origins of English liberty. ✉ *Great Russell St.,* ☎ *0171/636–1555; 0171/580–1788 (recorded information).* 🎟 *Free.* ⏲ *Mon.–Sat. 10–5, Sun. 2:30–6.*

★ ❹❷ **Sir John Soane's Museum.** On the border of London's legal district, this museum, stuffed with antique busts and myriad decorative delights, is an eccentric, smile-inducing 19th-century collection of art and artifacts in the former home of the architect of the Bank of England. ✉ *13 Lincoln's Inn Fields,* ☎ *0171/405–2107.* 🎟 *Free.* ⏲ *Tues.–Sat. 10–5.*

The City and South Bank

The City, the commercial center of London, was actually once the site of the great Roman city of Londinium. Since those days, the City has been rebuilt innumerable times and, today, ancient and modern jostle each other elbow to elbow. Several of London's most famous attractions are here, along with the adjacent South Bank area, where Shakespeare's Globe has the starring role.

❹❺ **Barbican Centre.** A vast arts center built by the City of London, the Barbican takes its name from the watchtower that stood here during the Middle Ages. The arts center contains a concert hall, where the London Symphony Orchestra is based, two theaters, an art gallery, a cinema, and several restaurants. The theaters are the London home of the **Royal Shakespeare Company.** ✉ *Silk St.,* ☎ *0171/638–4141, 0171/628–0183 tour reservations, 0171/628–3351 RSC backstage tour.* 🎟 *Barbican Centre free, gallery £5, conservatory £1.* ⏲ *Barbican Centre Mon.–Sat. 9 AM–11 PM, Sun. noon–11; gallery Mon.–Sat. 10–7:30, Sun. noon–7:30; conservatory weekends noon–5:30 when not in use for private function (call first).*

❹❹ **Museum of London.** At **London Wall,** so called because it follows the line of the wall that surrounded the Roman settlement, the Museum of London enables you to get the history of London sorted out—although there's a great deal to sort out: Oliver Cromwell's death mask, Queen Victoria's crinolined gowns, Selfridge's Art-Deco elevator lifts, and the Lord Mayor's Coach are just some of the goodies here. ✉ *London Wall,* ☎ *0171/600–3699.* 🎟 *Free 4:30–5:50.* ⏲ *Tues.–Sat. 10–6, Sun. noon–6.*

❹❻ **St. Mary-le-Bow.** This church was rebuilt by Christopher Wren after the Great Fire; it was built again after being bombed during World War II. It is said that to be a true Cockney, you must be born within the sound of Bow bells. The church is a landmark of the **Cheapside** district. This was the marketplace of medieval London (the word *ceap* is Old English for "to barter"), as the street names hereabouts indicate: Milk Street, Ironmonger Lane, and so on. Despite rebuilding, many of the streets still run on the medieval pattern. ✉ *Cheapside.*

★ ❹❸ **St. Paul's Cathedral.** London's symbolic heart, St. Paul's is Sir Christopher Wren's masterpiece. Its dome—the world's third largest—can be seen from many an angle in other parts of the city. The cathedral was completed in 1710 following the Great Fire. Wren was the architect who was also responsible for designing 50 City parish churches to replace those lost in that disaster. Fittingly, he is buried in the crypt under a simple Latin epitaph, composed by his son, which translates as: "Reader, if you seek his monument, look around you." The cathedral has been the site of many famous state occasions, including the funeral of Winston Churchill in 1965 and the ill-fated marriage of the prince and princess of Wales in 1981. In the ambulatory (the area behind the high altar) is the American Chapel, a memorial to the 28,000 U.S. servicemen and women stationed in Britain during World War II who lost their lives while on active service. The greatest architectural glory of the cathedral is the dome. This consists of three distinct elements: an outer, timber-frame dome covered with lead; an interior dome built of brick and decorated with frescoes of the life of St. Paul by the 18th-century artist Sir James Thornhill; and, in between, a brick cone that supports and strengthens both. There is a good view of the church from the **Whispering Gallery,** high up in the inner dome. The gallery is so called because of its remarkable acoustics, whereby words spoken on one side can be clearly heard on the other, 107 ft away. Above this gallery are two others, both external, from which there are fine views over the City and beyond. ✉ *St. Paul's Churchyard, Paternoster Sq.,* ☎ *0171/236–4128.* ⏲ *Cathedral open for visits Mon.–Sat. 8:30–4:30; ambulatory, crypt, and galleries open Mon.–Sat. 9:30–4:15.*

★ 47 **Shakespeare's Globe.** This spectacular theater is a replica of Shakespeare's open-roof Globe Playhouse (built in 1599; incinerated in 1613), where most of the playwright's great plays premiered. It stands 200 yards from the original, overlooking the Thames. It has been built with the use of authentic Elizabethan materials, down to the first thatch roof in London since the Great Fire. Plays are presented in natural light (and sometimes rain), to 1,000 people on wooden benches in the "bays," plus 500 "groundlings," standing on a carpet of filbert shells and clinker, just as they did nearly 4 centuries ago. The theater season is only from June through September; throughout the year, you can tour the Globe through admission to the **museum** devoted to Shakespeare and his times on the premises. ✉ *New Globe Walk, Bankside (South Bank),* ☎ *0171/928–6406.* 🎟 *£5 to museum.* ⏲ *Daily 10–5. Call for performance schedule.*

★ 48 **Tower of London.** A guaranteed spine-chiller, this is one of London's most famous sights and one of its most crowded, too. Come as early in the day as possible and head for the Crown Jewels so you can see them before the crowds arrive. The tower served the monarchs of medieval England as both fortress and palace. Every British sovereign from William the Conqueror in the 11th century to Henry VIII in the 16th lived here, and it remains a royal palace, in name at least. The White Tower is the oldest and also the most conspicuous building in the entire complex. Inside, the Chapel of St. John is one of the few unaltered parts. The Royal Armories, England's national collection of arms and armor, occupies the rest of the White Tower.

The **History Gallery,** south of the White Tower, is a walk-through display designed to answer questions about the inhabitants of the tower and its evolution over the centuries. Among other buildings worth seeing is the **Bloody Tower.** The little princes in the tower—the boy-king Edward V and his brother Richard, duke of York, supposedly murdered on the orders of the duke of Gloucester, later crowned Richard III—certainly lived in the Bloody Tower, and may well have died here, too. In the **Wakefield Tower,** Henry VI is alleged to have been murdered in 1471 during England's medieval civil war, the Wars of the Roses. It was a rare honor to be beheaded in private inside the tower; most people were executed outside, on **Tower Hill,** where the rabble could get a much better view.

The **Crown Jewels** are a breathtakingly splendid collection of regalia, precious stones, gold, and silver. The Royal Scepter contains the largest cut diamond in the world. The Imperial State Crown, made for the 1838 coronation of Queen Victoria, contains some 3,000 precious stones, largely diamonds and pearls. The Jewels are housed in the Duke of Wellington's Barracks. Look for the ravens whose presence at the tower is traditional. It is said that if they leave, the tower will fall and England will lose her greatness. ⊠ *Tower Hill,* ☎ *0171/709–0765.* 🎟 *£8.50; small additional admission charge to Fusiliers Museum only.* ⏲ *Mar.–Oct., Mon.–Sat. 9:30–6:30, Sun. 2–6; Nov.–Feb., Mon.–Sat. 9:30–5. Yeoman Warder guides conduct tours daily from Middle Tower, no charge, but a tip is always appreciated. Subject to weather and availability of guides, tours are conducted about every 30 mins until 3:30 in summer, 2:30 in winter.*

Hampstead

Hampstead is a village within the city, where many famous poets and writers have lived. Today it is a fashionable residential area, with a main shopping street and some rows of elegant 18th-century houses. The heath is one of London's largest and most attractive open spaces.

34 **Abbey Road Studios.** Here, outside the legendary Abbey Road Studios (the facility is closed to the public), is the most famous zebra crossing in the world. Immortalized on the cover of the Beatles' *Abbey Road* album of 1969, this pedestrian crosswalk is a spot beloved to countless Beatlemaniacs and baby boomers, many of whom venture here to leave their signature on the white stucco fence that fronts the adjacent studio facility. Abbey Road is not in Hampstead but in adjacent St. John's Wood, an elegant residential suburb a 10-minute ride on the tube from central London. ⊠ *3 Abbey Rd.*

35 **Kenwood House.** Standing alone in its own landscaped grounds on the north side of the heath is Kenwood House, built during the 17th century and remodeled by Robert Adam at the end of the 18th century. The house contains a collection of superb paintings by such masters as Rembrandt, Turner, Reynolds, Van Dyck, and Gainsborough—and *The Guitar Player,* probably the most beautiful Vermeer in England. Unfortunately, only one grand Adam interior remains. The lovely landscaped grounds provide the setting for symphony concerts in summer. ⊠ *Hampstead La.,* ☎ *0181/348–1286.* 🎟 *Free.* ⏲ *Easter–Sept., daily 10–6; Oct.–Easter, daily 10–4.*

Greenwich

The historical and maritime attractions at Greenwich, on the Thames, some 8 km (5 mi) east of central London, make it an ideal destination for a day out. You can get to Greenwich by riverboat from Westminster and Tower Bridge piers, by ThamesLine's high-speed river buses, or by train from Charing Cross station. You can also take the Docklands Light Railway from Tower Gateway to Island Gardens and walk a short distance along a pedestrian tunnel under the river.

Cutty Sark. Now in dry dock is the glorious 19th-century clipper ship *Cutty Sark.* ⊠ *King William Walk,* ☎ *0181/858–3445.* 🎟 *£3.50.* ⏲ *Late-Mar.–Sept., Mon.–Sat. 10–6, Sun. noon–6; Oct.–late-Mar., Mon.–Sat. 10–5, Sun. noon–5.*

National Maritime Museum. A treasure house of paintings, maps, models, and, best of all, ships from all ages, this is a fascinating museum. Don't miss the ornate royal barges. ⊠ *Romney Rd.,* ☎ *0181/858–4422.* 🎟 *£5.* ⏲ *Mon.–Sat. 10–6, Sun. noon–6.*

Old Royal Observatory. Stand astride both hemispheres in the courtyard of the Old Royal Observatory, where the prime meridian—zero degrees longitude—is set. The Observatory is at the top of the hill, behind the National Maritime Museum and Royal Naval College, in **Green-**

Greenwich

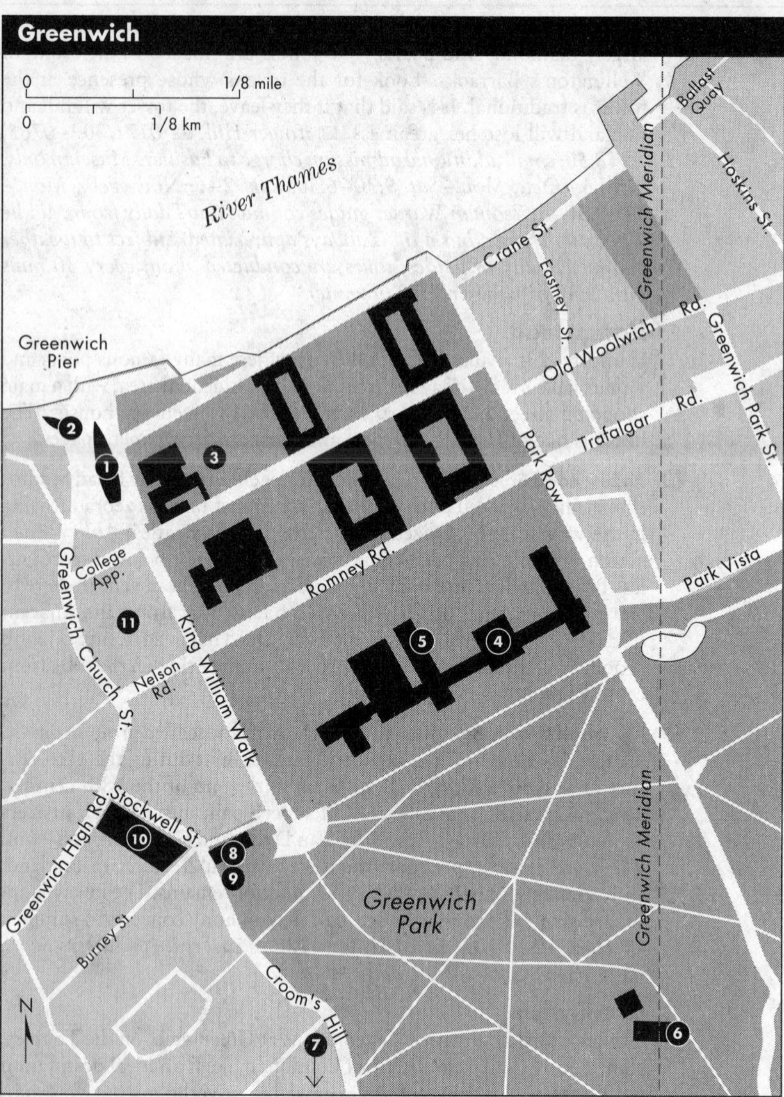

Covered Crafts Market, **11**
Cutty Sark, **1**
Fan Museum, **9**
Gipsy Moth IV, **2**
Greenwich Antique Market, **10**
Greenwich Theatre, **8**
National Maritime Museum, **5**
Old Royal Observatory, **6**
Queen's House, **4**
Ranger's House, **7**
Royal Naval College, **3**

wich Park, originally a royal hunting ground and today an attractive open space. The Observatory, founded in 1675, has original telescopes and other astronomical instruments on display. ✉ *Greenwich Park,* ☎ *0181/858–4422.* ⏲ *Mon.–Sat. 10–6, Sun. noon–6.*

Dining

For details and price-category definitions, *see* Dining *in* Great Britain A to Z, *above.*

Bloomsbury

$$ ✕ **Chez Gerard.** This purveyor of steak-*frîtes* (with french fries) and similarly simple Gallic offerings is reliable, relaxed, and usefully located near Oxford Street. ✉ *8 Charlotte St.,* ☎ *0171/636–4975. AE, DC, MC, V. Tube: Goodge St.*

$$ ✕ **Museum Street Café.** Convenient for British Museum lunches, and worth a special trip in the evening, the Mediterranean-tinged home cooking (spinach-and-olive tart; char-grilled leg of lamb; Valrhona chocolate cake), and minimalist white-wall decor in this little place are satisfying. ✉ *47 Museum St.,* ☎ *0171/405–3211. Reservations essential. MC, V. Closed weekends. Tube: Holborn.*

Chelsea

$$$$ ★ ✕ **La Tante Claire.** One of London's best restaurants, La Tante Claire is justly famous for Pierre Koffmann's superb haute cuisine: hot foie gras on shredded potatoes with a sweet wine and shallot sauce or his famous signature dish of pig's trotter stuffed with sweetbreads and wild mushrooms. The set-price lunch is a relative bargain. ✉ *68 Royal Hospital Rd.,* ☎ *0171/352–6045. Reservations essential 3 wks in advance. AE, DC, MC, V. Closed weekends, 2 wks at Christmas, 10 days at Easter, and 3 wks in Aug.–Sept. Tube: Sloane Sq.*

$$$–$$$$ ★ ✕ **Aubergine.** A table at Aubergine (warning: there are only 14) has been London's toughest reservation to score for almost as long as it's been open, because soccer star-turned-chef Gordon Ramsay has every table gasping in awe at his famous witty cappuccino of white beans with sauteéd girolles and truffles, followed by—well, anything at all. Reserve months ahead; go for lunch (£24) if money is an object. ✉ *11 Park Walk, SW10,* ☎ *0171/352–3449. Reservations essential. AE, DC, MC, V. Closed Sun. No lunch Sat. Tube: South Kensington.*

$$$ ✕ **Chutney Mary.** London's only Anglo-Indian restaurant provides a fantasy version of the British Raj, with colonial cocktails and authentic re-creations of comforting, rich dishes, such as Country Captain (chicken with almonds, raisins, chilis, and spices). ✉ *535 King's Rd.,* ☎ *0171/351–3113. AE, DC, MC, V. Tube: Fulham Broadway.*

$$ ✕ **Bluebird.** Here's Terence Conran's latest "gastrodome"—supermarket, brasserie, fruit stand, butcher shop, boutique, and café-restaurant, all housed in a snappy King's Road former garage. Go for the synergy and visual excitement—Conran's chefs share a tendency to promise more than they deliver. ✉ *350 King's Rd., SW3,* ☎ *0171/559–1000. Reservations essential. AE, DC, MC, V. Tube: Sloane Sq.*

The City

$$$ ✕ **St. John.** Resembling a stark monks' refectory crossed with an art gallery, this modern British innovator has equally uncompromising menus. Some loathe bone marrow and parsley salad, huge servings of braised pheasant with "black cabbage," or deviled crab, or organ meats any which way, with English puddings and Malmsey wine to follow, but newspaper journalists and swank architects love it. ✉ *26 St John St.,* ☎ *0171/251–0848. Reservations essential. No dinner Sun. Tube: Farringdon.*

Covent Garden

$$$ ★ ✕ **The Ivy.** The epitome of style without pretentiousness, this restaurant beguiles everybody, including media, literary, and theatrical movers and shakers. The menu's got it all—fish-and-chips, sausage-and-mash, squid-ink risotto, bang-bang chicken, sticky toffee pudding—and all are good. ✉ *1 West St.,* ☎ *0171/836–4751. Reservations essential. AE, DC, MC, V. Tube: Covent Garden.*

$$$ ★ ✕ **Rules.** This is probably the city's most beautiful restaurant—daffodil yellow 19th-century walls, Victorian oil paintings, and hundreds of framed engravings make up the history-rich setting—and certainly one of the oldest (it has been here since 1798). Rules is traditional from soup to nuts, or rather, from venison and Dover sole to trifle and Stilton. There's the odd nod to newer cuisines, but the clientele of expense-accounters and tourists in search of olde London Towne remains. Note there are three floors to this place, with the most opulent salons on the first floor. ✉ *35 Maiden La.,* ☎ *0171/836–5314. AE, DC, MC, V. Tube: Covent Garden.*

$$ ✕ **Christopher's.** It's a palatially good-looking slice of überurban USA, with a vaguely famous face at the neighboring table. Great shrimp, Maryland crab cakes, and steaks, of course. ✉ *18 Wellington St.,* ☎ *0171/240–4222. AE, DC, MC, V. Tube: Covent Garden.*

$–$$ ★ ✕ **Joe Allen.** This basement restaurant behind the Strand Palace Hotel follows the style of its New York counterpart, is descended on by packs of theatrical types after curtain, and is forever noisy. The menu, too, is straight from the Manhattan parent—Caesar salad, barbecue ribs with black-eyed peas and wilted greens, brownies with ice cream—and it's open late. ✉ *13 Exeter St.,* ☎ *0171/836–0651. Reservations essential. No credit cards. Tube: Covent Garden.*

$ ✕ **Food for Thought.** This is a simple downstairs vegetarian restaurant, with seats for only 50. The menu—stir-fries, casseroles, salads, and dessert—changes daily, and each dish is freshly made. No alcohol is served. ✉ *31 Neal St.,* ☎ *0171/836–0239. Reservations not accepted. No credit cards. Closed 2 wks at Christmas. Tube: Covent Garden.*

Kensington

$$$$ ★ ✕ **Bibendum.** Upstairs in the renovated 1911 Michelin building, this dining extravaganza continues to entice with a menu as Gallic and gorgeous as ever. From the scallops in citrus sauce to the passion-fruit *bavarois* (Bavarian cream), all the dishes are unpretentious but admirably done. The separate Oyster Bar, downstairs, is another way to go. ✉ *81 Fulham Rd.,* ☎ *0171/581–5817. Reservations essential. MC, V. Closed Sun. Tube: South Kensington.*

$$ ★ ✕ **Wódka.** This modern Polish restaurant in a quiet back street serves stylish food to a fashionable group and often has the relaxed atmosphere of a dinner party. Try herring blinis, roast duck with figs and port, and the several flavored vodkas. ✉ *12 St. Albans Grove,* ☎ *0171/937–6513. Reservations essential. AE, DC, MC, V. No lunch weekends. Tube: Kensington High St.*

Knightsbridge

$$$ ★ ✕ **Zafferano.** Princess Margaret, Eric Clapton, Joan Collins (she asked that the lights be turned down), and any number stylish folk have flocked to this Belgravia place, London's best exponent of *cucina nuova.* The fireworks are in the kitchen, not in the brick-wall-and-saffron-hued decor, but *what* fireworks: pumpkin ravioli with a splash of Amaretto, *mondeghini ai crostini di risotto* (minced pork wrapped in Savoy cabbage leaves), and monkfish with walnuts. Be sure to book early: even Al Pacino was turned away one night. ✉ *15 Lowndes St., SW1,* ☎ *0171/235–5800. Reservations essential. AE, MC, V. Tube: Knightsbridge.*

$–$$ ✕ **The Enterprise.** One of the new luxury breed of gastro-pubs, this is perhaps the chicest of the lot—near Harrods and Brompton Cross, it's filled with decorative types. The menu isn't overly pretty—char-grilled squid stuffed with almonds, entrecôte steak, salmon with artichoke hearts—but the ambience certainly is. ✉ *35 Walton St., SW3,* ☎ *0171/584–3148. AE, MC, V. No lunch weekends. Tube: South Kensington.*

$ ✕ **Stockpot.** Speedy service is the mark of this large, jolly restaurant full of students and shoppers. The food is filling and wholesome; try the homemade soups, the Lancashire hot pot, and the apple crumble. Breakfast is also served Monday–Saturday. ✉ *6 Basil St.,* ☎ *0171/589–8627. No credit cards. Tube: Knightsbridge.*

Mayfair

$$$$ ★ ✕ **Oak Room.** Bad boy Marco Pierre White enjoys Jagger-like fame from his TV appearances and gossip column reports of his complicated love life and random eruptions of fury. He should stick to his pans, say super-chef critics, meaning it literally in some cases. But, hype aside, Marco may be London's greatest chef and now gets to show off in his most spectacular setting yet—all belle epoque soaring ceilings and gilded bits, and palms and paintings. ✉ *Le Meridien, 21 Piccadilly W1,* ☎ *0171/734–8000. Reservations essential. Jacket and tie. AE, DC, MC, V. Tube: Piccadilly Circus.*

$$$ ✕ **Criterion.** A spectacular neo-Byzantine palace of gold mosaic, Christo-size turquoise drapes, and white tablecloths, the Criterion is under the aegis of Marco Pierre White, the bigmouthed, bigheaded wunderchef now at the helm of several of London's best restaurants. and features his style of haute-bistro French food: a rich, black squid-ink risotto; intricate assemblies of fish, and delicate salads. ✉ *Piccadilly Circus,* ☎ *0171/930–0488. AE, DC, MC, V. Tube: Piccadilly Circus.*

$–$$ ✕ **Villandry.** This foodie's paradise just moved to huge new premises—the food hall here is now even larger than the one at Harrods! French pâtés, Continental cheeses, fruit tarts, biscuits, and breads galore are for sale, and if you must indulge but can't wait to take a bite, there's a tearoom café and dining room that both serve exquisite lunches. Twice a month, dinners are offered, but they are among the hardest reservations to book in London. ✉ *170 Great Portland St., W1,* ☎ *0171/631–3131. AE, MC, V. Tube: Great Portland St.*

Notting Hill

$$$ ✕ **Clarke's.** There's no choice of dishes at dinner (and only a limited choice at lunch); chef Sally Clarke plans the meal according to what is freshest and best in the market each day. Her style is natural and unfussy West Coast cuisine. ✉ *124 Kensington Church St.,* ☎ *0171/221–9225. Reservations essential. MC, V. Closed weekends and 2 wks in Aug. Tube: Notting Hill Gate.*

$$$ ✕ **Kensington Place.** Trendy and loud, this ever-popular place features enormous plate-glass windows through which to be seen, and plenty of fashionable food. Try the foie gras with sweet-corn pancake, the rack of lamb, and the baked tamarillo with vanilla ice cream. ✉ *201 Kensington Church St.,* ☎ *0171/727–3184. MC, V. Tube: Notting Hill Gate.*

$$ ✕ **The Cow.** Slightly tucked away in the backwaters of trendy Portobello-land, this is the nicest of a trio of foodie pubs that feed the neighborhood arty hipsters and media stars. The Cow is the child of Tom Conran, son of Sir Terence (who owns half of London's restaurants). It pretends to be a pub in County Derry, serving oysters, crab salad, and other seafood with the beer, and heartier food in the cozy restaurant upstairs. ✉ *89 Westbourne Park Rd.,* ☎ *0171/221–0021. Reservations essential. MC, V. No dinner Sun. Tube: Westbourne Park.*

$$ ✕ **Pharmacy.** London's latest scene-arena, the Pharmacy looks just like its namesake, its wait staff is garbed like hospital orderlies, and even

its menu looks fab—but then Damien Hirst, artist extraordinaire, is involved. The menu highlights "comfort food" and ranges from fisherman's pie to spit-roast Landes duck, sauce aigre-doux. Don't you dare leave the bar without ordering a "Cough Syrup." ✉ *150 Notting Hill Gate, W11,* ☎ *0171/221–2442. Reservations essential. AE, MC, V. Tube: Notting Hill Gate.*

$ ✕ **Tootsies.** A useful burger joint characterized by loudish rock and vintage advertisements on the walls, Tootsies serves some of London's better burgers, as well as chili, chicken, BLTs, taco salad, apple pie, fudge cake, and ice cream. There are five other branches. ✉ *120 Holland Park Ave.,* ☎ *0171/229–8567. Reservations not accepted. MC, V. Tube: Holland Park.*

St. James's

$$$$ ✕ **The Ritz.** This Louis XVI marble, gilt, and trompe l'oeil treasure, with its view over Green Park, is known as London's most magnificent dining room. The latest chef retains the French accent and ingredients as rich as the decor, and also offers British specialties. Prix-fixe menus make the check more bearable, but the wine list is pricey. ✉ *Piccadilly,* ☎ *0171/493–8181. Jacket and tie. Reservations essential. AE, DC, MC, V. Tube: Green Park.*

$$$ ★ ✕ **Le Caprice.** Fabulously dark and glamorous, with its black walls and stark white tablecloths, Caprice is a perennial that does nothing wrong, from its kind, efficient, nonpartisan (famous folk eat here often) service to its pan-European menu (salmon fish cake with sorrel sauce; confit of goose with prunes). ✉ *Arlington House, Arlington St.,* ☎ *0171/629–2239. Reservations essential. AE, DC, MC, V. No lunch Sat. Tube: Green Park.*

Soho

$–$$$ ✕ **Mezzo.** Sir Terence Conran's 700-seater Mezzo isn't only London's biggest; it's the most gigantic restaurant in all of Europe—you could decant most of Soho inside its three levels. Downstairs is Mezzo, where the soaring, glass-walled kitchen abuts a bustling ocean liner of a dining room; here, the food is French-ish, with the usual Conran seafood platters, and there's a nifty jazz trio and dance floor. Upstairs, the "Mezzonine" and bar are informal, and less expensive. Finally, a separate café stays open till the wee hours. ✉ *100 Wardour St.,* ☎ *0171/314–4000. AE, DC, MC, V. Tube: Leicester Sq.*

$ ✕ **Crank's.** This restaurant belongs to a popular vegetarian chain that has weathered the storms of food fashion since the '60s, thanks to a certain worthiness of menu—mixed salads and thick soups; dense, grainy breads; and sugarless cakes. It is self-service, and many branches, though not this one, close at 8 PM. ✉ *8 Marshall St.,* ☎ *0171/437–9431. Reservations not accepted. AE, DC, MC, V. Closed Sun. Tube: Leicester Sq.*

South Bank

$$–$$$ ★ ✕ **OXO Tower Brasserie and Restaurant.** London finally has a room with a view, and *such* a view. On the eighth floor of the beautifully revived OXO Tower Wharf building, near the South Bank Centre, this elegant space has Euro food with this year's trendy ingredients (acorn-fed black pig charcuterie with tomato and pear chutney is one example). The ceiling slats turn and change from white to midnight blue, but who notices, with St. Paul's dazzling you across the water? ✉ *Bankside, SE1,* ☎ *0171/803–3888. AE, MC, V. Tube: Waterloo.*

Lodging

For details and price-category definitions, *see* Lodging *in* Great Britain A to Z, *above.* Note that although British hotels traditionally included breakfast in their nightly tariff, these days many of London's most expensive establishments charge extra for breakfast.

Bayswater

$$ **London Elizabeth.** Steps from Hyde Park and the Lancaster Gate tube, this family-owned gem has one of the prettiest hotel facades in London. The charm continues inside—foyer and lounge are crammed with coffee tables and chintz drapery, lace antimacassars, and little chandeliers. There is an exceptionally charming Anglo-Irish staff. ✉ *Lancaster Terrace, W2 3PF,* ☎ *0171/402–6641,* FAX *0171/224–8900. 55 rooms. Restaurant. AE, DC, MC, V. Tube: Lancaster Gate.*

$ **Columbia.** The public rooms in these five joined Victorians are as big as museum halls, painted in icy hues of powder blue and buttermilk, or paneled in dark wood. At one end of the day they contain the hippest band du jour drinking pints; at the other, there are sightseers sipping coffee. Rooms are clean, high-ceilinged, and sometimes very large—it's just a shame that teak veneer and avocado bathroom suites haven't made it back into the style bible yet. ✉ *95–99 Lancaster Gate, W2 3NS,* ☎ *0171/402–0021,* FAX *0171/706–4691. 103 rooms. Restaurant, bar. AE, MC, V. Tube: Lancaster Gate.*

$ ★ **Commodore.** This peaceful hotel of three converted Victorians has some amazing (especially for the price) rooms—as superior to the regular ones (which usually go to package tour groups) as Harrods is to K-Mart. Twenty are miniduplexes, with sleeping gallery. One (Number 11) is a real duplex, entered through a secret mirrored door, with a thick-carpeted, *very* quiet bedroom upstairs and its toilet below. ✉ *50 Lancaster Gate, W2 3NA,* ☎ *0171/402–5291,* FAX *0171/262–1088. 90 rooms. Bar. AE, MC, V. Tube: Lancaster Gate.*

Bloomsbury

$ **Morgan.** This charming family-run hotel in an 18th-century terrace house has rooms that are small and comfortably furnished, but friendly and cheerful. The tiny paneled breakfast room is straight out of a doll's house. The back rooms overlook the British Museum. ✉ *24 Bloomsbury St., WC1B 3QJ,* ☎ *0171/636–3735. 15 rooms with bath or shower. No credit cards. Tube: Russell Sq.*

$ **Ridgemount.** The kindly owners, Mr. and Mrs. Rees, make you feel at home in this tiny hotel by the British Museum. There's a homey, cluttered feel in the public areas and some bedrooms overlook a leafy garden. ✉ *65 Gower St., WC1E 6HJ,* ☎ *0171/636–1141. 34 rooms, 2 with bath. No credit cards. Tube: Russell Sq.*

Chelsea, Kensington, and Holland Park

$$$$ ★ **Blakes.** Patronized by musicians and film stars, this hotel is one of the most exotic in town. Its Victorian exterior contrasts with the rather 1980s ultrachic interior, an arty mix of Biedermeier and bamboo, four-poster beds, and chinoiserie, all lit as dramatically as film noir. The bedrooms have individual designs ranging from swaths of black moiré silk to an entirely pink suite. ✉ *33 Roland Gardens, SW7 3PF,* ☎ *0171/370–6701. 52 rooms. Restaurant. AE, DC, MC, V. Tube: Gloucester Rd.*

$$$$ ★ **Halcyon.** Discretion, decadent decor, and disco divas make this expensive, enormous, wedding-cake Edwardian desperately desirable. The Blue Room has moons and stars, the Egyptian Suite is canopied like a bedouin tent, on and on. All guest rooms are different but large, with the high ceilings and big windows of the Holland Park vernacular. ✉ *81 Holland Park, W11 3RZ,* ☎ *0171/727–7288,* FAX *0171/229–8516. 44 rooms. Restaurant. AE, DC, MC, V. Tube: Holland Park.*

$$$ ★ **The Gore.** Every wall of every room in this friendly and quiet hotel near the Albert Hall is smothered in prints and etchings, and antiques pepper the rooms. Some of these are spectacular follies—such as Tudor-

style Room 101, with its minstrel gallery and four-poster. The crowd here is elegant and arty. ✉ *189 Queens Gate, SW7 5EX,* ☎ *0171/584–6601,* FAX *0171/589–8127. 54 rooms. AE, DC, MC, V. Tube: Gloucester Rd.*

$$–$$$ **Portobello.** A faithful and chic core of visitors returns again and again to this eccentric hotel in a Victorian terrace near the Portobello Road antiques market. Some rooms are tiny, but the ambience of '60s swinging London, the ecclesiastical antiques, and the peaceful vista of the gardens in back make up for it. ✉ *22 Stanley Gardens, W11 2NG,* ☎ *0171/727–2777,* FAX *0171/792–9641. 25 rooms with bath or shower. Restaurant. AE, DC, MC, V. Tube: Ladbroke Grove.*

$ **Abbey House.** Standards are high (some rooms even feature orthopedic beds) and the rooms unusually spacious in this hotel in a fine residential block near Kensington Palace and Gardens. ✉ *11 Vicarage Gate, W8 4AG,* ☎ *0171/727–2594. 16 rooms without bath. No credit cards. Tube: Kensington High St.*

$ **The Vicarage.** This has long been a favorite for the budget-minded—family-owned, set on a leaf-shaded street just off Kensington Church Street, the Vicarage is set in a large white Victorian house. Bedrooms are traditional and comfortable, with solid English furniture. Definitely a charmer—but it is beginning to fray around the edges. ✉ *10 Vicarage Gate, W8 4AG,* ☎ *0171/229–4030. 19 rooms without bath. No credit cards. Tube: Kensington High St.*

Knightsbridge, Belgravia, and Victoria

$$$$ **The Lanesborough.** Brocades and Regency stripes, moiré silks and fleurs-de-lis, antiques, oils, and reproductions in gilded splendor—everything undulates with richness in this upscale conversion of the old St. George's Hospital at Hyde Park Corner. To register you just sign the book, then retire to your room to find a personal butler, business cards with your in-room fax and phone numbers, VCR and CD player, umbrella, robe, huge flacons of unguents for bath time, and a drinks tray. ✉ *1 Lanesborough Pl., SW1X 7TA,* ☎ *0171/259–5599,* FAX *0171/259–5606. 95 rooms. 2 restaurants. AE, DC, MC, V. Tube: Hyde Park Corner.*

$$$ **Basil Street.** Family-run for some 80 years, this is a gracious Edwardian hotel on a quiet street. The rooms are filled with antiques, as are the various lounges, hushed like libraries with polished wooden floors and Oriental rugs. It sounds swanky, but Basil Street is more like home. ✉ *Basil St., SW3 1AH,* ☎ *0171/581–3311,* FAX *0171/581–3693. 92 rooms, 72 with bath. 2 restaurants. AE, DC, MC, V. Tube: Knightsbridge.*

$$$ ★ **The Pelham.** Magnificent 18th-century pine paneling in the drawing room, glazed chintz and antique lace, four-posters in some rooms, fireplaces in others—this hotel run by Tim and Kit Kemp feels more like an elegant home. It's near the big museums, and 24-hour room service and business services are available. ✉ *15 Cromwell Pl., SW7 2LA,* ☎ *0171/589–8288,* FAX *0171/584–8444. 37 rooms. Restaurant. AE, MC, V. Tube: South Kensington.*

$ **London County Hall Travel Inn Capital.** Don't get too excited—this neighbor of the luxurious new Marriott in the County Hall complex lacks the fabled river view (it's at the back of the grand former seat of local government, on the south side of the Thames). Still, you get an incredible value, with the standard facilities of the cookie-cutter rooms of this chain, viz: TV, tea/coffeemaker, en suite bath/shower and—wow!—foldout beds that let you accommodate two children at no extra charge. You're looking at £50/night for a family of four, in the shadow of Big Ben. *That's* a bargain. ✉ *Belvedere Rd., SE1 7PB,* ☎ *01582/414341,* FAX *01582/400024. 312 rooms. Restaurant. AE, MC, V. Tube: Westminster.*

West End

$$$$ 🏨 **Brown's.** Close to Bond Street, Brown's is like a country house in the middle of town, with wood paneling, grandfather clocks, and large fireplaces. Founded in 1837 by Lord Byron's "gentleman's gentleman," James Brown, it has attracted Anglophilic Americans ever since. Both Roosevelts used to stay here. ✉ *34 Albemarle St., W1A 4SW,* ☎ *0171/493–6020,* FAX *0171/493–9381. 132 rooms. Restaurant. AE, DC, MC, V. Tube: Green Park.*

$$$$ ★ 🏨 **Claridge's.** This hotel has one of the world's classiest guest lists. The liveried staff is friendly, not at all condescending, and the rooms are luxurious. The hotel was founded in 1812, but the present decor is either 1930s Art Deco or country-house style. Have a drink or afternoon tea in the Foyer and hear the Hungarian mini-orchestra. The rooms are spacious, the sweeping staircase grand. Currently, the hotel is receiving a major renovation. ✉ *Brook St., W1A 2JQ,* ☎ *0171/629–8860,* FAX *0171/499–2210. 200 rooms. 2 restaurants. AE, DC, MC, V. Tube: Bond St.*

$$$$ ★ 🏨 **Covent Garden Hotel.** Clearly London's most relentlessly chic, extra-stylish hotel, this former 1880s-vintage hospital is located in the midst of the artsy Covent Garden district, and is now the London home-away-from-home for a melange of off-duty celebrities, actors, and style-mavens. Theatrically baronial, the public rooms will keep even the most picky atmosphere-hunter happy. Isn't that Helena Bonham Carter having tea in the drawing room? ✉ *10 Monmouth St., WC2H 9HB,* ☎ *0171/806–1000,* FAX *0171/806–1100. 46 rooms, 4 suites. Restaurant, minibars, room service, exercise room, laundry service. AE, MC, V. Tube: Covent Garden.*

$$$$ ★ 🏨 **Savoy.** This grand, historic, late-Victorian hotel has been the byword for luxury for just over a century. Hemingway loved its American Bar and Elizabeth Taylor spent her first honeymoon here. Spacious bedrooms have antiques and cream plasterwork, and the best ones overlook the Thames. More than a hint of dazzling 1920s style remains. ✉ *Strand, WC2R 0EU,* ☎ *0171/836–4343,* FAX *0171/240–6040. 202 rooms. 3 restaurants. AE, DC, MC, V. Tube: Aldwych.*

$$$ ★ 🏨 **Dorset Square.** The same husband (architect) and wife (interior designer) team who own the Pelham (☞ *above*) created this stunning, comfortable small hotel in a fine pair of Regency town houses north of Oxford Street almost a decade ago, but it remains sparklingly fresh. Service is personal and charming; you can be chauffeured in the owners' vintage Bentley on request. ✉ *39–40 Dorset Sq., NW1 6QN,* ☎ *0171/723–7874,* FAX *0171/724–3328. 37 rooms. Restaurant. AE, MC, V. Tube: Baker St.*

$$$ 🏨 **Dukes.** The refurbishment of this small Edwardian hotel in a cul-de-sac in St. James's has raised its popularity rating several notches. Top-floor suites are among the finds of London for peace, views, antiques, and hominess. ✉ *35 St. James's Pl., SW1A 1NY,* ☎ *0171/491–4840,* FAX *0171/493–1264. 62 rooms. Restaurant. AE, DC, MC, V. Tube: Green Park.*

$$$ 🏨 **Hazlitt's.** Still Soho's sole hotel, this, the last home of William Hazlitt, the essayist (1778–1830), is crammed with prints on every wall, Victorian claw-foot baths, assorted antiques, plants, and bits of art. There's no elevator, the sitting room is minuscule, floors can be creaky and bedrooms tiny, but Hazlitt's legion of devotees don't mind. And who needs room service when you live on Restaurant Row? ✉ *6 Frith St., W1V 5TZ,* ☎ *0171/434–1771,* FAX *0171/439–1524. 23 rooms. AE, DC, MC, V. Tube: Tottenham Court Rd.*

$$ 🏨 **Bryanston Court.** Three 18th-century houses have been converted into a traditional English family-run hotel with open fires and comfortable armchairs; the bedrooms are more contemporary. ✉ *56–60*

Great Cumberland Pl., W1H 7FD, ☎ *0171/262–3141,* FAX *0171/262–7248. 56 rooms with bath or shower. Restaurant. AE, DC, MC, V. Tube: Marble Arch.*

$$ **The Fielding.** Tucked away in a quiet alley, steps from the Royal Opera House, this cozy place is so adored by its regulars that you'd better book ahead. It's shabby-homey in decor and attitude—there's no elevator, only one room has a bathtub (most have showers), and there's no room service or restaurant, but it's cute and handy for the theater. ✉ *4 Broad Ct., Bow St., WC2B 5OZ,* ☎ *0171/836–8305,* FAX *0171/497–0064. 26 rooms, 1 with bath, 23 with showers. AE, DC, MC, V. Tube: Covent Garden.*

Nightlife and the Arts

The Arts

For a list of events in the London arts scene, visit a newsstand or bookstore to pick up the weekly magazine *Time Out*. The city's evening paper, the *Evening Standard*, carries listings, as do the major Sunday papers; the daily *Independent* and *Guardian;* and, on Friday, *The Times*. The London Tourist Board's *Visitor Call* service (calls cost 49p/min.; ☎ 0891/505440 for what's on this week) also offers listings for theater and other arts events.

BALLET

When its massive renovation program is complete, the Royal Opera House may once again host the **Royal Ballet.** Until 2000, however, the ballet will be performing at the Labatt's Apollo Hammersmith (☎ 0171/304–4000) and the Royal Festival Hall in the South Bank Arts Complex (☎ 0171/928–8800): check with the box office of the Royal Opera House (☎ 0171/304–4000) for complete information. The prices are slightly more reasonable than for the opera, but be sure to book well ahead. The **English National Ballet** and visiting companies perform at the Coliseum (☎ 0171/632–8300) but that theater, too, is scheduled for a renovation program lasting several seasons, and resident troupes will be performing elsewhere (call the Coliseum Box Office for further information). **Sadler's Wells Theatre** (☎ 0171/713–6000) hosts regional ballet and international modern dance troupes. Prices here are reasonable.

CONCERTS

Ticket prices for symphony orchestra concerts are still relatively moderate—between £5 and £25, although you can expect to pay more to hear big-name artists on tour. If you can't book in advance, arrive half an hour before the performance for a chance at returns.

The London Symphony Orchestra is in residence at the **Barbican Arts Centre** (☎ 0171/638–8891), although other top symphony and chamber orchestras also perform here. The **South Bank arts complex** (☎ 0171/928–8800), which includes the **Royal Festival Hall** and the **Queen Elizabeth Hall,** is another major venue for choral, symphonic, and chamber concerts. For less expensive concert going, try the **Royal Albert Hall** (☎ 0171/589–8212) during the summer Promenade season; special tickets for standing room are available at the hall on the night of performance. Note, too, that the concerts have begun to be jumbo-screen broadcast in Hyde Park, but even here a seat on the grass requires a paid ticket. Call 0171/589–82122 for further information. **The Wigmore Hall** (☎ 0171/935–2141) is a small auditorium, ideal for recitals. Inexpensive lunchtime concerts take place all over the city in smaller halls and churches, often featuring string quartets, vocalists, jazz ensembles, and gospel choirs. **St. John's, Smith Square** (☎ 0171/

222–1061), a converted Queen Anne church, is one of the more popular venues. It has a handy crypt cafeteria.

FILM

Most West End cinemas are in the area around Leicester Square and Piccadilly Circus. Tickets average £7.50. Matinees and Monday evenings are cheaper. Cinema clubs screen a wide range of films: classics, Continental, underground, rare, or underestimated masterpieces. A temporary membership fee is usually about £1. One of the best cinema clubs is the **National Film Theatre** (☎ 0171/928–3232), part of the South Bank arts complex.

OPERA

The **Royal Opera House** (☎ 0171/304–4000) ranks alongside the New York Met. It's one of the grandest sights in London, but, unfortunately, as of June 1997, the theater closed for a massive rebuilding program that is scheduled to last another year or two. The resident opera company will be performing at other venues during this period. For the 1998–99 season, most productions should be concentrated in the newly refurbished Sadler's Wells Theatre (☎ 0171/713–6000). For ongoing information check with the box office. The **Coliseum** (☎ 0171/632–8300) is the home of the English National Opera Company; productions are staged in English and are often innovative and exciting. The ticket price range is about £8 to £45. Call the box office for the latest information, as the Coliseum is also scheduled for a major renovation.

THEATER

London's theater life can more or less be divided into three categories: the government-subsidized national companies; the commercial, or "West End," theaters; and the fringe. The **Royal National Theatre Company** (NT) shares the laurels as the top national repertory troupe with the Royal Shakespeare Company. In similar fashion to the latter troupe, the NT presents a variety of plays by writers of all nationalities, ranging from the classics of Shakespeare and his contemporaries to specially commissioned modern works. The NT is based at the South Bank arts complex (box office: ☎ 0171/928–2252). The **Royal Shakespeare Company** (RSC) is based at the Barbican Arts Centre (box office: ☎ 0171/638–8891). At press time, the RSC announced it had terminated its summer season in London. That's a pity for summer visitors, but they can always book tickets at the spectacular new reconstruction of the famed Elizabethan-era **Globe Theatre** (box office: ☎ 0171/928–6406) on the South Bank, which only offers open-air, late-afternoon performances from June through September.

The **West End theaters** largely stage musicals, comedies, whodunits, and revivals of lighter plays of the 19th and 20th centuries, often starring television celebrities. Occasionally there are more serious productions, including successful productions transferred from the subsidized theaters, such as RSC's *Les Liaisons Dangereuses* and *Les Misérables*. The two dozen or so established **fringe theaters,** scattered around central London and the immediate outskirts, frequently present some of London's most intriguing productions, if you're prepared to overlook occasional rough staging and uncomfortable seating.

Most theaters have an evening performance at 7:30 or 8 daily, except Sunday, and a matinee twice a week (Wednesday or Thursday, and Saturday). Expect to pay from £10 for a seat in the upper balcony and at least £25 for a good seat in the stalls (orchestra) or dress circle (mezzanine)—more for musicals. Tickets may be booked in person at the theater box office; over the phone by credit card; or through ticket agents, such as **First Call** (☎ 0171/497–7941) or **Ticketmaster** (☎ 0171/

344–0055 or 800/775–2525 from the United States). In addition the **SOLT Kiosk** in Leicester Square sells half-price tickets on the day of performance for about 25 theaters; there is a small service charge. Beware of scalpers!

Nightlife

London's night spots are legion; here are some of the best known. For up-to-the-minute listings, buy *Time Out* magazine.

CABARET

The best comedy in town can be found in the big, bright, new-look **Comedy Store** (✉ Haymarket House, Oxendon St., near Piccadilly Circus, ☎ 01426/914433). **Madame Jo Jo's** (✉ 8 Brewer St., ☎ 0171/287–1414) is possibly the most fun of any London cabaret, with its outrageous, glittering drag shows. The place is luxurious and civilized.

JAZZ CLUBS

Blue Note (✉ 1 Hoxton Sq., ☎ 0171/729–8440), in an out-of-the-way warehouse on the northern edge of the City (the nearest tube is Old Street), is a cool jazz and world-beat club/restaurant that attracts a young crowd. **Ronnie Scott's** (✉ 47 Frith St., ☎ 0171/439–0747) is the legendary Soho jazz club where international performers regularly take the stage.

NIGHTCLUBS

Hanover Grand (✉ 6 Hanover Sq., ☎ 0171/499–7977) is a swank and opulent big West End club, which attracts TV stars and footballers whose exploits here you can later read about in the tabloids. The "Haute Couture" one-nighter takes over on Friday, while Saturday's glam disco "Malibu Stacey" pulls in all those who want to be seen. The lines outside get long, so dress up to impress the bouncers. **Ministry of Sound** (✉ 103 Gaunt St., ☎ 0171/378–6528) is more of an industry than a club, with its own record label, line of apparel, and, of course, DJs. Inside, there are chill-out rooms, dance floors, promotional Sony Playstations, Absolut shot bars—all the club kid's favorite things. If you are one, and you only have time for one night out, make it here. Glitzy **Stringfellows** (✉ 16–19 Upper St. Martin's La., ☎ 0171/240–5534) has an art deco upstairs restaurant, mirrored walls, and a dazzling light show in the downstairs dance floor.

ROCK

The Forum (✉ 9–17 Highgate Rd., Kentish Town, ☎ 0171/284–2200), a little out of the way, is a premier venue for medium-to-big acts. **100 Club** (✉ 100 Oxford St., W1, ☎ 0171/636–0933) is a basement dive that's always been there for R&B, rock, jazz, and beer. **The Shepherds Bush Empire** (✉ Shepherds Bush Green, W12, ☎ 0181/740–7474) is a major venue for largish acts in West London.

Shopping

Shopping is one of London's great pleasures. Different areas retain their traditional specialties, but there are also numerous pockets of local shops to explore, and it's fun to seek out the small crafts, antiques, and gift stores, designer-clothing resale outlets, and national department-store chains.

Shopping Districts

Chelsea. Centering on the King's Road, Chelsea was once synonymous with ultrafashion; it still harbors some designer boutiques, plus antiques and home furnishings stores.

Covent Garden. A something-for-everyone neighborhood, Covent Garden has numerous clothing chain stores, stalls selling crafts, and shops selling gifts of every type—bikes, kites, herbs, beads, hats, you name it.

Kensington. This area's main drag, Kensington High Street, is a smaller, classier version of Oxford Street (☞ *below*), with Barkers department store, and a branch of Marks & Spencer at the eastern end. Try Kensington Church Street for expensive antiques, plus a little fashion.

Knightsbridge. Kensington's neighbor, Knightsbridge has Harrods, of course, but also Harvey Nichols, the chicest clothes stop in London, and many expensive designers' boutiques along Sloane Street, Walton Street, and Beauchamp Place.

Mayfair. Bond Street, Old and New, is the elegant lure here, with the hautest of haute couture and jewelry outposts, plus fine art. South Molton Street offers high-price, high-style fashion—especially at Browns—and the tailors of Savile Row are of worldwide repute.

Oxford Street. Crowded and a bit past its prime, Oxford Street is lined with tawdry discount shops. However, Selfridges, John Lewis, and Marks & Spencer are wonderful department stores, and there are interesting boutiques secreted off Oxford Street, just north of the Bond Street tube stop, in little St. Christopher's Place and Gees Court.

Regent Street. Perpendicular to Oxford Street lies this noted shopping avenue—famous for its curving path—with possibly London's most pleasant department store, Liberty's, as well as Hamley's, the capital's toy mecca. Shops around once-famous **Carnaby Street** stock designer youth paraphernalia and at least 57 varieties of T-shirts.

St. James's. The fabled English gentleman buys much of his gear at stores in this area: handmade hats, shirts, and shoes, silver shaving kits, and hip flasks. Here is also the world's best cheese shop, Paxton & Whitfield. Don't expect any bargains in this neighborhood.

Street Markets

Street markets are one aspect of London life not to be missed. Here are some of the more interesting markets:

Bermondsey. Arrive as early as possible for the best treasure—that's what the dealers do. ✉ *Tower Bridge Rd., SE1.* ⏲ *Fri. 4AM–1 PM. Tube to London Bridge or Bus 15 or 25 to Aldgate and then Bus 42 over Tower Bridge to Bermondsey Sq.*

Camden Lock. The youth center of the world, apparently, it's good for cheap clothes and boots. The canalside antiques, crafts, and junk markets are also picturesque and very crowded. ✉ *Chalk Farm Rd., NW1.* ⏲ *Shops: Tues.–Sun. 9:30–5:30; stalls: weekends 8–6. Tube or Bus 24 or 29 to Camden Town.*

Camden Passage. The rows of little antiques stalls are a good hunting ground for silverware and jewelry. Stalls open Wednesday and Saturday, but there is also a books and prints market on Thursday. Surrounding shops are open the rest of the week. ✉ *Islington, N1.* ⏲ *Wed., Sat. 8:30–3. Tube or Bus 19 or 38 to Angel.*

Petticoat Lane. Look for budget-priced leather goods, gaudy knitwear, and fashions, plus cameras, videos, stereos, antiques, books, and bric-a-brac. ✉ *Middlesex St., E1.* ⏲ *Sun. 9–2. Tube to Liverpool St., Aldgate, or Aldgate East.*

Portobello Market. Saturday is the best day for antiques, though this neighborhood is London's melting pot, becoming more vibrant every year. Find fabulous small shops, the city's trendiest restaurants, and a Friday and Saturday flea market at the far end. ✉ *Portobello Rd., W11.* ⏲ *Fri. 5 AM–3 PM, Sat. 6 AM–5 PM. Tube or Bus 52 to Notting Hill Gate or Ladbroke Grove, or Bus 15 to Kensington Park Rd.*

London Essentials

Arriving and Departing

BY BUS

The **National Express** (✉ Victoria Coach Station, Buckingham Palace Rd., ☎ 0990/808080) coach service has routes to more than 1,200 major towns and cities in the United Kingdom. It's considerably cheaper than the train, although the trips usually take longer. National Express offers two types of service: ordinary service makes frequent stops for refreshment breaks (although all coaches have toilet and washroom facilities and reclining seats); Rapide and Flightlink service has stewardess and refreshment facilities on board. Day returns are available on both, but booking is advised on the Rapide service.

BY PLANE

International flights to London arrive at either Heathrow Airport, 24 km (15 mi) west of London, or at Gatwick Airport, 43 km (27 mi) south of the capital. Most flights from the United States go to Heathrow. Gatwick is London's second gateway. It has grown from a European airport into an airport that serves 21 scheduled U.S. destinations. A third, new, state-of-the-art airport, Stansted, is to the east of the city. It handles mainly European and domestic traffic, although there is a scheduled service from New York.

Carriers serving Great Britain include **American Airlines** (☎ 800/433–7300, ☎ 0181/572–5555 in London) to Heathrow, Gatwick; **British Airways** (☎ 800/247–9297, ☎ 0345/222111 in London) to Heathrow, Gatwick; **Continental** (☎ 800/231–0856, ☎ 0800/776464 in London) to Gatwick; **Delta** (☎ 800/241–4141, ☎ 0800/414767 in London) to Heathrow, Gatwick; **Northwest Airlines** (☎ 800/447–4747, ☎ 0990/561000 in London) to Gatwick; **United** (☎ 800/241–6522, ☎ 0845/8444777 in London) to Heathrow; **TWA** (☎ 800/892–4141, ☎ 0181/814–0707 or 01293/535535 in London) to Gatwick; and **Virgin Atlantic** (☎ 800/862–8621, ☎ 01293/747747 in London) to Heathrow, Gatwick.

Between the Airport and Downtown. The Piccadilly Line serves Heathrow (all terminals) with a direct Underground (subway) link. Two special buses also serve Heathrow: Airbus A1 leaves every 30 minutes for west and central London and Victoria Station; Airbus A2 goes to west and north London to Euston and King's Cross Station every 30 minutes. The new Heathrow Express train links the airport with Paddington station in only 15 minutes.

From Gatwick the quickest way to London is the nonstop rail Gatwick Express, costing (at press time) £9.50 one-way and taking 30 minutes to reach Victoria Station. Trains run every 15 minutes from 5:20 AM to 12:50 AM, then hourly 1:35 AM–4:35 AM. Hourly bus service (6:30 AM to 10 PM) is provided by Flightlink 777 to Victoria Coach Station. This takes about 90 minutes and costs £7.50 one-way.

Cars and taxis drive into London from Heathrow on M4; the trip can take more than an hour, depending on traffic. The taxi fare is about £40, plus tip. From Gatwick the taxi fare is at least £80, plus tip; traffic can be very heavy.

BY TRAIN

London is served by no fewer than 15 main-line train stations, so be absolutely certain of the station for your departure or arrival. All have Underground stops either in the train station or within a few minutes' walk from it, and most are served by several bus routes. The principal routes that connect London to other major towns and cities are on an InterCity network. Seats can be reserved by phone only with a credit card. You can, of course, apply in person to any British Rail Travel Centre or directly to the station from which you depart.

Fares. The fare structures are slowly changing as the formerly nationalized British Rail is sold off to various independent operators. Generally speaking, it is less expensive to buy a return (round-trip) ticket, especially for day trips not far from London, and you should always inquire at the information office to find out what discount fares are available for your route. You can hear a recorded summary of timetable and fare information to many destinations by calling the appropriate "dial and listen" numbers listed under British Rail in the telephone book. For travel inquiries call 0345/484950.

Below is a list of the major London rail stations and the areas they serve. One central telephone line gets you through to any of the stations: ☏ 0345/484950.

Charing Cross serves southeast England, including Canterbury, Margate, Dover/Folkestone, and ferry ports.

Euston/St. Pancras serves East Anglia, Essex, the Northeast, the Northwest, and North Wales, including Coventry, Stratford-upon-Avon, Birmingham, Manchester, Liverpool, Windermere, Glasgow, and Inverness, northwest Scotland.

King's Cross serves the east Midlands; the Northeast, including York, Leeds, and Newcastle; and north and east Scotland, including Edinburgh and Aberdeen.

Liverpool Street serves Essex and East Anglia.

Paddington serves the south Midlands, west and south Wales, and the west country, including Oxford.

Victoria serves southern England, including Gatwick Airport, Brighton, Dover/Folkestone and ferry ports, and the south coast.

Waterloo serves the southwestern United Kingdom, including Salisbury, Portsmouth, Southampton, and Isle of Wight.

Waterloo International is for the Eurostar to Europe.

Via the Channel Tunnel. If you're combining a trip to Great Britain with stops on the Continent, you can either drive your car onto a Le Shuttle train through the Channel Tunnel (35 minutes from Folkestone to Calais), or book a seat on the Eurostar high-speed train service that zips through the tunnel (3 hours from London's Waterloo International Station to Paris, 3¼ hours from London to Brussels). For details, *see* the Channel Tunnel *in* Chapter 1.

Getting Around

BY BUS

London's bus system consists of bright red double- and single-deckers, plus other buses of various colors. Destinations are displayed on the front and back, with the bus number on the front, back, and side. Not all buses run the full length of their route at all times. Some buses are still operated with a conductor whom you pay after finding a seat, but these days you will more often find one-person buses, in which you pay the driver upon boarding.

Buses stop only at clearly indicated stops. Main stops—at which the bus should stop automatically—have a plain white background with a red LT symbol on it. There are also request stops with red signs, a white symbol, and the word REQUEST added; at these you must hail the bus to make it stop. Smoking is not allowed on any bus. Although you can see much of the town from a bus, *don't* take one if you want to get anywhere in a hurry; traffic often slows travel to a crawl, and during peak times you may find yourself waiting at least 20 minutes for a bus and not being able to get on it once it arrives. If you intend to go by bus, ask at a Travel Information Centre for a free bus map.

Fares. Single fares start at 60p for short hops (90p in the central zone). Travelcards (☞ By Underground, *below*) are good for tube, bus, and British Rail trains in the Greater London Zones. There are also a number of bus passes available for daily, weekly, and monthly use, and prices vary according to zones. A photograph is required for weekly or monthly bus passes.

BY CAR

The best advice is to avoid driving in London because of the ancient street patterns and the chronic parking restrictions. One-way streets also add to the confusion.

BY TAXI

London's black taxis are famous for their comfort and for the ability of their drivers to remember the mazelike pattern of the capital's streets. Hotels and main tourist areas have ranks (stands) where you wait your turn to take one of the taxis that drive up. You can also hail a taxi if the flag is up or the yellow FOR HIRE sign is lighted. Fares start at £1.40 and increase by units of 20p per 281 yards or 55.5 seconds until the fare exceeds £8.60. After that, it's 20p for each 188 yards or 37 seconds. Surcharges are a tricky extra, which range from 40p for additional passengers or bulky luggage to 60p for evenings 8 PM until midnight, and until 6 AM on weekends and public holidays—at Christmas it zooms to £2 and there's 40p extra for each additional passenger. Note that fares are occasionally raised from year to year. As for tipping, taxi drivers should get 10%–15% of the tab.

BY UNDERGROUND

Known as "the tube," London's extensive Underground system is by far the most widely used form of city transportation. Trains run both beneath and above ground out into the suburbs, and all stations are clearly marked with the London Underground circular symbol. (A SUBWAY sign refers to an under-the-street crossing.) Trains are all one class; smoking is *not* allowed on board or in the stations.

There are 10 basic lines—all named. The Central, District, Northern, Metropolitan, and Piccadilly lines all have branches, usually taking you to the outlying sections of the city, so be sure to note which branch is needed for your particular destination. Electronic platform signs tell you the final stop and route of the next train, and some signs conveniently indicate how many minutes you'll have to wait for the train to arrive. Begun in the Victorian era, the Underground is still being expanded and improved. The East London line, which runs from Shoreditch and Whitechapel south to New Cross, is due to reopen after major reconstruction in 1998. September 1998 is the latest date for the opening of the Jubilee line extension: This state-of-the-art subway sweeps from Green Park to Southwark, with connections to Canary Wharf and the Docklands and the much hyped Milennium Experience megadome, and on to the east at Stratford.

From Monday through Saturday, trains begin running just after 5 AM; the last services leave central London between midnight and 12:30 AM. On Sunday trains start two hours later and finish about an hour earlier. The frequency of trains depends on the route and the time of day, but normally you should not have to wait more than 10 minutes. A pocket map of the entire tube network is available free from most Underground ticket counters. There should also be a large map on the wall of each platform, and the new computerized database, "Routes," is available at 14 London Transport (LT) Travel Information Centres (☞ *below*).

Fares. For both buses and tube fares, London is divided into six concentric zones; the fare goes up the farther afield you travel. Ask at Underground ticket counters for the LT booklet "Fares and Tickets," which gives all details; after some experimenting you'll soon know which ticket best serves your particular needs. You must buy a ticket before you travel; many types of travel cards can be bought from Pass Agents that display the sign: tobacconists, confectioners, newsagents, and National Railway stations.

Here is a summary of the major ticket categories, but note that these prices are subject to increases. Children (5–10) are usually half price.

Carnet. A convenient book of 10 single tickets to use in central zone 1 only; £10.

Singles and Returns. For one trip between any two stations, you can buy an ordinary single (one-way ticket) for travel anytime on the day of issue; if you're coming back on the same route the same day, then an ordinary return (round-trip ticket) costs twice the single fare. Singles vary in price from 60p for short hops (90p in the central zone) to £3.30 for a six-zone journey—not a good option for the sightseer who wants to make several journeys.

Travelcards. These allow unrestricted travel on the tube, most buses, and British Rail trains in the Greater London zones and are valid weekdays after 9:30 AM, weekends, and all public holidays. They cannot be used on airbuses, night buses, or for certain special services. There are different options available: a **One Day Travelcard** costs £3.50–£4.30; **Weekend Travelcards,** for the two days of the weekend and on any two consecutive days during public holidays, £5.20–£6.40. **Family Travelcards:** one-day ticket for one or two adults with one to four children costs £2.80–£3.40 with one child; extra children cost 60p each—adults do not have to be related to the children or even to each other!

Visitor's Travelcard. These are the best bet for visitors, but they must be bought before leaving home (they're available in both the United States and Canada). They are valid for periods of three, four, or seven days ($25, $32, $49 respectively) and can be used on the tube and virtually all buses and British Rail services in London. All these cards also include a set of money-saving discounts to many of London's top attractions. Apply to travel agents or to **BritRail Travel International** (✉ 1500 Broadway, New York, NY 10036, ☎ 212/382–3737).

For more information there are **LT Travel Information Centres** at the following tube stations: Euston, Hammersmith, King's Cross, Oxford Circus, Piccadilly Circus, St. James's Park, Victoria, and Heathrow (in Terminals 1, 2, and 4); open 7:15 AM–10 PM, with Terminal 4's TIC closing at 3 PM. For information on all London tube and bus times, fares, and so on, dial 0171/222–1234 (24 hours). For travelers with disabilities get the free leaflet, "Access to the Underground," ☎ 0171/918–3312.

Contacts and Resources

EMBASSIES

U.S. Embassy (✉ 24 Grosvenor Sq., W1A 1AE, ☎ 0171/499–9000).

Canadian High Commission (✉ McDonald House, 1 Grosvenor Sq., W1X 0AB, ☎ 0171/258–6600).

EMERGENCIES

Police, fire brigade, or ambulance: ☎ 999. **Late-night pharmacies: Bliss Chemist,** (✉ 5 Marble Arch, W1, ☎ 0171/723–6116) and **Boots** (✉ 44 Piccadilly Circus, W1, ☎ 0171/734–6126; ✉ 151 Oxford St., W1, ☎ 0171/409–2857).

GUIDED TOURS

By Bus. The **Original London Sightseeing Tour** (☎ 0181/877–1722) offers passengers a good introduction to the city from double-decker buses. Tours run daily every 12 minutes or so, departing from Baker Street (Madame Tussaud's), Marble Arch (Speakers' Corner), Piccadilly (Haymarket), or Victoria (Victoria Street). The 21 stops include most of the major sights, such as St. Paul's and Westminster Abbey, and you may hop off to view the sights and then get back on the next bus. Tickets (£12) can be bought from the driver. **The Big Bus Company** (☎ 0181/944–7810) runs a similar operation with a Red and Blue tour. The Red is a two-hour tour with 18 stops, and the Blue, one hour with 13. Both start from Marble Arch, Speakers' Corner. These tours include stops at such places as St. Paul's Cathedral and Westminster Abbey. Prices and pickup points vary according to the sights visited, but many pickup points are at major hotels. **Evan Evans** (☎ 0181/332–2222) offers good bus tours. Another reputable agency that operates bus tours is **Frames Rickards** (☎ 0171/837–3111).

By Canal. In summer narrow boats and barges cruise London's two canals, the Grand Union and Regent's Canal; most vessels operate on the latter, which runs between Little Venice in the west (the nearest tube is Warwick Ave. on the Bakerloo Line) and Camden Lock (about 200 yards north of Camden Town tube station). **Canal Cruises** (☎ 0171/485–4433) offers three or four cruises daily from March through October on the *Jenny Wren* and all year on the cruising restaurant *My Fair Lady.* **Jason's Trip** (☎ 0171/286–3428) operates one-way and round-trip narrow-boat cruises on this route. Trips last 1½ hours. The **London Waterbus Company** (☎ 0171/482–2660) operates this route year-round with a stop at London Zoo: trips run daily from April through October, and weekends only from November through March.

By River. All year boats cruise up and down the Thames, offering a different view of the London skyline. In summer (Apr.–Oct.) boats run more frequently than in winter—call to check schedules and routes. For trips from Charing Cross to Greenwich Pier, call **Catamaran Cruisers** (☎ 0171/839–3572) or **Westminster Passenger Boat Services** (☎ 0171/930–4097). **City Cruises** (☎ 0171/488–0344) go from Westminster to the Tower and the Thames Barrier, by **Thames Barrier Cruises** (☎ 0171/930–3373). A **Sail and Rail** ticket combines the modern wonders of Canary Wharf and Docklands development by Docklands Light Railway with the history of the riverside by boat. Tickets are available year-round from Westminster Pier or Tower Gateway (☎ 0171/363–9700). Upstream destinations include Kew, Richmond, and Hampton Court. Most of the launches have a public-address system and provide a running commentary on passing points of interest. Depending upon the destination, river trips may last from one to four hours. For more information call Tidal Cruises (☎ 0171/928–9009).

Excursions. LT, Evan Evans, and Frames Rickards (☞ By Bus, *above*) all offer day excursions (some combine bus and boat) to places of interest within easy reach of London, such as Windsor, Hampton Court, Oxford, Stratford-upon-Avon, and Bath. Prices vary and may include lunch and admission prices or admission only. Alternatively, make your own way, cheaply, to many of England's attractions on Green Line Coaches (☎ 0181/668–7261).

On Foot. One of the best ways to get to know London is on foot, and there are many guided and themed walking tours from which to choose. **The Original London Walks** (☏ 0171/624–3978), and **City Walks** (☏ 0171/700–6931) are just two of the better-known firms, but your best bet is to peruse the variety of leaflets at a London Tourist Information Centre. The duration of the walks varies (usually one–three hours), and you can generally find one to suit even the most specific of interests—Shakespeare's London, or a Beatles's Magical Mystery Tour, or, even—gasp!—a Jack the Ripper tour.

If you'd rather explore on your own, then the City of London Corporation has laid out a **Heritage Walk** that leads through Bank, Leadenhall, and Monument; follow the trail by the directional stars set into the sidewalks. A map of this walk can be found in *A Visitor's Guide to the City of London,* available from the City Information Centre across from St. Paul's Cathedral. The **Silver Jubilee Walkway** covers 16 km (10 mi) and is marked by a series of silver crowns set into the sidewalks; Parliament Square makes a good starting point. **The Thames Path** is a new National Trail, some 291 km (180 mi) from the river's source in Gloucestershire to the Thames Barrier; for information, call London Docklands Visitor Centre (☏ 0171/512–1111). Several guides offering further walks are available in bookshops. One of the latest and most fascinating is *Secret London* by Andrew Duncan (New Holland).

TRAVEL AGENCIES

American Express (✉ 6 Haymarket, SW1, ☏ 0171/930–4411; ✉ 89 Mount St., W1, ☏ 0171/499–4436). **Thomas Cook** (✉ 4 Henrietta St., WC2, ☏ 0171/379–0685; ✉ 1 Marble Arch, W1, ☏ 0171/724–9483).

VISITOR INFORMATION

London Tourist Information Centre (✉ Victoria Station Forecourt). **British Travel Centre** (✉ 12 Regent St., Piccadilly Circus, SW1).

Visitorcall is the London Tourist Board's 24-hour phone service—a premium-rate (39p–49p per minute) recorded information line, with different numbers for theater, events, museums, sports, getting around, and so on. To access the list of options call 0839/123456, or see the separate categories in the telephone directory.

WINDSOR TO BATH

The Thames, England's second-longest river, winds its way toward London through an accessible and gracious stretch of countryside. An excursion west from the capital, roughly following the river toward its source in the Cotswold Hills, allows you to explore such historic townships as Windsor, where the castle is still regularly used by the royal family; Oxford, home of the nation's oldest university; and Stratford-upon-Avon, Shakespeare's birthplace. Traveling south, you come to Bath, whose 18th-century streets recall an age more elegant than our own.

Windsor

★ **Windsor Castle,** 34 km (21 mi) west of London, has been a royal citadel since the days of William the Conqueror in the 11th century. During the 14th century Edward III revamped the old castle, building the Norman gateway, the great round tower, and new apartments. Almost every monarch since then has added new buildings or improved existing ones; over the centuries the medieval fortification has been transformed into the lavish royal palace the visitor sees today.

The devastating fire of November 1992, which started in the Queen's private chapel, totally gutted some of the State Apartments. A swift rescue response meant that, miraculously, hardly any works of art were

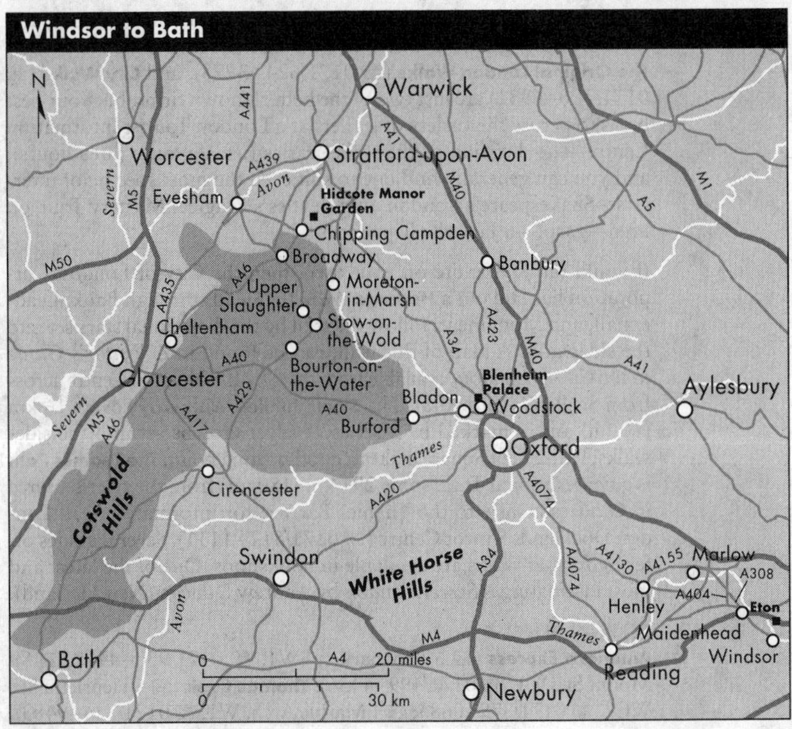

lost. In fact some were even discovered in the restoration process, with fragments of a 17th-century mural, done for Charles II by Antonio Verrio, surfacing during the renovation on St. George's Hall. Reopened to the public in December 1997 with grand fanfare, the castle has never looked more impressive. Costing a total of £37 million, phenomenal repair work has restored the **Grand Reception Room,** the **Green and Crimson Drawing Rooms,** and the **State and Octagonal Dining Rooms** to their former, if not greater, glory. The ceiling of St. George's Hall, where the Queen gives state banquets, was completely destroyed—today, a new green oak roof, the largest hammerbeam construction roof to have been built during the 20th century, now looms magnificently over the 600-year-old hall. The private chapel of the Royal Family has also been redesigned, with a new stained glass window commemorating the fire of 1992 and the restoration work that subsequently took place. All restored rooms, except the private chapel, are open to the public. Be aware that the State Apartments are sometimes closed when the Queen is in residence; call ahead to check.

St. George's Chapel, more than 230 ft long with two tiers of great windows and hundreds of gargoyles, buttresses, and pinnacles, is one of the noblest buildings in England. Inside, above the choir stalls, hang the banners, swords, and helmets of the Knights of the Order of the Garter, the most senior Order of Chivalry. The many monarchs buried in the chapel include Henry VIII and George VI, father of the present queen. (Note that St. George's Chapel is closed to the public on Sunday.)

The magnificent art collection at Windsor contains paintings by such masters as Rubens, Van Dyck, and Holbein; drawings by Leonardo da Vinci; and Gobelin tapestries. There are splendid views across to Windsor Great Park, the remains of a former royal hunting forest. Make time to view **Queen Mary's Dolls' House,** a charming toy country house

with every detail complete, including electricity, running water, and miniature books on the library shelves. It was designed in 1921 by the architect Sir Edwin Lutyens for the present queen's grandmother.

✉ *Windsor Castle,* ☎ *01753/868286.* 🎟 *£9.50, £21.50 family ticket; Dolls' House £1 extra (included in family ticket), or separately (including entry to the precincts).* ⏲ *Mar.–Oct., daily 10–5:30 (last admission at 4); Nov.–Feb., daily 10–4 (last entrance at 3).*

After seeing the castle stroll around the town and enjoy the shops; antiques are sold on cobbled Church Lane and Queen Charlotte Street.

A new attraction to delight children (of all ages) is a **Legoland** set in woodland 3¼ km (2 mi) outside Windsor. Hands-on activities both indoors and out include building, driving, and boating. For more information ask at the Windsor tourist office. ✉ *B3202, Bracknell/Ascot Rd.,* ☎ *0990/040404.* 🎟 *£16.* ⏲ *Mar.–June and Sept.–Nov., daily 10–6; July–Aug., daily 10–8.*

$$ ✕ **Ye Harte and Garter.** Right opposite Windsor Castle, in the hotel of the same name, this restaurant has a reasonably priced carvery offering a range of meats alongside the full à la carte menu. There is also a snack bar for sandwiches and light meals. ✉ *High St., Windsor,* ☎ *01753/863426. AE, DC, MC, V.*

$$$–$$$$ 🏨 **Oakley Court.** This relentlessly picturesque Victorian mock-castle is set in leafy grounds beside the river, just outside Windsor. Most of the bedrooms are in a bright wing of converted stables. It has the excellent Boulestin restaurant, plus sports facilities and a helipad. ✉ *Windsor Rd., Water Oakley, SL4 5UR,* ☎ *01628/609988,* FAX *01628/37011. 113 rooms. Restaurant, leisure center, heated indoor pool, sauna, 2 tennis courts. AE, DC, MC, V.*

$$$ 🏨 **Sir Christopher Wren's House.** As the name suggests, this house was built by the famous architect, though modern additions have been made to convert it into a hotel. There is a strong period flavor, though the faux-Baroque frills and flounces can be wearing. The restaurant overlooks the river, and cream teas are served on the terrace. ✉ *Thames St., Windsor, SL4 1PX,* ☎ *01753/861354,* FAX *01753/860172. 59 rooms. Restaurant. AE, DC, MC, V.*

Eton

Eton, Windsor Castle's equally historic neighbor, is home of the famous public school. (In Britain so-called public schools are private and charge fees.) Classes still take place in the distinctive redbrick Tudor-style buildings, the oldest of which are grouped around a quadrangle called School Yard. **The Museum of Eton Life** has displays on the school's history, and a guided tour is also available. ✉ *Brewhouse Yard,* ☎ *01753/671177.* ⏲ *Daily 2–5 during term, 10:30–4:30 on school holidays; guided tours Apr.–Sept., daily at 2:15 and 3:15.*

$$ ✕ **The Cockpit.** Cockfighting once took place in the courtyard of this smart 500-year-old oak-beam inn on Eton's quiet main street. Now a restaurant with a strong Italian flavor, its specialties include calves' liver and fresh fish. ✉ *47–49 High St., Eton,* ☎ *01753/860944. Reservations essential. AE, DC, MC, V. Closed Mon. No lunch Tues.*

Marlow

A relatively uncrowded route from Windsor to Oxford is along the river through Marlow and Henley on A308, then A4094, and A4155. In Marlow there are some stylish 18th-century houses on Peter and West streets, and several princes of Wales have lived in **Marlow Place** (✉ Station Rd.), which dates from 1721. Mary Shelley completed her celebrated horror story *Frankenstein* in the town.

Henley

Henley has been famous since 1839 for the rowing regatta it holds each year around the first Sunday in July. The social side of the regatta is as entertaining as the races themselves; elderly oarsmen wear brightly colored blazers and tiny caps, businessmen entertain wealthy clients, and everyone admires the ladies' fashions. The town is worth exploring for its small but good selection of specialty shops. The Red Lion Hotel near the 200-year-old bridge has been visited by kings, dukes, and writers. **St. Mary's Church** has a 16th-century "checkerboard" tower made of alternate squares of flint and stone. The **Chantry House,** built in 1420 as a school for poor boys, is an unspoiled example of the rare overhanging timber-frame design. ✉ *Hart St.,* ☎ *01491/577062.* 🎫 *Free.* ⏲ *For church services or by appointment.*

Oxford

Numbers in the margin correspond to points of interest on the Oxford map.

The surest way to absorb Oxford's unique blend of history and scholarliness is to wander around the tiny alleys that link the honey-color stone buildings topped by elegant "dreaming" spires, exploring the colleges where the undergraduates live and work. Oxford University, like Cambridge University, is not a single building but a collection of 35 independent colleges; many of their magnificent chapels and dining halls are open to visitors—times and (in some cases) entry charges are displayed at the entrance lodges. The main highways leading into Oxford are A4130 and A4074.

1 **Magdalen College** (pronounced "maudlin") is one of the most impressive, with cloisters more than 500 years old and lawns leading down to a
2 deer park and the River Cherwell. **St. Edmund Hall,** the next college up from Magdalen on High Street, has one of the smallest and most
3 picturesque quadrangles, with an old well in the center. **Christ Church,** on St. Aldate's, has the largest quadrangle, known as Tom Quad; hanging in the medieval dining hall are portraits of former students, including John Wesley, William Penn, and no fewer than 14 prime min-
4 isters. The doors between the inner and outer quadrangles of **Balliol College,** on Broad Street, still bear the scorch marks from the flames that burned Archbishop Cranmer and Bishops Latimer and Ridley at the stake in 1555 for their Protestant beliefs.

5 The **Oxford Story** on Broad Street is a multimedia presentation of the university's 800-year history. ✉ *Broad St.,* ☎ *01865/790055.* ⏲ *Apr.–June and Sept.–Oct., daily 9:30–5; Jul.–Aug., daily 9:30–7; Nov.–Mar., daily 10–4.*

6 The **Sheldonian Theatre,** which St. Paul's architect Christopher Wren designed to look like a semicircular Roman amphitheater, is one of Oxford's most distinctive buildings. Graduation ceremonies are held here. ✉ *Broad St.,* ☎ *01865/277299.* ⏲ *Mon.–Sat. 10–12:30 and 2–4:30; mid-Nov.–Feb. til 4. Closed 10 days at Christmas and Easter, also for student events.*

7 The **Ashmolean Museum,** which you encounter by turning right out of Broad Street into Magdalen Street, then taking the first left, is Britain's oldest public museum, holding priceless collections of Egyptian, Greek, and Roman artifacts; Michelangelo drawings; and European silverware. ✉ *Beaumont St.,* ☎ *01865/278000.* 🎫 *Free.* ⏲ *Tues.–Sat. 10–4, Sun. 2–4.*

8 Near the center of Oxford the 14th-century tower of the **University Church** (St. Mary the Virgin) provides a splendid panoramic view of

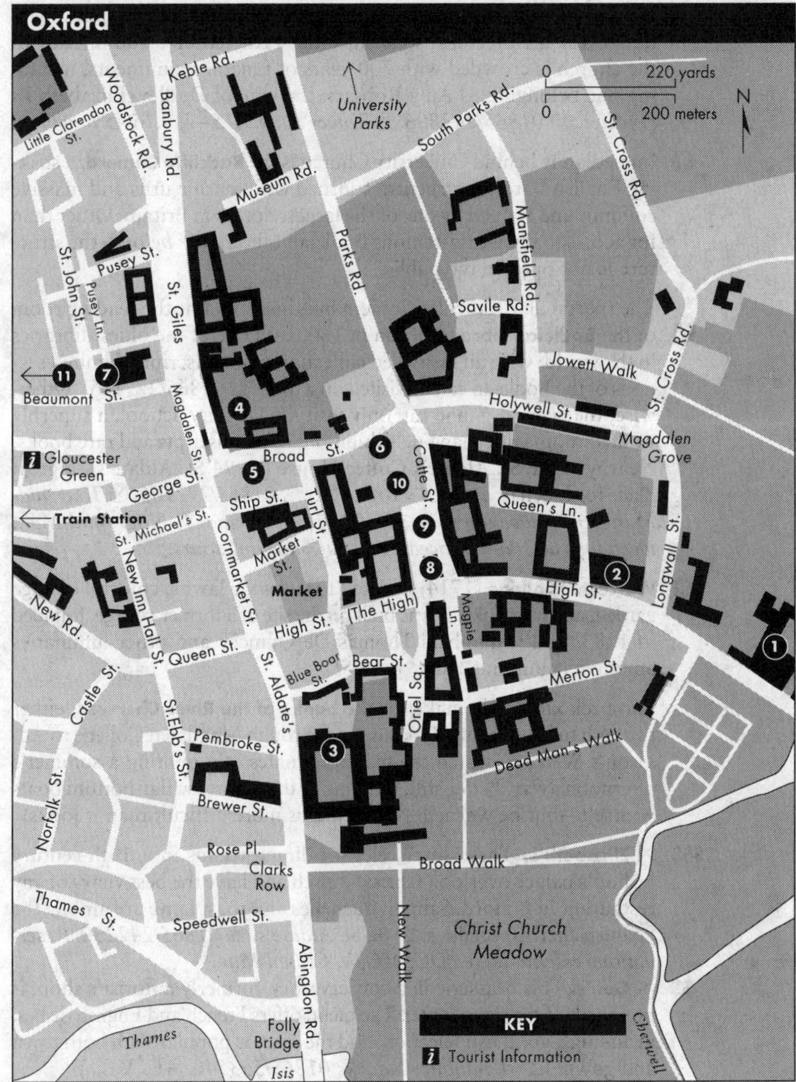

Ashmolean Museum, **7**
Balliol College, **4**
Bodleian Library, **10**
Christ Church, **3**
Magdalen College, **1**
Oxford Story, **5**
Radcliffe Camera, **9**
St. Edmund Hall, **2**
Sheldonian Theatre, **6**
University Church (St. Mary's), **8**
Worcester College, **11**

the city's famous skyline—the pinnacles, towers, domes, and spires spanning every architectural style since the 11th century. The interior of the church is crowded with 700 years of funeral monuments, including one belonging to Amy Robsart, the wife of Dudley, Elizabeth I's favorite. ☎ *01865/243806.* ⏲ *Tower daily 9:15–7, 9:15–5 in winter.*

9 Immediately behind University Church is the **Radcliffe Camera,** a striking English Baroque structure adorned with marble urns and massive columns and topped by one of the largest domes in Britain. Other than for access to the world-famous Bodleian Library (☞ *below*), the structure is not open to the public.

The spectacular Radcliffe Camera building contains the reading room
10 of the **Bodleian Library,** begun in 1602 and one of the oldest libraries in the world, with an unrivaled collection of manuscripts. Limited sections of the Bodleian can be visited on a tour (☎ 01865/277165). Otherwise, the general public can only visit the Divinity School, a superbly vaulted room with changing exhibitions of manuscripts and rare books. Nearby is the **St. Aldate's Coffee House** (✉ 94 St. Aldate's), a great place for lunch or coffee. ✉ *Broad St.,* ☎ *01865/277165.* ⏲ *Tour mid-Mar.–Oct., weekdays at 10:30, 11:30, 2, and 3; Nov.–mid-Mar., weekdays at 2 and 3; occasional Sat. morning tours.*

11 **Worcester College** (1714) is noted for its wide lawns, colorful cottage garden, and large lake. It was built on the site of a former college, founded in 1283, and it numbers Thomas De Quincey and other luminaries among its alumni. ✉ *Worcester St.*

For a relaxing walk make for the **banks of the River Cherwell,** either through the University Parks area or through Magdalen College to Addison's Walk, to watch the undergraduates idly punting a summer's afternoon away. Better still, rent one of these narrow flat-bottom boats yourself—but be warned: Navigating is more difficult than it looks!

$$$ ✕ **Elizabeth's.** These small, elegant dining rooms in a 16th-century bishop's palace overlook Christ Church and have the best views of any restaurant in Oxford. Salmon quenelles and roast lamb are among the Spanish chef's specialties. ✉ *82 St. Aldate's,* ☎ *01865/242230. Reservations essential. AE, DC, MC, V. Closed Mon.*

$$ ✕ **Gee's.** This brasserie in a conservatory, formerly a florist's shop, is just north of the town center. The menu offers French and English dishes, including a good fish selection, and the place is popular with both town and gown. ✉ *61 Banbury Rd.,* ☎ *01865/553540. AE, MC, V.*

$ ✕ **Munchy Munchy.** A constantly changing menu of spicy Indonesian dishes and a good selection of fresh fruit and vegetables make this a refreshing and popular spot. The surroundings are unpretentious and the prices are reasonable. ✉ *6 Park End St.,* ☎ *01865/245710. MC, V. Closed Sun., Mon.*

$$$$ 🏨 **Old Parsonage.** It's rare to find an attractive country house–hotel, with stone gables and mullion windows, in the middle of a city, but that is just what awaits at the Old Parsonage. It was established in 1660 and was completely restored and refurbished in 1991. Open fires, fascinating pictures, comfortable rooms, and immaculate service make this a hotel to remember. The rates are at the bottom of its price category. ✉ *1 Banbury Rd., OX2 6NN,* ☎ *01865/310210,* FAX *01865/311262. 30 rooms. Restaurant. AE, DC, MC, V.*

$$$–$$$$ 🏨 **The Randolph.** Oxford's only large central hotel has undergone extensive restoration of its beautiful Victorian Gothic interior (unfortunately, this has not extended to some of the very squeaky floorboards, an annoyance at night). It's across from the Ashmolean Museum. ✉

Beaumont St., OX1 2LN, ☎ 01865/247481, FAX 01865/791678. 104 rooms, 4 suites. Restaurant. AE, DC, MC, V.

$$$ **Eastgate Hotel.** This welcoming hotel has the traditional style of an inn. Flanked by ancient university buildings and colleges, it is a good place to get an insight into university life. ✉ *The High, OX1 4BE, ☎ 01865/248244, FAX 01865/791681. 62 rooms. Restaurant. AE, DC, MC, V.*

Woodstock

★ **Blenheim Palace,** about 13 km (8 mi) north of Oxford on A44 (Woodstock Road), is the most spectacular house in England, even beating Buckingham Palace and Windsor Castle for sheer grandeur and majesty. A vast pile of towers, colonnades, and porticoes, Blenheim was built in neoclassical style during the early 18th century by the architect Sir John Vanbrugh; it stands in 2,500 acres of beautiful gardens created later in the 18th century by the English landscape gardener "Capability" Brown. Soldier and statesman John Churchill, first duke of Marlborough, built the house on land given to him by Queen Anne as a reward for his defeat of the French at the Battle of Blenheim in 1704. The house is filled with fine paintings—don't miss the grand John Singer Sargent portrait of the 9th Duke and his wife, Consuelo Vanderbilt—tapestries, and furniture. Winston Churchill, a descendant of Marlborough, was born in the palace; some of his paintings are on display, and there is an exhibition devoted to his life. A cafeteria is on the grounds, as is a famous topiary maze, butterfly house, and other amusements. ✉ *Woodstock, ☎ 01993/811091. House, £8; grounds, £1. ⏲ Mid-Mar.–Oct., 10:30–4:45; grounds open year-round 9–4:45.*

Sir Winston Churchill (1874–1965) is buried in the nearby village of **Bladon.** His grave in the small tree-lined churchyard is all the more touching for its simplicity.

Just outside the back gates of Blenheim Palace is the village of **Woodstock**—extraordinarily civilized, it's filled with beautiful shops, some elegant 18th-century buildings, and exquisite hotels, such as The Bear (☎ 01993/811511), The Feathers (☎ 01993/812291), and the Blenheim Guest House and Tea Rooms (☎ 01993/811467), the last set just outside the imperial back gates of the palace. Stay here instead of in Oxford and take the 15-minute bus ride back and forth to the college town instead.

Stratford-upon-Avon

Numbers in the margin correspond to points of interest on the Stratford-upon-Avon map.

A34 runs northwest from Oxford and Blenheim across the Cotswold Hills to Stratford-upon-Avon, the hometown of William Shakespeare. Even without its most famous son, Stratford would be worth visiting. The town's timbered buildings bear witness to its prosperity during the 16th century, when it was a thriving craft and trading center. Attractive buildings from the 18th century add to the town's historic feel.

The main places of Shakespearean interest are run by the **Shakespeare Birthplace Trust** (☎ 01789/204016). They all have similar opening times, and you can get a combination ticket for them all—£10—or pay separate entry fees if you want to visit only one or two. *Shakespeare's Birthplace and Anne Hathaway's Cottage mid-Mar.–mid-Oct., Mon.–Sat. 9–5, Sun. 9:30–5; mid-Oct.–mid-Mar., Mon.–Sat. 9:30–4, Sun. 10–4. Nash's House, Hall's Croft, and Mary Arden's House mid-Mar.–mid-Oct., Mon.–Sat. 9:30–5, Sun. 10–5; mid-Oct.–mid-Mar., 10–4, Sun. 10:30–4. Last entry for all sights 30 mins before closing.*

★ 1 The **Shakespeare Birthplace and Centre** contains the costumes used in the BBC's versions of the plays and an exhibition of the playwright's life and work. ✉ *Henley St. A Shakespeare Birthplace Trust property.*

Originally a farmhouse, the girlhood home of Shakespeare's mother, 2 **Mary Arden's House,** is now an extensive museum of farming and country life, and it's beautifully evocative of the times in which Shakespeare lived. The black-and-white timbered house was built in the 16th century, and many of the original outbuildings are intact, together with a 600-nesting-hole dovecote. The garden is planted with trees mentioned in Shakespeare's plays. ✉ *Wilmcote (5.5 km/3½ mi northwest of Stratford, off A3400 and A46); reachable by train in a few minutes from Stratford. A Shakespeare Birthplace Trust property.*

★ 3 **Anne Hathaway's Cottage,** in Shottery on the edge of the town, is the early home of the playwright's wife. With a storybook thatched roof, this house is one of the most picturesque sights in all Britain. *A Shakespeare Birthplace Trust property.*

4 **Hall's Croft** is a fine Tudor town house that was the home of Shakespeare's daughter Susanna and her doctor husband; it is furnished in the decor of the day. The doctor's dispensary and consulting room can also be seen. ✉ *Old Town. A Shakespeare Birthplace Trust property.*

Along the main thoroughfare of Church Street are almshouses built by the Guild of the Holy Cross during the early 15th century. Farther
5 along is the **Guildhall Grammar School,** which Shakespeare probably attended as a boy, and which is—4 centuries later—still used as a school. ✉ *Church St., near Chapel La.,* ☎ *01789/293351.* ⏲ *Easter and summer school vacations, daily 10–6.*

6 Next to the Garrick Inn you'll find **Harvard House,** a half-timbered 16th-century structure that was home to Catherine Rogers, mother of the John Harvard who founded Harvard University in 1636. Unfortunately, the house is virtually unfurnished. ✉ *High St.* ⏲ *May–Sept. Contact the Shakespeare Centre for hours.*

7 The **Royal Shakespeare Theatre** occupies a perfect position on the banks of the Avon—try to see a performance if you can. The company (always referred to as the RSC) performs several Shakespeare plays each season, as well as scripts by a wide variety of other playwrights, between March and January. For a fascinating insight into how the theater operates, join one of the backstage tours, led twice daily (four times on Sunday). Beside the main theater is the smaller **Swan.** Modeled on an Elizabethan theater, the Swan stages productions in the round. The Swan also provides entry to the RSC Collection, comprising paintings, props, and memorabilia; visit it either on one of the backstage tours or on your own. It's best to book well in advance for RSC productions, but a very few tickets for the day of performance are always available, and it is also worth asking if there are any returns. ✉ *The Royal Shakespeare Theatre, Stratford-upon-Avon, Warwickshire CV37 6BB,* ☎ *01789/295623; programs available starting Feb.;* ☎ *01789/412602 for details on backstage tours and RSC Collection.*

8 A new auditorium for experimental productions, **The Other Place,** stands just down the street from the Royal Shakespeare Theatre. It is
9 in **Holy Trinity Church,** close to the Royal Shakespeare Theatre, that Shakespeare and his wife are buried.

$$$ ✕ **Box Tree Restaurant.** In the Royal Shakespeare Theatre, this elegant restaurant overlooks the river and is a favored spot for pre- and post-theater dining. Specialties include roast rack of lamb and grilled Scotch

Anne Hathaway's Cottage, **3**
Guildhall Grammar School, **5**
Hall's Croft, **4**
Harvard House, **6**
Holy Trinity Church, **9**
Mary Arden's House, **2**
The Other Place, **8**
Royal Shakespeare Theatre, **7**
Shakespeare Birthplace and Centre, **1**

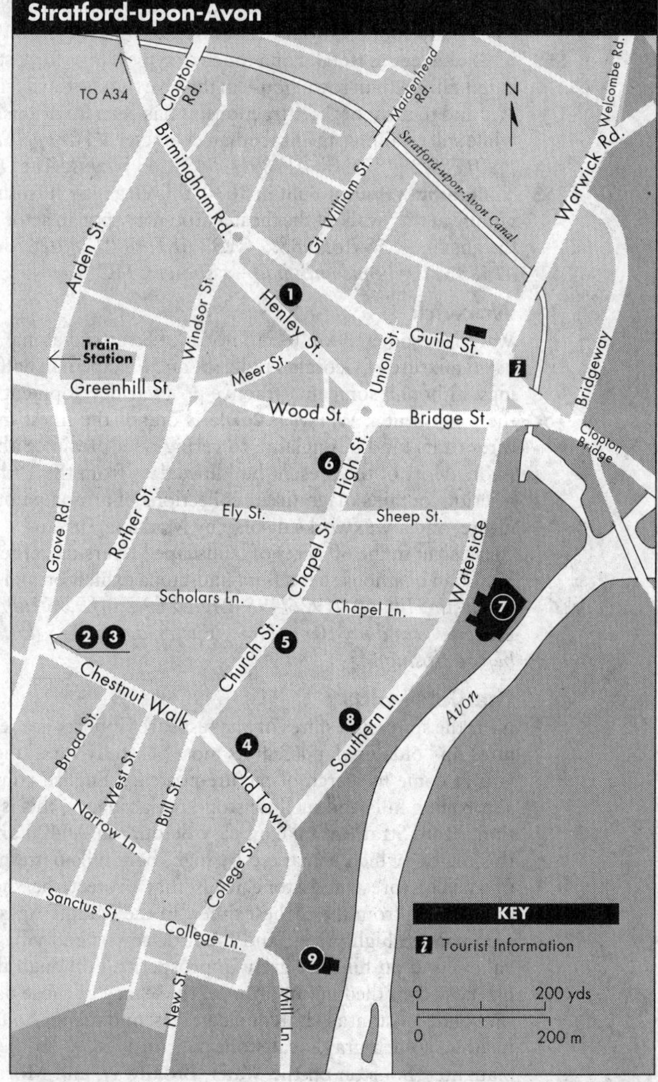

beef fillet. ✉ *Waterside,* ☏ *01789/293226. AE, MC, V. Closed when theater is closed.*

$$ ✕ **The Opposition.** Located near the Royal Shakespeare Theatre, the Opposition caters to the pre- and post-theater dining crowd (as do all sensible restaurants in Stratford). It is extremely popular with the locals, so book in advance. The American and Continental dishes change each month—if you're lucky there will be Cajun chicken. ✉ *13 Sheep St.,* ☏ *01789/269980. Reservations essential. MC, V.*

$ ✕ **The Slug and Lettuce.** Don't let the name put you off—this pine-paneled pub serves excellent meals. Long-standing favorites are chicken breast baked in avocado and garlic, and poached cushion of salmon. ✉ *38 Guild St.,* ☏ *01789/299700. Reservations essential. MC, V.*

$$$ 🏨 **Falcon Hotel.** Licensed as an alehouse since 1640, it still has a friendly inn atmosphere. The heavily beamed rooms in the older part are small and quaint; those in the modern extension are in standard international style. ✉ *Chapel St., CV37 6HA,* ☎ *01789/279953,* FAX *01789/414260. 73 rooms. Restaurant. AE, DC, MC, V.*

$$$ **Shakespeare Hotel.** For a touch of typical Stratford, stay at this timbered Elizabethan town house in the heart of the town, close to the theater and to most of the attractions. It has been luxuriously modernized while still retaining its Elizabethan character. ✉ *Chapel St., CV37 6ER,* ☎ *01789/294771,* FAX *01789/415411. 63 rooms. AE, DC, MC, V.*

$$ **Caterham House.** Built in 1830, this elegantly furnished building is within an easy walk of the theater. You may spot an actor or two among the guests. ✉ *58 Rother St., CV37 6LT,* ☎ *01789/267309,* FAX *01789/414836. 10 rooms with bath or shower. MC, V.*

Warwick

Warwick, some 13 km (8 mi) north of Stratford along A46, is an unusual mixture of Georgian redbrick and Elizabethan half-timber buildings, although some unattractive postwar developments have spoiled ★ the town center. **Warwick Castle** is one of the finest medieval structures of its kind in England, towering on a precipice above the River Avon. Most of the present buildings date from the 14th century. The interior contains magnificent collections of armor, paintings, and furniture, and a waxworks display by Madame Tussaud's. Outside, peacocks strut in the 60 acres of landscaped riverside gardens. A restored Victorian boathouse has a flora-and-fauna exhibition and a nature walk. ✉ *Castle Hill,* ☎ *01926/495421.* *£9.25 (£9.95 July and Aug.).* *Easter–Oct., daily 10–6; Nov.–Easter, daily 10–5 (last entry 30 mins before closing).*

The Cotswolds

Near the spires and shires of Shakespeare Country is a region that conjures up "olde Englande" at its most blissfully rural: the Cotwolds. If you've come in search of picture-postcard English countryside, with soft rolling hills and mellow stone-built villages, this is your destination, From Stratford take an easy detour via A3400 and B4632 into this region, which is marked by high, bare hills patterned by patches of ancient forest and stone walls that protect the sheep that have grazed here from the earliest times. In the Middle Ages English wool commanded high prices, and the little towns and villages nestling in valleys and on hillsides grew in prosperity. Although the wool trade has now dwindled in importance, the legacy of those days remains in the solid, substantial churches, cottages, and manor houses built of the mellow, golden-gray local stone. Burford, Stow-on-the-Wold, Upper Slaughter, Bourton-on-the-Water, Broadway, and Moreton-in-Marsh are just a few of the picturesque towns connected by pleasant country roads. The Old World atmosphere of the Cotswolds is as thick as honey, and as pleasant and sweet.

If you have time to visit only one Cotswold town, make it **Chipping Campden.** Its broad High Street is lined with houses in an attractive disarray of styles, many dating from the 17th century. Look for the group of almshouses built in 1624 and raised above street level and for the gabled **Market Hall** built three years later for the sale of local produce.

★ Six kilometers (4 mi) outside Chipping Campden is **Hidcote Manor Garden,** a 20th-century garden created around a Cotswold manor house (not open to the public). The lovely garden—which some connoisseurs consider the finest in Britain—consists of a series of open-air rooms divided by walls and hedges, each in a different style. ✉ *Hidcote Bartrim,* ☎ *01386/438333.* *Apr.–May and Aug.–Sept., Sat.–Mon., Wed., Thurs. 11–7; June–July, Sat.–Thurs. 11–7; Oct., Sat.–Mon., Wed., Thurs. 11–6. Last entrance 1 hr before sunset.*

B4632 runs along the western edge of the gently rolling Cotswold Hills as far as **Cheltenham,** once the rival of Bath in its Georgian elegance. Although it's now marred by modern developments, there are still some fine examples of the Regency style in its graceful secluded villas, lush gardens, and leafy crescents and squares.

Bath

Numbers in the margin correspond to points of interest on the Bath map.

Bath lies at the southern end of the Cotswolds (at the end of A46), some 113 km (70 mi) from Stratford. A perfect 18th-century city, perhaps the best preserved in all Britain, it is a compact place, easy to explore on foot; the museums, elegant shops, and terraces of magnificent town houses are all close to one another. After promenading through the town, stop at either the Pump Room (✉ Abbey Churchyard) for morning coffee or afternoon tea in grand surroundings (perhaps listening to the music of a string quartet), or Sally Lunn's (✉ North Parade Passage), where the famous Sally Lunn bun is still baked.

It was the Romans who first took the waters at Bath, building a temple in honor of their goddess Minerva and a sophisticated series of baths to make full use of the curative hot springs. To this day, these springs gush from the earth at a constant temperature of 115.7°F (46.5°C). In
1 the **Roman Baths Museum,** underneath the 18th-century Pump Room, you can see the excavated remains of almost the entire baths complex. ✉ *Abbey Churchyard,* ☎ *01225/477785.* 🎟 *£8.40 combined ticket for Roman Baths and Museum of Costume.* ⏲ *Apr.–July and Sept., daily 9–6; Aug., daily 9–6 and 8 PM–10 PM; Oct.–Mar., daily 9:30–5.*

2 Next to the Pump Room is the **Abbey,** built in the 15th century. There are superb fan-vaulted ceilings in the nave.

During the 18th century Bath became the fashionable center for taking the waters. The architect John Wood created a harmonious city from the mellow local stone, building beautifully executed terraces, crescents, and villas. The heart of Georgian Bath is the perfectly proportioned
3 **Circus,** begun in 1754, and the Royal Crescent, 1767–1774. A delightful
★ 4 peek into the gracious lifestyles of the Age of Enlightenment, **No. 1 Royal Crescent** is furnished as it might have been when Beau Nash, the master of ceremonies and arbiter of 18th-century Bath society, lived in the city. ☎ *01225/428126.* ⏲ *Mid-Feb.–Oct., Tues.–Sun. 10:30–5; Nov., Tues.–Sun. 10:30–4 (last admission 30 min before closing).*

5 Near the Circus are the **Assembly Rooms,** frequently mentioned by Jane Austen in her novels of early 19th-century life. Housed in a Neoclassical mansion, the salons now house a Museum of Costume that displays dress styles from Beau Nash's day to the present. ✉ *Bennett St.,* ☎ *01225/477785.* 🎟 *£8.40 combined ticket with Roman Baths.* ⏲ *Mon.–Sat. 10–5, Sun. 11–5.*

6 The **Theatre Royal** opened in 1805 and was restored in 1982. Next door the former home of Beau Nash—the dictator of fashion for mid-18th-century society in Bath—and his mistress Juliana Popjoy, is now a restaurant called Popjoy's (☞ Dining, *below*).

7 One of the most charming and picturesque sights in Bath is the **Pulteney Bridge,** an 18th-century span that was based on the Ponte Vecchio of Florence. Lined with little shops, the bridge is the only work of Robert Adam in the city. At the western end is the Victoria Art Gallery.

Abbey, **2**
Assembly Rooms, **5**
Circus, **3**
Holburne Museum and Crafts Study Centre, **8**
No. 1 Royal Crescent, **4**
Pulteney Bridge, **7**
Roman Baths Museum, **1**
Theatre Royal, **6**

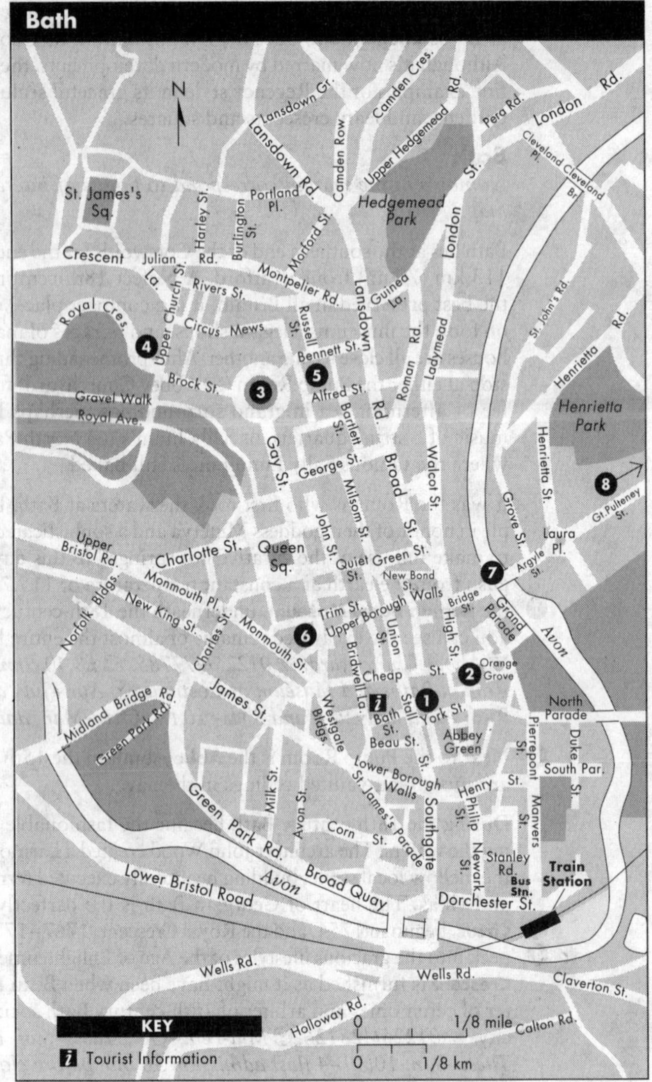

8 In an elegant 18th-century building the **Holburne Museum and Crafts Study Centre,** houses a superb collection of 17th- and 18th-century fine art, silverware, and decorative arts. ✉ *Great Pulteney St.,* ☎ *01225/466669.* ⏲ *Easter–mid-Nov., Mon.–Sat. 11–5, Sun. 2:30–5:30; mid-Nov.–mid-Dec. and mid-Feb.–Easter, Tues.–Sat. 11–5, Sun. 2:30–5:30.*

$$ ✕ **Number Five.** This candlelit bistro off Pulteney Bridge has a relaxed ambience and offers tasty homemade soups or more elaborate dishes, such as roast quail on wild rice and char-grilled loin of lamb. ✉ *5 Argyle St.,* ☎ *01225/444499. AE, DC, MC, V. Closed Sun. No lunch Mon.*

$$ ✕ **Popjoy's Restaurant.** Beau Nash entertained the best of 18th-century society here, and Popjoy's retains its air of elegance. Diners can choose between dining on the ground floor or upstairs in a lovely Georgian drawing room. ✉ *Sawclose,* ☎ *01225/460494. Reservations essential. AE, DC, MC, V. Closed Sun.*

$$ ✕ **Rascals.** In a mazelike cellar of interconnecting rooms just south of the abbey, Rascals is a cheerful bistro-style restaurant offering excellent food, fine wines at low prices, and a noisy, relaxed atmosphere. Chef and proprietor Nick Anderson provides an international range of dishes, such as poached veal with lentils and capers, though the menu changes regularly. ✉ *8 Pierrepoint Pl.,* ☎ *01225/330201. Reservations essential. MC, V. Closed Sun.*

$$$$ ★ **Royal Crescent.** The ultimate in luxury living, in a gracious, lavishly converted building, the hotel stands on one of England's most famous terraces. Each bedroom has been individually designed to recapture the elegance of Bath's heyday. The hotel's formal Dower House restaurant wins consistent praise. ✉ *16 Royal Crescent, BA1 2LS,* ☎ *01225/739955,* FAX *01225/339401. 25 rooms, 19 suites. Restaurant. AE, DC, MC, V.*

$$$ ★ **Queensberry Hotel.** In a quiet residential street near the Circus, this intimate, elegant hotel is in three 1772 town houses built by the architect John Wood for the Marquis of Queensberry. Renovations have preserved the Regency touches, and below stairs, the Olive Tree restaurant serves English and Mediterranean dishes. ✉ *Russell St., BA1 2QF,* ☎ *01225/447928,* FAX *01225/446065. 22 rooms with bath. Restaurant, bar. MC, V. Closed Dec. 24–30.*

$$ **Paradise House.** It's a steep uphill climb from the center of Bath, but you'll be rewarded by a wonderful prospect of the city from the upper stories of this Georgian guest house. It features open fires in winter and a lush, secluded garden for the spring and summer. ✉ *88 Holloway, BA2 4PX,* ☎ *01225/317723,* FAX *01225/482005. 8 rooms with bath or shower. AE, MC, V.*

Windsor to Bath Essentials

Getting Around

BY BUS

Regular long-distance services leave from Victoria Coach Station. **National Express** (☎ 0990/808080) has runs on the route. **Oxford Bus Company** (☎ 0181/668–7261) serves the region. The **Green Line** (☎ 0181/668-7261) bus leaves from Eccleston Bridge, behind London's Victoria train station, *not* from the Coach Station itself. Make sure you catch the fast direct service, which takes 45 minutes and runs hourly; the stopping services take up to 1 hour, 15 minutes.

BY CAR

M4 and M40 are the main highways out of London serving Oxford, the Cotswolds, and Bath. Once you're clear of London, take to the country roads and explore tiny villages and the best of the English countryside.

BY TRAIN

Windsor is easy to reach by train from London, either from Waterloo direct to Windsor and Eton Riverside (50 minutes), or from Paddington to Windsor Central, changing at Reading (45 minutes); there are two trains per hour on each route. Regular fast trains run from Paddington to Oxford and Bath, and less frequent and slower services requiring at least one change, to Stratford. For information, call 0345/484950. An alternative route to Stratford is from London's Euston Station to Coventry, from which there are hourly bus connections on the Stratford Blue line; call 01788/535555 for details.

Guided Tours

Evan Evans (☎ 0181/332–2222) operates daily one-day tours to Oxford, Stratford, and the Cotswolds. **Frames Rickards** (☎ 0171/837–3111) runs full-day sightseeing tours to Windsor, Stratford-upon-Avon, Oxford, and Bath. **Golden Tours** (☎ 0171/233–7030) runs four-day trips to Oxford, Stratford, and the Cotswolds from London. **Guide Friday** (Windsor and Oxford, ☎ 01865/790522; Stratford, ☎ 01789/294466) offers excellent open-top bus tours of Windsor, Oxford, the Cotswolds, and Shakespeare Country.

Visitor Information

Bath (✉ The Colonnades, 11–13 Bath St., ☎ 01225/477101). **Oxford** (✉ The Old School, Gloucester Green, ☎ 01865/726871). **Stow-on-the-Wold** (✉ Hollis House, The Sq., ☎ 01451/831082). **Stratford** (✉ Bridgefoot, next to Clopton Bridge, ☎ 01789/293127). **Warwick** (✉ The Court House, Jury St., ☎ 01926/492212). **Windsor** (✉ 24 High St., ☎ 01753/852010).

CAMBRIDGE

Cambridge, home of England's second-oldest university, is an ideal place to explore. There have been students here since the late 13th century, and virtually every generation after that then has produced fine buildings, often by the most distinguished architects of its day. The result is a compact gallery of the best of English architecture. There is also good shopping in the city, and you can enjoy relaxing riverside walks. Cambridge is 87 km (54 mi) north of London, 66 km (41 mi) northwest of Colchester, and 102 km (63 mi) southwest of Norwich.

Exploring Cambridge

Numbers in the margin correspond to points of interest on the Cambridge map.

The university is in the very heart of Cambridge. It consists of a number of colleges, each of which is a separate institution with its own distinct character. Undergraduates join an individual college and are taught by dons, who are known as "fellows." Each college is built around a series of courts, or quadrangles; because students and fellows live in these quadrangles, access is sometimes restricted, especially during examination weeks (April to mid-June). Visitors are not normally allowed into college buildings other than chapels, halls, and some libraries; some colleges levy an admission charge for certain buildings. Public visiting hours vary dramatically from college to college, and it's best to call ahead or to check first with the city tourist office. If you have time, there's no better way to absorb Cambridge's unique atmosphere than by hiring a punt at Silver Street Bridge or at Magdalene Bridge and navigating down past St. John's or upstream to Grantchester, the pretty village made famous by the poet Rupert Brooke.

10 **Emmanuel College.** Evident throughout much of Cambridge, the master hand of Christopher Wren designed the chapel and colonnade of Emmanuel College, founded in 1584. The college was an early center of Puritan learning; among the portraits of famous members of the college hanging in Emmanuel Hall is one of John Harvard, founder of Harvard University. ✉ *St. Andrew's St.,* ☎ *01223/334200.*

9 **Fitzwilliam Museum.** Cambridge's most renowned museum contains outstanding art collections (including paintings by Constable, Gainsborough, and the French Impressionists) and antiquities (especially from ancient Egypt). The coffee shop here is an excellent choice for a pastry or a light lunch. ✉ *Trumpington St.,* ☎ *01223/332900.* 🎫 *Free; donation requested.* ⏲ *Tues.–Sat. 10–5; Sun. 2:15–5.*

5 **Kettle's Yard.** Originally a private house owned by a former curator of London's Tate Gallery, Kettle's Yard is home to a fine permanent collection of 20th-century art, sculpture, furniture, and decorative

arts. A separate gallery provides space for a regular program of exhibitions. ⊠ *Castle St.,* ☎ *01223/352124.* ✉ *Free.* ⊙ *House, Tues.–Sun. 2–4; gallery, Tues.–Sat. 12:30–5:30, Sun. 2–5:30.*

★ 1 **King's College.** The high point of King's—and possibly of Cambridge—is its chapel, started by Henry VI in 1446, a masterpiece of late-Gothic architecture, with a great fan-vaulted ceiling supported only by a tracery of soaring side columns. Behind the altar hangs Rubens's painting, *Adoration of the Magi.* Every Christmas Eve the college choir sings the Festival of Nine Lessons and Carols, which is broadcast all over the world. The novelist E. M. Forster, who wrote *Howards End* and *A Passage to India,* studied at King's, as did the war poet Rupert Brooke. King's runs down to the **"Backs,"** the tree-shaded grounds on the banks of the River Cam, which is the background of many of the colleges. ⊠ *King's Parade,* ☎ *01223/331447.* ⊙ *Chapel, term time, Mon. 9:30–4:30, Tues.–Fri. 9:30–3:30, Sat. 9:30–3:15, Sun. 1:15–2:15; summer, Mon.–Sat.9:30–4:30, Sun. 1:15–2:15 and 5–5:30.*

4 **Magdalene College.** Across Magdalene (pronounced "maudlin") Bridge, a cast-iron 1820 structure, is Magdalene College, distinguished by pretty redbrick courts. It was a hostel for Benedictine monks for over 100 years before the college was founded in 1542. The college's **Pepys Library** (✉ free; ⊙ library: Apr.–Sept., Mon.–Sat. 11:30–12:30 and 2:30–5:30; Oct.–Mar., Mon.–Sat. 2:30–3:30) contains the books and desk of the 17th-century diarist, Samuel Pepys. ⊠ *Magdalene St.,* ☎ *01223/332100.*

7 **Pembroke College.** The first court of Pembroke College (1347), has some buildings dating from the 14th century. On the south side Christopher Wren's chapel—his first major commission, completed in 1665—looks like a distinctly modern intrusion. You can walk through the college, around a delightful garden, and past the fellows' bowling green. ⊠ *Trumpington St.,* ☎ *01223/338100.*

8 **Peterhouse College.** Cambridge's oldest college was founded in 1281 by the Bishop of Ely. Parts of the dining hall date from 1290; the chapel, in late Gothic style, dates from 1632. On the river side of the buildings is a large and tranquil deer park. ⊠ *Trumpington St.,* ☎ *01223/338200.*

6 **Queen's College.** One of the most eye-catching colleges, Queen's (1446) is named after the respective consorts of Henry VI and Edward IV. The college's Mathematical Bridge (best seen from the Silver Street road bridge) is an arched wooden structure that was originally held together by gravitational force; when it was taken apart to see how Isaac Newton did it, no one could reconstruct it without using nails. The present bridge, dating from 1902, is securely bolted. ⊠ *Queen's La.,* ☎ *01223/335511.* ⊙ *Daily 1:45–4:30.*

3 **St. John's College.** St. John's is Cambridge's second-largest college, founded in 1511 by Henry VII's mother, Lady Margaret Beaufort. The famous copy of the Bridge of Sighs in Venice is here, reaching across the Cam to the mock-Gothic New Court (1825). ⊠ *St. John's St.,* ☎ *01223/338600.* ⊙ *Weekdays 10–5:30, weekends 9:30–5:30.*

2 **Trinity College.** This is the largest college, with almost 700 undergraduates, established by Henry VIII in 1546. It has a handsome 17th-century Great Court, around which are sited the chapel, hall, gates, and a magnificent library by Christopher Wren—colonnaded and seemingly constructed as much of light as of stone. In the massive gate house is Great Tom, a large clock that strikes each hour and that figured in the race around the quadrangle at the heart of the movie *Char-*

Cambridge

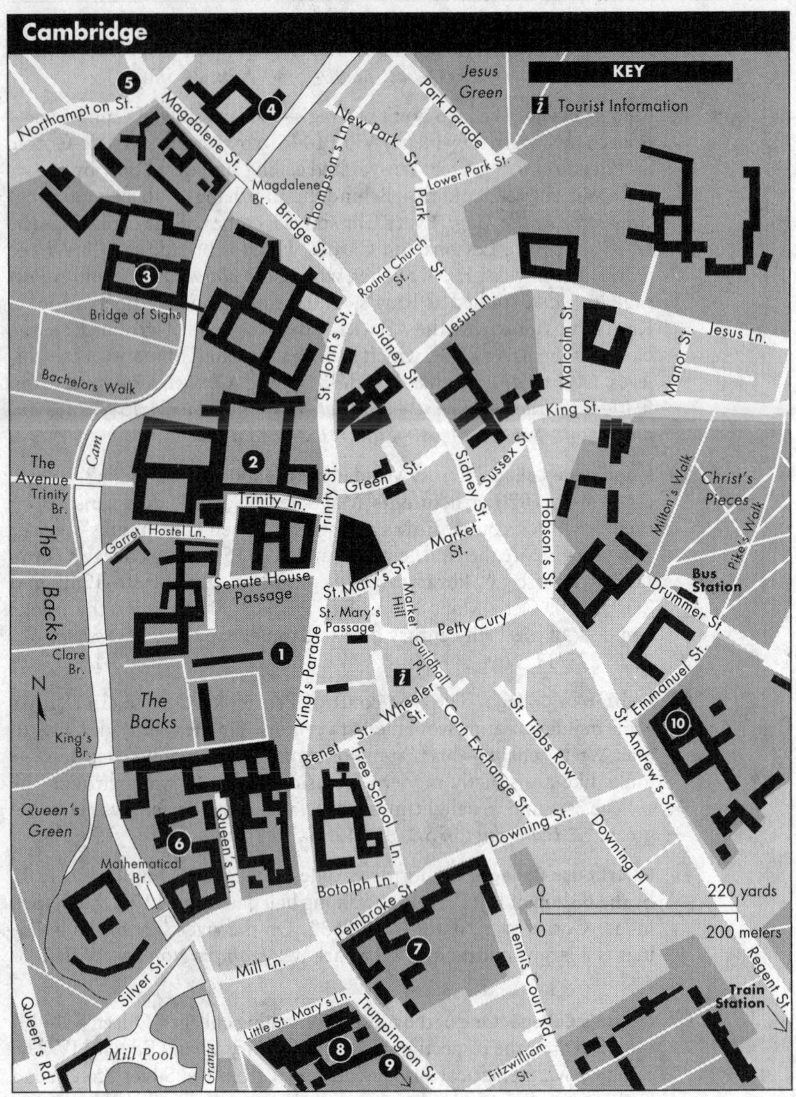

Emmanuel College, **10**
Fitzwilliam Museum, **9**
Kettle's Yard, **5**
King's College, **1**
Magdalene College, **4**
Pembroke College, **7**
Peterhouse College, **8**
Queen's College, **6**
St. John's College, **3**
Trinity College, **2**

iots of Fire. Prince Charles was an undergraduate here in the late 1960s. ✉ *St. John's St.,* ☎ *01223/338400.* ⏲ *College: daily 10–6; library: weekdays noon–2, Sat. in term time 10:30–12:30.*

$$–$$$ ★ ✕ **Midsummer House.** A classy restaurant set beside the River Cam, Midsummer House is lovely in summer. There's a comfortable conservatory. Set-price menus for lunch and dinner offer a selection of robust yet sophisticated European and Mediterranean dishes. Choices might include tender lamb or the best from the fish market adorned with inventively presented vegetables. ✉ *Midsummer Common,* ☎ *01223/369299. Reservations essential. AE, DC, MC, V. Closed Mon. No lunch Sat. No dinner Sun.*

$$ ✕ **Three Horseshoes.** This is an early 19th-century thatched cottage. The menu in the busy—sometimes crowded—pub-restaurant and conservatory sets out a tempting range of beautifully presented dishes. The emphasis is on modern British cuisine, for example, char-grilled meats or roast fish accompanied by sun-dried tomatoes, polenta, and olives. ✉ *Madingley (5 km/3 mi west of Cambridge),* ☎ *01954/210221. Reservations essential. AE, DC, MC, V. No dinner Sun.*

$–$$ ✕ **Brown's.** This huge, airy French-American style brasserie-diner was converted from the outpatient department of the old Addenbrooke's Hospital opposite the Fitzwilliam Museum. Large fans still keep things cool in the pale yellow dining room. The wide-ranging menu runs from toasted tuna sandwiches, steak-mushroom-and-Guinness pie, hamburgers, and salads to venison or gigot of lamb; check the daily specials, too—there's usually fresh fish and pasta. ✉ *23 Trumpington St.,* ☎ *01223/461655. AE, MC, V.*

$$$$ ★ 🏨 **Garden House Hotel.** Set among the colleges, this luxurious, modern hotel makes the most of its peaceful riverside location—it even rents out its own punts. Its gardens, lounge, cocktail bar, and conservatories all have river views, as do most of the smart guest rooms—if you want one, ask when you make your reservation. A leisure center incorporates an indoor swimming pool, a gym, a sauna, and a steam room. ✉ *Granta Pl., Mill La., CB2 1RT,* ☎ *01223/259988,* FAX *01223/316605. 118 rooms. Restaurant, pool. AE, DC, MC, V.*

$$$ 🏨 **Arundel House.** This hotel occupies a converted terrace of Victorian houses overlooking the river Cam and Jesus Green, while a pleasing conservatory and patio-garden out back offers a calm hideaway. The bedrooms are comfortably furnished with locally made mahogany furniture; Continental breakfast is included in the room rate, though a full breakfast is available for an extra charge. ✉ *53 Chesterton Rd., CB4 3AN,* ☎ *01223/367701,* FAX *01223/367721. 105 rooms with bath or shower. Restaurant. AE, DC, MC, V.*

Cambridge Essentials

Getting Around

BY BUS

There are 14 buses daily from Victoria Coach Station that take just under two hours. Call 0990/808080.

BY CAR

M11 is the main highway from London to Cambridge. The main car-rental companies have offices in Cambridge.

BY TRAIN

Half-hourly trains from London's Liverpool Street Station and King's Cross Station run to Cambridge. For information call 0345/484950. Average journey time varies from 50 minutes to 1½ hours, depending on the day of week or time of day.

Guided Tours

The **Cambridge Tourist Information Centre** offers two-hour guided walking tours of the city and the colleges daily; tickets (£5.75) are available up to 24 hours in advance from the city tourist information center. Various theme tours are also offered, including combined walking/punting tours and 1½-hour evening pub tours. Booking is essential—the tours are very popular. **Guide Friday** (☎ 01223/362444), in Cambridge, operates a city open-top bus tour every 15 minutes throughout the day (Oct.–May, half-hourly); tickets (£7.50) can be bought from the driver, the office at Cambridge train station, or Cambridge Tourist Information Center. You can join the tours at the station or at any of the specially marked bus stops throughout the city.

Visitor Information

Cambridge (✉ Wheeler St., off King's Parade, ☎ 01223/322640, FAX 01223/463385).

YORK

Once England's second city, the ancient town of York has survived the ravages of time, war, and industrialization to remain one of northern Europe's few preserved walled cities. It was King George VI, father of the present queen, who remarked that the history of York is the history of England. Even in a brief visit to the city, you can see evidence of life from every era since the Romans, not only in museums but also in the very streets and houses. York— 41 km (25 mi) northeast of Leeds, 133 km (82 mi) south of Newcastle—is surrounded by some of the grandest countryside England has to offer. A fertile plain dotted with ancient abbeys and grand aristocratic mansions leads westward to the hidden valleys and jagged, windswept tops of the Yorkshire Dales and northward to the brooding mass of the North York Moors. This is a land quite different from the south of England—it's friendlier, emptier, and less aggressively materialistic.

Exploring York

Numbers in the margin correspond to points of interest on the York map.

You can get a first, memorable overview of the city by taking a stroll along the **city walls.** Originally they were earth ramparts erected by York's Viking kings to repel raiders; the present stone structure dates from the 14th century. A narrow paved walk runs along the top (originally 5 km, or 3 mi, in circumference), passing over York's distinctive fortified gates or "bars" and providing delightful views across rooftops and gardens. Following an afternoon exploring the city, you can head for **Betty's,** on St. Helens Square—a York institution since 1912, it serves refreshing teas with a splendid selection of cakes.

★ 3 **Castle Museum.** A debtor's prison during the 18th century, this museum now offers a number of detailed exhibitions and re-creations, including a cobblestone Victorian street complete with crafts shops; a working water mill; and, most important, the Coppergate Helmet, a 1,200-year-old Anglo-Saxon helmet, one of only three ever found. ✉ *Clifford St.,* ☎ *01904/653611.* ⏲ *Apr.–Oct., Mon.–Sat. 9:30–5:30, Sun. 10–5:30; Nov.–Mar., Mon.–Sat. 9:30–4, Sun. 10–4.*

2 **Jorvik Viking Centre.** On this authentic Viking site, you can take another journey into history—whisked back in little "time cars" to the sights, sounds, and even the smells of a Viking street, which archaeologists have re-created in astonishing detail. ✉ *Coppergate,* ☎ *01904/*

653000. ⌚ *Apr.–Oct., daily 9–7; Nov.–Mar., daily 9–5:30; last admission 2 hrs before closing.*

❻ **Merchant Adventurers' Hall.** A superb medieval building (1357–68), this hall was built and owned by one of the richest medieval guilds; it contains the largest timber-frame hall in York. ✉ *Fossgate,* ☎ *01904/654818.* ⌚ *Mid-Mar.–mid-Nov., daily 8:30–5; mid-Nov.–mid-Mar., Mon.–Sat. 8:30–3.*

❼ **National Railway Museum.** Britain's national collection of locomotives forms part of this complex, the world's largest train museum. Among the exhibits are gleaming giants of the steam era, including *Mallard,* holder of the world speed record for a steam engine (126 mph). The museum lies just outside the city walls, by the train station. ✉ *Leeman Rd.,* ☎ *01904/621261.* ⌚ *Daily 10–6.*

★ ❹ **Shambles.** Within York's city walls the narrow streets still follow the complex medieval pattern. In the heart of the city is the Shambles, a particularly well-preserved example; the half-timbered shops and houses have such large overhangs that you can practically reach from one second-floor window to another.

❺ **Stonegate.** This is a narrow pedestrian street of 18th-century (and earlier) shops and courts. Along a narrow passage off Stonegate, at 52A, you will find the remains of a 12th-century Norman stone house—one of the very few surviving in England.

★ ❶ **York Minster.** The glory of York, this is the largest Gothic church in England and one of the finest in Europe. The 14th-century nave has soaring columns and intricate tracery, the choir screen portrays whimsical images of the kings of England, and the mighty rose window—just one of 128 stained-glass windows in the Minster—commemorates the marriage of Henry VII and Elizabeth of York. Visit the exquisite 13th-century **Chapter House** and the Roman and Saxon remains in the **Undercroft Museum and Treasury.** The 275 steps of the **Central Tower** lead to an unrivaled view of the city and the countryside beyond. The **Crypt** contains some of the cathedral's oldest and most valuable treasures, among them the Romanesque 12th-century statue of a heavy-footed Virgin Mary. ✉ *Duncombe Pl., York Minster Undercroft Museum and Treasury, Chapter House, Crypt, and Central Tower,* ☎ *01904/624426.* 🎟 *Minster free, donation appreciated.* ⌚ *Minster: summer, daily 7 AM–8:30 PM; winter, daily 7–6. Undercroft, Chapter House, Crypt, and Central Tower:* ⌚ *Summer Mon.–Sat. 10–5:30, Sun. 1–5:30; winter Mon.–Sat. 10–4:30, Sun. 1–4:30.*

$$–$$$ ★ ✕ **19 Grape Lane.** The narrow, slightly cramped restaurant is housed in a typically leaning timbered York building in the heart of town. It serves modern English food from a blackboard of such specials as grilled wild boar sausages, and the substantial puddings are always a treat. ✉ *19 Grape La.,* ☎ *01904/636366. MC, V. Closed Sun.*

$–$$ ✕ **Pierre Victoire.** At lunchtime in this airy brasserie you can feast on a set three-course menu of simple French food, one of the city's best bargains. At dinner prices increase, but not outrageously so, while the dishes become more elaborate: Choose from warming seasonal soups, confit of duck, or that old brasserie standby, *moules mariniere* (mussels). ✉ *2 Lendal,* ☎ *01904/655222. MC, V.*

$ ✕ **Pizza Express.** You eat in the grand salons of what used to be the York Gentleman's Club; a piano serenades evening diners from the lounge. The pizzas are not always all they could be, but lap up the good house wine and the upscale ambience and all is forgiven. ✉ *River House, 17 Museum St.,* ☎ *01904/672904. MC, V.*

York

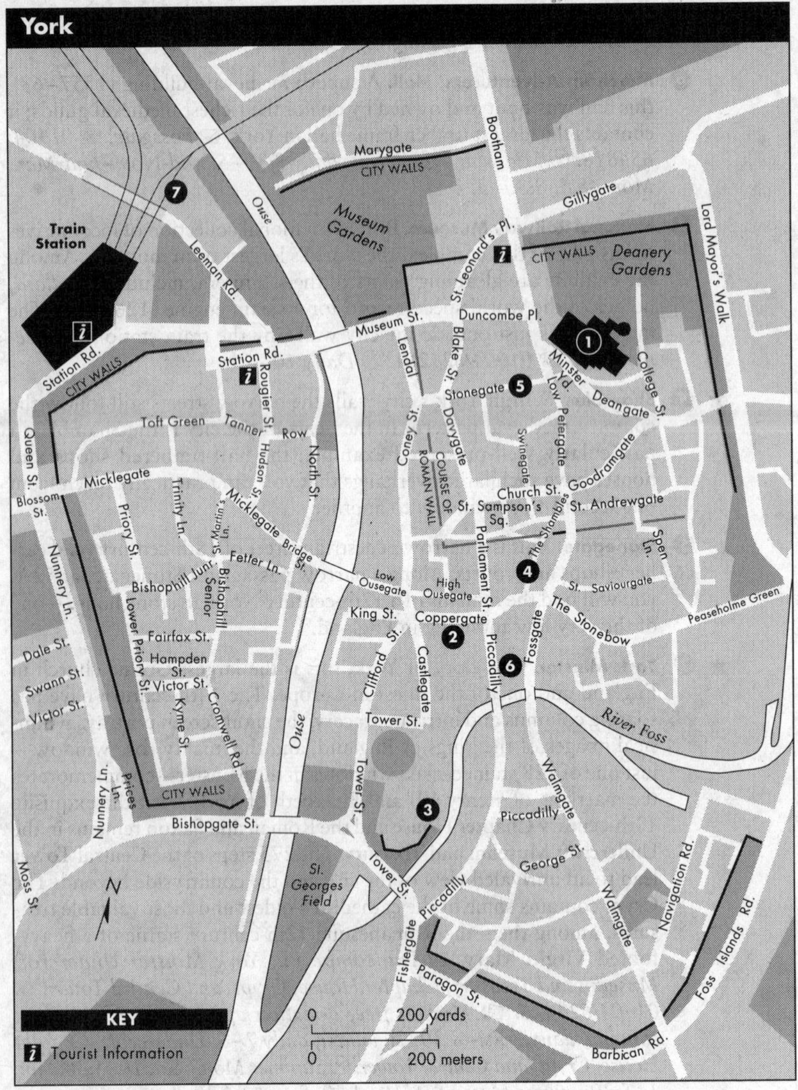

Castle Museum, **3**
Jorvik Viking Centre, **2**
Merchant Adventurers' Hall, **6**
National Railway Museum, **7**
Shambles, **4**
Stonegate, **5**
York Minster, **1**

$$$$ ★ ✕ 🏨 **Middlethorpe Hall.** This handsome, superbly restored 18th-century mansion is on the edge of the city, about 2½km (1½ mi) from the center, beside the racetrack. The individually decorated rooms, some in cottage-style accommodations around an 18th-century courtyard, are filled with antiques, paintings, and fresh flowers. The large garden grows fresh vegetables for the hotel's award-winning Anglo-French restaurant (reservations essential; jacket and tie), where you can eat in the original wood-paneled dining room by candlelight. ✉ *Bishopthorpe Rd., YO2 1QB,* ☎ *01904/641241,* ☎ *800/260–8338 in the U.S.,* FAX *01904/620176. 30 rooms. Restaurant. AE, DC, MC, V.*

$$$–$$$$ 🏨 **Dean Court.** This large Victorian house once provided accommodation for the clergy of York Minster, which looms just across the road. Refurbished to a high quality, it now has comfortably furnished rooms with plump sofas, TVs, and fine views overlooking the Minster. The restaurant serves good English cuisine, including a hearty Yorkshire breakfast. ✉ *Duncombe Pl., YO1 2EF,* ☎ *01904/625082,* FAX *01904/620305. 40 rooms. Restaurant. AE, DC, MC, V.*

$$–$$$ 🏨 **Savages.** Despite its name, this small hotel on a leafy road near the town center is eminently refined, with a reputation for attentive service. Once a Victorian home, it has a stylish and comfortable interior, and there's a bar in which to relax. ✉ *15 St. Peter's Grove, Clifton, YO3 6AQ,* ☎ *01904/610818,* FAX *01904/627729. 21 rooms with bath or shower. Restaurant. AE, DC, MC, V.*

$ 🏨 **Abbey Guest House.** This pretty, no-smoking, terraced guest house—formerly an artisan's house—is a 10-minute walk from the train station and town center. Although small, it's very clean and friendly, with a peaceful garden right on the river and ducks pottering about outside. Picnic lunches and evening meals can be arranged on request. ✉ *14 Earlsborough Terr., Marygate, YO3 7BQ,* ☎ *01904/627782. 7 rooms, 2 with bath. AE, MC, V.*

Side Trips: Fountains Abbey and Castle Howard

★ Thirty-two kilometers (21 mi) northwest of York, along B6265, you'll find that the majestic ruins of **Fountains Abbey,** with its own high tower and soaring 13th-century arches, make a striking picture on the banks of the river Skell. Founded in 1132, the abbey still possesses many of its original buildings, and the National Trust operates highly informative free guided tours around them (Apr.–Oct. only, usually at 2:30 and 3:30). The extensive ruins are set beside an 18th-century water garden and deer park, **Studley Royal,** combining lakes, ponds, and even a diverted river, while waterfalls splash around classical temples, statues, and a grotto. ✉ *Off B6265,* ☎ *01765/608888 or 01765/601005 (weekends).* ⏲ *Jan.–Mar., daily 10–5 (or dusk); Apr.–Sept., daily 10–7; Oct.–Dec., daily 10–5 (or dusk). Closed Fri. Nov.–Jan.*

Newby Hall—reached along pleasant country roads 5 km (3 mi) east of Fountains Abbey—has some restored interiors by the 18th-century master architect Robert Adam and some equally celebrated gardens with a collection of rare roses. There is a handy restaurant. ✉ *Skelton-on-Ure,* ☎ *01423/322583.* ⏲ *Apr.–Sept., Tues.–Sun., grounds 11–5:30, house noon–5.*

★ Nineteen kilometers (12 mi) southeast of Helmsley and 24 km (15 mi) northeast of York is **Castle Howard,** one of the grandest and most opulent stately homes in Britain. Its magnificent skyline is punctuated by stone chimneys and a graceful central dome. Many people know it best as Brideshead, the home of the Flyte family in Evelyn Waugh's tale of aristocratic woe, *Brideshead Revisited*; this was where much of the TV series was filmed. The audacity and confidence of the great Baroque house are startling, proclaiming the wealth and importance of the Howards and the utter self-assurance of its architect, Sir John Vanbrugh. Castle Howard took 60 years to build (1699–1759) and it was worth every year. A magnificent central hallway dwarfs all visitors, and there is no shortage of grandeur elsewhere: vast family portraits, delicate marble fireplaces, immense tapestries, and a great many marble busts. Outside, the stately theme continues in one of the most stunning Neoclassical landscapes in England. ✉ *Coneysthorpe,* ☏ *01653/648333.* 🎫 *House and gardens £7.* ⏲ *House mid-Mar.–Oct., daily 11–4:30; grounds daily 10–5.*

York Essentials

Getting Around

BY BUS

National Express (☏ 0990/808080) buses to York leave from London's Victoria Coach Station. Average travel time is 4½ hours to York.

BY CAR

Take the A1, the historic main route from London to the north, which branches east onto the A64 near Tadcaster for the final 19 km (12 mi) to York. Alternatively, take the M1, then M18, and finally the A1. The drive from London takes a minimum of four hours.

BY TRAIN

Great North-Eastern Railways (☏ 0345/484950) serves York from London King's Cross. Journeys on the fastest trains take two hours.

Guided Tours

Guide Friday (✉ De Grey Rooms, Exhibition Sq., ☏ 01904/640896) runs frequent city tours of York that allow you to get on and off the bus as you please (£7.50, £5.50 if booked in advance). It also conducts tours of the surrounding countryside, including Fountains Abbey and Castle Howard. **Yorktour** (☏ 01904-641737) also offers tours to Castle Howard. The **York Association of Voluntary Guides** (✉ De Grey Rooms, Exhibition Sq., ☏ 01904/640780) arranges short walking tours around the city each morning at 10:15, with additional tours at 2:15 PM from April through October, and one at 7 PM from July through August.

Visitor Information

De Grey Rooms (✉ Exhibition Sq., North Yorkshire, YO1 2HB, ☏ 01904/621756). **York railway station** (☏ 01904/621756). **Adjunct office** (✉ 6 Rougier St., ☏ 01904/620557).

THE LAKE DISTRICT

The poets Wordsworth and Coleridge can probably be held responsible for the development of the Lake District as a tourist destination. They, and other English men of letters, found it an inspiring setting for their work—and fashion, and thousands of visitors, have followed. The district, created in the 1970s as a national park from parts of the old counties of Cumberland, Westmorland, and Lancashire, combines so much that is magnificent in mountain, lake, and dales that new and entrancing vistas open out at each corner of the road. In addition to Wordsworth and Coleridge, other literary figures who made their homes in the region include De Quincey, Ruskin, Arnold, and the children's writer Beatrix Potter. Today, travelers find this region one of England's most peaceful destinations. Walking is perhaps the best way to discover the delights of this area.

The Lake District lies in the northwest of England, the entire region contained within the county of Cumbria. The major gateway from the south is Kendal; from the north, the gateway is Penrith—both are on the M6 motorway. The southern lakes and valleys contain the most popular destinations, notably the largest body of water, Windermere, as well as such quintessential Lake District towns and villages as Kendal, Bowness, Ambleside, Grasmere, Elterwater, Coniston, and Hawkshead. Among the northern lakes, south of Keswick and Cockermouth, you have the best chance to get away from the crowds and soak up the Lake District experience.

Kendal

The ancient town of Kendal—113 km (70 mi) north of Manchester—was one of the most important textile centers in northern England before the Industrial Revolution. Away from the busy main road, you'll discover narrow, winding streets and charming courtyards, many dating from medieval times.

Take a stroll along the River Kent, where—close to the Parish Church—you can visit the 18th-century **Abbott Hall.** Here the **Museum of Lakeland Life and Industry** offers interesting exhibits on blacksmithing, wheelwrighting, farming, weaving, printing, local architecture, and regional customs. ✉ *Kirkland,* ☎ *01539/722464.* ⏲ *Apr.–Oct., daily 10:30–5; Nov.–Mar., daily 10:30–4.*

At the northern end of town the **Kendal Museum** details splendidly the flora and fauna of the Lake District. It also contains displays on Alfred Wainwright, the region's most avid chronicler of countryside matters, who died in 1991. His multivolume Lake District walking guides are famous the world over; you'll see them in every local book and gift shop. ✉ *Station Rd.,* ☎ *01539/721374.* ⏲ *Apr.–Oct., daily 10:30–5; Nov.–Mar., daily 10:30–4.*

$$ ✕ **The Moon.** The good reputation here has been won with quality home-made dishes on a menu that changes monthly. There's always a strong selection of vegetarian dishes, and the cooking uses Mediterranean and Asian flourishes at times. ✉ *129 Highgate,* ☎ *01539/729254. MC, V. Closed Mon. in winter. No lunch.*

$ ✕▣ **The Punch Bowl Inn.** Hidden along a country road in the hamlet of Crosthwaite, 8 km (5 mi) west of Kendal, the Punch Bowl—formerly a 16th-century coaching inn—delights with its inspired Modern British food (reservations essential) and comfortable rooms. Fresh fish, local lamb, warming soups, and rich desserts all hit the spot. There are just three rooms; book well in advance. ✉ *Crosthwaite, near Kendal (off A5074), LA8 8HR,* ☎ *015395/68237,* FAX *015395/68875. 3 rooms. Restaurant. MC, V.*

Windermere

★ Windermere, 16 km (10 mi) northwest of Kendal on the A591, makes a natural touring base for the southern half of the Lake District—split between the part of town around the station (known as Windermere) and the prettier lakeside area ½ km (¼ mi) away, called Bowness-on-Windermere. A minibus (every 20 minutes in summer, hourly the rest of the year), leaving from outside Windermere train station, links the two. Although Windermere's marinas and piers have some charm, you can bypass the busier stretches of shoreline by walking beyond the boat houses, from where there's a fine view across the lake. A ferry crosses the water at this point to reach Far Sawrey and the road to Hawkshead; the crossing takes just a few minutes. ⏲ *Ferries run every 20 min Mon.–Sat. 6:50 AM–9:50 PM, Sun. 9:10 AM–9:50 PM; winter until 8:50 PM.*

The Lake District

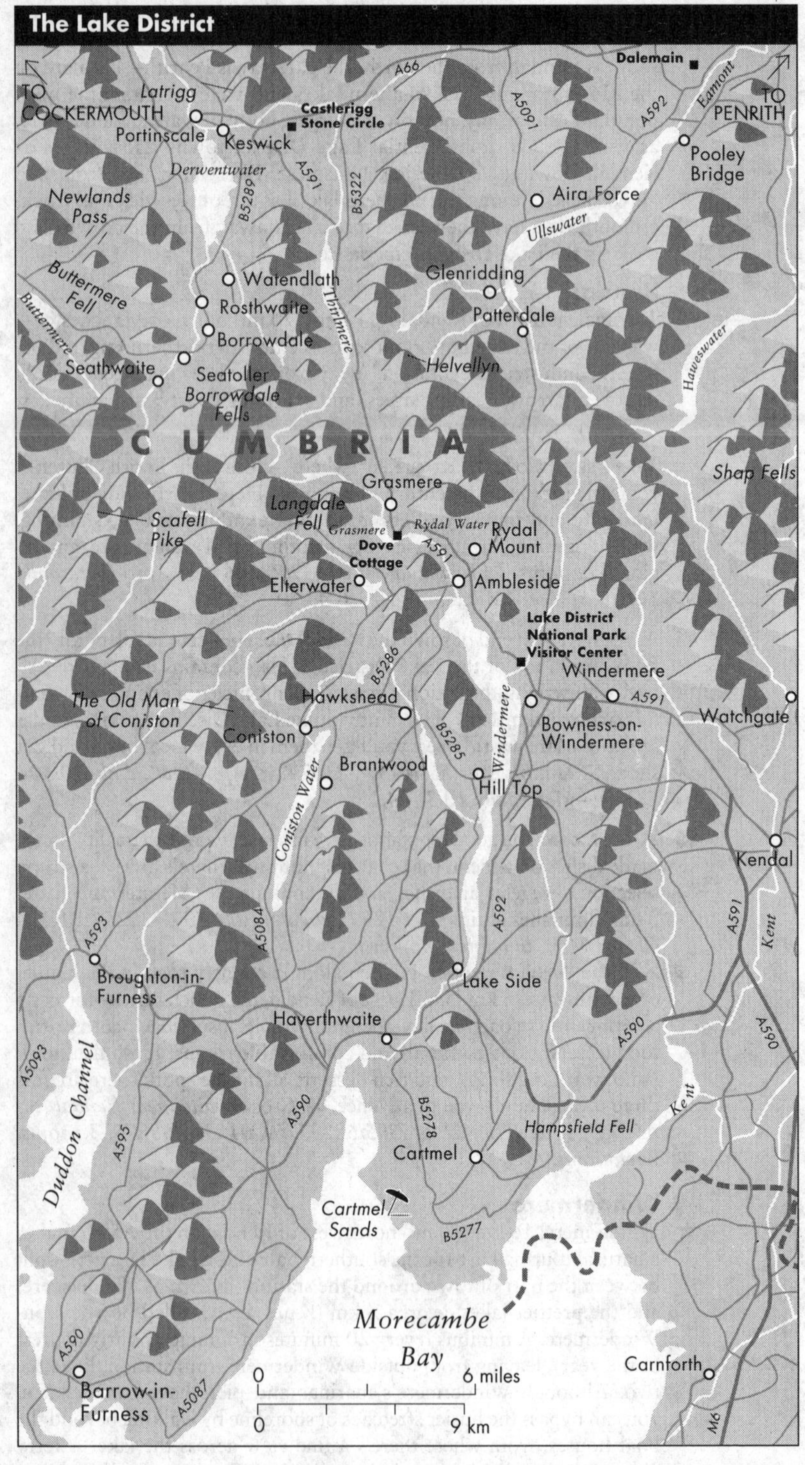

TO COCKERMOUTH
Latrigg
Portinscale
Keswick
Castlerigg Stone Circle
A66
Dalemain
A5091
A592
Eamont
TO PENRITH
Pooley Bridge
Derwentwater
A591
B5289
B5322
Newlands Pass
Aira Force
Ullswater
Buttermere Fell
Buttermere
Watendlath
Rosthwaite
Borrowdale
Seathwaite
Seatoller
Borrowdale Fells
Thirlmere
Glenridding
Patterdale
Helvellyn
Haweswater
C U M B R I A
Shap Fells
Grasmere
Langdale Fell
Scafell Pike
Grasmere
Dove Cottage
Rydal Water
Rydal Mount
A591
Elterwater
Ambleside
Lake District National Park Visitor Center
Windermere
B5286
Hawkshead
The Old Man of Coniston
Coniston
A591
Watchgate
Bowness-on-Windermere
Windermere
B5285
Brantwood
Coniston Water
Hill Top
Kendal
A592
A5084
A593
A591
Kent
Broughton-in-Furness
Lake Side
Haverthwaite
A590
A590
A5093
Duddon Channel
A590
B5278
A595
Hampsfield Fell
Kent
Cartmel
Cartmel Sands
B5277
Morecambe Bay
A590
Barrow-in-Furness
A5087
0
6 miles
0
9 km
Carnforth
M6

$$ ★ ✕ **Porthole Eating House.** In an intimate 18th-century house in the center of Bowness, the small restaurant has a largely Italian menu with homemade pasta and excellent meat and fish dishes. In winter a large open fire adds to the ambience. ✉ *3 Ash St., Bowness-on-Windermere,* ☎ *015394/42793. AE, DC, MC, V. Closed Tues. and mid-Dec.–late-Feb. No lunch Sat.*

$$$$ ★ ✕🏨 **Miller Howe.** This small, white Edwardian country house hotel is beautifully situated, with views across Windermere to the Langdale Pikes. The bedrooms have exceptional individual style—fresh and dried flowers are everywhere. The outstanding restaurant (reservations essential; jacket and tie) serves an imaginative set menu masterminded by John Tovey, renowned for his experimental British cuisine. The room rate includes breakfast and dinner. ✉ *Rayrigg Rd., Bowness-on-Windermere LA23 1EY,* ☎ *015394/42536,* FAX *015394/45664. 13 rooms. Restaurant. AE, DC, MC, V. Closed Dec.–Feb.*

$ 🏨 **Oakbank Hotel.** Right in the center of Bowness, the very friendly hillside Oakbank provides smart, well-equipped rooms (complete with TV and tea-making facilities), some with fine views over the lake, and all tastefully decorated in pale colors. ✉ *Helm Rd., Bowness-on-Windermere LA23 3BU,* ☎ *015394/43386. 11 rooms with shower. Breakfast room. MC, V.*

Brockhole

Five kilometers (3 mi) northwest of Windermere on the A591, a magnificent lakeside mansion houses the **Lake District National Park Visitor Centre,** which offers a fine range of exhibitions about the Lake District, including useful interpretative displays about the local ecology, flora, and fauna. The gardens are at their best in the spring, when floods of daffodils cover the lawns and the azaleas burst into bloom. ✉ *Ambleside Rd.,* ☎ *015394/46601.* 🎫 *Free.* ⏲ *Easter–late Oct., daily 10–4.*

Ambleside

The small town of Ambleside sits at the head of Lake Windermere—6½ km (4 mi) north of Brockhole, along the A591—making it a popular center for Lake District excursions. The town suffers terribly from tourist overcrowding in high season; Wednesday is particularly busy, when the local market takes place. However, it's easy enough to escape the crowds. Follow A593 west out of Ambleside and take the turning for the nearby village of **Elterwater,** a good stop for hikers. The B5343 continues west from here to **Langdale Fell,** where you can take one of several excellent walks: There are information boards at the various parking places and no more comforting resting place than the hiker's bar of the **Old Dungeon Ghyll Hotel** (✉ On B5343, west of Elterwater), where the roaring fireplace rapidly dries out wet walking gear.

$$ ✕ **Glass House.** This exciting conversion of an old watermill switches from a café by day to a thoroughly modern restaurant by night—with Mediterranean flavors, pan-fried fish, and char-grilled meats forming the mainstay of the menu. ✉ *Rydal Rd.,* ☎ *015394/32137. Reservations essential for dinner. MC, V. Closed Mon. Nov.–Easter.*

$$ ★ ✕🏨 **Britannia Inn.** The Britannia is a friendly inn in the heart of splendid walking country, with quaint little rooms and hearty homemade English food served in the bar. There's also a very popular four-course table d'hôte dinner served nightly (weekends only from November to mid-March). ✉ *Elterwater, on B5343, 6 km/4 mi west of Ambleside, LA22 9HP,* ☎ *015394/37210,* FAX *015394/37311. 13 rooms, 8 with shower. Restaurant. MC, V.*

Rydal Mount

If there's one poet associated with the Lake District, it is William Wordsworth, who made his home at Rydal Mount, 2 km (1 mi) northwest of Ambleside, from 1813 until his death 37 years later. Wordsworth and his family moved to these grand surroundings when he was nearing the height of his career, and his descendants still live here, surrounded by his furniture, portraits, and the 4½-acre garden laid out by the poet himself. ✉ *Rydal, Ambleside,* ☎ *015394/33002.* ⏲ *Mar.–Oct., daily 9:30–5; Nov.–Feb., Wed.–Mon. 10–4. Closed 3 wks in Jan.*

Grasmere

The heart of Wordsworth country, Grasmere is one of the most typical of Lake District villages, sited on a tiny, wood-fringed lake 2 km (1 mi) north of Dove Cottage, 6½ km (4 mi) northwest of Ambleside, and made up of crooked lanes lined with charming slate-built cottages. Since Wordsworth lived on the town's outskirts for almost 50 years—at Rydal Mount (☞ *above*) and Dove Cottage (☞ *below*), he, his wife Mary, his sister Dorothy, and his daughter Dora are buried in Grasmere churchyard.

★ **Dove Cottage** is the leading literary shrine of the Lake District. Located 2½ km (1½ mi) northwest of Rydal Mount, this was Wordsworth's home from 1799 until 1808, and the tiny house still contains many personal belongings. Dove Cottage is also headquarters of the Centre for British Romanticism, which documents the literary contributions made by Wordsworth and his sister Dorothy, Samuel Taylor Coleridge, Thomas De Quincey, and Robert Southey. ✉ *The Wordsworth Trust, Dove Cottage, Grasmere LA22 9SH,* ☎ *015394/35544.* ⏲ *Mid-Feb.–mid-Jan., daily 9:30–5.*

$$$ ✕🏨 **The Swan.** The handsome, flower-decked, 300-year-old Swan, a former coaching inn on the main road just outside Grasmere, keeps a fire in the lounge grate, an oak-beam restaurant ($$) serving Lake District specialties, and elegant guest rooms that combine space with fine views of the surrounding fells. ✉ *Grasmere, on the A591, LA22 9RF,* ☎ *015394/35551,* FAX *015394/35741. 36 rooms. Restaurant. AE, DC, MC, V.*

Coniston

Formerly a copper-mining village, Coniston is now a small lake resort and boating center at the foot of **The Old Man of Coniston** (2,635 ft), 13 km (8 mi) south of Grasmere. Tracks lead up from the village past an old mine to the peak, which you can reach in about two hours, though many experienced hikers include the peak in an enervating seven-hour circular walk from the village.

★ Just outside Coniston is **Brantwood,** the home of Victorian artist, critic, and social reformer John Ruskin (1819–1900). Here, in the rambling white 18th-century house, you'll find a collection of Ruskin's own paintings, drawings, and books. The extensive grounds were laid out by Ruskin himself. It's an easy drive to Brantwood from Coniston, but it's much more agreeable to travel here by ferry across the lake. Services are with either the Coniston Launch (Easter–Oct., hourly departures; fewer sailings in winter) or the steam yacht *Gondola* (Apr.–Oct., 4–5 trips daily), both departing from Coniston Pier. ✉ *Brantwood,* ☎ *015394/41396.* ⏲ *Mid-Mar.–mid-Nov., daily 11–5:30; mid-Nov.–mid-Mar., Wed.–Sun. 11–4.*

Hawkshead

Just outside the attractive village of Hawkshead, **Hill Top** was the home of children's author and illustrator Beatrix Potter, most famous for her *Peter Rabbit* stories. Now run by the National Trust, the tiny house is a popular—and often crowded—spot; admission has to be strictly controlled. Try to avoid visiting on summer weekends and during school vacations. The house is 3 km (2 mi) south of Hawkshead on the B5285, though you can also approach via the car ferry from Bowness-on-Windermere. ✉ *Near Sawrey, Ambleside,* ☎ *015394/36269.* ⏲ *Apr.–Oct., Sat.–Wed. 11–4:30.*

Ullswater

Hemmed in by towering hills, Ullswater, 10 km (6 mi) southwest of Penrith along A592, is the region's second-largest lake, enjoying a spectacular setting. Some of the finest views are from A592 as it hugs the lake's western shore, through Glenridding and Patterdale at the southern end. Here, you're at the foot of Helvellyn (3,118 ft), which lies to the west. Arduous footpaths run from the road between Glenridding and Patterdale and pass by Red Tarn, at 2,356 ft the highest Lake District tarn.

Aira Force, 8 km (5 mi) north of Patterdale, just off the A592, is a spectacular series of waterfalls pounding through a wooded ravine to feed into Ullswater. From the parking lot (parking fee charged), it's a 20-minute walk to the falls—bring sturdy shoes in wet weather. Just above Aira Force in the woods of Gowbarrow Park, William Wordsworth and his sister Dorothy were walking on April 15, 1802. Dorothy remarked that she had never seen "daffodils so beautiful." Two years later Wordsworth was inspired by his sister's words to write one of the best-known lyric poems in English, "I Wandered Lonely as a Cloud."

Keswick

The great Lakeland mountains of Skiddaw and Blencathra brood over the gray slate houses of Keswick (pronounced "Kezzick"), 22 km (14 mi) west of Ullswater, on the scenic shores of Derwentwater. As many of the best hiking routes radiate from here, it is more of a touring base than a tourist destination. People stroll the congested, narrow streets in boots and corduroy hiking trousers, and there are plenty of mountaineering shops in addition to hotels, guest houses, pubs, and restaurants.

★ To understand why **Derwentwater** is considered one of England's finest lakes, take a short walk from the town center to the lake shore, and follow the Friar's Crag path—about 15 minutes' level walk from the center of Keswick. This pine-tree-fringed peninsula is a favorite vantage point, with its view over the lake, the surrounding ring of mountains, and many tiny wooded islands. Ahead you will see the crags that line the **Jaws of Borrowdale** and overhang a dramatic mountain ravine—the perfect setting for a Romantic painting or poem. Between late March and November, cruises set off every hour in each direction from a wooden dock at the lake shore.

$ ✕ **Four in Hand.** This is a typical Cumbrian pub—once a stagecoach inn on the route between Keswick and Borrowdale—with a 19th-century paneled bar decorated with horse brasses and banknotes. The imaginative touches in its menu include hot asparagus rolled in ham; traditional dishes are steaks, meat pies, and Cumberland sausage. ✉ *Lake Rd.,* ☎ *017687/72069. No credit cards.*

$$$ ✕🏨 **Keswick Country House Hotel.** Built to serve railroad travelers during the 19th century, the Keswick has all the grandeur and style of that age, although it has been modernized. The room rate includes dinner, as well as breakfast, though you can opt for a stay without dinner if you wish. ✉ *Station Rd., CA12 4NQ,* ☎ *017687/72020,* FAX *017687/71300. 74 rooms. Restaurant. AE, DC, MC, V.*

Cockermouth

This attractive little town, 22 km (14 mi) northwest of Seatoller, at the confluence of the Derwent and Cocker rivers, is slightly larger than Keswick and has a maze of narrow streets that's a delight to wander. It was the birthplace of William Wordsworth and his sister Dorothy, whose childhood home, **Wordsworth House,** is a typical 18th-century north-country gentleman's home, now owned by the National Trust. ✉ *Main St.,* ☎ *01900/824805.* ⏲ *Apr.–Oct., weekdays 11–5; July–Aug., also Sat. 11–5.*

Lake District Essentials

Getting Around

BY BOAT

Windermere Lake Cruises (☎ 015394/43360) is the umbrella organization for two ferry operators on Lake Windermere: the Bowness Bay Boating Co. runs between Bowness and Ambleside, and Ambleside and Brockhole National Park Centre; while the Iron Steamboat Co. employs its fleet of vintage cruisers between Ambleside, Bowness, and Lakeside. A Freedom of the Lake ticket (£9) gives unlimited travel on any of the ferries for 24 hours.

BY BUS

National Express (☎ 0990/808080) serves the region from London's Victoria Coach Station. Average travel time to Kendal is just over 7 hours; to Windermere, 7½ hours; and to Keswick, 8¼ hours. **Stagecoach Cumberland** (☎ 01946/63222) operates year-round throughout the Lake District, with reduced service on weekends and bank holidays.

BY CAR

Take M1 north from London to M6, leaving at exit 36 and joining A590/A591 west (around the Kendal bypass to Windermere) or at exit 40, joining A66 directly to Keswick and the northern lakes. Travel time to Kendal is about four hours, to Keswick five–six hours. Car-rental companies are few and far between in the Lakes; rent in London or York before your trip.

Roads within the region are generally good, although many of the minor routes and mountain passes can be steep and narrow. Warning signs are normally posted if snow has made a road impassable. In July and August and during public holiday weekends, expect heavy traffic.

BY TRAIN

InterCity West Coast serves the region from London's Euston Station (☎ 0345/484950). Take an InterCity train bound for Carlisle, Edinburgh, or Glasgow, and change at Oxenholme for the branch line service to Kendal and Windermere. Average travel time to Windermere (including the change) is 4½ hours. The **Lakeside & Haverthwaite Railway Co.** (☎ 015395/31594) runs vintage steam trains in summer (and at Christmas) between Lakeside and Haverthwaite along Lake Windermere's southern tip.

ON FOOT

Every hamlet, village, and town provides scores of walking opportunities; stores throughout the region stock the right equipment, books, and maps. Always check on weather conditions before setting out, as mist or rain can roll in without warning. For short, local walks consult the tourist information centers, which can provide maps, guides, and advice. The other main source of information is the **Lake District National Park Visitor Information Centre** (☞ Brockhole, *above*).

Guided Tours

From Easter until October, the **National Park Authority** (☎ 015394/46601) at Brockhole, near Windermere, arranges half-day or full-day walks introducing you to the history and natural beauties of the Lake District. **Mountain Goat Holidays** (☎ 015394/45161) provides half- and full-day minibus sightseeing tours with skilled local guides.

Visitor Information

The Cumbria Tourist Board (✉ Ashleigh, Holly Rd., Windermere, Cumbria LA23 2AQ, ☎ 015394/44444). **Ambleside** (✉ The Old Courthouse, Church St., ☎ 015394/32582). **Grasmere** (✉ Red Bank Rd., ☎ 015394/35245). **Kendal** (✉ Town Hall, Highgate, ☎ 01539/725758). **Keswick** (✉ Moot Hall, Market Sq., ☎ 017687/72645). **Windermere** (✉ The Gateway Centre, Victoria St., ☎ 015394/46499).

EDINBURGH

Scotland and England *are* different—and let no Englishman tell you otherwise. Although the two nations have been united in a single state since 1707, Scotland retains its own marked political and social character, with, for instance, legal and educational systems quite distinct from those of England (a division that will become even greater, now that Edinburgh is once again to be the seat of a Scottish Parliament). And by virtue of its commanding position on top of a long-dead volcano and the survival of a large number of outstanding stone buildings carrying echoes of the nation's history, Edinburgh ranks among the world's greatest capital cities.

Exploring Edinburgh

Numbers in the margin correspond to points of interest on the Edinburgh map.

The key to understanding Edinburgh is to make the distinction between the Old and New Towns. Until the 18th century the city was confined to the rocky crag on which its castle stands, straggling between the fortress at one end and the royal residence, the Palace of Holyroodhouse, at the other. In the 18th century, during a civilizing time of expansion known as the "Scottish Enlightenment," the city fathers fostered the construction of another Edinburgh, one a little to the north. In 1767 the competition to design the New Town was won by a young and unknown architect, James Craig. His plan was for a grid of three east–west streets, balanced at each end by a grand square. The plan survives today, despite all commercial pressures. Princes, George, and Queen streets are the main thoroughfares, with St. Andrew Square at one end and Charlotte Square at the other. The mostly residential New Town, with elegant squares, classical facades, wide streets, and harmonious proportions, remains largely intact and lived-in today.

13 **Arthur's Seat.** The open grounds of Holyrood Park enclose Arthur's Seat, Edinburgh's distinctive, originally volcanic minimountain, with steep slopes and miniature crags. ✉ *Holyrood Park.*

★ 16 **Calton Hill.** Steps and a road lead up to splendid views north across the Firth (estuary) of Forth to the Lomond Hills of Fife, and south to the Pentland Hills. Among the various monuments on Calton Hill are a partial reproduction of Athens's **Parthenon,** begun in 1824 but left incomplete because the money ran out; the **Nelson Monument;** and the **Royal Observatory.** ✉ *North side of Regent Rd.*

11 **Canongate Kirk.** In the graveyard of this church, built in 1688, are buried some notable Scots, including the economist Adam Smith and the poet Robert Fergusson. ✉ *Canongate.*

18 **Charlotte Square.** The centerpiece of the New Town opens out at the western end of George Street. The palatial facade of the north side was designed by the great Scottish neoclassical architect, Robert Adam. The rooms of the elegant **Georgian House** are furnished to show the domestic arrangements of a prosperous late-18th-century Edinburgh

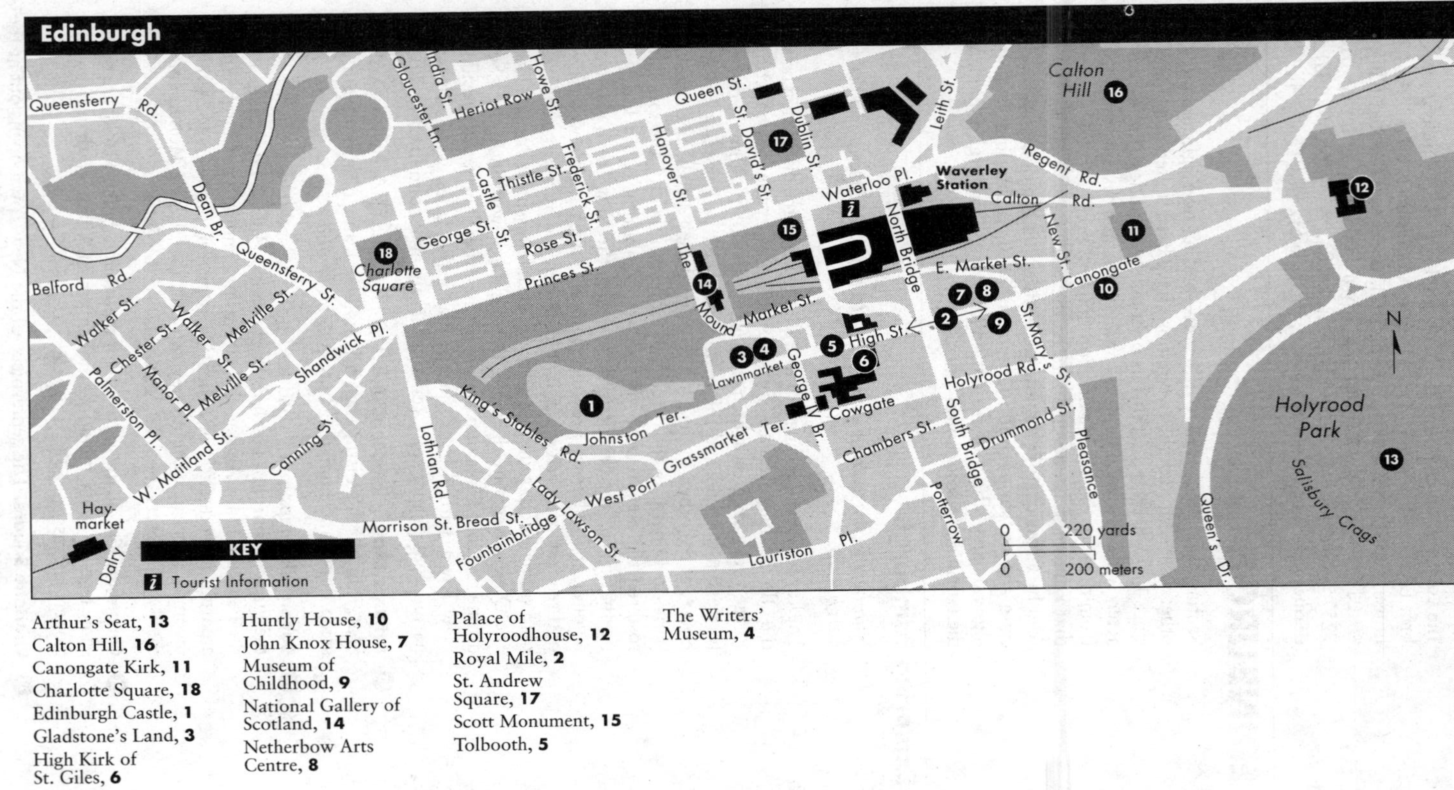

Arthur's Seat, **13**
Calton Hill, **16**
Canongate Kirk, **11**
Charlotte Square, **18**
Edinburgh Castle, **1**
Gladstone's Land, **3**
High Kirk of St. Giles, **6**
Huntly House, **10**
John Knox House, **7**
Museum of Childhood, **9**
National Gallery of Scotland, **14**
Netherbow Arts Centre, **8**
Palace of Holyroodhouse, **12**
Royal Mile, **2**
St. Andrew Square, **17**
Scott Monument, **15**
Tolbooth, **5**
The Writers' Museum, **4**

family. ⊠ *7 Charlotte Sq.,* ☎ *0131/225–2160.* 🎫 *£4.20.* ⏲ *Apr.–Oct., Mon.–Sat. 10–5, Sun. 2–5 (last admission 4:30).*

★ ❶ **Edinburgh Castle.** The brooding symbol of Scotland's capital and the nation's martial past, the castle dominates the city center. Its attractions include the city's oldest building—the 11th-century **St. Margaret's Chapel;** the **Crown Room,** where the Regalia of Scotland are displayed; **Old Parliament Hall;** and **Queen Mary's Apartments,** where Mary, Queen of Scots, gave birth to the future King James VI of Scotland (who later became James I of England). In addition military features of interest include the **Scottish National War Memorial** and the **Scottish United Services Museum.** The **Castle Esplanade,** the wide parade ground at the entrance to the castle, hosts the annual Edinburgh Military Tattoo—a grand military display staged during a citywide festival every summer (☞ The Arts, *below*). ⊠ *Castlehill,* ☎ *0131/668–8800.* 🎫 *£6.* ⏲ *Apr.–Sept., daily 9:30–5:15; Oct.–Mar., daily 9:30–4:15.*

❸ **Gladstone's Land.** This six-story tenement dates from 1620. It has an arcaded front and first-floor entrance typical of the period and is furnished in the style of a merchant's house of the time; there are magnificent painted ceilings. ⊠ *377B Lawnmarket,* ☎ *0131/226–5856.* 🎫 *£3.* ⏲ *Easter–Oct., Mon.–Sat. 10–5, Sun. 2–5 (last entrance 4:30).*

❻ **High Kirk of St. Giles.** Often called St. Giles's Cathedral, this historic structure dates back to the 12th century; the impressive choir was built during the 15th century. ⊠ *High St.* 🎫 *Suggested donation: £1.* ⏲ *Mon.–Sat. 9–5 (7 in summer), Sun. 1–5 and for services.*

❿ **Huntly House.** Built in 1570, this museum presents Edinburgh history and social life. ⊠ *142 Canongate,* ☎ *0131/529–4143.* 🎫 *Free.* ⏲ *Mon.–Sat. 10–5, Sun. during festival 2–5.*

❼ **John Knox House.** Its traditional connections with Scotland's celebrated religious reformer are tenuous, but this 16th-century dwelling gives a flavor of life in the Old Town during Knox's time. ⊠ *45 High St.,* ☎ *0131/556–2647.* ⏲ *Mon.–Sat. 10–5 (last admission 4:30).*

❾ **Museum of Childhood.** Even adults may well enjoy this celebration of toys. The museum was the first in the world to be devoted solely to the history of childhood. ⊠ *42 High St.,* ☎ *0131/529–4142,* FAX *0131/558–3103.* 🎫 *Free.* ⏲ *Mon.–Sat. 10–5, Sun. during festival 2–5.*

★ ⓮ **National Gallery of Scotland.** Works by the old masters and the French Impressionists and a good collection of Scottish paintings make this one of Britain's best national galleries. It is small enough to be taken in easily on one visit. There may be a charge for special exhibitions. ⊠ *The Mound,* ☎ *0131/556–8921.* 🎫 *Free.* ⏲ *Mon.–Sat. 10–5, Sun. 2–5. Print Room, weekdays 10–noon, 2–4, by arrangement.*

❽ **Netherbow Arts Centre.** In addition to the art gallery there are a theater and a café here. ⊠ *43 High St.,* ☎ *0131/556–9579.* 🎫 *£1.95.* ⏲ *Mon.–Sat. 10–5 (last admission 4:30).*

★ ⓬ **Palace of Holyroodhouse.** Still the Royal Family's official residence in Scotland, the palace came into existence originally as a guest house for the Abbey of Holyrood, founded in 1128 by Scottish king David I. It was extensively remodeled by Charles II in 1671. The state apartments, with their collections of tapestries and paintings, can be visited. ⊠ *East end of Cannongate,* ☎ *0131/556–7371, 0131/556–1096 (recorded information).* ⏲ *Apr.–Oct., daily 9:30–5:15; Nov.–Mar., daily 9:30–3:45; closed during royal and state visits.*

❷ **Royal Mile.** The backbone of the Old Town, the Royal Mile starts immediately below the Castle Esplanade (☞ **Edinburgh Castle,** *above*).

It consists of a number of streets running into one another—Castlehill, Lawnmarket, High Street, and Canongate—leading downhill to the **Palace of Holyroodhouse.** The many original Old Town "closes," narrow alleyways enclosed by high tenement buildings, reward exploration with a real sense of the former life of the city. ✉ *Between Edinburgh Castle and the Palace of Holyroodhouse.*

17 **St. Andrew Square.** The most notable building on this square at the eastward termination of George Street is the Georgian headquarters of the **Royal Bank of Scotland,** with a lavishly decorated central banking hall. ✉ *St. Andrew Sq.,* ☎ *0131/556–8555.* ⏲ *Mon., Wed.–Fri. 9:15–4:45, Tues. 10–4:45.*

15 **Scott Monument.** This unmistakable 200-ft-high Gothic spire was built in the 1840s to commemorate Sir Walter Scott (1771–1832), the celebrated novelist of Scots history. The monument is undergoing renovation, so it's best to call to make sure it's open. ✉ *Princes St.,* ☎ *0131/529–4068.* ⏲ *Apr.–Sept., Mon.–Sat. 9–6; Oct.–Mar., Mon.–Sat. 9–3.*

5 **Tolbooth.** A heart shape set in the cobbles of High Street marks the site of the 15th-century Tolbooth, the center of city life—and original inspiration for Sir Walter Scott's novel *The Heart of Midlothian*—until its demolition in 1817. ✉ *High St.*

4 **The Writers' Museum.** Housed in Lady Stair's House, a town dwelling of 1622, this museum recalls Scotland's literary heritage with exhibits on Sir Walter Scott, Robert Louis Stevenson, and Robert Burns. ✉ *Lady Stair's Close, Lawnmarket,* ☎ *0131/529–4901.* 🎫 *Free.* ⏲ *Mon.–Sat. 10–5, Sun. during festival 2–5.*

Dining and Lodging

Edinburgh's restaurants make the most of Scotland's excellent game, fish, shellfish, beef, and lamb. For details and price-category definitions, *see* Dining *in* Great Britain A to Z, *above.*

Much of Edinburgh's accommodation is very central, with New Town bed-and-breakfast establishments being especially convenient. For details and price-category definitions, *see* Lodging *in* Great Britain A to Z, *above.*

$$$$ ✕ **Le Pompadour.** The decor in this hotel-restaurant, with its subtle plasterwork and rich murals, is inspired by the France of Louis XV. A sophisticated French menu is accented with Scottish delicacies. ✉ *Caledonian Hotel, Princes St.,* ☎ *0131/459–9988. Reservations essential. Jacket and tie. AE, DC, MC, V. No lunch weekends.*

$$$ ★ ✕ **Jackson's Restaurant.** Set in the historic Old Town halfway down the Royal Mile, this intimate and candlelit spot offers good Scots fare. Aberdeen Angus steaks and Border lamb are excellent; there are vegetarian and seafood specialties, too. ✉ *2 Jackson Close, 209–213 High St.,* ☎ *0131/225–1793. Reservations essential. AE, MC, V.*

$$ ✕ **The Dome.** The splendid interior of this former bank—splendid is the word, thanks to the painted plasterwork and central dome—provides an elegant backdrop for relaxed dining. Or you just might opt for a drink at the central bar, a favored spot for sophisticates to wind down after work. The toasted BLT sandwiches are almost big enough for two, but if you're even more ravenous, the eclectic menu offers many other options.✉ *14 George St. EH2 2PF,* ☎ *0131/624–8624. AE, MC, V.*

$$ ✕ **Howie's.** Howie's is a simple neighborhood bistro. The steaks are tender Aberdeen beef, the Loch Fyne herring are sweet-cured to Howie's own recipe, and the clientele is lively. ✉ *75 St. Leonard's St.,* ☎ *0131/*

668–2917, MC, V, No lunch Mon.; ✉ 63 Dalry Rd., ☎ 0131/313–3334, MC, V, No lunch Mon.; ✉ 208 Bruntsfield Pl., ☎ 0131/221–1777, MC, V, No lunch Mon.

$–$$ ✕ **Pierre Victoire.** An Edinburgh success story with five in-town branches and franchises as far as London and Bristol, this bistro chain serves tasty, unpretentious French cuisine in excellent set menus, with especially good value at lunch. ✉ *38 Grassmarket,* ☎ *0131/226–2442, MC, V;* ✉ *10 Victoria St.,* ☎ *0131/225–1721, MC, V;* ✉ *8 Union St.,* ☎ *0131/557–8451, MC, V, Closed Mon.;* ✉ *17 Queensferry St.,* ☎ *0131/226–1890, MC, V, Closed Sun.;* ✉ *5 Dock Pl., Leith,* ☎ *0131/555–6178, MC, V, No dinner Sun.*

$ ★ ✕ **Beehive Inn.** One of the oldest pubs in the city, the Beehive snuggles in the Grassmarket, under the majestic shadow of the castle. The upstairs Rafters restaurant lies hidden in an attractive and spacious attic room, crammed with weird and wonderful junk. Open only for dinner, it features mostly steaks and fish: Try the charcoal-grilled trout with Drambuie. ✉ *18/20 Grassmarket,* ☎ *0131/225–7171. AE, DC, MC, V.*

$$$$ ★ **Caledonian Hotel.** "The Caley" echoes the days of the traditional great railway hotel, though the neighboring station has long since been demolished. The imposing Victorian decor has been lovingly preserved and embellished. There are also two excellent restaurants (☞ **Le Pompadour,** *above,* and **Carriages**, offering a less pricey Scottish menu). ✉ *Princes St., EH1 2AB,* ☎ *0131/459–9988,* FAX *0131/225–6632. 236 rooms. 2 restaurants. AE, DC, MC, V.*

$$$$ **George Intercontinental.** This imposing and extensively refurbished 18th-century building in the heart of the New Town retains some elegant Georgian features in its public areas, while the bedrooms are up-to-date and moderately luxurious. Though it's a busy place, the staff takes time to be helpful. ✉ *19–21 George St., EH2 2PB,* ☎ *0131/225–1251,* FAX *0131/226–5644. 195 rooms. 2 restaurants. AE, DC, MC, V.*

$$$ ★ **17 Abercrombie Place.** An exceptional standard is set at this Georgian terraced B&B in the center of the New Town. There are stunning views from the top-floor rooms. The host and the hostess both enjoy meeting guests and are very helpful. ✉ *17 Abercrombie Pl., EH3 6LB,* ☎ *0131/557–8036,* FAX *0131/558–3453. 9 rooms with bath or shower. Dining room. MC, V.*

$$ **Ellesmere Guest House.** This B&B is close to the King's Theatre and several good restaurants. You can relax in the comfortable sitting room with a good stock of brochures covering things to do in Edinburgh. The owners prefer no smoking. ✉ *11 Glengyle Terr., EH3 9LN,* ☎ *0131/229–4823,* FAX *0131/229–5285. 6 rooms, 1 with bath, 5 with shower. No credit cards; checks in dollars accepted.*

Nightlife and the Arts

The Arts

EDINBURGH FESTIVAL

The **Edinburgh International Festival,** a celebration of music, dance, and drama staged each summer (Aug. 15–Sept. 4 in 1999), draws international artists of the highest caliber. The **Festival Fringe** (information: ✉ 180 High St., ☎ 0131/226–5257or 0131/226–5259, FAX 0131/220–4205), the unruly child of the official festival, spills out of halls and theaters all over town, offering visitors a cornucopia of theatrical and musical events of all kinds—some so weird that they defy description. At the official festival you'll see top-flight performances by established artists, while at a Fringe event you might catch a new star, or a new art form, or a controversial new play. Advance information, programs, and ticket sales for the festival are available from the **Edinburgh International Festival Office** (✉ 21 Market St., ☎ 0131/226–4001, FAX 0131/225–1173).

The **Edinburgh Military Tattoo** (information: Edinburgh Military Tattoo Office, ✉ 32 Market St., EH1 1QB, ☎ 0131/225–1188, FAX 0131/225–8627) may not be art, but it is certainly entertainment. This celebration of martial music and skills (in 1999, held Aug. 6–28) is set on the Castle Esplanade. Dress warmly for late-evening shows. Even if it rains, the show most definitely goes on! Away from the August–September festival overkill, **Shoots and Roots** (☎ 0131/554–3092), the Edinburgh Folk Festival, takes place over Easter weekend (1999: April 2–5) and also the third weekend in November (in 1999: Nov. 18–22). This is the premier festival for Scottish folk music and folk/rock crossover.

The List, available from newsagents throughout the city; *The Day by Day List*; and *Events 1999,* available from the Information Centre, carry the most up-to-date details about cultural events. *The Scotsman,* an Edinburgh daily, also carries reviews in its arts pages on Monday and Wednesday.

Edinburgh Essentials

Arriving and Departing

BY BUS

Regular service is operated by **National Express** (☎ 0990/808080, FAX 0141/332–8055) between Victoria Coach Station, London, and St. Andrew Square bus station, Edinburgh, twice a day. The journey takes approximately eight hours.

BY CAR

London and Edinburgh are 656 km (407 mi) apart; allow a comfortable nine hours for the drive. The two principal routes to the Scottish border are A1 (mostly a small but divided road) or the eight-lane M1, then M6. From there, the choice is between the four-lane highway A74, which can be unpleasantly busy, followed by A701 or A702, or the slower but much more scenic A7 through Hawick. All the main car-rental agencies have offices in Edinburgh.

BY PLANE

British Airways (☎ 0345/222111) operates a shuttle service from London's Heathrow Airport to Edinburgh; reservations are not necessary, and you are guaranteed a seat. Flying time from London is one hour, 15 minutes. **British Midland** (☎ 0345/554554) also flies from Heathrow. **Air UK** flies from Gatwick (☎ 01293/535353) and Stansted (☎ 01279/680500) to Edinburgh (☎ 0345/666777). **EasyJet** (☎ 0990/292929) offers bargain fares from London Luton to Edinburgh. Transatlantic flights direct to Scotland use Glasgow Airport, with regular rail connections to Glasgow city center and on to Edinburgh.

BY TRAIN

Regular trains run from London's King's Cross Station (☎ 0345/484950) to Edinburgh Waverley (☎ 0131/557–3000 for recorded information); the fastest journey time is just over four hours.

Getting Around

BY BUS

Lothian Regional Transport (✉ 27 Hanover St., ☎ 0131/555–6363; ✉ Waverley Bridge, ☎ 0131/554–4494), operating dark-red-and-white buses, is the main operator within Edinburgh. A **Day Saver Ticket** (£2.20), allowing unlimited one-day travel on the city's buses, can be purchased in advance.

BY CAR

Driving in Edinburgh has its quirks and pitfalls, but competent drivers should not be intimidated. Metered parking in the center city is scarce and expensive, and the local traffic wardens are alert. Note that illegally parked cars are routinely wheel-clamped and towed away, and getting your car back will be expensive. After 6 PM the parking situation improves considerably, and you may manage to find a space quite near your hotel, even downtown. If you park on a yellow line or in a resident's parking bay, be prepared to move your car by 8 AM the following morning, when the rush hour gets under way.

BY TAXI

Taxi stands can be found throughout the downtown area, most conveniently at the west end of Princes Street, South St. David Street, and North St. Andrew Street (the latter two just off St. Andrew Sq.), Waverley Market, Waterloo Place, and Lauriston Place. You can also hail any taxi displaying an illuminated FOR HIRE sign.

Contacts and Resources

CONSULATE

U.S. Consulate General (✉ 3 Regent Terr., ☎ 0131/556–8315).

EMERGENCIES

Police, ambulance, fire (☎ 999). **Pharmacy. Boots** (✉ 48 Shandwick Pl., west end of Princes St., ☎ 0131/225–6757).

GUIDED TOURS

Orientation. Lothian Regional Transport (☞ Getting Around, By Bus, *above*) operates tours in and around the city.

Walking. The Cadies and Witchery Tours (✉ 352 Castlehill, 3rd floor, ☎ 0131/225–6745) offers a highly popular murder and mystery tour, and historical and other special-interest tours.

VISITOR INFORMATION

Edinburgh and Scotland Information Centre (✉ 3 Princes St., ☎ 0131/557–1700, FAX 0131/473–3881) is adjacent to Waverley Station.

14 Greece

Athens, the Northern Peloponnese, Mainland Greece, Corfu, the Aegean Islands

Conditioned by museums, textbooks, and college Greek, some travelers arrive in Athens and find it surprising to see the natives roaring around in sports cars and talking about the latest nouvelle restaurant. Shouldn't they look like the truncated statues in the British Museum and have brows habitually crowned with wild olive? Incongruous as it may seem, most Greeks have two arms and two legs attached to the torso in the normal places. Their countryside may be bleached and stony, but the Greeks themselves—as the lucky visitor will soon learn—provide the vibrant color that has long since vanished from classic monuments once saturated with pigment, blue, gold, and vermilion, under the eye-searing Aegean sun.

The land itself is a stunning presence, dotted with cypress groves, vineyards, and olive trees; carved into gentle bays or dramatic coves bordered with startling white sand; rolling hills and rugged mountain ranges that plunge into the sea. In Greece, indeed, you cannot travel far across the land without encountering the sea, or far across the sea without encountering one of its roughly 2,000 islands. Approximately equal in size to New York State, Greece has 15,019 km (9,312 mi) of coastline, more than any other country of its size. The sea is everywhere, not on three sides only but at every turn, reaching through the shoreline like a probing hand. This natural beauty and the sharp, clear light of sun and sea, combined with plentiful archaeological treasures, make Greece one of the world's most inviting and rewarding countries to visit.

Western poetry, music, architecture, politics, medicine, law—all had their birth centuries ago in Greece. Among the great mountains of mainland Greece are Mt. Olympus, whose cloud-capped peak was the fabled home of the Greek gods, and Mt. Parnassus, favorite haunt of the sun god, Apollo, and the nine Muses, goddesses of poetry, music, dance, history, and astronomy. Romantic and beautiful remains of the ancient past—the Acropolis and the Parthenon, the temples of Delphi, the Tombs of the Kings in Mycenae—and a later procession of Byzantine churches, Crusader castles and fortresses, and Turkish mosques are bountiful features throughout the country.

Of the many hundreds of islands and islets scattered across the Aegean Sea, in the east, and the Ionian Sea, in the west, fewer than 250 are still inhabited. This world of the farmer, fisherman, and seafarer has largely been replaced by the world of the tourist. More than 10 million vacationers visit Greece each year, almost doubling the entire native population; in fact, tourism has overtaken shipping as the most important element in the nation's economy. Once-idyllic beaches have become overcrowded and noisy, and fishing harbors have become flotilla-sailing centers. On some of the islands, the impact of the annual influx of visitors has meant the building of a new Greece, more or less in their image. But traditional Greece survives: Pubs and bars stand next door to *ouzeri* (informal eateries that serve appetizers and ouzo), *kafeneia* (Greek coffee houses) are as popular as discos, and pizza and hamburger joints must compete with tavernas.

Although mass tourism has transformed the main centers, it is still possible to strike out and discover your own place among the smaller islands and the miles of beautiful mainland coastline. Except for an occasional scarcity of accommodations, especially in high summer, this is the ideal way to see traditional Greece. Those who come only to worship the classical Greeks and gaze at their temples, seeing nothing but the glory that was, miss today's Greece. If you explore this fascinating country with open eyes, you'll enjoy it in all its forms: its slumbering cafés and buzzing tavernas; its elaborate religious rituals; its stark, bright beauty; and the generosity and curiosity of its people.

GREECE A TO Z

Customs on Arrival

For details on imports and duty-free limits, *see* Customs & Duties *in* Chapter 1. There's no duty on items for personal use, although you may bring in only one each of such expensive portable items as camcorders and computers. You should register these with Greek Customs upon arrival, to avoid any problems when taking them out of the country again. Bank notes amounting to more than $2,500 must be declared for re-export; foreign visitors may export no more than 100,000 dr. in Greek currency.

Dining

The principal elements of Greek cuisine are fresh vegetables, such as eggplant, tomatoes, and beans, inventively combined with lots of olive oil and seasoned with lemon juice, garlic, and oregano. The most common meat dishes are pork, lamb, and chicken, although occasionally goat is available. Fish is often the better, though more expensive, choice, particularly on the coast. Your best bet is to choose the tavernas and *estiatoria* (restaurants) that are frequented by the most Greeks. The estiatorio serves oven-baked dishes and stove-top stews called *magirefta,* prepared in advance and often served at room temperature; tavernas offer similar fare plus grilled meats and fish. Another alternative

Greece (Ellada)

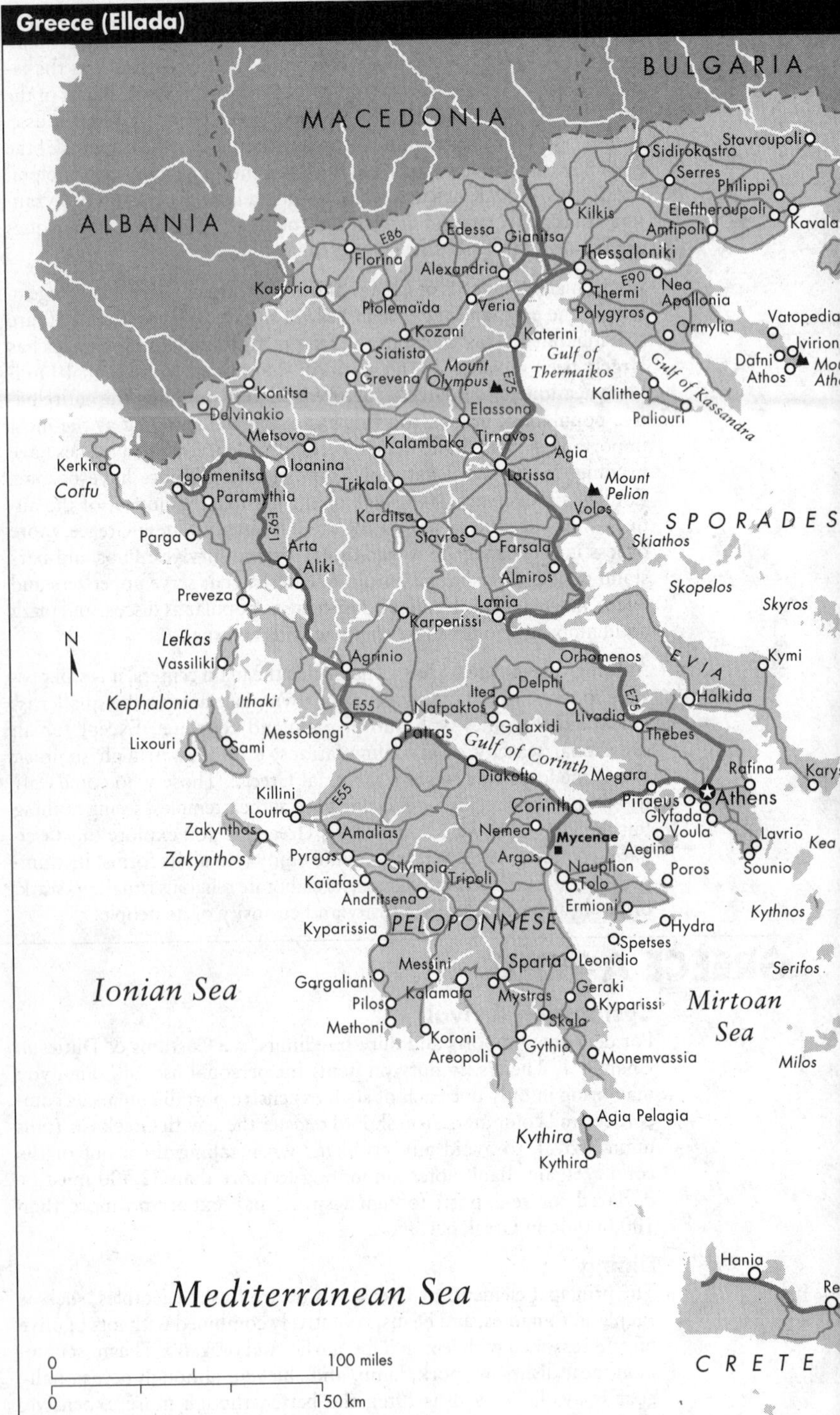

Black Sea
TURKEY
Kastanies
Xanthi
Komotini
Didymotiho
E90
THRACE
Istanbul
Avdira
Makri
Alexandroupoli
Sea of Marmara
Thassos
Samothrace
Mount Athos
Troy
Limnos
Lesvos
Mytilini
Plomari
TURKEY
Aegean Sea
Hios
Hios
Mesta
Pirgi
Izmir (Smyrna)
Andros
Andros
Ephesus
Samos
Samos
Pythagorio
Ikaria
Agios Kirykos
Tinos
Tinos
Ermoupoli
Syros
Mykonos
Delos
Patmos
Paros
Naxos
Leros
Bodrum (Halicarnassus)
Kos
Kos
CYCLADES
Amorgos
Ios
Astypalea
Nissyros
Symi
Oia
Fira
Santorini
Anafi
Tilos
Kameiros
Rhodes
Halki
Lindos
Rhodes
DODECANESE
Sea of Crete
Karpathos
Kassos
Heraklion
Mallia
Knossos
Siteia
Agios Nikolaos
Phaestos
Ierapetra

is an ouzeri or *mezedopolion,* where you order plates of appetizers, called *mezedes,* instead of an entrée. The decor of these establishments may range from simple to sophisticated, with prices to match.Traditional fast food in Greece consists of the gyro (slices of grilled meat with tomato and onions in pita bread), souvlakia (shish kebab), and pastries known as *pites,* filled with a variety of stuffings (spinach, cheese, or meat)—but hamburgers and pizzas are also found everywhere.

MEALTIMES

Lunch in Greek restaurants is served from 12:30 until 3. Dinner begins at about 9 and is served until 1 in Athens and until midnight outside Athens.

RATINGS

Prices are per person and include a first course, main course, dessert, VAT, and service charge. They do not include drinks or tip.

CATEGORY	ATHENS/THESSALONIKI/ MAIN ISLAND TOWNS	OTHER AREAS
$$$$	over 13,000 dr.	over 11,000 dr.
$$$	9,000 dr.–13,000 dr	7,000 dr.–11,000 dr.
$$	4,500 dr.–9,000 dr.	4,000 dr.–7,000 dr.
$	under 4,500 dr.	under 4,000 dr.

WHAT TO WEAR

Throughout the Greek islands you can dress informally for dinner, even at expensive restaurants; in Athens, jackets are appropriate at the top-price restaurants.

Language

English is widely spoken in hotels and elsewhere, especially by young people, and even in out-of-the-way places someone is always happy to lend a helping word. In this guide names are given in the Roman alphabet according to the Greek pronunciation.

Lodging

Greece offers a range of lodgings that accommodates most pocketbooks, from Spartan campgrounds to luxurious resorts complete with a pseudo village (bakery, church, café) on the premises. If you plan to visit during easter week (Catholic or Orthodox) or from mid-June through August, reserve well in advance. In August on the islands, even the most basic rooms are hard to find, as that's when most Greeks take their month-long vacation. Off season, you usually can negotiate room rates.

CAMPING

There are numerous privately owned campgrounds, with amenities ranging from basic to elaborate (those operated by the tourist organization are cushier than most). Contact the **Greek Camping Association** (✉ Solonos 102, Athens 10680, ☎ FAX 01/362–1560) or the Greek National Tourist Organization (EOT; ☞ Visitor Information *in* Athens Essentials, *below*) for more information.

HOTELS

Greek hotels are classified by the government as Luxury (L) and A–E. Within each category quality varies greatly, but prices usually don't. Still, you may come across an A-class hotel that charges less than a B-class, depending on facilities. In this guide hotels are classified according to price. All $$$$ and $$$ hotels are assumed to have air-conditioning and, unless indicated, all have private baths.

Prices quoted by hotels usually include service, local taxes, and VAT; many include breakfast. Often you can negotiate the price, sometimes by eliminating breakfast. The official price should be posted on the back of the door or inside a closet. Booking a room through a travel agency may reduce the price substantially. During high season larger resort hotels may insist that guests take half board. In Thessaloniki most room prices increase by about 40% during the two weeks of the International Trade Fair in September.

RATINGS

Prices quoted are for a double room in high season, including taxes and service, (with breakfast often included; inquire when booking).

CATEGORY	COST
$$$$	over 55,000 dr.
$$$	30,000 dr.–55,000 dr.
$$	17,000 dr.–30,000 dr.
$	under 17,000 dr.

RENTED ROOMS AND APARTMENTS

Most areas have family-run pensions and guest houses—usually clean, bright, and recently built—and self-catering apartments. Although in summer on the islands you will be approached by owners upon your arrival, you may want to pick up (at kiosks) an English-language copy of *Holiday Rentals in Greece: Rooms, Studios and Apartments* (published by Touristiki Ekdotiki), which includes photos and details on prices and facilities.

TRADITIONAL SETTLEMENTS

State-organized, these establishments house guests in buildings representative of the local architecture. Many settlements are described in a free brochure from the EOT (☞ Visitor Information *in* Athens Essentials, *below*), as well as in the English-language *Traditional Inns in Greece: Alternative Forms of Tourism* (published by Vertical Advertising-Publishing), available in foreign-language bookstores.

YOUTH HOSTELS

Hostels operate in major tourist areas but often close from season to season, so contact the **Greek Youth Hostel Organization** (✉ Damareos 75, Athens 11633, ☎ 01/751–9530, FAX 01/751–0616). The **YWCA** (✉ Amerikis 11, Athens 10672, ☎ 01/362–4291) puts up overnight female guests.

Mail

POSTAL RATES

Airmail letters and postcards for delivery within Europe cost 140 dr. for 20 grams and 220 dr. for 50 grams; for outside Europe 170 dr. for 20 grams and 260 dr. for 50 grams. All parcels must be inspected; bring them open and with wrapping materials to the nearest post office. In Athens parcels that weigh more than 2 kilograms (4½ pounds) must be brought to Mitropoleos 60 or to the Spiromiliou arcade off Voukourestiou Street.

RECEIVING MAIL

Mail service in Greece is slow, and letters often get lost; it's best to have important items registered or use a courier service. Most post offices are open weekdays 7:30–2. In Athens the **main offices** (Aeolou 100 and on Syntagma Square at Mitropoleos) stay open late (weekdays 7:30 AM–8 PM, Sat. 7:30–2, Sun. 9–2). You can have your mail addressed to "poste restante" and sent to any post office in Greece (in Athens: ✉ Aeolou 100, Athens 10200), where you can pick it up once you show your passport. Or have it mailed to American Express offices (✉

Ermou 2, Athens 10563). The service is free for holders of American Express cards or traveler's checks.

Money Matters

COSTS

Inflation in Greece has dropped to around 5% a year, but fluctuations in currency make it impossible to do accurate budgeting long in advance; watch the exchange rates. On the whole Greece offers good value compared with many other European countries. There are few regional price differences for hotels and restaurants. A modest hotel in a small town will charge only slightly lower rates than a modest hotel in Athens, with the same range of amenities. The same is true of restaurants. Car rentals are costly in Greece, but taxis, public transportation, and ferries are inexpensive even for long-distance runs.

CURRENCY

The Greek monetary unit is the drachma (dr.). Banknotes are in denominations of 100, 200, 500, 1,000, 5,000, and 10,000 dr.; coins, 5, 10, 20, 50, and 100. At press time (spring 1998), there were approximately 307 dr. to the U.S. dollar, 213 dr. to the Canadian dollar, 510 dr. to the pound sterling, 197 dr. to the Australian dollar, and 170 dr. to the New Zealand dollar. Daily exchange rates are prominently displayed in banks.

SAMPLE PRICES

At a central-city café you can expect to pay about 700–900 dr. for a cup of coffee (Greek coffee is always cheaper), 650–850 dr. for a bottle of beer, 450 dr. for a soft drink, and around 800 dr. for a grilled cheese sandwich. A 2-km (1½-mi) taxi ride costs about 175 dr. Admission to museums and archaeological sites is free on Sunday from mid-November to March. EU students enjoy free admission, students from other countries pay half the fee, and senior citizens frequently get a discount.

TIPPING

By law a service charge is figured into the price of a meal, but unless the waiter was rude or inept, it is customary to leave an additional 8%–10%. Tip porters 100 dr. per bag; in better hotels maids get about 200 dr. per day. For taxi drivers Greeks usually round off the fare to the nearest 50 dr. Hairdressers receive 10%. In legitimate theaters tip ushers 100 dr.; at the cinema give 100 dr. if you take a program. On cruises cabin and dining-room stewards get about 500 dr. per day; guides receive about the same.

National Holidays

January 1; January 6 (Epiphany); February 22 (Clean Monday); March 25 (Independence Day); April 9 (Good Friday); April 11 (Greek Easter Sunday); April 12 (Greek Easter Monday); May 1 (Labor Day); May 30 (Pentecost); August 15 (Assumption); October 28 (Ochi Day); December 25–26.

Opening and Closing Times

Office and shopping hours vary from season to season. Check with your hotel for up-to-the-minute information on opening and closing times.

Banks are open weekdays 8–2, except Friday, when they close at 1:30; they are closed weekends and public holidays. Even smaller towns have at least one bank with an ATM machine. **Museums and archaeological sites** are open 8:30–3 off season, or "winter," which runs October–mid-April. Depending on available personnel, sites usually stay open longer mid-April–September. Many museums are closed on Monday. **Shops** are usually open Tuesday, Thursday, and Friday 8:30–2 and

5–8:30; Monday, Wednesday, and Saturday 8:30–3. Supermarkets are open Monday–Saturday 8–8.

Shopping

Prices in large stores are fixed. Bargaining may take place in small, owner-managed souvenir and handicrafts shops and in antiques shops. In flea markets bargaining is expected.

EXPORT PERMITS

Antiques and Byzantine icons require an export permit (not normally given if the piece is of any value), but replicas can be bought fairly cheaply, although even these require a certificate stating they are copies.

SALES-TAX REFUNDS

Prices quoted in shops include the value-added tax (VAT). You may get a VAT refund on products worth 40,000 dr. or more (including VAT) bought in Greece from licensed stores, which usually display the Tax-Free Shopping sticker. Ask the shop to complete and give you a refund form called a Tax-Free check, which Greek Customs will stamp after viewing the item to make sure you are exporting it. Send the refund form back to the shop, with whom you should have made arrangements for the method of repayment.

Telephoning

COUNTRY CODE

The country code for Greece is 30. When dialing Greece from outside the country, drop the first zero in the regional telephone code.

INTERNATIONAL CALLS

Although you can buy phone cards (☞ *below*) with up to 1,000 units (11,300 dr., about one unit per local call), go to an OTE office for convenience and privacy if you plan to make several international calls. There is a three-minute minimum charge for operator-assisted station-to-station calls, a four-minute minimum for person-to-person connections. For an **AT&T** long-distance operator, dial 00/800–1311; **MCI,** 00/800–1211; **Sprint,** 00/800–1411. For operator-assisted calls in English, dial 161 or 162.

LOCAL CALLS

Many kiosks have pay telephones for local calls only. You pay the kiosk owner 20 dr. per call after you've finished. It's easier to buy a phone card from a Hellenic Telecommunications Organization office (OTE), kiosks, or convenience shops, and use it at the now-ubiquitous card phones. If you're calling within Greece, the price is reduced by about 30% weekdays 3 PM–5 PM and 10 PM–8 AM, and on weekends from 3 PM Saturday to 8 AM Monday.

Transportation

BY BOAT

Frequent car ferries and hydrofoils leave from Piraeus, the port of Athens, for the central and southern Aegean islands and Crete. Boats to such nearby islands as Andros and Tinos also leave from Rafina, east of Athens. Ships to the Ionian islands usually sail from Patras and Igoumenitsa. Travel agents and shipping offices in Athens and near all ports have details. Buy your tickets two or three days in advance, especially if you are traveling in summer or taking a car. Reserve your return journey or continuation soon after you arrive. Timetables change frequently, and boats may be delayed by weather conditions, so your plans should be flexible.

BY BUS

Bus travel is inexpensive, usually comfortable, and relatively fast. Bus timetables are available at tourist information offices. In summer and on holiday weekends, make reservations a few days before your planned trip. Railway-operated buses to Albania, Bulgaria, and Turkey (☎ 01/513–5768, –5769) leave from the Peloponnisos railway station in Athens (☞ Arriving and Departing by Train *in* Athens Essentials, *below*). All other buses leave Athens from one of two bus stations: Liossion 260, for Evia, eastern, and central Greece (including Delphi); Kifissou 100, for the Peloponnese and northern Greece.

BY CAR

Breakdowns. The **Automobile and Touring Club of Greece** (ELPA, ✉ Athens Tower, Messoghion 2–4, Athens 11525, ☎ 01/748–8800, FAX 01/778–6642; in an emergency, ☎ 104 throughout Greece) assists tourists with breakdowns free of charge if they belong to AAA or to ELPA (27,500 dr. per year, good throughout Europe); otherwise, there is a charge. ELPA also provides tourist information (☎ 174) to drivers.

Gasoline. At press time gas cost about 190 dr.–220 dr. a liter. Gas pumps and service stations are everywhere, and lead-free gas is widely available. In rural areas and on the islands many stations are closed evenings.

Parking. In Greece's half-dozen large cities, where downtown street parking and lots are hard to find—one of the reasons Athens continues installing more meters—buy a display sticker from the sidewalk boxes. It's often cheaper to leave your car at the hotel and take a cab or bus. Elsewhere, parking is easy.

Road Conditions. For the ratio of collisions to the number of cars on the road, Greece has one of the worst records in Europe. This is due, in part, to varied road conditions. Motorways tend to be good; tolls range from 250 dr. to 1,000 dr., depending on the distance. You need nerves of steel to drive in the cities, but many country roads, though narrow, are free of traffic.

Rules of the Road. Non-EU citizens must have an international driver's license. Driving is on the right, and although the vehicle on the right has the right-of-way, don't expect this or any other driving rule to be obeyed. The speed limit is 120 kph (74 mph) on the National Road though follow the temporary speed signs where it's under repair, 90 kph (54 mph) outside built-up areas, and 50 kph (31 mph) in town.

BY MOTORCYCLE AND BICYCLE

Dune buggies, bicycles, mopeds, and motorcycles can be rented on the islands. Use extreme caution. Helmets, technically compulsory for motorcyclists, are not usually available, and injuries are common.

BY PLANE

Olympic Airways (✉ Syngrou 96 or Fillelinon 15, near Syntagma, Athens, ☎ 01/966–6666 for reservations, ⏲ 7:20 AM–9:30 PM) has service between Athens and several cities and islands. Thessaloniki is also linked to the main islands, and there are a few inter-island connections. For information on arrivals and departures for Olympic Airways flights (West Terminal), call 01/936–3363, –3364, –3365, –3366; for other carriers (East Terminal), call 01/969–4466, –4467. In summer call for information on American-based charters at 01/969–4686, –4687; 01/997–2686, –2581 for other charters.

BY TRAIN

The **railway networks** are limited. The main line runs north from Athens, dividing into three lines at Thessaloniki. The main line continues to Belgrade, a second line goes east to the Turkish border and Istanbul, and a third line heads northeast to Bulgaria. The Peloponnese in the south is served by a narrow-gauge line dividing at Corinth into the Mycenae–Argos section and the Patras–Olympia–Kalamata section. ☎ *01/529–7777, for general information and timetables.* ⏲ *Daily 7 AM–9 PM.*

Visitor Information

There are **Greek National Tourist Organization (EOT)** offices throughout the country. **Tourist police** are in major cities and on the islands. Often more helpful are the **municipal tourism offices** that have been set up in the last decade (☞ Visitor Information *in each* Essentials *section, below*).

Weather

May, June, September, and October are the most temperate and least crowded tourist months to visit Greece. The heat can be unpleasant in July and August, especially in Athens, although the city's pollution is alleviated by the fact that half the residents have left for vacation. On the islands a brisk northwesterly wind, the *meltemi,* can make life more comfortable. The winter months tend to be damp and cold virtually everywhere.

CLIMATE

The following are the average daily maximum and minimum temperatures for Athens.

Jan.	55F	13C	**May**	77F	25C	**Sept.**	84F	29C
	44	6		61	16		67	19
Feb.	57F	14C	**June**	86F	30C	**Oct.**	75F	24C
	44	6		68	20		60	16
Mar.	60F	16C	**July**	92F	33C	**Nov.**	66F	19C
	46	8		73	23		53	12
Apr.	68F	20C	**Aug.**	92F	33C	**Dec.**	58F	15C
	52	11		73	23		47	8

ATHENS

Athens is essentially a village that outgrew itself, spreading outward from the original settlement at the foot of the Acropolis. Back in 1834, when it became the capital of modern Greece, the city had a population of fewer than 10,000. Now it houses more than a third of the entire Greek population—around 4.3 million. A modern concrete city has engulfed the old village and now sprawls for 388 square km (244 square mi), covering almost all the surrounding plain from the sea to the encircling mountains. The city is crowded and overwhelmingly hot during the summer. It also has an air-pollution problem, caused mainly by traffic fumes; in an attempt to lessen the congestion, it is forbidden to drive private cars in central Athens on alternate workdays. Still, Athens is an experience not to be missed. Its tangible vibrancy makes it one of the most exciting cities in Europe, and the sprawling cement has failed to overwhelm the astonishing reminders of the fabled ancient metropolis.

Although Athens covers a huge area, the major landmarks of the ancient Greek, Roman, and Byzantine periods are conveniently close to the modern city center. You can easily stroll from the Acropolis to the other sites, taking time to browse in shops and relax in cafés and tavernas along the way. From many quarters of the city one can glimpse "the glory that was Greece" in the form of the Acropolis looming above the horizon, but only by actually climbing that rocky precipice can you feel the impact of the ancient settlement. The Acropolis and Filopappou, two craggy hills sitting side by side; the ancient Agora (marketplace); and Kerameikos, the first cemetery, form the core of ancient and Roman Athens.

Exploring Athens

Numbers in the margin correspond to points of interest on the Athens map.

The central area of modern Athens is small, stretching from the Acropolis to Mt. Lycabettus, with its small white church on top. The layout is simple: Three parallel streets—Stadiou, Venizelou (a.k.a. Panepistimiou), and Akademias—link two main squares—Syntagma and Omonia. Try to wander off this beaten tourist track: Seeing the Athenian butchers in the central market near Monastiraki sleeping on their cold marble slabs during the heat of the afternoon siesta may give you more of a feel for the city than looking at hundreds of fallen pillars.

In summer closing times often depend on the site's available personnel, but throughout the year, arrive at least 30 minutes before the official closing time to ensure you can buy a ticket. Flash photography is forbidden in museums.

6 **Agios Eleftherios.** What's fascinating about the city's former cathedral is that the walls of this 12th-century Byzantine church incorporate reliefs—fanciful figures and zodiac signs—from buildings that date back to the Classical period. The church is also known as Little Mitropolis and Panagia Gorgoepikoos (Virgin Who Answers Prayers Quickly), based on its 13th-century icon, said to perform miracles. ✉ *Mitropolis Sq.,* ☎ *No phone.* 🎫 *Free.* ⏲ *Hours depend on services, but usually open daily 8–1.*

★ 1 **Akropolis.** After a 30-year building moratorium at the time of the Persian wars, the Athenians built this complex during the 5th century BC to honor the goddess Athena, patron of the city. It is now undergoing conservation as part of an ambitious 20-year rescue plan launched with international support in 1983 by Greek architects. The first ruins you'll see are the **Propylaia,** the monumental gateway that led worshipers from the temporal world into the spiritual world of the sanctuary; now only the columns of Pentelic marble and a fragment of stone ceiling remain. Above, to the right, stands the graceful **Naos Athenas Nikis** or **Apterou Nikis** (Wingless Victory). The temple was mistakenly called the latter because common tradition often confused Athena with the winged goddess Nike. Athenians claimed the sculptor had purposely omitted the wings on the temple's statue to ensure Victory would never fly away from the city. The elegant and architecturally complex **Erechtheion,** most sacred of the shrines of the Acropolis and later turned into a harem by the Turks, has finally emerged from extensive repair work. Dull, heavy copies of the Caryatids (draped maidens) now support the roof. The **Acropolis Museum** (☞ Museo Akropoleos, *below*) houses five of the six originals, their faces much damaged by acid rain. The sixth is in the British Museum in London.

The **Parthenonas** (Parthenon) dominates the Acropolis and indeed the Athens skyline. Designed by Ictinus, with Phidias as master sculptor, it was completed in 438 BC and is the most architecturally sophisticated temple of that period. Even with hordes of tourists wandering around the ruins, you can still feel a sense of wonder. The architectural decorations were originally painted vivid red and blue, and the roof was of marble tiles, but time and neglect have given the marble pillars their golden-white shine, and the beauty of the building is all the more stark and striking. The British Museum houses the largest remaining part of the original 532-ft frieze (the Elgin Marbles). The building has 17 fluted columns along each side and 8 at the ends, and these were cleverly made to lean slightly inward and to bulge, counterbalancing the natural optical distortion. The Parthenon has had a checkered history: It was made into a brothel by the Romans, a church by the Christians, and a mosque by the Turks. The Turks also stored gunpowder in the Propylaia. When this was hit by a Venetian bombardment in 1687, 28 columns of the Parthenon were blown out and a fire raged for two days, leaving the temple in its present condition. ✉ *Top of Dionyssiou Areopagitou,* ☎ *01/321–4172.* ⏲ *Weekdays 8–6:30 (8–4:30 in winter), weekends 8:30–2:30.*

❹ **Archaia Agora** (Ancient Agora). Now a sprawling confusion of stones, slabs, and foundations, this was the civic center and focal point of community life in ancient Athens, where Socrates met with his students while merchants haggled over the price of olive oil. It is dominated by the best-preserved Doric temple in Greece, the **Hephaisteion,** built during the 5th century BC. Nearby, the impressive Stoa Attalou (Stoa of Attalos II), reconstructed by the American School of Classical Studies in Athens with the help of the Rockefeller Foundation, houses the **Museo tis Agoras** (Museum of Agora Excavations). The museum offers a fascinating glimpse of everyday life in ancient Athens, its objects ranging from a terra-cotta chamber pot to the shards used in secret ballots to recommend banishment of powerful citizens (*ostraka,* from which the word "ostracism" is derived). ✉ *Three entrances: from Monastiraki, on Adrianou St.; from Thission, on Apostolos Pavlou St.; from Acropolis, on descent along Ag. Apostoli,* ☎ *01/321–0185.* ⏲ *Tues.–Sun. 8:30–2:45.*

❸ **Areios Pagos** (Areopagus). From this rocky outcrop, ancient Athens's supreme court, you can view the Propylaia, the Agora, and the modern city. Legend claims it was here that Orestes was tried for the murder of his mother, and much later St. Paul delivered his Sermon to the Unknown God, so moving that a senator named Dionysius was converted and became the first bishop of Athens. ✉ *Opposite Acropolis entrance.* 🎫 *Free.* ⏲ *Always open.*

★ ⓲ **Ethniko Archaiologiko Museo** (National Archaeological Museum). Though it's somewhat off the tourist route, a good 10-minute walk north of Omonia Square, this is a must for visitors. It houses one of the most exciting collections of antiquities in the world, including sensational archaeological finds made by Heinrich Schliemann at Mycenae; 16th-century BC frescoes from the Akrotiri ruins on Santorini; and the 6½-ft-tall bronze sculpture *Poseidon,* an original work of circa 470 BC, possibly by the sculptor Kalamis, which was found in the sea off Cape Artemision in 1928. ✉ *28 Oktovriou (Patission) 44,* ☎ *01/821–7717.* ⏲ *Mon. 12:30–7 (10:30–4:45 in winter), Tues.–Fri. 8–7 (8:30–3 in winter), weekends and holidays 8:30–3.*

★ ⓮ **Goulandri Museo Kikladikis ke Archaias Technis** (Goulandris Museum of Cycladic and Ancient Art). The collection spans 5,000 years, with nearly 100 exhibits of the Cycladic civilization (3000–2000 BC), including many of the slim marble figurines that so fascinated such artists as Picasso and Modigliani. ✉ *Neofitou Douka 4 or Irodotou 1,* ☎ *01/722–8321.* ⏲ *Mon. and Wed.–Fri. 10–4, Sat. 10–3.*

❽ **Irodion** (Odeon of Herod Atticus). This hauntingly beautiful 2nd-century AD theater was built Greek-style into the hillside but with typical Roman archways in its three-story stage building and barrel-vaulted entrances. Now restored, it hosts Athens Festival performances (☞ The Arts, *below*). ✉ *Dionyssiou Areopagitou St. across from Propylaia St.,* ☎ *01/323–2771.* ⏲ *Open only to Athens Festival audiences.*

★ ⓯ **Likavitos** (Mt. Lycabettus). Athens's highest hill is only a 10-minute walk northeast of Syntagma. It borders fashionable Kolonaki, a residential quarter worth a visit if you enjoy window-shopping and people-watching. A steeply inclined funicular climbs to the summit,

Agios Eleftherios, **6**
Akropolis, **1**
Archaia Agora, **4**
Areios Pagos, **3**
Ethniko Archaiologiko Museo, **18**
Goulandri Museo Kikladikis ke Archaias Technis, **14**
Irodion, **8**
Likavitos, **15**
Monastiraki, **5**
Museo Akropoleos, **2**
Panathinaïko Stadio, **12**
Pili tou Adrianou, **10**
Plaka, **7**
Stiles Olymbiou Dios, **11**
Syntagma, **16**
Theatro Dionyssou, **9**
Vivliothiki, Panepistimio, Akademia, **17**
Vizantino Museo, **13**

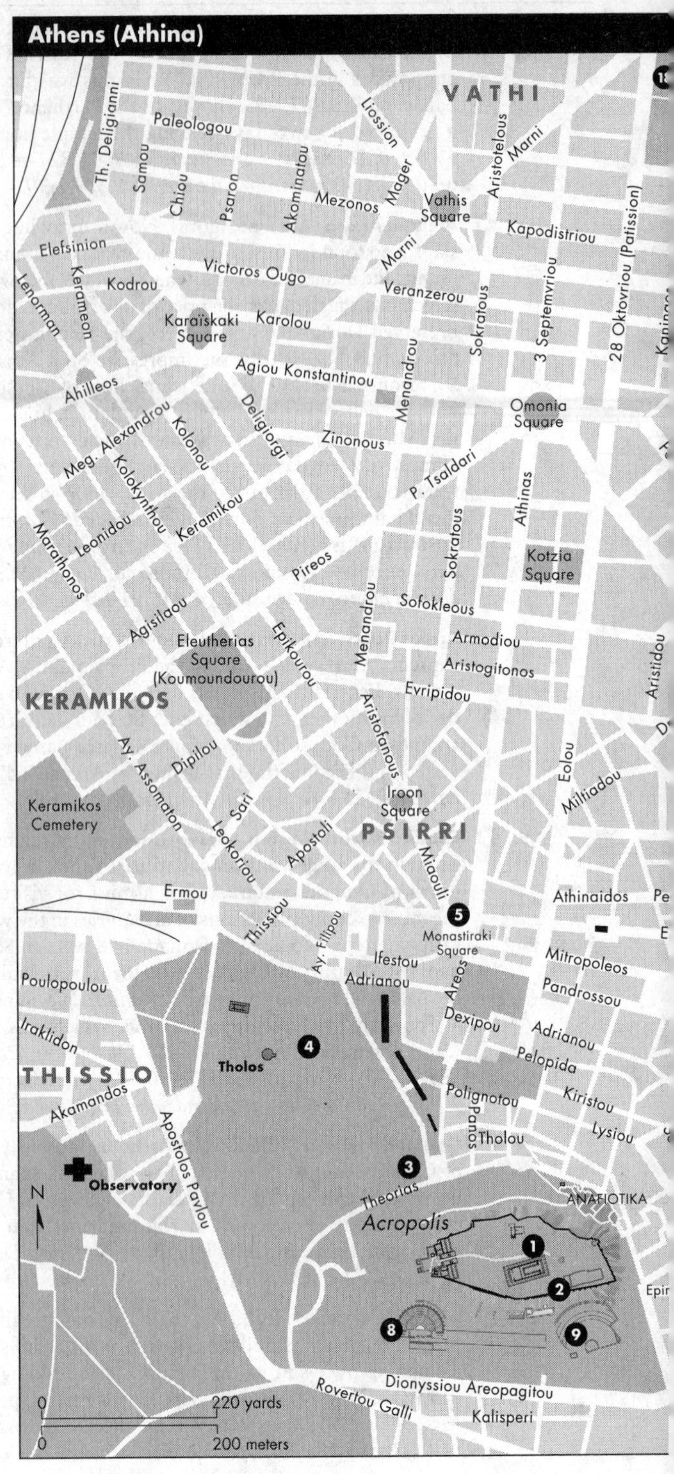

NEAPOLIS
Strefi
Tossitsa
Stournara
Solomou
Kapodistriou
Themistokleous
Em. Benaki
Kaningos
Kaningos Square
Zoodohou Pigis
Harilaou Trikoupi
Navarinou
Mavromichali
Ippokratous
Arachovis
Dervenion
Eressou
Methonis
Kallidromiou
Smolenski
Isavron
Tsimiski
Voulgaroktonou
Vatatzi
Laskareos
Sarantapichou
N. Ouranou
Dafnomili
LIKAVITOS
15
Agios Giorgos
Panepistimiou (Venizelou)
Akademias
Asklepiou
Municipal Cultural Center
Didotou
Skoufa
Chersonos
Massalias
Solonos
Sina
17
Stadiou
Aristidou
Korai
Omirou
Lykavitou
Anagnostopoulou
Marasli
Aristippou
Kleomenous
Loukianou
Spefsipou
Dragatsaniou
Klafthmonos Sq.
Paparigopoulou
Ch. Lada
Amerikis
Dimokritou
Voukourestiou
Pindarou
KOLONAKI
Patriarhou Ioakim
Ploutarchou
Alopekis
Karneadou
Ypsilantou
Irodotou
Praxitelous
Kolokotroni
Schliemann's Mansion
Kanari
Kolonaki Square
Merlin
Karageorgi Servias
Perikleos
Georgiou I
Vasilissis Sofias
Koumbari
14
13
Ermou
Syntagma Square
16
Parliament
Herod Atticus
Rigilis
6
Pendeli
Mitropoleos
Apollonos
Voulis
Nikis
Filellinon
Amalias
National Gardens
Vasileos Georgiou B'
Nikodimou
Souri
PLAKA
Adrianou
Scholiou
Kidathineon
7
Thespidos
Tripodon
Amalias Ave.
Zappion
Vasileos Konstantinou
Pafsaniou
Eratosthenous
Arianou
Epimenidou
Goura
Lysikratous
Vironos
Pitakou
10
Vasilissis Olgas
11
Agras
12
Ardittos Hill
Plastira Square

crowned by whitewashed Agios Giorgios chapel. The view from the top—pollution permitting—is the finest in Athens. ✉ *Funicular every 10 min from Ploutarchou 1 at Aristippou (take minibus 060 from Kolonaki Sq.),* ☎ *01/722–7065.* ⏲ *Fri.–Wed. 8:45 AM–midnight (12:30 AM in summer), Thurs. 10:30 AM–midnight (12:30 AM in summer).*

5 **Monastiraki.** The old Turkish bazaar area takes its name from Panayia Pantanassa Church, commonly called Monastiraki (Little Monastery); it once flourished as an extensive convent, perhaps dating from the 10th century. Near the church stands the Tzistarakis Mosque (1759), exemplifying the East-West paradox that characterizes Athens. But the district's real draw is the Sunday flea market, centered on tiny Abyssinia Square and running along Ifestou and Kynetou streets. Watching the interplay between Greeks, complete with wildly gesturing hands and dramatic facial expressions, will provide hours of entertainment. Everything's for sale, from gramophone needles to old matchboxes, from nose rings sold by young nomads to lacquered eggs and cool white linens from former USSR emigres. ✉ *South of intersection of Ermou and Athinas Sts.*

★ 2 **Museo Akropoleos** (Acropolis Museum). Tucked into one corner of the Acropolis, this institution contains superb sculptures, including the Caryatids and a collection of colored *korai* (statues of women dedicated by worshipers to Athena, patron of the ancient city). ☎ *01/323–6665.* ⏲ *Mon. 11–6:30 (11–4:30 in winter), Tues.–Fri. 8:30–6:30 (8:30–4:30 in winter), weekends 8:30–2:30.*

12 **Panathinaiko Stadio** (Panathenaic Stadium). A reconstruction of the ancient Roman stadium in Athens, this gleaming white marble structure was built for the first modern Olympic Games in 1896 and seats 80,000 spectators. ✉ *Near intersection Vas. Konstantinou and Vas. Olgas,* ☎ *No phone.* 🎫 *Free.* ⏲ *Daily 9–2 but can be viewed in its entirety from entrance.*

10 **Pili tou Adrianou** (Hadrian's Arch). Built in AD 131–32 by Emperor Hadrian to delineate ancient and imperial Athens, the Roman archway with Corinthian pilasters bears an inscription on the side facing the Acropolis, which reads, THIS IS ATHENS, THE ANCIENT CITY OF THESEUS. But the side facing the Temple of Olympian Zeus proclaims, THIS IS THE CITY OF HADRIAN AND NOT OF THESEUS. ✉ *Intersection Vas. Amalias and Dionyssiou Areopagitou.* 🎫 *Free.* ⏲ *Always open.*

★ 7 **Plaka.** Stretching east from the Agora, this is almost all that's left of 19th-century Athens, a lovely quarter with winding walkways, neoclassical houses, and such sights as the **Museo Ellinikis Laikis Technis** (Greek Folk Art Museum; ✉ Kidathineon 17, ☎ 01/322–9031, ⏲ Tues.–Sun. 10–2), with a collection dating from 1650, and the Roman Agora's **Aerides** (Tower of the Winds; ✉ Pelopidas and Aeolou, ☎ 01/324–5220, ⏲ Tues.–Sun. 8:30–2:45), a 1st-century BC water clock. The **Mnimeio Lysikratous** (Monument of Lysikrates; ✉ Herefondos and Lysikratous Sts.) is one of the few surviving tripods on which stood the award given to the producer of the best play in the Dionyssia festival. Above Plaka, at the northeastern base of the Acropolis is **Anafiotika,** the closest thing you'll find to a village in Athens. Take time to wander among its whitewashed, bougainvillea-framed houses and tiny churches, away from the city's bustle.

11 **Stiles Olymbiou Dios or Olymbion** (Temple of Olympian Zeus). This famous temple was begun during the 6th century BC, and, when it was finally completed 700 years later, it exceeded in magnitude all other temples in Greece. It was destroyed during the invasion of the Goths in the 4th century; only a few towering, sun-browned columns remain. ✉ *Vas. Olgas 1,* ☎ *01/922–6330.* ⏲ *Tues.–Sun. 8:30–3.*

16 **Syntagma** (Constitution Square). At the top of the square stands the **Vouli** (Parliament), formerly the royal palace, completed in 1838 for the new monarchy. From the Parliament you can watch the changing of the Evzone honor guard at the **Mnimeio Agnostou Stratiotou** (Tomb of the Unknown Soldier), with its text from Pericles's famous funeral oration and a bas-relief of a dying soldier modeled after a sculpture on the Temple of Aphaia in Aegina. The guard changes every few hours depending on the weather, but the most elaborate ceremony takes place on Sunday, when these sturdy young men don their *foustanellas* (kilts) with 400 pleats, one for each year of the Ottoman occupation. The procession usually arrives in front of Parliament at 11:15 AM. On the square's southern side sits the lush **Ethniko Kipo** (National Garden), offering a quick escape from the center's bustle. ✉ *Corner of Vas. Sofias and Vas. Amalias.*

9 **Theatro Dionyssou** (Theater of Dionyssos). In this theater dating from about 330 BC, the famous ancient dramas and comedies were performed in conjunction with bacchanalian feasts. The throne in the center was reserved for the priest of Dionyssos: It is adorned with regal lions' paws, and the back is carved with reliefs of satyrs and griffins. ✉ *Dionyssiou Areopagitou opposite Mitsaion St.,* ☎ *01/322–4625.* ⏲ *Daily 8:30–2:45.*

17 **Vivliothiki, Panepistimio, Akademia** (Old University complex). These three dramatic buildings belong to the University of Athens, designed by the Hansen Brothers in the period after independence and built of white Pentelic marble, with tall columns and decorative friezes. In the center is the Senate House of the university; on the right is the Academy, flanked by statues of Athena and Apollo; and on the left is the National Library. ✉ *Panepistimiou 28,* ☎ *Library 01/361–4413, Panepistimio 01/361–4301, Akademia 01/360–0207.* 🎫 *Free.* ⏲ *Library weekdays 9–9, others weekdays 9–2. Closed Aug.*

13 **Vizantino Museo** (Byzantine Museum). Housed in an 1848 mansion built by an eccentric French aristocrat, the museum is undergoing renovation. Not all its pieces are on display, but it has a unique collection of icons, re-creations of Greek churches throughout the centuries, and the very beautiful 14th-century Byzantine embroidery of the body of Christ, in gold, silver, yellow, and green. Sculptural fragments provide an excellent introduction to Byzantine architecture. ✉ *Vas. Sofias 22,* ☎ *01/721–1027.* ⏲ *Tues.–Sun. 8:30–2:50.*

Dining and Lodging

Search for places with at least a half dozen tables occupied by Athenians—they're discerning customers. For details and price-category information, *see* Dining *in* Greece A to Z, *above*.

It's always advisable to reserve a room. Hotels are clustered around the center of town and along the seacoast toward the airport. Modern hotels are more likely to be air-conditioned and to have double-glazed windows; the center of Athens can be so noisy that it's hard to sleep. Many hotels include breakfast within the room rate; inquire when booking. For details and price-category definitions, *see* Lodging *in* Greece A to Z, *above*.

$$$$ ★ ✕ **Bajazzo.** If you can splurge only once in Greece, this is the place, the only restaurant in Athens that has been accorded international praise. Chef Klaus Feuerbach changes the menu often, creating imaginative, beautifully presented dishes. The beef fillets with Metaxa sauce grilled in tobacco leaves, simple but flawless pork tenderloin with brie, intense smoked duck breast with foie gras and cherry froth, and the venison with bittersweet chocolate sauce are just some of the mouth-watering dishes. Try the herbed ice cream (rosemary, tarragon, dill) or the meringues filled with amaretto and crème anglaise for dessert. ✉ *Anapafseos 14, Mets,* ☎ *01/921–3013. Reservations essential. AE, DC, V. Closed Sun. No lunch.*

$$$$ ✕ **Vardis.** This grand restaurant is sometimes compared to the five-star Taillevent in Paris and a meal here is obviously worth the ride to the northern suburb of Kifissia. The award-winning chef is committed to the classics and to quality ingredients—he brings in sweetwater crayfish from Orhomenos and tracks down rare large shrimp from Thassos island. The clientele may be a little sedate, but the food is heavenly. Especially good are the warm foie gras with dried fig purée, the superb crayfish linguini, and the tournedos Rossini served with a demi-glace enriched with foie gras. ✉ *Diligianni 66 in Pentelikon Hotel, Kefalari, Kifissia,* ☎ *01/623–0650. Reservations essential. AE, DC, MC, V. Closed Sun. and Aug. No lunch.*

$$$–$$$$ ★ ✕ **Varoulko.** Acclaimed chef Lefteris Lazarou has joined forces with Fabrizio Buliani, and the results are magnificent as they try to outdo each other. Customers wait in line to sample such appetizers as sturgeon-filled phyllo triangles or carpaccio made from *petrobarbouno* (a kind of rock fish). Although the restaurant is most famous for its creative presentations of monkfish, there is a mind-boggling array of other seafood dishes. ✉ *Deligeorgi 14, Piraeus,* ☎ *01/411–2043,* ☎ FAX *01/411–1283. Reservations essential. AE, DC, V. Closed Sun. and Aug. No lunch.*

$$$ ★ ✕ **Boschetto.** The restaurant pampers diners with its park setting, expert maître d', and creative Italian nouvelle. The specialty here is fresh pasta, such as papardelle with wild mushrooms and quail-parmesan ragout, airy capellini with crab and sautéed tomatoes, or ravioli with crayfish, foie gras, and poppy seeds. End your meal with an unusual dessert of cream and chicken, followed by the finest espresso in Athens (cigars available). The tables tend to be close together; reserve near the window or in the courtyard during summer. ✉ *Alsos Evangelismos, Hilton area,* ☎ *01/721–0893. Reservations essential. AE, V. Closed Sun. and 2 wks in Aug. No lunch weekends.*

$$$ ✕ **Spondi.** You may feel like you're dining in a medieval wine cellar in this vaulted stone-interior restaurant with heavy candlesticks and massive wood furniture, but the cuisine is delightfully contemporary. Savor the grilled fresh foie gras with caramelized endive in mavrodafni sauce, together with a red wine chosen by the award-winning sommelier. When weather permits, diners sit in the bougainvillea-draped courtyard. ✉ *Pirronos 5, Pangrati,* ☎ *01/726–4021. Reservations essential. V. No lunch.*

$$–$$$ ✕ **Kollias.** Friendly owner Tassos Kollias creates his own dishes, ranging from the humble to the aristocratic: grilled scorpion fish flavored with mastic; lobster with lemon, balsamic vinegar, and a shot of honey; mussels stuffed with rice, grapes, and pine nuts. The large mixed salads include one with white beets, arugula, parsley, caper leaves, endive, and radishes. A fitting end to the meal: *loukoumades* (sweet fritters), best with the kumquat liqueur. ✉ *Stratigou Plastira 3, Piraeus,* ☎ *01/461–9150. Reservations essential weekends. AE, DC, MC, V. Closed Sun. and Aug. No lunch.*

$$ ✕ **Ta Tria Tetarta.** A bit more upscale than most mezedopolia, Tria Tetarta serves a large variety of unusual appetizers in a tri-level stone and wood house, decorated with eye-catching *objets* and antiques. Try the spicy feta sprinkled with red pepper and roasted in foil; spinach crepes with tomato, basil, and yogurt; skewered *seftalies* (seasoned meat dumplings); and the seafood pie. ✉ *Oikonomou 25, Exarchia,* ☎ *01/823–0560. Reservations essential. No credit cards. Closed Aug. No lunch Mon.–Sat.*

$$ ★ ✗ **Vitrina.** From the stenciled bread baskets to the door handles on the chair backs, it's obvious this restaurant concentrating on Aegean-inspired cooking is the creation of a fashion photographer. The combinations are bold: crayfish with coffee and coriander, scallops sautéed in mastic and lemon, grilled lamb ribs with grapefruit, honey, and buttermilk. If it's in season, sample the delicate chestnut mousse for dessert. Seating upstairs is best; downstairs is a bit claustrophobic. ✉ *Navarchou Apostoli 7, Psirri,* ☎ *01/321–1200. Reservations essential. No credit cards. Closed Mon. and mid-June–Sept. No lunch Tues.–Sat.; no dinner Sun.*

$$ ★ ✗ **Vlassis.** Relying on recipes from Thrace, Roumeli, Thessaly, and the islands, the chefs whip up Greek home cooking in generous portions. Musts are the *pastitsio* (baked minced lamb and macaroni) with bits of liver, the *lahanodolmades* (cabbage rolls), and the octopus *stifado* (stew), tender and sweet with lots of onions. The king-size *galaktobouriko* (custard in phyllo) will leave you with a smile on your face. ✉ *Paster 8, Platia Mavili (near American embassy),* ☎ *01/646–3060. Reservations essential. No credit cards. Closed Sun. and late July–mid-Sept. No lunch.*

$$ ✗ **Xynos.** Enter a time warp in this Plaka taverna: Athens in the '50s. The excellent food is still the same. Start with stuffed grape leaves, then move on to the taverna's forte, such cooked dishes as *tsoutsoukakia,* spicy meat patties with cinnamon. Nightly, a guitar duo drops by to charm the crowd with old Greek ballads. ✉ *Aggelou Geronta 4, Plaka (entrance down walkway next to Kafenion Glikis),* ☎ *01/322–1065. No credit cards. Closed weekends and July. No lunch.*

$ ✗ **Karavitis.** A neighborhood favorite, this taverna near the Olympic Stadium has warm-weather garden seating and a winter dining room decorated with huge wine casks. Classic Greek cuisine is well prepared here, including pungent *tzatziki* (yogurt-garlic dip), *bekri meze* (lamb chunks in a spicy red sauce), and *stamnaki* (beef baked in a clay pot). ✉ *Arktinou 35 and Pausaniou 4, Pangrati,* ☎ *01/721–5155. No credit cards. Closed a few days around Aug. 15. No lunch.*

$ ★ ✗ **O Platanos.** Set in a picturesque courtyard, this is one of Plaka's oldest yet least touristy tavernas. Don't miss the oven-baked potatoes, roast lamb, and exceptionally cheap but delicious barrel retsina. Although the waiters are helpful, not much English is spoken. ✉ *Diogenous 4, Plaka,* ☎ *01/322–0666. No credit cards. Closed Sun. and 2 wks in Aug.*

$ ✗ **Sigalas-Bairaktaris.** Run by the Bairaktaris family for more than a century, this is the best place to eat in Monastiraki Square. Order the tiny *tiropites* (cheese pies) sprinkled with sesame seeds and fried zucchini with garlicky dip for appetizers, then go to the window case to view the day's magirefta or sample the gyro platter. ✉ *Platia Monastiraki 2, Monastiraki,* ☎ *01/321–3036. AE, V.*

$ ✗ **To Ouzadiko.** If you're exploring Kolonaki's boutiques and museums, stop at this mezedopolion for the cozy interior (old posters, abundant wood, small marble tables), the friendly service, and the enticing mezedes. Depending on what the owner bought at market that morning, you may find delicious Thessaloniki mini meat pies called *tsigerosarmadakia* and juicy rooster with onions. Ouzadiko lives up to its name, serving 110 kinds of ouzo and tsipouro. ✉ *Karneadou 25–29 in Lemos shopping mall, Kolonaki,* ☎ *01/729–5484. Reservations essential. No credit cards. Closed Sun. and Aug. 10–31.*

$$$$ 🏨 **Andromeda Athens Hotel.** On a quiet street near the U.S. Embassy, this luxury hotel caters to business travelers, but all guests will relish the meticulous service and sumptuous decor. The spacious rooms have a salmon color scheme, modern amenities, and double-glazed windows. At press time the hotel was putting the finishing touches on a building across the street with 12 executive suites (one- and two-room apartments), which will include refrigerator, microwave, computer, and

pay TV system. ✉ *Timoleondos Vassou 22, Mavili Sq., 11521,* ☎ *01/643–7302,* FAX *01/646–6361. 20 rooms, 6 suites, 4 penthouses. Restaurant. AE, DC, MC, V.*

$$$$ **Astir Palace Vouliagmeni.** On a pine-studded promontory 25 km (16 mi) south of Athens, with a view of nearby islands, this 80-acre resort is a haven from the city center. Less expensive than the deluxe-category hotels in town, the complex is made up of three hotels: all three have been freshly decorated in the last few years. The private beach, sports, lovely landscaping, and sea views are bonuses. A shuttle transports guests to the center in the mornings. Buffet breakfast is included in the price. ✉ *Apollonos 40,Vouliagmeni 16671,* ☎ *01/890–2000,* FAX *01/896–2582;* ☎ *212/682–9191 in the U.S.,* FAX *212/682–9254 in the U.S. 458 rooms, 73 bungalows, 30 suites. 5 restaurants, 4 pools. AE, DC, MC, V.*

$$$$ **Athenaeum Inter-Continental.** The plush Inter-Continental has a marble atrium lobby that displays a private art collection and it is one of the few hotels in Athens with a health club. Its spacious rooms have sitting areas and marble bathrooms; ask for one with an Acropolis view. The hotel renovated the eighth and ninth floors to create the Club section, with private check-in, lounge, and library; complimentary breakfast, coffee, and evening cocktails. Shuttle service takes guests to the airport twice in the morning and to Syntagma Square throughout the day. ✉ *89–93 Syngrou, near Neos Kosmos 11745,* ☎ *01/920–6000,* FAX *01/924–3000. 548 rooms, 59 suites. 2 restaurants, pool. AE, DC, MC, V.*

$$$$ ★ **Athens Hilton.** A 200-year-old olive tree with a Turkish cannonball in its branches stands near what is still one of the city's top hotels after nearly 30 years. It is about a 20-minute walk from Syntagma, but a shuttle takes guests downtown during the day. The spacious rooms all have balconies and double-glazed windows, as well as fine views of either the Acropolis or Mt. Ymittos. The Galaxy bar, with its outdoor terrace and Athens panorama, is the ideal place to recoup from a hard day of sightseeing. ✉ *Vas. Sofias 46, 11528,* ☎ *01/725–0201,* FAX *01/725–3110. 453 rooms, 19 suites. 3 restaurants, pool. AE, DC, MC, V.*

$$$$ **Grande Bretagne.** The G. B., as it is known, has a prime location on Syntagma Square. A face-lift in 1992 restored the internationally famous landmark, and it remains a hub of Athenian social life. Ask for one of the coveted Syntagma rooms with large balconies and Acropolis views. The hotel has now added a no-smoking floor (the third) and "Smart" rooms, with desk, printer, fax, and photocopier, and a direct telephone line. ✉ *Vas. Georgiou A' 1, Syntagma, 10563,* ☎ *01/333–0000, 01/331–5555 for reservations,* FAX *01/322–8034, 01/322–2261 for reservations. 364 rooms, 23 suites. Restaurant. AE, DC, MC, V.*

$$$–$$$$ **Kefalari Suites.** Escape Athens' bustle among the neoclassical mansions and tree-lined boulevards of Kifissia suburb at this new hotel. Located in a turn-of-the-century building, the hotel offers imaginative suites at a range of prices lower than downtown deluxe hotels. You can opt for the Deck House (no need to go to sea), the chateau-inspired Malmaison, Aqaba, and the romantic Daphnes and Chloe. Suites include kitchenettes with utensils, refrigerators, minibars and verandas or balconies. Laptop computers with modem and faxes are available. ✉ *Pentelis 1 and Kolokotroni, Kefalari, Kifissia 14562,* ☎ *01/623–3333,* FAX *01/623–3330. 13 suites. AE, DC, MC, V.*

$$$ **Electra Palace.** At the edge of Plaka this hotel offers cozy rooms in warm hues and balconies for comparatively low prices. Rooms from the fifth floor up are smaller but have bigger balconies. The best feature is the rooftop pool with Jacuzzi and barbecue in summer. American breakfast is included in the price. ✉ *Nikodimou 18, Plaka 10557,* ☎ *01/324–1401 through 324–1410,* FAX *01/324–1875. 101 rooms, 5 suites. Restaurant, pool. AE, DC, MC, V.*

$$$ 🏨 **Novotel Athenes.** Although not central, this hotel is just a 10-minute walk from the rail station or the national archaeological museum. One of the city's better values, it has an elegant lobby and quiet rooms. The underground parking is free for guests, a bonus in this neighborhood. The rooftop pool is beside a Greek restaurant from which, in summer, you can watch the sun set behind the Acropolis. ✉ *M. Voda 4–8, Vathis Sq., 10439,* ☎ *01/825–0422,* FAX *01/883–7816. 189 rooms, 6 suites. 2 restaurants, pool. AE, DC, MC, V.*

$$ ★ 🏨 **Acropolis View Hotel.** This hotel in a quiet neighborhood below the Acropolis has agreeable rooms with balconies, about half with Parthenon views. Staff members in the homey lobby are friendly. ✉ *Webster 10, Acropolis 11742,* ☎ *01/921–7303, –7304, –7305,* FAX *01/923–0705. 32 rooms. Air-conditioning. AE, MC, V.*

$$ 🏨 **Austria.** This small, unpretentious hotel on Filopappou Hill, opposite the Acropolis, is ideal as a base for exploring the heart of ancient Athens. ✉ *Mouson 7, Filopappou 11742,* ☎ *01/923–5151 or 01/922–0777,* FAX *01/924–7350. 37 rooms. Air-conditioning. AE, DC, MC, V.*

$$ 🏨 **Castella Hotel.** Perched on the hill above picturesque Mikrolimano harbor, this is convenient if you have an early boat to catch. Rooms are fairly large; some have a sea view, as does the flower-filled roof garden, which looks out onto Mikrolimano and the yacht club. ✉ *Vasileos Pavlos 75, Castella, 18533,* ☎ *01/411–4735,* FAX *01/417–5716. 32 rooms. Restaurant, air-conditioning. AE, DC, MC, V.*

$ 🏨 **Aphrodite Hotel.** Halfway between Syntagma and Plaka, this perfectly comfortable hotel has quiet and tidy, if rather spare, rooms. With all the facilities of more costly hotels as well as a gracious, professional staff, it offers excellent value; about half the rooms have Acropolis views. ✉ *Apollonos 21, Syntagma, 10557,* ☎ *01/323–4357,* FAX *01/322–5244. 84 rooms. Air-conditioning. AE, DC, MC, V.*

$ ★ 🏨 **Art Gallery Pension.** On a peaceful side street not far from the Acropolis, this friendly place is prized by students and single travelers. The handsome house has an old-fashioned look, with family paintings on the muted white walls, comfortable beds, and ceiling fans. Many rooms have balconies with views of Filopappou or the Acropolis. ✉ *Erecthiou 5, Koukaki, 11742,* ☎ *01/923–8376, –1933,* FAX *01/923–3025. 19 rooms, 2 suites. No credit cards. Closed Nov.–Feb.*

$ 🏨 **Attalos Hotel.** The market area, where the Attalos is located, is full of life and color by day, but deserted at night. The hotel has a rooftop garden, and many rooms have fine views of the Acropolis or Lycabettus; about 12 include balconies. Try to get a room in the back, where street noise is less, though it's also reduced by double-glazed windows. ✉ *Athinas 29, Monastiraki, 10554,* ☎ *01/321–2801, –2802, –2803,* FAX *01/324–3124. 80 rooms. Air-conditioning. V.*

$ 🏨 **Marble House.** This friendly, popular pension, in a cul-de-sac about 15 minutes' walk from the Acropolis, has a steady clientele—even in winter, when it offers seasonally low monthly and weekly rates. Rooms are clean and quiet, with ceiling fans; at press time the owners were installing air-conditioning on the third floor. The courtyard is a lovely place to relax. Take Trolleys 1, 5, or 9 from Syntagma to the Zinni stop. ✉ *A. Zinni 35, Koukaki, 11741,* ☎ *01/923–4058 or 01/922–6461. 16 rooms, 11 with bath. No credit cards.*

Nightlife and the Arts

The Arts

The **Athens Festival** (box office, ✉ Arcade at Stadiou 4, ☎ 01/322–1459) runs from late June through September with concerts, opera, ballet, folk dancing, and drama. Performances are in various locations, including the theater of Herod Atticus (Irodion) below the Acropolis and Mt. Lycabettus. Tickets range in price from 4,000 dr. to 20,000 dr. and are available a few days before the performance.

Though rather corny, the **sound-and-light shows** (✉ Pnyx theater box office off Dionyssiou Areopagitou opposite Acropolis, ☎ 01/922–6210) beautifully display the Acropolis with dramatic lighting and a brief narrated history. Performances are given nightly from April through October, in English, at 9 PM, and admission is about 1,500 dr.

CONCERTS AND OPERAS

Greek and world-class international orchestras perform September through June at the **Megaron Athens Concert Hall** (✉ Vas. Sofias and Kokkali, ☎ 01/728–2333, FAX 01/728–2300). Information and tickets are available from the Megaron weekdays 10–4; prices range from 2,500 dr. to 20,000 dr. The Megaron also has a downtown box office (✉ Arcade at Stadiou 4).

DANCE

The lively **Dora Stratou Troupe** (✉ theater, Filopappou Hill, ☎ 01/921–4650; 01/324–4395 offices, FAX 01/324–6921; ⏲ performances mid-May–Sept., Tues.–Sun. 10:15 PM, also 8:15 PM Wed. and Sun.) performs Greek and Cypriot folk dances in authentic costumes. Tickets cost 3,000 dr. and are available from the box office before the show.

FILM

Almost all Athens cinemas now show foreign films; *The Athens News* and *Hellenic Times* list them in English. Tickets run about 1,800 dr.

Nightlife

Athens has an active nightlife: even at 3 AM the central squares and streets are crowded with revelers. In summer many downtown night spots move to the seaside. Ask your hotel for recommendations and check ahead for summer closings. For a uniquely Greek evening visit a club featuring *rembetika* music, a type of blues, or the popular *bouzoukia* (clubs with live bouzouki music). In the larger venues, where the food tends to be overpriced and second-rate, there is usually a per-person minimum or a prix-fixe menu; a bottle of whiskey costs about 29,000 dr.

BARS

Balthazar (✉ Tsoha 27, Ambelokipi, ☎ 01/644–1215 or 01/645–2278), in a neoclassical house, has a lush garden courtyard and subdued music. To enjoy Greek *kefi* (high spirits), visit the always-packed **Vareladiko** (✉ Distomou and E. Zanni 1, Piraeus, ☎ 01/422–7500) where you'll see some frenzied table dancing to Greek hits. Of the new bars for the under-40 crowd, **Kingsize** (✉ Amerikis 3, Syntagma, ☎ 01/323–2500) and **Plus Soda** (✉ Ermou 161, Thissio, ☎ 01/345–6187) are the most popular, playing techno, progressive, and house. With low-key music and a romantic park setting, **Parko** (✉ Eleftherias Park, Ilisia, ☎ 01/722–3784) is a summer favorite. **Folie** (✉ Eslin 4, Ambelokipi, ☎ 01/646–9852), has a friendly crowd of all ages dancing to jazz, blues, funk, and ethnic music. Ensconced in a 1940s arcade, **Stoa Cooper** (✉ Patission 101 and Kodrigtonos 19, ☎ 01/825–3932) lets you enjoy a quiet conversation in the glass-roofed hall or step into the fray of the split-level bar and dance to everything from rock to rembetika.

BOUZOUKIA

Diogenes Palace (✉ Syngrou 259, Nea Smyrni, ☎ 01/942–4267) is currently the "in" place with Athenians who want to hear Greece's singing stars, such as Antonis Vardis and Kaiti Garbi; it's also the most expensive. Decadence reigns at **Posidonio** (✉ Posidonios 18, Elliniko, ☎ 01/894–1033) as diners dance the seductive *tsifteteli* with enthusiasm.

LIVE ROCK, JAZZ, BLUES

Most big names in popular music perform at the informal **Rodon Live** (✉ Marni 24, Platia Vathis, ☎ 01/524–7427). Smaller groups play the sophisticated **Half Note** (✉ Trivonianou 17, Mets, ☎ 01/921–3310), the laid-back **Blues Hall** (✉ Ardittou 44, Mets, ☎ 01/924–7448), and the lively **Hi-Hat Cafe** (✉ Dragoumi and Krousovou 1, Hilton, ☎ 01/721–8171), which has hosted such artists as Guitar Shorty and Louisiana Red.

REMBETIKA CLUBS

Rembetika, the blues sung by Asia Minor refugees who came to Greece in the 1920s, still enthralls Greeks. At **Stathmos** (✉ Mavromateon 22, Pedion Areos, ☎ 01/883–2392), the band featuring the popular *rembetis* Bobis Goles usually starts off slowly, but by 1 AM is wailing to a packed dance floor. At **Stoa Athanaton** (✉ Sofokleous 19, Central Market, ☎ 01/321–4362 or 01/321–0342), in a renovated warehouse, the authentic music is enhanced by an infectious mood and the enthusiastic participation of the audience.

Shopping

Antiques

Pandrossou Street in Monastiraki is especially rich in shops selling small antiques and icons. Keep in mind that there are many fakes, and that you must have permission from the government to export objects from the Classic, Hellenistic, Roman, or Byzantine periods. Serious antiques collectors should head for **Martinos** (✉ Pandrossou 50, ☎ 01/321–2414). **Motakis** (✉ Abyssinia Sq. 3 in basement, ☎ 01/321–9005), run by members of the same family for more than 90 years, sells antiques and other beautiful old objects. At **Nasiotis** (✉ Ifestou 24, ☎ 01/321–2369) you may uncover interesting finds in a basement stacked with engravings, old magazines, and books, including first editions.

Flea Markets

The **Sunday morning flea market** (✉ Pandrossou and Ifestou Sts.) sells everything from secondhand guitars to Russian caviar. However little it costs, you should haggle. **Ifestou,** where coppersmiths have their shops, is interesting on weekdays; you can pick up copper wine jugs, candlesticks, and cookware for next to nothing.

Gift Ideas

Better tourist shops sell copies of traditional Greek jewelry; silver filigree; Skyrian pottery; onyx ashtrays and dishes; woven bags; attractive rugs, including flokatis; worry beads in amber or silver; and blue-and-white amulets to ward off the *mati* (evil eye). Reasonably priced natural sponges from Kalymnos also make good gifts. **George Goutis** (✉ Pandrossou 40, Monastiraki, ☎ 01/321–3212) has an eclectic assortment of costumes, embroidery, and old, handcrafted silver items. At **Riza** (✉ Voukourestiou 35 and Skoufa, Kolonaki, ☎ 01/361–1157) you can pick up wonderful handmade lace in romantic designs, unusual fabric at good prices, and such decorative items as handblown glass bowls. **Mati** (✉ Voukourestiou 20, Syntagma, ☎ 01/362–6238) has finely designed amulets to battle the evil eye, as well as a collection of monastery lamps and candlesticks. **Karamichos Mazaraki** (✉ Voulis 31–33, Syntagma, ☎ 01/323–9428) offers a large selection of flokatis that they will insure and ship to your home. **Pylarinos** (✉ Stadiou 6, Syntagma, ☎ 01/321–0384) carries Greek coins and stamps, as well as catalogs for collectors. For an inexpensive gift pick up some freshly ground Greek coffee at **Misseyiannis** (✉ Levendis 7, Kolonaki, ☎ 01/721–0136).

Handicrafts

The **National Welfare Organization** (✉ Vas. Sofias 135, across from Athens Tower, ☎ 01/646–0603; ✉ Ipatias 6 and Apollonos, Plaka, ☎ 01/321–8272) displays work by Greek craftspeople—stunning handwoven carpets, flat-weave kilims, tapestries from original designs, hand-embroidered tablecloths, ceramics, and flokatis. The **Center of Hellenic Tradition** (✉ Mitropoleos 59 or Pandrossou 36, Monastiraki, ☎ 01/321–3023) is another outlet for quality handicrafts. The Greek cooperative **EOMMEX** (✉ Mitropoleos 9, Syntagma, ☎ 01/323–0408) operates a showroom with folk and designer rugs made by more than 30 weavers around the country.

Jewelry

Prices for gold and silver are much lower in Greece than in many Western countries, and jewelry is of high quality. Many shops in Plaka carry original-design pieces available at a good price if you bargain hard enough. The more expensive **LALAoUNIS** (✉ Panepistimiou 6, Syntagma, ☎ 01/362–4354) showcases pieces by the world-famous Ilias Lalaounis, who takes his ideas from nature, biology, and ancient Greek pieces. **Zolotas** (✉ Pandronou 8, Plaka, ☎ 01/323–2413; ✉ Stadiou 9, Syntagma, ☎ 01/322–1222) is noted for its superb museum copies. The **Benaki Museum gift shop** (✉ Koumbari and Vas. Sofias, Kolonaki, ☎ 01/362–7367) has finely rendered copies of classical jewelry. The **Goulandris Cycladic Museum** (✉ Neofitou Douka 4, Kolonaki, ☎ 01/724–9706) carries good jewelry reproductions.

Side Trips

Mikrolimano

The pretty, crescent-shape harbor of Mikrolimano is famous for its many seafood restaurants. Although it has become increasingly touristy, its delightful atmosphere remains intact, and the harbor is crowded with elegant yachts. If you don't like seafood, you'll still be enchanted by the terraces of lovely houses tucked up against the hillsides. Take the Metro from Monastiraki Square to the Neo Faliron train station; it's only five minutes' walk from there.

Moni Kaisarini

★ Outside central Athens, on the slopes of Mt. Ymittos (ancient Mt. Hymettus), stands Moni Kaisarini (Kaisarini Monastery), one of the city's most evocative Byzantine remains. The well-restored 11th-century monastery, built on the site of a sanctuary of Aphrodite, has some beautiful frescoes dating from the 17th century. Nearby is a basilica and a picnic site with a superb panorama of the Acropolis and Piraeus. Take a taxi or bus 224 (in front of the Byzantine museum) to the end of the line, then walk 35 minutes along the paved road that climbs Mt. Ymittos. ✉ *Ethnikis Antistaseos,* ☎ *01/723–6619.* ⏲ *Monastery, Tues.–Sun. 8:30–2:45; grounds, daily sunrise–sunset.*

Athens Essentials

Arriving and Departing

BY BOAT

Most ships from the Greek islands dock at Piraeus (port authority ☎ 01/422–6000, 51–1311), 10 km (6 mi) from the center. From the main harbor you can take the nearby Metro right into Omonia Square. The trip takes 25 minutes and costs 150 dr. Alternatively, you can take a taxi, which takes longer because of traffic and costs around 1,700 dr. Often the driver will wait until he fills the taxi with several passengers headed in the same direction. It's faster to walk to the main street and hail a cab from there. If you arrive by hydrofoil in the smaller port of

Zea Marina, take Bus 905 or Trolley 20 to the Metro. At Rafina port (☎ 0294/22–300), which serves some of the closer Cyclades, you will have difficulty finding a taxi. Take a KTEL bus instead (slightly uphill from the port); they leave every 30 minutes from 5:40 AM until 9:30 PM, 460 dr.

BY BUS

Greek buses arrive either at Terminal A (✉ Kifissou 100, ☎ 01/512–4910) or Terminal B (✉ Liossion 260, you must call each regional counter for information; EOT provides a phone list ☞ Visitor Information, *below*). From Terminal A, take Bus 051 to Omonia Square; from Terminal B, take Bus 24 downtown. To get to the stations, catch Bus 051 at Zinonos and Menandrou off Omonia Square and Bus 024 on Amalias Avenue in front of the National Gardens. International buses drop their passengers off on the street, usually in the Omonia or Syntagma Square areas or at Stathmos Peloponnisos.

BY CAR

Whether you approach Athens from the Peloponnese or from the north, you enter by the Ethniki Odos (or National Road, as the main highways going north and south are known) and then follow signs for the center. Leaving Athens, routes to the National Road are well marked; signs usually name Lamia for the north and Corinth or Patras for the southwest.

BY PLANE

All travel visitors arrive by air at **Ellinikon Airport** (✉ Vas. Georgiou B' 1, ☎ 01/936–3363 for West Terminal, ☎ 01/969–4466 for East Terminal). The airport lies about 10 km (6 mi) from the city center. Olympic Airways flights, international and domestic, use the West Terminal, and all other flights arrive and depart from the East Terminal.

Between the Airport and Downtown. A **bus** service connects the two air terminals, Syntagma Square, Omonia Square, and Piraeus. Between the terminals and Athens, the express bus (No. 091) runs around the clock, about every 30 minutes during the day, hourly at night. You can catch the bus on Syntagma Square in front of McDonalds or off Omonia Square on Stadiou and Aeolou. From the airport terminals to Piraeus (Karaiskaki Sq.), the express bus (No. 019) leaves about every hour, day and night. The fare is 200 dr., 400 dr. after midnight (check with EOT, ☞ *below,* for night schedules). It's easier to take **taxis**: about 2,000 dr. to Piraeus; 1,000 dr. between terminals; 2,200 dr. to the center, more if there is traffic. The price goes up by about two thirds between midnight and 5 AM.

BY TRAIN

Athens has two railway stations, side by side, not far from Omonia Square. International trains from the north use **Stathmos Larissis** (☎ 01/823–7741). Take Trolley 1 from the terminal to Omonia Square. Trains from the Peloponnese use the marvelously ornate **Stathmos Peloponnisos** (☎ 01/513–1601). To Omonia and Syntagma squares take Bus 057. As the phones are almost always busy, it's easier to get departure times from the main information phone service (☞ By Train *in* Transportation, *above*) or buy tickets at a **railway office** downtown. ✉ *Sina 6,* ☎ *01/362–4402, –4403, –4404, –4405, –4406;* ✉ *Filellinon 17,* ☎ *01/323–6747, –6273; or* ✉ *Karolou 1,* ☎ *01/522–4302 for the Peloponnese, 01/522–2491 for northern Greece.*

Getting Around

Many of the sights and most of the hotels, cafés, and restaurants are within a fairly small central area. It's easy to walk everywhere, though sidewalks are often obstructed by cars parked by desperately frustrated drivers.

BY BUS

EOT (☞ Visitor Information, *below*) can provide bus information, as can the Organization for Public Transportation (✉ Metsovou 15, ☎ 01/883–6076, ⊙ weekdays 7:30–3, and Metsovou 185, ⊙ weekdays 7:30–3 and 7 PM–9 PM). The fare on buses and trolleys is 100 dr., and monthly passes are sold at the beginning of each month for 6,000 dr. (bus and trolley). Purchase tickets beforehand at curbside kiosks or from booths at terminals. Validate your ticket in the orange machines when you board to avoid a fine. Buses run from the center to all suburbs and nearby beaches from 5 AM until about midnight. For suburbs beyond central Kifissia, change at Kifissia. Most buses to the east Attica coast, including those for Sounion (☎ 01/823–0179; 1,150 dr. inland route, 1,200 dr. on coastal road) and Marathon (☎ 01/821–0872; 700 dr.), leave from the KTEL terminal (✉ Platia Aigyptiou, corner Mavromateon St. and Alexandras Ave.).

BY METRO

An electric (partially underground) railway runs from Piraeus to Omonia Square and then on to Kifissia, with downtown stops at Thission, Monastiraki, Omonia, and Platia Victorias (near the National Archaeological Museum). The standard fare is 100 dr. or 150 dr., depending on the number of zones traveled. You can buy a monthly pass covering the Metro, buses, and trolleys for 8,000 dr. at the beginning of each month. Validate your ticket by stamping it in the orange machines at the entrance to the platforms, or you will be fined.

BY TAXI

Although you will eventually find an empty taxi, it's often faster to call out your destination to one already carrying passengers; if the taxi is going in that direction, the driver will pick you up. Most drivers speak basic English. The meter starts at 200 dr., and even if you join other passengers, you must add this amount to your final charge. There is a basic charge of 66 dr. per km (½ mi); this increases to 130 dr. between midnight and 5 AM. There are surcharges for holidays (100 dr.), pickups from, not to, the airport (300 dr.) and from the port, train stations, and bus terminals (160 dr.) There is also a 55 dr. charge for each suitcase over 10 kilograms (22 pounds). Waiting time is 2,200 dr. per hour. Some drivers overcharge foreigners; make sure they turn on the meter and use the high tariff ("Tarifa 2") only after midnight. You can also call a radio taxi, which charges an additional 400 dr. for the pickup. Some reliable services are Kosmos (☎ 1300), Ermis (☎ 01/411–5200 and 01/411–5660), and Parthenon (☎ 01/581–4711 and 01/582–1292).

Contacts and Resources

EMBASSIES

United States (✉ Vasilissis Sofias 91, ☎ 01/721–2951).

Canadian (✉ Gennadiou 4, ☎ 01/725–4011). **United Kingdom** (✉ Ploutarchou 1, ☎ 01/723–6211).

EMERGENCIES

Police: Tourist police (✉ Dimitrakopoulou 77, Koukaki, ☎ 171); for auto accidents call city police (☎ 100). **Fire** (☎ 199). **Ambulance** (☎ 166, but a taxi is often faster). Not all hospitals are open nightly (☎ 106 for a Greek listing); ask your hotel to check for you. **Doctor:** Most hotels will call one for you; or contact your embassy. A Greek recording (☎ 105) lists doctors available 2 PM–7 AM, Sunday, and holidays. **Dentist:** Ask your hotel or embassy. **Pharmacy:** Many pharmacies in the central area have someone who speaks English. Try **Mantika** (✉ Stadiou 41 between Omonia and Syntagma, ☎ 01/331–2060, –2061). For information on late-night pharmacies dial 107 (Greek) or check the *Athens News*.

ENGLISH-LANGUAGE BOOKSTORES

Booknest (✉ Folia tou Bibliou, Panepistimiou 25–29, ☎ 01/322–9560). **Compendium** (✉ Nikis 28, upstairs, ☎ 01/322–1248). **Eleftheroudakis** (✉ Nikis 4, near Syntagma, ☎ 01/322–9388; and their main store at ✉ Panepistimiou 17, ☎ 01/331–4180). **Pantelides** (✉ Amerikis 9–11, ☎ 01/362–3673).

GUIDED TOURS

Excursions. The choice is almost unlimited. A one-day tour to Delphi will cost 19,500 dr., with lunch included, 17,000 without lunch; a two-day tour to Mycenae, Nauplion, and Epidaurus, around 30,400 dr., including half board in first-class hotels; and a full-day cruise from Piraeus, visiting the islands of Aegina, Poros, and Hydra costs around 18,000 dr., including buffet lunch on the ship (☞ Guided Tours *in* Mainland Greece, *below*).

Orientation. All tour operators offer a four-hour morning bus tour of Athens, including a guided tour of the Acropolis and its museum (9,300 dr.). Make reservations at your hotel or at a travel agency; many are situated around Filellinon and Nikis streets off Syntagma Square.

Personal Guides. All the major tourist agencies can provide English-speaking guides for personally organized tours, or call the **Union of Guides** (✉ Apollonas 9A, ☎ 01/322–9705, FAX 01/323–9200). Hire only those licensed by the EOT.

Special-Interest. For folk dancing take a four-hour evening tour (April–October; 9,000 dr.) that begins with a sound-and-light show of the Acropolis and then goes on to a performance of Greek folk dances in the open-air theater nearby. Another tour offers a dinner show at a taverna in the Plaka area, after the sound and light, for around 12,500 dr. Any travel agency can arrange these tours—and the excursions below—for you, but for the most efficient service, go first to **CHAT Tours**(☞ Travel Agencies, *below*). For those who want organized adventure travel, contact **Trekking Hellas** and **F-Zein**(☞ Travel Agencies, *below*).

Travel Agencies

American Express (✉ Ermou 2, ☎ 01/324–4975, FAX 01/322–7893). **CHAT Tours** (✉ Stadiou 4, ☎ 01/322–2886, FAX 01/323–5270). **Condor Travel** (✉ Stadiou 43, ☎ 01/321–2453 or 01/321–6986, FAX 01/321–4296). **Key Tours** (✉ Kallirois 4, ☎ 01/923–3166, FAX 01/923–2008). **Travel Plan** (✉ Christou Lada 9, ☎ 01/323–8801, FAX 01/322–2152). **Trekking Hellas** (✉ Fillelinon 7, 3rd floor, ☎ 01/331–0323, FAX 01/323–4548; offices also in Thessaloniki and Kalambaka). **F-Zein** (✉ Syngrou 132, 5th floor, ☎ 01/921–6285, FAX 01/922–9995.

Visitor Information

EOT (✉ Amerikis 2, near Syntagma, ☎ 01/331–0561; ✉ East Terminal—Arrivals—of Ellinikon Airport, ☎ 01/961–2722 and 01/969–4500; ✉ Piraeus, EOT Building, 1st floor, Zea Marina, ☎ 01/452–2591).

THE NORTHERN PELOPONNESE

Suspended from the mainland of Greece like a large leaf, the ancient land of Pelops offers beautiful scenery—rocky coasts, sandy beaches, mountains—and a fascinating variety of ruins: temples, theaters, mosques, churches, palaces, and medieval castles built by crusaders. Legend and history meet a few miles south of the isthmus of Corinth, in Mycenae, where Agamemnon, Elektra, and Orestes played out their grim family tragedy. This city dominated the entire area from the 18th through the 12th centuries BC and may even have conquered Minoan

Crete. According to Greek mythology, Paris, son of the king of Troy, in Asia Minor, abducted the beautiful Helen, wife of Menelaus, king of Sparta (Agamemnon, king of Mycenae, was Menelaus's brother). The abduction led to the Trojan War and the defeat of Troy—the story is told in Homer's *Iliad.* After Heinrich Schliemann's excavations in 1874 uncovered gold-filled graves and a royal palace, Mycenae became a world-famous archaeological site.

Begin your tour in Athens, heading west across the Corinth Canal (84 km/52 mi) to ancient Corinth. Head south to Mycenae (4 km/2½ mi off the road at Fichtion), and then turn off at Argos via Tiryns for Nauplion (63 km/39 mi from Corinth). The ancient theater of Epidauros is another 26 km (16 mi) west. From Epidauros you can return to Athens, joining the National Road at Corinth, or backtrack to Argos, where the road continues through the rugged mountains of Arcadia to ancient Olympia (191 km/118 mi from Argos). North of Olympia (122 km/76 mi) lies Patras, from where you can catch a ferry to Italy or return to Athens on the National Road, an exceptionally beautiful drive along the sea. If you want to go on to Delphi (☞ Mainland Greece, *below*), cross the gulf at Rion-Antirion en route.

Exploring the Northern Peloponnese

Corinth

★ When you cross the **Gefira Isthmou** or **Isthmos** (Corinth Canal), you will have entered the Peloponnese. The ancients once winched their ships across a paved slipway nearby, then talked for centuries about carving a canal through the limestone. The modern thruway was completed in 1893; you can watch the ships go by from the narrow bridge, 60 m (197 ft) above the water.

At the site of **Archaia Korinthos** (Ancient Corinth), you'll see remains of the Doric **Naos Apollonos** (Temple of Apollo), built during the 6th century BC and one of the few buildings that still stood when Julius Caesar decided to restore Corinth. In AD 51 St. Paul fulminated against the sacred prostitutes who served Aphrodite on the Acrocorinth, the peak behind the ancient city. A **museum** beside the ruins contains finds from the excavations. ☒ *13 km (8 mi) west of Corinth,* ☎ *0741/31–207.* ⏲ *Daily 8–5.*

Looming over ancient Corinth, the limestone **Acrocorinthos** (Acrocorinth) was one of the best naturally fortified citadels in Europe, where citizens retreated in times of invasions and earthquakes. Built on ancient foundations, the remains indicate the many additions made by Romans, Franks, Venetians, and Turks. *Take a taxi from ancient Corinth (about 1,300 dr.) or follow the signs by car.* ☎ *0741/31–443.* 🎫 *Free.* ⏲ *Daily 8:30–7 (8:30–5 in winter).*

Mycenae

★ When Ancient Mykines (Mycenae) was the fabulous stronghold of the Achaean kings of the 13th century BC. Destroyed in 468 BC, it was forgotten until 1874 when German archaeologist Heinrich Schliemann, who had discovered the ruins of ancient Troy, uncovered the remains of this fortress city. Mycenae was the seat of the doomed House of Atreus—of King Agamemnon and his wife, Clytemnestra (sister of Helen of Troy), and of their ill-fated children, Orestes and Elektra. When Schliemann uncovered six shaft graves (so named because the kings were buried standing up) of the royal circle, he was certain that one was the tomb of Agamemnon. The gold masks and diadems, daggers, jewelry, and other treasures found in the graves are now in the National Archaeological Museum in Athens; the new local museum is dedicated to ar-

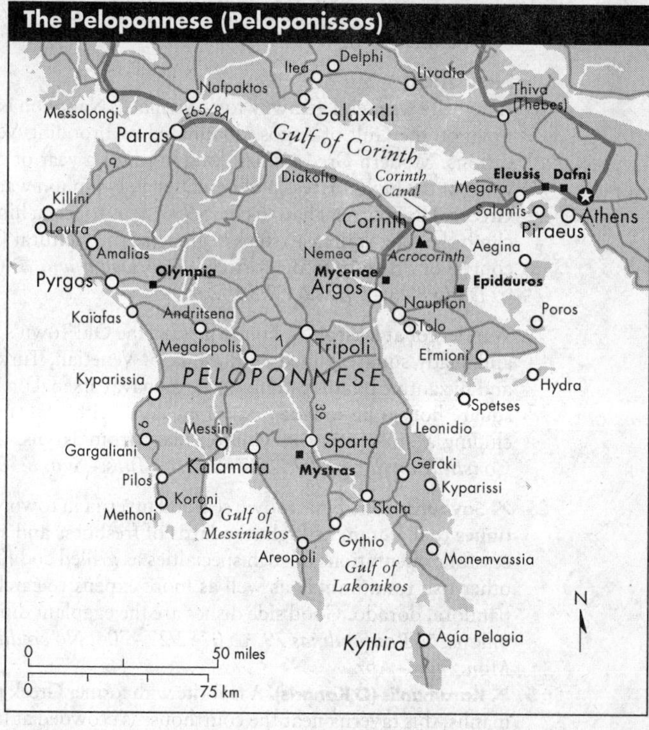

chaeological studies. You'll also see the monumental **Pili ton Leonton (Lion Gate)**, dating from 1250 BC, the castle ruins crowning the bleak hill, and the astounding beehive tomb **Thisavros tou Atrea** (Treasury of Atreus), built into the hillside outside the massive fortification walls, all remnants of the first great civilization in continental Europe. ☎ *0751/76–585.* ⏲ *Weekdays 8–7 (winter 8–5).*

Argos

One of the oldest continuously inhabited towns in Greece and prominent during the 8th century BC, Argos is unremarkable except for its grand central square and the **archaeological museum,** which includes Neolithic pottery, Roman objects, and finds from the Mycenaean tombs. ✉ *Off Platia Argos on Vas. Olgas,* ☎ *0751/68–819.* ⏲ *Tues.–Sun. 8:30–2:45.*

$ ✕ **I Spilia.** This countryside taverna is known for its specialty, *bogana,* baby lamb slow-cooked in a wood-burning oven that is sealed airtight with mud, giving the meat a wonderful smoky flavor. (Call ahead to make sure the chef saves you some.) He makes over 30 local specialties, including artichoke salad and succulent baby or goat livers basted with lemon-olive oil sauce. ✉ *Tripoleos 165, 3 km (2 mi) from Argos on old national road to Tripolis,* ☎ *0751/62–300; 0751/29–913 before 5 PM. No credit cards. No lunch Sun.*

Tiryns

Homer described Tirintha (Tiryns) as "the wall-girt city" for its Cyclopean ramparts, built of gigantic limestone blocks (the largest weighs 15 tons), which ancients thought could be handled only by giants. One version of the legend claims Tiryns was the birthplace of Hercules. The remains, including the walls, date mostly from the 13th century BC, when Tiryns was one of the most important Mycenaean cities. ✉ *On a low hill, just past the suburbs of Nauplion,* ☎ *0752/22–657.* ⏲ *Weekdays 8–7 (winter 8–5).*

Nauplion

★ A favorite weekend getaway for Athenians, Nauplion is a picturesque town on the Gulf of Argos, dominated by brooding Venetian fortifications. Modern Greece's first king lived for a year or two within the walls of the high fortress, **Palamidi,** when Nauplion was the capital of Greece. His courtiers had to climb 999 steps to reach him; you can still climb the long staircase (steps begin near the Cultural Center and the courts) or drive up to the fortress. ✉ *Above town,* ☎ *0752/28–036.* ⏲ *Daily 8–6:45 (winter 8:30–2:45).*

Wander for at least a few hours through the Old Town's narrow streets and shady squares, lined with a mix of Venetian, Turkish, Frankish, and Byzantine buildings. The Venetian naval arsenal on the main town square houses an **archaeological museum** with Mycenaean finds, including a 7th-century BC Gorgon mask from Tiryns. ✉ *East side of Constitution Sq.,* ☎ *0752/27–502.* ⏲ *Tues.–Sun. 8:30–3.*

$$ ✕ **Savouras.** The best-known seafood taverna in town, Savouras continues to maintain its high standards of freshness and simple but successful presentations of such specialties as grilled cod (usually fried at other fish restaurants), as well as more expensive catch—red mullet, pandora, dorado. Good side dishes are the eggplant dip and fava with onions. ✉ *Bouboulinas 79,* ☎ *0752/27–704. No credit cards. Closed Mon. Nov.–Apr.*

$ ✕ **Karamanlis (O Kanaris).** A favorite with former Greek president Karamanlis, this taverna near the courthouse is crowded at lunch with civil servants who come for its tasty magirefta. The fish soup makes a good appetizer, as do the melt-in-your-mouth *gigantes yiachni* (giant beans with fresh tomato), followed by savory beef yiouvetsi, stuffed squash, and oven-roasted potatoes. Fresh fish is also available. ✉ *Bouboulinas 1,* ☎ *0752/27–668. No credit cards. Closed Easter and elections.*

$ ✕ **Omorfo Tavernaki.** Snug and inviting, this mezedopolion serves up such appetizers as *tiroboukies* (cheese "bites") and croquettes made from wild greens, as well as some unusual dishes, such as Constantinople (politiko) souvlaki, marinated in yogurt and garlic, and a dish named after a hero from the Revolution, Kolokotronaiko pork, which is pan-fried with rosemary, garlic, and onion and extinguished with local wine. ✉ *Vas. Olgas and Kotsonopoulou 1,* ☎ *0752/25–944, Reservations essential weekends. No credit cards. No lunch.*

$$$$ ★ 🏨 **Candia House.** This beautifully decorated hotel 17 km (10½ mi) south of Nauplion on Candia Beach weds good taste with comfort. Fresh flowers, antiques, paintings by Greek artists, and handcrafted mirrors are just some of the special touches. All suites have balconies; four include fireplaces. Other facilities include massage in summer, a playroom with board games, and a gym. ✉ *Candia-Irion, 21100,* ☎ *0752/94–060,* FAX *0752/94–480; off-season,* ☎ *01/347–1503 and 094/841–864,* FAX *01/347–4732. 10 suites. Restaurant, pool. AE, DC, MC, V. Closed Nov.–Mar. except Christmas week.*

$$$ 🏨 **Amalia.** The Amalia occupies a fine neoclassical building in large gardens 3 km (2 mi) outside town, on the sea, on the way to ancient Tiryns. The public rooms are spacious and comfortable, and service is attentive. The beach is nearby. A buffet breakfast is included. ✉ *National Rd. to Argos outside Nauplion, 21100,* ☎ *0752/24–401,* FAX *0752/24–400; reservations,* ☎ *01/323–7301,* FAX *01/323–8792. 174 rooms and 1 suite. 2 restaurants, pool. AE, DC, MC, V.*

$–$$ 🏨 **Byron.** This lovely hotel in the old town is in a rose-and-blue 18th-century house. Rooms include minibars, hair dryers, and optional TV

(1,500 dr. daily). The owners have now added another building (yellow with green shutters), with four rooms that have Jugendstil furniture, TV, and air-conditioning. Guests eat breakfast on a terrace overlooking the town and the gulf. ✉ *Platonos 2, Platia Agios Spiridonos, 21100,* ☎ *0752/22–351,* ☎ FAX *0752/26–338. 18 rooms. Air-conditioning. AE, MC, V. Closed 3 wks in Nov.*

$ **Dioscouri.** With a fine view across the gulf of Nauplion and to the fort from its hillside location, this family-run hotel is cool and quiet, the best choice for a stay in the Old Town at the lowest prices. Continental breakfast is included. ✉ *Zigomala-Byronas 6, 21100,* ☎ *0752/28–550,* FAX *0752/21–202. 51 rooms. Restaurant. V.*

Epidauros

Epidauros was the sanctuary of Asklepios, the Greek god of healing. You can visit the foundations of the temples and ancient hospital, but ★ the site you must not miss is the ancient **open-air theater,** which seats 14,000. In summer, during the Festival of Ancient Drama, plays are staged here (☞ Nightlife and the Arts, *below*), but it merits a visit at any time of year. The acoustics are so good that you can sit in the top row and hear a whisper on stage. ☎ *0753/22–009.* ⏲ *Theater, daily 8–6 (8–5 in winter); museum, Tues.–Sun. 8–6 (8–5 in winter), Mon. noon–6, (noon–5 in winter).*

Olympia

★ The site of **Archaia Olympia** (Ancient Olympia) lies a few miles from the sea, northwest of Megalopolis, where a huge assembly hall was built to hold the 10,000 representatives of the Arcadian League. The Olympic Games were first held in 776 BC and continued to be celebrated every four years until AD 393, when the Roman emperor Theodosius I, with his Christian sensibility, banned these "pagan rites." Women were excluded from watching the games under penalty of death, although no one was ever executed; women's games were held a few weeks earlier. Archaeologists still uncover statues and votive offerings among the pine trees surrounding the **stadium,** the imposing ruins of the **Naos Dios** (Temple of Zeus), and the **Heraion** (Temple of Hera) within the sacred precinct. *Stadium/site:* ☎ *0624/22–517, museum:* ☎ *0624/22–742.* ⏲ *Site: weekdays 8–7 (8–5 in winter), weekends 8–3; museum: Mon. noon–7 (noon–5 in winter), Tues.–Fri. 8–7 (8–5 in winter), weekends 8–3.*

$$ ★ ✕ **O Kladeos.** Named for the river it borders, this *koutouki* (what the Greeks call a tiny eatery) is big with locals. Sit near the fireplace in winter, in the shade of the plane tree in summer. The food is simple but classic Greek: codfish with garlic dip, fried squid, lamb in oil-oregano sauce, and *patsa,* a tripe soup said to cure all ills. ✉ *Ancient Olympia beside river,* ☎ *0624/23–322. No credit cards. Closed Nov.–Feb. No lunch.*

$$ ✕ **Thraka.** This family-run taverna has a large variety of home-cooked food including *lahanodolmades* (cabbage leaves stuffed with minced meat), pastitsio, and beef stifado made with vinegar and garlic. The two kinds of baklava are from the family's pastry shop. ✉ *Vasiliou Bakopanou and Praxitelis Kondili,* ☎ *0624/22–575, 0624/22–475 off-season. AE, MC, V. Closed Nov.–Mar. (meals by special arrangement).*

$ ✕ **Bacchus.** If you're at the ancient site and want to break for lunch, follow signs to the nearby village of Miraka. You can try such hearty dishes as rooster with handmade noodles called *hilopites* (order one day before), charcoal-broiled chicken, goat in oregano sauce, and spit-roasted meats on weekends. ✉ *Miraka, 3 km (2 mi) outside Olympia, turnoff on Tripolis Rd.,* ☎ *0624/22–498. V. Closed Dec.–Mar.*

$$ **Hotel Europa.** Run by the gracious Spiliopoulos family, this Best Western hilltop hotel overlooks ancient Olympia, the mountains of Arcadia, Alfios Valley, and the distant sea. Rooms have flokati rugs, marble bathrooms, hair dryers, and TVs; most face the pool. ✉ *Off road to ancient Olympia, at Oikismou Drouba, 27065,* ☎ *0624/22–650,* FAX *0624/23–166. 42 rooms. Restaurant, pool . AE, DC, MC, V.*

$$ **Olympic Village.** Recently renovated and popular with groups, the hotel has simple rooms with views of the countryside, all new beds, wooden furniture, and comfortable public spaces. American breakfast is included. ✉ *On Pyrgos-Olympia road (about 300 yds from site), 27065,* ☎ *0624/22–211,* FAX *0624/22–812. 51 rooms. Restaurant, air-conditioning, pool. AE, V. Closed Nov.–Feb.*

$ **Pelops.** The Australian owner, who asserts that "from the moment he walks in, the client is the boss," has taken a standard '60s Greek hotel, situated across from the main church, and decorated each room differently, with knickknacks, chintz, and lace curtains, producing an old-fashioned feel. Rooms have orthopedic mattresses and telephones; most have balconies. ✉ *Varela 2, 27065,* ☎ *0624/22–543,* FAX *0624/22–213. 25 rooms. Restaurant. MC, V. Closed Nov.–Feb.*

Patras

Patras, the third-largest city in Greece and its main western port, is the business hub of the Peloponnese. The city's prettiest features are its arcaded streets and its squares surrounded by neoclassical buildings. The Byzantine **Kastro** (fortress), built on the site of the ancient acropolis, affords a fine view along the coast. **Agiou Andrea** (Cathedral of St. Andrew; ✉ West side of harbor at end of Agiou Andreou St., ☎ 061/330–644, ⏲ daily 7:30 AM–8 PM), reputedly the largest in Greece and built on the site of the crucifixion of St. Andrew, is also worth exploring. Its treasure is the saint's silver-mounted skull, returned to Patras in 1964 after 500 years in St. Peter's Cathedral, Rome.

Seven kilometers (4 mi) outside Patras is the **Achaia Clauss Winery,** founded in the mid-1800s by Baron von Klauss. You can take a tour and sample the area's famous *mavrodafni* (Black Daphne) wine, a heady dessert wine named after the Baron's love, who died prematurely. ✉ *Achaia; take Bus 7 from Kanakari St., get off at Kato Filagio stop and walk 900 yds, or taxi (about 1,100 dr.);* ☎ *061/325–051.* 🎟 *Free.* ⏲ *Daily 9–5.*

$$ ★ **Ditis.** When the diver-owner closes up shop in summer to indulge his love of the sea, locals mourn the loss of his cooking. The humble decor of his fish taverna belies the masterful seafood he prepares. Besides such occasional oddities as eel and limpets, the fresh local fish includes sargus, pandora, and gildhead, depending on the season, and all delectable. ✉ *Norman and Gambetta 44,* ☎ *061/432–554. No credit cards. Closed Sun. and July–Aug.*

$$ **Majestic.** Diners choose from an eclectic mix of Greek, French, and Italian dishes at this restaurant on one of Patras's main squares. Fresh seafood, such as dorado and swordfish, top the list, while other reliables include pork chops simmered in wine, rooster baked with noodles, and octopus marinated in vinaigrette. ✉ *Agiou Nikolaou 2, Platia Trion Simmachon,* ☎ *061/222–792. AE, DC, MC, V.*

$$ ★ **Petrino.** Wood, stone, and a live palm tree dominate this restaurant, which has finally brought creative Mediterranean cuisine to Patras. Try the chicken Narcissus, which is stuffed with shrimp wrapped in a spinach leaf and sprinkled with poppy seeds. In summer the restaurant moves to the Mosaitika area on nearby Rio beach. ✉ *Agiou Nikolaou 17,* ☎ *061/620–255. DC, V.*

$ ✕ **Lavyrinthos.** This classic taverna with wine barrels, old lamp fixtures, and a cozy loft, serves reliable, such traditional Greek dishes as rabbit in lemon and pungent homemade potato salad. After your meal be sure to try a shot of *detoura,* a local liqueur similar to cognac and flavored with cinnamon and clove. ✉ *Poukevil 44 near Platia Vas. Olgas,* ☎ *061/226–436. No credit cards.*

$$$ **Astir.** This large, pleasant hotel enjoys an excellent location on the waterfront near the center of town and has such amenities as a bar, a roof garden, and a sauna. ✉ *Ag. Andreou 16, 26223,* ☎ *061/277–502,* FAX *061/271–644. 120 rooms. 2 restaurants, pool. AE, DC, MC, V.*

$$$ ★ **Porto Rio Hotel and Casino.** Play a set of tennis or a round of beach volleyball, go for an afternoon dip, then head for the casino at this beachside hotel complex at Rion, about 8 km (5 mi) from Patras. There's a varied selection of rooms and bungalows; most rooms have outstanding views. ✉ *Rio-Patroon National Rd., 26500,* ☎ *061/992–212,* FAX *061/992–115. 235 rooms, 13 suites, 48 bungalows. Restaurant, pool. AE, DC, MC, V.*

$$ **Rannia.** Another recently renovated, reasonably priced hotel, the Rannia has a great location on Queen Olga Square, the loveliest plaza in Patras. It's also just two blocks from the waterfront and within walking distance of the bus and train stations. The clean, quiet rooms all have balconies and TVs. ✉ *Riga Fereou 53, Platia Vas. Olgas, 26221,* ☎ *061/220–114,* ☎ FAX *061/220–537. 30 rooms. Air-conditioning. V.*

Nightlife and the Arts

The **Festival of Ancient Drama** in the theater at Epidauros takes place from mid-July to mid-September; a smaller theater nearby simultaneously hosts **concerts and dance performances**; it's known as the Micro Theatro (Little Theater) of ancient Epidauros. Tickets can be bought at both theaters before performances (☎ 0753/22–006 for box office) or in advance from the festival box office in Athens (✉ Stadiou 4, ☎ 01/322–1459). Recently a new venue modeled on an ancient theater but with state-of-the-art lighting and sound opened less than a kilometer (½ mi) from the Olympia sanctuary; it hosts the summer **Festival Olympias,** featuring an eclectic mix of performances ranging from Paco Pena to the White Oak Dance Project. Ticket booths are located throughout the region or call the Floca community offices (☎ 0624/22–751). Patras also stages a **summer arts festival** July through August. Check with the Patras International Festival office (✉ Koryllon 2, Old Municipal Hospital, Old Town, ☎ 061/279–008) for details. A few weeks before Greek Orthodox Lent, Patras holds **Carnival** celebrations, including Sunday's Grand Parade, with entrants competing for the best costume. Buy tickets for Grand Parade seats (3,000 dr. and 5,000 dr.) at the kiosk in Vas. Georgiou Square or at the Carnival office in the Municipal Cultural Center (✉ Koryllon 2, Old Municipal Hospital, Old Town, ☎ 061/226–063).

Northern Peloponnese Essentials

Getting Around

BY BOAT

In summer hydrofoils leave Zea Marina in Athens for Nauplion.

BY BUS

The regional bus associations (KTEL) run frequent service from Athens to Nauplion (where you change for Mycenae), Epidauros, Corinth, Patras, and Olympia.

BY CAR

The roads are fairly good, and driving can be the most enjoyable (if not economical) way to see the area.

BY TRAIN

You can take a train from Athens to Corinth, where the route splits, heading either south to Argos, Mycenae, and Nauplion, or west along the coast to Patras, and then south to Pyrgos and the branch line to Olympia. If you will be returning to Athens, buy a round-trip ticket; there is a substantial discount.

Guided Tours

Available tours include one-day (with lunch, 19,500 dr.) or two-day (30,400 dr.) trips to Mycenae, Nauplion, and Epidauros; four-day trips to those sites, as well as Olympia and Delphi (97,000 dr.); and a six-day excursion to all major sites in the Peloponnese, including Astros, Sparta, and the Diros caves (155,000 dr.). **CHAT Tours** (✉ 4 Stadiou, Athens, ☎ 01/322–2886, FAX 01/323–5270). **Key Tours** (✉ Kallirois 4, Athens, ☎ 01/923–3166, FAX 01/923–2008).

Visitor Information

Nauplion: tourist information (✉ 25th Martiou across from OTE, ☎ 0752/24–444); tourist police, ✉ P. Koundourioti 14, ☎ 0752/28–131). **Olympia:** municipal tourist information office (✉ Kondili 75, ☎ 0624/23–100); tourist police (✉ Spiliopoulou 5, ☎ 0624/22–550). **Patras:** EOT (✉ Filopimenos 26, ☎ 061/620–353); tourist police (✉ Norman-Iroon Politechniou—harbor welcome station—☎ 061/451–833); Olympic Airlines (✉ Aratou 17–19, Platia Vas. Olgas, ☎ 061/222–901); Automobile and Touring Club of Greece (✉ Patroon Athinon 18, ☎ 061/425–411).

MAINLAND GREECE

The dramatic rocky heights of mainland Greece provide an appropriate setting for humanity's attempt to approach divinity. The ancient Greeks placed their gods on snowcapped Mt. Olympus and chose the precipitous slopes of Parnassus, "the navel of the universe," as the site for Delphi, their most important religious center. Many centuries later, pious Christians built a great monastery (Hosios Loukas) in a remote mountain valley. Others settled on the rocky peninsula of Athos, the Holy Mountain. Later, devout men established themselves precariously on top of strange, towerlike rocks and, to be closer to God, built such monasteries as those at Meteora, which remain among the most spectacular sights in Greece.

En route to Delphi from Athens via the National Road, take the turnoff for the ancient city of Thiva (Thebes, 90 km/56 mi from Athens). After detouring to the monastery of Hosios Loukas (turn off at Distomo village, 20 km/12 mi from Livadia), continue to Delphi. The road climbs a spur of Mt. Parnassus, past Arahova, known for its handmade rugs of brightly colored wools. From there it's a short, spectacular drive through the Pleistos gorge to the ancient site (179 km/111 mi from Athens). After Delphi the road descends in sharp bends to lackluster Lamia (another 82 km/51 mi), then heads northwest to Kalambaka and Meteora (139 km/86 mi from Lamia).

Exploring Mainland Greece

Thiva

Thiva (Thebes), of which little remains, was the birthplace of legendary Oedipus, who unwittingly fulfilled the prophecy of the Delphic Oracle by slaying his father and marrying his mother.

Hosios Loukas

★ Nestled in a serene upland valley is **Moni Osiou Louka** (Monastery of Hosios Loukas), a fine example of Byzantine architecture and decoration. Built during the 11th century to replace the earlier shrine of a local saint, it has some of the world's finest Byzantine mosaics. ☏ *0267/22–797.* ⏲ *May–mid-Sept., daily 8–2 and 4–7; mid-Sept.–mid-Nov., and Mar.–Apr., daily 8–6; mid-Nov.–Feb., daily 8–5.*

Delphi

★ At the edge of Delphi loom the Phaedriades, twin cliffs split by the Castalian spring. It was here that pilgrims to the Delphic Oracle came for purification. To the ancient Greeks Delphi was the center of the universe, because two eagles released by the gods at opposite ends of earth met here. For hundreds of years the worship of Apollo and the pronouncements of the oracle made Delphi the most important religious center of ancient Greece. When first excavated in 1892, most of the ruins were found to date from the 5th through the 3rd centuries BC. As you walk up the **Iera Odos** (Sacred Way) to the **Naos Apollonos** (Temple of Apollo), the **theater,** and the **stadium,** you'll see Mt. Parnassus above; silver-green olive trees below; and, in the distance, the blue Gulf of Itea. East of the main site, about 150 m (500 ft) down the road, is the area with the temple of **Athena Pronaia,** from which many of the museum's best sculptures came; the **gymnasium;** and the **Tholos,** the rotunda so familiar from postcards, though archaeologists still haven't discovered its purpose. This is one of Greece's most striking sites; if you come here in the early morning or evening, avoiding the busloads of tourists, you will feel the power and beauty of the place. ☏ *0265/82–312.* ⏲ *Weekdays 7:30–7:30 (9–3:30 in winter), weekends 8:30–3.*

Don't miss the world-famous bronze charioteer (early 5th century BC) in the **Delphi Museum.** Other works of art here include a statue of Antinoüs, Emperor Hadrian's lover; fragments of a 6th-century BC silver-plated bull, the largest example of an ancient statue in precious metal, and the stone *omphalos,* representing the navel of the earth. Also note the statues of Kleobis and Viton, who, according to legend, pulled their mother across a vast expanse of countryside by chariot to the Temple of Hera, then died when the goddess rewarded them with eternal sleep. It was said of them, "Those whom the gods love die young." ☏ *0265/82–312.* ⏲ *Weekdays 7:30–7:30 (9–3:30 in winter), weekends 8:30–3.*

$$ ✕ **Iniochos.** This excellent restaurant offers many local specialties, with an emphasis on appetizers: zucchini croquettes, roast feta, bekri meze. In winter warm yourself at the fireplace; in summer dine on the veranda overlooking Delphi. ✉ *Vas. Pavlou and Friderikis 19,* ☏ *0265/82–710,* FAX *0265/82–764. Reservations essential. AE, DC, MC, V.*

$ ✕ **Sunflower.** You'll find the classic Greek dishes well prepared here and reasonably priced—dolmades, tzatziki, a rich bean soup called *fassolada*—but the restaurant is known for its savory *bourekakia,* pastries stuffed with cheese and minced meat. ✉ *Vas. Pavlou and Friderikis 33,* ☏ *0265/82–442. AE, V. Closed weekdays in Nov.*

$$ ✕🏨 **Kastalia.** Simple rooms with paintings of the area offer views over Mt. Parnassus or to the Gulf of Itea. The restaurant serves traditional Greek food, sometimes with a twist; lamb fricassee, for example, has lettuce rather than the typical cabbage. In a separate new wing called Villa Apollonia, more luxurious, larger rooms have air-conditioning and TVs. ✉ *Vas. Pavlou and Friderikis 13, 33054,* ☏ *0265/82–205; reservations: 0265/82–919,* FAX *0265/82–208; Villa Apollonia,* ☏ *0265/82–325,* FAX *0265/82–609. Kastalia, 26 rooms; Villa Apollonia, 12 rooms. Restaurant. AE, DC, MC, V.*

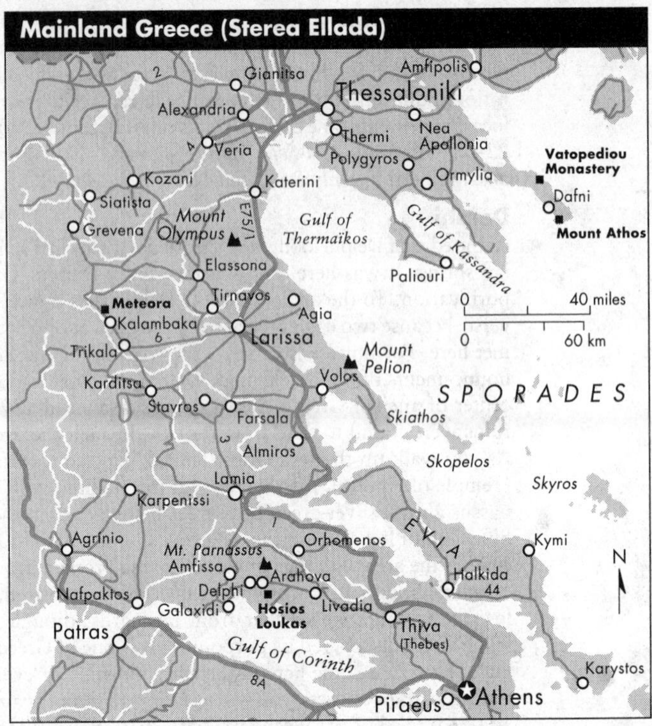

$$$ ★ 🏨 **Hotel Vouzas.** The hotel sits on the edge of a gorge and has wonderful views from every room; it is also the closest one (about 500 m/1,600 ft) to Delphi itself. A fantastic new veranda, where breakfast is served half the year overlooks the gorge, olive groves, and the Pleistos. The cozy living room with a fireplace fills up on winter weekends with Athenians who come to ski Mt. Parnassus. ✉ *Vas. Pavlou and Friderikis 1, 33054,* ☎ *0265/82–232,* FAX *0265/82–033. 58 rooms, 1 suite. Restaurant. MC, V.*

$$ 🏨 **Villa Filoxenia-Apollo.** Rustic, charming and lovingly decorated by the same people who own the Apollo hotel, Delphi's newest addition has such amenities as electronic keys and air-conditioning, a game area, and a lounge with fireplace, despite its price at the low end of its category. Rooms include TVs, minibars, and hair dryers; most have balconies and a view. Full breakfast is included. ✉ *Vas. Pavlou and Friderikis 15, 33054,* ☎ *0265/83–114,* FAX *0265/82–455. 14 rooms. Air-conditioning, games room. MC, V. Closed weekdays Jan.–mid-Mar.*

$ ★ 🏨 **Acropole.** This friendly, family-run hotel has a garden and a spectacular view—dramatic mountainside and a sea of olive groves—so that guests feel as though they're completely secluded. The rooms are freshly furnished with carved Skyrian furniture, traditional linens, and paintings, strangely enough, of the islands. Ten rooms have air-conditioning, all have satellite TV, direct-dial phones, and hair dryers. ✉ *Filellinon 13, 33054,* ☎ *0265/82–675,* FAX *0265/83–171. 42 rooms. AE, DC, MC, V.*

Meteora

Kalambaka serves as the base for visits to the monasteries of Meteora, which sit atop gigantic pinnacles that tower almost 1,000 ft above the plain. Monks and supplies once reached the top on ladders or in baskets; now steps are cut into the rocks, and some of the monasteries can easily be reached by car. Of the original 24 monasteries, only six can now be visited. Appropriate dress for women requires skirts to the knee (not shorts), and men should wear long pants. The fortresslike **Varlaam** monastery (☎ 0432/22–277; closed Fri., Thurs.–Fri. in winter) is easy to reach and has beautiful Byzantine frescoes. To get a better idea of what living in these monasteries was like 300 years ago, climb the steep rock steps to the **Megalo Meteoron** (☎ 0432/22–278; closed Tues., Tues.–Wed. in winter), the largest of them. Make sure that you allow time for the trek up if it's nearing midday or evening closing time. ⏲ *Daily 9–1 and 3:20–6 (3–5 in winter).*

In Kalambaka stop at the **Koimisis tis Theotokou** (Dormition of the Virgin), built during the first half of the 12th century by Emperor Manuel Comnenos, though some historians believe it was founded during the 7th century on the site of a temple of Apollo (classical drums and other fragments are incorporated into the walls). The latter theory explains the church's paleo-Christian features. The church also has vivid 16th-century frescoes. ✉ *North end of town, follow signs from Platia Riga Fereou,* ☎ *0432/24–962.* ⏲ *Daily 7 AM–10 AM and 3:30 PM–7 PM.*

$$ ★ ✕ **Restaurant Meteora.** A local favorite since 1925, this family restaurant on the upper square relies on the cooking of matriarch Ketty Gertzou, who prepares such dishes as tsoutsoukakia, lamb fricassee, stifado, *ladera* (vegetables cooked in olive oil), and chicken or pork in wine with green peppers and garlic. ✉ *Ekonomou 4, on Platia Dimarchiou,* ☎ *0432/22–316. No credit cards. Closed Nov.–Mar. No dinner.*

$–$$ ✕ **Ziogas.** The Kalambaka area is renowned for its meats, and here master-griller Grigoris chooses only the freshest local meats and barbecues them to perfection over burning wood—try the pork chops, the lamb ribs, or the succulent kokkoretsi. ✉ *On Patriarchou Dimitriou (the road from Kalambaka to Meteora), Kastraki,* ☎ *0432/22–286. No credit cards. Closed lunch Mon.–Sat. and Sun. dinner.*

$$$ 🏨 **Hotel Divani.** Popular with groups, Divani is close to Meteora and offers professional staff, large, comfortable public spaces, a pool surrounded by greenery, and rooms with subtle colors and new furnishings, half with views of the pinnacles. The receptionist can arrange for a taxi driver to take you to the various monasteries. ✉ *Trikalon 1, 42200,* ☎ *0432/22–583, 0432/22–330,* FAX *0432/23–638. 165 rooms. Restaurant, pool. AE, DC, MC, V.*

$$ 🏨 **Hotel Antoniadi.** This reliable hotel, priced at the low end of its category, has pastel-hued rooms with carpeting, minibars, color TVs, and hair dryers, and many have a view of the Meteora rocks. During the sweltering summers the hotel opens its rooftop pool. ✉ *Trikalon 148, 42200,* ☎ *0432/24–387,* FAX *0432/24–319, 23–419. 69 rooms. Restaurant, air-conditioning, pool. V.*

$ ★ 🏨 **Kastraki.** Open your window, step out on the balcony, and bid good morning to the massive rocks that seem to loom over this great little hotel, located in a village on the winding road from Kalambaka to Meteora. The area's best value in terms of the quality-price ratio, Kastraki is efficiently run by a pair of friendly and helpful brothers. ✉ *On Patriarchou Dimitriou, road between Kalambaka and Meteora, Kastraki, 42200,* ☎ *0432/75–336,* ☎ FAX *0432/75–335. 28 rooms. V.*

Mainland Greece Essentials

Getting Around

Although it's easiest to visit the region by **car,** there is very good **train** and **bus** service between the main towns, and between each town and Athens. The itinerary can also be done by guided tour (☞ Guided Tours, *below*); your best bet is to book a three-day trip that includes Delphi and Meteora, then leave the tour at Trikala and pick up a train to Thessaloniki, returning to Athens by plane, train, or bus.

Guided Tours

Call travel agencies in Athens for tours of mainland Greece, such as a three-day trip to Delphi and Meteora (73,000 dr.) and a six-day excursion to northern Greece including Delphi, Meteora, Thessaloniki and its outlying archaeological sites (191,500 dr.) (☞ Travel Agencies *in* Athens Essentials, *above*). **Trekking Hellas** (✉ Rodou 11, Kalambaka, ☎ FAX 0432/75–214) offers numerous outdoor travel excursions, ranging from canyoning to rafting.

Visitor Information

Delphi: municipal tourist office (✉ Vas. Pavlou and Friderikis 12, ☎ 0265/82–900); tourist police (✉ Aggelos Sikelianou 3, ☎ 0265/82–220). **Meteora:** tourist information office (✉ Kondili 38, as well as a station at Platia Dimarchiou, Kalambaka, ☎ 0432/75–306); tourist police (✉ Pindou and Ioanninon, Kalambaka, ☎ 0432/22–813).

CORFU

Temperate, multihued Corfu—of emerald mountains; turquoise waters lapping rocky coves; ocher and pink buildings; shimmering silver olive leaves; puffed red, yellow, and orange parasails; scarlet roses, bougainvillea, and lavender wisteria and jacaranda spread over cottages—could have inspired Impressionism. The island—which lies strategically in the northern Ionian Sea at the entrance to the Adriatic, off the western edge of Greece—has a history equally as colorful, reflecting the commingling of Corinthians, Romans, Goths, Normans, Venetians, French, Russians, and British. Today, over a million visitors a year—most from England and many from Europe—enjoy, and in summer, crowd its evocative capital city, isolated beaches, stylish restaurants, and resorts. The entire island has gracefully absorbed its many layers of history, and combines neoclassic villas and eco-sensitive resorts, horse-drawn carriages and Jaguars—simplicity and sophistication—in an alluring mix. But desirability comes at a price: Corfu is expensive. If price is a consideration, beware. The island of Corfu is small enough to cover completely in a few days. Roads vary from gently winding to spiraling, but they're generally well marked, and all lead to Corfu town, which, as some poets observe, is reminiscent of a stage set for a Verdi opera.

Exploring Corfu

If you arrive from Igoumenitsa or Patras, on mainland Greece, your ferry will dock at the **Old Port** on the north side of town, west of the **New Fortress** (1577–1578) (✉ on a promontory northwest of the old fortress and medieval town), built by the Venetians and added to by the French and the British to protect the town from a possible Turkish invasion. You can now wander through the maze of tunnels, moats, and fortifications.

The **Esplanade** (✉ between the Old Fortress and old town), the huge open parade ground on the land side of the canal, is central to the life of the town, and, many feel, the most beautiful *spianada* (esplanade) in Greece. It is bordered on the west by a street lined with seven- and eight-story Venetian and English Georgian houses, and arcades, called the **Liston** (modeled on the Parisian Rue de Rivoli, by the French, under Napoléon). Cafés spill out onto the passing scene, and Corfiot celebrations, games, and trysts occur in the sun and shadows.

Just past the Palace of St. Michael and St. George is the oldest cultural institution in modern Greece, the **Corfu Reading Society,** with archives (dating back several centuries) of the Ionian islands. One of the loveliest buildings in Corfu, it has an exterior staircase leading up to a loggia. ✉ *Kapodistriou.* ⏲ *Daily 9–1, Thurs. and Fri. 5–8.*

Visit the **Garrison Church of St. George** (1830), with its Doric portico. In summer there's folk dancing, and in August sound-and-light shows relate the fortress's history. The views from here, east to the Albanian coast and west over the town, are splendid. ✉ *In middle of Old Fortress.* 🎫 *Free.* ⏲ *8–7.*

$$$ ✕ **Aegli.** This 35-year-old restaurant on the Liston serves more than 100 different dishes, both local and international. The tables in front overlook the nonstop parade on the promenade. ✉ *Liston,* ☎ *0661/31949. AE, DC, MC, V. Closed Dec.–Feb.*

$$$ ✕ **The Venetian Well.** On the most charming little square in the old town, built around a 17th century well, this romantic restaurant—its staff tiptoes around lingering lovers—seems too evocative and perfect to be true. The dining rooms in the handsome Venetian building are painted the classic Greek blue. Creative entrées might include duck with kumquats or wild boar. ✉ *Across from Church of the Panayia; Kremasti Sq.,* ☎ *0661/44761. AE, DC, MC, V.*

$ ✕ **O Yiannis.** One of the nicest in Corfu, this restaurant is unpretentious and full of locals. It's also cheap: You'll be hard-pressed to tally up 2,000 dr. on the great barrel wine and wonderful food. Check out the ancient photos of Corfu's old-timers. ✉ *Sophia Kremona and Iassonos-Sossipatrou 30, Anemomilos,* ☎ *0661/31066. Reservations not accepted. No credit cards.*

$$$$ 🏨 **Corfu Palace.** Overlooking the bay, 100 yards from the center of town, this elegant hotel is one of the most beautiful in all of Greece. Tasteful and comfortable best describe its Old World grandeur. The spacious rooms, furnished in various styles (Louis XIV and Empire) have TVs and wide balconies with splendid views. The hotel also has two of Corfu's most luxurious restaurants. ✉ *Leoforos Democratias 2, 49100,* ☎ *0661/39485,* FAX *0661/31749. 110 rooms with bath. 2 restaurants, 2 bars, minibars, room service, outdoor saltwater pool, indoor saltwater pool, health club, shops, baby-sitting, meeting rooms. AE, DC, MC, V.*

$$$ 🏨 **Cavalieri Hotel.** In this venerable, eight-story building on the arcade of the Liston, get a room on the fourth and fifth floors with a number ending in 2, 3, or 4 for a breathtaking view of the Old Fort. The building is swank, yet graceful and chock-full of history. Have a drink at the usually empty but delightful English-style wood-paneled bar. Best of all is the roof garden, which offers light meals and the most remarkable view in town. ✉ *4 Kapodistriou, 49100,* ☎ *0661/39041,* FAX *0661/39336. 50 rooms with bath. Restaurant, bar. AE, DC, MC, V.*

$ 🏨 **Hotel Konstantinoupoulis.** A hotel for more than 200 years, this can be most ambitiously called traditional. But rooms are reasonably clean and acceptable if you're on a budget. It's opposite the dock for car ferries to the islands, with a great view of the old port. ✉ *Zavitsianou 11, Old Port, 49100,* ☎ *0661/39826. 44 rooms share bath. No credit cards.*

Outside Corfu town, at Kanoni, the site of the ancient capital, you may behold the most famous view on Corfu. A French cannon once stood in this hilly landscape, which is now built up and often noisy because of the nearby airport. From Kanoni, against the backdrop of the green slopes of Mount Ayia Deka, is the serene view of two tiny islets: one, **Moni Viahernes,** is reached by causeway. The other islet, **Pontikonisi,** called Mouse Island, has a **white convent** and, beyond, tall cypresses guarding the **13th-century chapel.** You can take a little launch or pedal boat to visit it—or even swim there. Elsewhere in the environs outside Corfu town are two fabled palaces and gardens open to visitors: **Mon Repos** and, in the village of Gastouri, **Achilleion,** the Greek retreat of Empress Elizabeth of Austria.

Corfu Essentials

Getting Around

You can get to Corfu by passenger ship, bus, car, and plane. Passenger ships stop at Corfu twice a week, April to October. **Minoan Lines** (✉ Akti Poseidonos 28, Piraeus, ☎ 01/411–8211 through 8216, FAX 01/411–8631) runs the ship service. Ferries from Igoumenitsa on the mainland leave every hour in summer and every two hours off-season, landing in Corfu town (two hours) and in Lefkimmi, at the southern tip of Corfu (45 minutes). **KTEL Corfu** buses (☎ 0661/39985 or 0661/37186) leave Athens (☎ 01/512–9443) three or four times a day. By car, the best route from Athens is the national road via Corinth to the Rion/Antirion ferry, then to Igoumenitsa (472 km/274 mi), where you take the ferry to Corfu. Call the **Touring Club of Greece** (☎ 104) for information.

Bus travel on Corfu is inexpensive, and the bus network covers the island. The **Spilia** (✉ Avramiou St., ☎ 0661/30627) bus company's terminal is at the New Port. Buses also run from the **San Rocco** (✉ San Rocco Sq., ☎ 0661/31595) bus company's depot. Many agencies run half-day tours of Old Corfu town, and tour buses go daily to all the sights on the island. Tickets and information are available at travel agencies all over town.

Visitor Information

Greek National Tourist Organization (GNTO or EOT; ✉ Kapodistriou 1, ☎ 0661/37520, 0661/37638, or 0661/37639, FAX 0661/30298).

Tourist Police: ✉ Kapodistriou 1, ☎ 0661/30265.

THE AEGEAN ISLANDS

The islands of the Aegean have colorful legends of their own—the Minotaur in Crete; the lost continent of Atlantis, which some believe was Santorini; and the Colossus of Rhodes, to name a few. Each island has its own personality. Mykonos has windmills, dazzling whitewashed buildings, hundreds of tiny churches and chapels on golden hillsides, and small fishing harbors. Visitors to volcanic Santorini sail into what was once a vast volcanic crater and anchor near the island's forbidding cliffs. Crete, with its jagged mountain peaks, olive orchards, and vineyards, contains the remains of the Minoan civilization. In Rhodes a bustling modern town surrounds a walled community with a medieval castle.

Exploring the Aegean Islands

Mykonos

Mykonos is the name of the island and also of its chief village—a colorful maze of narrow, paved streets lined with whitewashed houses, many with bright blue doors and shutters. Every morning women scrub the sidewalks and streets in front of their homes, undaunted by the donkeys that pass by each day. During the 1960s the bohemian jet set discovered Mykonos, and many old houses along the waterfront are now restaurants, bars, and discos—both gay and straight—all blaring music until early morning; a quiet café or taverna is hard to find. Mykonos is a favorite anchorage with the international yacht set, as well as being *the* holiday destination for the young, lively, and liberated—finding yourself alone on any of its beaches is unlikely.

If you stay more than a day, pay a quick visit to the **archaeological museum** to get a sense of the island's history; the most significant local find is a 7th-century BC *pithos* (storage jar) showing the Greeks emerging from the Trojan Horse. ✉ *East end of port,* ☎ *0289/22–325.* ⏲ *Tues.–Sun. 8:30–3.*

From the museum stroll down to the esplanade, where islanders promenade in the evening, or meander through the town, whose confusing layout was designed to foil attacking pirates. In a much-visited neighborhood called **Venetia** (Little Venice) at the southwest end of the port, a few of the old houses have been turned into stylish bars, and colorful balconies hang over the water. In the distance, lined up like toy soldiers on the high hill, are the famous **Mykonos windmills,** vestiges of a time when wind power was used to grind the island's grain.

★

Mykoniots claim that 365 churches and chapels dot their landscape, one for each day of the year. The best known of these is **Paraportiani** (Anargon St.), a whitewashed mix of Byzantine and vernacular idiom that has been described as a confectioner's dream gone mad.

$$$ ✕ **Chez Catherine.** This restaurant's interior combines the whitewashed walls and archways of the Cyclades with the feeling of a French château. Among the well-prepared French and Greek dishes are tournedos langoustine and a moussaka superior to most. The restaurant (the sign outside reads "Katrin") is known for its ace sommelier who maintains a discriminating wine list. ✉ *Delos and Drakopoulou, opposite St. Gerasimos's church,* ☎ *0289/22–169. Reservations essential. AE, MC, V. Closed Nov.–Apr. No lunch.*

$$ ✕ **Chrisanthos.** The clean lines of this sparkling white taverna with red shutters and blue chairs reflect the exquisite simplicity of its food: tomatoes stuffed with capers, risotto with cuttlefish ink, homemade french fries cooked in olive oil, and spaghetti *thanatos* made with female lobster. ✉ *Ftelia,* ☎ *0289/71–535. V. Closed Nov.–Apr.*

$$ ✕ **Spilia.** Tucked into a seaside cave on a rock ledge, this family operation (dad fishes, mom cooks) lets you choose lobster and other live seafood kept in the nearby tide pool to go with appetizers like grilled octopus, crunchy cheese pies, or mussels in cream with fennel. If you're on foot and not pulling up in your yacht, follow the signs from the beach off the fishing hamlet of Kalafati. ✉ *Kalafati below Hotel Anastassia,* ☎ *0289/71–205. No credit cards. Closed Nov.–Apr.*

$$$$ ★ ✕🏨 **Kivotos ClubHotel.** If you're going to splurge in Mykonos, this is the place: the hotel, a member of the Small Luxury Hotels of the World, has rooms that view the yachts on Ornos bay (about 3 ½ km/2 mi from Chora), its own beach, fitness center, squash court, and even a schooner you can rent for the day. Built on several levels, the hotel has beautifully decorated public spaces. At the restaurant, dishes are artfully presented—the chicken stuffed with feta and tomato comes with a spoon each of fava, lentils, and tzatziki. ✉ *Ornos Bay, 84600,* ☎ *0289/24–094,* FAX *0289/22–844; Athens,* ☎ *01/724–6766,* FAX *01/724–9203. 26 rooms, 4 suites. Restaurant, pool. AE, DC, MC, V. Closed mid-Oct.–Apr.*

$$$$ ★ 🏨 **Cavo Tagoo.** This medley of cream-color cubical suites perched above a small beach has been cited for its unique architecture in several international competitions. The hotel is about 10 minutes' walk from the port; all rooms have balconies or terraces with superb sea views. ✉ *700 m (400 yds) from town on road to Ayios Stefanos, Chora, 84600,* ☎ *0289/23–692,* FAX *0289/24–923; Athens,* ☎ *01/643–0233,* FAX *01/*

The Aegean Islands (Ta Nissia tou Aegaiov)

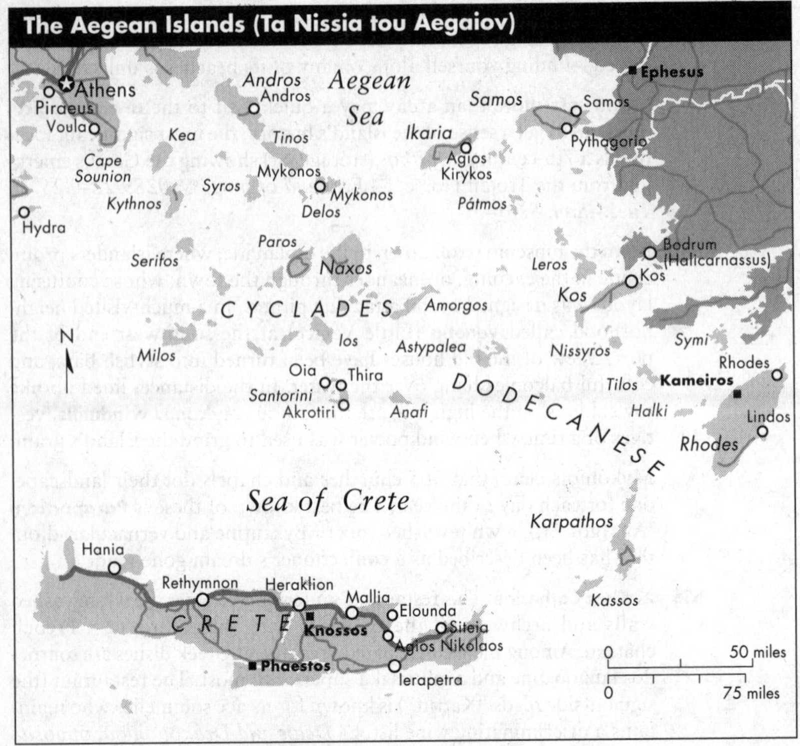

644–5237. 67 rooms, 5 suites. Restaurant, seawater pool. DC, MC, V. Closed Nov.–mid-Apr.

$$ **Kouneni Hotel.** The Kouneni is a casual, family-run hotel in the town center that's quieter than most. It is set in a cool green garden, an ideal place to linger over the full breakfast that's included in the price. Rooms are fairly large and look out on the garden. The owner will provide transportation from the harbor or airport. ✉ *Tria Pigadia, opposite public school, 84600,* ☎ *0289/22–301 or 0289/23–311,* FAX *0289/26–559. 19 rooms. No credit cards.*

$ **Philippi.** With a lovely flower garden whose scent permeates the immaculate rooms, this hotel is in Chora's center. Whether they have a private bathroom or not, rooms are the same price, so book early. ✉ *Kalogera 35, Chora 84600,* ☎ *0289/22–294,* FAX *0289/24–680. 13 rooms, 4 with bath. Air-conditioning. No credit cards. Closed Nov.–Mar.*

Delos

About 30 minutes by boat from Mykonos is the isle of Delos, the legendary sanctuary of Apollo. ★ Its **Exedra ton Leonton** (Terrace of the Lions), a remarkable group of nine Naxian marble sculptures from the 7th century BC, is worth the trip. Another highlight is a group of houses of the Roman period, with their fine floor mosaics. The best of these mosaics are in the **archaeological museum.** *Boats leave Mykonos several times daily in summer and once every morning in winter, depending on the winds.* ☎ *0289/22–259.* ⏲ *Tues.–Sun. 8:30–3.*

Santorini

The best way to approach Santorini is to sail into its harbor, once the vast crater of the volcano, and dock beneath its black and red cliffs, which rise up to 1,000 ft above the sea. The houses and churches of ★ the main town, **Thira** (Fira), cling inside the rim in dazzling white contrast to the somber cliffs. Most passenger ferries now use the new port,

Athinios, where visitors are met by buses, taxis, and donkey service to Thira, as well as by small-hotel owners hawking rooms. The bus ride into Thira takes about a half hour, and from there you can make connections to **Oia,** the serene town at the northern tip. Despite being packed with visitors in summer, the tiny town is charming and has spectacular views (as does Thira). While on Santorini, be sure to try the local wines. The volcanic soil produces a unique range of flavors, from light and dry to rich and aromatic.

The island's volcano erupted in the 15th century BC, destroying its Minoan civilization. At **Akrotiri,** on the south end of Santorini, the remains of a Minoan city buried by volcanic ash are being excavated. The site, believed by some to be part of the legendary Atlantis, is well worth visiting. ☎ *0286/81–366.* ⏲ *Tues.–Sun. 8:30–3.*

At **Archaia Thira** (Ancient Thira), a clifftop site on the east coast of the island, a well-preserved town in existence since before the 9th century BC has a theater and agora, houses, fortifications, and ancient tombs. ☎ *No phone.* *Free.* ⏲ *Tues.–Sun. 8:30–3.*

$$$ ★ ✕ **Domata.** Named for the revered Santorini tomato, this sleek restaurant has Aegean-inspired cuisine created by the same chef who spends winters at Vitrina, a noted Athens restaurant. Start with the mussels in white sauce and capers, or onions stuffed with sun-dried tomatoes, then move on to such entrées as crayfish with saffron or the heartier ribs marinated in fennel seed, ouzo, and yogurt. ✉ *Monolithos,* ☎ *0286/32–069. MC, V. Closed Sept.–May.*

$$$ ✕ **Selene.** At this longtime island favorite, the creative cooking combines nouvelle cuisine with traditional Santorini fare. Two dishes based on local recipes are the *apochti* (dried pork, like prosciutto) with fava and caper leaves and rabbit *tiravgoulo* (stew) cooked with fresh green onion, cheese, and eggs. The extensive Greek wine list complements the more than 30 dishes. ✉ *Thira,* ☎ *0286/22–249. MC, V. Closed Nov.–Mar.*

$$ ★ ✕ **Camille Stefani.** If you spend the day at Kamari beach or are exploring ancient Thira nearby, consider lingering a while longer at one of the island's best restaurants. It serves seafood and Greek and Continental cuisine. Begin with the *lahanodolmades,* a plate of fava, and moist tomato croquettes, followed by one of the 16 versions of beef, pork, or chicken fillet. Be sure to try at least a glass of the mellow Santorini Lava red wine. ✉ *Beach road, Kamari,* ☎ *0286/31–716. AE, DC, MC, V. Closed Dec.–mid-Feb., lunch Mon.–Thurs. and Fri.–Sat.*

$ ✕ **Neptune (Poseidonas).** Oia isn't known for its fine cuisine, but you'll never go wrong with the food served here: mouth-watering chicken souvlaki, flaky pies with spinach or squash, stews like lamb with oregano sauce, or pork with lemon. Ask for a table on the terrace so you can savor the stunning view. ✉ *Off Platia Plasanis on main pedestrian lane, Oia,* ☎ *0286/71–294. MC, V. Closed mid-Nov.–mid-Apr.*

$ ★ ✕ **Nikolas.** This simple, congenial taverna, visited by all who visit the island, is one of the few places in town that stays open in winter. Arrive early, as the cook runs out of food around midnight. The menu on the chalkboard offers barrel wine and a limited but delicious choice of classic Greek dishes, including stifado, stuffed cabbage rolls, and mountain greens. ✉ *Erithrou Stavrou, Thira,* ☎ *0286/24–550. No credit cards.*

$$$$ **Perivolas Traditional Houses.** Built into the cliff side at the outskirts of beautiful Oia, these authentic cave houses, some of them 200 and 300 years old, have been restored and individually decorated in Cycladic style. They overlook the sea and offer comfortable accommo-

dations complete with kitchenettes and terraces. ✉ *Oia 84702,* ☎ *0286/71–308,* FAX *0286/71–309. 16 houses. Pool. No credit cards. Closed Nov.–Mar.*

$$$ ★ **Kavalari Hotel.** A former captain's house, this inviting hotel is built into the cliff side. Each room is different; a few resemble small caves, accented with colorful blankets and interesting local handicrafts. Some rooms have kitchenettes; all have access to flower-decked terraces. ✉ *Follow signs from Hypapantis walkway, Box 17, Thira 84700,* ☎ *0286/22–455,* FAX *0286/22–603. 18 rooms. MC, V. Closed Nov.–mid-Apr.*

$$$ **Oia's Sunset.** At this complex of streamlined apartments with blue and green accents you'll find a mesmerizing sea view from the verandas and the pool bar. Though there is no air-conditioning, some apartments have living rooms; all the accommodations have fully equipped kitchens and direct-dial phones. ✉ *Platia Oia, Oia 84702,* ☎ *0286/71–490,* FAX *0286/71–421; Athens,* ☎ *01/364–1874,* FAX *01/363–1223. 8 studios, 7 apartments. Pool. AE, DC, MC, V. Closed mid-Oct.–mid-Apr.*

$–$$ **Delfini II.** Near Thira's center this hotel has rooms decorated with old handcrafted objects and ceramics. Rooms include refrigerators; apartments have kitchens and private balconies. Guests in the rooms make use of the terrace with sea view, umbrella pergola, and sun beds. ✉ *Thira, between cathedral and Ayios Minas church, 84700,* ☎ *0286/22–780,* FAX *0286/22–780 (0286/22–371 off-season). 4 rooms, 3 apartments. No credit cards. Closed Nov.–Mar.*

Rhodes

The large island of Rhodes, 11 km (7 mi) off the coast of Turkey, is the chief island of the Dodecanese. The northern end is one of Greece's major vacation centers. The **old walled city** is full of crooked, cobbled streets and echoes of antiquity. It's also full of the trappings of tourism, mainly evident in pubs and bars that cater to the large European market. The island as a whole is not so beautiful, but it has fine beaches and an excellent climate. It makes a good base for visiting other islands of the Dodecanese, with their mixture of Aegean and Turkish architecture.

The town of Rhodes has an attractive harbor with fortifications; the gigantic bronze statue of the Colossus of Rhodes, once supposed to have straddled the entrance, was one of the wonders of the ancient world. The fascinating **Old Town of Rhodes** was built by crusaders—the Knights of St. John—on the site of an ancient city. The knights ruled the island from 1309 until they were defeated by the Turks in 1522. On the Street of the Knights stands the Knights' Hospital. Behind it ★ the **archaeological museum** has ancient pottery and sculpture, including two famous statues of Aphrodite. ✉ *Platia Mouseou (Museum Square), reached by the wide staircase from the Hospital,* ☎ *0241/27–657.* ⏲ *Tues.–Fri. 8 AM–9 PM (winter until 2:40), weekends 8:30–3.*

The medieval **Palati ton Ippoton** (Palace of the Knights), destroyed in 1856 by a gunpowder explosion, was restored by the Italians as a summer retreat for Mussolini. It is now a museum. Note its splendid Hellenistic and Roman floor mosaics. ✉ *Ippoton St.,* ☎ *0241/23–359.* ⏲ *Tues.–Fri. 8–7 (8:30–2:40 in winter), weekends 8:30–3.*

★ The **walls** of Rhodes's Old Town are among the greatest medieval monuments in the Mediterranean. For 200 years the knights strengthened them, making them up to 40 ft thick in places and curving the surfaces to deflect cannonballs. You can take a walk on about half of the 4-km (2½-mi) road along the top of the fortifications. The tour begins from the courtyard of the Palace of the Knights at the end of Ippoton street.

☒ *Old town,* ☏ *0241/23–359.* ⊙ *Tours Tues. and Sat. 2:45 (arrive at least 15 mins early).*

★ The enchanting village of **Lindos** ornaments the eastern coast. Put on your comfortable shoes to climb the winding path to the ruins of the ancient acropolis, **Akropoli tis Archaias Lindou.** The sight of its beautiful colonnade with the sea far below is unforgettable. Look for little St. Paul's Harbor, beneath the cliffs of the acropolis; seen from above, it appears to be a lake, as the entrance from the sea is obscured by rocks. ☒ *Above town,* ☏ *0244/31–258.* ⊙ *Tues.–Sun. 8–6 (8:30–2:40 in winter).*

$$$$ ★ ✕ **Alexis.** The owners spare no effort to bring the enthusiastic clientele (Onassis was a big fan) the very best seafood—whether fresh lobster, mussels from nearby Simi steamed with onion, fennel, and white wine, or such specialties as sea urchin, limpets, and sea snail. ☒ *Sokratous 18, Old Town,* ☏ *0241/29–347. Reservations essential. AE, MC, V. No lunch Jun.–Aug.*

$$$$ ✕ **Ta Kioupia.** Antique farm implements hang on the walls at this Rhodes landmark, and tables are elegantly set with linens, fine china, and crystal. Food arrives on large platters, and for a fixed price you select what pleases your eye: carrot bread, pine-nut salad, oven-baked meatballs with leeks, *tiropites* (four-cheese pie), and rooster kebab. ☒ *Tris, about 7 km (4¼ mi) from Rhodes town,* ☏ *0241/91–824. Reservations essential. AE, V. Closed Jan. No lunch.*

$$ ✕ **Dinoris.** Housed in a cavernous hall built in 1530 as a stable for the knights, this establishment has long specialized in fish. For mezes try the variety platter, which includes their *psarokeftedakia* (fish balls made from a secret recipe) as well as mussels, shrimp, and lobster. ☒ *Platia Mouseou 14A, Old Town,* ☏ *0241/25–824. Reservations essential Mar.–Sept. AE, MC, V.*

$$ ★ ✕ **Palia Istoria.** Ensconced in an old house with genteel murals, this mezedopolion is a visual treat. Entrées include pork tenderloin in wine, fresh salmon in champagne sauce, and shrimp ouzo with orange juice. ☒ *Mitropoleos 108 and Dendrinou, Ayios Dimitrios area (about 700 dr. by taxi from center),* ☏ *0241/32–421. Reservations essential. MC, V. Closed Dec. 15–Jan. 15. No lunch.*

$ ✕ **Taverna Nisiros.** Once the home of an Aga, this simple taverna dishes up traditional Greek fare in the large courtyard or in the cozy interior decorated with sheep bells and kilims. Sample the strong barrel wine or a fiery liqueur like souma or tsipouro. ☒ *Ayiou Fanouriou 45–47, Old Town,* ☏ *0241/31–471. AE, MC, V.*

$$$$ ★ 🏨 **Grecotel Rhodos Imperial.** The buildings zigzag down the hillside like stacked red, blue, and yellow boxes. Linked by a pedestrian tunnel to the beach, the hotel offers good value for a resort set just 4 km (2½ mi) from Rhodes town. Guests can play tennis, jet ski and windsurf, rent a mountain bike, or just amble along in pedal boats. The crisp, modern rooms all have balconies, about two-thirds of them with sea views (about 9,000 dr. more). ☒ *Ialyssou Ave., Box 316, Ixia 85100,* ☏ *0241/75–000,* FAX *0241/76–690; Athens,* ☏ *01/725–0920,* FAX *01/725–7671. 402 rooms, 42 suites. 3 restaurants, 3 pools (1 indoor). AE, DC, MC, V. Closed Nov.–mid-Mar.*

$$$–$$$$ 🏨 **Grand Hotel.** This resort hotel in Rhodes town offers easy access to the beach across the street and the casino next door, the Old Town (20 minutes on foot), and the New Town's vibrant nightlife. Although about three-fourths of the rooms have been renovated, the best are in the newer wings. Rooms have balconies with either a sea or a garden view, there are a tennis court and exercise room, and the main pool is Olympic-size. ☒ *Akti Miaouli 1, Rhodes 85100,* ☏ *0241/26–284,* FAX *0241/32–217;* ☏ *01/291–7027 in Athens,* FAX *01/291–7672* *in Athens. 379 rooms, 18 suites. 2 restaurants, 4 pools (1 indoor, 1 children's). AE, DC, MC, V.*

$$$ **S. Nikolis' Hotel.** This small hotel within the Old Town is away from the most crowded tourist area. The rooms, in several 14th-century buildings, are outfitted with dark, rustic furniture, TV, hair dryers, air-conditioning (except in the apartments, which have fans), and refrigerators; they look out toward the spacious courtyard or the old city walls. The apartments have kitchen facilities. Depending on the suite, different "honeymoon" features include a Jacuzzi, king- or queen-size beds, bathtub, loft, and balconies. A roof terrace lets guests enjoy a buffet breakfast with a view over the town. ✉ *Ippodamou 61, Rhodes 85100,* ☎ *0241/34–561,* FAX *0241/32–034. 10 rooms, 8 suites, 4 apartments. Restaurant. AE, DC, MC, V.*

$$ **Spartalis Hotel.** Convenient if you have to catch a boat from the harbor, this is in Rhodes's New Town. Many rooms in the simple but lively hotel have balconies overlooking the bay, and there is a terrace for breakfast. The rooms on the street are noisy. ✉ *Plastira 2, Rhodes 85100,* ☎ *0241/24–371,* FAX *0241/20–406. 79 rooms. AE, DC, MC, V. Closed Nov.–Mar.*

Crete

Greece's largest island, lying in the south Aegean, was the center of Europe's earliest civilization, the Minoan, which flourished from about 2000 BC to 1200 BC. Crete was struck a mortal blow in about 1450 BC by an unknown cataclysm, now thought to have been political.

★ The most important Minoan remains are in the **archaeological museum** in Heraklion, Crete's largest (and least attractive) city. The museum's treasures include the frescoes and ceramics from Knossos and Agia Triada depicting Minoan life, and the Phaestos disc. In 1996 an archaeologist proposed that its undecipherable scribblings are actually Greek in a code used by cult members, pushing the language's first appearance back another 200 years to 1700 BC. ✉ *Xanthoudidou 1, Platia Eleftherias,* ☎ *081/226–092.* ⏲ *Mon. 12:30–7 (12:30–5 in winter), Tues.–Sun. 8–7 (8–5 in winter).*

Not far from Heraklion is the partly reconstructed, sublimely evocative palace of **Knossos.** ★ Note the simple throne room, which contains the oldest throne in Europe, and the bathrooms with their efficient plumbing. The palace was the setting for the legend of the Minotaur, a monstrous offspring of Queen Pasiphae and a bull, which King Minos confined to the labyrinth under the palace. ☎ *081/231–940.* ⏲ *Daily 8–7 (8–5 in winter).*

In addition to archaeological treasures, Crete boasts beautiful mountain scenery and many beach resorts along the north coast. One is **Mallia,** which contains the remains of another Minoan palace and has good sandy beaches. Two other beach resorts, Ayios Nikolaos and the nearby Elounda, lie farther east.

Western Crete, with soaring mountains, deep gorges, and rolling olive orchards, is much less overrun by tourists. The region is rich in Byzantine churches, Venetian monasteries, and interesting upland villages. ★ The town of **Rethymnon** is dominated at its western end by the **Fortezza,** one of the largest and best-preserved Venetian castles in Greece. Wandering through the town's old section, you will come across carved-stone Renaissance doorways belonging to vanished mansions; fountains; wooden Turkish houses; and one of the few surviving minarets in Greece. It belongs to the **Neratzes mosque,** and you can climb its 120 steps for a panoramic view. Don't miss the carefully restored Venetian **loggia,** the clubhouse of the local nobility. The small Venetian **harbor,** with its 13th-century lighthouse, comes to life in summer, with restaurant tables cluttering the quayside.

★ **Hania** is one of the most attractive towns in Greece. Work your way through the covered market, then through the maze of narrow streets to the waterfront. Walk along the inner harbor, past the Venetian arsenals and around to the old lighthouse, for a magnificent view of the town with the White Mountains looming beyond. Behind the outer harbor, Theotokopoulou and Zambeliou streets lead you into the alleys where almost all the houses are Venetian or Turkish, and to the **archaeological museum.** The finds come from all over western Crete: The painted Minoan clay coffins and elegant Late Minoan pottery indicate the wealth of the region during the Bronze Age. ✉ *Halidon 24,* ☎ *0821/90–334.* ⏲ *Tues.–Sun. 8:30–7 (8:30–3 in winter).*

In summer boat service operates along the southwest coast, stopping at **Paleochora,** the area's main resort. **Elafonissi** islet has white sand beaches and black rocks set in a turquoise sea (to get there you wade across a narrow channel). A good road on the west coast from Elafonissi north accesses beaches that are rarely crowded even in summer, ★ including **Falasarna,** near Crete's northwest tip.

$$ ★ ✕ **Vaonakis.** The lively owner is known for his *leventia,* loosely translated as pluck or generosity of heart, and his taverna's fine cooking: memorable Cretan mezedes, like handmade dolmades with tomato and carrot; fried *galantera,* made with the intestines of milk-fed lamb; pepper croquettes with white cheese, fried eggplants, and baby squash, and excellent saganaki. Leave room for the *mizithrokalitsouna,* Cretan pastries filled with sweet cheese and served hot with honey. ✉ *Pigianos Kambos near El Greco Hotel, Rethymnon,* ☎ *0831/72–252. No credit cards. Closed for lunch weekdays Oct.–Mar.*

$$ ✕ **Vassilis.** Watch the boats bobbing along the jetty at this congenial taverna. Don't miss the daily fish soup and such Cretan dishes as *koukouvayia* (a local roll soaked in wine, tomato, oil, and herbs). The owners also make their own rosé. ✉ *Nearchou 10, old harbor, Rethymnon,* ☎ *0831/22–967. V.*

$–$$ ✕ **Samaria.** The taverna has a loyal clientele who yearn for Greek food the way their grandmothers used to make it: stamnas, tzoutzoukakia, stuffed tomatoes, and creamy pastitsio (try a quarter kilo), ideal with the barrel retsina. The taverna stays open until very late. ✉ *El. Venizelou 39–40, Rethymnon,* ☎ *0831/24–681. V.*

$ ✕ **Kyriakos.** This popular taverna with pink tablecloths and green chairs offers fish and such Cretan specialties as snail stew with *pligouri* (cracked wheat), artichokes with broad beans, small eggplants with feta, and *tiropitakia* (pies with honey and creamy, mild Cretan cheese). ✉ *Leoforos Dimokratias 53, Heraklion,* ☎ *081/224–649. AE, DC, V. No dinner Sun. June–Sept., no dinner Wed. Oct.–May.*

$$ ✕🏨 **Doma.** This converted 19th-century mansion on the outskirts of Hania has the welcoming atmosphere of a private home: The sitting room has a fireplace and armchairs with embroidered scarlet bolsters. The dining room, where the owner serves dinner on request (lamb cooked with white wine and Cretan mountain herbs, for example), has a memorable view across the bay to the old town. Many rooms have air-conditioning; ask for one overlooking the garden to reduce street noise. ✉ *E. Venizelou 124, Hania 73100,* ☎ *0821/51–772,* FAX *0821/41–578. 25 rooms, 3 suites. Dining room. MC, V. Closed Nov.–Mar.*

$$$$ ★ 🏨 **Elounda Beach.** This is one of Greece's most renowned seaside resorts, 9 km (7 mi) north of Ayios Nikolaos. The complex, set in beautiful grounds—the pool is cleverly landscaped among carob trees—includes a miniature Greek village, complete with kafenion and

church, minigolf, two beaches, and a disco. Many of the suites—bliss!—have their own swimming pool. ✉ *Elounda Beach, 72053,* ☎ *0841/41–412,* FAX *0841/41–373; Athens,* ☎ *01/360–7120,* FAX *01/360–3392. 120 rooms, 43 bungalows, 37 suites, 27 suite-bungalows. 4 restaurants, pool, 4 tennis courts, health club, disco. AE, DC, MC, V. Closed Nov.–Mar.*

$$–$$$ **Mythos Suites Hotel.** A former 16th-century manor, this hotel near the cathedral has hardwood floors and beam ceilings, ceramic tiles, and remnants of the original massive stonework. The air-conditioned rooms are traditionally furnished, with brass beds in the two-floor maisonettes. All rooms, which overlook the small sunny courtyard pool, include a fully equipped kitchen. Only the maisonettes have balconies. ✉ *Platia Karaoli-Dimitriou 12, 74100 Rethymnon,* ☎ *0831/53–917,* ☎ FAX *0831/51–036. 1 apartment, 3 studios, 6 maisonettes. Pool. AE, DC, MC, V. Closed Nov.–Mar.*

$$ **Atrion.** Nestled in a quiet street behind Heraklion's historical museum, this well-run hotel has rooms done in shades of blue with heavy wood furniture and TVs. Drinks are served evenings in the tiny patio-garden. ✉ *Chronaki 9, Heraklion 71202,* ☎ *081/229–225,* FAX *081/223–292. 65 rooms. Restaurant, air-conditioning. AE, DC, MC, V.*

$$ ★ **Casa Delfino.** This tranquil hotel in the heart of Hania's old town was once part of a Venetian Renaissance palace; you can still see the original stonework throughout the building and the beautiful pebble mosaic in the atrium. Set around a courtyard, the rooms are decorated in cool pastel colors. Four apartments, available at a higher price, are decorated with 17th-century objects and may have such features as a private terrace, sea view, or hydromassage. ✉ *Theofanous 9, Palio Limani, Hania 73100,* ☎ *0821/93–098,* FAX *0821/96–500. 16 rooms. Air-conditioning. AE, DC, MC, V.*

$ ★ **Nostos.** Dating from the 1400s, this colorful, award-winning building seems to have housed all the peoples who passed through Hania: the renovated Venetian palazzo contains remains of an Ottoman bath and living quarters; it was also the site of the town's first Orthodox church. The roof garden is resplendent with abundant honeysuckle, bougainvillea, and grapes. Antique kitchenware adorns the breakfast room. All rooms have balconies and fans; two have sea views. ✉ *Zambeliou 42–46, Palio Limani, Hania 73131,* ☎ FAX *0821/94–740. 12 studios. MC, V.*

Aegean Islands Essentials

Getting Around

The simplest way to visit the Aegean Islands is by **cruise ship.** These usually stop at the four most popular islands—Mykonos, Rhodes, Crete, and Santorini. Car and passenger **ferries** sail to these destinations from Piraeus. Boats for Mykonos also leave from Rafina, 32 km (20 mi) north of Athens. En route you will pass one of the great sights of Greece: the Temple of Poseidon looming on a hilltop at Cape Sounion. There is also frequent **air** service from Athens to each island, but in summer and on holidays it's vital to book well in advance.

Guided Tours

AEGEAN CRUISES

From April through October many cruises go to the islands from Piraeus. Try **Golden Sun Cruises** (✉ Akti Miaouli 71, Piraeus, ☎ 01/428–7894, FAX 01/428–7898), or **Royal Olympic Cruises** (✉ Akti Miaouli 87, Piraeus, ☎ 01/429–0700 for reservations, FAX 01/429–0638). Most cruise agencies also have downtown Athens representatives.

Visitor Information

Crete: EOT (✉ Kriari 40, Megaron Pantheon building, Hania, ☎ 0821/92–943, ☎ FAX 0821/92–624; ✉ Xanthoudidou 1, Heraklion, ☎ 081/244–462, 228–225, 228–203; ✉ El. Venizelou beach road, Rethymnon, ☎ 0831/29–148); tourist police (✉ Karaiskaki 60, Hania, ☎ 0821/73–333; ✉ Dikaiosinis 10, Heraklion, ☎ 081/283–190, 289–614; ✉ El. Venizelou beach road next to EOT, Rethymnon, ☎ 0831/28–156); ELPA (✉ G. Papandreou 46–50 and Knossou, Heraklion, ☎ 081/289–440). **Mykonos:** Hotel Reservations office (✉ port, next to tourist police, ☎ 0289/24–540); Association of Rental Rooms and Apartments (✉ port, next to tourist police, ☎ 0289/24–860); tourist police (✉ Port, ☎ 0289/22–482). **Rhodes:** EOT (✉ Archbishop Makarios and Papagou, Rhodes town, ☎ 0241/23–655); municipal tourism office (✉ Platia, Rimini, ☎ 0241/35–945; closed Nov.–Mar.); tourist police (✉ Archbishop Makarios and Papagou, entrance on Karpathou, Rhodes town, ☎ 0241/27–423). **Santorini:** tourist police (✉ next to KTEL bus station, ☎ 0286/22–649).

15 Hungary

Budapest, the Danube Bend, Lake Balaton

Hungary sits, proudly but precariously, at the crossroads of Central Europe, having retained its own identity despite countless invasions and foreign occupation by great powers of the East and West. Its industrious, resilient people have a history of brave but doomed uprisings: against the Turks in the 17th century, the Hapsburgs in 1848, and the Soviet Union in 1956. Each has resulted in a period of readjustment, a return to politics as the art of the possible.

The '60s and '70s saw matters improve politically and materially for most Hungarians. Communist party leader János Kádár remained relatively popular at home and abroad, allowing Hungary to improve trade and relations with the West. The bubble began to burst during the 1980s, however, when the economy stagnated and inflation escalated. The peaceful transition to democracy began when young reformers in the party shunted aside the aging Mr. Kádár in 1988 and began speaking openly about multiparty democracy, a market economy, and cutting ties with Moscow. Events quickly gathered pace, and by spring 1990, as the Iron Curtain disappeared, Hungarians went to the polls in the first free elections in 40 years. A center-right government took office, sweeping away the Communists and their renamed successor party, the Socialists, who finished fourth. Ironically, four years later, in the nation's next elections, Hungarians voted out the ailing center-right party in favor of none other than the Hungarian Socialist party, which now rules in coalition with the Free Democrats. *Plus ça change . . .* Elections in spring of 1998 determine who will lead Hungary into the next century. At press time the ruling Socialist party was ahead in the polls and was likely to be chosen for another term.

In bald mathematical terms, the total area of Hungary (Magyarország) is less than that of Pennsylvania. Two rivers cross the country: the Duna (Danube) flows from the west through Budapest on its way to the southern frontier, the smaller Tisza from the northeast across the Great Plain (Nagyalföld). Western Hungary is dominated by the largest lake in Central Europe, Lake Balaton. Although overdevelopment is advancing, the northern lakeshore is still dotted with Baroque villages and Old World spas, and the surrounding hills are covered with vineyards. In eastern Hungary, the Nagyalföld is steeped in the romantic culture of the Magyars (the Hungarians' name for themselves), with its spicy food, strong wine, and proud *csikós* (horsemen).

However, it is Budapest, a city of more than 2 million people, that draws travelers from all over the world. Bisected by the Danube, the city has a split personality; villas and government buildings cluster in the hills of Buda to the west, whereas an imposing array of hotels, restaurants, and shopping areas crowd the flatlands of Pest.

Hungarians, known for their hospitality, love talking with foreigners. Hungarians of all ages share a deep love of music, and wherever you go you will hear it, whether it's opera performed at Budapest's imposing opera house or simply Gypsy violinists serenading you at dinner.

HUNGARY A TO Z

Customs

Objects for personal use may be imported freely. If you are over 16, you may also bring in 500 cigarettes or 100 cigars or 500 grams of tobacco, plus 1 liter of wine, 1 liter of spirits, 5 liters of beer, and 0.25 liters of perfume. A customs charge is made on gifts valued in Hungary at more than 21,000 Ft.

Keep receipts of any purchases from Konsumtourist, Intertourist, or Képcsarnok Vállalat. A special permit is needed for works of art, antiques, or objects of museum value. You are entitled to a VAT refund on new goods (i.e., not works of art, antiques, or objects of museum value) valued at more than 25,000 Ft.; *see* Shopping, *below*.

For further customs information, inquire at **Intel Trade Rt.** (✉ Budapest I, Csalogány u. 6–10, ☎ 1/356–9800) or the **Hungarian Customs Office** (✉ Budapest IX, Mester u. 7, ☎ 1/218–0017). If you have trouble communicating, ask **Tourinform** (☎ 1/317–9800) for help.

Dining

Although prices are steadily increasing, plenty of good, affordable restaurants offer a variety of Hungarian dishes. Meats, rich sauces, and creamy desserts predominate, but you can also find salads, even out of season. Bypass the usual red-or-white question and order *Egri Bikavér,* or "bull's blood," Hungary's best-known red wine, with any meal. A regular restaurant is likely to be called either a *vendéglő* or an *étterem.* You also have the option of eating in a *büfé* (snack counter), an *eszpresszó* (café), or a *söröző* (pub). Be sure to visit a *cukrászda* (pastry shop). Keep in mind that typical Hungarian breakfasts consist of cold cuts and bread; if the start of your day requires specially prepared omelets or blueberry muffins, be sure to inquire about your hotel's breakfast offerings ahead of time.

One caveat: many restaurants have a fine-print policy of charging for each slice of bread consumed from the bread basket. General overcharging is not unheard of, either. Authorities in Budapest, however, have been cracking down on establishments reported for overcharging. Don't order from menus without prices, and don't accept dining or drinking invitations from women hired to lure people into shady situations.

Hungary (Magyarország)

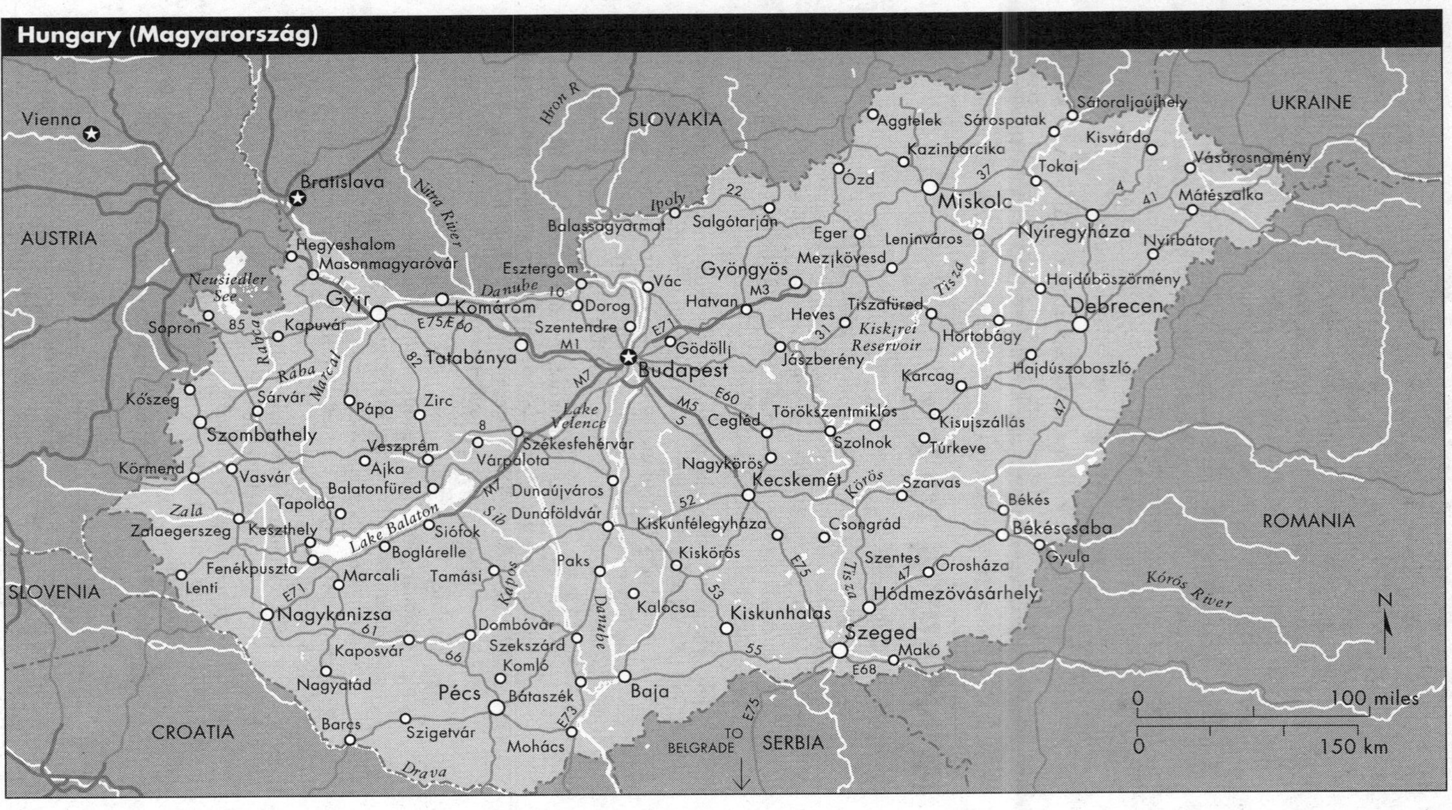

MEALTIMES

Hungarians eat dinner early—you risk offhand service and cold food after 9 PM. Lunch, the main meal for many, is served from noon to 2. Some restaurants are introducing simple breakfast menus catering to western travelers and expats.

RATINGS

Prices are per person and include a first course, main course, and dessert, but no wine or tip. Prices in Budapest tend to be a good 30% higher than elsewhere in Hungary.

CATEGORY	COST
$$$$	over 3,200 Ft.
$$$	2,300 Ft.–3,200 Ft.
$$	1,400 Ft.–2,300 Ft.
$	under 1,400 Ft.

WHAT TO WEAR

At most moderately priced and inexpensive restaurants, casual but neat dress is acceptable. In more expensive establishments, especially in Budapest, a jacket and a tie are sometimes required.

Language

Hungarian (Magyar) tends to look and sound intimidating at first because it is not an Indo-European language. Generally, older people speak some German, and many younger people speak at least rudimentary English, which has become the most popular language to learn. It's a safe bet that anyone in the tourist trade will speak at least one of the two languages.

Lodging

Lodging ranges from sophisticated hotels to guest houses, private rooms, and campsites. Unless otherwise noted, rooms include bath.

CAMPING

Most of the some 300 campsites in Hungary are open from May through September. As rates are no longer regulated, prices vary. An average rate is about 800 Ft. a day per site in Budapest and the Balaton region, slightly less elsewhere, plus an accommodations fee—about 500 Ft. per person per night. Children under 14 often get a 50% reduction. Camping is forbidden except in designated areas. For information contact travel agencies or **Tourinform** (☞ Visitor Information, *below*), where you can pick up a detailed map locating campsites around the country.

GUEST HOUSES AND PRIVATE LODGINGS

Also called *panziók* (pensions), small guest houses lying just outside the heart of the city or town provide simple accommodations well suited to people on a budget. These usually include a private bathroom, and many also offer breakfast. A room for two in Budapest with breakfast and private bath will run around $26–$65 per night in peak season, less at other times. Arrangements can be made through local tourist offices or travel agents abroad.

In the provinces rooms that you are offered directly are likely to be clean and in a relatively good neighborhood; the prospective landlord will probably not cheat you. Look for a placard reading either SZOBA KIADÓ or—in German—ZIMMER FREI (room for rent). The rate per night for a double room in Budapest or at Lake Balaton is around $23 (which usually includes the use of a bathroom but not breakfast). Reservations can also be made by any tourist office.

HOTELS

Don't expect a bargain on your hotel room in Budapest: High-season rates at established hotels rival those of most western capitals. There are few expensive hotels outside Budapest, but the moderately priced hotels are generally comfortable and well run. Unless otherwise noted, breakfast is not included.

YOUTH HOSTELS

Most hostels in Budapest are in university dorms and open only when school is not in session (typically July and August). Hostels have no age limits or membership requirements, and they offer a 10% discount to HI cardholders. Most have no curfews and offer 24-hour reception service. The **Hungarian Youth Hostel Federation** (✉ VI, Bajcsy-Zsilinszky út 31, 2nd floor, #3, ☎ FAX 1/331–9705) in Budapest publishes an informative, annual directory of hostels throughout the country and provides information. Budapest's two main hostel agencies are **Universum Ltd.** (✉ Báthory László u. 18, H–1029 Budapest, ☎ FAX 1/275–7046) and **Travellers' Youth Hostels** (TYH; ✉ Dózsa György út 152, H–1134 Budapest, ☎ 1/340–8585 or 1/329–8644, ☎ FAX 1/320–8425). Both companies operate year-round hostels, as well as summer-only. Be sure to book in advance in summer.

Hostels are uncommon outside Budapest, but some towns open their university dorms to travelers during July and August; inquire at the local tourist office. The atmosphere and price at these dorms is about the same as at a hostel.

RATINGS

The following price categories are for a double room with bath and breakfast, VAT included, during the peak season; rates are markedly lower off-season and in the countryside, sometimes under $20 for two. For single rooms with bath, count on about 80% of the double-room rate. Most large hotels require payment in hard currency.

CATEGORY	BUDAPEST	BALATON AND DANUBE BEND
$$$$	over $200	over $70
$$$	$140–$200	$50–$70
$$	$80–$140	$30–$50
$	under $80	under $30

During the peak season (June through August), full board may be compulsory at some of the Lake Balaton hotels, although this is increasingly rare. During the off-season (in Budapest, September through March; at Lake Balaton and the Danube Bend, May and September), rates can be considerably lower than those given above.

RENTALS

Apartments in Budapest and cottages at Lake Balaton, available for short- and long-term rental, can make the most economic lodging for families. Contact tourist offices in Hungary and abroad for rates and reservations. A Budapest apartment may cost anywhere from $30 to $60 a day; a luxury cottage for two on Lake Balaton costs about the same. You can make bookings in Budapest at the **IBUSZ Welcome Hotel Service** (✉ V, Apáczai Csere János u. 1, ☎ 1/318–3925 or 1/318–5776, FAX 1/117–9099), which is open 24 hours a day. Although some enterprising locals stand outside the IBUSZ office and offer tourists their apartments for lower than official rates, it's less risky if you go the official route. Other rental agencies in Budapest are **IBUSZ's main office** (✉ V, Ferenciek tere 10, ☎ 1/318–6866) and **Cooptourist** (✉ I, Attila u. 107, ☎ 1/375–2846 or 1/375–2937). **Amadeus Apartments** (Üllői út 197, ☎ 30/422–893, FAX 1/302–8268) oversees five apartments that cost roughly $40 a night (two-night minimum), including airport transport.

Mail

Two post offices, Keleti (Eastern; ✉ VII, Baross tér 11c) and Nyugati (Western; ✉ VI, Teréz körút 51), are open 24 hours. Each is near one of Budapest's main train stations.

POSTAL RATES

Postage for an airmail letter to the United States costs about 125 Ft; an airmail letter to the United Kingdom and elsewhere in Western Europe costs about 115 Ft. Airmail postcards to the United States cost about 85 Ft and to the United Kingdom and elsewhere in Western Europe, about 80 Ft.

RECEIVING MAIL

General delivery service is available through any post office in Budapest, including the main downtown branch (✉ Magyar Posta 4. sz., H-1052 Budapest, Városház utca 18); the envelope should have your name written on it, as well as "posta maradó" (poste restante) in large letters. The roman numeral prefix listed in a Budapest address refers to one of the city's 22 districts.

Money Matters

BANK MACHINES AND TRAVELER'S CHECKS

Eurocheque holders can cash personal checks in all banks and in most hotels. Many banks now also cash American Express and Visa traveler's checks. American Express has a full-service office in Budapest (✉ V, Deák Ferenc u. 10, ☎ 1/267–2020, 1/267–2313, or 1/266–8680; FAX 1/267–2029); two smaller branches on Castle Hill—in the Budapest Hilton Hotel (☎ 1/214–0118) and the Sisi Restaurant (☎ 1/264–0118)—offer mostly only currency exchange. Hungary's first Citibank (✉ V, Vörösmarty tér 4) offers full services to account holders, including a 24-hour ATM.

Hundreds of other ATMs have recently appeared throughout the capital and in other major towns. Some accept Plus network bank cards and Visa credit cards, others Cirrus and MasterCard. You can withdraw forints only (automatically converted at the bank's official exchange rate) directly from your account; most levy a 1% or $3 service charge. Many cash-exchange machines, into which you feed paper currency for forints, have also sprung up.

COSTS

The forint was significantly devalued over the last few years and continues its decline, but inflation has decreased to just under 20% from an annual rate of more than 25%. Although you receive more forints for your dollar, prices have risen to keep up with inflation. Nevertheless, even with inflation and the 25% value-added tax (VAT) in the service industry, enjoyable vacations with all the trimmings remain less expensive than in nearby Western European cities such as Vienna.

CREDIT CARDS

Most credit cards are accepted, but don't rely on them in smaller towns or less expensive accommodations and restaurants. The full-service American Express office (☞ Bank Machines and Traveler's Checks, *above*) in Budapest also dispenses cash to its cardholders.

CURRENCY

The unit of currency is the forint (Ft.). There are bills of 200, 500, 1,000, 2,000, 5,000, and 10,000 forints and coins of 1, 2, 5, 10, 20, 50, 100, and 200 forints. Note that a redesigned, small, two-tone 100-forint coin is now in co-circulation with the much larger, earlier version. At press time (spring 1998) the exchange rate was approximately 209 Ft. to the U.S. dollar, 145 Ft. to the Canadian dollar, 347 Ft. to the pound sterling, 134 Ft. to the Australian dollar, and 116 Ft. to the New Zealand dollar. Note that official exchange rates are adjusted at frequent intervals.

There is still a black market in hard currency, but changing money on the street is risky and illegal, and the bank rate almost always comes close. Stick with banks and official exchange offices.

SAMPLE PRICES

Cup of coffee, 100 Ft.; bottle of beer at a bar or restaurant, 300 Ft.–400 Ft.; soft drinks, 100 Ft.; ham sandwich, 150 Ft.; 2–km (1-mi) taxi ride, 150 Ft.; museum admission 100–250 Ft.

TIPPING

Four decades of socialism didn't alter the Hungarian habit of tipping generously. Cloakroom and gas-pump attendants, hairdressers, waiters, and taxi drivers all expect tips. At least 10% should be added to a restaurant bill or taxi fare. If a Gypsy band plays exclusively for your table, you can leave a few hundred forints in the plate provided.

National Holidays

January 1; March 15 (Anniversary of 1848 Revolution); April 4–5 (Easter and Easter Monday); May 1 (Labor Day); May 23–24 (Pentecost); August 20 (St. Stephen's and Constitution Day); October 23 (1956 Revolution Day); December 24–26.

Opening and Closing Times

Banks are generally open weekdays 8–2 or 3, often with a one-hour lunch break around noon; most close at 1 on Friday. **Museums** are generally open daily 10–6 and are closed on Monday; many stop selling admission 30 minutes before closing. Note that some museums change their opening and closing times by an hour or so at the beginning and end of peak seasons based on visitor traffic; it's prudent to double-check hours. Many have free admission one day a week; see individual listings in tours below, but double-check, as the days tend to change. **Department stores** are open weekdays 10–5 or 6, Saturday until 1. **Grocery stores** are generally open weekdays 7–6 or 7, Saturday until 1; **"non-stops"** or *éjjeli-nappali* (24-hour convenience stores) are (theoretically) open 24 hours.

Shopping

SALES-TAX REFUNDS

You are entitled to a VAT refund on new goods (i.e., not works of art, antiques, or objects of museum value) valued at more than 25,000 Ft. (VAT inclusive). Cash refunds are given only in forints. If you made your purchases by credit card, you can file for a credit to your card or to your bank account (again in forints), but this process is slow at best. If you intend to apply for the credit, make sure you get customs to stamp the original purchase invoice before you leave the country. For more information pick up a tax refund brochure from any tourist office or hotel, or contact **Intel Trade Rt.** (✉ Budapest I, Csalogány u. 6-10, ☎ 1/201–8120 or 1/356–9800).

Telephoning

COUNTRY CODE

The country code for Hungary is 36.

INTERNATIONAL CALLS

Direct calls to foreign countries can be made from Budapest and all major provincial towns by dialing 00 and waiting for the international dialing tone; on pay phones the initial charge is 60 Ft. To reach an **AT&T** long-distance operator, dial 00–800–01111; for **MCI**, dial 00–800–01411; for **Sprint**, dial 00–800–01877.

LOCAL CALLS

The cost of a three-minute local call is 20 Ft. Pay phones use 10, 20, and 50 Ft. coins. Most towns in Hungary can be dialed direct—dial 06 and wait for the buzzing tone, then dial the local number. It is unnecessary to use the city code, 1, when dialing within Budapest.

Gray, card-operated telephones are common in Budapest and the Balaton region. The cards—available at post offices, newsstands, and kiosks—come in units of 50 (800 Ft.) and 120 (1,800 Ft.) calls. A flock of children may gather around while you talk on your pay phone—collecting and trading used phone cards is a raging fad.

As Hungary's outmoded telephone system is being modernized, phone numbers are subject to change—usually without forewarning and sometimes several times. Thousands of phone numbers in Budapest alone will be changed over the next few years; sometimes a recording in Hungarian and English provides the new number. If you're having trouble getting through, ask your concierge to check the number.

OPERATORS

International calls can be made through the operator by dialing 09; for operator-assisted calls within Hungary, dial 01. Dial 198 for directory assistance throughout the country. Operators are unlikely to speak English. A safer bet is to consult *The Phone Book,* an English-language yellow pages–style telephone directory that also has cultural and tourist information; it's free in most major hotels, at many restaurants, and at English-language bookstores.

Transportation

Roman numeral prefixes in Budapest addresses refer to one of the city's 22 districts. (Full postal addresses do not cite a Roman numeral, as the district is indicated by the zip code.) Getting around is easier if you learn a few basic terms: *utca* (abbreviated *u.*) and *út,* which mean "street" and "road," respectively; *tér* or *tere* (square); and *körút* (ring).

BY BICYCLE

A land of rolling hills and flat plains, Hungary lends itself to bicycling. For brochures and general information on bicycling conditions and suggested routes, try Tourinform (☞ Visitor Information, *below*) or contact the **Magyar Kerékpáros Túrázók Szövetsége** (Bicycle Touring Association of Hungary; ✉ V, Bajcsy-Zsilinszky út 31, 2nd floor, apt. 3, H-1052 Budapest, ☎ 1/332–7177).

BY BOAT

Boat travel is possible in many parts of Hungary. Budapest, of course, straddles a major international waterway—the Danube. Vienna is six hours away by hydrofoil, and many Hungarian resorts are accessible by either hydrofoil or boat. For information about excursions or pleasure cruises, contact **MAHART Tours** (✉ V, Belgrád rakpart, H-1056 Budapest, ☎ 1/318–1704 or 1/318–1586).

BY BUS

Long-distance buses link Budapest with many main cities in Eastern and Western Europe. Services to the eastern part of the country leave from Népstadion station (✉ IX, Hungária körút 46–48, ☎ 1/252–4496). Buses to the west and south leave from the main Volán bus station (✉ V, Erzsébet tér, ☎ 1/317–2318) in the Inner City. Buses are inexpensive and tend to be crowded, so reserve your seat.

BY CAR

To drive in Hungary, U.S. and Canadian visitors are supposed to have an International Driver's License—although their domestic licenses are usually accepted—and U.K. visitors may use their own domestic licenses.

Breakdowns. The Magyar Autó Klub (Hungarian Automobile Club; ✉ Budapest XIV, Francia út 38/B, ☎ 088) runs a 24-hour "Yellow Angels" breakdown service.

Gasoline. Gas stations are plentiful in and around major cities, and major chains have opened modern full-service stations on highways in the provinces. A gallon of *ólommentes benzin* (unleaded gasoline) costs about 170 Ft. per liter and is usually available at all stations, as is diesel.

Road Conditions. There are three classes of roads: highways or "motorways" (designated by the letter M and a single digit), secondary roads (designated by a two-digit number), and minor roads (designated by a three-digit number). Highways and secondary roads are generally well maintained. Minor roads vary; tractors and horse-drawn carts may slow you down in rural areas. Tolls on major highways help fund the upgrading of many of the country's motorways. The M1 from Budapest to Vienna charges about 1,400 Ft. per car for the final section between the city of Győr and the Austrian border, making it the most expensive road to travel in Europe. Other toll roads are the M5, from Budapest to just south of Kecskemét (and eventually on through Szeged to Serbia), which costs around 1,100 Ft., and the M3 (incomplete and still free at press time, spring 1998), from Budapest to Slovakia.

Rules of the Road. Drive on the right. Unless otherwise noted, the speed limit in developed areas is 50 kph (30 mph), on main roads 80–100 kph (50–62 mph), and on highways 120 kph (75 mph). Keep alert: speed limit signs are scarce compared to those in the United States. Seat belts are compulsory and drinking alcohol is prohibited—there is a zero tolerance policy, and the penalties are severe.

BY TRAIN

Travel by train from Budapest to other large cities or to Lake Balaton is cheap and efficient. Remember to take a *gyorsvonat* (express train) and not a *személyvonat* (local), which can be extremely slow. A *helyjegy* (seat reservation), which costs about 300 Ft., is advisable for all Inter-City trains, which provide rapid, express service among Hungary's major cities.

Only Hungarian citizens are entitled to student discounts; non-Hungarian senior citizens (men over 60, women over 55), however, are eligible for a 20% discount. For more information about rail travel contact the MÁV Passenger Service (✉ Budapest VI, Andrássy út 35, ☎ 1/322-8275; ☎ 1/342-9150 international information; ☎ 1/322-7860 domestic information).

Visas

Only a valid passport is required of U.S., British, and Canadian citizens. For additional information contact the **Hungarian Embassy** in the United States (✉ 3910 Shoemaker St. NW, Washington, DC 20008, ☎ 202/362-6730), in Canada (✉ 299 Waverley St. Ottawa, Ontario K2P 0V9, ☎ 613/230-9614), in London (✉ 35b Eaton Pl., London SW1X 8BY, ☎ 0171/235-5218), or in Australia (✉ 17 Beale Crescent Deakin Act., Canberra 2600, ☎ 6126/282-3226).

Visitor Information

Tourinform (✉ Sütő u. 2, H-1052 Budapest, ☎ 1/317-9800.

Weather

Many of Hungary's major fairs and festivals take place in the spring and fall. During July and August, Budapest can be hot and the resorts at Lake Balaton crowded, so spring (May) and the end of summer (September) are the ideal times to visit.

CLIMATE

The following are average daily maximum and minimum temperatures for Budapest.

Jan.	34F	1C	**May**	72F	22C	**Sept.**	73F	23C
	25	−4		52	11		54	12
Feb.	39F	4C	**June**	79F	26C	**Oct.**	61F	16C
	28	−2		59	15		45	7
Mar.	50F	10C	**July**	82F	28C	**Nov.**	46F	8C
	36	2		61	16		37	3
Apr.	63F	17C	**Aug.**	81F	27C	**Dec.**	39F	4C
	45	7		61	16		30	−1

BUDAPEST

Exploring Budapest

Budapest, lying on both banks of the Danube, unites the hills of Buda and the wide boulevards of Pest. Though it was the site of a Roman outpost during the 1st century, the modern city was not actually created until 1873, when the towns of Óbuda, Pest, and Buda were joined. The resulting capital is the cultural, political, intellectual, and commercial heart of the nation; for the 20% of the nation's population who live here, anywhere else is just "the country."

Much of the charm of a visit to Budapest consists of unexpected glimpses into shadowy courtyards and long vistas down sunlit cobbled streets. Although some 30,000 buildings were destroyed during World War II and in 1956, the past lingers on in the often crumbling architectural details of the antique structures that remain and in the memories and lifestyles of Budapest's citizens.

The principal sights of the city fall roughly into three areas, each of which can be comfortably covered on foot. The Budapest hills are best explored using public transportation. Many street names have been changed since 1989 to purge all reminders of the communist regime—you can sometimes still see the old name, negated with a victorious red *x*, next to the new. The 22 districts of Budapest are referred to in addresses with Roman numerals, starting with I for the Várhegy (Castle Hill) district; V, VI, and VII indicate the main downtown areas.

Várhegy (Castle Hill)

Numbers in the margin correspond to points of interest on the Budapest map.

Most of Buda's main sights are on Várhegy (Castle Hill), a long, narrow plateau laced with cobblestone streets, clustered with beautifully preserved baroque, Gothic, and Renaissance houses, and crowned by the stately Royal Palace. Painstaking reconstruction work has been in progress here since the area was nearly leveled during World War II.

5 **Hadtörténeti Múzeum** (Museum of Military History). The collection here includes uniforms and regalia, many belonging to the Hungarian generals who took part in the abortive uprising against Austrian rule in 1848. Other exhibits trace the military history of Hungary from the

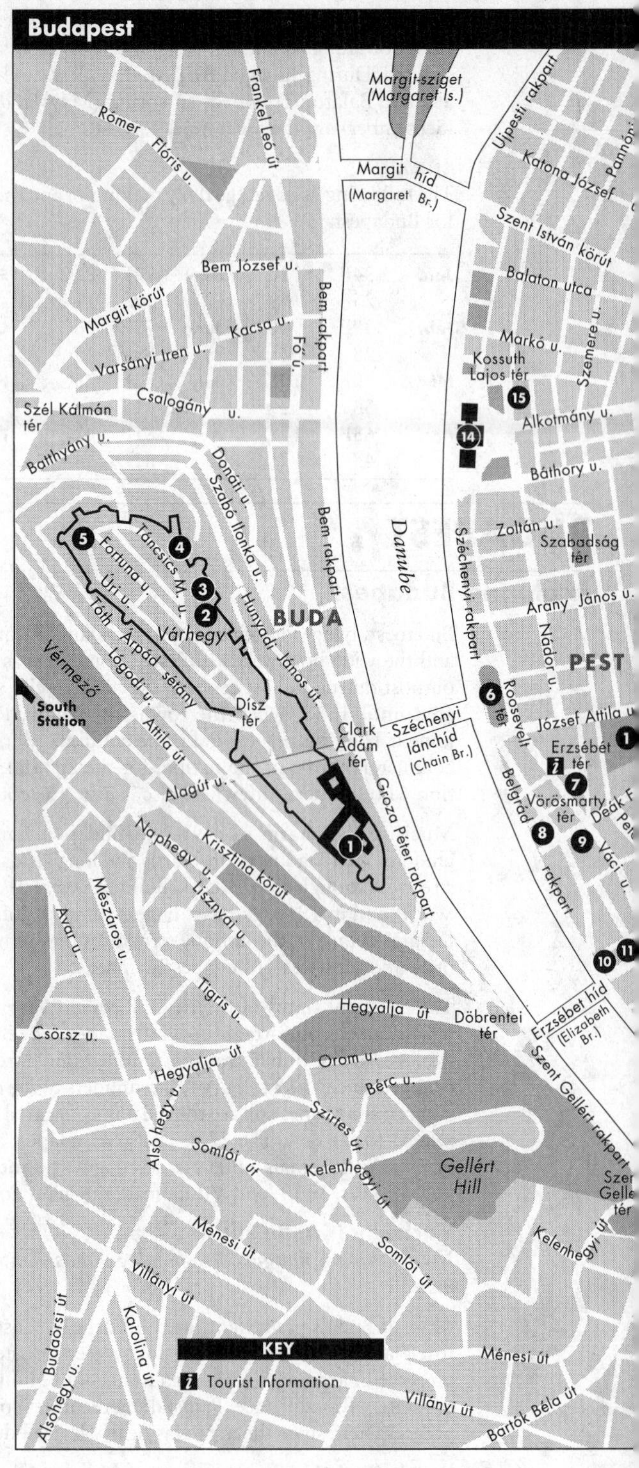
Budapest
Margit-sziget (Margaret Is.)
Margit híd (Margaret Br.)
Rómer Flóris u.
Frankel Leó út
Újpesti rakpart
Katona József
Szent István körút
Balaton utca
Bem József u.
Margit körút
Kacsa u.
Bem rakpart
Fő u.
Varsányi Iren u.
Csalogány u.
Markó u.
Szemere u.
Kossuth Lajos tér
Alkotmány u.
Szél Kálmán tér
Batthyány u.
Báthory u.
Donáti u.
Szabó Ilonka u.
Zoltán u.
Szabadság tér
Danube
Széchenyi rakpart
Táncsics M. u.
Fortuna u.
Úri u.
Tóth Árpád sétány
Hunyadi János út
BUDA
Várhegy
Arany János u.
Nádor u.
PEST
Vérmező
Lógodi u.
South Station
Dísz tér
Roosevelt tér
Attila út
Clark Ádám tér
Széchenyi lánchíd (Chain Br.)
József Attila u.
Erzsébet tér
Vörösmarty tér
Deák F.
Alagút u.
Belgrád rakpart
Groza Péter rakpart
Naphegy u.
Krisztina körút
Váci u.
Mészáros u.
Lisznyai u.
Avar u.
Tigris u.
Hegyalja út
Döbrentei tér
Erzsébet híd (Elizabeth Br.)
Csörsz u.
Orom u.
Bérc u.
Szent Gellért rakpart
Alsó hegy u.
Szirtes út
Somlói út
Kelenhegyi út
Gellért Hill
Szent Gellért tér
Ménesi út
Villányi út
Budaörsi út
Karolina út
KEY
Tourist Information
Alsóhegy u.
Bartók Béla út

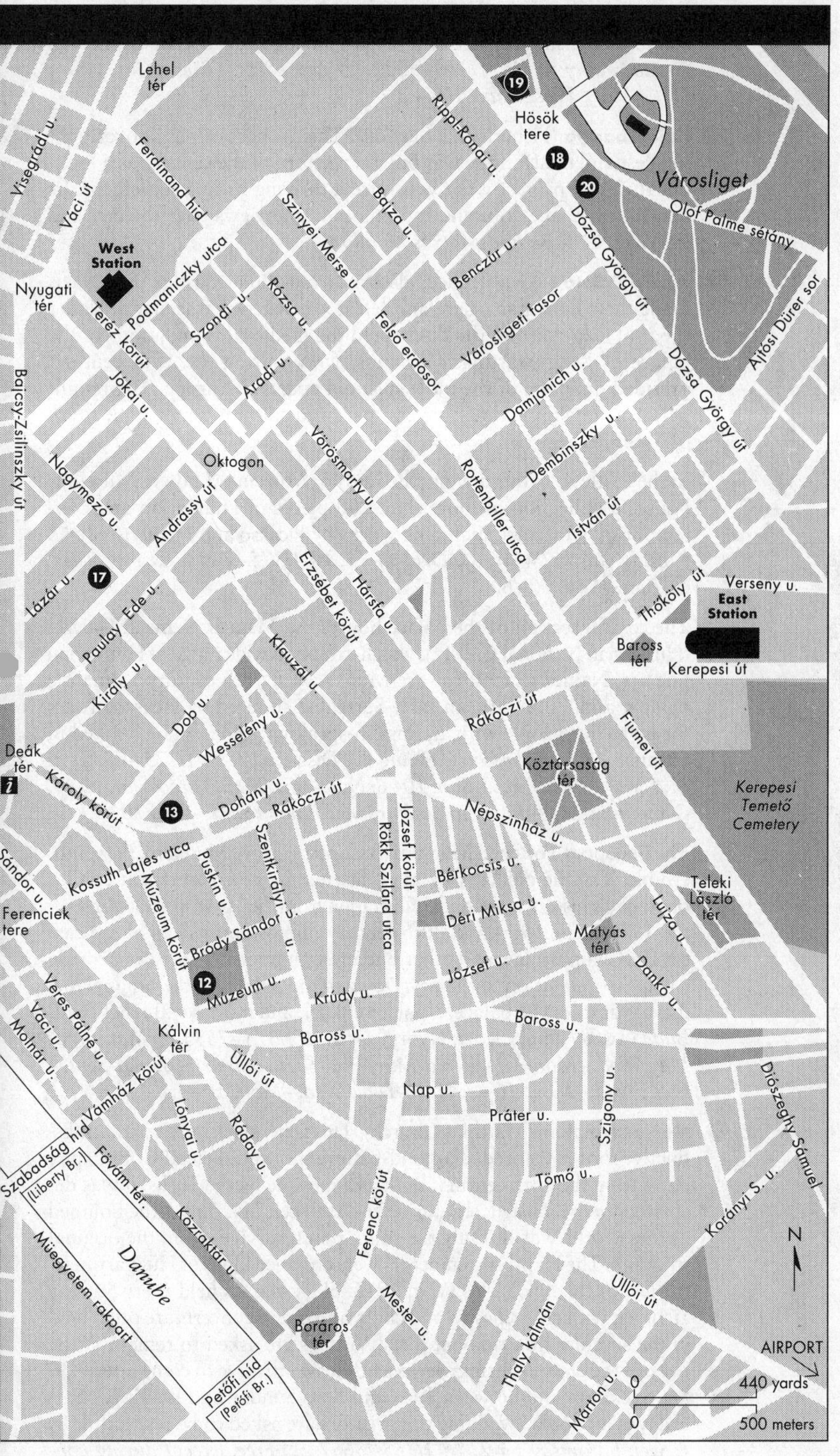

Lehel tér
Visegrádi u.
Váci út
Ferdinand híd
West Station
Nyugati tér
Teréz körút
Podmaniczky utca
Szondi u.
Rózsa u.
Szinyei Merse u.
Bajza u.
Rippl-Rónai u.
Hösök tere
Városliget
Olof Palme sétány
Dózsa György út
Benczúr u.
Felső erdősor
Városligeti fasor
Ajtósi Dürer sor
Bajcsy-Zsilinszky út
Jókai u.
Aradi u.
Oktogon
Vörösmarty u.
Damjanich u.
Dembinszky u.
Rottenbiller utca
Nagymező u.
Andrássy út
István út
Lázár u.
Paulay Ede u.
Erzsébet körút
Hársfa u.
Thököly út
Verseny u.
East Station
Baross tér
Kerepesi út
Király u.
Klauzál u.
Dob u.
Wesselény u.
Rákóczi út
Fiumei út
Deák tér
Károly körút
Dohány u.
Köztársaság tér
Kerepesi Temető Cemetery
Népszínház u.
Kossuth Lajos utca
Puskin u.
Szentkirályi u.
József körút
Rökk Szilárd utca
Bérkocsis u.
Sándor u.
Ferenciek tere
Múzeum körút
Déri Miksa u.
Teleki László tér
Lujza u.
Bródy Sándor u.
Mátyás tér
Danko u.
József u.
Múzeum u.
Krúdy u.
Veres Pálné u.
Váci u.
Kálvin tér
Baross u.
Molnár u.
Üllői út
Vámház körút
Nap u.
Szigony u.
Diószeghy Sámuel
Lónyai u.
Ráday u.
Práter u.
Szabadság híd (Liberty Br.)
Fővám tér
Tömő u.
Ferenc körút
Közraktár u.
Danube
Korányi S. u.
N
Műegyetem rakpart
Mester u.
Üllői út
Boráros tér
Thaly Kálmán
AIRPORT
Petőfi híd (Petőfi Br.)
Márton u.
0
440 yards
0
500 meters

original Magyar conquest in the 9th century up to the middle of this century. English-language tours can be arranged in advance. ✉ *I, Tóth Árpád sétány 40,* ☎ *1/356–9522.* ⏲ *Apr.–Sept., Tues.–Sun. 10–6; Oct.–Mar., Tues.–Sun. 10–4.*

★ ❸ **Halászbástya** (Fishermen's Bastion). This wondrous porch overlooking Pest and the Danube was built at the turn of the century as a lookout tower to protect what was once a thriving fishing settlement. Its neo-Romanesque columns and arches frame views over the city and the river. ✉ *I, Behind Mátyás templom.*

★ ❶ **Királyi Palota** (Royal Palace, also known as Buda Castle). The Nazis made their final stand here and left it a blackened wasteland. Under the rubble archaeologists discovered the medieval foundations of the palace of King Matthias Corvinus, who, during the 15th century, presided over one of the most splendid courts in Europe. The rebuilt palace is now a vast museum complex and cultural center. ✉ *I, south of Szent György tér.*

In the castle's northern wing, the **Ludwig Múzeum** (Ludwig Museum) houses a collection of more than 200 pieces of Hungarian and contemporary world art, including works by Picasso and Lichtenstein. ✉ *I, Buda Castle (Wing A), Dísz tér 17,* ☎ *1/375–7533.* 🎫 *Free Tues.* ⏲ *Tues.–Sun. 10–6.*

The central section of the palace houses the **Magyar Nemzeti Galéria** (Hungarian National Gallery), which exhibits a wide range of Hungarian fine art. Names to look for are Munkácsy, a 19th-century Romantic painter, and Csontváry, an early Surrealist admired by Picasso. Tours for up to five people with an English-speaking guide can be booked in advance. ✉ *I, Buda Castle (Wing C), Dísz tér 17,* ☎ *1/175–7533.* ⏲ *Mid-Mar.–Oct., Tues.–Sun. 10–6; Nov.–mid-Mar., Tues.–Sun. 10–4. (Note: mid-Jan.–mid-Mar., may reduce hours to Fri.–Sun. 10–4.)*

The **Budapesti Történeti Múzeum** (Budapest History Museum), the southern block of the palace, displays a fascinating new permanent exhibit of the city's history from Buda's liberation from the Turks in 1686 through the 1970s. The 19th- and 20th-century photos and videos of the castle, the Chain Bridge, and other Budapest monuments here can provide a helpful orientation to the city. Down in the cellars are the original medieval vaults of the palace, a palace chapel, and more royal relics. ✉ *I, Buda Castle (Wing E), Szt. György tér 2,* ☎ *1/375–7533.* ⏲ *Mar.–mid-May, Wed.–Mon. 10–6; mid-May–mid-Sept., daily 10–6; mid-Sept.–Oct., Wed.–Mon. 10–6; Nov.–Feb., Wed.–Mon. 10–4.*

★ ❷ **Mátyás templom** (Matthias Church). This venerable church with its distinctive roof of colored, diamond-pattern tiles and skeletal Gothic spire dates from the 13th century. Built as a mosque by the Turks, it was destroyed and reconstructed during the 19th century, only to be bombed during World War II. Only the south porch survives from the original structure. The Hapsburg emperors were crowned kings of Hungary here, the last of them, Charles IV, in 1916. High mass is held every Sunday at 10 AM with an orchestra and choir, and organ concerts are often held in the summer on Friday at 8 PM. Visitors are asked to remain at the back of the church during services (it's least intrusive to come after 9:30 AM weekdays and between 1 PM and 5 PM Sunday and holidays). Saturday is a popular wedding day; visitors are asked to be respectful. ✉ *I, Szentháromság tér 2,* ☎ *1/355–5657.* 🎫 *Free, except during concerts.* ⏲ *Church: Daily 7 AM–8 PM; Treasury: Daily 9:30–5:30.*

❹ **Zenetörténeti Múzeum** (Museum of Music History). The handsome, 18th-century gray-stone palace that once belonged to the noble Erdődy family hosts intimate recitals of classical music and displays rare manuscripts and antique instruments. ✉ *I, Táncsics Mihály u. 7,* ☎ *1/214–6770.* ⏲ *Mid-Nov.–late Dec. and 1st 2 wks of Mar., Tues.–Sun. 10–5; mid-Mar.–mid-Nov., Tues.–Sun. 10–6.*

The Heart of the City

Pest fans out from the Belváros (Inner City), which is bounded by the Kiskörút (Little Ring Road). The Nagykörút (Grand Ring Road) describes a wider semicircle from the Margaret Bridge to the Petőfi Bridge.

⓫ **Belvárosi plébánia templom** (Inner-City Parish Church). The oldest church in Pest dates from the 12th century. The structure incorporates a succession of Western architectural styles as well as preserving a Muslim prayer niche from the time when the Turks ruled the country. Liszt, who lived only a few yards away, often played the organ here. ✉ *V, Március 15 tér 2.*

★ **Korzó.** This elegant promenade runs south along the river, providing views of Castle Hill, the Chain Bridge, and Gellért Hill on the other side of the Danube. ✉ *V, from Eötvös tér to Március 15 tér.*

★ ⓱ **Magyar Állami Operaház** (Hungarian State Opera House). Flanked by a pair of marble sphinxes, this 19th-century neo-Renaissance treasure was the crowning achievement of architect Miklós Ybl. It has been restored to its original ornate glory—particularly inside. The best way to view the inside is to attend a ballet or opera, but there are no performances from around mid-July to late September, except for the week-long BudaFest international opera and ballet festival in mid-August. ✉ *VI, Andrássy út 22,* ☎ *1/331–2550, ext. 156 for tours. Foreign-language tours (45 min.) daily, 3 PM and 4 PM, meet in front of opera house.*

⓬ **Magyar Nemzeti Múzeum** (Hungarian National Museum). The stern, classical edifice was built between 1837 and 1847. On its steps, on March 15, 1848, Petőfi Sándor recited his revolutionary poem, the *"Nemzeti Dal"* ("National Song"), declaring "By the God of Magyar, / Do we swear, / Do we swear, chains no longer / Will we wear." This poem, along with the "12 Points," a formal list of political demands by young Hungarians, called upon the people to rise up against the Hapsburgs. Celebrations of the national holiday—long banned by the communist regime—are now held here (and throughout the city) every year on March 15. The museum's most sacred treasure, the Szent Korona (Holy Crown)—the one that looks like a great golden soufflé resting on a Byzantine band of enamel, pearls, and other gems—lies with a host of other royal relics in the domed Hall of Honor. The museum's epic Hungarian history exhibition includes exhibits chronicling the end of communism and the much-celebrated exodus of the Russian troops. ✉ *IX, Múzeum körút 14–16,* ☎ *1/338–2122.* ⏲ *Mid-Mar.–mid-Oct., Wed.–Sun. 10–6; mid-Oct.–mid-Mar., Wed.–Sun. 10–5. Museum may open Tues. also; call ahead to confirm.*

❿ **Március 15 tér** (March 15 Square). This square is not particularly picturesque, but it commemorates the 1848 struggle for independence from the Hapsburgs with a statue of the poet Petőfi Sándor, who died in a later uprising. On March 15, the national holiday commemorating the revolution, the square is packed with patriotic Hungarians. ✉ *V, end of Apácai Csere János u. just north of Erzsébet Bridge.*

⓭ **Nagy Zsinagóga** (Great Synagogue). Europe's largest synagogue was built between 1844 and 1859 in a Byzantine-Moorish style. Desecrated by German and Hungarian Nazis, it underwent years of massive restorations, completed in fall of 1996. Liszt and Saint-Saëns are among the great musicians who have played the synagogue's grand organ. ✉ *VII, Dohány u. 2–8,* ☎ *1/342–1335.* ⊙ *Weekdays 10–3, Sun. 10–1. Closed Jewish holidays.*

★ ⓯ **Néprajzi Múzeum** (Museum of Ethnography). Elegant both inside and out, this museum has impressive, exhaustive exhibits—captioned in English—of folk costumes and traditions. These are the authentic pieces you can't see in tourist shops. ✉ *V, Kossuth Lajos tér 12,* ☎ *1/332–6340.* 🎫 *Free Tues.* ⊙ *Mid-Mar.–mid-Oct., Tues.–Sun. 10–6; mid-Oct.–mid-Mar., Tues.–Sun. 10–4.*

⓮ **Országház** (Parliament). The riverfront's most striking landmark is the imposing neo-Gothic Parliament, now minus the red star on top. Still a workplace for the nation's legislators, it is open for tours only. ✉ *V, Kossuth Lajos tér. For tours: IBUSZ Tours,* ☎ *1/319–7520.*

❻ **Roosevelt tér** (Roosevelt Square). On this picturesque square opening onto the Danube you'll find the 19th-century neoclassical **Magyar Tudományos Akadémia** (Hungarian Academy of Sciences), and the 1907 **Gresham Palota** (Gresham Palace), a crumbling temple to the age of Art Nouveau. ✉ *V, at Pest end of Széchenyi lánchíd (Chain Bridge).*

★ **Széchenyi lánchíd** (Chain Bridge). The most beautiful of the Danube's eight bridges, the Széchenyi lánchíd was built twice: once in the 19th century and again after it was destroyed by the Nazis. Luckily, its classic, symmetrical design was left unchanged. ✉ *Spanning the Danube between I, Clark Ádám tér, and V, Roosevelt tér.*

⓰ **Szent István Bazilika** (St. Stephen's Basilica). Dark and massive, the 19th-century basilica is one of the chief landmarks of Pest. It was planned early in the 19th century as a neoclassical building, but by the time it was completed more than 50 years later, it was decidedly neo-Renaissance. During World War II the most precious documents from the municipal archives were placed in the basilica's bombproof cellar. The mummified right hand of St. Stephen, Hungary's first king and patron saint, is preserved in the Szent Jobb chapel; the guard will illuminate it for you for a minimal charge. A climb up to the cupola (or a lift on the elevator) affords a sweeping city view. As restorations are under way, with a target completion date of 2010, some part of the structure is likely to be under scaffolding when you visit. ✉ *V, Szt. István tér,* ☎ *1/317–2859.* 🎫 *Free.* ⊙ *Church: Mon.–Sat. 7–7, Sun 1–7. Szt. Jobb Chapel: Apr.–Sept., Mon.–Sat. 9–5, Sun. 1–5; Oct.–Mar., Mon.–Sat. 10–4, Sun. 1–4. Cupola: Apr. and Sept.–Oct., daily 10–5; May–Aug., daily 9–6.*

❾ **Váci utca** (Váci Street). Lined with expensive boutiques and dozens of souvenir shops, this pedestrian-only thoroughfare is Budapest's most upscale shopping street, and one of its most touristy areas. Váci utca's stretch south of Kossuth Lajos utca was recently transformed into another pedestrian-only zone, making the total length extend from Vörösmarty tér to the Szabadság Bridge. ✉ *V, south fromVörösmarty tér.*

❽ **Vigadó tér** (Vigadó Square). This square, opening onto a grand Danube view, is named for the **Vigadó concert hall** (☞ Nightlife and the Arts, *below*). The hall was built in an eclectic mix of Byzantine, Moorish, and Romanesque styles; the façade even draws upon the ceremonial knots from the uniforms of the Hungarian hussars. Liszt, Brahms, and Bartók all performed here. Completely destroyed during World War II, it has been faithfully rebuilt. ✉ *V, off the Korzó, between Vigadó u. and Deák Ferenc u.*

7 **Vörösmarty tér** (Vörösmarty Square). In this handsome square in the heart of the Inner City, street musicians and sidewalk cafés combine to make one of the liveliest, albeit sometimes too touristy, atmospheres in Budapest. It's a great spot to sit and relax—but prepare to be approached by caricature artists and money changers. ✉ *V, at northern end of Váci u.*

Hősök tere (Heroes' Square) and Városliget (City Park)

18 **Hősök tere** (Heroes' Square). Budapest's grandest boulevard of music and mansions, Andrássy út, ends appropriately at this sweeping piazza flanked by the Szépművészeti Múzeum (☞ *below*) and the Műcsarnok (☞ *below*). In the center stands the 120-ft bronze **Millenniumi Emlékmű** (Millennium Monument), begun in 1896 to commemorate the 1,000th anniversary of the Magyar Conquest and now newly shining in celebration of yet another 100 years. Statues of Árpád and six other founders of the Magyar nation occupy the base of the monument, while Hungary's greatest rulers and princes stand between the columns on either side. ✉ *VI, Andrássy út at Dózsa György út.*

20 **Műcsarnok** (Palace of Exhibitions). This striking 1895 structure on Heroes' Square schedules exhibitions of contemporary Hungarian and international art and a rich series of films, plays, and concerts. ✉ *XIV, Dózsa György út 37,* ☎ *1/343–7401.* *Free Tues.* ⏲ *Tues.–Sun. 10–6.*

★ 19 **Szépművészeti Múzeum** (Fine Arts Museum). An entire section of this Heroes' Square museum is devoted to Egyptian, Greek, and Roman artifacts, including many rare pieces of Greco-Roman ceramics. The institution's collection of Spanish paintings is among the best of its kind outside Spain. ✉ *XIV, Dózsa György út 41,* ☎ *1/343–9759.* ⏲ *Tues.–Sun. 10–5:30.*

★ **Városliget** (City Park). Just behind Heroes' Square, this 1-square-km (⅓-square-mi) park harbors Budapest's zoo, the state circus, an amusement park, and the outdoor swimming pool of the Széchenyi mineral baths. Inside is **Vajdahunyad Vár** (Vajdahunyad Castle), an art historian's Disneyland, created for the millennial celebration in 1896 and incorporating architectural elements typical of various periods of Hungary's history all in one complex. ✉ *XIV, between Dózsa György út and Hungária körút, and Vágány u. and Ajtósi Dürer sor.*

Elsewhere in the City

Aquincum. The reconstructed remains of the capital of the Roman province of Pannonia, dating from the 1st century AD, lie in northern Budapest's Óbuda district. A varied selection of artifacts and mosaics have been unearthed, giving a tantalizing inkling of what life was like on the northern fringes of the Roman empire. The on-site **Aquincum Museum** displays the dig's most notable finds. ✉ *III, Szentendrei út 139,* ☎ *1/250–1650. Grounds:* ⏲ *Mid-Apr.–end Apr. and Oct., Tues.–Sun. 9–5; May–Sept., Tues.–Sun. 9–6.*

Jánoshegy (János Hill). A *libegő* (chairlift) will take you to the summit, the highest point in Budapest, where you can climb a lookout tower for the best view of the city. ✉ *Take Bus 158 from Moszkva tér to last stop, Zugligeti út,* ☎ *1/395–6494 or 1/376–3764.* ⏲ *Mid-May–mid-Sept., daily 9–5; mid-Sept.–mid-May (depending on weather), daily 9:30–4. Closed alternate Mon.*

Szobor Park (Statue Park). For a look at Budapest's too-recent Iron Curtain past, make the 30-minute trip out to this open-air exhibit cleverly nicknamed "Tons of Socialism." Forty-two communist statues and memorials that once dominated the city have been exiled here since the political changes in 1989. You can wander among mammoth figures of Lenin and Marx while listening to songs from the Hungarian and Russian workers' movement blaring from loudspeakers. ✉ *XXII, Balatoni út, corner of Szabadkai út,* ☎ FAX *1/227–7446.* ⏲ *Mid-Apr.–Oct., daily 8–8; Nov.–mid-Apr., weekends 10–dusk.*

Dining and Lodging

Private restaurateurs are breathing excitement into the Budapest dining scene. You can choose from Chinese, Mexican, Italian, French, Indian, or various other cuisines—there are even vegetarian restaurants. Or you can stick to solid, traditional Hungarian fare. Be sure to check out the less expensive spots favored by locals. If you get a craving for sushi or tortellini, consult the restaurant listings in *The Budapest Sun* or *Budapest Week* (☞ Visitor Information, *below*). For details and price-category definitions, *see* Dining *in* Hungary A to Z, *above.*

Some 30 million tourists come to Hungary every year, and the boom has encouraged hotel building; yet there is sometimes a shortage of rooms, especially in summer. If you arrive in Budapest without a reservation, go to the 24-hour IBUSZ Welcome Hotel Service or to one of the tourist offices at any of the train stations or at the airport. For details and price-category definitions, *see* Lodging *in* Hungary A to Z, *above.*

$$$$ ✕ **Vadrózsa.** The name means "wild rose," and there are always fresh ones on the table at this restaurant in a romantic old villa in Buda's exclusive Rózsadomb district. It's elegant to the last detail—even the service is white-glove—and the garden is delightful in summer. Kitchen fortés include venison and a variety of grilled fish, and the house specialty, grilled goose liver, is exquisite. ✉ *II, Pentelei Molnár u. 15,* ☎ *1/326–5817. Reservations essential. AE, DC, MC, V.*

$$$–$$$$ ✕ **Kacsa.** Hungarian and international dishes with a focus on duck are done with a light touch, with quiet chamber music in the background, in this small, celebrated restaurant just a few steps from the river. Try the crisp wild duck stuffed with plums. ✉ *II, Fő u. 75,* ☎ *1/201–9992. Reservations essential. AE, DC, MC, V. Dinner only.*

$$$–$$$$ ✕ **Múzeum.** Named for its location just steps from the National Museum, this elegant salon with mirrors, mosaics, and swift-moving waiters serves authentic Hungarian cuisine with a lighter touch. The salads are generous, the Hungarian wines excellent, and the chef dares to be creative. ✉ *VIII, Múzeum körút 12,* ☎ *1/267–0375. AE. Closed Sun.*

$$$ ★ ✕ **Gundel.** George Lang, Hungary's best-known restaurateur, showcases his country's cuisine at this lauded turn-of-the-century palazzo in City Park. Dark-wood paneling, rich navy-blue and pink fabrics, paintings by exemplary Hungarian artists, and tables set with Zsolnay porcelain make the oversize dining room plush and handsome. Violinist György Lakatos, of the Lakatos Gypsy musician dynasty, strolls from table to table playing folk music, adding to the sensory extravagance. Waiters in black tie serve traditional favorites such as tender veal in a paprika-and-sour-cream sauce and carp *Dorozsma* (panfried with mushrooms). ✉ *XIV, Állatkerti út 2,* ☎ *1/321–3550. Reservations essential. AE, DC, MC, V.*

$$$ ✕ **Kisbuda Gyöngye.** This Budapest favorite, hidden away on a small street in Óbuda, is filled with mixed antique furniture, and its walls are covered with a patchwork of antique carved wooden cupboard doors. Try the fresh trout smothered in cream sauce with mushrooms and capers. ✉ *III, Kenyeres u. 34,* ☎ *1/368–6402 or 1/368–9246. Reservations essential. AE, DC, MC, V. Closed Sun.*

$$$ ★ ✕ **Lou Lou.** Since it opened in 1995, this convivial bistro tucked onto a side street near the Danube has been the hottest restaurant in Budapest. Framed prints, low lighting, and candles conjure a tasteful, elegantly romantic atmosphere. Blending local and Continental cuisines, the menu includes excellent rack of lamb—flown in fresh from New Zealand, and succulent fresh salmon with lemongrass; the Dijon-spiced venison fillets with wild berry sauce are a standout. At press time, Lou Lou was planning to relocate to a larger venue; check with Tourinform (☞ Visitor Information, *below*) for the latest information. ✉ *V, Vigyázó Ferenc u. 4,* ☎ *1/312–4505. Reservations essential. AE. Closed daily 3–7; Sat. lunch; Sun.*

$$$ ✕ **Müvészinas.** Walls hung with framed vintage prints and photos, antique vitrines filled with old books, and tall slender candles on the tables create a romantic, old-world ambience in this bustling, bistrolike restaurant in the heart of Pest. Dozens of Hungarian specialties fill the long menu; beef, veal, and poultry are each prepared a half-dozen ways, from sirloin "Budapest style" (smothered in a goose-liver, mushrooms, and sweet-pepper ragout) to spinach-stuffed turkey breast in fragrant garlic sauce. Poppy-seed crepes with plum sauce are a sublime dessert. ✉ *VI, Bajcsy-Zsilinszky út 9,* ☎ *1/268–1439. Reservations essential. AE, MC, V.*

$$ ✕ **Bagolyvár.** George Lang opened this restaurant next door to his gastronomic palace, Gundel (☞ *above*), in 1993. The immaculate dining room with soaring beamed ceilings has a familial yet professional atmosphere, and the kitchen produces first-rate daily menus of home-style Hungarian specialties. Soups, served in shiny silver tureens, are particularly good. Musicians entertain with cimbalom music nightly from 7 PM. In warm weather there is outdoor dining on a roomy back patio. ✉ *VI, Állatkerti körút 2,* ☎ *1/343–0217. AE, DC, MC, V.*

$$ ✕ **Náncsi Néni.** "Aunt Nancy's" restaurant is a perennial favorite, despite its out-of-the-way location. Irresistibly cozy, the dining room feels like a country kitchen: Chains of paprikas and garlic dangle from the low wooden ceiling and shelves along the walls are crammed with jars of home-pickled vegetables, which you can purchase to take home. On the home-style Hungarian menu (large portions!), turkey dishes are given a creative flair, such as breast fillets stuffed with apples, peaches, mushrooms, cheese, and sour cream. Special touches include an outdoor garden in summer and free champagne for all couples in love. ✉ *II, Ördögárok út 80,* ☎ *1/397–2742. AE, MC, V.*

$ ✕ **Fészek.** Hidden away inside the 100-year-old Fészek Artists' Club in downtown Pest is this large, neoclassical dining room. In summer, you can dine outdoors in a Venetian-style courtyard. The extensive menu proffers heavy Hungarian classics such as turkey stuffed with goose liver and a variety of game dishes; the venison stew with tarragon is outstanding. Guests must pay a 150-Ft. Artists' Club cover charge upon arrival; if you've reserved a table in advance, the fee will be added to your bill instead. ✉ *VII, Kertész u. 36 (corner of Dob u.),* ☎ *1/322–6043. AE, DC, MC, V.*

$ ★ ✕ **Tüköry Söröző.** At this traditional Hungarian spot, courageous carnivores can sample the beefsteak tartar, topped with a raw egg; many say it's the best in town. ✉ *V, Hold u. 15,* ☎ *1/269–5027. MC, V. Closed weekends.*

$$$$ ★ 🏨 **Budapest Hilton.** Built in 1977 around a 13th-century monastery adjacent to the Matthias Church, this perfectly integrated architectural wonder overlooks the Danube from the best site on Castle Hill. Every ample, contemporary room has a remarkable view; all are being further improved by complete renovations during 1999. Service is of the highest caliber. ✉ *I, Hess András tér 1–3, H-1014,* ☎ *1/214–3000,*

800/445–8667 in U.S. and Canada, FAX *1/156–0285. 295 rooms, 27 suites. 3 restaurants, air-conditioning. AE, DC, MC, V.*

$$$$ ★ **Budapest Marriott.** At this sophisticated yet friendly hotel near downtown Pest, every detail sparkles, including the marble floors and dark-wood paneling in the lobby. Stunning vistas open from every guest room, the ballroom, and even the fitness room. Most rooms have a balcony. Fitness facilities are outstanding. ✉ *V, Apáczai Csere János u. 4, H-1364,* ☎ *1/266–7000, 800/831–4004 in U.S. and Canada,* FAX *1/266–5000. 362 rooms, 20 suites. 3 restaurants, air-conditioning. AE, DC, MC, V.*

$$$$ **Danubius Hotel Gellért.** Built in 1918 in the *Jugendstil* (Art Nouveau style), this grand old lady with its double-deck rotunda sits regally at the foot of Gellért Hill. One of Hungary's most prized spa hotels, it also houses wonderfully ornate thermal baths—free to guests. Rooms range from palatial suites to awkward, tiny spaces and have either early 20th-century furnishings, including some authentic Jugendstil pieces, or newer, more basic contemporary decor. Rooms that face the building's inner core are drastically less expensive, but cramped and viewless. Now part of the Danubius hotel chain, the Gellért began an ambitious three- to four-year overhaul—including the addition of air-conditioning and refurnishing of all rooms in the mood of the original Eclectic-flourished Jugendstil style—in 1998. If you prefer them, inquire about completed rooms when reserving. Breakfast is included in the room rates. ✉ *XI, Gellért tér 1, H-1111,* ☎ *1/385–2200,* FAX *1/466–6631. 199 rooms, 13 suites. Restaurant, 2 pools. AE, DC, MC, V.*

$$$$ **Hotel Intercontinental Budapest.** Formerly the Forum Hotel, this boxy, modern riverside hotel consistently wins applause for its gracious appointments, friendly service, and gorgeous views across the Danube to Castle Hill. (Half the rooms look onto the street, so be sure to request one facing the river.) The hotel café, Bécsi Kávéház, is locally renowned for its pastries—and the fitness facilities similarly excellent. ✉ *V, Apáczai Csere János u. 12–14, Box 231, H-1368,* ☎ *1/327–6333,* FAX *1/327–6357. 392 rooms, 16 suites. 2 restaurants, pool, air-conditioning. AE, DC, MC, V.*

$$$$ ★ **Kempinski Hotel Corvinus Budapest.** Afternoon chamber music sets the tone at this sleek luxury hotel, a favorite of visiting VIPs. Rooms are spacious, with elegant contemporary decor featuring geometric blond-and-black Swedish inlaid woods. Large, sparkling bathrooms, most with tubs and separate shower stalls, are the best in Budapest. ✉ *V, Erzsébet tér 7–8,H-1051,* ☎ *1/266–1000, 800/426–3135 in the U.S. and Canada,* FAX *1/266–2000. 337 rooms, 28 suites. 2 restaurants, air-conditioning, pool. AE, DC, MC, V.*

$$$ **Danubius Grand Hotel.** Set on a car-free island in the Danube and connected to a bubbling thermal spa (free for guests), the Danubius (formerly Ramada) Grand feels removed from the city but is still only a short taxi- or bus-ride away. This venerable hotel, built in 1873, has been completely modernized, yet retains its period look, with high ceilings and Old-World furnishings. Room prices include breakfast. ✉ *XIII, Margit-sziget, H-1138,* ☎ *1/329–2300; 1/353–3029 for reservations;* FAX *1/153–3029. 164 rooms, 10 suites. Restaurant, pool. AE, DC, MC, V.*

$$$ **Danubius Thermal Hotel Helia.** Sleek Scandinavian design and a relatively tranquil location upriver make this spa hotel on the Danube a change of pace from its Pest peers. The neighborhood is nondescript, but the hotel is minutes from town and has thermal baths, spa, and special health packages. On-site tennis courts are a plus, and breakfast is included in the room rates. ✉ *XIII, Kárpát u. 62–64, H-1133,* ☎ *1/270–3277, 800/223–5652 in the U.S. and Canada,* FAX *1/270–2262. 254 rooms, 8 suites. Restaurant, pool. AE, DC, MC, V.*

$$ **Alba Hotel.** Tucked behind an alleyway at the foot of Castle Hill, this spotless, modern hotel is a short walk via the Chain Bridge from business and shopping districts. Rooms are snug and quiet, with white and pale-gray contemporary decor and quintessentially Budapestian views over rooftops and chimneys. Half of the rooms have bathtubs. A buffet breakfast is included in the room price. ✉ *I, Apor Péter u. 3, H-1011,* ☎ *1/375–9244,* FAX *1/375–9899. 50 rooms with bath, 45 with shower. Air-conditioning. AE, DC, MC, V.*

$$ **Astoria.** Revolutionaries and intellectuals once gathered in the marble-and-gilt Art Deco lobby here. Rooms are Empire-style and renovations have not obscured their charm. Rather, they added comforts—most notably soundproofing, which is essential as the Astoria stands at a busy downtown intersection. Breakfast is included in the room rates. ✉ *V, Kossuth Lajos u. 19–21, H-1053,* ☎ *1/317–3411,* FAX *1/318–6798. 25 rooms, 5 suites. Restaurant. AE, DC, MC, V.*

$$ ★ **Victoria.** The stately Parliament building is visible from every room of this relatively young establishment right on the Danube. The absence of conventioneers is a plus, and the location—an easy walk from Castle Hill and downtown Pest—couldn't be better. Room rates include breakfast. ✉ *I, Bem rakpart 11, H-1011,* ☎ *1/457–8080,* FAX *1/457–8088. 27 rooms, 1 suite. Air-conditioning. AE, DC, MC, V.*

$ ★ **Kulturinnov.** One wing of a magnificent 1902 neo-Baroque castle now houses basic budget accommodations. Rooms come with two or three beds and are clean and delightfully peaceful; breakfast is included in the rates. The neighborhood—one of Budapest's most famous squares in the luxurious castle district—is magical. ✉ *I, Szentháromság tér 6, H-1014,* ☎ *1/355–0122 or 1/375–1651,* FAX *1/375–1886. 16 rooms. AE, DC, MC, V.*

$ **Molnár Panzió.** Fresh air, peace, and quiet reign at this immaculate guest house high above Buda on Széchenyi Hill. Rooms in the octagonal main house are polyhedral, clean, and bright; most have distant views of Castle Hill and Gellért Hill, and some have balconies. Service is both friendly and professional, and the restaurant is first-rate. A Finnish sauna and garden setting add to the pension's appeal. ✉ *XII, Fodor u. 143, H-1124,* ☎ *1/395–1873,* ☎ FAX *1/395–1872. 23 rooms. Restaurant, air-conditioning in 8 rooms. AE, DC, MC, V.*

Nightlife and the Arts

The Arts

The English-language *The Budapest Sun* and *Budapest Week* list the week's entertainment and cultural events. Hotels and tourist offices distribute the monthly *Programme,* which contains details of all cultural events in the city. The monthly *Where Budapest,* free at most hotels, is another good resource in English. Buy tickets at venue box offices, your hotel desk, many tourist offices, or ticket agencies, among them the **National Philharmonic Ticket Office** (✉ V, Vörösmarty tér 1, ☎ 1/318–0281) and the **Central Theater Booking Office** (✉ VI, Andrássy út 18, ☎ 1/312–0000).

Arts festivals begin to fill the calendar in early spring. The season's first and biggest, the **Budapest Spring Festival** (early to mid-March), showcases Hungary's best opera, music, theater, fine arts, and dance, as well as visiting foreign artists. The weeklong **BudaFest** opera and ballet festival (mid-August) takes place at the Opera House. Information and tickets are available from ticket agencies (☞ *above*).

CONCERTS AND MUSICALS

Several excellent orchestras, such as the Budapest Festival Orchestra, are based in Budapest. Concerts frequently include works by Hungarian composers Bartók, Kodály, and Liszt. **Liszt Ferenc Zeneakadémia** (Franz Liszt Academy of Music; ✉ VI, Liszt Ferenc tér 8, ☎ 1/342–0179) is Budapest's premier classical concert venue; orchestra and chamber music performances take place in its splendid main hall. Classical concerts are also held at the **Pesti Vigadó** (Pest Concert Hall; ✉ V, Vigadó tér 2, ☎ 1/318–9167). The **Régi Zeneakadémia** (Old Academy of Music; ✉ VI, Vörösmarty u. 35, ☎ 1/322–9804) is a smaller venue for chamber music. The 1896 **Vígszínház** (Comedy Theater; ✉ XIII, Pannónia út 1, ☎ 1/269–5340) presents mostly musicals. Operettas and Hungarian renditions of popular Broadway musicals are staged at the **Operett Színház** (Operetta Theater; ✉ VI, Nagymező u. 19, ☎ 1/332–0535).

OPERA AND DANCE

Budapest has two opera houses, one of which is the gorgeous neo-Renaissance **Magyar Állami Operaház** (Hungarian State Opera House; ✉ VI, Andrássy út 22, ☎ 1/331–2550). There's also the plainer **Erkel Színház** (Erkel Theater; ✉ VIII, Köztársaság tér, ☎ 1/333–0540).

Displays of Hungarian folk dancing take place at the **Folklór Centrum** (Folklore Center; ✉ XI, Fehérvári út 47, ☎ 1/203–3868). The Hungarian State Folk Ensemble performs regularly at the **Budai Vigadó** (✉ I, Corvin tér 8, ☎ 1/201–5846). There are regular participatory folk-dance evenings—with instructions for beginners—at district cultural centers; consult the entertainment listings of *The Budapest Sun* or *Budapest Week* for schedules and locations, or check with a hotel concierge.

Nightlife

Budapest is a lively city by night. Establishments stay open well past midnight and Western European–style bars and British-style pubs have sprung up all over the city. For quiet conversation, hotel bars are a good choice, but beware of the inflated prices. Expect to pay cash for your night on the town. The city also has its share of seedy go-go clubs and "cabarets," some of which have been shut down for scandalously excessive billing and physical intimidation and assault. Avoid places where women lingering nearby "invite" you in, and never order without first seeing the price.

BARS

The most popular of Budapest's Irish pubs and a favorite expat watering hole is **Becketts** (✉ V, Bajcsy-Zsilinszky út 72, ☎ 1/311–1035), where Guinness flows freely amid polished-wood and brass decor. A hip, low-key crowd mingles at the stylish **Café Incognito** (✉ VI, Liszt Ferenc tér 3, ☎ 1/351–9428), with low lighting and funky music kept at a conversation-friendly volume by savvy DJs. **Café Pierrot** (✉ I, Fortuna u. 14, ☎ 1/375–6971), an elegant café and piano bar on a small street on Castle Hill, is well suited for a secret rendezvous.

CASINOS

Most casinos are open daily from 2 PM until 4 or 5 AM and offer gambling in hard currency—usually dollars—only. Sylvester Stallone is alleged to be an owner of the popular **Las Vegas Casino** (✉ V, Roosevelt tér 2, ☎ 1/317–6022), in the Atrium Hyatt Hotel. The **Gresham Casino** (✉ V, Roosevelt tér 5, ☎ 1/317–2407) is in the Gresham Palace at the Pest end of the Chain Bridge. In an 1879 building designed by prolific architect Miklós Ybl, who also designed the Hungarian State Opera House, the **Várkert Casino** (✉ I, Miklós Ybl tér 9, ☎ 1/202–4244) is the most attractive in the city.

JAZZ AND ROCK CLUBS

Established Hungarian jazz headliners and young up-and-comers play nightly at **The Long Jazz Club** (✉ VII, Dohány u. 22–24, ☎ 1/322–

0006; closed Sun.). **Made Inn** (✉ VI, Andrássy út 112, ☎ 1/311–3437), in an old stone mansion near Heroes' Square, has elaborate decor, a large outdoor bar, and a disco dance floor packed with local and international beautiful people. With wrought-iron and maroon-velvet decor, the stylish but unpretentious **Fél 10 Jazz Club** (✉ VIII, Baross u. 30, ☎ 06/60–318–467) has a dance floor and two bars on three open levels.

Shopping

You'll find plenty of expensive boutiques, folk art and souvenir shops, and classical record shops on or around **Váci utca,** Budapest's pedestrian-only promenade. Browsing among some of the smaller, less touristy, more typically Hungarian shops in Pest—on the **Kiskörút** (Small Ring Boulevard) and **Nagykörút** (Great Ring Boulevard)—may prove more interesting and less pricey. Artsy boutiques are springing up in the section of district V south of Ferenciek tere toward the Danube and around Kálvin tér. **Falk Miksa utca,** north of Parliament, is home to some of the city's best antiques stores. You'll also encounter Transylvanian women dressed in colorful folk costume standing on busy sidewalks selling their own handmade embroideries and ceramics at rock-bottom prices. Look for them at **Moszkva tér, Jászai Mari tér,** outside the **Kossuth tér Metro,** and around **Váci utca.**

The popular, modern **Skála-Metro** department store (✉ VI, Nyugati tér 1–2) near the Nyugati train station sells a little bit of not entirely everything; its Buda branch, Skála-Budapest (✉ XI, Október 23 u. 6–10), is larger and usually has a large open-air market out front.

Markets

The magnificent, cavernous, three-story **Vásárcsarnok** (Central Market Hall; ✉ IX, Vámház körút 1–3) teems with shoppers browsing among stalls packed with salamis, red paprika chains, and other enticements. Upstairs you can buy folk embroideries and souvenirs.

A good way to find bargains (and adventure) is to make an early morning trip out to **Ecseri Piac** (✉ IX, Nagykőrösi út—take Bus 54 from Boráros tér), a vast, colorful, chaotic flea market on the outskirts of Budapest. Try to go Saturday morning when by far the most vendors are out. Foreigners are a favorite target for overcharging, so prepare to be tough when bargaining.

Budapest Essentials

Arriving and Departing

BY BUS

Most buses to Budapest from the western region of Hungary and from Vienna arrive at **Erzsébet tér station** (✉ V, Erzsébet tér, ☎ 1/317–2318) downtown.

BY CAR

The main routes into Budapest are the M1 from Vienna (via Győr), the M5 from Kecskemét, the M3 from near Gyöngyös, and the M7 from the Balaton region.

BY PLANE

The only nonstop service between Budapest and the United States is aboard **Malév** (☎ 1/235–3535; 06/80–212–121 toll free or 1/235–3804 for tickets).

Hungary's international airport, **Ferihegy** (☎ 1/296–9696), is about 22 km (14 mi) southeast of the city. All **Lufthansa** and **Malév** flights operate from the newer Terminal 2; other airlines use Terminal 1. For same-day flight information call the airport authority (☎ 1/296–7155), where operators theoretically speak some English.

Between the Airport and Downtown. Minibuses marked LRI CENTRUM-AIRPORT-CENTRUM leave every half hour from 5:30 AM to 9:30 PM for the Erzsébet tér station (Platform 1) in downtown Budapest. The trip takes 30–40 minutes and costs around 700 Ft. The modern minivans of the reliable **LRI Airport Shuttle** (☎ 1/296–8555 or 1/296–6283) take you to any destination in Budapest, door to door, for around 1,300 Ft., even less than the least expensive taxi—and most employees speak English. At the airport buy tickets at the LRI counter in the arrivals hall near baggage claim; for your return trip call ahead for a pick-up. There are also approved **Airport Taxi** (☎ 1/282–2222) stands outside both terminals, with fixed rates based on which district you are going to. The cost to the central districts is about 3,500 Ft. Going to the airport, the cost is 1,999 Ft.; call one day ahead to arrange for a pick-up.

BY TRAIN

There are three main train stations in Budapest: **Keleti** (Eastern; ✉ VII, Rákóczi út, ☎ 1/313–6835), **Nyugati** (Western; ✉ V, Nyugati tér, ☎ 1/331–5346), and **Déli** (Southern; ✉ XII, Alkotás u., ☎ 1/375–6593). Trains for Vienna usually depart from Keleti station, those for Lake Balaton from Déli.

Getting Around

Budapest is best explored on foot. The maps provided by tourist offices are not very detailed, so arm yourself with one from any of the bookshops in Váci utca or from a stationery shop or newsstand.

BY BICYCLE

On Margaret Island in Budapest, **Bringóhintó** (✉ Hajós Alfréd sétány 1, across from the Thermal Hotel, ☎ 1/329–2072) rents four-wheeled pedaled contraptions called *Bringóhintós,* as well as traditional two-wheelers; standard bikes cost about 450 Ft. per hour, 600–1,000 Ft. for 24 hours. For more information about renting in Budapest, contact **Tourinform** (✉ V, Sütő u. 2, ☎ 1/317–9800).

BY PUBLIC TRANSPORTATION

The Budapest Transportation Authority (BKV) runs the public transportation system—the Metro (subway) with three lines, buses, streetcars, and trolleybuses—and it's cheap, efficient, and simple to use. Most of it closes down around 11:30 PM, but certain trams and buses run on a limited schedule all night. A *napijegy* (day ticket) costs about 600 Ft. (three-day "tourist ticket," around 1,200 Ft.) and allows unlimited travel on all services within the city limits. Metro stations or newsstands sell single-ride tickets for about 70 Ft. You can travel on all trams, buses, and on the subway with this ticket, but you can't change lines or direction.

Bus, streetcar, and trolleybus tickets must be canceled on board—watch how other passengers do it. Metro tickets are canceled at station entrances. Plainclothes agents wearing red armbands do frequent spot checks, often targeting tourists, and you can be fined several hundred forints if you don't have a canceled ticket.

BY TAXI

Taxis are plentiful and are a good value, but make sure that they have a working meter. The average initial charge is 50 Ft.–75 Ft., to which is added about 110 Ft. per km (½ mi) plus 30 Ft. per minute of waiting time. Avoid unmarked "freelance" taxis; stick with those affiliated with an established company. Your safest bet is to do what the locals do and order a taxi by phone. Simply provide the phone number you're calling from and they will know where you are; a car will arrive in about 5 to 10 minutes. The best rates are offered by **Citytaxi** (☎ 1/211–1111), **Fôtaxi** (☎ 1/222–2222) and **6 X 6** (☎ 1/266–6666).

Contacts and Resources

EMBASSIES

United States (✉ V, Szabadság tér 12, ☎ 1/267–4400). **Canadian** (✉ Mailing address: XII, Budakeszi út 32; ✉ street address: XII, Zugligeti út 51–53, ☎ 1/275–1200). **United Kingdom** (✉ V, Harmincad u. 6, ☎ 1/266–2888). **Australian** (✉ XII, Királyhágó tér 8–9, ☎ 1/201–8899).

EMERGENCIES

Police (☎ 107). **Ambulance** (☎ 104 or 1/200–0100 private, English-speaking). **Doctor** (☎ 1/325–9999 private, English-speaking). **24-hour pharmacies** (**Gyógyszertár,** in Pest, ☎ 1/311–4439; in Buda, ☎ 1/355–4691).

ENGLISH-LANGUAGE BOOKSTORES

Bestsellers (✉ V, Október 6 u. 11, ☎ 1/312–1295). **Central European University Academic Bookshop** (✉ V, Nádor u. 9, ☎ 1/327–3096).

GUIDED TOURS

Boat. From late March through October boats leave from the quay at Vigadó tér on 1½-hour cruises between the railroad bridges north and south of the Árpád and Petőfi bridges, respectively. The trip, organized by **MAHART Tours** (☎ 1/318–1704), runs only on weekends and holidays until late April, then once or twice a day, depending on the season; the trip costs around 800 Ft.

Excursions. Excursions farther afield include day-long trips to the *Puszta* (Great Plain), the Danube Bend, and Lake Balaton. **IBUSZ Travel** (☞ Visitor Information, *below*) offers trips to the Buda Hills and stays in many of Hungary's historic castles and mansions.

Orientation. Year-round, **IBUSZ Travel** (☞ Visitor Information, *below*) sponsors three-hour bus tours of the city that cost about 4,000 Ft. Starting from Erzsébet tér, they take in parts of both Buda and Pest. **Gray Line Cityrama** (✉ V, Báthori u. 22, ☎ 1/302–4382) also offers a three-hour city bus tour (about 4,000 Ft. per person).

Special-Interest. IBUSZ Travel (☞ Visitor Information, *below*), Gray Line Cityrama (☞ Orientation, *above*), and Budapest Tourist (☞ Visitor Information, *below*) organize a number of unusual tours, including horseback riding, bicycling, and angling, as well as visits to the National Gallery. These tour companies will provide personal guides on request. Also check at your hotel's reception desk.

The Chosen Tours (✉ XII, Zolyomi lépcső 27, ☎ 1/319–3427 or ☎ FAX 1/319–6800) offers a three-hour combination bus and walking tour (about 3,400 Ft.), "Budapest Through Jewish Eyes," highlighting the sights and cultural life of the city's important Jewish community.

TRAVEL AGENCIES

American Express (✉ V, Déak Ferenc u. 10, ☎ 1/266–8680). **Getz International** (✉ V, Falk Miksa u. 5, ☎ 1/269–3728 or 1/312–0649). **Vista** (✉ VI, Andrássy út 1, ☎ 1/269–6032, 1/269–6033, or 1/267–8603).

VISITOR INFORMATION

Tourinform (✉ V, Sütő u. 2, ☎ 1/317–9800. **Tourism Office of Budapest** (✉ V, Március 15 tér 7, ☎ 1/117–5964, 1/266–0479; ✉ VI, Nyugati pályaudvar, ☎ 1/302–8580). **IBUSZ Travel** (main branch, ✉ V, Ferenciek tere 10, ☎ 1/318–6866; tours and programs, ✉ Rubin Aktiv Hotel, XI, Dajka Gábor u. 3, Budapest, ☎ 1/319–7510 main, 1/319–7520 program information). **IBUSZ Welcome Hotel Service** (✉ V,

Apáczai Csere János u. 1, ☎ 1/318–3925 or 1/118–5776). **Budapest Tourist** (✉ V, Roosevelt tér 5, ☎ 1/317–3555).

The English-language weeklies *The Budapest Sun* and *Budapest Week* cover news, business, and culture and carry tips for visitors.

The Tourism Office of Budapest (☞ *above*) has developed the **Budapest Card,** which entitles holders to unlimited travel on public transportation; free admission to many museums and sights; and discounts on various purchases, entertainment events, tours, meals, and services from participating businesses. The cost is 2,000 Ft. for two days, 2,500 Ft. for three days; one card is valid for an adult plus a child under 14.

THE DANUBE BEND

About 40 km (25 mi) north of Budapest, the Danube abandons its eastward course and turns abruptly south toward the capital, cutting through the Börzsöny and Visegrád hills. In this area, the Danube Bend, are the Baroque town of Szentendre, the hilltop castle ruins and town of Visegrád, and the cathedral town of Esztergom.

Here, in the heartland, are traces of the country's history—the remains of the Roman empire's frontiers, the battlefields of the Middle Ages, and relics of the Hungarian Renaissance. Just 40 minutes from Budapest, Szentendre is a popular day trip. Although the entire area can be covered by car in a day—the round-trip from Budapest is only 124 km (77 mi)—two days, with a night in Visegrád or Esztergom, would be a better way to savor its charms.

Szentendre

★ The lively, flourishing artists' colony of Szentendre was first settled by Serbs and Greeks fleeing the advancing Turks during the 14th and 17th centuries. The narrow cobbled streets are lined with cheerfully painted houses, many now containing art galleries. Unfortunately, tacky souvenir shops have appeared, and in summer, the streets swarm with tourists. Part of the town's artistic reputation can be traced to the ceramic artist Margit Kovács, whose pottery blended Hungarian folk art traditions with motifs from modern art. The **Kovács Margit Múzeum** (Margit Kovács Museum), in a small, 18th-century merchant's house, is devoted to her work. ✉ *Vastag György u. 1,* ☎ *26/310–244.* ⏲ *Mid-Mar.–early Oct., daily 10–6; early Oct.–mid-Mar., Tues.–Sun. 10–4.*

The **Szabadtéri Néprajzi Múzeum** (Open-Air Ethnography Museum) re-creates Hungarian peasant life and folk architecture of the 19th century. Crafts demonstrations are held in summer. ✉ *Szabadság Forrás út,* ☎ *26/312–304.* ⏲ *Apr.–Oct., Tues.–Sun. 10–5.*

$$ ✕ **Rab Ráby.** This popular restaurant, decorated with wood beams and equestrian gear, is a great place for fish soup and fresh grilled trout. ✉ *Péter Pál u. 1,* ☎ *26/310–819. Reservations essential in summer. No credit cards.*

$$ 🏨 **Bükkös Panzió.** Impeccably clean, this stylishly modernized old house is on a small canal just a few minutes' walk from the town center. The narrow staircase and small rooms give it a homey feel. ✉ *Bükkös part 16, H-2000,* ☎ *26/312–021 or* ☎ FAX *26/310–782. 16 rooms. Restaurant. MC, V.*

Visegrád

This hilly village presided over by a mountaintop fortress was the seat of the kings of Hungary during the 14th century. The ruins of the palace of King Matthias on the main street have been excavated and recon-

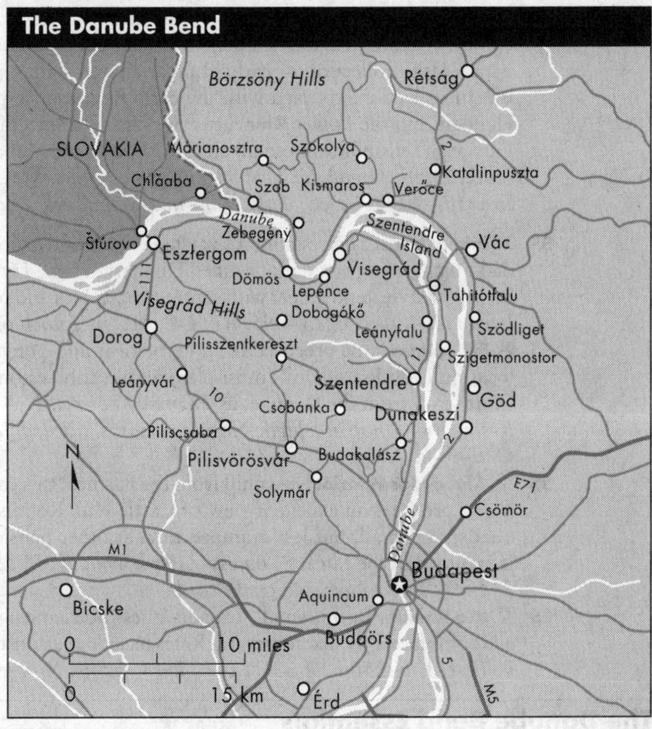

structed; there are jousting tournaments on the grounds of the fortress in June and a medieval festival in July. A winding road leads up to the haunting late-medieval fortress, **Fellegvár** (Citadel), from which you have a fine view of the Danube Bend. ☎ *26/398–101.* ⏲ *Mid-Mar.–mid-Nov., daily 9–5.*

$$$ 🏨 **Silvanus.** Set high up on Fekete hill, this hotel is renowned for its spectacular views and offers hiking trails through the forest. Rooms are bright and clean. A buffet breakfast is included in the rates. ✉ *Fekete-hegy, H-2025,* ☎ FAX *26/398–311 or 26/398–170. 88 rooms, 5 suites. Restaurant. AE, MC, V.*

$ 🏨 **Haus Honti.** This intimate, alpine-style pension, named for its owner, József Honti, is in a quiet residential area far from the main highway but close to the Danube ferry. A stream running near the house amplifies the country atmosphere. ✉ *Fő u. 66 H-2025,* ☎ *26/398–120. 7 rooms. No credit cards.*

Esztergom

This primarily Baroque town stands on the site of a Roman fortress. St. Stephen, the first Christian king of Hungary, was crowned here in the year 1000. The kings are long gone, but Esztergom is still the home of the archbishop of Esztergom, the cardinal primate, head of the Catholic church in Hungary.

★ Thousands of pilgrims visit the imposing **Bazilika** (basilica), the largest in Hungary, which stands on Vár-domb (Castle Hill) overlooking the town. It was here that the anticommunist cleric, Cardinal József Mindszenty, was finally reburied in 1991, ending an era of religious intolerance and persecution. The cathedral also houses a valuable collection of ecclesiastical art. ✉ *Szt. István tér,* ☎ *33/411–895.* 🎫 *Free.* ⏲ *Apr.–late-Oct., daily 7–6; late-Oct.–Mar., weekdays, 7–4, weekends 7–5.*

The **Keresztény Múzeum** (Museum of Christian Art) is in the Prímási Palota (Primate's Palace). It is one of the finest art galleries in Hungary, with a large collection of early Hungarian and Italian paintings. The Italian collection, coupled with the early Renaissance paintings from Flanders and the Lower Rhine, provides insights into the transition of European sensibilities from medieval Gothic to the humanistic Renaissance. ✉ *Mindszenty tér 2,* ☎ *33/413–880.* ⏲ *Mid-Mar.–Sept., Tues.–Sun. 10–6; Oct.–Dec.; early Mar.–mid-Mar., Tues.–Sun. 10–5.*

$$ ✕ **Prímáspince.** This restaurant's vaulted ceilings and exposed brick walls make a charming setting for refined Hungarian fare. Try the tournedos Budapest style, tender beef with sautéed vegetables and paprika. ✉ *Szt. István tér 4,* ☎ *33/313–495. AE, DC, MC, V. Lunch only Jan.–Feb.*

$ ✕ **Fili Falatozó.** Be prepared for a hefty meat-and-potatoes meal. The location is on Esztergom's most pleasant old cobblestone street, just a short stroll from the Danube. ✉ *Pázmány Péter u. 1,* ☎ *33/312–534. Reservations not accepted. No credit cards. Closed Jan. and Mon. Oct.–Mar.*

$$ 🏨 **Alabárdos Panzió.** Downhill from the Basilica, this cozy, remodeled house provides an excellent view of Castle Hill. Rooms (doubles and quads) are small, but less cramped than at other pensions. Breakfast is included in the rates. ✉ *Bajcsy-Zsilinszky u. 49, H-2500,* ☎ FAX *33/312–640. 21 rooms. No credit cards.*

$$ 🏨 **Ria Panzió.** In this small, friendly guest house near the cathedral, all rooms face a garden courtyard. Rates include breakfast. ✉ *Batthyány u. 11–13, H-2500,* ☎ *33/313–115. 13 rooms. No credit cards.*

The Danube Bend Essentials

Getting Around

The best way to get around on the Danube is by boat or hydrofoil. The three main centers—Szentendre, Esztergom, and Visegrád—all have connections with one another and with Budapest. Contact MAHART Tours (☎ 1/118–1704) for schedules. Regular bus service connects all three with one another and with Budapest. Szentendre is most easily reached by HÉV commuter rail, departing from the Batthyány tér Metro in Budapest; the trip takes about 40 minutes and costs around 180 Ft.

Guided Tours

IBUSZ Travel (✉ XI, Dajka Gábor u. 3, ☎ 1/319–7520 or 1/319–7519) organizes daylong bus trips from Budapest along the Danube stopping in Esztergom, Visegrád, and Szentendre. IBUSZ also runs full-day boat tours to Szentendre and Visegrád from May through September on Saturday. Both tours include lunch and admission fees.

Visitor Information

Budapest (Tourinform, ✉ V, Sütő u. 2, ☎ 1/117–9800). **Esztergom** (Grantours, ✉ Széchenyi tér 25, ☎ FAX 33/413–756; IBUSZ, ✉ Kossuth L. u. 5, ☎ 33/312–552; Komtourist, ✉ Lőrinc u. 6, ☎ 33/312–082). **Szentendre** (Tourinform, ✉ Dumsta J. u. 22, ☎ FAX 26/317–965.

LAKE BALATON

Lake Balaton, the largest lake in Central Europe, stretches 80 km (50 mi) across western Hungary. It is within easy reach of Budapest. Sometimes known as the nation's playground, it helps to make up for Hungary's much-lamented lack of coastline. On its hilly northern shore, ideal for growing grapes, is Balatonfüred, the country's oldest spa town.

Lake Balaton

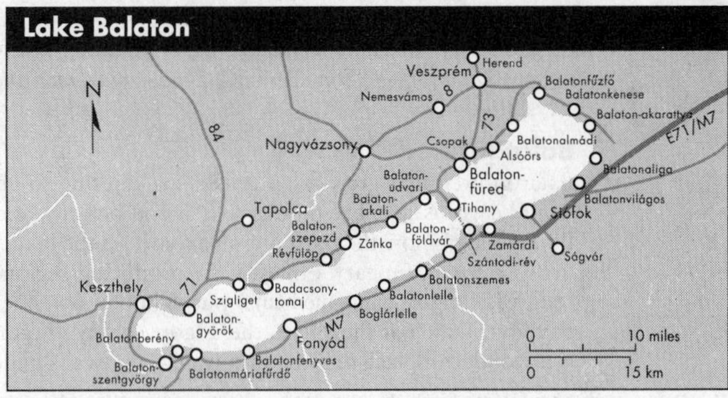

The national park on the Tihany Peninsula is just to the south, and regular boat service links Tihany and Balatonfüred with Siófok on the southern shore. This shore is flatter and more crowded with resorts, cottages, and high-rise hotels once used as communist trade-union retreats. The south shore's waters are even shallower than those of the north: you can walk out for nearly 2 km (1 mi) before they deepen.

The region grows more crowded every year (July and August are the busiest times), but a few steps along any side road will still lead you to a serene landscape of vineyards and old stone houses. A circular tour taking in Veszprém, Balatonfüred, and Tihany could be managed in a day, but two days, with a night in Tihany or Balatonfüred, would be more relaxed and allow for detours to Herend and its porcelain factory, or to the castle at Nagyvázsony.

Veszprém

Hilly Veszprém, though not on the lake itself, is the center of cultural life in the Balaton region. ★ **Veszprémi Várhegy** (Castle Hill) is the most attractive part of town, north of Szabadság tér. **Hősök Kapuja** (Heroes' Gate), at the entrance to the Castle, houses a small exhibit on Hungary's history. Just past the gate and down a little alley to the left is the **Tűztorony** (Fire Tower); note that the lower level is medieval while the upper stories are Baroque. There is a good view of the town and surrounding area from the castle balcony. Tower: ⏲ *May–Oct., daily 10–6.*

Vár utca, the only street in the castle area, leads to a small square in front of the **Püspök Palota** (Bishop's Palace) and the cathedral; outdoor concerts are held here in summer. Vár utca continues past the square up to a terrace erected on the north staircase of the castle. Stand beside the modern statues of St. Stephen and his queen, Gizella, for a far-reaching view of the old quarter of town.

$ ✕ **Club Skorpio.** This city-center eatery might look like an Alpine hut, but the excellent menu offers grilled meats and specialties such as pheasant soup and steamed wild duck. ✉ *Virág Benedek út 1,* ☎ *88/420–319. No credit cards.*

$ ★ ✕ **Diana.** Just a little southwest of the town center, it's worth the trip if you want to experience the old-fashioned charm of a small provincial Hungarian restaurant. The fish and game specialties are always good. There is also a 10-room pension on the premises. ✉ *József Attila u. 22,* ☎ *88/421–061. No credit cards.*

Herend

Herend is the home of some of Hungary's most renowned hand-painted porcelain. The Herendi Porcelángyár factory, founded in 1839, displays many rare pieces in its **museum.** ✉ *Kossuth Lajos u. 144,* ☎ *88/261–144.* ⏲ *Apr., weekdays 8:30–4, Sat. 9–4:30; May–Oct., Mon.–Sat. 8:30–4, Sun. 9–4:30; Nov.–mid-Dec. and Mar., weekdays 10–3.*

Balatonfüred

Balatonfüred first grew famous as a spa catering to people suffering from heart disease, but thanks to its good beaches and proximity to Budapest, it's now the most popular resort on the lake. The town also lies in one of Hungary's finest wine-producing regions. In the main square, strong-smelling medicinal waters bubble up under a colonnaded pavilion. Down at the shore, the Tagore sétány (Tagore Promenade) is a wonderful place to stroll and watch the swans glide by.

$$ ✕ **Baricska Csárda.** From its perch atop a hill at the southwestern end of town, this rambling, reed-thatched inn overlooks vineyards toward the river. The hearty fare includes roasted trout and *fogas* (a freshwater fish of the Balaton region), and desserts crammed with sweet poppyseed filling. In summer colorful Gypsy wedding shows are held nightly. ✉ *Baricska dülő, off Rt. 71 (Széchenyi út) behind the Shell station,* ☎ *87/343–105. AE, V. Closed mid-Nov.–mid-Mar.*

$$ ✕ **Tölgyfa Csárda** (Oak Tree Tavern). A prime hilltop location gives the tavern breathtaking views over the steeples and rooftops of Balatonfüred and the Tihany peninsula. The menu and decor are the equals of a first-class Budapest restaurant, and there's live Gypsy music in the evening. ✉ *Meleghegy hill (at end of Csárda u.),* ☎ *87/343–036. No credit cards. Closed late-Oct.–mid-Apr.*

$$$$ 🏨 **Annabella.** The cool, spacious guest quarters in this Miami-style highrise are especially pleasant in summer. Overlooking the Tagore Promenade and Lake Balaton, it has access to excellent water-sports facilities and is just around the corner from the main square in town. Room rates include breakfast. ✉ *Deák Ferenc u. 25, H-8230,* ☎ *87/342–222,* FAX *87/483–029. 383 rooms, 5 suites. 3 restaurants, 2 pools, air-conditioning in 5 suites. AE, DC, MC, V. Closed mid-Oct.–mid-Apr.*

$$$$ 🏨 **Marina.** The spiffy 12-story beachfront Marina skyscraper has less character than its refurbished and more pricey Lido wing, but the two share good facilities. ✉ *Széchenyi út 26, H-8239,* ☎ *87/343–644,* FAX *87/343–052. 291 rooms, 58 suites. Restaurant, pool. AE, DC, MC, V. Closed Oct.–late-Apr.*

$ 🏨 **Blaha Lujza.** This sober summer house in the historic section of town, built in classic Roman-villa style, was formerly owned by renowned Hungarian actress Blaha Lujza. Today it's a friendly, unassuming inn with clean, functional rooms. Breakfast is included in the room rates. ✉ *Blaha Lujza u. 4, H-8230,* ☎ FAX *87/343–094. 19 rooms. Restaurant. No credit cards. Closed Oct.–mid-Apr.*

Tihany

★ A short trip by boat or car takes you from Balatonfüred to the **Tihanyi fél-sziget** (Tihany Peninsula), a national park rich in rare flora and fauna. As you walk from the ferry port, follow green markers to the Oroszkút (springs) or red ones to the top of Csúcs-hegy, where there is a great view of the lake.

The village of Tihany, with its **Bencés Apátság** (Benedictine Abbey), is on the lake's northern shore. The abbey building houses a **museum** with exhibits related to the Balaton area. Also worth a look are the pink angels floating on the ceiling of the abbey church. Organ concerts are held weekend nights in July and early August. ✉ *Első András tér 1, Abbey:* ☎ *87/448–405; museum:* ☎ *87/448–650.* ⏲ *May–Sept., Mon.–Sat. 9–5:30, Sun. 11–5:30; Nov.–Mar., Mon.–Sat. 10–3, Sun.*

11–3; Apr. and Oct., Mon.–Sat. 10–4:30, Sun. 11–4:30; open holidays year-round from 11 (after mass).

$$ ✕ **Halásztanya.** The location on a twisting, narrow street and evening Gypsy music contribute to the popularity of this restaurant, which specializes in fish. ✉ *Visszhang u. 11,* ☏ *87/448–771. Reservations not accepted. No credit cards. Closed Nov.–Mar.*

$$ ✕ **Pál Csárda.** Two thatched cottages house this simple restaurant, where cold fruit soup and fish stew are the specialties. You can eat in the garden, which is decorated with gourds and strands of peppers. ✉ *Visszhang u. 19,* ☏ *87/448–605. Reservations not accepted. No credit cards. Closed Dec.–Mar.*

$$$$ ★ **Kastely.** Lush landscaped gardens surround this stately mansion on the water's edge. Inside, it's all understated elegance; rooms have balconies and beautiful views. A newer, less attractive building houses the Kastely's sister, the Park Hotel, which has less expensive rooms. Breakfast is included in the rates. ✉ *Fürdötelepi út 1, H-8237,* ☏ *87/448–611,* FAX *87/448–409. Kastely, 26 rooms; Park, 44 rooms. Restaurant. AE, DC, MC, V. Closed mid-Oct.–mid-Apr.*

$$ **Kolostor.** Cozy, wood-paneled rooms are built into an attic above a popular restaurant and brewery in the heart of Tihany village. Rates include breakfast. ✉ *Kossuth u. 14, H-8237,* ☏ FAX *87/448–009. 5 rooms. Restaurant. MC, V. Closed Nov.–Mar.*

Nagyvázsony

The small town of Nagyvázsony, a short drive inland from Lake Balaton, is primarily known for its **castle,** which dates from the early 15th century. The 92-ft-high keep is the oldest part, and its upper rooms now house the Kinizsi vár műzeum (Kinizsi Castle Museum), which displays armor, weapons, and other artifacts relating to the castle's history. Try to get to the highest balcony in late afternoon for the best view. The shops and homes surrounding the castle are preserved in their original style. ✉ *Vár u. 9,* ☏ *88/364–318.* ⏲ *Mar.–mid-Oct., daily 8–6.*

Lake Balaton Essentials

Getting Around

Trains from Budapest serve all the resorts on the northern shore; a separate line links the resorts of the southern shore. Highway 71 runs along the northern shore; M7 covers the southern. Buses connect most resorts, and regular ferries link the major ones. On summer weekends traffic can be heavy, and driving around the lake can take quite a while; because of the crowds, you should also book bus and train tickets in advance. In winter, schedules are curtailed, so check before making plans.

Guided Tours

IBUSZ Travel has several tours to Balaton from Budapest; inquire at the main office in Budapest (☞ Visitor Information *in* Budapest Essentials, *above*). Other tours more easily organized from hotels in the Balaton area include boat trips to vineyards and folk music evenings.

Visitor Information

Budapest (Balatontourist, ✉ V, Váci u. 7, ☏ 1/267–2726). **Balatonfüred** (Balatontourist, ✉ Tagore sétány 1, ☏ 87/343–471 or 87/342–822; Tourinform, ✉ Petőfi u. 8, ☏ 87/342–237). **Tihany** (Tourinform, ✉ Kossuth u. 20, ☏ 87/448–804; Tihany Tourist, ✉ Kossuth u. 11, ☏ 87/448–481). **Veszprém** (Tourinform, ✉ Rákóczi út 3, ☏ 88/404–548).

16 Iceland

Reykjavík, the Countryside

Don't be fooled by its name. Iceland is anything but icy, with only about 10% of the country covered by glaciers. Considering the high latitude, summers in Iceland are relatively warm, and the winter climate is milder than New York's. Coastal farms lie in green, pastoral lowlands where cows, sheep, and horses graze alongside raging streams.

Iceland's chilly name can be blamed on Hrafna-Flóki, a 9th-century Norse settler who failed to store up enough fodder to see his livestock through their first winter. Leaving in a huff, he passed a fjord filled with pack ice and cursed the country with a name that has stuck for 1,100 years.

The second-largest island in Europe, Iceland lies in the middle of the North Atlantic, where the warm Gulf Stream from the south meets cold currents from the north, creating a choice breeding ground for fish, which provide the nation with 80% of its export revenue. Iceland itself emerged from the bed of the Atlantic Ocean as a result of volcanic activity, which is still going on. Every five years, on average, this fire beneath the earth breaks the surface in the form of an eruption, sometimes even below glaciers. The fiery forces also heat the hot springs and geysers that bubble and spout in many parts of the country. The springs, in turn, provide hot water for public swimming pools and heating for most homes and buildings, helping to keep the air smogless. Hydropower, generated by harnessing some of the country's many rivers, is another main energy source, so pollution from fossil fuels is at a minimum.

Except for fish and agricultural products, almost all consumer goods are imported, making the cost of living high. Economic stability and reforms in recent years, however, have been bringing prices down to make them competitive with the rest of Scandinavia and not so different from those of Europe in general.

The first permanent settlers came from Norway in 874, though a handful of Irish monks are thought to have arrived a century earlier. In 1262, Iceland came under foreign rule, by Norway and later Denmark, and did not regain full independence until 1944. Today, almost 60% of the country's 267,000 people live in the greater Reykjavík area.

ICELAND A TO Z

Customs on Arrival

Tourists can bring in 6 liters of beer or 1 liter of wine containing up to 21% alcohol, 1 liter of liquor with up to 47% alcohol, and 200 cigarettes.

Dining

Restaurants are small and diverse. You can expect superb seafood and lamb, and the fresh fish is not to be missed—surely some of the best you'll ever have. Besides native cuisine, ethnic eateries range from Asian, Mexican, and Indian to French and Italian. Pizzas, hamburgers, and a tasty local version of the hot dog, with fried onions, are widely available. Most restaurants accept major credit cards.

MEALTIMES

Dinner, served between 6 and 9, is the main meal. A light lunch is usually served between noon and 2. Most restaurants are open from midmorning until midnight.

RATINGS

The following ratings are for a three-course meal for one person. Prices include taxes and service charges but not wine or cocktails.

CATEGORY	REYKJAVÍK	OTHER AREAS
$$$	over IKr4,000	over IKr3,500
$$	IKr3,000–IKr4,000	IKr2,500–IKr3,500
$	under IKr3,000	under IKr2,500

WHAT TO WEAR

Neat, casual dress is acceptable in all but the most expensive restaurants, where a jacket and tie are recommended.

Language

The official language is Icelandic, a highly inflected North Germanic tongue that is little changed from that originally spoken by the island's Norse settlers. English is widely understood and spoken, particularly by the younger generations.

Lodging

Hotels are clean, quiet, and friendly. Reykjavík and most villages also have guest houses and private accommodations.

If you tour Iceland on your own, get a list of hotels and guest houses in the various regions from the **Tourist Information Center** and additional lodging information from the **Iceland Tourist Bureau** (ITB; ☞ Visitor Information, *below*). The ITB actually operates its own chain of tourist-class hotels, now in combination with Icelandair. However, many are open in summer only. A Sleep-As-You-Please voucher is available from **Samvinn Travel** (✉ Austurstræti 12, IS-101 Reykjavík, ☎ 569–1010 or 569–1070), entitling holders to stay at a selection of hotels and guest houses all over Iceland; it costs IKr10,000 for seven nights.

FARM HOLIDAYS

Farm holidays are an excellent way to become acquainted with Iceland: Some 120 participating farms are listed with **Icelandic Farm Holidays** (✉ Bændahöllin, v/Hagatorg, IS-107 Reykjavík, ☎ 562–3640,

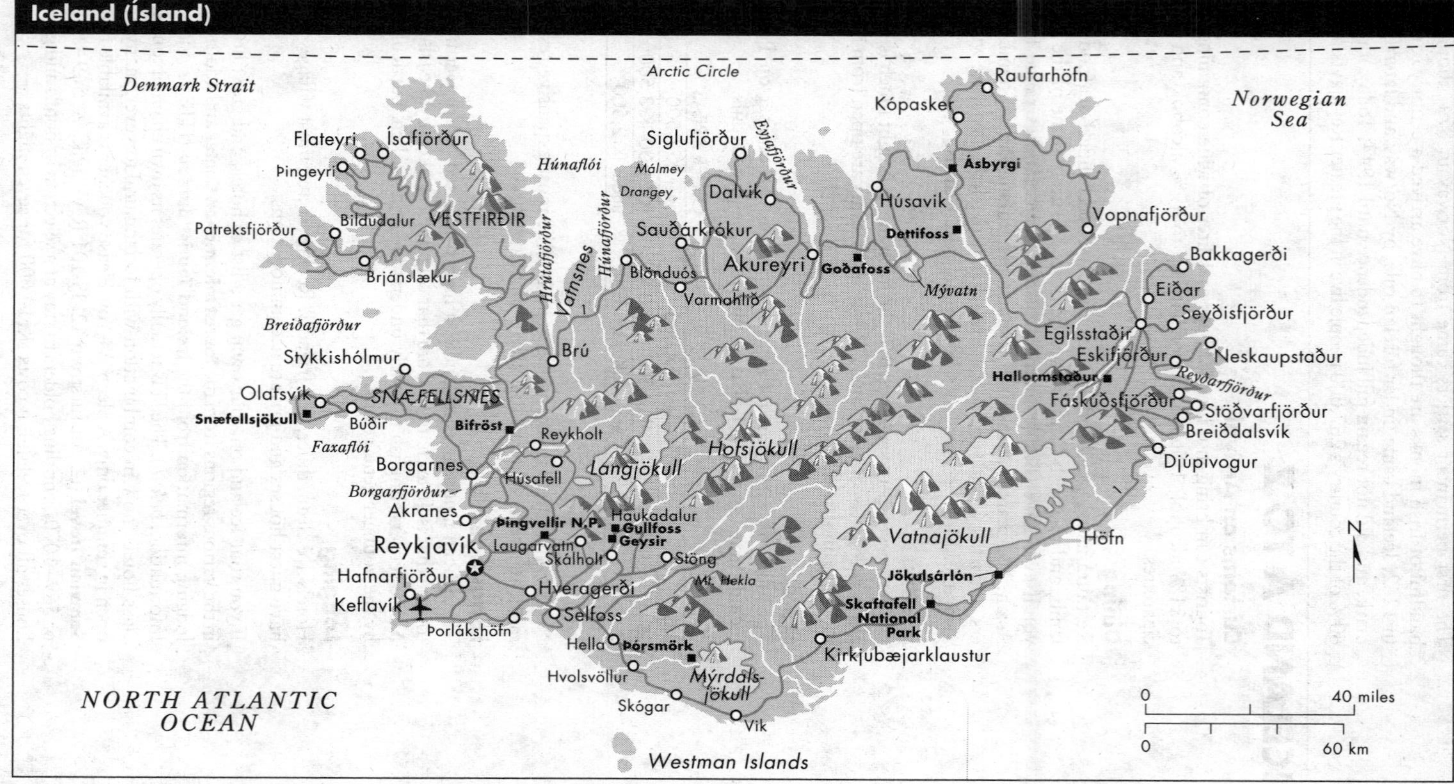
Iceland (Ísland)
Arctic Circle
Denmark Strait
Norwegian Sea
Raufarhöfn
Kópasker
Flateyri
Ísafjörður
Þingeyri
Húnaflói
Siglufjörður
Eyjafjörður
Málmey
Drangey
Ásbyrgi
Dalvík
Húsavík
Patreksfjörður
Bíldudalur
VESTFIRÐIR
Hrútafjörður
Húnafjörður
Sauðárkrókur
Dettifoss
Vopnafjörður
Brjánslækur
Vatnsnes
Blönduós
Akureyri
Goðafoss
Bakkagerði
Varmahlíð
Mývatn
Eiðar
Seyðisfjörður
Breiðafjörður
Egilsstaðir
Brú
Stykkishólmur
Eskifjörður
Neskaupstaður
Hallormstaður
Reyðarfjörður
Olafsvík
SNÆFELLSNES
Fáskrúðsfjörður
Stöðvarfjörður
Snæfellsjökull
Búðir
Bifröst
Breiðdalsvík
Reykholt
Hofsjökull
Faxaflói
Djúpivogur
Borgarnes
Langjökull
Húsafell
Borgarfjörður
Akranes
Haukadalur
Þingvellir N.P.
Gullfoss
Höfn
Vatnajökull
Reykjavík
Laugarvatn
Geysir
Skálholt
Stöng
Jökulsárlón
Hafnarfjörður
Mt. Hekla
Hveragerði
Keflavík
Skaftafell National Park
Selfoss
Þorlákshöfn
Hella
Þórsmörk
Kirkjubæjarklaustur
Hvolsvöllur
Mýrdalsjökull
NORTH ATLANTIC OCEAN
Skógar
Vík
N
0 40 miles
0 60 km
Westman Islands

562–3642, or 562–3643, FAX 562–3644). Many offer fishing, guided tours, and horseback riding.

HOSTELS

Information on the 30 hostels around the country can be obtained from the **Icelandic Youth Hostel Association** (✉ Sundlaugavegur 34, IS-105 Reykjavík, ☎ 553–8110, FAX 588–9201).

HUTS

Outside Reykjavík, the **Icelandic Touring Club** (✉ Mörkin 6, IS-108 Reykjavík, ☎ 568–2533, FAX 568–2535) operates several huts for mountaineers and hikers in remote areas, available all year except spring; club members get discounts and have priority.

RATINGS

Prices are for two people sharing a double room.

CATEGORY	REYKJAVÍK	OTHER AREAS
$$$	over IKr11,000	over IKr9,000
$$	IKr8,000–IKr11,000	IKr6,000–IKr9,000
$	under IKr8,000	under IKr6,000

Mail

POSTAL RATES

Airmail letters cost IKr65 to the United States and IKr45 to Europe.

RECEIVING MAIL

You can have your mail sent to the post office in any town or village in Iceland. In Reykjavík, have mail sent to the downtown post office (✉ R/O Pósthússtræti, IS-101 Reykjavík).

Money Matters

COSTS

As with many islands, Iceland is on the expensive side. Hotels and restaurants cost about 20% more in Reykjavík than elsewhere in the country. Ironically, though, prestige goods, like Armani clothes, Rolex watches, and top fashion labels in perfumes and jewelry are often cheaper once the value-added tax is refunded. The built-in airport departure tax is IKr1,340.

CURRENCY

The Icelandic monetary unit is the króna (plural krónur), which is equal to 100 aurar, and is abbreviated kr locally and IKr internationally. Coins are the IKr1, 5, 10, 50, and 100. There are krónur bills in denominations of 500, 1,000, 2,000, and 5,000. At press time (spring 1998), the rate of exchange was IKr71 to the U.S. dollar, IKr50 to the Canadian dollar, IKr118 to the pound sterling, IKr46 to the Australian dollar, and IKr39 to the New Zealand dollar, but some fluctuation occurs. No limitations apply to the import and export of currency. Foreign currency is easily exchanged for krónur at Icelandic banks. In fact, krónur are essentially unavailable abroad, so attempts to exchange at home are bound to be futile. Major credit cards are widely accepted.

SAMPLE PRICES

Cup of coffee or soft drink, IKr150; bottle of beer, IKr300; sandwich or snack, IKr300; 2-mi taxi ride, IKr500.

TIPPING

Tipping is not customary in Iceland.

National Holidays

January 1; April 1–5 (Easter); April 22 (first day of summer); May 1 (Labor Day); May 13 (Ascension); May 23–24 (Pentecost); June 6 (Seamen's Day, usual Sunday closings); June 17 (National Day); August 2 (public holiday); December 24–26; December 31(New Year's Eve, half-day off).

Opening and Closing Times

Banks are open weekdays 9:15–4. Some branches are also open Thursday 5–6.The **bank at Hotel Loftleiðir** (☒ Reykjavík Airport, IS-101 Reykjavík, ☎ 505–0900) is open weekends for foreign exchange only. Currency Exchange is provided by **The Change Group** (☒ Bankastræti 2, Reykjavík, ☎ 552–3735; open May–Sept., daily 8:30–8, and Oct.–Apr., 8:30–6). **Museums** are usually open 1–4:30, but some open as early as 10 and others stay open until 7. Some may be closed Monday. **Shops** are open weekdays 9–6 and Saturday 9–noon, and shopping malls Monday–Saturday 10–6. Grocery stores stay open later, including Sunday afternoon.

Shopping

SALES-TAX REFUNDS

A 24.5% *virðisaukaskattur,* (value-added tax or VAT) abbreviated VSK, applies to most goods and services. It is usually included in prices; if not, that fact must be stated explicitly. Foreign visitors can claim a partial refund on the VAT, which accounts for 19.68% of the purchase price of most goods and services. Fifteen percent of the purchase price for goods is refunded, providing you buy at least IKr5,000 worth of goods at one time. Souvenir stores issue "tax-free checks" that allow foreign visitors to collect the VAT rebates; these rebates are obtained when departing, in the duty-free store at Keflavík Airport. To qualify, keep your purchases in tax-free packages (except woolens), and show them to customs officers at the departure gate along with a passport and the tax-free check.

Telephoning

COUNTRY CODE

The country code for Iceland is 354. Iceland has only one area code, built in to the system; dial the 7-digit number immediately after the country code, without any extra numbers. All numbers outside Reykjavík begin with the number 4; numbers starting with 85 or 89 indicate mobile phones, which may have iffy reception.

INTERNATIONAL CALLS

For assistance with overseas calls dial 115; for direct international calls dial 00. To reach a long-distance operator in the United States from Iceland, you can use an international access code: **AT&T** (☎ 800–9001); **MCI** (☎ 999–002); **Sprint** (☎ 800–9003).

LOCAL CALLS

Pay phones, found in hotels, shops, bus stations, and post offices, take IKr10 and IKr50 coins. Outdoor telephone booths in towns and villages are sparse. Phone cards cost IKr500 and are sold at post offices, hotels, and some stores. For operator assistance with local calls dial 119; for information dial 118; for collect calls dial 115.

Transportation

BY BOAT

The few scheduled ferries travel mainly to the Westman Islands, from Þorlákshöfn on the south coast, and to Akranes, from Reykjavík.

The East. In summer the North Atlantic ferry ***Norröna*** sails from the Faroe Islands, Denmark, and Norway to Seyðisfjörður (720 km/450 mi east of Reykjavík). For information contact **Smyril Line Passenger Department** (☒ Box 370, FR-110 Torshavn, Faroes). **Norröna ferðaskrif-**

stofan (✉ Laugavegur 3, IS-101 Reykjavík, ☎ 562–6362, FAX 552–9450) also provides information.

BY BUS

An extensive network of buses serves most parts of Iceland; services are intermittent in winter, and some routes are operated only in summer. The bus network is operated from **Bifreiðastöð Íslands** (BSÍ, ✉ Vatnsmýrarvegur 10, ☎ 552–2300, FAX 552–9973); its terminal is on the northern rim of Reykjavík Airport. Guided bus tours are a good option (☞ Guided Tours *in* Reykjavík Essentials, *below*).

BY CAR

An international driver's license is required. Most of the Ring Road, which encircles the island, is two-lane asphalt. Other roads can be bumpy, often along gravel, dirt, or lava track—but the scenery is worth it. Be alert for loose livestock. Although service stations and garages are few and far apart, the main roads are patrolled, and fellow motorists are helpful. A four-wheel-drive vehicle is vital for remote roads such as those in the highlands, which may not be passable at all until early July. If you drive over the highlands, it is best to travel in convoy, especially when crossing unbridged rivers. For information on road conditions and the availability of gasoline off the beaten track, call **Vegagerð Ríkisins** (Public Roads Administration) at 563–1500.

There are car rental agencies at Keflavík International Airport, in Reykjavík, and in many towns.

BY PLANE

Daily flights go to most of the larger towns. Although plane travel is a bit expensive, special family fares and vacation tickets are available, and stiffening competition had prices declining at press time.

Visitor Information

Tourist Information Center (✉ Bankastræti 2, IS-101 Reykjavík, ☎ 562–3045, FAX 562–3057; ⏲ June–Aug., weekdays 8:30–6, Sat. 8:30–2, Sun. 10–2; Sept.–May, weekdays 9–5, Sat. 10–2). **Iceland Tourist Bureau** (✉ Skógarhlíð 18, IS-101 Reykjavík, ☎ 562–3300, FAX 562–5895). **Icelandic Tourist Board** (✉ Gimli, Lækjargata 3, IS-101 Reykjavík, ☎ 552–7488, FAX 562–4749).

Weather

Although it is a great year-round destination, Iceland is best for visiting from May to mid-November. From June through July, the sun barely sets. In December the sun shines for only three hours a day, but on clear, cold evenings any time from September through March you may see the Northern Lights dancing among the stars.

Weather in Iceland is unpredictable: in June, July, and August, sunny days alternate with spells of rain showers, crisp breezes, and driving winds. Winter temperatures fluctuate wildly—it can be as high as 50°F (10°C) or as low as –14°F (–10°C).

CLIMATE

Iceland enjoys a temperate ocean climate with cool summers and relatively mild winters. The climate in the north is stable and continental, the south fickle and maritime.

Below are average daily maximum and minimum temperatures for Reykjavík.

Jan.	35F	2C	**May**	50F	10C	**Sept.**	52F	11C
	28	− 2		39	4		43	6
Feb.	37F	3C	**June**	54F	12C	**Oct.**	45F	7C
	28	− 2		34	7		38	3
Mar.	39F	4C	**July**	57F	14C	**Nov.**	39F	4C
	30	− 1		48	9		32	0
Apr.	43F	6C	**Aug.**	56F	14C	**Dec.**	36F	2C
	33	1		47	8		29	− 2

REYKJAVÍK

Reykjavík has a small, safe city center, clean air, and plenty of open spaces. Their diet of fresh local seafood from the pollution-free waters may give a clue to Icelanders' longevity and attractiveness as a people. For a city of 110,000, Reykjavík offers an astonishingly wide range of artistic events—the main cultural season is winter, but there's always plenty going on in summer as well. Reykjavík hosts a two-week arts festival in June (in even-numbered years), with a strong international flavor. Most nightlife is in or near the city center; it's liveliest on weekends, when crowds hang around long after bars close at 3 AM.

Exploring Reykjavík

Numbers in the margin correspond to points of interest on the Reykjavík map.

Old Midtown, the capital's original core, is the city's highlight, with classic buildings, a park, museums, shops, galleries, and a plethora of cafés. Between the Second World War and the mid-'60s, a middle belt of residential neighborhoods, such as Vesturbæ, was established. Extending from the once separate community of Seltjarnarnes, well west of Old Midtown, to the salmon-populated Elliðaá River in the east, these areas have small, inviting parks. Many larger homes have established gardens with lovely flower beds and large trees, by Icelandic standards. Since the late '60s, distant suburbs, such as the intimidating Breiðholt, have sprung up as far as 8 km (5 mi) from the center of town. Recognizable by their large, modern apartment buildings, auto repair garages, office furniture stores, and the occasional small collections of convenience shops, these austere areas offer few attractions.

Old Midtown can be easily browsed on foot; if you prefer, the city's bus system is an efficient option. Sight-seeing tours are also available.

16 **Árbæjarsafn** (Open-Air Folk Museum). This authentic "village" of 18th- and 19th-century houses, 20 minutes southeast of downtown, is well worth the trip. ✉ *Árbær (Bus 10 from Hlemmur Bus Station),* ☎ *577–1111.* ⊙ *June–Aug., Tues.–Sun. 10–6, and by appointment.*

12 **Arnarhóll.** A statue of the Viking **Ingólfur Arnarson,** Iceland's first settler in 874, dominates this hill, from which you can share his view of Reykjavík more than 1,100 years after his arrival. To the north is the ultramodern, glossy-black **Seðlabanki** (Central Bank). Behind Ingólfur is the copper-green High Courts building nestled beside the old **National Library** building, which dates from the beginning of the 20th century. ✉ *Arnarhóll Hill.*

15 **Ásmundarsafn** (Ásmundur Sveinsson Sculpture Museum). Some originals by this sculptor, depicting ordinary working people, myths, and folktale episodes, are exhibited in the museum's gallery and studio and in the surrounding garden. ✉ *v/Sigtún (5-min ride from Hlemmur Sta-*

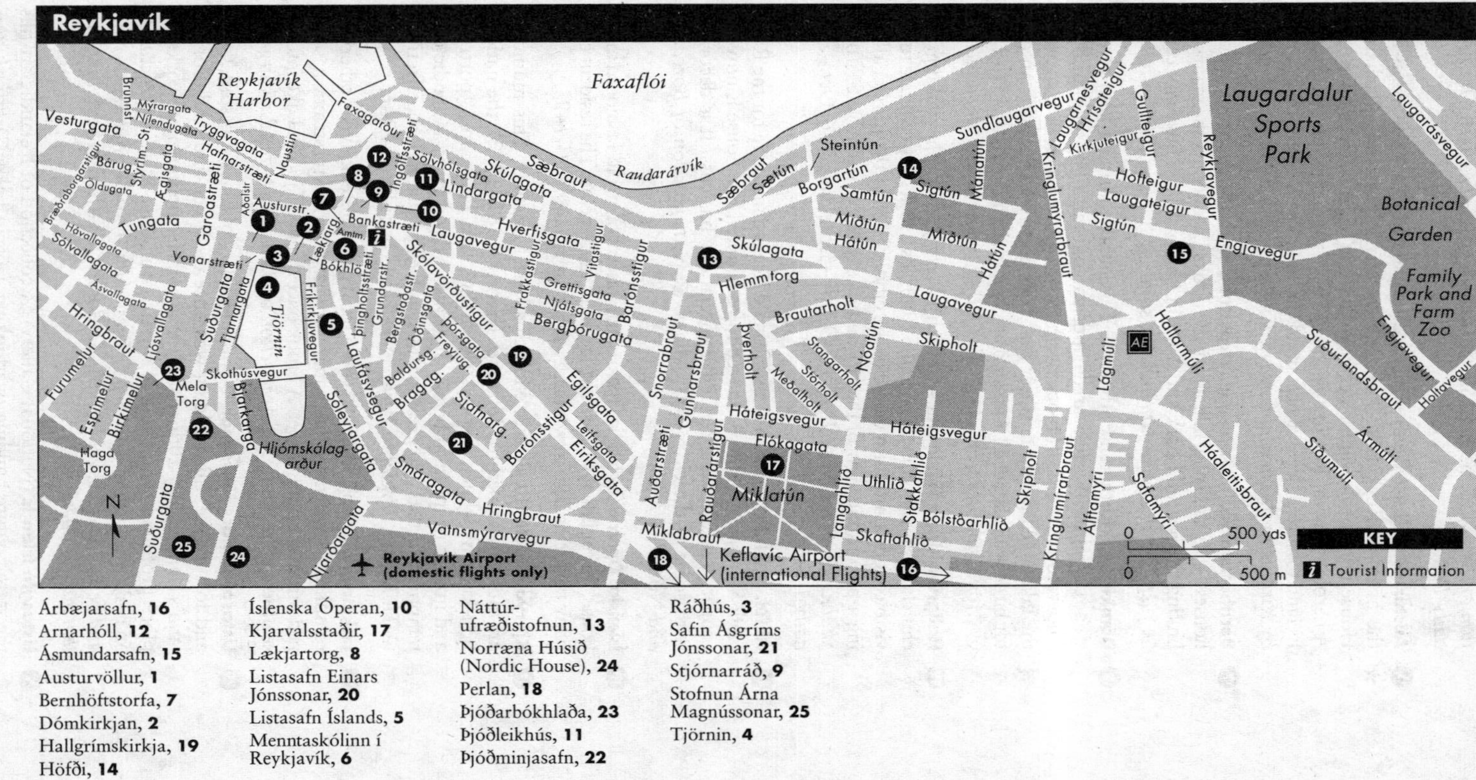

Árbæjarsafn, **16**
Arnarhóll, **12**
Ásmundarsafn, **15**
Austurvöllur, **1**
Bernhöftstorfa, **7**
Dómkirkjan, **2**
Hallgrímskirkja, **19**
Höfði, **14**
Íslenska Óperan, **10**
Kjarvalsstaðir, **17**
Lækjartorg, **8**
Listasafn Einars Jónssonar, **20**
Listasafn Íslands, **5**
Menntaskólinn í Reykjavík, **6**
Náttúrufræðistofnun, **13**
Norræna Húsið (Nordic House), **24**
Perlan, **18**
Þjóðarbókhlaða, **23**
Þjóðleikhús, **11**
Þjóðminjasafn, **22**
Ráðhús, **3**
Safin Ásgríms Jónssonar, **21**
Stjórnarráð, **9**
Stofnun Árna Magnússonar, **25**
Tjörnin, **4**

tion on Bus 5), ☎ *553–2155.* ⏲ *June–Sept., daily 10–4; Oct.–May, daily 1–4.*

1 ★ **Austurvöllur** (East Field). This small square in Old Midtown is truly the heart of Reykjavík. The 19th-century **Alþingishús** (Parliament House), one of the oldest stone buildings in Iceland, faces the square. A heroic statue of Jón Sigurðsson (1811–79), the nationalist who led Iceland toward independence, stands in the square's center. ⊠ *Bounded by Kirkjustræti, Thorvaldsstræti, Vallarstræti, and Pósthússtræti.*

7 **Bernhöftstorfa.** Picturesque, two-story, mid-19th-century wooden houses typify this small hill, which overlooks Lækjargata, the main street linking the peaceful park and Tjörnin Lake with the busy city center. ⊠ *Just east of Lækjargata and just south of Bankastræti.*

2 **Dómkirkjan** (Lutheran Cathedral). This small, charming 18th-century stone church, with a treasured baptismal font carved by sculptor Bertel Thorvaldsen, is a short block north from Tjörnin Lake. One corner of the lake is fed by warm water that does not freeze, creating an oasis for birds year-round. ⊠ *Austurvöllur Square (East Field),* ☎ *551–2113.* ⏲ *Mon. and Tues.–Fri. 9–5, Wed. 10–5 unless in use for services.*

19 **Hallgrímskirkja** (Hallgrím's Church). Forty years in the making, this church was finally completed in the 1980s. Its 210-ft gray concrete tower, visible from almost anywhere in the city, is open to the public, allowing a panoramic view of the city and its expansive suburbs. ⊠ *Top of Skólavörðustígur,* ☎ *551–0745.* ⏲ *May–Sept., daily 9–6; Oct.–Apr., daily 10–6.*

14 **Höfði.** Mikhail Gorbachev and Ronald Reagan met here for the Reykjavík Summit of 1986. Rumored to be haunted, the house is now city property, serving as a venue for special city business. It is decorated with some of the city's art holdings. ⊠ *Near junction of Borgartún and Nótún.*

10 **Íslenska Óperan** (Icelandic Opera). Reminiscent of an old-fashioned movie house, this building was, in fact, Iceland's first cinema. The resident company performs here in winter. ⊠ *Ingólfsstræti,* ☎ *551–1475.*

17 **Kjarvalsstaðir** (Reykjavík Municipal Art Museum). This municipal art museum named for Jóhannes Kjarval (1885–1972), the nation's best-known painter, displays the artist's lava landscapes, portraits, and images of mystical beings. It also shows works by Icelandic contemporary artists and great masters, as well as visiting art collections. ⊠ *Flókagata, Miklatún Park,* ☎ *552–6131.* ⏲ *Daily 10–6.*

8 **Lækjartorg** (Brook Square). Now a focal point in Reykjavík's otherwise rambling city center, this square opens onto **Austurstræti,** a semi-pedestrian shopping street. A brook once drained Tjörnin Lake into the sea (hence the name). ⊠ *At junction of Bankastræti and Lækjargata.*

20 **Listasafn Einars Jónssonar** (National Gallery of Einar Jónsson). Cubic and fortresslike, this building was once the home and studio of Iceland's leading early 20th-century sculptor. His monumental works explore profound symbolic and mystical subjects. ⊠ *Njarðargata,* ☎ *551–3797.* ⏲ *June–mid-Sept., Tues.–Sun. 1:30–4; mid-Sept.–Nov. and Feb.–May, weekends 1:30–4. Closed Dec.–Jan.* ⏲ *Sculpture garden always open.*

5 **Listasafn Íslands** (National Gallery). A collection of Icelandic art fills the stately white building overlooking Tjörnin Lake. ⊠ *Fríkirkjuvegur 7,* ☎ *562–1000.* ⏲ *Tues.–Sun. noon–6.*

6 **Menntaskólinn í Reykjavík** (Reykjavík Grammar School). Many graduates from the country's oldest educational institution, established in 1846, have gone on to dominate political and social life in Iceland. ✉ *Corner of Amtmannsstígur and Lækjargata.*

13 **Náttúrufræðistofnun** (Museum of Natural History). One of the last great auks is on display here, as well as several exhibits that focus on Icelandic natural history. It is just across from the west entrance to the Hlemmtorg terminus of the city's bus system. ✉ *Hlemmtorg, Hverfisgata 116,* ☎ *562–9822.* ⏲ *Tues., Thurs., and weekends 1:30–4.*

24 **Norræna Húsið** (Nordic House). Designed by Finnish architect Alvar Aalto, this blue-and-white Scandinavian cultural center has exhibitions, lectures, concerts, and a coffee shop. ✉ *Sæmundargata,* ☎ *551–7030.* ⏲ *Coffee shop, daily 9–5; exhibitions, daily 2–7.*

18 **Perlan.** The gleaming glass dome perches like a space station high on a hill atop six huge hot-water towers that provide hot water for much of the capital area. The wooded slopes of the hill are especially popular among walkers and runners and are home to Iceland's only population of rabbits, who have escaped from or been released by their owners. Inside you'll find a balcony with splendid views, a coffee shop, an ice cream bar, and a fine restaurant with the same name (☞ Dining and Lodging, *below*). ✉ *Öskjuhlíð Hill,* ☎ *562–0200.* ⏲ *Daily 11:30–10.*

23 **Þjóðarbókhlaða** (National and University Library). Clad in red aluminum, this edifice—completed in 1994—is hard to miss. It houses the voluminous collection from the now-closed Landsbókasafnið (Old National Library). ✉ *Arngrímsgata, on the corner of Suðurgata and Hringbraut,* ☎ *563–5600.* ⏲ *Weekdays 9–7, Sat. 10–5.*

11 **Þjóðleikhús** (National Theater). The interior of this basalt-black structure reflects the natural polygonal lava columns occurring in Iceland. It is a venue for the biennial June Reykjavík Arts Festival and, from fall to spring, diverse cultural events and theatrical presentations. ✉ *Hverfisgata 19,* ☎ *551–1200.*

22 **Þjóðminjasafn** (National Museum). On display are Viking artifacts, national costumes, weavings, carvings, and silver works. ✉ *Suðurgata 141,* ☎ *552–8888.* ⏲ *Mid-May–mid-Sept., Tues.–Sun. 11–5; late Sept.–early May, Tues., Thurs., and weekends noon–5.*

3 **Ráðhús** (Reykjavík City Hall). Inside are a tourist information desk, a large-scale relief map of Iceland, and a coffee shop. Modern architecture and nature meet here—not only at Tjörnin Lake (☞ *below*), but at the entrance from Vonarstræti; water seeping down one wall mimics nature, and moss clings to the stone structure. ✉ *Bounded by Fríkirkjuvegur, Vonarstræti, and Tjarnargata,* ☎ *563–2000.* ⏲ *Weekdays 8:20–4:15; coffee shop, weekdays 11–6, weekends noon–6.*

21 **Safn Ásgríms Jónssonar** (Ásgrímur Jónsson Collection). Works by this well-regarded post–Impressionist-period painter are displayed in his house, left otherwise untouched since his death in 1958. ✉ *Bergstaðastræti 74,* ☎ *551–3644.* ⏲ *June–Aug., Tues.–Sun. 1:30–4; Sept.–Nov. and Feb.–May, weekends 1:30–4. Closed Dec.–Jan.*

25 **Stofnun Árna Magnússonar** (Árni Magnússon Manuscript Institute). Here you'll find what is arguably Iceland's greatest cultural treasure trove—priceless manuscripts, some quite ornate, containing many of the sagas and much of the mythical poetry that established medieval Icelandic literature as some of the greatest in the world. ✉ *Suðurgata, University of Iceland,* ☎ *525–4010.* ⏲ *Mid-June–Sept., Mon.–Sat. 2–6 or by appointment.*

9 **Stjórnarráð** (Government House). Ironically once a jail, this white, 18th-century building now houses the offices of Iceland's prime minister. ✉ *At Lækjartorg (Brook Square), on seaward side of Bankastræti.*

4 **Tjörnin.** On the southeast end of this natural lake is **Hljómskálagarður** Park, a fine spot to relax and breathe in the fresh air. ✉ *Bounded by Tjarnargata on the west, Fríkirkjuvegur/Sóleyjargata on the east, and traversed by Skothúsvegur.*

Dining and Lodging

Most Reykjavík restaurants offer excellent seafood and lamb dishes. Evening reservations are necessary on weekends in the better restaurants. Some offer discount lunch or tourist menus. For details and price-category definitions, *see* Dining *in* Iceland A to Z, *above*.

Hotels run the gamut from elegant to simple, classic to modern. For details and price-category definitions, *see* Lodging *in* Iceland A to Z, *above*.

$$$ ✕ **Gallery at Hótel Holt.** The walls of this distinguished hotel dining room are covered with Icelandic art from the owner's private collection. Diners indulge in such mouthwatering seafood as gravlax and grilled halibut, and there's a fabulous wine list to match. ✉ *Holt Hotel, Bergstaðastræti 37,* ☎ *552–5700. AE, DC, MC, V.*

$$$ ★ ✕ **Perlan.** In this rather formal revolving restaurant under the Perlan dome, you may pay a bit more for the food—including Icelandic fish and lamb dishes—but the splendid view, especially at sunset, more than justifies the expense. ✉ *Öskjuhlíð,* ☎ *562–0200. No lunch. AE, DC, MC, V.*

$$ ✕ **Oðinsvé.** On the ground floor of a hotel with the same name, this cozy restaurant serves Scandinavian-French–style fare, mostly seafood and lamb. ✉ *Oðinstorg,* ☎ *552–5090. AE, DC, MC, V.*

$$ ✕ **Þrír Frakkar Hjá Úlfari.** Housed in an unassuming red building in an older part of town, this restaurant offers great beef dishes and unique seafood, including whale meat. The bright annex looks upon a tiny tree-filled park. ✉ *Baldursgata 14,* ☎ *552–3939. DC, MC, V.*

$$ ✕ **Við Tjörnina.** The imaginative Icelandic seafood here includes marinated cod cheeks and *tindabikkja* (starry ray) with grapes, capers, and Pernod. It's on the second floor of a typical early 20th-century corrugated-iron–clad house. ✉ *Templarasund 3,* ☎ *551–8666. AE, MC, V.*

$ ✕ **Hornið.** Pizzas and pasta are the draw, but good meat and fish dishes are also served at this cosmopolitan bistro. ✉ *Hafnarstræti 15,* ☎ *551–3340. AE, DC, MC, V.*

$ ✕ **Potturinn og Pannan.** The service at this small restaurant on the edge of the downtown area is efficient and friendly. Lamb, fish, and American-style salads are the best bets. ✉ *Brautarholt 22,* ☎ *551–1690. AE, MC, V.*

$$$ 🏨 **Hótel Borg.** Elegant art deco rooms retain their original unique style but are equipped with many handy gadgets, including CD players and coffeemakers. ✉ *Pósthússtræti 11, IS-101,* ☎ *551–1440,* FAX *551–1420. 26 rooms, 4 suites. Restaurant, bar. AE, D, MC, V.*

$$$ 🏨 **Hótel Holt.** One of Reykjavík's finest, the Holt has excellent service and an excellent restaurant (☞ *above*). Rooms are on the small side but warmed by works of leading Icelandic artists. It's in a central residential neighborhood. ✉ *Bergstaðastræti 37, IS-101,* ☎ *552–5700,* FAX *562–3025. 40 rooms, 14 suites. Restaurant. AE, DC, MC, V.*

$$$ 🏨 **Hótel Reykjavík.** Offering quality at modest prices, this hotel is convenient to the Reykjavík Municipal Art Museum. Under the same roof are a Korean café and a steak house—both are good. ✉ *Rauðarárstígur 39, IS-105,* ☎ *562–6250,* FAX *562–6350. 53 rooms, 7 jr. suites. 2 restaurants. AE, DC, MC, V.*

$$$ **Hótel Saga.** All the rooms above the fourth floor in this business-oriented hotel have spectacular views. There is a full range of services, and the location is convenient to most museums, shops, and restaurants. ✉ *Hagatorg, IS-107,* ☎ *552–9900,* FAX *562–3980. 216 rooms. Restaurant. AE, DC, MC, V.*

$$$ **Icelandair Hótel Esja.** Renovated in 1997, this hotel, with its Planet Pulse health facility, puts a strong emphasis on pampering its guests and is unique in offering a wide variety of exercise and spa-like therapies, even personal trainers. ✉ *Suðurlandsbraut 2, IS-108,* ☎ *505–0950,* FAX *505–0955. 172 rooms, including 12 jr. suites and 6 singles. Restaurant. AE, DC, MC, V.*

$$ **City Hotel.** On a quiet street, this private hotel is handy to midtown. ✉ *Ránargata 4A, IS-101,* ☎ *511–1155,* FAX *552–9040. 31 rooms. Restaurant. AE, DC, MC, V.*

$$ **Garður.** A student residence, it is open as a hotel only in summer when students flee. Its basic, modernized rooms are ideal for travelers on a tight budget; it is convenient to the National Museum, downtown, and other attractions. ✉ *Hringbraut, IS-107,* ☎ *551–5656. 44 rooms with shared bath and shower. AE, DC, MC, V. Closed in winter (book through Hótel Örk,* ☞ *Hveragerði, below**).*

$$ **Hotel Leifur Eiríksson.** Adjacent to the hilltop Hallgrim's Church, this utilitarian hotel is an easy walk from all the city's main attractions. ✉ *Skólavörðustígur 45, IS-101,* ☎ *562–0800,* FAX *562–0804. 29 rooms. Restaurant, bar. AE, DC, MC, V.*

$$ **Lind.** The Lind indulges in few frills but offers plenty of clean rooms. It's near the Hlemmur Station and is a 10-minute walk from downtown. ✉ *Rauðarárstígur 18, IS-105,* ☎ *562–3350,* FAX *562–3351. 44 rooms. Restaurant. AE, DC, MC, V.*

$ **Smárar Guest House.** Rooms here are simple and clean, with washbasins and access to a fully equipped kitchen. ✉ *Snorrabraut 52, near Hlemmur Station, IS-105,* ☎ *562–3330. 18 rooms without bath. MC, V.*

Shopping

The main shopping street starts at Lækjatorg (say, *Like*-ya-torg) (Brook Square), heads up the hill as Bankastræti, and continues on to become Laugavegur, where Skólavörðustígur angles in, descending from the huge Hallgrímskirkja. Skólavörðustígur has been pleasantly reborn as a center for distinctive custom jewelry, Icelandic-designed fashions, arts, crafts, and leatherwork. Attractive Icelandic woolen goods and handicrafts are sold in shops on Aðalstræti, Hafnarstræti, and Vesturgata.

The Icelandic Handicrafts Center (✉ Falcon House, Hafnarstræti 3, ☎ 551–1785) carries Icelandic woolens, knitting and tapestry materials, pottery, glassware, and jewelry. **Rammagerðin** (✉ Hafnarstræti 19, ☎ 551–7910) stocks a wide range of Icelandic clothes and souvenirs. For bargain woolens, it might well be worth a trip of about 25 minutes north out of Reykjavík to the **Álafoss Factory Store** (✉ follow Vesturlandsvegur out of town and turn right at the second traffic circle in the town of Mossfelsbær, ☎ 566–6303). At the **Handknitting Association of Iceland** (✉ Skólavörðustígur 9, ☎ 552–1890), you can buy high-quality hand knits through a knitters' cooperative. **The Kringlan Mall** (✉ Intersection of Miklabraut and Kringlumýrarbraut) is an option for homesick mall rats. For bargains, try the weekend **flea market** (✉ Kolaportið, at harborside in the rear of the Customs House on Geirsgata) between 11 and 5.

Reykjavík Essentials

Arriving and Departing

BY PLANE

Flights from the United States and Europe arrive at **Keflavík Airport** (☎ 505–0500), 50 km (31 mi) south of Reykjavík. **Reykjavík Airport** (☎ 569–4100) is the central hub of domestic air travel in Iceland. For reservations and information, contact Air Iceland (☎ 570–3030) or Íslandsflug (☎ 561–6060).

Between Keflavík Airport and Downtown. Buses connect with all flights to and from Keflavík. The drive takes 45 minutes and costs IKr600. **Flybus,** from **Reykjavík Excursions,** has terminals at Hótel Loftleiðir and Hótel Esja. **Taxis** are also available; they cost at least IKr4,500.

Getting Around

BY BUS

Midtown Reykjavík is served by two main bus stops: Lækjatorg (Brook Square) and Hlemmur Station. These punctuate the popular shopping street, Laugavegur, at its beginning and midpoint, and are stops on routes to the suburbs and neighboring metro communities.

Buses run from 7 AM to around midnight, some slightly later on weekends. The flat fare for Reykjavík and suburbs is IKr120 for adults. Exact change is required. Strips of tickets are available from bus drivers and at bus stations. If you need to change buses (once, within a half hour), ask for a *skiptimiða* (free transfer ticket, pronounced *skiff*-tee-mee-tha).

BY TAXI

Rates start at about IKr300; few in-town taxi rides exceed IKr700. **Hreyfill** (☎ 588–5522). **BSR** (☎ 561–0000 or 561–1720). **Bæjarleiðir** (☎ 553–3500).

Contacts and Resources

EMBASSIES AND CONSULATES

United States (✉ Laufásvegur 21, IS-101, ☎ 562–9100). **Canadian Consulate** (✉ Suðurlandsbraut 10, IS-101, ☎ 568–0820). **United Kingdom** (✉ Laufásvegur 31, IS-108, ☎ 550–5100).

EMERGENCIES

Police, ambulance, and fire (☎ 112). **Doctors and dentists** (☎ 569–6600, 552–1230). **Pharmacies** operate in shifts at night and on weekends; for information, ☎ 551–8888.

ENGLISH-LANGUAGE BOOKS

Eymundsson-Penninn (✉ Austurstræti 18, ☎ 511–1130 or 511–1140; ✉ Kringlan 4-6 [South Mall], ☎ 533–1130). **Mál og menning** (✉ Laugavegur 18, ☎ 552–4240).

GUIDED TOURS

For some, guided bus tours are preferable to driving the rougher roads. Day excursions and longer journeys by coach and/or plane are an excellent way to relax and enjoy Iceland's spectacular scenery. Destinations include Akureyri, Mývatn, Höfn, Snæfellsnes, the Westman Islands, and the West Fjords.

Most longer tours operate between June and September and cost from IKr25,000 to IKr150,000 per person, including accommodations and three meals a day. On some tours you'll stay in hotels; on others you'll sleep in tents. Tours typically last from 3 to 19 days.

Tours can be booked from abroad through **Icelandair** (☎ 505–0200) or travel agencies. The **Iceland Tourist Bureau** (✉ Skógarhlíð 18, IS-101, ☎ 562–3300, FAX 562–5895) is a well-established agency.

Guðmundur Jónasson Travel (✉ Borgartún 34, IS-105, ☎ 511–1515) is also an experienced agency. For information on other tour operators, contact the **Icelandic Tourist Board** (✉ Gimli, Lækjargata 3, IS-101, ☎ 552–7488, FAX 562–4749).

TRAVEL AGENCIES

Samvinn Travel (✉ Austurstræti 12, IS-101, ☎ 569–1010 or 569–1070, FAX 569–1095 or 552–7796). **Úrval–Útsýn Travel** (✉ Lágmúli 4, IS-108, ☎ 569–9300, FAX 588–0202).

VISITOR INFORMATION

Tourist Information Center (✉ Bankastræti 2, IS-101, ☎ 562–3045, FAX 562–3057). **Iceland Tourist Bureau** (✉ Skógarhlíð 18, IS-101, ☎ 562–3300, FAX 562–5895).

THE COUNTRYSIDE

Incredible natural contrasts appear throughout Iceland's beautiful countryside. Magnificent and diverse fjords impart a scenic wrinkle to all coasts excepting the south, which is marked with sprawling plains, foothills, and bizarre black sands crowned by pristine white glaciers. The interior highlands, a challenge to reach, are raw wonderlands of panoramas and solitude. You are never far from cool waterfalls, spurting hot springs, or snow-capped summits.

The amount of countryside you can cover naturally depends on time. Day trips from Reykjavík can easily be expanded to a few rewarding days in the neighboring southern or western regions. To circle the country via the Ring Road (Road 1), allow at least a week—this will give you time to explore some of the spectacular attractions along the way. There can be up to 80 km (50 mi) between towns and accommodations.

The South

You reach the rich piedmont and coastal farmlands of the south by descending the plateau east of Reykjavík along the Ring Road. Look sharp offshore toward the southeast on your way down, and you may see the Vestmannaeyjar (Westman Islands) in the distance on the horizon. This region, laced by major rivers with some of the country's best-known waterfalls, like majestic Gullfoss and wide-open Skógafoss, is charged with numerous hot springs, including Geysir, the original namesake of the spouting natural wonders.

Crowning the countryside are many noteworthy peaks. Mt. Hekla, once said to be where lost souls were banished, is alive and well—it last erupted in 1991. Also active is the volcanic network under Europe's largest glacier, Vatnajökull. Resulting meltwater from a 1996 eruption created a peculiar, though temporary sculpture garden of ice. Still remaining are huge boulders and the vast, expanded black sands of Skeiðarásandur, which cover a sizable part of the central south coast. Skiers, snowmobilers, and ice climbers need not despair, as Vatnajökull is larger than all of mainland Europe's glaciers combined. Don't miss the unique geology and flora and fauna of Skaftafell National Park, Iceland's first, with Mt. Hvannadalshnjúkur, Iceland's highest peak, just beyond its borders.

Hveragerði

Hveragerði, about 40 km (25 mi) east of Reykjavík, has hot springs and fruit and vegetable greenhouses. An unabashed tourist stop is **Eden,** where homegrown bananas have astonished visitors for years. A newly opened art gallery, **Listaskálinn** (✉ Austurmörk 2, ☎ 483–5071) shows local and traveling art and is a nice stop for coffee.

$$$ **Hótel Örk.** The rooms here are expensive, but meals in the ground-floor restaurant are reasonable. Three- to seven-day "spa cure" retreat packages are worthwhile. ✉ *Breiðamörk 1, IS-810,* ☎ *483–4700,* FAX *483–4775. 81 rooms. Restaurant, pool. AE, DC, MC, V.*

$ **Ból Youth Hostel.** Rooms in this standard youth hostel have one to five beds and kitchen facilities. There is also a guest house with doubles and a shower. ✉ *Hveramörk 14, IS-810,* ☎ *483–4198,* FAX *483–4088. 20 beds. MC, V. Closed mid-Sept.–mid-May.*

Selfoss

Selfoss, on the turbulent Ölfusá River, is the south's largest community. With many diverse services, it is home to the nation's largest dairy plant.

$$$ **Hótel Selfoss.** Just off the river, this hotel is a perfect base for sojourns to inland sites or to the coast. Their restaurant is the town's best eatery. ✉ *Eyravegur 2, IS-800,* ☎ *482–2500,* FAX *482–2524. 20 rooms. Restaurant. AE, DC, MC, V.*

Skógar

Skógar, 120 km (75 mi) east of Selfoss, is a small crossroads settlement near one of the country's many spectacular waterfalls, **Skógafoss.** What you see from the roadside is actually the last in a long series of cascades and plunging rapids that reward the hiker.

$$ **Hótel Edda.** Close to the Skógafoss waterfall, this airy summer hotel has views of the sea, mountains, and glaciers. ✉ *Skógar, IS-861 Hvolsvöllur,* ☎ *487–8870,* FAX *187–8870. 34 rooms without bath. Restaurant. AE, MC, V. Closed Sept.–May.*

Kirkjubæjarklaustur

Aptly named Kirkjubæjarklaustur (or church farmstead cloister) was the site of a medieval convent. When the volcano Láki erupted in 1783, it produced the greatest amount of lava from a single eruption in recorded history, its deposits greatly shaping the landscape. Two waterfalls and an August chamber music festival are among local attractions; contact the Community Center (☞ Visitor Information, *below*) for information.

$$ **Hotel Kirkjubæjarklaustur, Icelandair Hotel.** This is an excellent facility and one of the few in the chain open year-round. For liquid and mealtime refreshment, head to the restaurant and bar in the newer building. ✉ *Klausturvegur 6, IS-880,* ☎ *487–4799,* FAX *487–4614. 73 rooms, 57 with shower. Restaurant, pool. AE, MC, V.*

Skaftafell National Park

From the foot of the Skaftafellsjökull you can pass over lowland sands into lush foothills to Svartifoss, with its polygonal lava sides, and up to hidden glacial canyons and stunning mountaintops. If you're lucky, you will glimpse Iceland's highest summit, Mt. Hvannadalshnjúkur, rising 6,950 ft just outside the park borders. About 32 km (20 mi) east of the park is the adventure world of the **Jökulsárlón;** you can tour the glacial lagoon's eerie ice floes by boat (☞ Guided Tours *in* The Countryside Essentials, *below*).

$$ **Hótel Skaftafell.** Few hotels in Iceland can match this one's setting—near breathtaking Skaftafell National Park. Three price options for rooms are available: contemporarily furnished with private bath; spartan rooms without bath, and, lastly, similar rooms without bed linens where you provide a sleeping bag. The latter two groups share bathrooms, but kitchen facilities are a plus. A travel shop, a gas station, and a campsite are also on the property. ✉ *Skaftafell, Fagurhólsmýri, IS-785,* ☎ *478–1945,* FAX *478–1946. 53 rooms, 33 with bath. Restaurant. MC, V.*

$ ⛺ **Skaftafell National Park Campground and Service Center.** This sprawling campground has excellent facilities. ✉ *Skaftafell National Park,* ☎ *478–1627. MC, V. Closed Sept.–June.*

Höfn

Höfn, the major port community of the southeast, offers a fine view of Europe's largest glacier, **Vatnajökull,** and the adjacent mountains.

$$$ **Hótel Höfn.** A prominent hilltop location gives splendid views either to nearby mountains or the sea, from rooms furnished in contemporary Scandinavian decor. This clean and comfortable hotel has a restaurant with good service and tasty dishes, especially the lobster. You can order fast food at the grill. ✉ *Hornafjörður, IS-780,* ☎ *478–1240,* FAX *478–1996. 40 rooms, 32 rooms with bath. Restaurant, grill. AE, DC, MC, V.*

$$$ **Hótel Vatnajökull.** Though only in its second year, this hotel with spectacular views of the glacier already has a nationwide reputation for quality accommodations and excellent food, including fine meat and seafood. ✉ *Lindarbakka, Hornafjörður, IS-780,* ☎ *478–2555,* FAX *478–2444. 26 rooms. Restaurant. AE, DC, MC, V.*

Westman Islands

This cluster of islets off Iceland's south coast includes the isle of **Surtsey,** which, since 1963, has been closed to visitors as an ecological research preserve. Most of the 5,000 residents of the main isle of **Heimaey** have returned since the 1973 evacuation when the local volcano erupted. Heimaey has one of Iceland's best natural history museums, with an excellent aquarium. On the first weekend of August, islanders celebrate the 1874 grant of Icelandic sovereignty with a huge festival in the town of Vestmannaeyjar, on Heimaey. The population moves into a tent city in the **Herjólfsdalur** (Herjólf's Valley), a short distance west of town, for an extended weekend of bonfires, dance, and song.

The East

Numerous busy fishing towns and villages dot Iceland's east coast north of Höfn. As the names Stöðvarfjörður, Fáskrúðsfjörður, and Reyðarfjörður testify, each village has its own fjord. Farming thrives in the valleys, which enjoy almost Continental summers. The Ring Road ties the inland hub Egilsstaðir to the southeastern coastal villages, and secondary roads make outlying communities accessible.

Djúpivogur

Some of the oldest buildings in Djúpivogur, a fishing village since about 1600, date from the 1788–1920 Danish monopoly. Nearby, basaltic Mt. Búlandstindur, legendary as a force of mystical energy, rises to 6,130 ft.

$ **Berunes Youth Hostel** This small summer hostel offers lodging for 25 people in two-, three-, and four-person rooms. There are two separate cottages for five and seven people. ✉ *Beruneshreppur, IS-765,* ☎ FAX *478–8988. 32 beds. No credit cards. Closed mid-Sept.–mid-May.*

$ **Hótel Framtíð.** The friendly dining room in this small harborside hotel serves great home-style food. ✉ *Vogaland 4, IS-765,* ☎ *478–8887,* FAX *478–8187. 10 rooms without bath. Restaurant. AE, MC, V.*

Breiðdalsvík

Trade in this tiny village of a few hundred kindred souls dates from 1883. Hugging the shore on its own small inlet, the hamlet is gradually growing, thanks to its good harbor.

$$ **Hótel Bláfell.** The small hotel has a cozy, rustic interior and an award-winning seafood restaurant. ✉ *Sólvellir 14, IS-760,* ☏ *475–6770,* FAX *475–6668. 15 rooms, 7 with bath. Restaurant. AE, MC, V.*

Seyðisfjörður

Although it may be hard to believe now, the quaint village of Seyðisfjörður was one of Iceland's major trade ports in the 1800s, when tall sailing ships plied the crowded fjord. A number of beautiful wooden houses and buildings in Norwegian style attest to its affluent past. Nowadays, the ferry *Norröna* (☞ Transportation *in* Iceland A to Z, *above*) cruises into the harbor regularly during summer, disgorging visitors and vehicles from Europe.

$$ **Hótel Snæfell.** This hotel in an old wooden house has a glassed-in restaurant with a dramatic view of the fjord. ✉ *Austurvegur 3, IS-710,* ☏ *472–1460,* FAX *472–1570. 9 rooms. Restaurant. AE, MC, V.*

Egilsstaðir

Egilsstaðir is the major commercial hub of the eastern sector, with an airport approved for international flights. The town straddles the Ring Road and lies on the eastern shore of Lake Lögurinn, the reputed home of a wormlike serpent that guards a treasure chest.

During summer at nearby **Eiðar**—just north of Egilsstaðir on the Borgarfjörður Road, a local theater and dance troupe performs weekly in an intimate, open-air setting. Performances are in Icelandic, but English summaries are available. For information contact Philip Vogler (✉ Dalskógar 12, IS-700 Egilsstaðir, ☏ 471–1673, FAX 471–2190). The nation's largest forest, **Hallormsstaðarskógur,** is 25 km (15 mi) south of Egilsstaðir. Native birch and planted aspen, larch, and spruce have grown tall here. As with the entire region, it is ideal for hikers and horseback riders.

$$ **Foss Hotel Hallormsstaður.** New in 1998, this hotel is set in one of Iceland's largest forests and is part of the year-round Foss chain. ✉ *IS-707 Hallormsstaður,* ☏ *562–3350. 36 rooms. Restaurant. AE, MC, V.*

$$ **Hótel Hérað, Icelandair Hotel.** Opened in 1998, this hotel is one in the growing number of pleasant, year-round hotels in the chain. In a valley with views of the nearby countryside, it's convenient to Egilsstaðir's shopping center and pool. ✉ *IS-700Egilsstaðir,* ☏ *471–2770,* FAX *471–2771. 36 rooms. Restaurant. AE, MC, V.*

The North

The entire length of the north coast is deeply gouged by fjords, from Vopnafjörður in the east to Hrútafjörður (Rams' Fjord) at the western end. In fact, Eyjafjörður, the country's longest, dips far inward to Akureyri, the "Capital of the North." In the region's midsection, large, well-established farms, some dating from Viking times, have thrived in the shelter of long fertile valleys, whose rivers attract salmon fishers.

Húsavík

Huśsavík is a charming port on the north coast with a bustling harbor and a timber church dating from 1907. Handy to a nearby winter ski area, it is also a good base for summer hiking. Whale watchers have had amazing success on tours aboard a restored oak boat (☞ Guided Tours *in* The Countryside Essentials, *below*).

The true jewel of this area is **Mývatn,** 54 km (33 mi) southeast of Húsavík, with its fascinating "false craters" and varied, abundant birdlife. Among the species, the harlequin duck and barrow's goldeneye are found nowhere else in Europe. Bring head nets if you visit in summer, because the lake is rightly named for midges, huge swarms of which are essential in the bird food chain and a bit of a nuisance to humans.

Not far from Mývatn, shrub lands, lava barrens, and black sands are traversed in places by rivers with impressive waterfalls. At **Goðafoss** (Waterfall of the Gods), 52 km (32 mi) southwest of Húsavík, looping north along the Tjörnes Peninsula, the last Viking follower of the pagan Norse faith tossed his icons into the waterfall when forced to accept Christianity. Thundering **Dettifoss,** on the Jökulsá (Glacier River) 97 km (60 mi) southeast of Húsavík via the Tjörnes Peninsula, is Europe's most powerful waterfall, and its canyon is a national park. Also protected is the nearby promontory **Ásbyrgi,** which, according to legend, is a giant hoofprint left by Sleipnir, the eight-legged horse of the ancient Norse god Óðinn.

$$$ **Hótel Reynihlíð.** This popular hotel provides a helpful tourist information service and a restaurant for hungry travelers. Guests' comfort and convenience are paramount in this beautiful setting. ✉ *Mývatn, IS-660 Reykjahlíð,* ☎ *464–4170,* FAX *464–4371. 41 rooms. Restaurant. AE, DC, MC, V.*

$$ **Hótel Húsavík.** A favorite of skiers, this sizable hotel has 10 rooms with balconies and many that have views to either the sea or the mountains. Car rental, whale-watching tours, and a host of seasonal activities can be booked from the hotel. Delicious seafood dishes are cooked up in the restaurant. ✉ *Ketilsbraut 22, IS-640,* ☎ *464–1220,* FAX *464–2161. 44 rooms. Restaurant. MC, V.*

$$ **Hótel Reykjahlíð.** This small, peaceful hotel south of Húsavík near Mývatn has a prime lakeside location, meaning bird-watchers can spot most of the lake's main species right from their windows. All rooms are good-sized with baths and essential furnishings, but it is nature that supplies the luxury here. ✉ *Mývatn, IS-660 Reykjahlíð,* ☎ *464–4142,* FAX *464–4336. 9 rooms. Restaurant. MC, V.*

Akureyri

Akureyri's natural surroundings are unrivaled by those of any other Icelandic town. Several late-19th-century wooden houses give the city center a sense of history, as well as architectural variety. **Lystigarðurinn** (Arctic Botanic Gardens) has more than 400 species of Arctic flora native to Iceland. ✉ *Eyrarlandsvegur.* ⏲ *Daily 8* AM*–11* PM.

With the northernmost 18-hole golf course in the world, Akureyri hosts the **Arctic Open Golf Tournament** each year around midsummer. For information, call the Iceland Tourist Bureau (☞ Visitor Information *in* Iceland A to Z *or* Reykjavík Essentials, *above*).

$$$ **Fosshótel KEA.** This centrally located, first-class hotel has an excellent ground-level restaurant, Rósagarðarin, serving haute cuisine, plus an inexpensive cafeteria on the lower level. ✉ *Hafnarstræti 87-89, IS-602,* ☎ *460–2000,* FAX *460–2060. 95rooms. Restaurant. AE, DC, MC, V.*

$$$ **Hótel Norðurland.** Rooms here are pleasantly decorated with Danish furnishings. A sitting room has an impressive view. ✉ *Geislagata 7, IS-600,* ☎ *462–2600,* FAX *462–7962. 38 rooms. Restaurant. AE, DC, MC, V.*

$$ **Hótel Edda.** This summer hotel in a school dormitory is known for its quality service. ✉ *Menntaskólinn, IS-600,* ☎ *461–1434. 79 rooms, 7 with bath. Restaurant. AE, MC, V. Closed Sept.–mid-June.*

$ **Lónsá Farm Holidays.** This accommodation is spartan, but kitchen facilities are available. ✉ *Glæsibæjarhreppur, IS-601 ,* ☎ FAX *462–5037. 14 rooms without bath. MC, V.*

Sauðárkrókur

In summer, boat trips from the large coastal town of Sauðárkrókur to Drangey and the Málmey Islands offer striking views of the fjord and bird cliffs.

$$ **Hótel Áning.** Views from the tidy, though bare, rooms of this good-size summer hotel are of either the nearby mountains or the fjord. Hiking, golf, horseback riding, boat tours, and river rafting can be arranged from here. ✉ *Sæmundarhlíð, IS-550,* ☎ *453–6717 or 453–5940,* FAX *453–6087. 65 rooms. Restaurant. MC, V.*

Blönduós

The largest town on the west end of the north coast is nestled beneath gently rolling hills at the mouth of the glacially chalky Blanda. Though unsightly shrimp and shellfish processing plants and small industrial businesses mark the landscape here, from Blönduós it is an easy drive to neighboring picturesque valleys.

$$ **Gistihús Sveitasetrið, Blönduós.** This small hotel, in the old center of town, is a stone's throw from the seashore. Fresh trout and salmon are specialties at the large restaurant. ✉ *Aðalgata 6, IS-540,* ☎ *452–4126,* FAX *452–4989. 18 rooms, 11 with shower. Restaurant. AE, MC, V.*

The West

The west is dramatically diverse. It encompasses the northwest dragon head—the rugged Vestfirðir (West Fjords) where, at Europe's westernmost part, seabirds vastly outnumber people. Due south is the long arm of the Snæfellsnes Peninsula, with awe-inspiring Snæfellsjökull at its tip. South of the peninsula is Borgarfjörður, where rich farmlands steeped in the history of the Viking sagas still fire visitors' imaginations.

Ísafjörður

The uncrowned capital of the West Fjords and one of the most important fishing towns in Iceland hosts a renowned Easter week ski meet. This is a convenient jumping-off point for tours to Hornstrandir, the splendidly peaceful and desolate land north of the 66th parallel inhabited by millions of seabirds.

$$$ **Hótel Ísafjörður.** This hotel is great for families. The restaurant offers a wide variety of tasty seafood. ✉ *Silfurtorg 2, IS-400,* ☎ *456–4111,* FAX *456–4767. 32 rooms. Restaurant. AE, MC, V.*

Stykkishólmur

Stykkishólmur is an active port community on the peninsula's north coast, with a well-sheltered natural harbor. Classic timber houses, dating from as early as 1828, reveal its distinguished past, when many of the now-abandoned islets of Breiðafjörður were settled.

Snæfellsjökull

Literally the high point on the Snæfellsnes Peninsula is Snæfellsjökull, entry point in Jules Verne's novel *Journey to the Center of the Earth.* This beautiful glacier-covered conical summit, according to local legend, possesses mysterious energies and is home to hidden folk.

$$ **Hótel Búðir.** This rustic hotel is under the magical Snæfellsjökull and close to a beach of black lava and golden sand. The stellar restaurant here specializes in nouveau interpretations of seafood and regional lamb—all laced with herbs and veggies. ✉ *Staðarsveit, IS-355 Snæfellsnes,* ☎ *435–6700,* FAX *435–6701. 26 rooms, 6 with bath. Restaurant. MC, V. Closed Oct.–Apr.*

Ólafsvík

Commerce has been carried on in this small village, under the north shoulder of Snæfellsjökull, since 1687. From here you can hike to the top of the glacier or arrange snowmobile tours. Call the Tourist Information Center (☏ 436–1543).

$$ **Höfði Guest house.** This family-style, harborside hotel has a small restaurant that serves up fresh local fare such as trout and halibut. ✉ *Ólafsbraut 20, IS-355,* ☏ *436–1650,* FAX *436–1651. 14 rooms without bath. Restaurant. AE, MC, V.*

Borgarnes

Borgarnes, the major town of the Borgarfjörður district, is unique in Iceland as being the only sizeable coastal town that does *not* rely on fishing for its livelihood, turning instead to commerce and agriculture-related businesses.

$$$ **Hótel Borgarnes.** Daylight through large windows fills the neutral-color interiors of the newer rooms of this hotel. A number of south-facing rooms overlook the fjord, with views of nearby mountains. It's a good bet for dependable food and service. ✉ *Egilsgata 14–16, IS-310,* ☏ *437–1119,* FAX *437–1443. 75 rooms. Restaurant. AE, DC, MC, V.*

The Countryside Essentials

Dining and Lodging

Because most restaurants outside Reykjavík are in hotels, there are no separate restaurant listings in the regional coverage. For details and price-category definitions, *see* Dining *and* Lodging *in* Iceland A to Z, *above.*

Guided Tours

THE SOUTH

Glacier Tours (✉ Box 66, IS-780 Hafnarbraut, ☏ 478–1000) offers various adventure tours from Höfn in Hornafjörður. **Topp Ferðir** (✉ Lindarbakka, Höfn in Hornafjörður, ☏ 478–2666), has glacier jeep tours leaving from Hotel Vatnajökull. **Jórvik Aviation** (✉ Box 5308, Reykjavík, ☏ 562–5101) offers spectacular sight-seeing flights to Skaftafell National Park and environs. Boat tours can be arranged on arrival at the **Jökulsárlón** glacial lagoon (call Fjölnir Torfason, ☏ 478–1065, or Skaftafell National Park, ☏ 478–1627).

Westman Islands Travel Service (✉ Herjólfsgötu 4, Westman Islands, ☏ 481–2922) offers informative, reasonably priced sight-seeing trips by boat and bus in the Westman Islands. **Öræfaferðir** (✉ 785 Fagurhólsmýri, Hofsnes-Öræfi, Fagurhólsmýri, ☏ 478–1682), a father-son outfit, puts together tours ranging from introductory ice climbing to assaults on the summit of Iceland's highest mountain to bird-watching.

THE NORTH

In Húsavík, **Norður Sigling** (✉ Laugarbrekka 21, Húsavík, ☏ 464–1741) offers whale-watching aboard a classic oak ship.

THE WEST

West Tours (✉ Box 37, Ísafjörður, ☏ 456–5111) runs hiking and mountaineering trips to the inhabitable parts of Strandasýsla. Snowmobile trips to the top of Snæfellsjökull for groups can be arranged at **Snjófell** (✉ Arnarstapi, ☏ 435–6783). **Eyjaferðir** (✉ Egilshús, Stykkishólmur, ☏ 438–1450) runs boat tours.

Visitor Information

Akureyri (✉ Hafnarstræti 82, ☎ 462–7733). **Egilsstaðir** (✉ Egilsstaðir Campsite, ☎ 471–2320). **Höfn** (✉ Höfn Campsite, Hafnarbraut, ☎ 478–1701). **Húsavík** (✉ Safnarhús Húsavíkur Library/Museum, ☎ 464–1173). **Ísafjörður** (✉ Hafnarstræti 6, ☎ 456–5121). **Kirkjubæjarklaustur** (✉ Community Center, Klausturvegur 10, ☎ 487–4620).

Mývatn (✉ Eldá Travel, Mývatnssveit, ☎ 464–4220); June–August contact Reykjahlíðarskóli School (☎ 464–4390), 9 AM–10 PM. **Ólafsvík** (☎ 436–1543). **Selfoss** Tryggvaskáli (✉ next to Ölfusá River bridge, ☎ 482–1704). **Seyðisfjörður** Austfar (✉ Fjarðargata 8, ☎ 472–1111).

17 Ireland

Dublin, Dublin to Cork, Cork to Galway, the Northwest

For a small island country (just over half the size of New York State) isolated on the westernmost extreme of the continent, Ireland has nevertheless managed to strut its way around the European stage. Economically it has traditionally been a mere understudy to the great European powers (especially Great Britain); politically its influence is minimal, and yet everyone knows of the Irish, and they all cast a slightly envious eye at this mysterious island of romance.

No more so than now. A major influx of money from the European Union over the last decade has substantially enlivened Ireland's economy, particularly in the booming capital city of Dublin. One-third of the country's very young population lives in the city, which is as much a college town as a center of government. Galleries, art-house cinemas, elegant shops, coffeehouses, and a stunning variety of restaurants are springing up on virtually every street, transforming the provincial capital that once suffocated Joyce into a city every bit as cosmopolitan as the Paris to which he fled.

The heart of Dublin culture remains the public house, or pub, where the Irish can be found at their sharpest and most convivial, while seated in fast-talking, welcoming circles around tables supporting the almost sacred black stout, Guinness. Even if you do not usually frequent bars at home, attendance at the ritual of the Irish hostelry will add greatly to your visit.

Dublin's small city center is easy to navigate and strikingly beautiful, with recent renovations to Trinity College, Dublin Castle, and many of the magnificent granite public buildings and distinctive Georgian squares adding to its intimate grandeur. The pace of life outside the capital is even more relaxed—too bad there isn't an Irish-language equivalent of *mañana*. Indeed, the farther you travel from the metropolis, the more you will be inclined to linger. Apart from such sporting attractions as championship golf, horse racing, angling, and the native games of hurling and Gaelic football, the thing to do in Ireland is to stop, take a deep breath of some of the best air in the western world, and look around.

The lakes of Killarney—a chain of azure lakes surrounded by wild, boulder-strewn mountains—are justifiably among the country's most famous attractions. The Ring of Kerry is a gift from the gods to touring motorists, an out-and-back, daylong adventure through lush green mountain and valley, and on down to the sea. By contrast the lunar landscape of County Clare's eerie limestone desert, the Burren, must be explored on foot if you're to enjoy its rare alpine and Mediterranean flowers. Likewise, if you want to stand on the summit of the Cliffs of Moher to watch the Atlantic breakers bite into the ancient rocks 712 ft below, you'll have to get out of your car—even in the rain, and it often rains in Clare. The history buff will delight in the castles and great stately houses peppering the banks of the old River Shannon, the spine of the nation. Throughout the country, prehistoric and early Christian ruins and remains hint at the awesome age of civilization on this ancient island. Alternatively you could just visit a bookstore and pick up anything by the great writers of Ireland; let James Joyce, William Butler Yeats, John Millington Synge, or Seamus Heaney be your travel guide, as you seek out the places made famous in their works.

IRELAND A TO Z

Customs on Arrival

For details on imports and duty-free limits, *see* Customs & Duties *in* Chapter 1.

Dining

To the surprise of most visitors, Ireland is in the throes of a food revolution. Not far out of Dublin you begin to see some of the reasons all around you: livestock grazing in impossibly green fields, clear waters to spawn fish, and acres of produce thriving in the temperate climate. But it's Irish chefs who are the stars of the rapidly changing food scene. Many of them are young, they have traveled widely and absorbed the best influences of Europe, North America, and the Pacific Rim, resulting in a pan-European, postmodern cuisine. This new Irish cuisine has moved beyond the age-old roast-beef-and-Yorkshire-pudding habit of the old Anglo-Irish country houses. In its place an innovative, indigenous style is emerging, marrying simple treatments of traditional courses—black pudding, nettle soup, oysters, wild salmon—with more exotic, complicated dishes that feature unusual combinations of the best local, often organic ingredients.

Despite the new sophistication, there are many examples of traditional cooking, particularly in pubs serving lunches of Irish stew, boiled bacon and cabbage, or steamed mussels. Pubs are one of the pillars of Irish society, worth visiting as much for conversation and music as for drinking. The national drink, Guinness, is a pitch-black, malted stout, one of the great beers of the world; try it with raw oysters and tabasco for a melding of opposites. (If you're really adventurous, add a half-pint of milk to a half-pint of Guinness!)

Hotel dining rooms vary in quality, but the best country-house hotels offer some of the finest dining in Europe, and most of these will welcome guests whether they are overnighters or not.

MEALTIMES

Always check breakfast times in advance. It is usually 8–10, but some hotels serve from 7 to 11. Most offer a full Irish breakfast, with cereals, followed by bacon, eggs, sausage, and sometimes, black pudding. Lunch, from noon to 2 (or even 3), is a leisurely affair. Some hotels serve afternoon tea and scones. Most people go out for dinner after 8; if you want to eat earlier, watch for "early bird" menus, typically served from 6:30–7:30.

RATINGS

Prices are per person and include an appetizer, main course, and dessert, but no wine or tip. Many restaurants also have à la carte menus allowing you to select only the main course or even two appetizers. Sales tax is included in the price. Many places add a 10%–15% service charge—if not, a 10% tip is fine.

CATEGORY	COST
$$$$	over IR£25
$$$	IR£20–IR£25
$$	IR£15–IR£20
$	under IR£15

WHAT TO WEAR

People dress up for dinner at the top restaurants, but a jacket is ordinarily sufficient. Ties are rarely essential. Good casual wear is usually acceptable.

Language

Officially, Irish (Gaelic) is the first language of the Republic, but the everyday language of the vast majority of Irish people is English. Except for the northwest and parts of Connemara, where many signs are not translated, most signs in the country are written in Irish with an English translation underneath. There is one important exception to this rule, with which all visitors should familiarize themselves: FIR (pronounced fear) and MNÁ (pronounced muh-*naw*) translate, respectively, into "men" and "women." The *Gaelteacht* (pronounced *gale*-tocked)—areas in which Irish *is* the everyday language of most people—comprises only 6% of the land, and all its inhabitants are, in any case, bilingual.

Lodging

Accommodations in Ireland range all the way from deluxe castles and renovated stately homes to thatched cottages and farmhouses to humble bed-and-breakfasts. Standards everywhere are high, and they—and, make special note, prices—continue to rise. The days of considering Ireland your basic bargain destination are long gone. Pressure on hotel space reaches a peak between June and September, but it's a good idea to make reservations in advance at any time of the year, particularly at the more expensive spots. Rooms can be reserved directly from the United States; ask your travel agent for details. Bord Fáilte (the Irish Tourist Board, pronounced Board *Fall*-cha) has a Central Credit Card Reservations Service (✉ Suffolk St., Dublin 2, ☎ 01/605–7777, FAX 01/605–7787) that can make reservations, as can local tourist board offices.

Bord Fáilte has an official grading system and publishes a detailed price list of all approved accommodations, including hotels, guest houses, farmhouses, B&Bs, and hostels. No hotel may exceed this price without special authorization from Bord Fáilte; prices must also be displayed in every room. Don't hesitate to complain either to the manager or to Bord Fáilte, or both, if prices exceed this maximum.

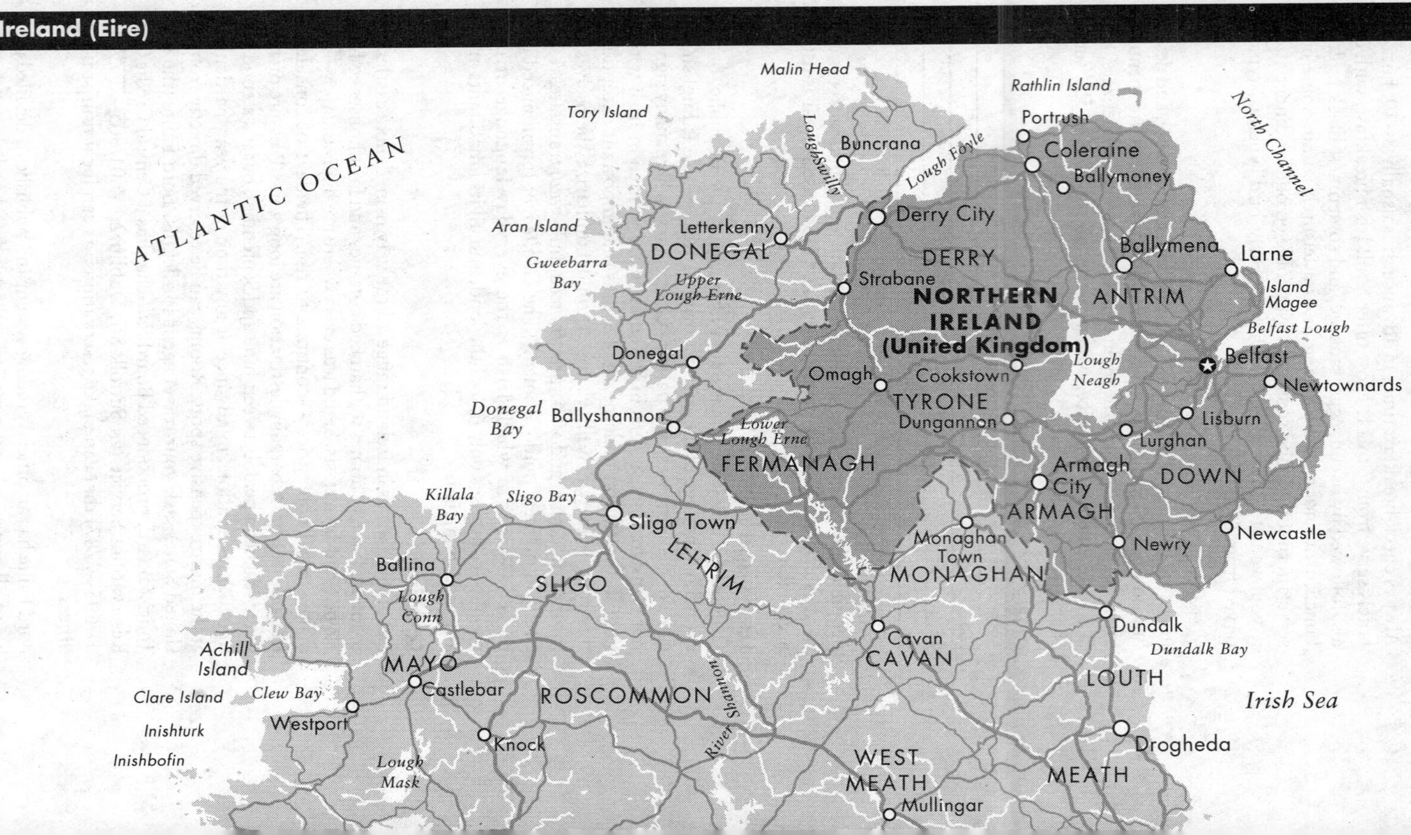
Ireland (Eire)
ATLANTIC OCEAN
Malin Head
Tory Island
Rathlin Island
North Channel
Portrush
Coleraine
Ballymoney
Buncrana
Lough Swilly
Lough Foyle
Derry City
Aran Island
Letterkenny
DONEGAL
Gweebarra Bay
Upper Lough Erne
Strabane
DERRY
NORTHERN IRELAND (United Kingdom)
Ballymena
ANTRIM
Larne
Island Magee
Belfast Lough
Belfast
Newtownards
Donegal
Omagh
Cookstown
Lough Neagh
TYRONE
Dungannon
Lisburn
Lurghan
Donegal Bay
Ballyshannon
Lower Lough Erne
FERMANAGH
Armagh City
ARMAGH
DOWN
Newcastle
Newry
Killala Bay
Sligo Bay
Sligo Town
LEITRIM
Monaghan Town
MONAGHAN
Ballina
Lough Conn
SLIGO
Cavan
CAVAN
Dundalk
Dundalk Bay
Achill Island
MAYO
Castlebar
Clare Island
Clew Bay
Westport
ROSCOMMON
River Shannon
LOUTH
Irish Sea
Inishturk
Inishbofin
Knock
Lough Mask
WEST MEATH
MEATH
Drogheda
Mullingar

GALWAY
Lough Corrib
Galway City
Ballinasloe
Athlone
DUBLIN
Dublin
Dun Laoghaire
REPUBLIC OF IRELAND
OFFALY
Naas
Bray
Galway Bay
Aran Islands
Birr
Portlaoise
KILDARE
Wicklow Town
LAOISE
Athy
WICKLOW
CLARE
Roscrea
Ennis
Nenagh
Arklow
CARLOW
Kilrush
KILKENNY
Thurles
Gorey
Limerick City
TIPPERARY
Kilkenny Town
LIMERICK
Cashel
Mouth of the Shannon
Listowel
Newcastle West
Tipperary
WEXFORD
Clonmel
Carrick-on-Suir
Wexford Town
Tralee
Dingle Peninsula
WATERFORD
Waterford City
Mallow
Killarney
Fermoy
Dingle Bay
Blasket Islands
KERRY
CORK
Dungarvan
Cork City
Youghal
Iveragh Peninsula
Midleton
Cobh
N
St. George's Channel
Skellig Rocks
Bandon
Kenmare Bay
Bantry Bay
Clonakilty
Skibbereen
Mizen Head
0
40 miles
0
60 km

In general, hotels charge per person. In most cases (but not all, especially in more expensive places), the price includes a full breakfast. VAT is included, but some hotels—again, usually the more expensive ones—add a 10%–15% service charge. This should be mentioned in their price list. If it's not, a tip of between 10% and 15% is customary—if you think the service is worth it. In $$ and $ hotels, be sure to specify whether you want a private bath or shower; the latter is cheaper. Off-season (October–May) prices are reduced by as much as 25%.

BED-AND-BREAKFASTS

Bed-and-breakfast means just that. The bed can vary from a four-poster in the wing of a castle to a feather bed in a whitewashed farmhouse or the spare bedroom of a modern cottage. Rates are generally around IR£16 per person, though these can vary significantly. Although many larger B&Bs offer rooms with bath or shower, in some you'll have to use the bathroom in the hall and, in many cases, pay 50p–IR£1 extra for the privilege.

CAMPING

There are a variety of beautifully sited campgrounds and trailer parks, but be prepared for wet weather! All are listed in *Caravan and Camping in Ireland,* available from Bord Fáilte.

GUEST HOUSES

Some smaller hotels are graded as guest houses. To qualify, they must have at least five bedrooms, but in major cities they often have many more. A few may have restaurants; those that do not will often provide evening meals by arrangement. Few will have a bar. Otherwise these rooms can be as comfortable as those of a regular hotel, and in major cities they offer very good value for the money, compared with the $ hotels.

RATINGS

Prices are for two people in a double room, based on high season (June–September) rates.

CATEGORY	COST
$$$$	over IR£180
$$$	IR£140–IR£180
$$	IR£100–IR£140
$	under IR£100

Mail

POSTAL RATES

Airmail rates to the United States, Canada, and the Commonwealth are 52p for the first 10 grams, air letters 45p, and postcards 38p. Letters to Britain and continental Europe cost 32p, postcards 28p.

RECEIVING MAIL

A general delivery service is operated free of charge from Dublin's **General Post Office** (✉ O'Connell St., Dublin 1, ☎ 01/705–7000).

Money Matters

COSTS

Dublin is one of Europe's most expensive cities—an unfortunate state of affairs that manifests itself most obviously in hotel rates and restaurant menus. You can generally keep costs lower if you visit Ireland on a package tour. Alternatively, consider staying in a guest house or one of the multitude of B&Bs; they provide an economical and atmospheric option (☞ Lodging, *above*). The rest of the country—with the exception of the better-known hotels and restaurants—is less expensive than Dublin. That the Irish themselves complain bitterly about the high cost of living is partly attributable to the high rate of value-added tax (VAT)—a stinging 21% on "luxury" goods and 12½% on hotel accommodations. Some sample costs make the point. For instance, while a double room in a moderately priced Dublin hotel will cost about IR£90, with breakfast sometimes another IR£9 per person, the current rate for a country B&B is around IR£16 per person. A modest small-town hotel will charge around IR£25 per person.

CURRENCY

The unit of currency in Ireland is the pound, or punt (pronounced poont), written as IR£ to avoid confusion with the pound sterling. The currency is divided into the same denominations as in Britain, with IR£1 divided into 100 pence (written *p*). There is likely to be some variance in the rates of exchange between Ireland and the United Kingdom (which includes Northern Ireland). Change U.K. pounds at a bank when you get to Ireland (pound coins not accepted); change Irish pounds before you leave.

Although the Irish pound is the only legal tender currency in the Republic, U.S. dollars and British currency are often accepted in large hotels and shops licensed as bureaux de change. Banks give the best rate of exchange. The rate of exchange at press time (spring 1998) was 70 pence to the U.S. dollar, 48 pence to the Canadian dollar, IR£1.17 to the British pound sterling, 45 pence to the Australian dollar, and 39 pence to the New Zealand dollar.

SAMPLE PRICES

Cup of coffee, 70p; pint of beer, IR£2.10; Coca-Cola, 95p; a sandwich, IR£1.80; 2-km (1-mi) taxi ride, IR£3.50.

National Holidays

January 1 (New Year's); March 17 (St. Patrick's Day); March 28 (Good Friday); March 31 (Easter Monday); May 1 (May Day); May 19 (Whit Monday); August 5 (August Holiday); October 28 (October Holiday); and December 25–26 (Christmas and St. Stephen's Day). If you're planning a visit at Easter, remember that theaters and cinemas are closed for the last three days of the preceding week.

Opening and Closing Times

Banks are open weekdays 10–4, and until 5 on Thursday. In small towns they may close for lunch from 12:30–1:30. **Museums** are usually open weekdays 10–5, Saturday 10–1, and Sunday 2–5. Always make a point of checking, however, as hours can change unexpectedly. **Shops** are open Monday–Saturday 9–5:30, closing earlier on Wednesday, Thursday, or Saturday, depending on the locality. Most shops will, however, remain open until 9 PM on Thursday for late shopping.

Shopping

SALES-TAX REFUNDS

Visitors from outside Europe can take advantage of the "cash-back" system on value-added tax (VAT) in two ways. The first is by having your invoice receipt stamped by customs on departure and mailing it back to the store for VAT refund. You must, however, verify at the time of purchase that the store operates by this system. The second and more popular option is by using one of the private cash-back companies, which charge a commission. **Europe Tax-free Shopping** offers customers their cash back at Dublin and Shannon airports when they present a Europe Tax-free Shopping voucher that has been filled out by the retailer at the point of sale. Other companies operate a cash-back system whereby you return your voucher just before you depart or when you arrive home, and you receive the VAT refund by mail, or it can be credited directly to your credit card.

Telephoning

COUNTRY CODE

The country code for the Republic of Ireland is 353.

INTERNATIONAL CALLS

For calls to the United States and Canada, dial 001 followed by the area code. For calls to the United Kingdom, dial 0044 followed by the number, dropping the beginning zero. To reach an **AT&T** long distance operator, dial 1–800/550–000. For **MCI,** dial 1–800/551–001. For **Sprint,** dial 1–800/552–001.

LOCAL CALLS

There are pay phones in all post offices and most hotels and bars, as well as in street booths. Local calls cost 20p for three minutes, calls within Ireland cost about 50p for three minutes, and calls to Britain cost about IR£1.75 for three minutes. Telephone cards are available at all post offices and most newsagents. Prices range from IR£2 for 10 units to IR£8 for 50 units. Card booths are as common as coin booths. Rates go down by about a third after 6 PM and all day Saturday and Sunday.

Tipping

Other than in upscale hotels and restaurants, the Irish are not really used to being tipped. Some hotels and restaurants will add a service charge of about 12% to your bill, so tipping isn't necessary unless you've received particularly good service.

Tip taxi drivers about 10% of the fare if the taxi has been using its meter. For longer journeys, where the fare is agreed in advance, a tip will not be expected unless some kind of commentary (solicited or not) has been provided. In luxury hotels porters and bellhops will expect IR£1; elsewhere, 50p is adequate. Hairdressers normally expect a tip of about IR£1. You don't tip in pubs, but if there is waiter service in a bar or hotel lounge, leave about 20p.

Transportation

BY BICYCLE

Biking can be a great way to get around Ireland. Details of bicycle rentals are available from the Bord Fáilte. Rates average IR£7.50 per day or IR£35 per week. You must pay a IR£30 deposit. Be sure to make reservations, especially in July and August. If you rent a bike in the Republic, you may *not* take it into Northern Ireland; nor may you take a bike rented in Northern Ireland into the Republic.

BY BOAT

Exploring Ireland's lakes, rivers, and canals is a delightful, offbeat way to get to know the country. Motor cruisers can be chartered on the Shannon, the longest river in the British Isles. Bord Fáilte has details of the wide choice of trips and operators available.

For drifting through the historic Midlands on the Grand Canal and River Barrow, contact **Celtic Canal Cruisers** (✉ 24th Lock, Tullamore, Co. Offaly, ☎ 0506/21861).

BY BUS

For the strictly independent traveler, the 15-day **Rambler** ticket gives unlimited travel by bus and is an excellent value at IR£98. It can be purchased from any city bus terminal and is valid for travel on any 15 days in a 30-day period. The provincial bus system operated by Bus Eireann is widespread—more so than the train system—although service can be infrequent in remote areas. But the routes cover the entire country and are often linked to the train services. *See* By Train, *below,* for details of combined train and bus discount tickets.

BY CAR

Parking. Despite the relative lack of traffic, parking in towns can be difficult. Signs with the letter P indicate parking lots, but if there's a stroke through the P, keep away or you'll collect a stiff fine, normally around IR£15. After 6 PM, restrictions are lifted. Give lot attendants about 50p when you leave.

Road Conditions. Ireland is one country in which a car is more or less essential for successful travel. Despite improvements in public transportation, both the train and bus networks are limited, and many of the most intriguing regions are accessible only by car. Roads are reasonable, though the absence of turnpikes means that trip times can be long; on the other hand, you'll soon find that driving past an ever-changing and often dramatic series of unspoiled landscapes can be very much part of the fun. There's a bonus in the fact that traffic is normally light, though you can easily find yourself crawling down country lanes behind an ancient tractor or a flock of sheep. This is not a country for those with a taste for life in the fast lane.

All principal roads are designated by the letter *N*, meaning National Primary Road. Thus, the main highway north from Dublin is N1, the main highway northwest is N2, and so on. Brand-new divided highways, or motorways—designated by blue signs and the letter *M*—take the place of some N roads. They are the fastest way to get from one point to another, but use caution, as they can end as abruptly as they begin. Road signs are usually in both Irish and English; in the northwest and Connemara, most are in Irish only, so make sure you have a good road map. A sensible rule to follow at unmarked intersections is: Keep going straight if there's no sign directing you to do otherwise. Distances on the new green signposts are in km; the old white signposts give distances in mi.

Rules of the Road. Driving is on the left. There is a general speed limit of 96 kph (60 mph) on most roads; in towns, the limit is 48 kph (30 mph). In some areas, the limit is 64 kph (40 mph); this is always clearly posted. At traffic circles (roundabouts), which are the main form of interchange, traffic from the right takes priority.

Seat belts must be worn by the driver and front-seat passengers. Children under 12 must ride in the back. The new (and controversial) drunk-driving laws are strict, restricting the driver to less than one pint of beer.

BY PLANE

Distances are not great in Ireland, so airplanes play only a small role in internal travel. There are daily flights from Dublin to Shannon, Cork, Waterford, Kerry, Knock, and Galway; all flights take about 30 minutes. There is frequent service to the Aran Islands, off Galway Bay, from Connemara Airport, Galway. The flight takes five minutes.

BY TRAIN

Iarnód Eireann (Irish Rail) and **Bus Eireann** (Irish Bus) are independent components of the state-owned public transportation company **Coras Iompair Eireann** (CIE). The rail network, although much cut back in the past 25 years, is still extensive, with main routes radiating from Dublin to Cork, Galway, Limerick, Tralee, Killarney, Westport, and Sligo; there is also a line for the north and Belfast. All trains are diesel; cars on principal expresses are air-conditioned. There are two classes on many trains—Super Standard (first class) and Standard (second class). Dining cars are carried on main expresses. There are no sleeping cars.

Speeds are slow in comparison with those of other European trains. Dublin, however, has a modern commuter train—the DART (Dublin Area Rapid Transit)—that runs south from the suburb of Howth through the city to Bray on the Wicklow coast and makes many stops along the way.

Fares. An **Explorer** ticket (rail and bus) is valid for any eight days in a 15-day period. One- and four-day round-trip train tickets are also available at discounted rates. The **Irish Rover** ticket includes travel in Northern Ireland via rail; it is good for five days' travel out of 15 consecutive days.

Visitor Information

The main **Bord Fáilte** visitor information office in Dublin is on Suffolk Street, just off Grafton Street (☎ 01/602–4000, ⏲ July–Sept., Mon.–Sat. 8:30–6, Sun. 11–5:30; Oct.–June, daily 9–6).

Weather

June to mid-September is Ireland's high season, but the country's attractions are not as dependent on the weather as those in most other northern European countries, and the scenery is just as attractive in the off-peak times of fall and spring. Accommodations are more economical in winter, although some—particularly in the west and the northwest—are closed from October through March. In all seasons the visitor can expect to encounter rain, although the sun is often out moments after a squall passes.

CLIMATE

Winters are mild though wet; summers can be warm and sunny, but there's always the risk of a sudden shower. No one ever went to Ireland for a suntan. The following are the average daily maximum and minimum temperatures for Dublin.

Jan.	46F	8C	**May**	60F	15C	**Sept.**	63F	17C
	34	1		43	6		48	9
Feb.	47F	8C	**June**	65F	18C	**Oct.**	57F	14C
	35	2		48	9		43	6
Mar.	51F	11C	**July**	67F	19C	**Nov.**	51F	11C
	37	3		52	11		39	4
Apr.	55F	13C	**Aug.**	67F	19C	**Dec.**	47F	8C
	39	4		51	11		37	3

DUBLIN

Today, Europe's most intimate capital has become a boom town—the soul of the new Ireland is in the throes of what may be the nation's most dramatic period of transformation since the Georgian era. Dublin is riding the back of the Celtic Tiger (as the roaring Irish economy has been nicknamed) and massive construction cranes are hovering over both shiny new hotels and old Georgian houses. Irish culture is hot: patriot Michael Collins has become a Hollywood box-office star, Frank McCourt's *Angela's Ashes* has conquered American best-seller lists, and *Riverdance* has become a worldwide tear-jerking old Irish mass-jig. Because of these and other attractions, travelers are coming to Dublin in ever-greater numbers, so don't be surprised if you stop to consult your map in Temple Bar—the city's most happening neighborhood—and are swept away by the ceaseless flow of bustling crowds. Dublin has become a colossally entertaining, engaging city—all the more astonishing considering its gentle size.

Exploring Dublin

Numbers in the margin correspond to points of interest on the Dublin map.

Originally a Viking settlement, Dublin is situated on the banks of the River Liffey, which divides the city north and south. The liveliest round-the-clock spots, including Temple Bar and Grafton Street, are both on the south side, although a variety of construction projects on the north side are helping to reinvigorate areas that have not typically been on visitors' paths. The majority of the city's most notable buildings date from the 18th century—the Georgian era—and, although many of its finer Georgian buildings disappeared in the redevelopment of the '70s, enough remain, mainly south of the river, to recall the elegant Dublin of centuries past. Literary Dublin can still be recaptured by those who follow the footsteps of Leopold Bloom's progress, as described in James Joyce's *Ulysses.* Trinity College, alma mater of Oliver Goldsmith, Jonathan Swift, and Samuel Beckett, among others, is a green, Georgian oasis, alive with young students scurrying to and fro, just like generations of aspiring scholars before them.

Trinity and St. Stephen's: The Georgian Heart of Dublin

"In Dublin's fair city—where girls are so pretty" went the centuries-old ditty about Ireland's historic capital. If Dublin is still one of the most charming cities in Europe, redolent in parts of the dignity and elegance of the 18th century, it is due to the elegant Georgian style of art and architecture, which flowered in the city between 1714 and 1820 during the English reigns of the three Georges. South of the Liffey are graceful squares and fashionable terraces from Dublin's elegant heyday and, interspersed with some of the city's leading sights, this area is perfect for an introductory city tour. Many travelers begin at O'Connell Bridge—as Dublin has no central focal point, most natives regard it as the city's Piccadilly Circus or Times Square—then head south down Westmoreland Street to Parliament House. When you pass 12 Westmoreland Street, drop in on **Bewley's Coffee House,** an institution that has been supplying Dubliners with coffee and buns since 1842. Open Monday–Saturday 9–5:30, its historic interior evokes the Dublin of everyone's dreams. Continue on to Trinity College—the Book of Kells, Ireland's greatest artistic treasure, is on view here—then eastward to Merrion Square and the National Gallery, south to St. Stephen's Green and Fitzwilliam Square, then head west to Dublin's two beautiful cathedrals— Christ Church and St. Patrick's—before heading back north for supper in a Temple Bar restaurant overlooking the Liffey.

2 **Bank of Ireland.** With a grand facade that is a veritable forest of marble columns, the Bank of Ireland is one of Dublin's most striking buildings. Located across the street from the front entrance to Trinity College, the Georgian structure was once the home of the Irish Parliament. Built in 1729, it was bought by the Bank of Ireland in 1803. Hurricane-shape rosettes adorn the coffered ceiling in the pastel-hued, colonnaded, clerestoried main banking hall, once the Court of Requests where citizens' petitions were heard. Just down the hall is the original House of Lords, with tapestries, an oak-panel nave, and a 1,233-piece Waterford glass chandelier; ask a guard to show you in. Visitors are welcome during normal banking hours; a brief guided tour is given every Tuesday at 10:30, 11:30, and 1:45. ✉ *2 College Green,* ☎ *01/677–6801.* ⏲ *Weekdays 10–4; Thurs. until 5.*

27 **Christ Church Cathedral.** Although St. Patrick's Cathedral is Dublin's grandest house of worship, Christ Church is actually the flagship of

Abbey Theatre, **4**
Bank of Ireland, **2**
Christ Church Cathedral, **27**
City Hall, **13**
Civic Museum, **15**
Custom House, **5**
Dublin Castle, **14**
Dublin Writers Museum, **8**
Four Courts, **30**
Geneaological Office, **18**
General Post Office, **6**
Grafton Street, **16**
Guinness Brewery, **28**
Ha'penny Bridge, **11**
Hugh Lane Municipal Gallery of Modern Art, **9**
Leinster House, **21**
Marsh's Library, **25**
Merrion Square, **23**
National Gallery of Ireland, **22**
National Library, **19**
National Museum, **20**
O'Connell Bridge, **3**
Old Jameson Distillery, **31**
Parnell Square, **7**
Phoenix Park, **32**
Rotunda Hospital, **10**
Royal Hospital Kilmainham, **29**
Royal Irish Academy, **17**
St. Patrick's Cathedral, **26**
St. Stephen's Green, **24**
Temple Bar, **12**
Trinity College, **1**

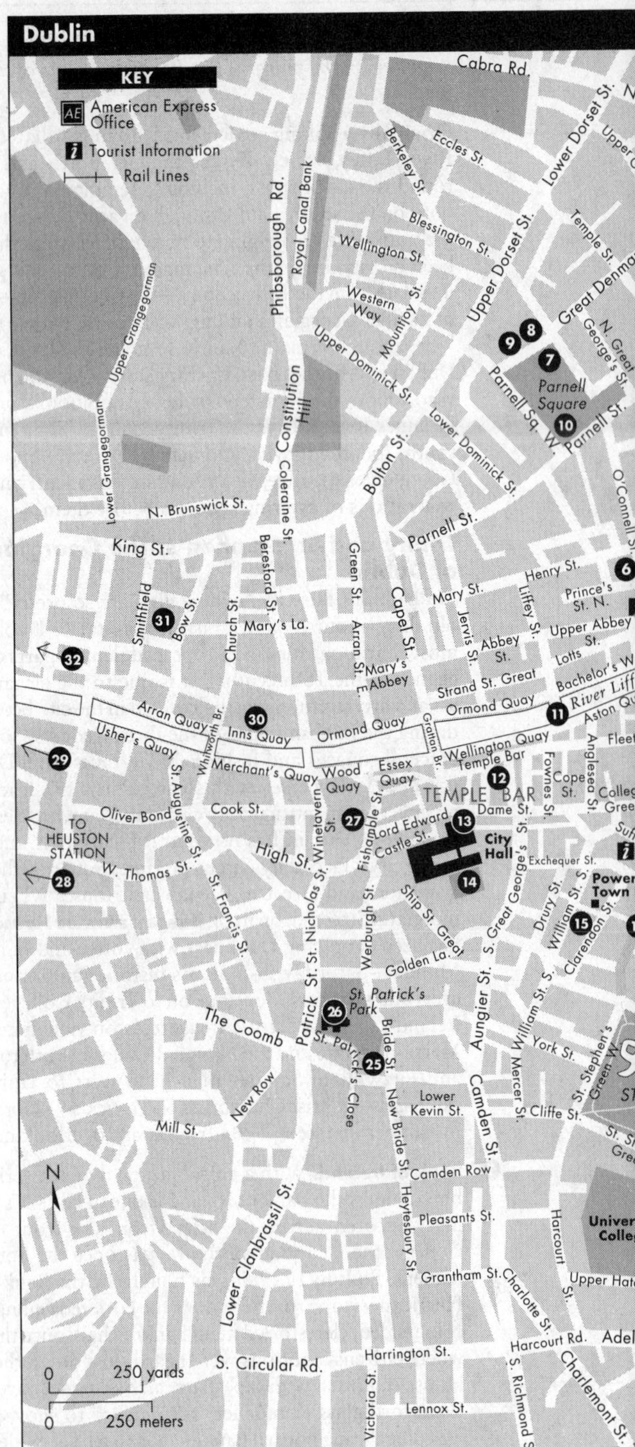

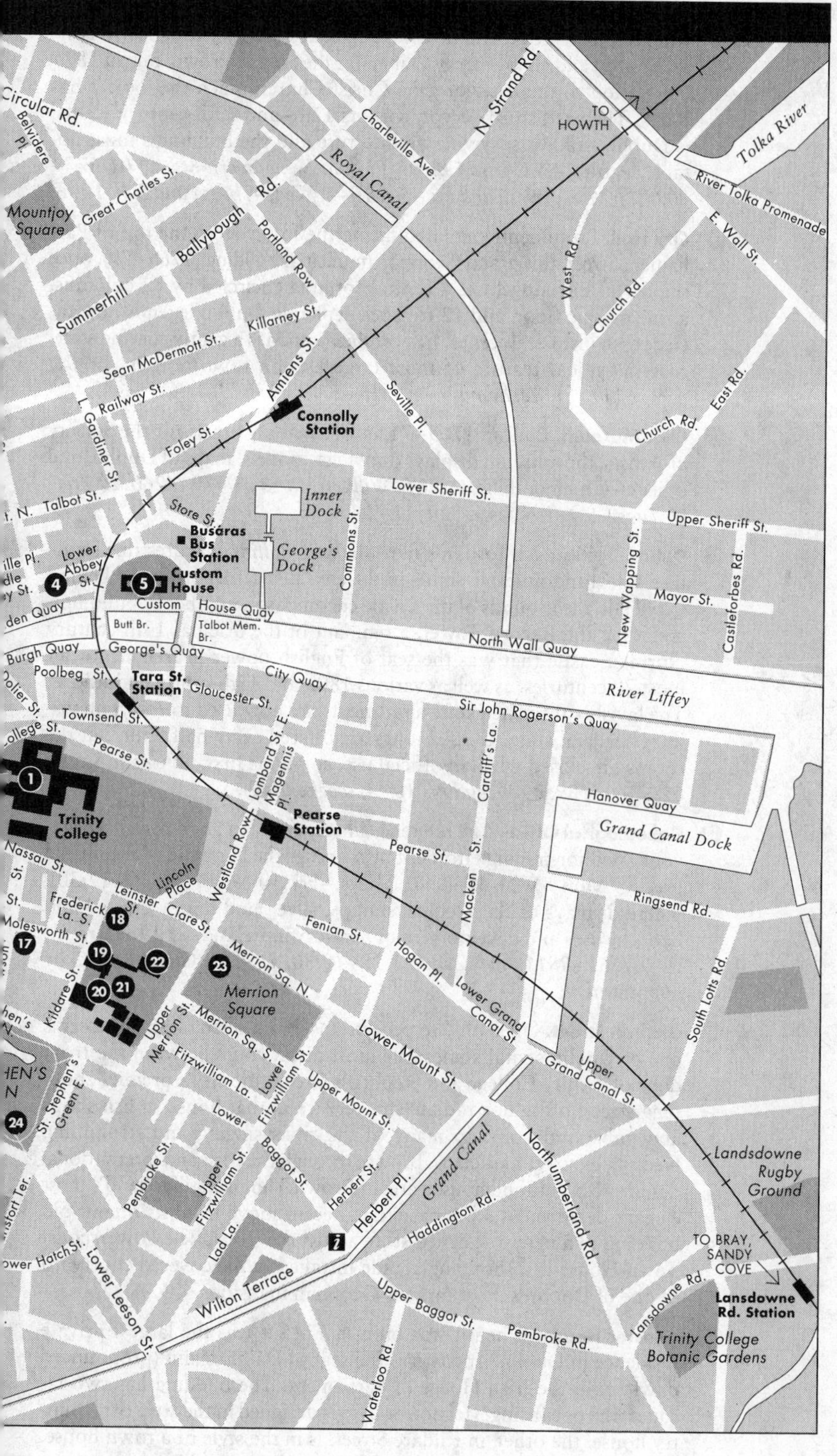

Circular Rd.
Belvidere Pl.
Charleville Ave.
N. Strand Rd.
TO HOWTH
Tolka River
Royal Canal
River Tolka Promenade
Great Charles St.
Ballybough Rd.
Mountjoy Square
E. Wall St.
Portland Row
West Rd.
Church Rd.
Summerhill
Killarney St.
Sean McDermott St.
Amiens St.
East Rd.
Railway St.
Seville Pl.
L. Gardiner St.
Connolly Station
Church Rd.
Foley St.
Lower Sheriff St.
N. Talbot St.
Inner Dock
Store St.
Upper Sheriff St.
Busáras Bus Station
Commons St.
New Wapping St.
Castleforbes Rd.
George's Dock
Lower Abbey St.
Custom House
Mayor St.
Custom House Quay
Butt Br.
Talbot Mem. Br.
North Wall Quay
Burgh Quay
George's Quay
Poolbeg St.
City Quay
Tara St. Station
Gloucester St.
River Liffey
Townsend St.
Sir John Rogerson's Quay
College St.
Pearse St.
Lombard St. E.
Magennis Pl.
Cardiff's La.
Hanover Quay
Trinity College
Pearse Station
Grand Canal Dock
Westland Row
Pearse St.
Nassau St.
Lincoln Place
Macken St.
Ringsend Rd.
Leinster St.
Clare St.
Frederick La. S.
Fenian St.
Molesworth St.
Hogan Pl.
Merrion Sq. N.
South Lotts Rd.
Lower Grand Canal St.
Kildare St.
Merrion Square
Upper Merrion St.
Merrion Sq. S.
Lower Mount St.
Upper Grand Canal St.
Fitzwilliam La.
Lower Fitzwilliam St.
Upper Mount St.
St. Stephen's Green E.
Lower Baggot St.
Grand Canal
Northumberland Rd.
Landsdowne Rugby Ground
Pembroke St.
Upper Fitzwilliam St.
Herbert St.
Herbert Pl.
Haddington Rd.
Lad La.
TO BRAY, SANDY COVE
Lower Hatch St.
Lower Leeson St.
Wilton Terrace
Lansdowne Rd.
Lansdowne Rd. Station
Upper Baggot St.
Pembroke Rd.
Trinity College Botanic Gardens
Waterloo Rd.

the Church of Ireland—it, not St. Paddy's, stood initially within the walls of the city. Construction was begun in 1172 by Strongbow, a Norman baron and conqueror of Dublin for the English crown, but an 1875 renovation to the exterior gave Christ Church much the look it has today. The vast, sturdy **crypt,** with its 12th- and 13th-century vaults, is Dublin's oldest surviving architecture and the building's most notable feature. ✉ *Christ Church Pl. and Winetavern St.,* ☎ *01/677–8099.* ⏲ *Mon., Tues., and Fri.–Sat. 10–5; Wed.–Thurs., and Sun. 10–6.*

13 **City Hall.** Prominently situated facing the Liffey from the top of Parliament Street, this grand Georgian municipal building (1769–79), once the Royal Exchange, has a central rotunda encircled by 12 columns, a fine mosaic floor, and 12 frescoes depicting Dublin legends and ancient Irish historical scenes. Just off the rotunda is a gently curving staircase, a typical feature of most large Dublin town houses. ☎ *01/679–6111.* ⏲ *Weekdays 9–1, 2:15–5.*

15 **Civic Museum.** Built in 1765–71 as an assembly house for the Society of Artists, the museum displays drawings, models, maps of Dublin, and other civic memorabilia. ✉ *58 S. William St.,* ☎ *01/679–4260.* 🎫 *Free.* ⏲ *Tues.–Sat. 10–5:45, Sun. 11–2.*

14 **Dublin Castle.** Neil Jordan's film *Michael Collins* captures this structure's near-indomitable status in the city. Just off Dame Street behind City Hall, the grounds of the Castle encompass a number of buildings, including the **Record Tower,** a remnant of the original 13th-century Norman castle that was the seat of English power in Ireland for almost 7½ centuries, as well as various 18th- and 19th-century additions. The lavishly furnished **state apartments** are now used to entertain visiting heads of state. Guided tours are offered every half hour, but the rooms are closed when in official use, so phone first. ✉ *Castle St.,* ☎ *01/677–7129.* ⏲ *Weekdays 10–5, weekends 2–5.*

18 **Genealogical Office.** The reference library here is a good place to begin your ancestor-tracing efforts. It also houses the **Heraldic Museum** (🎫 Free. ⏲ Mon.–Wed, 10–8:30, Thurs.–Fri. 10–4:30, Sat. 10–12:30), where displays of flags, coins, stamps, silver, and family crests highlight the uses and development of heraldry in Ireland. ✉ *2 Kildare St.,* ☎ *01/661–8811.* ⏲ *Weekdays 10–12:30, 2–4:30. Guided tours by appointment.*

★ 16 **Grafton Street.** Open only to pedestrians, brick-lined Grafton Street is one of Dublin's vital spines: the most direct route between the front door of Trinity College and Stephen's Green; the city's premier shopping street, off which radiate smaller streets that house stylish shops and pubs; and home to many of the city's singing and strumming buskers, or street musicians. Browse through the Irish and international designer clothing and housewares at **Brown Thomas,** still Ireland's most elegant department store despite its recent move from its quaint old building to a newly designed store across the street. The **Powerscourt Town House** is a shopping arcade installed in the covered courtyard of one of Dublin's most famous Georgian mansions.

21 **Leinster House.** When it was built in 1745 it was the largest private residence in Dublin. Today it is the seat of Dáil Eireann (pronounced dawl Erin), the Irish House of Parliament. The building has two facades: the one facing Merrion Square is designed in the style of a country house; the other, in Kildare Street, is in the style of a town house. ✉ *Kildare St.,* ☎ *01/678–9911.* ⏲ *Tours: Mon. and Fri. by prior arrangement (when Parliament is not in session). Dáil visitors' gallery: Access with an introduction from a member of Parliament.*

25 **Marsh's Library.** A short walk west from Stephen's Green and accessed through a tiny but charming cottage garden lies a gem of old Dublin: the city's—and Ireland's—first public library, opened in 1701 to "All Graduates and Gentlemen." Its interior has been left practically unchanged since it was built—it still contains "cages" into which scholars who wanted to peruse rare books were locked. (The cages were to discourage students who, often impecunious, may have been tempted to make the books their own.) ✉ *St. Patrick's Close,* ☎ *01/454–3511.* ⏲ *Mon. and Wed.–Fri. 10–12:45 and 2–5, Sat. 10:30–12:45.*

★ 23 **Merrion Square.** This tranquil Georgian square is lined on three sides by some of Dublin's best-preserved Georgian town houses, many of which have brightly painted front doors over which sit intricate fanlights. Even when the flower gardens are not in bloom, the vibrant green grounds, dotted with sculpture and threaded with meandering paths, are worth a walk-through. **No. 1,** at the northwest corner, was the home of Sir William and Sperenza Wilde, Oscar's parents. ✉ *East end of Nassau St.* ⏲ *Daily sunrise–sunset.*

★ 22 **National Gallery of Ireland.** On the west side of Merrion Square, this 1854 building contains the country's finest collection of old masters—great treasures include Vermeer's incomparable *Woman Writing a Letter* (twice stolen from Sir Alfred Beit and now safe at last), Gainsborough's *Cottage Girl,* and Caravaggio's recently rediscovered *The Arrest of Christ.* The gallery's restaurant is one of the city's best spots for an inexpensive, top-rate lunch. ✉ *Merrion Sq. (W),* ☎ *01/661–5133.* 🎫 *Free.* ⏲ *Mon.–Sat 10–5:30, Thurs. until 8:30, Sun. 2–5.*

19 **National Library.** The collections here include first editions of every major Irish writer. Temporary exhibits are held in the entrance hall, off the colonnaded rotunda. The recently renovated main reading room, opened in 1890, has a dramatic dome ceiling. ✉ *Kildare St.,* ☎ *01/661–8811.* 🎫 *Free.* ⏲ *Mon. 10–9, Tues.–Wed. 2–9, Thurs.–Fri. 10–5, Sat. 10–1.*

20 **National Museum.** Situated on the other side of Leinster House from the National Library, the museum is most famous for its spectacular collection of Irish artifacts from 6000 BC to the present, including the Tara Brooch, the Ardagh Chalice, the Cross of Cong, and a fabled hoard of Celtic gold jewelry. There is also an important collection of Irish decorative arts. ✉ *Kildare St.,* ☎ *01/660–1117.* 🎫 *Free.* ⏲ *Tues.–Sat. 10–5, Sun. 2–5.*

3 **O'Connell Bridge.** Strange but true: the main bridge spanning the Liffey is wider than it is long. The north side of the bridge is dominated by an elaborate memorial to Daniel O'Connell, "The Liberator," erected as a tribute to the great 19th-century orator's achievement in securing Catholic Emancipation in 1829. Today **O'Connell Street** is less a street to loiter in than to pass through on your way to elsewhere. **Henry Street,** to the left just beyond the General Post Office, is, like Grafton Street, a busy pedestrian thoroughfare where you'll find throngs of Dubliners out doing their shopping. A few steps down Henry Street off to the right is the colorful **Moore Street Market,** where street vendors recall their most famous ancestor, Molly Malone, by singing their wares—mainly flowers and fruit—in the traditional Dublin style.

17 **Royal Irish Academy.** The country's leading learned society houses important manuscripts in its 18th-century library. Just below the academy is the **Mansion House,** the official residence of the Lord Mayor of Dublin. Its Round Room, the site of the first assembly of Dáil Eireann in Jan-

uary 1919, is now used mainly for exhibitions. ✉ *19 Dawson St.,* ☎ *01/676–2570.* 🎫 *Free.* ⏲ *Weekdays 9:30–5.*

26 **St. Patrick's Cathedral.** Legend has it that St. Patrick baptized many converts at a well on the site of the cathedral during the 5th century. The building dates from 1190 and is mainly early English Gothic in style. At 305 ft, it is the longest church in the country. During the 17th century Oliver Cromwell, dour ruler of England and no friend of the Irish, had his troops stable their horses in the cathedral. It wasn't until the 19th century that restoration work to repair the damage was begun. St. Patrick's is the national cathedral of the Anglican church in Ireland and has had many illustrious deans. The most famous was Jonathan Swift, author of *Gulliver's Travels,* who held office from 1713 to 1745. Swift's tomb is in the south aisle; a corner at the top of the north transept commemorates him. Memorials to many other celebrated figures from Ireland's past line the walls. ✉ *Patrick St.,* ☎ *01/475–4817.* ⏲ *Weekdays 9–5:15, weekends 9–5.*

24 **St. Stephen's Green.** Dubliners call it simply Stephen's Green; green it is—strikingly so, year-round (you can even spot a palm tree or two). The north side is dominated by the magnificent **Shelbourne Hotel** (☞ Lodging, *below*), which lives up to its billing as "the best address in Dublin." A drink in one of its two bars, thronged after work, or afternoon tea in the elegant Lord Mayor's Room (IR£9 per person, including sandwiches and cakes), is the most financially painless way to soak in the old-fashioned luxury and genteel excitement.

★ 12 **Temple Bar.** Dublin's hippest neighborhood—bordered by Dame Street to the south, the Liffey to the north, Fishamble Street to the west, and Westmoreland Street to the east—is the city's version of the Latin Quarter, the playing ground of "young Dublin." Representative of the improved fortunes of the area, with its narrow, winding pedestrian-only cobblestone streets, is the **Clarence** (✉ 6–8 Wellington Quay, ☎ 01/670–9000), a favorite old Dublin hotel now owned and understatedly renovated in 1996 by Bono and the Edge of U2. The area is chock-full of small, hip stores, art galleries, and inexpensive restaurants and pubs. The **Irish Film Centre** (✉ 6 Eustace St., ☎ 01/679–5744), with a full program of new independent films and revivals, is emblematic of the area's vibrant mix of high and alternative culture.

★ 1 **Trinity College.** A must for every visitor, Ireland's oldest and most famous college is the heart of college-town Dublin. Trinity College, Dublin (familiarly known as TCD), was founded by Elizabeth I in 1592 and offered a free education to Catholics—providing they accepted the Protestant faith. As a legacy of this condition, until 1966 Catholics who wished to study at Trinity had to obtain a dispensation from their bishop or face excommunication. Today more than 70% of Trinity's students are Catholics, an indication of how far away those days seem to today's generation.

The pedimented, neoclassical Georgian facade, built between 1755 and 1759, consists of a magnificent portico with Corinthian columns. The design is repeated on the interior, so the view from outside the gates and from the quadrangle inside is the same. On the quad's lawn are statues of two of the university's illustrious alumni—statesman Edmund Burke and poet Oliver Goldsmith. Other famous students include the philosopher George Berkeley (who gave his name to the northern California city), Jonathan Swift, Thomas Moore, Oscar Wilde, John Millington Synge, Bram Stoker, Edward Carson, and Samuel Beckett. The 18th-century building on the left, just inside the entrance, is the **chapel.** There's an identical building opposite, the **Examination Hall.**

The oldest buildings are the library in the far right-hand corner and a row of redbrick buildings known as the **Rubrics,** which contain student apartments; both date from 1712.

Ireland's largest collection of books and manuscripts is housed in **Trinity College Library,** entered through the library shop. Its principal treasure is the Book of Kells, generally considered the most striking manuscript ever produced in the Anglo-Saxon world. Only a few pages from the 682-page, 9th-century gospel are displayed at a time, but there is an informative exhibit that reproduces many of them. At peak hours you may have to wait in line to enter the library; it's less busy early in the day. Don't miss the grand and glorious Long Room, an impressive 213 ft long and 42 ft wide, which houses 200,000 volumes in its 21 alcoves. ☎ *01/677–2941.* ⏲ *Mon.–Sat. 9:30–4:45, Sun. noon–4:30.*

In the Thomas Davis Theatre in the Arts Building, the **"Dublin Experience"** is an audiovisual presentation devoted to the history of the city over the last 1,000 years. ☎ *01/677–2941.* ⏲ *May–Oct., daily 10–5; shows every hr on the hr.*

North of the Liffey

The Northside city center is a mix of densely thronged shopping streets and run-down sections of once genteel homes. Nevertheless, there are some classic sights here, including some gorgeous Georgian monuments—the Custom House, the General Post Office, Parnell Square, and the Hugh Lane Gallery—and two landmarks of literary Dublin, the Dublin Writers Museum and the James Joyce Cultural Center, hub of Bloomsday celebrations. Most travelers begin heading up O'Connell Street to Parnell Square and the heart of James Joyce Country.

4 **Abbey Theatre.** Ireland's national theater was founded by W. B. Yeats and Lady Gregory in 1904. The original building was destroyed in a fire in 1951; the present theater was built in 1966. It has some noteworthy portraits and mementos in the foyer. Seats are usually available for about IR£8–12; all tickets are IR£8 for Monday performances. ✉ *Lower Abbey St.,* ☎ *01/878–7222*

5 **Custom House.** Extending 375 ft on the north side of the Liffey, this is the city's most spectacular Georgian building, the work of James Gandon, an English architect who arrived in Ireland in 1781 when construction commenced here (it continued for 10 years). The central portico is linked by arcades to the pavilions at each end. A statue of Commerce tops the graceful copper dome; statues on the main facade are based on allegorical themes. Republicans set the building on fire in 1921, but it was completely restored; it now houses government offices but there is a visitors center that is open to the public. ✉ *Custom House Quay,* ☎ *01/679–3377.* 🎫 *IR£2.* ⏲ *Weekdays 9:30–4, weekends 2–5.*

★ 8 **Dublin Writers Museum.** Two restored 18th-century town houses on the north side of Parnell Square, an area rich in literary associations, lodge one of Dublin's finest cultural sights. Rare manuscripts, diaries, posters, letters, limited and first editions, photographs and other mementos commemorate the lives and works of the nation's greatest writers (and there are *many* of them, so leave plenty of time) including Joyce, Shaw, Wilde, Yeats, and Beckett. Readings are held in the upstairs drawing rooms, gorgeously decorated with paintings and bas-relief wall decorations. The bookshop and café make this an ideal place to spend a rainy afternoon. ✉ *18–19 Parnell Sq. N,* ☎ *01/872–2077.* ⏲ *Mon.–Sat. 10–5, Sun. 11–5.*

30 **Four Courts.** Today the seat of the High Court of Justice of Ireland, the Four Courts are James Gandon's second Dublin masterpiece, built be-

tween 1786 and 1802. Like the Custom House and other buildings lining the north side of the Liffey, the courts were destroyed during the "Troubles" of the '20s and restored by 1932. Its distinctive copper-covered dome atop a colonnaded rotunda makes this one of Dublin's most instantly recognizable buildings. Visitors are allowed to listen in on court proceedings, which can often be interesting, educational, even scandalous. ✉ *Inns Quay,* ☎ *01/872–5555.* ⏲ *Daily 10:30–4.*

❻ **General Post Office.** The GPO (1818) is one of the great civic buildings of Dublin's Georgian era, but its fame derives from the role it played during the Easter Rising. Here, on Easter Monday, 1916, the Republican Forces stormed the building and issued the Proclamation of the Irish Republic. After a week of shelling, the GPO lay in ruins; 13 rebels were ultimately executed. Most of the original building was destroyed; only the facade—in which you can still see the scars of bullets on its pillars—remained. It is still a working post office, with an attractive two-story central gallery. ✉ *O'Connell St.,* ☎ *01/872–8888.* ⏲ *Mon.–Sat. 8–8, Sun. 10:30–6:30.*

⓫ **Ha'penny Bridge.** This heavily trafficked footbridge crosses the Liffey at a prime spot: Temple Bar is on the south side, and the bridge provides the fastest route to the thriving Mary and Henry Street shopping areas to the north. Until early in this century, a half-penny toll was charged to cross it. Yeats was one among many Dubliners who found this too high a price to pay—more a matter of principle than of finance—and so made the detour via O'Connell Bridge.

★ ❾ **Hugh Lane Municipal Gallery of Modern Art.** The imposing Palladian facade of this town house, once the home of the Earl of Charlemont, dominates the north side of Parnell Square. Sir Hugh Lane, a nephew of Lady Gregory (Yeats's patron), collected Impressionist paintings and 19th-century Irish and Anglo-Irish works. Among them are canvases by Jack Yeats (W. B.'s brother) and Paul Henry. ✉ *Parnell Sq.,* ☎ *01/874–1903.* 🎫 *Free.* ⏲ *Tues.–Thurs. 9:30–6, Fri.–Sat. 9:30–5, Sun. 11–5.*

㉛ **Old Jameson Distillery.** The birthplace of one of Ireland's best whiskeys has been fully restored and offers a fascinating insight into the making of *uisce batha,* or "holy water," as whiskey is known in Irish. There is a guided tour of the old distillery, an audiovisual tour, and a complimentary tasting where you get to sample five top-name Irish whiskeys. ✉ *Bow St.,* ☎ *01/872–5566.* ⏲ *Tours: May–Oct., weekdays 11, 2:30, and 3:30, Sat. 2:30 and 3:30, Sun. 3:30; Nov.–Apr., weekdays 3:30. Also by appointment.*

❼ **Parnell Square.** This is the north side's most notable Georgian square and one of Dublin's oldest. Because the first-floor reception rooms of the elegant brick-face town houses on the square were designed as reception rooms—fashionable hostesses liked passersby to be able to peer in and admire the distinguished guests at their luxurious, candlelit soireés—their windows are much larger than the others.

❿ **Rotunda Hospital.** Founded in 1745 as the first maternity hospital in Ireland or Britain, it is now most worth a visit for its **chapel,** with elaborate plasterwork, appropriately honoring motherhood. The **Gate Theater** (☞ Nightlife and the Arts, *below*), housed in an extension, attracts large crowds to its fine repertoire of classic Irish and European drama. ✉ *Parnell St.,* ☎ *01/873—0700*

Dublin West

If you're not an enthusiastic walker, hop a bus or find a cab to take you to these sights in westernmost Dublin.

★ 28 **Guinness Brewery.** Founded by Arthur Guinness in 1759, Ireland's all-dominating brewery is situated on a 60-acre spread to the west of Christ Church Cathedral; it is the most popular tourist destination in town. The brewery itself is closed to the public, but the **Hop Store,** part museum and part gift shop, puts on an 18-minute audiovisual show. After the show visitors get two complimentary glasses (or one pint) of the famous black stout. ✉ *Crane St.,* ☎ *01/453–3645.* ⏲ *Apr.–Sept., Mon.–Sat. 9:30–5, Sun. 10:30–4:30; Oct.–Mar., Mon.–Sat. 9:30–4, Sun. noon–4.*

★ 32 **Phoenix Park.** Europe's largest public park, extending about 3 mi along the Liffey's north bank, encompasses 1,752 acres of verdant lawns, woods, lakes, playing fields, a zoo, a flower garden (the **People's Garden,** to the right as you enter the park on Chesterfield Avenue), and two residences—those of the president of Ireland and the American ambassador. A 210-ft-tall obelisk, built in 1817, commemorates the Duke of Wellington's defeat of Napoléon. It is a jogger's paradise, but Sunday is the best time for everyone to visit: Games of cricket, soccer, polo, baseball, hurling—a combination of lacrosse, baseball, and field hockey—or Gaelic football are likely to be in progress.

★ 29 **Royal Hospital Kilmainham.** A short ride by taxi or bus from the city center, this is regarded as the most important 17th-century building in Ireland. Completed in 1684 as a hospice for soldiers, it survived into the 1920s as a hospital. The ceiling of the Baroque chapel is extraordinary. It now houses the **Irish Museum of Modern Art,** opened in 1991, which displays works by such non-Irish greats as Picasso and Miró but concentrates on the work of Irish artists. ✉ *Kilmainham La.,* ☎ *01/612–9900.* 🎫 *Free.* ⏲ *Exhibitions: Tues.–Sat. 10–5:30, Sun. noon–5:30; museum tours: Wed., Fri. 2:30, Sat. 11:30; historical tours: Sun. 2–4:30.*

Dining and Lodging

Dublin's restaurateurs are key players in the Irish food revolution now under way. You can still order up a traditional John Dory fillet, but more and more diners are opting for such nouvelle novelties as Dublin Bay prawns with Japanese sushi rice, pear, and a sweet soy chilli sauce. In dozens of spots adventurous young chefs are challenging older establishments on price and quality; many are taking advantage of the magnificent fresh livestock and fish that Ireland has in such abundance. If you want to browse beyond the restaurants recommended here, the area between Grafton Street and South Great George's Street has many to offer, as does Temple Bar, just across Dame Street. You'll find a pub—if not two or three—on virtually every block (☞ Nightlife and the Arts, *below,* for additional pub listings). For details and price-category definitions, *see* Dining *in* Ireland A to Z, *above.*

On the lodging front Dublin is in the midst of a major hotel boom. New hotels are being built in all parts of the city, though especially in some of the areas slightly outside the city center, in neighborhoods like Ballsbridge. In order to stay competitive many older hotels have been updating their facilities and refurbishing rooms. Still, as in most major cities, there is a shortage of mid-range accommodations. For value try one of the registered guest houses; in most respects they are indistinguishable from small hotels. B&Bs are the most economical option. Both guest houses and B&Bs tend to be in suburban areas—generally a 10-minute bus ride from the center of the city. This is not in itself a great drawback, and savings can be significant.

Bord Fáilte (☞ Visitor Information, *below*) can usually help if you find yourself without reservations. For details and price-category definitions, *see* Lodging *in* Ireland A to Z, *above*.

$$$$ ★ ✕ **Le Coq Hardi.** John Howard has been running one of Dublin's best restaurants here for many years. He has one of the most extensive wine lists in the country. Service is friendly and relaxed, and there is an air of quiet elegance about the Georgian dining room. Appetizer "smokies" are served in a ramekin of smoked haddock with a sauce of tomato, double cream, and cheese. A house speciality is the bacon-wrapped Coq Hardi chicken, with potatoes, apples, and ham, all in an Irish whiskey sauce. ✉ *35 Pembroke Rd., Ballsbridge,* ☎ *01/668–9070. AE, DC, MC, V. Closed Sun.*

$$$$ ✕ **Patrick Guilbaud.** Everything is French here, including the eponymous owner, his chef, the maître d' and the two Michelin stars that make it Ireland's highest-rated restaurant. Guillaume Le Brun's cooking is a fluent expression of modern French cuisine—not particularly flamboyant, but coolly professional. Expect superb foie gras, confit of Landaise duck in a delicate phyllo pastry, roe deer with junipers—and also some homage to Irish dishes, from Connemara lobster in season to braised pig's trotters. ✉ *Hotel Merrion, Merrion St.,* ☎ *01/676–4192. AE, DC, MC, V. Closed Sun., Mon., and Dec. 24–Jan. 14.*

$$$$ ★ ✕ **Peacock Alley.** Ireland's most bravura chef-owner is Conrad Gallagher, who ran away from school at 12 to be a cook. By 18 he was sous chef at the Plaza in New York, and at 19 *chef de cuisine* at the Waldorf-Astoria's Peacock Alley. Elegantly set white-linen-covered tables set the stage for the dazzling fare; Gallagher builds up the food on the plate and dabs multicolor oils and garnishes with painterly precision. His strikingly inventive dishes include an appetizer of smoked salmon with basmati rice, pear, preserved ginger, soy sauce, and quesadilla; an intensely flavored roast chestnut soup; deep-fried crab cakes with *katifi* (shredded phyllo pastry); daube of pot-roasted beef; and pan-seared red snapper with pureé of pumpkin. ✉ *47 South William St.,* ☎ *01/662–0760. AE, DC, MC, V. Closed Sun.*

$$$$ ★ ✕ **Thornton's.** Chef-owner Kevin Thornton is as restrained and classical in his approach as Conrad Gallagher is flamboyant, yet like Gallagher, he is a naturally gifted chef. Thornton's is in a renovated house with pine floors on the north bank of the Grand Canal, a long walk or short ride southwest of Stephen's Green. Service is French and quite formal. The cooking style is light, and the dishes are small masterpieces of structural engineering. In season Thornton marinates legs of partridge and cooks them separately, then removes the insides of the bird and purees them before stuffing and reforming the bird with the deboned breasts presented as a crown. ✉ *1 Portobello Rd.,* ☎ *01/454–9067. AE, DC, MC, V. Closed Sun. No lunch.*

$$$ ✕ **The Commons Restaurant.** This is a large elegant room with French windows in the basement of Newman House, where James Joyce was a student at the original premises of University College Dublin. The seasonal menu offers a light treatment of classical themes—steamed sea bass with sevruga caviar in an oyster emulsion; panfried foie gras in ginger bread crumbs, accompanied by a glass of walnut wine; and venison cutlet with red-wine mashed pototoes and blueberry pudding. ✉ *85–86 St. Stephen's Green,* ☎ *01/478–0530. AE, DC, MC, V. Closed Sun. No lunch Sat.*

$$$ ✕ **Cooke's Café.** Johnny Cooke has turned this city-center, Californian–Mediterranean-style bistro into a cool spot for visiting movie stars. Specialties tend toward fresh seafood (except Monday) and game: Cooke does a crab salad with spinach, coriander, mango salsa, and lime dressing; lobster grilled with garlic herb butter; and in season, a selection

of roast game including wild mallard and teal, sliced venison, and wood pigeon. It's busy and service can be slow; the outdoor seating on nice summer days is a consolation. ✉ *14 S. William St.,* ☎ *01/679–0536. AE, DC, MC, V. No lunch.*

$$$ ★ ✕ **L'Ecrivain.** Chef-owner Derry Clarke's sense of humor is sometimes tested by tipsy patrons who fall over a life-size sculpture of the writer Brendan Behan on their way out of his elegant restaurant. Paintings of Beckett and other Irish writers hang on the walls. The food is serious—disciplined and restrained, with the emphasis on fresh Irish produce. Starters may include grilled goat cheese with eggplant and charcoal-grilled Mediterranean vegetables. Cured, marinated lamb with prune stuffing is superb. ✉ *109a Lower Baggot St.,* ☎ *01/661–1919. AE, DC, MC, V. Closed Sun.*

$$ ✕ **Adrian's.** When Adrian Holden's daughter Catriona is in the kitchen, this unpretentious waterfront restaurant in the fishing village of Howth (30 minutes north of Dublin by commuter train or taxi) really starts to sing. A specialty are six varieties of spiced seafood—from the nearby fishing pier, of course—over cous-cous. ✉ *3 Abbey St., Howth,* ☎ *01/839–0231. AE, DC, MC, V.*

$$ ✕ **Chapter One.** Housed in the vaulted, stone-walled basement of the engrossing Dublin Writers Museum, just down the street from the Hugh Lane Municipal Gallery (☞ *above*), this is one of the most notable restaurants in north-side Dublin. Dishes include pressed duck and black pudding terrine with a pear chutney; grilled black sole with poached ravioli stuffed with salmon mousse; and pork with a confit of spiced pork belly. ✉ *18–19 Parnell Sq.,* ☎ *01/873–2266. AE, DC, MC, V. Closed Sun. No lunch Sat., no dinner Mon.*

$–$$ ✕ **La Mére Zou.** Eric Tydgadt is Belgian and his wife Isabelle is from Paris, so it's not surprising that their basement restaurant is Continental in emphasis. The menu includes six king-size plates; one of them, "La Belge," has a 6-ounce charcoal-grilled rump steak with french fries, and a salad with salami, country ham, chicory, and mayonnaise. ✉ *22 St. Stephen's Green,* ☎ *01/661–6669. AE, DC, MC, V. Closed Jan. 1–10. No lunch weekends.*

$ ✕ **Caviston's.** The Cavistons have been dispensing recipes for years from their fish counter and delicatessen in Sandycove, just south of the ferry port of Dun Laoghaire, 30 minutes by taxi or DART train south of Dublin. The fish restaurant next door is a lively and intimate place, with appetizers such as a phyllo pastry basket with prawns and twice-baked gorgonzola soufflé with a green salad. Typical entrées include panfried scallops served in the shell with a Thermidor sauce, and steamed Dover sole with mustard sauce. ✉ *59 Glasthule Rd., Dun Laoghaire,* ☎ *01/280–9120. MC, V. Closed Sun., Mon., and Dec. 23–Jan. 2. No dinner.*

$ ✕ **Milano.** This is a well-designed room with lots of brio and a tempting array of flashy pizzas. Expect to find thinner pizza crust than in the United States, with such combinations as tomato and mozzarella, ham and eggs, Cajun with prawns and tabasco, spinach and egg, or ham with anchovies. The owners opened a second restaurant in Temple Bar in late 1997. ✉ *38 Dawson St.,* ☎ *01/670–7744. AE, MC, V.*

$ ✕ **The Side Door.** The five-star Shelbourne Hotel has a stylish budget restaurant with oak floors, cream walls, and art deco–style tables and chairs. You can start off with a bowl of Thai soup, a grilled chicken risotto, or Mediterranean vegetable pizza. Main dishes include supreme of chicken marinated in honey, or charcoal-grilled rib eye of beef. Designer beers and a good wine list complement the food nicely. ✉ *27 St. Stephen's Green,* ☎ *01/676–6471. AE, DC, MC, V.*

Pub Food

Most pubs serve food at lunchtime, some throughout the day. The pub is at the heart of Irish social life—a center of good *craic,* good talk, and general fun. Food ranges from hearty soups and stews to chicken curries, smoked salmon salads, and sandwiches. Expect to pay IR£4–IR£5 for a main course. Many pubs do not take credit cards.

✕ **Davy Byrne's.** James Joyce immortalized Davy Byrne's in his sprawling novel *Ulysses.* Nowadays it's more akin to a cocktail bar than a Dublin pub, but it's good for fresh and smoked salmon, salads, and a hot daily special. Food is available at lunchtime and in the early evening. ✉ *21 Duke St.,* ☎ *01/671–1298.*

✕ **John M. Keating.** For a real Irish pub lunch, this old-timer at the corner of Mary and Jervis streets can't be beat. Upstairs you can sit at a low table and chat with locals as you warm up with a bowl of soup and nibble on a sandwich. ✉ *14 Mary St./23 Jervis St.,* ☎ *01/873–1567.*

✕ **Kitty O'Shea's.** Kitty O'Shea's cleverly, if a little artificially, re-creates the atmosphere of old Dublin. ✉ *23–25 Grand Canal St.,* ☎ *01/660–9965.*

✕ **Old Stand.** Located conveniently close to Grafton Street, the Old Stand offers grilled food, including steaks. ✉ *37 Exchequer St.,* ☎ *01/677–0823.*

✕ **Porterhouse.** Ireland's first brew pub has an open kitchen and offers a dazzling range of beers—from pale ales to dark stouts. ✉ *16–18 Parliament St.,* ☎ *01/679–8847.*

✕ **Stag's Head.** Recognized by Egon Ronay as serving the best pub lunch in the city, the Stag's Head is a favorite of Trinity students and businesspeople alike. ✉ *1 Dame Court,* ☎ *01/679–3701.*

Cafés

While Dublin has nowhere near as many cafés as pubs, it's easier than ever to find a good cup of coffee at most hours of the day or night.

✕ **Bewley's Coffee House.** The granddaddy of the capital's cafés, Bewley's has been supplying Dubliners with coffee and buns for more than a century. The aroma of coffee is irresistible, and the dark interior—with marble-top tables, original wood fittings, and stained-glass windows—evokes a more leisurely Dublin of the past. The Grafton Street location houses a museum. ✉ *78 Grafton St., 13 S. Great George's St., and 12 Westmoreland St.; all* ☎ *01/677–6761.*

✕ **Kaffe Moka.** One of Dublin's hottest haunts for the caffeine-addicted, this spot has three hyper-stylish floors and a central location in the heart of the city center. ✉ *39 S. William St.,* ☎ *01/679–8475.*

✕ **Thomas Read's.** By day it's a café, by night a pub. Its large windows overlooking a busy corner in Temple Bar make it a great spot for people-watching. The menu includes hot bagels, danishes, and baguette sandwiches. The coffees are particularly good. ✉ *123 Parliament St.,* ☎ *01/677–1487.*

$$$$ **Berkeley Court.** The most quietly elegant of Dublin's large modern hotels, Berkeley Court is in Ballsbridge—a leafy suburb about a 10-minute cab ride from the center of town. The Conservatory restaurant is a fresh and spacious spot for informal meals; recent additions to the hotel include five luxury suites, each with its own Jacuzzi. ✉ *Lansdowne Rd., Ballsbridge, Dublin 4,* ☎ *01/660–1711,* FAX *01/661–7238. 157 rooms, 29 suites. 2 restaurants, bar, health club. AE, DC, MC, V.*

CHASE

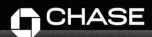

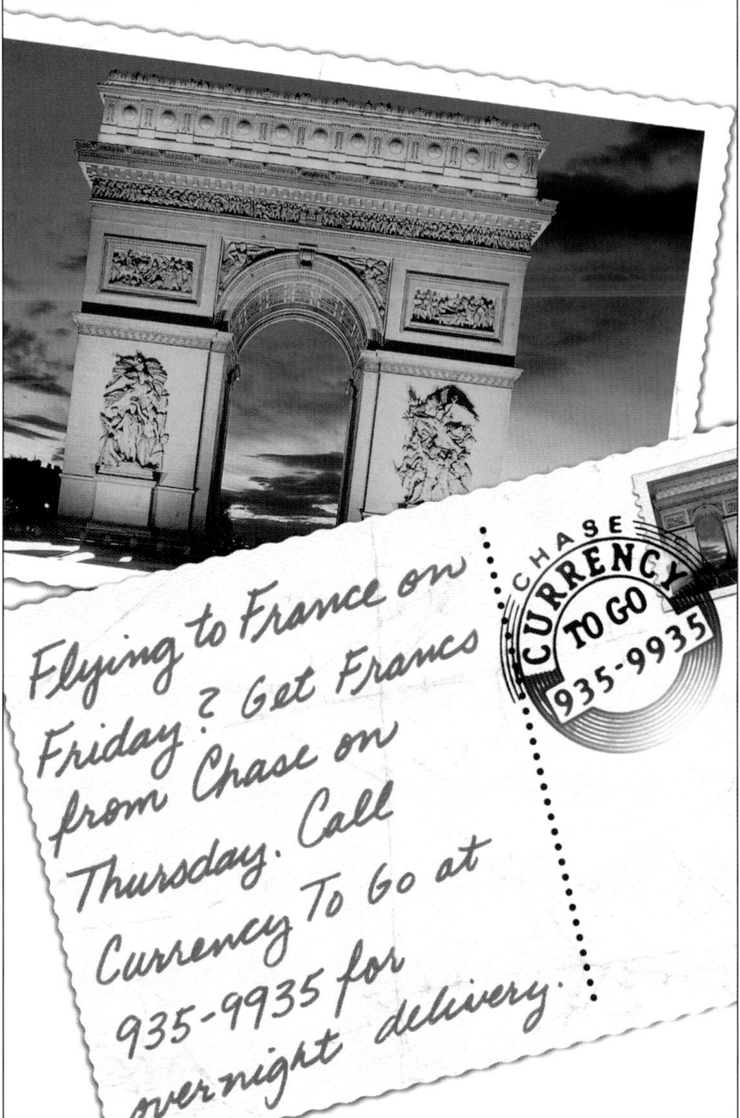

Or pounds for London. Or Deutschmarks for Düsseldorf. Or any of 75 foreign currencies. Call **Chase Currency To Go℠ at 935-9935** in area codes 212, 718, 914, 516 and Rochester, N.Y.; all other area codes call 1-800-935-9935. We'll deliver directly to your door.* Overnight. And there are no exchange fees. Let Chase make your trip an easier one.

CHASE. The right relationship is everything.℠

*$10 fee for overnight home delivery (subject to change).

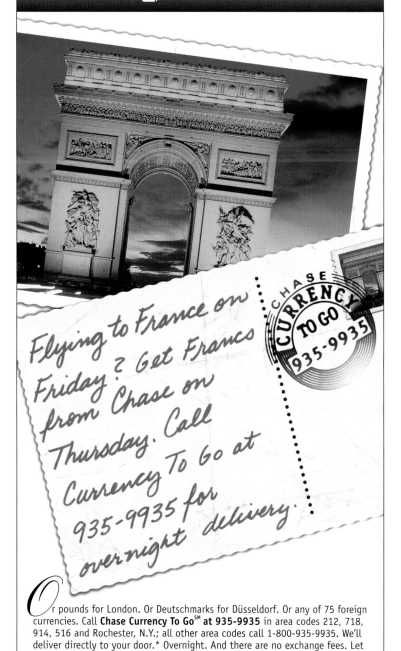

$$$$ **Conrad.** A subsidiary of Hilton Hotels, the Conrad is firmly aimed at the international business executive. The seven-story redbrick and smoked-glass building is well located just off Stephen's Green. The spacious rooms are decorated in light brown and pastel shades of green, and the bathrooms are fitted in Spanish marble. Alfie Byrne's, the main bar, attempts to re-create the traditional Irish pub atmosphere in spite of its high-powered clientele. There is a fitness room. ✉ *Earlsfort Terrace, Dublin 2,* ☎ *01/676–5555,* FAX *01/676–5424. 182 rooms, 9 suites. 2 restaurants, bar, exercise room. AE, DC, MC, V.*

$$$$ ★ **Shelbourne Hotel.** Old-fashioned luxury prevails at this magnificent showplace—one of Europe's grand old hotels, which has presided over Stephen's Green since 1824. Each room is unique; all have fine, carefully selected furniture and luxurious drapes. Those in front overlook the green and the Dublin mountains in the distance, but rooms in the back, without a view, are quieter. Downstairs, the public rooms are awhirl with life: The restaurant, 27 The Green, is one of the most elegant rooms in Dublin; Lord Mayor's Room, off the lobby, is a perfect rendezvous spot and offers a lovely afternoon tea; the two bars overflow with prosperous local business types. ✉ *27 Stephen's Green, Dublin 2,* ☎ *01/676–6471,* FAX *01/661–6006. 194 rooms, 9 suites. 2 restaurants, 2 bars, indoor pool, sauna, exercise room. AE, DC, MC, V.*

$$$$ **Westbury.** This comfortable, modern hotel has an excellent location right off the city's buzzing shopping mecca, Grafton Street. The spacious main lobby on the mezzanine level is furnished with attractive antiques and large sofas, on which guests sit to take afternoon tea. Bedrooms are rather utilitarian with pastel color schemes; the suites, which combine European decor with Japanese prints and screens, are more inviting. The flowery Russell Room serves formal lunches and dinners; the Sandbank, a ground-floor seafood bar, is less enticing. ✉ *Grafton St., Dublin 2,* ☎ *01/679–1122,* FAX *01/679–7078. 203 rooms, 8 suites. 2 restaurants, bar. AE, DC, MC, V.*

$$$ **Hibernian.** An early 20th-century Edwardian nurses' home was converted into this hotel in 1993. The distinctive red-and-amber brick facade has been retained, and every room is a different shape, decorated in light pastel shades with deep-pile carpets. The public rooms are slightly small, but are attractively done in cheerful chintz and stripes. There is a library off the lobby and a small restaurant that provides intimate dinners and lunches. ✉ *Eastmoreland Pl., off Upper Baggot St., Dublin 4,* ☎ *01/668–7666,* FAX *01/660–2655. 40 rooms. Restaurant, bar. AE, DC, MC, V.*

$$$ **Jurys.** This lively, fashionable spot has more atmosphere than most comparable modern hotels. It's a short cab ride from the center of town. Bedrooms are relatively spacious, and each comes with a picture-window view of town. Exclusive facilities for businesspeople are provided in the 100-room Towers annex. A cabaret runs May–October. ✉ *Ballsbridge, Dublin 4,* ☎ *01/660–5000,* FAX *01/660–5540. 400 rooms, 8 suites. 3 restaurants, indoor/outdoor pool. AE, DC, MC, V.*

$$ ★ **Ariel Guest House.** This is Dublin's leading guest house, a block from the elegant Berkeley Court, a 10-minute walk from Stephen's Green, and close to a DART stop. Rooms in the main house are lovingly decorated with antiques; 13 rooms at the back of the house are more spartan. All are immaculately kept. A crystal chandelier hangs over the comfortable leather and mahogany furniture in the gracious, fireplace-warmed drawing room. Breakfast is served in the airy, glass-enclosed dining room. Owner Michael O'Brien and manager Marion Garry are extraordinarily helpful. ✉ *52 Lansdowne Rd., Dublin 4,* ☎ *01/668–5512,* FAX *01/668–5845. 28 rooms. Breakfast room, wine bar, MC, V.*

$$ **Lansdowne.** In the leafy suburb of Ballsbridge, southeast of the city center, but within walking distance, this small establishment offers a very friendly ambience. The cozy rooms have recently been completely refurbished in the Georgian style. The basement bar is a popular hangout for local businesspeople and fans of the international rugby matches held at nearby Lansdowne Road. Parker's Restaurant specializes in steaks and seafood. ✉ *27 Pembroke Rd., Dublin 4,* ☎ *01/668–2522,* FAX *01/668–5585. 39 rooms. Restaurant. AE, DC, MC, V.*

$$ **Temple Bar.** Previously a city-center bank, these premises were converted into this well-appointed hotel in 1993. Although the decor is unexceptional, the triangular shape of the building on the corner of two streets makes the layout rather interesting. It is just around the corner from Trinity College and on the edge of Temple Bar. Busker's Pub is a popular street-level bar, and there is also a quieter lounge bar and a conservatory-style restaurant and coffee shop. ✉ *Fleet St., Temple Bar, Dublin 2,* ☎ *01/677–3333,* FAX *01/677–3088. 108 rooms. Restaurant, 2 bars, coffee shop. AE, DC, MC, V.*

$ **Dublin International Youth Hostel.** Housed in a converted convent, it offers dormitory accommodations (up to 25 people per room) and also family-size rooms that can take up to four people. This is a spartan, low-cost alternative to hotels. Nonmembers of the youth hostelling organization can stay for a small extra charge. The hostel is north of Parnell Square, near the Mater Hospital. ✉ *61 Mountjoy St., Dublin 1,* ☎ *01/830–1766,* FAX *01/830–1600. 380 beds. Restaurant. MC, V.*

$ **Jurys Christchurch Inn.** Expect few frills at this functional budget hotel (part of an otherwise upscale hotel chain), but it does offer good value for sharers, with a fixed room rate for up to three adults or two adults and two children. The biggest plus: the pleasant location, facing Christ Church Cathedral and within walking distance of most city-center attractions. The rooms are decorated in pastel colors with utilitarian furniture. A bar offers a pub lunch, and the restaurant serves breakfast and dinner. ✉ *Christchurch Pl., Dublin 8,* ☎ *01/454–0000,* FAX *01/454–0012. 182 rooms. Restaurant, bar. AE, DC, MC, V.*

$ **Mount Herbert Guest House.** Located close to the swank luxury hotels in the tree-lined inner suburb of Ballsbridge, a 10-minute bus ride from Dublin's center, the Mount Herbert is popular with budget-minded American visitors in the high season. Bedrooms are small, but all have 10-channel TVs and hair dryers. There is no bar on the premises, but there are plenty to choose from nearby. ✉ *7 Herbert Rd., Ballsbridge, Dublin 4,* ☎ *01/668–4321,* FAX *01/660–7077. 200 rooms. Restaurant, bar. AE, DC, MC, V.*

$ ★ **Number 31.** Two Georgian mews strikingly renovated in the early '60s by Ireland's leading modern architect as his own home are now connected via a small garden to the grand town house they once served; together they now form a marvelous guest house a short walk from Stephen's Green. Proprietors Mary and Brian Bennett offer gracious hospitality and made-to-order breakfasts. ✉ *31 Leeson Close, Dublin 2,* ☎ *01/676–5011,* FAX *01/676–2929. 19 rooms. AE, MC, V.*

Nightlife and the Arts

Dublin has undergone a small nightlife revolution. Sophisticated, internationally acclaimed dance clubs have taken the place of discos. The bar-pub scene has also gone upmarket, with bright, European-style café-bars nestling side by side with older, more traditional pubs. Still, Dublin's pub scene retains its celebrated charm and camaraderie.

The fortnightly magazine *In Dublin* (at newsstands) contains comprehensive details of upcoming events, including ticket availability. *The Event Guide* also lists events, and is given away free at many pubs and cafés. In peak season consult the free Bord Fáilte leaflet "Events of the Week."

Cabarets

The following all offer Irish cabaret. They are open only in peak season (roughly May–October; call to confirm):

Burlington Hotel (✉ Upper Leeson St., ☎ 01/660–5222). **Jurys Hotel** (✉ Ballsbridge, ☎ 01/660–5000). **Abbey Tavern** (✉ Howth, Co. Dublin, ☎ 01/839–0307).

Music

The **National Concert Hall** (✉ Earlsfort Terrace, ☎ 01/475–1666), just off Stephen's Green, is the place to go for classical concerts.

Nightclubs

Lillie's Bordello (✉ Grafton St., ☎ 01/679–9204) is a favorite with celebs and their admirers. **The Kitchen** (✉ Essex St., ☎ 01/677–6635) is part-owned by U2 and attracts a young, vibrant clientele.

Velure (✉ The Gaiety, South King St., ☎ 01/677–1717) attracts crowds every Saturday night to this elegant theater-cum-nightclub.

Pubs

Check advertisements in evening papers for "sessions" of folk, ballad, Irish traditional or jazz music. Listings below with telephone numbers offer some form of musical entertainment. For details on pubs that serve food, *see* Dining and Lodging *in* Dublin, *above*.

The **Brazen Head** (✉ 20 Lower Bridge St., ☎ 01/677–9549)—Dublin's oldest pub, dating from 1688—has music every night. President Bill Clinton dropped in at **Cassidy's** (✉ 42 Lower Camden St.) for a pint of stout during his visit to Dublin. **Doheny & Nesbitt's** (✉ 5 Lower Baggot St., ☎ 01/676–2945) is frequented by local businesspeople, politicians, and legal eagles. In the **Horseshoe Bar** (✉ Shelbourne Hotel, St. Stephen's Green) you can eavesdrop on Dublin's social elite and their hangers-on. **Kehoe's** (✉ 9 S. Anne St.) is popular with students, artists, and writers. Locals and visitors bask in the theatrical atmosphere of **Neary's** (✉ 1 Chatham St.). **O'Donoghue's** (✉ 15 Merrion Row, ☎ 01/661–4303) features some form of musical entertainment on most nights. The **Palace Bar** (✉ 21 Fleet St.) is a journalists' haunt. William Ryan's (✉ 28 Parkgate St.) is a beautifully preserved Victorian gem.

Theaters

Ireland has a rich theatrical tradition. The **Abbey Theatre** (✉ Marlborough St., ☎ 01/878–7222) is the home of Ireland's national theater company, its name forever associated with J. M. Synge, W. B. Yeats, and Sean O'Casey. The **Peacock Theatre** (same address and phone) is the Abbey's more experimental small stage. The **Gate Theatre** (✉ Cavendish Row, Parnell Sq., ☎ 01/874–4045) is an intimate spot for modern drama and plays by Irish writers. The **Gaiety Theatre** (✉ South King St., ☎ 01/677–1717) features musical comedy, opera, drama, and revues. The **Olympia Theatre** (✉ Dame St., ☎ 01/677–7124) has seasons of comedy, vaudeville, and ballet. The **Project Arts Centre** (✉ 39 E. Essex St., ☎ 01/679–6622) is an established fringe theater.

Shopping

Although the rest of the country is well supplied with crafts shops, Dublin is the place to seek out more specialized items—antiques, traditional sportswear, haute couture, designer ceramics, books and prints, silverware and jewelry, and designer hand-knit items.

Department Stores

The shops north of the river—many of them chain stores and lackluster department stores—tend to be less expensive and less design-conscious. Things may be changing, though, with the opening in fall 1996 of the **Jervis Shopping Center** (☒ Jervis St. at Mary St., ☎ 01/878–1323), the city's newest major shopping center. Also on the north side, **Clery's** (☒ O'Connell St., directly opposite the GPO, ☎ 01/878–6000) was once the city's most fashionable department store and is still worth a visit, despite its rapidly aging decor.

In the heart of Grafton Street is **Brown Thomas** (☒ Grafton St., ☎ 01/605–6666), Dublin's most elegant department store, offering many international and Irish designers. **Arnotts** (☒ Henry St., ☎ 01/805–0400) is Dublin's largest department store and has a good range of cut crystal.

Shopping Districts

Grafton Street is the most sophisticated shopping area in Dublin city center. **Molesworth** and **Dawson streets** are the places to browse for antiques. **Nassau** and **Dawson streets** are for books; the smaller side streets for jewelry, art galleries, and old prints. The pedestrianized **Temple Bar** area, with its young, offbeat ambience, has a number of small art galleries, specialty shops (including music and books), and inexpensive and adventurous clothes shops. The area is further enlivened by buskers (street musicians) and street artists. **St. Stephen's Green Center** contains 70 stores, large and small, in a vast Moorish-style glass-roof building. ☒ *St. Stephen's Green,* ☎ *01/478–0888.* ⊙ *Mon.–Sat. 9–6, Sun. noon–6.*

Books

Fred Hanna's (☒ 29 Nassau St., ☎ 01/677–1255) sells old and new books, with a good choice of books on travel and Ireland. **Hodges Figgis** (☒ 56–58 Dawson St., ☎ 01/677–4754) is Dublin's leading independent, with a café on the first floor. **Waterstone's** (☒ 7 Dawson St.,☎ 01/679–1415) is the Dublin branch of the renowned British chain.

Crystal, Ceramics, Jewelry, and Housewares

Kilkenny Shop (☒ Nassau St., ☎ 01/677–7066) is good for contemporary Irish-made ceramics, pottery, and silver jewelry. **McDowell** (☒ 3 Upper O'Connell St., ☎ 01/874–4961), in business for over 100 years, is a jewelry shop popular among Dubliners.

Tweeds and Woolens

Kevin & Howlin (☒ Nassau St., ☎ 01/677–0257) has ready-made tweeds for men. The **Blarney Woollen Mills** (☒ Nassau St., ☎ 01/671–0068) has a good selection of tweed, linen, and woolen sweaters in all price ranges. The **Dublin Woolen Mills** (☒ Metal Bridge Corner, 41 Lower Ormond Quay, ☎ 01/677–0301) at Ha'penny Bridge, has a good selection of hand-knit and other woolen sweaters at competitive prices.

Dublin Essentials

Arriving and Departing

BY BUS

The central bus station, **Busaras,** is at Store Street near the Custom House. Some buses terminate near O'Connell Bridge. Call 01/873–4222 for information on city services (Dublin Bus); dial 01/836–6111 for express buses and provincial services (Bus Eireann).

BY CAR

The main access route from the north is N1; from the west, N4; from the south and southwest, N7; from the east coast, N11. On all routes there are clearly marked signs indicating the center of the city: AN LÁR. The new M50 motorway encircles the city from Dublin Airport in the north to Tallaght in the south.

BY PLANE

All flights arrive at Dublin Airport, 10 km (6 mi) north of town.

Between the Airport and Downtown. Buses leave every 20 minutes from outside the Arrivals door for the central bus station in downtown Dublin. The ride takes about 30 minutes, depending on the traffic, and the fare is IR£2.50. A taxi ride into town will cost from IR£10 to IR£14, depending on the location of your hotel; be sure to ask in advance if the cab has no meter (☞ Getting Around By Taxi *below*).

BY TRAIN

There are three main stations: **Heuston Station** (✉ at Kingsbridge) is the departure point for the south and southwest; **Connolly Station** (✉ at Amiens St.), for Belfast, the east coast, and the west; and **Pearse Station** (✉ on Westland Row), for Bray and connections via Dun Laoghaire to the Liverpool/Holyhead ferries. Call 01/836–6222 for information.

Getting Around

Dublin is small as capital cities go—the downtown area is compact—and the best way to see the city and soak in the full flavor is on foot.

BY BUS

Most city buses originate in or pass through the area of O'Connell Street and O'Connell Bridge. If the destination board indicates AN LÁR, that means that the bus is going to the city center. Timetables (IR£2.50) are available from the **Dublin Bus** office (✉ 59 Upper O'Connell St., ☎ 01/873–4222) and give details of all routes, times of operation, and price codes. The minimum fare is 55p.

BY TAXI

Official licensed taxis, metered and designated by roof signs, do not cruise; they are beside the central bus station, at train stations, at O'Connell Bridge, Stephen's Green, College Green, and near major hotels. The initial charge is IR£2; the fare is displayed in the cab. (Make sure the meter is on.) A 1-mi trip in city traffic costs about IR£3.50. Hackney cabs, which also operate in the city, have neither roof signs nor meters, and will sometimes respond to hotels' requests for a cab. Negotiate the fare before your journey begins.

BY TRAIN

An electric train commuter service, **DART,** serves the suburbs out to Howth, on the north side of the city, and to Bray, County Wicklow, on the south side. Fares are about the same as for buses. Street-direction signs to DART stations read STAISIUN/STATION. The **Irish Rail** office is at 35 Lower Abbey Street; for rail inquiries, call 01/836–6222.

Contacts and Resources

EMBASSIES

United States (✉ 42 Elgin Rd., Ballsbridge, ☎ 01/668–8777). **Canadian** (✉ 65 St. Stephen's Green, ☎ 01/478–1988). **United Kingdom** (✉ 29 Merrion Rd., ☎ 01/205–3700).

EMERGENCIES

Police (☎ 999). **Ambulance** (☎ 999). **Doctor** (☎ 01/679–0700). **Dentist** (☎ 01/662–0766). **Pharmacy** (✉ Hamilton Long, 5 Upper O'Connell St., ☎ 01/874–8456).

GUIDED TOURS

Orientation. Both **Dublin Bus** (☎ 01/873–4222) and **Gray Line Sightseeing** (☎ 01/661–9666) offer bus tours of Dublin and its surrounding areas. Both also offer three- and four-hour tours of the main sights in the city center. In summer Dublin Bus has a daily three-hour city-center tour using open-top buses in fine weather (IR£8). From mid-April through September Dublin Bus runs a continuous guided open-top bus tour (IR£5) that allows you to hop on and off the bus as often as you wish and visit some 15 sights along its route.

Special-Interest. Elegant Ireland (☎ 01/475–1665) organizes tours for groups interested in architecture and the fine arts; these include visits with the owners of some of Ireland's stately homes and castles.

Walking. Most tourist offices have leaflets giving information on a selection of walking tours, including "Literary Dublin," "Georgian Dublin," and "Pub Tours." **Bord Fáilte** (☞ *below*) has a "Tourist Trail" walk, which takes in the main sites of central Dublin and can be completed in about three hours, and a "Rock 'n Stroll" tour, which covers the city's major pop and rock music sites.

Excursions. Bus Eireann (☎ 01/836–6111) and **Gray Line Sightseeing** (☎ 01/661–9666) offer daylong tours into the surrounding countryside and longer tours elsewhere; the price includes accommodations, breakfast, and admission costs. **CIE Tours International** (☎ 01/703–1888) offers vacations lasting from 5 to 10 days that include touring by luxury coach, accommodations, and main meals. Costs range from about IR£299 (IR£400 including round-trip airfare from London) to IR£580 (IR£680 from London) for an eight-day tour in July and August.

TRAVEL AGENCIES

American Express (✉ 116 Grafton St., ☎ 01/677–2874). **Thomas Cook** (✉ 118 Grafton St., ☎ 01/677–1721).

VISITOR INFORMATION

In addition to the main office (☞ Ireland A to Z, *above*), there are visitor information offices in the entrance hall of the **Bord Fáilte** headquarters (✉ Baggot St. Bridge, ☎ 01/676–5871; ⏲ weekdays 9:15–5:15); **Dublin Tourism** also has visitor information at the airport (arrivals level, ⏲ daily 8–10 PM); and at the Ferryport, Dun Laoghaire (⏲ daily 10–9 PM).

DUBLIN TO CORK

Ireland can be covered in three itineraries that, taken together, form a clockwise tour of the country, starting and ending in Dublin. Distances in Ireland seem short—the total mileage of the three itineraries combined is less than 960 km (596 mi)—but roads are narrow and often twisty and hilly, and side attractions are numerous, so you should aim for a daily mileage of no more than 240 km (149 mi). The consistently dazzling scenery, intriguing ruins, and beguiling villages will lead to many impromptu stops and explorations along the way. (We have tried to provide full addresses for hotels, restaurants, and sights, though many of Ireland's villages and towns are so tiny they barely have street names, much less house numbers. If in doubt, just ask for directions.)

The first tour takes you southwest from Dublin to hilly Cork, the Republic's second-largest city. On the way, you'll see the lush green fields of Ireland's famous stud farms and imposing Cashel, where Ireland built its reputation as the "Land of Saints and Scholars" while most of Europe was slipping into the Dark Ages.

Dublin to Cork

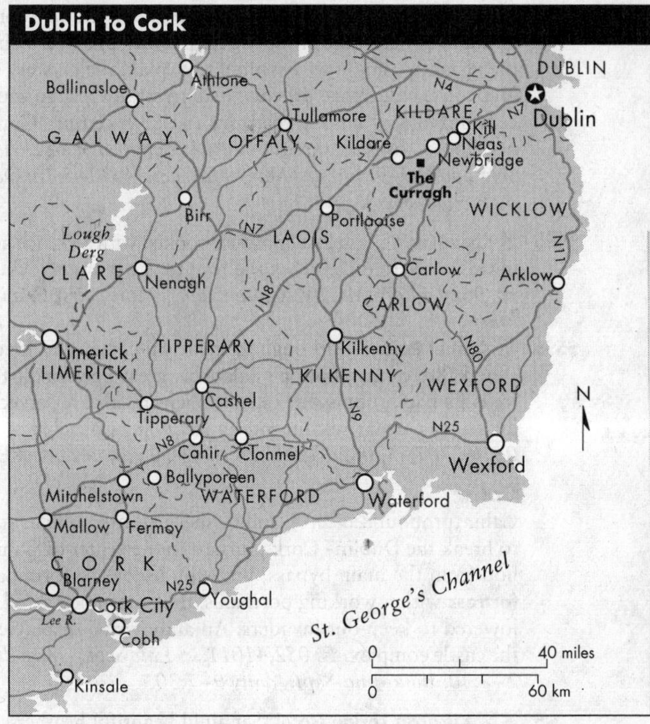

Exploring Dublin to Cork

Naas

The road to Naas (pronounced *nace*), passes through the area known as The Pale—that part of Ireland in which English law was formally acknowledged up to Elizabethan times. The road takes you to the center of the Irish racing world. **Goff's Kildare Paddocks** sells more than 50% of all Irish-bred horses. Naas has its own racecourse and lies just 4.8 km (3 mi) from Punchestown, famous for its steeplechases.

The Curragh

The Curragh, 8 km (5 mi) southwest of Naas just beyond the end of the bypass M7 and bisected by the main N7 road, is the biggest area of common land in Ireland, containing about 31 square km (12 square mi) and devoted mainly to grazing. You will see the **Curragh Racecourse,** home of the Irish Derby, on your right-hand side; to your left is the training depot of the Irish army.

Kildare

Horse-breeding is the basis of Kildare's thriving economy. It is also the traditional home of St. Brigid; St. Brigid's Cathedral, with a stocky square tower, is a restoration of a building that dates from the 13th century. The **National Stud and Horse Museum,** where breeding stallions are stabled, is a main center of Ireland's racing industry. ★ The elegant **Japanese Gardens,** laid out between 1906 and 1910 and considered among the finest in Europe, symbolically trace human life from birth to death. ☎ 045/521617. ⏲ *Feb.–Nov., daily 9:30–6. Tours on request.*

Cashel

★ Your first glimpse of the famous **Rock of Cashel** should be an unforgettably majestic sight: It rises imposingly to a height of 200 ft above the plains and is crowned with a group of magnificent gray stone ruins. The kings of Munster held it as their seat for about 7 centuries, and it was here that St. Patrick reputedly plucked a shamrock from the ground, using it as a symbol to explain the mystery of the Trinity, giving Ireland, in the process, its universally recognized symbol. The central building among the ruins is a 13th-century Gothic cathedral; next to it is the Romanesque Cormac's chapel. ☎ *062/61437.* ⏲ *June–Sept., daily 9–7:30; mid-Mar.–May, daily 9:30–5:30; Oct.–mid-Mar., daily 9:30–4.30.*

$$$ ✕ **Chez Hans.** Fresh local produce cooked with a French accent is served in this converted chapel at the foot of the famous rock. ✉ *Rockside,* ☎ *062/61177. MC, V. Closed Sun., Mon., first 3 wks in Jan. No lunch.*

$$$$ 🏨 **Cashel Palace.** Although in the town center, this magnificently restored 18th-century bishop's palace has great views of the Rock of Cashel from its back rooms. Inexpensive light meals are served all day in its bistro-style cellar restaurant. ✉ *Main St., Cashel, Co. Tipperary,* ☎ *062/62707,* FAX *062/61521. 26 rooms. 2 restaurants. AE, DC, MC, V.*

Cahir

Cahir (pronounced *care*), and Cashel are both popular stopping places to break the Dublin–Cork journey. In the center of Cahir, just a short hop from the main bypass, you will discover a formidable **medieval fortress** with a working portcullis, the gruesome barred gate that was lowered to keep out invaders. An audiovisual display can be seen in the castle complex. ☎ *052/41011.* ⏲ *Late Sept.–May, daily 10–1 and 2–4:30; June–mid-Sept., daily 9–7:30.*

$ ✕🏨 **Kilcoran Lodge Hotel.** Set amid beautiful heather-covered slopes on the main road 6 km (4 mi) south of Cahir, this handsome 19th-century house is an ideal place to break the journey with coffee or a simply cooked lunch. It occupies a scenic site on the southern slope of the Galtee Mountains. ✉ *Cahir, Co. Tipperary, on N8,* ☎ *052/41288,* FAX *052/41994. 23 rooms. Restaurant, indoor pool. AE, DC, MC, V.*

Cork City

The road enters Cork City along the banks of the River Lee. In the center of Cork, the Lee divides in two, giving the city a profusion of picturesque quays and bridges. The name Cork derives from the Irish *corcaigh* (pronounced *corky*), meaning a marshy place. The city received its first charter in 1185 and grew rapidly during the 17th and 18th centuries with the expansion of its butter trade. It is the major metropolis of the south and, with a population of about 133,250, the second-largest city in Ireland.

The main business and shopping center of Cork lies on the island created by the two diverging channels of the Lee, and most places of interest are within walking distance of the center. **Patrick Street** is the focal point of Cork; here you will find the city's two major department stores, **Roches** and **Cash's,** the latter of which has a good selection of Waterford crystal.

The famous 120-ft **Shandon Steeple,** the bell tower of **St. Anne's Church,** is on a hill across the river to the north of Cork's main shopping area. Shaped like a pepper pot, it houses the bells immortalized in the song "The Bells of Shandon." Visitors can climb the tower, read the inscriptions on the bells, and, on request, have them rung over Cork. ⏲ *May–Oct., Mon.–Sat. 9:30–5; Nov.–Apr., Mon.–Sat. 10–3:30.*

The liveliest place in town to shop is the pedestrian-only **Paul Street** area, to the west of Patrick Street, near the city center parking lot. **Meadows & Byrne** of Academy Street stocks the best in modern Irish design, including tableware, ceramics, furniture, and glass. The **Donegal Shop** in Paul Street Piazza specializes in made-to-order tweed suits and rainwear. At the top of Paul Street is the **Crawford Art Gallery,** which has an excellent collection of 18th- and 19th-century views of Cork and mounts adventurous exhibitions by modern artists. ✉ *Emmet Pl.,* ☎ *021/273377.* *Free.* *Weekdays 10–5, Sat. 9–1.*

$$$ ✕ **The Ivory Tower.** Seamus O'Connell, the young chef-owner of this first-floor restaurant off Patrick Street, concocts such adventurous dishes as tagliatelle of flashed squid, wild pheasant tamale, and salad of warmed duck confit. The bare boards and stick-back chairs are enlivened by original works of art, but the real star here is the brilliantly eclectic menu. ✉ *35 Princes St.,* ☎ *021/274665. MC, V. Closed Sun., Mon.*

$ ★ ✕ **Isaac's.** In an old warehouse with cast-iron pillars, this popular brasserie-style spot has modern art on the walls and Mediterranean-influenced food. Excellent local produce is used in such starters as warm potato salad with smoked bacon and black pudding. It's worth a try, whatever your budget. ✉ *48 MacCurtain St.,* ☎ *021/503805. MC, V.*

$$$ ★ ✕ **Arbutus Lodge.** This exceptionally comfortable hotel has an outstanding restaurant and panoramic views of the city and the river. The restaurant is acclaimed throughout Ireland, not least for its excellent wine list. There is a tennis court. ✉ *Middle Glanmire Rd., Montenotte,* ☎ *021/501237,* FAX *021/502893. 20 rooms. Restaurant. AE, DC, MC, V. Closed 1 wk at Christmas.*

$$$$ **Hayfield Manor.** This fine, luxury hotel, opened in 1996, is built to resemble an old country house. It is beside the university campus, five minutes' drive from the city center. The facilities include a sauna and health club. ✉ *Perrott Ave., College Rd.,* ☎ *021/315600,* FAX *021/316839. 53 rooms. Restaurant, indoor pool, sauna, health club. AE, DC, MC, V. Closed Dec. 24–27.*

$$ **Rochestown Park.** Set in beautiful wooded grounds 5 km (3 mi) south of the city, this hotel has been built around a Victorian manor house. The health center specializes in thalassotherapy—seaweed wraps and baths. ✉ *Rochestown Rd., Douglas,* ☎ *021/892233,* FAX *021/892178. 115 rooms. Restaurant, bar, pool, sauna, health club. AE, DC, MC, V.*

$ **Victoria Lodge.** Originally built in the early 20th century as a Capuchin monastery, this exceptionally well-appointed B&B is a five-minute drive from the town center; it is also on several bus routes. The rooms are simple but comfortable, with views over the lodge's own grounds. Breakfast is served in the spacious old refectory. ✉ *Victoria Cross,* ☎ *021/542233,* FAX *021/542572. 30 rooms with bath. Restaurant (wine license only). MC, V.*

Cobh

If you're American and have Irish roots, chances are your ancestors were among the thousands who sailed from Cork's port, the Cove of Cork, on Great Island, down the harbor. Cobh (pronounced *cove*), as it is known nowadays, can be reached by train from Kent Station, and the trip provides excellent views of the magnificent harbor. An attractive, hilly town, it is dominated by its 19th-century cathedral. It was the first and last European port of call for transatlantic liners, one of which was the ill-fated *Titanic.* Cobh has other associations with shipwrecks: It was from here that destroyers were sent out in May 1915 to search for survivors of the *Lusitania,* torpedoed by a German submarine with the loss of 1,198 lives. Cobh's maritime past and its links with emigration are documented in a new IR£2-million heritage center known as ★ **The Queenstown Project,** which opened in the town's old railway station in 1993. ☎ *021/813591.* *Feb.–Nov., daily 10–6.*

Part of the **Fota Estate,** on the Cork side of Cobh, consists of a magnificent arboretum (freely accessible). Also within the Fota Estate, the 238-square-km (70-acre) **Fota Wildlife Park** is an important breeding center for cheetahs and wallabies. ☎ *021/812678.* ⏲ *Mar. 17–Sept. 30, daily 10–6.*

$$$ ★ ✕🏨 **Ballymaloe House.** One of Ireland's best known and loved country houses, Ballymaloe has, for 50 years, been the home of Myrtle and Ivan Allen, who welcome guests with gracious aplomb. Each guest room is elegantly decorated in variations on the country-house style. Myrtle, the doyenne of Irish cooking, presides over the outstanding dining room. ✉ *Shanagarry, Midleton,* ☎ *021/652531,* FAX *021/652021. 32 rooms. Restaurant, pool. AE, DC, MC, V. Closed Dec. 24–27.*

Blarney

Most visitors to Cork want to kiss the famous **Blarney Stone** in the hope of acquiring the "gift of the gab." Blarney itself, should not, however, be taken too seriously as an excursion. ★ All that is left of **Blarney Castle** is its ruined central keep containing the celebrated stone. This is set in the battlements, and to kiss it, you must lie on the walk within the walls, lean your head back, and touch the stone with your lips. Nobody knows how the tradition originated, but Elizabeth I is credited with giving the word *blarney* to the language when, commenting on the unfulfilled promises of Cormac MacCarthy, Lord Blarney of the time, she remarked, "This is all Blarney; what he says, he never means." There are several good crafts shops in Blarney village, and the outing provides a good opportunity to shop around for traditional Irish goods at competitive prices. ✉ *Blarney Castle,* ☎ *021/385252.* ⏲ *Mon.–Sat. 9 to sundown, Sun. 9–5:30.*

Dublin to Cork Essentials

Getting Around

BY BICYCLE

Bicycles can be rented from **Isaac's** (✉ 48 MacCurtain St., Cork, ☎ 021/505399).

BY BUS

The main bus terminal in Cork is at Parnell Place (☎ 021/508188).

BY CAR

All the main car-rental firms have desks at Cork Airport. Be sure to get a map of Cork's complicated one-way street system.

BY TRAIN

The terminal at Cork is Kent Station. There are direct services from Dublin and Tralee and a suburban line to Cobh; call 021/506766 for information.

Guided Tours

Bus Eireann operates a number of trips from Parnell Place in Cork (☎ 021/506066).

Visitor Information

Tourist House (✉ Grand Parade, Cork, ☎ 021/273251, FAX 021/273504).

CORK TO GALWAY

The trip from Cork to Galway is about 300 km (186 mi) and includes stops in Killarney (87 km/54 mi west of Cork City) and Limerick. Killarney and the mysterious regions of the Burren are two very different

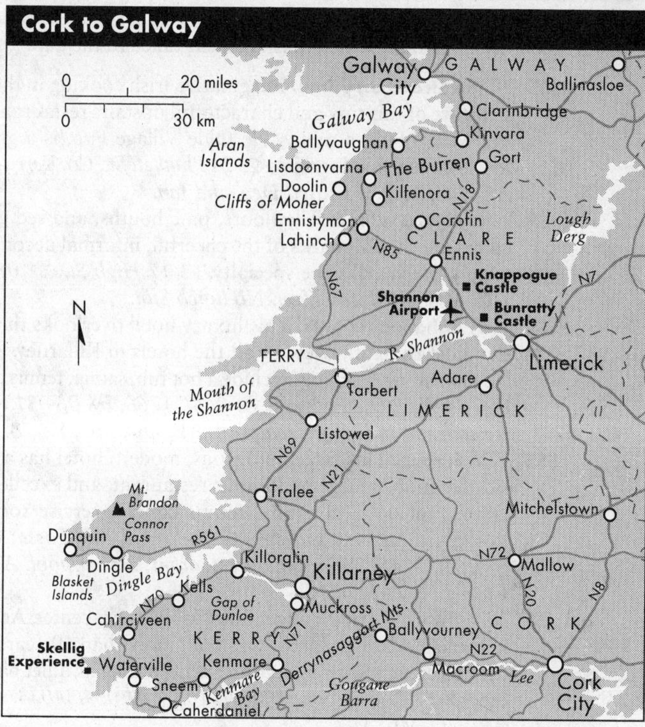

areas of outstanding natural beauty. The Shannon region around Limerick is littered with castles, both ruined and restored.

Beyond Macroom, the main Cork–Killarney road passes through the west-Cork **Gaelteacht**—a predominantly Irish-speaking region—and begins its climb into the Derrynasaggart Mountains. A detour to the left at Macroom will take you to the lake of **Gougane Barra,** source of the River Lee and now a national park. The 6th-century monk St. Finbarr, founder of Cork, had his cell on an island in the lake; this island can now be reached by causeway.

Killarney

Killarney itself is an undistinguished market town, well developed to handle the crowds that gather here in peak season. They come to drink in the famous scenery, located out of town toward the lakes that lie in a valley running south between the mountains. Part of Killarney's lake ★ district is within **Killarney National Park.** The 10,000-acre **Muckross Estate** (⏲ daily, daylight hours) is at the heart of the Killarney National Park. Cars are not allowed in the estate, so if you don't want to walk, rent a bicycle in town or take a trip in a jaunting car—a small two-wheel horse-drawn cart whose operators can be found at the gates to the estate and in Killarney. At the center of the estate is **Muckross House,** a 19th-century manor that contains the **Kerry Country Life Experience.** On the adjoining grounds is an Old World farm. ☎ *064/31440.* ⏲ *Sept.–June, daily 9–5:30; July–Aug., daily 9–7. Closed 1 wk. at Christmas.*

To get an idea of the splendor of the lakes and streams—and of the massive glacial sandstone and limestone rocks and lush vegetation that characterize the Killarney district—take one of the daylong tours ★ of the **Gap of Dunloe, the Upper Lake, Long Range, Middle and Lower lakes,** and **Ross Castle.** The central section, the Gap of Dunloe, is not suitable for cars, but horses and jaunting cars are available at **Kate Kearney's Cottage**, which marks the entrance to the gap.

$$$ ✕ **The Strawberry Tree.** Imaginative Irish cooking in the rustic style is a feature of this tiny and characterful upstairs restaurant. Downstairs, Yer Man's Pub, a minuscule Olde Village Pub, is a good choice for lunchtime bar-food specials. ✉ *24 Plunkett St., Co. Kerry,* ☎ *064/32688. AE, DC, MC, V. Closed Dec. and Jan.*

$$ ✕ **Gaby's Seafood.** Tile floors, pine booths, and red gingham tablecloths are the hallmarks of the cheerful, informal decor. Fresh seafood simply prepared is the specialty. ✉ *17 High St.,* ☎ *064/32519. AE, DC, MC, V. Closed Mon. No lunch Sun.*

$$$$ ★ ✕🏨 **Aghadoe Heights.** This luxury hotel overlooks the lakes and has the most romantic view of all the hotels in Killarney. The restaurant is outstanding. Facilities include a hot tub, sauna, tennis court, and fishing. ✉ *Aghadoe Heights,* ☎ *064/31766,* FAX *064/31345. 57 rooms. Restaurant, indoor heated pool. AE, DC, MC, V.*

$$$ ✕🏨 **Europe.** This large, luxurious, modern hotel has a secluded lakeside location, a large panoramic restaurant, and excellent sporting facilities, including a sauna, tennis court, exercise room, horseback riding, fishing, and bicycles. ✉ *Killorglin Rd., Fossa,* ☎ *064/31900,* FAX *064/32118. 205 rooms. Restaurant, indoor pool. AE, DC, MC, V. Closed Nov.–Mar. 15.*

$$ 🏨 **Arbutus.** A good budget hotel in the town center, Arbutus has been in the same family since it was built more than 60 years ago; rooms in the newer second-story section are desirable. Its quiet bar draws a local crowd. ✉ *College St.,* ☎ *064/31037,* FAX *064/34033. 44 rooms. Bar. AE, DC, MC, V.*

Ring of Kerry

In good weather the Ring of Kerry, which is a daylong scenic drive (a 176 km/109 mi round-trip from Killarney), provides a pleasant experience, despite its popularity with the tour-bus trade. Leave Killarney by the N71 Kenmare Road.

Kenmare

Kenmare is a small, mainly 19th-century market town at the head of Kenmare Bay. Across the water, as you drive out along the Iveragh Peninsula, are views of the gray-blue mountain ranges of the Beara Peninsula.

$$$$ ★ ✕🏨 **Park.** Spacious bedrooms individually decorated with late-Victorian antiques and Italian-marble-tile bathrooms distinguish the guest rooms at what is considered one of Ireland's finest country-house hotels. Local ingredients and seafood star on the restaurant's sophisticated Irish-Continental menu. Outdoor enthusiasts will appreciate the 18-hole golf course, tennis court, fishing, and bicycles. ☎ *064/41200,* FAX *064/41402. 50 rooms. Restaurant. Jacket and tie. AE, DC, MC, V.*

Sneem

Sneem, on the estuary of the River Ardsheelaun, is one of the prettiest villages in Ireland. Beyond the next village, Caherdaniel, is **Derrynane House,** home of the 19th-century politician and patriot Daniel O'Connell, "The Liberator," and remodeled by him in 1825. It still contains much of its original furniture. ☎ *066/75113.* ⏲ *Jan.–Mar., Nov., Dec., weekends 1–5; Apr. and Oct., Tues–Sun. 1–5; May–Sept., Mon.–Sat. 9–6, Sun. 11–7. Park:* 🎫 *Free.* ⏲ *Year-round.*

Dingle

If time and the weather are on your side, turn off the main Killorglin–Tralee road and make a tour of the **Dingle Peninsula**—one of the wildest and least spoiled regions of Ireland—taking in the **Connor Pass,**

Mount Brandon, the **Gallarus Oratory,** and stopping at **Dunquin** to hear some of Ireland's best traditional musicians. For an adventure off ★ the beaten path, arrange for a boat ride to the **Blasket Islands** and spend a few blissful hours wandering along the cliffs. **Dingle Town** is a handy touring base, with a surprisingly wide choice of good restaurants, open Easter–October.

$$ ✕ **Beginish.** The best of several small but sophisticated restaurants in town, this relaxing place serves local meat and seafood in a generous version of nouvelle cuisine. ✉ *Green St.,* ☎ *066/51588. AE, DC, MC, V. Closed Mon. and mid-Nov.–mid–Mar.*

$ ✕🏨 **Doyle's Seafood Bar.** Dingle's best-known seafood restaurant specializes in simply prepared local fish and shellfish. Eight comfortable rooms in the adjoining town house are also available. ✉ *John St.,* ☎ *066/51174,* FAX *066/51816. 8 rooms. Restaurant. DC, MC, V. Closed Sun. and mid-Nov.–early Mar.*

$ 🏨 **Greenmount House.** This impeccably kept, modern B&B a short walk from the town center is renowned for its imaginative breakfasts. ✉ *Gortanora, Dingle, Co. Kerry,* ☎ *066/51414,* FAX *066/51974. 12 rooms. MC, V.*

Tralee

In September the "Rose of Tralee" is selected from an international lineup of young women of Irish descent. The rest of the year Tralee is the commercial center of Kerry and home to the **Kerry County Museum,** which traces the history of Kerry's people from 5000 BC to the present day. ☎ *066/27777.* ⏲ *Mon.–Sat. 10–6, 10–8 in Aug.*

Limerick

Limerick is the fourth-largest city in the Republic, with a population of 60,000; economic investment and the world-wide phenomenon of Frank McCourt's *Angela's Ashes,* published in 1996, is helping it lose its image as an unattractive city marked by high unemployment. The Newtown area is dominated by mid-18th century buildings with fine Georgian proportions. The **Hunt Museum** is a treasure trove of art works from ancient Irish metalworks to Egyptian antiquities and 18th-century objets d'art that has recently found a new home in the noble Old Custom House on the banks of the River Shannon. ✉ *Rutland St.,* ☎ *061/312833.* 🎫 *IR£3.90.* ⏲ *Tues.–Sat. 10–5, Sun. 2–5.*

$$$$ ★ 🏨 **Castletroy Park.** High standards of comfort are the rule at this well-designed modern hotel on the outskirts of town. A hot tub, sauna, steam room, and exercise room are among the amenities. ✉ *Dublin Rd.,* ☎ *061/335566,* FAX *061/331117. 107 rooms. 2 restaurants, indoor pool. AE, DC, MC, V.*

$$ 🏨 **Greenhills.** This suburban, modern low rise is convenient for Shannon Airport and also makes a good touring base. The friendly owner-manager welcomes families. A hot tub, sauna, steam room, tennis court, and exercise room will appeal to the fitness-conscious. ✉ *Ennis Rd.,* ☎ *061/453033,* FAX *061/453307. 55 rooms. Restaurant, indoor heated pool. AE, DC, MC, V.*

Adare

★ As it turns out, not far from once-unsightly Limerick is Adare, one of Ireland's most picture-perfect towns. A bit of England in the Old Sod, it features storybook thatch-roof cottages and Tudor-style churches; here, too, are some delightful hotels, including one of Ireland's grandest. Visit the **Adare Heritage Centre** for a look back at the town's picturesque history. A seasonal tourist office also is open here from May through October. ✉ *Main St.,* ☎ *061/396666.* 🎫 *IR£2.* ⏲ *May–June, Sept.–Oct., daily 9–6; July–Aug., daily 9–7.*

$$$$ 🏨 **Adare Manor.** Set on the banks of the River Maigue, this somewhat spooky Tudor-Gothic fantasia of a castle is set within a magnificent 800-acre estate. The former home of the earls of Dunraven, it offers everything you'd want in an Irish manor-hotel, with baronial ballrooms, antiques-filled bedrooms, and such modern musts as a first-class restaurant and Robert Trent Jones–designed golf course. Too bad readers say the reception can be chilly—perhaps they should have stayed at the cozier Dunraven Arms on Adare's Main Street. ✉ *Adare, Limerick,* ☎ *061/396566,* FAX *061/396124. 64 rooms with bath. Restaurant, 2 bars, indoor pool, 18-hole golf course, horseback riding, fishing. AE, DC, MC, V.*

Bunratty

★ **Bunratty Castle,** a famous landmark midway between Limerick and Shannon Airport, is one of four castles in the area that offer nightly medieval banquets, which, though as fake as they come, at least offer some fairly uninhibited fun. The castle, once the stronghold of the princes of Thomond, is the most complete and—despite its ye-Olde-World banquets—authentic medieval castle in Ireland, restored in such a way as to give an idea of life during the 15th and 16th centuries. The **Folk Park** on its grounds has farm buildings and crafts shops typical of the 19th century. ☎ *061/361511.* ⏲ *Daily 9:30–dusk (last entry 1 hr before closing).*

Ennis

West of Shannon Airport is County Clare and its principal town, Ennis, the campaigning base of Eamon de Valera, the New York–born politician whose character and views dominated the Republic from independence until the mid-'50s. Just beyond Ennis, a 19 km (12 mi) signposted detour to Corofin will take you to the **Clare Heritage Center,** which explains the traumatic story of Ireland during the 19th century, a story of famines and untold misery that resulted in the mass emigrations of the Irish to England and the United States. ☎ *065/37955.* ⏲ *Apr.–Oct., daily 10–6; Nov.–Mar. by appointment.*

$$$ 🏨 **Old Ground.** This rambling creeper-clad building in the town center, dating from the early 18th century and much added-to over the years, is a comfortable, well-established hotel that serves as a popular base for golfers. Most of the hotel was renovated in 1997; bedrooms facing the gardens are quietest. ✉ *O'Connell St.,* ☎ *065/28127,* FAX *065/28112. 85 rooms. Restaurant. AE, DC, MC, V.*

$$ ★ 🏨 **Aberdeen Arms.** Golfers abound among the clientele of this comfortably refurbished Victorian seaside hotel. There are 10 tennis courts. ✉ *Lahinch, Co. Clare,* ☎ *065/81100,* FAX *065/81228. 55 rooms. 2 restaurants. AE, DC, MC, V.*

Lisdoonvarna

Lisdoonvarna, a small spa town with several sulfurous and iron-bearing springs with radioactive properties, is an excellent base for touring the Burren. It has developed something of a reputation over the years as a matchmaking center, with bachelor farmers and single women converging here each year around harvest time for a **Bachelors' Festival.**

$ 🏨 **Ballinalacken Castle.** It's not a castle, but a converted Victorian shooting lodge on the very edge of the Burren, commanding a breathtaking view of the Atlantic. Rooms are modest but full of character. ✉ *Co. Clare,* ☎ *065/74025,* FAX *065/74025. 12 rooms. Restaurant. MC, V. Closed early Nov.–Easter.*

$ 🏨 **Sheedy's Spa View.** Expect well-cared-for and spotlessly clean rooms at this friendly, family-run establishment with open turf fires and an excellent restaurant. ✉ *Lisdoonvarna,* ☎ *065/74026,* FAX *065/74555. 10 rooms with bath. Restaurant. AE, DC, MC, V.*

The Burren

Located in the northwest corner of county Clare, the Burren (from the Irish word for "stony rock") is a strange, rocky, limestone district—and a superb nature reserve, with a profusion of wildflowers that are at their best in late May. Huge colonies of puffins, kittiwakes, shags, guillemots, and razorbills nest along its coast. The **Burren Display Center** at Kilfenora explains the extraordinary geology and wildlife of the area in a simple audiovisual display. ☎ *065/88030.* ⏲ *Mid-Mar.–May and Sept.–Oct., daily 10–5; June–Aug., daily 10–6.*

The Cliffs of Moher

★ The dramatic **Cliffs of Moher** rise vertically out of the sea in a wall that stretches 8 km (5 mi) and varies in height from 710 ft to 1,440 ft. **O'Brien's Tower** is a defiant, broody sentinel built at their highest point. A visitor center at the base of the cliffs, beside the parking lot, is a good refuge from passing rain squalls (⏲ mid-Feb.–Apr., daily 10–5; May, June, and Sept., daily 10–6; July–Aug., daily 9:30–6:30). On a clear day the Aran Islands are visible from the cliffs, and in summer there are regular day trips to them from **Doolin,** a tiny village that claims three of the best pubs in Ireland for traditional music.

Ballyvaughan

A pretty waterside village with views of Galway Bay and the Aran Islands, Ballyvaughan makes a good base for exploring the Burren. At nearby **Ailwee Cave,** you can take a guided tour into the underworld of the Burren, where 3,415 ft of cave, formed millions of years ago, can be explored. ☎ *065/77036.* ⏲ *Early Mar.–June and Sept.–early Nov., daily 10–6 (last tour 5:30); July–Aug., daily 10–7 (last tour 6:30).*

$$ ★ ✕🏨 **Hyland's Hotel.** They have been looking after travelers for 250 years at this comfortable, family-run coaching inn in a seaside village in the heart of the Burren. The cheerful, unpretentious dining room specializes in local seafood and lamb. ✉ *Co. Clare,* ☎ *065/77037.* FAX *065/77131. 31 rooms. Restaurant. AE, MC, V. Closed Jan.*

Clarinbridge

The coast road continues into County Galway, through the pretty fishing village of **Kinvara.** Galway City is approached through **Clarinbridge,** the village that hosts Galway's annual Oyster Festival, which is held in September and features the superlative products of the village's oyster beds.

$ ✕ **Moran's of the Weir.** This waterside traditional thatched cottage is one of Ireland's simplest yet most famous seafood eateries. The specialty here is oysters, but they also serve crab, prawns, mussels, and smoked salmon. ✉ *The Weir, Kilcolgan, Co. Galway,* ☎ *091/96113. AE, MC, V.*

Cork to Galway Essentials

Getting Around

BY BICYCLE

You can rent bicycles from **Killarney Rent-A-Bike** (✉ Market Cross, Killarney, ☎ 064/32578).

BY BUS

Buses offer more flexible service than do trains; details are available from local visitor information offices.

BY CAR

All major rental companies have facilities at Shannon Airport. **Avis** (☎ 064/36655) and **Budget** (☎ 064/34341) also have facilities in Killarney. Taxis do not operate on meters; agree on the fare beforehand.

BY TRAIN

Trains run from Cork to Tralee, via Killarney, and from Cork to Limerick, changing at Limerick Junction.

Guided Tours

Bus Eireann offers day tours by bus from the Killarney and Tralee train stations; check with the tourist office or rail station for details. **Shannon Castle Tours** (☎ 061/360788) and **Destination Killarney** (☎ 064/32638) also operate tours.

Visitor Information

All visitor information offices are open weekdays 9–6 and Saturday 9–1: **Killarney** (✉ Town Hall, ☎ 064/31633, FAX 064/34506); **Limerick** (✉ Arthur's Quay, ☎ 061/317522, FAX 061/317939); **Shannon Airport** (☎ 061/471664); and **Tralee** (✉ Ashe Memorial Hall, ☎ 066/21288).

THE NORTHWEST

This route from Galway to Sligo and then back to Dublin, via Kells, takes you through the rugged landscape of Connemara to the fabled Yeats country in the northwest and then skirts the borders of Northern Ireland before returning to Dublin. The entire trip is about 400 km (250 mi) and although it passes through some of the wildest, loneliest, and most dramatic parts of Ireland, it takes in Galway City, which today has become a hip and happening mini-Dublin.

Galway City

A favorite weekend getaway of many native Irish, Galway City is a compact, bustling university town. Particularly in and around its main pedestrian-oriented street (the name of which changes from Williamsgate to William to Shop to High to Quay), the city's medieval heritage is everywhere apparent—in the intimate two- and three-story stucco buildings, the windy streets and narrow passageways, the cobblestones underfoot. **Eyre Square,** at the center of the city, is home to **Kennedy Park. Lynch's Castle** on Shop Street, now a bank, is the finest example of a 16th-century fortified house—fortified because the neighboring Irish tribes persistently raided Galway City, whose commercial life excluded them. **Naughton's** pub (☎ 091/566172), on the corner of Quay and Cross streets, offers excellent, inexpensive bar food at lunchtime and is a great place to mingle with locals. Across the River Corrib, in the northwestern corner of the city, **University College** is a center for Irish culture; its subdued 1848 Tudor-Gothic–style quadrangle is worth ★ a visit. In early summer you can stand on the **Weir Bridge** beside the town's cathedral and watch thousands of salmon as they leap and twist through the narrow access to the inner lakes.

On the west bank of the Corrib estuary, just outside of the Galway town walls, is **Claddagh,** said to be the oldest fishing village in Ireland. **Salthill Promenade,** with its lively seaside amenities, is the traditional place "to sit and watch the moon rise over Claddagh, and see the sun go down on Galway Bay"—in the words of the city's most famous song.

$$$ ★ ✕ **Drimcong House.** A 300-year-old lakeside house 13 km (8 mi) from Galway City is the home of one of Ireland's most highly regarded restaurants. Chef-owner Gerry Galvin fashions the finest local, organic ingredients into extraordinarily inventive dishes. The service is exceptional;

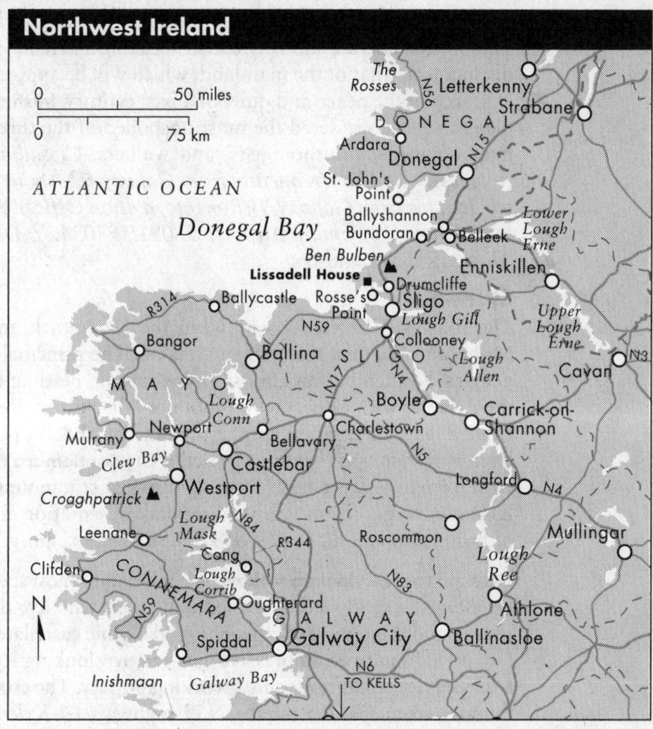

the dining room, elegant and understated. ✉ *Northwest on N59,* ☎ *091/555115. AE, DC, MC, V. Closed Sun., Mon., and Christmas–mid-Mar. No lunch.*

$$$ ✕ **Nimmo's.** Swiss chef Stephan Zeltner presides over a spacious second-floor dining room (a separately run wine bar is downstairs) in an old stone riverside building. Appropriately, fresh fish is a feature of the menu, as are hearty meat dishes and local produce. ✉ *Spanish Arch, Galway,* ☎ *091/563565. AE, DC, MC, V. Closed Sun. No lunch.*

$$ ✕ **Malt House.** This cheerful pub-restaurant tucked away in an alley off High Street in the center of old Galway has long been popular for good food—steaks, rack of lamb, prawns panfried in garlic butter—served in pleasantly informal surroundings. ✉ *Olde Malte Mall, High St., Galway,* ☎ *091/563993. AE, DC, MC, V. Closed Sun. Oct.–Apr.*

$$$ 🏨 **Galway Great Southern.** Expect to rub elbows with many native Irish visiting Galway at this grand, old-fashioned hotel whose limestone facade presides over the southeastern side of Eyre Square. Rooms have high ceilings and windows and Georgian-style furniture. A pianist often graces the spacious lobby, which, like the two bars, is a popular gathering spot. ✉ *Eyre Sq.,* ☎ *091/564041,* FAX *091/566704. 115 rooms. Restaurant, 2 bars, indoor pool. AE, DC, MC, V.*

$$ ★ 🏨 **Ardilaun House.** Top-floor, even-numbered rooms in this lovely, 19th-century house, set in pleasant grounds midway between Galway City and the seaside suburb of Salthill, have bay views, but even those without are just as pleasant. ✉ *Taylors Hill,* ☎ *091/521433,* FAX *091/521546. 89 rooms. AE, DC, MC, V.*

Aran Islands

Connemara is a land of romantic, underpopulated landscapes, and rugged craggy coastlines, where the Irish language is still used by many people. **Rossaveale,** a port on the coast road beyond Spiddal, is the handiest port for a trip to the Aran Islands, 48 km (30 mi) off the coast, where J. M. Synge drew the inspiration for his play *Riders to the Sea.* The Aran Islands are still 100% Irish-speaking and retain an atmosphere distinct from that of the mainland, which will be appreciated by those ★ in search of the peace and quiet of a past century. **Inishmaan,** the middle island, is considered the most unspoiled of the three and will delight botanists, ornithologists, and walkers. ✉ *Sailings daily from Rossaveale and less frequently from Galway.* 🎫 *About IR£12 round-trip (details from Galway Visitor Information Office). Also accessible by air from Connemara Airport;* ☎ *091/593034.* ⏲ *Daily flights.* 🎫 *About IR£35 round-trip.*

Clifden

The road to Clifden runs between the Maamturk and the Cloosh Mountains beside a string of small lakes. The principal town of Connemara, Clifden has an almost alpine setting, nestling on the edge of the Atlantic with a spectacular mountain backdrop. Recently, it's become a favored vacation spot, and numerous B&Bs, pubs, and shops have moved in. Just beyond Clifden is the **Connemara National Park,** with its many nature trails offering views of sea, mountain, and lake. Its visitor center features an audiovisual presentation and a collection of farm furniture. ☎ *095/41054.* ⏲ *Mar.–Sept., daily 10–6.*

Demand to see **Kylemore Abbey,** one of Ireland's most spectacular country estates, recently led the Benedictine nuns who live there to open it year-round. Built in 1868, this Baronial Gothic castellated mansion offers period interiors, impressive gardens overlooking Kylemore Lake, a self-service restaurant, and a working pottery. The estate is about 15 minutes from Clifden on the N59 highway. ✉ *Kylemore,* ☎ *095/41146.* 🎫 *IR£1.50.* ⏲ *Oct.–May 10–4, June–Sept. 9–6.*

$$$ ★ ✕🏨 **Renvyle House.** An extraordinary natural setting—a lake is at the front door and the Atlantic Ocean is at the back—distinguishes this country house, once owned by famed poet Oliver St. John Gogarty. Surrounded by a wild countryside, this hotel offers a host of outdoor activities. Elegantly decorated rooms all have breathtaking views. The cheerful, softly lit restaurant's table d'hôte menu emphasizes fresh local fish and lamb, cooked in traditional country house style. Facilities include a tennis court, a nine-hole golf course, fishing, and horseback riding. ✉ *Renvyle, Co. Galway,* ☎ *095/43511,* FAX *095/43515. 56 rooms. Restaurant, pool. AE, DC, MC, V. Closed Jan.–Feb.*

$–$$ ★ ✕🏨 **Quay House.** A roaring turf fire in the sitting room greets visitors to this three-story Georgian house, Clifden's oldest building (from 1820) and a short walk from the busy town center. All rooms but one have sea views. The restaurant is open for guests only. ✉ *Clifden, Connemara, Co. Galway,* ☎ *095/21369,* FAX *095/41168. 7 rooms. Restaurant. MC, V. Closed Nov.–mid-Mar.*

Westport

Westport is a quiet, mainly 18th-century town overlooking Clew Bay—a wide expanse of water studded with nearly 400 islands. The distinctive silhouette of **Croagh Patrick,** a 2,540-ft mountain, dominates the town. Today some 25,000 pilgrims climb it on the last Sunday in July in honor of St. Patrick, who is believed to have spent 40 days fasting on its summit in AD 441. Whether he did or not, the climb is an exhilarating experience and can be completed in about three hours; it should be attempted only in good weather, however.

$$ ✕ **Asgard.** On the Quay, a short distance from the town center, this pub serves award-winning food in both its downstairs bar and its more formal, second-floor restaurant. ✉ *The Quay, Westport,* ☎ *098/25319. AE, DC, MC, V.*

$$ ★ ✕🏨 **Delphi Lodge.** In the heart of what is arguably Mayo's most spectacular mountains-and-lakes scenery, this attractive sporting lodge is heavily stocked with fishing paraphernalia The owner, Peter Mantle, is a valuable storehouse of information and stories. Guests dine together; there is a wine list and a self-service bar. ✉ *4 mi. off the N59, northwest of Leenane, Co. Mayo,* ☎ *095/42211,* FAX *095/42296. 12 rooms. Restaurant, bar. MC, V.*

$$ 🏨 **Hotel Westport.** A modern low rise, this quiet hotel is five minutes' walk from the town center and overlooks the grounds of Westport House. ✉ *Newport Rd., Co. Mayo,* ☎ *098/25122,* FAX *098/26739. 49 rooms. Restaurant, indoor pool. AE, DC, MC, V.*

Sligo

County Sligo is noted for its seaside resorts, the famous golf course at Rosses Point (just outside Sligo Town), and its links with Ireland's most famous 20th-century poet, W. B. Yeats. An important collection of paintings by the poet's brother, Jack B. Yeats, can be seen in the **Sligo Library, Museum and Art Gallery** (✉ Stephen St., Sligo Town, ☎ 071/42212), which also has memorabilia of Yeats, the poet. Take a boat ★ from Sligo up to **Lough Gill** and see the **Lake Isle of Innisfree** and other places immortalized in Yeats's poetry. His grave is at Drumcliffe, beneath the slopes of Ben Bulben, just north of the town. Nearby is **Lissadell House,** a substantial mansion dating from 1830 that features prominently in his writings. It was the home of Constance Gore-Booth, later Countess Markeviecz, who took part in the 1916 uprising. ☎ *071/63150.* ⏲ *June–mid-Sept., Mon.–Sat. 10:30–12:30, 2–4:30.*

$ ✕ **Bistro Bianconi.** The decor is all white: blond wood and white-tile floors. The color comes from the page-long selection of gourmet pizzas, baked in the wood-burning oven with toppings both traditional and innovative. ✉ *44 O'Connell St., Sligo,* ☎ *071/41744. AE, MC, V. No lunch.*

$$$ ✕🏨 **Markree Castle.** A pastoral 1,000-acre estate is home to this 17th-century, family-owned castle, which also houses the elegant Knockmuldowney Restaurant. The common rooms share a comfortable informality; rooms are idiosyncratically decorated. ✉ *Off N4, south of Sligo Town,* ☎ *071/67800, 800/223–6510 in the U.S.,* FAX *071/67840. 30 rooms. Restaurant. AE, DC, MC, V.*

Donegal

With its central triangular "square," Donegal Town is the gateway to the magnificent northwest, with its rugged coastline and dramatic highlands, home to the "tweed villages" on the coast at the Rosses, where the famous Donegal tweed is woven.

$$$ ★ ✕🏨 **Rathmullan House.** This rambling, 18th-century country house, has light-filled, antiques-decorated rooms; three elegant, comfortable sitting rooms; and lawns that stretch down to a deserted, sandy beach. ✉ *Rathmullan, Co. Donegal,* ☎ *074/58188,* FAX *074/58200. 23 rooms with bath or shower. Dining room, indoor pool. AE, DC, MC, V. Closed Nov.–Easter.*

$ ✕🏨 **Castle Murray House Hotel.** The original house has been extended and modernized to take full advantage of the exceptional panoramic views of the bay and distant mountains. The restaurant is renowned for its superb French cuisine. ✉ *13 mi. west of Donegal Town, Dunkineely,* ☎ *073/37022,* FAX *073/37330. 8 rooms with shower, 2 with bath. Restaurant. MC, V. Closed mid-Jan.–mid-Feb.; Nov.–mid-Mar., most Mon. and Tues.*

Belleek

This route heads back to Dublin through Belleek, on the borders of Counties Donegal and Fermanagh, known for its fragile, lustrous china; a factory visit can be arranged (☎ 08036/565–501). For the remaining towns on this tour, *see* the Ireland country map.

From Belleek, the A46 skirts the shores of Lower Lough Erne in Northern Ireland, and passes **Tully Castle.** On Christmas Eve in 1641, Rory Maguire and a band of supporters stormed the castle, which had been built on land that had been seized from his clan. The residents were spared, but 75 other occupants were killed. It was burned and never lived in again. Take in the delightful lake and island views from within the ruins.

Kells

The N3 returns you to Dublin by way of Kells, in whose 8th-century abbey the Book of Kells was completed; a facsimile can be seen in **St. Columba's Church.** Among the remains of the abbey are a well-preserved round tower and a rare example of a stone-roof church dating from the 9th century. There are five richly sculptured stone crosses in Kells. The **Hill of Tara,** southeast of Navan, was the religious and cultural capital of Ireland in ancient times. Its importance waned with the arrival of Christianity during the 5th century, and today its crest is, appropriately enough, crowned with a statue of the man who brought Christianity to Ireland—St. Patrick.

The Northwest Essentials

Getting Around

BY BICYCLE

You can rent bikes from **Celtic Cycles** (✉ Victoria Pl., Galway City, ☎ 091/566606), **John Mannion** (✉ Railway View, Clifden, ☎ 095/21160), or **Gary's Cycles** (✉ Quay St., Sligo, ☎ 071/45418).

BY BUS

Bus Eireann (☎ 01/836–6111) runs bus services throughout the country. **McGeehan Coaches** (☎ 075/46150) services Co. Donegal locally.

BY CAR

In Galway, cars can be rented from **Avis** (☎ 091/568886), **Budget** (☎ 091/566376 or 091/564570), or **Murray's** (☎ 091/562222). Taxis do not operate on meters; agree on the fare beforehand.

BY TRAIN

Trains to Galway, Westport, and Sligo operate from Dublin's Heuston or Connolly (Sligo) stations. There is no train service north of Sligo.

Guided Tours

CIE Tours International operates day tours of Connemara out of Galway City and bus tours into the Donegal highlands from Sligo train station; details are available from local tourist offices. **CIE/Bus Eireann** (☎ 01/830–2222) and **Gray Line** (☎ 01/661–9666) offer tours of the Boyne Valley and County Meath out of Dublin.

Visitor Information

All offices are open weekdays 9–6 and Saturday 9–1: **Galway** (✉ off Eyre Sq., ☎ 091/563081, FAX 091/565201); **Sligo** (✉ Temple St., ☎ 071/61201, FAX 071/60360); **Westport** (✉ The Mall, ☎ 098/25711, FAX 098/26709).

18 Italy

Rome, Florence, Tuscany, Milan, Venice, Campania

Where else in Europe can you find the blend of great art, delicious food and wine, and sheer verve that awaits you in Italy? This Mediterranean country has made a profound contribution to Western civilization, producing some of the world's greatest thinkers, writers, politicians, saints, and artists. Impressive traces of their lives and works can still be seen in Italy's great buildings and lovely countryside.

The whole of Italy is one vast attraction, but the triangle of its most-visited cities—Rome (Roma), Florence (Firenze), and Venice (Venezia)—represents the great variety found here. In Rome and Florence, especially, you can feel the uninterrupted flow of the ages, from the Classical era of the ancient Romans to the bustle and throb of contemporary life being lived in centuries-old settings. Venice, by contrast, seems suspended in time, the same today as it was when it held sway over the eastern Mediterranean and the Orient. Each of these cities reveals a different aspect of the Italian character: the Baroque exuberance of Rome, Florence's serene stylishness, and the dreamy sensuality of Venice.

Trying to soak in Italy's rich artistic heritage poses a challenge. The country's many museums and churches draw hordes of visitors, all wanting to see the same thing at the same time. From May through September, the Sistine Chapel, Michelangelo's *David,* Piazza San Marco, and other key sights are more often than not swamped by mobs of tourists. Try to see the highlights at off-peak times. If they are open during lunch, this is often a good time. Again, relax: Seeing some attractions—such as the scrubbed facades of Rome's glorious Baroque churches—entails no opening hours and no lines at all.

It's important to be attentive to matters of personal security in certain parts of the country; always be on guard against pickpockets and purse snatchers in the main tourist cities and in Naples. Especially in Rome and Florence, watch out for bands of gypsy children, expert at lifting wallets. Keep the children at a distance, and don't be shy about shouting at them to stay away. Small cities and towns are usually safe.

Making the most of your time in Italy doesn't mean rushing through it. To gain a rich appreciation for Italy, don't try to see everything all at once. Practice the Italian-perfected *il dolce far niente*—the sweet art of idleness—which might mean skipping a museum to sit at a table in a pretty café, enjoying the sunshine and a cappuccino. Art—and life—are to be enjoyed, and the Italians can show you how.

ITALY A TO Z

Customs

For details on imports and duty-free limits, *see* Customs & Duties *in* Chapter 1.

Dining

Generally speaking, a *ristorante* pays more attention to decor and service than does a *trattoria,* which is simpler and often family run. An *osteria* used to be a simple tavern, though now the term may be used to designate a chic and expensive eatery. A *tavola calda* offers hot dishes and snacks, with seating. A *rosticceria* offers the same to take out.

The menu is always posted in the window or just inside the door of an eating establishment. Check to see what is offered, and note whether there are charges for *coperto* (cover) and *servizio* (service), which will increase your check. The coperto charge has been abolished in many eating places. Many restaurants offer a *menu turistico,* usually a complete dinner, limited to a few entrées, at a reasonable price (including taxes and service, with beverages extra). Tap water is safe in large cities and almost everywhere else unless noted *non potabile.* Bottled mineral water is available everywhere, *gassata* (with bubbles) or *non gassata* (without bubbles). If you prefer tap water, ask for *acqua semplice.* Note that many restaurants close from Christmas through the first week in January and for a good part of August.

MEALTIMES

Lunch is served in Rome from 1 to 3, dinner from 8 to 10 and sometimes later. Service begins and ends a half hour earlier in Florence and Venice, later in the south. Practically all restaurants close one day a week; some close for winter or summer vacations.

RATINGS

Prices are per person and include first course, main course, dessert or fruit, and house wine, where available.

CATEGORY	ROME, MILAN*	OTHER AREAS
$$$$	over 120,000 lire	over 100,000 lire
$$$	70,000 lire–120,000 lire	60,000 lire–80,000 lire
$$	40,000 lire–70,000 lire	30,000–60,000
$	under 40,000 lire	under 30,000 lire

**Note that restaurant prices in Venice can be slightly higher than those in Rome and Milan; in small cities prices are usually lower.*

WHAT TO WEAR

Except for restaurants in the $$$$ and occasionally in the $$$ categories, where jacket and tie are advisable, casual attire is acceptable.

Language

Italy is accustomed to English-speaking tourists, and in major cities you will find that many people speak at least a little English. In smaller hotels and restaurants and on public transportation, a basic knowledge or knowing just a few phrases of Italian come in handy.

Lodging

Italy, especially Rome, Florence, and Venice, offers a good choice of accommodations, though rooms tend to be small. Room rates are on a par with those of most European capitals, although porters, room service, and in-house laundering are disappearing in all but the most elegant hotels. Taxes and service are included in the room rate. Although breakfast is usually quoted in the room rate, it's actually an extra charge that you can decline. The desk might not be happy about it, but make your preference clear when booking or checking in. Air-conditioning also may be an extra charge. Rooms, except where noted, have a private bath with shower. Specify if you care about having either a bathtub or shower, as not all rooms have both. In $$ and $ places showers may be the drain-in-the-floor type guaranteed to flood the bathroom. In older hotels room quality may be uneven; if you don't like the room you're given, ask for another. This applies to noise, too; some front rooms are bigger and have views but get street noise. Rail stations in major cities have hotel-reservation service booths.

CAMPING

Italy has a wide selection of campgrounds, and the Italians themselves have taken to camping, which means that beach or mountain sites will be crammed in July and August. An international camping *carnet* (permit) is required; get one from your local association before leaving home. You can buy a campsite directory such as the detailed guide published by the Touring Club Italiano (available in bookstores) or obtain the free directory of campsites published by the Federazione Italiana del Campeggio (✉ Casella Postale 23, 50041 Calenzano, Florence, ☎ 055/882391, FAX 055/8825918) in tourist information offices or by mail from the organization if you send three international reply coupons.

HOTELS

Italian hotels are classified by regional tourist boards from five-star (deluxe) to one-star (modest hotels and small inns). The established price of the room appears on a rate card on the back of the door of your room or inside the closet door, though you may be able to get a lower rate by asking. Any variations above the posted rate should be cause for complaint and should be reported to the local tourist office. Sheraton, Forte, Jolly, Space, Atahotels, Best Western, Holiday Inn, and Italhotels are among the reliable chains or groups operating in Italy. Several Relais & Châteaux hotels are noted for individual atmosphere, personal service, and luxury; they are also expensive. The AGIP chain is found mostly on main highways. The Family Hotels group, composed mostly of small $$ and $ family-run hotels, offers good value, reliability, and special attention to families. Standards in one-star hotels are very uneven. At best, rooms are usually spotlessly clean but basic, with shower and toilets down the hall.

Low-season rates do not officially apply in Rome, Florence, and Milan, but you can usually bargain for discounted rates in Rome and Milan in summer (when business travelers are few) and in Florence in winter. Ask for *"la tariffa scontata."* You can save on hotel accommodations in Venice and in such resorts as Sorrento and Capri during their low seasons—the winter, early spring, and late-autumn months.

RATINGS

The following price categories are determined by the cost of two people in a double room.

Italy (Italia)

Rome
Tivoli
Anzio
Gaeta
Cassino
Isernia
MOLISE
Termoli
Gargano Peninsula
Foggia
PUGLIA
Bari
Brindisi
Lecce
Taranto
Golfo di Taranto
BASILICATA
Potenza
CAMPANIA
Naples
Vesuvius
Salerno
Paestum
Capri
CALABRIA
Cosenza
Catanzaro
Crotone
Reggio
Messina
Ionian Sea
Tyrrhenian Sea
Aeolian Islands
SICILY
Palermo
Etna
Catania
Siracusa
Agrigento
SARDINIA
Olbia
Sassari
Cagliari
Mediterranean Sea
TUNISIA
Tunis
ALGERIA
0 100 miles
0 150 km

CATEGORY	ROME, MILAN*	OTHER AREAS
$$$$	over 600,000 lire	over 450,000 lire
$$$	350,000 lire–600,000 lire	300,000 lire–450,000 lire
$$	250,000 lire–350,000 lire	200,000 lire–300,000 lire
$	under 250,000 lire	under 200,000 lire

**As with restaurant prices, the cost of hotels in Venice may be slightly more than those shown here.*

RENTALS AND AGRITOURISM

Short or long rental stays in town apartments or in rural villas or farms are a good option for families traveling with children and others who value independence and want a taste of living Italian-style. Agritourism, or staying on a working farm, usually for a week or more, is growing in popularity in rural areas throughout Italy, especially in Tuscany and Umbria. Agritourism accommodations range in style from rustic simplicity to country chic, and prices vary accordingly. Contact local APT tourist offices and the three main agritourist agencies (Agriturist, ✉ Piazza San Firenze 3, 50122, Florence, ☎ 055/295163; Terranostra, ✉ Via dei Magazzini 2, 50122, Florence, ☎ 055/280539; Turismo Verde, ✉ Via Verdi 5, 50127, Florence, ☎ 055/2344925).

Mail

The Italian mail system is notoriously erratic and can be excruciatingly slow. Until a trend toward greater efficiency is confirmed, allow up to 15 days for mail to and from the United States and Canada, almost as much to and from the United Kingdom, and much longer for postcards.

POSTAL RATES

Airmail letters to the United States cost 1,300 lire for up to 20 grams; postcards with a short greeting and signature cost 1,100 lire, but are charged at the letter rate if the message is lengthy. Airmail letters to the United Kingdom cost 800 lire, postcards 650 lire.

RECEIVING MAIL

You can have mail sent to American Express offices; service is free if you are a card member. You can send mail to Italian post offices, marked "fermo posta" and addressed to you c/o Palazzo delle Poste, with the name of the city in which you will pick it up. In either case you must show your passport and pay a small fee.

Money Matters

COSTS

Rome, Milan, and Venice are the more expensive Italian cities to visit. Taxes are usually included in hotel bills; a cover charge may appear as a separate item in restaurant checks, as does the service charge, usually about 15%, if added. There is a 19% tax on car rentals, usually included in the rates.

CURRENCY

The unit of currency in Italy is the lira (plural, lire). There are bills of 1,000, 2,000, 5,000, 10,000, 50,000, 100,000, and 500,000 lire (impossible to change, except in banks); coins are worth 50, 100, 200, and 500 lire. In 1999 the euro will be used as a banking currency, but the lire will still be the currency in use on a day-to-day basis. At press time the exchange rate was about 1,798 lire to the U.S. dollar, 1,266 lire to the Canadian dollar, and 2,943 lire to the pound sterling.

When your purchases run into hundreds of thousands of lire, beware of being shortchanged, a dodge that is practiced at ticket windows, toll booths, and cashiers' desks, as well as in shops and even in banks. *Always count your change before you leave the counter.* Always carry some smaller-denomination bills for sundry purchases; you're less likely to be shortchanged, and you won't have to face the eye-rolling dismay of cashiers reluctant to change large-denomination bills.

Credit cards are generally accepted in shops and hotels, but may not always be welcome in restaurants, so always look for card logos displayed in windows or ask when you enter to avoid embarrassing situations. When you wish to leave a tip beyond the 15% service charge that is usually included with your bill (☞ Tipping, *below*), leave it in cash rather than adding it to the credit card slip.

SAMPLE PRICES

A cup of espresso enjoyed while standing at a bar costs from 1,200 to 1,400 lire, the same cup served at a table, triple that. A bottle of beer costs from 2,500 to 3,800 lire, a soft drink about 2,200 lire. A *tramezzino* (small sandwich) costs about 2,200 lire, a more substantial one about 3,500. You will pay about 10,000 lire for a short taxi ride. Admission to a major museum is about 12,000 lire; a three-hour sightseeing tour, about 45,000 lire.

TIPPING

Tipping practices vary depending on where you are. Italians tip smaller amounts in small cities and towns, often not at all in cafés and taxis north of Rome. The following guidelines apply in major cities.

In restaurants a 15% service charge is usually added to the total; it's customary to give the waiter an additional 5%. Charges for service are included in all hotel bills, but smaller tips to staff members are appreciated. In general, in a $$ hotel, chambermaids should be given about 1,000 lire per room per day, 4,000–5,000 lire per week; bellhops 1,000–2,000 lire. Tip a minimum of 1,000 lire for room service and valet service. Tip breakfast waiters 500 lire per day per table (at end of stay). These amounts should be increased by 40% in $$$ hotels, doubled in $$$$ hotels. Give the concierge about 15% of the bill for services. Tip doormen about 500 lire for calling a cab.

Taxi drivers are happy with 5%–10%. Porters at railroad stations and airports charge a fixed rate per suitcase; tip an additional 500 lire per person, more if the porter is very helpful. Tip service-station attendants 1,000 lire if they are especially helpful. Tip guides about 2,000 lire per person for a half-day tour, more if they are very good.

National Holidays

January 1; January 6 (Epiphany); April 4–5 (Easter Sunday and Monday); April 25 (Liberation Day); May 1 (May Day); August 15 (Assumption, known as Ferragosto); November 1 (All Saints' Day); December 8 (Immaculate Conception); December 25–26.

Opening and Closing Times

Banks are open weekdays 8:30–1:30 and 2:45–3:45. **Churches** are usually open from early morning to noon or 12:30, when they close for about two hours or more, opening again in the afternoon until about 7 PM. **National museums** are usually open from 9 AM until 2 and are often closed on Monday, but there are many exceptions, especially at major museums. **Non-national museums** have entirely different hours, which may vary according to season. Most major archaeological sites are open every day, except some holidays. At all museums and sites, ticket offices close an hour or so before official closing time. Always check with the local tourist office for current hours and holiday closings. **Shops** are open, with individual variations, from 9 to 1 and from 3:30 or 4 to 7 or 7:30. They are open from Monday through Saturday, but close for a half day during the week; for example, in Rome most shops (except food shops) are closed on Monday morning (also Saturday afternoon in July and August), though a 1995 ordinance allows greater freedom. Some tourist-oriented shops and department stores—in downtown Rome, Florence, and Venice—are open all day, every day.

Shopping

SALES-TAX REFUNDS

Getting a refund of Italy's value-added tax is complicated. Foreign tourists who have spent more than 300,000 lire (before tax) in one store can take advantage of it, however. At the time of purchase, with passport or ID in hand, ask the store for an invoice describing the article or articles and the total lire amount. If your destination when you leave Italy is a non-EU country, you must have the invoice stamped at customs upon departure from Italy; if your destination is another EU country, you must obtain the customs stamp upon departure from that country. Once back home—and within 90 days of the date of purchase—you must send the stamped invoice back to the store, which should forward the IVA rebate directly to you. If the store participates in the Europe Tax-Free Shopping System (those that do display a sign to the effect), things are simpler. The invoice provided is a Tax-Free Check in the amount of the tax refund, which can be cashed at the Tax-Free Cash Refund window in the transit area of major airports and border crossings.

Telephoning

COUNTRY CODE

The country code for Italy is 39.

INTERNATIONAL CALLS

To place international calls many travelers go to the TELECOM telephone exchange, where the operator assigns you a booth, can help place your call, and collects payment when you have finished. To place an international call, insert a phone card, dial 00, then the country code, area code, and phone number. The cheaper and easier option, however, will be to use your AT&T, MCI, or Sprint calling card. For **AT&T USADirect,** dial access number ☎ 172–1011; for **MCI Call USA,** access number ☎ 172–1022; for **Sprint Express,** access number ☎ 172–1877. You will be connected directly with an operator in the United States. You can make collect calls from any phone by dialing ☎ 172–1011, which will get you an English-speaking operator. For information and operators in Europe and the Mediterranean area, dial ☎ 15; for intercontinental service, dial ☎ 170.

LOCAL CALLS

For all local calls, you must now dial area codes, even in cities. Most local calls cost 200 lire for two minutes. Pay phones take either 100-, 200-, or 500-lire coins or *schede telefoniche* (phone cards), purchased in bars, tobacconists, post offices, and TELECOM offices in either 5,000- 10,000-, or 15,000-lire denominations. For information and operators in Europe and the Mediterranean area, dial 15; for intercontinental service, dial 170.

Transportation

BY BOAT

Ferries connect the mainland with all the major islands. Car ferries operate to Sicily, Sardinia, Elba, Ponza, Capri (though taking a car here is not advised), and Ischia, among others. Lake ferries connect the towns on the shores of the Italian lakes: Como, Maggiore, and Garda.

BY BUS

Regional bus companies provide service throughout Italy. Route information and timetables are usually available at tourist information offices and travel agencies, or at bus company ticket offices. One of the interregional companies providing long-distance service is **SITA** (✉ Viale Cadorna 105, Florence, ☎ 055/47821).

BY CAR

The Autostrada del Sole (A1, A2, and A3) crosses the country from north to south, connecting Milan to Reggio Calabria. The A4 from west to east connects Turin to Trieste.

Breakdowns. Dial 116 for towing and repairs; breakdown service (emergency repairs and towing on an autostrada) is free for tourists with foreign license plates or with cars rented in Italy that have breakdown insurance. Dial 113 for an ambulance and highway police.

Gasoline. Gas, which costs the equivalent of more than $4 per U.S. gallon, or about 1,700 lire per liter, should be less expensive by 1999, when the gas tax will be lower. Except on the autostrade, most gas stations are closed Sunday; they also close from 12:30 PM to 3:30 PM and at 7 PM for the night. Self-service pumps can be found in most cities and towns.

Parking. Check with your hotel to determine the best place to park. Parking is greatly restricted in the center of most cities. Parking in a "Zona Disco" is for limited periods. City garages cost up to 30,000 lire per day.

Road Conditions. The extensive autostrada network (toll superhighways) connecting all major towns is complemented by equally well-maintained but toll-free *superstrade* (express highways), *strade statali* (main roads), and *strade provinciali* (secondary roads). All are clearly signposted and numbered. The ticket issued on entering an autostrada must be returned on leaving, along with the toll. On some shorter autostrade, mainly connections, the toll is payable on entering. Have small bills and change handy for tolls; shortchanging is a risk, so always count your change before leaving the toll booth. If you will be using autostrade extensively, buy a Viacard—an automatic toll card—for 50,000 or 100,000 lire at autostrada locations. Some automatic booths also take an array of credit cards.

Rules of the Road. Driving is on the right. The speed limit on an autostrada is 130 kph (81 mph). It is 110 kph (70 mph) on state and provincial roads, unless otherwise marked. Other regulations are largely as in the United States except that the police have the power to levy severe on-the-spot fines. Italians drive fast and impatiently; don't be surprised when, on a windy two-lane highway, drivers zip into the ongoing-traffic lane to pass you if you are going too slowly.

BY PLANE

Alitalia and its domestic affiliate **ATI,** plus some privately owned companies such as **Meridiana** and **Air One** in addition to other European airlines, provide service throughout Italy. Most of them offer several types of discount fares; inquire at travel agencies or at Alitalia agencies in major cities.

BY TRAIN

The fastest trains on the FS (Ferrovie dello Stato), the state-owned railroad, are the Eurostar trains, for which you pay a supplement and for which seat reservations are required in both first and second class and are included in the cost of the ticket. Also fast are Intercity (IC) and Eurocity (EC) trains, for which you pay a supplement in both classes and for which reservations may be required. Trains designated *Interregionale* are slower, making more stops. *Regionale* trains are locals, serving a single region. Throughout Italy, call ☎ 1478/880880 toll free daily 7 AM–9 PM for train information.

You can buy tickets and make seat reservations at travel agencies displaying the FS symbol up to two months in advance, thereby avoiding long lines at station ticket windows. **All tickets must be date-stamped in the small yellow or red machines near the tracks before you board.** Once stamped, your ticket is valid for six hours if your destination is within 200 km (124 mi) and for 24 hours for destinations beyond that; you can get on and off at will for the duration of the ticket's validity. If you don't stamp your ticket in the machine, you must actively seek out a conductor to validate the ticket on the train, paying an extra 10,000 lire for the service. If you merely wait in your seat for him to collect your ticket, you must pay at least a 30,000 lire fine. You will pay a hefty surcharge if you purchase your ticket on board the train. Tickets for destinations within a 100-km (62-mi) range can be purchased at any *tabacchi* (tobacconist). There is a refreshment service on all long-distance trains. Tap water on trains is not drinkable. Carry compact bags for easy overhead storage. Trains are very crowded at holiday times; always reserve, at all times of year.

Visitor Information

In Italy regional and local agencies, either the **Azienda di Promozione Turismo** (APT or AST) or the **Ente Provinciale per il Turismo** (EPT), as well as municipal tourist offices and others known as **Pro Loco** in small towns, provide helpful information.

Weather

The best months for good-weather sightseeing are April, May, June, September, and October, generally pleasant and not too hot. In general the northern half of the peninsula and the entire Adriatic Coast, with the exception of Apulia, are rainier than the rest of Italy.

CLIMATE

The hottest months are July and August, when brief afternoon thunderstorms are common in inland areas. Winters are relatively mild in most places on the tourist circuit, but there are always some rainy spells. The following are average daily maximum and minimum temperatures for Rome and Milan.

ROME

Jan.	52F	11C	**May**	74F	23C	**Sept.**	79F	26C
	40	5		56	13		62	17
Feb.	55F	13C	**June**	82F	28C	**Oct.**	71F	22C
	42	6		63	17		55	13
Mar.	59F	15C	**July**	87F	30C	**Nov.**	61F	16C
	45	7		67	20		49	9
Apr.	66F	19C	**Aug.**	86F	30C	**Dec.**	55F	13C
	50	10		67	20		44	6

MILAN

Jan.	40F	5C	**May**	74F	23C	**Sept.**	75F	24C
	32	0		57	14		61	16
Feb.	46F	8C	**June**	80F	27C	**Oct.**	63F	17C
	35	2		63	17		52	11
Mar.	56F	13C	**July**	84F	29C	**Nov.**	51F	10C
	43	6		67	20		43	6
Apr.	65F	18C	**Aug.**	82F	28C	**Dec.**	43F	6C
	49	9		66	16		35	2

ROME

Antiquity is taken for granted in Rome, where successive ages have piled the present on top of the past—building, layering, and overlapping their own particular segments of Rome's 2,500 years of history to form a remarkably varied urban complex. Most of the city's major sights are in the fairly small *centro* (center). At its heart lies ancient Rome, site of the Foro Romano and Colosseo. It was around this core that the other sections of the city grew up through the ages: medieval Rome, which covered the horn of land that pushes the Tiber toward the Vatican and extended across the river into Trastevere; and Renaissance Rome, which was erected upon medieval foundations and extended as far as the Vatican, with beautiful villas created in what were then the outskirts of the city.

Exploring Rome

Numbers in the margin correspond to points of interest on the Rome map.

The layout of the centro is highly irregular, but several landmarks serve as orientation points to identify the areas that most visitors come to see: The Colosseo (Colosseum), the Pantheon and Piazza Navona, the Basilica di San Pietro (St. Peter's Church), the Scalinata di Piazza di Spagna (Spanish Steps), and Villa Borghese. You'll need a good map to find your way around; newsstands offer a wide choice. Energetic sightseers will walk a lot, a much more pleasant way to see the city now that some traffic has been barred from the centro during the day; others might choose to take taxis, buses, or the Metro. If you are in Rome during a hot spell, do as the Romans do: Start out early in the morning, have a light lunch and a long siesta during the hottest hours, then resume sightseeing in the late afternoon and end your evening with a leisurely meal outdoors, refreshed by cold Frascati wine and the *ponentino,* the cool evening breeze.

Ancient Rome

7 **Arco di Costantino** (Arch of Constantine). The best-preserved of Rome's triumphal arches, this 4th-century BC monument is covered with reliefs depicting Constantine's victory over Maxentius at the Milvian Bridge. Just before this battle in AD 312, Constantine had a vision of a cross in the heavens and heard the words: "In this sign thou shalt conquer." The victory led not only to the construction of this majestic marble arch but also to a turning point in the history of Christianity: Soon afterward a grateful Constantine decreed that it was a lawful religion and should be tolerated throughout the empire. ✉ *Piazza del Colosseo at end of Via di San Gregorio.*

2 **Campidoglio** (Capitol Square). In the square on the Capitoline Hill, the majestic ramp and beautifully proportioned piazza are the handiwork of Michelangelo (1475–1564), who also worked on the three palaces, two of which house the Capitoline Museums. Palazzo Senatorio, at the center, is still the ceremonial seat of Rome's city hall; it was built over the Tabularium, where ancient Rome's state archives were kept. The statue at the center of the square is a copy of an ancient Roman bronze of Marcus Aurelius (AD 120–180). ✉ *Piazza del Campidoglio.*

★ 6 **Colosseo** (Colosseum). Massive and majestic, this ruin is ancient Rome's most famous monument, inaugurated in AD 80 with a program of games and shows that lasted 100 days. On opening day alone some 5,000 wild animals perished in the arena. The Colosseum could hold more than 50,000 spectators; it was faced with marble, decorated with stuccos, and had

Arco di Costantino, **7**
Basilica di San Pietro, **22**
Campidoglio, **2**
Campo dei Fiori, **33**
Castel Sant' Angelo, **20**
Chiesa del Gesù, **26**
Colosseo, **6**
Fondazione Keats-Shelley Memorial, **14**
Fontana delle Tartarughe, **25**
Fontana di Trevi, **15**
Foro Romano, **5**
Galleria Borghese, **19**
Galleria Doria Pamphili, **27**
Giardini Vaticani, **23**
Isola Tiberina, **35**
Musei Capitolini, **3**
Musei Vaticani, **24**
Museo Etrusco di Villa Giulia, **11**
Palazzo Altemps, **30**
Palazzo Barberini, **17**
Palazzo Farnese, **34**
Pantheon, **29**
Piazza Barberini, **16**
Piazza del Popolo, **9**
Piazza di Spagna, **12**
Piazza Navona, **32**
Piazza San Pietro, **21**
Piazza Venezia, **1**
San Luigi dei Francesi, **31**
Santa Maria dell'Aracoeli, **4**
Santa Maria della Concezione, **18**
Santa Maria del Popolo, **10**
Santa Maria sopra Minerva, **28**
Scalinata di Piazza di Spagna, **13**
Terme di Caracalla, **8**

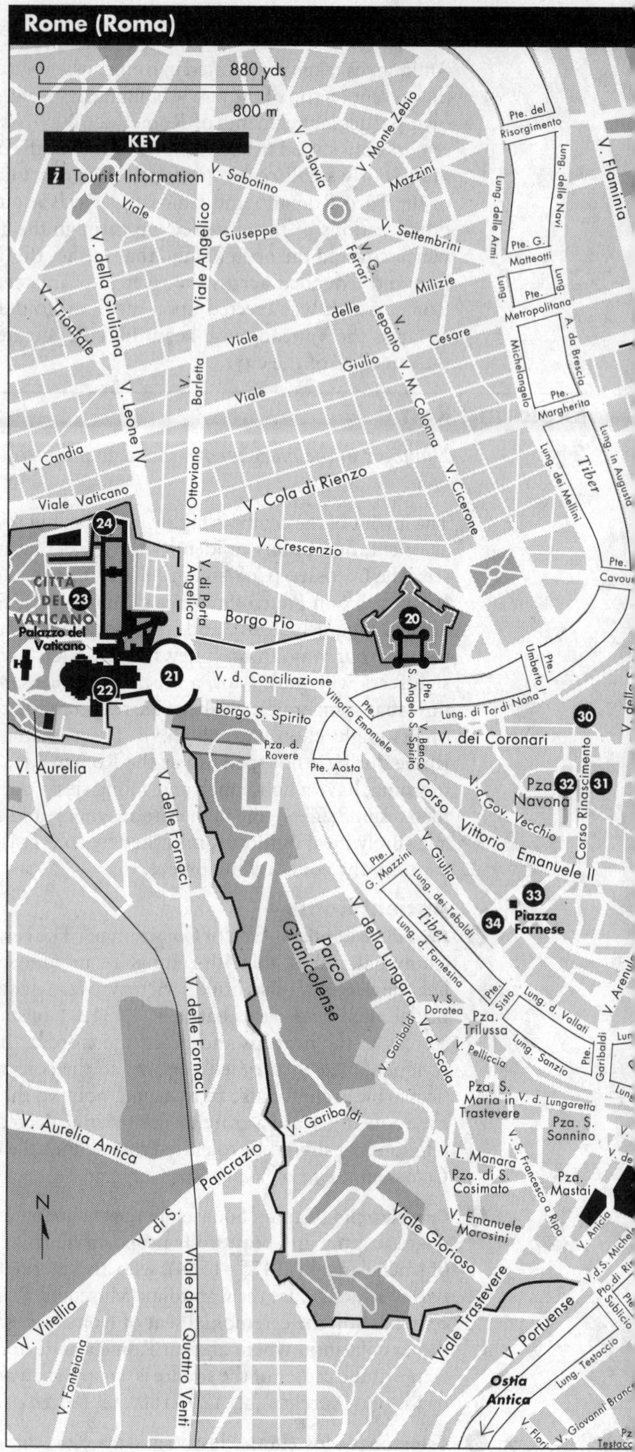

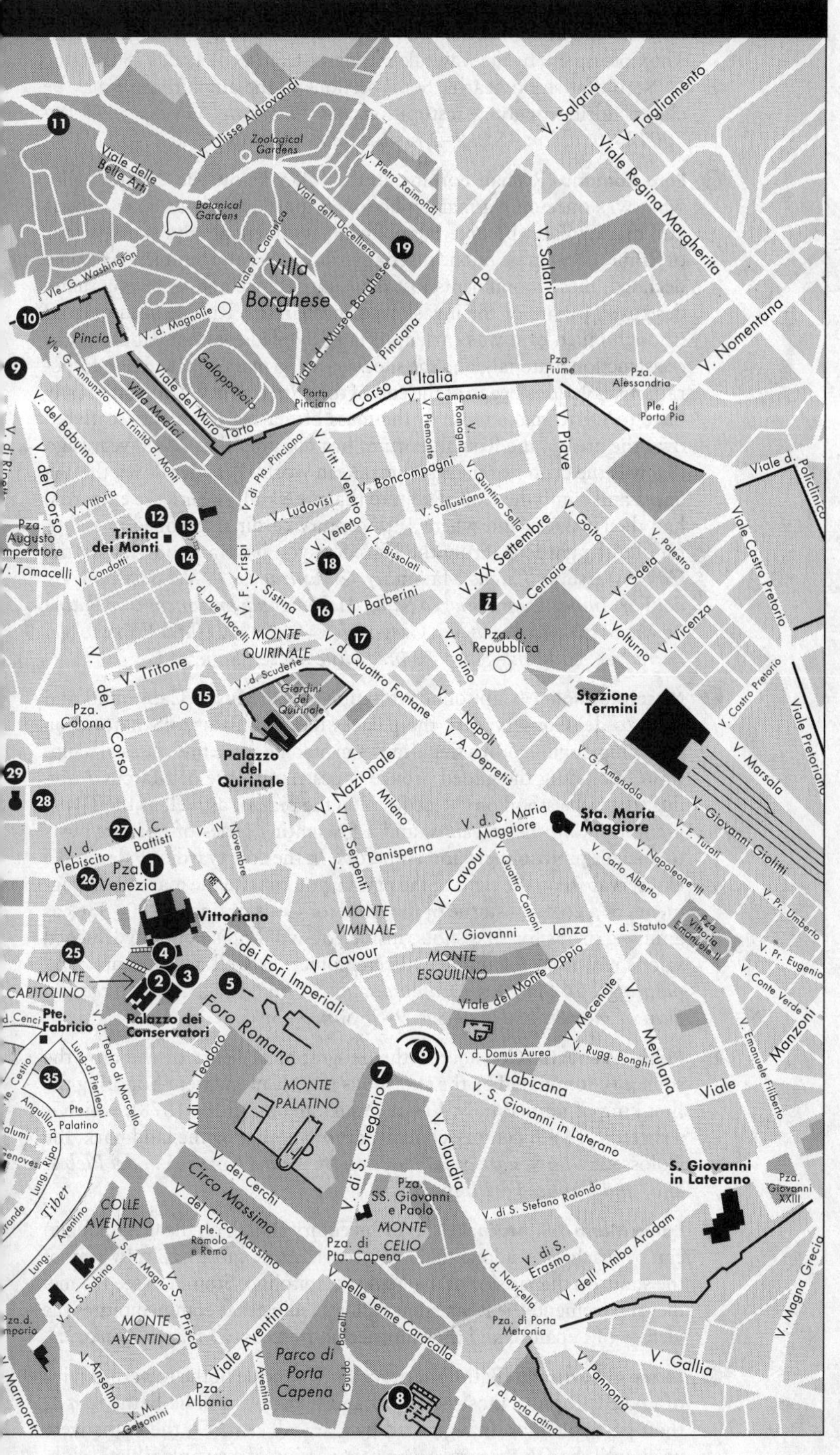

Villa Borghese
Zoological Gardens
Botanical Gardens
V. Ulisse Aldrovandi
Viale delle Belle Arti
Vle. G. Washington
Viale P. Canonica
V. d. Magnolie
Pincio
Vle. G. Annunzio
Villa Medici
Viale del Muro Torto
Galoppatoio
Viale dell' Uccelliera
Viale d. Museo Borghese
V. Pietro Raimondi
V. Pinciana
Porta Pinciana
Corso d'Italia
V. Po
V. Salaria
V. Tagliamento
Viale Regina Margherita
V. Nomentana
Pza. Fiume
Pza. Alessandria
Ple. di Porta Pia
V. Campania
V. Piemonte
V. Romagna
V. Quintino Sella
V. Piave
Viale d. Policlinico
Viale Castro Pretorio
V. di Ripetta
V. del Babuino
V. Trinità d. Monti
V. del Corso
V. Vittoria
Pza. Augusto Imperatore
V. Tomacelli
V. Condotti
Trinita dei Monti
V. di Pta. Pinciana
V. Vitt. Veneto
V. Ludovisi
V. Boncompagni
V. Sallustiana
V. L. Bissolati
V. XX Settembre
V. Goito
V. Palestro
V. Gaeta
V. Cernaia
V. Volturno
V. Vicenza
V. F. Crispi
V. Sistina
V. d. Due Macelli
V. Barberini
MONTE QUIRINALE
V. d. Quattro Fontane
V. Torino
Pza. d. Repubblica
Stazione Termini
V. Castro Pretorio
Viale Pretoriano
V. Marsala
V. Tritone
V. d. Scuderie
Giardini del Quirinale
Pza. Colonna
Palazzo del Quirinale
V. Nazionale
V. Napoli
V. A. Depretis
V. G. Amendola
V. Giovanni Giolitti
V. F. Turati
V. Milano
V. d. Serpenti
V. Panisperna
V. d. S. Maria Maggiore
Sta. Maria Maggiore
V. Carlo Alberto
V. Napoleone III
V. C. Battisti
V. IV Novembre
V. d. Plebiscito
Pza. Venezia
Vittoriano
V. Cavour
V. Quattro Cantoni
MONTE VIMINALE
V. Giovanni Lanza
V. d. Statuto
Pza. Vittorio Emanuele II
V. Pr. Umberto
V. Pr. Eugenio
V. Conte Verde
MONTE CAPITOLINO
V. dei Fori Imperiali
MONTE ESQUILINO
Viale del Monte Oppio
V. Mecenate
V. Merulana
V. Emanuele Filiberto
Viale Manzoni
Palazzo dei Conservatori
Pte. Fabricio
Foro Romano
V. d. Domus Aurea
V. Rugg. Bonghi
V. Labicana
V. S. Giovanni in Laterano
V. Teatro di Marcello
Lung. d. Pierleoni
V. di S. Teodoro
MONTE PALATINO
V. di S. Gregorio
V. Claudia
Pte. Palatino
Lung. Ripa
Tiber
V. dei Cerchi
Circo Massimo
V. del Circo Massimo
Pza. SS. Giovanni e Paolo
MONTE CELIO
S. Giovanni in Laterano
Pza. Giovanni XXIII
V. di S. Stefano Rotondo
V. dell' Amba Aradam
V. di S. Erasmo
V. d. Navicella
COLLE AVENTINO
Lung. Aventino
Ple. Romolo e Remo
Pza. di Pta. Capena
V. delle Terme Caracalla
V. S. A. Magno
V. d. S. Sabina
V. S. Prisca
MONTE AVENTINO
Pza. di Porta Metronia
V. Magna Grecia
V. Gallia
V. Pannonia
Viale Aventino
V. Aventina
Parco di Porta Capena
V. Guido Baccelli
V. d. Porta Latina
V. Anselmo
V. M. Gelsomini
Pza. Albania
V. Marmorata
Pza.d. Emporio
1
2
3
4
5
6
7
8
9
10
11
12
13
14
15
16
17
18
19
25
26
27
28
29
35

an ingenious system of awnings to provide shade. Try to see it both in daytime and at night, when yellow floodlights make it a magical sight. The Colosseum, by the way, takes its name from a colossal, 118-ft statue of Nero that stood nearby. Some sections of the amphitheater may be closed during ongoing restorations. ✉ *Piazza del Colosseo,* ☎ *06/7004261.* ⏲ *Mon.–Sat. 9–2 hrs before sunset, Sun. 9–1.*

5 **Foro Romano** (Roman Forum). In the valley below the Campidoglio, what was once only a marshy hollow important only as a crossroads and marketplace, became the political, commercial, and social center of Rome, containing public meeting halls, shops, and temples. As Rome declined, these monuments lost their importance and were eventually destroyed by fire or the invasions of barbarians. Rubble accumulated (though much of it was carted off later by medieval home builders as construction material), and the site reverted to marshy pastureland; sporadic excavations began at the end of the 19th century. You don't really have to try to make sense of the mass of marble fragments scattered over the area of the Roman Forum. Just consider that 2,000 years ago this was the center of the Mediterranean world. Wander down the **Via Sacra** and climb the **Colle Palatino** (Palatine Hill), where the emperors had their palaces and where 16th-century cardinals strolled in elaborate Italian gardens. From the belvedere you have a good view of the **Circo Massimo** (Circus Maximus). ✉ *Entrances to Via Sacra on Via dei Fori Imperiali and Piazza Santa Maria Nova; entrances to Palatine on Via Sacra and Via di San Gregorio,* ☎ *06/6990110.* *Entry to Via Sacra free.* ⏲ *Mon.–Sat. 9–2 hrs before sunset, Sun. 9–1.*

3 **Musei Capitolini** (Capitoline Museums). The **Museo Capitolino** and **Palazzo dei Conservatori,** the palaces flanking Palazzo Senatorio on the Campidoglio, form a single museum holding some fine classical sculptures, including the gilded bronze equestrian statue of Marcus Aurelius that once stood on the pedestal in the piazza, as well as the *Dying Gaul,* the *Capitoline Venus,* and a fascinating series of portrait busts of ancient philosophers and emperors. In the courtyard of Palazzo dei Conservatori on the right of the piazza, you can use the mammoth fragments of a colossal statue of the emperor Constantine (c.280–336) as amusing props for snapshots. Inside you will find splendidly frescoed salons still used for municipal ceremonies, as well as sculptures and paintings. ✉ *Piazza del Campidoglio,* ☎ *06/67102071.* *Free last Sun. of month.* ⏲ *Tues.–Sat. 9–7, Sun. 9–6:45.*

1 **Piazza Venezia.** Considered the geographical heart of the city, the square is dominated by the enormous marble monument honoring the first king of unified Italy, Victor Emmanuel II (1820–1878), which is a rhetorical 19th-century counterpart of another Rome landmark, the Colosseum. ✉ *Square at intersection of Via del Corso, Via del Plebiscito, and Via del Fori Imperiali.*

4 **Santa Maria dell'Aracoeli.** The 13th-century church on the Campidoglio can be reached by a long flight of steep stairs or, more easily, by way of the stairs on the far side of the Museo Capitolino. Stop in to see the medieval pavement, the Renaissance gilded ceiling that commemorates the victory of Lepanto, and the Pinturicchio frescoes. ✉ *Piazza Aracoeli.*

8 **Terme di Caracalla** (Baths of Caracalla). The scale of the towering ruins of ancient Rome's most beautiful and luxurious public baths hint at their past splendor. Inaugurated by Caracalla in 217, the baths were used until the 6th century. An ancient version of a swank athletic club, the baths were open to all, though men and women used them separately; citizens could bathe, socialize, and exercise in huge pools and richly decorated halls and libraries. ✉ *Via delle Terme di Caracalla.*

⏲ *Apr.–Sept., Tues.–Sat. 9–6, Sun.–Mon. 9–1; Oct.–Mar., Tues.–Sat. 9–3, Sun.–Mon. 9–1.*

Piazzas and Fountains

14 **Fondazione Keats-Shelley Memorial** (Keats and Shelley Memorial House). To the right of the Spanish Steps is the house where Keats (1795–1821) died; the building is now a museum of Keats memorabilia and it also houses a library of works by Romantic authors. ✉ *Piazza di Spagna 26,* ☎ *06/6784235.* ⏲ *June–Sept., weekdays 9–1 and 3–6; Oct.–May, weekdays 9–1 and 2:30–5:30.*

★ 15 **Fontana di Trevi** (Trevi Fountain). A spectacular fantasy of mythical sea creatures and cascades of splashing water, this fountain is one of Rome's Baroque greats. The fountain as you see it was completed in the mid-1700s, but there had been a drinking fountain on the site for centuries. Pope Urban VIII almost sparked a revolt when he slapped a tax on wine to cover the expenses of having the fountain repaired. Legend has it that visitors must toss a coin into the fountain to ensure their return to Rome. ✉ *Piazza di Trevi.*

19 **Galleria Borghese** (Borghese Gallery). At the northeast corner of Villa Borghese, a park studded with pines and classical statuary, is this gallery created by Cardinal Scipione Borghese in 1613 as a showcase for his fabulous collection of ancient sculpture. One of the noteworthy additions to the collections over the centuries, the reclining statue of Pauline Borghese by Canova continues to seduce visitors. Among some extraordinary works by Bernini (1598–1680), the unforgettable *Apollo and Daphne* shows how the artist transformed marble into flesh and foliage. The picture collection is no less impressive, with works by Caravaggio (1573–1610), Raphael (1483–1520), and Titian (c.1488–1576). ✉ *Piazzale Scipione Borghese, Villa Borghese,* ☎ *06/8548577. Reservations essential.* ☎ *06/84241607.* ⏲ *Tues.–Sat. 9–7, Sun. 9–1.*

11 **Museo Etrusco di Villa Giulia** (Etruscan Museum of Villa Giulia). Pope Julius III built this gracious Renaissance villa as a summer retreat. It now holds a world-class museum where you can delve into the world of the Etruscans, who inhabited Italy in pre-Roman times and have left fascinating evidence of their relaxed, sensual lifestyle. You'll observe smiles as enigmatic as that of the Mona Lisa on deities and other figures in terra-cotta, bronze, and gold. Ask especially to see the Castellani collection of ancient jewelry (and copies) hidden away on the upper floor. And see the full-scale replica of an Etruscan temple in the garden. ✉ *Piazza di Villa Giulia 9,* ☎ *06/3201951.* ⏲ *Tues.–Sat. 9–7, Sun. 9–2.*

17 **Palazzo Barberini** (Barberini Palace). Rome's most splendid 17th-century palace houses the **Galleria Nazionale di Arte Antica.** Its gems include Raphael's *Fornarina* and many other fine paintings, some lavishly frescoed ceilings, and a charming suite of rooms decorated in 1782 on the occasion of the marriage of a Barberini heiress. ✉ *Via delle Quattro Fontane 13,* ☎ *06/4814591.* ⏲ *Tues.–Sat. 9–7, Sun. 9–1.*

16 **Piazza Barberini.** This busy crossroads has two fountains by Bernini: the jaunty **Fontana del Tritone** (Triton) in the middle of the square and the **Fontana delle Api** (Bees) at the corner of Via Veneto. Decorated with the heraldic Barberini bees, this latter shell-shape fountain bears an inscription that was immediately regarded as an unlucky omen by the superstitious Romans, for it erroneously stated that the fountain had been erected in the 22nd year of the reign of Pope Urban VIII, who commissioned it, whereas in fact the 21st anniversary of his election was still some weeks away. The wrong numeral was hurriedly erased, but to no avail: Urban died eight days before the beginning of his 22nd

year as pontiff. ⊠ *Square at intersection of Via del Tritone, Via Vittorio Veneto, and Via Barberini.*

9 **Piazza del Popolo.** Designed by neoclassic architect Giuseppe Valadier in the early 1800s, this square is one of the largest and airiest in Rome. The 3,000-year-old obelisk in the middle was brought to Rome from Egypt by the emperor Augustus, and it once stood in the Circus Maximus. ⊠ *Square at southern end of Via Flaminia and northern end of Via del Corso.*

12 **Piazza di Spagna** (Spanish Square). The square is the heart of Rome's chic shopping district and a popular rendezvous spot, especially for the young people who throng the Spanish Steps on evenings and weekend afternoons. In the center of the elongated square, at the foot of the Spanish Steps, is Bernini's Fontana della Barcaccia (Old Boat), around which passersby cool themselves on hot summer nights. ⊠ *Southern end of Via del Babuino and northern end of Via Due Macelli.*

18 **Santa Maria della Concezione.** In the crypt under the main Capuchin church skeletons and scattered bones of some 4,000 dead Capuchin monks are arranged in odd decorative designs, a macabre practice peculiar to the Baroque age. ⊠ *Via Veneto 27,* ☎ *06/462850.* 🎫 *Free (donations encouraged).* ⏲ *Daily 9–noon and 3–6.*

10 **Santa Maria del Popolo.** This medieval church rebuilt by Bernini in Baroque style is rich in art; the pièces de résistance: two stunning Caravaggios in the chapel to the left of the main altar. You'll find it tucked away in the corner of Piazza del Popolo next to the monumental Renaissance city gate. ⊠ *Piazza del Popolo.*

★ 13 **Scalinata di Piazza di Spagna** (Spanish Steps). The 200-year-old staircase got its name from the Spanish Embassy to the Holy See (the Vatican), though the staircase was built with French funds in 1723, as the approach to the French church of **Trinità dei Monti** at the top of the steps. The steps are banked with blooming azaleas from mid-April to mid-May. ⊠ *Piazza di Spagna and Piazza Trinità dei Monti.*

Castel Sant'Angelo and the Vatican

★ 22 **Basilica di San Pietro** (St. Peter's Basilica). In all of its staggering grandeur and magnificence, St. Peter's Basilica is best appreciated as the lustrous background for ecclesiastical ceremonies thronged with the faithful. The original basilica was built during the early 4th century AD by the emperor Constantine, above an earlier shrine that supposedly marked the burial place of St. Peter. After more than a thousand years, the old basilica was so decrepit it had to be torn down. The task of building a new, much larger one took almost 200 years, and employed the architectural geniuses of Alberti (1404–72), Bramante (1444–1514), Raphael, Peruzzi, Antonio Sangallo the Younger (1483–1546), and Michelangelo, who died before the dome he had planned could be completed. The structure was finally finished in 1626.

Among the most famous works of art is Michelangelo's *Pietà* (1498), seen in the first chapel on the right just as you enter the basilica. Michelangelo carved four statues of the Pietà; this one is the earliest and best known, two others are in Florence, and the fourth, the *Rondanini Pietà,* is in Milan. At the end of the central aisle is the bronze statue of St. Peter, its foot worn by centuries of reverent kisses. The bronze throne above the altar in the apse was created by Bernini to contain a simple wood-and-ivory chair once believed to have belonged to St. Peter. Bernini's bronze baldachin over the papal altar was made with metal stripped from the portico of the Pantheon at the order of Pope Urban VIII, one of the powerful Roman Barberini family. His practice of plundering ancient monuments for material with which to carry out his grandiose schemes inspired the famous quip, "*Quod non fecerunt barbari, fecerunt Barberini*" ("What the barbarians didn't do, the Barberini did").

As you stroll up and down the aisles and transepts, observe the fine mosaic copies of famous paintings above the altars, the monumental tombs and statues, and the fine stucco work. Stop at the **Treasury** (Historical Museum), which contains some priceless liturgical objects. ✉ *Historical Museum entrance in the Sacristy .* ⏲ *Apr.–Sept., daily 9–6:30; Oct.–Mar., daily 9–5:30.*

The entrance to the so-called **Grotte Vaticane** (Vatican Grottoes), crypts containing chapels and the tombs of various popes, is in one of the huge piers at the crossing. It's best to leave this visit for last, as the crypt's only exit takes you outside the church. It occupies the area of the original basilica, over the necropolis, the ancient burial ground where evidence of what may be St. Peter's burial place has been found. ✉ *Vatican Grottoes entrance at piers at the crossing.* 🎫 *Free.* ⏲ *Apr.–Sept., daily 7–6; Oct.–Mar., daily 7–5.*

To see the roof and dome of the basilica, take the elevator or climb the stairs in the courtyard near the exit from the Vatican Grottoes. From the roof you can climb a short interior staircase to the base of the dome for an overhead view of the basilica's interior. Then, only if you are in good shape should you attempt the very long, strenuous, and claustrophobic climb up the narrow stairs to the balcony of the lantern atop the dome, where you can look down on the Vatican Gardens and out across all of Rome.✉ *Entrance in courtyard to the left as you leave the basilica.* ⏲ *Apr.–Sept., daily 8–6; Oct.–Mar., daily 8–5.*

Free 60-minute tours of St. Peter's Basilica are offered in English daily (usually starting about 10 AM and 3 PM, and at 2:30 PM Sun.) by volunteer guides. They start at the information desk under the basilica portico. At the Ufficio Scavi (☞ *below*) you can book special tours of the necropolis. Note that entry to St. Peter's, the Vatican Museums, and the Gardens is barred to those wearing shorts, miniskirts, sleeveless T-shirts, and otherwise revealing clothing. Women can cover bare shoulders and upper arms with scarves; men should wear full-length pants or jeans. ✉ *Piazza San Pietro,* ☎ *06/69884466.* ⏲ *Apr.–Sept., daily 7–7; Oct.–Mar., daily 7–6. Necropolis (left beyond Arco delle Campane entrance to Vatican),* ☎ *06/69885318. Apply a few days in advance to Ufficio Scavi, or try in morning for the same day. Office hrs Mon.–Sat. 9–5; closed Sun.*

20 **Castel Sant'Angelo** (Sant'Angelo Castle). Transformed into a formidable fortress, this castle was originally built as the tomb of Emperor Hadrian (AD 76–138) in the 2nd century AD. In its early days it looked much like the Augusteo (Tomb of Augustus), which still stands in more or less its original form across the river. Hadrian's Tomb was incorporated into the city's walls and served as a military stronghold during the barbarian invasions. According to legend it got its present name in the 6th century, when Pope Gregory the Great, passing by in a religious procession, saw an angel with a sword appear above the ramparts to signal the end of the plague that was raging. Enlarged and fortified, the castle became a refuge for the popes, who fled to it along the Passetto, an arcaded passageway that links it with the Vatican.

Inside the castle you see ancient corridors, medieval cells, and Renaissance salons, a museum of antique weapons, courtyards piled with stone cannonballs, and terraces with great views of the city. There's a pleasant bar with outdoor tables. The highest terrace of all, under the bronze statue of the legendary angel, is the one from which Puccini's heroine Tosca threw herself to her death. **Ponte Sant'Angelo,** the ancient bridge spanning the Tiber in front of the castle, is decorated with lovely Baroque angels designed by Bernini. ✉ *Lungotevere Castello 50,* ☎ *06/68300183.* ⏲ *Daily 9–7. Closed 2nd and 4th Tues. of month.*

23 **Giardini Vaticani** (Vatican Gardens). The attractively landscaped gardens can be seen in a two-hour tour that shows you a few historical monuments, fountains, and the lovely 16th-century house of Pius IV designed by Pirro Ligorio, as well as the Vatican's mosaic school. Vistas from within the gardens give you a different perspective of the basilica itself. Tickets: ✉ *Information office, on left side of St. Peter's Square,* ☎ *06/69884466.* ⏲ *Mon.–Sat. 8:30–7. Garden tour:* 🎫 *16,000 lire.* ⏲ *Mon., Tues., and Thurs.–Sat. 10 AM.*

24 **Musei Vaticani** (Vatican Museums). The accumulated collections of humanity's artistic history are housed here, from the Egyptians to the present, boasting such masterpieces as Michelangelo's frescoes in the Sistine Chapel. The collections cover nearly 8 km (5 mi) of displays, so if you are visiting St. Peter's and the museums on the same day, save yourself the 15-minute walk between the two by taking the shuttle bus (2,000 lire) that operates during museum opening hours, except on Wednesday. The ride gives you a glimpse of the Giardini Vaticani (☞ *above*). Posters at the museum entrance plot out a choice of four color-coded itineraries; the shortest takes about 90 minutes, the longest more than four hours, depending on your rate of progress. No matter ★ which tour you take, it will include the famed **Cappella Sistina** (Sistine Chapel). In 1508 Pope Julius II commissioned Michelangelo to paint the more than 10,000 square ft of the chapel's ceiling. For four years Michelangelo dedicated himself to painting in the fresco technique, over fresh plaster, and the result was a masterpiece. Cleaning has removed centuries of soot and revealed the original and surprisingly brilliant colors of the ceiling and the *Last Judgment.* You can try to avoid the tour groups by going early or late, allowing yourself enough time before the closing hour. In peak season the crowds definitely detract from your appreciation of this outstanding artistic achievement. To make sense of the figures on the ceiling, buy an illustrated guide or rent an audio guide. A pair of binoculars also helps.

Some of the highlights that might be of interest on your first tour are the reorganized Egyptian collection and the *Laocoön,* the *Belvedere Torso,* which inspired Michelangelo, and the *Apollo Belvedere.* The Raphael Rooms are decorated with masterful frescoes, and there are more of Raphael's works in the *Pinacoteca* (Picture Gallery). At the Quattro Cancelli, near the entrance to the Picture Gallery, a rather spartan cafeteria provides basic refreshments. ✉ *Viale Vaticano,* ☎ *06/69883041.* 🎫 *Free last Sun. of the month.* ⏲ *Easter wk and mid-Mar.–Oct., weekdays 8:45–3:45, Sat. 8:45–12:45; Nov.–mid-Mar., Mon.–Sat. 8:45–12:45. Last Sun. of the month 8:45–12:45. Closed Sun., except last Sun. of the month.*

21 **Piazza San Pietro** (St. Peter's Square). Completed in 1667, the vast, oval-shape square in front of St. Peter's basilica opens at the western end of Via della Conciliazione, the broad avenue created by Mussolini's architects by razing blocks of old houses. This opened up a vista of the basilica, giving the eye time to adjust to its mammoth dimensions, and thereby spoiling the effect Bernini sought. He enclosed his huge square in the embrace of mammoth quadruple colonnades. Look for the stone disks in the pavement halfway between the fountains and the obelisk. From these points the colonnades seem to be formed of a single row of columns all the way around. The square was designed to

accommodate crowds, and it has held up to 400,000 people at one time. At noon on Sunday when he is in Rome, the pope appears at his third-floor study window in the **Palazzo Vaticano,** to the right of the basilica, to bless the crowd in the square.

Since the Lateran Treaty of 1929, Vatican City has been an independent and sovereign state, which covers about 108 acres and is surrounded by thick, high walls. Its gates are watched over by the Swiss Guards, who still wear the colorful dress uniforms designed by Michelangelo. Sovereign of this little state is John Paul II, 264th pope of the Roman Catholic Church. For many visitors a **papal audience** is the highlight of a trip to Rome. Mass audiences take place on Wednesday morning in a modern audience hall (capacity 7,000) off the left-hand colonnade or in St. Peter's Square. Tickets are necessary, but you can also see the Pope when he appears at the window of the Vatican Palace to bless the crowd in the square below at noon on Sunday. He also blesses the public on summer Sundays when he's at the papal residence at Castel Gandolfo (☞ Guided Tours *in* Rome Essentials, *below*). For audience tickets write or fax well in advance indicating the date you prefer, language you speak, and hotel in which you will stay. Or, apply for tickets in person on the Monday or Tuesday before the Wednesday audience. ✉ *Prefettura della Casa Pontificia, 00120 Vatican City,* ☎ *06/69883017,* FAX *06/69885863.* ⏲ *Mon. and Tues. 9–1.*

Old Rome

33 **Campo dei Fiori** (Field of Flowers). This square is the site of a crowded and colorful daily morning market. The hooded bronze figure brooding over the piazza is philosopher Giordano Bruno, who was burned at the stake here for heresy. ✉ *Piazza Campo dei Fiori.*

26 **Chiesa del Gesù.** This huge 16th-century church is a paragon of the Baroque style and the tangible symbol of the power of the Jesuits, who were a major force in the Counter-Reformation in Europe. Its interior gleams with gold and precious marbles, and it has a fantastically painted ceiling that flows down over the pillars, merging with painted stucco figures to complete the three-dimensional illusion. ✉ *Piazza del Gesù.*

25 **Fontana delle Tartarughe** (Turtles). This pretty 16th-century bronze fountain by Giacomo della Porta (the turtles were added probably by Bernini in 1658) is in the heart of Rome's former Jewish Ghetto, a neighborhood with medieval inscriptions and friezes on the old buildings on Via Portico d'Ottavia, and the remains of the Teatro di Marcello (Theater of Marcello), a theater built by Julius Caesar to hold 20,000 spectators. ✉ *Piazza Mattei.*

27 **Galleria Doria Pamphili.** You can visit this rambling palazzo, still the residence of a princely family, to view the gallery housing the family's art collection and also some of the magnificently furnished private apartments. ✉ *Piazza del Collegio Romano 2, near Piazza Venezia,* ☎ *06/6797323.* ⏲ *Fri.–Wed. 10–5; guided tours of private apartments mornings only.*

35 **Isola Tiberina** (Tiberina Island). Built in 62 BC, Rome's oldest bridge, the **Ponte Fabricio,** links the Ghetto neighborhood on the Tiber's left bank to this little island, home to the city hospital and the church of San Bartolomeo. The island has been dedicated to healing ever since a temple to Aesculapius was erected here in 291 BC. **Ponte Cestio** links the island with the Trastevere section on the right bank.

OFF THE BEATEN PATH

Ostia Antica – (Ancient Ostia). The well-preserved Roman port city of Ostia Antica, near the sea, is a parklike archaeological site analogous with Pompeii and much easier to get to from Rome. There's a regular train service from the Ostiense Station (Piramide Metro stop). ✉ *Via dei Romagnoli, Ostia Antica,* ☎ *06/5651405.* ⊙ *Daily 9–1 hr before sunset.*

30 **Palazzo Altemps.** A 15th-century patrician dwelling, the palace has been beautifully restored and is now a showcase for the sculpture collection of the Museo Nazionale Romano. Informative labels in English make it easy to appreciate such famous sculptures as the amazingly intricate carved reliefs on the *Ludovisi Sarcophagus* and the *Galata,* representing the heroic death of a barbarian warrior. ✉ *Piazza Sant'Apollinare 46,* ☎ *06/6833759.* ⊙ *Tues.–Sun. 10–5.*

34 **Palazzo Farnese.** Now the French Embassy, one of the most beautiful of Rome's many Renaissance palaces dominates Piazza Farnese, where Egyptian marble basins from the Terme di Caracalla have been transformed into fountains. ✉ *Piazza Farnese.*

29 **Pantheon.** Originally built in 27 BC by Augustus's general Agrippa and totally rebuilt by Hadrian in the 2nd century AD, this is one of Rome's finest, best-preserved, and perhaps least appreciated ancient monuments. You don't have to look far past the huge columns of the portico and the original bronze doors to find the reason for its astounding architectural harmony: the diameter of the soaring dome is exactly equal to the height of the walls. The hole in the ceiling is intentional: the oculus at the apex of the dome signifies the "all-seeing eye of heaven." In ancient times the entire interior was encrusted with rich decorations of gilt bronze and marble that were plundered by later emperors and popes. ✉ *Piazza della Rotonda.* ⊙ *Mon.–Sat. 9–6:30, Sun. 9–1.*

★ 32 **Piazza Navona.** This elongated 17th-century piazza traces the oval form of the underlying Circus of Diocletian. At the center Bernini's lively **Fontana dei Quattro Fiumi** (Four Rivers) is a showpiece. The four statues represent rivers in the four corners of the world: the Nile, with its face covered in allusion to its then unknown source; the Ganges; the Danube; and the River Plate, with its hand raised. And here we have to give the lie to the legend that this was Bernini's mischievous dig at Borromini's design of the facade of the church of **Sant'Agnese in Agone,** from which the statue seems to be shrinking in horror. The fountain was created in 1651; work on the church's facade began a year or two later. The piazza dozes in the morning, when little groups of pensioners sun themselves on the stone benches and children pedal tricycles around the big fountain. In the late afternoon the sidewalk cafés fill up for the aperitif hour, and in the evening, especially in good weather, the piazza comes to life with a throng of street artists, vendors, tourists, and Romans out for their evening *passeggiata* (promenade). ✉ *North of Corso Vittorio Emanuele and west of Corso Rinascimento.*

31 **San Luigi dei Francesi.** The clergy of San Luigi considered Caravaggio's roistering and unruly lifestyle scandalous enough, but his realistic treatment of sacred subjects—seen in three paintings in the last chapel—was just too much for them. They rejected his first version of the altarpiece and weren't particularly happy with the other two works either. Thanks to the intercession of Caravaggio's patron, an influential cardinal, they were persuaded to keep them—a lucky thing, since they are now recognized to be among the artist's finest paintings. Have a few hundred-lire coins handy for the light machine. ✉ *Via della Dogana Vecchia.* ⊙ *Fri.–Wed. 7:30–12:30 and 3:30–7, Thurs. 7:30–12:30.*

28 **Santa Maria sopra Minerva.** Rome's only major Gothic church takes its name from the temple of Minerva over which it was built. Inside there are some beautiful frescoes by Filippo Lippi (1457–1504); out-

side there is a charming elephant by Bernini with an obelisk on its back. ✉ *Piazza della Minerva.*

Dining and Lodging

There is an abundance of restaurants in Rome, generally serving various Italian regional cuisines. The most expensive restaurants usually offer interpretations of Italian and international specialties with a flourish of linen and silver, followed up by a whopping *conto* (check). If you want typical Italian cooking and lower prices, try a more moderately priced ristorante or a trattoria, usually a smallish and unassuming, often family-run place. Fast-food places, many with Italian fare, and Chinese restaurants are proliferating in Rome. During August many restaurants close for vacation. For details and price-category information, *see* Dining *in* Italy A to Z, *above*.

Hotels listed are within walking distance of at least some sights and handy to public transportation. Those in the $$ and $ categories do not have restaurants but serve Continental breakfast. Rooms facing the street may get traffic noise throughout the night, and few hotels in the lower price categories have double-glazed windows. Ask for a quiet room—or bring earplugs. Always make reservations, even if only a few days in advance, by phone or fax. Always inquire about special low rates. Should you find yourself in the city without reservations, however, contact **HR** (✉ Termini Station; Aeroporto Fiumicino, ☎ 06/6991000), a hotel reservation service, or **EPT** (✉ Via Parigi 5, ☎ 06/48899253, FAX 06/4819316; ✉ Near Piazza della Repubblica; Aeroporto Fiumicino, ☎ 06/65956074; ✉ Stazione Termini, ☎ 06/4871270). The Rome municipal tourist information booths will also help you find a room (☞ Visitor Information *in* Rome Essentials, *below*). For details and price-category definitions, *see* Lodging *in* Italy A to Z, *above*.

$$$$ ★ ✕ **La Pergola.** High atop Monte Mario, the Cavalieri Hiltonís (☞ *below*) rooftop restaurant commands sweeping views onto the city below. The warmly elegant dining room has trompe l'oeil ceilings, handsome wood paneling, and large windows. Celebrated Wunder-chef Heinz Beck is a skilled technician, and brings Rome its finest example of Mediterranean *alta cucina* (haute cuisine). ✉ *Cavalieri Hilton, Via Cadlolo 101,* ☎ *06/3509221. Reservations essential. Jacket and tie. AE, DC, MC, V. Closed Sun.–Mon. No lunch.*

$$$$ ★ ✕ **La Rosetta.** In 1992 chef-owner Massimo Riccioli took the nets and fishing gear off the classic cherry-wood walls of his parents' trattoria to create what is widely known as the place to go in Rome to eat first-rate fish. Start with *ricci di mare* (sea urchins), *vongole veraci* (sautéed clams), or a variety of delicately marinated fish; move on to perfectly grilled seafood or a poached fillet. Desserts (made in house) are worth saving room for. ✉ *Via della Rosetta 9,* ☎ *06/6861002. Dinner reservations essential. AE, DC, MC, V.*

$$$ ✕ **Checchino dal 1887.** Literally carved out of a hillside made of potsherds from Roman times, Checchino serves the most traditional Roman cuisine—carefully prepared and served without fanfare—in a clean, sober environment. The slaughterhouses of the Testaccio quarter are long gone, but you can still try the variety of meats that make up the soul of Roman cooking, including *trippa* (tripe), and *coratella* (sweetbreads). There's also plenty to choose from for those uninterested in innards. Desserts are very good. ✉ *Via di Monte Testaccio 30,* ☎ *06/5746318. AE, DC, MC, V. Closed Mon., Aug., and during Christmas. No dinner Sun.*

$$$ ✕ **Da Checco er Carettiere.** Maybe this is what all Italian restaurants once looked like: an aging doorman, garlic braids hanging from the ceiling, black-and-white photos in small frames lining the wood-paneled walls. At this third-generation, family-run Trastevere institution you'll find all the Roman standards, solidly prepared with good-quality ingredients, plus plenty of local vegetables and an unusually good selection of fish. ✉ *Via Benedetta 10,* ☎ *06/5817018. AE, DC, MC, V. Closed Mon. No dinner Sun.*

$$–$$$ ✕ **Dal Bolognese.** This classic restaurant is a trendy choice for a leisurely lunch between sightseeing and shopping. An array of contemporary paintings decorate the dining room but the real attraction is the lovely piazza—prime people-watching real estate. As the name of the restaurant promises, the cooking here adheres to the hearty tradition of Bologna, with delicious homemade *tortellini in brodo* (filled pasta in broth), fresh pastas in creamy sauces, and *bollito misto* (steaming trays of boiled meats). ✉ *Piazza del Popolo 1,* ☎ *06/3611426. AE, MC, V. Closed Mon. and Aug.*

$$ ✕ **Colline Emiliane.** Behind an opaque glass facade not far from Piazza Barberini are a couple of plain dining rooms, where you are served light homemade pastas, *tortelli di zucca* (pumpkin-filled ravioli), and meats ranging from *giambonetto di vitello*(roast veal) to *cotoletta alla bolognese* (fried veal cutlet with cheese and prosciutto). Family-run, it's quiet and soothing. ✉ *Via San Nicolò da Tolentino 26,* ☎ *06/4818564. Reservations essential. AE, DC, MC, V. Closed Sun. and Aug.*

$$ ✕ **Il Cardinale.** This serene little restaurant turns out fanciful, lightened-up Roman fare, beautifully presented on king-size plates. Oil paintings and enlarged old photos of Roman landmarks are hung against golden damask wall coverings, and chairs and couches are covered in a pretty floral print. The menu speaks of composed salads, vegetable soups, and such pastas as *vermicelli cacio e pepe* (pasta with pecorino cheese and black pepper) or *ravioli di borragine* (ravioli filled with borage leaves), and various vegetable *sformati* (flans). ✉ *Via delle Carceri 6,* ☎ *06/6869336. AE, DC, MC, V. Closed Sun.*

$$ ★ ✕ **Myosotis.** Myosotis is the sequel to a successful restaurant on the outskirts of town run by the Marsilis. The menu rides that delicate line between tradition and innovation, focusing more on the freshness and quality of the ingredients than on elaborate presentation. Fresh pasta gets special attention: it's rolled out by hand to order for the *stracci alla delizia di mare* (pasta with seafood). There's a wide choice of fish, meat, and seasonal veggies to choose from. ✉ *Via della Vaccarella 3/5,* ☎ *06/2053943. Closed Mon. and 2 wks in Aug. AE, DC, MC, V.*

$$ ✕ **Papá Baccus.** Italo Cipriani, owner of Rome's best Tuscan restaurant, takes his meat as seriously as any Tuscan, using real Chianina beef for the house special, *bistecca alla fiorentina* (grilled, thick bone-in steak). Cipriani brings many ingredients from his home town in northern Tuscany. Try the sweet and delicate prosciutto from Pratomagno. The welcome here is warm, the service excellent. ✉ *Via Toscana 36,* ☎ *06/42742808. AE, DC, MC, V. Closed Sun., 2 wks in Aug., and during Christmas. No lunch Sat.*

$–$$ ★ ✕ **Antico Arco.** Run by three friends with a passion for wine and fine food, the Antico Arco has quickly won the hearts of Roman foodies with great invention and moderate prices. Particularly good are such starters as *sformato di finocchi in salsa d'arancia* (fennel flan with orange sauce) and such second courses as *petto d'anatra con salsa di lamponi* (duck breast with raspberry sauce). Don't miss dessert. ✉ *Piazzale Aurelio 7,* ☎ *06/5815274. Closed Mon. No lunch Tues.–Sat. AE, DC, MC, V.*

$ ★ ✕ **Dal Toscano.** The hallmarks of this great family-run Tuscan trattoria near the Vatican are friendly and speedy service, an open wood-fired grill, and such classic dishes as *ribollita* (a dense bread and vegetable soup), and the prized bistecca alla fiorentina. Wash it all down with a strong Chianti. All desserts are yummy and homemade. ✉ *Via Germanico 58,* ☎ *06/39725717. DC, MC, V. Closed Mon., Aug., and 2 wks in Dec.*

$ ✕ **Dar Poeta.** Romans drive across town for great pizza from this neighborhood joint in Trastevere. Maybe it's the dough—it's made from a secret blend of flours reputed to be easier to digest than the crust of the competition. For dessert try the unusual calzone with Nutella and ricotta. ✉ *Vicolo del Bologna 45,* ☎ *06/5880516. Reservations not accepted. AE, MC, V. Closed Mon. No lunch.*

$ ✕ **Il Simposio di Costantini.** At the classiest wine bar in town—wrapped in wrought-iron vines, wood paneling, and velvet—choose from about 30 wines in *degustazione* (available by the glass) or order a bottle from a list of over a thousand Italian and foreign labels sold in the shop next door. Food is appropriately fancy: marinated and smoked fish, composed salads, fine salami and cured meats (classical and wild), terrines and pâtes, and stellar cheeses. ✉ *Via Appia Antica 139,* ☎ *06/7880494. AE, MC, V. Closed Thurs.*

$ ✕ **L'Osteria dell'Ingegno.** This trendy *enoteca* (wine bar), infused with a hip modern decor and happening groove, seems almost out of place among the ruins of the old town. The short menu—a sampling of simple dishes that emphasize fine ingredients—changes weekly. Service is fast. ✉ *Piazza di Pietra 45,* ☎ *06/6780662. AE, D, MC, V. Closed Sun.*

$ ✕ **Perilli.** A bastion of authentic Roman cooking and trattoria charm since 1911 (the decor has changed very little), this is the place to go to try *rigatoni con pajata* (rigatoni with baby veal's intestines)—if you're into that sort of thing. Otherwise the carbonara and *all'amatriciana* (spicy tomato sauce with pancetta) are classics. The house wine is a golden nectar from the Castelli Romani. ✉ *Via Marmorata 39,* ☎ *06/5742415. No credit cards. Closed Wed.*

$$$$ 🏨 **Cavalieri Hilton.** Though it is outside the main part of Rome and a taxi or courtesy shuttle-bus ride to wherever you are going, this is a large, comfortable, elegant hotel, fresh from a stylish renovation and set in its own park, with two excellent restaurants. ✉ *Via Cadlolo 101, 00136,* ☎ *06/35091,* FAX *06/35092241. 358 rooms, 18 suites. 2 restaurants, pool. AE, DC, MC, V.*

$$$$ ★ 🏨 **Eden.** Under the aegis of the Forte hotel group, the historic Eden, a haunt of Hemingway, Ingrid Bergman, and Fellini, merits superlatives for dashing elegance and stunning vistas of Rome from the rooftop restaurant and bar (also from some of the most expensive rooms). Precious but discreet antique furnishings, sensuous Italian fabrics, fine linen sheets, and marble baths whisper understated opulence. ✉ *Via Ludovisi 49, 00187,* ☎ *06/478121,* FAX *06/4821584. 101 rooms, 11 suites. Restaurant. AE, DC, MC, V.*

$$$$ 🏨 **Hassler.** You can expect a cordial atmosphere and superb service at this hotel at the top of the Spanish Steps. The public rooms have an extravagant, somewhat dated decor, especially the clubby winter bar, garden bar, and the glass-roofed lounge, with gold marble walls and hand-painted tile floors. Elegant bedrooms are decorated in a variety of classic styles (the best feature frescoed walls). ✉ *Piazza Trinità dei Monti 6, 00187,* ☎ *06/699340,* FAX *06/6789991. 85 rooms, 15 suites. Restaurant. AE, MC, V.*

$$$ 🏨 **Dei Borgognoni.** This quietly chic hotel near Piazza Colonna is as central as you could want, yet the winding byway stage set gives you a sense of being off the beaten track. The centuries-old building provides spacious lounges, a glassed-in garden, and rooms well arranged to create an illusion of space, though they are actually compact. The hotel has a garage (fee), a rarity in such a central location. ✉ *Via del Bufalo 126, 00187,* ☎ *06/69941505,* FAX *06/69941501. 50 rooms. AE, DC, MC, V.*

$$$ ★ **Farnese.** A turn-of-the-century mansion, the Farnese is in a quiet but central residential district. Furnished in art deco style, with enchanting fresco decorations, it has compact rooms, plenty of lounge space, and a roof garden. ✉ *Via Alessandro Farnese 30, 00184,* ☎ *06/3212553,* FAX *06/3215129. 21 rooms, 2 suites. AE, DC, MC, V.*

$$ ★ **Britannia.** A quiet locale off Via Nazionale is only one of the attractions of this small and special hotel, where you will be coddled with luxury touches such as English-language dailies and local weather reports delivered to your room each morning. The well-furnished rooms (two with a rooftop terrace), frescoed halls, and lounge (where a rich breakfast buffet is served) attest the management really cares about superior service and value. ✉ *Via Napoli 64, 00184,* ☎ *06/4883153,* FAX *06/4882343. 33 rooms, 1 suite. AE, DC, MC, V.*

$$ **D'Este.** Within hailing distance of Santa Maria Maggiore and close to Termini Station, the hotel occupies a roomy 19th-century building. The fresh, pleasing decor evokes turn-of-the-century comfort with brass bedsteads and lamps and walnut furniture. Rooms are quiet, light, and spacious; many can be adapted to suit families. The attentive owner-manager sometimes offers special rates, particularly during the slack summer months. ✉ *Via Carlo Alberto 4/b, 00185,* ☎ *06/4465607,* FAX *06/4465601. 37 rooms. AE, DC, MC, V.*

$$ **La Residenza.** A converted town house near Via Veneto, this hotel offers good value and first-class comfort at reasonable rates. Public areas are spacious and furnished nicely and have a private-home atmosphere. Guest rooms are comfortable and have large closets and TVS. The hotel's clientele is mainly American, and rates include a generous buffet breakfast. ✉ *Via Emilia 22, 00187,* ☎ *06/4880789,* FAX *06/485721. 21 rooms, 7 suites. AE, MC, V.*

$$ **Scalinata di Spagna.** An old-fashioned pensione loved by generations of romantics, this tiny hotel is booked solid for months ahead. Its location at the top of the Spanish Steps, inconspicuous little entrance, quaint hodgepodge of old furniture, and view from the terrace where you breakfast make it seem like your own special, exclusive inn. ✉ *Piazza Trinità dei Monti 17, 00187,* ☎ *06/6793006,* FAX *06/69940598. 15 rooms. MC, V.*

$ **Amalia.** Near the Vatican and the Cola di Rienzo shopping district, this small, former *pensione* is owned and operated by the Consoli family—Amalia and her brothers. On several floors of a 19th-century building, it has 21 renovated rooms with gleaming marble bathrooms. The Ottaviano stop of Metro A is a block away. ✉ *Via Germanico 66, 00192,* ☎ *06/39723354,* FAX *06/39723365. 25 rooms, 4 without bath. AE, MC, V.*

$ ★ **Margutta.** Near the Spanish Steps and Piazza del Popolo, this small hotel has an unassuming lobby but bright, attractive bedrooms with wrought-iron bedsteads and modern baths. ✉ *Via Laurina 34, 00187,* ☎ *06/3223674. 21 rooms. AE, DC, MC, V.*

$ **Romae.** Near Termini Station, this mid-size hotel has clean, spacious rooms with light-wood furniture and small but bright bathrooms. The congenial, helpful management offers special winter rates and welcomes families. Low rates that include breakfast make this a good deal. ✉ *Via Palestro 49, 00185,* ☎ *06/4463554,* FAX *06/4463914. 20 rooms. AE, MC, V.*

Nightlife and the Arts

You will find information on scheduled events and shows at EPT and municipal tourist offices or booths. The biweekly booklet "Un Ospite a Roma," free from concierges at some hotels, is another source of information, as is "Wanted in Rome," published on Wednesday, available at newsstands. There are listings in English in the back of the weekly "Roma c'è" booklet, with handy bus information for each listing; it is published on Thursday and sold at newsstands. If you want to go to the opera, the ballet, or a concert, it's best to ask your concierge to get tickets for you. They are sold at box offices only, just a few days before performances.

The Arts

CONCERTS

The main concert hall is the **Accademia di Santa Cecilia** (✉ Via della Conciliazione 4, ☎ 06/68801044). There are many concerts year-round; look for posters or for schedules in the publications mentioned above.

FILM

The only English-language movie theater in Rome is the **Pasquino** (✉ Vicolo del Piede, just off Piazza Santa Maria in Trastevere, ☎ 06/5803622). The program is listed in Rome's daily newspapers. Several other movie theaters show films in English on certain days of the week; the listings in "Roma c'è" are reliable.

OPERA

The opera season runs from November or December through May, and performances are staged in the **Teatro dell'Opera** (✉ Via del Viminale, ☎ 06/4817003; toll-free in Italy 167016665). From May through August, the spectacular performances are held in the open air. After having been evicted from the ancient ruins of the Terme di Caracalla, performances have been held temporarily in Villa Pepoli, a parklike area adjacent to the ruins of the baths. Tickets go on sale at the opera box office two days in advance.

Nightlife

Rome's "in" nightspots change like the flavor of the month, and many fade into oblivion after a brief moment of glory. The best places to find an up-to-date list are the weekly entertainment guide "Trovaroma," published each Thursday in the Italian daily *La Repubblica,* and "Roma c'è," the weekly guide sold at newsstands.

BARS

Jacket and tie are in order in the elegant **Blue Bar** (✉ Via dei Soldati 25, ☎ 06/6864250) of the Hostaria dell'Orso. One of the grandest places for a drink in well-dressed company is **Le Bar** (✉ Via Vittorio Emanuele Orlando 3, ☎ 06/482931) of Le Grand Hotel. **Jazz Club** (✉ Via Zanardelli 12, ☎ 06/6861990), near Piazza Navona, is an upscale watering hole. **Flann O'Brien** (✉ Via Napoli 29, ☎ 06/4880418), one of a plethora of pubs that now monopolize the bar scene in Rome, has the feel of a good Irish pub but also serves a decent cappuccino. **Trinity College** (✉ Via del Collegio Romano 6, near Piazza Venezia, ☎ 06/6786472) has two floors of Irish pub trappings, with plenty o' gift of the gab and music until 2 AM.

DISCOS AND NIGHTCLUBS

Testaccio's three-floor **The Saint** (✉ Via Galvani 46, ☎ 06/5747945) has two discos designated "Paradiso" and "Inferno" (Heaven and Hell). You might spot an American celeb at **Gilda** (✉ Via Mario dei Fiori 97, ☎ 06/6784838), with a disco, piano bar, and live music. It's closed Monday and jackets are required. Just as exclusive is **Bella Blu** (✉ Via Luciani 21, ☎ 06/3230490), a Parioli club that caters to Rome's thirtysomething elite.

MUSIC CLUBS

For the best live music, including jazz, blues, rhythm and blues, African, and rock, go to **Big Mama** (✉ Vicolo San Francesco a Ripa 18, ☎ 06/

5812551). Live performances of jazz, soul, and funk by leading musicians draw celebrities to **Alexanderplatz** (✉ Via Ostia 9, in the Vatican area, ☎ 06/39742171). The music starts about 10 PM, and you can have supper while you wait.

WINE BARS

Informal enoteche (wine bars) are popular with Romans who like to burn the midnight oil but don't dig disco music. They usually serve light meals or snacks. **Spiriti** (✉ Via Sant'Eustachio 5, ☎ 06/6892499), near the Pantheon, serves light lunches at midday and is open until 1:30 AM. At family-run **Trimani Wine Bar** (✉ Via Cernaia 37/b, ☎ 06/4469630), you can sample some great wines at the counter or with a light, fixed-price meal at an upstairs table. **Il Simposio di Costantini** (✉ Via Appia Antica 139, near the Vatican, ☎ 06/7880494), wrapped in wrought iron vines, wood paneling, and velvet, offers about 30 wines by the glass.

Shopping

Via Condotti, directly across from the Spanish Steps, and the streets running parallel to Via Condotti, as well as its cross streets, form the most elegant and expensive shopping area for clothes and accessories in Rome. Lower-price fashions may be found on display at shops on **Via Frattina** and **Via del Corso.** Romans in the know do much of their shopping along **Via Cola di Rienzo** and **Via Nazionale.** For prints browse among the stalls at **Piazza Fontanelle Borghese** or stop in at the shops in the Pantheon area. For minor antiques **Via dei Coronari** and other streets in the Piazza Navona area are good. The most prestigious antiques dealers are situated in **Via del Babuino** and its environs. The open-air markets at **Campo dei Fiori** and in many neighborhoods throughout the city provide an eyeful of great local color.

Rome Essentials

Arriving and Departing

BY PLANE

Rome's principal airport is **Aeroporto Leonardo da Vinci** usually known as **Fiumicino** (✉ 29 km/18 mi southeast of Rome, ☎ 06/65953640 for flight information). The smaller **Ciampino** (✉ on the edge of Rome, ☎ 06/794941 for flight information) is used as an alternative by international and domestic lines, especially for charter flights.

Between the Airport and Downtown. To get to downtown Rome from **Fiumicino** you have a choice of two trains. Ask at the airport (at EPT or train information counters) which one takes you closest to your hotel. The nonstop Airport–Termini express takes you directly to Track 22 at Termini Station, Rome's main train terminal, well served by taxis and the hub of Metro (subway) and bus lines. The ride to Termini takes 30 minutes; departures are hourly, beginning at 7:50 AM, with the final departure at 10:05 PM. Tickets cost 13,000 lire. The other airport train (FM1) runs to Tiburtina station in Rome and beyond to Monterotondo, a suburban town to the east. The main stops in Rome are at the Trastevere, Ostiense, and Tiburtina stations. At each of these you can find taxis and bus and/or Metro connections to various parts of Rome. This train runs from 6:35 AM to 12:15 AM, with departures every 20 minutes. The ride to Tiburtina takes 40 minutes. Tickets cost 7,000 lire. For either train you buy your ticket at an automatic vending machine (you need Italian currency). There are ticket counters at some stations (Termini Track 22, Trastevere, Tiburtina). Remember to **date-stamp your ticket in one of the yellow machines near the track.**

A taxi to or from Fiumicino costs about 70,000 lire, including supplements. At a booth inside the terminal you can hire a four- or five-passenger car with driver for a little more. If you decide to take a taxi, use only the yellow or the newer white cabs, which must wait outside the terminal; make sure the meter is running. Gypsy cab drivers solicit your business as you come out of customs; they're not reliable, and their rates may be rip-offs. **Ciampino** is connected with the Anagnina Station of the Metro A by bus (runs every half hour). A taxi between Ciampino and downtown Rome costs about 35,000 lire.

BY TRAIN

Termini Station is Rome's main train terminal, although the Tiburtina, Ostiense, and Trastevere stations serve some long-distance trains, many commuter trains, and the FM1 line to Fiumicino Airport. For train information call ☎ 06/4775, ☎ 1478/88088 toll free, or try the English-speaking personnel at the Information Office in Termini, or at any travel agency. Tickets and seats can be reserved and purchased at travel agencies bearing the FS (Ferrovie dello Stato) emblem. Tickets can be purchased up to two months in advance. Short-distance tickets are also sold at tobacconists and ticket machines in the stations.

Getting Around

Rome's integrated Metrebus transportation system includes buses and trams (ATAC), Metro and suburban trains and buses (COTRAL), and some other suburban trains (FS) run by the state railways. A ticket valid for 75 minutes on any combination of buses and trams and one admission to the Metro costs 1,500 lire (time-stamp your ticket when boarding the first vehicle; you're supposed to stamp it again if you board another vehicle just before the ticket runs out, but few do). Tickets are sold at tobacconists, newsstands, some coffee bars, automatic ticket machines in Metro stations, some bus stops, and at ATAC and COTRAL ticket booths. A BIG tourist ticket, valid for one day on all public transport, costs 6,000 lire. A weekly ticket (Settimanale, also known as CIS) costs 24,000 lire and can be purchased only at ATAC and Metro booths.

BY BICYCLE

Pedaling through Villa Borghese, along the Tiber, and through city center when traffic is light is a pleasant way to see the sights, but remember: Rome is hilly. Rental concessions are at the Piazza di Spagna and Piazza del Popolo Metro stops, and at Largo San Silvestro and Largo Argentina. You will also find rentals at Viale della Pineta and Viale del Bambino on the Pincio. **I Bike Rome** (✉ underground parking lot Sector III at Villa Borghese, ☎ 06/3225240) leases bikes. **St. Peter's Motor Rent** (✉ Via di Porta Castello 43, near St. Peter's, ☎ 06/6875714) also rents bikes.

BY BUS

Orange ATAC (☎ 06/46954444) city buses (and a few streetcar lines) run from about 6 AM to midnight, with night buses (indicated N) on some lines. When entering a bus, remember to board at the rear and exit at the middle. Bus lines 117 and 119, with compact electric vehicles, makes a circuit of limited but scenic routes in downtown Rome. They can save you from a lot of walking, and you can get on and off as you please.

BY CAR

If you come by car, put it in a parking space (and note that parking in central Rome is generally either metered or prohibited) or a garage, and use public transportation. If you plan to drive into or out of the city, take time to study your route, especially on the GRA (Grande Raccordo Anulare, a beltway that encircles Rome and funnels traffic into the city, not always successfully). The main access routes to Rome from the north are the A1 autostrada from Florence and Milan, and the Aurelia highway (SS 1) from Genoa. The principal route to or from points south, such as Naples, is the A2 autostrada.

BY METRO

The Metro is the easiest and fastest way to get around, but the network has limited stops. It opens at 5:30 AM, and the last train leaves each terminal at 11:30 PM. Metro A runs from the eastern part of the city to Termini Station and past Piazza di Spagna and Piazzale Flaminio to Ottaviano-S. Pietro, near St. Peter's and the Vatican museums. Metro B serves Termini, the Colosseum, and Tiburtina Station (where the FM1 Fiumicino Airport train stops).

BY MOPED

You can rent a moped or scooter and mandatory helmet at **Scoot-a-Long** (✉ Via Cavour 302, ☎ 06/6780206). **St. Peter Moto** (✉ Via di Porta Castello 43, ☎ 06/6875714) also rents equipment.

BY TAXI

Taxis wait at stands and, for a small extra charge, can also be called by telephone. The meter starts at 4,500 lire; there are supplements for service after 10 PM, on Sunday and holidays, and for each piece of baggage. Use the yellow or the newer white cabs only, and be very sure to check the meter. To call a cab dial ☎ 06/3570, 06/5551, 06/4994, or 06/88177.

Contacts and Resources

EMBASSIES

United States (✉ Via Veneto 121, ☎ 06/46741). **Canadian** (✉ Via Zara 30, ☎ 06/445981). **United Kingdom** (✉ Via Venti Settembre 80a, ☎ 06/4825441).

EMERGENCIES

Police (☎ 113). **Ambulance** (☎ 1188 or 06/5510) Say "Pronto Soccorso" and be prepared to give your address. **Doctor** and **dentist: Salvator Mundi Hospital** (☎ 06/588961). **Rome American Hospital** (☎ 06/22551). **Pharmacies** are open 8:30–1 and 4–8. Some stay open all night, and all open Sunday on a rotation system; a notice of the pharmacies open in the neighborhood is posted at each pharmacy.

ENGLISH-LANGUAGE BOOKS

Economy Book and Video Center (✉ Via Torino 136, ☎ 06/4746877). **Anglo-American Bookstore** (✉ Via della Vite 102, ☎ 06/6795222). **Corner Bookstore** (✉ Via del Moro 48, Trastevere, ☎ 06/5836942).

GUIDED TOURS

Excursions. Most operators offer half-day excursions to Tivoli to see the Villa d'Este's fountains and gardens; Appian Line's and CIT's half-day tours to Tivoli also include Hadrian's Villa and its impressive ancient ruins. Most operators have all-day excursions to Assisi, to Pompeii and/or Capri, and to Florence. For do-it-yourself excursions to Ostia Antica and other destinations, pick up information at the EPT information offices (☞ *below*).

Orientation. Three-hour tours in air-conditioned buses with English-speaking guides cover Rome with four separate itineraries: "Ancient Rome," "Classic Rome," "Christian Rome," and the "Vatican Museums and Sistine Chapel." Most tours cost about 53,000 lire, though the Vatican Museums tour is about 60,000 lire. **American Express** (☎ 06/67641) tours depart from Piazza di Spagna. **CIT** (☎ 06/47941) depart from Piazza della Repubblica. **Appian Line** (☎ 06/4884151) picks up sightseers at their hotels. Though operators and names change, there is usually some kind of bus tour following a continuous circle route through the city center, stopping at important sites where you can get on and off at will. Check with the EPT for the name of the current operator and schedules. The least expensive organized bus tour (three hours) on the special 110 bus is run by **ATAC,** the municipal bus company. Book tours for about 15,000 lire at the ATAC information booth in front of Termini Station. There is at least one tour daily, departing at 2:30 (3:30 in summer).

Papal Audience. You can make your own arrangements (at no cost) to attend a public papal audience in the Vatican or to be at the Sunday blessing at the Pope's summer residence at Castel Gandolfo. Tour operators will make the arrangements for you, for a price. **CIT** (☎ 06/47941). **Appian Line** (✉ Via Barberini 109, ☎ 06/4884151). **Carrani** (✉ Via V. E. Orlando 95, ☎ 06/4880510).

Walking. Secret Walks (✉ Viale Medaglie d'Oro 127, 00136 Rome, ☎ 06/39728728 and 06/39728728) conducts small groups on theme walks led by English-speaking city experts; they can also arrange excursions. **Scala Reale** (✉ Via Varese 52, 00185 Rome, ☎ 06/44700898) also has English-language tours. For more information contact city tourist offices.

TRAVEL AGENCIES

American Express (✉ Piazza di Spagna 38, ☎ 06/67641). **CIT** (✉ Piazza della Repubblica 64, ☎ 06/47941). **CTS** (youth and budget travel, discount fares; ✉ Via Genova 16, ☎ 06/46791; ☎ 06/4679271 for information).

VISITOR INFORMATION

EPT (Rome Provincial Tourist) main office (✉ Via Parigi 5, 00185, ☎ 06/48899253; ✉ Termini Station; ✉ Fiumicino Airport). **City tourist information booths** (✉ Largo Goldoni, corner of Via Condotti; Via del Corso in the Spanish Steps area; Via dei Fori Imperiali, opposite the entrance to the Roman Forum; Via Nazionale, at Palazzo delle Esposizioni; Piazza Cinque Lune, off the north end of Piazza Navona).

FLORENCE

One of Europe's preeminent treasures, Florence draws visitors from all over the world. Its architecture is predominantly Early Renaissance and retains many of the implacable, fortresslike features of pre-Renaissance palazzi, whose facades were mostly meant to keep intruders out rather than to invite sightseers in. With the exception of a very few buildings, the classical dignity of the High Renaissance and the exuberant invention of the Baroque are not to be found here. The typical Florentine exterior gives nothing away, as if obsessively guarding secret treasures within. The treasures, of course, are very real. And far from being a secret, they are famous the world over. The city is an artistic treasure trove of unique and incomparable proportions. A single historical fact explains the phenomenon: Florence gave birth to the Renaissance.

Exploring Florence

Numbers in the margin correspond to points of interest on the Florence map.

Founded by Julius Caesar, Florence was built in the familiar grid pattern common to all Roman colonies that makes it easy to explore. Except for the major monuments, which are appropriately imposing, the buildings are low and unpretentious and the streets are narrow. At times Florence can be a nightmare of mass tourism. Plan, if you can, to visit the city in late fall, early spring, or even in winter, to avoid the crowds. For 15,000 lire you can purchase a special museum ticket valid for six months at six city museums, including the Palazzo Vecchio and the Museum of Santa Maria Novella. Inquire at any city museum.

Piazza del Duomo and Piazza della Signoria

★ ❸ **Battistero** (Baptistery). In front of the Duomo is the octagonal baptistery, one of the city's oldest and most beloved edifices, where since the 11th century Florentines have baptized their children. The interior dome mosaics are famous but cannot outshine the building's renowned gilded bronze east portal (facing the Duomo). Crafted by Lorenzo Ghiberti (1378–1455), it is the most splendid of the Baptistery's three portals. They were dubbed the "Gates of Paradise" by Michelangelo. A gleaming copy replaces the original, removed to the Museo dell'Opera del Duomo (☞ *below*). ✉ *Piazza del Duomo.* ⏲ *Mon.–Sat. 1:30–6:30, Sun. 8:30–1:30.*

❷ **Campanile** (Bell tower). Giotto (1266–1337) designed the early 14th-century bell tower, richly decorated with colored marbles and sculpture reproductions (the originals are in the Museo dell'Opera del Duomo (☞ *below*). The 414-step climb to the top is less strenuous than that to the cupola. ✉ *Piazza del Duomo.* ⏲ *Apr.–Oct., daily 9–7:30; Nov.–Mar., daily. 9–5.*

★ ❶ **Duomo.** Cattedrale di Santa Maria del Fiore is dominated by a cupola representing a touchstone in the history of architecture. The cathedral itself was begun by master sculptor and architect Arnolfo di Cambio in 1296, and its construction took 140 years to complete. Gothic architecture predominates; the facade was added in the 1870s but is based on Tuscan Gothic models. Inside, the church is cool and austere, a fine example of the architecture of the period. Take a good look at the frescoes of equestrian figures on the left wall; the one on the right is by Paolo Uccello (1397–1475), the one on the left by Andrea del Castagno (1421–57). The dome frescoes by Vasari take second place to the dome itself, Brunelleschi's greatest architectural and technical achievement. It was also the inspiration behind such later domes as the one Michelangelo designed for St. Peter's in Rome and even the Capitol in Washington. You can visit early medieval and ancient Roman remains of previous constructions excavated under the cathedral. And you can climb to the cupola gallery, 463 exhausting steps up between the two layers of the double dome for a fine view. ✉ *Piazza del Duomo.* ⏲ *Weekdays 10–5 (1st Sat. of month 10–3:30), Sun. 1–5. Cupola (entrance in left aisle of cathedral):* ⏲ *Weekdays 8:30–6:20, Sat. 9:30–5 (1st Sat. of month 9:30–3:20).*

★ ❾ **Galleria degli Uffizi** (Uffizi Gallery). The Uffizi Palace was built to house the administrative offices of the Medici, onetime rulers of the city. Later their fabulous art collection was arranged in the Uffizi Gallery on the top floor, which was opened to the public in the 17th century—making this the world's first modern public gallery. It houses Italy's most important collection of paintings. The emphasis is on Italian art of the Gothic and Renaissance periods. Make sure you see the works by Giotto, and look for the Botticellis (1445–1510) in Rooms X–XIV, Michelangelo's *Holy Family* in Room XXV, and the works by Raphael next door. In addition to its art treasures, the gallery offers a magnificent close-up view of the Palazzo Vecchio tower from the little coffee bar at the end of the corridor. Notoriously long lines can be avoided by purchasing tickets in advance from Consorzio ITA. ✉ *Loggiato Uffizi 6,* ☎ *055/23885; advance tickets, Consorzio ITA 055/2347941.* ⏲ *Tues.–Sat. 8:30–6:50, Sun. 8:30–1:50.*

❽ **Loggia del Mercato Nuovo** (Loggia of the New Market). Tiers of souvenirs and straw and leather goods are crammed into this historic open-air marketplace. Along with the goods, a main attraction is Pietro Tacca's bronze Porcellino (Piglet) fountain, a 17th-century copy of an ancient Roman work now in the Uffizi. Rubbing its snout is said to bring good luck. ✉ *Via Calimala.* ⏲ *Mon.–Sat. 8–7 (closed Mon. AM).*

★ ❹ **Museo dell'Opera del Duomo** (Cathedral Museum). The museum contains some superb sculptures by Donatello (c.1386–1466) and Luca della Robbia (1400–82)—especially their *cantorie,* or singers' galleries—and an unfinished *Pietà* by Michelangelo, which was intended for his own tomb. ✉ *Piazza del Duomo 9,* ☎ *055/2302885.* ⏲ *Mar.–Oct., Mon.–Sat. 9–7:30; Nov.–Feb., Mon.–Sat. 9–7.*

❿ **Museo di Storia della Scienza** (Museum of Science History). You don't have to know a lot about science to appreciate the antique scientific instruments presented here in informative, eye-catching exhibits. From astrolabes and armillary spheres to some of Galileo's own instruments, the collection is one of Florence's lesser-known treasures. ✉ *Piazza dei Giudici 1,* ☎ *055/2398876.* ⏲ *Mon., Wed., Fri. 9:30–1 and 2–5; Tues., Thurs., Sat. 9:30–1.*

❺ **Orsanmichele.** For centuries this was an odd combination of first-floor church and second-floor granary of one of Florence's craft guilds. The statues in the niches on the exterior (many of which are now copies) constitute an anthology of the work of eminent Renaissance sculptors, including Donatello, Ghiberti, and Verrocchio (1435–88). The tabernacle inside is an extraordinary piece by Andrea Orcagna. Some of the original statues can be seen in the Museo Nazionale del Bargello (☞ *below*) and the Palazzo della Signoria (☞ *below*). ✉ *Via Calzaiuoli.* ⏲ *Daily 9–noon and 4–6.Closed 1st and last Mon. of month.*

❼ **Palazzo Vecchio** (Old Palace). Also called Palazzo della Signoria, this massive, fortresslike city hall was begun in 1299 and was taken over, along with the rest of Florence, by the Medici family. Inside, the impressive, frescoed salons and the Medici *Studiolo* (Study) are the main attractions. ✉ *Piazza della Signoria,* ☎ *055/2768465.* 🎫 *Free Sun.* ⏲ *Mon.–Wed. and Fri.–Sat. 9–7, Sun. 8–1.*

❻ **Piazza della Signoria.** This is the heart of Florence and the city's largest square. In the pavement in the center of the square a slab marks the spot where Savonarola, the reformist monk who urged the Florentines to burn their pictures, books, musical instruments, and other worldly objects, was hanged and then burned at the stake as a heretic in 1498. The square, the Fontana di Nettuno (Neptune) by Ammanati (1511–92), and the surrounding cafés are popular gathering places for Florentines and for tourists who come to admire the Palazzo della Signoria, the copy of Michelangelo's *David* standing in front of it, and the sculptures in the 14th-century Loggia dei Lanzi, including a copy of Cellini's famous bronze *Perseus Holding the Head of Medusa.*

San Marco, San Lorenzo, Santa Maria Novella, Santa Croce

★ ⓰ **Cappelle Medicee** (Medici Chapels). These extraordinary chapels, part of the San Lorenzo complex, contain the tombs of practically every member of the Medici family, and there were a lot of them, for they guided Florence's destiny from the 15th century to 1737. Cosimo I, a Medici whose acumen made him the richest man in Europe, is buried in the crypt beneath the Chapel of the Princes, and Donatello's tomb is next to that of his patron. The **Cappella dei Principi** upstairs displays a dazzling array of colored marble panels. Michelangelo's **Sagrestia Nuova** tombs of Giuliano and Lorenzo de' Medici are adorned with the justly

- Battistero, **3**
- Campanile, **2**
- Cappelle Medicee, **16**
- Duomo (Cattedrale di Santa Maria del Fiore), **1**
- Galleria degli Uffizi, **9**
- Galleria dell'Accademia, **11**
- Giardino di Boboli, **24**
- Loggia del Mercato Nuovo, **8**
- Museo Archeologico, **12**
- Museo dell'Opera del Duomo, **4**
- Museo dell'Opera di Santa Croce e Cappella dei Pazzi, **21**
- Museo di San Marco, **13**
- Museo di Santa Maria Novella, **18**
- Museo di Storia della Scienza, **10**
- Museo Nazionale del Bargello, **19**
- Orsanmichele, **5**
- Palazzo Medici-Riccardi, **14**
- Palazzo Pitti, **23**
- Palazzo Vecchio, **7**
- Piazza della Signoria, **6**
- Ponte Vecchio, **22**
- San Lorenzo, **15**
- San Miniato al Monte, **27**
- Santa Croce, **20**
- Santa Maria del Carmine, **26**
- Santa Maria Novella, **17**
- Santo Spirito, **25**

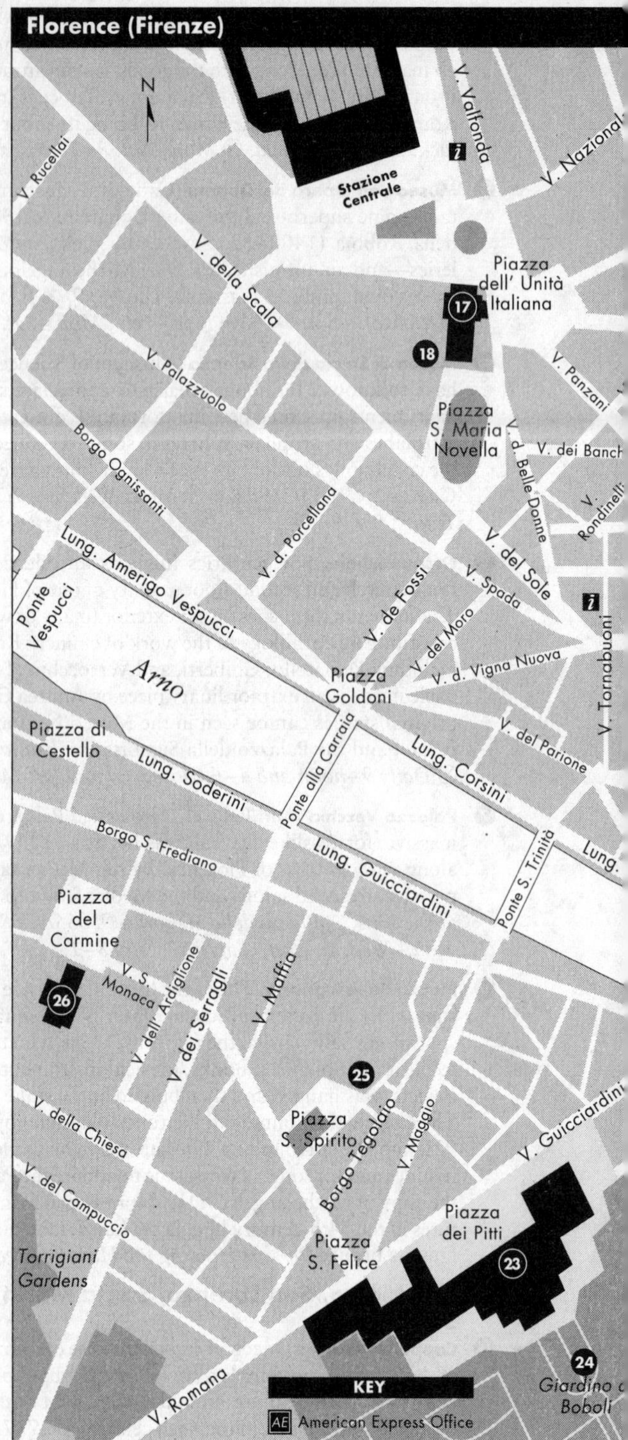

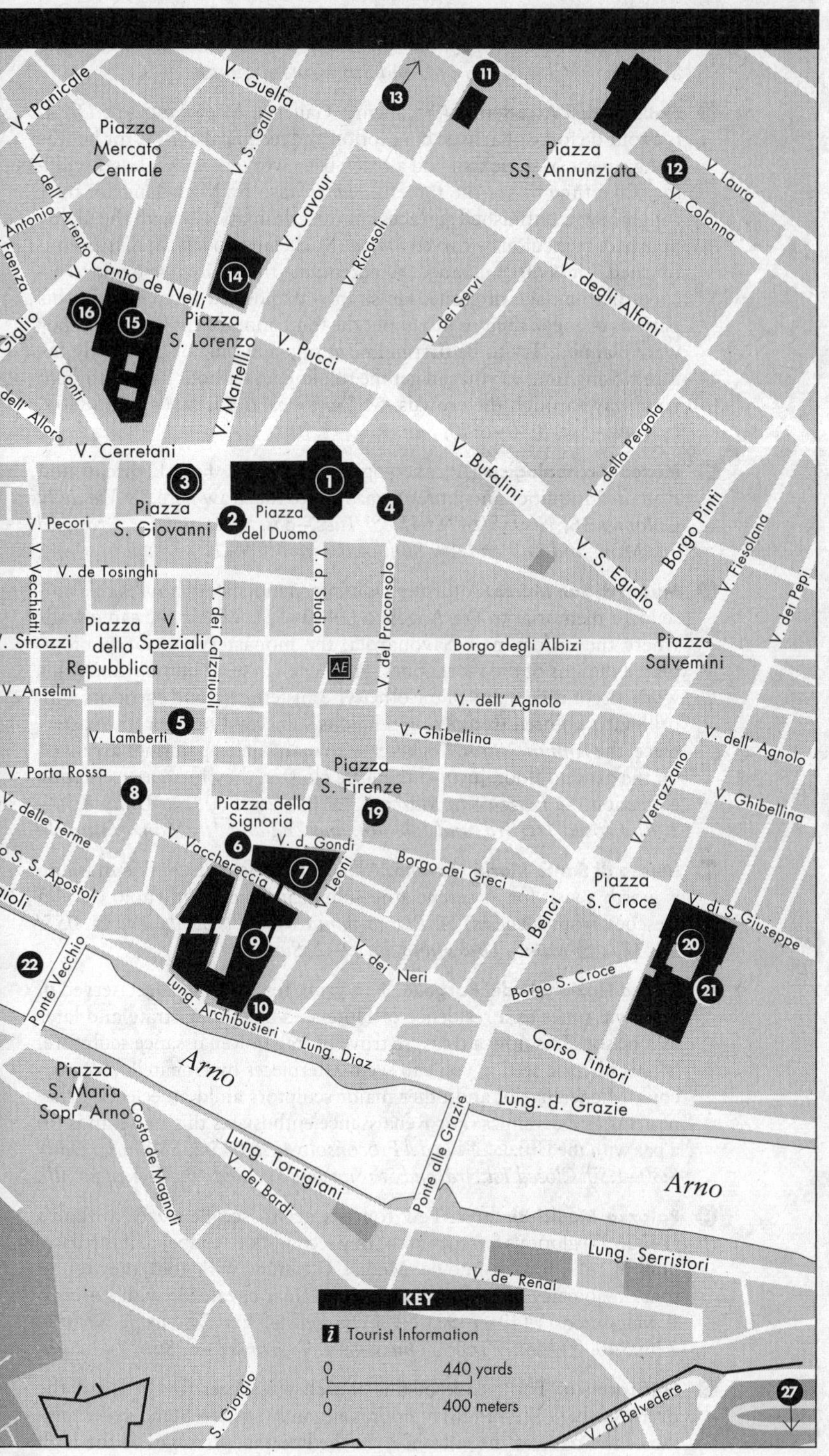
V. Panicale
V. Guelfa
Piazza
Mercato
Centrale
V. S. Gallo
13
11
Piazza
SS. Annunziata
12
V. Laura
V. Colonna
V. dell' Ariento
Antonio
Faenza
V. Cavour
V. Ricasoli
V. Canto de Nelli
14
V. degli Alfani
16
15
Piazza
S. Lorenzo
V. dei Servi
Giglio
V. Conti
V. Pucci
dell' Alloro
V. Martelli
V. Bufalini
V. della Pergola
V. Cerretani
3
1
Piazza
S. Giovanni
2
Piazza
del Duomo
4
V. Pecori
V. Vecchietti
V. de Tosinghi
V. dei Calzaiuoli
V. d. Studio
V. del Proconsolo
V. S. Egidio
Borgo Pinti
V. Fiesolana
V. dei Pepi
V. Strozzi
Piazza
della
Repubblica
V.
Speziali
AE
Borgo degli Albizi
Piazza
Salvemini
V. Anselmi
5
V. Lamberti
V. dell' Agnolo
V. Ghibellina
V. dell' Agnolo
V. Porta Rossa
8
Piazza
S. Firenze
V. Verrazzano
V. Ghibellina
V. delle Terme
Piazza della
Signoria
19
6
V. d. Gondi
V. Vacchereccia
7
V. Leoni
Borgo dei Greci
Piazza
S. Croce
o S. S. Apostoli
V. di S. Giuseppe
V. Benci
9
20
22
Ponte Vecchio
V. dei Neri
Borgo S. Croce
21
Lung. Archibusieri
10
Lung. Diaz
Corso Tintori
Arno
Piazza
S. Maria
Sopr' Arno
Lung. d. Grazie
Costa de Magnoli
Lung. Torrigiani
V. dei Bardi
Ponte alle Grazie
Arno
Lung. Serristori
V. de' Renai
KEY
Tourist Information
0
440 yards
0
400 meters
S. Giorgio
V. di Belvedere
27

famed sculptures of *Dawn* and *Dusk, Night* and *Day.* ✉ *Piazza Madonna degli Aldobrandini, San Lorenzo,* ☎ *055/2388602.* ⏲ *Daily 8:30–1:50. Closed 1st, 3rd, and 5th Mon. of month.*

★ ⓫ **Galleria dell'Accademia** (Accademia Gallery). Michelangelo's *David* is a tour de force of artistic conception and technical ability, for he was using a piece of stone that had already been worked on by a lesser sculptor. Take time to see the forceful *Slaves,* also by Michelangelo; their rough-hewn, unfinished surfaces contrast dramatically with the highly polished, meticulously carved *David.* Michelangelo left the *Slaves* "unfinished," it is often claimed, to accentuate the figures' struggle to escape the bondage of stone. He simply abandoned them because his patrons changed their minds about the tomb monument for which they were planned. Try to be first in line at opening time or go shortly before closing time so you can get the full impact without having to fight your way through the crowds. ✉ *Via Ricasoli 60,* ☎ *055/2388609.* ⏲ *Tues.–Sat. 8:30–6:50, Sun. 8:30–1:50.*

⓬ **Museo Archeologico** (Archaeological Museum). Fine Etruscan and Roman antiquities and a pretty garden are the draw here. ✉ *Via della Colonna 36,* ☎ *055/2478641.* ⏲ *Tues.–Sat. 9–2, and 1st, 3rd, and 5th Mon. and 2nd and 4th Sun. of the month 9–1.*

⓭ **Museo di San Marco.** A former Dominican monastery houses this museum, a memorial to Fra Angelico (1400–55). Within the same walls where the unfortunate Savonarola, the monastery's prior, contemplated the sins of the Florentines, Fra Angelico went humbly about his work, decorating many of the otherwise austere cells and corridors with brilliantly colored frescoes on religious subjects. Look for his masterpiece, the *Annunciation.* Together with many of his paintings arranged on the ground floor, just off the little cloister, they form a fascinating collection. ✉ *Piazza San Marco 1,* ☎ *055/2388608.* ⏲ *Daily 8:30–1:40. Closed 1st, 3rd, and 5th Sun. and 2nd and 4th Mon. of month.*

⓲ **Museo di Santa Maria Novella.** Adjacent to the church, this museum is worth a visit for its serene atmosphere and the faded Paolo Uccello frescoes from Genesis. ✉ *Piazza Santa Maria Novella 19,* ☎ *055/282187.* ⏲ *Mon.–Thurs. and Sat. 9–2, Sun. 8–1.*

★ ⓳ **Museo Nazionale del Bargello.** This grim, fortresslike palace served in medieval times as a residence of Florence's chief magistrate and later as a prison. It is now a treasure trove of Italian Renaissance sculpture. In this historic setting you can see masterpieces by Donatello, Verrocchio, Michelangelo, and other major sculptors amid an eclectic array of arms and ceramics. For Renaissance enthusiasts this museum is on a par with the Uffizi. ✉ *Via del Proconsolo 4,* ☎ *055/2388606.* ⏲ *Daily 8:30–1:50. Closed 1st, 3rd, and 5th Sun. and 2nd and 4th Mon. of month.*

⓮ **Palazzo Medici-Riccardi.** Few tourists get to see Benozzo Gozzoli's (1420–97) glorious frescoes in the tiny second-floor chapel of this palace, built in 1444 for Cosimo de' Medici. Gleaming with gold, they represent the journey of the Magi as a spectacular cavalcade with Lorenzo Il Magnifico (1449–1492) on a charger. ✉ *Via Cavour 1,* ☎ *055/2760340.* ⏲ *Mon.–Tues., Thurs.–Sat. 9–1 and 3–6, Sun. 9–1.*

⓯ **San Lorenzo.** The facade of this church was never finished, but the Brunelleschi (1377–1446) interior is elegantly austere. Stand in the middle of the nave at the entrance, on the line that stretches to the high altar, and you'll see what Brunelleschi wanted to achieve with the grid of inlaid marble in the pavement. Every architectural element in the church is placed to achieve a dramatic effect of single-point perspective. The **Sagrestia Vecchia,** decorated with stuccoes by Donatello, is attributed to Brunelleschi. ✉ *Piazza San Lorenzo.*

★ 20 **Santa Croce.** The mighty church of Santa Croce was begun in 1294 and has become a kind of pantheon for Florentine greats; monumental tombs of Michelangelo, Galileo (1564–1642), Machiavelli (1469–1527), and other Renaissance luminaries line the walls. Inside are two chapels frescoed by Giotto and another painted by Taddeo Gaddi (c. 1330–66), as well as an *Annunciation* and crucifix by Donatello. But it is the scale of this grandiose church that proclaims the power and ambition of medieval Florence. ✉ *Piazza Santa Croce,* ☎ *055/244619.* ⏲ *Apr.–Sept., Mon.–Sat. 8–6:30, Sun. 3–5; Oct.–Mar., Mon.–Sat. 8–12:30 and 3–6:30, Sun. 3–5.*

17 **Santa Maria Novella.** A Tuscan interpretation of the Gothic style, this handsome church should be viewed from the opposite end of Piazza Santa Maria Novella for the best view of its facade. Inside are some famous paintings, especially Masaccio's (1401–28) *Trinity,* a Giotto crucifix in the sacristy, and Ghirlandaio's frescoes in the choir chapel. ✉ *Piazza Santa Maria Novella,* ☎ *055/210113.* ⏲ *Sun.–Fri. 7–12:15 and 3–6, Sat. 7–12:15 and 3–5.*

Oltrarno

24 **Giardino di Boboli** (Boboli Garden). The main entrance to this garden on a landscaped hillside is in the right wing of Palazzo Pitti. The garden was laid out in 1550 for Cosimo de' Medici's wife, Eleanor of Toledo, and was further developed by later Medici dukes. ✉ *Piazza dei Pitti,* ☎ *055/213440.* ⏲ *Daily (except 1st and last Mon. of month) 9–1 hr before sunset.*

21 **Museo dell'Opera di Santa Croce e Cappella dei Pazzi** (Museum of Santa Croce and Pazzi Chapel). From the cloister of the monastery adjacent to Santa Croce you can visit the small museum and see what remains of the Giotto crucifix irreparably damaged by a flood in 1966, when water rose to 16 ft in parts of the church. The **Cappella dei Pazzi** in the cloister is an architectural gem by Brunelleschi. The interior is a lesson in spatial equilibrium and harmony. ✉ *Piazza Santa Croce,* ☎ *055/244619.*⏲ *Apr.–Sept., Thurs.–Tues. 10–12:30 and 2:30–6:30; Oct.–Mar., Thurs.–Tues. 10–12:30 and 3–5.*

23 **Palazzo Pitti.** This enormous palace is a 15th-century extravaganza the Medici acquired from the Pitti family shortly after the latter had gone deeply into debt to build the central portion. The Medici enlarged the building, extending its facade along the immense piazza. Solid and severe, it looks like a Roman aqueduct turned into a palace. The palace houses several museums: The **Museo degli Argenti** (Silver Museum) displays the fabulous Medici collection of objects in silver and gold; another has the collections of the **Galleria d'Arte Moderna** (Gallery of Modern Art). The most famous museum, though, is the **Galleria Palatina** (Palatine Gallery), with an extraordinary collection of paintings, many hung frame-to-frame in a clear case of artistic overkill. Some are high up in dark corners, so try to go on a bright day. ✉ *Piazza Pitti,* ☎ *055/210323. Museo degli Argenti and Galleria d'Arte Moderna:* ⏲ *Daily 8:50–1:50. Closed 2nd and 4th Sun. and 1st, 3rd, and 5th Mon. of month. Galleria Palatina:* ⏲ *Tues.–Sat. 8:50–6:50, Sun. 8:30–1:50.*

★ 22 **Ponte Vecchio** (Old Bridge). Florence's oldest bridge appears to be just another street lined with goldsmiths' shops until you get to the middle and catch a glimpse of the Arno below. Spared during World War II by the retreating Germans (who blew up every other bridge in the city), it also survived the 1966 flood. It leads into the **Oltrarno dis-**

trict, where the atmosphere of old-time Florence is preserved amid fascinating crafts workshops. ✉ *East of Ponte Santa Trinita and west of Ponte alle Grazie.*

27 **San Miniato al Monte.** One of Florence's oldest churches, this charming green-and-white marble Romanesque edifice is full of artistic riches, among them the gorgeous Renaissance chapel where a Portuguese cardinal was laid to rest in 1459 under a ceiling by Luca della Robbia. ✉ *Viale Michelangelo, or take stairs from Piazzale Michelangelo.*

26 **Santa Maria del Carmine.** The church is of little architectural interest but of immense significance in the history of Renaissance art. It contains the celebrated frescoes painted by Masaccio in the **Cappella Brancacci.** The chapel was a classroom for such artistic giants as Botticelli, Leonardo da Vinci (1452–1519), Michelangelo, and Raphael, since they all came to study Masaccio's realistic use of light and perspective and his creation of space and depth. ✉ *Piazza del Carmine,* ☎ *055/2382195.* ⏲ *Mon. and Wed.–Sat. 10–5, Sun. 1–5.*

25 **Santo Spirito.** Its plain, unfinished facade is less than impressive, but this church is important as one of Brunelleschi's finest architectural creations. It contains some superb paintings, including a *Madonna* by Filippo Lippi. Santo Spirito is the hub of a colorful, trendy neighborhood of artisans and intellectuals. An outdoor market enlivens the square every morning except Sunday; in the afternoon, pigeons, pet owners, and pensioners take over. ✉ *Piazza Santo Spirito.* ⏲ *Thurs.–Tues. 8–noon and 4–6, Wed. 8–noon.*

Dining and Lodging

Mealtimes in Florence are 12:30 to 2 and 7:30 to 9 or later. Many $$ and $ places are small, and you may have to share a table. Reservations are always advisable; to find a table at inexpensive places, get there early. For details and price-category definitions, *see* Dining *in* Italy A to Z, *above.*

With mass tourism and trade fairs, hotel rooms are at a premium in Florence for most of the year. Reserve well in advance. If you arrive without a reservation, the **Consorzio ITA** office in the train station (✉ Stazione Centrale di Santa Maria Novella), open 8:20 AM–9 PM can help you, but there may be a long line (take a number and wait). Now that much traffic is banned in the downtown area, many central hotel rooms are quieter. Local traffic and motorcycles can still be bothersome, however, so check the decibel level before you settle in. From November through March ask for special low winter rates. For details and price-category definitions, *see* Lodging *in* Italy A to Z, *above.*

$$$$ ★ ✕ **Enoteca Pinchiorri.** A sumptuous Renaissance palace with high, frescoed ceilings and bouquets in silver vases is the setting for this restaurant, one of the best and most expensive in Italy. A Tuscan menu and a special degustation menu, plus a variety of fish, game, and meat dishes à la carte are always on offer. Of the splendid combinations, a favorite is the *ignudi*—ricotta and cheese dumplings with a lobster and coxcomb fricassee. ✉ *Via Ghibellina 87,* ☎ *055/242777. Reservations essential. AE, MC, V. Closed Sun., Aug., and 10 days during Christmas. No lunch Mon. or Wed.*

$$$ ✕ **Alle Murate.** This sophisticated restaurant features creative versions of classic Tuscan food, along with such specialties as *lasagne con mozzarella al pomodoro fresco* (lasagna with mozzarella and fresh tomatoes). In the smaller room called the *vineria,* the menu and service are simpler and prices lower. ✉ *Via Ghibellina 52/r,* ☎ *055/240618. AE, DC, MC, V. Closed Mon. No lunch.*

$$ ✕ **Cammillo.** This bustling trattoria just on the other side of the Arno has been in the capable hands of the Masiero family for three generations, and in its present venue since 1945. Their farm in the country supplies the olive oil and wines for the restaurant, which marry nicely with the wide-ranging list of Tuscan specialities on the menu. Reservations are advised. ✉ *Borgo Sant'Jacopo 57/r,* ☎ *055/212427. AE, DC, MC, V. Closed Wed., 15 days in Aug., and 15 days Dec.–Jan.*

$$$ ★ ✕ **Cibrèo.** The food here is fantastic, from the first bite of seamless, creamy *crostini di fegatini* (savory Tuscan chicken liver spread on grilled bread) to the last bite of one of the melt-in-your-mouth-good desserts. If you thought you'd never try tripe, let alone like it, this is the place to lay any doubts to rest: the cold tripe salad with parsley and garlic is an epiphany. ✉ *Via dei Macci 118/r,* ☎ *055/2341100. Reservations essential. AE, DC, MC, V. Closed Sun., Mon., July 25–Sept. 5, and Dec. 31–Jan. 7.*

$$ ★ ✕ **La Giostra.** La Giostra, which means "carousel" in Italian, serves unusually good pastas requiring some explanation from Dimitri or Soldano, the owner's good-looking twin sons. In perfect English they'll describe a favorite dish, delicious *gnocchetti alla tibetana,* little potato dumpling morsels with mint and basil pesto. Leave room for dessert: this might be the only show in town with a sublime tiramisu and a wonderfully gooey Sacher torte. ✉ *Borgo Pinti 12/r,* ☎ *055/241341. AE, MC, V.*

$$ ✕ **Le Fonticine.** This restaurant is a welcome oasis in the culinary Siberia near the train station. The cheery interior is filled with the Brucis' painting collection, and you dine very well on Tuscan and Emilia-Romagnan dishes. Start with the mixed vegetable antipasto before moving on to their *osso buco alla fiorentina* (veal shanks in a hearty tomato sauce). ✉ *Via Nazionale 79/r,* ☎ *055/282106. AE, DC, MC, V. Closed Sun., Mon., and July 25–Aug. 25.*

$$ ✕ **Pallottino.** With its tile floor, photograph-filled walls, and wooden tables, Pallottino is the quintessential Tuscan trattoria, with such hearty, heartwarming classics as *pappa al pomodoro* (a tomato and bread soup) to *peposo alla toscana* (beef stew laced with black pepper). Their lunch special—*primo, secondo,* and *dolce* (first, second, and dessert courses)—could be, at 13,000 lire, the best bargain in town. ✉ *Via Isola delle Stinche 1/r,* ☎ *055/289573. AE, DC, MC, V. No credit cards at lunch. Closed Mon. and Aug. 1–20.*

$$ ✕ **Toscano.** A small table attractively set in a shop window identifies this restaurant near Palazzo Medici-Riccardi. It lives up to its name with Tuscan ambience and food, beamed ceilings, and a cold-cuts counter at the entrance. The kitchen prides itself on top-quality meat; try *spezzatino peposo* (beef stew with black pepper and a wine sauce). The prix-fixe menu is a good value. ✉ *Via Guelfa 70/r,* ☎ *055/215475. AE, DC, MC, V. Closed Tues. and Aug.*

$ ✕ **Baldovino.** This lively, brightly hued trattoria across the street from Santa Croce is the brainchild of David Gardner and Catherine Storrar, two Scottish expats. In addition to turning out fine, thin-crust pizzas, Baldovino offers some tasty antipasti (like their plate of smoked salmon and tuna), *insalatone* ("big salads"), as well as various pasta dishes and grilled meats—and they do it till the wee hours. It's a good idea to reserve ahead. ✉ *Via S. Guiseppe, 22/r,* ☎ *055/241 773, AE, DC, MC, V. Closed Mon. and last week Nov.–first week Dec.*

$ ✕ **La Maremmana.** The owners and chef here have been working together for 18 years, and it shows. The space is light and cheery—with white walls, tile floor, and pink tablecloths, giving the place a warm glow. Dead center is an impressive array of antipasti, which whet the taste buds for the glories that follow, such as spaghetti *alla vongole* (with tiny clams) and grilled meats. ✉ *Via dei Macci 77/r,* ☎ *055/241226. MC, V. Closed Sun.*

$$$$ **Excelsior.** The neo-Renaissance Excelsior, housed in a 13th-century convent that once was the residence of Josephine Bonaparte, has painted wooden ceilings, stained glass, and acres of Oriental carpets strewn over marble floors in the public rooms. Opulent furnishings adorn the guest rooms, some with elegant balconies overlooking the river or a Florentine panorama. ✉ *Piazza Ognissanti 3, 50123,* ☎ *055/264201,* FAX *055/210278. 168 rooms.* ✉ *Restaurant. AE, DC, MC, V.*

$$$$ ★ **Grand.** Facing its sister hotel, the smaller Excelsior (☞ *above*), across the expanse of Piazza Ognissanti, the Grand exudes old-world grace with its posh amenities. Sumptuous Renaissance style prevails, enriched with distinctive Florentine fabrics. Guest rooms are imperial or Florentine in style, many with frescoes or canopied beds. Bathrooms are swathed in marble. ✉ *Piazza Ognissanti 1, 50123,* ☎ *055/288781,* FAX *055/217400. 107 rooms. Restaurant, bar. AE, DC, MC, V.*

$$$$ **Hotel Lungarno.** During the Florence fashion weeks, this hotel—bought by the fashionable Ferragamo family in1995—buzzes with fashion industry glitterati. Guest rooms are large, and the blue- and white-trimmed white furnishings (the family colors are blue and white) are crisp and comfortable. Two of the guest rooms are in a medieval tower with exposed stone walls. The lobby bar, filled with oversize white sofas, has one of the most beautiful river views in Florence, and is a lovely place to stop in for a drink, even if you're not a guest. ✉ *Borgo San Jacopo 14, 50125,* ☎ *055/27261,* FAX *055/268437. 61 rooms, 11 suites. Bar. AE, DC, MC, V.*

$$$$ ★ **Plaza Hotel Lucchesi.** Elegant without being ostentatious, this hotel is right on the Arno near Santa Croce. Bedrooms are spacious and quiet (double glazing throughout), and the lounges and piano bar are a favorite rendezvous for Florentines. Front bedrooms have views of the river; rear rooms on the top floor have balconies and knockout views of Santa Croce. ✉ *Lungarno della Zecca Vecchia 38, 50122,* ☎ *055/26236,* FAX *055/2480921. 97 rooms. Restaurant. AE, DC, MC, V.*

$$$$ **Regency.** One of the Ottaviani family's small, select hotels, the Regency has the intimate and highly refined atmosphere of a private villa, luxuriously furnished with antiques and decorated with great style. Just outside the historic center of the city, it has a charming garden and the pleasant Le Jardin restaurant. ✉ *Piazza Massimo d'Azeglio 3, 50121,* ☎ *055/245247,* FAX *055/2346735. 34 rooms. Restaurant. AE, DC, MC, V.*

$$$$ **Villa Cora.** In a residential area on a hill overlooking Oltrarno, the Villa Cora is a converted private villa. Furnishings are exquisite and the atmosphere is quietly elegant. There are gardens to loll in, and a formal but charming restaurant. A Mercedes shuttle will whisk you into the centro. ✉ *Viale Machiavelli 18, 50125,* ☎ *055/2298451,* FAX *055/229086. 48 rooms. Restaurant, pool. AE, DC, MC, V.*

$$$ ★ **Brunelleschi.** This unique hotel in the heart of Florence encompasses a Byzantine tower, medieval church, and an 18th-century palazzo. Sections of ancient stone walls and brick arches set off the tasteful contemporary decor in the public rooms. Bedrooms have textured, coordinated fabrics in soft colors; the beige marble bathrooms are stately. ✉ *Piazza Sant'Elisabetta, Via dei Calzaiuoli, 50122,* ☎ *055/290311,* FAX *055/219653. 94 rooms. Restaurant. AE, DC, MC, V.*

$$$ ★ **Monna Lisa.** Staying here is like living in an aristocratic palace in the heart of Florence. American visitors in particular are fond of its smallish but homey bedrooms and sumptuously comfortable sitting rooms. Ask for a room on the quiet 17th-century courtyard, especially the one with the delightful balcony. A lavish buffet breakfast is included in the price. Reserve well in advance. ✉ *Borgo Pinti 27, 50121,* ☎ *055/2479751,* FAX *055/2479755. 30 rooms. AE, DC, MC, V.*

$$ **Hermitage.** Comfort and charm are the attributes of this hotel occupying the top six floors of a palazzo next to the Ponte Vecchio and the Uffizi. The inviting living room overlooking the Arno, flowered roof terrace, and well-lighted bedrooms are as lovely as a well-kept Florentine home. Double glazing and attentive maintenance sustain the relaxing ambience. ✉ *Vicolo Marzio 1, Piazza del Pesce, Ponte Vecchio, 50122,* ☎ *055/287216,* FAX *055/212208. 28 rooms. AE, MC, V.*

$$ **Hotel Ritz.** Set amid a row of buildings facing the Arno, this family-managed hotel has been decorated to make you feel as if you are a guest in a pretty, 19th-century Florentine home with 20th century amenities. Most of the rooms have lovely views of either the Arno or the domed, red-roofed "skyline" of Florence. ✉ *Lungarno Zecca Vecchia, 24, 50122,* ☎ *055/2340650,* FAX *055/240863. 30 rooms. AE, DC, MC, V.*

$$ **Hotel Torre Guelfa.** Hidden just 50 meters from the Ponte Vecchio, this small hotel has guest rooms in a Florentine palazzo and rooftop bar in its 13th-century tower. The owners have worked to make it feel like home, complete with canopy beds in some of the guest rooms. ✉ *Borgo S.S. Apostoli, 8, 50123,* ☎ *055/2396338,* FAX *055/2398577. 12 rooms. AE, MC, V.*

$$ ★ **Loggiato dei Serviti.** You'll find the Loggiato dei Serviti tucked under an arcade in one of the city's quietest and most attractive squares. With its vaulted ceilings and tasteful antique furnishings, this 19th-century town house hotel is a real find if you want to get the genuine Florentine feel while enjoying modern creature comforts. ✉ *Piazza Santissima Annunziata 3, 50122,* ☎ *055/2398280,* FAX *055/289595. 29 rooms. AE, DC, MC, V.*

$$ ★ **Morandi alla Crocetta.** This charming and distinguished residence near Piazza Santissima Annunziata was once a monastery, and access is up a flight of stairs. It is furnished in the classic style of a gracious Florentine home, and guests feel like privileged friends of the family. Small and exceptional, it is also a good value and must be booked well in advance. ✉ *Via Laura 50, 50121,* ☎ *055/2344747,* FAX *055/2480954. 9 rooms. AE, DC, MC, V.*

$$ **Pendini.** The atmosphere of an old-fashioned Florentine pensione is intact here, though most bedrooms have been renovated, with floral wallpaper, pastel carpeting, and modern baths. Public rooms have a turn-of-the century look, with some antiques. It's central, and off-season rates here are a real bargain. ✉ *Via Strozzi 2, 50123,* ☎ *055/211170,* FAX *055/281807. 42 rooms. AE, DC, MC, V.*

$$ **Porta Faenza.** A hospitable Italian-Canadian couple owns and manages this conveniently positioned hotel near the station. Spacious rooms in Florentine style and gleaming new bathrooms that, though compact, have such amenities as hair dryers make this a good value. The staff is helpful and attentive to guests' needs. ✉ *Via Faenza 77, 50123,* ☎ *055/284119,* FAX *055/210101. 15 rooms. AE, DC, MC, V.*

$$ **Villa Azalee.** In a residential area about five minutes from the train station, this century-old mansion is set in a large garden. It has a private-home atmosphere and comfortable living rooms. Rooms are decorated individually and are air-conditioned. ✉ *Viale Fratelli Rosselli 44, 50123,* ☎ *055/214242,* FAX *055/268264. 24 rooms. AE, DC, MC, V.*

$ **Alessandra.** The location, a block from the Ponte Vecchio, and clean, ample rooms make this a good choice for basic accommodations at reasonable rates. The English-speaking staff make sure guests are happy. ✉ *Borgo Santi Apostoli 17, 50123,* ☎ *055/283438,* FAX *055/210619. 25 rooms, 9 without bath. AE, MC, V. Closed Dec. 15–26.*

$ ★ **Bellettini.** Very central, this small hotel occupies two floors of an old but well-kept building near San Lorenzo, in an area with many inexpensive eating places. Rooms are ample, with Venetian or Tuscan decor, and bathrooms are modern. The management is friendly and helpful. ✉ *Via dei Conti 7, 50123,* ☎ *055/213561,* FAX *055/283551. 27 rooms, 23 with bath. AE, DC, MC, V.*

$ **Nuova Italia.** Near the main train station and within walking distance of the sights, this homey hotel in a dignified palazzo is run by a genial English-speaking family. Rooms are clean and simply furnished, and they have triple-glazed windows to ensure restful nights. ✉ *Via Faenza 26, 50123,* ☎ *055/268430,* FAX *055/210941. 20 rooms. AE, DC, MC, V.*

Nightlife and the Arts

The Arts

FILM

English-language films are shown Tuesday through Sunday evenings at the **Cinema Astro** (✉ Piazza San Simone near Santa Croce), and on Monday at the **Odeon** (✉ Piazza Strozzi) and the **Goldoni** (✉ Via dei Serragli).

MUSIC

Most major musical events are staged at the **Teatro Comunale** (✉ Corso Italia 16, ☎ 055/2779236). The box office (closed Sunday and Monday) is open from 9 to 1, and a half hour before performances. It's best to order your tickets by mail, however, as they're difficult to come by at the last minute. Amici della Musica (Friends of Music) puts on a series of concerts at the **Teatro della Pergola** (✉ Box office, Via della Pergola 10a/r, ☎ 055/2479652). For program information contact the **Amici della Musica** directly (✉ Via Sirtori 49, ☎ 055/608420).

Nightlife

BARS

The bar in the lobby of the **Excelsior** (✉ Piazza Ognissanti 3, ☎ 055/264201) attracts locals as well as business travelers and tourists. **The Jazz Club** (✉ Via Nuova dei Caccini 3, ☎ 055/2479700) offers good live jazz in a surprisingly well-ventilated club near the Duomo.

NIGHTCLUBS

The River Club (✉ Lungarno Corsini 8, ☎ 055/282465; closed Sun.) has winter-garden decor and a large dance floor. **Meccanò** (✉ in the Cascine park at Viale degli Olmi 1, ☎ 055/331371; closed Sun.) offers a multimedia experience, with videos, art, and music in a high-tech disco with a late-night restaurant, the Pomodoro d'Acciaio. **Hurricane Roxy** (✉ Via Il Prato 58/r, ☎ 055/2103999) serves a light lunch during the day but in the evening there's a deejay, good music, and welcoming atmosphere. **Jackie O** (✉ Via dell'Erta Canina 24a, ☎ 055/2342442; closed Wed.) is a glittering art deco disco with lots of mirrors and marble and a trendy clientele. **Space Electronic** (✉ Via Palazzuolo 37, ☎ 055/2393082; closed Mon., except Mar.–Sept.) is exactly what its name implies: ultramodern and psychedelic. **Yab** (✉ Via Sassetti 5/r, ☎ 055/282018; closed Sun. and Mon.) is another futuristic disco popular with the young jet set.

Shopping

Markets

The **Mercato di San Lorenzo** (✉ Piazza San Lorenzo and Via dell'Ariento; ⏲ Tues.–Sat. 8–7, Sun. in summer) is a fine place to browse for buys in leather goods and souvenirs. Don't miss the indoor, two-story **Mercato Centrale** (✉ Piazza del Mercato Centrale), near San Lorenzo, open in the morning Monday–Saturday.

Shopping Districts

Via Tornabuoni is the high-end shopping mecca. **Via della Vigna Nuova** is just as fashionable. Goldsmiths and jewelry shops can be found on and around the **Ponte Vecchio** and in the **Santa Croce area,** where there is also a high concentration of leather shops and inconspicuous shops selling gold and silver jewelry at prices much lower than those of the elegant jewelers near Ponte Vecchio. The monastery of **Santa Croce** (⊠ entrances at Via San Giuseppe 5/r and Piazza Santa Croce 16) houses a leather-working school and showroom. Antiques dealers can be found in and around the center, but are concentrated on **Via Maggio** in the Oltrarno area. **Borgo Ognissanti** is also home to shops selling period decorative objects.

Florence Essentials

Arriving and Departing

BY PLANE

The airport that handles most arrivals is **Aeroporto Galileo Galilei** (⊠ Pisa, ☎ 050/500707), more commonly known as Aeroporto Pisa-Galilei. Some domestic and European flights use Florence's **Aeroporto Vespucci** (⊠ Peretola, ☎ 055/333498).

Between the Airport and Downtown. Pisa-Galilei Airport is connected to Florence by train direct to the Stazione Centrale di Santa Maria Novella. Service is hourly throughout the day and takes about 60 minutes. When departing, you can buy train tickets for the airport and check in for all flights leaving from Aeroporto Pisa-Galilei at the Florence Air Terminal at Track 5 of Stazione Centrale di Santa Maria Novella. Aeroporto Vespucci is connected to downtown Florence by SITA bus.

BY TRAIN

The main station is **Stazione Centrale di Santa Maria Novella** (☎ 1478/88088 toll free). Florence is on the main north–south route between Rome, Bologna, and Milan or Venice. High-speed Eurostar trains reach Rome in less than two hours and Milan in less than three.

Getting Around

BY BICYCLE

Alinari (⊠ Via Guelfa 85/r, ☎ 055/280500). **Motorent** (⊠ Via San Zanobi 9/r, ☎ 055/490113).

BY BUS

Bus maps and timetables are available for a small fee at the Azienda Transporti Autolinee Fiorentine (ATAF, ⊠ near Stazione Centrale di Santa Maria Novella; Piazza del Duomo 57/r) city bus information booths. The same maps may be free at visitor information offices. **ATAF** city buses run from about 5:15 AM to 1 AM. Buy tickets before you board the bus; they are sold at many tobacco shops and newsstands. The cost is 1,500 lire for a ticket good for one hour, 2,500 lire for 2 hours, and 5,800 lire for four one-hour tickets, called a *multiplo.* A 24-hour tourist ticket (*turistico*) costs 6,000 lire. For excursions outside Florence, for instance, to Siena, you take **SITA** (bus terminal, ⊠ Via Santa Caterina da Siena 17, near the Stazione Centrale di Santa Maria Novella). The **CAP** bus terminal (⊠ Via Nazionale 13) is also near the train station.

BY CAR

The north–south access route to Florence is the Autostrada del Sole (A1) from Milan or Rome. The Florence–Mare autostrada (A11) links Florence with the Tyrrhenian coast, Pisa, and the A12 coastal autostrada. Parking in Florence is severely restricted.

BY MOPED

Try **Alinari** or **Motorent** (☞ By Bicycle, *above*).

BY TAXI

Taxis wait at stands and you can call them (☎ 055/4798 or 055/4390). Use only authorized cabs, which are white with a yellow stripe or rectangle on the door. The meter starts at 4,500 lire, with extra charges for nights, holidays, or radio dispatch.

ON FOOT

It is easy to find your way around in Florence with the help of the many landmarks. Major sights can be explored on foot, as they are packed into a relatively small area. Wear comfortable shoes. The system of street addresses is unusual, with commercial addresses (those with an *r* in them, meaning *rosso,* or red) and residential addresses numbered separately (32/r might be next to or a block away from plain 32).

Contacts and Resources

CONSULATES

United States (✉ Lungarno Vespucci 38, ☎ 055/2398276). **Canadian** (citizens should refer to their embassy in Rome; ☞ Rome Essentials, *above*). **United Kingdom** (✉ Lungarno Corsini 2, ☎ 055/284133).

EMERGENCIES

Police (☎ 113). **Ambulance** (☎ 118 or 055/212222). **Tourist Medical Service** (✉ Viale Lorenzo Il Magnifico, ☎ 055/475411). **Pharmacies** are open Sunday and holidays by rotation. Signs posted outside pharmacies list those open all night and on weekends. The pharmacy at Santa Maria Novella train station is always open.

ENGLISH-LANGUAGE BOOKSTORES

Seeber (✉ Via Tornabuoni 68, ☎ 055/215697). **Paperback Exchange** (✉ Via Fiesolana 31/r, near Santa Croce, ☎ 055/2478154). **BM Bookshop** (✉ Borgo Ognissanti 4/r, ☎ 055/294575).

GUIDED TOURS

Excursions. Operators offer a half-day excursion to Pisa, usually in the afternoon, costing about 48,000 lire, and a full-day excursion to Siena and San Gimignano, costing about 68,000 lire. Pick up a timetable at ATAF information offices near the train station, at SITA (✉ Via Santa Caterina da Siena 17, ☎ 055/214721), or at the APT tourist office (☞ *below*).

Orientation. A bus consortium (through hotels and travel agents) offers tours in air-conditioned buses covering the important sights in Florence with a trip to Fiesole. The cost is about 48,000 lire for a three-hour tour, including entrance fees, and bookings can be made through travel agents.

Special-Interest. Inquire at travel agents or at **Agriturist Regionale** (✉ Piazza San Firenze 3, ☎ 055/287838) for visits to villa gardens around Florence from April through June, or for visits to farm estates during September and October.

TRAVEL AGENCIES

American Express (✉ Via Guicciardini 49/r, ☎ 055/288751; ✉ Via Dante Alighieri 20/r, ☎ 055/50981). **CIT** (✉ Via Cavour 54/r, ☎ 055/294306). **Wagons-Lits** (✉ Via del Giglio 27/r, ☎ 055/218851).

VISITOR INFORMATION

Azienda Promozione Turistica (APT; ✉ Via Manzoni 16, 50121, ☎ 055/2346284).

TUSCANY

Tuscany is a blend of rugged hills, fertile valleys, and long stretches of sandy beach that curve along the west coast of central Italy and fringe the pine-forested coastal plain of the Maremma. The gentle, cypress-studded green hills may seem familiar: Leonardo and Raphael often painted them in the backgrounds of their masterpieces. Cities and towns here were the cradle of the Renaissance, which during the 15th century flourished in nearby Florence. Come to Tuscany to enjoy its unchanged and gracious atmosphere of good living, and, above all, its unparalleled artistic treasures, many still in their original tiny old churches and patrician palaces.

Prato

Since the Middle Ages, Prato, 21 km (13 mi) northwest of Florence, has been Italy's major wool-producing center, and it remains one of the world's largest manufacturers of cloth. Ignore the drab industrial outskirts and devote some time to the fine old buildings in the downtown area, crammed with artwork commissioned by Prato's wealthy merchants during the Renaissance. Though in ruins, the formidable **Castello** (Castle) built for Frederick II Hohenstaufen, adjacent to Santa Maria delle Carceri, is an impressive sight, the only castle of its type to be seen outside southern Italy. ✉ *Piazza Santa Maria delle Carceri.* 🎫 *Free.* ⏲ *Mon. and Wed.–Sat. 9:30–11:30 and 8:30–12:30 and 3–5:30, Sun. 9–11:30.*

The **Duomo,** erected during the Middle Ages, was decorated with paintings and sculptures by some of the most illustrious figures of Tuscan art. Among them was Fra Filippo Lippi (1406–69), who executed scenes from the life of St. Stephen on the left wall and scenes from the life of John the Baptist on the right in the *cappella maggiore* (main chapel). Bring a flashlight—there's no illumination provided. ✉ *Piazza del Duomo.* ⏲ *Daily 7–noon and 3:30–6:30.*

In the former bishop's palace, now the **Museo dell'Opera del Duomo** (Cathedral Museum), you can see the original reliefs by Donatello for the Pulpit of the Holy Girdle (Mary's belt, supposedly given to the apostle Thomas as evidence of her assumption into heaven; the relic is kept in a chapel of the cathedral). ✉ *Piazza del Duomo 49,* ☎ *0574/29339.* 🎫 *5,000 lire* ⏲ *Mon. and Wed.–Sat. 9:30–12:30 and 3–6:30, Sun. 9:30–12:30.*

The church of **Santa Maria delle Carceri** was built by Giuliano Sangallo in the 1490s, and is a landmark of Renaissance architecture. ✉ *Piazza Santa Maria delle Carceri, off Via Cairoli and southeast of the cathedral.*

$$ ✕ **Baghino.** In the heart of the historic center, Baghino serves typical Tuscan fare as well as such atypical Tuscan fare as spaghetti all'amatriciana and penne with clams and curry. You can dine in the lovely outdoor terrace in the summer. ✉ *Via dell'Accademia 9,* ☎ *055/27920, AE, DC, MC, V. No dinner Sun., no lunch Mon.*

Pistoia

A floricultural capital of Europe, Pistoia—about 15 km (9 mi) northwest of Prato—is surrounded by greenhouses and plant nurseries. Flowers aside, Pistoia's main sights are all in the historic center with superb examples of Romanesque architecture. The Romanesque **Duomo** is flanked by a bell tower begun in the 12th century and faces the unusual Gothic baptistery. Inside the cathedral in a side chapel dedicated to San Jacopo (St. James, the patron saint of Pistoia), there's a massive **silver altar** that alone makes the stop in Pistoia worthwhile. Nearly

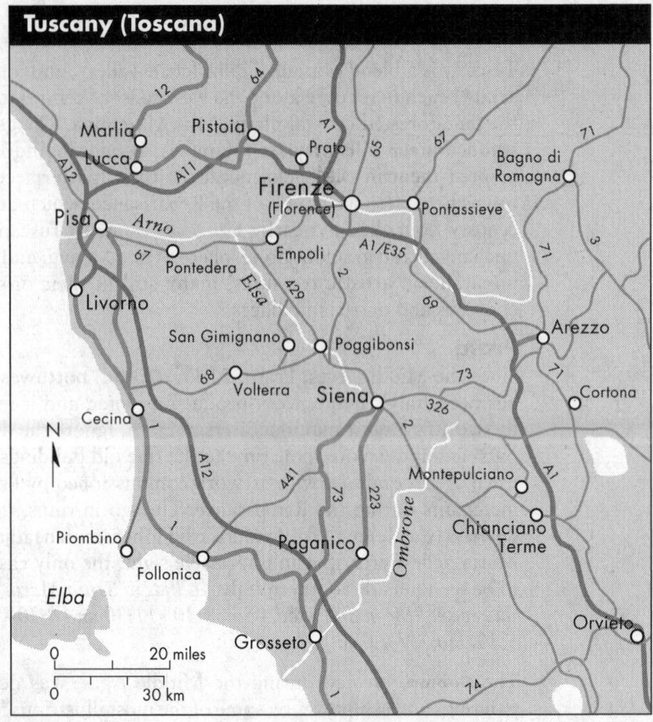

200 years in the making, it's an incredible piece of workmanship, begun in 1287. ✉ *Piazza del Duomo.*

North of the cathedral, the **Ospedale del Ceppo** (Hospital of the Tree Trunk), founded in the 13th century, gets its name from the hollow trunk in which offerings were placed. On the facade is a superb frieze by the workshop of Santi and Benedetto Buglioni, which was completed by Giovanni della Robbia (c. 1400–82) in 1527. ✉ *Piazza dell'Ospedale, Via delle Pappe.*

An architectural gem revealed in green-and-white marble, the medieval church of **San Giovanni Fuorcivitas** holds a *Visitation* by Luca della Robbia, a painting attributed to Taddeo Gaddi, and a holy-water font that may have been executed by Giovanni Pisano. ✉ *Via Cavour.*

Though it is not as grand as the silver altar in the cathedral, many consider Pistoia's greatest art treasure to be Giovanni Pisano's powerfully sculpted pulpit executed between 1298 and 1301 in the church of **Sant'Andrea.** ✉ *Via Sant'Andrea.*

$$ ✕ **Corradossi.**The food in this pan-Italian restaurant is elegant yet simple, service quick and attentive, and the prices more than reasonable. Start with the *trofia e gamberi,* corkscrew-shape pasta sauced with perfectly cooked shrimp and sliced baby zucchini, then follow with their *fritte miste*—little sea critters crisply fried. ✉ *Via Frosini 112* ☎ *0573/25683. AE, DC, MC, V. Closed Sun.*

$$ ✕ **S. Jacopo.** This charming restaurant near the Duomo has white walls, tile floors, and a gracious host in Bruno Lottini. The food is as welcoming as he: bread, flecked with olives, is baked on the premises and arrives hot. Regional favorites include *maccheroni S. Jacopo,* wide ribbons of house-made pasta with a duck *ragù* (sauce), and they can turn out perfectly grilled squid as well. Save room for dessert, especially the apple strudel. ✉ *Via Crispi 15,* ☎ *0573/27786. AE, DC, MC, V. Closed 15 days in Aug. No lunch Mon. and Tues.*

Lucca

Any tour of Tuscany should include Lucca, with its handful of marvelously elaborate Romanesque churches and late 19th-century and early 20th-century Liberty facades along the Fillungo, its main shopping thoroughfare. Because few cars are allowed in the historic center, the city is easy to get around in—and a pleasure. For that very reason it's an excellent alternative to, or side trip from, Pisa, just 22 km (14 mi) away. First enjoy the views of Lucca and countryside from the parklike 16th-century ramparts. Then explore the churches that look suspiciously like oversize marble wedding cakes. A forest of columns fronts the 11th-century **Duomo;** inside is the 15th-century tomb of Ilaria del Carretto by Jacopo della Quercia (1374–1438). ✉ *Piazza San Martino.*

Piazza del Mercato preserves the oval form of the Roman amphitheater over which it was built; an outdoor market bustles here on weekdays. The church of **San Frediano** is graced with an austere facade ornamented by 13th-century mosaic decoration. Inside, check out the exquisite reliefs by Jacopo della Quercia in the last chapel on the left and the bizarre mummy of St. Zita, patron saint of domestic servants. ✉ *Piazza San Frediano.*

One of the most fanciful facades in central Italy can be seen on the front of the church of **San Michele in Foro,** adorned with a marriage of arches and columns crowned by a statue of St. Michael. The church is an exceptional example of the Pisan Romanesque style and the decorative flair peculiar to Lucca. ✉ *Piazza San Michele.*

The **Villa Reale** (Royal Villa), at Marlia, 8 km (5 mi) west of Lucca, was once the home of Napoléon's sister, and has been restored by the Counts Pecci-Blunt. It is celebrated for its spectacular gardens, designed during the 18th and 19th centuries. Gardening buffs adore the legendary *teatro di verdura*, a theater carved out of hedges and topiaries; a music festival is usually held here during July and August. ✉ *Via Villa Reale, Marlia,* ☎ *0583/30108.* ⏲ *Guided visits on the hr, July–Sept., Tues.–Sun. at 10, 11, 4, 5, and 6; Oct.–Nov. and Mar.–June, Tues.–Sun. at 10, 11, 3, 4, and 5. Closed Dec.–Feb.*

$$–$$$ ✕ **La Mora.** You'll need a car or a taxi to get to this charming old way station 10 km (6 mi) outside Lucca, but its authentic local cooking is worth every effort. It is widely considered to be one of the best regional restaurants in Italy. Reservations are advised. ✉ *Via Sesto di Moriano 1748, Ponte a Moriano,* ☎ *0583/406402,* FAX *0583/406135. AE, DC, MC, V. Closed Wed. and Oct. 10–30.*

$$ ★ ✕ **Buca di Sant'Antonio.** Buca di Sant'Antonio has been around for more than 2 centuries, and it's easy to see why. A white-walled interior adorned with copper pots, expertly prepared food, and an able staff make dining here a real treat. The menu offers something for everyone, from simple pasta dishes to more daring dishes such as roast *capretto* (kid) with herbs. ✉ *Via della Cervia 3,* ☎ *0583/55881. AE, DC, MC, V. Closed Mon. and last 3 wks in July. No dinner Sun.*

$$ ✕ **Il Giglio.** Off vast Piazza Napoleone, Il Giglio has a quiet, turn-of-the-century charm and a dignified atmosphere. In summer the tables outdoors have a less formal air. The menu is classic: crostini di fegatini, steaks, and seafood. ✉ *Piazza del Giglio 3,* ☎ *0583/494058. AE, DC, MC, V. Closed Wed. and 2 wks in Feb. No dinner Tues.*

$–$$$ ★ 🏨 **Villa La Principessa.** This pretty 19th-century country mansion, 3½ km (2 mi) outside Lucca, is an exclusive hotel with a deluxe annex, Locanda L'Elisa. All rooms are individually and tastefully decorated.

Antique floors, furniture, and portraits set the tone, and the restaurant is known for its fine Tuscan dishes. ✉ *Massa Pisana, 55050,* ☎ *0583/370037,* FAX *0583/379136. 40 rooms. Restaurant, outdoor pool. AE, DC, MC, V. Closed Nov. 1–Mar. 31.*

$ **La Luna.** There's an aura of Old World charm in this family-run hotel on one of Lucca's most central and historic streets. Extensive renovations have endowed the establishment with gleaming modern bathrooms, leaving the atmosphere intact. A plus for anyone touring by car is the hotel's own garage and parking area. ✉ *Corte Compagni 12 (corner of Via Fillungo), 55100,* ☎ *0583/493634,* FAX *0583/490021. 30 rooms. AE, DC, MC, V. Closed last 3 wks in Jan.*

$ **Piccolo Hotel Puccini.** Just a few steps away from the busy square and church of San Michele, this little hotel is quiet and calm. It also offers parking (which must be reserved in advance) at a reasonable fee, which is a great advantage. ✉ *Via di Poggio, 9, 55100,* ☎ *0583/55421,* FAX *0583/55421. 14 rooms. AE, DC, MC, V.*

Pisa

If you cut through the kitschy atmosphere around the Leaning Tower, Pisa has much to offer. Its cathedral-baptistery-tower complex in Piazza dei Miracoli is among the most dramatic in Italy, and the Piazza dei Cavalieri is a superb example of a Renaissance piazza. Pisa's treasures are more subtle than Florence's, to which it is inevitably compared. Pisa usually emerges the loser, and it shouldn't. Though it sustained heavy damage during World War II, many of its beautiful Romanesque structures are still preserved and are well worth seeking out.

The **Battistero** (baptistery) in front of the cathedral is known mainly for its graceful form and for the pulpit carved by Giovanni Pisano's father, Nicola (1220–78). The baptistery was begun in 1153 but not completed until 1400. Ask one of the ticket takers if he'll sing for you inside the baptistery. The acoustics are remarkable; a tip of 5,000 lire is appropriate. ✉ *Piazza dei Miracoli.* 🎫 *15,000 lire for baptistery, Duomo, and Leaning Tower.* ⏲ *Apr.–Sept. 8–7:40; Oct.–Mar. 9–4:40.*

The Camposanto (Cemetery) is said to be filled with earth brought back from the Holy Land by Crusaders. Important frescoes, notably the *Drunkenness of Noah* by Renaissance artist Benozzo Gozzoli and a 14th-century *Triumph of Death,* are within. ✉ *Piazza dei Miracoli.* 🎫 *15,000 lire for baptistery, Duomo, and Leaning Tower.* ⏲ *Apr.–Sept., daily 8–7:40; Oct.–Mar., daily 9–5:40.*

★ **Pisa's Duomo** is elegantly simple, its facade decorated with geometric and animal shapes. The cavernous interior is supported by a series of 68 columns, while the pulpit is a prime example of Giovanni Pisano's work and one of the major monuments of the Italian Gothic style. Be sure to note the suspended lamp that hangs across from the pulpit. Known as Galileo's Lamp, it's said to have inspired his theories on pendular motion. ✉ *Piazza del Duomo.* 🎫 *15,000 lire for baptistery, Duomo, and Leaning Tower.* ⏲ *Apr.–Sept., Mon.–Sat. 10–7:40, Sun. 1–5; Oct.–Mar., daily 10–12:30 and 3–5:30.*

$$ ✕ **Bruno.** A country-inn look, with beam ceilings and soft lights, makes Bruno a pleasant place to lunch on classic Tuscan dishes, from *zuppa alla pisana* (vegetable soup) to *baccalà con porri* (cod with leeks). It's just outside the old city walls and only a short walk from the bell tower and cathedral. ✉ *Via Luigi Bianchi 12,* ☎ *050/560818. AE, DC, MC, V. Closed Tues. No dinner Mon.*

$$ ✕ **Osteria dei Cavalieri.** This charming white-walled osteria, a few steps from Piazza dei Cavalieri, is reason enough to come to Pisa. On offer are exquisitely grilled fish dishes, vegetarian dishes, and *tagliata,* thin slivers of rare beef, four different ways. Finish your meal with a lemon sorbet bathed in Prosecco, and walk away feeling like you've eaten like a king at plebeian prices. ✉ *Via San Frediano 16,* ☎ *055/580858, AE, DC, MC, V. Closed Sun. and July 25–Aug. 25. No lunch Sat.*

Siena

One of Italy's best-preserved medieval towns, Siena is rich both in works of art and in expensive antiques shops. Built on three hills, Siena is not an easy town to explore, for everything you'll want to see is either up or down a steep hill or stairway and many hotels are outside the old walls. But it is worth every ounce of effort. Siena really gives you the chance of seeing and feeling what the Middle Ages must have been like: dark fortresslike stone palaces, Gothic church portals, and narrow streets leading to airy squares. Siena was a center of learning and art during the Middle Ages, and almost all the public buildings and churches in the town have enough artistic or historical merit to be worth visiting. You can buy a combined ticket for admission to the Biblioteca Piccolomini and Museo dell'Opera Metropolitana.

One of the finest Gothic cathedrals in Italy, Siena's **Duomo** is unique in displaying a mixture of religious and civic ornamentation on both its interior and exterior. The unique inlaid marble floors and Nicola Pisano's pulpit, carved about 1265, are highlights. The animated frescoes of papal history in the Piccolomini Library (with an entrance off the left aisle of the cathedral) were painted by Pinturicchio. ✉ *Piazza del Duomo. Library:* ⏲ *Mar. 15–Oct. 31, daily 9–7:30; Nov. 1–Mar. 15, daily 10–1 and 2:30–5.*

The **Museo dell'Opera Metropolitana** (Cathedral Museum) contains some fine works of art, notably a celebrated *Maestà* by Duccio di Buoninsegna. ✉ *Piazza del Duomo,* ☎ *0577/283048.* ⏲ *Mid-Mar.–Sept., daily 9–7:30; Oct., daily 9–6; Nov.–Dec., daily 9–1:30; Jan.–mid-Mar., daily 9–1:30.*

★ The 13th-century **Palazzo Pubblico** (City Hall) dominates Piazza del Campo and houses the Museo Civico (Civic Museum), where there are noteworthy frescoes. ✉ *Piazza del Campo,* ☎ *0577/292263.* ⏲ *Mar.–Apr., Mon.–Sat. 9:30–6:30; Nov.–early Jan., Mon.–Sat. 9:30–1:30.*

★ Fan-shape, sloping **Piazza del Campo** is Siena's main center of activity, with 11 streets leading into it. Farsighted planning has preserved it as a medieval showpiece. This is the venue for the famous **Palio,** a breakneck, 90-second horse race that takes place twice each year, on July 2 and August 16. The **Torre del Mangia** (Bell Tower) of the Palazzo Pubblico (☞ *above*), offers a wonderful view (you'll have to climb 503 steps to reach it, however). ✉ *Piazza del Campo.* ⏲ *Daily 10–1 hr before sunset.*

$$ ✕ **Osteria Le Logge.** Just off Piazza del Campo, this is a fine choice for an informal but memorable meal. Get there early to claim a table. Among the specialties are *malfatti all'Osteria* (ricotta and spinach dumplings in cream sauce) and tagliata *alla rucola* (sliced steak with arugula). ✉ *Via del Porrione 33,* ☎ *0577/48013. AE, DC, MC, V. Closed Sun., 2 wks in June and Nov.*

$$ ✕ **Tullio Tre Cristi.** To find this historic trattoria, take Via dei Rossi from Via Banchi di Sopra. Even though it was discovered by tourists long ago, it remains true to typical Sienese cooking and atmosphere. Try spaghetti *alle briciole,* a poor-man's pasta with bread crumbs, tomato, and garlic. ✉ *Vicolo di Provenzano 1,* ☎ *0577/280608. MC, V. Closed Tues.*

$ ✕ **Le Tre Campane.** Conveniently set between Piazza del Campo and the Duomo, this small trattoria displays the colorful banners of Siena's 17 districts. Popular with the locals, it specializes in Tuscan fare and a *trittico* (trio) of pastas. ✉ *Piazzetta Bonelli 2,* ☎ *0577/286091. AE, DC, MC, V. Closed Tues. and 1 wk in July.*

$$$ ✕🏨 **La Suvera.** In this luxurious hotel in the Tuscan countryside, 27 km (17 mi) from Siena and 56 km (35 mi) from Florence, you can savor living on an aristocratic estate that was once owned by Pope Julius II. Rooms and suites are magnificently furnished with antiques and fitted with up-to-the-minute comforts. With salons, a library, Italian garden, swimming pool, and L'Oliviera restaurant (serving estate wines) to enjoy, guests find it hard to tear themselves away. There's even a helipad. ✉ *Off Rte. 541, Pievescola (Casola d'Elsa), 53030,* ☎ *0577/960300,* FAX *0577/960220. 22 rooms, 13 suites. Restaurant, pool. AE, DC, MC, V.* ⊗ *Open Easter–Oct.*

$$$$ ★ 🏨 **Certosa di Maggiano.** A 14th-century Carthusian monastery less than a mile southeast of Siena has been converted into a sophisticated oasis furnished in impeccable style. The bedrooms have every comfort, and the atmosphere is that of an aristocratic family villa. In warm weather breakfast is served on the patio next to the garden aburst with roses, zinnias, and other blessed friends. ✉ *Strada di Certosa 82, 53100,* ☎ *0577/288180,* FAX *0577/288189. 18 rooms. Restaurant, pool. AE, DC, MC, V.*

$$$$ 🏨 **Park Hotel.** Just outside the walls of the old city, this is a handsome and sprawling 15th-century villa on its own well-equipped grounds, with a 9-hole golf course. The furnishings in the public areas strike an elegant balance between antique charm and patrician comfort. Comfortable guest rooms might seem familiar, with their bold, dark fabrics, mirrors, and modern appointments. ✉ *Via di Marciano 18, 53100,* ☎ *0577/44803,* FAX *0577/49020. 69 rooms. Restaurant, pool. AE, DC, MC, V.*

$$ 🏨 **Antica Torre.** A cordial young couple runs this hotel in a restored centuries-old tower a 10-minute walk from Piazza del Campo. Rooms are smallish and are furnished sparingly but in good taste. Beam ceilings throughout and original brick vaults here and there are reminders of the tower's venerable history. ✉ *Via Fieravecchia 7, 53100,* ☎ FAX *0577/222255. 8 rooms. AE, MC, V.*

$–$$ ★ 🏨 **Duomo.** Occupying the top floor of a 17th-century building in the center of Siena, near Piazza del Campo, the hotel is quiet and is furnished in a neat contemporary style, with traces of the past showing in the artfully exposed brickwork in the breakfast room. Many rooms have superb views of the city's towers and the hills beyond. ✉ *Via Stalloreggi 38, 53100,* ☎ *0577/289088,* FAX *0577/43043. 23 rooms. AE, DC, MC, V.*

San Gimignano

San Gimignano-of-the-Beautiful-Towers—to use its original name—is perhaps the most delightful of the Tuscan medieval hill towns, 31 km (20 mi) northwest of Siena. There were once more than 70 tall towers here, symbols of power for the wealthy families of the Middle Ages. Fourteen still stand, giving the town its unique skyline. The main street leads directly from the city gates to Piazza della Cisterna, with a quaint wellhead, and Piazza del Duomo.

The walls of the **Collegiata** (Church), and those in the **Cappella della Santa Fina** chapel dedicated to Santa Fina, are decorated with radiant frescoes by Domenico Ghirlandaio. (Have plenty of 100-lire coins at hand for the light machines; to get a closer look at the chapel frescoes, buy a ticket for the Municipal Museum in Palazzo del Popolo.) From the steps of the church you can observe the town's countless crows as they circle the tall towers. In the pretty courtyard on the right as you descend the church stairs, there's a shop selling Tuscan and Deruta ceramics, which you'll also find in other shops along the Via San Giovanni. ✉ *Piazza del Duomo,* ☎ *0577/940316.* ⏲ *Daily 9:30–12:30 and 3–5:30.*

$$$ ✕ **Bel Soggiorno.** Bel Soggiorno is attached to a small hotel. It has fine views, refectory tables set with linen and candles, and leather-covered chairs. Specialties are *zuppa medioevale* (soup of mushrooms, truffle, grain, and potatoes) and *sorpresa in crosta* (spicy rabbit stew in a bread crust). ✉ *Via San Giovanni 91,* ☎ *0577/940375. AE, DC, MC, V. Closed Mon. and Jan.–Feb.*

$$ ✕ **La Mangiatoia.** In this rustic trattoria off Via San Matteo prices are more moderate than at places with a view. The kitchen turns out simple country cooking. ✉ *Via Mainardi 5,* ☎ *0577/941528. MC, V. Closed Tues., 3 wks in Nov., and 1 wk in Jan.*

$$ 🏨 **Pescille.** This rambling stone farmhouse, about 3 km (2 mi) outside San Gimignano, with a good view of the town, has been restored as a hotel and furnished in attractive chic rustic style. ✉ *Località Pescille, 53037,* ☎ *0577/940186,* FAX *0577/940186. 40 rooms. Pool. AE, DC, MC, V. Closed Nov. 15–Feb.*

Arezzo

To appreciate Arezzo you have to delve into the town's historic core, ignoring the industrialized suburbs. The city is one of Italy's three major gold jewelry production centers. In the old, upper town are an array of medieval and Renaissance buildings and a piazza that is a compendium of several eras. Tuscan art treasures abound in Arezzo, including frescoes by Piero della Francesca, stained glass, and ancient Etruscan pottery. In the old part of Arezzo, the poet Petrarch (1304–74), the artist Vasari (1511–74), and the satirical author Pietro Aretino (1492–1556) all lived.

The fine Gothic **Duomo** is decorated with richly colored 16th-century stained glass windows and an eye-level fresco of a tender Magdalen by Piero della Francesca next to the large marble tomb near the organ. ✉ *Piazza del Duomo.*

Next to what's left of an ancient **Roman amphitheater** and near the train station is the **Museo Archeologico** (Archaeological Museum), with a rich collection of Etruscan art, artifacts, and pottery. Reproductions of the latter by contemporary Arezzo artisans are sold in local ceramic shops. ✉ *Via Margaritone 10,* ☎ *0575/20882.* ⏲ *Mon.–Sat. 9–2, Sun. 9–1.*

★ In the church of **San Francesco** are famous frescoes by Piero della Francesca, painted between 1452 and 1466 and depicting *The Legend of the True Cross* on three walls of the choir. Unfortunately, part of the frescoes may be hidden from view while restoration work takes place. ✉ *Via Cavour.*

Piazza Grande is an attractive, sloping square where an extensive open-air fair of antiques and old bric-a-brac is held the first weekend of every month. The shops around the piazza also specialize in antiques, with prices lower than those you will encounter in Florence. The colonnaded apse and bell tower of the Romanesque church of **Santa Maria della Pieve** grace one end of this pleasant piazza.

$$ ★ ✕ **Buca di San Francesco.** Travelers and passing celebrities come to this rustic and historic cellar restaurant for the 13th-century cantina atmosphere, but locals love it for the food, especially ribollita and *sformato di verdure* (vegetable flan). ✉ *Piazza San Francesco 1,* ☎ *0575/23271. AE, DC, MC, V. Closed Tues. and 2 wks in July. No dinner Mon.*

$$ ✕ **L'Agania.** The main draw to this central osteria is not its plain wood paneling and cheap furniture, but its good, inexpensive dishes such as boar meat, both as a second course and in a savory sauce with pasta. Also try the *griffi,* which is actually veal cheek, but tasty in a sauce with tomatoes and spices. ✉ *Via Mazzini 10,* ☎ *0575/295381. AE, DC, MC, V. Closed Mon. and 2nd wk in June.*

$$ **Continental.** The circa-1950 Continental has fairly spacious rooms decorated in white and bright yellow, gleaming bathrooms, and the advantage of a central location within walking distance of all major sights. ✉ *Piazza Guido Monaco 7, 52100,* ☎ *0575/20251,* FAX *0575/350485. 74 rooms. AE, DC, MC, V.*

Cortona

Cortona, about 30 km (19 mi) south of Arezzo, has a peculiarly Tuscan brand of charm. This well-preserved, unspoiled medieval hill town is known for its excellent small picture gallery and a number of fine antiques shops, as well as for its colony of foreign residents. The approach to Cortona from the east passes the Renaissance church of **Santa Maria del Calcinaio.** The heart of Cortona is formed by **Piazza della Repubblica** and the adjacent **Piazza Signorelli.**

Picturesque **Palazzo Pretorio** (Praetorian Palace) houses a museum with a representative collection of Etruscan bronzes. Climb its centuries-old stone staircase to the **Museo dell'Accademia Etrusca** (Gallery of Etruscan Art). ✉ *Piazza Signorelli 9,* ☎ *0575/630415.* ⏲ *Apr.–Sept., Tues.–Sun. 10–1 and 4–7; Oct.–Mar., Tues.–Sun. 9–1 and 3–5.*

The **Museo Diocesano** (Diocesan Museum) houses an impressive number of large and splendid paintings by native son Luca Signorelli, as well as a beautiful *Annunciation* by Fra Angelico, a delightful surprise in this small, eclectic town. ✉ *Piazza del Duomo 1,* ☎ *0575/62830.* ⏲ *Apr.–Sept., Tues.–Sun. 9:30–1 and 3:30–7; Oct.–Mar., Tues.–Sun. 10–1 and 3–5.*

$$ ★ ✕ **Tonino.** The place to eat in Cortona, it's known for its delicious antipasto and for succulent steaks of Chiana Valley beef. It's best on weekdays, when it's quieter. Both service and food have a touch of class. The dining rooms, on two floors, have large picture windows overlooking the valley. ✉ *Piazza Garibaldi,* ☎ *0575/630500. AE, DC, MC, V. Closed Tues.*

Tuscany Essentials

Getting Around

BY BUS

Buses are a good alternative to driving; the region is crisscrossed by bus lines, which in some cases offer more frequent local service than trains, especially from Florence to Prato, a half-hour trip, and from Florence to Siena, which can take from 1¼ (by express bus) to 2 hours.

BY CAR

The best way to see the region is by car, taking detours to hill towns and abbeys. Roads throughout Tuscany are in good condition, though often narrow. The A1 autostrada links Florence with Arezzo and Chiusi (where you turn off for Montepulciano). A toll-free superstrada links Florence with Siena. For Chianti wine country scenery, take the S222 south of Florence through the undulating hills between Strada in Chianti and Greve in Chianti.

BY TRAIN

The main train network connects Florence with Arezzo and Prato. Another main line runs to Pisa, and a secondary line goes from Prato to the coast via Lucca. Trains also connect Siena with Pisa, a two-hour ride. Call ☎ 1478/88088 toll free for train information.

Guided Tours

American Express (✉ Via Guicciardini 49/r, ☎ 055/288751) operates one-day excursions to Siena and San Gimignano out of Florence. **CIT** (✉ Via Cavour 54/r, ☎ 055/294306) operates regional tours, too.

Visitor Information

Arezzo (✉ Piazza della Repubblica 28, ☎ 0575/377678). **Cortona** (✉ Via Nazionale 72, ☎ 0575/630352). **Lucca** (✉ Piazzale Verdi, ☎ 0583/419689). **Pisa** (✉ Piazza del Duomo 8, ☎ 050/560464). **Pistoia** (✉ Palazzo dei Vescovi, ☎ 0573/21622). **Prato** (✉ Via Cairoli 48, ☎ 0574/24112). **San Gimignano** (✉ Piazza del Duomo, ☎ 0577/940008).

MILAN

Milan, capital of all that is new in Italy, has a history spanning back at least 2,500 years. Its fortunes ever since, both as a great commercial trading center and as the object of regular conquest and occupation, are readily explained by its strategic position at the center of the Lombard Plain.

Exploring Milan

Numbers in the margin correspond to points of interest on the Milan map.

Virtually every invader in European history—Gaul, Roman, Goth, Longobard, and Frank—as well as every ruler of France, Spain, and Austria, has taken a turn at ruling the city and the region. So if you are wondering why so little seems to have survived from Milan's antiquity, the answer is simple—war. Thanks to the great family dynasties of the Visconti and the Sforza, however, there are still great Gothic and Renaissance treasures to be seen, including Leonardo's unforgettable *The Last Supper.* And thanks to new lords—Valentino and Armani among them (and alas a martyr: Versace's tragic murder has done little to stem the tide of his influence)—the city now dazzles as the design and fashion center of the world. Old and new come together at Milan's La Scala—Europe's most important opera house—where audiences continue to set sail for passion on the high C's.

5 **Castello Sforzesco.** Surrounded by a moat, this building is a somewhat sinister 19th-century reconstruction of the imposing 15th-century fortress built by the Sforzas, who succeeded the Viscontis as lords of Milan. It now houses wide-ranging collections of sculptures, antiques, and ceramics, including Michelangelo's *Rondanini Pietà,* his last work, left unfinished at his death. ✉ *Piazza Castello,* ☎ *02/62083191.* 🎫 *Free.* ⏲ *Tues.–Sun. 9:30–5:30.*

★ 1 **Duomo.** The massive Duomo, a mountain of marble fretted with statues, spires, and flying buttresses, sits—in all its Gothic drama—in the heart of Milan. The **Madonnina,** a gleaming gilt statue on the highest spire, is a city landmark. Take the elevator or walk up 158 steps to the roof for a view of the Lombard Plain and the Alps beyond. Dating from the 4th century, the **Baptistery** ruin is beneath the piazza; enter through the Duomo. ✉ *Piazza del Duomo.* ⏲ *Mar.–Oct., daily 9–5:30; Nov.–Feb., daily 9–4:30.*

★ 2 **Galleria Vittorio Emanuele.** In this spectacularly extravagant late-19th-century, glass-top, barrel-vaulted tunnel, Milanese and visitors stroll,

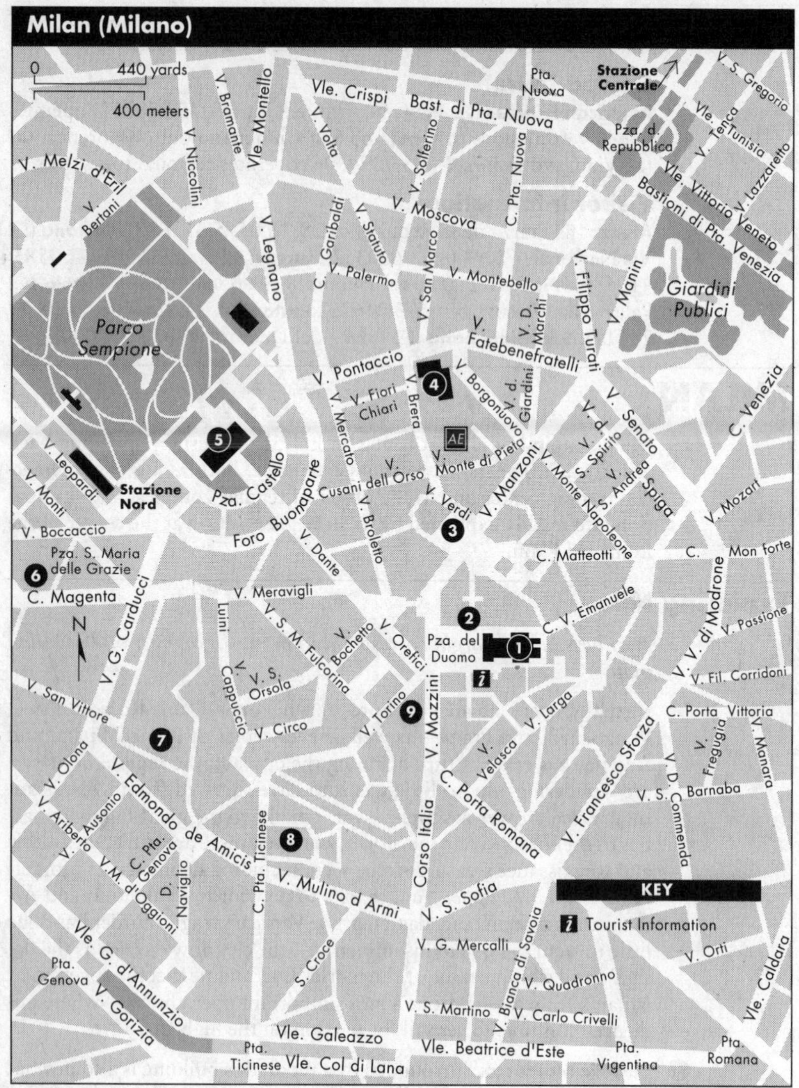

Castello Sforzesco, **5**
Duomo, **1**
Galleria Vittorio Emanuele, **2**
Pinacoteca di Brera, **4**
San Lorenzo Maggiore, **8**
San Satiro, **9**
Sant'Ambrogio, **7**
Santa Maria delle Grazie, **6**
Teatro alla Scala, **3**

window shop, and sip pricey cappuccinos at trendy cafés. ✉ *Piazza del Duomo, beyond the northern tip of cathedral's facade.*

★ ❹ **Pinacoteca di Brera** (Brera Painting Gallery). One of Italy's great fine art collections includes works by Mantegna (1431–1506), Raphael, and Titian. Most are of a religious nature, confiscated during the 19th century when many religious orders were suppressed and their churches closed. ✉ *Via Brera 28,* ☎ *02/722631.* ⏲ *Tues.–Sat. 9–5:30, Sun. 9–12:45.*

❽ **San Lorenzo Maggiore** (Older San Lorenzo). Sixteen ancient Roman columns line the front of this sanctuary; 4th-century mosaics still survive in the Chapel of St. Aquilinus. ✉ *Corso di Porta Ticinese.*

❾ **San Satiro** (St. Satyr). This church is another architectural gem in which Bramante's perfect command of proportion and perspective, characteristic of the Renaissance, made a small interior seem extraordinarily spacious and airy. ✉ *Via Torino.*

❼ **Sant'Ambrogio** (St. Ambrose). Noted for its medieval architecture, the church was consecrated by St. Ambrose in AD 387, and is the model for all Lombard Romanesque churches. Ancient pieces inside include a remarkable 9th-century altar in precious metals and enamels and some 5th-century mosaics. ✉ *Piazza Sant'Ambrogio.*

★ ❻ **Santa Maria delle Grazie** (Madonna of Grace). Although portions of this church were designed by Bramante, it plays second fiddle to the **Cenacolo Vinciano,** the former rectory next door, where, over a three-year period, Leonardo da Vinci painted his megafamous *The Last Supper.* The fresco has suffered more than its share of disasters, beginning with the experiments of the artist, who used untested pigments that soon began to deteriorate. *The Last Supper* is now a mere shadow of its former self, despite meticulous, slow restoration. Visitors are limited in time and number; lines can be long. ✉ *Piazza Santa Maria delle Grazie 2,* ☎ *02/4987588.* ⏲ *Tues.–Sun. 8–1:45; hrs may vary, call to confirm.*

❸ **Teatro alla Scala.** In this world-famous institution, Verdi established his reputation and Maria Callas sang her way into opera lore. Its rich history is displayed in the attached **Museo Teatrale alla Scala.** ✉ *Piazza della Scala,* ☎ *02/8053418.* ⏲ *Mon.–Sat. 9–noon and 2–6; plus May–Oct., Sun. 9:30–noon and 2:30–5. Closed occasionally during rehearsals.*

Dining and Lodging

Lombardy is home to some of Italy's freshest waters and in the south some of the best pasture land, so you can be sure restaurants have choice selections of meats and fish. All are paired nicely with the crisp wines of the region. For details and price-category information, *see* Dining *in* Italy A to Z, *above.*

If Rome is the administrative and political capital of Italy, Milan is the bustling business heart. As such, hotels are plentiful, with efficient service and for those hotels in the $$ and up categories, excellent standards. Stay as close to the city center as possible and always book well in advance. For details and price-category information, *see* Lodging *in* Italy A to Z, *above.*

$$$$ ★ ✕ **Savini.** Red carpets and cut-glass chandeliers characterize this typical old-world Milanese restaurant with dining rooms spread over three floors. There's also a "winter garden" from which patrons can people-watch Galleria shoppers. The Milanese *risotto al salto* (rice cooked as a pancake, tossed in the pan) is excellent here, as is the *co-*

toletta di vitello (breaded veal cutlets). ✉ *Galleria Vittorio Emanuele,* ☎ *02/72003433. AE, DC, MC, V. Closed Sun. and 10 days in Aug.*

$$$–$$$$ ★ ✕ **Boeucc.** Milan's oldest restaurant is not far from La Scala and is subtly lighted, with fluted columns, chandeliers, thick carpet, and a garden for warm-weather dining. You'll savor typical Milanese foods and such exotica as *penne al branzino e zucchine* (penne with sea bass and zucchini sauce) and *gelato di castagne con zabaglione caldo* (chestnut ice cream with hot zabaglione). ✉ *Piazza Belgioioso 2,* ☎ *02/76020224. Reservations essential. AE. Closed Sat., Aug., and Dec. 24–Jan. 2. No lunch Sun.*

$$ ✕ **Al Cantinone.** Opera goers still go to the Cantinone bar for a drink after the final curtain, just as they did a century ago. The decor is basic, the atmosphere lively, the service fast, and the food reliable. The proprietor stocks 240 different wines. Try the *cotoletta al Cantinone* (veal cutlets with mushrooms, olives, and a cream and tomato sauce). ✉ *Via Agnello 19,* ☎ *02/86461338. AE, MC, V. Closed Sun., Aug., and Dec. 24–Jan. 5. No lunch Sat.*

$$ ✕ **Antica Trattoria della Pesa.** The turn-of-the-century decor and atmosphere, dark wood paneling, and old-fashioned lamps still look much as they must have when this eatery opened 100 years ago. This is authentic Old Milan, and the menu is right in line, with risotto, minestrone, and osso buco. ✉ *Viale Pasubio 10,* ☎ *02/6555741. AE, DC, MC, V. Closed Sun., 2 wks in Aug., and Dec. 23–Jan. 6.*

$$ ✕ **Nabucco.** This is a smart, tastefully furnished restaurant in the Brera district. Menu highlights include *risotto con porcini,* an excellent range of salads, and homemade pastries and desserts. The prix-fixe lunch is a particularly good value. ✉ *Via Fiori Chiari 10,* ☎ *02/860663. AE, DC, MC, V. Closed Tues.*

$$ ✕ **Trattoria Milanese.** Between the Duomo and the Basilica of Sant' Ambrogio, this small, popular trattoria has been run by the same family for more than 60 years. It's invariably crowded, especially at dinner, when the regulars love to linger. Food is classic regional in approach, with risotto and *cotoletta alla milanese* (veal Milanese style) good choices. ✉ *Via Santa Marta 11,* ☎ *02/86451991. DC, MC, V. Closed Tues., Aug., and Dec. 24–Jan. 6.*

$–$$ ✕ **Bistrot di Gualtiero Marchesi/Brunch.** Atop the Rinascente department store off Piazza del Duomo, this brunch eatery, bar, and bistro is supervised by the well-known chef Gualtiero Marchese and offers a variety of menus with a full range of prices. A bonus is a great view of the Duomo's spires. ✉ *La Rinascente, Piazza Duomo,* ☎ *02/877120. AE, DC, MC, V. Closed Sun. No lunch Mon.*

$ ✕ **La Bruschetta.** A winning partnership of Tuscans and Neapolitans runs this tiny, busy, and first-class pizzeria near the Duomo. It features the obligatory wood-burning oven, though there are plenty of other dishes to choose from as well—try the *spaghetti alle cozze e vongole* (spaghetti with clams and mussels) or the grilled and skewered meats. ✉ *Piazza Beccaria 12,* ☎ *02/8692494. MC, V. Closed Mon., 3 wks in Aug., and Dec. 24–Jan. 3.*

$ ✕ **La Giara.** This tavern with bare wooden tables and benches features a limited selection of southern Italian specialties, notably a varied vegetable antipasto. Meat is grilled on a range at the front of the restaurant and served with crusty bread and dense olive oil from the Puglia region. You may be asked to share a table. ✉ *Viale Monza 10, near Piazzale Loreto,* ☎ *02/26143835. No credit cards. Closed Wed., Aug., and Dec. 23–Jan. 6. No lunch Tues.*

$$$$ ★ 🏨 **Duomo.** Just 20 yards from the cathedral, this hotel's first- through third-floor rooms all look out onto the church's Gothic gargoyles and pinnacles. The rooms are spacious and snappily furnished in contemporary style. ✉ *Via San Raffaele 1, 20121,* ☎ *02/8833,* FAX *02/86462027. 153 rooms. Restaurant. AE, DC, MC, V.*

$$$$ **Four Seasons.** The elegant restoration of a 14th-century monastery on an exclusive shopping street in the center of Milan has produced a precious gem—with the highest rates in the city. The hotel blends European class with American comfort. Individually furnished rooms have opulent marble bathrooms; most rooms face the quiet courtyard. Il Teatro serves dinner only. ✉ *Via Gesù 8, 20121,* ☎ *02/77088,* FAX *02/77085000. 98 rooms. 2 restaurants. AE, DC, MC, V.*

$$$$ ★ **Palace.** This truly elegant hotel, part of ITT-Sheraton's Luxury Collection, is one of the finest the city has to offer, with a personalized, attentive service to match, and elegantly outfitted and upholstered guest rooms. ✉ *Piazza della Repubblica 20, 20124,* ☎ *02/6336,* FAX *02/654485. 216 rooms. Restaurant, bar. AE, DC, MC, V.*

$$$$ **Pierre.** Luxury keynotes rooms individually furnished with elegant fabrics and an assortment of modern and antique furniture. Electronic gadgetry controls curtains and lights. You'll find the Pierre near the medieval Sant'Ambrogio church. ✉ *Via De Amicis 32, 20123,* ☎ *02/72000581,* FAX *02/8052157. 49 rooms. Restaurant. AE, DC, MC, V.*

$$$$ ★ **Principe di Savoia.** The pulse of the most fashionable and glitzy hotel in Milan is largely driven by the fashion and expense-account set. Dark-wood paneling and period furniture, brass lamps, and a stucco lobby are all reminiscent of early 1900s Europe. ✉ *Piazza della Repubblica 17, 20124,* ☎ *02/6230,* FAX *02/6595838. 287 rooms. Restaurant. AE, DC, MC, V.*

$$ **Canada.** This friendly, small, rather nondescript hotel close to Piazza del Duomo offers standard hotel trappings at a nice price. ✉ *Via Santa Sofia 16, 20122,* ☎ *02/58304844,* FAX *02/58300282. 35 rooms. AE, DC, MC, V.*

$$ **Casa Svizzera.** A faithful clientele considers this one of Milan's best moderately priced small hotels, so it's advisable to make early reservations. The location, adjacent to the Duomo and a few yards from the Galleria, is central and handy to Metro and bus lines. The soundproofed rooms burst forth with cheery floral prints. ✉ *Via San Raffaele 3, 20121,* ☎ *02/8692246,* FAX *02/72004690. 45 rooms. AE, DC, MC, V. Closed Aug. and Dec. 24–Jan. 6.*

$$ **Gritti.** This bright, clean hotel has a cheerful feel. Rooms are adequate, with picturesque views from the upper floors over the tile roofs to the gilt Madonnina atop the Duomo, only a few hundred yards away. ✉ *Piazza Santa Maria Beltrade 4 (north end of Via Torino), 20123,* ☎ *02/801056,* FAX *02/8901099. 48 rooms. AE, DC, MC, V.*

$ **London.** Close to the Duomo, the London has clean, good-size, simply furnished rooms and an English-speaking staff. ✉ *Via Rovello 3, 20121,* ☎ *02/72020166,* FAX *02/8057037. 29 rooms. MC, V. Closed Aug. and Dec. 23–Jan. 3.*

$ **San Francisco.** In a residential area between the central station and the university, this medium-size pension is handy to subway and bus lines. It also has the advantages of a friendly management, rooms that are bright and clean, and a charming garden. ✉ *Viale Lombardia 55, 20131,* ☎ *02/2361009,* FAX *02/26680377. 31 rooms. AE, DC, MC, V.*

Nightlife and The Arts

The Arts

Milan's most famous spectacle, **Teatro alla Scala** (✉ Piazza della Scala, Ufficio Biglietteria, Via Filodrammatici 2, ☎ 02/72003744) presents some of the world's most impressive operatic productions. The opera season begins December 7 (St. Ambrose Day) and ends in May. The concert season runs from May to the end of June and from September through November. There is a brief ballet season in September. Programs are available at principal travel agencies and tourist information offices in Italy and abroad.

Tickets are usually hard to come by, but your hotel may be able to help obtain them. For information on schedules, ticket availability, and how to buy tickets, the **Infotel Scala Service** (FAX 02/8607787 or 02/861778) operates (with English-speaking staff) at the ticket office, and is open daily noon–6. Telephone bookings are not accepted, but travelers from abroad can book in advance—within a short specified period before each presentation (these dates are published at the beginning of the season)—through postal bookings, for which a certain percentage of tickets are set aside, allocated on a first-come, first-served basis. Apply for a reservation by mail (☞ *above*) or fax with return fax number (also denoting time and date of transmission). You may also be able to book at CIT (☞ Contacts and Resources *in* Milan Essentials, *below*) or other travel agencies (no more than 10 days before performance) for a 15% advance booking charge.

Nightlife

El Brellin (✉ Vicolo Lavandai at the corner of Alzaia Naviglio Grande, ☎ 58101351) is one of many bars in the Navigli district; it's closed Sunday. Upscale, intimate nightcaps are sipped at **Momus** (✉ Via Fiori Chiari 8, ☎ 02/8056227) in the Brera quarter; it is closed Monday. **Le Scimmie** (✉ Via Ascanio Sforza 49, ☎ 02/89402874) delivers cool jazz in a relaxed atmosphere. The pricey nightclub **Stage** (✉ Galleria Manzoni, off Via Monte Napoleone, ☎ 02/76021071) serves dinner on Tuesday in digs great for dancing; it's closed Sunday. **Hollywood** (✉ Via Como 15/c, ☎ 02/6598996) is the in place for the fashion set.

Shopping

As one of the most renowned fashion centers in the world, it comes as no surprise that the majority of shops sell clothing—designer names with designer price tags. Milan's most elegant shopping streets are **Via Monte Napoleone, Via Manzoni, Via della Spiga,** and **Via Sant'Andrea.** Head for **Corso Buenos Aires,** near the central train station, if the chic goods of other areas are a shock to your purse.

Milan Essentials

Arriving and Departing

As Lombardy's capital and the most important financial and commercial center in northern Italy, Milan is well connected with Rome and Florence by fast and frequent rail and air service. Flights in and out of Milan during winter months are often prone to delay due to heavy fog.

BY CAR

From Rome and Florence take the A1 Autostrada. From Venice take the A4. Due to bans on parking throughout Milan center, it's easier to park on the outskirts and use public transportation.

BY PLANE

Aeroporto Milano Linate (✉ 11 km/7 mi east of Milan, ☎ 02/74852200) handles mainly domestic and European flights. **Aeroporto Malpensa** (✉ 50 km/30 mi northwest of the city, ☎ 02/74852200) services intercontinental flights. For air-traffic information for both airports and information on connections with Milan, call ☎ 02/74851.

Between the Airport and Downtown. Buses connect both airports with Milan, stopping at the central station and at the Porta Garibaldi station. Fare from Linate is 5,000 lire on the special airport bus or 1,500 lire on municipal Bus 73 (to Piazza San Babila); from Malpensa, 13,000 lire. A taxi from Linate to the center of Milan costs about 30,000 lire; from Malpensa, about 130,000 lire.

BY TRAIN

Milano Centrale (✉ Piazzale Duca d'Aosta, (☎ 1478/88088). Several smaller stations handle commuter trains. Rapid Intercity trains connect Rome and Milan daily, stopping in Florence and/or Bologna; a nonstop Intercity leaves Rome or Milan morning and evening, taking about four hours.

Getting Around

BY BUS AND STREETCAR

Buy tickets at newsstands, tobacco shops, and bars. The fare is 1,400 lire. One ticket is valid for 75 minutes on all surface lines and one subway trip. Daily tickets valid for 24 hours on all public transportation lines are sold at the Duomo Metro station ATM (city transport authority) information office, and at Milano Centrale Metro station. Twenty-four-hour tickets cost 5,000 lire; 48-hour tickets 9,000 lire.

BY METRO

Milan's subway network, the Metropolitana, is modern, fast, and easy to use. MM signs mark Metropolitana stations. There are, at present, three lines. The ATM has an information office (✉ mezzanine of the Duomo Metro station, ☎ 02/875495). Tickets are sold at newsstands at every stop, and in ticket machines *for exact change only.* The fare is 1,500 lire, and the subway runs from 6:20 AM to midnight.

BY TAXI

Use yellow cabs (☎ 02/6767, 02/8585, or 02/8388) only. They wait at stands or can be called in advance.

Contacts and Resources

CONSULATES

United States (✉ Via Principe Amedeo 2, ☎ 02/290351). **Canadian** (✉ Via Pisani 19, ☎ 02/6697451). **United Kingdom** (✉ Via San Paolo 7, ☎ 02/723001).

EMERGENCIES

Police (☎ 02/113). **Carabinieri** (☎ 02/112). **Ambulance** (☎ 02/7733). **Hospital and Doctor** (☎ 02/113).

GUIDED TOURS

Excursions. April–September, **Autostradale** (✉ Via Pompeo Marchesi 55, ☎ 02/48203177) offers an all-day tour of Lake Maggiore, including a boat trip to the Borromean Islands and lunch. The cost is about 130,000 lire. **Autostradale Viaggi** (✉ Piazza Castello 1, ☎ 02/166845010) operates similar tours.

Orientation. Three-hour morning or afternoon sightseeing tours depart Tuesday–Sunday from Piazzetta Reale (✉ Next to the Duomo); they cost about 50,000 lire and tickets can be purchased from APT offices (☞ Visitor Information, *below*) or aboard the bus.

TRAVEL AGENCIES

Compagnia Italiana Turismo (CIT) (✉ Galleria Vittorio Emanuele, ☎ 02/863701). **American Express Travel Agency** (✉ Via Brera 3, ☎ 02/809645).

VISITOR INFORMATION

Main tourist offices (✉ Stazione Centrale, ☎ 02/72524370). **APT Offices** (✉ Palazzo del Turismo, Via Marconi 1, ☎ 02/72524301).

VENICE

Venice—La Serenissima, the Most Serene—is disorienting in its complexity, an extraordinary labyrinth of narrow streets and waterways, opening now and again onto an airy square or broad canal. The majority of its magnificent palazzi are slowly crumbling; though this sounds like a recipe for a down-at-the-heels slum, somehow in Venice the shabby, derelict effect is magically transformed into one of supreme beauty and charm, rather than horrible urban decay. The place is romantic, especially at night when the lights from the vaporetti and the stars overhead pick out the gargoyles and arches of the centuries-old facades. For hundreds of years Venice was the unrivaled mistress of trade between Europe and the Orient, and the staunch bulwark of Christendom against the tide of Turkish expansion. Though the power and glory of its days as a wealthy city-republic are gone, the art and exotic aura remain.

Exploring Venice

Numbers in the margin correspond to points of interest on the Venice map.

To enjoy the city you will have to come to terms with the crowds of day-trippers, who take over the center around San Marco from May through September. Hot and sultry in summer, Venice is much more welcoming in early spring and late fall. Romantics like it in the winter, when prices are much lower, the streets are often deserted, and the sea mists impart a haunting melancholy to the *campi* (squares) and canals. Piazza San Marco is the pulse of Venice, but after joining with the crowds to visit the Basilica di San Marco and the Doge's Palace, strike out on your own and just follow where your feet take you—you won't be disappointed.

San Marco, Dorsoduro, and San Polo

★ 3 **Basilica di San Marco** (St. Mark's Basilica). Half Christian church, half Middle Eastern mosque, this building was conceived during the 11th century to hold the relics of St. Mark the Evangelist, the city's patron saint. Its richly decorated facade is surmounted by copies of four famous gilded bronze horses (the originals are in the basilica's upstairs museum). Inside, golden mosaics cover walls and vaults, lending an extraordinarily exotic aura. Be sure to see the **Pala d'Oro,** an eye-filling 10th-century altarpiece in gold and silver studded with precious gems and enamels. From the atrium climb the steep stairway to the museum: The bronze horses alone are worth the effort. ✉ *Piazza San Marco. Basilica:* ⏲ *Mon.–Sat. 9:30–5:30 (Oct.–Apr. until 5), Sun. 2–5:30 (Oct.–Apr. until 5).* 🎫 *Free. Pala d'Oro and Treasury:* ☎ *041/5225205.* ⏲ *same as basilica, last entry 30 min before closing. Gallery and Museum:* ⏲ *same as basilica, last entry 30 min before closing.*

★ 5 **Campanile di San Marco** (St. Mark's Bell Tower). This bell tower is a reconstruction of the 1,000-year-old tower that collapsed one morning in 1912, practically without warning. For a pigeon's-eye view of Venice, you can now take the elevator up to the top of this bell tower. Fifteenth-century clerics found guilty of immoral acts were suspended in wooden cages from the tower, sometimes to live on bread and water for as long as a year, sometimes to die of starvation and exposure. Look for them in Carpaccio's paintings of the square that hang in the Accademia. ✉ *Piazza San Marco,* ☎ *041/5224064.* ⏲ *June–Sept., daily 9:30–7, Oct.–May, daily 9:30–3:45. Closed 2 wks Jan.*

❻ **Collezione Peggy Guggenheim.** The late heiress's exceptional modern art collection—with works by Picasso, Kandinsky, Ernst, Pollock, and Motherwell—is housed in the incomplete Palazzo Venier dei Leoni. ✉ *Calle San Cristoforo, 701 Dorsoduro,* ☎ *041/5206288.* ⏲ *Wed.–Mon. 11–6.*

★ ❼ **Galleria dell'Accademia** (Accademia Gallery). Hanging in this museum is unquestionably the most extraordinary collection of Venetian art in the world. Works range from 14th-century Gothic to the Golden Age of the 15th and 16th centuries, including oils by Giovanni Bellini (1430–1516), Giorgione (1477–1511), Titian, and Tintoretto (1518–94), and superb later works by Veronese (1528–88) and Tiepolo (1696–1770). ✉ *Campo della Carità, Dorsoduro,* ☎ *041/5222247.* ⏲ *Mon.–Sat. 9–7, Sun. 9–2.*

❷ **Museo Correr.** Upstairs here you will find an eclectic collection of historical objects and a picture gallery of fine 13th- to 17th-century paintings. ✉ *Piazza San Marco, Ala Napoleonica,* ☎ *041/5225625.* ⏲ *Apr.–Oct., daily 9–5; Nov.–Mar., daily 9–7, last entry 1 hr before closing.*

★ ❹ **Palazzo Ducale** (Doge's Palace). During Venice's heyday, this was the epicenter of its great empire. More than just a palace, it was a combination White House, Senate, Supreme Court, torture chamber, and prison. The building's exterior is striking; the lower stories consist of two rows of fragile-seeming arches, while above rests a massive pink-and-white marble wall whose solidity is barely interrupted by its six great Gothic windows. The interior is a maze of vast halls, monumental staircases, secret corridors, and sinister prison cells. The palace is filled with frescoes, paintings, and a few examples of statuary by some of the Renaissance's greatest artists. Don't miss the famous view from the balcony, overlooking the piazza and St. Mark's Basin and the church of San Giorgio Maggiore across the lagoon. ✉ *Piazzetta San Marco,* ☎ *041/5224951.* ⏲ *Apr.–Oct., daily 9–7; Nov.–Mar., daily 9–5. Last entry 1½ hrs before closing time.*

★ ❶ **Piazza San Marco.** In the most famous piazza in Venice, pedestrian traffic jams clog the surrounding byways and even pigeons have to fight for space. Despite the crowds, San Marco is the logical starting place from which to explore the city. The short side of the square opposite the Basilica of San Marco is known as the Ala Napoleonica, a wing built by order of Napoléon to complete the much earlier palaces on either side of the square, enclosing it to form what he called "the most beautiful drawing room in all of Europe."

❾ **Santa Maria Gloriosa dei Frari.** This vast, soaring Gothic brick church known simply as I Frari contains a number of the most sumptuous, important pictures in Venice. Paradoxically, as the principal church of the Franciscans it is austere in design, suitably reflecting the order's vows of poverty. Chief among the works are the magnificent Titian altarpiece, the immense *Assumption of the Virgin* over the main altar. Titian was buried here at the ripe old age of 88, the only one of 70,000 plague victims to be given a personal church burial. ✉ *Campo dei Frari, San Polo,* ☎ *041/5222637.* ⏲ *Mon.–Sat. 9–noon and 3–6, Sun. 3–6.*

❽ **Scuola Grande di San Rocco** (School of St. Rocco). In the 1500s Tintoretto embellished the school with more than 50 canvases; they are an impressive sight, dark paintings aglow with figures hurtling dramatically through space amid flashes of light and color. The *Crucifixion* in the Albergo (the room just off the great hall) is held to be his masterpiece. ✉ *Campo di San Rocco, San Polo,* ☎ *041/5234864.* ⏲ *Nov.–Mar., weekdays 10–1 and weekends 10–4; Apr.–Oct., daily 9–5:30.*

North of San Marco and Ponte Rialto

★ 13 **Ponte Rialto** (Rialto Bridge). Street stalls hung with scarves and gondolier's hats signal the heart of Venice's shopping district. Cross over the bridge, and you'll find yourself on the edge of the famous market. Try to visit the Rialto market (⏲ Tues.–Sat. mornings; fish market closed Mon.) when it's in full swing, with fruit and vegetable vendors hawking their wares in a cacophony of sights and sounds. Not far beyond is the fish market, where you'll probably find sea creatures you've never seen before (and possibly won't want to see again). Ruga San Giovanni and Ruga del Ravano, beside the market, will bring you face to face with scores of shops. Start from the Salizzada San Giovanni side of the bridge.

11 **Santa Maria dei Miracoli.** Perfectly proportioned and sheathed in marble, the church embodies all the classical serenity of the early Renaissance. The interior of this late-15th-century building is decorated with marble reliefs by the church's architect, Pietro Lombardo, and his son Tullio. ✉ *Campo dei Miracoli.* ☎ *041/5235293.* ⏲ *Mon.–Sat. 10–5:30 and Sun. 3–6.*

10 **Santa Maria Formosa.** This graceful white marble church built by Mauro Coducci in 1492, was grafted onto 11th-century foundations. Inside is a hodgepodge of Renaissance and Baroque styles. A small vegetable market bustles in the square weekday mornings. ✉ *Campo Santa Maria Formosa,* ☎ *041/5234645.* 🎫 *Free.* ⏲ *Mon.–Sat. 10–5, Sun. 2–5.*

12 **Santi Giovanni e Paolo.** A massive Dominican church of Santi Giovanni e Paolo—known in the slurred Venetian dialect as San Zanipolo—is the twin (and rival) of the Franciscan Santa Maria Gloriosa dei Frari. The church is a kind of pantheon of the doges (25 are buried here), and contains a wealth of artwork. Outside in the campo stands Verrocchio's magnificent equestrian monument of **Bartolomeo Colleoni** (1400–75) who fought for the Venetian cause during the mid-1400s. ✉ *Campo San Giovanni e Paolo,* ☎ *041/5237510.* 🎫 *Free.* ⏲ *Mon.–Sat. 8–12:30 and 3–6, Sun. 3–6.*

Grand Canal, Cannareggio, and Dorsoduoro

Set off on a boat tour along the **Grand Canal,** which serves as Venice's main thoroughfare. The canal winds in the shape of a backwards S for more than 3½ km (2 mi) through the heart of the city, past some 200 Gothic and Renaissance palaces. Your vaporetto tour will give you an idea of the opulent beauty of the palaces and a peek into the side streets and tiny canals where the Venetians go about their daily business. ✉ *Just off Piazzetta di San Marco (the square in front of the Doge's Palace) you can catch Vaporetto 1 at either the San Marco or San Zaccaria landing stages (on Riva degli Schiavoni).*

16 **Ca' d'Oro.** The most flowery palace on the canal now houses the Galleria Franchetti. ✉ *Galleria Franchetti, Calle della Ca' d'Oro, 3933 Cannaregio,* ☎ *041/5238790.* ⏲ *Daily 9–2.*

15 **Ca' Foscari.** This 15th-century Gothic structure was once the home of Doge Foscari, who was unwillingly deposed and died the following day! Today it's the headquarters of Venice's university. ✉ *Fondamenta Ca'Foscari.*

★ 14 **Ca' Rezzonico.** The most spectacular palace in all of Venice was built between the mid-17th and 18th centuries and is now a museum of sumptuous 18th-century Venetian paintings and furniture. At press time (spring 1998) only the first floor was open. ✉ *Fondamenta Pedrocco, 3136 Dorsoduro,* ☎ *041/2410100.* ⏲ *Sat.–Thurs. 10–4.*

18 **Palazzo Labia.** Within the walls of this sumptuous palazzo you'll find the prettiest ballroom in Venice, magnificently adorned with Giambattista Tiepolo's 18th-century frescoes of Anthony and Cleopatra. This palace, once the home of Venice's most ostentatiously rich family, is now the Venetian headquarters of RAI, Italy's National Broadcasting Corporation, which occasionally hosts concerts in the Tiepolo ballroom. ✉ *Campo San Geremia, near the train station,* ☎ *041/5242812.* 🎫 *Free ballroom only Mon., Thurs., and Fri. 3–4.*

17 **Palazzo Vendramin Calergi.** This opulent Renaissance structure is noted as the place Wagner (1813–83) died. It's also the winter home of the municipal casino. ✉ *2040 Cannaregio, 30133.* ☎ *041/5297111.*

Elsewhere in Venice

Torcello. Discover the Venetian equivalent of World's End on this magical island in the Venetian lagoon. Settled 1,500 years ago and a thriving city during the Byzantine era, the island is now deserted, but art lovers still make pilgrimages to it because of its two great 11th-century churches. The cathedral of **Santa Maria Assunta** has a world-famous mosaic of the Virgin. Locanda Cipriani, a restaurant favored by Hemingway and the Duke of Windsor, still lures gourmands. Katharine Hepburn and Rossanzo Brazzi fell in love during a picnic on Torcello in the film classic *Summertime.* ✉ *Take Vaporetto 12 from Fondamente Nuove.*

Dining and Lodging

Venetians love seafood, and it figures prominently on most restaurant menus, sometimes to the exclusion of meat dishes. Fish is generally expensive, however, and you should bear this in mind when ordering: The price given on menus for fish as a main course is often per 100 grams, not the total cost of what you are served, which could be two or three times that amount. City specialties also include pasta e fagioli, risotto, and the delicious *fegato alla veneziana* served with grilled polenta. For details and price-category definitions, *see* Dining *in* Italy A to Z, *above*.

Space in the time-worn, but renovated palaces-cum-hotels are at a premium in this city, and even in the best hotel rooms can be small and offer little natural light. Preservation restrictions on buildings often preclude the installation of such things as elevators and air-conditioning systems. So don't come to Venice expecting to find the standard modern hotel room. On the other hand, Venice's luxury hotels can offer rooms of fabulous opulence and elegance, and even in the more modest hotels you can find comfortable rooms of great charm and character, sometimes with stunning views. Venice attracts visitors year-round, although the winter months are generally much quieter, and most hotels offer lower rates during this period. It is always worth booking in advance, but if you haven't, AVA (Venetian Hoteliers Association) booths (☞ Contacts and Resources *in* Venice Essentials, *below*) will help you find a room after your arrival in the city. For details and price-category definitions, *see* Lodging *in* Italy A to Z, *above*.

$$$$ ★ ✕ **Grand Canal.** The Hotel Monaco and Grand Canal's restaurant is a favorite among Venetians, who enjoy the sunny canal-side terrace, with views across the mouth of the Grand Canal to Giorgio Maggiore, and the cozy dining room in winter. Chef Fulvio De Santa turns out well-prepared Venetian seafood specialties, such as *scampi alla Ca' d'Oro* (shrimp in cognac sauce, served with rice), and savory meats. Pasta is made fresh daily on the premises, as is the marinated smoked salmon. ✉ *Hotel Monaco and Grand Canal, Calle Vallaresso 1325, San Marco,* ☎ *041/5200211. Jacket required. AE, DC, MC, V.*

Venice (Venezia)

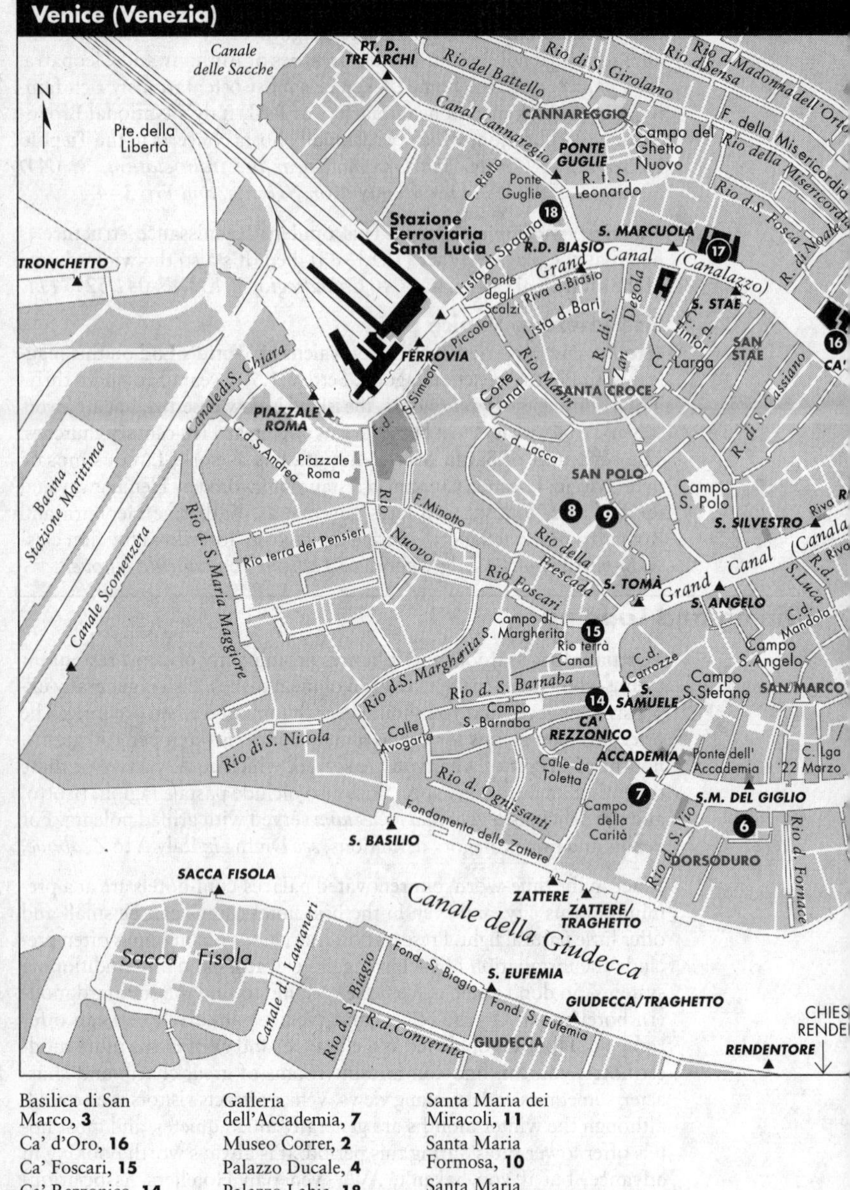

Basilica di San Marco, **3**
Ca' d'Oro, **16**
Ca' Foscari, **15**
Ca' Rezzonico, **14**
Campanile di San Marco, **5**
Collezione Peggy Guggenheim, **6**
Galleria dell'Accademia, **7**
Museo Correr, **2**
Palazzo Ducale, **4**
Palazzo Labia, **18**
Palazzo Vendramin Calergi, **17**
Piazza San Marco, **1**
Ponte Rialto, **13**
Santa Maria dei Miracoli, **11**
Santa Maria Formosa, **10**
Santa Maria Gloriosa dei Frari, **9**
Santi Giovanni e Paolo, **12**
Scuola Grande di San Rocco, **8**

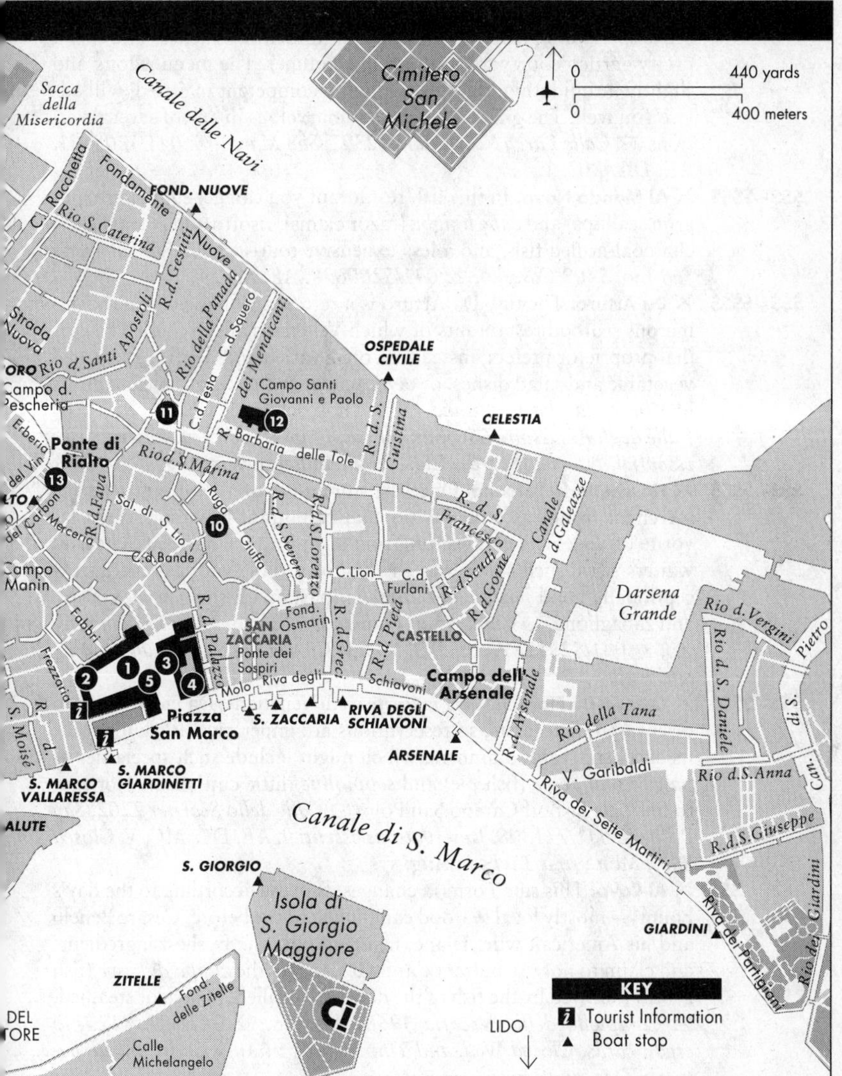
Cimitero San Michele
440 yards
400 meters
Sacca della Misericordia
Canale delle Navi
Fondamente Nuove
FOND. NUOVE
C. Racchetta
Rio S. Caterina
R.d. Gesuiti
Rio della Panada
C.d.Squero
dei Mendicanti
Strada Nuova
Rio d. Santi Apostoli
OSPEDALE CIVILE
Campo d. Pescheria
Campo Santi Giovanni e Paolo
C.d.Testa
R. d. S. Giustina
CELESTIA
Erberia
Ponte di Rialto
Rio d.S.Marina
R. Barbaria delle Tole
del Vin
del Carbon
Mercerie
R.d.Fava
Sal. di S. Lio
Ruga Giuffa
R.d.S.Severo
R.d.S.Lorenzo
R. d. S. Francesco
Canale d.Galeazze
C.d.Bande
Campo Manin
C.Lion
C.d. Furlani
R.d.Scudi
R.d.Gorne
Darsena Grande
Rio d.Vergini
Fabbri
R. d. Palazzo
Fond. Osmarin
R. d.Greci
R.d. Pietà
CASTELLO
SAN ZACCARIA
Ponte dei Sospiri
Rio d. S. Daniele
Pietro
Frezzaria
Molo
Riva degli Schiavoni
Campo dell' Arsenale
R.d.Arsenale
Rio della Tana
di S.
Piazza San Marco
S. ZACCARIA
RIVA DEGLI SCHIAVONI
R. d. S. Moisè
ARSENALE
V. Garibaldi
Rio d.S.Anna
Can.
S. MARCO VALLARESSA
S. MARCO GIARDINETTI
Riva dei Sette Martiri
Canale di S. Marco
R.d.S.Giuseppe
ALUTE
S. GIORGIO
Rio dei Giardini
Isola di S. Giorgio Maggiore
GIARDINI
Riva dei Partigiani
ZITELLE
Fond. delle Zitelle
KEY
Tourist Information
Boat stop
DEL ORE
Calle Michelangelo
LIDO
1
2
3
4
5
10
11
12
13

$$$$ ✕ **La Caravella.** La Caravella is reminiscent of an old Venetian sailing ship's dining saloon, with lots of authentic touches, and has a pretty garden courtyard used during summer. The menu is long and slightly intimidating, though the highly competent maître d' will advise you well. The *granseola* (crab) is marvelous in any of several versions. ✉ *Calle Larga XXII Marzo 2397, San Marco,* ☎ *041/5208901. AE, DC, MC, V.*

$$$–$$$$ ✕ **Al Mondo Novo.** In this fish restaurant you can get *cape sante* (pilgrim scallops) and *cape longhe* (razor clams), risotto and pasta dishes, charcoal-grilled fish, and a less-expensive tourist menu. ✉ *Salizzada San Lio, 5409 Castello,* ☎ *041/5200698. AE, MC, V.*

$$$–$$$$ ✕ **Da Arturo.** The tiny Da Arturo is a refreshing change from the numerous seafood restaurants of which Venetians are so fond. The cordial proprietor prefers, instead, to offer varied and delicious seasonal vegetable and salad dishes, or tasty, tender and generous meat courses like *braciola alla veneziana* (pork chop schnitzel with vinegar). ✉ *Calle degli Assassini 3656, San Marco,* ☎ *041/5286974. Reservations essential. No credit cards. Closed Sun. and 4 wks in Aug.*

$$$–$$$$ ✕ **Fiaschetteria Toscana.** Once the storehouse of a 19th-century wine merchant from Tuscany, this popular restaurant has long been a favorite of Venetians and visitors from terra firma. Courteous, cheerful waiters serve such specialties as *rombo* (turbot) with capers, an exceptionally good *pasta alla buranella* (pasta with shrimp, au gratin), and zabaglione. ✉ *Campo San Giovanni Crisostomo, 5719 Cannaregio,* ☎ *041/5285281. AE, DC, MC, V. Closed Tues. and 4 wks in July and Aug.*

$$$–$$$$ ★ ✕ **Osteria Da Fiore.** Long a favorite with Venetians, Da Fiore has been discovered by tourists, so reservations are imperative. It's known for its excellent seafood dinners, which might include such specialties as *pasticcio di pesce* (fish pie) and *seppioline* (little cuttlefish). Not easy to find, it's just off Campo San Polo. ✉ *Calle dello Scaleter 2202, San Polo,* ☎ *041/721308. Reservations essential. AE, DC, MC, V. Closed Sun., Mon., first 3 wks in Aug.*

$$$ ✕ **Al Covo.** This small osteria changes its menu according to the day's bounty—mostly local seafood caught just hours before. Cesare Benelli and his American wife, Diane, insist on only the freshest ingredients and claim to not use butter or animal fats. Try the *zuppa di pesce* (fish broth) followed by the fish of the day either grilled, baked, or steamed. ✉ *Campiello della Pescaria 3968, Castello,* ☎ *041/5223812. No credit cards. Closed Wed. and Thurs., 1 wk in Aug., and 1 month between Dec. and Jan.*

$$$ ✕ **Locanda Montin.** Peggy Guggenheim used to wine and dine the greatest artists of the 20th century here. Since those days, Montin has become more of an institution, less a bohemian hangout. Service can be erratic, but crowds still pack the place to enjoy the *rigatoni ai quattro formaggi* (rigatoni with four cheeses, mushrooms, and tomato) and antipasto Montin. ✉ *Fondamenta di Borgo, 1147 Dorsoduro,* ☎ *041/5227151. AE, DC, MC, V. Jan. 7–26, closed Tues. dinner and Wed.; closed 15 days in Aug.*

$$ ✕ **Vini da Gigio.** An attractive, friendly, and family-run establishment, this trattoria is found on the quayside of a canal, just off the Strada Nuova. Customers appreciate the affable service and tasty homemade pasta, fish, and meat dishes, and good draft wine. The barroom is pleasant and casual for lunch. ✉ *Fondamenta de la Chiesà, 3628A Cannaregio,* ☎ *041/5285140. AE, DC, MC, V. Closed Mon., 2 wks in Jan.–Feb., and 2 wks in Aug. No dinner Sun.*

$ ✕ **L'Incontro.** This trattoria has a faithful clientele drawn in by good food (excellent meat, but no fish) at reasonable prices. Menu choices include freshly made Sardinian pastas, juicy steaks, wild duck, boar, and (with advance notice) roast suckling pig. L'Incontro is between San Barnaba and Campo Santa Margherita. ✉ *Rio Terrá Canal, 3062A Dorsoduro, ☎ 041/5222404. MC, V. Closed Mon., 2 wks in Jan. and 2 wks. in Aug.*

$$$$ 🏨 **Cipriani.** A sybaritic oasis of stunningly decorated rooms and suites with marble baths and Jacuzzis, the Cipriani is located across St. Mark's Basin on the island of Giudecca, offering a panorama of romantic views of the entire lagoon. Some rooms have pretty garden patios. The subtly integrated 17th-century-style Palazzo Vendramin, an annex of seven suites and three double rooms, is open all year. ✉ *Giudecca 10, 30133, ☎ 041/5207744, FAX 041/5203930. 104 rooms. Restaurant, indoor pool. AE, DC, MC, V. Closed Dec.–mid-Mar.*

$$$$ 🏨 **Danieli.** Parts of this rather large hotel are built around a 15th-century palazzo bathed in sumptuous Venetian colors. The down side is the Danieli also has several modern annexes that some find bland and impersonal and the lower-price rooms can be exceedingly drab. Still, celebrities and English-speaking patrons crowd its sumptuous four-story-high lobby, chic salons, and dining terrace with a fantastic view of St. Mark's Basin. ✉ *Riva degli Schiavoni, 4196 Castello, 30122, ☎ 041/5226480, FAX 041/5200208. 219 rooms, 11 suites. Restaurant. AE, DC, MC, V.*

$$$$ ★ 🏨 **Gritti Palace.** This haven of pampering is like an aristocratic private home, with fresh flowers, fine antiques, lavish appointments, and Old World service. The dining terrace overlooking the Grand Canal is best in the evening when boat traffic dies down. ✉ *Campo Santa Maria del Giglio, 2467 San Marco, 30124, ☎ 041/794611, FAX 041/5200942. 87 rooms, 6 suites. Restaurant. AE, DC, MC, V.*

$$$ 🏨 **Londra Palace.** You get the obligatory view of San Giorgio and St. Mark's Basin at this distinguished hotel whose rooms are decorated in dark paisley prints, with such sumptuous touches as canopied beds. A neoclassical touch has been imparted into the rooms, with light pastel colors and plenty of marble. French chefs preside over Les Deux Lions restaurant, and the piano bar is open late. ✉ *Riva degli Schiavoni, 4171 Castello, 30122, ☎ 041/5200533, FAX 041/5225032. 36 rooms, 17 suites. Restaurant. AE, DC, MC, V.*

$$$ ★ 🏨 **Metropole.** Guests can step from their water taxi or gondola into the lobby of this small, very well-run hotel, rich in precious antiques, just five minutes from Piazza San Marco. Many rooms have a view of the lagoon, others overlook the garden at the back, but all are furnished with style. ✉ *Riva degli Schiavoni, 4149 Castello, 30122, ☎ 041/5205044, FAX 041/5223679. 77 rooms, 7 suites. Restaurant. AE, DC, MC, V.*

$$ ★ 🏨 **Accademia.** Hidden within the heart of Venice, this miniature Palladian villa—complete with canal-side garden—is the city's most enchanting hotel. There's plenty of atmosphere here, with just a touch of romance. Many rooms overlook the gardens, where you can sit in warm weather. ✉ *Fondamenta Bollani, 1058 Dorsoduro, 30123, ☎ 041/5210188, FAX 041/5239152. 27 rooms, 2 without bath. AE, DC, MC, V.*

$$ 🏨 **Ala.** The Ala is between San Marco and Santo Stefano, a few steps from the Santa Maria del Giglio vaporetto stop. Some rooms are large with coffered ceilings and old-style furnishings; smaller ones have more modern decor and orthopedic beds. Breakfast is served in a beautiful room overlooking a small canal. ✉ *2494 San Marco, 30124, ☎ 041/5208333, FAX 041/5206390. 85 rooms. AE, DC, MC, V.*

$$ 🏨 **American.** One of the smartest hotels in its class, the American is resplendent with beautiful terraces—teeming with red geraniums—that overlook the canal. The decor is stylish, from the treatment of wood in the reception area to the period furniture in the bar lounge. Most rooms have views and balconies on the canal and are nicely appointed,

drapes to carpets. ✉ *Rio San Vio, 628 Dorsoduro, 30123,* ☎ *041/5204733,* FAX *041/5204048. 29 rooms. AE, MC, V.*

$$ **Wildner.** Right between the super deluxe Danieli and Londra hotels, this pleasant family-run, unpretentious pensione enjoys the same views. Rooms are spread over four floors (no elevator), half with a view of San Giorgio, the others (cooler and quieter in summer) look out onto Campo San Zaccaria. ✉ *Riva degli Schiavoni, 4161 Castello, 30122,* ☎ *041/5227463,* FAX *041/5265615. 16 rooms. AE, DC, MC, V.*

$ **Bucintoro.** Whistler once stayed here, and today the Bucintoro is still favored by artists, drawn by the lagoon views from every room. Slightly off the tourist track, this friendly, family-run hotel has clean and simple rooms. The price is unbeatable for such spectacular vistas. ✉ *Riva San Biagio, 2135 Castello, 30122,* ☎ *041/5223240,* FAX *041/5235224. 28 rooms, 10 without bath. Restaurant. No credit cards. Closed Jan.–mid-Feb.*

$ **Locanda Fiorita.** Just off Campo Sant Stefano, near the Accademia Bridge, you'll find this welcoming hotel tucked away in a sunny little square (where breakfast is served in summer). The rooms have beamed ceilings and are simply furnished. ✉ *Campiello Novo o dei Morti, 3457/A San Marco, 30124,* ☎ *041/5234754,* FAX *041/5228043. 18 rooms, 4 without bath. AE, MC, V. Closed Jan. through Carnival.*

$ **Paganelli.** The lagoon views here so impressed Henry James that he wrote the Paganelli up in the preface to his *Portrait of a Lady.* This charming, small hotel on the waterfront has an annex on the quiet square of Campo San Zaccaria, and is tastefully decorated in Venetian style. ✉ *Riva degli Schiavoni, 4687 Castello, 30122,* ☎ *041/5224324,* FAX *041/5239267. 20 rooms, 1 without bath. AE, MC, V.*

Nightlife and the Arts

Your hotel concierge may be able to secure you tickets (or advice on how to get them) for some arts events going on around town.

The Arts

The **Biennale,** a cultural institution, organizes many events throughout the year, including the film festival, which begins at the end of August. The big Biennale international art exhibition, usually held from mid-June to the end of September, has been held since 1993 on odd-numbered years at the **Giardini di Castello** (Castello Gardens).

CONCERTS

Regular concerts are held at the Pietà Church, with an emphasis on Vivaldi, and at San Stae and San Barnaba. Concerts, sometimes free, are also held by visiting choirs and musicians in other churches. For information on these often impromptu events, ask at the APT office and look for posters on walls and in restaurants and shops. **Kele e Teo Agency** (✉ Ponte dei Bareteri, 4930 San Marco, ☎ 041/5208722, FAX 041/5208913) handles tickets for many musical events. You can often get them at **Box Office** (✉ Calle Loredan 4127, off Salizzada San Luca, ☎ 041/988369), too.

OPERA

Because of the devastating fire that destroyed **Teatro La Fenice** in January 1996, opera and concert performances were rescheduled in various venues. Although plans are being made to restore the building, performances are not forecast to recommence until the year 2000. Check with the APT (☞ Visitor Information *in* Venice Essentials, *below*) for current performances.

Nightlife

The Martini Scala Club (✉ Calle del Cafetier, 2077 San Marco, ☎ 041/5224121) is an elegant piano bar with a restaurant. Tunes start at 10 PM and go until the wee hours; it's closed Tuesday. For dancing try the **Disco Club Piccolo Mondo** (✉ 1056 Dorsoduro, ☎ 041/5200371), near the Accademia Gallery. **Fiddler's Elbow** (✉ Strada Nuova, Cannareggio 3847, ☎ 041/5239930) offers all the typical trappings of an Irish pub: gab, grub, and frothy Guinness.

Shopping

At **La Scialuppa** (✉ Calle delle Saoneri, 2695 San Polo) you'll find hand-carved wooden models of gondolas and their graceful oar locks known as *forcole*. **Norelene** (✉ Calle della Chiesa 727, in Dorsoduro, near the Guggenheim) has stunning hand-painted fabrics that make wonderful wall hangings or elegantly styled jackets and chic scarves. **Venetia Studium** (✉ Calle Larga XXII Marzo, 2430 San Marco) is famous for Fortuny-inspired lamps, furnishings, clothes, and accessories.

Glass

There's a lot of cheap Venetian glass for sale; if you want something better, try **l'Isola** (✉ Campo San Moisè 1468, near Piazza San Marco), where Carlo Moretti's chic, contemporary designs are on display. **Domus** (✉ Fondamenta dei Vetrai, Murano) has a good selection of glass and is on the island of Murano.

Shopping Districts

Le Mercerie, along with the Frezzeria and Calle dei Fabbri are some of Venice's busiest streets, which lead off from Piazza San Marco (☞ Ponte Rialto *in* Exploring Venice, *above*).

Venice Essentials

Arriving and Departing

BY CAR

If you bring a car to Venice, you will have to pay for a garage or parking space during your stay. Warning: Do not be waylaid by illegal con artists often wearing fake uniforms who may try to flag you down and offer to arrange parking and hotels. Continue on until you reach the automatic ticket machines.

Parking at **Piazzale Roma** (✉ Autorimessa Comunale, end of S11 road) costs between 15,000 and 25,000 lire. The private **Garage San Marco** (✉ Piazzale Roma, end of S11 road) costs between 34,000 and 46,000 lire per 24 hours, depending on the size of the car. To reach the privately run **Tronchetto** parking area, follow the signs to turn right before Piazzale Roma. Parking here costs 25,000 lire per 24 hours. (Do not leave valuables in the car. There is a left-luggage office, open daily 8–8, next to the Pullman Bar on the ground floor of the municipal garage at Piazzale Roma.) The AVA (☞ Visitor Information, *below*) has arranged a discount of around 5,000 lire per day for hotel guests who use the official Tronchetto parking facility. Ask for a voucher on checking into your hotel. Present the voucher at Tronchetto when you pay the parking fee.

A vaporetto (No. 82) runs from Tronchetto to Piazzale Roma and Piazza San Marco (also to the Lido in summer). In thick fog or when tides are extreme, a bus runs instead to Piazzale Roma, where you can pick up a vaporetto.

BY PLANE

Aeroporto Marco Polo (✉ 10 km/6 mi northeast of Venice on the mainland, flight information ☎ 041/2609260).

Between the Airport and Downtown. The most direct way is by the **Cooperativa San Marco** (✉ just off Piazza San Marco, ☎ 041/5222303) launch, with regular scheduled service throughout the day, until midnight; it takes about an hour to get to the landing, stopping at the Lido on the way, and the fare is 17,000 lire per person, including bags. Blue **ATVO** buses make the 25-minute trip in to Piazzale Roma, where the road to Venice terminates; the cost is 5,000 lire. From Piazzale Roma visitors will most likely have to take a vaporetto to their hotel (☞ Getting Around, *below*). **Water taxis** (slick high-power motorboats called *motoscafi*) should cost about 87,000 lire. **Land taxis** are available, running the same route as the buses; the cost is about 60,000 lire.

BY TRAIN

Make sure your train goes all the way to the **Stazione Ferroviaria Santa Lucia** (✉ Venice's northwest corner; ☎ 1478/88088 toll free). Some trains leave passengers at the **Stazione Ferroviaria Venezia-Mestre** (✉ on the mainland; ☎ 1478/880880 toll free). All trains traveling to and from Santa Lucia stop at Mestre, so to get from Mestre to Santa Lucia, or vice versa (a 10-minute trip), take the first available train, remembering there is a *supplemento* (extra charge) for traveling on Intercity, Eurocity, and Eurostar trains, and that if you board one of these trains without having paid in advance for this part of the trip, you are subject to a hefty fine. Since most tourists arrive in Venice by train, tourist services are conveniently located at Santa Lucia, including an **APT** information booth (☎ 041/5298727) and baggage depot. If you need a hotel room, the station has an **AVA** booth (☞ *below*). Directly outside the train station are the main vaporetto landing stages; from here, vaporetti can transport you to your hotel's general neighborhood. Be prepared with advance directions from the hotel and a good map.

Getting Around

First-time visitors find that getting around Venice presents some unusual problems: The complexity of its layout (the city is made up of more than 100 islands, all linked by bridges); the bewildering unfamiliarity of waterborne transportation; the apparently illogical house numbering system and duplication of street names in its six districts; and the necessity of walking whether you enjoy it or not. It's essential to have a good map showing all street names and water bus routes; buy one at any newsstand.

BY GONDOLA

If you mustn't leave Venice without treating yourself to a gondola ride, take it in the quiet of the evening when the churning traffic on the canals has died down and at high tide, the palace windows are illuminated, and the only sounds are the muted splashes of the gondolier's oar. Make sure he understands that you want to see the *rii,* or smaller canals, as well as the Grand Canal. There's supposed to be a fixed minimum rate of about 120,000 lire for 50 minutes, and a nighttime supplement of 30,000. Come to terms with your gondolier *before* stepping into his boat.

BY TRAGHETTO

Few tourists know about the two-man gondolas that ferry people across the Grand Canal at various fixed points. It's the cheapest and shortest gondola ride in Venice, and it can save a lot of walking. The fare is 700 lire, which you hand to one of the gondoliers when you get on. Look for TRAGHETTO signs.

BY VAPORETTO

ACTV water buses run the length of the Grand Canal and circle the city. There are several lines, some of which connect Venice with the major and minor islands in the lagoon. The fare is 4,500 lire on all lines. A 24-hour tourist ticket costs 15,000 lire, a three-day ticket 30,000 lire, and a seven-day ticket 55,000 lire; these are especially worthwhile if you are planning to visit the islands. ACTV information is available by calling ☎ 041/5287886, daily from 7:30 AM–8 PM. Free timetables are available at the ticket office at Piazzale Roma. Timetables are posted at every landing stage, but there is not always a ticket booth operating. After 9 PM, tickets are available on the boats, but you must immediately inform the controller that you need a ticket. For this reason it may be useful to buy a *blocchetto* (book of tickets) in advance. Landing stages are clearly marked with name and line number, but check before boarding, particularly with the 52 and 82, to make sure the boat is going in your direction.

Line 1 is the Grand Canal local, calling at every stop, and continuing via San Marco to the Lido. (It takes about 45 minutes from the station to San Marco.) **Line 52** runs from the railway station to San Zaccaria via Piazzale Roma and Zattere, and continues to the Lido. **Line 52/** (note the difference) goes along the same route but makes stops along the Giudecca instead of Zattere and continues to Fondamente Nuove (where boats leave for the islands of the northern Lagoon) and Murano. **Line 82** runs in a loop from San Zaccaria to Giudecca, Zattere, Piazzale Roma, the train station, Rialto, (with fewer stops along the Grand Canal than Line 1), and back to San Zaccaria (and out to the Lido in the afternoon).

BY WATER TAXI

Motoscafi, or taxis, are excessively expensive, and the fare system is as complex as Venice's layout. A minimum fare of about 50,000 lire gets you nowhere, and you'll pay three times as much to get from one end of the Grand Canal to the other. *Always agree on the fare before starting out.* It's probably worth considering taking a water taxi only if you are traveling in a small group.

ON FOOT

This is the only way to reach many parts of Venice, so wear comfortable shoes. Invest in a good map that names all the streets, and count on getting lost more than once.

Contacts and Resources

CONSULATES

United Kingdom (✉ Campo della Carità 1051, Dorsoduro, ☎ 041/5227207). There is no U.S. or Canadian consular service in Venice. The nearest consulates are in Milan (☞ Contacts and Resources *in* Milan Essentials, *above*).

EMERGENCIES

Police (☎ 113). **Carabinieri** (☎ 112). **Ambulance** (☎ 118). **Doctor** (emergency room, Venice's hospital, ☎ 041/5230000). **Red Cross First Aid Station** (✉ Piazza San Marco 55, near Caffè Florian, ☎ 041/52286346).

Pharmacies are open weekdays 9–12:30 and 3:45–7:30; Saturday 9–12:45; a notice telling where to get late-night and Sunday service is posted outside every pharmacy. **Farmacia Italo-Inglese** (✉ Calle della Mandola, ☎ 041/5224837). **Farmacia Internazionale** (✉ Calle Larga XXII Marzo, ☎ 041/5222311).

GUIDED TOURS

Excursions. The **Cooperativa San Marco** (✉ just off San Marco, ☎ 041/5222303) organizes tours of the islands of Murano, Burano, and Torcello departing daily at 9:30 and 2:30 from the landing stage in front of Giardini Reali near Piazza San Marco; tours last about 3½ hours and cost about 25,000 lire. However, tours tend to be annoyingly commercial and emphasize glass factory showrooms where you are pressured to buy, often at higher than standard prices. **American Express** (✉ Salizzada San Moisè, 1471 San Marco, ☎ 041/5200844, FAX 041/5229937) books a day trip to Padova by boat along the Brenta River, with stops at three Palladian villas. The tours run three days a week from March to November; the cost is about 120,000 lire per person, and bookings need to be made the day before.

Orientation. American Express (☞ *above*) and other operators offer two-hour walking tours of the San Marco area, taking in the basilica and the Doge's Palace. The cost is about 36,000 lire, including admission. From April 25 through November 15, American Express offers an afternoon walking tour that ends with a short gondola ride (about 40,000 lire).

Personal Guides. American Express (☞ *above*) can provide guides for walking or gondola tours of Venice, or cars with driver and guide for excursions on the mainland. Pick up a list of licensed guides and their rates from the main **APT** office (✉ Calle dell'Ascensione 71C, ☎ 041/5226356, FAX 041/5298730).

Special-Interest. Some tour operators offer group gondola rides with a serenade. The cost is about 40,000 lire. During the summer free guided tours of the Basilica di San Marco are offered by the Procuratoria; information is available at a desk in the atrium of the church. From June through August there are several tours daily, except Sunday, and some tours are in English, including one at 11 AM.

TRAVEL AGENCIES

American Express (✉ Salizzada San Moisè 1471, ☎ 041/5200844, FAX 041/5229937). **Wagons-Lits Turismo** (✉ Piazzetta dei Leoncini 289, ☎ 041/5223405, FAX 041/5228508).

VISITOR INFORMATION

Main APT (✉ Calle dell'Ascensione 71C, Palazzetto Selva off Piazza San Marco, ☎ 041/5226356 or 041/5298730, FAX 041/5230399; ⊙ Mon.–Sat. 9:40–3:20). **APT booths** (✉ Santa Lucia Station, ☎ 041/5298727, ⊙ daily 8:10–6:50; ✉ on the Lido, Gran Viale S. M. Elisabetta 6A, ☎ 041/5265721, FAX 041/5298720; ⊙ summer only).

AVA (Venetian Hoteliers Association, ✉ train station, ☎ 041/715016 or 1678/43006; ⊙ daily 8 AM–9 PM). Satellite locations at airport, Municipal parking garage, and Piazzale Roma.

CAMPANIA

Campania, the region comprised of Naples, the Amalfi coast, and sun-drenched points south is where most people's preconceived ideas of Italy become a reality. You'll find lots of beaches, good food that relies heavily on tomatoes and mozzarella, acres of classical ruins, and gorgeous scenery. The exuberance of the locals doesn't leave much room for efficient organization, however, and you may have to revise your concept of real time; here minutes dilate into hours at the drop of a hat.

Once a city that rivaled Paris as a brilliant and refined cultural capital, Napoli (Naples) is afflicted by acute urban decay and chronic delinquency. You need patience, stamina, and a healthy dose of cau-

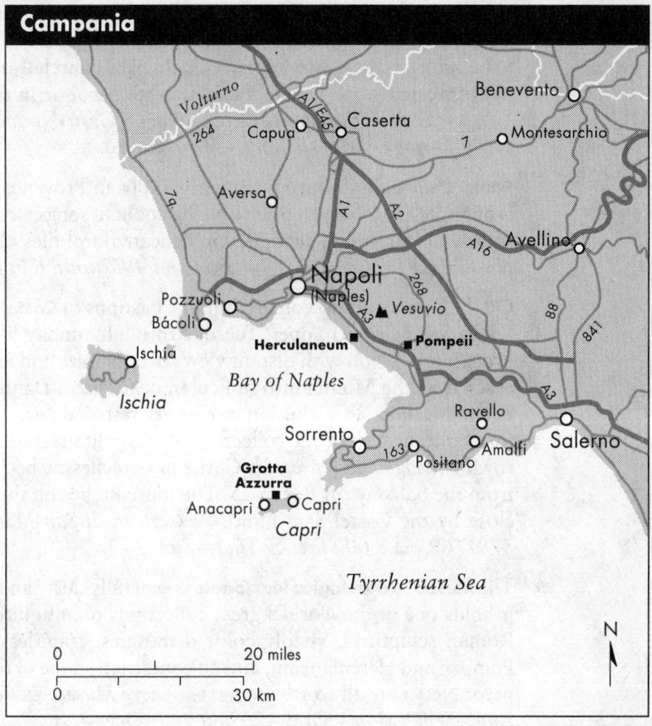

tion to visit Naples on your own, but it's worth it for those who have a sense of adventure and the capacity to discern the enormous riches the city has accumulated in its 2,000-year history.

If you want the fun without the hassle, skip Naples and head for Sorrento, Capri, and the Amalfi coast, legendary haunts of the sirens who tried to lure Odysseus off course. Sorrento is touristy but has some fine old hotels and beautiful views; it's a good base for a leisurely excursion to Pompeii. Capri is a pint-size paradise, though sometimes too crowded for comfort, and the Amalfi coast offers enchanting towns and spectacular scenery.

Naples

Founded by the Greeks, Naples became a playground of the Romans and was ruled thereafter by a succession of foreign dynasties, all of which left traces of their cultures in the city and its environs. The most splendid of these rulers were the Bourbons, who were responsible for much of what you will want to see in Naples. Among the greatest relics of Bourbon powers in Naples is the 17th-century **Palazzo Reale** (Royal Palace), still furnished in the lavish Baroque style that suited them so well. ✉ *Piazza del Plebiscito,* ☎ *081/5808111.* ⏲ *Apr.–Oct., Tues.–Sun. 9–7:30; Nov.–Mar., Sun.–Tues. 9–1:30, Thurs.–Sat. 9–6.*

Also known as the Maschio Angioino, the massive stone **Castel Nuovo** was built by the city's Aragon rulers during the 13th century; inside, the city's **Museo Civico,** comprises mainly local artworks from the 15th to the 19th centuries, and there are also regular exhibitions. The windows offer views over the piazza and the port below. ✉ *Castel Nuovo, Piazza Municipio.* ⏲ *Mon.–Sat. 9–7, Sun. 9–1.*

Via Toledo (✉ runs north–south connecting Piazza Dante, Piazza del Gesù, and Piazza del Plebiscito), also known as Via Roma, is great for strolling and watching the antics of the Neapolitans, whose daily lives are fraught with theatrical gestures and fiery speeches. They all seem to be actors in their own human comedy. The church **Gesù Nuovo,** with oddly faceted stone facade and elaborate Baroque interior, is off Via Toledo. ✉ *Via Benedetto Croce, Piazza Gesù Nuovo.* 🎫 *Free.* ⏲ *Daily 7–noon and 4–7 (Oct.–Mar. until 6).*

Santa Chiara, built during the early 1300s in Provençal Gothic style, is opposite Gesù Nuovo. A favorite Neapolitan song celebrates the quiet beauty of its cloister, decorated in delicate floral tiles. ✉ *Piazza Gesù Nuovo.* 🎫 *Free.* ⏲ *Daily 7–noon and 4–7 (until 6 in winter).*

On the heights of the Vomero hill, the bastions of **Castel Sant'Elmo** (✉ Largo San Martino), open Tuesday through Sunday 9–2, occupy an evocative position with distant views over Naples and its bay. You can reach it by the **Montesanto funicular,** near Piazza Dante. The **Certosa di San Martino,** a Carthusian monastery restored during the 17th century, contains an eclectic collection of Neapolitan landscape paintings, royal carriages, and *presepi* (Christmas crèches). Check out the view from the balcony off Room 25. The museum lies on the Vomero Hill, close by the Castel Sant'Elmo. ✉ *Certosa di San Martino,* ☎ *081/5781769.* 🎫 *8,000 lire.* ⏲ *Tues.–Sun. 9–2.*

★ The **Museo Archeologico Nazionale** is generally dusty and unkempt, but it holds one of the world's great collections of antiquities. Greek and Roman sculptures, vividly colored mosaics, countless objects from Pompeii and Herculaneum, and an equestrian statue of the Roman emperor Nerva are all worth seeing. ✉ *Piazza Museo,* ☎ *081/440166.* ⏲ *Aug.–Sept., Mon.–Sat. 9–7, Sun. 9–1; Oct.–July, Wed.–Mon. 9–2.*

★ The **Museo di Capodimonte** is housed in an 18th-century palace built by Bourbon king Charles III, and surrounded by a vast park that affords sweeping views of the bay. The picture gallery is devoted to work from the 13th to the 18th centuries, including many familiar masterpieces by Dutch and Spanish masters, as well as by the great Italians. Other rooms contain an extensive collection of porcelain and majolica from the various royal residences, some produced in the Bourbons' own factory right here on the grounds. ✉ *Parco di Capodimonte,* ☎ *081/7441307.* ⏲ *Tues.–Sat 10–7, Sun. 10–2.*

$$$ ✕ **La Sacrestia.** This lovely restaurant above Mergellina has a fine view from the delightful summer terrace. Traditional Neapolitan specialties of the day might be baked or steamed sea bass and *linguine in salsa di scorfano* (linguine with scorpion-fish sauce). ✉ *Via Orazio 116,* ☎ *081/7611051. AE, DC, MC, V. Closed Mon. lunch and Sun. dinner (Sept.–June), Sun. (July–Aug.), and 2 wks in mid-Aug.*

$$ ✕ **Ciro a Santa Brigida.** This no-frills restaurant is a favorite with businesspeople, artists, and journalists. Tables are arranged on two levels, and the decor is classic trattoria. This is the place to try traditional Neapolitan *sartù di riso* (a rich rice dish with meat and peas) and *melanzane alla parmigiana* or *scaloppe alla Ciro* (eggplant or veal with prosciutto and mozzarella). There's pizza, too. ✉ *Via Santa Brigida 71, off Via Toledo,* ☎ *081/5524072. AE, DC, MC, V. Closed Sun. and 2 wks in Aug.*

$$$$ 🏨 **Excelsior.** On the shore drive the Excelsior has splendid views of the bay from its front rooms. Spacious bedrooms are well furnished in informal floral prints or more formal Empire style; all have a comfortable, traditional air. The salons are formal, with chandeliers and wall paintings, and the excellent Casanova restaurant is elegant. ✉ *Via Partenope 48, 80121,* ☎ *081/7640111,* FAX *081/7649743. 102 rooms. Restaurant. AE, DC, MC, V.*

$$$ ★ **Jolly Ambassador.** This hotel occupies the top 14 floors of a downtown skyscraper, and its rooms and roof restaurant have wonderful views of Naples and the bay. It's furnished in the functional, modern style typical of this reliable chain, which promises comfort and efficiency in a city where these are scarce commodities. ✉ *Via Medina 70, 80133,* ☎ *081/416000,* FAX *081/5518010. 251 rooms. Restaurant. AE, DC, MC, V.*

$$–$$$ **Rex.** This hotel occupies a fairly quiet spot near the Santa Lucia waterfront. On the first two floors of an art nouveau building, the hotel reveals a haphazard collection of 1950s modern, fake period pieces, and even some folk art. ✉ *Via Palepoli 12, 80132,* ☎ *081/7649389,* FAX *081/7649227. 38 rooms. Bar. AE, DC, MC, V.*

Herculaneum

★ Hercules is reputed to have founded Herculaneum (Ercolano), just 10 km (6 mi) southeast of Naples. The elite Roman resort was devastated by the same volcanic eruption that buried Pompeii in AD 79. Excavations have revealed that many died on the shore in an attempt to escape, as a slow-moving mud slide embalmed the entire town by covering it with a 36-ft-deep blanket of volcanic ash and ooze. While that may have been unfortunate for Herculaneum's residents, it has helped to preserve the site in pristine condition for nearly two millennia. ✉ *Corso Ercolano,* ☎ *081/7390963.* ⏲ *Daily 9–1 hr before sunset (ticket office closes 2 hrs before sunset).*

Pompeii

★ An estimated 2,000 of Pompeii's residents perished on that fateful August day. The ancient city of Pompeii was much larger than Herculaneum, and excavations have progressed to a much greater extent (though the remains are not as well preserved, due to some 18th-century scavenging for museum-quality artwork, most of which you are able to see at Naples's Museo Archeologico Nazionale. This prosperous Roman city had an extensive forum, lavish baths and temples, and patrician villas richly decorated with frescoes. It's worth buying a detailed guide of the site to gain an understanding of the ruins and their importance. Be sure to see the **Villa dei Misteri** (Villa of the Mysteries), with frescoes some 1,900 years old that still retain rich detail and color depth. Have lots of small change handy to tip the guards at the more important houses so they will unlock the gates for you. ✉ *Pompeii Scavi,* ☎ *081/8610744.* ⏲ *Daily 9–1 hr before sunset (ticket office closes 2 hrs before sunset).*

Sorrento

In the not-too-distant past, small Sorrento was a genteel resort for the fashionable elite. Now the town, 28 km (17 mi) southwest of Pompeii, has spread out along the crest of its fabled cliffs. The once secret haunts for the few tourists who came for the magnificent coastline have been long discovered, now ravaged by package tours. But truly, nothing can dim the delights of the marvelous climate and view of the Bay of Naples. For the best views go to the **Villa Comunale,** near the old church of San Francesco (in itself worth a visit). **Museo Correale,** in an attractive 18th-century villa, retains a collection of decorative arts and paintings of the Neapolitan school. ✉ *Via Correale.* ⏲ *Mar.–Oct., Mon. and Wed.–Sat. 9–12:30 and 5–7, Sun. 9–12:30; Nov.–Feb., Wed.–Mon. 9–1:30.*

$$ ✕ **Antica Trattoria.** Garden dining at this homey, hospitable spot is a joy in summer. Classic *pennette al profumo di bosco* (mini-penne with a creamy mushroom and ham sauce), sometimes pricey fish, and *gamberetti freschi Antica Trattoria* (shrimp in a tomato sauce) are typical house specialties. ✉ *Via Giuliani 33,* ☎ *081/8071082. AE, MC, V. Closed Mon. and 4 wks Jan.–Feb.*

$$ ✕ **Gigino.** Just off the central Piazza Tasso, this is one of Sorrento's best inexpensive and informal eateries. The fixed-price menu at lunch is especially good value. ✉ *Via degli Archi 15,* ☎ *081/8781927. MC, V. Closed Tues.*

$$ ✕ **Parrucchiano.** One of the town's best and oldest, Parrucchiano features greenhouse-type dining rooms dripping with vines and dotted with plants. Among the antipasti, try the *panzerotti* (pastry crust filled with mozzarella and tomato), and for a main course, the scaloppe *alla sorrentina,* again with mozzarella and tomato. ✉ *Corso Italia 71,* ☎ *081/8781321. MC, V. Closed Wed. Nov.–May.*

$$$$ **Bellevue Syrene.** This exclusive hotel is set in a cliff-top garden close to the center of Sorrento. It retains its solid, old-fashioned comforts and sumptuous charm, with Victorian nooks and alcoves, antique paintings, and exuberant frescoes. ✉ *Piazza della Vittoria 5, 80067,* ☎ *081/8781024,* FAX *081/8783963. 73 rooms. Restaurant, bar. AE, DC, MC, V.*

$$$$ **Excelsior Vittoria.** In the heart of Sorrento, this hotel right on the cliff has Art Nouveau furnishings, some very grand, though faded. Tenor Enrico Caruso's bedroom is preserved as a relic; guest bedrooms are spacious and elegant in a turn-of-the-century way. ✉ *Piazza Tasso 34, 80067,* ☎ *081/8071044,* FAX *081/8771206. 109 rooms. Restaurant, pool. AE, DC, MC, V.*

$$$–$$$$ **Imperial Hotel Tramontano.** Incorporating the birthplace of the poet Torquato Tasso—the first of an impressive list of literary credentials—this palatial villa lies within a semitropical garden in the center of Sorrento. The sumptuous furnishings and belle epoque tone are set off by the spectacular views out to sea. ✉ *Via Veneto 1, 80067,* ☎ *081/8782588,* FAX *081/8072344. 120 rooms. Restaurant. AE, MC, V. Closed Dec.–Feb.*

$$ **Eden.** Fairly quiet and central, the Eden has bright but undistinguished bedrooms; the lounge and lobby have more character. Renovation work in 1998 will add seven mini-apartments. Prices are low in this category. ✉ *Via Correale 25, 80067,* ☎ *081/8781909,* FAX *081/8072016. 63 rooms. Restaurant, pool. MC, V.*

$ **City.** The central position and excellent value for money are the best reasons to stay in this modest establishment, close to the bus and train stations. Bedrooms are small and functional, but it's relaxed and the management is always ready with information and advice. ✉ *Corso Italia 221, 80067,* ☎ FAX *081/8772210. 13 rooms. AE, MC, V.*

Capri

No matter how many day-trippers crowd onto the island, no matter how touristy certain sections have become, Capri remains one of Italy's loveliest places. Incoming visitors disembark at Marina Grande, from where you can take some time out for an excursion to the **Grotta Azzurra** (Blue Grotto). Be warned that this must rank as one of the country's all-time great rip-offs: Motorboat, rowboat, and grotto admissions are charged separately, and if there's a line of boats waiting, you'll have little time to enjoy the grotto's marvelous colors. At Marina Grande you can also take a boat excursion around the island. A cog railway or bus service takes you up to the deliberately commercial and self-consciously picturesque **Capri Town**, where you can stroll through the **Piazzetta,** a choice place from which to watch the action, and window-shop expensive boutiques. The **Giardini di Augusto** (Gardens of Augustus; ✉ Via Matteotti), have gorgeous views. To get away from the ★ crowds, hike to **Villa Jovis,** one of the many villas that Roman emperor Tiberius built on the island. The walk takes about 45 minutes, with pretty views all the way and a final spectacular vista of the entire Bay of Naples and part of the Gulf of Salerno. ✉ *Villa Jovis, Via Tiberio.* ⏲ *Daily 9–1 hr before sunset.*

You can take the bus or a jaunty open taxi to **Anacapri** and look for the little church of **San Michele** (✉ Off Via Orlandi, ⏲ Easter–Oct., daily 7–7, and Nov.–Easter, daily 10–3), where a magnificent hand-painted majolica tile floor shows you an 18th-century vision of the Garden of Eden. **Villa San Michele** is the charming former home of Swedish scientist-author Axel Munthe. ✉ *Via Axel Munthe.* ⏲ *May–Sept., daily 9–6; Nov.–Feb., daily 10:30–3:30; Mar., daily 9:30–4:30; Apr. and Oct., daily 9:30–5.*

$$–$$$ ✕ **La Capannina.** Only a few steps away from Capri's social center, the Piazzetta, La Capannina has a delightful vine-hung courtyard for summer dining and a reputation as one of the island's best eating places. Antipasto features fried ravioli and eggplant stuffed with ricotta, and house specialties include chicken, scaloppini, and a refreshing, homemade lemon liqueur called *limoncello.* ✉ *Via Botteghe 14,* ☎ *081/8370732. AE, DC, MC, V. Closed mid-Nov.–mid-Mar.*

$$ ★ ✕ **Al Grottino.** This small family-run restaurant, with a handy location near the Piazzetta, displays autographed photographs of celebrity customers. House specialties are gnocchi with tomato sauce and mozzarella, and *linguini con gamberini* (linguini with shrimp sauce). ✉ *Via Longano 27,* ☎ *081/8370584. AE, MC, V. Closed Tues. and Nov. 3–Mar. 20.*

$$ ✕ **Da Gemma.** One of Capri's favorite places for a homey atmosphere and a good meal, Da Gemma features pappardelle all'aragosta and fritto misto. If you're on a budget, forgo the fish that you pay for by weight—it's always expensive. Pizza makes a great starter. ✉ *Via Madre Serafina 6,* ☎ *081/8370461. AE, DC, MC, V. Closed Mon. Oct.–Apr.*

$$$$ 🏨 **Quisisana.** One of Italy's poshest hotels is right in the center of the town of Capri. The rooms are spacious, and many have arcaded balconies with views of the sea; the decor is traditional or contemporary, with some antique accents. From the small terrace at the entrance you can watch all Capri go by, but the enclosed garden and pool in the back are perfect for getting away from it all. The bar and restaurant are casual in a terribly elegant way. ✉ *Via Camerelle 2, 80073,* ☎ *081/8370788,* FAX *081/8376080. 143 rooms. Restaurant, pool. AE, DC, MC, V. Closed Nov.–mid-Mar.*

$$$ ★ 🏨 **Villa Brunella.** The glassed-in bar of this family-run hotel is on the lane leading to Punta Tragara and the Faraglioni. From that level you descend to the restaurant, and then to the rooms and the pool on lower levels. Furnishings are tastefully casual and comfortable, the views serendipitous. Be prepared to climb stairs; there's no elevator. ✉ *Via Tragara 24, 87003,* ☎ *081/8370122,* FAX *081/8370430. 18 rooms. Restaurant, pool. AE, DC, MC, V. Closed Nov.–Mar.*

$$$ 🏨 **Villa Sarah.** Just a 10-minute walk from the Piazzetta, the Sarah is a whitewashed Mediterranean villa with bright, simply furnished rooms. There's a garden and small bar, but no restaurant. ✉ *Via Tiberio 3/A, 87003,* ☎ *081/8377817,* FAX *081/8377215. 20 rooms. AE, DC, MC, V. Closed Nov.–Mar.*

Positano

★ Positano's jumble of pastel houses, topped by whitewashed cupolas, clings to the mountainside above the sea. The town—the prettiest along this stretch of coast—attracts a sophisticated group of visitors and summer residents who find that its relaxed and friendly atmosphere more than compensates for the sheer effort of moving about this exhaustingly vertical town, most of whose streets are stairways. This former fishing village has now opted for the more regular and lucrative rewards of tourism and commercialized fashion. Practically every other shop is a boutique displaying locally made casual wear. The beach is the town's main focal point, with a little promenade and a multitude of café-restaurants.

$$ ✕ **'O Capurale.** Among all the popular restaurants on the beach promenade, 'O Capurale (just around the corner) has the best food and lowest prices. Tables are set under vines on a breezy sidewalk in the summer, upstairs and indoors in winter. Spaghetti con melanzane and crepes al formaggio are tasty. ✉ *Via Regina Giovanna 12,* ☎ *089/875374. AE, DC, MC, V. Closed Nov.–mid-Feb.*

$$$$ **Le Sirenuse.** The most fashionable hotel in Positano, in an 18th-century villa, has been in the same family for eight generations. The hotel is set into the hillside overlooking Positano's harbor. Most of the bedrooms face the sea—these are the best. Because of the hotel's location, the dining room is like a long, closed-in terrace overlooking the village of Positano. The cuisine ranges from acceptable to excellent. ✉ *Via Cristoforo Colombo 30, 84017,* ☎ *089/875066,* FAX *081/811798. 60 rooms. Restaurant, bar. AE, DC, MC, V.*

$$$$ **Palazzo Murat.** The location is perfect, in the heart of town, near the beachside promenade and set within a walled garden. The old wing is a historic palazzo, with tall windows and wrought-iron balconies; the newer wing is a whitewashed Mediterranean building with arches and terraces. Guests can relax in antiques-strewn lounges or on the charming vine-draped patio. ✉ *Via dei Mulini 23, 84017,* ☎ *089/875177,* FAX *089/811419. 32 rooms. Restaurant, bar. AE, DC, MC, V. Closed Jan.–Mar.*

$$$$ **San Pietro.** Perched on the side of a cliff, this opulent hotel offers unparalleled views of the sea and the Amalfi coast. It's eclectic and airy, with unusual antiques and, everywhere, hanging bougainvillea. The guest rooms are tastefully appointed but the window views steal the show. Verdant with plants, the light, open dining room offers fine Italian cuisine. An elevator takes guests to the hotel's small beach area. ✉ *Via Laurito 2, 84017,* ☎ *089/875455,* FAX *089/811449. 60 rooms. Restaurant. AE, DC, MC, V. Closed Nov.–Mar.*

$$–$$$ ★ **La Fenice.** Paradise found. This tiny and unpretentious hotel beckons with bougainvillea-laden vistas, castaway cottages, and a turquoise pool, all perched over a private beach. Guest rooms—accented with coved ceilings, whitewashed walls, and native folk art—are simple havens of tranquility (book the best, those closest to the sea, only if you can handle *very* steep walkways). Situated on the peaceful outskirts of town, this is happily open year-round. ✉ *Via G. Marconi 4, 84017,* ☎ *089/875513,* FAX *089/811309. 10 rooms. Pool. No credit cards.*

Amalfi

The coastal drive down to the resort town of Amalfi provides some of the most dramatic and beautiful scenery you'll find in all of Italy. Amalfi itself is a charming maze of covered alleys and narrow byways straggling up the steep mountainside. The **piazza** just below the cathedral forms the town's heart—a colorful assortment of pottery stalls, cafés, and postcard shops grouped around a venerable old fountain. The exterior of the **cathedral** is its most impressive feature. The **cloisters,** with whitewashed arches and palms, are worth a glance, and the small **museum** in the adjoining crypt could really inspire you to climb up all those stairs.

$$ ✕ **La Caravella.** Tucked away under some arches lining the coast road, the Caravella has a nondescript entrance but a pleasant interior decorated with paintings of old Amalfi. It's small and intimate, and proprietor Franco describes the cuisine as *"sfiziosa"* (taste tempting).

Specialties include *linguini al pesto amalfitano* (pasta with pesto) based on a medieval recipe and *calamari ripieni* (stuffed squid). ✉ *Via M. Camera 12,* ☎ *089/871029. AE, MC, V. Closed Nov. and Tues. (except Aug.).*

$$$$ ★ 🏨 **Santa Caterina.** A large mansion perched above terraced and flowered hillsides on the coast road just outside Amalfi proper, the Santa Caterina is one of the best hotels on the entire coast. The rooms are tastefully decorated, and most have small terraces or balconies with great views. There are lounges and terraces for relaxing, and an elevator whisks guests down to the seaside saltwater pool, bar, and swimming area. Amid lemon and orange groves are two romantic villa annexes. ✉ *Strada Amalfitana 9, 84011,* ☎ *089/871012,* FAX *089/871351. 54 rooms. Restaurant, pool. AE, DC, MC, V.*

Ravello

★ Ravello is not actually on the coast, but on a high mountain bluff overlooking the sea 8 km (5 mi) north of Amalfi. The road up to it is a series of switchbacks, and the village itself clings precariously on the mountain spur. The village flourished during the 13th century and then fell into a tranquility that has remained unchanged for the past 6 centuries. The town center is Piazza del Duomo, with its **cathedral,** founded in 1087. Note the fine bronze 12th-century doors and, inside, two pulpits richly decorated with mosaics: one depicting the story of Jonah and the whale; the other—more splendid—carved with fantastic beasts and resting on a pride of lions. Composer Richard Wagner once stayed in Ravello, and today there is a Wagner festival every summer on the garden terrace of the 11th-century **Villa Rufolo.** There is a Moorish cloister with interlacing pointed arches, beautiful gardens, an 11th-century tower, and a belvedere with a fine view of the coast. ✉ *Piazza del Duomo.* ⏲ *Summer, daily 9–8; winter, daily 9–6 or sunset.*

At the entrance to the **Villa Cimbrone** complex is a small cloister that looks medieval but was actually built in 1917, with two bas-reliefs: one representing nine Norman warriors, the other illustrating the seven deadly sins. Then, the long avenue leads through peaceful gardens scattered with grottoes, small temples, and statues to a belvedere and terrace where, on a clear day, the view stretches out over the Mediterranean Sea. ⏲ *Daily 8:30–1 hr before sunset.*

$$$$ 🏨 **Hotel Palumbo.** Of all the hotels on the Amalfi coast, the Hotel Palumbo is the most genteel—and one of the most costly. Occupying a 12th-century patrician palace furnished with antiques and provided with modern comforts, this hotel has an elegant, warm atmosphere. You won't quickly forget the lovely garden terraces, breathtaking views, and sumptuous upstairs dining room. Some of the bedrooms are small, but they are full of character. The rooms facing the sea are the choice ones—and the more expensive (those in the modern annex are considerably cheaper). ✉ *Via Toro 28, 84010,* ☎ *089/857244,* FAX *089/858133. 8 rooms. Restaurant. AE, DC, MC, V.*

Campania Essentials

Getting Around

BY BOAT

Most boats and hydrofoils for the islands and the Sorrento peninsula leave from the Molo Beverello Pier (✉ Near Naples's Piazza Municipio); there's also a hydrofoil station at Mergellina Pier.

Hydrofoils. Caremar (☎ 081/5513882). **Linee Marittime Veloci** (LMV, ☎ 081/5527209. **SNAV** (✉ leaves from Mergellina pier only, ☎ 081/7612348).

Passenger and Car Ferries. Service is frequent. **Caremar** (☞ *above*). **Linee Marittime Veloci** (LMV, ☎ 081/5527209).

BY BUS

SITA (☎ 081/5522176 for information).

BY CAR

The Naples–Pompeii–Salerno toll road has exits at Herculaneum and Pompeii, and connects with the tortuous coastal road to Sorrento and the Amalfi coast at the Castellammare exit. Parking within Naples is not recommended: Window smashing and robbery are not uncommon.

BY HELICOPTER

From May through September there's direct helicopter service (☎ 081/5841481 for information) between Capodichino and Capri or Ischia.

BY PLANE

There are several daily flights between Rome and Naples's **Aeroporto Capodichino** (✉ 8 km/5 mi north of downtown Naples, ☎ 081/7896111).

BY TRAIN

Stazione Centrale (✉ Piazza Garibaldi, ☎ 147/888088 for toll-free information). A great number of trains run between Rome and Naples every day; Intercity trains make the journey in less than two hours. There are several stations in Naples, and a network of suburban trains connects the city with diverse points of interest in Campania, most usefully the **Circumvesuviana line** (☎ 081/7722444), which runs to Herculaneum (Ercolano), Pompeii, and Sorrento. Naples has a **Metropolitana** (subway); though it's old and trains are infrequent, it beats the traffic. The fare is 1,500 lire.

Guided Tours

One-, two-, or three-day guided tours of the area depart from Rome. **American Express** (☎ 06/67641). **Carrani** (☎ 06/4880510 and 06/4742501). **Appian Line** (☎ 06/4884151). From Naples you can choose from a wide range of half-day and all-day tours on the mainland and to the islands. **Tourcar** (✉ Piazza Matteotti 1, ☎ 081/5523310). **STS** (✉ Piazza Medaglie d'Oro 41, ☎ 081/5789292).

Visitor Information

Capri (✉ Marina Grande pier, ☎ 081/8370634; ✉ Piazza Umberto I, Capri Town, ☎ 081/8370686). **Naples EPT** (✉ Piazza dei Martiri 58, ☎ 081/405311; ✉ Stazione Centrale, ☎ 081/268779; ✉ Stazione Mergellina, ☎ 081/7612102; ✉ Aeroporto Capodichino, ☎ 081/7805761). **Azienda Autonoma di Soggiorno, Cura e Turismo** (AASCT, ✉ Piazza del Gesù, ☎ 081/5523328). **Sorrento** (✉ Via De Maio 35, ☎ 081/8074033).

19 Luxembourg

When you try to locate Luxembourg on a map, look for "Lux." at the heart of Western Europe. Even abbreviated, the name runs over—west into Belgium, east into Germany, south into France—as the country's influence has done for centuries. The Grand Duchy of Luxembourg is a thriving, Rhode Island–size land that contains variety and contrasts out of all proportion to its size.

It has a wild and beautiful highland country studded with castles, rich in history. It has legendary vineyards producing great wines and a lovely farmland called Le Bõn Pays. And, of course, it has its capital, with an ancient fortress towering above the south central plain. Seen through early morning mists, Luxembourg City revives the magic of Camelot. Yet it is actually the nerve center of a thousand-year-old seat of government, a bustling and important element of the European Union (EU), a spot where the past still speaks, the present interprets, and the future listens.

One of the smallest countries in the United Nations, Luxembourg comprises only 2,587 square km (999 square mi). It is dwarfed by its neighbors, yet from its history of invasion, occupation, and siege, you might think the land covered solid gold. Starting in AD 963, when Charlemagne's descendant Sigefroid started to build his castle atop the promontory of the Bock, the duchy encased itself in layer upon layer of fortifications until by the mid-19th century its very impregnability was considered a threat. The Castle of Luxembourg was ultimately dismantled in the name of peace, its neutrality "guaranteed" by the 1867 Treaty of London. But the Grand Duchy was to be invaded twice again, in 1914 and 1940. Its experiences during World War II convinced Luxembourg of the necessity to cooperate with all its neighbors to avoid conflicts. The entire country now flaunts new wealth, new political muscle, and the highest per capita income in Europe. Luxembourg bristles with international banks—enough to rival Switzerland—and just outside the Old City, a new colony has been populated by *fonctionnaires* of the EU, the successor of the Common Market.

There is an old saying that describes the life of the Luxembourgers—or *Luxembourgeois,* if you prefer the more elegant French appellation: "One Luxembourger, a rose garden; two Luxembourgers, a kaffeeklatsch; three Luxembourgers, a band." This is a country of parades and processions, good cheer, and a hearty capacity for beer and Moselle wine. In its traditions, values, and politics, Luxembourg remains more conservative than its neighbors. This may occasionally seem stifling to the younger generation of Luxembourgeois, but to the majority of their elders these attitudes express the age-old national motto, *Mir wëlle bleiwe wat mir sin* ("We want to remain what we are").

LUXEMBOURG A TO Z

Customs on Arrival

For information on customs regulations, *see* Chapter 1.

Dining

Restaurants in Luxembourg combine Gallic quality with Teutonic quantity. The best deals are to be found at lunch, when you can find a plat du jour or *menu* (two or three courses included in the price) at bargain rates. Pizzerias, found everywhere, offer an inexpensive alternative.

MEALTIMES

Most hotels serve breakfast until 10. Luxembourgers shut down their computers at noon to rush home for a two-hour lunch. Dinner is eaten a bit earlier than in neighboring countries, generally between 7 and 10.

RATINGS

Prices quoted are per person and include a first course, main course, and dessert, but not wine. Service (10%) and sales tax (3%) are included in quoted prices.

CATEGORY	COST
$$$$	OVER FLUX 3,000
$$$	FLUX 1,500–FLUX 3,000
$$	FLUX 750–FLUX 1,500
$	UNDER FLUX 750

WHAT TO WEAR

Stylish, casual dress is expected in most restaurants; when in doubt, err on the side of formality. In expensive French restaurants, formal dress (jacket and tie) is taken for granted.

Language

Native Luxembourgers speak three languages fluently: Luxembourgish, German, and French. Many also speak English.

Lodging

CAMPING

The Grand Duchy is probably the best-organized country in Europe when it comes to camping. It offers some 120 sites, all with full amenities. Listings are published annually by the National Tourist Office (☞ Visitor Information, *below*).

HOTELS

Most hotels in Luxembourg City are relatively modern and range from the international style to smaller, family-run establishments. Weekdays, Luxembourg City hotels are often full of business travelers, who depart on Friday; many hotels accordingly offer reduced rates on weekends.

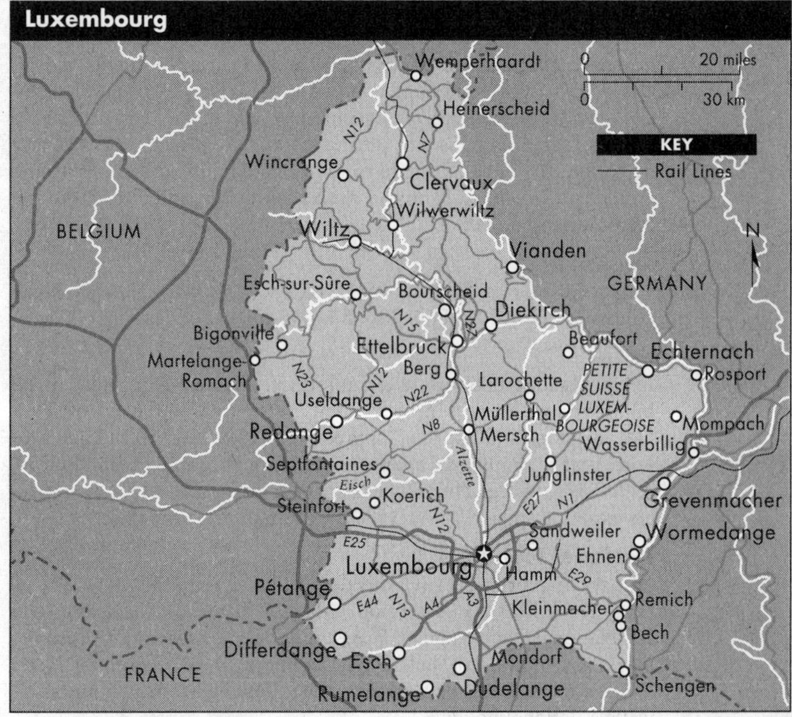

RATINGS

Price categories are for a double room. Service (10%) and sales tax (3%) are included in posted rates. Check for special rates when making reservations.

CATEGORY	COST
$$$$	OVER FLUX 8,000
$$$	FLUX 5,000–FLUX 8,000
$$	FLUX 2,500–FLUX 5,000
$	UNDER FLUX 2,500

YOUTH HOSTELS

Inexpensive youth hostels are plentiful; many are housed in historic buildings. For information contact **Centrale des Auberges Luxembourgeoises** (✉ Rue du Fort Olisy 2, L-2261, Luxembourg City, ☎ 225588).

Mail

POSTAL RATES

Airmail postcards and letters to North America weighing less than 20 grams cost Flux 25. Letters and postcards to the United Kingdom cost Flux 16.

RECEIVING MAIL

Mail can be sent in care of American Express (✉ Avenue de la Porte-Neuve 34, L-2227 Luxembourg City). This service is free for holders of American Express credit cards or traveler's checks.

Money Matters

COSTS

Luxembourg is a highly developed and sophisticated country with a high standard and cost of living. Prices in the countryside are slightly lower than in Luxembourg City.

CURRENCY

In Luxembourg, as in Belgium, the unit of currency is the franc (abbreviated *Flux*). Luxembourg issues its own currency in bills of 100, 1,000, and 5,000 francs and coins of 1, 5, 20, and 50 francs. Belgian currency can be used freely in Luxembourg, and the two currencies have the same value. At press time (spring 1998), the exchange rate was Flux 37 to the U.S. dollar, Flux 26 to the Canadian dollar, Flux 60 to the pound sterling, Flux 23 to the Australian dollar, and Flux 20 to the New Zealand dollar.

SAMPLE PRICES

Cup of coffee, Flux 50–Flux 65; glass of beer, Flux 40–Flux 60; movie admission, Flux 200–Flux 220; 5-km (3-mi) taxi ride, Flux 600.

TIPPING

In hotels and restaurants, taxes and service charges are included in the bill. If you wish to tip further, round off the total to the nearest Flux 100. Bellhops and doormen appreciate a tip of Flux 50 to Flux 100. Porters at the railway station (whose services can be reserved on ☎ 4990 5574) charge Flux 50 per bag, max charge Flux 150. Taxi drivers expect a tip; add about 15% to the amount on the meter.

National Holidays

January 1; February 15 (Carnival); April 5 (Easter Monday); May 1 (May Day); May 13 (Ascension); May 24 (Pentecost Monday); June 23 (National Day); August 15 (Assumption); November 1 (All Saints' Day); November 2 (All Souls' Day); December 25–26 (Christmas). Note: When a holiday falls on a Sunday, the following Monday is automatically a national holiday.

Opening and Closing Times

Banks are generally open weekdays 8:30–4:30, though some close for lunch (noon–2). In Luxembourg City, an automatic exchange machine located in the Rue de la Reine accepts banknotes of most foreign currencies. **Museums'** opening hours vary, so check individual listings. Most are closed Monday, and in the countryside some also close for lunch (noon–2). **Shops** and department stores are generally open Monday 2–6 and Tuesday–Saturday 9–6. Some close for lunch (noon–2). A few small family businesses are open Sunday 8–noon.

Shopping

SALES-TAX REFUNDS

Purchases of goods for export may qualify for a Value Added Tax refund of 15%. For more information, *see* Money *in* Chapter 1.

Telephoning

COUNTRY CODE

The country code for Luxembourg is 352. Note that there are no area codes within the Grand Duchy.

INTERNATIONAL CALLS

The cheapest way to make an international call is to dial direct from a public phone. To reach an **AT&T** long-distance operator, dial 0800–0111; for **MCI,** dial 0800–0112; for **Sprint,** dial 0800–0115.

LOCAL CALLS

You can find public phones on the street and in city post offices. A local call costs a minimum of Flux 5 from a public phone (slightly more from restaurants and gas stations). Post offices sell Telekaart, in denominations from Flux 250 to Flux 750, which can be used in nearly half the country's phone booths. To place operator-assisted calls, dial 0010.

Visitor Information

Office Nationale du Tourisme (National Tourist Office; main branch, ✉ Gare Centrale, ☎ 481199; head office, ✉ B.P. 1001, L-1010 Luxembourg City, ☎ 428282–1, FAX 4282–8238; airport branch, ☎ 4282–8221).

Weather

The main tourist season in Luxembourg is from early May through October, with spring and fall the most rewarding seasons. In the hilly north there is frequently snow in winter.

CLIMATE

In general, temperatures in Luxembourg are moderate. Be sure to pack rain gear. The following are the average daily maximum and minimum temperatures for Luxembourg.

Jan.	37F	3C	**May**	65F	18C	**Sept.**	66F	19C
	29	– 1		46	8		50	10
Feb.	40F	4C	**June**	70F	21C	**Oct.**	56F	13C
	31	– 1		52	11		43	6
Mar.	49F	10C	**July**	73F	23C	**Nov.**	44F	7C
	35	1		55	13		37	3
Apr.	57F	14C	**Aug.**	71F	22C	**Dec.**	39F	4C
	40	4		54	12		32	0

LUXEMBOURG CITY

As you arrive in the capital of Luxembourg from the airport and cross the vast span of the Grande Duchesse Charlotte Bridge, you're greeted by an awe-inspiring panorama of medieval stonework fortifications fronted by massive gates. Then, after a left turn that swings you into the Boulevard Royal, you're back in the 20th century of BMW and Mercedes cars and glittering glass-and-concrete office buildings. A block away, in the Old City, the sedate pace of a provincial picture-book town delightfully returns.

Exploring Luxembourg City

Numbers in the margin correspond to points of interest on the Luxembourg City map.

The military fortifications and the Old Town, with its cobbled streets and inviting public squares, make for terrific exploring. In 1994 the United Nations Educational, Scientific, and Cultural Organization (UNESCO) declared these areas part of the world's cultural heritage.

★ 13 **Bock.** This stony promontory is Luxembourg's raison d'être. Jutting up dramatically above the valley, the Bock once supported the castle built by the first Duke of Luxembourg in AD 963. Taking in vertiginous views of the valley, you'll see the **Plateau du Rham** across the way, on the right, and before it, the massive towers of Duke Wenceslas's fortifications, which were built in 1390. The blocklike *casernes* (barracks) were added during the 17th century by the French. From the Bock you can gain access to fascinating 18th-century military tunnels. At the entrance, the **Crypte Archéologique du Bock** (Archaeological Crypt) offers an audiovisual presentation providing a brief history of Luxembourg from the 10th to the 15th centuries. ✉ *Montée de Clausen,* ☎ *226753.* ⏲ *Mar.–Oct., daily 10–5.*

8 **Boulevard Royal.** Luxembourg's mini–Wall Street, once the site of the fortress's main moat, curves around the west and north sides of the

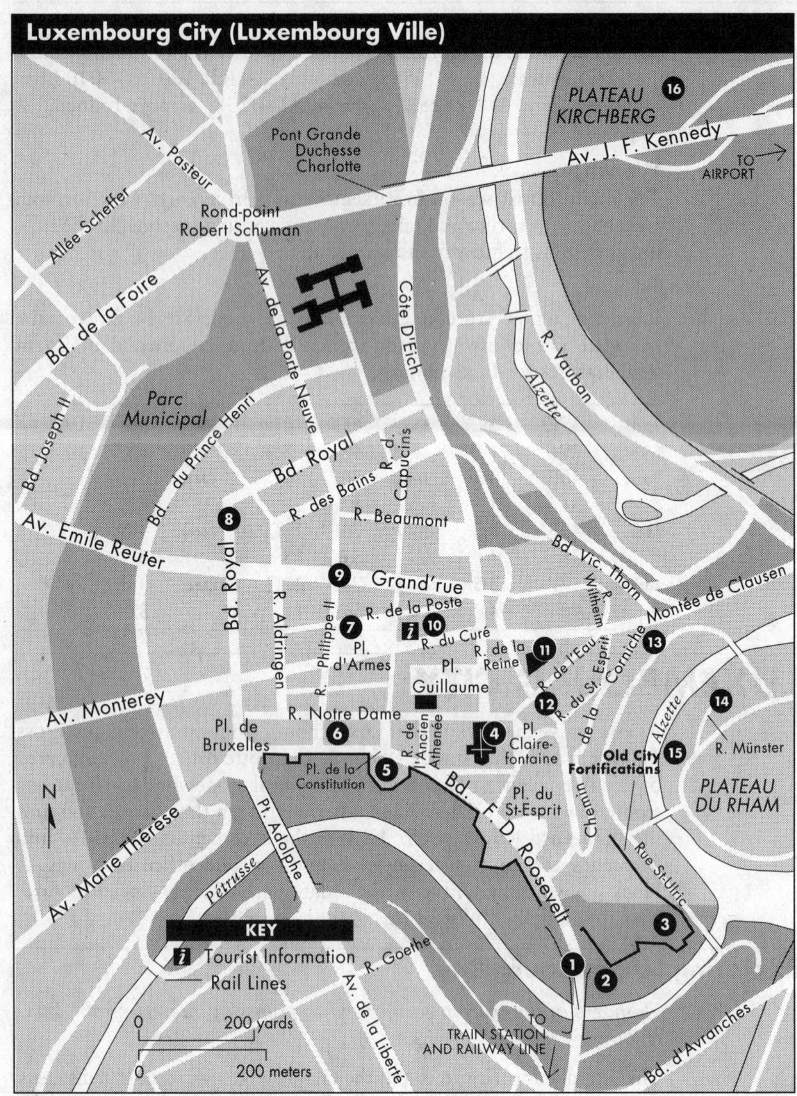

Bock, **13**
Boulevard Royal, **8**
Casemates de la Pétrusse, **5**
Casino Luxembourg, **6**
Cathédrale Notre-Dame, **4**
Citadelle du St-Esprit, **3**
Eglise de St-Jean Baptiste, **14**
Grand'Rue, **9**
Maquette de la Forteresse, **10**
Monument de la Solidarité Nationale, **2**
Musée d'Histoire de la Ville de Luxembourg, **12**
Le Natur Musée au Grund, **15**
Palais Grand-Ducal, **11**
Place d'Armes, **7**
Plateau Kirchberg, **16**
Viaduc, **1**

Old City. It is lined with as many of the duchy's 225 financial institutions as could be crowded into five blocks.

5 **Casemates de la Pétrusse** (Pétrusse casemates). During the many phases of the fortress-city's construction, the rock itself was hollowed out to form a honeycomb of underground passages. Those facing the Pétrusse Valley go back to the Spanish occupation during the 17th century. ✉ *Pl. de la Constitution.* ⏲ *July–Sept., daily 11–4.*

6 **Casino Luxembourg.** Far from being a gaming establishment, this gracious hall, where Liszt played his last public concert, is now a gallery where contemporary art exhibitions are mounted. ✉ *Rue Notre-Dame 41,* ☎ *225045.* ⏲ *Wed.–Mon. 11–6 (Thurs. until 8).*

4 **Cathédrale Notre-Dame.** Luxembourg's 17th-century cathedral is still the scene of national pilgrimage during the two weeks beginning on the third Sunday after Easter. It has an extravagantly carved portal and a fine Baroque organ gallery, both the work of Daniel Muller. In the crypt are the tombs of members of the present ruling dynasty as well as that of John the Blind (1296–1346), the gallant count of Luxembourg and king of Bohemia who fell at the Battle of Crécy in France during the Hundred Years' War. ✉ *Rue Notre-Dame (Crypt entrance Bd. F. D. Roosevelt).* 🎫 *Free. Crypt:* ⏲ *Easter–Oct., weekdays 10–5, Sat. 8–6, Sun. 10–6; Nov.–Easter, weekdays 10–11:30 and 2–5, Sat. 8–11:30 and 2–5, Sun. 10–5.*

3 **Citadelle du St-Esprit** (Citadel of the Holy Spirit). This 17th-century citadel was built during a French occupation by Maréchal Vauban (1633–1707), Louis XIV's chief military engineer, in the typical style of thrusting wedges. From the "prow" you have a panoramic view of the three spires of the cathedral, the Alzette River, and the white tower of the European Parliament secretariat. ✉ *Plateau du St-Esprit.*

14 **Eglise de St-Jean Baptiste** (Church of St. John the Baptist). This Baroque church on the shore of the Alzette River was formerly part of a Benedictine abbey. Among its treasures are a cycle of the Stations of the Cross made of Limoges enamel and a Black Madonna once thought to provide protection against the plague. The riverside passageway outside the church has an awe-inspiring view of the cliffs. ✉ *Rue Münster.*

9 **Grand'Rue.** The city's main upscale shopping street runs west to east from Boulevard Royal to Rue du Fossé. The pedestrian mall is lined with luxury boutiques and tempting patisseries, adding to the Luxembourg bourgeois touch.

10 **Maquette de la Forteresse** (Scale Model of the Fortress). This model is a copy of one (now in Paris) made of the fortress-city for Napoléon in 1804, when the fortified complex was at the peak of its glory. ✉ *Rathskeller, Rue du Curé,* ☎ *222809.* ⏲ *School holidays (Easter weeks, Whitsun week, mid-July–mid-Sept.), daily 10–5:45.*

2 **Monument de la Solidarité Nationale** (Monument to National Unity). Luxembourg was the only occupied country during World War II to stage a general strike against its occupiers. Hitler annexed the Grand Duchy and drafted its young men into the German army. This moving memorial honors Luxembourg's World War II casualties. Within the stark walls is a small, stained-glass chapel housing a symbolic tombstone. ✉ *Kanounenhiwel, Plateau du St-Esprit.*

★ 12 **Musée d'Histoire de la Ville de Luxembourg** (Luxembourg City Historical Museum). Oft postponed, this exciting, interactive museum opened in 1996 to rave reviews. It explores the wealth of the city's history over 1,000 years, and visitors are provided with electronic cards to use the many touch-sensitive screens in their language of choice. A successful marriage of ancient buildings and contemporary technology, the museum invites visitors to descend in time and space in a panoramic elevator the size of an exhibition hall. ✉ *Rue du St-Esprit 14,* ☎ *229050-1 (direct information line).* ⌚ *Tues.–Sun. 10–6 (Thurs. until 8).*

★ ⓯ **Le Natur Musée au Grund** (Museum of Nature). The newest of Luxembourg's museums, opened in 1996, was until recently a women's prison. The building, dating from 1308, now houses collections and displays that help visitors situate themselves in relation to their environment, past and present. The museum stands on the bank of the Alzette River in the heart of the **Grund;** to get here in comfort, take the elevator from the Plateau du St-Esprit. ✉ *Rue Münster 23,* ☎ *462233-1 (direct information line).* ⌚ *Tues.–Thurs. 2–6, Fri.–Sat. 10–6.*

⓫ **Palais Grand-Ducal** (Palace of the Grand Duke). This restored palace was the former residence of the royal family. Parts date from the 16th century, notably the section that once served as the town hall; a distinct Spanish-Moorish influence is obvious in the elaborate facade. Tickets for guided tours (often sold out) are available only at the City Tourist Office (☞ Visitor Information *in* Contacts and Resources, *below*). ✉ *Rue du Marché-aux-Herbes.* ⌚ *Guided tours only; mid-July–early Sept., in English, Mon., Tues., Thurs.–Sat., 4.*

❼ **Place d'Armes.** Lined with symmetrical plane trees and strung with colored lights, this is the city's liveliest and most welcoming square. A bandstand (concerts are often held here on summer evenings), sidewalk cafés, fast-food joints, and a twice-monthly flea market constantly lure natives and tourists alike. From its southeast corner, a passage leads to the more dignified **Place Guillaume,** with the Hôtel de Ville (Town Hall); there's a farmers' market Wednesday and Saturday mornings. Next, continuing southeasterly, comes the elegant, sloping **Place Clairefontaine,** adorned with a graceful statue of the much-loved Grande Duchesse Charlotte, who ruled from 1919 to 1964.

⓰ **Plateau Kirchberg.** Several European Union institutions as well as some major banks lie in this district. The most prominent structure—at 23 stories, Luxembourg's only skyscraper—is home to the secretariat of the European Parliament. ✉ *Across Grande Duchesse Charlotte Bridge. Bus 18 (direction Domaine du Kiem) from Bd. Royal loops around the area.*

❶ **Viaduc.** The 19th-century bridge is also known as the *Passerelle* (footbridge), although it carries vehicular traffic from the railway station. A good starting point for exploring Luxembourg City, it spans the valley of the Pétrusse (now more a brook than a river), which has become a beautiful park. ✉ *From Av. de la Gare to Pl. St-Esprit.*

Dining and Lodging

Today, leading chefs are taking traditional Luxembourg specialties—*jambon d'Ardennes* (pearly pink raw-smoked ham served cold with pickled onions), *treipen* (blood pudding), and *écrevisses* (crayfish)—and giving them all a newer-than-now nouvelle spin. In the process, Luxembourg City is becoming a true capital *gastronomique.* Keep in mind that many upscale places offer a reasonably priced menu at lunch. For more details and price-category definitions, *see* Dining *in* Luxembourg A to Z, *above.*

Hotels in the city center are more conveniently located for exploring than those clustered around the train station. There are also large, modern hotels near the airport and on the Plateau Kirchberg. For details and price-category definitions, *see* Lodging *in* Luxembourg A to Z, *above.*

$$$$ ★ ✕ **Clairefontaine.** The tastefully discreet luxury of this dining spot on the city's most attractive square draws government ministers, visiting dignitaries, and well-heeled gourmands. Chef-owner Tony Tintinger's inspirations include a showcase of foie gras specialties, innovative fish dishes (soufflé of langoustines perfumed with anise), and such game offerings as tournedos of doe with wild mushrooms. ✉ *Pl. de Clairefontaine 9,* ☎ *462211. Reservations essential. Jacket and tie. AE, DC, MC, V. Closed Sun., 3 wks in Aug., 1st wk in Nov. No lunch Sat.*

$$$ ★ ✕ **Jan Schneidewind.** The chef/owner of this bandbox bistro serves excellent stuffed crab with lobster coulis, saffron-flavored monkfish, and other seafood specialties. In August, this is virtually the only top-rank restaurant in town that stays open. ✉ *Rue du Curé 20,* ☎ *222618. AE, DC, MC, V. Closed Mon., 3 wks in Feb. No lunch Sat.*

$$$ ✕ **La Lorraine.** Outstanding seafood is the specialty of this restaurant strategically situated on the place d'Armes. A retail shop around the corner shows off the freshness of its wares. Baked skate (in hazelnut butter with capers) and puff pastry with sole and morels are good bets. ✉ *Pl. d'Armes 7,* ☎ *474620. Jacket required. AE, DC, MC, V. Closed Sun., 2nd ½ of Aug.*

$$ ✕ **Ancre d'Or.** This tidy, friendly brasserie, just off Place Guillaume, has a wide variety of old-time Luxembourg specialties. Try their *judd mat gardebounen* (smoked pork with broad beans). Portions are generous, service is friendly, and the clientele is local. ✉ *Rue du Fossé 23,* ☎ *472973. MC, V. Closed Sun.*

$$ ★ ✕ **Lëtzebuerger Kaschthaus.** One of the country's great chefs, Lea Linster, owns this farmhouse-restaurant, which celebrates local culinary traditions: green-bean soup, sweetbreads vol-au-vent, sausage with savory lentils. Pretty print linens, stenciled wallpaper, and original ceramic flooring add up to a comfortable, retro setting. Its authenticity makes the special trip worthwhile. ✉ *Rte. de Bettembourg 4, Hellange (10 km/6 mi south of the city),* ☎ *516573. Reservations essential. AE, DC, MC, V. Closed Tues., 3 wks in Aug./Sept. No lunch Wed.*

$$ ✕ **Mousel's Cantine.** Right next to the great Mousel brewery, this fresh, comfortable café serves up heaping platters of local specialties—braised and grilled ham, sausage, broad beans, and fried potatoes—accompanied by crockery steins of creamy *Gezwickelte Béier* (unfiltered beer). ✉ *Montée de Clausen 46,* ☎ *470198. MC, V. Closed Sun.*

$$ ✕ **Times.** On a pedestrian street of art galleries and boutiques you'll also find excellent-value food. The narrow dining room lined with glass and Canadian cherry wood is often crowded with artists and journalists. The cuisine tends toward such ambitious creations as fillet of suckling pig flavored with tea. ✉ *Rue Louvigny 8,* ☎ *222722. AE, DC, MC, V.*

$ ★ ✕ **Ems.** Everybody in Luxembourg vies for one of the vinyl booths in this unpretentious but lively establishment. Its vast portions of mussels in a rich wine-and-garlic broth are best accompanied by french fries and a bottle of sharp, cold, and inexpensive Auxerrois or Rivaner. Ems is open until 1 AM. ✉ *Pl. de la Gare 30,* ☎ *487799. Reservations not accepted. AE, DC, MC, V. No lunch Sat.*

$ ✕ **Oberweis.** Luxembourg's most famous patisserie also serves light lunches. You select your meal at the counter (quiche lorraine, spinach pie, and the like), and it is served at your table. ✉ *Grand'Rue 19–20,* ☎ *470703. Reservations not accepted. AE, DC, MC, V. Closed Sun.*

$$$$ ★ 🏨 **Le Royal.** In the city center, on Luxembourg's Wall Street and within steps of parks, shopping, and the Old Town, Le Royal is the best choice for luxury. It's solid, modern, and sleek, with pleasant lobbies

on each floor. A new (1997) wing has been added, with an exotic winter garden and a deluxe restaurant, La Pomme Cannelle. ✉ *Bd. Royal 12, L-2449,* ☎ *416161,* FAX *225948. 190 rooms, 20 suites.. 2 restaurants, bar, indoor pool, beauty salon, health club. AE, DC, MC, V.*

$$$ **Cravat.** This charming Luxembourg relic straddles the valley and the Old Town in the best location in the city. Though corridors have a dated air, guest rooms are fresh and welcoming in a variety of tastefully retro styles. The art deco coffee shop has been freshened up but still draws fur-hatted ladies of a certain age. The prime minister and his cabinet can be found in the hotel tavern most Friday afternoons. ✉ *Bd. F. D. Roosevelt 29, L-2011,* ☎ *221975,* FAX *226711. 58 rooms. 2 restaurants. AE, DC, MC, V.*

$$$ **Parc Belair.** This privately owned, family-run hotel a few blocks from the city center stands on the edge of the Parc de Merl. Rooms are a warm beige; those on the park are the quietest. The complex includes a separate restaurant with outdoor café. A substantial buffet breakfast is included. The restaurant serves dinner only. ✉ *Av. du X Septembre 109, L-2551,* ☎ *442323,* FAX *444484. 45 rooms, 7 suites. Restaurant. AE, DC, MC, V.*

$$ **Auberge le Châtelet.** At the edge of a quiet residential area, this pleasant hotel has stone and terra-cotta floors, double windows, Oriental rugs, and tropical plants. Rooms are furnished in knotty pine and have new tile baths. The nine rooms in the adjoining annex cost slightly less. ✉ *Bd. de la Pétrusse 2, L-2320,* ☎ *402101,* FAX *403666. 32 rooms. Restaurant. AE, DC, MC, V.*

$$ ★ **La Cascade.** A turn-of-the-century villa has been converted into a hotel of considerable charm and elegance. There's a good Italian restaurant and a lovely terrace overlooking the Alzette River. A bus stops outside to take you to the city center, just over a mile away. ✉ *Rue de Pulvermuhl 2, L-2356,* ☎ *428736,* FAX *4287–8888. 8 rooms. Restaurant. AE, DC, MC, V.*

$$ **Italia.** This is a find: a former private apartment house converted into hotel rooms, some with plaster detailing and vintage cabinetry. Rooms are solid and freshly furnished, all with tile bathrooms. The restaurant downstairs is one of the city's better Italian eateries. ✉ *Rue d'Anvers 15-17, L-1130,* ☎ *486626,* FAX *480807. 20 rooms. Restaurant. AE, DC, MC, V.*

$$ **Sieweburen.** At the northwestern end of the city is this attractively rustic hotel, opened in 1991; the clean, large rooms have natural-wood beds and armoires. There's a playground in front and woods in the back. The brasserie-style tavern, older than the rest of the property, is hugely popular, especially when its terrace is open. ✉ *Rue des Septfontaines 36, L-2534,* ☎ *442356,* FAX *442353. 13 rooms. Restaurant. Closed 3 wks late Dec.–early Jan. AE, DC, MC, V.*

$–$$ **Ibis.** The Luxembourg franchise of this French hotel chain is across the street from the airport, with direct access to the motorway. You can walk or use the free shuttle. Ibis hotels may not be strong on personality but provide honest value for the money. Family rooms sleeping up to four are available. The forest begins just behind the hotel. ✉ *Rte. de Trèves, L-2632 Findel,* ☎ *438801,* FAX *438802. 120 rooms. Restaurant. AE, DC, MC, V.*

$ **Carlton.** In this vast 1918 hotel near the train station, you'll find roomy, quiet quarters. The beveled glass and the oak parquet and terrazzo floors are original—but so are the toilets, all down the hall. Each room has antique beds, floral-print comforters, and a sink; wooden floors, despite creaks, are white-glove clean. ✉ *Rue de Strasbourg 9, L-2561,* ☎ *299660,* FAX *299664. 50 rooms without toilet, 8 with shower. No credit cards.*

Shopping

Luxembourg City's principal shopping area comprises the **Grand'Rue** and its side streets. Jewelry and designer fashions are particularly well represented. Luxembourg chocolates, called *knippercher,* are popular purchases at the best pastry shops. Luxembourg's most famous product is porcelain from **Villeroy & Boch** (✉ Rue du Fossé 2, ☎ 4682–1216). Feast your eyes on their tableware, crystal, and cutlery at the glitzy main store, then buy—at a 20% discount—at the excellent second-quality factory outlet to the northwest of the city center (✉ Rue Rollingergrund 330).

Side Trips

The northern highlands that comprise the celebrated Ardennes plateau were the hunting ground of emperors and dukes and have been fought over from time immemorial to World War II. Castles punctuate its hills and dominate the valleys; rocky rivers and streams pour off its slopes. In contrast, the Petite Suisse, to the northeast of the capital, presents a more smiling face. It's a hilly area of leafy woods, rushing brooks, and old farms, ideal for rustic picnics and great hiking. An easy hour's drive from Luxembourg City will take you to any of the towns except Clervaux, which is a bit farther.

Diekirch

In the Ardennes, Diekirch has a lovely little Romanesque church, **Eglise St-Laurent** (St. Lawrence's), with Merovingian tombs, and (south of town) the Devil's Altar, a Celtic dolmen. The **Musée National d'Histoire Militaire** (National Military History Museum) mainly commemorates the Battle of the Bulge, the last German counter-offensive, which began just before Christmas, 1944. ✉ *Bamertal 10,* ☎ *808908.* ⏲ *Apr.–Oct., daily 10–6; Nov.–Mar., daily 2–6.*

Vianden

★ The medieval **Château de Vianden** is the most romantic sight in the Grand Duchy. Rearing up on a hill above the tiny village, and replete with conical spires and massive bulwarks, it vividly recalls Luxembourg's feudal past. This was the last bit of Luxembourg soil to be liberated by U.S. troops toward the end of World War II. ✉ *Grand-rue,* ☎ *849291.* ⏲ *Apr.–Sept., daily 10–6; Mar. and Oct., daily 10–5; Nov.–Feb., daily 10–4.*

Clervaux

Surrounded by deep-cleft hills, the town is noted for the 12th-century **Château de Clervaux,** which has become the permanent home for Luxembourg-born Edward Steichen's "Family of Man," arguably the greatest photographic exhibit ever assembled. Franklin Delano Roosevelt's ancestor, Philip de Lannoi, set forth from this castle in 1621 to seek his fortune in America. ✉ *Grand-rue,* ☎ *522–4241.* ⏲ *Mar.–Dec., Tues.–Sun. 10–6.*

Bourscheid

★ The romantic ruins of the **Château de Bourscheid** loom 500 ft above the River Sûre, commanding three valleys. Restorations have made the rambling towers and walls more accessible. ✉ *Bourscheid Moulin-Plage,* ☎ *90570.* ⏲ *Apr., daily 11–5; May–June and Sept., daily 10–6; July–Aug., daily 10–7; Oct., daily 11–4; rest of year, weekends 11–4.*

Müllerthal

This small village has given its name to the entire district, also known as the Petite Suisse. It's covered with dense fir and beech forests, with high limestone bluffs and twisting brooks, and many an inviting inn along the way. Follow routes E27 and 121 to vantage points for panoramic views of the River Sûre.

Echternach

Echternach's cobbled market square is a mix of Gothic arcades and medieval town houses. The River Sûre here forms the border with Germany, and large numbers of tourists cross over on weekends. The surrounding woods attract hikers heading to the rock formation known as the Gorge du Loup (Wolf's Gorge). Some 15,000 pilgrims participate every year in a dancing procession on the Tuesday after Pentecost, ending at the **Basilique St-Willibrord,** whose crypt (⏲ daily 9:30–6:30) contains the tomb of the great English missionary St. Willibrord (658–739). Painstakingly detailed reproductions of the illuminated manuscripts of the Echternach School are displayed in the **Musée de l'Abbaye** (Abbey Museum). ✉ *Parvis de la Basilique 11,* ☎ *727472.* ⏲ *Apr.–Oct., daily 10–noon and 2–6; Nov.–Mar., weekends 2–5.*

Luxembourg City Essentials

Arriving and Departing

BY PLANE

All international flights arrive at Luxembourg's **Findel Airport,** 6 km (4 mi) northeast of the city.

Between the Airport and Downtown. Bus 9 links the airport, the city center, and the main bus depot, next to the train station. Tickets cost Flux 40. A taxi costs Flux 700–Flux 800. If you are driving, follow the signs for the CENTRE VILLE (city center).

BY TRAIN

Luxembourg is served by frequent direct trains from Paris (four hours) and Brussels (three hours). From Amsterdam (six hours), the journey is via Brussels. There are connections from most German cities via Koblenz. Outside Luxembourg City, three major train routes extend to the north, south, and east. All services are from the **Gare Centrale** (☎ 4990 4990).

Getting Around

BY BICYCLE

Bicycling is an excellent way to see the city and outlying areas. Bikes can be rented in Luxembourg City at **Velo en Ville** (✉ Bisserwee 8, ☎ 4796–2383) from April through October.

BY BUS

Luxembourg City has highly efficient bus service (for information: Aldringen Center, underground station off Boulevard Royal; 10-ride ticket, Flux 320).

BY CAR

On-street parking in Luxembourg City is difficult. If you're in Luxembourg for a day, use one of the underground parking lots or park at the Parking Glacis next to the Municipal Theater, five minutes' walk from the city center. If you arrive from the west, use the free Parking Stade (opposite the Stadium) on Route d'Arlon and take the shuttle bus (Flux 40) to town. If you arrive from France, look for the park-and-ride facility Sud; from Germany, look for Kirchberg- FIL. You need local currency for the bus ride.

BY TAXI

Taxi (☎ 480058 or 482233) stands are near the Gare Centrale and the main post office; it is almost impossible to hail one in the street.

Contacts and Resources

EMBASSIES

United States (✉ Bd. Emmanuel Servais 22, ☎ 460123). **Canadian:** In Belgium (✉ Av. de Tervuren 2, 1040 Brussels, ☎ 00322/741–0611). **United Kingdom** (✉ Bd. F. D. Roosevelt 14, ☎ 229864).

EMERGENCIES

Police (☎ 113). **Ambulance, Doctor, Dentist** (☎ 112). **Pharmacies** in Luxembourg stay open nights on a rotation system; see signs listing late-night facilities outside each pharmacy.

ENGLISH-LANGUAGE BOOKS

For books and magazines in English, try **Magasin Anglais** (✉ Allée Scheffer 13, ☎ 224925).

GUIDED TOURS

Orientation. Sales-Lentz (☎ 650065-1, direct information line) runs 1½-hour city bus tours (June–Sept.) and 2¼-hour city and environs tours (Apr.–mid-Nov.) from the war memorial on Place de la Constitution. A guided walking tour leaves daily at 2:30 from Place d'Armes (Easter–Oct.). **Luxembourg Live** (☎ 461617) guided minitrain tours of the Old Town and the Pétrusse Valley operate from the Place de la Constitution (Apr.–Oct.).

★ **Special Interest.** The **Wenzel Walk** allows visitors to experience 1,000 years of history in 100 minutes. The walk starts at the Bock promontory and leads over medieval bridges and past ancient ruins. The City Tourist Office (☞ Visitor Information, *below*) can provide a guide.

Self-Guided Tours. The **Luxembourg Card** provides free admission to 31 major attractions in the capital and countryside and free use of public transport throughout the Grand Duchy. For one person it costs Flux 300 for one day, 500 for two, and 700 for three days; family cards are twice the price. Cards can be bought in hotels and tourist offices.

TRAVEL AGENCIES

American Express (✉ Av. de la Porte-Neuve 34, ☎ 228555). **Carlson/Wagonlit** (✉ Grand'Rue 99, ☎ 460315). **Sotour** (including youth travel; ✉ Pl. du Théâtre 15, ☎ 461514).

VISITOR INFORMATION

Luxembourg City Tourist Office (✉ Pl. d'Armes, ☎ 222809). **Beaufort** (✉ Rue de l'Eglise 9, ☎ 836081). **Bourscheid** (✉ Château, ☎ 90564). **Clervaux** (✉ Château, ☎ 920072). **Diekirch** (✉ Esplanade 1, ☎ 803023). **Echternach** (✉ Porte St-Willibrord, Basilique, ☎ 720230). **Vianden** (✉ Maison Victor Hugo, Rue de la Gare 37, ☎ 834257).

20 Malta

Valletta, Around the Islands

Hulking megalithic temples, ornate Baroque churches, narrow old-world streets, and hilltop citadels are Malta's human legacy. Dizzying limestone cliffs, sparkling Mediterranean seas, and charming rural landscapes make up its natural beauty. Its three main islands—Malta, Gozo, and Comino—offer history, swimming, spectacular coastal views, and culinary delights.

In its 7,000 years of human habitation, Malta has been overrun by every major Mediterranean power: Phoenicians, Carthaginians, Romans, Byzantines, and Arabs; French, Germans, Aragonians, and the Knights of the Order of St. John of Jerusalem; Napoléon, the British, and now European tourists. The Germans and Italians tried to take it in World War II—their air raids were devastating—but could not.

The islands' history with the Knights of the Order of St. John has given them their lasting character. Charles V of Spain, 410 years before the Axis powers' assault, granted Malta to the Knights after the Ottoman Turks chased the military order of hospitalers out of Rhodes. In 1565, when the forces of Suleyman the Magnificent laid siege to the islands, it was the Knights' turn, with the faithful backing of the Maltese, to send the Turks packing.

The handsome limestone buildings and fortifications that the wealthy Knights left behind are all around the islands. Malta has plenty of modern overdevelopment, too—all the more reason to stick to the historic sights on Malta and head to quieter Gozo to relax and to enjoy the sea. You'll need at least four days to see Malta and Gozo; allow two or more for taking in Malta's splendid past, then make your way to Gozo for a few days of the good life.

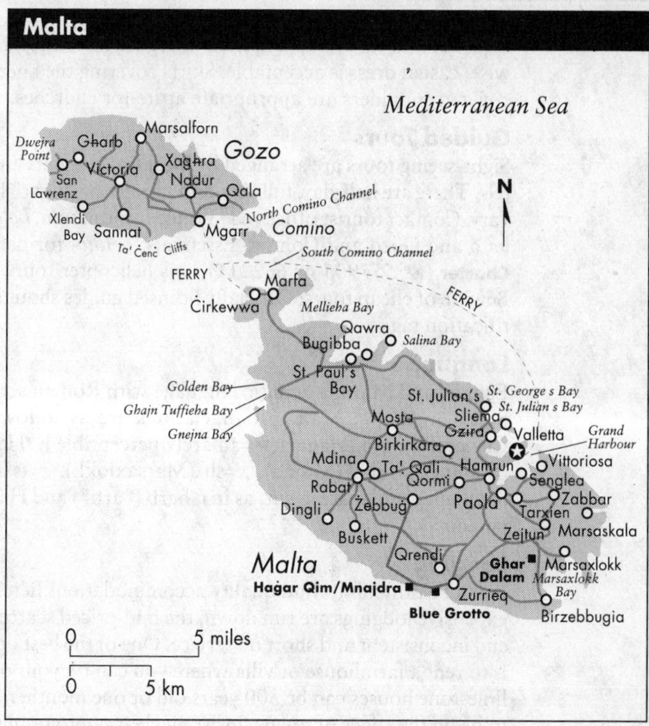

MALTA A TO Z

Customs on Arrival

You may bring into Malta, duty-free, 200 cigarettes, one bottle of liquor, one bottle of wine, and one bottle of perfume. Up to Lm 50 in currency may be brought in.

Dining

Traditional Maltese cuisine is Sicilian and Moorish in origin, but Italian food is on most restaurant menus as well. Locally caught fish is a specialty. The national dish is *fenek* (rabbit); *braġjoli* (beef olives) and lampuki (fish) pie are runners-up. Pastry coats fish, vegetables, cheese, and pasta dishes. Soups, *minestra* (minestrone) and *aljotta* (fish soup) especially, are common, delicious with daily baked crusty Maltese bread. Capers, the buds of the *caperis specicum* shrub that is native to the islands, are widely used. Nativė wine is abundant and inexpensive; look for medium-dry whites. Ċisk lager is a local favorite, and Blue Label ale is a slightly heartier brew.

RATINGS

Prices are per person for a three-course meal, not including wine and tip.

CATEGORY	COST
$$$$	OVER LM 10
$$$	LM 7–LM 10
$$	LM 4–LM 7
$	UNDER LM 4

WHAT TO WEAR

A jacket and tie are appropriate in higher-priced restaurants. Otherwise, casual dress is acceptable. Skirts covering the knees or pants and covered shoulders are appropriate attire for churches.

Guided Tours

Sight-seeing tours are arranged by local travel agents and the large hotels. There are half-day, full-day, and "Malta by Night" bus tours; rates vary. Contact tourist offices (☞ Visitor Information, *below,* and in Valletta and Gozo and Comino Essentials, *below*) for details. **Malta Air Charter** (☎ 557905 or 662211) runs helicopter tours of the islands. Beware of cheap tours: Officially licensed guides should wear an identification tag.

Language

English and Malti, a Semitic language with Roman script, are the official languages. Malti pronunciations are as follows: *ċ*=ch (as in Ċirkewwa), *ġ*=j (Haġar), *ħ*=a barely perceptible h (Hal Saflieni), *j*=y (Dwejra), *M*=im (Mdina), *x*=sh (Marsaxlokk), *ż*=ts (Żebbuġ), and the plain *g* and *q* are silent, as in Għarb ("arb") and Haġar Qim ("*ha*-jar eem").

Lodging

It can be difficult to find quality accommodations here. Often, the inexpensive lodgings are run down, the mid-priced scarce, and the high-end inconsistent and short on service. One of the best options on Gozo is to rent a farmhouse or villa where you can fix your own meals. The limestone houses can be 300 years old or one month; newer ones tend to be on the edges of towns. Insist on clear photographs and details in writing before sending a deposit.

RATINGS

Prices are for two people sharing a double room.

CATEGORY	COST
$$$$	OVER LM 50
$$$	LM 25–LM 50
$$	LM 12–LM 25
$	UNDER LM 12

Mail

Airmail letters to the United States and Canada cost 22¢; postcards cost 22¢. Airmail letters and postcards to the United Kingdom cost 16¢.

Money Matters

COSTS

Malta is among the least expensive holiday destinations in Europe, though with the rapid development of tourism, prices are inevitably rising. Prices in Sliema and in Valletta, the capital, are slightly higher than those elsewhere in the islands.

CURRENCY

The unit of currency is the Maltese lira (Lm), also sometimes referred to as the pound; it's divided into 100 cents. There are Lm 2, 5, 10, and 20 bills. The 1¢ coin is bronze, and other coins—2¢, 5¢, 10¢, 25¢, 50¢, and Lm 1—are silver. At press time (spring 1998) the exchange rate was Lm 2.55 to the U.S. dollar, Lm 1.77 to the Canadian dollar, Lm 4.24 to the pound sterling, Lm 1.63 to the Australian dollar, and Lm 1.39 to the New Zealand dollar.

SAMPLE PRICES

In Maltese currency: cup of coffee, 30¢; bottle of beer, 30¢; Coca-Cola, 25¢; sandwich, 90¢; individual pizza, Lm 1.70.

TIPPING

A tip of 10% is expected when a service charge is not included.

National Holidays

January 1; February 10 (St. Paul's Shipwreck); March 19 (St. Joseph's Day); March 31 (Freedom Day); April 2 (Good Friday); May 1 (Worker's Day); June 7 (Commemoration of First Maltese Nationalist Protest); June 29 (Sts. Peter and Paul); August 15 (Assumption, or Santa Marija); September 8 (Our Lady of Victories); September 21 (Independence Day); December 8 (Immaculate Conception); December 13 (Republic Day); December 25.

Opening and Closing Times

Banks are open weekdays 8–12:45; in summer also Friday 2:30–4, Saturday 8–11:30; in winter also Tuesday and Friday 2:30–4, Saturday 8:30–noon. Banks in tourist areas are also open in the afternoon. The currency-exchange booth at the airport is open 24 hours, and there are ATMs in tourist areas. **Museums** run by the Museums Department (☏ 233821) are open as follows: October–mid-June, Monday–Saturday 8–5; Sunday 8–4:15; mid-June–September, daily 7:45–2. Gozo Museums: October–March, Monday–Saturday 8:30–4:30, Sunday 8:30–3; April–mid-June and mid–end September, Monday–Saturday 8:30–6:30, Sunday 8:30–3; mid-June–mid-September, Monday–Saturday 8:30–7, Sunday 8:30–3. All museums are closed on public holidays. Other museums' hours may vary slightly, so check locally. **Shops** are open Monday–Saturday 9–1 and 4–7.

Telephoning

COUNTRY CODE

The country code for Malta is 356.

INTERNATIONAL CALLS

Overseas operator, 194. **International dialing access code,** 00. For an **AT&T** long-distance operator, dial 0800–890110.

LOCAL CALLS

Operator, 190. Public phones are mostly operated by phone cards, which may be purchased at many shops for Lm 2.

Transportation

BY BOAT

Daily car and passenger **ferries** (☏ 243964 in Malta, 556114 or 556743 in Gozo) run year-round from Ċirkewwa (northwest Malta) to Mġarr Harbor on Gozo. One service leaves weekdays from Pietà (near Valletta) to Gozo. Commuter ferry service links Sliema to Valletta. An express **hydrofoil** service operates from Pietà.

BY BUS

Most routes across the island start at Valletta (Terminal: Triton Fountain Sq. just outside main City Gate, ☏ 225916). Local fares on Malta's pied fleet of new and retro buses are a remarkably cheap: 11¢. Bus routes are marked on the tourism bureau's map of the islands.

BY CAR

Driving is on the left, and in spite of the well-signposted routes, challenging. Speed limits are 40 kph (25 mph) in towns, 65 kph (40 mph) elsewhere. British driver's licenses are acceptable; Americans must have international licenses.

BY HELICOPTER

Malta Air Charter (☏ 557905 or 662211) makes the 10-minute flight to and from Gozo several times daily.

Visitor Information

National Tourism Organization–Malta (✉ 280 Republic St., Valletta CMR 02, ☎ 224444/5).

Weather

Late April into June and late September through October have pleasantly warm weather, and the sea is delightful. Mid-June to early September is too hot for comfort; November through March tends to be cool and occasionally rainy.

CLIMATE

The following are the average daily maximum and minimum temperatures for Valletta.

Jan.	58F	14C	**May**	71F	22C	**Sept.**	81F	27C
	50	10		61	16		7	22
Feb.	59F	15C	**June**	79F	26C	**Oct.**	75F	24C
	51	11		67	19		66	19
Mar.	61F	16C	**July**	84F	29C	**Nov.**	67F	20C
	52	11		72	22		60	16
Apr.	65F	18C	**Aug.**	85F	29C	**Dec.**	61F	16C
	56	13		73	23		54	12

VALLETTA

Malta's capital, the minicity of Valletta, has ornate palaces and museums protected by massive fortifications of honey-color stone. Houses along the narrow streets have overhanging wooden balconies for people-watching from indoors. Generations ago they gave house-bound women a window on the world of the street.

Exploring Valletta

The main entrance to town is through the City Gate (where all bus routes end), which leads onto Triq Repubblika (Republic Street), the spine of the grid-pattern city and the main shopping street. Triq Sala Mercante (Merchant Street) parallels Repubblika to the east and is also good for strolling. From these two streets, cross-streets descend toward the water; some are stepped.Valletta's compactness makes it ideal to explore on foot. Before setting out along Republic Street, stop at the tourist information office for maps, brochures, and a copy of *What's On.*

Barrakka ta' Fuq (Upper Barrakka Gardens). Where Knights once honed their fencing skills under a covered loggia (now open to the sky), a troupe of cats and some greenery occupy this lofty lookout over the Grand Harbor and the Three Cities across the water. ✉ *Southeastern heights of city off Castile Square.* ⏲ *Dawn to dusk.*

★ **Casa Rocca Piccola.** The exquisitely cultured current owners, Nicolas and Frances De Piro d'Amico Inguanez, host tours of the last of the patrician houses still nobly occupied. The treasures inside chart the history of the house, from a portable baroque chapel for baptisms to a painting of "Miss Electricity," commissioned to mark the local contribution of an ambitious ancestor. ✉ *74 Triq Repubblika,* ☎ *231796.* ⏲ *Guided tours Mon.–Sat. 10, 11, noon, 1.*

Forti Sant'Iermu (Fort St. Elmo). Built in 1552 by the knights to defend the harbor, it was completely destroyed during the siege of 1565 and rebuilt by succeeding military leaders. Today part of the fort houses the **War Museum** (☎ 222430), with its collection of military objects related to World War II, including an Italian E-Boat and one of the three Gloster Gladiator biplanes that defended the island. ✉ *St. Elmo Pl., Valletta. Fort:* ☎ *226400.* 🎫 *Free.* ⏲ *mid-June–Sept., daily 7:45–2; Oct.–mid-June, Mon.–Sat. 8:15–5; Sun. 8:15–4:15.*

★ **Konkatidral ta' San Gwann** (St. John's co-Cathedral). Functional in design but lavishly decorated, the Order of St. John's own church (1578) is Malta's most important treasure. The Knight's colored-marble tombstones on the floor are gorgeous. Each of the side chapels was decorated by a national auberge of the Knights. Many of the paintings and the decoration scheme are by the island's beloved 17th-century painter Mattia Preti (b. 1613). The cathedral **museum** has illuminated manuscripts and a rich collection of Flemish tapestries. ✉ *Pjazza San Gwann.* ⏲ *Weekdays 9:30–4:30, weekends 9:30–1.*

★ **Muzew Arkejologiku** (National Museum of Archaeology). Housed in the Auberge de Provence (the hostel of the knights from Provence), the museum has a fine collection of finds taken from Malta's many prehistoric sites—Tarxien, Haġar Qim, and the Hypogeum at Paola. ✉ *Triq Repubbklika,* ☎ *233821.* ☞ Opening and Closing Times, *above.*

Manoel Theater. If you are here in opera season, don't miss a show at the third-oldest theater in Europe, which had its opening night on January 9, 1732. Intimate and splendidly decorated, it was designed after Palermo's theater at the time. ✉ *Old Theater St. at Old Bakery St.,* ☎ *246389.* ⏲ *Guided tours weekdays 10:45 and 11:30, Sat. 11:30.*

★ **St. Paul's Shipwreck Church.** The importance of the Apostle Paul to the Maltese explains the work lavished on this Baroque marvel—its raised central vault, oval dome, and marble columns. The *os brachii* (arm bone) relic of San Pawl is in a chapel on the right, a splendid gated chapel is on the left, and a baptismal font stands by the door. ✉ *Triq San Pawl just north of Triq Santa Lucija.* ☞ *Opening and Closing Times,* above.

★ **Palazz tal-Gran Mastri** (Grand Masters' Palace). Malta's parliament meets here, and Malta's president sometimes uses one of the palace rooms. Upstairs, friezes in the sumptuously decorated state apartments depict scenes from the history of the knights. A gallery displays Gobelin tapestries, and the coffered wooden ceilings are remarkable. At the back of the building is the **Armoury of the Knights,** with exhibits of arms and armor down through the ages. ✉ *Palace Sq., Triq Repubblika,* ☎ *221221.* ☞ *Opening and Closing Times, above.*

Sacra Infermeria (Hospital of the Knights). This gracious building near the seawall has been converted into the Mediterranean Conference Center. For an introduction to the island, see the "Malta Experience," a multimedia presentation on the history of Malta that is given here daily on the hour. ✉ *Mediterranean St.,* ☎ *243776.* ⏲ *Weekdays 9–4.*

Dining and Lodging

$$$$ ✕ **The Carriage.** It feels like a prohibition-era secret when you ride the private elevator to the top floor, where you seem to be joining a stylish international party. Window tables have splendid views. Warm service brings you ambitious fare that sometimes disappoints. ✉ *22/5 Valletta Bldgs., South St.,* ☎ *247828. Reservations essential. Jacket and tie. AE, DC, MC, V. Closed Sun., Mon. No dinner Tues., Wed. No lunch Sat.*

$$$ ✕ **Giannini.** Atop the quiet west end of Valletta's mighty bastions, this is among the city's most reserved and elegant restaurants. Leading politicians and the fashionable set dine here on haute Maltese-Italian cuisine. There is a lounge downstairs; the restaurant is on the fifth floor.

✉ *23 Windmill St.,* ☎ *237121. Reservations essential. AE, DC, MC, V. No dinner Sun.–Thurs., no lunch weekends.*

$$ ★ ✕ **Caffe Cordina.** On the ground floor of the original treasury of the Knights is Malta's finest café. Since 1837, this ornate, vaulted confectionery has produced hot, savory breakfast pastries, *Gaquata-ghasel* (honey rings), and dozens of other mouth-watering treats—as well as the best espresso and cappuccino on the island. Bear with the sulky teenagers behind the counter—it's worth it. ✉ *244/45 Triq Republika,* ☎ *234385.*

$$ ✕ **Trattoria Palazz.** In a golden limestone cellar beneath the city's public library, which the Knights of Malta built over 270 years ago, this tiny, romantic hideaway cooks up tasty Maltese/Italian dishes. Specials and recommendations are your best bet here. ✉ *43 Old Theater St.,* ☎ *226611. Reservations essential. AE, DC, MC, V. Closed Sun.*

$ ✕ **Lantern.** Two brothers run this friendly spot. The interior of this 18th-century town house on Valletta's western heights is spare but chummy, and the traditional Maltese food is tasty. ✉ *20 Sappers St.,* ☎ *237521. V. Closed Sun.*

$ ✕ **Pizzeria Bologna.** This very casual spot serves delicious pizza and at lunch creative sandwiches on local ftjra ("ftee-ra," a wide sandwich roll)—with what the owner calls the "freshest and finest quality food possible." ✉ *60 Triq Repubblika,* ☎ *238014. No credit cards. Closed Sun.*

$$$$ **Hotel Phoenicia.** The grande dame of Malta is just outside Valletta's City Gate and across from the busy bus terminus. Nonetheless, you can enjoy attractive lounges, a stunning dining room, and very well-appointed guest rooms (standard rooms can be small). Service is inconsistent—from professional to haughty and surly. ✉ *The Mall, Floriana, VLT 16,* ☎ *225241, FAX 235254. 136 rooms. 2 restaurants, 2 bars, pool, shops. AE, DC, MC, V.*

$$ **Castille.** In a 16th-century former palazzo, this slightly worn—sagging mattresses and not-so-nice bathrooms—is by far the best bet for inexpensive accommodations in Valletta. Rooms are spacious, with good windows, and the staff is friendly. Book at least three months ahead. ✉ *Castille Sq., VLT 07,* ☎ *243677, 243678, FAX 243679. 38 rooms. Rooftop restaurant, café. AE, V.*

$$ **Osborne.** In budget-hotel-starved Valletta, the Osborne provides a foothold within the city walls. The spacious lounge downstairs and the rooftop sundeck are filled with adventuresome European travelers, but the rooms are smoked-in, dark, and worn. ✉ *50 South St., VLT 11,* ☎ *243656, FAX 232120. 60 rooms. Restaurant. AE, DC, V.*

Shopping

Valletta's main shopping street, **Triq Repubblika,** is lined with touristy shops—pick up postcards and film here, then venture onto side streets for a gander at everyday Maltese wares. The **Government Craft Center** (✉ Pjazza San Gwann) has traditional handmade goods. At the **open-air market** (Triq Sala Mercate), with some haggling you may snap up a good bargain.

Valletta Essentials

Arriving and Departing

BY BOAT

Virtú (☎ 318854, FAX 345221) runs express passenger ferries (Lm 21–Lm 36) most days of the week between Malta and Catania, Syracusa, and Pozzallo (separately) on Sicily. Summer and winter schedules vary.

BY PLANE

Air Malta runs a weekly direct flight from New York in conjunction with **Balkan Airlines** and, along with several other airlines, regular flights from London, Paris, Frankfurt, Athens, and Rome to Luqa Airport (☎ 249600), 6 km (4 mi) south of Valletta.

Between the Airport and Downtown. Local Bus 8 (11¢) passes through Luqa on its way to Valletta, with a stop at the airport every 10 or 15 minutes. Taxis (Lm 8–Lm 10) are also available.

Getting Around

BY BUS

Bus 98 (11¢) circles the perimeter of the city every hour from the terminus by the City Gate. Buses do not run on streets within the city.

BY TAXI

Metered taxis are plentiful. Be sure the meter is switched on when your trip starts, or bargain first. Tip the driver 10%.

Contacts and Resources

CONSULATES AND HIGH COMMISSIONS

British High Commission (✉ 7 St. Anne St., Floriana, ☎ 233134). **U.S. Embassy** (✉ 2nd Floor, Development House, St. Anne St., Floriana, ☎ 235960).

EMERGENCIES

Police (☎ 191). **Ambulance** (☎ 196). **Fire Brigade** (☎ 199). **Hospital: St. Luke's** (Gwardamangia, ☎ 241251).

GUIDED TOURS

Orientation. One-hour boat tours of Valletta's Grand Harbour leave regularly from Sliema jetty. Buy tickets at most travel agencies or on the boat.

Personal Guides. Licensed guides can be hired through local travel agencies.

TRAVEL AGENCIES

American Express (representative; ✉ Brockdorff, 14 Zachary St., Valletta, ☎ 232141). **Thomas Cook** (✉ Il-Pjazzetta, Tower Rd., Sliema, ☎ 344225). Local agencies have desks at most hotels.

VISITOR INFORMATION

Valletta (✉ 1 City Gate Arcade, ☎ 237747; ✉ Luqa Airport, ☎ 249600; or ✉ 280 Republic St., ☎ 224444 or 228282). **St. Julian's** (✉ Ballutta Bay, ☎ 342671 or 342672).

AROUND MALTA

The conurbanization around Valletta varies in character. The Three Cities area has its Old World charms, while the semi-urban sprawl of Sliema and St. Julian's bears an unfortunate resemblance to Floridian overdevelopment. Southern and eastern Malta has prehistoric sites, as well as the stunning cliffs and waters around the Blue Grotto. The ancient walled city of Mdina rises out of the center of the island. On the way to the ferry on the northwest end, parallel rift valleys alternate fertile terrain with barren, exposed hills, and sandy or rocky coastline. Alas, the cities in this direction, such as Buġibba, Qawra, and Mellieha, have largely been done in by interchangeable international resorts with no real Maltese character.

The Three Cities

East across the Grand Harbor from Valletta, the three cities of **Vittoriosa, Senglea, and Conspicua** are where the Knights of the Order of St. John first settled—and where crucial fighting took place in the Great Seige of the Turks in 1565. Vittoriosa, also called Birgu, is named for the victory over the Turkish navy. The 5 km (3 mi) of great walls around the cities are the Cotonera Lines, built in the 1670s.

In **Vittoriosa/Birgu** in early October, hundreds of actors stage a Grand Master's crossing of the harbor and monastery doors on Triq San Lawrenz open to the public for the **Birgu Festa.** On the narrow streets north of the main square you can loop from the Triq La Vallette to the Triq Majjistral on the right. Triq It-Tramuntana takes you past Baroque doorways, the Knights' Auberge d'Angleterre (Inn of England), and a Saracen-style house that is thought to be from the 1200s.

Below Birgu's main square, **Knisja ta' San Lawrenz** is the city's finest church, with Mattea Preti's *Martyrdom of San Lawrenz.*

The displays in the **Inquisitor's Palace,** on Birgu's Triq San Lawrenz, reveal less discussed aspects of less-tolerant times in Malta.

At the tip of **Senglea, Gardjola Garden,** once a high fort, has great views and a turret carved with a vigilant eye and ear.

Sliema and St. Julian's

Sliema's shoreline is an almost-flashy commercial strip—a hint of what St. Julian's is all about. Heavily trafficked Paceville, just beyond St. Julian's, is where Malta's club-goers rock at night. The town of Ta' Xbiex is equipped for yachts.

$$$$ ✕ **Barracuda.** Perched precariously on columns and commanding a superb view of St. Julian's Bay, this old house holds one of Malta's most delightful and efficiently run restaurants. Seafood is the drawing card here—choose from a variety caught the same day served with such sauces as cucumber and mint or tomatoes, black olives, and capers. ✉ *194/5 Main St., St. Julian's.* ☎ FAX *331817. AE, DC, MC, V.*

$$$$ ✕ **San Giuliano.** The large second-story dining room overlooking Spinola Bay in St. Julian's makes for some of the swankiest dining in Malta. The Italian chef prepares a delicious array of antipasti and knows that truly fresh fish caught the same day needs little fussing. ✉ *Spinola Bay, St. Julian's,* ☎ *332000. Reservations essential. AE, DC, MC, V. No lunch Mon.*

$$ ✕ **Ta' Kolina.** The only point of culinary interest on Sliema's waterfront, this untrendy spot serves traditional Maltese dishes—such as *timpana* (baked pasta covered with pastry), fresh cheese salad, bragioli, and octopus. ✉ *151 Tower Rd., Sliema,* ☎ *335106. AE, DC, MC, V. No lunch.*

Paola and Tarxien

★ Here the **Hal Saflieni Hypogeum,** a massive labyrinth of underground chambers, was used for burials more than 4,000 years ago. Many of the chambers are decorated with red ocher or fine carvings. ✉ *On the road to Santa Licija,* ☎ *233821.* ⏲ *By appointment.*

The three interconnecting **Tarxien Temples** have curious carvings, oracular chambers, and altars, all dating from about 2800 BC. Nearby are remains of an earlier temple from about 4000 BC. ✉ *Behind Paola's Church of Christ the King.* ☞ *Opening and Closing Times,* above.

Marsaxlokk

At the fishing and resort town Marsaxlokk on the southeast coast you can see the *luz zu,* Malta's photogenic traditional fishing boat, up close. Its vertical prow has Phoenician ancestry.

$$ ✕ **Ix-Xlukkajr.** Seafood is the draw at the seemingly unpronounceable, harborside "Ish-Shlu-Kayre." Octopus marinated in garlic sauce is a wonderful cold starter. Try the whole-fish specials and for dessert, home-

made prickly pear and kiwi ice creams. ✉ *Village Sq.,* ☎ *612109. MC, V. Closed Wed.*

Għar Dalam

The semifossilized remains of long-extinct species of dwarf elephants and hippopotamuses that roamed the island some 125,000 years ago were found in a **cave** here. The fossils are now on display in the small **museum** (☞ Opening and Closing Times, *above*).

Birżebbuġia

On the eastern side of Marsaxlokk harbor, this town has the only sandy beach in the region, on Pretty Bay.

Zurrieq

On the way to Zurrieq from Valletta you will pass limestone quarries, which make for windless fruit tree orchards after their limestone is exhausted. On the far side of town, **Wied-iz-Zurrieq** (valley) runs along the road to a lookout over the towering walls of the Blue Grotto's bay. Across the water, tiny **Filfla,** flat-topped from British Air Force target practice, is the smallest of the Maltese islands.

★ The turn-off for the **Blue Grotto** is 1 km (½ mi) beyond the lookout. A steep road takes you to the rocky inlet where noisy boats (Lm 2.50) leave for the grottoes (there are many) and the stained-glass-blue waters that splash their walls. Bring a bathing suit in case the water is calm enough for swimming. ✉ *Coast Rd.*

★ The 4,800-year-old **Haġar Qim** ("ha-jar eem") gives a clear picture of the massive scale of Malta's ancient sandstone temples. The altars are well preserved, but the decoration (some of which is a reproduction)
★ is pitted. From the temple of **Mnajdra** ("mna-ee-dra"), on the edge of a hill by the sea, views are superb. The temple is encircled by hard corraline limestone walls and has the typical, cloverlike trefoil plan. ✉ *Coast Rd.* ☞ Opening and Closing Times, *above*.

Dingli

With a car, you can drive south from Mdina to Dingli for a tour of the countryside, a look at the cliffs, and a tree fix at **Buskett Gardens.** Buskett Gardens surround **Verdala Castle,** which the Knights built as a hunting lodge during the 16th century. Now the President of Malta uses it to host distinguished visitors. It is not open to the public. ✉ *Buskett Rd.* ⏲ *Daily (gardens).*

Mdina

★ In Malta's ancient, walled capital—the longtime stronghold of Malta's nobility—traffic is limited to residents' cars, and the noise of the world outside doesn't penetrate the thick, golden walls. The quiet streets are lined with sometimes block-long, still-occupied noble palaces.

★ At the serene, Baroque **Il-Katidral Ta' l-Imdina** (Cathedral of St. Peter and St. Paul) you can view Mattia Preti's 17th-century painting, *The Shipwreck of St. Paul.* In the **Cathedral Museum** there are Dürer woodcuts and illuminated manuscripts. ✉ *Archbishop Sq.,* ☎ *454679.* ⏲ *Mon.–Sat. 9–1 and 1:30–4.*

Rabat

The town's name means suburb—of Mdina, in this case. The beautiful **Knysja San Pawl** (St. Paul's Church, ✉ Parish Sq.) stands above a grotto where St. Paul reputedly took refuge after his shipwreck on Malta.

Catacombs run under much of Rabat. Up Triq Santa Agatha from Parish Square, the **Catacombs of St. Paul** are clean of bones but full of carved-out burial troughs. Don't forget the way out when you set off to explore. **St. Agatha's Crypt and Catacombs,** farther up the street, were beautifully frescoed between 1200 and 1480, then defaced (literally) by Turks in 1551. ✉ *St. Agatha St.* ☞ *Opening and Closing Times, above.*

Mosta

The **Church of St. Mary,** or the Rotunda, has one of the largest unsupported domes in Europe, after St. Peter's in Rome and Hagia Sophia in Istanbul. A German bomb fell through the roof during World War II—without detonating. ✉ *Rotunda Sq. (Buses 53 and 57).*

GOZO AND COMINO

Gozo is a place to relax. Spend a morning in the walled, hilltop Citadella, stroll around Victoria's narrow limestone-walled streets, look inside splendid local churches, then head down for a swim at Ramla Bay or a boat ride from the Inland Sea at Dwejra ("dway-ra"). You can take great walks along the cliffs of Ta' Ċenċ ("ta chench") and San Lawrenz/Dwejra or hike past the centuries-old salt pans west of Marsalforn at Qbajjar.

Gozo has some superb restaurants, and local bakeries turn out tasty, crusty round loaves. The island's traditional craft is lace making, still practiced by a diminishing number of older women who still make time for the intricacy of this labor of love. Gozitan men love to hunt, and native and migratory birds are either caged or shot. Most of the waist-high stone structures that dot Gozo's fields are blinds, and on autumn hunting season mornings you'll hear the sporadic pop of rifles. The ferry docks at Mgarr Harbour, but this part of Gozo is unrepresentative. Go elsewhere.

Xagħra

The parish **Church of Our Lady of Victories** has two clock towers. One clock has the correct time, the other is deliberately wrong to fool the devil. In the cliffs to the west is reputedly **Calypso's Cave,** of Homer's *Odyssey* fame, viewable only from a platform a good distance away.

★ Imagine domes rising from the heavy stone walls of eastern Xagħra's 5,800-year-old **Ġgantija Temples,** and you will get a sense of their original power. Each bears the classic five-apse plan that is the signature of Maltese megalithic temples. ✉ *Xagħra plateau.* ☞ Opening and Closing Times, *above.*

$$ ★ ✕ **Oleander.** Mario Attard prepares sophisticated, authentic local food at this village square restaurant. The fresh tomato soup and pasta with anchovies, tomatoes, and black olives are spectacular. ✉ *10 Victory Sq.,* ☎ *557230. AE, MC, V. Closed Mon.*

$ ★ ✕ **Gester Restaurant.** This old-time luncheonette is run by sisters Gemma and Ester, who serve delicious, homey Gozitan food. Try peppered local sheep's milk cheese, rabbit in rich tomato sauce, lasagna, and the meadlike local "wine." For dessert have Mr. Rapa's ice cream, from down the street; it's the best in Malta. ✉ *8th September Ave.,* ☎ *556621. No credit cards. Closed Sun. Lunch only.*

$$$ 🏨 **Cornucopia.** This sprawling complex of hotel rooms, bungalows, and farmhouses lies on the western flank of town. Valley view rooms (24 and 47 are the best), bungalows, and farmhouses are spacious and pleasant. Avoid all others. ✉ *10 Gnien Imrik St., Xagħra XRA 102,* ☎ *556486, 553866,* FAX *552910. 45 rooms, 2 suites, 11 bungalows, 2 farmhouses, 2 apts. Restaurant, 3 pools. AE, DC, MC, V.*

Nadur

Gozo's second-largest town has a substantial parish church with a colored Italian marble interior and French stained-glass windows.

★ Baker Joe at **Mekren's Bakery** (✉ Triq Tal-Hanaq, 50 yards down the road to Ramla after first intersection in Nadur) makes some of Gozo's best bread—for Lm 11¢ a loaf—and occasionally whips up sweet pastry or pizza.

Outside Nadur are two small beaches that were once considered secret. Anything but that now, tiny **San Blas Bay** to the north is accessed by a *very* steep descent on foot past citrus groves. **Hondoq Bay,** to the east through the town of Qala, faces Comino. The beach isn't gorgeous, but the swims to rocky inlets are delightful.

Ramla Bay

The ochre-color sands at Ramla Bay cover Gozo's largest and most popular beach, which is ideal for swimming.

$ ✕ **Il-Werqa.** When the sunshine and the sea are no longer enough at this popular beach, take a few steps over to the fish shack with the cactus sign for its "special fish dinner," in which only today's catch is served. ✉ *Ramla Bay Beach,* ☎ *559723. No credit cards. Closed Nov.–Easter.*

Victoria

Gozo's capital is a charming old city with warrens of narrow streets, a hilltop Cittadella, and two main squares—Pjazza Independenza beneath the Cittadella and Pjazza San Franġisk. The splendid Baroque **Bażilika San Ġorġ,** down Triq San Ġużepp from Pjazza Indepenża, has the most beautiful interior on Gozo. The original city here is the walled, hilltop **Cittadella.** It has steep, winding streets and great views from its ramparts. The **katidral**'s dome fell in a 1693 earthquake; it is now simulated by a trompe l'oeil painting. A museum displays the cathedral's ceremonial silver. Up the street to the left of the church, then left onto Triq Milite Bernardo, the intriguing **Folklore Museum** occupies three medieval houses. The **Archaeological Museum** (✉ Triq il-Katidral, ☞ Opening and Closing Times, *above*) exhibits objects from various ancient periods.

Take the street to the left of the katidral to this one-stop shop for high-quality local lacework and nicely packaged food items. The **Cittadella Boutique** (✉ 4 Fosse St., ☎ 555953; closed Sun.) also serves light lunches of tomatoes, cheese, bread, and wine.

$$$ ✕ **Brookie's.** In a stone farmhouse under the western walls of the Citadella, Brookie's prepares some of the island's priciest and richest fare (cream is a favorite ingredient). A popular bar is on site, as well as a terrace and patio for drinks. Service can be erratic. ✉ *½ Triq Wied Sara,* ☎ *559524. AE, DC, MC, V. Closed Mon.*

$$–$$$ ★ **Paradise Travel and Property Services, Ltd.** This realtor has stunning farmhouses to rent. Be specific with your request: number of guests, old or new farmhouse, necessity of pool (usually unheated), telephone service, size of town, and so on. Linen and weekly maid service is provided. Paradise can also arrange car rentals. ✉ *38 St. Sabina Sq., VCT 102,* ☎ *562025,* FAX *562026. 15 self-catering farmhouses. AE, MC, V.*

Sannat

Sannat is a quiet town due south of Victoria where lace makers work along the streets and the church is Baroque. Beyond town, park your car along the dirt road and continue north and west for the spectacular Ta' Ċenċ cliffs and wildflowers in the fields around them.

Palazzo Palina (☎ 556474), to the right of the Hotel Ta' Ċenċ (☞ *below*) entrance, an early 18th-century manor house built in the time of Grand Master Ramon Perellos Y Rocaful, contains some of its original furnishings. Tours can be arranged for hotel guests, or stop by in the morning to see if a caretaker is in.

$$$$ **Hotel Ta' Ċenċ.** Near the windy southern cliffs of Gozo, the understated hotel has an exclusivity unique for Malta. In spite of poorly lit rooms, not enough staff, and the unkempt peripheries of the property, the hotel is a quiet, memorable place to relax for a few days. There is private swimming at a rocky inlet a 10-minute drive away. ✉ *Ta' Ċenċ, near Sannat, VCT 112,* ☎ *556819 or 556830,* FAX *558199. 59 rooms, 21 suites, 4 apts. Restaurant, 2 pools. AE, DC, MC, V.*

Xlendi Bay

The miniature, fjordlike Xlendi Bay (that's "shlendi") is home to fishermen and an abundance of holiday flats that have come close to spoiling this splendid place. The promenade along the water is lined with cafés, and on Sunday families traditionally parade here in their finest.

Ghajn il-Kbira (The Great Fountain; ✉ Fontana, between Victoria and Xlendi Bay) was built during the 15th century to provide fresh spring water and laundry facilities for nearby Gozitans. Today, though it is still used for its original intent, you're just as likely to see a car being washed.

Malta's history, geography, and clear blue sea provide excellent opportunities for underwater exploration. Contact **St. Andrew's Divers' Cove Ltd.** (✉ St. Simon St., Xlendi Bay, and Shore St., Mġarr Harbour, ☎ 551301, FAX 561548).

$$$ ★ **St. Patrick's Hotel.** This well-maintained midsize hotel stands steps away from the bay. Newly rebuilt, it is architecturally consistent with its surroundings in town, even to the balconied facade. Harbor view rooms are the best; avoid claustrophobic courtyard rooms. ✉ *Xlendi Bay VCT 115,* ☎ *562951 or 562952,* FAX *556598. 40 rooms, 4 penthouse rooms. Restaurant. AE, MC, V.*

Marsalforn and Qbajjar

On a bay north of Victoria, this former fishing village is a tourist factory out of character with the rest of the island. On the coast west of Marsalforn, past Qbajjar ("by-*jar*"), is a stretch of salt pans dating from the time of the Knights. June through September, troughs cut into the limestone flats are filled with seawater, left to evaporate, then scraped for the salt left behind. The coarse crystals are excellent for cooking. In season you can buy salt along the road here from the gatherers.

$$$$ ✕ **Auberge Ta' Frenċ.** In an atmospheric limestone farmhouse, this French-inspired restaurant has Gozo's most refined service and classic cuisine. Seafood dishes are best here. ✉ *Marsalforn Rd.,* ☎ *553888. Reservations essential. AE, DC, MC, V. Closed Tues. and weekdays Jan.–Feb.*

Għarb

This far-west island village is one of the prettiest on Gozo. Its central square has a particularly handsome church. If the privately owned, 28-room **Għarb Folklore Museum** (✉ 99 Pjazza il-Knisja, ☎ 561929) isn't busy, chances are you'll see the quirky owner on the street flagging down cars.

$$–$$$ ★ ✕ **Jeffrey's.** Chef/owner Jeffrey's interpretations of Gozitan classics in this romantic find are superb: a delicate brine-free fish soup, succulent braciola, and rabbit in a white wine and garlic sauce. Jeffrey harvests produce from his own farm and herbs from outside the kitchen. ✉ *10 Triq L-Għarb,* ☎ *561006. Reservations essential. AE, MC, V. Closed Sun. and Nov.–Easter. No lunch.*

San Lawrenz and Dwejra

The **cliffs of San Lawrenz and Dwejra** ("dway-ra") are spectacular—especially at sunset. From Għarb, follow signs for the hamlet of San

Lawrenz. Park where the road turns to dirt at the town's end and follow the road for a km (½ mi) or so.

★ A must on Gozo is a ride (Lm 5 per boat) from the tiny **Inland Sea** through a natural tunnel under the cliffs out to the sea. Have the boatman loop around Dwejra Point to see the **Azure Window and Fungus Rock.** You can also walk to the window and the rock.

Comino

The 1-square-mi island is populated by a handful of people year-round. Day trippers walk the dirt paths and swim in the beautiful but overcrowded **Blue Lagoon,** whose underwater grottoes scuba divers love to explore.

$$$$ **Comino Hotel.** Functionally modern, the Comino is the only hotel on the island. In spite of its private beach, abundant water sports, and a spirited new manager, the hotel needs to update rooms, public spaces, and furnishings. Day use of facilities is also available. ✉ *Gozo Channel, SPB 10,* ☏ *529821,* FAX *529826. 95 rooms, 45 bungalows. Restaurant, 2 pools. AE, DC, MC, V.*

Gozo and Comino Essentials

Getting Around

BY BOAT

Hourly ferries leave from Ċirkewwa on Malta for Mġarr Harbour on Gozo. Passenger fares are Lm 1.75; car fares are Lm 5.75. Less frequent ferries go to Comino from Ċirkewwa and from Mġarr Harbor on Gozo for Lm 2.

BY BUS

A rather unreliable bus service (☏ 562040) connects Victoria with the major towns in Gozo. A bus from the harbor to Victoria runs according to the ferry schedule.

BY TAXI OR RENTAL CAR

Mario's Taxi and Rent a Car (✉ Victoria, ☏ 557242, FAX 551827). **Mġarr Rent a Car** (✉ Mġarr Harbour, ☏ 556081 or 556098).

Contacts and Resources

EMERGENCIES

Police (☏ 191). **Ambulance** (☏ 196). **Fire Brigade** (☏ 199). **Hospital: Craig Hospital** (☏ 561600).

GUIDED TOURS

Xlendi Pleasure Cruises' 40-ft *Gozo Princess* circles Gozo and Comino, stopping at scenic spots. Lm 10.50 includes buffet meals, and you can swim from the boat. ✉ *Xlendi Bay,* ☏ *559967,* FAX *555667.*

VISITOR INFORMATION

Mġarr Harbour (✉ Mġarr Harbor, ☏ 553343); **Victoria** (✉ Palm St., ☏ 561419).

21 The Netherlands

Amsterdam; Historic Holland; The Hague, Delft, and Rotterdam

The bucolic images of windmills and wooden shoes that brought tourism here in the decades after World War II have little to do with the Netherlands of the '90s. Sure, tulips grow in abundance in the bulb district of Noord and Zuid Holland provinces, but today's Netherlands is no backwater operation: This tiny nation has an economic strength and cultural wealth that far surpass its size and population.

Sophisticated, modern Netherlands has more art treasures per square mile than any other country on earth, as well as a large number of ingenious, energetic citizens with a remarkable commitment to quality, style, and innovation. The 41,526 square km (15,972 square mi) of the Netherlands are just about half the area of the state of Maine, and its population of 15 million is slightly less than that of the state of Texas. Formerly home to the most successful seafaring merchants, the country is still one of the world's most important distribution and transport hubs, and the banks have invested this wealth around the world. The country encourages internal accomplishments as well, particularly of a cultural nature. In the country, within a 120-km (75-mi) radius, are 10 major art museums and several smaller ones that together contain the world's richest and most comprehensive collection of art masterpieces from the 15th to the 20th centuries. In the same small area are a half dozen performance halls offering music, dance, and internationally known performing arts festivals.

The marriage of economic power and cultural wealth is nothing new to the Dutch; during the 17th century, for example, money raised through their colonial outposts overseas was used to buy or commission portraits and paintings by young artists such as Rembrandt, Hals, Vermeer, and Van Ruysdael. But it was not only the arts that were encouraged: The Netherlands was home to the philosophers Descartes, Spinoza, and Comenius; the jurist Grotius; the naturalist Van Leeuwenhoek, inventor of the microscope; and others like them who flourished in the country's enlightened tolerance. The Netherlands continues to subsidize its artists and performers, supporting an educational system in which creativity in every field is respected and nourished.

The Netherlands is the delta of Europe, located where the great Rhine and Maas rivers and their tributaries empty into the North Sea. Near the coast, it is a land of flat fields and interconnecting canals; in the center it is surprisingly wooded, and in the far south are rolling hills. About half of the Netherlands is below sea level.

Amsterdam is the focal point of the country's culture, as well as of a 60-km (37½-mi) circle of cities, known as the Randstad (agglomeration of cities), that includes The Hague (the Dutch seat of government and the world center of international justice), Rotterdam (the industrial center of the Netherlands and the world's largest port), and the historic cites of Haarlem, Leiden, Delft, and Utrecht.

The northern and eastern provinces are rural and quiet; the southern provinces that hug the Belgian border are lightly industrialized and sophisticated. The great rivers that cut through the heart of the country provide both geographical and sociological borders. The area "above the great rivers," as the Dutch phrase it, is peopled by tough-minded and practical Calvinists; to the south are more ebullient Catholics. A tradition of tolerance pervades this densely populated land; aware that they cannot survive alone, the Dutch are bound by common traits of ingenuity, personal honesty, and a bold sense of humor.

THE NETHERLANDS A TO Z

Customs

For imports and duty-free limits, *see* Customs & Duties *in* Chapter 1.

Dining

The Dutch enjoy a wide variety of cuisines from traditional Dutch to Indonesian—the influence of the former Dutch colony. Breakfast includes several varieties of bread, butter, jam, ham, cheese, chocolate, boiled eggs, juice, and steaming coffee or tea. Lunch tends to be a *broodje* (sandwich) from the great selection of delicatessens. Dutch specialties for later meals include *erwtensoep* (rich, thick pea soup with pieces of tangy sausage or pigs' knuckles) and *stamppot* (mashed potatoes and greens with *worst* [sausage]); both are usually served only in winter. *Haring* (herring) is particularly popular, especially the "new herring" caught between May and September and served raw, with a garnish of onions and pickles. At Indonesian restaurants, where the chief item is *rijsttafel* (rice table), a meal made up of rice and 20 or more small meat, seafood, or vegetable dishes, many of which are hot and spicy. Eating places range from snack bars, fast-food outlets, and modest local cafés to gourmet restaurants of international repute. Of special note are the *bruin cafés* (brown cafés), characterful, traditional pubs that normally serve snack-type meals.

The indigenous Dutch liquor is potent and warming *jenever* (gin), both "old" (matured) and "young." Dutch liqueurs and beers are also popular.

MEALTIMES

Lunchtime in this grab-a-broodje culture is between 12:30 and 1. The Dutch eat dinner at around 6 or 7 PM, especially in the country and smaller cities, so many restaurants close at about 10 PM and accept final orders at 9. In larger cities dining hours vary, and some restaurants stay open until midnight.

The Netherlands (Nederland)

RATINGS

Prices are per person including three courses (appetizer, main course, and dessert), service, and sales tax but not drinks. For budget travelers, many restaurants offer a tourist menu at an officially controlled price, currently Fl. 25.

CATEGORY	AMSTERDAM/ MAIN CITIES	OTHER AREAS
$$$$	over Fl. 100	over Fl. 85
$$$	Fl. 70–Fl. 100	Fl. 55–Fl. 85
$$	Fl. 40–Fl. 70	Fl. 35–Fl. 55
$	under Fl. 40	under Fl. 35

WHAT TO WEAR

Jacket and tie are advised for restaurants in the $$$$ and $$$ categories. The tolerant Dutch accept casual outfits in most eateries.

Language

Dutch is a difficult language for foreigners, but the Dutch are fine linguists, so almost everyone speaks at least some English, especially in larger cities and tourist centers.

Lodging

The Netherlands has a wide range of accommodations, from the luxurious Dutch-owned international Golden Tulip hotel chain to traditional, small-town hotels and family-run guest houses. For young or adventurous travelers, the provinces abound with modest hostels, campgrounds, and rural bungalows. Bed-and-breakfast establishments are in short supply and must be booked well ahead at local tourist offices.

HOTELS

Dutch hotels are generally clean, if not spotless, no matter how modest their facilities, and service is normally courteous and efficient. There are many moderate and inexpensive hotels, most of which are relatively small. In the provinces, the range of accommodations is more limited, but there are friendly, inexpensive family-run hotels that are usually centrally located. Some have good—if modest—dining facilities. Hotels generally quote room prices for double occupancy, and rates often include breakfast, service charges, and VAT.

To book hotels in advance, you can use the free **Netherlands Reservation Center** (✉ Box 404, 2260 AK Leidschendam, ☎ 070/3202500, FAX 070/3202611; ⏲ Weekdays 8–8, Sat. 8–2). For a small fee, tourist offices can usually make reservations at short notice. Bookings must be made in person, however.

B&B RESERVATION AGENCIES

VVV (☞ Visitor Information, *below*) provides lists of B&B and "pension" accommodation. **Bed & Breakfast Holland** (✉ Theophile de Bockstraat 3,1058 TV, Amsterdam, ☎ 020/6157527) also provides a selection of B&B addresses.

RATINGS

Prices are for two persons sharing a double room.

CATEGORY	AMSTERDAM/ MAIN CITIES	OTHER AREAS
$$$$	over Fl. 500	over Fl. 350
$$$	Fl. 300–Fl. 500	Fl. 200–Fl. 350
$$	Fl. 200–Fl. 300	Fl. 150–Fl. 200
$	under Fl. 200	under Fl. 150

Mail

POSTAL RATES

The Dutch postal system is as efficient as the telephone network. Airmail letters to the United States cost Fl. 1.60 for the first 20 grams; postcards cost Fl. 1.60; aerograms cost Fl. 1.30. Airmail letters to the United Kingdom cost Fl. 1 for the first 20 grams; postcards cost Fl. 1; aerograms cost Fl. 1.30.

RECEIVING MAIL

If you're uncertain where you'll be staying, have mail sent to "poste restante, Hoofd Postkantoor" in major cities along your route (making sure that your name and initials are clear and correctly spelled), or to American Express offices, where a small fee is charged on collection to non–American Express customers.

Money Matters

COST

The Netherlands is a prosperous country with a high standard of living, so overall costs are similar to those in other northern European countries. Prices for hotels and services in major cities are 10% to 20% higher than those in rural areas. Amsterdam and The Hague are the most expensive. Hotel and restaurant service charges and the 6% value-added tax (VAT) are usually included in the prices quoted.

The cost of eating varies widely, from a snack in a bar or a modest restaurant offering a *dagschotel* (day special) or "tourist menu" at around Fl. 25 to the considerable expense of gourmet cuisine. A traditional Dutch breakfast is often included in the overnight hotel price.

CURRENCY

The unit of currency in the Netherlands is the guilder, written as NLG (for Netherlands guilder), Fl., or simply F. (from the centuries-old term for the coinage, florin). Each guilder is divided into 100 cents. Bills are in denominations of 10, 25, 50, 100, 250, and 1,000 guilders. Denominations over Fl. 100 are rarely seen, and many shops refuse to change them. Coins are 1, 2.5, and 5 guilders and 5, 10, and 25 cents. Don't confuse the 1- and 2.5-guilder coins and the 5-guilder and 5-cent coins. Bills have a code of raised dots that can be identified by touch.

At press time (spring 1998), the exchange rate for the guilder was Fl. 2 to the U.S. dollar, Fl. 1.39 to the Canadian dollar, Fl. 3.32 to the pound sterling, Fl. 1.29 to the Australian dollar, and Fl. 1.10 to the New Zealand dollar.

MUSEUM ADMISSIONS

The **Museumjaarkaart,** which can be purchased from most museums and all VVV tourist offices, provides a year's free or discounted admission to about 450 museums. It costs Fl. 55, Fl. 45 if you're over 55, and Fl. 25 if you're under 18. A photo and passport are required for purchase. Not all museums participate.

SAMPLE PRICES

Half bottle of wine, Fl. 25; glass of beer, Fl. 3.50; cup of coffee, Fl. 3; ham and cheese sandwich, Fl. 5; 2-km (1-mi) taxi ride, Fl. 12.

TIPPING

Hotels and restaurants almost always include 10%–15% service and 6% VAT in their charges. Give a doorman Fl. 3 for calling a cab. Bellhops in first-class hotels should be tipped Fl. 2 for each bag they carry. Hat-check attendants expect at least Fl. 1, and washroom attendants get 50¢. Taxis in almost every town have a tip included in the meter charge, but you round the fare to the nearest guilder nevertheless.

National Holidays

January 1; April 4–5 (Easter); April 30 (Queen's Day; shops are open unless it falls on Sunday); May 5 (Liberation); May 13 (Ascension); June 23–24 (Pentecost); December 25–26.

Opening and Closing Times

Banks are open weekdays 9–4. GWK Border Exchange Offices at major railway stations and Schiphol Airport are open Monday–Saturday 8–8 and Sunday 10–4. GWK offices in major cities or at border checkpoints are open 24 hours. **Museums** in Amsterdam are open all week. Elsewhere they close on Monday, but there are exceptions, so check with local tourist offices. In rural areas, some museums close or operate shorter hours during winter. Usual hours are 10–5. **Shops** are open weekdays and Saturday 8:30 or 9–5:30 or 6, but outside the cities some close for lunch. Department stores and most shops, especially in shopping plazas (in The Hague and Amsterdam) do not open on Monday until 1 PM. Late-night shopping usually can be done until 9 PM on Thursday or Friday. Sunday opening, from noon to 5, varies from city to city. In larger cities, major department stores and chain and mall stores will probably be open.

Shopping

SALES-TAX REFUNDS

Purchases of goods in one store on one day amounting to Fl. 300 or more qualify for a value-added tax, called BTW (VAT) refund of 17.5%, which can be claimed at the airport or main border crossing when you leave the Netherlands, or by mail. This arrangement is only valid if you export the goods within 30 days. Ask the salesperson for a VAT refund form when you buy anything that may qualify.

Telephoning

COUNTRY CODE

The country code for the Netherlands is 31. When dialing a number in the Netherlands from outside the country, drop the initial 0 from the local area code.

INTERNATIONAL CALLS

Direct-dial international calls can be made from any phone booth. To reach an **AT&T** long-distance operator, dial 0800/022–9111; for **MCI,** dial 0800/022–9122; for **Sprint,** dial 0800/022–9119.

LOCAL CALLS

All towns and cities have area codes that are used only when you are calling from outside the area. All public phone booths require phone cards. Phone cards may be purchased from post offices, railway stations, and newsagents for Fl. 10 or Fl. 25. Pay phones in bars and restaurants take 25¢ or Fl. 1 coins, but rates are often hiked. Dial 0800/0410 for an English-speaking operator.

Transportation

BY BICYCLE

The Netherlands is a cyclist-friendly country with specially designated cycle paths, signs, and picnic areas. Bikes can be rented at train stations in most cities and towns, and Dutch trains are cycle-friendly, too, with extra-spacious entryways designed to accommodate bicycles. You will need an extra ticket for the bike, however. There are some restrictions on carrying bicycles on trains, so check first. Advice on rentals and routes is available from offices of the Netherlands Board of Tourism in North America or in the Netherlands (☞ Visitor Information, *below*), or from local tourist offices.

BY BUS

The Netherlands has an excellent bus network between and within towns. Bus excursions can be booked on the spot and at local tourist offices. In major cities, the best buy is a strippenkaart ticket (Fl. 11), which can be used for all bus, tram, and metro services. Each card has 15 strips, which are canceled either by the driver as you enter the bus or by the stamping machine at each door of the tram. More than one person can travel on a strippenkaart—it just gets used up more quickly. You can buy it at train stations, post offices, some tourist offices, in Amsterdam at the national bus system (GVB) ticket office in the plaza in front of the central railway station, and at many newsagents. A dagkaart, a travel-anywhere ticket (Fl. 12, one day; Fl. 16, two days; Fl. 19.75, three days), covers all urban bus/streetcar routes. National public transport information is available from ☎ 0900/9292, at a cost of 75¢ per minute.

BY CAR

Breakdowns. Experienced, uniformed mechanics of the **Wegenwacht** patrol the highways in yellow cars 24 hours a day. Operated by the Royal Dutch Touring Club (ANWB), they will help if you have car trouble. On major roads, ANWB also maintains phone boxes from which you can call for assistance. To use these services, you may be asked to take temporary membership in ANWB.

Gasoline. Gas, *benzine* in Dutch, costs around Fl. 2.29 per liter for regular, Fl. 2.23 for super unleaded, and Fl. 1.52 for diesel.

Parking. Parking in the larger towns is difficult and expensive, with illegally parked cars quickly towed away or subject to a wheel clamp. Fines for recovery can top Fl. 300. Consider parking on the outskirts and using the efficient public transportation.

Road Conditions. The Netherlands has one of the best road systems in Europe, and even the longest trips between cities take only a few hours. Multilane expressways (toll-free) link major cities, but the smaller roads and country lanes provide more picturesque routes. In towns, many of the streets are narrow, and you'll have to contend with complex one-way systems and cycle lanes. Be particularly vigilant for cyclists; they're ubiquitous, and they assume you'll give them the right of way. Information about weather and road conditions can be obtained by calling ☎ 0900/9622 (50¢ per minute).

Rules of the Road. The speed limit on expressways is 120 kph (75 mph); on city streets and in residential areas it is 50 kph (30 mph) or less, according to the signs. Driving is on the right.

BY PLANE

KLM Royal Dutch Airlines, under the banner of CityHopper, operates several domestic services connecting major cities. In this small country, however, you'd probably travel just as fast by car or train.

BY TRAIN

Fast, frequent, comfortable trains operate throughout the country. All trains have first- and second-class cars, and many intercity trains have buffet or dining-car services. Sometimes one train contains two separate sections that divide during the trip, so be sure you are in the correct car for your destination.

At railway stations, look for blue columns marked REISWIJZER ("Route Finder"). For Fl. 1.25, paid with a telephone card, you can get a printout in English with door-to-door travel information that includes stops and connections on trains, buses, and trams.

Fares. To get the best value out of rail travel, purchase a pass. The Benelux Tourrail can be bought abroad, but the other passes are available only in the Netherlands. A Holland Rail Pass (known in the Netherlands as a Euro Domino Holland) ticket allows unlimited travel throughout the Netherlands for 3, 5, or 10 days within any 30-day period. A Transport Link ticket, which offers free travel on buses and trams as well, may be bought in conjunction with the Holland Rail Pass. Your rail pass is also valid on Interliner, a fast bus network that operates 16 intercity lines. Other options are a Dagkaart (one-day, travel-anywhere ticket) and, from June through August, a Zomertoer (summer tour) ticket for 3 days' travel in a 10-day period offers excellent value. The Netherlands Board of Tourism's (NBT) and Netherlands Railways offices abroad have information on train services. Your passport may be needed when you purchase these tickets. Rail Idee tickets include entry to tourist attractions with train, boat, and bus transportation, usually with a reduction of 20%. Ask about these fares at railway information bureaus or local tourist offices.

Visitor Information

Netherlands Board of Tourism (✉ Box 404, 2260 AK Leidschendam, Holland, ☎ 070/3175454, FAX 070/3202611). **VVV** (acronym for national tourist offices; telephone inquiries, ☎ 0900/34034066, 75¢ per minute) has branches even in smaller towns.

Weather

The prime tourist season in the Netherlands runs from April through October and peaks during school vacation periods (Easter, July, and August), when hotels may impose a 20% surcharge. Dutch bulb fields bloom from late March to the end of May; hotels tend to fill up then, too. June is the ideal time to catch the warm weather and miss the crowds, but every region of the Netherlands has its season. Delft is luminous after a winter storm, and fall in the Utrecht countryside can be as dramatic as it is in New England.

CLIMATE

Summers are generally warm, but beware of sudden showers and blustery coastal winds. Winters are chilly and wet but are not without clear days. If the canals freeze over, then they immediately fill with keen skaters, the learners pushing along chairs. After a cloudburst, notice the watery quality of light that inspired Vermeer and other great Dutch painters. The following are the average daily maximum and minimum temperatures for Amsterdam.

Jan.	40F	4C	**May**	61F	16C	**Sept.**	65F	18C
	34	1		50	10		56	13
Feb.	41F	5C	**June**	65F	18C	**Oct.**	56	13C
	34	1		56	13		49	9
Mar.	47F	8C	**July**	70F	21C	**Nov.**	47F	8C
	38	3		59	15		41	5
Apr.	52F	11C	**Aug.**	68F	20C	**Dec.**	41F	5C
	43	6		59	15		36	2

AMSTERDAM

Amsterdam is a gem of a city for the visitor. Small and densely packed with fine buildings, many dating from the 17th century or earlier, it is easily explored on foot or by bike.

Exploring Amsterdam

The old heart of the city consists of canals, with narrow streets radiating out like the spokes of a wheel. The hub of this wheel and the most convenient point to begin sight-seeing is Centraal Station. Across the street, in the same building as the Old Dutch Coffee House, is a tourist information office. The Rokin, once an open canal, is the main route from Centraal Station via the Dam to the Muntplein. Amsterdam's key points of interest can be covered within two or three days, including visits to one or two of the important museums and galleries. The city center is broken up into districts that are easily covered on foot.

Around the Dam

Numbers in the margin correspond to points of interest on the Amsterdam map.

★ 14 **Anne Frankhuis** (Anne Frank House). Immortalized by the poignant diary kept by the young Jewish girl from 1942 to 1944, when she and her family hid here from the German occupying forces, it also holds a small exhibition on the Holocaust. ✉ *Prinsengracht 263,* ☎ *020/5567100.* ⏲ *June–Aug., Mon.–Sat. 9–7, Sun. 10–7; Sept.–May, Mon.–Sat. 9–5, Sun. 10–5.*

10 **Beurs van Berlage** (Berlage's Stock Exchange). This impressive building, completed in 1903, dominates the Damrak between Centraal Station and the Dam. It was designed by Hendrik Petrus Berlage (1856–1934), whose principles were to guide modernism; the building's function was fundamental to the design. The sculpture and rich decoration of the plain brick interior are among modernism's embryonic masterpieces. It now houses two concert halls, a large exhibition space, and its own museum, which also offers the chance to climb the 39-m- (138-ft-) high tower for its superb views. ✉ *Damrak 277,* ☎ *020/6265257.* ⏲ *Museum: Tues.–Sun. 10–4.*

1 **Centraal Station** (Central Station). The flamboyant redbrick and stone portal was designed by P. J. H. Cuijpers (1827–1921) and built in 1884–89. It provides an excellent viewpoint for both the Beurs van Berlage and the Scheepvaartshuis, two of the city's best examples of early 20th-century architecture. Compare it with Cuijpers's other significant contribution to Amsterdam's architectural heritage—the Rijksmuseum. ✉ *Stationsplein.*

11 **Dam** (Dam Square). This is the broadest square in the old section of the town. Fishermen used to come here to sell their catch. Today it is a busy crossroads, circled with shops and bisected by traffic; it is also a popular spot for outdoor performers. At one side of the square stands a simple monument to Dutch victims of World War II. Eleven urns contain soil from the 11 provinces of the Netherlands, while a 12th contains soil from the former Dutch East Indies, now Indonesia. ✉ *Jct. Rokin, Damrak, Moses en Aaronstraat, and Paleisstraat.*

6 **De Waag** (The Weighhouse). Dating from 1488, this turreted, redbrick monument dominates the Nieuwmarkt (New Market) in the oldest part of Amsterdam. Once the headquarters for ancient professional guilds, the building now is home to the Society for Old and New Media, which hosts occasional exhibitions in the magnificently restored **Theatrum Anatomicum,** up the winding stairs. ✉ *Nieuwmarkt,* ☎ *020/5579844.*

13 **Het Koninklijk Paleis te Amsterdam** (Royal Palace in Amsterdam). The vast, well-proportioned classical structure dominating the Dam was completed in 1655. It is built on 13,659 pilings sunk into the marshy soil. The great pediment sculptures are an allegorical representation of Amsterdam surrounded by Neptune and mythological sea crea-

tures. Filled with opulent 18th- and early 19th-century furnishings, it is the official royal residence but is used only on high state occasions. ☒ *Dam,* ☎ *020/6248698.* ⊙ *Tues.–Thurs. 1–4; daily 12:30–5 in summer. Sometimes closed for state events.*

9 **Museum Amstelkring.** The facade carries the inscription "*Ons Lieve Heer Op Solder*" ("Our Lord in the Attic"). In 1578 Amsterdam embraced Protestantism and outlawed the church of Rome. The municipal authorities were so tolerant that secret Catholic chapels were allowed to exist; at one time there were 62 in Amsterdam alone. One such chapel was established in the attics of these three neighboring canalside houses, built around 1661. The lower floors were used as ordinary dwellings, while services were held in the attics regularly until 1888, the year the St. Nicolaaskerk was consecrated for Catholic worship. Of interest are the Baroque altar with its revolving tabernacle, the swinging pulpit that can be stowed out of sight, and the upstairs gallery with its displays of religious artifacts. ☒ *Oudezijds Voorburgwal 40,* ☎ *020/6246604.* ⊙ *Mon.–Sat. 10–5, Sun. 1–5.*

3 **NewMetropolis** (Science and Technology Museum). This stunning, modern science and technology center was designed by Renzo Piano, architect of the Pompidou Center in Paris. The building's colossal, copper-clad volume rises from the harbor waters like the hull of a ship. Hands-on exhibits for young and old range from elementary physics to the latest technological gadgets. The rooftop terrace offers a superb panoramic view across the city. ☒ *Oosterdok 2, Prins Hendrikkade,* ☎ *020/5313233.* *Fl. 23.50.* ⊙ *Mon.–Thurs. 10–6, Fri.–Sun. 10–9.*

12 **Nieuwe Kerk** (New Church). This huge Gothic structure stands next to the royal palace, in a corner of the Dam. It was gradually expanded until 1540, when it reached its present size. Gutted by fire in 1645, it was reconstructed in an imposing Renaissance style, as interpreted by strict Calvinists. The superb oak pulpit, the 14th-century nave, the stained-glass windows, and the great organ (1645) are all shown to great effect on national holidays, when the church is bedecked with flowers. As befits the Netherlands' national church, the Nieuwe Kerk is the site of all coronations, most recently that of Queen Beatrix in 1980. In democratic Dutch spirit, the church is also used as a meeting place and has a lively café, temporary exhibitions, and concerts. ☒ *Dam,* ☎ *020/6268168.* *Free, except for special exhibitions.* ⊙ *Daily 11–5; exhibitions daily 10–6.*

8 **Oude Kerk** (Old Church). The city's oldest house of worship dates from the early 14th century but it was badly damaged by iconoclasts after the Reformation. The church still retains its original bell tower and a few remarkable stained-glass windows. The tower overlooks a typical view of Old Amsterdam. Rembrandt's wife, Saskia, is buried here. ☒ *Oudekerksplein 23,* ☎ *020/6258284.* ⊙ *Mon.–Sat. 11–5, Sun. 1–5.*

5 **Rijksmuseum Nederlands Scheepvaart** (State Museum of Netherlands Shipping). This former naval warehouse maintains a collection of restored vessels, including a replica of a three-masted VOC (Verenigde Oostindische Compagnie—Dutch East India Company) trading ship from 1749. The museum explains the whole history of Dutch shipping, from dugout canoes right through to modern container ships, with maps, paintings, and models. The Prins Hendrikkade and the Eastern Harbor were the hub of shipping activity during the Netherlands' Golden Age. ☒ *Kattenburgerplein 1,* ☎ *020/5232222.* ⊙ *Mon.–Sat. 10–5, Sun. 1–5.*

7 **Rosse Buurt** (red-light district). This area is defined by two of the city's oldest canals. In the windows at canal level, women in sheer lingerie slouch, stare, or do their nails. Although the area can be shocking, with

Amsterdam Historisch Museum, **16**
Anne Frankhuis, **14**
Beurs van Berlage, **10**
Begijnhof, **17**
Bloemenmarkt, **21**
Centraal Station, **1**
Concertgebouw, **32**
Dam, **11**
De Waag, **6**
Engelse Kerk, **17**
Gouden Bocht, **19**
Het Koninklijk Paleis te Amsterdam, **13**
Jodenbreestraat, **23**
Joods Historisch Museum, **27**
Jordaan, **35**
Leidseplein, **34**
Muiderstraat, **25**
Munttoren, **20**
Museum Amstelkring, **9**
Museum het Rembrandthuis, **24**
Museum Willet-Holthuysen, **22**
Muziektheater/ Stadhuis, **28**
NewMetropolis, **3**
Nieuwe Kerk, **12**
Oude Kerk, **8**
Portugese Israelitische Synagoge, **26**
Rijksmuseum, **29**
Rijksmuseum Nederlands Scheepvaart, **5**
Rijksmuseum Vincent van Gogh, **30**
Rosse Buurt, **7**
Scheepvaartshuis, **4**
Schreierstoren, **2**
Spui, **18**
Stedelijk Museum, **31**
Vondelpark, **33**
Westerkerk, **15**

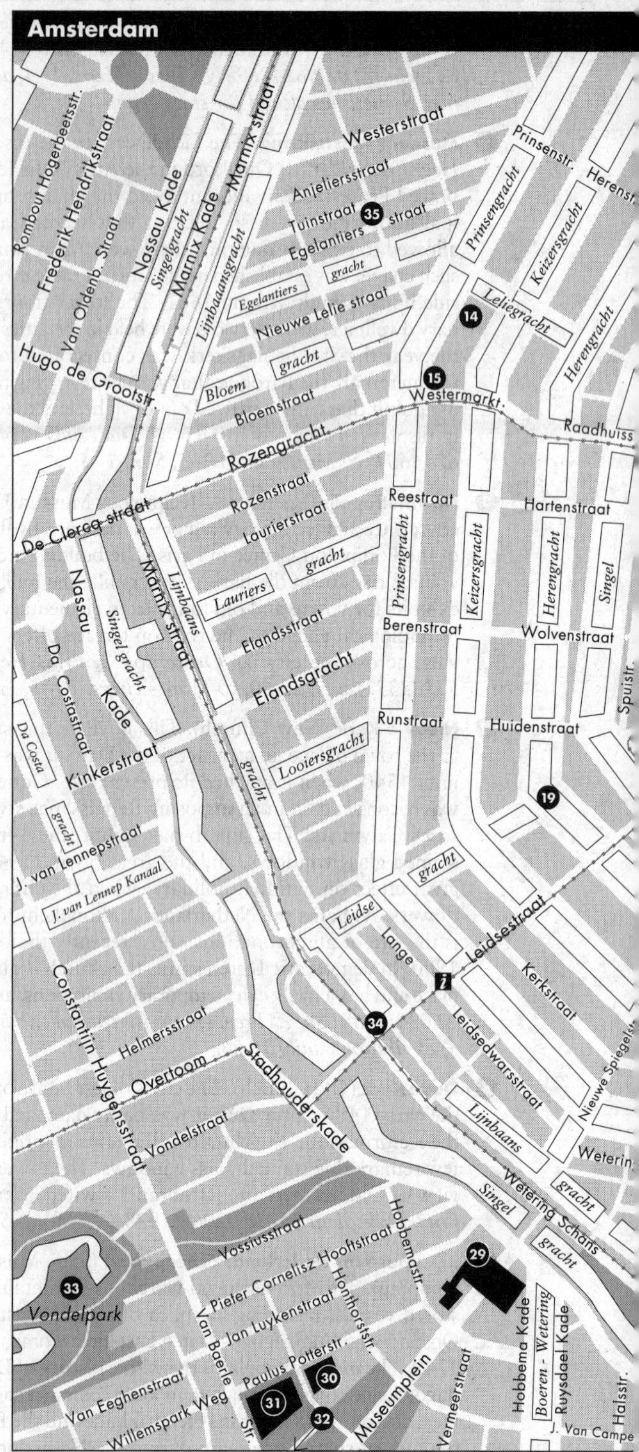

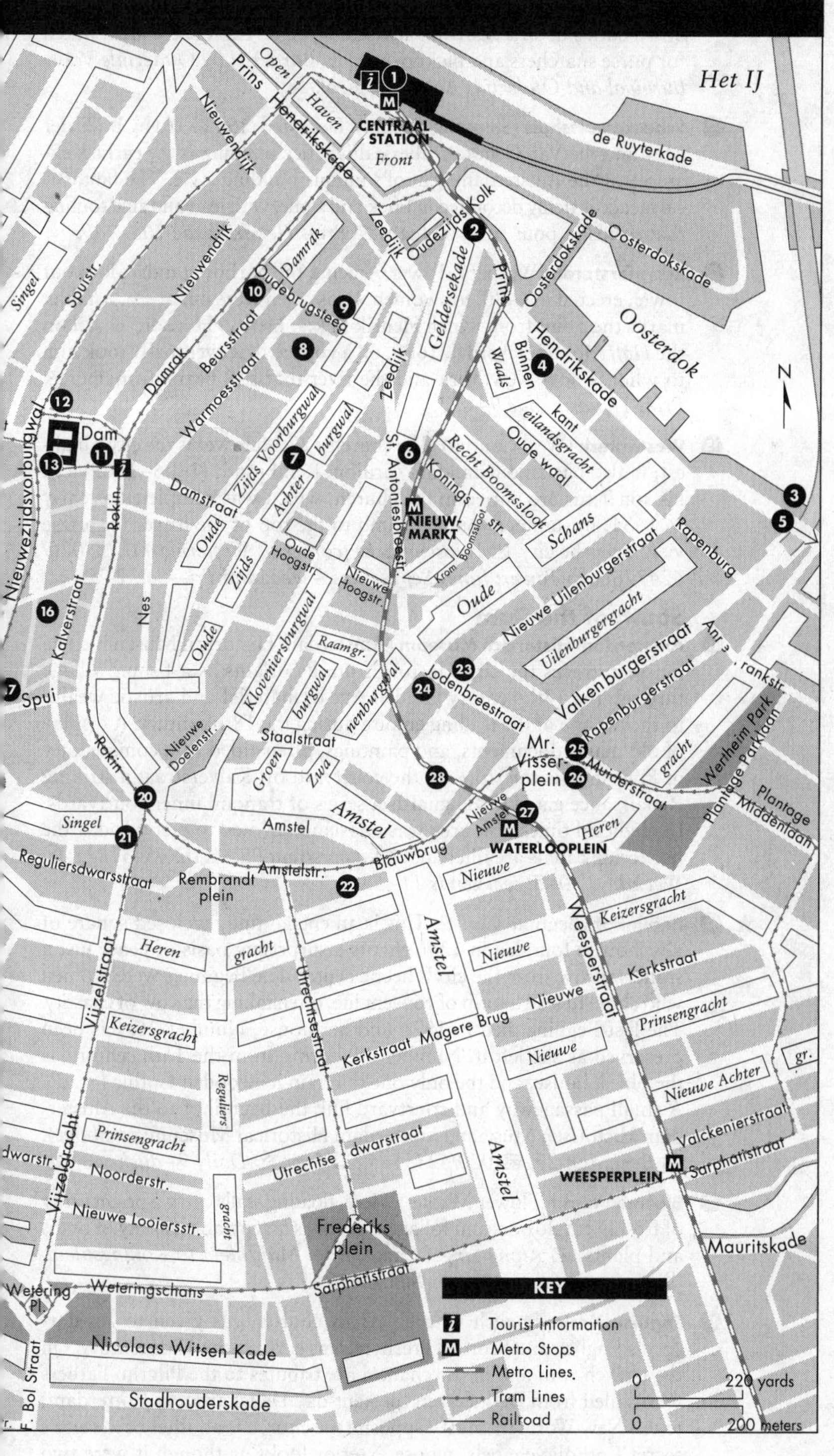

Het IJ
Open
Haven
Front
CENTRAAL STATION
Prins Hendrikskade
de Ruyterkade
Nieuwendijk
Oudezijds Kolk
Zeedijk
Geldersekade
Oosterdokskade
Oosterdok
Prins Hendrikskade
Binnen
Waals
Singel
Spuistr.
Damrak
Oudebrugsteeg
Beursstraat
Warmoesstraat
Nieuwezijdsvoorburgwal
Dam
Rokin
Damstraat
Zijds Voorburgwal
Achter burgwal
Oude
Zijds
St. Antoniesbreestr.
Recht Boomssloot
Konings str.
Kromboomssloot
NIEUWMARKT
Kant eilandsgracht
Oude waal
Schans
Rapenburg
Oude Hoogstr.
Nieuwe Hoogstr.
Nieuwe Uilenburgerstraat
Uilenburgergracht
Kalverstraat
Nes
Kloveniersburgwal
Raamgr.
Jodenbreestraat
Valkenburgerstraat
Rapenburgerstraat
Spui
Nieuwe Doelenstr.
Staalstraat
Groen
Zwa
nenburgwal
Mr. Visser-plein
Muiderstraat
gracht
Wertheim Park
Plantage Parklaan
Plantage Middenlaan
Amstel
Singel
Nieuwe Amstel
Heren
WATERLOOPLEIN
Reguliersdwarsstraat
Rembrandt plein
Amstelstr.
Blauwbrug
Nieuwe
Keizersgracht
Weesperstraat
Heren gracht
Vijzelstraat
Utrechtsestraat
Kerkstraat
Magere Brug
Prinsengracht
Keizersgracht
Reguliers
Nieuwe Achter
gr.
Prinsengracht
Valckenierstraat
dwarstr.
Noorderstr.
Utrechtse dwarsstraat
WEESPERPLEIN
Sarphatistraat
Nieuwe Looiersstr.
Vijzelgracht
Frederiks plein
Mauritskade
Wetering Pl.
Weteringschans
Sarphatistraat
Nicolaas Witsen Kade
Stadhouderskade
F. Bol Straat
KEY
Tourist Information
Metro Stops
Metro Lines
Tram Lines
Railroad
0 220 yards
0 200 meters
N

its sex shops and porn shows, it is generally safe, but midnight walks down dark side streets are not advised. If you do explore the area, watch for purse snatchers and pickpockets. ✉ *Bordered by Oudezijds Voorburgwal and Oudezijds Achterburgwal.*

❹ **Scheepvaartshuis** (Shipping Offices). Designed (1911–16) by J. M. der Mey and the Van Gendt brothers, this office building is the earliest example of the Amsterdam School's unique building style. The fantastical facade is richly decorated in brick and stone, with lead and zinc roofing that seems to pour from on high. ✉ *Prins Hendrikkade 108–119.*

❷ **Schreierstoren** (Weepers' Tower). Facing the harbor stands a lookout tower, erected in 1480, for women whose men were out at sea. A tablet marks the point from which Henrik (a.k.a. Henry) Hudson set sail on the *Half Moon* on April 4, 1609, on a voyage that eventually took him to what is now New York and the river that still bears his name. ✉ *Prins Hendrikkade 94–95.*

⓯ **Westerkerk** (West Church). The church's 279-ft tower is the city's highest; it also has an outstanding carillon. Rembrandt (1606–1669) and his son Titus are buried in the church, which was completed as early as 1631. In summer you can climb to the top of the tower for a fine view over the city. ✉ *Prinsengracht (corner of Westermarkt),* ☎ *020/6247766.* ⏲ *Tower: June–Sept., Tues.–Wed. and Fri.–Sat. 2–5.*

South of the Dam

⓰ **Amsterdam Historisch Museum** (Amsterdam Historical Museum). The museum traces the city's history from its origins as a fishing village through the 17th-century Golden Age of material and artistic wealth to the decline of the trading empire during the 18th century. A display of old maps, documents, and paintings, often aided by a commentary in English tells the story. In the courtyard off Kalverstraat a striking Renaissance gate (1581) guards a series of tranquil inner courtyards. In medieval times, this area was an island devoted to piety. Today the bordering canals are filled in. ✉ *Kalverstraat 92,* ☎ *020/5231822.* ⏲ *Weekdays 10–5, weekends 11–5.*

★ ⓱ **Begijnhof** (Beguine Court). This is an enchanting, enclosed square of almshouses founded in 1346 that is a surprising oasis of peace just a stone's throw from the city's hectic center. The Beguines were women who chose to lead a form of convent life, often taking the vow of chastity. The last Beguine died in 1974 and her house, Number 26, has been preserved as she left it. Number 34, dating from the 15th century, is the oldest house, and the only one to retain its wooden Gothic facade. A small passageway and courtyard link the Begijnhof to the Amsterdam Historisch Museum (Amsterdam Historical Museum; ☞ *above*). ✉ *Begijnhof 29,* ☎ *020/6233565.* 🎫 *Free.* ⏲ *Daily 9–dusk.*

㉑ **Bloemenmarkt** (Flower Market). Here, floating stalls carry a bright array of freshly cut flowers and foliage, as well as an enviable variety of bulbs and plants. ✉ *Along Singel Canal, from Muntplein to Koningsplein.* ⏲ *Mon.–Sat. (occasionally Sun.) 9:30–5.*

⓱ **Engelse Kerk** (English Church). This church was given to Amsterdam's English and Scottish Presbyterians early in the 17th century. On the church wall and in the chancel are tributes to the Pilgrim Fathers who sailed from Delftshaven (present-day Delfshaven, in Rotterdam) to the New World in 1620. Opposite the church is another of the city's secret Catholic chapels, whose exterior looks as though it were two adjoining houses, built in 1671. ✉ *Begijnhof (☞ above).*

★ ⓳ **Gouden Bocht** (Golden Bend). The Herengracht (Gentlemen's Canal) is the city's most prestigious canal. The stretch of the canal from Leidsestraat to Huidenstraat is named for the sumptuous patrician houses with double staircases and grand entrances that line it. Seventeenth-century merchants moved here from the Amstel River to escape the byproducts of their wealth: noisy warehouses, unpleasant brewery smells, and the risk of fire in the sugar refineries. These houses display the full range of Amsterdam architectural detailing, from gables in a variety of shapes to elaborate Louis XIV–style cornices and frescoed ceilings. They are best seen from the east side of the canal. For more gables turn down Wolvenstraat into the Keizersgracht (the Emperor's Canal). ✉ *Herengracht—Leidsestraat to Huidenstraat.*

20 **Munttoren** (Mint Tower). Built in 1620 at this busy crossroads, the graceful tower that was later added to this former royal mint has a clock and bells that still seem to mirror the Golden Age. There are frequent carillon recitals. ✉ *Muntplein.*

22 **Museum Willet-Holthuysen.** Built in 1690, the elegant residence was bequeathed to the city of Amsterdam, on condition that it be retained as a museum. It provides a peek into the lives of the city's well-heeled merchants. The rooms are elegantly furnished in an opulent Louis XVI style. ✉ *Herengracht 605,* ☎ *020/5231870.* ⏲ *Weekdays 10–5, weekends 11–5.*

18 **Spui** (sluice). In the heart of the university area, the lively square was a center for revolutionary student rallies in 1968. Now you'll find bookstores and bars, including cozy brown cafés. ✉ *Jct. Nieuwe zijds Voorburgwal, Spuistraat, and Singel Canal.*

Jewish Amsterdam

The original settlers in the Jodenbuurt (old Jewish Amsterdam) were wealthy Sephardic Jews from Spain and Portugal, later followed by poorer Ashkenazic refugees from Germany and Poland. At the turn of the century this was a thriving community of Jewish diamond polishers, dyers, and merchants.

23 **Jodenbreestraat.** During World War II this street marked the southwestern border of the *Joodse wijk* (Jewish neighborhood), by then an imposed ghetto. The character of the area was largely destroyed by highway construction in 1965 and more recently by construction of both the Metro and the Muziektheater/Stadhuis complex (☞ *below*).

27 **Joods Historisch Museum** (Jewish Historical Museum). A complex of three ancient synagogues, places of worship that once served a community of 100,000 Jews, shrunk to fewer than 10,000 after 1945, is now a museum. Founded by American and Dutch Jews, it displays religious treasures in a clear cultural and historical context. As the synagogues lost most of their treasures in the war, their architecture and history are more compelling than the exhibits. ✉ *Jonas Daniël Meijerplein 2–4,* ☎ *020/6269945.* ⏲ *Daily 11–5.*

25 **Muiderstraat.** This pedestrianized area east of Waterlooplein retains much of the neighborhood's historic atmosphere. Notice the gateways decorated with pelicans, symbolizing great love; according to legend, the pelican will feed her starving young with her own blood. ✉ *Muiderstraat/Waterlooplein.*

★ 24 **Museum het Rembrandthuis** (Rembrandt's House). From 1639 to 1658, Rembrandt (1606–1669) lived at Jodenbreestraat 4. For more than 20 years the ground floor was used by the artist as living quarters; the sunny upper floor was his studio. It contains a superb collection of his etchings as well as work by his contemporaries. The modern new wing next door houses a multimedia auditorium, two new exhibition spaces, and a shop. From St. Antonies Sluis bridge, just by the house, there is a canal view that has barely changed since Rembrandt's time. ✉ *Jodenbreestraat 4–6,* ☎ *020/6249486.* ⏲ *Mon.–Sat. 10–5, Sun. 1–5.*

㉘ **Muziektheater/Stadhuis** (Music Theater/Town Hall complex). Amsterdammers come to the town hall section of the building by day to obtain driver's licenses, pick up welfare payments, and get married. They return by night to the rounded, marble-clad facade overlooking the Amstel river to see opera and ballet performed by the Netherlands' finest companies. You can wander into the town hall for a look at some interesting sculptures and other displays. A guided tour of the Muziektheater takes you around the dressing rooms, dance studios, backstage, and even to the wig department. ✉ *Amstel 3,* ☎ *020/5518054.* ⏲ *Guided tours Wed. and Sat. at 3.*

★ ㉖ **Portugese Israelitische Synagoge** (Portuguese Israelite Synagogue). As one of Amsterdam's four neighboring synagogues, this was part of the largest Jewish religious complex in Europe. The beautiful, austere interior of the 17th-century building is still intact, even if the building itself is marooned on a traffic island. ✉ *Mr. Visserplein 3,* ☎ *020/6245351.* ⏲ *Apr.–Oct., Sun.–Fri. 10–12:30 and 1–4; Nov.–Mar., Mon.–Thurs. 10–12:30 and 1–4, Fri. 10–12:30 and 1–3, Sun. 10–noon.*

The Museum Quarter

㉜ **Concertgebouw** (Concert Hall). The sounds of the country's foremost orchestra, the world-famous Concertgebouworkest, resonate in this imposing, classical building. The smaller of the two auditoriums is used for chamber music and solo recitals. The main hall hosts world-class concerts. ✉ *Concertgebouwplein 2–6,* ☎ *020/6718345.*

㉞ **Leidseplein.** This lively square is the pulsing heart of the city's nightlife. During the summer you can enjoy the entertainment of street performers on the many café terraces.

★ ㉙ **Rijksmuseum** (State Museum). Allow at least an hour or two to explore the main collection of Dutch paintings at the most important of Dutch museums, and a whole morning or afternoon if you want to visit other sections. It was founded in 1808, but the current, rather lavish building dates from 1885, designed by the architect of Centraal Station, P. J. H. Cuijpers. As well as Italian, Flemish, and Spanish paintings, there are also vast collections of furniture, textiles, ceramics, sculpture, and prints. The museum's fame, however, rests on its unrivaled collection of Dutch 16th- and 17th-century masters. Of Rembrandt's masterpieces, *The Nightwatch,* concealed during World War II in caves in Maastricht, was misnamed because of its dull layers of varnish; in reality it depicts the Civil Guard in daylight. Also worth searching out are Frans Hals's family portraits, Jan Steen's drunken scenes, Van Ruysdael's romantic but menacing landscapes, and Vermeer's glimpses of everyday life bathed in his limpid light. The recently refurbished Zuid Vleugel (South Wing) houses an impressive treasure trove of Eastern art. ✉ *Stadhouderskade 42,* ☎ *020/6732121.* ⏲ *Daily 10–5.*

★ ㉚ **Rijksmuseum Vincent van Gogh** (Vincent van Gogh State Museum). This museum contains the world's largest collection of the artist's works—200 paintings and nearly 500 drawings—as well as works by some 50 of his contemporaries. There are usually very well presented temporary exhibitions. The modern, airy building was designed by Gerrit Rietvelt (1888–1964) and completed in 1972. The low entrance foyer opens into a high, skylit exhibition space. From September 1998 through the end of 1999 the museum is being extended and renovated. Van Gogh's most important works will be exhibited in the South Wing of the Rijksmuseum (☞ *above*). ✉ *Paulus Potterstraat 7,* ☎ *020/5705200.* ⏲ *Daily 10–5.*

31 **Stedelijk Museum** (Municipal Museum). The museum has a stimulating collection of modern art and ever-changing displays of the works of contemporary artists. Before viewing the paintings of Cézanne, Chagall, Kandinsky, and Mondriaan, check the list of temporary exhibitions in Room 1. Museum policy is to trace the development of the artist rather than merely to show a few masterpieces. Don't forget the museum's restaurant overlooking a garden filled with modern sculptures. ✉ *Paulus Potterstraat 13,* ☎ *020/5732911.* ⏲ *Daily 11–5.*

33 **Vondelpark.** Amsterdam's central park is an elongated rectangle of paths, lakes, and pleasant, shady greenery. A monument honors the 17th-century epic poet Joost van den Vondel, after whom the park is named. There is also an open-air sculpture by Picasso. In-line skaters duck and weave around Sunday strollers, and there are special children's areas with paddling pools and sandboxes. From June through August, free outdoor concerts and plays are performed in the park from Wednesday through Sunday. ✉ *Stadhouderskade.*

The Jordaan

35 **Jordaan.** In this old part of Amsterdam the canals and side streets are named for trees, flowers, and plants. When it was the French quarter of the city, the area was known as *le jardin* (the garden), a name that over the years has become Jordaan. The best time to explore the district is on a Sunday morning or in the evening. The Jordaan has attracted many artists and is something of a bohemian quarter, where run-down buildings are being converted into restaurants, antiques shops, boutiques, and galleries. ✉ *Bordered by Prinsengracht, Lijnbaansgracht, Brouwersgracht, and Raadhuisstraat.*

Dining and Lodging

Amsterdammers are less creatures of habit than are the Dutch in general. Even so, health-conscious citizens prefer set menus and early dinners. The blue-and-white TOURIST MENU sign in a restaurant guarantees an economical (Fl. 25) yet imaginative set menu created by the head chef. For traditionalists the NEDERLANDS DIS soup tureen sign is a promise of regional recipes and seasonal ingredients. "You can eat in any language" is the city's proud boast, so when Dutch restaurants are closed, Indonesian, Chinese, and Turkish restaurants are often open. For details and price-category definitions, *see* Dining *in* The Netherlands A to Z, *above.*

Accommodations are tight from Easter to summer, so early booking is advised. As few hotels have parking lots, cars are best abandoned in a multistory parking garage for the duration of your stay. For details and price-category definitions, *see* Lodging *in* The Netherlands A to Z, *above.*

$$$$ ★ ✕ **La Rive.** This world-class restaurant is fit for royalty. The French cuisine, with an awe-inspiring "truffle menu" of dishes prepared with exotic (and expensive) ingredients, can be tailored to meet your every whim. Epicureans should inquire about the "chef's table": With a group of six you can sit at a table alongside the open kitchen and watch chefs prepare and describe each of your courses. ✉ *Amstel Inter-Continental Hotel (☞ below), Professor Tulpplein 1,* ☎ *020/6226060. Jacket and tie. AE, DC, MC, V.*

$$$$ ★ ✕ **'t Swarte Schaep.** The Black Sheep is named after a proverbial 17th-century sheep that roamed the area. With its creaking boards and array of copper pots, the interior is reminiscent of a ship's cabin. The Dutch chef uses seasonal ingredients to create classical, gastronomic dishes with regional flourishes. Choices include scallops wrapped in

bacon for starters and fillet of beef with hazelnuts as a filling main course. ✉ *Korte Leidsedwarsstraat 24,* ☎ *020/6223021. Reservations essential. Jacket and tie. AE, DC, MC, V.*

$$$–$$$$ ★ ✕ **Excelsior.** The restaurant at the Hôtel de l'Europe (☞ *below*) offers a varied menu of French cuisine based on local ingredients prepared by chef Jean Jacques Menanteau. There is a splendid selection of no less than 15 set menus. Service is discreet and impeccable, and the view over the Amstel River, to the Muntplein on one side and the Muziektheater on the other, is the best in Amsterdam. ✉ *Hôtel de l'Europe, Nieuwe Doelenstraat 2–4,* ☎ *020/6234836. Reservations essential. Jacket and tie. AE, DC, MC, V. No lunch Sat.*

$$$ ★ ✕ **De Silveren Spiegel.** In an alarmingly crooked 17th-century house, you can have an outstanding meal while you enjoy the personal attention of the owner at one of just a small cluster of tables. Local ingredients such as Texel lamb and wild rabbit are cooked with subtlety and flair. ✉ *Kattengat 4–6,* ☎ *020/6246589. Jacket and tie. AE, MC, V.*

$$$ ✕ **Le Tout Court.** This small, meticulously appointed restaurant serves seasonal specialties (spring lamb, summer fruits, game in autumn and winter) personally prepared by owner-chef John Fagel, who mixes generous Dutch helpings with rich sauces. Lighter main courses include poached turbot. The restaurant is popular with Amsterdam's media set. ✉ *Runstraat 13,* ☎ *020/6258637. AE, DC, MC, V. Closed Sun.–Mon.*

$$–$$$ ✕ **Dynasty.** Surrounded by luxurious oriental furniture and murals, you can savor subtly spiced Pan-Asian dishes from Thailand, Malaysia, and China. Main-course delicacies include mixed seafood in banana leaves and succulent duck and lobster on a bed of watercress. In one of the city's most active nightlife areas, it can get very busy, but service is always impeccable. ✉ *Reguliersdwarsstraat 30,* ☎ *020/6268400. Jacket required. AE, DC, MC, V. Closed Tues. No lunch.*

$$–$$$ ✕ **Eerste Klas.** Amsterdam's best-kept secret is in the most obvious of places: the former first-class waiting lounge of the central train station. Classic dark-wood paneling and soft interior lighting create the perfect hideaway from the city's hustle and bustle. A continental brasserie-like menu includes tasty salads, steaks, and fish dishes. ✉ *Stationsplein 15, Spoor 2b,* ☎ *020/6250131. Jacket and tie. AE, DC, MC, V.*

$$–$$$ ★ ✕ **Lonny's.** Lonny Gerungan's family have been cooks on Bali for generations—even preparing banquets for visiting Dutch royals. His plush restaurant in Amsterdam, draped in silky fabrics, serves the finest authentic Indonesian cuisine. Staff are dressed in exuberant traditional Balinese costumes. Even the simplest rijsttafel is a feast of more than 15 delicately spiced dishes. ✉ *Rozengracht 46–48,* ☎ *020/6238950. Reservations essential. AE, DC, MC, V.*

$$–$$$ ✕ **Lucius.** Outstanding fish and seafood are simply served in an informal brasserie setting. Choices range from grilled lobster to more adventurous creations such as sea bass with buckwheat noodles and mushrooms. This may not be the place for the queasy, though—as you tuck into your fish, its live cousins eye you from a tank along the wall. ✉ *Spuistraat 247,* ☎ *020/6241831. AE, DC, MC, V. Closed Sun. No lunch.*

$$–$$$ ✕ **Oesterbar.** The Oyster Bar specializes in seafood, grilled, baked, or fried. The upstairs dining room is more formal than the downstairs bistro, but prices don't vary. The sole is prepared in four different ways, or you can try the local specialties such as halibut and eel; oysters are a stimulating, if pricey, appetizer. ✉ *Leidseplein 10,* ☎ *020/6232988. AE, DC, MC, V.*

$$–$$$ ★ ✕ **Pier 10.** Perched on the end of a pier behind Centraal Station, this intimate restaurant was built in the '30s as a shipping office. Water laps gently just beneath the windows, and the harbor lights twinkle in the distance. The chef's special salads are lavish affairs, and the vegetable side orders are carefully steamed to perfection. Other culinary adventures might include a handsome platter of dove, duck, and partridge with cranberry sauce. ✉ *De Ruyterkade Steiger 10,* ☎ *020/6248276. Reservations essential. AE, MC, V. No lunch.*

$$ ✕ **De Knijp.** Traditional Dutch food is served here in a traditional Dutch environment. The mezzanine level is especially cozy. Alongside tamer dishes, there are seasonal game specialties including wild boar ham with red cabbage and fillet of hare. After-midnight dinner draws concert goers from the neighboring Concertgebouw. ✉ *Van Baerlestraat 134,* ☎ *020/6720077. AE, DC, MC, V.*

$$ ✕ **De Waag.** The lofty, beamed interior below the Theatrum Anatomicum (☞ De Waag *in* Exploring Amsterdam, *above*) has been converted into a grand café and restaurant. The reading table harbors computer terminals for Internet enthusiasts. Dinnertime brings a seasonal selection of generous, French-influenced continental cuisine to be savored by candlelight. ✉ *Nieuwmarkt 4,* ☎ *020/5579844. AE, MC, V.*

$$ ✕ **Kantjil en de Tijger.** This lively Indonesian restaurant is a favorite with the locals and close to the bars on the Spui. The menu is based on three different rijsttafel, with a profusion of meat and vegetable dishes varying in flavor from coconut-milk sweetness to peppery hot. ✉ *Spuistraat 291/293,* ☎ *020/6200994. AE, DC, MC, V. No lunch.*

$$ ✕ **Rose's Cantina.** A perennial favorite of the sparkling set, it offers spicy Tex-Mex food, lethal cocktails, and a high noise level. Pop in for a full meal or a late afternoon drink. ✉ *Reguliersdwarsstraat 38,* ☎ *020/6259797. Weekend reservations essential. AE, DC, MC, V.*

$$ ★ ✕ **Toscanini.** This cavernous, noisy Italian restaurant has superb cuisine. Try antipasti followed by fresh pasta or the simple fish and meat dishes, all expertly prepared with the day's best fresh produce. Top it off with a sumptuous dessert. ✉ *Lindengracht 75,* ☎ *020/6232813. Reservations essential. No credit cards. No lunch.*

$ ✕ **Het Gasthuys.** In this bustling restaurant you'll be served handsome portions of traditional Dutch home cooking, choice cuts of meat with excellent fries and piles of mixed salad. Sit at the bar or take a table high up in the rafters at the back. In summer there is an enchanting terrace on the canal side.✉ *Grimburgwal 7,* ☎ *020/6248230. No credit cards.*

$ ✕ **Pancake Bakery.** Here's a chance to try a traditionally Dutch way of keeping eating costs down. The name of the game is pancakes—laden with savory cheese and bacon or fruit and liqueur. The Pancake Bakery is not far from the Anne Frankhuis (☞ Exploring Amsterdam, *above*). ✉ *Prinsengracht 191,* ☎ *020/6251333. Reservations not accepted. AE, MC, DC, V.*

$$$$ ★ 🏨 **Amstel Inter-Continental.** Amsterdam's grande dame opened in 1867 and was spectacularly renovated in late 1992. The interior creates a Dutch atmosphere with a European touch. The spacious rooms have Oriental rugs, brocade upholstery, Delft lamps, and a color scheme that borrows from the warm tones of Makkum pottery. The Amstel is frequented by many of the nation's top businesspeople and sometimes hosts members of the royal family. ✉ *Professor Tulpplein 1, 1018 GX,* ☎ *020/6226060,* FAX *020/6225808. 79 rooms. 2 restaurants, pool. AE, DC, MC, V.*

$$$$ 🏨 **Golden Tulip Barbizon Palace.** The newest Golden Tulip hotel in Amsterdam combines past and present with fantasy and flair. The modern entrance blends in with the 17 neighboring monumental houses that the hotel occupies; inside, a towering atrium stretches across the length of the hotel. The Restaurant Vermeer serves haute cuisine. ✉ *Prins Hendrikkade 59–72, 1012 AD,* ☎ *020/5564564,* FAX *020/6243353. 274 rooms, 6 suites, 11 apartments. 2 restaurants. AE, DC, MC, V.*

$$$$ **Grand Amsterdam.** In 1991 Amsterdam's former city hall was converted into a luxury hotel. Parts of this elegant building date from the 16th century, but most of it belongs to the early 20th, when the country's best artists and architects were commissioned to create a building the city could be proud of. Reception areas and the rooms are palatially luxurious and have hosted Michael Jackson as well as visiting presidents. The kitchen of the brasserie-style restaurant, Café Roux, is supervised by the incomparable Albert Roux. ✉ *Oudezijds Voorburgwal 197, 1001 EX,* ☎ *020/5553111,* FAX *020/5553222. 182 rooms. Restaurant, pool. AE, DC, MC, V.*

$$$$ ★ **Hôtel de l'Europe.** Behind the stately facade of this building dating from the end of the 19th century is a full complement of modern facilities, as befits a hotel often ranked among the world's best. The rooms are larger than usual for Amsterdam, and each is decorated according to its shape and location. Bright rooms overlooking the Amstel are done in pastel colors; others have warm, rich colors and antiques. Apart from its world-renowned Excelsior restaurant (☞ Dining, *above*), the hotel houses a sophisticated leisure complex. ✉ *Nieuwe Doelenstraat 2–8, 1021 CP,* ☎ *020/6234836,* FAX *020/6242962. 80 rooms, 20 suites. 2 restaurants, lap pool. AE, DC, MC, V.*

$$$ ★ **Ambassade.** With its beautiful canal-side location, its Louis XV–style decoration, and its Oriental rugs, the Ambassade seems more like a stately home than a hotel. Service is attentive and room prices include breakfast. For other meals, the neighborhood has a good choice of restaurants. ✉ *Herengracht 341, 1016 AZ,* ☎ *020/6262333,* FAX *020/6245321. 51 rooms, 6 suites, 1 apartment. AE, DC, MC, V.*

$$$ **Grand Hotel Krasnapolsky.** The fine Old World hotel is enhanced by the Winter Garden restaurant ($$), which dates from 1818. In 1995 the hotel expanded into the building next door, increasing its size by half and replacing the bland decor with stylish period furnishings. The cosmopolitan atmosphere carries through all the rooms, with decor ranging from Victorian to Art Deco. ✉ *Dam 9, 1012 JS,* ☎ *020/5548080,* FAX *020/6261570. 429 rooms, 14 apartments. 4 restaurants. AE, DC, MC, V.*

$$$ ★ **Pulitzer.** The Pulitzer is one of Europe's most ambitious hotel restorations, using the shells of a block of 24 17th-century merchants' houses. Inside, the refined atmosphere is sustained by the modern art gallery, the lovingly restored brickwork, oak beams, and split-level rooms: No two are alike. Redecoration during 1996 replaced much of the modern furniture with pieces in a more appropriate period style. ✉ *Prinsengracht 315–331, 1016 GZ,* ☎ *020/5235235,* FAX *020/6276753. 218 rooms, 7 suites, 5 apartments. Restaurant, pool. AE, DC, MC, V.*

$$ **Atlas Hotel.** Known for its friendly atmosphere, this small hotel is in Amsterdam's most prestigious neighborhood, just a block from the Vondelpark (☞ Exploring Amsterdam, *above*). The moderate-size rooms are decorated in a comfortable, modern style. The main museums are within easy walking distance. ✉ *Van Eeghenstraat 64, 1071 GK,* ☎ *020/6766336,* FAX *020/6717633. 23 rooms. Restaurant. AE, DC, MC, V.*

$$ **Canal House Hotel.** The American owners opt for antiques rather than televisions as furnishings in this canal-side hotel to create a real sense of sleeping in the 17th century. Spacious rooms overlook the canal or the illuminated garden. A hearty Dutch breakfast is included in the price. ✉ *Keizergracht 148, 1015 CX,* ☎ *020/6225182,* FAX *020/6241317. 26 rooms with bath or shower. AE, DC, MC, V.*

$–$$ ★ **Agora.** The cheerful bustle of the nearby Singel flower market is reflected in this small hotel in an 18th-century house. Rooms are light and spacious, some decorated with vintage furniture; the best overlook the canal or the university. The Agora has a considerate staff, and a relaxed neighborhood ensures the hotel's popularity. Book well in advance. ✉ *Singel 462, 1017 AW,* ☎ *020/6272200,* FAX *020/6272202. 15 rooms, 13 with bath or shower. AE, DC, MC, V.*

$–$$ 🏨 **Hotel Seven Bridges.** Named for the view from its front steps, this small canal-house hotel has rooms decorated with individual flair. Oriental rugs warm wooden floors, and there are comfy antique armchairs and marble washstands. The Rembrandtsplein is nearby. For a stunning view, request a canal-side room. One of the pleasures here is breakfast in bed. ✉ *Reguliersgracht 31, 1017 RK,* ☎ *020/6231329. 6 rooms. AE, MC, V.*

$ 🏨 **Amstel Botel.** The floating hotel moored near Centraal Station is an appropriate place to stay in watery Amsterdam. The rooms are small and basic, but the large windows offer fine views across the water to the city. Make sure you don't get a room on the land side of the vessel, or you'll end up staring at a postal sorting office. ✉ *Oosterdokskade 224, 1011 AE,* ☎ *020/6264247,* FAX *020/6391952. 176 rooms with shower. AE, DC, MC, V.*

$ 🏨 **Hotel de Filosoof.** On a quiet street near Vondelpark, the hotel attracts artists, thinkers, and people looking for something a little unusual. Each room is decorated in a different philosophical or cultural motif—there's an Aristotle room and a Goethe room adorned with texts from *Faust.* ✉ *Anna van den Vondelstraat 6, 1054 GZ,* ☎ *020/6833013,* FAX *020/6853750. 25 rooms. AE, MC, V.*

$ 🏨 **Hotel Washington.** On a peaceful street, the hotel is just a few blocks from the Museumplein and the Concertgebouw (☞ The Museum Quarter *in* Exploring Amsterdam, *above*). Many of the world's top musicians find it the ideal place to reside when in Amsterdam. Period furniture and attentive service lend this small establishment a homely feel. All, except the cheaper upper-floor rooms, have bath or shower and toilet. ✉ *Frans van Mierisstraat 10, 1071 RS,* ☎ *020/6796754,* FAX *020/6734435. 21 rooms, 1 apartment. AE, DC, MC, V.*

Nightlife and the Arts

The Arts

The arts flourish in cosmopolitan Amsterdam. The best sources of information about performances are the *Time Out Amsterdam* listings on the Internet (http://www.timeout.nl). *De Uit Krant* is available in Dutch and covers practically every event. The biweekly *What's On in Amsterdam* is published by the tourist office, where you can also secure tickets for the more popular events. Tickets must be booked in person from Monday through Saturday, 10–4. You can also book at the **Amsterdam Uit Buro** (✉ Stadsschouwburg, Leidseplein 26, ☎ 020/6211211).

CLASSICAL MUSIC

The **Concertgebouw** (✉ Concertgebouwplein 2–6, ☎ 020/6718345) is the home of one of Europe's finest orchestras. A smaller auditorium in the same building is used for chamber music, recitals, and even jam sessions. While ticket prices for international orchestras are fairly high, most concerts are good value, and the Wednesday lunchtime concerts are free.

FILM

The largest concentration of movie theaters is around Leidseplein and near Muntplein. Most foreign films are subtitled rather than dubbed, which makes Amsterdam a great place to catch up on movies you missed at home. The largest theater (seven screens) in the city is the **City 1–7** (✉ Kleine Garmanplantsoen 13–25, ☎ 020/6234579). The Art Deco–

era **Tuschinski** (✉ Reguliersbreestraat 26, ☎ 020/6262633) is the most beautiful cinema house.

OPERA AND BALLET

The Dutch national ballet and opera companies are housed in the **Muziektheater** (✉ Waterlooplein, ☎ 020/6255455). Guest companies from other countries perform here during the three-week Holland Festival in June. The country's smaller regional dance and opera companies usually include performances at the **Stadsschouwburg** (Municipal Theater; ✉ Leidseplein 26, ☎ 020/624 2311) in their schedules.

THEATER

Young American comedians living in Amsterdam have created **Boom Chicago** (✉ Leidsepleintheater, Leidseplein 12, ☎ 020/5307300), improvised comedy with a local touch. You can munch pizzas and salad during performances. For experimental theater, dance, and colorful cabaret in Dutch, catch the shows at **Felix Meritis House** (✉ Keizersgracht 324, ☎ 020/6231311). Along the **Nes** you'll find a phenomenal selection of performance spaces for theater and dance. The main theater ticket booking office is at the **De Brakke Grond** (✉ Nes 45, ☎ 020/6229014), which is also the Flemish Cultural Center.

Nightlife

Amsterdam has a wide variety of dance clubs, bars, and exotic shows. The more respectable—and expensive—after-dark activities are in and around Leidseplein and Rembrandtsplein; fleshier productions are on Oudezijds Achterburgwal and Thorbeckeplein. Most bars and clubs are open every night from 5 PM to 2 AM or 5 AM. On weeknights very few clubs charge admission, though the more lively ones sometimes ask for a "club membership" fee of Fl. 20 or more.

CAFÉS AND BARS

Amsterdam, and particularly the Jordaan (☞ Exploring Amsterdam, *above*), is renowned for its brown cafés, so named because of the rich wooden furnishings and—some say—the centuries-old pipe-tobacco stains on the ceilings. There are also a variety of grand cafés, with spacious interiors, snappy table service, and well-stocked reading tables. Two other variants of Amsterdam's buzzing bar are the *proeflokalen* (tasting houses) and *brouwerijen* (breweries). "When in Rome, do as the Romans do," could be applied to the Dutch tolerance of the dreaded weed, to be enjoyed in one of the many "coffee shops" with the green leaves of the marijuana plant showing in the window.

At the **Rooie Nelis** (✉ Laurierstraat 101, ☎ 020/6244167), you can spend a rainy afternoon chatting with friendly strangers over homemade meatballs and a beer or apple tart and coffee. **De Gijs** (✉ Lindegracht 249, ☎ 020/6380740) is a characterful example of the brown café. More fashionable cafés include **Caffe Esprit** (✉ Spui 10, ☎ 020/6221967), serving delicious burgers and fine lunches. It is often used as a venue for radio and television interviews. **De Jaren** (✉ Nieuwe Doelenstraat 20, ☎ 020/6255771), a spacious café with a canal-side terrace, attracts smart young businesspeople, arts and media workers, and trendy types. The beamed interior of **De Admiraal Proeflokaal en Spijhuis** (✉ Herengracht 319, ☎ 020/6254334) is an intimate setting to enjoy the head-warming selection of award-winning *genevers* (gins). If Continental lagers no longer tickle your fancy, then the home-brewed selection of beers at **Maximiliaan Amsterdams Brouwhuis** (✉ Kloveniersburgwal 6, ☎ 020/6266280) are well worth sampling. **Tweede Kamer** (✉ Heisteeg 6, just off the Spui, ☎ no phone), named for parliament's lower house, offers draughts, chess, and backgammon in a convivial, civilized atmosphere permeated with the smoke of hemp.

CASINO

Holland Casino (✉ Max Euweplein 62, ☎ 020/6201006), just off Leidseplein, has blackjack, roulette, and slot machines in elegant, canal-side surrounds. There are also glamorous, but pricey, cabaret dinner arrangements. You'll need your passport to get in; the minimum age is 18.

DANCE CLUBS

Dance clubs tend to fill up after midnight. The cavernous **Escape** (✉ Rembrandtsplein 11–15, ☎ 020/6221111) has shrugged off its mainstream image and taken on a much hipper mantle. The **It** (✉ Amstelstraat 24, ☎ 020/6250111) is gay on Saturday. It's primarily straight on Thursday, Friday, and Sunday—but could never be accused of being straitlaced. **RoXY** (✉ Singel 465, ☎ 020/6200354) is the current hot spot, though you need to be a member or impressively dressed to get in. **Seymour Likely Too** (✉ Nieuwezijd Voorburgwal 161, ☎ 020/4205663) was opened by a group of artists in the wake of their success with the Seymour Likely Lounge, a popular bar across the road. This club is guaranteed to have a lively, trendy crowd hopping to the latest music.

GAY AND LESBIAN BARS

Amsterdam has a vibrant gay and lesbian community, concentrated principally on Warmoesstraat, Reguliersdwarsstraat, Amstelstraat, and Kerkstraat near Leidseplein. The **Gay & Lesbian Switchboard** (☎ 020/6236565, ⏲ 10–10) has friendly operators who provide information on the city's nightlife and other advice for gay or lesbian visitors. The **COC** (✉ Rozenstraat 14, ☎ 020/6263087), the Dutch lesbian and gay political organization, operates a coffee shop and weekend discos.

JAZZ CLUBS

Café Meander (✉ Voetboogsteeg 5, ☎ 020/6258430) caters to a younger crowd with traditional jazz to the latest in hip-hop and experimental crossover streams. The **Bimhuis** (✉ Oude Schans 73–77, ☎ 020/6233373, ⏲ Thurs.–Sat. from 9 PM), in a converted warehouse, has long offered the best jazz and improvised music in town. Ticket holders can sit in the adjoining BIM café and enjoy a magical view across the Oude Schans canal.

ROCK CLUBS

Melkweg (✉ Lijnbaansgracht 234, ☎ 020/6248492), a big draw in the flower-power era, is making a comeback as a major rock and pop venue with its large, new auditorium; it also has a gallery, theater, cinema, and café. The **Paradiso** (✉ Weteringschans 6–8, ☎ 020/6264521), converted from a church, has become a vibrant venue for rock, New Age, and even contemporary classical music.

Shopping

Amsterdam is a cornucopia of interesting markets, quirky specialty shops, antiques, art, and diamonds.

Department Stores

De Bijenkorf (✉ Dam 1), the city's number-one department store, is excellent for contemporary fashions and furnishings. **Maison de Bonneterie en Pander** (✉ Rokin 140–142; ✉ Beethovenstraat 32) is the Queen Mother of department stores—gracious, genteel, and understated. The well-stocked departments of **Vroom and Dreesmann** (✉ Kalverstraat 201) carry all manner of goods.

Gift Ideas

DIAMONDS

Since the 17th century, "Amsterdam cut" has been synonymous with perfection in the quality of diamonds. You can see this craftsmanship at any of the diamond-cutting houses. The cutters explain how the diamond's value depends on the four *c*s—carat, cut, clarity, and color—before encouraging you to buy. There is a cluster of diamond houses on the Rokin.

PORCELAIN

The Dutch have been producing Delft, Makkum, and other fine porcelain for centuries. **Focke and Meltzer** (✉ P. C. Hooftstraat 65–67, ☎ 020/6642311) stores have been selling it since 1823. Available pieces range from affordable, newly painted tiles to expensive Delft blue-and-white pitchers.

Markets

Antiekmarkt de Looier (✉ Elandsgracht 109; ⏲ Sun.–Wed. 11–5, Thurs. 11–9) is a bustling covered market that's great for antiques, especially silver and toys. In summer, you'll find etchings, drawings, and watercolors at the Sunday **art markets** on Thorbeckeplein and the Spui. On Saturday the Noordermarkt and Nieuwmarkt host an **organic farmers' market,** with essential oils and other New Age fare alongside oats, pulses, and vegetables. Amsterdam's lively **Waterlooplein flea market** (⏲ Mon.–Sat. 9:30–4) next to the Muziektheater is the ideal spot to rummage for secondhand clothes, inexpensive antiques, and other curiosities. The **Bloemenmarkt** (flower market) on the Singel has bulbs and cut flowers. A small but choice **stamp market** (⏲ Wed. and Sat. 1–4) is held on the Nieuwezijds Voorburgwal.

Shopping Districts

The Jordaan and the quaint streets crisscrossing the main ring of old canals are a treasure trove of trendy small boutiques and unusual crafts shops. Leidsestraat, Kalverstraat, Utrechtsestraat, and Nieuwendijk are Amsterdam's chief shopping districts, which have largely been turned into **pedestrian-only areas.** The imposing new **Kalvertoren** shopping mall (✉ Kalverstraat, near Munt) offers covered shopping and a rooftop restaurant with magnificent views of the city. **Magna Plaza** shopping center (✉ Nieuwezijds Voorburgwal 182), built inside the glorious old post office behind the Royal Palace, is *the* place for A-to-Z shopping in a huge variety of stores. The **Spiegelkwartier** (✉ Nieuwe Spiegelstraat and Spiegelgracht), just a stone's throw from the Rijksmuseum, is Amsterdam's antiques center, with galleries for wealthy collectors, as well as old curiosity shops. **P. C. Hooftstraat,** and also Van Baerlestraat and Beethovenstraat, are the homes of haute couture and other fine goods. **Rokin** is hectic with traffic and houses a cluster of boutiques and renowned antiques shops selling 18th- and 19th-century furniture, antique jewelry, Art Deco lamps, and statuettes. **Schiphol Airport** tax-free shopping center is often lauded as the world's best.

Amsterdam Essentials

Arriving and Departing

BY PLANE

Most international flights arrive at Amsterdam's Schiphol Airport. Immigration and customs formalities on arrival are relaxed, with no forms to be completed.

Between the Airport and Downtown. The best transportation between the airport and the city center is the direct rail link to the central train station, where you can get a taxi or tram to your hotel. The train runs every 10 to 15 minutes throughout the day and takes about a half hour. Make sure you buy a ticket before boarding: ruthless conductors will happily impose a fine. Second-class single fare is Fl. 6.25. Taxis from the airport to central hotels cost about Fl. 60.

BY TRAIN

The city has excellent rail connections with the rest of Europe, including the high-speed **Thalys** service to Brussels and Paris (☏ 0900/9228, 50¢ per minute) with a journey time of just over four hours. Other fast links include Cologne and Hannover. It is now possible to travel by train to London, by either the Eurostar channel tunnel link or the High Speed Sea service, in less than seven hours. Centraal Station (✉ Stationsplein; international service information, ☏ 0900/9296, 50¢ per minute, long wait) is in the center of town.

Getting Around

BY BICYCLE

Rental bikes are widely available for around Fl. 10 per day with a Fl. 50–Fl. 200 deposit. Several rental companies are close to the central train station, or ask at tourist offices for details. Lock your bike whenever you park it, preferably to something immovable. Also, check with the rental company to see what your liability is under their insurance terms.

BY BOAT

The **Canalbus** (🎫 Fl. 19.50 for a hop-on, hop-off day card) travels between the central train station and the Rijksmuseum. The **Museum Boat** (🎫 Fl. 22; ☞ Guided Tours, *below*), makes seven stops near major museums.

BY CAR

The city's concentric ring of canals, one-way systems, and lack of parking facilities continue to plague drivers. It's best to put your car in one of the parking lots on the edge of the old center and abandon it for the rest of your stay.

BY METRO, TRAM, AND BUS

A zonal fare system is used. Tickets (starting at Fl. 3) are available from automatic dispensers on the Metro or from the drivers on trams and buses; or buy a money-saving strippenkaart (☞ Getting Around, By Bus, *in* The Netherlands A to Z, *above*). Even simpler is the dagkaart, which covers all city routes for Fl. 12. These discount tickets can be obtained from the main GVB ticket office (weekdays 7–7, weekends 8–7) in front of Centraal Station and from many newsstands, along with route maps of the public transportation system. A new alternative for visitors is the Circle Tram 20, which goes both ways around a loop that passes close to most of the main sights and offers a hop-on, hop-off ticket for one–three days.

BY TAXI

Taxis are expensive: A 5-km (3-mi) ride costs around Fl. 15. Taxis are not usually hailed on the street but are picked up at stands near stations and other key points. Alternatively, you can dial 020/6777777. Water taxis (☏ 020/6222181) are more expensive: Standard-size water taxis—for up to eight people—cost Fl. 90 for a half hour, including pick-up charge, and Fl. 30 per 15 minutes thereafter.

ON FOOT

Amsterdam is a compact city of narrow streets and canals, ideal for exploring on foot. The tourist office issues seven excellent guides in English that detail walking tours around the center. The best are "The Jordaan," a stroll through the lively canal-side district, and "Jewish

Amsterdam," a walk past the symbolic remains of Jewish housing and old synagogues.

Contacts and Resources

CONSULATES

United States (✉ Museumplein 19, ☎ 020/6645661). **Canadian** (✉ 7 Sophialaan, The Hague, ☎ 070/3614111). **United Kingdom** (✉ Koningslaan 44, ☎ 020/6764343).

EMERGENCIES

Police (☎ 112). **Ambulance** (☎ 112). **Central Medical Service** (☎ 0900/35032042, Fl. 1 per minute), will give you names and opening hours of pharmacists and dentists as well as doctors.

ENGLISH-LANGUAGE BOOKSTORES

American Book Center (✉ Kalverstraat 185, ☎ 020/6255537). **Athenaeum Boekhandel** (✉ Spui 14, ☎ 020/6233933). **English Bookshop** (✉ Lauriergracht 71, ☎ 020/6264230). **Waterstone's** (✉ Kalverstraat 152, ☎ 020/6383821).

GUIDED TOURS

Bike. From April through October, guided bike tours are an excellent way to discover Amsterdam. There are also supervised tours to the idyllic countryside and quaint villages just north of the city. The three-hour city tour costs Fl.30, and the 6½-hour countryside tour costs Fl.42.50, arranged by **Yellow Bike Guided Tours** (✉ Nieuwezijds Kolk 29, ☎ 020/6206940).

Boat. The most enjoyable way to get to know Amsterdam is on a boat trip along the canals. Departures are frequent from points opposite Centraal Station, along the Damrak, and along the Rokin and Stadhouderskade (near the Rijksmuseum). For a tour lasting about an hour, the cost is around Fl. 12.50, but the student guides expect a small tip for their multilingual commentary. A candlelight dinner cruise costs upward of Fl. 39.50. Trips can be booked through the tourist office.

At **Canal-Bike** locations (✉ corner Leidsestraat and Keizersgracht, Leidsekade, Stadhouderskade opposite Rijksmuseum, Prinsengracht opposite Westerkerk; ☎ 020/6239886), a pedal boat for four costs FL. 20.50 per hour.

The **Museum Boat** (✉ Stationsplein 8, ☎ 020/6222181) combines a scenic view of the city with seven stops near 20 museums. Tickets, good for the entire day, are Fl. 22.

Bus. Guided bus tours also provide an excellent introduction to Amsterdam. A bus-and-boat tour includes the inevitable trip to a diamond factory. Costing Fl. 25–Fl. 35, the comprehensive 3½-hour tour can be booked through **Lindbergh** (✉ Damrak 26–27, ☎ 020/6222766) or **Key Tours** (✉ Dam 19, ☎ 020/6235051).

Travel Agencies

American Express (✉ Damrak 66, ☎ 020/5207777; ✉ Van Baerlestraat 39, ☎ 020/6738550). **Holland International** (✉ Leidseplein 23, ☎ 020/6262660). **Key Tours** (✉ Dam 19, ☎ 020/6235051). **Reisburo Arke** (✉ Damrak 90, ☎ 020/5550888). **Thomas Cook** (Bureau de Change, ✉ Leidseplein 31a, ☎ 020/6267000; ✉ Damrak 1, ☎ 020/6203236).

Visitor Information

VVV Amsterdam Tourist Office (✉ Stationsplein 10, in front of Centraal Station in Old Dutch Coffee House; ☎ 0900/4040400, Fl. 1 per minute—electronic queue—you may end up paying for a long wait).

HISTORIC HOLLAND

Between the historic towns, you'll see some of the Netherlands' windmill-dotted landscape and pass through centers of tulip growing and cheese production. Highlights are the historic cities of Leiden and Utrecht and the major museums in Haarlem.

Apeldoorn is 90 km (56 mi) east of Amsterdam along highway A1, where the national park and royal palace are day trips in themselves. Amersfoort is an optional stop-off on the way. Arnhem is 15 km (9 mi) south of Apeldoorn on the A90, for trips to the open-air museum with children during summer months. The historically important centers of Utrecht, Gouda, and Leiden form an arc from the Groene Hart (Green Heart) of Holland toward the coast. Utrecht is 40 km (25 mi) southeast of Amsterdam on the A2. West of Utrecht, 36 km (22 mi) along the A12, you'll come to Gouda. Heading north on N11, you'll come to the ancient city of Leiden. The bulb fields of Lisse are halfway between Haarlem and Leiden, taking the N208 or the H206 coastal route. Haarlem is 20 km (12 mi) directly west of Amsterdam on the A5.

Amersfoort

Although Amersfoort, east of Amsterdam on the way to Apeldoorn, is now a major industrial town, it has managed to retain much of its medieval character and charm. It is also the birthplace of the modern painter Piet Mondriaan (1872–1944). A double ring of canals surrounds the town's old center. The **Hovik** canal was once the harbor and loading quay. The **Koppelport** (⊠ Kleine Spui), an imposing water gate across the Eem, dates from 1400. The turreted **Kamperbinnenpoort** (⊠ Langstraat) is a land gate surviving from the 15th century. The graceful 335-ft-high **Onze Lieve Vrouwetoren** (Tower of Our Lady; ⊠ Breestraat) on a Gothic church has musical chimes that can be heard every Friday between 10 and 11 AM.

Museum Flehite, with its unusual medieval collections, gives a fascinating insight into the history of the town, augmented by a large model of the Old Town. In the associated **St. Pieters-en-Bloklands Gasthuis,** a hospice founded in 1390, you can visit the chapel and a medieval room. ⊠ *Westsingel 50,* ☎ *033/4619987.* ⏲ *Tues.–Fri. 10–5, weekends 2–5.*

The **Culinair Museum Mariënhof** (Culinary Museum) traces the history of eating and drinking, from prehistoric hunters and early agriculture, via the Roman period, through to the present day. The Mariënhof was a convent during the 16th century. ⊠ *Kleine Haag 2,* ☎ *033/4631025.* ⏲ *Tues.–Fri. 10–5, weekends 2–5.*

Apeldoorn

★ The main attraction at Apeldoorn is the **Rijksmuseum Paleis Het Loo** (Het Loo Palace National Museum). Built during the late 17th century for William III, this former royal palace was the summer residence for the House of Orange from 1684 to 1972. It has been beautifully restored to illustrate the domestic surroundings enjoyed by the House of Orange for more than 3 centuries. The museum, housed in the stables, has a fascinating collection of royal memorabilia, including cars and carriages, furniture and photographs, and silver and ceramics. The formal gardens and the surrounding parkland have attractive walks. ⊠ *Amersfoortseweg 1,* ☎ *055/5772400.* ⏲ *Tues.–Sun. 10–5.*

★ The **Nationale Park De Hoge Veluwe** (Hoge Veluwe National Park) is an area of moorlands, dense woods, and open meadows lying in the triangle formed by Arnhem, Apeldoorn, and Ede. At the entrance to the park are free white bikes for everybody's use or touring cars cost-

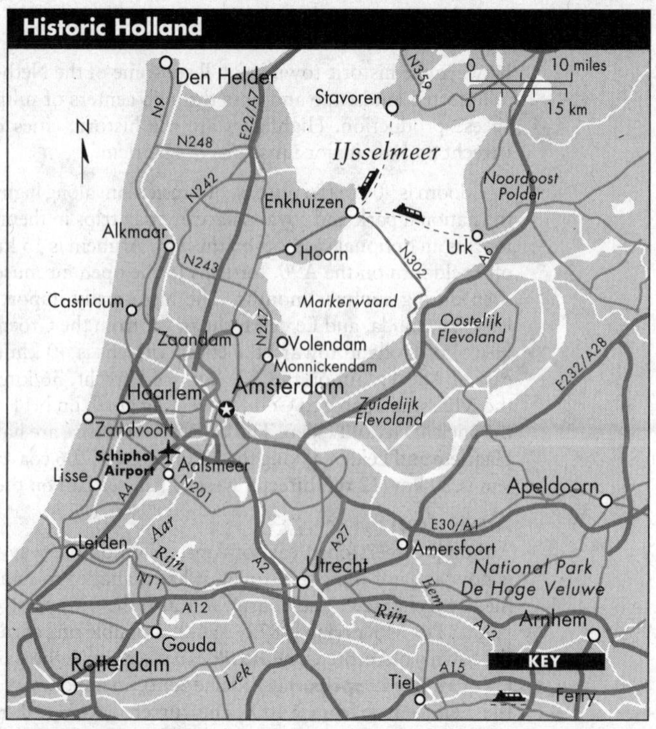

ing Fl. 25. ✉ *5 km (3 mi) from Apeldoorn on N304.* ⏲ *Oct.–Mar., daily 9–6; Apr.–May, daily 8–8; June–Sept., daily 8* AM*–10* PM*.*

★ The **Kröller-Müller Museum** lies in the woods in the middle of the Hoge Veluwe park. The museum displays one of the finest collections of modern art in the world. It possesses 278 works by Vincent van Gogh, as well as paintings, drawings, and sculptures by such masters as Seurat, Redon, Braque, Picasso, and Mondriaan. The building, too, is part of the experience; it seems to bring the museum's wooded setting right into the galleries with you. ✉ *National Park De Hoge Veluwe, 5 km (3 mi) from Apeldoorn on N304,* ☎ *0318/591241.* ⏲ *Tues.–Sun. 10–5, sculpture garden closes ½ hour earlier and is closed Nov.–Mar.*

$$$$ ✕ **De Echoput.** Near Rijksmuseum Paleis Het Loo (☞ *above*), this delightful restaurant is a member of the Alliance Gastronomique Nederlandaise, a guarantee of an excellent meal. Game from the surrounding forest is a specialty. An attractive terrace overlooks fountains and greenery for summer dining. ✉ *Amersfoortseweg 86,* ☎ *055/5191248. Reservations essential. Jacket and tie. AE, DC, MC, V. Closed Mon. No lunch Sat.*

$$$ 🏨 **Bilderberg Hotel de Keizerskroon.** In style and amenities it is a business hotel; in comfort and cordiality, a traveler's hotel; and in setting—at the edge of the town on a quiet street leading toward the woods—a weekend getaway inn. Three of the suites have an open hearth and a Jacuzzi. ✉ *Koningstraat 7, 7315 HR,* ☎ *055/5217744,* FAX *055/5214737. 91 rooms, 6 suites. Restaurant, room service, indoor pool, sauna, steam room, exercise room, laundry service, free parking. AE, DC, MC, V.*

Arnhem

If you have children in tow, consider a visit to the **Nederlands Openlucht Museum** (Open-Air Museum) in Arnhem. In a 44-acre park, the curators have brought together original buildings and furnishings from all over the Netherlands to establish a comprehensive display of Dutch rural architectural styles and to depict traditional ways of living. There are farmhouses and barns, workshops, and windmills—animals, too. ✉ *Schelmseweg 89,* ☎ *026/3576111.* ⏲ *Apr.–Oct., daily 10–5.*

Utrecht

The city of Utrecht was formerly the academic and religious center of the Netherlands. The gabled houses of Nieuwegracht, the canals with their sluice gates, the 13th-century wharves and storage cellars of Oudegracht, and an abundance of Gothic churches are just some of the city's key attractions. Utrecht hosts a number of internationally respected festivals, especially the annual Holland Festival of Early Music in the last week of August. If you arrive by rail, you pass through the enormous and ugly Vredenburg shopping center on the way to the beautiful, tree-lined old town.

The main cathedral square is a good point for orientation. The **Domkerk** is a late-Gothic cathedral with a series of fine stained-glass windows. The Domtoren (cathedral tower; ⏲ Apr.–Oct., weekdays 10–5, weekends noon–5; Nov.–Mar., weekends noon–5) opposite was connected to the cathedral until a hurricane hit in 1674. The bell tower is the country's tallest, and its 465 steep steps lead to a magnificent view. A guide is essential in the tower's labyrinth of steps and passageways. ✉ *Domplein,* ☎ *030/2310403.* 🎫 *Free.* ⏲ *Tours on the hr; May–Sept., weekdays 10–5, Sat. 10–3:30, Sun. 2–4; Oct.–Apr., weekdays 11–4, Sat. 11–3:30, Sun. 2–4.*

★ The **Rijksmuseum van Speelklok tot Pierement** (National Museum of Mechanical Musical Instruments) is devoted solely to music machines—from music boxes to street organs and even musical chairs. During the guided tour music students play some of the instruments. ✉ *Buurkerkhof 10,* ☎ *030/2312789.* ⏲ *Tues.–Sat. 10–5, Sun. 1–5.*

The **Rijksmuseum Het Catharijneconvent** (The Catherine's Convent State Museum) contains the country's largest display of medieval art in addition to its collection of holy relics and vestments. ✉ *Nieuwegracht 63,* ☎ *030/2317296.* ⏲ *Tues.–Fri. 10–5, weekends 11–5.*

The **Centraal Museum** houses a rich collection of contemporary art, especially applied arts, and exhibits about the city. Amid the clutter is a Viking ship (discovered in 1930) and a 17th-century doll house with period furniture, porcelain, and miniature old master paintings. ✉ *Agnietenstraat 1,* ☎ *030/2362362.* ⏲ *Tues.–Sat. 10–5, Sun. noon–5.*

An important part of the museum's collection is a 15-minute walk away in Utrecht's eastern suburbs, the **Rietveld-Schröderhuis** (Rietveld-Schröder House). In 1924 architect Gerrit Rietveld (1888–1964), working with Truus Schröeder, designed what is considered to be the architectural pinnacle of de Stijl (The Style). The use of primary colors (red, yellow, blue) and black and white, as well as the definition of interior space, is unique and innovative even today. ✉ *Prins Hendriklaan 50a,* ☎ *030/2362310.* ⏲ *Wed.–Sat. 11–4:30, Sun. 1:30–4:30; by appointment only.*

$$ ✕ **Polman's Huis.** An incredibly high ceiling, painted with cherubs, welcomes you to this spacious restaurant. Attentive service accompanies well-prepared international cuisine, influenced by Asian as well as European palates. Vegetables are either steamed to perfection or given an exotic twist. ✉ *Keistraat 2,* ☎ *030/2313368. AE, DC, MC, V.*

$ ✕ **De Soepterrine.** This snug restaurant offers ten varieties of steaming homemade soups, including Dutch specialties such as thick *erwten-*

soep (green pea soup). Each bowl comes with crusty bread and herb butter. Quiches and generous salads fill up extra corners. ✉ *Zakkendragerssteeg 40,* ☎ *030/2317005. Reservations not accepted. AE, MC, DC, V.*

$$ 🏨 **Malie Hotel.** The Malie is in a 19th-century row house on a quiet, leafy street a 15-minute walk from the old center. Rooms are brightly decorated though simply furnished. The attractive breakfast room overlooks a garden and terrace. ✉ *Maliestraat 2–4, 3581 SL,* ☎ *030/2316424,* FAX *030/2340661. 29 rooms with bath or shower. AE, DC, MC, V.*

Gouda

Gouda is famous for its cheese. Brightly colored farm wagons are loaded high with cheeses for the morning **Kaasmarkt** (Cheese Market; ⏲ July–Aug., Thurs. 10–noon). In the ornate Baroque **Waag** (weigh house) overlooking the marketplace, the **Kaasexposeum** (cheese exhibition) explains the history of cheese and dairy products. ✉ *Markt 35–6,* ☎ *0182/529996.* ⏲ *Apr.–Oct., Mon.–Sat. 10–5, Sun. noon–5.*

Sint Janskerk (Church of St. John) on the market square holds carillon concerts (⏲ July–Aug., daily at 12:30) in summer. The structure you see today was built during the 16th century. It has the longest nave in the country and 64 glorious stained-glass windows, the oldest of which is from 1555. ✉ *Achter de Kerk 16,* ☎ *0182/512684.* ⏲ *Mar.–Oct., Mon.–Sat. 9–5; Nov.–Feb., Mon.–Sat. 10–4.*

The **Stedelijk Museum Het Catharina Gasthuis** (The Catharina Hospice Municipal Museum) is a former hospital. In it are many unusual exhibits, including a fearsome medieval torture chamber and an equally horrific operating room. ✉ *Oosthaven 10/ Achter de Kerk 14,* ☎ *0182/588440.* ⏲ *Mon.–Sat. 10–5, Sun. noon–5.*

$$ ✕ **Goudsche Salon.** Wooden floors and a big table of newspapers and magazines contribute to the friendly atmosphere here. A good-value, seasonally changing set menu may include such delights as peppery rabbit stew. ✉ *Wijdstraat 13,* ☎ *0182/512330. MC, V. Closed Tues.*

Leiden

Leiden is renowned for its spirit of religious and intellectual tolerance and for its university and royal connections. The university was founded by William the Silent as a reward to Leiden for its victory over the Spanish in the 1573–74 siege. During the war the dikes were opened and the countryside flooded so that the rescuing navy could sail right up to the city walls. The unusual **De Burcht** (The Keep; ✉ Burgsteeg 14), a man-made mound that formed part of the city's early fortifications, affords a spectacular view of the city.

The Pilgrim Fathers stayed in Leiden before they set out for Delftshaven on the first stage of their arduous voyage to the New World. Documents relating to their stay are now kept in the vaults of **Museum De Lakenhal** (☞ *below*). The Public Reading Room of the **Stadsarchief** (City Record Office), however, has facsimiles of documents and other material of historical interest. ✉ *Dolhuissteeg 7,* ☎ *071/5120191 or 071/5165355.* ⏲ *Weekdays 9:30–5, Sat. 9–12:15.*

The recently opened **Leiden American Pilgrim Museum** houses a historic furniture collection in a 16th-century house. ✉ *Beschuitsteeg 9,* ☎ *071/5122413.* ⏲ *Wed.–Sat. 1–5.*

Founded in 1590, the **Hortus Botanicus** (botanical gardens) are among the oldest in the world. The highlights are ancient trees, a faithful reconstruction of a 16th-century garden, an herb garden, and an orangery. ✉ *Rapenburg 73,* ☎ *071/5277249.* ⏲ *Mon.–Sat. 9–5, Sun. 10–5.*

Museum De Lakenhal (Cloth Hall Museum), a textile and antiques museum and art gallery, occupies a classical building constructed in 1639 for cloth merchants. Pride of place in the collection goes to the 16th- and 17th-century Dutch paintings, with works by Steen, Dou, Rembrandt, and, above all, Lucas van Leyden's *Last Judgment* (1526)—the first great Renaissance painting executed in what is now the Netherlands. Other rooms are devoted to furniture and to the history of Leiden's medieval guilds: the drapers, tailors, and brewers. ✉ *Oude Singel 28–32,* ☎ *071/5165360.* ⏲ *Tues.–Fri. 10–5, weekends noon–5.*

★ **Molenmuseum de Valk** (Windmill Museum) is housed in a windmill built in 1747, which was worked by 10 generations of millers until 1964. The seven floors contain the original workings, an old forge, and living quarters. ✉ *2e Binnenvestgracht 1,* ☎ *071/5165353.* ⏲ *Tues.–Sat. 10–5, Sun. 1–5.*

St. Pieterskerk (St. Peter's Church, ✉ Pieterskerkhof 1a) is associated closely with the Pilgrim Fathers, who worshiped here, and with their spiritual leader, John Robinson, who is buried here. An imposing structure, inside and out, it is surrounded by quaint, cobbled streets. A narrow street by the **Persijnhofje** alms house (✉ Kloksteeg 21), dating from 1683, leads to the gracious, tree-lined Rapenburg canal, crossed by triple-arch bridges and bordered by stately 18th-century houses.

The **Rijksmuseum van Oudheden** (National Museum of Antiquities) is the country's leading archaeological museum. The prize exhibit is the entire 1st-century Temple of Taffeh, donated by the Egyptian government. There is also a floor devoted to finds in the Netherlands. ✉ *Rapenburg 28,* ☎ *071/5163163.* ⏲ *Tues.–Sat. 10–5, Sun. noon–5.*

$$ ✕ **Stadscafé Restaurant van der Werff.** The imposing Art Nouveau interior has a romantic view of the De Valk windmill across the water. A café throughout the day, it becomes a restaurant in the evening, with an appetizing and adventurous dinner menu based on traditional Dutch cuisine. ✉ *Steenstraat 2,* ☎ *071/5130335. AE, DC, MC, V.*

$–$$ ✕ **Annie's Verjaardag.** A vaulted cellar full of students and a canal-side terrace make Annie's attractive in all weather. The selection of salads and baguettes is usually accompanied by a daily special, such as mussels or jugged hare. ✉ *Oude Rijn 1a,* ☎ *071/5125737. Reservations not accepted. No credit cards.*

$–$$ ✕ **Nieuw Minerva.** This family-run hotel is a conversion of eight 15th-century buildings. The original part of the hotel is decorated in Old Dutch style; the newer part is better equipped but has slightly less character. Many rooms overlook a quiet tributary of the Rhine. The restaurant caters to most tastes and pockets; the excellent three-course tourist menu has vegetarian as well as meat and fish selections. ✉ *Boommarkt 23, 2311 EA,* ☎ *071/5126358,* FAX *071/5142674. 38 rooms, 30 with bath or shower. Restaurant. AE, DC, MC, V.*

$$ **Hotel De Doelen.** The spartan decor of this small hotel is in keeping with its origins as a 17th-century patrician's house, but the rooms are comfortable and modern, some still furnished in period style. ✉ *Rapenburg 2, 2311 EV,* ☎ *071/5120527,* FAX *071/5128453. 15 rooms with bath or shower. AE, DC, MC, V.*

Lisse

The **Keukenhof,** a 70-acre park and greenhouse complex, is planted each year to create a special exhibition of flowering bulbs (in spring only) between Leiden and Haarlem. The world's largest flower show draws huge spring crowds to its regimental lines of tulips, hyacinths, and daffodils. (A lazier way to see the flowers is from the windows of the Leiden–Haarlem train.) ✉ *N208, Lisse,* ☎ *0252/465555.* 💵 *Fl. 17.* ⏲ *Late Mar.–late May, daily 8–7:30.*

Aalsmeer

Flowers are big business to the Dutch, and the Netherlands has the world's largest complex of flower auction houses. The biggest of these facilities (it also is the single largest in the world) is the **Bloemenveiling** (flower auction) in Aalsmeer, close to Schiphol International Airport and Amsterdam. In a building the size of three football fields, three auction rooms function simultaneously. Get there early; it's all over by 10 AM. ✉ *Legmeerdijk 313,* ☎ *0297/334567.* ⏲ *Weekdays 7:30 AM–11:30 AM. Closed weekends and public holidays.*

Haarlem

With buildings notable for their secret inner courtyards and pointed gables, Haarlem can resemble a 17th-century canvas, even one painted by Frans Hals, the city's greatest painter. The area around the **Grote Markt** (market square) provides an architectural stroll through the 17th and 18th centuries. Some of the facades are adorned with such homilies as, "The body's sickness is a cure for the soul."

The **Vleeshal** (meat market), close to the Stadhuis (town hall), has an especially fine gabled front. This dates from the early 1600s and is now used as the **Archeologisch Museum Haarlem** (Haarlem Archaeological Museum), with local history and computer simulations of reconstructed finds. ✉ *Grote Markt 16.* 💵 *Free.* ⏲ *Wed.–Sun. 1–5.*

The **Grote Kerk** (cathedral) is also known as the St. Bavo, to whom it is dedicated. Built between 1400 and 1550, it houses one of the world's finest organs, which has 5,000 pipes and was played by both Mozart and Handel. An annual organ festival is held here in July. ✉ *Grote Markt,* ☎ *023/5330877.* ⏲ *Apr.–Aug., Mon.–Sat. 10–4; Sept.–Mar., Mon.–Sat. 10–3:30.*

The **Teylers Museum** claims to be the oldest museum in the country. It was founded by a wealthy merchant in 1778 as a museum of science and the arts; it now houses a fine collection of the Hague school of painting as well as drawings and sketches by Michelangelo, Raphael, and other non-Dutch masters. As the canvases in this building are shown in natural light, try to visit on a sunny day. ✉ *Spaarne 16,* ☎ *023/5319010.* ⏲ *Tues.–Sat. 10–5, Sun. 1–5.*

The **Frans Hals Museum,** in what was a 17th-century hospice, contains a marvelous collection of works by Hals (1585–1666); his paintings of the guilds of Haarlem are particularly noteworthy. The museum also has works of the artist's 17th-century contemporaries. ✉ *Groot Heiligland 62,* ☎ *023/5164200.* ⏲ *Mon.–Sat. 11–5, Sun. 1–5.*

$$ ✕ **Café Restaurant Brinkman.** This elegant, classic grand café overlooks the magnificent Grote Kerk. You can while away the afternoon over a single coffee or choose from a wide menu of casseroles and grills with salad. ✉ *Grote Markt 9–13,* ☎ *023/5323111. AE, DC, MC, V.*

$$$ 🏨 **Golden Tulip Lion d'Or.** Just five minutes from the old city center and conveniently near the railway station, this comfortable but unprepossessing hotel offers all the luxuries associated with a Golden Tulip hotel. Special weekend deals include reduced room rates, gourmet evening meals, and free cocktails. ✉ *Kruisweg 34–36, 2011 LC,* ☎ *023/5321750,* FAX *023/5329543. 32 rooms, 2 suites. Restaurant. AE, DC, MC, V.*

Historic Holland Essentials

Getting Around

The most convenient way to explore the countryside is by rented car out of Amsterdam. All the towns listed above can also be reached by bus or train. Check with the tourist office in Amsterdam for help in planning your trip, or inquire at Centraal Station.

Guided Tours

The towns of Historic Holland are covered, in various combinations, by organized bus tours out of Amsterdam. Brochures for tour operators are available from the **VVV Amsterdam Tourist Offices** (☞ Visitor Information *in* Amsterdam Essentials, *above*).

The VVV office in Utrecht (☞ *below*) organizes several excursions, including a boat trip along the canals and a sight-seeing flight over the city. There are also day trips to country estates, castles, and gardens.

Visitor Information

In towns such as Apeldoorn and Gouda, which have few good hotels, B&B accommodations, booked through the VVV tourist office, make more interesting choices.

Amersfoort (⊠ Stationsplein 9–11, ☎ 033/4635151). **Apeldoorn** (⊠ Stationstraat 72, ☎ 0900/91681636). **Gouda** (⊠ Markt 27, ☎ 0182/513666). **Haarlem** (⊠ Stationsplein 1, ☎ 0900/32024043). **Leiden** (⊠ Stationsplein 210, ☎ 071/5146846). **Lisse** (⊠ Grachtweg 53a, ☎ 0252/414262). **Utrecht** (⊠ Vredenburg 90, ☎ 0900/34034085).

THE HAGUE, DELFT, AND ROTTERDAM

The royal, diplomatic, and governmental seat of Den Haag or 's-Gravenhage (The Hague) is the Netherlands' most dignified and spacious city. Its close neighbor is the leading North Sea beach resort of Scheveningen. Also nearby are Delft, a historic city with many canals and ancient buildings, and the energetic and thoroughly modern international port city of Rotterdam. The latter is known to the Dutch as "Manhattan on the Maas," for its office towers as well as its cultural attractions.

There are excellent train connections between all these cities. The Hague and Delft, only 14 km (9 mi) from each other, are both about 60 km (37 mi) southwest of Amsterdam and can be reached within an hour by fast, frequent trains. Rotterdam is only a quarter of an hour farther.

By road The Hague is 50 km (31 mi) southwest of Amsterdam using the A4, then the A44. Delft is 60 km (37 mi) southwest of Amsterdam on the A4, then the A13, via The Hague. The A13 is also the trunk road to Rotterdam, 13 km (8 mi) farther south. Rotterdam is just 73 km (45 mi) south of Amsterdam.

The Hague

During the 17th century, when Dutch maritime power was at its zenith, The Hague was known as "the Whispering Gallery of Europe" because it was thought to be the secret manipulator of European politics. The Hague remains a powerful world diplomatic and juridical capital, as well as the seat of government for the Netherlands.

The city's heart is the **Hofvijver** (court pond), a still, reflecting pond filled with water lilies. It was originally a moat to protect the gracious ★ **Binnenhof** (Inner Court or Parliament Buildings) complex. The Hague was established in 1250, when William II built a castle on this site. At the center is the medieval **Ridderzaal** (Knights' Hall). Inside are vast beams spanning a width of 59 ft, flags, and stained-glass windows. A sense of history pervades the 13th-century great hall, now used mainly for ceremonies. The two government chambers sit separately in buildings on either side of the Ridderzaal; they can be visited by guided tour only when Parliament is not in session. Tours in English are conducted by Stichting Bezoekerscentrum Binnenhof (Binnenhof Visitors Center), just to the right of the Ridderzaal. ✉ *Binnenhof 8a,* ☎ *070/3654779 for tours. Reservations required.* 🎫 *Parliament exhibition: free.* ⏲ *Mon.–Sat. 10–4.*

★ The **Mauritshuis** (Maurits House), a small, well-proportioned palace on the far side of the Binnenhof, dates from 1644. This former royal residence is one of the finest small art museums in the world. It contains a feast of art from the 17th century, including six works by Rembrandt van Rijn (1606–1669); of these the most powerful is *The Anatomy Lesson of Dr. Tulp,* a theatrical work depicting a dissection of the lower arm. Also here are the celebrated *Girl Wearing a Turban* and the glistening *View of Delft* by Jan Vermeer (1632–1675). ✉ *Korte Vijverberg 8,* ☎ *070/3469244.* ⏲ *Tues.–Sat. 10–5, Sun. 11–5.*

Lange Voorhout is a large L-shape boulevard close to the monumental surroundings of the Mauritshuis and Parliament buildings. During the 19th century, horse-drawn trams clattered along its cobbles and deposited dignitaries outside the various palaces. The **Hoge Raad** (Supreme Court; ✉ Lange Voorhout 34) once belonged to William I, the first king of the Netherlands. With its clumsy skewed gable, **the headquarters of the Dutch Red Cross** at No. 6 seems out of place on this stately avenue.

The **Kloosterkerk** (cloister church; ✉ Lange Voorhout 4, corner Parkstraat), built in 1400, is The Hague's oldest church. In spring the adjoining square is covered with yellow and purple crocuses; on Thursday in summer it is the setting for a colorful antiques market.

Panorama Mesdag is a 400-ft painting-in-the-round that shows the nearby seaside town of Scheveningen as it looked in 1880. Hendrik Mesdag (1831–1915), a late-19th-century marine painter, used the muted colors of the Hague school in his calming seascape, as well as special perspective techniques. ✉ *Zeestraat 65,* ☎ *070/3642563.* ⏲ *Mon.–Sat. 10–5, Sun. noon–5.*

Rijksmuseum H. W. Mesdag (H. W. Mesdag National Museum), the painter's former home, contains works by Mesdag and members of the Hague school interspersed with those of Corot, Courbet, and Rousseau. These delicate landscapes represent one of the finest collections of Barbizon School painting outside France. ✉ *Laan van Meerdervoort 7f,* ☎ *070/3621434.* ⏲ *Tues.–Sun. noon–5.*

The **Vredespaleis** (Peace Palace), near Laan van Meerdervoort, is a monument to world peace through negotiation. Following the first peace conference at The Hague in 1899, the Scottish-American millionaire Andrew Carnegie donated $1.5 million for the construction of a building to house a proposed international court. Today the **International Court of Justice,** currently in session for the trial of war criminals from former Yugoslavia, has its headquarters here. There are guided tours when the court is not in session. ✉ *Carnegieplein 2,* ☎ *070/3469680.* ⏲ *June–Sept., weekdays 10–4; Oct.–May, weekdays 10–3. Guided tours at 11, 2, and 3.*

The **Haags Gemeentemuseum** (Hague Municipal Museum) is the home of the world's largest collection of the work of Piet Mondriaan (1872–

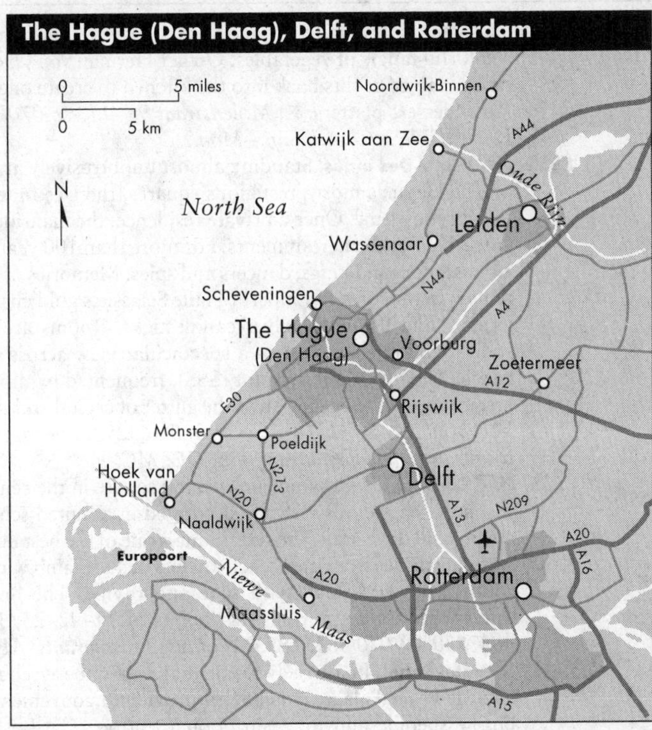

1944). It traces the development of his style from figurative painting to refined, minimalist abstraction. There are also two vast collections of musical instruments—European and non-European. H.P. Berlage's 1935 building itself is a fascinating example of the International Style in modern architecture. ✉ *Stadhouderslaan 41,* ☏ *070/3381111.* ⏲ *Tues.–Sun. 11–5.*

👆 The IMAX theater **Omniversum** is housed in a cylindrical building with a 75-ft dome that acts as a screen for the projection of 6–10 daily video presentations about outer space and nature. ✉ *President Kennedylaan 5,* ☏ *070/3545454 (reservations and show times).* 🎫 *Fl. 17.50.* ⏲ *Shows Tues.–Thurs. hourly 11–4, Fri.–Sun. hourly 11–9 (except 6).*

$$$ ✕ **Da Roberto.** Popular with politicians and The Hague's business elite, Roberto's is a quiet and comfortable restaurant where all the adventure goes into the cuisine. Italian standards and some ambitious variations are treated to elegant nouvelle cuisine presentation. ✉ *Noordeinde 196,* ☏ *070/3464977. AE, DC, MC, V. Sun.*

$$–$$$ ★ ✕ **Bistromer.** A notch above most other seafood restaurants in The Hague, Bistromer has a menu that ranges from the North Sea to the Mediterranean. Portions are generous, and the food is cooked to perfection. There's a wood-paneled dining room for snug winter meals and an attractive glassed-in porch for the summer. ✉ *Javastraat 9,* ☏ *070/3607389. AE, DC, MC, V. Weekend lunch.*

$$–$$$ ✕ **Djawa.** Whether or not it is a result of the city's diplomatic heritage is unknown, but The Hague is said to have the Netherlands' highest concentration of Indonesian restaurants. Among them is this cozy, family-run neighborhood restaurant not far from the center. ✉ *Mallemolen 12a,* ☏ *070/3635763. AE, DC, MC, V. No lunch.*

$$–$$$ ✕ **Le Haricot Vert.** What was built in 1638 as a staff house for the nearby palace is nowadays an intimate, candlelit restaurant in the city center.

Succulent meats swimming in sauce appear on large white plates with a colorful tangle of vegetables. Owner Herman van Overdam chats at diners' tables or flits back into the kitchen to create one of his sinfully laden dessert platters. ✉ *Molenstraat 9a–11,* ☎ *070/3652278. AE, DC, MC, V. No lunch Sun.–Mon.*

$$$$ ✕ **Hotel Des Indes.** Standing almost unobtrusively at the end of one of The Hague's most prestigious squares, the Des Indes is grace and gentility supreme. Once a private residence, the mansion was built for grand balls and entertainments. For more than 100 years it has hosted ambassadors and kings, dancers and spies. Memories of famous guests remain in the form of Emperor Haile Selassie's gold chair and the ballerina Anna Pavlova's silver candlesticks. Rooms are spacious and stylish, and one suite offers a spectacular view across the city to the beach. The historic restaurant ($$$), frequented by diplomats, serves memorable haute cuisine amid the glitter of crystal and silver. ✉ *Lange Voorhout 54–56, 2514 EG,* ☎ *070/3632932,* FAX *070/3451721. 69 rooms, 6 suites. Restaurant. AE, DC, MC, V.*

$$$ ✕ **Corona.** Overlooking a charming square in the center of the city, this hotel has rooms restfully decorated in a muted scheme of white, cream, and dove gray. The restaurant is one of the best in town; mouth-watering dishes from the French kitchen include lamb with forest mushrooms and wild duck with sage and thyme. The brasserie serves sandwiches and light meals. ✉ *Buitenhof 39–42, 2513 AH,* ☎ *070/3637930,* FAX *070/3615785. 26 rooms. 2 restaurants. AE, DC, MC, V.*

$–$$ **Hotel Sebel.** In a largely residential district between the city center and the Peace Palace, Hotel Sebel provides a convenient stopover for businesspeople and for visitors on vacation. The freshly decorated rooms are invitingly spacious and have marble bathrooms. ✉ *Zoutmanstraat 38, 2518 GR,* ☎ *070/3608010,* FAX *070/3455855. 30 rooms. Bar, breakfast room. AE, DC, MC, V.*

Scheveningen

Scheveningen is adjacent to The Hague along the North Sea coast, with the **Scheveningse Bosjes** (Scheveningen Woods) separating it from the city. A fishing village since the 14th century, Scheveningen became a popular beach resort during the 19th century. The beach itself, protected from tidal erosion by stone jetties, slopes gently into the sea in front of a high promenade that protects the boulevard and everything behind it from winter storms. The surface of the beach is fine sand, and you can bicycle or walk for miles to the north.

The **Pier,** completed in 1962, stretches 1,220 ft into the sea. Its four circular end buildings contain a sun terrace and restaurant, an observation tower, an amusement center with a children's play area, and an underwater panorama. ✉ *Northern end of Boulevard.*

The **Sea Life Center** on the beachfront is an ingeniously designed aquarium complex with a transparent underwater tunnel. You walk through it as if you were on the sea floor, with sharks, rays, eels, and octopuses swimming inches above your head. ✉ *Strandweg 13,* ☎ *070/3542100.* ⊙ *Sept.–June, daily 10–6; July–Aug., daily 10–9.*

Madurodam, between The Hague and Scheveningen, is a miniature Netherlands where the country's important buildings are duplicated at a scale of 1:25. No detail has been forgotten, from the lighthouse and 4½-km (3-mi) train track to the hand-carved furniture in the gabled houses. ✉ *Haringkade 175, Scheveningen,* ☎ *070/3553900.* *Fl. 19.50, children up to 11 years Fl. 15.* ⊙ *Apr.–Sept., daily 9 AM–11 PM; Oct.–Mar., daily 9–5.*

$$$$ **Kurhaus Hotel.** At the turn of the century this imposing spa hotel stood alone at the center of the beach as a fashionable resort. Now it is modern and bustling, with a casino among its new attractions. There is a fancifully painted ceiling over the large central court and a buffet restaurant. Rooms have tasteful neoclassical furnishings. ✉ *Gevers Deynootplein 30, 2586 CK,* ☎ *070/4162636,* FAX *070/4162646. 231 rooms, 10 suites. 2 restaurants. AE, DC, MC, V.*

Delft

Probably no town in the Netherlands is more intimate, more attractive, or more traditional than this minimetropolis, whose famous blue-and-white earthenware is popular throughout the world. Compact and easy to explore despite its web of canals, Delft is best discovered on foot—although canal-boat excursions are available April through October, and horse-drawn trams leave from the marketplace. Every street is lined with attractive Gothic and Renaissance houses.

In the marketplace, the only lively spot in this tranquil town, is the **Nieuwe Kerk** (New Church), built during the 14th century, with its tall Gothic spire and a 48-bell carillon. The crypt contains the remains of members of the Orange-Nassau line, including all members of the royal family since King William I ascended the throne in the mid-16th century. ✉ *Markt,* ☎ *015/2123025.* ⏲ *Tower: Mar.–Oct., Mon.–Sat. 9–6; Nov.–Feb., Mon.–Sat. 11–4.*

The **Stedelijk Museum Het Prinsenhof** (Prinsenhof Municipal Museum) was formerly the Convent of St. Agatha, founded in 1400. The chapel inside dates from 1471; its interior is remarkable for the wooden statues under the vaulting ribs. Today the Prinsenhof is a museum that tells the story of the liberation of the Netherlands after 80 years of Spanish occupation (1568–1648). ✉ *St. Agathaplein 1,* ☎ *015/2602358.* ⏲ *Tues.–Sat. 10–5, Sun. 1–5.*

The **Oude Kerk** (Old Church), a vast Gothic monument from the 13th century, overlooks the Oude Delft canal, the city's oldest waterway. The beautiful tower, surmounted by a brick spire, lists somewhat alarmingly. ✉ *Heilige Geest Kerkhof,* ☎ *015/2123015.* ⏲ *Apr.–Nov., Mon.–Sat. 10–5.*

The timbered rooms of the **Lambert van Meerten Museum** are filled with the country's most complete collection of old Dutch tiles and Delft pottery. ✉ *Oude Delft 199,* ☎ *015/2602358.* ⏲ *Tues.–Sat. 10–5, Sun. 1–5.*

Decorated porcelain brought to the Netherlands from China on East India Company ships during the 17th century became so popular that Dutch potters felt their livelihood was being threatened. They therefore set about creating pottery to rival Chinese porcelain. This resulted in the famous local specialty—Delftware. Only two manufacturers still make hand-painted Delftware: **De Delftse Pauw** (✉ Delftweg 133, ☎ 015/2124920; ⏲ Apr.–mid-Oct., daily 9–4:30; mid-Oct.–Mar., weekdays 9–4:30, weekends 11–1) and **De Porceleyne Fles** (✉ Rotterdamsweg 196, ☎ 015/2560234; ⏲ Apr.–Oct., Mon.–Sat. 9–5, Sun. 9:30–5; Nov.–Mar., Mon.–Sat. 9–5).

$$$ ✕ **L'Orage.** This fresh, classically designed canal-side restaurant serves up delicious fish steeped in tantalizing sauces. The award-winning chef/owner, Jannie Munk, bases many of her dishes on recipes from her native Denmark. ✉ *Oude Delft 111b,* ☎ *015/2123629. Reservations essential. Jacket and tie. AE, DC, MC, V. Closed Mon.*

$–$$ ✕ **Spijshuis De Dis.** Seafood is a house specialty at this favorite neighborhood spot, where a friendly staff serves typically Dutch cuisine. The mussels with garlic sauce are delicious, and you can try such delicacies as roast quail. ✉ *Beestenmarkt 36,* ☎ *015/2131782. AE, MC, V. Wed. Lunch by reservation only.*

$ ★ **Hotel de Plataan.** Converted in 1994 from a rather grand old post office building, Hotel de Plataan was decorated by a local artist in 1950s-style cream and green. Most rooms have a kitchen nook. You can also have meals in Het Establissement, an excellent restaurant that serves meaty casseroles as well as imaginative vegetarian dishes. ✉ *Doelenplein 9–10, 2611 BP,* ☎ *015/2126046,* FAX *015/2157327. 23 rooms, 2 suites. Restaurant. AE, DC, MC, V.*

$$–$$$ **Hotel De Ark.** This bright, airy hotel in the center of old Delft comprises three canal houses joined so that nearly every room has a view of either the canal or the large garden in back. Rooms are clean and modern. ✉ *Koornmarkt 59–65, 2611 EC,* ☎ *015/2157999,* FAX *015/2144997. 16 rooms, 9 apartments. AE, DC, MC, V.*

$$ **Hotel Leeuwenbrug.** On one of the prettiest canals in Delft, this traditional Dutch family-style hotel is in a former patrician mansion and an annex. The mansion is simpler, with smaller rooms; the annex is more contemporary and businesslike. You can breakfast overlooking the canal; rooms on the top floor of the annex overlook the city. ✉ *Koornmarkt 16, 2611 EE,* ☎ *015/2147741,* FAX *015/2159759. 38 rooms. AE, MC, V.*

Rotterdam

Rotterdam is one of the few thoroughly modern cities in the Netherlands and the site of the world's largest and busiest port. Art lovers know the city for its extensive and outstanding collection of art; philosophers recall it as the city of Erasmus. Representative of the city's adventuresome modern architecture is the **Erasmusbrug** (Erasmus Bridge), an extraordinary, single-span pylon bridge over the Meuse river. This forms the main link with the **Kop van Zuid,** Rotterdam's phenomenal ongoing development project in former docklands on the south bank.

In the city center a most intriguing series of cube-shape apartments balance on a tall stem. One of these precarious-looking houses, the **Kijk-Kubus** (literally, viewing cube), just east of the center, is open to the public. ✉ *Overblaak 70,* ☎ *010/4142285.* ⏲ *Mar.–Nov., daily 11–5; Dec.–Feb., Fri.–Sun. 11–5.*

The biggest surprise in Rotterdam is the remarkable 48-km- (30-mi-) long **Europoort** (Europort; ✉ Willemsplein), which handles more than 250 million tons of cargo every year and more ships than any other port in the world. It is the delta for three of Europe's most important rivers (the Rhine, the Waal, and the Meuse/Maas). You can get to the piers by tram or Metro (blue line to the Leuvehaven station) from the train station. The 1¼-hour harbor tour (☞ Boat Trips *in* Guided Tours, *below*) illuminates Rotterdam's vital role in world trade.

You can also survey the harbor from the vantage point of the **Euromast** observation tower. Get there via the RET Metro red line to Dijkszicht. ✉ *Parkhaven 20,* ☎ *010/4364811.* ⏲ *Mar.–June and Sept., daily 10–7; July and Aug., Sun. and Mon. 10–7, Tues.–Sat. 10AM–10:30 PM; Oct.–Feb., daily 10–5.*

IMAX Rotterdam is a gigantic movie theater in which films are projected onto a six-story screen. There are earphones for English translation. ✉ *Leuvehaven 77,* ☎ *010/4048844.* ⏲ *Shows Tues.–Sun. 2, 3, and 4; Mon. also during holiday periods.*

The inner harbor's hodgepodge of cranes, barges, steamships, and old shipbuilding machinery looking like a maritime junkyard is a work in progress: Volunteers are restoring the vessels and machinery. The open-air museum of shipbuilding, shipping, and communications is part of the **Maritiem Museum Prins Hendrik** (Prince Henry Maritime Museum), housed in a large gray building at the head of the quay. Moored in the inner harbor adjacent to the museum is the historic 19th-century Royal Dutch Navy warship, *De Buffel.* Within the museum are exhibits devoted to the history and activity of the great port outside. ✉ *Leuvehaven 1,* ☎ *010/4132680.* ⏲ *Tues.–Sat. 10–5, Sun. 11–5.*

The **Museumpark,** an easy stroll along the canal from Eendrachtsplein Metro station, is a welcome contrast to the industrial might of the Europoort and the Netherlands' maritime history. Three of Rotterdam's ★ art institutions are sited around these landscaped gardens. The **Boymans–van Beuningen Museum** has an Old Arts section that includes the work of Bruegel, Bosch, and Rembrandt, as well as a renowned print gallery with works by artists such as Dürer and Cézanne. Dali and Magritte mix with the Impressionists in the Modern Arts collection. ✉ *Museumpark 18–20,* ☎ *010/4419400.* ⏲ *Tues.–Sat. 10–5, Sun. 11–5.*

The **Nederlands Architectuurinstituut** (Netherlands Institute of Architecture), designed by Jo Coenen, hosts innovative exhibitions and lectures in the field of architecture, town and country planning, and interior design from the 1800s to the present. ✉ *Museumpark 25,* ☎ *010/4401200.* ⏲ *Tues.–Sat. 10–5, Sun. 11–5.*

The **Kunsthal** (Art Hall) in Museumpark mounts all manner of major temporary exhibitions, usually on modern subjects—from Andy Warhol retrospectives to rows of compact cars. ✉ *Kunsthal: Westzeedijk 341,* ☎ *010/4400300.* ⏲ *Tues.–Sat. 10–5, Sun. 11–5.*

Delfshaven—spelled Delftshaven when the Pilgrims set sail from here—is the last remaining nook of old Rotterdam. Rows of gabled buildings and a windmill line the waterfront. Today Delfshaven is an up-and-coming area of trendy galleries, cafés, and restaurants. ✉ *From the station, double back along Schiedamseweg, then turn right down Aelbrechtskolk.*

$$$ ✕ **Loos.** The stylish brasserie is in one of the city's few remaining old neighborhoods. The fare is adventurous French-influenced Dutch, with such dishes as quail with caramelized apples. ✉ *Voorhaven 3,* ☎ *010/4775181. AC, MC, V. No lunch weekends.*

$–$$$ ✕ **Heerenhuis De Heuvel.** Resplendent beside a lake in the city's Maas Park, this airy 19th-century building has the sunniest terrace in town. In one wing is a restaurant serving such tantalizing dishes as cod with sesame seeds. In the café on the other side of the building, the same kitchen serves inexpensive, lighter meals. ✉ *Baden-Powelllaan 12,* ☎ *010/4364249. AE, DC, MC, V.*

$$ ✕ **Inn the Picture.** This trendy café offers a wide selection of typical Dutch fare. The salads are especially inviting. In summer tables afford a view of passing crowds in the shopping district. ✉ *Karel Doormanstraat 294,* ☎ *010/4117723. AE, DC, MC, V.*

$$–$$$ ✕🏨 **Hotel New York.** The twin towers of the Hotel New York have been a feature of Rotterdam's skyline for almost a century. Some rooms retain the original walnut paneling and restored Art Nouveau carpets, while others are modern in design. Downstairs, the huge café-restaurant serves everything from English afternoon tea to a choice of five different types of oysters. The hotel is a 15-minute walk from the Rijnhaven Metro station, or you can take one of the hotel's water taxis direct from Veerhaven or Leuvehaven. ✉ *Koninginnenhoofd 1, 3072 AD,* ☎ *010/4390500,* FAX *010/4842701. 71 rooms with shower or bath, 1 apartment. Restaurant. AE, DC, MC, V.*

$ **Hotel Van Walsum.** This pleasant, family-run hotel is just around the corner from Rotterdam's main museums and has an apartment as one of the options. The small restaurant overflows into the garden in good weather. ✉ *Mathenesserlaan 199–201, 3014 HC,* ☎ *010/4363275,* FAX *010/4364410. 25 rooms, 1 apartment. Restaurant. AE, DC, MC, V.*

The Hague, Delft, and Rotterdam Essentials

Getting Around

The heart of The Hague and Delft are compact enough to be explored on foot. Scheveningen is reached from The Hague's center by bus or tram; public transportation is more convenient than driving because of severe parking problems at the resort. The RET Metro is an easy-to-use option for getting around Rotterdam; the two main branches (north–south and east–west) cross in the heart of the business district at a major transfer center.

Guided Tours

ORIENTATION

Sight-seeing tours of **The Hague** can be arranged by or through the main VVV tourist office next to the train station (☞ Visitor Information, *below*). The 2½- to 3-hour "Royal Bus Tour" from outside the office at 1 PM every day from April through September takes passengers past Queen Beatrix's residences. **Scheveningen** is for walkers. The Scheveningen VVV office (☞ Visitor Information, *below*) has information about coastal strolls. **Delft** is best seen on foot. The VVV Delft Tourist Office (☞ Visitor Information, *below*) organizes tours. From April through September daily two-hour bus tours of **Rotterdam** are conducted by the VVV Rotterdam Tourist Office (☞ Visitor Information, *below*) from the office at 1:30 PM.

BOAT

From **The Hague,** various boat companies run short day trips and longer candlelight dinner cruises. These can be booked at The Hague tourist office (☞ Visitor Information, *below*) or through De Haagse Rederij (✉ Spui 256, ☎ 070/3462473). In **Scheveningen** there are fishing-boat tours around the Dutch coast; contact Sportsviscentrum Trip 30 (☎ 070/3541122). In **Delft,** the tourist office (☞ Visitor Information, *below*) organizes boat tours along the unspoiled canal system. You can cruise the port of **Rotterdam** on a basic tour of 1¼ hours (year-round) or choose one that lasts as long as nine hours (midsummer only). Spido Havenrondvaarten (✉ Willemsplein, ☎ 010/4135400), the main boat company, also operates 1¼-hour summer evening music-and-dinner cruises of the inner harbor. The pier can be reached by taking the RET Metro blue line toward Spijkenisse to the Leuvehaven station and walking to the end of the boulevard.

Visitor Information

If you're planning to spend a few days in The Hague or Rotterdam, ask for the VVV brochure on city events and entertainment. Tickets for concerts and other activities can be reserved in person at the VVV.

Delft (✉ Markt 83–85, ☎ 015/2126100). **The Hague** (✉ Babylon Center, Koningin Julianaplein 30, next to the train station, ☎ 0900/34035051). **Rotterdam** (✉ Coolsingel 67, ☎ 0900/34034065). **Scheveningen** (✉ Gevers Deynootweg 1134, ☎ 0900/34035051).

22 Norway

Oslo; the Coast Road to Stavanger; Through Telemark to Bergen; Above Bergen: the Far North

On Norway's dramatic west coast, deep fjords knife into steep mountain ranges. Inland, cross-country ski trails follow frozen trout streams, and downhill trails slice through forests carpeted with wildflowers and berries in summer. In older villages, wooden houses spill down toward docks where Viking ships were once moored. Small fishing boats and pleasure craft and large industrial oil tankers dot the maritime horizon.

Inhabited since 1700 BC, Norway is today a peaceful nation, but from the 8th to the 10th century AD, apart from vicious infighting at home, the Vikings marauded as far afield as Seville and the Isle of Man. This fierce spirit remained, despite Norway's subsequent centuries of subjugation by the Danes and Swedes. Independence came early in the 20th century but was tested during World War II, when the Germans occupied the country. Norwegian Resistance fighters rose to the challenge, eventually sabotaging Nazi efforts to develop atomic weapons.

The foundations for modern Norwegian culture were laid in the 19th century, during the period of union with Sweden, which lasted until 1905. Oslo blossomed at this time, and Norway produced its three greatest men of arts and letters: composer Edvard Grieg (1843–1907), playwright Henrik Ibsen (1828–1906), and painter Edvard Munch (1863–1944). Other notable Norwegians of this period were the polar explorers Roald Amundsen and Fridtjof Nansen.

All other facts aside, Norway is most famous for its fjords, formed during an ice age a million years ago. The ice cap burrowed deep into existing mountain-bound riverbeds, creating enormous pressure. There was less pressure along the coast, so the entrances to most fjords are shallow, about 500 ft, while inland depths reach as much as 4,000 ft. Although Norway's entire coastline is notched with fjords, the most breathtaking sights are on the west coast between Stavanger and Trondheim, and the northern Helgeland coastline to the Lofoten Islands. From the sheltered villages deep in fjord country to the wildest windswept plateaus in Finmark, Norwegians remain outdoor fanatics, firmly in the grip of their country's natural beauty.

NORWAY A TO Z

Customs

Residents of non-European countries who are over 18 may import duty-free into Norway 400 cigarettes or 500 grams of other tobacco products. Residents of European countries who are over 18 may import 200 cigarettes or 250 grams of other tobacco goods. Anyone can bring in souvenirs, gifts, perfume, and eau de cologne to a value of NKr 5,000 after being out of the country for more than 24 hours. Within 24 hours, you may bring in goods duty free valued up to NKr 2,000. Anyone over 20 may bring in 1 liter of liquor, 1 liter of wine, and 2 liters of beer or 2 liters of wine and 2 liters of beer. Travelers who have reached 18 years may bring in 2 liters of wine and 2 liters of beer.

Dining

The Norwegian diet emphasizes protein and carbohydrates. Breakfast is usually a large buffet of smoked fish, cheeses, sausage, cold meats, and whole-grain breads accompanied by tea, coffee, or milk. Lunch is simple, usually *smørbrød* (open-face sandwiches). Restaurant and hotel dinners are usually three-course meals, often starting with soup and ending with fresh fruit and berries. Meals are generally expensive, so take hotel breakfast when it's offered. Spirits are not served on Sunday, although beer and wine are available in most establishments. Alcohol is very expensive and, except in restaurants, is sold only during strictly regulated hours at state-owned *vinmonopol* stores. When dining out, take note that laws relating to drinking and driving are very strict; you should never drink without having a designated driver.

MEALTIMES

Lunch is from noon to 3 at restaurants featuring a *koldtbord*—a Scandinavian buffet, primarily for special occasions and visitors. Dinner has traditionally been early, but in hotels and major restaurants it is now more often from 6 to 11.

RATINGS

Prices are per person and include a first course, main course, and dessert, without wine or tip. (☞ Tipping, *below*).

CATEGORY	COST
$$$$	over NKr 450
$$$	NKr 300–Nkr 450
$$	NKr 150–NKr 300
$	under NKr 150

WHAT TO WEAR

Unless otherwise indicated, jacket and tie or high-fashion casual wear are recommended for restaurants in the $$$$ and $$$ price categories; during the summer, neat casual dress is acceptable in most places.

Language

There are two official forms of the Norwegian language—*bokmål* and *nynorsk*—plus many dialects. As is typical of Scandinavian languages, Norwegian's additional vowels—æ, ø, and å—come at the end of the alphabet in the phone book.

English is the main foreign language taught in schools, and movies, music, and TV reinforce its popularity. It is widely spoken by people in larger cities and most commercial establishments.

Norway (Norge)

0
200 miles
0
300 km
North Cape
Vardø
Vadsø
Hammerfest
Kirkenes
ATLANTIC OCEAN
Alta
Masi
Tromsø
Kantokeino
FINLAND
Bardu
Narvik
Norwegian Sea
Svolvoer
Lofoten
Vestfjorden
Bodø
Fauske
Saltdal
Arctic Circle
Mo i Rana
Umbukta
Sandnessjøen
Mosjøen
E6
Brønnøysund
SWEDEN
Gulf of Bothnia
Vikna
Namsos
Steinkjer
Trondheim
Meråker
Støren
Kristiansund N.
70
Oppdal
Røros
Ålesund
Tynset
E69
Dombås
Otta
Nordfjord
Koppang
Florø
Jostedalsbreen
Rena
Lillehammer
Sognefjorden
Lake Mjøsa
Hamar
Voss
E68
Eidsvoll
Bergen
Hardangerfjorden
7
Hønefoss
40
Oslo
11
Kongsberg
Baltic Sea
Drammen
Sarpsborg
Oslofjord
Haugesund
Larvik
Fredrikstad
Skien
Sandefjord
Stavanger
39
Arendal
Evje
Egersund
Grimstad
Skagerrak
Kattegat
Mandal
Kristiansand S.

Lodging

CAMPING

There are 1,160 registered campsites in the country, many in spectacular surroundings. Prices vary according to the facilities provided: A family with a car and tent can expect to pay about NKr 100 per night. Some campsites have log cabins available from between NKr 250 and NKr 600 per night. *Camping Norway* is available from tourist offices and the **Norges Automobil Forbund** (NAF; ✉ Storgt. 2, 0155 Oslo, ☎ 22341400).

HOTELS

Accommodations in Norway are usually spotless, and smaller establishments are often family run. Service is thoughtful and considerate, right down to blackout curtains to block out the midnight sun. The **Fjord Pass** (✉ Fjord Tours, Box 1752, 5024 Bergen, ☎ 55326550), which costs about $11, is valid for discounts at 250 establishments. Hotels in larger towns have special summer rates from late June to early August, and some chains have their own discount offers—see Norway's annual accommodation guide at tourist offices. Discounts in smaller hotels are offered to guests staying several days; meals are then included in the rate.

RATINGS

Prices are summer rates for two people in a double room with bath, and include breakfast, service, and taxes.

CATEGORY	MAJOR CITIES	OTHER AREAS
$$$$	OVER NKR 1,300	OVER NKR 1,000
$$$	NKR 1,000–NKR 1,300	NKR 850–NKR 1,000
$$	NKR 800–NKR 1,000	NKR 650–NKR 850
$	UNDER NKR 800	UNDER NKR 650

RENTALS

Norwegians escape to *hytter* (mountain cabins) whenever they have the chance. Stay in one for a week or two and you'll see why—magnificent scenery, pure air, edible wild berries, and a chance to hike, fish, or cross-country ski. For information on renting cabins, farms, or private homes, write to **Den Norske Hytteformidling A.S.** (✉ Box 3404, Bjølsen, 0406 Oslo, ☎ 22356710), or get the brochure "Norsk Hytteferie" from tourist offices. An unusual alternative is to rent a *rorbu* (fisherman's dwelling) in the northerly Lofoten Islands. Contact **Destination Lofoten** (✉ Box 210, 8301 Svolvær, ☎ 76073000).

YOUTH HOSTELS

Norway has about 100 youth hostels; some are schools or farms in winter. Members of the Youth Hostel Association (YHA) get a discount. Contact **Norske Vandrerhjem** (NoVa; ✉ Dronningensgt. 26, 0154 Oslo, ☎ 23139300). International YHA guides are available to members in the United Kingdom and North America (☞ Students *in* Chapter 1). There are no age restrictions for membership.

Mail

Opening times for post offices can vary throughout the country, but in general they are open weekdays 9–5 and Saturday 10–2. They cash traveler's checks and exchange foreign currency as well as offering postal services.

POSTAL RATES

Letters and postcards to the United States cost NKr 6.00 for the first 20 grams. The rate is NKr 5.00 for the first 20 grams for the United Kingdom.

RECEIVING MAIL

If you're uncertain about where you'll be staying, have your mail marked "poste restante" and sent to the town where you plan to pick it up. Your last name should be underlined. The service is free; letters are directed to the nearest main post office, where you'll need your passport to pick up your mail. American Express offices will also hold mail (nonmembers pay a small fee on collection).

Money Matters

COSTS

Norway has a high standard—and cost—of living, but there are ways to save money by taking advantage of special offers for accommodations and travel during the tourist season and on weekends.

CURRENCY

The unit of currency in Norway is the krone, written as Kr. on price tags but officially NOK (bank designation), NKr, or kr. The krone is divided into 100 øre. Bills of NKr 50, 100, 200, 500, and 1,000 are in general use. Coins are in denominations of 50 øre and 1, 5, 10, and 20 kroner. Credit cards are accepted in most hotels, stores, restaurants, and many gas stations and garages, but generally not in smaller shops and inns in rural areas. The exchange rate at press time (spring 1998) was NKr 7.35 to the U.S. dollar, NKr 5.12 to the Canadian dollar, NKr 12.22 to the pound sterling, NKr 4.72 to the Australian dollar, and NKr 4.06 to the New Zealand dollar.

SAMPLE PRICES

Cup of coffee, NKr 12–NKr 25; ½ liter of beer, NKr 35–NKr 50; soft drink, NKr 10–NKr 25; ham sandwich, NKr 20–NKr 50; taxi base rates in Oslo: Nkr 24–Nkr 47, depending on time of day and whether you phone for or hail the cab.

TIPPING

A 10%–12% service charge is added to most bills at hotels and restaurants. If you have had exceptional service, then give an additional 5%–10% tip. Round off a taxi fare to the next higher unit, or a little more if the driver has been particularly helpful with luggage. If the porter helps with your luggage, give Nkr 15–20. Tip with kroner only.

National Holidays

January 1; March 28 (Palm Sunday); April 1–2, 4–5 (Easter); May 1 (Labor Day); May 13 (Ascension), May 17 (Constitution Day); May 23–24 (Pentecost); December 25–26.

Opening and Closing Times

Banks are open weekdays 8–3:30, in summer 8:15–3. **Museums** are usually open Tuesday–Sunday 10–3 or 4. **Shops** are usually open weekdays 9 or 10–5 (Thursday until 7) and Saturday 9–1 or 2, though times vary. Shopping malls are often open until 8 on weeknights.

Shopping

GIFT IDEAS

Prices of handmade articles are government-controlled, and selection is widest in Oslo, so that's the best place to do your shopping: Pewter, silver, glass, sheepskin, leather, painted wood decorations, kitchenware, and knitwear all make special souvenirs.

SALES-TAX REFUNDS

Much of the 23% Norwegian value-added tax (VAT) will be refunded to visitors who spend more than NKr 300 in any single store. Ask for a special tax-free check and show your passport to confirm that you are not a resident. All purchases must be sealed and presented together with the tax-free check at the tax-free counter at foreign ferry ports and at airports and border posts. The VAT will be refunded, minus a service charge. General information about the tax-free system is available by calling 67149901.

Telephoning

Domestic rates are reduced 5 PM–8 AM weekdays and all day on weekends. Cheap rates for international calls apply only after 10 PM. Avoid using room phones in hotels. In the public booths you can find card phones or coin phones. Be sure to read the instructions; some phones require the coins to be deposited before dialing, some after. You can buy telephone cards at Narvesen kiosks or at the post office. The largest coins generally accepted are NKr 10, although some new phones take NKr 20 coins. Most older phones take only NKr 1 or NKr 5 coins. The minimum deposit is NKr 2 or NKr 3, depending on the phone.

COUNTRY CODE

The international country code for Norway is 47.

INTERNATIONAL CALLS

These can be made from any pay phone. For calls to North America, dial 00–1, then the area code and number. When dialing the United Kingdom, omit the initial zero of the area code (for Central London you would dial 00 followed by 44, then 171 and the local number). To reach an **AT&T** long-distance operator, dial 80019011.

LOCAL CALLS

Area codes are not used in Norway. The cost of calls within the country varies according to distance: In Oslo, the cost goes up according to the amount of time used after the three-minute flat fee. The Oslo phone book has dialing information in English.

OPERATORS AND INFORMATION

For local information, dial 180. For international information, dial 181. For international collect calls, dial 115.

Transportation

The Norwegian words for street (gate or gata), road (veien), avenue (aveny), and square (plass) are abbreviated gt., vn., av., and pl.

BY BUS

The Norwegian bus network makes up for some limitations of the country's train system, and several routes are particularly scenic. For example, the **Nord-Norge Buss Service** (Northern Norway bus service; ✉ 8400 Sortland, ☎ 76111111), starting at Fauske (on the train line to Bodø), goes right up to Kirkenes on the Russian-Norwegian border, covering the 1,000 km (625 mi) in four days. Buses leave the Oslo area from **Bussterminalen** (Bus Terminal; ✉ Galleri Oslo, Schweigaardsgt. 10, ☎ 23002400), close to Oslo's Sentralstasjonen (Oslo S or Central Station).

BY CAR

Breakdowns. Norges Automobil Forbund patrols main roads and has emergency telephones on mountain roads. For NAF 24-hour service, dial 81000505.

Gasoline. Gas costs 8–9 NKr per liter and diesel costs 7.17–7.36 NKr per liter. Gas stations are not hard to find in remote areas.

Parking. Street parking in cities and towns is clearly marked. There are also municipal parking lots. You cannot park on main roads or on bends. Check the leaflet *Parking in Oslo,* available free from the tourist office, at toll stations, and at the City Hall; or ask at your hotel.

Road Conditions. Away from the major routes, roads are narrow and winding, so don't expect to average more than 50–70 kph (30–40 mph), especially in fjord country. Even the best roads suffer from frost, and mountain passes may be closed in winter. Snow tires (preferably studded) are advised in winter in most areas; if you're renting a car, choose a smaller model with front-wheel drive.

Rules of the Road. Driving is on the right. The speed limit is 90 kph (55 mph) on highways, 80 kph (50 mph) on main roads, 50 kph (30 mph) in towns, and 30–40 kph (18–25 mph) in residential areas. The use of headlights at all times is mandatory. For assistance contact Norges Automobil Forbund (NAF)—the Norwegian Automobile Association (✉ Storgt. 2, 0155 Oslo, ☎ 22341400). It is important to remember to yield to the vehicle approaching from the right. Passing areas on narrow roads are marked with a white *M* (for *møteplass*) on a blue background.

BY FERRY

Norway's long, fjord-indented coastline is served by an intricate and essential network of ferries and passenger ships. A wide choice of services is available, from simple hops across fjords (saving many miles of traveling) and excursions among the thousands of islands to luxury cruises and long journeys up the coast. Most ferries carry cars. Reservations are required on journeys of more than one day but are not needed for simple fjord crossings. Fares and exact departure times depend on the season and the availability of ships. Contact **Nortra** (Norwegian Travel Association) or the **Norway Information Center** for details (☞ Visitor Information, *below.*)

One of the world's great sea voyages is aboard one of the mail-and-passenger Hurtigruten ships that run up the Norwegian coast from Bergen to Kirkenes, well above the Arctic Circle. Contact the **Bergen Line** (✉ 405 Park Ave., New York, NY 10022, ☎ 800/323–7436; Tromsø Main Office, ☎ 77648200).

BY PLANE

Fares are high, so be sure to ask about the special rates available year-round within Norway. For longer distances, flying can be cheaper than driving a rented car, given the cost of gas and incidentals. Inquire about "Visit Norway" passes, which provide relatively cheap domestic-flight coupons. Norwegian airlines can be contacted at the following addresses: **SAS** (✉ Oslo City, Stenersgt. 1A, 0184 Oslo, ☎ 81003300). **Braathens SAFE AS** (✉ Haakon VII's Gt. 2, 0161 Oslo, ☎ 67597000 or 67586000). **Norsk Air** (✉ Torp Airport, Sandefjord, ☎ 33482600). **Widerøe** (✉ Volls vei 6, 1324 Lysaker, ☎ 67596600).

BY TRAIN

Trains are punctual and comfortable, and most routes are scenic. Lines fan out from Oslo and leave the coastline (except in the south) to buses and ferries. Reservations are required on all *ekspresstog* (express trains) and night trains. The Oslo–Bergen route is especially beautiful, and the Oslo–Trondheim–Bodø route takes you within the Arctic Circle. Do not miss the side trips from Myrdal to Flåm from the Oslo–Bergen line, and Dombås to Åndalsnes from the Oslo–Trondheim line. **NSB** (Norwegian rail system; ☎ 81500888) trains leave Oslo from Sentralstasjonen (Oslo S or Central Station; ✉ Jernbanetorget, beginning of Karl Johans Gt.).

Fares. In addition to the Europe-wide passes (Eurail and Inter-Rail), **ScanRail passes,** good in Norway, Sweden, Denmark, and Finland, are also available. ScanRail passes offer unlimited travel in a set number of travel days within a specified period. They are available in the

United States through Rail Europe (☎ 914/682–2999) and DER Travel Service (☎ 310/479–4411). A **Norway Rail Pass** is available with a choice of one or two weeks' unlimited rail travel or three travel days within a month within Norway. In the United States the ticket is available through DER Travel Service, Rail Europe, and ScanAm (☎ 201/835–7070 or 800/545–2204), and in London through NSB Travel. **Reduced fares** during off-peak times ("green" routes) are also available if booked in advance. These can be purchased in Norway only.

Visitor Information

Nortra (Norwegian Travel Association; ✉ Drammensveien 40, Postboks 2893, Sentrum, 0230 Oslo, ☎ 22925200). **Norway Information Center** (✉ Vestbanepl. 1, 0250 Oslo, ☎ 22830050; ✉ Oslo Sentralstasjonen/Central Station, East of Strandgt). **Trafikanten** (✉ Oslo Sentralstasjonen/Central Station, East of Strandgt., ☎ 22177030 or 177: public transportation).

Weather

Norway is an important winter sports center. January, February, and early March are good skiing months, and hotel rooms are plentiful then. Avoid late April, when sleet, rain, and repeated thaws and refreezings may ruin the good skiing snow and leave roads—and spirits—in bad shape. The country virtually closes down for the five-day Easter holiday, when Norwegians make their annual migration to the mountains. If you plan to visit at this time, reserve well in advance. May is one of the best times to visit—the days are long and sunny, cultural life is still going strong, and *Syttende mai* (Constitution Day, May 17), with all its festivities, is worth a trip in itself. Norwegians tend to take their vacations in July and the first part of August. Summers are generally mild. With the midnight sun, even in the "southern" city of Oslo, night seems more like twilight around midnight, and dawn comes by 2 AM. The weather can be fickle, and rain gear and sturdy waterproof shoes are recommended even in summer.

CLIMATE

The following are the average daily maximum and minimum temperatures for Oslo.

Jan.	28F	– 2C	**May**	61F	16C	**Sept.**	60F	16C
	19	– 7		43	6		46	8
Feb.	30F	– 1C	**June**	68F	20C	**Oct.**	48F	9C
	19	– 7		50	10		38	3
Mar.	39F	4C	**July**	72F	22C	**Nov.**	38F	3C
	25	– 4		55	13		31	– 1
Apr.	50F	10C	**Aug.**	70F	21C	**Dec.**	32F	0C
	34	1		54	12		25	– 4

OSLO

Although it's one of the world's largest capital cities in area, Oslo has only about 500,000 inhabitants. In recent years the city has become more lively: shops are open later, and pubs, cafés, and restaurants are crowded at all hours.

Exploring Oslo

Numbers in the margin correspond to points of interest on the Oslo map.

The downtown area is compact, but the city limits include forests, fjords, and mountains, giving Oslo a pristine airiness that complements its urban dignity. Explore downtown on foot, then venture beyond via bus, streetcar, or train.

★ 10 **Aker Brygge** (Aker Wharf). The quayside shopping and cultural center, with a theater, cinemas, and galleries among the stores, restaurants, and cafés, is a great place to linger late into summer nights. It's in the central harbor—the heart of Oslo and head of the fjord. ✉ *Off Dokkveien.*

8 **Akershus Slott** (Akershus Castle). This fortified harborfront castle was built during the Middle Ages and restored in 1527 by Christian IV of Denmark (Denmark then ruled Norway) after it was damaged by fire. He laid out the present city of Oslo (naming it Christiania, after himself) around his new residence; Oslo's street plan still follows his design. Some rooms are open for guided tours, and the grounds form a park. Also on the grounds are the **Forsvarsmuséet** (Defense Museum; ☎ 23093582) and **Hjemmefrontmuséet** (Resistance Museum; ☎ 23093138). Both give you a feel for the Norwegian fighting spirit throughout history and especially during the German occupation, when the Nazis set up headquarters on this site and had a number of patriots executed here. ✉ *Festningspl.; castle,* ☎ *22412521; Forsvarsmuséet,* ☎ *29093582; Hjemmefrontmuséet,* ☎ *23093138.* ⏲ *Castle, May–mid-Sept., Mon.–Sat. 10–4, Sun. 12:30–4; Sept. and Apr., Sun. 12:30–4; guided tours May–Sept., Mon.–Sat. 11, 1, and 3, Sun. 1 and 3. Forsvarsmuséet, June–Aug., weekdays 10–3, weekends 11–4; Sept.–May, weekdays 10–6, weekends 11–4. Hjemmefrontmuséett, mid-Apr.–mid-June, Mon.–Sat. 10–4, Sun. 11–4; mid-June–Aug., Mon., Wed., Sat. 10–5, Tues., Thurs. 10–6, Sun. 11–5; Sept., Mon.–Sat. 10–4, Sun. 11–4; Oct.–mid-Apr., Mon.–Sat. 10–3, Sun. 11–4.*

21 **Barnekunst Muséet** (The International Museum of Children's Art). The museum displays drawings, paintings, ceramics, sculptures, tapestry, and handcrafts collected from more than 180 countries. There is also a Children's Workshop. ✉ *Lille Frens vei 4,* ☎ *22468573.* ⏲ *Mid-Jan.–June and mid-Sept.–mid-Dec., Tues.– Thurs. 9:30–2, Sun. 11–4; July–mid-Aug. Tues.–Thurs., Sun. 11–4. Closed mid-Aug.–1st week of Sept., mid-Dec.–mid-Jan., and 1 wk during Easter.*

Bygdøy. In summer, ferries make the seven-minute run from Rådhusbryggen (City Hall Wharf) across the fjord to the Bygdøy peninsula, where there are several museums (☞ Fram-Muséet, Kon-Tiki Muséet, Norsk Folkemuseum, Vikingskiphuset, *below*) and some popular beaches. You can also take bus 30 (from the National Theater or the Central Station) ⏲ *Ferries run May–Sept., daily every half hr 8:15–5:45.*

18 **Ekebergsletta Parken.** The oldest traces of human habitation in Oslo are the 5,000-year-old carvings on **runic stones** across the road from the park, marked by a sign reading FORTIDSMINNE. ✉ *Karlsborgveien; take Trikk 18 or 19 east from National theater or Central Station to Sjømannsskolen stop.*

15 ***Fram*-Muséet** (*Fram* Museum). Housed in a triangular building, the museum is devoted to the polar ship *Fram,* the wooden vessel that belonged to explorer Fridtjof Nansen. In 1893 Nansen led an expedition that reached latitude 86°14′N, farther north than any European had been at that time. Active in Russian famine-relief work, Nansen received a Nobel Peace Prize in 1922. You can board the ship and imagine yourself in one of the tiny berths with a force-9 gale blowing outside and the temperature dozens of degrees below freezing. ✉ *Bygdøynes,* ☎ *22438370.* ⏲ *Mar.–Apr., daily 11–2:45; May and Sept., daily 10–4:45; June–Aug., daily 9–5:45; Oct., daily 10–2:45; Nov., weekends 11–2:45; Dec.–Feb., weekends 11–3:45.*

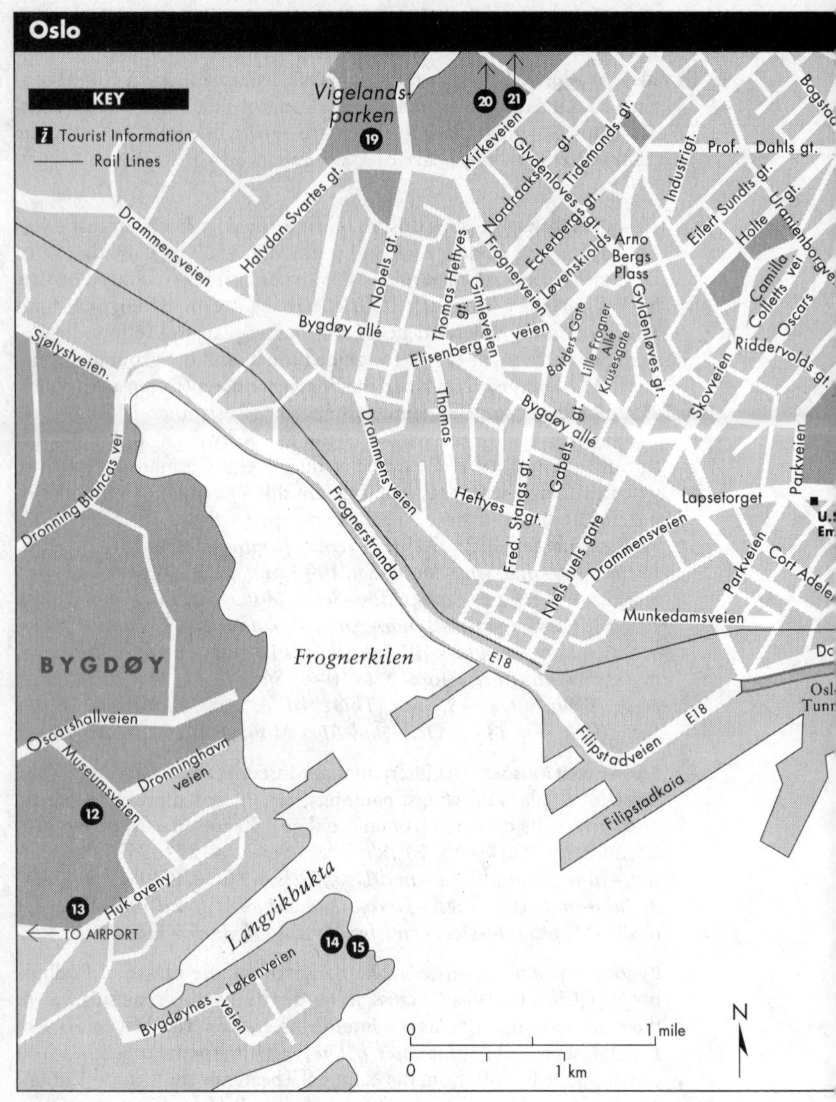
Oslo
KEY
Tourist Information
Rail Lines
Vigelandsparken
Drammensveien
Halvdan Svartes gt.
Kirkeveien
Glydenløves gt.
Tidemands gt.
Industrigt.
Prof. Dahls gt.
Bogstad
Nordraaksens gt.
Eckerbergs gt.
Løvenskiolds
Arno Bergs Plass
Eilert Sundts gt.
Holte gt.
Uranienborgve.
Camilla Colletts vei
Oscars
Nobels gt.
Thomas Heftyes gt.
Gimleveien
Frognerveien
Bygdøy allé
Elisenberg veien
Balders Gate
Lille Frogner Allé
Krusesgate
Gyldenløves gt.
Riddervolds gt.
Skovveien
Sjølystveien
Thomas
Drammensveien
Bygdøy allé
Gabels gt.
Parkveien
Frognerstranda
Heftyes gt.
Fred. Stangs gt.
Lapsetorget
U.S. Em
Niels Juels gate
Drammensveien
Parkveien
Cort Adeler
Munkedamsveien
Dronning Blancas vei
BYGDØY
Frognerkilen
E18
Oslo Tunn
Oscarshallveien
Museumsveien
Dronninghavn veien
Filipstadveien
E18
Filipstadkaia
Huk aveny
TO AIRPORT
Langvikbukta
Løkenveien
Bygdøynes veien
0
1 mile
0
1 km
N
19
20
21
12
13
14
15

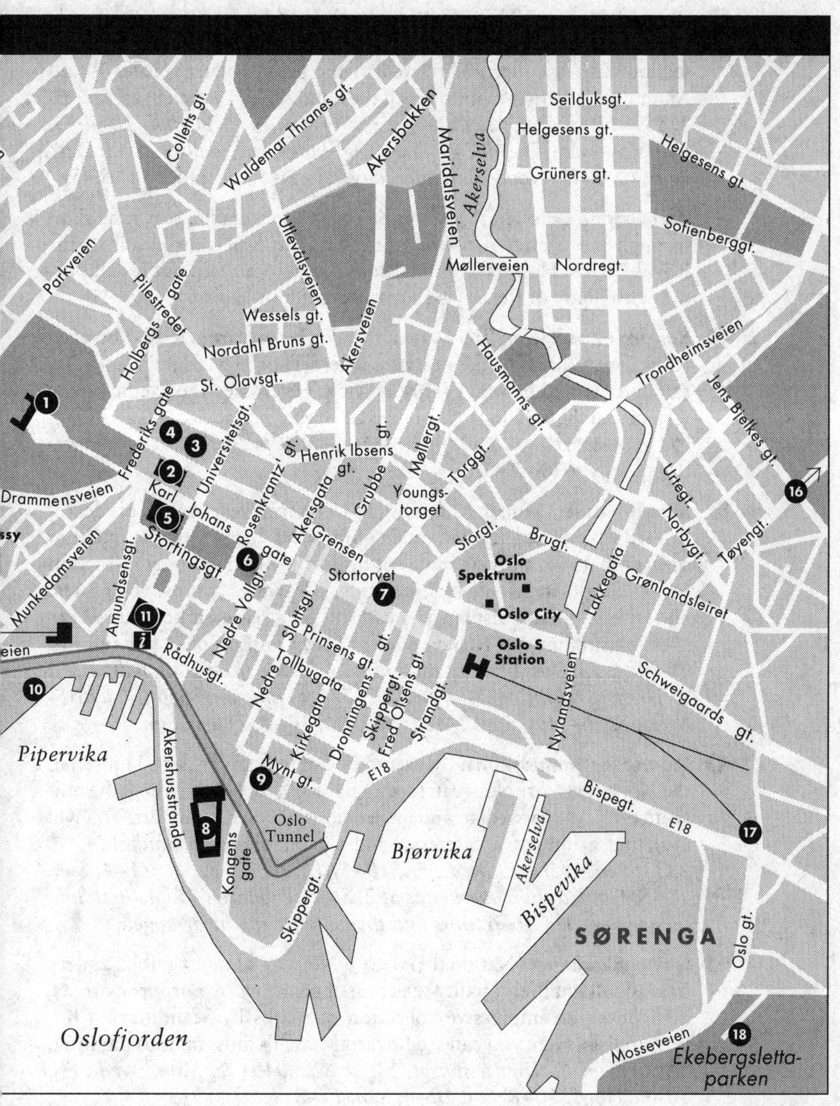

Seilduksgt.
Helgesens gt.
Grüners gt.
Helgesens gt.
Sofienberggt.
Akerselva
Maridalsveien
Akersbakken
Waldemar Thranes gt.
Colletts gt.
Ullevålsveien
Møllerveien
Nordregt.
Parkveien
Pilestredet
Holbergs gate
Wessels gt.
Nordahl Bruns gt.
Akersveien
Hausmanns gt.
Trondheimsveien
Jens Bjelkes gt.
St. Olavsgt.
Frederiks gate
Universitetsgt.
Rosenkrantz' gt.
Henrik Ibsens gt.
Møllergt.
Grubbe gt.
Torggt.
Youngstorget
Urtegt.
Norbygt.
Tøyengt.
Drammensveien
Karl Johans gate
Akersgata
Grensen
Storgt.
Brugt.
Stortingsgt.
Munkedamsveien
Amundsensgt.
Nedre Vollgt.
Sloltsgt.
Stortorvet
Oslo Spektrum
Oslo City
Lakkegata
Grønlandsleiret
Oslo S Station
Rådhusgt.
Prinsens gt.
Nedre Tollbugata
Kirkegata
Dronningens gt.
Skippergt.
Fred Olsens gt.
Strandgt.
Nylandsveien
Schweigaards gt.
Pipervika
Mynt gt.
E18
Akershusstranda
Oslo Tunnel
Kongens gate
Bispegt.
E18
Bjørvika
Akerselva
Bispevika
Skippergt.
SØRENGA
Oslo gt.
Oslofjorden
Mosseveien
Ekebergsletta-parken
1
2
3
4
5
6
7
8
9
10
11
16
17
18

❹ **Historisk Museum** (Historical Museum). In addition to displays of daily life and art from the Viking period, the museum has an ethnographic section with a collection related to the great polar explorer Roald Amundsen, the first man to reach the South Pole. ✉ *Frederiksgt. 2,* ☎ *22859912.* ⏲ *Apr., daily 11–3:45; early May and Sept, daily 10–4:45; mid-May–mid-June, daily 9–5:45; mid-June–Aug., daily 9–6:45; Oct., daily 10–3:45; Nov.–Mar., weekdays 11–2:45, weekends 11–3:45.*

Karl Johans Gate (Karl Johan's Street). Oslo's main street runs right through the center of town, from the Oslo S Station uphill to the Royal Palace. Half its length is closed to automobiles but it still bustles with many of the city's shops and outdoor cafés.

★ ⓮ ***Kon-Tiki* Muséet** (*Kon-Tiki* Museum). Take the ferry from Rådhusbryggen (City Hall Wharf) to the museum where Thor Heyerdahl's *Kon-Tiki* raft and his reed boat *RA II* are on view. He crossed the Pacific on the former and the Atlantic in the latter. ✉ *Bygdøynesvn. 36,* ☎ *22438050.* ⏲ *Oct.–Mar., daily 10:30–4; Apr.–May and Sept., daily 10:30–5; June–Aug., daily 9:30–5:45.*

★ ⓰ **Munch-Muséet** (Munch Museum). In 1940, four years before his death, Edvard Munch bequeathed much of his work to the city; the museum opened in 1963, the centennial of his birth. Although only a fraction of its 22,000 items—books, paintings, drawings, prints, sculptures, and letters—are on display, you can still get a sense of the tortured expressionism that was to have such an effect on European painting. ✉ *Tøyengt. 53; Bus 29 from Rådhuset or T-bane from Nationaltheatret to Tøyen in northeast Oslo,* ☎ *22673774.* ⏲ *June–mid-Sept., daily 10–6; late Sept.–May, Tues., Wed., Fri., Sat. 10–4, Thurs., Sun. 10–6.*

❾ **Muséet for Samtidskunst** (Museum of Contemporary Art). Housed in the Norwegian Art Nouveau former Bank of Norway building, the museum displays Norwegian and international contemporary art. You will also find a library, a cafeteria, and a book shop. ✉ *Bankpl. 4,* ☎ *22335820.* ⏲ *Tues., Wed., Fri. 10–5, Thurs. 10–8, Sat. 11–4, Sun. 11–5. Guided tours weekends at 2. Special children's tours first Sun. in month at 1. Group tours and theme tours can be arranged.*

❸ **Nasjonalgalleriet** (National Gallery). Norway's largest public gallery has a small but high-quality selection of paintings by European artists, and there's an impressive collection of works by Scandinavian Impressionists. Here you can see Edvard Munch's most famous painting, *The Scream.* ✉ *Universitetsgt. 13,* ☎ *22200404.* ⏲ *Mon., Wed., Fri. 10–6, Thurs. 10–8, Sat. 10–4, Sun. 11–3.*

❺ **Nationaltheatret** (National Theater). Statues of Bjørnstjerne Bjørnson, the nationalist poet who wrote Norway's anthem, and Henrik Ibsen, who wrote the plays *Peer Gynt, A Doll's House, Hedda Gabler,* and other classics, watch over Nationaltheatret. Ibsen worried that his works, packed with allegory, myth, and sociological and emotional angst, might not have appeal outside Norway. As it happened, they changed the face of modern theater around the world. ✉ *Stortingssgt. 15,* ☎ *22/412710.*

★ ⓬ **Norsk Folkemuseum** (Norwegian Folk Museum). Take the ferry from Rådhusbryggen (City Hall Wharf) and walk up a well-marked road to see this large park where centuries-old historic farmhouses have been collected from all over the country and reassembled. A whole section of 19th-century Oslo was moved here, as was a 12th-century wooden stave church. ✉ *Museumsvn. 10,* ☎ *22123700.* ⏲ *Jan.–mid-May, Mon.–Sat. 11–3, Sun. 11–4; mid-May–mid-June, daily 10–5; mid-June–Aug., daily 10–6; early Sept., daily 10–5; mid-Sept.–Dec., Mon.–Sat. 11–3, Sun. 11–4.*

7 **Oslo Domkirke** (Oslo Cathedral). Consecrated in 1697 and subsequently much renovated, this staid cathedral is modest compared to those of other European capitals, but the interior is rich with treasures, such as the Baroque carved wooden altarpiece and pulpit. The ceiling frescoes by Hugo Lous Mohr were done after World War II. Behind the cathedral is an area of arcades, small restaurants, and street musicians. ✉ *Stortorvet 1.* ⏲ *Weekdays 10–4.*

17 **Oslo Ladegård** (The Manor). Now owned by the city council, this museum has scale models of old Oslo on the site of the 13th-century Bispegård (Bishop's Palace). ✉ *St. Hallvards Plass, Oslogt. 13,* ☎ *22194468.* ⏲ *May–Sept.; guided tours Wed. at 6 and Sun. at 1, and on request; book in advance.*

11 **Rådhuset** (City Hall). The impressive redbrick city hall stands on the waterfront. Designed by architects Arnstein Arnesen and Magnus Paulsson it opened officially on May 5, 1950. Friezes in the courtyard depict scenes from Norwegian folklore, but the exterior is dull compared to the marble-floored inside halls, where murals and frescoes bursting with color depict daily life, historical events, and Resistance activities in Norway. The elegant main hall has been the venue for the Nobel Peace Prize Ceremony since 1991. ✉ *Rådhuspl.,* ☎ *22861600.* 🎫 *Free.* ⏲ *May–Aug., Mon.–Sat. 9–5, Sun. noon–4; Sept.–Apr., Mon.–Sat. 9–3:30. Tours weekdays 10, noon, and 2.*

★ 1 **Slottet** (Royal Palace). This neoclassical structure, completed in 1848, is as sober, sturdy, and unpretentious as the Norwegian character. The surrounding park is open to the public, though the palace is not. The changing of the guard takes place daily at 1:30. When the king is in residence—signaled by a red flag—the Royal Guard strikes up the band. ✉ *Drammensvn. 1,* ☎ *22048700.*

6 **Stortinget** (Parliament). Built in 1866 by Swedish architect Emil Langelot, this bow-front, yellow-brick building stretched across the block is open to visitors by request when Parliament is not in session. A guide will take you around the frescoed interior and into the debating chamber. ✉ *Karl Johans Gt. 22,* ☎ *22313050.* 🎫 *Free.* ⏲ *Guided tours July–Aug.; public gallery, weekdays when parliament is in session.*

2 **Universitet** (University). The University's main hall, the *Aula* (hall), is decorated with murals by the Norwegian artist Edvard Munch (1863–1944). It is open only in summer and for public concerts and lectures during the rest of the year. ✉ *Karl Johans Gt. 47.* ⏲ *Last wk of June–mid-Aug., weekdays 10–2:45.*

★ 19 **Vigelandsparken** (Frogner Park/Vigeland's Park). Gustav Vigeland's sculptures *Wheel of Life,* a circle in stone depicting the stages of human life, and *The Monolith,* nearly 50 ft high and covered with more than 100 linked human forms, are the focal point of Vigelandsparken, in northwest Oslo, which is filled with Vigeland's works. The park contains 192 sculptures with a total of 650 figures. Open-air restaurants, tennis courts, and swimming pools provide additional diversions. ✉ *Kirkevn. and Middelthunsgt.; Trikk 12 or 15 or T-bane trains 1, 2, 3, 4, 5, or 8 to Majorstuen.*

★ 13 **Vikingskiphuset** (Viking Ship Museum). Three remarkably intact 9th-century ships last used by Vikings on the shores of the Oslofjord as royal burial chambers are the treasures of this cathedral-like museum. Also on display are riches that accompanied the royal bodies on their last voyage. The ornate craftsmanship evident in the ships and jewelry dispels any notion that the Vikings were skilled only in looting and pillaging. ✉ *Huk aveny 35.* ⏲ *Nov.–Mar., daily 11–3; Apr. and Oct., daily 11–4; May–Aug., daily 9–6; Sept., daily 11–5.*

Elsewhere in Oslo

20 At 203 ft above ground level, Holmenkollen's **Holmenkollbakken** (Holmenkollen Ski Museum and Ski Jump) is one of the world's highest jumps and the site of an international contest each March. Carved into the rock at the base is the Ski Museum. The ½-hour train ride from downtown Oslo out to the jump sweeps from underground up to 1,322 ft above sea level. ✉ *Kongevn. 5, Holmenkollen; Frognerseter/Holmenkollen T-bane train from Nationaltheatret, to Holmenkollen; walk uphill to the jump;* ☎ *22/923200.*

Dining and Lodging

Oslo's chefs are gaining recognition worldwide. Norwegian cuisine, based on products from the country's waters and farmland, is now firmly in the culinary melting pot. Menus change daily, weekly, or according to the season in many Oslo restaurants. For details and price-category information *see* Dining *in* Norway A to Z, *above.*

Lodging in the capital is expensive. Prices for downtown accommodations are high, even for B&Bs, although just about all hotels have weekend, holiday, and summer rates (25%–50% reductions). Taxes and service charges, unless otherwise noted, are included. Breakfast is usually included also, but be sure to ask before booking your room. If you arrive and need a hotel the same day, ask about last-minute prices, which are generally discounted. The helpful accommodations bureau of the **Norway Information Center** (☞ Visitor Information *in* Oslo Essentials, *below*) in Oslo's Sentralstasjonen (Oslo S or Central Station) can help you find a room; apply in person and pay a fee of NKr 20. If you are planning your trip from home, call **ScanAm** (in the U.S., ☎ 201/835–7070 or 800/545–2204) and ask about the Oslo Package, which combines an Oslo Card (☞ Getting Around *in* Oslo Essentials, *below*) with discounted room rates for almost all of Oslo's better hotels. For details and price-category information, *see* Lodging *in* Norway A to Z, *above.*

$$$$ ★ ✕ **Bagatelle.** Bagatelle was the first restaurant with a Norwegian chef serving Norwegian food to receive international recognition. Choose the seven-course menu for the full range of chef Hellstrøm's talents. The chairs are comfortable, service is impeccable, and Norwegian contemporary art adorns the walls. ✉ *Bygdøy allé 3,* ☎ *22446397. AE, DC, MC, V. Closed Sun. No lunch.*

$$$$ ★ ✕ **D'Artagnan.** Stellar French-inspired food and excellent service make this a place to remember. Try chef Freddie Nielsen's copious Grand Menu if you're famished. Otherwise, try the beef; you can literally cut it with a fork. A Touch of France (☎ 22425697, $$), downstairs from D'Artagnan, is a French-style brasserie run by the same chef. The bouillabaisse is outstanding. ✉ *Øvre Slottsgt. 16,* ☎ *22415062. Reservations essential. AE, DC, MC, V.*

$$$$ ★ ✕ **De Fem Stuer.** Chef Frank Halvorsen prepares food that is even better than the view from this restaurant near the Holmenkollen ski jump. Modern versions of Norwegian classics focus on fish and game. ✉ *Holmenkollen Park Hotel, Kongevn. 26,* ☎ *22922734. AE, DC, MC, V.*

$$$$ ✕ **Feinschmecker.** In the fashionable Frogner area, only minutes from the center of town, this restaurant specializes in modern Scandinavian cuisine. ✉ *Balchensgt. 5,* ☎ *22441777. Reservations essential. AE, DC, MC, V. Closed Sun.*

$$$ ✕ **Babette's Gjestehus.** This intimate restaurant has an international menu with a French accent. ✉ *Rådhuspassasjen,* ☎ *22416464. Reservations essential. AE, DC, MC, V. Closed Sun. No lunch.*

$$$ ★ ✕ **Theatercafeen.** One of the last Viennese-style cafés in northern Europe, this is a favorite with the literary and entertainment crowd. The pastry chef here also makes desserts for Norway's royal family. ✉ *Hotel Continental, Stortingsgt. 24/26,* ☎ *22824050. AE, DC, MC, V.*

$$ ✕ **Det Gamle Raadhus.** The "old city hall," Oslo's oldest restaurant, is in a building that dates from 1641. Specialties include seafood casserole. ✉ *Nedre Slottsgt. 1,* ☎ *22420107. AE, DC, MC, V. Closed Sun.*

$$ ★ ✕ **Dinner.** Though its name does not identify the restaurant as specializing in Szechuan-style cuisine, this is the best place for Chinese food, both hot and not so pungent. The mango pudding dessert is wonderful. ✉ *Stortingsgt. 22,* ☎ *22426890. AE, DC, MC, V. No lunch.*

$$ ✕ **Frognerseteren.** This restaurant specializing in fish and reindeer looks down on the city from just above the Holmenkollen ski jump. The upstairs room has the same view as the more expensive panorama veranda, and there is an outdoor café. ✉ *Holmenkollenvn. 200,* ☎ *22140550. DC, MC, V.*

$$ ✕ **Kastanjen.** The short menu at this stylish neighborhood bistro changes often and offers all seasonal ingredients. The three-course prix-fixe dinner is an excellent value. ✉ *Bygdøy allé 18,* ☎ *22434467. AE, DC, MC, V. Closed Sun. and 2 wks in July.*

$ ✕ **Lofotstua.** This rustic fish restaurant has a cozy atmosphere and good food. Typical specialties include fresh cod and seafood from the Lofoten Islands in northern Norway. ✉ *Kirkevn. 40,* ☎ *22469396. AE, DC, MC, V. Closed Sat. and July.*

$ ✕ **Vegeta.** The all-you-can-eat specials at this vegetarian spot are a great value. The restaurant is next to the Nationaltheatret bus and trikk station. ✉ *Munkedamsvn. 3B,* ☎ *22834020. Reservations not accepted. AE, DC, V.*

$$$$ ★ 🏨 **Grand Hotel.** It's hard to beat the Grand's site on Oslo's main street, opposite Parliament. The hotel has comforts and history to match its name. Palmen, just off the lobby, is where Oslo matrons sip afternoon tea. ✉ *Karl Johans Gt. 31, 0159,* ☎ *22429390,* FAX *22421225. 287 rooms, 50 suites. 3 restaurants, indoor pool. AE, DC, MC, V.*

$$$$ ★ 🏨 **Holmenkollen Park Rica.** The imposing building in the old romantic folkloric style stands near the ski jump in Holmenkollen. The rooms are bright, and most have balconies with excellent views of the city and the fjord. ✉ *Kongevn. 26, 0390,* ☎ *22922000,* FAX *22141692. 221 rooms. 2 restaurants, indoor pool. AE, DC, MC, V.*

$$$$ ★ 🏨 **Hotel Continental.** The Brockmann family, owners since 1900, have succeeded in combining the rich elegance of the turn of the century with modern, comfortable living. Antique furniture and shiny white porcelain fixtures add a distinctive touch to the impeccably decorated rooms. ✉ *Stortingsgt. 24–26, 0161,* ☎ *22824000,* FAX *22429689. 159 rooms, 19 suites. 3 restaurants. AE, DC, MC, V.*

$$$$ 🏨 **Radisson SAS Scandinavia Hotel.** The SAS, across from the Royal Palace, is a comfortable business hotel with impeccable service, including an airport bus that stops right outside. The rooftop lunch bar, Summit 21, has views of the entire city. ✉ *Holbergs Gt. 30, 0166,* ☎ *22113000,* FAX *22113017. 491 rooms, 3 suites. 2 restaurants, indoor pool. AE, DC, MC, V.*

$$$ 🏨 **Bondeheimen.** Established to provide "down-home" accommodations for farmers on business in the big city, this may be Oslo's most Norwegian hotel. The rooms are simple and comfortable. ✉ *Rosenkrantz' Gt. 8, 0159,* ☎ *22429530,* FAX *22419437. 81 rooms. Restaurant. AE, DC, MC, V.*

$$$ 🏨 **Radisson SAS Park Royal Hotel.** Fifteen minutes from Oslo's center, this hotel is clean, efficient, and convenient to Fornebu Airport. The top-class facilities, including direct airport check-in, are well suited to business stays. ✉ *Fornebuparken, Box 1324, 1324 Lysaker,* ☎ *67120220,* FAX *67120011. 254 rooms, 14 suites. Restaurant. AE, DC, MC, V.*

$$ ★ 🏨 **Ambassadeur.** On a quaint residential street, this hotel has individually designed rooms and personalized service. ✉ *Camilla Colletts vei 15, 0266,* ☎ *22441835,* FAX *22444791. 41 rooms, 8 suites. Indoor pool. AE, DC, MC, V.*

$$ 🏨 **Rainbow Cecil Tulip Hotel.** Known for its copious breakfast table, this hotel is right in the heart of town near the Parliament building. ✉ *Stortingsgt. 8, 0130,* ☎ *22427000,* FAX *22422670. 112 rooms. AE, DC, MC, V.*

$$ 🏨 **Stefan.** The service is cheerful and accommodating in this hotel in the center of Oslo. One of its main attractions is the popular restaurant on the top floor, where Oslo's best buffet lunch, featuring traditional Norwegian dishes, is served. ✉ *Rosenkrantz' Gt. 1, 0159,* ☎ *22429250,* FAX *22337022. 138 rooms. Restaurant. AE, DC, MC, V.*

$ 🏨 **Gabelshus Hotel.** Only five minutes from the center of town on an attractive side street in Frogner, Gabelshus has the feel of a large country house. The rooms are spacious and airy. ✉ *Gabels Gt. 16, 0272,* ☎ *22552260,* FAX *22442730. 43 rooms. Restaurant. AE, DC, MC, V.*

$ 🏨 **Munch.** This B&B, near the National Gallery, is a five-minute walk from the city center. The rooms are large but basic. ✉ *Munchsgt. 5, 0165,* ☎ *22424275,* FAX *22206469. 180 rooms. AE, DC, MC, V.*

$ 🏨 **Oslo Vandrerhjem Haraldsheim.** Oslo's youth hostel is one of Europe's largest. Most rooms have four beds; those in the new wing all have showers. Breakfast is included. ✉ *Haraldsheimvn. 4, 0409; Trikk 10 or 11 to Sinsen;* ☎ *22222965,* FAX *22221025. 270 beds. V.*

$ 🏨 **Rainbow Gyldenløve.** Freshly decorated rooms are offered here at a reasonable price. Just outside are many shops and cafés. ✉ *Bogstadvn. 20, 0355,* ☎ *22601090,* FAX *22603390. 168 rooms. AE, DC, MC, V.*

Nightlife and the Arts

The Arts

Considering the city's small population, Oslo has a surprisingly rich arts scene. Check the monthly "What's On in Oslo," available at the Tourist Information Center (☞ Visitor Information *in* Oslo Essentials, *below*).

FILM

All films are screened in the original language with Norwegian subtitles. Oslo has one of Europe's best cinema collections, with 30 screens; call ☎ 82030000 for schedules for: **Coloseum** (✉ Fr. Nansensv. 6, Majorstua); **Eldorado** (✉ Torggt.9); **Felix** (✉ Bryggetorget, Akerbrygge); **Saga** (✉ Stortingsgt. 28); **Klingenberg** (✉ Olav V'sgt. 4). For alternative and classic films, try **Cinemateket** (✉ Dronningensgt. 16, ☎ 22474505), the city's only independent cinema.

MUSIC

Oslo's modern **Konserthuset** (✉ Munkedamsvn. 14, ☎ 22833200) is the home of the Oslo Philharmonic. A smaller hall in the same building has folk dancing, held Monday and Thursday at 9 in July and August. At **Den Norske Opera** (The Norwegian Opera House; ✉ Storgt. 23, ☎ 22429475), performances usually start at 7:30; it's closed in July and August. **Cosmopolite Club** (✉ Industrigaten 36, ☎ 22690198) has international acts regularly, ranging from folk to jazz. **Rockefeller Music Hall** (✉ Torggt. 16, ☎ 22203232) has concerts featuring well-known pop and rock acts. **Oslo Spektrum** (✉ Sonja Henies plass 2, ☎ 22178050) is a large indoor show and concert venue.

THEATER

Winter is *the* cultural season, when the **Nationaltheatret** (National Theater; ☞ Exploring Oslo, *above*) presents modern plays (all in Norwegian), classics, and a good sampling of Ibsen. **Det Norske Teatret** (The Norwegian Theater; ✉ Kristian IV's Gt. 8, ☎ 22424344), one of Europe's most modern theater complexes, has musicals and plays (all in Norwegian).

Nightlife

NIGHTCLUBS AND BARS

Karl Johans Gate is a lively and drunken place into the wee hours, with loads of music cafés and clubs, as well as more conventional nightspots. **Barock-Restauranthuset** (✉ Universitetsgt. 26, ☎ 22424420), complete with elegant chandeliers and blaring techno pop, is where Oslo's young and beautiful people choose to dance. **Smuget** (✉ Rosenkrantz' Gt. 22, ☎ 22425262) is a combination discotheque and bar with live rock and blues bands almost every night of the week. **Lipp** (✉ Olav V's Gt. 2, ☎ 22414400), a popular pre-dinner drinks bar (for people over 24), also has a restaurant with an international kitchen. Media people and students hang out at **Kristiania** (✉ Kristian IV's Gt. 12, ☎ 22425660), a three-story disco with live music sessions on the third floor. **Baronen og Baronessen** (✉ Stortingsgt. 10, ☎ 22420470), a combination discotheque, piano bar, and restaurant, is one of the few places serving food until 4 AM. Students frequent the informal and intimate **Ett Glass** (✉ Karl Johansgt. 23, ☎ 22334079) café.

Outdoor Activities and Sports

The forests within Oslo's vast city limits include 11 sports chalets geared toward exercise and the outdoors. The areas around **Skullerudstua** and **Skistua** have outstanding walking and skiing trails. Small passenger ferries run between Vippetangen and the islands that dot Oslo fjord, including **Hovedøya,** which has the ruins of a medieval monastery and swimming possibilities. On Bygdøy you will find **Huk,** the area's most popular beach. Contact **Oslo Kommune** (✉ Forestry Services, Skogvesenet, ☎ 22082200) for more information. For winter or summer "safaris" through the forest by Land Rover, contact the **Norway Information Center** (☞ Visitor Information *in* Oslo Essentials, *below*).

Shopping

Many of the larger stores are in the pedestrian-only areas between Stortinget and the cathedral. Shops stay open until 5 or 6 on weekdays, 2 or 3 on Saturday, and 7 or 8 on Thursday. Stores hold extended hours the first Saturday of the month, known as "Super Saturday." The **Basarhallene** (✉ at back of the cathedral) is an art and handicrafts boutique center just around the corner from the many outdoor vendors and shops that line the pedestrian part of Karl Johans Gate. One of Oslo's newest shopping areas, **Aker Brygge** (✉ waterfront), a complex of booths, offices, and sidewalk cafés, is especially lively in summer and spring. Check out the many shops and galleries on **Bogstadveien/Hegdehaugsveien** (✉ runs from Majorstua to Parkveien).

Department Stores and Malls

Glasmagasinet (✉ Stortorvet 9, ☎ 22908900; ⏲ weekdays 10–7, Sat. 10–6) has a large assortment of wares in 50 different stores, including souvenirs and silver and pewter jewelry. **Paléet** (✉ Karl Johans Gt., ☎ 22417086; ⏲ weekdays 10–8, Sat. 10–5) is an elegant indoor shopping center with 45 shops and 13 restaurants. Oslo's largest shopping mall, **Oslo City** (✉ opposite Sentralstasjonen/Central Station, ☎ 22938050; ⏲ weekdays 9–9, Sat. 9–7) has more than 100 stores and businesses including a bank, a travel agency, and a grocery store on the lower level. **Steen & Strøm** (✉ Kongengsgt. 23, ☎ 22004000; ⏲ weekdays 10–7, Sat. 10–6) is an exclusive department store with six floors and 58 different shops plus a cafeteria. **Gunerius** (✉ Storgt.32, ☎ 22170571; ⏲ weekdays 9–7, Sat. 9–6) has 21 shops, including a big low-price grocery store in the cellar and a restaurant.

Flea Markets

Every Saturday during spring, summer, and fall, there is a flea market at **Vestkanttorget** (✉ two blocks east of Frogner Park, junction of Professor Dahls Gt. and Eckerbergs Gt.) Check the papers for local *loppemarkeder* (flea markets) in schools and outdoor squares around town.

Side Trips

Høvikodden

Just outside Oslo is the **Henie-Onstad Kunstsenter** (Henie-Onstad Art Center), which displays an impressive collection of important works by Leger, Munch, Picasso, Bonnard, and Matisse. The center was a gift from the Norwegian Olympic skater Sonja Henie and her husband, shipowner Niels Onstad. ✉ *About 12 km (7 mi) southwest of Oslo on E18,* ☎ *67543050.* ⏲ *Mon. 9–5, Tues.–Fri. 9–9, weekends 11–9.*

Vinterbro

Tusenfryd is Norway's largest amusement park, with more than 50 attractions, including carousels, a roller coaster, games, an outdoor stage, shops, and restaurants. Don't miss **Vikingelandet** (Viking Land), which re-creates life during the time of the Vikings, with trading centers, boat building, a blacksmith, jewelry making, and farm animals. One of the "Vikings" will also help you try your talent as an archer, or you can join "Leif Eriksson" on an expedition in the depths of a mountain cave. ✉ *1433 Vinterbro, about 20 km (12 mi) southeast of Oslo on E18,* ☎ *64946363.* ⏲ *Tusenfryd: May–early June and mid-Aug.–mid-Sept., weekends 10:30–7; June 6–mid-Aug., daily 10:30–7. Vikingelandet: 2 wks in mid-June, weekdays 10:30–3, weekends 1–7; last wk in June–mid-Aug., daily 1–7.*

Lillehammer

At the top of the long finger of Lake Mjøsa, Lillehammer is reached by train from the Sentralstasjonen (Central Station) in about two hours. A paddle steamer, D/S *Skibladner,* travels the length of the lake (six hours each way) in summer, making several stops. At the site of the 1994 Winter Olympics, Lillehammer's **Hunderfossen,** the Olympic bobsled track (✉ about 5 km/3 mi north of town) is open for runs. You can book at the **Lillehammer Tourist Office** (✉ Lilletorget, ☎ 61259299). Lillehammer is also home of **Maihaugen** (✉ Maihaugvn. 1, ☎ 61288900), one of the largest open-air museums in northern Europe. More than 100 old buildings have been relocated here, along with workshop interiors, antique tools, and the like.

Oslo Essentials

Arriving and Departing

BY PLANE

Gardermoen Airport (✉ 37 km/23 mi north of Oslo), is Oslo's main airport.

Between the Airport and Downtown. Taxis between downtown and Gardermoen cost between Nkr 700 and Nkr 800. **Flybussen** (airport bus; ☎ 67/596220) takes about 40 minutes from Galleri Oslo shopping center, stopping at Jernbanetorget (Central Station); fare is Nkr 80. The high-speed **Airport Express Train** carries passengers from Central Station to Gardermoen in just 19 minutes; fares run about Nkr 150.

BY TRAIN

Trains on international or domestic long-distance and express routes arrive at Oslo's **Sentralstasjon** (Oslo S or Central Station; ⊠ east of Strandgt.). Suburban trains depart from the Sentralstasjon, Stortinget, and the Nationaltheatret stations.

Getting Around

BY PUBLIC TRANSPORTATION

Oslo Kortet (the Oslo Card)—valid for one, two, or three days—entitles you to free entrance to museums, public swimming pools, and the racetrack; unlimited travel on the Oslo transport system and Norwegian Railways commuter trains within the city limits; free parking on the street and in some lots; and discounts at various stores, cinemas, and sports centers. You can get the card at Oslo's tourist information offices and hotels (☞ Visitor Information, *below*). A one-day card costs Nkr 150; two-day, Nkr 220; three-day, Nkr 250.

If you're using public transportation only occasionally, you can get tickets (Nkr 18) at bus and subway (T-bane) stops. For Nkr 40, the **Tourist Kort** (Tourist Ticket) gives 24 hours' unlimited travel on all public transportation, including the summer ferries to Bygdøy, Hovedøya, Langøya, and Gressholmen. The **Flexikort** gives you eight subway, bus, or trikk rides for Nkr 100, including transfers.

BY TAXI

Taxis can be hailed on the street when the roof light is on, found at taxi stands, or ordered by phone (☎ 22388090), though during peak hours you may have to wait.

Contacts and Resources

EMBASSIES AND CONSULATE

United States (⊠ Drammensvn. 18, ☎ 22448550). **Canadian** (⊠ Oscarsgt. 20, ☎ 22466955). **United Kingdom** (⊠ Thos. Heftyesgt. 8, ☎ 23132700). **Australian Consulate** (⊠ Jernbanetorget 2, 0106 Oslo, ☎ 22414433.

EMERGENCIES

Police (☎ 112 or 22669050). **Ambulance** (☎ 113 or 94208000). **Dentist** (☎ 22176566). **Emergency Clinic: Oslo Legevakt** (☎ 22118080). **Pharmacy: Jernbanetorgets Apotek** (☎ 22412482; ⏲ 24 hrs).

ENGLISH-LANGUAGE BOOKSTORES

Tanum Libris (⊠ Karl Johans Gt. 37–41, ☎ 22411100). **Erik Qvist** (⊠ Drammensvn. 16, ☎ 22542600, near U.S. Embassy).

GUIDED TOURS

Forest. The Norway Information Center (☎ 22/830050; ☞ Visitor Information, *below*) can arrange four- to eight-hour motor safaris through the forests surrounding Oslo.

Orientation. HMK Sightseeing (⊠ Hegdehaugsvn. 4, ☎ 22/208206) offers several bus tours in and around Oslo. **Båtservice Sightseeing** (⊠ Rådhusbryggen 3, ☎ 22/200715) has a bus tour, five cruises, and one combination tour.

Personal Guides. The Norway Information Center can provide an authorized city guide for your own private tour. **OsloTaxi** (⊠ Trondheimsvn. 100, ☎ 22388070) also gives private tours.

Sleigh Rides. You can ride an old-fashioned sleigh or a horse through Oslomarka, the woods surrounding the city, through **Vangen Skistue** (✉ Laila and Jon Hamre, Fjell, 1404 Siggerud, ☎ 64/865481).

Street Train. Starting at noon and continuing at 45-minute intervals until 10 PM, the **Oslo Train,** which looks like a chain of dune buggies, leaves Aker Brygge for a 30-minute ride around the town center. Ask at the Norway Information Center (☞ Visitor Information, *below*).

POST OFFICE

The **Oslo Hoved Post Kontor** (Oslo Main Post Office; ✉ Dronningensgate 15) is open weekdays 8–6, Saturday 10–3.

TRAVEL AGENCIES

Winge (American Express, ✉ Karl Johans Gt. 33/35, ☎ 22004500). **Bennett** (✉ Linstowsgt. 6, ☎ 22697100). **NSB Reisebyr AS** (✉ Storgt. 10 b, ☎ 23151550).

VISITOR INFORMATION

Nortra (Norwegian Travel Association; ✉ Drammensveien 40, Postboks 2893, Sentrum, 0230 Oslo, ☎ 22925200). **Norway Information Center** (✉ Vestbanepl. 1; Sentralstasjon/Central Station, east of Strandgt., ☎ 22830050). For information on public transportation call **Trafikanten** (✉ Oslo Sentralstasjonen/Central Station, east of Strandgt., ☎ 22177030 or 177).

THE COAST ROAD TO STAVANGER

Route E18 parallels the Sørlandet coast south of Oslo toward the busy port of Kristiansand. Beyond the city, the coast curves west and north to Stavanger. After Flekkefjord, follow the coast road (Route 44) past the fishing port of Egersund to Ogna, and then on to Stavanger. Sørlandet is an area where whaling has given way to canneries, lumber, paper production, and petrochemicals. Yet the beauty of this 608-km (380-mi) route remains, and you'll find seaside towns, rocky headlands, and stretches of forest (fjord country does not begin until north of Stavanger). Travel between towns takes less than an hour in most cases. South of Stavanger is flat and stony Jæren, the largest expanse of level terrain in this mountainous country. The mild climate and the absence of good harbors caused the people here to turn to agriculture, and the miles of stone walls are a testament to their labor. It is also possible to reach Stavanger on an inland route through Telemark.

Drammen

Drammen lies on the shore of the wide Drammen River, 45 km (28 mi) long, and popular for its salmon and trout fishing. The river was the city's main street during the centuries when the production of wood products (paper and cellulose) were the chief industries in Drammen. From May 10 through August you can join a five-hour guided tour aboard the 114-year-old sailing ship ***Christiane,*** which sails south from Drammen to the attractive little village of Holmsbu.

The center of Drammen has a great variety of shops and restaurants. **Bragernes Torg** is home to a sizable farmer's market. This large square is lined by several buildings dating from just after 1866, when a huge fire devastated the entire district. **Drammen Theater,** also built after the great fire, has an impressive collection of ceiling paintings and crystal chandeliers. Designed by Emil Langlet, it was completed in 1870.

$$ ✕ **Spiraltoppen Café.** You'll find excellent views and food here atop Bragernes Hill. ✉ *Bragernesåsen,* ☎ *32837815. Reservations not accepted. AE, DC, MC, V.*

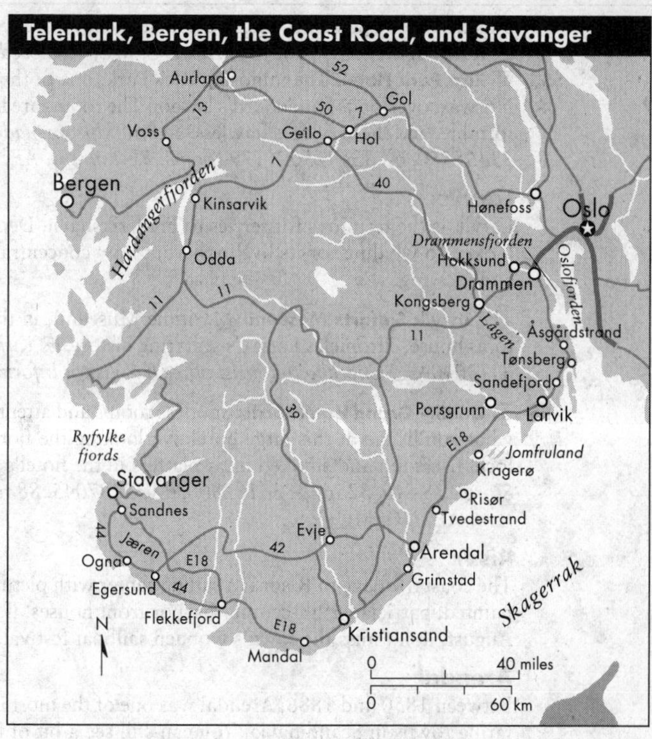

$$ 🏨 **Rica Park Hotel.** This comfortable and central hotel has traditional Norwegian decor. ✉ *Gamle Kirkepl. 3, 3019,* ☎ *32838280,* FAX *32893207. 96 rooms, 2 suites. 2 restaurants. AE, DC, MC, V.*

Åsgårdstrand

Edvard Munch painted many of his best works in Åsgårdstrand, where he spent seven summers in a small yellow frame house. **Munchs lille hus** is open to visitors during the summer. ✉ *Munchsgt.,* ☎ *33/031708.*

Tønsberg

Tønsberg is Norway's oldest town, founded in 871 during the Viking Age, or possibly earlier; it is the site of the Oseberg Viking ship, discovered in 1903. Shipping, commerce, and culture prospered in Tønsberg from the Viking Age until the rise of Oslo as Norway's capital during the 14th century. Later, Tønsberg had a resurgence as a thriving whaling port during the 1700s. Today, on the steep **Slottsfjellet** (Castle Hill; ✉ next to Tønsberg train station), the ruins of **Tønsberghus,** an extensive fortress and abbey, evokes the Middle Ages, when Tønsberg was the administrative center for the Norwegian kings. A model of Tønsberghus stands in the lookout tower, finished in 1888 to commemorate the town's millennium. The tower also affords a panoramic view of Oslo fjord and the surrounding mountains.

Sandefjord

Attractive Sandefjord is a port that served as the base for the Norwegian whaling fleet until after World War II, when large-scale competition from the Soviet Union and Japan made the operation uneconomical. The port remains a busy depot for timber shipping.

$$–$$$ ✕ **Ludl's Gourmet Odd Ivar Solberg.** Chef Solberg has taken over chef
★ Ludl's duties preparing fish specialties in one of the best restaurants

outside Oslo. The eight- and five-course menus are excellent choices. ✉ *Rådhusgt. 7,* ☎ *33462741. AE, DC, MC, V. Closed Sun.*

$$$ ★ **Rica Park Hotel.** The imposing Rica Park, one of the best hotels in Norway, overlooks Sandefjord's harbor. The rooms are large and comfortable, and the service is flawless. ✉ *Strandpromenaden 9, 3200,* ☎ *33465550,* FAX *33447500. 179 rooms. Restaurant. AE, DC, MC, V.*

Larvik

Larvik is the terminus for ferries to Frederikshavn, Denmark. It once looked to whaling for its livelihood but now concentrates on lumber and ferrying.

The **Larvik Sjøfarts Museum** (Maritime Museum), in the former customs house, chronicles Larvik's seafaring history. ✉ *Kirkestredet 5,* ☎ *33130404.* ⏲ *Check with tourist office (*☞ *Visitor Information, below**).*

$$ **Quality Grand Hotel Farris.** Spotless rooms and attentive service are what you'll find at this large hotel overlooking the fjord. Sample the local fish soup and smoked meat platters in the hotel's restaurant. ✉ *Storgt. 38–40, 3256,* ☎ *33187800,* FAX *33187045. 88 rooms. Restaurant. AE, DC, MC, V.*

Risør

The coastal village of Risør is a sailing center with picturesque, white-painted, patrician 19th-century harbor-front houses. If you're here in August, don't miss the town's wooden sailboat festival.

Arendal

Between 1850 and 1886, Arendal was one of the most important seafaring towns in Scandinavia. You can still see a bit of that era in the tidy cottages and grandiose captains' houses all within shouting distance of the docks. Explore Arendal's **Tyholmen quarter,** the oldest part of the town, for a glimpse into this 19th-century world.

Arendals Rådhus (Arendal's City Hall) was created by the Danish architect Peder Krog Bonsach Jessen and constructed between 1812 and 1815. Originally built as a private home for one of Arendal's wealthy ship owners, it was converted to City Hall in 1844.

$$ ✕ **Madam Reiersen.** Good, traditional Norwegian food is served at this informal waterfront restaurant. ✉ *Nedre Tyholmsvn. 3,* ☎ *37021900. Reservations essential on weekends. AE, DC, MC, V.*

$$$$ **Clarion Tyholmen Hotel.** This maritime hotel is in the heart of the old town, which is filled with well-preserved, brightly painted houses. The views of the fjord are splendid. ✉ *Teaterpl. 2, 4801,* ☎ *37026800,* FAX *37026801. 60 rooms. 2 restaurants. AE, DC, MC, V.*

Kristiansand

The largest town in Sørlandet, Kristiansand has important air, sea, road, and rail links. It was laid out during the 17th century in a grid pattern, with the imposing **Christiansholm Festning** (fort) guarding the eastern harbor approach.

The open-air **Vest-Agder Fylkesmuseum** (county museum) has 30 old buildings and farms rebuilt in the local style of the 18th and 19th centuries. ✉ *Kongsgård; Rte. E18, east of Kristiansand;* ☎ *38090228.* ⏲ *Sept.–mid-June, Sun. noon–5 or by appointment.*

Kristiansand Cannon Museum has the last remaining 38-cm caliber cannon in the world. The huge cannon installations were built by the Germans during World War II. ✉ *South of town, off E 39,* ☎ *38085090.* ⏲ *May–Oct., Thurs.–Sun. 11–6; mid-June–Aug., daily 11–6.*

Children love the **Kristiansand Dyrepark** (Kristiansand Zoo), with five separate parks, including a water park, a forested park, an entertainment park, and a zoo. There's also **Kardemomme By** (Cardamom Town), a replicated village. ✉ *4609 Kardemomme By,* ☎ *38049700.* *NKr 175.* *Jan.–mid-June and mid-Aug.–Dec., daily 10–3; mid-June–mid-Aug., daily 9–6.*

$$ ✕ **Sjøhuset.** Seafood and fish are the best bets in this rustic waterfront restaurant. ✉ *Østre Strandgt. 12a,* ☎ *38026260. Reservations not accepted. AE, DC, MC, V.*

$$$ **Rica Travel Hotel.** Only a stone's throw from the town hall and cathedral, this hotel is also close to the harbor beach. Breakfast and evening buffet are included. ✉ *Dronningens Gt. 66, 4602,* ☎ *38021500,* FAX *38020119. 47 rooms. Restaurant. AE, DC, MC, V.*

Mandal

Norway's most southerly town is famous for its beach, salmon, and 18th- and 19th-century houses. Every year, seafood lovers flock here for the shellfish festival the second weekend in August.

Flekkefjord

The road climbs and weaves its way through steep, wooded hills before descending to the fishing port of Flekkefjord, with its charming **Hollenderbyen,** or Dutch Quarter.

Ogna

Ogna is known for the stretch of beautiful and unspoiled sandy beach that has inspired so many Norwegian artists, among them Kitty Kjelland.

★ Stavanger

Stavanger is a former trading town that became a focus (some environmentalists say victim) of the oil boom. It is now the fourth-largest city in Norway. Drilling platforms and oil tankers take the place of fishing boats in the harbor. In sharp contrast to the new high-rise complexes, there is an old quarter with narrow, cobbled lanes and clapboard houses at odd angles. The town is believed to date from the 8th century.

Stavanger's Anglo-Norman **Domkirke** (cathedral), next to the central market, was established in 1125 by the English bishop of Winchester. Norway and England had strong trading and ecclesiastical links throughout the Middle Ages. ✉ *City center, next to pond, Breiavatnet.*

Ledaal is a fine patrician mansion where the royal family resides when visiting Stavanger. ✉ *Eiganesvn. 45,* ☎ *51520618.* *Mid-June–mid-Aug., daily 11–4; mid-Aug.–mid-June, Sun. 11–4.*

Breidablikk manor house (designed by the architect Henrik Nissen) was built by a Norwegian shipping magnate between 1881 and 1882. An outstanding example of Norwegian "Swiss style" architecture, it has been perfectly preserved. ✉ *Eiganesvn. 40A,* ☎ *51523115.* *Mid-June–mid-Aug., daily 11–4; mid-Aug.–mid-June, Sun. 11–4.*

Ullandhaug is a reconstructed Iron Age farm. ✉ *Grannesvn., Ullandhaug,* ☎ *51534140.* *Mid-June–Aug., daily 11–4; early May–mid-June and Sept., Sun. noon–4.*

The **Norsk Hermetikkmuseum** (Canning Museum) in the heart of Old Stavanger is a reconstructed sardine factory that was in use between 1890 and 1920. ✉ *Øvre Strandgt. 88A,* ☎ *51534989.*

The **Utvanndrings Sentre** (Norwegian Emigration Center) specializes in genealogy and family research, helping to bridge the gap between

Norway and the families of emigrants. ✉ *Nedre Strandgt. 31,* ☎ *51538860,* FAX *51538863.* ⏲ *Weekdays 9–3.*

The **Ryfylke fjords** north and east of Stavanger form the southern end of the fjord country. The city is a good base for exploring this region, with the "white fleet" of low-slung sea buses making daily excursions into even the most distant fjords of Ryfylke. Great for a heart-stopping view is Prekestolen (Pulpit Rock), a huge cube of rock with a vertical drop of 2,000 ft. You can join a tour to get here or you can do it on your own from mid-June to late August by taking the ferry from Fiskepiren across Hildefjorden to Tau, riding a bus to the Pulpit Rock Lodge, and walking 1½–2 hours to the rock.

$$$ **Comfort Hotel Grand.** On the edge of the town center, this hotel doesn't aim to be fancy: Rooms are comfortable and bright, done in white and pastels. In summer the rates drop significantly. ✉ *Klubbgt. 3, 4012,* ☎ *51895800,* FAX *51895710. 92 rooms. AE, DC, MC, V.*

$$–$$$ **Skagen Brygge.** In three rehabilitated old sea houses, almost all rooms are different, from modern to old-fashioned maritime with exposed beams and brick-and-wood walls. The hotel can make reservations for you at any of 14 restaurants in the area and put the tab on your bill. ✉ *Skagenkaien 30, 4006,* ☎ *51894100,* FAX *51895883. 106 rooms. Turkish bath. AE, DC, MC, V.*

The Coast Road to Stavanger Essentials

Getting Around

BY BUS

Local buses cover the entire route, but they take much longer than the train. For details on fares and schedules, check with the tourist offices listed below or the Norway Information Center in Oslo (☞ Visitor Information *in* Oslo Essentials, *above*).

BY CAR

Driving gives you the chance to stop at coastal villages that are either not served by trains or have only sporadic service. The route is simple: E18 as far as Flekkefjord, then Route 44 to Stavanger.

BY TRAIN

The Sørland line leaves from Oslo Central Station and goes all the way to Stavanger via Kristiansand. It has five departures daily to Kristiansand; three continue to Stavanger. The Oslo–Drammen stretch is an engineering feat that includes Norway's longest tunnel, an 11-km (7-mi) bore through sheer rock.

Guided Tours

In summer a daily boat excursion sets out from Oslo southwest to the coastal resorts of Kragerø, Jomfruland, and Risør. You return the same day, and refreshments are served on board. Contact the Norway Information Center (☞ Visitor Information *in* Oslo Essentials, *above*).

Visitor Information

Arendal (✉ Friholmsgt. 1, ☎ 37022193). **Drammen** (✉ Rådhuset, ☎ 32806210). **Flekkefjord** (✉ Main St., ☎ 38321260). **Kristiansand** (✉ Dronningensgt. 2, ☎ 38026065). **Larvik** (✉ Storgt. 48, ☎ 33130100). **Mandal** (✉ Bryggetgt., ☎ 38260820). **Risør** (✉ Strandgaten, ☎ 37158560). **Stavanger** (✉ Rosenkildehuset, Rosenkildetorget 1, ☎ 51859200). **Tønsberg** (✉ Nedre Langgt. 36B, ☎ 33310220).

THROUGH TELEMARK TO BERGEN

Bergen is Norway's second-largest city. To get here from Oslo, drive west through Telemark, a region marked by steep valleys, pine forests, lakes, and fast-flowing rivers full of trout. Morgedal, the cradle of skiing, is here. At the Haukeligrend crossroads, Route 11 really begins to climb, and you'll see why the Norwegians are so proud of keeping this route open all year. Hardangervidda, a wild mountain area and national park, was the stronghold of Norway's Resistance fighters during World War II. Farther west is the beautiful Hardangerfjord. Few places on earth match western Norway—the fabled land of the fjords—for spectacular scenic beauty.

Fjord transportation is good, as crossing fjords is a necessary as well as scenic way to travel in Norway. Hardangerfjorden, Sognefjord, and Nordfjord are three of the deepest and most popular.

Kongsberg

Kongsberg, founded in 1624 next to the fast-flowing Lågen River as a silver-mining town, is one of the gateways to Telemark. Forests give way to rocky peaks and desolate spaces farther into the plateau. Although there is no more mining, the old mines at Saggrenda are open for guided tours; contact the tourist office (☞ Visitor Information, *below*). In the town center is an 18th-century rococo church, which reflects the town's former source of wealth—silver. The **Norsk Bergverksmuseum** (Norwegian Mining Museum) includes the **Silver Mines Collection,** the **Ski Museum,** and the **Royal Mint Museum.** ✉ *Hyttegt. 3,* ☎ *32733260.* ⏲ *Mid-May–mid-Aug., weekdays 10–6, weekends 10–4; mid–late Aug., daily 10–4; Sept., daily noon–4; Oct.–mid-May, Sun. noon–4. Otherwise by appointment.*

$$ ✕ **Gamle Kongsberg Kro.** Hearty Norwegian dishes are served at this café near Nybrofossen (the Nybro waterfall). ✉ *Thornesvn. 4,* ☎ *32731633. DC, MC, V.*

★ Heddal

Heddal is the first stop in Telemark. Here you'll find the **Heddal Kirke** (Heddal Church), Norway's largest stave church, built in 1147. Stave churches are built with wooden planks staked vertically into the ground or base and usually have some carved ornamentation on the doors and around the aisle. These churches date from the medieval period and are found almost exclusively in southern Norway. ☎ *35020400.*

Seljord

The attractive village of Seljord, on a lake of the same name, has ornamented wooden houses and a medieval church. The countryside by the lake is richer than that on the Telemark plateau; meadows and pastureland run down to the lakefront. Before you descend toward Seljord, you'll see the Lifjell area's highest peak, **Røydalsnuten** (4,235 ft), on the left.

Morgedal

It was here in the 19th century that Sondre Nordheim developed the Telemark method of skiing. You can get the full story of that development at **Olav Bjåland Museum** (✉ opposite Morgedal Turisthotell, ☎ 35054250), named for the south polar explorer and ski hero.

Kinsarvik

The attractive village of Kinsarvik is on the Sørfjord. For the best view of the junction of the Sørfjord and the mighty Hardangerfjord, take the ferry to Utne. On the dramatic 30-minute ferry crossing, you will come to understand why this area was such a rich source of inspiration for Romantic composer Edvard Grieg.

$$$$ ★ **Utne Hotel.** The white frame house dates from 1722, making this hotel one of the oldest in Norway. The wood-paneled, hand-painted dining room is decorated with copper pans, old china, and paintings. ✉ *5797 Utne,* ☎ *53666983,* FAX *53666950. 22 rooms with bath or shower. Restaurant. AE, DC, MC, V.*

$$$ **Best Western Kinsarvik Fjord Hotel.** This handsome hotel near the busy ferry port offers good views of Hardangerfjord and the glacier. The rooms are bright and spacious. ✉ *5780 Kinsarvik,* ☎ *53663100,* FAX *53663374. 70 rooms. Restaurant. AE, DC, MC, V.*

★ Bergen

The road descends tortuously into Bergen, the capital of the fjords and Norway's second-largest city (pop. 219,000), which is the EU's European Culture Center for the year 2000. The town was founded in 1070, and before oil brought an influx of foreigners to Stavanger, Bergen was the most international Norwegian city, having been an important trading and military center when Oslo was still an obscure village. A member of the medieval Hanseatic League, it offered an ice-free harbor and convenient trading location on the west coast. Natives of Bergen still think of Oslo as a dour provincial town.

Despite numerous fires in its past, much of medieval Bergen has survived. Seven surrounding mountains set off the weathered wooden houses, cobbled streets, and Hanseatic-era warehouses of **Bryggen** (the harbor area).

The best way to get a feel for Bergen's medieval trading heyday is to visit the **Hanseatisk Museum.** One of the oldest and best-preserved of Bergen's wooden buildings, it is furnished in 16th-century style. ✉ *Bryggen,* ☎ *55316710.* ⏲ *May–Aug., daily 10–4; Sept.–Apr., weekdays 11–3, Sat. noon–3, Sun. noon–4.*

Rosenkrantztårnet (the Rosenkrantz tower) is part of the **Bergenhus Festning** (Bergenhus Fortress), the 13th-century fortress guarding the harbor entrance. The tower and fortress were destroyed during World War II but were meticulously restored during the 1960s and are now rich with furnishings and household items from the 16th century. ✉ *Bergenhus,* ☎ *55314380.* ⏲ *Mid-May–mid-Sept., daily 10–4; mid-Sept.–mid-May, Sun. noon–3, or upon request.*

From behind Bryggen you can walk through the meandering back streets to the popular **Fløybanen** (Fløyen Funicular), which climbs a steep 1,070 ft to the top of Fløyen, one of the seven mountains guarding the city. ✉ *Øvregt..* ⏲ *May–Sept., weekdays every ½ hour 7:30 AM–11 PM, Sat. 8 AM–midnight, Sun. 9 AM–midnight.*

★ **Troldhaugen** (Troll Hill) manor on Nordås Lake, once home to Edvard Grieg, is now a museum that incorporates a new chamber-music hall. Recitals are held from late June to mid-August (Wed. and Sun. 7:30 PM, Sat. 2). ✉ *Troldhaugsvn, Hop,* ☎ *55910710.* ⏲ *Jan.–Mar., weekdays 10–2; early Apr. and Oct.–Nov., weekdays 10–2, Sat. noon–4, Sun. 10–4; mid-Apr.–Sept., daily 9–6. Closed Dec.*

$$$$ ✕ **Lucullus.** This French-inspired seafood restaurant is, appropriately enough, in the Hotel Neptun. It has an excellent wine cellar, with special emphasis on white wines to go with the fish. ✉ *Walckendorffsgt. 8,* ☎ *55901000,* FAX *55233202. AE, DC, MC, V. Closed Sun.*

$$$ ★ ✕ **Finnegaardstue.** This classic Norwegian restaurant near Bryggen has four snug, intimate rooms. Some of the timber interior dates from the 18th century. The emphasis here is on seafood, but the venison and

reindeer are outstanding. Traditional Norwegian desserts, such as cloudberries and cream, are irresistible. ✉ *Rosenkrantzgt. 6,* ☎ *55550300,* FAX *55315811. AE, DC, MC, V. Closed Sun.*

$$–$$$ ★ ✕ **Munkestuen Café.** This tiny mom-and-pop place is a hometown legend. Try the monkfish with hollandaise sauce or the fillet of roe deer with morels. Reserve a table early; they can be booked up to four weeks in advance. ✉ *Klostergt. 12,* ☎ *55902149. Reservations essential. AE, DC, MC, V. Closed weekends and 3 wks in July. No lunch.*

$$$$ **Augustin.** This small but excellent hotel in the center of town has been restored to its original late–Art Nouveau character, complete with period furniture in the lobby. ✉ *C. Sundtsgt. 22–24, 5004,* ☎ *55230025,* FAX *55304010. 82 rooms. Restaurant. AE, DC, MC, V.*

$$–$$$$ **Radisson SAS Hotel.** This hotel on the harbor is near a section of old, well-preserved warehouses and buildings. Ravaged by nine fires since 1170, the warehouses have been rebuilt each time in the same style, which SAS has incorporated into its design. ✉ *Bryggen, 5003,* ☎ *55543000,* FAX *55324808. 273 rooms. 2 restaurants. AE, DC, MC, V.*

$–$$ **Rainbow Hotel Bryggen Orion.** Facing the harbor in the center of town, the hotel is surrounded by Bergen's most famous sights. The rooms are decorated in warm, sunny colors. ✉ *Bradbenken 3, 5003,* ☎ *55318080,* FAX *55329414. 229 rooms. Restaurant. AE, DC, MC, V.*

Through Telemark to Bergen Essentials

Getting Around

BY BUS

Buses in the region rarely run more than twice a day; schedules are available at tourist offices or **Nor-Way Bussekspress** (✉ Bussterminalen, Galleri Oslo, ☎ 81544444). All buses serving the Bergen region depart from Bergen's **central bus station** (✉ Strømgaten 8, ☎ 177).

BY CAR

E18 goes from Oslo to Drammen and Route 11 from Drammen to Haukeli. From Haukeli to Kinsarvik you take Route 13. After the ferry crossing, Kinsarvik–Utne–Kvandal, you follow Route 7 to Bergen.

BY PLANE

Flesland Airport is 20 km (12 mi) south of Bergen.

BY TRAIN

For Bergen, the ***Bergensbanen*** has five departures daily, plus an additional one on Sunday, in both directions on the Oslo–Bergen route. The only train service in the southern part of Telemark is the Oslo–Stavanger line (via Kristiansand).

Guided Tours

Bergen is the gateway to the fjords, and excursions cover most towns in the western part of the region as well as the fjords farther north. Contact the tourist information offices (☞ *below*) for details of these constantly changing tours.

Visitor Information

Bergen (✉ Bryggen 7, ☎ 55321480). **Kinsarvik** (✉ Public Library bldg./mid-June–mid-Aug., ☎ 53663112). **Kongsberg** (✉ Storgt. 35, ☎ 32735000).

ABOVE BERGEN: THE FAR NORTH

The fjords continue northward from Bergen all the way to Kirkenes, at Norway's border with the Republic of Russia. in the north you can hike, climb, fish, bird-watch (seabirds), see Samiland—the land of the Sami ("Lapps")—or experience the unending days of the midnight sun in June and July. The Lofoten Islands present the grand face of the "Lofoten Wall"—a rocky massif surrounded by the sea and broken into six pieces. Svolvær, the most populated island, has a thriving summer artists' colony. It's also known for Lofotfisket, a winter cod-fishing event.

The major towns north of Bergen are Ålesund, Kristiansund, Molde, and Trondheim. In Northern Norway the major towns are Bodø, Narvik, Harstad, Tromsø, Hammerfest, and Kirkenes. Cheaper accommodations are the rule in the north, whether you stay in hotels, cabins, campsites, guest houses, or *rorbuer*—fishermen's huts next to the sea with modern facilities.

★ Ålesund

Ålesund's pride is its unique, internationally recognized collection of Art Nouveau–style buildings constructed between 1904 and 1907 after The Great Fire. Medieval in style, romantic, and colorful, with towers and ornaments from the Viking Age, these buildings line the narrow streets of the old town. This area on the west coast of Norway was one of the first places exposed after the Ice Age. Excavations in the Skjonghelleren cave on the nearby island of Valderøy have given evidence of stone-age settlements living off the rich fishing grounds. Even today, much of the town's income derives from the fishing industry. *Klipfisk* (split, dried cod), which is exported worldwide, is the main ingredient for *bacalao,* a popular local dish whose name derives from the Portuguese for salted cod, the preparation of which west-coast Norwegians learned from Portuguese fishermen.

$$ ✕ **Fjellstua.** This mountaintop restaurant has tremendous views over the surrounding peaks, islands, and fjords. The main dining room serves the widest variety of dishes and homemade desserts. ✉ *Fjellstua,* ☎ *70126582. AE, DC, MC, V. Closed Dec.–early Feb.*

$$ ✕ **Sjøbua.** On an old wharf at Brunholmen, Sjøbua offers an excellent seafood selection. You can even pick your own dinner from a saltwater aquarium. ✉ *Brunholmgt. 1,* ☎ *70127100. AE, DC, MC, V.*

$$$ 🏨 **Comfort Home Hotel Bryggen.** This dockside warehouse converted into a hotel has splendid views over the water. ✉ *Apotekergt. 1–3, 6004,* ☎ *70126400,* FAX *70121180. 85 rooms. AE, DC, MC, V.*

$$ 🏨 **Quality Scandinavie Hotel.** The impressive building dates from 1905. The rooms are decorated in blue, peach, and green, with reproduction Biedermeier furniture. ✉ *Løvenvoldgt. 8, 6002,* ☎ *70123131,* FAX *70132370. 65 rooms. 2 restaurants. AE, DC, MC, V.*

Trondheim

Trondheim sits at the southern end of Norway's widest fjord, Trondheimsfjord. This water-bound city, the third largest in the country, is where Norwegian rulers are traditionally crowned. It has a historic fish market worth seeing, as well as Scandinavia's two largest wooden buildings. One is a student dormitory and the other is the rococo **Stiftsgården,** built between 1774 and 1778, which became a royal palace in 1906. It is one of the highlights of Norwegian architecture, but the architect is unknown. Construction of Scandinavia's largest medieval building, **Nidaros Domkirke** (Nidaros Cathedral), started here in 1320 but was not completed until the early 1920s. For centuries this was a pilgrimage church. ✉ *Kongsgårdsgt. 2,* ☎ *73538480.*

$$$ ★ ✕ **Bryggen.** A feast of Norwegian specialties is served at this popular restaurant near the Gamle Bybro (Old Town Bridge). There's also a creperie and a wine and cheese room. ✉ *Ø Bakklandet 66,* ☎ *73520230. AE, DC, MC, V.*

$$ ✕ **Hos Magnus.** This old-fashioned, cozy restaurant is in the new part of the Bryggen section of town. The menu includes such dishes as rosette

of salmon cured and marinated with aquavit and brandy sauce and lamb roulade stuffed with cheese and mushrooms. ✉ *Kjøpmannsgt. 63,* ☎ *73524110. AE, DC, MC, V.*

$$ ★ ✕ **Tavern på Sverresborg.** Outside the city, at the open-air Folk Museum, this restaurant serves Norwegian specialties. ✉ *Sverresborg,* ☎ *73520932. AE, DC, MC, V.*

$$$ **Radisson SAS Royal Garden Hotel.** Trondheim's finest hotel has excellent facilities for sports and fitness, as well as many features useful to guests with disabilities. ✉ *Kjøpmannsgt. 73, 7010,* ☎ *73521100,* FAX *73531766. 297 rooms. Restaurant, indoor pool. AE, DC, MC, V.*

$$ ★ **Comfort Home Hotel Bakeriet.** Built as a bakery in 1863, the hotel opened in 1991. Few rooms look alike, but all are large and stylish in their simplicity, with natural wood furniture and beige-and-red textiles. A light evening meal is included in the room rate. ✉ *Brattørgt. 2, 7010,* ☎ *73525200,* FAX *73502330. 110 rooms. AE, DC, MC, V.*

$–$$ **Hotel Ambassadeur.** Take in the dramatic view of fjord and coastline from the roof terrace of this hotel, about 300 ft from the market square. Breakfast and a light evening meal are included. ✉ *Elvegt. 18, 7013,* ☎ *73527050,* FAX *73527052. 34 rooms. AE, DC, MC, V.*

Bodø

Bodø, the first major town above the Polar Circle is, with its 40,000 inhabitants, the second-largest city in Northern Norway and the last stop on the European rail system. Bodø's modern airport has frequent flights daily serving most of the country. *Hurtigruten* (the Coastal Express ship) calls in twice a day, and a ferry will take you from Bodø straight to the Lofoten islands. For boat excursions to coastal bird colonies on **Værøya,** Bodø is also the best base. The city was bombed by the Germans in 1940. Today you'll find a bustling modern city center including lively shopping streets, a marina, and good restaurants and accommodations. The stunning, contemporary **Bodø Cathedral,** its spire separated from the main building, was built after the war. Inside are rich modern tapestries; outside is a war memorial. **Norsk Luftfarts Museum** (the Norwegian Aviation Museum) is divided into military and civilian sections. Among the attractions are an American U-2 spy plane, a Junkers 52, a Catalina anti-submarine aircraft, and the mosquito bomber. Try the flight simulator. ✉ *Olav V's gt.* *Kr 65.* *Mid-June–mid-Aug., weekdays and Sun. 10–8, Sat. 10–5; mid-Aug.–mid June, Mon., Tues., Thurs., Fri. 10–4, Wed. 10–7, Sat. 10–5, Sun. 11–6.*

Saltstraumen, the world's strongest tidal current, has inspired tales of ships' being sucked down in its maelstrom (whirlpool). It is one of nature's wonders as well as a paradise for anglers. A new visitor's center opened here in 1996. ✉ *33 km (20 mi) south of Bodø.*

Kjærringøy Gamle Handelssted (Kjærringøy Old Trading Post) is 40 km (25 mi) north of Bodø. It has one of Norway's most important collections of buildings preserved from the 19th century, capturing part of the history of north Norwegian coastal life and culture. The Norwegian author Knut Hamsun developed a special relationship to Kjerringøy, which became the basis for some of his best literary descriptions. For more information contact Destination Bodø AS (✉ Box 514, Sjøgt 21, 8001 Bodø, ☎ 75526000).

$$ ✕ **Turisthytta.** This mountaintop lodge, accessible only by car, is a fine place to have a meal while basking in the midnight sun. There is a good range of dishes, from snacks and open-face sandwiches to fresh fish. ✉ *Turisthytta,* ☎ *75/583300. No credit cards.*

$$ **Norrø na.** This bed-and-breakfast is comfortable, with a grand location. ✉ *Storgt. 4B, 8006,* ☎ *75/525550,* FAX *75/523388. 99 rooms. AE, DC, MC, V.*

$$ 🏨 **Radisson SAS Hotel.** This grandiose hotel pulses with life and has enough amenities to keep you entertained nearly around the clock. The rooms have all the amenities, and the service is impeccable. ✉ *Storgt. 2, 8006, ☎ 75/524100, FAX 75/527493. 194 rooms. Restaurant. AE, DC, MC, V.*

★ Lofoten Islands

The Lofoten Islands are a 190-km (118-mi) chain of mountaintops rising from the bottom of the sea north of Bodø. In summer their farms, fjords, and fishing villages become a major tourist magnet. Between January and March, thousands of fishermen from all over the country head for Lofoten to the annual Lofotfisket, the world's largest annual cod fishing event. **Svolvær,** the main town and administrative center for the villages on Lofoten Islands, is connected with the other islands by express boat and ferry and by coastal steamer and air to Bodø. It has a thriving summer art colony. **Lofotr** (Viking Museum of Borg; ✉ 8360 Høstad, ☎ 76004900), 67 km (42 mi) south of Svolvær on Route E10, has the only reconstruction of a Viking chieftain's homestead in Norway. The year 900 is re-created once you enter the building, with its flickering fireplace and cod liver oil lamps. You may also bump into the chieftain himself; he tells many stories of raids and expeditions. The **midnight sun** is visible in Lofoten from May 27 to July 17. The best places to view it are Unstad and Eggum on **Vestvågøy** and Gimsøy and Laukvik on **Vågan.**

Narvik

Narvik is a rebuilt city, an ice-free seaport, and a major iron ore shipping center. An excellent railway connects it to the mines across the Swedish border. **Krigsminnemuseet** (the War Memorial Museum) has gripping displays on wartime intrigue and suffering. ✉ *Kongensgt., near the main square, ☎ 76944426. ⏲ Mar.–mid-June and mid-Aug.–Sept., daily 11–2; mid-June–mid-Aug., daily 10–10. Closed Oct.–Feb. except for group tours arranged in advance.*

$$$ 🏨 **Grand Royal Hotel.** An eager-to-please staff serves you at this handsome hotel near the train station. There are many possibilities for skiing and fishing nearby. ✉ *Kongensgt. 64, 8500, ☎ 76941500, FAX 76945531. 107 rooms. 2 restaurants. AE, DC, MC, V.*

Harstad

Northeast of Lofoten on Hinnøya, Norway's largest island, is Harstad, where the population of 22,000 swells to 42,000 during the annual June cultural festival and the July deep-sea fishing festival.

Tromsø

Farther north on the mainland is Tromsø, self-dubbed "the Paris of the North" for its nightlife inspired by the midnight sun. Looming over the remote arctic university town are 6,100-ft peaks with permanent snowcaps. Tromsø trails off into the islands: Half the 50,000 inhabitants of the town live offshore. Be sure to see the spectacular **Ishavskatedral** (Arctic Cathedral), with its eastern wall made entirely of stained glass. Coated in aluminum, the **Tromsø bridge** has triangular peaks that make a bizarre mirror for the midnight sun.

Part of Tromsø University, **Tromsø Museum** concentrates on science, the Sami, and northern churches. ✉ *Lars Thøringsvei 10, Folkeparken; take Bus 20; ☎ 77645000. ⏲ June–Aug., daily 9–9; Sept.–May, weekdays 8:30–3:30, Sat. noon–3, Sun. 11–4.*

$$$–$$$$ 🏨 **Radisson SAS Hotel Tromsø.** Rooms in this hotel in the center of town have spectacular views over the shoreline. ✉ *Sjøgt. 7, 9001, ☎ 77600000, FAX 77685474. 195 rooms. 3 restaurants. AE, DC, MC, V.*

$$$ **Comfort Saga Hotel.** On a pretty town square, this hotel has quiet and comfortable, if basic, rooms. Its restaurant serves affordable, hearty meals. ✉ *Richard Withs Pl. 2, 9008,* ☎ *77681180,* FAX *77682380. 66 rooms, 3 suites. Restaurant. AE, DC, MC, V.*

Hammerfest

Hammerfest is the world's northernmost town, founded in 1789, an elegant, festive-looking port despite having been razed twice in its history. In the late 19th century fire leveled it, and years later, defeated German troops destroyed the town as they retreated. Modern Hammerfest is a natural starting point for exploring Finmark.

In the Sami settlements surrounding Hammerfest, you can discover **Sami culture** and traditional Sami food, visit a Sami camp, and spend a night in a *lavo* (Sami tent) through Hammerfest Turist AS (☎ 78412185). The city is also home to **Isbjørn Klubben** (the Royal and Ancient Polar Bear Society), which has taxidermic displays of polar bears and other Arctic animals. ✉ *Town Hall basement,* ☎ *78413100.* *Free.* *June–Aug., weekdays 8–8, weekends 10–5.*

The Far North Essentials

Getting Around

BY CAR

E6 and its feeder roads are the only routes available north of Trondheim, where the country narrows dramatically.

BY SHIP

One of the best ways to travel in northern Norway is aboard a **Hurtigruten** (coastal steamer; main office, Tromsø, ☎ 77648200), which starts out in Bergen and turns around 2,000 nautical km (1,250 mi) farther north at Kirkenes. Many steamers run this route, so you can stay in port for any length of time and pick up the next one coming through. Major tourist offices have schedules, and reservations are essential as far as a year in advance (☞ Visitor Information, *below*).

BY TRAIN

A major train route runs from Oslo to Trondheim to Bodø. From Bodø tours go to the Lofoten by ferry. To reach the Nordkapp (North Cape), the northernmost mainland point in Norway and Europe, you must continue your trip by bus from Fauske. With a Scanrailpass you get 50% discount on the buses. From Narvik a train to Sweden departs twice a day. In summer a special day trip through wild and beautiful scenery takes you to the Swedish border.

Visitor Information

Ålesund (✉ Rådhuset, ☎ 70121202). **Bodø** (✉ Sjøgt. 21, ☎ 75526000). **Hammerfest** (✉ 9600, ☎ 78412185). **Harstad** (✉ Torvet 8, ☎ 77063235). **Lofoten** (✉ 8300 Svolvær, ☎ 76073000). **Narvik** (✉ Kongensgt. 66, ☎ 76943309). **Tromsø** (✉ Storgt. 61, ☎ 77610000). **Trondheim** (✉ Munkegt. 19, ☎ 73929394).

23 Poland

Warsaw, Kraków and Environs, Gdańsk and the North

Poles are fond of quoting, with a wry grimace, the old Chinese curse, "May you live in interesting times." The times are certainly interesting in 1990s Poland, the home of the Solidarity political/labor/social movement that sent shock waves through the Soviet Bloc in 1980, and the first Eastern European state to shake off communist rule. But as the grimace implies, being on the firing line of history—something that the Poles are well used to—can be uncomfortable.

You will be constantly reminded that the return to free-market capitalism after more than 45 years of state socialism is an experiment on an unprecedented scale that has brought hardships for millions but also benefits for a growing percentage of the population. With 39 million inhabitants living in a territory of 318,400 sq km (121,000 sq mi), Poland in the 1990s is suspended between the Old World and the New, and the images can be confusing. Bright, new, privately owned shops with smiling assistants carry on business in shabby buildings that have not been renovated for decades. Billboards advertise goods that most Poles cannot afford. Many key public services, such as health care and education, have deteriorated as local authorities make valiant attempts to satisfy an increasingly demanding electorate with woefully insufficient funds.

The official trappings of the communist state were quickly dismantled after the Solidarity victory in the 1989 elections. But communism never sat easily with the Poles. It represented yet another stage in their age-old struggle to retain their identity in the face of pressure from large and powerful neighbors to the west and east. Since its foundation as a unified state on the great north European plain during the 10th century, Poland has lain at the heart of Europe, precisely at the halfway point on a line drawn from the Atlantic coast of Spain to the Ural Mountains. This has never been an enviable position. During the Middle Ages Poland fought against German advance; in the Golden Age of Polish history during the 16th and 17th centuries—of which you will be reminded by splendid Renaissance buildings in many parts of the country—Poland pushed eastward against her Slavic neighbors, taking Kiev and dreaming of a kingdom that stretched from the Baltic to the Black Sea. By the end of the 18th century Poland's territories were divided among the Austrian, Prussian, and Russian empires.

During the 20th century Poland fell victim to peculiarly vicious forms of dictatorship—from both the right and the left: the brutal Nazi occupation and imposition of soviet rule. Poland's ancient cities—Kraków, Warsaw, Gdańsk—tell much of the tale of European history and culture. Its countryside offers unrivaled opportunities to escape from the 20th century. Paradoxically, communism—which after 1956 dropped attempts to collectivize agriculture and left the Polish farmer on his small, uneconomical plot—has left rural Poland in something of a time warp. Despite pollution, cornflowers still bloom, storks perch atop untidy nests by cottage chimneys, and horsepower still frequently comes in the four-legged variety. While the Poles have a certain wary reserve, they will win you over with their strong individualism—expressed through their well-developed sense of humor and their capacity for conviviality.

As the Polish transformation from communism approaches the 10-year mark, Poland is increasingly becoming a "normal" European country with "normal" problems. It's likely to take several generations before the physical and psychological traces of 45 years of Soviet rule fade and at least 20 years until Poland "catches up" with the poorest EU member in terms of standard of living. Nevertheless, the country has undergone enormous changes since 1989. One measure of how far Poland has come is that it is expected to become a NATO member in 1999. Parliamentary elections in fall 1997 returned a center-right coalition with deep roots in the Solidarity movement to power, where it "cohabits" with a post-communist President.

POLAND A TO Z

Customs

Persons over 18 may bring in duty-free: personal belongings, including musical instruments, one computer, one radio, one camera with 24 rolls of film; up to 250 cigarettes or 50 cigars, ½ liter of spirits and 2 liters of wine; and goods with a total value of $200. Foreign currency over the value of $2,500 may be brought in but must be declared on arrival. Further customs information can be obtained in Warsaw by calling 022/650–28–73.

Dining

Polish food and drink are basically Slavic with Baltic overtones. The emphasis is on soups and meat (especially pork), as well as freshwater fish. Cream is a staple, and pastries are rich and often delectable. The most popular soup is *barszcz* (known to many Americans as borscht), a clear beet soup often served with such Polish favorites as sausage, cabbage, potatoes, sour cream, coarse rye bread, and beer. Other typical dishes are *pierogi,* which may be stuffed with savory or sweet fillings; *gołąbki* (cabbage leaves stuffed with minced meat); *bigos* (sauerkraut with meat and mushrooms); and *flaki* (a tripe soup). Polish beer is excellent; vodka is a specialty and is often downed before, during, and after meals.

Zajazdy (roadside inns) and *bar mleczny* (milk bars), which are often less expensive than regular restaurants, serve more traditional food. As elsewhere in Central Europe, cafés are a way of life in Poland and often serve delicious, homemade pastries and ice cream.

Poland (Polska)

MEALTIMES

Poles eat their main meal at around 2 PM with a light supper at about 8 PM. Restaurants—especially in major cities—open around noon for lunch and serve dinner between 7 PM and 10 PM. Although many restaurants in the provinces close around 10 PM, more cosmopolitan establishments stay open until 11 PM or later. Most hotel restaurants serve the evening meal until 10:30.

RATINGS

Prices are per person and include three courses and service but not drinks.

CATEGORY	WARSAW/KRAKÓW	OTHER AREAS
$$$$	zł 100–200	over zł 60
$$$	zł 50–zł 100	zł 40–zł 60
$$	zł 25–zł 50	zł 20–zł 40
$	under zł 25	under zł 20

WHAT TO WEAR

In Warsaw and Kraków formal dress is customary at $$$ and $$$$ restaurants. Casual dress is appropriate elsewhere.

Language

Polish is a Slavic language that uses the Roman alphabet but has several additional characters and diacritical marks. Because it has a high incidence of consonant clusters, most English speakers find it a difficult language to decipher, much less pronounce. Many older Poles speak German; the younger generation usually knows some English. In larger cities English is increasingly common, especially in hotels, but you may have difficulty in the countryside.

Lodging

There was a time just a few years ago when travelers in Poland were unlikely to find acceptable lodging except in major cities or near major tourist attractions. Now acceptable lodging can be found even in remote corners of the country. For luxurious, world-class accommodations you'll have to wait several more years before being satisfied with offerings outside Warsaw.

HOTELS

The government rates hotel accommodations with from one to five stars. Orbis hotels, owned by the state tourist office and currently undergoing privatization, have almost all been accorded four or five stars and guarantee a reasonable standard of cleanliness and service (although many travelers find them characterless). Most of them range in price from $$ to $$$$; the chain includes a number of foreign-built luxury hotels. In recent years Orbis hotels have faced competition from a growing number of privately owned lodgings, often part of international chains and mostly in the top price range.

Municipal hotels and Dom Turysty hotels are run by local authorities or the Polish Tourist Association. They are often rather old and can have limited bath and shower facilities. Standards are improving as many undergo renovations; prices are in the $$ category.

PRIVATE ACCOMMODATIONS

Rooms can be arranged either in advance through a travel agent or on the spot at the local tourist information office. Villas, lodges, rooms, or houses are available. Daily rates vary from about $6 for a room to more than $150 for a villa.

RATINGS

The following chart is based on a rate for two people in a double room with bath or shower and breakfast. These prices are in U.S. dollars; many hotels in Poland quote prices in American dollars or German marks because of the fluctuations in Polish currency.

CATEGORY	COST
$$$$	over $200
$$$	$100–$200
$$	$50–$100
$	under $50

ROADSIDE INNS

Many roadside inns are quite attractive, offering inexpensive food and guest rooms at moderate rates.

Mail

POSTAL RATES

Airmail letters abroad cost about zł 1.50 (depending on weight); postcards, gr 90. Post offices are open weekdays 8–8. At least one post office is open 24 hours in every major city. In Warsaw the 24-hour post office is at ✉ ul. Świętokrzyska 31.

Money Matters

COSTS

Poland is one of the more expensive countries of Eastern Europe, and inflation is high by Western standards, although the rate has fallen to about 10% annually. Prices are highest in the big cities, especially Warsaw. The farther you stray from the tourist track, the cheaper your vacation will be.

CURRENCY

The monetary unit in Poland is the złoty (zł), which is divided into 100 groszy (gr). Since the currency reform of 1994, there are notes of 10, 20, 50, 100, and 200 złotys, and coins in values of 1, 2, and 5 złotys and 1, 2, 5, 10, and 50 groszys. At press time (spring 1998), the exchange rate was zł 3.4 to the U.S. dollar, zł 2.4 to the Canadian dollar, zł 5.6 to the pound sterling, zł 2.16 to the Australian dollar, and zł 1.86 to the New Zealand dollar.

The złoty is exchangeable at a free-market rate in banks and at *kantory* (private exchange bureaus), which sometimes offer slightly better rates than do banks and are often open 24 hours a day. There are also cash machines throughout the country that accept most major credit cards as long as you have a PIN number (Bankomat currently has 500 machines in Poland).

CREDIT CARDS

Major credit cards are accepted in all major hotels, in the better restaurants and nightclubs, and for other tourist services. In small cafés and shops, especially in the provinces, credit cards are not likely to be accepted.

SAMPLE PRICES

A cup of coffee, zł 4–zł 8; a bottle of beer, zł 3–zł 5; a soft drink, zł 2–zł 4.5; a ham sandwich, zł 32–zł 5; a 2-km (1-mi) taxi ride, zł 5.

TIPPING

If service is not included, waiters get a standard 10% of the bill. On smaller bills round upward to the nearest zł or two. Hotel porters and doormen get about zł 2 per bag.

National Holidays

January 1; April 4–5 (Easter); May 1 (Labor Day); May 3 (Constitution Day); May 29 (Corpus Christi); August 15 (Assumption); November 1 (All Saints' Day); November 11 (Independence Day; rebirth of the Polish state in 1918); December 25, 26 (Christmas and Boxing Day).

Opening and Closing Times

Banks are open weekdays 8 or 9–3 or 6. **Museum** hours vary greatly but are generally Tuesday–Sunday 9–5. Among **shops,** food shops are open weekdays 7–7, Saturday 7–1 or 2; many are now open on Sunday, and there are a few all-night stores in most central shopping districts. Other stores are open weekdays 11–7 and Saturday 9–1 or 2.

Precautions

Tap water in major cities is unsafe to drink, so ask for bottled mineral water. Beware of meat dishes served in cheap snack bars.

Telephoning

COUNTRY CODE

The international country code for Poland is 48. When dialing a number in Poland from outside the country, drop the initial 0 from the local area code.

INFORMATION

For local directory information, dial 913; for Poland-wide directory information and dialing codes, dial 912; for international information and codes, dial 908.

INTERNATIONAL CALLS

Post offices and first-class hotels have booths at which you can use your calling card or pay after completing your call. To place a call via **AT&T** USA Direct, dial 0–0800–111–1111. For **MCI,** dial 0–0800–111–2122. For **Sprint Global One,** dial 0–0800–111–3115.

LOCAL CALLS

Increasingly many phones in Poland now take phone cards, which can be used for either local or long-distance calls. The cards, which cost zł 7.5 or zł 15, are sold at kiosks and post offices. When making a long-distance call, first dial 0, wait for the dial tone, then dial the rest of the number. To place a domestic long-distance call to a number without a direct-dial facility, dial 900.

Transportation

BY BUS

PKS (☎ 9433) is the national bus company. **Polski Express** (☎ 022/620–03–30) is private and much nicer. Both offer long-distance service to most cities. Express buses, on which you can reserve seats, are somewhat more expensive than trains but often—except in the case of a few major intercity routes—get to their destinations more quickly. For really out-of-the-way destinations, the bus is often the only means of transportation. Bus stations are usually quite near railway stations. Tickets and information are best obtained from any travel agency, hotel, or the bus station itself.

BY CAR

Breakdowns. Poland's **Motoring Association** (PZMot) offers breakdown, repair, and towing services to members of various international insurance organizations; check with Orbis (☞ Travel Agencies *in* Warsaw, *below*) before you leave home. Carry a spare-parts kit. For emergency road help call 981.

Car Rentals. You can rent cars at international airports or through most travel agents. Rates tend to be high, due to the lack of competition, but vary according to season, car model, and mileage. Fly-drive vacations are also available.

Gasoline. The price of gas is about zł 22 for 10 liters of high octane. Filling stations are located every 30 km (19 mi) or so and are usually open 6 AM–10 PM. More and more bright, clean, full-service 24-hour stations are opening each year.

Road Conditions. Despite the extensive road network, driving conditions, even on main roads, have deteriorated greatly during the 1990s, owing to a major increase in traffic and the lack of divided highways, making driving in Poland extremely dangerous. Minor roads tend to be narrow, and drivers frequently encounter horse-drawn carts, bicycles, and pedestrians. If you're in a hurry, stick to roads marked E (express roads that in theory lead to a border of Poland) or A (domestic express roads).

Rules of the Road. Driving is on the right. The speed limit on highways is 110 kph (68 mph) and on roads in built-up areas, 60 kph (37 mph). A built-up area is marked by a white rectangular sign with the name of the town on it.

BY PLANE

LOT, Poland's national airline, operates daily flights linking eight main cities: Warsaw, Kraków, Gdańsk, Wrocław, Szczecin, Poznań, Katowice, and Rzeszów. Fares begin at about $80 round-trip from Warsaw. Tickets and information are available from LOT or any travel agent. Be sure to book well in advance, especially for the summer season.

BY TRAIN

Poland's **PKP** railway network is extensive and relatively inexpensive. Most trains have first- and second-class accommodations, but Western visitors usually prefer to travel first-class. You should arrive at the station well before departure time. The fastest trains are intercity and express trains, which require reservations. Orbis and other travel agents furnish information, reservations, and tickets. If you're traveling on overnight trains, reserve a berth in a first-class sleeping car or second-class couchette. Long-distance trains carry buffets.

Fares. Polish trains run at three speeds—*ekspresowy* (express), *pośpieszny* (fast), and *osobowy* (slow)—and fares vary accordingly. You pay more for intercity and express, and round-trip tickets are priced at precisely double the one-way fare.

Visas

Citizens of the United States and the United Kingdom do not need visas for entry to Poland; Canadian citizens and citizens of other countries that have not yet abolished visas for Poles must pay the equivalent of $34 (more for multiple-entry visas). Apply to the Polish Consulate General in any country. Visitors from Canada and other countries that require visas must complete one application form and provide two photographs; allow about two weeks for processing. Such visas are issued for 90 days but can be extended in Poland through the local county police headquarters.

You can contact the Polish Consulate General at the following addresses. **United States** (✉ 233 Madison Ave. New York, NY 10016, ☎ 212/889–8360; ✉ 1530 N. Lake Shore Dr., Chicago, IL 60610, ☎ 312/337–8166; ✉ 2224 Wyoming Ave. NW, Washington DC 20008, ☎ 202/232–4517). **Canada** (✉ 1500 Pine Ave West., Montréal, Québec H3G 1B4, ☎ 514/937–9481; ✉ 2603 Lakeshore Blvd. W, Toronto, Ontario M8V 1G5, ☎ 416/252–5471). **United Kingdom** (✉ 73 New Cavendish St., London W1N 7RB, ☎ 0171/580–0475). **Australia** (✉ 7 Turrana St., Yarralumla, Canberra, ACT 2600, ☎ 06/273–1208; ✉ 10 Trelawney St., Woollahra, Sydney, NSW 2025, ☎ 02/9363–9816.

Visitor Information

There is no national tourist office in Poland. State-run tourist offices are listed in individual cities' Essentials (☞ *below*).

Weather

The main tourist season runs from May through September. The best times for sightseeing are late spring and early fall. Major cultural events usually take place in the cities during the fall. The early spring is often wet and windy.

CLIMATE

Below are the average daily maximum and minimum temperatures for Warsaw.

Jan.	32F	0C	**May**	67F	20C	**Sept.**	66F	19C
	22	– 6		48	9		49	10
Feb.	32F	0C	**June**	73F	23C	**Oct.**	55F	13C
	21	– 6		54	12		41	5
Mar.	42F	6C	**July**	75F	24C	**Nov.**	42F	6C
	28	– 2		58	16		33	1
Apr.	53F	12C	**Aug.**	73F	23C	**Dec.**	35F	2C
	37	3		56	14		28	– 3

WARSAW

At the end of World War II Warsaw lay in ruins, a victim of systematic Nazi destruction. Only one-third of its prewar population survived the German occupation. The experience is visible everywhere in the memorial plaques describing mass executions of civilians and in the bullet holes still on the facades of some buildings. However, Warsovians painstakingly rebuilt their beloved Old Town, reconstructing it from old prints and paintings. The result, an area whose buildings are painted in warm pastel colors, is remarkable. Surrounding the old districts, however, is the modern Warsaw, built since the war in utilitarian Socialist-Realist and later styles, giving it a certain "soviet" feel.

Exploring Warsaw

Numbers in the margin correspond to points of interest on the Warsaw map.

The sights of Warsaw are all relatively close to one another, making most attractions accessible on foot. A walking tour of the old historic district takes about two hours. A walk along the former Royal Route—the Trakt Królewski—which stretched south from Castle Square down Krakowskie Przedmieście, through Nowy Świat and on along Aleje Ujazdowskie, which is considered by many locals to be Warsaw's finest street, is also worthwhile. Lined with magnificent buildings and embassies, it has something of a French flavor. The Muranów district is the site of Jewish Warsaw.

Stare Miasto (Old Town) and Nowego Miasto (New Town)

7 **Barbakan** (Barbican). This pinnacled redbrick gate is a fine example of a 16th-century defensive fortification. From here you can see the partially restored wall that was built to enclose the Old Town and enjoy a splendid view of the Vistula River, with the district of Praga on its east bank. ⊠ *Ul. Freta.*

3 **Bazylika Świętego Jana** (Cathedral of St. John). The oldest church in Warsaw, it dates from the 14th century. Several Polish kings were crowned here. ⊠ *Ul. Świętojańska 8.*

10 **Kościół Najświętszej Marii Panny** (St. Mary's Church). This is the oldest church in the New Town, built as a parish church for the district by the princes of Mazovia in the early 15th century. St. Mary's has been destroyed and rebuilt many times throughout its history. The Gothic bell tower dates from the early 16th century. Note the houses with curiously stark and formalized wall paintings on the nearby ulica Kościelna. ⊠ *Przyrynek 2.*

6 **Muzeum Historyczne Warszawy** (Historical Museum of Warsaw). This excellent museum detailing the history of the city has a 20-minute movie, *Warsaw Remembers,* describing the history of Warsaw, mostly made up of old footage. It is shown in English at noon. ⊠ *Rynek Starego*

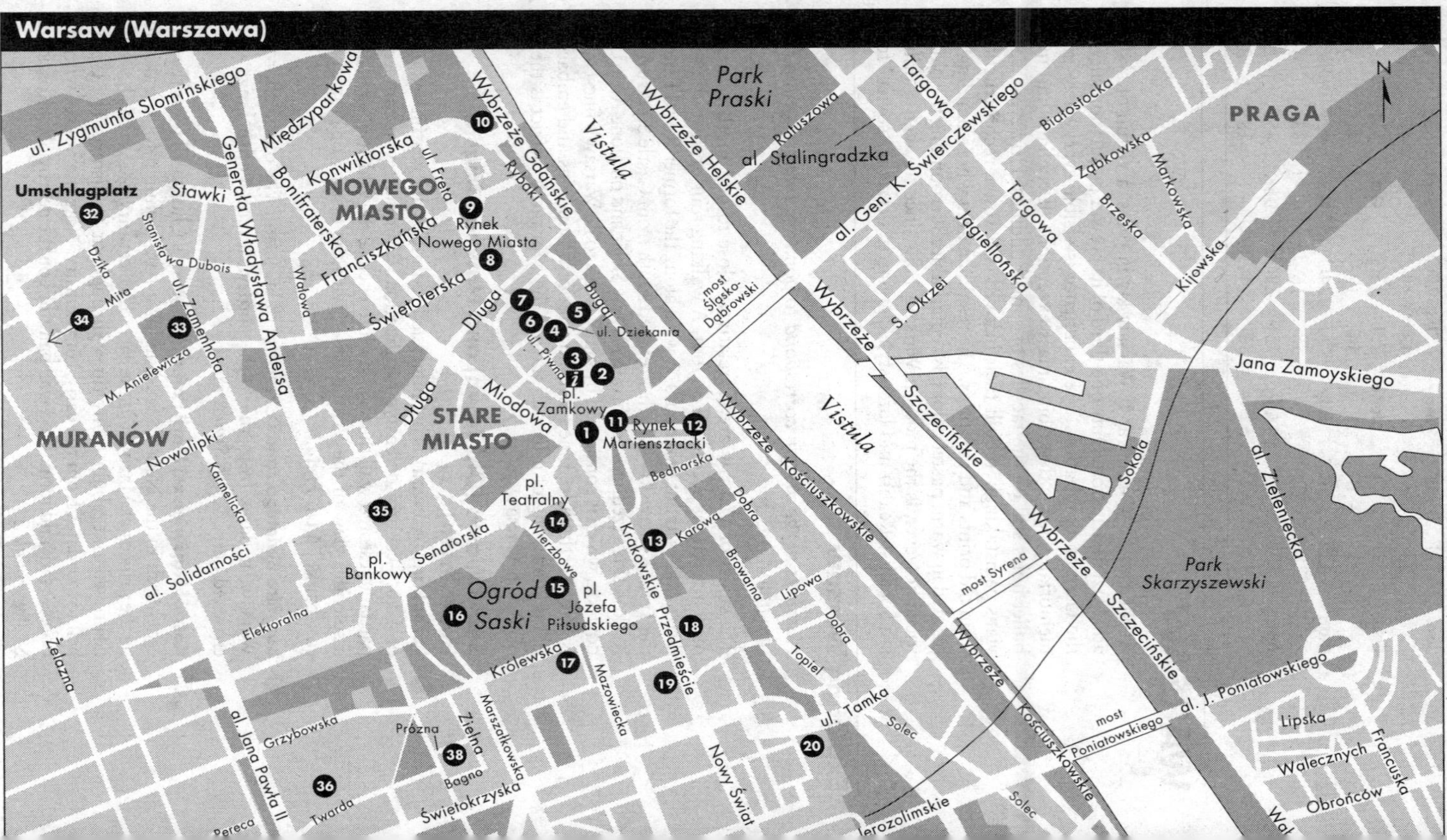
Warsaw (Warszawa)
N
PRAGA
Park Praski
Vistula
Wybrzeże Helskie
Wybrzeże Gdańskie
Wybrzeże Szczecińskie
Wybrzeże Kościuszkowskie
most Śląsko-Dąbrowski
most Syrena
most Poniatowskiego
al. Stalingradzka
al. Gen. K. Świerczewskiego
Targowa
Jagiellońska
Ratuszowa
Białostocka
Ząbkowska
Markowska
Brzeska
Kijowska
S. Okrzei
Sokola
Jana Zamoyskiego
al. Zieleniecka
Park Skarzyszewski
al. J. Poniatowskiego
Francuska
Lipska
Walecznych
Obrońców
Solec
Jerozolimskie
ul. Tamka
Dobra
Lipowa
Topiel
Browarna
Karowa
Bednarska
Rynek Mariensztacki
pl. Zamkowy
Miodowa
ul. Piwna
ul. Dziekania
Bugaj
Rybaki
Długa
STARE MIASTO
NOWEGO MIASTO
Rynek Nowego Miasta
ul. Freta
Świętojerska
Franciszkańska
Bonifraterska
Konwiktorska
Międzyparkowa
Wałowa
Krakowskie Przedmieście
Nowy Świat
pl. Teatralny
Wierzbowe
Senatorska
pl. Józefa Piłsudskiego
Ogród Saski
Królewska
Mazowiecka
Marszałkowska
Świętokrzyska
Zielna
Bagno
Próżna
Twarda
Grzybowska
Pereca
pl. Bankowy
Elektoralna
al. Solidarności
Karmelicka
Nowolipki
al. Jana Pawła II
Żelazna
MURANÓW
M. Anielewicza
ul. Zamenhofa
Stanisława Dubois
Dzika
Miła
Stawki
Umschlagplatz
ul. Zygmunta Słomińskiego
Generała Władysława Andersa
1
2
3
4
5
6
7
8
9
10
11
12
13
14
15
16
17
18
19
20
32
33
34
35
36
38

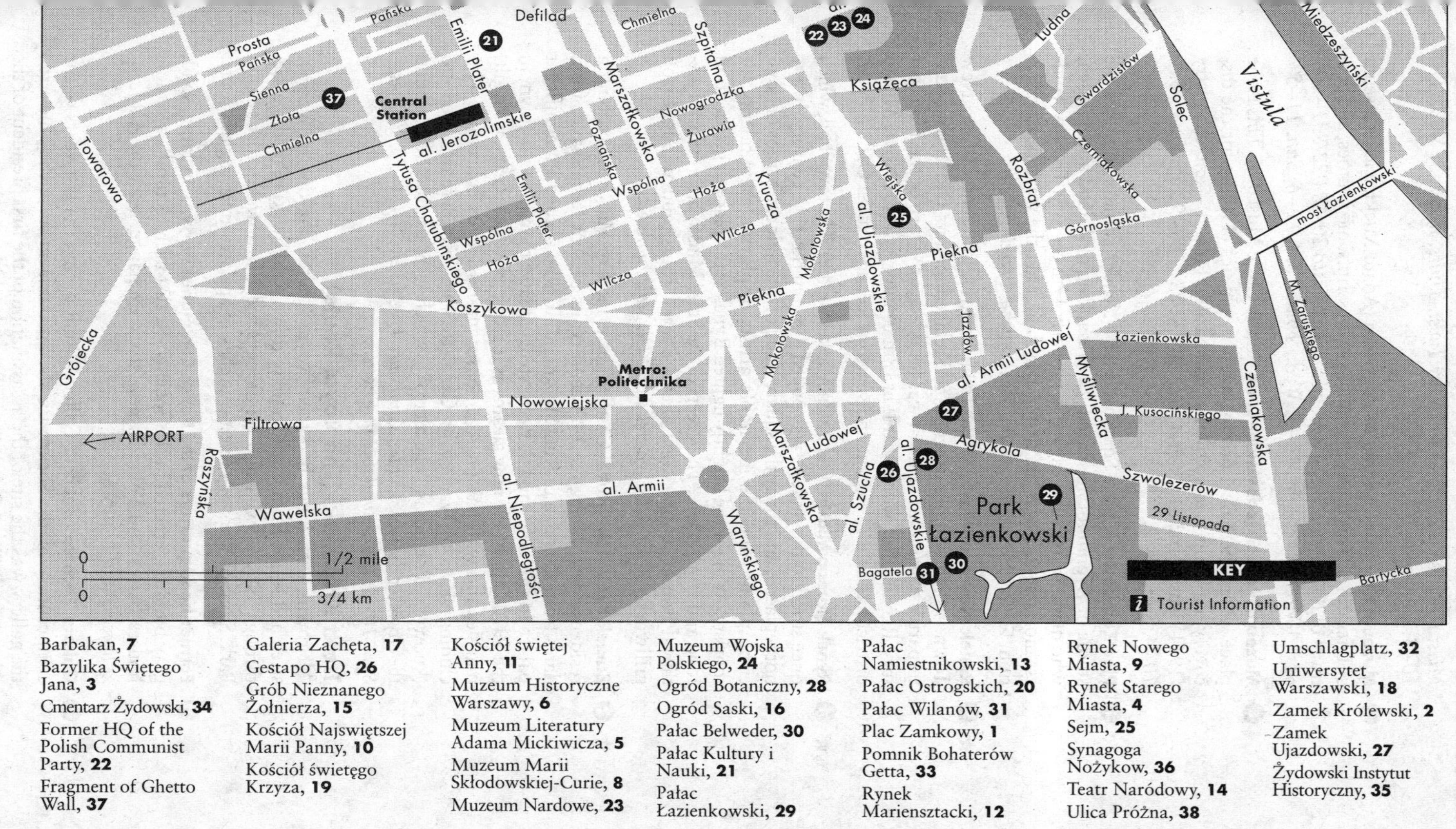
Vistula
Miedzeszyński
most Łazienkowski
M. Zaruskiego
Solec
Czerniakowska
Gwardzistów
Ludna
Rozbrat
Górnośląska
Łazienkowska
J. Kusocińskiego
Myśliwiecka
Szwolezerów
29 Listopada
Bartycka
KEY
Tourist Information
Park Łazienkowski
Agrykola
al. Armii Ludowej
Jazdów
al. Ujazdowskie
Wiejska
Książęca
Piękna
Mokotowska
Krucza
Szpitalna
Chmielna
Defilad
Emilii Plater
Pańska
Prosta
Sienna
Złota
Central Station
al. Jerozolimskie
Nowogrodzka
Żurawia
Marszałkowska
Poznańska
Wspólna
Hoża
Wilcza
Tytusa Chałubinskiego
Towarowa
Grójecka
Koszykowa
Metro: Politechnika
Nowowiejska
Filtrowa
AIRPORT
Raszyńska
Wawelska
al. Niepodległości
al. Armii
Ludowej
Waryńskiego
al. Szucha
Bagatela
1/2 mile
3/4 km
0
Barbakan, 7
Bazylika Świętego Jana, 3
Cmentarz Żydowski, 34
Former HQ of the Polish Communist Party, 22
Fragment of Ghetto Wall, 37
Galeria Zachęta, 17
Gestapo HQ, 26
Grób Nieznanego Żołnierza, 15
Kościół Najswiętszej Marii Panny, 10
Kościół świętego Krzyza, 19
Kościół świętej Anny, 11
Muzeum Historyczne Warszawy, 6
Muzeum Literatury Adama Mickiwicza, 5
Muzeum Marii Skłodowskiej-Curie, 8
Muzeum Nardowe, 23
Muzeum Wojska Polskiego, 24
Ogród Botaniczny, 28
Ogród Saski, 16
Pałac Belweder, 30
Pałac Kultury i Nauki, 21
Pałac Łazienkowski, 29
Pałac Namiestnikowski, 13
Pałac Ostrogskich, 20
Pałac Wilanów, 31
Plac Zamkowy, 1
Pomnik Bohaterów Getta, 33
Rynek Mariensztacki, 12
Rynek Nowego Miasta, 9
Rynek Starego Miasta, 4
Sejm, 25
Synagoga Nożykow, 36
Teatr Naródowy, 14
Ulica Próżna, 38
Umschlagplatz, 32
Uniwersytet Warszawski, 18
Zamek Królewski, 2
Zamek Ujazdowski, 27
Żydowski Instytut Historyczny, 35

Miasta 28, ☎ *022/635–16–25.* ⊙ *Tues., Thurs. noon–5; Wed., Fri. 10–3; weekends 10:30–4:30.*

5 **Muzeum Literatury Adama Mickiewicza** (Adam Mickiewicz Museum of Literature). This museum contains manuscripts, mementoes, and portraits of Polish writers. ✉ *Rynek Starego Miasto 20,* ☎ *022/831–40–61.* ⊙ *Mon., Tues., Fri. 10–3; Wed., Thurs., Sat. 11–6; Sun. 11–5.*

8 **Muzeum Marii Skłodowskiej-Curie** (Marie Curie Museum). This is the place where the Nobel prize winner for physics (1903)—for the discovery of radium and polonium (named after Poland)—and chemistry (1911) was born. ✉ *Ul. Freta 16,* ☎ *022/831–80–92.* ⊙ *Tues.–Sat. 10–4, Sun. 10–2.*

1 **Plac Zamkowy** (Castle Square). Here a slender column supports the **statue of Zygmunt (Sigismund) III Wasa,** king of Poland and Sweden, who made Warsaw his capital in the early 17th century. The city's oldest monument, it was the first to be rebuilt after the wartime devastation. ✉ *Jct. Ul. Miodowa and Krakowskie Przedmieście.*

★ 9 **Rynek Nowego Miasta** (New Town Square). The center of the New Town is slightly more irregular and relaxed than its Old Town counterpart (☞ *below*). The town was founded at the turn of the 15th century. Rebuilt after World War II in 18th-century style, the **Nowe Miasto** district has a more elegant and spacious feeling to it. ✉ *Off Ul. Freta.*

★ 4 **Rynek Starego Miasta** (Old Town Market Square). The town hall, which once stood in the middle, was pulled down in the 19th century. It was not replaced, and today the square is full of open-air cafés, tubs of flowering plants, and the inevitable artists displaying their talents for tourists. At night the brightly lighted Rynek is the place to go for good food and atmosphere. The streets of the **Stare Miasto** have colorful medieval houses, cobblestone alleys, uneven roofs, and wrought-iron grillwork. ✉ *Jct. Ul. Piedarska and Ul. Swiętojańska.*

★ 2 **Zamek Królewski** (Royal Castle). The princes of Mazovia first built a residence here during the 14th century; its present Renaissance form dates from the reign of King Sigismund III, who needed a magnificent palace for his new capital. Reconstructed later than the Old Town, in the 1970s, the castle now gleams as it did in its earliest years, with gilt, marble, and wall paintings; it houses impressive art collections—including views of Warsaw by Canaletto's nephew Bernardo Bellotto (known in Poland as "Canaletto"), which were used to help rebuild the city after the war. ✉ *Plac Zamkowy 4,* ☎ *022/657–21–70.* ⊙ *Tues.–Sun. 10–3; tours available in English.*

Trakt Królewski (The Royal Route)

All towns with kings had their Royal Routes; the one in Warsaw stretched south from Castle Square down Krakowskie Przedmieście, through Nowy Świat and on along Aleje Ujazdowskie to Łazienki Park. Some of Warsaw's finest churches and palaces are along this route.

22 **Former headquarters of the Polish Communist Party.** This large, solid, gray building, erected in the Socialist-Realist architectural style, now houses banks and Poland's new stock exchange. ✉ *Cor. Al. Jerozolimskie and Nowy Świat.*

17 **Galeria Zachęta** (Zachęta Gallery). Built during the last years of the 19th century by the Society for the Encouragement of the Fine Arts, the gallery was the site of the assassination of the first president of the post–World War I Polish Republic, Gabriel Narutowicz, by a right-wing fanatic in 1922. It has no permanent collection but organizes thought-provoking special exhibitions (primarily modern art) in high,

well-lit halls. ✉ *Pl. Małachowskiego 3,* ☎ *022/827–69–09.* ⏲ *Tues.–Sun. 10–6.*

㉖ **Gestapo Headquarters.** Now the Ministry of National Education, the building also houses a small museum that recalls the horrors that took place behind its peaceful facade. ✉ *Al. Szucha 25,* ☎ *022/629–49–19.* ⏲ *Wed.–Sun. 10–4.*

⑮ **Grób Nieznanego Żołnierza** (Tomb of the Unknown Soldier). The only surviving fragment of an early 18th-century Saxon palace, which was blown up by the Nazis in 1944, now honors Poland's war dead. Ceremonial changes of the guard take place here at noon on Sunday; the Polish Army still uses the goose step. ✉ *Plac Piłsudskiego.*

⑲ **Kościoł świętego Krzya** (Holy Cross Church). Inside is a pillar in which the heart of the great Polish composer Frédéric Chopin is entombed. Opposite the church is a statue of Nicolaus Copernicus, the astronomer, who was born in Poland. ✉ *Ul. Krakowskie Przedmieście 3.*

⑪ **Kościół świętej Anny** (St. Anne's Church). Originally built in 1454, it was rebuilt in high Baroque style during the 17th century. Thanks to recent redecoration and regilding, it once again glows in its Baroque splendor. A plaque on the wall outside marks the spot where Pope John Paul II celebrated mass in 1980, during his first visit to Poland after his election to the papacy. ✉ *Ul. Krakowskie Przedmieście 68.*

★ ㉓ **Muzeum Narodowe** (National Museum of Warsaw). The museum has an impressive collection of Polish and European paintings, Gothic icons, and works from antiquity. ✉ *Al. Jerozolimskie 3,* ☎ *022/621–10–31.* ⏲ *Tues., Wed., Fri.–Sun. 10–4, Thurs. noon–5.*

㉔ **Muzeum Wojska Polskiego** (Polish Army Museum). With exhibits of weaponry, armor, and uniforms tracing Polish military history across the past 10 centuries, it captures the romance of the subject. Heavy armaments stand guard outside. ✉ *Al. Jerozolimskie 3,* ☎ *022/629–52–71.* ⏲ *Wed.–Sun. 10–4.*

㉘ **Ogród Botaniczny** (Botanical Gardens). These beautiful plantings belonging to the University were laid out in 1818. Note the neoclassic Observatory. ✉ *Al. Ujazdowskie 4.*

⑯ **Ogród Saski** (Saxon Gardens). The palace park was designed by French and Saxon landscape gardeners; the gardens still contain 18th-century sculptures, a man-made pond, and a sundial. ✉ *Corner ul. Marszałkowska and ul. Królewska.*

㉚ **Pałac Belweder** (Belvedere Palace). This 18th-century former residence and office of the President is now a state guest house. ✉ *Ul. Belwederska 2.*

㉑ **Pałac Kultury I Nauki** (Palace of Culture and Science). With ironic humor, locals tell you that the best vantage point from which to admire their city is atop the 37-story Palace of Culture and Science. Why? Because it is the only point from which you can't see the Palace of Culture and Science. This wedding-cake-style skyscraper was a personal gift from Stalin. Although Poles dislike it as a symbol of Soviet domination, it does afford a panoramic view and is Warsaw's best example of early 1950s "Socialist Gothic" architecture. ✉ *Plac Defilad,* ☎ *022/656–67–77.* ⏲ *Daily 9–4, Sun. 10–4.*

★ ㉙ **Pałac Łazienkowski** (Łazienki Palace). Set inside the wonderfully landscaped French-style **Park Łazienkowski** (Łazienki Park), the palace, a gem of the Polish neoclassical style, was the private residence of Stanisław August Poniatowski, the last king of Poland. It overlooks a lake stocked with huge carp. At the impressionistic Chopin monument nearby, you can stop for a rest and, on summer Sundays, listen to a wonderful open-air concert. ✉ *Ul. Agrykola 1,* ☎ *022/621–62–41.* ⏲ *Tues.–Sun. 9:30–3.*

13 **Pałac Namiestnikowski** (Namiestnikowski Palace). Built during the 17th century by the Radziwiłł family (into which Jacqueline Kennedy's sister, Lee, later married), this palace at one time functioned as the administrative office of the tsarist occupiers. In 1955 the Warsaw Pact was signed here, and now the palace serves as the official residence of Poland's president. In the forecourt is an equestrian statue of Prince Józef Poniatowski, a nephew of the last king of Poland, and one of Napoléon's marshals. ✉ *Krakowskie Przedmieście 46–48.*

20 **Pałac Ostrogskich** (Ostrogski Palace). Headquarters of the Chopin Society, the 17th-century mansion towers impressively above the street. The best approach is along the steps from ulica Tamka. During the 19th century the Warsaw Conservatory was housed here (Paderewski was one of its students); now used for Chopin concerts, it has a small museum with mementoes of the composer. ✉ *Ul. Okólnik 1,* ☎ *022/827–54–71.* ⏲ *Wed.–Mon. 10–2.*

★ 31 **Pałac Wilanów** (Wilanow Palace). Built by King Jan Sobieski, who in 1683 stopped the Ottoman advance on Europe at the Battle of Vienna, the palace later passed into the hands of Stanisław Kostka Potocki. Potocki amassed a major art collection and was responsible for the layout of the palace gardens. He opened Poland's first public museum here in 1805. Potocki's neo-Gothic tomb can be seen to the left of the driveway as you approach the palace. The palace interiors still hold much of the original furniture; there's also a striking display of 16th- to 18th-century Polish portraits on the first floor. Outside, to the left of the main entrance, is a romantic park with pagodas, summer houses, and bridges overlooking a lake. There's also a **gallery** of contemporary Polish art on the grounds, and the stables to the right of the entrance now house a **poster museum** that is well worth visiting. ✉ *Ul. Wiertnicza 1, 10 km (6 mi) from town center,* ☎ *022/42–07–95.* ⏲ *Wed.–Mon. 9:30–2:30.*

12 **Rynek Mariensztacki** (Mariensztat Square). At the bottom, and to the left of, a steeply sloping, cobbled street is a quiet, leafy 18th-century square that is worth a detour. ✉ *Ul. Bednarska.*

25 **Sejm.** The Polish Houses of Parliament, with their round, white debating chamber, were built during the 1920s, after the rebirth of an independent Polish state. ✉ *Ul. Wiejska 4–6.*

14 **Teatr Narodowy** (Opera House and National Theater). The Opera House and the National Theater were built in the 1820s and reconstructed after World War II. ✉ *Plac Piłsudskiego,* ☎ *022/826–32–88.*

18 **Uniwersytet Warszawski** (University of Warsaw). Established in 1816, the university has always been a center for independent political thinking, and most student protests have started here. In 1968 it was the scene of student demonstrations directed against communist influence in Polish culture. Not far from the university, next to the Bristol Hotel on Krakowskie Przedmieście, in the small garden opposite ulica Bednarska, stands a monument to the great Polish poet Adam Mickiewicz. It was here that Warsaw University students gathered in March 1968, after a performance of Mickiewicz's until-then banned play, *Forefathers' Eve,* and set in motion the events that led to the toppling of Poland's longtime communist leader Władysław Gomułka. ✉ *Krakowskie Przedmieście 26–28,* ☎ *022/620–03–81.*

27 **Zamek Ujazdowski** (Ujazdów Castle). Reconstructed in the 1980s, it is now a museum that hosts a variety of exhibitions by contemporary Polish, European, and North American artists. The building has a terrace at the back looking over formal gardens laid out down to the Vistula. ✉ *Al. Ujazdowskie 6,* ☎ *022/628–12–71.* ⏲ *Tues.–Sun. 11–5.*

The Muranów District

The Muranów district is the historic heart of the old prewar Warsaw Jewish district and ghetto under the Nazi regime. In April 1943 the Jewish resistance began the Warsaw Ghetto uprising, which was put down by the Nazis with unbelievable ferocity; the Muranów district was flattened. Today there are only bleak gray apartment blocks here.

34 **Cmentarz Żydowski** (Jewish Cemetery). This active cemetery is an island of continuity amid destruction. The cemetery survived the war, and although badly neglected during the postwar period, it is gradually being restored. Fine 19th-century headstones testify to the Jewish community's important role in Polish history and culture. Ludwik Zamenhof, the creator of Esperanto, is buried here. ✉ *Ul. Okopowa 49–51.*

37 **Fragment of Ghetto Wall.** In the courtyard of this building, through the archway on the right, stands a 3-m- (9½-ft-) tall fragment of the ghetto wall that existed for one year from November 1940. ✉ *Ul. Złota 60.*

33 **Pomnik Bohaterów Getta** (Heroes of the Warsaw Ghetto). The simple monument to the heroes of the Warsaw Ghetto is a slab of dark granite with a bronze bas-relief. A monument also marks the site of the house at ulica Miła 18 in which the command bunker of the uprising was concealed. ✉ *Ul. Zamenhofa, between ul. Anielewicaz and ul. Lewartowskiego.*

36 **Synagoga Nożykow** (Nozyk Synagogue). Founded in 1900 by Zelman and Ryfka Nożyk, the synagogue survived the war and is now the only active synagogue in Warsaw. ✉ *Ul. Twarda 6.*

38 **Ulica Próżna**(Próżna Street). This is the only street in Jewish Warsaw where tenement buildings have been preserved on both sides of the street. The Lauder foundation plans to restore the street to its original state. No. 9 belonged to Zelman Nożyk.

32 **Umschlagplatz.** From this rail terminus, hundreds of thousands of the ghetto's inhabitants were shipped in cattle cars to the extermination camp of Treblinka, about 100 km (60 mi) northeast of Warsaw. The school building to the right of the square was used to detain those who had to wait overnight for transport, and the beginning of the rail tracks survives on the right. At the entrance to the square is a **symbolic gateway,** erected in 1988 as a memorial on the 45th anniversary of the uprising. ✉ *Corner ul. Stawki and ul. Dzika.*

35 **Żydowski Instytut Historyczny** (Jewish Historical Institute). Some 3 million Polish Jews were put to death by the Nazis during World War II, ending the enormous Jewish contribution to Polish culture, tradition, and achievement. The Institute houses the Ronald S. Lauder Foundation Genealogy Project, which acts as a clearinghouse of information on available archival sources and on the history of towns and villages in which Polish Jews lived. English-speaking staff are available weekdays after 10 AM. The Institute also houses a **museum,** currently under renovation, which has photographic exhibitions and displays of mementoes and artifacts that recall a lost world. The nearby Sony building stands on the site of Warsaw's largest synagogue, which was blown up by the Nazis in May of 1943 as a triumphal finale to the liquidation of the Jewish ghetto. ✉ *Ul. Tłomackie 3/5,* ☎ *022/827–92–21.* ⏲ *Weekdays 9–3.*

Dining and Lodging

More and more interesting restaurants have opened up throughout the city, but some of the most atmospheric dining rooms are still to be found on and around the Rynek Starego Miasta (Old Town Square) in the Old Town. Reservations for dinner can be made by telephone (by your hotel receptionist if you don't speak Polish); in the case of expensive and fashionable restaurants, this is essential. For details and price-category definitions, *see* Dining *in* Poland A to Z, *above*.

Orbis hotels are reliable, offering standardized, functional rooms. Most show signs of wear, but bathrooms have often been renovated to Western European standards. Private accommodations are cheap and hospitable. Information and reservations are available through the Center for Tourist Information (☞ Visitor Information *in* Warsaw Essentials, *below*), or through Syrena (✉ ul. Krucza 17, ☎ 022/628–75–40). Some hotels have lower prices during the winter months. For details and price-category definitions, *see* Lodging *in* Poland A to Z, *above*.

$$$$ ★ ✕ **Belvedere.** Housed in the elegant, romantic, 19th-century orangery in Łazienki Park, the restaurant has tables set among palms and waterfalls. The overpriced menu offers many traditional dishes, such as saddle of hare in nut sauce. ✉ *Łazienki Królewskie, entrance from ul. Parkowa,* ☎ *022/41–48–06. Reservations essential. AE, DC, MC, V.*

$$$ ✕ **Bazyliszek.** Dimly lighted, the Bazyliszek excels in boar, venison, and duck. A good café and snack bar are downstairs. ✉ *Rynek Starego Miasta 3/9,* ☎ *022/831–18–41. AE, DC, MC, V.*

$$$ ✕ **Café Ejlat.** Try the meat pierogis or the daily special, prepared under the watchful eye of Stanisław Pruszyński, who escaped from Poland in 1955, became a successful restauranteur in Canada, and returned to Poland after communism collapsed. It's a gathering spot for expats and hip Warsovians for afternoon tea as well. ✉ *Al. Ujazdowskie 47,* ☎ *022/628–54–72. AE, DC, MC, V.*

$$$ ✕ **Opus One.** For a change from Polish food, try this popular Austrian restaurant for hot pretzels, huge wiener schnitzel, and homemade potato salad. These, along with a pianist and occasional live jazz, attract Polish yuppies. ✉ *Pl. Młynarskiego 2,* ☎ *022/827–51–00. Reservations essential. AE, DC, MC, V.*

$$$ ✕ **Pod Samsonem.** This simple, pre-war Jewish-style (nonkosher) restaurant serves traditional Polish food. Specialties include fried trout and loin of beef with vegetables, mushrooms, and potatoes. ✉ *Ul. Freta 3/5,* ☎ *022/31–17–88. AE, DC, MC, V.*

$$ ✕ **Czytelnik.** Intellectuals and politicians who drop in from the Parliament next door hang out at this cafeteria-style restaurant/café with homemade food. ✉ *Ul. Wiejska 12a,* ☎ *022/628–14–41. No credit cards. Closed dinner.*

$$ ✕ **Kamienne Schodki.** This intimate, candlelit restaurant is in one of the Rynek Starego Miasta's restored medieval houses. Its specialty is duck; be sure to try the pastries as well. ✉ *Rynek Starego Miasta 26,* ☎ *022/831–08–22. AE, DC, MC, V.*

$$ ✕ **Menora.** Poland's only kosher restaurant stands on the dilapidated Plac Grzybowski, opposite the Jewish Theater and synagogue. Among the traditional dishes are kreplach (crepes with meat filling) and apple cake. ✉ *Plac Grzybowski 2,* ☎ *022/620–37–54. AE, DC, MC, V.*

$$ ✕ **Qchnia Artystyczna.** This artsy place at the back of the Ujazdowski Castle is not for the stodgy. The service is terrible, but the food, such as the vegetarian *naleśniki* (crepes with sweet cheese or fruit filling), and the view overlooking the park more than make up for it. ✉ *Ujazdowski Castle, Al. Ujazdowskie 6,* ☎ *022/625–76–27. AE, DC, MC, V.*

$$$$ ★ **Bristol.** Since reopening in 1992 after a decade of renovation, Warsaw's most famous hotel has reclaimed its tradition of luxury and elegance. Built in 1901 and once partially owned by Ignacy Paderewski, the pianist who was Poland's prime minister in 1919–1920, the Bristol remains at the center of Warsaw's social life. ✉ *Krakowskie Przedmieście 42–44, 00–325,* ☎ *022/625–25–25,* FAX *022/625–25–77. 163 rooms, 43 suites. 2 restaurants, pool. AE, DC, MC, V.*

$$$$ **Marriott.** This Marriott was completed in 1989, and at 40 stories (20 make up the hotel; the rest are set aside for office and retail shopping space), the building is among the tallest in Warsaw. ✉ *Al. Jerozolimskie 65–79, 00–697,* ☎ *022/630–63–06,* FAX *022/830–00–50. 488 rooms, 34 suites. 3 restaurants, pool. AE, DC, MC, V.*

$$$$ ★ **Sheraton.** Finished in 1996, this hotel stands near the Parliament and Embassy Row. The tastefully decorated rooms overlook a beautiful square. Hotel service is impeccable, and there are excellent exercise facilities in the basement. ✉ *Ul. Prusa 2, 00–493,* ☎ *022/657–61–00,* FAX *022/657–62–00. 331 rooms, 19 suites. 2 restaurants. AE, DC, MC, V.*

$$$$ **Victoria Inter-Continental.** The main advantage of this large 1970s hotel is its location near the Old Town. It has the full range of Inter-Continental facilities. Ask for a room facing Victory Square. ✉ *Ul. Królewska 1, 00–065,* ☎ *022/657–80–11,* FAX *022/657–80–57. 347 rooms, 13 suites. 3 restaurants, pool. AE, DC, MC, V.*

$$$ **Hotel Europejski.** This late-19th-century hotel has views overlooking the Royal Route and the Tomb of the Unknown Soldier. Rooms are spacious, and the location is so good that you may not mind the slightly shabby furnishings. ✉ *Krakowskie Przedmieście 13, 00–065,* ☎ *022/826–50–51,* FAX *022/826–11–11. 233 rooms, 5 suites. Restaurant. AE, DC, MC, V.*

$$ **Dom Chłopa.** This renovated 1950s hotel has bright, pine-furnished rooms with gleaming bathrooms. It is a five-minute walk from the primary shopping streets and the National Philharmonic. If you don't mind the noisy clientele of the nightclub on the ground floor, it's good value. ✉ *Plac Powstańców Warszawy 2, 00–030,* ☎ *022/827–49–43,* FAX *022/ 625–15–45. 282 rooms. Restaurant. AE, DC, MC, V.*

$$ **MDM.** The rooms are slightly dreary, with brown bedspreads, but the place is clean and the bathrooms are up to Western standards. For a downtown hotel, you can't beat the price. The breakfast is outstanding. ✉ *Plac Konstytucji 1, 00-647,* ☎ *022/621–62–11,* FAX *022/621–41–73. 105 rooms, 5 suites. Restaurant. AE, DC, MC, V.*

Nightlife and the Arts

The Arts

The *Warsaw Insider,* available at most major hotels, is the best English-language source. If you read Polish, *Gazeta Wyborcza* and the monthly *IKS (Informator Kulturalny Stolicy)* have extensive listings. Cultural information is available over the telephone (☎ 022/629–84–89). Tickets can be ordered at your hotel, at the theater itself, or through the ticket office **Zasp** (✉ Al. Jerozolimskie 25, ☎ 022/621–94–54).

CONCERTS

The **National Philharmonic** (✉ Ul. Sienkiewicza 10, ☎ 022/826–57–12) is Poland's best concert hall. Another hall with outstanding acoustics is the **Studio Koncertowe Polskiego Radia** (Polish Radio Concert Studio; ✉ Woronicza 17, ☎ 022/645–52–52). **The Royal Castle** (✉ Plac Zamkowy 4, ☎ 022/65–72–170) has regular concerts in its stunning Great Assembly Hall. In summer free Chopin concerts are held at the Chopin monument in **Łazienki Park** on Sunday. Summer Chopin concerts are held at **Żelazowa Wola** (☎ 046/863–6300), the composer's birthplace, 58 km (36 mi) west of Warsaw.

OPERA

Teatr Wielki (✉ Pl. Teatralny 1, ☎ 022/826–32–88) hosts the Grand Theater of Opera and Ballet. Its stage is one of Europe's largest. The beautiful, intimate **Opera Kameralna** (✉ Al. Solidarności 76b, ☎ 022/831–22–40) theater is not to be missed.

THEATERS

There are still 17 major theaters in Warsaw, despite large cuts in state funding, attesting to Poles' love of this art form. The **Globe Theatre Group** (☎ 022/620–44–29) has a varied contemporary English-language repertory. **Teatr Narodowy** (✉ Plac Teatralny 1, ☎ 022/826–32–88) is the oldest in Poland (it opened in 1765). **Współczesny** (✉ ul. Mokotowska 13, ☎ 022/25–59–79) presents contemporary works. **Żydowski Theater** (✉ Plac Grzybowski 12/16, ☎ 022/620–70–25), Warsaw's Jewish Theater, stages performances in Yiddish; headsets are available for translations into English.

Nightlife

BARS

Harenda (✉ Krakowskie Przedmieście 4/6, ☎ 022/826–29–00), with an outdoor terrace in summer, is open until 3 AM. **The John Bull Pub** (✉ ul. Zielna 37, ☎ 022/620–06–56) is open until midnight and serves English draft beers.

CABARET

Arena (✉ ul. Marszałkowska 104, ☎ 022/827–50–91) has boisterous floor shows. Major hotels have nightclubs that are popular with some visitors and present striptease and jazz. Check listings in the press.

CAFÉS

Warsaw's *kawiarnia* (cafés), which move outdoors in summer, are busy meeting places, serving coffee and pastries in Central European style. **Café Blikle** (✉ Nowy Świat 35, ☎ 022/826–66–19) is a traditional, fashionable hangout on Warsaw's main shopping street. **E. Wedel** (✉ ul. Szpitalna 8, ☎ no phone), a venerable Warsaw institution, under new ownership in 1996 added tea, coffee, and soft drinks to the beverage menu after having served nothing but thick, incredibly rich hot chocolate for 100 years. **Nowe Miasto** (✉ Nowego Miasta 13/15, ☎ 022/831–43–79), a vegetarian café-cum-restaurant, is on the restored, quiet New Town Square. The large, bustling **Nowy Świat** (✉ Nowy Świat 63, ☎ 022/826–58–03) is good for people-watching and has a good selection of foreign-language newspapers. Tiny **Pożegnanie z Afrika** (Out of Africa; ✉ Ul. Freta 4/6, ☎ no phone) café has good coffee from all over the world; forget the food. **Słodkie Fukier** (✉ ul. Mokotowska 45, ☎ 022/622–49–34) serves delicious pastries and good coffee.

DANCE CLUBS

Ground Zero (✉ ul. Wspólna 62, ☎ 022/625–43–80), a former bomb shelter, has a torrid scene. The popular **Hades** (✉ Al. Niepodległośi 162, ☎ 022/49–12–51), in the basement of Poland's best business school, the Main School of Commerce, has plenty of seating space. **Panorama Club** (✉ Al. Jerozolimskie 65/79, ☎ 022/630–74–35), on the top floor of the Marriott, is elegant and very expensive; hotel guests have priority for admission. **Riviera Remont** (✉ ul. Waryńskiego 12, ☎ 022/25–74–97) is one of the hottest places in town. There is a well-established disco at the student club **Stodoła** (✉ ul.Batorego 10, ☎ 022/25–86–25). **Tango** (✉ ul. Smolna 15, ☎ 022/622–19–19) is an upmarket disco and cabaret where high entrance charges on Wednesday—zł 85—include a buffet supper.

JAZZ CLUBS

Akwarium (✉ ul. Emilii Plater 49, ☎ 022/620–50–72) is a popular jazz club. **Kawiarnia Literacka,** (✉ Krakowskie Przedmieście 87/89, ☎ 022/826–57–84), overlooking Castle Square, has classic jazz on weekends.

Shopping

Nowy Świat, Krakowskie Przedmieście, and ulica Chmielna are lined with boutiques selling good-quality leather goods, silver jewelry, clothing, and trinkets. For the best selection of Polish wood carvings, including animals and nativity scenes, go to **Arex** (✉ ul. Chopina 5B, ☎ 022/629–66–24). Try the **Cepelia** stores (✉ Plac Konstytucji 5, ☎ 022/621–26–18, and ✉ Rynek Starego Miasta 10, ☎ 022/831–18–05) for handicrafts such as glass, enamelware, amber, and hand-woven wool rugs. **Desa** (✉ ul. Marszałkowska 34, ☎ 022/621–66–15) specializes in antiques (those from before 1945 cannot be legally exported). **Galeria Plakatu** (✉ Rynek Starego Miasta 23, ☎ 022/831–93–06) has an excellent selection of Polish posters, which were world famous during the 1970s and '80s.

Warsaw Essentials

Arriving and Departing

BY BUS

Warsaw's central **bus terminal** is at ✉ aleje Jerozolimskie 144.

BY CAR

Seven main access routes lead to the center of Warsaw. Highways E30 and E77 are the main arteries from the West.

BY PLANE

All international flights arrive at Warsaw's modern **Okęcie Airport** (Port Lotniczy) just southwest of the city. Terminal 1 serves international flights; Terminal 2, next door, serves domestic flights. For flight information contact the airlines, or call the airport at 022/650–42–20.

Between the Airport and Downtown. The airport–city bus (leaves the airport about every 20 minutes from Platform 4 and costs zł 6) and public Bus 175 (leaves the airport every 15 minutes and costs zł 1.40) run past almost all major downtown hotels. The trip takes about 25 minutes.

Avoid at all costs taxi drivers who approach you in the arrivals hall and who are parked outside the arrivals hall. Your best bet is to go upstairs to the departure drop-off and flag down a taxi (if he refuses, ask him to call one) or call 919 for a radio taxi (fare about zł 35). Some of the hotels will also pick you up (fare about zł 45).

BY TRAIN

Trains to and from Western Europe arrive at **Dworzec Centralny** (Central Station; ✉ Al. Jerozolimskie 54, ☎ 022/620–03–61, local train information; 022/620–45–12, international train information) in the center of town. For tickets contact a travel agent or your hotel or go to the train station.

Getting Around

BY BUGGY

Horse-drawn carriages can be rented at a negotiated price at the Old Town Market Square or Castle Square.

BY SUBWAY

Warsaw's subway opened in spring 1995. At present there is only one line, which runs 11 mi from the southern suburbs to the city center (Natolin to Plac Politechniki with an extension to the Palace of Culture and Science due to open in April 1998), but it is clean and fast, costs the same as the tram and bus, and uses the same tickets, which you cancel at the entrance to the station. Trains run every 5 minutes during rush hours, every 15 minutes during off-peak hours.

BY TAXI

Taxis are still relatively cheap—about zł 3.60 for the first kilometer (½ mile) and zł 1.40 for each additional kilometer (½ mile)—and are readily available at taxi stands. Most major hotels have their own monogrammed fleets, but expect to pay more than you would for the efficient radio taxi service (☎ 919, English spoken), which is also considerably cheaper than taxis at stands.

BY TRAM AND BUS

Though often crowded, they are the cheapest way of getting around. Trams and buses (including express buses) cost zł 1.40. The bus fare goes up to zł 4.20 between 11 PM and 5:30 AM. Tickets must be bought in advance from **Ruch** newsstands. You must cancel your own ticket in a machine on the tram or bus when you get on; watch how others do it. Beware of very professional pickpockets.

Contacts and Resources

EMBASSIES

United States (✉ Al. Ujazdowskie 29–31, ☎ 022/628–30–41). **Canadian** (✉ Ul. Matejki 1/5, ☎ 022/629–80–51). **United Kingdom** (✉ Al. Róż 1, ☎ 022/628–10–01). **U.K. Consulate** (✉ Ul. Emilii Plater 28, ☎ 022/625–30–30). **Australian** (✉ ul. Estońska 3/5,☎ 022/617–6081/5).

EMERGENCIES

Police (☎ 997). **Ambulance** (☎ 999). **Doctor** (☎ 999, your embassy; or **The American Medical Center** (AMC; ☎ 060/2243–024 [24 hours]). **Pharmacies** in Warsaw stay open on a rotational system. Signs listing the nearest open facility are posted outside every pharmacy.There is also a **24-hour pharmacy** upstairs in the Central Train Station (✉ Al. Jerozolimskie 54, ☎ 022/25–69–84).

ENGLISH-LANGUAGE BOOKSTORES

American Bookstore (✉ Krakowskie Przedmieście 45, ☎ 022/826–01–61). **Empik** (✉ ul. Marszałkowska 116/122, ☎ 022/827–79–89).

GUIDED TOURS

Bus tours of the city depart in the morning and afternoon from major hotels. **Mazurkas Travel** (✉ ul. Długa 8/14, ☎ 022/635-66–33) offers an excellent selection of tours around the city. **Orbis** (☞ Travel Agencies, *below*) also has half-day excursions into the surrounding countryside. These usually include a meal and some form of traditional entertainment. **Our Roots** (☞ Travel Agencies, *below*) offers four-hour tours of Jewish Warsaw.

TRAVEL AGENCIES

American Express (✉ Krakowskie Przedmieście 11, ☎ 022/635–20–02; Marriott Hotel, ✉ Al. Jerozolimskie 65/79, ☎ 022/630–69–52; 24-hour ☎ 022/625–40–30). **Carlson Wagonlit Travel** (✉ Ul. Nowy Świat 64, ☎ 022/826–04–31). **Orbis** (✉ ul. Bracka 16, ☎ 022/826–02–71; ✉ ul. Marszałkowska 142, (☎ 022/827–80–31). **Our Roots–Jewish Information and Tourist Bureau** (✉ ul. Twarda 6, ☎ 022/620–05–56).

VISITOR INFORMATION

The **Center for Tourist Information** (✉ Plac Zamkowy 1, ☎ 022/ 635–18–81).

KRAKÓW

Kraków, once the capital of the country (before losing the honor to Warsaw in 1611) and seat of the country's oldest university, is one of the few Polish cities that miraculously escaped devastation during World War II. Today Kraków's fine ramparts, towers, facades, and churches, illustrating 7 centuries of Polish architecture, make it a major attraction for visitors. Kraków's Old Town is listed by UNESCO as one of the 12 great historic cities of the world.

Its location—about 270 km (167 mi) south of Warsaw—also makes it a good base for hiking and skiing trips in the mountains of southern Poland. Within exploring range from Kraków are, in addition, the famous Polish shrine to the Virgin Mary at Częstochowa, and, at Auschwitz (Oświęcim), a grim reminder of man's capacity for inhumanity.

Exploring Kraków

Numbers in the margin correspond to points of interest on the Kraków map.

It seems a miracle that the marvelous old city of Kraków escaped World War II virtually undamaged. The city has three basic districts for touring: the Old Town, the Jewish quarter, and the Wawel. Each area can be seen in a half day or so, but more time can easily be spent.

2 **Barbakan** (The Barbican). This imposing, round, redbrick 15th-century fortress was part of the old city defense system. It stands in Planty Park, which, circling the Old Town, replaces the old walls of the town, which were torn down in the mid-19th century. ✉ *Ul. Basztowa.*

1 **Brama Floriańska** (St. Florian's Gate). The surviving fragment of the city wall opposite the Barbakan, where students and amateur artists like to hang their paintings for sale in the summer, contains the renaissance Municipal Arsenal. ✉ *Ul. Pijarska.*

9 **Collegium Maius** (Greater College). The pride of the oldest building of the world-renowned **Jagiellonian University**, founded in 1364, is the Italian-style arcaded courtyard. A **museum** here contains the Copernicus globe, the first on which the American continents were shown, as well as astronomy instruments belonging to Kraków's most famous graduate. ✉ *Ul. Świętej Anny 8,* ☎ *012/422–05–49 (museum).* ⏲ *Mon.–Sat. 8–6 (courtyard); 11–1:30 (museum, by appointment only).*

5 **Kościół Mariacki** (Church of the Virgin Mary). Every hour, four short bugle calls drift down from the spire of this church. The notes are a centuries-old tradition that honors a trumpeter whose throat was pierced by an enemy arrow as he was warning his fellow citizens of an impending Tartar attack. Inside the church is a 15th-century wooden altarpiece—the world's largest—carved by Veit Stoss. The saints' faces are reputedly those of local burghers. ✉ *Rynek Główny.*

11 **Kościół na Skałce** (Church on the Rock). This Pauline Church is the center of the cult of St. Stanisław, an 11th-century bishop and martyr. Starting in the 19th century, it also became the last resting place for well-known Polish writers and artists; among those buried here are the composer Karol Szymanowski and the poet and painter Stanisław Wyspiański. ✉ *Ul. Skałeczna and ul. Paulińska.*

Kraków

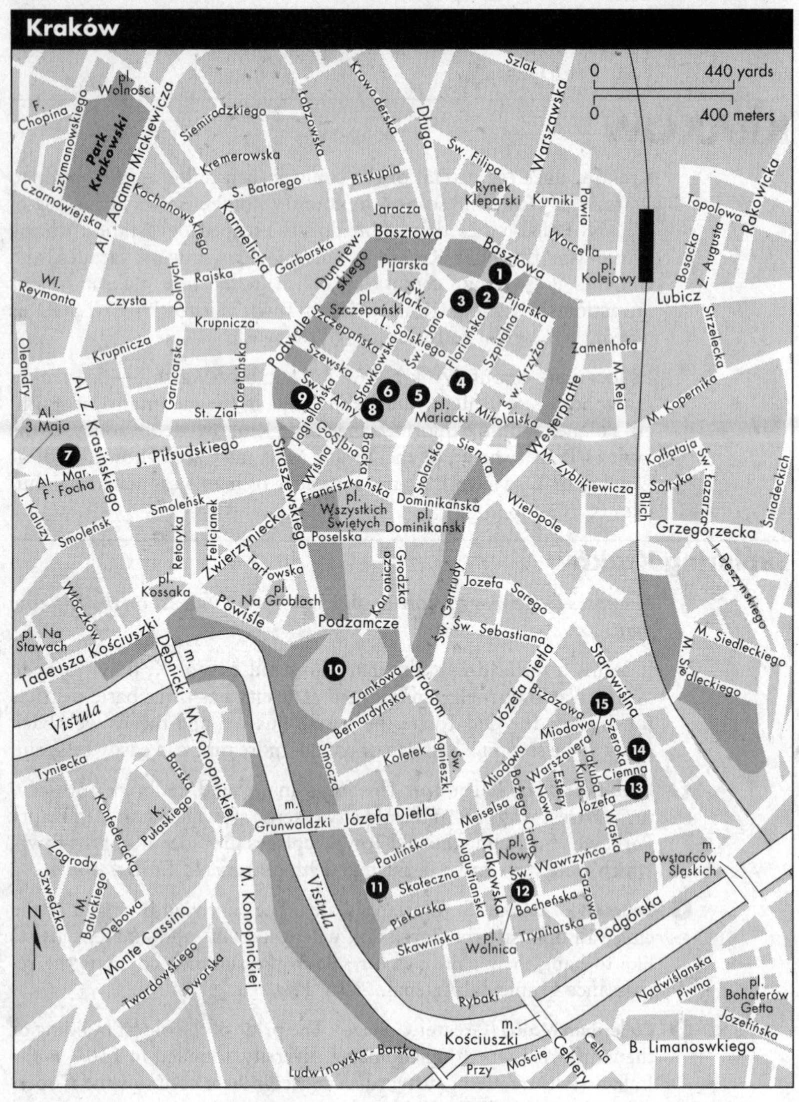

Barbakan, **2**
Brama Floriańska, **1**
Collegium Maius, **9**
Kościół Mariacki, **5**
Kościół na Skałce, **11**
Muzeum Narodowy, **7**
Pałac Czartoryskich, **3**
Ratusz, **12**
Rynek Główny, **4**
Stara Synagoga, **14**
Sukiennice, **6**
Synagoga Remuh, **15**
Synagoga Wyoska, **13**
Wawel, **10**
Wieża Ratuszowa, **8**

7 **Muzeum Narodowy** (National Museum). The highlights of this museum are Polish Art Nouveau and 20th-century painting, as well as historic arms and uniforms. ✉ *Al. 3 Maja 1,* ☎ *012/634–33–37.* ⏲ *Tues.–Sun. 10–3:30, Wed. 10–6.*

★ 3 **Pałac Czartoryskich** (Czartoryski Palace). This branch of the National Museum, partially housed in the **Municipal Arsenal,** is one of the best art collections in Poland. Highlights include Leonardo da Vinci's *Lady with an Ermine.* ✉ *Ul. Św. Jana 19,* ☎ *012/422–55–66.* ⏲ *Tues.–Sun. 10–3, Fri. 10–5.*

12 **Ratusz** (City Hall of Kazimierz). The building is in the Kazimierz district of Kraków, which was once a town in its own right, chartered in 1335 and named for its founder, Kazimierz the Great. After 1495, when they were expelled from Kraków by King John Albert, this was the home of Kraków's Jews. The 15th-century town hall on the town square, now the **Muzeum Etnograficzne** (Ethnographic Museum), displays a well-mounted collection of regional folk art. ✉ *Pl. Wolnica,* ☎ *012/656–28–63.* ⏲ *Mon. 10–6, Wed., Thurs., and Fri. 10–3, weekends 10–2.*

4 **Rynek Główny** (Main Market Square). This is one of the largest and finest Renaissance squares in Europe. ✉ *Center of old town at ul. Floriańska and Św. Anny.*

14 **Stara Synagoga** (Old Synagogue). This synagogue was built during the 15th century and reconstructed in Renaissance style following a fire in 1557. Here, in 1794, Tadeusz Kościuszko successfully appealed to the Jewish community to join in the national insurrection. The synagogue now houses the **Museum of the History and Culture of Kraków Jews.** ✉ *Ul. Szeroka 23,* ☎ *012/422–09–62.* ⏲ *Wed., Thurs. 9–3:30, Fri. 11–6, weekends 9–3. Closed 1st weekend of month; open following Mon. and Tues.*

6 **Sukiennice** (Cloth Hall). In the center of the main square stands a covered market hall built during the 14th century but remodeled during the Renaissance. The ground floor (⏲ Mon.–Sat. 10–6, Sun. 10–5) is still in business, selling trinkets and folk-art souvenirs. On the second floor, in a branch of the **National Museum,** you can view a collection of 19th-century Polish painting. ✉ *Rynek Główny,* ☎ *012/422–11–66.* ⏲ *Tues.–Sun. 10–3:30, Thurs. 10–5:30.*

15 **Synagoga Remuh** (Remuh Synagogue). This 16th-century synagogue is still used for worship. The cemetery, used by the Jewish community from 1533 to 1799, is the only well-preserved Renaissance Jewish burial ground in Europe. The so-called New Cemetery (✉ ul. Miodowa), which contains many old headstones, was established in the 19th century. ✉ *Ul. Szeroka 40.*

13 **Synagoga Wysoka** (High Synagogue). This late-16th-century synagogue has a prayer room on the second floor. ✉ *Ul. Józefa 38.*

★ 10 **Wawel.** This impressive castle complex of Gothic and Renaissance buildings stands on fortifications dating from the 8th century. Inside the castle is a **museum** with an exotic collection of Oriental tents that were captured from the Turks at the Battle of Vienna in 1683 and rare 16th-century Flemish tapestries. **Katedra Wawelska** (Wawel Cathedral) is where, until the 18th century, Polish kings were crowned and buried. Until 1978 the cathedral was the principal church of Archbishop Karol Wojtyła, now Pope John Paul II. ✉ *Ul. Grodzka,* ☎ *012/422–51–55.* ⏲ *Tues.–Sun. 9:30–3.*

8 **Wieża Ratuszowa** (Town Hall Tower). Across from the Cloth Hall is all that remains of the 16th-century town hall. The tower now houses

a branch of the **Muzeum historii i kultury żydowstwa krakowskiego** (Museum of Jewish Kraków) and has a panoramic view of the Old Town. ✉ *Rynek Główny.* ⏲ *June–Sept., Fri.–Wed. 9–3, Thurs. noon–5. Closed 2nd weekend of every month.*

Dining and Lodging

For details and price-category definitions, *see* Dining and Lodging *in* Poland A to Z, *above*.

There is a serious shortage of hotel rooms in Kraków, especially during the busy summer tourist season, when it is absolutely essential to book well in advance. Kraków lacks centrally located and reasonably priced, first-class hotels. Rooms facing the street in the old town are often noisy at night.

$$$$ ✕ **Hawelka.** Established in 1876 by a merchant, Antoni Hawelka, this restaurant specializes in Polish cuisine. The restaurant on the ground floor is casual and cheaper than the one upstairs. ✉ *Rynek Główny 34,* ☎ *012/422–47–53. AE, DC, MC, V.*

$$$$ ✕ **Wierzynek.** It was in a restaurant on this site, after a historic meeting in 1364, that the king of Poland wined and dined the Holy Roman Emperor Charles IV, five kings, and a score of princes. The current establishment serves traditional Polish specialties and excels in soups and game. ✉ *Rynek Główny 15,* ☎ *012/422–10–35. AE, DC, MC, V.*

$$$ ★ ✕ **Pod Aniołami.** In summer the restaurant is in a courtyard; in winter it moves into a cozy cellar. It's a favorite place for lunch with Kraków's consular corps. The salads and homemade bread are especially good. ✉ *Ul. Grodzka 35,* ☎ *012/421–39–99. No credit cards.*

$$$ ✕ **Staropolska.** Traditional Polish cuisine is served in a medieval setting. Try the pork, duck, or sautéed carp. ✉ *Ul. Sienna 4,* ☎ *012/422–58–21. AE, DC, MC, V.*

$$ ✕ **Jama Michalikowa.** Kraków's most famous café serves good coffee and excellent ice cream. ✉ *Ul. Floriańska 45,* ☎ *012/422–15–61.*

$ ✕ **Kabaret Loch Camelot.** This little café is on a small street right off the main square. It's a good place to get a glass of wine or to listen to a recital (on Friday or Saturday at 8 PM). It's also open in the morning for coffee. ✉ *Ul. Tomasza 17,* ☎ *No phone. No credit cards.*

$$$ ✕🏨 **Cracovia.** Large and Orbis-run, this five-story 1960s hotel is one of the few likely to have space during the busy summer months. The rooms are small and standardized but comfortable. It also has one of the better restaurants in town. The chef specializes in an internationalized Polish cuisine. Try the *krem z pieczarek* (thick and creamy mushroom soup), followed by chateaubriand. ✉ *Al. Marszałka F. Focha 1, 30–111,* ☎ *012/422–86–66,* FAX *012/421–95– 86. 427 rooms. Restaurant. AE, DC, MC, V.*

$$$ 🏨 **Continental.** The first Holiday Inn in Eastern Europe, this high-rise hotel is bland but comfortable. Its location, on the far side of Kraków Common, makes it a good choice if you want to combine sightseeing with a little exercise. ✉ *Ul. Armii Krajowej 11, 30–150,* ☎ *012/637–50–44,* FAX *012/637–59–38. 305 rooms. Restaurant, pool. AE, DC, MC, V.*

$$$ 🏨 **Forum.** Opened in 1988, this charmless Orbis hotel stands on the south bank of the Vistula, commanding a fine view of Wawel Castle. It's a bit far from the Old Town but has good exercise facilities. ✉ *Ul. Marii Konopnickiej 28, 30–302,* ☎ *012/266–95–00,* FAX *012/266–58–27. 280 rooms. Restaurant, pool. AE, DC, MC, V.*

$$$ 🏨 **Francuski.** This small, turn-of-the-century hotel is just inside the Old Town's ramparts. It has an intimate atmosphere and friendly service, and the rooms are small but elegant in a homey, Eastern European way.

The restaurant is tranquil and plush. ✉ *Ul. Pijarska 13, 31–015,* ☎ *012/422–51–22,* FAX *012/422–52–70. 42 rooms. Restaurant. AE, DC, MC, V.*

$$$ ★ 🏨 **Grand.** An air of Regency elegance predominates at this late-19th-century hotel in the Old Town, although some Art Nouveau stained-glass windows have been preserved on the first floor. Rooms have reproduction period furniture and modern bathrooms and facilities. ✉ *Ul. Sławkowska 5–7, 31–014,* ☎ *012/421–72–55,* FAX *012/421–83–60. 56 rooms. Restaurant. AE, DC, MC, V.*

$$ 🏨 **Pollera.** This 150-year-old hotel is a bit on the shabby side but is good value because of its location. The bathrooms are ancient. ✉ *Ul. Szpitalna 30, 31–024,* ☎ *012/422–10–44,* FAX *012/422–13–89. 42 rooms. Restaurant. AE, DC, MC, V.*

$ 🏨 **Saski.** In this Old World, centrally located hotel, a stupendous prewar elevator takes you to your room. ✉ *Ul. Sławkowska 3, 31–014,* ☎ *012/421–42–22,* FAX *012/421–48–30. 63 rooms. AE, DC, MC, V.*

Side Trips

Oświęcim (Auschwitz)

About 50 km (30 mi) west of Kraków is Oświęcim, better known by its German name, Auschwitz. Here 4 million victims, mostly Jews, were executed by the Nazis in the Auschwitz and Birkenau concentration camps. **Auschwitz** is now a museum, with restored crematoria and barracks housing dramatic displays of Nazi atrocities. The buildings at Birkenau, a 15-minute walk away, have been left just as they were found in 1945 by the Soviet Army. Oświęcim itself is an industrial town with good connections from Kraków; buses and trains leave Kraków periodically, and signs in Oświęcim direct visitors to the former camp. ✉ *Ul. Więźniów Oświęcimia 20,* ☎ *033/4321–33.* ⏲ *Nov.–Mar., daily 8–3; Apr. and Oct., daily 8–5; May and Sept., daily 8–6; June–Aug., daily 8–7. Birkenau:* ⏲ *Daily, sunrise–sunset.*

Wieliczka

About 8 km (5 mi) southeast of Kraków is the oldest salt mine in Europe, in operation since the 13th century. The mine is on the Unesco World Cultural Heritage list and is famous for its magnificent underground chapel hewn from crystal rock, the **Chapel of the Blessed Kinga** (Queen Kinga was a 14th-century Polish queen, later beatified). ✉ *Ul. Daniłowicza 10,* ☎ *012/278–73–34.* ⏲ *Daily 8–4.*

Częstochowa

About 120 km (70 mi) from Kraków and reachable by regular trains and buses, Częstochowa is the home of the holiest shrine in a country that is some 95% Catholic. Inside the 14th-century **Pauline Monastery** on Jasna Góra (Light Hill) is the *Black Madonna,* a painting of Our Lady of Częstochowa attributed by legend to St. Luke. It was here that an invading Swedish army met heroic resistance from the Poles in 1655.

$ 🏨 **Polonia.** The Polonia makes a good base for exploring the Monastery, and as most of the guests are pilgrims, the atmosphere is a mixture of piety and good fun. ✉ *Ul. Piłsudskiego 9, 42–200,* ☎ *034/24–40–67,* FAX *034/65–11–05. 62 rooms. Restaurant. AE, DC, MC, V.*

Wadowice

About 40 km (25 mi) southwest of Kraków is the little town of Wadowice, birthplace of Pope John Paul II. You can visit the **Muzeum Wadowice** (Wadowice Museum), dedicated to his life, in the house where he grew up. ✉ *Ul. Kościelna 7,* ☎ *033/326–62.* ⏲ *Tues.–Sun. 9–noon, 2–5.*

Kraków Essentials

Consulate

United States (✉ Ul. Stolarska 9, ☎ 012/421–67–67, 012/422–97–64, or 012/422–14–00).

Getting Around

Kraków can be reached by **air** with direct flights from many major European cities and most Polish cities (Airport information, ☎ 012/116–700.) By car the city can be reached by major **highways**—E7 direct from Warsaw and E40 from Częstochowa. **Trains** link Kraków with most major destinations in Poland; the station, Kraków Główny (✉ Plac Kolejowy 1, ☎ 012/422–22–48, international information) is in the city center near the Old Town. The **bus** station is across the street.

Guided Tours

Bus or walking tours of Kraków and its environs are provided by Orbis and other travel agencies (☞ *below*). Jordan Tours (☞ *below*) specializes in "Schindler's List" tours (*Schindler's List,* Steven Spielberg's award-winning 1993 film, inspired visitors to Kraków to retrace the steps of German industrialist Oskar Schindler, who saved the lives of more than 1,200 Jews during the Holocaust by hiring them to work in his enamel factory at ulica Lipowa 4.) Horse-drawn carriages can be rented at the main market square for a negotiated price.

Travel agencies

Jordan Tours (✉ Ul. Szeroka 2, ☎ 012/421–71–66). **Orbis** (✉ Rynek Glówny 41, ☎ 012/422–40–35; ✉ Al. Marszałka F. Focha 1, ☎ 012/421–98–80).

Visitor Information

Częstochowa: Częstochowa Informacja Turystyczna (✉ Al. Najświętszej Marii Panny 64, ☎ 034/24–13–60). **Kraków**: Wawel Tours (✉ Ul. Pawia 8, ☎ 012/421–77–06).

GDAŃSK AND THE NORTH

In contrast to Kraków and the south, Poland north of Warsaw is a land of castles, dense forests and lakes, and fishing villages and beaches. If you don't have a car, consider going straight to Gdańsk and making excursions from here.

Exploring Gdańsk and the North

By car from Warsaw, follow routes E77 and E62 through Płock. Continue through Włocławek to Toruń, where you can stay overnight. The route leading north from Toruń to Gdańsk passes through some of the oldest towns in Poland. Along the way are many medieval castles, manor houses, and churches that testify to the wealth and strategic importance of the area. Two short detours are a must: One is to Kwidzyń, to see the original 14th-century castle and cathedral complex, which is open to the public. The other is to Malbork (☞ *below*).

For a different route back to Warsaw, follow highway E77 southeast along the outer edge of Poland's scenic lake district. The area is rich in natural and historic attractions. A side trip 42 km (26 mi) east of Ostróda takes you to the medieval town of Olsztyn. Another diversion, 17 km (10½ mi) west of Olsztynek, is the site of the Battle of Grunwald.

Gdańsk

Gdańsk, once the Free City of Danzig, contains another of Poland's beautifully restored old towns, displaying a rich heritage of Gothic, Re-

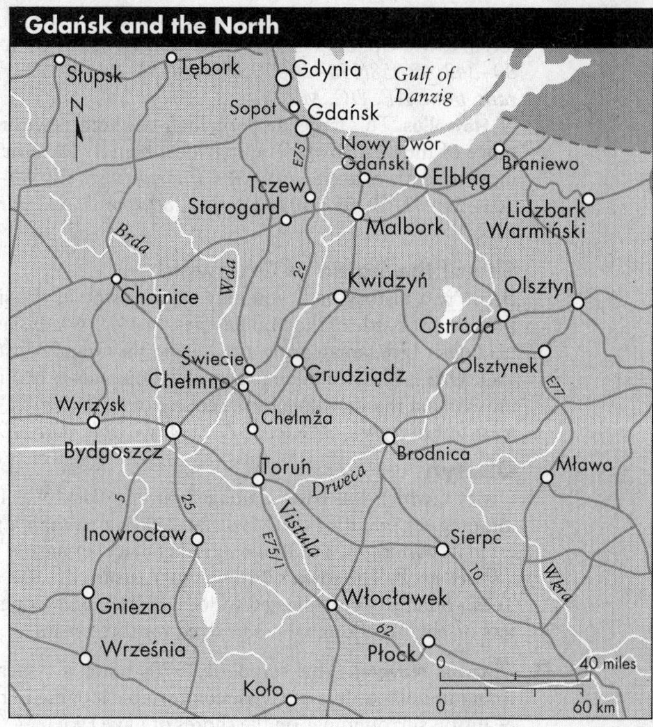

naissance, and Mannerist architecture. In 1997 Gdańsk celebrated its 1,000th anniversary. This is where the first shots of World War II were fired and where the first free trade union in the Soviet bloc, Solidarity, was born after strikes in August 1980. The city's Old Town has a wonderful collection of historic town houses and narrow streets. Splendid **ulica Długa** (best for shopping) and Długi Targ are great starting points for walks into other districts. The evocative **Solidarity Monument**—erected in honor of workers killed by the regime during strikes in 1970—stands outside the former Lenin shipyards. The nearby town of **Sopot** is Poland's most charming pre-war seaside resort.

$$$ ✕ **Major.** This restaurant, superbly located on Gdańsk's main pedestrian shopping street, specializes in seafood but also serves traditional Polish meat dishes. ✉ *Ul. Długa 18,* ☎ *058/301–10–69. AE, DC, MC, V.*

$$$ ✕ **Pod Łososiem.** The name of this restaurant refers to salmon, which, if available on the day you visit, is highly recommended. Other fish and wild fowl such as duck and pheasant are good choices, too. The famous Gdańsk liqueur "Goldwasser" used to be made in the basement. ✉ *Ul. Szeroka 54,* ☎ *058/301–76–52. AE, DC, MC, V.*

$$ ★ ✕ **Tawerna.** This well-established restaurant overlooking the river serves traditional Polish and Germanic dishes such as pork cutlets and seafood. Yes, it's touristy, but the food is delicious. ✉ *Ul. Powroźnicza 19–20, off Długi Targ,* ☎ *058/301–92–48. AE, DC, MC, V.*

$$$ 🏨 **Grand.** With its magnificent location on the Bay of Gdańsk in the charming German-era seaside resort of Sopot, this pre-war hotel is well worth the short commute. The rooms could have been restored more authentically, but the view from the restaurant is great. ✉ *Ul. Powstańców Warszawy 12/14, 81–718 Sopot,* ☎ *058/551–00–41,* FAX *058/551–61–24. 112 rooms. Restaurant. AE, DC, MC, V.*

$$$ **Marina.** Built in 1982, this large high-rise is one of the better hotels in town. Upper floors have splendid views. ✉ *Ul. Jelitkowska 20, 80–342,* ☎ *058/553–20–79,* FAX *058/553–04–60. 193 rooms. Restaurant, pool. AE, DC, MC, V.*

$$ **Hewelius.** This large, modern, high-rise hotel is within walking distance of the Old Town. The spacious, blandly furnished rooms have most modern conveniences. ✉ *Ul. Heweliusza 22, 80–861,* ☎ *058/301–56–31,* FAX *058/301–19–22. 280 rooms. Restaurant. AE, DC, MC, V.*

Site of the Battle of Grunwald

If you're a history buff, you may want to stop at the site of possibly the greatest battle of the Middle Ages. In 1410 Władysław Jagiełło and his Polish-Lithuanian army annihilated the Grand Master of the Teutonic Order, Ulrich von Jungingen, and thousands of his knights. A small museum on the site explains the course of the battle. ✉ *17 km (11 mi) west of Olsztynek off Rte. 537.* ⏲ *May–Sept., daily 10–6.*

Olsztyn

Olsztyn, which was badly damaged during World War II, is more of a jumping off point for the Mazurian Lakes area than a place of interest in its own right. The **Rynek** (market place) in the old town is worth a short stroll. The town's 14th-century **castle** contains a **museum** (⏲ Tues.–Sun. 10–4) dedicated to local culture and **Copernicus's quarters** on the first floor, where he lived for three years.

$$ **Orbis Novotel.** This standard 1970s hotel is typical of the kind found in Poland. It is the most comfortable lodging in the area, set in beautiful surroundings on the shores of Lake Ukiel. ✉ *Ul. Sielska 4A, 10–802,* ☎ *089/527–40–81,* FAX *089/527–54–03. 97 rooms. Restaurant. AE, DC, MC, V.*

Olsztynek

This otherwise drab town contains the **Muzeum Budownictwa Ludowego** (Museum of Folk Buildings, or Skansen), a collection of historic timber buildings from different parts of the country. ✉ *ul. Sportowa 21,* ☎ *089/519–21–64.* ⏲ *mid-Apr.–Aug., daily 9–3; Sept., Tues.–Sun. 9–3.*

★ Malbork

This huge, redbrick, turreted castle was one of the most powerful strongholds in medieval Europe. From 1308 to 1457 it was the residence of the Grand Masters of the Teutonic Order. The Teutonic Knights were a thorn in Poland's side until their defeat at the Battle of Grunwald in 1410. Inside Malbork Castle is a museum with beautiful examples of amber—including lumps as large as melons and pieces containing perfect specimens of prehistoric insects. ✉ *Rte. 50, 58 km (36 mi) southeast of Gdańsk,* ☎ *055/72–33–64.* ⏲ *Oct.–Apr., Tues.–Sun. 9–3; May–Sept., Tues.–Sun. 9–5.*

Płock

Once you get through Płock's industrial area, you will find a lovely medieval city that was, for a short time, the capital of Poland. The 12th-century **Katedra** (cathedral), where two Polish kings are buried, has a **Muzeum Diecezjalne** (Diocesan Museum). In the remains of the dramatic 14th-century **Teutonic castle** is the **Muzeum Mazowieckie** (Mazovian Museum), with one of the best Art Nouveau collections in Poland.

Toruń

Toruń, birthplace of Nicolaus Copernicus, is a medieval city that grew wealthy due to its location on the north–south trading route along the

Vistula. In 1998 Torun was placed on the Unesco World Cultural Heritage List. Its **Old Town** district is a remarkably successful blend of Gothic buildings—churches, the town hall, and burghers' homes—and Renaissance and Baroque patrician houses. The town hall tower (1274) is the oldest in Poland. Don't leave without trying some of Toruń's famous gingerbread and honey cakes.

$$$ ✕ **Pod Kurantem.** The cuisine is regional in this attractive old wine cellar. Slow service is the penalty for popularity. ✉ *Rynek Staromiejski 29,* ☎ *No phone. No credit cards.*

$$ ✕ **Zajazd Staropolski.** Excellent meat dishes and soups are served in a restored 17th-century interior. ✉ *Ul. Żeglarska 10/14,* ☎ *056/260–60. AE, DC, MC, V.*

$$$ 🏨 **Helios.** This friendly, medium-size Orbis hotel in the city center has a good restaurant. ✉ *Ul. Kraszewskiego 1, 87–100,* ☎ *056/250–33,* FAX *056/235–65. 108 rooms. Restaurant. AE, DC, MC, V.*

$$ 🏨 **Kosmos.** A functional 1960s hotel, Kosmos has recently had a facelift. It is near the river, in the city center. ✉ *Ul. Popiełuszko 2, 87–100,* ☎ *056/270–85,* FAX *056/213–41. 59 rooms. Restaurant. AE, DC, MC, V.*

Gdańsk and the North Essentials

Getting Around

Gdańsk is a major transportation hub, with an international airport just outside town (and good bus connections to downtown) and major road and rail connections with the rest of the country.

Guided Tours

Orbis, and other travel agencies, (☞ Travel Agencies *in* Warsaw Essentials, *above*) arrange group and individual package tours of Warsaw, Toruń, Gdańsk, Poznań, and the surrounding areas.

Visitor Information

Gdańsk (Orbis, ✉ ul. Heweliusza 22, ☎ 022/301–45–44). **Olsztyn** (Orbis, ✉ ul. Dąbrowszczaków 1, ☎ 089/527–46–74). **Płock** (✉ Hotel Tetropol, Al. Jachowicza 49, ☎ 024/262–94–97). **Toruń** (✉ ul. Piekary 37/39, ☎ 056/237–46; Orbis, ✉ ul. Mostowa 7, ☎ 056/217–14).

24 Portugal

Lisbon; the Portuguese Riviera, Sintra, and Queluz; the Algarve

Clinging to the western cusp of the continent, insulated from Spain's arid plains and burning sun, Portugal is one of Europe's great surprises. Although you'll find fine food and wine, spectacularly sited castles, medieval hilltop villages, and excellent beaches, Portugal is a land of myriad and delightful distinctions.

It's far more lush than Spain—the landscape unfolds in astonishing variety from a mountainous, green interior to a sweeping coastline—and Celtic and Moorish influences are evident in the land, its people, and their tongue. Given its long Atlantic coastline, it isn't surprising that Portugal has been a maritime nation for most of its tumultuous history. From the charting of the Azores archipelago in 1427 to the discovery of Japan in 1542, Portuguese explorers unlocked the major sea routes to southern Africa, India, eastern Asia, and the Americas. This great era of exploration, known as the *descobrimentos,* reached its height during the 15th century under the influence of Prince Henry the Navigator. The glories of the Portuguese empire were relatively short-lived, however, and the next several centuries saw dynastic instability, extravagant spending by feckless monarchs, natural disasters, and foreign invasion. The 20th century brought little change, and not until a bloodless coup in 1974 deposed the ruling right-wing dictatorship was democracy established and the process of modernization begun.

Today Portugal is a stable country, its people keen to share in the prosperity offered by developments within the European Union (EU). Given the relatively short time since the revolution, this stability demonstrates the inherent strengths of the Portuguese psyche. Political confidence couldn't have been maintained without improvements in the economy, and there have been great strides forward since 1974—the highway system, in particular, has been completely overhauled as money from Brussels has been used to modernize the country's infrastructure. One effect of this regeneration is that Portugal has become more expensive over the last few years.

Following its 1994 stint as European City of Culture, Portugal's capital city—Lisbon—moved firmly into the international limelight during 1998 when it hosted the World Exposition (Expo '98), the last great world expo of the 20th century. A startling regeneration program has improved the city center, its transportation, and public buildings. Meanwhile, over at the former Expo site—reclaimed dockland a little northeast of the city's center—the new development called Expo Urbe continues to take shape. Here you're encouraged to tour the stupendous Lisbon Oceanarium, the expo's erstwhile centerpiece.

Most visitors are drawn to the country's south, including Lisbon, its coastal and wooded environs, and the beaches and low-lying plains of the Algarve. The Algarve coast is one of Europe's most popular vacation areas, and Lisbon, Portugal's sophisticated capital, has the trappings of a modern commercial center, with skyscrapers wedged in among turn-of-the-century buildings. Off the beaten track, you'll be rewarded with glimpses of a traditional life and culture shaped by memories of empire and tempered by the experience of revolution.

PORTUGAL A TO Z

Customs on Arrival

See Customs *in* Chapter 1.

Dining

Seafood is a staple, and *sardinhas assadas* (fresh-grilled sardines) are a local favorite. There are said to be as many ways to prepare *bacalhau* (dried salt cod) as there are days in the year. Freshly caught lobster, crab, shrimp, tuna, sole, and squid are widely available. *Caldeirada* is a piquant seafood stew; in an *arroz de marisco,* seafood stew is mixed with rice. In the Algarve *cataplana* is a must—a mouthwatering mixture of clams, ham, tomatoes, onions, garlic, and herbs, named for the covered copper pan in which it's cooked. Meat lovers wax rhapsodic over char-grilled *frango* (chicken)—usually served with very hot *piri-piri* (chili) sauce—northern-style *leitão da bairrada* (roast suckling pig); *coelho á caçadora* (rabbit with potatoes, onions, garlic, and a splash of wine); and the tasty *linguiça* (spiced sausages) and *presunto* (cured) ham. *Porco alentejana* (pork with clams) is a tasty southern specialty that's found all over the country; *cozido a Portuguesa* (Portuguese stew) is similarly ubiquitous, though more of an acquired taste—a boiled selection of meat, offal, and root vegetables. Desserts include *doces de ovos* (egg-and-sugar confections), *pudim flan* (egg custard), egg and almond tarts, and fruit. Water is safe, but you may prefer bottled water—*sem gas* for still, *com gas* for fizzy.

Unless noted, reservations are not necessary. Less expensive meals in Portugal are served in a *churrascaria* (grill house), a *tasca* (tavern), or a *cervejaria* (beer hall–restaurant). A seafood specialist is a *marisqueira.* In *adegas típicas* (wine cellars), you dine on Portuguese specialties, drink wine, and listen to traditional *fado* music. At all restaurants be wary of eating anything brought as an appetizer that you didn't order. You'll be charged extra, even if you eat just one olive.

MEALTIMES

Most hotels serve breakfast until 10. Lunch usually begins around 1 PM; dinner is served at about 8 PM.

RATINGS

Prices are per person, without alcohol. Taxes and service are usually included, but a tip of 5%–10% is always appreciated.

Portugal

0
50 miles
0
50 km
N
ATLANTIC
OCEAN
SPAIN
Minho
Valença
Viana
do Castelo
Lima
Serra do Gerês
N103
N101
Bragança
Chaves
Barcelos
Braga
Póvoa de Varzim
Guimarães
Tâmega
A3/IP1
A4/IP4
Mirandela
Vila do Conde
Amarante
Vila Real
N102/IP2
Mogadouro
Oporto
Penafiel
Douro
Sabor
Douro
Lamego
Douro
Espinho
Oliveira
dos Azeméis
Moimenta
da Beira
S. Pedro
do Sul
Vouga
Albergaria-a-Velha
Aveiro
Viseu
Pinhel
IP5
Sta. Comba
Dão
Mealhada
Mondego
Guarda
Mira
Cantanhede
Serra da Estrêla
Coimbra
Covilhã
Figueira
da Foz
Arganil
Fundão
Zêzere
A1/IP1/E1
N10
Penamacor
N109
Pombal
Serra da
Gardunha
N233
Leiria
Proença-
a-Nova
Castelo
Branco
Nazaré
Batalha
Ourém
Tomar
Alcobaça
Fátima
IP2
Sra. do Aire
IP6
Abrantes
Nisa
Caldas
da Rainha
N118
Tagus
Torres
Novas
Obidos
Portalegre
Aveiras de Cima
Santarém
Torres Vedras
Ponte
de Sor
Mafra
Tejo
Vila Franca
de Xira
N8
Sorraia
Avis
Sintra
Lisbon
N10
Estremoz
Elvas
Cascais
Arraiolos
Estoril
A6/IP1
Montemor-
o-Novo
Sra. de Ossa
Guadiana
A2/IP1
Seixal
Vila
Viçosa
Setúbal
Sado
Évora
Cabo
Espichel
Alcácer
do Sal
Reguengos
N2
IP2
TO THE
AZORES
IP1/E1
Ferreira do
Alentejo
Moura
Sines
Beja
Santiago
do Cacem
Vilaverde de Ficalho
Cabo de
Sines
N122
Serpa
Castro
Verde
Chança
Odemira
Ourique
Mértola
Guadiana
TO MADEIRA
ISLAND
N120
Mira
Almodovar
Monchique
ALGARVE
Portimão
EN125
IP1
S. Brás de Alportel
Vila do Bispo
Lagos
Albufeira
Tavira
Vila Real de
S. António
Cabo de
S. Vicente
Sagres
Faro
Olhão

CATEGORY	COST
$$$$	over 6,000$00
$$$	4,500$00–6,000$00
$$	3,000$00–4,500$00
$	under 3,000$00*

WHAT TO WEAR

Neatness will suffice for all but the most formal occasions; jacket and tie are advised for city restaurants in the $$$$ categories; otherwise, casual dress is acceptable.

Language

Portuguese is difficult to pronounce and understand (most people speak quickly and elliptically); if, however, you have a fair knowledge of a Latin language, you may be able to read a little Portuguese. Just be aware that, with some cognates, appearances can be deceptive—it's best to double-check terms in a pocket Portuguese–English dictionary. In large cities and major resorts many people speak English and, occasionally, French.

Lodging

Portugal has many lodging options and some of the lowest rates in Europe. The government grades hotels with one to five stars; there are also small, family-owned, city-center *pensões* (pensions); rooms in country manor houses; villas, holiday apartments, and campsites ; and luxury *pousadas* (tourist hotels) in historic buildings. Rates depend on location and time of year. In the Algarve in winter, particularly January–March, room prices drop by as much as 40%. In high season (summer, Easter, and Christmas) you'll need to book ahead, especially in the Algarve.

Tourist offices can help with reservations and will provide lists of the local hostelries without charge. In Lisbon there are hotel reservations desks at the airport and at the downtown tourist information center. If you arrive at a holiday resort in summer without a reservation, you may be offered an inexpensive *quarto* (room) at a rail or bus station—quartos are usually simply furnished; always see the room before agreeing to take it.

CAMPING

There are more than 150 campsites throughout the country, with a large concentration in the Algarve. The main operating chain is **Orbitur** (✉ Rua Diogo do Couto 1–8, 1100 Lisbon, ☎ 01/815–4871); most local tourist offices can direct you to specific sites. For additional information contact **Federação Portuguesa do Campismo** (✉ Av. Cel. Ed. Galhardo 24, 1170 Lisbon, ☎ 01/812–6900).

COUNTRY AND MANOR HOUSES

Many splendid country homes, manor houses, and historic buildings are accessible through a variety of programs in which private homeowners offer you a room, breakfast, and sometimes dinner (on request). Properties are inspected and approved by the government and then advertised by a variety of private agencies. The Portuguese National Tourist Office in your home country (☞ Visitor Information *in* Chapter 1) can provide more information in advance of your trip; in Portugal tourist offices can advise about the most attractive local possibilities.

HOTELS AND POUSADAS

As well as regular hotels, many towns also have smaller inns called *estalagems* or *albergarias,* which usually provide breakfast only.

The 39 state-subsidized pousadas, most of which are in castles or old monasteries or in newer buildings on sites that have a particularly fine view, are five-star luxury properties—though rates in low season can make them a remarkably good value. For more information contact **Enatur Pousadas de Portugal** (✉ Av. Santa Joana Princesa 10, 1700 Lisbon, ☎ 01/848–1221, FAX 01/840–5846), or the national tourist organization in your home country (☞ *also* Tour Operators *in* Chapter 1).

PENSIONS

The mainstay of budget accommodation in Portugal is the *pensão,* or pension, rated up to four stars and sometimes including meals in the price; depending on the rating, size, and location, pensão rooms come with or without private baths or showers; air-conditioning is standard only in the higher-category accommodations. A *residencial* (between a pensão and a hotel) has similar facilities and, again, is found in most towns and larger villages; breakfast is usually included.

RATINGS

Prices quoted are for two people in a double room based on high-season rates, including tax and service.

CATEGORY	COST
$$$$	over 35,000$00
$$$	25,000$00–35,000$00
$$	15,000$00–25,000$00
$	under 15,000$00

Mail

In Lisbon the post office in the Praça dos Restauradores is open daily 8 AM–10 PM, and there's a 24-hour post office at the airport. Main post offices in towns are open weekdays 8:30–6; offices in rural areas close for lunch and at 6 PM on weekdays and aren't open on weekends.

You can have mail sent care of American Express (✉ Top Tours, Av. Duque de Loulé 108, 1000Lisbon, ☎ 01/315–5885, FAX 01/315–5873). Elsewhere in the country, post offices in major towns offer "held mail" services (you simply have letters sent to you labeled "poste restante" at a particular post office address).

Money Matters

COSTS

The most expensive areas are Lisbon, the Algarve, and the tourist resorts along the Tagus estuary; the least expensive are country towns. A sales, or value-added, tax (called IVA) of either 5% (for basic foodstuffs, medicines, and accommodation), 12% (restaurant bills), or 17% (other goods and services, including car rentals) is included in the price of most items.

CURRENCY

The unit of currency in Portugal is the escudo, which is divided into 100 centavos. Escudos come in bills of 500$00, 1,000$00, 2,000$00, 5,000$00, and 10,000$00. (In Portugal the dollar sign stands between the escudo and the centavo.) Owing to the complications of dealing with millions of escudos, 1,000$00 is always called a *conto,* so 10,000$00 is referred to as 10 contos. Coins come in denominations of 1$00, 2$50, 5$00, 10$00, 20$00, 50$00, 100$00, and 200$00.

At press time (spring 1998), the exchange rate was about 182$00 to the U.S. dollar, 125$00 to the Canadian dollar, and 298$00 to the pound sterling. You can change money in hotels and in larger shops and restaurants, but banks and *cambios* (exchange offices) usually give better rates.

SAMPLE PRICES

Cup of coffee, 100$00–200$00; bottle of beer, 150$00; soft drink, 125$00–175$00; bottle of house wine, 600$00–800$00; 2-km (1-mi) taxi ride, 450$00; city bus ride, 150$00; museum entrance, 250$00–500$00.

TIPPING

Service is included in bills at hotels and most restaurants. In hotels give the porter who carries your luggage 200$00 and leave the maid who cleans your room 200$00 a day. If you dine regularly in the hotel, give your waiter between 500$00 and 1,000$00 at the end of your stay; give the wine waiter somewhat less if you order wine with every meal. Otherwise tip 5%–10% on restaurant bills, except at inexpensive establishments, where you may just leave any coins given in change. Taxi drivers get 10%; cinema and theater ushers who seat you, 50$00; train and airport porters, 100$00 per bag; hairdressers, around 10%.

National Holidays

January 1; April 2 (Good Friday); April 25 (Anniversary of the Revolution); May 1 (Labor Day); June 3 (Corpus Christi); June 10 (National Day); August 15 (Assumption); October 5 (Day of the Republic); November 1 (All Saints' Day); December 1 (Independence Day); December 8 (Immaculate Conception); December 25.

Opening and Closing Times

Banks are open weekdays 8:30–3. There are automatic currency-exchange machines in Lisbon (around the Praçado Comércio and Praça dos Restauradores) and in other cities. **Museums** are usually open 10–12:30 and 2–5. Most close on Sunday afternoon, and all close Monday. Most **palaces** close on Tuesday. **Shops** are open weekdays 9–1 and 3–7, Saturday 9–1. Shopping malls in Lisbon and other cities remain open until 10 PM or midnight and are often open on Sunday.

Shopping

Bargaining is not the practice in city stores or shops, though it is sometimes possible in flea markets and antiques shops. The **Centro de Turismo Artesanato** (✉ Rua Castilho 61, 1200 Lisbon, ☎ 01/386–0879) will ship goods abroad even if they weren't bought in Portugal. By air to the United States, parcels take about three weeks; by sea, two months.

SALES-TAX REFUNDS

For non-EU residents, the IVA tax paid on individual items that cost more than 11,700$00 can be reclaimed when buying in a tax-free associated shop. Ask for a special *Tax-Free Shopping Cheque* at the shop and get it stamped by airport customs, and the money will be refunded at the tax-free desk at Lisbon airport. You can also have the check stamped at any border crossing and receive the refund by mail or credit card. Shops that specialize in IVA-refund purchases are clearly marked, and shop assistants can help with the forms.

Telephoning

During the last two years or so Portugal has been updating its phone system, causing phone numbers to change throughout the country. The changes made up to press time (spring 1998) have been incorporated, but some 2% of the country's phone numbers are still slated to change. The good news is that, if you dial an old number, there will be a recording stating the new number; the bad news is that, unless you're dialing a large tourism-oriented establishment or major international corporation, the message will only be given in Portuguese.

COUNTRY CODE

The country code for Portugal is 351. When dialing a number in Portugal from outside the country, drop the initial 0 in the regional code.

INTERNATIONAL CALLS

You can make international and collect calls from most public phones as well as from main post offices, which almost always have a supply of phone cabins (you're assigned a booth, and you pay at the end of the call). In larger towns you may be able to charge calls that cost more than 500$00 to your MasterCard or Visa. Some phone booths accept international calls. For the operator, dial 099 (Europe, Algeria, Morocco, and Tunisia) or 098 (rest of the world). Access numbers to reach American long-distance operators are: for **AT&T,** 050–171288; for **MCI,** 050–171234; for **Sprint,** 050–171877.

LOCAL CALLS

Older-style pay phones take 10$00, 20$00, and 50$00 coins; the newer models (with instructions in English) take 100$00 and 200$00 coins as well; 10$00 is the minimum payment for short local calls. PORTUGAL TELECOM card phones will accept plastic phone cards of 50 or 120 units; you can buy these cards at post and phone offices and most tobacconists and newsagents.

Transportation

BY BUS

Several private operators provide regular service from Lisbon's main **bus terminal** (✉ Av. Casal Ribeiro 18, ☎ 01/354–5439) to destinations throughout Portugal.One major company, **Renex** (✉ Rua dos Arameiros 15, ☎ 01/888–2829), operates from a different address and offers services to northern towns and the Algarve. At either terminal it's wise to buy tickets a day in advance. It's three hours to Oporto and five hours to the Algarve. For information on particular routes, contact the main tourist office in Lisbon; for tickets visit the terminals themselves or any travel agency(☞ *also* Lisbon Essentials, *below*).

BY CAR

Breakdowns. All large garages in and around towns have breakdown services, and you'll see orange emergency (SOS) phones along turnpikes and highways. The national automobile organization, **Automóvel Clube de Portugal** (✉ Rua Rosa Araújo 24/26, 1200 Lisbon, ☎ 01/356–3931) provides reciprocal membership with AAA and other European automobile associations.

Gasoline. Gas prices are among the highest in Europe: around 185$00 per liter for super, 165$00 for regular, and 160$00 for unleaded. Many gas stations are self-service, and credit cards are widely accepted.

Parking. Parking lots and underground garages abound in major cities, but those in Lisbon and Oporto are no longer cheap. It's often difficult to find a parking space near city-center hotels, though increasingly common parking meters are improving the situation.

Road Conditions. The turnpikes and main highways that link Lisbon with Cascais, the Algarve, Oporto, and other main cities are in good shape. Minor roads are often poor and winding with unpredictable surfaces. The local driving may be faster and less forgiving than you're used to, and other visitors in rental cars on unfamiliar Algarve roads can cause problems: Drive carefully.

EN 125, the principal east–west Algarve highway, has been widened and resurfaced, and construction of the new IP1 Algarve highway, from the Spanish border to Albufeira, has eliminated many of the formerly horrendous bottlenecks. In the north the IP5 shortens the drive from Aveiro to the border with Spain, near Guarda, but should be driven on with great care. A major re-vamp is scheduled to eliminate dangerous hills and curves. IP4 connects Oporto through Vila Real to once-remote Bragança.

The A2-A6 turnpike system south from Lisbon currently reaches just past Montemor-o-Novo on its way to the Spanish frontier at Badajoz and Alcacer do Sal en route to the Algarve. There's good, fast access to Setúbal and to Évora and other Alentejo towns, though rush hour traffic on the 25 de Abril bridge across the Tagus can be frustrating. An alternative is to take the 17-km- (11-mi-) long Vasco da Gama bridge (opened 1998 and Europe's second-longest water crossing after the Chunnel) across the Tagus estuary to Montijo and then link up with southbound and eastbound roads.

Rules of the Road. Driving is on the right. At the junction of two roads of equal size, traffic coming from the right has priority. Vehicles already in a traffic circle have priority over those entering it from any point. The use of seat belts is obligatory. Horns should not be used in built-up areas, and a reflective red warning triangle, for use in a breakdown, must be carried. The speed limit on turnpikes is 120 kph (74 mph); on other roads it is 90 kph (56 mph), and in built-up areas, 50 kph–60 kph (30 mph–36 mph).

BY PLANE

The internal air services of **TAP Air Portugal** (✉ Praça Marquês de Pombal 3, 1200 Lisbon, ☎ 01/386–4080) are good. Other internal services are provided by **Portugália** (☎ 01/848–4759) and **SATA-Air Açores** (☎ 096/22311)—which flies to the Azores—both of whose schedules change according to season. Any travel agent can provide up-to-date prices and timetables.

BY TRAIN

For such a small country Portugal has a very extensive rail system. Trains are clean and leave on time, but there are few express runs except the one between Lisbon and Oporto, which takes just over three hours for the 338-km (210-mi) journey, and the one between Lisbon and the Algarve (four hours to Faro, five hours to Lagos). You should buy tickets and reserve seats (at stations or through travel agents) two or three days in advance. Advance reservations are essential on Lisbon–Oporto express trains; on the Algarve rail line you can simply buy tickets on the day of travel. Timetables are generally the same on weekends as on weekdays, except on suburban lines.

International Services. Trains to Madrid, Paris, and other parts of Europe depart from the Santa Apolonia Station in Lisbon, Campanhã in Oporto, and Coimbra (Paris only).

Train Passes. Special **tourist passes** are available through travel agents or at main train stations, valid for periods of 7, 14, or 21 days for first- and second-class travel on any domestic train service; mileage is unlimited. At press time (spring 1998), the cost was 18,000$00 for 7 days, 30,000$00 for 14 days, and 42,000$00 for 21 days.

Weather

The tourist season runs from spring through autumn, but some parts of the country—especially the Algarve, which has 3,000 hours of sunshine annually—are balmy even in winter. Hotel prices are greatly reduced between November and February, except in Lisbon, where business visitors keep rates uniformly high throughout the year.

CLIMATE

Portugal's climate is temperate year-round. Even in August, the hottest month, the Algarve and the Alentejo are the only regions where the midday heat may be uncomfortable, but in these regions you can go to the beaches to swim and soak up the sun. What rain there is falls from November through March; December and January can be chilly at times, even on the Algarve, and very wet to the north, but there's no snow except in the mountains of the Serra da Estrela in the northeast. The almond blossoms and vivid wildflowers that cover the countryside start to bloom early in February.

The following are the average daily maximum and minimum temperatures for Lisbon.

LISBON

Jan.	57F	14C	**May**	71F	21C	**Sept.**	79F	26C
	46	8		55	13		62	17
Feb.	59F	15C	**June**	77F	25C	**Oct.**	72F	22C
	47	8		60	15		58	14
Mar.	63F	17C	**July**	81F	27C	**Nov.**	63F	17C
	50	10		63	17		52	11
Apr.	67F	20C	**Aug.**	82F	28C	**Dec.**	58F	15C
	53	12		63	17		47	9

LISBON

Spread out over a string of hills to the north of the Tagus River estuary, Portugal's capital presents unending treats for the eye. Its wide boulevards are bordered by black-and-white mosaic sidewalks made of tiny cobblestones called *calçada.* Modern, pastel-color apartment blocks vie for attention with art nouveau structures covered with decorative tiles. Winding, hilly streets provide scores of *miradouros,* vantage points that offer spectacular views of the river and the city.

With a population of around a million, Lisbon is a small capital by European standards. Its center stretches north from the spacious Praça do Comércio, one of the largest riverside squares in Europe, to the Rossío, a smaller square lined with shops and sidewalk cafés. This district, known as the Baixa (Lower Town), is one of the earliest examples of town planning on a large scale. The grid of parallel streets between the two squares was built after an earthquake and tidal wave destroyed much of the city in 1755. The Alfama, the old Moorish quarter that survived the earthquake, lies just east of the Baixa, and the Bairro Alto—an 18th-century quarter of restaurants, bars, and clubs—just to the west; Belém, a district containing many royal palaces and museums, lies another 5 km (3 mi) to the west. A similar distance northeast of the center, the riverside Expo site has the Lisbon Oceanarium—Europe's largest aquarium—as its major attraction.

Lisbon is not easy to explore on foot. The steep inclines of many streets present a tough challenge to the casual visitor, and places that appear to be close to one another on a map are sometimes on different levels. Yet the effort is worthwhile—judicious use of trams, the funicular railway, and the majestic city-center *elevador* (vertical lift) make walking tours enjoyable even on the hottest summer day.

Castelo de São Jorge and the Alfama

Numbers in the margin correspond to points of interest on the Lisbon map.

The Moors, who imposed their rule on most of the southern Iberian Peninsula during the 8th century, left their mark on Lisbon. Their most visible traces are the imposing castle, set on one of the city's highest hills, and the Alfama, a district of narrow streets that wind up toward it. This jumble of steep, stepped alleys and whitewashed houses with flower-laden balconies and red-tile roofs is notoriously easy to get lost in, though it's relatively compact. Its down-to-earth charm is most apparent in June, during the festivals of the *Santos Populares* (Popular Saints), when the entire quarter turns out to eat, drink, and be merry. The best way to tour the area is to take Tram 28, Bus 37, or a taxi up to the castle and then walk down.

★ 1 **Castelo de São Jorge** (St. George's Castle). Although the castle is Moorish in construction, it stands on the site of a fort used by the Visigoths as early as the 5th century. The main walls enclose the ruins of a Muslim palace that served as the residence of Portuguese kings until the 16th century; the outer walls encompass the (restored) medieval church of Santa Cruz, a few simple houses, and souvenir shops. Inside the main gate are well-tended grounds and terraces with panoramic city views. There are entrances to the castle from Largo do Chão da Feira or Largo do Menino de Deus. ✉ *Rua da Costa do Castelo,* ☏ *no phone.* 🎟 *Free.* ⏲ *Apr.–Sept., daily 9–9; Oct.–Mar., daily 9–7.*

2 **Miradouro de Santa Luzia.** Hop off Tram 28 at the miradouro for one of the most sweeping views of the Alfama and the Tagus River. The little terrace garden by the Santa Luzia Church catches the sun all day, while a nearby café provides outdoor seats and welcome drinks. ✉ *Largo da Santa Luzia.*

3 **Museu da Marioneta** (Puppet Museum). The intricate workmanship that went into the creation of the puppets on display here is remarkable. ✉ *Largo Rodrigues de Freitas 19,* ☏ *01/886–5794.* ⏲ *Tues.–Sun. 10–12:30 and 2–6.*

4 **Museu de Artes Decorativas** (Museum of Decorative Arts). Housed in a splendid 18th-century mansion with period furnishings, the museum puts on temporary exhibitions of its art and furniture and conducts more than 20 workshops that teach threatened handicrafts—bookbinding, carving, and cabinetmaking. ✉ *Largo das Portas do Sol 2,* ☏ *01/886–2183.* ⏲ *Tues.–Sun. 10–5.*

★ 5 **Sé** (Cathedral). Founded in 1150 to commemorate the defeat of the Moors three years earlier, the Sé has an austere Romanesque interior and a beautiful 13th-century cloister. The treasure-filled sacristy contains the relics of the martyr St. Vincent, carried—according to legend—from the Algarve to Lisbon in a ship piloted by ravens. ✉ *Largo da Sé,* ☏ *01/886–6752.* 🎟 *Free.* ⏲ *Cathedral: daily 9–noon and 2–6. Sacristy:* ⏲ *Daily 10–1 and 2–6.*

The Baixa and the Modern City

The neoclassical grid design of the city rebuilt under the direction of the Marquês de Pombal after the 1755 earthquake can be seen perfectly today in the Baixa, Lisbon's main shopping and banking district. This opens on its northwestern end into the Praça dos Restauradores, the beginning of modern Lisbon, with Avenida da Liberdade running northwest to the green expanses of the Parque Eduardo VII.

8 **Avenida da Liberdade.** A stroll along the city's main avenue, from the Praça dos Restauradores to the Parque Eduardo VII, takes about 30 minutes, though you may want to stop at an open-air café in the esplanade that runs down the center of the tree-lined avenue. ✉ *Between Praça dos Restauradores and Parque Eduardo VII.*

6 **Baixa** (Lower Town). The Baixa's various streets once housed trades and crafts now reflected in the street names: Rua dos Sapateiros (Cobblers' Street), Rua da Prata (Silversmiths' Street), and Rua Aurea (Gold-

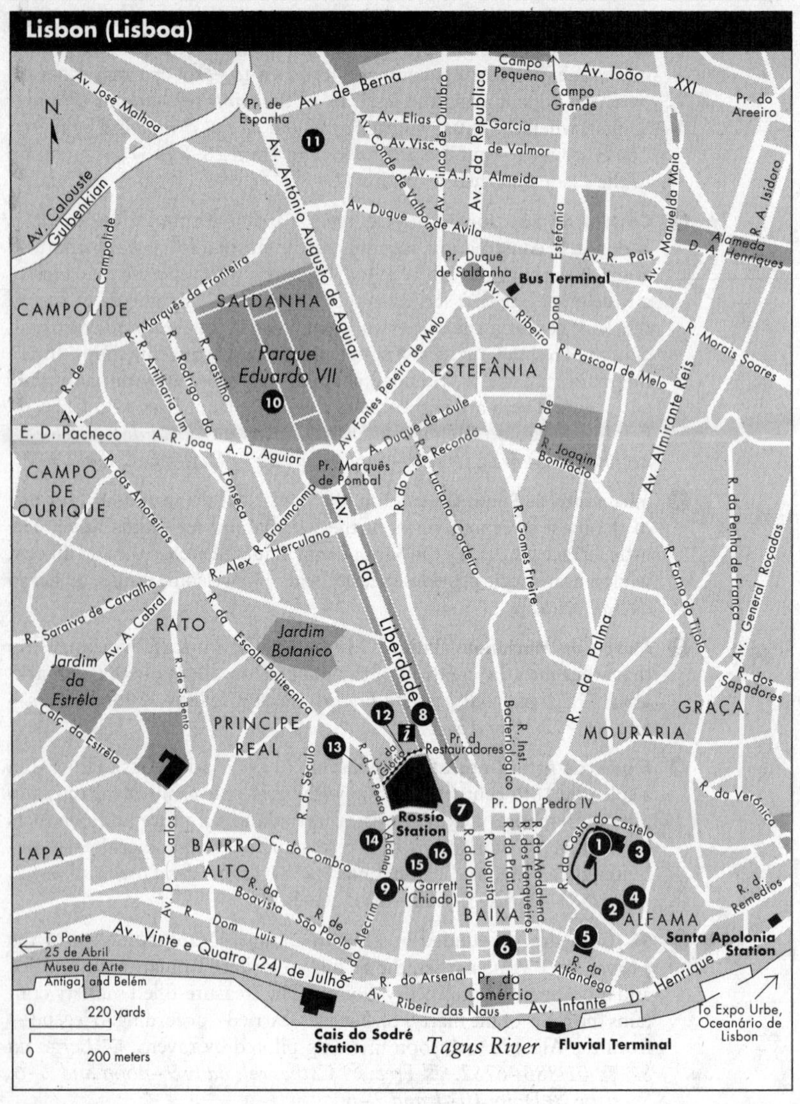

Avenida da Liberdade, **8**
Baixa, **6**
Castelo de São Jorge, **1**
Chiado, **9**
Elevador da Glória, **12**
Elevador de Santa Justa, **16**
Fundação Calouste Gulbenkian, **11**
Igreja de São Roque, **14**
Igreja do Carmo, **15**
Instituto do Vinho do Porto, **13**
Miradouro de Santa Luzia, **2**
Museu da Marioneta, **3**
Museu de Artes Decorativas, **4**
Parque Eduardo VII, **10**
Rossío, **7**
Sé, **5**

smiths' Street). Scattered throughout are shoe shops, glittering jewelry stores, and a host of cafés and delicatessens that sell wines, cheeses, and pastries. ✉ *Between the river and Rossío.*

9 **Chiado.** This chic district is home to some of the city's most fashionable shops. Rua Garrett, in particular, the Chiado's principal street, is lined with old department stores and a series of comfortable, turn-of-the-century, wood-paneled coffee shops. Most famous is the **Brasileira** (✉ Rua Garrett 120, ☎ 01/346–9541; ⏲ closed Sun.), which has a life-size statue of Fernando Pessoa, Portugal's national poet, seated at one of the sidewalk tables. ✉ *Western side of Baixa.*

★ 11 **Fundação Calouste Gulbenkian** (Calouste Gulbenkian Foundation). This cultural trust, one of the country's real treasures, houses a museum of art and artifacts collected by Armenian oil magnate Calouste Gulbenkian (1869–1955). It displays superb Greek and Roman coins, Persian carpets, Chinese porcelain, and paintings by such old masters as Rembrandt and Rubens, as well as impressionist and pre-Raphaelite works. The complex also houses a good modern art museum and two concert halls that host music and ballet festivals in winter and spring. ✉ *Av. de Berna 45 (Metro: Palhavã),* ☎ *01/795–0236.* 🎫 *Free Sun.* ⏲ *June–Sept., Tues., Thurs., Fri., and Sun. 10–5, Wed. and Sat. 2–7:30; Oct.–May, Tues.–Sun. 10–5.*

10 **Parque Eduardo VII** (Edward VII Park). The city's main park was named in honor of King Edward VII of England, who visited Lisbon in 1903. Rare flowers, trees, and shrubs thrive in both the *estufa fria* (cold greenhouse) and the *estufa quente* (hot greenhouse). ✉ *Parque Eduardo VII (Metro: Rotunda),* ☎ *01/388–2278.* ⏲ *Apr.–Sept., daily 9–6; Oct.–Mar., daily 9–5.*

7 **Rossío.** Lisbon's main square since the Middle Ages is officially known as Praça Dom Pedro IV (whom the central statue commemorates). Renowned sidewalk cafés line the east and west sides of the square. ✉ *Praça Dom Pedro IV.*

Bairro Alto

Lisbon's Bairro Alto (Upper Town) is largely made up of 18th- and 19th-century buildings that house a mixture of restaurants, theaters, nightclubs, churches, bars, and antiques shops. It's an appealing area to explore on foot. Two novel ways to approach and leave the neighborhood are by funicular railway and by street elevator.

12 **Elevador da Glória.** One of the finest approaches to the Bairro Alto is via the funicular railway on the western side of Avenida da Liberdade, by Praça dos Restauradores. The ascent takes about a minute; passengers are let out at the São Pedro de Alcântara miradouro, a viewpoint that faces the castle and the Alfama. ✉ *Calçada da Glória,* ☎ *01/363–2044.* ⏲ *Daily 7 AM–midnight.*

16 **Elevador de Santa Justa.** The extraordinary street elevator—enclosed in a Gothic-style tower created by Raul Mesnier, a Portuguese protégé of Gustave Eiffel—connects the Bairro Alto with Rua da Santa Justa in the Baixa. ✉ *Largo do Carmo,* ☎ *01/363–2044.* ⏲ *Daily 7 AM–midnight.*

14 **Igreja de São Roque** The highly decorative Church of St. Roque is best known for its flamboyant 18th-century **Capela de São João Baptista** (Chapel of St. John the Baptist), adorned with rare stones and mosaics that resemble oil paintings. The **Museu de Arte Sacra** (Museum of Sacred Art) next door displays a collection of 16th- to 18th-century paintings. ✉ *Largo Trinidade Coelho,* ☎ *01/346–0361.* 🎫 *Church*

and museum free. ⏲ *Church daily 8:30–5; museum Tues.–Sun. 10–1 and 2–5.*

15 **Igreja do Carmo** (Carmelite Church). The sacristy and nave of this church, the only sections to survive the 1755 earthquake, house the quirky **Museu Arqueológico** (Archaeological Museum), filled with everything from Roman coins to medieval sarcophagi. ✉ *Largo do Carmo,* ☎ *01/346–0473.* 🎫 *500$00.* ⏲ *Apr.–Sept., daily 10–6; Oct.–Mar., daily 10–1 and 2–5.*

13 **Instituto do Vinho do Porto** (Port Wine Institute). Inside the cozy, club-like lounge you can sample more than 300 types and vintages of Portugal's most famous beverage—from extra-dry white varieties to the older ruby-red vintages. ✉ *Rua S. Pedro de Alcântara 45,* ☎ *01/342–3307.* ⏲ *Mon.–Sat. 10–10.*

Belém

Numbers in the margin correspond to points of interest on the Belém map.

To see the best examples of that uniquely Portuguese, late-Gothic architecture known as Manueline, head for Belém, at the southwestern edge of Lisbon. If you're traveling in a group of three or four, taxis are the cheapest way to get here; otherwise take Tram 15 from the Praça do Comércio for a more scenic, if bumpier, journey.

19 **Monumento dos Descobrimentos** (Monument to the Discoverers). Erected in 1960, the tall, white, angular slab at the water's edge—a modern tribute to the seafaring explorers—stands at what was the departure point for many a voyage. A mosaic, surrounded by an intricate wave pattern of black and white stones, lies at its foot. Take the elevator to the top for river views. ✉ *Av. de Brasília,* ☎ *no phone.* ⏲ *Tues.–Sun. 9:30–7.*

★ 17 **Mosteiro dos Jerónimos** (Jerónimos Monastery). This impressive structure was conceived and planned by King Manuel I at the beginning of the 16th century to commemorate the discoveries of Vasco da Gama. Construction, begun in 1502, was largely financed by treasures brought back from the Portuguese "discoveries" in Africa, Asia, and South America. The stunning double cloister has arches and pillars heavily sculpted with marine motifs. ✉ *Praça do Império,* ☎ *01/362–0034.* 🎫 *Church free; cloister free Sun.* ⏲ *June–Sept., Tues.–Sun. 10–6:30; Oct.–May, Tues.–Sun. 10–1 and 2:30–5.*

18 **Museu da Marinha** (Maritime Museum). The huge collection here reflects Portugal's long seafaring tradition. The exhibits range from early maps, model ships, and navigational instruments to fishing boats and royal barges. ✉ *Praça do Império (at west end of Jerónimos Monastery),* ☎ *01/362–0010.* 🎫 *Free Sun. 10–1.* ⏲ *Tues.–Sun. 10–6.*

23 **Museu Nacional de Arte Antiga** (National Museum of Ancient Art). Occupying a 17th-century palace in the wealthy district of Lapa, halfway between Belém and the Bairro Alto, this museum was founded in 1884 and fully restored in 1994. It has a beautifully displayed collection of Portuguese art, mainly 15th–19th centuries, whose highlight is the St. Vincent Altarpiece (1467–1470) by Nuno Gonçalves. ✉ *Rua das Janelas Verdes (Bus 27 and Bus 49),* ☎ *01/396–4151.* ⏲ *Tues. 2–6, Wed.–Sun. 10–6.*

21 **Museu Nacional dos Coches** (National Coach Museum). One of the largest collections of coaches in the world is housed in a former riding school. The oldest conveyance on display was made for Philip II

Monumento dos Descobrimentos, **19**
Mosteiro dos Jerónimos, **17**
Museu da Marinha, **18**
Museu Nacional de Arte Antiga, **23**
Museu Nacional dos Coches, **21**
Palácio da Ajuda, **22**
Torre de Belém, **20**

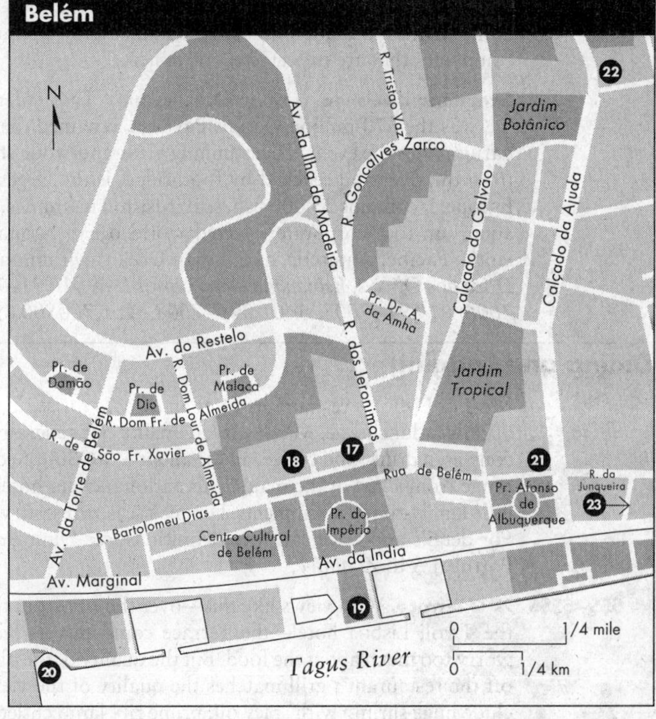

of Spain in the late 16th century, but the most stunning exhibits are three golden baroque coaches made in Rome for King John V in 1716. ✉ *Praça Afonso de Albuquerque,* ☎ *01/361–0850.* 🎫 *Free Sun. 10–1.* ⏲ *June–Sept., Tues.–Sun. 10–1 and 2:30–6:30; Oct.–May, Tues.–Sun. 10–1 and 2:30–5:30.*

❷❷ **Palácio da Ajuda** (Ajuda Palace). Once a royal residence, this impressive building now contains a collection of 18th- and 19th-century paintings, furniture, and tapestries. ✉ *Calçada da Ajuda,* ☎ *01/363–7095.* 🎫 *Free Sun. 10–2. Guided tours arranged on request.* ⏲ *Thurs.–Tues. 10–5.*

★ ❷⓿ **Torre de Belém** (Belém Tower). The balconies and domed turrets of the fanciful Torre de Belém make this perhaps the purest Manueline structure in the country. Although it was built during the early 16th century on an island in the middle of the Tagus River, the tower now stands near its north bank—the river has changed course over the centuries. ✉ *Av. da India,* ☎ *01/301–6892.* ⏲ *June–Sept., Tues.–Sun. 10–6:30; Oct.–May, Tues.–Sun. 10–1 and 2:30–5.*

Expo Urbe

Expo Urbe—an ambitious urban renewal project 5 km (3 mi) northeast of the city center—is building on the infrastructure left in place after Expo '98. To put the Tagus River back at the heart of the city, planners have revitalized a 5-km- (3-mi-) long stretch of riverfront, which is easy to reach via the Oriente train or—coming from the east—via the 16-km (9-mi) Ponte Vasco de Gama suspension bridge that now spans the Tagus. In addition to the Oceanarium (*see below*) there are apartment buildings, restaurants, shops, an exhibition center, a theater, a marina, and acres of landscaped parkland. Work on the project will continue for another decade; when it's finished Expo Urbe should be home to around 25,000 inhabitants and employ a similar number in companies that are expected to move here.

Oceanário de Lisboa. (Lisbon Oceanarium). The centerpiece of Expo '98 was the $70-million Oceans Pavilion, renamed the Lisbon Oceanarium after the event. This stunning glass-and-stone structure, rising from the river and reached by footbridge, is the largest aquarium in Europe. It contains 25,000 fish, seabirds, and mammals, and is the first aquarium to incorporate selected world ocean habitats (North Atlantic, Pacific, Antarctic, and Indian Ocean) within one complex. ✉ *Doca dos Olivais, Esplanada Dom Carlos I,* ☎ *01/891–7002, 01/891–7006, 01/891–7007, or 01/891–7008.* 🎫 *1,700$00.* ⏲ *Daily 10–8.*

Dining and Lodging

Most of Lisbon's restaurants offer an *ementa turistica* (tourist menu), usually at lunchtime. Meals vary in quality but generally include three courses, a drink, and coffee, all for about 3,000$00. Accommodations range from some of the major international chain hotels to charming little family-run establishments. For peak season reserve well in advance. For details and price-category definitions, *see* Dining *and*Lodging *in* Portugal A to Z, *above*.

$$$–$$$$ ✕ **O Terraço.** With views like this—over the city from the top floor of the Tivoli Lisboa hotel—the Terrace could put its feet up and not worry too much about the food. But the quality of the dishes that come off the restaurant's grill matches the quality of the view. Choices include huge shrimp with spicy oil, prime rib, lamb cutlets, or the freshest of fish. ✉ *Av. da Liberdade 185,* ☎ *01/353–0181. Reservations essential. AE, DC, MC, V.*

$$$–$$$$ ★ ✕ **Sua Excêlencia.** There's no written menu in this cozy Lapa district restaurant. The English-speaking owner talks you through the outstanding Portuguese dishes available. ✉ *Rua do Conde 34,* ☎ *01/390–3614. MC, V. Closed Wed. and Sept. No lunch weekends.*

$$$–$$$$ ✕ **Tagide.** Delicious Portuguese food and wine are served in this fine old tiled house that looks out over the Baixa and the river. Try to secure a window table. ✉ *Largo Academia das Belas Artes 18–20, at bottom of Rua Ivens,* ☎ *01/346–0570. Reservations essential. AE, DC, MC, V. Closed weekends.*

$$$–$$$$ ★ ✕ **Tavares Rico.** A seasonal, French-inspired menu, an excellent wine list, and handsome Edwardian furnishings have made this dining room (established as a café in the 18th century) one of Lisbon's most famous restaurants. ✉ *Rua Misericórdia 37,* ☎ *01/342–1112. Reservations essential. AE, DC, MC, V. Closed Sat. No lunch Sun.*

$$–$$$$ ✕ **Gambrinus.** Noted for its fish and shellfish, it is among Lisbon's older restaurants. To enter you pass through an inconspicuous door off a busy street and into one of its small, wood-paneled dining rooms. ✉ *Rua das Portas de S. Antão 23–25,* ☎ *01/346–8974 or 01/342–1466. AE, DC, MC, V.*

$$–$$$$ ★ ✕ **Pap' Açorda.** Art and media types scramble for the closely packed tables in this former bakery at the heart of the Bairro Alto. It's now one of the district's most happening restaurants, serving cutting-edge versions of Portuguese classics—grilled sea bass, breaded veal cutlets, and, *açorda,* a bread-based stew rich in seafood. ✉ *Rua da Atalaia 57,* ☎ *10/346–4811. Reservations essential. AE, DC, MC, V.*

$$–$$$$ ✕ **Solmar.** This large restaurant near Restauradores is best known for its seafood, but try the wild boar or venison in season. ✉ *Rua das Portas de S. Antão 108,* ☎ *01/342–3371. AE, DC, MC, V.*

$-$$$ ★ ✕ **Bota Alta.** This tiny, wood-paneled tavern is one of the Bairro Alto's oldest eating places; lines form outside the door by 8 PM. The menu is strong on traditional Portuguese dishes—bacalhau cooked in cream, homemade sausages, steaks in wine sauce, or grilled fish. ✉ *Travessa da Queimada 37,* ☎ *01/342–7959. MC, V. Closed Sun. No lunch Sat.*

$-$$$ ✕ **O Madeirense.** In Lisbon's only Madeiran restaurant, a rustic-style room, the *espedata* is famously traditional: A skewer of fillet steak is hung from a stand above the table so that you can serve yourself. ✉ *Loja 3027, Amoreiras Shopping Center, Av. Eng. Duarte Pacheco,* ☎ *01/381–3147. AE, DC, MC, V.*

$$ ✕ **Comida de Santo.** Lively Brazilian music and excellent Brazilian food served in an attractive, brightly painted dining room ensure a steady repeat clientele. ✉ *Calçada Eng. Miguel Pais 39,* ☎ *01/396–3339. Reservations essential. AE, DC, MC, V.*

$-$$ ✕ **Bonjardim.** Known as "Rei dos Frangos" (King of Chickens), it specializes in the spit-roasted variety. Just off the Restauradores, it's very crowded at peak hours. ✉ *Travessa S. Antão 11,* ☎ *01/342–4389. AE, DC, MC, V.*

$-$$ ✕ **Cantinho da Paz.** This joyful mom-and-pop establishment on the edge of the Bairro Alto specializes in the cuisine of Goa. The shrimp curry is rich in coconut and cream; the *balichão* shrimp is tangier and hotter. ✉ *Rua da Paz 4, off Rua dos Poiais de São Bento,* ☎ *01/396–9698. Dinner reservations essential Sun. V. Closed Mon.*

$-$$ ★ ✕ **Cervejaria Trindade.** Prepare for hearty Portuguese cuisine served in a 19th-century Lisbon beer hall adorned with colorful tiles. It specializes in seafood and has a garden for summer dining. ✉ *Rua Nova da Trindade 20,* ☎ *01/342–3506. AE, DC, MC, V.*

$-$$ ✕ **Sinal Vermelho.** This Bairro Alto restaurant updates the traditional Lisbon adega. Start with a plate of clams drenched in oil and garlic and follow with the fresh fish, which is rarely disappointing. ✉ *Rua das Gáveas 89,* ☎ *01/346–1252. Weekend reservations essential. AE, MC, V. Closed Sun.*

$-$$ ✕ **Vá e Volta.** This is a splendid place for one-plate Bairro Alto fare—fried or grilled meat or fish dishes served with gusto and good humor. ✉ *Rua do Diario de Notícias 100,* ☎ *01/342–7888. AE, MC, V. Closed Mon.*

$ ✕ **As Barrigas.** Here the house specialty is a rich *arroz de polvo* (rice with octopus). There are also steaks, fish of the day, and other Bairro Alto tavern standards. And the name? It means "the stomachs," which you'll appreciate once you've feasted on the large portions. ✉ *Travessa da Queimada 31,* ☎ *01/347–1220. V.*

$$$$ 🏨 **Lisboa Sheraton and Towers.** A typical Sheraton hotel, it has a huge reception area and medium-size rooms. The deluxe units in the Towers section, which has a separate reception desk and a private lounge, are about the same size but more luxuriously appointed and have better views. ✉ *Rua Latino Coelho 1, 1000,* ☎ *01/357–5757,* FAX *01/354–7164. 381 rooms. 2 restaurants, pool. AE, DC, MC, V.*

$$$$ ★ 🏨 **Ritz Four Seasons.** One of the finest hotels in Europe, the Ritz is renowned for its excellent service. The large, handsomely decorated guest rooms all have terraces, and the public rooms are elegantly appointed with tapestries, antique reproductions, and fine paintings. The best rooms are in the front overlooking Parque Eduardo VII. ✉ *Rua Rodrigo da Fonseca 88, 1070,* ☎ *01/383–2020,* FAX *01/383–1783. 304 rooms. Restaurant. AE, DC, MC, V.*

$$$–$$$$ **Park Atlantic.** The rooms in this distinctive luxury hotel are on the small side, but they're soundproof and attractively decorated; those on the front overlook the Parque Eduardo VII. ✉ *Rua Castilho 149, 1070,* ☎ *01/383–0400,* FAX *01/383–3231. 330 rooms. Restaurant. AE, DC, MC, V.*

$$$–$$$$ ★ **Tivoli Lisboa.** Facing Lisbon's main avenue, this comfortable, well-run establishment has a large public area furnished with inviting armchairs and sofas. The guest rooms are all pleasant, but those in the rear are quieter. ✉ *Av. da Liberdade 185, 1250,* ☎ *01/353–0181,* FAX *01/357–9461. 327 rooms. Restaurant, pool. AE, DC, MC, V.*

$$$ ★ **As Janelas Verdes.** This late-18th-century mansion has marvelously restored, individually furnished rooms. You can eat breakfast in an ivy-covered patio garden. Reservations are vital at this hotel; it's as popular as it is small. ✉ *Rua das Janelas Verdes 47, 1200,* ☎ *01/396–8143,* FAX *01/396–8144. 17 rooms. Dining room. AE, DC, MC, V.*

$$$ **Fenix.** At the top of Avenida da Liberdade, this elegant hotel has large guest rooms—many with fine views over the restored square in front—and a pleasant basement Spanish restaurant. ✉ *Praça Marquês de Pombal 8, 1250,* ☎ *01/386–2121,* FAX *01/386–0131. 119 rooms. Restaurant. AE, DC, MC, V.*

$$$ **Lisboa Plaza.** At this comfortable family-owned hotel behind Avenida da Liberdade, the staff is friendly and helpful. Pastel colors, prints on the walls, dried flower arrangements, and smart, well-stocked bathrooms all add to the charm. An excellent buffet breakfast is included in the room rate. ✉ *Travessa do Salitre 7, 1250,* ☎ *01/346–3922,* FAX *01/347–1630. 106 rooms. Restaurant. AE, DC, MC, V.*

$$$ ★ **York House.** This residential, built as a convent in the 17th century, is in a shady garden at the top of a long flight of steps. It has a good restaurant, and full or half board is available. Book well in advance: this atmospheric place is small and has a loyal following. ✉ *Rua das Janelas Verdes 32, 1200,* ☎ *01/396–2435,* FAX *01/397–2793. 34 rooms. Restaurant. AE, DC, MC, V.*

$$ ★ **Albergaria Senhora do Monte.** Four of the rooms in this unpretentious little hotel, in the oldest part of town near St. George's Castle, have terraces that offer some of the loveliest views of Lisbon—though these rooms fall into a higher price category. Other rooms are less exalted, but the top-floor grill has a picture window. ✉ *Calçada do Monte 39, 1100,* ☎ *01/886–6002,* FAX *01/887–7783. 28 rooms. Restaurant. AE, DC, MC, V.*

$$ **Flamingo.** A good-value choice near the top of the Avenida da Liberdade, this hotel has simply furnished, slightly old-fashioned rooms; those in the front are noisy. ✉ *Rua Castilho 41, 1250,* ☎ *01/386–2191,* FAX *01/386–1216. 39 rooms. Restaurant. AE, DC, MC, V.*

$$ **Principe Real.** There's a real old-fashioned warmth and charm—from the rattling elevator to the lovely antique furniture in the rooms—at this small hotel close to the botanical gardens. And each day starts with the glorious views accompanying the complimentary buffet breakfast in the top-floor restaurant. ✉ *Rua da Alegria 53, 1250,* ☎ *01/346–0116,* FAX *01/342–2104. 23 rooms. Restaurant. AE, DC, MC, V.*

$ **Aljubarrota.** An effusive welcome awaits in this fourth-floor pensão (no elevator) in the Baixa. The small rooms have linoleum floors, but they're carefully maintained, and antique tiles and old bedsteads add character. Tiny little balconies in some offer neck-craning views over the rooftops to the castle. ✉ *Rua da Assunção 531100,* ☎ *01/346–0112. 15 rooms. No credit cards.*

$ **Casa de São Mamede.** One of the first private houses to be built in Lisbon after the 18th-century earthquake, São Mamede has been handsomely restored and transformed into a relaxed guest house. Only breakfast is served, but you're just a 10-minute walk away from the Bairro

Alto. ✉ *Rua da Escola Politécnica 159, 1250,* ☎ *01/396–3166,* FAX *01/395–1896. 28 rooms. MC, V.*

$ **Hotel Borges.** This dependable, old-fashioned Chiado district hotel has good service, a breakfast room, and a charm that transcends its limited facilities. ✉ *Rua Garrett 108–110, 1200,* ☎ *01/346–1951,* FAX *01/342–6617. 99 rooms. Breakfast room. MC, V.*

Nightlife and the Arts

Lisbon has an extensive arts-and-nightlife scene. You'll find listings of music, theater, film, and other entertainment in the monthly *Agenda Cultural* booklet, available from the tourist office. The Friday editions of the *Diario de Notícias* and *O Independente* newspapers also contain listings magazines.

The Arts

Plays are performed in Portuguese at the **Teatro Nacional de D. Maria II** (✉ Praça Dom Pedro IV, ☎ 01/347–2246) from August through June. Classical music, opera, and ballet are presented in the beautiful **Teatro Nacional de Opera de São Carlos** (✉ Rua Serpa Pinto 9, ☎ 01/346–5914). Classical music and ballet are also staged from autumn through summer by the **Fundação Calouste Gulbenkian** (✉ Av. Berna 45, ☎ 01/793–5131). Of particular interest is the annual Early Music and Baroque Festival presented in churches and museums around Lisbon every spring. The **Centro Cultural de Belém** (✉ Praça do Império, ☎ 01/361–2400) hosts a full range of concerts and exhibitions. Free recitals take place regularly at the Igreja do Carmo and Igreja de São Roque in the Bairro Alto, and at the Sé. The **Nova Filarmônica,** one of Portugal's national orchestras, performs concerts around the country throughout the year; look also for performances by the **Orquestra Metropolitana de Lisboa** (Lisbon Metropolitan Orchestra).

All films shown in Lisbon appear in their original language with Portuguese subtitles. There are dozens of movie houses throughout the city, including a selection on Avenida da Liberdade. A modern cinema complex, in the **Amoreiras shopping center** (✉ Av. Eng. Duarte Pacheco, ☎ 01/383–1275), has 10 screens. There's also a multiscreen cinema at the **Colombo shopping center** (✉ Av. Col. Militar, Benfica, ☎ 01/711–3200).

Nightlife

DANCE CLUBS AND BARS

The main areas for bars and discos are the Bairro Alto or along Avenida 24 de Julho, northwest of Cais do Sodré Station. Fashionable, late-opening bars have also sprung up in the converted warehouses of the Doca de Santo Amaro in the Alcântara district, next to the Ponte 24 de Abril. In the Bairro Alto, the best place to start a night out is the refined **Instituto do Vinho do Porto** (✉ Rua de São Pedro de Alcântara 45, ☎ 01/347–5707), where you choose from a menu of port wines. **Pavilhão Chines** (✉ Rua Dom Pedro V 89, ☎ 01/342–4729) is decorated with bric-a-brac from around the world. Typical of the more youthful Bairro Alto joints is the boisterous **Três Pastorinhos** (✉ Rua da Barroca 111–113, ☎ 01/341–4301). Many find their way to the dockside development near Cais do Sodré, where restaurant-bars like **Rock City** (✉ Rua Cintura do Porto de Lisboa, Armazém 225, ☎ 01/342–8636) are the rage; this one has a garden and is open until 4 AM for steaks, drinks, and live music. The **Kapital** (✉ Av. 24 de Julho 68, ☎ 01/395–5963) attracts trendy Lisboetas. **Trumps** (✉ Rua Imprensa Nacional 104b, ☎ 01/397–1059) is the city's biggest gay dance club. **Memorial** (✉ Rua Gustavo Sequeira 42, ☎ 01/396–8891) is also popular with gay and lesbian visitors.

MUSIC CLUBS

The most popular nightspots in Lisbon are the adegas típicas or wine cellars, where you can not only drink wine but also dine on Portuguese specialties and listen to haunting fado melodies. Most of these are scattered throughout the Alfama and Bairro Alto districts. The singing starts at 10 PM, and reservations are advised. The **Adega do Machado** (✉ Rua do Norte 91, ☎ 01/342–8713) is a reliable fado spot in the Bairro Alto. For reasonable food, as well as entertaining singing by a number of people, including one of the cooks, visit the **Adega do Ribatejo** (✉ Rua Diário de Notícias 23, Bairro Alto, ☎ 01/346–8343). In the Alfama **Parreirinha d'Alfama** (✉ Beco do Espírito Santo 1, ☎ 01/886–8209) is considered one of the best fado clubs. Lisbon's top spot for live jazz is **The Hot Clube** (✉ Praça da Alegria 39, ☎ 01/346–7369; closed Sun.–Wed.), where sessions don't usually begin until 11 PM.

Shopping

Flea Markets

A **Feira da Ladra** (flea market) takes place on Tuesday morning and all day Saturday in the Largo de Santa Clara behind the Church of São Vicente, near the Alfama district.

Gift Ideas

HANDICRAFTS

For embroidered goods and baskets from the Azores, try **Casa Regional da Ilha Verde** (✉ Rua Paiva de Andrade 4 , Chiado). **Casa Ribeiro da Silva** (✉ Travessa Fiéis de Deus 69, Bairro Alto) is the place to go for hand-crafted pottery. **Fábrica Sant'Ana** (✉ Rua do Alecrim 95, Bairro Alto) sells wonderful hand-painted ceramics and tiles. For fine porcelain visit **Vista Alegre** (✉ Largo do Chiado 18 and Rua Ivens 52, Bairro Alto). **Viúva Lamego** (✉ Largo do Intendente and Calçada do Sacramento 29) has the largest selection of tiles and pottery.

JEWELRY AND ANTIQUES

Most of the antiques shops are along the Rua Escola Politénica, Rua Dom Pedro IV, Rua da Misericórdia, and Rua do Alecrim. **Antonio da Silva** (✉ Praça Luis de Camões 40), at the top of the Chiado, specializes in antique silver and jewelry. Look for Portuguese gold and silver filigree work at **Sarmento** (✉ Rua Aurea 251), in the Baixa.

LEATHER GOODS

Shoe stores abound in Lisbon, and the better shops can make shoes to order on short notice. You can buy leather gloves at a variety of specialty shops on Rua do Carmo and Rua Aurea. Fine leather handbags and luggage are sold at **Casa da Siberia** (✉ Rua Augusta 254, Baixa). Visit **Ulisses** (✉ Rua do Carmo 87, Chiado) for a fine selection of gloves.

Shopping Districts

Since the fire that destroyed much of the **Chiado** in 1988, an extensive reconstruction project has made great progress. Downtown restoration is best exemplified by the beautifully renovated **Eden** building (✉ Av. da Liberdade), an Art Deco triumph containing a Virgin Megastore and a small shopping center. Another important shopping area is in the **Baixa** quarter (between the Rossío and the River Tagus). On Avenida Engeneiro Duarte Pacheco, west of Parque Eduardo VII, the blue-and-pink towers of the **Amoreiras,** a huge shopping center, dominate the Lisbon skyline. For the very latest shopping experience visit **Colombo,** in the suburb of Benfica and reached directly by metro (Col. Militar–Luz)—it's the largest shopping mall on the Iberian peninsula.

Lisbon Essentials

Arriving and Departing

BY BUS

International buses, and most from the north or the Algarve, arrive at the city's **main bus terminal** (✉ Av. Casal Ribeiro 18, ☎ 01/354–5439), a few minutes' walk from Saldanha metro station; taxis line up outside the terminal. You may also arrive at the **Renex bus terminal** (✉ Campo Cebolas, ☎ 01/887–4871) near the cathedral. From it you can walk down to the main Avenida Infante d'Henrique and catch Bus 9, 39, 46, or 90 to the central Praça dos Restauradores.

BY PLANE

Lisbon's **Portela Airport** (☎ 01/841–3700 or 01/840–2262) is about a 20-minute drive north of the city.

Between the Airport and Downtown. A special bus, the **Aerobus 91,** runs every 20 minutes, 7 AM–9 PM, from outside the airport into the city center; tickets, available from the driver, cost 430$00 or 1,000$00 and provide one and three days' travel, respectively, on all of Lisbon's buses and trams. **Taxis** here are so cheap that it's worth taking one straight to your destination. The cost into Lisbon is about 1,500$00–2,000$00, and to Estoril or Sintra, 6,000$00. If you put luggage in the trunk, add another 300$00. There are no trains or subways between the airport and the city, but there are car-rental desks at the airport.

BY TRAIN

International trains from Paris and Madrid arrive at **Santa Apolonia Station** (☎ 01/888–4025), just east of the city center. There's a tourist office at the station and plenty of taxis and porters are available, but you won't find any car-rental firms. To get to the central Praça dos Restauradores by public transport, take the metro from the station or Bus 9, 39, 46, or 90.

Getting Around

Lisbon is a hilly city, and the sidewalks are paved with cobblestones, so walking can be tiring, even when you're wearing comfortable shoes. However, buses, trams, and the metro (subway) system connect all parts of the city. A pass for unlimited rides on buses or trams costs 430$00 for one day's travel (*bilhete um dia*), 1,000$00 for three days (*bilhete tres dias*); the four-day (1,600$00) or seven-day (2,265$00) **Passe Turistico** (Tourist Pass) is also valid on the metro and the elevador. You can buy Tourist Passes at the Cais do Sodré Station train station, Restauradores metro station, and other terminals. Otherwise, you pay a flat fee of 150$00 to the driver every time you ride a bus, tram, or the elevador; it's better to buy your ticket in advance from a kiosk, in which case the 150$00 ticket is valid for two separate journeys.

The **Lisboa Card** costs 1,700$00 (24 hrs), 2,800$00 (48 hrs), or 3,600$00 (72 hrs) and gives free, unlimited travel on the city's public transportation system, as well as free entrance to the city's museums. Buy it from the **Municipal Council Tourist Office** (✉ Rua Jardim do Regedor 51, ☎ 01/343–3672) or at the **Jerónimos Monastery** in Belém (☞ Exploring, *above*).

BY BUS AND TRAM

Buses and trams operate 6:30 AM–midnight. Try Tram 28 for an inexpensive tour of the city; buses to Costa da Caparica and Setúbal cross the Tagus bridge. In summer old-fashioned trams run on tours through the city (2,800$00 per person), departing from Praçca do Comércio; call the public transportation company, **Carris** (☎ 01/363–9343).

BY FERRY

Ferries cross the Tagus River from the Fluvial Terminal, adjacent to Praça do Comércio, to the suburb of Cacilhas, famous for its fish restaurants; the 10-minute crossing (daily 7 AM–9:30 PM) costs 90$00. Ferries run to Cacilhas all night from the quay at Cais do Sodré. For details about two-hour cruises on the Tagus River, contact **Transtejo** (☎ 01/887–5058). Services operate from April through October, and the price is 3,750$00.

BY SUBWAY

The subway, called the **Metropolitano** (☎ 01/355–8457), operates 6:30 AM–1 AM. It has recently been extended to connect Santa Apolónia and Cais do Sodré train stations with the rest of the network, and now it also runs out to the Oriente station at the former Expo site. Individual tickets cost 70$00; a 10-ticket strip, a *caderneta,* is 550$00. Watch out for pickpockets during rush hour.

BY TAXI

Taxis have a lighted sign on their green roofs. There are stands in the main squares, or you can flag one cruising by, though this can be difficult late at night. Taxis are metered and take up to four passengers at no extra charge. Rates start at 300$00, with an extra charge for luggage.

Contacts and Resources

EMBASSIES

United States (✉ Av. Forças Armadas, ☎ 01/727–3300). **Canadian** (✉ Av. da Liberdade 144-3, ☎ 01/347–4892). **United Kingdom** (✉ Rua São Bernado 33, ☎ 01/392–4000).

EMERGENCIES

SOS Emergencies (☎ 115). **Police** (☎ 01/346–6141). **Ambulance** (☎ 01/301–7777 or 01/942–1111). **Doctor:** British Hospital (✉ Rua Saraiva de Carvalho 49, ☎ 01/395–5067). **Pharmacies:** Open weekdays 9–1 and 3–7, Sat. 9–1; a notice on the door indicates the nearest one open on weekends or after hours; a similar list appears in Lisbon's daily newspapers.

GUIDED TOURS

Orientation and Excursions. A half-day tour of Lisbon will cost about 6,000$00; a full-day trip north to Obidos, Nazaré, and Fatima will run about 15,000$00 (including lunch), as will a full day east along the "Roman Route" to Évora and Monsaraz. As the tours are so similar, several companies have joined together in one organization: **Citirama** (✉ Av. Praia da Vitória 12-b, ☎ 01/355–8569 or 01/355–8564) has details about all the possible excursions. You can make reservations through Citirama or any travel agent or hotel.

Personal Guides. Contact the main **Lisbon Tourist Office** (☞ Visitor Information, *below*) or the **Syndicate of Guide Interpreters** (✉ Rua do Telhal 4, ☎ 01/346–7170). The front desk at your hotel may also have a list of bilingual guides. Beware of unauthorized guides who try to "guide" you to a particular shop or restaurant.

TRAVEL AGENCIES

Abreu (✉ Av. da Liberdade 158–160, ☎ 01/347–6441). **Marcus & Harting** (✉ Rossío 45–50, ☎ 01/346–9271). **Top Tours** (✉ Av. Duque de Loulé 108, ☎ 01/315–5877).

VISITOR INFORMATION

Lisbon Tourist Office: main (Palácio Foz, Praça dos Restauradores, at Baixa/Lower Town end of Avenida da Liberdade, ☎ 01/346–3643); airport (☎ 01/849–3689).

THE PORTUGUESE RIVIERA, SINTRA, AND QUELUZ

Extending 32 km (20 mi) west of Lisbon is a stretch of coast known as the Portuguese Riviera. Over the years the Casino at Estoril and the beaches, both there and in Cascais, have served as playgrounds for the wealthy. To the north of Cascais and Estoril lie the lush mountains of Sintra and, to the northeast, the historic town of Queluz, dominated by its 18th-century rococo palace and formal gardens. The villas, châteaus, and luxury *quintas* (country properties) of Sintra contrast notably with Cascais and Estoril, where life revolves around the sea.

Sporting possibilities abound: golf courses, horseback riding, fishing, tennis, squash, swimming, Grand Prix racing, mountain climbing, and country walks. Beaches vary both in quality and cleanliness, though more and more display the blue Council of Europe flag, which signals a high standard of unpolluted water and sands. The waters off Cascais and Estoril are calm, though sullied as a result of their proximity to the mouth of Lisbon's Tagus River. To the north, around Guincho's rocky promontory and along the Praia de Maçãs coast, the Atlantic is often windswept and rough, but provides good surfing and windsurfing. The 30-minute train journey to Cascais affords splendid sea views.

Estoril

Estoril, 26 km (16 mi) west of Lisbon, is filled with grand homes and gardens, and many of its large mansions date from the last century, when the town was a favorite with the European aristocracy. People-watching is the favored pastime, and one of the best places for it is on the seafront Tamariz esplanade. The best and longest local beach is at adjacent Monte Estoril, which adjoins Estoril's beach.

The town's famous **casino** also houses a restaurant, bar, theater, and art gallery. A major open-air handicrafts and ceramics fair is held here from July through September, and many concerts and ballets are staged here during the Estoril Festival each summer. Admission to the casino complex is free, though it costs 500$00 to enter the gaming rooms; taking in dinner and a floor show can cost up to 9,000$00. ✉ *Parque do Estoril,* ☏ *01/468–4521.* ⏲ *Casino and restaurant 3 PM–3 AM, floor show nightly, 11.*

$$–$$$$ ✕ **A Choupana.** Just outside town toward Lisbon, this restaurant overlooks the beach, putting its picture windows to good use with views of Cascais Bay. You can sample high-quality fresh seafood and other local dishes such as the cataplana of chicken and clams. ✉ *Estrada Marginal, São João de Estoril,* ☏ *01/468–3099. AE, DC, MC, V. Closed Mon.*

$$–$$$$ ✕ **The English Bar.** This mock-Tudor establishment serves good Portuguese and French-influenced cuisine in friendly, comfortable surroundings. There are beautiful views over the beach to Cascais and an excellent wine list. ✉ *Av. Saboia, off Av. Marginal Monte Estoril,* ☏ *01/468–0413. AE, DC, MC, V. Closed Sun.*

$–$$$ ✕ **Restaurante Frolic.** The friendly restaurant-bar has a covered, outdoor terrace. Try the delectable cakes, or stop longer for a Portuguese meal or a pizza. ✉ *Av. Clotilde,* ☏ *01/468–1219. AE, DC, MC, V.*

$$$$ ★ ✕🏨 **Hotel Palácio.** During World War II exiled European aristocrats came here to wait out the war in grand style. Rooms are splendidly appointed, and those on the first, third, and fifth floors have balconies; public areas are decorated with monumental columns, tiled floors, and chandeliers. The elegant Four Seasons restaurant ($$–$$$$) serves buffets around the garden pool in summer and seeks perfection with

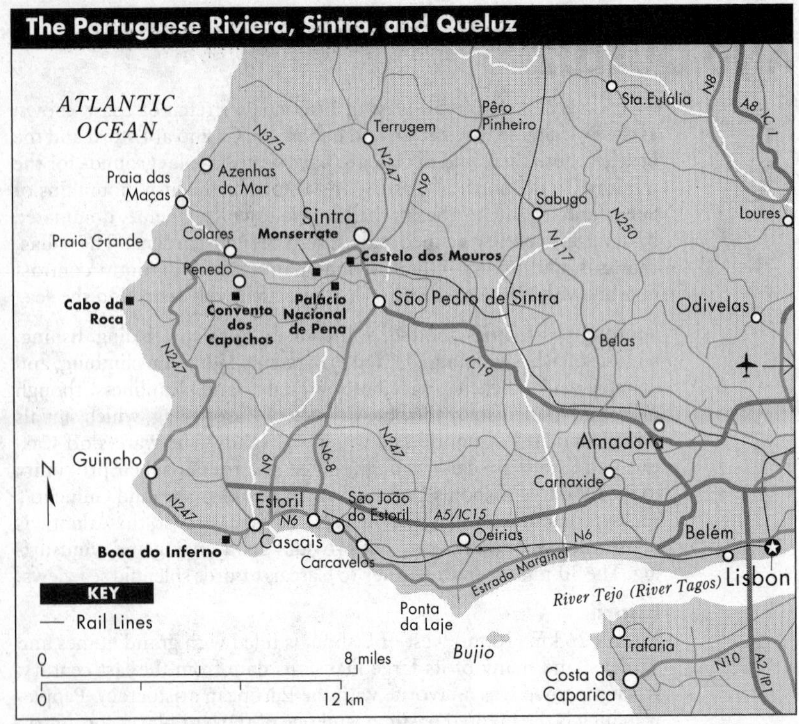

the freshest of foods—the menu changes with the season. ✉ *Parque do Estoril, 2765,* ☎ *01/468–0400,* FAX *01/468–4867. 162 rooms. Restaurant, pool. AE, DC, MC, V.*

★ Cascais

Once a mere fishing village, Cascais (3¼ km/2 mi west of Estoril)—with three small, sandy bays—is now a heavily developed resort area. Even so, it has retained some of its small-town character, seen at its best around the harbor and in the streets and squares off Largo 5 Outubro, where you'll find lace shops, cafés, and restaurants galore.

The most visited local attraction is the forbiddingly named **Boca do Inferno** (Mouth of Hell), just 2 km (1¼ mi) west of Cascais, where the sea pounds into an impressive natural grotto. ✉ *Estrada da Boca do Inferno.* 🎫 *Free.*

The **Igreja de Nossa Senhora da Assunção** (Church of Our Lady of the Assumption) has paintings by Portuguese artist Josefa de Óbidos. ✉ *Largo da Assunção,* ☎ *no phone.* 🎫 *Free.* ⏲ *Daily 9–1 and 5–8.*

One of Cascais's elegant 19th-century town houses now serves as the charming **Museu Conde de Castro Guimarães** (Museum of the Counts of Guimarães), which displays 18th- and 19th-century paintings, ceramics, furniture, and archaeological artifacts that were excavated nearby. It's set in the attractive grounds of the **Parque do Marechal Carmona** (Marechal Carmona Park, ⏲ daily 9–6), in which you'll find a shallow lake, a café, and a small zoo. ✉ *Estrada da Boca do Inferno,* ☎ *no phone.* 🎫 *Free Sun.* ⏲ *Tues.–Sun. 11–12:30 and 2–5.*

$–$$$$ ✕ **Beira Mar.** Tucked behind the fish market, the Beira Mar serves a wide variety of fish and meat dishes—be careful when choosing shellfish as it's sold by weight and can be very pricey. The atmosphere is comfortable and unpretentious. ✉ *Rua das Flores 6,* ☎ *01/483–0152. AE, DC, MC, V. Closed Tues.*

$–$$$ ✕ **João Padeiro.** This town center restaurant serves the best sole in the region—and other seafood as well—in cheerful surroundings. ✉ *Rua Visconde da Luz 12,* ☎ *01/483–0232. AE, DC, MC, V. Closed Sun.*

$$$$ ★ ✕🏨 **Hotel Albatroz.** On a rocky outcrop, this attractive old house, converted from an aristocrat's summer residence, is the most luxurious of Cascais's hotels. Though enlarged and modernized, it has retained its character, with charming bedrooms and a pleasant terrace bar. The restaurant ($$–$$$$) offers superior sea views; it specializes in fish dishes, such as local grilled sole or baked cod stuffed with ham. ✉ *Rua Frederico Arouca 100, 2750,* ☎ *01/483–2821,* FAX *01/484–4827. 40 rooms. Restaurant, pool. AE, DC, MC, V.*

$ 🏨 **Solar Dom Carlos.** This delightful inn tucked into a quiet backstreet is the most appealing budget bet in town. Dating from the 16th century, it was formerly a nobleman's mansion and any lingering mustiness is the smell of history, not neglect—the traditionally tiled floors and walls positively gleam. ✉ *Rua Latina Coelho 8, 2750,* ☎ *01/482–8115,* FAX *01/486–5115. 18 rooms. MC, V.*

Guincho

There's a superb, wide beach (overlooked by several seafood restaurants) at Guincho (11 km/7 mi northwest of Cascais), where rollers from the Atlantic pound onto the sand even on the calmest of days, providing perfect conditions for windsurfing. But beware: the undertow at Guincho beach is notoriously dangerous, and even the best swimmers should take heed.

Cabo da Roca

The windswept Cabo da Roca (20 km/12 mi northwest of Cascais; 15 km/9 mi west of Sintra) and its lighthouse mark continental Europe's westernmost point. As with many similar places, tourist stalls take advantage of its popularity and offer shell souvenirs and other gimmicks, while an information desk and gift shop sells a certificate that verifies your visit.

★ Convento dos Capuchos

In 1560 Franciscan monks built the Convento dos Capuchos (Capuchin Convent) deep in the hills of the Serra de Sintra (Sintra Mountains) 6 km (4 mi) northeast of Cabo da Roca, 9 km (5½ mi) southwest of Sintra. The tiny friary, whose 12 diminutive cells are hacked out of solid rock, is lined with cork for warmth and insulation—hence its nickname of "Cork Convent." ✉ *Signposted off Rte. N247,* ☎ *01/923–0137.* ⌚ *June–Sept., daily 10–6; Oct.–May, daily 10–5.*

Monserrate

This botanical wonderland 5 km (3 mi) northeast of Convento dos Capuchos and 4 km (2½ mi) west of Sintra was laid out by Scottish gardeners in the mid-1800s. It surrounds an exotic and architecturally extravagant domed Moorish-style palace (closed to visitors). In addition to a dazzling array of other plant species, the gardens have one of the largest collections of fern varieties in the world. ✉ *Estrada da Monserrate,* ☎ *01/923–1201.* ⌚ *June–Sept., daily 9–7; Oct.–May, daily 10–5.*

★ Sintra

One of Portugal's oldest towns, beautiful Sintra (30 km/19 mi northwest of Lisbon, 13 km/8 mi north of Estoril) should not be missed. It was the summer residence of early Portuguese kings and aristocrats; by the 18th and 19th centuries its charms became widely known as English travelers, poets, and writers—including an enthusiastic Lord

Byron—were drawn by the region's beauty. If you're in the area on the second or fourth Sunday of the month, visit the **Feira de Sintra** (Sintra Fair) in the nearby village of São Pedro de Sintra, 2 km (1¼ mi) to the southeast.

★ At the center of the Old Town stands the 14th-century **Palácio Nacional de Sintra** (Sintra Palace). This twin-chimney building, a combination of Moorish and Gothic architectural styles, was once the summer residence of the House of Avis, Portugal's royal line. Today it's a museum (guided tours only) exhibiting some fine examples of Moorish-Arabic *azulejos* (tiles). ✉ *Largo Rainha D. Amelia,* ☎ *01/923–0085.* *Free Sun.* AM. ⏲ *Thurs.–Tues. 10–1 and 2–5.*

The 8th-century **Castelo dos Mouros** (Moors' Castle) defied hundreds of invaders until it was conquered by Dom Afonso Henriques in 1147. Follow the steep, partially cobbled road up to the ruins, or rent a horse-drawn carriage in Sintra. From the castle's serrated walls, you can see why its Moorish architects chose the site: The views falling away on all sides are breathtaking. ✉ *Estrada da Pena.* *Free.* ⏲ *June–Sept., daily 10–7; Oct.–May, daily 10–5.*

★ The **Palácio Nacional de Pena** (Pena Palace), a Wagnerian-style extravaganza built by the king consort Ferdinand of Saxe-Coburg in 1840, is a cauldron of clashing styles, from Arabian to Victorian, and was home to the last kings of Portugal. It's surrounded by a park filled with trees and flowers brought from every corner of the Portuguese empire by Dom Fernando, consort to Dona Maria II, in the 1840s. It's a long but pleasant walk to the palace from Sintra (about 1½ hours), although there's also hourly bus service from Sintra train station and town center. ✉ *Estrada da Pena,* ☎ *01/923–0227.* *Free Sun. 10–2.* ⏲ *June–Sept., Tues.–Sun. 10–6:30; Oct.–May, Tues.–Sun. 10–1 and 2–5.*

$$–$$$$ ✕ **Solar de São Pedro.** Highly recommended by its habitués, this restaurant specializes in Portuguese and French country cooking. Its English-speaking host adds to the warm, friendly atmosphere. ✉ *Largo da Feira 12, São Pedro de Sintra,* ☎ *01/923–1860. AE, DC, MC, V. Closed Wed.*

$–$$ ✕ **Alcobaça.** Classic Portuguese cooking is offered at this central, very reasonably priced restaurant. Try the grilled chicken or the arroz de marisco. ✉ *Rua das Padarias 7–11,* ☎ *01/923–1651. MC, V.*

$$$$ ★ **Palácio de Seteais.** This luxurious former palace set on its own grounds a kilometer (half mile) from Sintra was built by the Dutch consul in Portugal during the 18th century. Its stately rooms are decorated with delicate wall and ceiling frescoes, and it houses a splendid restaurant. ✉ *Rua Barbosa do Bocage 8, 2710,* ☎ *01/923–3200,* FAX *01/923–4277. 30 rooms. Restaurant, pool. AE, DC, MC, V.*

$$ ★ **Quinta das Sequóias.** Reservations are essential at this lovely old antiques-filled manor house set on gardens down a side road. It's just over a kilometer (half mile) from Sintra and makes an excellent touring base; time in the Jacuzzi or the sauna here is a wonderful way to unwind from a day of sightseeing. Dinner is served if ordered in advance. ✉ *Apartado 4, 2710,* ☎ FAX *01/923–0342. 6 rooms. Pool. AE, DC, MC, V.*

$$ **Tivoli Sintra.** From its perch in the center of Sintra, the Tivoli has views over the nearby valleys. The smart rooms provide space and comfort in equal measure. ✉ *Praça da República, 2710,* ☎ *01/923–3505,* FAX *01/923–1572. 75 rooms. Restaurant. AE, DC, MC, V.*

Queluz

The town of Queluz, 15 km (9 mi) east of Sintra and 15 km (9 mi) northwest of Lisbon, is accessible by train directly from Lisbon or by way of the IC19/N249 road, which runs between Lisbon and Sintra.

★ Once you turn off the main road, it's hard to miss the magnificent **Palácio Nacional de Queluz** (Queluz Palace). Inspired in part by Versailles, this salmon-pink rococo palace was begun by Dom Pedro III in 1747, and took 40 years to complete. The formal landscaping and waterways surrounding it are the work of the French designer Jean-Baptiste Robillon. Restored after a fire in 1934, the palace is now used for formal banquets and music festivals and as housing for visiting heads of state. You can walk through its more elegant rooms, among them the Music Salon, the Hall of the Ambassadors, and the mirrored Throne Room with its crystal chandeliers and gilt trim. ✉ *Rte. IC19,* ☎ *01/435–0039.* ⏲ *Wed.–Mon. 10–1 and 2–5.*

$$$ ★ ✕🏨 **Pousada de Dona Maria I.** The old servants' quarters, beneath the clock tower opposite the Queluz palace, have undergone a stunning refurbishment: marble hallways lined with prints of old Portugal give way to high-ceiling rooms whose reproduction furniture carefully follows 18th-century fashion. Across the road in the old palace kitchens, the Restaurante de Cozinha Velha ($$–$$$$, reservations essential) takes full advantage of its heritage. The cooking hits the mark; a spicy cataplana of salmon, monkfish, clams, and shrimp is just one superb main course. ✉ *Rte. IC19 2745,* ☎ *01/435–6158,* FAX *01/435–6189. 24 rooms. Restaurant. AE, DC, MC, V.*

The Portuguese Riviera, Sintra, and Queluz Essentials

Getting Around

Although the best way to reach Cascais, Estoril, and Sintra is by train from Lisbon, there are some useful bus connections between towns. The area is served by three main roads: the often congested four-lane coastal road (the N6 Avenida Marginal), the IC19/N249 to Sintra, and the A5 expressway, which links Lisbon with Cascais.

A commuter train leaves every 15 to 30 minutes (5:30 AM–2:30 AM) from Cais do Sodré Station in Lisbon for the trip to Estoril and on to Cascais, four stops farther. A one-way ticket costs 185$00. Trains from Lisbon's Rossío station run every 15 minutes to Queluz (155$00), taking 20 minutes, and on to Sintra (185$00), which takes 40 minutes. For current information about train services, call 01/888–4025.

At Cascais the bus terminal (☎ 01/483–6357) outside the train station operates regular summer services to Guincho (journey time 15 min) and Sintra (40 min). From the bus terminal outside the Sintra train station, there's regular year-round service to Cascais and Estoril (1 hr). There's also a daily bus service from the Sintra train station to the Moorish Castle and Pena Palace.

Guided Tours

Most travel agents and guided-tour operators (☞ Lisbon Essentials, *above*) can reserve you a place on a guided tour, or you can contact the reception desk of your hotel. Half-day trips to Queluz, Sintra, or Estoril, or a tour of the area's royal palaces, cost around 8,000$00; nine-hour tours of Mafra, Sintra, and Cascais cost 13,000$00, including lunch; and there's even an evening visit to Estoril's casino for 13,000$00, including dinner.

Visitor Information

Cascais (✉ Rua Visconde da Luz 14, ☎ 01/486–8204). **Estoril** (✉ Arcadas do Parque, ☎ 01/466–3813). **Sintra** (✉ Praça da República 3, ☎ 01/923–1157 or 01/924–1700 and train station ☎ 01/924–1623).

THE ALGARVE

The Algarve, Portugal's southernmost region, encompasses some 240 sun-drenched km (150 mi) of coastline, making it a top destination for foreign visitors. During the past three decades it has been heavily developed and in certain areas, apartment complexes, hotels, and restaurants sprout from every bay and cliff top. There are, however, still fishing villages and secluded beaches that remain untouched, while the attractions in even the most developed resorts are well known—clean, sandy beaches; excellent sports facilities; championship golf courses; and plenty of color in the local markets, cafés, and restaurants. The drive to Albufeira from Lisbon takes about four hours; allow another hour to reach either Faro or Lagos. (Note that regional authorities are currently working to improve the clarity and quality of directional signs along roads—welcome news for visitors to the Algarve.)

Monte Gordo

Pine woods and orchards break up the flat landscape around Monte Gordo, a town of brightly colored houses with extensive tourist facilities 4 km (2½ mi) west of Vila Real de Santo António, a town—laid out in an 18th-century grid pattern similar to that of the Baixa district in Lisbon—near the Spanish border. There's a long stretch of beach here. Other local beaches to the west, such as Praia Verde and Manta Rota, are equally attractive—you should have little trouble finding a spot on the sand, perhaps having a lunch of grilled sardines at one of the numerous beach bar-restaurants.

$ ✕ **Mota.** The Mota is a lively, unpretentious seafood restaurant with a covered terrace right on the ocean. It often has live music in the evening. ✉ *On the beach at Monte Gordo,* ☎ *081/512340. No credit cards.*

$$ 🏨 **Alcazar.** This attractive hotel has unusual architecture and interior design—the sinuous arches and low molded ceilings suggest the inside of a cave or an Arab tent. ✉ *Rua de Ceuta 9, 8900,* ☎ *081/512184,* FAX *081/512242. 95 rooms. Restaurant, pool. AE, DC, MC, V.*

Tavira

A tuna-fishing port at the mouth of the River Gilão 20 km (12 mi) west of Monte Gordo, Tavia has numerous attractions: cobbled old town streets, a seven-arch Roman bridge, old Moorish defense walls crowning the central hill, and a series of interesting churches—not least, **Santa Maria do Castelo** (St. Mary of the Castle), which was built on the site of a former mosque. There are good sand beaches on nearby **Ilha da Tavira** (Tavira Island), which you can reach by ferry from the jetty at Quatro Águas. ✉ *2 km (1¼ mi) east of town center.* 🎫 *180$00 round-trip.* ⏲ *May–mid-Oct., every 30–60 min.*

Olhão

Founded during the 18th century, the fishing port and market town of Olhão, 22 km (14 mi) west of Tavira, is notable for its North African–style architecture (cube-shape whitewashed buildings) and some of the best food markets in the Algarve (next to the harbor). There are also ferries from Olhão to the nearby sandy islands of **Armona** and **Culatra,** both of which have excellent beaches. ✉ *Jetty east of the town gardens.* 🎫 *Round-trip: 160$00 Armona, 200$00 Culatra.* ⏲ *July–Aug., ferries run hourly; Sept.–June, 3 or 4 ferries daily. Schedule available at tourist office.*

Faro

Founded by the Moors, Faro—provincial capital of the Algarve—was taken by Afonso III in 1249, ending the Arab domination of Portugal.

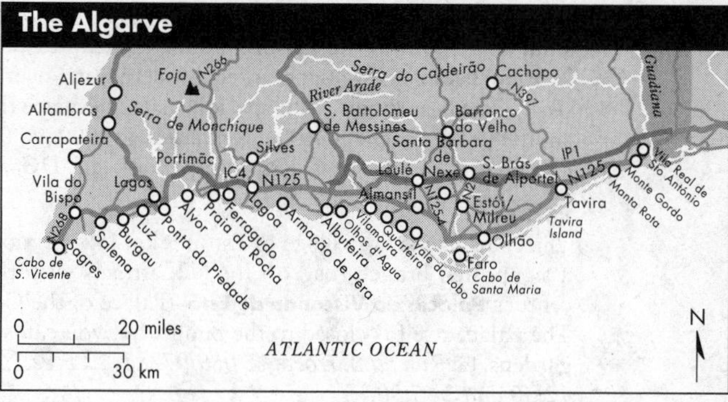

The Algarve

It's a modern center 9 km (6 mi) west of Olhão, full of restaurants that offer international cuisines. There's also a smart marina.

★ In the older district, the **Cidade Velha,** you can see remnants of medieval walls and gates. One of the old gates, the **Arco da Vila,** with a white marble statue of St. Thomas Aquinas in a niche at the top, leads to the grand Largo da Sé (Cathedral Square). Surrounded by orange trees in the square, you'll find the restored Gothic Sé (Cathedral) whose stunning interior is decorated with 17th-century tiles. ✉ *Largo da Sé.* ⏲ *Mon.–Sat. 10–noon and 2–5, Sun. 8–1.*

The old town's **Museu Municipal** (Municipal Museum), housed in a former convent, has a section devoted to the Roman remains found at nearby Milreu (☞ Estói, *below*). ✉ *Largo D. Afonso III,* ☎ *089/822042.* ⏲ *Mon.–Sat. 9–5.*

Perhaps the most fascinating museum in town is the **Museu Regional do Algarve** (Algarve Regional Museum), which displays an ethnographical collection showing just how much the Algarve has changed since the 1960s. There are displays relating to lace making, embroidery, and fishing, plus the restored interior of an old-time general store. ✉ *Rua do Pé da Cruz,* ☎ *no phone.* ⏲ *Weekdays 10–6.*

★ The best of the sights is surely the **Capela dos Ossos** (Chapel of the Bones) in the **Igreja do Carmo** (Carmelite Church), decorated with human bones taken from the monks' cemetery. ✉ *Largo do Carmo,* ☎ *no phone.* ⏲ *Mon.–Sat. 10–1 and 3–5.*

There's a large sand beach on Faro Island, the **Praia de Faro,** which is connected by road (Bus 16 from the harbor gardens). Or you can take the ferry from the jetty below the old town to the beach at Farol on Culatra Island (☞ Olhão, *above*).

$$$ ✕ **Cidade Velha.** Occupying an 18th-century house inside the old town walls, this intimate restaurant serves excellent international cuisine. ✉ *Rua Domingos Guieiro 19,* ☎ *089/27145. AE, MC, V. Closed Sun. No lunch June–Sept.*

$$ ✕ **Dois Irmãos.** A friendly staff in this central, cheery setting serves up an array of cataplana dishes. Save room for the homemade *pudim caseiro* (creme caramel). ✉ *Largo do Terreiro do Bospo 14–15,* ☎ *089/823337. AE, DC, MC, V.*

$$$$ ★ ✕🏨 **Hotel La Reserve.** This intimate luxury hotel in the hills, 10 km (6 mi) inland from Faro and set in a 6-acre park, offers high-class apartment accommodations, including small duplexes with verandas and sea views. Don't pass up the restaurant (reservations essential; closed Tues.; no lunch), which serves elegant cuisine with a French accent; local game is a specialty, and the wine list is very good. ✉ *Santa Bar-*

bara de Nexe, 8000, ☎ 089/90234 or 089/90474, FAX 089/90402. 12 studios, 8 duplexes. Restaurant, pool. No credit cards.

$$ **Hotel Eva.** This well-appointed, modern hotel overlooks the yacht basin. The best rooms, with spacious balconies, face the sea; there's a shuttle to the beach. ✉ *Av. da República 1, 8000, ☎ 089/803354, FAX 089/802304. 150 rooms. Restaurant, pool. AE, DC, MC, V.*

Estói

The charming small village of Estói, 9 km (5½ mi) north of Faro, on a signposted branch road off the N2, attracts visitors with its 18th-century **Palácio do Visconde de Estói** (Palace of the Counts of Estói). The palace itself is closed to the public, but you can stroll around its gardens. ✉ *Rua da Barroca, ☎ 089/97282. Free. Tues.–Sat. 9–12:30 and 2–5:30.*

A 10-minute walk down the main road from town, there are extensive 1st-century **Roman ruins** at **Milreu.** ✉ *Estói, ☎ 089/91620. Free. Tues.–Sun. 10–noon and 2–5.*

Loulé

This little market town in the hills 17 km (10 mi) northwest of Faro, along the N125–4, was once a Moorish stronghold and is now best known for its crafts and the decorative white chimneys of its houses. In its narrow streets you can usually see coppersmiths and leather workers toiling in their workshops. You can also visit the partially restored ruins of a medieval Saracen **castle,** inside of which is the town's **museum.** ✉ *Largo D. Pedro I. Free. Daily 9–12:30 and 2:30–5.*

The 13th-century **parish church,** decorated with handsome tiles and wood carvings, contains an unusual wrought-iron pulpit. ✉ *Largo Pr. C. da Silva. Free. Mon.–Sat. 9–noon and 2–5:30.*

Almansil/Vale do Lobo/Quinta do Lago

East of the nondescript town of Almansil, 13 km (8 mi) west of Faro, the 18th-century Baroque chapel of **São Lourenço** (St. Lawrence) surprises you with its blue-and-white tile panels and intricate gilt work. The cottages beside it have been transformed into a lovely art gallery. ✉ *On the N125, ☎ 089/395451. Mon.–Sat. 10–1 and 2–5.*

The nearest beach is about 6 km (4 mi) to the southwest, where the upscale resort of **Vale do Lobo** sits in exclusive isolation.To the southeast is the equally grand **Quinta do Lago** resort known for its golf, leisure activities, and hotel.

$$$$ **Le Meridien Dona Filipa.** The Dona Filipa has a lavish interior, pleasant rooms, and first-rate service. Set on extensive, beautifully landscaped grounds near the beach, the hotel houses a chic restaurant that offers an excellent international menu. Discount fees for nearby golf courses are available. ✉ *Vale do Lobo, 8235 Almansil, ☎ 089/394141, FAX 089/394288. 147 rooms. Restaurant, pool, tennis court. AE, DC, MC, V.*

Vilamoura

Vilamoura, 10 km (6¼ mi) west of Almansil, is a highly developed resort area. In addition to its modern luxury hotels and a casino, it has a large yacht marina, several golf courses, a major tennis center, one of Europe's largest shooting centers, and other sports facilities. The beach is a splendid stretch, and there's more good sand just 4 km (2½ mi) to the east at the neighboring market town of Quarteira, once a quiet fishing village but now a bustling high-rise resort.

$$$ **Hotel Dom Pedro Golf.** In the heart of this successful vacation complex, the Dom Pedro is close to the casino and not far from the beach.

Each room is attractively furnished and has its own balcony, and you can take advantage of golf privileges, tennis courts, and the hotel's own health club. ✉ *Vilamoura, 8125 Quarteira,* ☎ *089/389650,* FAX *089/315482. 263 rooms. Restaurant, pool, health club. AE, DC, MC, V.*

Albufeira

Once an attractive fishing village, Albufeira, 10 km (6¼ mi) west of Vilamoura, has long since mushroomed into a large, brash resort. But with its steep, narrow streets and hundreds of whitewashed houses clutching the slopes, Albufeira retains a distinctly Moorish flavor. Among its attractions are a lively fish market (held daily), stunning caves and grottoes along the local coast, and plenty of nightlife.

$$$ ✕ **Cabaz da Praia.** This long-established restaurant has a spectacular view of the main beach from its cliff-side terrace. There's fine French-Portuguese cooking here—fish soup, imaginatively served fish plates, and chicken with seafood. ✉ *Praça Miguel Bombarda 7,* ☎ *089/512137. AE, MC, V. Closed Thurs. No lunch Sat.*

$$$ ✕ **La Cigale.** Nine kilomters (5½ mi) east of Albufeira, overlooking its own little beach, this restaurant—one of the best—offers both French and Portuguese cuisine. ✉ *Olhos d'Agua,* ☎ *089/501637. DC, MC, V. Closed Dec.–Feb.*

$$–$$$ ✕ **A Ruina.** A rustic restaurant on the beach, built on several levels, this is the place for good views and charcoal-grilled seafood. ✉ *Cais Herculano, Praia dos Pescadores,* ☎ *089/512094. No credit cards.*

$$$$ ★ 🏨 **Sheraton Algarve.** This luxury hotel occupies a spectacular cliff-top site 8 km (5 mi) east of town. It overlooks the sea and has direct access to a very fine beach via an exterior elevator. The architecture and decor blend traditional Moorish-style courtyards, fountains, and terraces with fine Portuguese tiles and furnishings. Up-to-the-minute facilities include a sauna, a nine-hole golf course, tennis courts, and an exercise room. An excellent buffet breakfast is included in the room rate. ✉ *Praia da Falésia, 8200 Albufeira,* ☎ *089/500100,* FAX *089/501950. 215 rooms. Restaurants, 3 pools, sauna, 3 tennis courts, exercise room, beach. AE, DC, MC, V.*

$$$ 🏨 **Hotel Cerro Alagoa.** The smartly decorated guest rooms here have private balconies; be sure to request a sea view. It's a 10-minute walk to the town center, but there's courtesy bus service to both Albufeira and the local beaches. ✉ *Via Rápida, 8200,* ☎ *089/588261,* FAX *089/580–2199. 310 rooms. Restaurant, pool. AE, DC, MC, V.*

Armação de Pêra

The straggling resort of Armação de Pêra, 14 km (8 mi) west of Albufeira, has one of the longest beaches in the Algarve, a wide sandy strand with a pretty promenade. Local boats take sightseers on cruises to the caves and grottoes along the shore.

$$ ✕ **A Santola.** This well-established restaurant overlooking the beach is the best in town. Try the excellent cataplana. ✉ *Largo da Fortaleza,* ☎ *082/312332. MC, V. Closed Sun.*

$$$–$$$$ 🏨 **Vila Vita Parc.** The pampering begins as soon as you pass through the wrought-iron gates. Gentle colors, fireplaces, dark woods, and the feel of an exclusive oasis run throughout this superb cliff-top resort. Landscaped gardens wind down to two sequestered beaches. ✉ *Alporchinhos (Box 196)8365,* ☎ *082/315310,* FAX *082/315333. 65 rooms, 8 suites. 6 restaurants, 3 pools, 9-hole golf course, 5 tennis courts, beach. AE, DC, MC, V.*

$–$$$ 🏨 **Hotel Garbe.** The bar, lounge, and restaurant—all with terraces that provide views of the sea—take full advantage of the superb location of this squat, white, central hotel. Rooms are modern and smartly furnished, and steps lead from the hotel down to the beach. ✉ *Av.*

Marginal, 8365, ☎ *082/315187,* FAX *082/315087. 152 rooms. Restaurant, pool. AE.*

Portimão

Portimão, 15 km (9 mi) west of Armação de Pêra, is the most important fishing port in the Algarve; it's cheerful and busy with shops and open-air cafés. There was a settlement here at the mouth of the River Arade even before the Romans arrived. Restaurants along the quay are pleasant spots to sample the local specialty: charcoal-grilled sardines with chewy fresh bread and red wine.

$$ ✕ **A Lanterna.** This well-run restaurant is just over the bridge at Parchal, on the Ferragudo side of town. Its specialty is duck, but you might also try the exceptional fish soup or smoked fish. ✉ *Parchal,* ☎ *082/414429. MC, V. Closed Sun. No lunch.*

$$$$ ★ **Le Meridien Penina.** This impressive golf hotel, on 360 well-maintained, secluded acres off the main road between Portimão and Lagos, has spacious, elegant public rooms, pleasant guest rooms (many with balconies), and attentive service. Rooms in the back of the hotel face the Serra de Monchique and have the best views. The excellent golf courses were designed by Henry Cotton, and greens fees are waived for hotel guests, who also have full use of an impressive range of activities and facilities. ✉ *Montes de Alvor, 8500,* ☎ *082/415415,* FAX *082/415000. 192 rooms. Restaurant, pool, sauna, golf privileges, tennis court, horseback riding, beach. AE, DC, MC, V.*

Praia da Rocha

Now dominated by high-rise apartments and hotels, this was the first spot in the Algarve (3 km/2 mi south of Portimão) to be developed as a resort. It has an excellent beach, made more interesting by its wall of huge, colored rocks worn into odd shapes by sea and wind.

$$ ✕ **Safari.** This lively Portuguese seafront restaurant has a distinctly African flavor. Seafood and delicious Angolan recipes are the specialties. ✉ *Rua António Feu,* ☎ *082/23540. AE, DC, MC, V.*

$$–$$$$ **Hotel Algarve-Casino.** A modern hotel, the Algarve-Casino is perched atop a cliff. Decorated in Moorish style, it has good-size rooms and an attentive staff. Leisure facilities are particularly comprehensive here, and there's easy access to the fine beach below. The on-site casino has international shows and gaming rooms. ✉ *Av. Tomás Cabreira, 8500,* ☎ *082/415001,* FAX *082/415999. 209 rooms. Restaurant, 2 pools, beach, casino. AE, DC, MC, V.*

$–$$ **Hotel Bela Vista.** Tasteful decor and such magnificent appointments as traditional tiles and stained-glass panels help to make this small beachfront hotel the delight that it is. Relax on the terrace that overlooks the beach; in summer the hotel has live music performances. ✉ *Av. Tomás Cabreira, 8500,* ☎ *082/24055,* FAX *082/415369. 14 rooms. Beach. AE, DC, MC, V.*

Silves

Once the Moorish capital of the Algarve, Silves, 18 km (11 mi) northeast of Portimão, along the N124-1, ceased to be important after it was almost completely destroyed by the 1755 earthquake. The 12th-century sandstone ★ **castelo** (castle), with its impressive parapets, was restored in 1835 and still dominates the town. ✉ *Castelo do Silves,* ☎ *082/445624.* 🎫 *Free.* ⏲ *Daily 9–7.*

Below the fortress stands the 12th- to 13th-century **Santa Maria da Sé** (Cathedral of St. Mary), which was built on the site of a Moorish mosque. ✉ *Rua da Sé.* 🎫 *Free.* ⏲ *Mon.–Sat. 8:30–6, Sun. 8:30–1.*

The excellent **Museu Arqueológico** (Archaeological Museum), below the cathedral, displays artifacts from prehistoric times through the 17th century. ✉ *Rua das Portas de Loulé 14,* ☎ *082/442020.* ⏲ *Mon.–Sat. 10–12:30 and 2–6.*

Lagos

Lagos—western terminus of the coastal railway that runs from Vila Real de Santo António—is a bustling holiday resort, whose main pedestrian streets are lined with shops, restaurants, and bars. It's still an important fishing port, too, with an attractive harbor and a modern marina, though it's the amazing nearby cove beaches that attract the holiday crowds. The prettiest, the Praia de Doña Ana, is just a 30-minute walk away, along the cliff top. Lagos has a venerable history (Henry the Navigator maintained a base here) most evident in its imposing **city walls,** which still survive, and its 17th-century harborside fort at **Ponta da Bandeira.** ✉ *Av. dos Descobrimentos.* ⏲ *Tues.–Sat. 10–1 and 2–6, Sun. 10–1.*

The 18th-century baroque **Igreja de Santo António** (Church of St. Anthony) is renowned for its exuberant carved and gilt wood decoration. The **Museu Regional** (Regional Museum) at the church houses an extraordinary jumble of exhibits, including mosaics and archaeological and ethnographical items. ✉ *Rua General Alberto Silveira,* ☎ *082/762301.* ⏲ *Tues–Sun. 9:30–12:30 and 2–5.*

$$$ ★ ✕ **Dom Sebastião.** Portuguese cooking and charcoal-grilled specials are the main attractions at this cheerful restaurant. It has a wide range of aged Portuguese wines. ✉ *Rua 25 de Abril 20,* ☎ *082/762795. AE, DC, MC, V. Closed Sun. in winter.*

$$$ ✕ **No Patio.** You'll find some fine food, indeed, at this cheerful restaurant with an attractive patio. It's run by a Danish couple, Bjarne and Gitte, and the fare is international with a Scandinavian accent. Specialties include tenderloin of pork with a Madeira and mushroom sauce. ✉ *Rua Lançarote de Freitas 46,* ☎ *082/763777. AE, MC, V.*

$$$ ★ **Hotel de Lagos.** This modern hotel stretches out at the eastern edge of the Old Town, within easy walking distance of all the sights and restaurants. From its terraced rooms you look down at the pool or across the river to the coast. Traditional tiles are effectively used throughout, even on lamps and tabletops. A shuttle bus runs to the beach, where the hotel has outstanding club facilities. ✉ *Rua Nova da Aldeia, 8600 Lagos,* ☎ *082/769967,* FAX *082/769920. 317 rooms. 2 restaurants, 2 pools. AE, DC, MC, V.*

Sagres

On the windy headland at Sagres, 30 km (19 mi) west of Lagos (take the N268 south from the N125 at Vila do Bispo) some contend that Prince Henry established his famous school of navigation—the first of its kind—in the 15th century. A small road leads across a promontory hundreds of feet above the sea, through the tunnel-like entrance to the ★ **Fortaleza de Sagres.** Here you can experience the crashing of the waves, the howl of the wind, and centuries of nautical history at the site where Henry The Navigator's memory is preserved. Recent renovations transformed the on-site youth hostels into an exhibition center and cafeteria, restored the 16th century church, and created parking areas outside the fort. The fishermen still come here to tempt fate and cast their long lines from the surrounding cliffs. ☎ *082/620140.* ⏲ *May–Sept. daily 10–8:30; Oct.–Apr. 10–6:30.*

$–$$ ★ ✕ **Pousada do Infante.** Housed in a sprawling structure with a red-tile roof, this pousada affords spectacular views of the sea and craggy rock cliffs. The moderate-size rooms are well appointed and have small balconies. The restaurant offers excellent fresh fish, good desserts, and more marvelous sea views. ✉ *8650 Sagres,* ☎ *082/624222,* FAX *082/624225. 39 rooms. Restaurant, pool. AE, DC, MC, V.*

★ Cabo de São Vicente

There are spectacular views from Cabo de São Vicente (Cape St. Vincent), 6 km (4 mi) west of Sagres. This point, the most southwesterly tip of Europe, is sometimes called *o fim do mundo* (the end of the world). The lighthouse at Cabo de São Vicente is said to have the strongest reflectors in Europe, casting a beam some 96 km (60 mi) out to sea; it's open to the public. It was probably at this breathtaking spot that Pedro Álvares Cabral, Vasco da Gama, Ferdinand Magellan, and other great explorers learned their craft 500 years ago.

Algarve Essentials

Getting Around

The main east–west highway in the Algarve is the two-lane N125, which extends from Vila Real de Santo António, on the Spanish border, to Sagres. This road doesn't run right along the coast, but turnoffs to beachside destinations are posted along the route. A four-lane motorway, the IP1/E1, is several miles inland and runs parallel to the coast from the suspension bridge at the Spanish border west to Albufeira, where it joins the main road to Lisbon. Daily bus and rail service connects Lisbon with the major towns in the Algarve; trips take four–six hours.

TAP Air Portugal and Portugalia have daily flights to Faro, the capital of the Algarve, from Lisbon (a 45-minute trip; ☞ *also* Transportation *in* Portugal A to Z, *above*), and there are frequent flights to Faro from most European capitals.

Guided Tours

Organized guided bus tours of some of the more noteworthy villages and towns depart from Faro, Vilamoura, Albufeira, Portimão, and Lagos.

Visitor Information

Albufeira (✉ Rua 5 de Outubro, ☎ 089/585279), **Armação de Pêrá** (✉ Av. Marginal, ☎ 082/312145), **Faro** (✉ Rua da Misericórdia 8/12, ☎ 089/803604; airport branch, ☎ 089/818582), **Lagos** (✉ Largo Marquês de Pombal, ☎ 082/763031), **Loulé** (✉ Edifico do Castelo, ☎ 089463900), **Monte Gordo** (✉ Av. Marginal, ☎ 081/544495), **Olhão** (✉ Rua Martins Mestre, 6A, ☎ 089/713936), **Portimão** (✉ Largo 1 de Dezembro, ☎ 082/419131), **Praia da Rocha** (✉ Av. Tomás Cabreira, ☎ 082/419132), **Silves** (✉ Rua 25 de Abril, ☎ 082/442255), and **Tavira** (✉ Rua da Galeria 9, ☎ 081/322511).

25 Romania

Bucharest, the Black Sea Coast and Danube Delta, Transylvania

Though Romania can be a challenging destination, it may well be the most beautiful country in Eastern Europe. Its natural attractions are varied, from the summer resorts on the Black Sea coast to the winter ski resorts in the rugged Carpathian Mountains. The many medieval towns and rural villages of Romania are among the most unspoiled in Europe.

Romania is made up of the provinces of Walachia, Moldavia, and Transylvania, and borders Ukraine, Moldova, Bulgaria, Serbia, and Hungary. With a population of 23 million, Romania is a "Latin island" in a sea of Slavs and Magyars—its people are the descendants of the Dacian tribe and of the Roman soldiers who garrisoned this easternmost province of the Roman Empire. Barbarian invasions, struggles against the Turks, the Austro-Hungarian domination of Transylvania, and a strong French cultural influence have all played a part in the evolution of Romanian culture. Famous natives of what is now Romania include Androcles (famed for his care of a lion), writer and Nobel Peace Prize winner Elie Wiesel, and the sculptor Constantin Brancusi.

Romania's largest metropolis, Bucharest, may appear unwelcoming, but its wide, tree-lined avenues and hidden charm can outweigh the effects of rows of drab buildings and depressing neighborhoods. Elsewhere in the country are the painted monasteries of Bucovina and the Romanian Riviera on the Black Sea, with the spectacular wildlife sanctuaries of the nearby Danube Delta. Transylvania is famous for the Dracula legend and its related sights, but the region is also home to Hungarian and German populations with distinctive folk traditions.

The overthrow of the Ceauşescu regime in December 1989 started the country moving toward Western-style democracy and a market economy. Shortages are easing, and the range of available goods and services is increasing, though rising prices have hit many Romanians hard. Romanian standards are often quite different from those in the West.

As Romania is among the poorest countries in Europe, it is useful to keep certain precautions in mind. Petty theft remains a widespread problem. If you are traveling independently, you may wish to take some food supplies with you. If you are a vegetarian, note that only a limited range of produce is available (especially in winter). You should use water purification tablets or boil your tap water, as hepatitis is a danger. Alternatively, bottled mineral water is readily available. You should bring an emergency supply of toilet paper, a full first-aid kit, a flashlight for poorly lighted streets and corridors, and, in summer, insect repellent. As medical facilities do not meet Western standards, it is best to take along your own vitamins and medication (including needles and syringes for injections if you need them).

Romania is likely to remain underexplored until the serious problems caused by the overthrown Ceauşescu regime are resolved. In the meantime, whether you're on a controlled package vacation or fearlessly trekking alone, you will experience a part of Europe that has, for better or worse, largely escaped the complexities of the late 20th century.

ROMANIA A TO Z

Customs on Arrival

You may bring in a personal computer and printer, 2 cameras, 10 rolls of film, 1 small camcorder/video camera and VCR, 10 rolls of video film, a typewriter, binoculars, a radio/tape recorder, a small television set, a bicycle, a stroller for a child, 200 cigarettes, 2 liters of liquor, and 4 liters of wine or beer. Gifts are permitted, though you may be charged duty on some electronic goods. Declare video cameras, personal computers, and expensive jewelry on arrival. Souvenirs and gifts may be taken out of Romania, provided their value does not exceed 50% of the currency you have changed legally—so keep all receipts.

Dining

Standards have improved to a point that many hotels and restaurants provide quality cuisine and varied menu choices. Traditional Romanian foods are *mamaliga* (corn porridge), *sarmale* (cabbage rolls filled with meat and rice), *ciorbă* (a slightly spicy and sour soup stock), and sheep-milk cheeses. Favored meats are usually pork or beef. Away from the bigger restaurants with printed menus, overcharging is a hazard, so you may want to ask for prices before you eat. For snacks, there are always the street vendors and their fragrant offerings such as *covrigi* (giant pretzels) and roasted chestnuts.

MEALTIMES

Outside Bucharest and the Black Sea and Carpathian resorts, many restaurants will have stopped serving by 9 PM, although an increasing number have begun staying open until 11 PM or later.

RATINGS

Prices are per person and include first course, main course, and dessert. Because high inflation means local prices frequently change, ratings are given in U.S. dollars, which remain constant. Your bill will be in lei.

CATEGORY	COST
$$$$	over $30
$$$	$20–$30
$$	$10–$20
$	under $10

WHAT TO WEAR

Jacket and tie are advised for the best restaurants and business lunches and dinners. Casual dress is appropriate at other times.

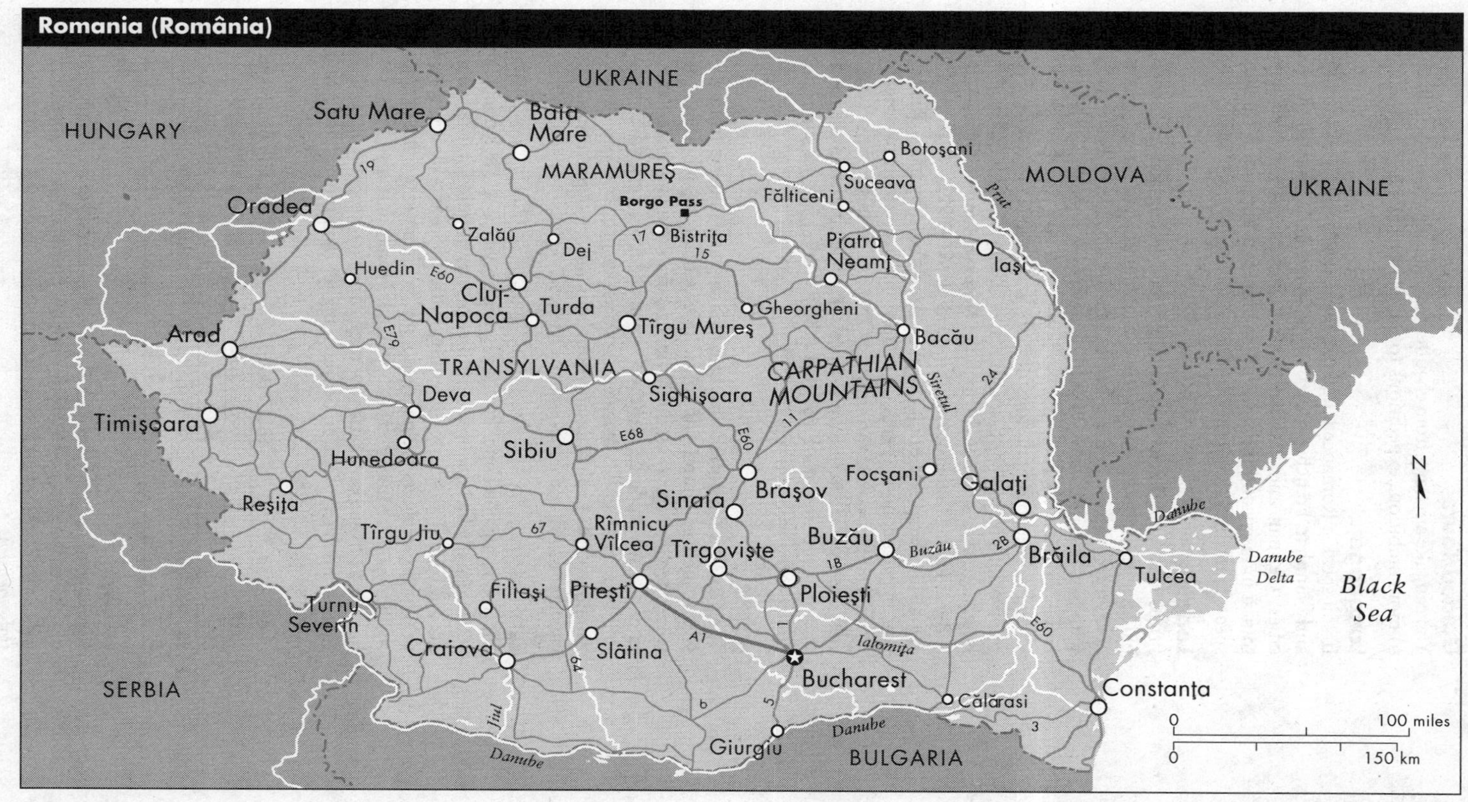
Romania (România)
UKRAINE
HUNGARY
MOLDOVA
UKRAINE
SERBIA
BULGARIA
Black Sea
MARAMUREŞ
TRANSYLVANIA
CARPATHIAN MOUNTAINS
Borgo Pass
Satu Mare
Baia Mare
Oradea
Zalău
Dej
Bistriţa
Huedin
Cluj-Napoca
Turda
Tîrgu Mureş
Gheorgheni
Arad
Timişoara
Deva
Hunedoara
Sibiu
Sighişoara
Reşiţa
Botoşani
Suceava
Fălticeni
Piatra Neamţ
Iaşi
Bacău
Focşani
Galaţi
Brăila
Tulcea
Danube Delta
Constanţa
Călărasi
Braşov
Sinaia
Buzău
Tîrgovişte
Ploieşti
Bucharest
Giurgiu
Tîrgu Jiu
Rîmnicu Vîlcea
Piteşti
Slâtina
Filiaşi
Turnu Severin
Craiova
Prut
Siretul
Buzău
Ialomiţa
Jiul
Danube
E60
E68
E79
A1
N
0 100 miles
0 150 km

Guided Tours

You can take anything from chauffeured sight-seeing drives in Bucharest to more ambitious expeditions to the Danube Delta.

Language

If you speak a Romance language, Romanian is likely to sound pleasantly familiar. French is widely spoken and understood in Romanian cities, German and Russian less so. Romanians involved with the tourist industry and the staff in most hotels and major resorts usually speak English.

Lodging

Prices are highly variable depending on booking arrangements. Prepaid arrangements through travel agencies abroad often benefit from discounted prices. Some schemes, such as fly-drive holidays, come with bed-and-breakfast accommodation vouchers. Most state-run facilities take vouchers; in deluxe hotels you pay a little extra. Otherwise, book accommodations directly with hotels (which may require reservations by fax) or through travel agencies. Bookings in state-run hotels can also be made through the **National Tourism Office—ONT** (✉ 7 B-dul Gen. Magheru, Bucharest, ☎ 01/6141922, FAX 01/3123907). Avoid the cheap and often cheerless hotels used by many Romanians; you may encounter perilous conditions. Rooms in private homes, which can be booked through the ONT office and some private agencies, are a good alternative to hotels. Private citizens come to railway stations and offer spare rooms in their homes, but use discretion and be prepared to bargain.

HOTELS

The ONT ranks hotels with one to five stars, ranging from inexpensive to deluxe. Standards of facilities, including plumbing and hot water, decline rapidly through the categories and may not be ideal even in expensive accommodations. Ask at the front desk when hot water will be available. No matter what class of property you choose, you should not leave valuables in your room and, on departure, you should check your bill for unnecessary charges.

RATINGS

The following hotel price categories are for two people in a double room. Rates usually include breakfast. Because of inflation, ratings are given according to hard-currency equivalents. There is a dual price system in which foreigners are charged a much higher rate than Romanians; the higher price may not be displayed. Hotels may also insist on your buying lei from them (at a low exchange rate) to pay your bill. Room rates in Bucharest tend to be much higher than those in the rest of the country.

CATEGORY	BUCHAREST	OUTSIDE BUCHAREST
$$$$	over $200	over $80
$$$	$125–$200	$50–$80
$$	$70–$125	$30–$50
$	under $70	under $30

RENTALS

Rustic cottages may be rented at such ski resorts as Sinaia and Predeal. Details are available from Romanian tourist offices abroad or local offices in Bucharest (☞ Contacts and Resources *in* Bucharest Essentials, *below*).

Mail

Postal codes are not used in Romania. Rates increase regularly, so check before you post.

Money Matters

COSTS

Hotel and restaurant prices can be as high as those in Western Europe. Prices of basic items, artificially low from communism, have increased dramatically and are now often as high as or higher than prices found in the West.

CREDIT CARDS

Major credit cards are welcome in larger hotels and restaurants in the Bucharest area. Though they are becoming more common, they are not accepted in most independent establishments or in the countryside.

CURRENCY

The unit of currency is the leu (plural lei). There are coins of 20, 50, and 100 lei. Banknotes come in denominations of 200, 500, 1,000, 5,000, 10,000, and 50,000 lei (introduced in 1997). Do not expect to be given change of less than 100 lei. Inflation and frequent price increases are expected to continue; costs are therefore best calculated in convertible hard currencies such as U.S. dollars, German marks, or Swiss francs. As U.S. dollars are the most readily negotiated currency, it is a good idea always to keep some with you, especially in smaller denominations. At press time (spring 1998), the official exchange rate was approximately 8,100 lei to the U.S. dollar, 5,350 lei to the Canadian dollar, and 12,500 lei to the pound sterling.

An increasing number of licensed *casă de schimb* (exchange offices) compete to offer rates far better than the official rate available at banks, the airport, the train station, or in hotels. Do not deal with the dangerous black market. Retain all exchange receipts, as you may need to prove your money was changed legally, and you must produce these receipts to exchange lei back into hard currency upon departure from Romania. By law, foreigners must pay for everything except air tickets in lei, though hard currency is widely accepted. You may not import or export lei.

SAMPLE PRICES

Museum admission usually costs less than 10,000 lei; a bottle of imported beer in a restaurant, around 20,000 lei; a 2-km (1-mi) taxi ride, about 5,000 lei.

TIPPING

Most Romanians do not tip, but it is generally expected of foreigners. A 10% tip is welcomed and appreciated (especially by taxi drivers).

National Holidays

January 1–2 (New Year's); April 20 (Orthodox Easter Monday—this date changes yearly according to the Orthodox calendar); May 1 (Labor Day); December 1 (National Day); December 25–26 (Christmas); December 31 (New Year's Eve).

Opening and Closing Times

Banks are open weekdays 9–12:30. Exchange office hours vary, but most are open weekdays 9–5 and Saturday 9–1; some are open until 7 on Saturday and 1 on Sunday. **Museums** are usually open 10–6, closed on Monday (and sometimes Tuesday). **Shops** are generally open weekdays 10–6. Most state-owned shops close at 2 on Saturday, though an increasing number of private shops are staying open later.

Shopping

Private shops are beginning to bring extra style and choice to Romania. Bargains can be found on Oriental-style and flat-weave rugs, as well as on crystal, porcelain, and glassware. Traditional folk crafts, such as painted eggs, handmade lace, and embroidered items, are especially attractive. Keep receipts of all purchases, regardless of their legal export status.

Telephoning

COUNTRY CODE

The country code for Romania is 40. When dialing Romania from outside the country, drop the initial 0 from the regional code.

INTERNATIONAL CALLS

Direct-dial international calls can be made from hotels, the train station, the phone company building on Bucharest's Calea Victoriei, and local post offices (☞ Local Calls, *below*). To place long-distance calls out of Romania, dial 00, then the country code and number. To place a call from Romania via an **AT&T** USADirect international operator, dial 01–800–4288; for **MCI,** dial 01–800–1800; for **Sprint,** dial 01–800–0877. For international information, dial 971.

LOCAL CALLS

The Romanian telephone system is antiquated and overextended: Local calls can be dialed directly, but you may have to wait for long-distance calls. Coin-operated telephones at roadsides, airports, and train stations usually work only for local calls; most older phones use the hard-to-find 20-lei coins, although some require 50- or 100-lei coins. Many new orange phones installed around Bucharest require the use of a phone card, which can be purchased at post offices and in some hotels. Long-distance calls can also be made at the post office: Order your call and pay at the counter. When your call is ready, the town you are phoning is announced along with the cabin number you should proceed to for your call. In larger towns, private business offices offer phone, fax, and telex services.

The area code for Bucharest is 01, and telephone numbers in the city have 2, 3, 6, or 7 as a prefix, followed by a six-digit number. Long-distance calls within Romania should be prefixed with a 0 followed by the area code for the county or region. For information in Romania, your hotel's front desk or phone book is often your best bet. In Bucharest, try dialing 931; for internal long distance, dial 991; for local information, dial 951 (the operators sometimes speak English, though they are not always friendly).

Transportation

BY BOAT

Regular passenger services operate on various sections of the Danube; tickets are available at the ports (e.g., Giurgiu, Turnu Severin). The Black Sea Ferry operates between Istanbul and Constanţa; tickets are available through most travel agencies, or from **Danubius** ✉ (Str. Ferdinand 22/36, Constanţa, ☎ 041/615836).

BY BUS

Bus stations, or *autogara,* are usually near train stations. Buses are generally crowded and far from luxurious. Tickets go on sale at stations up to two hours before departure.

BY CAR

An International Driver's Permit is required for all drivers from outside the country for stays of more than 30 days.

Gasoline. State gas stations, usually at the edge of towns on main roads, remain scarce. There are many new private gas stations that charge a bit more than the state stations. Most gas stations sell regular (90-octane), premium (98-octane), *motorina* (diesel), and *fară plumb* (unleaded). Although prices recently increased by approximately 40%, they still remain low compared to those of Western Europe.

Car Rentals. A number of international car rental companies have opened offices in Bucharest and other major towns. **Avis** is at Bucharest's Otopeni Airport (☎ 01/2300054), and in various hotels. **Budget** is in the Hotel Dorobanţi (✉ Calea Dorobantilor 1–7, Bucharest, ☎ 01/2102867) and at Otopeni Airport. **Hertz** is in the Hotel Dorobanţi (✉ ☞ *above*, ☎ 01/2115450) and at Otopeni Airport. **Europcar** is in the ONT Carpaţi Building (✉ B-dul Gen. Magheru 7, ☎ 01/6131540).

Road Conditions. A network of main roads covers the country, though the majority only allow for a single lane in each direction. Potholes are common, and a few roads have not been paved at all. Farm machinery, slow-moving trucks, horses and carts, or herds of animals often block roads. At night poorly lighted or unlighted roads and vehicles are the norm.

Rules of the Road. Driving is on the right and road signs are the same as in much of Western Europe. Speed limits are 60 kph (37 mph) in built-up areas and 80 kph–90 kph (50 mph–55 mph) on all other roads. Driving after drinking any alcohol is prohibited. Seat belts are compulsory. Spot checks are frequent; police can levy on-the-spot fines.

BY PLANE

Tarom operates daily flights to major Romanian cities from Bucharest's Baneasa Airport. In summer additional flights link Constanţa with major cities, including Cluj and Iaşi. Be prepared for delays and cancellations. For domestic flights, go to Piaţa Victoriei 1, Bucharest (☎ 01/6594125). International flights can be booked at the central reservations office (✉ Str. Brezoianu 10, Bucharest ☎ 01/6150499 or 6134295, FAX 01/6130363) and at some major hotels.

BY TRAIN

Romanian Railways (CFR) operates an extensive network of trains. *Rapid* and *accelerat* trains are the fastest, with limited stops; *Personal* trains are slow and have many stops. *Expres* designates special international express trains, such as the Dacia Expres to Vienna. First class is worth the extra cost. A *vagon de dormit* (sleeper) or cheap *cuşeta,* with bunk beds is available on longer journeys. It is always advisable to reserve a seat, but you cannot buy the ticket itself at a train station more than one hour before departure. If your reserved seat is already occupied, it may have been sold twice. To buy a ticket ahead of time in Bucharest, contact either a travel agency or the CFR Advance Booking Office (✉ Str. Brezoianu 10, ☎ 01/614 5528). You will be charged a small commission, but the process is less time-consuming than buying your ticket at the station.

Visas

U.S. citizens need only a valid passport to enter Romania for up to 30 days, but border guards may try to extort money from you anyway: Be firm. If you're traveling on a British, Australian, or New Zealand passport, you must pay $31 for a 30-day tourist card when you cross the border. Canadians must pay $33. There is no application, you don't need any photos—just hand the border guard your money. They prefer U.S. dollars but will accept British pounds or German marks.

Visitor Information

ONT (formerly the Romanian National Tourist Office, now privatized; ✉ B-dul Gen. Magheru 7, Bucharest, ☎ 01/3122598, FAX 01/3122594; Otopeni Airport; Gara de Nord); office signs in most Romanian towns read AGENŢIA DE TURISM).

Weather

Bucharest is at its best during the spring and fall. The Black Sea resorts open in mid- to late May and close at the end of September. Developed ski resorts in the Carpathians such as Poiana Braşov, Predeal, and Sinaia, are increasingly popular in winter months.

CLIMATE

The Romanian climate is temperate and generally free of extremes, but snow as late as April is not unknown, and the lowlands can be very hot in midsummer. The following are the average daily maximum and minimum temperatures for Bucharest.

Jan.	34F	1C	**May**	74F	23C	**Sept.**	78F	25C
	19	− 7		51	10		52	11
Feb.	38F	4C	**June**	81F	27C	**Oct.**	65F	18C
	23	− 5		57	14		43	6
Mar.	50F	10C	**July**	86F	30C	**Nov.**	49F	10C
	30	− 1		60	16		35	2
Apr.	64F	18C	**Aug.**	85F	30C	**Dec.**	39F	4C
	41	5		59	15		26	− 3

BUCHAREST

The name Bucureşti was first used officially in 1459 by Vlad Ţepeş, the real-life Dracula. Two centuries later, this citadel on the Dîmboviţa River became the capital of Walachia, and after another 200 years, it was named the capital of Romania. Bucureşti gradually developed into a place of bustling trade and gracious living, with ornate and varied architecture, landscaped parks, busy, winding streets, and wide boulevards. The city was known before World War II as the Paris of the Balkans, but its glory now lies buried under decades of neglect and political turmoil.

Nicolae Ceauşescu's megalomaniacal drive to redevelop the capital involved the forced displacement of thousands of people and the demolition of many priceless early houses, churches, synagogues, and other irreplaceable buildings. Piaţa Unirii was the hub of his enormously expensive and impractical vision. Construction cranes now stand eerily idle above unfinished tower blocks with colonnaded, white marble facades. They flank a lengthy boulevard leading to the enormous, unfinished Palace of Parliament. After such a massive diversion of resources, it is not surprising that the infrastructure is weakened, but the city is currently directing its efforts to remedying the situation. Happily, Bucharest still has places of historical interest, cafés, cinemas, and performance halls.

Exploring Bucharest

The high-rise Hotel Inter-Continental dominates the main intersection at Piaţa Universităţii; northward, up the main shopping streets Bulevardul Nicolae Bălcescu, Bulevardul General Magheru, and Bulevardul Ana Ipătescu, only the occasional older building survives. However, along Calea Victoriei, the flavor of Bucharest's grander past can be savored, especially at the former royal palace opposite the Romanian Senate (formerly Communist Party headquarters) in Piaţa Revoluţiei and near the domed National Library. South along Calea Victoriei is the busy Lipscani trading district, a remnant of the Old City.

Historic Bucharest

Numbers in the margin correspond to points of interest on the Bucharest map.

❹ **Biserica din Curtea Veche** (Church of the Princely Court). Founded in the 16th century beside the Princely Court, this beautiful basilica remains an important center of worship. ✉ *Str. Selari.*

❺ **Curtea Veche** (Princely Court). The Princely Court now houses **Muzeul Curtea Veche–Palatul Voievodal,** a museum exhibiting the remains of the palace built by Vlad Ţepeş during the 15th century. The site was under renovation in 1998, and the museum was not expected to be accessible until 1999. ✉ *Str. Iuliu Maniu 31.*

❸ **Hanul lui Manuc** (Manuc's Inn). This renovated 19th-century inn, arranged in the traditional Romanian fashion around a courtyard, now houses a small hotel and restaurant. Manuc was a wealthy Armenian merchant who died in Russia—poisoned by a famous French fortuneteller who, having forecast Manuc's death on a certain day, could not risk ruining her reputation. The 1812 Russian-Turkish Peace Treaty was signed here. ✉ *Str. Iuliu Maniu 62–64,* ☎ *01/6131415.*

★ ❷ **Palatul Cotroceni** (Cotroceni Palace). On the Dîmboviţa River corniche near the Botanical Gardens, this grand building was once the royal residence. It now offers an intimate view into the lives of Romania's former ruling families. Reservations are required for visitors. ✉ *B-dul. Geniului 1,* ☎ *01/2211200.*

★ ❶ **Palatul Parlamentului** (Parliament Palace). This is among the largest buildings in the world. As deep as it is high, the mammoth building was originally meant to house Ceauşescu and his government offices. The unfinished structure is currently the home of the Romanian parliament. Tours are available, although the building is often closed to visitors during conferences and other government functions. ✉ *South entrance.* ⏲ *Daily 10–4.*

Lipscani District

❼ **Biserica Stavropoleos** (Stavropoleos Church). This small, exquisite church combines late-Renaissance and Byzantine styles with elements of Romanian folk art. Inside are superb wood and stone carvings and a richly ornate iconostasis (the painted screen that partitions off the choir). ✉ *Str. Stavropoleos.*

❽ **Lipscani** is a bustling bazaar of narrow streets, open stalls, and small artisans' shops. In Hanul cu Tei, off Strada Lipscani, you'll find many galleries and shops dealing in traditional crafts and gifts. ✉ *Str. Lipscani.*

❻ **Muzeul Naţional de Istorie** (National History Museum). This vast, somewhat dreary museum contains an enormous collection dating from the Neolithic period to the 1920s. The Treasury has a stunning hoard of objects in gold and precious stones—royal crowns, weapons, plates, and jewelry—dating from the 4th millennium BC through the 20th century. ✉ *Calea Victoriei 12,* ☎ *01/6157056.* ⏲ *Treasury, Tues.–Sun. 10–5, last ticket at 4PM; museum, Wed.–Sun. 10–4.*

Around Bucharest

⓮ **Arcul de Triumf.** The Arcul de Triumf was built in 1922 to commemorate the Allied victory in World War I. Originally constructed of wood and stucco, it was rebuilt during the 1930s and carved by some of Romania's most talented sculptors. ✉ *Head of Şos. Kiseleff.*

❿ **Ateneul Român** (Romanian Athenaeum). The Ateneul concert hall, with its Baroque dome and Greek columns, has survived much upheaval since 1888 and is still home to the George Enescu Philharmonic Orchestra. ✉ *Str. Franklin 1,* ☎ *01/6156875.*

⓫ **Muzeul Colecţiilor de Artă** (Museum of Art Collections). This small museum affiliated with the National Art Museum houses an impressive

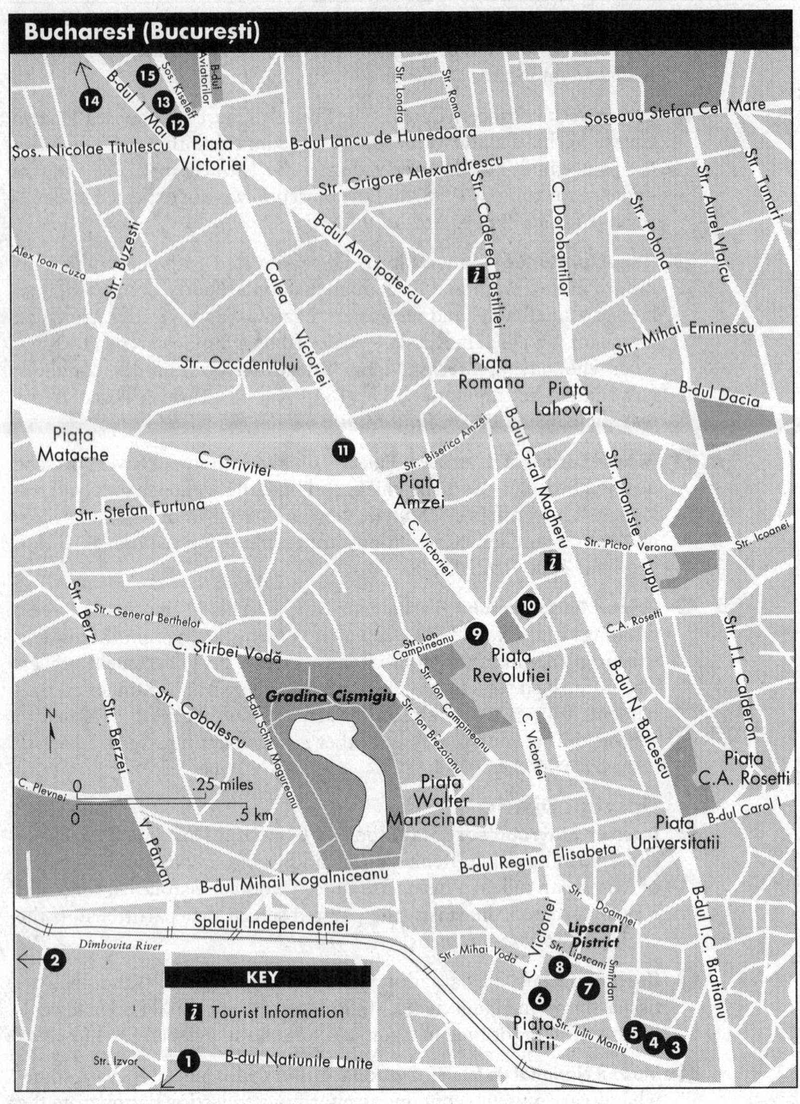

Arcul de Triumf, **14**
Ateneul Român, **10**
Biserica din Curtea Veche, **4**
Biserica Stavropoleos, **7**
Curtea Veche, **5**
Hanul lui Manuc, **3**
Lipscani, **8**
Muzeul Colecțiilor de Artă, **11**
Muzeul de Artă al României, **9**
Muzeul de Științe Naturale Grigore Antipa, **12**
Muzeul National de Istorie, **6**
Muzeul Satului Romanesc, **15**
Muzeul Țăranului Român, **13**
Palatul Cotroceni, **2**
Palatul Parlamentului, **1**

collection of Romanian Art from the 19th and 20th centuries as well as carpets, furniture, and icons painted on glass. ✉ *Str. Calea Victoriei 111,* ☎ *01/6506132.* 🎫 *Free Wed.* ⏲ *Wed.–Sun. 10–6; last admission at 5.*

9 **Muzeul de Artă al României** (National Art Museum). Once the royal palace, this building houses a fine collection that includes pieces by the sculptor Brancusi and marvelous works from the Bruegel school. The building was undergoing restoration in 1998 but was scheduled to be completed in 1999. ✉ *Calea Victoriei 49,* ☎ *01/6155193.* 🎫 *Free Wed.* ⏲ *Wed.–Sun. 10–6, Last admission at 5.*

12 **Muzeul de Științe Naturale Grigore Antipa** (Natural History Museum). Natural wildlife exhibits from around Romania and the rest of the world are on display in realistic settings. ✉ *Șos. Kiseleff 1,* ☎ *01/4100581.* ⏲ *Tues.–Sun. 10–5.*

★ 15 **Muzeul Satului Romanesc** (Romanian Village Museum). This fabulous open-air museum near Herăstrău Lake is home to more than 300 representations of folk style and architecture taken from peasant villages of different regions and periods. ✉ *Șos. Kiseleff 28,* ☎ *01/2229110.* ⏲ *Oct.–mid-May, daily 8–4; mid-May–Sept., daily 9–7.*

★ 13 **Muzeul Țăranului Român** (Museum of the Romanian Peasant). This enchanting museum has beautiful displays of costumes, icons, carpets, and other artifacts from rural life, including reconstructed interiors from two 19th-century wooden churches. ✉ *Șos. Kiseleff 3,* ☎ *01/6505360.* ⏲ *Tues.–Sun. 10–6.*

Dining and Lodging

The number of restaurants and fast-food chains in Bucharest has increased dramatically in the past few years. Food kiosks, cafés, grills, and restaurants are ubiquitous, and many serve good, inexpensive food. Be sure to check your bill, as it is not uncommon for restaurants to try to overcharge foreigners. Some places will serve wine and water only by the bottle and not by the glass. Romanian coffee is served with grounds; instant coffee is called *ness.*

More private hotels are appearing throughout Bucharest. Competition has inspired more attention to service as well as an improvement in amenities. Hotels are often heavily booked during the tourist season as well as during expositions. For details and price-category definitions, *see* Dining *and* Lodging *in* Romania A to Z, *above.*

$$$$ ✕ **Korea House.** One of the few Asian restaurants in Bucharest serves spicy and very authentic food. The fish and seafood are particular favorites, especially the squid, which is prepared in a piquant brown sauce. ✉ *Str. Cimpina 53,* ☎ *01/6665283. No credit cards.*

$$$$ ✕ **Velvet.** Among the first deluxe restaurants in Bucharest, it offers lobster, shrimp dipped in sauces, duck, pheasant, and lamb. The atmosphere is definitely formal. ✉ *Știrbei Vodă 2–4,* ☎ *01/3111736. Reservations essential. AE, DC, MC, V.*

$$$ ✕ **Café de Paris.** The food here matches the splendid ambience. Though the pasta servings are not generous enough for a full meal, the fresh salad together with the steak and chicken Café de Paris make a good meal. The reasonably priced Sunday brunch is also worthwhile. ✉ *Str. Jean-Louis Calderon 33,* ☎ *01/3127013. Reservations essential. AE, MC, V.*

$$$ ★ ✕ **La Premiera.** Just behind the National Theater, this appealing restaurant offers a superb mix of international cuisine. The walls are decorated with scenes of Bucharest during the 1920s and '30s. ✉ *Str. Tudor Arghezi 16,* ☎ *01/3124397. Reservations essential. AE, MC, DC, V.*

$$ ★ **Bistro Atheneu.** This charming restaurant, a favorite among both Romanians and expatriates, offers Romanian cuisine such as liver in mushroom sauce, steak, and grilled chicken. Local musicians play classical music. ✉ *Str. Episcopiei 3,* ☎ *01/6134900. Reservations essential. No credit cards.*

$$ ★ **Piccolo Mondo.** Among menu items here are kebabs, hummus, tabouleh, chicken, and a variety of other Middle Eastern dishes, as well as a sampling of Italian and Romanian items. ✉ *Str. Clucerului,* ☎ *01/2229046. No credit cards.*

$$ **Sydney.** Lighting up Piaţa Victoriei, this Australian bar and restaurant offers a variety of grilled meats, a salad bar, and generous Mexican dishes. There is a wide choice of drinks, including many imported beers. ✉ *Calea Victoriei 222,* ☎ *01/6594207. AE, V.*

$$ **Tandoori.** This is one of a handful of restaurants that have smoking and no-smoking sections. The menu here concentrates on tasty Indian dishes, many involving chicken and vegetables prepared in spicy sauces. ✉ *Str. Budai Deleanu 4,* ☎ *01/6234147. Reservations essential. No credit cards.*

$–$$ **Casa Veche.** At this cozy restaurant specializing in wood-oven pizza the selection is large and innovative. ✉ *Georges Enescu Str. 15–17,* ☎ *01/6156821. Reservations essential. AE, MC, V.*

$$$$ **Athenée Palace Hilton.** After five years of construction and anticipation, this hotel has finally reopened under Hilton management as the only top-ranking hotel in Romania. Its immaculate, spacious rooms are the best in Bucharest, and the hotel's long history and central location add to its many advantages. ✉ *Str. Episcopiei 1–3,* ☎ *01/3151212,* FAX *01/3152121. 257 rooms, 15 suites. 3 restaurants. AE, DC, MC, V.*

$$$$ **Lido.** In the center of the city, this prewar hotel has been privatized and renovated to offer comfortable rooms and good facilities. ✉ *B-dul Gen. Magheru 5,* ☎ *01/6144930,* FAX *01/3126544. 107 rooms, 12 suites. Restaurant, pool. AE, DC, MC, V.*

$$$$ ★ **Sofitel.** On the edge of the city en route to the airport, the Sofitel is a Western oasis in Bucharest. Every room is spotless. Those on the front side have a beautiful view of Herăstrău Park. ✉ *B-dul Expoziţiei 2,* ☎ *01/2234000.* FAX *01/2224650. 91 rooms, 12 suites. 2 restaurants. AE, DC, MC, V.*

$$$ ★ **Minerva.** Renovated in 1992, this state-run hotel is comfortable and clean. All rooms come with air-conditioning and television, and the staff is anxious to please. ✉ *Str. Gheorghe Manu 2–4,* ☎ *01/3111550,* FAX *01/3123963. 70 rooms, 13 suites. Restaurant. AE, DC, MC, V.*

$$ ★ **Casa Victor.** Though very simple, this is one of the better inexpensive alternatives to the drab, government-run hotels or expensive newer hotels. The room rate includes cable television, a refrigerator, and an ample breakfast served at any hour. It's within walking distance of the Arcul de Triumf, Herăstrău Park, and the metro. ✉ *Emanoil Porumbaru Str. 44,* ☎ *01/22291830,* FAX *01/2229436. 12 rooms, 8 suites. Restaurant. No credit cards.*

$ **Triumf.** This economical, comfortable hotel is on a small park near the Arcul de Triumf. It once served the Communist elite. The more expensive rooms are mini-apartments. ✉ *Şos. Kiseleff 12,* ☎ *01/2223172,* FAX *01/2232411. 97 rooms, 3 suites. Restaurant. V.*

Nightlife and the Arts

The Arts

The **Romanian Athenaeum** (✉ Str. Franklin 1, ☎ 01/6156875) is Bucharest's concert hall. Here, the George Enescu Philharmonic Orchestra performs regularly. Inside the **Teatrul Naţional** (National Theater; ✉ Piaţa Universitatii, ☎ 01/6151502), the **Ion Dacian Operetta** performs. The **Opera Română** (✉ B-dul Mihail Kogălniceanu 70, ☎ 01/6131857) opera house has some good productions. At the **Radio Hall** (✉ Str. Gen. Berthelot 62–64, ☎ 01/2224714) you can hear classical music performed by a variety of local and visiting musicians.

Nightlife

For a Romanian feel, head to the Lipscani district and the subterranean **Club A** (✉ Str. Blanari 14, ☎ 01/6156853), where university students come to enjoy the crowded dance floor and the inexpensive beer. The **Dubliner** (✉ B-dul N. Titulescu 18, ☎ 01/2229473) is a hot spot for the local expatriate community; it serves a variety of imported beers. For a lively Romanian bar with good music, try the **Laptaria Enache** (Milk Bar; ✉ Teatrul Naţional, ☎ 01/6158508) after 11 PM. If you enjoy participating in the evening's entertainment, go to the **Manhattan Club** (✉ B-dul Expoziţiei 2, ☎ 01/6686290) for a karaoke show. If dancing is part of your plan, head to the **Salsa You and Me** (✉ Str. 11 Iunie 51, ☎ 3355640) to finish the night moving to a Latin beat surrounded by all ages and nationalities. Since its opening in 1997, the **White Horse** (✉ Str. George Călinescu 4A, ☎ 01/6797796) English pub has drawn both foreigners and Romanians.

One of the older and better known of Bucharest's 16 casinos is the **Casino Victoria** (✉ Calea Victoriei 174, ☎ 01/6505865), which also offers a dinner show.

Shopping

The **Apollo** gallery, in the National Theater building (☞ The Arts *in* Nightlife and the Arts, *above*), sells art that you may legally take home with you. The galleries in the fascinating **Hanul cu Tei** (✉ Off Str. Lipscani) also sell art that can be exported.

For local folklore arts and crafts watch for *Artizanat* stores, specializing in crafts made by Romanian peasants, such as embroidered decorations, dolls, and masks. Try the one in the **Muzeul Satului Romanesc** (Şos. Kiseleff 28, ☎ 01/2229110). There's a good Artizanat store in the **Muzeul Ţăranului Român** (✉ Şos. Kiseleff 3, ☎ 01/6505360). In the Lipscani area, be sure to look at the carpets, ceramics, and figurines in the **Magazin Amintiri** (✉ Str. Gabroveni 20).

Romania is well known for its handmade woven carpets. For export they must be purchased from an authorized retailer such as **Covoare** (✉ B-dul Unirii 13, ☎ 01/3362174).

Crystal, porcelain, and china can be great values in Romania. **Sticerom S.A.** (✉ Str. Selari 9–11, ☎ 01/6157504, and ✉ Str. Soarelui 3-5, ☎ 01/6144066) has a good selection, specializing in magnificent, high-quality items with unbelievably low prices.

The **World Trade Center** (✉ B-dul Expoziţiei 2) is a small version of a Western shopping mall. **Mario Plaza** (✉ 12 Calea Dorobantilor) also provides a modern alternative to traditional Bucharest shopping.

The main food market is **Piaţa Amzei,** offering a variety of cheeses, fruits, and flowers and providing a glimpse of animated Romanians bargaining for food.

Bucharest Essentials

Arriving and Departing

BY CAR

Three main routes lead into the city—E70 from the Hungarian border to the west, E60 via Braşov from the north, and E70/E85 from Bulgaria and the south. Bucharest has few street signs and many one-way systems.

BY PLANE

All international flights to Romania land at Bucharest's **Otopeni Airport** (☎ 01/2300042), 16 km (9 mi) north of the city.

Between the Airport and Downtown. Express **Bus** 783 leaves the airport every 30 minutes between 7 AM and 10 PM, stopping in the main squares before terminating in Piaţa Unirii. The journey takes an hour and costs 6,000 lei round-trip. A shuttle service connects the airport to the center of Bucharest: For $10 a person, **Sky Services** (☎ 01/2329691) takes passengers to Bucharest's main hotels and the train station. Your hotel can arrange transport by **car** from the airport. **Taxi** drivers at the airport seek business aggressively and usually demand payment in dollars; the cost is about $20–$30 with tip, so bargain.

BY TRAIN

There are five main stations in Bucharest; international lines operate from **Gara de Nord** (✉ B-dul Gara de Nord, ☎ 01/952). For tickets and information, go to the **CFR Advance Booking Office** (✉ Str. Brezoianu 10 , ☎ 01/614 5528).

Getting Around

Bucharest is spacious and sprawling. Though the old heart of the city and the two main arteries running the length of it are best explored on foot, long, wide avenues and vast squares make some form of transportation necessary. It is generally safe on the streets at night, but watch out for unlighted vehicles and hidden potholes.

BY BUS, TRAM, AND TROLLEY BUS

Surface transit may sometimes be uncomfortable and crowded, but service is extensive. A one-way ticket can be purchased for 1,200 lei (spring 1998) from kiosks near bus stops or from tobacconists; validate your ticket when you board. There are also *abonaments* (day and week passes). More expensive **maxi taxis** (minibuses that stop on request) and **express buses** take fares on board. The system shuts down at midnight, though buses become scarce around 11 PM.

BY SUBWAY

Three subway lines serve the city. Change is available from kiosks inside stations. The present price is 2,700 lei for one round-trip ticket. The system closes at 11 PM.

BY TAXI

Hail a cab in the street, or dial 01/953, 941, 945, 985—the operators may speak English. A taxi is relatively inexpensive, but be sure there is a meter or negotiate a price before getting in.

Contacts and Resources

EMBASSIES AND CONSULATE

United States (✉ Tudor Arghezi, ☎ 01/2104042). **United Kingdom** (✉ Str. J. Michelet 24, ☎ 01/3120303). **Canadian** (✉ Str. N. Iorga 36, ☎ 01/2229845). **Australian** (Honorary Consular Section, ✉ 124A Str. Mihai Eminescu, 3rd floor, Apt. 8, Bucharest, ☎ 041/210-6027).

EMERGENCIES

Police (☎ 955). **Ambulance** (☎ 961). **Fire** (☎ 981). Each sector of Bucharest is required to have a 24-hour pharmacy; ask at your hotel or call 961.

GUIDED TOURS

Carpatours (✉ B-dul 1 Mai 16, ☎ 01/2120643).

MAIL

Bucharest Central Post Office (✉ Matei Millo 10, ☎ 01/6144054).

TRAVEL AGENCIES

Magellan Tourism (✉ B-dul Gen. Magheru 12–14, ☎ 01/2119650, FAX 01/2104903). **Medair Travel and Tourism** (✉ Str. N. Bălcescu 16, ☎ 01/3113190, FAX 01/3121688). **Romantic Travel** (✉ Str. Mamulari 4, ☎ 01/3100401, ☎ FAX 01/3123056).

VISITOR INFORMATION

ONT (✉ B-dul Gen. Magheru, ☎ 01/3122598). Front desks in main hotels also dispense brochures and information.

THE BLACK SEA COAST AND DANUBE DELTA

The southeastern Dobrogea region, only 45 minutes by air from Bucharest (210 km/130 mi by road), has been important throughout Romania's long history. Within a clearly defined area are the historic port of Constanţa; the Romanian Riviera pleasure coast; the Murfatlar vineyards; Roman, Greek, and earlier ruins; and the Danube Delta, which has become one of Europe's leading wildlife sanctuaries. The rapid development of the resorts and increasing interest in the delta region have led to improvement of tourist facilities and transport. You're likely to enter the region through the port of Constanţa and then continue to one of the many resort areas or journey north to the Danube Delta.

Constanţa

Romania's second-largest city has the busy, polyglot flavor characteristic of so many seaports. The poet Ovid was exiled here from Rome in AD 8; a statue of him presides over one of the city's squares.

The **Muzuel Naţional de Istorie şi Arheologie** (National History and Archaeological Museum) displays statues from the Neolithic Hamangian culture (4000–3000 BC) as well as Greek and Roman artifacts. ✉ *Piaţa Ovidiu 12,* ☎ *041/618763.* ⏲ *Tues.–Sun. 10–6.*

The **Edificiu Roman cu Mozaic** (✉ Piaţa Ovidiu 1) is a Roman complex of warehouses and shops from the 4th century that has a large mosaic floor. The **Parcul Arheologic** (Archaeology Park; ✉ B-dul Republicii) contains artifacts from the 3rd and 4th centuries, including the remains of Roman baths. Modern attractions in Constanţa include the **Acvariul** (Aquarium; ✉ Str. Februarie 16) and the **Delfinariul** (Dolphinarium; ✉ B-dul Mamaia 265).

$$$ ✕ **Cazinou.** The turn-of-the-century former casino near the aquarium is decorated in ornate 20th-century style; there's an adjoining bar by the sea. Seafood dishes are the house specialties. ✉ *Str. Februarie 16,* ☎ *041/617416. No credit cards.*

$$ ★ ✕ **Veneţia.** This quaint and friendly Italian restaurant right off Piaţa Ovidiu is decorated with scenes from Venice. A variety of pasta dishes is available here. ✉ *Str. Mircea cel Batrin 5,* ☎ *041/617390. No credit cards.*

$$$ 🏨 **Palace.** Near the city's historic center, this large and gracious renovated old hotel has a good restaurant. A terrace overlooks the sea and the tourist port of Tomis. ✉ *Str. Remus Opreanu 5–7,* ☎ *041/614696,* FAX *041/617532. 102 rooms, 9 suites. Restaurant. No credit cards.*

Eforie Nord, Neptun, Jupiter, Venus, Saturn, and Mangalia

A string of seaside resorts lies just south of Constanţa. Eforie Nord is an up-to-date thermal treatment center. The names of several resorts

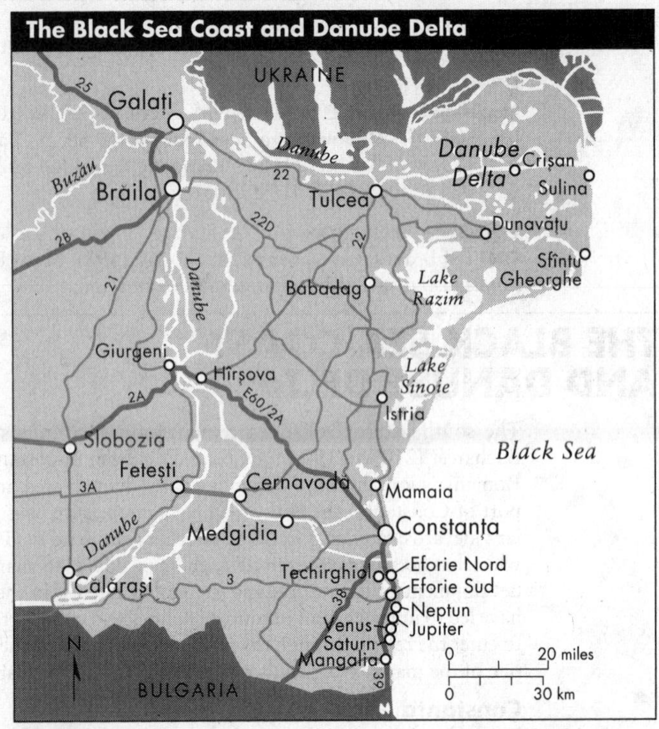

built during the 1960s evoke the coast's Greco-Roman past—Neptun, Jupiter, Venus, and Saturn. Not typically Romanian, these resorts offer good amenities for relaxed seaside vacations. The old port of Mangalia is the southernmost resort.

You can take excursions from the seaside resorts to the **Podgorile Murfatlar** (Murfatlar Vineyards) for wine tasting. Visits to the ruins of the Roman town at **Tropaeum Trajani** can also be arranged.

$$$ ★ ✕🏨 **Panoramic.** Right on the beach, this hotel is among the nicer ones in the area. Seaside rooms have a magnificent view. The restaurant offers very good Romanian cuisine. ✉ *Olimp–Neptun,* ☎ *041/731356. 418 rooms. Restaurant, pool. AE, MC, V.*

$ 🏨 **Moldova.** One of many inexpensive hotels near the beach, it has somewhat run-down rooms, but they are clean and the staff is friendly. ✉ *Olimp–Neptun,* ☎ *041/731916. 466 rooms. Restaurant. No credit cards.*

Mamaia

The largest of the Black Sea resorts, Mamaia is on a strip of land bordered on one side by the Black Sea and fine beaches and on the other by the fresh waters of Mamaia Lake. All the resorts along this stretch of the coast have high-rise modern apartments, villas, restaurants, nightclubs, and discos. There are cruises down the coast to Mangalia and along the new channel that links the Danube with the Black Sea near Constanţa. Sea-fishing expeditions can also be arranged for early risers, with all equipment provided.

Just 60 km (37 mi) north of Mamaia is **Istria,** which was founded in 600 BC by Greek merchants from Miletus. There are traces of early Christian churches, baths, and even entire neighborhoods here.

Between Mamaia and the Danube Delta town of Tulcea lies **Babadag.** It was here, according to local legend, that Jason and the Argonauts cast anchor during their search for the mythical Golden Fleece.

$$$ ★ **Rex.** A former residence of King Carol, this is the largest and grandest of all the hotels in Mamaia. The rooms are spacious and clean, while the staff is very attentive. ✉ *Mamaia,* ☎ *041/831595,* FAX *041/831690. 90 rooms. Restaurant, outdoor pool . AE, DC, MC, V.*

$ **Lido.** One of many newly built and moderately priced hotels, it stands next to an outdoor pool near the beach at the north end of the resort area of Mamaia. ✉ *Mamaia,* ☎ *041/831555. 129 rooms. Restaurant, pool. No credit cards.*

Tulcea

Tulcea is the main town of the Danube Delta and the gateway to the region. Built on seven hills and influenced by Turkish architectural styles, this former market town is now an important sea and river port. It is the center of the Romanian fish industry, famous for processing caviar-bearing sturgeon.

The **Muzeul Deltei Dunării** (Danube Delta Museum) provides a good introduction to the flora, fauna, and way of life of the communities in the region. ✉ *Str. Grigore Antipa 2,* ☎ *040/515866.* ⏲ *Tues.–Sun. 11–4.*

$$ **Delta.** On the bank of the Danube, this spacious, modern hotel has good facilities. ✉ *Str. Isaacei 2,* ☎ *040/514720,* FAX *040/516260. 117 rooms. Restaurant. V.*

The Danube Delta

The **Delta Dunării** (Danube Delta) is Europe's largest wetlands reserve, covering 4,357 square km (1,676 sq mi), with a sprawling, watery wilderness that stretches from the Ukrainian border to a series of lakes north of the Black Sea resorts. Romanians have committed themselves to the restoration of this treasure. The Danube Delta is a refuge for hundreds of species of migratory birds, some from as far away as China and India, and home to birds such as the pelican. Unfortunately, many of these birds have been frightened away; in order to find the beauty of this sanctuary, it is necessary to venture some distance from frequented tourist areas.

As the Danube approaches the Delta Dunării, it divides into three branches. The northernmost branch forms the border with Ukraine, the middle arm leads to the busy port of Sulina, and the southernmost arm meanders gently toward the little port of Sfintu Gheorghe, a simple holiday spot. From these channels, countless canals widen into tree-fringed lakes and water-lily pools; there are sand dunes and lush forests.

$$ **Lebăda.** This not-very-comfortable hotel is the only one convenient for fishing trips into the more remote parts of the delta. ✉ *Sulina Canal, mi 14.5, Crişan,* ☎ *040/543778. 74 rooms. Restaurant. No credit cards.*

Black Sea Coast and Danube Delta Essentials

Getting Around

Travel in this area involves several hours on the road; allow more than one day for a substantive trip.

Guided Tours

Most hotels in the Black Sea region arrange guided tours throughout the area. Individual and group tours can also be prearranged through travel agencies in Bucharest.

Visitor Information

Constanța (Danubius; ✉ B-dul Ferdinand 22/36, ☎ 041/615836). **Mamaia** (ATI—Carpaţi; ✉ B-dul Tomis 46, ☎ 041/614861, FAX 041611429). **Tulcea** (Europolis; ✉ Str. Pacii 20, ☎ 040/512443).

TRANSYLVANIA

Transylvania, Romania's western province, contains some of Europe's most beautiful and unspoiled villages and rural landscapes. The Carpathian Mountains, which separate Transylvania from Walachia and Moldavia, shielded the province from the Turks and Mongols during the Middle Ages. Germans and Hungarians settled here during this period, building spectacular castles, towns, and churches. Since the 1980s many ethnic Germans have emigrated, but Transylvania, which was ruled by Hungary until 1920, is still home to a large Hungarian minority and to many of Romania's 2 million ethnic Gypsies. The dearth of amenities outside the main towns makes traveling in the region difficult. One solution is to base yourself in a major town such as Sibiu, Sinaia, or Braşov and take day trips into the countryside.

Sinaia

Prior to World War II and the abdication of the royal family, Sinaia was a summer retreat for Romania's aristocracy. On the mountainside stand many grand summer homes from this period, as well as the **Sinaia Minastire,** a practicing monastery since 1695.

One of the best-preserved royal palaces in Europe, **Castelul Peleş** (Peles Palace) served as the summer residence of the first Hohenzollern king of Romania, Carol I. ✉ *2 Peleşului Str.; take Strada Manastirii uphill and follow signs to the Castle.*

Castelul Pelisor, the summer home of the second Hohenzollern king, Ferdinand, is not as grand as Peles Palace, but it is elegantly decorated and much more comfortably furnished. Tours in English are available upon request. ✉ *Str. Peleşului,* ☎ *044/310918.* ⏲ *Wed.–Sun. 9–3.*

$$$$ ★ ✕🏨 **Mara Sinaia.** Opened in 1996, this is easily one of the grandest hotels in Romania outside Bucharest. The elegant restaurant provides Romanian fare. ✉ *Str. Toporasilor 1A,* ☎ *044/310440,* FAX *044/310651. 142 rooms, 6 suites. Restaurant, pool. AE, MC, V.*

$ ✕🏨 **Economat.** This hotel was built in the same Bavarian style as the nearby Peleş Palace. Surrounded by mountains, it is very simple, comfortable, and ideally located. Its flavorful restaurant offers traditional French cuisine in a very Germanic town. Menu items include fondue, quiche, onion soup, and other delicious treats. ✉ *On grounds of Peleş Palace,* ☎ *044/311151,* FAX *044/313555. 40 rooms. Restaurant. V.*

Bran

Castelul Bran (Castle Bran) is beautifully preserved. It is claimed to be the castle of Vlad Ţepeş, though in reality his castle lies in ruins farther west in Transylvania, and Bran was actually a trading point during the Middle Ages. In the parking area is a market where local peasants sell hand-woven sweaters and other crafts. ✉ *Str. Principală (Rte. DN 73).* ⏲ *Tues.–Sun., 8–4:30.*

Braşov and Poiana Braşov

To really enjoy Braşov, you must go to the center of the city, **Piaţa Sfatului,** a large cobblestone square where you can find peddlers of different wares, occasionally a musician, and colorful Gypsies and beggars. This is the heart of the old Germanic city, which was once an important medieval trade center. **Casa Sfatului** (⏲ Tues.–Sun., 8–4) in the center of Piaţa Sfatului, was once the town hall of old Braşov. Built in

1420, it now houses a historical museum. Just off Piaţa Sfatului is the spiraling tower of the **Biserica Neagră** (Black Church), a Gothic masterpiece that was built during the early 15th century. It acquired its name after a fire in 1689 left it black and charred. Currently it is undergoing massive renovation, and scaffolding covers almost every inch of the exterior. Opposite the Black Church is **Strada Republicii,** a walking street that provides a wealth of opportunities for shoppers.

For a breathtaking, panoramic view of Braşov, ride the **Telecabina Timpa** (✉ Str. Romer, ⏲ Tues.–Sun. 10–6), a cable car that runs to the top of Mount Timpa. To find the cable car, hike through the old section of the city: Leave Piaţa Sfatului on Strada Apollonia Hirscher; take a left on to Strada Castelului; the next right is Strada Romer. Follow this to the cable car. Just below the entrance to Telecabina Timpa are some of the remains of the old Braşov city wall. A stroll along the wall will take you to the **Bastionul Ţesătorilor** (Weaver's Bastion), which now holds a museum that is occasionally open to the public.

A 10-minute drive, or bus ride (No. 2), from Braşov on St. Stejărişului brings you to **Poiana Braşov.** The mountaintop ski resort has several good restaurants and hotels. In winter Poiana Braşov offers some of the best skiing in Romania, though trails are not groomed and ski lifts are limited. In summer you can follow well-marked hiking trails along the spectacular mountainsides. Riding the cable car to the top of the mountain gives you a view of the Transylvania Plains. Local peasants sell handmade wool sweaters in the central parking lot for incredibly low prices. ✉ *Agenţa Poiana Braşov,* ☎ *068/262389.*

$$ ★ ✕ **Coliba Haiducilor.** In this classic Romanian-rustic lodge, the walls are decorated with hunting trophies. The large fireplace, waiters dressed in peasant costume, and traditional song and dance transport you to an earlier era. The menu includes boar, bear, venison, chicken, and other delights. ✉ *Poiana Braşov,* ☎ *068/262137. No credit cards.*

$$ ★ ✕ **Sura Dacilor.** Built to look like a traditional Romanian hunting lodge, it offers garlic chicken, mixed grill, salad, and ciorba. ✉ *Poiana Braşov,* ☎ *068/262327. No credit cards.*

$$$$ 🏨 **Aro Palace.** Architecturally a typical Communist-era hotel built in the 1950s, the Aro Palace lacks charm but is comfortable and has good facilities. ✉ *B-dul Eroilor 27, Braşov,* ☎ *068/142840,* FAX *068/150427. 292 rooms, 15 suites. 3 restaurants, pool. AE, DC, MC, V.*

$$ ★ 🏨 **Casa Viorel.** This private hotel opened in 1995 is a true paradise. Every room is immaculate, with a balcony and view of the mountains, and the service is superb. ✉ *Poiana Braşov,* ☎ *068/262024,* FAX *068/262148. 10 rooms, 2 suites. No credit cards.*

$$ 🏨 **Centrul De Echitatie** (Equitation Center). The resort is home to a stable that provides opportunities for wagon and sleigh rides and horseback riding through the mountainous countryside. Several clean villas are available for rent. Backwoods barbecues can also be arranged. It is on the bus line to Braşov, and within walking distance of all facilities in Poiana Braşov. ✉ *Poiana Braşov,* ☎ *068/262161. 10 1- and 2-bedroom villas. No credit cards.*

Sighişoar

Sighişoara's enchanting towers and spires can be seen from a great distance. Above the modern town is a medieval **citadel** and quarter that are among the loveliest and least spoiled in Europe. Walking up from the city center of Sighişoara, you enter the citadel through the 60-m- (195-ft-) tall **Bastionul de Ceas** (clock tower), which dates from the 14th century. The clock still works, complete with rotating painted wooden figures, one for each day of the week. The tower houses the town's **Muzeul de Istorie** (History Museum), which includes some moving photographs of the 1989 revolution that led to the execution of Nicolae and Elena Ceauşescu. From the wooden gallery at the top of the tower, you can look out over the town with its terra-cotta roofs and painted houses. ✉ *Pta. Muzeului.* ⏲ *Tues.–Sun. 9–3:30.*

Along narrow, cobbled streets lined with faded pink, green, and ocher houses, you'll come to a covered staircase. This leads to a 14th-century **Berglorcje** (Gothic Church) and the **Cimitir de Germania** (German cemetery), a testament to the town's settlers, which extends over the hilltop beyond the city walls.

$–$$ ✕ **Restaurentul Cetaţe (Casa Vlad Dracul).** Occupying a house where the father of Vlad Ţepeş (Count Dracula) once lived, this pleasant bar and restaurant is the best place in town for a meal. The first floor serves draft beer at wooden tables. Upstairs, a cozy restaurant with fittingly Gothic-style furniture serves good soups and traditional Romanian dishes. ✉ *Str. Cositorarilor 5,* ☎ *065/771596. No credit cards.*

$ 🏨 **Rex.** This new hotel has added a much-needed clean and modern establishment to the town. Though a few minutes walk from the center, it is definitely the most appealing hotel in the city. ✉ *Str. Dumbravei 18,* ☎ FAX *065/166615 24 rooms. Restaurant. No credit cards.*

Sibiu

Known as Hermannstadt to the Germans, who founded the city in 1143, Sibiu was the Saxons' main town in Transylvania. It still has a distinctly German or Central European feel to it even though there are few ethnic Germans left. The old part of the town centers around the magnificent **Piaţa Mare** (Great Square) with its painted 17th-century town houses. The **Biserica Romano Catolică** (Roman Catholic Church) on the square is a splendid high-Baroque building. The **Brukenthal Museum,** also on the square, housed in the palace of its founder, Samuel Brukenthal, Hapsburg governor from 1777 to 1787, has one of the most extensive collections of silver, paintings, and furniture in Romania.

The second center of the old town is **Piaţa Mica** (Small Square), next to which stands the Cathedral, a massive 14th- to 15th-century edifice with a simple, stark interior.

$$$ ★ 🏨 **Continental.** At this hotel, you'll find the nicest accommodations Sibiu has to offer. ✉ *Calea Dumbravii 2–4,* ☎ *069/218100,* FAX *069/210125. 182 rooms. Restaurant. MC, V.*

Transylvania Essentials

Getting Around

Travel by car is the best way to explore Transylvania's rich rural life. Regular rail travel is available to most Transylvanian towns, and air flights are possible to larger towns such as Braşov and Sibiu (☞ Transportation *in* Romania A to Z, *above*).

Guided Tours

Many travel agencies in Bucharest, and those in many hotels throughout Transylvania, offer guided tours of the region. The **Transylvanian Society of Dracula** (✉ Str. George Călinescu 20, Apt. 28, Bucharest, ☎ FAX 01/2314022) arranges unique "Dracula" tours that combine locations figuring in Bram Stoker's *Dracula* with those associated with the historical figure on whom the novel is based.

Visitor Information

Braşov (✉ Aro-Palace, B-dul Eroilor 9, ☎ 068/142840, FAX 01/150427). **Sibiu** (✉ Str. Cetăţii 1, ☎ 069/211788, FAX 01/211933).

26 Slovakia

Bratislava, the High Tatras and Eastern Slovakia

Despite more than 70 years of common statehood with the Czech Republic, not to mention centuries spent under Hungarian and Hapsburg rule, Slovakia has shaped a distinct cultural profile. The country's farmlands stretch to an important mountain range. Its culture, steeped in folk tradition, is particularly rich.

Although they speak a language closely related to Czech, the Slovaks have a strong sense of national identity. United with the Czechs during the 9th century as part of the Great Moravian Empire, the Slovaks were conquered a century later by the Magyars and remained under Hungarian domination until 1918. The Hungarians were not alone in infiltrating the country; after the Tartar invasions of the 13th century, many Saxons were invited to resettle the land and develop the economy. During the 15th and 16th centuries, Romanian shepherds migrated from Wallachia through the Carpathians into Slovakia. The merging of these varied groups with the resident Slavs further enriched the native folk culture.

Bratislava, the capital of Hungary for nearly 250 years until 1784, and now the capital of the new Slovak republic, was once a city filled with picturesque streets and Gothic churches. Forty years of communist rule hid its ancient beauty behind hulking, and now dilapidated, futuristic structures. The streets of the Old Town, however, are now undergoing rapid revitalization.

The peaks of the High Tatras are a major draw. The smallest Alpine range in the world, the Tatras rise magnificently from the foothills of northern Slovakia. Hikers and skiers are the chief visitors here. The area's subtler attractions—the exquisite medieval towns of the Spiš region below the Tatras and the beautiful 18th-century wood churches farther east—are definitely worth the trip.

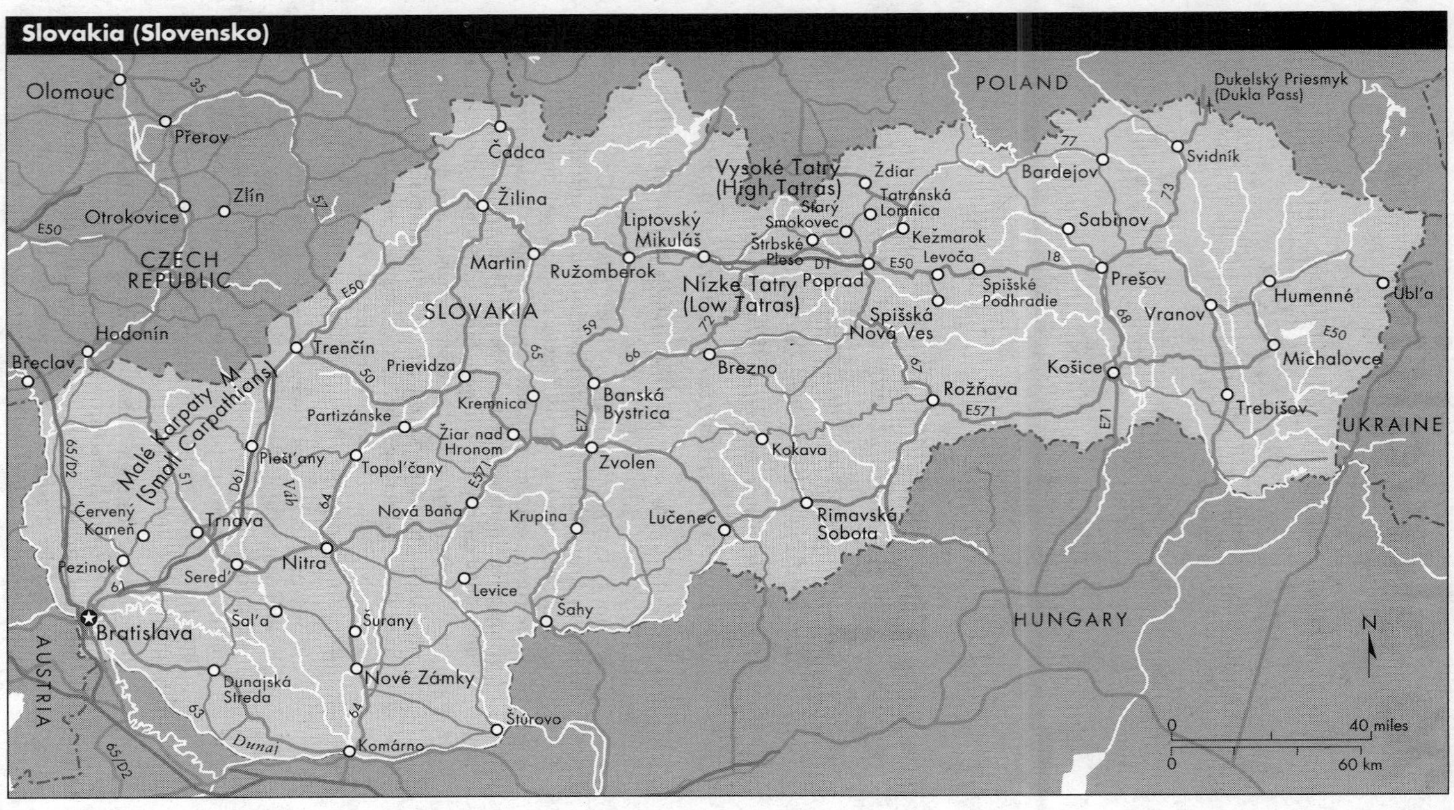

Slovakia (Slovensko)
POLAND
UKRAINE
HUNGARY
AUSTRIA
CZECH REPUBLIC
SLOVAKIA
Dukelský Priesmyk (Dukla Pass)
Olomouc
Přerov
Zlín
Otrokovice
Čadca
Žilina
Martin
Ružomberok
Liptovský Mikuláš
Vysoké Tatry (High Tatras)
Ždiar
Tatranská Lomnica
Starý Smokovec
Štrbské Pleso
Kežmarok
Levoča
Poprad
Nízke Tatry (Low Tatras)
Spišské Podhradie
Spišská Nová Ves
Bardejov
Svidník
Sabinov
Prešov
Vranov
Humenné
Ubl'a
Michalovce
Košice
Trebišov
Rožňava
Brezno
Banská Bystrica
Zvolen
Kokava
Rimavská Sobota
Lučenec
Krupina
Šahy
Levice
Nová Baňa
Kremnica
Žiar nad Hronom
Prievidza
Partizánske
Topoľčany
Trenčín
Hodonín
Břeclav
Malé Karpaty M (Small Carpathians)
Piešťany
Váh
Červený Kameň
Trnava
Pezinok
Sereď
Nitra
Bratislava
Šaľa
Šurany
Nové Zámky
Dunajská Streda
Dunaj
Komárno
Štúrovo
E50
E571
E71
E77
D1
D61
65/D2
18
35
50
51
57
59
61
63
64
65
66
67
68
72
73
77
N
0
40 miles
60 km

SLOVAKIA A TO Z

Customs

Enter valuable items such as jewelry or laptops on arrival on your customs declaration, so that you encounter no problems with customs officials on departure. U.S. or EU citizens over 18 years old can bring in 250 cigarettes (or their equivalent in tobacco), 2 liters of wine, 1 liter of spirits, and ½ liter of eau de cologne.

There is no limit on the amount of goods purchased for noncommercial use, but to be on the safe side, keep all receipts. You can only export antiques bought at specially designated shops, with special approval by a commission at the National Relic and Landscape Center (Bratislava, ☏ 07/374444). Commission approval is based on a court-expert opinion submitted by you; for a list of court experts, call the Historical Museum (Bratislava Castle, ☏ 07/5311444).

Dining

In Slovakia you can choose from a variety of ambiences—restaurants, *vináreň* (wine cellars), beer taverns, cafeterias, and a growing number of coffee shops and snack bars. Most restaurants are remarkably inexpensive, but privatization is pushing up prices.

Typical main dishes are roast pork, duck, or goose, served with sauerkraut and some type of dumpling or potatoes, generally with a rich gravy. Peppers frequently spice up bland entrées. Look for *bryndzové halušky,* a tasty Slovak noodle dish with sheep cheese. Fresh green vegetables and salads are still rare, but there are plenty of the pickled variety. Be sure to try *palacinky,* a delicious treat of crepes stuffed with fruit and cream or jam.

MEALTIMES

Lunch is usually from 11:30 to 2 or 3; dinner from 6 to 9:30 or 10. Some places are open all day, and in Bratislava it may be easier to find a table during off-hours.

RATINGS

Prices are reasonable by American standards, even in the more expensive restaurants. The following prices are for meals made up of a first course, main course, and dessert (excluding wine and tip).

CATEGORY	COST
$$$$	OVER 600 SK
$$$	400 SK–600 SK
$$	200 SK–400 SK
$	UNDER 200 SK

WHAT TO WEAR

A jacket is suggested for higher-priced restaurants. Otherwise, casual dress is acceptable.

Language

Slovak, a western-Slavic tongue related to both Czech and Polish, is the official language of Slovakia. English is popular among young people, but German is still the most useful language for visitors.

Lodging

Slovakia's hotel industry has reacted slowly to the political and economic changes that began in 1989. There are a few new hotels, and the state holds a majority ownership in many of the older hotels. Bratislava and the High Tatras have the highest hotel rates in Slovakia—but prices drop dramatically in the rest of the country. Many older properties are gradually being renovated. Shortages of hotel rooms are common during the peak season, so make reservations well in advance. Many private room agencies are in operation, and as long as you arrive in a city before 9 PM, you should be able to get a room. Brace yourself for inconveniences from faulty plumbing to indifferent reception clerks. Unless otherwise noted, rooms include bath.

CAMPING

In summer signs that announce *Autokemping* (campsites) crop up along major highways like mushrooms after rain. Campsites open year-round are extremely scarce. Plumbing is often primitive, and hot water is a blessing, not a given. The main Satur Tours and Travel office in Bratislava (☞ Visitor Information, *below*) has a rudimentary country-wide directory.

HOTELS

Satur Tours and Travel, the country's largest travel agency (☞ Visitor Information, *below*) officially grades hotels from one to five stars. The Interhotels—often owned by Satur—fall mainly in the three- to five-star categories; most of their rooms have baths or showers.

PRIVATE ACCOMMODATIONS

Satur (☞ Visitor Information, *below*) can help you find a private room in Bratislava and other large cities. These accommodations are invariably cheaper (around $20) and often more comfortable than hotels, though you may have to sacrifice some privacy. You can also wander the main roads looking for signs reading ROOM FREE, or more frequently, in German, ZIMMER FREI or PRIVATZIMMER.

RATINGS

Prices are for double rooms, generally not including breakfast. Prices at the lower end of the scale apply off-season. At certain periods, such as Easter or during festivals, rates may increase by 15%–25%.

CATEGORY	COST
$$$$	OVER 3,200 SK
$$$	1,600 SK–3,200 SK
$$	480 SK–1,600 SK
$	UNDER 480 SK

Mail

POSTAL RATES

First-class (airmail) letters to the United States and Canada cost 16 Sk up to 20 grams, postcards 10 Sk. Airmail (first-class) letters to the United Kingdom cost 12 Sk up to 20 grams, postcards 7 Sk.

RECEIVING MAIL

Mail can be marked "poste restante" and sent to the main post office in Bratislava (✉ Hlavná posta, Nám. SNP 5, ☎ 07/533–1241); there's no charge.

Money Matters

COSTS

Costs are highest in Bratislava and only slightly less in the High Tatra resorts and main spas. The least expensive areas are central and eastern Slovakia.

CURRENCY

The unit of currency in Slovakia is the crown, or koruna, written as Sk, and divided into 100 halierov. There are bills of 20, 50, 100, 200, 500, 1,000, and 5,000 Sk, and coins of 10, 20, and 50 halierov and 1, 2, 5, and 10 Sk.

At press time (spring 1998), the rate of exchange was 34 Sk to the U.S. dollar, 24 Sk to the Canadian dollar, 56 Sk to the pound sterling, 21 Sk to the Australian dollar, and 18 Sk to the New Zealand dollar.

SAMPLE PRICES

Cup of coffee, 10 Sk–15 Sk; beer (½ liter), 15 Sk; Coca-Cola, 10 Sk–15 Sk; ham sandwich, 30 Sk; 2-km (1-mi) taxi ride, 150 Sk. Admission to museums and castles ranges from 10 Sk to 50 Sk.

TIPPING

Although many Slovaks still tip in restaurants by rounding up the bill to the nearest multiple of 10, higher tipping is beginning to catch on. For good service, 10% is considered an appropriate gratuity on very large tabs. Tip porters and room service 20 Sk. In taxis round up the bill to the nearest multiple of 10. Give tour guides and helpful concierges between 20 Sk and 30 Sk for services rendered.

National Holidays

January 1 (day of founding of the Slovak Republic); January 6 (Twelfth Night); April 2 and 5 (Good Friday and Easter Monday); May 1 (Labor Day); May 8 (Liberation of the Republic); July 5 (Sts. Cyril and Methodius); August 29 (anniversary of the Slovak National Uprising); September 1 (Constitution Day); September 15 (Our Lady of Sorrows); November 1 (All Saints' Day); December 24–26 (Christmas holiday).

Opening and Closing Times

Banks are open weekdays 8–3; they remain open through the general lunch hour. **Museums** are usually open Tuesday–Sunday 10–5. **Shops** are generally open weekdays 9–6 and stay open slightly later on Thursday; some close between noon and 2. Many are also open Saturday 9–noon (department stores, 9–4).

Passport and Visa information

Entry without a visa is permitted for citizens of the United States (up to 30 days), United Kingdom (6 months), and Canada (90 days). Citizens of Australia and New Zealand need a visa for visits of up to 30 days.

Telephoning

If you plan to make several local or out-of-town calls, buy a phone card. You can buy one at most newsstands or at any post office for 100 Sk; the cards can be used for both local and out-of-town calls.

COUNTRY CODE

The country code for Slovakia is 421. When dialing a number from outside the country, drop the initial zero from the regional code.

INTERNATIONAL CALLS

You can automatically dial many countries, including North America and the United Kingdom, from public pay phones. You can also call from Telefón/Telegraf (✉ Kolárska 12, Bratislava, ☎ 07/363400), a public communications office with phone booths inside and out. It's open daily 24 hours. For international inquiries dial 0139 or 0149 for the United States, Canada, or the United Kingdom. To place a call via an **AT&T USA Direct** international operator, dial 00–421–00101; for **MCI,** dial 001–881–422–0042; for **Sprint,** dial 001–881–824–9242.

LOCAL CALLS

These cost 2 Sk from a pay phone. Public phones on street corners are often out of order. Try a hotel if you're stuck. At press time phone numbers in Bratislava are being changed gradually to an 8-digit format, except 3-digit emergency numbers. For information call 120.

Transportation

The most common words you'll find on street signs are *ulica* (street, abbreviated *ul.*) and *námestie* (square, abbreviated *nám.*).

BY BUS

Bus and tram service in Bratislava is very cheap and reasonably frequent, and you can use it to reach any of the places in the tours below. The timetables can be confusing, so be sure to confirm your itinerary.

The bus network in the rest of Slovakia is dense, but service to the smaller towns can be infrequent.

BY CAR

Breakdowns. In Bratislava contact the 24-hour repair service (☎ 07/154). The *Auto Atlas SR* (available at any bookstore) has a list of emergency road-repair numbers in various towns. If you have an accident and need an ambulance, call the emergency number (☎ 155).

Gasoline. Gasoline is expensive. Service stations are usually along main roads on the outskirts of towns and cities. Finding a station in Bratislava can be difficult, so fill up on the freeway as you approach the city. Lead-free gasoline, known as "natural," is still available only at select stations.

Road Conditions. Main roads are often narrow but adequate. Traffic is light, especially away from main centers. Outside Bratislava, a car is especially useful in central and eastern Slovakia, where many of the sights are difficult to reach by public transportation.

Rules of the Road. Drive on the right. Speed limits are 60 kph (37 mph) in built-up areas, 90 kph (55 mph) on open roads, 110 kph (68 mph) on expressways, and 130 kph (80 mph) on highways. Seat belts are compulsory; drinking and driving is strictly prohibited.

BY PLANE

Tatra Air Slovakia (☎ 07/292306) has flights from Bratislava to Košice twice on weekdays and once on Sunday.

BY TRAIN

Train service is erratic to all but the largest cities—Bratislava, Poprad, Prešov, Košice, and Banská Bystrica. Make sure to take the express trains marked R or the fast Intercity trains. Reliable, if slow, electric rail service connects Poprad with the resorts of the High Tatras. If you're going just to the Tatras, an electric train will get you there.

Visitor Information

Satur Tours and Travel (main office, ✉ Jesenského 5, Bratislava, ☎ 07/323816 or 07/367645, FAX 07/323816; ⏲ Oct.–May, weekdays 9–6; June–Sept., weekdays 9–6, Sat. 9–noon)—the country's largest travel agency, with 54 offices all around Slovakia—can set you up with hotel, tour, and transportation reservations and tickets.

Weather

Organized sightseeing tours generally run from April or May through October. Some monuments, especially castles, either close entirely or have shorter hours in winter. Hotel rates drop off-season except during festivals. In winter (December–February), skiers from all over Eastern Europe crowd the slopes and resorts of the High Tatra mountains. Visit the mountains in late spring (May or June) or fall and you'll have the hotels and restaurants pretty much to yourself.

CLIMATE

The following are the average daily maximum and minimum temperatures for Bratislava.

Jan.	36F	2C	**May**	70F	21C	**Sept.**	72F	22C
	27	− 3		52	11		54	12
Feb.	39F	4C	**June**	75F	24C	**Oct.**	59F	15C
	28	− 2		57	14		45	7
Mar.	48F	9C	**July**	79F	26C	**Nov.**	46F	8C
	34	1		61	16		37	3
Apr.	61F	16C	**Aug.**	79F	26C	**Dec.**	39F	4C
	43	6		61	16		32	0

BRATISLAVA

In Bratislava you'll find high-rise housing projects, faded supermodern structures, and less-than-inspiring monuments. But Europe's newest capital city is changing. Everywhere you look new shops are opening and older buildings are under renovation—as if the city's residents are trying to forget as quickly as possible the past 40 years of playing second fiddle to Prague.

Exploring Bratislava

Numbers in the margin correspond to points of interest on the Bratislava map.

Despite its charms, there's no denying that Bratislava is intensely industrial. Avoid the newer, and shabbier, parts of the city and head toward the Danube River to discover the peace and beauty of the **Staré Mesto** (Old Town) and its Gothic and Renaissance architectural treasures. Walking between the major sites will take just an hour or two.

10 **Dóm svätého Martina** (St. Martin's Cathedral). Construction of this massive Gothic church, with its 280-ft gold-trimmed steeple, began during the 14th century. Between the 16th and 19th centuries, 17 Hungarian monarchs were crowned here. ✉ *Rudnayovo nám.*, ☎ *07/5331359.* ⏲ *Weekdays 10–11:30 and 2–6, Sat. 10–noon, Sun. 2–4:30.*

7 **Hlavné námestie** (Main Square). This enchanting square in Old Town is lined with old houses and palaces that represent architectural styles from Gothic (No. 2), through Baroque (No. 4) and Rococo (No. 7), to a wonderfully decorative example of Art Nouveau (No. 10). ✉ *Bordered by Radničná ul. and Rybárska ul.*

9 **Hrad** (Castle). Bratislava's castle has been continually rebuilt since its original fortifications were laid in the 9th century. The Hungarian kings expanded the castle into a royal residence, and the Hapsburgs turned it into a very successful defense against the Turks. Its current design, square with four corner towers, stems from the 17th century, although the existing castle had to be completely rebuilt after a disastrous fire in 1811. In the castle you'll find the **Slovenské národné múzeum** (Slovak National Museum). The exhibits cover crafts, historic furniture and clocks, and silver treasure. ✉ *Zámocká ul.*, ☎ *07/5311444.* ⏲ *Castle and museum: Tues.–Sun. 9–5.*

2 **Hurbanovo námestie** (Hurban Square). This busy square hides the entrance to the Old Town. A small bridge, decorated with statues of St. John Nepomuk and St. Michael, takes you over the old moat, now blossoming with trees and fountains, into the intricate barbican and past Michalská brána (Michael's Gate; ☞ *below*).

4 **Jezuitský kostol** (Jesuit Church). Wild with Baroque detailing on the inside, this church was originally built by Protestants who, in 1636, were granted an imperial concession to build a place of worship on

Dóm svätého Martina, **10**
Hlavné námestie, **7**
Hrad, **9**
Hurbanovo námestie, **2**
Jezuitský kostol, **4**
Kostol Klarisiek, **8**
Michalská brána, **3**
Námestie SNP, **1**
Nový Most, **11**
Primaciálny palác, **5**
Stará radnica, **6**

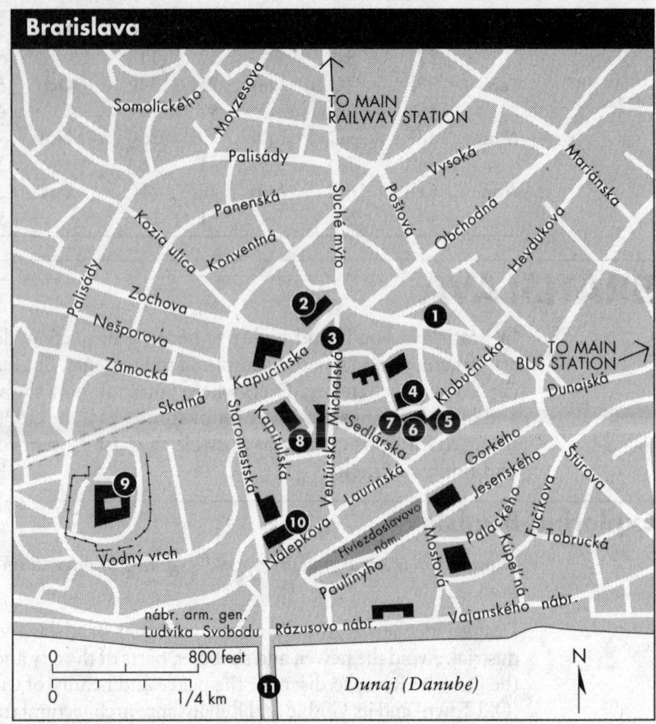

the strict condition that it have no tower. ✉ *Hlavné nám,* ☎ *no phone.* ⏲ *Mass: weekdays 6:30, 3:15, 4, and 6; Sun. and holidays at 7, 9, 11, 5, and 6.*

❽ **Kostol Klarisiek** (Church and Monastery of the Poor Clares). Go through the arched passageway at the back of the Baroque Palác Uhorskej kráľovskej komory (Hungarian Royal Chamber) on Michalská ulice and you'll come to this church and convent on a tiny square. The one-nave, Gothic church is small but still imposing, due to its richly decorated spire. ✉ *Farská ul.,* ☎ *no phone.*

❸ **Michalská brána** (Michael's Gate). Topped with a copper onion dome and a statue of St. Michael, this 500-year-old gate at one entrance to Old Town is the only remainder of Bratislava's three original city gates. ✉ *Hurbanovo nám.*

❶ **Námestie SNP** (SNP Square). An abbreviation for *Slovenské Národné Povstanie* (Slovak National Uprising), "SNP" appears on streets, squares, bridges, and posters throughout Slovakia. The anti-Nazi resistance movement, organized partly by the Communists, involved partisan fighting in Slovakia's mountainous areas during the final years of World War II. On the monument that commemorates it in this square, you can often see the Slovak flag (red, blue, and white with a double cross) flying from a partisan's gun. In 1992 the square was the center for demonstrations in support of Slovak independence. ✉ *Bordered by Obchodná ul. and Poštová ul.*

❶❶ **Nový Most** (New Bridge). This futuristic bridge, opened in 1972, was formerly known as Most SNP. The steps under the passageway and up the other side lead in the direction of the historic castle. *Between Staromestská ul. and Panónska ul.*

5 **Primaciálny palác** (Primates' Palace). Go through the back entrance of the Old Town Hall (☞ *below*) to find the **Primaciálne námestie** (Primates' Square), which is dominated by the glorious pale pink, classical elegance of the Palace. In the dazzling Hall of Mirrors Napoléon and Hapsburg Emperor Francis I signed the Peace of Bratislava of 1805, following Napoléon's victory at the Battle of Austerlitz. ✉ *Primaciálne nám. 1,* ☎ *07/5331407.* ⏲ *Tues.–Sun. 10–5.*

6 **Stará radnica** (Old Town Hall). A colorful jumble of Gothic and Renaissance arcades, archways, and audience halls makes up the Old Town Hall. Walk through the vaulted passageway with early Gothic ribbing into a cheerful Renaissance courtyard. (The hall's interior is not open to the public.) Toward the back of the courtyard, you'll find the entrance to the **Mestské múzeum** (City Museum), which documents Bratislava's rocky past. ✉ *Primaciálne nám. Museum:* ☎ *5335800.* ⏲ *Tues.–Sun. 10–5.*

Dining and Lodging

When it's time to eat, you can be happy that you're in Bratislava. The long-shared history with Hungary gives Slovak cuisine an extra fire. Bratislava's proximity to Vienna, moreover, has lent a bit of grace and charm to the city's eateries. You'll find a variety of meat dishes, all spiced to enliven the palate and served (if you're lucky) with the special noodles Slovaks call *halušky.* Keep in mind that the city's many street stands offer a price-conscious alternative to restaurant dining. Try some *langoš*—flat, deep-fried, and delicious pieces of dough, which can be seasoned with garlic and other toppings. For details and price-category definitions, *see* Dining *in* Slovakia A to Z, *above.*

On the whole, Bratislava's hotels are no bargain, and new properties are few and far between. If you're on a budget, investigate the accommodation services at the Bratislava Tourist Information branch in the main train station (✉ Hlavná stanica, Predstaničné nám., ☎ 07/395906)—but stay near the city center, as the fringe areas are a vast sea of block housing. For details and price-category definitions, *see* Lodging *in* Slovakia A to Z, *above.*

$$$$ ✕ **Arkadia.** At the threshold of Bratislava Castle, Arkadia's several dining rooms range from intimate to boisterous and are decorated with period 19th-century furnishings. Come here by taxi and after fortifying yourself with steak or shish kebab, enjoy the 15-minute and mostly downhill walk back into town. ✉ *Zámocké schody,* ☎ *07/5335650. AE, DC, MC, V.*

$$$ ★ ✕ **Kláštorná Vináreň.** This Old Town monastery offers subterranean meals in its vaulted cellars. When ordering *čikós tokáň* (a fiery mixture of pork, onions, and peppers), keep a glass of mellow red wine and a fire hose on hand. *Bravčové ražniči* (a tender pork shish kebab with fried potatoes) is milder. It is the only downtown place with live cimbal and violin folk music at night. ✉ *Františkánska ul. 2,* ☎ *07/5330430. AE, MC, V. Closed Sun.*

$$ ✕ **Modrá Hviezda.** A small, privately owned wine cellar, the "Blue Star" eschews the international standards in favor of regional fare. Try the *Bryndzový posúch* (baked sheep-cheese pie) and *Mamičkina špecialita* (my mother's favorite dish; stewed beef with sour-cream sauce, potato-dough fritters, and cranberries). ✉ *Beblavého 14,* ☎ *07/5332747. No credit cards.*

$ ✕ **Pekná Brána.** The wide selection at this old-fashioned, cozy restaurant includes Chinese and vegetarian cuisines as well as traditional Slovak specialties. In the back rooms and the cellar you can enjoy a fireplace and dishes hot off an open roast grill. ✉ *Vysoká ul. 39,* ☎ *07/323008. AE, MC, V.*

$ ✕ **Stará Sladovňa.** This beer hall is known lovingly, and fittingly, as "Mamut" (the word for Mammoth, a huge and ungainly beast) to Bratislavans. Locals come here for the Bohemian beer on tap and for inexpensive, filling meals. The place, which has billiards and slot machines on two floors, seats almost 1,000, so don't worry about reservations. ✉ *Cintorínska ul. 32,* ☎ *07/321151. No credit cards.*

$$$$ ★ **Danube.** Opened in 1992, this French-run hotel on the bank of the Danube has superior facilities and service. The modern rooms are done in tasteful pastels; the public areas gleam. ✉ *Rybné nám. 1, 81338,* ☎ *07/5340000,* FAX *07/5314311. 264 rooms, 4 compartments, and 12 suites. 2 restaurants, pool. AE, DC, MC, V.*

$$$$ **Hotel Forum Bratislava.** The Forum opened in 1989 in downtown Bratislava offering top facilities. It houses three restaurants—French, Slovak, and Hungarian—and several cafés and bars. Rooms are bright and, thanks to twice-daily maid service, very clean. Request a room with a view of the castle or Old Town. ✉ *Hodžovo nám. 2, 81625,* ☎ *07/5348111,* FAX *07/5314645. 226 rooms, 10 suites. 3 restaurants, pool. AE, DC, MC, V.*

$$ ★ **Grémium.** This small, bright, affordable pension is in the center of Bratislava's Old Town. The friendly staff serves a terminally arty clientele. A Continental breakfast is included in the room rate. Rooms have showers, not tubs. ✉ *Gorkého ul. 11, 81103,* ☎ *07/321818,* FAX *07/5330653. 5 rooms, 1 suite. Restaurant. AE, MC, V.*

$$ **Hotel Turist.** Modern, no-frills, and pleasant, this hotel is a short hop from the city center. A winter stadium and a swimming pool (open in summer) are nearby. Rooms have showers, not tubs. ✉ *Ondavská ul. 5, 82647,* ☎ *07/5262789,* FAX *07/5438263. 95 rooms. AE, MC, V.*

Nightlife and the Arts

For listings of events look in Bratislava's English-language newspaper, *The Slovak Spectator,* or ask at **Bratislava Tourist Information** (BIS; ☞ Visitor Information, *below*).

The **Slovak Philharmonic Orchestra** puts on excellent concerts at the Reduta (✉ Medená 3, ☎ 07/5333351 or 07/5333352). **Slovenské Národné Divadlo** (Slovak National Theater; ✉ Hviezdoslavo nám. 1, ☎ 07/5333083 and 5333890) offers high-quality opera and ballet performances at bargain prices.

Bratislava hosts an annual jazz festival in the fall, but the city lacks a good venue for regular jazz gigs. That said, the **Čierny Havran Club** (Black Raven, ✉ Biela ul. 6, ☎ 07/5333159) occasionally has local jazz acts. **Hysteria Pub** (✉ Odbojárov 9, ☎ 07/5254495) plays rock and dancefloor. An American style hard rock bar is the **Harley-Davidson Club** (✉ Rebarborova ul. 1, ☎ 07/5523585); take trolley-bus 220 from behind the Tesco department store and get off at Ružinovský cintorín (Ružinov Cemetery). If you prefer to stay dowtown, go to the **Diskobar Centrum Pub** (✉ Župné nám. 3, no phone). Good Guiness beer is served at the **Irish Pub** (✉ Sedlárska ul. 6, ☎ 07/5310706) which has a non-smoking corner.

Shopping

You will find plenty of folk art and souvenir shops along **Obchodná ulica** (Shopping Street) as well as on Námestie SNP (☞ Exploring Bratislava, *above*). Stores tend to come and go in this fast-changing city.

There are several **Dielo** (✉ Obchodná 27, Obchodná 33, Nám. SNP 12) stores that sell works by Slovak artists and craftspeople at reasonable prices. **Folk, Folk** (✉ Rybárska Brána 2) has a large collection of Slovak folk art, including crystal, pottery, hand-woven tablecloths, wooden articles, and dolls in folk costumes. **ÚĽUV** (✉ Nám. SNP 12) has a nice selection of hand-painted table pottery and vases, wooden figures, and folk costumes.

Bratislava Essentials

Arriving and Departing

BY BUS

Buses run frequently between Prague and Bratislava; the trip costs around 300 Sk and takes about five hours. From Vienna there are four buses a day from Autobusbahnhof Wien-Mitte; the trip takes between 1½ and 2 hours. The **Autobusová Stanica** (Bus Station; ✉ Mlynské nivy ul., ☎ 07/5267231) in Bratislava is outside the city center; take Trolleybus 217 to Mierové námestie in the direction of the Hrad (Castle), or Trolleybus 220 to Tesco department store.

BY CAR

Good freeways link Prague and Bratislava via Brno (D1 and D2); the 315-km (195-mi) journey takes about 3½ hours. From Vienna take the A4 and then Route 8 to Bratislava. The 60-km (37-mi) trip takes about 1½ hours.

BY PLANE

As few international airlines land in Bratislava, the most convenient international airport for Slovakia is Vienna's Schwechat Airport, approximately 60 km (37 mi) from Bratislava. Four buses a day stop at Schwechat en route to Bratislava, or you can even take a taxi; the journey takes just over an hour, depending on the border crossing. From Prague's Ruzyně Airport you can take a ČSA flight to Bratislava; the flight takes about an hour. A Tatra Air flight from Zürich to Bratislava takes about two hours.

BY TRAIN

Bratislava's train station is **Hlavná stanica** (✉ Predstaničné nám., ☎ 07/5484484). The tourist information office here provides traveling tips and helps find accommodation in the city; you can contact the bureau by calling the station's general number. Reasonably efficient train service connects Prague and Bratislava (five–six hours). Unless you crave adventure, take the Intercity trains for their speed and safety. There are several trains a day to and from Vienna (just over an hour).

Getting Around

BY BUS

Bus, trolleybus, and tram service in Bratislava is cheap, fairly frequent, and convenient for getting to the main sights. Buy tickets ahead of time at any newsstand or at automatic ticket dispensers for 7 Sk each and stamp them when you enter the bus, trolleybus, or tram.

BY CAR

Driving can be difficult in Bratislava and parking spaces are at a premium in the city center; foot power is the most effective way to see the sights. If you do need to rent a car, you can do so either at Satur (☞ Visitor Information, *below*) or at the Forum Bratislava and Danube hotels (☞ Dining and Lodging, *above*). Watch out for no-parking zones or you get the boot and have to pay a hefty fine to have it removed.

Contacts and Resources

EMBASSIES

United States (✉ Hviezdoslavovo nám. 4, ☎ 07/5330861, FAX 07/5318861). **Canadian** (✉ Mišíkova 28/d, ☎ 07/352175 or 07/352177,

FAX 07/399995). **United Kingdom** (✉ Panská 16, ☎ 07/5317688 or 07/5319633, FAX 07/5310002).

EMERGENCIES

Police (☎ 158). **Ambulance** (☎ 155). **Pharmacies:** Lekáreň pod Manderlom (✉ Nám. SNP 20, ☎ 07/363731); Lekáreň (✉ Palackého 10, ☎ 07/5319665).

Lekárne (pharmacies) take turns staying open late or on Sunday. Look for the list posted on the front door of each pharmacy. For after-hours service, ring the bell; you will be served through a little hatch-door.

ENGLISH-LANGUAGE BOOKSTORES

Big Ben (✉ Michalská 1, ☎ 07/5333632).

GUIDED TOURS

The best tours of Bratislava are offered by Bratislava Tourist Information (BIS; ☞ Visitor Information, *below*), which can arrange a tour in a vintage coach or a tour with an individual guide for a very reasonable price. Both BIS and Satur (☞ Visitor Information, *below*) offer worthwhile one-day tours of castles and the Small Carpathian mountains close to Bratislava.

VISITOR INFORMATION

Bratislava Tourist Information (BIS, ✉ Klobučnícka 2, ☎ 07/5334370). **Satur Tours and Travel** (main office, ✉ Jesenského 5, ☎ 07/367645).

THE HIGH TATRAS AND EASTERN SLOVAKIA

Outside Bratislava the High Tatras region is particularly visitor-friendly for Slovakia; you'll find some of the best hotels in the country (often with saunas to pamper tired skiers), good orientation tours, and stunning mountain scenery laced with well-marked walking trails, though finding a satisfying meal in the Tatras can be difficult, especially in late fall, when some restaurants close completely. One bright spot is shish kebab made on a *koliba* (open-faced grill). Both an electric train network and a winding highway (Route 537) link the industrial center of Poprad with the resorts spread about on the lower slopes of the High Tatras.

In the brooding towns of the Spiš region just south and east of the High Tatras (on a map look for the prefix "Spišský" preceding a town name) isolation and economic stagnation have preserved a striking mix of Gothic and Renaissance architecture—Gothic churches with Renaissance bell towers attached are typical of the area. These towns do tend to be short on creature comforts.

East of Spiš, the Šariš region is permeated with a unique legacy of both Orthodox and Greek Catholic (Uniate) churches. The splendid walled town of Bardejov makes the best center from which to set out on a journey. Be prepared, though, to get lost along some rough minor roads while seeking out 17th- and 18th-century wooden churches—and the right person to open them up for you. In stark contrast to the general tranquillity are the Nazi and Soviet tanks, trenches, and planes, kept as a reminder of the fighting that took place here in 1944; these are concentrated near the Slovakia–Poland border at the Dukelský Priesmyk (Dukla Pass).

Spišská Sobota

The beautiful medieval suburb of Spišská Sobota seems light-years away from the Communist apartment blocks of its industrial neighbor Poprad. Once a hub of the historic Spiš empire, the village is rife with

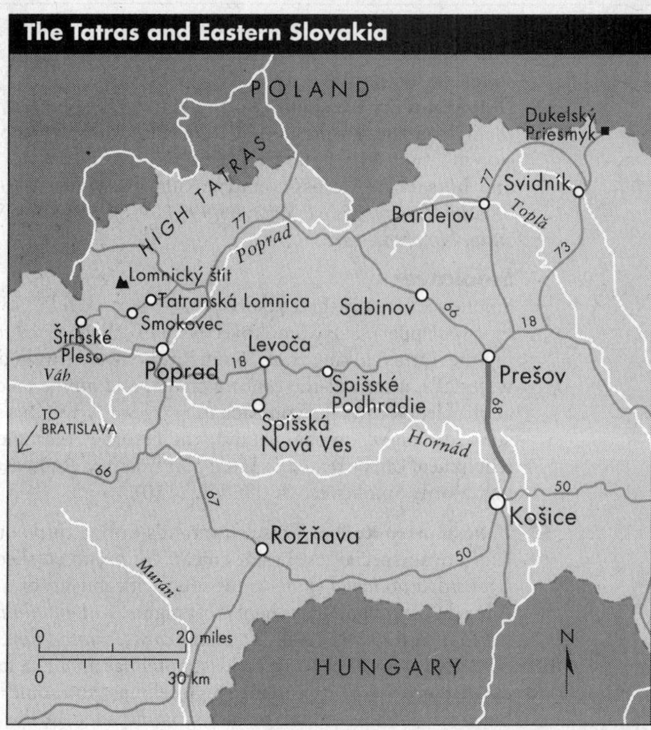

steep shingled roofs, high timber-framed gables, and arched brick doorways. The lovely old square—a nearly perfect ensemble of Renaissance houses—has a Romanesque church, **Kostol svätého Juraja** (St. George's Church; ✉ Sobotské nám., ☎ no phone), rebuilt during the early 16th century. The church's ornate altar is the work of Pavol of Levoča, one of the great wood-carvers of the 16th century. Getting into the church, however, can be tricky; ask for admittance at the neighboring **Múzeum** (museum). The museum's collection focuses on local history, including the career of Pavol of Levoča. ✉ *Sobotské nám. 33,* ☎ *no phone,* ⏲ *Tues.–Sun. 9–4.*

★ Levoča

One of the most famous Spiš towns is Levoča, whose layers of Renaissance-on-Gothic architecture are undergoing the pains of restoration. The row of facades in Námestie Majstra Pavla, the main square, is particularly striking, especially those of Nos. 43, 45, 47, and 49. **Kostol s vätého Jakuba** (St. Jacob's Church) on the main square has an astounding concentration of Gothic religious art, including some of the most impressive work by Spiš artist Pavol of Levoča. His carved-wood high altar is monumental in size and exquisite in detail. At press time the church's exterior and organ were undergoing extensive renovation. ✉ *Nám. Majstra Pavla,* ☎ *no phone.*

Just 16 km (10 mi) east from Levoča along Route 18 is one of the largest castles in Europe: **Spišský hrad** (Spiš Castle). The beautiful views relieve the grim atmosphere of the museum's display of torture devices. There are also exhibits on local history. ✉ *On hill above the town of Spišské Podhradie,* ☎ *0966/512786.* ⏲ *June–Aug., daily 9–6; May, Sept., and Oct., Tues.–Sun. 9–5*

$$$ ✕🏨 **Hotel Satel.** Inside in an 18th-century mansion, the Satel centers around a picturesque courtyard that conjures up all the charm of fairy-tale Levoča. The guest rooms are bright and modern. ✉ *Nám. Majstra Pavla 55, 05401,* ☎ *0966/512943,* FAX *0966/514486. 21 rooms, 2 suites. Restaurant. AE, DC, MC, V.*

$$ **Hadušovský Penzión.** A half mile from the Spiš Castle and 12 km (8 mi) from the downhill skiing resort Plejsy near Krompachy, this pension in a two-story family house offers cozy rooms, horseback-riding, and horse-driven cross-country skiing in winter. ✉ *Hodkovce 14, Spišské Vlachy, 05361,* ☎ *0965/495129,* FAX *0965/495546. 1 room, 1 suite. No credit cards.*

Smokovec

Smokovec is really three resorts in one: Starý (Old), Nový (New), and Horný (Upper). Starý Smokovec is an excellent place to start exploring the Tatras' hiking trails. Some of the more traveled paths lead to waterfalls, a turn-of-the-century chalet, and alpine lakes. A funicular at Hrebienok can take you back to Starý Smokovec. As soon as there's sufficient snow on the ground, the resort is crammed with skiers (equipment can be rented at Tatrasport Adam & Andrea: ✉ Tatra building, Horný Smokovec, ☎ 0969/422110).

$$ ✕ **Restaurant Koliba.** This restaurant's koliba turns out some excellent Slovak specialties. Besides meat, try *bryndza* (sheep cheese) and *kapustová polievka* (sauerkraut soup with mushrooms and sausage). A local Gypsy band plays here most nights. ✉ *Downhill from the train station,* ☎ *0969/422204. No credit cards. Closed Sun.*

$$$ ★ **Grand Hotel.** The town's oldest hotel has an air of faded fin de siècle elegance. Large rooms have high ceilings, and some have their own balcony. A filling buffet breakfast is included in the rate. ✉ *Starý Smokovec, 06201,* ☎ *0969/422154,* FAX *0969/422157. 78 rooms, 5 suites, some with bath. Restaurant, pool. AE, DC, MC, V.*

Tatranská Lomnica

Tiny out-of-the-way Tatranská Lomnica is a peaceful, but still convenient, spot for hiking and skiing. The **Magistrale** trail (24 km/15 mi) begins behind the Grandhotel Praha (☞ *below*). Skirting the tree line, you'll see dwarf pines and spectacular views—with relatively little exertion. At the **Múzeum Tatranského Národného Parku** (Museum of the Tatra National Park), startlingly realistic mounted animals dominate the first floor, while exhibits on local peasant life are found upstairs. ☎ *0969/467951.* ⏲ *Weekdays 8–noon and 1–4:30, weekends 8–noon.*

$$ ✕ **Zbojnícka Koliba.** This tavern offers a small range of Slovak specialties prepared over an open fire amid rustic decor and accompanied by folk music. *Near Grandhotel Praha,* ☎ *0969/467267. No credit cards. Dinner only.*

$$$ ★ **Grandhotel Praha.** The multiturreted, turn-of-the-century hotel has spacious, traditionally decorated guest rooms. The restaurant still has an air of elegance unusual in Slovakia. ✉ *Tatranská Lomnica, 05960,* ☎ *0969/467941,* FAX *0969/467891. 83 rooms, 7 suites. Restaurant. AE, DC, MC, V.*

Bardejov

Once astride the trade routes between Poland and Russia, Bardejov still revolves around its beautiful main square. On the south side of the square is the **Šarišské múzeum** (Šariš Museum), filled with 16th- to 19th-century religious art taken from local Russian Orthodox churches. ✉ *Radničné nám. 13,* ☎ *0935/746038.* ⏲ *Daily except Mon., 8–noon, 12:30–4.*

Kostol svätého Egídia (St. Egidium Church), on the main square, is an almost purely Gothic building inside and out. Nearly a dozen perfectly preserved Gothic side altars line the nave. ✉ *Radničné nám.,* ☎ *0935/722595.* ⏲ *Tues.–Sun., summer 9–5:30, winter 10–4 .*

$$ 🏨 **Republika.** Socialist architecture aside, this hotel's big advantage is location—a few steps from Bardejov's beautiful main square. ✉ *Radičné nám. 50, 08631 Bardejov,* ☎ *0935/722721,* FAX *0935/722567. 30 rooms, half with shower. Restaurant. No credit cards.*

🏨 **Roland.** This pension is right at the main square, on the second floor of a brick municipal building. It is nevertheless quiet at night. ✉ *Radničné nám. 22, 08501 Bardejov,* ☎ *0935/186. 3 suites. Restaurant. No credit cards.*

$ 🏨 **Športhotel.** A rectangular hotel with a gray facade built in 1989, it sits on the Topľa River bank, among tennis and volleyball playgrounds, just seven minutes from Bardejov's beautiful main square. ✉ *Kutuzovova. 34, 08501 Bardejov,* ☎ *0935/724949,* FAX *0935/728208. 20 rooms, only showers, no tubs. Restaurant. No credit cards.*

The High Tatras and Eastern Slovakia Essentials

Getting Around

Many of the towns in this region have no formal street names; instead, they usually have signs pointing to hotels, restaurants, and museums.

BY CAR

Driving is the quickest and most convenient way to see eastern Slovakia—sometimes it's the only way to reach small villages. Route 537 is the main road between Poprad and the High Tatras resort towns.

BY PLANE

If you want to travel by plane, ČSA's 40-minute flights from Bratislava to Poprad connect with services from Prague and are reasonably priced. Tatra Air Slovakia has flights from the capital to Košice (☞ Transportation *in* Slovakia A to Z, *above*).

BY TRAIN OR BUS

Trains and buses run frequently, but service is cut back sharply on weekends. The electric trains that run between Poprad and the resort towns in the High Tatras leave from the upper platforms of Poprad's main train station, Železničná stanica Poprad-Tatry (✉ Wolkerova 496, ☎ 092/62509).

Guided Tours

Satur's (☞ Visitor Information *in* Bratislava Essentials, *above*) seven-day Grand Tour of Slovakia, which leaves from Bratislava every other Saturday from June through September, stops in the High Tatras and a few other towns in eastern Slovakia. The Satur office in Starý Smokovec (☎ 0969/422710 or 0969/422597) is also helpful in arranging tours of the Tatras and the surrounding area. **TLS Air** (Poprad airport, ☎ 092/63875) offers a biplane flight over the Tatras from Poprad airport, complete with champagne.

Visitor Information

Bardejov (✉ Radničné nám. 21, ☎ 0935/186). **Smokovec** (✉ Starý Smokovec, ☎ 0969/186). **Tatranská Lomnica** (☎ 0969/967951).

27 Slovenia

Surging peaks, mysterious caves, and a coast dotted with well-preserved Venetian cities of old are the attractions of Slovenia. The combination of alpine, plain, and coastal geography allows both morning skiing high in the Julian Alps and views of sunset on the Adriatic on the same day. Slovenes' love of their natural surroundings is reflected in the motto they use for their country: A Green Piece of Europe (fully half of which is covered by forests).

Slovenia's northern border is lined with the jagged peaks of the Karavanke Mountains. The Julian Alps, capped by majestic Mt. Triglav (Three Heads), which rises to 9,393 ft, dominate the northwest. Eastward, the mountains gradually descend to the great Hungarian plain. Lovely lakes nestle in thickly wooded mountain valleys, and vineyards cover low-lying hills farther east.

Slovenia has from earliest times been a frontier region. The Romans came from the coast and marched north; Germanic tribes propelled themselves south. Later Slovenia became a province of Charlemagne's empire; next it served as the Hapsburg empire's bulwark against the Turks. The years during World War II, when Slovenia was annexed by Hitler and Mussolini, were filled with both heroic and unspeakable acts. After World War II, as part of Yugoslavia, Slovenia was at the vanguard of the movement toward democracy and self-determination following Tito's death.

The 2 million Slovenes held a national referendum on December 23, 1990, voting for independence and sovereignty from Yugoslavia, and proclaimed their independence on June 26, 1991. Slovenia gained recognition from other nations and soon set about becoming an active member of the family of European states. Following 500 years as part the Austro-Hungarian Empire, Slovenes have perfectly combined Austrian efficiency and organization with a genuine and captivating

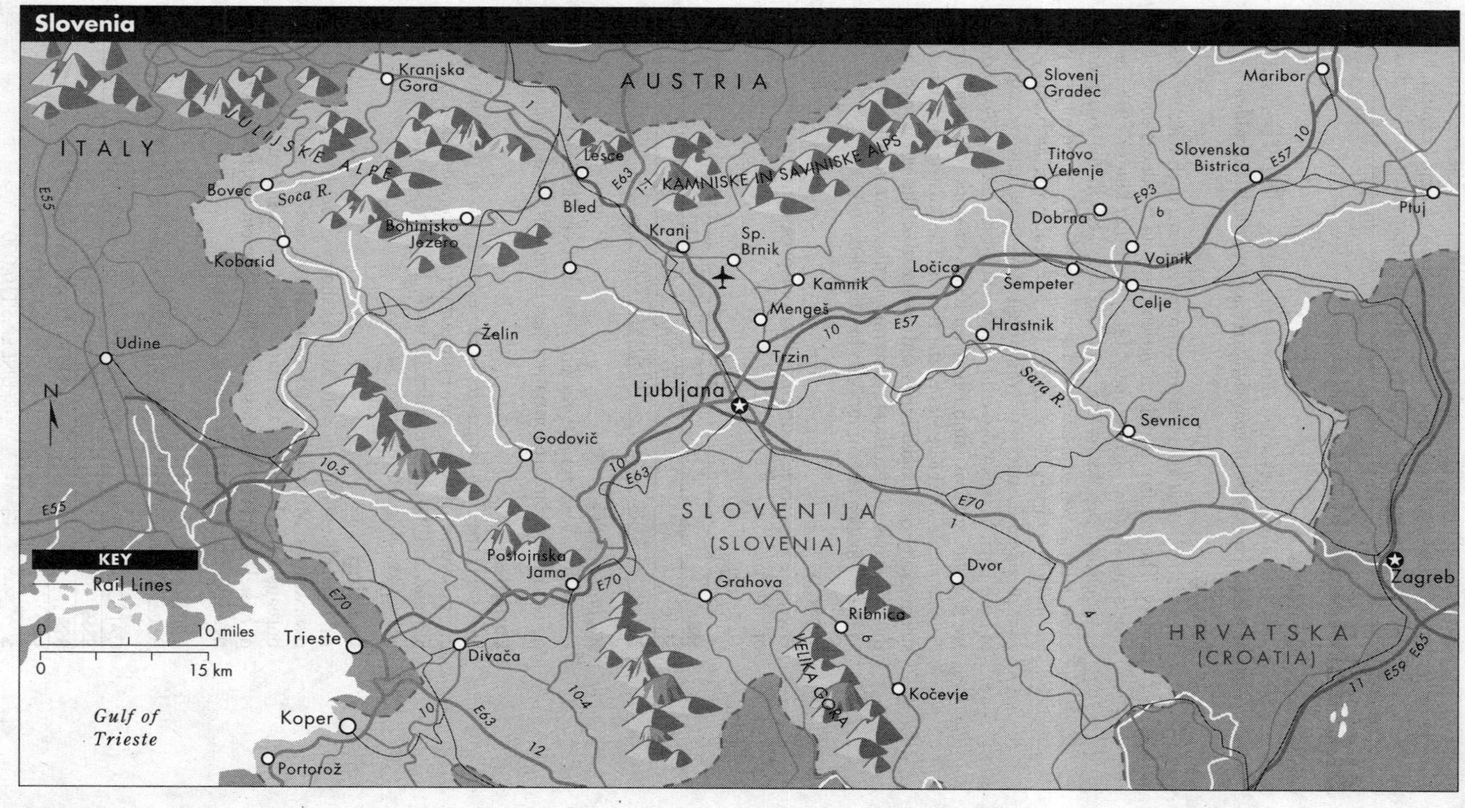
Slovenia
AUSTRIA
ITALY
JULIJSKE ALPE
KAMNISKE IN SAVINJSKE ALPS
Kranjska Gora
Slovenj Gradec
Maribor
Lesce
Titovo Velenje
Slovenska Bistrica
Bovec
Soca R.
Bled
Dobrna
Ptuj
Bohinjsko Jezero
Kranj
Sp. Brnik
Vojnik
Kobarid
Kamnik
Ločica
Šempeter
Celje
Menges
Hrastnik
Želin
Trzin
Udine
Ljubljana
Sara R.
Sevnica
N
Godovič
SLOVENIJA
(SLOVENIA)
E55
KEY
Rail Lines
Postojnska Jama
Grahova
Dvor
Zagreb
Ribnica
0
10 miles
Trieste
Divača
HRVATSKA
(CROATIA)
0
15 km
VELIKA GORA
Kočevje
Gulf of Trieste
Koper
Portorož
E57
E63
E65
E59
E70
E93
10
10.4
10.5
11
12
1
1-1
6
4

Slavic friendliness. Slovenia's small size (about half the area of Switzerland) can be an advantage: From the centrally located capital, Ljubljana, everything in the country is no more than a three-hour drive.

SLOVENIA A TO Z

Customs

Duty-free allowances are: 1 carton of cigarettes, 1 liter of spirits, 2 liters of wine.The export of historical artifacts is strictly forbidden.

Dining

Slovenia has some 40 different culinary regions, each with its specific dishes. The country is rich in agriculture and produces some of Europe's finest wines. Trout, charr, pike, and other kinds of fish abound in mountain brooks, rivers, and lakes. In season there is plentiful game, such as venison, hare, and quail; non-factory-bred quality poultry, including turkey, duck, and goose; and veal, pork, lamb, and young goat prepared in ingenious traditional ways. Frog legs are a specialty of Ljubljana. You can also enjoy zesty Swiss-type cheeses. Roast dishes are popular, such as lamb ribs with beans or pork roast with applesauce made from the apples of the region. The Austrian influences result in exceptional baked goods and fine pastries. The best way to sample this bounty is to visit local restaurants called *gostilna;* reserve ahead, as many smaller restaurants can be crowded.

RATINGS

Prices are for a three-course meal for one person, not including drinks or tip.

CATEGORY	COST
$$$	OVER SIT4000
$$	SIT2500–SIT4000
$	UNDER SIT2500

WHAT TO WEAR

Casual dress is acceptable in many restaurants in Slovenia, but Slovenes do tend to dress more formally when going out for the evening.

Language

Slovene is the chief language. In the eastern part of the country signs are posted in Slovene and Hungarian; on the Adriatic coast both Slovene and Italian are officially used. English, German, and Italian are spoken in many places.

Lodging

All hotels listed have private bath or shower, but check when making reservations. Most have at least partial air-conditioning. Local tourist bureaus can help to find alternative accommodations in private rooms or hostels. During the high season (June–September), many hotels, particularly on the coast, become fully booked.

RATINGS

Prices are for two people sharing a double room and include breakfast.

CATEGORY	COST
$$$$	OVER SIT25,000
$$$	SIT18,000–SIT25,000
$$	SIT10,000–SIT18,000
$	UNDER SIT10,000

Mail

A 20-gram airmail letter to the United States costs SIT118, a postcard, SIT70. To Europe a 20-gram letter costs SIT80, and a postcard SIT70.

Post offices are open weekdays 8–6 and Saturday 8–noon. Stamps are also sold at hotels, newsstands, and kiosks.

Money Matters

COSTS

A cup of coffee or tea costs SIT150–SIT200; a glass of beer, SIT250–SIT300; a slice of cake, around SIT250–SIT300; a bottle of local wine, SIT1,500–SIT2,000. Admission to museums costs SIT300–SIT400.

CURRENCY

The monetary unit in Slovenia is the Slovenian tolar (SIT). One Slovenian tolar is divided into 100 stotin. There are notes of SIT10,000, SIT5,000, SIT1,000, SIT500, SIT500, SIT200, SIT200, SIT100, SIT50, SIT20, and SIT10 and coins of 2 and 1 Slovenian tolar and 50 stotin. At press time (spring 1998) the rate of exchange was SIT164 to the U.S. dollar, SIT113 to the Canadian dollar, SIT267 to the pound sterling, SIT102 to the Australian dollar, and SIT88 to the New Zealand dollar.

TIPPING

Tax is already included in listed prices. As tips are not included in bills, a 10% tip is customary; if service is especially good, tip 15%.

National Holidays

January 1–2 (New Year's); February 8 (Preseren Day, Slovene cultural day); April 4–5 (Easter Sunday and Monday); April 27 (National Resistance Day); May 1 (May Day); May 24 (Pentecost Monday); June 25 (Slovenia National Day); August 15 (Assumption); October 31 (Reformation Day); November 1 (All Saints' Day); December 25; December 26 (Independence Day).

Opening and Closing Times

Banks are open weekdays 8:30–12:30 and 2–4:30, Saturday 8–11. You can also change money at exchange desks in hotels, gas stations, tourist agencies, supermarkets, and small exchange offices. **Museums** are open Tuesday–Sunday 10–6. **Shops** are open weekdays 7–7 and Saturday. 7:30–1.

Telephoning

COUNTRY CODE

The country code for Slovenia is ☎ 386.

INTERNATIONAL CALLS

To make international calls, dial 00 and then the appropriate country code. International calls can be made from local telephones or at the post office.

LOCAL CALLS

Pay phones take telephone cards. These have values of SIT900, SIT1,500, or SIT2,600 and can be purchased at post offices and kiosks. Lower rates apply from 10 PM to 7 AM and all day Sunday. For telephone information dial 988 in all towns.

Transportation

In Slovenian the words for street (ulica) and drive (cesta) are abbreviated ul. and c. The word for square is trg.

BY BOAT

Between Easter and the last week of September the ***Prince of Venice*** (Kompas Turizem, ✉ Prazakova 4, Ljubljana, ☎ 061/133–4180) catamaran makes regularly scheduled trips between Venice and Potoroz.

BY BUS

This is the cheapest form of transportation in urban areas; a token costs SIT70 and can be purchased at kiosks and post offices. If you board a bus without a token the cost is SIT 100. Buses operate every half hour and cover an extensive network. Intercity bus fares range from SIT700 to SIT1,000. For information on intercity routes call the **Ljubljana bus station** (✉ Trg OF, ☎ 061/1336136).

BY CAR

An international license is required in Slovenia. Main roads between large towns are comparable to those in Western Europe. On toll roads tolls range from SIT100 to SIT500 depending on route and distance traveled. The main highways between Ljubljana and the Austrian and Italian borders have recently been widened. A tunnel speeds traffic through the Karavanke Alps between Slovenia and Austria. From Vienna the passage is by way of Maribor to Ljubljana, with a highway from Graz to Celje. Slovenia's roads also connect with Italy's autostrada. Minor roads can be unsurfaced, narrow, and winding. Gas costs SIT120 per liter. Cars may be rented from SIT11,000 per day with no seasonal variation in prices.

BY PLANE

There are no direct flights between Slovenia and the United States. Adria Airways, the Slovene national airline, offers regular flights to most major European cities. Austrian Airlines has daily flights from Vienna. Aeroflot and Swissair also have good connections.

BY PRIVATE TAXI

Private taxis operate 24 hours a day throughout the country. Telephone from your hotel or hail one in the street. Taxis have an initial charge of SIT150 and charge SIT100 per kilometer (½ mi). Drivers are bound by law to display and run a meter.

BY TRAIN

Daily trains link Slovenia with Austria, Italy, Hungary, and Croatia. Many are overnight trains with sleeping compartments.

Visas

No visas are necessary for holders of valid passports from the United States, Canada, the United Kingdom, or mainland European countries.

VISITOR INFORMATION

Ljubljana (national tourist office, ✉ Dunajska 156, ☎ 61/1891840.

Weather

The tourist season runs throughout the year, though prices tend to be lower from November through March. Late spring and fall are best, usually warm enough for swimming but not uncomfortably hot.

CLIMATE

Weather in Slovenia can vary greatly depending upon what part of the country you are in. Temperatures are colder and precipitation tends to be higher in the alpine regions, while the summers on the coast can be quite hot. Ljubljana and the Pannonian plain have less extreme variations in weather. The following are the average temperatures for Ljubljana.

Jan.	32F	0C	**May**	59F	14.5C	**Sept.**	59F	15C
Feb.	37F	2.5C	**June**	65F	18C	**Oct.**	49F	9C
Mar.	43F	6C	**July**	70F	20C	**Nov.**	40F	4C
Apr.	49F	9C	**Aug.**	68F	19C	**Dec.**	32F	0C

LJUBLJANA

The capital of the republic of Slovenia is on occasion referred to as "Ljubljana the beloved," a play on words: *Ljubljena* means "beloved"; change one letter, and you have the name Ljubljana.

In 34 BC, the Romans founded Emona on this site. Traces of the Roman occupation have been preserved in sections of walls and a complex of foundations complete with mosaics. The original Roman town was destroyed by the barbarian hordes during the 5th century. Slovenes settled here in the 7th century. Later, under the German name Laibach, this became the capital of the Duchy of Carniola, which in 1335 passed into the hands of the House of Hapsburg. From then until the end of World War I Ljubljana remained part of the Hapsburg monarchy. In 1849 the railway linking Vienna and Trieste reached Ljubljana, establishing it as a major center of commerce, industry, and culture.

Influences from the past are apparent in the Ljubljana of today, although you will have to pass through concentric circles like the age lines of a tree in order to reach the romantic heart of the original old town. Vast industrial complexes and high-rise apartments form the outermost ring. "Downtown," composed mainly of modern office buildings, is also spread out.

To reach the old, romantic Ljubljana, follow one of the city's main commercial streets, Miklosiceva Cesta, south from the railway station, eventually passing a series of palatial three- and four-story structures in a florid Art Nouveau style (Jugendstil), topped by cupolas, spires, and ornate statuary, facades adorned with extravagant arches, balustrades, and curlicue details. Miklosiceva reaches the River Ljubljanica at Presernov Trg, the square named for Slovenia's greatest poet, France Preseren, whose bronze statue stands here. This expansive, traffic-free square, the banks of the river, and old Ljubljana are the places where this lively city is at its most animated. The narrow cobblestone passageways through the medieval quarter and its 19th-century adjuncts evoke a calmer, quieter time. Here students pedal bicycles to and from classes. Along Mestni and Stari Trg green hills rise straight up behind the curve of steeply pitched tile roofs.

Exploring Ljubljana

1. The most glorious of all the Vienna Secessionist-style buildings, the **Centromerkur** department store, was created by a Viennese architect in 1903. The building has a flaring iron butterfly-wing portal and is topped by a statue of Mercury. Inside, extraordinarily graceful curved wrought-iron stairways lead to upper floors. *Trubaljeva 1; Presernov Trg, corner of Miklosiceva and Trubarjeva;* ☎ *61/126–3170.*

2. The massive **Franciskanska Cerkev** (Franciscan Church) was built in high-Baroque style between 1646 and 1660. The main altar is by Francesco Robba, dating from 1736. The three sets of stairs in front serve as a popular meeting place for students. *Presernov Trg 4.* ⏲ *Daily 8–6.*

3. The **Tromostovje** (Triple Bridge) leads over the Ljubljanica to the old town, with the fortress on 1,233-ft-high Grajski Hrib (Castle Hill) as its backdrop. The three bridges started as a single span, but in 1929–1931 the two graceful outer arched bridges, designed by architect Joze Plecnik (1872–1957), were added.

4. The big and bustling flower, fruit, and vegetable market on **Vodnikov Trg** (Vodnikov Square) is held six days a week; on Sunday a flea market takes its place. An elegant riverside colonnade designed by Plecnik

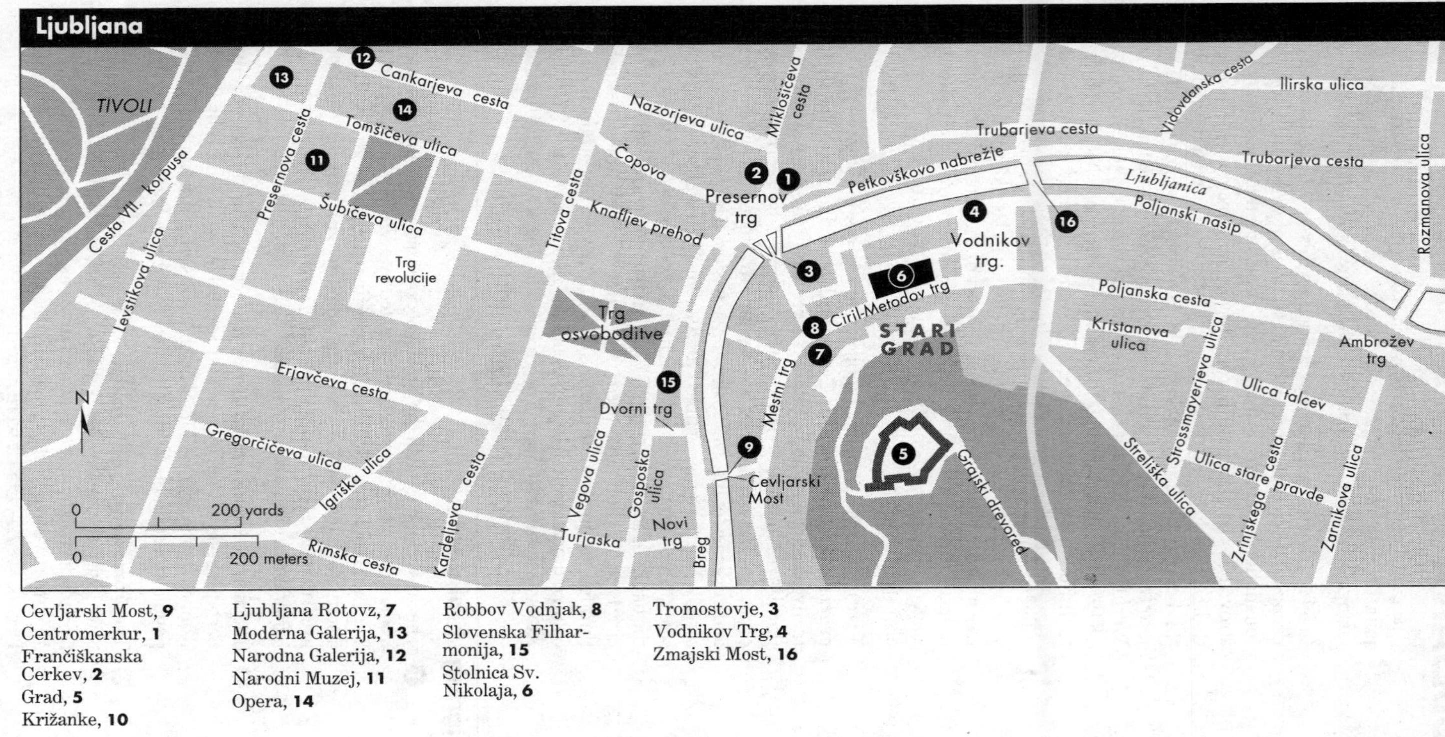

Cevljarski Most, **9**
Centromerkur, **1**
Frančiškanska Cerkev, **2**
Grad, **5**
Križanke, **10**
Ljubljana Rotovz, **7**
Moderna Galerija, **13**
Narodna Galerija, **12**
Narodni Muzej, **11**
Opera, **14**
Robbov Vodnjak, **8**
Slovenska Filharmonija, **15**
Stolnica Sv. Nikolaja, **6**
Tromostovje, **3**
Vodnikov Trg, **4**
Zmajski Most, **16**

runs the length of the market, and a bronze statue of Valentin Vodnik, the first Slovene poet, for whom the square is named, overlooks the scene. *Resljeva c. and Poljanska c.,* ⏲ *7–6.*

5 The **Grad** (Castle) dates from the early 16th century. Its courtyard is used for occasional concerts, and the ramparts shelter a restaurant and a café. The tower was added in the mid-19th century; a park on the castle hill was landscaped in the 1930s by Plecnik. The magnificent setting affords splendid views down across the old town, with its red roofs, spires, and green cupolas, and the river, with its bridges, all silhouetted against the backdrop of the Julian Alps. *Ljubljanski Gric; marked* STUDENTOVSKA ULICA *at its start opposite the Vodnik statue at the center of Vodnikov Trg, alongside Krekov Trg, narrow paved path that changes name several times on the way up leads to Grad; second footpath leads up from Gornji Trg; roundabout route starting from Streliska ul. leads up by car.* ☎ *061/1327216.* ⏲ *Apr.–Oct., daily 10–8; Nov.–Mar., daily 10–5.*

6 The **Stolnica Sv. Nikolaja** (Cathedral of St. Nicholas), a Baroque single-nave church with twin steeples, was built between 1701 and 1708. The cupola was added in 1836; the richly decorated interior has been renovated several times. ✉ *Dolnicarjeva 1, Vodnikov Trg,* ☎ *061/310684.*

From the cathedral, **Ciril-Metodov Trg** (lined with fine old palaces, such as those at Nos. 1, 21, and 27) leads to the heart of old Ljubljana.

Cobbled, traffic-free **Mestni Trg** extends into the oldest part of the city, past onetime town houses and patrician palaces now divided into functional apartments but still presenting marvelously ornate facades; carved oak doors with great brass handles are framed within columns, and second and third floors are decorated with balustrades, statuary, and intricate ironwork. Narrow passageways connect with inner courtyards in one direction and run to the riverfront in the other. Street-level floors contain boutiques, antiques shops, or art galleries.

7 Behind the facade of the **Ljubljana Rotovz,** also referred to as the **Magistrat** (Town Hall), a passage leads to a central courtyard with a statue of Hercules and a fountain with a Narcissus figure. On the sides murals depict historic battles for the town. ✉ *Mestni trg 1.*

8 The 1751 **Robbov Vodnjak** (Robba's Fountain) ranks as the masterpiece of the Baroque sculptor Francesco Robba (1698–1757). It is an allegorical representation of the three main Kranjska rivers—the Sava, the Krka, and the Ljubljanica—that flow through Slovenia. ✉ *Mestni trg.*

Stari Trg (Old Square), the continuation of Mestni Trg, funnels into a narrow slot lined with cafés and small restaurants; in good weather tables are set out on the cobblestones. ✉ *Mestni Trg and Cankarjevo nab.*

9 **Cevljarski Most** (Shoemaker's Bridge) was at one time a wide wooden bridge with huts for craftsmen where cobblers plied their trade. The original span has been replaced several times; the present ferroconcrete structure, with more than a dozen Corinthian columns topped by stone spheres, was built in 1931 to plans by Plecnik. ✉ *Pod Tranco.*

In late afternoon and early evening, as the bridge's (☞ *above*) globular lights come on and are reflected in the water, **Jurcicev Trg** (Jurcicev Square), a small square rimmed with boutiques and several cafés, is Ljubljana at its brightest and most appealing. ✉ *West end of Cevljarski Most.*

10 The **Krizanke** (Monastery of the Holy Cross) occupies an entire block. From the 13th through the 20th centuries it was the seat of a local branch of the Knights of the Teutonic Order. The complex was adapted in the

1930s by Joze Plecnik to contain an open-air stage. ✉ *Beside Trg Franc. Revolucije.*

Trg Franc. Revolucije (French Revolution Square) is dominated by Plecnik's **Ilirski Steber** (Illyrian Column), erected in 1929 to commemorate the brief tenure of Napoléon's Illyrian Provinces regime in Slovenia. ✉ *Rimska c. and Vegova c.*

Trg Republike (Republic Square), the heart of Ljubljana's cultural life, is where old and new parts of the city merge in an unlikely mix of glass-and-steel skyscrapers and the city's chief cultural institutions (museums, concert halls, small theaters) on the north side and the preserved remains of the ancient city of **Emona** (between Erjavceva Cesta and Gregorciceva ul.) on the south. ✉ *Subiceva ul. and Valvazorjeva ul.*

11 At the **Narodni Muzej** (National Museum), the city's oldest museum, the greatest treasure is the Vace Situle, a bronze urn discovered in Vace in Slovenia. Dating from the 5th century BC, it is a wonderful example of Illyrian workmanship. ✉ *Muzejski 1, north of Trg Republike,* ☎ *061/218886.* ⏲ *Tues.–Sat. 10–6, Sun. 10–1.*

12 The **Narodna Galerija** (National Gallery), in an imposing turn-of-the-century structure, contains a survey of Slovene art from the 13th through the early 20th century. ✉ *Cankarjeva 20, north of Trg Republike,* ☎ *061/1263109.* ⏲ *Tues.–Sat. 10–6, Sun. 10–1.*

13 The **Moderna Galerija** (Modern Gallery), in a strikingly modern one-story structure, displays a selection of paintings, sculpture, and prints by Slovenian 20th-century artists. In odd-numbered years it also hosts the International Biennale of Graphics. ✉ *Cankarjeva 15, north of Trg Republike,* ☎ *061/214106.* ⏲ *Tues.–Sat. 10–6, Sun. 10–1.*

14 The **Opera,** a neo-Renaissance palace with an ornate facade topped by an allegorical sculpture group, was erected in 1892. ✉ *Zupanciceva 1, 1000,* ☎ *061/1254840.* ⏲ *Weekdays 11–1, and 1 hr before performances.*

Wolfova Ulica, which runs from Presernov Trg parallel to the river, is a delightful small street with pleasant cafés and smart shops on one side, the greenery of parks on the other.

15 The **Slovenska Filharmonija** (Slovenian Philharmonic Hall) was built in 1891 for one of the oldest music societies in the world, established in 1701, among whose associates were Hadyn, Brahms, Beethoven, and Paganini. *Kongresni trg 10,* ☎ *61/311–892.*

16 The spectacular **Zmajski Most** (Dragon's Bridge) has a fire-breathing winged dragon (reputedly descended from the Ljubljana coat of arms) at each of its four corners. ✉ *Resljeva ul.*

Dining and Lodging

$$$ ✕ **Vinoteka.** At the fairgrounds, this fine restaurant offers the best national dishes, such as grilled seafood with lemon, as well as vegetarian food. It also serves a great selection of Slovenian wines. ✉ *Dunajska 18,* ☎ *61/1315015. AE, DC, MC, V. Closed Sun.*

$$ ✕ **Nostalgia.** This restaurant is crammed with relics of former Socialist Yugoslavia and Slovenia; ask your neighbors at other tables to explain the meaning of some of the decorations. ✉ *Stari trg 9,* ☎ *61/222682. No credit cards.*

$$ ✕ **Pivnica Kratchowill (Pub Brewery).** This unpretentious restaurant is next door to the train station and is open until midnight and on Sunday. It serves typical Central European fare: Try the cordon bleu or pork schnitzel with a Union beer. ✉ *Kolodvorska 14,* ☎ *061/1333114. AE, DC, MC, V.*

$$ ✕ **Rotovz.** In the old quarter, this restaurant has tables beneath umbrellas on the cobblestones in summer and serves meals in the dark wood interior in colder weather. Order *pastrmka* (trout) with parsley potatoes or a frog-leg specialty, along with crisp salad and a bottle of first-rate Slovenian wine. ✉ *Mestni trg 2,* ☎ *61/212839. AE, DC, MC, V. Closed Sun.*

$$ ✕ **Spajza.** Tucked into a rose-color building in the old section, this restaurant has the best decor in the city in a winding series of rooms full of color and knickknacks. Excellent food selections may include venison in cognac sauce with fresh asparagus or pasta with mushrooms and zucchini. ✉ *Gornji trg 28,* ☎ *61/1253094. AE, DC, MC, V. Closed Sun.*

$$$$ **Grand Hotel Union.** This turn-of-the-century hotel occupies a magnificent Jugendstil structure. The lobby and the main-floor café have been tastefully renovated, as have the rooms. ✉ *Miklosiceva 1, 1000,* ☎ *061/1254133,* FAX *061/217910. 233 rooms, 6 suites. 2 restaurants. AE, DC, MC, V.*

$$$$ **Holiday Inn.** Close to the center of town, it has excellent views of the castle hill and the surrounding mountains. Pluses include a spacious lobby, enough elevators, and a basement garage. You can also count on a sizable bed with a firm mattress. ✉ *Miklosiceva Cesta 3, 1000,* ☎ *061/1255051,* FAX *061/1250323 . 127 rooms, 6 suites. Restaurant, indoor pool. AE, DC, MC, V.*

$$$$ **Intercontinental Lev.** Convenient to the bus and train station and renovated in 1998, it has modern decor. Pavorotti stayed here during his concert in Ljubljana. ✉ *Vosnjaska 1, 1000,* ☎ *061/1332155,* FAX *061/321994. 147 rooms, 6 suites. Restaurant. AE, DC, MC, V.*

$$$ **Austrotel Kompas.** This small, modern hotel is well managed and has a popular steak restaurant. ✉ *Miklosiceva Cesta 9, 1000,* ☎ *061/1326133,* FAX *061/301181. 62 rooms, 5 suites. Restaurant. AE, DC, MC, V.*

$$$ **Best Western Slon Hotel.** Close to the river, this older hotel was completely renovated in 1996. It is on the site of a famous mid-16th-century inn and maintains an atmosphere of traditional hospitality. The breakfast here is among the finest in the city. The rooms are comfortable but not special. ✉ *Slovenska 34, 1000,* ☎ *061/1701100,* FAX *061/217164. 185 rooms. 2 restaurants. AE, DC, MC, V.*

$$ **Hotel Turist.** The rooms are basic, but this hotel is conveniently in the city center. Service is satisfactory at best. ✉ *Dalmatinova 15, 1000,* ☎ *061/1322343,* FAX *061/319291. 190 rooms. 2 restaurants. AE, DC, MC, V.*

Ljubljana Essentials

Arriving and Departing

BY CAR

☞ Transportation *in* Slovenia A to Z, *above.*

BY PLANE

Ljubljana's airport is at **Brnik** (☎ 064/222700), 22 km (14 mi) north of the city. A shuttle bus runs between the airport and Ljubljana and other nearby destinations.

BY TRAIN

The **train station** (✉ Trg OF, ☎ 61/131–5167), close to the city center, has a tourist information office to help travelers find accommodations in hotels, pensions, and apartments.

Getting Around

BY BUS

In Ljubljana buses run 3 AM–midnight. (☞ Transportation *in* Slovenia A to Z, *above.*)

BY TAXI

☞ Transportation *in* Slovenia A to Z, *above.*

Contacts and Resources

EMBASSIES AND CONSULATES

U.S. Embassy (✉ SI–1000, Prazakova 4, ☎ 061/301485, FAX 61/301401). **Consulate of Canada** (✉ Miklosiceva 19, ☎ 61/1303570, FAX 61/1303575). **British High Commission** (✉ SI–1000, Trg republike 3/IV, ☎ 61/1257191, FAX 61/1250174).

EMERGENCIES

Ambulance, fire brigade (☎ 112). **Police** (☎ 113). **Doctor:** Ljubljana Emergency Medical Services (☎ 61/323060). **Pharmacies:** Open 24 hours (☎ 61/314558).

GUIDED TOURS

Contact the Tourist Office (☞ *below*).

VISITOR INFORMATION

Tourist Office (✉ Kresija building, next to Triple Bridge, ☎ 061/1330111).

WESTERN SLOVENIA

From Ljubljana a toll road (E-63) runs 42 km (26 mi) northwest past Kranj; from there a recently reconditioned road (E-651) takes you to the resorts of Bled and Kranjska Gora. A drive of 52 km (32 mi) west from Ljubljana on the toll road (marked A-10) will bring you to the karst region and to Postojnska Jama, the caves that are among Slovenia's foremost natural attractions. To the southwest, 125 km (78 mi) from Ljubljana (via the A-10), lies the Adriatic Coast. Once under the control of the Republic of Venice, this region has rich vineyards, karst caves, and elegant Venetian cities. The four towns of Koper, Izola, Piran, and Potoroz dominate the 42 km (26 mi) of coastline. Koper is Slovenia's largest port for seagoing vessels and cargo ships. Potoroz and the smaller medieval city of Piran are the resort centers.

Bled

Bled, 50 km (31 mi) northwest of Ljubljana, is among the most magnificently situated mountain resorts in Europe. The healing powers of its thermal springs were known during the 17th century, but most early visitors were pilgrims from within a fairly narrow radius on their way to the little island church in its lake. By the early 19th century the aristocracy arrived to bask in Bled's tranquil Alpine setting.

Since the mid-1970s a spate of new hotels and a wide range of recreational facilities have sprung up in Bled, including an 18-hole golf course. Rowing, hiking, swimming, boating, biking, tennis, and horseback riding are important here. In winter there's skiing and ice skating at the nearby high-altitude resort of Zatrnik.

Blejsko Jezero (Lake Bled), surrounded by forests, is nestled within a rim of mountains, with a castle on one side and a promenade beneath stately chestnut trees on the other. Horse-drawn carriages clip-clop along the promenade while swans glide on the lake. On a minuscule island the lovely **Cerkov Svetega Martina** (St. Martin's) pilgrimage church rises from within a circle of red roofs and trees. Graceful, old-fashioned canopied wooden boats called *pletna,* propelled by oarsmen standing aft, carry passengers to the island.

The stately 16th-century **Grad** (Castle) perches above the lake at the summit of a steep cliff, against the backdrop of the Julian Alps and Mt. Triglav. You can climb up to the castle for fine views of the lake, the resort, and the surrounding countryside. ☎ *64/741–230.* ⏲ *Mar.–Oct., daily 8–7; Nov.–Feb., daily 9–4.*

The **Vintgar Gorge** was cut between precipitous cliffs by the clear river Radovna, which flows down numerous waterfalls and through pools and rapids. The trip in the gorge leads over bridges and along wooden walkways and galleries. ✉ *5 km (3 mi) northeast of Bled on road to Pokljuka/Zg. Gorje.*

$$$ ✕ **Gostilna Lectar.** At this restaurant with a cozy country-inn atmosphere, you can choose from an impressive array of Slovenian national dishes and wines. Try the pumpkin soup, the "peasant's plate" (buckwheat dumplings, mixed smoked meats, potatoes, and fresh steamed vegetables), and the apple strudel topped with handmade apple ice cream, for a cross-section of local cuisine. ✉ *Linhartov trg 2, Radovljica, 9 km/5½ mi south of Bled on Rte. E61,* ☎ *064/715642. AE, DC, MC, V.*

$$$ ✕ **Okarina.** Occupying the street level and expanded courtyard of a home overlooking the lake, Okarina is the best place to dine in Bled. The fresh fish grilled with natural herbs and lemon or truffles in cream sauce over noodles are memorable; the service can become hectic in summer. ✉ *Riklijeva 9,* ☎ *064/741458. AE, DC, MC, V.*

$$ ✕ **Ribic.** At this small restaurant the fish selection is excellent and very fresh. Service is warm and inviting. ✉ *Cesta Svobode 27,* ☎ *064/77866. AE, DC, MC, V.*

$$$$ 🏨 **Vila Bled.** Yugoslavia's late president Tito used this former royal residence on the lake as a hunting lodge. It was converted into a luxurious small-scale hotel in 1984 and became part of the Relais et Chateaux association in 1987. Among the elegant touches are hand-embroidered linen sheets, Art Deco furnishings, antique rugs, Oriental vases, and original art. ✉ *C. Svobode 26, 4260,* ☎ *064/7915,* FAX *064/741320. 10 rooms, 20 suites. Restaurant. AE, DC, MC, V.*

$$$ 🏨 **Grand Hotel Toplice.** This elegant, old-fashioned, ivy-covered resort hotel has been favored by British visitors since the '20s. Directly on the lake, the main building has balconies and big windows that offer dramatic views of the castle and the Julian Alps. The rooms, the lounges, and the bar are all furnished with antiques and heirloom rugs. ✉ *Cesta Svobode 20, 4260,* ☎ *061/7910,* FAX *061/741841. 206 rooms. Restaurant, indoor pool. AE, DC, MC, V.*

$$$ 🏨 **Park Hotel.** This severely modern hotel in the center of the resort faces the lake. Spacious rooms with one glass wall and big balconies look out on the lake and the castle. ✉ *C. Svobode 15, 4260,* ☎ *064/7930,* FAX *064/741505. 215 rooms. Restaurant, indoor pool. AE, DC, MC, V.*

$$–$$$ 🏨 **Golf Hotel.** Set back from the lake, the modern, boxlike structure has unexceptional rooms. In an annex to the hotel, Golf Apartments, under a ski-lodge–style sloping roof, sleep up to five persons each; you can do your own cooking or take meals at the Golf Hotel. ✉ *Cankarjeva 6, 4260,* ☎ *064/7920,* FAX *064/741768. 150 rooms, 60 apartments. Restaurant, outdoor and indoor pools. AE, DC, MC, V.*

Bohinjsko Jezero

A 26-km (16-mi) drive west from Bled will take you to Bohinjsko Jezero (Lake Bohinj) in **Triglavski Narodni Park** (Triglav National Park). In a valley surrounded by the steep walls of the Julian Alps, at an altitude of 1,715 ft, this deep-blue, 4½-km- (3-mi-) long lake is even more dramatically situated than Bled, and not nearly as developed.

At the lakeside, the small, exquisite 15th-century Gothic church of **Sveti Janez** (St. John), with a fine bell tower, contains a number of notable 15th- and 16th-century frescoes.

At the opposite end of the lake a cable car leads up **Mt. Vogel** to a height of 5,035 ft. Here you have spectacular views of the Julian Alps massif and the Bohinj valley and lake. The cable car is old and slow; you may have to wait in line up to two hours to board. From the cable-car base the road continues 5 km (3 mi) beyond the lake to the point where the waters of the Savica make a tremendous leap over a 195-ft waterfall.

Kranjska Gora

Kranjska Gora, 39 km (24 mi) northwest of Bled, is one of the largest winter tourist centers in Slovenia, in the dramatic setting of some of the country's highest peaks. In summer the resort caters mainly to hiking and mountaineering enthusiasts.

A spectacular side trip from Kranjska Gora is the drive over the **Vrsic Pass,** at 5,252 ft, and the descent into the beautiful Soca Valley, winding through the foothills to the west of Mt. Triglav, occasionally plunging into tunnels along the way. You reach the rustic mountain resort of **Bovec** after 44 km (27 mi). From here the road follows the magnificent turquoise-color Soca River (Isonzo, in Italian) running parallel to the border.

Postojnska Jama

The Postojnska Jama (Postojna Caves) are among the largest and most extraordinary caves in the world, with 23 km (14 mi) of labyrinthine underground passageways and chambers on two levels, of which the first 7 km (4½ mi) are easily accessible and illuminated by electric light. The passage by train and on foot takes you through a succession of extraordinary rock formations of rare beauty and color. In keeping with the strangeness of this underground world are the snakelike creatures, the size of a pencil, called Proteus Anguineus, on view in a floodlit aquarium in the Great Hall. Eyeless and colorless because of countless millennia of life in total darkness, the proteus is both fish and mammal, a biological conundrum that can live up to 60 years. The cave temperature averages 8°C (46°F) year-round; in summer it can seem chilly. You can rent woolen cloaks at the entrance. One-and-a-half-hour tours leave every half hour in summer, hourly the rest of the year. ✉ *Jamska c. 30, Postojna,* ☎ *67/25–041.* 🎫 *SIT1,900.* ⏲ *May–Sept., daily 8:30–6; Apr. and Oct., daily 8:30–5; Nov.–Mar., weekdays 9:30–1:30, weekends 9:30–3.*

Skocjanske Jame

The Skocjanske Jame (Skocjan Caves) are included in UNESCO's list of World Natural and Cultural Heritage sites. These caves require walking, but the beauty of the caverns makes the effort worthwhile. One-hour tours leave hourly. ✉ *Matavun 12, 26 km (16 mi) southwest of Postonjska Jama along A–10 and Rte. 10; look for signs;* ☎ *067/60122.* 🎫 *SIT1700.* ⏲ *June–Sept., daily 10–6; May, Apr., Oct., tours daily 10, 1, and 5; Nov.–Mar., tours weekdays 10, weekends 10 and 3.*

Potoroz

Known for its thermal spas, Potoroz has a pleasant Mediterranean climate. Its situation on a south-facing slope keeps the city warm and blocks cold northern air even in winter. In summer vacationers fill the town in pursuit of the pleasures of the sea and the healing spas.

$$$ 🏨 **Hotel Palace.** At this modern hotel resort complex the elegant thermal spa recreation center offers massages and medical treatments. Rooms are comfortable and service professional. ✉ *Obala 45, 6320,*

☎ 066/747380, FAX 066/747002. 150 rooms. Restaurant, outdoor and indoor pools. AE, DC, MC, V.

Piran

★ The medieval walled Venetian city of Piran is the jewel of the Slovenian coast, perched on a small, triangular peninsula pointing into the Adriatic Sea. Its narrow, winding, covered walkways are hardly wider than the span of outstretched arms. The charming inner harbor and grand plaza are crowned by a Romanesque church at the top of a hill.

Western Slovenia Essentials

Getting Around

Passenger ships connect the Slovenian coast (Potoroz) with other ports and cities along the Istrian and Dalmatian coasts and the Adriatic Sea. There are four marinas (Izola, Koper, Piran, and Potoroz) to choose from if you arrive on a private or rented yacht.

Visitor Information

Bled (✉ C. svabode 15, ☎ 64/741122). **Postojna** (Jamska c. 30, ☎ 067/25041). **Potoroz** (✉ Obala 16, ☎ 66/747015).

EASTERN SLOVENIA

Maribor

Eastern Slovenia's chief city is next to the Austrian border, 128 km (79 mi) from Ljubljana. Straddling the Drava River, Maribor was founded during the 11th century under the name Marburg an der Drau (Marburg on the Drava). For centuries it served as a bastion against the repeated tides of Turkish conquest that swept into Central Europe. The old town north of the Drava has retained its pre-20th-century look, with ornate 18th- and 19th-century town houses and patrician palaces typical of Imperial Austria. Traffic-free narrow streets lead down to the riverside, where a number of fine old buildings have recently been restored and much of the waterfront along the former defensive walls outfitted with bars, terrace cafés, restaurants, and boutiques. On the far side of the river, high-rise and industrial Maribor stretches south into the countryside. Beyond the apartment complexes, factories, and smokestacks, this is a land of vineyards and apple orchards.

Along the left bank of the river stands a restored ancient tower, **Sodni Stolp** (Tower of Justice). Near the tower, the facade of the **Stara Trta** (Vojasniska Ulica 8) inn is covered with grapevines said to be the oldest continuously producing vines in Europe, from which a small quantity of wine has been made annually for more than 400 years. Their yearly production is measured at no more than a few gallons, bottled as Somotska Crnina. A second historic tower, **Vodni Stolp** (Water Tower), now houses the **Vinoteka Slovenskih**, the wine shop of the regional wine-producing cooperative, where you can sample and purchase the best of local wines.

One street back from the waterfront, the **Kuzno Znamenje** (Plague Memorial) stands before the 16th-century **Razstavni** (Town Hall; Glavni Trg), which has an unusual Renaissance balcony. A passage through the Town Hall courtyard leads to the **Stolnica** (cathedral) in a small park next to the pedestrian precinct.

The **Grad** (castle) has Renaissance and Baroque elements grafted onto its original Gothic core, built in 1478. The castle houses the **Pokrajinski Muzej** (Regional Museum), with archaeological and ethnographic exhibits, collections of regional costumes and uniforms, Roman relics, an art gallery, and a collection of arms and armor. The main salon, where Franz Liszt gave recitals, is decorated with frescoes and ceiling paintings. ✉ *Grajska ul. 2,* ☎ *062/21851.* ⏲ *Apr. 15–Dec. 1, Tues.–Sat. 9–5, Sun. 10–2.*

$$$ **Best Western Slavija.** This modern white high-rise hotel qualifies as the best by far in Maribor, with a spacious lobby and comfortably decorated rooms. ✉ *Vita Kraigherja 3, 2000,* ☎ *062/213661,* FAX *062/222857. 120 rooms. Restaurant. AE, DC, MC, V.*

$$ **Hotel Orel.** The four-story prewar building on the main square has a pleasant restaurant at street level. The rooms are acceptable and the service is friendly. ✉ *Grajski trg 3a, 2000,* ☎ *062/26171,* FAX *062/28497. 146 rooms, 7 suites. Restaurant. AE, DC, MC, V.*

Ptuj

The small medieval town of Ptuj (pronounced pt-tooey), 25 km (15 mi) southeast of Maribor, began as a powerful Roman military camp. Later it served as a stronghold in the Austrian line of defense against the Turks. The core of this undefeated medieval town is extremely compact, huddled between the wide Drava and the turreted castle above it. The narrow cobblestone streets are crowded with old secular and religious red-roof buildings that have Gothic, Renaissance, and Baroque features.

The gingerbread **Rotovz** (Town Hall), a turn-of-the-century re-creation of an earlier building on this spot, is balanced on the opposite corner of the square by the powerful **Florjanov Spomenik** (Saint Floria Monument). ✉ *Mestni Trg.*

A giant marble 2nd-century tombstone forms the **Orfejev Spomenik** (Orpheus Pillar), its surface carved with scenes from the Orpheus myth. During the Middle Ages the monument served as a pillory. ✉ *Mestni Trg.*

The mighty onion-dome **Mestni Stolp** (Town Tower) has Roman tombstones incorporated into its lower walls. Around the square on which it stands and on adjoining streets are a number of beautifully preserved old patrician residences. ✉ *Slovenski Trg.*

Presernova Ulica, the main artery of the city, lined with historic buildings, winds its way in a gentle curve around the castle hill. It leads past the **Dominikanski Samostan** (Dominican Monastery), with its fine facade, to the town gate, the medieval entrance to the castle.

The **Grad** (castle), surrounded by defensive towers and ramparts, appears more imposing from the outside than from within. A good part of the building has been turned into a museum, with rooms furnished as they were by the last owners, the family of the countess of Herbertstein, who bought the property in 1873 and had the castle thoroughly restored. It has been open to the public since 1945. The Knight's Hall holds a collection of weapons spanning 4 centuries. Visits are in the company of an English-speaking guide. ✉ *Grajska Raven.* ⏲ *Tues.–Sat. 9–noon and 2–5, Sun. 9–noon.*

Ptuj is famous for its **carnival** in the last days before Lent, when the people of the town dress up as Kurent figures (carnival figures symbolizing harbingers of spring) in strange costumes made of long sheepskin coverings, horned headgear, painted leather masks, and cowbells hanging from belts, in a tradition that may go as far back as the 6th century.

Eastern Slovenia Essentials

Visitor Information

Maribor (✉ Glavni trg 15, ☎ 062/211262). **Ptuj** (✉ Slovenski trg 14, ☎ 062/771569).

28 Spain

Madrid, Around Madrid, Barcelona, Moorish Spain, Costa del Sol, Excursion to Morocco, Canary Islands

Spain is much more than flamenco, bullfighting, and white hillside villages—it is soaring cathedrals, narrow lanes twisting through medieval towns, delicious food, spirited nightlife, and great art. Spain's masters range from El Greco, Velázquez, and Goya to Picasso, Miró, and Dalí.

As any Spaniard is quick to point out, Spain is really several countries in one, each with its own proud character, its own distinctive cuisine, and sometimes even its own language. Andalusia, in the south, comes closest to postcard images of Spain: rolling hills dotted with whitewashed villages and olive trees. Andalusia's capital, Seville, is known for flamenco music and dance; for the girls dressed in ruffled polka-dot dresses at its April Fair; and for the solemn processions of penitents during Semana Santa (Holy Week). The region is also marked by its Moorish heritage, and remnants of its Islamic past abound, from the red-and-white striped arches of Córdoba's mosque to Spain's most important monument, Granada's Alhambra Palace. Andalusia is known more for tapas than for gourmet cuisine; provincial specialties include mounds of fried fish and shellfish called *frituras,* olives, cured ham, and the sherries of Jerez. On the Andalusian coast, the famed Costa del Sol, you can join the jet set at Marbella or, if you're feeling adventurous, cross the Strait of Gibraltar to explore northern Morocco.

Spain's vast center is still shaped by its role as a great battlefield for centuries of contests between Moorish and Christian armies. Turreted castles look out over the bleak plains of Castile–La Mancha, the land of Don Quixote, and Castile-Leon, once known as Old Castile. Castile is home to Toledo, where Jews, Moors, and Christians lived and worked together before the Christian Reconquest of the 15th century. The province also has medieval jewels like Segovia; the university city of Salamanca; and the fortress town of Ávila. The people of Castile are as simple, warm, and hearty as their cuisine—huge portions of roast lamb or suckling pig washed down with red wine from the Valdepeñas or Ribera del Duero regions.

At the hub of it all is Madrid, one of the liveliest capitals in Europe. Madrid is the seat of the Spanish government, a center for the national media, and the home of dozens of embassies, but its sophisticated shine is just a veneer. Scratch the surface, and beyond Madrid's designer boutiques and chic restaurants you'll find a simple Castilian town. Life here is lived in cafés and rustic taverns; all it takes to become a local is to duck inside.

Madrid is also a magnet for art lovers, with three world-class museums—the Prado, the Reina Sofía, and the Thyssen-Bornemisza—all along a 1-km (½-mi) stretch of leafy promenade. The city's restaurants serve good food from all of Spain's regions, but are probably best known for their seafood, which arrives daily from the coasts and has earned landlocked Madrid an affectionate reputation as Spain's biggest port.

Catalonia—with a population of 3 million Catalan-speakers—is Spain's richest and most industrial region. Its capital, Barcelona, rivals Madrid for power and is generally regarded as the winner in culture and chic. Barcelona's tree-lined streets, Art Nouveau architecture, and renovated waterfront still gleam from the scouring they received for the 1992 Summer Olympics—an event that not only focused the world's attention on this Mediterranean port, but also provided the city with new museums, sports facilities, and restaurants. The spirit of turn-of-the-century modernist architect Antoni Gaudí lives on both in his Sagrada Familia cathedral, which is still unfinished, and in the Catalans' general passion for stylish design.

Since Franco died in 1975, and since the country joined the European Union in 1986, Spain has been forced to modernize. The most obvious improvements for the traveler are the fast new nationwide network of superhighways and the high-speed AVE train linking Seville and Córdoba to Madrid. Happily, though, Spain's uniqueness has not been tossed aside in the rush toward the 21st century. Fewer Spaniards take a siesta these days, but shops still close at midday, and three-hour lunches are commonplace. Young adults still live with their parents until marriage. Bullfight fans are not giving in to animal-rights activists. And flamenco is making a comeback with young rock-and-rollers.

Most exciting for anyone vacationing in Spain is the Spaniards' insistence on enjoying life. This may mean strolling in the park with the family on a Sunday afternoon, lingering over a weekday lunch, or socializing with friends until dawn. A zest for living life to its fullest is Spain's greatest contribution to Europe.

SPAIN A TO Z

Customs

For details on imports and duty-free limits, *see* Customs & Duties *in* Chapter 1.

Dining

Spain offers a choice of restaurants, tapas bars, and cafés. Restaurants are strictly for lunch and dinner; they do not serve breakfast. Tapas bars are ideal for a glass of wine or beer accompanied by an array of appetizers. Cafés, called *cafeterías,* are basically coffee shops that serve snacks, light meals, tapas, and pastries along with coffee, tea, and alcoholic drinks. They also serve breakfast and are perfect for afternoon tea or a cup of thick, creamy hot chocolate.

MEALTIMES

Mealtimes in Spain are much later than in any other European country. Lunch begins between 1 and 2:30, usually around 2, and around 3 on

Sunday. Dinner is usually available from 8:30 on, but it's more often taken at 10, especially in larger cities and resorts. Lunch, rather than dinner, is the main meal. Tapas bars are busiest between noon and 2 and from 8 PM on. Cafés are usually open from around 8 AM to midnight.

PRECAUTIONS

Tap water is safe to drink in all but the remotest villages. In Madrid tap water is excellent; in Barcelona it's safe and getting tastier. However, most Spaniards drink bottled mineral water; ask for either *agua sin gas* (without bubbles) or *agua con gas* (with bubbles). A good paella should be served only at lunchtime and should be prepared to order (usually 30 minutes); beware paella dinners (tourist traps) or prices that look too good to be true.

RATINGS

Spanish restaurants are officially classified from five forks down to one fork, with most places earning two or three forks. In our rating system, prices are per person and include a first course, main course, and dessert, but not wine or tip. Sales tax (IVA) is usually included in the menu price; check the menu for *IVA incluído* or *IVA no incluído.* When it's not included, an additional 7% will be added to your bill. Most restaurants offer a prix-fixe menu called a *menú del día;* however, this is often offered only at lunch, and at dinner tends to be a reheated version of the same. *Menús* are usually the cheapest way to eat; à la carte dining is more expensive. Service charges are never added to your bill; leave around 10%, less in $ restaurants and bars. Major centers such as Madrid, Barcelona, Marbella, and Seville tend to be a bit more expensive.

CATEGORY	COST
$$$$	over 9,000 ptas.
$$$	6,000 ptas.–9,000 ptas.
$$	3,000 ptas.–6,000 ptas.
$	under 3,000 ptas.

TYPICAL DISHES

Paella—a mixture of saffron-flavored rice with seafood, chicken, sausage, and vegetables—is Spain's national dish. Gazpacho, a cold soup usually made of crushed garlic, tomatoes, and olive oil and garnished with diced vegetables, is a traditional Andalusian dish, served mainly in summer. Galicia and the Basque country are the country's gourmet centers, and both serve outstanding fish and seafood; if you can spend time in these northern provinces, indulge in a *fuente de marisco* (mixed shellfish/seafood platter). Asturias is famous for its *fabadas* (bean stews), cider, and dairy products; Extremadura for its hams and sausages; and Castile for its roasts, especially *cochinillo* (suckling pig), *cordero* (lamb), and *perdiz* (partridge). The best wines are those from the Rioja and Penedés regions. Valdepeñas is a pleasant table wine, and most restaurants serve a perfectly acceptable house wine; ask for *vino de la casa* (say *tinto* for red and *blanco* for white). *Un café solo* is a small, black espresso coffee, and the tasty *café con leche* is coffee with cream, somewhat like *café au lait*. Weaker, black, American-style coffee is hard but not impossible to come by; ask for a *café americano* (watered-down espresso) or instant coffee.

WHAT TO WEAR

In $$$$ and $$$ restaurants, jacket and tie are the norm. Elsewhere, casual dress is appropriate.

Language

Spanish (called Castellano, or Castilian) is not the principal language throughout Spain. The Basques speak Euskera; in Catalonia, you'll hear

Spain (España)

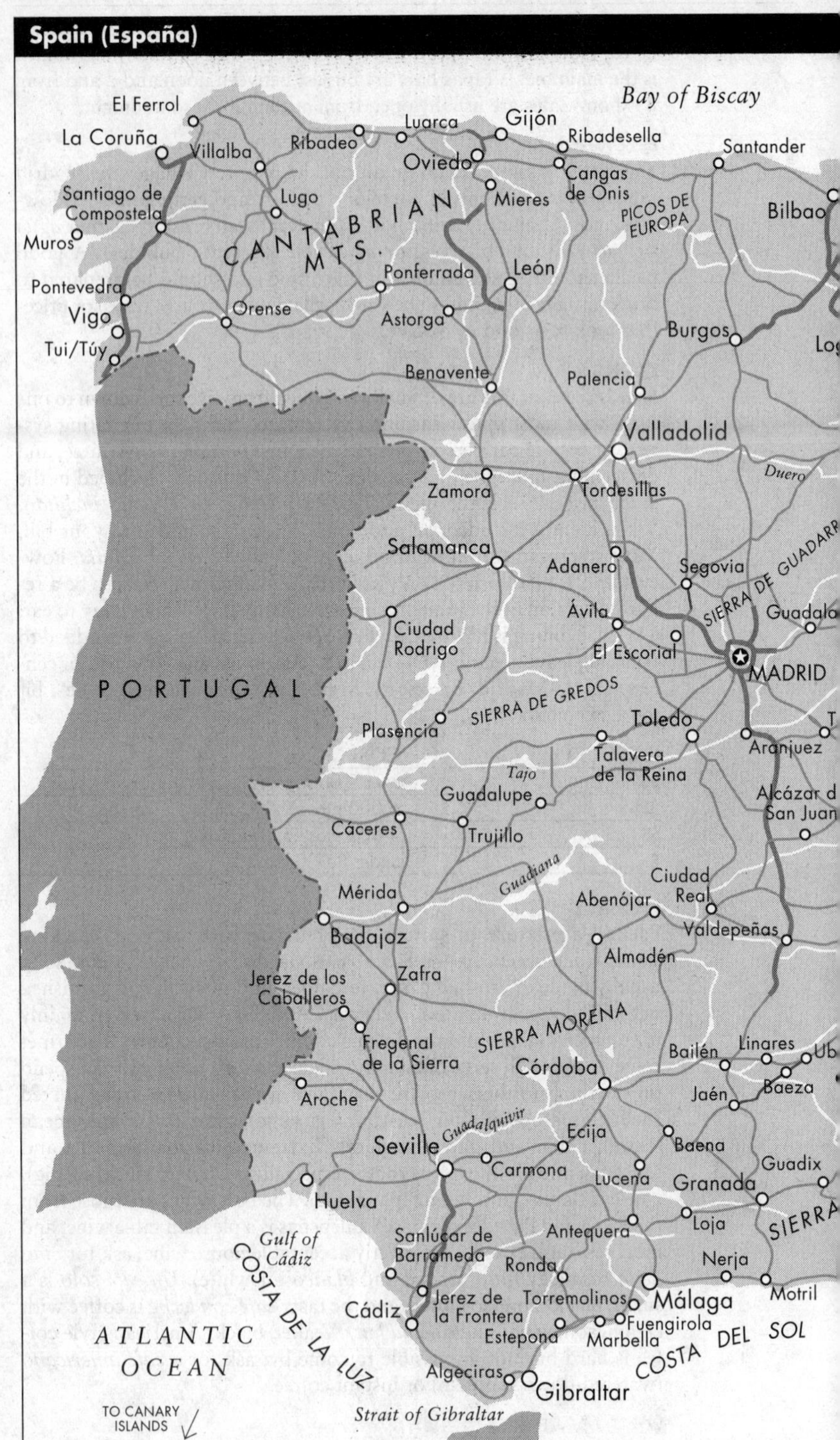

Bay of Biscay
El Ferrol
La Coruña
Villalba
Ribadeo
Luarca
Gijón
Ribadesella
Santander
Oviedo
Cangas de Onis
Mieres
Santiago de Compostela
Lugo
CANTABRIAN MTS.
PICOS DE EUROPA
Bilbao
Muros
Pontevedra
Vigo
Tui/Túy
Orense
Ponferrada
León
Astorga
Burgos
Benavente
Palencia
Valladolid
Duero
Zamora
Tordesillas
Salamanca
Adanero
Segovia
SIERRA DE GUADARRAMA
Ávila
Ciudad Rodrigo
El Escorial
MADRID
PORTUGAL
SIERRA DE GREDOS
Toledo
Plasencia
Talavera de la Reina
Aranjuez
Tajo
Guadalupe
Alcázar de San Juan
Cáceres
Trujillo
Guadiana
Ciudad Real
Mérida
Abenójar
Badajoz
Valdepeñas
Almadén
Jerez de los Caballeros
Zafra
SIERRA MORENA
Fregenal de la Sierra
Bailén
Linares
Córdoba
Baeza
Aroche
Jaén
Guadalquivir
Ecija
Seville
Baena
Guadix
Carmona
Lucena
Granada
Huelva
Antequera
Loja
Gulf of Cádiz
Sanlúcar de Barrameda
Nerja
COSTA DE LA LUZ
Ronda
Motril
Jerez de la Frontera
Torremolinos
Málaga
Cádiz
Fuengirola
Estepona
Marbella
ATLANTIC OCEAN
COSTA DEL SOL
Algeciras
Gibraltar
TO CANARY ISLANDS
Strait of Gibraltar

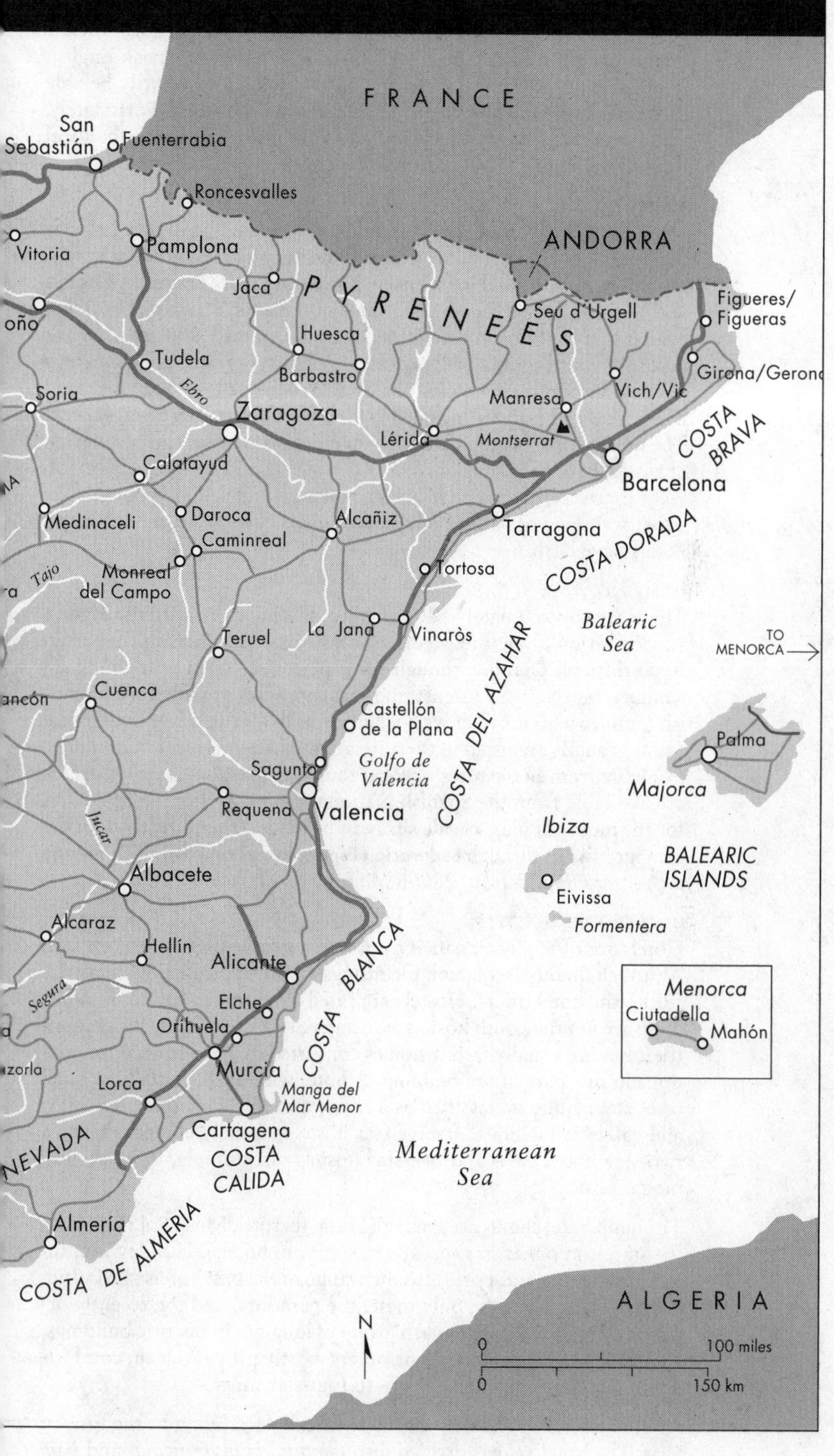
FRANCE
San Sebastián
Fuenterrabia
Roncesvalles
Vitoria
Pamplona
ANDORRA
Jaca
PYRENEES
Seu d'Urgell
Figueres/ Figueras
Huesca
Tudela
Barbastro
Girona/Gerona
Ebro
Soria
Zaragoza
Manresa
Vich/Vic
Lérida
Montserrat
COSTA BRAVA
Barcelona
Calatayud
Medinaceli
Daroca
Alcañiz
Caminreal
Tarragona
Tajo
Monreal del Campo
Tortosa
COSTA DORADA
La Jana
Vinaròs
Balearic Sea
TO MENORCA
Teruel
Cuenca
Castellón de la Plana
COSTA DEL AZAHAR
Palma
Sagunto
Golfo de Valencia
Majorca
Requena
Valencia
Ibiza
Jucar
BALEARIC ISLANDS
Albacete
Eivissa
Formentera
Alcaraz
Hellín
Alicante
COSTA BLANCA
Menorca
Ciutadella
Mahón
Segura
Elche
Orihuela
Murcia
Lorca
Manga del Mar Menor
Cartagena
COSTA CALIDA
Mediterranean Sea
Almería
COSTA DE ALMERIA
ALGERIA
N
0
100 miles
0
150 km

Catalan; and in Galicia, Gallego. However, almost everyone in these regions also speaks and understands Spanish. If your Spanish breaks down, you should have no trouble finding people who speak English in major cities and coastal resorts, but you won't necessarily be able to count on the bus driver or the passerby on the street. Fortunately, Spanish is fairly easy to pick up, and your efforts to speak the local tongue are bound to be graciously received.

Lodging

Spain has a wide range of accommodations, including luxury palaces, medieval monasteries, converted 19th-century houses, modern hotels, coastal high-rises, and inexpensive hostels in family homes. All hotels and hostels are listed with their rates in the annual *Guía de Hoteles,* available from bookstores and kiosks for around 1,200 ptas., or for perusal in local tourist offices. Rates are always quoted per room, not per person. Single occupancy of a double room costs 80% of the usual price. Breakfast is rarely included in the quoted room rate; always check. The quality of rooms, particularly in older properties, can be uneven; always ask to see your room *before* you sign the acceptance slip. If you want a private bathroom in a less expensive hotel, state your preference for shower or bathtub; the latter usually costs more, though many hotels have both.

CAMPING

There are approximately 540 campgrounds in Spain, with the highest concentration along the Mediterranean coast. The season runs from April through October, though some places are open year-round. In summer, especially in August, the best campsites are filled with Spanish families who move in with what seems like their entire household. Campgrounds are listed in the annual publication *Guía de Campings,* available from bookstores or local tourist offices, and further details are available from the Spanish National Tourist Office. Reservations for the most popular seaside sites can be made either directly with the campground or through **Federación Española de Campings,** ✉ *Príncipe de Vergara 85, 2°-dcha, 28006 Madrid,* ☎ *91/562–9994.*

HOTELS AND HOSTELS

Hotels are officially classified from five stars (the highest) to one star. Although quality is a factor, the ratings mainly indicate how many facilities the hotel offers. Hostels are rated from three stars to one star; these are not the youth hostels associated with the word in most countries, but are usually family homes converted to provide accommodations in one part of the building. A hotel with an *R* on its blue hotel or hostel plaque is classified as a *residencia,* and may offer breakfast and cafeteria facilities. A three-star hostel is usually comparable to a two-star hotel; two- and one-star hostels offer simple, basic accommodations.

The main hotel chains are Barceló, Husa, Iberotel, Meliá Sol, Tryp, and the state-run *paradores* (paradors; state-run hotels). Holiday Inn, InterContinental, and Forte also own some of the best hotels in Madrid, Barcelona, and Seville; only these, the paradors, and the recently organized Estancias de España, a group of lodgings in historic buildings, have any special character. The others mostly provide clean, comfortable accommodation in the two- to four-star range.

At many hotels, rates can vary dramatically according to the time of year. The hotel year is divided into *temporada alta, media,* and *baja* (high, mid-, and low season); high season usually covers summer, Easter, and Christmas plus the major fiestas. IVA is rarely included in the quoted room rates, so expect an additional 7% to be added to your bill. Service charges are not included.

PARADORS

Spain has about 100 state-owned and -run paradors, many of which are in magnificent medieval castles or convents. Most of these are relatively luxurious and are priced accordingly. All have restaurants that serve some regional specialties, and you can stop in for a meal or a drink without spending the night. Breakfast, however, is an expensive buffet, and you'll do better to go down the street for a cup of coffee and a roll. Paradors are often booked far in advance; for more information or to make reservations, contact **Paradores** (✉ Requena 3, 28013 Madrid, ☎ 91/516–6666, FAX 91/516–6657), **Marketing Ahead Inc.** (✉ 433 5th Ave., New York, NY 10016, ☎ 212/686–9213 or 800/223–1356, FAX 212/686–0271), or **Keytel International** (✉ 402 Edgware Rd., London W2 1ED, ☎ 0171/402–8182, FAX 0171/724–9503). These firms also have extensive information on—and can reserve—other fine lodgings.

RATINGS

Prices are for two people in a double room, not including breakfast.

CATEGORY	MAJOR CITY	OTHER AREAS*
$$$$	over 20,000 ptas.	over 18,000 ptas.
$$$	14,000 ptas.–20,000 ptas.	12,000 ptas.–18,000 ptas.
$$	9,000 ptas.–14,000 ptas.	7,000 ptas.–12,000 ptas.
$	under 9,000 ptas.	under 7,000 ptas.

**In Gibraltar, $$$: £65–£75 ($104–$120); $$: £40–£46 ($64–$74); not including tax.*

VILLAS

Villas are plentiful all along the Mediterranean coast, and cottages in Cantabria and Asturias on the north coast are available from a few agencies. Several agencies in both the United States and United Kingdom specialize in renting property; check with the Spanish National Tourist Office.

Mail

POSTAL RATES

At press time (spring 1998) the following rates were in effect: To the United States, airmail letters up to 20 grams and postcards each cost 115 ptas. To the United Kingdom and other European countries (both EU and non-EU), letters up to 20 grams and postcards each cost 70 ptas. Within Spain, letters and postcards each cost 35 ptas. Mailboxes are yellow with red stripes; use the slot marked EXTRANJERO for mail going abroad. Buy your *sellos* (stamps) at a *correos* (post office) or in an *estanco* (tobacco shop).

RECEIVING MAIL

Because mail delivery in Spain can be slow and unreliable, it's best to have your mail sent to American Express. An alternative is to have mail held at a Spanish post office; have it addressed to *lista de correos* (poste restante) in a town you'll be visiting. The address should include the name of the province in parentheses—e.g., Marbella (Málaga). You'll need to show your passport to claim your mail. American Express charges $2 per letter for noncardholders.

Money Matters

CHANGING MONEY

The word to look for is CAMBIO (exchange). Most Spanish banks take a 1½% commission, though some less scrupulous places charge more; always check, as rates can vary widely. To change money in a bank, you need your passport and plenty of patience, because filling out the forms takes time. Hotels offer rates lower than banks, but they rarely charge a commission, so you may well break even. Restaurants and stores, with the exception of those catering to the tour-bus trade, generally do not accept payment in dollars or traveler's checks. If you have a credit card with a Personal Identification Number (PIN), you'll most likely be able to get cash advances at cash machines.

COSTS

The days when Spain was the bargain basement of Europe are truly over; the cost of living in Spain is now on a par with that of most other European nations. In recent years, however, currency fluctuations have increased the buying power of visitors from North America and the United Kingdom.

CREDIT CARDS

Most hotels, restaurants, and stores accept payment by credit card. Visa is the most widely accepted card, followed by MasterCard (called EuroCard in Spain). More-expensive establishments may also take American Express and Diners Club.

CURRENCY

Spain's unit of currency is the peseta (pta.). Bills are worth 10,000, 5,000, 2,000, and 1,000 ptas.; coins are worth 500, 200, 100, 50, 25, 10, 5, and 1 pta. At press time (spring 1998), Europe's currency markets were rather unstable; the Spanish exchange rate was about 150 ptas. to the U.S. dollar, 105 ptas. to the Canadian dollar, and 250 ptas. to the pound sterling.

CURRENCY REGULATIONS

Visitors may take any amount of foreign currency in bills or traveler's checks into Spain, as well as any amount of pesetas. When leaving Spain you may take out only 100,000 ptas. per person in Spanish banknotes and foreign currency up to the equivalent of 500,000 ptas., unless you can prove you declared the excess at customs on entering the country.

SAMPLE PRICES

A cup of coffee costs between 125 ptas. (if you're standing) and 150 ptas. (if you're seated); a Coca-Cola, 150 ptas.; a small draft beer, 125 ptas.; a glass of wine in a bar, 100 ptas.; a ham sandwich 300–450 ptas.; a local bus or subway ride 125–200 ptas.; a 1-mi taxi ride, about 400 ptas.

TIPPING

Spaniards appreciate being tipped, but they don't expect American rates. By law, restaurants and hotels are not allowed to add a service charge to your bill, but, confusingly, your bills for both will probably say *servicios e impuestos incluídos* (service and tax included). In restaurants ignore this unhelpful snippet and leave 10% if you've had a full meal. In humbler eateries, bars, and cafés, leave 5%–10%, or round the bill up to the nearest 100 ptas. Tip taxi drivers about 5%–10% when they use the meter, otherwise *nothing*—they'll have seen to it themselves. Train and airport porters usually operate on a fixed rate of 60 ptas.–100 ptas. a bag. Hotel porters get 100 ptas.–150 ptas. for carrying bags, and waiters get the same for bringing room service. If you stay in a hotel for more than two nights, it's customary to tip the maid 100 pts. per night.

National Holidays

January 1; January 6 (Epiphany); Good Friday (April 2); Easter (April 4); May 1 (May Day); July 25 (St. James's Day); August 15 (Assumption); October 12 (National Day); November 1 (All Saints' Day); December 6 (Constitution); December 8 (Immaculate Conception); December 25. Other holidays include May 2 (Madrid Day) and March

19 (St. Joseph's Day); these are not celebrated in every region, so inquire locally.

Opening and Closing Times

Banks are open Monday–Saturday 9–2 from October through June; in summer they are closed on Saturday. Hours for **museums and churches** vary; most are open in the morning, but most museums close one day a week, often Monday. **Stores** are open weekdays from 9 or 10 until 1:30 or 2, then in the afternoon from around 5 to 8. In some cities, especially in summer, stores close on Saturday afternoon.

Shopping

SALES-TAX REFUNDS

Value-added tax, called IVA, is levied on most goods and services; it's 7% at hotels and restaurants (except on the Canary Islands, where it's 4%) and 16% on car rentals. A number of shops, particularly large stores and boutiques in holiday resorts, offer a 16% IVA refund on purchases of over 15,000 ptas.: You show your passport, fill out a form, and the store mails the refund to your home. The receipt must detail the purchase and the amount of IVA, must be signed by both vendor and customer, and must then be sealed. You can also present your original receipt in the IVA office at the airport (the Barcelona and Madrid airports have booths near the duty-free shops); customs signs the original and gives it back to you to mail to the vendor. The vendor then mails you the refund.

Telephoning

COUNTRY CODE

The country code for Spain is 34. When calling Spain from outside the country, drop the initial 9 from the regional code.

INTERNATIONAL CALLS

You can call abroad from any pay phone marked TELÉFONO INTERNACIONAL. Use 50-pta. (or 100-pta., if the phone takes them) coins initially, then coins of any denomination to prolong your call. Dial 07 for international, wait for the tone to change, then dial 1 for the United States, 0101 for Canada, or 44 for the United Kingdom, followed by the area code and number. For lengthy international calls, go to the *telefónica,* a phone office found in all sizable towns: here, an operator assigns you a private booth and collects payment at the end of the call. This is the cheapest and by far the easiest way to call overseas, and you can charge calls costing more than 500 ptas. to your Visa or MasterCard.

LOCAL CALLS

There are three types of pay phones in Spain, all of them bright green or dull blue. The most common kind has a digital readout, so you can see your money ticking away. You need at least 25 ptas. for a local call, 75 ptas. to call another province. Insert coins and wait for a dial tone. (At older models you line coins up in a groove on top of the dial, and they drop down as needed.)

Newer pay phones take only phone cards, which can be purchased at any tobacco shop in denominations of 1,000 or 2,000 ptas.

Note that to call anywhere within Spain—even locally—from any kind of phone, you need to dial the area code first. All provincial codes begin with a 9.

OPERATORS AND INFORMATION

For the operator and information for any part of Spain, dial 003. The international information and assistance operator is at 025 (some operators speak English). If you're in Madrid, dial 008 to make collect calls to countries in Europe; 005 for the rest of the world. Private long-distance companies have special access numbers: **AT&T** (☎ 900/99–00–11), **MCI** (☎ 900/99–00–14), and **Sprint** (☎ 900/99–00–13).

Transportation

BY BUS

Spain has an excellent bus network, but there is no national or nationwide bus company; the network simply consists of numerous *empresas* (private regional bus companies), and there are thus no comprehensive bus passes. Buses tend to be more frequent than trains, are sometimes cheaper, and often allow you to see more of the countryside. Some of the buses on major routes are now quite luxurious, though it's worth mentioning that, although they designate no-smoking seats, it's hard to cordon smoke in a bus; so you may be in for a smokier ride than you're used to. On major routes and at holiday times, it's a good idea to buy your ticket a day or two in advance. Some cities have central bus stations, but in many of these, including Madrid and Barcelona, buses leave from various boarding points; always check with the local tourist office. Unlike train stations, bus stations usually have facilities for luggage storage.

BY CAR

Gasoline. At press time gas cost 120 ptas. per liter for super (octane) and 115 ptas. per liter for regular. *Sin plomo* (unleaded) gas is now available at a steadily increasing number of pumps. Most pumps have attendant service, but there's no need to tip for a simple fill-up. Most gas stations accept credit cards.

Parking. Parking restrictions should be checked locally. In many cities a blue line on the street indicates parking for residents only; other cars are towed promptly. Thefts are common, so it's safer to leave your car in one of the many staffed parking lots; charges are reasonable.

Road Conditions. Roads marked *A* (*autopista*) are toll roads. *N* stands for national or main roads, and C for country roads. Spain's huge road-improvement scheme has been largely completed, but many N roads are still single-lane, and the going can be slow. Tolls vary but are high; for example: Bilbao–Zaragoza 3,010 ptas., Salou–Valencia 2,150 ptas., Seville–Jerez 610 ptas., and Santiago–La Coruña 510 ptas.

Rules of the Road. Driving is on the right. The use of horns and high-beam headlights is forbidden in cities. Front seat belts are compulsory. Children under age 10 may not ride in front seats. At traffic circles, give way to traffic coming from the right unless your road has priority. Your home driver's license is essential and must be carried with you at all times, along with your car insurance and vehicle registration. If you are bringing your own car into Spain, you will also need an International Driving License and a proof-of-insurance Green Card. Speed limits are 120 kph (74 mph) on *autopistas,* 100 kph (62 mph) on N roads, 90 kph (56 mph) on C roads, and 60 kph (37 mph) in cities unless otherwise signposted.

BY PLANE

Iberia and its subsidiary **Aviaco** operate a wide network of domestic flights, linking all of Spain's major cities and the Balearic Islands. Domestic airfares are high by U.S. standards, although deregulation is pushing prices lower. A frequent shuttle service connects Madrid and Barcelona. Iberia has its own offices in most major Spanish cities and acts as agent for Aviaco. In Madrid, Iberia headquarters are at Velázquez 130 (☎ 91/411–1011 for domestic reservations, ☎ 91/329–4353 for international, or call Info-Iberia for flight information, ☎ 91/329–5767). You can also book flights at most travel agencies. **Air Europa** (☎ 91/

305–8159 and 91/559–1500) and **Spanair** (☎ 91/393–6735) offer slightly cheaper service between Madrid and Barcelona as well as flights to the Canary Islands. For information on other airlines' flights to and within Spain, call the airline itself, or call the Madrid airport (☎ 91/305–8343, -44, -45, or -46) and ask for your airline.

BY TRAIN

The Spanish railroad system—usually known by its initials, RENFE—has greatly improved in recent years. It operates several different types of trains—Talgo (ultramodern), electric unit expresses (ELT), diesel rail cars (TER), and ordinary *expresos* and *rápidos*. Fares are determined by the kind of train you travel on as well as the distance traveled. Of the long-distance trains, Talgos are by far the quickest, most comfortable, and most expensive; *expresos* and *rápidos* are the slowest and cheapest. The high-speed Alto Velocidad Español (AVE) runs between Madrid and Seville in just 2½ hours, with a stop in Córdoba; fares vary, but the AVE can cost almost as much as flying. A few lines, such as the narrow-gauge FEVE routes along the north coast from San Sebastián to El Ferrol and on the Costa Blanca around Alicante, do not belong to the national RENFE network and do not accept international rail passes.

The **RENFE Tourist Card,** on sale to anyone who lives outside Spain, buys you unlimited distance over 3, 5, or 10 days' travel. Contact the Spanish National Tourist Office for a list of agencies or call RENFE in Madrid at ☎ 011–34/1–563–0202.

Visitor Information

For the Tourist Office of Spain in your home country, *see* Visitor Information *in* Chapter 1. For general information on travel within Spain, call Turespaña's information line (☎ 901/300600). For regional and city tourist offices, *see* Visitor Information *in* the Essentials directory for the relevant geographic region, *below*.

Weather

The tourist season runs from Easter to mid-October. The best months for sightseeing are May, June, September, and early October, when the weather is usually pleasant and sunny without being unbearably hot. In July and August, try to avoid Madrid and the inland cities of Andalusia, where the heat can be stifling and many places close down at 1 PM. Air conditioning is not widely used. The one exception to Spain's high summer temperatures is the north coast, where the climate is similar to that of northern Europe.

Seasonal events can clog parts of the country, and major fiestas, such as Pamplona's running of the bulls (July 6–15), cause prices to soar. In 1999 Semana Santa (Holy Week) spans the end of March and the beginning of April; this is the time to catch some of Spain's most spectacular fiestas.

CLIMATE

The following are the average daily maximum and minimum temperatures for Madrid.

Jan.	47F	9C	**May**	70F	21C	**Sept.**	77F	25C
	35	2		50	10		57	14
Feb.	52F	11C	**June**	80F	27C	**Oct.**	65F	18C
	36	2		58	15		49	10
Mar.	59F	15C	**July**	87F	31C	**Nov.**	55F	13C
	41	5		63	17		42	5
Apr.	65F	18C	**Aug.**	85F	30C	**Dec.**	48F	9C
	45	7		63	17		36	2

MADRID

Smack in the heart of Spain at 2,120 ft above sea level, Madrid is the highest capital in all of Europe. Fittingly, it is also one of Europe's most vibrant cities. Madrileños are vigorous, joyful people, famous for their apparent ability to defy the need for sleep; they embrace their city's cultural offerings and make enthusiastic use of its cafés and bars. If you can match this energy, you'll take in Madrid's museum mile, with more masterpieces per meter than anywhere else in the world; regal Madrid, with its sumptuous palaces and posh boutiques; medieval Madrid, with its dark, narrow lanes, and Madrid after midnight, where today's action is.

Exploring Madrid

Numbers in the margin correspond to points of interest on the Madrid map.

You can see important parts of the city in one day if you stop only to visit the Prado and Royal Palace. Two days should give you time for browsing. You can begin in the Plaza Atocha (Glorieta del Emperador Carlos V), at the bottom of the Paseo del Prado.

★ 1 **Centro de Arte Reina Sofía** (Queen Sofía Arts Center). Spain's Queen Sofía opened this center in 1986, and it quickly became one of Europe's most dynamic venues—a Spanish rival to Paris's Pompidou Center. A converted hospital, the center houses painting and sculpture, including works by Joan Miró and Salvador Dalí as well as Picasso's *Guernica,* the painting depicting the horrific April 1937 carpet bombing of the Basque country's traditional capital by Nazi warplanes aiding Franco in the Spanish Civil War. ✉ *Main entrance, C. de Santa Isabel 52,* ☎ *91/467–5062.* 🎫 *Free Sat. 2:30–9 and Sun.* ⏲ *Mon., Wed.–Sat. 10–9; Sun. 10–2:30.*

10 **Convento de las Descalzas Reales** (Convent of the Royal Barefoot Nuns). Founded by Juana de Austria, daughter of Charles V, this convent is still in use. Over the centuries, the nuns—daughters of royalty and nobility—have endowed it with an enormous wealth of jewels, religious ornaments, superb Flemish tapestries, and the works of such master painters as Titian and Rubens. A bit off the main track, it's one of Madrid's better-kept secrets. Guided tours in English are led once a day; your ticket includes admission to the nearby, but less interesting, **Convento de la Encarnación.** ✉ *Plaza de las Descalzas,* ☎ *91/559–7404.* ⏲ *Tues.–Thurs., Sat. 10:30–12:30 and 4–5:30; Fri. 10:30–12:30, and Sun. 11–1:30.*

7 **Fuente de la Cibeles** (Cybele's Fountain). Cybele, the Greek goddess of fertility and unofficial emblem of Madrid, languidly rides her lion-drawn chariot here, watched over by the mighty Palacio de Comunicaciónes, a splendidly pompous, cathedral-like post office. Fans of the home football team, Real Madrid, used to celebrate major victories by splashing in the fountain, but police now blockade it during big games. The fountain stands in the center of **Plaza de la Cibeles,** one of Madrid's great landmarks, at the intersection of the city's two main arteries. ✉ *Meeting of Castellana and Calle de Alcalá.*

★ 2 **Museo del Prado** (Prado Museum). On the old cobblestone section of the Paseo del Prado you'll find Madrid's number-one cultural site, one of the world's most important art museums. Plan to spend at least a day here; it takes at least two days to view the museum's treasures properly. Brace yourself for crowds. The greatest treasures—the Velázquez, Murillo, Zurbarán, El Greco, and Goya galleries—are all on the upper floor. Two of the best works are Velázquez's *Surrender of Breda* and his most famous work, *Las Meninas,* awarded a room of its own. The Goya galleries contain the artist's none-too-flattering royal portraits, his exquisitely beautiful *Marquesa de Santa Cruz,* and his famous *Naked Maja* and *Clothed Maja,* for which the 13th duchess of Alba was said to have posed. Goya's most moving works, the *Second of May* and the *Fusillade of Moncloa* or *Third of May,* vividly depict the sufferings of Madrid patriots at the hands of Napoléon's invading troops in 1808. Before you leave, feast your eyes on Hieronymus Bosch's flights of fancy, *Garden of Earthly Delights* and the triptych *The Hay Wagon,* both on the ground floor. ✉ *Paseo del Prado s/n,* ☎ *91/330–2800.* 🎫 *Free Sun.* ⏲ *Tues.–Sat. 9–7, Sun. 9–2.*

❹ **Museo Thyssen-Bornemisza.** Opened in 1992 in the elegantly renovated Villahermosa Palace, this museum has plenty of airy spaces and natural light. The ambitious collection—800 paintings—attempts to trace the history of Western art through examples from each important movement, beginning with 13th-century Italy. Among the museum's gems are the *Portrait of Henry VIII,* by Hans Holbein (purchased from the late Princess Diana's grandfather, who used the money to buy a new Bugatti sports car). Two halls are devoted to the Impressionists and post-Impressionists, with many works by Pissarro as well as Renoir, Monet, Degas, Van Gogh, and Cézanne. The more recent paintings include some terror-filled examples of German expressionism, but these are complemented by some soothing Georgia O'Keeffes and Andrew Wyeths. ✉ *Paseo del Prado 8,* ☎ *91/369–0151.* ⏲ *Tues.–Sun. 10–7.*

★ ⓭ **Palacio Real** (Royal Palace). This magnificent granite-and-limestone pile was begun by Philip V, the first Bourbon king of Spain, who was always homesick for his beloved Versailles and did his best to re-create its opulence and splendor. To judge by the palace's 2,800 rooms, with their lavish rococo decorations, precious carpets, porcelain, timepieces, mirrors, and chandeliers, his efforts were successful. From 1764, when Charles III first moved in, until the coming of the Second Republic and the abdication of Alfonso XIII, in 1931, the Royal Palace proved a very stylish abode for Spanish monarchs; today, King Juan Carlos, who lives in the far less ostentatious Zarzuela Palace outside Madrid, uses it only for official state functions. Allow 1½–2 hours for a visit that includes the Royal Pharmacy and other outbuildings. The **Royal Carriage Museum,** which belongs to the palace, has a separate entrance on Paseo Virgen del Puerto. One of its highlights is the wedding carriage of Alfonso XIII and his English bride, Victoria Eugenia (granddaughter of Queen Victoria), which was damaged by a bomb tossed in the Calle Mayor during the couple's wedding procession in 1906. Another is the chair that carried the gout-stricken Emperor Charles V to his retirement at the remote monastery of Yuste. The museum has been closed for several years for restoration; inquire at the Royal Palace about its reopening. ✉ *Bailén s/n,* ☎ *91/559–7404.* ⏲ *Mon.–Sat. 9:30–5, Sun. 9–3. Closed during official functions.*

★ ❺ **Parque del Retiro** (Retiro Park). Once a royal retreat, Retiro is Madrid's prettiest park. Visit the beautiful rose garden, **La Rosaleda;** enjoy street musicians and magicians; row a boat around El Estanque; and wander past the park's many statues and fountains. Look particularly at the monumental **statue of Alfonso XII,** one of Spain's least notable kings (though you wouldn't think so from the statue's size), or wonder at the **Monument to the Fallen Angel**—Madrid claims the dubious honor of being the only capital to have a statue dedicated to the Devil. The **Palacio de Velázquez** and the beautiful, glass-and-steel **Palacio de**

Centro de Arte Reina Sofía, **1**
Convento de las Descalzas Reales, **10**
Fuente de la Cibeles, **7**
Museo del Prado, **2**
Museo Thyssen-Bornemisza, **4**
Palacio Real, **13**
Parque del Retiro, **5**
Plaza de la Villa, **12**
Plaza Mayor, **11**
Puerta de Alcalá, **6**
Puerta del Sol, **9**
Real Academia de San Fernando, **8**
Ritz, **3**
Teatro Real, **14**

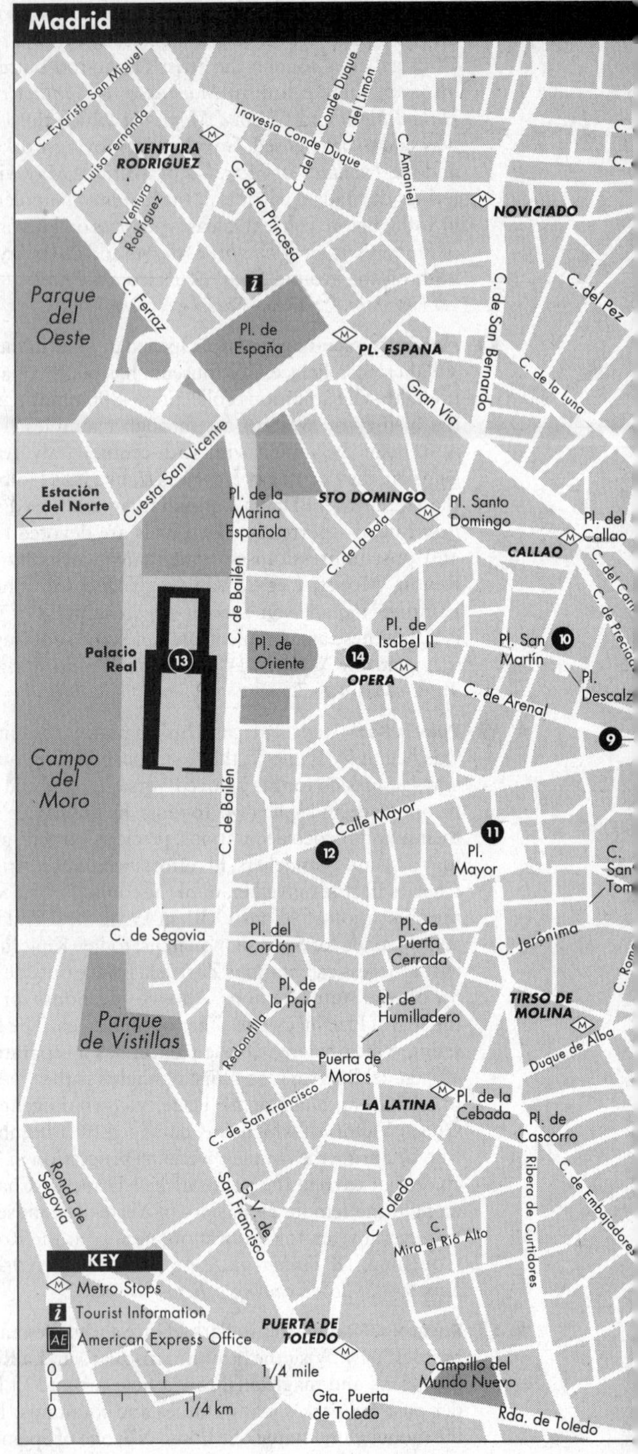

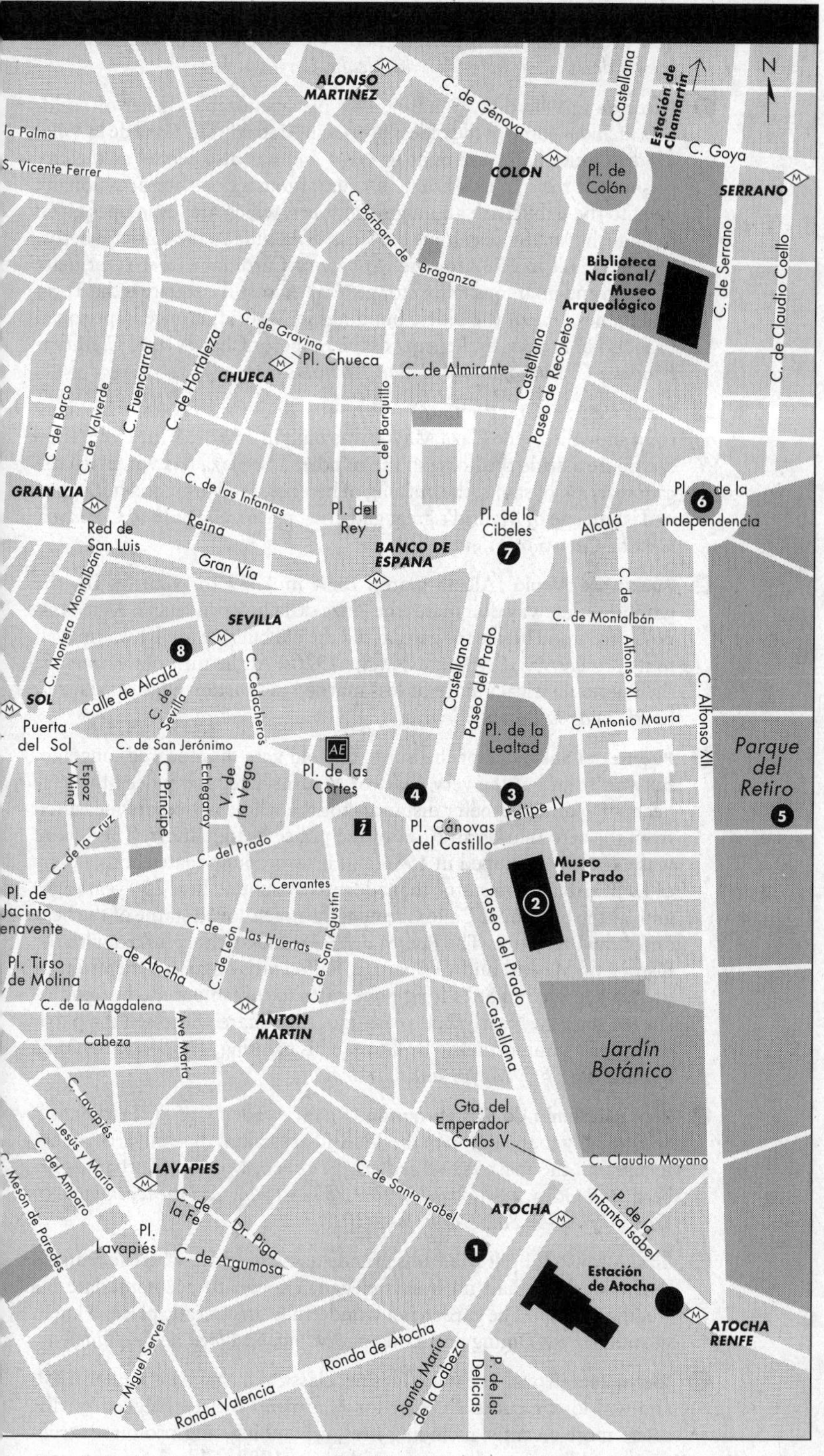
ALONSO MARTINEZ
C. de Génova
Castellana
Estación de Chamartín
N
la Palma
S. Vicente Ferrer
COLON
Pl. de Colón
C. Goya
SERRANO
C. Bárbara de Braganza
Biblioteca Nacional/ Museo Arqueológico
C. de Serrano
C. de Claudio Coello
C. de Gravina
Pl. Chueca
CHUECA
C. de Almirante
Castellana
Paseo de Recoletos
C. del Barco
C. de Valverde
C. Fuencarral
C. de Hortaleza
C. del Barquillo
GRAN VIA
C. de las Infantas
Reina
Pl. del Rey
Pl. de la Cibeles
Alcalá
Pl. de la Independencia
Red de San Luis
BANCO DE ESPANA
Gran Vía
C. Montera Montalbán
SEVILLA
C. de Montalbán
C. de Alfonso XI
C. Cedacheros
Castellana
Paseo del Prado
C. Alfonso XII
SOL
Calle de Alcalá
C. de Sevilla
Puerta del Sol
C. de San Jerónimo
Pl. de la Lealtad
C. Antonio Maura
Parque del Retiro
AE
Pl. de las Cortes
Espoz y Mina
C. Príncipe
Echegaray
V. de la Vega
Felipe IV
C. de la Cruz
Pl. Cánovas del Castillo
C. del Prado
Museo del Prado
Pl. de Jacinto Benavente
C. Cervantes
C. de León
las Huertas
C. de San Agustín
Paseo del Prado
Pl. Tirso de Molina
C. de Atocha
C. de la Magdalena
Ave María
ANTON MARTIN
Castellana
Cabeza
Jardín Botánico
C. Lavapiés
C. Jesús y María
C. del Amparo
Gta. del Emperador Carlos V
C. Claudio Moyano
C. Mesón de Paredes
LAVAPIES
C. de Santa Isabel
C. de la Fe
ATOCHA
P. de la Infanta Isabel
Pl. Lavapiés
Dr. Piga
C. de Argumosa
Estación de Atocha
ATOCHA RENFE
C. Miguel Servet
Ronda de Atocha
Santa María de la Cabeza
P. de las Delicias
Ronda Valencia

Cristal, built as a tropical plant house during the 19th century, now host occasional art exhibits. ✉ *Between C. Alfonso XII and Avda. de Menéndez Pelayo below C. de Alcalá. Daylight hrs.*

12 **Plaza de la Villa** (City Square). This plaza's notable cluster of buildings includes some of the oldest houses in Madrid. The **Casa de la Villa,** Madrid's city hall, was built in 1644 and has also served as the city prison and the mayor's home. Its sumptuous salons are occasionally open to the public; ask about guided tours, which are sometimes given in English. An archway joins the Casa de la Villa to the **Casa Cisneros,** a palace built in 1537 for the nephew of Cardinal Cisneros, primate of Spain and infamous inquisitor general. Across the square is the **Torre de Lujanes,** one of the oldest buildings in Madrid; it once imprisoned Francis I of France, archenemy of the Emperor Charles V. ✉ *C. Mayor between C. Santiago and C. San Nicholas.*

★ 11 **Plaza Mayor** (Great Square). Without a doubt the capital's architectural showpiece, the Plaza Mayor was built in 1617–19 for Philip III—the figure astride the horse in the middle. The plaza has witnessed the canonization of saints, the burning of heretics, fireworks, and bullfights, and is still one of Madrid's great gathering places. ✉ *South of C. Mayor, west of Cava San Miguel.*

6 **Puerta de Alcalá** (Alcalá Gate). Built in 1779 for Charles III, the grandiose gateway dominates the Plaza de la Independencia. A customs post once stood beside the gate, as did the old bullring until it was moved to its present site, Las Ventas, in the 1920s. At the turn of the century, the Puerta de Alcalá more or less marked the eastern edge of Madrid. ✉ *Plaza de la Independencia.*

9 **Puerta del Sol** (Gate of the Sun). The old gate disappeared long ago, but you're still at the very heart of Madrid here, and indeed the very heart of Spain: kilometer distances for the whole nation are measured from the zero marker in front of the police headquarters. The square was expertly revamped in 1986 and now accommodates both a copy of **La Mariblanca** (a statue that adorned a fountain here 250 years ago) and, at the bottom of Calle Carmen, the much-loved statue of the **bear and strawberry tree.** The Puerta del Sol is inextricably linked with the history of Madrid and of Spain; a half century ago, a generation of literati gathered in Sol's long-gone cafés to thrash out the burning issues of the day. Nearly 200 years ago, the square witnessed the patriots' uprising immortalized by Goya in his painting, *The Second of May.* ✉ *Meeting of C. Mayor and C. Alcalá.*

8 **Real Academia de San Fernando** (Royal Academy of St. Ferdinand). Second only to the Prado in the Madrid art stakes, this fine-arts gallery focuses on the masters: Velázquez, El Greco, Murillo, Zurbarán, Ribera, and Goya. ✉ *Alcalá 13,* ☎ *91/532–1546.* 💳 *Free weekends.* ⏲ *Tues.–Fri. 9–9; Sat.–Mon. 9–2:30.*

3 **Ritz.** Alfonso II built Madrid's grande dame in 1910, when he realized that his capital had no hotels elegant enough to accommodate his wedding guests. The garden is a wonderfully aristocratic place to lunch in summer. ☞ Dining and Lodging, *below.* ✉ *Plaza de Lealtad 5.*

14 **Teatro Real** (Royal Theater). This neoclassical theater was built in 1850 and was long a cultural center for *Madrileño* society. Plagued by disasters more recently, including fires, a bombing, and profound structural problems, the house went dark in 1988. Closed for almost a decade for restoration, it reopened to worldwide fanfare in October 1997. Now replete with golden balconies, plush seats, and state-of-the-art stage

equipment for operas and ballets, the theater is a modern showpiece with its vintage appeal intact. ✉ *Plaza de Isabel II.* ☏ *91/516–0606.*

Bullfighting

Madrid's bullfighting season runs from March through October. Fights are held on Sunday and sometimes also on Thursday; starting times vary between 4:30 and 7 PM. The height of taurine spectacle comes with the San Isidro festivals, in May, which usher in three weeks of daily bullfights. The bullring is at **Las Ventas,** formally known as the Plaza de Toros Monumental (✉ Alcalá 237, ☏ 91/356–2200, metro: Ventas). You can buy your ticket here shortly before the fight or, for a 20% surcharge, at the agencies that line Calle Victoria, just off Carrera San Jerónimo and Puerta del Sol.

Dining and Lodging

For details and price-category definitions, *see* Dining *and* Lodging *in* Spain A to Z, *above.* Note that some restaurants in Madrid close for Holy Week.

$$$$ ★ ✕ **Horcher.** In a luxurious mansion at the edge of Retiro Park, this classic restaurant is renowned for its hearty but elegant fare, served with impeccable style in an intimate dining room. Specialties include wild boar, venison, and roast wild duck with almond croquettes. The star appetizer is lobster salad with truffles. Other dishes, such as stroganoff with mustard, pork chops with sauerkraut, and a chocolate-covered fruit-and-cake dessert called *baumkuchen,* reflect the restaurant's German roots. A wide selection of French and German wines rounds out the menu. ✉ *Alfonso XII 6,* ☏ *91/522–0731. Reservations essential. AE, DC, MC, V. Closed Sun. No lunch Sat.*

$$$$ ✕ **Viridiana.** The trendiest of Madrid's haute cuisine restaurants, Viridiana is decorated in black and white and has the relaxed atmosphere of a bistro. Iconoclast chef Abraham García creates a new menu every two weeks, dreaming up such varied fare as red onions stuffed with *morcilla* (black pudding); soft flour tortillas wrapped around marinated fresh tuna; and filet mignon in white-truffle sauce. The tangy grapefruit sherbet for dessert is a marvel. ✉ *Juan de Mena 14,* ☏ *91/531–5222. Reservations essential. AE, MC, V. Closed Sun. and Aug.*

$$$$ ✕ **Zalacaín.** A deep-apricot color scheme, set off by dark wood and gleaming silver, makes this restaurant look like an exclusive villa. Zalacaín introduced nouvelle cuisine to Spain and continues to set the pace after 20 years at the top—splurge on such dishes as prawn salad in avocado vinaigrette, scallops and leeks in Albariño wine, and roast pheasant with truffles. A prix-fixe tasting menu allows you to sample the restaurant's best for about 6,500 ptas. Service is somewhat stuffy. ✉ *Alvarez de Baena 4,* ☏ *91/561–5935. Reservations essential. AE, DC, V. Closed Sun. and Aug. No lunch Sat.*

$$$ ★ ✕ **El Cenador del Prado.** The Cenador's innovative menu has French and Asian touches, as well as exotic Spanish dishes that rarely appear in restaurants. Dine in a baroque salon or a less-formal, plant-filled conservatory. The house specialty is *patatas a la importancia* (sliced potatoes fried in a sauce of garlic, parsley, and clams); other possibilities include shellfish consommé with ginger ravioli, veal and eggplant in béchamel, or wild boar with prunes. For dessert try the *cañas fritas,* a cream-filled pastry once served only at Spanish weddings. ✉ *C. del Prado 4,* ☏ *91/429–1561. AE, DC, MC, V. Closed Sun. and Aug. 1–15. No lunch Sat.*

$$$ ✕ **Gure-Etxea.** In the heart of Old Madrid, on the Plaza de Paja, this is one of the capital's most authentic Basque restaurants. The ground-

floor dining room is airy, high-ceilinged, and elegant; brick walls line the lower level, giving it a rustic, farmhouse feel. As in the Basque country, you are waited on only by women. Classic dishes include *bacalao al pil-pil* (spicy cod fried in garlic and oil—making the "pil-pil" sound), *rape en salsa verde* (monkfish in garlic-and-parsley sauce), and for dessert *leche frita* (fried custard). On weekdays the lunch menu includes a hearty and inexpensive daily special. ✉ *Plaza de Paja 12,* ☎ *91/365–6149. AE, DC, V. Closed Sun. and Aug. No lunch Mon.*

$$$ ✕ **La Trainera.** La Trainera is all about fresh seafood—the best money can buy. This informal restaurant, with its nautical decor and maze of little dining rooms, has reigned as the queen of Madrid's seafood houses for decades. Crab, lobster, shrimp, mussels, and a dozen other types of shellfish are served by weight in *raciones* (large portions). Although many Spanish diners share several plates of these delicacies as their entire meal, the grilled hake, sole, or turbot makes an unbeatable second course. Skip the listless house wine and go for a bottle of Albariño from the cellar. ✉ *Lagasca 60,* ☎ *91/576–8035. AE, MC, V. Closed Sun. and Aug.*

$$ ★ ✕ **Casa Botín.** Just off the Plaza Mayor, Madrid's oldest and most famous restaurant has been catering to diners since 1725. Its decor and food are traditionally Castilian, as are the wood-fire ovens used for cooking. *Cochinillo asado* and *cordero asado* are the specialties. The restaurant was a favorite of Hemingway's and is somewhat touristy, but it's still fun. Try to get a table in the basement or the upstairs dining room. ✉ *Cuchilleros 17,* ☎ *91/366–4217. Reservations essential. AE, DC, MC, V.*

$$ ✕ **Casa Vallejo.** With its homey dining room, friendly staff, creative menu, and reasonable prices, this restaurant is a well-kept secret of Madrid's budget gourmets. To start, try the tomato, zucchini, and cheese tart or the artichokes and clams; then move on to duck breast in prune sauce or meatballs made with lamb, almonds, and pine nuts. The fudge-and-raspberry pie is worth a trip in itself. ✉ *San Lorenzo 9,* ☎ *91/308–6158. Reservations essential. AE, DC, MC, V. Closed Sun. No dinner Mon.*

$$ ★ ✕ **La Gamella.** American-born chef Dick Stephens has created a new reasonably priced menu at this hugely popular spot. The sophisticated rust-red dining room, batik tablecloths, oversize plates, and attentive service remain the same, but much of the nouvelle cuisine has been replaced by more traditional fare, such as chicken in garlic, beef bourguignon, or steak tartare à la Jack Daniels. A few signature dishes—such as sausage-and-red-pepper quiche and, for dessert, bittersweet chocolate pâté—remain, and the lunchtime *menú del día* is a great value at 1,700 ptas. ✉ *Alfonso XII 4,* ☎ *91/532–4509. AE, DC, MC, V. Closed Sun., Mon., and Aug. 15–31. No lunch Sat.*

$$ ✕ **Nabucco.** Had enough Spanish food for the moment? With pastel-washed walls and subtle lighting from gigantic, wrought-iron candelabras, this pizzeria and trattoria is a trendy but elegant haven in gritty Chueca. Fresh bread sticks and garlic olive oil show up within minutes of your arrival. The spinach, ricotta, and walnut ravioli is heavenly, and this may be the only Italian restaurant in Madrid where you can order (California-style?) barbecued-chicken pizza. Considering the ambience and quality, the bill is a pleasant surprise. ✉ *Hortaleza 108,* ☎ *91/310–0611. AE, MC, V.*

$$ ✕ **Nicolas.** One of Madrid's hottest restaurants, Nicolas serves updated versions of traditional Spanish classics in a chic brasserie setting, at reasonable prices. Specialties include garlic soup, a stew of garbanzos and baby squid, sea bass with shrimp, and red peppers stuffed with pork. ✉ *Villalar 4,* ☎ *91/431–7737. AE, DC, MC, V. Closed Sun. and Mon.*

$ ✕ **La Biotika.** A vegetarian's dream, this small, cozy restaurant in the heart of the bar district (just east of Plaza Santa Ana) serves macrobiotic vegetarian cuisine every day of the week. Enormous salads, hearty soups, fresh bread, and creative tofu dishes make dining here a flavorful experience. A small market at the entrance sells macrobiotic groceries. ✉ *Amor de Dios 3,* ☎ *91/429–0780. No credit cards.*

$ ★ ✕ **Casa Mingo.** Resembling an Asturian cider tavern, Casa Mingo is built into a stone wall beneath the Norte train station. It's a bustling place where the only dishes offered are succulent roast chicken, sausages, and salad, all washed down with endless bottles of *sidra* (hard cider). Normally, you'll share long plank tables with other diners; in summer small tables appear on the sidewalk. ✉ *Paseo de la Florida 2,* ☎ *91/547–7918. No credit cards.*

$$$$ **Palace.** Long a favorite with celebrities, this dignified turn-of-the-century hotel opposite parliament and the Prado emerged in 1997 from the most massive renovation in its history. It's as charming and stylish as ever; the Belle Epoque decor—especially the glass dome over the lounge—has always been superb, but now double-glazed windows keep street noise at bay. ✉ *Plaza de las Cortes 7, 28014,* ☎ *91/429–7551,* FAX *91/429–8266. 436 rooms, 20 suites. Restaurant. AE, DC, MC, V.*

$$$$ ★ **Ritz.** Spain's most exclusive hotel is elegant and aristocratic, with beautiful rooms, spacious suites, and sumptuous public salons furnished with antiques and handwoven carpets. The restaurant is justly famous, and the garden terrace is the perfect setting for summer dining. Weekend brunch is accompanied by harp music, and weekend tea or supper by chamber music from February through May. Near the Retiro Park and overlooking the Prado, the Ritz offers unadulterated luxury. ✉ *Plaza Lealtad 5, 28014,* ☎ *91/521–2857,* FAX *91/532–8776. 158 rooms. Restaurant. AE, DC, MC, V.*

$$$$ **Tryp Ambassador.** Once the palace of the Dukes of Granada, this hotel sits on a quiet old street near the Royal Palace. You enter through a magnificent front door backed by a three-story spiral staircase; inside, the rooms are large and luxurious, with separate sleeping and sitting areas. ✉ *Cuesta de Santo Domingo 5, 28013,* ☎ *91/541–6700,* FAX *91/559–1040. 182 rooms. Restaurant. AE, DC, MC, V.*

$$$$ **Villamagna.** Renowned in the early '90s as the favorite of visiting financiers and reclusive rock stars, the Villamagna has been humbled by competition, and its reputation for ultra exclusivity has faded with the decor of its green-and-white lobby. Still, it's one of Madrid's top luxury hotels, its modern facade belying an exquisite interior furnished with 18th-century antiques. Set in a delightful garden, it offers all the amenities you'd expect from an internationally known hotel. ✉ *Paseo de la Castellana 22, 28046,* ☎ *91/576–7500,* FAX *91/575–9504. 164 rooms, 18 suites. Restaurant. AE, DC, MC, V.*

$$$$ **Villa Real.** English antiques and 19th-century Aubusson tapestries set the tone in the lobby of this very personal hotel. The emphasis is on service and luxurious details, such as three telephones in every room and teletext service on TV. Decor in the rooms is somewhat clubby, with leather sofas and dark-red floral fabrics. The hotel looks over the Plaza de las Cortes and is convenient to almost everything. ✉ *Plaza de las Cortes 10, 28014,* ☎ *91/420–3767,* FAX *91/420–2547. 94 rooms, 20 suites. AE, DC, MC, V.*

$$$ **El Prado.** Wedged in among the classic buildings of Old Madrid, this slim hotel is within stumbling distance of Madrid's best bars and nightclubs. Rooms are soundproofed with double-pane glass and are surprisingly spacious. Appointments include pastel floral prints and gleaming marble baths. ✉ *C. Prado 11, 28014,* ☎ *91/429–0234,* FAX *91/429–2829. 47 rooms. AE, DC, MC, V.*

$$$ ★ **Reina Victoria.** One of Madrid's most historic and best-loved hotels, the Reina Victoria faces two of the city's liveliest squares. Once a haven for bullfighters, the hotel now attracts a more upscale clientele, who are treated to large, comfortable rooms with magnificent views. ✉ *Plaza del Angel 7, 28014,* ☎ *91/531–4500,* FAX *91/522-0307. 110 rooms. AE, DC, MC, V.*

$$ **Carlos V.** If you like to be right in the center of things, hang your hat at this classic hotel on a pedestrian street: It's just a few steps away from the Puerta del Sol, Plaza Mayor, and Descalzas Reales convent. A suit of armor guards the tiny lobby, while crystal chandeliers add elegance to the second-floor lounge. All rooms are bright and carpeted, and the price is right. ✉ *Maestro Victoria 5, 28013,* ☎ *91/531–4100,* FAX *91/531–3761. 67 rooms. AE, DC, MC, V.*

$$ **Inglés.** The Inglés is a long-standing budget favorite, once frequented by writers and artists such as Virginia Woolf. Though dreary, the rooms are comfortable enough, and the location is key: You're a short walk from the Puerta del Sol in one direction, the Prado in the other. Inexpensive restaurants and distinctive bars are close at hand. ✉ *Echegaray 10, 28014,* ☎ *91/429–6551,* FAX *91/420–2423. 58 rooms. AE, DC, MC, V.*

$$ ★ **Paris.** You can't get more central than this: for a remarkably fair price, the Paris offers delightful Old World charm right at the corner of the busy Puerta del Sol and Calle de Alcalá. The odd-shape rooms are clean, spacious, and decked out in orange bedspreads and curtains. The lobby is dark, woody, and somehow redolent of times long past. There's no bar, but three meals are served in the bright, second-floor restaurant. All in all, it's an unusual deal. ✉ *Alcalá 2, 28014,* ☎ *91/521–6496,* FAX *91/531–0188. 114 rooms. Restaurant. MC, V.*

$ **Hotel Villar.** All of these rooms are pleasant, clean, and tastefully furnished, with antique beds and armoires, but the real attractions are the eight rooms with balconies. Laden with flowers, the balconies overlook lively Calle Príncipe and have corner views of the Plaza Santa Ana, including the well-heeled crowds arriving at the Teatro Español. The best bargain in the area, Villar is on the second floor of a beautiful old building with a marble foyer and winding staircase. ✉ *Calle Príncipe 18, 28014,* ☎ *91/531–6600,* FAX *91/521-5073. 34 rooms, 18 with bath. AE, DC, MC, V.*

$ **Mora.** Right across the Paseo del Prado from the Botanical Garden, the Mora rewards your journey with a sparkling, faux-marble lobby and bright, carpeted hallways. Rooms are simple but large and comfortable. Those on the street have great views of the garden and Prado through soundproof, double-pane windows. ✉ *Paseo del Prado 32, 28014,* ☎ *91/420–1569,* FAX *91/420–0564. 61 rooms. AE, DC, MC, V.*

Nightlife and the Arts

The Arts

Details of all cultural events are listed in the daily newspaper *El País* or in the weekly *Guía del Ocio.*

CONCERTS AND OPERA

Madrid's main concert hall is the **Auditorio Nacional de Madrid** (✉ Príncipe de Vergara 146, ☎ 91/337–0100, metro: Cruz del Rayo). For ballet or opera, catch a performance at the legendary **Teatro Real** (✉ Plaza de Isabel II, ☎ 91/516-0606), whose splendid facade dominates the Plaza de Oriente. After a lengthy restoration the theater reopened on a grand scale in October 1997 (☞ Exploring, *above*).

FILM

Foreign films are mostly dubbed into Spanish, but movies in English are listed in *El País* or *Guía del Ocio* under "VO" (*versión original*). A dozen or so theaters now show films in English. **Alphaville** (✉ Martín de los Heroes 14, off Plaza España, ☎ 91/559–3836) and **Cines Renoir** (✉ Martín de los Heroes 12, off Plaza España, ☎ 91/559–5760) are good bets for VO films. The **Filmoteca** (✉ Santa Isabel 3, ☎ 91/369–1125) is a city-run institution showing different classic VO films every day.

THEATER

If language is no problem, check out the fringe theaters in Lavapiés and the Centro Cultural de la Villa (☎ 91/575–6080), beneath the Plaza Colón, and the open-air events in Retiro Park. The **Círculo de Bellas Artes** (✉ Marqués de Casa Riera 2, off Alcalá 42, ☎ 91/531–7700) is a leading theater. The **Teatro Español** (✉ Príncipe 25 on Plaza Santa Ana, ☎ 91/429–6297) stages Spanish classics. The **Teatro María Guerrero** (✉ Tamayo y Baus 4, ☎ 91/319–4769), the home of the Centro Dramático Nacional, stages plays by García Lorca. Most theaters have two curtains, at 7PM and 10:30 PM, and close on Monday. Tickets are inexpensive and often easy to come by on the night of the performance.

ZARZUELA

Zarzuela, a combination of light opera and dance that's ideal for non–Spanish speakers, is performed at the **Teatro Nacional Lírico de la Zarzuela** (✉ Jovellanos 4, ☎ 91/524–5400). The season runs from October through July.

Nightlife

BARS AND CAFÉS

Mesónes. The most traditional and colorful taverns are on Cuchilleros and Cava San Miguel, just west of Plaza Mayor, where you'll find a whole array of *mesónes* with such names as Tortilla, Champiñón, and Boqueron.

Old Madrid. Wander the narrow streets between Puerta del Sol and Plaza Santa Ana—most are packed with traditional tapas bars. The **Cervecería Alemana** (✉ Plaza Santa Ana 6, ☎ 91/429–7033) is a beer hall founded over 100 years ago by Germans and patronized, inevitably, by Ernest Hemingway. **Los Gabrieles** (✉ Echegaray 17, ☎ 91/429–6261) has magnificent ceramic decor and becomes something of a disco late at night. For a more tranquil atmosphere try **Viva Madrid** (✉ Fernández y González 7, ☎ 91/429–3640), a lovely old bar.

Calle Huertas. This street is lined with fashionable bars with turn-of-the-century decor and guitar or chamber music, often live. **La Fídula** (✉ Calle Huertas 57, ☎ 91/429–2947) is one of the best. **Casa Alberto** (✉ Calle Huertas 18) is a quieter tavern with brick walls, a good selection of draft beers, and tapas in the early evening.

Plaza Santa Bárbara. This area just off Alonso Martínez is packed with fashionable bars and beer halls. Stroll along Santa Teresa, Orellana, Campoamor, or Fernando VI and take your pick. The **Cervecería Santa Bárbara** (☎ 91/319–0449), in the plaza itself, is one of the most colorful, a popular beer hall with a good range of tapas.

Cafés. Madrid has no lack of old-fashioned cafés, with dark-wood counters, brass pumps, marble-top tables, and plenty of atmosphere. **Café Comercial** (✉ Glorieta de Bilbao 7, ☎ 91/521–5655) is a typical spot in the classic style. **Café Gijón** (✉ Paseo de Recoletos 21, ☎ 91/521–5425) is a former literary hangout and the most famous of the old cafés; it's now just one of many terrace cafés that line the Castellana. **Café León** (✉ Alcalá 57) is just up from Cibeles. **El Espejo** (✉ Paseo de Recoletos 31, ☎ 91/308–2347) has art-nouveau decor and an outdoor terrace in summer. For a late-night coffee, or something stronger, stop in at the baroque **Palacio de Gaviria** (✉ Arenal 9, ☎ 91/526–8089), a restored 19th-century palace on a tawdry commercial street. It allegedly once housed an unofficial royal consort.

CABARET

Florida Park (☎ 91/573–7805), in Retiro Park, offers dinner and a show with ballet, flamenco, or Spanish dance; it is open Monday–Saturday from 9:30 PM (shows are at 10:45 PM). **Berlin** (✉ Costanilla de San Pedro 11, ☎ 91/366–2034) opens at 9:30 for a dinner that's tasty by most cabaret standards, followed by a show and dancing until 4 AM. **La Scala** (✉ Rosario Pino 7, ☎ 91/571–4411), in the hotel Meliá Castilla, is Madrid's finest nightclub, with dinner, dancing, cabaret at 8:30 and a second, less expensive show around midnight. Most night tours hit this club.

DISCOS AND NIGHTCLUBS

Nightlife—or *la marcha,* as the Spanish fondly call it—reaches legendary heights in Spain's capital. Smart, trendy dance clubs filled with well-heeled Madrileños are everywhere. For more adventurous exploring, try the scruffy bar district in Malasaña, around the Plaza Dos de Mayo, where smoke-filled hangouts line Calle San Vicente Ferrer, or the notorious haunts of Chueca, where tattoo studios and street-chic boutiques break up the endless alleys of techno and after-hours clubs.

Amadis (✉ Covarrubias 42, under the Luchana Cinema, ☎ 91/446–0036) has telephones on every table, encouraging people to call each other with invitations to dance. You must be over 25 to enter. The well-heeled crowd likes **Archy's** (✉ Marqués de Riscal 11, ☎ 91/308–3162). Salsa has become a fixture in Madrid; check out the most spectacular moves at **Azucar** (Sugar; ✉ Paseo Reina Cristina 7, ☎ 91/501–6107). Madrid's hippest new club is a three-story bar, disco, and cabaret called **Bagelus** (✉ María de Molina 25, ☎ 91/561–6100). **Joy Eslava** (✉ Arenal 11, ☎ 91/366–3733), a downtown disco in a converted theater, is an old standby. **Pacha** (✉ Barceló 11, ☎ 91/466–0137), one of Spain's infamous chain discos, is always energetic. **Siroco** (✉ San Dimas 3, ☎ 91/593–3070) offers two different types of music Tuesday through Saturday: live Spanish pop downstairs, disco and acid jazz upstairs. **Space of Sound** (✉ Plz. Estacion de Chamartin, in the train station, ☎ 91/733-3505) almost fails to qualify as a nightclub: it's open Saturday and Sunday mornings from dawn until noon, full of drag queens and club kids who refuse to let the night end. **Torero** (✉ Cruz 26, ☎ 91/523–1129) is for the beautiful people—quite literally: a bouncer allows only those judged *gente guapa* (beautiful people) to enter.

FLAMENCO

Madrid offers an array of flamenco shows. Some are good, but many are aimed at the tourist trade. Dinner tends to be mediocre and overpriced, but it ensures the best seats; otherwise, opt for the show and a *consumición* (drink) only, usually starting around 11 PM and costing 3,000 ptas.–3,500 ptas. **Arco de Cuchilleros** (✉ Cuchilleros 7, ☎ 91/364–0263) is one of the better and cheaper venues. **Café de Chinitas** (✉ Torija 7, ☎ 91/559–5135) is reasonably authentic. **Casa Patas** (✉ Canizares 10, ☎ 91/369–0496) is a major showplace; it offers good, if somewhat touristy, flamenco and tapas to boot, all at reasonable prices. **Corral de la Morería** (✉ Morería 17, ☎ 91/365–8446) serves dinner à la carte and invites well-known flamenco stars to perform with the resident group. Since the Corral opened its doors in 1956, visiting celebrities such as the late Frank Sinatra and Ava Gardner have left their autographed photos for the walls.

JAZZ CLUBS

The city's best-known jazz venue is **Café Central** (✉ Plaza de Angel 10, ☎ 91/369–4143). **Café del Foro** (✉ San Andrés 38, ☎ 91/445–3752) is a friendly club with live music nightly. Another well-known spot is **Clamores** (✉ Albuquerque 14, ☎ 91/445–7938). **Populart** (✉ Huertas 22, ☎ 91/429–8407) features blues, Brazilian music, and salsa. Seasonal citywide festivals also present excellent artists; check the local press for listings and venues.

Shopping

The main shopping area in central Madrid surrounds the pedestrian streets Preciados and Montera, off the Gran Vía between Puerta del Sol and Plaza Callao. The **Salamanca** district, just off the Plaza de Colón, bordered roughly by Serrano, Goya, and Conde de Peñalver, is more elegant and expensive; just west of Salamanca, the shops on and around Calle Argensola, just south of Calle Génova, are on their way upmarket. Calle Mayor and the streets to the east of Plaza Mayor are lined with fascinating old-fashioned stores straight out of the 19th century.

Antiques

The main areas for antiques are the Plaza de las Cortes, the Carrera San Jerónimo, and the Rastro flea market, along the Ribera de Curtidores and the courtyards just off it.

Boutiques

Calle Serrano has the widest selection of smart boutiques and designer fashions—think Prada, Armani, and Donna Karan New York, as well as renowned Spanish designers such as Josep Font-Luz Diaz. Worth special trips are several posh boutiques. **Seseña** (✉ De la Cruz 23, ☎ 91/531–6840), has outfitted Hollywood stars (and Hillary Rodham Clintón) since the turn of the century. **Sybilla** (✉ Jorge Juan 12, ☎ 91/578–1322) is the studio of Spain's best-known woman designer, whose fluid dresses and hand-knit sweaters in natural colors and fabrics have made her a favorite with model Helena Christensen. **Adolfo Dóminguez** (✉ Serrano 96, ☎ 91/576–7053; ✉ C. Orense, ☎ 91/576–0084), one of Spain's top designers, has several boutiques in Madrid. **Loewe** (✉ Serrano 26, ☎ 91/577–6056; ✉ Gran Vía 8, ☎ 91/522–6815) is Spain's most prestigious leather store.

Several upscale shopping centers group a variety of exclusive shops stocked with unusual clothes and gifts: **Galerías del Prado** (✉ Plaza de las Cortes 7, on the lower level of the Palace Hotel); **Los Jardines de Serrano** (✉ corner of Calle Goya and Claudio Coello); and **Centro Comercial ABC** (✉ Paseo de la Castellana 34). South of the city center an old factory building has been transformed into the ultraslick, government-subsidized **Mercado Puerta de Toledo** (✉ Ronda de Toledo 1). For street-chic fashion closer to medieval Madrid, check out the window displays at the **Madrid Fusion Centro de Moda** (✉ Plaza Tirso de Molina, 15, ☎ 91/369–0018), where up-and-coming Spanish labels like Instinto, Kika, and Extart fill five floors with faux furs, funky jewelry, and the city's most eccentric selection of shoes.

Department Stores

El Corte Inglés (✉ Preciados 3, ☎ 91/532–8100; ✉ Goya 76, ☎ 91/577–7171; ✉ Goya 87, ☎ 91/432–9300; ✉ Princesa 42, ☎ 91/542–4800; ✉ Serrano 47, ☎ 91/432–5490; ✉ La Vaguada Mall, ☎ 91/387–4000; ✉ Parquesur Mall, ☎ 91/558–4400; ✉ Raimundo Fernández Villaverde 79, ☎ 91/556–2300) is Spain's biggest, brightest, and most successful chain store. **Marks & Spencer** (✉ C. Serrano 52,

☎ 91/431–6760), a British department store, specializes in woolen goods, underwear, and gourmet foods.

Food and Flea Markets

The **Rastro,** Madrid's most famous flea market, operates on Sunday from 9 to 2 around the Plaza del Cascorro and the Ribera de Curtidores. A **stamp and coin market** is held on Sunday morning in the Plaza Mayor. Mornings, take a look at the colorful food stalls inside the 19th-century glass-and-steel **San Miguel** market, also near the Plaza Mayor. There's a **secondhand-book market** most days on the Cuesta Claudio Moyano, near Atocha Station.

Gift Ideas

No special crafts are associated with Madrid itself, but traditional Spanish goods are sold in many stores. El Corte Inglés (☞ *above*) stocks a good selection of Lladró **porcelain,** as do several specialty shops on the Gran Vía and the Plaza de España, behind the Plaza Hotel. Department stores stock good displays of **fans,** but for superb examples, try the long-established Casa Diego, in Puerta del Sol. Two stores opposite the Prado on Plaza Cánovas del Castillo, Artesanía Toledana and El Escudo de Toledo, have a wide selection of **souvenirs,** especially Toledo swords, inlaid marquetry ware, and pottery. Carefully selected **handicrafts** from all over Spain—ceramics, furniture, glassware, rugs, embroidery, and more—are sold at **Artespaña** (✉ Hermosilla 14, ☎ 91/435–0221).

Madrid Essentials

Arriving and Departing

BY BUS

Madrid has no central bus station. Check with the tourist office for departure points for your destination. The **Estación del Sur** (✉ Canarias 17, ☎ 91/468–4200, metro: Palos de la Frontera) serves Toledo, La Mancha, Alicante, and Andalucía. **Auto-Rés** (✉ Plaza Conde de Casal 6, ☎ 91/551–7200, metro: Conde de Casal) serves Extremadura, Cuenca, Salamanca, Valladolid, Valencia, and Zamora. Auto-Rés has a central ticket and information office at Salud 19 (☎ 91/551–7200), just off Gran Vía, near the Hotel Arosa. The Basque country and most of north-central Spain are served by **Auto Continental** (✉ Alenza 20, ☎ 91/533–0400, metro: Ríos Rosas). For Àvila, Segovia, and La Granja, use **Empresa La Sepulvedana** (✉ Paseo de la Florida 11, ☎ 91/530–4800, metro: Norte). **Empresa Herranz** (✉ Calle Fernández de los Ríos s/n, ☎ 91/543–8167, metro: Moncloa) serves El Escorial and the Valley of the Fallen. **La Veloz** (✉ Avda. Mediterraneo 49, ☎ 91/409–7602, metro: Conde de Casal) serves Chinchón.

BY CAR

The main roads are: north–south, the Paseo de la Castellana and Paseo del Prado; east–west, Calle de Alcalá, Gran Vía, and Calle de la Princesa. The M30 ring road circles Madrid, and the M40 is an outer ring road about 12 km (7 mi) further from the city. For Burgos and France, drive north up the Castellana and follow the signs for the N I. For Barcelona, head up the Castellana to Plaza Dr. Marañón, then right onto María de Molina and the N II; for Andalusia and Toledo, head south down Paseo del Prado, then follow the signs to the N IV and N401, respectively. For Segovia, Ávila, and El Escorial, head west along Princesa to Avenida Puerta de Hierro and onto the N VI–La Coruña.

BY PLANE

All international and domestic flights arrive at Madrid's Barajas Airport (☎ 91/305–8343), 16 km (10 mi) northeast of town just off the N II Barcelona highway. For information on arrival and departure times, call **Info-Iberia** (☎ 91/329–5767) or the airline concerned (☞ Air Travel *in* Chapter 1).

Between the Airport and Downtown. Buses leave the national and international terminals every 15 minutes from 5:40 AM to 2 AM for the downtown bus terminal at Plaza de Colón, just off the Paseo de la Castellana. The ride takes about 20 minutes, and the fare at press time was 450 ptas. Most city hotels are then only a short taxi or metro ride away. The fastest and most expensive route into town is by taxi (usually about 1,500 ptas., but up to 2,000 ptas. plus tip in traffic). Pay the metered amount plus the 350-pta. surcharge and 150 ptas. for each suitcase. By car take the N II (which becomes Avenida de América) into town, then head straight into Calle María de Molina and left on either Calle Serrano or the Castellana.

BY TRAIN

Madrid has three railroad stations. **Chamartín** (✉ Avda. Pío XII), in the northern suburbs beyond the Plaza de Castilla, is the main station, with trains to France and the north (including Barcelona, Ávila, Salamanca, Santiago, and La Coruña). Most trains to Valencia, Alicante, and Andalusia leave from Chamartín but stop at Atocha station as well. **Atocha station** (✉ Glorieta del Emperador Carlos V, southern end of Paseo del Prado) sends trains to Segovia, Toledo, Granada, Extremadura, and Lisbon. A convenient metro stop (Atocha RENFE) connects the Atocha rail station to the city subway system. The old Atocha station, designed by Eiffel, is Madrid's terminal for high-speed AVE service to Córdoba and Seville. **Norte** (or Príncipe Pío; ✉ Paseo de la Florida, above Campo del Moro) serves the residential suburbs.

For all train information call or visit the **RENFE offices** (✉ Alcalá 44, ☎ 91/563–0202 Spanish; 91/328–9020 English, if speaker is available; ⏲ weekdays 9:30–8). There's another RENFE office in the International Arrivals Hall at Barajas Airport, or you can purchase tickets at any of the three main stations or from travel agents displaying the blue and yellow RENFE sign.

Getting Around

Madrid is a fairly compact city, and most of the main sights can be visited on foot. If you're staying in one of the modern hotels in northern Madrid, however, off the Castellana, you may need to use the bus or subway. Some rough guidelines: the walk from the Prado to the Royal Palace at a comfortable sightseeing pace, but without stopping, takes around 30 minutes; from Plaza del Callao on Gran Vía to the Plaza Mayor, about 15 minutes.

BY BUS

City buses are red and generally run from 6 AM to midnight (some stop earlier). The flat fare is 130 ptas. Route plans are displayed at *paradas* (bus stops), and a map of the entire system is available from Empresa Municipal de Transportes (EMT) booths on Plaza de la Cibeles, Callao, or Puerta del Sol. You can save money by buying a **Bonobus** (660 ptas.), good for 10 rides, from EMT booths or any tobacco shop.

BY METRO

The metro offers the simplest and quickest means of transport and operates from 6 AM to 1:30 AM. Metro maps are available from ticket offices, hotels, and tourist offices. The flat fare at press time was 130 ptas. a ride; a 10-ride ticket, 660 ptas. Carry some change (5, 25, 50, and 100 ptas.) for the ticket machines, especially after 10 PM; the machines make change and allow you to skip long ticket lines.

BY TAXI

Madrid has more than 18,000 taxicabs, and fares are low by New York or London standards. The meter starts at 170 ptas.; each additional km (½ mi) costs 70 ptas. The average city ride costs about 500 ptas., and there is a surcharge of 150 ptas. between 11 PM and 6 AM and on holidays. A supplemental fare of 150 ptas. applies to trips to the bullring or football matches, and there is an additional charge of 150 ptas. per suitcase. The airport surcharge is 350 ptas. Cabs available for hire display a LIBRE sign during the day and a green light at night. They hold four passengers. Make sure the driver turns the meter on when you start your ride; tip 5%–10% of the fare. To radio a cab call **Tele-Taxi** (☎ 91/445–9008 or 91/448–4259).

Contacts and Resources

EMBASSIES

United States (✉ Serrano 75, ☎ 91/577–4000). **Australia** (✉ Paseo de la Castellana 143, ☎ 91/579–0428). **Canada** (✉ Núñez de Balboa 35, ☎ 91/431–4300). **New Zealand** (✉ Plaza de La Lealtad 2, ☎ 91/523–0226). **United Kingdom** (✉ Fernando el Santo 16, ☎ 91/319–0200).

EMERGENCIES

112 is the **general emergency number** in all E.U. nations (akin to 911 in the U.S.). **Police** (emergencies, ☎ 091; Municipal Police, ☎ 092 for towed cars or traffic accidents). **Ambulance** (☎ 061, 91/522–2222 or 91/588–4400). **Emergency clinics:** Hospital 12 de Octubre (☎ 91/390–8000), La Paz Ciudad Sanitaria (☎ 91/358–2600). **English-speaking doctors:** British-American Medical Unit (☎ 91/435–1823). **Pharmacies:** List of pharmacies open 24 hours (*farmacias de guardia*) published daily in El País.

ENGLISH-LANGUAGE BOOKS

Booksellers (✉ José Abascal 48, ☎ 91/442–8104). **The International Bookshop** (✉ Campomanes 13, ☎ 91/541–7291). **Turner's English Bookshop** (✉ Génova 3, ☎ 91/319–0926).

GUIDED TOURS

Orientation. Julià Tours (✉ Gran Vía 68, ☎ 91/559–9605). **Pullmantur** (✉ Plaza de Oriente 8, ☎ 91/541–1807). **Trapsatur** (✉ San Bernardo 23, ☎ 91/302–6039). All three run the same tours, conducted in Spanish and English. Reserve directly with the offices above, through any travel agent, or through your hotel. Departure points are the addresses above, though you can often arrange to be picked up at your hotel. Tours leave in morning, afternoon, and evening and cover various selections of sites and activities. Trapsatur also runs the Madridvision bus, which makes a one-hour tour of the city with recorded commentary in English. No reservation is necessary; catch the bus in front of the Prado every 1½ hours beginning at 10 AM, from Tuesday through Sunday. There are no buses on Sunday afternoon. A round-trip ticket costs 1,500 ptas., and a two-day pass, 2,200 ptas. If you want a personal tour with a local guide, contact the **Asociación Profesional de Informadores** (✉ Ferraz 82, ☎ 91/542–1214 or 91/541–1221).

Walking and Special-Interest. The **ayuntamiento** (city hall) has a popular selection of Spanish bus and walking tours under the title "Discubre Madrid." Walking tours depart most mornings and visit many hidden corners as well as major sights; options include "Madrid's Railroads," "Medicine in Madrid," "Goya's Madrid," and "Commerce and Finance in Madrid." Schedules are listed in the "Discubre Madrid" leaflet available from the municipal tourist office. Tickets can be purchased at the Patronato de Turismo (✉ C. Mayor 69, ☎ 91/588–2906).

Excursions. Julià Tours, Pullmantur, and **Trapsatur** (☞ *above*) run full- or half-day trips to El Escorial, Ávila, Segovia, Toledo, and Aranjuez, and in summer to Cuenca and Salamanca. Summer weekends, the popular *Tren de la Fresa* (Strawberry Train) takes passengers from the old Delicias Station to Aranjuez (known for its production of strawberries) on a 19th-century train. Tickets can be obtained from RENFE offices (☞ Arriving and Departing by Train, *above*), travel agents, and the Delicias Station (⊠ Paseo de las Delicias 61). Other one- or two-day excursions by train are available on summer weekends. Contact RENFE for details.

TRAVEL AGENCIES

American Express (⊠ Plaza de las Cortes 2, ☎ 91/322–5445). **Pullmantur,** across the street from the Royal Palace (⊠ Plaza de Oriente 8, ☎ 91/541–1807). **Carlson Wagons-Lits** (⊠ Paseo de la Castellana 96, ☎ 91/563–1202).

VISITOR INFORMATION

Madrid tourist office (⊠ Ground floor, Torre de Madrid, Plaza de España, near Calle de la Princesa, ☎ 91/541–2325) is the best place for comprehensive information. The **Madrid Provincial Tourist Office** (⊠ Duque de Medinacelli 2, ☎ 91/429–4951) is also helpful. The **municipal tourist office** (⊠ Plaza Mayor 3, ☎ 91/366–5477) is centrally located, but hordes of tourists tend to deplete its stock of brochures. The **airport tourist office** (⊠ International Arrivals Hall, Barajas Airport, ☎ 91/305–8656) has a convenient visitors' center.

AROUND MADRID

The beauty and romantic histories of the small cities near Madrid rank them among Spain's most inspiring sights. Ancient Toledo, Spain's former capital; the great palace-monastery of El Escorial; Segovia's Roman aqueduct and fairy-tale Alcázar; the imposing medieval walls of Ávila; and the magnificent Plaza Mayor of the old university town of Salamanca all lie within an hour or two of the capital.

All of these towns, with the possible exception of Salamanca, can easily be visited on day trips from Madrid. But if you've had your fill of Spain's booming capital, you'll find it far more rewarding to leave Madrid altogether and tour from one town to another, spending a night or two in classically Spanish Castile. After the day-trippers have gone home, you can enjoy the real charm of these provincial communities and wander at leisure through their medieval streets.

Toledo

If you're driving, head south from Madrid on the N401. About 20 minutes from the capital, look left for a prominent rounded hill topped by a statue of Christ. This is **El Cerro de los Angéles** (Hill of the Angels), the geographical center of the Iberian Peninsula. After 90 minutes of drab, industrial scenery, the unforgettable silhouette of Toledo suddenly rises before you, with the imposing bulk of the Alcázar and the slender spire of the cathedral dominating the skyline. This former capital, where Moors, Jews, and Christians once lived in harmony, is now a living national monument, holding all the elements of Spanish civilization in hand-carved, sun-mellowed stone. For a stunning view, and to capture the beauty of Toledo as El Greco knew it, begin with a panoramic drive around the Carretera de Circunvalación, crossing over the Alcántara bridge and returning by way of the bridge of San Martín. As you gaze at the city rising like an island in its own bend of the Tagus, you may notice how little its skyline has changed in the four centuries since El Greco painted *Storm over Toledo*.

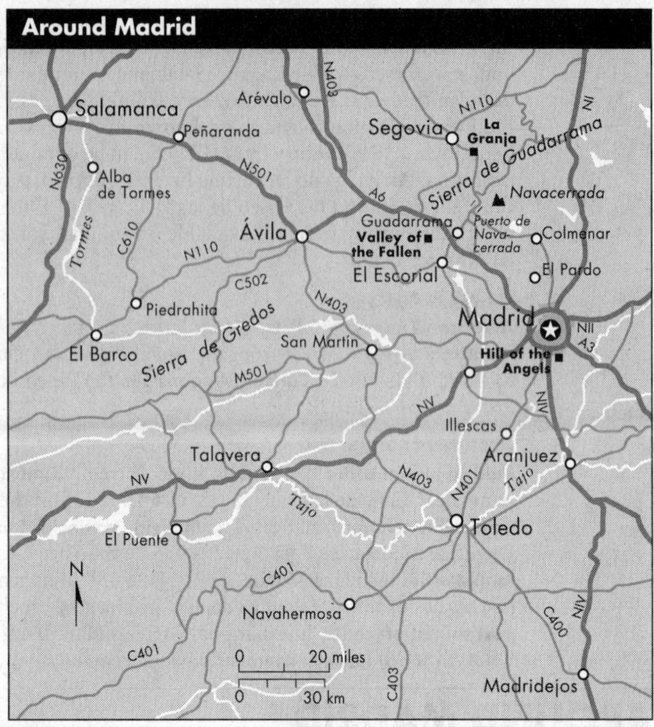

Toledo is a small city steeped in history and full of magnificent buildings. It was the capital of Spain under both Moors and Christians until Philip II moved the capital to Madrid in 1561. Begin your visit with a drink in one of the many terrace cafés on the central **Plaza Zocódover;** study a map and try to get your bearings, for a veritable labyrinth confronts you as you try to find your way to Toledo's great treasures. While here search the square's pastry shops for Toledo's typical *mazapanes* (marzipan candies).

Toledo's 13th-century **cathedral** is the seat of the Cardinal Primate of Spain, and one of the country's great cathedrals. Somber but elaborate, it blazes with jeweled chalices, gorgeous ecclesiastical vestments, historic tapestries, some 750 stained-glass windows, and paintings by Tintoretto, Titian, Murillo, El Greco, Velázquez, and Goya. The cathedral has two surprises: a **Mozarabic chapel,** where Mass is still celebrated on Sunday according to an ancient Mozarabic rite handed down from the days of the Visigoths (AD 419–711); and its unique **Transparente,** an ornate Baroque roof that gives a theatrical glimpse into heaven as the sunlight pours down through a hole to a mass of figures and clouds. ☎ *925/222241.* ⏲ *Mon.–Sat. 10:30–1 and 3:30–6 (7 in summer), Sun. 10:30–1:30 and 4–6 (7 in summer).*

In the tiny chapel of **Santo Tomé,** which houses El Greco's (1541–1614) masterpiece, *The Burial of the Count of Orgaz,* you can capture some of the incredible spirit of the Greek painter who adopted Spain, and in particular Toledo, as his home. Do you recognize the sixth man from the left among the painting's earthly contingent? Or the young boy in the left-hand corner? The first is El Greco himself, the second his son Jorge Manuel—embroidered on the boy's handkerchief you'll see *1578,* the year of his birth. ✉ *C. de Santo Tomé,* ☎ *925/210209.* ⏲ *Daily 10–1:45 and 3:30–5:45 (6:45 in summer).*

Casa de El Greco (El Greco's House) contains copies of his works. ✉ *Off C. de San Juan de Dios,* ☎ *925/224046.* ⏲ *Tues.–Sat. 10–2 and 4–6, Sun. 10–2.*

The splendid **Sinagoga del Tránsito** (Tránsito Synagogue) was commissioned in 1366 by Samuel Levi, chancellor to Peter the Cruel. The synagogue bears Christian and Moorish as well as Jewish influences in its architecture and decoration; notice the stars of David interspersed with the arms of Castile and León. The small **Museo Sefardí** (Sephardic Museum) chronicles Toledo's former Jewish community. ✉ *C. Samuel Levi s/n, corner of Reyes Católicos,* ☎ *925/223665.* ⏲ *Tues.–Sat. 10–1:45 and 4–5:45, Sun. 10–1:45.*

Santa María la Blanca (St. Mary the White) was originally a synagogue, founded in 1203. Stormed during the early 15th century by a Christian mob led by St. Vincent Ferrer, it was then consecrated as a church. Except for the 16th-century altarpiece, however, the architecture is neither Jewish nor Christian but Moorish; the interior has five naves, horseshoe arches, and capitals decorated with texts from the Koran. ✉ *C. del Ángel,* ☎ *925/227257.* ⏲ *Daily 10–1:45 and 3:30–5:45 (7 in summer).*

Ferdinand and Isabella began **San Juan de los Reyes,** a beautiful Gothic church with fine cloisters, in 1476. The iron manacles on the outer walls were placed there for posterity by Christians freed by the Moors. The Catholic Monarchs originally intended to be buried here, but their great triumph at Granada in 1492 changed their plans. ✉ *C. de los Reyes Católicos,* ☎ *925/223802.* ⏲ *Daily 10–1:45 and 3:30–5:45 (6:45 in summer).*

The **Museo de la Santa Cruz** (Museum of the Holy Cross) contains a collection of splendid El Grecos. ✉ *Off Plaza de Zocódover,* ☎ *925/221036.* ⏲ *Mon. 10–2 and 4–6:30, Tues.–Sat. 10–6:30, Sun. 10–2.*

In the **Hospital de Tavera** (Tavera Hospital), outside the city walls, you can see El Greco's *Baptism of Christ* and Alonso de Berruguete's exquisitely carved tomb of Cardinal Tavera. ✉ *Paseo de Madrid,* ☎ *925/220451.* ⏲ *Daily 10–1:30 and 3:30–6.*

$$$ ★ ✕ **Asador Adolfo.** Toledo's most famous restaurant, near the cathedral, is known for its gratifying combination of good food, service, and Old-World charm. Parts of the building date from the 14th century; the dining room retains its original wood-beam ceiling and traces of original murals. Try the superb roast meat and the *tempura de flor de calabacín* (zucchini-flower tempura). ✉ *C. de la Granada 6 and Hombre de Palo 7,* ☎ *925/227321. AE, DC, MC, V. No dinner Sun.*

$$$ ★ ✕ **Hostal del Cardenal.** Up against the city ramparts, in the 17th-century palace of Cardinal Lorenzana, this restaurant has five dining rooms and a delightful garden for summer dining. Both the food and the service are excellent; try the *cochinillo asado.* ✉ *Paseo de Recaredo 24,* ☎ *925/220862. Reservations essential. AE, DC, MC, V.*

$$ ✕ **La Abadía.** Perfect for a light lunch, a sandwich, or a round of tapas, this stylish bar-restaurant has vaulted stone ceilings and a huge, old wooden door. The dining room downstairs specializes in shish kebabs, grilled meats, and salads. ✉ *Plaza San Nicolás 3,* ☎ *925/251140. MC, V. No dinner.*

$$ ✕ **Venta de Aires.** This century-old inn on the edge of town, not far from the Tajo River, is where Toledanos go to eat partridge. Steaks and lamb are also expertly prepared. ✉ *Circo Romano 35,* ☎ *925/220545. AE, DC, MC, V.*

$$$ ★ 🏨 **Parador Conde de Orgaz.** The best and most expensive hotel in Toledo, the Conde de Orgaz is one of Spain's most highly respected paradors. It's a modern structure built in the traditional Toledan style;

perched on a hill across the river (a 15-minute drive from the city center), it commands magnificent views of the city. Book well in advance. ✉ *Cerro del Emperador s/n, 45001,* ☎ *925/221850,* FAX *925/225166. 77 rooms. Pool. AE, DC, MC, V.*

$$ **Hostal del Cardenal.** Built during the 18th century as a summer palace for a cardinal, this quiet and beautiful hotel has some rooms that overlook a wooded garden. It's hard to believe that the highway is so close by. ✉ *Paseo de Recaredo 24, 45004,* ☎ *925/224900,* FAX *925/222991. 27 rooms. Restaurant. AE, DC, MC, V.*

$$ **Pintor El Greco.** Next door to the famous painter's house/museum, this friendly hotel fills a building that was once a 17th-century bakery. The interior is warm and modern, with some antique touches such as exposed brick vaulting and terra-cotta tile floors. ✉ *Alamillos del Tránsito 13, 45002,* ☎ *925/214250,* FAX *925/215819. 33 rooms. AE, DC, MC, V.*

El Escorial

In the foothills of the Guadarrama Mountains, 50 km (31 mi) northwest of Madrid, and 120 km (74 mi) from Toledo, stands the Monastery of San Lorenzo del Escorial, the burial place of Spanish kings and queens. Built by the religious fanatic Philip II as a memorial to his father, Charles V, El Escorial is a vast, rectangular structure, conceived and executed with a monotonous magnificence worthy of the Spanish royal necropolis: It was designed by Juan de Herrera, Spain's greatest Renaissance architect. The **Pantéon Real** (Royal Pantheon) contains the tombs of all the monarchs since Carlos I save three. Only those queens who bore sons who were later crowned lie in the same crypt; the others, along with royal sons and daughters who never ruled, lie in the nearby **Pantéon de los Infantes** (Princes' Pantheon). The monastery's other highlights are Philip II's magnificent **library,** with 40,000 rare volumes and 2,700 illuminated manuscripts, including the diary of St. Teresa, and the **royal apartments.** Compare the spartan private apartment of Philip II, including the simple bedroom in which he died in 1598, with the beautiful carpets, porcelain, and tapestries with which his less austere successors embellished the rest of his somber commission. ✉ *Jct. Rtes. C600 and M505, NW of Madrid,* ☎ *91/890–5905.* ⏲ *Tues.–Sun. 10–6 (7 in summer), last entry 45 min before closing time.*

$$$ ★ ✕ **Charolés.** This elegant restaurant has a terrace above the street for summer dining. Its meat dishes are famous throughout the region; try the *charolés a la pimienta* (peppered steak). Fresh fish is brought in daily from Spain's north coast. ✉ *Floridablanca 24,* ☎ *91/890–5975. Reservations essential. AE, DC, MC, V.*

$$ ✕ **El Candil.** One of the best of the many middle-range restaurants in El Escorial, El Candil is perched above a bar on the corner of Plaza San Lorenzo on the village's main street. In summer you can dine outdoors in the square, a delightful spot. ✉ *Reina Victoria 12,* ☎ *91/890–4103. AE, DC, MC, V.*

$$ ✕ **Mesón de la Cueva.** Founded in 1768, this atmospheric *mesón* has several small, rustic dining rooms. It's a must for ambience—and the food is tasty, too. ✉ *San Antón 4,* ☎ *91/890–1516. No credit cards. Closed Mon.*

$$$ **Victoria Palace.** The rooms at the back of this grand old hotel near the monastery have balconies and a splendid view toward Madrid. There's also a garden. ✉ *Juan de Toledo 4, 28200,* ☎ *91/890–1511,* FAX *91/890–1248. 89 rooms. Pool. AE, DC, MC, V.*

$$ **Miranda Suizo.** With its dark-wood fittings, marble café tables, and main-street locations, this charming hotel is straight out of the 19th century. The guest rooms are comfortable. ✉ *Floridablanca 20, 28200,* ☎ *91/890–4711,* FAX *91/890–4358. 52 rooms. AE, DC, MC, V.*

Valle de los Caídos (Valley of the Fallen)

Eight kilometers (5 mi) along the road from El Escorial to Segovia, the mighty cross of the Valley of the Fallen looms up on your left. Hewn out of sheer granite, the vast basilica beneath was built by General Franco between 1940 and 1959 as a monument to those who perished in the Civil War. Buried here are 43,000 war dead and Franco himself, who died in 1975. A funicular to the top of the monument costs 350 ptas. ✉ *Rte. C600,* ☎ *91/890–5611.* ⏲ *Tues.–Sun. 10–6 (9:30–7 in summer).*

En Route The local road from here to Segovia offers a spectacular drive up through the Guadarrama Mountains by way of the **Puerto de Navacerrada** (Navacerrada Pass) at 6,000 ft. The steep descent through pine forests via the hairpin bends of the *Siete Revueltas* (Seven Curves) brings you straight into La Granja.

La Granja

El Palacio de La Granja (La Granja Palace), with its splendid formal gardens and fountains, was built between 1719 and 1739 by the homesick Philip V, first Bourbon king of Spain and grandson of France's Louis XIV, to remind him of his beloved Versailles. The whole place is like an exquisite piece of France in a Spanish wood, and it's small wonder that Philip chose to be buried here in the splendor of his own creation rather than in the austerity of El Escorial. The exquisite gardens are open until dusk, and you can stroll around them for free except when the fountains are running. ✉ *Rte. N601, 11 km (7 mi) SE of Segovia,* ☎ *921/470020.* ⏲ *Tues.–Sun. 10–6; winter, Tues.–Sat. 10–1:30 and 3–5, Sun. 10–2.*

★ Segovia

The golden-stone market town of Segovia has outstanding medieval and Roman monuments, embroideries and textiles, and excellent cuisine.

The majestic **Roman aqueduct,** its huge granite blocks held together without mortar, greets you at the entrance to Segovia. At its foot is a small bronze statue of Romulus and the wolf, presented by Rome in 1974 to commemorate the 2,000-year history of Spain's greatest surviving Roman monument.

The **Ronda de Santa Lucía** leads to the most romantic view of the Alcázar, perched high on its rock like the prow of a mighty ship. Return via the Carretera de los Hoyos for yet another magical view, this time of the venerable cathedral rising from the ramparts.

Calle Real, the main shopping street, passes the Romanesque church of San Martín, with a porticoed outer gallery.

Plaza Mayor, with colorful ceramic shops (good bargains) and pleasant cafés, is set against a backdrop of ancient arcaded houses and one of the loveliest Gothic cathedrals in Spain.

Segovia's **cathedral** was the last Gothic cathedral to be built in Spain (the first was in nearby Ávila). Begun in 1525 by order of Charles V, it has a golden and harmonious interior, illuminated by 16th-century Flemish windows. Its museum, off the cloister, has the first book printed in Spain (1472) and a 17th-century ceiling paneled in white and gold, a splendid example of Mudéjar *artesonado* work. ✉ *Plaza Mayor,* ☎ *911/435325.* ⏲ *Daily 9–6 in winter, 9–7 in summer.*

The turreted **Alcázar** is largely a fanciful re-creation from the 1880s; the original 13th-century castle was destroyed by fire in 1862. However, the view from its ramparts—and, even better, from its tower if you can manage the 156 steps—is breathtaking. The Alcázar served as a major residence of the Catholic Monarchs; here Isabella met Ferdinand, and from here she set out to the Plaza Mayor to be crowned Queen of Castile. The interior successfully illustrates the dawn of Spain's Golden Age. ✉ *Plaza del Alcázar,* ☎ *911/460759.* ⏲ *Daily 10–6 in winter, 10–7 in summer.*

$$–$$$ ✕ **Casa Duque.** At the end of Segovia's main shopping street, this restaurant has several floors of beautifully decorated traditional dining rooms. It is the main rival to the famous Mesón de Cándido. There's plenty of local atmosphere, and the food is pure Castilian—roasts are the house specialty. ✉ *Cervantes 12,* ☎ *921/430537. AE, DC, MC, V.*

$$–$$$ ★ ✕ **Mesón de Cándido.** Segovia's most prestigious restaurant has seven dining rooms filled with medieval atmosphere, decorated with Castilian memorabilia and photos of the dignitaries who have dined here over the years. Specialties are *cochinillo asado* and *cordero asado,* both succulent. ✉ *Plaza Azoguejo 5,* ☎ *921/425911. Reservations essential. AE, DC, MC, V.*

$$ ✕ **La Oficina.** Just off the Plaza Mayor, traditional Castilian dishes are served in two delightful dining rooms that date back to 1893. ✉ *Cronista Lecea 10,* ☎ *921/460286. AE, DC, MC, V.*

$$ 🏨 **Infanta Isabel.** Right on a corner of the Plaza Mayor, this small, central hotel has a Victorian feel and great views of the cathedral. Guest rooms are feminine and light, with painted white furnishings. ✉ *Isabel la Católica, 40001,* ☎ *921/461300,* FAX *921/462217. 29 rooms. AE, DC, MC, V.*

$$ 🏨 **Los Linajes.** With an 11th-century facade and quiet, medieval surroundings, Los Linajes is a pleasure to come home to. Rooms are basic and comfortable, some with balconies and superb views. ✉ *Dr. Velasco 9, 40003,* ☎ *921/460475,* FAX *921/460479. 53 rooms. Bar, breakfast room, nightclub. AE, DC, MC, V.*

$$ ★ 🏨 **Parador Nacional de Segovia.** To the north of town, this modern parador offers comfortable, spacious rooms and pools. The views of the city are magnificent, especially at night. The food in the restaurant is superior. ✉ *Carretera de Valladolid s/n (off the N601 toward Valladolid), 40003,* ☎ *921/443737,* FAX *921/437362. 106 rooms. Restaurant, indoor and outdoor pools. AE, DC, MC, V.*

Ávila

At nearly 4,100 ft above sea level, Ávila is the highest provincial capital in Spain. Alfonso VI and his son-in-law, Count Raimundo de Borgoña, rebuilt the town and walls in 1090, bringing it permanently under Christian control. It is these walls, the best-preserved military installations of their kind in Spain, that give Ávila its special medieval quality. Thick and solid, with 88 towers tufted with untidy storks' nests, they stretch for 2½ km (1½ mi) around the entire city and make an ideal focus for the start of your visit. For a superb overall view, drive out to the **Cuatro Postes** (Four Posts), ¾ km (½ mi) out on the road to Salamanca.

The spirit of St. Teresa the Mystic, to whom Ávila is dedicated, lives as vividly today as it did during the 16th century. Several institutions associated with Teresa's life are open to visitors; the most popular is the **Convento de Santa Teresa,** on the site of the saint's birthplace. There's an ornate baroque chapel, a small gift shop, and a museum with some of Teresa's relics: her rosary, books, walking stick, sandal sole, and preserved ring finger, wearing her wedding ring. ✉ *Plaza de la Santa, inside the southern gate,* ☎ *920/211030.* 🎟 *Free.* ⏲ *Daily 9:30–1:30 and 3:30–8:30 (until 9 in summer).*

Ávila's oldest and most rewarding ecclesiastical monuments predate St. Teresa. The impregnable hulk of the **cathedral** resembles a fortress as much as a house of God. Though of Romanesque origin—the Romanesque sections are recognizable by their red-and-white stonework—

it is usually cited as Spain's first Gothic cathedral. Inside is the ornate alabaster tomb of Cardinal Alonso de Madrigal, a 15th-century bishop whose swarthy complexion earned him the nickname of "El Tostado" (the toasted one). ✉ *Plaza de la Catedral,* ☎ *920/211641.* ⏲ *Daily 10–1:30 and 3:30–6:30.*

The **Basílica de San Vicente,** just outside the walls, is one of Ávila's finest Romanesque churches, erected on the spot where St. Vincent and his sisters Sabina and Cristeta were martyred in AD 306. Here, too, St. Teresa is said to have experienced the vision that told her to reform the Carmelite order. ✉ *Plaza de San Vicente,* ☎ *920/255230.* ⏲ *Tues.–Sun. 10–2 and 4–8.*

You can relax in the pleasant **Plaza de Santa Teresa,** with outdoor cafés and a statue of the saint erected for Pope John Paul's visit in 1982.

The **Monasterio de Santo Tomás** was built between 1482 and 1493 by Ferdinand and Isabella, who used it as a summer palace. It houses the tomb of their only son, Prince Juan, who died at the age of 19 while a student at Salamanca; and the tomb of the notorious Inquisitor General Tomás de Torquemada. ✉ *Plaza Granada,* ☎ *920/220400.* 🎫 *Monastery free.* ⏲ *Daily 11–1 and 4–6.*

$$ ✕ **El Fogón de Santa Teresa.** Traditional Castilian roasts, lamb chops, and trout head the menu at this attractive restaurant in the vaults of the Palacio de Valderrábaños. ✉ *Alemania 3,* ☎ *920/211023. AE, DC, MC, V.*

$$ ★ ✕ **El Molino de la Losa.** On a quiet spit of land in the Adaja River, this restaurant occupies a restored 15th-century mill and has splendid views of Ávila's walls. In summer you can have a drink and enjoy some tapas outside by the duck pond. Specialties include lamb roasted in a medieval-style wood oven and fresh river trout. ✉ *Bajada de la Losa 12,* ☎ *920/211101. AE, MC, V. Closed Mon. in winter.*

$$ ★ ✕ **Mesón del Rastro.** This ancient inn tucked into the city walls is Ávila's most atmospheric place to dine. Local specialties include *ternera* (veal) and *yemas de Santa Teresa,* a dessert made from candied egg yolks. ✉ *Plaza del Rastro 4,* ☎ *920/211218. AE, DC, MC, V.*

$$$ ★ 🏨 **Meliá Palacio de los Velada.** A beautifully restored 16th-century palace houses Ávila's top hotel, ideally located in the heart of the city, beside the cathedral. You can relax between sightseeing excursions in the lovely palace courtyard. The attractive rooms are modern and comfortable, and have all the amenities. ✉ *Plaza de la Catedral 10, 05001,* ☎ *920/255100,* FAX *920/254900. 85 rooms. Restaurant. AE, DC, MC, V.*

$$$ 🏨 **Parador Raimundo de Borgoña.** Superbly set in a 15th-century palace just inside the city's northern walls, this parador has rooms decorated in traditional Castilian style and spacious, gleamingly modern bathrooms. Some rooms also have four-poster beds and views of the city walls. The attractive dining room serves local dishes, including the inevitable *yemas,* and the garden sometimes permits access to the walls. ✉ *Marqués Canales de Chozas 2, 05001,* ☎ *920/211340,* FAX *920/226166. 62 rooms. Restaurant. AE, DC, MC, V.*

Alba de Tormes

From Ávila it's straight sailing all the way to Salamanca. If you're a devotee of St. Teresa, however, you can take a small detour to the old ducal town of Alba de Tormes to visit the **Convento de Carmelitas** (Carmelite Convent, ⏲ daily 9–2 and 4–8), where the saint is buried.

★ Salamanca

Salamanca is an ancient and gorgeous city, and even your first glimpse of it is bound to be unforgettable. In the foreground as you approach is the sturdy 15-arch Roman bridge, and above this—dominating the view—soar the city's old houses and the golden walls, turrets, and domes of its plateresque cathedrals. The word *plateresque* comes from *plata* (silver), implying that the stone is chiseled and engraved as intricately as that delicate metal.

The west facade of the Dominican **Monasterio de San Estebán** (Monastery of St. Stephen) is a superb example of the plateresque style. ✉ *Plaza Basilios,* ☎ *923/215000.* ⌚ *Daily 9–1 and 4–7 (5–8 in summer).*

Salamanca has two distinct, adjoining **cathedrals,** the **Catedral Vieja** (Old Cathedral) and the grandly carved **Catedral Nueva** (New Cathedral). Inside the sturdy Romanesque walls of the old cathedral is a stunning altarpiece with 53 painted panels. Within the splendid **cloister** are a worthy collection of religious art and the **Capilla de Santa Bárbara** (Chapel of St. Barbara, or Degree Chapel) where anxious students sought help the night before their final exams. ✉ *Plaza de Anaya,* ☎ *923/217476.* *New cathedral free.* ⌚ *Old Cathedral and cloisters: daily 10–12:30 and 4–5:30; new cathedral: daily 10–1 and 4–6.*

Founded by Alfonso IX in 1218, the **universidad** (university) of Salamanca is to Spain what Oxford University is to England. On the famous facade of the **Escuelas Mayores**, a profusion of plateresque carving surrounds the medallions of Ferdinand and Isabella. See if you can find the famous frog and skull, said to bring good luck to students in their examinations. Inside, the **Sala de Fray Luis de León** (Friar Luis's lecture room) has remained untouched since the days of that great scholar, and the prestigious **library** boasts some 50,000 parchment and leather-bound volumes. ✉ *C. Traviesa,* ☎ *923/294400, ext. 1150.* ⌚ *Weekdays 9:30–1:30 and 4–7:30, Sat. 9:30–1:30 and 4–7, Sun. 10–1.*

The elegant, 18th-century **Plaza Mayor** is Salamanca's crowning glory. Built by Alberto and Nicolás Churriguera, it is widely thought the most beautiful Plaza Mayor in Spain. Here you can browse in stores offering typical *charro* jewelry (silver and black flower heads), head down the adjoining streets in search of colorful tapas bars, or just relax and watch the world go by at an outdoor café.

$$ ★ ✕ **Chapeau.** This chic spot offers both meat and fish carefully roasted in its wood-fire ovens. Try the *pimientos rellenos* and, for dessert, the orange mousse. ✉ *Gran Vía 20,* ☎ *923/271833. AE, DC, MC, V. No dinner Sun.*

$$ ✕ **El Mesón.** There's plenty of color and plenty of good, traditional Castilian food in this typical mesón, just off the Plaza Mayor, beside the Gran Hotel. ✉ *Plaza Poeta Iglesias 10,* ☎ *923/217222. AE, MC, V. No dinner Sun.*

$$ ✕ **Río de la Plata.** This tiny, long-standing basement restaurant just off Calle de San Pablo retains a warm, old-fashioned character with a fireplace and a local crowd. The food—good-quality fish and meat—is simple but carefully prepared. ✉ *Plaza del Peso 1,* ☎ *923/219005. AE, MC, V. Closed Mon. and July.*

$$$–$$$$ **Gran Hotel.** The grande dame of Salamanca's hotels offers stylishly baroque lounges and refurbished, yet old-fashioned, oversize rooms just steps from the Plaza Mayor. ✉ *Poeta Iglesias 5, 37001,* ☎ *923/213500,* FAX *923/213501. 137 rooms. Restaurant. AE, DC, MC, V.*

$$$ **Palacio de Castellanos.** Opened in 1992 in an immaculately restored 15th-century palace, this hotel is a welcome alternative to Salamanca's national parador (probably the ugliest of them all). There is an exquisite interior patio and an equally beautiful restaurant. ✉ *San Pablo 58, 37001,* ☎ *923/261818,* FAX *923/261819. 63 rooms. Restaurant. AE, DC, MC, V.*

$$–$$$ 🏨 **Las Torres.** This Plaza Mayor hotel has modern, comfortable rooms. Be sure to ask for one with a balcony on the plaza itself. ✉ *Plaza Mayor 26 and Concejo 4, 37001,* ☎ *923/212100,* FAX *923/212101. 44 rooms. AE, DC, MC, V.*

Around Madrid Essentials

Arriving and Departing

Trains to Toledo leave from Madrid's Atocha Station; to Salamanca from Chamartín Station; and to Ávila, Segovia, and El Escorial from both stations, although sometimes more frequently from Chamartín. For schedules and reservations call RENFE (☎ 91/328–9020).

Getting Around

BY BUS

All towns are linked by buses; local tourist offices can advise on schedules. Each town has a central bus station. **Ávila** (✉ Avda. de Madrid, ☎ 920/220154). **Salamanca** (✉ Filiberto Villalobos 71, ☎ 923/236717). **Segovia** (✉ Paseo Ezequiel González, ☎ 921/427707). **Toledo** (✉ Ronda de Castilla la Mancha, off the road from Madrid, ☎ 925/215850).

BY CAR

The N403 from Toledo to Ávila passes through spectacular scenery in the Sierra de Gredos, as does the C505 from Ávila to El Escorial. From El Escorial to Segovia, both the Puerto de León and Puerto de Navacerrada mountain passes offer magnificent views. The N501 from Ávila to Salamanca takes you across the tawny plain of Castile.

BY TRAIN

There's a direct train line between El Escorial, Ávila, and Salamanca; otherwise, train connections are poor, and you'll do better to go by bus.

Visitor Information

Ávila (✉ Plaza de la Catedral 4, ☎ 920/211387). **El Escorial** (✉ Floridablanca 10, ☎ 91/890–1554). **Salamanca** (✉ Casa de las Conchas, Rúa Mayor s/n, ☎ 923/268571; information booth, ✉ Plaza Mayor). **Segovia** (✉ Plaza Mayor 10, ☎ 921/460334). **Toledo** (✉ Puerta de Bisagra, ☎ 925/220843).

BARCELONA

Barcelona, capital of Catalunya (Catalonia), thrives on its business acumen and industrial muscle. The hardworking citizens of this thriving metropolis are proud to have and use their own language—street names, museum exhibits, newspapers, radio programs, and movies are all in Catalan. An important milestone here was the city's long-awaited opportunity to host the Olympic Games, in summer 1992; the Olympics were of singular importance in Barcelona's modernization. Their legacy includes a vastly improved ring road and several other highways; four new beaches; and an entire new neighborhood in what used to be the run-down industrial district of Poble Nou. In addition, the promontory of Montjuïc has a new sports stadium, several swimming pools, and an adjoining marina. Few cities can rival the medieval atmosphere of the Gothic Quarter's narrow alleys, the elegance and distinction of the Moderniste (Art Nouveau) Eixample, or the many fruits of Gaudí's whimsical imagination. Extraordinarily endowed with 2,000 years of art and architecture, Barcelona remains a world center for design.

Exploring Barcelona

Numbers in the margin correspond to points of interest on the Barcelona map.

It should take you two full days of sightseeing to complete the following tour. The first part covers the Gothic Quarter, the Picasso Museum, and the Rambla. The second part takes you to Passeig de Gràcia and the church of the Sagrada Família; and the third, to Montjuïc.

The Barri Gòtic (Gothic Quarter) and La Rambla

★ 1 **Catedral de la Seu** (Cathedral). Citizens of Barcelona gather on Sunday morning to dance the *sardana,* a symbol of Catalan identity, on Plaça de la Seu, in front of the cathedral. The elaborate Gothic structure was built between 1298 and 1450, though the spire and Gothic facade were not added until 1892. Inside, highlights are the beautifully carved **choir stalls;** Santa Eulàlia's tomb, in the crypt; the battle-scarred crucifix from Don Juan's galley in the naval battle of Lepanto, in the **Capella de Lepanto** (Lepanto Chapel); and the cloisters. ⊠ *Plaça de la Seu,* ☎ *93/315–1554.* *Free.* *Daily 7:45–1:30 and 4–7:45.*

12 **Gran Teatre del Liceu.** Barcelona's famous opera house was tragically gutted by fire in 1994 and is scheduled to reopen in early 1999. Built between 1845 and 1847, the Liceu claims to be the world's oldest opera house and was also one of the world's most beautiful, with ornamental gilt and plush red-velvet fittings. Anna Pavlova danced here in 1930, and Maria Callas sang here in 1959. If the theater is still closed, you can arrange a visit to the rooms that were not damaged. ⊠ *Rambla, corner of C. de Sant Pau,* ☎ *93/318–9122.*

9 **Monument a Colom** (Columbus Monument). You can ride an elevator to the top for a commanding view of the city and port. Columbus faces out to sea, pointing, ironically, east toward Naples. Nearby you can board the cable car to cross the harbor to Barceloneta or catch it in the other direction up Montjuïc. ⊠ *Bottom of the Rambla.* *Tues.–Sat. 10–2 and 3:30–6:30, Sun. 10–7.*

15 **Museu d'Art Contemporani** (MACBA; Museum of Contemporary Art). Designed by American Richard Meier, the new contemporary-art museum is an important addition to Barcelona's treasury of art and architecture. Located in the city's once (and still) rough-and-tumble Raval district, it and the neighboring **Centre de Cultura Contemporànea (CCCB)** (Center for Contemporary Culture) have reclaimed important buildings and spaces as part of the city's renewal of its historic quarters and traditional neighborhoods. ⊠ *Plaça dels Àngels 1,* ☎ *93/412–0810.* *Tues.–Fri. noon–8, weekends 10–3.*

2 **Museu Frederic Marès.** Here you can browse for hours among the miscellany assembled by sculptor/collector Frederic Marès, including everything from polychrome crucifixes to hat pins, pipes, and walking sticks. ⊠ *Plaça Sant Iu 5,* ☎ *93/310–5800.* *Free 1st Sun. of month.* *Tues.–Sat. 10–5, Sun. 10–2.*

10 **Museu Marítim** (Maritime Museum). Housed in the 13th-century Drassanes Reiales (Royal Shipyards), this museum is packed with ships, figureheads, and nautical paraphernalia. You can pore over early navigation charts, including a map by Amerigo Vespucci and the 1439 chart of Gabriel de Valseca, the oldest chart in Europe. ⊠ *Plaça Portal de la Pau 1,* ☎ *93/318–3245.* *Free 1st Sun. of every month.* *Tues.–Sat. 10–2 and 4–7, Sun. 10–2.*

★ 5 **Museu Picasso.** Two 15th-century palaces provide a striking setting for these collections of Picasso's early art, donated in 1963 and 1970 by

Picasso's secretary and then by the artist himself. The works range from childhood sketches to exhibition posters done in Paris shortly before the artist's death. In rare abundance are the Rose Period and Blue Period paintings and the variations on Velázquez's *Las Meninas.* ✉ *Carrer Montcada 1519,* ☎ *93/319–6310.* *Free 1st Sun. of the month.* ⏲ *Tues.–Sat. 10–8, Sun. 10–3.*

★ ❹ **Palau de la Música** (Palace of Music). Attend a performance at Domènech i Montaner's fantastic Moderniste concert house. ✉ *Sant Francesc de Paula 2, off Via Laietana,* ☎ *93/268–1000.*

⓮ **Palau de la Virreina.** Built by a one-time Spanish viceroy to Peru in 1778, this building is now a major exhibition center. Check to see what's showing while you're in town. ✉ *Rambla de les Flors 99,* ☎ *93/301–7775.* ⏲ *Tues.–Sat. 10–2 and 4:30–9, Sun. 10–2, Mon. 4:30–9. Last entrance 30 min before closing.*

★ ⓫ **Palau Güell.** Gaudí built this mansion between 1885 and 1890 for his patron, Count Eusebi de Güell. It's the only Gaudí house open to the public and one of the highlights on the Ruta Modernista. ✉ *Nou de la Rambla 3.* ⏲ *Tues.–Sat. 10–1:30 and 4–7:30.*

⓰ **Plaça de Catalunya.** This intersection is the business center and transport hub of the modern city. ✉ *Top of the Rambla.*

❸ **Plaça del Rei.** Several historic buildings surround what is widely considered the most beautiful square in the Gothic Quarter. Following Columbus's first voyage to America, the Catholic Kings received him in the **Saló de Tinell,** a magnificent banquet hall built in 1362. Other ancient buildings around the square are the **Palau del Lloctinent** (Lieutenant's Palace); the 14th-century **Capella de Santa Àata** (Chapel of St. Agatha), built right into the Roman city wall; and the **Palau Padellàs** (Padellàs Palace), which houses the **Museu d'Historia de la Ciutat** (City History Museum). ✉ *Plaça del Rei,* ☎ *93/315–1111,* ⏲ *Tues.–Sat. 10–2 and 4–8, Sun. 10–2.*

❽ **Plaça Reial.** In this splendid 19th-century square, arcaded houses overlook the wrought-iron **Font de les Tres Gràcies** (Fountain of the Three Graces) and lampposts designed by a young Gaudí in 1879. Despite the preponderance of substance users, abusers, and peddlers here, Plaça Reial retains its elegance; the most colorful time to come is Sunday morning, when crowds gather at the stamp and coin stalls and listen to soapbox orators. ✉ *C. Colom, off Rambla.*

❼ **Plaça Sant Jaume.** This impressive square in the heart of the Gothic Quarter was built in the 1840s, but the two imposing buildings facing each other across it are much older. The 15th-century **ajuntament** (city hall), has an impressive black and gold mural (1928) by Josep María Sert (who also painted the murals in New York's Waldorf-Astoria) and the famous **Saló de Cent,** the first European parliament, from which the Council of One Hundred ruled the city from 1372 to 1714. To visit the interior, you'll need to arrange permission in the protocol office. The **Palau de la Generalitat,** seat of the Autonomous Catalonian Government, is a 15th-century palace open to the public on special days or by arrangement. ✉ *Meeting of C. de Ferràn and C. Jaume I.*

⓭ **Rambla St. Josep.** This stretch of the boulevard is one of the most fascinating. The colorful paving stones on the Plaça de la Boquería were designed by Joan Miró. Glance up at the swirling Moderniste dragon and the Art Nouveau street lamps; then take a look inside the bustling **Boquería Market** and the **Antiga Casa Figueras,** a vintage pastry shop on the corner of Petxina, with a splendid mosaic facade. ✉ *Between Pl. de la Boquería and Rambla de les Flors.*

Casa Milà, **18**
Catedral de la Seu, **1**
Fundació Miró, **21**
Gran Teatre del Liceu, **12**
Mançana de la Discòrdia, **17**
Monument a Colom, **9**
Museu d'Art Contemporani, **15**
Museu Frederic Marès, **2**
Museu Marítim, **10**
Museu Nacional d'Art de Catalunya, **20**
Museu Picasso, **5**
Palau de la Música, **4**
Palau de la Virreina, **14**
Palau Güell, **11**
Plaça de Catalunya, **16**
Plaça del Rei, **3**
Plaça Reial, **8**
Plaça Sant Jaume, **7**
Rambla St. Josep, **13**
Santa Maria del Mar, **6**
Temple Expiatori de la Sagrada Família, **19**

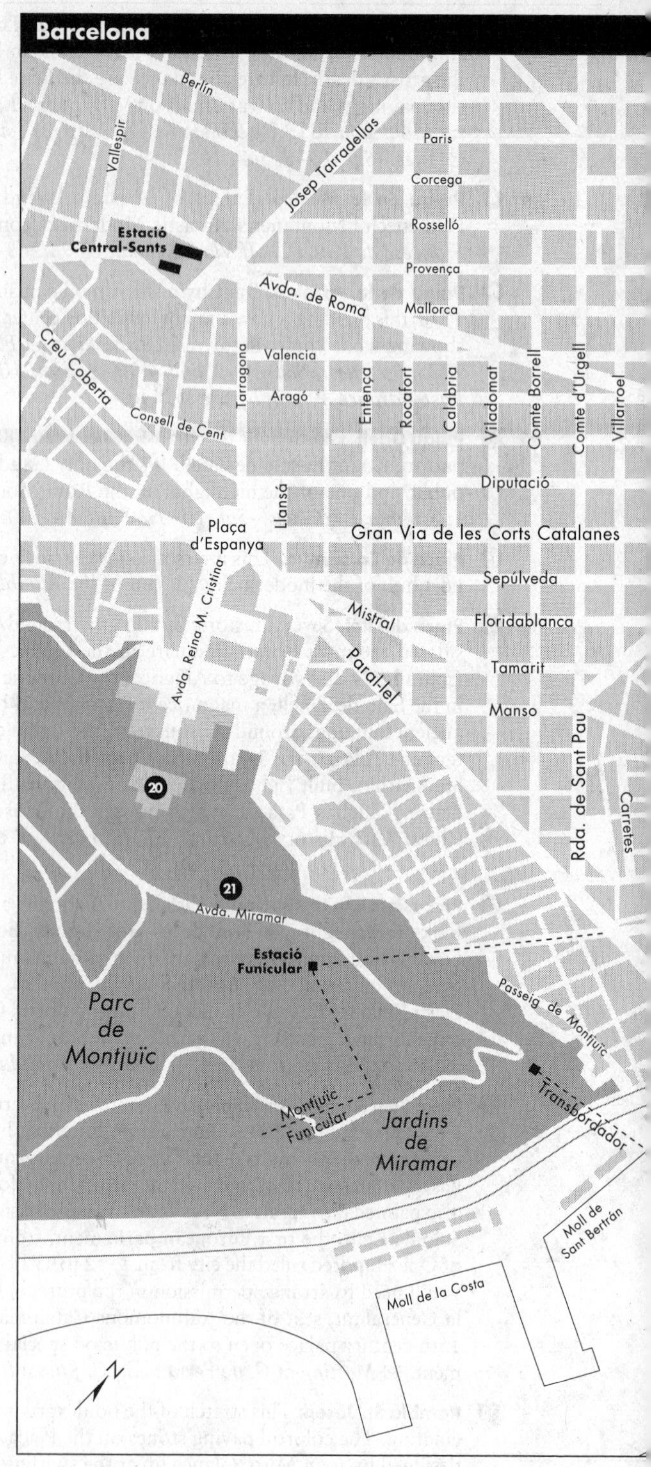

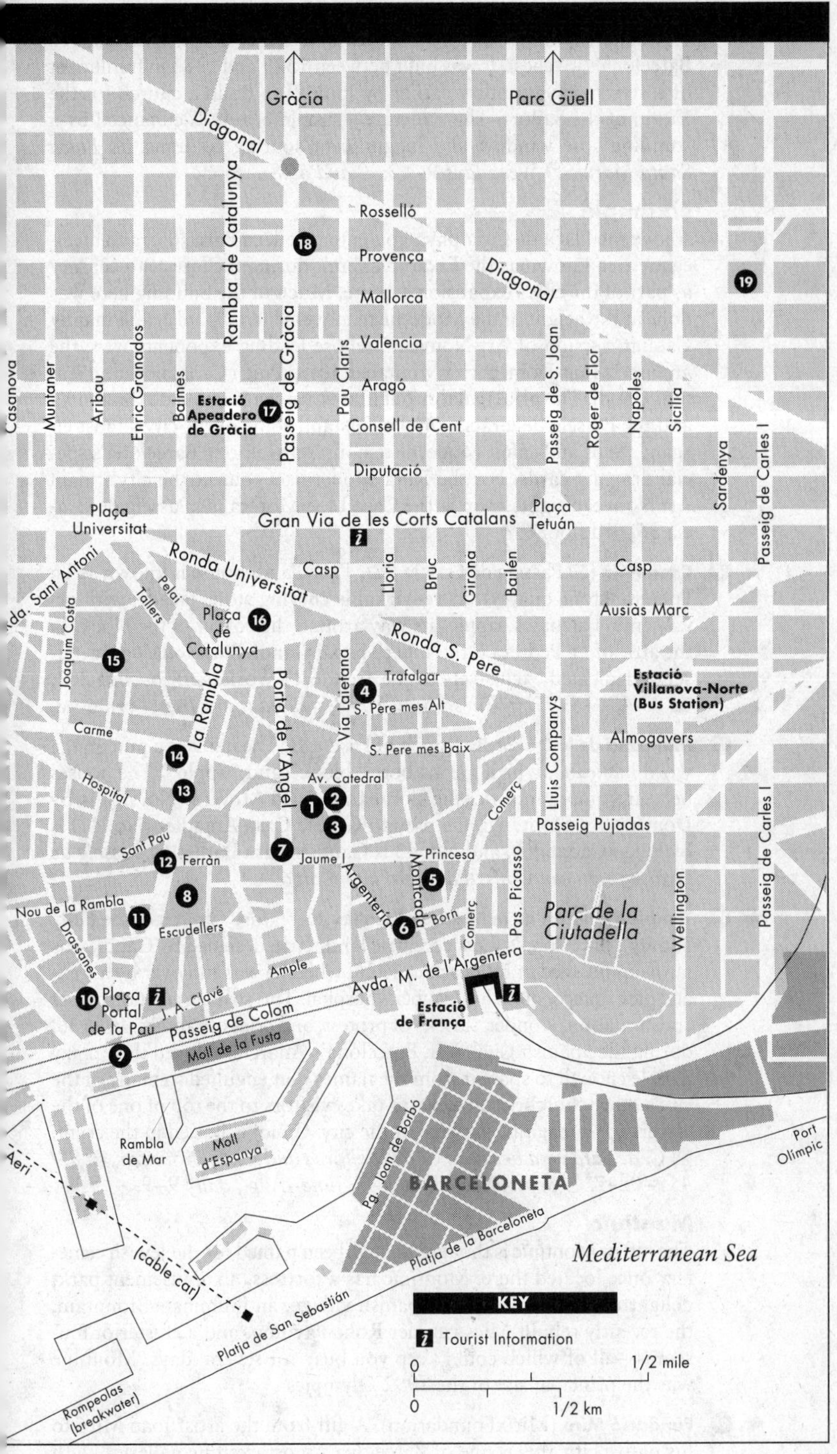
Gràcia
Parc Güell
Diagonal
Rambla de Catalunya
Rosselló
Provença
Mallorca
Valencia
Aragó
Consell de Cent
Diputació
Gran Via de les Corts Catalans
Casanova
Muntaner
Aribau
Enric Granados
Balmes
Estació Apeadero de Gràcia
Passeig de Gràcia
Pau Claris
Passeig de S. Joan
Roger de Flor
Napoles
Sicilia
Sardenya
Passeig de Carles I
Plaça Universitat
Plaça Tetuán
Ronda Universitat
Ronda Sant Antoni
Casp
Lloria
Bruc
Girona
Bailén
Ausiàs Marc
Pelai
Tallers
Joaquim Costa
Plaça de Catalunya
Ronda S. Pere
Porta de l'Angel
Via Laietana
Trafalgar
S. Pere mes Alt
S. Pere mes Baix
Estació Villanova-Norte (Bus Station)
Almogavers
Lluis Companys
La Rambla
Carme
Hospital
Av. Catedral
Comerç
Passeig Pujadas
Sant Pau
Ferràn
Jaume I
Princesa
Montcada
Argenteria
Born
Pas. Picasso
Parc de la Ciutadella
Wellington
Nou de la Rambla
Escudellers
Drassanes
Ample
Avda. M. de l'Argentera
Plaça Portal de la Pau
J. A. Clavé
Passeig de Colom
Estació de França
Moll de la Fusta
Rambla de Mar
Moll d'Espanya
Pg. Joan de Borbó
BARCELONETA
Port Olímpic
Aeri
(cable car)
Platja de la Barceloneta
Platja de San Sebastián
Mediterranean Sea
Rompeolas (breakwater)
KEY
Tourist Information
0
1/2 mile
0
1/2 km
1
2
3
4
5
6
7
8
9
10
11
12
13
14
15
16
17
18
19

★ 6 **Santa Maria del Mar** (St. Mary of the Sea). Simply the best example of Mediterranean Gothic architecture, this church is widely considered Barcelona's loveliest. It was built between 1329 and 1383 in fulfillment of a vow made a century earlier by James I to build a church for the Virgin of the Sailors. The structure's simple beauty is enhanced by a stunning rose window and magnificent soaring columns. ✉ *Plaça Santa Maria.* ⏲ *Weekdays 9–12:30 and 5–8.*

Eixample

Above the Plaça de Catalunya you enter modern Barcelona and an elegant area known as the Eixample, built during the late 19th century as part of the city's expansion scheme. Much of the building here was done at the height of the Moderniste movement, a Spanish and mainly Catalan version of Art Nouveau, whose leading exponents were the architects Luís Domènech i Montaner, Josep Puig i Cadafalch, and Antoni Gaudí. The principal thoroughfares are the Rambla de Catalunya and the Passeig de Gràcia, on which stand some of the city's most elegant shops and cafés. Moderniste houses are among Barcelona's special drawing cards. For the Ruta Modernista tour of the city's main Art Nouveau sights, stop at the Casa Lleó Morera (✉ Passeig de Gràcia 35, 3rd floor).

★ 18 **Casa Milà** (✉ Passeig de Gràcia 92). This Gaudí house is known as **La Pedrera** (stone quarry). Its remarkable curving stone facade, with ornamental balconies, ripples its way around the corner of the block. In the attic of La Pedrera is the superb **Espai Gaudí,** Barcelona's only museum dedicated exclusively to the architect's work. ✉ *Provença 261,* ☎ *93/484–5995.* ⏲ *Tues.–Sun. 10–8; guided tours Tues.–Fri. 6 PM.*

17 **Mançana de la Discòrdia** (Block of Discord). The name is a pun on the word *mançana,* which means both "block" and "apple." The houses here are quite fantastic: the floral **Casa Lleó Morera** (No. 35) is by Domènech i Montaner, the pseudo-Gothic **Casa Amatller** (No. 41) is by Puig i Cadafalch, and No. 43 is Gaudí's **Casa Batlló.** ✉ *Passeig de Gràcia, between Consell de Cent and Aragó.*

★ 19 **Temple Expiatori de la Sagrada Família** (Expiatory Church of the Holy Family). Barcelona's most eccentric landmark, designed by Gaudí, was far from finished at his death in 1926, when he was run over by a tram and died unrecognized in a pauper's hospital. This striking creation causes consternation, wonder, shrieks of protest, and cries of rapture. In 1936, during the Spanish Civil War, Barcelona's Anarchists loved their crazy temple enough to spare it from the flames that engulfed so many of the city's other churches. An elevator takes visitors to the top of one of the towers for a magnificent view of the city. Gaudí is buried in the crypt. ✉ *C. de Sardenya between C. de Mallorca and C. de Provença,* ☎ *93/455–0247.* ⏲ *Sept.–May, daily 9–7; June–Aug., daily 9–9.*

Montjuïc

The hill of Montjuïc is thought to have been named for the Jewish cemetery once located there. Montjuïc has a fortress, an amusement park, delightful gardens, a model Spanish village, an illuminated fountain, the recently rebuilt Mies van der Rohe Pavilion, and a cluster of museums—all of which could keep you busy for several days. Montjuïc was the principal site of the 1992 Olympics.

★ 21 **Fundació Miró** (Miró Foundation). A gift from the artist Joan Miró to his native city, this is one of Barcelona's most exciting galleries, with many of its exhibition spaces devoted to Miró's droll, colorful works. ✉ *Av. de Miramar,* ☎ *93/329–1908.* ⏲ *Tues., Wed, Fri., Sat. 11–7, Thurs. 9:30–7, Sun. 10:30–2:30.*

★ 20 **Museu Nacional d'Art de Catalunya** (National Museum of Catalan Art). In the **Palau Nacional** atop a long flight of steps up from the Plaça Espanya, the collection of Romanesque and Gothic art treasures, medieval frescoes, and altarpieces—most from small churches and chapels in the Pyrenees—is simply staggering. The museum's last renovation was directed by architect Gae Aulenti, who also remodeled the Musée d'Orsay, in Paris. ✉ *Montjuïc,* ☎ *93/423–7199.* ⏲ *Tues–Sat. 10–7; Thurs. 10–9; Sun. 10–2:20.*

Elsewhere in Barcelona

★ **Parc Güell.** This park at the north end of town is Gaudí's magical attempt at creating a garden city. ✉ *C. D'Olot s/n,* ⏲ *May–Aug., daily 10–9; Sept.–Apr., daily 10–7.*

Gràcia. This small, once-independent village within the city is a warren of narrow streets whose names change at every corner. Here you'll find tiny shops that sell everything from old-fashioned tin lanterns to feather dusters. ✉ *Around C. Gran de Gràcia above Diagonal.*

Barceloneta. Take a stroll around the old fishermen's quarter, built in 1755. There are no-frills fish restaurants on the Passeig Joan de Borbó. Hike out to the end of the *rompeolas* (breakwater), extending 4 km (2½ mi) southeast into the Mediterranean, for a panoramic view of the city and a few breaths of fresh air. The modernized port is home to the Aquarium, one of Europe's best; the Maregmagnum shopping center; the IMAX wide-format cinema; the newly opened World Trade Center; and numerous bars and restaurants. The 1992 Olympic Village, now a hot tapas and nightlife spot, is up the beach to the north and is easily identifiable by the enormous, gold, Frank Gehry–designed fish sculpture next to the Hotel Arts. ✉ *Below Estació de França and Ciutadella Park.*

Bullfighting

Barcelona's bullring is the **Monumental** (✉ Gran Via and Carles I), where bullfights are held on Sunday between March and October; check the newspaper for details. For tickets with no markup, go to the official ticket office (✉ Muntaner 24, near Gran Via, ☎ 93/453–3821). There's a **Bullfighting Museum** at the ring (⏲ Mar.–Oct., daily 10–1 and 5:30–7).

Dining and Lodging

For details and price-category definitions, *see* Dining *in* Spain A to Z, *above.*

Hotels around the Rambla and in the Gothic Quarter have a generous helping of Old-World charm but are weaker on creature comforts; those in the Eixample are mostly '50s or '60s buildings, often recently renovated; and the newest hotels are out along the Diagonal or beyond, in the residential districts of Sarriá and Pedralbes, with the exception of the Hotel Arts, in the Olympic Port. There are hotel reservation desks at the airport and Sants Station. For details and price-category definitions, *see* Lodging *in* Spain A to Z, *above.*

$$$$ ✕ **Beltxenea.** There's an air of intimacy in this redecorated Eixample apartment, now converted into a series of elegant dining rooms. In summer you can dine outside, in the formal garden. Chef Miguel Ezcurra's excellent cuisine makes for one of Barcelona's top Basque dining opportunities; a specialty is his *merluza con kokotxas y almejas* (hake and clams fried in garlic, then simmered in stock). ✉ *Mallorca 275,* ☎ *93/215–3024. AE, DC, MC, V. Closed Sun. and July–Aug. No lunch Sat.*

$$$$ ✕ **Jean Luc Figueras.** Every restaurant that Jean Luc Figueras has touched has shot straight to the top of the charts, so it's no surprise that the first to bear his name has done likewise. This one, installed in a Gràcia town house that was once couturier Cristóbal Balenciaga's studio, may be the best of all. For an extra $20 or so, the taster's menu is the best choice. ✉ *C. Santa Teresa 10,* ☎ *93/415–2877. Reservations essential. AE, DC, MC, V. Closed Sun. No lunch Sat.*

$$$ ✕ **Agut d'Avignon.** This venerable Barcelona institution takes a bit of finding; it's near the junction of Ferràn and Avinyó, in the Gothic Quarter. The ambience is rustic, the clientele often businesspeople and politicians from the nearby Generalitat. The cuisine is traditional Catalan; try one of the game specialties in season. ✉ *Trinitat 3,* ☎ *93/317–3693. Reservations essential. AE, DC, MC, V.*

$$$ ✕ **La Cuineta.** This intimate restaurant, in a 17th-century house just off Plaça Sant Jaume, has a sister behind the cathedral; both specialize in Catalan nouvelle cuisine. The decor is elegant and traditional; the service, professional; and the cuisine, impeccable. ✉ *Paradis 4,* ☎ *93/315–0111;* ✉ *Pietat 12,* ☎ *93/315–4156. AE, DC, MC, V. Closed Mon.*

$$$ ✕ **Quo Vadis.** Just off the Rambla, near the Boquería Market and Betlem Church, is an unimpressive facade camouflaging one of Barcelona's most respected restaurants. The much-praised cuisine includes such delicacies as *hígado de ganso con ciruelas* (goose liver with plums). ✉ *Carme 7,* ☎ *93/317–7447. AE, DC, MC, V. Closed Sun.*

$$$ ★ ✕ **Tram-Tram.** With chef Isidro Soler at the helm in the kitchen and Reyes Lizán as hostess and pastry chef, Tram-Tram is one of Barcelona's culinary highlights. The excursion northwest to the villagelike suburb of Sarrià is a delight. Order the taster's menu and let Isidro take care of you—you won't regret it. ✉ *Major de Sarrià 121,* ☎ *93/204–8518. AE, MC, V. Closed Sun. and Dec. 24–Jan. 6.*

$$ ✕ **Can Culleretes.** This picturesque old restaurant began life as a pastry shop in 1786; today it's one of the most atmospheric and reasonably priced restaurants in Barcelona. Tucked into an alley between Ferràn and Boquería, it has three dining rooms decorated with photos of visiting celebrities; the kitchen serves real Catalan cooking and is very much a family concern. Don't be put off by the street life that might be raging outside. ✉ *Quintana 5,* ☎ *93/317–3022. AE, MC, V. Closed Mon. No lunch Sun.*

$$ ✕ **Los Caracoles.** Just below the Plaça Reial is Barcelona's best-known tourist haunt, crawling with Americans having a terrific time. Its walls are hung thick with photos of bullfighters and visiting celebrities; its specialties are mussels, paella, and of course, *caracoles* (snails). ✉ *Escudellers 14,* ☎ *93/309–3185. AE, DC, MC, V.*

$$ ★ ✕ **Set Portes.** With plenty of Old-World charm, this delightful restaurant near the waterfront has been going strong since 1836. The cooking is Catalan, the portions enormous, and specialties are paella *de pescado* (with seafood) and *zarzuela Set Portes* (a mixed grill of seafood). The restaurant serves nonstop from 1 PM to 1 AM. ✉ *Passeig Isabel II 14,* ☎ *93/319–3033. AE, DC, MC, V.*

$$ ✕ **Sopeta Una.** Dining in this delightful, small restaurant, with old-fashioned decor and intimate atmosphere, is more like eating in a private home—and you're right near the Palau de la Músicañ. All the dishes are Catalan, and the atmosphere is genteel and middle-class. For dessert try the traditional Catalan *música*, a plate of raisins, almonds, and dried fruit served with a glass of muscatel. ✉ *Verdaguer i Callis 6,* ☎ *93/319–6131. V. Closed Sun.*

$ ★ ✕ **Agut.** Simple, hearty Catalan fare awaits you in this unpretentious restaurant in the lower reaches of the Gothic Quarter. Founded in 1924, Agut has kept its popularity. There's plenty of wine to go with the traditional home cooking, along with a family warmth that always makes the place exciting. ✉ *Gignàs 16,* ☎ *93/315–1709. AE, MC, V. Closed Mon. and July. No dinner Sun.*

$ ★ ✕ **Egipte.** This small, friendly restaurant hidden behind the Boquería Market is a real find, known better to locals than to visitors. Its traditional Catalan home cooking, huge desserts, and swift, personable service all make it a good value. ✉ *Jerusalem 12,* ☎ *93/301–6208. Reservations not accepted. AE, DC, MC, V. Closed Sun.*

$ ✕ **La Fonda.** This is one of three Camós family restaurants that offer top dining value. The other two locations are in neighboring Plaça Reial: Les Quinze Nits (✉ Plaça Reial 6) and Hostal de Rita (✉ Carrer Arago 279, near the corner of Arago and Pau Claris). Be early (1 for lunch, 8 for dinner), as long lines tend to form. ✉ *Escudellers 10,* ☎ *93/301–7515. Reservations not accepted. AE, DC, MC, V.*

$$$$ ★ **Condes de Barcelona.** The Condes is one of Barcelona's most popular hotels, so rooms must be booked well in advance. The decor is stunning, with marble floors and columns, an impressive staircase, and an outstanding bar area. Guest rooms are on the small side. ✉ *Passeig de Gràcia 75, 08008,* ☎ *93/484–8600,* FAX *93/488–0614. 183 rooms. Restaurant. AE, DC, MC, V.*

$$$$ **Hotel Arts.** This luxurious skyscraper, a Ritz-Carlton property, overlooks Barcelona from the new Olympic Port, providing unique views of the Mediterranean, the city, and the mountains behind. A short taxi ride from the center of the city, the hotel is virtually a world of its own. Rooms are ultramodern, with pale wood, Bang & Olufsen CD players, and Frette linens. The hotel has three restaurants that serve, variously, Mediterranean cuisine, Californian cooking, and tapas, like *gambas al ajillo* (baby shrimp fried in garlic). At press time, rumors had a grand casino opening directly beneath the hotel. ✉ *C. de la Marina 1921, 08005,* ☎ *93/221–1000,* FAX *93/221–1070. 455 rooms and suites. 3 restaurants, pool. AE, DC, MC, V.*

$$$$ **Hotel Claris.** Widely considered Barcelona's best hotel, the Claris is a fascinating mélange of design and tradition. The rooms come in 60 different layouts, all decorated in a classical, 18th-century English style. Wood and marble furnishings and decorative details are everywhere, and you can dip into a Japanese water garden, a first-rate restaurant, and a rooftop pool—all near the center of Barcelona. ✉ *Carrer Pau Claris 150, 08009,* ☎ *93/487–6262,* FAX *93/215–7970. 124 rooms and suites. Restaurant, pool. AE, DC, MC, V.*

$$$$ **Princesa Sofía.** The most convenient hotel to the airport, the Sofía is removed from the hue and cry of downtown. For business and convenience, it's one of the city's best options. ✉ *Plaça Pius XII 4, 08028,* ☎ *93/330–7111,* FAX *93/411–2106. 505 rooms. 3 restaurants, 2 pools. AE, DC, MC, V.*

$$$$ ★ **Rey Juan Carlos I–Conrad International.** Towering over the western end of Barcelona's Avinguda Diagonal, this modern skyscraper is an exciting commercial complex as well as a luxury hotel. Jewelry, furs, caviar, art, flowers, fashions, and even limousines are for sale or hire on site. The lush garden, including a swan-dappled pond, has an Olympic-size swimming pool; the green expanses of Barcelona's finest in-town country club, El Polo, spread luxuriantly out beyond. There are two restaurants: Chez Vous, with French cuisine, and Café Polo, with a sumptuous buffet and an American bar. ✉ *Av. Diagonal 661671, 08028,* ☎ *93/448–0808,* FAX *93/448–0607. 375 rooms, 40 suites. 2 restaurants, pool. AE, DC, MC, V.*

$$$$ ★ **Ritz.** This classic hotel has new management and has maintained or even heightened its splendor. The entrance lobby is awe-inspiring; the rooms spacious, and furnished with Regency furniture; and the service excellent. ✉ *Gran Via 668, 08010,* ☎ *93/318–5200,* FAX *93/318–0148. 158 rooms. Restaurant. AE, DC, MC, V.*

$$$ ★ **Colón.** This cozy, older hotel has a unique charm and intimacy reminiscent of an English country hotel. Rooms are comfortable and tasteful. The location, right in the heart of the Gothic Quarter, is ideal, and front rooms overlook the cathedral and square. ✉ *Avda. Catedral 7, 08002,* ☎ *93/301–1404,* FAX *93/317–2915. 147 rooms. Restaurant. AE, DC, MC, V.*

$$ **España.** This hotel has large, modern bedrooms—the best and quietest overlooking the bright interior patio—and stunning Art Nouveau public rooms. The high-ceilinged ground level has a breakfast room decorated with mermaids; elaborate woodwork; and, in the cafeteria, an Eusebio Arnau Art Nouveau sculpted chimney. The neighborhood is seedy but safe. ✉ *Sant Pau 911, 08001,* ☎ *93/318–1758,* FAX *93/317–1134. 76 rooms. Restaurant. AE, DC, MC, V.*

$$ **Gran Vía.** Architectural features are the special charm of this 19th-century mansion, close to the main tourist office. The original chapel has been preserved, and you can have breakfast in a hall of mirrors, climb the hotel's Moderniste staircase, and make calls from elaborate Belle Epoque phone booths. ✉ *Gran Vía 642, 08007,* ☎ *93/318–1900,* FAX *93/318–9997. 53 rooms. AE, DC, MC, V.*

$$ ★ **Oriente.** Barcelona's oldest hotel opened in 1843. Its public rooms are a delight—the ballroom and dining rooms have lost none of their 19th-century magnificence—though the bedrooms are rather bland. It's just below the Liceu, and its terrace café is the perfect place for a drink. ✉ *Rambla 45, 08002,* ☎ *93/302–2558,* FAX *93/412–3819. 142 rooms.Restaurant. AE, DC, MC, V.*

$ **Continental.** Something of a legend among cost-conscious travelers, this comfortable hostel with canopied balconies stands at the top of the Rambla, just below Plaça Catalunya. The rooms are homey and comfortable, the staff is friendly, and the location is ideal. Buffet breakfasts are a plus. ✉ *Rambla 138, 08002,* ☎ *93/301–2508,* FAX *93/302–7360. 35 rooms. AE, DC, MC, V.*

$ **Jardí.** With views over the charming and traffic-free squares, Plaça del Pi and Plaça Sant Josep Oriol, this hotel's bedrooms are small but have gleaming bathrooms and powerful showers. The quietest rooms are the highest, but you have to walk up to them; there's no elevator. ✉ *Plaça Sant Josep Oriol 1, 08002,* ☎ *93/301–5900,* FAX *93/318–3664. 40 rooms. AE, DC, MC, V.*

Nightlife and the Arts

The Arts

To find out what's on, look in the daily papers or the weekly *Guía del Ocio,* available at newsstands all over town. *Actes a la Ciutat* is a weekly list of cultural events published by the *ajuntament* and available from its information office on Plaça Sant Jaume, or at the Palau de la Virreina (☞ Exploring, *above*). The daily *El Pais* lists all events of interest on its *agenda* page.

CONCERTS

Catalans are great music lovers. Their main concert hall is the **Palau de la Música** (☞ Exploring, *above*), whose ticket office is open weekdays 11–1 and 5–8 and Saturday 5–8 only. You can usually buy tickets just before the concert. Sunday-morning concerts (11 AM) are a local tradition. Musical events are also held (free) in the Town Hall's Saló de Cent on Thursday at 8, as well as in some of Barcelona's best architectural venues, such as the church of Santa Maria del Mar and others. Barcelona's opera house, the newly rebuilt **Liceu,** should open in early 1999.

DANCE

L'Espai de Dansa i Mùsica de la Generalitat de Catalunya (✉ Travessera de Gràcia 63, ☎ 93/414–3133), usually listed simply as "L'Espai" (The Space), is now Barcelona's prime venue for ballet and contemporary dance. **El Mercat de les Flors** (✉ Lleida 59, ☎ 93/426–1875), not far from Plaça d'Espanya, always has a rich program of modern dance and theater. The **Teatre Victoria** (✉ Avda. Parallel 67, ☎ 93/443–2929) also has a good selection of dance and theater, as does the **Teatre Nacional de Catalunya** (Plaça de les Arts 1, ☎ 93/306–5706), in the Olympic Port.

FILM

More and more theaters in Barcelona regularly show foreign movies in their original languages—indicated by "v.o.," or *versión original.* Some of the most important are the Olympic Port's 15-screen **Icaria Yelmo** (Salvador Espriu 61, 93/221–7585), **Capsa** (Pau Claris 134, 93/215–7393), or the happening Gràcia neighborhood's **Verdi** (✉ Verdi 32, Gràcia, ☎ 93/237–0516).

THEATER

Most plays are in Catalan, but Barcelona is also known for its experimental theater and its mime troupes. The best-known modern theaters are the **Teatre Lliure** (✉ Montseny 47, Gràcia, ☎ 93/218–9251), **El Mercat de les Flors** (☞ Dance, *above*), **Teatre Romea** (✉ Hospital 51, ☎ 93/317–7189), **Teatre Tívoli** (✉ Casp 10, ☎ 93/412–2063), **Teatre Poliorama** (✉ Rambla Estudios 115, ☎ 93/317–7599), and **Teatre Nacional de Catalunya** (Plaça de les Arts 1, ☎ 93/900–121133).

Nightlife

BARS

Champagne Bars. *Xampanyerías,* serving sparkling Catalan *cava,* are something of a Barcelona specialty. **El Xampanyet** (✉ Montcada 22, ☎ 93/319–7003), just down from the Picasso Museum, has cider, cava, and tapas in a lively setting. **La Cava del Palau** (✉ Verdaguer i Callis 10, ☎ 93/310–0938), near the Palaù de la Música, has a wide selection of cavas, wines, and cocktails. **La Folie** (✉ Bailén 169, ☎ 93/457–4449) is one of the best.

Cocktail Bars. The **Passeig del Born,** near the Picasso Museum, is lined with bars. **Dry Martini** (✉ Aribau 162, ☎ 93/217–5072) has more than 80 different gins. **El Copetin** (✉ Passeig del Born 19) has exciting decor and good cocktails. **El Paraigua** (Plaça Sant Miquel, Gothic Quarter, behind City Hall, ☎ 93/217–3028), serves cocktails in a stylish setting with classical music. **Ideal Cocktail Bar** (✉ Aribau 89, ☎ 93/453–1028) has good malt whiskeys. **Miramelindo** (✉ Passeig del Born 15, ☎ 93/319–5376) offers a large selection and often jazz.

Tapas Bars. Cal Pep (✉ 8 Plaça de les Olles, ☎ 93/319–6183), near Santa Maria del Mar, is a popular spot, with the best and freshest selection of tapas. **Euskal Etxea** (✉ Placeta Montcada 13, ☎ 93/310–2185), a Basque bar, has excellent tapas and atmosphere. **Carrer de la Mercé** is all tapas bars, just across from the Moll de la Fusta, from Correos (the post office) down to the Iglesia de la Mercé. **Alt Heidelberg** (✉ Ronda Universitat 5, ☎ 93/318–1032) has German beer on tap and German sausages. **Casa Tejada** (Tenor Viñas, near Plaça Francesc Macià, ☎ 93/200–7341) has some of the finest tapas in Barcelona. The tapas establishments along Passeig de Gràcia look inviting, but serve mainly prepared and microwaved fare. **Tramoia,** at the corner of Rambla de Catalunya and Gran Via, is a happy exception.

CABARET

Barcelona City Hall (✉ Rambla de Catalunya 2-4 [access through New Canadian Store], ☎ 93/317–2177) offers sophisticated shows in a beautifully decorated music hall. **Starlets** (✉ Av. Sarrià 44, ☎ 93/430–9156) has cabaret nightly.

CAFÉS AND TEAROOMS

Carrer Petritxol (from Portaferrissa to Plaça del Pi) is famous for its *chocolaterías* (serving hot chocolate, tea, coffee, and pastries) and tearooms. The **Café de l'Opera** (✉ Rambla 74, ☎ 93/317–7585; ⏲ daily 10AM–2AM), across from the Liceu opera house, is a perennial hangout. **Els Quatre Gats** (✉ Montsió 3, ☎ 93/302–4140) draws a devoted crew of regulars. The traditional **Salón de Té Libre i Serra** (✉ Ronda Sant Pere 3, ☎ 93/318–9183) has a good selection of pastries. **Salón de Té Mauri** (✉ corner of Rambla de Catalunya and Provença, ☎ 93/215–8146) is a traditional tearoom. Near the Picasso Museum, don't miss the hip **Textil Café** (✉ Montcada 1214, ☎ 93/268–2598), in the Museu Textil's lovely medieval courtyard.

DISCOS AND NIGHTCLUBS

At **Luz de Gas** (✉ Muntaner 246, ☎ 93/209–7711), guitar and soul performances are followed by wild abandon. **Otto Zutz** (✉ Lincoln 15, just below Via Augusta, ☎ 93/238–0722) is a top-ranked spot. **Up and Down** (✉ Numancia 179, ☎ 93/280–2922), pronounced "pendow," is a lively classic. **Oliver and Hardy** (✉ Diagonal 593, next to Barcelona Hilton, ☎ 93/419–3181), **La Tierra** (✉ Aribau 230, ☎ 93/200–7346), and **El Otro** (✉ Valencia 166, ☎ 93/323–6759) welcome all ages, even those over 35.

FLAMENCO

El Patio Andaluz (✉ Aribau 242, ☎ 93/209–3378) is a solid option but rather expensive. **Los Tarantos** (✉ Plaça Reial 17, ☎ 93/318–3067) was the most happening flamenco spot at press time. **Tablao del Carmen** (✉ Arcs 9, Poble Espanyol, ☎ 93/325–6895) is a solid runner-up.

JAZZ CLUBS

The **Barcelona Pipa Club** (✉ Plaça Reial 3, ☎ 93/302–4732) hosts such visiting artists as Jordi Rossy and Billy McHenry. The Gothic Quarter's **Harlem Jazz Club** (✉ Comtessa Sobradiel 8, ☎ 93/310–0755) veritably sizzles. **Jamboree** (✉ Plaça Reial 17, ☎ 93/301–7564), downstairs from Los Tarantos (☞ Flamenco, *above*), has regular jazz performances. **La Cova del Drac** (✉ Vallmajor 33, ☎ 93/200–7032) is still hot.

Ports and Beaches

The Barcelona waterfront has undergone a major overhaul since 1992. The **Port Vell** (Old Port) now includes an extension of the Rambla, the **Rambla de Mar,** crossing the inner harbor from just below the Columbus Monument. This boardwalk connects the Rambla with the **Moll d'Espanya,** which comprises a shopping mall, a dozen restaurants, an aquarium, a cinema complex, and Barcelona's two yacht clubs. A walk around the Port Vell leads past the marina to Passeig Joan de Borbó, both lined with restaurants and their outdoor tables. From here you can go south out to sea along the *rompeolas,* a 3-km (2-mi) excursion, or north (left) down the San Sebastián beach to the Passeig Marítim, which leads to the **Port Olímpic.** Except for the colorful inner streets of Barceloneta, the traditional fisherman's quarter, this new construction is largely devoid of local character. Take the Golondrinas boat (☞ Getting Around, By Boat, *below*) to the end of the breakwater and walk into Barceloneta for some paella.

Beaches

Barcelona's beaches have improved and proliferated. Starting at the southern end of the city (to the right looking out to sea) is the **Platja (Beach) de Sant Sebastià,** a nudist enclave, followed by **La Barceloneta, Passeig Marítim, Port Olímpic, Nova Icaria, Bogatell,** and, at the northern tip, the **Mar Bella.** Topless bathing is the rule. Water quality is officially tested and rated as acceptable, but you should still have a careful look before you dive; some days are better than others.

Shopping

Elegant shopping districts are the Passeig de Gràcia, Rambla de Catalunya, and the Diagonal. For more affordable, old-fashioned, and typically Spanish-style shops, explore the area between the Rambla and Via Laietana, especially around Carrer de Ferràn. The area around Plaça del Pi from Boquería to Portaferrisa and Canuda is well stocked with youthful fashion stores and imaginative gift shops.

Barcelona has several shopping plazas: **Les Glories** (✉ Avda. Diagonal 208, Plaça de les Glories, ☎ 93/486–0639), **L'Illa** (✉ Diagonal 545, between Numancia and Entenza, ☎ 93/444–0000), and **Maremagnum** (✉ Moll d'Espanya s/n, Port Vell, ☎ 93/225–8100). Try **Carrer Tuset,** north of Diagonal between Aribau and Balmes, for small boutiques.

Antiques

Carrer de la Palla and Banys Nous, in the Gothic Quarter, are lined with antiques shops where you'll find old maps, books, paintings, and furniture. An **antiques market** is held every Thursday in front of the Cathedral. The **Centre d'Antiquaris** (✉ Passeig de Gràcia 57, ☎ 93/215–4499), has some 75 antiques stores. **Gothsland** (✉ Consell de Cent 331, ☎ 93/488–1922) specializes in Moderniste designs.

Boutiques

Fashionable boutiques line Passeig de Gràcia and Rambla de Catalunya. Others are on Gran Via between Balmes and Pau Claris, and on the Diagonal between Ganduxer and Passeig de Gràcia. **Adolfo Domínguez** (✉ Passeig de Gràcia 89, Valencia 245, ☎ 93/487–3687) is one of Spain's top clothing designers. **Loewe** (✉ Passeig de Gràcia 35, Diagonal 570, ☎ 93/216–0400) is Spain's top leather store. **Joaquín Berao** (✉ Rosselló 277, ☎ 93/218–6187), is a top jewelry designer. **Zapata** (✉ Buenos Aires 64, at Diagonal, ☎ 93/430–4785), is a top jewelry dealer.

Department Stores

El Corte Inglés (✉ Plaça de Catalunya 14, ☎ 93/302–1212; ✉ Diagonal 617, near the María Cristina metro stop, ☎ 93/419–2828) is Barcelona's—and Spain's—great consumer emporium. L'Illa (☞ *above*) contains a **Marks & Spencer** and an **FNAC.**

Food and Flea Markets

The **Boquería Market** (✉ on Rambla between Carme and Hospital) is a superb, colorful food market, held every day except Sunday. **Els Encants** (✉ end of Dos de Maig, on the Plaça Glòries Catalanes), Barcelona's wild-and-woolly flea market, is held every Monday, Wednesday, Friday, and Saturday, 8–7. **Sant Antoni Market** (✉ end of Ronda Sant Antoni), is an old-fashioned food and clothes market, best on Sunday when there's a secondhand **book market** with old postcards, press cuttings, lithographs, and prints. There's a **stamp and coin market** (✉ Plaça Reial) on Sunday morning. An **artists' market** (✉ Placeta del Pi, just off Rambla and Boquería) sets up on Saturday morning.

Gift Ideas

No special handicrafts are associated with Barcelona, but you'll have no trouble finding typical Spanish goods anywhere in town. **Xavier Roca i Coll** (✉ Sant Pere mes Baix 24, off Via Laietana, ☎ 93/215–1052) specializes in silver models of Barcelona's buildings.

If your friends back home are into fashion and jewelry, you're in the right city—Barcelona makes all the headlines on Spain's booming fashion front. Barcelona and Catalonia passed along a playful sense of design even before Antoni Gaudí began creating shock waves over a century ago. A number of stores and boutiques specialize in design items (jewelry, furnishings, knickknacks). **Bd** (Barcelona Design; ✉ Mallorca 291293, ☎ 93/458–6909) offers reproduction furniture from many designers. **Dos i Una** (✉ Rosselló 275, ☎ 93/217–7032) is a good source of clever gifts. **Vinçon** (✉ Passeig de Gràcia 96, ☎ 93/215–6050) has a huge selection of stylish housewares.

Barcelona Essentials

Arriving and Departing

BY BUS

Barcelona has no central bus station, but all buses operate either from the old Estació Vilanova, generally known as **Estació del Norte** (✉ end of Av. Vilanova, ☎ 93/893–5312) or from the **Estació Autobuses de Sants** (✉ C. Viriato, next to Sants Central train terminal, ☎ 93/490–0202). **Julià** (✉ Ronda Universitat 5, ☎ 93/317–6454) runs buses to Zaragoza and Montserrat. **Alsina Graëlls** (✉ Ronda Universitat 4, ☎ 93/265–6866) runs to Lérida and Andorra.

BY PLANE

All international and domestic flights arrive at **El Prat de Llobregat** airport (☎ 93/478–5000 or 93/478–5032), 14 km (8½ mi) south of Barcelona just off the main highway to Castelldefels and Sitges. For information on arrival and departure times, call the airport or Info-Iberia (☎ 93/412–5667).

Between the Airport and Downtown. The airport-to-city **train** leaves every 30 minutes between 6:30 AM and 11 PM, costs about 350 ptas., and reaches the Barcelona Central (Sants) Station in 15 minutes and Plaça de Catalunya, in the heart of the old city (at the head of La Rambla), in 20–25 minutes. From there a short taxi hop of 350–500 ptas. will take you from Plaça Catalunya to most of central Barcelona's hotels. The **Aerobus** service connects the airport with Plaça Catalunya every 15 minutes between 6:25 AM and 11 PM; the fare of 475 ptas. can be paid with all international credit cards. RENFE also provides a bus service to the Central Station during the night hours. A **taxi** from the airport to your hotel, including airport and luggage surcharges, will cost about 3,000 ptas.

BY TRAIN

The **Sants Central Station** (✉ Plaça Països Catalans, ☎ 93/490–0202, 24-hr RENFE information line) is Barcelona's main train station, serving international and national destinations as well as suburban areas. The old and elegant **Estació de França** (✉ Av. Marquès de l'Argentera, ☎ 93/490–0202, 24-hr RENFE information) now serves as the main terminal for certain trains to France and some express trains to points in Spain. Inquire at the tourist office (☞ Visitor Information, *in* Contacts and Resources, *below*) for current travel information and to find out which station you need. Many trains also stop at the **Passeig de Gràcia underground station** (✉ Passeig de Gràcia and C. Aragó, ☎ 93/488–0236); this station is closer to the Plaça de Catalunya and Rambla area than Sants. Tickets and information are available here, but luggage carts are not.

Getting Around

Modern Barcelona, the Eixample—above the Plaça de Catalunya—is built on a grid system, but there's no helpful numbering scheme. The Gothic Quarter from the Plaça de Catalunya to the port is a warren of narrow streets. You'll need a good street map to get around. Almost all sightseeing can be done on foot, but you may need to use taxis, the metro, or buses to link certain sightseeing areas, depending on how much time you have. From mid-May to mid-October look for **Bus Turistic 100** for low-cost transport to Barcelona's main sites.

BY BOAT

Golondrinas boats operate short harbor trips from the Portal de la Pau near the Columbus Monument daily 10–8 in summer, 10 AM–1:30 PM, weekends only, in winter. A one-way ticket lets you off at the end of the breakwater for a 4-km (2½-mi) stroll, surrounded by the Mediterranean, back into Barceloneta.

BY BUS

City buses run from about 5:30 or 6 AM to 10:30 PM, though some stop earlier. There are also night buses to certain destinations. The flat fare is 155 ptas. Route plans are displayed at bus stops. You can purchase a **tarjeta multiviatge,** good for 10 rides, at the transport kiosk on Plaça de Catalunya (750 ptas.).

BY CABLE CAR AND FUNICULAR

Montjuïc Funicular (⏲ summer, noon–2:45 and 4:30–9:25; winter, 11–8:15) is a cog railroad that runs from the junction of Avenida Parallel and Nou de la Rambla to the Miramar Amusement Park on Montjuïc. A **teleferic** (cable car; summer, daily noon–8; winter, weekends 11–7:30) runs from the amusement park up to Montjuïc Castle.

The **Transbordador Aeri Harbor Cable Car** (🎫 1,500 ptas.; ⏲ Oct.–June, weekdays noon–5:45, weekends noon–6:15; June–Oct., daily 11–9) runs from Miramar on Montjuïc to the Torre de Jaume I across the harbor on Barcelona *moll* (quay), and on to the Torre de Sant Sebastià at the end of Passeig Joan de Borbó in Barceloneta. You can board at either stage.

To reach Tibidabo summit, take either Bus 58 or the Ferrocarrils de la Generalitat train from Plaça de Catalunya to Avenida Tibidabo, then the *tramvía blau* (blue tram) to Peu del Funicular, and the **Tibidabo Funicular** from there to the Tibidabo Fairground. The funicular runs every half hour from 7:15 AM to 9:45 PM.

BY METRO

The subway is the fastest and easiest way to get around. You can pay a flat fare of 150 ptas. or buy a **tarjeta multiviatge,** good for 10 rides (780 ptas.). Maps of the system are available at main metro stations and branches of the Caixa savings bank.

BY TAXI

Taxis are black and yellow. When available for hire, they show a LIBRE sign in the daytime and a green light at night. The meter starts at 315 ptas., and there are supplements for luggage (100 ptas. per case), and for rides from the airport, a station, or the port (varies according to zone). There are cab stands all over town; cabs may also be flagged down on the street. Taxi drivers in Barcelona are nearly always pleasant, helpful, and fair, and don't care much about tips one way or the other.

Contacts and Resources

CONSULATES

United States (✉ Pg. Reina Elisenda 23, ☎ 93/280–2227). **Australia** (✉ Gran Viá Carles III 98, ☎ 93/330–9496). **Canada** (✉ Via Augusta 125, ☎ 93/209–0634). **New Zealand** (✉ Travessera de Gràcia 64, ☎ 93/209–0399). **United Kingdom** (✉ Diagonal 477, ☎ 93/419–9044).

EMERGENCIES

112 is the **general emergency number** in all EU nations (akin to 911 in the U.S.). **Police** (National Police, ☎ 091; Municipal Police, ☎ 092). **Medical emergencies** (☎ 061). **Pharmacies** (☎ 010). **Tourist Attention** (✉ La Rambla 43, ☎ 93/317–7016, 24-hour assistance for crime victims).

ENGLISH-LANGUAGE BOOKSTORES

BCN Books (✉ Aragó 277, ☎ 93/487–3123) is one of Barcelona's top spots for books in English. **Come In** (✉ Provença 203, ☎ 93/253–1204) is another good option for English books. **El Corte Inglés** (☞ Department Store, *in* Shopping, *above*) sells English guidebooks and novels, but the selection is limited. For variety, try **The English Bookshop** (✉ Entençan 63, ☎ 93/425–4466). The bookstore at the **Palau de la Virreina** (☞ Exploring, *above*) has good books on art, design, and Barcelona.

GUIDED TOURS

Orientation. City sightseeing tours are run by **Julià Tours** (✉ Ronda Universitat 5, ☎ 93/317–6454). **Pullmantur** (✉ Gran Viá de les Corts Catalanes 635, ☎ 93/318–5195) also has city sightseeing. Tours leave from the above terminals, though you may be able to arrange a pickup at your hotel. Both agencies offer the same tours at the same prices. A morning sightseeing tour visits the Gothic Quarter and Montjuïc; an afternoon tour concentrates on Gaudí and the Picasso Museum. You can visit Barcelona's Olympic sites from May through October.

Excursions. Trips out of town are run by Julià Tours and Pullmantur (☞ *above*). The principal attractions are a half-day tour to Montserrat to visit the monastery and shrine of the famous Black Virgin; a full-day trip to the Costa Brava resorts, including a boat cruise to the Medes Isles; and, from June through September, a full-day trip to Andorra for tax-free shopping.

SPECIAL-INTEREST AND WALKING TOURS

La Ruta del Modernismo (the Route of Modernism), created by Barcelona's *ayuntamiento,* connects some 50 key sites in the city's rich trove of Art Nouveau architecture. Everything from Gaudí's first lamppost to the colossal Sagrada Família to the odd Moderniste pharmacy or bakery is included, along with guided visits of key sites not open to the general public. The Palau Güell (✉ Carrer Nou de Rambla 3–5, ☎ 93/317–3974) is "kilometer zero" for the tour; you can also buy the multiple ticket at the Casa Lleó Morera (✉ Passeig de Gràcia 35, 3rd floor, ☎ 93/488–0139). Tickets are 1,500 ptas. adults, 800 ptas. students and seniors. Both offices are open Monday–Saturday 10–7.

TRAVEL AGENCIES

American Express (✉ Roselló 257, corner of Passeig de Gràcia, ☎ 93/217–0070). **Bestours** (✉ Diputación 241, ☎ 93/487–8580). **Viajes Iberia** (✉ Rambla 130, ☎ 93/317–9320). **Wagons-Lits Cook** (✉ Passeig de Gràcia 8, ☎ 93/317–5500).

VISITOR INFORMATION

Information on Barcelona: Centre d'Informació Turistic de Barcelona (Plaça de Catalunya 17, lower level, ☎ 93/304–3135, FAX 93/304–3155).

Sants train station (☎ 93/491–4431). **França** train station (☎ 93/319–5758). **El Prat Airport** (☎ 93/478–4704). **Ajuntament** (✉ Plaça Sant Jaume, ☎ 93/402–7000, ext. 433). **Palau de la Virreina** (cultural information; ✉ Rambla 99, ☎ 93/301–7775). **Palau de Congressos** (during special events and conferences; ✉ Avda. María Cristina, ☎ 93/423–3101, ext. 8356). **Information on Catalonia and Spain: El Prat Airport** (☎ 93/478–4704). **Centre d'Informació Turística** (Palau Robert, Passeig de Gràcia 107, at Diagonal, ☎ 93/238–4000). **General information: dial 010.**

MOORISH SPAIN

Stretching from the dark mountains of the Sierra Morena in the north, west to the plains of the Guadalquivir valley, and south to the mighty, snowcapped Sierra Nevada, Andalucía (Andalusia) rings with echoes of the Moors. Creating a kingdom they called Al-Andalus, these North African Muslims ruled southern Spain for almost 800 years, from their conquest of Gibraltar in 711 to their expulsion from Granada in 1492. To this day the cities and landscapes of Andalusia are rich in their legacy: Córdoba's breathtaking mosque, Granada's magical Alhambra Palace, and Seville's landmark Giralda tower were the inspired creations of Moorish architects and craftsmen working for Al-Andalus's Arab emirs. Outside the cities, brilliant white villages—with narrow streets, heavily grilled windows, and whitewashed facades, all clustered around cool private patios—and the wailing songs of flamenco, vaguely reminiscent of the muezzin's call to prayer, all stem from centuries of Moorish occupation.

The downside to a visit here, especially to Seville, is that petty crime is not uncommon, and thieves often prey on tourists. Purse-snatching and thefts from cars, even when drivers are in them, are depressingly familiar. *Always* keep your car doors *and* trunk locked. *Never* leave valuables in your car. Leave your passport, traveler's checks, and credit cards in your hotel's safe, *never* in your room. Don't carry expensive cameras or wear jewelry. Take only the minimum amount of cash with you. There comes a time, of course—if your windshield is smashed or your bag is snatched, for example—when all the precautions in the world are beside the point. If you're unlucky, it's an equally depressing fact that the police, again especially in Seville, often take a distinctly casual attitude to such thefts, combining indifference to beleaguered tourists with rudeness in about equal measure.

Seville

Numbers in the margin correspond to points of interest on the Seville map.

Lying on the banks of the Guadalquivir River, 538 km (334 mi) southwest of Madrid, Sevilla (Seville)—Spain's fourth-largest city and the capital of Andalusia—is one of the most alluring cities in Europe. Famous in the arts as the home of the sensuous Carmen and the amorous Don Juan—and celebrated in real life for its spectacular Semana Santa (Holy Week) processions and April Fair—Seville is the urban embodiment of Moorish Andalusia.

★ 1 Begin your visit in the **cathedral,** which was begun in 1402, a century and a half after Ferdinand III seized Seville from the Moors, and took more than a century to build. It's the largest and highest cathedral in Spain, the largest Gothic building in the world, and the world's third-largest church after St. Peter's in Rome and St. Paul's in London. As if that weren't enough, it has the world's largest carved wooden altarpiece. Despite all this, the inside can be dark and gloomy, with too

many overly ornate Baroque trappings. Seek out the beautiful Virgins by Murillo and Zurbarán and reflect on the history enshrined in these walls. In a silver urn before the high altar rest the precious relics of Seville's reconquerer, Ferdinand III. You may want to pay your respects to Christopher Columbus, whose mortal vestiges are said to be enshrined in the flamboyant mausoleum in the south aisle. Borne aloft by statues representing the four medieval kingdoms of Spain, perhaps the great voyager has found peace at last, after the transatlantic quarrels that carried his body from Valladolid to Santo Domingo and from Havana to Seville. ✉ *Plaza Virgen de los Reyes,* ☏ *95/421–4971.* ⏲ *Mon.–Sat. 10:30–5, Sun. 2–4, and mass.*

★ ❷ Adjacent to the cathedral is the **Giralda,** a splendid example of Moorish art and now a symbol of Seville. Originally the minaret of Seville's great mosque, the Giralda was incorporated by the Christians into their new cathedral after the Reconquest and later topped by a bell tower and weather vane. In place of steps, 35 sloping ramps climb the 230 ft to the viewing platform; St. Ferdinand is said to have ridden his horse to the top to admire the view of the city he had just conquered. Seven centuries later, your view of the Golden Tower and shimmering Guadalquivir is just as beautiful. Try to see the Giralda at night, too, when floodlights cast a different magic on this Islamic gem. ✉ *Plaza Virgen de los Reyes,* ☏ *95/456–3321.* ⏲ *Mon.–Sat. 11–5, Sun. 10–1:30 and 2–4.*

★ ❸ The high fortified walls of the **Alcázar** belie the exquisite delicacy of the palace's interior. It was built by Peter the Cruel—so known because he murdered his stepmother and four of his half brothers—who lived here with his mistress, María de Padilla, from 1350 to 1369. Don't mistake this for a genuine Moorish palace, as it was built more than 100 years after the reconquest of Seville; rather, its style is Mudéjar—

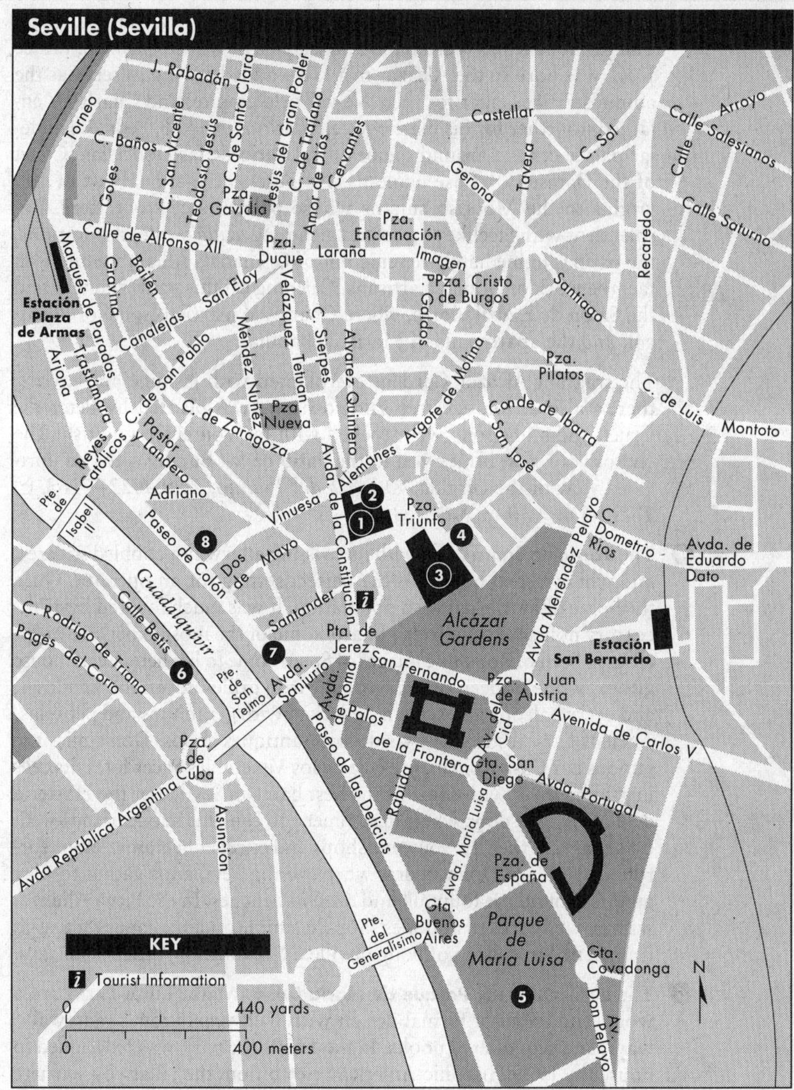

Alcázar, **3**
Barrio de Santa Cruz, **4**
Calle Betis, **6**
Cathedral, **1**
Giralda, **2**
Maestranza Bullring, **8**
Parque de María Luisa, **5**
Torre de Oro, **7**

built by Moorish craftsmen working under orders of a Christian king. The Catholic Kings (Ferdinand and Isabella)—whose only son, Prince Juan, was born in the Alcázar in 1478—added a wing to serve as the administrative center for their New World empire, and Charles V enlarged it further for his marriage celebrations in 1526. Pedro's Mudéjar palace centers around the beautiful **Patio de las Doncellas** (Court of the Damsels), whose name pays tribute to the annual gift of 100 virgins to the Moorish sultans whose palace once stood here. Resplendent with lacelike stucco and gleaming *azulejo* (tile) decorations, the patio is immediately reminiscent of Granada's Alhambra and is in fact the work of Granada artisans. Opening off this patio you will find the **Salón de Embajadores,** where Charles V married Isabel of Portugal, and the apartments of María de Padilla.

The fragrant **Alcázar Gardens** are planted with jasmine and myrtle; there's also an orange tree said to have been planted by Peter the Cruel, and a lily pond well stocked with fat, contented goldfish. The end of your visit brings you to the **Patio de las Banderas** for an unrivaled view of the Giralda. ✉ *Plaza del Triunfo,* ☎ *95/422–7163.* ⏲ *Tues.–Sat. 9:30–5, Sun. 9:30–1.*

★ ❹ The **Barrio de Santa Cruz,** with its twisting alleyways, cobbled squares, and whitewashed houses, is the perfect setting for an operetta. Once the home of Seville's Jewish population, it was much favored by 17th-century noblemen and today boasts some of the most expensive properties in Seville. Romantic images of Spain come to life here: Every house gleams white or deep ocher, wrought-iron grilles adorn the windows, and every balcony and patio is bedecked with geraniums and petunias. Ancient bars nestle side-by-side with antiques shops. Don't miss the famous bar **Casa Román,** in Plaza de los Venerables Sacerdotes, its ceilings hung thick with some of the best hams in Seville; or the **Hostería del Laurel,** next door, where in summer you can dine in one of the loveliest squares in the city. Souvenir shops and excellent ceramic shops surround the **Plaza Doña Elvira,** where young Sevillanos gather to play guitars around the fountain and *azulejo* benches. In the **Plaza Alianza,** with its well-stocked antiques shops, a simple crucifix hangs on a wall, framed in a profusion of bougainvillea. ✉ *North of Alcázar Gardens.*

❺ The gardens of the **Parque de María Luisa** (María Luisa Park) are a wonderful blend of formal design with wild vegetation, shady walkways, and sequestered nooks. In the 1920s the park was redesigned to house the 1929 Hispanic-American exhibition; the villas you see here today are the fair's remaining pavilions. The centerpiece of the exhibition was the grandiose pavilion of Spain at the monumental **Plaza de España.** At the opposite end of the park you can feed the hundreds of white doves that gather around the fountains of the lovely **Plaza de América.** Two of the pavilions here now house the **Museo Arqueológico** (Archaeological Museum; ☎ 95/423–2401; ⏲ Tues.–Sat. 9–8) and the **Museo de Artes y Costumbres Populares** (Museum of Folklore; ☎ 95/423–2576; ⏲ Tues.–Sun. 9–2:30). ✉ *Park entrance, Glorieta San Diego.*

❻ An early evening stroll along the **Calle Betis,** on the far side of the Guadalquivir, is a delight that few foreigners taste. The vista of sparkling water and palm-lined banks is stunning. ✉ *Between San Telmo and Isabel II bridges.*

❼ From this side of the river you can see the **Torre de Oro** (Tower of Gold), a 12-sided structure built by the Moors in 1220. During the day you can enjoy a nice view from the tower, which also houses a small naval museum. ✉ *Paseo de Colón, between C. Santander and C. Almirante Lobo,* ☎ *95/422–2419.* ⏲ *Tues.–Fri. 10–2, weekends 11–2.*

8 Farther along the Paseo de Colón, visit the **Maestranza Bullring,** one of Spain's oldest and most beautiful, for a bit of the bullfighting history for which Andalusia is famous. *Corridas* are held here, usually on Sunday, from Easter through October; the best are during the April Fair. Buy tickets in advance at the ring or from the kiosks on Calle Sierpes (these charge a commission). You can visit the ring and the small **museum** year-round. ✉ *Paseo de Colón 12,* ☎ *95/422–4577.* ⏲ *Weekdays 10–1:30 and 4–5:30; weekends 10–1:30.*

Seville's regular flamenco clubs cater largely to tourists and cost a little over 3,000 ptas. per person, but their shows are colorful and serve as a good introduction for the uninitiated. **El Arenal** (✉ Rodo 7, ☎ 95/421–6492) is a flamenco club in the back of the picturesque Mesón Dos de Mayo. **Los Gallos** (✉ Plaza Santa Cruz 11, ☎ 95/421–6981), an intimate club in the heart of the Barrio Santa Cruz, offers fairly pure flamenco. Catch flamenco and other regional dances nightly at **El Patio Sevillano** (✉ Paseo de Colón 11, ☎ 95/421–4120), which mainly serves tour groups.

$$$ ★ ✕ **Egaña-Oriza.** Egaña-Oriza is one of Seville's most fashionable and acclaimed restaurants. The Basque specialties include *merluza con almejas en salsa verde* (white fish and clams in green sauce) and *tostón de hígado de oca gratinada* (goose liver on toast au gratin). ✉ *San Fernando 41,* ☎ *95/422–7211. AE, DC, MC, V. Closed Sun. and Aug. No lunch Sat.*

$$$ ✕ **La Albahaca.** Set in an attractive old house in the heart of the Barrio Santa Cruz, the Albahaca offers plenty of style and atmosphere and original, imaginative cuisine. Specialties are *suprema de lubina con almejas negras* (sea bass with venus clams) and *filetitos de ciervo con salsa de hongos* (venison with wild mushroom sauce). ✉ *Plaza Santa Cruz 12,* ☎ *95/422–0714. AE, DC, MC, V. Closed Sun.*

$$$ ✕ **La Isla.** In the center of town between the cathedral and the Convent of La Caridad, La Isla has long been famous for its superb seafood and paella. ✉ *Arfe 25,* ☎ *95/421–5376. AE, DC, MC, V.*

$$$ ✕ **San Marco.** The brothers Ramacciotti serve Italian-influenced cuisine in an 18th-century mansion with a classic Andalusian patio—a wonderful spot for a summer meal. Try the ravioli *relleños de lubina en salsa de almejas* (stuffed with sea bass in a clam sauce), *cordero relleño de espinacas y setas* (lamb with spinach and forest mushrooms), or any of a delectable array of desserts. ✉ *Cuna 6,* ☎ *95/421–2440. AE, DC, MC, V. Closed Mon. and Aug.*

$$ ★ ✕ **Enrique Becerra.** This small, cozy restaurant is a short walk from the cathedral. Its lively, crowded bar decorated with Sevillian ceramic tiles is a meeting place for locals, who enjoy its excellent selection of tapas. The menu concentrates on traditional Andalusian home-cooked dishes. ✉ *Gamazo 2,* ☎ *95/421–3049. AE, DC, MC, V. Closed Sun.*

$$ ★ ✕ **La Judería.** This bright, modern restaurant near the Hotel Fernando III is fast gaining recognition for the quality of its Andalusian and international cuisine and reasonable prices. Fish dishes from the north of Spain and meat from Ávila are specialties. Try *cordero lechal asado* (roast baby lamb) or *urta a la Roteña* (a bream dish from Rota, on the Costa de la Luz—cooked with brandy, peppers, onions, and tomatoes). ✉ *Cano y Cueto 13,* ☎ *95/441–2052. Reservations essential. AE, DC, MC, V. Closed Mon. and Aug.*

$$ ★ ✕ **Mesón Don Raimundo.** In an old convent close to the cathedral, the Mesón has deliberately Sevillian atmosphere and decor. Its bar is the perfect place to sample some splendid tapas, and the restaurant, when

not catering to tour groups, is one of Seville's most delightful. ✉ *Argote de Molina 26,* ☎ *95/422–3355. AE, DC, MC, V. No dinner Sun.*

$–$$ ✕ **El Bacalao.** This popular fish restaurant, opposite the church of Santa Catalina, is in an Andalusian house decorated with ceramic tiles. As the name suggests, the house specialty is *bacalao* (salt cod); try it *con arroz* (with rice) or *al pil-pil* (fried in garlic and oil—making the "pil-pil" sound). ✉ *Plaza Ponce de León 15,* ☎ *95/421–6670. AE, DC, MC, V. Closed Sun., end of July, and beginning of Aug.*

$$$$ ★ **Alfonso XIII.** This ornate Mudéjar-style palace was built for King Alfonso XIII's visit to the 1929 exhibition. It's worth a visit just for its splendid Moorish decor, including beautiful stained glass and the colorful ceramic tiles typical of Seville. ✉ *San Fernando 2, 41004,* ☎ *95/422–2850,* FAX *95/421–6033. 127 rooms, 19 suites. Restaurant, pool. AE, DC, MC, V.*

$$$$ ★ **Tryp Colón.** The rooms and suites have been very comfortably modernized while retaining much of their old-fashioned style. You're right in the heart of town, near the main shopping area; and on the premises you can dine in the elegant El Burladero restaurant or the more casual La Tasca. ✉ *Canalejas 1, 41001,* ☎ *95/422–2900,* FAX *95/422–0938. 204 rooms, 14 suites. 2 restaurants. AE, DC, MC, V.*

$$$ **Doña María.** Near the cathedral, the Doña María is one of Seville's most charming hotels. Some rooms are small and plain; others are tastefully furnished with antiques. Room 310 has a four-poster double bed, 305 has two single four-posters, and both have spacious bathrooms. There's no restaurant, but a breakfast buffet is served. The rooftop pool has a good view of the Giralda, just a stone's throw away. ✉ *Don Remondo 19, 41004,* ☎ *95/422–4990,* FAX *95/421–9546. 69 rooms. Pool. AE, DC, MC, V.*

$$ **Bécquer.** Conveniently near the main shopping areas, this relatively modern hotel prides itself on attentive service. It's one of the best mid-range options, with comfortable rooms decorated in traditional Spanish style. There's also a parking garage. ✉ *Reyes Católicos 4, 41001,* ☎ *95/422–8900,* FAX *95/421–4400. 116 rooms, 2 suites. AE, DC, MC, V.*

$$ **Giralda.** The Giralda is comfortable and functional, with spacious, light rooms decorated in typical Castilian style. It lies on the edge of the old city, in a cul-de-sac off Avenida Menéndez Pelayo, and caters largely to tour groups. Rooms on the fifth floor are best. ✉ *Sierra Nevada 3, 41003,* ☎ *95/441–6661,* FAX *95/441–9352. 96 rooms, 5 suites. Restaurant. AE, DC, MC, V.*

$$ **Murillo.** This picturesque hotel in the heart of the Barrio Santa Cruz has small, simple rooms, but the setting is a virtue. You can't reach the hotel by car, but porters with trolleys will fetch your luggage from your taxi. ✉ *Lope de Rueda 7, 41004,* ☎ *95/421–6095,* FAX *95/421–9616. 57 rooms. AE, DC, MC, V.*

$ **Internacional.** If you want an inexpensive alternative, head for this Old-World, family-run hotel in the narrow streets of the old town, near the Casa de Pilatos. The rooms are very plain, but the service is friendly. ✉ *Aguilas 17, 41003,* ☎ FAX *95/421–3207. 24 rooms. DC, MC, V.*

Carmona

Thirty kilometers (19 mi) east of Seville, the N IV brings you to Carmona. This unspoiled Andalusian town of Roman and Moorish origin has a wealth of Mudéjar and Renaissance churches and its streets of whitewashed houses. Most worthwhile is the church of **San Pedro,** begun in 1466, whose extraordinary interior is an unbroken mass of sculptures and gilded surfaces, and whose tower, erected in 1704, is an unabashed imitation of Seville's Giralda. Carmona's most affecting monument is its splendid **Roman necropolis,** where in huge underground chambers some 900 family tombs, dating between the 2nd and 4th centuries AD, were chiseled out of the rock. ✉ *C. Enmedio,* ☎ *95/414–0811.* ⏲ *Summer, Tues.–Fri. 9–2 , Sat. 10–2; winter, Tues.–Fri. 10–2 and 4–6, weekends 10–2.*

$$$$ ★ **Casa de Carmona.** If you want to relax like royalty, do it at one of the most stunning hotels in all of Spain. The 16th-century palace of Lasso de la Vega was renovated in the late 1980s, and today you'll find beautifully furnished rooms decorated with fine art, rich fabrics, and antiques. ✉ *Plaza de Lasso 1, 41410,* ☎ *95/414–3300,* FAX *95/414–3752. 30 rooms. Restaurant, pool. AE, DC, MC, V.*

$$$ ★ **Parador Alcázar del Rey Don Pedro.** The beauty of this modern parador—scheduled to reopen in mid-1998 after a complete renovation—is its splendid, peaceful setting, in the ruins of the old Moorish Alcázar on top of the hill above Carmona. The views across the vast fertile plain below are magnificent. ✉ *Alcázar, 41410,* ☎ *95/414–1010,* FAX *95/414–1712. 63 rooms. Restaurant, pool. AE, DC, MC, V.*

Jerez de la Frontera

One hundred kilometers (60 mi) south of Seville, Jerez is world headquarters for **sherry.** The word *sherry,* first heard in Great Britain in 1608, is in fact an English corruption of this town's old Moorish name, Xeres; today, names such as González Byass and Domecq are just as inextricably linked with Jerez. The town's wine-making tradition dates from Roman times and continued under the Moors despite the Koran's condemnation of alcohol.

At any given time more than a million barrels of sherry are maturing in Jerez's vast, aboveground wine cellars. Most **bodegas** (wineries) welcome visitors, but it's wise to phone ahead for an appointment. If you take a tour, a guide will explain the *solera* method of blending old wine with new, and the importance of the *flor* (a sort of yeast that forms on the surface of the wine as it ages) in determining the kind of sherry. You can finish by sampling generous amounts of pale, dry fino, nutty amontillado, or rich, deep oloroso, and of course you'll be welcome to purchase a few bottles at interesting prices in the shop.

Founded in 1730, **Domecq** (☎ 956/151000) is Jerez's oldest *bodega* and makes the world's best-selling brandy, Fundador, as well as sherry. Other wineries worth visiting are **Sandeman** (☎ 956/301100), **Harveys** (☎ 956/151000), and **Wisdom and Warter** (☎ 956/184306). If you only have time for one, tour the prestigious **González Byass,** home of Tío Pepe (☎ 956/357000).

The **Real Escuela Andaluza del Arte Ecuestre** (Royal Andalusian School of Equestrian Art) stands on the grounds of the Recreo de las Cadenas, a splendid 19th-century palace. Every Thursday the Cartujana horses—a cross between the native Andalusian workhorse and the Arabian—and skilled riders in 18th-century riding costume demonstrate intricate dressage techniques and jumping in the spectacular show "Como Bailan los Caballos Andaluces." ✉ *Avda. Duque de Abrantes,* ☎ *956/307798.* ⏲ *Thurs. 11–1 (reservations essential).*

Dining and Lodging

$$$ ✕ **La Mesa Redonda.** Just off Avenida Alvaro Domecq, this small, friendly restaurant serves classic Jerez dishes in what feels like a family dining room. There are only eight tables; the round one at the end of the room gives the restaurant its name. The menu changes constantly; your best bet is to take the advice of the chef's wife, Margarita—who also has an encyclopedic knowledge of Spanish wines. ✉ *Manuel de la Quintana 3,* ☎ *956/340069. AE, DC, MC, V. Closed Sun.*

$$$ ✕ **Gaitán.** Within walking distance of the riding school, Gaitán's white walls and brick arches are adorned with colorful ceramic plates and photos of famous diners. The menu is Andalusian, with a few Basque dishes. In season, *setas* (wild mushrooms) make a delicious starter. ✉ *Gaitán 3,* ☎ *956/345859. AE, DC, MC, V. No dinner Sun.*

$$$ ✕🏨 **Jerez.** This luxury hotel is a low, white building in the residential neighborhood north of town. The bar and elegant restaurant overlook the terrace, pool, and big, leafy garden, and all public rooms are light and airy. The best bedrooms overlook the pool and garden. ✉ *Avda. Alvaro Domecq 35, 11405,* ☎ *956/300600,* FAX *956/305001. 116 rooms, 4 suites. Restaurant, pool. AE, DC, MC, V.*

$–$$ 🏨 **Ávila.** Centrally located but tucked away on a side street, this friendly hotel is a good value. Guest rooms have basic furnishings and tile floors, with beds on the small side. The lobby is joined by a TV lounge and bar, providing a convenient break spot. ✉ *Ávila 3, 11401,* ☎ *956/334808,* FAX *956/336807. 32 rooms. Bar, breakfast room. AE, DC, MC, V.*

Córdoba

Numbers in the margin correspond to points of interest on the Córdoba map.

Ancient Córdoba (138 km [86 mi] northwest of Seville), city of the caliphs and one of Spain's oldest cities, is the greatest urban embodiment of Andalusia's Moorish heritage. Moorish emirs and caliphs held court here from the 8th to the 11th centuries, and the city became one of the Western world's greatest centers of art, culture, and learning. Moors, Christians, and Jews lived together in peace here.

★ ❶ Córdoba is especially famous for its **Mezquita** (mosque), one of the finest ever built by the Moors. Founded by Abd ar-Rahman I (756–788), it was completed by Al Mansur (976–1002) around 987. As you step inside you'll face a forest of gleaming pillars of precious marble, jasper, and onyx, rising to the red-and-white horseshoe arches characteristic of Moorish architecture. Not even the heavy Baroque cathedral that Charles V built in its midst—and later regretted—can detract from the extraordinary art of the Moorish craftsmen. The mosque once housed the original copy of the Koran and a bone from the arm of the prophet Mohammad, relics that drew thousands of pilgrims before St. Ferdinand reconquered Córdoba for the Christians in 1236. The building opens onto the **Patio de los Naranjos** (Orange Tree Courtyard) and the bell tower, which was the mosque's minaret. ✉ *Torrijos and Cardinal Herrero,* ☎ *957/470512.* ⏲ *May–Sept., daily 10–7; Oct.–Apr., daily 10–6.*

Near the mosque, the streets of Torrijos, Cardenal Herrero, and Deanes are lined with tempting souvenir shops specializing in local handicrafts, especially the filigree silver and embossed leather for which Córdoba is known.

❷ In her niche on Cardenal Herrero, the **Virgen de los Faroles** (Virgin of the Lanterns) stands demurely behind a lantern-hung grille.

❸ The **Judería,** or Jewish quarter, is packed with houses, museums, and monuments that best typify Córdoba's storied past. The municipal tourist office is on the **Plaza Judá Leví.** ✉ *Around C. Judíos.*

❹ Two delightful old mansions house the **Museo Taurino** (Museum of Bullfighting), with a well-presented collection of memorabilia, paintings, and posters by early 20th-century Córdoban artists, and rooms dedicated to great Córdoban *toreros*—even the hide of the bull that killed the legendary Manolete in 1947. ✉ *Plaza Maimónides,* ☎ *957/201056.* ⏲ *May–Sept., Tues.–Sat. 9:30–1:30 and 5–8, Sun. 9:30–1; Oct.–Apr., Tues.–Sat. 10–2 and 5–7, Sun. 10–1.*

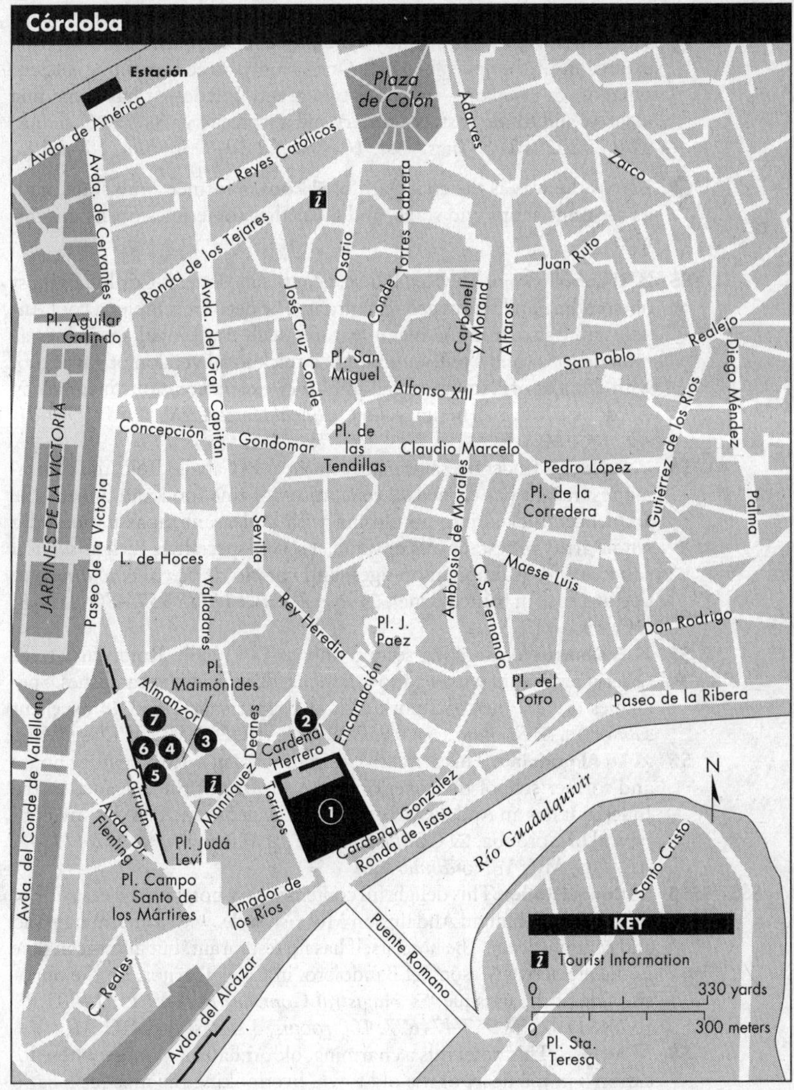

El Zoco, **7**
Judería, **3**
Maimónides, **5**
Mezquita, **1**
Museo Taurino, **4**
Synagogue, **6**
Virgen de los Faroles, **2**

5 A statue of the great Jewish philosopher **Maimónides** stands in Plaza
6 Tiberiades. Nearby is the only **synagogue** in Andalusia to survive the expulsion of the Jews in 1492. One of only three remaining ancient synagogues in Spain—the other two are in Toledo—it has some fine Hebrew and Mudéjar stucco tracery and a women's gallery. ✉ *C. Judíos,* ☎ *957/202918.* ⏲ *Tues.–Sat. 10–2 and 3:30–5:30, Sun. 10–1:30.*

7 Across the way is the courtyard of **El Zoco,** a former Arab souk, with its pleasant shops and stalls, and a bar that sometimes opens in summer.

$$$ ★ ✕ **El Caballo Rojo.** The Red Horse, near the mosque, is Córdoba's most outstanding and renowned restaurant. The decor resembles a cool Andalusian patio, and the menu features such traditional specialties as *rabo de toro* (bull's tail); *salmorejo,* a thick local version of gazpacho, with chunks of ham and egg; and other exotic creations inspired by Córdoba's Moorish heritage. ✉ *Cardenal Herrero 28,* ☎ *957/478001. AE, DC, MC, V.*

$$ ✕ **El Blasón.** Under the same management as El Caballo Rojo, this charming restaurant has earned its reputation for fine food and unbeatable ambience. Tucked into an old inn with a pleasant tapas patio and a whole array of restaurants upstairs, it serves specialties such as *salmón con naranjas* (salmon in oranges) and *musclo de oca al vino afrutado* (leg of goose in fruited wine). ✉ *José Zorrilla 11,* ☎ *957/480625. AE, DC, MC, V.*

$$ ★ ✕ **El Churrasco.** Ranking second only to El Caballo Rojo, this atmospheric restaurant with a patio is famous for its grilled meat dishes. Specialties are *churrasco,* a pork dish in pepper sauce, and an excellent *salmorejo.* ✉ *Romero 16,* ☎ *957/290819. AE, DC, MC, V. Closed Aug.*

$$ ✕ **La Almudaina.** This attractive restaurant is in a 15th-century house and former school that overlooks the Alcázar at the entrance to the Judería. It has an Andalusian patio, and the decor and cooking are both typical of Córdoba. ✉ *Campo Santo de los Mártires 1,* ☎ *957/474342. AE, DC, MC, V. No dinner Sun.*

$$$–$$$$ ★ 🏨 **Conquistador.** This delightful contemporary hotel on the east side of the mosque is built in Andalusian Moorish style, with a charming patio and ceramic decor. The hotel itself has no restaurant, but guests can dine in the attractive Mesón del Bandolero, in Calle Torrijos, on the opposite side of the mosque. ✉ *Magistral González Francés 15, 14003,* ☎ *957/481102,* FAX *957/474677. 100 rooms, 3 suites. AE, DC, MC, V.*

$$ 🏨 **Marisa.** This hotel fills a charming, old Andalusian house whose location—in the heart of the old town, overlooking the mosque's Patio de los Naranjos—is its prime virtue. The decor is quaint and charming, and the rates reasonable. ✉ *Cardenal Herrero 6, 14003,* ☎ *957/473142,* FAX *957/474144. 28 rooms. AE, DC, MC, V.*

OFF THE BEATEN PATH

If you're traveling between Córdoba and Granada, you might want to stop for a drink and wander the narrow streets and squares of **Baena,** a picturesque Andalusian town of white houses clustered on a hillside. ✉ *Rte. N432, 63 km (39 mi) southeast of Córdoba.*

Granada

Numbers in the margin correspond to points of interest on the Granada map.

The graceful city of Granada, 166 km (103 mi) southeast of Córdoba, rises onto three hills dwarfed by the mighty snowcapped peaks of the Sierra Nevada, on which lie the highest roads in Europe. Atop one of these hills, the pink-gold Alhambra Palace, at once terribly imposing yet infinitely delicate, gazes out across the rooftops and gypsy caves of the Sacromonte to the fertile plain, rich in orchards, tobacco fields, and poplar groves. Granada was the Moors' last stronghold, their most cherished city; it fell finally to the Catholic Kings in January 1492.

★ 1 Begin your visit at the **Capilla Real** (Royal Chapel). This ornate Gothic masterpiece is the burial shrine of Ferdinand and Isabella, who have lain side-by-side here since 1521, later joined by their daughter Juana la Loca, mother of Holy Roman Emperor Charles V. ⊠ *Calle Oficios,* ☎ *958/229239.* ⏲ *Mar.–Sept., daily 10:30–1 and 4–7; Oct.–Feb., daily 10:30–1 and 3:30–6:30.*

2 Next door is the **cathedral,** commissioned in 1521 by Charles V, who thought the Royal Chapel "too small for so much glory." It is a grandiose and gloomy monument, not completed until 1714 but still surpassed in beauty and historic value by the neighboring Royal Chapel—which, despite the emperor's plans, still houses the tombs of his grandparents and mother. ⊠ *Gran Vía de Colón 5,* ☎ *958/222959.* ⏲ *Mar.–Sept., Mon.–Sat. 10:30–1 and 4–7, Sun. 4–7; Oct.–Feb., Mon.–Sat. 10:30–1:30 and 3:30–6, Sun. 3:30–6.*

3 The neighboring streets of the **Alcaicería,** the old Arab silk exchange,
draw souvenir hunters. Across the Gran Vía de Colón, Granada's main
4 shopping street, the narrow streets wind up the slopes of the **Albaicín,**
the old Moorish quarter, a fascinating mixture of dilapidated white houses
and beautiful *cármenes,* luxurious villas with fragrant gardens.

★ 5 Make your way up to the small plaza in front of the church of **San Nicolás** for an unforgettable view of the Alhambra—particularly at night, when the palace is floodlit. ⊠ *Cam. Nuevo de S. Nicolás.*

From the Plaza Nueva the Cuesta de Gomérez climbs steeply toward
★ 6 the **Alhambra,** the grandest and most stunning Moorish monument in
all of Andalusia. Your visit begins on a promenade where the Duke of Wellington planted shady elms and Washington Irving tarried among the gypsies, from whom he learned the Moorish legends so evocatively recounted in his *Tales of the Alhambra.* Continue through the **Puerta de la Justicia** (Gate of Justice), above which the hand of Fatima, her fingers evoking the five laws of the Koran, beckons you inside. Once you are inside, the legends of the Patio of the Lions, the Hall of the Two Sisters, and the murder of the Abencerrajes spring to life amid a profusion of lacy walls, frothy stucco, gleaming tiles, and ornate domed ceilings. Here in this realm of myrtles and fountains, festooned arches, and careful inscriptions, every corner holds its secret. Here the emirs installed their harems, awarded their favorites the most lavish of courts, and bathed in marble baths. In the midst of so much delicacy, the Baroque palace of Charles V would seem an intrusion—heavy and incongruous—were it not for its splendid acoustics, which make it the perfect setting for Granada's summer music festival. Wisteria, jasmine, and roses line your route from the Alhambra to the **Generalife,** the caliphs' summer retreat, where crystal drops shower from slender fountains against a background of stately cypresses. The sweeping view includes the clustered white houses of the Albaicín; the Sacromonte, riddled with gypsy caves; and the bulk of the Alhambra towering above the city. ⊠ *Enter on Cuesta de Gomérez,* ☎ *958/221503 and 958/220915.* ⏲ *Nov.–Feb., daily 9–7, Mar.–Oct., daily 9–8. Floodlit visits Tues., Thurs., and Sat. 10 PM–midnight (Sat. 8–10 PM in winter). Ticket office opens 30 min before opening time, closes 1 hr before closing.*

The province of Granada was also the home of the poet Federico García Lorca. García Lorca was born on June 5, 1898, in the village of **Fuentevaqueros,** 10 km (6 mi) west of Granada; his childhood home is now a **museum** (⊠ Poeta García Lorca 4, ☎ 958/516453). On the outskirts of Granada is the Lorca family's summer residence, **Huerta**

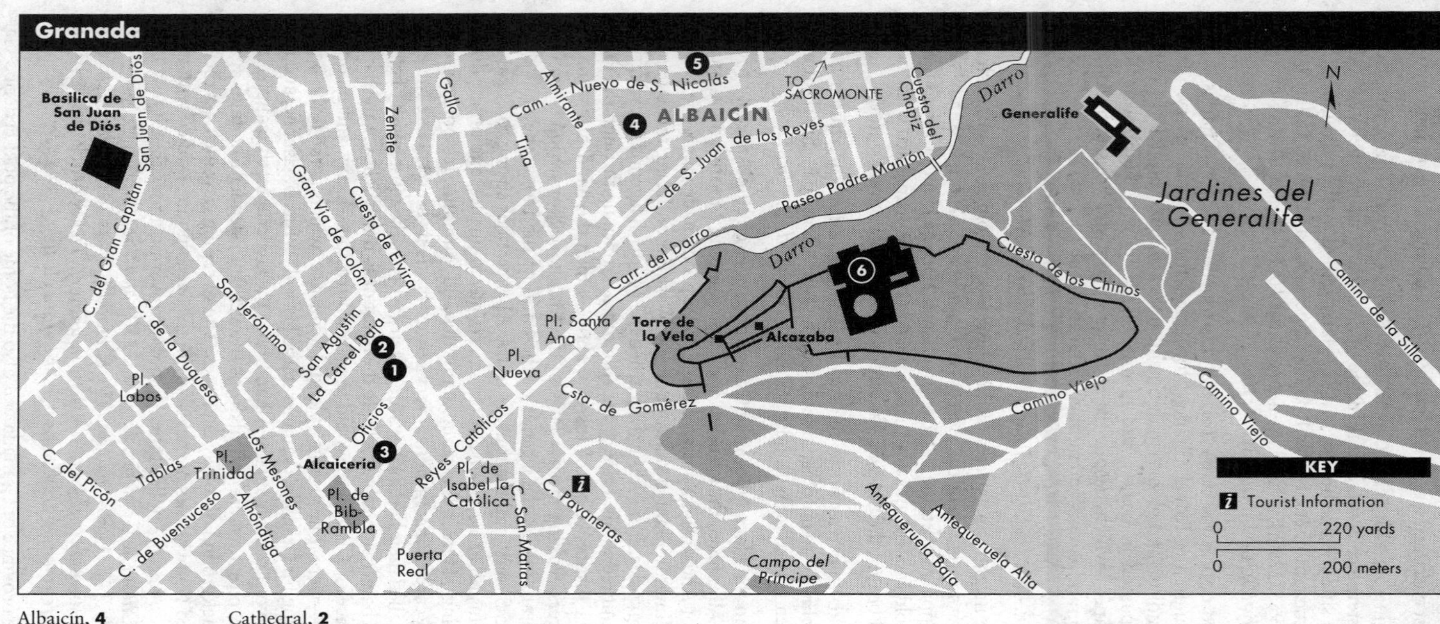

Albaicín, **4**
Alcaicería, **3**
Alhambra, **6**
Capilla Real, **1**
Cathedral, **2**
San Nicolás, **5**

del San Vicente, now also a museum and a cultural center putting on exhibitions on Lorca and his time (✉ C. de la Virgen Blanca, ☎ 958/258466). You can also make the short trip to **Viznar,** 9 km (5½ mi) northeast of Granada—just outside this village is the spot where the poet was executed at the outbreak of the Spanish Civil War, in 1936, and where he is probably buried in a common grave. A memorial park commemorates him.

There are several "impromptu" flamenco shows in the caves of the Sacromonte, but these can be little more than tourist traps. Go only if you're accompanied by a Spanish friend who knows his or her way around or with a tour organized by a local agency. **Jardines Neptuno** (✉ C. Arabial, ☎ 958/522533) is a colorful flamenco club catering mainly to tourists. **Reina Mora** (✉ Mirador de San Cristóbal, no phone), though somewhat smaller than Jardines Neptuno, offers regular flamenco shows known as *tablaos.*

$$$ ✕ **Carmen de San Miguel.** The crux of this restaurant is its superb setting, perched on the Alhambra hill (beside the Hotel Alhambra Palace) in a villa with an outdoor terrace and magnificent views over Granada. The food is average continental cuisine. ✉ *Paseo Torres Bermejas 3,* ☎ *958/226723. AE, DC, MC, V. Closed Sun.*

$$$ ✕ **Cunini.** Right in the center of town, near the cathedral, this restaurant has long been valued for the quality of its seafood. Try one of the mixed-fish platters, either fried (*fritura mixta*) or grilled (*parrillada*). The long tapas bar up front is popular with locals, the dining room in back small and cozy. ✉ *Pescadería 9,* ☎ *958/250777. AE, DC, MC, V. Closed Mon.*

$$ ✕ **Los Manueles.** This old inn is one of Granada's long-standing traditions. The walls have ceramic tiles, and the ceiling is hung with hams. There's lots of atmosphere, good old-fashioned service, and plenty of traditional Granadan cooking. ✉ *Zaragoza 2,* ☎ *958/223413. AE, DC, MC, V.*

$$ ✕ **Sevilla.** A colorful restaurant in the Alcaicería, beside the cathedral, it has a superb tapas bar at the entrance. The dining room is picturesque, if rather small and crowded. The menu can be somewhat tourist-oriented, but the *sopa sevillana* (fish soup) is excellent. ✉ *Oficios 12,* ☎ *958/221223. AE, DC, MC, V. Closed Mon. No dinner Sun.*

$$$$ 🏨 **Parador de San Francisco.** Magnificently set in an old convent within the Alhambra precincts, San Francisco is the most popular parador in Spain. Queen Isabella was entombed here before the completion of the Royal Chapel. The rooms in the old section are the most elaborate; all need to be reserved four–six months in advance. ✉ *Alhambra, 18008,* ☎ *958/221440,* FAX *958/222264. 36 rooms. Restaurant. AE, DC, MC, V.*

$$$–$$$$ ★ 🏨 **Alhambra Palace.** This flamboyant, ocher-red, Moorish-style palace was built around 1910 and sits halfway up the hill to the Alhambra. The mood is busier than at the more isolated parador, but the decor offers rich carpets, tapestries, and Moorish tiles. The best rooms overlook the town. The terrace is the perfect place for an early evening drink as the sun sets over the Sierra Nevada. ✉ *Peña Partida 2, 18009,* ☎ *958/221468,* FAX *958/226404. 122 rooms, 12 suites. Restaurant. AE, DC, MC, V.*

$$ 🏨 **América.** Here's a simple but charming hotel within the Alhambra precincts: the location is magnificent, and you can linger over breakfast on a delightful patio. It's popular, so reserve months in advance. ✉ *Real de la Alhambra 53, 18009,* ☎ *958/227471,* FAX *958/227470. 14 rooms. Restaurant. No credit cards. Closed Nov.–Feb.*

$$ ★ 🏨 **Victoria.** An absolute gem of an Old-World hotel, the Victoria overlooks the Puerta Real—where noise can be a disadvantage. The carpeted bedrooms have dark, polished furniture. ✉ *Puerta Real 3, 18005,*

☎ *958/257700,* FAX *958/263108. 68 rooms, 2 suites. 2 restaurants. AE, DC, MC, V.*

$ **Inglaterra.** At this period house just two blocks above the Gran Vía de Colón, Old-World charm outweighs creature comforts, though accommodations are perfectly adequate for the reasonable rates. ✉ *Cetti Meriem 4, 18010,* ☎ *958/221559,* FAX *958/227100. 36 rooms. AE, DC, MC, V.*

Moorish Spain Essentials

Arriving and Departing

Seville, Córdoba, and Granada all lie on direct train routes from Madrid. Service is frequent from both Chamartín and Atocha stations in Madrid, and includes overnight trains (to Seville and Granada), slower day trains, and express Talgos. In addition the high-speed AVE train connects Seville, Córdoba, and Atocha station on entirely new track; it's more expensive than any other train, but it's a pleasant whiz of a ride and cuts the inter-province travel time down to 2½ hours. Most bus service from Madrid to Andalusia operates out of the Estación del Sur (☞ Arriving and Departing *in* Madrid, *above*). If you have a car, follow the N IV, which takes you through the scorched orange plains of La Mancha to Córdoba, then along the Guadalquivir River to Seville. The N323 road, which splits from the N IV at Bailén, takes you past lovely olive groves and rolling hills to Granada.

Getting Around

BY BUS

Seville has two bus stations, **Estación del Prado de San Sebastián** (✉ C. Manuel Vázquez Sagastizábal s/n, ☎ 95/441–7111), and **Estación Plaza de Armas** (✉ Cristo de la Expiración, by Cachorro Bridge, ☎ 95/490–8040), closer to downtown. Check with the tourist office to determine which one you'll need. In Granada, the main bus station is on ✉ Carretera de Jaén, ☎ 958/185011). Córdoba has no central bus depot, so check at the tourist office for the appropriate company.

BY CAR

Driving in Moorish Spain, long anathema to travelers, was transformed by improvements in the early 1990s. If you enjoy winding roads and gorgeous landscapes, consider renting a car.

BY TRAIN

Seville and Córdoba are linked by direct train service. Buses are a better choice between either of them and Granada, as trains are relatively slow and infrequent and often involve a time-consuming change. Seville's main train station is **Santa Justa** (✉ Avda. Kansas City, ☎ 95/454–0202; RENFE office: ✉ Zaragoza 29, ☎ 95/454–7998). Granada's train station is at the end of Avenida Andaluces (RENFE office: ✉ Reyes Católicos 63, ☎ 958/271272). Córdoba's train station is on the Glorieta Conde de Guadalorce (RENFE office: ✉ Ronda de los Tejares 10, ☎ 957/475884).

Guided Tours

Guided tours of Seville, Córdoba, and Granada are run by **Julià Tours** (☎ 91/571–8696), **Pullmantur** (☎ 91/541–1807), and **Trapsatur** (☎ 91/542–6666), departing from either Madrid or from Costa del Sol resorts; check with travel agents. In Seville you may find group excursions to the sherry *bodegas* and equestrian museum in Jerez de la Frontera.

Visitor Information

Córdoba (✉ Plaza de Judá Leví, ☎ 957/200522). **Granada** (✉ Plaza Mariana Pineda 10, ☎ 958/226688; ✉ Corral del Carbón, C. Mariana Pineda, ☎ 958/225990). **Jerez** (✉ Larga 35, ☎ 956/331150). **Seville** (✉ Avda. Constitución 21, ☎ 95/422–1404; Costurero de la Reina: ✉ Paseo de las Delícias 9, ☎ 95/423–4465).

COSTA DEL SOL

Ah, the Costa del Sol, where impoverished fishing villages of the 1950s are now retirement colonies and package-tour havens for northern Europeans and Americans. Fear not; behind the hideous concrete monsters are old cottages, villas, and gardens resplendent with jasmine and bougainvillea. The sun still sets over miles of beaches, and the lights of small fishing craft still twinkle in the distance. The primary diversion here is indolence—swimming and sunning—but when you need something to do, you can head inland to historic Ronda and the perched white villages of Andalusia or take a day trip to Gibraltar or Tangier.

Exploring the Costa del Sol

Nerja

Nerja is a small but expanding resort town that so far has escaped the worst excesses of development. Its growth has been largely confined to village-style complexes outside town, such as El Capistrano. There's ★ pleasant bathing here, though the sand is gray and gritty. The **Balcón** ★ **de Europa** is a fantastic lookout, high above the sea. The **Cuevas de Nerja** (a series of stalactite caves) lie off the road to Almuñecar and Almería; a kind of vast underground cathedral, they contain the world's largest known stalactite (203 ft long). ☎ *95/252–9520.* ⏲ *Sept.–June, daily 10–2:30; July–Aug., daily 10:30–2 and 4–8.*

$$ ✕ **Casa Luque.** One of the most authentically Spanish of Nerja's restaurants occupies a charming old Andalucian house behind the church of Balcón de Europa. ✉ *Plaza Cavana 2,* ☎ *95/252–1004. AE, DC, MC, V. Closed Mon. and Feb.*

$$ ✕ **Udo Heimer.** A genial German is your host at this Art Deco villa; his menu is a combination of traditional German dishes and local produce. Try pumpkin stuffed with ham or prawns wrapped in bacon and served in a curried banana sauce. ✉ *Pueblo Andaluz 27,* ☎ *95/252–0032. AE, DC, MC, V. Closed Wed. and Jan.–Feb. No lunch.*

$$$ 🏨 **Mónica.** Spacious and luxurious, the hotel has cool, Moorish-style architecture and acres of marble. Popular with package tours, it's within walking distance of the center of town. ✉ *Playa Torrecilla, 29780,* ☎ *95/252–1100,* FAX *95/252–1162. 234 rooms. 2 restaurants, 2 pools. AE, DC, MC, V.*

$$$ ★ 🏨 **Parador de Nerja.** A modern structure surrounded by a leafy garden on the cliff's edge, this parador offers rooms with balconies overlooking the garden and, obliquely, the sea; those in the newer, single-story wing open onto their own patios. An elevator takes you down to the beach. ✉ *Almuñecar, 8, Nerja 29780,* ☎ *95/252–0050,* FAX *95/252–1997. 73 rooms. Restaurant, pool. AE, DC, MC, V.*

Málaga

Málaga (544 km [337 mi] south of Madrid) is a busy port city with ancient streets and lovely villas surrounded by exotic foliage. The central Plaza de la Marina, overlooking the port, is a pleasant place for a drink. The main shops are along the Calle Marqués de Larios.

Málaga's **cathedral,** built between 1528 and 1782 on the site of the former mosque, is unfinished, its construction funds having mysteriously dried up. (One story has it that the money was donated instead to the American Revolution.) Because it's missing one of its twin tow-

Costa del Sol

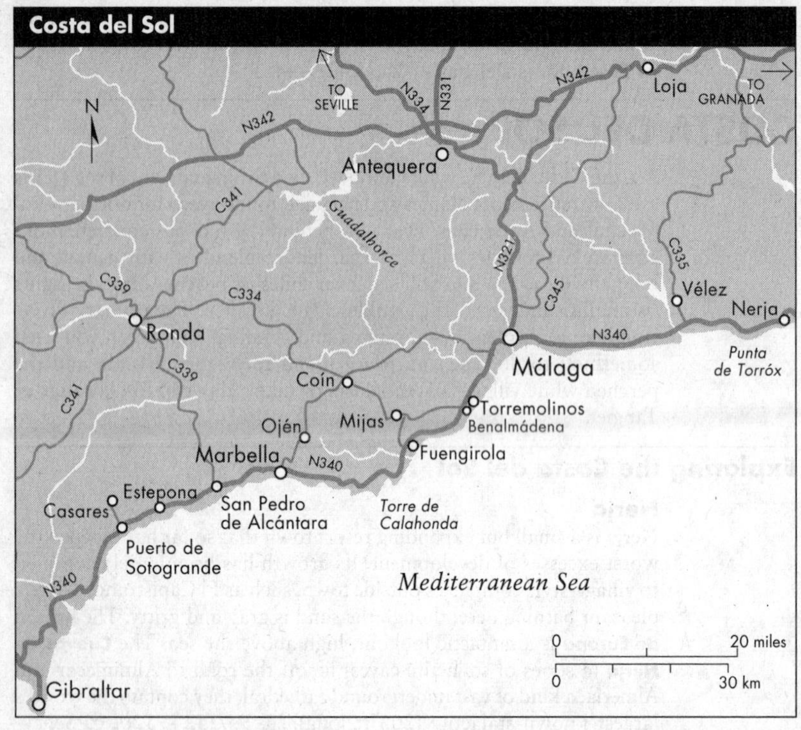

ers, the cathedral is known as *La Manquita* (the one-armed lady). The lovely, enclosed choir, which somehow survived the burnings of the civil war, is the work of the great 17th-century artist Pedro de Mena. The adjoining **museum** has art and religious artifacts. ✉ *Calle de Molina Larios,* ☎ *95/221–5917.* ⏲ *Mon.–Sat. 10–12:30 and 4–6:30.*

The **Alcazaba** (fortress) was begun during the 8th century, when Málaga was the most important port in the Moorish kingdom. Both the fortress and the ruins of the Roman amphitheater at its entrance will be undergoing restoration throughout 1998; inquire about which parts are open to the public. The inner palace dates from the 11th century, when the Moorish emirs camped out here for a time after the breakup of the caliphate in Córdoba. ✉ *Entrance on Alcazabilla.* ⏲ *Open Wed.–Mon. 9:30–8.*

★ It takes some energy to climb through the Alcazaba gardens to the summit of **Gibralfaro.** (You can also drive, by way of Calle Victoria, or take the parador minibus that leaves roughly every 1½ hours from near the cathedral on Molina Lario.) Gibralfaro's fortifications were built for Yusuf I in the 14th century—the Moors called it Jebelfaro, which means "rock of the lighthouse," after the beacon that stood here to guide ships into the harbor and warn of invasions by pirates. The beacon is gone, but there's a small parador that makes a delightful place for a drink or a meal and has some stunning views.

$$$ ✕ **Café de Paris.** The owner of this stylish restaurant in the Paseo Marítimo area was once a chef at Maxim's in Paris and La Hacienda in Marbella. The *menú de degustación* (tasting menu) lets you try a little of everything. Specialties include *rodaballo con espinacas* (turbot and spinach). ✉ *Vélez Málaga 8,* ☎ *95/222–5043. Reservations essential. AE, DC, MC, V. Closed Sun.*

$$ ✕ **Casa Pedro.** Casa Pedro can get crowded—Malgueños have been flocking to this no-frills fish restaurant for more than 50 years. In the seaside suburb of El Palo, the restaurant has a huge, bare dining room that overlooks the ocean. Try joining the local families who come for lunch on Sunday. ✉ *Quitapenas 121, El Palo beach,* ☎ *95/229–0013. AE, DC, MC, V. Closed Nov. No dinner Mon.*

$$ ✕ **Rincón de Mata.** This is one of the best of many restaurants in the pedestrian shopping streets between Calle Larios and Calle Nueva. The menu is more original than most, with house specialties such as *tunedor* (calf in sauce). In summer tables appear on the sidewalk. ✉ *Esparteros 8,* ☎ *95/222–3135. AE, DC, MC V.*

$ ✕ **La Cancela.** At this colorful restaurant in the center of town, just off Calle Granada, you can dine indoors or alfresco. ✉ *Denís Belgrano 5,* ☎ *95/222–3125. AE, DC, MC, V.*

$$$ **Larios.** Málaga's newest hotel opened in 1994, in an elegant, restored building on the central Plaza de la Constitución. ✉ *Marqués de Larios 2, 29005,* ☎ *95/222–2200,* FAX *95/222–2407. 34 rooms, 6 suites. Restaurant, meeting room. AE, DC, MC, V.*

$$$ ★ **Parador de Málaga-Gibralfaro.** In a small wood on top of Gibralfaro—3½ km (2 mi) above the city—this cozy parador offers spectacular views over the city and bay. Guest rooms have a pleasant mixture of modern comforts and Spanish charm. ✉ *Monte de Gibralfaro, 29016,* ☎ *95/222–1903,* FAX *95/222–1904. 38 rooms. Restaurant, pool. AE, DC, MC, V.*

$$ **Las Vegas.** In a pleasant, if somewhat tumultuous, part of town just east of the center, this convenient hotel has a dining room overlooking the Paseo Marítimo, a pool, and a large leafy garden. Rooms at the back enjoy fine ocean views. ✉ *Paseo de Sancha 22, 29016,* ☎ *95/221–7712,* FAX *95/222–4889. 107 rooms. Restaurant, pool. AE, DC, MC, V.*

$ **Victoria.** This small, renovated hostel in an old house just off Calle Larios offers excellent budget accommodations in a central location. ✉ *Sancha de Lara 3, 29015,* ☎ FAX *95/222–4224. 14 rooms. AE, DC, MC, V.*

Torremolinos and Benalmádena

As you approach Torremolinos through an ocean of concrete blocks, it's hard to grasp that it was once an inconsequential fishing village. Today this grossly overdeveloped resort is a prime aesthetic example of 20th-century tourism run amok, despite a helpful cleanup in 1996. The town center, with its brash Nogalera Plaza, is full of overpriced bars and restaurants. Far more attractive is the district of La Carihuela, farther west, below the Avenida Carlota Alexandra—here you'll find some old fishermen's cottages, a few excellent seafood restaurants, and a traffic-free esplanade for an enjoyable stroll on a summer evening. La Carihuela merges with the coastal resort of Benalmádena-Costa, which has a lively yacht harbor and marina; at the western end of the resort is the Torrequebrada casino and golf course, while inland is the surprisingly unspoiled village of Benalmádena itself.

$$$ ✕ **Ventorillo de la Perra.** This old inn (built in 1785) is 3 km (2 mi) from the center of Torremolinos, on the road inland to Arroyo de la Miel. A cozy, rustic atmosphere prevails in both the dining room and the bar; the ceiling in the latter is hung with hams. The menu mixes Malagueño specialties and general Spanish fare with international favorites. ✉ *Avda. Constitución, Arroyo de la Miel,* ☎ *95/244–1966. AE, DC, MC, V. Closed Mon.*

$$ ✕ **Casa Guaquin.** Casa Guaquin is widely known as the best seafood restaurant in the area. Changing daily catches and stalwarts like *coquinas al ajillo* (wedge-shell clams in garlic sauce) are served on a sea-

side patio. ✉ *Paseo Marítimo 63,* ☎ *95/238–4530. AE, MC, V. Closed Thurs. and mid-Dec.–mid-Jan.*

$$ ✕ **Europa.** A short walk from the Carihuela, this villa has pleasant dining in leafy surroundings—it's in the middle of a large garden. On Sunday local families flock here for a leisurely lunch. ✉ *Via Imperial 32,* ☎ *95/238–8022. AE, DC, MC, V.*

$$ ✕ **Juan.** Juan is a good place to enjoy seafood in summer, with a sunny outdoor patio facing the sea. Specialties include the great Costa del Sol standbys: *sopa de mariscos* (shellfish soup), *dorada al horno* (oven-roasted giltheads), and *fritura malagueña* (Málaga's fried fish). ✉ *Paseo Marítimo 29, La Carihuela,* ☎ *95/238–5656. AE, DC, MC, V.*

$$$ **Cervantes.** This busy, cosmopolitan hotel in the heart of town has comfortable rooms, good service, and a well-known dining room on the top floor. ✉ *Las Mercedes s/n, 29620,* ☎ *95/238–4033,* FAX *95/238–4857. 397 rooms. Restaurant, 2 pools. AE, DC, MC, V.*

$$ **Tropicana.** On the beach at the far end of the Carihuela is this comfortable, relaxing resort hotel, with several good restaurants nearby. ✉ *Trópico 6, 29620,* ☎ *95/238–6600,* FAX *95/238–0568. 86 rooms. Pool. AE, DC, MC, V.*

$ ★ **Miami.** Set in an old Andalusian villa in a shady garden to the west of the Carihuela, Miami is something of an oasis in the desert of concrete. ✉ *Aladino 14, 29620,* ☎ *95/238–5255. 26 rooms. Pool. No credit cards.*

Fuengirola and Mijas

Head west from Torremolinos for the similar but more staid resort of Fuengirola, a retirement haven for Britons and Americans. A short drive from Fuengirola up into the mountains takes you to the picturesque ★ and oft-photographed village of **Mijas.** Though the vast and touristy main square may seem like an extension of the Costa's tawdry bazaar, Mijas does have hillside streets of whitewashed houses whose authentic village atmosphere survived the tourist boom of the '60s largely unscathed. You can visit the bullring, the nearby church, and the chapel of Mijas's patroness, the Virgen de la Peña (to the side of the main square) and shop for quality gifts and souvenirs.

$$ ✕ **Portofino.** This lively restaurant, one of Fuengirola's best, is camouflaged among the brash souvenir shops and fast-food joints on the seafront promenade, just east of the port. The menu is international. ✉ *Paseo Marítimo 29,* ☎ *95/247–0643. AE, DC, MC, V. Closed Mon.; no lunch July–mid-Sept.*

$$ ✕ **Mirlo Blanco.** Here, in a large Andalusian townhouse overlooking the square, you can sample Basque dishes, such as *txangurro* (crab) and *merluza a la vasca* (hake with asparagus, eggs, and clam sauce). The decor and ambience are both pleasantly busy, and in warm weather, you can dine on the terrace overlooking the square. ✉ *Plaza Constitución 13,* ☎ *95/248–5700. AE, DC, MC, V.*

$$$$ ★ **Byblos Andaluz.** You won't miss any comforts in this luxury spa hotel, set in a huge garden of palms, cypresses, and fountains. The restaurant, Le Nailhac, is known for its French cuisine and can also provide special, low-calorie meals. ✉ *Mijas-Golf, Fuengirola, 29640,* ☎ *95/247–3050,* FAX *95/247–6783. 111 rooms, 33 suites. 2 restaurants, indoor and outdoor pools. AE, DC, MC, V.*

$$$ **Mijas.** This beautifully situated hotel at the entrance to Mijas has views of the hillsides stretching down to Fuengirola and the Mediterranean. ✉ *Urb. Tamisa, 29650,* ☎ *95/248–5800,* FAX *95/248–5825. 98 rooms, 3 suites. Restaurant, 2 pools. AE, DC, MC, V.*

Marbella and Estepona

Marbella is the most fashionable resort area on the Costa del Sol. It does smack a bit of the Florida land boom, and the town's otherwise charming ancient Moorish quarter is crowded with both upmarket boutiques and modern, T-shirt-and-fudge shops; but when people speak of Marbella, they refer both to the town and to the resorts, some more exclusive than others. These sretch some 8 km (5 mi) east of town, between the highway and the beach, and west to San Pedro de Alcántara and Estepona. If you're vacationing in southern Spain, this is the place to stay: in one place you've got championship golf courses and tennis courts, yacht harbors, fashionable waterfront cafés, and trendy shopping arcades.

Marbella's Golden Mile (which is, in fact, 3 mi), with its mosque, Arab banks, and residence of Saudi Arabia's King Fahd, illustrates the ever-growing influence of wealthy Arabs in this playground of the rich. In the plush marina, **Puerto Banús,** flashy yachts, fashionable people, and expensive restaurants form a glittering parade that outshines even St. Tropez.

Estepona, which until recently marked the end of the urban sprawl of the Costa del Sol, is set back from the main highway and lacks the hideous high-rises of Torremolinos and Fuengirola. It's not hard to see the original outlines of this old fishing village. Wander the streets of the Moorish village, around the central food market and the church of **San Francisco,** and you'll find a pleasant contrast to the excesses higher up the coast.

$$$$ ★ ✕ **La Hacienda.** Owned by the family of the late Paul Schiff, former chef, La Hacienda belongs to the Relais Gourmand group and is one of the best-known and highest-rated restaurants in Spain. The menu reflects both Schiff's native Belgium and his adopted home, Andalusia: It's a combination of European and Spanish cuisine, orchestrated by Schiff's daughter, Cathy. The *menú de degustación,* at around 7,000 ptas., lets you sample Galvez's very best creations. ✉ *Urb. Las Chapas, Carretera N340, km 193, 12 km (7 mi) east of Marbella on the road to Málaga,* ☎ *95/283–1276. Reservations essential. AE, DC, MC, V. Closed Mon., Tues., and mid-Nov.–mid-Dec.*

$$$$ ✕ **La Meridiana.** A favorite with the local jet set, La Meridiana is just west of town, toward Puerto Banús, and is famous for its original Bauhaus architecture and the superb quality and freshness of its ingredients. ✉ *Camino de la Cruz,* ☎ *95/277–6190. Reservations essential. AE, DC, MC, V. Closed Jan. No lunch June–Aug., or Mon.–Tues. Sept.–May.*

$$$ ✕ **Santiago.** This busy place is known as the best fish restaurant in Marbella, but you can pursue excellent meat dishes as well. ✉ *Paseo Marítimo 5,* ☎ *95/277–0078. AE, DC, MC, V. Closed Nov.*

$$$$ ✕🏨 **Las Dunas.** This spectacular hotel, brand-new in 1997, rises like a multicolor apparition next to the beach midway between Estepona and Marbella. The setting is palatial, with trickling fountains and generous use of exotic plants. ✉ *La Boladilla Baja, Ctra de Cádiz Km. 163, 29689,* ☎ *95/279–4345,* FAX *95/279–4825. 36 rooms, 39 suites, 33 apartments. 2 restaurants, pool, fitness center. AE, DC, MC, V.*

$$$$ ★ 🏨 **Los Monteros.** On the road to Málaga, 2½ km (1¼ mi) east of Marbella, this deluxe hotel offers top-notch facilities, including golf, tennis, pools, horseback riding, and gourmet dining in the famous El Corzo Grill. It's the third-most-expensive hotel in Spain, after the Ritz and Villamagna in Madrid. Eighty percent of the guests are British, which may explain the somewhat starched formality of the rooms. ✉ *Urb. Los Monteros, Carretera N340, Km 187, 29600,* ☎ *95/277–1700,* FAX

95/282–5846. 158 rooms, 10 suites. 3 restaurants, 1 indoor and 2 outdoor pools. AE, DC, MC, V.

$$$$ 🏨 **Marbella Club.** The grande dame of Marbella tends to attract an older clientele. The bungalow-style rooms run from small to spacious, and the decor varies considerably, so specify the type you prefer. The grounds are exquisite. Breakfast is served on a patio where songbirds flit through the vegetation. ✉ *Carretera de Cádiz, Km 178, 29600,* ☎ *95/282–2211,* FAX *95/282–9884. 83 rooms, 36 suites, 10 bungalows. Restaurant, 2 pools. AE, DC, MC, V.*

$$$$ ★ 🏨 **Puente Romano.** A spectacular, modern hotel and apartment complex of low, white stucco buildings 3¼ km (2 mi) west of Marbella (on the road to Puerto Banús), this "village" has a Roman bridge in its beautifully landscaped grounds as well as two pools, a tennis club, squash courts, and a nightclub. ✉ *Carretera de Cádiz, Km 177, 29600,* ☎ *95/282–0900,* FAX *95/277–5766. 152 rooms, 77 suites. 2 restaurants, 2 pools. AE, DC, V.*

$$–$$$ 🏨 **El Fuerte.** The best of the few hotels in the center of Marbella, this one has simple, adequate rooms. The 1950s-style building sits in a large garden with an outdoor pool. ✉ *Avda. El Fuerte s/n, 29600,* ☎ *95/286–1500,* FAX *95/282–4411. 261 rooms, 25 suites. Restaurant, indoor and outdoor pools. AE, DC, MC, V.*

Ronda

You arrive in Ronda (61 km [38 mi] northwest of Marbella) via a spectacular mountain road from San Pedro de Alcántara, between Marbella and Estapona. Ronda is one of the oldest towns in Spain and the last stronghold of the storied Andalusian bandits. The town's most dramatic feature is its ravine, known as ★ **El Tajo,** which is 915 ft across and divides the old Moorish town from the "new town" of El Mercadillo. Spanning the gorge is the amazing **Puente Nuevo,** built between 1755 and 1793, whose parapet offers dizzying views of the River Guadalevin, far below. Ronda's breathtaking setting and ancient houses are its chief attractions. Stroll the old streets of **La Ciudad;** drop in at the historic **Reina Victoria** hotel, built by the English from Gibraltar as a fashionable resting place on their Algeciras-Bobadilla railroad line. Visit the **bullring,** one of the oldest and most beautiful in Spain; Ronda's most famous native son, Pedro Romero (1754–1839), father of modern bullfighting, is said to have killed 5,600 bulls here during his 30-year career. The **museum** inside has posters dating back to the very first fights held in this ring in May 1785. The ring is privately owned now, but three or four fights are still held in the summer; tickets are exceedingly difficult to come by (☎ 95/287–4132; ⏲ daily 10–6:30, 10–8 in summer). Above all, don't miss the clifftop walk and the gardens of the **Alameda del Tajo** (Tajo Park), where you can feast on one of the most dramatic views in all of Andalusia.

$$$ ✕ **Don Miguel.** Near the Puente Nuevo, this restaurant's terrace offers spectacular views of the ravine. The house specialty is lamb—*asado de cordero lechal Don Miguel*—reared on the owner's farm. ✉ *Villanueva 4,* ☎ *95/287–1090. AE, DC, MC, V. Closed mid-Jan.–mid-Feb.; Sun. and Wed. in June, July, Aug.*

$$ ✕ **Pedro Romero.** Located opposite the bullring, this restaurant is, not surprisingly, packed with colorful taurine decor. The restaurant serves traditional regional recipes; the *tocinillo del cielo al coco* (sweet caramel custard flavored with coconut) is a treat. ✉ *Virgen de la Paz 18,* ☎ *95/287–1110. AE, DC, MC, V.*

$$$ ✕🏨 **Parador de Ronda.** Spain's newest parador stands at the very edge of the Tajo gorge, with a modern interior concealed within the shell of the old town hall. The rooms are spacious and comfortable, and

the restaurant is justifiably famous. ✉ *Plaza de España, 29400,* ☎ *95/287–7500,* FAX *95/287–8188. 62 rooms, 8 suites. Restaurant, pool, meeting room. AE, DC, MC, V.*

$$ **Polo.** A cozy, old-fashioned hotel in the center of town, Polo has a reasonably priced restaurant. The staff is friendly, and the rooms are simple but comfortable. ✉ *Mariano Souvirón 8, 29400,* ☎ *95/287–2447,* FAX *95/287–2449. 33 rooms. Restaurant. AE, DC, MC, V.*

Casares

Nineteen kilometers (11¾ mi) northwest of Estepona, the mountain village of Casares lies high in the Sierra Bermeja. Streets lined with ancient white houses perch on the slopes beneath a ruined Moorish castle. Stop for a breather, admire the view of the Mediterranean, and check out the village's thriving ceramics industry.

Between Estepona and Gibraltar the highway is flanked by new and prosperous vacation developments known as *urbanizaciones*. The architecture here is much more in keeping with traditional Andalusian style than the earlier, concrete stuff. Near Gibraltar, Sotogrande—a millionaires' paradise—is the home of the Puerto de Sotogrande Marina and the Valderrama golf course, which hosted the 1997 Ryder Cup.

Gibraltar

Numbers in the margin correspond to points of interest on the Gibraltar map.

To enter Gibraltar simply walk or drive across the border at **La Línea** and show your passport. In theory, drivers need an International Driver's License, insurance certificate, and registration book; play it safe and bring these documents with you to avoid a possible hefty fine. In practice, these requirements are usually waived. Flights leave London for Gibraltar daily; as yet there are no flights from Spanish airports, but there are plenty of bus tours from Spanish cities. Julià Tours, Pullmantur, and many smaller agencies run daily tours to Gibraltar (except Sunday) from most Costa del Sol resorts. Portillo runs an inexpensive daily tour to Gibraltar from the Torremolinos bus station, and you can always take the regular Portillo bus to La Línea and walk across the border. Once you reach Gibraltar the official language is English, and the currency is the British pound, but Spanish and pesetas are also widely accepted.

The Rock of Gibraltar acquired its name in AD 711, when it was captured by the Moorish chieftain Tarik at the beginning of the Arab invasion of Spain. It became known as Jebel Tariq (Rock of Tariq), later corrupted to Gibraltar. After successive periods of Moorish and Spanish domination, Gibraltar was captured by an Anglo-Dutch fleet in 1704 and ceded to the British by the Treaty of Utrecht in 1713. This tiny British colony, whose impressive silhouette dominates the strait between Spain and Morocco, is a rock just 5⅘ km (3⅗ mi) long, ¾ km (½ mi) wide, and 1,394 ft high.

Upon entering Gibraltar by car, you have to cross the airport runway on the narrow strip of land that links the Rock with La Línea, in Spain.
1 If you turn left (east) at Devil's Tower Road, you'll reach **Catalan Bay,** a small fishing village founded by Genoese settlers during the 18th century and now one of the Rock's most picturesque resorts. The road continues on, beneath water catchments that supply the colony's drink-
2 ing water, to another resort, **Sandy Bay.** A right (west) turn at Devil's Tower Road will bring you to the town of Gibraltar itself. Several minibus tours are readily available here.

3 Bypassing the town, you reach the Rock's southernmost tip, **Punta**
Grande de Europa (Europa Point). Stop here to admire the view across
the strait to the coast of Morocco, 22½ km (14 mi) away. You are standing on what in ancient times was called one of the two Pillars of Hercules. (The second pillar was just across the water, in Morocco—a
mountain between the cities of Ceuta and Tangier.) Plaques explain the
history of the gun installations here, and nearby, on Europa Flats, you
4 can see the **Nun's Well,** an ancient Moorish cistern. Also here is the
5 **Shrine of Our Lady of Europe,** venerated by sailors since 1462.

6 High on the western slopes, Europa Road winds its way above **Rosia**
Bay, to which Admiral Nelson's flagship, HMS *Victory,* was towed after
the Battle of Trafalgar, in 1805. Aboard were the battle's casualties,
now buried in Trafalgar Cemetery on the southern edge of town, and
the body of Nelson himself, preserved in a barrel of rum. Nelson was
taken to London for burial.

7 Continue on Europa Road as far as the **Stakis International Casino** (⊠
Europa Rd., ☎ 9567/76666), above the Alameda Gardens. Make a
8 sharp right here up Engineer Road to **Jews' Gate,** an unbeatable lookout point over the docks and Bay of Gibraltar to Algeciras, in Spain.
Here you can access the **Upper Nature Preserve,** which includes St.
Michael's Cave, the Apes' Den, the Great Siege Tunnel, and the Moorish Castle (☞ *below*). The preserve is open daily 10–sunset. Queens
9 Road leads to **St. Michael's Cave,** a series of underground chambers
adorned with stalactites and stalagmites—a wonderful setting for concerts, ballet, and drama.

10 Drive down Old Queen's Road to the **Apes' Den,** near the Wall of Charles
V. The famous Barbary apes are a breed of cinnamon-color, tailless mon-
keys, natives of the Atlas Mountains in Morocco. Legend holds that
as long as the apes remain, the British will continue to hold the Rock.
Winston Churchill himself ordered the maintenance of the ape colony
when its numbers began to dwindle during World War II.

Passing under the cable car that runs to the Rock's summit, drive up to
11 the **Great Siege Tunnel,** at the northern end of the Rock. These huge
galleries were carved out during the Great Siege of 1779–83. In 1878
the Governor, Lord Napier of Magdala, entertained ex-President Ulysses
S. Grant here at a banquet in St. George's Hall. From here the Holy-
land Tunnel leads out to the east side of the Rock, above Catalan Bay.

12 The last stop before the town is at the **Moorish Castle,** on Willis Road,
built by chieftain Tarik's successors. The present **Tower of Homage**
was rebuilt by the Moors in 1333. Admiral Rooke hoisted the British
flag from its top when he captured the Rock in 1704, and it has flown
here ever since.

13 Willis Road leads steeply down to the colorful, congested **town of Gibral-**
tar, where Britain's dignified Regency architecture blends with the
shutters, balconies, and patios of southern Spain. Apart from the attraction of shops, restaurants, and pubs on Main Street, you'll want
to visit some of the following: the **Governor's Residence;** the **Law**
Courts, where the famous case of the *Mary Celeste* sailing ship was
heard in 1872; the Anglican **Cathedral of the Holy Trinity;** and the
Catholic **Cathedral of St. Mary the Crowned.** The exhibits of the re-
14 cently refurbished **Gibraltar Museum** recall the history of the Rock
throughout the ages. ⊠ *Bomb House La.,* ☎ *9567/74289.* ⏲ *Week-*
days 10–6, Sat. 10–2.

15 Finally, the **Nefusot Yehudada Synagogue** on Line Wall Road is worth
16 a look for its inspired design. If you're interested in guns, the **Koehler**

Apes' Den, **10**
Catalan Bay, **1**
Gibraltar Museum, **14**
Great Siege Tunnel, **11**
Jews' Gate, **8**
Koehler Gun, **16**
Moorish Castle, **12**
Nefusot Yehudada Synagogue, **15**
Nun's Well, **4**
Punta Grande de Europa, **3**
Rosia Bay, **6**
St. Michael's Cave, **9**
Sandy Bay, **2**
Shrine of Our Lady of Europe, **5**
Stakis International Casino, **7**
Town of Gibraltar, **13**

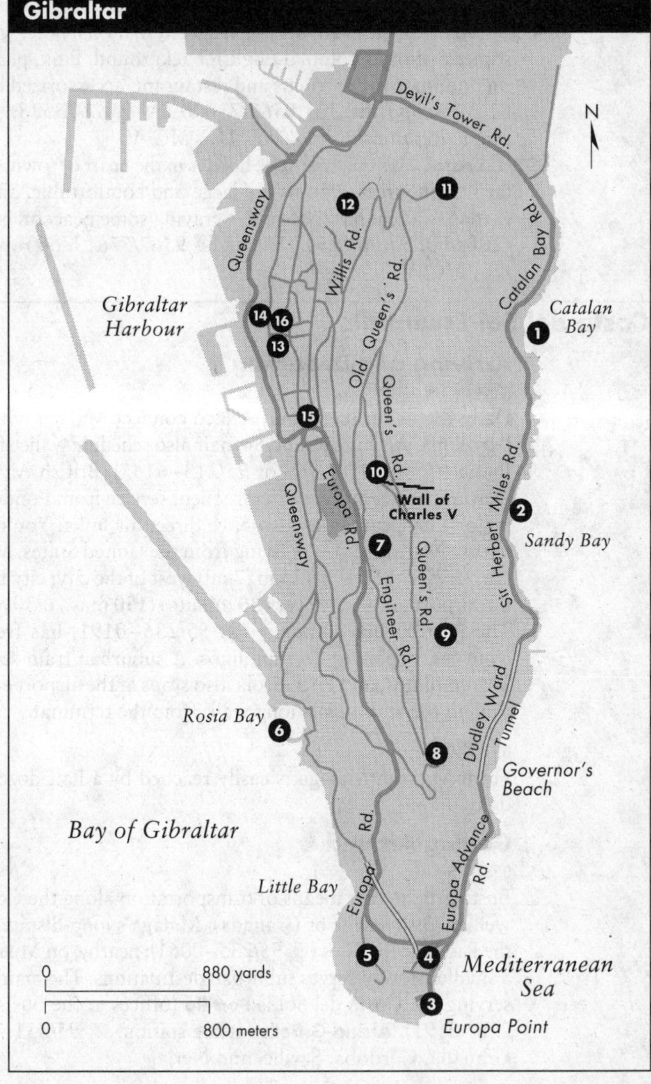

Gun, in Casemates Square at the northern end of Main Street is an impressive example of the type of gun developed during the Great Siege.

$$$ ✕ **La Bayuca.** One of the Rock's best-established restaurants, La Bayuca is renowned for its onion soup and Mediterranean dishes. Prince Charles and Prince Andrew have dined here while on naval service. ✉ *21 Turnbull's La.,* ☎ *9567/75119. AE, DC, MC, V. Closed Tues. No lunch Sun.*

$–$$ ✕ **Strings.** This popular bistro serves an English-style menu, with daily specials chalked up on a blackboard. ✉ *44 Cornwall's La.,* ☎ *9567/78800. AE, MC, V. Closed Sun.*

$$$$ 🏨 **The Eliott.** The Rock's most modern hotel, the Eliott is right in the center of the town in what used to be the Gibraltar Holiday Inn. The rooms are functional and comfortable. ✉ *2 Governor's Parade,* ☎ *9567/70500,* FAX *9567/70243. 122 rooms, 8 suites. Pool, sauna. AE, DC, MC, V.*

$$$ ★ **The Rock.** Overlooking the town and harbor, the refurbished Rock is spiffy enough to qualify as a truly international hotel while preserving something of its colonial English background. Pink, peach, and beach predominate in the rooms and restaurant, accessorized by ceiling fans. ✉ *3 Europa Rd.,* ☎ *9567/73000,* FAX *9567/73513. 102 rooms, 8 suites. Restaurant, pool. AE, DC, MC, V.*

$$ **Bristol.** This colonial-style hotel is in the heart of town, just off Gibraltar's main street. Rooms are large and comfortable, and the tropical garden is a real haven if you're craving some peaceful isolation. ✉ *10 Cathedral Sq.,* ☎ *9567/76800,* FAX *9567/77613. 60 rooms. Pool. AE, DC, MC, V.*

Costa del Sol Essentials

Arriving and Departing

BY PLANE

Daily flights on Iberia and Aviaco connect Málaga with Madrid and Barcelona. Air Europa and Spanair also schedule wallet-friendly flights. Iberia (☎ 95/213–6166 or 95/213–6167), British Airways, and numerous charter airlines offer frequent service from London; most other major European cities also have direct air links. You'll have to connect in Madrid if you're flying from the United States. **Málaga Airport** (☎ 95/224–8804) is 12 km (7 mi) west of the city; city buses run from the airport to the city every 30 minutes (150 ptas., 6:30 AM–midnight). The Portillo bus company (☎ 95/236–0191) has frequent service from the airport to Torremolinos. A suburban train serving Málaga, Torremolinos, and Fuengirola also stops at the airport every half hour, though the station is a long walk from the terminal.

BY TRAIN

From Madrid, Málaga is easily reached by a half dozen rapid trains daily.

Getting Around

BY BUS

Buses are the best means of transportation along the Costa del Sol (as well as from Seville or Granada). Málaga's long-distance station is on the Paseo de los Tilos (☎ 95/235–0061); nearby, on Muelle de Heredía, a smaller station serves suburban destinations. The main bus company serving the Costa del Sol is **Portillo** (offices at the bus station, ☎ 95/236–0191). **Alsina-Gräells** (at the station, ☎ 95/231–8295) goes to Granada, Córdoba, Seville, and Nerja.

BY TRAIN

The train station in Málaga (✉ Explanada de la Estación, ☎ 95/236–0202) is a 15-minute walk from the city center, across the river. The **RENFE** office (✉ Strachan 2, ☎ 95/221–4127) is more convenient for tickets and information.

Guided Tours

Numerous companies, including **Julià Tours** and **Pullmantur,** lead one- and two-day excursions from all Costa del Sol resorts to such places as Seville, Granada, Córdoba, Ronda, Gibraltar, and Tangier. Your hotel desk or any travel agent can arrange a reservation.

Visitor Information

The most helpful tourist offices (by far) are in Málaga and Marbella. The Málaga office covers the entire province.

Estepona (✉ Paseo Marítimo Pedro Manrique, ☎ 95/280–0913). **Fuengirola** (✉ Avda. Jesús Santos Rein 6, ☎ 95/246–7457). **Gibraltar** (✉ Cathedral Sq., ☎ 9567/74950). **Málaga** (✉ Pasaje de Chinitas 4, ☎ 95/

221–3445, and at the airport in both national and international terminals). **Marbella** (✉ Glorieta de la Fontanilla, ☎ 95/282–2818). **Nerja** (✉ Puerta del Mar 2, ☎ 95/252–1531). **Ronda** (✉ Plaza de España 1, ☎ 95/287–1272). **Torremolinos** (✉ Plaza Pablo Picasso, ☎ 95/237–1159).

EXCURSION TO MOROCCO

The crossing to Morocco, just 14 km (9 mi) across the Strait of Gibraltar, may be the longest short trip on the globe: a 90-minute boat ride from Algeciras to Tangier replaces a Europe on the brink of the 21st century with seemingly timeless North Africa.

Islam is the state religion here, and Arabic is the official language, but you'll also hear French, Berber, Spanish, and English. Berbers, Romans, Vandals, and Arabs inhabited Morocco in the country's early history, but incessant conflict between Arabs and Berbers left Morocco ripe for invasion. After expelling the Moors from the Iberian Peninsula, Spain and Portugal attacked the Moroccan coast. Other European countries, including Germany and France, fought for control of Morocco until 1956, when all foreign rights were relinquished except for those to the Western Sahara, which is still disputed territory.

Tangier

In Tangier, walk up the Rue Portugal, just right of the port entrance, skirting the left-hand edge of the medina. Continue up the hill through a small gate in the medina wall to the **Fondouk Market,** where you will be surrounded by the color and vitality—men and women with bright *djellabas* (full-length robes with pointed hoods)—that inspired Delacroix, Regnault, Fortuny, and so many others to make Morocco a leitmotif. A left on Rue de la Liberté leads up to Place de France and the sumptuous **French consulate.** Another left on Boulevard Pasteur takes you down past a belvedere to the **tourist office.**

Walk down the **Grand Socco** (large market) through the pointed archway to the Petit Socco (small market) into the heart of Tangier's old city and artisan district. Uphill to the left is the **Place de la Kasbah,** where a belvedere has views over the port across to Tarifa.

$$$$ ✕🏨 **El Minzah Hotel.** Ask any native where the best place in town is—for either dining *or* lodging—and the immediate answer will be the El Minzah. Lovely studded wooden doors, hotel staff in Ottoman costumes, and fine views over the Mediterranean to the Iberian Peninsula prove them right. ✉ *85 Rue de la Liberté,* ☎ *09/935885,* FAX *09/934546. 100 rooms. Restaurant, pool. AE, DC, MC, V.*

$$ 🏨 **Hotel Continental.** Overlooking the port from the edge of the medina, this wonderful palace, built in 1888, is the best buy in Tangier for aesthetes and dreamers—and really, who else goes to Morocco? Bertolucci stayed in Room 108 while shooting *The Sheltering Sky.* Monsieur Abdessalam is a gracious host. ✉ *36 Rue Dar el Baroud,* ☎ *09/931024,* FAX *09/931143. 15 rooms with bath, 30 rooms share 10 baths. AE, DC, MC, V.*

$ 🏨 **Hotel Muniria.** William Burroughs wrote *Naked Lunch* in Room 9, now the home of Madame Rabia, the lovely owner. Room 8 overlooks the Bay of Tangier. Rue Magellan can be tricky to find. ✉ *2 Rue Magellan,* ☎ *09/935337. 6 rooms with bath, 2 rooms share a bath. No credit cards.*

Casablanca

Casablanca, a booming metropolis of 3.5 million, is bound to disappoint cineasts and romantics hoping to bump into Bergman and Bogart. The closest they'll get: At the counterfeit Rick's Bar, in the Hyatt

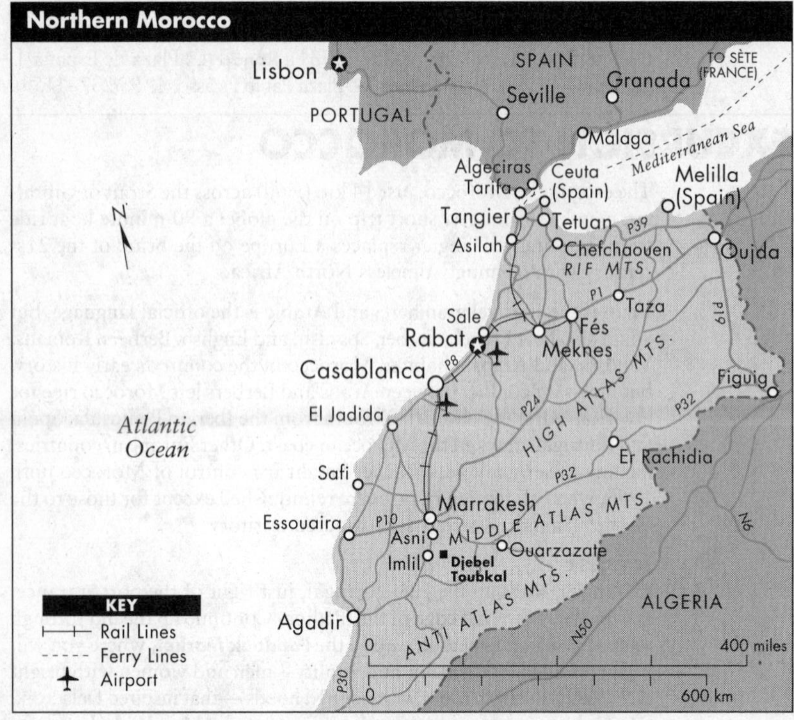

Regency, waiters take orders in trench coats and fedoras. The **Grande Mosquée Hassan II,** however, will not disappoint. Opened in 1994, it's second in size only to the mosque in Mecca, with room for 25,000 worshipers inside—where the glass floor reveals the ocean below—and 80,000 in the courtyard. The 650-ft minaret is Morocco's tallest structure. Casablanca's **Corniche** is a pleasant promenade; the **spice market** in the medina is another attraction.

$$ ✕ **Al Mounia.** The best spot in Casablanca for authenticity and value, Al Mounia serves the classic Moroccan specialties: *pastilla* (pigeon pie), *harira* (lentil, chickpea, and meat soup), *tajines* (meat or fish stewed in almonds, plums, and/or vegetables), *mechoui* (roast lamb), and couscous. ✉ *95 Rue du Prince Moulay Abdallah,* ☎ *02/222669. AE, DC, MC, V. Closed Sun.*

$$$$ ✕🏨 **Royal Mansour.** One of Morocco's top hotels, the Royal Mansour is a treat: fabulous food is served in a lush garden courtyard to live Cole Porter tunes, and a rooftop *hammam* (Turkish bath). ✉ *27 Av. des F.A.R.,* ☎ *02/313011,* FAX *02/312583. 159 rooms, 23 suites. 3 restaurants. AE, DC, MC, V.*

$$ 🏨 **Hotel Moussafir.** New, impeccably clean, and well situated near the Casa-Voyageurs train station, the Moussafir is about one-tenth as expensive as the Royal Mansour and not nearly as far removed in quality. ✉ *Bd. Bahmir,* ☎ *02/401984,* FAX *02/400799. 99 rooms. Restaurant. AE, DC, MC, V.*

Marrakesh

The tumultuous and panoramic **Djemâa el Fna** (Assembly of the Dead) square, the highlight of a visit to Marrakesh, is a sensorial feast. Great clouds of aromatic smoke from the outdoor kitchens in the center of the square combine with the sounds of Berber musicians and storytellers, the muezzin's eerie call to prayer, snake charmers' flutes, and water vendors' bells. Scribes and clients confer intimately in the shade of umbrellas, tooth pullers are surrounded by even rows of molars, the snowcapped Atlas peaks rise behind the 800-year-old Kotoubia minaret, and the warmth of the fires meets the cool evening breeze from the mountains (Marrakesh is equidistant from the Atlantic and the Sahara).

$$$$ ✕ **Dar Marjana.** You'll feel like you've walked into a Delacroix painting. Excellent cuisine, beautiful surroundings, Nubian waiters uniformed in rich greens, belly dancing, and folk music combine for a true tour de force. ✉ *15 Derb Sidi Ali Tair, Bab Doukkala,* ☎ *04/445773. MC, V. Closed Tues. No lunch.*

$$$$ ✕🏨 **La Mamounia.** Everyone from Winston Churchill to Bryan Ferry has loved this unique oasis within an oasis. One of the most famous hotels in the world, La Mamounia is worth every one of the many nickels it costs. The grounds, facilities, service, and taste are sensational, and you're walking distance from Djemâa el Fna square. ✉ *Av. Bab Jdid,* ☎ *04/448981,* FAX *04/444940. 171 rooms, 57 suites, 3 villas. 5 restaurants, pool. AE, DC, MC, V.*

Fez

Traditionally considered Morocco's intellectual and spiritual capital, Fez can at first seem almost too quiet after tumultuous Marrakesh. Whereas the latter is a crossroads between the Berber Sahara and black Africa from one direction and Islam and the Orient from the other, Fez is more refined, Islamic, Mediterranean, even Andalusian. The 9th-century medina, **Fez el Bali** (Old Fez), is a labyrinth of mosques (360 of them), *medersas* (medieval residential colleges), shops, and artisans. Nowhere in Morocco is a good guide more indispensable.

Fez's architectural treasures are many: carving and tilework, the **water clock**, the **Kairaouine Mosque**, and **Kairaouine University**, which, founded during the 9th century, predates Bologna's university by 200 years and Oxford's by 300. The souks and *fondouks* are all hauntingly ancient and aesthetically perfect.

$$ ✕ **Al Andalus.** On the airport road in the modern part of town, this excellent spot is a local secret. Owner Hilali Fouad's collection of curios and antiques is as enticing as the food. ✉ *34 Rte. d'Immouzzer,* ☎ *05/603162,* FAX *05/600548. AE, DC, MC, V.*

$$$$ ✕🏨 **Hotel Merinides.** This spectacular hotel is usually booked well in advance. The views over Fez el Bali from the pool, nicely raised above the fray, are unique. ✉ *Borj Nord,* ☎ *05/646040,* FAX *05/645225. 79 rooms, 11 suites. 2 restaurants, pool. AE, DC, MC, V.*

$$–$$$$ 🏨 **Palais Jamai.** This elegant palace, 120 years old, was once the residence of the Vizir Jamai. There are views over the medina, and you're close to Fez el Bali. ✉ *Bab Guissa,* ☎ *05/634331,* FAX *05/635096. 123 rooms, 14 suites. 2 restaurants, pool. AE, DC, MC, V.*

Morocco Essentials

You will not need a visa, you *can* drink the water, and the time is usually one hour behind Spain. Women traveling alone or without men will have difficulty and should hire a reputable guide, wear conservative clothing, and be on guard at all times. The country code for Morocco is 212; drop the zero in the area code when calling from outside the country.

Getting Around

BY BOAT

From Algeciras to Tangier, **Transmediterranea** (✉ Recinto del Puerto s/n, Algeciras, ☎ 95/666–3850). **Madrid** (✉ C. Pedro Muñoz Seca 2, ☎ 91/431–0700). **Tangier** (✉ 31 Av. de la Résistance, ☎ 09/941101) has a 90-minute hydrofoil and a two-hour car ferry. The slow boat is bigger, more stable, and offers better views than the somewhat claustrophobic hydrofoil. Having your passport stamped and getting your yellow exit card before you leave the boat can save you an hour or more.

BY BUS

Bus stations: **Casablanca** (✉ 23 Rue Leon l'Africain, ☎ 02/268061). **Fez** (✉ Av. Mohammed V, ☎ 05/622041). **Marrakesh** (✉ Bab Doukkala, ☎ 04/433993). **Tangier** (✉ Av. des F.A.R., ☎ 09/932415).

BY CAR

Moroccan roads are free-for-alls. In addition to the poor surfaces, there is a bumper-car, helter-skelter confusion from which, miraculously, most people emerge unscathed. If you choose to brave the roads in search of freedom from set schedules, international car-rental agencies are well represented. **Casablanca: Budget** (✉ Torres de los Habous, Av. des F.A.R., ☎ 02/313945) and **Hertz** (✉ 25 Rue Foucault, ☎ 02/484710). **Fez: Avis** (✉ 50 Bd. Chefchaouen, ☎ 05/626746), Budget (✉ Bureau Grand Hotel, Av. Chefchaouen, ☎ 05/620919), and **Hertz** (✉ Hotel de Fez, Av. des F.A.R., ☎ 05/622812). **Marrakesh: Budget** (✉ 213 Av. Mohammed V, ☎ 04/434604) and **Hertz** (✉ 157 Av. Mohammed V, ☎ 04/434680). **Tangier: Budget** (✉ 79 Av. du Prince, Moulay Abdallah, ☎ 09/937994) and **Hertz** (✉ 36 Av. Mohammed V, ☎ 09/933322).

BY PLANE

Royal Air Maroc (☎ 800/344–6726 in the U.S. outside NY, ☎ 212/750–6071 in the U.S. in NY; ☎ 91/547–7905 in Madrid) and **Iberia Airlines** (☎ 800/772–4642 in the U.S., 902/400500 in Spain) fly to Casablanca from Madrid in 90 minutes. The former has comprehensive domestic service.

BY TRAIN

Trains from Tangier to Casablanca leave at 4 PM and arrive six hours later. There are two stations in **Casablanca,** the Gare du Port (also called Casa–Port, ☎ 02/223011) and the Gare des Voyageurs (also called Casa–Voyageurs, ☎ 02/243818). The latter serves Marrakesh and the south. **Fez** (☎ 05/625001), **Marrakesh** (☎ 04/447768), and **Tangier** (☎ 09/931201) have their own stations as well.

Guided Tours

Most Moroccan cities have a swarm of very insistent, unofficial "guides." The best way to get rid of these volunteers, who may falsely assure you that all hotels are full and take you to shops where they get commissions on purchases, is to ignore them and pretend you know exactly where you're going. If you do want a guide, hire a cheaper and better one at the local tourist office.

Visitor Information

United States (✉ 20 E. 46th St., Suite 1201, New York, NY 10017, ☎ 212/557–2520). **United Kingdom** (✉ 205 Regent St., W1R 7DE, London, ☎ 44171/437–0073). **Madrid** (✉ C. Ventura Rodríguez, 28008, ☎ 91/542–7431). **Casablanca** (✉ 55 Rue Omar Slaoui, ☎ 02/271177). **Fez** (Place de la Résistance, ☎ 05/623460). **Marrakesh** (✉ 176 Bd. Mohammed V, ☎ 04/432097; ✉ Place Abdel–Moumen Ben Ali, ☎ 04/431088). **Tangier** (✉ 29 Bd. Pasteur, ☎ 09/938239).

CANARY ISLANDS

Closer to North Africa than to mainland Spain, the ruggedly exotic Canary Islands are becoming a year-round destination for sunseekers and nature lovers alike. The Canaries lie 112 km (70 mi) off the coast of southern Morocco and enjoy mild, sunny weather throughout the year, except for the north coast of Tenerife. Each of the seven volcanic islands in this archipelago is distinct: some have lush tropical vegetation, poinsettias as tall as trees, and banana plantations, while others are so arid as to resemble an exotic moonscape of lava rock and sand dunes. Between them the islands are home to six national parks and dozens of other protected ecological zones; Tenerife has Spain's highest peak, Mt. Teide (12,198 ft), snowcapped for much of the year. Depending on the island, you can explore caves once inhabited by ancient tribal dwellers called the Guanches, hike through mist-shrouded forests of virgin laurel trees, eat meats grilled over the heat of a volcanic crater, or scuba dive off long stretches of unspoiled coastline.

Tenerife

Of all the Canary Islands, Tenerife is the most popular and has the greatest variety of scenery. Its beaches are small, though, with volcanic black sand or sand imported from the Sahara Desert.

Most tourists stay in the south coast's **Playa de las Americas,** in the island's most arid and barren zone. Chock-a-block with hotels, it's popular with young couples and singles, and offers little apart from sprawling hotel pools and sizzling nightlife.

An hour northeast by superhighway is Tenerife's capital, **Santa Cruz.** No whitewashed villas or sleepy streets here; instead, imagine all the traffic, action, and crowds of an important shipping port. Santa Cruz throws one of Spain's wildest pre-Lenten Carnival fiestas.

The **Museo Arqueológico Provincial** (Provincial Museum of Archaeology) contains ceramics and mummies from the Stone Age Guanches, the native people who inhabited the islands before they were conquered and colonized by the Spanish during the 15th century. The **tourist office** is just around the corner in the same building. ✉ *Palacio Insular, Bravo Murillo 5, 3rd floor,* ☎ *922/242090.* ⏲ *Tues.–Sun. 10–8.*

The best sight in Santa Cruz is the colorful weekday-morning market, **Mercado de Nuestra Señora de Africa,** where you can buy everything from tropical fruits and flowers to canaries and parrots. ✉ *Avda. de San Sebastín.* ⏲ *Mon.–Sat. 5 AM–noon.*

Santa Cruz's beach, **Las Teresitas,** is about 7 km (4½ mi) northeast of the city, near the town of San Andrés, and is especially popular with local families. It was created with imported white sand from the Sahara.

Also north of Santa Cruz are the university town of La Laguna and the island's first resort village, **Puerto de la Cruz.** High-rise hotels and hawkers of plastic bananas are encroaching on the village's atmosphere, but it still has a tropical, flower-filled central square.

Inland, the road from Orotava rises through banana plantations, almond groves, and pine forests to the entrance to ★ **Mt. Teide National Park.** The visitors' center, open daily 9–4, offers trail maps, guided hikes, educational videos, and bus tours. Before arriving at the foot of the mountain, you pass through a stark landscape called Las Cañadas del Teide, a violent jumble of rocks and minerals created by millions of years of volcanic activity. For 1,800 ptas., a cable car will take you within 534 ft of the top of Mt. Teide, where you'll have good views of the southern part of the island and neighboring Gran Canaria. The cable car operates daily 9–5; the last trip leaves at 4.

The north-coast town of **Icod de los Vinos** boasts a 3,000-year-old, 57-ft-tall dragon tree once worshipped by the ancient Guanches, and a plaza surrounded by typical Canarian houses with wooden balconies.

Farther west, **Garachico** is the most peaceful and best preserved village on this touristy isle.

$$$$ ★ ✕ **El Coto de Antonio.** One of the finest restaurants in the Canaries, El Coto de Antonio puts a gourmet spin on local dishes. In a setting as cozy as a tavern, you can relax over an earthenware pot of succulent seafood stew enhanced with potatoes, yams, blanched *gofio* (a traditional corn-and-barley pudding), and cheese; or the house specialty: *pejines* (similar to sardines) dried in the sun, soaked in liquor, and served flambé at your table. ✉ *General Goded 13,* ☎ *922/272105. AE, MC, V. Closed Mon.*

$$ ✕ **La Masia del Mar.** There's no menu here; you simply point and choose from a vast array of fresh fish and shellfish in a big refrigerated case. Add a salad and a bottle of white wine to the order, and then find a seat on the wide terrace overlooking Las Caletas cove (about 5 km/3 mi west of Playa de las Americas), and enjoy a simple feast of the best food the Canaries have to offer. ✉ *Caleta de Adeje,* ☎ *922/710241. MC, V.*

$$$$ **Hotel Gran Melia Bahia del Duque.** This sprawling hotel is a jumble of pastel houses and palaces, with Renaissance windows, loggias, and quiet courtyards. Rooms have oversize beds, summery wicker and pine furnishings, and rich architectural details such as scalloped plasterwork and hand-painted ceramics. ✉ *Carretera Bajada la Caleta, km 2, Costa Adeje, 38670,* ☎ *922/713000,* FAX *922/712369. 362 rooms. 5 restaurants, 4 pools. AE, MC, V.*

$$ **Hotel Monopol.** One of Puerto de la Cruz's first inns, this hotel has welcomed guests for over a century. Before that it was a private home (built in 1742) in the Canarian patio style. Tropical plants fill the center courtyard. Rooms are simple but have good views of the sea or the main plaza. ✉ *Quintana 15, Puerto de la Cruz, 38400,* ☎ *922/384611,* FAX *922/370310. 110 rooms. Restaurant, pool. AE, MC, V.*

Gran Canaria

The place to be in the '60s and '70s, Gran Canaria has better beaches than Tenerife. Most visitors base themselves in the south-coast resorts **Playa del Inglés** and **Maspalomas,** where the white-sand beach extends for 4 km (2½ mi).

Gran Canaria's central highlands provide a glimpse of rural island life: The road passes through numerous villages, and it's common to see farmers walking along the road laden with burlap sacks of potatoes.

The highest point on the island, **Mirador Los Pechos,** offers magnificent vistas.

Gran Canaria's capital, **Las Palmas,** the largest city in the Canaries, is a multicultural whirlwind of a place, overrun with sailors, tourists, traffic jams, diesel-spewing buses, and hordes of shoppers. Despite the somewhat seedy center, Las Palmas does have an interesting and beautiful old quarter, La Vegueta. Here you can wander cobblestone streets and visit the **Casa Museo Colón** (Columbus House and Museum), where the great explorer is said to have stayed when he stopped to repair the mast on the *Pinta.* ✉ C. *Colón 1,* ☎ *928/311255.* *Free.* *Sept.–July, weekdays 9–6, weekends 9–3.*

It's quite a walk to the other end of town and the beach, so you may want to jump on one of the many canary-yellow buses, named *guaguas* (pronounced "wawas") in honor of the ancestral Guanches. Take the *guagua* to **Parque Santa Catalina**; lines 2, 3, and 30 link the old town and the port. The real jewel of the capital is **Las Canteras beach,** a sparkling-clean strand of white sand perfect for swimming or strolling.

$$ ✕ **Tenderete II.** Local cuisine is cherished at this unassuming little restaurant in a shopping center, one of the few in the Canaries to serve *gofio,* a traditional corn-and-barley pudding. Typical Canarian soups and stews are always available for the first course; the main course is

always fish, grilled or baked in rock salt. ✉ *Avda. de Tirajan, Edificio Aloe, Maspalomas,* ☎ *928/761460. AE, DC, MC, V.*

$$$ 🏨 **Hotel Palm Beach.** The Palm Beach, one of the islands' most sophisticated and luxurious hotels, rests in the middle of a 1,000-year-old palm oasis at the edge of Maspalomas Beach. The spacious rooms have dark bamboo furniture, large marble baths, and terraces overlooking the sea or the pool. ✉ *Avda. del Oasis s/n, Maspalomas, 35106,* ☎ *928/140806,* FAX *928/141808. 358 rooms. Restaurant, pool. AE, MC, V.*

Lanzarote

Stark and dry, with landscapes of volcanic rock, Lanzarote enjoys good beaches and tasteful architecture—low-rise, with a green-and-white color scheme– the latter due to the efforts of the late artist César Manrique, a Lanzarote native revered for single-handedly saving the island from mass development.

★ In Costa Teguise the **Jameos del Agua** (water cavern) is a natural wonder created when molten lava streamed through an underground tunnel and hissed into the sea. The site features an auditorium with fantastic acoustics, and a restaurant and bar. ✉ *Rte. GC710, 21 km (13 mi) north of Arrecife,* ☎ *928/835010.* ⏲ *Daily 11–6:45, Tues. and Sat. also 7 PM–3 AM.*

★ The **Parque National Timanfaya,** popularly known as the "fire mountains," takes up much of the southern part of the island. Here you can have a camel ride, take a guided coach tour of the volcanic zone, and eat lunch at one of the world's most unusual restaurants, El Diablo (☎ *928/840057*), where meat is cooked over the crater of a volcano using the earth's natural heat.

$–$$ ✕ **La Era.** One of only three buildings to survive the eruption of the volcano that wiped out the town of Yaiza in 1730, this farmhouse restaurant offers country-style tabletops arranged around a center patio. It's a great place to try regional dishes such as goat stew, or Canarian cheeses. ✉ *Barranco 3, behind the city hall (Ayuntamiento), Yaiza,* ☎ *928/830016. AE, DC, MC, V.*

$$$$ ✕🏨 **Meliá Salinas.** A stunning hotel built around an interior tropical garden, the Meliá Salinas offers a chance to rub elbows with vacationing business and political leaders from all over Europe. Rooms have a tropical feel, and all have large, flower-filled terraces that face the sea. The hotel's restaurant, La Graciosa—Lanzarote's poshest dining spot—overlooks the garden. A German chef prepares international dishes from fresh island ingredients: think giant prawns, duck breast in plum sauce, and halibut wrapped in chard. ✉ *Costa Teguise, 35509,* ☎ *928/590040,* FAX *928/590390. 310 rooms. 2 restaurants, pool. AE, DC, MC, V.*

Fuerteventura

The island of Fuerteventura was only recently discovered by tourists—mostly Germans—who now come to windsurf, and to enjoy the dunes of Corralejo and the endless white-sand beaches of the Sotovento coast. Diving is good along the lengthy and lonely Jandía Peninsula, while the arid interior is largely the domain of goatherds.

La Palma

Known as the garden isle, La Palma has luxuriant foliage, tropical storms, rainbows, and black crescents of beach, the most popular of which is ★ **Los Cancajos.** The capital, **Santa Cruz de la Palma,** was burned to the ground by pirates in 1533; it was rebuilt with royal assistance, and today remains one of the most beautiful and harmonious examples of Spanish colonial architecture.

Canary Islands Essentials

Arriving and Departing

BY BOAT

Transmediterranea (☎ 91/431–0700 in Madrid) operates a slow, comfortable ferry between Cádiz and the Canary Islands.

BY PLANE

Iberia and its sister carrier **Aviaco** have several direct flights daily to Tenerife, Gran Canaria, and Lanzarote from most cities in mainland Spain. The other islands can be reached by connecting flights or hydrofoil. **Air Europa** and **Spanair** serve the Canaries from Madrid and Barcelona at slightly lower prices.

From the United States, **Air Europa** (☎ 212/888–7010 in New York) flies directly to Tenerife once a week.

Getting Around

BY BOAT

Transmediterranea operates inter-island car ferries. Trips often take all night; ferries have sleeping cabins. The company also runs a passenger-only hydrofoil service three times a day between Las Palmas and Tenerife. One hydrofoil a day links southern Fuerteventura with Las Palmas and Tenerife.

BY BUS

In Tenerife buses meet all arriving Iberia flights at Reina Sofía airport and transfer passengers to the bus terminal in the outskirts of Santa Cruz de Tenerife.

BY CAR

Most people rent a car or Jeep for at least part of their stay, as driving is by far the best way to explore the countryside. Reservations are necessary only during the Christmas and Easter holidays. **Hertz** and **Avis** have representatives on all the islands, though you'll get better rates from the Spanish company **Cicar** (☎ 928/802790), with offices at all the airports.

BY PLANE

All the Canary Islands except La Gomera are served by air. Tenerife has two airports: Reina Sofía, in the south, and Los Rodeos, in the north. As a general rule long-distance flights arrive at the southern terminal and inter-island flights use the northern one. Driving time from one airport to the other is 1½ hours.

Airport information: **Tenerife** (✉ Reina Sofía, ☎ 922/759200; ✉ Los Rodeos, ☎ 922/635800). **Gran Canaria** (☎ 928/579000). **Lanzarote** (☎ 928/811450). **Fuerteventura** (☎ 928/860500). **La Palma** (☎ 922/411540).

Guided Tours

One-day tours of Tenerife and sightseeing excursions to other islands can be arranged through **Viajes Insular** (☎ 922/380262 in Puerto de la Cruz), which has branches on all islands except La Gomera and El Hierro.

Visitor Information

Each of the Canary Islands has its own tourist office. **Tenerife** (✉ Plaza de España 1, Santa Cruz, ☎ 922/605592). **Gran Canaria** (✉ Parque Santa Catalina, Las Palmas, ☎ 928/264623). **Lanzarote** (✉ Parque Municipal, Arrecife, ☎ 928/80157). **La Palma** (✉ Palacio Salazar, C. Real s/n, Santa Cruz de la Palma, ☎ 922/412106).

29 Sweden

Stockholm, Uppsala and the Folklore District, the West Coast, and the Glass Country

The natural beauty of Sweden, with its glaciered mountains, vast forest tracts, thousands of lakes and rivers, and unspoiled archipelagoes, stands in stark contrast to the cosmopolitan lifestyle of Swedish towns and cities.

Covering an area of 457,013 square km (173,665 square mi), making it the fourth largest in Europe, the country is nearly 1,600 km (1,000 mi) long, covering an environment that changes dramatically as you travel from the barren Arctic north to the fertile plains of the south. Still, Sweden is home to only 8.9 million people. The main centers of population lie south of the province of Dalarna, less than halfway up the country. The railway line that runs 2,128 km (1,322 mi) from Trelleborg, in the far south, to Riksgränsen in the north, is the world's longest stretch of continuously electrified track. Traveling it takes more than 35 hours.

Sweden is a land of contrasts. It has short, warm summers and long, dark, cold winters. Ancient Viking rune stones and 19th-century landmarks coexist with modern skyscrapers. Socialism exists side by side with staunch royalism. Shop windows, full of the latest in consumer goods, attract shoppers who are as at home in the city as they are in the countryside. Swedes seem to like this diversity, big-city living contrasting with the silence of the countryside. Sweden is also a clean country; it is possible to fish for salmon, trout, and the odd sturgeon right in the center of Stockholm, just a stone's throw away from the Royal Palace. In Göteborg's busy harbor, you can watch fish jump out of the water—fish that are also sold at the local market. In downtown Malmö, startlingly large hares hop around in the parks.

Once the dominant power of the Nordic region, Sweden has always been politically independent. During the Cold War, it was largely successful in retaining its position as a neutral trading partner of both superpowers. The economic recession of the late 1980s forced Sweden to rethink its comprehensive welfare system, making changes down to its very foundations. When the country developed one of Europe's largest budget deficits, the fragile conservative coalition that had defeated the long-incumbent Social Democrats in 1991 attempted further cutbacks.

The Social Democrats' power was restored in 1994, but cutbacks have continued at an ever-increasing pace. Sweden joined the European Union (EU) in January 1995, following a closely won referendum preceded by a heated debate. While the domestic benefits of membership have been slow in showing themselves, Sweden has quickly become an influential and respected member of this often divided organization.

SWEDEN A TO Z

Customs

For details on imports and duty-free limits, *see* Customs & Duties *in* Chapter 1.

Dining

Traditional Swedish restaurants are giving way to myriad international culinary influences. Fast-food outlets abound, but there is an impressive range of eateries—from top-class establishments to less expensive places for lunch or a snack—to suit even the most fickle palates and every budget.

Restaurants all over the country specialize in *husmanskost* (home cooking), based on traditional Swedish recipes. Sweden is world famous for its *smörgåsbord,* a word now internationally used as a synonym for diversity. This tempting buffet of hot and cold dishes, usually with a strong emphasis on seafood, notably herring, has something to tickle all taste buds. You can usually find an authentic smörgåsbord, and eat as much as you wish, for SKr 200–300. Hotels sometimes serve a smörgåsbord-style breakfast, often included in the room price.

MEALTIMES

Swedes eat early. Lunch is served from 11 AM, and outside the main cities restaurants often close at 9 PM or don't even open for dinner. In the large cities there are plenty of places to eat, although it is advisable to make reservations at the more popular establishments, especially on weekends.

RATINGS

Prices are per person and include a first course and main course, but no drinks. Service charges and *moms* (value-added tax) are included in the check, but it is common to tip 5%–10%.

CATEGORY	COST
$$$$	OVER SKR 350
$$$	SKR 250–SKR 350
$$	SKR 120–SKR 250
$	UNDER SKR 120

WHAT TO WEAR

Except for the most formal restaurants, where a jacket and a tie are preferable, casual—or casual chic—attire is perfectly acceptable. Swedish dress is generally more conservative than that of Americans.

Language

Swedish is closely related to Danish and Norwegian. After "z," the Swedish alphabet has three extra letters, "å," "ä," and "ö." Also, *v* and *w* are interchangeable. Most Swedes speak English.

Lodging

Sweden offers a variety of accommodation from simple bed-and-breakfasts, campsites, and hostels to hotels of the highest international standard. Major hotels in larger cities cater mainly to business clientele and can be expensive; weekend rates are more reasonable. Prices are normally on a per-room basis and include all taxes and service charges

Sweden (Sverige)
N
0 50 miles
0 75 km
Riksgränsen
Kiruna
Gällivare
Luleälven
Jokkmokk
400
Arctic Circle
Norwegian Sea
Arjeplog
Tärnaby
Töre
Torneå
Kalix
Arvidsjaur
E79
Sorsele
Luleå
95
Piteå
Storuman
Lycksele
Skellefteå
342
Umeälven
Åsele
92
Umeå
Strömsund
90
Åre
Östersund
E75
Tännäs
Sundsvall
FINLAND
NORWAY
84
Ljungan
Gulf of Bothnia
Idre
Hudiksvall
70
Bollnäs
Mora
Söderhamn
Klarälven
62
Falun
Gävle
80
Borlänge
Avesta
E4
Fagersta
Uppsala
Åland
Karlstad
Västerås
E18
Stockholm
Mälaren
Gulf of Finland
Mellerud
Örebro
Strömstad
Vänern
Uddevalla
Trollhättan
Norrköping
Gotska Sandön
ESTONIA
Göteborg (Gothenburg)
Vättern
Linköping
Baltic Sea
40
Jönköping
Borås
Nässjö
E66
Visby
Gulf of Riga
Falkenberg
E6
Värnamo
Oskarshamn
Gotland
Halmstad
Växjö
23
Kalmar
Öland
LATVIA
Helsingborg
Karlskrona
Malmö
Kristianstad
DENMARK
LITHUANIA
Trelleborg
Ystad

and usually breakfast. Apart from the more modest inns and the cheapest budget establishments, private baths and showers are standard. Whatever their size, Swedish hotels provide scrupulously clean accommodation and courteous service. Sweden virtually shuts down during the entire month of July, so make your hotel reservations in advance, especially if you're staying outside the city areas during July and early August.

CAMPING

Camping is popular in Sweden. About 750 officially approved sites dot the country, most next to the sea or a lake and offering such activities as windsurfing, horseback riding, and tennis. They are generally open between June 1 and September 1, although some stay open year-round. A free, abbreviated list of sites is published in English by the **Sveriges Campingvårdernas Riksforbünd** (Swedish Campsite Owners' Association, ✉ Box 255, 451 17 Uddevalla, ☎ 0522/642440, FAX 0522/642430).

CHALET RENTAL

At 250 chalet villages with high standards, accommodations can often be arranged on the spot at tourist offices. **Scandinavian Seaways** (☎ 031/650600) in Göteborg arranges package deals that combine a ferry trip from Britain across the North Sea and a stay in a chalet village.

HOTELS

Major hotel groups have their own central reservations services. **Scandic** (☎ 08/6105050). **Best Western** (☎ 08/330600 or 020/792752). **Sweden Hotels** (☎ 08/7898900). **Radisson SAS** (☎ 020/797592).

The official annual guide, *Hotels in Sweden*, published by and available free from the Swedish Travel and Tourism Council (☞ Visitor Information, *below*), gives comprehensive information about hotel facilities and prices. The **Sweden Hotels** group has about 100 independently owned hotels and its own classification scheme—*A*, *B*, or *C*—based on facilities. **Hotellcentralen** (✉ Central Station, 111 20, ☎ 08/7892456, FAX 08/7918666) is an independent agency that makes advance telephone reservations for hotels in Stockholm. **Countryside Hotels** (✉ Box 69, 830 13 Åre, ☎ 0647/51860, FAX 0647/51920), 35 select resort hotels, may be restored manor houses or centuries-old inns.

RATINGS

Prices are for two people in a double room, based on standard rates; tax and breakfast are included.

CATEGORY	COST
$$$$	OVER SKR 1,200
$$$	SKR 970–SKR 1,200
$$	SKR 725–SKR 970
$	UNDER SKR 725

Mail

POSTAL RATES

Airmail letters and postcards to the United States and Canada weighing less than 20 grams cost SKr 8. Postcards and letters within Europe cost SKr 5.

RECEIVING MAIL

If you're uncertain where you will be staying, have your mail addressed to "poste restante" and sent to ✉ S-101 10 Stockholm. Collection is at Post Office Stockholm 1 (✉ Drottningg. 53, ☎ 08/7814682). American Express (☞ Travel Agencies *in* Stockholm Essentials, *below*) offers a poste-restante service free to cardholders and for a small fee to others.

Money Matters

COSTS

Sweden is looked upon as an expensive country, although prices are generally in line with the European average. Restaurant prices can be high, but bargains exist: In cities look for the lunch *dagens rätt* (dish of the day), about SKr 60–SKr 70. Also, check for a recommended two- or three-course menu. Hotels are at their priciest fall through spring; many have special low summer and weekend winter rates. Heavy taxes and excise duties make liquor prices among the highest in Europe.

CURRENCY

The unit of currency in Sweden is the krona (plural kronor), which is divided into 100 öre and is written as SKr, SEK, or kr. Coins come in values of 50 öre and 1, 5, or 10 kronor; bills in denominations of 20, 100, 500, and 1,000 kronor. Traveler's checks and foreign currency can be exchanged at banks all over Sweden and at post offices displaying the NB EXCHANGE sign. At press time (spring 1998), the exchange rate was SKr 7.72 to the U.S. dollar, SKr 5.33 to the Canadian dollar, SKr 12.61 to the pound sterling, SKr 4.83 to the Australian dollar, and SKr 4.11 to the New Zealand dollar.

SAMPLE PRICES

Cup of coffee, SKr 15–SKr 25; beer, SKr 30–SKr 49; soda, SKr 15–SKr 25; ham sandwich, SKr 25–SKr 50; 1-mi taxi ride, SKr 40–SKr 70 (depending on the taxi company, day and time).

TIPPING

Tipping in Sweden has become more common in recent years. At hotels it is customary to tip the porter about SKr 5 per item. For taxi rides, SKr 5 to SKr 10 is usual. A niggling feature of the Swedish restaurant scene is that you often must check your coat or sports jacket whether you want to or not; the tip for this is usually SKr 10.

National Holidays

January 1; January 6 (Epiphany); April 2 (Good Friday); April 5 (Easter Monday); May 1 (Labor Day); May 13 (Ascension); June 25 (Midsummer Evening); June 26 (Midsummer Day); November 6 (All Saints' Day); December 25–26. Hotels and restaurants may close for some of these holidays and for the week between Christmas and New Year's.

Opening and Closing Times

Banks are open weekdays 9:30–3; some stay open until 5 in larger cities. Banks at Stockholm's Arlanda Airport and Göteborg's Landvetter Airport are open every day, with extended hours. Forex and Valuta Specialisten **currency-exchange offices** operate in downtown Stockholm, Göteborg, and Malmö, also with extended hours. **Museum** hours vary widely, but most are open weekdays 10–4 or 10–5, weekends 11–4, but may close on Monday. **Shops** are generally open weekdays 9 or 9:30–6 and Saturday 9–1 or 9–4. Some department stores remain open until 8 or 9 on certain evenings, and some are also open Sunday noon–4 in major cities. Many supermarkets open on Sunday.

Shopping

Swedish goods are internationally renowned for their style and quality. Best buys are glassware, jewelry, stainless steel, pottery and ceramics, leather goods, and textiles. You will find a wide selection of goods in such major stores as NK, PUB, and Åhléns, which have branches all over the country.

For glassware at bargain prices, head for the Kingdom of Crystal (☞ The West Coast and the Glass Country, *below*). The major glassworks have large factory outlets where you can pick up seconds at prices well below normal retail. For clothing, the best centers are Borås and Ullered, not far from Göteborg, where you can find bargains from the leading mail-order and discount companies. In rural areas, head to the local Hemslöjd craft centers for high-quality clothing, woodwork, and needlework.

SALES-TAX REFUNDS

Many Swedish shops participate in the tax-free shopping program, enabling visitors to claim a refund of most of the *moms* (value-added tax) paid, a rate of about 25%. Participating shops display a distinctive black, blue, and yellow sticker in the window. (Some stores offer the service only on purchases amounting to more than SKr 200.) The cashier will wrap and seal your purchase and give you a "Tax-Free Shopping Check" equivalent to the tax paid minus a handling charge. This check can be cashed when you leave Sweden and show your unopened packages, either at the airport or aboard ferries. If you're packing your purchases in a suitcase, you can show them at the "Tax-Free" counter at Arlanda airport's check-in lobby and get your refund before you check your luggage. You need your passport when making your purchase and claiming your refund.

Telephoning

COUNTRY CODE

The country code for Sweden is 46. When dialing Sweden from outside the country, drop the first zero in the regional telephone code.

INTERNATIONAL CALLS

These can be made from any pay phone. For calls to the United States and Canada, dial 0Q9, then 1 (the country code), then wait for a second dial tone before dialing the area code and number. When dialing the United Kingdom, omit the initial zero on area codes (for Central London you would dial 009 followed by 44, wait for the second tone, then dial 171 and the local number). You can make international calls from **Telebutik** offices. To reach an **AT&T** long-distance operator, dial 020/795611; for **MCI,** 020/795922; and for **Sprint,** 020/799011.

LOCAL CALLS

Sweden has plenty of pay phones; to use them you'll need SKr 1, 5, or 10 coins, as a local call costs SKr 2. You can also purchase a *telefonkort* (telephone card) from a Telebutik, hospital, or *Pressbyrån* store for SKr 35, SKr 60, or SKr 100. The card can provide a savings if you make numerous domestic calls and is indispensable when you're faced with one of the many public phones that accept only cards. Telephone numbers beginning with 020 are toll-free within Sweden.

OPERATORS AND INFORMATION

For international calls, the operator assistance number is 0018; directory assistance, which costs SKr 15 per minute, is 07977. Within Sweden, dial 90130 for operator assistance and 07975 for directory assistance (this service is free from public phones).

Transportation

The basic street sign terms you'll come across are *gatan* (street, abbreviated to *g.*), *vägen* (road, abbreviated to *v.*) and *gränd* (lane, shortened to *gr.*).

BY BICYCLE

Cycling is popular in Sweden, and the country's uncongested roads and many cycle paths make it ideal for extended bike tours. Bicycles can be rented throughout the country; inquire at tourist information offices. Rental costs average around SKr 80 per day or SKr 400 per week. The **Swedish Touring Club** (STF) in Stockholm (✉ Kungsg. 2, Box 25,

101 20, ☎ 08/4632200 or 020/292929, FAX 08/6781958) can give you information about cycling packages that include bike rental, overnight accommodation, and meals. **Cykelfrämjandet** (National Cycle Association, ✉ Torsg. 31, Box 6027, 102 31 Stockholm, ☎ 08/321680, FAX 08/310503) has information in English and German about cycling trips around Sweden.

BY BOAT

A classic Swedish boat trip is the four-day journey along the Göta Canal between Göteborg and Stockholm, operated by **Göta Canal Steamship Company** (✉ Box 272, 401 24 Göteborg, ☎ 031/806315, FAX 031/158311). Children must be at least 8 years old to ride aboard the steamship.

BY BUS

Sweden has excellent express bus services that provide inexpensive and relatively speedy transportation around the country. An information and booking office is at the front of Stockholm's station, **Cityterminalen** (✉ Klarabergsviadukten 72, bookings, ☎ 020/640640). **Swebus** and **Wasatrafik** run daily; other private companies operate weekends only. In the far north, postal buses delivering mail to remote areas also carry passengers, providing an offbeat, inexpensive journey.

BY CAR

Breakdowns. The Larmtjänst organization, run by a confederation of Swedish insurance companies, provides 24-hour breakdown service. Its phone numbers are listed in the Yellow Pages.

Gasoline. Sweden has some of the highest gasoline prices in Europe, about SKr 8 per liter, depending on the grade. Gas stations are self-service: pumps marked SEDEL are automatic and accept SKr 20 and SKr 100 bills; pumps marked KASSA are paid for at the cash desk; the KONTO pumps are for customers with Swedish gas credit cards.

Parking. Park on the right-hand side of the road, but if you want to park overnight, particularly in suburban areas, be sure not to do so the night the street is being cleaned; circular signs with a red border indicate when this occurs. Timed ticket machines and, sometimes, meters operate in larger towns, usually between 8 AM and 6 PM. Parking is free on weekends. The fee varies from about SKr 5 to SKr 30 per hour. Parking garages in urban areas are mostly automated, often with machines that accept credit cards; LEDIGT on a garage sign means space is available. On the street, a circular sign with a red border and a red diagonal on a blue background means parking is prohibited; a yellow rectangle with a red border means restricted parking. Beware: fines for parking violations are very high in Sweden. City "Trafikkarta" maps, available at many gas stations, include English explanations of parking signs and systems.

Road Conditions. Sweden has an excellent network of more than 80,000 km (50,000 mi) of highways. The fastest routes are those with numbers prefixed with an *E* (for "European"). Road E4, for instance, covers the entire distance from Helsingborg, in the south, to Stockholm, and on to Sundsvall and Umeå, in the north, finishing at Haparanda, on the Finnish border. All main and secondary roads are well surfaced, but some minor roads, particularly in the north, are gravel.

Rules of the Road. Drive on the right and, no matter where you sit in a car, you must wear a seat belt. You must also have at least low-beam headlights on at all times. Signs indicate five basic speed limits, ranging from 30 kph (19 mph) in school or playground areas to 110 kph (68 mph) on long stretches of *E* roads.

BY PLANE

Most major cities are served by **SAS** (☎ 020/727000) and smaller, independent airlines. From Stockholm, there are flights to more than 30 points around the country. SAS offers cut-rate round-trip fares every day on selected flights.

BY TRAIN

Frequently, trains link Stockholm with Göteborg and Malmö. First- and second-class cars are provided on all main routes, and sleeping cars are available in both classes on overnight trains. Most long-distance trains have a buffet car and a playground car for kids. Seat reservations are advisable, and on some trains—indicated with *R, IN,* or *IC* on the timetable—mandatory. Reservations (☎ 020/757575, Swedish recorded message, wait to be served by operator) can be made right up to departure. Couchette reservations on the regular train cost SKr 95 and beds from SKr 180. The Swedish rail network also operates high-speed **X2000** trains from Stockholm to Göteborg, Falun, Malmö, Jönköping and Sundsvall, and from Göteborg to Malmö.

For SKr150 you can buy a **Reslustkort** (wanderlust card), which gets you 50% reductions on *röda platser* ("Red," or off-peak, seats). Red seats have to be booked at least seven days in advance. **ScanRail** passes allow unlimited train travel throughout Sweden, as well as Denmark, Finland, and Norway. Limited ferry passage in and beyond Scandinavia is also included. The pass is available for 21 days or five days of travel within 15 days. In the United States, call RailEurope (☎ 800/438–7245), or DER (☎ 800/782–2424).

Visitor Information

Swedish Travel and Tourism Council (✉ Box 3030, Kungsg. 36, 103 61 Stockholm, ☎ 08/7255500, FAX 08/7255531).

Weather

The tourist season runs from mid-May through mid-September; many attractions, however, close in late August, when the schools reopen at the end of the Swedish vacation season. The weather can be glorious in the spring and fall, when fewer visitors are around.

CLIMATE

Sweden has typically unpredictable north European summer weather, but, as a general rule, it is likely to be warm but not hot from May until September. In Stockholm, the weeks just before and after midsummer offer almost 24-hour light, while in the far north, above the Arctic Circle, the sun doesn't set between the end of May and the middle of July.

The following are the average daily maximum and minimum temperatures for Stockholm.

Jan.	30F	– 1C	**May**	58F	14C	**Sept.**	60F	15C
	23	– 5		43	6		49	9
Feb.	30F	– 1C	**June**	67F	19C	**Oct.**	49F	9C
	22	– 5		51	11		41	5
Mar.	37F	3C	**July**	71F	22C	**Nov.**	40F	5C
	26	– 4		57	14		34	1
Apr.	47F	8C	**Aug.**	68F	20C	**Dec.**	35F	3C
	34	1		55	13		28	– 2

STOCKHOLM

Stockholm stands on 14 islands surrounded by water so clean that you can fish and swim in the heart of the city. This cultivated, civilized city has many parks, squares, and wide streets, providing welcome calm in what has become a bustling metropolis. Modern glass and steel buildings abound in the city center, but you are seldom more than a five-minute walk from twisting, medieval streets and water views.

The first written mention of Stockholm dates from 1252, when a powerful regent named Birger Jarl built a fortified castle here. This strategic position, where the fresh waters of Lake Mälaren meet the brackish Baltic Sea, prompted King Gustav Vasa to take over the city in 1523, and King Gustavus Adolphus to make it the heart of an empire a century later.

During the Thirty Years' War (1618–48), Sweden became an important Baltic trading state, and the city gained a reputation as a commercial center. But by the beginning of the 18th century, Swedish influence had begun to wane, and Stockholm's development slowed. It did not pick up again until the Industrial Revolution, when the hub of the city moved north from the Gamla Stan (Old Town) area.

Exploring Stockholm

Numbers in the margin correspond to points of interest on the Stockholm map.

Stockholm's main attractions are concentrated in a relatively small area, and the city itself can be explored in just a few days. If you have only limited time in Stockholm, give priority to a tour of Stockholm's Gamla Stan (Old Town), a labyrinth of narrow medieval streets, alleyways, and quiet squares on the island just south of the city center. Be sure to visit the large island of Djurgården. Although it's only a short walk from the city center, the most pleasant way to approach it is by ferry from Skeppsbron, in Gamla Stan.

11 **Gröna Lund Tivoli.** Stockholm's only amusement park is a family favorite, with traditional rides and new attractions on the waterfront each season. ⊠ *Djurgårdsv.,* ☎ *08/6707600.* ⏲ *Late Apr.–early Sept. Prices and hours are subject to change; call ahead.*

14 **Historiska Museet** (Historical Museum). The museum houses some remarkable gold and silver treasures dating from the Swedish Viking era. ⊠ *Narvav. 13–17,* ☎ *08/7839400.* ⏲ *Tues.–Sun. 11–5, Thurs. 11–8. Closed Mon.*

★ 8 **Junibacken.** This fairy-tale house lets you travel in small carriages through the world of children's book writer Astrid Lindgren, creator of the irrepressible character Pippi Longstocking. ⊠ *Galärvarsv.,* ☎ *08/6600600.* ⏲ *Daily 10–6.*

★ 3 **Kungliga Slottet** (Royal Palace). Visit at noon and watch the time-honored, yet now superfluous changing of the smartly dressed guards. You can wander at will into the palace courtyard and the building itself. The **Livrustkammaren** (Royal Armory), has an outstanding collection of weaponry and royal regalia. The **Skattkammaren** (Treasury) houses the Swedish crown jewels, including the regalia used for the coronation of King Erik XIV in 1561. You can also visit the **Representationsvånengen** (State Apartments), where the king swears in each successive government. ⊠ *Gamla Stan,* ☎ *08/6664466.* *SKr 35 daytime, SKr 40 evening, not including coupons or passes for rides.* ⏲ *Late Apr.–early Sept. Prices and hrs subject to change; call ahead.*

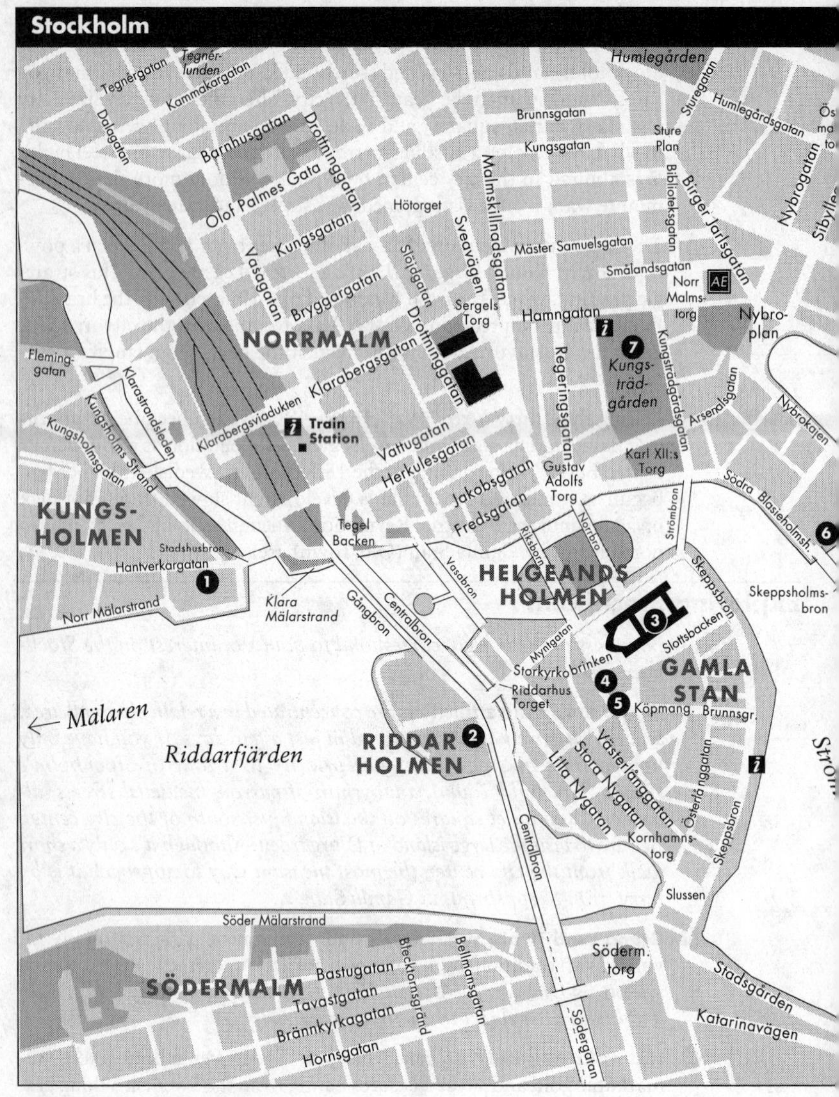

- Gröna Lund Tivoli, **11**
- Historiska Museet, **14**
- Junibacken, **8**
- Kungliga Slottet, **3**
- Kungsträdgården, **7**
- National Museet, **6**
- Nordiska Museet, **13**
- Riddarholmskyrkan, **2**
- Skansen, **12**
- Stadshuset, **1**
- Storkyrkan, **4**
- Stortorget, **5**
- Vasamuseet, **10**
- Waldemarsudde, **9**

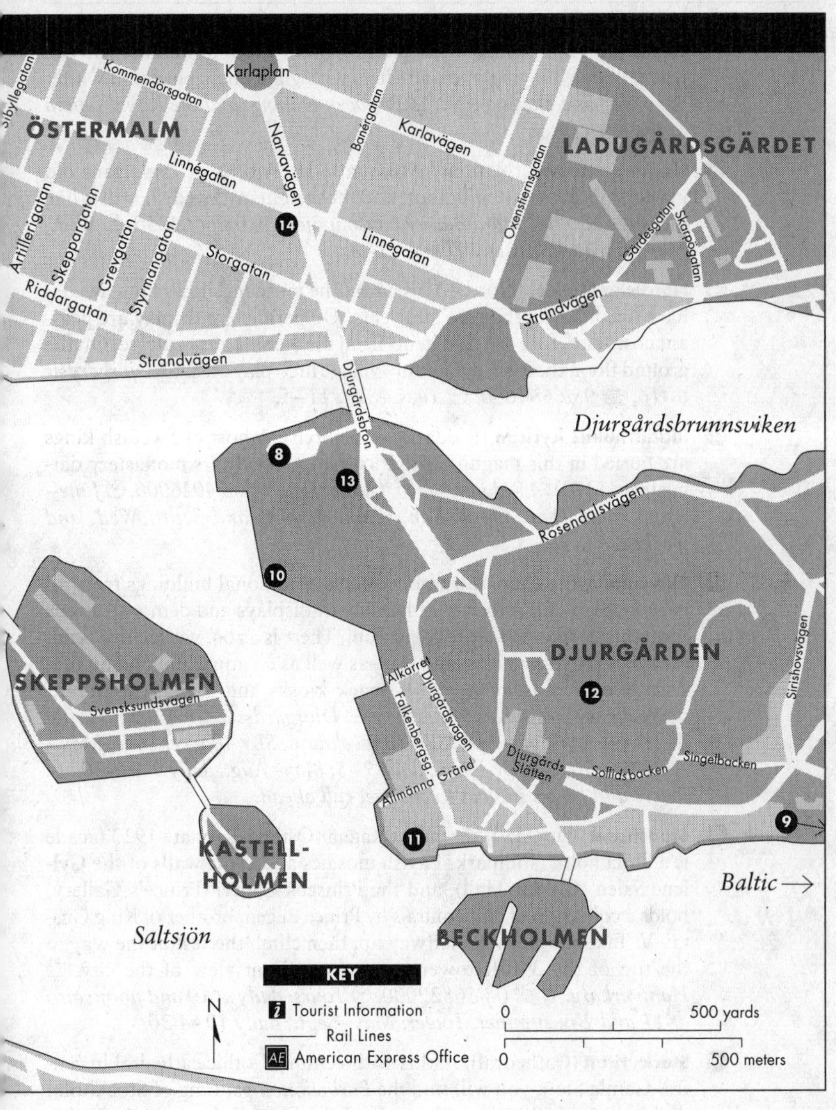
Karlaplan
Kommendörsgatan
Sibyllegatan
ÖSTERMALM
Narvavägen
Banérgatan
Karlavägen
LADUGÅRDSGÄRDET
Oxenstiernsgatan
Linnégatan
Artillerigatan
Skeppargatan
Grevgatan
Styrmangatan
Storgatan
Riddargatan
Gärdesgatan
Skarpögatan
Strandvägen
Djurgårdsbron
Djurgårdsbrunnsviken
Rosendalsvägen
SKEPPSHOLMEN
Svensksundsvägen
DJURGÅRDEN
Sirishovsvägen
Alkarret
Djurgårdsvägen
Falkenbergsg.
Djurgårds Slätten
Solidsbacken
Singelbacken
Allmänna Gränd
KASTELL-HOLMEN
Baltic
Saltsjön
BECKHOLMEN
KEY
Tourist Information
Rail Lines
American Express Office
500 yards
500 meters
8
13
10
14
12
11
9

7 **Kungsträdgården** (King's Garden). Originally built as a royal kitchen garden, this was turned into a public park in 1562. In summer you can watch people playing open-air chess with giant chess pieces. In winter the park has a skating rink. ⊠ *Between Hamng. and the Royal Opera in the city center.*

6 **National Museet** (National Museum). The works of important old masters, including Rembrandt, and those of many Swedish artists line the walls here. ⊠ *Södra Blasieholmshamnen,* ☎ *08/6664250.* ⊙ *Wed., Fri.–Sun. 11–5, Tues., Thurs. 11–8.*

13 **Nordiska Museet** (Nordic Museum). The museum shows how Swedes have lived during the past 500 years. On permanent display are peasant costumes, folk art, and items from the Sami (Lapp) culture. On the ground floor, there's a delightful "village life" play area. ⊠ *Djurgårdsv. 6–16,* ☎ *08/6664600.* ⊙ *Tues.–Sun. 11–5.*

2 **Riddarholms kyrkan** (Riddarholm Church). A host of Swedish kings are buried in this magnificent sanctuary, a Greyfriars monastery dating from 1270. ⊠ *Riddarholmen, Gamla Stan,* ☎ *08/4026000.* ⊙ *June–Aug., Mon.–Sat. 11–4, Sun. noon–4; May and Sept., Wed. and weekends noon–3.*

★ 12 **Skansen.** More than 150 reconstructed traditional buildings from all over Sweden and a variety of handicraft displays and demonstrations form this large, open-air folk museum. There is a zoo, with native Scandinavian lynxes, wolves, and elks, as well as an aquarium and an old-style *tivoli* (amusement park). Snack kiosks and a nicer restaurant make it easy to spend a whole day. ⊠ *Djurgårdsslätten 49–51,* ☎ *08/4428000.* *Sept.–Apr., SKr 30 weekdays, SKr 40 weekends; May–Aug., SKr 50.* ⊙ *Sept.–Apr., daily 9–5; May–Aug., daily 9 AM–10 PM. Prices and hours subject to change; call ahead.*

★ 1 **Stadshuset** (City Hall). Architect Ragnar Östberg's ornate 1923 facade is a Stockholm landmark. Lavish mosaics adorn the walls of the **Gyllene Salen** (Golden Hall), and the **Prinsens Galleri** (Prince's Gallery) holds a collection of large murals by Prince Eugen, brother of King Gustav V. Take the elevator halfway up, then climb the rest of the way to the top of the 348-ft tower for a magnificent view of the city. ⊠ *Hantverkarg. 1,* ☎ *08/50829000.* ⊙ *Tours: daily at 10 and noon; also at 11 and 2 in summer. Tower: May–Sept., daily 10–4:30.*

4 **Storkyrkan** (Cathedral). In this 15th-century Gothic cathedral in central Gamla Stan, you will find the *Parhelion,* a painting of Stockholm dating from 1520, the oldest in existence. ⊠ *Trångsund 1,* ☎ *08/7233000.*

5 **Stortorget.** Danish King Christian II ordered a massacre in this square in 1520 that triggered a revolt and the founding of the sovereign state of Sweden. ⊠ *Gamla Stan, just southwest of Kungliga Slottet.*

★ 10 **Vasamuseet.** The 17th-century warship *Vasa* sank ignominiously in Stockholm Harbor on its maiden voyage in 1628 because it was not carrying sufficient ballast. Forgotten for centuries, the largely intact vessel was recovered from the sea in 1961 and now stands sentinel over the harbor in this striking museum; the museum also has film presentations and displays. ⊠ *Galärvarvet,* ☎ *08/6664800.* ⊙ *Thurs.–Tues. 10–5, Wed. 10–8.*

Västerlånggatan. The main street of Gamla Stan brims with boutiques and antiques shops.

9 **Waldemarsudde.** Once the summer residence of Prince Eugen, this museum offers an important collection of Nordic paintings dating from

1880 to 1940, as well as the prince's own works. ✉ *Prins Eugens väg 6,* ☎ *08/6622800.* 🎫 *SKr 50.* ⏲ *June–Aug., Wed. and Fri.–Sun. 11–5, Tues. and Thurs. 11–8; Sept.–May, Tue.–Sun. 11–4. Prices and hrs subject to change; call ahead.*

Elsewhere in Stockholm

You can admire the world's largest display of water lilies at the **Bergianska Botaniska Trädgården** (Bergianska Botanical Garden), north of the city center. There are plants from all over the world at the Victoria House. ✉ *Frescati,* ☎ *08/162853.* 🎫 *Free to park.* ⏲ *Greenhouse daily 11–5; herbal garden daily 8–5; Victoria House May–Sept., daily 11-5; park always open.*

Just shy of 508 ft, the **Kaknästornet** (the Kaknäs TV Tower) on Gärdet is the tallest structure in Scandinavia. From its top you have a magnificent view of the city and the surrounding archipelago. Facilities include a cafeteria, restaurant, and gift shop. ✉ *Ladugårdsgärdet, Bus 69 from Sergels Torg,* ☎ *08/7892435.* ⏲ *10–9 year-round.*

Dining and Lodging

Stockholm has one of the highest densities of restaurants per capita in Europe. Lunch is generally served between 11 and 2; if you're looking for value dining, make lunch your big meal. For details and price-category information, *see* Dining *in* Sweden A to Z, *above.*

Stockholm has plenty of hotels in higher price brackets, but summer rates—some as much as 50% off—can make even very expensive hotels affordable. The major chains also offer bargain plans on weekends throughout the year and weekdays in summer. For details and price-category information, *see* Lodging *in* Sweden A to Z, *above.*

More than 50 hotels offer the "Stockholm Package," providing one night's lodging at between SKr 398 and SKr 890 per person and including breakfast and a Stockholmskortet (☞ Getting Around, *below*). The package is available June through mid-August, at Christmas and Easter, and Friday through Monday year-round; get details from Hotellcentralen (☞ Lodging *in* Sweden A to Z, *above*) and travel agencies (☞ Contacts and Resources *in* Stockholm Essentials, *below*). If you arrive in Stockholm without a hotel reservation, Hotellcentralen can arrange accommodation for you.

$$$$ ✕ **Operakällaren.** One of Stockholm's best-known traditional restaurants is found in the elegant Opera House. With both Scandinavian and Continental cuisine on its menu, it is famed for its smörgåsbord, available from June 1st, with seasonal variations, through Christmas. In summertime you can dine on the veranda. ✉ *Operahuset, Jakobs Torg 2,* ☎ *08/6765801. AE, DC, MC, V. Main dining room closed July.*

$$$$ ✕ **Ulriksdals Värdshus.** Top-notch service, a beautiful location—in a castle park on the outskirts of town—and a noteworthy Swedish and international menu highlighting a lunchtime smörgåsbord all make this worth a splurge. Built in 1868, the restaurant was once a country inn, and it hasn't lost a bit of its country hospitality. ✉ *Ulriksdals Slottspark, Solna,* ☎ *08/850815. AE, DC, MC, V. No dinner Sun.*

$$$$ ★ ✕ **Videgåard.** One of Stockholm's best restaurants offers delicious, original meat and fish dishes. The decor is subtly modern and the staff well versed with the contents of the varied menu. ✉ *Regeringsg. 111,* ☎ *08/4116153. AE, DC, MC, V.*

$$$ ★ ✕ **Clas på Hörnet.** Just outside the city center, this small, intimate establishment occupies the ground floor of a restored 200-year-old town house, now a hotel (☞ *below*). It serves international and Swedish cuisine. ✉ *Surbrunnsg. 20,* ☎ *08/165136. AE, DC, MC, V. Closed July.*

$$$ ★ ✕ **Den Gyldene Freden.** Once a favorite haunt of Stockholm's artists and composers, this restaurant, dating from 1722, has an Old Town ambience. Every Thursday, the Swedish Academy meets for lunch on the second floor. The menu offers a tasteful combination of French and Swedish cuisines. ✉ *Österlångg. 51,* ☎ *08/249760. AE, DC, MC, V. Closed Sun. and July. No lunch except Sat.*

$$$ ✕ **Il Conte.** A warm, Italian-style restaurant close to Stockholm's most elegant avenue, Strandvägen, Il Conte has delicious Italian dishes and wines served by an attentive staff. The restaurant is tastefully decorated to create an alluring, refined atmosphere. ✉ *Grevg. 9,* ☎ *08/6612628. Reservations essential. AE, DC, MC, V. Call for closing dates.*

$$$ ★ ✕ **Stallmästaregården.** This historic inn with an attractive courtyard and garden sits in Haga Park, just north of Norrtull, about 15 minutes by car or slightly longer by bus from the city center. In summer fine French and Swedish cuisine is served in the courtyard overlooking Brunnsviken lake. ✉ *Norrtull, near Haga, Bus 52 to Stallmästaregården.* ☎ *08/6101300. AE, DC, MC, V. Closed Sun.*

$$$ ✕ **Wedholms Fisk.** You can only get fresh fish and shellfish at this open, high-ceiling restaurant near Berzelli Park, across from the Royal Dramatic Theater. The tartare of salmon and the grilled sole are noteworthy, and portions are generous. The Scandinavian artwork on display is part of the owner's personal collection. ✉ *Nybrokajen 17,* ☎ *08/6117874. AE, DC, MC, V. Closed Sun. and July.*

$$ ★ ✕ **Calle P.** Palm leaves function as plates at this trendy restaurant, which has an unusual menu of exotic dishes. On the edge of a small park, it draws a younger crowd for people-watching and music. ✉ *Berzelli Park,* ☎ *08/6782120. AE, DC, MC, V. Closed Sun.*

$$ ✕ **Eriks Bakficka.** A favorite among locals, Eriks is a block from elegant Strandvägen and a few steps down from street level. The restaurant serves a wide variety of Swedish dishes; the pub section has a lower-priced menu. The same owner operates Eriks in Gamla Stan, one of Stockholm's most exclusive restaurants. ✉ *Frederikshovsg. 4,* ☎ *08/6601599. AE, DC, MC, V. Closed July.*

$$ ✕ **Gondolen.** Suspended under the gangway of the Katarina elevator at Slussen square, Gondolen has a magnificent view over the harbor, Mälaren, and the Baltic. The cuisine is international with a range of prix-fixe menus available. ✉ *Stadsgården 6,* ☎ *08/6417090. AE, DC, MC, V. Closed Sun.*

$$ ✕ **Martini.** This Italian restaurant is a great place to eat; patrons line up for a seat in summer, when the terrace is open. The main restaurant is below street level, but light colors and a bustling atmosphere make it cheerful. ✉ *Norrmalmst. 4,* ☎ *08/6798220. AE, DC, MC, V.*

$$ ✕ **Nils Emil.** Frequented by members of the Swedish royal family, this elegant but unpretentious restaurant is noted for its delicious Swedish cuisine and generous helpings. Paintings of the Stockholm archipelago decorate the walls. ✉ *Folkungag. 122, Södermalm,* ☎ *08/6407209. Reservations essential. AE, DC, MC, V. Closed July. No lunch Sat.*

$$ ✕ **Sturehof.** Opened before the turn of the century, Sturehof is one of Sweden's oldest fish restaurants. It has a refurbished (1996) bistro/pub, but the nautically inspired ambience of the main restaurant has been preserved. ✉ *Stureplan 2,* ☎ *08/6798750. AE, DC, MC, V.*

$ ✕ **Örtagården.** One floor up from Östermalms Saluhall market is this attractive, vegetarian buffet of soups, salads, hot dishes, and homemade bread plus a 5-SKr bottomless cup of coffee—in a turn-of-the-century atmosphere. ✉ *Nybrog. 31,* ☎ *08/6621728. AE, MC, V.*

$$$$ 🏨 **Amaranten.** Not far from the central train station, Amaranten is a large, modern hotel. Rooms with air-conditioning and soundproofing are available at a higher rate. ✉ *Kungsholmsg. 31, 104 20,*

☎ *08/6541060,* FAX *08/6526248. 410 rooms. Restaurant, pool. AE, DC, MC, V.*

$$$$ **Berns Hotell.** This cozy, yet subtly ultramodern hotel is in a mid-19th century building that was turned into a hotel in 1989. Its Art Deco, Italian-inspired design means no carpets, just exquisite wooden floors. ✉ *Näckströmsg. 8, 111 47,* ☎ *08/6140700,* FAX *08/6115175. 65 rooms. Restaurant. AE, DC, MC, V.*

$$$$ **Continental.** In the city center across from the train station, the Continental is a reliable hotel that's especially popular with Americans. ✉ *Klara Vattugränd 4, 101 22,* ☎ *08/244020,* FAX *08/4113695. 268 rooms. Restaurant. AE, DC, MC, V.*

$$$$ ★ **Diplomat.** This elegant hotel near the city center, Djurgården, and the open-air museum Skansen offers magnificent views over central Stockholm. The turn-of-the-century town house was used by embassies in the 1930s; in 1966 it was converted into a hotel. Try the Teahouse Restaurant and the upstairs bar. ✉ *Strandv. 7C, 104 40,* ☎ *08/6635800,* FAX *08/7836634. 133 rooms. Restaurant. AE, DC, MC, V.*

$$$$ **Grand.** The Grand is a large, Old World–style hotel dating from 1874 that stands opposite the Royal Palace on the waterfront in the center of town. Most of its rooms have waterfront views. The two restaurants—French and Swedish—offer harbor views, and the bar serves light snacks. ✉ *Blasieholmshamnen 8, 103 27,* ☎ *08/6793500,* FAX *08/6118686. 319 rooms. 2 restaurants. AE, DC, MC, V.*

$$$$ ★ **Lady Hamilton.** As charming, desirable, and airily elegant as its namesake, the Lady Hamilton opened in 1980 as a modern hotel inside a 15th-century building. Swedish antiques accent the light, natural-tone decor in all the guest rooms and common areas. The subterranean sauna rooms provide a chance to take a dip in the building's original, medieval well. ✉ *Storkyrkobrinken 5, 111 28,* ☎ *08/234680,* FAX *08/4111148. 34 rooms. AE, DC, MC, V.*

$$$$ **Radisson SAS Strand.** This gracious, Old World hotel was built in 1912 and modernized in 1983. No two rooms are the same; all are furnished with antiques. The hotel's Italian restaurant has a superb wine list. ✉ *Nybrokajen 9, 103 27,* ☎ *08/6787800,* FAX *08/6112436. 148 rooms. Restaurant. AE, DC, MC, V.*

$$$$ **Reisen.** This 17th-century building, on the waterfront in Gamla Stan, has been a hotel since 1819; it has a fine restaurant, a grill, tea and coffee service in the library, and a good piano bar. The swimming pool was installed beneath surviving medieval arches in the structure's foundations. ✉ *Skeppsbron 12–14, 111 30,* ☎ *08/223260,* FAX *08/201559. 114 rooms. 3 restaurants, pool. AE, DC, MC, V.*

$$$$ **Scandic Crown.** A modern hotel with a panoramic view of Gamla Stan and City Hall, the Scandic Crown is on Stockholm's trendy south side. Two big attractions are the Couronne d'Or French eatery and a cellar with wines for tasting, some dating from 1650. ✉ *Guldgr. 8, 104 65,* ☎ *08/7022500,* FAX *08/6428358. 264 rooms. 2 restaurants, pool. AE, DC, MC, V.*

$$$ **Birger Jarl.** Just outside the city center, this contemporary, conservative, thickly carpeted refuge is for business travelers, conferences, and tourists requiring unfussy comforts. Breakfast is an extensive buffet just off the lobby, but room service is also available. Rooms are not large, but they are well furnished; four family-style rooms have extra floor space and sofa beds. ✉ *Tuleg. 8, 104 32, Bus 46 to Stureplan,* ☎ *08/6741000,* FAX *08/6737366. 225 rooms. AE, DC, MC, V.*

$$$ ★ **Clas på Hörnet.** An 18th-century inn converted into a small hotel in 1982, Clas på Hörnet is not far from the city center. Its rooms, furnished with period antiques, go quickly. If you can't reserve a night's lodging, at least have a meal in the excellent restaurant (☞ *above*). ✉

Surbrunnsg. 20, 113 48, ☎ 08/165130, FAX 08/6125315. 10 rooms. Restaurant. AE, DC, MC, V.

$$$ **Gamla Stan.** This quiet, cozy hotel is in one of Gamla Stan's 17th-century houses. Each room is uniquely decorated. ✉ *Lilla Nyg. 25, 111 28, ☎ 08/244450, FAX 08/216483. 51 rooms. AE, DC, MC, V.*

$$$ **Lydmar Hotel.** Just opposite Hummlegården in the center of Stockholm lies this modern hotel, a 10-minute walk from the downtown hub of Sergels Torg. The lobby lounge is alive on weekends with the latest jazz sounds. ✉ *Stureg. 10, 114 36, ☎ 08/56611300, FAX 08/56611301. 61 rooms, 5 junior suites. AE, DC, MC, V.*

$$$ **Prize.** This sleek hotel has ultramodern rooms as compactly efficient as overnight train compartments. Some have no windows but are fitted with backlit shoji screens to simulate daylight. The hotel occupies part of the World Trade Centre, above one end of the Central Train Station, but a shock-absorbent base eliminates noise and vibrations from the trains below. ✉ *Kungsbron 1, 111 22, ☎ 08/56622200, FAX 08/56622444. 158 rooms. AE, DC, MC, V.*

$$$ **Sergel Plaza.** This basic, modern downtown hotel has a relaxing atmosphere, a piano bar just behind the light, spacious lobby, and an executive floor, a casino, and a body care center. The restaurant offers international haute cuisine. ✉ *Brunkebergstorg. 9, 103 27, ☎ 08/226600, FAX 08/215070. 406 rooms, 12 suites. Restaurant. AE, DC, MC, V.*

$$ **Alexandra.** Serving a business clientele in the Södermalm area, this small hotel is only five minutes by subway from the city center. The rooms are light and airy; 40 rooms were renovated in 1997. ✉ *Magnus Ladulåsg. 42, 118 27, ☎ 08/840320, FAX 08/7205353. 74 rooms. AE, DC, MC, V.*

$$ **Arcadia.** On a hilltop near a large waterfront nature preserve, this converted dormitory is still within 15 minutes of downtown by bus or subway, or 30 minutes on foot along pleasant shopping streets. Rooms are furnished in a spare, neutral style, with plenty of natural light. ✉ *Körsbärsv. 1, 114 89, Bus 43 to Körsbärsvägen, ☎ 08/160195, FAX 08/166224. 82 rooms. Restaurant. AE, DC, MC, V.*

$$ **August Strindberg.** A narrow, frescoed corridor leads from the street to the flagstone courtyard, into which the hotel's restaurant expands in summer. New parquet flooring and high ceilings distinguish the rooms, which are otherwise plainly furnished. Kitchenettes are available; some rooms can be combined into family apartments. The four floors have no elevator. ✉ *Tegnérg. 38, 113 59, ☎ 08/325006, FAX 08/209085. 19 rooms. Restaurant. AE, DC, MC, V.*

$$ **Långholmen.** Formerly a prison (built in 1724), this was converted into a combined hotel and hostel in 1989. The island on which it sits has popular beaches and a prison museum. ✉ *Långholmen, Box 9116, 102 72, ☎ 08/6680500, FAX 08/7208575. 101 rooms. 3 restaurants. AE, DC, MC, V.*

$$ ★ **Örnsköld.** Just behind the Royal Dramatic Theater in the heart of the city, this gem has the atmosphere of an old private club, with a brass-and-leather lobby and Victorian-style furniture in the moderately spacious, high-ceiling rooms. Rooms over the courtyard are quieter, but those facing the street are sunnier. ✉ *Nybrog. 6; 114 34, ☎ 08/6670285, FAX 08/6676991. 30 rooms. AE, MC, V.*

$$ **Stockholm Plaza Hotel.** On one of Stockholm's foremost streets for shopping and entertainment, the building, dating from the turn of the century is furnished in an old-style, elegant manner and has reasonably sized rooms. ✉ *Birger Jarlsg. 29, 103 95, ☎ 08/145120, FAX 08/103492. 151 rooms. AE, DC, MC, V.*

$ ***Gustav af Klint.*** A "hotel ship" moored at Stadsgården quay, near Slussen subway station, the *Gustav af Klint* is divided into a hotel and a hostel. You can dine on deck in summer. ✉ *Stadsgårdskajen 153, 116 45,* ☎ *08/6404077,* FAX *08/6406416. 8 hotel cabins; 100 hostel beds. Restaurant. AE, MC, V.*

Nightlife and the Arts

The Arts

Stockholm's theater and concert season runs from September through May, so you won't find many big-name artists in summer except during the Stockholm Water Festival in August. For a list of events, pick up the free booklet *Stockholm This Week,* available from hotels and tourist information offices. For tickets to theaters and shows try **Biljettdirekt** at Sweden House (☞ Visitor Information *in* Stockholm Essentials, *below*) or any **post office.**

CONCERTS

The city's main concert hall is **Konserthuset** (✉ Hötorget 8, ☎ 08/102110), home of the Stockholm Philharmonic Orchestra. Also look in the local press for events at **Berwaldhallen** (✉ Strandv. 69, ☎ 08/7845000). In summer many city parks have free concerts; listings appear in the "Events" section of *Stockholm This Week.*

FILM

English and American films predominate, screened with the original soundtrack and Swedish subtitles. Programs are listed in the local evening newspapers, although movie titles are usually given in Swedish. **Filmstaden Sergel** (✉ Hötorget, ☎ 08/7896060) has 18 cinemas under one roof. Most cinemas take reservations over the phone, and the latest releases may well be sold out. The city's annual **Stockholms Filmfestival** is held in early November, screening new and classic films from all over the world.

OPERA

Operan (the Royal Opera House; ✉ Jakobs Torg 2, ☎ 08/248240) lies just across the water from Slottet. The season runs from mid-August to early June and offers world-class performances. The exquisite **Drottningholms Slottsteater** (Drottningholm Court Theater, ✉ Drottningholm, ☎ 08/6608225) offers opera, ballet, and orchestral music from May to early September; the original 18th-century stage machinery is still used in these productions. Drottningholm, the royal residence, is reached by subway and bus or by special theater-bus (which leaves from the Grand Hotel or opposite the Central Train Station). Boat tours run here in summer (☞ Contacts and Resources *in* Stockholm Essentials, *below*).

THEATER

Stockholm has some 20 theaters. **Kungliga Dramatiska Teatern** (Dramaten: the Royal Dramatic Theater, ✉ Nybroplan, ☎ 08/6670680), with great gilded statues at Nybroplan, stages international productions in Swedish. **Vasa Teatern** (✉ Vasag. 19–21, ☎ 08/102363) offers whimsical Swedish comedies. Musicals are presented regularly at several city theaters. Productions by the **English Theatre Company** are occasionally staged at various venues in Stockholm; check the local press for details.

Nightlife

CABARET

Stockholm's biggest nightclub, **Börsen** (✉ Jakobsg. 6, ☎ 08/7878500), has high-quality Swedish and international cabaret. **Wallmans Salonger** (✉ Teaterg. 3, ☎ 08/6116622) offers an unforgettable cabaret experience; reservations are essential.

BARS AND NIGHTCLUBS

Café Opera (✉ Operahuset, Gustav Adolfs Torg, ☎ 08/4110026) is a favorite meeting place of the suit and tie set; at the waterfront end of Kungsträgården, it has the longest bar in town, plus dining, roulette, and dancing after midnight. Royalty and other dignitaries mingle at **Riche** (✉ Birger Jarlsg. 4, ☎ 08/6117022); the grand bar's pedigree stretches back to 1893. **Birger Bar** (✉ Birger Jarlsg. 5, ☎ 08/6797210) is a bar, eatery (Italian), and night club. The **Clipper Club** at the Hotel Reisen (✉ Skeppsbron 12–14, ☎ 08/223260) is a hot spot. Not to be forgotten is the renovated restaurant/bar **Berns' Salonger** (✉ Berzelli Park 9, ☎ 08/6140550); the Red Room, on the second floor, is where playwright August Strindberg once held court. **Sture Compagniet** (✉ Stureg. 4, ☎ 08/6117800) is good for drinking and dancing. **Mushrooms** (✉ Berzelli Park) is the bar for trendy night owls.

Pubs now abound in Stockholm. Watch for happy hour when drinks are cheap. **Limerick** (✉ Tegnérg. 10, ☎ 08/6734398) is a favorite Hibernian spot. Irish beer enthusiasts rally at **Dubliner** (✉ Smålandsg. 8, ☎ 08/6797707). **The Tudor Arms** (✉ Grevg. 31, ☎ 08/6602712) is just as popular as when it opened in the '70s.

DANCING

Penny Lane (✉ Birger Jarlsg. 29, ☎ 08/201411) pulls in all ages with music from the '70s. **Karlson & Co** (✉ Kungsg. 56, ☎ 08/203339) is a pub, restaurant, and nightclub. **Bäckahästen** (✉ Kungsg. 56, ☎ 08/4115180) is lively on weekends.

JAZZ CLUBS

Fasching (✉ Kungsg. 63, ☎ 08/216267) is Stockholm's largest, with a varied jazz and soul offering. **Stampen** (✉ Stora Nyg. 5, ☎ 08/205793) runs out of seats early; reservations are useful.

Shopping

Department Stores

NK (✉ Hamng. 18–20, ☎ 08/7628000) is a high-class galleria. **PUB** (✉ Hötorget, ☎ 08/239915) has 42 boutiques. **Åhléns City** (✉ Klarabergsg. 50, ☎ 08/246000) is a traditional department store.

Food and Flea Markets

One of the largest flea markets in northern Europe, the **Loppmarknaden,** is held in the parking garage of the Skärholmen shopping center, a 20-minute subway ride from downtown. (SKr 10 on weekends; weekdays 11–6, Saturday 9–3, and Sunday 10–3). Beware of pickpockets. For a real Swedish food market with such specialties as marinated salmon and reindeer try **Östermalms Saluhall** (✉ at Hötorget; Mon. 10–6, Tues. 9–6, and Sat. 9–3; from late June through Aug., the Sat. market is open 9–2). Another good bet is **Hötorgshallen** (✉ at Hötorget; ⏲ Aug.–Apr., Mon.–Thur. 10–6, Fri. 10–6:30, and Sat. 10–4, and May–July, weekdays 10–6 and Sat. 10–1), under Filmstaden Sergel (☞ Film *in* Nightlife and the Arts, *above*).

Gift Ideas

Stockholm shops have the best in Swedish design and elegance. The choice and price of Swedish and international brand name items, particularly glass, porcelain, furs, jewelry, and leather goods, makes a day's shopping a must (☞ Shopping *in* Sweden A to Z, *above*).

Glassware

For the best buys try **Nordiska Kristall** (✉ Kungsg. 9, ☎ 08/104372). **Gustavsbergs Fabriksbod** (✉ Odelbergs Väg 13, Gustavsberg, ☎ 08/

57035655) just outside the city is a factory shop of quality. **Duka** (✉ Sveav. 24/26, ☎ 08/104530) specializes in crystal as well as porcelain.

Handicrafts

A good center for all kinds of Swedish wood and metal handicrafts is **Svensk Hemslöjd** (✉ Sveav. 44, ☎ 08/232115). For elegant home furnishings and timeless fabrics, try **Svenskt Tenn** (✉ Strandv. 5A, ☎ 08/6701600), best known for its selection of designer Josef Franck's furniture and fabrics. **Svenskt Hantwerk** (✉ Kungsg. 55, ☎ 08/214726) has Swedish folk costumes and handicraft souvenirs from different parts of Sweden.

Shopping Districts

Shop till you drop means hitting the stores along **Hamngatan** with a vengeance. The **Gamla Stan** area is best for antiques shops, bookshops, and art galleries. **Sturegallerian** (✉ Stureg.) is an elegant covered shopping gallery on the site of the former public baths at Stureplan.

Side Trips

★ Skärgården

You could sail forever among the 24,000 islands of Stockholm's Skärgården (archipelago). But if you don't have a boat, then purchase the Båtluffarkortet (Inter-Skerries Card, 🎫 SKr 250) from early June to mid-August, which gives you 16 days' unlimited travel on Waxholmsbolaget (Waxholm Steamship Company) boats. Get the card at Excursion Shop at Sweden House or at the Waxholm Steamship Company terminal (☞ Stockholm Essentials, *below*).

Fjäderholmarna

The group of four islands known as Fjäderholmarna (the Feather Islets) lies only 20 minutes by boat from the city center. They were formerly a restricted military zone but are now a haven of restaurants, cafés, a museum depicting life in the archipelago, an aquarium with many species of Baltic marine life, handicraft studios, shops, and a pirate-ship playground. Boats leave from Slussen, Strömkajen, and Nybroplan (Apr. 29–Sept. 17); contact the **Strömma Canal Company** (☎ 08/4117023) or Fjäderholmarna information (☎ 08/7180100).

Mariefred

In Mariefred, on the southern side of Lake Mälaren about 64 km (40 ★ mi) from Stockholm, **Gripsholm Slott** (Gripsholm Castle), with its drawbridge and four massive round towers, is one of Sweden's most romantic castles. Following the destruction of a castle from the 1380s, King Gustav Vasa built the present structure in 1577. It now houses the state portrait collection, some 3,400 paintings. ☎ *0159/10194.* ⏲ *Apr.–Sept., Tues.–Sun. 10–3; Oct.–Mar., weekends noon–3.*

An unforgettable boat journey on the recently restored vintage steamer ***Mariefred,*** the last coal-fired ship on Lake Mälaren, is the best way to get to Gripsholm, but you can also take the train. ✉ *Boat departs quay next to City Hall,* ☎ *08/6698850.* 🎫 *SKr 160 round-trip.* ⏲ *Mid-June–late Aug., Tues.–Sun. 10 AM (returns 4:30).*

Skokloster

Built by the Swedish field marshal Carl Gustav Wrangel, **Skokloster Slott** (Skokloster Palace) contains many of his trophies from the Thirty Years' War. The palace, about 70 km (44 mi) from Stockholm in Skokloster, also displays one of the largest private collections of arms in the world, as well as some magnificent Gobelin tapestries. Next door to the palace is a **motor museum** housing Sweden's largest collection of

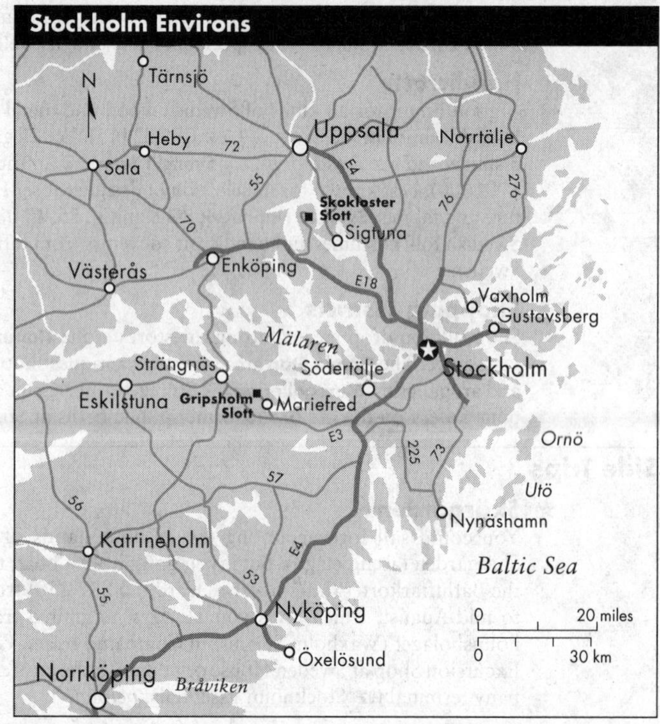

vintage cars and motorcycles. ☎ *018/386077.* ⏲ *May–Aug. 11–4 daily, Sept. and Oct. weekdays 1–2, Sat. and Sun. 1–4.*

Skokloster is easily reached by boat. The route follows the narrow inlets of Lake Mälaren along the "Royal Waterway." It stops at **Sigtuna,** an ancient trading center. You can get off the boat here to visit the town, which has medieval ruins and an 18th-century town hall. For boat information contact the **Strömma Canal Company.** ✉ *Boats depart from Stadshusbron (City Hall Bridge,* ☎ *08/4117023).* 🎫 *SKr 165 round-trip.* ⏲ *Early June–mid.-Aug. Tues.–Thurs. and weekends.*

Stockholm Essentials

Arriving and Departing

BY BUS

All major bus lines arrive at the **Cityterminalen** (✉ Next to the train station). Bus tickets are also sold at the railroad reservations office.

BY CAR

One of the two main access routes from the west and south is the **E20** main highway from Göteborg The other is the **E4** from Helsingborg, continuing as the main route to Sundsvall, the far north, and Finland. All routes to the CENTRUM (city center) are well marked.

BY PLANE

International flights arrive at **Arlanda Airport** (✉ 40 km/25 mi north of the city). For information on arrival and departure times, call the individual airlines.

Between the Airport and Downtown. The airport is linked to Stockholm by a major highway. Buses depart for **Cityterminalen** from the international and domestic terminals every 10–15 minutes between 6:30 AM and 11 PM. The ride costs SKr 60 per person. A bus-taxi package is available from the bus driver at prices ranging from SKr 160 per person to SKr 220; additional passengers in a group pay only the bus portion of the fare. Ask the bus driver for details. For bus information call the **Stockholm Transit Authority** (SL; ☏ 08/6001000). A **taxi** directly from the airport will cost around SKr 345 (be sure to ask the driver if he offers a "fixed-price" airport-to-city rate before you get into the taxi). Look for Taxi Stockholm and Taxi Kurir cabs and ask the cab line attendant for help. Illegal taxis abound. The **SAS limousine service** operates a shared taxi service at SKr 263 per person to any point in greater Stockholm. Limousine rental is SKr 616. The moms (VAT; ☞ Sales Tax Refunds *in* Sweden A to Z, *above*) will be deducted if the limousine is booked ahead of time through a travel agent in connection with an international arrival.

BY TRAIN

Both long distance and commuter trains arrive at Stockholm Central Station on Vasagatan, a main boulevard in the heart of the city. For train information and ticket reservations 6 AM–11 PM, call 020/757575 (recorded message, wait for assistance). There is a ticket and information office at the station where you can make reservations. Automatic ticket-vending machines are also available.

Getting Around

Maps and timetables for all city transportation networks are available from the **Stockholm Transit Authority** (SL) information desks (✉ Sergels Torg; Stockholm Central Station; Slussen in Gamla Stan; information ☏ 08/6001000).

Stockholmskortet (the Stockholm card) grants unlimited transportation on city subway, bus, and rail services, and free admission to 70 museums and several sightseeing trips. The card costs SKr 199 for 24 hours, SKr 398 for two days, and SKr 498 for three days. It is available at the tourist information centers at Sweden House, Kaknästornet (TV tower; ☞ Visitor Information, *below*), and at Hotellcentralen at the central train station (☞ Lodging *in* Sweden A to Z, *above*).

BY BOAT

Waxholmsbolaget (Waxholm Steamship Company) terminal (✉ Strömkajen, in front of Grand Hotel, ☏ 08/6795830). **Strömma Kanal Bolaget** (Strömma Canal Company; ✉ boats depart from Stadshusbron/City Hall Bridge, ☏ 08/4117023).

BY BUS AND SUBWAY

The SL operates both the bus and subway systems. Tickets for the two networks are interchangeable. The subway system, known as T-banan (*T* stands for tunnel), is the easiest and fastest way to get around. Station entrances are marked with a blue T on a white background. Trains run frequently between 5 AM and 2 AM. The comprehensive bus network serves out-of-town points of interest, such as Waxholm, with its historic fortress, and Gustavsberg, with its porcelain factory. In greater Stockholm there are a number of night-bus services.

Bus and subway fares are based on zones, starting at SKr 14, good for travel within one zone, such as downtown, for one hour. You pay more if you travel in more than one zone. Single tickets are available at station ticket counters, but it is cheaper to buy the **SL Tourist Card,** which is valid on buses and the subway and also gives free admission to a number of sights and museums (though not as many as the Stockholmskortet). It can be purchased at Pressbyrån newsstands and SL information desks and costs SKr 60 for 24 hours or SKr 120 for 72 hours. Also available from the Pressbyrån newsstands are SKr 95 coupons, good for at least 10 bus or subway rides in the central zone.

BY TAXI

Typically, a trip of 10 km (6 mi) will cost SKr 97 between 9 AM and 4 PM on weekdays, SKr 107 on weekday nights, and SKr 114 on weekends. Call **Taxi Stockholm** (☎ 08/150000), **Taxikurir** (☎ 08/300000), or **Taxi 020** (☎ 020/939393).

BY TRAIN

SL runs commuter trains from Stockholm Central Station to a number of nearby locales, including Nynäshamn, a departure point for ferries to the island of Gotland. Trains also run from the Slussen station to the fashionable seaside resort of Saltsjöbaden.

Contacts and Resources

EMBASSIES

Unietd States (✉ Strandv. 101, ☎ 08/7835300). **Canadian** (✉ Tegelbacken 4, ☎ 08/4533000). **United Kingdom** (✉ Skarpög. 6–8, ☎ 08/6719000). **Australian** (✉ Sergelstorg 12, ☎ 08/61323900).

EMERGENCIES

Police (☎ 08/4010000; 112, emergencies only). **Ambulance** (☎ 112). **Doctor** (Medical Care Information, ☎ 08/6449200). **Private clinic** (✉ City Akuten, ☎ 08/4122960). **Dentist** (8 AM–9 PM, ☎ 08/6541117, 9 PM–8 AM, ☎ 08/6449200). **24-hour Pharmacy** (C. W. Scheele, ☎ 08/4548130).

ENGLISH-LANGUAGE BOOKSTORES

Akademibokhandeln (✉ Mäster Samuelsg. 32, ☎ 08/6136100).

GUIDED TOURS

Boat. Take a trip through the **archipelago** with one of Waxholm Steamship Company and Strömma Kanal Bolaget's (Strömma Canal Company's) ships (☞ Getting Around, *above*). Trips range from one to three hours each way. One-day excursions include Waxholm, Utö, Sandhamn, and Möja. Conventional sightseeing tours include a one-hour **city tour** run by Strömma Kanal Bolaget and leaving from the Nybroplan quay every hour on the half hour between 10:30 and 5:30 in summer. Don't miss the boat trip to the 17th-century palace of **Drottningholm.** Trips depart every hour on the hour from 10 to 4 and at 6 PM during the summer from City Hall Bridge (Stadshusbron). Other trips go from Stadshusbron to the ancient towns of **Sigtuna and Vaxholm.** By changing boats you can continue to Uppsala to catch the train back to Stockholm. Information is available from the Strömma Canal Company (☞ Getting Around, *above*) or the Stockholm Tourist Centre at Sweden House (☞ Visitor Information, *below*).

Orientation. More than 35 different tours—by foot, boat, bus, or a combination of these—are available throughout the summer. Some take only 30 minutes, others an entire day. A 90-minute coach tour, costing SKr 120, runs daily. Tickets are available from the Excursion Shop at Sweden House (☞ Visitor Information, *below*).

Personal Guides. Guide Centralen (✉ Sweden House, Hamng. 27, Box 7542, 103 93, ☎ 08/7892496) at the Stockholm Information Service offers individual guides and group bookings.

Special-Interest. Special-interest tours in the Stockholm area include spending a weekend at a cabin in the archipelago, renting a small fishing or sailing boat, visiting the Gustavsberg porcelain factory, and more. Call the Tourist Centre at Sweden House (☞ Visitor Information, *below*) for details.

TRAVEL AGENCY

American Express (✉ Birger Jarlsg. 1, ☎ 08/6795200, FAX 08/6116214).

VISITOR INFORMATION

Stockholm Tourist Centre (✉ Sweden House, Kungsträdgården, Hamng. 27, ☏ 08/7892490). **Stockholm Information Service** (✉ Sweden House, Excursion Shop, Box 7542, 103 93, ☏ 08/7892415). **Stockholm Central Station** (✉ Vasag., ☏ 020757575). **City Hall** (summer only) (✉ Hantverkarg. 1, ☏ 08/50829000). **Kaknästornet** (TV Tower; ✉ Ladugårdsgärdet, ☏ 08/7892435). **Fjäderholmarna** (☏ 08/7180100).

UPPSALA AND THE FOLKLORE DISTRICT

The "Folklore District" is essentially the provinces of Dalarna and Värmland. With its rural ambience, it's the best place to discover some of the country's most interesting traditions. Dalarna, which has its own special style of handicrafts, can be reached via the ancient city of Uppsala. Return to Stockholm through the Bergslagen region, the heart of the centuries-old Swedish iron industry.

★ Uppsala

Uppsala is well worth exploring. **Gamla (Old) Uppsala** is dominated by three huge burial mounds dating from the 5th century. The first Swedish kings, Aun, Egil, and Adils, were all buried here. The church next to the burial mounds was the seat of Sweden's first archbishop, built on the site of a former pagan temple. At the adjacent Odinsborg restaurant you can sample local mead brewed from a 14th-century recipe. Check all prices and times listed below with the local tourist office, as they are subject to change.

The impressive **Domkyrka** (cathedral), with its twin towers that dominate the skyline, has been the seat of the archbishop of the Swedish church for 700 years. Its present appearance owes much to major restoration work completed during the late 19th century. At the **Cathedral Museum** (⏲ May–Aug., daily 9–4:30; Sept.–Apr., Sun. 12:30–3) in the north tower, you can see one of Europe's finest collections of ecclesiastical textiles. ✉ *Domkyrkoplan,* ☏ *018/187166. Cathedral:* ⏲ *Daily 8–6.*

Strategically positioned atop a hill, the impressive **Uppsala Slott** (Uppsala Castle) was built during the 1540s by King Gustav Vasa. Having broken his ties with the Vatican, the king was eager to show who was actually running the country; he even arranged to have the cannons aimed directly at the archbishop's palace. ✉ *Borggården,* ☏ *018/544810.* ⏲ *Mid-Apr.–mid-June, daily 11–3; mid-June–mid-Aug., daily 10–5.*

Uppsala Universitetet (Uppsala University) is Scandinavia's oldest, founded in 1477. Beneath the cupola of the university's venerable **Gustavianum**, near the cathedral, is the anatomical theater, where public dissections of executed convicts were a popular 17th-century tourist attraction. ✉ *Akademig. 3,* ☏ *018/4710000.* ⏲ *Mid-May–mid-Sept., 11–4 daily.*

One of the most famous people to emerge from Uppsala was Carl von Linné, known as Linnaeus. A professor of botany during the 1740s, he developed the system of plant and animal classification still used today. Visit the **gardens** he designed, as well as his former residence, Linni Trädgården, now a museum. ✉ *Svartbäcksg. 27. Garden* ☏ *018/109490;* ⏲ *May–Aug., daily 9–9; Sept., daily 9–7. Museum* ☏ *018/136540;* ⏲ *June–Aug., Tues.–Sun. noon–4; May and Sept., weekends noon–4.*

$$$ ★ ✕ **Domtrappkällaren.** One of the city's most popular restaurants, Domtrappkällaren is in a 14th-century cellar near the cathedral. The menu includes both French and Swedish fare. ✉ *St. Eriksgr. 15,* ☏ *018/*

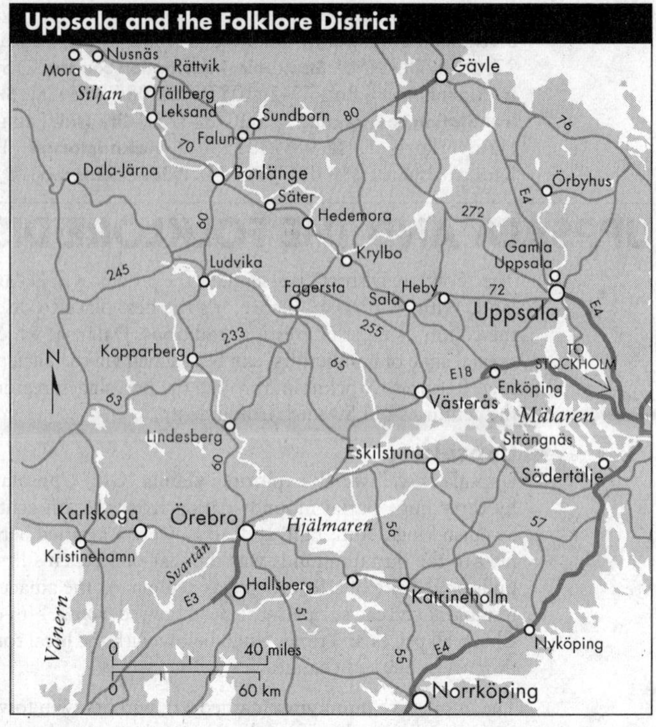

130955, FAX 018/101740. Reservations essential. AE, DC, MC, V.

$$$$ **Gillet.** Operated by the Sweden Hotels group, Uppsala's largest hotel was was opened in 1971 and renovated most recently in 1996. Its lobby is decorated with marble. ✉ *Dragarbrunnsg. 23, 751 42,* ☎ *018/155360,* FAX *018/153380. 160 rooms. 2 restaurants, pool. AE, DC, MC, V.*

$$ **Grand Hotel Hörnan.** An Old World hotel opened in 1906, the Grand Hotel Hörnan is in the city center near the train station, with a view of the castle and the cathedral. ✉ *Bangårdsg. 1, 753 20,* ☎ *018/139380,* FAX *018/120311. 37 rooms. AE, DC, MC, V. Closed July.*

Säter

Säter, one of the best-preserved wooden villages in Sweden, sits northwest of Uppsala on the way to Dalarna in farming country.

Falun

Probably the best place to stay in Dalarna is Falun, the province's capital. Here you can visit the **Falu Koppargruva** (Great Pit), a hole created in 1687, when an abandoned copper mine collapsed. There are actually still working mines in the area and guided tours (requiring good shoes) into some of the old shafts. ✉ *Ask at tourist board on Stora Torget (main square) for directions.* ⏲ *May–Aug., daily 10–4:30; Sept.–mid-Nov. and Mar.–Apr., weekends 12:30–4:30.*

The **Storamuseum** tells the story of the local mining industry. ☎ *023/15825 or 023/711475 .* ⏲ *May–Aug., daily 10–4:30, Sept.–Apr., daily 12:30–4:30.*

$$$ **Bergmästaren.** In the town center, this cozy hotel built in traditional Dalarna style, is filled with antique furnishings. ✉ *Bergskolegr. 7, 791 26,* ☎ *023/63600,* FAX *023/22524. 88 rooms. Restaurant. AE, DC, MC, V.*

$$ 🏨 **Hotel Falun.** This intimate-feeling hotel built in the 1950s is in the center of town. The front desk closes at 9 PM. ✉ *Centrumhuset, Trotzg. 16, 791 71,* ☎ *023/29180,* FAX *023/13006. 25 rooms, 16 with shower. AE, DC, MC, V.*

★ Sundborn

Just outside Falun, at Sundborn, is the former home of Swedish artist Carl Larsson, **Carl Larsson Gården.** Here, in an idyllic lakeside setting, you can see a selection of his paintings, which owe much to local folk-art traditions. His great-grandchildren still use the house on occasion. ✉ *Carl Larssonsv. 12,* ☎ *023/60053 in summer, 023/60069 in winter.* ⏲ *May–Sept., daily 10–5; Oct.–Apr., Tues. at 11; tours only, in groups of 15 every 10 minutes (may be a wait in summer).*

Tällberg

The real center of Dalarna folklore is the area around Lake Siljan, by far the largest of the 6,000 lakes in the province. The attractive lakeside village of Tällberg is a good starting point.

$$ ★ 🏨 **Åkerblads.** Near the shores of Lake Siljan, the hotel offers a genuine experience of rural Sweden. In a typical Dalarna farmstead, parts of which date from the 16th century, it is run by the 19th generation of the Åkerblad family and has been a hotel since 1910. ✉ *Sjögatu, 793 70,* ☎ *0247/50800,* FAX *0247/50652. 58 rooms with bath, 6 rooms with shared WC/shower. Restaurant. AE, DC, MC, V.*

Mora

Mora is the home of the artist Anders Zorn (1860–1920), famous for his distinctive and tasteful paintings of robust, naked women in rural surroundings. His house and **Zorn Museet** (the Zorn Museum), exhibiting his paintings, are open to the public. ✉ *Vasag. 36,* ☎ *0250/16560.* ⏲ *House, guided tours only; call for information and times. Museum, May 15–Sept. 15, Mon.–Sat. 9–5, Sun. 11–5; Sept. 16–May 14, Mon.–Sat. noon–5, Sun. 1–5.*

$$ ★ 🏨 **Siljan.** Named for the nearby lake, the Siljan is a small but up-to-date hotel. ✉ *Morag. 6, 792 01,* ☎ *0250/13000,* FAX *0250/13098. 43 rooms with shower, 2 with WC only. Restaurant. AE, DC, MC, V.*

Rättvik

At midsummer in Rättvik, hundreds of people wearing traditional costumes arrive in longboats to attend midsummer church services—a time-honored tradition. Twelve-man longboat races are held in summer. The *Gustav Vasa* vintage steamboat has trips with nightly dancing and prawn dinners.

★ Nusnäs

Nusnäs is the home of the brightly colored Dalarna wooden horses, known as *Dalahästar.* Handmade, red or blue painted with traditional floral patterns, the only real Dala horses are made here. One of the biggest workshops is Nils Olsson (✉ Edåkersv. 17, ☎ 0250/37200).

Ludvika

This important center of the old Bergslagen mining region stretches from the forests of Värmland in the west to the coastal gorges in the east. Ludvika has a notable open-air mining museum, the **Gammelgården.** ✉ *Nilsnilsg. 7,* ☎ *0240/10019.* ⏲ *June 1–Sept. 3, daily 11–6.*

The **Lokmuseet** (Railway Engine Museum) showcases three steam turbine–driven engines once used to pull trains filled with iron ore, the only ones of their kind in the world. ✉ *Signposted,* ☎ *0240/20493.* ⏲ *June 1–Sept. 3, daily 10–6.*

The poet Dan Andersson lived in **Luosastugan** (Luosa Cottage) in the early part of the century. Music and poetry festivals are held in Andersson's memory in nearby towns. ✉ *Signposted,* ☏ *0240/86050 (tourist office).* ⏲ *mid-May–Aug., daily 11–5.*

$$$ **Grand.** A modern-style hotel, the Grand enjoys a central location. ✉ *Eriksg. 6, 771 31,* ☏ *0240/18220,* FAX *0240/611018. 102 rooms. Restaurant. AE, DC, MC, V.*

$ **Rex.** The Rex is a basic, modern hotel near the city center. It was built in 1960. ✉ *Engelbrektsg. 9, 771 30,* ☏ *0240/13690. 28 rooms, 15 with shower. AE, DC, MC, V. Closed 1 wk in July.*

Örebro

Örebro nestles on the western edge of Lake Hjälmaren. It received its charter during the 13th century, becoming an important trading center for the farmers and miners of the Bergslagen region. Rising from a small island in the Svartån (Black River), right in the center of town, is the imposing **Örebro slott** (Örebro castle), parts of which date from the 13th century. The castle is now the residence of the regional governor and has an excellent restaurant, Slottskrogen. ✉ *Kanslig.,* ☏ *019/212121 (Örebro Tourist Information).* ⏲ *Call ahead.*

In the **Wadköping** district, just east of the castle, a number of old houses and crafts workshops have been painstakingly preserved. At the north end of town is **Svampen** (the Mushroom), a 193-ft-tall water tower. From the top (reached by elevator), you can enjoy a magnificent view of the surrounding countryside. ⏲ *Apr. 30–Sept. 4, daily 10–8.*

$$ ✕ **Cajsa Warg.** This excellent restaurant is named after the Swedish woman who reportedly wrote one of the earliest Swedish cookbooks about 250 years ago. Some of her recipes can be sampled here. ✉ *Kanslig.,* ☏ *019/168020. AE, DC, MC, V.*

$$$ **Scandic Grand.** In the heart of town, the Grand is Örebro's largest hotel. Built in 1985, it offers all the modern comforts. ✉ *Fabriksg. 23, 70008,* ☏ *019/150200,* FAX *019/185814. 219 rooms. 2 restaurants. AE, DC, MC, V.*

$$$ **Stora Hotellet.** Across the street from the castle on the Svartån, this Best Western hotel is one of the oldest in Sweden, dating from 1858. It has a cozy 13th-century cellar restaurant, the Slottskällaren, and an English pub, the Bishop's Arms. ✉ *Drottningg. 1, 701 45,* ☏ *019/124360,* FAX *019/6117890. 103 rooms. Restaurant. AE, DC, MC, V.*

Uppsala and the Folklore District Essentials

Getting Around

The train from Stockholm to Uppsala takes only 50 minutes, and service is fairly frequent. For information about bus travel, call Dalatrafik (☏ 020/232425). A car will give you the flexibility to explore some of the attractions not so easily accessible by public transportation; the drive to Uppsala, via the E4, is about 71 km (44 mi).

Guided Tours

Uppsala is compact enough to explore on foot, and guided sightseeing tours are available; call the Guide Service (Uppsala Tourist Information office, ☏ 018/274800). For guided tours of the district, contact the Falun tourist office (☞ *below*), which has both package tours and personalized services.

Visitor Information

Falun (✉ Stora Torget, ☏ 023/83637). **Ludvika** (✉ Fredsg. 10, ☏ 0240/86050). **Mora** (✉ Ångbåtskajen, ☏ 0250/26550). **Örebro** (✉ Slottet,

☎ 019/212121). **Rättvik** (✉ Torget, ☎ 0248/70200). **Uppsala** (✉ Fyris Torg 8, ☎ 018/274800).

THE WEST COAST AND THE GLASS COUNTRY

A shipping city on the North Sea, Göteborg (Gothenburg) is an important port to Sweden. Nearby is Sweden's scenic western coast. Inland lies the Glass Country and the medieval fortress town of Kalmar, on the east coast.

Göteborg

This attractive harbor city is Sweden's second largest, well worth a stop. A quayside jungle of cranes and warehouses attests to the city's industrial life, yet within a 10-minute walk of the waterfront is an elegant, modern city of broad avenues, green parks, and gardens. As in Stockholm, the major attractions are gathered in an accessible central area. There is an excellent streetcar network and in summer, sightseeing tours on a vintage open-air streetcar.

Once known as "Little London" because British merchants invested heavily in developing Göteborg during the 19th century, it could have more accurately been called "Little Amsterdam," for the city was in fact laid out during the 17th century by Dutch architects, who gave it its extensive network of straight streets divided by canals. Only one major canal survives, which can be explored by sightseeing boat. Gothenburgians fondly refer to these short and squat (so that they can pass under the city's 20 low bridges) boats as *paddan* (toads). Passengers embark for the one-hour boat tour at the **Paddan terminal.** ✉ *Kungsportsplatsen.* ⏲ *Departures: late Apr.–late June and mid-Aug.–early Sept., daily 10–5; late June–mid-Aug., daily 10–9; early Sept.–Oct. 1, daily noon–3; closed Oct.–late Apr.*

★ Running through the heart of Göteborg is **Kungsportsavenyn,** commonly called Avenyn (the Avenue). This broad, tree-lined boulevard is lined with many brand-name stores, boutiques, and eateries making for a very Continental atmosphere, especially in summer. Avenyn ends at **Götaplatsen,** where there is a **grand theater,** a **concert hall,** an **art museum,** and a **library** that has a wide selection of English-language newspapers. Just a stone's throw away from Götaplatsen is the **Liseberg amusement park** (✉ Öregrytev. 5).

Trädgårdsföreningen (The Garden Association) maintains an attractive park with a magnificent Palm House, built in 1878 and recently restored, and a butterfly house containing 40 different species. ✉ *Just off Kungsportsavenyn. Park* ⏲ *daily 7–8. Palm House* ⏲ *daily 10–4. Butterfly House:* ☎ *031/611911.* ⏲ *Oct.–Mar., Tues.–Sun. 10–3; Apr., Tues.–Sun. 10–4; May and Sept., daily 10–4; June–Aug., daily 10–5.*

For shopping, try **Nordstan** (✉ entrances on Köpmansg., Nils Ericsonsg., Kanaltorgsg., and Östra Hamng.), a covered complex of shops near the train station.

The **Maritima Centrum** (Maritime Centre), at the harbor near the Nordstan shopping complex, provides a chance to explore a number of historic vessels, among them a destroyer, a lightship, a trawler, and several tugboats. ✉ *Packhuskajen 8,* ☎ *031/105950.* ⏲ *Mar.–Apr. and Sept.–Nov., daily 10–4; May–June, daily 10–6; July, daily 10–9; Aug., daily 10–6.*

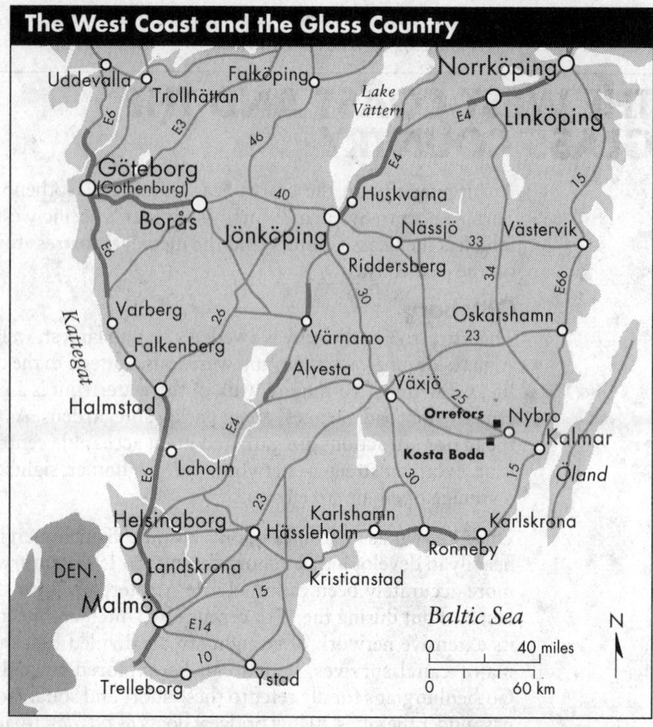

$$$$ ★ ✕ **Sjömagasinet.** In a renovated 200-year-old shipping warehouse, this waterfront restaurant has a view of the harbor and the suspension bridge; in summer an outdoor terrace provides even better views. The regular menu features seafood. ✉ *Klippanskulturreservat,* ☎ *031/246510,* FAX *031/245539. Reservations essential. AE, DC, MC, V.*

$$$ ★ ✕ **Räkan.** The informal Räkan makes the most of an unusual gimmick. The tables are arranged around a long tank, and if you order shrimp, the house specialty, they arrive at your table in radio-controlled boats you navigate yourself. ✉ *Lorensbergsg. 16,* ☎ *031/169839,* FAX *031/186418. Reservations essential. AE, DC, MC, V. No lunch weekends.*

$$$$ ★ **Sheraton Hotel and Towers.** Opened in 1986, this is Göteborg's most modern and spectacular international-style hotel. It has an atrium lobby with a central fountain. The international-style restaurant changes its menu from French to Asian to Italian, for example, each month. ✉ *Södra Hamng. 59–65, 401 24,* ☎ *031/806000,* FAX *031/159888. 344 rooms. Restaurant. AE, DC, MC, V.*

$$$ ★ **Eggers.** Dating from 1859 (renovated in 1997), the Best Western Eggers has more Old World character than other hotels in the city. Most rooms are furnished with antiques. ✉ *Drottningtorget, 401 25,* ☎ *031/806070,* FAX *031/154243. 67 rooms. AE, DC, MC, V.*

$$$ **Liseberg Heden.** Not far from the Liseberg amusement park, this is a modern, family hotel. ✉ *Sten Stureg., 411 38,* ☎ *031/7506900,* FAX *031/7506930. 159 rooms. Restaurant. AE, DC, MC, V.*

Jönköping

Jönköping is an attractive town on the southern shore of Lake Vättern, Sweden's second-largest lake. The town is distinguished not only by its age—it celebrated the 700th anniversary of its founding in 1984—but also as the birthplace of the match-manufacturing industry, established here during the 19th century. **Tändsticksmuseet** (the Match Museum), built on the site of the first factory, has exhibits on the development and manufacture of matches. ✉ *Tändsticksgr. 7,* ☎ *036/105543.* ⏲ *June–Aug., weekdays 10–5, weekends 10–3; Sept.–May, Tues.–Thurs. noon–4, weekends 11–3.*

$$ ★ ✕ **Mäster Gudmunds Källare.** This particularly inviting restaurant is cozily nestled beneath the vaults of a 16th-century-style cellar and is only two minutes from the train station. The cuisine is typically Swedish. ✉ *Kapellg. 2,* ☎ *036/100640. AE, DC, MC, V.*

$$$ **John Bauer Hotel.** This modern Best Western, named for a local artist famous for his fairy-tale depictions of trolls and mystical landscapes, lies close to the center of town and overlooks Munksjön lake. ✉ *Södra Strandg. 15, 550 02,* ☎ *036/349000,* FAX *036/349050. 100 rooms. Restaurant. AE, DC, MC, V.*

Växjö

The nub of Sweden's Glass Country is Växjö, the main town in Kronoberg County. On the second Sunday in August, Växjö celebrates "Minnesota Day." Swedes and Swedish-Americans come together to commemorate their common heritage with American-style square dancing and other festivities. Some 10,000 Americans visit Växjö each year, drawn here by a desire to see where their ancestors emigrated from during the 19th century. The **Utvandrareshus** (Emigrants' House, ✉ Vilhelm Mosbergsg. 4, ☎ 0470/20120), in the town center, tells the story of the migration period, when close to a million Swedes—a fourth of the entire population—set sail for the promised land across the sea. The museum has exhibits about the rigors of their journey, and people of Swedish descent can trace their ancestry in an archive and research center.

★ Manufacture of Swedish **glass** dates from the middle of the 16th century, when Venetian glassblowers were first invited to the Swedish court. About 200 years passed before glassmaking became a major Swedish industry. Because the dense forests between Växjö and Kalmar offered an unlimited supply of wood for firing furnaces, the glass industry was centered here. All the major Swedish glass companies, including **Orrefors** (✉ follow signposts, ☎ 0481/34195 or 0481/34000 for tours), which celebrated its 100th anniversary in 1998, and **Kosta Boda** (✉ follow signposts, ☎ 0481/24030 or 0481/34500 for tours), still operate in this area, and their plants are open to the public; their factory shops sometimes give huge discounts. As there are no regular local bus services, you'll need a car to get around.

$$$ **Statt.** A conveniently located, traditional hotel, this Best Western attracts tour groups. The building dates from 1853; the rooms themselves are modern but classic and were completely renovated in 1996. The hotel has a cozy Irish pub and two restaurants. ✉ *Kungsg. 6, 352 33,* ☎ *0470/13400,* FAX *0470/44837. 124 rooms. 2 restaurants. AE, DC, MC, V.*

$ **Esplanad.** This small, central, family hotel offers the basic amenities. ✉ *Norra Esplanaden 21A, 352 31,* ☎ *0470/22580,* FAX *0470/26226. 27 rooms, most with shower. MC, V.*

Kalmar

★ In this bustling coastal town the imposing 12th-century **Kalmar Slott** (Kalmar Castle) stands as a reminder of the time when Kalmar was the "lock and key" of Sweden. Situated on the eastern coast, it was often attacked by Baltic raiders. Most of the present-day castle stems from the days of King Gustav Vasa, who rebuilt the fortress during the 16th century. ✉ *Slottsv.,* ☎ *0480/56450.* ⏲ *June–Sept., daily 10–4; Oct.–Mar., every second weekend 11–4.*

$$$$ **Slottshotellet.** Occupying a gracious old house on a quiet street, Slottshotellet faces a waterfront park and is a few minutes' walk from both the train station and Kalmar Castle. Inside, a host of modern facilities are wrapped in a 19th-century atmosphere. Restaurant service is offered on the terrace in summer. ✉ *Slottsv. 7, 392 33,* ☎ *0480/88260,* FAX *0480/88266. 36 rooms. Restaurant. AE, DC, MC, V.*

$$$ **Stadshotellet.** This Best Western in the town center is a large hotel done in traditional English style with freshly decorated rooms. The main building dates from 1907. ✉ *Stortorget 14, 392 32,* ☎ *0480/15180,* FAX *0480/15847. 139 rooms. Restaurant. AE, DC, MC, V.*

The West Coast and the Glass Country Essentials

Getting Around

The best and cheapest way to get around Göteborg is with the **Göteborg Card.** It provides free travel on all public transportation, free parking, and free admission to the Liseberg amusement park and all city museums. The card costs SKr 75 for 24 hours.

BY CAR

By car, Göteborg is 478 km (297 mi) west of Stockholm along the E20.

BY PLANE

SAS operates hourly flights to Göteborg from Stockholm's Arlanda Airport between 7 AM and 10 PM on weekdays, less frequently on weekends. The trip by air takes 55 minutes.

BY TRAIN

Regular train services depart from Stockholm's Central Station for Göteborg every hour. Normal travel time is about 4½ hours. Daily high-speed **X2000** trains also operate between the two cities. These shave a little more than an hour off the normal journey time, but cost more. Seat reservations are compulsory on all trains to Göteborg.

Guided Tours

Summer sightseeing tours around Göteborg usually begin at the city tourist office on Kungsportsplatsen 2 (reserve tickets at the office in advance). Tour boats run frequently in summer; a central reservations service (☎ 031/609660) will book you with either Paddans Sightseeing or Börjessons Sightseeing.

Visitor Information

Göteborg (✉ Kungsportsplatsen 2, ☎ 031/100740). **Kalmar** (✉ Larmg. 6, ☎ 0480/15350). **Växjö** (✉ Kungsg.11, ☎ 0470/41410).

30 Switzerland

Zürich, Geneva, Luzern, Lugano, Bern, Zermatt

The Swiss keep coziness under strict control: An electric eye beams open a sliding glass door into a room of carved wood, copper, and old-fashioned rafters. That is the paradox of the Swiss, whose primary impulses pitch high-tech urban efficiency against rustic Alpine comfort.

Alcohol here is measured with scientific precision into glasses marked for 1 or 2 centiliters (⅓ or ⅔ ounces), and the local wines come in graduated carafes reminiscent of laboratory beakers. And as for passion—well, the "double" beds have separate mattresses and sheets tucked firmly down the middle. Politically isolated, culturally self-contained, Switzerland remains economically aloof . . . even Europhobic. As their neighbors pull their wagons in a circle, sweeping away borders to present a unified front to the world, the Swiss continue to choose their apples from bins marked *Inland* (domestic), leaving the *Ausland,* or imported, varieties to humbly rot. Yet Switzerland is many different countries. Not far from the hum of commerce in the streets of Zürich you can listen to the tinkle of cowbells on the slopes of the Klewenalp. While befurred and bejeweled socialites shop in Geneva, the women of Appenzell, across the country, stand beside their husbands on the Landsgemeinde-Platz, raising their hands to vote—a right they won only in 1990.

Switzerland combines most of the attractions of its larger European neighbors—Alpine grandeur, urban sophistication, ancient villages, exhilarating ski slopes, and all-around artistic excellence. It's the heartland of the Reformation, the homeland of William Tell; its cities are full of historic landmarks, its countryside strewn with castles. The varied cuisine reflects French, Italian, and German influences.

All these assets have made Switzerland a major tourist destination, and the Swiss are delighted to pave the way. A welcoming if reserved people, many of them are well versed in English, and they have earned their age-old reputation for hospitality. Their hotels and inns are famous for cleanliness and efficiency, and the notoriously high prices do mirror the quality you'll receive in return.

Switzerland (Suisse, Schweiz, Svizzera)

SWITZERLAND A TO Z

Customs

For details on imports and duty-free limits, *see* Customs & Duties *in* Chapter 1.

Dining

Because the Swiss are so good at preparing everyone else's dishes, it is sometimes said that they have none of their own, but there definitely is a distinct and characteristic Swiss cuisine. Switzerland produces great cheeses—Gruyère, Emmentaler, Appenzeller, and Vacherin—that form the basis of many dishes. Raclette is cheese melted over a fire and served with potatoes and pickles. Fondue is either a bubbling pot of melted cheeses flavored with garlic and kirsch, into which you dip chunks of bread, or a pot of boiling broth into which you dip various meats. *Rösti* is shredded potato sauteed until golden brown. Other Swiss specialties are *geschnetzeltes Kalbfleisch* (veal bits in cream sauce with mushrooms), Italian-style polenta in the Ticino, and fine game in autumn. A wide variety of Swiss sausages makes for filling, inexpensive meals, and in every region the breads are varied and superb.

Dining options range from luxury establishments to modest cafés, Stübli, and restaurants specializing in local cuisine. In resorts especially, most restaurants are associated with hotels, and the half-pension plan includes a simple, hot meal in the room rate.

MEALTIMES

At home, the main Swiss meal of the day is lunch, followed by a light snack in the evening. Restaurants are open at midday and at night; often limited menus are offered all day. Watch for *Tagesteller* or *Plats du jour* (prix-fixe lunch platters or menus), enabling you to a taste of the best restaurants without paying high à la carte rates.

RATINGS

Prices are per person, including tip and taxes, but not wine and coffee.

CATEGORY	ZÜRICH/GENEVA	OTHER AREAS
$$$$	over 90 SF	over 70 SF
$$$	50 SF–90 SF	40 SF–70 SF
$$	30 SF–50 SF	20 SF–40 SF
$	under 30 SF	under 20 SF

WHAT TO WEAR

Jacket and tie are suggested for restaurants in the $$$$ and $$$ categories (except in more relaxed ski resorts); casual dress is acceptable elsewhere.

Language

French is spoken in the southwest, around Lake Geneva, and in the cantons of Fribourg, Neuchâtel, Jura, Vaud, and the western portion of Valais; Italian is spoken in the Ticino; and German is spoken everywhere else—in more than 70% of the country, in fact. The Romance language called Romansh has regained a firm foothold throughout the Upper and Lower Engadine regions of the canton Graubünden, where it takes the form of five different dialects. English, however, is spoken widely. Many signs are in English as well as in the regional language, and all hotels, restaurants, tourist offices, train stations, banks, and shops have at least a few English-speaking employees.

Lodging

Switzerland's accommodations range from the most luxurious hotels to more practical rooms in private homes. Pick up the free "Schweizer Hotelführer" (Swiss Hotel Guide) from Switzerland Tourism (☞ Visitor Information *in* Chapter 1). The guide lists all members of the Swiss Hotel Association (SHA).

Most hotel rooms have private bath and shower; those that don't, noted below, are usually considerably cheaper. Remember that the no-nonsense Swiss sleep in separate beds or, at best, a double with separate bedding. For a standard double bed, request a "French bed" or a *lit matrimoniale*. Service charges and taxes are included in the price quoted. Breakfast is usually included. In resorts especially, half pension (choice of a noon or evening meal) may be included in the room price. If you choose to eat à la carte or elsewhere, the management, if notified in advance, will usually reduce your price.

CHALETS

Off-season, per-day prices for a furnished chalet for four are around 50 SF per person; in peak season, prices double. You may save money if you write directly to the village or resort you wish to rent in. Pick up an illustrated brochure from the **Swiss Touring Club** (✉ Ch. de Blandonnet 4, C.P. 820, CH-1214 Vernier, ☎ 022/4172727, FAX 022/4172020). You can also get a brochure at **Uto-Ring AG** (✉ Beethovenstr. 24, CH-8002 Zürich, ☎ 01/4972727, FAX 01/4972721). In the United States write to **Interhome** (✉ 36 Carlos Dr., Fairfield, NJ 07006). In Britain, contact **Interhome** (✉ 383 Richmond Rd., Twickenham, Middlesex TW1 2EF).

HOTELS

The Swiss Hotel Association grades from one to five stars. Always confirm the price before you register, and check the posted price in your room. Often rates will be quoted on a per-person basis; single rooms are about two-thirds the price of doubles, but this can vary considerably. Romantik Hotels and Restaurants and Relais & Châteaux have premises in either historic houses or houses with some special character. First-class Relais du Silence hotels are usually isolated in a peaceful setting. The Check-In E and G (*einfach und gemütlich,* or "Cheap and Cozy") Hotels are dependable small hotels, boardinghouses, and mountain lodges.

RATINGS

Prices are for two people in a double room with bath or shower, including taxes, service charges, and breakfast.

CATEGORY	ZÜRICH/GENEVA	OTHER AREAS
$$$$	over 450 SF	over 300 SF
$$$	250 SF–450 SF	200 SF–300 SF
$$	120 SF–250 SF	120 SF–200 SF
$	under 120 SF	under 120 SF

Mail

POSTAL RATES

Mail rates are divided into first class "A" (air mail) and second class "B" (surface). Letters and postcards to the United States up to 20 grams cost 1.80 SF first class, .90 SF second class; to the United Kingdom, 1 SF first class, .80 SF second class.

RECEIVING MAIL

If you're uncertain where you'll be staying, you can have your mail, marked "poste restante" or "postlagernd," sent to any post office in Switzerland. The sender's name and address must be on the back, and you'll need identification to collect it. You can also have your mail sent to American Express. This service is free to those holding American Express cards or traveler's checks; others are charged a small fee.

Money Matters

Most major credit cards are generally, though not universally, accepted at hotels, restaurants, and shops. Traveler's checks are almost never accepted outside banks.

COSTS

Switzerland's high standard of living is reflected in its prices. You'll pay more for luxury here than in almost any other European country. Though annual inflation has been less than 2% for years, and the dollar has regained its strength against the SF, Switzerland's exorbitant cost of living makes travel noticeably expensive. You'll find plenty of reasonably priced digs and eats, however, if you look for them.

Zürich and Geneva are Switzerland's priciest cities, followed by Basel, Bern, and Lugano. Price tags at resorts—especially the better-known Alpine ski centers—rival those in the cities. Off the beaten track and in the northeast prices drop considerably.

CURRENCY

The unit of currency is the Swiss franc (SF), divided into 100 centimes (in Suisse Romande) or rappen (in German Switzerland). There are coins of 5, 10, 20, and 50 rappen/centimes and of 1, 2, and 5 francs. Bills come in denominations of 10, 20, 50, 100, 200, and 1,000 francs. At press time (spring 1998), the Swiss franc stood at 1.49 SF to the U.S. dollar, 1.03 SF to the Canadian dollar, .95 SF to the Australian dollar, .82 SF to the New Zealand dollar, and 2.46 SF to the pound sterling.

SAMPLE PRICES

Cup of coffee, 3 SF; bottle of beer, 3.50 SF; soft drink, 3.50 SF; sausage and Rösti, 16 SF; 1⅓-km (1-mi) taxi ride, 12 SF (more in Geneva, Lugano, or Zürich).

TIPPING

Although restaurants include service charges of 15% along with the taxes in bills, a small tip is still expected: 1 SF or 2 SF per person for a modest meal, 5 SF for a first-class meal, and 10 SF at an exclusive gastronomic mecca in the $$$$ range. When possible, tip in cash. Elsewhere, give bathroom attendants 1 SF and hotel maids 2 SF. Theater and opera-house ushers get 2 SF. Hotel porters and doormen should get about 2 SF per bag in an upscale hotel; 1 SF elsewhere. Airport porters receive 5 SF per bag.

National Holidays

January 1–2; April 2 (Good Friday); April 4–5 (Easter Sunday and Monday); May 13 (Ascension); May 23–24 (Whitsunday/Pentecost); August 1 (National Day); December 25–26. May 1 (Labor Day) is celebrated in French-speaking areas.

Opening and Closing Times

Banks are open weekdays 8:30–4:30 or 5 but are often closed at lunch. **Museum** times vary considerably, though many close on Monday. Check locally. **Shops** are generally open 8–noon and 1:30–6:30. Some close Monday morning and at 4 on Saturday. In cities, many large stores do not close for lunch. There is a trend toward late shop hours, usually on Thursday or Friday evening.

Shopping

SALES-TAX REFUNDS

A 6.5% value-added tax (VAT) is included in the price of all goods. Nonresidents spending at least 550 SF at one time at a particular store may get a VAT refund. To obtain a refund, pay by credit card; at the time of purchase, the store clerk should fill out and give you a red form and keep a record of your credit card number. When leaving Switzerland, you must hand deliver the red form to a customs officer—at the customs office at the airport, or, if leaving by car or train, at the border. Customs will process the form and return it to the store, which will refund the tax by crediting your card.

Telephoning

COUNTRY CODE

The country code for Switzerland and Liechtenstein is 41. When dialing Switzerland from outside the country, drop the initial zero from the area code.

INTERNATIONAL CALLS

To dial international numbers directly from Switzerland, dial 00 before the country's code. If a number cannot be reached directly, dial 114 for a connection. Dial 191 for international numbers and information. Calls from booths in train stations and post offices are far cheaper than those made from hotels. A phone card, available in 5 SF, 10 SF, and 20 SF units at the post office or train station, allows you to call from any adapted public phone. Note that fewer and fewer public phones accept coins. International access codes for the major telephone companies will put you directly in touch with an operator who will place your call: for **AT&T,** dial 155/0011; for **MCI,** dial 155/0222; for **Sprint,** dial 155/9777. Telephone rates are lower between 5 PM and 7 PM, after 9 PM, and on weekends. Calls to the United States cost 1.80 SF per minute, to the United Kingdom 1 SF per minute.

LOCAL CALLS

There is direct dialing to every location in Switzerland. For local and international codes, consult the pink pages of the telephone book.

Transportation

BY BICYCLE

Bikes can be rented at all train stations and returned to any station. Rates for standard bikes are 17 SF per half day, 22 SF per day, and 88 SF per week. Mountain bikes are 24 SF per half day, 30 SF per day, or 120 SF per week. Groups get reductions according to the number of bikes. Individuals must make a reservation by 6 PM the day before they plan to use the bike, groups a week in advance. There is a daily charge of 6 SF to transport a bicycle on local trains and 12 SF on intercity or long-range trains.

BY BOAT

Drifting across a Swiss lake and stopping off here and there at picturesque villages makes for a relaxing day trip, especially if you are lucky enough to catch one of the elegant old paddle steamers (although there is a supplemental charge). Trips are scheduled on most of the lakes, with increased service in summer. Unlimited travel is free to holders of the Swiss Pass (☞ *below*). For those not traveling by train, there is also a **Swiss Boat Pass** (35 SF), which allows half-fare travel on all lake steamers for the entire calendar year.

BY BUS

Switzerland's famous yellow postal buses link main cities with villages off the beaten track. Both postal and city buses follow posted schedules to the minute. Free timetables can be picked up at any post office.

The Swiss Pass (☞ *below*) allows you unlimited travel on postal buses, which venture well beyond the rail routes. "The Best River and Lakeside Walks," a free booklet available from Switzerland Tourism (☞ Visitor Information, *below*), describes 28 walks you can enjoy by hopping on and off postal buses. Most walks take about three hours.

BY CAR

Breakdowns. Assistance is available by telephone: Dial 140 and ask for *Strassenhilfe/Secours routier.*

Gasoline. *Sans plomb* or *bleifrei* (lead-free) gasoline costs 1.17 SF per liter; super costs 1.30 per liter. Leaded regular is no longer available.

Parking. Areas are clearly marked. Parking in public lots normally costs about 2 SF per hour.

Road Conditions. Conditions are usually excellent due to well-surfaced roads. Note that roads—especially in the mountains—wind about considerably. Don't plan to achieve high average speeds. When estimating likely travel times, look carefully at the map: There may be only 32 km (20 mi) between one point and another, but there could also be a mountain pass along the way. There is a well-developed highway network, though some notable gaps still exist in the south along an east–west line, roughly between Lugano and Sion. Under some mountain passes, there are tunnels through which cars are transported by train while passengers remain inside—an experience not unlike riding through the world's longest car wash. A combination of steep or winding routes and hazardous weather conditions may close some roads during the winter, especially over mountain passes. Dial ☎ 163 for bulletins and advance information on road conditions.

Rules of the Road. Drive on the right. In built-up areas, the speed limit is 50 kph (30 mph), and on main highways, it's 120 kph (75 mph). On other roads outside built-up areas, the limit is 80 kph (50 mph). Fines for speeding are exorbitant and foreigners are required to pay on the spot—in cash. Children under 12 are not permitted to sit in the front seat. The use of seat belts in both the front and rear seats is mandatory. Driving with parking lights is prohibited, and the use of headlights is mandatory during heavy rain and in road tunnels. To use the main highways, you must display a sticker or *vignette,* which you can buy for 40 SF from Switzerland Tourism (☞ Visitor Information, *below,* and *in* Chapter 1) before you leave home, at the border stations when you enter the country, or at post offices and most gas stations. Cars rented in Switzerland already have these stickers. Traffic going up a mountain has priority, except when postal buses are coming down (signs showing a yellow post horn against a blue background indicate that postal buses have right-of-way). During the winter, snow chains are advisable—sometimes mandatory. They can be rented in all areas, and snow-chain service stations have signs reading SERVICE DE CHAÎNES À NEIGE or SCHNEEKETTENDIENST.

BY PLANE

Swissair (☎ 800/221–4750 in the U.S.; 0171/434–7300 in the U.K.) connects airports in Zürich, Basel, and Geneva. The airline's in-house tour operator, **Swisspack,** arranges flexible packages (✉ 106 Calvert St., Harrison, NY 10528, ☎ 800/688–7947) for the independent traveler who flies at least one way between North America and Europe on Swissair. **Crossair** (☎ 0171/439–4144 in the U.K., ☎ 1553636 toll free within Switzerland) is Switzerland's domestic airline, servicing local airports and various Continental cities as well, including Rome, Barcelona, Berlin, Amsterdam, and London.

BY TRAIN

Swiss trains are swift (except through the mountains), immaculate, and punctual. Don't linger between international connections: Swiss Federal Railways (CFF/SBB) runs a tight ship. If you plan to use the trains extensively, get a comprehensive timetable (*Offizieles Kursbuch* or *Horaire*), which costs 16 SF, or a portable, pocket version called the

Fribo for 12 SF. A useful booklet "Switzerland by Rail," available from Switzerland Tourism (☞ Visitor Information, *below,* and *in* Chapter 1), describes passes, itineraries, and discounts available to rail travelers. Apply for tickets through your travel agent or **Rail Europe** (☎ 800/438–7245).

Inter-City or **Express** trains are the fastest, stopping only at principal towns. A ***Regionalzug/Train Régional*** is a local train, often affording the most spectacular views. Meals, snacks, and drinks are provided on most main services. Seat reservations are useful during rush hours and high season, especially on international trains and in second class.

Fares offer many extras for visitors. The **Swiss Pass** is the best value, offering unlimited travel on Swiss Federal Railways, postal buses, lake steamers, and the local bus and tram services of 30 cities. It also gives reductions on many privately owned railways, cable cars, and funiculars. Available from Switzerland Tourism (☞ Visitor Information, *below,* and *in* Chapter 1) and from travel agents outside Switzerland, the card is valid for 4 days (210 SF second class, 316 SF first class), 8 days (264 SF second class, 378 SF first class), 15 days (306 SF second class, 442 SF first class), or one month (420 SF second class, 610 SF first class). There is also a three-day **Flexi Pass** (210 SF second class, 316 SF first class), which offers the same unlimited travel options as a regular Swiss Pass for any three days within a 15-day period. In some popular tourist areas, **Regional Holiday Season Tickets,** issued for 15 days, give five days of free travel by train, postal buses, steamers, and mountain railways, with half fare for the rest of the validity of the card. Central Switzerland offers a similar pass for seven days, with two days of free travel. Prices vary widely, depending upon the region and period of validity. Travelers holding tickets or passes on Swiss Federal Railways can forward their luggage to their final destination.

Increasingly popular with tourists is a **Swiss Half-Fare Travel Card,** which allows half-fare travel for 30 days (90 SF) or one year (150 SF). The **Swiss Card,** which can be purchased in the United States through Rail Europe (✉ 226–230 Westchester Ave., White Plains, NY 10604, ☎ 800/438–7245) and at train stations at the Zürich and Geneva airports and in Basel, is valid for 30 days and grants full round-trip travel from your arrival point to any destination in the country, plus a half-price reduction on any further excursions during your stay (140 SF second class, 170 SF first class). For more information, get the free "Swiss Travel System" or "Discover Switzerland" brochures from Switzerland Tourism (☞ Visitor Information, *below,* and *in* Chapter 1). You can get information from **Swiss Federal Railways** by phone (☎ 1572222).

Visitor Information

Switzerland Tourism (✉ Bellariastr. 38, Postfach, CH-8027 Zürich, ☎ 01/2881111, FAX 01/2881205).

Weather

Switzerland attracts visitors year-round. Winter sports begin around Christmas and usually last until mid-April, depending on snow conditions. The countryside is a delight in spring, when wildflowers are in bloom, and foliage colors (and clear skies) in fall rival those in New England. In the Ticino, or the Italian-speaking region, and around Lake Geneva (Lac Léman), summer lingers late: There is often sparkling weather in September and October.

CLIMATE

Summer is generally warm and sunny, though the higher you go, the cooler it gets, especially at night. Winter is cold everywhere: In low-lying areas it is frequently damp and overcast; in the Alps, days are brilliantly clear but invariably cold and snowy—especially above 4,600 ft.

Summer and winter, some areas of Switzerland are subject to an Alpine wind that blows from the south and is known as the *Föhn.* It brings clear but somewhat oppressive weather, which the Swiss claim causes headaches. The only exception to these more general weather patterns is the Ticino; protected by the Alps, it has a positively Mediterranean climate—even in winter.

The following are the average daily maximum and minimum temperatures for Zürich.

Jan.	36F	2C	**May**	67F	19C	**Sept.**	69F	20C
	26	– 3		47	8		51	11
Feb.	41F	5C	**June**	73F	23C	**Oct.**	57F	14C
	28	– 2		53	12		43	6
Mar.	51F	11C	**July**	76F	25C	**Nov.**	45F	7C
	34	1		56	14		35	2
Apr.	59F	15C	**Aug.**	75F	24C	**Dec.**	37F	3C
	40	– 4		56	14		29	– 2

ZÜRICH

Zürich is not what you'd expect. Stroll around on a fine spring day and you'll ask yourself if this can really be one of the great business centers of the world: the glistening lake, swans on the river, sidewalk cafés, hushed old squares of medieval guild houses. There's not a gnome—a mocking nickname for a Swiss banker—in sight. For all its economic importance, this is a place where people enjoy life.

Zürich started in 15 BC as a Roman customs post on the Lindenhof overlooking the River Limmat, but its growth really began around the 10th century AD. It became a free imperial city in 1336, a center of the Reformation in 1519, and gradually assumed commercial importance during the 1800s. Today the Zürich stock exchange is fourth in the world, and the city's extraordinary museums and galleries and luxurious shops along the Bahnhofstrasse, Zürich's 5th Avenue, attest to its position as Switzerland's cultural—if not political—capital.

Exploring Zürich

Numbers in the margin correspond to points of interest on the Zürich map.

Although Zürich is Switzerland's largest city, it has a population of only 360,000 and is small by European standards. That's one of its nicest features: It's small enough to be explored comfortably on foot. The Limmat river, crisscrossed with lovely low bridges, bisects the city. On the left bank are the Hauptbahnhof, the main train station, and the Bahnhofplatz, a major urban crossroads and the source of the world-famous luxury shopping street, Bahnhofstrasse. The right bank constitutes the younger, livelier Old Town, also known as Niederdorf.

9 **Altstadt.** Zürich's Old Town is a maze of well-preserved medieval streets. Along Rindermart, Napfplatz, and Kirchgasse you'll find charming old houses. ✉ *Near the Rathaus.*

2 **Bahnhofstrasse.** Zürich's principal street and most glamorous boulevard is renowned for world-class shopping, cafés, and as the banking center. Below the Bahnhofstrasse, bank vaults house one of the world's great treasure troves: Zürich is a leading international precious-met-

als market, rivaled only by London, and much of the gold and silver lies heaped below. ✉ *Runs north–south, west of the Limmat.*

★ ❺ **Fraumünster.** Of the church spires that are Zürich's signature, the Fraumünster's is the most delicate, a graceful sweep to a narrow spire. The Romanesque, or pre-Gothic, choir is graced by stained-glass windows by Chagall. ✉ *Stadthausquai.* ⏲ *May–Sept., daily 9–noon and 2–6; Oct.–Apr., 10–noon and 2–5.*

⓬ **Graphische Sammlung** (Graphic Collection). This impressive collection of the Federal Institute of Technology displays portions of its vast holdings of woodcuts, etchings, and engravings by European masters such as Dürer, Rembrandt, Goya, and Picasso. ✉ *Rämistr. 101,* ☎ *01/6324046.* 🎫 *Free.* ⏲ *weekdays 10–5, Wed. until 8.*

★ ❿ **Grossmünster** (Large Church). During the 3rd century AD, St. Felix and his sister Regula were martyred nearby by the Romans. Legend maintains that having been beheaded, they then walked up the hill carrying their heads and collapsed on the spot where the Grossmünster now stands. On the south tower of this 11th-century structure you can see a statue of Charlemagne (768–814), who is said to have founded the church when his horse stumbled on the same site. In the 16th century, the Zürich reformer Huldrych Zwingli preached sermons here that were so threatening in their promise of fire and brimstone that Martin Luther himself was frightened. ✉ *Zwinglipl.,* ☎ *01/2526144.* ⏲ *Mar. 15–Oct., daily 9–6; Nov.–Mar. 14, daily 10–4.*

★ ⓫ **Kunsthaus.** With a varied, high-quality permanent collection of paintings—medieval, Dutch and Italian Baroque, and Impressionist, the Kunsthaus is Zürich's best art museum. Swiss artists—particularly Hodler—are well represented, and there are works from the origins of Dadaism, conceived in Zürich by French exile Hans Arp. ✉ *Heimpl. 1,* ☎ *01/2516765.* ⏲ *Tues.–Thurs. 10–9, Fri.–Sun. 10–5.*

❸ **Lindenhof.** On this quiet square are the remains of the original Roman customs house and fortress, and the imperial medieval residence. A fountain commemorates the day in 1292 when Zürich's women saved the city from the Hapsburgs. As the story goes, the town was on the brink of defeat when its women donned armor and marched to the Lindenhof. On seeing them, the enemy thought they were faced with another army and promptly beat a strategic retreat. ✉ *Bordered by Fortunag., to the west and intersected by Lindenhofstr.*

❽ **Rathaus** (Town Hall). Zürich's 17th-century Town Hall is strikingly Baroque, with its interior as well preserved as its facade. There's a richly decorated stucco ceiling in the Banquet Hall and a fine ceramic stove in the government council room. ✉ *Limmatquai 55. Closed to the public except for Mon. AM and Wed. PM cantonal and parliament meetings.*

❹ **St. Peters Kirche** (St. Peter's Church). Zürich's oldest parish church, with a 13th-century tower, has the largest clock face in Europe. ✉ *St. Peterhofstatt.* ⏲ *Daily 9–4.*

★ ❶ **Schweizerisches Landesmuseum** (Swiss National Museum). In a gargantuan neo-Gothic building, this museum possesses an enormous collection of objects dating from the Stone Age to modern times, including costumes, furniture, early watches, and a great deal of military history, including thousands of toy soldiers reenacting battles. ✉ *Museumstr. 2,* ☎ *01/2186511.* 🎫 *Free.* ⏲ *Tues.–Sun. 10:30–5.*

❼ **Wasserkirche** (Water Church). Next to one of Switzerland's most delicate late-Gothic structures is the **Helmhaus,** an exhibit space and fine art bookstore. ✉ *Limmatquai 31.* ⏲ *Daily 10–6.*

Altstadt, **9**
Bahnhofstrasse, **2**
Fraumünster, **5**
Graphische Sammlung, **12**
Grossmünster, **10**
Kunsthaus, **11**
Lindenhof, **3**
Rathaus, **8**
St. Peters Kirche, **4**
Schweizerisches Landesmuseum, **1**
Wasserkirche, **7**
Zunfthaus zur Meisen, **6**

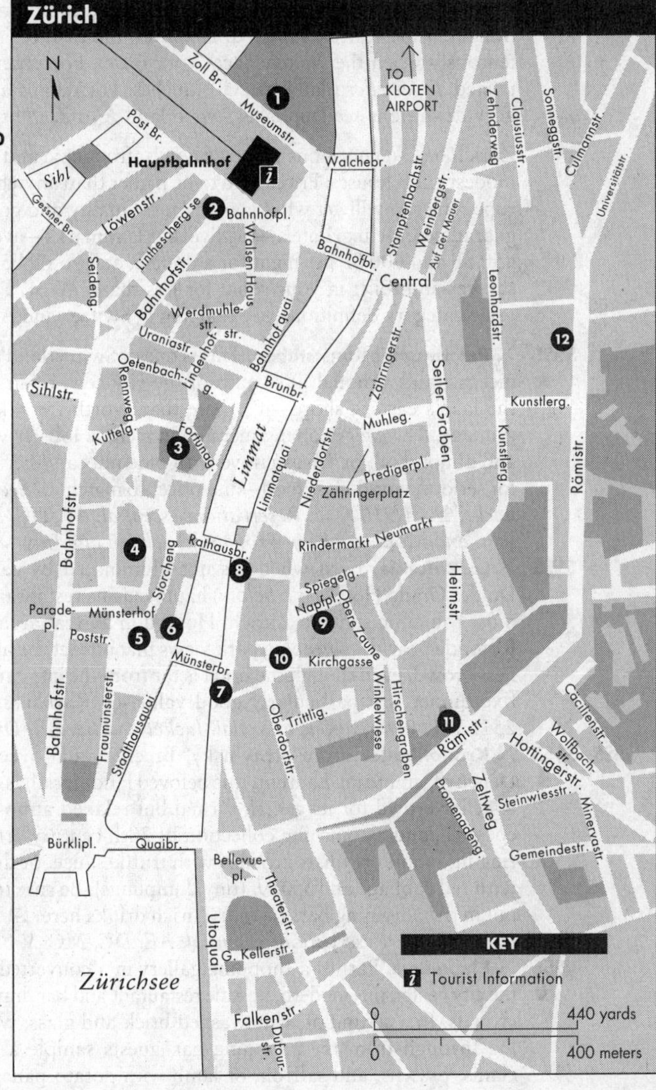

6 **Zunfthaus zur Meisen.** Erected for the city's wine merchants during the 18th century, this Baroque guildhall today houses the Landesmuseum's exquisite ceramics collection. ✉ *Münsterhof 20,* ☎ *01/2112144.* 🎟 *Free.* ⏲ *Tues.–Sun. 10:30–5.*

Elsewhere in Zürich

Museum Rietberg. A wonderful representation of art from India, China, Africa, Japan, and Southeast Asia is displayed in the neoclassic Villa Wesendonck, where Richard Wagner once lived (as in *Wesendonck Songs*). ✉ *Gablerstr. 15, take Tram 7 from city center,* ☎ *01/2024528.* ⏲ *Tues.–Sun. 10–5.*

Dining and Lodging

You're likely to be served seconds in Zürich's generous restaurants, where the rest of your Rösti and geschnetzeltes Kalbfleisch simmer in copper pans by your table while you relish the hefty first portion. This is a

Germanic city, but its status as a minor world capital means international cuisines can be sampled. However, the cash register rings portentously when the waiter places your order. For savings, watch for posted *Tagesteller* (daily special) lunches. For details and price-category definitions *see* Dining *in* Switzerland A to Z, *above*.

Zürich has an enormous range of hotels, from chic and prestigious to modest guest houses. Prices tend to be higher than anywhere else in Europe, but you will get what you pay for: Quality and good service are guaranteed. Deluxe hotels—the five-star landmarks—average between 450 SF and 600 SF per night for a double, and you'll be lucky to get a shower and toilet in your room for less than 140 SF. For details and price-category definitions, *see* Lodging *in* Switzerland A to Z, *above*.

$$$$ ★ ✕ **Petermann's Kunststuben.** This is one of Switzerland's gastronomic meccas, and although it's south of the city center—in Küssnacht on the lake's eastern shore—it's more than worth the 8-km (5-mi) pilgrimage. The ever-evolving menu may include lobster with artichoke and almond oil, or Tuscan dove with pine nuts and herbs. Come here for serious, world-class food—and prices to match. ✉ *Seestr. 160, Küssnacht,* ☏ *01/9100715. Reservations essential. AE, DC, MC, V. Closed Sun. and Mon., 2 wks in Feb., and 3 wks in late July–early Aug.*

$$$$ ✕ **La Rotonde.** Even when it's not illuminated by candlelight, the Dolder Grand Hotel's (☞ *below*) haute-cuisine restaurant is one of the most romantic spots in Zürich. Housed in a great arc of a room, La Rotonde provides sweeping park views that attract the lunchtime business crowd, even though the hotel is far from the city center. The prix-fixe dinner is a particularly good value. ✉ *Kurhausstr. 65,* ☏ *01/2516231. Reservations essential. Jacket and tie. AE, DC, MC, V.*

$$$–$$$$ ★ ✕ **Kronenhalle.** From Stravinsky, Brecht, and Joyce to Nureyev, Deneuve, and Saint-Laurent, this beloved landmark has always drawn a stellar crowd for its genial, formal but relaxed atmosphere, hearty cooking, and astonishing collection of 20th-century art. Try the herring in double cream, tournedos with truffle sauce, or duck *à l'orange* with red cabbage and *Spätzli* (tiny dumplings). Be sure to have a cocktail in the adjoining bar: *Le tout* Zürich drinks here. ✉ *Rämistr. 4,* ☏ *01/2516669. Reservations essential. AE, DC, MC, V.*

$$$ ★ ✕ **Blaue Ente.** Part of a shopping gallery in a converted mill south of the city center, this modern, upscale restaurant and bar draw well-dressed crowds. In a setting of whitewashed brick and glass, with jazz filtering through from the adjoining bar, guests sample a pot-au-feu of clams, prawns, and saffron, or lamb with potato pancakes and eggplant. Take Tram 2 toward Wildbachstrasse. ✉ *Seefeldstr. 223,* ☏ *01/4227706. Reservations essential. AE, DC, MC, V.*

$$$ ✕ **Veltliner Keller.** Though its rich, carved-wood decor borrows from Graubündner Alpine culture, this ancient dining spot is no tourist-trap transplant: The house, built in 1325 and functioning as a restaurant since 1551, has always stored Italian-Swiss Valtellina wines, which were carried over the Alps and imported to Zürich. There is a definite emphasis on the heavy and the meaty, but the kitchen is flexible and reasonably deft with more modern favorites as well: grilled salmon, veal steak with Gorgonzola, and dessert mousses. ✉ *Schlüsselg. 8,* ☏ *01/2254040. Reservations essential. AE, DC, MC, V.*

$$ ★ ✕ **Oepfelchammer.** This was once the haunt of Zürich's beloved writer Gottfried Keller, and it still draws unpretentious literati. The bar is dark and riddled with graffiti, with sagging timbers and slanting floors; the welcoming little dining rooms have carved oak paneling, coffered ceilings, and damask linens. The traditional meats—calf's liver, veal, tripe in white wine sauce—come in generous portions; salads are fresh and seasonal. It's always packed and service can be slow. ✉ *Rindermarkt 12,* ☎ *01/2512336. MC, V. Closed Sun.*

$$ ✕ **Opus.** Bathed in this restaurant's bookish hum, you can enjoy a chic supper of Italian-inspired specialties: olive risotto with shrimp, duck breast with orange and balsamic vinegar sauce. A three-course lunch menu is good value, especially the vegetarian version. On winter weekends, there's a hip salon/cabaret show between courses, with anything from Piaf to readings from Dorothy Parker (*auf Deutsch, natürlich*). ✉ *Pfalzg. 1,* ☎ *01/2115917. AE, DC, MC, V.*

$$ ★ ✕ **Zunfthaus zur Zimmerleuten/Käferstube.** While the pricier zunfthaus upstairs is often overwhelmed with conference crowds, at substreet level a cozy, candle-lit haven dubbed "coopers' pub" serves intimate, atmospheric meals in a dark-beamed, old-Zurich setting. Standard dishes have enough novelty to stand apart: roast hare with elderberry sauce, homemade cinnamon ice cream with wine-poached pear. *Limmatquai 40,* ☎ *01/2520834. AE, DC, MC, V.*

$–$$ ★ ✕ **Bierhalle Kropf.** Under the giant boar's head and century-old murals, businesspeople, workers, and shoppers crowd shared tables to feast on generous hot dishes and a great selection of sausages. The *Leberknödli* (liver dumplings) are tasty, *Apfelköchli* (fried apple slices) tender and sweet, and the service as wise-cracking-cranky as in a New York deli. ✉ *In Gassen 16,* ☎ *01/2211805. AE, DC, MC, V. Closed Sun.*

$–$$ ★ ✕ **Zeughauskeller.** Built as an arsenal in 1487, this enormous stone and beam hall offers hearty meat platters and a variety of beers and wines amid comfortable, friendly chaos. Waitresses are harried and brisk, especially at lunchtime, when crowds are thick with locals—don't worry, just roll up your sleeves and dig in. ✉ *Bahnhofstr. 28, at Paradepl.,* ☎ *01/2112690. AE, DC, MC, V.*

$ ✕ **Adler's Swiss Chuchi.** A bit of a shock in a black-leather-and-nose-ring neighborhood, this squeaky-clean, Swiss-kitsch restaurant features an airy, modern decor, with carved fir, Alpine-rustic chairs, Big Boy–style plastic menus and good home-cooked national specialties. Excellent lunch menus are rock-bottom cheap and served double-quick; nights are reserved for fondue. ✉ *Roseng. 10,* ☎ *01/2669696. AE, DC, MC, V.*

$ ✕ **Reithalle.** In this hip downtown theater complex behind the Bahnhofstrasse, an old military horse barn has been converted into a popular restaurant, with candles perched on the mangers and beams and heat ducts exposed. Young, street-smart locals sample French and Italian specialties, many vegetarian, and an excellent international blackboard list of open wines. Too bad it's closed Saturday and Sunday nights. ✉ *Gessnerallee 8 ,* ☎ *01/2120766. AE, MC, V.*

$$$$ ★ 🏨 **Baur au Lac.** This is the highbrow patrician of Swiss hotels, with luxurious but low-key facilities—like the Rolls-Royce limousine service. Its broad back is turned to the commercial center, while its front rooms overlook the lake, canal, and manicured lawns of the hotel's private park. The decor is posh, discreet, and firmly fixed in the Age of Reason. ✉ *Talstr. 1, CH-8022,* ☎ *01/2205020,* FAX *01/2205044. 125 rooms. 2 restaurants. AE, DC, MC, V.*

$$$$ ★ 🏨 **Dolder Grand.** A cross between Camp David and Maria Theresa's summer palace, this sprawling Victorian fantasy-palace sits high on a wooded hill over Zürich, quickly reached from Römerhof by funicular railway (free for guests). It's a picturesque hodgepodge of turrets, cupolas, half-timbering, and mansards; the uncompromisingly modern wing was added in 1964, but from inside the connection is seamless. Its restaurant La Rotonde excels in traditional French cuisine (☞ *above*). ✉ *Kurhausstr. 65, CH-8032,* ☎ *01/2516231,* FAX *01/2518829. 183 rooms. 2 restaurants, pool. AE, DC, MC, V.*

$$$$ ★ 🏨 **Widder.** The antithesis of tradition-bound, grande-dame hotels, this glossy architectural showcase revels in the present while preserving the past. Eight adjacent medieval houses were gutted and combined to create the Widder, tumbling together new and old, from the museum-perfect facade to the burnished cabinetry. Scotch-sampling and excellent live jazz lure a posh crowd to the bar. ✉ *Rennweg. 7, CH-8001,* ☎ *01/2242526,* FAX *01/2242424. 42 rooms, 7 suites. 2 restaurants. AE, DC, MC, V.*

$$$ ★ **Florhof.** This is an anti-urban-hotel, a gentle antidote to the bustle of downtown commerce. In a quiet residential area by the Kunstmuseum, this Romantik property pampers famous writers, theater directors, and visiting professors with its polished wood, blue-willow fabrics, and wisteria-sheltered garden. ✉ *Florhofsg. 4,* ☎ *01/2614470,* FAX *01/2614611. 33 rooms. Restaurant. AE, DC, MC, V.*

$$$ **Neues Schloss.** Now managed by the German-owned Arabella chain, this small, intimate hotel in the business district, southeast of Paradeplatz, offers a warm welcome, good service, and a new, jewel-tone room decor. Its airy, floral restaurant, Le Jardin, is popular at lunch. ✉ *Stockerstr. 17, CH-8022,* ☎ *01/2869400,* FAX *01/2869445. 58 rooms. Restaurant. AE, DC, MC, V.*

$$$ **Splügenschloss.** Befitting its age, this Relais & Châteaux property maintains its ornate, antiques-filled decor. Some rooms have been completely paneled in Alpine-style pine; others are decorated in fussy florals. Its location southeast of the Neues Schloss may be a little out of the way for tourists, but atmosphere buffs will find it worth the effort. ✉ *Splügenstr. 2, CH-8002,* ☎ *01/2899999,* FAX *01/2899998. 5 rooms. Restaurant. AE, DC, MC, V.*

$$$ ★ **Zum Storchen.** In a stunning central location, tucked between Fraumünster and St. Peters Kirche, this 600-year-old structure has become an impeccable modern hotel. It has warmly appointed rooms, some with French windows opening over the Limmat river, and a lovely restaurant with riverfront terrace seating. ✉ *Weinpl. 2, CH-8001,* ☎ *01/2115510,* FAX *01/2116451. 73 rooms. Restaurant. AE, DC, MC, V.*

$$ **Haus zum Kindli.** This charming little bijoux hotel could pass for a 3-D Laura Ashley catalogue, with every cushion and bibelot as artfully styled as a magazine ad. The result is welcoming, intimate, and a sight less contrived than most cookie-cutter hotel decors. At the Opus restaurant downstairs, guests earn 20% off menu prices to vie with crowds of locals. (☞ Dining, *above*). ✉ *Pfalzg. 1, CH-8001,* ☎ *01/2115917,* FAX *01/2116528. 21 rooms. AE, DC, MC, V.*

$$ **Rössli.** Though small and sometimes short on staff, this modern hotel offers a refreshing antidote to Zürich's medievalism. The chic decor pairs stone and wood textures with bold textiles and vivid lithographs. Extras include safes and bathrobes. Some singles are tiny, but all have double beds. The adjoining bar can be noisy; ask for a room facing the back. ✉ *Rösslig. 7, CH-8001,* ☎ *01/2522121,* FAX *01/2522131. 13 rooms, 1 suite. AE, DC, MC, V.*

$ **Leoneck.** From the cowhide-covered front desk to the edelweiss-print curtains, this budget hotel wallows in its Swiss roots, but balances this with no-nonsense conveniences: new tile baths (with cow shower curtains), murals, and built-in pine furniture. It's one stop from the Central tram stop, two from the Bahnhof. *Leonhardst. 1, CH-8001,* ☎ *01/2616070,* FAX *01/2616492. 65 rooms. AE, DC, MC, V.*

$ **Limmathof.** This spare but welcoming city hotel inhabits a handsome historic shell and is ideally placed on the Limmatquai, minutes from the Hauptbahnhof. Rooms have tile bathrooms and plump down quilts. There's an old-fashioned Weinstube as well as a new vegetarian restaurant that doubles as the breakfast room. ✉ *Limmatquai 142, CH-8023,* ☎ *01/2614220,* FAX *01/2620217. 62 rooms. Restaurant. AE, DC, MC, V.*

$ **St. Georges.** This simple former pension has a bright lobby and breakfast space; rooms are milky white-on-white. A few now offer full bathrooms, but the majority, under 100 SF, have shower and toilet down the hall. ✉ *Weberstr. 11, CH-8004,* ☎ *01/2411144,* FAX *01/2411142. 40 rooms, 11 with bath. AE, DC, MC, V.*

Nightlife and the Arts

Zürich has a lively nightlife scene, largely centered in the Niederdorf (☞ Exploring Zúrich, *above*). And despite its small population, Zürich is a big city when it comes to the arts; it supports a top-ranked orchestra, an opera company, and a theater. For information on goings-on, check *Zürich News,* published weekly in English and German. Also check "Züri-tip," a supplement to the Friday edition of the daily German-language newspaper *Tages Anzeiger.* For tickets to opera, concert, and theater events, contact **BiZZ** (✉ Billettzentrale Zürich, Kulturpavillon, Werdmühlepl., ☎ 01/2212283). Depending on the event, **Musik Hug** (✉ Limmatquai 28, ☎ 01/2611600) makes reservations. Also try **Jecklin** (✉ Rämistr. 30, ☎ 01/2515900).

The Arts

During July or August, the **Theaterspektakel** takes place, with circus tents housing avant-garde theater and experimental performances on the lawns by the lake at Mythenquai. The Zürich Tonhalle Orchestra, named for its concert hall **Tonhalle** (✉ Claridenstr. 7, ☎ 01/2063434), was inaugurated by Brahms in 1895 and enjoys international acclaim. Tickets sell out quickly, so book directly through the Tonhalle. The music event of the year is the **Züricher Festspiele** (International Festival), when, for four weeks in June, orchestras and soloists from all over the world perform, and plays and exhibitions are staged. Book well ahead. Details are available from Info- und Ticketoffice (✉ Postfach 6036, CH-8023, ☎ 01/2154030).

Nightlife

BARS AND LOUNGES

Champagnertreff in the Hotel Central (✉ Central 1, ☎ 01/2515555) is a popular neo–Art Deco piano bar with several champagnes available by the glass. The **Jules Verne Panorama Bar** (✉ Uraniastr. 9, ☎ 01/2111155) shakes up cocktails with a wraparound downtown view. The narrow bar at the **Kronenhalle** (✉ Rämistr. 4, ☎ 01/2516669) draws mobs of well-heeled locals and internationals for its prize-winning cocktails. Serving a young, arty set until 4 AM, **Odéon** (✉ Am Bellevue, ☎ 01/2511650) is a cultural and historic landmark (Mata Hari danced here) and a gay bar by night.

DISCOS

The medieval-theme **Adagio** (✉ Gotthardstr. 5, ☎ 01/2063666) offers classic rock, jazz, and tango to well-dressed thirtysomethings. **Kaufleuten** (✉ Pelikanstr. 18, ☎ 01/2011098) is a landmark dance club that draws a hip, well-dressed crowd. Tuesday nights are free. **Mascotte** (✉ Theaterstr. 10, ☎ 01/2524481) draws all ages on weeknights, a young crowd on weekends, for funk and soul.

JAZZ CLUBS

Casa Bar (✉ Münsterg. 30, ☎ 01/2612002) is, arguably, Zürich's most famous jazz club. The **Widder Bar** (✉ Widderg. 6, ☎ 01/2242411), in the Hotel Widder (☞ Dining and Lodging, *above*), attracts local celebrities with its 800-count "library of spirits" and international jazz groups.

Shopping

One of the broadest assortments of watches in all price ranges is available at **Bucherer** (✉ Bahnhofstr. 50, ☎ 01/2112635). **Heimatwerk** (✉ Rennweg 14 and Bahnhofstr. 2, ☎ 01/2115780) specializes in Swiss handicrafts, all of excellent quality. **Jelmoli** (✉ Seideng. 1, ☎ 01/2204411), Switzerland's largest department store, carries a wide range of tasteful Swiss goods. You can snag some of last season's fashions at deep discounts at **Lagerverkauf** (✉ Weinpl. 10, ☎ 01/2128318), which jumbles chichi brands on thrift-shop style racks. If you have a sweet tooth, stock up on truffles at **Sprüngli** (✉ Paradepl., ☎ 01/2244646). The renowned chocolatier **Teuscher** (✉ Storcheng. 9, ☎ 01/2115153) concocts a killer champagne truffle. For the latest couture, go to one of a dozen **Trois Pommes** (✉ Weggeng. 1) boutiques featuring top-name designers such as Versace, Armani, or Donna Karan .

Side Trip from Zürich: Liechtenstein

For an international day trip out of Zürich, dip a toe into tiny Liechtenstein: There isn't room for much more. Just 80 km (50 mi) southeast on the Austrian border, this miniature principality covers a scant 158 square km (61 square mi). An independent nation since 1719, Liechtenstein has a customs union with Switzerland, which means they share trains, currency, and diplomats—but not stamps, which is why collectors prize the local releases. It's easiest to get there by car, since Swiss trains pass through without stopping. If you're using a train pass, ride to Sargans or Buchs. From there, local postal buses deliver mail and passengers across the border to Liechtenstein's capital, Vaduz.

Exploring Liechtenstein

Green and mountainous, with vineyards climbing its slopes, greater Liechtenstein is best seen by car; however, the postal buses are prompt and their routes are extensive.

VADUZ

In fairy-tale Vaduz, Prince Johannes Adam Pius still lives in the Castle, a massive 16th-century fortress perched high on the cliff above the city. Only honored guests of the prince tour the interior, but its exterior and the views from the grounds are worth the climb. In the modern town center, head for the tourist information office to have your passport stamped with the Liechtenstein crown. Upstairs, the **Liechtensteinische Staatliche Kunstsammlung** (Liechtenstein State Museum of Art) showcases various segments of the vast collection. ✉ *Städtle 37,* ☎ *075/2322341.* ⏲ *Apr.–Oct., daily 10–noon and 1:30–5:30; Nov.–Mar., daily 10–noon and 1:30–5.*

On the same floor, the **Briefmarkenmuseum** (Stamp Museum) attracts philatelists from all over the world to see the 300 frames of beautifully designed and relatively rare stamps. ✉ *Städtle 37,* ☎ *075/2366105.* 🎟 *Free.* ⏲ *Apr.–Oct., daily 10–noon and 1:30–5:30; Nov.–Mar., daily 10–noon and 1:30–5.*

At press time (spring 1998), the **Liechtensteinisches Landesmuseum** (National Museum) was closed for structural repair. With luck it will open before 2000; this worthwhile museum houses church carvings, ancient coins, and arms. ✉ *Städtle 43,* ☎ *075/22310.* ⏲ *May–Sept., daily 10–noon and 1:30–5:30; Oct.–Apr., Tues.–Sun. 2–6.*

BEYOND VADUZ

In **Schaan,** just north of Vaduz, visit the Roman excavations and the parish church built on the foundations of a Roman fort. Or drive southeast of the capital to the chalets of picturesque **Triesenberg** for spectacular views of the Rhine Valley. **Malbun** is a sun-drenched ski bowl with comfortable slopes and a low-key ambience.

$ ★ ✕ **Wirthschaft zum Löwen.** It may be tiny, but Liechtenstein has a cuisine of its own, and this is the place to try it. In a farmhouse on the Austrian border, the friendly Biedermann family serves pungent *Sauerkäse* (sour cheese) and *Käseknöpfli* (cheese dumplings), plus lovely meats and the local crusty, chewy bread. ✉ *Schellenberg,* ☎ *075/3731162. No credit cards.*

$$$$ ★ ✕ **Real.** Surrounded by slick modern decor, you'll find rich, old-style Austrian-French cuisine in all its buttery glory. It's prepared these days by Martin Real, son of the unpretentious former chef, Felix Real—who, in his retirement, presides over the 20,000-bottle wine cellar. The menu offers game, seafood, soufflés, and an extraordinary wine list. Downstairs is a more casual Stübli for those who don't feel like getting dressed up. Upstairs is a baker's dozen of small, airily-decorated rooms. ✉ *Städtle 21, Vaduz FL-9490,* ☎ *075/2322222,* FAX *075/2320891. 11 rooms, 2 suites. Restaurant. AE, DC, MC, V.*

$$$$ **Park-Hotel Sonnenhof.** A garden oasis commanding a superb view of the valley and mountains beyond, this hillside retreat in a residential district offers discreet luxury minutes from downtown Vaduz. Some rooms open directly onto the lawns; others have balconies. The excellent restaurant, open only to guests, offers a five-course tasting menu for 100 SF, as well as more modest entrées. ✉ *Mareestr. 29, Vaduz FL-9490,* ☎ *075/2321192,* FAX *075/2320053. 17 rooms, 12 suites. Restaurant, indoor pool. AE, DC, MC, V.*

$$ **Engel.** On the main tourist street, its café bulging with bus-tour crowds, this simple hotel manages to maintain a local, comfortable ambience. ✉ *Städtle 13, Vaduz FL-9490,* ☎ *075/2320313,* FAX *075/2331159. 20 rooms. 2 restaurants. AE, DC, MC, V.*

$ **Alpenhotel.** This turn-of-the-century chalet, perched well above the mists of the Rhine in sunny Malbun, has added a modern wing. The old rooms are small and cozy; the higher-priced new rooms are modern and spare. The Vögeli family's welcoming smiles and good food have made it a local institution. ✉ *Triesen, Malbun FL-9497,* ☎ *075/2631181,* FAX *075/2639646. 21 rooms. 2 restaurants, indoor pool. AE, DC, MC, V.*

Liechtenstein Essentials

VISITOR INFORMATION

Tourist Office (✉ Städtle 37, Box 139, Vaduz FL-9490, ☎ 075/2321443).

Zürich Essentials

Arriving and Departing

BY BUS

All bus services to Zürich will drop you at the **Hauptbahnhof** (City center). There are also hotel bus services that charge 17 SF per person.

BY CAR

Highways link Zürich directly to France, Germany, and Italy. The quickest approach is from Germany.

BY PLANE

Zürich-Kloten (☎ 01/8127111) is Switzerland's most important airport. Several airlines fly directly to Zürich from major cities in the United States, Canada, and the United Kingdom. Swissair flies nonstop from major international cities. "Fly Rail Baggage" allows Swissair passengers departing Switzerland to check their bags at any of 120 rail or postal bus stations throughout the country; luggage is automatically transferred to the airplane. At eight Swiss railway stations, passengers may complete all check-in procedures for Swissair flights, including picking up their boarding pass and checking their bags.

BY TRAIN

Zürich is the northern crossroads of Switzerland, with swift and punctual trains arriving from Basel, Geneva, Bern, and Lugano. All routes lead to the Hauptbahnhof.

Getting Around

The city's transportation network is excellent.

BY BUS AND TRAM

VBZ Züri-Linie (Zürich Public Transport) buses and trams run from 5:30 AM to midnight, every six minutes on all routes at peak hours, and about every 12 minutes at other times. Before you board the bus, you must buy your ticket from one of the automatic vending machines found at every stop. An all-day pass is a good buy at 7.20 SF. Free route plans are available from VBZ offices and larger kiosks.

BY TAXI

Taxis are very expensive, with an 8 SF minimum, and should be avoided unless you have no other means of getting around.

Contacts and Resources

CONSULATES

Contact the **United States** embassy in Bern (✉ Jubiläumsstr. 93, ☎ 031/3577011). Contact the **Canadian** embassy in Bern (✉ Kirchenfeldstr. 88, ☎ 031/3526321). There is a **British** consulate in Zürich (✉ Dufourstr. 56, ☎ 01/2611520).

EMERGENCIES

Police (☎ 117). **Ambulance** (☎ 144). **Doctor/Dentist Referral** (☎ 01/2616100). **Pharmacy: Bellevue** (✉ Theaterstr. 14, ☎ 01/2525600) offers an all-night service and stocks many international brands.

ENGLISH-LANGUAGE BOOKS

English-language magazines are available at most large kiosks, especially in the Hauptbahnhof. **Payot** (✉ Bahnhofstr. 9, ☎ 01/2115452). **Stäehli** (✉ Bahnhofstr. 70, ☎ 01/2013312).

GUIDED TOURS

Orientation. Three bus tours are available. The daily "Sights of Zürich" tour (29 SF) gives a good general idea of the city in two hours. "In and Around Zürich" covers more ground and includes an aerial cableway trip to Felsenegg; it takes 2½ hours and costs 39 SF for adults. All tours start from the Hauptbahnhof. Contact the Tourist Office (☞ *below*) for reservations.

Walking. Daily from May to October, two-hour conducted walking tours (18 SF) start at the train station. This Tourist Office service also offers day trips by coach to Luzern, up the Rigi, Titlis, or Pilatus mountains, and the Jungfrau. Ask the Tourist Service at the station, or your hotel, for information.

TRAVEL AGENCIES

American Express (✉ Bahnhofstr. 20, ☎ 01/2118370). **Kuoni Travel** (✉ Bahnhofpl. 7, ☎ 01/2213411).

VISITOR INFORMATION

Tourist service (not to be confused with the Tourist Office; ☞ *below*) (✉ Bahnhof, ☎ 01/2114000). **Tourist Office** (✉ Bahnhofbrücke 1, ☎ 01/2111256, FAX 01/2113981). **Hotel reservations** (☎ 01/2154040, FAX 01/2154044).

GENEVA

Draped at the foot of the Jura and the Alps on the westernmost tip of Lake Geneva (or Lac Léman), Geneva is the most cosmopolitan and graceful of Swiss cities. Just a stone's throw from the French border, this French-speaking region's mansarded mansions stand guard beside the River Rhône, where yachts bob, gulls dive, and Rolls-Royces purr beside manicured promenades. The combination of Swiss efficiency and French savoir faire gives the city a chic polish, and the infusion of international blood from the United Nations adds a heterogeneity that is rare in cities with a population of only 180,000.

Headquarters of the World Health Organization and the International Red Cross, Geneva has always been a city of humanity and enlightenment, offering refuge to writers Voltaire, Hugo, and Stendhal, as well as to religious reformers Calvin and Knox. Byron, Shelley, Wagner, and Liszt all fled from scandal to Geneva.

A Roman seat for 500 years (from 120 BC), then home to early Burgundians, Geneva flourished under bishop-princes into the 11th century, fending off the greedy dukes of Savoy in conflicts that lasted into the 17th century. Under the guiding fervor of Calvin, Geneva rejected Catholicism and became a stronghold of Protestant reforms. In 1798 it fell to the French, but joined the Swiss Confederation as a canton in 1815, shortly after Napoléon's defeat. The French accent remains.

Exploring Geneva

Numbers in the margin correspond to points of interest on the Geneva map.

Geneva crowds along the tapering shores of Lake Geneva, which, at the Pont du Mont-Blanc, narrows back into the Rhône river. Thus Geneva is as much a river town as a lake town, and its Rive Droite (Right Bank, on the north side) and Rive Gauche (Left Bank, on the south side) have strong identities. Most of the central city's best is concentrated on the Rive Gauche, but the Rive Droite is where the waterfront and many handsome hotels are located. These elegant neighborhoods, and the time-frozen beauty of the Old Town, are easily toured on foot. To visit the International Area, a modern section well north of city center, you may need to take a bus or a cab.

★ ⑩ **Cathédrale St-Pierre** (St. Peter's Cathedral). Built during the 12th and 13th centuries in Gothic style, the cathedral's aesthetic balance was tipped when a sternly beautiful but incongruous neoclassic portico was added in the 18th century. Its austerity reflects its change of role—from a Catholic cathedral to a Protestant church, stripped of its ornaments by followers of Calvin. Climb the north and south towers; there's also the *site archéologique* (archaeological site) (☞ *below*) below the cathedral. ✉ *Pl. de la Taconnerie,* ☎ *022/3102929.* ⏲ *Oct.–May, Mon.–Sat. 9–7, Sun. 11–7; June–Sept., Tues.–Sat. 2–5, Sun. 10–noon and 2–5 (except during services).*

★ ⑭ **Collection Baur.** This graceful mansion exhibits businessman Alfred Baur's Asian object collection of rose and celadon porcelains from China, medieval Japanese stoneware, Samurai swords, and much more. ✉ *8 rue Munier-Romilly,* ☎ *022/3461729.* ⏲ *Tues.–Sun. 2–6.*

⑦ **Hôtel de Ville** (Town Hall). Dating from the 16th century, this still-active Town Hall shelters the Alabama Hall, where, on August 22, 1864, the Geneva Convention was signed by 16 countries, laying the foundation of the International Red Cross. ✉ *Rue de l'Hôtel-de-Ville,* ☎ *022/3192209.* ⏲ *Individual visits by request.*

★ ❽ **Maison Tavel** (Tavel House). In the oldest building in town, this gem of a museum presents a vivid, intimate re-creation of daily life and urban history. Several rooms have period furnishings, while others display arcane souvenirs of Geneva's past—including a guillotine and a garishly painted miter, worn by convicted pimps in Calvin's day. ✉ *6 rue du Puits-St-Pierre,* ☎ *022/3102900.* *Free.* ⏲ *Tues.–Sun. 10–5.*

★ ❹ **Monument de la Réformation** (Monument of the Reformation). Conceived on a grand scale between 1909 and 1917, this group of larger-than-life sculptures pays homage to such Protestant pioneers as Bèze, Calvin, Farel, and Knox. It's flanked by memorials to kingpins Ulrich Zwingli and Martin Luther. ✉ *Just off Pl. Neuve and Promenade des Bastions, in Parc des Bastions.*

★ ⓭ **Musée d'Art et Histoire** (Museum of Art and History). A mother lode of world culture, this 1910 landmark houses an enormous Beaux-Arts collection. Among its holdings are several masterworks of Maurice-Quentin de la Tour; and a full room of Alpine landscapes by Swiss Impressionist Ferdinand Hodler. There are also collections on archaeology—including Genevan pre-history—arms, and porcelain. ✉ *2 rue Charles-Galland,* ☎ *022/4182600.* *Free.* ⏲ *Tues.–Sun. 10–5.*

★ ❺ **Musée d'Art Moderne et Contemporain** (Museum of Modern and Contemporary Art). The concrete floors and fluorescent lighting from this former factory highlight the gritty museum collection of stark, mind-stretching, post-1965 artworks. The building's spare, bleak lines serve as a foil to the art, which includes works by Gordon Matta-Clark, Jenny Holzer, Sol Lewitt, and Jean Basquiat. Of particular interest is a permanent reconstruction of art collector Ghislain Mollet-Viéville's Paris apartment, where he lived in a state of pure modernism among works of Sol Le Witt and Carl André. To get here from city center, take Tram 12 toward Plaine de Plainpalais; at its main stop, get off and walk straight across the park. Head up rue des Vieux-Grenadiers and turn right into the entrance. ✉ *10 rue des Vieux-Grenadiers,* ☎ *022/3206122.* ⏲ *Tues.–Sun. noon–6; walking commentary in French Tues. 6:30.*

❾ **Musée Barbier-Mueller** (Barbier-Mueller Museum). Since 1907 Josef Mueller and his family have acquired a staggering number of fine "primitive" pieces from Africa, Oceania, Southeast Asia, and the Americas. A small, but exquisitely presented selection is on view at any given time; labels in English guide visitors from ivory fly-whisk handles from Zaire to massive carved masks from New Ireland. ✉ *10 rue Calvin,* ☎ *022/3120270.* ⏲ *Daily 11–5.*

★ ⓯ **Musée Internationale de la Croix-Rouge** (International Red Cross Museum). State-of-the-art media technology illuminates human kindness in the face of disaster, both natural and man-made. The sometimes grim displays include a reconstruction of a 3- by 2-m (10- by 6½-ft) concrete prison cell that once contained 17 political prisoners. The masterpiece of the exhibition is the astonishing Mur du Temps (Wall of Time), a simple time line that traces, year by year, wars and natural disasters that have killed 100,000 people or more. Young children may be upset by some imagery. The commentaries are in several languages, including English. ✉ *17 av. de la Paix,* ☎ *022/7345248 or 022/7332660 for recorded information.* *10 SF.* ⏲ *Tues.–Sun. 10–5.*

❷ **Musée Rath** (Rath Museum). Geneva's first art museum frequently installs new, top-notch exhibitions and the Russian lieutenant general Simon Rath's former art holdings. ✉ *Pl. Neuve,* ☎ *022/4183340.*

Up to 10 SF, depending on exhibition. ⏲ *Subject to change; check local listings; closed Mon.*

★ ⓰ **Palais des Nations** (Palace of Nations). The period detail alone—bronze torchères, allegorical murals by José Maria Sert—merit a visit to the home of the European branch of the United Nations. The Assembly Hall is where, in 1988, Yassir Arafat met with remaining UN delegates when denied a U.S. visa. ✉ *Palais des Nations,* ☎ *022/9074560.* ⏲ *Apr.–June and Sept.–Oct., daily 10–noon and 2–4; July–Aug., daily 9–6; Jan.–Mar. and Nov.–mid-Dec., weekdays 10–noon and 2–4. By appointment only, last 2 wks in Dec.*

★ ❻ **Place du Bourg-de-Four.** This sprawling Old-Town square once served as a Roman forum and a cattle and wheat market. It's now a charming mix of scruffy bohemia, genteel tradition, and slick gentrification. ✉ *At intersection of rue Verdaine and rue des Chaudronniers.*

❸ **Place Neuve.** At this major crossroads you'll see the **Grand Théâtre,** which hosts opera, ballet, and sometimes the Orchestre de la Suisse Romande (it also performs at nearby Victoria Hall), and the **Conservatoire de Musique.** ✉ *Intersection of bd. du Théâtre, rue de la Corraterie, and Parc des Bastions.*

★ ❶ **Pont du Mont-Blanc** (Mont-Blanc Bridge). From the middle of this bridge—spanning the westernmost point of Lac Léman as it squeezes back into the Rhône—you can see the snowy peak of Mont Blanc. From March through October you'll have a fine view of the **Jet d'Eau,** Europe's tallest fountain, gushing 475 ft up. ✉ *Joins rue du Mont-Blanc with quai Général-Guisan.*

❶❶ **Site archéologique** (archaeological site). In the 1980s the floors of the Cathédrale St-Pierre (☞ *above*) were lifted and the foundations of previous churches excavated. Walkways reveal remnants of a 4th-century Christian baptistery and a striking 5th-century mosaic floor. ✉ *Pl. de la Taconnerie, under the nave of Cathédrale St-Pierre (entrance outside),* ☎ *022/3102929.* ⏲ *June–Sept., Tues.–Sat. 11–5, Sun. 10–5; Oct.–May, Tues.–Sat. 2–5, Sun. 10–noon and 2–5.*

⓬ **Temple de l'Auditoire** (Protestant Lecture Hall). In this former Catholic chapel, Jean Calvin taught missionaries his doctrines of radical, puritanical reform; from 1556 to 1559, the Scots reformer John Knox also preached here. Today English and Dutch services are held Sunday; otherwise you'll find the temple closed to the public. ✉ *Pl. de la Taconnerie,* ☎ *022/3118533.*

Dining and Lodging

Connoisseurs of *haute gastronomie* will not be disappointed by this city that persuades great French chefs to cross the border with a wealthy, discerning clientele. But the traditional cuisine is earthy and rich, with dishes such as *pieds de cochon* (pigs' feet) and *fricassée* (savory wine-based stew) of chicken or pork. Other dishes to watch for are *omble chevalier* (a kind of salmon trout native to Lac Léman) and *cardon* (cardoon, an artichokelike vegetable) baked in a gratin with cream and Gruyère. Many restaurants close on weekends; almost all on Sunday. For details and price-category definitions, *see* Dining *in* Switzerland A to Z, *above*.

Hotels in Geneva are pricey, but there are pleasant, less-expensive choices. Since it's a popular convention center, blocks of rooms can be snatched up quickly. Book well in advance and brace yourself: You will have to pay more than 120 SF simply to have a toilet in your room. In the heart of town, opt for higher floors as a hedge against traffic

Cathédrale St-Pierre, **10**
Collection Baur, **14**
Hôtel de Ville, **7**
Maison Tavel, **8**
Monument de la Réformation, **4**
Musée d'Art et Histoire, **13**
Musée d'Art Moderne et Contemporain, **5**
Musée Barbier-Mueller, **9**
Musée Internationale de la Croix-Rouge, **15**
Musée Rath, **2**
Palais des Nations, **16**
Place du Bourg-de-Four, **6**
Place Neuve, **3**
Pont du Mont-Blanc, **1**
Site archéologique, **11**
Temple de l'Auditoire, **12**

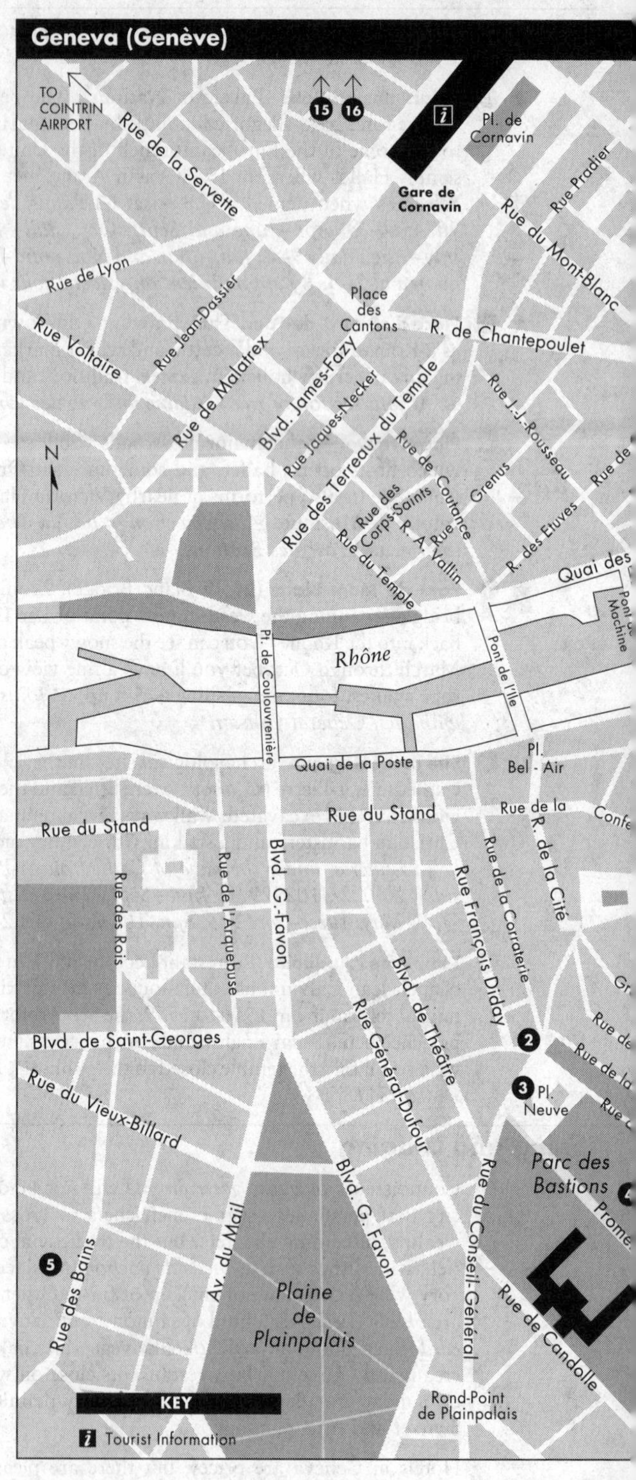

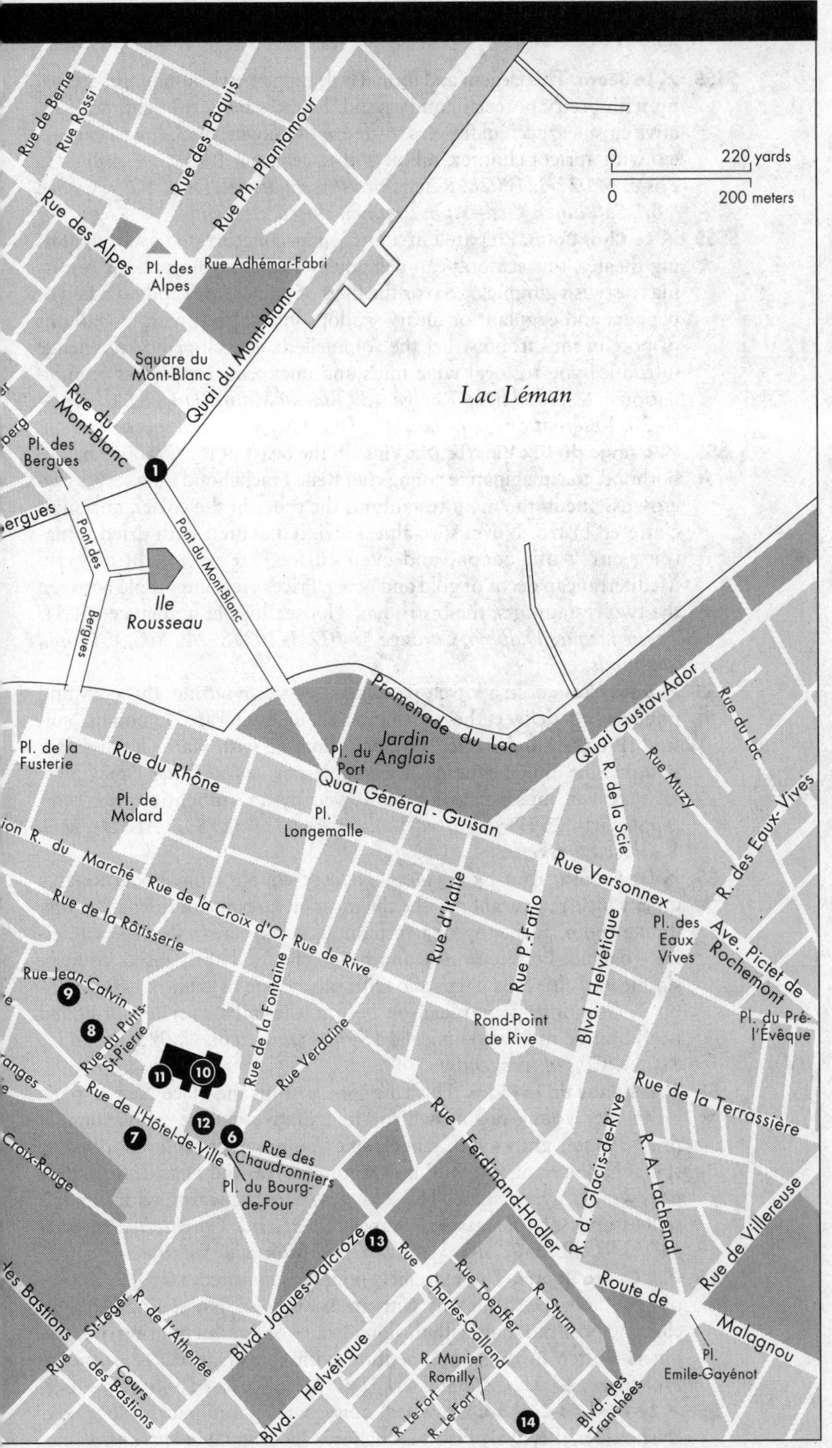

Rue de Berne
Rue Rossi
Rue des Pâquis
Rue Ph. Plantamour
Rue des Alpes
Pl. des Alpes
Rue Adhémar-Fabri
Square du Mont-Blanc
Quai du Mont-Blanc
Rue du Mont-Blanc
Pl. des Bergues
Pont des Bergues
Pont du Mont-Blanc
Ile Rousseau
Lac Léman
0
220 yards
0
200 meters
Promenade du Lac
Jardin Anglais
Pl. du Port
Quai Gustav-Ador
Pl. de la Fusterie
Rue du Rhône
Pl. de Molard
Quai Général - Guisan
Pl. Longemalle
R. de la Scie
Rue Muzy
Rue du Lac
R. des Eaux-Vives
Rue Versonnex
R. du Marché
Rue de la Croix d'Or
Rue de la Rôtisserie
Rue de Rive
Rue d'Italie
Rue P.-Fatio
Blvd. Helvétique
Pl. des Eaux Vives
Ave. Pictet de Rochemont
Pl. du Pré-l'Évêque
Rue Jean-Calvin
Rue du Puits-St-Pierre
Rue de la Fontaine
Rue Verdaine
Rond-Point de Rive
Rue de la Terrassière
Rue de l'Hôtel-de-Ville
Rue des Chaudronniers
Pl. du Bourg-de-Four
Croix-Rouge
Rue Ferdinand-Hodler
R. d. Glacis-de-Rive
R. A. Lachenal
Rue de Villereuse
Route de Malagnou
Pl. Emile-Gayénot
Rue Charles-Galland
Rue Toepffer
R. Sturm
R. Munier Romilly
R. Le-Fort
R. Le-Fort
Blvd. des Tranchées
Blvd. Jaques-Dalcroze
Blvd. Helvétique
R. de l'Athenée
Rue St-Leger
Cours des Bastions
des Bastions
1
6
7
8
9
10
11
12
13
14

noise. For details and price-category definitions, *see* Lodging *in* Switzerland A to Z, *above*.

$$$$ ✕ **Le Béarn.** This elegant and formal little Empire-style restaurant, dressed up with pretty porcelain and crystal, features modern, light, and creative cuisine: zucchini flowers stuffed with prawns, duck-breast carpaccio with apricot chutney, rabbit with sage and nettles. ✉ *4 quai de la Poste,* ☎ *022/3210028. Reservations essential. AE, DC, MC, V. Closed Sun., Sat. lunch Oct.–Apr.; summer, closed weekends.*

$$$$ ★ ✕ **Le Chat Botté.** Prepared in a kitchen as concentrated as an operating theater, this seafood can deliciously surprise you without resorting to stylish gimmicks. Savor the likes of pan-crisped cod on a bed of peppers and eggplant or meaty scallops interspliced with medallions of porcini mushrooms. Let the sommelier's encyclopedic knowledge introduce you to local wine finds and unexpected *mariages* (combinations). ✉ *Hotel Beau Rivage, 13 Quai du Mont-Blanc, tel. 022/71–6–20. Reservations required. AE, DC, MC, V. Closed weekends.*

$$$ ★ ✕ **L'Ange du Dix Vins/Le Dix Vins.** In the heart of the Carouge neighborhood, the imaginative young chef Réné Fracheboud now serves two crowds, one in the main restaurant, the other in the cozier, antiques-cluttered bistro. Novel specialties, vividly flavored with dried tomatoes, curry oil, cocoa, and even coffee, are served in a warm Mediterranean decor of gold and ocher. Prices are comparable between the two restaurants; the bistro has a looser, livelier ambiance. ✉ *31/29 rue Jacques Dalphin, Carouge,* ☎ *022/3420318. AE, MC, V. Closed weekends,*

$$ ★ ✕ **Boeuf Rouge.** In a kitsch-packed fin-de-siècle setting, this cozy and popular spot delivers the real thing: rich, unadulterated Lyonnaise cuisine. Try the hand-stuffed pistachio sausage with warm lentil salad; *boudin noir* (blood sausage) with apples; or *andouillettes* (spicy pork sausages) in mustard sauce—followed by an authentic *tarte Tatin* (apple tart). ✉ *17 rue Alfred-Vincent,* ☎ *022/7327537. AE, DC MC, V. Closed weekends.*

$$ ★ ✕ **La Favola.** Run by a young Ticinese couple from Locarno, this quirky little restaurant may be the most picturesque in town. The tiny dining room, at the top of a vertiginous spiral staircase, strikes a delicate balance between rustic and fussy. The food aptly mixes country simple and city chic: carpaccio with olive paste or white truffles, rabbit in Gorgonzola, and venison *bollito* (the Italian version of boiled beef) braised in Barolo wine. ✉ *15 rue Jean Calvin,* ☎ *022/3117437. MC, V. Closed weekends.*

$$ ★ ✕ **Les Fous de la Place.** This chic spot, just off the Place Neuve, pulls in an arty young-pro crowd for imaginative cuisine at reasonable prices: oyster gratin with fennel, spicy pumpkin gnocchi on a bed of spinach, pheasant and wild-mushroom tourte, and *tarte Tatin* (apple tart) with Gruyère cream. The setting is spare but warm, with slim red settees and saffron tasseled drapes. ✉ *21, rue Corraterie,* ☎ *022/3105340. AE, DC, MC, V. Closed Sun, Mon, and Sat. lunch.*

$$ ✕ **L'Opera Bouffe.** This extremely popular spot offers a small selection of light daily specials, many with an Asian twist. The setting is warm, chic and post-modern, with thrilling strains of Puccini pouring over the diners—often in direct competition with conversation. ✉ *5, av. de Frontenex,* ☎ *022/7366300. AE, DC, MC, V. Closed Sun. July–Aug.*

$$ ✕ **Le Pied-de-Cochon.** Crowded, noisy, smoky, and packed shoulder-to-shoulder, this lively bistro is anchored by original beams and a zinc-top bar. The staple among the good, simple fare is *pieds de cochon* (pigs' feet)—either grilled, with mushrooms, with lentils, or *désossés* (boned); there are also andouillettes, tripe, and salads. ✉ *4 pl. du Bourg-de-Four,* ☎ *022/3104797. AE, DC, MC, V. Closed Sun. May–Sept.*

$ ★ ✕ **Les Armures.** Everyone from workers to politicians comes to this restaurant in the picturesque and historic namesake hotel (☞ *below*) decorated with authentic arms from the Middle Ages. The broad menu of Swiss specialties ranges from fondue to *choucroute* (sauerkraut cooked with goose fat, onions, and white wine) to Rösti. ✉ *1 rue du Puits-St-Pierre,* ☎ *022/3103442. AE, DC, MC, V.*

$ ✕ **Taverne de la Madeleine.** Tucked into the commercial maze between the Rue de la Croix d'Or and the Old Town, this casual, alcohol-free café claims to be the oldest eatery in Geneva. Relax over homemade choucroute, fresh salads and vegetable plates, or fresh-baked fruit tarts in the charming Victorian dining room upstairs. Hot food is served until 6 PM in summer, only until 4 PM on Saturday. ✉ *20 rue Toutes-âmes,* ☎ *022/3106070. No credit cards. Closed Sun.*

$$$$ **Beau-Rivage.** Hushed and genteel, this grand old Victorian palace has been largely restored to its 1865 character: It's all velvet, parquet, and frescoes. Fabric-beswagged front rooms take in magnificent Right Bank views. In 1898, Empress Elizabeth of Austria died here after being stabbed only 300 ft away. ✉ *13 quai du Mont-Blanc, CH-1201,* ☎ *022/7166666,* FAX *022/7166060. 91 rooms, 6 suites. 3 restaurants. AE, DC, MC, V.*

$$$$ ★ **Des Bergues.** Having emerged from its chrysalis of renovation in 1997, this 1834 Right Bank landmark basks in attention—the mansard facade has been restored, bathrooms revamped, even the antique engravings in the rooms have been tastefully re-framed. The air is thick with discretion; registering guests are seated in the low-key marble lobby as if they were shopping for jewels. ✉ *33, que des Bergues, CH-1201,* ☎ *022/7315050,* FAX *022/7321989. 40 rooms, 10 suites. Restaurant. AE, DC, MC, V.*

$$$ ★ **Les Armures.** This 17th-century architectural treasure reveals charming original stonework, frescoes, and stenciled beams while still providing impeccable modern comforts. Intimate rooms are embellished with slick marble baths. Its casual restaurant is an Old Town must (☞ *above*). Approach by car can be difficult, and the nearest parking is three blocks away. ✉ *1 rue du Puits-St-Pierre, CH-1204,* ☎ *022/3109172,* FAX *022/3109846. 28 rooms. Restaurant. AE, DC, MC, V.*

$$$ **Métropole.** Built in 1855, Metropole has as much riverside splendor as its Right Bank sisters—at a lower price. There's a relaxed ambience despite the grand scale, with leather and hunting prints mixed in with discreet pastels. Riverside rooms are noisier, over traffic, but the view compensates; ask for the quieter third or fourth floors. ✉ *34 quai Général-Guisan, CH-1204,* ☎ *022/3183200,* FAX *022/3183300. 127 rooms. 3 restaurants. AE, DC, MC, V.*

$$ **Strasbourg-Univers.** A stylish oasis in the slightly sleazy train-station neighborhood, this mid-level retreat offers sleek decor (marble and faux–burled wood), convenience, and four-star quality at a three-star price. ✉ *10 rue Pradier, CH-1201,* ☎ *022/9065800,* FAX *022/7384208. 49 rooms. Restaurant. AE, DC, MC, V.*

$$ **Touring-Balance.** This hotel flashes a modern, contemporary look; ask to stay in the slick, solid, high-tech rooms on the higher floors, adorned with gallery-quality lithographs. You can't beat this location for shopping and sightseeing. At press time, it had been bought by the neighboring Cigogne, and renovations were in the works. ✉ *13 pl. Longemalle, CH-1204,* ☎ *022/3104045,* FAX *022/3104039. 64 rooms. 2 restaurants. AE, DC, MC, V.*

$ ★ **De la Cloche.** Think of yourself as a privileged border in the doily-trimmed flat of a sweet *dame d'un certain age.* The once-luxurious apartment has been carved into eight bedrooms, with toilets down the hall and a familial shower (two rooms have their own). The homey decor (flocked wallpaper, bookcase loaded with travel guides) matches the spirit of the place; feel free to make a cup of tea in the kitchen. ✉ *6 rue de la Cloche, CH-1201,* ☎ *022/7329481,* FAX *022/7381612. 8 rooms. AE, DC, MC, V.*

$ **Des Tourelles.** Once worthy of a czar, now host to the backpacking crowd, this fading Victorian offers enormous bay-window corner rooms, many with marble fireplaces and views over the Rhône. Most rooms now have a modern shower and toilet, and those on the street side have double-glazed windows and heavy drapes to keep the street noise out. The staff is young and friendly, and the breakfast an all-you-can-eat delight. ✉ *2 bd. James-Fazy, CH-1201,* ☎ *022/7324423,* FAX *022/7327620. 23 rooms, 20 with shower. AE, DC, MC, V.*

Nightlife and the Arts

Geneva Agenda, which has weekly listings of films, concerts, museum exhibitions and galleries, is available free in most hotels.

The Arts

The **Grand-Théâtre de Genève** (✉ pl. Neuve, ☎ 022/3112311) has concerts of classical music as well as opera, operetta, and dance; watch for listings of Sunday-morning chamber music recitals in the foyer. Recent productions have been displaced during a new renovation project; it may be reopened by publication time. The bijoux **Victoria Hall** (✉ 14 rue Général-Dufour, ☎ 022/3288121) is the main venue of L'Orchestre de la Suisse Romande, which was conducted for 50 years by Ernest Ansermet and through him had close links with Stravinsky. For information on the orchestra's season, call 022/3170017.

Nightlife

For a quiet drink, the bars of luxury hotels like the Métropole (☞ *above*) are hard to beat. For dancing, **Arthur's** (✉ 20 rte. de Pré-Bois, ☎ 022/7881600), in the Mövenpick hotel, is Switzerland's largest disco, with several dance areas. You can also prowl around the Quai du Seujet-try, where there are several nightspots. Try **L'Interdit** (✉ 18 quai du Seujet, ☎ 022/7389091) for classic disco; **Le Loft**(✉ 20 quai du Seujet, ☎ 022/7382828) is as much a gay bar as a dance club.

Geneva Essentials

Arriving and Departing

BY BUS

Long-distance buses generally use the **Gare Routière de Genève** (bus station, ✉ pl. Dorcière, just off rue du Mont-Blanc, ☎ 022/7320230).

BY CAR

Since Geneva sits on the border of the French Alps, near Annecy and not far from Lyon, entry from the French autoroutes is very convenient. From within Switzerland, enter from the north via the **A1** expressway from Lausanne.

BY PLANE

Cointrin (✉ northwest of city center, ☎ 022/7913111), Geneva's airport, is served by several airlines with direct flights from New York, Washington, Toronto, or London. Swissair also has flights from Chicago and Los Angeles. Swissair ticket holders departing from Cointrin can check their luggage through to the airplane from 120 rail and postbus stations, and also get their boarding passes at eight train stations.

Between the Airport and Downtown. Cointrin has a direct rail link with **Cornavin** (☎ 022/1572222; charge of 1.40 SF per minute; from outside Switzerland do not add the city code 22), the city's main train station in the center of town. Trains run about every 10 minutes from

5:30 AM to midnight. The trip takes about six minutes, and the second-class fare is 5 SF. There is also regular city **bus service** from the airport to the center of Geneva. The bus takes about 20 minutes, and the fare is 3 SF. Some hotels provide their own bus service. **Taxis** are plentiful and very expensive, charging at least 30 SF to the city center. Tips are expected only for luggage.

BY TRAIN

All services—domestic and international—use **Cornavin Station** (✉ city center; ☎ 022/1572222 for information, schedule, and reservations; charge of 1.40 SF per minute; from outside Switzerland do not add the city code 22).

Getting Around

BY BUS AND TRAM

There are scheduled services by local buses and trams every few minutes on all routes. Before you board, you must buy your ticket from one of the vending machines at the stop (they have English instructions). For 2.20 SF you can use the system for one hour, changing as often as you like. To save money and time, buy a ***carte journalière,*** a ticket for all-day unlimited city center travel for 5 SF; these are available at some newsstands. Travel with a **Swiss Pass** is free (☞ Transportation by Train *in* Switzerland A to Z, *above*).

BY TAXI

Taxis are extremely expensive; use them only if there's no alternative. There is a 5 SF minimum charge per passenger just to get into the cab, plus a 2.70 SF-per-km (½ mi) charge.

Contacts and Resources

CONSULATES

Australia (✉ rue de Moillebeau 56, ☎ 022/9182900). **Canada** (✉ 1 rue du Pré de la Bichette, ☎ 022/7339000). **New Zealand** (✉ Chemin du Petit-Saconnex, ☎ 022/7349530). **United Kingdom** (✉ 37 rue de Vermont, ☎ 022/9182400). **United States Mission** (✉ rte. de Pré-Bois 29, ☎ 022/7981615).

EMERGENCIES

Police (☎ 117). **Ambulance** (☎ 144). **Hospital** (✉ Hôpital Cantonal, rue Micheli-du-Crest 24, ☎ 022/3723311). **Doctor referral** (☎ 022/3202511). **Pharmacies** (☎ 111).

GUIDED TOURS

Boat. In good weather take one of the delightful day trips that stop at the villages on the vineyard-fringed lake: **Mouettes Genevoises** (☎ 022/7322944), **Swissboat** (☎ 022/7324747), or **Compagnie de Navigation** (☎ 022/3112521).

Orientation. Bus-walking tours around Geneva are operated by **Key Tours** (☎ 022/7314140). The two-hour tours leave from the bus station in place Dorcière (✉ city center, behind the English church) daily at 2 PM and also at 10 AM in high season. You may opt to transfer to a mini-train at Place Neuve and continue into the old town.

Walking. The **Tourist Office** (☞ *below*) offers a series of two-hour guided group walks following varying itineraries, from "Historic Edifices" to "International Geneva." Tours depart at 2:30 daily from the Hôtel de Ville (✉ Rue de l'Hôtel-de-Ville), June 15–September 30, and cost 35 SF per person (minimum two). The Tourist Office also provides **audio tours** (in English) of the Old Town, covering 26 points of interest, complete with map, cassette, and player; rental is 10 SF. A refundable deposit of 50 SF is required.

VISITOR INFORMATION

Office du Tourisme de Genève (Tourist Office; ✉ 3 rue du Mont-Blanc, ☎ 022/9097000). **Information booth** (✉ 4 pl. du Molard, on the Left Bank; Cornavin Station). **Mail information** (✉ 10 rte. de l'Aéroport, Case Postale 596, CH-1215, Genève 15, ☎ 022/9297000, FAX 022/9297011).

LUZERN

As you cruise down the leisurely sprawl of the Vierwaldstättersee, mist rising off the gray waves, mountains—great loaflike masses of forest and stone—looming above the clouds, it's easy to understand how Wagner could have composed his *Siegfried Idyll* in his mansion beside this lake. This is inspiring terrain, romantic and evocative. When the waters roil up you can hear the whistling chromatics and cymbal clashes of Gioacchino Rossini's thunderstorm from his 1829 opera, *Guillaume Tell.* It was on this lake, after all, that William Tell—the beloved, if legendary, Swiss national hero—supposedly leapt from the tyrant Gessler's boat to freedom. And it was in a meadow nearby that three furtive rebels and their cohorts swore an oath by firelight and planted the seed of the Swiss Confederation.

Exploring Luzern

Numbers in the margin correspond to points of interest on the Lucerne map.

Luzern's Old Town straddles the waters of the River Reuss where it flows out of the Vierwaldstättersee, its more concentrated section occupying the river's right bank. There are a couple of passes available for discounts for museums and sights in the city. One is a museum pass that costs 25 SF and grants free entry to all museums for one month. If you are staying in a hotel, you may also want to pick up a special visitor's card; once stamped by the hotel, it entitles you to discounts at most museums and other tourist-oriented businesses as well. You can get both passes at the tourist office (*see* Luzern Essentials, *below*).

Altes Rathaus (Old Town Hall). This relic facing the end of a modern bridge, the Rathaus-Steg, was built between 1599 and 1606 in the late-Renaissance style. ✉ *Rathausquai, facing the end of bridge, Rathaus-Steg.*

7 **Am Rhyn-Haus** (Am Rhyn House). Also known as the Picasso Museum, the compact Renaissance-style building has an impressive collection of late paintings by Picasso. ✉ *Furreng. 21,* ☎ *041/4101773.* 6 *SF.* ⏲ *Apr.–Oct., daily 10–6; Nov.–Mar., daily 11–1 and 2–4.*

8 **Bourbaki-Panorama.** An enormous conical wooden structure was created in 1876–1878 as a genuine, step-right-up tourist attraction. Its conical roof covers a sweeping, wraparound epic painting of the French Army of the East retreating into Switzerland at Verrières—a famous episode in the Franco-Prussian War. It is closed for renovations until mid-1999. ✉ *Löwenpl.,* ☎ *041/4109942.* ⏲ *May–Sept., daily 9–6; Mar., Apr., and Oct., daily 9–5.*

5 **Franziskanerkirche** (Franciscan Church). More than 700 years old, this church retains its 17th-century choir stalls and carved wooden pulpit despite persistent modernization. ✉ *Franziskanerpl., just off Münzg.*

10 **Gletschergarten** (Glacier Garden). The bedrock of this 19th-century tourist attraction was excavated between 1872 and 1875 and has been dramatically pocked and polished by Ice Age glaciers. A private mu-

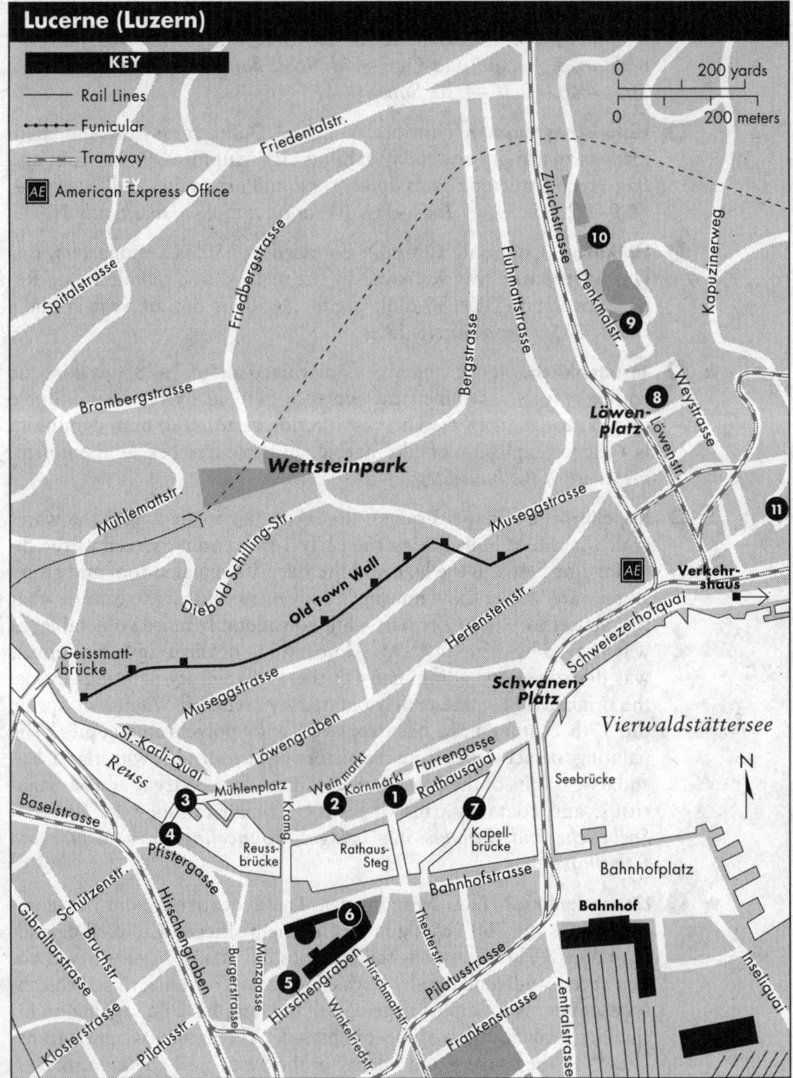

Am Rhyn-Haus, **1**
Bourbaki-Panorama, **8**
Franziskanerkirche, **5**
Gletschergarten, **10**
Historisches Museum, **4**
Hofkirche, **11**
Jesuitenkirche, **6**
Kapellbrücke, **7**
Löwendenkmal, **9**
Spreuerbrücke, **3**
Weinmarkt, **2**

seum on the site displays impressive relief maps of Switzerland. ✉ *Denkmalstr. 4,* ☎ *041/4104340.* 7 *SF.* ⏲ *May–mid-Oct., daily 8–6; Mar., Apr., and mid-Oct.–mid-Nov., daily 9–5; mid-Nov.–Feb., Tues.–Sat. 10:30–4:30, Sun. 10–5.*

4 **Historisches Museum** (Historical Museum). Dating from 1567, this building was an armory and today exhibits city sculptures, Swiss arms, and flags; reconstructed rooms depict rural and urban life. ✉ *Pfisterg. 24,* ☎ *041/2285424.* ⏲ *Tues.–Fri. 10–noon and 2–5, weekends 10–5.*

11 **Hofkirche** (Collegiate Church). Founded in 750 as a monastery, this Gothic structure was destroyed by fire in 1633 and rebuilt in late-Renaissance style. The 80-rank organ (1650) is one of Switzerland's finest. ✉ *St. Leodegarstr. 13.*

★ 6 **Jesuitenkirche** (Jesuit Church). Constructed in 1667–78, this Baroque edifice reveals a symmetrical entrance flanked by two onion-dome towers, added in 1893. The vast interior, restored to mint condition, is a rococo explosion of gilt, marble, and epic frescoes. ✉ *Banhofstr., just west of Rathaus-Steg.*

★ 7 **Kapellbrücke** (Chapel Bridge). It snakes diagonally across the water and, when first built during the early 14th century, served as the dividing line between the lake and the river. Its shingled roof and grand stone water tower (now housing a souvenir stand) are to Luzern what the Matterhorn is to Zermatt—but considerably more vulnerable, as was proved by a fire in 1993. Almost 80% of this fragile monument was destroyed, including many of the 17th-century paintings inside; the original 111 gable panels painted by Heinrich Wägmann during the 17th century have been replaced with polychrome copies. The paintings depict scenes from the history of Luzern and Switzerland, legendary exploits of the city's patron saints—St. Leodegar and St. Mauritius, and coats of arms of local patrician families. ✉ *Between Seebrücke and Rathaus-Steg bridges, connecting Rathausquai and Bahnhofstr.*

★ 9 **Löwendenkmal** (Lion Monument). The evocative monument commemorates the 760 Swiss guards and their officers who died defending Louis XVI of France at the Tuileries in Paris in 1792. Carved out of a sheer sandstone face by Lucas Ahorn of Konstanz, this 19th-century wonder is a simple image of a dying lion, his chin sagging on his shield, a broken stump of spear in his side. The Latin inscription translates: "To the bravery and fidelity of the Swiss." ✉ *Denkmalstr.*

3 **Spreuerbrücke.** This narrow, weathered, all-wood covered bridge dates from 1408. In its center is a lovely 16th century chapel looking back on the Old Town. Its interior gables hold a series of eerie, well-preserved paintings by Kaspar Meglinger of the *Dance of Death*; they date from the 17th century, though their style and inspiration—tracing to the plague that devastated Luzern and all of Europe during the 14th century—are medieval. ✉ *Between Geissmattbrücke and Reussbrücke bridges, connecting Zeughaus Reuss-Steg and Mühlenpl.*

2 **Weinmarkt** (Wine Market). One of the loveliest of Luzern's several fountain squares, this former site of the wine market drew visitors from across Europe from the 15th to the 17th century to witness its passion plays. Its Gothic central fountain depicts St. Mauritius, patron saint of warriors, and its surrounding buildings are flamboyantly frescoed in 16th-century style. ✉ *Sq. just west of Kornmarkt, north of Metzgerrainle.*

Elsewhere in Luzern

★ **Verkehrshaus.** The Swiss Transport Museum is one of Luzern's (if not Switzerland's) greater attractions. Easily reached by steamer, car, or Bus

WHEN WAS THE LAST TIME YOU FELT THIS GOOD IN THE AIR?